I0319480

Gustave Masson

A Compendious Dictionary of French Language

French-English

Gustave Masson

A Compendious Dictionary of French Language
French-English

ISBN/EAN: 9783337016364

Printed in Europe, USA, Canada, Australia, Japan

Cover: Foto ©Andreas Hilbeck / pixelio.de

More available books at **www.hansebooks.com**

A COMPENDIOUS

DICTIONARY OF THE FRENCH LANGUAGE

(French-English -:- English-French).

ADAPTED FROM THE DICTIONARIES OF
PROF. ALFRED ELWALL.

lowed by a List of the principal Diverging Derivations, and preceded by Chronological and Historical Tables.

BY
GUSTAVE MASSON,
ASSISTANT MASTER AND LIBRARIAN, HARROW SCHOOL.

NEW EDITION.

London:
MACMILLAN AND CO.
1880.

[redacted]

TO

THE REV. B. F. WESTCOTT, D.D.,

Canon of Peterborough, and Regius Professor in the University of Cambridge,

HIS VOLUME IS AFFECTIONATELY DEDICATED AS A SMALL TOKEN OF SINCERE AND RESPECTFUL FRIENDSHIP.

GUSTAVE MASSON.

PREFACE.

In preparing a Dictionary like the present one, a compiler ought not, I think, to aim at originality. Accuracy and completeness are the qualities he should attempt to realize. I have worked mainly on the lines of Prof. Elwall's Dictionaries (Paris: Delalain Frères. Two Vols.), and my constant endeavour has been to keep equally distant from exaggerated concision and over abundance of detail. There is one point, however, to which I would venture to call the attention of the reader, namely, the etymologies in the French-English part. They form a distinctive feature in my volume, and are given on the authority of Messrs. Littré, Schéler, and Brachet. The list of *diverging derivations,* together with the chronological, historical, and literary tables, will, I trust, be likewise found useful; and I shall be proud indeed if the Dictionary I now offer to the public is deemed worthy of the kind reception which my previous works have met with.

GUSTAVE MASSON.

HARROW-ON-THE-HILL.
November 1873.

CHRONOLOGICAL TABLES

OF THE

HISTORY OF FRENCH LITERATURE

FROM THE EARLIEST PERIOD TO THE PRESENT DAY.

In the following Tables the letters *b*, *fl.*, and *d* stand for *born*, *flourished*, and *dead*, respectively.

TABLE I.

THE MIDDLE AGES—FIRST PERIOD.

(From the Ninth to the Fourteenth Century.)

SYNCHRONISMS.

814. Charlemagne, *d.*
912. Conquest of Neustria by the Normans.
1066. The Normans in England.
1069. The Chronicle of the Pseudo-Turpin not much anterior to this date.
1071. William VI., count de Poitiers, *b.*
1091. Saint Bernard, *b.*
1095. First Crusade.
1100. Cercamons, *troubadour*, *b.?*
1112. Robert Wace, *b.*
1120. Pierre d'Auvergne, *troubadour*, *b.?*
1127. William VI., count de Poitiers, *d.*
1147. Giraud le Roux, *troub.*, *fl.*
1150. Geoffroy de Villehardoin, *b.*—The *cours d'amour*, *fl.*—Arnauld Daniel, *troub.*, *fl.*
1153. Saint Bernard, *d.*
1160. Bernard de Ventadour, *troub.*, *fl.*
1163. Folquet de Marseille, *troub.*, *b.?*
1174. Jordan Fantosme composes his historical poem.
1177. Garnier of Pont Saint Maxence composes his poem in honour of Thomas à Becket.
1180. Robert Wace, *d.*
1191. Chrestien de Troyes, *d.*
1194. Ermengarde, countess de Narbonne, *d.*
1200. Decay of the *cours d'amour.*—Geoffroy Rudel, *troub.*, *d.*
1201. Thibaut de Champagne, *d.*—Arnauld de Marveil, *d.?*
1209. Crusade against the Albigenses.
1210. Chronicle of the war against the Albigenses, *composed in the Langue d'Oc.*
1211. Bertrand de Born, *troub.*, *d.*
1213. Villehardoin, *d.*—*Jaufre et Brunissende*, a Provençal romance, composed about that time.
1222. Joinville, *b.*—Elias de Barjols, *troub.*, *fl.*
1229. End of the Crusade against the Albigenses.—Adenès le Roi, *b.?*—Sordello, *troub.*, *fl.*
1240. *Blandin de Cornouailles*, a Provençal romance, composed.—Guillaume de Lorris, *fl.*—Adam de la Halle, *b.*
1245. *L'image du monde*, composed.
1250. Marcabrus, *troub.*, *fl.*—Bertrand Carbonel, *troub.*, *fl.*
1253. Thibaut de Champagne, *d.*
1262. *Le jeu du mariage ou de la feuillée*, by Adam de la Halle.
1270. Saint Louis, *d.*
1275. *Berthe aux grands pieds*, a romance by Adenès le Roi, composed.
1284. *Le jeu de Robin et de Marion*, by Adam de la Halle.
1286. Adam de la Halle, *d.*
1300. The Provençal life of Saint Honorat, composed.
1319. Joinville, *d.*

I. Langue d'Oc.

The *Langue d'Oc* or *Provençale* literature was the first to flourish, and for a short time it shone with extraordinary splendour. The southern *Troubadours* during the eleventh and twelfth centuries were the poets of civilized society. They chiefly wrote lyrics, and their compositions may be classed under the following heads :—

1. *Vers*, including pieces of various styles generally divided into stanzas.
2. *Chansons*, amatory poems *always* divided into stanzas.
3. *Complaintes (plank)*, elegiac compositions usually written in lines of ten or twelve syllables.
4. *Tensons*, or *jeux partis*, poetical discussions or debates on certain points of war or of love. The *tenson* (contention) is made up of an even number of stanzas followed by two *envois*. When there are more than two interlocutors, the piece is called a *torneyamen*.
5. *Sirventes*, satirical compositions also divided into stanzas.
6. *Pastorelles*, eclogues introducing two or more characters.
7. *Ballads*.

A few *romances of chivalry* written in the Langue d'Oc may also be mentioned :—

Girard de Roussillon (beginning of the twelfth century); *Jaufre et Brunissende* (1213); *Ferabras* (1230? 1240?).

Finally, amongst the principal monuments of Provençal literature, we must not forget to name :—

A Chronicle (metrical) of the Crusade against the Albigenses (1210); a translation of the *De Consolatione* of Boetius, and a series of religious poems composed by the Vaudois.

The intellectual glory of Langue d'Oc perished in the thirteenth century with the political independence of Southern France. The Crusade against the Albigenses (1209–29) was its *coup de grâce*.

II. Langue d'Oïl.

I. Romances of Chivalry.—Religious enthusiasm, martial prowess, and, at a later period, love, are the three elements which predominate in these compositions.

The first French romance in point of antiquity is the *chanson de Roland* (eleventh century), erroneously supposed by some to be the work of a *Trouvère* called Théroulde or Thurold.

1. *The chansons de geste (gesta)*, representing more particularly the principles of war and religion, include :—

   (a) *Subjects belonging to national history*, written generally in monorhyme stanzas of decasyllabic or Alexandrine verses. Chief cycles of poems :—

   1. Geste du Roi.
   2. Geste de Doon de Mayence.
   3. Geste de Guillaume au Cort-nez.

   (b) *General subjects of an historical character*, often borrowed from ancient history or from the Apocrypha. Principal works :—

   1. Le chevalier au cygne.
   2. Les quatre fils Aymon.
   3. Amis et Amile.
   4. Le chanson d'Antioche (was recast by *Graindor de Douai*).
   5. Le roman d'Alexandre (by *Lambert le Cort* and *Alexandre de Bernay*).

2. *Romances of the Round Table.*—Celtic themes treated by Norman *Trouvères*. The subject of these poems is the creation of an order of chivalry instituted by King Arthur for the purpose of recovering the *Saint Graal*, or cup with which our Lord celebrated the Last Supper. This cycle includes works written in

Octosyllabic verses, thus:—

1. Le roman de la charrette.
2. Perceval le Gallois.
3. Eric et Enide.
4. Le chevalier au lion.

Prose, thus:—

1. Le roman du Saint Graal.
2. La quête du Saint Graal.
3. Tristan de Leonnois.
4. Lancelot du Lac.

II. Rhymed Chronicles, and Chronicles in Prose:—

Le roman de Rou, Le roman de Brut, both by Robert Wace.

La conquête de Constantinople, by Villehardoin.

Histoire de Saint Loys, by the Sire de Joinville.

Chronicles of Jehan Froissart

III. Fabliaux.—We include under this designation a number of didactic or satirical poems, which can be divided and classified according to the subjects treated.

1. *Lais.* Generally referring to some old Celtic narrative.—Marie de France.
2. *Dits.* Poems written in various metres, and enumerating the various qualities of the subjects or characters introduced. Thus, the *Dits du Gardecors* and *du Pélican*, by Baudoin de Condé.
3. *Fabliaux*, properly so called, satirical poems in octosyllabic lines, rhyming by couplets and directed against:—
   (*a*) The secular clergy. Thus, *Le provoire qui menga les mures.*
   (*b*) The monks. Thus, *Coquaigne, L'ordre de bel eyse.*
   (*c*) The knights and barons. Thus, *Le chevalier au barizel, Le vair palefroi.*
   (*d*) The *bourgeoisie*. Thus, *La bourse pleine de sens.*
   (*e*) The serfs. Thus, *Le vilain mire.*
4. *Débats* and *disputes*; rhymed dialogues.—*La desputoison du vin et de l'iaue.*
5. *Moral and religious poems.—Le enseignement d'un père à son fils*; the *Bibles* of Guiot de Provins and of the Seigneur de Berze; the poem on Sainte Léocade, by Gautier de Coinsi; the poems of Rutebeuf.
6. *Didactic poems, Cyclopædias.—L'image du monde.*
7. *Satirical and allegorical poems*:—
   (*a*) Le roman de Renart (*Renart le nouvel, Renart le contrefait, Couronnement de Renart*, etc.).
   (*b*) Le roman de la Rose, begun by Guillaume de Lorris, and continued by Jehan de Meung.
8. *Historical poems* are merely rhymed gazettes. Thus, *La complainte et le jeu de Pierre de la Broce.*
9. *Songs.* The principal *chansonniers* are Adam de la Halle, and Thibaut, count of Champagne.

IV. Sermon Writers:—

Saint Bernard of Clairvaux.

V. Origins of the French Stage:—

Mysteries, Miracle-plays, Moralities.—Jehan Bodel (*Jeu de Saint Nicolas*) Adam de la Halle (*Jeu de la feuillée*).

TABLE II.

THE MIDDLE AGES—SECOND PERIOD.

(Fourteenth and Fifteenth Centuries.)

SYNCHRONISMS.

1321. Dante Alighieri, *d.*
1323. Institution of the *Jeux Floraux* by Clémence Isaure.
1328. Philippe III. king of France, first of the Valois dynasty.
1331. Abul-Feda, Mussulman writer, *d.*
1332. Edward Balliol crowned king of Scotland.
1334. Giotto, *d.*
1337. Edward III., king of England, declares war against France.—Jehan Froissart, *b.*
1340. Naval victory gained by England at the Sluys.
1341. *Petrarch crowned at the Capitol.*
1346. Battle of Nevil's Cross.
1347. William of Ockham, *d.*
1354. Marino Faliero, doge of Venice.
1356. Battle of Poitiers.
1360. Peace of Brétigny.
1362. Pierre Bercheure, *d.*
1363. Christine de Pisan, *b.*—Gerson, *b.*
1374. Petrarch, *d.*
1375. Boccaccio, *d.*
1382. Nicolas Oresme, *d.*
1386. Alain Chartier, *b.*
1391. Charles, duke d'Orléans, *b.*
1400. Chaucer, *d.*
1402. The brotherhood of the *Confrères de la Passion* authorized.
1415. Battle of Agincourt.
1429. Joan of Arc at Orleans.
1442. The performances of the *Clercs de la Basoche* suspended.
1457. The first book bearing a printed date is published at Strasburg.
1460. Battles of Northampton and Wakefield.
1474. William Caxton prints his first book.
1483. Edward IV., king of England, *d.*
1495. First Greek edition of Aristotle printed by the Aldi, at Venice.

I. Chroniclers and Historians:—

Chronicles of Jehan Froissart.
Livres des faits et bonnes mœurs du Roi Charles V., by Christine de Pisan.
Chronicles of Philippe de Commynes.
Histoire du petit Jehan de Saintré, by Antoine de la Sale.

II. Sermon Writers:—

Jean Charlier de Gerson, Chancellor of the University of Paris.
Michel Ménot.
Oliver Maillart.

III. Satires, Tales, and Facetiæ in Prose and Verse:—

Le Curial, Le Quadriloge invectif, Le Livre des Quatre Dames, by Alain Chartier.
Continuation of the *Roman de la Rose*, by Jehan de Meung.
Jacquemin Gelée finishes the *Roman de Renart le Nouvel.*
An anonymous author, native of Champagne, writes the *Roman de Renart le Contrefait.*
Guillaume Coquillart—*Satire des Droits Nouveaux.*
Les Sérées, by Guillaume Bouchet, Sieur de Brocourt.
Les Bigarrures et Touches de Tabourot, Sieur des Accords.—*Les Escraignes Dijonnoises*, by the same.
Les Cent Nouvelles Nouvelles.
L'évangile des Quenouilles.
Les Quinze Joies du Mariage, by Antoine de la Sale.

IV. Origins of the French Stage:—

Mysteries, Miracles, and Moralities.—*Miracle of the Passion*, by the brothers Gréban.
Farces, or Pièces Farcies, originally performed by the Clercs de la Basoche.—*Farce de Patelin.*
Soties, performed by the Enfants sans Souci.—*Le jeu de Robin et de Marion.*—*Jeu du Prince des Sots*, by Gringoire.
Dits and Débats, performed by the successors of the old minstrels.

V. Miscellaneous Poetry:—

Eustache Deschamps.
Olivier Basselin (*Vaux-de-Vire*).
Charles, duc d'Orléans.
François Corbueil, surnamed Villon—*Le Petit Testament, Le Grand Testament.*

TABLE III.

THE REFORMATION AND THE RENAISSANCE.

(Sixteenth Century.)

SYNCHRONISMS.

1503. Michel de L'Hôpital, *b.*
1507. The *Mystère de la Passion* printed in Paris.
1509. Calvin, Estienne Dolet, *b.*—Martial d'Auvergne, *d.*
1513. Jacques Amyot, *b.*
1515. *François I. ascends the throne.*—Ramus, *b.*
1518. Michel Ménot, Leonardo da Vinci, *d.*
1519. Théodore de Bèze, *b.*
1520. Pierre Viret, *b.*—Raffaelle Sanzio, *d.*
1523. *The Memoirs of Philippe de Commynes published.*
1524. Joachim du Bellay, Ronsard, Hotman, *b.*
1527. Henri Estienne, Brantôme, *b.*
1529. Estienne Pasquier, *b.*—Machiavel, *d.*
1530. La Boétie, Bodin, *b.*—*Copernicus publishes his System.*
1531. La Noue, *b.*
1532. Estienne Jodelle, *b.*—*Gargantua* published.
1533. Montaigne, *b.* — Ariosto, Erasmus, *d.*
1534. *Foundation of the Society of the Jesuits.*
1536. Vauquelin de la Fresnaye, *b.*
1538. Amadis Jamyn, *b.*
1540. Guicciardini, *d.*—The *Inst. de la Relig. Christ.* published.
1544. Clément Marot, Despériers, *d.*—Du Bartas, *b.*
1545. Robert Garnier, *b.*
1546. Estienne Dolet, *d.* — Desportes, *b.*
1549. The *Illustr. de la Langue Françoise* published.
1550. Agrippa d'Aubigné, *b.*
1552. Rabelais, Herberay des Essarts, *d.*—Bertaut, *b.*
1556. Malherbe, *b.*
1558. *The Inquisition established.*—Mary Stuart, *d.*
1559. *Peace of Câteau-Cambrésis.*
1560. *Charles IX. king of France.*—Joachim du Bellay, *d.*
1561. Lord Bacon, *b.*
1562. *Massacre of Vassy.*
1563. *The Duc de Guise murdered.*
1564. Calvin, *d.*—Shakespeare, *b.*
1566. The *Apologie pour Hérodote* published.
1568. La Boétie, *d.*
1572. *Massacre of St. Bartholomew.*—Ramus, Jean Goujon, *d.*
1573. Jodelle, L'Hôpital, *d.*—Régnier, *b.*
1574. Charles IX., *d.*
1577. Blaise de Monluc, *d.*
1580. *First edition of Montaigne's Essays.*
1585. Amadis Jamyn, *d.*—Guarini's *Pastor fido.*
1587. Battle of Coutras.
1589. Ronsard, Hotman, Henri III., *d.*

The Revolution which took place during the Sixteenth Century was of a threefold character:—

1. RELIGIOUS:—Against the Abuses of the Papal System.

Jean Calvin—*Institution de la Religion Chrétienne, Sermons,* &c.
Pierre Viret—*Sermons.*
Théodore de Bèze—*Hist. Ecclésiast. des Eglises Réformées au royaume de France.*
Henri Estienne—*Apologie pour Hérodote,* &c.
Agrippa d'Aubigné—*Les Tragiques, Le Baron de Fæneste, Confession de Sancy.*
Clément Marot—*Poems.*

2. PHILOSOPHICAL:—Against the Traditions of Scholasticism.

François Rabelais—*Gargantua.*
Estienne Dolet.
Bonaventure Despériers—*Contes et joyeux devis, Cymbalum mundi.*
Michel de Montaigne—*Essais.*
Pierre Ramus.

3. LITERARY:—Against the Grammar and the Art of the Middle Ages.

Joachim du Bellay—*L'Illustration de la Langue Françoise.*
Pierre Ronsard—*La Franciade, Odes, Satires,* &c.
Amadis Jamyn—*Translation of part of the Iliad.*
Estienne Jodelle—*Cléopâtre,* tragedy; *Eugène,* comedy.
Pierre de Larivey—*Le Laquais, La Veuve, Les Esprits,* &c., comedies.
Remi Belleau—*Poems.*
Guillaume de Saluste du Bartas—*La Divine Sepmaine.*
Vauquelin de la Fresnaye—*Art Poëtique François.*
Pierre Bertaut—*Poems.*
Robert Garnier—*Tragedies.*
Philippe Desportes—*Poems.*

TRANSLATORS :—

Herberay des Essarts, *by his translation of "The Amadis," seems to protest in favour of the Middle Ages and of Chivalry.*
Jacques Amyot—*Translation of Plutarch.*

The Civil and Religious Dissensions of the Age produce a number of Publicists, Controversialists, Memoir Writers, &c. :—

Michel de L'Hôpital, Chancellor of France.
Estienne de la Boétie—*Contr'un, ou de la Servitude volontaire.*
Estienne Pasquier—*Recherches de la France,* &c.
Jean Bodin—*De la République.*
La Noue—*Discours Politiques et Militaires.*
Blaise de Monluc—*Commentaires.*
Pierre de Bourdeilles, Sieur de Brantôme—*Vies des Grands Capitaines,* &c.
François Hotman—*Franco-Gallia.*
La Satire Ménippée, by Gillot, Florent Chrestien, Nicolas Rapin, Pierre Pithou, Gilles Durand, and Passerat.

SATIRE. TRANSITION TO THE FOLLOWING EPOCH :—

Mathurin Régnier.

TABLE IV.

FIRST HALF OF THE SEVENTEENTH CENTURY.

(*Reigns of Henri IV., Louis XIII.*)

SYNCHRONISMS.

1590. Battle of Ivry.—Théophile de Viaud, *b.*—Du Bartas, *d.*
1591. La Noue, *d.*
1592. Michel de Montaigne, *d.*
1593. Jacques Amyot, *d.*
1594. Balzac, Saint Amand, *b.*—Tintoretto, Jean Bodin, *d.*
1595. Desmarets de St. Sorlin, *b.*—Tasso, *d.*—*Battle of Fontaine-Française.*
1596. Descartes, *b.*
1598. *Edict of Nantes.*—Voiture, *b.*
1600. Saint Pavin, *b.*—Giordano Bruno, *d.*—Shakespeare's *Hamlet.*
1601. Augustin Carrache, Robert Garnier, *d.* — Georges de Scudéry, *b.*
1603. Pierre Charron, *d.*—Sarrazin, *b.*
1605. Théodore de Bèze, *d.*—Godeau, *b.*
1606. Pierre Corneille, *b.*—Vauquelin de la Fresnaye, Philippe Desportes, *d.*
1607. Mdlle. de Scudéry, *b.*
1609. Rotrou, *b.*—Annibal Carrache, *d.*
1610. *Henri IV. murdered.*—Scarron, La Calprenède, *b.*
1612. Larivey, *d.*—Benserade, *b.*
1613. Régnier, *d.* — La Rochefoucauld, Saint-Evremont, *b.*
1614. Brantôme, *d.*—Cardinal de Retz, *b.*
1615. Pasquier, *d.*
1616. Shakespeare, *d.*
1617. *Pyrame et Thisbé* performed.
1618. Thirty Years' War.—Racan's *Bergeries* performed.
1619. Guarini, Louis Carrache, *d.*
1621. La Fontaine, *b.*
1622. Molière, *b.*—François de Sales, *d.*
1623. Pascal, *b.*
1624. Gombauld's *Endymion* published. — Ministry of Cardinal Richelieu.
1625. Charles I. king of England.—D'Urfé, Sarpi, Marini, *d.*
1626. Madame de Sévigné, Chapelle, *b.*—Théophile de Viaud, Lord Bacon, *d.*
1627. Siege of La Rochelle.—Bossuet, *b.*
1628. Malherbe, *d.*
1629. The *Académie Françoise* founded.
1630. Hardy, Agrippa d'Aubigné, *d.*
1632. *Battle of Lutzen.*—Fléchier, Bourdaloue, *b.*
1636. Corneille's *Le Cid* performed.—Boileau, *b.*
1637. Descartes' *Discours de la Méthode* published.
1638. Malebranche, Madame Des Houlières, *b.*
1639. Chaulieu, *b.*—*Horace, Cinna,* performed.
1640. *The Long Parliament.*—Rubens, *d.*
1642. Cardinal Richelieu, *d.*

Towards the beginning of this epoch, literature still shows traces of the agitation and confusion which had marked the previous era. The influence of Spanish taste manifests itself in the works of some authors—

Saint François de Sales—*Introduction à la Vie dévote*, etc.
Camus, Bishop of Bellay.

The success obtained by pastoral poetry in Italy (*L'Aminta, Il Pastor fido*) suggests to Honoré d'Urfé the idea of his novel *L'Astrée*.

PUBLICISTS, HISTORIANS, PHILOSOPHERS, DIPLOMATISTS:—

François Pithou—*De la Grandeur, Droits, etc., des Rois et Royaume de France.*
Pierre Pithou—*Les Libertés de l'Eglise Gallicane.*
Pierre Charron—*Traité de la Sagesse.*
Guillaume du Vair—*Méditations, Traité de l'Éloquence, Mémoires.*
Du Plessis-Mornay—*Mémoires.*
Le Président Jeannin—*Négociations.*
Cardinal Arnauld d'Ossat—*Letters and Despatches.*
Sully—*Les Œconomies Royales.*

RE-ESTABLISHMENT OF DISCIPLINE IN IMAGINATIVE LITERATURE:—

Malherbe—*Poésies diverses, Ode a Marie de Medicis.*

Malherbe's School:—

Le Marquis de Racan—*Les Bergeries.*
Le Président Maynard—*Poésies.*

THE SPIRIT OF SOCIABILITY IS DEVELOPED, AND CONTRIBUTES TO REGENERATE LITERATURE.

The Hôtel de Rambouillet:—

Italian Influence.—Vincent Voiture—*Lettres sur la Prise de Corbie, De la Carpe au Brochet*, &c.
Spanish Influence.—Guez de Balzac—*Le Socrate Chrétien, Le Prince*, &c.

Mademoiselle de Scudéry's "Saturdays"—"Précieux" and "Précieuses:"—

Miscellaneous Poetry.—Valentin Conrart. Chapelain—*La Pucelle.* Godeau. Sarrazin.
Heroic Romances.—Gombauld—*L'Endymion.* La Calprenède—*Cassandre.* The Scuderys—*La Clélie, Le Grand Cyrus.*

The "Cabarets d'Honneur"—"Bohème Littéraire:"—

Poetry.—Théophile de Viaud. Saint Amand—*Moïse sauvé.* Saint Pavin.
Burlesque Romances—Charles Sorel—*Francion.* Scarron—*Le Roman Comique, Virgile travesti.*

The Académie Française is founded by Cardinal Richelieu.

The Stage:—

The Popular Drama—Tragi-comedy.—Alexandre Hardy. Théophile de Viaud—*Pyrame et Thisbé.*

The Genteel Drama—Pastoral Tragedies.—Racan—*Les Bergeries.*

Reform of the Theatre—

Mairet—*Sophonisbe.*
"The Five Authors," collaborateurs of Richelieu.
Desmarets de Saint Sorlin—*Les Visionnaires*, comedy.
Rotrou—*Venceslas.*
Pierre Corneille. His first plays—*Mélite, Clitandre, La Veuve, La Galerie du Palais, Le Cid, Horace, Cinna, Le Menteur.*

Reform in Moral and Metaphysical Philosophy—

Descartes—*Discours de la Méthode.*

Port Royal des Champs, attempt made by Roman Catholics to reform their own Church—

The Abbé de Saint-Cyran. The Arnauld family.

TABLE V.

SECOND HALF OF THE SEVENTEENTH CENTURY.

(The Reign of Louis XIV.)

SYNCHRONISMS.

1643. Battle of Rocroy.—Louis XIII., *d.*
1645. Archbishop Laud, *murdered.*—Battle of Naseby.
1646. Anthony Hamilton, *b.*—Condé, *d.*
1648. Beginning of *La Fronde.*—Voiture, *d.*
1649. *Charles I., king of England, beheaded.*
1650. Descartes, Vaugelas, *d.*
1651. Fénelon, *b.*—Scarron's *Le Roman Comique* published.
1653. Pope Innocent X. condemns the *five propositions* of Jansenius. [d.
1655. Gassendi, Lesueur, Balzac,
1656. Pascal's *Lettres Provinciales* published.
1657. Monaldeschi murdered at Fontainebleau.
1658. *Oliver Cromwell, d.*
1659. Peace of the Pyrenees.—Molière's *Précieuses Ridicules* performed.
1660. Charles II. proclaimed king of England.—Scarron, *d.*
1661. Mazarin, *d.* — Bossuet preaches his first sermon.
1662. Pascal, *d.*—The manufacture of the *Gobelins* established.
1665. The Great Plague of London.—Nicholas Poussin, *d.*
1666. Fire of London.—Anne of Austria, *d.*
1667. The Cabal.—The *Paradise Lost* published.—Bochard, *d.*—*Tartufe* and *Andromaque* performed.
1668. Peace of Aix-la-Chapelle.—Le Sage, *b.*
1674. Lord Clarendon, Milton, *d.*
1677. Racine's *Phèdre* performed.
1683. Colbert, *d.*—Duquesne bombards Algiers.
1684. Pierre Corneille, *d.* — The *Dragonnades.*
1688. English Revolution.—Duquesne, Quinault, *d.*—Montesquieu, *b.*—Siege of Derry.
1691. Louvois, *d.*
1693. Bussy-Rabutin, Pelisson, Madame de La Fayette, *d.*
1694. Antoine Arnauld, *d.*—Voltaire, *b.*
1695. La Fontaine, Mignard, Nicole, *d.*
1696. Madame de Sévigné, *d.*
1697. Peace of Ryswick.—Charles XII. king of Sweden.—The Abbé Prévost, *b.*
1701. Bossuet, Bourdaloue, Mdlle. de Scudéry, *d.*
1706. Battle of Ramilies.
1707. Crébillon *fils*, *b.*
1709. The *Tatler* first started.
1712. Battle of Denain. — Jean Jacques Rousseau, *b.*
1715. Death of Louis XIV.—Malebranche, Fénelon, *d.*—*Gil Blas* published.

I. Literature of Opposition :—

Protestantism—

Sermons, theological works: Claude, Du Bosc, Mestrezat, Superville, Saurin.
Periodical literature, pamphlets: Bayle, Basnage, Desmaizeaux, Jurieu, Leclerc.

Jansenism.—Claude Lancelot, Du Guet (*L'Ouvrage des Six Jours, &c.*), Nicole (*Essais de Morale*), Le Maistre de Sacy, Quesnel (*Réflexions Morales sur le Nouveau Testament*).

Free-thinkers.—Saint-Evremont, Chapelle (*Poésies*), Chaulieu (*Poésies*), Hesnault, Madame Deshoulières, La Fontaine.

Politicians.—Cardinal de Retz (*Mémoires*), Guy Patin (*Letters*).

Great Dispute on the relative merits of Ancient and Modern Writers.—Perrault, Pradon.

II. A few Writers are conspicuous for Genius and Vigour :—

The Duc de la Rochefoucauld—*Maximes, Mémoires.*
Madame de Sévigné—*Letters.*
Madame de La Fayette—*Zaïde.* The Princesse de Clèves marked a revolution in novel writing.
Pierre Corneille composes his last tragedies—*Rodogune, Héraclius, Don Sanche d'Aragon, Nicomède, Agésilas, &c.*
Molière writes with much liberty in spite of the absolutism of Louis XIV. His chief productions are—*Le Tartufe, Le Misanthrope, Les Femmes Savantes, L'Avare, L'École des Maris, Le Bourgeois Gentilhomme, Les Fourberies de Scapin.*
Mézeray—*Histoire de France.*

III. The Majority are specially remarkable for Regularity, Harmony, and Taste :—

Boileau Despréaux—*Epîtres, Satires, L'Art Poétique, Le Lutrin.*
Quinault—*Atys, Armide, Roland* (operas).
Fléchier—*Oraisons funèbres.*
Bourdalone—*Sermons.*
Bossuet—*Sermons, Oraisons funèbres, Discours sur l'Histoire universelle, Histoire des Variations.*
Malebranche—*La Recherche de la Vérité.*
La Bruyère—*Les Caractères et Mœurs de ce Siècle.*
Racine, pre-eminently happy in delineating the passions of the human heart. Chief works—*La Thébaide, Alexandre, Andromaque, Bérénice, Bajazet, Mithridate, Britannicus, Iphigénie, Phèdre, Athalie, Esther, Les Plaideurs.*

IV. Transition to the following Epoch. *Liberal Ideas begin to manifest themselves :—*

Regnard—*Comedies: Le Joueur, Le Légataire universel.*
Le Sage—*Turcaret, Gil Blas, Le Diable boiteux.*
Fénelon—*Télémaque, Fables, Tales, Correspondence,* &c.'
Massillon—*Le Petit Carême, Oraisons funèbres.*
Saint Simon—His *Memoirs* are the most striking condemnation of the despotism of Louis XIV.

TABLE VI.

THE EIGHTEENTH CENTURY, DOWN TO THE OUTBREAK OF THE FRENCH REVOLUTION.

SYNCHRONISMS.

1717. Discussions about the Bull *Unigenitus.*
1718. Conspiracy of Cellamare.—Charles XII., *d.*
1719. Madame de Maintenon, *d.*
1721. Montesquieu's *Lettres Persanes* published.
1725. Peter the Great, *d.*
1726. Cardinal Fleury Prime Minister in France.
1727. Isaac Newton, *d.*—George II. king of England.
1728. Marmontel, *b.*—Swift publishes his *Gulliver's Travels.*
1732. Voltaire's tragedy *Zaïre* performed.
1734. Siege of Philipsburg. —Battle of Parma.
1735. Linnæus publishes his *Systema Naturæ.*
1738. Boerhaave, *d.*
1739. Capture of Porto Bello by the English.
1740. Frederick II. king of Prussia.
1742. Downfall of Robert Walpole's Cabinet.
1743. Cardinal Fleury, *d.*—Voltaire's *Mérope* performed.
1745. Battle of Fontenoy.—The Pretender in England.
1746. Battles of Culloden and of Rocoux.
1747. Battle of Lawfeld.—Siege of Bergen-op-Zoom. — Le Sage, *d.*
1748. *Clarissa Harlowe* published. —Treaty of Aix-la-Chapelle. —*L'Esprit des Lois* published.
1751. The first volume of the *Encyclopédie* published.—D'Aguesseau, *d.*
1754. Revolution in Corsica.
1755. Montesquieu, *d.* — Earthquake at Lisbon.
1756. Battle of Port-Mahon.—Admiral Byng tried.
1758. Pope Benedict XIV., *d.*
1759. Rousseau's *Nouvelle Héloïse* published.
1760. George II., king of England, *d.*
1761. Capitulation of Pondicherry.
1763. Trial of Wilkes.—Grenville Administration. — L'Abbé Prévost, *d.*
1764. Mdme. de Pompadour, *d.*—Xavier de Maistre, *b.*
1765. Rockingham Cabinet in England.
1766. Madame de Staël, *b.*
1767. Benjamin Constant, Fiévée, *b.*
1768. Captain Cook starts on his first voyage.
1769. Robertson's *History of Charles V.* published.—Napoléon Bonaparte, Cuvier, Châteaubriand, Soult, Wellington, Walter Scott, *b.*
1770. *Letters of Junius.*
1773. American Revolution.
1774. Louis XVI. king of France. —Clement XIV. (Ganganelli), *d.*
1775. Battle of Lexington.
1777. Albert von Haller, *d.*
1778. Lord Chatham, Voltaire, Linnæus, Rousseau, *d.*
1781. Lessing, *d.* — Kant publishes his *Critic of Pure Reason.*
1785. Trial of Warren Hastings.
1786. Moses Mendelssohn, *d.*
1788. Buffon, *d.*

With reference to the preceding age, the literature of the eighteenth century is at the same time :—

I. A feeble Continuation:—

COMEDY—

The School of Molière.—D'Allainval (*L'École des Bourgeois*).

Authors who endeavoured to move the feelings rather than to interest the mind.—Destouches (*Le Glorieux*), La Chaussée, Diderot, Beaumarchais (*Le Barbier de Séville—Le Mariage de Figaro*).

Analytical School.—Marivaux (*Le Legs—Les Jeux de l'Amour et du Hasard*).

TRAGEDY.—Voltaire, Crébillon, La Motte (*Inès de Castro*), La Noue (*Mahomet II.*).

PULPIT ELOQUENCE.—L'Abbé Poulle, L'Abbé de Boismont, Duguet.

LYRIC POETRY.—J. B. Rousseau (*Odes, Cantates, &c.*), Le Franc de Pompignan.

II. A Development:—

POETRY OF NATURE.—Saint Lambert (*Les Saisons*), Lemierre (*Les Fastes*), Roucher (*Les Mois*), Delille.

DIDACTIC POETRY.—Louis Racine (*La Religion—La Grâce*), Lemierre (*La Peinture*), Marmontel, Voltaire, Fontanes.

TALES AND NOVELS.—L'Abbé Prévost (*Manon Lescaut*), Marivaux, Diderot, Rousseau, Marmontel, Voltaire, Bernardin de St. Pierre.

LIGHT POETRY, FABLES, ETC.—Voltaire, Piron, Gresset (*Ver-Vert*), Florian, La Motte.

FORENSIC ELOQUENCE.—D'Aguesseau (*Mercuriales*), Gerbier, Servan, La Chalotais.

III. A Reaction against:—

ANTIQUITY.—La Motte (*Paradoxes Littéraires*), Fontenelle.

RELIGION—

With which is associated a system of philosophy :—

Applied to Ontological Facts.—Condillac.

Applied to the Study of Nature.—Buffon, Réaumur, the Jussieu family, B. de St. Pierre.

For which is substituted :—

Deism.—Voltaire, Rousseau, Duclos, Vauvenargues.

Atheism.—Helvétius, Diderot, D'Holbach, Lamettrie, Lalande, Condorcet.

SOCIAL INSTITUTIONS.—*Historical Studies are assiduously cultivated :*—

Erudition properly so called.—Calmet, Fréret, Ducange, the Daciers, the Benedictines.

Erudition applied to History.—Daniel (*Histoire de France*), Dubos (*Histoire de l'Établissement de la Monarchie*).

Philosophy applied to History.—Hénault, Montesquieu (*Grandeur et Décadence des Romains*) Raynal, Mably.

Descriptive History.—Vertot, Rollin, Voltaire (*Hist. de Charles XII.*), Rulhière.

Memoirs.—Madame de Staal, Madame de Caylus, Beaumarchais.

Political Science.—Montesquieu (*Lettres Persanes — Esprit des Lois*), Terrasson (*Sethos*). Quesnay, Voltaire, L'Abbé de St. Pierre.

LITERARY CRITICISM, ÆSTHETICS, ACADEMIC ELOQUENCE.—Grimm (*Correspondance*), La Harpe (*Lycée*), Fontenelle, Thomas (*Éloges*), D'Alembert, Diderot, Rollin, Montesquieu (*Essai sur le Goût*), Dubos, Morellet.

REIGN OF PUBLIC OPINION :—

Salons.—Madame du Deffand, Madame Geoffrin, Madame Necker, Mademoiselle de L'Espinasse, Madame de Lambert (*Avis d'une Mere à son Fils*), Baron d'Holbach (*Système de la Nature*).

Newspaper Literature.—Fréron, Desfontaines (*L'Année Littéraire—Le Mercure de France*).

The ENCYCLOPÉDIE, of which D'Alembert and Diderot were the chief editors, may be considered s the great literary manifesto of the eighteenth century in France.

TABLE VII.

FROM THE STORMING OF THE BASTILLE TO THE CONSULATE.

SYNCHRONISMS.

89. Opening of the States-General at Versailles.—Meeting in the Tennis-court. — Necker banished.—Taking of the Bastille.—Necker recalled.—The king returns to Paris.

90. Burke publishes his Reflections on the French Revolution.-Benjamin Franklin, *d.*

91. Mozart, *d.*—Mirabeau, *d.*—Vendean insurrection.—Opening of the French Legislative Assembly.

92. Rouget de l'Isle composes the *Marseillaise.*—Taking of the Tuileries by the mob.—Battles of Valmy and Jemmapes.—National Convention.—Proclamation of the French republic.-Gustavus III., king of Sweden, murdered.

1793. Louis XVI., beheaded.—Marie Antoinette, queen of France, beheaded.—Reign of Terror.

1794. Acquittal of Warren Hastings.-Lavoisier, André Chénier, Robespierre, beheaded.

1795. Battle of Loano.—End of the National Convention.—The metrical system of weights and measures established in France.

1796. Brilliant campaign of Bonaparte in Italy.—Battles of Millesimo, Lonato, Arcole. —Laplace publishes his *Exposition du Système du Monde.*

1797. Battle of Rivoli.—Treaty of Tolentino.—*Coup d'État* of Fructidor. — Treaty of Campo Formio. — General Hoche, *d.*

1798. French expedition to Egypt. — Battle of Aboukir. — Malthus publishes his work on population.

The era of theories which had prepared the way for reforms of every kind ends with the taking the Bastille; and to discussions of a merely intellectual character must now succeed political tion. The influence of thought makes itself felt through fresh channels; and whilst newspaper erature acquires a power of the most extraordinary kind, the debates of the *Assemblée Constituante*, e *Assemblée Legislative*, and the *Convention* give occasion to flights of eloquence which Demosthenes d Cicero never surpassed.

1. *Orators who represented more particularly the doctrines of Montesquieu and Voltaire :—*
   Mounier, Malouet, Lally-Tollendal, Condorcet.

2. *Orators chiefly identified with the theories of the Contrat Social :—*
   Adrien Duport, Lameth, Sieyès, Barnave, Vergniaud, Guadet, Gensonné.

3. The "Ancien Régime" has its orators in Maury and Cazalès.

4. Extreme revolutionists :—Robespierre, Marat.

Mirabeau standing apart like the genius of modern French eloquence.

URNALISTS.—The inexperience of these extemporized politicians was equal to their audacity.

1. *On the Revolutionary side :—*Camille Desmoulins (*Révolutions de France et de Brabant—Vieux Cordelier*), Loustalot (*Révolutions de Paris*), Marat (*L'Ami du Peuple*).

2. *On the Royalist side :—*Rivarol, Montlosier, Mallet du Pan (*Les Actes des Apôtres—La Quotidienne*).

Pamphlet-Writers.—Sieyès (*Qu'est-ce que le Tiers État?*), Mirabeau (*Essai sur le Despotisme*), Necker (*Compte-rendu au Roi*), Benjamin Constant (*De la Force du Gouvernement actuel, et de la Nécessité de s'y rallier*).

Madame Roland.—*Mémoires, Correspondance.*

Dramatic Literature.—Fabre d'Eglantine (*Le Philinte de Molière*), Collin d'Harleville (*L'Optimiste, le Vieux Célibataire*), Chamfort (*La jeune Indienne, Mustapha et Zéangir*), Andrieux (*Les Étourdis*).

Tragedies and comedies are very little else but dramatic pamphlets. Thus :—
Marie Joseph Chénier (*Charles IX., Henri VIII., Fénelon*). And on the Royalist side :—
Laya (*L'Ami des Lois*).

Lyric and Descriptive Poetry.—André Chénier, Roucher.—Marie Joseph Chénier is essentially the poet of the Revolution.—Andrieux, Écouchard Le Brun, Rouget de l'Isle (*La Marseillaise*).—Delille (*La Pitié*) represents Royalism in poetry.

Philosophy.—The doctrines of the Condillac School became the substratum of all *official* teaching throughout the French Republic; and it is from the sensationalist point of view that the "Écoles Normales" were founded.

Principal writers on metaphysics and science in general:—Garat, Volney (*Les Ruines, Catéchisme de la Loi naturelle*), Condorcet (*Esquisse d'un Tableau historique des Progrès de l'Esprit humain*), Berthollet, Haüy, Cabanis.

A strong reaction soon takes place against the tenets of the Revolutionists :—

(*a*) *From the mystical or religious point of view*:—St. Martin, *le philosophe inconnu* (*Des Erreurs et de la Vérité*), Joseph de Maistre (*Considérations sur la France*).

(*b*) *From the political point of view*: — Necker (*Histoire de la Révolution*), Mounier (*Recherches sur les Causes qui ont empêché les Français de devenir libres*), Mallet du Pan (*Considérations sur la Révolution française*), Morellet.

Napoleon Bonaparte.—Speeches and proclamations to his troops.

TABLE VIII.

THE CONSULATE AND THE EMPIRE.

SYNCHRONISMS.

1799. Storming of Seringapatam.—*Coup d'État* of Brumaire.—The Consulate.

1800. Battles of Marengo, Montebello, Hohenlinden. — Attempt upon the life of the First Consul.—Mallet du Pan, *d.*—Bichat publishes his *Recherches physiologiques sur la Vie et la Mort.*

1801. Treaty of Luneville.—Evacuation of Egypt by the French.—End of Pitt's first administration.—The French *Concordat* signed by the Pope. — Rivarol, *d.*—Alexander I., emperor of Russia.

1802. Peace of Amiens.—Napoleon created Consul for life.

1803. Herder, *d.*—The French invade Holland and Hanover.

1804. Conspiracy of Georges Cadoudal, Moreau, and Pichegru.—The Duke d'Enghien shot.—Proclamation of the Empire.

1805. Battles of Trafalgar and of Austerlitz. — Nelson, *d.*—Treaty of Presburg between France and Austria. — Madame de Staël publishes *Corinne.*

1806. W. Pitt, *d.*—Creation of the French university.—Battles of Jena and Auerstadt.—Fox, *d.*

1807. Defeat of the Grenville cabinet.—Battles of Eylau and of Friedland. — Treaty of Tilsit.—Sismondi publishes his *Histoire des Républiques Italiennes.*

1808. Invasion of Spain by the French. — Dupont capitulates at Baylen.—Interview between Napoleon and Alexander I. at Erfurth.

1809. Siege of Saragossa.—Battles of Talavera and of Wagram.—Châteaubriand publishes *Les Martyrs.*

1810. Napoleon marries the Archduchess Maria - Louisa.—Battles of Busaco and of Torres Vedras.—Bernadotte adopted by Charles XIII., king of Sweden, as heir to the throne.

1811. Battle of Albuera. — Increased despotism of Napoleon.

1812. Successes of Wellington in Spain.—Campaign of Russia.—The Pope transferred to Fontainebleau.—Conspiracy of General Mallet.

1813. European coalition against Napoleon.—Battles of Lutzen, Bautzen, Leipsic, &c.—Publication of Madame de Staël's *De l'Allemagne.*

1814. Invasion of France by the Allies.—Paris capitulates.—Louis XVIII. ascends the throne.

1815. The *hundred days.*—Battle of Waterloo.—Napoleon abdicates.—First Edition of Béranger's songs.

Despotism and real literature are incompatible. The reign of military force inaugurated on the 18th Brumaire put an end to all utterance of thought; and a censorship of the strictest character kept the press in complete check.

PHILOSOPHY:—

(a) Strict continuation of the School of Condillac:—Destutt de Tracy.

(b) Modified:—De Gérando—La Romiguière.

(c) Revival of idealism:—

1. *From the point of view of German thought*:—Charles Villers—Fr. Ancillon.

2. *From the point of view of the Scotch School* (Reid, Dugald-Stewart):—Royer Collard.

3. *From an independent point of view*:—Benjamin Constant—Maine de Biran.

4. *In connection with a religious revival*:—De Bonald (*Législation Primitive*), Joseph de Maistre (*Soirées de St. Pétersbourg*), Abbé Frayssinous (*Conférences*).

The *Société d'Auteuil*, consisting of sensationalist philosophers who met at the house of Madame Helvétius—Daunou, Ginguené, Destutt de Tracy, &c.—is the great centre of constitutional opposition to Bonaparte.

Writers on Scientific Subjects:—Georges Cuvier (*Recherches sur les Ossements fossiles*), Geoffroy St. Hilaire, Fourcroy, La Place (*Exposition du Système du Monde*), Lacépède (*Histoire naturelle des Quadrupèdes ovipares et des Serpents*).

Legislation and Administration:—Merlin (*Répertoire universel de Jurisprudence*), Portalis (*Discours et Rapports*), Roederer (*Journal d'Économie politique*), Regnault de St. Jean d'Angély.

History:—Daru (*Histoire de Venise*), Michaud (*Histoire des Croisades*), Lacretelle (*Histoire de France au XVIII. Siècle*), Sismondi (*Histoire de France*), Cardinal de Bausset (*Histoire de Bossuet*).

Criticism and Erudition:—Ginguené, Auger, Malte-Brun, Daunou, Dussault, Hoffmann, De Feletz, Geoffroy, Boissonade.

During the Empire the periodical press was kept under the severest control.

Le Publiciste (Mademoiselle de Meulan, Suard).

Le Mercure de France (La Harpe, Fontanes, De Bonald).

Le Journal des Débats (Bertin de Vaux).

POETRY.—Ceasing to be an inspiration, it becomes a trade ("on travaille des vers comme une broderie").

1. *Didactic and descriptive poetry reigns supreme*:—

Delille (*Les Jardins*), Fontanes (*Le Verger*), Castel (*Les Plantes*), Berchoux (*La Gastronomie*), Esménard (*La Navigation*).

2. *Epic poetry sinks into insignificance*:—

Parseval-Grandmaison (*Philippe-Auguste*), Baour-Lormian (*L'Atlantide*).

3. *The Drama*:—*Tragedy*. As genius is altogether absent, the vices of the pseudo-classical system are all the more conspicuous.

Raynouard (*Les Templiers*), De Jouy (*Sylla*), La Harpe (*Philoctète*), Briffaut (*Ninus II.*), Baour-Lormian (*Omasis*), M. J. Chénier (*Tibère*), Arnault (*Marius à Minturnes*), Lemercier (*Agamemnon*).

Ducis, divided between the inspiration of his genius and the influence of the age in which he lived, satisfied neither the one nor the other (*Hamlet*, *Le Roi Lear*, *Othello*, *Abufar*).

Letourneur's translation of Shakespeare proves that an epoch of reform is dawning for French tragedy.

4. *Comedy.*—The delineation of social foibles and ridicules is still successful.—Etienne (*Les Deux Gendres*), Alexandre Duval (*Le Tyran domestique*—*La Fille d'Honneur*), Picard (*Médiocre et Rampant*—*La Petite Ville*), Lemercier (*Pinto*).

5. *Lyric poetry* :—

Millevoye, Madame Dufrénoy (*Élégies*), Lebrun (*Odes*, *Élégies*, *Épîtres*).

NOVELS AND TALES :—

Fiévée (*La Dot de Suzette*), Madame Cottin (*Malek-Adhel*, *Malvina*, *etc.*), Madame de Souza (*Adèle de Sénanges*), Madame de Krüdner (*Valérie*).

The standard of reform in literature, philosophy, and politics is raised, on the Royalist side by Châteaubriand (*Atala*, *René*, *Le Génie du Christianisme*, *Les Martyrs*); on the Liberal side by Mme. De Staël (*Delphine*, *Corinne*, *De l'Allemagne*, *Considérations sur la Révolution française*).

TABLE IX.

THE RESTORATION AND THE REIGN OF LOUIS PHILIPPE.

SYNCHRONISMS.

1818. Bernadotte (Charles John XIV.), king of Sweden.
1819. James Watt, *d.*
1820. George III., king of England, *d.*—The Duke de Berry murdered by Louvel.—Birth of the Duke de Bordeaux.
1821. Congress of Laybach.—Death of Napoleon.—Insurrection in Greece.
1822. Shelley, *d.*—Lord Castlereagh, *d.*—M. de Villèle, Prime Minister of France.
1823. Invasion of Spain by the French.—Death of Pope Pius VII.
1824. Charles X., king of France.—Lord Byron, *d.*
1825. General Foy, *d.*—Augustin Thierry publishes his *Histoire de la Conquête de l'Angleterre par les Normands.*
1826. Jefferson, *d.*—Saint Simon, *d.*—John Adams, *d.*—Don Pedro, king of Portugal.
1827. Battle of Navarino. — M. Victor Hugo publishes his play of *Cromwell*.
1828. Downfall of M. de Villèle's cabinet in France.—M. Victor Hugo publishes his *Orientales.*
1829. Catholic Emancipation Bill in England.—Prince de Polignac forms an anti-liberal government in France.
1830. William IV., king of England.—Revolution in France.—Algiers taken by the French. — Benjamin Constant, *d.* — Revolution in Belgium.
1834. Lafayette, *d.*—Cabinets of Lord Melbourne and of Sir R. Peel.
1837. William IV., king of England, *d.*—Siege of Constantine by General Valée.—Treaty of La Tafna.
1838. Prince Talleyrand, *d.*
1840. Discussions between England and France on the Eastern Question.
1843. Anti-Corn-law League in England.
1844. Geoffroy St. Hilaire, *d.*—Bernadotte, *d.*—Battle of Isly.
1846. Polish insurrection.—Louis Napoleon Bonaparte escapes from the fortress of Ham.—Pius IX., Pope.
1848. Revolutions throughout the continent of Europe.—Châteaubriand, *d.*
1850. Louis Philippe, *d.*—Balzac the novelist, *d.*

This epoch is essentially one of transition. A general feeling prevails that social, political, and religious institutions must, as well as literature, be thoroughly modified.

PHILOSOPHY.—Materialism undergoes a complete transformation. Broussais (*De l'Irritation et de la Folie*) adheres strictly to the old traditions; but a union is attempted between philosophy and sociology.—MM. St.-Simon, Fourier, Auguste Comte (*Positivism*: MM. Littré, Taine, etc.), Jean Reynaud, Pierre Leroux.

IDEALISM is associated with the revival of religious opinions :—

(a) *Protestantism*:—Cellérier, Al. Vinet, Ath. Coquerel, Sam. Vincent, Ad. Monod.

(b) *Catholicism*:—Baron d'Eckstein, Droz, Ballanche.

The Abbé de Lamennais begins :—

(1) By exalting the power of the Church (*Essai sur l'Indifférence*).—*Chief Disciples*: Laurentie, De Genoude.

(2) He attempts to reconcile the Church with the Revolution. *École de la Chesnaie*: Lacordaire, Ozanam, Gerbet, Besson, Maurice de Guérin, Bautain (*Paroles d'un Croyant*), etc.

(3) He advocates the downfall of the Church (*Affaires de Rome, Le Livre du Peuple*).

(c) affects the form of eclecticism, and assumes a position independent of Christianity, but not hostile to it—Victor Cousin. The school is soon broken up.]

(d) *Deists*:—MM. Jules Simon, Garnier, Jouffroy, Damiron, Caro.

(e) *Scientific Freethinkers*:—MM. Havet, Renan, Vacherot.

Eclecticism gives a great impulse to historical researches.—MM. Matter (*Histoire du Gnosticisme*), Barthélémy St.-Hilaire, Bartholmess, De Rémusat (*Abélard, Anselme de Cantorbéry*), Ravaisson, Saisset, etc. M. Franck edits the *Dictionnaire des Sciences philosophiques*.

Oriental Studies:—MM. Champollion, Sylvestre de Sacy, Etienne Quatremère, Stanislas Julien, Eugène Burnouf, De Chézy, Abel Rémusat, Jules Oppert, Panthier, Munk, De Rougé.

Classical Erudition:—MM. Letronne, Thurot, Quicherat, Egger, Naudet, Leclerc, Patin, Charpentier, Raoul Rochette, Boissonade, etc.

Writers on Science:—MM. Flourens, Biot, Arago, Claude Bernard, Ampère, Poinsot, Alibert, Milne-Edwards, Thénard, Dumas, etc.

POLITICS, LEGISLATION, ADMINISTRATION.—*Pamphlets on the Royalist side*: MM. de Châteaubriand (*De Bonaparte et des Bourbons, La Monarchie selon la Charte*); De Montlosier (*Mémoire à consulter*). A little later on the *Liberal side*: Paul Louis Courier (*Pamphlet des Pamphlets*). Later still: M. de Cormenin, M. Génin, M. Michelet (*Des Jésuites*), M. de Girardin.

ELOQUENCE.—*Royalists*:—MM. de Châteaubriand, Royer-Collard, Berryer, De Villèle, De Martignac, De Montalembert.

Liberal Royalists:—MM. Camille Jordan, De Serre, Guizot, Thiers, Cousin, Dupin, the Duke de Broglie.

Republicans and Liberals:—General Foy, MM. Manuel, Odilon-Barrot, De Lamartine.

WRITERS ON POLITICAL ECONOMY, ETC.:—MM. Say, Michel Chevalier, De Tocqueville, Passy, Baudrillart, Louis Reybaud, Laboulaye.

NEWSPAPERS AND REVIEWS:—The *Revue Française*, published during the early period of the Restoration, is the organ of the *Doctrinaires* (MM. Guizot, De Broglie, Duvergier de Hauranne).

The *Globe* represents the Liberal party with socialist tendencies (MM. Dubois, Pierre Leroux, Sainte-Beuve).

The *Revue des deux Mondes* is established in 1829, and soon takes the lead.

Daily Papers:—

Le Constitutionnel, Liberal, Voltairean, and slightly Bonapartist.

Le Siècle, Liberal.

Le Journal des Débats, Conservative.

Le National, Republican (M. Armand Carrel).

LITERARY CRITICISM is particularly brilliant during this epoch. M. Villemain lectures at the Sorbonne on the history of French literature. M. Nisard (*Histoire de la Littérature française*); M. St.-Marc Girardin (*Cours de Littérature dramatique*); M. Sainte-Beuve (*Critiques et Portraits littéraires, Causeries du Lundi*); MM. de Sacy, Jules Janin, Ampère, Prévost-Paradol, Taine.

PRINCIPAL SALONS:—*Royalist and Catholic:* Madame Swetchine, Madame de Duras. *Protestant and Liberal:* The Duchess de Broglie. *Neutral:* Madame Récamier.

POETRY AND THE DRAMA.—Under the twofold influence of M. de Châteaubriand and Madame de Staël's teaching, supplemented by a more accurate knowledge of foreign literature, *La jeune France* seeks to break down for ever the barriers of the so-called classical school.

École Romantique.—"La Muse Française."—Leaders of the Movement: MM. Emile Deschamps, De Lamartine, Victor Hugo.

(*a*) *Religious Group:* MM. Turquety (*Amour et Foi*); Reboul, Sainte-Beuve (*Consolations, Pensées d'Août*); Guttinguer (*Mélanges Poétiques*); Duclésieux, Madame Tastu.

(*b*) *Independent Group:* MM. Alfred de Musset (*Contes d'Espagne et d'Italie*), Barbier (*Iambes*), Théophile Gautier, Barthélémy et Méry (*La Némésis, Napoléon en Égypte*), Alfred de Vigny (*Poèmes Antiques et Modernes*), Hégésippe Moreau, Brizeux (*Marie, Les Bretons*); Mesdames Emile de Girardin (*Napoline*) and Desbordes Valmore.

École Classique.—A few writers remain faithful to the old traditions: MM. Viennet, Alexandre Guiraud (*Les Maccabées*), Pierre Lebrun (*Poésies sur la Grèce*). MM. Béranger and Désangiers raise the French *chanson* to the proportions of an ode. The former represents the political, and the latter the epicurean side of French lyric poetry. MM. Casimir Delavigne (*Les Messéniennes*) and Alexandre Soumet form the transition between the *Classiques* and the *Romantiques*.

THE DRAMA is an attempt to introduce into France the style of Shakespeare, and also to place before the public, in a striking manner, extravagant and often dangerous ideas on social and political reform.

1. *Artistic Drama:*—MM. Victor Hugo (*Hernani, Lucrèce Borgia*, etc.). Alexandre Dumas (*Henri III. et sa Cour, Charles VII., Caligula*, etc.), Alfred de Vigny (*La Maréchale d'Ancre*).

2. *Philosophic Drama:*—MM. Alexandre Dumas (*Antony, Angèle*), Alfred de Vigny (*Chatterton*), Balzac (*Mercadet, Les Ressources de Quinola, Vautrin*).

Casimir Delavigne (*Les Enfants d'Édouard, Louis XI., Marino Faliero*) and Alexandre Soumet (*Jeanne d'Arc, Norma, Une Fête de Néron*) stand apart.

Comedy:—M. Scribe and his numerous *collaborateurs* give us slight and amusing sketches of society (*L'Intérieur d'un Bureau, Le Secrétaire et le Cuisinier, Bertrand et Raton, La Camaraderie*); MM. Alfred de Musset (*Comédies et Proverbes*) and Théodore Leclerc (*Proverbes*).

A reaction sets in about the year 1840, represented chiefly in tragedy by M. Ponsard (*Lucrèce, Agnès de Méranie, Charlotte Corday*), and in comedy by MM. Emile Augier (*La Ciguë, L'Aventurière, Philiberte*) and Jules Sandeau (*Le Gendre de Monsieur Poirier, Mademoiselle de la Seiglière*). The admirable talent of Mademoiselle Rachel helps considerably this return to classical traditions.

NOVELS AND ROMANCES:—

(a) *School of Châteaubriand.—Images:* MM. Victor Hugo (*Notre Dame de Paris*), Alfred de Vigny (*Cinq-Mars*), Mérimée (*Chronique de Charles IX.*), Alexandre Dumas, Théophile Gautier (*Le Capitaine Fracasse*).

(b) *School of Madame de Staël.—Ideas:* MM. de Balzac (*Eugénie Grandet, Le Père Goriot, Le Médecin de Campagne*), Emile Souvestre (*Le Mât de Cocagne, Riche et Pauvre, L'Homme et l'Argent*), Madame Georges Sand (*Lélia, Valentine, Consuelo, François le Champi*), Sainte-Beuve (*Volupté*).

(c) *Humorists:*—Xavier de Maistre (*Voyage autour de ma Chambre*), Topffer (*Nouvelles Genevoises*), Alphonse Karr (*Sous les Tilleuls, Fort en Thème, Fa Dièze*), Edmond About (*Le Roi des Montagnes, Les Mariages de Paris*).

(d) *Independent Group:*—Madame de Duras (*Ourika*), MM. Fiévée (*La Dot de Suzette*), Charles Nodier (*Jean Sbogar, Thérèse Aubert, Inès de las Sierras*), Delécluze (*Mademoiselle de Liron*), Alfred de Musset (*Nouvelles*), Saintine (*Picciola*), Madame Charles Reybaud (*Le Cadet de Colobrières, Mademoiselle de Malepeire*), M. Jules Sandeau.

HISTORY AND BIOGRAPHY:—

1. *Picturesque or Descriptive School:*—MM. de Ségur (*Histoire de Napoléon et de la Grande Armée*), De Barante (*Histoire des Ducs de Bourgogne*), Augustin Thierry, Amédée Thierry, Thiers, Michelet (*Histoire de France*).

2. *Philosophic School:*—MM. Guizot (*Histoire de la Civilisation*), Mignet (*Histoire de la Révolution*), Louis Blanc (*Histoire de la Révolution*), De Tocqueville, De Vielcastel, Duvergier de Hauranne (*Histoire de la Restauration*), Edgar Quinet (*La Révolution*), Henri Martin (*Histoire de France*).

3. *Biographies and Memoirs:*—M. Sainte-Beuve (*Port Royal*); Memoirs of Madame De Laroche Jaquelin, the Duchess d'Abrantès, etc.

A great impulse is given to historical studies. MM. Petitot and Monmerqué publish their collection of French Memoirs. M. Michaud brings out the *Biographie Universelle*. King Louis-Philippe's government orders the publication of a series of documents on the history of France.

A LIST OF THE

PRINCIPAL CHRONICLES AND MEMOIRS

ON THE

HISTORY OF FRANCE,

FROM THE DAYS OF VILLEHARDOUIN TO THE PRESENT TIME.

N.B.—The numbers thus enclosed [ ] give the extreme dates of the epoch over which the Memoirs extend; those enclosed thus ( ) represent the birth and death of the chronicler.

(1160—1213) Villehardouin (Geoffroy de), *De la conqueste de Constantinoble* [1198—1207]. "Son récit a de la simplicité et de la franchise."

(1224—1318) Joinville (Jean, Sire de), *Histoire de Saint-Louis* [1215—1270]. "Naïveté gracieuse et piquante."

(1320—1380) Guesclin (Bertrand du). Under his name various memoirs were composed during the fourteenth century which are not only interesting, but tolerably impartial.

(1337—1410) Froissart (Jean), *Chroniques* [1322—1400]. "N'a pas d'autre passion que celle de voir et de narrer."

(14th cent.) Cavelier (Robert), *Chronique de Bertrand du Guesclin.* In monorhyme stanzas.

(1363—1433) Pisan (Christine de), *Le Livre des fais et bonnes meurs du saige roi Charles V.* [1337—1380]. An authentic and touching narrative.

(1368—1421) Boucicault (Jean, dit le Maingre), *Le Livre des faits* [1368—1421]. A brilliant description of Boucicault's deeds, but very meagre from the political point of view.

(? 1390—1453) Monstrelet (Enguerrand de), *Chronique* [1400—1444]. Valuable especially for the original documents it gives.

(? —1433) Fénin (Pierre de), *Mémoires* [1407—1422]. Full of details about court affairs—a Burgundian—rather partial.

(? —1484) Cousinot (Guillaume), *Chronique de la Pucelle* [1422—1429]. Written in an interesting manner.

(? ?) Cochon (Pierre), *Chronique Normande* [1181—1430]. The author was a violent partisan of the Armagnac side.

(1420—1507) Molinet (Jean), *Chronique des ducs de Bourgogne* [1461—1469].—*Chronique métrique, avec celle de Châtelain* (George 1404—1475). A very interesting chronicle.

(1466—1527) Anton (Jean d'), *Chronique* [1499—1508]. On the reign of Louis XII.

(1426—1502) La Marche (Olivier de), *Mémoires* [1435—1492]. "Précieux pour l'histoire du temps."

(? 1420—1469) Duclercq (Jacques), *Mémoires* [144—1467]. Interesting details on the Duke of Burgundy.

(1445—1509) Commines (Philippe de), *Mémoires* [1464—1496]. The most valuable work we have on that epoch. The facts are too often estimated merely according to their results.

(? ?) Troyes (Jean de), *Chroniques de Louis XI.* Known by the name of "*Chronique scandaleuse.*"

(? ?) Villeneuve (Guillaume de), *Mémoires* [1494—1496]. Almost the only authentic account we have on the expedition of Charles VIII. into Italy.

(1476—1550) Bouchet (Jean), *Le panégyrique du chevalier sans reproche* (*Louis de la Trémouille*).

(? —1470) Chartier (Jean), *Chronique de Charles VII., roi de France* [1422—1461]. Heavy, dull, and badly written.

(1476—1524) Bayard (Pierre du Terrail, Seigneur de), *Histoire du Chevalier Bayard, composée par "le loyal serviteur"* (G. Champier).

(? —1559) Bellay (Martin du), *Mémoires.* Books 5–7 comprise fragments of the *Ogdoads* of Guillaume du Bellay (1491—1543).

(? 1190—1536) Fleurange (Robert III. de la Mark, Seigneur de), *Mémoires* [1419—1521].

(1476—1531) Savoie (Louise de), *Journal.* "Faits historiques assez curieux; détails domestiques intéressants."

(1502—1577) Monluc (Blaise de), *Commentaires* [1521—1572]. "Incomparable pour la description des batailles et pour les harangues militaires."

(1509—1573) Tavannes (Gaspar de Saulx, Sieur de), *Mémoires* [1530—1573]. Written by his son.

(1509—1571) **Vieilleville (François de Scépeaux, Sieur de), *Mémoires*.** Written by his secretary Vincent Carloix.
(? —1518) **Villars (François de Boyvin, Baron du), *Mémoires* [1550—1561].**
(? —1582) **Rabutin (François de), *Commentaires des dernières guerres*** (the wars under Henry II.).
(? —1589) **Salignac (Bernard de).** Has written a lucid account of the siege of Metz [1552].
(1517—1572) **Coligny (Gaspard de), *Discours, etc.*** on the siege of St. Quentin [1557].
(? 1527—1614) **Chartre (Claude de la), and Rochechouart (Guillaume de).** On the battle of Renty [1554].
(1520—1592) **Castelnau-Mauvissiere (Michel de), *Mémoires* [1559—1570].** Extremely valuable.
(1536—1613) **Mergey (Jean de).** His autobiography contains curious anecdotes related with much simplicity and *naïveté*.
(1531—1591) **Lanoue (François de), *Mémoires* [1562—1570].** "Haute impartialité; style vif et coloré."
flourished 1558 **Gamon (Achille), *Mémoires sur les guerres civiles du Haut-Vivarais* [155—156].** Impartial.
(? 1518—1599) **Philippi (Jean), *Mémoires* [1560—1590].** Written with too much precipitation.
(1555—1623) **Bouillon (Henri de la Tour d'Auvergne, Duc de), *Mémoires* [1555—1586].** Interesting.
(1563—1633) **Tavannes (Guillaume de), *Mémoires historiques* [1560—1596].**
(1528—1599) **Chiverny (Philippe Hurault, Comte de), *Mémoires d'état sous les rois Henri III. et Henri IV.* [1567—1599].** An invaluable statement of all the political transactions carried on for the defence of the throne.
(1579—1600) **Pont-le-Voy (Philippe Hurault, Abbé de), *Mémoires* [1599—1600].** "Style lourd et prolixe, mais naïf."
(1553—1615) **Valois (Marguerite de), *Mémoires* [1555—1582].** "S'est peinte en buste d'une plume légère."
(1530—1579) **Choisnin de Châtellerault (Jean), *Discours au vrai, etc.*** On the election of the Duke d Anjou to the crown of Poland [1573].
(1548—1590) **Merle (Matthieu), *Mémoires* [1574—1580].** His memoirs are the plain narrative of a brave party-chief.
(1525—1610) **Palma-Cayet (Pierre Victor), *Chronologie Novennaire* [1589—1598].** "Modèle de science et d'analyse."—***Chronologie Septennaire* [1598—1604].** "Fort intérieure."
(? ?) **Saint-Auban (Jacques Pape, Sieur de), *Mémoires* [1572—1587].** "Détails intéressants sur la Saint-Barthélemy et sur diverses entreprises militaires."
(1542—1617) **Villeroy (Charles de Neufville, Sieur de), *Mémoires d'état* [1567—1621].** A perfect school for diplomatists.
(1573—1650) **Angoulême (Charles de Valois, Duc d').** His autobiography contains an interesting and impartial appreciation of Henry IV.
(1540—1611) **Estoile (Pierre de l'), *Régistres journaux des règnes de Henri III. et Henri IV.*** The work of an honest and conscientious man, remarkably free from party-spirit.
(? —1619) **Gillot (Jean).** An account of the transactions connected with the regency of Marie de Medici.
(1551—1607) **Groulart (Claude), *Mémoires ou voyages faits en cour* [1588—1606].**
(1510—1580) **Marillac (Charles de).** His memoirs may be considered as the complement of those of Villeroy.
(1540—1614) **Brantôme (Pierre de Bourdeille, Sieur de), *Vies des grands capitaines, dames illustres, etc.*** A writer who combines *naïveté* with true Gascon vanity, and also with gross licentiousness.
(16th cent.) **Haton (Claude), *Mémoires* [1533—1582].** They refer chiefly to the state of Champagne and Brie, and are described as "*La version populaire de l'histoire des luttes du seizième siècle.*"
(1553—1641) **Sully (Maximilien de Béthune, Duc de), *Les economies royales* [1570—1628].** The style is obscure and diffuse, but the details given can always be relied upon.
(1549—1623) **Plessis-Marly (Philippe de Mornay, Sieur du), *Mémoires* [1571—1623].** Interesting for the history of the French Reformation.
(1540—1622) **Jeannin (Le Président), *Négociations*.** "Livre très estimé des diplomates."
(1550—1630) **Aubigné (Théodore Agrippa d'), *Mémoires* [1551—1562].** Published originally under the title of "***Histoire secrète.***"
(1583—1670) **Pontis (Louis de).** "Conte la vie et le temps de Louis XIII. avec naïveté et bonsens" (Madame de Sévigné).
(1573—1670) **Estrées (Annibal, Maréchal Duc d'), *Mémoires de la régence de Marie de Médicis*.**
(1569—1621) **Pontchartrain (Paul Phélyppeaux, Seigneur de), *Mémoires concernant les affaires de France sous le règne de Marie de Médicis*.**
(17th cent.) **Beauvais-Nangis (Marquis de), *Mémoires*.** Relates with impartiality the history of Richelieu's administration.
(1558—1652) **La Force (Jacques Nompar de Caumont, Duc de), *Mémoires et correspondance* [1572—1640].** "Renseignements précieux sur des points particuliers: décrit l'état de la ligue au midi de la France."
(1579—1638) **Rohan (Henri, Duc de) *Mémoires sur les guerres des réformés* [1610—1629]; *Mémoires sur la guerre de la Valteline*.**
(1579—1646) **Bassompierre (François, Maréchal de), *Mémoires* [1598—1631].** "Détails précieux sur les hommes et les événements de l'époque."
(1608—1660) **Orléans (Gaston, Duc d'), *Mémoires* [1608—1635].** "Offrent plusieurs particularités curieuses, et portent sur tout un grand caractère de vérité" (Petitot).
(1589—1674) **Arnauld d'Andilly (Robert), *Mémoires sur sa vie*.** "Il raconte, mais il abrège" (Sainte-Beuve).
(? 1608—1663) **Montrésor (Claude Bourdeilles, Comte de), *Mémoires*.** They are written with sincerity.
(1613—1663) **Campion (Henri de), *Mémoires* [1616—1660].** Essentially honest.
(? 1612—1673) **Chouppes (Aymar, Marquis de), *Mémoires*.** Interesting.
(1619—1684) **Navailles (Philippe de Montault de Bénac, Duc de), *Mémoires* [1630—1682].** Very sober and reserved in their appreciation of men and things.
(1621—1689) **Motteville (Françoise Berthauld, Dame de).** Her memoirs on Anne of Austria [1611—1666] are sincere, written in an agreeable manner, but somewhat too diffuse.
(1619—1692) **Tallemant des Réaux (Gédéon), *Historiettes*.** One of the wittiest of memoir writers. The stories he tells us are amusing, but too often of a *scabreux* character.
(1625—1678) **Gramont (Antoine, Maréchal Duc de), *Mémoires* [1630—1677].** "Narration vive et animée; a une certaine couleur Gasconne."
(1613— ?) **La Guette (Catherine Meurdrac, Dame de), *Mémoires* [1613—1672].** Interesting for the history of the Fronde.
(1618—1693) **Bussy (Roger de Rabutin, Comte de), *Mémoires* [1634—1666].** An excellent writer, but a man of no dignity of character.
(1616—1698) **Arnauld (Antoine), *Mémoires contenant quelques anecdotes sur la cour de France* [1634—1655].** "Agréable" (Ste.-Beuve).
(1610—1675) **Mouigiat (François de Paul de Clermont, Marquis de), *Mémoires* [1635—1660].** "Ses mémoires offrent des renseignements précieux."
(1594—1666) **Brienne (Henri Auguste de Loménie, Comte de), *Mémoires sur les règnes de Louis XIII. et Louis XIV.*** "Précieux par leur exactitude."

(1595—1652) Talon (Omer), *Mémoires.* One of the most distinguished French lawyers of the age.

(1613—1680) La Rochefoucauld (François, Duc de). "Ses mémoires (sur la régence d'Anne d'Autriche) expliquent pour une bonne part ses maximes" (Vinet).

(1614—1679) Retz (Jean François Paul de Gondi, Cardinal de), *Mémoires* [1628—1655]. "Incomparable dans ses portraits, qui sont moins des figures que des caractères" (Géruzez).

(? ?) Joly (Guy). "Ses mémoires [1648—1665] sont la contrepartie de ceux du Cardinal de Retz."

(1625—1707) Nemours (Marie d'Orléans, Duchesse de). "Mémoires piquants, spirituels, mais un peu secs" (St.-Beuve).

(? —1671) Lenet (Pierre), *Mémoires sur les guerres civiles des années 1649 et suivantes.* "Portent le cachet de la franchise."

(1603—1680) La Porte (Pierre de), *Mémoires* [1624—1666]. "Intéressants plutôt pour la connaissance de l'intérieur de la cour que pour les faits historiques" (Petitot).

(1620—1683) Tavannes (Jacques de Saulx, Comte de), *Mémoires* [1650—1652]. (?—?) Balthazar, *Histoire de la guerre de Guyenne* [1651—1653]. These memoirs, which complete one another show what influence the Fronde movement had over the government of Louis XIV.

(1630—1708) Cosnac (Daniel de), *Mémoires.* The autobiography of a clever man mixed up with all the intrigues of the court of Versailles.

(1627—1693) Montpensier (Anne Marie Louise d'Orléans, Duchesse de). "Ses mémoires [1627—1688] sont très intéressants et très véridiques" (Sainte-Beuve).

(1625—1703) Gourville (Hérauld de), *Mémoires* [1642—1678]. "Gil Blas supérieur, Figaro sans mauvais goût" (Sainte-Beuve).

(1648—1711) Feuquières (Antoine de Pas, Marquis de), *Mémoires sur la guerre.* Voltaire made considerable use of them whilst writing his *Siècle de Louis XIV.*

(1656—1733) Forbin (Claude, Comte de), *Mémoires.* Were compiled by Reboulet from Forbin's notes.

(1650—1725) Tessé (René de Froulay, Comte de), *Mémoires et lettres* [1698—1708]. "Intéressants sur les affaires d'Italie et d'Espagne."

(1618—1699) Pomponne (Simon Arnauld, Marquis de), *Mémoires* [1666-68]. Contain a large number of details which are to be found nowhere else on Pomponne's mission to Sweden.

(1617—1686) Coligny-Saligny (Jean, Comte de). His memoirs are very hostile to the Prince de Condé, of whom he thought he had reasons to complain.

(1655—1733) Le Gendre (Louis), *Mémoires.* Interesting to read; on the life of the notorious Archbishop of Paris, Harlay de Champvallon.

(1644—1724) Choisy (François-Timoléon de), *Mémoires pour servir à l'histoire de Louis XIV.* "Très vifs, très amusants, et . . . très fidèles quant à l'esprit et au ton des choses et des gens qu'il y représente" (Sainte-Beuve).

(1638—1720) Dangeau (Philippe de Courcillon, Marquis de), *Journal de la cour de Louis XIV.* [1681—1715]. Extremely valuable, but tedious.

(1673—1729) Caylus (Marguerite de Villette-Murçay, Marquise de), *Souvenirs.* "Ne lui demandez qu'une suite rapide de portraits et d'esquisses; elle y excelle." (Sainte-Beuve).

(1675—1755) Saint-Simon (Louis de Rouvrey, Duc de), *Mémoires* [1642—1723]. "Écrit *à la diable* pour l'immortalité" (Châteaubriand).

(1704—1772) Duclos (Charles Pineau), *Mémoires secrets des règnes de Louis XIV. et de Louis XV.* "Renferment des renseignements précieux."

(1673—1736) Duguay-Trouin (René), *Mémoires* [1689—1712]. "Très fautif."

(1665—1737) Marais (Mathieu), *Journal et Mémoires.* "Il est proprement un magasin à renseignements" (Sainte-Beuve).

(1684—1750) Staal (Madame Cordier de Launay, Baronne de), *Mémoires.* "Forment une des plus agréables lectures par les détails et par la manière dont ils sont écrits" (Vinet).

(1689—1771) Barbier (Edmond Jean François), *Journal historique et anecdotique du règne de Louis XV.* [1718—1762]. Full of interesting details on the history of the Paris Parliament, and on French society in general.

(1670—1734) Berwick (James Fitz-James, Duc de), *Mémoires.* Published by the Duke's grandson.

(1694—1757) Argenson (René-Louis, Marquis d'), *Mémoires et Journal* [1717—1757]. "Son bon sens est raboteux, mais robuste. Il choque, mais il instruit." (Sainte-Beuve).

(1695—1758) Luynes (Charles Philippe, Duc de), *Mémoires* [1735—1758]. "Se distinguent par l'impartialité autant que par l'exactitude."

(?1720— ?) Hausset (N . . . ., Dame du), *Mémoires.* "Écrits avec une sorte de naïveté et d'ingénuité qui s'est conservée assez honnête dans le voisinage du vice." (Sainte-Beuve).

(1753—1830) Ségur (Louis-Philippe, Comte de), *Mémoires, ou souvenirs et anecdotes.* Full of interest.

(1722—1791) Bésenval (Pierre-Victor, Baron de), *Mémoires.* "Raillerie, persiflage; la manie de se moquer de tout" (Sainte-Beuve).

(1739—1823) Dumouriez (Charles François), *Vie et ouvrages du Général Dumouriez.*

(1725—1793) Penthièvre (Louis Marie Joseph de Bourbon, Duc de), *Mémoires.* "Exacts."

(1753—1793) Pétion (Jérôme), *Mémoires.*

(1744—1818) Bertrand-Molleville (Antoine François, Marquis de), *Mémoires particuliers pour servir à la fin du règne de Louis XVI.* Written with strong partiality on the royalist side.

(1759—1809) Cléry (Jean Baptiste), *Journal de ce qui s'est passé à la tour du Temple pendant la captivité de Louis XVI.* A simple and touching narrative.

(1752—1822) Campan (Henriette Genest, Dame), *Mémoires sur la vie privée de Marie Antoinette.* "Écrits d'un style clair, naturel et élégant."

(1757—1834) La Fayette (Gilbert-Motier, Marquis de), *Mémoires et correspondance.* Written with taste and with a great desire to be thoroughly unprejudiced.

(1739—1800) Bouillé (François Claude Amour, Marquis de), *Mémoires sur la Révolution.*

(1749—1800) Mallet du Pan (Jacques), *Mémoires et correspondance.* "Doit être placé au premier rang des observateurs et des juges les plus éclairés du dernier siècle." (Sainte-Beuve).

(1772—1857) La Rochejaquelin (Marie Louise Victoire de Donnissan, Marquise de), *Mémoires.* The epic of the Vendean campaign.

(1746—1830) Genlis (Félicité Stéphanie Ducrest de St.-Aubin, Comtesse de). "Ses mémoires, quoique diffus, offrent des détails curieux."

(1769—1834) Bourienne (Fauvelet de). His memoirs are interesting, but disfigured by partiality.

(1754—1793) Roland (Manon Philipon, Dame), *Mémoires et correspondance.* Very one-sided; written with extraordinary freshness of style.

(1766—1837) Staël-Holstein (Anne-Louise-Germaine Necker, Baronne de), *Considérations sur la Révolution Française.—Dix ans d'exil.* "Désavoue les excès, avoue le principe de la révolution."

(1784—1838) Abrantès (Laure Permon, Duchesse d'), *Mémoires—Histoire des salons de Paris.* "Style facile, exposition amusante, anecdotes curieuses, portraits piquants."

(1769—1821) Napoléon Bonaparte, *Mémoires* (published par Montholon, Gourgaud, Bertrand). "Style simple et nu" (Sainte-Beuve).

(1762—1841) Miot de Mélito (André François, Comte). "Ses mémoires sont du plus haut mérite; on y voit partout l'honnête homme et une haute intelligence."

(1768—1848) Châteaubriand (François-Auguste, Vicomte de), *Mémoires d'outre-tombe.* "Pleins de génie et de passion" (de Loménie).

(1761—1835) Beugnot (Jean Claude, Comte), *Mémoires.* "Sa plume, au milieu de quelques défauts, a des qualités rares et des traits ineffaçables." (Sainte-Beuve).

(1740—1814) Malouet (Victor, Baron). His memoirs are well written, and the portraits he gives of some of the revolutionary leaders are capitally drawn.

(1783—1865) Dupin (André Marie Jean Jacques), *Mémoires.* Interesting as giving the history of the modern French bar in connection with political events.

(1774—1852) Marmont (Augustin Frédéric Louis Viesse de), Duc de Raguse. *Mémoires.* "Donnent une idée peu favorable de son caractère."

(1731—1813) Georgel (Jean François), *Mémoires* [1760—1806]. "Intéressants."

(1774—1833) Savary (René), Duc de Rovigo. *Mémoires.* "Sont au nombre des sources les plus importantes."

(1766—1834) Arnault (Antoine Vincent), *Souvenirs d'un sexagénaire.*

(1753—1837) Dumas (Mathieu), *Souvenirs—Précis des événements militaires* [1799—1807]. "Ouvrage capital."

(1766—1847) Grouchy (Emmanuel, Marquis de), *Fragments historiques.* Endeavours chiefly to justify his conduct at Waterloo.

(1758—1817) Masséna (André, Duc de Rivoli), *Mémoires.*

(1781—1824) Beauharnais (Eugène), *Mémoires et correspondance.*

(1768—1844) Bonaparte (Joseph), *Mémoires et correspondance.* "Jettent un grand jour sur l'histoire de l'Empire."

(1757—1819) Hue (François), *Dernières années de Louis XVI.*

(1756—1845) Vaublanc (Viénot, Comte de), *Mémoires sur la Révolution.*

(1735—1814) Ligne (Charles Joseph, Prince de), *Journal des guerres.*

(1727—1819) Morellet (André), *Mémoires.*

(1764—1830) Gouvion Saint-Cyr (Laurent), *Mémoires—Journaux.*

(1765—1854) Thibaudeau (Antoine), *Mémoires sur la convention, le directoire et le consulat.*

(1747—1793) Lauzun (Armand Louis de, Duc de Biron), *Mémoires.* Very scandalous; have been disowned by the family.

(1755—1830) Lévis (Gaston, Duc de), *Souvenirs et portraits.*

(1779—1869) Jomini (Antoine Henri), *Mémoires.*

(? —1805) Augeard (Joseph Marie), *Mémoires secrets* [1760—1800].

(1784—1867) Fézensac (Raymond Emery Philippe Joseph de Montesquiou, Duc de), *Mémoires—Journal—Souvenirs.*

(1780—1873) Ségur (Philippe Paul, Comte de), *Histoire et Mémoires.* Invaluable for the history of the Consulate and the Empire.

A Synoptical Table of the principal CHANSONS DE GESTE *composed in the Langue d'Oïl.*

(N.B.—ALL THE *CHANSONS* MARKED * HAVE BEEN PRINTED.)

		Date of the Composition.	*Author.*	*Subjects.*
1. GESTE DU ROI. (*The Knights of Northern France.*)	*Berthe aux grands pieds.**	About 1275.	Adenès le Roi.	Contains the legendary history of the mother of Charlemagne.
	Jean de Lanson.	13th century.	Unknown.	Describe Charlemagne's struggles with his rebellious vassals.
	*Huon de Bordeaux.**	Between 1180 and 1200.	—	
	Acquin.	End of the 12th century.	—	Charlemagne's expedition in Brittany.
	Aspremont.	13th century.	—	Roland's first exploits in Italy.
	*Fierabras.**	14th century.	—	
	*Otinel.**	Middle of the 13th century.	—	
	*Guy de Bourgogne.**	Beginning of the 13th cent.	—	
	*Prise de Pampelune.**	14th century.	—	Charlemagne's wars in Spain.
	Anseïs de Carthage.	Second half of the 13th cent.	Pierre du Riés.	
	*Chanson de Roland.**	Beginning of the 12th cent.	Unknown.	
	Conquête de l'Espagne.	Compilation (14th century).	Nicholas of Padua.	
	*Gaydon.**	After 1216.	Unknown.	
	*Les Saxons.**	13th century.	Jean Bodel.	Charlemagne's war against the Saxons.
	*Macaire.**	13th century.	Unknown.	Legendary history of Charlemagne's supposed wife Blanchefleur.
2. GESTE DE DOON DE MAYENCE. (*The Knights of Germany.*)	*Doon de Mayence.**	13th century.	Unknown.	Charlemagne and the Germans.
	*Gaufrey.**	End of the 13th century.	—	Charlemagne's wars against the Saracens.
	Les enfances Ogier.	13th century.	Adenès le Roi.	Charlemagne and the Lombards.
	La chevalerie Ogier.	12th century.	Raimbert de Paris. (?)	
	*Aye d'Avignon.**	13th century.	Unknown.	Charlemagne and the Saracens.
	Guy de Nanteuil.	13th and 14th centuries.	—	
	*Parise la Duchesse.**	13th century.	—	The origins of this poem are Germanic.
	Maugis d'Aigremont.	14th century.	—	Reminiscences of the wars against the Saracens.
	Vivier l'amachour de Monbranc.	13th and 14th centuries.	—	Charlemagne's wars against his rebellious vassals.
	Les Quatre fils Aimon.	13th century.	—	
3. GESTE DE GUILLAUME AU CORT NEZ. (*The Knights of Aquitaine.*)	*Garin de Monglane.*	13th century.	—	Struggles between the North and South of France.
	*Girart de Viane.**	13th century.	Bertrand de Bar-sur-Aube. (?)	Wars of the feudal lords against the king.
	Aimeri de Narbonne.	First half of the 13th cent.	Unknown.	Wars against the Saracens.
	Les enfances Guillaume.	13th century.	—	
	*Le couronnement Looys.**	13th century.	—	The last days of Charlemagne—partly imitated from Eginhard.
	*Le Charroi de Nismes.**	13th century.	—	Wars against the Saracens.
	*La prise d'Orange.**	13th century.	—	Supposed siege of Orange by the Saracens.
	Beuve de Comarchis.	Second half of the 13th cent.	Adenès le Roi.	
	Guibert d'Andernas.	13th century.	Unknown.	
	Mort d'Aimeri de Narbonne.	End of the 13th century.	—	
	Enfances Vivien.	12th century.	—	Expeditions of Charlemagne and of Louis I. into Spain.
	Chevalerie Vivien.	13th century.	—	The defence of Villedaigne-sur-l'Orbieux by Guillaume, Duke of Aquitaine, against the Saracens (793).
	*Aliscamps.**	13th century.	—	
	Rainoart.	End of the 12th century.	—	Wars against the Saracens.
	*Moniage Guillaume.**	13th century.	—	Legendary account of the last years of the Duke d'Aquitaine.
	Bataille Loquifer.	13th century.	Jendeus de Brie. (?)	Wars against the Saracens.
	Moniage Rainoart.	13th century.	Unknown.	Comic imitation of the "Moniage Guillaume."
	Renier.	13th century.	—	Has neither historical nor literary merit.
	*Foulque de Candie.**	13th century.	Herbert le Duc.	Wars in Spain.

Provinces	Dialect	Epoch / Region	Principal Texts	Principal Characteristics
Provinces of Maine...... " Brittany...... " Perche...... " Anjou...... " Poitou......	Normandy.	1. *Epoch of purity* (till 1200).	Laws of William the Conqueror.	1. *i* rejected from most of the syllables in *ie*, *ier*, *ai*, *air*, which are written either without *i*, as *derrere* (for *derrière*), or by putting the *i* in the preceding syllable, as *primer* (for *premier*). 2. Most of the syllables now in *o*, *ou*, *u*, *eu*, *oi*, *on*, *or*, and even a few in *a*, were spelt *u*. 3. The only diphthongs used were *ei*, *ui* (*ue*); at a later period *ou*. 4. Nasal sounds became weak, and often disappeared entirely. 5. Contractions fewer than in the other dialects. 6. Final *t* replaced by *d*. 7. Favourite vowels: (α) *e*, (β) *ei*, (γ) *u*, (δ) *ui*.
		2. *Epoch of modification*, through the Bourguignon element (1200–1250).	Roman de Rou (13th century). Voyage de Charlemagne à Jérusalem (1230–1250).	
		3. *Epoch of modification*. Picard element (1250–1320).	The acts and documents in Rymer's *Fœdera*. The poems of Marie de France (1260).	
Provinces of Artois...... " Flanders...... " Lower Maine " Champagne.. " Lorraine...... " Hainaut...... " Namur...... " Liége...... " South Brabant	Picardy.		Roman de Mahomet (13th century). Roman de la Violette ou de Gérars de Nevers (1234). Lai d'Ignaurès (13th century).	1. *Ch* always substituted for *s* or *c* weak: thus *tchi* (for *ici*). *k* or *g* generally put instead of *ch*: thus *kachier* (for *chasser*). 2. Fondness for *c*, *ch*, and final *g*. 3. *ou* substituted for *o* and *eu*; *eu* for *ou*; *oi* for *ei*. 4. *e* often put instead of *ai*, and *vice versâ*. 5. *r* often replaced by *s*. 6. *s* with the sound *ze* often replaced by *ss*, and *ss* by *s*. 7. *i* prefixed to *e*, or substituted for it. 8. *g* used instead of *j*. 9. Where the Bourguignon used *o* and *a*, the vowel *e* was substituted. 10. Favourite vowels: (α) *oi*, *ai*, *ie*; (β) *oi*, *ai*; (γ) *o*, *ou*, *eu*; (δ) *i*, *oi*, *oui*.
Provinces of Nivernais ... " Berry...... " Orléanais.... " Touraine.... " Lower Bourbonnais..... " Anjou...... " Ile de France " Champagne (*part*)...... " Lorraine (*part*) " Franche-Comté " Vaud...... " Neufchâtel... " Berne......	Burgundy.	(Burgundy proper.)	Sermons de Saint Bernard (about 1150). Roman de Gérars de Viane (13th century).	1. *i* added to almost all the initial, medial, or final syllables in *a* or *é*. 2. *o* pure of the French language (except when followed by *r*) was written *oi*. 3. *g* sometimes served to mark the nasal *n*. 4. *ç* and *s* soft replaced by *z*. 5. In some localities *l* soft was expressed by *ll*, *lz*, or *lg*. 6. Favourite vowels: (α) *oi*, *ai*, *ei*, *ie*; (β) *oi*, *ei*, *ai*; (γ) *o*; (δ) *ui*, *oi*, *eui*, *oui*.
		(Paris idiom.)	Maurice de Sully (Sermons), died in 1106. Partonopeus de Blois (13th century). Thibaut de Marly (13th century).	
		(Champagne.)	Roman de la Rose (13th century). Roman du Renart (11th century).	

A CHRONOLOGICAL LIST

OF THE

PRINCIPAL FRENCH NEWSPAPERS,

PUBLISHED DURING THE REVOLUTION AND THE FIRST EMPIRE.

N.B.—Re., Ro., and Ro.L. stand respectively for Republican, Royalist, and Royalist-Liberal.

Year.	*Name of Newspaper.*	*Ceased to appear.*		*Name of Editor.*
1772	Le Mercure de France	Dec. 10, 1792.	*Ro.L.*	Mallet du Pan, Pancoucke.
1777	Le Journal de Paris	June 1827.	*Ro.L.*	Garat, André Chénier, etc.
1789	Le Hérant de la Nation	June 30, 1789.	*Ro.*	Mangourit.
,,	La Gazette Universelle	Aug. 10, 1789.	*Ro.L.*	Cerisier.
,,	La Gazette Nationale ou Le Moniteur Universel	*still continued.*	*Ro.L.*	Pancoucke, La Harpe, Lacretelle, Andrieux, Garat, Ginguené, etc.
,, ,,	Le Journal général de la Cour et de la Ville (Le petit Gautier)	Aug. 10, 1792.	*Ro.L.*	Brune, Gautier.
,,	Les Actes des Apôtres	1791.	*Ro.*	Pelletier, Champcenetz, Rivarol, etc.
,,	La Chronique de Paris	Aug. 25, 1793.	*Re.*	Millin, Noël, Condorcet, etc.
,,	L'Ami du Peuple	Sept. 21, 1792.	*Re.*	Marat.
,,	Les Annales patriotiques et littéraires	June 4,	*Re.*	Mercier, Carra.
,,	L'Assemblée Nationale	Sept. 30, 1791.	*Ro.L.*	Beaulieu.
,,	Le Courrier de Brabant	Sept. 9, 1790.	*Re.*	Camille Desmoulins.
,,	Le Courrier de Provence	Sept. 30, 1791.	*Ro.L.*	Mirabeau.
,,	La Gazette de Paris	Aug. 9, 1792.	*Ro.*	Durozoy.
,,	Le Journal de Versailles	Dec. 31, 1790.	*Re.*	Regnault de St. Jean d'Angély.
,,	Le Journal des Débats et Decrets	Feb. 1800.	*Re.*	Barrère, Louvet, etc.
,,	L'Orateur du Peuple	1792.	*Re.*	Fréron, Marat, Labenette.
,,	Le Patriote français	1793.	*Re.*	Brissot de Warville.
,,	Les Révolutions de France et de Brabant	1791.	*Re.*	Camille Desmoulins.
,,	Les Révolutions de Paris	1794.	*Re.*	Prudhomme, Loustalot.
1790	L'Ami du Roi, des Français, etc.	Aug. 10, 1792.	*Ro.*	Royon, Montjoye, Crapart.
,,	La Bouche de Fer	1791.	*Re.*	Fauchet, Bonneville, Anacharsis Clootz.
,,	Grande Joie, Grande Colère du Père Duchêne	Feb. 1794.	*Re.*	Hébert.
,, ,,	Journal de la Société des Amis de la Constitution monarchique	June 18, 1791.	*Ro.L.*	Fontanes, Clermont Tonnerre.
,,	Journal de Louis XVI. et de son Peuple	Aug. 10, 1792.	*Ro.*	*Authors unknown.*
,,	Journal des Amis de la Constitution	Sept. 20, 1791.	*Re.*	Choderlos de Laclos.
,,	Journal du Soir	Sept. 30, 1811.	*Re.*	Feuillant, Chaigneau.
,,	Le Lendemain	June 19, 1791.	*Ro.L.*	Beffroy de Reigny (*Le Cousin Jacques*).
1791	La Chronique du Mois	July 1793.	*Re.*	Clavière, Condorcet, Dussault, etc.
,,	La Feuille du Jour	Aug. 10, 1792.	*Ro.*	Parisot.
,,	Journal des Débats des Amis de la Constitution	Dec. 14, 1796.	*Re.*	Defiers.
,,	Le Logographe	Aug. 17, 1792.	*Re.*	Lehodey.
,,	Le Thermomètre du Jour	Aug. 25, 1793.	*Re.*	Dulaure, etc.
1792	Annales de la République	1800.	*Re.*	*Authors unknown.*
,,	Bulletin de l'Assemblée Législative	Dec. 29, 1795.	*Re.*	*Authors unknown.*
,,	Bulletin de Minuit	Aug. 12, 1792.	*Ro.*	*Authors unknown.*
,,	Bulletin des Amis de la Vérité	April 30, 1795.	*Re.*	*Authors unknown.*
,,	Le Défenseur de la Constitution	Aug. 10, 1792.	*Re.*	Maximilien Robespierre.
,,	Journal de France	May 19, 1795.	*Re.*	Feuillant, Chaigneau.
,,	Journal de la Convention	June 30, 1793.	*Re.*	*Authors unknown.*
,,	Journal prophétique	October 1793.	*Re.*	Pierre Pontard.
,,	Nouvelles Politiques	Nov. 1, 1810.	*Ro.L.*	Suard, Dupont de Nemours, Guizot, Morellet, Lacretelle, etc.
,,	Le Républicain	Sept. 14, 1800.	*Re.*	Charles Duval, etc.
,,	La Révolution de 1792	May 8, 1794.	*Re.*	*Authors unknown.*
,,	La Sentinelle	Nov. 21, 1792.	*Re.*	Tallien.
1793	Journal de la Montagne	Nov. 18, 1794.	*Re.*	Lavaux, Th. Rousseau, etc.
,,	Le Rougyff	May 24, 1794.	*Re.*	Guffroy.
1794	Bulletin de la Convention	Oct. 26, 1795.	*Re.*	*Authors unknown.*
1795	Le Messager du Soir	Sept. 4, 1797.	*Re.*	Lunier, Isidore Langlois, etc.
1796	Le Point du Jour	Oct. 4, 1798.	*Re.*	Drouet.
1797	L'Accusateur Public	1799.	*Re.*	Richer-Serisy.
,,	La Clef du Cabinet des Souverains	Dec. 30, 1804.	*Ro.L.*	Garat, Fontanes, Pommereuil, etc.
,,	Le Spectateur du Nord	Sept. 1800.	*Ro.*	Baudus, Villers, Rivarol, etc.
1798	Le Courrier de l'Égypte	June 18, 1801.	*Re.*	*Authors unknown.*
1800	Journal de l'Empire	*still continued.*	*Ro.L.*	Bertin, Fiévée, Etienne, Geoffroy.
1814	Journal des Débats (*formerly* Journal de l'Empire)	*still continued.*	*Ro.L.*	Dussault, Hoffman, De Feletz.

CONCORDANCE OF THE
FRENCH REPUBLICAN CALENDAR WITH THE GREGORIAN.

Republican Month.	An. II. 1793—1794.	An. III. 1794—1795.	An. IV. 1795—1796.	An. V. 1796—1797.	An. VI. 1797—1798.	An. VII. 1798—1799.	An. VIII. 1799—1800.	An. IX. 1800—1801.	An. X. 1801—1802.	An. XI. 1802—1803.	An. XII. 1803—1804.	An. XIII. 1804—1805.	An. XIV. 1805—1806.
First Vendémiaire . . .	Sept. 22.	Sept. 22.	Sept. 22.	Sept. 22.	Sept. 22.	Sept. 22.	Sept. 23.	Sept. 23.	Sept. 23.	Sept. 23.	Sept. 23.	Sept. 23.	Sept. 23.
First Brumaire	Oct. 22.	Oct. 22.	Oct. 22.	Oct. 22.	Oct. 22.	Oct. 22.	Oct. 23.	Oct. 23.	Oct. 23.	Oct. 23.	Oct. 23.	Oct. 23.	Oct. 23.
First Frimaire	Nov. 21.	Nov. 21.	Nov. 21.	Nov. 21.	Nov. 21.	Nov. 21.	Nov. 22.	Nov. 22.	Nov. 22.	Nov. 22.	Nov. 22.	Nov. 22.	Nov. 22.
First Nivôse.	Dec. 21.	Dec. 21.	Dec. 21.	Dec. 21.	Dec. 21.	Dec. 21.	Dec. 22	Dec. 22.	Dec. 22.	Dec. 22.	Dec. 22.	Dec. 22.	Dec. 22.
First Pluviôse	Jan. 20.	Jan. 20.	Jan. 20.	Jan. 20.	Jan. 20.	Jan. 20.	Jan. 21.	Jan. 21.	Jan. 21.	Jan. 21.	Jan. 21.	Jan. 21.	
First Ventôse	Feb. 19.	Feb. 19.	Feb. 19.	Feb 10.	Feb. 19.	Feb. 10.	Feb. 20.	Feb. 20.	Feb. 20.	Feb. 20.	Feb. 21.	Feb. 21.	
First Germinal.	Mar. 21.	Mar. 21.	Mar. 21.	Mar. 21.	Mar. 21.	Mar. 21.	Mar. 22.	Mar. 22.	Mar. 22.	Mar. 22.	Mar. 22.	Mar. 22.	
First Floréal	Apr. 20.	Apr. 20.	Apr. 20.	Apr. 20.	Apr. 20.	Apr. 20.	Apr. 21.	Apr. 21.	Apr. 21.	Apr 21.	Apr. 21.	Apr. 21.	
First Prairial	May 20.	May 20.	May 20.	May 20.	May 20.	May 20.	May 21.	May 21.	May 21.	May 21.	May 21.	May 21.	
First Messidor	June 19.	June 19.	June 19.	June 10.	June 19.	June 10.	June 20.	June 20.	June 20.	June 20.	June 20.	June 20.	
First Thermidor	July 19.	July 19.	July 19.	July 19.	July 19.	July 19.	July 20.	July 20.	July 20.	July 20.	July 21.	July 20.	
First Fructidor	Aug. 18.	Aug. 18.	Aug. 18.	Aug. 18.	Aug. 18.	Aug. 18.	Aug. 19.	Aug. 19.	Aug. 19.	Aug. 19.	Aug. 19.	Aug. 19.	
First Complementary day.	Sept. 17.	Sept. 17.	Sept. 17.	Sept. 17.	Sept. 17.	Sept. 17.	Sept. 18.	Sept. 18.	Sept. 18.	Sept. 18.	Sept. 18	Sept. 18.	

Officially decreed on the 3rd of October, 1793, *and suppressed on the*

AUTUMN.			WINTER.		
VENDEMIAIRE. 1st Month.	BRUMAIRE. 2nd Month.	FRIMAIRE. 3rd Month.	NIVÔSE. 4th Month.	PLUVIÔSE. 5th Month.	VENTÔSE. 6th Month.
First Decade.	*First Decade.*	*First Decade.*	*First Decade.*	*First Decade.*	*First Decade.*
1. Grape.	1. Apple.	1. Rampion.	1. Turf.	1. Laurel.	1. Colt's-foot.
2. Saffron.	2. Celery.	2. Turnip.	2. Pit Coal.	2. Moss.	2. Cornelian.
3. Chestnut.	3. Pear.	3. Chicory.	3. Bitumen.	3. Holly.	3. Wallflower
4. Mead. Saffron.	4. Beetroot.	4. Medlar.	4. Sulphur.	4. Snowdrop.	4. Privet.
5. *Horse.*	5. *Goose.*	5. *Pig.*	5. *Dog.*	5. *Bull.*	5. *He-goat.*
6. Balsam.	6. Heliotrope.	6. Corn Salad.	6. Lava.	6. Thyme Laurel.	6. Asarum.
7. Carrot.	7. Fig.	7. Cauliflower.	7. Veget. Earth.	7. Tinder.	7. Evergreen-buckthorn.
8. Amaranthus.	8. Scorzonera.	8. Honey.	8. Dung.	8. Mezereon.	8. Violet.
9. Parsnip.	9. Beam-tree.	9. Juniper.	9. Saltpetre.	9. Poplar.	9. Willow.
10. *Tub.*	10. *Plough.*	10. *Pickaxe.*	10. *Flail.*	10. *Quince-tree.*	10. *Spade.*
Second Decade.	*Second Decade.*	*Second Decade.*	*Second Decade.*	*Second Decade.*	*Second Decade.*
11. Potato.	11. Salsify.	11. Wax.	11. Granite	11. Hellebore.	11. Narcissus.
12. Everlastings.	12. Water-lily.	12. Horse Radish.	12. Clay.	12. Broccoli.	12. Elm.
13. Pumpkin.	13. Jer. Artichoke.	13. Cedar.	13. Slate.	13. Laurel.	13. Fumitory.
14. Mignonette.	14. Endive.	14. Pine.	14. Grit.	14. Filbert-tree.	14. Hedge mustard.
15. *Ass.*	15. *Turkey.*	15. *Roebuck.*	15. *Rabbit.*	15. *Cow.*	15. *She-goat.*
16. Jalap.	16. Chervil.	16. Furze.	16. Silex.	16. Box.	16. Spinage.
17. Water-wort.	17. Cress.	17. Cypress.	17. Chalk.	17. Lichen.	17. Arnica.
18. Saracen.	18. Leadwort.	18. Ivy.	18. Lime.	18. Yew.	18. Chickweed.
19. Sunflower.	19. Pomegranate.	19. Savin.	19. Marble.	19. Lungwort.	19. Chervil.
20. *Wine-press.*	20. *Harrow.*	20. *Mattock.*	20. *Cribble.*	20. *Pruning-knife.*	20. *String.*
Third Decade.	*Third Decade.*	*Third Decade.*	*Third Decade.*	*Third Decade.*	*Third Decade.*
21. Hemp.	21. Bacchanal.	21. Sugar Maple.	21. Plaster.	21. Thlaspi.	21. Mandragora.
22. Peach.	22. Medlar.	22. Heath.	22. Salt.	22. Tiller.	22. Parsley.
23. Turnip.	23. Madder.	23. Reed.	23. Iron.	23. Dog's grass.	23. Spoonwort.
24. Amaryllis.	24. Orange.	24. Sorrel.	24. Copper.	24. Drag.	24. Easter Daisy.
25. *Ox.*	25. *Pheasant.*	25. *Cricket.*	25. *Cat.*	25. *Hare.*	25. *Tunny.*
26. Veg. Marrow.	26. Pistachio.	26. Pine Kernel.	26. Tin.	26. Woad.	26. Dandelion.
27. Allspice.	27. Quince.	27. Cork.	27. Lead.	27. Nut-tree.	27. Sylvia.
28. Tomato.	28. Service-tree.	28. Truffle.	28. Zinc.	28. Cyclamen.	28. Maidenhair.
29. Barley.	29. Magnolia.	29. Olive.	29. Quicksilver.	29. Celandine.	29. Ash-tree.
30. *Barrel.*	30. *Garden-roller.*	30. *Shovel.*	30. *Sieve.*	30. *Sledge.*	30. *Dibble.*

REPUBLICAN CALENDAR

9th of September, 1804 (*22nd of Fructidor, Year XIII.*)

SPRING.			SUMMER		
GERMINAL. 7TH MONTH.	FLOREAL. 8TH MONTH.	PRAIRIAL. 9TH MONTH.	MESSIDOR. 10TH MONTH.	THERMIDOR. 11TH MONTH.	FRUCTIDOR. 12TH MONTH.
First Decade	*First Decade.*	*First Decade.*	*First Decade.*	*First Decade.*	*First Decade.*
1. Primrose.	1. Rose.	1. Trefoil.	1. Rye.	1. Spelt.	1. Plum.
2. Plantain.	2. Oak.	2. Asphodel.	2. Oats.	2. Mullein.	2. Millet.
3. Asparagus.	3. Fern.	3. Clover.	3. Onion.	3. Melon.	3. Lycopodium.
4. Tulip.	4. Hawthorn.	4. Angelica.	4. Veronica.	4. Tare.	4. Barley.
5. *Hen.*	5. *Nightingale.*	5. *Duck.*	5. *Mullet.*	5. *Ram.*	5. *Salmon.*
6. Strawberry-blite.	6. Columbine.	6. Balm.	6. Rosemary.	6. Shavegrass.	6. Tuberose.
7. Birch.	7. Valley Lily.	7. Mountain Lily.	7. Cucumber.	7. Mugwort.	7. Pearl Barley.
8. Jonquil.	8. Mushroom.	8. Wild Thyme.	8. Shallot.	8. Cardamom.	8. Apocynium.
9. Alder-tree.	9. Hyacinth.	9. Wheat.	9. Wormwood.	9. Blackberry.	9. Liquorice.
10. *Forcing-frame.*	10. *Rake.*	10. *Scythe.*	10. *Sickle.*	10. *Watercan.*	10. *Ladder.*
Second Decade.	*Second Decade.*	*Second Decade.*	*Second Decade.*	*Second Decade.*	*Second Decade.*
11. Periwinkle.	11. Rhubarb.	11. Strawberry.	11. Coriander.	11. Parsnip.	11. Water Melon.
12. Yoke Elm.	12. Sainfoin.	12. Betony.	12. Artichoke.	12. Water Thistle.	12. Fennel.
13. Morel.	13. Gilliflower.	13. Pea.	13. Stock.	13. Apricot.	13. Barberry.
14. Beech.	14. Ground Ivy.	14. Acacia.	14. Lavender.	14. Sweet Basil.	14. Nut.
15. *Bee.*	15. *Silkworm.*	15. *Quail.*	15. *Chamois.*	15. *Sheep.*	15. *Trout.*
16. Lettuce.	16. Comfrey.	16. Pink.	16. Gooseberry.	16. Guimauve.	16. Citron.
17. Larch.	17. Pimpernel.	17. Elder.	17. Tobacc	17. Linseed.	17. Thistle.
18. Water Hemlock	18. Goosefoot.	18. Poppy.	18. Vetch.	18. Almond.	18. Buckthorn.
19. Radish.	19. Golden casket.	19. Lime.	19. Cherry.	19. Gentian.	19. Tacca.
20. *Hive.*	20. *Hoe.*	20. *Pitchfork.*	20. *Park.*	20. *Dam.*	20. *Panier.*
Third Decade.	*Third Decade.*	*Third Decade.*	*Third Decade.*	*Third Decade.*	*Third Decade.*
21. Judas tree.	21. Thrift.	21. Barbel.	21. Mint.	21. Carline Thistle.	21. Eglantine.
22. Cos-lettuce.	22. Fritillary.	22. Camomile.	22. Cummin.	22. Caper.	22. Filbert.
23. HorseChestnut.	23. Borage.	23. Honeysuckle.	23. Bean.	23. Lentil.	23. Hop.
24. Rooket.	24. Valerian.	24. Cheese rennet.	24. Orchis.	24. Alicampagne.	24. Sorgho.
25. *Pigeon.*	25. *Carp.*	25. *Tench.*	25. *Guinea-fowl.*	25. *Otter.*	25. *Crawfish.*
26. Anemone.	26. Spindle-tree.	26. Jessamine.	26. Sage.	26. Myrtle.	26. Seville Orange.
27. Lilac.	27. Civet.	27. Vervein.	27. Garlic.	27. Colza.	27. Golden rod.
28. Heart's-ease.	28. Bugloss.	28. Thyme.	28. Vetch.	28. Lupin.	28. Maize.
29. Myrtle.	29. Mustard.	29. Peony.	29. Corn.	29. Cotton.	29. Chestnut.
30. *Pruning-knife.*	30. *Crook.*	30. *Waggon.*	30. *Challletia.*	30. *Mill.*	30. *Basket.*

Festivals commemorative of Virtue, Genius, Work, Opinion, Rewards.

A LIST

OF THE PRINCIPAL SIGNS AND ABREVIATIONS

USED IN THIS BOOK.

§ liquid *l*, *gn*, or *ll*.
* Archaism.
¶ Neologism.
‡ Idiomatic words or phrases.
† Popular or slang words or expressions.
' *s* prefixed to words beginning with an aspirated 'h.'
agric. agriculture.
Ang.-Sax. Anglo-Saxon.
Ar. Arabic.
carp. carpentry.
Celt. Celtic.
chem. chemistry.
com. commerce.
comp. composition.
D. Dutch.
E. English.
F. French.
fam. familiar.
fig. figurative.
G. German.
Geol. Geology.
Gr. Greek.
gram. grammar.
Heb. Hebrew.
iron. ironical.
I. or *It.* Italian.
L. Latin.
L.L. Low Latin.
L.G. Low German.
med. medicine.
mec. mechanics.
mus. music.
nav. navigation.
O.D. Old Dutch.
O.F. Old French.
O.G. Old German.
O.H.G. Old High German.
O.M.G. Old Middle German.
pers. persons; *Pers.* Persian (in the etymological part).
pop. popular.
Prov. Provençal.
Scand. Scandinavian.
Sp. Spanish.
surg. surgery.
techn. technology.
th. things
univ. university.

N.B.—When the adverbs are formed regularly from the adjectives then they are not given, in order to save room but the corresponding adjectives are prefixed with the sign ‖. All words spelt alike in English and French will be found in the ENGLISH-FRENCH PART only.

TABLE OF

FRENCH COINS, MEASURES, AND WEIGHTS,

REDUCED TO ENGLISH MONEY, MEASURES, AND WEIGHTS.

Francs.	Centimes.	Shillings.	Pence.
Fr.	c.	s.	d.
0	05	0	0·48
0	10	0	0·96
0	25	0	2·4
0	50	0	4·8
1	00	0	9·6
2	00	1	7·2
3	00	2	4·8
4	00	3	2·4
5	00	4	0·0
6	00	4	9·6
7	00	5	7·2
8	00	6	4·8
9	00	7	2·4
10	00	8	0·0
11	00	8	9·6
12	00	9	7·2
13	00	10	4·8
14	00	11	2·4
15	00	12	0·0
16	00	12	9·6
17	00	13	7·2
18	00	14	4·8
19	00	15	2·4
20	00	16	0·0

ITINERARY MEASURE.

Mètre (ten-millionth part of the arc of a meridian between the pole and the equator)..	3·2808992	feet.
Décamètre (10 metres)	32·808992	feet.
Kilomètre (1,000 metres)	1093·633	yards.
Myriamètre (10,000 metres)	6·2138	miles.

LONG MEASURE.

Décimètre (10th of a metre)	3·937079	inches.
Centimètre (100th of a metre)	0·393708	inch.
Millimètre (1,000th of a metre)	0·03937	inch.

SUPERFICIAL MEASURE.

Are (100 square metres)	0·098845	rood.
Hectare (10,000 square metres)	2·471143	acres.
Centiare (1 square metre)	1·196033	square yard.

MEASURE OF CAPACITY.

Litre (1 cubic decimetre) . . .	1·760773	pint.
Décalitre (10 litres)	2·2009668	gallons.
Hectolitre (100 litres)	22·009668 / 2·7512	gallons *or* bushels.
Kilolitre, mètre cube (1,000 litres)	3·426	quarters.
Décilitre (10th of a litre).	0·1760773	pint.
Centilitre (100th of a litre).	0·01760773	pint.

SOLID MEASURE.

Stère (1 cubic metre)	1·31 cubic yard *or* 35 cubic feet, 547 cubic inches.
Décastère (10 steres).	13·1 cubic yards.
Décistère (10th of a stere)	3 cubic feet, 918·7 cubic inches.

WEIGHTS.

Gramme (weight of a cubic centimetre of water in its state of maximum density or 39½ Fahrenheit or 4 degrees centigrade)	15·4325	grains troy.
Décagramme (10 grammes)	6·43	pennyweight.
Hectogramme (100 grammes)	3·527 / 3·216	oz. avoirdupois *or* oz. troy.
Kilogramme (1,000 grammes)	2·2055 / 2·6803	lb. avoirdupois *or* lb. troy.
Quintal métrique (100 kilogrammes).	220·548	lb.
Millier, tonneau de mer (1,000 kilogrammes).	19 cwt. 12 oz. 5 dwt.	
Décigramme (10th of a gramme)	1·5432	grain.
Centigramme (100th of a gramme)	0·15432	grain.
Milligramme (1,000th of a gramme)	0·015432	grain.

THERMOMETER.

0° Centigrade	Melting ice	32°	Fahrenheit.
100° do.	Boiling water	212°	do.
0° Réaumur	Melting ice	32°	do.
80° do.	Boiling water	212°	do.

DICTIONNAIRE

FRANÇAIS-ANGLAIS.

A, sm. *a vowel, the first letter of the alphabet.* ‡ *Il ne sait ni A ni B*, he does not know A from B. ‡ *Il n'a pas fait une panse d'A*, he has not even set about it. ‡ *Être marqué à l'A*, to be a man of great merit

A, third pers. sing. pres. of the v. Avoir

A, pr. to, at, in, by, from, into, with, for, according to, on, under, and, of, 's. *C'est à moi, à mon frère*, it is mine, my brother's

Abaissement, sm. (*etym.* à, baisser), lowering, letting down, fall, abasement, disgrace, humiliation, couching

Abaisser, va. (*etym.* à, baisser), to lower, to pull down, to abase, to let fall; *s'*—, vr. to fall, to shrink, to subside, to condescend

Abajoue, sf. (*etym.* à, bajoue), a cheek-pouch

Abandon, sm. (*etym.* à, bandon, *or* ban, *O. F. and Prov. permission*), forsaking, abandonment, relinquishment, sincerity, easy grace. *A l'*—, unprotected, in confusion

Abandonné, e, a. adj. forsaken, lewd

Abandonnement, sm. (*etym.* abandonner), giving up, disorder, lewdness

Abandonner, va. (*etym.* abandon), to forsake, to abandon, to resign; *s'*—, vr. to give oneself up, to give way, to trust, to be disheartened

Abasourdir, va. (*etym.* à, bas, *a prefix indicating a bad disposition, and* sourd), to stun, to deafen, to bewilder

Abatage, sm. (*etym.* abattre), lopping, felling, slaughter

Abâtardir, va. (*etym.* à, bâtard), to corrupt; *s'*—, vr. to degenerate, to decay

Abâtardissement, sm. (*etym.* abâtardir), degeneracy, decay

Abatée, sf. (*etym.* abattre), falling off to leeward

Abat-faim, sm. (*etym.* abattre, faim), large joint of meat; *plur.* des abat-faim

Abatis, sm. (*etym.* abattre), felling, things thrown down, giblets, offal

Abat-jour, sm. (*etym.* abattre, jour), skylight, shade; *plur.* des abat-jour

Abattement, sm. (*etym.* abattre), despondency, lowness of spirits, dejection

Abatteur, sm. (*etym.* abattre), —*d'ouvrage*, hard-working man, (*fig.*) a doer of great things

Abattoir, sm. (*etym.* abattre), slaughter-house

Abattre, va. (*etym.* à, battre), to beat down, to fell, to slaughter, to dishearten, to allay, to show one's cards; *s'*—, to fall, to burst, to abate, to be disheartened, (*nav.*) to heave down, to swoop down

Abat-voix, sm. (*etym.* abattre, voix), sounding-board; *plur.* des abat-voix

Abbaye, sf. (*etym. L.* abbatia, *from* abbas), abbey

Abbé, sm. (*etym. L.* abbas, *from the Syriac*, abba, *father*), abbot, priest

Abbesse, sf. (*etym. L.* abbatissa, *from* abbas), abbess

Abcès, sm. (*etym. L.* ab, cedere), abscess. *Former un* —, to gather

Abdiquer, va. (*etym. L.* abdicare), to abdicate, to resign (the crown)

Abécédaire, sm. (*etym.* A. B. C. D.), spelling-book, primer, horn-book

§**Abeille**, sf. (*etym. L.* apicula, *dimin. of the subst.* apis), bee

Abêtir, va. n. (*etym.* à, bête), to dull, to blunt; *s'*—, vr. to grow stupid

Abhorrer, va. (*etym. L.* ab, horrere), to abhor, to hate, to detest; *s'*—, vr. to hate oneself, to hate each other

Abîme, sm. (*etym. Gr.* ἄβυσσος), gulf, abyss, the deep, hell

Abîmer, va. (*etym.* abîme), to swallow up, to destroy, to spoil. *Abîmé de dettes*, over head and ears in debt. *S'*—, vr. to be swallowed up, to be lost

‡**Abject, e**, adj. (*etym. L.* abjectus, *from* abjicere, *to cast down*), abject, base

Abjurer, va. (*etym. L.* abjurare, *to swear*), to abjure, to renounce

Ablatif, sm. (*etym. L.* ab, latus, *a word indicating the action of carrying*), ablative case

Able, Ablette, sf. (*etym. L. L.* abula, *from* albula, *a small kind of fish, from* albus, *white*) whitebait, bleak, bley

Ablégat, sm. (*etym. L.* ab, legatus), sublegate, ablegate

Aboi, Aboiement, sm. (*etym.* aboyer), bark, barking

Abois, sm. plur. bay. *Être aux* —, to be at bay, (*fig.*) to be driven to one's last shift

Abolir, va. (*etym. L.* ab, olescere, *to grow*), to abolish, to repeal, to destroy

Abolissement, sm., **Abolition**, sf. (*etym.* abolir), abolishment, abolition

¶**Abolitioniste**, adj. s. (*etym.* abolition), abolitionist

Abondance, sf. (*etym.* abondant), plenty, abundance. —*de bien ne nuit pas*, one can't have too much of a good thing. *D'*—, extempore

‡**Abondant, e**, adj. (*etym.* abonder), plentiful, abundant, copious

Abonder, vn. (*etym. L.* ab, unda, *water*), to abound. —*dans le sens de*, quite to agree with

Abonné, e, s. (*etym.* abonner), subscriber. *Être* —*à*, to be a subscriber to

Abonnement, sm. (*etym.* abonner), subscription

s'Abonner, vr. (*etym. L. L.* abonnare, *to limit*), to subscribe to

Abonnir, va., *s'*—, vr. (*etym.* à, bon), to improve

Abord, sm. (*etym.* à, bord), access; *plur.* outskirts, approaches. *Dès l'*—, from the outset. *D'*—, *de prime* —, adv. first, at first. *D'*—*que*, as soon as

Abordable, adj. (*etym.* abord), of easy access

Abordage, sm. (*etym.* abord), boarding

Aborder, vn. a. to land, to accost, to attack; (*fig.*) —*un sujet*, to enter upon

Aborigènes, sm. plur. (*etym. L.* ab, origo), aborigines

Abortif, ve, adj. (*etym. L.* abortivus, *from* ab, oriri, *to be born*), abortive

Abouchement, sm. (*etym.* aboucher), meeting, interview

Aboucher, va. (*etym.* à, bouche), to bring together; *s'*—, to have an interview

Aboutir, vn. (*etym.* à, bout), to tend, to end, to abut, to draw to a head, to gather

Aboutissant, adj. running, abutting

Aboutissants, sm. plur. circumstances. *See* Tenant

Aboyer, vn. (*etym. L.* a, baubari, *to bark*), to bark. *Chien qui aboie ne mord pas*, barking dogs don't fight

Aboyeur, sm. (*et.* aboyer), barker

Abrégé, sm. (*etym.* abréger), abridgment, abstract. *En* —, shortly, in a few words

Abréger, va. (*etym. L. L.* abbreviare, *from* ad, brevis, *short*), to abridge, to shorten

Abreuver, va. (*etym. L.* ad, bibere, *to drink; O. F.* abeuvrer), to water, to soak, to overwhelm

Abreuvoir, sm. (*etym.* abreuver), watering-place

Abri, sm. (*etym. L.* apricus, *exposed to the sun*), shade, shelter, screen, protection. *A l'*—*de*, under shelter. *Sans* —, unsheltered

Abricot, sm. (*etym. Sp.* albaricoque, *Ar.* al-birkouk, *Gr.* πραικόκιον, *L.* praecox), apricot

Abricotier, sm. (*etym.* abricot), apricot-tree

Abriter, va. (*etym.* abri), to shelter

Abrogation, sf. (*etym.* abroger), repeal, abrogation

Abroger, va. (*etym. L.* ab, rogare, *to ask*), to abrogate

‡**Abrupt, e**, adj. (*etym. L.* ab, ruptus, *broken*), rugged, abrupt, blunt

Abrutir, va. (*etym* à, brute), to besot, (*fig.*) to tire out. *C'est un travail abrutissant*, it is dry wearisome work. *S'*—, vr. to besot oneself, (*fig.*) to grow stupid

Abrutissement, sm. (*etym.* abrutir), brutishness, sottishness

Absent, e, adj. (*etym.* absence), absent, out of the way

s'Absenter, vr. (*etym.* absence), to absent oneself

Absinthe, sf. (*etym. Gr.* ἀψίνθιον), wormwood, bitters

‡**Absolu, e**, adj. (*etym. L.* absolutus), absolute, peremptory

¶**Absolutisme**, sm. (*etym.* absolu), absolute power

¶**Absolutiste**, sm. (*etym.* absolu), absolutist

Absorber, va. (*etym. L.* ab, sorbere, *to swallow*), to suck up, to absorb, to engross

Absoudre, va. (*etym. L.* absolvere), to absolve, to acquit

Absoute, sf. (*etym. L.* absolvere), general absolution

s'Abstenir, vr. (*etym. L.* abs, tenere, *to hold*), to abstain, to refrain

‡**Abstractif, ve,** adj. (*etym. L.* abstractivus), abstractive

Abstraction, sf. (*etym. L.* abstrahere, *to draw from*), abstraction, fit of absence

Abstraire, va. (*etym. L.* abstrahere), to abstract

‡**Abstrait, e,** adj. (*etym.* abstraire), abstruse, obscure, abstract

Abstrus, e, adj. (*etym. L.* abstrusus, *from* abs, trudere, *to push*), abstruse

‡**Absurde,** adj. (*etym. L.* absurdus), absurd, unreasonable

Absurdité, sf. (*etym.* absurde), absurdity

Abus, sm. (*etym. L.* abusus), abuse, error, bad use. *Appel comme d'—*, appeal to a secular court

Abuser, va. (*etym.* abus), to delude, to abuse, to impose on; — vn. to make a bad use, to misuse; *s'—*, vr. to be mistaken

Abuseur, sm. (*etym.* abus), deceiver

‡**Abusif, ve,** adj. (*etym.* abus), improper, wrong

Acabit, sm. (*etym. L.L.* acapita, *purchase*), quality, taste

Académicien, sm. (*etym.* académie), academician

Académie, sf. (*etym. L.* academia, *from the Gr.* ἀκαδημία), academy, cast, riding school

‡**Académique,** adj. (*etym.* académie), academical

‡**s'Acagnarder,** vr. (*etym.* à, cagnard), to grow lazy

Acajou, sm. mahogany, mahogany wood

Acanthe, sf. (*etym. L.* acanthus, *Gr.* ἄκανθος), acanthus

Acariâtre, adj. (*etym. O.F.* acarier, *to confront, from* à, cara, *face, visage; see* CHÈRE), peevish

Accablant, e, adj. (*etym.* accabler), overwhelming, oppressive

Accablement, sm. (*etym.* accabler), despondency, dejection

Accabler, va. (*etym.* à, *O.F.* caabler *or* chaabler, *to throw down*), to crush, to overwhelm, to dishearten, to tire out

Accaparement, sm. (*etym.* accaparer), monopoly, buying up

Accaparer, va. (*etym. L.* ac *for* ad, *L.L.* caparra, *from* capere, *to take*), to engross, to forestall, to monopolize

Accapareur, se, adj. (*etym.* accaparer), monopolist

Accéder, vn. (*etym. L.* accedere, *from* ad, cedere, *to go*), to agree, to accede

Accélérateur, trice, adj. (*etym.* accélérer), accelerating

Accéléré, e, adj. (*etym.* accélérer), fast, quick. *Pas—*, double-quick time

Accélérer, va. (*etym. L.* accelerare, *from* ad, celerare, *to quicken*), to hasten, to accelerate

Accent, sm. (*etym. L.* accentus, *from* ad, cantus, *a song*), accent, tone

Accentuer, va. (*etym.* accent), to accent, to accentuate. *Traits accentués*, marked features. *S'—*, vr. to receive the accent

Acceptation, sf. (*etym.* accepter), acceptation, acceptance

Accepter, va. (*etym. L.* ad, cipere *for* capere, *to take*), to accept, to receive

Accepteur, sm. (*etym.* accepter), acceptor

Acception, sf. (*etym.* accepter), acceptation, respect

Accès, sm. (*etym. L.* accessus, *approach*), access, fit. *D'un — si difficile*, of such difficult approach

Accession, sf. (*etym.* accès), accession, adhesion

‡**Accessoire,** adj. (*etym. L.* accessor), accessory, unessential; — sm. appendage, properties

Accident, sm. (*etym. L.* accidens, *pr. part. of* accidere, *to happen*), accident, casualty, effect, roughness

Accidenté, e, adj. (*etym.* accident), uneven, checkered. *Pays —*, hilly country, uneven ground

‡**Accidentel, le,** adj. (*etym.* accident), accidental

Acclamer, va. (*etym. L.* ad, clamare, *to shout*), to proclaim unanimously

Acclimatation, sf. (*etym.* à, climat), acclimation

Acclimatement, sm. (*etym.* à, climat), acclimating

Acclimater, va. (*etym.* à, climat), to acclimatize; *s'—*, vr. to get accustomed to a climate

Accointance, sf. (*etym. L.* ad, cognitus, *known*), dealings

Accolade, sf. (*etym.* à, col), hug, bracket. *Donner l'— à, recevoir l'—*, to dub a knight, to be dubbed a knight

Accoler, va. (*etym.* à, col), to join, to fasten, to tie up

Accommodage, sm. (*etym.* accommoder), dressing, sauce

Accommodant, e, adj. (*etym.* accommoder), easy to deal with

Accommodement, sm. (*etym.* accommoder), arrangement

Accommoder, va. (*etym. L.* ad, commodus, *convenient*), to fit up, to accommodate, to dress, to reconcile. *Le voilà bien accommodé!* he is in a pretty pickle! ‡ — *qq.'un de toutes pièces*, to speak horribly ill of. *S'—*, vr. to make oneself comfortable, to comply with, to be reconciled, to trick oneself out with

§**Accompagnateur, trice,** s. (*etym.* accompagner), accompanist

§**Accompagnement,** sm. (*etym.* accompagner), attendance, accompanying, (*mus.*) accompaniment, base

§**Accompagner,** va. (*etym.* à, *Rom. verb* companhar), to accompany, to attend on; *s'—*, vr. to take with one, to accompany oneself

Accompli, e, adj. (*etym.* accomplir), complete, accomplished, faultless, gone by

Accomplir, va. (*etym.* à, *O.F.* complir; *see* COMPLET), to accomplish, to fulfil, to realize; *s'—*, vr. to be realized

Accomplissement, sm. (*etym.* accomplir), accomplishment, realization

Accord, sm. (*etym.* accorder), concord, agreement, harmony, sweet sound, tune; *plur.* marriage settlements. *Être d'—*, to agree, to be agreed, to be in tune. *D'—*, granted. *Tomber d'— sur une chose*, to grant a thing

§**Accordailles,** sf. pl. (*etym.* accord), betrothal

Accordé, e, s. (*etym.* accorder), betrothed

Accorder, va. (*etym. L.* ad, cor, *heart*), to grant, to tune, to blend, to reconcile; *s'—*, vr. to agree, to tally, to be in tune

Accordeur, sm. (*etym.* accorder), tuner

Accordoir, sm. (*etym.* accorder), tuning-key

‡**Accort, e,** adj. (*etym. I.* accorto, *cunning, clever*), civil, sprightly

Accoster, va. (*etym. L.* ad, costa. *Joinville has the verb* acostoier), to accost, to come alongside

Accotement, sm. (*etym.* à, côte), side-way

s'Accoter, vr. (*etym.* à, *O.F.* cote *or* cotte), to lean

Accouchée, sf. (*etym.* accoucher), woman in childbirth

Accouchement, sm. (*et.* accoucher), confinement

Accoucher, vn. (*etym.* à, coucher), to be brought to bed. † *Accouchez donc!* out with it! — va. to attend, to deliver

Accoucheur, sm. (*etym.* accoucher), surgeon-accoucheur

Accoucheuse, sf. (*etym.* accoucher), midwife

s'Accouder, vr. (*etym. L.* accubitare, *from* ad, cubitus, *the elbow*), to lean on one's elbow

Accoudoir, sm. (*etym.* accouder), leaning-place

Accouplement, sm. (*etym.* à, couple), coupling, pairing

Accoupler, va. (*etym.* à, couple), to couple; *s'—*, vr. to pair, to match

Accourcir, s'Accourcir. *See* RACCOURCIR, etc.

Accourir, vn. (*etym.* à, courir), to run up, to hasten

Accoutrer, va. (*etym.* à, coudre?), to dress up, to rig out

Accoutumance, sf. (*etym.* accoutumer), habit, custom

Accoutumé, e, adj. (*etym.* accoutumer), usual, customary. *Avoir — de*, to be accustomed to

Accoutumer, va. (*etym.* à, coutume), to accustom; *s'—*, vr. to accustom oneself

Accréditer, va. (*etym.* à, crédit), to sanction, to give credit to, to obtain credit for; *s'—*, vr. to gain credit

Accroc, sm. (*etym.* à, croc; *pronounce* a-krô), rent, tear, hitch

Accroche-cœur, sm. (*etym.* accrocher, cœur), heart-breaker

Accrocher, va. (*etym.* accroc), to hang up, to hook, to tear, to grapple, to get hold of; *s'—*, vr. to catch at, to stick to

Accroire (en faire), vn. (*etym.* à, croire), to try to deceive; — (*s'en faire*), vr. to be self-conceited

Accroissement, sm. (*etym.* accroître), increase, extension, enlargement, growth

Accroître, va. (*etym. L.* ad, crescere, *to grow; see* CROÎTRE), to increase, to enlarge; *s'—*, vr. to increase, to grow

s'Accroupir, vr. (*etym.* à, croupe), to squat down, to cower

§**Accueil,** sm. (*etym.* accueillir), reception

§**Accueillir,** va. (*etym. L.* ad, colligere, *to collect*), to receive

Acculer, va. (*etym.* à, cul; *pronounce the* l), to bring to bay, to push; *s'— à*, vr. to lean one's back

Accumuler, va. (*etym.* à, cumuler), to heap up, to accumulate

Accusateur, trice, s. adj. (*etym.* accuser), accuser. *L'— public*, the attorney-general

Accusation, sf. (*etym.* accuser), accusation, imputation. *Chef d'—*, bill of indictment. *Mettre en —*, to arraign, to impeach

Accusé, e, s. adj. (*etym.* accuser), accused, prisoner. — *de réception*, sm. acknowledgment

Accuser, va. (*etym. L.* accusare), to accuse, to impeach, to complain, to own to. — *réception de*, to acknowledge (the receipt of). — *son jeu*, to call one's game. *S'—*, vr. to accuse oneself, to accuse each other

Acerbe, adj. (*etym. L.* acerbus), sharp, harsh, acerb

Acerbité, sm. (*etym.* acerbe), acerbity, sourness

Acéré, e, adj. (*etym.* acérer), sharp, cutting, keen

Acérer, va. (*etym.* acier), to steel, to temper

Acétate, sm. (*etym.* acide), acetate, acetite

Achalandage, sm. (*etym.* achalander), custom, practice

Achalander, va. (*etym.* à, chaland), to draw customers to. *Boutique bien achalandée*, shop well thronged with customers. *S'—*, vr. to draw customers

Acharné, e, pp. adj. (*etym.* acharner), eager, furious, bent

Acharnement, sm. (*etym.* acharner), rage, fury

Acharner, va. (*etym.* à, chair), to set on; *s'—*, vr. to be mad *or* maddened, to be bent on

Achat, sm. (*etym. see* ACHETER), purchase, acquisition

Ache, sf. (*etym. L.* apium, *from the Gr.* ἄπιον), smallage

Acheminement, sm. (*etym.* a, chemin), step

Acheminer, va. (*etym.* a, chemin), to forward, to despatch; *s'—*, vr. to bend one's steps, to progress well

Acheter, va. (*etym. L.* ad, caput, *head*), to buy, to purchase

Acheteur, se, smf. (*etym.* acheter), purchaser, buyer

Achevé, e, adj. (*etym.* achever), finished, thorough

Achèvement, sm. (*etym.* achever), completion, accomplishment

Achever, va. (*etym.* à, chef), to finish, to end, to complete, to despatch

Achoppement (pierre d'), sm. (*etym.* a, chopper), stumbling-block

Achromatique, adj. (*etym. Gr.* α priv., χρῶμα, *colour*), achromatic

Acide, sm. adj. (*etym. Gr.* ἀκή, *a point*), acid

Acidité, sf. (*etym.* acide), acidity, sourness, tartness

Acidulé, e, adj. (*etym.* acide), acidulous, sourish

Aciduler, va. (*etym.* acide), to acidulate

Acier, sm. (*etym. L.L.* aciarium, *from* acies, *a point*), steel, sword. — *poule*, carbonized steel

Aciérer, va. (*etym.* acier), to steel

Aciérie, sf. (*etym.* acier), steel-works

Acolyte, sm. (*etym. Gr.* ἀκόλουθος, *follower*), acolyte, follower

A-compte, sm. (*etym.* à, compte), instalment. *Par —*, by instalments. — loc. adv. on account

Aconit, sm. (*etym. Gr.* ἀκόνιτον), aconite, wolf's-bane

Acoquiner, va. (*etym.* à, coquin), to captivate, to allure; *s'—*, to attach oneself to

Acotylédone, sf. adj. (*etym.* à, cotylédon), acotyledon, acotyledonous

Acoustique, sf. (*etym. Gr.* ἀκουστικός, *from* ἀκούειν, *to hear*), acoustics. *Cornet —*, ear-trumpet. *Voûte —*, whispering-gallery

Acquéreur, sm. (*etym.* acquérir), acquirer, purchaser, buyer

Acquérir, va. (*etym. L.* acquirere, *from* ad, quærere, *to seek; see* QUÉRIR), to acquire, to get, to buy; — vn. to improve

Acquêt, sm. (*etym. L.* acquisitum), acquisition

Acquiescement, sm. (*etym.* acquiescer), compliance

Acquiescer, vn. (*etym. L.* acquiescere, *from* ad, quiescere, *to rest*), to acquiesce, to comply, to yield

Acquis, pp. adj. (*etym.* acquérir), acquired. *Je vous suis —*, I am wholly at your disposal. — sm. experience. *Avoir de l'—*, to have great acquirements

Acquit, sm. (*etym.* acquitter), receipt, acquittance, lead. *Pour —*, received. *Par manière d'—*, for form's sake

Acquit-à-caution, sm. cocket, permit

Acquittement, sm. (*etym.* acquitter), acquittal, release, discharge

Acquitter, va. (*etym. L.* ad, *L.L.* quittare, *to leave*), to acquit; *s'—*, to discharge, to perform, to fulfil

Âcre, adj. (*etym. L.* acer), sharp, bitter

Âcreté, sf. (*etym.* âcre), acrity, pungency

Acrimonie, sf. (*etym.* âcre), acrimony

Acrimonieux, se, adj. (*etym.* acrimonie), acrimonious

Acrobate, s. (*etym. Gr.* ἄκρος, *high*, βάτειν, *from* βαίνειν, *to walk*), rope-dancer

Acrostiche, sm. adj. (*etym. Gr.* ἀκρόστιχον, *from* ἄκρος, στίχος, *a line of poetry*), acrostic

Acte, sm. (*etym. L.* actus, *from* agere, *to act*), act, action, deed, certificate; *pl.* records, rolls

Acteur, sm. (*etym.* agir), actor

‡**Actif, ve**, adj. (*etym. L.* activus, *from* agere), active. *Des dettes —ves*, assets. — sm. capital, assets. *Mettre à l'—*, to credit capital with

Actinie, sf. (*etym. Gr.* ἀκτίς, *a ray*), sea-anemone

Action, sf. (*etym. L.* actionem, *from* agere), action, fight, lawsuit, share, stock. *Offrir des —s de grâce*, to return thanks. *Compagnie par —s*, joint-stock company

Actionnaire, sm. (*etym.* action), shareholder

Actionner, va. (*etym.* action), to bring an action against; *s'—*, to grow warm

Activer, va. (*etym.* actif), to hasten, to spur on

Activité, sf. (*etym.* actif), activity, nimbleness. *En — de service*, in active service

Actrice, sf. actress

Actualité, sf. (*etym.* actuel), actuality, reality; *pl.* things *or* persons of the day

‡**Actuel, le**, adj. (*etym. L.* actualis, *from* actus, *an act*), actual, real, for the time being

Acutangle, Acutangulaire, adj. (*etym. L.* acutus, angulus), acute-angled

Adage, sm. (*etym. L.* ad, agere, *to lead*), adage, maxim

Adamantin, e, adj. (*etym. L.* adamas, *diamond*), adamantine

Adapter, va. (*etym. L.* adaptare, *from* ad, aptare, *to fit*), to adapt, to apply

Addition, sf. (*etym. L.* addere, *to add*), addition, bill

Additionnel, le, adj. (*etym.* addition), additional

Additionner, va. (*etym.* addition), to cast up

Adepte, sm. (*etym. L.* adeptus, *from* adipisci, *to obtain*), adept, initiated

Adhérence, sf. (*etym.* adhérer), adhesion, adherence

Adhérent, e, adj. (*etym.* adhérer), adhesive, adherent, sticking; — sm. follower

Adhérer, vn. (*etym. L.* adhærere), to adhere, to stick

Adhésif, ve, adj. (*etym.* adhérer), adhesive

Adieu, sm. farewell, adieu. *Sans —*, I don't say good-bye. — *les beaux jours!* good-bye to the fine weather! — *—s!* about ship!

Adjacent, e, adj. (*etym. L.* adjacens, *from* ad, jacere, *to lie*), adjacent, neighbouring

Adjectif, sm. adj. (*etym. L.* adjicere, *to place near*), adjective

Adjectivement, adv. (*etym.* adjectif), adjectively

Adjoindre, va. (*etym. L.* adjungere, *to join to*), to associate, to join

Adjoint, sm. (*etym.* adjoindre), coadjutor, assistant. *L'— du maire*, Mr. deputy mayor

Adjonction, sf. (*etym.* adjoindre), adjunction

Adjudant, sm. (*etym. L.* adjuvare, *to help*), adjutant

Adjudicataire, sm. (*etym. L.* adjudicare, *to adjudge*), highest bidder. — *d'une fourniture*, contractor

Adjudication, sf. (*etym. L.* adjudicare), adjudging, contract

Adjuger, va. (*etym. L.* adjudicare), to adjudge, to award. ‡ *Adjugé!* that matter is settled then

Adjurer, va. (*etym. L.* adjurare), to adjure, to summon

Admettre, va. (*etym. L.* admittere), to allow of, to admit

Administrateur, sm. (*etym.* administrer), administrator, manager. *Les —s*, the board, the committee

‡**Administratif, ve**, adj. (*etym.* administrer), administrative

Administration, sf. (*etym.* administrer), administration, management

Administré, sm. (*etym.* administrer), who is under the charge of

Administrer, va. (*etym. L.* ad, ministrare, *to supply*), to administrate, to rule, to dispense, to administer

‡**Admirable**, adj. (*etym. L.* admirabilis), admirable. ‡ *Vous êtes — vraiment!* you are a pretty fellow, really!

Admirateur, trice, s. (*etym.* admirer), admirer

Admiratif, ve, adj. (*etym.* admirer), admiring

Admirer, va. (*etym. L.* admirari), to admire, to wonder at

Admission, sf. (*etym.* admettre), admittance, admission

Admonester, Admonéter, va. (*etym. L.* ad, monere, *to warn*), to reprimand

Adolescent, sm. (*etym.* adolescence), youth, lad

Adolescente, sf. girl, lass

Adoniser, va. (*etym. Gr.* Ἄδωνις), to bedizen; *s'—*, vr. to adonize

s'Adonner, vr. (*etym.* à, donner), to apply oneself, to become addicted

Adopter, va. (*etym. L.* adoptare, *from* ad, optare, *to choose*), to adopt, to choose

Adoptif, ve, adj. (*etym.* adopter), adoptive

Adorateur, sm. (*etym.* adorer), worshipper, votary

Adorer, va. (*etym. L.* adorare, *from* ad, orare, *to pray*), to worship, to adore, to dote upon

Ados, sm. (*etym.* à, dos), a shelving bank

Adosser, va. (*etym.* à, dos), to lean; *s'— à*, to lean one's back against

Adoucir, va. (*etym.* à, doux), to sweeten, to soften, to mitigate, to appease, to smooth; *s'—*, vr. to relent, to grow mild

Adoucissant, e, adj. (*etym.* adoucir), soothing, lenitive

Adoucissant, sm. emollient

Adoucissement, sm. (*etym.* adoucissant), softening, alleviation, comfort

Adresse, sf. (*etym.* adresser), dexterity, skill, address, craft. *Tour d'—*, sleight of hand trick; *see* TOUR. *Le mot est arrivé à son —*, (*fig.*) the arrow has hit the mark

Adresser, va. (*etym.* à, dresser; mettre à droit), to forward, to address; *s'—*, vr. to apply to, to be addressed to. ‡ *Vous vous adressez bien mal*, you have come to the wrong shop

‡**Adroit, e**, adj. (*etym.* à, droit; *L.* ad, directus), dexterous, shrewd, sharp

Adulateur, trice, s. (*etym. L.* adulator, *from* adulari, *to flatter*), flatterer, adulator

Aduler, va. (*etym. L.* adulari), to flatter meanly, to cringe to

Adulte, adj. (*etym. L.* adultus, *pp. of* adolere), grown up, adult

Adultère, adj. (*etym. L.* adulterium, *from* ad, ulter *for* alter), adulterous
Adultère, smf. adulterer (*m.*), adulteress (*f.*). — sm. adultery
Adultérer, va. (*etym.* adultère), to adulterate
Adultérin, adj. (*etym.* adultère). *Enfant* —, a child born in adultery
***Advenir,** vn. (*etym. L.* ad, venire), to happen, to occur. ‡ *Advienne que pourra,* come what may
Adverbe, sm. (*etym. L.* ad, verbum, *word*), adverb
Adversaire, sm. (*etym. L.* adversarius, adversus; *O.F.* aversier), adversary, antagonist
Adverse, adj. (*etym. L.* adversus, *from* ad, versus, *turned*), adverse, calamitous
Adversité, sf. (*etym. L.* adversitatem), adversity
Aérage, sm., **Aération,** sf. (*etym. L.* aer), airing, ventilation. *Puits d'aérage,* air-shaft
Aérer, va. (*etym. L.* aer), to air, to ventilate
Aérien, ne, adj. (*etym. L.* aer), aërial, of the air
Aéromètre, sm. (*etym. Gr.* ἀήρ, μέτρον, *measure*), aërometer
Aéronaute, sm. (*etym. Gr.* ἀήρ, ναύτης, *a sailor*), aëronaut
Aérostat, sm. (*etym. Gr.* ἀήρ, στατός, *who has stopped*), air-balloon
Affabilité, sf. (*etym.* affable), affability, courteousness
Affadir, va. (*etym.* à, fade), to make insipid, to sicken, to cloy
Affadissement, sm. (*etym.* affadir), sickening
Affaibli, e, adj. (*etym.* à, faible), weak, impaired
Affaiblir, va. to weaken, to enfeeble; *s'*—, vr. to grow weak
Affaiblissant, e, adj. (*etym.* affaiblir), debilitating
Affaiblissement, sm. (*etym.* affaiblir), decay, debilitation
Affaire, sf. (*etym.* à, faire), affair, concern, job, business, trade, contention, dispute, fight. ‡ *C'est l'— d'un instant,* it won't be long. *J'en fais mon* —, I take it upon myself. *Cela ne fait rien à l'*—, that has nothing to do with the business. *C'est une toute autre* —, it is quite another matter. *C'est une — faite,* it is as good as done. *Mêlez-vous de vos —s,* mind your own business. *Il connaît son* —, he knows what he's about. *Avoir — à,* to have to do with. *Il est dans les —s,* he is in business. *Faire de bonnes —s,* to get on well. *Être bien dans ses —s,* to be well off. *Homme d'*—, agent, steward. *Étude, bureau d'—s,* agency office. *Une — d'or,* a capital speculation. *C'est toute une* —, it is no trifle. *Ce n'est pas une* —, it is no such weighty matter. *Son — est faite,* his fortune is made. *Son — est bonne,* (*iron.*) he is in for it. *Il fera votre* —, he is the man for you. *Une — d'honneur,* a duel. *L'— était chaude,* the fight was a warm one. *Ce n'est pas le plus beau de son* —, it is not the best of his business. *En voilà une* —, here's a pretty piece of work. *Serrez mes —s,* put by my things
Affairé, e, adj. (*etym.* affaire), busy, bustling
Affaissement, sm. (*etym.* affaisser), subsiding, despondency, sinking
Affaisser, va. (*etym.* à, faix), to weigh down; *s'*—, vr. to sink. *Il s'affaissa sur lui-même,* he sank down on the ground
Affamé, e, adj. (*etym.* à, faim), starving, eager
Affamer, va. (*etym.* à, faim), to starve, to famish
Affecté, e, adj. (*etym.* affecter), affected, finical
Affecter, va. (*etym. L.* ad, factare, *frequent. of* facere; *O.F.* affaiter, affaitier), to affect; *s'*—, vr. to be affected
Affection, sf. (*etym. L.* affectio), affection, love
Affectionné, e, adj. (*etym.* affection), affectionate
Affectionner, va. (*etym.* affection), to be fond of, to have a liking for; *s'*—, vr. to take pleasure in
‖**Affectueux, se,** adj. (*etym. L.* affectuosus, *from* affectus, *an impression*), affectionate
Afférent, e, adj. (*etym. L.* ad, ferire, *to strike*), pertaining
Affermer, va. (*etym.* à, ferme, *sf.*), to farm, to rent
Affermir, va. (*etym.* à, ferme, *adj.*), to strengthen, to confirm, to harden; *s'*—, to grow stronger, to be confirmed
Affermissement, sm. (*etym.* affermir), strengthening, consolidation
Affêté, e, adj. (*etym. see* AFFECTER: *it is the same word*), affected, finical
Afféterie, sf. (*etym.* affecter), affectation, priminess
Affichage, sm. (*etym.* afficher), bill-sticking
Affiche, sf. (*etym. see* AFFICHER), bill. — *de théâtre,* play-bill
Afficher, va. (*etym.* à, ficher), to post up, to make a parade. *Défense d'*—, stick no bills. ‡ — *le bel esprit,* to set up for a wit. *S'*—, vr. to be stuck up, to forget all decency
Afficheur, sm. (*etym.* afficher), bill-sticker
Affidé, e, s. adj. (*etym. L.* ad, fides; *O.F.* affié), follower, trusty
Affilé, e, adj. (*etym.* à, fil), sharp, keen. ‡ *Une langue bien —e,* a sharp tongue
Affiler, va. to sharpen
Affiliation, sf. (*etym.* à, filiation), affiliation, admission
Affilié, e, adj. (*from* affilier), member
Affilier, va. (*etym. L.* ad, filius), to adopt, to initiate
Affiloir, sm. (*etym.* à, fil), whetstone, steel
Affinage, sm. (*see* AFFINER), refining
Affiner, va. (*etym.* à, fin, *adj.*), to refine, to trick
Affinerie, Affineur. *See* RAFFINERIE, &c.
Affinité, sf. (*etym. L.* affinis, *from* ad, finis, *end*), affinity, congeniality
†**Affiquets,** sm. plur. (*from* affique, *Pic. of* affiche; *lit. what is affixed, stuck on*), finery, trinkets
‖**Affirmatif, ve,** adj. (*etym.* affirmer), affirmative
Affirmer, va. (*etym. L.* affirmare, *from* ad, firmare), to affirm, to assert
Affleurement, sm. (*etym.* affleurer), level, (*mines*) end of a vein
Affleurer, va. (*etym.* à, fleur), to put on a level with, (*mines*) to crop out
Afflictif, ve, adj. personal
Affligé, e, adj. sorrowful
Affligeant, e, adj. grievous, afflicting
Affliger, va. (*etym. L.* affligere; *O.F.* aflire, *pp.* aflict), to grieve, to distress; *s'*—, vr. to grieve
Affluence, sf. (*etym. L.* affluens), affluence, crowd, concourse
Affluent, e, s. adj. tributary
Affluer, vn. (*etym. L.* affluere), to abound, to flow, to rush
Affolé, e, adj. (*etym.* à, fol), dotingly fond
s'Affoler, vr. to be infatuated
Affouage, sm. (*etym. L.L.* affoagium, *from* affocare, *to put on the hearth*), right to cut wood
Affourche (Ancre d'), sf. (*etym.* à, fourche), small bower anchor
Affourché, e, adj. astraddle
Affourcher, va., *s'*—, vr. to moor across
Affranchi, e, adj. (*etym.* à, franchir), freed, prepaid
Affranchir, va. to free, to frank; *s'*—, vr. to free oneself, to be prepaid
Affranchissement, sm. (*etym.* affranchir), enfranchisement, immunity, prepayment, postage
Affres, sf. pl. (*etym. O.H.G.* eiver, eipar, *sharp, rugged*), pangs (of death)
Affrètement, sm. (*etym.* affréter), freighting, chartering
Affréter, va. (*etym.* à, fréter), to freight, to charter
Affréteur, sm. freighter, charterer
‖**Affreux, se,** adj. (*see* AFFRES), ghastly, sad
Affriander, Affrioler, va. (*etym.* à, friand; frioler, *to fry slightly*), to make dainty, to allure
Affronter, va. (*etym.* affront), to affront, to encounter. *See* VOISINAGE
Affublement, sm. (*etym. L.* ad, fibula, *a buckle; O.F.* affibler), ridiculous dress, rig-out
Affubler, va. to dress up; *s'*—, vr. to dress oneself up, to trick oneself out
Affût, sm. (*etym.* à, fût, wood; "Af-fût, c'est *au bois,*" Littré), lurking-place. — *d'un canon,* gun-carriage. *Être, se tenir à l'— de,* to lie in wait for, to be on the watch for
Affûtage, sm. (*etym.* affûter), setting, mounting
Affûter, va. (*etym.* affût), to grind
Afin de, loc. prep. in order to, so as to
Afin que, conj. that, in order that
Agaçant, e, adj. (*etym. O.H.G.* hazjan, *to pursue, to worry? O.F.* agace?), tiresome, alluring
Agace *or* **Agasse,** sf. (*etym. L.L.* agasia), magpie
Agacement, sm. (*etym.* agacer), setting on edge, irritation
Agacer, va. to set on edge, to irritate, to allure; *s'*—, vr. to be set on edge, to be irritated
Agacerie, sf. (*etym.* agacer), enticing ways
Âge, sm. (*etym. L.L.* ætaticum, *from* ætas, *age*), age, time of life. *Quel — avez-vous?* how old are you? *D'un certain* —, elderly. *Entre deux —s,* middle-aged. *Le doyen d'*—, the senior member. ‡ *Il tire sur l'*—, he is getting old. *Au moyen* —, in the Middle Ages
Âgé, e, adj. (*etym.* âge), old
Agence, sf. (*etym.* agent), agency
Agencement, sm. (*etym.* agencer), ordering
Agencer, va. (*etym. L.L.* agentiare), to order
Agenda, sm. (*L.*) note-book, memorandum-book
§**s'Agenouiller,** vr. (*etym.* à, genouil, *O.F. for* genou), to kneel down
§**Agenouilloir,** sm. (*etym.* agenouiller), hassock, cushion
Agent, sm. (*etym. L.* agens). ‡ — *de change,* stockbroker. — *comptable,* accountant, (*mar.*) purser
Agglomérer, va., *s'*—, vr. (*etym. L.* agglomerare, *to heap up*), to agglomerate
Aggravant, e, adj. (*etym.* aggraver), aggravating
Aggraver, va. (*etym.* à, grave), to aggravate, to make worse; *s'*—, vr. to grow worse, to increase
‖**Agile,** adj. (*etym. L.* agilis), agile, active, light-footed
Agilité, sf. (*etym. L.* agilitas), agility, nimbleness
Agio, sm. (*etym. I.* aggio or agio, *ease; see* AISE), agio

Agiotage, sm. (*etym.* agioter), stockjobbing

Agioter, va. to gamble in the stocks

Agioteur, sm. stockjobber

Agir, vn. (*etym. L.* agere, *to act*), to act, to operate, to behave. ¦ *Faire* —, to call into action. *Bien* —, to behave well *or* handsomely. *Mal* —, to behave badly or unhandsomely

Agissant, e, adj. active, stirring

Agit (il s'), v. impers. the thing is, the question is, ... is the matter. ¦ *De quoi s'—-il?* what is the matter? *Voici ce dont il s'—*, this is what it is

Agitateur, sm. (*etym.* agiter), agitator

Agiter, va. (*etym. L.* agitare, *frequent. of* agere, *to act*), to agitate, to jolt, to toss, to consider, to deliberate upon

§**Agneau**, sm. (*etym. L.* agnus), lamb

§**Agneler**, va. to ewe

§**Agnelet**, sm. lambkin

§**Agneline**, sf. lamb's wool

§**Agnès**, sf. (*etym. Gr.* ἁγνής, *from* ἁγνός, *pure*), chaste and innocent girl, simpleton

Agonie, sf. (*etym. Gr.* ἀγωνία, *fight*), pangs, agony. ¦ *Être à l'—*, to be dying

†**Agonir**, va. to load with abuse, to call names

Agonisant, e, s. dying man *or* woman. *Prières des —s*, prayers for the dying

Agoniser, vn. to be at the last gasp

Agrafe, sf. (*etym.* à, *a root* graf *or* grap; *O.F.* agrappe), clasp, hasp. — *et porte*, hook and eye

Agrafer, va. to hook; *s'—*, vr. to be fastened, to fasten one's dress

Agraire, adj. (*etym. L.* agrarius, *from* ager, *field*), agrarian

Agrandir, va. (*etym.* à, grand), to enlarge, to increase, to promote, to exaggerate; *s'—*, vr. to grow larger, to increase, to grow rich

Agrandissement, sm. enlargement, aggrandizement

‡**Agréable**, adj. (*etym.* à, gré), agreeable, snug. ¦ *Avoir pour —*, to consent to

Agréé, sm. (*etym.* agréer), solicitor, attorney

Agréer, va. (*etym.* à, gré), to accept, to receive, to allow; — vn. to please

Agrégat, sm. (*etym. L.* aggregatum, *from* aggregare), aggregate

Agrégation, sf. (*etym.* agréger), aggregation, admission, fellowship. ¦ *Concours d'—*, competition for the fellowship

Agrégé, sm. fellow

Agréger, va. (*etym. L.* aggregare), to admit

Agrément, sm. (*etym.* à, gré), pleasantness, trimming, consent. ¦ *Les arts d'—*, accomplishments

Agrès, sm. plur. (*etym.* à, gréer), rigging

Agresseur, sm. (*etym. L.* aggressor, *from* aggredi, *to attack*), aggressor, assailant

Agressif, ve, adj. (*etym. see* AGRESSEUR), aggressive, hostile, provoking

Agreste, adj. (*etym. L.* agrestis, *from* ager, *a field*), wild, rural, ill-bred

Agricole, adj. (*etym. L.* agricola), agricultural

Agriculteur, sm. (*etym. L.* agricultor), husbandman, farmer

Agriculture, sf. (*etym. L.* agricultura), agriculture, husbandry

†**Agriffer**, va. (*etym.* à, griffe), to clutch, to gripe; *s'—*, vr. to clutch, to cling

Agronome, sm. (*etym. Gr.* ἀγρονόμος, *from* ἀγρός, *a field*, νόμος, *law*), agriculturist, writer on husbandry

Agronomie, sf. (*etym. see* AGRONOME), agricultural art

Agronomique, adj. (*etym. see* AGRONOME), agricultural

Aguerri, e, adj. (*etym.* à, guerre), warlike, inured to war

Aguerrir, va. (*etym. see* AGUERRI), to inure; *s'—*, vr. to get inured, to grow bold

Aguets, sm. plur. (*etym.* à, guet), watch. ¦ *Être aux —*, to be on the watch

***Ahaner**, vn. (*in O.F.* ahaner *means to cultivate the ground*), to toil

Aheurtement, sm. (*etym.* à, heurter), wrongheadedness

s'Aheurter, vr. (*etym. see* AHEURTEMENT), to be bent on, to persist

Ah! interj. oh! oh dear!

Ahurir, va. (*etym.* à, hure), to flurry, to dumbfound

Aï, sm. a kind of champagne

Aide, sf. (*etym. L.* adjuvare, *to help*), help, succour, subsidies. *A l'—!* help! *Dieu nous soit en —*, God help us

Aide, sm. aid, abettor. — *-major*, adjutant. — *-chirurgien*, surgeon's mate

Aider, va. to help, to aid, to abet; — vn. to forward, to further, to assist; *s'—*, vr. to help oneself, to make use of, to assist each other

Aïe! interj. oh!

‡**Aïeul**, sm. (*etym. L.* avus), grandfather, forefather. *Mes deux —s*, my two grandfathers. *Nos aïeux*, our forefathers

Aïeule, sf. grandmother

Aigle, sm. (*etym. L.* aquila), eagle, genius, lectern. — sf. a standard. ¦ *Ce n'est pas un —*, he is no genius

Aiglon, sm. eaglet, young eagle

‡**Aigre**, adj. (*etym. L.* acer, *sharp, tart*), sour, crabbed, shrill, brittle

Aigre-doux, adj. half-sour half-sweet

Aigrefin, sm. sharper

Aigrelet, Aigret, te, adj. (*etym. see* AIGRE), sourish, rather sour

Aigrette, sf. (*etym. O.H.G.* heigro? *see* HÉRON), egret, tuft of feathers, heron. *A —*, tufted

Aigretté, e, adj. (*etym. see* AIGRETTE), tufted

Aigreur, sf. (*etym. see* AIGRE), sourness, crabbedness, the heartburn. ¦ *Se dire des —s*, to say spiteful things to one another

Aigrir, va. (*etym. see* AIGRE), to sour, to turn sour, to exasperate; *s'—*, vr. to be soured, to be exasperated

Aigu, ë, adj. (*etym. L.* acutus, *sharp*), sharp, keen, acute, shrill

Aiguade, sf. (*etym. L.* aqua), watering-place

Aigue-marine, sf. (*etym. see* AIGUADE), beryl, aquamarina

Aiguière, sf. (*etym. see* AIGUADE), ewer, jug

§**Aiguille**, sf. (*etym.* aigu), needle, hand of a watch, spire, index, switches, points. *Ouvrage à l'—*, needlework. *Fusil à —*, needle-gun. — *à tricoter*, knitting-needle. — *à emballage*, packing-needle. — *d'inclinaison*, dipping-needle

§**Aiguillée**, sf. (*etym.* aiguille), needleful

§**Aiguillette**, sf. (*etym.* aiguille), point, shoulder-knot, tag, slice

§**Aiguilleur**, sm. (*etym. see* AIGUILLE), pointsman

§**Aiguillier**, sm. (*etym. see* AIGUILLE), needle-case, needle-maker

§**Aiguillon**, sm. (*etym. see* AIGUILLE), sting, goad, spur, incentive

§**Aiguillonner**, va. (*etym.* aiguillon), to goad, to urge on, to rouse

Aiguiser, va. (*etym. see* AIGU), to sharpen, to whet, to quicken

Ail (*plur.* **Aulx, Ails**), sm. (*etym. L.* allium or alium), garlic

Aile, sf. (*etym. L.* ala), wing, pinion, aisle, sail. *A tire d'—*, swiftly. ¦ *Il ne bat plus que d'une —*, he is almost done for

Ailé, e, adj. (*etym.* aile), winged, screw

Aileron, sm. (*etym.* aile), pinion, fin

§**Ailleurs**, adv. (*etym. L.* aliorsum), elsewhere. *D'—*, from somewhere else, from some one or something else, besides, after all

‡**Aimable**, adj. (*etym.* aimer), kind, amiable, gentle

Aimant, e, adj. (*etym.* aimer), affectionate

Aimant, sm. (*etym. L.* adamantem, *accus. of* adamas), loadstone, magnet

Aimantation, sf. (*etym.* aimant, *s.*), magnetizing

Aimanté, e, adj. (*etym.* aimant, *s.*), magnetic

Aimanter, va. (*etym.* aimant, *s.*), to touch with the loadstone

Aimer, va. (*etym. L.* amare), to love, to be fond of, to like

Aine, sf. (*etym. L.* inguen), groin

Aîné, e, s. adj. (*etym. L.* ante, natus), eldest, oldest, senior

Aînesse, sf. (*etym.* aîné), priority of birth, eldership. ¦ *Droit d'—*, law of primogeniture

Ainsi, adv. (*etym. L.* in, sic; *O.F.* insi, ensi), thus, so. — *done*, so then. — *de suite*, so on, so forth. *Pour — dire*, as it were, so to speak. *Comme...*, —..., as..., so... *Il en est — de*, it is so with

Ainsi que, conj. as well as, just as, like

Air, sm. (*etym. L.* aer), air, breeze, vapour, look, appearance, manner, likeness, tune. ¦ *Paroles en l'—*, idle talk. *Prendre l'—*, to take a walk. *Tout le monde est en l'—*, everybody is astir. *Coup d'—*, a cold. *Un courant d'—*, a draught. *Être entre deux —s*, to be in a draught. *Avoir l'air*, to look, to seem, to appear. *De quoi ai-je l'—?* what do I look like? *Se donner de grands —s*, to carry one's head too high. *Un — de famille*, a family look. *Un faux — de*, a sort of likeness to

Airain, sm. (*etym. L.* æs, *brass*), brass. ¦ *Un cœur d'—*, an unfeeling heart

Aire, sf. (*etym. L.* area), threshing-floor, area, point of the compass, eyry, nest

Airelle, sf. (*etym. Port.* airella), whortleberry, bilberry

Airer, vn. (*etym.* aire), to build its eyry

Ais, sm. (*etym. L.* assis, *a plank*), board, plank

Aisance, sf. (*etym.* aise), ease, competency. ¦ *Être dans l'—*, to have a competency

Aise, sf. (*etym. ? Goth.* azets, *easy*), gladness, ease, leisure. ¦ *Il n'en prend qu'à son —*, he takes his own time about it. *Vous en parlez bien à votre —*, you don't know what it is. *Mettre à l'—*, to set at ease. *Être à son —*, to be well off. *Être à l'—*, to be at one's ease

‡**Aisé, e**, adj. easy, in easy circumstances

Aisselle, sf. (*etym. L.* axilla), armpit

Ajonc, sm. (*etym. ? L.L.* adjotum, ajoncum), thorn-broom, reed

Ajournement, sm. (*etym.* ajourner), postponement, summons

Ajourner, va. (*etym.* à, jour), to postpone, to summon

Ajoutage, Ajutage, sm. (*etym.* ajouter), tube, end-pipe

Ajouter, va. (*etym. L.* ad, juxta), to add, to proceed, to go on saying. ¦ — *foi*, to give credit

Ajustage, sm. (*etym.* à, juste), adjusting

Ajustement, sm. (*etym.* à, juste), adjusting, settlement, dress, garb

Ajuster, va. (*etym.* à, juste), to adjust, to fit, to adapt, to settle, to reconcile, to attire, to take aim; *s'—*, vr. to fit together, to agree together, to attire oneself

Alambic, sm. (*etym. Ar.* al, anbiq, *from the Gr.* ἄμβιξ, *a vase*), alembic, still

Alambiqué, e, adj. (*etym.* alambic), far-fetched, strained

Alambiquer, va. to strain

Alanguir, va. (*etym.* à, languir), to enfeeble; *s'—*, to droop; to grow languid

Alarme, sf. (*etym.* à, l'arme), fright, alarm. ‡ *L'— est au camp,* (*fig.*) our rogues are in a pretty fright

Alarmer, va. to alarm, to frighten, to call to arms; *s'—*, vr. to take alarm, to be uneasy

¶**Alarmiste,** sm. alarmist

Albâtre, sm. (*etym. Gr.* ἀλάβαστρον), alabaster, whiteness

Albatros, sm. (*etym. Sp.* alcatraz), albatross

Alberge, sf. (*etym. Sp.* alberchigo, *from L.* albus), early peach

Albinos, sm. (*etym. from L.* albus; albinos *is the Sp. pl. of* albino), albino

Alcali, sm. (*etym. Ar.* al, cali, *soda*), alkali

Alcalin, e, adj. (*etym.* alcali), alkaline

Alchimie, sf. (*etym. from the Ar. art.* al, chimie), alchemy

Alchimiste, sm. (*etym.* alchimie), alchemist

Alcool, sm. (*etym. Ar.* al, qohl, *a kind of powder*), alcohol, spirits of wine

Alcoolique, adj. (*etym.* alcool), alcoholic

Alcooliser, va. (*etym.* alcool), to alcoholize

Alcyon, sm. (*etym. Gr.* ἀλκυών), kingfisher, halcyon

Aléatoire, adj. (*etym. L.* alea, *a die*), contingent, of chance

Alène, sf. (*etym. O.H.G.* alansa, *transpos.* alasna), awl

Alénois, adj.m. (*corrupt for* Orlénois, *from the neighbourhood of Orléans*). *Cresson —*, garden-cresses

Alentour, adv. (*etym.* tour), round about. ‡ *Le pays d'—*, the neighbouring country

Alentours, sm.plur. neighbourhood, adjacent parts, those about. *Aux —*, in the neighbourhood

‡**Alerte,** adj. (*etym. I.* all'erta), alert, brisk, watchful, shrewd. — sf. alarm, alert. *Donner l'—*, to rouse up. — interj. be on the look-out! to arms!

Alevin, sm. (*etym. O.F.* alever, *in the sense of* élever, *to bring up*), small fish

Alexandrin, sm. adj. (*etym.* Alexandre), alexandrine

Alezan, sm. adj. (*etym. Ar.* al, hasan, *the beautiful*), chestnut horse, sorrel horse

Algarade, sf. (*etym. Ar.* al, gharet, *a foray*), rating. *Faire une — à*, to rate

Algèbre, sf. (*etym. Ar.* al, djabroun, *reunion of parts*), algebra

Algue, sf. (*etym. L.* alga), sea-weed

Aliboron, sm. (*etym. O.H.G.* altheran, *the old enemy, the devil*), grizzle, long-ears, donkey

Alidade, sf. (*etym. L.L.* alidada, *from the Ar.* al, dada, *computation*), index, transom

Aliéné, e, adj. s. (*etym.* aliéner), lunatic, mad, alienated. *Maison d'—s*, lunatic asylum

Aliéner, va. (*etym. L.* alienare, *from* alius, *other*), to alienate, to transfer, to derange, to estrange; *s'—*, vr. to withdraw, to become deranged

§**Alignement,** sm. (*etym.* ligne), line, row, putting in a straight line, falling in; fall in! *Sortir de l'—*, to project. *A gauche — !* (*mil.*) eyes left, dress

§**Aligner,** va. (*etym.* ligne), to put in a straight line. ‡ *— des mots,* (*iron.*) to put black upon white

Aliment, sm. (*etym. L.* alere, *to feed*), food, sustenance, alimony

Alimentaire, adj. (*etym.* aliment), alimentary, alimental. *Pension —*, maintenance, alimony

Alimenter, va. (*etym.* aliment), to feed, to nourish, to supply, to furnish; *s'—*, to be fed

Alinéa, sm. (*etym. L.* a, linea, *a line*), paragraph

Alité, e, adj. (*etym.* aliter), confined to one's bed, bedridden

Aliter, va. (*etym.* lit), to confine to one's bed

Alizé, adj. (*etym. O.F.* alis, *regular, smooth*). *Vents —s*, trade-winds

Alizier, sm. (*etym. L.L.* aliorius: *the word is also spelt* alisier), lotus, lote-tree

Allaitement, sm. (*etym.* allaiter), suckling, nursing

Allaiter, va. (*etym.* lait), to suckle, to nurse

Allant, e, adj. (*etym.* aller), stirring, bustling

Allants, sm.pl. goers. ‡ *Les —s et venants*, the goers and comers

Allécher, va. (*etym. L.* allicere, *to attract*), to allure, to entice

Allée, sf. going, alley, walk, avenue. *Les —s et venues*, the goings and comings

Allége, sf. (*etym. L.L.* allegium; *O.F.* allevioire), lighter, tender

Allégeance, sf. (*etym. L.L.* allegiantia, *from* al *for* ad, lige, *faithful*), allegiance

Allégement, sm. (*etym.* alléger), lightening, alleviation

Alléger, va. (*etym. L.L.* allevare, *from* al *for* ad, levis, *light*), to lighten, to disburden, to relieve

Allégorie, sf. (*etym. Gr.* ἀλληγορία, *from* ἄλλος, *other*, ἀγορεύειν, *to say*), allegory

‡**Allégorique,** adj. (*etym.* allégorie), allegorical

Allégoriser, va.n. (*etym. L.* allegorizare, *from* allegoria), to allegorize

‡**Allègre,** adj. (*etym. I.* allegro, *from the L.* alacer?), lively

Allégresse, sf. (*etym.* allègre), joy, cheerfulness, alacrity

Alléguer, va. (*etym. L.* allegare, *from* al *for* ad, legare, *to send*), to allege, to declare

Allemand, e, s. adj. (*etym. O.* all, mann), German. ‡ *Une querelle d'—*, a groundless quarrel

Aller, vn. (*etym. L.* adnare, *to swim to*), to go, to walk, to be on the point of, to suit, to become, to match, to amount. ‡ *— à pied*, to walk. *— à cheval*, to ride. *— aux informations*, to inquire. *— aux voix*, to vote. *Cela va sans dire*, that's of course. *— de mal en pis*, to grow worse and worse. *Cet homme n'ira pas loin*, that man won't live long. *Comment cela va-t-il?* how are you? — (*faire*), va. to make go, to play a trick. — (*laisser*), va. to let go, to release. — (*se laisser*), vr. to yield, to take no care of oneself. — (*s'en*), to go away. *Va-t'en, allez-vous-en*, begone, get you gone. — (*y*), vn. to stake, to be at stake, to set about it. ‡ *Il y va de votre honneur*, your honour is at stake. *Il faut y — doucement*, you must go to work gently

Aller, sm. going. ‡ *Billet d'—*, simple ticket. *Billet d'— et de retour*, return ticket, ticket there and back. *Au pis —*, at the worst. ‡ *C'est un pis-aller*, it is a makeshift

Alleu, sm. (*etym. L.L.* alodium, *from the O.H.G.* all, od, *property*). *Franc —*, freehold

Alliage, sm. (*etym.* allier), alloy. *Règle d'—*, alligation

Alliance, sf. (*etym.* allier), marriage, alliance, covenant, wedding-ring

Allié, e, smf. (*etym.* allier), kinsman, kinswoman, ally

Allier, va. (*etym. L.* alligare, *from* al *for* ad, ligare, *to bind*), to alloy, to combine, to unite, to match; *s'—*, vr. to combine, to form an alliance

†**Allobroge,** sm. (*etym. name of a nation: Celt.* all, *other*, brô, *land, or* brog, *habitation*), a stupid man

Allocation, sf. (*etym. L.* ad, locare, *to let or hire*), grant, sum allowed

Allocution, sf. (*etym. L.* ad, loqui, *to speak*), address, allocution

Allodial, adj. (*etym. see* ALLEU), freehold

Allonge, sf. (*etym.* allonger), eking-piece

Allongé, e, adj. elongated

Allongement, sm. lengthening

Allonger, va. (*etym.* à, long), to lengthen, to protract. — *un coup*, to deal a blow. ‡ *Faire — le pas à*, to make go faster. *S'—*, vr. to stretch, to stretch one's limbs

Allons! interj. come! — *donc*, nonsense!

¶**Allopathe,** sm. (*etym. Gr.* ἄλλος, πάθος, *other, disease*), allopath

Allouer, va. (*etym. L.* ad, locare, *to place*), to allow, to grant

Allumer, va. (*etym. L.* ad, lumen), to kindle, to fire, to set on fire, to light up. — *le sang*, to fire the blood. *S'—*, vr. to kindle, to catch fire, to be inflamed. *La guerre civile s'allume*, civil war breaks out

Allumette, sf. (*etym.* allumer), match

Allumeur, sm. lighter

Allure, sf. (*etym.* aller), gait, way of walking, pace, way of dealing. — *d'une affaire*, turn

Almanach, sm. (*etym.* ? Eusebius has ἀλμενιχιακά), almanack. — *d'adresses*, directory

Almée, sf. (*etym. Ar.* âlmet, *learned from* alam, *learning*), almee, dancing-girl

Aloi, sm. (*etym.* à, loi), standard, quality, condition. *De bon —*, good. *De bas —*, bad, low-born. *De franc —*, true-hearted

Alors, adv. (*etym. I.* allora, *at the hour, then*), then, at that time, now, in that case. ‡ — *comme —*, time enough when that comes. — *que*, when

Alose, sf. (*etym. L.* alausa, alosa), shad, alose

Alouette, sf. (*etym. L.* alauda), lark. *Pied d'—*, larkspur

Alourdir, va. (*etym.* à, lourd), to make heavy; *s'—*, vr. to grow heavy

Aloyau, sm. (*etym. L.* ad, lumbus, *the back?*), loin, sirloin

Alpaga, Alpague, sm. alpaca

Alpestre, Alpin, e, adj. (*etym.* Alpes), Alpine

‡**Alphabétique,** adj. alphabetic

Altérant, e, adj. (*etym.* altérer), which makes thirsty

Altérateur, trice, adj. (*etym.* altérer), productive of change

Altération, sf. (*etym. see* ALTÉRER), alteration, change, great thirst

Altercation, sf. (*etym. L.* altercatio), wrangling, altercation

Altéré, e, adj. altered, changed, thirsty

Altérer, va. (*etym. L.* alterare, *from* alter, *other*), to alter, to change, to misrepresent, to make thirsty, to cause thirst; *s'—*, to undergo a change, to change, to be weakened, to grow thirsty

Alternat, sm. (*etym.* alterner), alternation, alternancy

‡**Alternatif, ve,** adj. alternate, done by turns

Alterne, adj. alternate

Alterner, vn. (*etym. L.* alternus, *from* alter, *other*), to alternate, to succeed each other

Altesse, sf. (*etym. L.* altus, *high*), highness. — *royale, sérénissime*, royal, serene highness

Altier, e, adj. haughty, overbearing

Alto, sm. tenor-violin, tenor

Alun, sm. (*etym. L.* alumen), alum

Alvéole, sm. (*etym. L.* alveolus, *dimin. of* alveus, *a bed, a hollow thing*), cell, socket, alveolus

Alvéolé, e, adj. cellular, with sockets

Amabilité, sf. amiableness, kindness

Amadou, sm. (*etym.* amadouer), tinder, touchwood

Amadouer, va. (*etym.* ? *Sc.* à, mata, *to feed*), to coax, to wheedle

Amaigri, e, adj. (*etym.* amaigrir), emaciated, spare

Amaigrir, va. (*etym.* à, maigrir), to emaciate, to reduce; — vn., *s'—*, vr. to grow thin, to fall away

Amaigrissement, sm. emaciation, thinness

Amalgame, sm. (*etym. Gr.* μάλαγμα, *the act of softening*), amalgam, medley

Amalgamer, va. to amalgamate; *s'—*, vr. to amalgamate, to agree together

Amande, sf. (*etym. Gr.* ἀμυγδάλη), almond, kernel. *Yeux fendus en —s*, almond-shaped eyes

Amandier, sm. (*etym.* amande), almond-tree

Amant, sm. (*etym. L.* amare, *to love*), lover, suitor, votary

Amante, sf. mistress

Amarante, sf. (*etym. Gr.* ἀμάραντος, *which does not fade*), amaranth

Amarante, adj. amaranthine

Amariner, va. (*etym.* à, marin), to man, to equip, to inure to sea

Amarrage, sm. (*etym.* amarre), mooring, making fast, anchoring

Amarre, sf. (*etym.* à, *and the D.* maaren), cable, hawser

Amarrer, va. to moor, to lash, to belay

Amas, sm. (*etym.* amasser), heap, store, great crowd, mob

Amasser, va. (*etym.* à, masse), to heap up, to gather, to store up, to collect. ‡ *Il ne songe qu'à —*, he thinks of nothing but heaping up money. *S'—*, vr. to heap up, to gather, to come together, to drift

Amateur, sm. (*etym. L.* amare), amateur, fond of. ‡ *Il travaille en —*, he works like a gentleman

Amazone, sf. (*etym. doubtful, see* Littré), amazon, riding-habit

Ambages, sf. plur. (*etym. L.* ambages), idle talk. ‡ *Sans —*, to the purpose

Ambassade, sf. (*etym. O.H.G.* ambaht, *a servant*), embassy

Ambassadeur, sm. ambassador, messenger

Ambassadrice, sf. ambassadress

‡**Ambigu, ë,** adj. (*etym. L.* ambiguus), ambiguous, obscure; — sm. a kind of collation, medley

Ambiguïté, sf. ambiguity

‡**Ambitieux, se,** adj. (*etym. L.* ambitiosus), ambitious, aspiring, far-fetched

Ambitionner, va. (*etym.* ambition), to aspire, to covet

Ambre, sm. (*etym. Ar.* anbar), amber. ‡ *Homme fin comme l'—*, a shrewd man

Ambregris, sm. ambergris

Ambrer, va. to scent with ambergris, to amber

Ambroisie, sf. (*etym. Gr.* ἀμβροσία), ambrosia

Ambulant, e, adj. strolling, itinerant. *Marchand —*, pedlar

Âme, sf. (*etym. L.* anima), soul, spirit, ghost, mind, feeling, conscience. — *d'un violin*, soundboard. — *de soulier*, sole. — *d'un fagot*, small wood. — *d'un canon*, bore, chamber. — *d'un soufflet*, clack. — *d'une devise*, motto. ‡ *Bonne —*, simple soul. — *basse*, — *de boue*, mean, grovelling soul. *Rendre l'—*, to give up the ghost. *Pauvre — en peine!* poor ghost! *Avoir charge d'—s*, to have cure of souls. — *qui vive*, a living soul. *Grandeur d'—*, highmindedness. *Avec —*, feelingly. — *damnée*, tool

***Amé, e,** adj. (*etym. L.* amatus), well-beloved

Amélioration, sf. (*etym.* améliorer), improvement, amelioration

Améliorer, va. (*etym. L.* ad, melior), to improve, to ameliorate; *s'—*, vr. to improve, to alter for the better

Aménagement, sm. (*etym.* aménager), parcelling out, disposition

Aménager, va. (*etym.* à, ménage), to parcel out, to dispose

Amendable, adj. (*etym.* amende), amenable to fine, open to amendment

Amende, sf. (*etym. L.* e, mendum, *a fault*), fine, penalty. ‡ *Mettre à l'—*, to fine. *Faire — honorable de*, to make a public confession of

Amendement, sm. amendment, improvement, manuring

Amender, va. to amend, to improve, to manure; *s'—*, vr. to amend, to improve

Amener, va. (*etym.* à, mener), to bring, to pull, to bring on. ‡ — *une affaire à bonne fin, à bien*, to bring a thing happily about. *Mandat d'—*, writ

Aménité, sf. (*etym. L.* amœnus, *pleasant*), amenity, pleasantness

Amenuiser, va. (*etym.* à, menu), to make thin

Amer, sm. bitter

‡**Amer, ère,** adj. (*etym. L.* amarus), bitter, grievous. *Avoir la bouche —e*, to have a bad taste in one's mouth

Amertume, sf. bitterness, acerbity

Améthyste, sf. (*etym. Gr.* ἀμέθυστος, *from* ἀ *priv.*, μεθύειν, *to intoxicate*), amethyst

Ameublement, sm. (*etym.* à, meuble), furniture, set of furniture

Ameublir, va. (*etym.* à, meuble, *adj.*), (*agric.*) to lighten

Ameuter, va. (*etym.* à, meute), to stir up, to urge on. *Des gens ameutés*, a mob. *S'—*, vr. to rise, to mutiny

Ami, sm., **Amie,** sf. (*etym. L.* amicus), friend, acquaintance. *Bon —*, lover, sweetheart. ‡ *Parler en —*, to speak like a friend. — *jusqu'à la bourse*, friend so far as the purse is not concerned. *Ma mie!* or rather *mamie!* (*fam.*) my love! *Les bons comptes font les bons —s*, (*prov.*) short reckonings make good friends

‡**Amiable,** adj. amicable. ‡ *Vendre à l'—*, to sell by private contract. *L'affaire s'est arrangée à l'—*, the business has been settled without going to law

Amiante, sm. (*etym. Gr.* ἀμίαντος, *from* ἀ *priv.*, μιαίνειν, *to soil*), asbestos, amianthus

‡**Amical, e,** adj. friendly, amicable

Amidon, sm. (*etym. Gr.* ἄμυλον), starch

Amidonner, va. to starch

Amidonnerie, sf. starch-manufactory

Amidonnier, sm. starch-maker

Amincir, va. (*etym.* mince), to make thinner; *s'—*, vr. to grow thinner

Amincissement, sm. (*etym.* amincir), thinning

Amiral, sm. (*etym. Ar.* amir, *L.Gr.* ἀμηρᾶς), admiral. *Contre- —*, rear-admiral. *Vaisseau —*, flagship

Amirauté, sf. (*etym.* amiral), admiralship, navy office

Amitié, sf. (*etym.* ami), friendship, kindness. ‡ *Prendre en —*, to take a liking to. *Faites-nous l'— de*, do us the kindness to. *Présentez mes —s à monsieur votre père*, remember me kindly to your father

Ammoniac, que, Ammoniacal, e, adj. (*etym.* ammoniaque), ammoniac, ammoniacal

Ammoniaque, sf. (*etym. Gr.* ἀμμωνιακός, *from* Ἄμμων, *because that substance used to be prepared in Libya, near the temple of Jupiter Ammon*), ammonia

Amnistie, sf. (*etym. Gr.* ἀμνηστία, *from* ἀ *priv.*, μνάομαι, *I remember*), amnesty

Amnistié, e, adj. person included in an amnesty

Amnistier, va. to grant a pardon to

Amoindrir, va. (*etym.* moindre), to lessen, to curtail; *s'—*, vr. to decrease, to decay

Amoindrissement, sm. lessening, decrease

Amollir, va. (*etym.* mol), to soften, to mollify; *s'—*, vr. to become soft, effeminate

Amollissement, sm. softening, effeminacy

Amonceler, va. (*etym.* monceau), to heap up, to accumulate; *s'—*, vr. to gather, to be heaped up

Amoncellement, sm. heaping up

Amont (d'), adv. (*etym.* à, mont), up the stream. *En —*, up the river

Amorce, sf. (*etym.* à, mordre), bait, allurement, priming of a firearm. ‡ *Sans brûler une —*, without firing a shot

Amorcer, va. to bait, to allure, to prime

Amorçoir, sm. borer

Amortir, va. (*etym.* à, mort), to deaden, to allay; ‡ — *une dette*, to redeem. *S'—*, vr. to be deadened, to be allayed, to be redeemed

Amortissable, adj. redeemable

Amortissement, sm. redemption, buying up. *Caisse, fonds d'—*, sinking-fund

Amour, sm. (*etym. L.* amor), love, fondness, deep affection. *Pour l'— de Dieu*, for God's sake. *Lacs d'—*, love-knots

s'Amouracher, vr. to be enamoured of

Amourette, sf. love, love-affair

‡**Amoureux, se,** adj. loving, amorous. — *fou de*, mad with love for

Amoureux, sm. lover. ‡ *Un — transi*, a whining lover

Amour-propre, sm. self-love, conceit

Amovibilité, sf. (*etym.* amovible), precariousness of tenure

Amovible, adj. (*etym. L.* a, movere), revocable, precarious

Amphibie, adj. (*etym. Gr.* ἀμφίβιος), amphibious

Amphigouri, sm. (*etym.?*) rigmarole

‖**Amphigourique**, adj. ludicrous, unmeaning

Amphithéâtre, sm. (*etym. Gr.* ἀμφί, *on both sides, and* θέατρον, *a theatre*), amphitheatre, first gallery

Amphitryon, sm. (*etym. Gr.* Ἀμφιτρύων, *name of a king of Thebes*), host, entertainer

Amphore, sf. (*etym. L.* amphora, *a jar with two handles*), amphora, urn, pitcher

‖**Ample**, adj. (*etym. L.* amplus), ample, spacious, copious. ‡ *A plus — informé*, for further information

Ampleur, sf. width, fulness, abundance

Ampliation, sf. duplicate

Amplifier, va. to amplify, to develop, to exaggerate

Ampoule, sf. (*etym. L.* ampulla, *a kind of vase*), phial, blister. *La sainte —*, the ampulla

Ampoulé, e, adj. turgid, high-flown

Amputer, va. (*etym. L.* amputare, *to cut*), to cut off, to amputate

Amulette, sf. (*etym. L.* amuletum), amulet

Amusant, e, adj. (*etym.* amuser), amusing, laughable

Amusement, sm. amusement, pastime, toy

Amuser, va. (*etym.* à, muser), to amuse, to divert, to delay, to befool; *s'—*, vr. to amuse, to be amused, to lose one's time, to befool

Amusette, sf. trifling amusement

Amygdale, sf. (*etym. L.* amygdala, *an almond*), tonsil, gland

Amygdalite, sf. mumps

An, sm. (*etym. L.* annus), year. ‡ *Le jour de l'—, le premier de l'—*, New Year's Day. *Bon —, mal —*, one year with another. *Service du bout de l'—*, year's end mass (for the dead)

Anachorète, sm. (*etym. Gr.* ἀνά, *far*, χωρεῖν, *to go*), anchorite

Analogie, sf. (*etym. Gr.* ἀναλογία; *see* ANALOGUE), analogy, resemblance

Analogique, adj. analogous, analogical

Analogue, adj. (*etym. Gr.* ἀνάλογος, *in accordance with reason*), analogous, similar

Analysable, adj. (*etym.* analyse), which may be resolved

Analyse, sf. (*etym. Gr.* ἀνάλυσις, *solution*), analysis, parsing, outline. ‡ *En dernière —*, after all

Analyser, va. to analyse, to parse, to give a sketch

‖**Analytique**, adj. analytical

Ananas, sm. (*etym. Peruv.* nanas, *name of the fruit*), pine-apple, pine-strawberry. ‡ *Serre à —*, pinery

Anarchie, sf. (*etym. Gr.* ἀναρχία, *from* ἀν *priv.*, ἀρχή, *rule*), anarchy, misrule

Anarchique, adj. anarchical

Anarchiste, sm. anarchist

Anathématiser, va. (*etym.* anathème), to anathematize, to curse

Anathème, sm. (*etym. Gr.* ἀνάθεμα, *exposition, person exposed*), anathema, curse, accursed person

Anatomie, sf. (*etym. Gr.* ἀνατομή, *dissection*), anatomy, anatomical figure

‖**Anatomique**, adj. anatomical

Anatomiser, va. to dissect, to anatomize

Anatomiste, sm. anatomist, dissector

Ancêtres, sm.plur. (*etym. L.* antecessor), forefathers, ancestors

Anchois, sm. (*etym. I.* acciuga), anchovy

‖**Ancien, ne**, adj. (*etym. L.L.* antianus, *from L.* ante, *before*), old, ancient, elder

Ancienneté, sf. ancient date, antiquity, oldness. *A l'—*, by seniority

Ancrage, sm. (*etym.* ancre), anchorage

Ancre, sf. (*etym. Gr.* ἄγκυρα, *a hook*), anchor. *— de salut*, (*fig.*) last resource. *Maîtresse —*, (*nav.*) sheet anchor. *Chasser sur ses —s*, to drag her anchors. *Être à l'—*, to lie at anchor. *Lever l'—*, to weigh anchor

Ancré, e, adj. at anchor. ‡ *Bien —*, (*fig.*) well grounded

Ancrer, va. to cast anchor; *s'—*, vr. to obtain a good footing

§**Andouille**, sf. (*etym. L.L.* inductilis), chitterlings, pigtail tobacco

§**Andouiller**, sm. (*etym. L.* ante, *before?* *and F.* œil?), antlers. *Les maîtres —s*, the brow antlers

§**Andouillette**, sf. (*etym. see* ANDOUILLE), forcemeat ball

Âne, sm. (*etym. L.* asinus), ass, donkey, dunce. *Bonnet d'—*, dunce's cap. ‡ *Des coq-à-l'—*, cock-and-bull stories. *Des contes de peau d'—*, child's stories. *Chemin à dos d'—*, shelving road

Anéantir, va. (*etym.* à, néant), to annihilate, to crush; *s'—*, vr. to come to nothing, to bow down to the dust

Anéantissement, sm. utter destruction, annihilation, prostration

‡**Ânerie**, sf. (*etym.* âne), gross ignorance

Ânesse, sf. she-ass

Anévrismal, e, adj. (*etym.* anévrisme), aneurismal

Anévrisme, sm. (*etym. Gr.* ἀνεύρυσμα, *dilatation*), aneurism

Anfractueux, se, adj. (*etym. L.* anfractus, *from* amb, frangere, *to break*), broken, rugged on all sides

Anfractuosité, sf. (*etym.* anfractueux; *used more particularly in the plural*), anfractuosity

Ange, sm. (*etym. G.* ἄγγελος, *messenger*), angel, heavenly spirit, chain-shot. ‡ *Être aux —s*, to be overjoyed

‖**Angélique**, adj. heavenly, angelical

Angélique, sf. angelica, lungwort

Angine, sf. (*etym. L.* angina, *from* angere, *to strangle*), quinsey, angina, sore-throat

Anglais, sm. (*etym. L.* Anglus), English, Englishman

Anglaise, sf. Englishwoman, hornpipe; *pl.* ringlets. *Lieux à l'—*, watercloset

Angleux, se, adj. thick-shelled

Anglicisme, sm. anglicism

¶**Anglomane**, adj. English-mad

¶**Anglomanie**, sf. anglomania

Angoisse, sf. (*etym. L.* angustia, *narrowness*), pang, anguish, agony. ‡ *Une poire d'—*, a gag, a chokepear. (*fig.*) a bitter draught

§**Anguillade**, sf. (*etym.* anguille), lash

§**Anguille**, sf. (*etym. L.* anguis, *a snake*), eel. ‡ *Il y a — sous roche*, there is treachery abroad

‖**Angulaire**, adj. (*etym.* angle), angular, pointed. *Pierre —*, corner-stone

Anguleux, se, adj. sharp, many-cornered

Anicroche, sf. (*formerly spelt* hanicroche; *from* hand? *and* croche, *a hook*), hitch, stoppage

Ânier, sm., **Ânière**, sf. (*etym.* âne), donkey-driver

Animal, sm. (*etym. L.* animal), animal, beast, blockhead, rude fellow

Animal, e, adj. animal, sensual

Animé, e, adj. animated, sprightly

Animer, va. (*etym. L.* anima, *soul*), to animate, to give life to; *s'—*, vr. to brighten up, to become animated, to cheer up, to encourage each other. *Son teint s'anime*, his colours glow

Animosité, sf. (*etym. see* ANIMER), animosity, enmity

Anis, sm. (*etym. Gr.* ἄνισον), anise, aniseed

Aniser, va. (*etym.* anis), to flavour with aniseed

Anisette, sf. anisette

Annales, sf.plur. (*etym. L.* annus), annals

Annates, sf.plur. (*etym. L.L.* annata), annats, yearly revenue

Anneau, sm. (*etym. L.* anellus), ring, link, curl, ringlet

Année, sf. (*etym.* an), year, twelvemonth. *— moyenne, une — dans l'autre*, one year with another. *Souhaiter la bonne — à*, to wish a happy New Year to

Annelé, e, adj. (*etym. O.F.* annel = anneau), annulated

Annelet, sm. (*etym.* annel), a small ring

Annexe, sf. (*etym. L.* annexus, *from* ad, nectere, *to join*), annex, schedule, chapel of ease

Annexer, va. to annex

Annihiler, va. (*etym. L.* ad, nihil, *nothing*), to annihilate, to cancel

Anniversaire, adj. (*etym. L.* annus, vertere, *to turn*), yearly, anniversary

Annonce, sf. (*etym. L.* ad, nuntius, *messenger*), advertisement, bill. *Voir aux —s*, see the advertisements

Annoncer, va. to give notice of, to announce, to advertise, to usher in; *s'—*, vr. to announce oneself, to promise. ‡ *L'affaire s'annonce bien*, the thing promises well

Annonciation, sf. annunciation, angel's message, Lady-day

Annotateur, sm. (*etym.* annoter), annotator

Annoter, va. (*etym.* note), to annotate

Annuaire, sm. (*etym. L.* annus), annuary, annual, directory

‖**Annuel, le**, adj. annual, once a year

Annuité, sf. annuity, yearly allowance. ‡ *Détenteur d'—s*, annuitant

Annulaire, adj. (*etym.* anneau), annular

Annulaire, sm. ring-finger

Annulation, sf. (*etym.* annuler), annulment, repeal

Annuler, va. (*etym.* nul), to annul, to repeal, to cancel

Anoblir, va. (*etym.* noble), to ennoble

Anoblissement, sm. ennobling. *Lettres d'—*, a patent of nobility

Anodin, e, adj. (*etym. Gr.* ἀνώδυνος, *painless*), anodyne, calming

Anomalie, sf. (*etym. Gr.* ἀνώμαλος, *irregular*), anomaly

Ânon, sm. (*etym.* âne), ass's colt

‡**Ânonnement**, sm. hemming and hawing

‡**Ânonner**, va. to stammer

Anonyme, adj. (*etym. Gr.* ἀνώνυμος, *nameless*), anonymous. *Société —*, joint-stock company

Anormal, e, adj. (*etym. Gr.* a *priv.*, *L.* norma, *a rule*), irregular

Anse, sf. (*etym. L.* ansa), handle, creek, bay. † *Faire le pot à deux —s*, to set one's arms akimbo. † *Faire le panier à deux —s*, to walk with a lady under each arm. ‡ *Faire danser l'— du panier*, to make good perquisites

Anspect, sm. (*pron.* anspek: *etym. E.* handspike), handspike, lever

Antagonisme, sm. (*etym. Gr.* ἀνταγώνισμα, *the act of fighting against*), antagonism

Antagoniste, sm. (*etym. Gr.* ἀνταγωνιστής), antagonist

Antarctique, adj. (*etym.* anti, arctique), antarctic, southern

Antécédent, sm. (*etym. L.* antecedere, *to go before*), antecedent. ‡ *Un homme sans —s,* an unknown man

‡**Antécédent, e,** adj. antecedent

Antechrist, sm. Antichrist

Antédiluvien, ne, adj. (*etym.* ante, diluvien), antediluvian, before the Flood

Antenne, sf. (*etym. L.* antenna), yard, feeler, horn

Antépénultième, adj. (*etym.* ante, pénultième), antepenultimate

‡**Antérieur, e,** adj. (*etym. L.* anterior), previous, prior, anterior

Antériorité, sf. priority

Anthère, sf. (*etym. Gr.* ἀνθηρός, *flowering*), anther, tip

Anthologie, sf. (*etym. Gr.* ἄνθος, *flower*), anthology

Anthropologie, sf. (*etym. Gr.* ἄνθρωπος, *man,* λόγος, *discourse*), anthropology, natural history of man

Anthropophage, adj. (*etym. Gr.* ἄνθρωπος, φαγεῖν, *to eat*), cannibal, anthropophagus

Anthropophagie, sf. cannibalism

Antichambre, sf. (*etym.* anti *for* ante, chambre), antechamber. ‡ *Faire faire — à,* to keep one waiting

Antichrétien, ne, adj. antichristian

Anticiper, va. (*etym. L.* anti *for* ante, capere, *to take*), to forestall, to be beforehand with; — vn. to anticipate, to encroach

Antidartreux, se, adj. (*etym.* anti, dartre), remedy against the ringworm, antiherpetic

Antidater, va. (*etym.* anti, dater), to antedate

Antienne, sf. (*etym. Gr.* ἀντίφωνα, *one voice singing against another*), anthem

Antilope, sm. (*etym. ?*), antelope

Antimoine, sm. (*etym. Ar.* athmoud *or* ithmid), antimony

Antipape, sm. (*etym.* anti, pape), antipope

Antipathie, sf. (*etym. Gr.* ἀντιπάθεια, *passion against*), antipathy

Antipathique, adj. (*etym.* antipathie), antipathetic

Antiphrase, sf. (*etym.* anti, phrase), antiphrasis

Antipodes, sm. plur. (*etym. Gr.* ἀντί, *against,* ποῦς, *foot*), antipodes, (*fig.*) the very opposite

§**Antiquaille,** sf. (*etym. I.* anticaglia), antiquated thing, old lumber

Antiquaire, sm. (*etym.* antique), antiquary, antiquarian

Antique, adj. (*etym. L.* antiquus), antique, old-fashioned

Antiquité, sf. (*etym.* antique), antiquity, ancientness. *Une —,* a piece of antiquity

Antiscorbutique, adj. (*etym.* anti, scorbutique), antiscorbutic

¶**Antisocial, e,** adj. (*etym.* anti, social), antisocial

Antithèse, sf. (*etym. Gr.* ἀντίθεσις), antithesis

Antre, sm. (*etym. L.* antrum, *a cave*), cavern, den

Anxiété, sf. (*etym. L.* anxietas), anxiety, uneasiness

Août, sm. (*etym. L.* Augustus), August. *La mi- —,* the middle of August

Aoûter, va. (*etym.* août), to ripen

Aoûteron, sm. (*etym.* août), harvest-labourer

Apaiser, va. (*etym.* paix), to appease, to pacify, to hush, to mitigate, to soothe; *s'—,* vr. to be pacified *or* appeased, to sober down, to abate

Apanage, sm. (*etym. L.* ad, panis, *bread*), appanage

Apanager, va. (*etym.* apanage), to endow with an appanage

Apanagiste, sm. (*etym.* apanage), prince endowed with an appanage

A part, loc. adv. apart, aside. ‡ *— moi,* to myself

Aparté, sm. (*etym. L.* a parte), words spoken aside

Apathie, sf. (*etym. Gr.* a *priv.,* πάθος, *passion*), apathy

Apathique, adj. (*etym.* apathie), apathetic

Apercevoir, va. (*etym.* percevoir), to perceive, to notice; *s'—,* vr. to perceive oneself, to perceive each other, to be seen, to notice

Aperçu, sm. (*past part. of* apercevoir), sketch, short notice, rough estimate, summary

Apéritif, ve, adj. (*etym. L.* aperire, *to open*), opening, aperient

Aphélie, sf. (*etym. Gr.* ἀπό, ἥλιος, *the sun*), aphelion, aphelium

Aphérèse, sf. (*etym. Gr.* ἀφαίρεσις, *from* ἀφαιρεῖν, *I remove*), aphæresis

Aphorisme, sm. (*etym. Gr.* ἀφορισμός), aphorism

Aphthe, sm. (*etym. Gr.* ἅπτω, *to burn*), ulcer

Api (Pomme d'), sf. (*etym. L.* Appianum), api

Apitoyer, va. (*etym.* pitié), to touch with pity, to move; *s'—,* vr. to bewail, to commiserate

Aplanir, va. (*etym. L.* planus, *even*), to smooth, to remove; *s'—,* vr. to grow smooth

Aplanissement, sm. (*etym.* aplanir), levelling, facilitating

Aplatir, va. (*etym.* plat), to flatten; *s'—,* vr. to be flattened

Aplatissement, sm. (*etym.* aplatir), flattening

Aplomb, sm. (*etym.* plomb), perpendicularity, self-possession, impudence. ‡ *D'—,* perpendicular, in equilibrium. *Avec —,* self-collectedly

Apocryphe, adj. (*etym. Gr.* ἀπόκρυφος), apocryphal

Apogée, sm. (*etym. Gr.* ἀπόγαιος), apogee, highest pitch

Apologétique, adj. (*etym. Gr.* ἀπολογητικός), apologetical, exculpatory

Apologie, sf. (*etym. Gr.* ἀπολογία), apology

Apologiste, sm. (*etym.* apologie), apologizer, defender

Apophthegme, sm. (*etym. Gr.* ἀπόφθεγμα), apophthegm, apothegm

Apoplectique, adj. (*etym. Gr.* ἀποπληκτικός), apoplectic, apoplectical

Apoplexie, sf. (*etym. Gr.* ἀποπληξία), apoplexy. *Coup d'— foudroyante,* apoplectic stroke

Apostasie, sf. (*etym. Gr.* ἀποστασία), apostasy, backsliding

Apostasier, va. (*etym.* apostasie), to apostatize

Apostat, sm. (*etym. Gr.* ἀποστάτης), apostate

Aposter, va. (*etym.* poster), to station, to put; *s'—,* vr. to place oneself

§**Apostille,** sf. (*etym. L.L.* postilla, *a note*), marginal note, recommendation

§**Apostiller,** va. to write notes, to recommend

Apostolat, sm. (*etym. Gr.* ἀπό, στέλλω, *I arrange*), apostleship

‡**Apostolique,** adj. (*etym. L.* apostolicus), apostolic, apostolical

Apostropher, va. (*etym.* apostrophe), to apostrophize

Apostume, sm. *corrupt for* Apostème, sm. (*etym. Gr.* ἀπόστημα), abscess, swelling

Apothéose, sf. (*etym. Gr.* ἀπό, θεός, *god*), apotheosis, deification, deifying

Apothicaire, sm. (*etym. Gr.* ἀποθήκη, *shop*), apothecary. ‡ *Mémoire d'—,* an extravagant bill

Apôtre, sm. (*etym. see* Apostolat), apostle. ‡ *Faire le bon —,* to play the hypocrite

Apparaître, vn. (*etym.* à, paraître), to appear

Apparat, sm. (*etym. L.* apparatus, *from* ad, parare, *to prepare*), pomp, ostentation, preparation. *Discours d'—,* a set speech

Apparaux, sm. (*plur. of* appareil), (*mar.*) appurtenances

§**Appareil,** sm. (*etym. see* Appareiller), show, equipage, preparation, apparatus, dressing, attire, garb

§**Appareillage,** sm. (*etym.* appareil), getting under sail

§**Appareillé, e,** adj. matched, mismatched

§**Appareillement,** sm. (*etym.* à, pareil), sorting, matching, pairing, yoking

§**Appareiller,** va. (*etym.* à, pareil), to match; — vn. (*mar.*) to get under sail; *s'—,* vr. to pair

Apparence, sf. (*etym. L.* apparentia), look, appearance, probability, show

‡**Apparent, e,** adj. (*etym. L.* apparens, *from* apparere), apparent, visible, seeming, good-looking

Apparenté, e, adj. (*etym.* à, parent), related, allied

S'Apparenter, vr. (*etym.* à, parent), to marry into

Appariement, sm. (*etym.* apparier), coupling, pairing

Apparier, va. (*etym.* à, paire), to couple, to match; *s'—,* vr. to pair, to couple

Appariteur, sm. (*etym. L.* apparitor, *one who is present*), apparitor, beadle

Apparition, sf. (*etym. L.* apparere), apparition, ghost, vision

Appartement, sm. (*etym. L.* ad, partiri, *to divide*), lodgings, apartments

Appartenance, sf. (*etym.* appartenir), appurtenance

Appartenir, vn. (*etym. L.* ad, pertinere), to belong to, to be the property of, to depend on; *s'—,* vr. to be one's own master

Appas, sm. plur. (appas *is really the plural of* appât), charms, attractions

Appât, sm. (*etym.* à, *and O.F.* past; *see* Paître), bait, allurement

Appâter, va. (*etym.* appât), to bait, to feed

Appauvrir, va. (*etym.* à, pauvre), to impoverish, to make poor; *s'—,* vr. to grow poor

Appauvrissement, sm. impoverishment

Appeau, sm. (*same word as* appel), bird-call, decoy-bird

Appel, sm. (*etym.* appeler), call, appeal, challenge, muster, levy

Appelant, e, adj. (*etym.* appeler), appellant, decoy-bird

Appeler, va. (*etym. L.* appellare), to call, to name, to challenge. *En — à,* to appeal to. *En — de,* to appeal from

Appellatif, ve, adj. (*etym. L.* appellativus), appellative

Appellation, sf. (*etym. L.* appellationem), appellation, appeal

Appendice, sm. (*etym. L.* appendix), appendix, appendage

Appendre, va. (*etym.* à, pendre), to hang up

Appentis, sm. (*etym. L.L.* appendicium), shed, outhouse

Appesantir, va. (*etym.* à, pesant), to make heavy, to weigh down; *s'—,* vr. to grow heavy, to dwell, to insist

Appesantissement, sm. (*etym.* appesantir), heaviness

Appétissant, adj. (*etym.* appétit), tempting, dainty

Appétit, sm. (*etym. L.* appetere), appetite, longing. *Demeurer sur son* —, to stay one's stomach

Applaudir, va. (*etym. L.* applaudere), to applaud, to cheer; *s'*—, vr. to congratulate oneself

Applaudissement, sm. (*etym.* applaudir), applause, cheering

Applique, sf. (*etym.* appliquer), charging. *Pièces d'*—, inlaid work

Appliqué, e, adj. (*fig.*) careful, studious

Appliquer, va. (*etym. L.* applicare, *from* ad, plicare, *to fold*), to apply, to adapt, to suit, to fit; *s'*—, vr. to apply, to be assiduous, to attribute to oneself

Appoint, sm. (*etym.* à, point), odd money

Appointement, sm. (*etym.* appointer), *pl.* salary. ‡ *Toucher de faibles* —*s*, to receive a low salary

Appointer, va. (*etym.* appoint), to punish, to equip, to give a salary

Apport, sm. (*etm.* apporter), dowry, share, deposit

Apporter, va. (*etym.* à, porter), to bring, to fetch, to allege

Apposer, va. (*etym.* à, poser), to set, to fix. — *sa signature*, to sign. — *les scellés*, to seal up

Appréciateur, trice, smf. (*etym.* apprécier), appraiser, he, she who appreciates

Appréciatif, ve, adj. (*etym.* apprécier), of appreciation. *État* —, estimate

Apprécier, va. (*etym. L.* appretiare, *from* ad, pretium), to appraise, to estimate, to appreciate

Appréhender, va. (*etym. L.* apprehendere, *from* ad, prehendere, *to take*), to dread, to apprehend, to arrest

Appréhensif, ve, adj. (*etym.* appréhender), apprehensive

Apprendre, va. (*etym. see* APPRÉHENDER), to learn, to teach, to apprise, to be apprised of. ‡ *Un mal appris*, an illbred person. *S'*—, vr. to be learnt, to teach one another

Apprenti, e, smf. (*etym.* apprendre), apprentice, novice

Apprentissage, sm. (*etym.* apprenti), apprenticeship, preparation

Apprêt, sm. (*etym. see* APPRÊTER), preparation, stiffness, cooking, dressing

Apprêté, e, adj. prepared, affected, dressed, cooked

Apprêter, va. (*etym.* à, *the adj.* prêt), to prepare, to dress, to cook; *s'*—, vr. to get ready, to prepare

Apprêteur, sm. (*etym.* apprêter), dresser

Apprivoisé, e, adj. tame

Apprivoiser, va. (*etym.* à, privé), to tame, to subdue; *s'*—, vr. to grow tame *or* familiar

Approbateur, trice, smf. (*etym. L.* approbator; *see* APPROUVER), approver

‖**Approbatif, ve,** adj. (*etym. L.* approbativus), approving

Approchant, e, adj. (*etym.* approcher), something like, of the same kind as

Approche, sf. (*etym. see* APPROCHER), approach, access. *Lunette d'*—, telescope

Approcher, va. (*etym.* à, proche; *O.F.* aproismer, *from L.* approximare), to bring near, to have access to; — vn. to approach, to go up to, to be like; *s'*—, vr. to approach, to go closer to

Approfondir, va. (*etym.* à, profond), to deepen, to search into, to investigate

Approprier, va. (*etym.* à, propre), to appropriate, to accommodate, to clean, to set to rights; *s'*—, vr. to appropriate to oneself, to embezzle

Approuver, va. (*etym. L.* approbare), to approve, to commend

Approvisionnement, sm. (*etym.* approvisionner), victualling, provisions

Approvisionner, va. (*etym.* à, provision), to victual, to stock, to provide; *s'*—, vr. to provide oneself, to lay in a stock

‖**Approximatif, ve,** adj. (*etym. L.* ad, proximus, *nearest*), approximate. *Devis* —, rough estimate

Appui, sm. (*etym. see* APPUYER), prop, stay, interest, help. *Point d'*—, fulcrum, prop. — *de fenêtre*, window-sill. *A hauteur d'*—, breast-high

Appui-main, sm. (*plur.* des appuis-main), maulstick, rest-paper

Appuyer, va. (*etym. L.L.* appodiare, *from* ad, podium, *height*), to prop up, to lean, to second, to back; — vn. to bear, to lean, to weigh, to lay great stress; *s'*—, vr. to lean, to recline, to confide, to allege

‖**Âpre,** adj. (*etym. L.* asper), rough, hard, bitter, harsh, eager, greedy. ‡ — *au gain*, — *à la curée*, (*fig.*) greedy of gain

Après, prep. (*etym.* à, près; *O.F.* empres), after, behind, about. — *le roi vint*…, next to the king came… ‡ *Il est toujours* — *moi*, he is always hanging about me. — adv. afterwards, what then? *Ci*-—, hereafter. — *coup*, too late. *D'*—, prep. from, after, according to. *D'*— *nature*, from nature

Après-midi, sf. afternoon

Âpreté, sf. (*etym.* âpre), asperity, roughness, harshness, greediness

Apte, adj. (*etym. L.* aptus), apt to, fit for

Apurement, sm. (*etym.* apurer), audit, closing

Apurer, va. (*etym.* à, pur), to audit, to close

Aquarelle, sf. (*etym. I.* acquerello, *dimin. of* acqua, *water*), water-colours, aquarelle. *A l'*—, in water-colours

Aquarelliste, sm. water-colour painter

Aquatique, adj. (*etym. L.* aquaticus, *from* aqua, *water*), marshy, watery

Aqueduc, sm. (*etym. L.* aqua, ducere, *to lead*), aqueduct, conduit

Aqueux, se, adj. (*etym. L.* aquosus, *from* aqua, *water*), watery, aqueous

Aquilin, adj. (*etym. L.* aquilinus, *from* aquila, *eagle*), aquiline, hooked

Aquilon, sm. (*etym. L.* aquilo, *north wind*), north wind

Arabe, sm. adj. Arab, Arabian, Arabic, (‡) an usurer

Arabique, adj. Arabic

Arabisant, sm. an Arabic scholar

Araignée, sf. (*etym. L.* arachnea, *from the Gr.* ἀράχνη), spider. *Toile d'*—, cobweb, spider's web

Aratoire, adj. (*etym. L.* arare), of husbandry, aratory

Arbalète, sf. (*etym. L.* arcuballista; *see* BALISTE), crossbow, (*nav.*) Jacob's staff

Arbalétrier, sm. (*etym.* arbalète), crossbowman, chief rafters

Arbitrage, sm. (*etym.* arbitre), arbitration

‖**Arbitraire,** adj. (*etym.* arbitre), arbitrary, absolute, optional

‖**Arbitral, e,** adj. (*etym.* arbitre), by arbitration. *Sentence* —*e*, award

Arbitre, sm. (*etym. L.* arbiter), umpire, arbiter, master. *Libre* —, freewill

Arbitrer, va. (*etym.* arbitre), to arbitrate, to estimate

Arborer, va. (*etym. L.* arbor, *a tree*), to erect, to hoist

Arborisé, e, adj. arborized

Arbouse, sf. (*etym. L.* arbutum), arbute-berry

Arbousier, sm. (*etym.* arbouse), arbute-tree

Arbre, sm. (*etym. L.* arbor), tree, (*mec.*) shaft, beam. *L'*— *de la Croix*, the Cross. *Grand* —, (*tech.*) shaft. — *moteur*, main shaft, driving axle. — *de couche*, crank axle, horizontal shaft. — *du tiroir*, excentric shaft. — *coudé*, crank axle. — *des roues*, paddle shaft

Arbrisseau, sm. (*etym. L.L.* arboricellus? *dimin. of* arbor), shrub

Arbuste, sm. (*etym. L.* arbustum), shrub

Arc, sm. (*etym. L.* arcus), bow, longbow, arch, curve, arc; *plur.* (*mec.*) staples. ‡ *Avoir plusieurs cordes à son* —, to have two strings to one's bow

Arcane, sm. (*etym. L.* arcanus, *secret, hidden in a box*, arca), arcanum

Arc-boutant, sm. (*etym.* arc, bouter), (*arch.*) buttress, flying buttress, (*nav.*) boom

Arc-bouter, va. to prop with buttresses

Arceau, sm. (*etym.* arc), small arch

Arc-en-ciel, sm. rainbow

Archaïque, adj. (*etym. see* ARCHAÏSME), archaic

Archaïsme, sm. (*etym. Gr.* ἀρχαϊσμός, *from* ἀρχαῖος, *ancient*), archaism

Archal (Fil d'), sm. (*etym. L.* aurichalcum, *from the Gr.* ὀρείχαλκος), brass wire

Archange, sm. (*etym. Gr.* ἀρχάγγελος, *from* ἄρχω, *I rule*, ἄγγελος), archangel

Arche, sf. (*etym. L.* arca), arch. — *de Noé*, Noah's ark. — *d'alliance*, ark of the Covenant

Archéologie, sf. (*etym. Gr.* ἀρχαιολογία, *from* ἀρχαῖος, *old*, λόγος, *speech*), archæology

Archéologique, adj. (*etym.* archéologie), archæological

Archéologue, sm. (*etym.* archéologie), archæologist

Archer, sm. (*etym.* arc), archer, bowman

Archet, sm. (*etym.* arc), bow, fiddlestick, turner's drill-bow

Archevêché, sm. (*etym.* archevêque), archbishopric, archbishop's palace

Archevêque, sm. (*etym. Gr.* ἀρχιεπίσκοπος, *from* ἄρχω, *I rule*, ἐπίσκοπος, *a bishop*), archbishop

Archi-, part. arch-, (*fam.*) downright. ‡ *Il est fou*, — *fou*, he is mad, downright mad

Archichancelier, sm. lord high chancellor

Archidiaconat, sm. archdeaconship, archdeaconry

Archidiaconé, sm. archdeaconry

Archidiacre, sm. archdeacon

Archiduc, sm. archduke

Archiducal, e, adj. archducal

Archiduché, sm. archdukedom

Archiduchesse, sf. archduchess

Archiépiscopal, e, adj. archiepiscopal

Archiépiscopat, sm. archbishopric

Archimandritat, sm. (*etym.* archimandrite), dignity of an archimandrite

Archimandrite, sm. (*etym. Gr.* ἀρχιμανδρίτης, *from* ἄρχω, μάνδρα, *an enclosure, a cloister*), archimandrite

Archipel, sm. (*etym. I.* arcipelago; *O.F.* archipelague), archipelago

Archiprêtre, sm. archpriest

Archiprêtré, sm. archpriesthood, archpriest's house

Architecte, sm. (*etym. Gr.* ἀρχιτέκτων), architect

Architectonique, sf. (*etym.* architecte), art of building; —adj. architectonic

Architrave, sf. (*etym. L.* archi, trabs, *a beam*), architrave

Archiviste, sm. (*etym.* archives), keeper of the records

Archivolte, sf. (*etym. L.* archi, voltum, *a roof*), archivault

Archontat, sm. (*etym.* archonte), office of archon

Archonte, sm. (*etym. Gr.* ἄρχω, *I rule*), archon

Arçon, sm. (*etym.* arc), holster, saddle-bow. *Pistolets d'—*, horse-pistols. ‡ *Perdre, vider les —s*, to be unhorsed, to be thrown, to be nonplussed. *Être ferme sur ses —s*, to sit well in one's saddle, (*fig.*) to be staunch to one's principles

Arctique, adj. (*etym. Gr.* ἀρκτικός, *from* ἄρκτος, *a bear*), arctic, northern

|**Ardent, e,** adj. (*etym. L.* ardere, *to burn*), fiery, burning, scorching, eager, sanguine, spirited, red. *Charbon —*, lighted charcoal. *Chambre —e*, Star Chamber. *Chapelle —e*, a large display of wax tapers burning round a coffin

Ardent, sm. Will o' the wisp, ignis fatuus

Ardeur, sf. (*etym. L.* ardorem), heat, earnestness, passion, fervour, activity, mettle

Ardoise, sf. (*etym. Celt.* arddu, ardwn, *very dark*), slate

Ardoisé, e, adj. slate-coloured

Ardoisier, sm. slate-worker; — adj. slaty

Ardoisière, sf. slate-quarry

Ardu, e, adj. (*etym. L.* arduus), arduous, difficult

Are, sm. (*etym. L.* area), are (rather more than 119 square yards)

Arène, sf. (*etym. L.* arena), sand, arena

Aréomètre, sm. (*etym. Gr.* ἀραιός, *small*, μέτρον, *measure*), areometer

Aréopage, sm. (*etym. Gr.* Ἀρειόπαγος), Areopagus

Arête, sf. (*etym. L.* arista), fish-bone, ridge, edge, prickle, (*arch.*) arris. *A vive —*, square-edged

Argent, sm. (*etym. L.* argentum), silver, money, coin. *— comptant*, ready money, cash, wealth, riches, (*herald.*) argent. *— blanc*, silver coin. *— vierge*, silver ore. *Vif —*, quicksilver. *Vaisselle d'—*, plate. ‡ *Un bourreau d'—*, a very spendthrift. *Jeter son — par la fenêtre*, to throw away one's money. *Manger son —*, to squander one's money. *Être à court d'—*, to be short of cash. *— en caisse*, cash in hand. *Il faut toujours avoir l'— à la main*, one is always paying money away. *Être cousu d'—*, to roll in riches. *De l'— bien placé*, money which brings in a good interest. *— mignon*, treasure. *Un — fou*, lots of money. *Vous en avez pour votre —*, you have had your money's worth. *Faire — de tout*, to turn everything into money. *Prendre pour — comptant*, to take for sterling truth. *Point d'—, point de Suisse*, no song, no supper. *Bon jeu, bon —*, all fair and above-board

Argenté, e, adj. plated, silvery

Argenter, va. to plate, (*fig.*) to silver; *s'—*, vr. to be plated, to shine like silver

Argenterie, sf. plate, silver-plate

Argenteur, sm. silver-washer

Argentier, sm. silversmith, house-steward, treasurer

Argentifère, adj. argentiferous, rich in silver

Argentin, e, adj. silvery, argentine. *Voix —e*, clear voice

Argentine, sf. wild tansy

Argenture, sf. silvering

Argile, sf. (*etym. Gr.* ἄργιλλος, *from* ἀργός, *white*), clay

Argileux, se, adj. clayey, argillaceous

Argilifère, adj. rich in clay, argilliferous

Argonaute, sm. (*etym. Gr.* Ἀργοναύτης), Argonaut, nautilus

Argot, sm. (*etym.* ? *see* Littré), slang, cant

Argousin, sm. (*etym. corrupt. of the Sp.* alguazil), convict-keeper, policeman

Arguer, va. (*etym. L.* argutare, argutari, *frequent. of* arguere), to argue, to infer, to urge, to plead, to accuse

Argument, sm. (*etym.* arguer), argument, reasoning, controversy, summary

Argumentant, sm. disputant, wrangler

Argumentateur, sm. arguer, opponent

Argumenter, vn. to argue, to infer

Argutie, sf. (*etym. L.* argutia, *from* arguere), cavil, quibble, sophistry

†**Aria,** sm. (*etym.* ?) ado. *Quel —!* what a fuss!

Arianisme, sm. (*etym. the proper name* Arius), Arianism, Arian heresy

Aride, adj. (*etym. L.* aridus), parched, dry, barren, arid, uninteresting

Aridité, sf. drought, aridity, barrenness, want of interest, unfeelingness

Arien, ne, adj. Arian

Ariette, sf. (*etym. I.* arietta), light air, arietta

Aristarque, sm. (*etym. Gr.* Ἀρίσταρχος), Aristarch, critic. ‡ *Se poser en —*, to play the critic

Aristocrate, adj. (*etym. see* ARISTOCRATIE), aristocratic, aristocrat

Aristocratie, sf. (*etym. Gr.* ἀριστοκρατία, *government exercised by the best*), aristocracy, nobility

Aristocratique, adj. aristocratical

Aristotélicien, ne, adj. (*etym.* Aristote), Aristotelian, peripatetic

Aristotélisme, sm. Aristotelism, doctrine of Aristotle

Arithméticien, sm. arithmetician

|**Arithmétique,** sf. (*etym. Gr.* ἀριθμός, *number*), arithmetic, ciphering. — adj. arithmetic

Arlequin, sm. (*etym. I.* arlecchino), harlequin

Arlequinade, sf. harlequin's trick, buffoonery

Armateur, sm. (*etym.* arme), ship-owner, captain, privateer

Armature, sf. iron bars, sheathing. *— des soupapes*, valve-gear

Arme, sf. (*etym. L.* arma), weapon, arm; *plur.* war, fencing, arms, coat of arms. ‡ *Suspension d'—s*, a truce. *Port d'—s*, licence to shoot. *—s à feu*, firearms. *Faire passer par les —s*, to condemn to be shot. *A l'— blanche*, with the bayonet. *Faire ses premières —s*, to be at one's first battle. *Homme d'—s*, man-at-arms. *Portez, présentez, reposez —s!* carry, present, ground arms! *Apprêtez —s!* ready! *—s au bras!* support arms! *Salle d'—s*, fencing-school

Armée, sf. army, host

Armement, sm. armament, accoutrements, fitting out

Armer, va. to arm, to rouse, to equip, to fit out. *— un fusil*, to cock. *— une poutre*, to sheathe. *La force armée*, the military. *A main armée*, by main strength. — vn. to take up arms. *S'—*, vr. to arm oneself, to fly to arms. *S'— de courage*, to muster courage

§**Armillaire,** adj. (*etym. L.* armilla, *bracelet*), armillary

Armoire, sf. (*etym. L.* armarium), cupboard, closet

Armoiries, sf. plur. (*etym. O.F.* armoier, *to make war*), coat of arms, escutcheon, armorial bearings

Armoise, sf. (*etym. Gr.* ἀρτεμισία, *from* Ἄρτεμις, *name of a goddess*), mugwort, wormwood

Armorial, sm. (*etym.* armoiries), book of heraldry

Armorier, va. to paint a coat of arms. *Carrosse armorié*, carriage with armorial bearings

Armure, sf. armour

Armurier, sm. gunsmith, armourer, sword-cutler

Aromate, sm. (*etym. Gr.* ἀρώματα, *plur. of* ἄρωμα), aroma, perfume

Aromatique, adj. aromatic, fragrant

Aromatiser, va. to scent, to aromatize

Arome, sm. aroma, scent

Aronde, sf. (*etym. L., see* HIRONDELLE), swallow. *A queue d'—*, dovetailed

Arpége, Arpégement, sm. (*etym. I.* arpeggio), arpeggio

Arpent, sm. (*etym. L.* arepennis *or* arapennis), between one and one and a half English acres

Arpentage, sm. land-measuring, land-surveying

Arpenter, va. to survey land, to stride along

Arpenteur, sm. land-surveyor

Arpenteuse, sf. citigrade spider

Arqué, adj. (*etym.* arc), arched, curved, crooked. ‡ *Aux jambes —es*, bandy-legged

Arquebuse, sf. (*etym. I.* archibuso), arquebuse

Arquebuser, va. to shoot

Arquebusier, sm. gunsmith, arquebusier

Arquer, va. to bend, to crook; *s'—*, vr. to be bent, to be bowed

Arrachement, sm. (*etym.* arracher), tearing away, extraction

‡**d'Arrache-pied,** adv. unremittingly, uninterruptedly

Arracher, va. (*etym. L.* eradicare), to tear out, to pluck away, to wrench, to wrest, to pull out, to extract. *— la vie à*, to take away (the life of). ‡ *Vous ne lui arracheriez jamais cela de la tête*, you would never get that idea out of his head. *S'—*, vr. to tear oneself. ‡ *On se l'arrache*, every one wishes to have him, there is quite a scramble after it

Arracheur, sm. tearer away, tooth-drawer. ‡ *Être menteur comme un — de dents*, to be a confirmed liar

Arrangeant, e, adj. (*etym.* arranger), easy to deal with

Arrangement, sm. arrangement, order, scheme, agreement. *Entrer en — avec ses créanciers*, to compound with one's creditors

Arranger, va. (*etym.* à, ranger), to put in order, to arrange, to settle, to make up, to suit. *— une lampe*, to trim. ‡ *Voilà qui m'arrange*, that suits me well. *Je l'arrangerai de la bonne manière*, I'll settle his business for him. *S'—*, vr. to arrange oneself, to dress, to settle oneself comfortably, to make shift, to come to an agreement. ‡ *Arrangez-vous*, do as you will

Arrérages, sm. plur. (*etym. O.F.* arrère, *for* arrière), arrears

Arrêt, sm. (*etym.* arrêter), sentence, award, execution, rest, (*mec.*) catch, stop-work. *Maison d'—*, jail, gaol. *Point d'—*, stop. *Un temps d'—*, a bit of rest. *Chien d'—*, pointer. *Tenir le gibier en* —, to stop (the game). *Envoyer aux* —*s*, to put under arrest. *Garder les* —*s*, *être aux* —*s*, to be put under arrest

Arrêté, sm. decision. — *de compte*, closing of an account

Arrêté, e, adj. decided, fixed

Arrêter, va. (*etym. L.* ad, restare), to stop, to fasten, to settle, to hire, to book, to arrest; — vn. to stop; *s'*—, vr. to stop, to stand still, to adopt, to dwell on. *Ne vous arrêtez pas en si beau chemin*, don't stop half way

Arrhes, sm.plur. (*etym. L.* arrha or arra), earnest-money, pledges

Arrière, adv. (*etym. L.* ad, retro), behind, backward. — interj. stand back! fall back! — (*en*), loc. adv. behind, backward, behindhand, in arrears. *Voyager en* —, to sit with one's back to the horses, to the engine. — sm. (*nav.*) stern. *Aller à l'*—, to go aft. *Vent* —, before the wind

Arrière-boutique, sf. (*in this and the eleven following words* arrière *does not take the plural*), back-shop

Arrière-cour, sf. back-yard

Arrière-garde, sf. rear-guard, rear

Arrière-goût, sm. after-taste

Arrière-main, sm. back-stroke. — *d'un cheval*, hind-quarters

Arrière-neveu, sm. grand-nephew; *pl.* remotest posterity

Arrière-pensée, sf. after-thought, by-end

Arrière-petit-fils, sm. great-grandson

Arrière-petite-fille, sf. great-granddaughter

Arrière-petits-enfants, sm.plur. great-grand-children

Arrière-plan, sm. back-ground

Arrière-saison, sf. autumn, decline of life

Arriéré, e, adj. in arrears, behindhand. — sm. arrears, work behindhand

Arriérer, va. to delay, to throw back; *s'*—, vr. to be behindhand

Arrimage, sm. (*etym.* arrimer), stowage, stowing

Arrimer, va. (*etym. Sp. and Port.* arrumar), to stow away

Arrivage, sm. arrival

Arrivant, sm. (*etym.* arriver), new-comer

Arrive (il), v.imp. to happen, to chance, to come to pass. *Quoi qu'il* —, no matter what happens. *Il — souvent que*, it often happens that

Arrivée, sf. arrival, (*nav.*) falling off

Arriver, vn. (*etym. L.L.* adripare), to come, to arrive, to reach, to land, to happen, to occur, to succeed

s'Arroger, vr. (*etym. L.* ad, rogare, *to ask, to claim*), to assume wrongfully, to arrogate, to lay claim to

Arrondir, va. (*etym.* rond), to round, to enlarge, to turn elegantly. ‡ — *sa pelote*, to make money. *S'*—, vr. to grow round, to grow wealthy

Arrondissement, sm. rounding, district

Arrosage, sm. (*etym.* arroser), watering, irrigation

Arrosement, sm. watering, sprinkling, paying all round

Arroser, va. (*etym. L.* ad, ros, *the dew*), to water, to bathe

Arrosoir, sm. watering-pot

Art, sm. (*etym. L.* ars), art, artifice, skill, cunning. *Maître ès* —*s*, master of arts. *See* HOMME

Artère, sf. (*etym. Gr.* ἀρτηρία), artery

Artériel, le, adj. arterial

Artésien, ne, adj. (*etym. L.L.* Artesianus, *an inhabitant of the province of Artois, in France*), Artesian

Artichaut, sm. (*etym. Ar.* ardhischoki), artichoke. *Cul d'*—, bottom of an artichoke. *Foin d'*—, choke

Article, sm. (*etym. L.* articulus), joint, articulation, knuckle, item, head, paper, article. — *de fond*, leading article. *A l'— de la mort*, at the point of death. ‡ *Faire l'*—, to praise one's own goods

Articulé, e, adj. articulate, distinct

Articuler, va. (*etym. L.* articulare), to utter, to articulate, to state

Artifice, sm. (*etym. L.* artificium, *from* ars, *facere*), artifice, contrivance. *Feu d'*—, fireworks

‖**Artificiel, le,** adj. artificial, fictitious

Artificier, sm. firework-maker

‖**Artificieux, se,** adj. artful, cunning

§**Artillerie,** sf. (*etym. L.* ars), artillery, ordnance, cannon

§**Artilleur,** sm. artillery-man, gunner

Artimon, sm. (*etym. Gr.* ἀρτέμων, *from* ἀρτάω, *to be suspended*). *Mât d'*—, mizzen mast. *Perroquet d'*—, mizzen-top mast

Artisan, sm. (*etym.* art), artisan, mechanic, maker

Artison, sm. (*etym.* ? *see* Littré), worm, wood-fretter

‖**Artiste,** s. artist, performer

Artistique, adj. relating to the arts

Aruspice, sm. (*etym. L.* aruspex *or* haruspex), sooth-sayer, aruspex

As, sm. (*etym. L.* as), ace, as

Asbeste, sm. (*etym. Gr.* ἄσβεστος, *unconsumed*), asbestos

Ascaride, sm. (*etym. Gr.* ἀσκαρίς, *from* ἀσκαρίζω, *to move*), ascaris

Ascendance, sf. (*etym. L.* ascendere), ascendency, superiority, descent

Ascendant, e, adj. ascending, ascendant. — sm. ascendant, ruling passion. *Les* —*s*, the progenitors

Ascensionnel, le, adj. of ascent, up ...

Ascète, sm. (*etym. Gr.* ἀσκητής, *a man who exercises himself*), ascetic

Ascétique, adj. ascetic

Ascétisme, sm. asceticism

Asile, sm. (*etym. L.* asylus), asylum, refuge, shelter. *École, salle d'*—, infant school

Asperge, sf. (*etym. L.* asparagus), asparagus. *Botte d'*—*s*, bundle of asparagus

Asperger, va. (*etym. L.* ad, spargere, *to scatter*), to sprinkle

Aspérité, sf. (*etym. L.* asperitas), asperity, roughness, ruggedness

Aspersion, sf. (*etym.* asperger), besprinkling

Aspersoir, sm. holy-water sprinkler

Asphalte, sm. (*etym. Gr.* ἄσφαλτος), bitumen, asphalt

Asphaltique, adj. bituminous

Asphodèle, sm. (*etym. Gr.* ἀσφοδελός), daffodil, asphodel

Asphyxie, sf. (*etym. Gr.* ἀσφυξία, *from* a priv., σφυγμός, *pulse*), suffocation

Asphyxié, e, adj. suffocated

Asphyxier, va. to suffocate, to stifle; *s'*—, vr. to be suffocated, to suffocate oneself

Aspic, sm. (*etym. Gr.* ἀσπίς), aspic. *Langue d'*—, slanderer

Aspirant, e, adj. (*etym.* aspirer), aspirating, sucking up. *Pompe* —*e*, suction-pump

Aspirant, sm. candidate. — *de marine*, midshipman

Aspirer, va. (*etym. L.* ad, spirare), to breathe hard, to inhale, to draw up, to suck up, to aspirate; — vn. to aspire, to aim

§**Assaillant,** sm. (*etym.* assaillir), assailant

§**Assaillir,** va. (*etym. L.* ad, salire, *to jump*), to assail, to assault

Assainir, va. (*etym. L.* ad, sanus, *healthy*), to cleanse, to purify; *s'*—, vr. to become healthy

Assainissement, sm. making healthy, cleansing

Assaisonnement, sm. (*etym.* assaisonner), seasoning, relish, flavour

Assaisonner, va. (*etym.* à, saison), to season, to flavour

Assassin, sm. (*etym. Ar.* haschisch; *liter. those who intoxicate themselves with haschisch*), assassin, murderer. —, —*e*, adj. killing, murderous

Assassinat, sm. murder, assassination

Assassiner, va. to kill, to murder, to be the death of, to bore to death

Assaut, sm. (*etym.* assaillir), assault, onset, storming, besetting. — *d'armes*, fencing match. ‡ *Faire — d'esprit*, to bandy words

Asséchement, sm. (*etym.* assécher), drainage

Assécher, va. (*etym.* à, sécher), to drain

Assemblage, sm. (*etym.* assembler), assemblage, junction, joining. *Boulon d'*—, holding bolt

Assemblée, sf. meeting, assembly. — *au tambour*, call

Assembler, va. (*etym. L.* ad, simul, *together*), to assemble, to call together; *s'*—, vr. to assemble, to meet

Assener, va. (*etym. L.* ad, signare), to deal, to strike

Assentiment, sm. (*etym.* à, sentiment), assent, approbation

Asseoir, va. (*etym.* à, seoir), to put on a seat, to set, to settle

Assermenter, va. (*etym.* à, serment), to swear. * *Prêtre assermenté*, priest having accepted the constitution

Assertion, sf. (*etym. L.* asserere, *to take or seize*), assertion

Asservir, va. (*etym.* à, servir), to enslave, to subdue; *s'*—, vr. to become a slave

Asservissant, e, adj. enslaving

Asservissement, sm. enslaving, slavery

Assesseur, sm. (*etym. L.* assessorem), assessor, assistant

Assez, adv. (*etym. L.* ad, satis), enough

‖**Assidu, e,** adj. (*etym. L.* assiduus), steady, assiduous, hardworking, attentive

Assiduité, sf. assiduity, steadiness, attention

Assiégé, e, adj. beleaguered, besieged

Assiégeant, e, adj. sm. besieging, besieger

Assiéger, va. (*etym.* à, siéger), to besiege

Assiette, sf. (*etym. L.* ad, sedere), plate, proper position, assessment. ‡ *Pique-* —, parasite. *Ne pas être dans son* —, to be out of sorts

Assiettée, sf. plateful

§* **Assignat,** sm. assignat

§**Assignation,** sf. assignment, writ, subpœna. *Signifier une — à*, to serve a writ on

§**Assigner,** va. (*etym. L.* ad, signare), to assign, to allot, to summon, to subpœna

Assimiler, va. (*etym. L.* ad, similis), to liken, to assimilate; *s'*—, vr. to liken oneself, to be assimilated

Assis, e, past part. sm. seated, sitting; *see* ASSEOIR. *Voter par — et levé*, to vote by sitting and standing

Assise, sf. layer, row. *Cour d'*—*s*, court of assize, assizes. — *de houille*, coal-measure

Assistance, sf. (*etym.* assister), attendance, company, audience, help

Assistant, e, adj. s. assistant. *Les —s*, the company

Assister, va. (*etym. L.* adsistere), to help, to assist, to succour; — vn. to be present

Association, sf. (*etym.* associer), association, partnership

Associé, sm. associate, accomplice, partner, fellow. — *commanditaire*, sleeping partner. — *gérant*, managing partner. — *principal*, senior partner

Associer, va. (*etym. L.* associare, *to join to*), to associate, to admit, to link together, to take into partnership; *s'—*, vr. to associate with, to take a share in, to enter into partnership with

Assombrir, va. (*etym.* à, sombre), to darken, to make gloomy; *s'—*, vr. to grow dark

†**Assommant, e**, adj. (*etym.* assommer), wearisome, tiresome

Assommer, va. (*etym.* somme, *a burden* ?), to fell to the ground, to beat to death, to tire out

Assommoir, sm. club, life-preserver. *Coup d'—*, dreadful blow

Assomption, sf. (*etym. L.* assumere, *to take to*), assumption

Assorti, e, adj. (*etym.* à, sorte), well matched, well furnished

Assortiment, sm. assortment, stock, set, suit

Assortir, va. to match, to sort, to stock; *s'—*, vr. to be matched, to get a good stock

Assoupi, e, adj. drowsy

Assoupir, va. (*etym. L.* ad, sopire, *to send to sleep*), to make drowsy, to lull, to quiet, to allay. — *une affaire*, to hush up. *S'—*, vr. to doze, to slumber, to be allayed

Assoupissant, e, adj. somniferous

Assoupissement, sm. drowsiness, doze

Assouplir, va. (*etym.* à, souple), to make supple, to unstiffen, to break; *s'—*, vr. to grow supple, to grow more tractable

Assourdir, va. (*etym.* à, sourd), to deafen, to stun, to muffle

Assourdissant, e, adj. deafening, stunning

Assouvir, va. (*etym. L. L.* assopire? as-sufficere?), to glut, to satiate; *s'—*, vr. to be glutted, to be satiated

Assouvissement, sm. glutting, gratifying

Assujettir, va. (*etym.* à, sujet), to subject, to enslave, to expose, to oblige, to fasten

Assujettissant, e, adj. which ties down, binding

Assujettissement, sm. subjection, constraint, tying down

Assumer, va. (*etym. L.* ad, sumere, *to take*), to assume, to take

Assurance, sf. (*etym.* assurer), assurance, conviction, security, boldness, insurance. *Compagnie d'— pour la vie, contre l'incendie*, fire and life insurance company

‡**Assuré, e**, adj. positive, certain, bold, impudent, insured

Assurer, va. (*etym.* à, sûr), to assert, to assure, to vouch for, to ensure, to steady, to fasten, to settle on, to insure; *s'—*, vr. to be assured of, to ascertain, to insure oneself, to make sure of, to arrest, to seize

Assureur, sm. insurer, underwriter

Astérisque, sm. (*etym. Gr.* ἀστερίσκος, *a small star*), asterisk, star

Asthmatique, adj. (*etym.* asthme), asthmatic

Asthme, sm. (*etym. Gr.* ἆσθμα, *breathing*), asthma

Asticot, sm. (*etym.* asticoter), worm, gentle

Asticoter, va. (*etym. G.* stechen, *to move*), to tease, to wriggle

Astiquer, va. (*etym. G.* stich, *a pointed thing*), to furbish up

Astragale, sm. (*etym. Gr.* ἀστράγαλος, *a small bone*), (*arch.*) astragal

Astre, sm. (*etym. L.* astrum), star

Astreindre, va. (*etym. L.* adstringere, *to seize hold of*), to constrain, to compel, to confine; *s'—*, vr. to bind oneself down, to confine oneself

Astrologie, sf. (*etym. Gr.* ἀστρολογία), astrology

Astrologique, adj. astrological

Astrologue, sm. astrologer

Astronome, sm. (*etym. Gr.* ἀστρονόμος), astronomer

Astronomie, sf. astronomy

Astronomique, adj. astronomical

Astuce, sf. (*etym. L.* astutia, *cunning*), guile, cunning, craftiness

‡**Astucieux, se**, adj. crafty, cunning

Atelier, sm. (*liter. a joiner's shop, from L. L.* hastella, *a small stick, or piece of wood*), workshop, workmen, gang, studio. *Chef d'—*, foreman

Atermoiement, sm. (*etym.* atermoyer), composition, compounding, delay

Atermoyer, va. (*etym.* à, terme), to put off, to defer payment; *s'—*, vr. to compound with one's creditors

Athée, sm. adj. (*etym. Gr.* ἄθεος, *from* a priv., θεός, *god*), atheist, atheistical

Athéisme, sm. atheism

Athénée, sm. (*etym. Gr.* Ἀθηναῖον, *temple of Minerva*), Athenæum

Athlétique, adj. (*etym. Gr.* ἀθλητής, *a wrestler*), athletic

Atmosphérique, adj. (*etym.* atmosphère *from the Gr.* ἀτμός, *vapour*, σφαῖρα, *sphere*), atmospherical. *Tuyau —*, vacuum tube

Atome, sm. (*etym. Gr.* ἄτομος, *which cannot be divided*), atom

Atone, adj. (*etym.* atonie), lacklustre, lifeless

Atonie, sf. (*etym. Gr.* ἀτονία), atony, debility

Atours, sm. plur. (*etym.* à, tourner), finery, attire. *Dame d'—*, lady of the chamber

Atout, sm. (*etym.* à, tout), trump, (†) knock, blow. *Couper avec l'—*, to trump

Atrabilaire, adj. (*etym. L.* ater, *black*, bilis, *bile*), atrabilious, splenetic

Âtre, sm. (*etym. O. H. D.* astrik, *G.* estrich, *the floor of a room*), fireplace, hearth

‡**Atroce**, adj. (*etym. L.* atrox), heinous, atrocious, excruciating

Atrocité, sf. atrocity, atrociousness

Atrophie, sf. (*etym. Gr.* ἀτροφία, *from* a priv., τρέφειν, *to feed*), atrophy, emaciation

s'Atrophier, vr. to grow or become emaciated

s'Attabler, vr. (*etym.* à, table), to sit down to table

Attachant, e, adj. (*from* attacher), engaging, pleasing, attractive, tying

Attache, sf. tie, link, tether, leash, bond

Attaché, sm. attaché

Attachement, sm. attachment, inclination, affection

Attacher, va. (*etym.* à, tacher), to tie, to fasten, to link, to tether, to endear, to interest, to move; *s'—*, vr. to cling to, to stick to, to love, to become attached to, to win the affection of, to strive, to apply oneself

Attaquable, adj. (*etym.* attaquer), assailable

Attaquant, sm. assailant

Attaque, sf. onset, attack, fit, stroke

Attaquer, va. (*is the northern pronunciation of* attacher), to attack, to encounter, to affront, to impeach, to begin, to contest; *s'—*, vr. to attack each other, to attack, to fall upon

Attarder, va. (*etym.* à, tard), to delay, to retard; *s'—*, vr. to set out late, to stop out late, to loiter

Atteindre, va. (*etym. L.* attingere), to hit, to reach, to harm, to overtake, to attain, to be a match for; — vn. to reach, to attain to

Atteinte, sf. blow, hurt, wrong, prejudice, slight attack. *Hors d'—*, out of reach. *Porter — à*, to wrong

Attelage, sm. (*etym.* atteler), set of horses, team, set of harness

Atteler, va. (*etym. O. F.* astele or astelet, *part of the collar of a horse*), to put to (the horses)

Attenant, e, adj. (*etym.* à, tenir), adjacent, adjoining, next to. — prep. adv. close by, hard by

Attendant (en), adv. (*etym.* attendre), meanwhile, in the meantime

Attendre, va. (*etym. L.* ad, tendere, *to aim at*), to wait, to expect, to look forward to. — *de pied ferme*, to be ready for. *Il se fait bien —*, he is a long while coming. *S'—*, vr. to expect, to look forward to

Attendrir, va. (*etym.* à, tendre), to soften, to mollify, to affect, to move to tears; *s'—*, vr. to become less tough, to be moved, to melt into tears

Attendrissant, e, adj. moving

Attendrissement, sm. emotion, tears, pity

Attendu que, loc. conj. since, whereas

Attentat, sm. (*etym.* attenter), criminal attempt, outrage

Attentatoire, adj. derogatory

Attente, sf. waiting, expectation, hope. *Salle d'—*, waiting-room

Attenter, vn. (*etym.* à, tenter), to make an attempt

‡**Attentif, ve**, adj. (*etym. see* ATTENTION), attentive, heedful, intent

Attention, sf. (*etym. L.* attentio, *from* attendere, *to stretch towards*), attention, kind notice

Atténuant, e, adj. (*etym. see* ATTÉNUER), extenuating, palliative. *Circonstances —es*, extenuating circumstances

Atténuation, sf. extenuation

Atténuer, va. (*etym. L.* ad, tenuis, *small or slender*), to palliate, to extenuate, to attenuate

Atterrer, va. (*etym.* à, terre), to throw to the ground, to subvert, to dishearten thoroughly

Attestation, sf. (*etym.* attester), attestation, evidence, warrant, voucher. — *sous serment*, affidavit

Attester, va. (*etym. L.* attestari, *from* ad, testis, *a witness*), to attest, to vouch for, to take to witness

Attiédir, va. (*etym.* à, tiède), to chill, to cool; *s'—*, vr. to grow cool, to become lukewarm

Attiédissement, sm. lukewarmness

†**Attifer**, va. (*etym.* à, *O. F.* tifer, *to dress the hair*), to bedizen, to bedeck; *s'—*, vr. to bedizen oneself out

Attique, sm. (*arch.*) attic. — adj. Attic, Athenian

§**Attirail**, sm. (*etym.* attirer) train, equipage, encumbrances, paraphernalia

Attirant, e, adj. attractive, pleasing

Attirer, va. (*etym.* à, tirer), to draw, to attract, to allure; *s'*—, vr. to attract one another, to bring on oneself, to incur

Attiser, va. (*etym. L.* ad, titio, *a brand*), to stir, to poke

Attisoir, sm. poker

Attitré, e, adj. (*etym.* à, titre), ordinary, appointed

Attouchement, sm. (*etym.* à, touche), touch, feeling. *Point d'*—, point of contact

Attractif, ve, adj. (*etym.* attraire), attractive

Attraire, va. (*etym. L.* attrahere, *to draw towards*), to attract

Attrait, sm. allurement, charm, attraction

Attrape, sf. (*etym.* à, trappe), trap, take-in, trick

Attraper, va. to catch, to entrap, to overreach, to trick, to hit off; *s'*—, vr. to overreach oneself, to overreach one another, to knock oneself

Attrapeur, sm. deceiver

Attrayant, e, adj. attractive, engaging

Attribuer, va. (*etym. L.* attribuere, *to grant to*), to ascribe, to attribute; *s'*—, vr. to claim

Attribut, sm. attribute, emblem, predicate

Attributif, ve, adj. attributive

Attristant, e, adj. (*etym.* attrister), sorrowful, sad

Attrister, va. (*etym. L.* ad, tristis), to grieve, to sadden; *s'*—, vr. to grieve at, to grow sad at

Attroupement, sm. (*etym. see* ATTROUPER), crowd, mob

Attrouper, va. (*etym.* à, troupe), to gather in crowds; *s'*—, vr. to gather in crowds, to flock together

Aubade, sf. (*etym.* aube), music at early dawn, (†) good scolding. *Donner une* — *à*, to play music under the windows of

Aubaine, sf. (*etym. doubtful, see* Littré), aubaine, alienage, windfall, godsend

Aube, sf. (*etym. L.* albus, *white*), dawn, break of day, alb, (*etym.* ?) float-board, paddle-board, paddles. *Roue à* —*s*, paddle-wheel. —*s mobiles*, feathering paddles

Aubépine, sf. (*etym. L.* alba, spina), hawthorn, may

Auberge, sf. (*etym. Prov.* albere, *lodging*), inn, tavern

Aubergine, sf. (*etym. L.* albus, *because the fruit is white*), mad-apple

Aubergiste, smf. innkeeper, tavern-keeper

‡**Aucun, e**, adj. pron. (*etym. L.* aliquis), any, any whatever, no, not any

Audace, sf. (*etym. L.* audacia), audacity, daring, impudence, sauciness. ‡ *Payer d'*—, to put a bold face on the matter

‡**Audacieux, se**, adj. daring, bold, audacious, impudent, saucy

Audiencier, sm. (*etym.* audience), crier

Auditeur, sm. auditor, hearer, councillor

Auditif, ve, adj. auditory

Auditoire, sm. assembly-room, session-house, hearers, congregation

Auge, sf. (*etym. L.* alveus, *a basin*), trough, horse-trough, hod

Auget, sm. trough

Augmentatif, ve, adj. augmentative

Augmenter, va. (*etym. L.* augmentare), to augment, to increase, to enlarge, to aggravate. — *un employé*, to raise the salary of. — *un domestique*, to raise the wages of. — vn., *S'*—, vr. to increase, to grow

Augure, sm. (*etym. L.* augurium), augury, omen, augur, soothsayer

Augurer, va. to augur, to conjecture

Auguste, adj. (*etym. L.* augustus), august, grand, imposing, holy

Augustin, sm. (*etym. the name of St. Augustine*), Augustine monk

Aujourd'hui, adv. (*etym.* au, jour, de, hui—*L.* hodie), to-day, in our days, nowadays. *D'— en huit, en quinze*, this day week, this day fortnight. *Il y a — huit jours, quinze jours*, a week ago, a fortnight ago

Aulique, adj. (*etym. L.* aula, *a court*), aulic

Aumône, sf. (*etym. Gr.* ἐλεημοσύνη, *pity, compassion*), alms. *Faire l'*—, to give alms

Aumônerie, sf. chaplaincy

Aumônier, sm. chaplain

Aumusse, sf. (*etym.* ?) amess

Aunage, sm. (*etym.* aune), measure by ells

Aunaie, sf. (*etym. L.* alnetum, *a plantation of alder-trees*), alder-plantation

Aune, sm. (*etym. L.* alnus), alder-tree

Aune, sf. (*etym. L.L.* alena, *from the Goth.* aleina), ell

Auner, va. to measure by ells

Auparavant, adv. (*etym.* au, par, avant), before, heretofore, ere now, first, first of all

Auprès, adv. (*etym.* au, près), close by, near. — *de*, prep. near, nigh, close to, in comparison with, in the service of

Auréole, sf. (*etym. L.* aureola [corona *understood*], *a crown of gold*), halo, crown of glory

Auriculaire, adj. (*etym. L.* auricula, *dimin. of* auris, *the ear*), auricular. — sm. little finger

Aurifère, adj. (*etym. L.* aurum, ferre, *to carry*), auriferous. *Terrain* —, gold-diggings

Aurore, sf. (*etym. L.* Aurora), Aurora, dawn, promise, the east, yellow, saffron. — adj. yellow, saffron-coloured

Ausculter, va. (*etym. L.* auscultare, *to listen*), to auscultate

Auspice, sm. (*etym. L.* auspicium), auspice, omen, auspices, patronage

Aussi, adv. (*etym. L.* aliud, sic; *O.F.* altresi), also, besides, so, therefore, such, as much, so much. — *bien*, after all, to tell the truth

Aussitôt, adv. forthwith, as soon. — *dit*, — *fait*, no sooner said than done

Austérité, sf. (*etym.* austère), austerity, harshness, sternness

Autan, sm. (*etym. L.* altanus, *south-west wind; see* Vitruvius), south wind, (*poet.*) bleak wind

Autant, adv. (*etym. L.* ad, tantum), as much, so much, so many. ‡ — *de fait*, so much done. — *dire*, one might as well say. — *que*, loc. conj. as much. *D'*— *que* (*parce que*), forasmuch as

Autel, sm. (*etym. L.* altare), altar; *pl.* religion. ‡ *Maître* —, high altar

Auteur, sm. (*etym. L.* auctor), author, creator, maker, authority, perpetrator. ‡ *Droits d'*—, copyright

Authenticité, sf. (*etym.* authentique), authenticity, genuineness

‡**Authentique**, adj. (*etym. L.* authenticus), authentic, true

Autochthones, sm. plur. (*etym. Gr.* αὐτός, *same*, χθών, *the earth*), aborigines

Autocrate, sm., **Autocratrice**, sf. (*etym. Gr.* αὐτός, κράτος, *strength*), autocrat

Autocratie, sf. (*etym.* autocrate), autocracy

Autocratique, adj. autocratic, autocratical

Autographe, sm. (*etym. Gr.* αὐτός, γράφειν, *to write*), autograph. — adj. autographic

Autographie, sf. facsimile

Autographier, va. to make a fac-simile of

Automate, sm. (*etym. Gr.* αὐτός, μάτος, *an effort*), automaton, simpleton

Automatique, adj. mechanical, automatous

Automatisme, sm. automatism

Automnal, e, adj. (*etym.* automne), autumnal, of autumn

Automne, sm. (*etym. L.* autumnus), autumn

Autopsie, sf. (*etym. Gr.* αὐτός, ὄψις, *sight, view*), post-mortem examination

Autorisation, sf. (*etym.* autoriser), authorization, licence

Autoriser, va. (*etym. L.* auctor), to empower, to authorize, to license; *s'*—, vr. to be encouraged, to avail oneself of

Autorité, sf. (*etym. L.* auctoritas), authority, rule, law, the authorities. ‡ *Jouer d'*— (*aux cartes*), to play without calling. *De mon — privée*, of my own free will

Autour, adv. (*etym.* au, tour), around. — *de*, prep. round, around, about

Autour, sm. (*etym. L.L.* astorius, *from* Astur, *because the bird originally came from the Asturias*), goshawk

Autre, ind. adj. (*etym. L.* alter), other, different, more. *Personne* —, *pas d'*—, no other, no one else. *Pas d'*— *chose*, nothing else. *Rien* — *chose*, nothing else

‡**Autre**, ind. pron. other. *L'un ou l'*—, either. *Ni l'un ni l'*—, neither. *L'un et l'*—, both. *L'un l'*—, each other, one another. ‡ *L'un portant l'*—, one with another. *Comme nous* —*s*, like us. *Comme dit cet* —, as the saying is. *Il n'en fait jamais d'*—*s*, it is just like him. *A d'*—*s!* you need not expect me to believe that!

Autrefois, adv. formerly, heretofore, in bygone times, in days of yore

Autruche, sf. (*etym. L.* avis, struthio; *liter. bird-ostrich*), ostrich

Autrui, ind. pron. (*etym. L.* alter, huic), others, our neighbour

Auvent, sm. (*etym. L.* ante, ventus), penthouse, awning

Auxiliaire, sm. adj. (*etym. L.* auxiliaris), auxiliary, aid

s'Avachir, vr. (*etym. G.* weich, *soft*), to get out of shape, to lose its freshness

Aval, sm. (*com.*) guarantee; *plur.* des avals

Aval (en), adv. (*etym.* à, val), down the river

Avalanche, sf. (*etym. L.L.* avalantia, *descent, fall*), avalanche

Avaler, va. (*etym.* à, val), to swallow, to quaff, to toss down. — *un discours*, to hear to the end. ‡ — *un affront*, to pocket an affront. ‡ *Il lui a fallu* — *le goujon*, he was obliged to swallow it down

Avaleur, sm. a man who is in the habit of swallowing greedily

Avaloire, sf. throat, swallow, breeching

Avance, sf. (*etym. see* AVANCER), advance, start, first steps, attention, projection. *Avoir de l'*— *sur*, to have the start of. *Faire de grandes* —*s*, to advance large sums

Avance (d', par), loc. adv. in advance, beforehand

Avancé, e, adj. advanced, spent, late, spoilt, forward, clever. *Ouvrage* —, (*mil.*) outwork. *Garde* —*e*, outpost. † *Vous voilà bien* —*!* you're no farther than before!

Avancement, *sm.* advance, improvement, progress, preferment, advantage

Avancer, *va.* (*etym.* avant), to advance, to move forward, to urge on, to promote. *Faire* —, to bring forward, to call (*a cab*). — *vn.* to advance, to go forward, to walk on, to project, to protrude. *S'*—, *vr.* to advance, to gain ground, to protrude, to project

Avanie, *sf.* (*etym. L.Gr.* ἀβανία, *affront; O.F.* vanie), ill-treatment

Avant, *prep.* (*etym. L.* ab, ante), before, in front of. — *adv.* before, far, deep. —*que*, *loc. conj.* ere, before. —*de*, *loc. prep.* before

Avant, *sm.* bow, prow, forepart. *Passagers de l'*—, forecabin passengers. ¦ *Aller de l'*—, to go ahead

Avantage, *sm.* (*etym. L.L.* abantaticum, *from L.* ab, ante), advantage, gain, upper hand, convenience, (*jurisp.*) gift, endowment. — *du vent*, weather-gage

Avantager, *va.* to favour, to gratify, to settle upon, to endow with

¦**Avantageux**, **se**, *adj.* advantageous, profitable, convenient, becoming, assuming

Avant-bras, *sm.* fore-arm; *plur.* des avant-bras

Avant-corps, *sm.* forepart; *plur.* des avant-corps

Avant-cour, *sf.* front yard; *plur.* des avant-cours

Avant-coureur, *sm.* forerunner, precursor, harbinger; *plur.* des avant-coureurs

Avant-courrière, *sf.* harbinger; *plur.* des avant-courrières

Avant-dernier, **ère**, *adj.* last but one

Avant-garde, *sf.* van, vanguard

Avant-goût, *sm.* foretaste, anticipation; *plur.* des avant-goûts

Avant-hier, *adv.* the day before yesterday

Avant-pied, *sm.* outer vamp; *plur.* des avant-pieds

Avant-port, *sm.* outer harbour; *plur.* des avant-ports

Avant-poste, *sm.* outpost, out-picket; *plur.* des avant-postes

Avant-propos, *sm.* preface, preliminary dissertation

Avant-scène, *sf.* stage-box; *plur.* des avant-scènes

Avant-toit, *sm.* eaves; *plur.* des avant-toits

Avant-train, *sm.* fore-wheels; *plur.* des avant-trains

Avant-veille, *sf.* the last day but one before

Avare, *sm. adj.* (*etym. L.* avarus), miser; covetous, miserly, grasping

Avarice, *sf.* (*etym. L.* avaritia), avarice, covetousness

Avarie, *sf.* (*etym. L.L.* avaria, havaria, *origin doubtful*), damage, injury

Avarié, **e**, *adj.* damaged

Avarier, *va.* to damage; *s'*—, *vr.* to be damaged, to be spoilt

A-vau-l'eau, *adv.* (*etym. see* Aval), down the stream. ¦ *Tout allait* —, everything was going to rack and ruin

Avec, **Avecque**, *prep.* (*etym. L.* apud hoc; *O.F.* avoec), with, along with, in spite of. *D'*—, from

†**Aveindre**, *va.* (*etym. L.* advenire), to reach after

Aveline, *sf.* (*etym. L.* nux avellana, *from* Avella, *a town in Campania*), filbert

Avenant, **e**, *adj.* (*etym.* à, venir), prepossessing, pleasing. *Quelque chose d'*—, something prepossessing. *A l'*—, *adv.* on the same scale, of a piece

Avènement, *sm.* accession, advent, coming. ¦ *Don de joyeux* —, benevolence

Avenir, *sm.* the future, futurity, prospects. ¦ *Jeune homme d'un grand* —, a youth of great promise

Avent, *sm.* Advent

Aventure, *sf.* (*etym. L.* adventurus, *from* advenire, *to happen, to come to pass*), adventure, accident, daring enterprise, intrigue, love affair. ¦ *Courir les* —*s*, to seek after adventures. *Tenter l'*—, to try one's fortune. *A l'*—, at random. *Par* —, *d'*—, by chance. *Mal d'*—, whitlow. *Se faire dire la bonne* —, to have one's fortune told. *Diseuse de bonne* —, fortune-teller, seer. *Grosse* —, (*com.*) bottomry

Aventuré, **e**, *adj.* uncertain, adventurous

Aventurer, *va.* to risk, to venture; *s'*—, *vr.* to venture, to risk oneself, to try the chance

Aventureux, **se**, *and* **Aventurier**, **ère**, *s. adj.* adventurous, daring, enterprising; adventurer, impostor

Avenu, **e**, *adj.* *Non* —, null and void

Avérer, *va.* (*etym. L.* a, verus, *true*), to prove. *C'est un fait avéré*, it is a fact

Averse, *sf.* (*etym. L.* a, vertere, *to turn*), shower, shower of rain

Avertir, *va.* to warn, to give notice, to admonish. *Un bon averti en vaut deux*, (*proverb*) forewarned, forearmed

Avertissement, *sm.* warning, admonition, notice, advertisement. — *préalable*, previous warning

Aveu, *sm.* (*etym.* à, vœu), avowal, confession, acknowledgment. *De l'— de tout le monde*, every one agrees that. *Homme sans* —, vagrant, vagabond

Aveugle, *adj.* (*etym. L.* ab, oculus), blind, sightless, implicit. *Un* — *-né*, a man born blind. *Crier comme un* —, to cry out, to shriek

Aveuglement, *sm.* blindness, delusion

Aveuglément, *adv.* blindly, foolishly, implicitly

Aveugler, *va.* to blind, to dazzle

Aveuglette (**à l'**), *adv.* gropingly, in the dark, blindly

¦**Avide**, *adj.* (*etym. L.* avidus), greedy, grasping, covetous

Avidité, *sf.* avidity greediness

Avilir, *va.* (*etym.* à, vil), to debase, to degrade, to disparage, to depreciate; *s'*—, *vr.* to debase oneself, to disgrace oneself, to lose its value, to fall in price

Avilissant, **e**, *adj.* degrading, worthless

Avilissement, *sm.* worthlessness, disgrace, debasement

Aviné, **e**, *adj.* (*etym.* à, vin), tipsy, drunken

Aviron, *sm.* (*etym.* à, viron; *see* Virer), oar, scull. *Jeu d'*—*s*, set of oars. *Coup d'*—, stroke of an oar

Avis, *sm.* (*etym.* à, vis, *from the L.* visum), opinion, way of thinking, advice, warning, notice. *A mon* —, in my opinion. *Sans* —, on a short notice, (*com.*) without advice. *Aller aux* —, to vote

Avisé, **e**, *adj.* wary, clear-sighted, prudent

Aviser, *va.* to espy, to advise. *Il faut* —, it must be seen to. *S'*—, *vr.* to bethink oneself of

§**Avitaillement**, *sm.* (*etym.* avitailler), victualling

§**Avitailler**, *va.* (*etym.* à, vitaille, victuaille), to victual, to provide with; *s'*—, *vr.* to provision oneself

Aviver, *va.* (*etym.* à, vif), to brighten, to heighten

Avocat, *sm.* (*etym. L.* advocare, *to call to*), lawyer, barrister, intercessor, advocate. — *général*, attorney-general

Avoine, *sf.* (*etym. L.* avena), oats

Avoir, *va.* (*etym. L.* habere), to have, to possess, to hold, to entertain. — *à*, to have to. *Faire* — *à*, to procure for

Avoir (**y**), *v.imp.* *Il ne saurait* —, there cannot be. *Qu'y a-t-il?* what's the matter? *Il y a*, there is, there are. *Il y a deux jours*, two days ago

Avoir, *sm.* substance, property, credit-side. *Tout son* —, all he had or possessed. *Compte par doit et* —, account by D^r and C^r. *Porter à l'*—*de*, to credit

Avoisinant, **e**, *adj.* (*etym.* voisin), adjacent

Avoisiner, *va.* to be close to, to be the neighbour of, to live close to

Avorté, **e**, *adj.* (*etym.* avorter), abortive

Avortement, *sm.* miscarriage, untimely birth, abortion, discomfiture

Avorter, *vn.* (*etym. L.* abortare), to miscarry, to be baffled, to fail

Avorton, *sm.* abortive child, abortion

Avoué, *sm.* (*etym. see* Avocat), solicitor, attorney. *Étude d'*—, solicitor's office

Avouer, *va.* (*etym.* à, vouer), to own, to avow, to acknowledge, to profess, to approve. ¦ *Faire* — *à*, to elicit from. *S'*—, *vr.* to own oneself

Avril, *sm.* (*etym. L.* aprilis), April. ¦ *Poisson d'*—, April fool. *Donner un poisson d'*— *à*, to make an April fool of

Axe, *sm.* (*etym. L.* axis), axis, diameter, axle, spindle. — *coudé*, crank. — *en T*, cross-axle

Axiome, *sm.* (*etym. Gr.* ἀξίωμα, *a proposition*), axiom, truism

Ayant cause, *sm.* representative, assignee, executor

Ayant droit, *sm.* rightful claimant

Azimut, *sm.* (*etym. Ar.* al, semt, *path*), azimuth

Azote, *sm.* (*etym. Gr.* a priv., ζάω, *I live*), azote

Azoté, **e**, *adj.* containing azote

Azur, *sm.* (*etym. Pers.* lâzur), lapis lazuli, azure, light blue

Azuré, **e**, *adj.* azure, blue, sky-coloured

Azyme, *adj.* (*etym. Gr.* a priv., ζύμη, *leaven*), unleavened. *Fête des* —*s*, feast of unleavened bread

B

B, *sm.* *the second letter of the alphabet*, b

Babil, *sm.* (*onomatop.*), chattering, babble, prattle, prating, cawing

§**Babillage**, *sm.* (*etym.* babil), idle prattle, silly talk

§**Babillard**, **e**, *s. adj.* chatterbox, babbler, prattler, tell-tale; talkative, yelping

§**Babillement**, *sm.* talkativeness

§**Babiller**, *vn.* to prattle, to chat, to talk idly, to chatter, to caw, to bark

Babiole, *sf.* (*etym. from a root* bab), bawble, gewgaw, trifle, plaything

Bâbord, *sm.* (*etym. G.* backbord), (*nav.*) larboard.

— interj. larboard the helm! port the helm! aport! — *tout*, hard aport!

Babouche, sf. (*etym. Ar.* bâboudj; *Pers.* papoch, *from* pa, *foot*, poch, *a wrap*), a sort of slipper

Babouin, sm. (*etym. G.* bäppe), baboon; — sm., —e, f. young monkey, hussey

Bac, sm. (*etym. L.L.* bachium, baccus, *a boat*), ferry-boat, trough

Baccalauréat, sm. (*etym. L.L.* bachalariatus, *a grade in ancient chivalry; see* BACHELIER), bachelor's degree, baccalaureate. — *ès lettres*, — *ès sciences*, baccalaureate of letters, of sciences

Bacchanal, sm. (*etym. the name of the god* Bacchus), uproar, row; —e, sf. bacchanal, drunken revelry; —es, sf.plur. Bacchanals, feast of Bacchus

Bâche, sf. (*etym.* bac, *in the sense of tank*), cart-tilt, hot-bed frame, drag-net, tank

Bachelier, sm. (*etym. from a root* bacal, bacel, bachel = vassal), bachelor. — *ès lettres*, — *ès sciences*, bachelor of letters, of sciences

Bâcher, va. (*etym.* bâche), to tilt

Bachique, adj. convivial, drinking

†**Bachot,** sm. (*etym.* bac), wherry

Bachotage, sm. wherrying

Bâcler, va. (*etym. Prov.* baclar, *to shut*), to bar, to patch up, to hurry over

Badaud, e, smf. (*etym. L.L.* badare, batare, *to gape*), cockney, gazer, idler

Badauder, vn. to go gaping about, to idle

Badauderie, sf. loitering, idling, silly talk

Badigeon, sm. (*etym.* ?) whitewash

Badigeonnage, sm. whitewashing

Badigeonner, va. to whitewash, to daub

Badigeonneur, sm. whitewasher, plasterer

Badin, e, adj. (*etym. same as* badaud), sprightly, playful

Badinage, sm. jesting, trifling, jocularity, mere trifle

Badine, sf. switch, light cane; *pl.* small tongs

Badiner, va.n. to jest, to be joking, to wave about. ‡ *Un homme qui ne badine pas*, a man who means what he says

Badinerie, sf. jesting

Bafouer, va. (*etym. O.D.* bap *or* baf, *a lip*), to scoff at, to scout, to jeer at

†**Bâfre,** sf. (*etym. same as* bafouer), a spread, a blow-out

†**Bâfrer,** vn. to stuff and swill

†**Bâfreur,** sm. a greedy person

Bagage, sm. (*etym. O.F.* bagues, sf.plur. *parcels*), luggage, baggage, wretched furniture. *Bureau des* —, luggage office. *Enregistrer son* —, to book one's luggage. ‡ *Plier* —, to be off, to die

Bagarre, sf. (*etym.* ?) stoppage, affray, brawl, squabble

Bagatelle, sf. (*etym. L.L.* baga; *O.F.* bagues), trifle, trash, bawble. ‡ *S'amuser à la* —, to waste one's time in trifles. — interj. nonsense! tush!

§**Bagne,** sm. (*etym. I.* bagno), bagnio, hulks, convicts' prison

†**Bagou,** sm. (*etym.* ba, gueule), gabble, gab, talk. † *Avoir du* —, to talk glibly and impudently

Bague, sf. (*etym. L.L.* bauca, bauga, *a bracelet*), ring. *Jeu de* —*s*, ring-tilting

‡**Baguenauder,** vn. (*etym.* ?) to trifle

Baguenaudier, sm. bladder-nut tree, ring-puzzle

Baguer, va. (*etym. Sp.* baga, *a rope*), to tack, to baste

Baguette, sf. (*etym. I.* bacchetta, *a rod*), switch, rod, wand, ramrod, drumstick, maulstick, bead, fillet. — *à gants*, glove-stretcher. ‡ *Faire marcher à la* —, to rule with a tight hand

Baguier, sm. (*etym.* bague), ring-casket, ring-cup

Bah! interj. tush! pooh! *Ah* —! really! you don't mean it!

Bahut, sm. (*etym.* ? *see* Littré), trunk, chest

Bai, e, adj. (*etym. L.L.* baius, bagus), bay. *Cheval* —, bay. — *châtain*, chestnut-coloured

Baie, sf. (*etym.* (1) Baie, *prop. name, a bay;* (2) *L.* bacca, *a berry;* (3) *L.L.* badare, *to gape*), bay, opening, berry, trick

§**Baignade,** sf. (*etym.* bain), bath, dip

§**Baigner,** va. to bathe, to dip; *se* —, vr. to take a bath, to bathe, to wade, to welter

§**Baigneur, se,** s. bather, bathkeeper

§**Baignoir,** sm. bathing-place

§**Baignoire,** sf. bath, a kind of box at a theatre

§**Bail,** sm. (*etm. L.L.* ballum), lease. — *à vie*, life lease. — *à terme*, lease for a term

§**Bâillement,** sm. (*etym.* bâiller), yawning, gaping, hiatus

§**Bâiller,** vn. (*etym. L.L.* badare; *O.F.* baailler), to yawn, to gape, to be ajar

§**Bailler,** va. (*etym. L.L.* bajulare, *to carry*), to give. † *Vous nous la baillez belle*, a pretty story you tell us there

§**Bâilleur, se,** s. yawner

§**Bailleur, eresse,** s. lessor. — *de fonds*, money-lender

§**Bailli,** sm. bailiff

§**Bailliage,** sm. bailiwick

§**Bâillon,** sm. gag

§**Bâillonner,** va. to gag, to stop the tongue of

Bain, sm. (*etym. L.* balneum, *a bath*), bath, bathing, bathing-rooms. — *de siège*, sitting bath. — *sur place*, bath taken in the establishment. — *à domicile*, bath sent to the house

Bain-marie, sm. (*etym.* ?) water-bath

Baïonnette, sf. (*etym.* Bayonne, *name of a town in France*), bayonet

Baisemain, sm. hand-kissing, levee, politeness. *Il y a eu* — *à la cour*, the queen has held a levee, a drawing-room

Baisement, sm. kissing the Pope's toe

Baiser, va. (*etym. L.* basiare), to kiss, to embrace; *se* —, vr. to kiss each other

Baiser, sm. kiss, embrace. — *de Judas*, a traitor's kiss. *Un gros* —, a hearty kiss

Baisse, sf. (*etym.* baisser), fall. *Jouer à la* —, to speculate on the fall of stock. *Les actions sont en* —, shares are at a discount

Baissé, e, adj. lowered, downcast. *Tête* —*e*, headlong, undauntedly, hanging down one's head. *Se retirer tête* —*e*, to sneak away

Baisser, va. (*etym.* bas, *adj.*), to lower, to let down, to drop. — *les yeux*, to look down. ‡ — *l'oreille*, to lose heart. — *pavillon*, to strike one's colours, to yield. — *un instrument*, to lower. *Faire* — *le ton à quelqu'un*, to bring down the tone of. — vn. to fall, to sink, to become low, to be falling, to be on the wane. *Se* —, vr. to stoop

¶**Baissier,** sm. (*à la Bourse*) bear

Bajoue, sf. (*etym.* ba, joue), chop, cheek, flabby chop

Bal, sm. (*etym.* balle, *because the game of ball was formerly accompanied by dancing*), ball

Baladin, sm. juggler, mountebank, merry-andrew

Baladinage, sm. buffoonery

Balafre, sf. (*etym.* ?) gash, slash, long scar

Balafré, e, adj. slashed, scarred

Balafrer, va. to slash, to give a cut over the face

Balai, sm. (*etym. Celt.* balaen, *a broom*), broom, besom. *Manche à* —, broomstick. *Donner un coup de* — *à une chambre*, to sweep a room slightly. ‡ *Il fait* — *neuf*, he's a new broom and sweeps well. † *Rôtir le* —, to drudge on in a low situation, to lead a disorderly life

Balais, adj. (*etym.* Balaschan, *name of a town in the neighbourhood of Samarkand*). *Rubis* —, balass ruby

Balance, sf. (*etym. L.* bilanx), balance, pair of scales, suspense, balance-sheet. — *d'essai*, assay-balance. *Emporter la* —, to turn the scale, to carry the day. *Faire pencher la* —, to turn the scale. *En* —, doubtful

Balancé, sm. setting, balancé

Balancement, sm. balancing, poising, swinging, rocking, wavering, uncertainty, choice of attitudes

Balancer, va. to balance, to poise, to rock, to move to and fro, to swing, to weigh, to counterbalance, to counterpoise, to group well. — vn. to move to and fro, to waver, to be unsettled. *Il n'y a pas à* —, there can be no doubt about the thing. *Se* —, vr. to swing, to go in a swing, to see-saw, to keep one's balance, to counterbalance each other, to hover

Balancier, sm. (*etym.* balancer), scale-maker, balance-maker, pendulum, balance, beam, coining-engine, pole

Balançoire, sf. (*etym.* balancer), swing

Balayage, sm. (*etym.* balayer), sweeping

Balayer, va. (*etym.* balai), to sweep, to put to flight

Balayeur, se, s. sweeper

Balayures, sf.plur. sweepings, dirt

Balbutiement, sm. (*pronounce* balbuciement), lisping, stammering, stuttering

Balbutier, vn. (*etym. L.* balbus, *a stammerer; pronounce* balbucier), to lisp, to stammer, to falter, to blunder, to stumble

Balcon, sm. (*etym. I.* balcone, *a scaffolding*), balcony, verandah, side-box seats, gallery

Baldaquin, sm. (*etym.* Baldaco, *a corrupt. of* Bagdad, *a city where rich silk hangings were made*), canopy. *Un lit à* —, a four-post bedstead

Baleine, sf. (*etym. L.* balæna), whale, whalebone. *Huile de* —, whale-oil. *Blanc de* —, spermaceti

Baleiné, e, adj. whalebone, with whalebone. *Corset* —, whalebone stays

Baleineau, sm. young whale

Baleinier, sm. whaler, whalebone dealer

Balise, sf. (*etym. doubtful*), beacon, buoy, a fruit

Baliste, sf. (*etym. Gr.* βάλλειν, *to throw*), ballista

Baliveau, sm. (*etym. L.* bajulus; *see* BAILLER, *to give*), staddle, standel

Baliverner, vn. to talk nonsense

Balivernes, sf.plur. (*etym. unknown*), idle talk. *Dire des* —, to talk nonsense

Ballade, sf. (*etym. O.F.* baller, *to dance*), ballad

Ballant, e, adj. dangling. *Marcher les bras* —*s*, to walk along with one's arms dangling by one's side

Balle, sf. (*etym. Celt.* ball), ball, bullet, shot, bale, pack, husk, chaff, boll, glume. *Jouer à la —*, to play at ball. *Rimeur de —*, paltry rhymer. ‡ *C'est un enfant de la —*, he is a chip of the old block. *Prendre la — au bond*, to seize occasion by the fore-lock. *A vous la —, c'est à vous de parler*, it's your turn now. *Renvoyer la —*, to give tit for tat. *Quand la — me viendra*, when my turn comes. *— morte*, spent ball. *— ramée*, chain-shot. *Charger à —*, to load with ball. *— d'avoine*, chaff

Ballon, sm. (*etym.* balle), football, balloon, (*fig.*) a man puffed up with pride

Ballonné, e, adj. distended, swollen

Ballonnement, sm. distension, tightness

Ballonner, va.n., *se —*, vr. to distend, to swell

Ballonnier, sm. football-maker, balloon-maker

Ballot, sm. (*etym.* balle), bundle, package, bale, pack

Ballottage, sm. ballot

Ballottement, sm. vote by ballot, tossing, shaking about

Ballotter, va. to ballot, to toss, to stir, to debate, to make fun of. *Être ballotté par la mort*, to hang between life and death. — vn. to shake, to be loose

Ballottin, sm. small bale

Balourd, e, s. (*etym. the pejorative syll.* ba, *and* lourd), dolt, dullard

Balourdise, sf. clownishness, blunder

Balsamine, sf. (*etym. Gr.* βαλσαμίνη), balsamine, balsam

Balsamique, adj. (*etym. Greek* βάλσαμον), balsamic, balmy

Balustre, sm. (*etym. Gr.* βαλαύστιον, *the flower of the pomegranate*), baluster, railing

†**Bambin**, sm. (*etym. I.* bambino), little chap, bantling

†**Bambochade**, sf. (*etym.* bamboche), scene of low life

†**Bamboche**, sf. (*etym. I.* bamboccio, *a doll*), puppet, spree, idle tales

†**Bambocher**, vn. to lead a riotous life

†**Bambocheur**, sm. loose fellow, scapegrace

Bambou, sm. (*etym. ?*) bamboo

Ban, sm. (*etym. O.H.G.* bannan), ban, bann. *Acheter des —s*, to get a licence

Banal, e, adj. (*etym.* ban), hackneyed, trite, common

Banalité, sf. hackneyed or commonplace saying

Banane, sf. banana-fig, plantain

Bananier, sm. (*etym.* banane), banana-tree

Banc, sm. (*etym. O.H.G.* banc, panc), bench, form, seat, pew, thwart. *Être sur les —s*, to be at school. — *d'œuvre*, churchwardens' pew. *— de rocher*, reef. *— de glace*, iceberg, field of ice. *— de poisson*, shoal of fish. *— d'huîtres*, bed of oysters. *Sur le — des accusés*, in the dock

Bancal, e, adj. (*etym. ?*) bandy-legged

Bandage, sm. (*etym.* bande), bandage, band, truss, hoop

Bandagiste, sm. truss-maker

Bande, sf. (*etym. G.* band), band, bandage, strip, slip, thong, (*billiards*) cushion, side, (*locom.*) strap, gang, set. *Faire — à part*, to keep aloof. *Donner à la —*, (*nav.*) to heel

Bandeau, sm. bandage, headband

Bandelette, sf. strip, slip, fillet

Bander, va. to bind up, to tie up, to bend, to cock, to stretch; — vn. to be tight

Banderole, sf. (*etym. diminut. of* bandière, *for* bannière), streamer, shoulder-belt

Bandoulière, sf. (*etym. I.* bandoliera), shoulder-belt, bandoleer. *En —*, over the shoulder

Banlieue, sf. (*liter.* lieue du ban), suburbs, outskirts

Banne, sf. (*etym. L.* benna, *a carriage*), tilt, awning, hamper

Banni, sm. (*etym.* ban), exile, banished man

Bannière, sf. banner, standard

Bannir, va. to banish, to exile; *se —*, vr. to banish oneself, to withdraw

Bannissement, sm. banishment, exile

Banque, sf. (*etym. I.* banca), banking business, bank. *Actions de la —*, bank-stock. *Faire la —*, to be a banker. *Faire sauter la —*, to break the bank

Banqueroute, sf. (*etym. I.* banca, rotta, *broken bench*), bankruptcy. *Faire —*, to become a bankrupt

Banqueroutier, sm. bankrupt

Banquette, sf. bench, form, outside, footpath

Banquier, sm. banker, money-dealer

Banquise, sf. (*etym.* banc, *Engl.* ice), field of ice, iceberg

Baptême, sm. (*etym. Gr.* βαπτίζειν), baptism, christening. *Tenir sur les fonts de —*, to stand godfather, godmother. *Nom de —*, Christian name

Baptiser, va. to baptize, to christen, to nickname

Baptiste, sm. baptist. *Saint Jean —*, Saint John the Baptist

Baptistère, sm. baptistery

Baquet, sm. (*diminut. of* bac), tub, bucket

‡**Baragouin, Baragouinage**, sm. (*etym. Br.* bara, *bread*, gwin, *wine*), gibberish, jargon

‡**Baragouiner**, va.n. to talk gibberish, to jabber

Baraque, sf. (*etym. Gael.* barrachad, *a hut, from* barrach, *branches of trees*), hut, field-barracks, booth, stall, cupboard

Baraquement, sm. hutting

Baraquer, va., *se —*, vr. to hut

Baraterie, sf. (*etym. O.F.* barat, *deceit*), barratry

Baratte, sf. (*etym. Bret.* baraz, *a tub*), churn

Barbacane, sf. (*etym. Ar.* bâbâk-khâneh, *a gallery*), barbican, loophole

Barbare, adj. (*etym. L.* barbarus), savage, barbarous, barbarian, untutored, unlettered, uncouth

Barbaresque, adj. of Barbary

Barbarie, sf. barbarousness, barbarism, barbarity

Barbarisme, sm. barbarism

Barbe, sf. (*etym. L.* barba), beard, whiskers, wattle, awn, lappet, pinner, barbles. *Faire sa —*, to shave. *Faire faire sa —*, to get shaved. *Plat, brosse à —*, shaving basin, shaving brush. *A sa —*, to his face. ‡ *Rire dans sa —*, to laugh in one's sleeve. *La sainte —*, the powder-room

Barbe, adj. sm. (*etym.* barbarie), (*horse*) barb

Barbeau, sm. (*etym.* barbe), barbel, (*bot.*) blue-bottle

Barbelé, e, adj. barbed, bearded

Barbet, sm. water-spaniel

Barbiche, sf. tuft (on the chin)

Barbichon, sm. lapdog

Barbier, sm. barber

‡**Barbifier**, va. to shave

§**Barbillon**, sm. little barbel, point

Barbon, sm. greybeard, dotard

Barboter, vn. (*etym. ?*) to dabble

§**Barbouillage**, sm. (*etym.* barbouiller), scrawl, daub

§**Barbouiller**, va.n.(*etym.* bar, *and* bouillie, *O.F. for mud*), to daub, to besmear, to blot, to bungle, to stammer out, to flounder. *— le cœur*, to make one sick

§**Barbouilleur**, sm.dauber, scribbler

Barbu, e, adj. bearded

Barbue, sf. dab, brill

Barcarolle, sf. (*etym.* barque), barcarolle

Barcelonnette, sf. (*etym.* berceau), swinging cradle

Bardane, sf. (*etym. L.L.* bardana), burdock, bur

Barde, sm. (*etym. Celt.* barz), bard

Barder, va. to lard. *Bardé de fer*, clad in armour. *Se —*, vr. to clothe oneself

Bardot, sm. mule, (*fig.*) drudge

Barème, sm. (*name of a man who published a work of that kind*), ready-reckoner

§**Barguigner**, va. (*etym. ? L.L.* barcaniare), to haggle

Baril, sm. (*etym. Celt.* bar, *branch of a tree*), barrel, cask, keg, tub. *Mettre en —*, to barrel

Bariolage, sm. (*etym.* barioler), motley, medley of colours

Bariolé, e, adj. variegated, streaked, motley

Barioler, va. (*etym.* ba, *and O.F.* riole, *a streak*), to paint with many colours

Baromètre, sm. (*etym. Gr.* βάρος, *weight*, μέτρον, *measure*), barometer, weather-glass

Barométrique, adj. barometrical

Baronne, sf. baroness

Baronnie, sf. barony

Baroque, adj. (*etym. Port.* barroco, *irregular*), odd, uncouth, whimsical

Barque, sf. (*etym. L.L.* barca, *a boat*), boat, barge. *Passer la —*, (*fig.*) to cross the Styx. ‡ *Conduire bien sa —*, (*fig.*) to manage one's business properly

Barrage, sm. (*etym.* barre), stopping up, barring, dam, toll-gate, turnpike, toll

Barre, sf. (*etym. Celt.* bar, *a branch*), bar, wedge, ingot, cross-bar, dash, stroke of the pen, (*nav.*) helm, boom; *plur.* prisoners' base. *— d'appui*, hand-rail. *C'est une — de fer*, (*fig.*) he is inflexible. ‡ *C'est de l'or en —*, it is as good as gold

Barré, e, adj. barred, scratched out, streaked

Barreau, sm. bar, grating

Barrer, va. to bar, to stop up, to scratch out, to draw a dash across

Barrette, sf. (*etym. L.* birrum *or* birrus, *a kind of cloth*), cap

Barricader, va. to barricade

Barrière, sf. (*etym.* barre), barrier, gate, stile, fence, hindrance, lists, starting-post

Barrique, sf. (*etym. see* Baril), cask, hogshead

Baryte, sf. (*etym. Gr.* βαρύς, *heavy*), baryta

Baryton, sm. (*etym. Gr.* βαρύς, τόνος, *tone*), barytone

Bas, Basse, adj. (*etym. L.* Bassus, *a surname expressing a certain conformation of the body*), low, shallow, mean, grovelling, worthless, abject, dark, gloomy, overcast, near. *Machine à basse pression*, low-pressure engine. *Les basses cartes*, the small cards. *Il a la vue basse*, he is short-sighted. *En — âge*, in infancy. *De — lieu*, of low birth, low-born. ‡ *Avoir l'oreille basse*, to look ashamed. † *Les eaux sont basses*, money is scarce with me. *Faire* *main basse sur*, to put to the sword, to lay hold of. *A voix basse*, in a whisper

Bas, sm. lower part, bottom, foot. *— de la jambe*, small. *— d'une robe*, hem, skirt. *Les hauts et les — de la vie*, the ups and downs of life

Bas, sm. stocking

Bas, adv. low. *Jeter à —, mettre à —*, to pull down. *A — !* down ! down with. *A — du lit*, out of bed. *En —*, down below. *Regarder du haut en —*, to look at with the utmost arrogance. *Ici-—*, here below. *— les armes*, down with your arms. *Chapeau —*, most respectfully. *Être bien —*, to be very ill. *Il est — dans ses affaires*, his business is in a bad state. ‡ *Porter — l'oreille*, to be abashed. *Mettre —*, to litter, to bring forth

Basalte, sm. (*etym. L.* basaltes), basalt

Basaltique, adj. basaltic

Basane, sf. (*etym. Ar.* bithanet, *prepared sheepskin*), sheepskin

Basané, e, adj. swarthy, dark, sunburnt

Bas-bleu, sm. blue-stocking

Bas-côté, sm. aisle, foot-path

Bascule, sf. (*etym.* battre, cul), swipe, weighing-machine, weigh-bridge, swing, rim. *Porte à —*, swing-gate. *Faire la —*, to kick up. *Faire faire la — à*, to upset

Base, sf. (*etym. Gr. βάσις, step, way of going*), base, basis, foundation, groundwork, principal ingredient

§**Baser,** va. to ground, to rest, to base; *se —*, vr. to take one's stand, to rest

Bas-fond, sm. piece of low ground, flat, (*nav.*) shallow, shoal

Basilic, sm. (*etym. Gr. βασιλίσκος, a small king*), basilisk, basil

Basilique, sf. (*etym. Gr. βασιλικός, royal*), stately pile, basilic

Basin, sm. (*etym. L.Gr. βαμβάκιον, made of silk; O.F.* bombasin), bombazeen, dimity

Basoche, sf. (*etym. L.* basilica), a legal tribunal which existed in France during the middle ages

Basque, sf. (*etym. L.* Vasco, *name of a people*), skirt

Bas-relief, sm basso-relievo

Basse, sf. (*mus.*) base, bass, violoncello. *— continue*, thorough-bass

Basse-contre, sf. lower tenor, counter-base

Basse-cour, Basse-fosse, Basse-lice, &c. *See* Cour, Fosse, &c.

Bassesse, sf. meanness, baseness, lowness, mean action, vulgarity. *Faire des —s*, to be guilty of meanness

Basset, sm. terrier

Basse-taille, sf. base voice

Bassin, sm. (*etym. Celt.* bac, *hollow*), basin, dock

Bassine, sf. large pan

Bassiner, va. to warm, to bathe, to foment, to water

Bassinet, sm. pan, skull-cap

Bassinoire, sf. warming-pan

Basson, sm. bassoon, bassoonist

Bast ! interj. (*etym. I.* basta), pshaw ! pooh ! nonsense !

§**Bastille,** sf. (*etym. L.L.* bastire, *to build*), castle

Bastingage, sm., **Bastingue,** sf. (*etym. ?*), netting. *Filets de —*, boarding-netting

Bastionné, e, adj. with bastions

Bastonnade, sf. (*etym.* bâton), bastinado, cudgelling

†**Bastringue,** sm. (*etym. ?*) a low dancing-place

Bas-ventre, sm. belly

Bât, sm. (*etym. a root* bat *or* bast, *meaning to prop up, to support*), pack-saddle. ‡ *Je sais où le — vous blesse*, I know where the shoe pinches you

†**Bataclan,** sm. (*a word arbitrarily compounded from* battre), rattle-traps, equipage

§**Bataille,** sf. (*etym.* battre), battle, fight, engagement, action. *Livrer — à*, to give battle to. *— rangée*, pitched battle. *Corps de —*, main body. *Cheval de —*, war-horse, charger, (*fig.*) hobby

§**Batailler,** vn. to struggle hard, to battle

§**Batailleur,** s. adj. quarrelsome person, contentious

§**Bataillon,** sm. battalion. *— carré*, square. *Chef de —*, major

Bâtard, e, adj. (*etym.* bât, *and* ard, *a syllable meaning kind, sort*), bastard, misbegotten, mongrel, degenerate. *Écriture —e*, sloping hand. *Porte —e*, house-door

Bâtardise, sf. bastardy

Bateau, sm. (*etym. Celt.* bâd; *O.F.* batel), boat, wherry, boatful. *Faire une partie de —*, to go a-boating. *Bois de —*, old boat timber

Batelet, sm. skiff, cock-boat

Bateleur, sm. (*etym. O.F.* basteau, *a small stick*), mountebank, tumbler

Batelier, sm. boatman, waterman

Batelière, sf. woman who rows a boat

Bâter, va. to saddle. ‡ *Un âne bâté*, a downright ass

Bâti, sm. frame, tacking, basting

Bâti, e, adj. made. *Bien —*, handsome. *Mal —*, ill-shaped. † *Être — par les Romains*, to be as strong as Samson. *Je suis ainsi —*, (*fig.*) such is my humour

Batifolage, sm. (*etym.* batifoler), toying, playing

Batifoler, vn. (*etym. I.* battifolle, *a rampart on which young men used to take a walk*), to toy, to play

Bâtiment, sm. (*etym.* bâtir), building, structure, ship, vessel

Bâtir, va. (*etym. same root as* bâton *and* bât), to build, to construct, to baste, to tack; *se —*, vr. to build for oneself, to be building

Bâtisse, sf. building

Bâtisseur, sm. builder

Batiste, sm. (*etym.* Baptiste, *name of the man who first manufactured cambric. His statue is at Cambray*), cambric, lawn

Bâton, sm. (*etym. see* Bât), stick, cudgel, prop, (*mus.*) straight bar. *— de commande*, truncheon. *— pastoral*, crosier. *— à deux bouts*, quarterstaff. *— ferré*, iron-tipped stick. *Mener le — haut*, to command harshly. ‡ *A —s rompus*, by fits and starts, on and off. † *Le tour du —*, perquisites. ‡ *Mettre, jeter des —s dans les roues*, to put spokes in the wheel. *Jouer du —*, to handle a cudgel

Bâtonner, va. to beat, to cane

Bâtonnet, sm. tip-cat, chopstick

Bâtonnier, sm. president of the corporation of barristers

Bâtonniste, sm. cudgel-player, quarterstaff-player

Batrachomyomachie sf. (*etym. Gr. βάτραχος, a frog; μῦς, a rat; μάχη, a fight*), Homer's battle of frogs and rats

Battage, sm. thrashing

Battant, sm. (*etym.* battre), clapper, fold. *Porte à deux —s*, folding-door

Battant, e, adj. quarrelsome. † *Tout — neuf*, bran new

Batte, sf. bat, beater. *— d'Arlequin*, Harlequin's wooden sword. *— à beurre*, churn staff

Battement, sm. throbbing, beating, clapping, stamping, flapping, fluttering

Batterie, sf. scuffle, kitchen utensils, battery. *— de navire*, broadside. *— de fusil*, hammer. *Faire feu de toutes ses —s*, to fire a broadside. *Changer de —s*, (*fig.*) to change one's plans

Batteur, sm. beater. *— d'estrade*, scout. † *— de pavés*, idle fellow. *— en grange*, thrasher

Battoir, sm. bat, racket

Battre, va. (*etym. L.L.* batere, *for* batuere, *to beat*), to beat, to strike, to thrash, to defeat. ‡ *— son plein*, to be in one's prime. *C'est — l'air*, it is labour in vain. † *— le pavé*, to idle about. ‡ *— à plates coutures*, to beat most soundly. *Se tenir pour battu*, to give up. — vn. to throb, to beat, to pant, to bang, to swing. *— des mains*, to clap one's hands. † *— froid à*, to treat coldly. *— en retraite*, to retreat, to fall back vr. to beat oneself, to scramble. *Se — les* lash one's sides, (*fig.*) gel one's brains. † *J bats l'œil*, I don't care for it

Battu, e, adj. pa (*etym.* battre), beaten *les oreilles —es et r d'une affaire*, to b tired of hearing a *Il a les yeux —s*, his heavy

Battue, sf. (*etym.* battue. *Faire une —* to beat up

Baudet, sm. (*etym* baud, *gay, contented*, donkey, tressle

Baudrier, sm. (*ety* balterarius, *from* ba belt), belt, baldrick

Baudruche, sf. *O.F.* baudrée, *an old leather*), goldbeater's

Bauge, sf. (*etym.* baugium, bugia), lai hole, pugging mortar

Baume, sm. (*etym.* samum, *Gr. βάλσαμο-* Baal, *prince, and* sc *oil*), balm, balsam

Bavard, sm. (*etym.* talkative person, gossi tale. —, *—e*, adj. tal loquacious, prating

Bavardage, sm. bavard), chattering, c gossiping

Bavarder, vn. (*ety* vard), to chatter, to bl

Bavaroise, sf. (*etym name* Bavière), bav milk-posset

Bave, sf. (*etym.* o *expressing the chat young children: com Gr. βαβάζειν*), slobber, foam, slime

Baver, va. (*etym.* ba slobber, to drivel, to fo

Bavette, sf. (*etym.* bib. † *Tailler des —s* to chatter, to gossip

Baveux, se, adj. bave), slobbering, drive

Bavolet, sm. (*etym.* bavoler, *to fly about*), c of a bonnet, cap

Bayadère, sf. (*etym.* bailadeira, *a female da* bayadere

Bayer, vn. (*etym.* Bailler), to gape, to h after. ‡ *— aux corneill* stand open-mouthed

Bazar, sm. (*etym.* bazâr, *market*), bazaar

Béant, e, adj. (*etym. part. of the O.F.* beer, *now* bayer), gaping, yawning

Béat, e, adj. (*ety* beatus, *happy*), sanc nious

Béatifier, va. (*etym.* to beatify

Beau, Bel, m., **Bell** adj. (*etym. L.* bellus), b ful, fine, handsome, l favourable, seemly, b ing. *Homme, femme d air*, courtier, woman fashion. ⁑ *Un — parleur*, an orator. *Il y a — jour que*, it is long since. *Il ferait — voir que . . . .*, it would be a pretty thing indeed if . . . *Le temps se met au —*, the weather is clearing up. *En conter de belles*, to tell a heap of stories. *De plus belle*, anew, afresh

Beau, sm. the beautiful, fop, dandy. *Le plus — de l'affaire*, the best part of the matter. ⁑ *Faire le —*, to strut about, (*anim.*) to play its best tricks. *En voilà du —*, that is strange news certainly

Beau, adv. *Tout —*, softly, gently, soho! *Donner —*, to give a good chance. *Avoir —*, it is in vain. *En —*, in a favourable light. *Bel et bon*, good

Beaucoup, adv. (*etym.* beau, coup), much, a great deal. *De —*, by far

Beau-fils, sm., **Belle-fille**, sf. (beau *is here used, as it often was in the Middle Ages, as a term of affection*), son-in-law, daughter-in-law, step-son, step-daughter

Beau-frère, sm., **Belle-sœur**, sf. brother-in-law, sister-in-law, step-brother, step-sister

Beau-père, sm., **Belle-mère**, sf. father-in-law, mother-in-law, step-father, step-mother

Beaupré, sm. (*etym.* G. bug, *the prow, and* spriet, *piece of wood*), bowsprit

Beauté, sf. (*etym.* beau), beauty, loveliness

Bec, sm. (*etym. Celt.* bec *or* beg; *Gael.* beig), beak, mouth, bill, nib, prow, burner, spout. *Blanc —*, younker. *Avoir — et ongles*, (*fig.*) to be armed with tooth and nail. *Il a bon —*, *le — bien affilé*, his tongue runs glib. *Coup de —*, peck, (*fig.*) taunt. *Tenir quelqu'un le — dans l'eau*, to keep one in suspense

Bécarre, s. adj. (*etym.* B *and* carré, *on account of its shape*), natural

Bécasse, sf. (*etym.* bec, *and* P. acée *or* assée, *name of a woodcock*), woodcock

Bécassine, sf. (*etym.* bécasse), snipe

Bec-de-corbin, sm. (*etym.* bec, *and* corbin *for* corbeau), bill-head. *A —*, bill-headed

Bec-de-lièvre, sm. hare-lip. *A —*, hare-lipped

Becfigue, sm. becafico

Bêche, sf. (*etym. see* BEC), spade

Bêcher, va. (*etym.* bêche), dig

Becquée, sf. (*etym.* bec), beakful, food

Becquet, sm. (*etym.* bec), beco

Becqueter, va. (*etym.* bec), peck

Bedaine, sf. (*etym. ?*), paunch, belly. *A grosse —*, big-bellied

Bedeau, sm. (*etym. O.H.G.* butil, *public crier*), beadle

Beffroi, sm. (*etym. O.H.G.* bervrit, *a tower of defence*), belfry, bell-tower

Bégaiement *or* **Bégayement**, sm. (*etym.* bégayer), stammering, stuttering

Bégayer, vn.a. (*etym.* bègue), to stammer, to stutter, to lisp

Bègue, adj. (*etym. a root* beg, *which denotes some mental or bodily infirmity*), stammering, stuttering

†**Bégueule**, sf. (*etym.* gueule, bec; *see* BEANT), prude

†**Bégueulerie**, sf. (*etym.* bégueule), prudery, prudishness

Béguin, sm. (*so named from the persons who wore it first*), a kind of cap

§**Beignet**, sm. (*etym. dimin. of the O.F.* bigne *or* beugne, *a tumour*), fritter

Bêlant, e, adj. (*etym.* bêler), bleating

Bêlement, sm. (*etym.* bêler), bleating

Bêler, vn. (*etym. L.* balare), to bleat

Belette, sf. (*etym. dimin. of the Celt.* bele, *a marten*), weasel

Bélier, sm. (*etym. L.L.* bella, *a bell. The* bélier *is properly the bell-wether*), ram

Belladone, sf. (*etym. I.* bella, donna), deadly nightshade

Belle, sf. fair one, beauty, the winning game

Belle-de-jour, sf. convolvulus

Belle-de-nuit, sf. marvel of Peru

Belligérant, e, adj. (*etym. L.* bellum, gerere, *to carry on war*), belligerent

Belliqueux, se, adj. (*etym. L.* bellicosus, *warlike*), warlike, martial

Belvédère, sm. (*etym. I.* bello, *fine*, vedere, *to see*), belvidere, terrace

Bémol, sm. adj. (*etym.* B, *and L.* mollis, *soft*), flat

Bénédictin, e, s. adj. (*etym. from the name of* St. Benedict), benedictine

Bénédiction, sf. (*etym. L.* benedictio, *a blessing*), blessing, benediction. *En — d*, blessed by. † *Il pleut que c'est une —*, it rains like the very deuce. *Il vous a donné des —s*, he cursed you nicely

Bénéfice, sm. (*etym. L.* beneficium), profit, gain, earnings, perquisites, living, benefit

Bénéficiaire, sm. adj. (*etym.* bénéfice), beneficiary

Bénéficier, sm. (*etym.* bénéfice), incumbent

Bénéficier, vn. to gain; — va. to work (*mines*)

Benêt, sm. (benêt *is the Norm. pronun. of* benoit, *for* béni), booby, noodle

Bénévole, adj. (*etym. L.* benevolus, *well-wisher*), gentle, kind, gratuitous

Béni, e, adj. past part. blessed

§**Bénignité**, f. (*etym. L.* benignitas), benignity

Bénin, **Bénigne**, adj. (*etym. L.* benignus), kind, soft, gentle, favourable

Bénir, va. (*etym. L.* benedicere), to bless

Bénit, e, adj. past part. blessed, consecrated. *Eau —e*, holy water. † *De l'eau —e de cour*, fair promises and nothing more

Bénitier, sm. (*etym.* bénit), holy water font

Benjoin, sm. (*etym. ?*), benzoin

§**Béquille**, sf. (*etym.* bec. *A stick ending in the form of a beak*), crutch

Bercail, sm. (*etym. L.L.* vervecale, *from* vervex (berbex), *a ram*), fold. † *Rentrer au —*, to go home again

Berceau, sm. (*etym. L.L.* berra, *a fence made of wicker-work*), cradle, birth, arbour, bower

Bercer, va. (*etym.* berceau), to rock, to lull to sleep, to beguile. *Avoir été bercé d'une histoire*, to have heard a story over and over again. *Se —*, vr. to swing, to lull oneself

Berceuse, sf. (*etym.* berceau), cradle-rocker, lullaby

Béret, sm. (*etym. see* BARRETTE), beret, flat cap, turban

Berge, sf. (*etym. G.* bergen, *to defend*), steep bank, beach

Berger, sm. (*etym. L.L.* berbix, *sheep*), shepherd, swain. *Étoile du —*, evening star, Venus. ⁑ *Heure du —*, the happy hour

Bergère, sf. shepherdess, easy-chair

Bergerette, sf. lass, country lass

Bergerie, sf. sheepfold

Bergeronnette, sf. (*etym.* berger), wagtail

Berline, sf. (*etym. from the city of* Berlin), berlin

Berlingot, sm. old chariot

Berlue, sf. (*etym. prefix pejor.* ber, *and* lue *from L.* lucere, *to shine*), dimness of sight

Berner, va. (*etym. O.F.* berne, *a kind of coarse cloth*), to toss in a blanket, to ridicule

Béryl, sm. (*etym. Gr.* βήρυλλος), beryl

Besace, sf. (*etym. see* BISSAC), wallet, bag. *Réduire à la —*, to reduce to beggary

Besicles, sf. plur. (*for* baricles, *from* beryllus), spectacles, barnacles

§**Besogne**, sf. (*etym. see* BESOIN), work, toil, task. † *Abattre de la —*, to get through a great deal of work. *Se mettre en —*, to set to work. *Donner, tailler de la — à*, to cut out work for

§**Besoigneux**, se, adj. (*etym.* besoin), needy, necessitous

Besoin, sm. (*etym. prefix* bes, *and* soin), want, need, hunger, longing for. *Avoir — de*, to want. *Au —*, in need. *Faire — à*, to be necessary to

Bestial, e, adj. (*etym. L.* bestia), beastly, bestial, brutish

Bestialité, sf. bestiality

†**Bestiasse**, sf. simpleton, ninny

Bestiaux, sm. plur. cattle

†**Bêta**, sm. blockhead, noodle

Bétail, sm. cattle, live-stock. *Gros —*, black cattle. *Menu —*, small cattle

‖**Bête**, sf. beast, animal, fool, loo. *—s à cornes*, cattle. *— à laine*, sheep. *— de somme*, beast of burden. *— de trait*, draught-horse, ass, mule, &c. † *Remonter sur sa —*, to get on one's legs again. *Faire la —*, to play the fool. ⁑ *C'est ma — noire*, he, she, it is my eyesore. *C'est une bonne —*, he, she is a good-natured fool. *— à bon Dieu*, lady-bird. † *La — du bon Dieu*, a good foolish creature. *Une fine —*, a shrewd one. *Morte la —, mort le venin*, dead dogs don't bite. — adj. stupid, silly, foolish. *Pas si —*, not such a fool as all that

⁑**Bêtise**, sf. (*etym.* bête), silliness, stupidity, nonsense, blunder, trifle

Betterave, sf. (*etym.* bette, rave; bette *from the L.* beta), beetroot

Beuglement, sm. (*etym.* beugler), bellowing, lowing

Beugler, vn. (*etym. L.* buculus, *dim. of* bos), to bellow, to low

Beurre, sm. (*etym. L.* butyrum, *from the Gr.* βούτυρον), butter. *Au — noir*, with fried butter, fried in butter. *— fin*, best butter. *— fort*, rancid butter. *Promettre plus de — que de pain*, to be lavish of promises

Beurré, sm. butter-pear

Beurrée, sf. slice of bread and butter

Beurrer, va. to butter

Bévue, sf. (*etym. pejor. pref.* bé, *and* vue), oversight, blunder. *Faire une —*, to commit an oversight

Biais, sm. (*etym. L.* bifax, *from* bis, *twice*, facies, *face*), slant, slope, bias, way, direction. *Prendre de —*, to take a slanting direction. *Prendre un bon —*, to go the right way

Biaiser, vn. to slant, to slope, to play fast and loose; — va. to force the bias of

Biberon, sm. (*etym. L.* bibere, *to drink*), feeding-bottle. *Élever au —*, to bring up by hand

Bibliographe, sm. (*etym. Greek* βιβλίον, *and* γράφειν, *to describe*), bibliographer

Bibliographie, sf. (*etym. Gr.* βιβλιογραφία, *description of books*), bibliography

Bibliographique, adj. (*etym.* bibliographie), bibliographical

Bibliomane, sm. (*etym. Gr.* βίβλιον, *and* μαίνεσθαι, *to be mad*), bibliomaniac

Bibliomanie, sf. bibliomania

Bibliophile, sm. (*etym. Gr.* βίβλιον, *and* φίλος, *loving*), book-lover

Bibliothécaire, sm. (*etym.* bibliothèque), librarian

Bibliothèque, sf. (*etym. Gr.* βιβλιοθήκη, *from* βίβλιον, *and* θήκη, *a place of deposit*), library, book-case

Biblique, adj. (*etym.* Bible), biblical, scriptural

Biche, sf. (*etym. doubtful: comp.* bique, *and E.* bitch), hind, darling, love

‡**Bichette,** sf. (*etym.* biche), darling

Bichon, ne, smf. (*etym. contract. from* barbichon), lapdog, darling

Bichonner, va. (*etym.* bichon), to curl, to make smart

Bicoque, sf. (*etym. I.* bicocca, *a small castle on a height*), small fortified town, hovel

Bidet, sm. (*etym. Gael.* bideach, *very small*), nag, cob, bidet

Bidon, sm. (*etym. see* BEDAINE), can, canteen

Bielle, sf. (*etym.* ?), connecting-rod

Bien, sm. (*etym. L.* bene), good, gift, virtue, property, goods and chattels, estate, landed estate. *Grand — vous fasse!* much good may it do you! *Les gens de —*, good people. *Le mieux est l'ennemi du —*, let well alone. — adv. well, right, very, most, much, comfortable, well off, good-looking, sufficient. *C'est — fait*, it serves you right. *Mener à —*, to bring to a happy end. *En —*, favourably. *En tout — tout honneur*, with honourable intentions. *Tant — que mal*, as well as may be. *Voilà qui est —*, that is something like

Bien que, conj. although, though

Bien! interj. well!

Bien-aimé, e, adj. beloved one, darling

Bien-dire, sm. fine talk. † *Se mettre sur son —*, to mind one's Ps and Qs

Bien-être, sm. well-being, welfare, small competency

Bienfaisance, sf. (*etym.* bien, faire), beneficence, bounty

Bienfaisant, e, adj. beneficent, kind, beneficial, salutary, acting well

Bienfait, sm. benefit, kindness, utility, good action

Bienfaiteur, trice, s. (*etym.* bien, faire), benefactor, benefactress

Bien-fonds, sm. (*etym.* bien, fonds, *used only in the plural*), estate, landed property

Bienheureux, se, adj. happy, blessed. *Les —*, the blessed, the blest

Biennal, e, adj. (*etym. L.* biennalis, *from* bi *for* bis, *and* annus, *year*), biennial

Bienséance, sf. (*etym.* bienséant), decorum, good manners, conveniency

Bienséant, e, adj. (*etym.* bien, séant, *pres. part. of* seoir), decorous, becoming

Bientôt, adv. soon, shortly. *A —*, I hope to see you soon

§**Bienveillance,** sf. (*etym.* bien, veillant), benevolence, goodwill

§**Bienveillant, e,** adj. (*etym.* bien, veillant *for* veuillant, *old pres. part. of* vouloir), kind

Bienvenu, e, adj. (*etym.* bien, venir), welcome. *Le —*, welcome

Bienvenue, sf. welcome, footing. *Payer sa —*, to pay one's footing

Bière, sf. (*etym. O.H.G.* bâra; *Ang.-Sax.* bær, bère), coffin, bier

Bière, sf. (*sometimes spelt* bierre; *etym. Ang.-Sax.* beor; *Scan.* bior), beer, malt liquor. *Ce n'est pas de la petite —*, it is no trifle

Biffer, va. (*etym. doubtful*), to scratch out, to erase

Bifteck, sm. (*pl.* biftecks), beefsteak. — *aux pommes*, beefsteak with potatoes

Bifurquer, vn. (*etym. L.* bifurcus, *from* bi *for* bis, *and* furca, *a fork*), to be forked, to branch off

Bigame, adj. (*etym. L.* bigamus, *from* bi *for* bis, *and* γάμος, *marriage*), guilty of bigamy

Bigamie, sf. bigamy

Bigarreau, sm. (*etym.* bigarré), whiteheart cherry

Bigarrer, va. (*etym. L.* bis, variare, *to diversify*), to checker, to variegate, to diversify

Bigarrure, sf. (*etym.* bigarrer), odd medley of colours, motley

Bigot, e, adj. (*etym.* ?), bigoted, over-devout

Bigoterie, sf., **Bigotisme,** sm. (*etym.* bigot), bigotry

Bijou, sm. (*etym. L.* bis, jocare? *lit. something which plays or shines on both sides*), jewel, trinket

Bijouterie, sf. (*etym.* bijoutier), jewelry

Bijoutier, sm. (*etym.* bijou), jeweller

Bilan, sm. (*etym. I.* bilancio, *balance*), balance-sheet. *Déposer son —*, to stop payment

Bilboquet, sm. (*etym.* ?), cup and ball, tumbler, giddy fellow, rubbishing work

Bile, sf. (*etym. L.* bilis), bile, wrath. *Décharger sa —*, to vent one's spleen. *Échauffer la — de*, to stir up the wrath of

Bilieux, se, adj. (*etym. L.* biliosus, *from* bilis), bilious, choleric

§**Billard,** sm. (*etym. from* bille, *a piece of wood, a billet.* Billard *was formerly the name of the cue*), billiards, billiard-table, billiard-room

§**Bille,** sf. (*etym. L.* billa = bulla, *a ball*), marble, billiard-ball, log, packer's stick. *Faire la —*, to hole the ball

§**Billet,** sm. (*etym. dim. from the L.L.* billa, *a rescript, a schedule*), note, letter, circular, bill, ticket. — *doux*, love-letter. — *de mariage, de décès*, invitation to a wedding, to a funeral. — *de complaisance*, accommodation bill. — *d'aller et de retour*, return ticket. — *de logement*, billeting ticket. — *de garde*, (*France*) order to mount guard

Billevesée, sf. (*etym. O.F.* bille, *a ball*, vesée, *full of wind*), nonsense, crotchet

§**Billon,** sm. (*etym. comp. the E.* bullion, *O.F.* billon = *mass*), copper coin, bad coin, ridge

§**Billot,** sm. (*etym.* bille, *piece of wood*), block, wedge, yoke, stick

Bimane, adj. (*etym. L.* bi *for* bis, *and* manus, *hand*), two-handed, bimanous

Bimbeloterie, sf. (*etym. Norm.* bimbelot, *a trousseau*), toy-trade

Bimbelotier, sm. (*etym.* bimbelot), toyman

Binage, sm. (*etym.* biner), second hoeing, saying two masses in one day in two different places

Binaire, adj. (*etym. L.* binarius, *from* bis), binary

Biner, va. (*etym. L.L.* binare, *from* binus, *twofold*), to hoe a second time, to say two masses in one day

Binette, sf. (*etym.* biner), hoe, (†) odd face (binette *in this sense means orig. a wig, from* Binet, *the name of Louis XIV.'s wig-maker*)

Binocle, sm. (*etym. L.* binus, oculus), telescope, double eyeglass

Binôme, sm. (*etym. L.* bis, *Gr.* νόμος, *division*), binomial

Biographe, sm. (*etym. Gr.* βίος, *life*, γράφειν, *to write*), biographer

Biographie, sf. (*etym.* biographe), biography, life

Biographique, adj. (*etym.* biographe), biographical

Bipède, adj. (*etym. L.* bi *for* bis, *and* pes, *foot*), biped, two-footed animal

Bique, sf. (*etym. I.* becco, *a ram*), she-goat

Bis, adj. (*etym. L.* byssinus, *of a cotton colour*), brown, swarthy

Bisaïeul, sm., **Bisaïeule,** sf. (*etym.* bis, aïeul), grandfather, grandmother; *plur.* les bisaïeuls

Bisannuel, le, adj. (*etym.* bis, annuel), biennial

‡**Bisbille,** sf. (*etym. I.* bisbiglio, *murmur*), tiff, bickering. *Être en —*, to have fallen out together

Biscaïen, sm. (*etym.* Biscay), long-barrelled musket, small cannon shot

Biscornu, e, adj. (*etym.* bis, cornu), with two horns, oddly-shaped, odd, whimsical

Biscotin, sm. (*etym. I.* biscottino, *dimin. of* biscotto), hard biscuit

Biscuit, sm. (*etym. L.* bis, coctus, *cooked*), biscuit, sponge cake, unvarnished porcelain, coloured lamps

Bise, sf. (*etym.* ?), cold bleak wind, winter

Biseau, sm. (*etym.* ?) basil, bevel, sidestick. *Taillé en —*, basiled, bevelled

Biset, sm. (*etym.* bis, *brown*), rock-dove, national guard on duty without his uniform

Bischof *or* **Bishop,** sm. negus, bishop

Bisque, sf. (*etym.* ?) crawfish soup, bisk

‡**Bisquer,** vn. (*etym. Scan.* bisk, *sour*), to be vexed

Bissac, sm. (*etym. L.* bisaccium), bag

Bissection, sf. (*etym.* bis, section), bisection

***Bisser,** va. (*etym.* bis), to encore

Bistouri, sm. (*etym. L.L.* bistoria, *a kind of weapon*), bistoury, incision-knife

Bitume, sm. (*etym. L.* bitumen), bitumen

Bituminer, Bitumer, va. (*etym.* bitume), to bituminate

Bitumineux, se, adj. (*etym.* bitume), bituminous

Bivac, Bivouac, sm. (bivouac *is more used: etym. G.* bei, wachen, *to watch near*), bivouac

Bivaquer, Bivouaquer, vn. to bivouac

‡**Bizarre,** adj. (*etym. Sp.* bizarro, *valiant*), odd, strange, whimsical, fantastical

Bizarrerie, sf. (*etym.* bizarre), oddness, strangeness, whim, caprice, extravagance

Blafard, e, adj. (*etym. O.H.D.* blei *or* bleih, *white*, faro, *colour*), pale, wan, dim, leaden-hued

Blague, sf. (*etym. Gael.* blagh, *to blow*), pouch, tobacco-pouch, (†) humbug, fudge

†**Blaguer,** va. (*etym.* blague), to humbug

†**Blagueur, se,** s. (*etym.* blague), humbug

Blaireau, sm. (*etym. L.L.* bladarellus, *dim. of* bladarius, *corn-merchant*), badger, badger-hair brush

Blâmer, va. (*etym. L.* blasphemare), to blame, to reprove, to find fault with; *se —*, vr. to blame oneself

Blanc, che, adj. (*etym. O.H.D.* blanch), white, clean,

hoary. *Argent* —, *monnaie blanche*, silver. *Armes blanches*, steel weapons. *Cartes blanches*, small cards. ¦ *Se faire — de son épée*, to make much of a power which one does not possess. *Donner carte blanche à quelqu'un*, to give a person full powers. *Nuit blanche*, sleepless night. *Sauce blanche*, melted butter

Blanc, sm. white, white man, white mark, margin, blank, whiting. *Voué au* —, consecrated to the Holy Virgin (being dressed always in white). *Tirer au* —, to shoot at a white mark. — *de volaille*, flesh of a fowl. — *d'Espagne*, whiting. *Chauffé à* —, heated excessively, red hot. *Saigner jusqu'au* —, to bleed plentifully. *Laisser en* —, to leave blank. *Mettre du noir sur du* —, to blacken paper

Blanc-bec, sm. (*etym.* blanc, bec), beardless youth, simpleton; *plur.* des blancs-becs

Blanchâtre, adj. whitish

Blanche, sf. white woman, white ball, minim

Blancheur, sf. whiteness, white

Blanchi, e, adj. (*etym.* blanchir), hoary, blanched

Blanchiment, sm. (*etym. sync. for* blanchissement, *from* blanchir), bleaching, blanching

Blanchir, va. to whiten, to clean, to bleach, to wash, to whitewash, to clear, to blanch, to scald; — vn. to grow white, old, grey, to foam; *se* —, vr. to whiten, to wash one's own linen, to clear oneself

Blanchissage, sm. (*etym.* blanchir), washing

Blanchissant, e, adj. foaming, blanching

Blanchisserie, sf. washerwoman's business, wash-house, bleaching-house

Blanchisseur, se, s. washerman, laundress, washerwoman. —*se en gros*, washerwoman. —*se en fin*, clear-starcher

Blanc-seing, sm. blank signature; *plur.* des blanc-seings

Blanquette, sf. (*etym.* blanc), small white wine, blanquette. — *de veau*, hashed veal, hash

Blaser, va. (*etym.* ? *Ang.-Sax.* blase or blaese, *a brand*), to pall, to dull, to blunt, to tire; — vr. to impair one's health, to get tired of, to have lost all relish for a thing

Blason, sm. (*etym.* ?), heraldry, blazonry, coat of arms, armorial bearings

Blasonner, va. to emblazon, to blazon

Blasphémateur, trice, adj. (*etym.* blasphémer), blasphemer

Blasphématoire, adj. (*etym.* blasphémer), blasphemous, blaspheming

Blasphème, sm. (*etym.* blasphémer), blasphemy

Blasphémer, vn. a. (*etym. Gr.* βλασφημεῖν, *to speak evil of*), to blaspheme

Blé, sm. (*etym. Celt.* blawd? *L.* ablata, *lit. things taken away?*), corn, wheat. — *noir*, buckwheat. — *de Turquie*, Indian corn, maize. ¦ *Manger son — en herbe*, to spend one's money before one gets it

Blême, adj. (*etym. Scand.* blámi, *of a blue colour*), pale, almost livid

Blêmir, vn. to turn pale

Blessant, e, adj. offensive, injurious

Blessé, e, s. wounded man or woman

Blesser, va. (*etym. O.G.* bletzen, *to patch up*), to hurt, to wound, to offend. *Blessé à mort*, mortally wounded. *Blessé au vif*, stung to the quick. *Se* —, vr. to hurt oneself, to hurt one another, to take offence, to offend each other

Blessure, sf. hurt, bruise, wound

Blet, te, adj. (*etym.* ?), over-ripe

Bleu, e, adj. (*etym. O.H.G.* blâo, blaw), blue, azure, cerulean, black and blue. ¦ *Des contes* —*s*, old woman's tales

Bleu, sm. blue, azure, cerulean blue. *Les* —*s*, the republican soldiers in the French Revolution

Bleuâtre, adj. bluish, rather blue

Bleuir, va. to blue, to make blue; — vn. to turn blue

Blindage, sm. (*etym.* blinder), blinding, blinds

Blindé, e, adj. (*etym.* blinder), steel-plated, iron-cased

Blinder, va. (*etym. Eng.* blind), to protect against artillery

Bloc, sm. (*etym. O.H.G.* bloc, bloch), block, log, lump. *En* —, in a lump

Blockhaus, sm. (*etym. G.* blockhaus), block-house

Blocus, sm. (*etym. G.* blockhaus), blockade, investment

Blond, e, adj. (*etym.* ?), light-complexioned, flaxen, fair, light

Blond, sm. fairness, flaxen colour, yellow. — *ardent*, sandy, carroty. — *cendré*, pale yellow. — *doré*, golden

Blonde, sf. (*etym.* ?), blonde, blond lace

Blondin, sm. fair-complexioned man, beau

Bloquer, va. (*etym.* bloc), to blockade, to block up, to invest

Blottir (se), vr. (*etym.* ?), to crouch, to creep

Blouse, sf. (*etym.* ?), smock-frock, pinafore, (*billiards*) hole, pocket

Blouser, va. (*etym.* ?), to hole, (?) to mislead; *se* —, vr. to make a mistake, to find oneself in the wrong box

Bluet, sm. (*etym.* bleu), corn-flower

Bluette, sf. (*etym. see* Berlue), slight production, spark, flash of wit

Blutage, sm. sifting

Bluter, va. (*etym.* bure; *O.F.* bureter), to pass through a sieve

Blutoir, *also* **Bluteau**, sm. bolting machine, mill

Bobèche, sf. (*etym.* ?), socket, sconce

Bobine, sf. (*etym.* ?), reel, bobbin

Bobinette, sf. (*etym.* bobine), string

Bobo, sm. (*childish onomat.*), sore, hurt, pain

Bocage, sf. (*etym. L.L.* boscaticum, *from* boscus), grove

Bocal, sm. (*etym. Gr.* βαυκάλις, *vase*), glass jar, glass globe, mouthpiece

Bœuf, sm. (*etym. L.* bos), ox, bullock, beef

¦ **Bohème**, sm. poor artist. *La grande* —, the lower order of artists

Bohémien, ne, s. (*etym.* Bohème), gipsy

Boire, va. (*etym. L.* bibere), to drink, to quaff, to put up with, to imbibe. *Faire — à la ronde*, to pass the bottle. — *d'un trait*, to toss off. *Ce papier boit*, this paper blots. *A boire!* some drink, ho! *Ici on donne à — et à manger*, good entertainment for man and beast. *Chanson à* —, drinking song. — *sec*, to drink hard, to be a hearty toper. ¦ *Qui a bu boira*, what is born in the bone is bred in the flesh. *Se* —, vr. to be drunk

Boire, sm. drink, liquor, drinking. *Le — et le manger*, food and drink

Bois, sm. (*etym. G.* busch), wood, forest, firewood, timber, horns, antlers. — *blanc*, deal wood. ¦ *Être du — dont on fait les généraux*, &c., to be of the stuff generals, &c. are made of. ¦ *Entre le — et l'écorce il ne faut pas mettre le doigt*, one must not meddle with family matters. *En plein* —, full in the ship's side, full in the hull

Boisé, e, adj. woody, woodland, wainscoted

Boisement, sm. planting with trees

Boiser, va. to wainscot

Boiserie, sf. (*etym.* boiser), wainscot, wainscoting

Boisseau, sm. (*etym. L.L.* bustellus; *O. F.* boiste ?), bushel

Boisson, sf. (*etym.* boire), drink, beverage, draught. *Être pris de* —, to be intoxicated

Boîte, sf. (*etym. Gr.* πυξίδα), box, case, mortar. — *à vapeur*, steam-chest. — *à soupapes*, free-valve box. ¦ *Dans les petites —s les bons onguents*, precious things are packed in small parcels

Boiter, vn. (*etym.* boîte, *in the sense of articulation*), to be lame, to limp, to hobble. — *tout bas*, to limp a great deal

Boiteux, se, adj. (*etym.* boiter), lame, crippled, limping, rickety. *Vers* —, line without the proper number of feet. *Le Diable* —, the Devil upon two sticks

Bol, sm. (*etym. Eng.* bowl), bowl, basin, bolus

Bolide, sm. (*etym. Gr.* βολίς, *a blow*), aerolith

Bombance, sf. (*etym. L.* bombus, *noise*), good cheer

Bombarde, sf. (*etym. L.* bombus), bombard, gunboat, full organ

Bombardement, sm. bombardment

Bombarder, va. (*etym.* bombard), to bombard

Bombasin, sm. (*etym. see* Basin), bombazine

Bombe, sf. (*etym. see* Bombarde), shell, bomb. *Gare la* — ! (*fig.*) look out!

Bombé, e, adj. (*etym.* bomber), convex, bulged

Bomber, vn., *se* —, vr. (*etym.* bombe), to be convex, to bulge

Bombyx, sm. (*etym. Gr.* βόμβυξ, *silkworm*), silkworm

¦ **Bon, ne**, adj. (*etym. L.* bonus), nice, good, kind, merciful, upright, virtuous, right, favourable. † *Courte et bonne*, a short life and a merry one. ¦ *Avoir — pied, — œil*, to be hale and hearty. *A quoi* —, what is the use of

Bon, sm. good, good people, the best part, the joke, order, check. *Il a du* —, he has some good qualities. — *du trésor*, treasury bond. — *pour la somme*, I.O.U. for the amount

Bon, adv. good, right. *Il fait — de*, it is very pleasant to. *Quand — vous semblera*, when you think proper. *Tout de* —, in earnest

Bon! interj. good!

Bonace, sf. (*etym.* bon), calm, calm weather

Bonasse, adj. (*etym.* bon), silly, simple, foolish

Bonbonnière, sf. (*etym.* bonbon), sweetmeat-box, snug little place

Bond, sm. (*etym.* bondir), rebound, bound, spring, capers. *Par sauts et par —s*, (*fig.*) by fits and starts. ¦ *Faire faux — à*, to disappoint

Bonde, sf. (*etym.* ?), sluice, flood-gate, bung, bung-hole, coarse cheese

Bondir, vn. (*etym. L. L.* bombitare, *to make a noise*), to bound, to rebound, to skip, to caper

Bondissant, e, adj. bounding

Bonheur, sm. happiness, bliss, felicity, good luck, success. *Avoir du* —, *jouer de* —, to be lucky. *Porter — à*, to bring good luck to. † *Au petit* —, I'll risk it

Bonhomie, sf. (*etym.* bonhomme), simplicity, good nature, foolish credulity

Bonhomme, sm. (*etym.* bon, homme), simple soul, old man, good man. — adj. of simplicity. *Un air* —, a look of simplicity

Boni, sm. (*etym. L.* aliquid boni, *something good*), bonus

Bonification, sf. (*etym.* bonifier), improvement

Bonifier, va. (*etym. L.* bonus, facere), to improve, to make good

Bonjour, sm. good morning, good day. *Souhaiter un* —, to wish a good morning. *Donner un petit* — *à*, to give a call

Bonne, sf. (*etym.* bon), housemaid, servant-girl. — *d'enfants*, nurse, nursery-maid. — *à tout faire*, maid-of-all-work

Bonnet, sm. (*etym. L.L.* boneta or bonetum, *a kind of cloth*), cap. — *de police*, foraging cap. — *d'âne*, dunce's cap. — *à poil*, bearskin cap. *Les gros* —*s*, the bigwigs. ‡ — *blanc et blanc* —, six of one and half a dozen of the other. ‡ *Avoir la tête près du* —, to be a fiery personage. ‡ *Mettre son* — *de travers*, to be very cross. ‡ *Jeter son* — *par-dessus les moulins*, not to care for the consequences. ‡ *Prendre sous son* —, to take into one's own head. ‡ *Être deux têtes sous un* —, when one says yes, the other says yes. ‡ *Être triste comme un* — *de nuit*, to be in the dumps

Bonneterie, sf. hosier's business, hosiery line

Bonnetier, sm. hosier

Bonsoir, sm. good evening, good night

Bonté, sf. (*etym. L.* bonitatem), goodness, kindness, good nature

Bord, sm. (*etym. O.H.G.* borr, *a board, a plank*), edge, brink, verge, border, skirt, hem, brim, rim, bank, side. *Vaisseau de haut* —, ship of the line. *Être du* — *de quelqu'un*, (*fig.*) to side with a person. *Faire feu des deux* —*s*, to fire both broadsides at once. *Livre de* —, log, ship's journal

Bordée, sf. broadside, tack. *Courir des* —*s*, to tack about

Border, va. to skirt, to border, to line, to trim, to fringe, to bind, to ship; *se* —, vr. to tuck in one's bedclothes

Bordereau, sm. (*dimin. of* bord), account, memorandum

Bordure, sf. (*etym.* border), border, skirt, trimming, fringe, binding

Boréal, e, adj. (*etym. L.* borealis, *from* Boreas), north, northern, northerly

Borée, sm. (*etym. L.* Boreas), Boreas, north wind

§**Borgne,** adj. (*etym.* ?), one-eyed, dark, blind, low

§**Borgnesse,** sf. one-eyed wretch

Borne, sf. (*the reg. form is* bodne, *from a Celt. root* bod), boundary, bound, limit, bourn

Borné, e, adj. (*etym.* borne), limited, narrow, shallow, narrow-minded

Borner, va. (*etym.* borne), to bound, to limit, to confine

Bosquet, sm. (*dimin. of* bois), little grove, shrubbery

Bosse, sf. (*etym. Celt.* bôs, bosen, *tumour*), hump, hump-back, bump, unevenness, bruise, bust, relievo

Bosseler, va. to emboss

Bossoir, sm. cat-head

Bossu, e, s. hunchback, humpback, crookback

Bossuer, va. to bruise, to batter, to dent

Bot, adj. (*etym. G.* butt: *only used in the masc.*), club-footed

Botanique, sf. (*etym. Gr.* βοτανική, *from* βοτάνη, *plant*), botany. — adj. botanical, botanic

Botaniste, sm. botanist

Botte, sf. (*etym. O.G.* bôzo, *a bundle*), bunch, bundle, truss, hank; (*Ang.-Sax.* butte, bytte, *a large vase*), cask, bottle, boot; (*Span.* botar, *to thrust*), lunge, thrust. —*s fortes*, jack-boots. —*s à revers*, top-boots. ‡ *A propos de* —*s*, about nothing. *Mettre en* —, to tie in a bundle. *Pousser une* —, to give a home-thrust

Botté, e, adj. booted

Botteler, va. to bottle, to truss

Botter, va. to make boots for, to help on with his boots; *se* —, vr. to put one's boots on

Bottier, sm. bootmaker

§**Bottillon,** sm. little bunch

Bottine, sf. half-boot, lady's boot

Bouc, sm. (*etym. Celt.* boc, bouk, byk), goat, he-goat. — *émissaire*, scapegoat

Boucan, sm. (*etym.* ?), place where the savages dry and smoke their meat, (‡) great noise

Boucaner, va. to dry and smoke meat or fish

Boucanier, sm. buccaneer

Bouche, sf. (*etym. L.* bucca, *from the Sans.* bhuj, *to eat*), mouth, muzzle. *Fermer la* — *à quelqu'un*, to silence a person. — *close!* mum is the word! *Dire tout ce qui vient à la* —, to say whatever comes uppermost. *Officiers de la* —, officers of the king's kitchen. ‡ *Être sur sa* —, to be greedy. *Faire la petite* —, to be dainty. *Prendre sur sa* —, to stint oneself. *Bonne* —, dainty morsel, tit-bit. *Pour la bonne* —, for the wind-up. — *à feu*, gun, cannon, piece of ordnance. — *de chaleur*, hot-air pipe

Bouché, e, adj. dull, unintelligent

Bouchée, sf. (*etym.* bouche), mouthful

Boucher, va. to stop up, to shut up. — *un trou*, to stop up a gap, (*fig.*) to pay a debt

Boucher, ère, s. (*etym.* bouc), butcher, butcher's wife

Boucherie, sf. butchery, butcher's shop, slaughter-house

Bouche-trou, sm. supernumerary; *plur.* des bouche-trous

Bouchon, sm. (*etym.* ? bouche, *mouth* ! *O.F.* bousche, *a bundle of branches* !), cork, bung, stopper, wisp of straw, tip-penny, low public-house. *Faire sauter le* —, to uncork, to have a drinking bout

Bouchonner, va. to rumple, to rub down

Boucle, sf. (*etym. L.L.* bucula), buckle, tie, ring, curl, ringlet, loop

Bouclé, e, adj. curled, in ringlets

Boucler, va. to buckle, to curl

Bouclier, sm. (*etym. L.L.* [clypeus] buccularius), shield, buckler. *Une levée de* —*s*, a general rising

Bouddhisme, sm. (*etym. Sans. prop. name* Buddha), Buddhism

Bouddhiste, sm. Buddhist, sectary of Buddha

Bouder, va.n. (*etym.* ?), to pout, to be sulky, not to have it. — *contre son ventre*, to punish oneself

Bouderie, sf. sulkiness

Boudeur, se, s. sulky person

Boudin, sm. (*etym.* ?), pudding

Boue, sf. (*etym. Celt.* baw, *mud*), mud, mire, dirt, filth. — *d'encre*, sediment. — *d'eaux minérales*, pool

Bouée, sf. (*etym. L.* boja, *chain*), buoy. — *de sauvetage*, life-buoy

Boueur, se, s. scavenger

Boueux, se, adj. muddy, dirty

Bouffant, e, adj. (*etym.* bouffer), ample, full-skirted

Bouffant, sm. hoop, full skirt

‡**Bouffarde,** sf. (*etym.* bouffer), a pipe

Bouffe, sm. (*etym. I.* buffa, *a joke*), comic actor, buffoon. *Les* —*s*, the opera Buffa

Bouffée, sf. puff, gust, whiff

Bouffer, vn. (*onomat.*), to puff up, to swell

Bouffi, e, adj. puffed up, swollen out, turgid, inflated

Bouffir, va.n. (*same word as* bouffer), to swell, to puff up, to bloat

Bouffissure, sf. puffiness, swelling, bombast

Bouffon, sm. buffoon, fool. —, —*ne*, adj. droll, comical

Bouffonnerie, sf. buffoonery, drollery

Bouge, sf. (*etym. L.L.* bodium, *small dwelling*), closet, dirty hole, low ale-house, bulge

Bougeoir, sm. (*etym.* bouger), chamber-candlestick

Bouger, vn. (*etym. prov.* bolegar, *to move*), to stir, to budge, to make a movement

Bougie, sf. (*etym.* Bougie, *town in Africa*), candle, wax candle, taper, bougie

†**Bougonner,** va.n. (*etym.* ?), to rate, to scold

§**Bouillant, e,** adj. boiling, scalding, fiery, hot-headed

§**Bouilli,** sm. piece of boiled beef. —, —*e*, adj. boiled. *Cuir* —, waxed leather

§**Bouillie,** sf. hasty-pudding, pap, pulp. ‡ *Faire de la* — *pour les chats*, to lose one's time altogether

§**Bouillir,** vn. (*etym. L.* bullire, *from* bulla), to boil, to be in ebullition, to ferment. *Cela fait* — *la marmite*, it keeps the pot boiling. *La tête me bout*, my head is on fire

§**Bouilloire,** sf. (*etym.* bouillir), kettle

§**Bouillon,** sm. (*etym.* bouillir), froth, foam, broth, flounce. *Bouillir à gros* —*s*, to boil fast. — *aux herbes*, herb-tea. — *coupé*, weak broth. *Court* —, fish-water. † — *pointu*, clyster. ‡ *Boire un* —, to drink a drop too much, to be unfortunate in business. † *Faire boire un* — *de onze heures à*, to administer poison to. *Des manches à* —*s*, full sleeves

§**Bouillonnant, e,** adj. foaming, frothy

§**Bouillonnement,** sm. gushing, foaming

§**Bouillonner,** vn. to be in ebullition, to foam

§**Bouillotte,** sf. (*etym.* bouillir), kettle, boiler, bouillotte

Boulanger, ère, s. (*etym.* boule), baker, baker-woman

Boulangerie, sf. bread-making, baker's trade, baker's shop

Boule, sf. (*etym. L.* bulla), bowl, ball. — *de neige*, snow-ball, guelder-rose

Bouleau, sm. (*etym. L.* betula), birch-tree, birch

Bouledogue, sm. bull-dog

Boulet, sm. (*etym.* boule), cannon-ball, shot, fetlock, pastern

Boulette, sf. (*etym.* boule), pellet, forcemeat ball, blunder

Boulevard, sm. (*etym. G.* bollwerk), bulwark, boulevard

Bouleversé, e, adj. upset, distracted, disturbed

Bouleversement, sm. subversion, total overthrow, commotion, consternation

Bouleverser, va. (*etym.*

boule, *and L.* versare, *to turn*), to overthrow, to subvert, to unsettle

Boulingrin, sm. (*etym. Eng.* bowling-green), lawn, grass-plot

‡**Boulot, te**, adj. (*etym.* boule), fat

Bouquet, sm. (*etym. see* BOSQUET), nosegay, bouquet, birthday compliment, sprig, bunch, cluster. *— d'arbres*, little grove, cluster of trees. *— de feu d'artifice*, crowning-piece in fireworks. *— du vin*, flavour

Bouquetière, sf. (*etym.* bouquet), flower-girl

Bouquin, sm. (*etym. Eng.* book), old book; (*etym.* bouc), old he-goat

Bouquiner, vn. to hunt after old books

Bouquiniste, sm. keeper of a book-stall

Bourbe, sf. (*etym. ?*), mire, mud, slough

Bourbeux, se, adj. miry, muddy

Bourdon, sm. (*etym. ?*), drone, humble-bee, staff, big bell

Bourdonnement, sm. buzz, hum, buzzing, humming

Bourdonner, vn. to buzz, to hum

Bourg, sm. (*etym. O.H.G.* burg, *Celt.* borg, *Gr.* πύργος), market-town, borough

Bourgade, sf. village

Bourgeois, sm. burgher, burgess, townsman, one who lives on his income, commoner, civilian, master. —, *—e*, adj. town, private, narrow-minded, vulgar. *En habits —*, in plain clothes. *Voiture —e*, private carriage. *Pension —e*, boarding-house. *Cuisine —e*, plain cookery. *—e*, sf. citizen's wife

Bourgeoisie, sf. the citizens, middle classes, freedom of the city. *La petite —*, the small tradesmen

Bourgeon, sm. (*etym. O.H.G.* burjan, *to raise*), bud, budding, shoot, pimple

Bourgeonné, e, adj. in buds, pimpled

Bourgeonner, vn. to bud, to sprout, to break out in pimples

Bourgeron, sm. (*etym.* berger ?), short smock-frock

Bourgmestre, sm. (*etym. G.* burgermeister), burgomaster

Bourrache, sf. (*etym. L.* borraginem), borage

Bourrade, sf. (*etym.* bourrer), blow, thrust, rating

Bourrasque, sf. (*etym. I. pat.* bora, *north wind ?*), squall, commotion

Bourre, sf. (*etym. L.L.* burra), hair, floss-silk, flock of wool, wadding, wad, down

Bourreau, sm. (*etym. prop. name* Borel ?), executioner, headsman, tormentor, unfeeling brute. *Valet de —*, deputy executioner. ‡ *— d'argent*, spendthrift

Bourrée, sf. (*etym.* bourre), brushwood, fagot, sort of jig

Bourreler, va. (*etym.* bourreau), to goad, to rack, to harrow. *Bourrelé de remords*, stung with remorse

Bourrelet, sm. (*etym. O.F.* bourrel, *dimin. of* bourre), a kind of stuffed cap worn by children, porter's knot, pad, padding

Bourrelier, sm. (*etym. O.F.* bourrel), harness maker

Bourrer, va. to stuff, to cram, to ram; *se —*, vr. to stuff, to cram oneself

Bourriche, sf. (*etym.* bourre), hamper, basket

Bourrique, sf. (*etym. L.L.* buricus *or* burricus, *a small horse*), donkey, she-ass, blockhead, dunce, handbarrow, sorry jade

Bourriquet, sm. donkey, ass's foal, blockhead, handbarrow

Bourru, e, adj. peevish, surly

Bourse, sf. (*etym. L.* byrsa, *Gr.* βύρσα), purse, pouch, Exchange, business, scholarship, hair-bag, an empty purse. ‡ *Sans — délier*, without any expense. *Coupe- —*, cutpurse. *La — ou la vie!* your money or your life!

†**Boursicaut**, sm. (*dim. of* bourse), little stock of money

Boursier, sm. treasurer, foundation scholar, stock-jobber

Boursouflage, sm. bombast, fustian

Boursouflé, e, adj. puffy, swollen, turgid, fustian

Boursoufler, va. (*etym.* bourse, souffler), to puff out, to blow out

Boursouflure, sf. puffiness, swelling, turgidness, pomposity

Bousculer, va. (*alter. of* boute, culer, *from* bouter *and* cul), to knock about, to hustle about

Bouse, sf. (*etym.* bœuf ?), the dung of an ox *or* a cow

†**Bousin**, sm. (*etym. ?*), uproar, noise

Boussole, sf. (*etym. I.* bossolo, *a small box*), compass, guide

Bout, sm. (*etym. I.* botto), end, extremity, scrap. *Mettre — à —*, to put endwise. *Joindre les deux —s*, to make the two ends meet. *Montrer le — de l'oreille*, (*fig.*) to give an insight *or* a glimpse into one's real character. ‡ *Être au — de son rouleau*, to be at one's wits' end. *Rire du — des dents, des lèvres*, to give a constrained laugh. *C'est tout le — du monde*, it is the utmost. *À —*, exhausted, spent. *À — de forces*, quite spent. *Pousser à —*, to confound, to exasperate. *Venir à — de*, to succeed in. *À tout — de champ*, every instant. *Au — du compte*, after all. *À — portant*, quite close. *Des —-rimés*, rhymes given

Boutade, sf. (*etym.* bouter), whim, freak, sally, bit of poetry. *Par —s*, by fits and starts

Boute-en-train, sm. merry companion, singing bird; *plur.* des boute-en-train

Boute-feu, sm. linstock, firebrand; *plur.* des boute-feu

§**Bouteille**, sf. (*etym. L.L.* buticula, *dimin. of* buta, *a small cask*), bottle. *Mettre en —*, to bottle. *Payer — à*, to treat to a bottle

***Bouter**, va. (*etym. M.H.G.* bôzen, *to knock*), to place, to put

Boute-selle, sm. signal to saddle

Boutique, sf. (*etym. Gr.* ἀποθήκη, *the storing of goods*), shop

Boutiquier, ère, adj. shop-keeper

Boutoir, sm. (*etym.* bouter), snout. *Un coup de —*, (*fig.*) a rough reply

Bouton, sm. (*etym.* bout), bud, pimple, button, knob, handle. *— d'arme à feu*, sight. *— à queue*, shank-button. *— double*, studs. *— d'or*, gold button. ‡ *Serrer le — à*, to press hard

Boutonné, e, adj. buttoned, pimpled, mysterious, close

Boutonner, vn. to bud; — va. to button

Boutonnerie, sf. button-trade

Boutonnière, sf. button-hole

Bouture, sf. (*etym.* bouter), slip, cutting

Bouvier, sm. (*etym.* bœuf), cowherd, drover, cattle-driver

Bouvreuil, sm. (*etym. dimin. of* bœuf), bullfinch

Bovine, adj.f. (*etym. L.* bovina, *from* bos), bovine, black

***Boxe**, sf. boxing, the ring

***Boxer**, vn., *se —*, vr. to box, to fight

***Boxeur**, sm. boxer, prize-fighter

Boyau, sm. (*etym. L.L.* botellus), bowels, hose, pipe, branch. *Corde à —*, catgut

Boyauderie, sf. a manufacture of fiddle-strings

Boyaudier, sm. a fiddle-string maker

Braconnage, sm. poaching

Braconner, vn. to poach

Braconnier, sm. (*etym.* braque, *a kind of dog*), poacher

Brahmane, Brahmine, sm. (*etym. Sans.* brâhmân), brahmin

§**Braillard, e, Brailleur, se**, adj. brawling, noisy, obstreperous

§**Brailler**, vn. (*etym.* braire, *like* criailler *from* crier), to bawl, to brawl, to squall

Braiment, sm. (*etym.* braire), braying

Braire, vn. (*etym. L.L.* bragire, *to neigh*), to bray, to squall

Braise, sf. (*etym. O.G.* bras, *fire*), burning embers, live coal, small charcoal

Braiser, va. to stew

Bramement, sm. belling

Bramer, vn. (*etym. O.H.D.* bremen, *to bellow: comp. the Gr.* βρέμειν), to bell

Brancard, sm. (*etym.* branche), handbarrow, shaft, shutter

Branchage, sm. boughs, branches

Branche, sf. (*etym. Celt.* brac, brech, *arm*), bough, branch

Brandir, va. (*etym. O.F.* brand), to brandish

Brandon, sm. (*etym. O.H.G.* brant), brand, firebrand, wisp of straw

Branlant, e, adj. shaky, tottering

Branle, sm. swinging, swing, impulse, hammock. *Mettre en —, donner le — à*, to set a-going. *Se mettre en —*, to begin a peal. *Mener le —*, to take the lead

Branle-bas, sm. signal for action. *Faire —*, to clear for action

Branlement, sm. swinging, shaking, tottering

Branler, vn. (*etym. ?*), to swing, to totter, to stir. ‡ *— dans le manche*, to shake in one's seat, to waver. — va. to swing, to shake

Braque, sm. (*etym. O.H.G.* bracko, *a hound*), brach-hound. ‡ — s. adj. cracked, half-crazed person

Braquemart, sm. (*etm. ?*), a short wide sword

Braquer, va. (*etym. ?*), to point. *— ses regards sur*, to rivet one's eyes on

Bras, sm. (*etym. L.* brachium, *arm*), arm, hands, handle. †*Avoir les — longs*, (*fig.*) to have a great deal of credit *or* influence. *— dessus — dessous*, arm in arm. *Être au — de quelqu'un*, to hold a person's arm. *Avoir quelqu'un sur les —*, to have to maintain, to be troubled with. *Les — m'en sont tombés*, I stood astounded. *À force de —*, by main strength. *À tour de —, à — raccourci*, with all one's might. *À — le corps*, in one's arms

Brasier, sm. (*etym. see* BRAISE), pan of burning coals, brazier

Brassage, sm. (*etym.* brasser), brewing, mixing

Brassard, sm. (*etym.* bras), brace, ribbon (on the arm)

Brasse, sf. (*etym. L.* brachia, *plur. of* brachium), fathom, stroke

Brassée, sf. (*etym.* brasse), armful, stroke

Brasser, va. (*etym. Celt.* brag, bracha, braig, *fermented grain*), to brew, to plot

Brasserie, sf. (*etym.* brasser), brewery, brew-house

Brasseur, sm. (*etym.* brasser), brewer

Brassières, sf.pl. (*etym.* bras), linen stays

Bravache, sm. (*etym. I.* bravaccio), braggadocio, bully

Bravade, sf. (*etym. I.* bravata), bravado

Brave, adj. (*etym. ?*), brave, gallant, manful, worthy, smart. — sm. brave man, worthy fellow, ruffian. ‡ — *à trois poils*, hard fighter

Braver, va. to dare, to brave, to defy, to face, to beard

Bravo! interj. sm. (*I.*), (*plur.* des bravos), bravo! applause; (*plur.* des bravi), a bravo, a bully

Bravoure, sf. bravery, manhood, valour

Brebis, sf. (*etym. L.* vervecem, *a ram*), ewe, sheep, † — *galeuse*, a person who is shunned

Brèche, sf. (*etym. O.H.G.* brecha, *the action of breaking*), gap, hole, opening, breach, notch

Brèche-dents, adj.s. gap-toothed, gap-toothed person; *plur.* des brèche-dents

§Bredouillement, sm. stuttering, stammering

§Bredouiller, vn. (*etym. ?*), to stutter, to stammer

§Bredouilleur, se, smf. stutterer, stammerer

Bref, Brève, adj. (*etym. L.* brevis), brief, short, succinct, quick. — adv. in a word, in short. — sm. brief, church calendar

Brelan, sm. (*etym. G.* bretling, *a small board*), brelan, gambling-house

Breloque, sf. (*etym. ?*), watch-seal, charm

Bretelle, sf. (*etym. ?*), brace, strap

Brette, sf. (*etym. Scand.* bredda, *sword*), long rapier

Bretteur, sm. known duellist, bully

Breuvage, sm. (*etym. L.L.* biberaticum), draught, drink, beverage

Brève, sf. (*etym. L.* brevis), short syllable, breve

Brevet, sm. (*dimin. of* bref), patent, commission, warrant, licence

Breveté, e, adj. patented, licensed

Breveter, va. to grant a patent to

Bréviaire, sm. (*etym. L.* breviarium, *from* brevis), breviary, vade-mecum

Bribe, sf. (*etym. ?*), scrap, crumb

Bric-à-brac, sm. (*etym. see* Broc), odds and ends, old stores; *plur.* des bric-à-brac

Brick, sm. (*etym. Eng.* brig), brig

Bricole, sf. (*etym. O.F.* bric *or* briche, *a snare*), breast-collar, strap

Bride, sf. (*etym. O.H.G.* brittil, brittl), bridle, check, strings, loop. ‡ *Tenir en* —, to keep a tight hand over. *Mettre la — sur le cou*, to allow full liberty. *Lâcher la* — *à*, to slacken the reins of. *Tourner* —, to turn back. *A toute* —, *à — abattue*, at full speed or gallop

Brider, va. to bridle, to curb; — vn. to wrinkle

Bridon, sm. snaffle-bridle

Brièvement, adv. (*etym. O.F.* brief), briefly

Brièveté, sf. (*etym. O.F.* brief), briefness, brevity, conciseness

Brigadier, sm. (*etym.* brigade), corporal

Brigand, sm. (*etym.* brigade), robber, brigand, ruffian

Brigandage, sm. plundering, extortion

Brigander, vn. to rob

Brigantin, sm. (*etym.* brigand), brigantine

Brigue, sf. (*etym. L.L.* briga, *quarrel*), underhand means, party, cabal

Briguer, va. to solicit, to canvass for

§Brillant, e, adj. (*etym.* briller), bright, brilliant, sparkling. — sm. brilliancy, brightness, brilliant

§Brillanter, va. to cut into a brilliant

§Briller, vn. (*etym. L.* beryllus, *a precious stone; see* Béryl), to shine, to be bright, to glare, to blaze

Brimborion, sm. (*etym. L.* breviarium, *corrupted into* briborion, brimborion), gewgaw, nicknack

Brin, sm. (*etym. ?*), blade, sprig, shoot, bit. ‡ *Beau — d'homme*, a tall handsome man

Brioche, sf. (*etym.* broyer), brioche, blunder

Brique, sf. (*etym. Ang.-Sax.* brice, *a fragment*), brick. *Four à —s*, brick-kiln

Briquet, sm. (*etym. see* Brique), steel, tinder-box, short sabre

Briquetage, sm. brick-work

Briqueter, va. to give the appearance of brick

Briqueterie, sf. brick-kiln, brick-field, brick-making

Briquetier, sm. brick-maker

Bris, sm. (*etym. see* Briser), breach, wreck

Brisants, sm.plur. (*etym.* briser), breakers

Brise, sf. (*etym. ?*), breeze

Brisées, sf.plur. scattered boughs, steps. ‡ *Aller sur les — de*, to try to oust

Brise-glace, sm. starling, ice-breaker, iceboat; *plur.* des brise-glaces

Brise-lame, sm. break-water; *plur.* des brise-lames

Brisement, sm. (*etym.* briser), breaking

Brise-mottes, sm. clod-crusher; *plur.* des brise-mottes

Briser, va.n. (*etym. Gael.* bruis, *a fragment*), to break, to shatter, to crush, to snap

Brise-tout, sm. mischievous child, awkward body; *plur.* des brise-tout

Briseur, sm. breaker

Brise-vent, sm. a screen; *plur.* des brise-vent *or* vents

Brisure, sf. (*etym.* briser), broken place, fold

Britannique, adj. British, Britannic

Broc, sm. (*etym.* broche), pitcher, jack

Brocantage, sm. (*etym.* brocanter), dealing in second-hand goods, dealing in curiosities

Brocanter, va. (*etym. ?*), to deal in second-hand goods, in curiosities

Brocanteur, se, smf. dealer in curiosities. *Magasin de* —, curiosity-shop

Brocard, sm. (*etym.* Burchard, *name of a bishop of Worms*), taunt, jeer, scoff

Brocarder, va. to taunt

Brocart, sm. (*etym.* brocher), brocade, flowered silk

Brochage, sm. (*etym.* brocher), stitching

Broche, sf. (*etym. L.* broccus *or* brochus, *a protruding tooth*), brooch, spit, spindle, knitting-needle, stem, peg, spigot

Brocher, va. (*etym.* broche), to work, to stitch, to hurry through. ‡ *Brochant sur le tout*, overtopping all the rest

Brochet, sm. (*etym.* broche), pike

Brochette, sf. (*etym.* broche), skewer, stick, a string of orders. ‡ *Élever à la* —, to bring up daintily

Brocheur, se, s. (*etym.* brocher), stitcher

Brochure, sf. stitching, pamphlet

Brodequin, sm. (*etym. Gr.* βύρσα, *a kind of leather ?*), sock, half-boot, lady's boot, boot

Broder, va. (*etym. Celt.* broud, brouda, brodio), to embroider, (*fig.*) to embellish

Broderie, sf. embroidery, (*fig.*) romance, embellishment

Brodeur, se, s. embroiderer

Broiement, sm. (*etym.* broyer), grinding, crushing

Broncher, vn. (*etym. O.F.* bronche, *trunch*), to stumble, to trip

Bronches, sf.plur. (*etym. Gr.* βρόγχος, *throat*), bronchia

Bronchite, sf. (*etym.* bronches), bronchitis

Bronzé, e, adj. bronzed, sunburnt, tanned

Bronzer, va. (*etym.* bronze), to bronze

Broquette, sf. (*etym.* broche), tack, small nail

Brossage, sm. (*etym.* brosse), brushing

Brosse, sf. (*etym. O.H.G.* burst, brustia), brush

Brossée, sf. brushing, thrashing

Brosser, va. to brush

Brosserie, sf. brush-trade, brush-manufactory

Brosseur, sm. an officer's man-servant, man, servant

Brouée, sf. (*etym. ?*), fog, mist

Brouet, sm. (*etym. Celt. and O.H.G.* brod), broth, brewis, caudle

Brouette, sf. (*etym. L.L.* birota, *a two-wheeled vehicle*), barrow, wheelbarrow, hand-barrow

Brouetter, va. to wheel in a barrow, to carry

Brouhaha, sm. (*etym. ?*), hubbub, uproar

§Brouillamini, sm. (*etym. ?*), confusion

§Brouillard, sm. (*etym.* brouée), fog, haze, mist, waste-book, blotting-paper

§Brouillasser, vn. (*etym.* brouillas, *old form for* brouillard), to drizzle

§Brouille, sf. (*etym.* brouiller), disagreement, coolness

§Brouillé, e, adj. in disorder, who has quarrelled. *Œufs —s*, buttered eggs

§Brouiller, va. (*etym. ?*), to mix, to mingle, to upset, to perplex, to set at variance. ‡ — *les cartes*, to make mischief

§Brouillerie, sf. (*etym.* brouiller), misunderstanding, broil

§Brouillon, sm. foul copy, rough draft, waste-book

§Brouillon, ne, s. blunderhead, meddling body

Brouir, va. (*etym. O.G.* bruejen, *to heat*), to blight

Brouissure, sf. (*etym.* brouir), blight, blast

§Broussailles, sf. plur. (*etym.* brousser), brushwood

Broussin, sm. (*dimin. of Celt.* broz *or* broc, *a knot*), a shoot, an excrescence

Brout, sm. (*etym. Ang.-Sax.* brustian, *to bud*), browse-wood

Brouter, va. (*etym. see* Brout), to browse

Broyer, va. (*etym. ?*), to grind, to pound, to crunch, to crush. *Machine à* —, crushing-mill. † — *du noir*, (*fig.*) to have the spleen. *Se* —, vr. to be ground

Bru, sf. (*etym. O.H.D.* brût, *bride*), daughter-in-law

§Brugnon, sm. (*etym. I.* brugna, prugna, *a plum*), nectarine

Bruine, sf. (*etym. ?*), drizzling rain, drizzle

Bruiner, vn. to drizzle

Bruire, va. (*etym. ?*), to rustle, to murmur

Bruissement, sm. rushing, rustling, murmur

Bruit, sm. (*etym.* bruire), noise, sound, uproar, clamour, murmur, fame, renown, mention. *Sans* —, noiselessly, quietly. *A grand* —, noisily, ostentatiously. *A petit* —, privately. *Il n'est — que de*, people talk of nothing but. *Le — court*, it is said that. *Faire courir un — que*, to spread abroad that

Brûlant, e, adj. burning, hot, glowing
Brûlé, e, adj. burnt. *Avoir un goût de* —, to taste as if it was burnt. *Sentir le* —, to smell of fire
†**Brûle-gueule,** sm. (*etm.* brûler, gueule), a short pipe; *plur.* des brûle-gueule
Brûle-pourpoint, adv. point-blank
Brûler, va. (*etym. L.L.* perustulare), to burn, to burn down, to set fire to, to inflame, to scorch, to dry up, to scald. ‡ — *le pavé*, to rattle along full speed. *La fièvre le brûle*, he is in a burning fever. *Nous avons brûlé nos vaisseaux*, there is no going back. — *à petit feu*, to burn by a slow fire. — vn. to burn, to be on fire, to glow, to be lighted, to long. *Les pieds lui brûlent*, he longs to be gone. *Se* —, vr. to burn oneself, to scald oneself
Brûle-tout, sm. save-all; *plur.* des brûle-tout
Brûlot, sm. (*etym.* brûler), fire-ship, fire-brand, incendiary
Brûlure, sf. (*etym.* brûler), burn, scald
Brume, sf. (*etym. L.* bruma, *winter solstice*), haze, thick fog, mist
Brumeux, se, adj. (*etym.* brume), hazy, foggy
Brun, sm. (*etym. O.H.G.* brûn), brown, dark-haired man, dark-featured man
Brun, e, adj. brown, dun, dusky, dark-featured
Brunâtre, adj. brownish
Brune, sf. dark-haired girl *or* woman, dusk
Brunet, te, s. dark person
Brunir, va. to brown, to darken, to burnish; — vn., *se* —, vr. to turn brown, to get dark
Brunissage, sm. (*etym.* brunir), burnishing
Brunisseur, se, s. burnisher
Brunissoir, sm. burnisher
Brunissure, sf. burnishing
Brusque, adj. (*etym. I.* brusco), abrupt, blunt, rough, hasty
Brusquer, va. to treat roughly, to be blunt with, to do quickly, to make a sudden attack on
Brusquerie, sf. abruptness, bluntness, roughness
Brut, e, adj. (*etym. L.* brutus), rough, unpolished, raw, coarse, brute, brutish, gross
Brutalement, adv. (*etym.* brutal), brutal
Brutaliser, va. (*etym.* brutal), to use roughly, to maltreat
Brutalité, sf. (*etym.* brutal), brutality, brutish passion
‡**Bruyant, e,** adj. (*etym.* bruire), noisy, clamorous, obstreperous, loud
Bruyère, sf. (*etym. Celt.* brwg, *a bush, hedge*), heath, furze, broom, common. *Terre de* —, garden mould. *Coq de* —, heath-cock, grouse
Buanderie, sf. (*etym.* buée), wash-house
Buandier, ère, smf. (*etym.* buée), washerman, washerwoman
Bubon, sm. (*etym. Gr.* βουβών, *tumour*), boil
Bucentaure, sm. (*etym. Gr.* βοῦς, *ox*, κένταυρος, *centaur*), Bucentaur
Bucéphale, sm. (*etym. Gr.* βοῦς, *ox*, κεφαλή, *head*), Bucephalus
Bûche, sf. (*etym. same as* bois), log, blockhead
Bûcher, sm. (*etym.* bûche), woodhouse, funeral pile, stake
Bûcher, va.n. (*etym.* bûche), to rough-hew, (‡) to work hard, to knock
Bûcheron, sm. (*dimin. of* bûche), woodcutter
Bucolique, adj. (*etym. Gr.* βουκολικός, *pastoral*), pastoral, bucolic
Budget, sm. (*etym. O.F.* boulgette, *small purse*), budget
Buée, sf. (*etym.* ?), steam, vapour
Buffet, sm. (*etym.* ?), sideboard, dresser, refreshment-room, service of plate, organ-case
Buffle, sm. (*etym. Gr.* βούβαλος), buffalo, buff
Buffleterie, sf. (*etym.* buffle), leathern accoutrements
Buis, sm. (*etym. Gr.* πύξος), box, box-wood
Buisson, sm. (*etym.* buis), bush, thicket
Buissonneux, se, adj. bushy
Buissonnier, ère, adj. bush, hedge. *Faire l'école* —*ère*, to play the truant
Bulbe, sm. (*etym. Gr.* βολβός, *onion*), bulb
Bulbeux, se, adj. (*etym.* bulbe), bulbous
Bulle, sf. (*etym. L.* bulla), bubble, bulla, bull
Bulletin, sm. (*etym.* bulle), vote-ticket, official report. — *de bagages*, luggage-ticket
Buraliste, sm. (*etym.* bureau), office-keeper
Bure, sf. (*etym. Gr.* πυρρός, *red*), drugget, coarse cloth, shaft
Bureau, sm. (*etym.* bure), desk, office, counting-house, ticket-office, committee, board. — *de poste*, post-office. — *d'arrondissement*, branch post-office. — *restant*, to be left till called for. — *de placement*, register-office. *Chef de* —, head-clerk. *Garçon de* —, porter. *Prendre l'air du* —, to go and see how things stand
*****Bureaucrate,** sm. (*etm.* bureaucratie), clerk in a Government office, an official personage
*****Bureaucratie,** sf. (*etm.* bureau, *and Gr.* κρατεῖν, *to rule; pronounce* bureaucracie), bureaucracy, official influence
*****Bureaucratique,** adj. (*etym.* bureaucrate), official
Burette, sf. (*dimin. of the O.F.* buire, *a vase*), vase, cruet, can
Burin, sm. (*etym. O.H.G.* borôn, *to pierce*), graving-tool, style of engraving
Buriner, va. to engrave, to write like copperplate
Burlesquement, adv. (*etym.* burlesque), in a burlesque manner
Burnous, sm. (*etym. Ar.* bornos), burnous
Busc, sm. (*etym. I.* busto, *the body; see* BUSTE), busk, whalebone
Buse, sf. (*etym. L.L.* busio, *from* buteo, *a hawk*), buzzard, noodle, ventilator
Busqué, e, adj. arched
Busquer, va. (*etym.* busc), to put a busk to, to slope
Buste, sm. (*etym. see* BUSC), bust, head and shoulders. *Portrait en* —, half-length portrait
But, sm. (*same word as* boot), mark, butt, aim, goal, target. *Tirer de* — *en blanc*, to shoot point-blank. *De* — *en blanc*, abruptly. *Toucher le* —, to hit the mark
Buter, va. (*etym.* but), to prop, to buttress, to anger, to stumble
Butin, sm. (*etym. Scand.* byti), booty, spoil, plunder
Butiner, vn.a. to plunder, to collect booty, to pilfer
Butor, sm. (*etym.* ?), bittern, booby
Butte, sf. (*same word as* but), knoll, mound, hillock. *Être en* — *à*, to be exposed to
Butter, vn. to stumble
Buvable, adj. (*etym.* buvant), drinkable, fit to be drunk
Buvard, sm. (*etym.* buvant), blotting-case. *Papier* —, blotting-paper
Buvetier, sm. (*etym.* buvant), man who keeps a refreshment-room
Buvette, sf. refreshment-room
Buveur, se, smf. (*etym. L.* bibitorem), guest, drinker, toper
Buvoter, vn. (*etym.* buveur), to sip, to tipple

C

C, sm. c; C, one hundred
Çà, pron.dem. (*etym. L.* ecce hoc; *see* CELA), that. *Comme* —, so, in this way, so so. — adv. here, hither. — *et là*, here and there. — interj. now come! *Or* —, now then, I say
Cabale, sf. (*etym. Heb.* kabala), cabal, cabala
Cabaler, vn. to cabal
Cabalistique, adj. cabalistic, cabalistical
Caban, sm. (*etym. Arab.* abâ, *a kind of cloak*), hooded cloak, pilot-coat
Cabane, sf. (*etym. Celt.* cab, *hut*), cottage, hut, cabin, flat-bottomed barge, breeding-cage
Cabanon, sm. cell
Cabaret, sm. (*etym.* ?), wine-shop, tavern, set of tea-things
Cabaretier, ère, smf. tavern-keeper
Cabas, sm. (*etym. L.* capax), basket, work-bag
Cabestan, sm. (*etym.* ?), windlass, capstan, capstern
§**Cabillaud,** sm. (*etym. Bas.* bacailaba, *cod*), cod-fish
Cabine, sf. (*same word as* cabane), cabin
Cabinet, sm. study, closet, cabinet, office, practice, business, collection. — *de lecture*, circulating library. — *de verdure*, summer-house. — *d'aisances*, water-closet. — *de toilette*, dressing-room. — *d'orgue*, chamber organ. *Homme de* —, a studious man
Câbleau, sm. a boat-rope
‡**Caboche,** sf. (*etym. L.* caput), pate, noddle, head, bob-nail
Cabotage, sm. coasting-trade
Caboter, vn. (*etym. Ital.* cabotaggio), to ply in the coasting-trade
Caboteur, sm. coaster
Cabotier, sm. coasting-vessel
‡**Cabotin, e,** smf. (*etym.* caboter ?), strolling player, bad actor
Cabrer, vn. (*etym. Sp.* cabra, *goat*), to prance, to rear, to fly into a passion
Cabri, sm. (*etym. L.L.* capritum, *goat*), kid
Cabriole, sf. (*etym.* cabri), caper
Cabrioler, vn. to cut capers
Cabriolet, sm. cabriolet, one-horse chaise
Cabus, adj. (*etym. L.* caput, *head*), headed
†**Cacade,** sf. (*etm. L.* cacare), failure, mess
Cacaotier, Cacaoyer, sm. (*etym.* cacao), cocoa-tree
Cacatois, sm. cockatoo, (*nav.*) royal
Cachalot, sm. (*etym. Bas.* cachau, *tooth*), spermaceti-whale
Cache, sf. (*etym. see* CACHER), hiding-place

Cache-cache, sm. hide and seek

Caché, e, adj. part. hidden, secret, dissembling, retired

Cachemire, sm. (*proper name of a kingdom in Asia*), cashmere

Cache-nez, sm. comforter; *plur.* des cache-nez

Cacher, va. (*etym. L.* coactare, *to squeeze, to press*), to hide, to conceal, to secrete, to dissemble

Cachet, sm. (*etym.* cacher), seal, stamp, signet, lesson. *— volant*, flying seal. *Lettre de —*, arbitrary order of imprisonment. ‡*Courir le —*, to give private lessons

Cacheter, va. to seal, to seal up. *Pain à —*, wafer

Cachette, sf. hiding-place. *En —*, privately, by stealth

Cachot, sm. dungeon, prison

Cachotterie, sf. making a secret of trifles, mystery

Cachottier, ère, adj. (*etm.* cachotterie), who affects mystery, close

Cacographie, sf. (*etym. Gr.* κακός, *bad*, γράφειν, *to write*), cacography

Cactus, Cactier, sm. (*etym. Gr.* κάκτος, *a thorny plant*), cactus

Cadastre, sm. (*etym. L.L.* capitastrum, *from L.* caput, *head*), Government survey of lands, the board of surveys, land register-book

Cadavéreux, se, adj. (*etym.* cadavre), cadaverous, death-like

Cadavre, sm. (*etym. L.* cadaver), corpse, dead body, carcase

Cadeau, sm. (*etym. L.* catellus, *small chain*), gift, present, boon, flourish

Cadenas, sm. (*etym. L.L.* catenacium, *from L.* catena, *chain*), padlock

Cadenasser, va. to padlock

Cadence, sf. (*etym. L.* cadere, *to fall*), cadence, trill, quaver, harmony, numbers, time. *Aller en —*, to keep time

Cadencé, e, adj. cadenced, harmonious, in time

Cadencer, va. to give a cadence to

Cadenette, sf. (*etym. prop. name* Cadenet), a truss of hair

***Cadène,** sf. (*etym. L.* catena), chain, chaingang

Cadet, te, adj. s. (*etym. L.* caput; *O.F.* capdet), younger, junior. *— de famille*, young man of good family

Cadran, sm. (*etym. L.* quadrantem), dial, dial-plate. *— solaire*, sun-dial

Cadrat, sm. (*etym. L.* quadratus), a quadrat

Cadratin, sm. an m quadrat

Cadre, sm. (*etym. I.* quadro, *frame*), frame, framework, plan, outline, staff of a regiment

Cadrer, vn. to agree, to tally, to square; — va. to quadrate, to square

Caduc, que, adj. (*etym. L.* caducus), decrepit, frail, crazy, lapsed

Caducée, sm. (*etym. Gr.* κηρύκειον, *the insignia of a herald*), caduceus, wand, staff

Caducité, sf. decrepitude, crazy state, decay, lapsing

Cafard, e, adj. (*etym. L.L.* caphardum, *a kind of dress*), canting, hypocritical

Cafarder, vn. sneak

Cafarderie, sf. cant, hypocrisy

Café, sm. (*etym. Ar.* cahveh), coffee, coffee-time, coffee-house

Cafetan, Caftan, sm. (*etym. Turk.* kaftân), caftan

Cafetier, sm. coffee-house keeper

Cafetière, sf. coffee-pot

Cafier, *or* **Caféier,** sm. coffee-tree

Cage, sf. (*etym. L.* cavea, *a hollow place*), cage, jail, shell, case, groove

Cagneux, se, adj. (*etym. O.F.* cagne, *bitch*; *L.* canis), bow-legged, crook-kneed

Cagot, e, smf. adj. (*etym. L.* canes, Gothi; *see* Littré), bigot, hypocrite; bigoted

Cagoterie, sf. bigotry, hypocrisy

Cagotisme, sm. bigotry, false piety

Cahier, sm. (*etym. L.* quaternarium), stitched book, paper book, copy-book, memorial. *— des charges*, specifications, conditions

Cahin-caha, adv. (*etym. L.* qua hinc, qua hac), so so, poorly

Cahot, sm. (*etym. ?*), jolt, jolting, shake. *Faire des —s*, to jolt

Cahotage, sm. jolting, shaking

Cahotant, e, adj. jolting

Cahoter, va. (*etym. ?*), to jolt, to shake, to toss about

Cahutte, Cahute, sf. (*etym. G.* kaue, *a small place*), hut, crib, hovel

§**Caille,** sf. (*etym. O.H.G.* wahtala), quail

§**Caillé,** sm. (*etym.* cailler), curds

§**Caillebotter,** va. (*etym.* cailler, botte), to curdle

§**Cailler,** va. (*etym. L.* coagulare), to curdle, to clot, to coagulate

§**Cailletage,** sm. (*etym.* caillette), gossip

§**Cailleter,** vn. (*etym.* caillette), to gossip

§**Cailleteau,** sm. (*etym.* caille), young quail

§**Caillette,** sf. (*etm.* cailler), rennet; (*etym.* caille), a gossip

§**Caillot,** sm. (*etym.* cailler), clot of blood

§**Caillou,** sm. (*etym. ?*), flint, pebble

§**Cailloutage,** sm. stones, stoning

§**Caillouter,** va. to stone

§**Caillouteux, se,** adj. stony, flinty, pebbly

§**Cailloutis,** sm. broken stone

Caisse, sf. (*etym. L.* capsa, *box*), case, chest, box, trunk, strong-box, cashier's office, cash, body, frame, drum. *Tenir la —*, to be cashier, to hold the strings of the purse. *Livre de —*, cash-book. *Compte de —*, cash-account. *Faire sa —*, to make up one's cash-book, to verify one's cash-account. *Passer à la —*, to go to the pay-office. *Avoir en —*, to have in hand. *— d'amortissement*, sinking-fund. *— d'épargne*, savings-bank. ‡ *Battre la —*, to beat the drum, to muster one's partisans. ‡ *Battre la grosse —*, to advertise in all the papers. *— à eau*, (*locom.*) water-tank

Caissier, sm. cashier

Caisson, sm. waggon, ammunition-waggon, powder-cart, box, locker, compartment, cassoon

Cajoler, va. (*etym. see* Cage), to wheedle, to coax, to cajole, to fawn upon

Cajolerie, sf. wheedling, coaxing, cajoling, fawning

Cajoleur, se, s. wheedler, deceiver, cajoler

Cal, Calus, sm. (*etym. L.* callus), callosity, callus

Calamité, sf. (*etym. L.* calamitas), calamity

‖**Calamiteux, se,** adj. (*etym. L.* calamitosus), calamitous

Calandre, sf. (*etym. ?*), calender, hotpress, weevil, calandra

Calandrer, va. to calender

Calandreur, se, smf. calenderer

Calcaire, adj. (*etym. L.* calcarius, *from* calx), chalky, calcareous. *Pierre —*, limestone

Calciner, va. (*etym. L.* calx), to calcine

Calcul, sm. (*etym. L.* calculus, *a pebble*), ciphering, arithmetic, accounts, reckoning, computation, calculus, stone

Calculateur, trice, adj. calculating

Calculer, va. to calculate, to reckon, to compute, to cipher

Cale, sf. (*etym. G.* keil, *wedge*), wedge, hold, stocks, slip, ducking. *A fond de —* at the bottom of the hold

Calebasse, sf. (*etym. Ar.* kerbah, *a water-bottle*), calabash, gourd

Calebassier, sm. calabash-tree, gourd

Calèche, sf. (*etym. Slav. Bohem.* kolassa), open carriage, calash, hood, garden-bonnet

Caleçon, sm. (*etym. L.L.* calcio, *sock*), pair of drawers

Calembour, sm. (*etym. prop. name* Calenberg; *see* Littré), pun

‡**Calembredaines,** sf. pl. (*etym. ?*), nonsense, idle talk

Calendes, sf. plur. (*etym. Gr.* καλεῖν, *to call*), kalends. *Renvoyer aux — grecques*, to put off till the day of judgment

Calendrier, sm. (*etym. L.* calendarium), calendar, almanack

Calepin, sm. (*etym. prop. name* Calepino), note-book, memorandum-book

Caler, va. (*etym.* cale), to prop. † *Il commence à — bas*, (*fig.*) he begins to sing another note

Calfat, sm. (*etym.* calfater), caulker

Calfatage, sm. caulking

Calfater, va. (*etym. Arab.* kalafa, *to stop up chinks with tow*), to caulk

Calfeutrage, sm. (*etym.* calfeutrer), stopping up of chinks

Calfeutrer, va. (*same word as* calfater), to stop up chinks

Calibre, sm. (*etym. Arab.* kâlab, *mould*), bore, calibre, size, rule

Calice, sm. (*etym. Gr.* κύλιξ, *drinking-cup*), chalice, communion-cup; (*etym. Gr.* κάλυξ, *covering*), calyx, cup

Calicot, sm. (*etym.* Calicut, *a town in India*), calico, shopman

Califat, sm. caliphate

Calife, sm. (*etym. Ar.* khalifa, *successor of Mahomet*), caliph

Califourchon, adv. (*etym. ?*), astride, astraddle

Câlin, e, adj. s. (*etym. L.* canis ?), wheedling, coaxing

Câliner, va. to coax, to caress; *se —*, vr. to take one's ease

Câlinerie, sf. coaxing, wheedling

Calleux, se, adj. (*etym. L.* callosus), callous, hard

Calligraphe, sm. (*etym. Gr.* κάλλος, *beauty*, γράφειν, *to write*), penman

Calligraphie, sf. penmanship, calligraphy

Callosité, sf. (*etym. L.* callositatem), callosity

Calmant, e, adj. soothing, composing. — sm. soothing draught

Calme, adj. (*etym. I.* calma), calm, still, quiet, serene, unruffled, cool, collected, dull, flat, heavy

‖**Calmer,** va. to calm, to still, to hush, to allay, to soothe, to assuage; — vn. to grow calm, to lull

Calomniateur, trice, s. adj. (*etym.* calomnie), slanderer, calumniator, backbiter; slanderous

Calomnie, sf. (*etym. L.* calumnia), slander, calumny

Calomnier, va. (*etym. L.* calumniari), to slander, to calumniate, to asperse, to accuse wrongfully, to revile

‖**Calomnieux, se,** adj. (*etym.* calomnie), calumnious, slanderous, defamatory

Calorifère, adj. sm. (*etym. L.* calor, *heat*, ferre, *to carry*), heat-bearing; house heating-apparatus

Calorifique, adj. (*etym. L.* calorificus, *heat-producing*), calorific

Calorique, sm. (*etym. L.* calor, *heat*), caloric, heat, warmth

Calotte, sf. (*dimin. of* cale), cap, coif, calotte, canopy, pan of the skull, box on the ear, the priesthood

†**Calotter**, va. (*etm.* calotte), to box a person's ears; *se* —, vr. to punch each other

†**Calottin**, sm. (*etm.* calotte), (*liter.*) he who wears a skull-cap, a priest

Calque, sm. (*etym. I.* calco), tracing, copy

Calquer, va. (*etym. I.* calcare), to trace, to copy

Calus, sm. (*etym. L.* callus), callosity

Calvaire, sm. (*etym. L.* calvaria, *from* calvus, *bald*), Mount Calvary

Calvinisme, sm. (*etym. prop. name* Calvin), Calvinism

Calviniste, adj. Calvinist, Calvinistic

Calvitie, sf. (*etym. L.* calvities, *from* calvus, *bald*; *pronounce* calvicie), baldness

Camaïeu, sm. (*etym. L.L.* camæus, *onyx*), cameo

Camarade, s. (*etym. Sp.* camara, *room*), comrade, partner, friend

Camaraderie, sf. companionship, coterie, coalition

Camard, e, adj. (*etym. see* Camus), snub-nosed, flat

Cambouis, sm. (*etym. prov.* camois, *mud*), cart-grease, coom, gome

Cambré, e, adj. arched, bent up

Cambrer, va. (*etym. L.* camera, *vault*), to arch

Cambrure, sf. bend, cambering

Cambuse, sf. (*etym. D.* kabuys, *the kitchen in a ship*), steward's room, store-room

Cambusier, sm. steward's mate, purser's mate

Camée, sm. (*etym. see* Camaïeu), cameo

Caméléon, sm. (*etym. Gr.* χαμαί, *on the ground*, λέων, *lion*), chameleon

Camellia, sm. (*etym. prop. name of* Father Camelli), camelia

Camelot, sm. (*etym. L.* camelus, *camel*), camlet

‡**Camelote**, sf. (*etym.* camelot), paltry wares, carelessly made goods, trash

Camérier, sm. (*etym. I.* camera, *room*), the Pope's chamberlain

Camériste, sf. (*etym. I.* camerista, *from* camera, *room*), maid of honour, lady's maid

Camion, sm. (*etymol. ?*), dray, truck, small pin

Camionnage, sm. cartage

Camionneur, sm. drayman, carter

Camisole, sf. (*etym. I.* camiciola, *small shirt*), morning jacket. — *de force*, strait-waistcoat

§**Camomille**, sf. (*etym. Gr.* χαμαίμηλον, *from* χαμαί, *on the ground, and* μῆλον, *apple*), camomile

Camouflet, sm. (*etym.* chaud, *and* moufiet, *dimin. of* muffle), puff of smoke, (‡) rap over the knuckles

Camp, sm. (*Picard, for* champ), camp, encampment

Campagnard, e, s. adj. (*etym.* campagne), countrywoman, countryman, clown; country, clownish. *Gentilhomme* —, country squire

Campagne, sf. (*etym. L.* campus, *field*), country, plain, fields, country house, country life, campaign, cruise. *Battre la* —, to beat up, to scour the country, (‡) to wander from one's subject, to be delirious. *Entrer en* —, to take the field. *En rase* —, in the plain. *Se mettre en* —, (*fig.*) to set to work. *Pièce de* —, field-piece

§**Campanille**, sm. (*etym. L.L.* campanile, *from L.* campana, *bell*), campanile

Campanule, sf. (*dim. of L.* campana), hare-bell, blue-bell, bell-flower

Campé, e, adj. firmly planted

Campêche, sm. (*prop. name*), logwood

Campement, sm. camping, encampment. *Effets de* —, tents, camp gear

Camper, vn. (*etym.* camp), to encamp, to be in a place for a short time; — va. to encamp, to camp, to give, to leave

Camphre, sm. (*etym. Ar.* kafur), camphor

Camphré, e, adj. camphorate

Camphrer, va. to camphor

Camus, e, adj. s. (*etym. ?*), flat, flat-nosed, put out, vexed; flat-nosed person

§**Canaille**, sf. (*etym. I.* canaglia, *from* cane, *dog*), rabble, mob, rascal. — adj. low, rascally

Canal, sm. (*etym. L.* canalis), canal, pipe, conduit, stream, bed, channel, straits, groove

Canaliser, va. to canalize

Canapé, sm. (*etym. Gr.* κωνωπεῖον, *a bed with curtains*), sofa, couch

Canard, sm. (*etym. see* Cane), duck, drake, (†) hoax, (‡) a lump of sugar dipped in coffee

Canarder, va. to fire on

Canardière, sf. decoy, fowling-piece, loophole

Canari, sm. (*etym. prop. name* Canary Islands), canary bird

Cancan, sm. (*etym. L.* quamquam), pother, idle stories, gossiping, (†) low kind of dance

Cancaner, vn. to tittle-tattle, (†) to dance the cancan

Cancanier, ère, smf. talebearer, regular gossip

Cancre, sm. (*same word as* chancre), sea-crab, (‡) stingy fellow, dunce, pitiful wretch

Candélabre, sm. (*etym. L.* candelabrum), chandelier, candelabrum, sconce, lamp-post

Candeur, sf. (*etym. L.* candor, *whiteness*), candour, purity, innocence, plain-dealing, sincerity

Candi, adj. (*etym. Sans.* khanda, *preparation of sugar*), candied

Candidat, sm. (*etym. L.* candidatus, *dressed in white*), candidate. *Se porter* — *pour*, to stand candidate for

Candidature, sf. candidature, candidateship

‡**Candide**, adj. (*etym. L.* candidus), candid, sincere, open-hearted, upright

Candir, va.n. (*etym.* candi), to candy

Cane, sf. (*etym. O.F.* ane, *from L.* anas, *duck*), duck

Caneton, sm. young duck, duckling

Canette, sf. (*etym.* cane), duckling; (*etym. L.L.* canna, *a vase*), can, jug

Canevas, sm. (*etym. L.L.* canevasium, *from L.* cannabis, *hemp*), canvas, ground-work, sketch

Caniche, sm. (*etym. L.* canis), poodle

Caniculaire, adj. (*etym. L.* canicularis), canicular

Canicule, sf. (*etym. L.* canicula, *a small bitch*), the dog-star, dog-days

Canif, sm. (*etym. Scan.* knifr, *knife*), penknife

Canin, e, adj. (*etym. L.* canis), canine. —*e*, sf. canine tooth

Canne, sf. (*etym. Gr.* κάννα, κάννη), cane, reed, walking-stick, single-stick, tube

Cannelé, e, adj. fluted, grooved

Canneler, va. (*etym.* cannelle, *dimin. of* canne), to flute, to groove

Cannelle, sf. (*etym.* canne), cinnamon, tap, cock. † *Être en* —, to be in pieces

Cannellier, sm. (*etym.* cannelle), cinnamon-tree

Cannelure, sf. (*etym.* canneler), fluting, key-groove

Cannibale, sm. (*etym. O.Am.* Canniba, *prop. name*), cannibal

Canon, sm. (*etym. I.* cannone, *from* canne), cannon, barrel, pipe, glass, socket, instep, cannon-bit. *Poudre à* —, gunpowder. (*etym. Gr.* κανών), law, rule. *Le droit* —, canon law

Canonicat, sm. (*etym. L.* canonicatus, *from* canonicus, a canon), canonry

‡**Canonique**, adj. (*etym. L.* canonicus), canonical

Canoniser, va. (*etym. Gr.* κανών, *rule, law, list*), to canonize

Canonnade, sf. cannonade, cannonading

Canonner, va. to cannonade

Canonnier, sm. gunner, artilleryman

Canonnière, sf. gunboat, popgun, gunner's tent

Canot, sm. (*etym. ?*), canoe

Canotier, sm. boatman, rower

Cantaloup, sm. (*etym. I. prop. name* Cantaluppo), cantaloup melon

Cantate, sf. (*etym. I.* cantata), cantata

Cantatrice, sf. (*etym. L.* cantare, *to sing*), singer

Cantharide, sf. (*etym. Gr.* κανθαρίς), cantharis, Spanish fly

Cantilène, sf. (*etym. I.* cantilena), cantilena

Cantine, sf. (*etym. L.* quintana, *camp-market*), bottle-case, canteen

Cantinier, ère, s. keeper of a canteen

Cantique, sm. (*etym. L.* canticum, *from* cantus, *song*), song, canticle

Cantonade, sf. (*etym. I.* cantonata, *from* cantone, *corner*), behind the scenes. *Parler à la* —, to speak to a person behind the scenes

Cantonnement, sm. (*etym.* canton), cantonment

Cantonner, va.n. to canton

Cantonnier, sm. road-mender, roadman, signal-man

Canule, sf. (*dimin. of* canne), clyster pipe, tap, faucet, canula

Caolin, *see* Kaolin

Cap, sm. (*etym. L.* caput), cape, headland, foreland, head. *Armé de pied en* —, armed cap-à-pie, armed from head to foot

Capable, adj. (*etym. L.L.* capabilis, *from L.* capere, *to contain*), able, fit, capable, apt, intelligent, of good abilities. *Un sujet* —, a man of good abilities. ‡ *Faire le* —, to play the man of capacity. *Avoir l'air* —, to wear a self-conceited look

Capacité, sf. (*etym. L.* capacitatem), capacity, capability, parts, abilities, burden, tonnage

Caparaçon, sm. (*augment. of the L.L.* capare, *cape or hood*), caparison

Caparaçonner, va. to caparison

Cape, sf. (*Picard, pronunc. of* chape), cape, cloak, try-sail. *N'avoir que la* — *et l'épée*, to have but one's cloak and sword. ‡ *Roman de* — *et d'épée*, a novel full of battles and adventures. *Rire sous* —, to laugh in one's sleeve. *Vendre sous* —, to sell secretly

Capétien, ne, adj. (*etym. proper name* Capet), Capetian

Capillaire, adj. (*etym. L.* capillaris, *from* capillus, *hair*), capillary. — sm. maiden's-hair, capillaire

Capillarité, sf. (*etym.* capillaire), capillarity, capillary attraction

Capilotade, sf. (*etym. Sp.*

cabirotada, *a cape*), hash, minced meat. ‡ *Mettre en —*, to beat to a mummy, to run down a person's reputation

Capitaine, sm. (*etym. L.L.* capitanus, capitaneus, *from L.* caput), captain, master, commander. — *au long cours*, captain, master of a merchant-vessel. *Le — des chasses*, the lord ranger

Capitainerie, sf. captainship

Capital, e, adj. (*etym. L.* capitalis), capital, main, chief, deadly. — sm. main point, capital, stock, cash. —*e*, sf. metropolis, capital

Capitalisation, sf. realization

Capitaliser, va. to realize

Capitaliste, sm. capitalist, moneyed man

Capitan, sm. (*etym. see* CAPITAINE), swaggerer

Capiteux, se, adj. (*etym. L.* caput), heady

Capitole, sm. (*etym. L.* Capitolium), the Capitol

Capitolin, e, adj. (*etym. L.* Capitolinus), Capitoline

Capitoul, sm. (*etym. Prov.* capitol, *chapter*), municipal magistrate of the city of Toulouse

Capitulaire, sm. (*etym. L.* capitularis, *from* capitulum, *chapter*), capitular

Capituler, vn. (*etym. L.* capitulum), to capitulate, to compound

Capon, sm. (*etym. see* CHAPON), (†) sneak, cat-tackle

Caponner, vn. (†) to cheat, to sneak, to cat

Caporal, sm. (*etym. I.* capo, *head*), corporal

Capot, adj. (*etym.* cape), capot, dumb. ‡ *Rester —*, to be struck dumb

Capote, sf. (*etym.* capot), capote, rough coat, watch-coat, light bonnet, hood

Câpre, sf. (*etym. Gr.* κάππαρις), caper

Caprice, sm. (*etym. I.* capriccio, *from* capra, *goat*), caprice, whim, freak, humour. *Travailler de —*, to work by fits and starts. *Avoir un — pour*, to take a liking to

‡**Capricieux, se**, adj. s. capricious, whimsical, fickle; a capricious person

Capricorne, sm. (*etym. L.* Capricornus), Capricorn

Câprier, sm. (*etym.* câpre), caper-bush

Capsule, sf. (*etym. L.* capsula, *dimin. of* capsa, *box*), pod, capsule, cap, percussion-cap, capsula

Captatoire, adj. undue

Capter, va. (*etym. L.* captare, *frequent. of* capere, *to take*), to obtain by underhand means

Captieux, se, adj. (*etym. L.* captiosus, *from* capere; *pronounce* capcieux), captious, insidious

Captif, ve, adj. s. (*etym. L.* captivus), captive, prisoner

Captiver, va. to captivate, to enslave, to bring under

Captivité, sf. (*etym. L.* captivitatem), captivity, bondage

Capturer, va. to capture, to apprehend

Capuce, *also* **Capuchon**, sm. (*etym. I.* capuccio, *augment. of* cappa), cowl, hood

Capuchonné, e, adj. hooded

Capucin, e, s. (*etym. I.* cappucino, *from* cappuccio), capuchin friar, nun

‡**Capucinade**, sf. dull sermon

Capucine, sf. nasturtium, ring of a gun, pipkin

Caque, sf. keg, barrel. ‡ *La — sent toujours le hareng*, what is bred in the bone will never come out of the flesh

Caquer, va. (*etym. D.* kaaken, *to take out the gills*), to barrel, to cure

Caquet, sm. (*etym. see* CAQUETER), cackling, chattering, prate, tittle-tattle. † *Rabattre le — de quelqu'un*, to make a person lower his tone. *Avoir bien du —*, to have a nimble tongue

Caquetage, sm. cackling, chattering, cackle, prating

Caqueter, vn. (*onomat.*), to cackle, to chatter, to prate

Caqueteur, se, smf. prattler

Car, conj. (*etym. L.* quare, *wherefore*), for, because

Carabin, sm. (*etym. L.* Calabricus, *from* Calabria), light cavalry in the tenth century. (†) medical student

Carabine, sf. rifle, carbine

Carabiné, e, adj. stiff. *Brise —e*, stiff gale of wind

Carabinier, sm. carabinier, rifleman

Caracoler, vn. to caracole, to wheel about

Caractère, sm. (*etym. L.* character), character, letter, type, spell, sign, badge, style, temper, strength of mind. *Avoir le — bien fait, mal fait*, to be good-tempered, bad-tempered. *Faire sortir de son —*, to put out of temper

Caractériser, va. to characterize, to distinguish; *se —*, vr. to show oneself in one's true light

Caractéristique, sf. adj. characteristic, peculiar

Carafe, sf. (*etym. Arab.* garâfa, *to draw out*), decanter

Carafon, sm. small decanter, half-pint

Carambolage, sm. cannon (*at billiards*)

Carambole, sf. (*etym. Sp.* carambola), cannon

Caramboler, va. to cannon, to make a cannon

Carapace, sf. (*etym. Sp.* carapacho), shell

Caraque, sf. (*etymol.* ?), carack

Caravane, sf. (*etym. Pers.* karouân, *a company of travellers*), caravan. † *Faire ses —s*, to lead a dissolute life

§**Caravansérail**, sm. (*etym. Pers.* karouan, sarâi, *a house*), caravansary

Caravelle, sf. (*etym. I.* caravella, *a boat*), caravel, carvel

¶**Carbonarisme**, sm. (*etym. I.* carbonari, *plur. of* carbonaro), carbonarism

Carbone, sm. (*etym. L.* carbo, *charcoal*), carbon

Carboné, e, adj. carbonated

Carbonifère, adj. (*etym. L.* carbo, ferre, *to bear*), carboniferous

Carbonique, adj. (*etym. L.* carbo), carbonic. *Gaz acide —*, carbonic acid gas

Carboniser, va. to carbonize

Carbure, sf. (*etym. see* CARBONE), carburet

Carburé, e, adj. carburetted

Carcan, sm. (*etym. O.H.G.* querca, *throat*), iron collar, pillory, carcanet, necklace

Carcasse, sf. (*etym. see* CARQUOIS), carcase, body, hulk, shape, frame, (*arch.*) shell, skeleton

Cardage, sm. carding

Carde, sf. (*etym. L.* carduus, *thistle*), card, comb, card-engine, chard

Carder, va. to card

Cardeur, se, s. wool-carder

Cardinalat, sm. cardinalship

Cardon, sm. cardoon

Carême, sm. (*etym. L.* quadragesima, *fortieth* [*day*]), Lent, Lent-sermons. *La Mi-—*, mid-lent. *Faire —*, to keep Lent. † *Une face de —*, a woe-begone countenance. *Comme Mars en —*, as regular as clockwork. *Comme marée en —*, just in the nick of time

Carême-prenant, sm. (*etym.* carême, prendre), carnival-time, mummer; *plur.* des carêmes-prenants

Carénage, sm. careening, careening-wharf

Carène, sf. (*etym. L.* carina), keel, ship's bottom, careen, careening

Caréner, va. to careen

Caressant, e, adj. affectionate, coaxing, caressing

Caresse, sf. (*etym. L.* carus, *dear*), caress, endearment, fondling, fawning

Caressé, e, adj. beautifully finished

Caresser, va. (*etym.* caresse), to caress, to fondle, to stroke, to wanton with, to smile on, to fawn upon, to make much of, to cherish

Caret, sm. (*etym.* ?), sea-tortoise, turtle; (*etym.* char), rope-maker's reel. *Fil de —*, rope-yarn

Cargaison, sf. (*etym.* carguer), cargo, lading

Carguer, va. (*same word as* charger), to reef, to clue up

Caricaturer, va. n. (*etym.* caricature), to caricature

Carie, sf. (*etym. L.* caries), caries, rottenness, cariosity, brown rust

Carier, va. to rot

§**Carillon**, sm. (*etym. L.L.* quadrilionem, *quaternion*), chime, peal, racket, square iron bars. *Faire un —*, to make a great noise

§**Carillonné, e**, adj. high festival

§**Carillonner**, vn. to ring a peal, to make a racket

§**Carillonneur**, sm. bell-ringer, bawler

Carlin, sm. (*etym.* ?), pug-dog

Carlingue, sf. (*etym.* ?), keelson, step

¶**Carliste**, s. adj. (*etym.* Charles, Carlos), Carlist

Carlovingien, ne, s. adj. (*etym. L.L.* Carlus, Carolus), Carlovingian

Carme, sm. (*etym.* Mount Carmel), Carmelite friar. — *déchaussé*, bare-footed Carmelite

Carmin, sm. (*etym. L.L.* carmesinus; *see* CRAMOISI), carmine

Carminatif, ve, adj. (*etym. L.L.* carminativus), good against flatulency

Carnassier, ère, adj. (*etym. L.* caro, carnis, *flesh*), carnivorous, flesh-eating, fond of meat

Carnassière, sf. game-bag

Carnaval, sm. (*etym. L.* carnis levamen, *indulgence of the flesh*), carnival, Shrovetide

Carne, sf. (*etym. L.* cardinem), corner of a stone, a table

Carnet, sm. (*etym. L.L.* quaternetum, *a set of four sheets of paper*), note-book

Carnier, sm. (*same word as* charnier), game-bag

Carnivore, s. adj. (*etym. L.* carnivorus, *from* caro, vorare, *to devour*), carnivorous animal, carnivorous

†**Carogne**, sf. (*etym. see* CHAROGNE), a disagreeable woman

Caronade, sf. carronade

Carotide, sf. adj. (*etym. Gr.* καρωτίδες, *from* καροῦν, *to send to sleep*), carotid

Carotte, sf. (*etym. L.* carota), carrot, roll. † *Tirer une — à quelqu'un*, to get something out of a person

†**Carotter**, vn. to play shabbily, to cheat

†**Carottier, ère, Carotteur, se**, s. a person who is in the habit of cheating

Carpe, sf. (*etym. Gr.* [illegible]), carp. *Le saut de —*, a summersault. † *Faire la — pâmée*, to sham a fainting fit

Carpeau, sm. young carp

Carpette, sf. (*etym. L.* carpere), packing-cloth, centre-carpet

§**Carpillon**, sm. very young carp

Carquois, sm. (*etym. L. Gr.* ταρκάσιον, *O.F.* tarquois), quiver

Carrare, sm. Carrara-marble

Carré, e, adj. (*etym. L.* quadratus), square. *Avoir des épaules —es*, to be broad-shouldered. ¦ *Une tête —e*, a clear-headed fellow. *Bonnet —*, doctor's cap. *Partie —e*, party of four. — sm. square, landing-place, floor, breast of mutton, (*arch.*) fillet, (*print.*) demy, printing demy

Carreau, sm. (*etym. L.* quadrum, *square*), tile, pavement, pane of glass, cushion, diamond (*at cards*), tailor's goose, stoppage of the bowels, quarry, bolt. *Coucher quelqu'un sur le —*, to lay one sprawling on the ground. *Le valet de —*, a knave of diamonds, (*fig.*) a pitiful fellow. *Garder à —*, to reserve a diamond, (*fig.*) to be ready for any emergency

Carrefour, sm. (*etym. L.* quadrifurcum, *from* quadri *for* quatuor, *and* furca, *a fork*), cross-road, place where four roads meet

Carrelage, sm. paving, pavement

Carreler, va. (*etym.* carrel, carreau), to pave with tiles, to cobble

Carrelet, sm. plaice, flounder, square fishing-net, ruler, awl

Carreleur, sm. pavier, travelling cobbler

Carrelier, sm. tilemaker

Carrément, adv. square, to the point, clearly

Carrer, va. (*etym. L.* quadrare), to square, to form into squares

Carrier, sm. (*etym. L.* quadratarius, *stone-cutter*), quarry-man

Carrière, sf. (*etym. L.L.* quadraria, *quarry*), quarry, course, race-ground, career, race. *Donner — à un cheval*, to give the reins to a horse

Carriole, sf. (*etym. I.* carriuola), tilted cart

Carrossable, adj. good for carriages. *Route —*, carriage-road

Carrosse, sm. (*etym. I.* carrozza, *dimin. of* carro, *car*), coach, carriage. *Avoir, rouler —*, to keep a carriage. *Cheval de —*, coach-horse, (*fig.*) a lubberly fellow

Carrossier, sm. coach-maker, coach-horse

Carrousel, sm. (*etym. I.* carosello), tilting-match, carousal, tilt-yard

Carrure, sf. (*etym. L.* quadratura, *from* quadrare; *see* Carrer), breadth of shoulders

Carte, sf. (*etym. L.* charta, *from Gr.* χάρτης), card, direction, pasteboard, ticket, map, chart, bill of fare. *Faire une partie de —s*, to have a game of cards. *—s peintes*, court-cards. *—s basses*, small cards. *Fausse —*, odd card. *Donner les —s*, to deal. *Battre, mêler les —s*, to shuffle the cards. *Vous êtes le premier en —s*, it is your lead. *Jouer —s sur table*, to show one's hand, (*fig.*) to deal fair. *Connaître le dessous des —s*, to be in the secret. † *Perdre la —*, (*fig.*) to get flurried. *Tirer les —s*, to tell fortunes by the cards. *Donner — blanche à*, to give full powers to. *Dîner à la —*, to dine by the bill of fare prices

Cartel, sm. (*etym. see* Carte), challenge, cartel, dial-case

Cartésianisme, sm. (*etym. see* Cartésien), Cartesianism

Cartésien, ne, s. adj. (*etym.* Cartesius, *Latin name of* Descartes), Cartesian

Cartilagineux, se, adj. (*etym. L.* cartilaginosus), cartilaginous, gristly

Cartomancie, sf. (*etym.* carte *and* mancie; *see* Mancie), cartomancy, fortune-telling by cards

Carton, sm. (*etym. I.* cartone, *augment. of* carta), pasteboard, pasteboard box, boards, cartoon, (*print.*) cancel

Cartonnage, sm. boards, putting in boards

Cartonné, e, adj. in boards, boards

Cartonner, va. to put in boards, to cancel

Cartonnier, sm. pasteboard-maker, bandbox-maker

Carton-pierre, sm. statuary pasteboard

Cartouche, sf. (*etym. I.* cartoccio, *from* carta), cartridge. — sm. cartouch. *— à poudre*, blank cartridge

Caryatide, sf. (*etym. Gr.* Καρυάτιδες, *prop. name*), caryatid

Cas, sm. (*etym. L.* casus), case, circumstance, state of things, accident, matter, high opinion, business. *Le — échéant*, if it should so happen. *Dans le — de*, able to, likely to. *Faire grand — de*, to think very highly of. *Un cas —*, a slight reflection. *En tout —*, at all events. *C'est le — de dire*, one may well say

Casanier, ère, adj. s. (*etym. L.L.* casanus, *from* casa, *house*), domestic, home-keeping

Casaque, sf. (*etym. L.* casa, *house*), coat, cassock. † *Tourner —*, to become a turncoat

Casaquin, sm. (*etym.* casaque), jacket. † *Donner sur le — à quelqu'un*, to give a thrashing to some one

Cascatelle, sf. (*etym. I.* cascatella), a small cascade

Case, sf. (*etym. L.* casa), hut, cabin, division, pigeon-hole, square, point

Casemater, va. (*etym.* casemate), to fortify with casemates

Caser, vn. (*etym.* case), to make a point; — va. to stow away, to put by, to procure a situation; *se —*, vr. to find a situation, to settle oneself, to be put away

Caserne, sf. (*etym. L.* casa), barracks

Casernement, sm. barracking

Caserner, va.n. to lodge in barracks

Casier, sm. (*etym.* case), pigeon-holes

Casimir, sm. (*corrupt. of* cachemire), kerseymere

Casoar, sm. (*etym. Mal.* casuwaris), cassowary

Casque, sm. (*etym. I.* casco, *skull*), helmet, casque, head-piece, hood, helmet-shell

Casquette, sf. cap

Cassandre, sm. (*etym. Gr. prop. name* Κάσσανδρος, Κασσάνδρα), dotard

Cassant, e, adj. brittle. ¦ *Prendre un ton —*, to speak arrogantly

Cassation, sf. (*etym.* casser), annulment, quashing. *La Cour de —*, the supreme court of appeal. *Moyen de —*, plea of proceedings in error. *Se pourvoir en —*, to lodge an appeal

Casse, sf. (*etym.* casser), breakage; (*Gr.* κασία), cassia; (*L.* capsa), case; (*O.H.G.* chezi, *pan*), case, ladle

Cassé, e, adj. broken, decrepit, worn out. ¦ *Payer les pots —s*, to pay the damage

Casse-cou, sm. breakneck place, rough rider, breakneck ladder; *plur.* des casse-cou *or* cous. — interj. danger!

Cassement, sm. trouble

Casse-noisette, Casse-noix, sm. nutcrackers; *plur.* des casse-noisettes, &c.

Casser, va. (*etym. L.* quassare, *to shake*), to break, to split, to wear out, to annul, to disband, to cashier, to dissolve. *— la tête à*, to knock a person's brains out, to quite stun. *— aux gages*, to dismiss. *— les vitres*, (*fig.*) to pass all bounds. *Qui casse les verres les paye*, who breaks pays. *Se —*, vr. to break, to be broken, to snap, to split, to be worn out. *Se — le cou*, (*fig.*) to fail lamentably. *Se — la tête*, to rack one's brain. *Il s'est cassé le nez*, he broke his nose, (*fig.*) he found himself disappointed

Casserole, sf. (*etym. dim. of* casse), saucepan, stewpan

Casse-tête, sm. tomahawk, life-preserver, din, tiring work, puzzle-brain, heady wine; *plur.* des casse-tête *or* têtes

Cassette, sf. (*dimin. of* casse *or* caisse), casket, money-box, private purse

Casseur, sm. breaker. † *— d'assiettes*, a bully, a quarrelsome fellow

Cassine, sf. (*etym. L.L.* cassina, *a cottage*), country-house, (†) hovel

Cassis, sm. (*etym.* ?), black currants, black currant bush, black currant brandy

Cassolette, sf. (*etym. Sp.* casoleta, *a pan*), perfume-box

Cassonade, sf. (*etym. Port.* cassonada), moist sugar, brown sugar

Cassure, sf. fracture, break

§**Castagnettes,** sf. plur. (*etym. Sp.* castañetas), castanets

Caste, sf. (*etym. Port.* casta), caste

***Castel,** sm. (*same word as* château), castle

§**Castille,** sf. (*etym. L.* castellum), bickering, altercation

Castor, sm. (*etym. L.* castor), beaver, castor, beaver-hat, fur-cloth

Casuiste, sm. (*etym. L.* casus), casuist

Casualité, sf. casualty, accident

Casuel, le, adj. (*etym. L.* casualis), casual, precarious. *Revenu —*, fees, perquisites. — sm. fees, perquisites. *Le — d'une cure*, the surplice fees

Catachrèse, sf. (*etym. Gr.* κατάχρησις, *abuse*), catachresis

Cataclysme, sm. (*etym. Gr.* κατακλυσμός, *action of wetting*), cataclysm

Catacombes, sf. plur. (*etym. L.L.* catacumba, *orig.* ?), catacombs

Catacoustique, sf. (*etym. Gr.* κατακουστικός, *liter. reflected acoustics*), catacoustics

Catafalque, sm. (*etym.* ?), catafalco

Catalepsie, sf. (*etym. Gr.* κατάληψις, *the action of taking in*), catalepsy, trance

Cataleptique, adj. s. (*etym.* catalepsie), cataleptic

Cataplasme, sm. (*etym. Gr.* κατάπλασμα, *application upon*), poultice, cataplasm

Catapulte, sf. (*etym. Gr.* καταπέλτης, *hurling against*), catapult

Cataracte, sf. (*etym. Gr.* καταράκτης, *sluice*), cataract, fall, waterfall. *Abaisser une —*, to couch a cataract

Catarrhe, sm. (*etym. Gr.* κατάρροος, *flowing down*), catarrh

Catarrheux, se, adj. catarrhal, afflicted with a catarrh

Catéchiser, va. (*etym. Gr.* κατηχίζειν), to catechize, to chapter

Catéchisme, sm. (*etym. Gr.* κατηχισμός), catechism. *Faire le — à*, to teach the catechism

Catéchiste, sm. (*etym. Gr.* κατηχιστής), catechist

Catéchumène, sm. (*etym. Gr.* κατηχούμενος), catechumen

Catégorie, sf. (*etym. Gr.* κατηγορία, *attribute*), category

Catégorique, adj. (*etym. Gr.* κατηγορικός), categorical, unequivocal

Cathédrale, sf. adj. (*etym. L.L.* cathedralis, *from* cathedra, *chair*), cathedral

Catholicisme, sm. (*etym.* catholique), catholicism

Catholicité, sf. catholicism, the catholics

Catholique, s. adj. (*etym. Gr.* καθολικός, *universal*), catholic, Roman catholic

Catir, sm. (*etym.* catir), gloss

Catimini, loc.adv. (*etym. ?*), secretly

†**Catin,** sf. (*etym.pop.abbrev. of* Catherine), harlot

Catir, va. (*etym. L.* coactus, *squeezed*), to press *or* gloss cloth

Catisseur, sm. cloth-presser

Catissage, sm. pressing

Catoptrique, sf.adj. (*etm. Gr.* κατοπτρικός, *from* κάτοπτρον, *mirror*), catoptrical, catoptrics

Cauchemar, sm. (*etym. L.* calcare, *to tread, and O.G.* mar, *an evil spirit*), nightmare, bore, bugbear

Caudataire, sm. (*etym. L.* candatarius *from* cauda, *tail*), train-bearer

Cauris, Coris, sm. (*Indian word*), cowry

Cause, sf. (*etym. L.* causa), cause, grounds, motive, suit. *En tout état de* —, in every case, at all events. *Pour* —, not without reason. *Prendre fait et* — *pour*, to side with. *Agir, parler avec connaissance de* —, to have good grounds for what one does or says. *Avocat sans* —, briefless barrister. *Être en* —, to be concerned in a thing. *Mettre hors de* —, to set aside. *Obtenir gain de* —, to carry the day

Causer, va. (*etym. L.* causari), to cause, to occasion, to bring about; — vn. to converse, to talk, to chat. — *de la pluie et du beau temps*, to talk about one thing and the other. † *Assez causé!* enough of that!

Causerie, sf. talk, chat, conversation

Causeur, se, talker, talkative person. — adj. talking, chatty, talkative

Causeuse, sf. sofa

Causticité, sf. (*etym.* caustique), causticity, caustic humour

Caustique, adj. (*etym. Gr.* καυστικός, *from* καίειν, *to burn*), caustic, biting

Caustique, sf. caustics, caustic curve

§**Cauteleux, se,** adj. (*etym. O.F.* cautèle, *from the L.* cautus, *prudent*), crafty, wily

Cautère, sm. (*etym. Gr.* καυτήριον, *from* καίειν), cautery, issue. † *Un* — *sur une jambe de bois*, a useless remedy

Cautérisation, sf. (*etym.* cautériser), cauterization

Cautériser, va. (*etym.* cautère), to cauterize, to burn, to sear

Caution, sf. (*etym. L.* cautionem), security, surety, bail. *Sous* —, under bail. *Sujet à* —, not to be depended upon *or* trusted

Cautionnement, sm. (*etym.* caution), security, bail

Cautionner, va. to stand security for

Cavale, sf. (*etym. L.* caballus, *horse*), mare

Cavalerie, sf. (*etym.* cavalier), cavalry, horse. *Grosse* —, heavy cavalry

Cavalier, sm. (*etym. see* CHEVALIER), horseman, rider, gentleman, partner, cavalier, knight. ‖ —, —*ère*, adj. flippant, free, cavalier

Cavalière, sf. horsewoman, rider

Cavatine, sf. (*etym. I.* cavatina), cavatina

Cave, sf. cellar, liqueur-case, boot of a carriage, mould, pool

Cave, adj. (*etym. L.* cavus, *hollow*), hollow, lunar

Caveau, sm. cellar, burial-vault

Caver, va. to hollow out, to stake

Caverne, sf. (*etym. L.* caverna, *from* cavus), cavern, cave, den

Caverneux, se, adj. hollow, cavernous

Caviar, sm. (*etym. M.Gr.* καυιάρι), caviare

Cavité, sf. (*etym.* cave), hollow, cavity

C', Ce, Cet, m., **Cette,** f., **Ces,** plur., pron.dem. this, that. *Ce . . . ci, cette . . . ci*, this; *ces . . . ci*, these. *Ce . . . là, cette . . . là*, that; *ces . . . là*, those. *Sur ce*, thereupon, whereupon

***Céans,** adv. (*etym. O.F.* çal, ens, *from L.* intus, *within*), here, within, in this house

Ceci, pron. this, this thing. *See* CELA

Cécité, sf. (*etym. L.* caecitatem, *blindness*), blindness, cecity

Céder, va. (*etym. L.* cedere, *to go*), to give up, to yield, to make over, to transfer; — vn. to give way, to yield, to relent

§**Cédille,** sf. (*etm. I.* zediglia, *dimin. of* zeta, *name of a Gr. letter*), cedilla

Cèdre, sm. (*etym. Gr.* κέδρος), cedar, cedar-tree

Ceindre, va. (*etym. L.* cingere, *to surround*), to gird, to bind, to encircle, to encompass; *se* —, vr. to gird on, to encircle with

Ceinture, sf. (*etym. L.* cinctura, *from* cingere), belt, girdle, zone, sash, waistband, waist, middle, inclosure, fence, cincture. *Bonne renommée vaut mieux que* — *dorée*, a good name is better than riches

Ceinturon, sm. (*etym.* ceinture), belt

Cela, pron. that, that thing. *C'est* —, that is it. *C'est bien* —, that is quite right. *Comme* —, so so. *C'est parler,* —! that is something like talking

Céladon, sm. (*prop.name*), sentimental swain. — adj. sea-green

Célébrant, sm. (*etym.* célébrer), officiating priest

Célèbre, adj. (*etym. L.* celeber), famous, renowned, celebrated

Célébrer, va. (*etym. L.* celebrare), to celebrate, to praise, to extol, to glorify

Célébrité, sf. (*etym. L.* celebritatem), celebrity, renown, fame

Celer, va. (*etym. L.* celare, *to hide*), to hide, to conceal, to keep secret. *Se faire* —, to deny oneself to visitors. *Se* —, vr. to conceal oneself

Céleri, sm. (*etym. I.* seleri, *L.* selinum, *and Gr.* σέλινον, *parsley*), celery. *Un pied de* —, a head of celery

Célérité, sf (*etym. L.* celeritatem), despatch, speed, celerity

Céleste, adj. (*etym. L.* coelestis), heavenly, celestial. *Bleu* —, sky-blue

Célestin, sm. (*etym. L. prop.n.* Cœlestinus), Celestine

Célibat, sm. (*etym. L.* coelibatus, *from* coelebs), a single life, celibacy

Célibataire, sm. bachelor, unmarried man

Cellérier, ère, smf. (*etym. see* CELLIER), cellarer

Cellier, sm. (*etym. L.* cellarium, *pantry*), store-room, cellar

Cellulaire, adj. cellular

Cellule, sf. (*etym. L.* cellula, *dimin. of* cella), cell

Celui, m., **Celle,** f., **Ceux, Celles,** plur., pron. (*etym.* celui, *L.* ecce, illius; *celle*, ecce, illa), he, she, one, they, those, him, her, the one

Celui-ci, m., **Celle-ci,** f., **Ceux-ci, Celles-ci,** pl., pron. this person, this one, the latter, these, these people

Celui-là, m., **Celle-là,** f., **Ceux-là, Celles-là,** plur., pron. that person, that one, those, those people, the former, the first

Cémenter, va. (*etym.* cément), to cement

Cénacle, sm. (*etym. L.* cœnaculum, *from* cœnare, *to sup*), guest-chamber

Cendre, sf. (*etym. L.* cinerem), ashes, cinders, dust, remains, death. *Le jour des* —*s*, Ash-Wednesday

Cendré, e, adj. ash-coloured, ashy. *Blond* —, pale, yellow

Cendrier, sm. ash-pan, dealer in ashes

§**Cendrillon,** sf. Cinderella

Cène, sf. (*etym. L.* cœna), the Lord's Supper

Cénobitique, adj. (*etym.* cénobite), cenobitical

Cénotaphe, sm. (*etym. Gr.* κενοτάφιον), empty tomb

Cens, sm. (*etym. L.* census), census, quit-rent, cense

§**Censé, e,** adj. (*etym. L.* censere, *to think*), deemed, reputed, looked upon as

Censeur, sm. (*etym. L.* censor), censor, critic, proctor

Censitaire, adj. (*etym.* cens), copyholder

Censure, sf. (*etym. L.* census), censorship, censure, vote of censure

Censurer, va. to censure; *se* —, vr. to censure oneself, to be censured

Cent, adj. (*etym. L.* centum), a hundred, cent. — sm. a hundred. *Un* — *pesant*, a hundredweight. *Un* — *de piquet*, a game of piquet

Centaine, sf. hundred

Centaure, sm. (*etym. Gr.* κένταυρος, *Sans.* Gandharva, *horse-headed deity*), centaur

Centaurée, sf. (*etym. L.* centaurea), centaury, knapweed

Centenaire, adj. (*etym. L.* centenarius, *from* centum), of a hundred years old, centenary

Centenier, sm. (*etym. L.* centenarius), centurion

Centi-, partic. centi-, a hundredth

Centième, sm. (*etym. L.* centesimus), hundredth, hundredth part

Centime, sm. (*etym. L.* centesimus), centime, (*fig.*) stiver, brass farthing

Centon, sm. (*etym. L.* cento, *patchwork covering*), fragments of verses taken from some author

¶**Centralisateur, trice,** adj. centralizing

¶**Centralisation,** sf. centralization

¶**Centraliser,** va. (*etym.* central), to centralize, to centre

Centrifuge, adj. (*etym. L.* centrum, fugere, *to flee from*), centrifugal

Centripète, adj. (*etym. L.* centrum, petere, *to seek*), centripetal

Cent-Suisse, sm. Swiss lifeguardsman

Centupler, va. (*etym. L.* centuplicare), to increase a hundredfold, to centuple

Centurie, sf. (*etym. L.* centuria), hundred, troop of a hundred men, century; *plur.* centuries, prophecies

Cep, sm. (*etym. L.* cippus, *trunk of a tree*), vine plant

Cépée, sf. (*etym.* cep), stump, tuft of shoots

Cependant, conj. in the meantime, however, nevertheless

Céramique, adj.sf. (*etym. Gr.* κέραμος, *clay*), ceramic, the potter's art

Cérat, sm. (*etym. L.* ceratum, *made of wax*), cerate

Cerbère, sm. (*etym. Gr. prop. n.* Κέρβερος), Cerberus

Cerceau, sm. (*etym. L.L.* circellus, *dimin. of* circus), hoop, hoop-net, pinions

Cerclage, sm. cooperage

Cercle, sm. (*etym. L.* circulus, *dimin. of* circus), circle, hoop, ring, assembly, company, club, clubhouse; *plur.* casks

Cercler, va. to hoop

Cercueil, sm. (*etym. L.L.* sarcus, *from O.H.G.* sarc, *a case*), coffin, bier, grave

Céréale, adj. (*etym. L.* cerealis, *from* Ceres), corn, cereal. —*s*, sf.plur. corn

Cérémonie, sf. (*etym. L.* cærimonia, *from* Cære, *prop. name*), ceremony

Cérémonieux, se, adj. ceremonious, formal

Cerf, sm. (*etym. L.* cervus), stag, hart

§Cerfeuil, sm. (*etym. Gr.* χαιρέφυλλον), chervil
Cerf-volant, sm. kite, paper kite, horn-beetle
Cerise, sf. (*etym. L.* Cerasus, *Gr.* Κέρασος, *prop. name*), cherry. — adj. cherry-colour, cherry-coloured
Cerisier, sm. cherry-tree
Cerné, e, past part. surrounded. *Yeux —s,* eyes surrounded with a black ring
Cerneau, sm. (*etym. O.F.* cerne, *a circle*), unripe walnut
Cerner, va. (*etym. L.* circinare, *to surround*), to invest, to beset, to hem in, to surround, to unshell
‖**Certain, e,** adj. (*etym. L.* certus), certain, sure, worthy of trust, settled, appointed, stated. *—s gens,* some people. — sm. certainty
Certes, adv. (*etym. L.* certus), truly, most certainly
Certificat, sm. (*etym. L.L.* certificare), certificate, voucher, testimonial. *— de bonne vie et mœurs,* a certificate of good moral conduct
Certifier, va. to certify, to attest, to vouch for, to assure; *se —,* vr. to be attested
Cerveau, sm. (*etym. L.* cerebellum), brain, mind, intelligence. ‡*Un — creux,* a visionary. †*Un — timbré,* a crack-brained fellow. ‡*Un — brûlé,* a hot-headed fellow. *Rhume de —,* a cold
Cervelas, sm. (*etym. I.* cervellata), Bologna sausage
Cervelle, sf. (*see* Cerveau), brain, mind, intelligence. *Tête sans —,* light-brained person. *Faire sauter la — à,* to knock out a person's brains. *— de palmier,* pith
Cervoise, sf. (*etym. L.* cervisia, *Celt.* cwrw), beer
Césarienne, adj. (*etym.* César), Cæsarian
Cessant, e, adj. (*etym.* cesser), set aside. *Toute affaire —e,* to the suspension of all other business
Cesse, sf. rest. *Je n'aurai point de — que,* I shall have no rest till
Cesser, vn.a. (*etym. L.* cessare), to leave off, to cease, to discontinue
Cessionnaire, adj. (*etym.* cession), assignee, cessionary
Ceste, sm. (*etym. L.* cæstus), cestus
Césure, sf. (*etym. L.* cæsura), cæsura
Cétacé, sm. adj. (*etym. L.* cete), whale, cetaceous animal; cetaceous
Chablis, sm. (*prop. name*), chablis wine, wind-fallen wood
Chacal, sm. (*etym. Turk.* schakal), jackal
Chacun, e, pron. (*etym.* chaque, un), each, every one, each one
Chafouin, e, adj. s. (*etym.* chat, fouine), pitiful, weasel-faced
Chagrin, sm. (*etym.* ?), grief, sorrow, trouble, chagrin, concern, vexation, peevishness; (*etym. I.* zigrino, *Turk.* sagri), shagreen. *Peau de —,* shagreen
Chagrin, e, adj. sorrowful, grieved, fretful, peevish
Chagrinant, e, adj. (*etym.* chagriner), vexatious, provoking
Chagriner, va. to grieve, to sadden, to vex, to provoke, to shagreen; *se —,* vr. to grieve, to be chagrined, to fret, to be provoked, to grieve each other
Chaîne, sf. (*etym. L.* catena), chain, fetters, shackles, gang of convicts, bondage, ridge, warp, (*arch.*) chain-course, belting-course, boom. *— anglaise,* (*dance*) right and left. *Mettre à la —,* to enchain, to fasten
Chaînette, sf. little chain, chain-stitch
Chaînon, sm. link
Chair, sf. (*etym. L.* carnem), meat, flesh, pulp, body, flesh-colour. *— à pâté,* minced meat. *— baveuse,* proud flesh. *Donner la — de poule,* to make one's flesh creep
Chaire, sf. (*etm. Gr.* καθέδρα), pulpit, chair, professorship. *En pleine —,* before the whole congregation
Chaise, sf. (*same word as* chaire), chair, seat, chaise, curb. *— à porteurs,* sedan-chair. *— longue,* invalid's chair. *— percée,* close-stool
Chaland, e, s. (*etym.* ?), customer. — sm. barge, lighter
Chaldaïque, adj. (*etym.* Chaldéen), Chaldaic, Chaldean
Chaldéen, ne, sm.f. (*etym. L.* Chaldæus, *Gr.* Χαλδαῖος), Chaldean, Chaldaic, the Chaldean tongue
Châle, sm. (*etym. Arab.* schâl, *a woollen dress*), shawl
Chalet, sm. (*etym.* ?), Swiss cottage
Chaleur, sf. (*etym. L.* calorem), heat, warmth, fire, earnestness, fervour
Chaleureux, se, adj. spirit-stirring, impassioned
Châlier, ère, adj. *L'industrie —ère,* the shawl-trade
Chaloupe, sf. (*etym. D.* sloep), boat, launch. *— canonnière,* gunboat
Chalumeau, sm. (*etym. L.* calamus, *reed*), straw, reed, pipe, blowpipe
Chamade, sf. (*etym. I.* chiamare, *L.* clamare, *to call*), parley
‡§**Chamailler,** vn. (*etym.* ?), to squabble, to wrangle
Chamarrer, va. (*etym. see* Simarre), to bedizen, to trim with lace; *se —,* vr. to bedizen oneself
Chamarrure, sf. medley, tinsel
Chambellan, sm. (*etym. O.H.G.* chamarling), chamberlain
Chambranle, sm. (*etm.* ?), door or window frame, chimneypiece
Chambre, sf. (*etym. L.* camera, camara), room, chamber, apartment, honeycomb, camera, lock. *Femme de —,* lady's maid. *Être en —,* to have a room to oneself (*in a school*)
Chambrée, sf. mess, ward, common room (of workmen), full house
Chambrette, sf. small room, snug little room
Chambrière, sf. chambermaid, long whip
Chameau, sm., **Chamelle,** sf. (*etym. L.* camelus, *Gr.* κάμηλος, *Arab.* djamal), camel
Chamelier, sm. camel-driver
Chamois, sm. (*etym. O.H.G.* gam-z, *G.* gemse), chamois, shamoy, buff
Champ, sm. (*etym. L.* campus), field, career, opportunity, space. *Loger aux —s,* to live in the country. *A travers —s,* across the country. *Être aux —s,* to be uneasy. *Battre aux —s,* to beat a salute. *Le — clos,* the lists. *Le — de repos,* the burial-ground. *Prendre du —,* to take one's room. *Avoir le — libre,* to have a clear field before one. *Poser de —,* to lay edgewise. *Sur-le- —,* on the spot, forthwith. *A tout bout de —,* ever and anon
§**Champagne,** sf. (*etym. see* Campagne), Champagne; sm. *— frappé,* iced champagne
Champenois, e, s. adj. (*etym.* Champagne), native of Champagne
Champêtre, adj. (*etym. L.* campestris), rustic, rural, country, sylvan
§**Champignon,** sm. (*etym. L.L.* campinio, *from L.* campus, *field*), mushroom, fungoid excrescence, cap-stand. *Couche de —s,* mushroom bed
§**Champignonnière,** sf. mushroom bed
Chance, sf. (*etym. L.L.* cadentia, *from L.* cadens, *falling*), chance, risk, hazard, luck, mishap. *Être en —,* to have a run of luck
Chancelant, e, adj. tottering, feeble, unsettled, unsteady
Chanceler, vn. (*etym. O.F.* eschanceler, *to get out of bonds*), to totter, to be unsettled
Chancelier, sm. (*etym. L.* cancellarius; *see* Littré), chancellor
Chancelière, sf. chancellor's lady, foot-bag
Chancellerie, sf. (*etym.* chancelier), chancellor's offices. *Style de —,* diplomatic language
Chanceux, se, adj. doubtful, uncertain, lucky, unlucky
Chancre, sm. (*etym. L.* cancer), canker, ulcer
Chandeleur, sf. (*etym. L.* candelarum), Candlemas
Chandelier, sm. (*etym.* chandelle), candlestick, tallow-chandler, (*locom.*) stanchions for guard. *— de fer,* crowbar
Chandelle, sf. (*etym. L.* candela), candle, tallow-candle, stay-supporter. *Travailler à la —,* to work by candle-light. ‡ *Économie de bouts de —,* economy of nothing at all. ‡*Le jeu ne vaut pas la —,* it is not worth the while. †*Voir trente-six —s,* to see all the stars of heaven
Chanfrein, sm. (*etym. L.L.* chamus, *bit*), chanfrin, chanfron, headpiece, chamfer
Change, sm. (*etym. see* Changer), exchange, change, barter, wrong scent, exchange office. *Agent de —,* stock-broker. *Lettre de —,* bill of exchange. *Le taux du —,* the rate of exchange. *Donner, faire prendre le — à,* to throw on the wrong scent
Changé, e, adj. changed, altered
Changeant, e, adj. changeable, fickle, unsettled, changing
Changement, sm. (*etym.* changer), change, alteration, shifting, changing
Changer, va. (*etym. L.L.* cambiare, *L.* cambire, *Gr.* κάμβειν, *to bend*), to change, to alter, to exchange, to shift; — vn. to change, to be unsteady, to be changed. *— du tout au tout,* to undergo a thorough change. *— en bien, en mal,* to change for the better, for the worse. *Pour —,* by way of change. *Se —,* vr. to change, to be changed, to alter, to amend
Changeur, se, sm.f. (*etym. L.L.* cambiatorem), money-changer
Chanoine, sm. (*etym. L.* canonicus), canon. *Vie de —,* an easy life
Chanoinesse, sf. canoness
Chanson, sf. (*etym. L.L.* cantionem, *the action of singing*), song, stuff, idle tales. *— à boire,* drinking song. *N'avoir qu'une —,* to be ever harping on the same string. *—s que tout cela!* stuff and nonsense!
Chansonner, va. to make songs on, to lampoon
Chansonnette, sf. little song
Chansonnier, sm. song-writer, song-book
Chant, sm. (*etym. L.* cantus), singing, song, tune, music, canto, warbling, chirruping
***Chantage,** sm. (*etm.* chanter), extortion of money
Chantant, e, adj. easy to be sung, tuneful
Chanter, vn. (*etym. L.* cantare, *frequent. of* canere), to sing, to warble. *— à pleine voix,* to sing to the top of one's voice. *C'est comme s'il*

chantait, it is as if he talked to the wind. *Se* —, vr. to be sung

Chanterelle, sf. (*etym.* chanter), first string, decoy bird, musical bottle

Chanteur, se, s. (*etym. L.* cantorem), singer, vocalist

Chantier, sm. (*etym. L.L.* cantarium, *cask-stand*), wood-yard, work-yard, shipbuilder's yard, dockyard, stock, stand

Chantonner, va. to hum a tune

Chantre, sm. (*etym. see* CHANTEUR), church-singer, chorister

Chantrerie, sf. precentor-ship, chantry

Chanvre, sm. (*etym. L.* cannabis, cannabus), hemp

Chape, sf. (*etym. see* CAPE), cope, cap, inner box, axle-bearing, coat. — *en fer*, iron strap

Chapeau, sm. (*etym. I.* cappello), hat, bonnet, cap. *Étui de* —, hatbox. *Un coup de* —, a bow. — *chinois*, Chinese bells

Chapelain, sm. (*etym. L.L.* capellanus), chaplain

Chapeler, va. (*etym. L.* capulare, *to strike*), to rasp, to chip

Chapelet, sm. (*etym. dim. of* chapel, *for* chapeau), string of beads, chaplet, chain-pump. ‡ *Défiler son* —, to tell one's story

Chapelier, ère, smf. (*etym.* chapeau), hatter, hat-maker

Chapelle, sf. (*etym. L.L.* capella), chapel, choir, reservoir. *Maître de* —, precentor

Chapellenie, sf. chaplaincy

Chapellerie, sf. hat-manufactory, hatter's shop

Chapelure, sf. raspings, chippings

Chaperon, sm. (*etym. see* CAPE), hood, chaperon, shoulder-knot, apron of a canon, coping, top

Chaperonner, va. to chaperon, to cope, to hoodwink

Chapiteau, sm. (*etym. L.L.* capitellum,) capital

Chapitre, sm. (*etym. L.* capitulum,) chapter, chapter-house. *Avoir voix au* —, to have a right to vote, (*fig.*) to enjoy great credit

Chapitrer, va. (*etym.* chapitre), to scold

Chapon, sm. (*etym. L.* caponem), capon, crust of bread rubbed with garlic

Chaque, adj. (*etym. L.* quisque), each, every

Char, sm. (*etym. L.* carrus), car, chariot. — *à bancs*, pleasure-van

Charançon, sm. (*etym. L.* calandrus, *a cricket*), weevil

Charbon, sm. (*etym. L.* carbonem), embers, charcoal, coals, carbuncle, anthrax, black rust, smut. *Boîte au* —, coal-scuttle. *Une voie de* —, a sack of charcoal

Charbonné, e, adj. charred, carbonized, daubed, rusty

Charbonner, va. to daub with charcoal; — vn., *se* —, vr. to char, to be charred

Charbonnerie, sf. coal-store, the Carbonari

Charbonneux, se, adj. carbuncled

Charbonnier, sm. charcoal-burner, charcoal-seller, coal-heaver, collier, coal-shed, charcoal-box. *La foi du* —, implicit faith. — *est maître chez lui*, a man's house is his castle

Charbonnière, sf. coal-woman, coalseller's wife, charcoal-oven

Charcuterie, sf. pork-butcher's business, pork-butcher's meat

Charcutier, ère, s. (*etym.* chair, cuit), pork-butcher

Chardon, sm. (*etym. L.* carduus), thistle, spikes, sea-urchin. — *à foulon*, teasel, fuller's thistle

Chardonneret, sm. (*etym.* chardon), goldfinch

Charge, sf. (*etym.* charger), load, weight, encumbrance, expenses, charge, office, dignity, imputation, caricature, extravagant joke. *Le navire est en* —, the ship is taking in her cargo. *A* —, burdensome. *Femme de* —, housekeeper. *Témoin à* —, witness for the prosecution. *Cahier de* —*s*, conditions. *A* — *d'autant*, on condition you let me do the same

Chargé, e, adj. part. laden, loaded, freighted, bowed down, deep, registered, foul

Chargement, sm. load, freight, cargo, bill of lading, registry. *Faire son* —, (*nav.*) to lade

Charger, va. (*etym. L.L.* carricare, *from L.* carrus), to load, to lade, to freight, to intrust, to charge, to register, to fill, to accuse, to fall on, to caricature, to write over; *se* —, vr. to load oneself with, to take charge of, to charge each other, to impute to each other, to be overcast

Chariot, sm. (*etym.* char), chariot, waggon, slide, (*loc.*) cradle, cistern

Charitablement, adv. (*etym.* charitable), charitably

Charité, sf. (*etym. L.* charitatem), charity, alms, alms-giving, forbearance. — *bien ordonnée commence par soi-même*, charity begins at home. *Dame de* —, visitor of the poor

Charivari, sm. (*etym. ?*), mock serenade, uproar, discordant music

Charlatanerie, sf., **Charlatanisme,** sm. (*etym.* charlatan), quackery, charlatanry

Charmant, e, adj. delightful, charming

Charme, sm. (*etym. L.* carmen), spell, charm, attraction; (*etym. L.* carpinus), yoke-elm

Charmé, e, adj. delighted

Charmer, va. to bewitch, to charm, to fascinate, to beguile

§**Charmille,** sf. row, hedge of young yoke-elms, grove

§**Charnel, le,** adj. (*etym. L.* carnalis), carnal-minded, lustful, carnal

Charnier, sm. (*etym. L.L.* carnarium, *from L.* caro, *flesh*), charnel-house, larder, scuttled cask

Charnière, sf. (*etym. L.L.* cardinaria, *from L.* cardo, *hinge*), hinge, joint

Charnu, e, adj. (*etym. L.* caro), fleshy, browny, pulpy

Charnure, sf. the fleshy part of the body

§**Charogne,** sf. (*etym. I.* carogna), carrion

Charpente, sf. (*etym. see* CHARPENTIER), beam, wood-work, framework

Charpenté, e, adj. built, constructed

Charpenter, va. to hack

Charpenterie, sf. carpenter's trade

Charpentier, sm. (*etym. L.* carpentarius, *chariot-builder*), carpenter, whale-cutter

Charpie, sf. (*etym. O.F.* charpir, *L.* carpere), lint. *Être en* —, to be done to rags

Charretée, sf. cart-load, waggon-load

Charretier, ère, s. carter

Charrette, sf. (*etym. dim. of* char), cart, truck

Charriage, sm. (*etym.* charrier), cartage, carting, carriage

Charrier, vn. (*etym. L.L.* carricare, *from L.* carrus), to cart, to carry, to drift. — *droit*, (*fig.*) to act uprightly. *Le fleuve charrie*, ice is drifting down the stream

Charroi, sm. cartage, carting, waggon-train

Charron, sm. wheelwright

Charronnage, sm. wheelwright's work. *Bois de* —, cart-timber

Charrue, sf. (*etym. L.* carruca, *kind of vehicle*), plough. *Garçon de* —, plough-boy. *Passer la* — *sur*, to plough up. *Mettre la* — *devant les bœufs*, to put the cart before the horse. *Tirer la* —, (*fig.*) to have a hard life of it

Charte, sf. (*etym. L.* charta), charter

¶**Chartiste,** sm. (*etym.* charte), Chartist

Chartre, sf. (*etym. L.* carcerem, *prison*), prison. *En* — *privée*, illegally detained

Chartreuse, sf. (*etym.* Chartreux), Charterhouse, Carthusian convent, Carthusian nun, isolated cottage

Chartreux, sm. (*etym. L.* Cartusiensis), a Chartreux, a Carthusian monk. *Un chat* —, a bluish-grey cat

Charybde, sm. (*etym. Gr. prop. n.* Χάρυβδις), Charybdis

Châsse, sf. (*etym. L.* capsa; *see* CAISSE), shrine, reliquary, frame, cheeks of a pair of scales

Chasse, sf. (*etym. see* CHASSER), hunting, the hunt, the chase, shooting, coursing, the huntsmen, play, driving out. *Capitaine des* —*s*, ranger. *Cheval de* —, hunter. *Chien de* —, hound

Chasselas, sm. (*etym. ?*), white garden grapes

Chasse-marée, sm. fish-cart; *plur.* des chasse-marée

Chasse-mouches, sm. fly-flap; *plur.* des chasse-mouches

Chasse-pierres, sm. guard-iron

Chasser, va. (*etym. L.L.* captare, *to hunt*), to hunt, to shoot, to chase, to drive away, to discharge, to send away, (*nav.*) to look out for the land; — vn. to hunt, to shoot, to carry far, to swing, (*print.*) to drive out, to drag the anchors. *Bon chien chasse de race*, he is a chip of the old block. *Il aime à* — *au plat*, he likes eating game better than shooting it

Chasseresse, sf. huntress

Chasseur, se, smf. hunter, huntress

Chassie, sf. bleareduess

Chassieux, se, adj. (*etym. L.* cæcus, *blind*), blear-eyed

Châssis, sm. (*etym.* châsse), frame, framework, sash

Chastement, adv. (*etym.* chaste), chastely

Chasteté, sf. (*etym. L.* castitatem), chastity

Chasublier, sm. (*etym.* chasuble), maker of sacerdotal robes

Chat, Chatte, s. (*etym. L.L.* catus, cattus), cat, dainty creature, cross-tag, catkins. — *botté*, Puss in boots. *A bon* — *bon rat*, tit for tat. *Appeler un* — *un* —, to call a spade a spade. *Acheter* — *en poche*, to buy a pig in a poke. *Il n'y a pas de quoi fouetter un* —, it is not worth mentioning

§**Châtaigne,** sf. (*etym. L.* castanea), chestnut

§**Châtaigneraie,** sf. chestnut-grove

§**Châtaignier,** sm. chestnut-tree

Châtain, adj. (*only used in the masc.*) nut-brown, chestnut

Chat-cervier, sm. lynx

Château, sm. (*etym. L.* castellum), castle, palace, country-seat, mansion. *Des* —*x en Espagne*, castles in the air

Châtelain, sm. governor of a castle, the lord of the manor

Châtelaine, sf. lady of the manor

Châtelet, sm. little castle, ribbon-weaver's frame

Châtellenie, sf. castle-ward, jurisdiction

Chat-huant, sm. (*etym. ?*), screech-owl

Châtiable, adj. worthy of punishment

Châtier, va. (*etym. L.* castigare), to chastise, to correct, to polish

Châtiment, sf. (*etym. L.* castigamentum), chastisement, correction, chastening

Chatoiement, sm. (*etym. see* CHATOYER), sparkling, play of colours

Chaton, sm. (*etym. L.* cista, *Gr.* κίστη, *box*), kitten, bezel, stone, ament

§**Chatouillement,** sm. tickling, titillation

§**Chatouiller,** va. (*etym. L.* catulire), to tickle, to please, to gratify

§**Chatouilleux, se,** adj. ticklish, touchy

Chatoyant, e, adj. sparkling

Chatoyer, vn. (*etym.* chat), to sparkle, to play in the light

Châtrer, va. (*etym. L.* castrare), to castrate, to geld

Chattemite, sf. (*etym.* chatte, *and L.* mitis, *gentle*), demure-looking person

Chatterie, sf. dainties, sweetmeats, coaxing words

§**Chaud, e,** adj. (*etym. L.* calidus, *hot*), hot, hasty, brisk, fresh. *Pleurer à —es larmes*, to cry bitterly. *Avoir la tête —e*, to be passionate

Chaud, sm. heat, warmth. *Avoir —, faire —*, to be hot, warm. *Il y fera —*, it will be warm work

Chaudière, sf. (*etym. L.* caldaria), copper, boiler

Chaudron, sm. (*etym.* chaudière), caldron

Chaudronnerie, sf. coppersmith's wares *or* trade

Chaudronnier, sm. coppersmith, brazier, boiler-maker

Chauffage, sm. heating, burning, fuel. *Bois de —*, firewood

Chauffe, sf. fire-box, furnace, heating

Chauffer, va. (*etym. L.* calefacere), to warm, to air, to keep in fuel, to urge on, (*mil.*) to open a brisk fire on; — vn. to warm, to be heating, to get up steam, to be coming on. ¦*Cela chauffe*, the affair is getting on bravely

Chaufferette, sf. chafing-pan

Chauffeur, sm. stoker, fireman

Chauffoir, sm. warming-room, stove, warm linen cloth

Chaufour, sm. (*etym.* chaux, four), lime-kiln

Chaufournier, sm. lime-burner

Chaulage, sm. liming

Chauler, va. (*etym.* chaux), to steep in lime-water

Chaume, sm. (*etym. L.* calamus), thatch, thatched roof

Chaumière, sf. thatched cottage

Chaumine, sf. hut, cot

Chausse, sf. (*etym. see* CHAUSSER), strainer, shoulder-knot, waste-pipe

Chaussée, sf. (*etym. L.* calceata [via], *road trodden down*), causeway, embankment, dyke

Chausse-pied, sm. shoe-horn; *plur.* des chausse-pieds

Chausser, va. (*etym. L.* calceare, *to tread*), to make *or* put on the shoes *or* boots of, to earth up; — va. to fit; *se —*, vr. to put on one's shoes *or* boots

Chausses, sf.plur. (*etym. L.* calceus), small clothes. ! *Tirer ses —s*, (*fig.*) to scamper away

Chausse-trape, sf. trap, caltrop; *plur.* des chausse-trapes

Chaussette, sf. sock

Chausson, sm. list-shoe, pumps, puff

Chaussure, sf. boots, shoes. ¦ *Trouver — à son pied*, to meet with something to one's liking, to meet with one's match

Chauve, adj. (*etym. L.* calvus), bald

Chauve-souris, sf. (*etym.* ?), bat

***Chauvinisme,** sm. (*etym. fictit. prop. name* Chauvin), blind patriotism

Chaux, sf. (*etym. L.* calx), lime, limestone, calx. *Four à —*, lime-kiln

Chavirer, vn.a. (*etym.* cha *for* cap, *head, and* virer), to capsize, to upset

Chef, sm. (*etym. L.* caput, *head*), head, leader, chief, head-cook, first actor, fag-end. *De son —*, of one's own head. *Du — de sa femme*, in right of his wife. *Au premier —*, in the highest degree

Chef-d'œuvre, sm. masterpiece, trial-piece; *plur.* des chefs-d'œuvre

Chef-lieu, sm. chief town, capital; *plur.* des chefs-lieux

Cheik, sm. (*etym. Arab.* schaikh, *old man*), sheik

Chemin, sm. (*etym. Celt.* kamm, cam, ceim, *step*), way, road, track. *— de traverse*, cross-road. *— détourné*, by-way. *Par voies et par —s*, highways and byways. *— de fer*, railway. *— de fer américain*, tram-road. ¦ *Ne pas aller par quatre —s*, to speak one's mind openly, to go roundly to work. † *Faire voir du — à*, to lead a person a pretty dance

Cheminée, sf. (*etym. L.* caminus, *hearth*), chimney, flue, nipple of a gun. *Garniture de —*, chimney ornaments. *Sous le manteau de la —*, under the rose

Cheminer, vn. to travel, to walk, to jog on

Chemise, sf. (*etym. L.L.* camisia), shirt, linen, shift, wrapper. *Devant de —*, shirt-front

Chemisette, sf. shirt-front, chemisette, tucker

Chemisier, ère, smf. (*etym.* chemise), shirt-maker

Chênaie, sf. (*etym.* chêne), oak-grove

Chenal, sm. (*etym. see* CANAL), narrow channel, mill-race

¦**Chenapan,** sm. (*etym. G.* schnapphahn, *he who catches a chicken*), scamp

Chêne, sm. (*etym. L.L.* casnus, *oak*), oak

Chenet, sm. (*etym.* chien), fire-dog

Chènevière, sf. (*etym.* chenevis), hemp-field

Chènevis, sm. (*etym. L.* cannabis, *hemp*), hemp-seed

Chenil, sm. (*etym. L.* canis), dog-kennel, hunting establishment, dirty hole

§**Chenille,** sf. (*etym. L.* canicula ?), caterpillar, grub, chenille. *Laid comme une —*, as ugly as sin

Chenu, e, adj. (*etym. L.* canus, *white*), hoary

Cheptel, sm. (*etym. L.* capitale), lease of cattle, leased-out cattle

Cher, Chère, adj. (*etym. L.* carus), dear, beloved

Cher, adv. dear, dearly. *Il fait — vivre*, living is dear

Chercher, va. (*etym. L.* circare, *to go round*), to look for, to seek, to fetch, to endeavour. *— des yeux*, to look for. *— noise, querelle à*, to pick a quarrel with. *Se —*, vr. to seek after oneself, to seek each other

Chercheur, se, s. seeker

Chère, sf. (*etym. L.L.* cara, *face; Gr.* κάρα, *head*), cheer, entertainment, fare

Chérif, sm. (*etym. Arab.* sharif, *noble*), sheriff

Chéri, e, adj. cherished, beloved

Chérir, va. (*etym.* cher), to cherish, to be fond of; *se —*, vr. to be in love with oneself, to love each other tenderly

Cherté, sf. dearness, high price

Chérubin, sm. (*etym. L.L.* cherubim), cherub

Chétif, ve, adj. (*etym. L.* captivus), puny, pitiful, paltry, wretched

Cheval, sm. (*etym. L.* caballus), horse, steed. *— de main*, led-horse. *— à deux fins*, a horse fit to ride or drive. *— entier*, a stallion. † *Un — échappé*, an ungovernable person. ¦ *Bon — de trompette*, not easily frightened. *Monter sur ses grands chevaux*, (*fig.*) to be all upon the high ropes. *Monter, aller à —*, to ride. *Être à — sur les principes*, to hold fast to the rule. *Être à — sur un fleuve*, (*mil.*) to hold both banks of a river. *Remède de —*, strong remedy. *Fièvre de —*, burning fever. ¦ *Lettre à —*, threatening letter. *A — donné on ne regarde pas à la bride*, you must not look a gift horse in the mouth

Chevaleresque, adj. (*etym. I.* cavalleresco), chivalrous, knightly, adventurous

Chevalerie, sf. (*etym.* chevalier), chivalry, knighthood

Chevalet, sm. wooden horse, easel, bridge, trestle, prop

Chevalier, sm. (*etym.* cheval), knight, sandpiper. *— d'industrie*, a sharper

Chevalière, sf. signet-ring

Chevaline, adj.f. of the horse species

Cheval-marin, sm. walrus

Chevaucher, vn. (*etym. L.L.* caballicare, *from L.* caballus), to ride, to overlap

Chevau-léger, sm. (*etym.* cheval, léger), light-horseman; *plur.* des chevau-légers

Chevelu, e, adj. (*etym.* cheveu), hairy, long-haired, comose. *Cuir —*, scalp

Chevelure, sf. (*etym. L.L.* capillatura, *from L.* capillus, *hair*), head of hair, scalp, foliage

Chevet, sm. (*dimin. of* chef), head of a bed, apsis of a church

Cheveu, sm. (*etym. L.* capillus), hair. *Être coiffé en —x*, not to wear a cap. *Tiré par les —x*, (*fig.*) far-fetched

§**Cheville,** sf. (*etym. L.* clavicula, *small key, from* clavis), ankle, ankle-bone, peg, bolt, pin, expletive. *— ouvrière*, main-spring. *Ne pas aller à la — de*, to be unworthy to tie one's shoes

§**Chevillé, e,** adj. fastened with pegs or bolts, full of expletives. ¦ *Avoir l'âme —e dans le corps*, to have as many lives as a cat

§**Cheviller,** va. to peg, to pin

§**Chevillette,** sf. small peg

***Chevir,** vn. (*etym.* chef), to conquer a person

Chèvre, sf. (*etym. L.* capra), goat

Chevreau, sm. kid

§**Chèvrefeuille,** sm. (*etym. L.* caprifolium), honeysuckle

Chevrette, sf. roe, doe, prawn, little andiron

§**Chevreuil,** sm. (*etym. L.* capreolus, *from* caper), roe-buck

Chevrier, sm. (*etym. L.* caprarius), goatherd

Chevron, sm. (*etym. L.* capra), stripes, rafter, joist, chevron

Chevrotant, e, adj. tremulous, quavering

Chevrotine, sf. slugs

Chez, prep. (*etym. L.* casa, *house*), to, at, to the house of, among, with

*¦**Chic,** sm. (*etym.* ?), style, knack

Chicane, sf. (*etym. L. Gr.* τζυκάνιον, *tennis*), pettifogging, quirks and quibbles of law, quarrel. *Chercher — à*, to pick a quarrel with

Chicaner, vn.a. to chicane,

to quibble, to quarrel with, to vex

Chicanerie, sf. quibbling

Chicaneur, se, Chicanier, ère, adj. quibbling, quarrelsome

Chiche, adj. (*etym. L.* ciccus, *small thing*), stingy, niggard

Chicorée, sf. (*etym. Gr.* κιχώριον), endive, chicory

‡**Chicot,** sm. stump

Chien, ne, s. adj. (*etym. L.* canis), dog, cur, bitch, cock of a gun, scrubbing-brush; miserly, wretched, villanous. *Qui m'aime aime mon —*, love me, love my dog. ‡*Jeter sa langue aux —s*, to give it up. † *Un temps de —*, wretched weather. ‡ *Entre — et loup*, in the dusk of the evening

Chien-dent, sm. dog's grass, couch-grass

Chiffe, sf., **Chiffon,** sm. (*etym. ?*), rag

Chiffonné, e, adj. rumpled, crumpled. *Minois —*, pleasant but irregular-featured countenance

Chiffonner, va. (*etym.* chiffon), to rumple, to crumple, to vex

Chiffonnier, ère, s. rag-gatherer

Chiffre, sm. (*etym. Arab.* çafar, *empty*), figure, digit, sum, marked price, cipher

Chiffrer, va.n. (*etym.* chiffre), to cipher, to mark the price of, to figure a bass

§**Chignon,** sm. (*same word as* chaînon), nape of the neck, back-hair

Chimère, sf. (*etym. Gr.* Χίμαιρα, *fabulous animal*), Chimæra, idle fancy, crotchet

Chimérique, adj. chimerical, fanciful, air-built

Chimie, sf. (*etym. Gr.* χυμία), chemistry

Chimique, adj. chemic, chemical

Chimiste, sm. chemist

Chimpanzé, sm. chimpanzee

Chiné, e, adj. (*etym.* Chine), variegated

Chinoiserie, sf. (*etym.* chinois), trinkets, baubles

Chiourme, sf. (*etym. I.* ciurma), galley-slaves, the convicts

†**Chiper,** va. (*etym. ?*), to pilfer

†**Chipie,** sf. (*O.F.* chipoe), finical creature

†**Chipoter,** vn. (*etym. ?*), to dispute about trifles

†**Chipotier, ère,** smf. (*etym.* chipoter), trifler

Chique, sf. (*etym. Span.* chico, *small*), quid of tobacco

Chiquenaude, sf. (*etm. ?*), fillip

†**Chiquer,** va. to chew tobacco, to eat and drink

Chirurgical, e, adj. (*etym.* chirurgie), surgical

Chirurgie, sf. (*etym. Gr.* χειρουργία, *from* χείρ, *hand, and* ἔργον, *work*), surgery, the surgical art

Chirurgien, sm. (*etym.* chirurgie), surgeon

Chlore, sf. (*etym. Gr.* χλωρός, *yellowish, greenish*), chlorine

¶**Chloroforme,** sm. (*etym.* chlore, formique), chloroform

¶**Chloroformer,** va. to chloroform

Chlorure, sf. chloride

Choc, sm. (*etym. I.* cioco, *stump of a tree*), shock, collision, clash, blow

Chocolat, sm. (*etym. I.* cioccolata), chocolate

Chocolatier, sm. chocolate dealer

Chocolatière, sf. chocolate pot

Chœur, sm. (*etym. L.* chorus), chorus, choir, choristers. *Enfant de —*, chorister

Choir, vn. (*etym. L.* cadere, *to fall*), to fall, to tumble

Choisi, e, adj. select, chosen, choice

Choisir, va. (*etym. Goth.* kausjan, *to taste, to try*), to choose, to select, to single out

Choix, sm. (*etym.* choisir), choice, choosing, option, selection. *Des marchandises de —*, choice articles

Cholérique, sm. adj. (*etym. L.* cholericus), cholera patient, choleric

Chômage, sm. (*etym.* chômer), stoppage of work, being without work, rest

Chômer, vn. (*etym. Celt.* choum, cum, *to stop, to cease*), to be out of work, to be at a standstill, to lie fallow; — va. to keep, to observe

Chope, sf. (*etym. G.* schoppen), pitcher, flagon, tankard

Chopine, sf. pint

Chopper, vn. (*etym. O.F.* chope, *stump of a tree*), to stumble

Choquant, e, adj. shocking, offensive, unpleasant

Choquer, va. (*etym.* choc), to shock, to strike against, to wound. *— de l'aile*, to strike with one's wing

Choral, e, adj. (*etm.* chœur), belonging to a chorus. — sm. kind of sacred music; *plur.* des chorals

Choriste, sm. (*etym.* chœur), chorister

Chorus (faire), va. to sing in chorus, to chime in with

Chose, sf. (*etym. L.* causa), thing, matter, business, one's own property

Chou, sm. (*etym. L.* caulis), kale, puff, knot of ribbon. — *pommé, frisé*, white-headed, savoy cabbage. *Trognon de —*, cabbage stump. † *J'en ferais volontiers mes —x gras*, I would willingly have it for myself. *Mon petit —*, my darling, little dear. — *blanc*, nothing. *Faire — blanc*, to miss one's blow

Chouan, sm. (*etym. ?*), insurgent of Vendée

Chouannerie, sf. the Vendean insurrection

Choucas, sm. (*etym. O.H.G.* chouch), jackdaw

Choucroute, sf. "sauerkraut"

Chouette, sf. owl, owlet, laughingstock, one against two

Chou-fleur, sm. cauliflower

Chou-rave, sm. turnip-cabbage

Choyer, va. (*etym. I.* soiare, *to flatter*), to pet, to take great care of, to fondle; *se —*, vr. to nurse oneself

Chrême (saint), sm. (*etym. Gr.* χρίσμα, *ointment*), chrism

Chrétien, ne, s. adj. (*etym. L.* christianus), Christian

Chrétienté, sf. (*etym. L.* christianitatem), Christendom

Christianiser, va. (*etym. L.* christianus), to christianize

Christianisme, sm. Christianity

Chromatique, sm. adj. (*etym. Gr.* χρῶμα, *colour*), chromatic

Chronique, sf. (*etym. L.* chronicus; *Gr.* χρονικός, *from* χρόνος, *time*), chronicle. — adj. chronic. *Passer à l'état —*, to become chronical

Chronologie, sf. (*etym. Gr.* χρονολογία, *discourse about time*), chronology

Chronologique, adj. (*etym. Gr.* χρονολογικός), chronological

Chronomètre, sm. (*etym. Gr.* χρόνος, μέτρον, *measure*), chronometer, timekeeper

Chrysalide, sf. (*etym. L.* chrysalidem), chrysalis, aurelia, grub

Chrysanthème, sm. chrysanthemum

Chrysocale, sm. (*etym. Gr.* χρυσός, *gold*, καλός, *fine*), pinchbeck

Chuchotement, sm., **Chuchoterie,** sf. (*etym.* chuchoter), whisper

Chuchoter, vn.a. (*onom.*), to whisper

Chut! interj. (*onom.*), hush!

Chute, sf. (*etym.* chu, *past part. of* choir), fall, falling, failure, dropping, lift, thrust. *Une — d'eau*, a waterfall. *A la — du jour*, at the close of the day

Ci, partic. (*etym. see* Ici), here, this. *Par — par là*, here and there, now and then

Cible, sf. (*etym. G.* scheibe, *target*), target

Ciboire (saint), sm. (*etym.* κιβώριον, *vase*), pyx, ciborium

Ciboule, sf. (*etym. L.* cæpulla, *dimin. of* cæpa, *onion*), scallion

Ciboulette, sf. (*dimin. of* ciboule), chives

Cicatrice, sf. (*etym. L.* cicatricem), scar, seam

Cicatriser, va. to close, to cicatrize, to scar, to heal; *se —*, vr. to close, to cicatrize, to skin over

Cicéro, sm. (*print.*), pica

Cid, sm. (*etym. Arab.* seid, *lord*), lord

Cidre, sm. (*etym. L.* sicera, *a kind of drink*), cider

Ciel, sm. (*etym. L.* cœlum; *plur.* des ciels, des cieux), heaven, the sky, the firmament, the heavens, climate, tester, roof, canopy. *A — ouvert*, open

Cierge, sm. (*etym. L.* cereus, *of wax*), taper, wax-taper

Cigale, sf. (*etym. L.* cicada), grasshopper, cicada

Cigare, sm. (*etym. Span.* cigarro), cigar

Cigogne, sf. (*etym. L.* ciconia), stork

Ciguë, sf. (*etym. L.* cicuta), hemlock

Cil, sm. (*etym. L.* cilium), eyelash

Ciliaire, adj. (*etym.* cil), belonging to the eyelashes, ciliary

Cilice, sm. (*etm. L.* cilicium), haircloth

Cime, sf. (*etym. Gr.* κῦμα, *a young shoot*), top, summit, cyma, cyme

Ciment, sm. (*etym. L.* cæmentum, *freestone*), cement. *Fait à chaux et à —*, strongly built

Cimenter, va. to cement, to strengthen

Cimeterre, sm. (*etym. I.* scimitarra, *Pers.* chimchir), scimitar

Cimetière, sm. (*etym. Gr.* κοιμητήριον), burial-ground, cemetery

Cimier, sm. (*etym. L.L.* cimeria, cimerium, *top*), buttock, haunch

Cinéraire, adj. (*etym. L.* cinerarius, *from* cinis, *ash*), cinerary. — sf. cineraria

Cingler, vn. (*etym. O.H.G.* segelên, *to set sail*), to sail, to steer; — va. (*etym. L.* cingulum, *from* cingere, *to surround*), to cut, to deal a blow, to lash

Cinname, sm. (*etym. Gr.* κίνναμον), cinnamon

Cinq, adj. (*etym. L.* quinque), five

Cinquantaine, sf. (*etym.* cinquante), fifty. *S'approcher de la —*, to be nearly fifty years old

Cinquante, adj. (*etym. L.* quinquaginta), fifty

Cinquantième, adj. sm. (*etym.* cinquante), fiftieth

Cinquième, adj. sm. fifth

Cintre, sm. (*etym. L.L.* cintrum, *from L.* cingo ?), arch, wooden frame. *En plein —*, semicircular. *Loges du —*, the highest tier of boxes

Cintrer, va. to arch

Cipaye, sm. (*etym. Pers.* sipâhi), sepoy, sipahi

Cirage, sm. (*etym.* cirer), blacking, waxing

Circoncire, va. (*etym. L.* circumcidere), to circumcise

Circoncis, e, smf. person circumcised

Circoncision, sf. (*etym. L.* circumcisionem), circumcision

Circonférence, sf. (*etym. L.* circumferentia), circumference

Circonflexe, adj. (*etym. L.* circumflexus), circumflex
Circonlocution, sf. (*etym. L.* circumlocutionem), circumlocution
Circonscription, sf. (*etym. L.* circumscriptionem), circumscription, bounds
Circonscrire, va. (*etym. L.* circumscribere), to circumscribe
§**Circonspect,** adj. (*etym. L.* circumspectus), circumspect, wary, cautious, prudent
Circonspection, sf. (*etym. L.* circumspectionem), wariness, circumspection, guardedness
Circonstance, sf. (*etym. L.* circumstantia), circumstance, appurtenances. *Pièce de* —, play written for the occasion. *L'homme de la* —, the very man we want
Circonstancié, e, adj. circumstantial
Circonstancier, va. (*etym.* circonstance), to detail
Circonvenir, va. (*etym. L.* circumvenire), to impose upon, to circumvent, to overreach
Circonvoisin, e, adj. (*etym. L.* circum, *and* voisin), adjacent, neighbouring
Circonvolution, sf. (*etym. L.* circumvolutus), circumvolution
§**Circulaire,** adj. (*etym. L.* circularis), circular
Circulant, e, adj. (*etym.* circuler), circulating, in circulation
Circulatoire, adj. (*etym. L.* circulatorius), circulatory
Circuler, vn. (*etym. L.* circulari), to circulate, to revolve, to move, to spread abroad, to be current
Cire, sf. (*etym. L.* cera), wax
Ciré, e, adj. waxed. *Toile* —*e*, oil-cloth
Cirer, va. (*etym.* cire), to wax, to black, to polish, to clean
Ciron, sm. (*etym. L.L.* sirines), flesh-worm
Cirque, sm. (*etym. L.* circus), circus
§**Cisaille,** sf. (*etym.* ciseau), parings, clippings, shears
Cisalpin, e, adj. (*etym. L.* cisalpinus), cisalpine
Ciseau, sm. (*etym. L.* cæsus, *action of cutting*), chisel; *pl.* scissors
Ciseler, va. to chisel, to carve, to chase, to enchase
Ciseleur, sm. chiseler, carver, chaser
Ciselure, sf. chiselling, carving, chasing
Citadelle, sf. (*etym. I.* cittadella, *dimin. of* città, *city*), citadel, tower
Citadin, e, smf. (*etym. I.* cittadino), townsman, citizen
Citateur, trice, adj. (*etym.* citer), a person who quotes
Cité, sf. (*etym. L.* civitatem), city
Citer, va. (*etym. L.* citare), to quote, to cite, to name, to summon

Citerne, sf. (*etym. L.* cisterna), cistern, tank
Citoyen, ne, s. (*etym. L.L.* civitadanus, *from L.* civitas), citizen
Citrique, adj. (*etym. L.* citrus), citric
Citronnier, sm. (*etym.* citron), lemon-tree
§**Citrouille,** sf. (*etym. L.* citrus), pumpkin
Civet, sm. (*etym. L.* cæpatum, *from* cæpa, *onion*), jugged hare
Civette, sf. (*etym. Arab.* zabâd), civet-cat, civet, chives
Civière, sf. (*etym. L.L.* ceno-vehum, *from L.* cœnum, *mud, and* vehere, *to carry*) handbarrow
Civilisateur, trice, adj. (*etym.* civiliser), civilizing
Civilisation, sf. (*etym.* civiliser), civilization
Civiliser, va. to civilize
Civilité, sf. civility, urbanity
Civique, adj. (*etym. L.* civicus), civic
Civisme, sm. (*etym.* civique), civism
Clabauder, vn. (*etym.* clabaud, *a kind of dog*), to bark, to brawl
Clabauderie, sf. clamour, outcry, brawling
Clabaudeur, se, s. clamourer, brawler
Claie, sf. (*etym. Celt.* cliath, clwyd, cluit), hurdle, wattle, riddle
]**Clair, e,** adj. (*etym. L.* clarus), clear, bright, obvious, perspicuous. — sm. light. *Tirer à* —, *au* —, to strain, (*fig.*) to make out. — adv. clearly, plainly, openly
Clairet, adj. pale-coloured wine
Claire-voie, sf. opening
Clairière, sf. glade, thin place
Clair-obscur, sm. light and shade
Clairon, sm. (*etym. L.* clarus), clarion
Clair-semé, e, adj. (clair *is invariable*), thinly sown, set far apart
Clairvoyance, sf. (*etym.* clairvoyant), clearsightedness, clearheadedness, perspicacity
Clairvoyant, e, adj. (*etym.* clair, voir), clearsighted, clearheaded, acute, shrewd
Clameur, sf. (*etym. L.* clamorem), clamour, outcry
!**Clampin,** sm. (*etym.* ?), idler, lag
]**Clandestin, e,** adj. (*etym. L.* clandestinus), clandestine, private, underhand
Clapet, sm. (*etym. Germ.* klappen, *to make a noise in falling*), clack-valve, blow-valve
Clapier, sm. (*etym. L.L.* clapus, *a heap of stones*), burrow, hutch
Clapoter, vn. (*etym. G.* klappen), to splash, to chop
Clapoteuse, adj. f. swelling. *Une mer* —, a heavy or chopping sea

Clapotis, sm., **Clapotage,** sm. (*etym. G.* klappen), splashing, chopping
Claque, sf. (*onomat.*), slap, smack, clapping; *plur.* clogs. — sm. opera-hat
Claquement, sm. clacking, clapping, snapping, chattering, crack
Claquemurer, va. to coop up
Claquer, va.n. to slap, to crack, to smack, to clap, to galoche, to clap, to snap. *Faire* — *son fouet*, to smack one's whip, (*fig.*) to talk glibly
Claqueur, sm. (*etym.* claquer), clapper, applauder
Clarifier, va. (*etym. L.* clarificare), to clarify, to clear; *se* —, vr. to settle, to grow clear
Clarinette, sf. (*etym.* clair), clarionet
Clarté, sf. (*etym. L.* claritatem), light, clearness, brightness, perspicuity
Classe, sf. (*etym. L.* classis), class, rank, order, rate, school, school-time, school-room
Classement, sm. (*etym.* classer), classing
Classer, va. to class
Classique, adj. classic, classical
Claveau, sm. (*etym. L.* clavellus, *small nail*), key-stone, rot
Clavelée, sf. (*etym. see* CLAVEAU), rot
Clavecin, sm. (*etym. I.* clavicembalo), harpsichord
Clavicule, sf. (*etym. L.* clavicula, *small key*), collar-bone, clavicle
Clavier, sm. (*etym. L.* clavis), key-board
Clef, sf. (*etym. L.* clavis), key. *Fermer une porte à* —, to lock a door. *Donner un tour de* —, to turn the key. *Mettre sous* —, to lock up. — *forée*, piped key. *Mettre la* — *sous la porte*, (*fig.*) to remove secretly
Clématite, sf. (*etym. Gr.* κληματίς, *small branch*), clematis
Clémence, sf. (*etym. L.* clementia), mercy, clemency
Clepsydre, sf. (*etym. L.* clepsydra), clepsydra, water-clock
Clerc, sm. (*etym. L.* clericus), clerk, clergyman, scholar. *Maître* —, head-clerk. *Petit* —, junior clerk. ! *Faire un pas de* —, to commit a blunder
Clergé, sm. (*etym. L.* clericatus), the clergy
Clichage, sm. (*etym.* clicher), stereotyping, stereotype
Cliché, sm. stereotype-plate
Clicher, va. (*etym.* ?), to stereotype
Clicheur, sm. stereotyper
Clientèle, sf. (*etym. L.* clientela), train of dependants, protection, connection, custom, business

§**Clignement,** sm., **Clignotement,** sm. (*etym.* cligner), winking, blinking
§**Cligne-musette,** sf. (*etym.* cligne, *and O.F.* musette, *hiding-place*), hide and seek
§**Cligner,** va.n., **Clignoter,** vn. (*etym. L.L.* clinare, *to lower*), to wink, to blink, to twinkle
Climat, sm. (*etym. Gr.* κλίμα, *inclination*), climate, clime
Climatérique, adj. (*etym. Gr.* κλιμακτήρ, *step of a ladder*), climacteric
Clin, sm. (*etym. see* CLIGNER), wink. — *d'œil*, the twinkling of an eye, a twinkling, a trice
Clinique, adj. (*etym. Gr.* κλίνη, *bed*), clinic, clinical. — sf. clinical surgery, clinical hospital
Clinquant, sm. (*etym. D.* klinken, *to sound*), tinsel, false glitter
Clique, sf. (*same word as* claque), set, gang
Cliquetis, sm. (*etym. O.F.* cliqueter, *to make a noise*), clashing, clash, clanking, jingling
Cloaque, sm. (*etym. L.* cloaca), sink, common sewer, cesspool
Cloche, sf. (*etym.* ?), bell, glass bell, stew-pan, dish-cover
Clochement, sm. hobble, hobbling, limp
Cloche-pied, adv. on one foot, hopping
Clocher, sm. (*etym.* cloche), steeple, bell-tower. *Course au* —, steeple-chase. *Parler pour son* —, (*fig.*) to speak up for one's own interest. *Intérêts de* —, local interests
Clocher, vn. (*etym. L.L.* cloppicare, *from* cloppus, *lame*), to be lame, to hobble along
Clocheton, sm. bell-turret
Clochette, sf. little bell, hand-bell, bell-flower
Cloison, sf. (*etym. L.* claudere), partition, (*nav.*) bulk-head
Cloisonnage, sm. partition-work
Cloître, sm. (*etym. L.* claustrum), cloister, convent, monastery
Cloîtré, e, adj. cloistered, mewed up
Cloîtrer, va. to shut up in a convent, to immure; *se* —, to enter a monastery *or* convent, to shut oneself up
Clopin-clopant, adv. (*see* CLOCHER, vn.), with a hobbling gait
Cloporte, sm. (*etym.* ?), wood-louse
Clore, va. (*etym. L.* claudere), to close, to shut up, to stop
Clos, sm. close, enclosure. — *de vigne*, vineyard
Clos, e, adj. closed, shut up, fenced. *A huis* —, with shut doors. *Ce sont là lettres* —*es*,

it is a secret. — *et couvert*, in good repair. *A la nuit —e*, when it was quite dark

Closerie, sf. small garden

Clôture, sf. (*etym. L.* claudere), enclosure, fence, closing, seclusion. *Incessamment la —*, to be closed shortly

Clôturer, va. to close

Clou, sm. (*etym. L.* clavus), nail, stud, boil. — *à crochet*, tenter-hook. *River le — à*, to give a clincher. — *de girofle*, clove

Clouer, va. to nail, to nail down, to fasten down

Clouterie, sf. nail-manufactory

Cloutier, sm. nail-maker, nail-seller

Cloyère, sf. (*etym.* claie), basket of oysters

¶**Clubiste**, sm. clubbist

Clysopompe, sf. (*etm. Gr.* κλύζειν, *to wash, and* pompe), clysopomp, syringe

Clystère, sm. (*etym. Gr.* κλύζειν, *to wash*), clyster

Coaccusé, e, smf. (*etym.* co, accusé), fellow-prisoner

Coadjuteur, trice, smf. (*etym. L.* coadjuvare, *to help in common*), coadjutor, fellow-helper

Coadjutorerie, sf. a coadjutor's duty

Coaguler, va. (*etym. L.* coagulare), to curdle, to clot, to coagulate

Coaliser, va. (*etym. L.* coalescere), to unite, to form in a coalition; *se —*, vr. to form a coalition

Coassement, sm. croaking, croak

Coasser, vn. (*etym. L.* coaxare), to croak

Coassocié, e, s. (*etym.* co, associé), fellow-partner

§**Cocagne**, sf. (*etym. L.* coquere, *to cook*), Cockaigne. *Un pays de —*, a land of plenty. *Mât de —*, greased pole

Cocarde, sf. (*etym. O.F.* cocard, *cock*), cockade, ventilator

†**Cocasse**, adj. (*etym.* ?), droll, funny

Coccinelle, sf. (*etym. L.* coccus, *red grain*), lady-bird

Coche, sm. (*etym. L.* concha, *shell, vase*), public coach, barge. *Être, faire la mouche du —*, (*fig.*) to be about as useful as the fly on the coach wheel

Coche, sf. (*etym.* ?), a notch

§**Cochenille**, sf. (*etm. I.* cocciniglia, *from L.* coccinus, *scarlet*), cochineal

§**Cochenillier**, sm. cochineal-tree

Cocher, sm. (*etym.* coche), coachman, driver, cabman

Cochet, sm. (*etym.* coq), a small cock

Cochon, sm. (*etym.* ?), pig, hog, swine, pork, dirty fellow, beast, (*manuf.*) sow. *Gardeur de —s*, swineherd. — *de lait*, sucking-pig. — *d'Inde*, guinea-pig

Cochonner, vn. to farrow, to bungle, to mess

†**Cochonnerie**, sf. nastiness

Coco, sm. cocoa-nut, stick-liquorice water

Cocon, sm. (*etym.* coque), cocoon

Cocote, sf. (*etym.* coq), chicken, saucepan, egg-boiler

Cocotier, sm. (*etym.* coco), cocoa-nut tree

Codébiteur, sm. joint-debtor

Codétenteur, sm. joint-holder

Codétenu, sm. (*etym.* co, détenu), fellow-prisoner

§**Codicille**, sm. (*etym. L.* codicillus, *dimin. of* codex), codicil

Coercitif, ve, adj. coercive

Coéternel, le, adj. coeternal

Cœur, sm. (*etym. L.* cor), heart, stomach, soul, bosom, spirit, heartiness, core, height, depth. *De —, de bon —*, heartily, with a will. *A contre- —*, reluctantly. *Sans —*, poor-spirited, heartless. *Avoir mal au —*, to be sick. *Un spectacle à soulever le —*, a heartsickening sight. *Un homme de —*, a gallant-minded man. *Avoir le — gros*, to have one's heart full, to sob. *N'avoir pas le — au métier*, to have no taste for one's work. *Remettre du — au ventre à*, to cheer up. *Faire contre fortune bon —*, to keep a good heart. *Le — ne lui en dit pas*, it goes against his stomach. *Faire la bouche en —*, to purse one's mouth. *A — joie*, to one's heart's delight. *Dîner par —*, to go without dinner

Coexistant, e, adj. coexistent

Coexistence, sf. (*etym.* coexister), coexistence

Coexister, vn. (*etym.* co, exister), to coexist

Coffre, sm. (*etym. L.* cophinus), chest, trunk, box, seat, coffer, body, (*print.*) coffin, drum. ‡ *Avoir le — bon, solide*, to have good lungs

†**Coffrer**, va. (*etym.* coffre), to send to prison

Coffret, sm. (*dimin. of* coffre), little chest, casket

§**Cognassier**, sm. (*etym.* coing), quince-tree

§**Cognée**, sf. (*etym. L.* cuneus, *wedge*), axe, hatchet

§**Cogner**, va. (*see* COGNÉE), to knock in, to thump

Cohabiter, va. (*etym. L.* cohabitare), to cohabit

Cohéritier, ère, s. (*etym.* co, héritier), coheir, coheiress

Cohorte, sf. (*etm. L.* cohors), cohort, crowd, crew

Cohue, sf. (*etym. L.L.* cohua), rout, press, crowd

***Coi, te**, adj. (*etym. L.* quietus), snug, still, quiet, close. *Se tenir —, demeurer —*, to keep snug

Coiffe, sf. (*etym.* ?), cap, coif, hood, lining, caul

Coiffé, e, adj. past part. dressed, arranged, quite taken with

Coiffer, va. (*etym.* coiffe), to put on one's head, to dress a person's hair, to become, to cap, to infatuate with, (*nav.*) to lay aback, (*hunt.*) to seize; — vn. to dress hair, to fit well, to become, (*nav.*) to be taken aback; *se —*, vr. to dress one's hair, to put on, to be infatuated with

Coiffeur, se, s. hair-dresser

Coiffure, sf. coiffure

Coin, sm. (*etym. L.* cuneus), corner, nook, wedge, clock, stamp

Coïncider, vn. (*etym.* co, *L.* incidere, *to fall*), to coincide

Coing, sm. (*etym. L.* Cydonium, *Gr.* Κυδωνία, *from* Cydon, *prop. name*), quince

Cointéressé, e, smf. (*etym.* co, intéressé), partner

Col, sm. (*etym. see* COU), neck, collar, stock

Colback, sm. (*etym. Turk.* kolbak), kind of bearskin cap

Coléoptère, sm. adj. (*etym. Gr.* κολεόπτερος, *from* κολεός, *case, and* πτερόν, *wing*), coleopter

Colère, sf. (*etym. Gr.* χολέρα), anger, passion, wrath, pet, rage, fury. — adj. hasty, passionate, irascible

‖**Colérique**, adj. (*etym.* colère), choleric

Colibri, sf. (*etym.* ?), humming-bird

Colifichet, sm. (*etym.* colle, ficher), trinket, bawble, gewgaw, trifle

Colimaçon, sf. (*etym.* limaçon), snail

§**Colin-maillard**, sm. (*etym.* colin, maillard, maillot ?), blindman's buff

Colique, sf. (*etym. Gr.* κωλικός), stomach-ache, colic. — *de miséréré*, volvulus

Colis, sm. (*etym. I.* colli, *burdens*), package

Colisée, sm. (*etym. L.L.* coliseum, *for* colosseum), coliseum

Collaborateur, sm. (*etym. L.* collaborare), fellow-labourer, contributor

Collaboration, sf. (*etym. L.* collaborare), contribution. *Ouvrage fait en —*, work composed by more than one author

Collage, sm. (*etym.* coller), pasting, paper-hanging, sizing, clarifying

Collant, e, adj. (*etm.* coller), sticking, sticky, tight

Collatéral, e, smf. adj. (*etym.* co, latéral), collateral relation, collateral

Collation, sf. (*etym. L.* collationem), collation, lunch, luncheon

Collationner, va. (*etym.* collation), to collate; — vn. to make a slight meal, to lunch

Colle, sf. (*etym. L.* colla), paste, (†) fib, crack, (†) examination. — *forte*, glue. — *à bouche*, lip-glue. — *de peau*, size. — *de poisson*, isinglass

Collecte, sf. (*etym. L.* collectus), collection, collect

Collecteur, sm. (*etym. L.* collectorem), collector, tax-gatherer

‖**Collectif, ve**, adj. sm. (*etm. L.* collectivus), collective, collective noun

Collége, sm. (*etym. L.* collegium), school, grammar-school, college

Collégien, sm. (*etym.* collége), schoolboy, collegian

Collègue, sm. (*etym. L.* collega), colleague, fellow-member

Coller, va. (*etym.* colle), to paste, to stick, to glue, to size, to clarify, to stump, to cushion the ball. *Il avait les yeux collés sur*, his eyes were fastened on. *Se —*, vr. to stick together

Collerette, sf. (*dimin. of* collier), collar, frill, involucre. — *du grand piston*, duplicate piston ring

Collet, sm. (*dimin. of* col), collar, cape, snare, neck, scrag. *Prendre au —*, to collar. — *montant*, stand-up collar. ‡ — *monté*, prudish

Colleter, va. n. (*etym.* collet), to collar, to set snares for

Colleur, sm. (*etym.* colle), sizer, paper-hanger, bill-sticker

Collier, sm. (*etym. L.* collare, *from* collum, *neck*), collar, necklace, carcanet. *Cheval de —*, draught-horse. *Être franc du —*, to draw freely, (‡) to be hearty and sincere. *Un coup de —*, a strong effort. ‡ — *de misère*, drudgery

Colline, sf. (*etym. L.* collis), hill, eminence

Colloque, sf. (*etym. L.* colloquium), colloquy

Colloquer, va. (*etym. L.* cum, locare), to place

Collusion, sf. (*etym. L.* collusionem), collusion

‖**Collusoire**, adj. (*etym.* collusion), collusive

Collyre, sm. (*etym. L.* collyrium), collyrium, eye-salve

Colombe, sf. (*etym. L.* columba), dove; (*etym. L.* columna), upright joist

Colombier, sm. (*etym.* colombe), dove-cot, pigeon-cot, columbier; *pl.* pigeon-holes, gaps

Colon, sm. (*etym. L.* colonus), colonist, planter

Colonie, sf. (*etym. L.* colonia), colony, settlement, the colony, the colonists

Colonisateur, trice, adj. (*etym.* coloniser), colonizing

Colonisation, sf. (*etym.* coloniser), colonization, colonizing, settlement

Coloniser, va. (*etym.* colonie), to colonize, to settle

Colonnade, sf. (*etym.* colonne), colonnade

Colonne, sf. (*etym. L.* columna), pillar, column

Colonnette, sf. small column

Colophane, sf. (*etym. L.* Colophonia, *belonging to the town of* Colophon), rosin, colophony

Coloquinte, sf. (*etym. Gr.* κολοκυνθίς, *pumpkin*), colocynth, (†) the head

Colorant, **e**, adj. colouring

Coloré, **e**, adj. coloured, ruddy, specious, glowing

Colorer, va. (*etym. L.* colorare), to colour, to tinge, to give a specious colour to

Colorier, va. (*etym.* colori, *past part. of O.F.* colorir), to colour, to stain

Colorié, **e**, adj. coloured, stained, camleted

Coloris, sm. (*etym. see* Colorier), colouring, colours, hue, freshness

Coloriste, sm. (*etm.* coloris), colourist, print-colourer

Colosse, sm. (*etym. L.* colossus), colossus

Colportage, sm. (*etym.* colporter), hawker's business, hawking

Colporter, va. (*etym.* col, porter), to hawk, to retail, to spread abroad

Colporteur, sm. hawker, newsman, retailer

Colza, sm. (*etym. D.* koolzaad, *cabbage-seed*), rapeseed, rape

Combat, sm. (*etym.* combattre), fight, battle, combat, engagement. *Hors de* —, disabled

Combattant, sm. fighting-man, combatant, warrior

Combattre, va. (*etym. L.* cum, *and* battre), to fight, to combat, to strive with, to oppose, to contend; *se* —, vr. to fight, to combat each other, to have its remedy

Combien, adv. (*etym. O.F.* com, comme, *and* bien), how much, how many. — *y a-t-il!* how much is there? how many are there? how long is it? how far is it? *De* —, how much? by how much? — sm. the price

Combinaison, sf. (*etym.* combiner), combination, contrivance

Combiné, **e**, adj. combined

Combiner, va. (*etym. L.* combinare), to combine, to contrive

Comble, sm. (*etym. L.* cumulus), top, roof, heaping, over-measure, the summit, the depth, shed. — adj. full. *Salle* —, full house

Combler, va. to fill up to the brim, to fulfil, to gratify, to overwhelm, to make good

Combustibilité, sf. (*etm.* combustible), combustibility

Comédie, sf. (*etym. Gr.* κωμῳδία), comedy, play, the company, theatre, playhouse, farce, sham. *La haute* —, true comedy. ‡ *Le secret de la* —, everybody's secret

Comédien, **ne**, s. comedian, performer, hypocrite

Comestible, s. adj. (*etym. L.L.* comestibilis), eatable. *Magasin de* —*s*, Italian warehouse

Comète, sf. (*etym. Gr.* κομήτης), comet

Comice, sm. (*etym. L.* comitium), comitia, the electors

‖**Comique**, sm. (*etym. L.* comicus), comedy, the comic art, comic author, comic actor, comic effect. — adj. comic, humorous, comical, droll, laughable

Comité, sm. (*from the Engl.*), committee. *En petit* —, a small party. — *de lecture*, greenroom committee

Commandant, **e**, smf. (*etym.* commander), commander, commanding officer, major. — *de place*, captain of the place

Commande, sf. (*etym. see* Commander), order. *Ouvrage de* —, work bespoken. *Maladie de* —, feigned illness

Commandement, sm. (*etym.* commander), command, bidding, commandment, word of command, writ. *Avoir à* —, to have at command. *Secrétaire des* —*s*, private secretary

Commander, va.n. (*etym. L.* cum, mandare), to command, to have the command of, to require, to order, to bespeak, to overlook; *se* —, vr. to have a command over oneself, to be subject to one's will

Commanderie, sf. commandery

Commandeur, sm. commander

Commanditaire, sm. adj. (*etym.* commandite), sleeping partner

Commandite, sf. (*etym.* commander), limited liability. *Société en* —, limited liability company

Commanditer, va. to supply the funds for

Comme, adv. (*etym. L.* quo modo), how. — *cela*, middling, so so. — *quoi*, how. *C'est tout* —, it's all the same thing. — conj. as, when, since, whereas

‡**Commémoratif**, **ve**, adj. (*etym.* commémoration), commemorative

Commençant, **e**, adj. beginner, novice

Commencer, va.n. (*etym. L.* cum, initiare), to begin, to commence, to set about, to enter upon, to initiate

Commensal, sm. (*etym.* com, *and L.* mensa), guest, boarder

Comment, adv. (*etym. L* quomodo, inde), how, why, how is it that? what? —, interj. how! what! indeed! — sm. the why, the wherefore

Commentaire, sm. (*etym. L.* commentarius), comment, commentary, remark. *Point de* —*s!* no remarks!

Commentateur, sm. (*etym. L.* commentator), commentator

Commenter, va. (*etym. L.* commentari), to comment; — vn. to comment, to criticize, to exaggerate; *se* —, vr. to be commented

Commérage, sm. (*etym.* commère), idle gossip, gossiping

Commerçant, **e**, adj. commercial, mercantile, trading. — sm. merchant, tradesman, dealer

Commerce, sm. (*etym. L.* commercium), trade, business, commerce, intercourse, connection, conversation, correspondence, intrigue

Commercer, vn. to trade with

‡**Commercial**, **e**, adj. commercial, trading

Commère, sf. (*etym.* co, mère), godmother, gossip, shrewd woman. ‡ *Faire la* —, to gossip

Commettant, sm. constituent, employer

Commettre, va. (*etym. L.* committere), to commit, to be guilty of, to perpetrate, to intrust, to confide, to risk, to set at variance; *se* —, vr. to be committed, to commit oneself

Comminatoire, adj. (*etm.* commination), comminatory

Commis, sm. (*past part. of* commettre), clerk, shopman. — *voyageur*, commercial traveller. — *de l'octroi*, toll-clerk. — *des vivres*, purser's clerk

Commissaire, sm. (*etym. L.* commissus), commissioner, commissary, steward. — *de police*, police magistrate. *Bureau du* —, police office. *Juge*- —, delegate. — -*priseur*, auctioneer, appraiser. *Sous*- —, issuing commissary

Commission, sf. (*etym. L.* commissio), commission, warrant, charge, power, errand, message, committee. *Avoir* — *de*, *pour*, to be commissioned, empowered to. *Faire une* —, *aller en* —, to go on an errand. *Faire la* —, to be a commission agent. *Maison de* —, commission agency

Commissionnaire, sm. commission-agent, factor, carrier, porter

Commissionner, va. to commission

Commode, adj. (*etym. L.* commodus), convenient, commodious, snug, pleasant, easy, fit, proper, good-natured, accommodating. *Un homme peu* —, an ugly customer. *N'être pas* — *à vivre*, not to be over easy to deal with

Commode, sf. chest of drawers

Commodément, adv. (*etm.* commode), conveniently, comfortably

Commodité, sf. convenience, conveniency, comfort, accommodation, commodiousness, ease, opportunity; *plur.* watercloset. *A votre* —, when best suits you

Commuable, adj. (*etym.* commuer), commutable

Commuer, va. (*etym. L.* commutare), to commute

Commun, **e**, adj. (*etym. L.* communis), common, one, general, usual, plentiful, rife, low, vulgar. *Année* —*e*, one year with another. *Maison* —*e*, town-hall. *Faire vie* —*e*, to live together. *D'un* — *accord*, unanimously

Commun, sm. the generality, the bulk, the common stock, prayers for the saint's day, outhouses, privy. *Un homme du* —, a man of low birth. *Vivre sur le* —, to live at the expense of the public. *Comme le* — *des martyrs*, (*fig.*) like most people

Communal, **e**, adj. (*etym.* commun), communal, of the parish, parish

Communauté, sf. (*etym.* communal), community

Communaux, sm. plur. the parish pasture and forest grounds

Commune, sf. (*etym.* commun), the commons, parish, the parishioners

Communément, adv. (*etym.* commun), commonly, usually, generally

Communiant, **e**, s. communicant

Communicatif, **ve**, adj. (*etym.* communiquer), communicative

Communication, sf. (*etym. L.* communicatio), communication, intercourse, message, producing of documents. *Prendre* — *de*, to take cognizance of

Communier, vn. (*etym. L.* communicare), to communicate, to receive the holy Sacrament. — *sous les deux espèces*, to communicate in both kinds. — va. to administer the holy Sacrament to

Communion, sf. (*etym. L.* communio), the holy Communion, the Lord's Supper, fellowship

Communiquer, va. (*etm. L.* communicare), to communicate, to impart, to acquaint, to show; — vn. to be in communication, to confer, to communicate

¶**Communisme**, sm. (*etym.* commun), communism

¶**Communiste**, sm. communist

Compacte, adj. (*etym. L.* compactus), compact

§**Compagne**, sf. (*etym. see* Compagnon), partner, companion, helpmate, consort, mate

§**Compagnie**, sf. company, fellowship, partnership

§**Compagnon**, sm. (*etym. L.* cum, panis), companion,

attendant, mate, consort, journeyman. *Joyeux* —, jolly fellow

§**Compagnonnage,** sm. (*etym.* compagnon), journeyman's time, trade-union

Comparaison, sf. (*etym. L.* comparatio), comparison, likening, simile. *Sans* —, incomparably. *Hors de toute* —, beyond compare

Comparaître, vn. (*etym.* com, paraître), to appear

‖**Comparatif, ve,** adj. (*etym. L.* comparativus), comparative

Comparer, va. (*etym. L.* comparare), to liken, to compare; *se* —, vr. to compare *or* liken oneself, to be compared *or* likened

Comparse, sm. (*etym. I.* comparsa, *act of appearing*), figurant, supernumerary

Compartiment, sm. (*etym. O.F.* compartir, *to divide*), compartment, panel, rib-wall. *A* —*s*, with compartments. *Exploitation par* —*s*, panel-work

Comparution, sf. (*etym.* comparaître), (*law*) forthcoming, appearance

Compas, sm. (*etym.* com, pas), pair of compasses, dividers, mariner's compass. *Par* — *et par mesure*, by rule and compass. — *de proportion*, sector

Compasser, va. (*etym.* compas), to measure, to lay out symmetrically, to weigh. *Être compassé*, to be formal *or* precise

Compatibilité, sf. (*etym.* compatible), compatibility, compatibleness

Compatir, vn. (*etym. L.* cum, pati, *to suffer with*), to feel for, to sympathize with, to agree, to be compatible with

Compatissant, e, adj. compassionate, feeling

Compatriote, s. (*etym. L.* cum, *L.L.* patriota), fellow-countryman, countrywoman

‖**Compendieux, se,** adj. (*etym. L.* compendiosus), abridged

Compensateur, trice, sm. adj. (*etym.* compenser), compensating, compensator

Compenser, va. (*etym. L.* cum, pensare, *to weigh*), to compensate, to counterbalance; *se* —, vr. to compensate each other

Compérage, sm. (*etym.* compère), spiritual relationship between godfather and godmother, trickery

Compère, sm. (*etym.* com, père), godfather, crony, gossip, neighbour, cunning fellow

Compétence, sf. (*etym. L.* competentia), competence, competency, cognisance, province

Compéter, vn. (*etym. L.* competere), to belong by virtue of certain rights

Compétiteur, sm. (*etym. L.* competitor), competitor

Compilateur, sm. (*etym. L.* compilator), compiler

Compiler, va. (*etym. L.* compilare), to compile

Complainte, sf. (*past part. of the O.F. verb* complaindre), lament, wailing, bemoaning, complaint

Complaire, vn. (*etym. L.* cum, placere), to please, to humour

Complaisance, sf. (*etym.* complaisant), complaisance, compliance, complacency, accommodation. *C'est par trop de* —, that is really too kind

‖**Complaisant, e,** adj. s. complaisant, obliging; fawner, toad-eater

Complément, sm. (*etym. L.* complementum), complement, objective case, object

Complémentaire, adj. necessary to complete, completing

§**Complet, ète,** sm. adj. (*etym. L.* completus), complete, total, utter. *Être au grand* —, to have a full muster

Compléter, va. to complete

Complexe, adj. (*etym. L.* complexus), complex, compound, complicated

Complexion, sf. (*etym. L.* complexio), constitution, humour, disposition

Complice, adj. s. (*etym. L.* complex), a party to; accomplice, abettor

Complicité, sf. (*etym.* complice), participation, share

Complies, sf. plur. (*etym. L.* horæ completæ, *complete hours*), compline

Complimenter, va. (*etm.* compliment), to compliment

Complimenteur, se, s. complimenter

Compliqué, e, adj. complicated, intricate

Compliquer, va. (*etym. L.* cum, plicare, *to fold with*), to complicate, to render intricate; *se* —, vr. to get complicated

Complot, sm. (*etym. ?*), plot

Comploter, va. to plot

Componction, sf. (*etym. L.* compunctio), compunction, contrition

Comporter, va. (*etym. L.* comportare), to allow of, to admit of, to allow, to suffer; *se* —, vr. to behave, to demean oneself

Composé, e, adj. (*etym.* composer), compound, complicate, composite, formal, stiff. *Société bien* —*e*, fashionable society. — sm. compound

Composer, va. (*etym.* com, poser), to compose, to write, to make up; — vn. to compose, to compound, to come to an agreement; *se* —, vr. to be composed, to be made up, to compose (one's demeanour, &c.)

Compositeur, sm. (*etym.* ‖*L.* compositor), composer, compositor, compounder

Composition, sf. (*etym. L.* compositio), composition, compound. *Homme d'une* — *facile, difficile*, an easy-tempered man, a man hard to satisfy. *Entrer en* —, to compound

Compote, sf. (*etym. O.F.* compost, *from the L.* compositus), kind of stew. *En* —, reduced to nothing. † *Avoir un œil en* —, to have a black eye

Compotier, sm. stewed-fruit dish

Comprendre, va. (*etym. L.* comprehendere), to understand, to comprehend

Compresse, sf. (*etym. L.* compressus), bolster, compress

Comprimé, e, adj. compressed, flattened

Comprimer, va. (*etym. L.* comprimere), to compress, to squeeze, to curb, to repress; *se* —, vr. to be compressed, to be kept down, to be curbed

Compris, e, past part. *Y* — *mon frère*, including my brother. *Mon frère* —, *non* —, my brother included, without reckoning my brother

Compromettre, va. (*etm. L.* compromittere), to compromise, to implicate, to forfeit; *se* —, vr. to commit, compromise, *or* injure oneself

Compromis, sm. compromise. *Mettre en* —, to compromise

Comptabilité, sf. (*etym.* comptable), accounts, book-keeping, the accountant's office. *Chef de* —, general accountant

Comptable, adj. (*etym.* compter), accountable, amenable. *Agent* —, accountant. — sm. accountant

Comptant, adj. m. (*etym.* compter), ready money, in cash. — sm. ready money, cash. *Au* —, in ready money

Compte, sm. (*etym. L.* computus), account, reckoning, calculation, right sum, right quantity, interest, purpose, value, regard. *A* —, on account. *A bon* —, cheap. *Au bout du* —, after all. *En fin de* —, in fine, at last. — *rond*, in round numbers. — *courant*, running account. *De* — *fait*, on computation. — *de vente*, account-sales. *Cour des* —*s*, audit office. *Livre de* —*s*, account-book. *Pour le* — *de*, for the account of. *Être de* — *à demi avec*, to go halves with a person in. *Être en* — *avec*, to have an account open with. *Être de bon* —, to be exact. *Être loin de son* —, to be out in one's reckoning. *Avoir une chose en* —, to have to account for a thing. *Devoir* — *de*, to be accountable for. *Porter en* —, to carry to account. *Faire entrer en ligne de* —, (*fig.*) to take into account or consideration. *Tenir* — *de*, to make up, to take into account. *Faire, tenir* — *de*, to value. *Faire bon* — *de*, to care little for. *Cela ne fait pas mon* —, that is not what I want. *Prendre sur son* —, to take upon oneself. *Avoir bon* — *de*, to obtain what one wants. *Donner son* — *à*, to discharge, to serve a person out. *Faire* — *sur*, to rely on. *A ce* — *-là*, in that case, at that rate. — *rendu*, report, return. *Les bons* —*s font les bons amis*, short reckonings make long friends

Compté, e, adj. considered, counted. *Tout bien* —, all things considered. *Marcher à pas* —*s*, to walk slowly

Compter, va. (*etym. L.* computare), to count, to reckon, to pay, to charge for, to comprise, to include; — vn. to count, to reckon, to be reckoned, to cast accounts, to cipher, to purpose, to intend, to rely, to depend, to calculate

Compteur, se, smf. (*etym.* compter), reckoner, tell-tale, meter, click

Comptoir, sm. (*etym.* compter), counter, cashier's desk, bar, tap, counting house, factory

Compulser, va. (*etym. L.* compulsare, *to force, to oblige*), to go through

Comte, sm. (*etym. L.* comes), count, earl

Comté, sm. (*etym. L.* comitatus), county, earldom

Comtesse, sf. (*etym. L.* comitissa), countess

Concasser, va. (*L.* conquassare), to break, to crush

Concavité, sf. (*etym. L.* concavitas), concavity

Concéder, va. (*etym. L.* concedere, *to yield*), to grant, to concede. *Se faire* —, to obtain the grant of

Concentré, e, adj. uncommunicative, repressed, smothered, concentrated

Concentrer, va. (*etym.* con, centre), to concentrate, to suppress, to dissemble; *se* —, vr. to concentrate, to centre, to wrap oneself up in oneself

Concentrique, adj. (*etm.* see CONCENTRER), concentric

Concernant, prep. concerning, relating to

Concerner, va. (*etym. L.* concernere), to concern, to relate to

Concert, sm. (*etym. I.* concerto), concert, melody, concert-room, chorus, lays, union, strains. *De* —, in concert, jointly, by a common consent. — *spirituel*, concert of sacred music

Concerter, va. to concert, to settle. *Homme concerté*, a man made up of affectation. *Se* —, vr. to concert matters

Concessionnaire, sm. (*etym.* concession), grantee, patentee

Concetti, sm. plur. (*Ital. word*), conceits

Concevable, adj. (*etym.* concevoir), conceivable

Concevoir, va. (*etym. L.* concipere), to conceive, to entertain, to imagine, to comprehend, to understand

Concierge, s. (*etym. L.L.* conservius, *from L.* cum and servire?), door-keeper

Conciergerie, sf. place of doorkeeper, porter's lodge

Concile, sm. (*etym. L.* concilium), council of the church

Conciliabule, sm. (*etym. L.* conciliabulum), clandestine meeting, cabal

Conciliant, e, Conciliateur, trice, adj. conciliating, conciliatory

Concilier, va. (*etym. L.* conciliare), to conciliate, to reconcile

Concis, e, adj. (*etym. L.* concisum), concise, brief

Concision, sf. (*etym. L.* concisio), conciseness, brevity

Concitoyen, ne, s. (*etym.* con, citoyen), fellow-citizen

Conclaviste, sm. (*etym.* conclave), a priest whose duty it is to wait upon a cardinal during the conclave

Concluant, e, adj. (*etym.* conclure), conclusive

Conclure, va. (*etym. L.* concludere), to conclude, to settle, to decide upon, to infer; — vn. to move, to declare for, to pronounce, to be conclusive; *se* —, vr. to be concluded, to be brought to a conclusion, to be inferred

Conclusion, sf. (*etym. L.* conclusio), conclusion, close, inference, motion. *Prendre ses* —*s*, to make a motion

Concombre, sm. (*etym. L.* cucumerem), cucumber

Concordance, sf. (*etym.* concordant), concordance, concord

Concordant, e, adj. agreeing

Concordat, sm. (*etym. L.* concordatum, *from* concordare), concordat, composition, bankrupt's certificate

Concorde, sf. (*etym. L.* concordia), concord, good understanding

Concorder, vn. (*etym. L.* concordare), to live in concord, to agree, to concur

Concourir, vn. (*etym. L.* concurrere), to concur, to contribute, to conspire, to compete, to meet

Concours, sm. (*etym. L.* concursus), concurrence, concourse, combination, meeting, competition

Concret, ète, adj. (*etym. L.* concretus), concrete

Concurrence, sf. (*etym.* concurrent), competition, concurrence, opposition. *Jusqu'à* — *de*, to the amount of. *Entrer en* —, to set up an opposition

||**Concurrent, e**, s. (*etym. L.* cum, currere), competitor

Concussion, sf. (*etym. L.* concussio, *shake*), peculation, extortion, bribery

Concussionnaire, sm. (*etym.* concussion), peculator, extortioner, guilty of bribery

Condamnable, adj. (*etym.* condamner), condemnable

Condamnation, sf. (*etym. L.* condemnatio), condemnation, doom, judgment, sentence. *Passer* —, to pass sentence. *Subir sa* —, to undergo one's sentence

Condamner, va. (*etym. L.* condemnare), to condemn, to sentence, to doom, to give over, to block up, to stop up; *se* —, vr. to condemn oneself, to plead guilty, to condemn each other, to be shut up

Condensabilité, sf. (*etym.* condensable), condensability

Condensable, adj. (*etym.* condenser), which can be condensed

Condensateur, sm. (*etym.* condenser), condenser

Condensation, sf. (*etym. L.* condensatio), condensation, condensing. *Auget de* —, condensing cistern

Condenser, va. (*etym. L.* condensare), to condense; *se* —, vr. to condense, to be condensed

Condescendance, sf. (*etym.* condescendre), condescension, compliance

Condescendre, vn. (*etym. L.* condescendere), to condescend, to comply, to bear

Condisciple, sm. adj. (*etym. L.* cum, discipulus), fellow-disciple, schoolfellow, fellow-student

Condition, sf. (*etym. L.* conditio), condition, state, terms, rank, quality, line of life, service, situation, place. *A* — *que*, *sous* — *que*, on condition that. *A* — *de*, on condition of. *Vendre à* —, *sous* —, to sell upon condition. *Sans* —*s*, without any condition, unconditional

Conditionné, e, adj. conditioned

||**Conditionnel, le**, adj. (*etym.* condition), conditional. *Clause* —*le*, proviso

Condoléance, sf. (*etym. L.* cum, dolere, *to mourn with*), condolence. *Faire ses compliments de* — *à*, to condole with

Conducteur, trice, adj. (*etym. see* CONDUIRE), conducting. *Fil* —, conducting rod. — sm. leader, conductor, guide, driver, drover, guard, superintendent, manager, foreman, assistant engineer. — sf. conductress, guide

Conductibilité, sf. (*etym.* conductible), conductibility

Conduire, va. (*etym. L.* conducere), to lead, to conduct, to guide, to drive, to carry, to be conducive, to attend, to carry out, to manage, to be at the head of. *Difficile à* —, untractable. *Se* —, vr. to find one's way, to be led, to behave, to conduct oneself, to go on

Conduit, sm. (*etym. L.* conductus), conduit, pipe, tube. — *de la vapeur*, steam-port. — *de vent*, blast pipe. — *en entonnoir*, tunnel pipe. — *de distribution*, delivery pipe. — *de détente*, expansion pipe

Conduite, sf. (*etym.* conduit), guidance, leading, driving, conveyance, distribution, disposition, management, plan, direction, charge, care, command, behaviour, dealings, forecast, discretion. *Avoir de la* —, to be steady, well-behaved. *Ses camarades lui ont fait la* —, his comrades saw him a short way on his journey

*__Confabulation__, sf. (*etym.* confabuler), familiar conversation

*__Confabuler__, vn. (*etym. L.* confabulari), to talk familiarly, to chat

Confection, sf. (*etym. L.* confectionem), execution, making, drawing up, confection, electuary. *Magasin de* —, ready-made clothes warehouse

Confectionner, va. to make, to draw up, to complete; *se* —, vr. to be made

Confédéré, e, past part. confederate

Confédérer, va. (*etym. L.* confoederare), to confederate

Conférence, sf. (*etym. L.* conferentia), comparison, collation, conference, debating society

Conférer, va.n. (*etym. L.* conferre), to collate, to compare, to confer

Confesse, sf. (*etym. see* CONFESSER), confession

Confesser, va. (*etym. L.* confessum, *supine of* confiteri), to confess, to acknowledge, to own

Confesseur, sm. (*etym. L.* confessor), confessor

Confession, sf. (*etym. L.* confessionem), confession. *On lui aurait donné le bon Dieu sans* —, one would have trusted him implicitly

Confiance, sf. (*etym.* confiant), trust, reliance, dependence, confidence, security, self-conceit. *Abus de* —, breach of trust. *Homme de* —, confidential man

Confiant, e, adj. (*etym.* confier), confiding, confident, unsuspicious, self-conceited

Confidemment, adv. (*etym.* confident), in all confidence

Confidence, sf. (*etym. L.* confidentia), confidence, disclosure, secret

||**Confidentiel, le**, adj. (*etym.* confidence), confidential

Confier, va. (*etym.* con, fier), to entrust, to confide, to trust; *se* —, vr. to be entrusted *or* confided, to confide to each other, to unbosom oneself, to trust, to put one's trust in

Confiner, vn. (*etym. see* CONFINS), to border upon, to be contiguous; — va. to confine, to shut up; *se* —, vr. to confine oneself, to shut oneself up

Confins, sm. plur. (*etym. L.* confinis), confines, borders

Confire, va. (*etym. L.* conficere, *to finish*), to preserve, to pickle, to steep, to soak

Confirmatif, ve, adj. (*etym. L.* confirmativus), confirmatory, confirmative

Confirmer, va. (*etym. L.* confirmare), to confirm, to strengthen; *se* —, vr. to prove true, to be confirmed

Confiseur, se, s. (*etym.* confire), confectioner

Confisquer, va. (*etym. L.* confiscare), to confiscate, to forfeit

Confit, e, adj. (*etym.* confire), dried, preserved, pickled, steeped, undone. — *en malice*, perfect master of mischief

Confiture, sf. (*often employed in the plur.*; *etym.* confire), preserves, jam

Conflit, sm. (*etym. L.* conflictus), conflict

Confluent, sm. confluence

Confluer, vn. (*etym. L.* confluere), to meet

Confondre, va. (*etym. L.* confundere), to mingle, to blend, to mix, to huddle together, to confuse, to disturb, to involve, to mistake, to abash; *se* —, vr. to be blended, to blend, to mingle, to mix together, to be confused, to be lost, to be lost in apologies

Conforme, adj. (*etym. L.* conformis), conformable to, true to, agreeable with. *Pour copie* —, conformable to the original

Conformément, adv. conformably to, in compliance with

Conformer, va. (*etym. L.* conformare), to conform. *Mal conformé*, badly made. *Se* —, vr. to conform to, to comply with, to submit

Conformité, sf. (*etym.* conforme), conformity, congenialness, consistency

Confraternité, sf. (*etym.* con, fraternité), brotherhood, fellowship, confraternity

Confrère, sm. (*etym.* con, frère), brother, brother-member, fellow-...

Confrérie, sf. brotherhood, sisterhood, fraternity

Confronter, va. (*etym.* con, front), to confront, to compare

Confus, e, adj. (*etym. L.* confusus), confused, jumbled together, intricate, abashed, ashamed

Confusément, adv. confusedly, indistinctly

Congé, sm. (*etym. L.* commeatus, *from* commeare, *to go, to pass away*), leave, discharge, furlough, holiday, warning, notice to quit, clearance, paying off, apophyge, apophysis. *Avoir fait un* —, to have served one's time. *Être en* —, to be absent on furlough, to have a holiday. *Donner* —, to give warning

Congédier, va. (*etym.* congé), to dismiss, to discharge, to pay off

Congélation, sf. (*etym.* congeler), congelation, congealment, freezing

Congeler, va. (*etym. L.* congelare), to congeal; *se* —, vr. to congeal

Congestion, sf. (*etym. L.* congestionem), congestion, determination of blood. — *cérébrale*, congestion of the brain

Conglomérer, va. (*etym. L.* conglomerare), to conglomerate

Congratuler, va. (*etym. L.* congratulari), to congratulate

Congre, sm. (*etym. L.* conger), conger-eel

Congréganiste, sm. (*etym.* congrégation), lay member

Congrès, sm. (*etym. L.* congressus), congress

‖**Congru, e**, adj. (*etym. L.* congruus), sufficient, proper

Conique, adj. conic, tapering

‖**Conjectural, e**, adj. (*etym. L.* conjecturalis), conjectural, speculative, of mere conjecture

Conjecturer, va. (*etym.* conjecture), to conjecture, to guess, to surmise

‖**Conjoint, e**, adj. (*etm.* com, joint), wedded, of partnership, conjoint, joined. —*s*, sm. plur. the husband and wife, the wedded couple

‖**Conjonctif, ve**, adj. (*etym. L.* conjunctivus), conjunctive

Conjonction, sf. (*etym. L.* conjunctionem), union, conjunction

Conjoncture, sf. (*etym.* conjoindre), conjuncture

Conjugaison, sf. (*etym.* conjuguer), conjugation

‖**Conjugal, e**, adj. (*etym. L.* conjugalis), conjugal, connubial

Conjuguer, va. (*etym. L.* conjugare), to conjugate; *se* —, vr. to be conjugated

Conjurateur, sm. (*etym. L.* conjurare), conjuror

Conjuration, sf. conspiracy, plot, incantation, conjuration, entreaty, fervent prayer. *Faire, tramer une* —, to form a conspiracy, to conspire or plot

Conjuré, e, adj. confederate. — sm. conspirator

Conjurer, va.n. (*etym. L.* conjurare), to conspire, to plot, to conjure, to charm away, to avert, to adjure, to beseech; *se* —, vr. to conspire together

Connaissance, sf. (*etym.* connaissant), knowledge, notion, learning, information, attainments, acquaintance, stag's footmark, cognizance. *Prendre* — *de*, to look into, to study, to take cognizance of. *Parler, agir avec* — *de cause*, to speak, to act upon good grounds. *Il est à ma* — *que*, I know well that. *Un homme de profondes* —*s*, a man of great learning. *Perdre* —, to swoon or faint away. *Tomber sans* —, to fall senseless. *Faire* — *avec, faire la* — *de*, to become acquainted with. ‡ *Se trouver en pays de* —, to feel quite at home

Connaissement, sm. (*etym.* connaitre), bill of lading

Connaisseur, se, s. connoisseur, good judge

Connaître, va. (*etym. L.* cognoscere), to know, to acquire information, to be acquainted with, to be skilled, to be aware of. — *son monde*, to know what people are. *Se* —, vr. to know oneself, to know each other, to be acquainted, to be a connoisseur, to understand. *Il s'y connaît*, he understands the thing. *Ne plus s'y* —, to be quite beside oneself

Connétable, sm. (*etym.* comes stabuli, *count of the stable*), constable. *Le grand* —, the lord high constable

Connétablie, sf. constable's office or jurisdiction

Connexion, Connexité, sf. (*etym. L.* connexionem, connexitatem), connexion

Connivег, va. (*etym. L.* connivere, *to wink*), to connive, to wink

Connu, sm. the known. ‡ — ! the trick is stale

Conquérant, e, s. adj. conqueror, conquering

Conquérir, va. (*etym. L.* conquirere), to conquer, to subdue, to overcome; *se* —, vr. to win

Conquête, sf. (*etym. L.* conquisita, *past part. fem. of* conquirere), conquest

Consacrant, adj. sm. (*etm.* consacrer), consecrating, consecrator

Consacré, e, adj. proper, right

Consacrer, va. (*etym. L.* consecrare), to consecrate, to dedicate, to give up wholly, to ordain, to devote, to sanctify, to sanction; *se* —, vr. to devote oneself, to set apart for oneself

Consanguin, e, adj. (*etym. L.* consanguineus), by the father's side

Consanguinité, sf. (*etm. L.* consanguinitas), consanguinity

Conscience, sf. (*etym. L.* conscientia), conscience, consciousness, conscientiousness, work paid by the day, compositors on the establishment. *Se faire* — *de quelque chose*, to scruple to do a thing. *En toute sûreté de* —, with a safe conscience. *Pour l'acquit de sa* —, for conscience' sake. *Avoir de la* —, to be conscientious. *Être homme de* —, to be a conscientious man

‖**Consciencieux, se**, adj. (*etym.* conscience), conscientious

Conscrit, sm. (*etym. L.* conscriptus), conscript, raw recruit, freshman, new boy. — adj. conscript

Consécrateur, adj. sm. (*etym. L.* consecrator), he who consecrates

‖**Consécutif, ve**, adj. (*etm. L.* consecutivus), consecutive

Conseil, sm. (*etym. L.* consilium), advice, counsel, resolution, course, adviser, council, board, committee. *C'est un homme de bon* —, he is a sensible man. ‡ *La nuit porte* —, take advice of your pillow

§**Conseiller, ère**, s. (*etym.* conseil), adviser, counsellor

§**Conseiller**, va. to advise, to counsel, to give advice; *se* —, vr. to seek advice, to be advised

Consentement, sm. consent, assent. *De mon* —, with my consent

Consentir, vn. (*etym. L.* consentire), to consent, to assent, to allow. *Qui ne dit mot consent*, silence gives consent

Conséquence, sf. (*etym. L.* consequentia), conclusion, consequence, inference. *Cela tire à* —, this might be drawn into a precedent. *Cela ne tire pas à* —, that proves nothing. *Cela est sans* —, that is immaterial

‖**Conséquent, e**, adj. (*etm. L.* consequens), consistent. — sm. consequent

Conservateur, trice, s. adj. (*etym. L.* conservator), preserver, guardian, commissioner, keeper, conservative

Conservation, sf. (*etym. L.* conservationem), state of preservation, guardianship, commissionership, jurisdiction. — *d'hypothèques*, registration

Conservatoire, sm. (*etm.* conserver), conservatory

Conserve, sf. (*etym.* conserver), preserves, pickles, consort, convoy, glasses, preservers. *Naviguer de* —, to keep company. *Perdre sa* —, to part from her consort

Conservé, e, past part. adj. preserved. *Être bien* —*e*, to bear one's age well, to look young

Conserver, va. (*etym. L.* conservare), to preserve, to keep, to maintain, to guard, to save, to lay by, to pickle, (*nav.*) to keep within sight of; *se* —, vr. to reserve for oneself, to keep, to look young, to look well for one's age, to preserve oneself, to remain, to be kept up.

‖**Considérable**, adj. (*etm.* considérer), notable, considerable, weighty, momentous

Considérant, sm. (*etym.* considérer), preamble, clause, grounds

Considération, sf. (*etym.* considérer), wariness, consideration, grounds, respect, weight, regard, respectability. *La prise en* — *d'une loi*, the second reading of a bill. *A la* — *de, en* — *de, par* — *pour*, out of regard for, on account of

§**Considéré, e**, adj. much respected, well looked upon

Considérer, va. (*etym. L.* considerare), to gaze on, to look at, to consider, to ponder on, to examine. † *Tout bien considéré*, all things duly considered. *Se* —, vr. to behold oneself, to gaze on *or* look at each other, to value oneself, to have a consideration for each other

§**Consignataire**, sm. (*etym.* consigner), depositary, consignee

§**Consignation**, sf. (*etym.* consigner), consignment, deposit. *La caisse des dépôts et* —*s*, the Government deposit and consignment office. *Faire une* — *de*, to consign

§**Consigne**, sf. (*etym.* consigner), orders, instructions, regulation, gate-keeper. *Forcer la* —, to force a sentry, to break through orders. *Lever la* —, to revoke orders

§**Consigner**, va. to deposit, to consign, to record, to confine, to keep in. *On a consigné la troupe*, the soldiers are confined to their barracks. *Je l'ai consigné à ma porte*, I have given orders not to admit him

Consistance, sf. (*etym.* consistant), consistency, firmness, stability, credit, consideration, nature. *Esprit sans* —, an unsteady mind. *Étoffe sans* —, a flimsy stuff. *N'avoir pas de* —, to be unsettled. *Avoir peu de* —, not to be depended on

Consistant, e, adj. consistent, consisting

Consister, vn. (*etym. L.* consistere), to consist

Consistoire, sm. (*etym. L.* consistorium, *from* consistere), consistory

‖**Consistorial, e**, adj. (*etym.* consistoire), belonging to a consistory

Consolant, e, adj. consoling, consolatory, comforting, comfortable

Consolateur, trice, s. adj. (*etym. L.* consolator), consoler, consoling

Consolation, sf. (*etym.* consoler), comfort, consolation, solace. ‡ *Une fiche de* —, a forfeit, a bit of comfort

Consoler, va. (etym. L. consolari), to comfort, to console, to solace; se —, vr. to be comforted, to be consoled, to console oneself, to get over. — d'un refus, to get over a refusal

Consolidé, e, adj. consolidated. Le tiers —, the three per cent. consols. La dette —e, the funded debt

Consolider, va. (etym. L. consolidare), to consolidate, to fund, to heal up; se —, vr. to consolidate, to be strengthened by, to gather strength from, to take root

Consommateur, sm. (etym. consommer), consumer, perfecter

Consommation, sf. (etym. consommer), consumption, waste, consummation, end, completion. Jusqu'à la — des temps, till the end of time

Consommé, e, sm. adj. gravy soup, jelly broth; consummate, perfect, accomplished, used up

Consommer, va. (etym. L. consummare), to consummate, to complete, to fill up the measure of, to consume

Consomption, sf. (etym. L. consumptionem), consumption, decline

Consonnance, sf. (etym. L. consonantia), consonance

Consonne, sf. (etym. L. consonus), consonant

Consorts, sm. plur. (etym. L. consors, sharing the same lot), associates, company

Conspirateur, trice, smf. (etym. conspirer), conspirator

Conspiration, sf. (etym. L. conspiratio), conspiracy, plot

Conspirer, va.n. to conspire, to plot, to hatch treason

Conspuer, va. (etym. L. conspuere, from cum, and spuere, to spit), to treat with scorn, to point one's finger at

Constance, sf. (etym. L. constantia), constancy, steadfastness, firmness of purpose, patience

Constant, e, adj. (etym. L. constans), constant, steadfast, unshaken, steady, lasting, uninterrupted, undoubted

Constater, va. (etym. L. cum, status), to aver, to prove, to ascertain, to verify

Consterné, e, adj. of dismay or consternation, dismayed, struck with consternation

Consterner, va. (etym. L. consternere, to throw down), to strike with consternation, to dismay

Constipé, e, adj. constipated, costive

Constiper, va. (etym. L. constipare, from cum, and stipare, to condense), to bind, to constipate

Constituant, e, adj. (etym. constituer), constituent

Constitué, e, adj. constituted, established. Les corps —s, the bodies corporate. Enfant bien, mal —, a healthy child, an unhealthy child

Constituer, va. (etym. L. constituere), to constitute, to make up, to appoint, to empower

Constitutif, ve, adj. (etym. constituer), constitutive

Constitution, sf. (etym. L. constitutio), constitution, settlement, annuity, declaration of powers

Constitutionnalité, sf. (etym. constitutionnel), constitutionality

Constitutionnel, le, adj. (etym. constitution), constitutional

Constructeur, sm. (etym. L. constructor), builder, constructor

Construire, va. (etym. L. construere), to build, to construct, to erect, to make, to frame; se —, vr. to build oneself, to construct for oneself, to be constructed

Consubstantiel, le, adj. (etym. L. consubstantialis), consubstantial

Consulaire, sm. adj. a man of consular rank, consular

Consulat, sm. (etym. L. consulatus), consulship, consulate

Consultant, adj. (etym. consulter), advising. Avocat —, chamber counsel. Médecin —, consulting physician

Consultatif, ve, adj. (etym. consulter), consultative, deliberative. Avoir voix —ve, to be admitted to give one's opinion, but not to vote

Consulter, va. (etym. L. consultare), to consult, to advise with

Consumant, e, adj. consuming, devouring, wasting

Consumer, va. (etym. L. consumere), to consume, to destroy, to wear out; se —, vr. to be consumed or worn out or wasted, to pine away, to exhaust oneself, to squander away one's fortune, to undermine one's health, to waste one's time

Contagieux, se, adj. (etym. L. contagiosus), infectious, contagious, catching

Conte, sm (etym. see Conter), tale, story. —s bleus, à dormir debout, idle tales. — fait à plaisir, story of one's own invention. — en l'air, unlikely story

Contemplateur, trice, s. (etym. L. contemplator), contemplator, contemplative man or woman

Contemplatif, ve, adj. (etym. L. contemplativus), contemplative, thoughtful, musing, dreamy

Contempler, va. (etym. L. contemplari), to contemplate, to behold, to gaze on, to muse on; se —, vr. to look at oneself, to gaze upon each other, to admire oneself

Contemporain, e, adj. (etym. L. contemporaneus), contemporary

Contempteur, trice, adj. s. (etym. L. contemptor, from contemnere), he or she who despises

Contenance, sf. (etym. contenir), capaciousness, extent, burden, countenance, demeanour. Cela sert de —, that keeps one in countenance. Ne savoir quelle — tenir, faire, to be at a loss how to look. Faire bonne —, to put a good face on the matter. Perdre —, to be put out of countenance, to stand abashed

Contenant, e, adj. containing. — sm. container

Contenir, va. (etym. L. continere), to hold, to contain, to confine, to keep back or in, to curb; se —, vr. to keep down one's anger or joy, to restrain oneself

Content, e, adj. (etym. L. contentus), glad, cheerful, contented, pleased, satisfied

Contentement, sm. (etym. contenter), satisfaction, contentedness, cheerfulness, content. — passe richesse, content is beyond riches

Contenter, va. to content, to satisfy, to humour, to please; se —, vr. to indulge oneself

Contentieux, sm. (etym. L. contentiosus), affairs in litigation, disputed claims office. Chef du —, director of litigious affairs

Contention, sf. (etym. L. contentio), wrangling, contention, heat, warmth, intenseness of thought

Contenu, sm. contents

Conter, va. (etym. L. computare, to count), to relate, to tell stories. — ses peines, to confide one's sorrows. En —, to deceive. En — de belles, to tell fine stories. Se —, vr. to be told or related, to tell each other

Conteste, sf. (etym. contester), dispute. Sans —, indisputably

Contester, va. (etym. L. contestari), to contest, to call in question, to dispute; — vn. to wrangle, to quarrel; se —, vr. to be contested, to contest each other

Conteur, sm. (etym. conte), story-teller

Contexte, sm. (etym. L. contextus), context

Contigu, ë, adj. (etym. L. contiguus), contiguous, adjoining, adjacent. Être — à, to border upon

Contiguïté, sf. (etym. contigu), contiguity, contiguousness

Contingence, sf. (etym. contingent), contingency

Continu, e, adj. (etym. L. continuus), continuous, continual, continued. — sm. matter, a body

Continuateur, trice, s. (etym. continuer), continuator, continuer

Continuel, le, adj. (etym. continu), continual

Continuer, va. (etym. L. continuare), to continue, to go on with, to persevere in, to prolong

Continuité, sf. (etym. L. continuitas), continuity, continuance, series, continuousness

Contondant, e, adj. (etym. L. contundere), blunt

Contorsion, sf. (etym. L. contorsio), contortion, grin, distortion

Contour, sm. (etym. see Contourner), contour, outline, folds, circumference

Contourné, e, adj. distorted

Contourner, va. (etym. con, tourner), to distort, to deform; se —, vr. to grow crooked

Contractant, e, adj. (etym. see Contracter), contracting

Contracté, e, adj. contracted

Contracter, va. (etym. L. contractus), to contract. — une maladie, to catch a disease

Contractilité, sf. (etym. contractile), contractility

Contradicteur, sm. (etym. L. contradictor), contradicter, opponent

Contradictoire, adj. (etym. see Contradicteur), contradictory, after hearing both parties

Contraindre, va. (etym. L. constringere), to constrain, to compel, to lay or impose a restraint upon; se —, vr. to constrain oneself, to lay a restraint upon oneself

Contraint, e, adj. constrained, stiff, ill at ease. Un aveu —, a reluctant confession. Un silence —, an awkward silence

Contrainte, sf. (etym. contraindre), constraint

Contraire, adj. (etym. L. contrarius), contrary, unfavourable, adverse. — sm. contrary; pl. things of the most opposite nature, contraries. Aller au — de, to go against, to gainsay

Contrariant, e, adj. (etym. contrarier), cross, provoking, annoying, vexatious. Que c'est —! how provoking!

Contrarier, va. (etym. L. contrarius), to thwart, to cross, to be contrary to, to contradict, to vex; se —, vr. to thwart, to contradict, to tease each other

Contrariété, sf. (etym. L. contrarietas), contradiction, contrariety, annoyance

Contraste, sm. (etym. see Contraster), contrast

Contraster, va.n. (etym. L. contra, stare), to contrast

Contrat, sm. (*etym. L.* contractus, *past part. of* contrahere), contract, deed. — *de mariage*, marriage settlements

Contravention, sf. (*etym.* contrevenir), infraction, offence. *Être en* —, to infringe the regulations

Contre, adv. sm. (*etym. L.* contra), close to, near, over against. *Le pour et le* —, the pros and cons

Contre-allée, sf. (contre *is invariable in this and all similar compounds*), sidewalk, side-alley

Contre-amiral, sm. rear-admiral

Contre-appel, sm. second call

Contre-balancer, va. to make up for, to counterbalance, to countervail; *se* —, vr. to counterbalance one another

Contrebande, sf. (*etym. I.* contrabbando, *from* contra, *and* bando, *decree, order*), smuggling, contraband, smuggled goods. *Faire la* —, to be a smuggler. *Faire entrer en* —, *passer en* —, to smuggle in. *De* —, smuggled. *Vaisseau de* —, smuggler

Contrebandier, ère, s. smuggler

Contre-bas, adv. downwards

Contrebasse, sf. double bass

Contre-batterie, sf. counter-battery, counterplot

Contrecarrer, va. to thwart, to cross, to counteract; *se* —, vr. to cross one another

Contre-cœur, adv. reluctantly, grudgingly, against one's will

Contre-coup, sm. rebound, glancing off, counterblow, consequence

Contredanse, sf. quadrille

Contredire, va. (*etym. L.* contradicere), to contradict, to gainsay, to be inconsistent with, to disprove; *se* —, vr. to contradict oneself, to contradict each other, to be contradictory, to be inconsistent

Contredit, sm. contradiction. *Sans* —, unquestionably

Contrée, sf. (*etym. It.* contrada), country

Contrefaçon, sf. counterfeiting, counterfeit, forgery, piracy

Contrefacteur, sm. counterfeiter, pirate, imitator

Contrefaire, va. to counterfeit, to mimic, to ape, to pretend to be, to forge, to pirate; *se* —, vr. to disguise oneself, to play the counterfeit, to dissemble

Contrefait, e, adj. counterfeited, deformed

Contre-fort, sm. counterfort, stiffener, lesser range

Contre-jour, sm. false light. *A* —, in a false light

Contre-lettre, sf. counter-deed, defeasance

Contre-maître, sm. master's mate, boatswain's mate, overseer, foreman

Contre-marche, sf. counter-march, counter-movement

Contre-marque, sf. counter-mark, (*theat.*) check

Contre-partie, sf. counterpart, reverse

Contre-pente, sf. descent

Contre-pied, sm. back-scent, reverse

Contre-poids, sm. counterpoise, counterbalance

Contre-poil, sm. wrong way. *A* —, against the hair *or* grain, the wrong way

Contre-poison, sm. antidote, counter-poison

¶**Contre-rail,** sm. guard-rail

Contrescarpe, sf. (*etym.* contre, escarpe), counterscarp

Contre-sens, sm. wrong meaning, opposite meaning, misconstruction, misconception, contrary to common sense, wrong side. *A* —, in a wrong sense. *Prendre le* — *de*, to put a wrong construction on. *Faire des* —, to make faults of translation. † *Jouer à* —, (*theat.*) to act quite wrong

Contre-signer, va. to countersign

Contre-temps, sm. disappointment, untoward accident, unseasonable act, counter-measure. *A* —, out of season

Contrevenant, sm. offender, transgressor

Contrevenir, vn. to infringe, to transgress, to offend

Contrevent, sm. shutter, straining piece

Contre-vérité, sf. irony, ironical speech

Contribuable, adj. (*etym.* contribuer), tax-payer

Contribuer, vn. (*etym. L.* contribuere), to contribute, to have a share, to be accessory, to conduce, to tend, to be laid under contribution

Contribution, sf. (*etym. L.* contributio), contribution, share, tax, average, average share. — *foncière*, land-tax. —*s directes*, *indirectes*, assessed taxes, excise revenue. *Mettre à* —, to lay under contribution

Contrister, va. (*etym. L.* contristare), to grieve, to pain, to cast a gloom over, to sadden. *Un visage contristé*, a woebegone countenance. *Se* —, vr. to feel grieved

Contrit, e, adj. (*etym. L.* contritus, *from* cum, *and* tritus, *ground down*), contrite, penitent, grieved

Contrôle, sm. (*contract. for* contre, rôle), control, counter-register, stamp, controller's office, stamp office, check-taker's office, lists, rolls

Contrôler, va. (*contract. for* contre, rôler), to control, to find fault with, to register, to check, to stamp, to try

Contrôleur, se, s. (*etym.* contrôler), comptroller, fault-finder

Controuver, va. (*etym.* con, trouver), to devise, to forge, to invent

Controverse, sf. (*etym. L.* controversia), controversy

Controversé, e, adj. controverted

Contumace, sf. adj. (*etym. L.* contumax), contumacy, contumacious

Contumax, adj. (*etym. L.* contumax), contumacious

¶**Contusionner,** va. (*etm.* contusion), to bruise

Convaincant, e, adj. convincing

Convaincre, va. (*etym. L.* convincere), to convince, to convict; *se* —, vr. to convince or satisfy oneself, to be convinced

‖**Convenable,** adj. (*etym.* convenir), proper, suitable, seasonable, convenient, beseeming, worthy, decent, well-bred, unobjectionable, respectful. *D'un ton* —, in a proper tone

Convenance, sf. (*etym. L.* convenientia), relation, similarity, decency, propriety, decorum, good breeding. *Mariage de* —, suitable marriage. *Blesser les* —*s*, to break through all decorum

Convenir, vn. (*etym. L.* convenire), to agree, to own, to acknowledge, to grant, to settle, to suit, to be right, to be proper; *se* —, vr. to suit each other, to agree

Conventicule, sm. (*etym. L.* conventiculum), conventicle

‖**Conventionnel, le,** adj. (*etym.* convention), conventional

Convenu, e, adj. settled, agreed. *C'est* —, it is a settled thing

Converger, vn. (*etym. L.* convergere), to converge

Convers, e, adj. s. (*etym. L.* conversus), lay (brother *or* sister)

Conversation, sf. (*etym. L.* conversatio), conversation, talk, discourse, chat. *Être en* — *avec*, to be talking with. *Être à la* —, to attend to the conversation

Converser, vn. (*etym. L.* conversari), to converse, to talk, to hold a conversation with, to chat

Conversion, sf. (*etym. L.* conversio), conversion, turning, change

Converti, e, s. convert

Convertir, va. (*etym. L.* convertere), to convert, to bring over, to turn, to change; *se* —, vr. to become converted, to be changed, to be convertible

Convertissement, sm. (*etym.* convertir), conversion

Convertisseur, sm. (*etm.* convertir), a person anxious to convert others to his own way of thinking, an exchange agent

Convexe, adj. (*etym. L.* convexus), convex

Convexité, sf. (*etym. L.* convexitas), convexity

Conviction, sf. (*etym. L.* convictio), conviction, convincing proof. *Pièces de* —, articles produced in evidence

Convié, e, s. (*etym. see* CONVIER), guest

Convier, va. (*etym. I.* convitare), to invite, to desire, to urge, to impel

Convive, sm. (*etym. L.* conviva), guest, table-companion

Convoi, sm. (*etym. see* CONVOYER), funeral train, funeral, convoy, train. *Suivre le* —, to attend the funeral. — *d'aller*, *de retour*, down-train, up-train. — *de grande vitesse*, *de petite vitesse*, fast train, slow train

Convoiter, va. (*etym. L.L.* cupiditia), to covet, to long for

Convoitise, sf. longing, covetousness

Convoler, vn. (*etym. L.* convolare), to marry again

Convoquer, va. (*etym. L.* convocare), to summon, to convoke, to call together

Convoyer, va. (*etym. L.* cum, via), to convoy, to escort

‖**Convulsif, ve,** adj. (*etym. L.* convulsus), convulsive, convulsed

Convulsionnaire, adj. (*etym.* convulsion), convulsionary

Coopérateur, trice, s. (*etym. L.* cooperator), fellow-labourer

Coopérer, vn. (*etym. L.* cooperari), to cooperate, to concur, to conduce

Coordonner, va. (*etym.* co, ordonner), to arrange in order

Copartageant, e, s. (*etym.* co, partager), copartner

Copeau, sm. (*etym.* couper), shaving, chip

Copie, sf. (*etym. L.* copia), copy

Copier, va. to copy, to mimic

‖**Copieux, se,** adj. (*etym. L.* copiosus), plentiful, copious, abundant

Copiste, sm. (*etym.* copier), copyist, amanuensis

Copropriétaire, sm. (*etym.* co *for* com, *and* propriétaire), joint-owner

‖**Copulatif, ve,** adj. (*etym. see* COPULE), copulative

Copule, sf. (*etym. L.* copula), copula

Coq, sm. (*onomat.*), cock, ship's cook, weather-cock. ‡ *Être comme un* — *en pâte*, to live in clover. — *d'Inde*, turkey, turkey-cock. — *d-l'âne*, nonsense, cock and bull story

Coque, sf. (*etym. L.* concha, *shell*), shell, egg-shell, cocoon, hull. *Œufs à la* —, boiled eggs. *Au sortir de la* —, as soon as hatched

Coquecigrue, sf. (*etym. ?*), a kind of fabulous animal; *plur.* (*fig.*) nonsense, idle stories

Coquelicot, sm. (*etym. ?*), poppy, corn-poppy

Coqueluche, sf. (*etym. L.L.* cuculuccia, *hood*), cowl, hooping-cough, (‡) darling

Coquerico, sm. (*onomat.*), cock-a-doodle-doo

‖**Coquet, te,** adj. (*etym.* coq), coquettish

Coqueter, vn. to coquet

Coquetier, sm. (*etym.* coque), egg-merchant, poulterer, egg-cup

Coquette, sf. coquette, flirt, jilt. *C'est une franche* —, she is a downright flirt

Coquetterie, sf. (*etym.* coqueter), coquetry, coquettishness, flirtation, finicalness, affectation

§**Coquillage,** sm. (*etym.* coquille), shell, shell-fish, shell-work

§**Coquille,** sf. (*etym. L.* conchylia, *plur. of* conchylium), shell, spandrel, wrong letter, small-post, foot-board, movable kitchen-grate. *Rentrer dans sa* —, to draw in one's horns. *Épée à poignée en* —, basket-hilted sword

Coquin, sm. (*etym. L.* coquinus, *from* coquus), rascal, rogue, knave, scoundrel. *Vie de* —, lazy life. — adj. easy, lazy. —*e*, sf. hussy, jade, slut

Coquinerie, sf. piece of knavery, deed of rascality

Cor, sm. (*etym. L.* cornu), corn (*on the feet*), horn, bugle, French horn. *Donner, sonner du* —, to blow the horn. *A* — *et à cri*, with hue and cry. *Demander à* — *et à* —, to clamour for

§**Corail,** sm., **Coraux,** plur. (*etym. L.* corallium), coral. *Banc de* —, coral reef

Corbeau, sm. (*etym. L.L.* corvellus, *dimin. of L.* corvus), crow, raven, corbel, grappling-iron

§**Corbeille,** sf. (*etym. L.* corbicula, *dimin. of* corbis, *basket*), basket, flower-bed, corbel. — *de mariage*, wedding presents

§**Corbillard,** sm. (*etym. prop. name* Corbeil), hearse, young raven

§**Corbillon,** sm. (*etym.* corbeille), basket

Corbin, sm. (*etym. L.* corvinus, *from* corvus), crow. *A bec de* —, bill-headed

Cordage, sm. (*etym.* corde), rope, cord, cordage, rigging, coil of rope

Corde, sf. (*etym. L.* chorda), rope, cord, string, twine, packthread, whipcord, clothes-line, halter, the gallows, chord, point, thread, twist, chorda, span. *Mériter la* —, to deserve hanging. †*Friser la* —, narrowly to escape hanging. ‡*Un homme de sac et de* —, a downright villain. *Instrument à* —*s*, stringed instrument. — *à boyau*, catgut. *Flatter la* —, to run one's fingers lightly over the strings. *La* — *sensible*, the sensitive part. *Habit usé jusqu'à la* —, *qui montre la* —, a coat worn threadbare

Cordeau, sm. (*etym.* corde), line. *Tirer au* —, to lay out by the line

Cordelier, sm. (*etym.* cordelle, *dimin. of* corde), Franciscan, Franciscan monk

Cordelière, sf. cordelier's girdle, knotted rope

Corder, va. to twist, to cord

Corderie, sf. rope-making, ropery, rope-walk, store-room, rope-selling

Cordial, sm. (*etym. L.* cor, cordis, *heart*), cordial. ‖—, —*e*, adj. hearty, cordial, sincere, strengthening

Cordialité, sf. cordiality, heartiness

Cordier, sm. rope-maker

Cordon, sm. yarn, twist, string, strand, ribbon, check-string, bow-string, girdle, band, line, milled edge. ‡— *bleu*, first-rate cook

Cordonnerie, sf. (*etym.* cordonnier), boot and shoe making, shoe-maker's trade, shoe-room

Cordonnet, sm. (*etym.* cordon), twist, silk-twist, braid, milled edge

Cordonnier, sm. (*etym. O.F.* cordoan, *leather from* Cordoue [Cordova], *a town in Spain*), boot and shoe maker

Coreligionnaire, sm. (*etym.* co, religion), coreligionist

Coriace, adj. (*etym. L.* corium, *leather*), tough, close-fisted

Coriandre, sf. (*etym. L.* coriandrum), coriander

Corinthien, ne, adj. (*etym.* Corinthe), Corinthian

Corme, sm. (*etym. L.* cornum), fruit of the service-tree

Cormier, sm. sorb-apple tree, service-tree

Cormoran, sm. (*etym.* cor *for* corb, *crow, and Bret.* môrvran, *from* mor, *sea, and* vran, *crow*), cormorant

Cornaline, sf. (*etym. L.* cornu), cornelian

Corne, sf. (*etym. L.* cornu), horn, hoof, outer rind, corner, dog's-ear. — *d'abondance*, cornucopia. — *d'amorce*, priming horn. — *d'Ammon*, ammonite. *Chapeau à trois* —*s*, cocked hat, three-cornered hat. *Faire des* —*s à un livre*, to dog's-ear a book. — *d'artimon*, (*nav.*) gaff

Cornée, sf. (*etym.* corne), cornea

§**Corneille,** sf. (*etym. L.* cornicula, *dimin. of* cornix), rook, crow

Cornemuse, sf. (*etym.* corne, *in the sense of* cor, *and* muse, musette), bagpipe

Corner, va. to trumpet about; — vn. to sound the horn, to blow the horn badly, to speak through an ear-trumpet, to tingle, to sing. *Les oreilles me cornent*, I have got a singing in my ears

Cornet, sm. (*dimin. of* corne), cornet, horn, ink-horn, dice-box, box, calamary. — *à bouquin*, cowherd's horn. — *à piston*, cornopean. — *acoustique*, ear-trumpet

Cornette, sf. (*etym.* cornet), mob-cap, commodore's pendant, cornet. — sm. cornet

Corniche, sf. (*etym. I.* cornice, cornicione), cornice. *A* —, surbased

Cornichon, sm. (*etym.* corne), gherkin, pickled gherkin, small horn, (‡) ninny

§**Cornouiller,** sm. (*etym.* cornouille, *from the L.* corniculum), cornelian-tree

Cornu, e, adj. (*etym. L.* cornutus), horned, preposterous

Cornue, sf. retort

Corollaire, adj. sm. (*etym. L.* corollarium), corollary

Corolle, sf. (*etym. L.* corolla), corolla

‖**Corporel, le,** adj. (*etym. L.* corporalis), corporeal, bodily, corporal

Corps, sm. (*etym. L.* corpus), body, substance, volume, corps, trunk, frame, main point, consistency, corporation, depth, barrel. *Se tuer le* — *et l'âme*, (*fig.*) to work one's life and soul out. *Répondre* — *pour* —, to be personally answerable for. †*Un pauvre* —, a poor creature. †*Un drôle de* —, a queer fellow. *N'avoir rien dans le* —, to have eaten nothing for several hours, to have no mettle. *A* — *perdu*, headlong, with might and main. *A son* — *défendant*, in self-defence, reluctantly, against one's will. *A mi-* —, in the middle of the body. *Lutter* — *à* —, to fight hand to hand. *Le vaisseau avait péri* — *et biens*, the ship had been utterly lost. — *de bâtiment*, building. *Faire* — *avec*, to be one body with. *Aller en* —, to go in a body. *Il est l'honneur de son* —, he is an honour to his company. — *de délit*, main evidence. — *de preuves*, whole body of evidence. — *de garde*, the guard, guard-house

Corpulence, sf. (*etym. L.* corpulentia), stoutness, corpulency

Correcteur, trice, s. (*etym. L.* correctorem), corrector, correctress, reader of the proofs

‖**Correctif, ve,** adj. sm. (*etym.* correction), corrective

‖**Correctionnel, le,** adj. relative to misdemeanours. *Le tribunal de police* —*le*, the police court

‖**Corrélatif, ve,** adj. sm. (*etym.* co, relatif), correlative

Corrélation, sf. (*etym.* co, relation), correlativeness

Correspondance, sf. (*etym.* correspondant), correspondence, letter-writing, letters, connections, intercourse, return. *Voiture de* —, branch coach

Correspondant, e, adj. sm. (*etym.* correspondre), corresponding, correspondent

Correspondre, vn. (*etym. O.F.* co, respondre), to correspond, to be in correspondence, to communicate; *se* —, vr. to correspond, to be well matched

Corriger, va. (*etym. L.* corrigere), to correct, to rectify, to set right, to cure, to soften, to temper; *se* —, vr. to correct oneself, to cure oneself

Corroborant, e, *also* **Corroboratif, ve,** adj. (*etym.* corroborer), strengthening, tonic, corroborative

Corroborer, va. (*etym. L.* cum, roborare), to strengthen, to corroborate, to confirm

Corroder, va. (*etym. L.* corrodere), to corrode, to canker

Corrompre, va. (*etym. L.* corrumpere), to corrupt, to taint, to spoil, to rot, to destroy, to deprave, to vitiate, to bribe; *se* —, vr. to be corrupted, to grow corrupt, to spoil

Corrompu, e, adj. past part. corrupt, corrupted, depraved, dissolute, spoilt

Corrosif, ve, sm. adj. (*etym. L.* corrosivus), corrodent; corrosive, corroding

Corroyer, va. (*etym. O.F.* conroi, *the act of preparing*), to curry, to dress, to puddle with clay, to hammer, to plane, to roll, to weld

Corroyeur, sm. (*etym.* corroyer), currier, leather-dresser

Corrupteur, trice, s. adj. (*etym. L.* corruptor), corruptive, corrupting, fraught with corruption

Corruptibilité, sf. (*etym. L.* corruptibilitatem), corruptibility

Cors, sm. pl. (*etym. L.* cornu), (*hunt.*) starts, branches. *Un cerf dix* —, a full-grown stag

Corsage, sm. (*etym.* corps), shape, bust, chest, boddice

Corsaire, sm. (*etym. I.* corsa, *course*), privateer, captain of a privateer, corsair, pirate

‡**Corsé, e,** adj. (*etym.* corps), strong, racy

Corselet, sm. corselet

Corset, sm. stays

‡**Corsetière,** sf. staymaker

Cortége, sm. (*etym. I.* corteggio, *from* corte, *court*), retinue, train, troop, crowd

Corvéable, adj. s. (*etym.* corvée), bound to do villein service

Corvée, sf. (*etym. L.L.* corvata), villein service, duty service, (*milit.*) work (sweeping, carrying, &c.), (*fig.*) drudgery

Cosse, sf. (*etym. Fl.* schosse, *a cod*), pod, cod, husk, shell, rind

Cossu, e, adj. (*etym.* cosse), podded, husked, (†) substantial, wealthy

Costumé, e, adj. dressed, in a fancy dress

Costumer, va. to dress; *se* —, vr. to dress as

Costumier, sm. fancy-dress dealer, property-keeper

Cote, sf. (*etym. L.* quota), quota, share, price-current, quotation of exchanges, number. ‡ *Faire une — mal taillée*, to take one with the other

Côte, sf. (*etym. L.* costa), rib, coast, shore, hill, declivity, fillet. *Bas à —s*, ribbed stockings. *Faire* —, to run ashore

Côté, sm. (*etym. L.* costa), side, part, quarter, way, beam-ends. *Le bas — d'une église, d'une route*, the aisle of a church, the lower side of a road

Côteau, sm. hill

Côtelette, sf. chop, cutlet

Coter, va. (*etym.* cote), to number, to endorse, to quote

Coterie, sf. (*etym. L.L.* coteria, *from* cota, *a cottage*), circle, coterie, a set, a club

Cothurne, sm. buskin

Côtier, ère, adj. sm. (*etym.* côte), coasting, coaster

§**Cotillon**, sm. (*etym.* cotte), petticoat, (*danc.*) cotillon

Cotisation, sf. (*etym.* cotiser), assessment, subscription, clubbing

Cotiser, va. (*etym.* cote), to rate; *se* —, vr. to club together, to open a subscription

Coton, sm. (*etym. Ar.* gothon), cotton, down. — *filé*, cotton yarn, spun cotton. — *plat*, darning cotton. ‡ *Élever un enfant dans du* —, to bring up a child in lavender. ‡ *Filer, jeter un mauvais* —, (*fig.*) to be going down in the world, to be going fast

Cotonnade, sf. cotton stuffs, cotton goods

Cotonneux, se, adj. downy, nappy, mealy

Cotonnier, sm. cotton-tree

Cotonnier, ère, adj. (*etym.* coton), cotton

Côtoyer, va. to walk by the side of, to coast along

Cotret, sm. (*etym. L.L.* costeretum, *a bundle, a load*), small fagot. ‡ *Huile de* —, stirrup oil

Cotte, sf. (*etym. L.L.* cotta), petticoat, — *d'armes*, coat of arms

Cotuteur, sm. (*etym.* co, tuteur), joint-guardian

Cou, *also* **Col**, sm. (*etym. L.* collum), neck. ‡ *Prendre ses jambes à son* —, to take to one's heels

‖**Couard, e**, adj. sm. (*etym. L.* cauda, *tail*), cowardly, coward

Couardise, sf. (*etym.* couard), cowardice

Couchage, sm. (*etym.* coucher), bed, night's bed, bedding

Couchant, adj. m. (*etym.* coucher), setting. *Chien* —, setter, (*fig.*) toad-eater, fawner. — sm. the setting sun, the western heaven, wane, decline

Couche, sf. (*etym. Prov.* colga), bed, couch, delivery, linen, stratum, layer, seam, coating. *Faire ses —s*, to be confined. *Une fausse* —, a miscarriage

Couchée, sf. (*etym.* couché, *from* coucher), stopping for the night, night's lodging

Coucher, va. (*etym. L.* collocare, *to place with*), to put to bed, to undress, to lay down, to bend down, to write down, to stake; — vn. to sleep, to go to bed. — *à la belle étoile*, to sleep in the open air. *Se* —, vr. to go to bed, to lie down, to set, to go to roost

Coucher, sm. going to bed, bedtime, sunset

Couchette, sf. bedstead

Coucheur, se, s. bed-fellow

Couci-couci, loc. adv. (*etym. I.* cosi, cosi), so so, middling

Coucou, sm. cuckoo, Dutch clock, cowslip, barren strawberry plant

Coude, sm. (*etym. L.* cubitus), elbow, turn, bend. † *Lever le* —, to tipple

Coudé, e, adj. (*etym.* coude), bent, cranked

Coudée, sf. cubit. *Avoir ses —s franches*, to have elbow-room, to be at perfect liberty

Cou-de-pied, sm. instep

Coudoyer, va. (*etym.* coude), to jostle, to elbow

Coudre, va. (*etym. L.* consuere, *to sew with*), to sew, to stitch, to tack

Coudrier, sm. (*etym. L.* corylus, *nut-tree*), hazel-tree, nut-tree

Couenne, sf. (*etym. L.* cutis, *skin ?*), rind, sward, coat, buffy coating

Couenneux, se, adj. (*etym.* couenne), swardlike, buffy. *Angine —se*, diphtheria

Coulage, sm. (*etym.* couler), leakage, waste, scalding of linen

Coulant, e, adj. (*etym.* couler), running, flowing, fluent, smooth. ‡ *Homme — en affaires*, a man pleasant to deal with. — sm. diamond slide, slide

Coulée, sf. (*etym.* couler), running hand, tapping

Couler, vn. (*etym. L.* colare, *to filter*), to flow, to run, to trickle, to glide away; — va. to spend, to pass, to strain, to slip, to slur, to cast, to sink, to scald linen. † *Un homme coulé*, a ruined man. *Se* —, vr. to creep, to glide, to slip, to do for oneself

Couleur, sf. (*etym. L.* colorem), colour, hue, dye, complexion, brown, character, paint, pretence, suit, colours. *Haut en* —, florid. *Reprendre* —, to come to life again. *Les pâles —s*, the green sickness. *Prendre* —, to brown, to look well, to declare oneself openly. *Donner de la* —, to follow suit

Couleuvre, sf. (*etym. L.* colubra), adder, snake. ‡ *Avaler des —s*, to put up with mortifications

Coulevrine, sf. (*etym.* couleuvre), culverine

Coulis, sm. (*etym.* couler), "coulis," cullis. — adj. *Un vent* —, a draught

Coulisse, sf. (*etym.* coulis), groove, slide, side-scenes, side-walks, running string, galley. ‡ *Faire les yeux en* —, to look sideways

¶**Coulissier**, sm. side-walk, stockbroker

Couloir, sm. (*etym.* couler), lobby, passage, strainer

Coulure, sf. dropping, falling off, running out

Coup, sm. (*etym. Gr.* κόλαφος, *a blow*), blow, stroke, knock, shock, wound, discharge, resolution, draught, aim, throw, move, thrust

‖**Coupable**, s. adj. (*etym. L.* culpabilis), guilty, culpable, wrongful

Coupant, e, sm. adj. edge; sharp, sharp-edged

Coupe, sf. (*etym. L.L.* cuppa, *cup*), cup, goblet, basin, crater; (*etym.* couper), cutting, cutting down, shape, profile, section, plan, cut. ‡ *Faire sauter la* —, to make the pass

Coupé, sm. chariot, front seats, (*danc.*) coupee

Coupé, e, adj. intersected, diversified, loose, diluted

Coupe-gorge, sm. cut-throat place, den of thieves; *plur.* des coupe-gorges

Coupe-jarret, sm. cut-throat, ruffian; *plur.* des coupe-jarrets

Couper, va. (*etym.* coup), to cut, to fell, to lop off, to chop off, to clip, to divide, to cross, to chap, to break in upon, to intercept, to dilute, to mix, to trump; — vn. to be sharp, to cut well, to take a short cut, to trump; *se* —, vr. to cut oneself, to cut each other's throat, to be cut, to intersect, to contradict oneself, to be chafed

Couperet, sm. chopper, cleaver

Couperose, sf. (*etym. ?*), copperas, red pimples

Couperosé, e, adj. blotched and pimpled, mottled with red

Coupeur, se, s. cutter, player

Couple, sf. (*etym. L.* copula), couple, brace, leash. — sm. pair, couple

Coupler, va. to couple together

Couplet, sm. stanza, verse

Coupoir, sm. large knife

Coupole, sf. (*etym. I.* cupola), cupola, dome

Coupon, sm. remnant, part, dividend warrant, coupon, box-ticket

Coupure, sf. cut, suppression, erasure, intrenchment

Cour, sf. (*etym. L.L.* curtis, cortis), court-yard, court, cabinet

Courage, sm. (*etym. L.L.* coraticum, *from L.* cor, *heart*), courage, daring, gallantry, spirit. ‡ *Prendre son — à deux mains*, to summon up all one's courage

‖**Courageux, se**, adj. courageous, manful, gallant

Courant, e, adj. (*etym.* courir), running, present, current. *Chien* —, hound, beagle. *Les affaires —es*, the every-day business. *Main —e*, waste-book, sm. stream

Courante, sf. courant, (†) looseness of the bowels

Courbatu, e, adj. (*etym.* court, battu), who has got the lumbago, knocked up, (*of a horse*) foundered

Courbature, sf. lumbago, foundering

Courbe, adj. (*etym. L.* curvus), bent, crooked, curved. — sf. curve, bend, curb

Courber, va. to bend, to bow, to make crooked; *se* —, vr. to be bent, to stoop, to bend

Courbette, sf. curvet, cringing

Courbure, sf. curve, bend

Coureur, se, smf. runner, racer, gadabout

Courge, sf. gourd, pumpkin

Courir, vn. (*etym. L.* currere, *to run*), to run, to race, to gad about, to hasten, to spread over, to be prevalent, to sail. *Par le temps qui court*, as times go. — *vent arrière*, to scud before the wind. — *vent devant*, to spoon. — va. to pursue, to run after, to hunt, to course. *Une nouvelle qui court les rues*, stale news

Courlis, *also* **Courlieu**, sm. (*onomat.*), curlew

Couronne, sf. (*etym. L.* corona), crown

Couronnement, sm. (*etym.* couronner), coronation, crowning, coping, top, taffrail

Couronner, va. (*etym. L.* coronare), to crown, to cap; *se* —, vr. to crown oneself, to be crowned, to decay at the top. *Cheval couronné*, broken-kneed horse

Courre, va. (*etym. see* COURIR), to hunt, to chase

Courrier, sm. (*etym.* courre), messenger, courier, mail, post, correspondence. — *par* —, by return of post. *Faire son* —, to write one's letters for the post

Courroie, sf. (*etym. L.* corrigia, *a thong*), thong, strap. ¦ *Allonger la* —, to make a penny go a great way, to strain the rope

Courroucé, e, adj. angry, wrathful, enraged

Courroucer, va. (*etym. ?* *see* Littré), to anger; *se* —, vr. to be wroth, to rage

Courroux, sm. (*etym. ?*), wrath, anger, rage

Cours, sm. (*etym. L.* cursus), course, current, stream, flow, scope, play, path, track, currency, vogue, range of stones, public walk

Course, sf. (*etym.* cours), running, run, race, course, walk, distance, errand, fare, privateering, length of piston stroke, coursing. *Vaisseau armé en* —, privateer. *Faire la* —, to go privateering

Coursier, sm. steed, courser, bow-gun, float-board

Court, e, adj. short, short-lived, curt, scanty. ¦ —*e et bonne*, a short life and a merry one. — adv. short. *Être à* — *de*, to be short of. *Rester, demeurer, se trouver* —, to stop short, to be nonplussed

Courtage, sm. (*etym.* courtier), broker's business, brokerage

Courtaud, sm. thick-set person, crop-eared horse. *Un* — *de boutique*, a shopman. —, —*e*, adj. thick-set, crop-eared

Courte-pointe, sf. (*should be* coulte-pointe; *etym. L.* culcita, puncta), counterpane, quilt

Courtier, sm. (*etym. L.L.* curatarius, *from L.* curare, *to take care*), broker. — *marron*, unlicensed broker

Courtine, sf. (*etym. L.L.* cortina, *a small yard*), curtain

Courtisan, sm. (*etym. I.* cortigiano), courtier

Courtisane, sf. courtesan

Courtiser, va. (*etym. see* Courtois), to court, to pay one's court to

Courtois, e, adj. (*etym. L.L.* curtis, *a yard*), courteous, civil

Courtoisie, sf. courtesy, civility

Couru, e, adj. part. sought after

Cousin, e, s. (*etym. L.* consobrinus), cousin, crony, good friend. — sm. (*etym. L.* culex), gnat

Cousinière, sf. musquito-net

Coussin, sm. (*etym. L.* culcita, *a bed*), cushion, pillow

Coussinet, sm. pad, small cushion, iron wedge, (*railway*) chair

Cousu, e, past part. (*etym.* coudre), sewed, stitched. ¦ *Être tout* — *d'or*, to be all over gold. ¦ *Bouche* —*e!* mum's the word

Coût, sm. cost, charge

Coûtant, adj. (*etym.* coûter), cost. *Au prix* —, at cost price

Couteau, sm. (*etym. L.* cultellus), knife, short sword. ¦ *Être à* —*x tirés*, to be at daggers drawn. *Il faut jouer des* —*x*, we must draw our daggers

Coutelas, sm. cutlass, hanger

Coutelier, ère, s. cutler, cutler's wife

Coutellerie, sf. cutlery

Coûter, vn. (*etym. L.* constare, *to be with*), to cost, to stand in, to be expensive. ¦ — *gros, les yeux de la tête*, to cost tremendously dear

¦**Coûteux, se,** adj. (*etym.* coûter), expensive, costly

Coutil, sm. (*etym. O.F.* coutte, *a bed*), ticking, drill, duck

Coutre, sm. (*etym. L.* culter), coulter

Coutume, sf. (*etym. L.L.* costuma), custom, habit, wont. *Une fois n'est pas* —, one act is not a habit

Coutumier, ère, adj. customary. *Droit* —, common law. *Pays* —, country where common law obtains. *Être* — *du fait*, to be an old offender

Couture, sf. (*etym. L.* consutum, *supine of* consuere), needlework, sewing, seam

Couturer, va. to seam, to scar

Couturière, sf. (*etym.* couture), sempstress, dressmaker

Couvaison, sf. (*etym. L.* cubatio), brooding season

Couvée, sf. (*etym.* couver), brood, covey

Couvent, sm. (*etym. L.* conventus), convent

Couver, va. (*etym. L.* cubare), to hatch, to brood on. — *une maladie*, to be breeding a distemper. — vn. to brood, to lie smouldering; *se* —, vr. to be brooding or hatching

Couvercle, sm. (*etym. L.* cooperculum), lid, cover, cap

Couvert, e, past part. covered, clothed, clad, secret, obscure, cloudy. — sm. the cloth, knife and fork, cover, covert, shelter, lodging, shady spot. *Mettre le* —, to lay the cloth. *Être à* —, to be under cover, to have security

Couverture, sf. cover, covering, blanket, security. *Faire la* —, to turn down the bedclothes

Couveuse, sf. (*etym.* couver), brooding hen

¦**Couvre-chef,** sm. (*etym.* couvrir, chef), hat, cap; *plur.* des couvre-chefs

Couvre-feu, sm. (*etym.* couvrir, feu), curfew, fire-plate; *plur.* des couvre-feu

Couvre-pieds, sm. (*etym.* couvrir, pieds), quilt, counterpane; *plur.* des couvre-pieds

Couvreur, sm. (*etym.* couvrir), tiler, slater, thatcher

Couvrir, va. (*etym. L.* cooperire, *from* cum, operire, *to cover*), to cover, to spread, to wrap up, to tile, to slate, to thatch, to load, to palliate, to obliterate, to defray; *se* —, vr. to wrap oneself up, to put one's hat on, to be overcast, to grow dark, to conceal oneself, to reimburse oneself

Crabe, sf. (*etym. Gr.* κάραβος), crab

Crac, interj. (*onomat.*), crack! in a twinkling

Crachat, sm. spittle, badge of an order of knighthood

Craché, e, adj. just like. † *C'est son père tout* —, he is the very image of his father

Crachement, sm. (*etym.* cracher), spitting

Cracher, vn. (*etym. Scand.* hrâki, *spittle*), to spit, to sputter

Crachoir, sm. spittoon

Craie, sf. (*etym. L.* creta), chalk

Craindre, va. (*etym. L.* tremere), to fear, to dread

Crainte, sf. fear, dread, apprehension

¦**Craintif, ve,** adj. fearful, timorous

Cramoisi, e, adj. sm. (*etym. Arab.* karmesi, *crimson*), crimson, crimson hue

Crampe, sf. (*etym. O.G.* krampf), cramp

Crampon, sm. (*etym. G.* krampe), cramp-iron, calkin, frostnail

Cramponner, va. to cramp, to rough-shoe; *se* —, vr. to cling

Cran, sf. (*etym. L.L.* crena, *a notch*), notch, nick

Crâne, sm. (*etym. Gr.* κράνιον, *a skull*), skull, cranium, (¦) swaggerer. ¦ *Faire le* —, to swagger and bluster, to act the swaggerer

¦**Crânement,** adv. downright, and no mistake

¦**Crânerie,** sf. blustering, swaggering

Crapaud, sm. (*etym. Ang.-Sax.* creopan), toad, mortar-carriage, (*nav.*) goose-neck

Crapaudine, sf. a kind of stone, grating to keep frogs out. *A la* —, broiled

Crapule, sf. (*etym. L.* crapula), low debauchery, low debauched people

¦**Crapuleux, se,** adj. (*etym.* crapule), grossly debauched

Craquement, sm. cracking, creaking, gnashing

Craquer, va. (*onomat.?*), to crack, to creak, to gnash

Craqueter, vn. to crackle, to gabble

Crassane, sf. (*etym. L.* crassus?), a sort of pear

Crasse, sf. (*etym. L.* crassus, *fat*), dirth, filth, rusticity, uncouth manners, stinginess, slag, hammer-slag. — adj. gross

Crasser, va. to dirt, to foul

Crasseux, se, adj. dirty, squalid, stingy

Cravache, sf. (*etym. Slav.* karabâc, *whip*), riding-whip

Cravate, sf. (*etym.* Croate, *Croatian*), neckcloth, cravat, tassel

Crayeux, se, adj. (*etym.* craie), chalky

Crayon, sm. (*etym.* craie), pencil, lead-pencil, crayon, pencil drawing, sketch

Crayonner, va. to pencil out, to sketch

Créance, sf. (*etym. same as* croyance), debt, book-debt, trust, credence, confidence, credit, command. *Lettre de* —, letter of credit; *plur.* credentials

Créancier, ère, s. creditor

Créateur, trice, s. adj. (*etym. L.* creatorem), maker, creator, first author; creative

Créature, sf. (*etym. L.* creatura), creature, being

Crécelle, sf. (*etym. ?*), rattle

Crécerelle, sf. (*etym. ?*), kestrel

Crèche, sf. (*etym. G.* krippe), crib, manger, infant school

Crédibilité, sf. (*etym. L.* credibilis), credibility

Crédit, sm. (*etym. L.* credere), credit. *A* —, on credit, without proof. — *à*, to give credit. *Passer une somme au* — *d'une personne*, to credit a person for a sum

Créditer, va. to credit

¦**Crédule,** adj. (*etym. L.* credulus), credulous, easy of belief, unsuspecting

Crédulité, sf. (*etym. L.* credulitatem), credulity, credulousness

Créer, va. (*etym. L.* creare), to make, to create; *se* —, vr. to create oneself

§**Crémaillère,** sf. (*etym. ?*), pot-hanger, rack. ¦ *Pendre la* —, to give a house-warming. *Chaise à* —, spring-back chair

Crème, sf. (*etym. L.L.* cremum), custard, cream, the best

Crément, sm. (*etym. L.* crementum), increment

Crémerie, sf. dairy

Crémier, ère, s. milkman, milkwoman

Créneau, sm. (*etym.* cran), battlement

Créneler, va. to embattle, to indent, to cog, to mill the edge of

Crêpe, sm. (*etym. L.* crispus), crape, pall. — sf. pancake

Crêper, va., *se* —, vr. to crisp, to crape

Crépine, sf. fringe

Crépir, va. to rough-cast, to grain, to crisp

Crépu, e, adj. frizzled, woolly

Crépuscule, sm. (*etym. L.* crepusculum), twilight, dawn

Cresson, sm. (*etym. L.* crescere?), cress

Crétacé, e, adj. (*etym. L.* cretaceus, *from* creta, *chalk*), cretaceous, chalky

Crête, sf. (*etym. L.* crista), cock's comb, tuft, crest, top, ridge

Cretin, sm. (*etym. G.* kreidling), cretin, idiot

Crétinisme, sm. idiocy

Cretonne, sf. (*etym. name of the first manufacturer*), stout calico

Creuser, va.n. to dig, to hollow, to excavate, to sift, to search; *se* —, vr. to dig for oneself

Creuset, sm. (*etym. L.L.* crucibulum), crucible, test

§**Creux, se**, adj. (*etym. L.L.* crosum), deep, hollow, sunken, empty, unsubstantial. ‡ *Une tête —se*, a visionary. — adv. hollow. — sm. hollow, cavity, excavation

Crevasse, sf. (*etym.* crever), crack, crevice, chap, chink, cranny, cleft, flaw

Crevasser, va., *se* —, vr. to crack, to crevice, to chap

Crève-cœur, sm. (*etym.* crever, cœur), sad disappointment, heart-sore; *plur.* des crève-cœur

Crever, va. (*etym. L.* crepare), to burst, to break, to tear, to cram, to work to death; — vn. to burst, to die; *se* —, vr. to burst

Crevette, sf. (*etym. G.* krabbe), shrimp, prawn

Cri, sm. (*etym. I.* grido), cry, shout, clamour, outcry, scream, shriek, barking, yelping, howl, howling, whining, squeak, squeal, chirp

Cri-cri, sm. (*onom.*), cricket

§**Criailler**, vn. to bawl, to squall, to be ever complaining

§**Criaillerie**, sf. bawling, squalling, scolding

§**Criailleur, se**, s. brawler, squaller

Criant, e, adj. glaring, crying, shameful

Criard, e, adj. brawling, noisy, squalling, clamorous, harsh-sounding, shrill, troublesome

Crible, sm. (*etym. L.* cribrum), sieve, riddle

Cribler, va. to sift, to riddle, to overwhelm. *Criblé de dettes*, over head and ears in debt

Cric, sm. (*onomat.*), screw-jack, lifting-jack

Criée, sf. public sale

Crier, vn. to cry out, to shriek, to screech, to scold, to inveigh against; — va. to cry, to hawk about, to put up for sale; *se* —, vr. to be cried

Crieur, se, s. brawler, crier

Crime, sm. (*etym. L.* crimen), crime, guilty deed

Criminel, le, adj. s. (*etym. L.* criminalis), criminal, guilty; criminal proceedings

Crin, sm. (*etym. L.* crinis), horse-hair, hair, bristles, mane

‡**Crin-crin**, sm. (*onomat.*), fiddler, fiddle

Crinière, sf. (*etym.* crin), mane, horse-tail

Crise, sf. (*etym. Gr.* κρίσις), crisis, fit

Crispation, sf. (*etym.* crisper), shrivelling, nervous irritation, fidgets

Crisper, va. (*etym. L.* crispare), to shrivel, to give the fidgets; *se* —, vr. to shrivel up, to move convulsively

Cristal, sm. (*etym. Gr.* κρύσταλλος), crystal, cut-glass

Cristallin, e, adj. (*etym.* cristal), crystalline. — sm. crystalline

Cristalliser, va.n., *se* —, vr. to crystallize

Critiquable, adj. (*etym.* critiquer), open to criticism

Critique, sm. (*etym. Gr.* κριτικός), critic. — sf. criticism, critique. — adj. critical, criticizing

Critiquer, va.n. to criticize, to animadvert upon, to reflect upon; *se* —, vr. to criticize oneself *or* one another, to be criticized

Critiqueur, sm. criticizer, shallow critic

Croassement, sm. (*etym.* croasser), croaking, croak

Croasser, vn. (*onomat.*), to croak

Croc, sm. (*onomat.*), hook, drag-hook, tusk, fang, curled-up moustaches. ‡ *Pendre au* —, to hang up, to lay by

Croc-en-jambe, sm. trip up; *plur.* des crocs en-jambe

Croche, adj. crooked. — sf. quaver

Crochet, sm. (*etym.* croc), hook, tenter, hasp, pick-lock, steel-yard, dog-tooth, a kind of porter's knot, turn, bend, bracket, crotchet, needle, pronged hoe. *Clou à* —, tenter-hook. *Broder au* —, to chain-stitch. ‡ *Faire un* —, to turn out of one's way

Crocheter, va. to pick a lock

Crocheteur, sm. porter. — *de serrures*, housebreaker, pick-lock

Crochu, e, adj. crooked. ‡ *Avoir les mains —es*, to be light-fingered

Croire, va. (*etym. L.* credere), to believe, to credit, to trust; *se* —, vr. to believe oneself, to think that one is, to consult oneself, to depend upon oneself

Croisade, sf. (*etym.* croiser), crusade

Croisé, sm. crusader

Croisé, e, adj. crossed, double-milled, alternate

Croisée, sf. window, casement

Croisement, sm. (*etym.* croiser), crossing

Croiser, va. (*etym.* croix), to cross, to thwart, to cross out; — vn. to cross; *se* —, vr. to cross each other, to be crossed, to take the cross

Croiseur, sm. cruiser

Croisière, sf. cruise, cruising-station, intersection of two lines. ‡ *Tenir la* —, to be on a cruise

§**Croisillon**, sm. (*etym.* croix), cross-bar

Croissance, sf. (*etym. L.* crescentia), growth, growing

Croissant, sm. (*pres. part. of* croître), crescent, pruning-hook. —, —e, adj. growing, increasing

Croître, vn. (*etym. L.* crescere), to grow, to increase, to thrive, to lengthen, to swell

Croix, sf. (*etym. L.* crux), cross, sorrows, tribulation. ‡ — *de par Dieu*, horn-book. — *ou pile*, head or tail

Croquant, sm. (*etym.* ?), peasant, poor wretch

Croquant, e, adj. (*etym.* croquer), crisp, crackling, crunching

Croquemitaine, sm. (*etym.* ?), old bogy

†**Croque-mort**, sm. (*etym.* croquer, mort), undertaker's man; *plur.* des croque-morts

†**Croque-note**, sm. (*etym.* croquer, note), a poor musician; *plur.* des croque-notes

Croquer, vn.a. (*onomat.* croc), to be crisp, to crunch, to eat, to sketch, to slur over. † — *le marmot*, to dance attendance. ‡ *Enfant gentil à* —, a lovely child

Croquet, sm. hard almond *or* spice cake

Croqueur, se, s. eater, gormandizer

§**Croquignole**, sf. (*etym.* croquer), cracknel, fillip

Croquis, sm. sketch, outline

Crosse, sf. (*etym. L.* crux), crosier, butt-end, hockey stick

Crotte, sf. (*etym. G.* kloss ?), dirt, mud, squalid poverty

Crotter, va. to dirt; *se* —, vr. to dirty one's clothes, to get dirty

Crottin, sm. dung

Croulant, e, adj. falling, tottering, sinking

Croulement, sm. falling in

Crouler, vn. (*etym. L.L.* corotulare), to fall, to sink

Croupe, sf. (*etym. G.* kropf, *protuberance*), crupper, rump, buttock, back, ridge

Croupier, sm. partner, "croupier"

Croupière, sf. crupper. ‡ *Tailler des —s à*, to cut out work for . . .

Croupion, sm. rump

Croupir, vn. (*etym.* croupe), to stagnate, to rot, to wallow

Croupissant, e, adj. stagnant

§**Croustillant, e**, adj. crisp, crusty

§**Croustiller**, va.n. (*etym.* croûte), to munch pieces of crust

§**Croustilleux, se**, adj. smutty, free

Croûte, sf. (*etym. L.* crusta), crust, scab, coat, (‡) daub, (†) old fool

Croûton, sm. (*etym.* croûte), crust, sippet, (‡) dauber

Croyable, adj. (*etym.* croire), credible, worthy of belief

Croyance, sf. creed, belief, expectation

Croyant, e, s. adj. (*etym.* croire), believer, faithful

Crû, sm. (*past part. of* croître), growth, country, vineyard

Cru, e, adj. (*etym. L.* crudus), raw, uncooked, crude, indigestible, hard, harsh, crabbed, coarse. ‡ *A* —, on the bare skin

Cruauté, sf. (*etym. L.* crudelitatem), cruelty, cruel deed

Cruche, sf. (*etym. O.H.G.* cruoc, *pitcher*), pitcher, jug, jar, (†) blockhead

Cruchon, sm. small jug, (†) booby

Crucifère, adj. sf. (*etym. L.* crux, *cross*, fero, *I bear*), cruciferous, cross-bearer

Crucifiement, sm. crucifixion

Crucifier, va. (*etym. L.* crux, figere, *to fix*), to crucify

Crudité, sf. (*etym. L.* cruditatem), crudeness, crudity, coarse expression

Crue, sf. (*etym.* crû), rising, swelling, growth

§**Cruel, le**, adj. (*etym. L.* crudelis), cruel, unmerciful, painful, grievous

Crustacé, e, adj. s. (*etym. L.* crusta), crustaceous, crustacean

Cubage, sm. (*etym.* cube), cubature

Cuber, va.n. (*etym.* cube), to cube

§**Cueillette**, sf. (*same word as* collecte), gathering, collection, (*nav.*) miscellaneous cargo

§**Cueillir**, va. (*etym. L.* colligere), to gather, to pluck, to pick, to cull; *se* —, vr. to be gathered

§**Cuiller**, *also* **Cuillère**, sf. (*etym. L.* cochleare), spoon, ladle. — *à bouche*, table-spoon. — *à café*, tea-spoon. — *à potage*, soup-ladle. — *à pot*, ladle. — *à ragoût*, gravy-spoon

§**Cuillerée**, sf. (*etym.* cuiller), spoonful

Cuir, sm. (*etym. L.* corium), hide, skin, leather, strop, (‡) incorrect speaking. ‡ *Entre — et chair*, under the skin, (*fig.*) in private. — *de laine*, double-milled cloth

Cuirasse, sf. (*etym.* cuir), cuirass, breastplate. *Au défaut de la* —, in the vulnerable point

Cuirassé, e, adj. past part. armed with a cuirass, (*fig.*) casehardened, close

Cuirasser, va. (*etym.* cuirasse), to arm with a cuirass, to harden; *se* —, vr. to put on one's cuirass, to harden oneself

Cuire, va. (*etym. L.* coquere), to cook, to dress, to do, to burn, to digest. *Vin cuit*, sweet wine. — vn. to be cooked, to smart, to be sore. ‡ *Il vous en cuira*, you shall smart for it

Cuisant, e, adj. sharp, smarting, poignant, bitter

Cuisine, sf. (*etym. L.* coquina), kitchen, fare, cheer, cooks, cookery, spice-box. ¦ *Du latin de* —, dog Latin
¦**Cuisiner**, va. to cook
Cuisinier, sm. cook. —*-ère*, sf. cook, Dutch oven
¦**Cuissard**, sm. (*etym.* cuisse), armour for the thigh
Cuisse, sf. (*etym. L.* coxa), thigh, leg
Cuisson, sf. (*etym. L.* coctionem), cooking, dressing, burning, smarting
Cuistre, sm. (*O.F.* coustre, *sacristan, from L.* custos), college scout, (¦) vulgar pedant, low-minded fellow
Cuite, sf. (*etym.* cuire), burning, baking, ovenful
Cuivre, sm. (*etym. L.L.* cuprum), copper, copper coin, copper plate, (*plur.*) brass instruments
Cul, sm. (*etym. L.* culus), bottom. —*blanc*, wheat-ear, fallow-finch. —*d'artichaut*, bottom of an artichoke —*-de-jatte*, cripple. —*-de-lampe*, (*arch.*) bracket, (*print.*) tail-piece. —*-de-sac*, blind alley
Culasse, sf. (*etym.* cul), breech
Culbute, sf. (*etym. see* CULBUTER), somersault, tumble
Culbuter, va. (*etym.* cul, buter, bouter), to throw down, to upset, to rout: — vn. to fall head over heels, to be upset, to be done up; *se* —, vr. to be upset, to throw down each other
Culée, sf. (*etym.* cul), abutment
Culinaire, adj. (*etym. L.* culinarius), culinary
Culminant, e, adj. culminating, highest
Culminer, vn. (*etym. L.* culminare), to reach the culminating point
Culotte, sf. (*etym.* cul), breeches, rump, buttock
Culotter, va. to breech, (†) to season a pipe
Culottier, sm. breeches-maker
Culpabilité, sf. guilt, culpability
Culte, sm. (*etym. L.* cultus), worship, religion, creed
Cultivateur, sm. (*etym.* cultiver), husbandman, cultivator, farmer
Cultiver, va. (*etym. L.* cultus), to till, to cultivate, to improve, to exercise
Cultivé, e, adj. cultivated
Culture, sf. (*etym. L.* cultura), tillage, cultivation, culture, improvement
Cumul, sm. plurality of offices
Cumuler, va. (*etym. L.* cumulare), to hold more than one office
¦**Cupide**, adj. (*etym. L.* cupidus), covetous, greedy, grasping
Cupidité, sf. (*etym. L.* cupiditatem), cupidity, covetousness
Curage, sm. (*etym.* curer), cleaning out, cleansing
Curateur, trice, s. (*etym. L.* curatorem), trustee
Curatif, ve, adj. (*etym. L.* curare, *to take care*), curative, healing
Cure, sf. (*etym. see* CURÉ), living, curacy, vicarage, cure; (*etym. L.* cura), care
Curé, sm. (*etym. L.* curatus), parish priest, curate
Cure-dent, sm. tooth-pick; *plur.* des cure-dents
Curée, sf. (*etym.* cuir), quarry, appetite
§**Cure-oreille**, sm. (*etym.* curer, oreille), ear-pick; *plur.* des cure-oreilles
Curer, va. (*etym. L.* curare), to clean out, to cleanse; *se* —, vr. to pick one's teeth
Curie, sf. (*etym. L.* curia), curia, ward
¦**Curieux, se**, adj. s. (*etym. L.* curiosus), curious, inquisitive, eager, careful, dainty, fond; connoisseur, inquisitive person, busybody, virtuoso
Curiosité, sf. (*etym. L.* curiositatem), curiosity, inquisitiveness, rarity
¦**Cursif, ve**, adj. (*etym. L.* cursus), cursive
§**Curviligne**, adj. (*etym. L.* curva, linea), curvilineal, curvilinear
Cutané, e, adj. (*etym. L.* cutis, *skin*), cutaneous
Cuve, sf. (*etym. L.* cupa, *tub*), vat, tub, copper
Cuvée, sf. vatful, tubful
Cuver, vn. to ferment, to work
Cuvette, sf. (*dimin. of* cuve), basin, cistern
Cyclopéen, ne, adj. (*etym.* Cyclope), Cyclopean, Cyclopic
§**Cygne**, sm. (*etym. L.* cycnus), swan, cygnus
Cylindre, sm. cylinder, roller, barrel of an organ
Cylindrique, adj. (*etym. Gr.* κυλινδρικός), cylindrical
Cymaise, sf. ogee, cyma
Cymbale, sf. (*etym. Gr.* κύμβαλον), cymbal
Cymbalier, sm. cymbal-player
Cynique, sm. adj. (*etym. Gr.* κυνικός), cynic, cynical
Cynisme, sm. (*etym. Gr.* κυνισμός), cynicism
Cyprès, sm. (*etym. L.* cupressus), cypress
Cytise, sm. (*etym. Gr.* κύτισος), cytisus, laburnum
Czar, Czarine. *See* TSAR. (*Czar* is the Polish form)

D

D, sm. d; D, five hundred
Dactyle, sm. (*etym. Gr.* δάκτυλος, *finger*), dactyl
¦**Dada**, sm. horse, cock-horse, hobby
¦**Dadais**, sm. ninny, booby
Dague, sf. (*etym.* ?), dagger, dirk, dags (of a brocket)
Daguerréotyper, va. (*etym.* daguerréotype), to daguerreotype
§**Daigner**, va. (*etym. L.* dignus), to vouchsafe, to deign, to condescend
Daim, sm., **Daine**, sf. (*etym. L.* dama), deer
Dais, sm. (*etym. L.* discus, *a dining table*), canopy
Dallage, sm. (*etym.* daller), flagging, flagstone pavement
Dalle, sf. (*etym.* ?), flag, flagstone, slab, slice, piece (of copper)
Daller, va. to pave with flagstones
Dalmatique, sf. (*etym. L.* Dalmatica) dalmatic
Dalot, sm. (*etym.* dalle), scupper
*****Dam**, sm. (*etym. L.* damnum), damage, detriment
Damas, sm. (*etym.* Damascus, *a town*), damask, diaper, Damascus blade damson
Damasquiner, va. (*etym.* damas), to damaskeen
Damasser, va. to damask
Dame, sf. (*etym. L.* domina), lady, dame, (*cards*) queen, dam; —*s*, draughts. — interj. why, nay, forsooth, egad
Dame-jeanne, sf. demijohn; *plur.* des dames-jeannes
Damer, va. (*etym.* dame), to crown. ¦ — *le pion*, to outdo
Dameret, sm. fop, lady's man
Damier, sm. draught-board
Damner, va. (*etym. L.* damnare; *pronounce* dâner), to damn, to doom to hell fire
Damné, e, adj. damned, in hell, hateful, infernal
*****Damoiseau**, sm. (*etym. L.L.* dominicellus, *dimin. of L.* dominus), gentle youth, page, fop, spark
*****Damoiselle**, sf. (*fem. of* damoiseau), damsel
Dandinement, sm. swinging about one's body
Dandiner, vn., *se* —, vr. (*etym. Eng.* to dandle), to swing about one's body
¦**Dangereux, se**, adj. (*etym.* danger), dangerous
Dans, prep. (*etym. L.* de, intus), in, into, within, during, according to
Dansant, e, adj. dancing
Danse, sf. (*etym. see* DANSER), dancing, the dance, step, (†) beating, drubbing. † *Avoir l'air à la* —, to look ready to do a thing. *La — de Saint-Guy*, Saint Vitus's dance
Danser, vn. a. (*etym. O.H.G.* danson, *to draw, to stretch*), to dance. † *Faire* —, to make one smart for it. ¦ *Ne savoir sur quel pied* —, (*fig.*) not to know which way to turn. — *sur la corde*, to dance on the tight rope
Danseur, se, s. dancer
Dard, sm. (*etym. Ang.-Sax.* daradh, darodh), dart, sting, forked tongue, spindle
Darder, va. to dart, to hurl
Dartre, sf. (*etym. Bass.* dardru), ringworm. — *farineuse*, scurvy eruption
Dartreux, se, adj. s. (*etym.* dartre), scabby, of the ringworm, that has got the ringworm
Date, sf. (*etym. L.* data, *things given*), date
Dater, va. n. to date, to reckon
Datif, sm. (*etym. L.* dativus), dative
Datte, sf. date (*fruit*)
Dattier, sm. date-tree
Daube, sf. (*see* DAUBER), a kind of stew
¦**Dauber**, va. (*etym. O.G.* dubban, *Eng.* to dub), to cuff, to jeer at
Dauphin, sm. (*etym. L.* delphinus), dolphin, the Dauphin
Dauphine, sf. the Dauphiness
Davantage, adv. (*etym.* de, avantage), more, any more, any longer
De, prep. (*etym. L.* de), of, some, any, from, out of, to, with, by, on
Dé, sm. (*etym. L.* datum), die; (*etym. L.* digitale), thimble. *A vous le* —, it is your turn to play. ¦ *Tenir le — dans la conversation*, to have all the talk to oneself
Débâclage, sm. clearing
Débâcle, sf. breaking up of the ice, (¦) downfall, hurry-skurry
Débâcler, va. to clear, to unfasten; — vn. (†) to break up
Déballage, sm. unpacking
Déballer, va. (*etym.* dé, balle, *a parcel, a bale*), to unpack
Débandade, adv. helter-skelter, confusion
Débander, va. (*etym.* dé, bander), to unbind, to unbend, to unbrace, to uncock; *se* —, vr. to unbend, to disband, to leave the ranks
Débaptiser, va. to unchristen; *se* —, vr. to change one's name

§**Débarbouiller,** va. to wash the face of, to clean; *se* —, vr. to wash one's face

Débarcadère, sm. (*etym. see* DÉBARQUER), terminus, landing-place

Débarder, va. to unlade floated wood

Débardeur, sm. river-porter, one who carries wood ashore

Débarquement, sm. landing, disembarking

Débarquer, va. (*etym.* dé, barque), to land, to disembark. *Un nouveau débarqué,* (*fig.*) a raw countryman. — vn. to land, to go on shore

Débarras, sm. (*etym.* dé, barre), riddance

Débarrasser, va. (*etym.* débarras), to rid of, to free from, to ease, to clear; *se* —, vr. to get rid of, to shake off

Débarrer, va. (*etym.* dé, barre), to unbar, to undo the bars of

Débat, sm. (*etym. see* DÉBATTRE), altercation, strife, debate, discussion

Débâter, va. (*etym.* dé, bâter), to unsaddle

Débattre, va. (*etym.* dé, battre), to argue, to debate, to disown; *se* —, vr. to be argued, to struggle, to flounder about

Débauche, sf. (*etym. see* DÉBAUCHER), debauch, drunken revelry, jollification, lewdness

Débauché, e, s. adj. (*etym.* débaucher), a debauchee, a rake; debauched

Débaucher, va. (*etym.* dé, *O.F.* bauche, *a place for work*), to debauch, to lead into wrong courses, to entice from one's duty; *se* —, vr. to follow ill courses, to go astray

Débet, sm. (*etym. L.* debet, *he owes*), debit, balance

‖**Débile,** adj. (*etym. L.* debilis), weak, feeble

Débilitant, e, adj. (*etym.* débiliter), debilitating, weakening

Débilité, sf. (*etym. L.* debilitatem), debility, weakness, feebleness

Débiliter, va. (*etym. L.* debilitare), to impair, to weaken, to debilitate

†**Débine,** sf. poverty

Débit, sm. (*etm. L.* debitum), sale, market, retail warehouse, licence to sell, cutting up, delivery

Débitant, e, s. (*etym.* débiter), dealer, retailer

Débiter, va. (*etym.* débit), to sell, to retail, to cut out, to deliver, to spread about, to debit; *se* —, vr. to be sold, to be uttered

Débiteur, trice, s. (*etym. L.* debitor), debtor

Débiteur, se, s. (*etym.* débiter), retailer, hawker

Déblai, sm. clearing away, excavation, rubbish, (*mines*) gobbing

Déblatérer, vn. (*etym. L.* de, blaterare, *to cry*), to rail

Déblayer, va. (*etym. L.L.* debladare, *to remove the corn*), to take away, to clear away the rubbish from

Débloquer, va. (*etym.* dé, bloquer), to raise the blockade, (*print.*) to turn back

Déboire, sm. (*etym.* dé, boire), nasty taste, mortification

¶**Déboisement,** sm. (*etm.* déboiser), the action of cutting down woods *or* forests

¶**Déboiser,** va. (*etym.* dé, bois), to destroy the woods *or* forests

Déboîter, va. (*etym.* dé, boîte), to disjoint

Débonder, va. (*etym.* dé, bonde), to take out the bung of, to open the sluice of; — vn., *se* —, vr. to gush out, to sluice out, to give vent to

Débonnaire, adj. (*etym.* de, bon, aire; *see* Littré), easy, easy-tempered, good-natured

Débordement, sm. (*etm.* déborder), overflowing, overflooding, inroad, irruption, flood, outburst, dissoluteness

Déborder, vn. (*etym.* dé, bord), to overflow, to be flooded, to burst forth, to jut out, to lap over, (*nav.*) to sheer off; — va. to unborder, to undo, to overtop, to leave behind, to outflank

Débotter, va. (*etym.* dé, botte), to pull off a person's boots; *se* —, vr. to pull off one's boots

Débouché, sm. (*etym.* déboucher), outlet, issue, market, contrivance

Débouchement, sm. (*etym.* déboucher), disemboguement, uncorking, issue, market

Déboucher, va. (*etym.* dé, bouche), to clear, to open, to uncork; — vn. to emerge, to debouch, to empty itself

Déboucler, va. (*etym.* dé, boucle), to unbuckle, to uncurl; *se* —, vr. to come unbuckled or out of curl

Débourber, va. (*etym.* dé, bourbe), to clear mud away, to take a thing out of the mud

Débourrer, va. (*etym.* dé, bourre), to draw out the wadding of, to unstop, (†) to polish (*a man*), to break in (*a horse*)

Déboursés, Débours, sm. plur. money laid out, expenses

Débourser, va. (*etym.* dé, bourse), to lay out, to disburse

Debout, adv. (*etym.* de, bout), on end, upright, standing. — interj. up! rise! get up!

Débouter, va. (*etym.* dé, bouter), to nonsuit

Déboutonner, va. (*etym.* dé, boutonner), to unbutton; *se* —, vr. to unbutton one's clothes, to come unbuttoned, (†) to unbosom oneself

§*se* **Débrailler,** vr. (*etym.* dé, braies, *O.F.* breeches), to uncover one's breast. ‡ *Un air débraillé,* (*fig.*) a rakish look

Débrider, va. (*etym.* dé, bride), to unbridle, to despatch, to hurry through

Débris, sm. (*etym.* dé, briser), fragment, broken bit, remains, wreck, ruins

§**Débrouillement,** sm. (*etym.* débrouiller), unravelling

§**Débrouiller,** va. (*etym.* dé, brouiller), to unravel, to disentangle, to disembroil; *se* —, vr. to be unravelled, to be set to rights

Débrutir, va. (*etym.* dé, brut), to rough-polish

Débusquer, *also* **Débûcher,** va. (*etym.* dé, bûche *or* busche, bois), to drive, to dislodge

Début, sm. (*etym.* dé, but), lead, first throw, outset, beginning

Débutant, e, s. (*etym.* débuter), new performer, beginner

Débuter, vn. (*etym.* début), to lead, to play first, to begin, to make one's first appearance

Deçà, prep. adv. on this side of

Décacheter, va. to unseal

Décadence, sf. decay, decline, downfall

Décalquer, va. (*etym.* dé, calquer), to countertrace

Décampement, sm. (*etym.* décamper), decampment

Décamper, vn. (*etym.* dé, camp), to decamp, to move off

Décanter, va. (dé, *L.* canthus), to decant

Décapiter, va. (*etym.* dé, *L.* caput), to behead, to decapitate

Décarreler, va. (*etym.* dé, carrel, carreau), to take up a tile *or* brick floor

Décasyllabe, adj. (*etym. Gr.* δέκα, *and* syllabe), decasyllabic

Décatir, va. (*etym.* dé, catir), to sponge, to ungloss

Décatissage, sm. (*etym.* décatir), sponging

Décaver, va. (*etym.* dé, cave), to win the stake of

Décédé, e, adj. (*etym.* décéder), deceased

Décéder, vn. (*etym. L.* decedere), to die, to depart this life

Déceler, va. (*etym.* dé, celer), to disclose, to reveal, to betoken; *se* —, vr. to betray oneself, to tell against each other

Décembre, sm. (*etym. L.* December), December

Décence, sf. (*etym.* décent), decency, decorum, propriety

Décennal, e, adj. (*etym. L.* decennalis), decennial

‖**Décent, e,** adj. decent, decorous

Décerner, va. to award, to bestow, to confer

Décès, sm. (*etym. L.* decessus), decease, death. *Acte de* —, death-certificate

Décevant, e, adj. deceitful, deceptive

Décevoir, va. (*etym. L.* decipere), to beguile, to delude, to disappoint

Déchaîné, e, adj. past part. let loose, unchained, wild, raging

Déchaînement, sm. unbridling, unloosening, outburst

Déchaîner, va. (*etym.* dé, chaîne), to unshackle, to unbind, to let loose; *se* —, vr. to break loose, to inveigh against

Déchanter, vn. (*etym.* dé, chanter), to lower one's key. *Faire* —, to lower the tone of

Décharge, sf. unloading, unlading, discharge, volley, drain, outlet, lumber-room, release, evidence, acquittal. *Porter en* —, (*com.*) to credit

Déchargement, sm. (*etym.* décharger), unloading, unlading

Décharger, va. (*etym.* dé, charger), to unload, to unlade, to lighten, to relieve, to shoot, to exonerate, to ease, to open, to acquit, to release, to strike out; — vn. to unload, to unlade, (*print.*) to come off; *se* —, vr. to throw down, to throw upon, to leave the care of, to empty itself, to unburden one's heart, to burst out, to go off by itself, to fade

Décharné, e, adj. (*etym.* décharner), fleshless, gaunt, thin, bony

Décharner, va. (*etym.* dé, chair), to pick, to strip the flesh off

Déchaussement, sm. (*etym.* déchausser), baring the root *or* the foundations, gumlessness

Déchaussé, e, adj. barefooted, laid bare, gumless

Déchausser, va. (*etym.* dé, chausser), to pull off the boots, to lay bare the foot of, to wear away the gums, to lay bare; *se* —, vr. to pull off one's shoes, boots, stockings, to lie bare, to be gumless

Déchéance, sf. (*etym.* déchoir), forfeiture, dethronement, falling off

Déchet, sm. (*etym.* déchoit, *old past part. of* déchoir), loss, waste, falling off

Décheveler, va. (*etym.* dé, cheveu), to dishevel

Déchiffrable, adj. (*etym.* déchiffrer), decipherable, legible

Déchiffrement, sm. (*etym.* déchiffrer), deciphering

Déchiffrer, va. (*etym.* dé, chiffrer), to make out, to decipher; *se* —, vr. to be deciphered *or* made out

Déchiqueter, va. (*etym.* dé, chiqueter, *to tear to pieces*), to cut up, to slash, to pink, to tear

Déchirant, e, adj. (*etym.* déchirer), heartrending, harrowing

Déchirement, sm. (*etym.* déchirer), tearing, rending, rent

Déchirer, va. (*etym.* dé, *O.H.G.* skerran, *to tear*), to tear, to rend, to rip up, to revile, to slander, to grate upon, to bite; *se* —, vr. to be torn, to rend oneself

Déchirure, sf. (*etym.* déchirer), rent, tear, break, cleft

Déchoir, vn. (*etym.* dé, choir), to fall away, to decline, to sink, to forfeit

‖**Décidé, e,** adj. (*etym.* décider), decided, bold, strong-minded

Décider, va.n. (*etym.* *L.* decidere, *to cut*), to decide, to settle, to induce; *se* —, vr. to come to a decision, to make up one's mind, to declare for

Décimer, va. (*etym.* *L.* decimare), to decimate, to carry off

‖**Décisif, ve,** adj. (*etym.* décider), decisive, peremptory, positive

Déclamateur, sm. adj. declaimer; declamatory, of declamation

Déclamatoire, adj. declamatory

Déclamer, va.n. (*etym.* *L.* declamare), to declaim, to recite, to inveigh

Déclaré, e, adj. declared, open

Déclarer, va. to declare, to disclose; *se* —, vr. to declare oneself, to appear, to break out

Déclasser, va. (*etym.* dé, classer), to unclass

Déclin, sm. (*see* DÉCLINER), decline, close, wane, trigger

Déclinaison, sf. (*etym.* *L.* declinationem), declension, declination, variation

Décliner, vn. (*etym.* *L.* declinare), to decline, to wane apace, to decay; — va. to decline, to tell one's name

Déclivité, sf. (*etym.* *L.* declivitas), slope, declivity

Déclouer, va. (*etym.* dé, clouer), to unnail, to take up; *se* —, vr. to come unnailed

Décocher, va. (*etym.* dé, coche), to let fly, to dart

Décoiffer, va. (*etym.* dé, coiffer), to take off the head-dress, to undress a person's hair, to undo; *se* —, vr. to take off one's head-dress, to undress one's hair

Décoller, va. (*etym.* *L.* de, collum), to behead, to undo, (*etym.* colle), to unpaste, to unglue, to drive away; *se* —, vr. to come off, to open

Décolleter, va. (*etym.* dé, collet), to cut down a dress low, to bare the neck and shoulders. *Être décolletée*, to wear a low dress. ‡ *Langage décolleté*, free language

Décolorer, va. (*etym.* dé, colorer), to discolour; *se* —, vr. to lose one's colour, to fade

Décombres, sm. plur. (*etym.* de, *O.F.* combres), rubbish

Décommander, va. (*etym.* dé, commander), to countermand

Décomposer, va. (*etym.* dé, composer), to decompose, to discompose, to distort; *se* —, vr. to be decomposed *or* discomposed, to undergo a change

Décompte, sm. (*etym.* dé, compte), discount, abatement, disappointment

Décompter, va.n. (*etym.* dé, compter), to abate, to reckon off, to be disappointed

Déconcerter, va. (*etym.* dé, concerter), to disconcert, to baffle, to foil; *se* —, vr. to be disconcerted

Déconfit, e, past part. (*etym.* dé, confit), discomfited

Déconfiture, sf. (*etym.* déconfire), discomfiture, havoc

§**Déconseiller,** va. (*etym.* dé, conseiller), to dissuade from

Déconsidération, sf. (*etym.* dé, considération), disrepute, discredit

Déconsidérer, va. (*etym.* dé, considérer), to bring into disrepute

Déconstruire, va. (*etym.* dé, construire), to take to pieces

Décontenancer, va. (*etym.* dé, contenance), to put out of countenance, to abash; *se* —, vr. to lose countenance

Déconvenue, sf. (*etym.* dé, convenir), mishap, ill luck

Décor, sm. (*see* DÉCORER), decoration, scenery of a theatre, scenes. *Peintre en* —*s*, house *or* scene-painter

Décorateur, sm. (*etym.* *L.* decorator), decorator

Décoration, sf. (*etym.* décorer), decoration, scenery, badge, insignia

Décoré, e, adj. wearing a badge *or* star, decorated

Décorer, va. (*etym.* *L.* decorare, *from* decus), to decorate, to bedeck, to dignify, to confer the insignia of an order of knighthood; *se* —, vr. to bedeck oneself

Découcher, va.n. (*etym.* dé, coucher), to sleep from home, to lie out, turn out of one's bed

Découdre, va. (*etym.* dé, coudre), to unsew, to unstitch, to rip up. † *En* —, to fight it out. *Se* —, vr. to come unsewn

Découler, vn. (*etym.* dé, couler), to trickle down, to drop, to flow, to proceed

Découper, va. (*etym.* dé, couper), to cut up, to carve, to cut out

Découplé, e, adj. strapping. *Gaillard bien* —, big strapping fellow

Découpler, va. (*etym.* dé, coupler) to uncouple

Découpure, sf. (*etym.* dé, couper), cutting out, paper-cutting

Décourageant, e, adj. discouraging, disheartening

Découragement, sm. discouragement, dejection

Décourager, va. (*etym.* dé, courage), to dishearten, to discourage, to deter, to discountenance; *se* —, vr. to lose heart, to be disheartened, to despond

Décousu, e, past part. adj. (*etym.* dé, cousu), unsewn, desultory, unconnected. — sm. unconnectedness

Découvert, sm. deficit, uncovered balance. —, —*e*, adj. past part. uncovered, bare, discovered, open

Découverte, sf. (*etym.* découvert), discovery

Découvrir, va. (*etym.* dé, couvrir), to uncover, to unroof, to unwrap, to expose, to unguard, to discover, to disclose

Décrasser, va. (*etym.* dé, crasse), to rub the dirt off, to clean, (‡) to brush up. ‡ — *ses écus*, to rub off the plebeian rust from one's money-box. *Se* —, vr. to clean the dirt off one's skin *or* hands, (†) to turn gentleman

Décréditer, va. (*etym.* dé, crédit), to discredit

Décret, sm. (*etym.* *L.* decretus), decree, writ, warrant

Décréter, va. (*etym.* décret), to decree, to enact, to issue a warrant

Décrié, e, adj. in bad repute, disreputable

Décrier, va. (*etym.* dé, crier), to cry down, to bring into disrepute

Décrire, va. (*etym.* *L.* describere), to describe; *se* —, vr. to be described

Décrocher, va. (*etym.* dé, croc), to unhook, to take down; *se* —, vr. to come unhooked

Décroissement, sm. (*etym.* décroître), decrease, wane

Décroître, vn. (*etym.* dé, croître), to decrease, to fall, to wane

Décrotter, va. (*etym.* dé, crotte), to brush, to clean. ‡ *Se faire* —, to have one's boots *or* clothes brushed. *Se* —, vr. to brush one's boots *or* clothes

Décrotteur, sm. shoe-black

Décrottoir, sm. scraper, door-scraper

Décrottoire, sf. (*etym.* décrotter), hard brush

Décrue, sf. (*etym.* décru, *past part. of* décroître), fall, decrease

Décupler, va. (*etym.* *L.L.* decuplare), to increase tenfold

Décurie, sf. (*etym.* *L.* decuria), decuria

§**Dédaigner,** va. (*etym.* *L.* dedignari), to scorn, to disdain, to look down upon

§**Dédaigneux, se,** adj (*etym.* dédaigner), scornful, disdainful

Dédain, sm. (*etym.* dédaigner), scorn, disdain

Dédale, sm. (*etym.* *prop. name* Dædalus), maze, labyrinth

Dedans, adv. prep. (*etym.* de, dans), inside, within, in. † *Mettre* —, to take in. *Là* —, in there. *Au* —, *en* —, within, inside. *Par* —, through. — sm. inside, interior

Dédicace, sf. (*etym.* *L.* dedicare, *to dedicate*), dedication

Dédicatoire, adj. (*etym.* *L.* dedicatorius), dedicatory

Dédier, va. (*etym.* *L.* dedicare), to dedicate; *se* —, vr. to dedicate oneself

Dédire, va. (*etym.* dé, dire), to gainsay; *se* —, vr. to recall what one has said, to recant, to withdraw

Dédit, sm. (*past part.* dédire), unsaying, forfeit, bond

Dédommagement, sm. (*etym.* dédommager), damages, amends

Dédommager, va. (*etym.* dé, dommage), to make up to, to indemnify for; *se* —, vr. to indemnify oneself, to be indemnified

Dédorer, va. (*etym.* dé, dorer), to ungild, to rub off the gilding; *se* —, vr. to come ungilt

Dédoubler, va. (*etym.* dé, doubler), to take out the lining, (*nav.*) to unsheath

Déduire, va. (*etym.* *L.* deducere), to take off, to deduct to deduce, to infer

Déesse, sf. (*etym.* Dieu), goddess

§**Défaillance,** sf. (*etym.* défaillant), fainting fit, swoon, decay, despondency

§**Défaillant, e,** adj. (*etym.* défaillir), decaying, expiring

§**Défaillir,** vn. (*etym.* dé, faillir), to fail, to be wanting, to decay, to faint

Défaire, va. (*etym.* dé, faire), to undo, to unmake, to unpack, to defeat, to overthrow, to rid of, to disturb, to discompose; *se* —, vr. to come undone, untied, unfastened, to spoil, to weaken, to get rid of, to leave off

Défait, e, part. adj. undone, untied, defeated, thin, rid, discomposed, awry

Défaite, sf. (*etym.* défaire), defeat, rout, sale, evasion, plea

Défalquer, va. (*etym.* *L.* de, falx, *a scythe*), to take off, to defalcate

se Défausser, vr. (*etym.* dé, faux), to play a card of another suit

Défaut, sm. (*etym.* dé, faillir), fault, blemish, defect, deficiency, break, default. ‡ *Le — de la cuirasse*, (*fig.*) the weak side

Défaveur, sf. (*etym.* dé, faveur), disfavour

‖**Défavorable,** adj. (*etym.* dé, favorable), unfavourable, disadvantageous
‖**Défectif, ve,** adj. (*etym. L.* defectivus), defective
‖**Défectueux, se,** adj. (*etym. L.* defectus), defective, imperfect, deficient
Défectuosité, sf. (*etym.* défectueux), defect, flaw
Défendable, adj. (*etym.* défendre), defensible, tenable
Défendeur, eresse, s. (*jurisp.*) defendant
Défendre, va. (*etym. L.* defendere), to defend, to safeguard, to uphold, to vindicate, to forbid, to interdict; *se* —, vr. to defend oneself, to resist, to vindicate oneself
Défendu, e, adj. past part. defended, forbidden
Défense, sf. (*etym. L.* defensum), defence, safeguard, works, shelter, prohibition, tusk
Défenseur, sm. (*etym. L.* defensorem), defender, upholder, counsel
‖**Défensif, ve,** adj. (*etym. L.* defensum), defensive
Déférer, va. (*etym. L.* deferre), to bestow, to tender, to report, to refer to; — vn. to defer, to comply with
Déferler, va. (*etym.* dé, ferler), to unfurl; — vn. to break heavily
Déferrer, va. (*etym.* dé, fer), to take off the tip of, to unshoe, to knock the irons off; *se* —, vr. to lose its tip, to come unshod, to get rid of one's irons
§**Défeuiller,** va. (*etym.* dé, feuille), to strip of its leaves
Défi, sm. (*etym.* défier), defiance, challenge
Défiance, sf. (*etym.* défiant), mistrust, distrust, suspicion, diffidence, wariness, discretion
Défiant, e, adj. mistrustful, distrustful, wary
Défier, va. (*etym.* dé, fier), to dare, to defy, to challenge; *se* —, vr. to defy one another, to distrust, to be diffident
Défigurer, va. (*etym.* dé, figure), to disfigure, to distort, to mangle; *se* —, vr. to disfigure oneself, to become disfigured
Défilé, sm. (*etym.* défiler), pass, defile, strait, filing off
Défiler, vn. (*etym.* dé, file), to file off, to defile, (†) to go off; — va. to unthread, to unstring; *se* —, vr. to come unthreaded, unstrung
Défini, e, adj. definite
Définir, va. (*etym.* dé, finir), to appoint, to decree, to define, to portray; *se* —, vr. to define oneself, to be defined
‖**Définitif, ve,** adj. (*etym. L.* definitivus), definitive
Défleurir, vn. (*etym.* dé, fleurir), to shed its blossoms; — va. to nip the blossoms, to take off the bloom of
Déflorer, va. (*etym. L.* deflorare), to deflower

Défoncement, sm. (*etym.* défoncer), staving, breaking in
Défoncer, va. (*etym.* dé, fond), to stave, to beat in, to dig up
Déformer, va. (*etym. L.* deformare), to deform; *se* —, vr. to be deformed or out of shape
Défourner, va. (*etym.* dé, four), to take out of the oven
Défrayer, va. (*etym.* dé, *and O.F.* frayer, *to spend*), to defray
Défrichement, sm. (*etym.* défricher), clearing
Défricher, va. (*etym.* dé, friche), to clear, to polish
Défriser, va. (*etym.* dé, friser), to uncurl, (†) to put out
Défroncer, va. (*etym.* dé, froncer), to unplait, to unknit one's brow
Défroque, sf. (*etym.* défroquer), cast-off clothes, wardrobe
Défroquer, va. (*etym.* dé, froc), to unfrock
Défunt, e, s. adj. (*etym. L.* defunctus, *dead*), deceased, defunct
Dégagé, e, past part. graceful, slender, easy, flippant, free, emancipated, (*arch.*) with a private entrance
Dégagement, sm. (*etym.* dégager), disengagement, release, redemption, unconcern, (*arch.*) a private entrance
Dégager, va. (*etym.* dé, gage), to disengage, to redeem, to take out of pledge, to call back, to withdraw, to clear, to make a private entrance to, to extricate, to evolve; *se* —, vr. to be disengaged, to get free, to get clear, to be cleared
Dégainer, va. (*etym.* dé, gaine), to unsheath
Déganter, va., *se* —, vr. (*etym.* dé, gant), to unglove
Dégarnir, va. (*etym.* dé, garnir), to strip, to untrim, to unrig, to thin; *se* —, vr. to part with, to strip oneself, to become empty
Dégât, sm. (*etym.* dé, *and O.F.* gast, *waste*), damage, havoc, waste
Dégel, sm. (*etym.* dégeler), thaw
Dégeler, va.n., *se* —, vr. to thaw
Dégénéré, e, adj. degenerate
Dégénérer, vn. (*etym. L.* degenerare), to degenerate
¶**Dégénérescence,** sf. (*etym. L.* degenerare), degeneracy
Dégingandé, e, adj. (*etym.* dé, *and* gigues-jambes), tall and ungainly
Dégluer, va., *se* —, vr. (*etym.* dé, glu), to unglue
Dégoiser, va.n. (*etym.* dé, gosier), to chirrup, to rattle on, (†) to spin a yarn
Dégommer, va. (*etym.* dé, gomme), to ungum, (†) to oust out of

Dégonflement, sm. (*etym.* dégonfler), reduction, emptying
Dégonfler, va. (*etym.* dé, gonfler), to reduce, to empty; *se* —, vr. to collapse, to subside
Dégorgement, sm. (*etym.* dé, gorger), outflow, flow, scouring
Dégorger, va. (*etym.* dé, gorge), to clear, to unstop, to disgorge, to scour; — vn. to disgorge; *se* —, vr. to disgorge, to empty oneself
Dégourdi, e, adj. restored to warmth, (‡) sharp, forward, with the chill off
Dégourdir, va. (*etym.* dé, *and O.F.* gourd, *cold*), to take off the numbness from, to restore warmth to, to sharpen the wits of, to take the chill off; *se* —, vr. to feel warmer, to feel more lively
Dégourdissement, sm. (*etym.* dégourdir), cessation of numbness, brightening up, taking the chill off
Dégoût, sm. (*etym.* dé, goût), loathing, distaste, disgust
‖**Dégoûtant, e,** adj. disgusting, loathsome, nauseous, filthy
Dégoûté, e, adj. squeamish, fastidious. ‡ *Faire le* — to be squeamish
Dégoûter, va. (*etym.* dégoût), to disgust with; *se* —, vr. to be disgusted with
Dégouttant, e, adj. (*etym.* dégoutter), dripping
Dégoutter, vn. (*etym.* dé, goutte), to trickle, to drop, to be dripping
Dégradant, e, adj. degrading, disgraceful
Dégrader, va. (*etym. L.* de, gradus), to degrade, to debase, to damage, to dilapidate; *se* —, vr. to degrade oneself, to be damaged *or* dilapidated
Dégrafer, va. (*etym.* dé, graf; *see* A-GRAF-ER), to unclasp, to unhook
Dégraissage, sm. (*etym.* dégraisser), cleaning, scouring
Dégraisser, va. (*etym.* dé, graisse), to skim, to clean, to scour
Dégraisseur, se, s. (*etym.* dégraisser), scourer
Degré, sm. (*etym. L.L.* degradus, *from L.* de, gradus, *step*), step, stairs, degree, stage
Dégréer, va. (*etym.* dé, gréer), to unrig
Dégrèvement, sm. (*etym.* dégrever), reduction
Dégrever, va. (*etym.* dé, grever), to reduce, to disburden
Dégringoler, vn. (*etym. ?*), to run down, to tumble down
Dégriser, va. (*etym.* dé, griser), to sober
Dégrossir, va. (*etym.* dé, gros), to rough-hew, to make a rough sketch
Dégrossissage, *also* **Dégrossissement,** sm. (*etym.* dégrossir), roughening down

§**Déguenillé, e,** adj. s. (*etym.* dé, guenille), ragged, tattered, ragamuffin, tatterdemalion
Déguerpir, vn. (*etym.* dé, *and O.F.* guerpir, *to abandon*), to pack off
Déguisement, sm. (*etym.* déguiser), disguise
Déguiser, va. (*etym.* dé, guise), to disguise, to dissemble, to cloak; *se* —, vr. to disguise oneself
¶**Dégustateur,** sm. (*etym.* déguster), taster
¶**Dégustation,** sf. (*etym. L.* degustatio), tasting
¶**Déguster,** va. (*etym. L.* degustare), to taste
Déhanché, e, adj. (*etym.* dé, hanche), hipshot, ungainly
Déharnachement, sm. (*etym.* déharnacher), unharnessing
Déharnacher, va. (*etym.* dé, harnacher), to unharness
Déhonté, e, adj. (*etym.* dé, honte), shameless, unblushing
Dehors, adv. (*etym.* de, hors), out, without, outside
Déifier, va. (*etym. L.* deificare), to deify
Déisme, sm. (*etym. L.* deus) deism
Déiste, s. adj. (*etym. L.* deus), deist, deistical
Déjà, adv. (*etym.* dès, jà), already
se **Déjeter,** vr. (*etym. L.* dejectare), to warp, to deviate
Déjeuner, vn. (*etym.* dé, jeûner), to breakfast
Déjoindre, va. (*etym. L.* disjungere), to disjoin
Déjouer, va. (*etym.* dé, jouer), to foil, to baffle, to thwart
Delà, prep. (*etym.* de, là), beyond, on the other side, further than
Délabrement, sm. (*etym.* délabrer), dilapidation, decay
Délabrer, va. (*etym. ?*), to shatter, to dilapidate, to reduce to tatters
Délacer, va. (*etym.* dé, lacer), to unlace; *se* —, vr. to unlace oneself, to come unlaced
Délai, sm. (*etym. L.* dilatum, *supine of* differre), delay
Délaissement, sm. (*etym.* délaisser), forlorn state, destitution
Délaisser, va. (*etym.* dé, laisser), to forsake, to cast off, to desert
Délassement, sm. (*etym.* dé, lasser), refreshment, relaxation, distraction
Délasser, va. (*etym.* dé, las), to refresh, to unbend, to relax; *se* —, vr. to refresh oneself, to unbend one's mind
Délateur, trice, s. (*etym. L.* delator), informer
Délayer, va. (*etym. L.* dilatare), to dilute, to spin out
Délecter, va. (*etym. L.* delectare, *frequent. of* delicere), to delight; *se* —, vr. to delight

Délégué, e, s. adj. delegate, deputy; delegated

Déléguer, va. (*etym. L.* delegare), to depute, to delegate, to entrust, to assign

Délétère, adj. deleterious, deadly

Délibérant, e, adj. deliberative

‖**Délibératif, ve,** adj. deliberative

‖**Délibéré, e,** adj. bold, resolute. ‡ *De propos* —, designedly

Délibéré, sm. (*Jurispr.*) deliberation

Délibérer, vn. (*etym.* dé, libérer), to deliberate, to resolve

‖**Délicat, e,** adj. (*etym. L.* delicatus = deliquatus, *liquid, soft*), delicate, weak, soft, gentle, dainty, touchy

Délicatesse, sf. (*etym.* délicat), delicacy, weakness, tenderness, niceness, fastidiousness

Délice, sm., —*s*, sf. pl. (*etym. L.* deliciæ), delight, delights

‖**Délicieux, se,** adj. (*etym. L.* deliciosus), delicious, delightful

Délié, e, adj. (*etym. L.* delicatus), slender, slim, fine, shrewd, subtle, glib, voluble; — sm. thin stroke, up stroke

Délier, va. (*etym.* dé, lier), to untie, to loosen; *se* —, vr. to unbind oneself, to get loose

¶**Délimitation,** sf. (*etym.* délimiter), fixing the boundary, boundary

¶**Délimiter,** va. (*etym. L.L.* delimitare), to fix the boundary of

Délinquant, e, s. (*etym. L.* delinquere), offender, delinquent

Délirant, e, adj. raving, delirious

Délire, sm. (*etym. L.* delirium), delirium

Délirer, vn. (*etym. L.* delirare), to rave

Délit, sm. (*etym. L.* delictum), misdemeanour, offence. *En flagrant* —, in the very act

Délivrance, sf. (*etym.* délivrer), delivery, deliverance, rescue, confinement

Délivrer, va. (*etym.* dé, libre), to deliver, to release, to rescue; *se* —, vr. to shake off, to set oneself free

Déloger, va.n. (*etym.* dé, loger), to remove, to move, to turn out, to oust

§**Déloyal, e,** adj. (*etym.* dé, loyal), disloyal, faithless, unfair

Déloyauté, sf. (*etym.* déloyal), disloyalty, falseness

Déluré, e, adj. (*etym.* leurre), disenchanted

Démagogie, sf. (*etym. Gr.* δημαγωγία), demagogy

§**Démagogique,** adj. (*etym. Gr.* δημαγωγικός), demagogical, factious

§**Démailloter,** va. (*etym.* dé, maillot), to unswathe

Demain, adv. (*etym. L.* de, mane), to-morrow

Démancher, va.n. (*etym.* dé, manche), to take off the handle of, to shift

Demande, sf. (*etym.* demander), question, inquiry, request, claim

Demander, va. (*etym. L.* demandare, *to confide*), to ask, to beg, to crave, to sue

Demandeur, eresse, s. (*jurisp.*) plaintiff, applicant

Démangeaison, sf. (*etym.* démanger), itching, itch

Démanger, vn. (*etym.* dé, manger), to itch

Démanteler, va. (*etym.* dé, mantel, manteau), to dismantle

Démantibuler, va. (*etym.* dé, mandibule), to break the jaw, (†) to break anything. *Se* — *la mâchoire*, to break one's jaw

Démarche, sf. (*etym.* dé, marche), gait, walk, bearing, proceeding, application

Démarquer, va. (*etym.* dé, marque), to unmark

Démarrer, va.n. (*etym.* dé, [a]marrer), to unlash, to unbend, to leave moorings

Démasquer, va. (*etym.* dé, masquer), to unmask; *se* —, vr. to unmask oneself

Démâter, va. (*etym.* dé, mât), to dismast

Démêlé, sm. (*etym.* démêler), quarrel, contest

Démêler, va. (*etym.* dé, mêler), to disentangle, to part, to unravel, to make out, to discover, to have to do with; *se* —, vr. to be unravelled, to clear up, to stand out

Démêloir, sm. (*etym.* démêler), comb

Démembrement, sm. (*etym.* démembrer), dismemberment

Démembrer, va. (*etym. L.* demembrare), to tear limb from limb, to dismember

Déménagement, sm. (*etym.* déménager), removing, removal, moving

Déménager, va.n. (*etym.* dé, ménage), to remove, to move, to march off

Démence, sf. (*etym. L.* dementia), insanity, madness

se Démener, vr. (*etym.* dé, mener), to struggle, to labour hard

Démenti, sm. (*etym.* démentir), lie, contradiction, disappointment

Démentir, va. (*etym.* dé, mentir), to give the lie to, to contradict flatly, to gainsay, to belie; *se* —, vr. to contradict oneself *or* each other, to discontinue, to fall off

Démérite, sm. (*etym.* dé, mérite), demerit, unworthiness

Démériter, vn. (*etym.* dé, mériter), to do amiss, to forfeit the esteem

‖**Démesuré, e,** adj. (*etym.* dé, mesuré), huge, immoderate, unbounded

Démettre, va. (*etym.* dé, mettre), to dislocate, to dismiss, to overrule; *se* —, vr. to dislocate, to put out of joint, to be put out of joint, to resign

Démeubler, va. (*etym.* dé, meuble), to strip of furniture

Demeurant (Au), loc. adv. (*etym.* demeurer), after all, however

Demeure, sf. (*etym.* demeurer), abode, dwelling, residence. *Mettre quelqu'un en* — *de*, to call upon a person to. *Il y a péril en la* —, the thing brooks no delay

Demeurer, vn. (*etym. L.* demorari), to live, to dwell, to reside

Demi, e, adj. (*etym. L.* dimidius), half, semi

Démission, sf. (*etym. L.* dimissio), resignation

Démissionnaire, adj. s. (*etym.* démission), that has resigned

Démocrate, sm. (*etym.* see DÉMOCRATIE), democrat

Démocratie, sf. (*etym. Gr.* δημοκρατία), democracy

‖**Démocratique,** adj. (*etym. Gr.* δημοκρατικός), democratical

Demoiselle, sf. (*etym. L.L.* dominicella), damsel, young lady, maiden, spinster, single woman, dragon-fly, beetle

Démolir, va. (*etym. L.* demoliri), to pull down, to demolish, to overthrow

Démolisseur, sm. (*etym.* démolir), puller down

Démonétisation, sf. (*etym.* démonétiser), calling in of the coin

Démonétiser, va. (*etym. L.* de, moneta, coin), to call in

Démoniaque, adj. s. (*etym. Gr.* δαιμονιακός), demoniacal, madman

Démonstrateur, sm. (*etym. L.* demonstrator), demonstrator

‖**Démonstratif, ve,** adj. (*etym. L.* demonstrativus), demonstrative

Démonter, va. (*etym.* dé, monter), to unhorse, to dismount, to take to pieces, to unset, to supersede, to baffle; *se* —, vr. to fall to pieces, to get unsettled

Démontrer, va. (*etym. L.* demonstrare), to show, to demonstrate; *se* —, vr. to be shown

Démoraliser, va. (*etym.* dé, moraliser), to demoralise; *se* —, vr. to be demoralised

Démordre, vn. (*etym.* dé, mordre), to let go, to swerve from

Démunir, va. (*etym.* dé, munir), to deprive of provisions; *se* —, vr. to part with

Démuseler, va. (*etym.* dé, museau), to unmuzzle

Dénaturé, e, adj. unnatural

Dénaturer, va. (*etym.* dé, nature), to change the nature of, to distort, to misrepresent, to disguise

Dénégation, sf. (*etym. L.L.* denegatio), denial

Déni, sm. (*etym.* see DÉNIER), refusal, denial

Déniaiser, va. (*etym.* dé, niais), to make a person less stupid, (*iron.*) to deceive, to make a fool of

Dénicher, va. (*etym.* dé, nicher), to take out of a nest, (*etym.* dé, niche) of a niche, to hunt, to ferret out; — vn. to fly away, to be afoot, to be off

Dénicheur, sm. (*etym.* dénicher), birdsnester, hunter after, groper for

Denier, sm. (*etym. L.* denarius), denarium, denier, penny, farthing, mite, sum, revenue, interest. *Le* — *de saint Pierre*, Peter's pence. ‡ — *à Dieu*, earnest money. ‡ *Au* — 20, 25 (at the rate of one franc for 20 or 25), 5 per cent., 4 per cent.

Dénier, va. (*etym. L.* denegare), to deny

Dénigrement, sm. (*etym.* dénigrer), disparagement

Dénigrer, va. (*etym. L.* denigrare, *black*), to disparage, to sneer at

Dénombrement, sm. (*etym.* dénombrer), numbering, census, catalogue

Dénominateur, sm. (*etym. L.L.* denominator), denominator

‖**Dénominatif, ve,** adj. (*etym. L.L.* denominativus), denominative

Dénoncer, va. (*etym. L.* denuntiare), to denounce, to declare, to inform against

Dénonciateur, trice, s. (*etym. L.* denuntiatorem), denunciator

Dénonciation, sf. (*etym. L.* denuntiationem), denunciation

Dénoter, va. (*etym. L.* denotare), to denote, to betoken

Dénouer, va. (*etym. L.L.* denodare), to untie, to loosen, to unravel; *se* —, vr. to come untied, to be unravelled, to unravel, to wind up, to shoot, to grow

Dénoûment, sm. (*etym.* dénouer), issue, event, end

Denrée, sf. (*etym. L.* denarius), provisions, article of food, commodity, ware

Densité, sf. (*etym. L.* densitas), density

Dent, sf. (*etym. L.* dens), tooth, fang, cog, burnisher. ‡ —*s de lait, de sagesse*, first teeth, wisdom-teeth. *Faire ses* —*s*, to cut one's teeth. *Coup de* —, bite. *Avoir les* —*s longues*, to be very hungry. *Il n'en cassera que d'une* —, he shall not have any. *A belles* —*s*, ravenously, eagerly. *Être sur les* —*s*, to be quite tired out. *Parler, prononcer du bout des* —*s*, to talk in a lisping tone. *Rire du bout des* —*s*, to force oneself into a laugh. *Avoir une* — *contre quelqu'un*, to have a grudge against a person. *Montrer les grosses* —*s*, to speak sharply. — *-de-lion*, dandelion

Denté, e, adj. (*etym. L.* dentatus), cogged, toothed, denticulated

Dentelé, e, adj. (*etym.* dentelle), denticulated, jagged

Dentelle, sf. (*etym. L.* denticulus, *dimin. of* dens), lace, lace-work

Dentelure, sf. (*etym.* dentelle), indentation, denticulation

Dentiste, sm. (*etym.* dent), dentist

Denture, sf. (*etym.* dent), a set of teeth, the cogs of a wheel

¶**Dénuder,** va. (*etym. L.* denudare), to lay bare, to denude

Dénué, e, adj. destitute

Dénuer, va. (*etym. L.* denudare), to strip, to bereave; *se* —, vr. to strip oneself

Dénûment, sm. (*etym.* dénuer), destitution, bereavement

§**Dépareillé, e,** adj. incomplete

§**Dépareiller,** va. (*etym.* dé, pareil), to make imperfect, to spoil a set

Déparer, va. (*etym.* dé, parer), to disfigure, to spoil the look of

Déparler, va. (*etym.* dé, paire), to take away one, to part

Départ, sm. (*etym.* départir), departure, leaving

Département, sm. (*etym.* départir), department

Départir, va. (*etym.* dé, partir, *in the sense of* partager), to distribute, to dispense, to bestow, to endow; *se* —, vr. to desist, to give up

Dépasser, va. (*etym.* dé, passer), to go beyond, to pass, to overshoot, to excel

Dépaver, va. (*etym.* dé, paver), to unpave

Dépayser, va. (*etym.* dé, pays), to send abroad, to send from home, to give new habits to, to bewilder; *se* —, vr. to leave the country, to leave one's home

Dépecer, va. (*etym.* dé, pièce), to cut up, to carve

Dépêche, sf. (*etym. see* DÉPÊCHER), despatch

Dépêcher, va. (*etym. I.* dispacciare), to despatch, to make haste with, to forward; *se* —, vr. to make haste

Dépeindre, va. (*etym. L.* depingere), to paint, to depict

§**Dépenaillé, e,** adj. (*etym.* dé, *and O.F.* penaille, *a rag*), ragged, soiled

Dépendance, sf. (*etym.* dépendant), dependence, dependency, appendage, outer premises

Dépendant, e, adj. (*etym.* dépendre, *v.n.*), dependent

Dépendre, va. (*etym.* dé, pendre), to take down; — vn. (*etym. L.* dependere), to depend, to be dependent, to proceed, to result, to be in the gift, to belong

Dépens, sm. plur. (*etym. L.* depensum, *supine of* dependere), expense, costs

Dépense, sf. (*etym. L.* depensum), expense, expenditure, waste, larder, pantry

Dépenser, va. (*etym.* dépense), to spend, to lay out, to waste

Dépensier, ière, adj. (*etym. L.* dispensare), extravagant, a spendthrift. — sm. a bursar

Dépérir, vn. (*etym. L.* deperire), to decay, to pine away

Dépérissement, sm. dépérir), decay, withering, decline

se **Dépêtrer,** vr. (*etym. O.F.* dé, pestrer, *from the L.L.* pastorium, *a fastening put to a horse*), to get out, to get rid

Dépeuplement, sm. depopulation

Dépeupler, va. (*etym.* dé, peupler), to unpeople, to depopulate, to thin; *se* —, vr. to become unpeopled *or* unstocked

Dépilatoire, adj. (*etym.* dépiler), which makes the hair fall

Dépiler, va. (*etym. L.* de, pilus), to make the hair fall; *se* —, vr. to lose its hair

Dépister, va. (*etym.* dé, piste), to track, to hunt out

Dépit, sm. (*etym. L.* despectus), spite, rancour

Dépiter, va. (*etym. L.* despectare), to vex, to fret, to provoke; *se* —, vr. to be vexed with, to be vexed, to fret

Déplacé, e, past part. adj. (*etym.* déplacer), misplaced, unbecoming

Déplacement, sm. removal, displacing

Déplacer, va. (*etym.* dé, place), to displace, to remove; *se* —, vr. to change one's abode *or* one's place

Déplaire, vn. (*etym. L.* displicere), to displease, to offend. ‡ *N'en déplaise à*, with due deference to. *Se* —, vr. to be displeasing to oneself, to dislike each other

§**Déplaisant, e,** adj. unpleasant, displeasing

Déplaisir, sm. (*etym.* déplaire), displeasure, sorrow, trouble

Déplanter, va. (*etym.* dé, planter), to displant

Déplier, va. (*etym.* dé, plier), to unfold, to open, *se* —, vr. to come unfolded

Déplisser, va. (*etym.* dé, plisser), to unplait

Déploiement, sm. (*etym.* déployer), unfolding, display, show

Déplorer, va. (*etym L.* deplorare), to bewail, to deplore

Déployer, va. (*etym.* dé, ployer), to unfold, to spread open, to unfurl, to deploy. ‡ *Rire à gorge déployée*, to laugh boisterously. *Enseignes déployées*, colours flying. *Se* —, vr. to be unfolded, to unroll itself, to be spread to the wind, to stretch out, to deploy

Dépolir, va. (*etym.* dé, polir), to take off the polish of. ‡ *Du verre dépoli*, rough glass

Dépopulariser, va. (*etym.* dé, populariser), to render unpopular; *se* —, vr. to lose one's popularity

Déportation, sf. (*etym. L.* deportatio), transportation

Déportement, sm. (*etym.* déporter), behaviour, good or bad; scandalous behaviour

Déporter, va. (*etym. L.* deportare), to transport. *Les déportés*, the convicts

Déposant, sm. (*etym.* déposer), deponent, depositor

Déposer, va. (*etym.* dé, poser), to lay down, to put down, to deposit, to entrust, to commit, to depose; — vn. to give evidence, to prove, to settle

Dépositaire, sm. (*etym. L.* depositarius), depositary, guardian, confidant

Déposséder, va. (*etym.* dé, posséder), to dispossess, to strip

Dépôt, sm. (*etym. L.* depositum), depositing, trust, deposit, depository, office, agency, depôt, lock-up house. *Mandat de* —, writ of imprisonment. — *de mendicité*, workhouse

§**Dépouille,** sf. (*etym. L.* de, spolium), slough, skin, remains

§**Dépouillé, e,** past part. despoiled, bare

§**Dépouillement,** sm. (*etym.* dépouiller), privation, giving up, abstract, summing up

§**Dépouiller,** va. to skin, to take off the skin of, to strip, to despoil, to rob, to lay aside, to make an abstract of, to sum up

Dépourvu, e, adj. (*etym.* dé, pourvu), unprovided, destitute. ‡ *Au* —, unawares

Dépraver, va. (*etym. L.* depravare), to deprave, to vitiate, *se* —, vr. to become depraved

Déprécier, va. (*etym. L.* de, pretium), to underrate, to depreciate

Déprédateur, sm. (*etym. L.* deprædator), depredator, plunderer

Déprimé, e, past part. flattened

Déprimer, va. (*etym. L.* deprimere), to depress, to detract from the merit of

Depuis, prep., **Depuis que,** conj. (*etym.* de, puis), for, during, from

Députation, sf. (*etym. L.L.* deputationem), deputation, a seat in the House, the deputies

Député, sm. (*etym.* député), deputy

Députer, va.n. (*etym. L.* deputare), to depute

Déracinement, sm. (*etym.* déraciner), rooting up, uprooting

Déraciner, va. (*etym.* dé, racine), to root up, to extirpate, to eradicate; *se* —, vr. to be uprooted

§**Déraillement,** sm. (*etym.* dérailler), running off the rails

§**Dérailler,** vn. (*etym.* dé, *Eng.* rail), to run off the rails

Déraison, sf. (*etym.* dé, raison), irrationality, nonsense, folly

‖**Déraisonnable,** adj. (*etym.* dé, raisonnable), unreasonable, irrational

Déraisonnement, sm. (*etym* déraisonner), unreasonableness

Déraisonner, vn. (*etym.* dé, raisonner), to talk incoherently, to talk nonsense

Dérangé, e, part. adj. unsettled, disordered

Dérangement, sm. (*etym.* déranger), derangement, disturbance, disorder, inconvenience

Déranger, va. (*etym.* dé, ranger), to derange, to displace, to move, to upset, to disturb

†**Dératé, e,** adj. (*etym.* dé, rate), lively

Derechef, adv. (*etym.* de, re, *and* chef tête), once again

Déréglé, e, adj. irregular, out of order, lawless, profligate

Dérèglement, sm. (*etym.* dé, régler), irregularity, profligacy

Dérégler, va. (*etym.* dé, règle), to put out of order; *se* —, vr. to get out of order, to lead an irregular life

Dérider, va. (*etym.* dé, rider), to unwrinkle, to cheer up; *se* —, vr. to smooth one's brow

Dérisoire, adj. (*etym. L.* derisorius), derisive

Dérive, sf. (*etym. Engl.* to drive), leeway drift. *Aller en* —, to drift

Dérivé, e, adj sm. (*etym.* dé, rive), derivative

Dériver, vn. to leave the shore, to drift; (*etym. L.* derivare), to be derived; — va. (*etym.* dé, river), to unrivet

‖**Dernier, ère,** adj. (*etym. L.* de, retro), last, latter, farthest

Dérobé, e, adj. past part. private, back, spare, leisure. *A la dérobée*, by stealth

Dérober, va. (*etym.* dé, *O.F.* rober, *to rob*), to steal from, to screen, to shield; *se* —, vr. to steal away, to escape, to shun, to be hidden, to sink

Dérogatoire, adj. (*etym. L.* derogatorius), derogatory

Dérogeant, e, adj derogating

Déroger, vn. (*etym. L.* derogare), to derogate, to stoop

§**Dérouiller,** va. (*etym.* dé, rouille), to take or rub the rust off, to brighten up; *se* —, vr. to lose one's rust, to brighten up

Dérouler, va. (*etym.* dé, rouler), to unfold, to unroll;

se —, vr. to unroll, to unfold itself, to open to one's view

Déroute, sf. (*etym.* *O.F.* derout *or* deront, *from the L.* disruptus), rout, defeat, disorder, ruin

Dérouter, va. (*etym.* déroute), to lead astray, to baffle

Derrière, adv. prep. sm. (*etym.* *L.* de, retro), back, behind, hind part, breech, bottom, backside, rear

Derviche, Dervis, sm. (*etym.* *Pers.* derouich, *poor*), dervise *or* dervish

Dès, prep. (*etym.* *L.* de, ex), from, since, even in

se Désabonner, vr. (*etm.* dès, abonner), to leave off subscribing

Désabuser, va. (*etym.* dès, abuser), to undeceive, to disabuse; *se* —, vr. to be disabused, to undeceive oneself

Désaccord, sm. (*etym.* dès, accord), disagreement, variance

Désaccoutumer, va. (*etym.* dès, accoutumer), to disaccustom, to break; *se* —, vr. to break oneself, to leave off

Désaffection, sf. (*etym.* dès, affection), disaffection

Désaffectionner, va. (*etym.* désaffection), to disaffect; *se* —, vr. to lose the affection of

‖**Désagréable,** adj. (*etym.* dès, agréable), unpleasant, disagreeable

Désagrément, sm. (*etym.* dès, agrément), unpleasantness, disagreeableness, discomfort, vexation

Désaltérer, va. (*etym.* dès, altérer), to quench the thirst of, to refresh; *se* —, vr. to quench one's thirst

Désappointement, sm. (*etym.* désappointer), disappointment

Désappointer, va. (*etym.* dès, appointer), to disappoint

Désapprendre, va. (*etm.* dès, apprendre), to unlearn

Désapprobateur, trice, adj. disapproving, of disapproval, fault-finding

Désapprobation, sf. (*etym.* dès, approbation), disapprobation

Désappropriation, sf. (*etym.* désapproprier), giving up property

Désapproprier, va. (*etm.* dès, approprier), to strip a person of his property; *se* —, vr. to divest oneself

Désapprouver, va. (*etm.* dès, approuver), to disapprove, to dislike

Désarçonner, va. (*etym.* dès, arçon), to unhorse, to run down

Désargenter, va. (*etym.* dès, argenter), to unplate, to drain of cash; *se* —, vr. to lose its plating, to empty one's pocket

Désarmé, e, adj. unarmed, disarmed

Désarmement, sm. (*etym.* désarmer), disarming

Désarmer, va. (*etym.* dès, armer), to unarm, to disarm, to strip, to pay off, to uncock a gun; *se* —, vr. to unarm, to disarm

Désarroi, sm. (*etym.* dès, *O.F.* arroi), confusion, disorder

Désassorti, e, adj. past part. (*etym.* dès, assorti), mismatched, ill-matched

Désastre, sm. (*etym.* dès, astre), disaster

‖**Désastreux, se,** adj. (*etym.* désastre), disastrous

Désavantage, sm. (*etym.* dès, avantage), disadvantage, detriment

‖**Désavantageux, se,** adj. (*etym.* désavantage), disadvantageous, detrimental, unfavourable

Désaveu, sm. (*etym.* dès, aveu), disavowal

Désavouer, va. (*etym.* dès, avouer), to disown, to disavow

Désceller, va. (*etym.* dès, sceller), to unfasten, to loosen, to unseal

Descendance, sf. (*etym.* descendant), descent, lineage

Descendant, e, adj. (*etym.* descendre), descending, down, ebb

Descendre, vn. (*etym.* *L.* descendere), to go down, to get down, to descend, to alight, to make a descent, to ebb, to slope down, to lead down; — va. to take down, to reach down

Descente, sf. (*etym.* descendre), descent, going down, declivity, hill-side, search, funnel, down-stroke, rupture

Descriptif, ve, adj. (*etym.* *L.* descriptus), descriptive

Désembarquement, sm. (*etym.* désembarquer), landing, disembarking

Désembarquer, va. to land, to disembark, to unship

Désemparer, va. (*nav.*) to disable; — vn. to quit, to leave. *Sans* —, without leaving off

Désemplir, va. (*etym.* dès, emplir), to empty a little; — vn. to be less full; *se* —, vr. to get empty

Désenchantement, sm. (*etym.* désenchanter), disenchantment

Désenchanter, va. (*etym.* dès, enchanter), to disenchant

Désenclouer, va. (*etym.* dès, enclouer), to unnail, to unspike

Désenfler, va. (*etym.* dès, enfler), to reduce a swelling, to take the wind out of; — vn., *se* —, vr. to be less swollen

se Désenivrer, vr. (*etym.* dès, enivrer), to get sober again

Désennuyer, va. (*etym.* dès, ennuyer), to divert, to drive away dulness from; *se* —, vr. to divert one's thoughts

Désensorceler, va. (*etym.* dès, ensorceler), to unbewitch

Désert, e, adj. (*etym.* *L.* desertus), desert, wild, uninhabited. — sm. wilderness, desert

Déserter, va.n. (*etym.* désert), to forsake, to desert

Déserteur, sm. (*etym.* *L.* desertor), deserter

Désespérant, e, adj. dispiriting, most provoking

‖**Désespéré, e,** past part. adj. (*etym.* désespérer), in despair, disconsolate, much vexed

Désespérer, vn. (*etym.* dès, espérer), to despair, to give up all hope; — va. to drive to despair, to vex beyond expression; *se* —, vr. to despair, to despond

Désespoir, sm. (*etym.* dès, espoir), despair, hopelessness, desperate act, despondency. *Coup de* —, desperate attempt. *En* — *de cause*, as a last shift

§**Déshabillé,** sm. (*etym.* déshabiller), dishabille, an undress

§**Déshabiller,** va. (*etym.* dès, habiller), to undress, to strip; *se* —, vr. to take off one's clothes, to undress

Déshabituer, va. (*etym.* dès, habituer), to break, to disaccustom; *se* —, vr. to break oneself of

Déshériter, va. (*etym.* dès, hériter), to disinherit

Désheurer, va. (*etym.* dès, heure), to interfere with the time of certain stated occupations; *se* —, vr. to be irregular as to time

Déshonnête, adj. (*etym.* dès, honnête), immodest, unseemly

Déshonneur, sm. (*etym.* dès, honneur), dishonour, disgrace

Déshonorant, e, adj. dishonourable, shameful

Déshonorer, va. (*etym.* dès, honorer), to dishonour, to disgrace; *se* —, vr. to dishonour oneself

§**Désigner,** va. (*etym.* *L.* designare), to designate, to point out, to denote, to betoken

¶**Désillusionner,** va. (*etym.* dès, illusion), to destroy the illusions of

Désinfecter, va. (*etym.* dès, infecter), to disinfect, to cleanse, to purify

Désinfection, sf. (*etym.* dès, infection), disinfection

Désintéressé, e, adj. uninterested

Désintéressement, sm. (*etym.* désintéresser), disinterestedness

Désintéresser, va. (*etym.* dès, intéresser), to indemnify, to repay

Désinvolture, sf. (*etym.* *I.* disinvoltura), ease of motion, easy carriage

Désir, sm. desire, longing, wish

Désirer, va. (*etym.* *L.* desiderare), to desire, to wish for, to long for. *Laisser à* —, to be unsatisfactory

Désireux, se, adj. (*etym.* désir), desirous

Désistement, sm. (*etym.* désister), desistance

se Désister, vr. (*etym.* *L.* desistere), to desist

Désobéir, vn. (*etym.* dès, obéir), to disobey, to transgress

Désobéissance, sf. (*etym.* désobéir), disobedience

Désobéissant, e, adj. disobedient, undutiful, froward

Désobligeance, sf. (*etym.* désobligeant), ungraciousness

‖**Désobligeant, e,** adj. disobliging

Désobliger, va. (*etym.* dès, obliger), to disoblige

Désœuvré, e, adj. s. (*etym.* dès, œuvre), unemployed, idle; idler

Désœuvrement, sm. idleness

Désolant, e, adj. distressing, annoying, tiresome

Désolé, e, past part. adj. laid waste, desolate, disconsolate

Désoler, va. (*etym.* *L.* desolare), to lay waste, to grieve, to annoy; *se* —, vr. to be disconsolate

Désopiler, va. (*etym.* dès, *L.* oppilare, *to stop up*), to remove obstructions. *Se* — *la rate*, to laugh immoderately

Désordonné, e, adj. disorderly, lawless, ungovernable, inordinate, wild

Désordonner, va. (*etym.* dès, ordonner), to disorder

Désordre, sm. (*etym.* dès, ordre), disorder, bustle, uproar, discomposure, disturbance

Désorganisateur, trice, adj. (*etym.* désorganiser), disorganizing

Désorganisation, sf. (*etym.* désorganiser), disorganization

Désorganiser, va. (*etym.* dès, organiser), to disorganize; *se* —, vr. to become disorganized

Désorienter, va. (*etym.* dès, orienter), to put out of one's reckoning, to bewilder

Désormais, adv. (*etym.* dès, *and O.F.* ores, mais), hereafter, henceforward

Désosser, va. (*etym.* dès, os), to unbone, to dissect

Despote, sm. despot

‖**Despotique,** adj. despotic, despotical

Despotisme, sm. despotism

se Dessaisir, vr. (*etym.* des, saisir), to let go, to disseize

Dessaler, va. (*etym.* des, saler), to unsalt

Dessangler, va. (*etym.* des, sangler), to ungirth

Desséchant, e, adj. drying, withering

Desséchement, sm. (*etym.* des, sécher), draining, drying up, state of emaciation

Dessécher, va., *se* —, vr. (*etym.* des, sec), to dry, to drain, to waste away, to wither

Dessein, sm. (*etym. see* DESSIN), design, view, purpose

Desserrer, va. (*etym.* des, serrer), to loosen, to slacken. ‡ — *les dents*, to open one's mouth

Dessert, sm. (*etym.* desservir), dessert

Desserte, sf. leavings, parochial duty

Desservant, sm. (*etym.* desservir), officiating clergyman, curate

Desservir, va. (*etym.* des, servir), to remove the cloth, to officiate at, to put down and take up passengers, to do an ill turn to

Dessiccatif, ve, adj. (*etym. L.L.* desiccativus), desiccative

§**Dessiller,** va. (*etym.* des, cil), to unseal, to open a person's eyes

Dessin, sm. (*etym. see* DÉSIGNER), drawing, sketch, pattern, draught. *A* —, figured. *A grand* —, of a large pattern

Dessinateur, sm. (*etym.* dessiner), draughtsman, pattern-drawer

Dessiner, va. to draw, to sketch, to plan

Dessouder, va. (*etym.* des, souder), to unsolder; *se* —, vr. to come unsoldered

Dessous, adv. (*etym.* des, sous), beneath, below, underneath

Dessus, adv. (*etym.* des, *sus or* sur), on, upon, above, uppermost. ‡ *Sens* — *dessous*, upside down. *En avoir par-* — *la tête*, to be worried out of one's life. — sm. top, upper part, right side, lid, cover, direction. — *de porte*, frieze-panel. — *de vent*, (*nav.*) weather-gage, wind

Destin, sm. (*etym. see* DESTINER), fate, destiny, doom, career

Destinataire, sm. (*etym.* destiner), person to whom it is addressed

Destination, sf. (*etym. L.* destinationem), destination. *A* —, to one's destination. *A* — *de*, (*nav.*) bound for

Destinée, sf. (*etym.* destiner), destiny, fate, doom

Destiner, va. (*etym. L.* destinare), to destine, to design, to doom; *se* —, vr. to be destined

Destitué, e, adj. destitute, devoid

Destituer, va. (*etym. L.* destituere), to dismiss

Destructeur, trice, s. adj. (*etym. L.* destructorem), destroyer, destroying

Destructif, ve, adj. (*etym. L.* destructivus), destructive

Désunion, sf. (*etym.* dés, union), disjunction, disunion

Désunir, va. (*etym.* dés, unir), to disunite; *se* —, vr. to be disunited

Détaché, e, adj. detached, loose

Détachement, sm. (*etym.* détacher), unconcern, indifference, disengagement, detachment

Détacher, va. (*etym.* dé, tache), to take out the stains of, to unfasten, to untie, to undo, to take down, (*mus.*) to staccato, to win over; *se* —, vr. to come unfastened, to fall, to break off, to be disengaged, to stand out

§**Détail,** sm. detail, particular, retail

§**Détaillant, e,** adj. retail dealer, retailer

§**Détailler,** va. (*etym.* dé, tailler), to cut up, to retail,

Détaler, va. (*etm.* dé, étaler), to pack up, to scamper away

Déteindre, va. (*etym.* dé, teindre), to take out the colour of; —, vn., *se* —, vr. to fade, to lose its colour, to leave a mark

Dételer, va. (*etym.* dé, atteler), to take out the horses, to unyoke

Détendre, va. (*etym.* dé, tendre), to unbend, to relax, to slacken, to take down; *se* —, vr. to be slackened, to unbend

Détenir, va. (*etym.* dé, tenir), to withhold, to detain

Détente, sf. (*etym.* détendre), trigger, detent, expansion. † *Dur à la* —, a tight-fisted hand

Détenteur, sm. (*etym. L.* detentorem), a holder of property

Détenu, e, past part. (*etym. see* DÉTENIR), prisoner

Déterger, va.n. (*etym. L.* detergere), to clean

Détériorer, va. (*etm. L.* deterior, *worse*), to deteriorate, to spoil; *se* —, vr. to get spoilt

Déterminant, e, adj. determinative, conclusive

‖**Déterminatif, ve,** adj. determinative

Déterminé, e, adj. (*etym.* déterminer), determinate, appointed, keen, resolute. *Un* —, a desperate fellow

Déterminer, va. (*etym. L.* determinare), to determine, to induce, to persuade; *se* —, vr. to determine, to make up one's mind

Déterrer, va. (*etym.* dé, terre), to dig up, to unearth, to ferret out

Détester, va. (*etym. L.* detestari), to hate, to loathe, to detest; *se* —, vr. to loathe oneself, to detest each other

Détoner, vn. (*etym. L.* detonare), to detonate

Détonner, vn. (*etym.* dé, ton), to sing out of tune

Détordre, va. (*etym.* dé, tordre), to untwist, to unwring

§**Détortiller,** va. (*etym.* dé, tortiller), to untwist

Détour, sm. (*etym.* dé, tour), turn, bend, winding, wile, shift, roundabout way

Détourné, e, adj. by, unfrequented, out of the way, circuitous

Détournement, sm. (*etym.* détourner), turning aside, embezzlement

Détourner, va. (*etym.* dé, tourner), to turn away, to divert, to avert, to ward off, to embezzle, to make away with, to wrest; *se* —, vr. to go out of one's way

Détracteur, sm. (*etym. L.* detractor), detracter, traducer, sneerer

Détraquer, va. (*etym.* dé, traquer), to spoil the paces of, to put out of order. ‡ *Une tête détraquée*, a disordered brain

Détrempe, sf. water-colours. *A la* —, in water-colours

Détremper, va. (*etym.* dé, tremper), to dilute, to soften

Détresse, sf. (*etym. L.* districtum), distress

Détriment, sm. (*etym. L.* detrimentum), detriment, (*nat. hist.*) remains

Détroit, sm. (*etym. L.* districtus), straits, pass

Détromper, va. (*etym.* dé, tromper), to undeceive; *se* —, vr. to be undeceived

Détrôner, va. (*etym.* dé, trône), to dethrone

Détrousser, va. (*etym.* dé, trousse), to let down, to rifle

Détruire, va. (*etym. L.* destruere), to destroy, to overthrow, to subvert, to ruin; *se* —, vr. to fall into decay, to make away with oneself, to destroy each other

Dette, sf. (*etym. L.* debitum), debt, duty

§**Deuil,** sm. grief, mourning. *En* —, in mourning. *Mener le* —, to be the chief mourner

Deutéronome, sm. Deuteronomy

Deux, adj. sm. (*etym. L.* duo), two, deuce

‖**Deuxième,** adj. (*etym.* deux), second

Dévaliser, va. (*etym.* dé, valise), to plunder, to rifle, to strip

Devancer, va. (*etym.* de, avant), to go before, to get the start of

Devancier, ière, s. (*etym.* devancer), predecessor, forefathers, ancestors

Devant, adv. (*etym.* de, avant), before, in front of. *Au-* — *de*, before. *Par-* —, before

Devanture, sf. (*etym.* devant), front

Dévastateur, trice, s. adj. ravager, despoiler, destroyer

Dévaster, va. (*etym. L.* devastare), to devastate

Déveine, sf. (*etym.* de, veine), a series of unfavourable chances at play

Développement, sm. (*etym.* développer), unfolding, development, expansion, deploying

Développer, va. (*etym.* ?), to unwrap, to undo, to unfold, to develop; *se* —, vr. to develop oneself, to expand, to enlarge, to thrive, to be unfolded, to stretch out

Devenir, vn. (*etym. L.* devenire), to become, to grow

Dévergondage, sm. (*etym.* dévergondé), shamelessness, licentiousness

Dévergondé, e, adj. s. (*etym.* de, vergogne = *L.* verecundia), shameless

Devers, prep. (*etym.* de, vers), before, by

Déverser, va.n. to overflow, to incline

se **Dévêtir,** vr. (*etym.* dé, vêtir), to divest oneself

Dévider, va. (*etym.* dé, vide), to wind

Dévidoir, sm. (*etym.* dévider), reel, winder

Dévier, vn., *se* —, vr. (*etm. L.* deviare), to deviate, to swerve

Devin, eresse, s. (*etym. L.* divinus), soothsayer, conjurer

Deviner, va. (*etym.* devin), to foretell, to divine, to find out, to fathom; *se* —, vr. to understand each other

Devis, sm. (*etym. L.* divisum), estimate

Dévisager, va. (*etym.* dé, visage), to scratch the face of, to stare at

Devise, sf. motto, device

Deviser, va. (*etym.* devise), to chat

Dévisser, va. (*etym.* dé, vis), to unscrew

Dévoiement, sm. (*etym.* dévoyer), looseness of the bowels

Dévoiler, va. (*etym.* dé, voile), to unveil, to display, to disclose; *se* —, vr. to unveil, to be unveiled

Devoir, va. (*etym. L.* debere), to owe, to be indebted to, to be obliged, to be necessary

Devoir, sm. duty, task, workmen's union. *Se mettre en* — *de*, to set about. *Rendre ses* —*s*, to pay one's respects

Dévolu, sm. (*etym. L.* devolutus), lapse of right, provision. † *Jeter son* — *sur*, to make choice of

Dévorant, e, adj. devouring, ravenous

Dévorateur, trice, s. adj. (*etym. L.* devoratorem), devourer, devouring

Dévorer, va. (*etym. L.* devorare), to devour, to eat up, to squander away, to prey upon; *se* —, vr. to devour each other

‖**Dévot, e,** adj. (*etym. L.* devotus), devout, sanctimonious

Dévotion, sf. (*etym. L.* devotionem), devoutness, devotion. *Être en* —, to be at prayers

Dévouement, sm. (*etym.* dévouer), self-sacrifice, devotion, devotedness

Dévouer, va. (*etym.* dé, vouer), to devote, to consign; *se* —, vr. to devote oneself

se Dévoyer, vr. (*etym.* dé, voie), to lose one's way

Dextérité, sf. (*etym. L.* dexteritas), dexterity, expertness, skill

‖**Diable**, sm. (*etym. Gr.* διάβολος), devil. *Au — soit de, le — emporte*, the deuce take. *Ce n'est pas le* —, it is no great things. *Faire le — à quatre*, to play the deuce

Diablerie, sf. (*etym.* diable), devilry

Diablesse, sf. (*etym.* diable), she-devil

Diablotin, sm. (*dimin. of* diable), imp of the devil

Diabolique, adj. (*etym. Gr.* διαβολικός), diabolical, devilish

Diaconat, sm. (*etym. L.L.* diaconatus), deaconship, deaconry, diaconate

Diacre, sm. (*etym. Gr.* διάκονος), deacon

Diadème, sm. (*etym. Gr.* διάδημα), diadem

Diagnostique, adj. (*etym. Gr.* διαγνωστικός), diagnostical

Dialecte, sm. (*etym. Gr.* διάλεκτος), dialect

Dialecticien, sm. (*etym.* dialectique), dialectician

‖**Dialectique**, adj. sf. (*etym.* διαλεκτική), dialectic, dialectics

Diamant, sm. (*etym. L.* adamantem), diamond

‖**Diamétral, e**, adj. (*etym.* diamètre), diametrical

Diamètre, sm. (*etym. Gr.* διάμετρος), diameter

Diane, sf. (*etym. L.* dies, day), reveille, morning gun

‖**Diantre**, sm. (*etym. euphemism for* diable), the deuce

Diaphane, adj. (*etym. Gr.* διαφανής), transparent, diaphanous

Diarrhée, sf. diarrhœa

Dictateur, sm. (*etym. L.* dictator), dictator

Dictature, sf. (*etym. L.* dictatura), dictatorship

Dictée, sf. (*etym.* dicter), dictation

Dicter, va. (*etym. L.* dictare), to dictate

Dictionnaire, sm. (*etym.* diction), dictionary

Dicton, sm. (*etym. L.* dictum), saying, old saw, by-word

‖**Didactique**, adj. smf. (*etym. Gr.* διδακτικός), didactic, didactical; didactic order

Dièse, adj. sm. (*etym. Gr.* δίεσις), sharp, diesis

Diète, sf. (*etym. Gr.* δίαιτα), diet

Dieu, sm. (*etm. L.* Deus), God

Diffamant, e, adj. defamatory

Diffamateur, trice, adj. (*etm.* diffamer), slanderer, asperser

Diffamatoire, adj. (*etym.* diffamer), slanderous, defamatory

Diffamer, va. (*etym. L.* diffamare), to defame, to slander

Différemment, adv. (*etym.* différent), differently, unlike

Différencier, va. (*etym.* différence), to distinguish

Différend, sm. (*etym.* différer), difference. *Être en — sur*, to differ about

Différentiel, le, adj. differential

Différentier, va. (*etym.* différence), to differentiate

Différer, va.n. (*etym. L.* differre), to put off, to defer, to procrastinate, to be unlike, to disagree

‖**Difficile**, adj. (*etym. L.* difficilis), difficult, hard, troublesome, painful, unaccommodating, fastidious, trying

Difficulté, sf. (*etym. L.* difficultatem), difficulty

‖**Difficultueux, se**, adj. that is ever starting difficulties

Difforme, adj. (*etym. L.* difformis), deformed, ugly

Difformité, sf. (*etym.* difforme), deformity, crookedness

Diffus, e, adj. (*etym. L.* diffusus), diffuse

Digérer, va. (*etym. L.* digerere), to digest, to concoct

Digeste, sm. (*etym. L.* digesta), digest

Digestif, ve, adj. sm. (*etym. L.L.* digestivus), digestive

Digitale, sf. (*etym. L.* digitalis), foxglove, digitalis

***Digne**, adj. (*etym. L.* dignus), worthy, deserving, dignified

***Dignitaire**, sm. (*etym.* dignité), dignitary

§‖**Dignité**, sf. (*etym. L.* dignitatem), dignity

Digue, sf. (*etym. G.* deich, *Gael.* dig), dike, dam, embankment

Dilapidateur, trice, s. adj. (*etym.* dilapider), dilapidator, dilapidating

Dilapider, va. (*etym. L.* dilapidare, *to cast stones about*), to dilapidate

Dilater, va., *se* —, vr. (*etym. L.* dilatare), to dilate, to expand

Dilatoire, adj. dilatory

Dilemme, sm. dilemma

Diligemment, adv. (*etm.* diligent), steadily, diligently, carefully

Diligence, sf. (*etym. L.* diligentia), expedition, speed, diligence, care, stage-coach

Diluvien, ne, adj. (*etym. L.* diluvium), diluvian, of the flood

Dimanche, sm. (*etym. L.* [dies] dominica), Sunday

Dîme, sf. (*etym. L.* decimus), tithe

Dîmer, va.n. (*etym. L.* decimare), to collect the tithes

Diminuer, va.n. (*etym. L.* diminuere), to diminish, to lessen, to curtail, to lower, to impair

‖**Diminutif, ve**, adj. sm. (*etm. L.L.* diminutivus), diminutive

¶**Dînatoire**, adj. (*etym.* dîner), dinner. *Déjeuner* —, a late substantial breakfast

Dinde, sf. (*etym.* de, Inde), turkey-hen

Dindon, sm. (*etym.* dinde), turkey-cock

Dindonneau, sm. (*etym.* dindon), young turkey

Dindonnier, ère, smf. (*etym.* dindon), keeper of turkeys

Dînée, sf. (*etym.* dîner), dinner, inn where we dine

Dîner, vn. (*etym. L.L.* dicœnare ?), to dine. — sm. dinner

Dînette, sf. (*etym.* dîner), doll's dinner. *Faire la* —, to play at dinner

Diocésain, s. adj. (*etym.* diocèse), diocesan

Diocèse, sm. (*etym. Gr.* διοίκησις), diocese

Dioptrique, sf. adj. (*etym.* διοπτρικός), dioptrics, dioptrical

Diphthongue, sf. (*etym. Gr.* δίφθογγος), diphthong

Diplomate, sm. adj. (*etym.* diplôme), diplomatist, politician; diplomatic

Diplomatie, sf. (*etym.* diplomate), diplomacy, roundabout ways. ‡ *Faire de la* —, to have recourse to wiles

‖**Diplomatique**, adj. (*etym.* diplomate), diplomatic

Diplôme, sm. diploma

Dire, va. (*etym. L.* dicere), to say, to tell, to express, to declare. ‡ *Se moquer du qu'en dira-t-on*, not to care for what people say. ‡ *Comme qui dirait*, as if you said. *Si le cœur vous en dit*, if you have a mind for it. *Se* —, vr. to say to oneself, to be said. — sm. saying, words, statement, account. *A votre* —, by what you say

Directeur, sm. (*etym. L.L.* director), director, manager, governor. — *spirituel*, father-confessor

Directoire, sm. (*etym. L.L.* director), directory

Directrice, sf. (*etym. L.* directrix), directrix, directress

Dirigeant, e, adj. leading, directing

Diriger, va. (*etym. L.* dirigere), to direct, to guide, to manage, to be at the head of; *se* —, vr. to proceed, to move on, to conduct oneself, to be guided

Dirimant, e, adj. (*etym. L.* dirimere), which nullifies

Discernement, sm. (*etm.* discerner), distinction, discernment, acuteness

Discerner, va. (*etym. L.* discernere), to discern, to descry

Disciplinaire, adj. disciplinary

Discipliner, va. (*etym.* discipline), to discipline; *se* —, vr. to be disciplined

Discontinuer, va.n. (*etm.* dis, continuer), to discontinue, to leave off

Disconvenance, sf. (*etym.* disconvenant), unsuitableness

Disconvenir, vn. (*etym.* dis, convenir), to deny, to disown

Discorde, sf. (*etym. L.* discordia), discord, strife

Discoureur, se, s. great talker

Discourir, vn. (*etym. L.* discurrere), to discourse, to descant

Discours, sm. (*etym. L.* discursus), language, words, speech, discourse, treatise

Discourtois, e, adj. (*etym.* dis, courtois), discourteous

Discréditer, va. (*etym.* discrédit), to discredit

‖**Discret, ète**, adj. (*etym. L.* discretus), discreet, judicious

Disculper, va. (*etym.* dis, *L.* culpa), to exculpate, to exonerate; *se* —, vr. to exonerate oneself

Discussion, sf. (*etym. L.* discussionem), discussion. ‡ *Mettre en* —, to discuss

Discuter, va. (*etym. L.* discutere), to discuss, to argue

‖**Disert, e**, adj. (*etym. L.* disertus), eloquent

Disette, sf. (*etym.* ?), dearth, scarcity, want

Diseur, se, s. (*etym.* dire), sayer, teller

Disgrâce, sf. (*etym.* dis, grâce), disgrace, awkwardness, clumsiness, ungraciousness

Disgracier, va. (*etym.* disgrâce), to disgrace. *Disgracié, disgracié de la nature*, ill-favoured

‖**Disgracieux, se**, adj. (*etym.* dis, gracieux), ungraceful

Disjoindre, va. (*etym. L.* disjungere), to disjoin, to sever; *se* —, vr. to fall to pieces

Disjonctif, ve, adj. sf. disjunctive

Disjonction, sf. (*etym. L.* disjunctio), disjunction, separation

Disloquer, va. (*etym. L.* dis, locare), to dislocate, to put out of joint, to break up; *se* —, vr. to dislocate, to be broken up

Disparaître, vn. (*etym.* dis, paraître), to disappear, to vanish

Disparate, sf. (*etym. L.* disparatus), incongruity, unlikeness. — adj. unlike, incongruous

Disparité, sf. (*etym.* dis, parité), disparity

Disparition, sf. (*etym. see* DISPARAÎTRE), disappearance

‖**Dispendieux, se**, adj.

(*etym. L.* dispendiosus), expensive

Dispensaire, sm. (*etym. see* DISPENSER), dispensatory, dispensary

Dispensateur, trice, s. (*etym. L.* dispensatorem), dispenser, ruler, dispensator

Dispense, sf. (*etym.* dispense), dispensation

Dispenser, va. (*etym. L.* dispensare), to dispense, to bestow, to exempt; *se* —, vr. to be dispensed, to excuse oneself from

Disperser, va. (*etym. L.* dispersum), to scatter, to disperse; *se* —, vr. to disperse, to spread, to be scattered

Disponibilité, sf. (*etym.* disponible), disposal. *En* —, (*milit.*) on the unattached list

Disponible, adj. (*etym. L.* disponere), disposable, at one's disposal

Dispos, adj. m. (*etym. L.* dispositus), nimble, alert, hale and hearty, cheerful

Disposer, va. (*etym.* dis, poser), to dispose, to order, to make ready, to incline, to ordain, to value; *se* —, vr. to make ready, to prepare, to place oneself, to put oneself in an attitude

Dispositif, sm. (*etym.* disposer), recital, enacting part

Disposition, sf. (*etym. L.* dispositionem), disposition, arrangement, ordering, mood, frame of mind, taste, abilities, propensity, disposal, stipulation

Disproportionné, e, adj. (*etym.* disproportion), disproportionate, inadequate, unequal

Disputer, vn. (*etym. L.* disputare), to dispute, to argue, to vie with; — va. to dispute, to stand up for, to deny, to contend; *se* —, vr. to dispute, to strive with each other for, to contend for

Disputeur, adj. sm. (*etym.* disputer), disputatious

Disque, sm. (*etym. L.* discus), quoit, disk

‖**Dissemblable,** adj. (*etym.* dis, semblable), unlike, dissimilar

Dissemblance, sf. (*etym.* dis, semblance), dissimilarity

Disséminer, va. (*etym. L.* disseminare), to disseminate, to spread

Dissentiment, sm. (*etym. O.F.* dissentir), dissent

Disséquer, va. (*etym. L.* dissecare), to dissect

Disserter, vn. (*etym. L.* dissertare), to dissert, to descant

Dissidence, sf. (*etym. L.* dissidentia), dissent, difference, schism

Dissident, e, adj. (*etym. L.* dissidens), dissenting; — s. dissenter

Dissimulé, e, adj. dissembling

Dissimuler, va. (*etym. L.* dissimulare), to dissemble, to conceal, to disguise; *se* —, vr. to hide from oneself *or* from each other, to be concealed

Dissipateur, trice, s. adj. (*etym. L.* dissipator), squanderer, waster; wasteful

Dissipé, e, adj. dissipated, idle

Dissiper, va. (*etym. L.* dissipare), to dispel, to dissipate, to scatter, to waste, to idle away, to entertain; *se* —, vr. to be dispelled, to vanish, to be squandered away, to take some distraction

‖**Dissolu, e,** adj. (*etym. L.* dissolutus), dissolute, lewd

Dissolvant, e, adj. sm. (*etym. L.* dissolvens), solutive, dissolvent

Dissoudre, va. (*etym. L.* dissolvere), to dissolve; *se* —, vr. to dissolve, to be dissolved

Dissuader, va. (*etym. L.* dissuadere), to dissuade

Dissyllabe, Dissyllabique, adj. (*etym. L.* disyllabus), dissyllabic

Distancer, va. (*etym.* distance), to leave behind, to outdistance

Distension, sf. (*etym. L.* distentionem), stretching, distension

Distillateur, sm. (*etym. L.* distillare), distiller

Distiller, va. (*etym. L.* distillare), to distil, to discharge, to vent; — vn. to fall drop by drop

Distillerie, sf. (*etym. O.F.* distilleur = distillateur), distillery, still

‖**Distinctif, ve,** adj. (*etym.* distinct), distinctive, of distinction

Distinction, sf. (*etym. L.* distinctionem), distinction, gentility, good breeding

Distingué, e, adj. of distinction, distinguished, genteel

Distinguer, va. (*etym. L.* distinguere), to distinguish; *se* —, vr. to win distinction, to be eminent, to be descried

Distique, sm. distich

Distraire, va. (*etym. L.* distrahere), to separate, to take away, to distract, to divert, to entertain; *se* —, vr. to divert one's attention, to take some relaxation

‖**Distrait, e,** adj. absent, heedless

Distribuer, va. (*etym. L.* distribuere), to distribute, to deal out, to lay out; *se* —, vr. to be distributed, to share among themselves

Distributeur, trice, s. (*etym. L.* distributorem), bestower, distributer

Distributif, ve, adj. (*etym. L.L.* distributivus), distributive

Distribution, sf. (*etym. L.* distributionem), distribution, delivery, (*theat.*) cast

Dit, sm. (*etym. L.* dictum), saying

Diurne, adj. (*etym. L.* diurnus), diurnal

‖**Divagation,** sf. (*etym.* divaguer), straying, wandering, rambling

Divaguer, va. (*etym. L.* divagari), to go astray, to ramble from the point

Divergence, sf. (*etym.* divergent), divergency, difference

‖**Divers, e,** adj. (*etym. L.* diversus), various, diverse, sundry. — sm. plur. sundries

Diversifier, va. (*etym. L.* diversus), to diversify; *se* —, vr. to be diversified

Diversité, sf. (*etym. L.* diversitatem), diversity, variety

Divertir, va. (*etym. L.* divertere), to divert, to entertain, to purloin, to misapply; *se* —, vr. to divert oneself, to make merry

Divertissant, e, adj. diverting, entertaining

Divertissement, sm. (*etym.* divertir), entertainment

Dividende, sm. (*etym. L.* dividendus), dividend. — *arriéré*, unclaimed dividend

‖**Divin, e,** adj. (*etym. L.* divinus), divine, heavenly

Divinatoire, adj. (*etym.* divination), divining, divinatory

Diviniser, va. (*etym.* divin), to deify

Divinité, sf. (*etym. L.* divinitatem), godhead, divinity

Diviser, va. (*etym. L.* divisum), to divide; *se* —, vr. to be divided

Diviseur, sm. (*etym. L.* divisor), divisor

Divisionnaire, adj. (*etym.* division), divisionary

Divorcer, vn. (*etym. L.L.* divortiare), to divorce

Divulguer, va. (*etym. L.* divulgare), to divulge, to let out

Dix, adj. sm. (*etym. L.* decem), ten

‖**Dixième,** adj. sm. (*etym. L.* decimus), tenth, tenth part

Dizain, sm. (*etym.* dix), decastich, ten packs of cards

Dizaine, sf. (*etym.* dix), ten

Docilité, sf. (*etym. L.* docilitas), docility

Docimasie, sf. (*etym. Gr.* δοκιμασία, *trial*), docimasia

‖**Docte,** adj. (*etym. L.* doctus), learned

Docteur, sm. (*etym. L.* doctorem), doctor. — *ès lettres, ès sciences*, doctor in letters, in sciences

Doctorat, sm. (*etym. see* DOCTEUR), doctor's degree, doctorship

Doctrinaire, sm. (*etym.* doctrine), doctrinary

Dodécaèdre, sm. (*etym. Gr.* δωδεκάεδρος), dodecahedron

Dodécagone, sm. (*etym. Gr.* δωδεκάγωνος), dodecagon

Dodu, e, adj. (*etym.* ?), plump

Dogaresse, sf. (*etym. I.* dogaressa), wife to the doge

‖**Dogmatique,** adj. (*etym. Gr.* δογματικός), dogmatical, dogmatic

Dogmatiser, va. n. (*etym.* dogme), to dogmatize

Dogmatiste, sm. (*etym.* dogmatiser), dogmatist

Dogme, sm. (*etym. Gr.* δόγμα), tenet, dogma

Dogue, sm. (*etym. Eng.* dog), bulldog, dog

Doigt, sm. (*etym. L.* digitus), finger, toe, claw, finger's breadth. ‡ *Mettre le — dessus*, to hit the nail on the head. *Faire toucher du bout du —*, to make it as clear as day. *Être comme les deux —s de la main*, to be hand and glove together. † *Un — de vin*, a drop of wine

Doigté, Doigter, sm. (*etym.* doigt), fingering

Doit, sm. (*etym. see* DEVOIR), debit-side

Dol, sm. (*etym. L.* dolus), deceit

Doléance, sf. (*etym. O.F.* doléant, dolent), complaint, wailing, grievance

Dolent, e, adj. (*etym. L.* dolens), doleful, mournful

Dolman, *also* **Doliman,** sm. (*etym. Turk.* thoulîmet, *a kind of dress*), hussar's pelisse, pelisse

Dolmen, sm. (*etym. Gael.* tolmen, *a stone-table*), Druid's stone

Doloire, sf. (*etym. L.* dolabra), cooper's adze

Domaine, sm. (*etym. L.L.* domantum), domain, demesne, estate

Domesticité, sf. (*etym.* domestique), domesticity, the household, the retainers

Domestique, adj. (*etym. L.* domesticus), household, domestic, family, private. — sm. man-servant, servant, domestic, the household. — sf. woman-servant. — *à tout faire*, maid of all work

Domicile, sm. (*etym. L.* domicilium), residence, dwelling

Domiciliaire, adj. (*etym.* domicile), domiciliary

Domicilié, e, adj. (*etym.* domicile), settled, residing

Dominant, e, adj. (*etym.* dominer), ruling, prevailing, predominant

Dominateur, trice, s. adj. (*etym. L.* dominator), ruler, master; ruling, domineering

Dominer, va. n. (*etym. L.* dominari), to rule, to have dominion, to take the lead, to domineer, to tower above

Dominicain, adj. sm. (*etym. L.* Dominicus, *proper name*), Dominican

Dominicaine, sf. Dominican nun

Dommage, sm. (*etym. L.* domare, *to tame*), wrong, prejudice, damage, injury, loss. *Demander des —s-intérêts*, to sue for damages

Dommageable, adj. (*etym.* dommage), prejudicial
Dompter, va. (*etym. L.* domitare), to subdue, to quell, to master; *se* —, vr. to quell one's passions
Dompteur, sm. (*etym.* dompter), subduer, tamer
Don, sm. (*etym. L.* donum), gift, boon, bounty
Donateur,trice, s.(*etym. L.* donator), donor
Donc, conj. (*etym.* ?), then, therefore
†**Dondon,** sf. (*etym.* ?), a fat, buxom woman
Donjon, sm.(*etym.* ?),castle-keep, turret
Donnant, e, adj. (*etym.* donner), giving. ‡ *Il n'est guère* —, he is not very fond of giving
Donnée, sf. (*etym.* donner), given quantity, datum, idea, notion
Donner, va. (*etym. L.* donare), to give, to give away, to present, to grant, to hand, to gift with, to ascribe, to deal, to yield. ‡ *Vous me la donnez belle*, a pretty story you tell me there. ‡ *Donnant donnant*, give and take. — vn. to strike, to knock, to run, to stumble, to believe, to be fond, to charge, to front, to open into, to sell well. *Ne savoir où — de la tête*, not to know which way to turn. — *du cor*, to blow the horn. *Se* —,vr. to give oneself up,to become addicted, to give oneself. † *S'en* —, to have a treat. ‡ *Se — de garde de*, to mistrust, to beware of
Dont, pron. rel. (*etym. L.* de, unde), of whom, whereof, whose
Donzelle, sf. (*etym. L.L.* dominicella), wench
Dorade, sf. (*etym.* dorer), dorado, gold fish
Doré, e, adj. gilt, golden, deceitful, winning. — *sur tranche*, gilt-edged
Dorénavant, adv. (*etym.* de, *O.F.* ores = heure, en, avant), henceforward, henceforth
Dorer, va. (*etym. L.* deaurare), to gild; *se* —, vr. to be gilt
Doreur, se, s. (*etym.* dorer), gilder
Dorique, adj. s. Doric
Dorloter, va. to coddle, to nurse; *se* —, vr. to coddle oneself
Dormant, e, adj. (*etym.* dormir), sleeping, asleep, stagnant, fixed
Dormeur, se, s. (*etym.* dormir), sleeper, sleepyhead
Dormir, vn. (*etym. L.* dormire), to sleep, to slumber, to be asleep, to lie dormant, to be stagnant, to smoulder; — va. — *un somme*, to take a nap
Dormitif, ve, adj. (*etym. L.* dormire), dormitive
Dortoir, sm. (*etym. L.* dormitorium), dormitory, bedroom
Dorure, sf. (*etym.* dorer), gilding, gilt
‖**Dos,** sm. (*etym. L.* dorsum), back, ridge. — *rond*, broad-shouldered. † *Faire le gros* —, to assume an air of consequence. ‡ *Se mettre quelqu'un à* —, to bring upon one's back. ‡ *Chaussée à — d'âne*, shelving road
Dossier, sm. (*etym. L.L.* dorsarium), back, brief, notes, papers. *Dépouiller le — de*, to examine the notes of
Dot, sf. (*etym. L.* dotem), portion, dowry, dower
Dotation, sf.(*etym. L.L.* dotationem), endowment
Doter, va. (*etym. L.* dotare), to portion, to endow
Douaire, sm. (*etym. L.L.* dotarium), jointure, marriage-settlement
Douairière, sf. (*etym.* douaire), dowager
Douane, sf. (*etym.* ?), the customs, the custom-house
Douanier, sm. (*etym.* douane), custom-house officer
‖**Double,** adj. (*etym. L.* duplex), double, twofold, arrant, double-minded
Doubler, va.(*etym.* double), to double, to heighten, to double up, to fold in two, (*theat.*) to act as substitute for, to line, to outsail. *Doublé en cuivre*, copper-bottomed. — vn. to double
Doublon, sm. (*etym. Sp.* doblon), doubloon, (*print.*) double
Doublure, sf. (*etym.* doubler), lining, (*theat.*) double
Douceâtre, adj. (*etym.* doux), sweetish, sweet, insipid
‖**Doucereux, se,** adj. (*etym.* douceur), sweetish, mawkish
‖**Doucet, te,** adj. (*dimin. of* doux), demure
Douceur, sf. (*etym.* dulcorem), sweetness, sweet things, smoothness, melodiousness, gentleness. *Dire des —s*, to say all sorts of kind things
Douche, sf. (*etym. I.* doccia, *gutter*), shower-bath
Doucher, va.(*etm.* douche), to give a shower-bath
Doucine, sf. (*etym.* ?), doucine, cyma, ogee
Douer, va. (*etym. L.* dotare), to endow, to gift
§**Douillet, te,** adj. (*etym. O.F.* douille, *L.* dulcis), soft, downy
§**Douillette,** sf. an overcoat *or* dress in wadded silk
Douleur, sf. (*etym. L.* dolorem), pain, ache, painfulness, sorrow
*se **Douloir,** vr. (*etym. L.* dolere), to feel pain *or* sorrow
‖**Douloureux, se,** adj. (*etym. L.* dolorosus), painful, sore, tender, mournful
Doute, sm. (*etym.* douter), doubt, doubtfulness, misgiving
Douter, vn. (*etym. L.* dubitare), to doubt, to question, to scruple; *se* —, vr. to suspect
‖**Douteux, se,** adj. doubtful, dubious, questionable, in doubt
Douve, sf. (*etym. L.L.* doga, *conduct, passage*), stave, (*bot.*) spearwort
‖**Doux, ce,** adj. (*etym. L.* dulcis), sweet, fresh, not salt enough, unfermented, soft, smooth, gentle, mild. *Filer* —, to be very humble. — adv. gently, softly. *Tout* —! gently!
Douzaine, sf.(*etym.* douze), dozen
Douze, adj. (*etym. L.* duodecim), twelve, twelfth
‖**Douzième,** sm.adj. (*etym.* douze), twelfth, twelfth part
Doyen, sm. (*etym. L.* decanus), the senior member, elder, dean
Doyenné, sm. (*etym.* doyen), deanery, Carlisle pear
Drachme, sf. (*etym. Gr.* δραχμή), drachm, dram
Dragée, sf. (*etym. Gr.* τραγήματα, *sweetmeats*), sugar-plum, comfit, pill, small shot, (*agric.*) meslin. ‡ *Tenir la — haute à*, to keep a high hand over
Dragon, sm. (*etym. L.* draconem), dragon, termagant, dragoon
Dragonnades, sf. plur. (*etym.* dragon), dragoonades
Dragonne, sf. (*etym.* dragon), sword-knot
Drague, sf. (*etym. Eng.* drag), dredging-machine
Draguer, va.(*etym.* drague), to dredge, to drag
Dragueur, sm. (*etym.* draguer), dredging-machine
***Drainer,** va. (*etym. Eng.* drain), to drain
‖**Dramatique,** adj. (*etym. Gr.* δραματικός), dramatic, dramatical
Dramaturge, sm. (*etym. Gr.* δραματουργός), playwright, dramatist
Drame, sm. (*etym. Gr.* δρᾶμα), drama, play
Drap, sm. (*etym.* ?), cloth, sheet. *Tailler en plein* —, to cut and hew. *Le voilà en de beaux —s*, a pretty pickle he is in
Drapeau, sm.(*etym.* drap), flag, colours, banner, ensign. *Sous les —x*, in active service
Draper, va. (*etym.* drap), to cover with mourning cloth, to hang, to arrange tastefully, to rail at; *se* —, vr. to wrap oneself up, to strut
Draperie, sf. drapery, woollen stuffs, cloth manufactory
Drapier, sm. adj. (*etym.* drap), clothier, woollen-draper; cloth
Drèche, sf. (*etym. O.H.G.* drescan, *to thresh the corn*), malt
Dresser, va. (*etym. L.* directus), to straighten, to raise, to hold up, to prick up, to pitch, to lay out, to draw up, to train; — vn. to stand on end; *se* —, vr. to stand, to rise
Dressoir, sm. (*etym.* dresser), dresser
§**Drille,** sm. (*etym. O.H.G.* drigil, *a servant*), a foot-soldier. ‡ *Un bon* —, a boon companion
Drogman, sm. (*etym. L. Gr.* δραγούμανος), dragoman, interpreter
Drogue, sf. (*etym.* ?), drug, rubbish
Droguer, va.(*etym.* drogue), to physic; *se* —, vr. to physic oneself
Droguet, sm.(*etym.* drogue), drugget
Droguiste, sm. (*etym.* drogue), druggist
‖**Droit, e,** adj. (*etym. L.* directus), right, straight, upright, straightforward. — sm. right, claim, power, righteousness, the law, duty, tax, fee, commission. *De* —, *de plein* —, by right. *A bon* —, justly. *A qui de* —, to those whom it may concern
Droite, sf. the right hand, the right, straight line
Droiture, sf. (*etym.* droit), uprightness, rectitude
Drôle, adj. (*etym.* ?), queer, odd, droll. — sm. rogue, knave
Drôlerie, sf. (*etym.* drôle), drollery, trash
Drôlesse, sf. a lewd woman
Dromadaire, sm. dromedary
Dru, e, adj. (*etym.* ? *Gael.* drùth, *self-willed*), full-fledged, brisk, lusty, thick. — adv. briskly
Druide, esse, s. (*etym. Celt.* derf or derv, *oak*), druid, druidess
Druidique, adj. (*etym.* druide), druid's, druidical
Druidisme, sm. (*etym.* druide), druidism
Dryade, sf. (*etym. Gr.* δρυάς), dryad, wood-nymph
Dû, sm. (*etym. L.* debere), due, duty
‖**Dubitatif, ve,** adj.(*etym. L.* dubitativus), dubitative
Duc, sm. (*etym. L.* dux), duke, horned owl
Ducaton, sm. (*etym.* ducat), ducatoon
Duché, sm. (*etym. L.* ducatus), duchy, dukedom
Duchesse, sf. (*etym.* duc), duchess
Ductilité, sf. (*etym.* ductile), ductility
§**Duègne,** sf. (*etym. Sp.* dueña), duenna
Duel, sm. (*etym. L.* duellum), duel, dual
Duelliste, sm. (*etym.* duel), duellist
Dulcinée, sf. (*etym. L.* dulcis), Dulcinea
Dunes, sf. plur. (*etym. Celt.* dûn, *a hill*), downs
Dunette, sf. (*etym.* dune), poop
Duper, va. (*etym.* dupe), to fool, to dupe
Duperie, sf. (*etym.* duper), imposition, cheat
Duplicata, sm. (*etym. L.*

duplicata, *pl.n.of* duplicatus), duplicate
Duplicité, sf. (*etym. L.* duplicitas), duplicity
§**Dur, e**, adj. (*etym. L.* durus), hard, tough, stale, stiff, harsh. — *au travail*, hard-working. —*e*, sf. *Coucher sur la —e*, to lie on the bare ground
Durant, prep. (*etym.* durer), during, for.

Durcir, va. (*etym.* dur), to harden, to toughen; — vn., *se* —, vr. to harden, to grow hard *or* tough
Durcissement, sm. (*etym.* durcir), hardening
Durée, sf. (*etym. L.* durare), duration, continuance, endurance, solidity
Durer, vn. (*etym. L.* durare), to last, to endure, to hold out

Dureté, sf. (*etym. L.* duritatem), hardness, toughness, obduracy, roughness, stiffness, unkindness
§**Durillon**, sm. (*etym.* dur), callosity, corn
Duvet, sm. (*etym. L.* dumetum), down
Dynamique, sf. adj. (*etym. Gr.* δυναμικός), dynamics, dynamic

Dynastie, sf. (*etym. Gr.* δυναστεία), dynasty
Dynastique, adj. (*etym.* dynastie), dynastic
Dyspepsie, sf. (*etym. Gr.* δυσπεψία), dyspepsy
Dysphagie, sf. (*etym. Gr.* δυς, φαγεῖν, *to eat*), dysphagia, difficulty of swallowing
Dyssenterie, sf. (*etym. Gr.* δυσεντερία), dysentery

E

E, sm. e
Eau, sf. (*etym. L.* aqua), water, wet, watering-place, perspiration, tears, gloss, track. — *-de-vie*, brandy. — *-de-vie de riz*, arrack. † *Tenir le bec dans l'—*, to keep some one in suspense. *Faire —*, (*nav.*) to be leaky. *Faire de l'—*, to take in fresh water. *Faire venir l'— au moulin*, to bring grist to the mill. *Porter de l'— à la rivière*, to carry coals to Newcastle. *Le temps est à l'—*, it threatens rain
Ébahi, e, past part. wonder-struck, amazed
s'Ébahir, vr. (*etym. O.F.* bair, *to astonish*), to be wonder-struck
Ébahissement, sm. (*etym.* ébahir), amazement, wonder
Ébat, sm. sport, (*plur., fig.*) sports, frolics
s'Ébattre, vr. (*etym.* é, *for O.F.* es, battre), to skip about, to gambol
Ébaubi, e, adj. (*etym.* é, *for O.F.* es, *L.* balbus), wonder-struck
Ébauche, sf. (*etym. see* Ébaucher), rough-draught, rude outline
Ébaucher, va. (*etym.* é, *for O.F.* es, bauche, *a kind of cement*), to rough-draw, to sketch the outline of
Ébauchoir, sm. (*etym.* ébauche), a kind of chisel
Ébène, sm. (*etym. L.* ebenus), ebony, ebon
Ébénier, sm. (*etym.* ébène), ebony-tree
Ébéniste, sm. (*etym.* ébène), cabinet-maker
Ébénisterie, sf. (*etym.* ébéniste), cabinet-making, cabinet-work
Éblouir, va. (*etym. ?*), to dazzle
Éblouissant, e, adj. dazzling
Éblouissement, sm. (*etym.* éblouir), dazzling
§**Éborgner**, va. (*etym.* é, borgne), to put out a person's eye
Éboulement, sm. (*etym. see* Ébouler), falling in, fall
Ébouler, vn., *s'—*, vr. (*etym.* é, boule), to fall in
Ébouriffé, e, adj. (*etym.* bourre), in disorder
Ébrancher, va. (*etym.* é, branche), to lop, to trim

Ébranlement, sm. (*etym.* ébranler), shaking, tottering, shock, perturbation, emotion
Ébranler, va. (*etym.* é, branler), to shake, to cause to totter, to unsettle; *s'—*, vr. to be shaken, to totter, to move forward
Ébrécher, va. (*etym.* é, brèche), to notch, to make a gap in; *s'—*, vr. to be notched
Ébruiter, va. (*etym.* é, bruit), to noise *or* rumour abroad; *s'—*, vr. to take wind
§**Écaille**, sf. (*etym. G.* schale, *scale*), scale
§**Écailler**, va., *s'—*, vr. to scale, to peel off
§**Écailler, ère**, s. oyster-man *or* woman
§**Écailleux, se**, adj. scaly
Écale, sf. (*etym. L.* scala), the peel of green walnuts
Écaler, va. (*etym.* écale), to peel walnuts
Écarlate, adj. sf. (*etym. L.* Galaticus [rubor], *red from Galatia*), scarlet
:§**Écarquiller**, va., *s'—*, vr. (*etym. ?*), to open wide
Écart, sm. (*etym.* écarter), stepping aside, strain, flight, digression, error, cards discarded. *A l'—*, in a lonely place, aside
Écarteler, va. (*etym. L.* ex, *L.L.* quartillus, *dimin. of L.* quartus), to quarter
Écartement, sm. (*etym.* écarter), opening, separation
Écarter, va. (*etym.* é, carte), to open, to remove, to set aside, to scatter, to dispel; *s'—*, vr. to widen, to separate, to deviate, to ramble, to wander
Ecchymose, sm. (*etym. Gr.* ἐγχύμωσις), ecchymosis
Ecclésiastique, adj. sm. ecclesiastical, ecclesiastic
Écervelé, e, adj. (*etym.* é, cervelle), hare-brained, giddy-brained
Échafaud, sm. (*etym. L.L.* scafaldus), scaffold, scaffolding, stage, framework
Échafaudage, sm. (*etym.* échafaud), scaffolding, preparations
Échafauder, va. (*etym.* échafaud), to make a scaffolding, to pile up
Échalas, sm. (*etym. L.L.* [illegible]

carratium), (†) as thin as a lath, hop-pole
Échalote, sf. (*etym. L.* Ascalonia, *from the proper name* Ascalon), shalot
Échancrer, va. (*etym.* é, chancre), to cut deep, to hollow out
Échancrure, sf. (*etym.* échancrer), hollowing out, deep cut, indentation
Échange, sm. (*etym.* é, change), exchange, barter
Échanger, va. (*etym.* échange), to barter, to exchange
Échanson, sm. (*etym. O.H.G.* scencan, *to pour out to drink*), cupbearer
§**Échantillon**, sm. (*etym.* é, *and O.F.* cant, *corner*), sample, pattern, specimen
Échappatoire, sf. (*etym.* échapper), hole to creep out of
Échappée, sf. (*etym.* échapper), prank, frolic, vista, accidental light. ‡ *Par —s*, by snatches
Échappement, sm. (*etym.* échapper), escape, escapement, (*arch.*) space to turn in a staircase
Échapper, vn. (*etym. L. L.* excappare), to escape, to break out of, to slip, to drop away. *Un échappé des petites maisons*, a madman. — va. to escape. *L'— belle*, to have a narrow *or* hairbreadth escape. *S'—*, vr. to escape, to get away, to burst, to forget oneself
Écharpe, sf. (*etym. O.H.G.* scherpe, *pocket*), scarf, sling. *En —*, over the shoulders, in a sling, slanting
Écharper, va. (*etym.* écharpe), to cut and slash, to cut to pieces
Échasses, sf. plur. (*etym. O.Fl.* schaetse, *stilts*), stilts
Échassier, sm. a bird of the family of Grallæ
Échaudé, sm. (*etym.* échauder), sort of cake
Échauder, va. (*etym.* é, chaud), to scald; *s'—*, (*fig.*) to burn one's fingers
Échauffant, e, adj. sm. (*etym.* échauffer), heating, too exciting, over-exciting remedy *or* food
Échauffement, sm. (*etym.* échauffer), heating, over-excitement

Échauffer, va. (*etym.* é, chauffer), to heat, to warm, to inflame. † — *la bile, les oreilles*, to provoke. *S'—*, vr. to get warm, to overheat oneself, to grow angry
Échauffourée, sf. (*etym.* chaud, fourrer ?), affray, fray, skirmish
Échéance, sf. (*etym.* échoir), expiration, falling due. *A l'—*, when due. *A courte, longue —*, short-dated, long-dated
Échec, sm. (*etym. O.H.G.* schâh, *booty*), check, repulse, loss, failure. *Faire — et mat*, to checkmate. *Tenir en —*, to keep in check. —*s*, plur. chess, chessmen
Échelle, sf. (*etym. L.* scala), ladder, scale, (*plur.*) the ports of the Levant. — *de corde, de siége*, rope-ladder, scaling-ladder. *Faire la courte —*, to let a person get upon one's back. ‡ *Après lui il faut tirer l'—*, there's no coming near him
Échelon, sm. (*etym.* échelle), round, step
Échelonner, va. (*etym.* échelon), to draw up; *s'—*, vr. to be drawn up
§**Écheniller**, va. (*etym.* é, chenille), to clear from caterpillars
Écheveau, sm. (*etym. L.L.* scapellus, *dim. of L.* scapus, *a roll*), skein. *Grand —*, hank
Échevelé, e, adj. (*etym. L.L.* excapillare), dishevelled
Échevin, sm. (*etym. Sax.* scepeno), alderman
Échine, sf. (*etym. Celt.* chein, *back*), backbone, back, (*arch.*) echinus
Échiner, va. (*etym.* échine), to break one's back, to knock on the head, to commit, to work to death; *s'—*, vr. to sprain one's back, (†) to work oneself to death, to knock oneself up
Échiquier, sm. (*etym.* échec), chess-board, the exchequer, square net. *En —*, checkerwise, (*nav.*) in a bow and quarter line
Échoir, vn. (*etym. L.* ex, cadere), to fall to the lot, to fall due. *Le cas échéant*, should it so befall
Échoppe, sf. (*etym. O.H.G.* schupfa, *shop*), stall, scorper

Échouer, vn. (*etym.* ?), to run aground, to strand, to founder, to miscarry; — va. to run aground; *s'*—, vr. to run one's ship aground

Éclabousser, va. (*etym.* ?), to splash

Éclaboussure, sf. (*etym.* éclabousser), splash, bit broken off

Éclair, sm. (*etym. see* ÉCLAIRER), flash of lightning, flashing, flash of fire

Éclairage, sm. (*etym.* éclairer), lighting, lights. — *au gaz*, gas-light

Éclaircie, sf. (*etym.* éclaircir), bright spot, glade

Éclaircir, va. (*etym.* é, clair), to clear up, to brighten, to thin, to solve, to illustrate, to sift; *s'*—, vr. to clear up, to clear, to brighten, to be cleared up, to be elucidated, to inquire

Éclaircissement, sm. (*etym.* éclaircir), explanation, insight

Éclairer, va. (*etym.* é, clair), to enlighten, to brighten, to give light to, to throw a light upon, to send out scouts. *Être logé et éclairé*, to have bed and candles. — vn. to give light, to light, to lighten; *s'*—, vr. to derive instruction

Éclaireur, sm. (*etym.* éclairer), scout

Éclat, sm. fragment, bit, splinter, burst, noise, rupture, brilliancy, lustre, glare

Éclatant, e, adj. (*etym.* éclater), bright, shining, glittering

Éclater, vn. (*etym. O.H.G.* skleizan, *to break*), to shiver, to splinter, to burst, to blow up, to break out, to be exposed

Éclectique, sm. adj. eclectic

Éclectisme, sm. (*etym.* éclectique), eclecticism

Éclipser, va. (*etym.* éclipse), to eclipse, to throw into the shade; *s'*—, vr. to be eclipsed, (†) to disappear, to be off

Écliptique, sf. adj. ecliptic

Éclisse, sf. (*etym. O.H.G.* kliozan, *to split*), splint, splinter, cheese-wattle, split-wood

Éclopé, e, adj. (*etym.* é, *O.F.* clop), limping, lame, quite lame

Éclore, vn. (*etym. L.* excludere), to be hatched, to hatch, to blow, to open, to dawn, to come to light

Écluse, sf. (*etym. L.* exclusa [aqua]), lock, sluice, flood-gate, mill-dam

Éclusier, sm. lock-keeper

École, sf. (*etym. L.* schola), school, the school-house, the scholastic philosophy, a blunder. *Sentir l'*—, to savour of pedantry

Écolier, ère, s. (*etym. L.* scholaris), pupil, scholar

Éconduire, va. (*etym. L.* ex, conducere), to show out, civilly to deny

Économat, sm., *etym.* économe), stewardship, bursarship, steward's office

Économe, adj. (*etym. Gr.* οἰκονόμος), thrifty, saving, sparing. — s. steward, bursar, stewardess

Économie, sf. (*etym. Gr.* οἰκονομία), good husbandry, economy, savings

‡**Économique**, adj. (*etym. Gr.* οἰκονομικός), economic, economical

Économiser, va. (*etym.* économie), to manage well, to husband, to save

Économiste, sm. (*etym.* économie), economist

Écorce, sf. (*etym. L.* cortex), bark, rind, peel, crust

Écorcher, va. (*etym. L.L.* excorticare), to flay, to skin, to graze, to peel the bark off, to taste rough, to speak broken English, French, &c., to grate on, to fleece; *s'*—, vr. to rub one's skin off

Écorchure, sf. (*etym.* écorcher), excoriation

Écorner, va. (*etym.* é, corne), to break the horn off, to chip, to dog's-ear, to make a hole in one's income

Écornifleur, se, s. (*etym.* écorner), trencher-friend

Écornure, sf. (*etym.* écorner), chip, piece broken off

Écosser, va. (*etym.* é, cosse), to shell

Écot, sm. (*etym. Eng.* scot, shot), share, score, reckoning, party. *Parlez à votre* —, speak to the people of your set

Écoulement, sm. flow, flowing out, drainage, emanation, sale

s'Écouler, vr. (*etym.* é, couler), to run out, to flow out, to glide on, to elapse, to disperse, to sell

Écourter, va. (*etym. L.L.* excurtare), to crop, to dock, to curtail

Écoute, sf. listening-place, (*nav.*) sheet. *Se tenir aux* —*s*, to stand listening

Écouter, va. (*etym. L.* auscultare), to listen to, to hearken to, to mind, to overhear; *s'*—, vr. to hearken to one's own voice, to be over-anxious

Écouteur, se, s. (*etym. L.* auscultatorem), eavesdropper

§**Écoutille**, sf. (*etym.* ?), hatchway, hatch

§**Écouvillon**, sm. (*etym. O.F.* escoube, *broom*), sponge, scovel

Écran, sm. (*etym.* ?), screen, fire-screen

Écrasé, e, adj. flat, crushed in, squat

Écrasement, sm. (*etym.* écraser), the action of crushing

Écraser, va. (*etym. O.Scan.* krassa, *to crush*), to crush, to quash, to tread out, to throw into the shade, to overwhelm

Écrémer, va. (*etym.* é, crème), to cream, to skim

Écrevisse, sf. (*etym. O.H.G.* schepiz, *crab*), crab, crawfish

s'Écrier, vr. (*etym.* é, crier), to cry out, to exclaim

Écrin, sm. (*etym. L.* scrinium), casket

Écrire, va. (*etym. L.* scribere), to write, to pen, to advise; *s'*—, vr. to be written, to sign oneself

Écrit, sm. writing, paper, note of hand, agreement

Écriteau, sm. (*etym.* écrit), bill. *Mettre un* —, to stick up a bill

Écritoire, sf. (*etym. L.* scriptorium), ink-horn, ink-stand

Écriture, sf. (*etym. L.* scriptura), writing, hand, (*plur.*) accounts, books, the Holy Scriptures. *Commis aux* —*s*, counting-house clerk

§**Écrivailleur**, **Écrivassier**, sm. (*etym.* écrire), scribbler

Écrivain, sm. (*etym. L.L.* scribanus), writer, author, scrivener

Écrou, sm. (*etym. Germ.* schraube), screw-nut, entry in the gaol-book. *Contre-* —, counter-nut. *Livre d'*—, gaol-book

Écrouelles, sf. plur. (*etym. L.L.* scrofellæ, scrofulæ), the king's evil, scrofula

Écrouer, va. (*etym.* écrou), to enter in the gaol-book, to put into gaol

Écroulé, e, past part. fallen

Écroulement, sm. (*etym.* écrouler), falling down, crash, fall

s'Écrouler, vr. (*etym.* é, crouler), to fall down, to sink in, to crumble away

Écru, e, adj. (*etym.* cru), raw, unbleached

Écu, sm. (*etym. L.* scutum), shield, escutcheon, (*money*) crown

Écubier, sm. (*etym.* ?), hawse-hole

§**Écueil**, sm. (*etym. L.* scopulus), rock, reef, stumbling-block

Écuelle, sf. (*etym. L.* scutella), porringer. † *Mettre tout par* —*s*, to treat sumptuously. *Qui s'attend à l'*— *d'autrui a souvent mal dîné*, it is ill waiting for dead men's shoes

Éculer, va. (*etym.* é, cul), to tread down at heels; *s'*—, vr. to wear down at heel

Écumant, e, adj. (*etym.* écumer), foaming

Écume, sf. (*etym. O.H.G.* scûm), foam, froth, yeast, scum. *Pipe d'*— *de mer*, meerschaum

Écumer, va. (*etym.* écume), to skim, to scum, to scour; — vn. to foam, to froth

Écumeur, sm. (*etym.* écumer), skimmer of the seas, rover

Écumeux, se, adj. (*etym.* écume), frothy, yeasty

Écumoire, sf. (*etym.* écumer), skimmer

Écurer, va. (*etym. L.* ex, curare), to scour, to clean out

§**Écureuil**, sm. (*etym. L.L.* squiriolus), squirrel

Écurie, sf. (*etym. O.H.G.* skûra, skura), stable, stud. *Garçon d'*—, ostler

Écusson, sm. (*dimin. of* écu), escutcheon. *En* —, by gem

Écuyer, sm. (*etym. L.L.* scutarius), squire, shield-bearer, riding-master, horseman, equerry, hand-rail. *Le grand* —, the master of the horse

Écuyère, sf. horsewoman. *Bottes à l'*—, riding boots

Édenter, va. (*etym.* é, dent), to break out the teeth of

Édifiant, e, adj. (*etym.* édifier), edifying

Édifier, va. (*etym. L.* ædificare), to build, to edify; *s'*—, vr. to edify each other

Édilité, sf. (*etym. L.* ædilitas), ædileship

Édit, sm. (*etym. L.* edictum), edict, decree

Éditer, va. to publish, to edit

Éditeur, sm. (*etym. L.* editor, *from* edere), publisher, editor

Édredon, sm. (*etym. Scand.* eider, *goose, and* dun, *down*), eider-down, eider-down coverlet

‡**Éduquer**, va. (*etym. L.* educare), to bring up

Effacer, va. (*etym.* e, face), to scratch out, to blot out, to efface, to wipe out, to wash out, to throw into the shade; *s'*—, vr. to be *or* become effaced, to wash out, to come out, to stand sideways, to keep in the background

Effarer, va. (*etym. L.* efferare), to scare, to affright; *s'*—, vr. to be scared or affrighted

Effaroucher, va. (*etym.* e, farouche), to scare, to startle, to fright away; *s'*—, vr. to be scared, to take fright, to fly off

‡**Effectif**, ve, adj. sm. (*etym. L.* effectivus), effective, effective force

Effectuer, va. (*etym. L.* effectus), to effectuate, to effect, to bring about; *s'*—, vr. to be brought about *or* effected

Efféminé, e, adj. (*etym. L.* effeminare), effeminate, womanish, womanly

Efféminer, va. to effeminate, to unman

Effet, sm. (*etym. L.* affectus), effect, performance, power, (*com.*) bill, (*plur.*) effects, goods. *Chose à* —, clap-trap. —*s à payer, à recevoir*, bills payable, bills receivable. *À l'*— *de*, with the intent to

§**Effeuiller**, va. (*etym.* ef, *L.* folium), to pluck the leaves of; *s'*—, vr. to shed its leaves

‡**Efficace**, adj. (*etym. L.* efficacem), efficacious, effectual

Efficacité, sf., *also* **Efficace**, sf. (*etym. L.* efficax), efficacy

Effigie, sf. (*etym. L.* effigies), effigy

Effilé, e, adj. sm. (*etym.* ef,

fil), slender, slim; fringed linen, trimming
Efflanqué, e, adj. lean
Efflanquer, va. (*etym.* ef, flanc), to reduce to a pitiful plight
Effleurer, va. (*etym.* ef, fleurer), to graze, to touch slightly, to glance at
Effluve, sm. (*etym.* L. effluvium), effluvium
Effondrer, va. (*etym.* ef, fond), to dig up and manure, to break up; s'—, vr. to fall in, to sink down
s'Efforcer, vr. (*etym.* L.L. exfortiare), to strive, to endeavour, to exert oneself
Effort, sm. (*etym.* see Efforcer), effort, endeavour, strain
Effraction, sf. (*etym.* L.L. effractionem), breaking into
Effrayant, e, adj. frightful, fearful, appalling. — *de laideur*, frightfully ugly
Effrayer, va. (*etym.* see Frayeur), to frighten, to startle, to dismay; s'—, vr. to take fright, to be scared
Effréné, e, adj. (*etym.* L. effrenatus), unbridled, wild, ungovernable
Effroi, sm. (*etym.* see Frayeur), fright, dread, dismay
Effronté, e, adj. (*etym.* ef, front), saucy, bold, shameless, unblushing
Effronterie, sf. (*etym.* effronté), effrontery, sauciness. *Payer d'—*, to brazen it out
‖**Effroyable,** adj. (*etym.* effroi), frightful, dreadful, ghastly, tremendous
Effusion, sf. (*etym.* L. effusionem), pouring out, effusion. — *de sang*, bloodshed
‖**Égal, e,** adj. (*etym.* L. æqualis), adequate, equal, even, level. — s. equal, peer, fellow
Égaler, va. (*etym.* égal), to equal, to level, to match, to smooth; s'—, vr. to equal, to liken oneself
Égaliser, va. (*etym.* égal), to equalize, to level
¶**Égalitaire,** adj. (*etym.* égalité), fond of equality
Égalité, sf. (*etym.* L. æqualitatem), equality, parity, evenness
Égard, sm. (*etym.* O.F. esgarder), regard, respect, account. *Sans avoir — à*, regardless of. *En — à*, in consideration of. *Avoir —, des —s*, to show regard to. *Par — pour moi*, for my sake
Égarement, sm. (*etym.* see Égarer), error, aberration, disorder, wildness
Égarer, va. (*etym.* é, garer), to lead astray, to mislead, to bewilder, to mislay. *Un air égaré*, a wild look. *S'—*, vr. to lose one's way, to go astray, to wander, to fall into error
Égayer, va. (*etym.* é, gai), to enliven, to divert, to cheer up; s'—, vr. to brighten up, to be cheerful, to make oneself merry
Égide, sf. (*etym.* Gr. αἰγίς, *the shield of Athene*), ægis, shield
Églantier, sm. (*etym.* O.F. aiglant, *from the L.* aculeus), wild-briar, dog-rose
Église, sf. (*etym.* Gr. ἐκκλησία), church
Églogue, sf. (*etym.* Gr. ἐκλογαί, *select pieces*), eclogue
Égoïsme, sm. (*etym.* L. ego), selfishness, egotism
‖**Égoïste,** s. adj. egotist, selfish person; selfish, egotistical
Égorger, va. (*etym.* é, gorge), to cut the throat of, to butcher, to slaughter; s'—, vr. to cut each other's throats
§**s'Égosiller,** vr. (*etym.* é, and O.F. gosillier = gosier), to bawl oneself sore, to chirp loudly
Égout, sm. (*etym.* see Égoutter), dripping, sewer, drain
Égoutter, va., s'—, vr. (*etym.* é, goutte), to drain dry
§**Égratigner,** va. (*etym.* é, and gratiner, O.F. for gratter), to scratch oneself
§**Égratignure,** sf. (*etym.* égratigner), scratch
Égrener, va. (*etym.* é, grain), to pick. — *un chapelet*, to tell one's beads. — *des perles*, to unstring pearls
§**Égrillard, e,** adj. (*etym.* é, grille), sprightly, brisk, pert
Éhonté, e, adj. (*etym.* é, honte), shameless, brazen-faced
Éjaculer, va. (*etym.* L. ejaculari), to ejaculate, to spurt out
Élaborer, va. (*etym.* L. elaborare), to elaborate, to work out
Élaguer, va. (*etym.* é, and O.H.G. lah, *incision*), to lop off, to cut away
Élan, sm. (*etym.* O.H.G. elaho, *elk*), elk, moose deer, spring, bound, flight, outbreak, buoyancy
Élancé, e, adj. straight, tall, well-shaped, slim
Élancement, sm. (*etym.* élancer), twinge, transport
Élancer, va.n. (*etym.* é, lancer), to pain, to shoot; s'—, vr. to spring, to rush, to dash
Élargir, va. (*etym.* é, large), to widen, to enlarge, to stretch. *Faire —*, to order a prisoner to be set at large. *S'—*, vr. to widen
Élargissement, sm. (*etm.* élargir), widening, enlarging
Élasticité, sf. (*etym.* élastique), elasticity
Élastique, adj. (*etym.* Gr. ἐλαστικός), elastic, springy, buoyant
Électeur, sm. (*etym.* L. elector), elector
Électif, ve, adj. (*etym.* L.L. electivus), elective
Électricité, sf. (*etym.* électrique), electricity
Électrique, adj. (*etym.* L. electrum), electric
Électriser, va. (*etym.* électrique), to electrify; s'—, vr. to be electrified
Électromètre, sm. (*etym.* électro, mètre), electrometer
Élégamment, adv. (*etym.* élégant), elegantly
Élégiaque, adj. (*etym.* élégie), elegiac
Élégie, sf. (*etym.* L. elegia), elegy
Élémentaire, adj. elementary
Élevage, sm. breeding of cattle
Élévation, sf. (*etym.* L. elevationem), raising, elevation, height, view, rise, preferment, loftiness
Élève, sm. (*etym.* see Élever), pupil, scholar
Élevé, e, adj. high, lofty, exalted, brought up, bred
Élever, va. (*etym.* L. e, levare), to raise, to lift up, to set up, to elevate, to exalt, to extol, to bring up, to rear; s'—, vr. to rise up, to soar, to ascend, to stand, to tower, to climb, to exalt oneself, to amount
Éleveur, sm. (*etym.* élever), cattle-breeder
Élider, va. (*etym.* L. elidere, *to crush*), to cut out, to elide
Éliminer, va. (*etym.* L. eliminare), to eliminate, to strike out
Élire, va. (*etym.* L. eligere), to elect, to choose
Élite, sf. (*etym.* élit, *old past part. of* élire), flower, choicest. *Troupes d'—*, choice troops
Elle, Elles, pron. pers. (*etym.* L. illa), she, they, her, them, it
Ellébore, sm. (*etym.* Gr. ἐλλέβορος), hellebore
Ellipse, sf. (*etym.* Gr. ἔλλειψις), ellipsis
Elliptique, adj. (*etym.* Gr. ἐλλειπτικός), elliptical
Éloge, sm. (*etym.* L. elogium), praise, commendation, eulogy
Élogieux, se, adj. (*etym.* éloge), full of praise
§**Éloigné, e,** adj. far, remote, distant
§**Éloignement,** sm. (*etym.* éloigner), removal, departure, withdrawal, retirement, dislike, distance, background
§**Éloigner,** va. (*etym.* é, loin), to remove, to send away, to dismiss, to divert, to avert; s'—, vr. to go away, to remove, to leave, to withdraw, to stand aloof, to become remote
Éloquemment, adv. (*etm.* éloquent), eloquently
Élu, e, s. adj. (*etym.* élire), the elected, the chosen, elect
Élucubration, sf. (*etym.* L. elucubrationem), lucubration
Élucubrer, va. (*etym.* L. elucubrari), to compose a laborious work
Éluder, va. (*etym.* L. eludere), to elude, to evade
Élysée, sf. (*etm.* L. Elysium), Elysium
§**Émail,** sm. (*etym.* O.H.G. smelzan, *to melt*), enamel
§**Émailler,** va. (*etm.* émail), to enamel, to adorn
Émanciper, va. (*etym.* L. emancipare), to emancipate; s'—, vr. to make too free
Émaner, vn. (*etym.* L. emanare), to emanate
Émargement, sm. (*etym.* émarger), signature in the margin on receiving one's salary
Émarger, va. (*etym.* é, marge), to sign in the margin
Emballage, sm. (*etym.* emballer), packing. *Toile d'—*, wrapper
Emballer, va. (*etym.* en, balle), to pack up
Emballeur, sm. (*etym.* emballer), packer
¶**Embarcadère,** sm. (*etm.* Sp. embarcadero), wharf, terminus
Embarcation, sf. (*etym.* Sp. embarcacion), boat, craft
Embardée, sf. (*etym.* ?), yaw, lurch. *Faire une —*, to lurch
Embarquement, sm. (*etym.* embarquer), embarcation, shipping
Embarquer, va. (*etym.* en, barque), to embark; s'—, vr. to embark, to go on board
Embarras, sm. (*etym.* en, barre), encumbrance, clog, hindrance, stoppage, obstruction, trouble. *Faire des —*, to make a great fuss
Embarrassant, e, adj. troublesome, embarrassing, cumbersome
Embarrasser, va. (*etym.* embarras), to stop up, to clog, to obstruct, to encumber, to embarrass, to perplex, to ensnare; s'—, vr. to get entangled, to get mixed up with, to trouble one's head about, to be at a loss
Embauchage, sm. (*etym.* embaucher), hiring, enticing away
Embaucher, va. (*etym.* en, bauche, bauge), to hire, to entice away
Embaumement, sm. (*etym.* embaumer), embalming
Embaumer, va. (*etym.* en, baume), to perfume, to embalm
Embéguiner, va. (*etym.* en, béguin), to cover the head with a piece of linen; s'—, vr. to have one's head covered, (?) to be infatuated with
Embellir, va. (*etym.* en, beau), to embellish, to beautify, to adorn; — vn., s'—, vr. to grow handsomer, to improve
Embellissement, sm. (*etym.* embellir), embellishment
†**Embêtant, e,** adj. very tiresome
†**Embêtement,** sm. (*etym.* embêter), worry
†**Embêter,** va. (*etym.* en, bête), to worry; s'—, vr. to be worried, to be dull
Emblée, loc. adv. (*etym.* O.F. embler = enlever), at the first onset, without opposition

Emblématique, adj. (*etym.* emblème), emblematical
Emblème, sm. (*etym. Gr.* ἔμβλημα), emblem
Emboîtement, sm. (*etym.* emboîter), jointing, fitting in
Emboîter, va., s'—, vr. to fit in, to joint. — *le pas*, to tread in another's footsteps
Embonpoint, sm. (*etym.* en, bon, point), stoutness, plumpness
Embossage, sm. (*etym.* embosser), bringing the broadside to bear
Embosser, va. (*etym.* en, bosse), to bring the broadside to bear on
Emboucher, va. (*etym.* en, bouche), to put one's mouth to, to bit a horse, to give the cue
Embouchure, sf. (*etym.* emboucher), mouth, mouthpiece
Embouquer, vn. (*etym.* en, bouque, bouche), to enter a strait
Embourber, va., s'—, vr. (*etym.* en, bourbe), to stick fast in the mud or mire
Embranchement, sm. (*etym.* en, branche), branching-off, branch-road, branch-line
Embrasement, sm. (*etym.* embraser), conflagration
Embraser, va. (*etym.* en, braise), to set on fire, to kindle, to burn; s'—, vr. to take fire, to kindle, to glow
Embrassade, sf., *also* **Embrassement**, sm. (*etym.* embrasser), embrace, hug
Embrasser, va. (*etym.* en, bras), to embrace, to clasp in one's arms, to hug, to kiss, to encompass, to encircle, to comprise; s'—, vr. to embrace each other, to be embraced
Embrasure, sf. (*etym.* ?), embrasure, port-hole, window-recess
Embrigader, va. (*etym.* en, brigade), to divide into brigades, to enlist
Embrocher, va. (*etym.* en, broche), to spit
§**Embrouillement**, sm. (*etym.* embrouiller), embroiling, intricacy, confusion
§**Embrouiller**, va. (*etym.* en, brouiller), to embroil, to throw into confusion; s'—, vr. to get perplexed, to become intricate
Embruiné, e, adj. (*etym.* en, bruine), misty, hazy
Embûche, sf. snare, ambush
Embuscade, sf. (*etym. I.* imboscata), ambush, ambuscade
Embusquer, va. (*etym.* en, *and root* bosc; *see* Bois), to place in ambush; s'—, vr. to place oneself in ambush, to hide oneself
Émeraude, sf. (*etym. L.* smaragdus), emerald
Émerger, vn. (*etym. L.* emergere), to emerge
Émeri, sm. (*etym. Gr.* σμύρις, σμίρις), emery
§**Émerillon**, sm. (*etym. L.* merula), merlin, (*nav.*) iron swivel
§**Émerillonné, e**, adj. (*etym.* émerillon), lively, brisk
Émérite, adj. (*etym. L.* emeritus), emerited
§**Émerveiller**, va. (*etym.* é, merveille), to strike with wonder, to amaze; s'—, vr. to marvel, to wonder, to be wonder-struck
Émétique, sm. adj. (*etym. Gr.* ἐμετικός), emetic
Émettre, va. (*etym.* é, mettre), to issue, to utter, to emit, to throw out
§**Émeute**, sf. (*etym. O.F.* esmeu, ému), riot, disturbance
§**Émeutier**, sm. (*etym.* émeute), rioter
Émietter, va., s'—, vr. (*etym.* é, miette), to crumble
Émigrer, vn. (*etym. L.* emigrare), to emigrate
Éminemment, adv. eminently
Émissaire, sm. (*etym. L.* emissarius), emissary
Emmagasinage, sm. (*etym.* emmagasiner), warehousing
Emmagasiner, va. (*etym.* en, magasin), to warehouse, to house
§**Emmailloter**, va. (*etym.* en, maillot), to swathe, to swaddle
Emmancher, va. (*etym.* en, manche), to put a handle to, to begin; s'—, vr. to fit on, to be done
Emmêler, va. (*etym.* en, mêler), to entangle
Emménagement, sm. (*etym.* emménager), moving in, accommodations, berths, stowage-room
Emménager, va., s'—, vr. (*etym.* en, ménage), to move in
Emmener, va. (*etym.* en, mener), to take away, to lead away
Emmieller, va. (*etym.* en, miel), to sweeten with honey
§**Emmitoufler**, va. (*etym.* en, *and O.F.* moufle, *glove*), to wrap or muffle up; s'—, vr. to muffle oneself up
Émoi, sm. (*etym.* é, *and O.H.G.* magan, *to be able*), anxiety, flutter, stir, rumour
Émonder, va. (*etym.* é, *and L.* mundus, *clean*), to prune
Émoudre, va. (*etym. L.* emolire), to grind
Émouleur, sm. (*etym.* émoudre), grinder
Émoulu, e, past part. adj. (*etym.* émoudre), sharp-edged. ‡ *Frais — de*, just fresh from
Émousser, va. (*etym.* é, mousse), to blunt, to dull, to deaden; s'—, vr. to become blunt or dull
§**Émoustiller**, va. (*etym.* é, moustille), to stir up, to rouse, to exhilarate
Émouvoir, va. (*etym. L.* emovere), to move, to chafe, to be rough, to stir up, to rouse, to impassion
§**Empaillage**, sm. (*etym.* empailler), stuffing
§**Empailler**, va. (*etym.* en, paille), to put straw bottoms to, to pack in straw, to stuff
§**Empailleur, se**, s. (*etym.* empailler), chairmender, naturalist
Empaler, va. (*etym.* en, pale), to empale
Empan, sm. (*etym. Germ.* spannen, *to extend*), span
Empanacher, va. (*etym.* en, panache), to plume
Empaqueter, va. (*etym.* en, paquet), to make up into a bundle, to pack together; s'—, vr. to wrap oneself up, to huddle themselves together
S'Emparer, vr. (*etym. I.* imparare, *to learn*), to seize, to take possession, to lay hold
Empâter, va. (*etym.* en, pâte), to make clammy or sticky, to fatten, to impaste, to work up
Empêché, e, past part. adj. pre-engaged, perplexed, embarrassed
Empêchement, sm. (*etym.* empêcher), impediment, hindrance, obstruction, objection. — *dirimant*, absolute impediment
Empêcher, va. (*etym. L.* impedicare), to prevent, to hinder, to impede, to stop; s'—, vr. to help, to forbear, to refrain
Empenner, va. (*etym. L.* in, penna, *feather*), to feather
Empereur, sm. (*etym. L.L.* imperatorem), emperor
Empesé, e, adj. starched, stiff
Empeser, va. (*etym.* empois), to starch, to stiffen
Empester, va. (*etym.* en, peste), to infect, to taint, to stink
Empêtrer, va. (*etym. L.L.* partorium, partoria, *impediments*), to entangle, to hamper. ‡ *L'air empêtré*, a sheep-faced look. S'—, vr. to get entangled, to hamper oneself with
Emphase, sm. (*etym. Gr.* ἔμφασις), emphasis, pomposity
§**Emphatique**, adj. (*etym. Gr.* ἐμφατικός), emphatic, pompous
Emphytéose, sf. (*etym. Gr.* ἐμφύτευσις), emphyteusis, long lease
Emphytéotique, adj. (*etym.* emphytéose), emphyteutic
Empierrement, sm. (*etym.* empierrer), ballasting, stoning
Empierrer, va. (*etym.* en, pierre), to stone, to ballast
Empiètement, sm. (*etym.* empiéter), encroachment, encroaching
Empiéter, va. (*etym.* en, pied), to encroach
‡**Empiffrer**, va. (*etym.* en, piffre), to stuff with food, to fatten
Empiler, va. (*etym.* en, pile), to pile up, to stack
Empire, sm. (*etym. L.* imperium), empire, reign, control, sway, ascendency
Empirer, va. (*etym.* en, pire), to aggravate; — vn. to grow worse and worse
Empirique, adj. sm. (*etym. Gr.* ἐμπειρικός), empiric
Empirisme, sm. (*etym. see* EMPIRIQUE), empiricism
Emplacement, sm. (*etym.* en, placer), site, situation, place
Emplâtre, sm. (*etym. Gr.* ἔμπλαστρον), plaster, (‡) sickly creature, (‡) mere drone
Emplette, sf. (*etym. L.L.* implicare, *to spend*), purchase
Emplir, va., s'—, vr. (*etym. L.* implere), to fill
Emploi, sm. use, employment, appropriation, place, department. *Chef d'—*, chief actor in his line of characters
Employé, e, sm. adj. clerk; busy, occupied
Employer, va. (*etym. L.* implicare, *to fold in*), to employ, to use, to appropriate, to lay out, to spend; s'—, vr. to be employed, to busy oneself, to use one's credit
Empocher, va. (*etym.* en, poche), to pocket, to pouch
§**Empoigner**, va. (*etym.* en, poigne), to clutch
Empois, sm. (*etym.* en, poix), starch
Empoisonnement, sm. (*etym.* empoisonner), poisoning
Empoisonner, va. (*etym.* en, poison), to poison, to infect, to embitter, to corrupt; s'—, vr. to poison oneself, to be poisoned
Empoisonneur, se, s. (*etym.* empoisonner), poisoner
Empoissonnement, sm. (*etym.* empoissonner), stocking with fish
Empoissonner, va. (*etym.* en, poisson), to stock with fish
Emporté, e, adj. hasty, passionate, fiery
Emportement, sm. (*etym.* emporter), transport, burst, passion, dissoluteness
Emporte-pièce, sm. (*etym.* emporter, pièce), punch, (‡) a cutting remark
Emporter, va. (*etym.* en, porter), to carry away, to bear off, to take away, to imply, to involve, to entail. *L'—*, to get the better of, to carry the day, to prevail, to excel, to outweigh. ‡ — *la pièce*, to cut to the quick. *Autant en emporte le vent*, these are mere words. S'—, vr. to fall into a passion, to fire up, to get heated, to run away
Empoter, va. (*etym.* en, pot), to pot, to put in pots

Empourprer, va. (*etym.* en, pourpre), to tinge with purple

Empreindre, va. (*etym.* L. imprimere), to impress, to imprint, to tincture, to tinge; s'—, vr. to leave a trace, to be stamped

Empreinte, sf. (*etym.* empreindre), impress, impression, stamp, mark

Empressé, e, adj. (*etym.* empresser), eager, forward, earnest

Empressement, sm. (*etym.* empresser), eagerness, alacrity, obligingness, cordiality, assiduity

s'Empresser, vr. to be eager, to hasten, to be studious of pleasing, assiduously attentive, to flock

Emprisonnement, sm. (*etym.* emprisonner), imprisonment. — *cellulaire*, solitary confinement

Emprisonner, va. (*etym.* en, prison), to imprison, to enclose, to confine

Emprunt, sm. (*etym.* emprunter), borrowing, loan. *Contracter un* —, to raise a loan. *Visage d'* —, false face

Emprunté, e, adj. fictitious, awkward

Emprunter, va. (*etym.* L.L. impromutuare), to borrow, to assume

Emprunteur, se, s. (*etym.* emprunter), borrower

Empuantir, va. (*etym.* en, puant), to infect with a bad smell

Empyrée, sm. (*etym.* Gr. ἐν, πῦρ, fire), the empyrean

Émule, s. (*etym.* L. æmulus), emulator, rival, competitor

En, prep. (*etym.* L. in), in, into, to, through, like a, as a. — *roi*, like a king. *Une maison — briques*, a brick house

En, pers. pron. (*etym.* L. inde), of him, of her, of them, of it, thence

Encâblure, sf. (*etym.* en, câble), cable's length

Encadrement, sm. (*etym.* encadrer), framing, frame

Encadrer, va. (*etym.* en, cadre), to frame, to encircle, to surround, to introduce

Encaisse, sf. (*etym.* en, caisse), cash in hand, metallic reserve fund

Encaissement, sm. (*etym.* encaisser), packing in a box, collection, paying in, embankment

Encaisser, va. (*etym.* en, caisse), to case, to pack in cases *or* boxes, to receive, to embank

Encan, sm. (*etym.* L. in, quantum), auction. *A l'* —, by auction

§**s'Encanailler**, vr. (*etym.* en, canaille), to keep low company

Encaustique, sf. (*etym.* Gr. ἐγκαυστικὴ [τέχνη]), encaustic painting

Encaver, va. (*etym.* en, cave), to cellar

Enceindre, va. (*etym.* L. incingere), to encircle, to begird, to encompass

Enceinte, sf. (*etym.* L. incinctus), circuit, fence, walls, circle. — part. f. with child, pregnant, in the family way

Encens, sm. (*etym.* L. incensum, *burnt*), incense, flattery

Encensement, sm. (*etym.* encenser), incensing

Encenser, va. (*etym.* encens), to burn incense on, to incense, to bow the knee to, to flatter

Encenseur, sm. (*etym.* encenser), flatterer

Encensoir, sm. (*etym.* encenser), censer. † *Donner de l'* —, to flatter grossly. † *A coups d'* —, with fulsome flattery

Enchaînement, sm. (*etym.* enchaîner), chain, concatenation, train

Enchaîner, va. (*etym.* en, chaîne), to chain, to enchain, to fetter, to bind, to wed, to hold in restraint; s'—, vr. to be linked together, to link oneself

Enchanté, e, adj. enchanted, delightful

Enchantement, sm. (*etym.* L. incantamentum), enchantment, spell, charm

Enchanter, va. (*etym.* L. incantare), to enchant, to bewitch, to delight

Enchanteur, teresse, s. (*etym.* L. incantatorem), enchanter, enchantress. — adj. enchanting

Enchâsser, va. (*etym.* en, châsse), to enshrine, to enchase

Enchère, sf. (*etym.* L.L. incheriare), bidding, bid, auction. *Folle* —, resale at any price

Enchérir, va. (*etym.* enchère), to bid for, to outbid for, to raise the price of; — vn. to outbid, to improve on, to go beyond, to become dearer

Enchérissement, sm. (*etym.* enchérir), dearness

Enchérisseur, sm. (*etym.* enchérir), bidder. ‡ *Le plus offrant et dernier* —, the highest bidder

Enchevêtrer, va. (*etym.* en, chevêtre), to entangle; s'—, vr. to get entangled

Enchifrènement, sm. (*etym.* enchifrener), cold in the head

Enchifrener, va. (*etym.* en, chanfrein), to give a cold in the head

Enclave, sf. (*etym.* see ENCLAVER), a land surrounded by other lands

Enclaver, va. (*etym.* L. in, clavus, *nail*), to enclose, to take into, to lock in

Enclin, e, adj. (*etym.* L. inclinis), inclined to, prone

Enclitique, sf. (*etym.* Gr. ἐγκλιτικός), enclitic

Enclore, va. (*etym.* L.L. inclaudere), to enclose, to fence in

Enclos, sm. enclosure, close, paddock

Enclouer, va. (*etym.* L.L. inclavare), to prick a horse's foot

Enclouure, sf. (*etym.* enclouer), prick of a nail, hitch

Enclume, sf. (*etym.* L. incudinem, *an anvil*), anvil

§**Encoignure**, sf. (*etym.* en, coin), corner

Encolure, sf. (*etym.* en, col), chest and shoulders, look, mien

Encombre, sm. (*etym.* L.L. incombrum), hindrance, cross accident

Encombrement, sm. (*etym.* encombrer), encumbering

Encombrer, va. (*etym.* encombre), to stop up, to obstruct, to encumber

Encontre, loc. adv. (*etym.* en, contre), against. *Aller à l'— de, à l'* —, to run counter to

Encore, adv. (*etym.* L. hanc horam), still, yet, as yet, again, anew, more, still more, another, longer, besides

Encorné, e, adj. (*etym.* en, corne), horned

Encourageant, e, adj. encouraging, inspiriting

Encouragement, sm. (*etym.* encourager), encouragement, incentive, incitement

Encourager, va. (*etym.* en, courage), to encourage, to inspirit, to embolden, to countenance

Encourir, va. (*etym.* L. incurrere), to incur, to draw upon oneself

Encrasser, va. (*etym.* en, crasse), to cover with dirt; s'—, vr. to cover oneself with dirt, (*f*) to marry below one's position

Encre, sf. (*etym.* L. encaustum), ink. — *de Chine*, Indian ink. † *C'est la bouteille à l'* —, it is rather obscure

Encrier, sm. (*etym.* encre), inkstand, inktrough

Encroûter, va. (*etym.* L. incrustare), to give a coating of; s'—, vr. to be crusted over, to grow rusty

Encyclique, adj. sf. (*etym.* Gr. ἐγκύκλιος), encyclical, encyclical letter

Encyclopédie, sf. encyclopedia

Encyclopédiste, sm. (*etym.* encyclopédie), encyclopedist

Endémique, adj. (*etym.* Gr. ἐνδημία), endemic, endemical

Endetter, va. (*etym.* en, dette), to make one run into debt; s'—, vr. to incur debts

Endêver, vn. (*etym.* ?), to be mad. *Faire* —, to drive mad, to plague

Endiablé, e, adj. (*etym.* en, diable), possessed of the devil, (*fig.*) mad

s'Endimancher, vr. (*etym.* en, dimanche), to put on one's Sunday clothes

Endoctriner, va. (*etym.* en, doctrine), to indoctrinate, to teach one his lesson

Endolori, e, adj. (*etym.* en, douleur), aching, sore, painful

Endommager, va. (*etym.* en, dommage), to damage, to injure

Endormeur, sm. (*etym.* endormir), deceiver, wheedler

Endormi, e, adj. asleep, sleeping, drowsy, benumbed

Endormir, va. (*etym.* en, dormir), to send to sleep, to lull, to beguile, to benumb; s'—, vr. to fall asleep, to go to sleep, to be lulled into security, to grovel, to die

Endos, Endossement, sm. (*etym.* en, dos), endorsement

Endosser, va. (*etym.* endos), to put on, to don, to endorse, to saddle

Endosseur, sm. (*etym.* endosser), endorser

Endroit, sm. (*etym.* en, droit), spot, place, passage, right side. *A l'— de*, with respect to

Enduire, va. (*etym.* L. inducere), to lay on a coat of

Enduit, sm. coating, coat, plaster

Endurant, e, adj. enduring, meek-minded

Endurcir, va. (*etym.* en, durcir), to harden, to inure to steel; s'—, vr. to toughen to inure oneself, to grow hardened

Endurcissement, sm. (*etym.* endurcir), hardening, obduracy, hardness of heart

Endurer, va. (*etym.* en, durer), to endure, to undergo

Énergie, sf. (*etym.* Gr. ἐνέργεια), energy, strength, pithiness

Énergique, adj. energetic, energetical, pithy

Énergumène, sm. (*etym.* Gr. ἐνεργούμενος), energumen, demoniac

Énerver, va. (*etym.* L. enervare), to enervate, to unnerve; s'—, vr. to become enerved *or* enervated

Enfance, sf. (*etym.* L. infantia), infancy, babyhood, childhood, childish thing, dotage

Enfant, s. (*etym.* L. infantem), infant, baby, small child, child. *Petits—s*, grandchildren. — *trouvé*, foundling. *Les —s perdus*, (*milit.*) the forlorn hope. *Un bon* —, a good fellow, a simpleton. *Les —s de France*, the princes and princesses of France

Enfantement, sm. (*etym.* enfanter), childbirth, conception

Enfanter, va. (*etym.* enfant), to bring forth, to bear, to give birth to

§**Enfantillage**, sm. (*etym.* L. infantilis), child's play, childishness

Enfantin, e, adj. (*etym.* enfant), infantine, childish

Enfariner, va. (*etym.* en,

farine), to sprinkle with flour; *s'*—, vr. to get all over flour

Enfer, sm. (*etym. L.* infernus), hell. *Un jeu d'*—, ruinous play

Enfermer, va. (*etym.* en, fermer), to shut up *or* in, to coop up, to put away, to hide, to contain, to harbour. *Sentir l'enfermé*, to smell musty. *S'*—, vr. to shut oneself up *or* in

Enferrer, va. (*etym.* en, fer), to run through the body; *s'*—, vr. to run oneself through, to run one another through the body, (*fig.*) to get embarrassed

Enfilade, sf. (*etym.* enfiler), suite of rooms, long string, raking fire

Enfiler, va. (*etym.* en, fil), to thread, to string pearls, to pick straws, to go down, to run down *or* through, to enter upon, to rake fore and aft; *s'*—, vr. to be threaded, to be strung

Enfin, adv. (*etym.* en, fin), at last, at length, lastly, in short

Enflammer, va. (*etym. L.* inflammare), to set fire to, to set in a blaze, to inflame, to heat, to rouse, to incense; *s'*—, vr. to take fire, to be inflamed, to fire up, to be smitten with

Enflé, e, past part. adj. swollen, bloated, puffed up, inflated

Enfler, va. (*etym. L.* inflare), to swell, to inflate, to bloat, to raise; *s'*—, vr. to be swollen, to swell, to rise, to be puffed up

Enflure, sf., *also* **Enflement**, sm. (*etym.* enfler), swelling, bloatedness, pride, inflation

Enfoncé, e, past part. adj. broken open, deep, sunken

Enfoncement, sm. (*etym.* enfoncer), breaking open *or* down *or* through, sinking, nook, recess

Enfoncer, va. (*etym.* en, foncer), to thrust, to drive in, to break open, to do for; — vn. to sink down; *s'*—, vr. to go deep *or* far, to strike, to sink, to bury oneself, (†) to make a mess of it

Enfonceur, sm. (*etym.* enfoncer), † — *de portes ouvertes*, doer of nothings

Enforcir, va. (*etym.* en, force), to strengthen; — vn., *s'*—, vr. to grow stronger

Enfouir, va. (*etym. L.* infodare), to bury, to hide in the ground; *s'*—, vr. to earth *or* bury oneself

Enfouissement, sm. (*etym.* enfouir), burying, hiding in the ground

Enfourcher, va. (*etym.* en, fourche), to bestride

Enfourchure, sf. (*etym.* enfourcher), fork

Enfourner, va. (*etym.* en, four), to put in the oven

Enfreindre, va. (*etym. L.* infringere), to infringe, to pass over, to break

s'Enfuir, vr. (*etym.* en, fuir), to flee, to take to flight, to run

Enfumer, va. (*etym.* en, fumer), to smoke, to fill with smoke

Engageant, e, adj. engaging, winning, prepossessing

Engagement, sm. (*etym.* engager), engagement, pledging, pawning, mortgage, enlisting, bounty, attachment

Engager, va. (*etym.* en, gage), to pledge, to pawn, to engage, to bind, to be binding on, to urge, to induce, to hire, to enlist, to entangle, to involve; *s'*—, vr. to engage, to enter into an engagement, to be bound for, to get involved, to enlist

Engeance, sf. (*etym. O.F.* enger, *to provide*), breed, brood

Engelure, sf. (*etym.* en, geler), chilblain

Engendrer, va. (*etym. L.* ingenerare), to beget, to engender, to give rise to; *s'*—, vr to be engendered, to spring up

Engin, sm. (*etym. L.* ingenium), skill, engine, tool, snare

Englober, va. (*etym.* en, globe), to unite, to lump together

Engloutir, va. (*etym. see* Glouton), to swallow, to swallow up, to ingulf, to engross; *s'*—, vr. to be swallowed up

Engluer, va. (*etym.* en, glu), to lime; *s'*—, vr. to get entangled in the birdlime, to be ensnared

Engorgement, sm. (*etym.* engorger), choking up, stoppage, congestion

s'Engorger, vr. (*etym.* en, gorge), to be choked up *or* congested

Engouement, sm. (*etym.* engouer), sort of choking, infatuation, extravagant fondness

Engouer, va. (*etym.* en, *and a root* gav, *throat*), to choke up, (*fig.*) to infatuate; *s'*—, vr. to half-choke oneself, to be infatuated with

s'Engouffrer, vr. (*etym.* en, gouffre), to rush into, to be lost *or* ingulfed

Engourdir, va. (*etym.* en, gourd), to benumb, to dull, to blunt; *s'*—, vr. to become numb, to grow dulled

Engourdissement, sm. (*etym.* engourdir), numbness, torpor, sluggishness

Engrais, sm. (*etym. see* Engraisser), fat pasture, fattening food, manure

Engraissement, sm. (*etym.* engraisser), fattening, corpulence

Engraisser, va. (*etym. L.* incrassare), to fatten, to manure; — vn. to grow fat *or* stout, to thrive; *s'*—, vr. to grow fat, to fatten

Engraver, va.n., *s'*—, vr. (*etym.* en, *and a root* grav, *sand*), to strand; (*etym.* en, graver), to engrave on

Engrenage, sm. (*etym.* engrener), cogged wheels, gear

Engrener, vn., *s'*—, vr. (*etym.* en, grain), (*mech.*) to put in gear

Enhardir, va. (*etym.* en, hardir), to embolden; *s'*—, vr. to grow bold, to make bold

Enharnacher, va. (*etym.* en, barnache), to harness, to accoutre

Énigmatique, adj. (*etym.* énigme), enigmatical

Énigme, sm. (*etym. Gr.* αἴνιγμα), enigma, riddle

Enivrant, e, adj. intoxicating, inebriating

Enivrement, sm. (*etym.* enivrer), intoxication, raptures

Enivrer, va. (*etym. L.* inebriare), to intoxicate, to inebriate, to enrapture; *s'*—, vr. to get drunk, to glut oneself, to be enraptured

Enjambée, sf. stride

Enjambement, sm. (*etym.* enjamber), running of the sense into the next verse

Enjamber, va. (*etym.* en, jambe), to get over, to take at a stride; — vn. to take a stride, to stride along, to project, to encroach

Enjeu, sm. (*etym.* en, jeu), stake

Enjoindre, va. (*etym. L.* injungere), to enjoin, to direct

Enjôler, va. (*etym.* en, geôle), to wheedle, to inveigle

Enjôleur, se, s. (*etym.* enjôler), wheedler

Enjolivement, sm. (*etym.* enjoliver), embellishment

Enjoliver, va. (*etym.* en, joli), to adorn, to embellish

Enjoué, e, adj. (*etym.* en, jouer), playful, sportive, cheerful

Enjouement, sm. (*etym.* en, jouer), playfulness, cheerfulness

Enlacement, sm. (*etym.* enlacer), entwining, interweaving

Enlacer, va. (*etym.* en, lacs), to lace, to entwine, to wind round; *s'*—, vr. to entwine, to wind oneself round

Enlaidir, va. (*etym.* en, laid), to disfigure, to make ugly; — vn. to grow ugly

Enlaidissement, sm. (*etym.* enlaidir), disfigurement

Enlèvement, sm. (*etym.* enlever), removal, carrying away, kidnapping, rape, elopement

Enlever, va. (*etym.* en, lever), to raise, to lift up, to heave up, to remove, to clear away, to carry away, to kidnap; *s'*—, vr. to be raised *or* lifted up, to be taken up, to be taken away, to come off, to fly into a passion

Enluminer, va. (*etym.* en, *L.* luminare), to colour, to illuminate; *s'*—, vr. to paint one's face, to put on rouge

Enlumineur, se, s. (*etym.* enluminer), colourer, illuminator

Enluminure, sf. (*etym.* enluminer), colouring, ambitious elegance

Ennemi, e, s. adj. (*etym. L.* inimicus), enemy, foe, the opposite; hostile, unfriendly, inimical, opposite, hurtful

Ennoblir, va. (*etym.* en, noble), to ennoble, to exalt; *s'*—, vr. to be ennobled

Ennui, sm. (*etym.* ?), wearisomeness, tediousness, annoyance, care

Ennuyant, e, adj. tiresome

Ennuyé, e, past part. adj. wearisome, sick and tired, bored

Ennuyer, va. (*etym.* ennui), to tire, to weary, to annoy, to bore, to bother; *s'*—, vr. to feel quite dull, to be weary

Ennuyeux, se, adj. s. (*etym.* ennui), tedious, wearisome, annoying; a bore, a tiresome body

Énoncé, sm. statement, assertion, wording

Énoncer, va. (*etym. L.* enunciare), to word, to express, to state; *s'*—, vr. to express oneself, to be worded *or* expressed

Énonciation, sf. (*etym. L.* enunciationem), statement, enunciation

s'Enorgueillir, va. (*etym.* en, orgueil), to make proud, to puff up; *s'*—, vr. to pride oneself, to be proud of, to be puffed up

Énorme, adj. (*etym. L.* enormis), enormous, heinous, preposterous

Énormément, adv. (*etym.* énorme), enormously

Énormité, sf. (*etym. L.* enormitas), hugeness, enormity

s'Enquérir, vr. (*etym. L.* inquirere), to inquire, to make inquiries

Enquête, sf. (*etym. L.* inquisita), inquiry, inquest, inquisition

Enraciner, va. (*etym.* en, racine), to implant, to root; — vn., *s'*—, vr. to take root, to root, to grow

Enragé, e, adj. mad, rabid, enraged, raging

Enrager, vn. (*etym.* en, rage), to go mad, to be mad, to be enraged

Enrayer, va. (*etym.* en, rai), to put spokes to, to put the drag on, to rein up, to trace the first furrow

Enrégimenter, va. (*etym.* en, régiment), to form into regiments

Enregistrement, sm. (*etym.* en, registrar), registration, recording, entry. *Receveur d'*—, registrar

Enregistrer, va. (*etym.* en, registre), to register, to enter, to record

Enrhumer, va. (*etym.* en,

rhume), to give a cold. *Être enrhumé du cerveau*, to have a cold in one's head. *S'*—, vr. to catch a cold

Enrichir, va. (*etym.* en, riche), to enrich, to make wealthy; *s'*—, vr. to grow rich, to thrive

Enrichissement, sm. (*etym.* enrichir), enriching, ornament

Enrôlement, sm. (*etym.* enrôler), enlistment

Enrôler, va. (*etym.* en, rôle), to enrol, to enlist; *s'*—, vr. to enrol oneself, to enlist

Enroué, e, adj. hoarse

Enrouement, sm. (*etym.* enrouer), hoarseness

Enrouer, va. (*etym.* en, *L.* raucus), to make hoarse; *s'*—, vr. to get hoarse

§**Enrouiller**, va. (*etym.* en, rouille), to rust, to grow rusty; *s'*—, vr. to grow rusty

Enroulement, sm. (*etym.* enrouler), rolling, scroll, volution, twisting

Enrouler, va. (*etym.* en, rouler), to roll, to roll up; *s'*—, vr. to roll, to twine

Ensablement, sm. (*etym.* ensabler), sandbank, ballasting, gravelling

Ensabler, va., *s'*—, vr. to run on a sandbank

Ensanglanté, e, adj. bloody, stained *or* smeared with blood

Ensanglanter, va. (*etym.* en, sanglant), to stain with blood

§**Enseigne**, sf. (*etym.* *L.* in, signum), sign, token, proof, ensign, colours, ensigncy. † *A bonnes —s*, on sure grounds. ‡ *Être logé à la même —*, (*fig.*) to be in the same predicament. — sm. ensign. *— de vaisseau*, senior midshipman. *— de première classe*, second lieutenant

§**Enseignement**, sm. (*etym.* enseigner), teaching, instruction, tuition, lesson

§**Enseigner**, va. (*etym.* *L.L.* insignare), to teach, to instruct, to show

Ensemble, adv. (*etym.* *L.* in, simul), together, at the same time. — sm. whole, harmony. *Morceau d'—*, a piece of music for several voices. *Mettre de l'— dans*, to go well together in

Ensemencement, sm. sowing

Ensemencer, va. (*etym.* en, semence), to sow

Enserrer, va. (*etym.* en, serrer), to lock in

Ensevelir, va. (*etym.* *L.* in, sepelire), to bury, to entomb, to swallow up; *s'*—, vr. to bury oneself, to be buried

Ensevelissement, sm. (*etym.* ensevelir), burial

Ensorceler, va. (*etym.* en, sorcier), to bewitch

Ensorcellement, sm. (*etym.* ensorceler), bewitchment, bewitchery

Ensuite, adv. (*etym.* en, suite), afterwards, next

§'**Ensuivre**, vr. (*etym.* en, suivre), to follow, to ensue, to spring

Entablement, sm. (*etym.* en, table), entablature, entablement

Entacher, va. (*etym.* en, tacher), to taint, to infect

§**Entaille**, sf. (*etym.* *see* ENTAILLER), notch, gash, slash

§**Entailler**, va. (*etym.* en, tailler), to notch, to jag

Entamer, va. (*etym.* *L.L.* intaminare), to begin to cut, to touch, to graze, to enter upon, to fathom

Entassement, sm. (*etym.* entasser), heap, accumulation

Entasser, va. (*etym.* en, tas), to heap up, to heap, to huddle together; *s'*—, vr. to huddle together, to be huddled together

Entendement, sm. (*etym.* entendre), understanding, sense, judgment

Entendeur, sm. (*etym.* entendre), who understands. *A bon — salut!* a word to the wise

Entendre, va. (*etym.* *L.* intendere), to hear, to overhear, to understand, to expect, to intend, to mean; *s'*—, vr. to hear one's own voice, to hear each other's voices, to know what one means, to understand each other, to be a thing of course, to be skilled in, to know. — *comme larrons en foire*, to be as thick as thieves

Entendu, e, part. adj. (*etym.* entendre), heard, understood

Entente, sf. (*etm.* entendre), meaning, knowledge, skill, understanding

Enter, va. (*etym.* *Gr.* ἐμφύτευω), to graft

Enterrement, sm. (*etym.* enterrer), burial, interment

Enterrer, va. (*etym.* en, terre), to bury in the ground, to inter; *s'*—, vr. to bury oneself

Entêté, e, adj. extravagantly fond, prepossessed with, bent on, stubborn, self-willed, obstinate

Entêtement, sm. (*etym.* entêter), stubbornness

Entêter, va. (*etym.* en, tête), to give the headache, to intoxicate, to put into the head of, to prepossess; *s'*—, vr. to be prepossessed with, to grow stubborn

Enthousiasme, sm. (*etm.* *Gr.* ἐνθουσιασμός), enthusiasm, rapture

Enthousiasmer, va. (*etm.* enthousiasme), to enrapture; *s'*—, vr. to be in raptures

Enthousiaste, s. adj. (*etm.* *see* ENTHOUSIASME), enthusiast; enthusiastic, filled with enthusiasm

Enticher, va. (*etym.* en, tache), to taint, to infect; *s'*—, vr. to get infected, to cling to

§**Entier, ère**, adj. (*etym.* *L.* integrum), whole, entire, total, (*fig.*) headstrong, opinionated. — sm. whole number, integer

Entomologie, sf. (*etym.* *Gr.* ἔντομον, λόγος), entomology

Entomologique, adj. entomological

Entomologiste, sm. entomologist

Entonner, va. (*etym.* en, tonne), to tun, to barrel, to give out the tune, to strike up; *s'*—, vr. to rush, to blow

Entonnoir, sm. (*etym.* entonner), funnel

Entorse, sf. (*etym.* en, tors), sprain, sprained ankle, shock

§**Entortillement**, sm. (*etym.* entortiller), twining, winding, twisting, perplexity

§**Entortiller**, va. (*etym.* en, tortiller), to wrap up, to twine, to twist, to entangle, to perplex, *s'*—, vr. to twist oneself round, to wind round oneself

Entourage, sm. (*etym.* entourer), mounting, railing, those about, advisers

Entourer, va. (*etym.* en, tours), to surround, to encompass, to gather round, to beset

Entournure, sf. (*etym.* *O.F.* entourner), sloping. *Gêné dans les —s*, tight in the sleeves

Entours, sm. plur. (*etym.* en, tour), parts round, adjacent parts, those about

Entr'acte, sm. (*etym.* entre, acte), interval between the acts

§**Entrailles**, sf. plur. (*etym.* *L.* interanea), bowels, entrails, feeling

Entrain, sm. (*etym.* en, train), spirits, high spirits

Entraînant, e, adj. overpowering, winning

Entraînement, sm. (*etym.* entraîner), enthusiasm, impulse, sway, seduction

Entraîner, va. (*etym.* en, traîner), to draw along, to carry along, to lead away, to inspirit, to gain over, to win, to urge; (*etym.* en, *and Eng.* to train), to train

§**Entraîneur**, sm. (*etym.* entraîner), trainer

Entrant, sm. comer in, goer in

Entrave, sf. (*etym.* *L.* in, trabes), fetters, trammels, hindrance

Entraver, va. (*etym.* entrave), to fetter, to trammel, to hinder

Entre, prep. (*etym.* *L.* inter), between, among, in, through

Entre-bâiller, va. (*etym.* entre, bâiller), to half-open

Entrechat, sm. (*etym.* *I.* intrecciato), caper, cut. *Battre, faire des —s*, to cut capers

*s'*Entrechoquer, vr. (*etym.* entre, choquer), to knock against each other, to encounter each other, to jar, to conflict

Entre-colonne, Entre-colonnement, sm. (*etym.* entre, colonne), intercolumniation

Entre-côte, sm. (*etym.* entre, côte), meat between the ribs

Entrecouper, va. (*etym.* entre, couper), to intersect, to traverse, to diversify

*s'*Entre-déchirer, vr. (*etym.* entre, déchirer), to tear each other, to malign each other

*s'*Entre-détruire, vr. (*etym.* entre, détruire), to destroy each other

Entre-deux, sm. (*etym.* entre, deux), space between, partition

Entrée, sf. entrance, entry, opening dance, free access, entrance-money, a seat, occasion, town-dues

Entrefaites, sf. pl. *used only as an* adv. (*etym.* entre, fait). *Sur ces —*, meanwhile, in the interim

Entrelacement, sm. (*etym.* entrelacer), interweaving, wreathing

Entrelacer, va. (*etym.* entre, lacer), to interweave, to entwine, to blend; *s'*—, vr. to twine *or* twist round each other, to entwine

Entrelarder, va. (*etym.* entre, larder), to interlard

§**Entre-ligne**, sm. (*etym.* entre, ligne), space between the lines, (*print.*) space-line, lead

Entreluire, vn. (*etym.* entre, luire), to glimmer

Entremêler, va. (*etym.* entre, mêler), to intermingle, to intermix, to intersperse; *s'*—, vr. to intermingle, to meddle

Entremets, sm. (*etym.* entre, mets), side-dish

Entremetteur, se, s. (*etym.* entremettre), intermediate agent, go-between

*s'*Entremettre, vr. (*etym.* entre, mettre), to interpose, to go between

Entremise, sf. (*etym.* entremettre), interposition, mediation, medium

Entrepont, sm. (*etym.* entre, pont), between the decks

Entreposer, va. (*etym.* entre, poser), to warehouse, to put in bond

Entreposeur, sm. (*etym.* entreposer), warehouse-keeper. — *de tabacs*, manager of a tobacco store

Entrepôt, sm. (*etym.* entreposer), store-room, bonding-warehouse, emporium

Entreprenant, e, adj. enterprising, adventurous

Entreprendre, va. (*etym.* entre, prendre), to undertake, to venture, to contract, to attempt, to try, to seize; — vn. to intrench, to encroach

Entrepreneur, se, s. (*etym.* entreprendre), contractor

Entreprise, sf. (*etym.* entreprendre), undertaking, enterprise, contract, office, intrenchment, encroachment, attempt [illegible]

Entrer, vn. (*etym. L.* intrare), to enter, to go in, to come in, to partake of, to have a share in, to fit

Entresol, sm. (*etym.* entre, sol), apartments between the ground-floor and the first story

Entretenir, va. (*etym.* entre, tenir), to hold together, to keep in good repair, to maintain, to preserve, to keep, to entertain, to converse with; *s'*—, vr. to hold each other together, to be maintained, to be kept up, to subsist, to keep oneself, to defray one's own expenses, to converse

Entretien, sm. (*etym.* entretenir), maintenance, keep, repair, keeping in repair, preservation

Entrevoie, sf. (*etym.* entre, voie), space between the rails

Entrevoir, va. (*etym.* entre, voir), to catch a glimpse of, to foresee

Entrevue, sf. interview, meeting

Entr'ouvrir, va. (*etym.* entre, ouvrir), to half-open; *s'*—, vr. to gape, to open

Énumérer, va. (*etym. L.* enumerare), to enumerate, to go over

Envahir, va. (*etym. L.* invadere), to invade, to overrun, to break in upon

Envahissement, sm. (*etym.* envahir), invasion, encroachment, infringement

Envahisseur, sm. (*etym.* envahir), invader

Enveloppe, sf. (*etym. see* ENVELOPPER), wrapper, covering, envelope, exterior. *Une — épaisse,* (*fig.*) a rude exterior

Envelopper, va. (*etym.* en, *and O.F.* voleper), to wrap up, to cover, to envelop, to fold up, to invest, to involve. *Esprit enveloppé,* sluggish mind. *S'*—, vr. to wrap oneself up, to envelop oneself, to be involved

Envenimé, e, adj. envenomed

Envenimer, va. (*etym.* en, venin), to envenom, to inflame, to exasperate; *s'*—, vr. to rankle, to fester, to be *or* grow envenomed

Enverguer, vn. (*etym.* vergue), to bend sails

Envergure, sf. (*etym.* en, vergue), length, breadth, spread of wing

Envers, prep. (*etym.* en, vers), towards, to. ‡ — *et contre tous,* against the whole world. — sm. (*etym. L.* inversus), wrong side, inside out. *Avoir l'esprit à l'*—, to be half-mad

Envi, loc. adv. (*etym. L.* invitus), with emulation of each other, vying with each other

Envie, sf. (*etym. L.* invidia), envy, spite, spleen, a mind, wish, fancy, longing, mark, agnail (hangnail). *Se passer l'— de,* to indulge oneself with. *Faire passer l'— de ... à,* to sicken a person with

§**Envieillir,** vn. (*etym.* en, vieillir), to grow old in

Envier, va. (*etym. L.L.* invidiare), to envy, to long for, to like, to fancy

Envieux, se, adj. (*etym. L.* invidiosus), envious

Environ, adv. (*etym.* en, *and O.F.* viron = autour), about

Environnant, e, adj. surrounding

Environner, va. (*etym.* environ), to surround, to environ, to encompass

Environs, sm. plur. (*etym.* environ), environs, vicinity

Envisager, va. (*etym.* en, visage), to look at, to look in the face, to look upon, to weigh well; *s'*—, vr. to eye each other

Envoi, sm. (*etym. see* ENVOYER), expedition, parcel, present, consignment, envoy. *Lettre d'*—, letter of advice

Envoisiné, e, adj. (*etym.* en, voisin), that has neighbors

s'Envoler, vr. (*etym.* en, voler), to fly away, to take flight

Envoyé, sm. messenger, envoy

Envoyer, va. (*etym. L.* in, via), to send, to forward, to despatch, to emit. † — *promener paître,* (*reg.*) to send about one's business

Envoyeur, sm. adj. (*etym.* envoyer), sender, despatching

Éolien, ne, adv. (*etym. Gr.* Αἰολεύς, *for the dialect; prop. name* Éole, *for the harp*), Eolian, Eolic

Épacte, sm. (*etym. Gr.* ἐπακτός, add-ed), epact

§**Épagneul, e,** s. (*etym.* Espagnol), spaniel

Épais, se, adj. (*etym. L.* spissus), thick, dense, stout, coarse, heavy-witted, dull, muddy, turbid

Épaisseur, sf. (*etym.* épais), thickness, denseness, stoutness, coarseness, heaviness, dulness

Épaissir, va. n. (*etym.* épais), to thicken, to grow stout; *s'*—, vr. to thicken, to grow thick *or* stout, to grow duller

Épaississement, sm. (*etym.* épaissir), thickening, increasing bigness *or* dulness

Épanchement, sm (*etym.* épancher), discharge, overflow, outburst, effusion

Épancher, va. (*etym. same as* épandre), to pour out, to open, to vent; *s'*—, vr. to be effused, to pour itself out, to unbosom oneself

Épandre, va. (*etym. L.* expandere), to pour out, to spread over, to spill, to shed, to scatter; *s'*—, vr. to spread, to stretch

Épanouir, va. (*etym. see* ÉPANDRE), to cause to blow, to brighten up, to expand; *s'*—, vr. to expand its leaves, to blow, to bloom, to brighten up

Épanouissement, sm. (*etym.* épanouir), blowing, opening, brightness, expansion

§**Épargnant, e,** adj. thrifty, saving

§**Épargne,** sf. thriftiness, saving, savingness. *Caisse d'*—, savings-bank

§**Épargner,** va. (*etym.* ?), to be sparing of, to spare, to husband; *s'*—, vr. to spare oneself, to spare one another, to deny oneself

§**Éparpillement,** sm. (*etym.* éparpiller), scattering, frittering away

§**Éparpiller,** va. (*etym.* é, *and I.* parpaglione, *butterfly*), to scatter, to fritter away, to be scattered about

Épars, e, adj. (*etym. L.* sparsus), scattered, dispersed

Épaté, e, adj. (*etym.* é, patte), broken-footed, flat. *Au nez* —, flat-nosed

Épaule, sf. (*etm. L.* spathula), shoulder. *A larges —s,* broad-shouldered. ‡ *Donner un coup d'— à,* to give a lift

Épaulement, sm. (*etym.* épaule), shoulder

Épauler, va. (*etym.* épaule), to break the shoulder of, to back, to help, to cover

Épaulette, sf. (*etym.* épaule), epaulet, shoulder-piece

Épave, adj. (*etym. L.L.* expavus), strayed, stray. — sf. waif, wrecks

Épée, sf. (*etym. L.* spatha), sword. *Homme d'*—, soldier. *Une bonne* —, a good swordsman. *Coup d'— dans l'eau,* useless effort. *N'avoir que la cape et* —, to be a soldier of fortune. *Se faire blanc de son* —, to boast. — *de chevet,* thing which one makes constant use of. *Mettre quelque chose du côté de l'*—, to lay something by

Épeler, va. (*etym. O.H.G.* spellôn, *to relate*), to spell

Éperdu, e, adj. (*etym. past part. of the O.F.* éperdre), bewildered, distracted, dismayed

Éperlan, sm. (*etym. Germ.* spierling), sprat, smelt

Éperon, sm. (*etym. O.H.G.* sporo), spur, prow, rostrum. *Donner de l'— à,* to set spurs to

Éperonner, va. (*etym.* éperon), to spur, to spur on

Épervier, sm. (*etym. O.H.G.* sparvari), hawk, sparrow-hawk, sweep-net

Éphémère, adj. (*etym. Gr.* ἐφήμερος), ephemeral. — sm. ephemera

Éphore, sm. (*etym. Gr.* ἔφορος), ephor

Épi, sm. (*etym. L.* spica), ear of corn, &c., cluster

Épice, sf. (*etym. L.* species), spice, fees. *Pain d'*—, gingerbread

Épicer, va. (*etym.* épice), to spice

Épicerie, sf. (*etym.* épice), grocery, grocer's business

Épicier, ère, s. (*etym.* épice), grocer

Épicurien, ne, adj. s. (*etym.* Épicure), Epicurean, epicure

Épicurisme, sm. Epicureanism

Épidémie, sf. (*etym. Gr.* ἐπιδήμιος), epidemical disease, epidemic

Épidémique, adj. (*etym.* épidémie), epidemical, epidemic

Épiderme, sm. (*etym. Gr.* ἐπιδερμίς), scarf-skin, epidermis

Épier, vn. (*etym. L.* spicare), to ear; — va. (*etym. O.H.G.* spehôn), to spy, to watch

Épieu, sm. (*etym. L.* spiculum), boar-spear, hunting-pole

Épigastre, sf. (*etym. Gr.* ἐπιγάστριον), epigastrium

Épigastrique, adj. (*etym.* épigastre), epigastric

Épigrammatique, adj. (*etym.* épigramme), epigrammatical

Épigrammatiste, sm. (*etym.* épigramme), epigrammatist

Épigramme, sf. (*etym. Gr.* ἐπίγραμμα), epigram

Épigraphe, sf. (*etym. Gr.* ἐπιγραφή), inscription, motto

Épilepsie, sf. (*etym. Gr.* ἐπιληψία), epilepsy, falling sickness

Épileptique, s. adj. epileptic

Épiler, va. (*etym.* é, *and L.* pilus, *hair*), to depilate; *s'*—, vr. to take out one's grey hair

Épiloguer, vn. a. (*etym.* épilogue), to carp at, to find fault with

Épilogueur, sm. (*etym.* épiloguer), fault-finder

Épinards, sm. plur. (*etym.* épine), spinage. *Épaulette à graines d'*—, major's or colonel's epaulet (made of large bullion)

Épine, sf. (*etym. L.* spina), thorn, prickle, spine, backbone. — *blanche,* hawthorn, may. — *noire,* black thorn, sloe-tree

Épinette, sf. (*etym.* épine), spinet

Épineux, se, adj. (*etym. L.* spinosus), thorny, braky, knotty, intricate, over-particular

Épine-vinette, sf. (*etm.* ?), barberry-bush

Épingle, sf. (*etym. L.* spinula), pin, pin-money. ‡ *Tirer son — du jeu,* to get out of the scrape. † *Être tiré à quatre —s,* to look as if one came out of a bandbox

Épinglette, sf. (*etym.* épingle), priming-wire, piercer

Épinglier, ère, s. pin-maker

Épinière, adj. (*etym.* épine), spinal

Épiphanie, sf. (*etym. Gr.* ἐπιφάνεια, *manifestation*), Epiphany, Twelfth-day

Épique, adj. (*etym. Gr.* ἐπικός), epic, heroic

Épiscopat, sm. (*etym. L.*

F

episcopatus), episcopacy, bishopric, the bishops

†**Épisodique,** adj. (*etym.* épisode), episodical

Épispastique, adj. epispastic

Épisser, va. (*etym. O.H.G.* splitzan), to splice

Épissoir, sm. (*etym.* épisser), (*nav.*) marling-spike

Épistolaire, adj. s. (*etym. L.* epistolaris), epistolary, letter-writer

Épitaphe, sf. (*etym. Gr.* ἐπιτάφιος), epitaph

Épithalame, sm. (*etym. Gr.* ἐπιθαλάμιος), epithalamium

Épithète, sf. (*etym. Gr.* ἐπίθετος), epithet

Épitoge, sf. (*etym. L.L.* epitogium), a kind of silk ornament worn by members of the French university, and corresponding to the academical hood

Épître, sm. (*etym. L.* epistola), epistle

Épizootie, sf. (*etym. Gr.* ἐπί, ζῶον, *animal*), murrain, epizooty

Épizootique, adj. epizootic

Éploré, e, adj. (*etym.* é, *O.F.* plorer = pleurer), in tears, weeping

Éplucher, va. (*etym.* é, *L.* pilare, *to pluck out the hair*), to pick, to scan, to sift

Éplucheur, se, s. (*etym.* éplucher), picker of words

Épluchures, sf. plur. parings

Épointer, va. (*etym.* é, pointe), to break the point of; s'—, vr. to break off its point

Éponge, sf. (*etym. L.* spongia), spunge, sponge

Éponger, va. (*etym.* éponge), to spunge up, to spunge

Épopée, sf. (*etym. Gr.* ἔπος, ποιεῖν, *to make*), epopee

Époque, sf. (*etym. Gr.* ἐποχή), epoch, time, period

Époumoner, va., s'—, vr. (*etym.* é, poumon), to tire one's lungs

§**Épousailles,** sf. pl. (*etym. L.* sponsalia), nuptials, espousals

Épouse, sf. (*etym.* see Époux), wife, spouse

Épousée, sf. bride

Épouser, va. (*etym. L.* sponsare), to marry, to wed, to espouse; s'—, vr. to marry

Épouseur, sm. (*etym.* épouser), suitor, husband

Épousseter, va. (*etym.* é, *and* pousse = poussière), to dust, (*fig.*) to dust a person's jacket for him; s'—, vr. to wipe off the dust from

†**Épouvantable,** adj. (*etym.* épouvanter), frightful, dreadful, appalling

§**Épouvantail,** sm. (*etym.* épouvanter), scarecrow, bugbear

Épouvante, sf. dismay, dread, fright, panic

Épouvantement, sm. (*etym.* épouvanter), the action of frightening

Épouvanter, va. (*etym. L.* expaventem), to appal, to strike with terror, to frighten, to waste; s'—, vr. to be terrified, to tremble

Époux, sm. (*etym. L.* sponsus), husband, spouse, married couple

s'Éprendre, vr. (*etym.* é, prendre), to be enamoured, to be smitten with

Épreuve, sf. (*etym.* see Éprouver), trial, test, proof, proof-sheet. *Seconde* —, revise. *Troisième* —, second revise

Éprouver, va. (*etym.* é, prouver), to try, to experiment, to prove, to experience

Éprouvette, sf. (*etym.* éprouver), test-tube, gauge, steam-gauge

Épuisement, sm. (*etym.* épuiser), exhaustion, draining off. *Tuyau d'*—, exhausting pipe

Épuiser, va. (*etym.* é, puiser), to exhaust, to drain, to waste; s'—, vr. to be exhausted, to exhaust oneself

Épuration, sf. (*etym.* épurer), purifying, refining, improvement

Épure, sf. (*etym.* é, pur), clean draught

Épuré, e, adj. chastened, pure, chaste

Épurer, va. (*etym.* é, pur), to purify, to refine, to clarify, to weed; s'—, vr. to be purified, to become pure

Équarrir, va. (*etym.* é, carré), to square, to cut up

Équarrissage, sm. squareness, squaring, cutting up

Équarrisseur, sm. knacker

Équateur, sm. (*etym. L.* æquatorem), the equator

Équation, sf. equation. — *du premier, du second degré*, simple equation, quadratic equation

Équerre, sm. (*etym. L.* ex, quadrare), square. — *de fer*, iron knee

Équestre, adj. (*etym. L.* equestris), equestrian

Équiangle, adj. (*etym.* équi, *and L.* angulus), equiangular

Équilibre, sm. (*etym. L.* æquilibrium), equilibrium, balance, perpendicular

Équilibrer, va. to poise, to place in equilibrium

Équilibriste, smf. a juggler

Équinoxe, sm. (*etym. L.L.* æquinoctium), the equinox

Équinoxial, e, adj. (*etym.* æquinoctialis), equinoctial

Équipage, sm. (*etym.* équiper), equipage, carriage, garb, plight, crew. *Maître d'*—, boatswain

Équipe, sf. (*etym.* see Équiper), set, gang, train of boats

Équipée, sf. (*etym.* équiper), freak, frolic

Équipement, sm. (*etym.* équiper), outfit, equipment. *Effets d'*—, accoutrement

Équiper, va. (*etym.* esquif), to equip, to fit out, to man; s'—, vr. to equip oneself, to fit oneself out, to rig oneself out

Équitablement, adv. (*etym.* équitable), equitably, fairly

Équitation, sf. (*etym. L.* equitationem), horsemanship, riding. *Maître, école d'*—, riding master, riding school

Équité, sf. (*etym. L.* æquitatem), equity, even-handed dealing

Équivaloir, vn. (*etym.* équi, valoir), to be equivalent

Équivoque, adj. (*etym. L.* æquivocus), equivocal, of doubtful character, suspicious

Équivoque, sf. equivocation, quibble, error, mistake

Équivoquer, vn. to equivocate, to quibble; s'—, vr. to make a mistake

Érable, sm. (*etym. L.* acer, arbor), maple

Érafler, va. (*etym.* é, rafler), to graze, to scratch

Éraflure, sf. scratch

§**Éraillé, e,** adj. puckered up, wrinkled

§**Érailler,** va. (*etym. L.* es, rallum, *a scraper*), to fray, to fret, to chafe

§**Éraillure,** sf. fret

Ère, sf. (*etym. L.* æra), era, æra

Érèbe, sm. (*etym. Gr.* ἔρεβος, *obscurity*), Erebus

Éreinter, va. (*etym.* é, rein), to break one's back, to tire out, (†) to lash away at; s'—, vr. to break one's back, to tire oneself out

Érésipèle, Érysipèle, sm. (*etym. Gr.* ἐρυσίπελας), erysipelas

Ergot, sm. (*etym.* ?), spur, (*agric.*) smut. † *Monter sur ses* —*s*, to ride one's high horse

Ergoter, vn. (*etym. L.* ergo ?), to cavil, to quibble

Ergoteur, se, s. (*etym.* ergoter), caviller, quibbler

Ériger, va. (*etym. L.* erigere), to erect, to raise, to set up; s'—, vr. to set up for

Ermitage, sm. (*etym.* ermite), hermitage

Ermite, sm. (*etym. Gr.* ἐρημίτης), hermit

Érotique, adj. (*etym. Gr.* ἐρωτικός), erotic

Erpétologie, *better* **Herpétologie,** sf. (*etym. Gr.* ἑρπετόν, λόγος), erpetology

Errant, e, adj. (*etym. O.F.* errer = *L.* itinerare), wandering, roving, vagrant, erratic

Errements, sm. plur. (*etm. O.F.* errer), track, ways

Errer, vn. (*etym. L.L.* iterare, *to travel*), to wander, to rove, to ramble; (*etym. L.* errare), to err, to be mistaken

Erreur, sf. (*etym. L.* errorem), error, mistake, wanderings

Erroné, e, adj. (*etym. L.* erroneus), erroneous, wrong

Érudit, e, adj. (*etym. L.* eruditus), erudite, learned

†**Esbroufe,** sm. (*etym.* ?), fuss. *Faire de l'*—, *faire ses* —*s*, to make a fuss

Escabeau, sm., **Escabelle,** sf. (*etym. L.* scabellum), stool

Escadre, sm. (*etym. Ital.* squadra, *brigade*), squadron. *Chef d'*—, commodore

§**Escadrille,** sf. small squadron

Escadron, sm. squadron, troop. *Chef d'*—, major

Escalader, va. (*etym.* escalade), to scale, to climb over

Escale, sf. (*etym. I.* scala, *ladder*), port, putting in, trading-station. *Faire* — *à*, to touch at

Escalier, sm. (*etym. L.* scala), staircase, stairs

Escamotage, sm. (*etym.* escamoter), juggling

Escamoter, va. (*etym. Sp.* escamotar), to juggle away, to convey away, to filch

Escamoteur, sm. (*etym.* escamoter), conjurer, juggler, thimble-rigger, pilferer

†**Escampativos,** sm. plur. (*etym.* ?), escape. *Faire des* —, to run away furtively

†**Escampette,** sf. (*etm. O.F.* escampe), escape. *Prendre la poudre d'*—, to run away

Escapade, sf. (*etym. I.* scappata), prank, frolic, trick

§**Escarbilles,** sf. pl. (*etym. L.* carbo), coal-cinders

Escarbot, sm. (*etym. L.* scarabæus), black-beetle

Escarboucle, sf. (*etym. L.* carbunculus), carbuncle

Escarcelle, sf. (*etym. L.L.* excarpsus), purse

Escargot, sm. (*etym. Sp.* carncol, *snail*), snail

Escarmouche, sf. (*etym. O.H.G.* skerman, *to fight*), skirmish, brush

Escarmoucher, vn. to skirmish

Escarole, sf. (*etym.* ?), scarrol

Escarpe, sf. (*etym. O.H.G.* scarp), scarp

Escarpement, sm. escarpment, steep side, steep

Escarpé, e, adj. steep, rugged

Escarpin, sm. (*etym. L.L.* scarpus), pump

Escarpolette, sf. (*etym.* ?), swing

Escarre, *better* **Eschare,** sf. (*etym. Gr.* ἐσχάρα), eschar, scab

Escient, sm. (*etym. L.* scientem), knowledge. *A bon, à son* —, knowingly

Esclandre, sm. (*etym. L.* scandalum), scandal

Esclavage, sm. (*etym.* esclave), slavery, bondage, thraldom

Esclave, adj. s. (*etym. L.* Slavus, *Slavonian*), slavish, slave, bondsman, thrall, drudge

Escobarderie, sf. (*etym. prop. n.* Escobar), shuffling, prevarication

†**Escoffier,** va. (*etym. L.* ex, conficere), to kill

Escogriffe, sm. (*etym.* ?), shark; tall, shabby, ill-looking fellow
Escompte, sm. (*etym. see* ESCOMPTER), discount. *Règle d'—*, rebate *or* discount. *Sous —*, with a discount. *Comptoir d'—*, discounting bank. *Faire l'—*, to discount bills
Escompter, va. (*etym.* es, compter), to discount, to cash, to turn some news to profit beforehand
Escopette, sf. (*etym. L.L.* sclopus, sclopus), carbine, blunderbuss
Escorte, sf. (*etym. I.* scorta), escort, guard, convoy
Escorter, va. to escort
Escouade, sf. (*etym. I.* squadra), small party, squad
Escourgeon, sm. (*etym. L.L.* scario), winter barley
Escrime, sf. (*etym. see* ESCRIMER), fencing
Escrimer, va. (*etym. O.H.G.* skirm, skerm, *shield*), to fence; *s'—*, vr. to battle together, to strive hard, to be a tolerable hand
Escrimeur, sm. fencer
Escroc, sm. (*etym. O.H.G.* scurgo, *rogue*), swindler, cheat, sharper
Escroquer, va. to swindle, to obtain undeservedly
Escroquerie, sf. swindling
Escroqueur, se, s. stealer
Espace, sm. (*etym. L.* spatium), space. — sf. (*print.*) space
Espacement, sm. (*etym.* espacer), interspace, interval, spacing
Espacer, va. to leave a space between, to space
Espadon, sm. (*etym. I.* spadone), back-sword, sword-fish
Espagnolette, sf. (*etym.* espagnol), fastening, baize
Espalier, sm. (*etym. I.* spalliere, *support for the shoulders*), wall-fruit trees
Espars, sm. plur. (*etym. G.* sparren), spars
Espèce, sf. (*etym. L.* species), species, kind, sort, particular case, elements. *Communier sous les deux —s*, to receive the Communion in both kinds
Espérance, sf. (*etym. I.* speranza), hope, expectation
Espérer, va. (*etym. L.* sperare), to hope, to expect, to trust
Espiègle, adj. (*etym. G.* eulenspiegel), sprightly, arch, mischievous
Espièglerie, sf. trick, prank, arch saying
Espingole, sf. (*etym. G.* springen), blunderbuss
Espion, ne, smf. (*etym.* épier), spy
Espionnage, sm. (*etym.* espionner), espionage
Espionner, va. to spy
Espoir, sm. (*etym. L.* spes), hope
Esprit, sm. (*etym. L.* spiritus), spirit, Ghost, breath, the mind, the intellect, wits, fancy, wit, sense, humour, temper, a genius, a turn, meaning. — *rude*, aspirate. — *doux*, soft breathing. *Le bel —*, wit. *Faire de l'—*, to try to be witty. *Un — fort*, a person above prejudice, free-thinker. *Avoir l'— mal fait*, to be of a cantankerous disposition
Esquif, sm. (*etym. O.H.G.* skif), skiff, bark
§**Esquille,** sf. (*etym. Gr.* σχίδιον, *fragment*), splinter
Esquinancie, sf. (*etym. Gr.* κυνάγχη, *sore throat*), quinsy
Esquisse, sf. (*etym. Gr* σχέδιος, *done quickly*), sketch, outline
Esquisser, va. to sketch
Esquiver, va. (*etym. O.H.G.* skiuhan, *to be frightened*), to evade, to escape; *s'—*, vr. to slip away, to escape
Essai, sm. (*etym. L.* exagium, *weighing*), trial, essay, test, sample
Essaim, sm. (*etym. L.* examen), swarm, bevy
Essaimer, vn. to swarm
Essayer, va. (*etym.* essai), to try, to prove, to assay; *s'—*, vr. to try one's hand, to learn
Essayeur, sm. assayer
Essence, sf. (*etym. L.* essentia), essence, species
‡**Essentiel, le,** adj. (*etym. L.* essentialis), essential. — sm. the essential, the main point
Essieu, sm. (*etym. L.* axiculus), axle-tree, axle, spindle. — *coudé*, cranked axle. — *menant*, leading axle-tree
Essor, sm. (*etym. O.F.* essorer = *L.L.* exaurare), flight, soaring, scope, play
§**Essorillé, e,** adj. (*etym. L.* ex, auris), crop-eared
Essouffler, va. (*etym.* es, souffler), to put out of breath; *s'—*, vr. to put oneself out of breath
Essuie-main, sm. (*etym.* essuyer, main), towel; *plur.* des essuie-main *or* mains
Essuyer, va. (*etym. L.* exsiccare), to wipe, to wipe away, to dust, to dry, to endure, to undergo; *s'—*, vr. to wipe one's face, hands, clothes, &c.
Est, sm. (*etym. G.* ost), the east
Estacade, sf. (*etym. I* steccata), stockade
Estafette, sf. (*etym. I.* staffetta, *small stirrup*), express, estafette
Estafier, sm. (*etym. I.* staffiere), servant
Estafilade, sf. (*etym. I.* staffilata, *a blow given with a thong*), gash, cut, rent
Estaminet, sm. (*etym.* ?), coffee-house with smoking-room
Estampe, sf. (*etym. I.* stampa), print, engraving
Estamper, va. to stamp
§**Estampille,** sf. (*etym.* estampe), stamp
§**Estampiller,** va. to stamp
Ester, vn. (*etym. L.* stare), to appear in court
Esthétique, sf. (*etym. Gr.* αἰσθητικός), æsthetics
Estimateur, sm. (*etym. L.* æstimatorem), appraiser, esteemer, appreciator
Estimatif, ve, adj. (*etym.* estimer), of estimation. *Devis, état —*, estimate
Estime, sf. (*etym.* estimer), esteem, estimation, dead-reckoning
Estimer, va. (*etym. L.* æstimare), to estimate, to value, to appraise, to account, to reckon; *s'—*, vr. to estimate oneself, to esteem oneself, to have a mutual esteem for each other, to deem oneself
Estoc, sm. (*etym. G.* stock), point of a sword. *Frappant d'— et de taille*, cutting and thrusting
Estocade, sf. a thrust
Estomac, sm. (*etym. Gr* στόμαχος), stomach, body
Estompe, sf. (*etym. G.* stumpf), stump
Estomper, va. to stump
Estrade, sf. (*etym. L.* strata, *paved road*), country, raised platform, dais. ‡ *Battre l'—*, to beat up the country
Estragon, sm. (*etym. L.* draconem), tarragon
Estramaçon, sm. (*etym. L.L.* scramasaxus, *a kind of cutlass*), a long two-edged sword
Estrapade, sf. (*etym. I* strappata), strappado
Estropier, va (*etym.* ?), to cripple, to maim, to mangle, to mutilate; *s'—*, vr. to maim oneself
Esturgeon, sm. (*etym. O.H.G.* sturio), sturgeon
Et, conj. and
Étable, sf. (*etym. L.* stabulum), stable, cattle-shed
Établi, sm. work-bench
Établir, va. (*etym. L* stabilire), to set up, to set, to ground, to establish, to erect, to settle; *s'—*, vr. to settle oneself, to stay, to set up in business, to obtain
Établissement, sm. (*etym.* établir), setting up, fixing, establishment, foundation, settlement, cantonment, time of high water. *Dans l'—*, on the premises
Étage, sm. (*etym. L.* stare), story, floor, pair of stairs, row, layer, rank. *De bas —*, of low degree
Étagère, sf. (*etym.* étage), set of shelves
Étai, sm. (*etym. Fl.* staede), prop, stay
Étain, sm. (*etym. L.* stannum), tin, pewter
Étal, sm. (*etym. O.H.G.* stal, *stall*), stall, butcher's stall
Étalage, sm. (*etym.* étaler), show, display
Étalagiste, sm. (*etym.* étalage), huckster, stall-keeper
Étaler, va. (*etym.* étal), to spread out, to lay out, to display, to show off; *s'—*, vr. to stretch oneself out, to lie sprawling
Étalier, sm. (*etym.* étal), butcher's boy
Étalon, sm. (*etym. L.L.* stalo, stallo), standard. (*etym. L.L.* stallum, *stable*), stallion
Étamage, sm. (*etym.* étamer), tinning, quicksilvering
Étamer, va. (*etym.* étain), to tin, to quicksilver
Étameur, sm. tinman, tinker
Étamine, sf. (*etym. O.F.* estame), thin-stuff, bolting, cloth; (*etym. L.* stamina), stamen
Étanche, adj. (*etym. see* ÉTANCHER), water-tight, air-tight, steam-tight
Étanchement, sm. (*etym.* étancher), stopping
Étancher, va. (*etym.* ?), to stop, to stanch, to quench, to slake
Étançon, sm. (*etym. O.F.* estance, *prop*), shore, stay
Étançonner, va. (*etym.* étançon), to prop
Étang, sm. (*etym. L.* stagnum), pond, pool
Étape, sf (*etym. L.L.* stapula), station, allowance, stage, halting-place. ‡ *Brûler l'—*, to pass through without stopping
État, sm. (*etym. L.* status), state, condition, position, plight, statement, account, return, muster-roll, business, craft, trade, calling, dominions. *Faire — de*, to have a regard for. *Faire — de*, to intend to. *Faire — que*, to reckon that
État-major, sm. the staff, the staff-officers. *Chef d'—*, Brigade-Major
Étau, sm. (*etym.* ?), vice
Étayer, va. (*etym.* étai), to prop up, to shore; *s'—*, vr to be propped up, to maintain one's fortune
Été, sm. (*etym. L.* æstatem), summer
§**Éteignoir,** sm. (*etym.* éteindre), extinguisher
Éteindre, va (*etym. L.* exstinguere), to put out, to extinguish, to quench, to dim, to obscure, to slake, to root out, to allay, to exterminate; *s'—*, vr to go out, to be extinguished *or* quenched, to be dimmed, to cool, to perish, to be lost, to die peaceably
Étendard, sm. (*etym. L.* extendere), flag, standard, colours
Étendre, va. (*etym. L.* extendere), to spread, to extend, to lay on, to stretch, to lengthen out, to expand; *s'—*, vr. to stretch oneself, to lay oneself, to spread oneself, to branch out
Étendu, e, past part. adj. stretched out, extended, spread out, lying, extensive, large
Étendue, sf. extent, duration, compass
‡**Éternel, le,** adj. (*etym. L.* æternalis), lasting, eternal, endless

Éterniser, va. (*etym. L.L.* æternisare), to eternize, to make endless, to make for ever famous; *s'—*, vr. to last for ever

Éternité, sf. (*etym. L.* æternitatem), eternity

Éternuement, sm. (*etym.* éternuer), sneeze, sneezing

Éternuer, vn. (*etym. L.* sternutare), to sneeze

Étésien, adj. m. (*etym. Gr.* ἐτησίαι, *annual winds*), Etesian

Éthéré, e, adj. (*etym. L.* æthereus), ethereal

Éthique, sf. (*etym. Gr.* ἠθικός), ethics

Ethnographique, adj. (*etym. Gr.* ἔθνος, γράφειν), ethnographical

Étiage, sm. (*etym. L.L.* æstivaticum), low-water mark

Étincelant, e, adj. sparkling, glittering, flashing, gleaming

Étinceler, vn. to sparkle, to glitter, to gleam, to twinkle, to flash

Étincelle, sf. (*etym. L.* scintilla), spark

Étincellement, sm. sparkling, twinkling

Étiolement, sm. (*etym.* étioler), etiolation

Étioler, va., *s'—*, vr. (*etym. O.F.* étiule, *straw*), to etiolate

Étique, adj. (*etym. see* Hectique), consumptive, hectic, meagre

Étiqueter, va. (*etym.* étiquette), to label, to docket

Étiquette, sf. (*etym.* ?), label, etiquette. ‡ *Juger sur l'— du sac*, to judge of things by the appearance

Étirer, va. (*etym.* é, tirer), to stretch, to draw out, to wire-draw; *s'—*, vr. to stretch oneself

Étoffe, sf. (*etym. L.* stupa), stuff, materials

Étoffer, va. to put enough stuff in, to stuff. *Robe étoffée*, ample gown. *Personne bien étoffée*, person well to do in the world. *Cheval étoffé*, stout-made horse

Étoile, sf. (*etym. L.* stella), star, destiny, crack. — *de mer*, star-fish

Étoilé, adj. starred, studded with stars, cracked

Étole, sf. (*etym. L.* stola), stole

‖**Étonnant**, e, adj. wonderful, astonishing, surprising

Étonnement, sm. (*etym.* étonner), wonder, amazement, astonishment

Étonner, va. (*etym. L.* extonare), to astonish, to amaze; *s'—*, vr. to be astonished, to wonder, to marvel

Étouffant, e, adj. suffocating, stifling, sultry

Étouffement, sm. (*etym.* étouffer), suffocation

Étouffer, va. (*etym.* ? *Gr.* τῦφος, *vapour*), to stifle, to smother, to choke, to hush up

Étoupe, sf. (*etym. L.* stuppa), tow, stuffing, oakum

Étourderie, sf. (*etym.* étourdir), giddiness, heedlessness

‖**Étourdi**, e, adj. s. giddy, heedless, giddy-head, blunderer

Étourdir, va. (*etym. L.L.* stordatus), to make giddy, to stun, to stagger, to astound, to benumb; *s'—*, vr. to shake off the thoughts

Étourdissant, e, adj. (*etym.* étourdir), deafening, stunning, obstreperous

Étourdissement, sm. giddiness, stupefaction

Étourneau, sm. (*etym. L.* sturnellus), starling, giddy-brains

‖**Étrange**, adj. (*etym. L.* extraneus), strange, odd, queer, uncouth

Étranger, ère, adj. s. (*etym.* étrange), foreign, extraneous, unknown, foreigner. — sm. foreign lands

Étrangeté, sf. (*etym.* étrange), strangeness

Étranglement, sm. (*etym.* étrangler), strangulation

Étrangler, va. (*etym. L.* strangulare), to strangle, to throttle, to choke, to narrow too much, to slur over. — vn. to be choking; *s'—*, vr. to strangle oneself, to choke oneself

Étrangleur, sm. strangler

Être, sm. (*etym. L.* esse), being, existence, frame, the way about the house. — vn. to be, to exist, to belong. *Où en êtes-vous?* how far have you got? *J'en suis pour mon argent*, I have lost my money. *Comme si de rien n'était*, as if nothing was the matter. *Vous y êtes*, you have hit it

Étrécir, **s'Étrécir**, &c., see **Rétrécir**, &c.

Étreindre, va. (*etym. L.* stringere), to bind, to clasp, to grasp. *Qui trop embrasse mal étreint*, (*prov.*) grasp all, lose all

Étreinte, sf. (*etym.* étreindre), tie, embrace, clasp, grasp

Étrenne, sf. (*etym. L.* strena), New Year's gift, handsel

Étrenner, va. n. to give a New Year's gift, to handsel, to take handsel

Êtres, sm. plur. (*etym.* ?), the various parts of a house

Étrier, sm. (*etym. O.H.G.* strëban, *to lean*), stirrup, stirrup-bandage, (*arch.*) strap. *A franc —*, full speed. *Coup de l'—*, stirrup-cup. *Faire vider les —s à*, to unhorse

§**Étrille**, sf. (*etym. L.* strigilis), curry-comb

§**Étriller**, va. (*etym.* étrille), to curry, to comb † — *quelqu'un*, to give a thrashing

Étriqué, e, adj. (*etym.* ?), scanty, poor

Étrivière, sf. (*etym. O.F.* estrif, *stirrup*), stirrup-leather

‖**Étroit**, e, adj. (*etym. L.* strictus), narrow, tight, shallow, close, strict

Étrusque, adj. Etruscan

Étude, sf. (*etym. L.* studium), study, acquirements, study-room, (*arts*) figure, office, practice. *Maître d'—*, usher. *Mettre à l'—*, (*theat.*) to put in rehearsal, to order a survey. *Tête d'—* a head

Étudiant, sm. student

Étudié, e, adj. studied, elaborate

Étudier, va. (*etym. L.* studium), to study, to watch; *s'—*, vr. to study one's own temper, to make it one's study

Étui, sm. (*etym. M.H.G.* stûche, *a kind of sheath*), case, box, sheath, needle-case. — *de mathématiques*, box of mathematical instruments

Étuve, sf. (*etym. O.H.G.* stupa, *stove*), hot-bath, vapour-bath, drying stove

Étuvée, sf. stew

Étymologie, sf. (*etym. Gr.* ἐτυμολογία), etymology, derivation

Étymologique, adj. (*etym.* étymologie), etymological

Étymologiste, sm. etymologist

Eucharistie, sf. (*etym. Gr.* εὐχαριστία), the Eucharist, the Lord's Supper

Eucharistique, adj. Eucharistical

Eucologe, sm. (*etym. Gr.* εὐχολόγιον), Roman breviary

Eunuque, sm. (*etym. Gr.* εὐνοῦχος, *keeper of the bed*), eunuch

Euphémisme, sm. (*etym. Gr.* εὐφημισμός), euphemism

Euphonie, sf. (*etym. Gr.* εὐφωνία), euphony

‖**Euphonique**, adj. (*etym.* euphonie), euphonic

Euphuisme, sm. (*etym. Gr.* εὐφυής, *in good taste*), euphuism

Eux, pron. m. plur. they, them

Évacuer, va. (*etym. L.* evacuare), to evacuate

s'Évader, vr. (*etym. L.* evadere), to evade, to slip away, to break loose

Évaluation, sf. (*etym.* évaluer), valuation, estimate

Évaluer, va. (*etym.* é, value), to value, to rate; *s'—*, vr. to be valued *or* rated

‖**Évangélique**, adj. (*etym. L.* evangelicus), evangelical

Évangéliser, va. (*etym. L.* evangelizare), to preach the Gospel, to evangelize

Évangéliste, sm. (*etym. L.* evangelista), evangelist

Évangile, sf. (*etym. L.* evangelium = *Gr.* εὐαγγέλιον), the Gospel

s'Évanouir, vr. (*etym.* é, *L.* vanescere), to faint, to swoon, to vanish, to pass away. *Faire —*, to dispel, (*alg.*) to eliminate

Évanouissement, sm. (*etym.* évanouir), swoon, fainting fit

Évaporé, e, adj. giddy-headed

Évaporer, va. (*etym. L.* evaporare), to evaporate, to give vent to; *s'—*, vr. to evaporate, (*fig.*) to get heedless

Évasé, e, adj. (*etym.* é, vase), wide, wide-opened

Évasement, sm. widening, opening, width

Évaser, va. (*etym.* é, vase), to widen, to extend

‖**Évasif**, ve, adj. (*etym.* évasion), evasive, shuffling

Évasion, sf. (*etym. L.* evasionem), escape, flight

Évêché, sm. (*etym. L.* episcopatus), bishopric, bishop's palace

§**Éveil**, sm. (*etym.* éveiller), a hint, warning, alert

§**Éveillé**, e, adj. awake, waking, sprightly, sharp

§**Éveiller**, va. (*etym. L.* evigilare), to awake, to wake, to rouse; *s'—*, vr. to awake, to wake

Événement, sm. (*etym. L.* evenire), event, occurrence, emergency, issue, end, incident. ‡ *A tout —*, whatever may befall. † *Faire —*, to create a sensation

Évent, sm. (*etym.* éventer) smack, flatness, vapidness, air-hole, (*artil.*) windage

§**Éventail**, sm. (*etym.* éventer), fan

§**Éventailliste**, sm. fan-maker, fan-seller

Éventaire, sm. (*etym.* évent), fruit or fish woman's basket

Éventé, e, adj. flat, vapid, giddy-brained

Éventer, va. (*etym.* é, vent) to fan, to air, to injure, to make flat, to discover, to scent; *s'—*, vr. to fan oneself, to be spoiled, to grow flat, to take wind

Éventrer, va. (*etym.* é, ventre), to rip up, to rip open; *s'—*, vr. to rip one's belly open

Éventualité, sf. (*etym.* éventuel), contingency, uncertainty

‖**Éventuel**, le, adj. (*etym. L.* eventus), contingent, uncertain. — sm. extra fees

Évêque, sm. (*etym. L.* episcopus), bishop

Éversif, ve, adj. (*etym. L.* evertere), subversive

s'Évertuer, vr. (*etym.* é, vertu), to exert oneself, to struggle hard

Éviction, sf. (*etym. L.* evictionem), ejection

Évidemment, adv. (*etym.* évident), evidently, obviously

Évidence, sf. (*etym. L.* evidentia), obviousness, evidence. *Mettre en —*, to expose to view. *Se mettre en —*, to put oneself forward

Évider, va. (*etym.* é, vide) to hollow, to scoop out, to groove, to unstarch

Évier, sm. (*etym. L.* aquarium), sink

Évincer, va. (*etym. L.* evincere), (*jurispr.*) to evict, (*fig.*) to oust

Évitement, sm. (*etym.* éviter), passing. *Gare d'—* sidings

Éviter, va. (*etym. L.* evitare), to avoid, to shun, to eschew, to spare; *s'—*, vr. to shun or avoid each other, to spare oneself; —vn. to swing, to stem

Évoquer, va. (*etym. L.* evocare), to raise up, to start, to evoke

Exact, e, adj. (*etym. L.* exactus, *careful*), punctual, exact, strict, accurate, correct

Exacteur, sm. (*etym. L.* exactorem), extortioner, exactor

Exactitude, sf. (*etym.* exact), punctuality, exactness, accurateness

Exagérateur, trice, s. adj. (*etym. L.* exaggeratorem), given to exaggeration, exaggerating

Exagération, sf. (*etym. L.* exaggerationem), exaggeration

Exagérer, va. (*etym. L* exaggerare, *to heap up earth*), to exaggerate, to overrate

Exalter, va. (*etym. L.* exaltare), to exalt, to extol, to over-excite, to work up; *s'—*, vr. to grow heated

Examen, sm. (*etym. L.* examen), examination

Examinateur, trice, s (*etym. L.* examinatorem), examiner

Examiner, va. (*etym. L.* examinare), to examine, to inspect, to scan; *s'—*, vr. to examine oneself

Exarchat, sm. (*etym.* exarque), exarchate

Exarque, sm. (*etym. Gr.* ἔξαρχος), exarch

Exaspérer, va. (*etym. L.* exasperare), to exasperate, to incense

Exaucer, va. (*etym. see* EXHAUSSER), to hear, to grant

Excédant, e, adj. exceeding, over and above, (*fig.*) tiring. —sm. overplus, surplus, excess

Excéder, va. (*etym. L.* excedere), to exceed, to weary, to surfeit; *s'—*, vr. to over-fatigue oneself

Excellentissime, adj. (*etym. L.* excellentissimus), most excellent

Exceller, vn. (*etym. L.* excellere), to excel, to outdo

Excentricité, sf. (*etym.* excentrique), eccentricity

†**Excentrique**, adj. (*etym. L.* excentricus), eccentric

Excepter, va. (*etym. L.* exceptare), to except

†**Exceptionnel, le**, adj. (*etym.* exception), exceptional, contrary to use

Excès, sm. (*etym. L.* excessus), excess, riot

†**Excessif, ve**, adj. (*etym.* excès), excessive, unreasonable

Exciper, va. (*etym. L.* excipere), to plead an exception

Excitant, e, adj. sm. exciting, stimulating, stimulant

Exciter, va. (*etym. L.* excitare), to urge, to impel, to excite, to inspirit, to rouse; *s'—*, to work oneself up, to excite each other

Exclamatif, ve, adj. (*etym.* exclamation), of exclamation

Exclure, va. (*etym. L.* excludere), to exclude, to shut out; *s'—*, vr. to exclude each other

†**Exclusif, ve**, adj. (*etym.* exclusion), exclusive

Excommunier, va. (*etym. L.* excommunicare), to excommunicate

Excorier, va. (*etym. L.* excoriare), to excoriate

Excroissance, sf. (*etym. L.* excrescens), excrescence

Excuser, va. (*etym. L.* excusare), to excuse, to apologize for; *s'—*, vr. to excuse oneself, to apologize, to lay the blame on another, to beg to be excused

Exécrer, va. (*etym. L.* exsecrari), to execrate

Exécutable, adj. (*etym.* exécuter), feasible, practicable

Exécutant, sm. performer, musician

Exécuter, va. (*etym. L.* executum), to execute, to carry out, to fulfil, to distrain; *s'—*, vr. to sell off one's property, to comply, to be done

Exécuteur, trice, s (*etym. L.* executorem), executor, executioner, hangman

†**Exécutif, ve**, adj. (*etym. see* EXÉCUTER), executive

Exécution, sf. (*etym. L.* executionem), execution, fulfilment, carrying out. *En — de*, in pursuance of. *Homme d'—*, an enterprising man

Exécutoire, adj. sm. (*etym. see* EXÉCUTER), executory, writ of execution

Exégèse, sf. (*etym. Gr.* ἐξήγησις), exegesis

†**Exemplaire**, sm. (*etym. L.* exemplare), copy. —adj. (*etym. L.* exemplaris), exemplary

Exemple, sm. (*etym. L.* exemplum), example, copy. *Par —*, loc. adv. for example, for instance

Exempt, e, adj. (*etym. L.* exemptus), exempt, free. —sm. * police officer

Exempter, va. (*etym.* exempt), to exempt, to free, to dispense; *s'—*, vr. to exempt or free oneself, to dispense with

Exercer, va. (*etym. L.* exercere), to exercise, to train, to inure, to drill, to try; *s'—*, vr. to exercise oneself, to practise

Exercice, sm. (*etym. L.* exercitium), exercise, training, practice, drill, (*financ.*) budget

Exergue, sm. (*etym. Gr.* ἐξ, ἔργον, *out of the work*), exergue, superscription

Exhalaison, sf. (*etym. L.* exhalationem), exhalation

Exhaler, va. (*etym. L.* exhalare), to exhale, to emit, to breathe out; *s'—*, vr to be exhaled, to be breathed out

Exhaussement, sm. raising, height

Exhausser, va. (*etym. L.* exaltare), to raise, to run up

Exhiber, va. (*etym. L.* exhibere), to exhibit, to produce

Exhorter, va. (*etym. L.* exhortari), to exhort

Exhumer, va. (*etym. L.* exhumare), to disinter, to take up, to bring to light

Exigeant, e, adj. particular, exacting, unreasonable

Exigence, sf. (*etym. L.* exigentia), unreasonableness, demand, exigency, need

Exiger, va. (*etym. L.* exigere), to exact, to require

Exigibilité, sf. (*etym. see* EXIGIBLE), exigibility

Exigible, adj. (*etym.* exiger), due, demandable

Exigu, ë, adj. (*etym. L.* exiguus), small, slender, scanty

Exiguïté, sf. (*etym. L.* exiguitatem), smallness, slenderness, scantiness

Exil, sm. (*etym. L.* exilium), exile

Exilé, e, smf. exile

Exiler, va. (*etym.* exil), to exile, to banish; *s'—*, vr. to go into exile, to exile oneself, to seclude oneself

Existant, e, adj. existing, existent

Exister, vn. (*etym. L.* existere), to exist, to be, to be extant, to prevail

Exode, sm. (*etym. Gr.* ἔξοδος), the Book of Exodus, Exodus

Exorbitamment, adv. (*etym.* exorbitant), exorbitantly

Exorciser, va. (*etym. L.* exorcizare), to exorcise, to cast out

Exorcisme, sm. (*etym. L.* exorcismus), exorcism

Exorciste, sm. (*etym. L.* exorcista), exorcist

Exorde, sm. (*etym. L.* exordium), exordium, (*fig.*) beginning

Exotique, adj. (*etym. L.* exoticus), exotic, foreign

Expansibilité, sf. (*etym.* expansible), expansibility

Expansif, ve, adj. (*etym* expansion), expansive, diffusive, unreserved

Expansion, sf. (*etym. L.* expansionem), spread, expansion. *Avoir de l'—*, to be expansive

Expatrier, va. (*etym. L.* ex, patria), to expatriate; *s'—*, vr. to leave one's native land, to go abroad

Expectative, sf. (*etym. L.* exspectare), expectation

Expectorer, va. (*etym. L.* expectorare), to expectorate

Expédient, sm. (*etym. L.* expedire), expedient, shift, device, way

Expédier, va. (*etym. L.* expedire), to despatch, to send off, to forward, to expedite, to draw up

Expéditeur, sm. (*etym.* expedier), sender, shipper

†**Expéditif, ve**, adj. (*etym.* expedier), expeditious, speedy

Expédition, sf. (*etym. L.* expeditionem), despatch, expedition, *plur.* despatches, copy

Expéditionnaire, sm. (*etym.* expédition), commissioner, sender, copying clerk

Expérience, sf. (*etym. L.* experientia), experiment, experience

Expérimenté, e, adj. experienced, expert

Expérimenter, va. (*etym. L.* experimentare), to experiment, to experience

†**Expert**, sm. (*etym. L.* expertus), one skilled in an art, appraiser, surveyor. *A dire d'—s*, according to official estimation

Expertise, sf. (*etym.* expert), report, survey, estimation

Expiatoire, adj (*etym. L.* expiatorius), of atonement, expiatory

Expier, va. (*etym. L.* expiare), to atone for, to expiate

Expirant, e, adj. expiring, dying

Expirer, va. (*etym. L.* expirare), to expire, to breathe out; — vn. to breathe one's last, to die

†**Explétif, ve**, adj. (*etym. L.* expletivus), expletive

Explicateur, sm. (*etym. L.* explicatorem), guide, exhibitor

Explicatif, ve, adj. (*etym. L.* explicativus), explanatory

Explication, sf (*etym. L.* explicationem), explanation, construing

†**Explicite**, adj. (*etym. L.* explicitus), explicit, express

Expliquer, va. (*etym. L.* explicare), to explain, to expound, to illustrate, to account for, to construe; *s'—*, vr. to speak plain, to explain oneself, to account for, to come to an explanation

Exploit, sm. (*etym. L.L.* explecta), achievement, deed, exploit, writ. — *de saisie*, writ of distrainment

Exploitable, adj. (*etym. L.L.* explectabilis), that may be distrained, improvable, which may be worked

Exploitant, sm. district writ-serving, farmer, cultivator, manager, speculator

Exploitation, sf. (*etym. L.L.* explectationem), cultivation, growing, working, farm. *Matériel d'—*, working stock. *Mettre en —*, to begin to work

Exploiter, va. (*etym. L.* explicare), to farm, to cultivate, to work, to turn to one's own profit; — vn. to serve writs

Explorateur, sm. (*etym. L.* exploratorem), explorer

Explorer, va. (*etym. L.* explorare), to explore, to search into

Exportateur, sm. (*etym. L.* exportatorem), exporter

Exporter, va. (*etym. L.* exportare), to export

Exposant, sm. petitioner, expositor, exponent, index

Exposé, sm. statement, account

Exposer, va. (*etym.* ex, poser), to expose, to exhibit, to lay out, to lay bare; *s'*—, vr. to lay oneself open, to expose oneself

Exposition, sf. (*etym. L.* expositionem), exhibition, exposing, exposure, statement, exposition, expounding

‖**Exprès, esse,** adj. (*etym. L.* expressus), express. — sm. express, courier. — adv. on purpose, purposely

‖**Expressif, ve,** adj. (*etym.* expression), expressive, full of expression

Exprimable, adj. expressible, to be expressed

Exprimer, va. (*etym. L.* exprimere), to squeeze out, to express, to utter, to betoken; *s'*—, vr. to express oneself, to be expressed

Expropriation, sf. (*etym.* exproprier), dispossession

Exproprier, va. (*etym. L.* ex, propre), to dispossess

Expulser, va. (*etym. L.* expulsare), to expel, to drive out, to eject

Expurger, va. (*etym. L.* expurgare), to expurgate

‖**Exquis, e,** adj. (*etym. L.* exquisitus), exquisite

Extase, sf. (*etym. Gr.* ἔκστασις), trance, ecstasy, rapture

s'Extasier, vr. to fall into ecstasies *or* raptures

Extatique, adj. ecstatic

Extensibilité, sf. (*etym.* extensible), extensibility

Extensif, ve, adj. (*etym. L.* extensivus), of extension, of expansion

Exténuer, va. (*etym. L.* extenuare), to debilitate, to weaken, to extenuate; *s'*—, vr. to wear oneself out

‖**Extérieur, e,** adj. (*etym. L.* exteriorem), outer, outward, exterior, foreign, outside. — sm. outside, exterior, outer part, foreign countries

Exterminateur, trice, adj. (*etym. L.* exterminatorem), exterminating, destroying. — sm. exterminator, destroyer

Exterminer, va. (*etym. L.* exterminare), to exterminate, to root out, to utterly destroy; *s'*—, vr. to exterminate each other

Externat, sm. (*etym.* externo), day-school

Externe, s. (*etym. L.* externus), day-scholar; — adj. external, outer

Extinction, sf. (*etym. L.* exstinctionem), extinction, extinguishment, putting out, prescription

Extirpateur, sm. (*etym.* extirper), rooter out, extirpator

Extirper, va. (*etym. L.* exstirpare), to pluck up by the roots

Extorquer, va. (*etym. L.* extorquere), to wring, to extort, to wrest

Extorsion, sf. (*etym. L.* extorsionem), extortion

Extraire, va. (*etym. L.* extrahere), to extract, to draw out, to dig out

Extrait, sm. (*etym. L.* extractus), spirit, extract, abstract, certificate, single number

‖**Extrajudiciaire,** adj. (*etym.* extra, judiciaire), extrajudicial

Extra-muros, adj. without the walls, suburban

‖**Extraordinaire,** adj. (*etym. L.* extraordinarius), extraordinary, unusual, odd, singular. — sm. the extraordinary

Extravaguer, va. (*etym. L.* extra, vagari), to talk nonsense, to be light-headed

s'Extravaser, vr. (*etym. L.* extra, vas), to be extravasated

‖**Extrême,** adj. (*etym. L.* extremus), extreme, utmost, furthest. — sm. extreme. *Les —s se touchent*, extremes meet

Extrême-onction, sf. (*etym.* extrême, onction), extreme unction

Extrémité, sf. (*etym. L.* extremitatem), extremity, end, tip, point, last moment, utmost distress

‖**Extrinsèque,** adj. (*etym. L.* extrinsecus), extrinsic

Exulter, vn. (*etym. L.* exsultare), to exult, to display much joy

Ex-voto, sm. votive offering

F.

F, s. sixth letter of the alphabet, f

Fa, sm. (*mus.*) F. *Clef de* —, bass, bass-clef

Fable, sf. (*etym. L.* fabula), fable, mythology, untruth, laughing-stock, common talk

Fabliau, sm. (*etym. O.F.* fabiel), a mediæval tale in verse

Fablier, sm. (*etym.* fable), an author, a collection of fables

Fabricant, sm. manufacturer, maker

Fabricateur, sm. (*etym. L.* fabricatorem), coiner, forger

Fabrique, sf. (*etym. L.* fabrica), manufacture, make, fabrication, coining, manufactory, factory, structure, fabric

Fabriquer, va. (*etym. L.* fabricare), to manufacture, to make, to coin, to forge, to fabricate

‖**Fabuleux, se,** adj. (*etym. L.* fabulosus), fabulous

Fabuliste, sm. (*etym. L.* fabula), fabulist

Façade, sf. (*etym. I.* facciata), front

Face, sf. (*etym. L.* facies), face, countenance, front, aspect, posture, bearings. *De* —, in front. *En* —, adv. in the face, in front. *Faire* — *à*, to face, to meet, to cope with

Facétie, sf. (*etym. L.* facetia), facetiousness, merry conceit, joke, jest

‖**Facétieux, se,** adj. droll, facetious, jocular

Facette, sf. (*etym. dimin. of* face), facet, face

Fâché, e, part. adj. angry, displeased

Fâcher, va. (*etym. Prov.* fastigar), to make angry, to offend, to anger; *se* —, vr. to get angry, to be offended

Fâcherie, sf. (*etym.* fâcher), quarrel, bickering

‖**Fâcheux, se,** adj. (*etym. L.* fâcher), vexatious, unpleasant, grievous, to be regretted, rugged, tedious, tiresome. *Un* —, a bore

‖**Facile,** adj. (*etym. L.* facilis), easy, natural, free, ready, indulgent

Facilité, sf. (*etym. L.* facilitatem), facility, ease, easiness, freedom, fluency, easy temper, accommodation

Faciliter, va. (*etym.* facile), to facilitate, to make easy

Façon, sf. (*etym. L.* factionem, *the power of doing*), fashion, make, shape, cut, workmanship, ceremony. *Avoir bonne* —, to look handsome. *Sans* —, without ceremony. *Faire des —s*, to stand upon ceremony

Faconde, sf. (*etym. L.* facundia), eloquence, glibness of tongue, flow of words

Façonner, va. (*etym.* façon), to work, to fashion, to shape, to dress; *se* —, vr. to improve, to form, to grow familiar with

Façonnier, ère, adj. (*etym.* façon), ceremonious

"**Factage,** sm. (*etym. see* FACTEUR), porterage

Facteur, sm. (*etym. L.* factorem), manufacturer, maker, factor, agent, postman, carrier, porter. *Un — d'orgues*, an organ builder

‖**Factice,** adj. (*etym. L.* factitius), factitious

‖**Factieux, se,** adj. (*etym. L.* factiosus), factious

Faction, sf. (*etym. L.* factionem), guard, sentry, faction. *Des soldats en* —, soldiers on guard. *Être en* —, to be on guard. *Faire* —, (*fig.*) to stand kicking one's heels

Factionnaire, sm. (*etym.* faction), sentinel, sentry

Factorerie, Factorie, sf. (*etym.* facteur), factory

Facture, sf. (*etym. L.* factura), invoice, bill of parcels, composition

‖**Facultatif, ve,** adj. (*etym. L.* facultatem), optional

Faculté, sf. (*etym. L.* facultatem), faculty, mind, property

Fadaise, sf. (*etym.* fade), twaddle. *Dire des —s*, to twaddle

‖**Fade,** adj. (*etym. L.* fatuus, *insipid*), tasteless, unsavoury

Fadeur, sf. (*etym.* fade), tastelessness, insipidity

Fagot, sm. (*etym. L.* fax, *torch*), faggot, bundle of wood, (†) idle story. *Sentir le* —, to smell of the stake

Fagoter, va. to bind up in faggots, to jumble up, to dress absurdly; *se* —, vr. to make a fright of oneself

Fagotin, sm. (*etym.* fagot), Pug, Jack-Pudding

‖**Faible,** adj. (*etym. L.* flebilis, *to be mourned for*), feeble, weak, faint, poor, slender. — sm. the weak, the helpless, frailty, foible, partiality

Faiblesse, sf. (*etym.* faible), feebleness, weakness, fainting fit, partiality, fondness

Faiblir, vn. (*etym.* faible), to grow weak, to give way, to yield, to slacken, to flag

Faïence, sf. (*etym.* Faenza, *a town in Italy*), crockery, earthenware, delft

Faïencier, ère, s. (*etym.* faïence), crockery-merchant

§**Failli,** sm. bankrupt

§**Faillibilité,** sf. (*etym.* faillible), fallibility

§**Faillible,** adj. (*etym.* faillir), liable to error, fallible

§**Faillir,** vn. (*etym. L.* fallere, *to deceive*), to err, to transgress, to be mistaken, to give way

§**Faillite,** sf. failure

Faim, sf. (*etym. L.* fames), starvation, hunger. † *Un meurt-de-* —, a starveling

Faine, sf. (*etym. L.* faginea (glans)), mast

Fainéant, e, adj. (*etym.* faire, néant), slothful, lazy, sluggish

Fainéanter, vn. to idle

Fainéantise, sf. sloth, laziness, sluggishness

Faire, va. (*etym.* L. facere), to do, to act, to make, to work, to perform, to travel, to have, to lay, to play, to counterfeit. *N'avoir que — de*, to have no need for. *Ne — que*, to do nothing but. *Ne — que de*, to have just. — vn. to do, to look, to contrive, to deal. *Se —*, vr. to be done, to be made, to happen, to turn, to pretend to be, to get used, to reconcile oneself to

Faisable, adj. (*etym.* faire), feasible, practicable, allowable

Faisan, de, or **e**, s. (*etym.* L. phasianus, *from* Phasis, *a river in Asia Minor*), pheasant

se Faisander, vr. to get high

Faisanderie, sf. (*etym.* faisander), pheasantry

Faisceau, sm. (*etym.* L.L. fascellus), bundle, sheaf, stack, pile, pencil, cone, cluster

Faiseur, se, s. (*etym.* faisant), doer, maker, author, (†) charlatan

Fait, e, past part. done, made, full-grown, experienced, seasoned. *C'en est —*, it is done now

Fait, sm. (*etym.* L. factum), deed, act, fact. *Prendre — et cause pour*, to take up the quarrel. *Je lui ai bien dit son —*, I told him a piece of my mind. *Si —*, yes indeed, I beg your pardon

Faite, sm. (*etym.* L. fastigium, *top*), top, roof, pinnacle

Faix, sm. (*etym.* L. fascia, *bundle*), weight, burden, load

Falaise, sf. (*etym.* H.G. felisa, *rock*), cliff

Falbala, sm. (*etym.* ? *comp the Engl.* furbelow), furbelow

|**Fallacieux, se**, adj. (*etm.* L. fallaciosus), fallacious, deceitful

Falloir, vn. imp. (*etym. see* FAILLIR), must, to be obliged *Comme il faut*, as it should be, genteel

Falot, e, adj. (*etym.* ?), funny, grotesque

Falot, sm. (*etym* Gr. φανός, *brilliant*), cresset, lantern

Falourde, sf. (*etym.* ?), large fagot

Falsificateur, sm. (*etym.* falsifier), falsifier, adulterator, debaser

Falsifier, va. (*etym.* L. falsificare), to falsify, to adulterate, to debase

Famé, e, adj. (*etym.* O F fame = L. fama), famed

Famélique, adj sm. (*etym.* L famelicus), starving, starveling

|**Fameux, se**, adj. (*etym.* L. famosus), famous, famed, renowned

Familiariser, va. (*etym.* familier), to familiarise; *se —*, vr. to grow familiar, to become familiarised

Familiarité, sf. (*etym.* L. familiaritatem), familiarity, (*plur.*) liberties

§**Familier, ère**, adj. (*etym.* L. familiaris), familiar

§**Famille**, sf. (*etym.* L. familia), family, kindred, the household

Fanal, sm. (*etym.* L.L. fanale), light, lantern, beacon

Fanatique, adj. (*etym.* L. fanaticus), fanatic, fanatical

¶**Fanatiser**, va. (*etym.* fanatique), to fanaticize

Fanatisme, sm. (*etym.* fanatique), fanaticism

Faner, va. (*etym.* L. fœnum, *hay*), to make hay, to spread, to wither, to dry up, to fade; *se —*, vr. to fade away, to wither, to droop

Faneur, se, s. (*etym.* faner), hay-maker

Fanfan, sm. (*for* enfant), darling, ducky

Fanfare, sf. (*onomatop.*), flourish of trumpets

Fanfaron, sm. adj. (*etym.* fanfare), boaster, braggart, swaggerer, bragging, boasting, blustering

Fanfaronnade, sf. (*etym.* fanfaron), boasting

Fanfaronnerie, sf. boasting

Fanfreluche, sf. (*etym.* L.L. famfaluca, *bubble*), bauble, gewgaw

Fange, sf. (*etym.* L.L. famix, *mud*), mire, mud, filth, low condition, filth of debauch

Fangeux, se, adj. (*etym.* fange), miry, muddy, marshy

Fanon, sm. (*etym.* L.L fano, *a strip*), dewlap, fin, bone, fetlock

Fantaisie, sf. (*etym.* Gr. φαντασία), fancy, mind, whim, liking, fantasy, floss-silk

Fantasmagorie, sf. (*etm.* Gr. φάντασμα, *ghost*, ἀγορεύειν, *to speak*), phantasmagoria, dissolving view

Fantasmagorique, adj. phantasmagorical

!**Fantasque**, adj. (*etym.* L. fantasticus), fantastical, fanciful, whimsical

Fantassin, sm. (*etym.* I. fantaccino), foot-soldier

|**Fantastique**, adj. (*etym.* L. fantasticus), fantastic, fantastical

Fantôme, sm. (*etym.* Gr. φάντασμα), phantom, ghost

Faon, sm. (*pronounc.* fan; *etym.* L. fœtus ?), fawn

Faquin, sm. (*etym.* I. facchino, *porter*), scoundrel, puppy

Faraud, sm. (*etym.* ?), a man proud of his fine clothes

Farce, sf. (*etym.* L.L. farsus, farce, interlude, drollery, trick, prank, joke, stuffing, forcemeat. *Faire une — à*, to play a trick on. *Faire ses —s*, to play tricks, to be wild

Farceur, se, smf. (*etym.* farce), comic actor, joker

Farcir, va. to stuff; *se —*, vr. to cram, to stuff

Fard, sm. (*etym.* ?), paint, rouge, deceit, disguise

Fardeau, sm. (*etym.* ?), burden, load, fardel

Farder, va. (*etym.* fard), to paint, to rouge, to gloss, to put the best uppermost, to deceive; *se —*, vr. to use paint; — vn. (*etym.* fardeau), to give way

Farfadet, sm. (*etym.* ?) hobgoblin

Faribole, sf. (*etym.* ?), idle story, trifle

Farine, sf. (*etym.* L. farina), flour

Farineux, se, adj. (*etym.* L. farinosus), mealy, white with flour, scurfy

Farouche, adj. (*etym.* L. ferocem), wild, fierce, grim, surly, unsociable

Fascine, sf. (*etym.* L. fascina, *a bundle*), fascine, faggot, lavin

Fasciner, va. (*etym.* L. fascinare), to fascinate

Faste, sm. (*etym.* L. fastus), pomp, ostentation, display

Fastes, sm. plur. (*etym.* L. fasti [libri]), fasti, (*fig.*) records, annals

|**Fastidieux, se**, adj. (*etm.* L. fastidiosus), dull, tedious, irksome

!**Fastueux, se**, adj. (*etym.* L. fastuosus), pompous, gorgeous, ostentatious, showy

Fat, adj. (*etym.* L. fatuus, *silly*), self-conceited, foppish. — sm. coxcomb, fop, puppy

Fatalisme, sm. (*etym.* fatal), fatalism

Fataliste, sm. fatalist

Fatalité, sf. (*etym.* L. fatalitatem), fatality

Fatidique, adj. (*etym.* L. fatidium), prophetic, fatidical

Fatigant, e, adj. tiring, fatiguing, wearisome

Fatigue, sf. (*etym.* fatiguer), toil, fatigue, hardship, weariness. *Habits de —*, working-clothes

Fatiguer, va. (*etym.* L. fatigare), to tire, to weary, to fatigue, to impoverish; — vn. to work hard, to be tiring; *se —*, vr. to fatigue oneself, to be tired

Fatras, sm. (*etym.* ?), rubbish, trash, stuff

Fatuité, sf. (*etym.* L. fatuitatem), self conceitedness, puppyism, foppishness

Faubourg, sm. (*etym.* L. foris, burgum), suburbs, outskirts

Faubourien, ne, adj. smf. (*etym.* faubourg), suburban, inhabitant of a faubourg

Fauchage, sm. (*etym.* faucher), mowing

Faucher, va. (*etym.* faux), to mow, to cut down

Faucheur, sm. mower

Faucheur, Faucheux, sm. shepherd-spider

§**Faucille**, sf. (*etym. dimin. of* faux), sickle, reaping-hook

Faucon, sm. (*etym.* L. falco), falcon, hawk

Fauconneau, sm. jackhawk, (*artill.*) falconet

Fauconnerie, sf. (*etym.* faucon), falconry, hawking

Fauconnier, sm. falconer

Faufiler, va. (*etym.* faux, fil), to tack, to baste; *se —*, vr. to slip in, to ingratiate oneself with

Faune, sm. (*etym.* L. *prop. name* Faunus), faun, forest-butterfly. — sf. the fauna, the animals

Faussaire, sm. (*etym.* L.L. falsarius), forger

Fausser, va. (*etm.* L. falsare), to bend, to twist, to dint, to force, to warp. *— compagnie à*, to give the slip, to break one's promise; *se —*, vr. to be bent, warped

Fausset, sm. (*etym.* I. falsetto), falsetto, spigot, faucet, ventpeg

Fausseté, sf. (*etym.* L. falsitatem), falseness, falsity, untruth, story

Faute, sf. (*etym.* L. fallere), fault, shortcomings, trespass, sin, flaw, oversight, want. *Faire — à*, to fail. *— de*, for want *or* lack of

§**Fauteuil**, sm. (*etym.* L.L. faldistorium), elbow-chair, arm-chair

Fauteur, trice, s. (*etym.* L. fautorem), abettor, upholder

Fautif, ve, adj. (*etym.* faute), faulty, bad, full of blemishes

Fauve, adj. (*etym.* O.H.G. falo, *tawny*), fallow, tawny. — sm. fawn-colour

Fauvette, sm. (*etym.* fauve), warbler

Faux, sf. (*etym.* L. falcem), scythe

|**Faux, sse**, adj. false, untrue, deceitful, wrong, mistaken, forged, out of tune. — adv. falsely, wrongfully, out of tune. *Porter à —*, to be out of the perpendicular, (*fig.*) to be inapplicable, to be groundless. — sm. falsehood, the false, forgery. *Arguer de —*, to tax false. *Faire un —*, to commit forgery

Faux-fuyant, sm. (*etym.* faux, fuyant), byway, subterfuge

Faux-monnayeur, sm. coiner

Faveur, sf. (*etm.* L. favorem), favour, kindness, good-will, vogue, bit of ribbon

|**Favorable**, adj. (*etym.* L. favorabilis), favourable

Favori, ite, s. (*past part. of the O.F. verb* favorir), favourite, darling, (*plur.*) whiskers

Favoriser, va. (*etym.* favour), to favour, to befriend, to countenance

¶**Favoritisme**, sm. (*etym.* favori), favouritism

*****Féal, e**, adj. (*etym.* O.F. *for* fidèle), trusty, liege

Fécale, adj. f. (*etym.* L. fæcalis). *Matière —*, excrements

|**Fécond, e**, adj (*etym.* L. fecundus), prolific, fertile, fruitful

Fécondant, e, adj. (*etym.* féconder), fertilizing, genial

Féconder, va. (*etym.* L. fecundare), to fecundate, to inuuvenate, to fertilise

Fécondité, sf. (*etym. L.* fecunditatem), fruitfulness, fecundity

Fécule, sf. (*etym. L.* fæcula), fecula

¶**Fédéraliste**, sm. (*etym.* fédéral), federalist

¶**Fédératif, ve**, adj. (*etym.* fédéré), federative

Fédération, sf. (*etym. L.* fœderationem), confederation

¶**Fédéré, e**, adj. (*etym. L.* fœderare), confederate

Fée, sf. (*etym. L.* fata), fairy, elf, fay

Féerie, sf. (*etym.* fée), fairy art, magic art

Féerique, adj. (*etym.* féerie), fairy. *Pièce* —, pantomime

Feindre, va.n. (*etym. L.* fingere), to feign, to counterfeit, to suppose, to scruple; *se* —, vr. to pretend to be

Feint, e, past part. adj. feigned, pretended, assumed

Feinte, sf. dissimulation, pretence, feint, fiction, friar, slight

Feld-maréchal, sm. (*etym. G.* feldmarschall), a field-marshal

Fêler, va., *se* —, vr. (*etym.* ?), to crack

Félicité, sf. (*etym. L.* felicitatem), bliss, felicity, blessedness, happiness

Féliciter, va. (*etym. L.* felicitare), to congratulate, to felicitate; *se* —, vr. to congratulate oneself, to wish each other joy

Félon, ne, adj. s. (*etym. L.L.* felo), caitiff

Félonie, sf. (*etym.* félon), treason

Félouque, sf. (*etym. Ar.* faluka, *a boat*), felucca

Fêlure, sf. (*etym.* fêler), crack

Femelle, sf. (*etym. L.* femella), female

Féminin, e, adj. (*etym. L.* femininus), feminine, womanly, womanish

Femme, sf. (*etym. L.* fœmina), woman, female, wife. *Ce que — veut Dieu le veut*, a woman must have her way. *Prendre* —, to take a wife

Femmelette, sf. (*etym.* femme), silly woman

Fenaison, sf. (*etym. L.* fœnum, *hay*), hay-making

Fendeur, se, s. (*etym.* fendre), cleaver, splitter

Fendre, va. (*etym. L.* findere), to split, to cleave, to rip up, to cut open, to crack, to rend, to squeeze through. *Geler à pierre* —, to freeze as hard as can be. — vn. to be ready to split, to ache. *Se* —, vr. to split, to be split, to crack

Fendu, e, past part. adj. split, cloven, cracked

Fenêtre, sf. (*etym. L.* fenestra), window, casement, lattice

§**Fenouil**, sm. (*etym. L.* fœniculum), fennel

Fente, sf. (*etym.* fendre), chink, crack, cranny, slit, cleft

Féodal, e, adj. (*etym. see* FIEF), feudal

Féodalité, sf. (*etym.* féodal), feodality

Fer, sm. (*etym. L.* ferrum), iron, iron tip, tag, head, point, steel, sword, horse-shoe, chain, fetters. — *battu*, wrought iron. —*s à repasser, à papillotes*, irons, curling irons. *Mettre un* — *à*, to shoe. *Perdre un* —, to cast a shoe. † *Tomber les quatre* —*s en l'air*, to fall sprawling on the ground

Fer-blanc, sm. (*etym.* fer, blanc), tin, tin-plate

Ferblanterie, sf. (*etym.* ferblantier), tin wares

Ferblantier, sm. (*etym.* ferblanc), tinman

Férie, sf. (*etym. L.* feria), feria, holy day

Férié, e, adj. (*etym. L.* feriatus), ferial

Férir, va. (*etym. L.* ferire, *to strike*), to strike. *Sans coup* —, without a blow

Ferler, va. (*etym. Engl.* to furl), to furl

Fermage, sm. rent

Ferme, adj. (*etym. L.* firmus), firm, steady, strong, fast, obligatory. — adv. firmly, hard, fast. — ! steady !

Ferme, sf. (*etym. L.* firma), farm, farm-house, farming. *Donner à* —, to let out to farm. *Prendre à* —, to farm

Fermé, e, past part. shut, closed

Fermenter, vn. (*etym. L.* fermentare), to ferment, to work

Fermer, va. (*etym. L.* firmare), to shut, to close. — vn., *se* —, vr. to shut, to close

Fermeté, sf. (*etym. L.* firmitatem), firmness, hardness, strength, vigour

Fermeture, sf. (*etym. L.* fermer), fastening, closing, shutting

Fermier, sm. (*etym.* ferme), farmer

Fermière, sf. farmer's wife

Fermoir, sm. (*etym.* fermer), clasp

Féroce, adj. (*etym. L.* ferocem), fierce, ferocious, wild

Férocité, sf. (*etym. L.* ferocitatem), ferocity, ferociousness

§**Ferraille**, sf. (*etym.* fer), old iron

§**Ferrailler**, vn. to fence, to draw, to tilt, to wrangle

§**Ferrailleur**, sm. dealer in old iron, bully

Ferrant, adj.m. *Maréchal* —, farrier

Ferré, e, past part. roughshod, (*fig.*) a complete master

Ferrement, sm. (*etym. L.* ferramentum), iron tool, iron work

Ferrer, va. (*etym. L.* ferrare), to bind with iron, to shoe, to tag, to put a ferrule to. — *à glace*, to rough-shoe.

Ferronnerie, sf. (*etym.* fer), iron-foundry

Ferronnier, ère, s. (*etym.* fer), ironmonger

Ferronnière, sf. (*etym.* ?), frontlet

Ferrugineux, se, adj. (*etym. L.* ferrugo, *rust*), ferruginous

Ferrure, sf. (*etym.* ferrer), iron-work, shoeing a horse

Fertiliser, va. (*etym.* fertile), to fertilize

Fertilité, sf. (*etym. L.* fertilitatem), fertility, fruitfulness

Férule, sf. (*etym. L.* ferula, *from* ferire, *to strike*), ferule, cane, rod

Ferveur, sf. (*etym. L.* fervorem), earnestness, fervour, fervency

Fesse-Mathieu, sm. (*etym.* fesser, Mathieu, *i.e. to beat Matthew* [*the usurer*] *for the purpose of getting money out of him*), skin-flint

Festin, sm. (*etym. see* FESTINER), feast, entertainment, banquet

Festiner, va.n. (*etym. L.* festivum), to feast

Feston, sm. (*etym. L.* festum), festoon

Festonner, va. (*etym.* feston), to festoon, to cut in festoons

***Festoyer**, vn. (*etym.* fête), to feast

Fête, sf. (*etym. L.* festum), festival, feast, holy day, holiday. *La* — *-Dieu*, Corpus Christi day. *Ce n'est pas tous les jours* —, Christmas comes but once a year. *Faire* — *de quelque chose à quelqu'un*, to hold out hopes of. *Faire* — *à quelqu'un*, to receive with open arms

Fêter, va. (*etym.* fête), to keep, to observe, to receive with open arms, to feast

Fétiche, sm. adj. (*etym. Port.* fetisso, *an enchanted thing*), fetich

Fétichisme, sm. fetichism

Fétide, adj. (*etym. L.* fœtidus), fetid, offensive

Fétu, sm. (*etym. L.* festuca), straw

Feu, sm. (*etym. L.* focus), fire, heat, the stake, homestead, family. — *de joie*, bonfire. *Un* — *d'artifice*, fireworks. *Je n'y vois que du* —, I can make nothing out of it. — *de paille*, sudden blaze. *Faire* — *qui dure*, to take care of one's health. *Mettre le* — *aux étoupes*, to add fuel to flame. *Faire le coup de* —, to handle a gun. *Faire long* —, to hang fire. *Faire* — *des quatre pieds*, to do one's utmost. *N'avoir ni* — *ni lieu*, to have neither house nor home. — *follet*, Will-o'-the-wisp

Feu, e, adj. (*etym. L.* functus?), deceased, defunct, late

Feudataire, s. (*etym. O.F.* feud, feod = fief), feudatory

§**Feuillage**, sm. (*etym.* feuillet), foliage, leaves

§**Feuillant, tine**, s. (*etym.* Feuillans, *prop. name of a small town*), monk and nun of the order of St. Bernard

§**Feuille**, sf. (*etym. L.* folium), leaf, sheet, list, way-bill

§**Feuillée**, sf. (*etym.* feuille), bower

§**Feuillet**, sm. (*etym.* feuille), leaf, third stomach

§**Feuilleter**, va. (*etym.* feuillet), to turn over the pages of, to make puff-paste. *Gâteau feuilleté*, puff-paste

¶§**Feuilleton**, sm. (*etym.* feuillet), the lower part of a newspaper containing generally reviews of new books, tales, poetry, and critical articles

¶§**Feuilletoniste**, sm. a writer of *feuilletons*

§**Feuillette**, sf. (*etym. L.L.* folietta), a half hogshead

Feutre, sm. (*etym. L.L.* filtrum), felt, felt hat

Fève, sf. (*etym. L.* faba), bean-stalk, bean. — *d'Espagne*, scarlet-runners. *Le roi de la* —, the king of Twelfth-night

Féverole, sf. (*etym.* fève), horse-bean, kidney-bean

Février, sm. (*etym. L.* Februarius), February

Fi ! interj. (*etym. L.* fi ! phi ! phy !), fie, for shame. *Faire* — *de*, to turn up one's nose at

Fiacre, sf. (*etym. prop. n. of St. Fiacre*), hackney-coach

§**Fiançailles**, sf. (*etym.* fiancer), betrothal

Fiancé, e, s. betrothed

Fiancer, va. (*etym. O.F.* fiance), to betroth, to affiance

Fibre, sf. (*etym. L.* fiber), fibre, string. *Avoir la* — *sensible*, to be of a melting mood, to be touchy

Fibreux, se, adj. (*etym.* fibre), fibrous, stringy

Ficeler, va. (*etym.* ficelle), to tie up

Ficelle, sf. (*etym. L.* fiscella, *a small basket*; filicellum, *dimin. of* filum ?), string, packthread, twine

Fiche, sf. (*etym.* ficher), pin, fish, -

Ficher, va. (*etym. L.L.* figitare? fixicare ?), to stick in the ground, to fix, to mix

†**Fichu, e**, adj. (*etym.* ?), ridiculous, impertinent, disagreeable. *Un homme* —, a man done for; — sm. (*etym.* ?), kerchief

¶**Fictif, ve**, adj. (*etym.* fiction), fictitious

Fidéicommis, sm. (*etym. L.* fideicommissum), trustee, trust

¶**Fidèle**, adj. (*etym. L.* fidelis), faithful, true, loyal, accurate, retentive. — sm. trusty follower

Fidélité, sf. (*etym. L.* fidelitatem), fidelity, faithfulness, true-heartedness, loyalty, accuracy

Fiduciaire, sm. (*etym. L.* fiduciarius), fiduciary, in trust

Fief, sm. (*etym. Goth.* faihu, *property*), fief, fee. *Arrière-* —, rere-fee

Fieffé, e, adj. (*etym.* fief), arrant, downright, regular

Fiel, sm. (*etym. L.* fel), gall, spleen, malice

Fiente, sf. (*etym. L.* fimus, *dung*), dung

Fier, va., *se* —, vr. (*etym. L.* fidus), to trust, to rely, to depend

‖**Fier, ère,** adj. (*etym. L.* ferus), proud, imperious, haughty, boastful, lofty, high-minded, spirited. *Un fier-à-bras*, a bully, a Hector

Fierté, sf. (*etym. L.* feritatem), pride, haughtiness, loftiness, high-mindedness, boldness

Fièvre, sf. (*etym. L.* febris), fever. † *Une — de cheval*, a violent fever. ‡ *Tomber de — en chaud mal*, to fall out of the frying-pan into the fire

Fiévreux, se, adj. (*etym.* fièvre), fever-giving, liable to fever, feverish

Fifre, sm. (*etym. O.H.G.* pfîfa, *whistle*), fife, fifer

Figer, va., *se* —, vr. (*etym. L.* figere), to congeal, to coagulate

Figue, sf. (*etym. L.* ficus), fig

Figuier, sm. (*etym.* figue), fig-tree, fig-eater

Figurant, e, s. figurant, supernumerary

‖**Figuratif, ve,** adj. (*etym. L.* figurativus), figurative, typical, characteristic

Figure, sf. (*etym. L.* figura), figure, form, shape, face, court-card

Figuré, e, past part. adj. figured

Figurer, va. (*etym. L.* figurare), to figure, to be a figure of; — vn. to look well, to match well together, to figure; *se* —, vr. to figure to oneself, to fancy

Figurine, sf. (*etym.* figure), little figure

Fil, sm. (*etym. L.* filum), thread, yarn, web, wire, edge, stream, current. — *de la Vierge*, gossamer. *De droit* —, straight, right against. — *à plomb*, plumb line. *Donner du — à retordre*, to give a great deal of trouble. *De — en aiguille*, from one thing to another. *Avoir le* — (*fig.*) to be a sharp one

Filage, sm. (*etym.* fil), spinning

***Filandière,** sf. (*etym.* filer), a woman whose business it is to spin. *Les sœurs —s*, the Fates

Filandreux, se, adj. (*etym.* filer), fibrous, stringy

Filant, e, adj. flowing. *Étoile —e*, falling star

Filasse, sf. (*etym.* fil), tow

Filateur, sm. (*etym.* filer), spinning-mill owner

Filature, sf. (*etym.* filer), spinning-mill, factory

File, sf. (*etym.* fil), row, file, rank. *Par — à droite*, right file

Filer, vn. to spin, to wire-draw, to conduct, to pay out, to veer, to play a wrong card; — vn. to rope, to give in, to file off, to be off, to purr. ‡ — *doux*, to keep quiet

Filet, sm. thread, string, fillet, filament, chine, rule, net, snaffle. *Coup de* —, haul

Fileur, se, s. spinner

Filière, sf. (*etym.* fil), draw-plate, screw-plate, purlin. *Passer par la* —, to go through the regular channel

Filigrane, sf. (*etym. I.* filigrana), filigree, watermark

§**Fille,** sf. (*etym. L.* filia), daughter, child, girl, maiden, nun

§**Fillette,** sf. (*etym.* fille), lass, maiden

§**Filleul,** sm. (*etym. L.* filiolus), godson

§**Filleule,** sf. goddaughter

Filon, sm. (*etym.* fil), vein, lode

Filou, sm. (*etym.* ?), pickpocket

Filouter, va. to filch, to cheat

Filouterie, sf., *also* **Filoutage,** sm. cheating

Fils, sm. (*etym. L.* filius), son, boy

Filtre, sm. (*etym. same word as* feutre), filter, strainer

Filtrer, va.n., *se* —, vr. (*etym.* filtre), to filter

Fin, sf. (*etym. L.* finis), end, conclusion, close, aim. — *de non-recevoir*, plea of exception

‖**Fin, e,** adj. (*etym. L.* finitus), slender, fine, thin, delicate, nice, real, acute, shrewd, keen, artful. — sm. main point, gist. — *contre* —, diamond cut diamond. *Jouer au* —, to finesse

Finance, sf. (*etym. I.* finanza), cash, ready money, finances, exchequer, money-matters

‡**Financer,** vn. (*etym.* finance), to come down, to pay

Financier, sm. (*etym.* finance), financier, moneyed-man. —, *ère*, adj. financial

***Finaud, e,** adj. (*etym.* fin), artful, cunning

Finesse, sf. (*etym.* fin), slenderness, fineness, delicacy. *Entendre — à*, to give a malicious construction to. *Je n'y entends pas* —, I see nothing in it

Finette, sf. (*etym.* fin), thin tissue

Fini, e, past part. ended, finished, done, broken down, finite. — sm. the finite, the finish

Finir, va. (*etym. L.* finire), to end, to finish, to conclude. — vn. to end, to come to a conclusion. *En* —, to have done with it

Fiole, sf. (*etym. L.* phiala), phial, vial

Fioritures, sf. plur. (*etym. I.* fioriture), graces

Fisc, sm. (*etym. L.* fiscus), treasury, fisc

Fiscal, e, adj. sm. (*etym.* fisc), fiscal

Fistule, sf. (*etym. L.* fistula), fistula

Fixation, sf. fixing, appointing, settling, assessment

‖**Fixe,** adj. (*etym. L.* fixus), fixed, stationary, regular. — sm. regular salary, settled weather, fixed bodies. *Au beau* —, at set fair. — interj. (*milit.*), eyes front!

Fixer, va. (*etym.* fixe), to fix, to fasten, to rivet; *se* —, vr. to fasten on, to stick on

Fixité, sf. (*etym.* fixe), fixedness, stability

Flacon, sm. (*etym. L.* vasculum), bottle, case-bottle, scent-bottle

Flageller, va. (*etym. L.* flagellum, *a whip*), to scourge, to flagellate; *se* —, vr. to scourge oneself

Flageoler, vn. (*etym.* flageolet?), to tremble beneath him, her, it

Flagorner, va.n. (*etym.* ?), to palaver, to flatter

Flagornerie, sf. (*etym.* flagorner), palaver, flattery

Flagorneur, se, s. wheedler, sycophant

Flair, sm. (*etym. see* FLAIRER), scent

Flairer, va. (*etym. L.* fragrare), to smell, to scent

Flamant, sm. (*etym.* flamber) flamingo

Flambant, e, adj. blazing, flaming

***Flambé, e,** adj. done for, knocked on the head

Flambeau, sm. (*etym. O.F.* flambe), torch, flambeau, candlestick

Flamber, vn. (*etym.* flambe), to blaze, to blaze up; — va. to disinfect, to singe

Flamberge, sf. (*etym.* flanc; *G.* bergen, *to cover*), sword. *Mettre — au vent*, to draw

Flamboyant, e, adj. blazing, flashing

Flamboyer, vn. (*etym.* flamber), to blaze, to flash

Flamme, sm. (*etym. L.* flamma), flame, blaze, glow, passion, pendant, fleam

Flammèche, sf. (*etym.* flamme), spark, flake of fire

Flan, sm. (*etym. L.* flare, *to blow*), custard, disk

Flanc, sm. (*etym. L.* flaccus? *soft*), flank, side. ‡ *Se battre les —s*, to lash one's sides, (*fig.*) to exert oneself. *Prêter le* —, to lay oneself open. *Par le — droit!* to the right about

Flandrin, e, adj. (*etym. prop. name* Flandre, *from* Flanders), (‡) a tall, spare man

Flanelle, sf. (*etym. L.* flamineum, *woollen stuff*), flannel

Flâner, vn. (*etym.* ?), to loiter, to lounge about, to stroll

Flânerie, sf. (*etym.* flâner), loitering, idling, lounge, stroll

Flâneur, se, s. idler, lounger, loiterer

Flanquer, va. (*etym.* flanc), to flank; (*etym. same word as* flaquer), (‡) to deal, to give

Flaque, sf. (*etym. Flem.* vlacke, *a pool*), puddle, pool

Flaquer, va. (*etym.* flaque), to throw a liquid

Flasque, adj. (*etym. L.* flaccidus), pithless, feeble, flabby

Flatter, va. (*etym. O.H.G.* flaz, *flat*), to flatter, to fawn upon, to caress, to stroke; *se* —, vr. to flatter oneself, to flatter each other

Flatterie, sf. flattery

‖**Flatteur, se,** adj. (*etym.* flatter), flattering, pleasing, insinuating. — s. flatterer

Fléau, sm. (*etym. L.* flagellum, *a scourge*), flail, scourge, beam, door-bar

Flèche, sf. (*etym. M.H.G.* flitsch, *arrow*), arrow, bolt, spire, flitch

Fléchir, va. (*etym. L.* flectere, *to bend*), to bend, to bow; — vn. to bend, to give way, to sink

Fléchissement, sm. (*etym.* fléchir), bending, bowing

‖**Flegmatique,** adj. (*etym. L.* phlegmaticus), phlegmatic

Flegme, sm. (*etym. Gr.* φλέγμα), phlegm

Flétrir, va. (*etym.* ?), to wither, to fade, to blight; *se* —, vr. to wither, to fade, to disgrace oneself

Flétrissant, e, adj. dishonouring, disgraceful

Flétrissure, sf. withering, fading, brand of shame

Fleur, sf. (*etym. L.* florem), flower, blossom, bloom, prime. *La fine — de*, the pink of. *A — de*, even with, on a level with

Fleuraison, Floraison, sf. (*etym.* fleur), bloom, blooming, the season

Fleur-de-lis, sm. flower-de-luce

Fleurdeliser, va. to brand, to adorn with flower-de-luces

Fleuret, sm. (*etym.* fleur), ferret, foil

Fleurette, sf. (*etym.* fleur), floweret, pretty things. *Conter — à*, to make love to

Fleuri, e, past part. adj. blooming, in bloom *or* flower

Fleurir, vn. (*etym.* fleur), to bloom, to blow, to flower, to flourish; — va. to give a nosegay *or* a flower to

Fleuriste, sm. (*etym.* fleur), flower-gardener, florist, artificial flower-maker

Fleuron, sm. flower, floret

Fleuve, sm. (*etym. L.* fluvius), river, large river

Flexibilité, sf. (*etym. L.* flexibilitatem), flexibility, pliability

Flibustier, sm. (*etym. was spelt originally* fribustier = *freebooter*), freebooter, filibuster

Flocon, sm. (*etym. L.* floccus), flock, tuft, flake

Floconneux, se, adj. (*etym.* floccus), flaky

†**Flonflon,** sm. (*onomat.*), tol-de-rol

Florissant, e, adj. (*etym. see* FLEURIR), flourishing, blooming

Flot, sm. (*etym. L.* fluctus), wave, billow, surge

Flottaison, sf. (*etym.* flotter), water-line

Flottant, e, adj. floating, buoyant, waving, wavering

Flotte, sf. (*etym. L.* fluctus), fleet, float

Flotter, vn. (*etym.* flot), to float, to be buoyed up, to swim

§**Flottille,** sf. flotilla

Flou, sm. a light style of painting or engraving —**e,** adj. (*etym. O.F.* flo, *weak*), light, graceful, too light

¶‖**Flouer,** va.(*etm.* flouter?), to steal, to cheat

¶‖**Flouerie,** sf.(*etm.* flouer), cheat, act of cheating

Fluet, te, adj. (*etym.* flou), slender, delicate, spare

‖**Fluide,** adj. sm. (*etym. L.* fluidus), fluid

Fluidité, sf. (*etym.* fluide), fluidity

Flûte, sf. (*etym. I.* flauto), flute, flute-player, roll; (*etym. D.* fluit), a kind of ship. *Ce qui vient de la — s'en retourne au tambour,* light come, light go

Flûté, e, adj. (*etym.* flûte), softly shrill, fluted

Fluvial, e, adj. (*etym. L.* fluvialis), river, fluvial, fluviatic

Flux, sm. (*etym. L.* fluxus), flood, flow, rising, flux

Fluxion, sf. (*etym. L.* fluxionem), inflammation. — *de poitrine,* inflammation on the chest

Foc, sm. (*etym. G.* fock), jib, stay-sail. *Grand —,* standing jib. *Petit —,* fore stay-sail. *Bâton de —,* jib-boom. *Contre—,* foretop-gallant stay sail. *Second —,* middle jib

Foi, sf. (*etym. L.* fides), faith, belief, creed, trust. *Faire —,* to be admitted in evidence. *En — de quoi,* in witness whereof

Foie, sm. (*etym. L.* [jecur] ficatum, *liver fattened with figs*), liver

Foin, sm. (*etym. L.* fœnum, *hay*), hay, choke. † *Mettre du — dans ses bottes,* to feather one's nest

Foin! interj. (*etym.* fouin = fouine, *a pole-cat*), plague take

Foire, sf. (*etym. L.* feria), fair, market

Fois, sf. (*etym. L.* vices, *times*), time. *A la —,* at once. *Une —,* once. *Deux —,* twice

Foison, sf. (*etym. L.* fusionem), plenty. *A —,* in abundance

Foisonner, vn. to be plentiful

Folâtre, adj. (*etym.* fou, fol), playful, sportful, wanton, frisky

Folâtrer, vn. to frolic, to sport, to dally, to toy

Folâtrerie, sf. dalliance, toying

Folie, sf. (*etym.* fou, fol), folly, madness, distraction, foolish thing, a piece of folly

Follet, te, adj. (*etym.* fou, fol), playful, foolish. *Esprit —,* sprite, elf. *Poil —,* downy hair

Folliculaire, sm. (*etym.* folliculo, *small sheet of paper*), scribbler

Fomenter, va. (*etym. L.* fomentare), to foment

Foncé, e, adj. deep, dark

Foncer, va. (*etym.* fond), to deepen, to sink

Foncier, ère, adj. (*etym.* fonds), landed

Fonction, sf. (*etym. L.* functionem), duty, office, function

Fonctionnaire, sm.(*etm.* fonction), functionary

Fonctionner, vn. to work

Fond, sm. (*etym. L.* fundus), bottom, back, back part, fund, depth, groundwork, seating, main point. *Faire — sur,* to rely upon. *A —,* thoroughly. *Faire une charge à — de train,* to charge right down upon. *Au —, dans le —,* in the main

Fondamental, e, adj. (*etym.* fondement), fundamental

Fondateur, trice, s. founder

Fondation, sf. (*etym. L.* fundationem), foundation

Fondement, sm. (*etym. L.* fundamentum), foundation, substructure, groundwork, reliance, trust, (*anat.*) fundament

Fonder, va. (*etym. L.* fundare), to build, to lay the foundations of, to found. *Fondé de pouvoirs,* attorney. — *quelqu'un de procuration,* to give a power of attorney; *se —,* vr. to rely, to be founded or grounded

Fonderie, sf. foundry, melting-house, casting, founding

Fondeur, sm. founder

Fondre, va.n. (*etym. L.* fundere), to melt, to thaw, to smelt, to found, to cast, to blend, to convert, to sink in, to rush, to fall, to make a sudden stoop at; *se —,* vr. to melt, to be founded or cast, to fuse

Fondrière, sf. (*etym.* fond), bog, quagmire

Fonds, sm. (*etym. see* FOND), ground, piece of land, landed estate, funds, stocks, stock in trade. *Être en —,* to be in cash. *Mettre, vendre à — perdus,* to sink

Fontaine, sf. (*etym. L.L.* fontana), spring, fountain, fount

Fontainier, Fontenier, sm. fountain-maker, turncock

Fonte, sf. (*etym.* fondre), melting, smelting, thawing, casting, cast, fount; (*etym. L.L.* funda, *purse*), holster

Fonts, sm. plur. (*etym. L.* fons), font

***For,** sm. (*etym. L.* forum), tribunal. *Le — intérieur,* one's conscience

Forage, sm. (*etym.* forer), boring

Forain, e, adj. (*etym. L.L.* foraneus), alien. *Marchand —,* strolling trader, hawker

Forban, sm. (*etym. L.* foris, bannum), freebooter, pirate

Forçat, sm. (*etym.* force), convict

Force, sf. (*etym. L.L.* forcia, fortia), strength, force, power, might, skill, proficiency, efficacy, virtue. *Tour de —,* feat of strength, a clever thing. *A — de,* by strength of, by means of. *A toute —,* by all manner of means. *Être de première —,* to be very clever. *Être, n'être pas de — à,* to be capable of, unable to. *Être en —,* to muster strong. — *m'est,* I am obliged. *Maison de —,* county-jail. *Avoir — de chose jugée,* to be a decided thing

‖**Forcé, e,** past part. adj. forced, unnatural, cramped, far-fetched

Forcené, e, adj. (*etym. L.* foris, *out of, G.* sinn, *sense*), mad

Forcer, va. (*etym.* force), to force open, to break open, to take by force, to storm, to compel. — *la main à quelqu'un,* to drive a person to do a thing. — *de voiles,* to crowd all sail. *Se —,* vr. to exert oneself too much, to strive

Forer, va. (*etym. L.* forare, *to pierce*), to bore, to perforate

Forestier, ère, adj.(*etym. L.L.* foresta), forest. *Garde —,* ranger, forest-ranger

Forêt, sf.(*etym. L.L.* foresta), forest

Foret, sm. (*etym. L.* forare), drill, gimlet

Forfaire, vn. (*etym. L.L.* forisfacere), to forfeit, to prevaricate

Forfait, sm. (*etym. L.L.* forisfactum), heinous crime, contract

Forfaiture, sf. (*etym.* forfaire), forfeiture, prevarication

Forfanterie, sf. (*etym. I.* furfanteria, *a rascally action*), boasting, bragging

Forge, sf. (*etym. L.* fabrica), smithy, forge, iron-mill

Forger, va. to forge, to coin, to invent; — vn. to overreach; *se —,* vr. to conjure up, to picture to oneself

Forgeron, sm. (*etym.* forger), blacksmith, smith

Forgeur, sm. forger, coiner

se Formaliser, vr. to take exception at

Formaliste, adj. sm. (*etym.* formel), precise, formal, formalist

Formalité, sf. (*etym.* formel), formality, ceremony

Format, sm. (*etym. L.* formatus), size

Forme, sf. (*etym. L.* forma), form, shape, figure, aspect, (*plur.*) manners. *Mettre des —s,* to be polite

‖**Formel, le,** adj. (*etym. L.* formalis), explicit, formal

Former, va. (*etym. L.* formare), to form, to make; *se —,* vr. to form, to make to oneself, to be formed

Formulaire, sm. (*etym.* formule), formulary

Formule, sf. (*etym. L.* formula), form, formula

Formuler, va. to draw up, to express

***Fors,** prep. (*etym. L.* foris *out of*), except, but, save

Fort, e, adj. (*etym. L.* fortis), strong, stout, proficient, hard. — sm. the strong man, the strong side, the main point, fort, stronghold, porter. — adv. hard, stoutly, very

Forteresse, sf. fortress

Fortifiant, e, adj. strengthening, invigorating. — sm. tonic

Fortifier, va. (*etym. L.* fortificare), to strengthen, to invigorate, to fortify; *se —,* vr. to grow stronger, to strengthen oneself, to improve, to fortify oneself

‖**Fortuit, e,** adj. (*etym. L.* fortuitus), fortuitous, chance

Fortune, sf. (*etym. L.* fortuna), fortune, risk, chance, luck. *A la — du pot,* potluck. *Homme à bonnes —s,* lady-killer. *Demi- —,* one horse carriage

Fortuné, e, adj. (*etym. L.* fortunatus), fortunate

Fosse, sf. (*etym. L.* fossa), pit, large hole, grave, (*nav.*) boatswain's store-room

Fossé, sm. (*etym.* fosse), moat, trench, ditch

Fossette, sf. (*dimin. of* fosse), pitch in the hole, dimple

Fossile, adj. sm. (*etym. L.* fossilis), fossil

Fossoyeur, sm. (*etym.* fosse), sexton, grave-digger

Fou, or **Fol, Folle,** adj. (*etym. L.L.* follis, *foolish*), mad, insane, distracted, crazy, wild. *Les —s rires,* wild laughter. —s, madman, madwoman, fool, madcap gannet, booby, (*chess*) bishop. *Plus on est de —s, plus on rit,* the more, the merrier

§†**Fouailler,** va. (*etym.* fouet), to whip

Foudre, sf. (*etym. L.* fulgur), lightning, thunder, thunderbolt. — sm. (*fig.*) thunderbolt; (*etym. G.* fuder), a large cask

Foudroiement, sm.(*etm.* foudroyer), striking with thunder, utter destruction

Foudroyant, e, adj. thundering, thunder-striking, dreadful

Foudroyer, va. (*etym.* foudre), to strike with lightning, to batter down, to beat down, to crush

Fouet, sm. (*etym. O.F.* fou = *L.* fagus, *beech* ?), thong, whip-cord, lashes, stripes, flogging, cat, (*artill.*) horizontal fire. † *Faire claquer son* —, to sound one's own trumpet

Fouetter, va. to whip, to flog. ‡ *Avoir bien d'autres chiens à* —, to have other fish to fry. *Il n'y a pas de quoi* — *un chat*, it is not worth while spending breath about it; — vn. to beat, to patter, to sweep

Fougère, sf. (*etym. L.* filix, *fern*), fern, brake

Fougue, sf. (*etym. L.* focus), fury, passion, fire, impetuosity, mettle

|**Fougueux, se,** adj. (*etym.* fougue), fiery, headlong, unruly, fierce

§**Fouille,** sf. (*etym.* fouiller), excavation, digging

§**Fouiller,** va.n. (*etym. L.* fodicare, *frequent. of* fodere, *to dig*), to dig, to excavate, to search, to dive into; *se* —, vr. to fumble in one's pockets, to search one another

§**Fouillis,** sm. (*etym.* fouiller), mess, confusion, litter

Fouine, sf. (*etym. L.* faginus, *belonging to the beech-tree*), pole-cat, pitchfork, fish-spear

Fouir, va. (*etym. L.* fodere), to dig, to sow

Foulard, sm. (*etym. ?*), silk-handkerchief

Foule, sf. (*etym. see* FOULER), crowd, throng, concourse, mob, rabble. *Faire* —, to draw crowds

Fouler, va. (*etym. L. root* full; *thus* FUL-CIRE, FULL-O), to tread upon, to press, to crush, to gall, to sprain. *Avoir le pied* —*é*, to have a sprained ankle; *se* —, vr. to sprain one's foot, wrist, &c.

Foulon, sm. (*etym. L.* fullo), fuller

Foulure, sf. sprain, fulling, treading, follings

Four, sm. (*etym. L.* furnus), oven, bake-house, furnace, kiln, kidnapping-house. *Des petits* —*s*, fancy biscuits. ‡ *Faire* —, to give back the money

Fourbe, sf. (*etym. I.* furbo), imposture, cheat, piece of villany. — adj. knavish, cheating, crafty. — sm. knave, cheat, cozener

Fourbir, va. (*etym. O.H.G.* furban, *to polish*), to furbish, to rub up, to burnish

Fourbisseur, sm. furbisher, sword cutler

Fourbissure, sf. furbishing

Fourbu, e, adj. (*etym. past part. of the O.F.* forboire, *to drink to excess*), foundered, over-fatigued

Fourche, sf. (*etym. L.* furca), pitchfork. *En* —, forked

Fourcher, vn., *se* —, vr. (*etym.* fourche), to fork, to branch off, to trip. *La langue lui a fourché*, he has made a slip of the tongue

Fourchette, sf. fork, table-fork, prop, breast-bone, frog

Fourchu, e, adj. (*etym.* fourche), forked, cross, cloven. *Au pied* —, cloven-footed

Fourgon, sm. (*etym. ?*), van, waggon, oven-rake, poker

Fourgonner, va. to poke, to stir

Fourmi, sf. (*etym. L.* formica), ant, emmet. † *Avoir des* —*s dans les jambes*, to have pins and needles in one's legs

Fourmilier, sm. ant-bear

Fourmilière, sf. ant-hill, swarm

§**Fourmillement,** sm. tingling, pins and needles, swarm

§**Fourmiller,** vn. (*etym.* fourmi), to swarm, to tingle, to feel pins and needles

Fournaise, sf. (*etym. L.* fornacem), furnace

Fourneau, sm. (*etym. L.* furnus), kitchen-stove, furnace, bowl, chamber. *Haut* —, blast furnace

Fournée, sf. (*etym.* four), batch, baking, kiln

Fourni, e, past part. stocked, furnished, thick

Fourniment, sm. (*etym.* fournir), accoutrements

Fournir, va.n. (*etym. O.H.G.* frumjan, *to finish*), to supply, to furnish, to provide, to stock, to draw; *se* —, vr. to deal with, to be supplied by, to provide oneself

Fournisseur, sm. contractor, tradesman

Fourniture, sf. supply, provision, remittance, trimmings, garnish

Fourrage, sm. (*etym. O.F.* feurre, fourre, *straw*), fodder, provender, forage, (*artill.*) wad

Fourrager, vn.a. to forage, to ravage, to plunder

Fourragère, adj.f. fit for fodder

Fourrageur, sm. forager

Fourré, sm. thicket. —, e, past part. adj. furry, furred, warmly lined, wooded. ‡ *Paix* —*e*, patched-up peace. ‡ *Coup* —, secret thrust

Fourreau, sm. (*etym. O.F.* fuere, *sheath*), sheath, scabbard, case, cover, child's frock

Fourrer, va. (*etym. O.F.* fuere), to thrust, to poke, to cram, to beat, to stuff, to line with fur; *se* —, vr. to thrust oneself, to intrude, to wrap oneself up warm

Fourreur, sm. (*etym.* fourrer), furrier, dealer in furs

Fourrier, sm. (*etym. L.L.* fodrarius, *from* fodrum, *fodder*), quarter-master

Fourrière, sf. (*etym. O.F.* feurre), pound

Fourrure, sf. (*etym.* fourrer), fur, (*nav.*) service

Fourvoyer, va. (*etym. L.* foris, *out of*, via, *way*), to lead astray; *se* —, vr to go astray, to make an egregious blunder

Foyer, sm. (*etym. L.L.* focarium, *hearth*), hearth, hearth-stone, fireside, homestead, native land, furnace, fire-grate, (*theat.*) saloon, green room, focus

Frac, sm. (*etym. G.* frack), frock-coat, dress-coat

Fracas, sm. (*etym. I.* fracasso), crash, din, uproar, fuss, bustle

Fracasser, va. to shatter, to break; *se* —, vr to be shattered to pieces

Fraction, sf. (*etym. L.* fractionem), breaking, fraction, part

Fractionnaire, adj (*etm.* fraction), fractional

Fracturer, va., *se* —, vr. (*etym.* fracture), to fracture

Fragilité, sf. (*etym. L.* fragilitatem), brittleness, fragility, unstableness, frailty

Frai, sm. (*etym. O.F.* froier, *to rub*), spawn, spawning season, fry, wear

Fraicheur, sf. (*etym.* frais), coolness, cool, chill, freshness, sweetness, bloom, flaw of wind

Fraichir, vn. (*etym.* frais), to freshen

Frairie, sf. (*etym. L.* fratria, *college, brotherhood*), merry-making, feast

|**Frais, Fraiche,** adj. (*etm. O.H.G.* frisc), cool, fresh, cold, bracing, untainted, sweet, new, (*iron.*) in a pretty plight. — sm. cool, freshness, gale. *Mettre au* —, to put to cool. *Prendre, respirer le* —, to breathe the fresh air. — adv. cool, freshly, fresh. *Boire* —, to take care the wine is not warm

Frais, sm. plur. (*etym. L.L.* fredum, *fine*), expenses, outlay. *Faux* —, incidental expenses. *Tous* — *faits*, clear of all expenses. *Sur de nouveaux* —, anew, afresh. *Se mettre en* —, to go to great expense

Fraise, sf. (*etym. L.* fragum), strawberry, ruffle, ruff, ruffs, start

Fraisier, sm. (*etym.* fraise), strawberry-plant

Framboise, sf. (*etym. O.H.G.* brâmberi), raspberry

Framboisier, sm. (*etym.* framboise), raspberry bush

Framée, sf. (*etym. L.* framea), framea

Franc, sm. (*etym.* franc), frank. *Le décime pour* —, 10 per cent.

|**Franc, Franche,** adj. (*etym. L.* francus), free, frank, open-hearted, downright, ingenuous, very, pure, ungrafted. *Qui a son* — *-parler*, accustomed to speak his mind. — adv. frankly, plainly, fully

Franc, Franque, s. Frank

Franchir, va. to leap over, to clear, to cross, to overstep, to overcome

Franchise, sf. franchise, immunity, freedom, ingenuousness. *En* —, duty free

Franciscain, s. (*etym.* St. Francis of Assisi), monk of the order of St. Francis

Franciser, va. (*etym.* Français), to make French, to frenchify; *se* —, vr. to become French

Francisque, sf. (*etym. L.L.* francisca, *from* Francus), battle-axe

Franc-maçon, sm. (*etym.* franc, maçon), freemason

Franc-maçonnerie, sf. freemasonry

Frange, sf. (*etym. L.* fimbria, *fringe*), fringe

Franger, va. to fringe

Franger, Frangier, sm. fringe-maker

Frangipane, sf. (*etym. proper name of the Marquis* de Frangipani, *who invented the perfume*), a kind of scent, a cake half custard and half almond, a sort of pear

‡**Franquette,** sf. (*etym.* franc). ‡ *A la bonne* —, frankly, sincerely

Frappant, e, adj. striking

Frappé, e, adj. spirited, forcible, well-wrought, iced

Frappement, sm. (*etym.* frapper), striking

Frapper, va. (*etym. D.* flappen, *to give a blow*), to strike, to hit, to meet, to stamp, to beat, to coin, to beat against; — vn. to strike, to hit, to knock, to rap; *se* —, vr. to hit *or* knock one's head, &c., to beat, to strike each other

Frappeur, se, s. knocker

Frasque, sf. (*etym. I.* frasca), trick, prank

|**Fraternel, le,** adj. (*etym. L.* fraternus), brotherly, fraternal

Fraterniser, vn. (*etym. L.* fraternus), to fraternize

Fraternité, sf. (*etym. L.* fraternitatem), brotherhood, fraternity

Fraude, sf. (*etym. L.* fraudem), fraud, deceit, fraudulency, knavery. *Faire la* —, to smuggle. *Entrer quelque chose en* —, to smuggle in

Frauder, va. (*etym.* fraude), to defraud

Fraudeur, sm. (*etym.* frauder), smuggler

|**Frauduleux, se,** adj. (*etym. L.* fraudulosus), fraudulent

Fraxinelle, sf. (*etym. L.* fraxinus), fraxinella

Frayé, e, adj. beaten, trodden

Frayer, va. (*etym.* frai), to open, to prepare, to show, to rub, to graze; — vn. to milt, to associate with, to agree; *se* —, vr. to open to oneself

Frayeur, sf. (*etym. L.* frigorem), fright, terror

Fredaine, sf. (*etym. ?*), wild prank, frolic

Fredonnement, Fredon, sm. (*etym. ?*), trill, humming

Fredonner, va.n. (*etym.* fredon), to hum

Frégate, sf. (*etym. L.* fabricata ?), frigate, frigate-bird

Frein, sm. (*etym. L.* frenum), bit, curb, check, frenum, drag, break. *Serrer le* —, to put on the break

Frelatage, sm., **Frelaterie**, sf. (*etym.* frelater), adulteration, sophistication

Frelaté, e, past part. adulterated, sophisticated, spurious

Frelater, va. (*etym. D.* verlaten, *to decant*), to adulterate, to sophisticate

Frelateur, sm. sophisticator, adulterator

Frêle, adj. (*etym. L.* fragilis), frail, weak

Frelon, sm. (*etym.* frêle), hornet, drone

‡**Freluquet**, sm. (*etym. O.F.* freluche, *trifle*), puppy, prig

Frémir, vn (*etym. L.* fremere), to shudder, to quake, to quiver, to rustle, to simmer

Frémissant, e, adj. shuddering, quivering, trembling, rustling, simmering, boiling

Frémissement, sm. shudder, thrill, trembling, quivering, rustling, simmering

Frêne, sm. (*etym. L.* fraxinus), ash-tree, ash

Frénésie, sf. (*etym. L.* phrenesis, *from the Gr.* φρήν, *thought*), frenzy, madness, distraction

Frénétique, adj. (*etym. L.* phreneticus), frantic, frenetic

Fréquence, sf. (*etym. L.* frequentia), frequency, quickness

Fréquenter, va.n. (*etym. L.* frequentare), to frequent, to associate with

Frère, sm. (*etym. L.* frater), brother, friar. — *de lait*, foster-brother. *Faux* —, traitor

Fresque, sf. (*etym. I.* al fresco), fresco

Fret, sm. (*etym. G.* fracht, *freight*), freight

Fréter, va.n. (*etym.* fret), to freight, to charter

Fréteur, sm. (*etym.* fréter), freighter

§**Frétillant, e**, adj. wriggling

§**Frétillement**, sm. (*etym.* frétiller), wriggling, frisking

§**Frétiller**, vn. (*etym. L.L.* fritillare, *to pound pepper*), to wriggle, to jump about, to frisk about

Fretin, sm. (*etym. L. L.* freto, *a small coin*), fry, young fish, trash. *Menu* —, small fry

Friabilité, sf. (*etym.* friable), friability, friableness

Friand, e, adj. (*etym.* frire), dainty, nice, partial to

Friandise, sf. (*etm.* friand), daintiness, epicurism, dainties

Fricasser, va. (*etym. ?*), to fricassee, to squander away

Friche, sf. (*etym. L.L.* friscum), waste land

†**Fricot**, sm. (*etym. ?*), stew, grub

†**Fricoter**, va.n. (*etym.* fricot), to cook, to treat oneself

Frictionner, va. (*etym.* friction), to rub; *se* —, vr. to rub oneself

Frigidité, sf. (*etym. L.* frigidus), frigidity

Frigorifique, adj. (*etym. L.* frigorificus), frigorific

Frileux, se, adj. (*etym. L.* frigidulosus ?), chilly, sensible of cold

Frimas, sm. (*etym. O.F.* frimer, *to freeze*), hoar-frost, rime

†**Frime**, sf. (*etym. L.* frumen ?), pretence, show

†**Frimousse**, sf. (*etym.* frime), face

†**Fringale**, sf. (*etm. corrupt of the O.F.* faim-valle), sudden and craving hunger

Fringant, e, adj. (*etym. O.F.* fringuer, *to jump about*), smart, frisky, dapper

Fripé, e, adj. rumpled, shabby, worn out

Friper, va. (*etym. ?*), to rumple, to crumple, to wear out, to squander away, (†) to guzzle; *se* —, vr. to get rumpled

Friperie, sf. (*etym.* friper), old clothes, frippery, rubbish

Fripier, sm. second-hand clothes seller, dealer in old furniture, plagiarist

Fripon, ne, s. adj. (*etym.* friper), rogue, knave, cheat, roguish

Friponner, va. to filch, to pilfer, to cozen

Friponnerie, sf. (*etym.* friponner), roguery, knavery

Frire, va.n. (*etym. L.* frigere, *to fry*), to fry

Frise, sf. (*etym. prop. name* Frise), frieze

Friser, va.n. (*etym. ?*), to curl, to frizzle, to crisp, to border upon, to be near. — *la quarantaine*, to be getting near forty; *se* —, vr. to curl, to fall into curl, to curl one's hair

Frisson, sm. (*etym. L.* frictionem), shivering, cold chill, shudder, thrill

Frissonnement, sm. (*etym.* frisson), shivering, shiver, thrill, shudder

Frissonner, vn. to shiver, to shudder, to feel a thrill

Frisure, sf. (*etym.* friser), curls, curling, head-dress

Frit, e, past part. fried, (*fig.*) done for, eaten up

Friture, sf. (*etym.* frire), frying, grease, dish of fried fish

‖**Frivole**, adj. (*etym. L.* frivolus), flimsy, frivolous, trifling

Frivolité, sf. (*etym. L.* frivolitatem), frivolousness, frivolity, trifle

Froc, sm. (*etym. L.L.* froccus, *coat*), monk's frock. *Prendre le* —, to be a monk. *Quitter le* —, *jeter le* — *aux orties*, to throw off the cowl

‖**Froid**, sm. (*etym. L.* frigidum), cold, cold weather, chill, chilliness, coldness, unconcern. *Il y a du* — *entre eux*, there is a coldness between them. —, e, adj. cold, dispassionate, untouched, cool, dull. *Faire de l'enthousiasme à* —, to get up a mock enthusiasm

Froideur, sf. (*etym.* froid), coldness, chill, ice, lifelessness, unfeelingness

Froidure, sf. cold, winter

Froissement, sm. (*etym.* froisser), bruising, rumpling, clashing

Froisser, va. (*etym. L.* frustum, *broken piece*), to bruise, to rub, to rumple, to clash with, to offend

Frôlement, sm. (*etym.* frôler), grazing, rustling

Frôler, va. (*etym. ?*), to graze

Fromage, sm. (*etym. L.L.* formaticum), cheese

Fromagerie, sf. cheese-dairy

Froment, sm. (*etym. L.* frumentum), wheat

Fronce, sf. (*etym. see* FRONCER), gather

Froncement, sm. (*etym.* froncer), puckering. — *des sourcils*, frown

Froncer, va. (*etym. L.* frons ?), to wrinkle, to contract, to gather. — *les sourcils*, to frown; *se* —, vr. to contract, to wrinkle

Fronde, sf. (*etym. L.* funda, *the O.F. was* fonde), a sling

Fronder, va. (*etym.* fronde), to sling, to hurl, to animadvert on, to jeer at

Frondeur, sm. (*etym.* fronder), slinger, fault-finder

Front, sm. (*etym. L.* frontem), forehead, brow, face, boldness, impudence, front. *A — découvert*, undisguisedly. *Avoir du* —, to be as bold as brass. *Avoir le — de*, to have the face to. *Faire* —, to face about. *Sur le — de bandière*, on the lines. *De* —, loc. adv. in front, abreast, at a time

Frontière, sf. adj. frontier, border

Fronton, sm. (*etym.* front), pediment

Frottage, sm. rubbing, waxing and polishing

Frottement, sm. (*etym.* frotter), friction, rubbing

Frotter, va.n. (*etym. L.* frictum), to rub, to wax and polish, to drub. † — *les oreilles à quelqu'un*, to warm one's ears for him; *se* —, vr. to rub oneself, to associate, to meddle

Frotteur, sm. (*etym.* frotter), rubber, floor-polisher

¶†**Frou-frou**, sm. (*onomat.*) rustling of silk. *Faire du* —, to display great luxury

Fructifiant, e, adj. fructifying

Fructifier, vn. (*etym. L.* fructificare), to fructify, to bear fruit

‖**Fructueux, se**, adj. (*etym. L.* fructuosus), fruitful, fructuous, profitable, lucrative

Frugalité, sf. (*etym. L.* frugalitatem), frugality

Frugivore, adj. (*etym. L.* fruges, vorare), frugivorous

Fruit, sm. (*etym. L.* fructus), fruit, dessert, benefit, profit, offspring. —*s d'espalier*, wall-fruit. † *Être* — *sec*, to be plucked

Fruiterie, sf. (*etym.* fruit), fruit-loft, fruit-trade

Fruitier, ère, adj. s. (*etym.* fruit), fruit, fruiterer, greengrocer. — sm. orchard, fruit-loft

Fruste, e, adj. (*etym. L.* frustum, *piece*), defaced, worn away

Frustrer, va. (*etym. L.* frustrari), to defraud, to disappoint, to frustrate

‖**Fugitif, ve**, adj. (*etym. L.* fugitivus), fugitive, runaway, fleeting, transient

Fugue, sf. (*etym. L.* fuga), fugue, (*fig.*) wild prank. † *Faire une* —, to run away from home

Fuir, vn. (*etym. L.* fugere), to flee, to fly, to take flight, to run away, to glide, to run, to leak; — va. to flee from, to shun; *se* —, vr. to avoid each other, to fly from oneself

Fuite, sf. (*etym. past part.* fui), flight, running away, escape, avoiding, shunning, shift, leakage

¶**Fulmi-coton**, sm. (*etym. L.* fulmen, coton), gun-cotton

Fulminant, e, adj. thundering, fulminating

Fulminer, va.n. (*etym. L.* fulminare), to thunder, to storm, to fulminate

Fumant, e, adj. smoking, steaming, fretting and fuming

Fumée, sf. (*etym. see* FUMER), smoke, steam, bubble, conceit, fumes

Fumer, va.n. (*etym. L.* fumare), to smoke, to reek, to steam, to fret and fume; (*etym. see* FUMIER), to manure, to dung

Fumeron, sm. smoky bit of charcoal

Fumet, sm. (*etym.* fumer), flavour

Fumeur, sm. (*etym.* fumer), smoker

‖**Fumeux, se**, adj. (*etym. L.* fumosus), heady, fumy

Fumier, sm. (*etym. L.L.* fimarium, *from* fimus, *manure*), dunghill, muck

Fumigatoire, adj. (*etym. L.* fumus), fumigating

Fumiste, sm. (*etym.* fumée), chimney-builder

¶**Fumivore**, adj. sm. (*etym. L.* fumus, vorare), smoke-consuming, smoke-consumer

¶**Fumoir**, sm. (*etym.* fumer), smoking-room

Funambule, sm. (*etym. L.* funambulus), rope-dancer

‖**Funèbre**, adj. (*etym. L.* funebris), funeral, dismal, gloomy

§**Funérailles**, sf. pl. (*etym. L.* funeralia), funeral

Funéraire, adj. (*etym. L.* funerarius), funeral, funereal

‡**Funeste**, adj. (*etym. L.* funestus), fatal, baleful, disastrous

Fur, sm. (*etym. L.* forum). *Au — et à mesure*, in proportion, by degrees

Furet, sm. (*etym. L.* fur, *thief*), ferret, Paul Pry

Fureter, va.n. to hunt with a ferret, to rummage, to pry about

Fureteur, se, s. (*etym.* fureter), a person who hunts with a ferret, (*fig.*) an inquisitive person

Fureur, sf. (*etym. L.* furorem), madness, fury, furiousness, height

Furibond, e, adj. (*etym. L.* furibundus), mad with rage, furious

Furie, sf. (*etym. L.* furia), fury, rage, madness, intensity

‡**Furieux**, se, adj. (*etym. L.* furiosus), furious, mad, wild. — sm. madman

Furoncle, sm. (*etym. L.* furunculus), boil

‡**Furtif**, ve, adj. (*etym. L.* furtivus), stealthy, furtive, secret

Fusain, sm. (*etym.* fuseau), spindle-tree, prickwood, charcoal-pencil

Fuseau, sm. (*etym. L.* fusellus), spindle, distaff. † *Jambes de —*, spindle-shanks

Fusée, sf. (*etym.* fuseau), spindle-full, (*fig.*) intrigue, rocket, fusee

Fusibilité, sf. (*etym.* fusible), fusibility

Fusil, sm. (*etym. I.* fucile, focile), steel, hammer, gun, musket. — *de chasse*, fowling-piece. — *de munition*, musket. — *à aiguille*, needle-gun. — *à vent*, air-gun. — *à deux coups*, double-barrelled gun

Fusilier, sm. (*etym.* fusil), fusilier, fusileer

§**Fusillade**, sf. (*etym.* fusiller), firing, volley of musketry

§**Fusiller**, va. (*etym.* fusil), to shoot; *se —*, vr. to fire at each other

Fustiger, va. (*etym. L.* fustigare), to whip, to flog; *se —*, vr. to scourge oneself

Fût, sm. (*etym. L.* fustis, *stick*), stock, shaft, cask

Futaie, sf. (*etym.* fût), forest, wood

§**Futaille**, sf. (*etym.* fût), cask, barrel

Futaine, sf. (*etym. prop. name* Fostat, *a suburb of Cairo*), fustian

Futé, e, adj. (*etym.* fût), crafty, cunning

Futilité, sf. (*etym. L.* futilitatem), futility

Futur, e, adj. (*etym. L.* futurus), future, to come. — s. accepted lover or mistress. — sm. the future, futurity

Fuyant, e, adj. tapering, flattened, flying

Fuyard, e, adj. (*etym.* fuir), easily scared, flying, fugitive

G

G, sm. g

Gabare, sf. (*etym.* ?), lighter, store-ship, drag-net

°**Gabelle**, sf. (*etym. O.G.* giban, *to give*), tax upon salt, salt magazine

†**Gabelou**, sm. (*etym.* gabelle), a clerk of the gabelle, a clerk of the custom-house

Gabier, sm. (*etym. I.* gabbiare), top-man

Gabionner, va. (*etym.* gabion), to cover with gabions

Gâche, sf. (*etym.* ?), staple

Gâcher, va. (*etym.* gâche), to mix, (*fig.*) to bungle at, to make a mess of

Gâchette, sf. (*etym.* gâche), tumbler, follower

Gâcheur, sm. bricklayer's man, bungler

Gâcheux, se, adj. splashy, sloppy, miry

Gâchis, sm. (*etym.* gâcher), dirt, litter, mess

Gaffe, sf. (*etym. Gael.* gaf), boat-hook, gaff

Gage, sm. (*etym. L.L.* vadium), pledge, pawn, security, forfeit, wages. *Prêter sur —s*, to be a pawnbroker. *Homme à —s*, a hired servant

Gager, va. (*etym.* gage), to wager, to bet, to give wages to

Gageure, sf. wager, bet

§**Gagnant**, adj. sm. winning, winner

§**Gagne-pain**, sm. (*etym.* gagner, pain), means of subsistence; *plur.* des gagne-pain

§**Gagne-petit**, sm. (*etym.* gagner, petit), knife-grinder; *plur* des gagne-petit

§**Gagner**, va. (*etym. O.H.G* weidanjan, *to turn out to graze*), to gain, to get, to win, to earn, to bribe, to catch. — *de vitesse*, to outstrip. — vn. to spread, to reach, to improve; *se —*, vr. to be gained, to be earned, to be catching

‡**Gai**, e, adj. (*etym. O.H.G.* gâhi, *prompt*), merry, blithesome, cheerful, gaudy. *Avoir le vin —*, to be merry in one's cups. *Être un peu —*, to be a little flustered. — adv. merrily, cheerly

Gaieté, **Gaîté**, sf. (*etym.* gai), merriment, mirth, gaiety, mettlesomeness. *De — de cœur*, wantonly. *Grosse —*, boisterous mirth

‡§**Gaillard**, e, adj. (*etym. Gael.* galach, *courage*), jovial, jolly, merry, free, spirited, gallant. — sm. fellow, blade, jovial fellow, gallant fellow. *Un — résolu*, a determined dog. *Petit —*, sly dog. *Maître du — d'avant*, captain of the forecastle. — sf. wench, (*print.*) galliard, bourgeois

§**Gaillardise**, sf. (*etym.* gaillard), jollity, (*pl.*) smutty things

Gain, sm. (*etym. see* GAGNER), gain, profit

Gaine, sf. (*etym. L.* vagina), sheath, (*archit.*) terminal

Gainier, sm. sheath-maker

Gala, sm. (*etym. O.F.* gale, *rejoicing*), gala. *Jours de —*, gala-days

‡**Galant**, e, adj. (*etym. O.F.* gale), honest, tasteful, genteel, gallant. *En — homme*, like an honest man, like a gentleman. *Un vert —*, a lover of the ladies. — sm. gallant, lover

Galanterie, sf. politeness, gallantry, compliment

Galbe, sm. (*etym. I.* garbo), (*archit.*) entasis, swell, contour

Gale, sf. (*etym.* ?), itch, scab, mange, scurf. † *Méchant comme la —*, a very demon

Galère, sf. (*etym. I.* galera), galley, (*plur.*) galleys, hard labour. *Vogue la —*, happen what may! *C'est une vraie —*, it is downright drudgery

Galerie, sf. (*etym. L.L.* galeria), gallery, drift, the company, the lookers-on

Galérien, sm. (*etm.* galère), convict, galley-slave

Galet, sm. (*etym. O.F.* gal, *pebble*), shingle, beach, shovel-board

Galetas, sm. (*etym. prop. name* Galata, *a suburb of Constantinople*), garret, attic

Galette, sf. (*etym.* galet), kind of cake, (†) an old fool

Galeux, se, adj. (*etym.* gale), infected with the itch, scabby, mangy, scurfy

‡**Galimafrée**, sf. (*etym.* ?), a stew made of broken meat

Galimatias, sm. (*etym.* ?), gibberish

Galion, sm. (*etym.* galée, *in the sense of a galley*), galleon

Galiote, sf. (*etym.* galée), galiot. — *à bombes*, bomb-ketch

Galle, sf. (*etym. L.* galla), gall. — *de chêne*, oak-apple. *Noix de —*, oak-gall

Gallicisme, sm. (*etym. L.* Gallicus), gallicism

Gallinacé, e, adj. (*etym. L.* gallinaceus), gallinaceous

Gallique, adj. (*etym.* galle), gallnut; (*etym. L.* Gallicus), gallic

Galoches, sf. plur. (*etym. L.* gallicæ, *shoes worn in Gaul*), galoshes, clogs. *Menton de —*, turned up chin

Galon, sm. lace

Galonner, va. to lace

Galop, sm. gallop

Galopade, sf. gallop

Galoper, vn. (*etym. Goth.* hlaupan, *to run*), to gallop, to run about; — va. to put on a gallop, to gallop after

Galopin, sm. (*etym.* galoper), errand-boy, scullion, urchin, blackguard

Galoubet, sm. (*etym.* ?), three-holed flute

§**Galvanique**, adj. (*etym.* galvanisme), galvanic

Galvaniser, va. (*etym.* galvanisme), to galvanize

Galvanisme, sm. (*etym. prop. name* Galvani), galvanism

Galvauder, va. (*etym.* ?), to scold, to upset, to disgrace

Gambade, sf. (*etym. O.F.* gambe = jambe), gambol, antics

Gambader, vn. to gambol

Gamelle, sf. (*etym. L.* camella, *a wooden porringer*), porringer, platter

Gamin, sm. (*etym.* ?), urchin, boy, young vagabond

Gamme, sf. (*etym. Gr.* Γ, *γάμμα*), gamut, scale. *Changer de —*, to alter one's tone

Ganache, sf. (*etym. Gr.* *γένυς, chin*), lower jaw of a horse, (*fig.*) blockhead, low easy chair

°**Gandin**, sm. (*etym. name of a character in a play*), a ridiculous dandy

Gangrène, sf. (*etym. Gr.* *γάγγραινα*), mortification, gangrene, corruption, canker

se Gangrener, vr. (*etym.* gangrène), to mortify, to grow corrupted. *Âme gangrenée*, soul cankered to the core

Gangréneux, se, adj. (*etym.* gangrène), gangrenous

Gangue, sf. (*etym. G.* gang, *a way, path*), gangue, veinstone

Ganse, sf. (*etym.* ?), ribbon, string, loop

Gant, sm. (*etym. L.L.* wantus), glove. *Aller comme un —*, to fit to a T. *Se donner des —s*, (*fig.*) to give oneself airs

Gantelet, sm. (*etym.* gant), gauntlet, hand-bandage, hand-leather

Ganter, va.n. (*etym.* gant), to glove; *se —*, vr. to put on one's gloves

Ganterie, sf. (*etym.* ganter), glove-trade, glove-making

Gantier, ère, s. (*etym.* ganter), glover

Garance, sf. (*etym.* ?),

madder. — adj. madder-coloured, red

Garancière, sf. (*etym.* garance), field of madder

Garant, e, s. (*etym. O.H.G.* worên, *to furnish, to pledge*), guarantee, answerable, bail, warrant, voucher, (*nav.*) tackle-fall

Garantie, sf. (*etym.* garantir), warranty, indemnity, warranting, pledge, voucher, security. *Bureau de* —, assay office

Garantir, va. (*etm.* garant), to guarantee, to warrant, to be security for, to secure; *se* —, vr. to screen oneself, to avoid, to keep clear

Garcette, sf. (*etym.* ?), gasket. — *de ris*, reef-line. *Coupes de* —, stripes with a rope

Garçon, sm. (*etym. L.L.* garcio), lad, boy, bachelor, journeyman, workman, waiter. — *de bureau*, office-porter. *Les* —*s d'honneur*, the bridesmen. *Faire le mauvais* —, to ruffle it. — *de caisse, de recette*, money-collector

Garde, sf. (*etym.* garder), guard, keeping, hilt, ward, fly-leaf, nurse. *Soldats de* —, guard. *Être de bonne* —, to keep a sharp look-out, to keep well. *La grand'garde*, the main-guard. *Être de* —, to be on duty. *A la* —*!* watch! *Prendre* —, to take care, to mind, to beware of. *Se donner bien* — *de*, to be cautious how. *N'avoir* — *de, soin de ne pas*, to take good heed not to. —sm. guard, guardsman, keeper, guardian. — *du corps*, — *royal*, lifeguardsman. — *à cheval*, horse-guard. — *-magasin*, store-keeper. — *champêtre*, rural. — *de commerce*, sheriff's officer, bailiff

Garde-chasse, sm. game-keeper

Garde-chiourme, sm. convict-keeper

Garde-feu, sm. fire-guard

Garde-fou, sm. rail, hand-rail, parapet

Garde-frein, sm. brakes-man

Garde-malade, sm. f. nurse

Garde-manger, sm. larder, pantry, buttery

Garde-meuble, sm. lumber-room, store-room

Garder, va. (*etym. O.H.G.* wartên, *to take care*), to keep, to hold back, to withhold, to look after, to take care of, to nurse; *se* —, vr. to keep, to last, to beware, to take care, to guard

Garde-robe, sf. wardrobe, closet

Gardeur, se, s. (*etym.* garder), keeper

Garde-vue, sm. screen

Gardien, ne, s.adj. (*etym.* garder), keeper, guardian

Gardon, sm. (*etym. L.L.* gardio), roach

Gare! interj. (*imperat. of the verb* garer), get out of the way, look out

Gare, sf. (*etym.* garer), station, form, terminus, basin. *Chef de* —, superintendent. *Livrable en* —, to be given when called for

Garenne, sf. (*etym.* warenna), warren, rabbit-warren

Garer, va. (*etym. H.G.* warnôn, *to take care*), to stop, to moor; *se* —, vr. to get out of the way, to guard against, to stop at a siding-place, to arrive at the station

se Gargariser, vr. (*etym. Gr.* γαργαρίζειν), to gargle one's throat

Gargarisme, sm. (*etym.* gargariser), gargarism, gargle

†**Gargote**, sf. (*etym.* gargoter, *to make a noise in boiling*), cook-shop

†**Gargotier, ère**, s. (*etym.* gargote), keeper of a cook-shop, bad cook

§**Gargouille**, sf. (*etym. L.L.* gargula, *throat*), gurgoyle, water spout, water shoot

§**Gargouillement**, sm. (*etym.* gargouille), gurgling

Gargousse, sf. (*etym. corrupt. of* cartouche), cannon-cartridge

Garigue, sf. (*etym. Prov.* garric, *oak*), moor, heath

Garnement, sm. (*etym.* garnir), scapegrace

Garni, e, adj. furnished. *Hôtel* —, lodging-house. *Maison* —*e*, private lodging-house. *Loger, louer en* —, to live in furnished lodgings, to let lodgings

Garnir, va. (*etym. O.H.G.* warnôn, *to take care*), to furnish, to stock, to garnish, to stuff, to fledge; *se* —, vr. to provide oneself, to provide

Garnisaire, sm. (*etym.* garnir), bailiff's man

Garnison, sf. (*etym.* garnir), garrison, bailiff's men

Garniture, sf. (*etym.* garnir), furniture, ornaments, trimming, set

Garrot, sm. (*etym.* ?), withers

Garrotte, sf. (*etym.* garrot), garotte

Garrotter, va. (*etym.* garrotte), to pinion, to bind

Gars, sm. (*etym. see* GARÇON), lad

Gascon, sm. (*etym. L. prop. name* Vasco), Gascon, braggar

Gasconnade, sf. (*etym.* Gascon), gasconade. ‡ *Dire des* —*s*, to draw the long bow

Gasconner, vn. to speak with a Gascon accent, to brag

§**Gaspillage**, sm. (*etym.* gaspiller), squandering, wasting

§**Gaspiller**, va. (*etm. O.H.G.* gaspildan, *to waste*), to waste, to squander away

§**Gaspilleur**, sm. (*etym.* gaspiller), squanderer

Gastralgie, sf. (*etym. Gr.* γαστραλγία), gastralgia

Gastrique, adj. (*etym. Gr.* γαστήρ, *stomach*), gastric

Gastrite, sf. (*etym. Gr.* γαστήρ), gastritis

Gastronome, sm. (*etym.* gastronomie), epicure

Gastronomie, sf. (*etym.* γαστρονομία), gastronomy

Gastronomique, adj. gastronomic

Gâteau, sm. cake, honey-comb. — *des rois*, twelfth-cake. ‡ *Avoir part au* —, to have a share of the profit

Gâte-métier, sm. spoil-trade

Gâter, va. (*etym. M.H.G.* wastel, *cake*), to spoil, to pet, to taint; *se* —, vr. to spoil, to get spoiled

Gâte-tout, sm. mar-all

†**Gauche**, adj. (*etym. O.H.G.* welk, *weak*), left, crooked, ill-shaped, awkward, bashful. — sf. left hand, left wing. — sm. awkwardness

Gaucher, ère, adj. (*etym.* gauche), left-handed

Gaucherie, sf. awkward thing, clumsiness

Gauchir, va. (*etym. O.H.G.* wankjan, *to yield*), to turn aside, to flinch, to shuffle, to warp

Gaude, sf. (*etym. G* waude), weld, dyer's weed, hasty pudding

Gaudriole, sf. (*etym. O.F.* gaudir, *to make merry*), jolly song, broad jest

Gaufre, sf. (*etym. G.* waffel), honey-comb, waffle, wafer

Gaufrer, va. (*etym.* gaufre), to goffer

Gaufreur, sm. (*etym.* gaufrer), gofferer

Gaule, sf. (*etym.* Fries. walu, *pole*), pole, switch

Gauler, va. (*etym.* gaule), to beat, to knock down

se Gausser, vr. (*etym.* ?), to jeer at, to make game of

Gavotte, sf. (*etym. prop. name* Gavots, *the inhabitants of the district of Gap, in France*), kind of dance

Gaz, sm. (*etym. G.* geist), gas. *Usine à* —, gasworks

Gaze, sf. (*etym. prop. name* Gaza, *a town*), gauze

Gazéiforme, adj. (*etym.* gaz), gasiform

Gazer, va. (*etym.* gaze), to cover with a gauze, to veil, to gloss over

Gazetier, sm. (*etym.* gazette), gazetteer

Gazette, sf. (*etym. I.* gazzetta, *a small coin*), newspaper

Gazeux, se, adj. (*etym.* gaz), gaseous

Gazomètre, sm. (*etym.* gaz, *Gr.* μέτρον, *measure*), gasometer

Gazon, sm. (*etym. O.H.G.* waso), grass, greensward

Gazonner, va. (*etym.* gazon), to cover with grass

§**Gazouillement**, sm. (*etym.* gazouiller), warbling, chirping, prattling

§**Gazouiller**, vn. (*etym. Bret.* geiz, geld, *murmur*), to warble, to twitter, to chirrup, to babble, to prattle; — va. to warble out, to lisp out

Geai, sm. (*etym.* gai ?), jay

Géant, e, s. (*etym. L.* gigantem), giant, giantess

Géhenne, sf. (*etym. Heb.* geia, hinnom, *valley of Hinnom*), Gehenna

Geindre, va. (*etym. L.* gemere), to moan, to whine

Gélatine, sf. (*etym. L.* gelare, *to freeze*), gelatin

Gélatineux, se, adj. (*etym.* gélatine), gelatinous, gelatine

Gelée, sf. (*etym.* geler), frost, jelly. — *blanche*, hoar-frost

Geler, va.n., *se* —, vr. (*etym. L.* gelare), to freeze

Gelinotte, sf. (*etym. O.F.* geline = *L.* gallina), pullet. — *des bois*, hazel-hen

Gémeaux, sm. plur. (*etym. L.* gemini), the Gemini, the Twins

Gémir, vn. (*etym. L.* gemere), to groan, to moan, to wail, to coo

Gémissant, e, adj. groaning, moaning, wailing

Gémissement, sm. (*etym.* gémir), groan, moan, wail, cooing

Gemme, sf. adj. (*etym. L.* gemma), gem. *Pierre* —, gem. *Sel* —, rock salt

Gémonies, sf. plur. (*etym. L.* gemoniæ [scalæ]), gemoniæ. *Traîné aux* —, (*fig.*) vowed to execration

Gênant, e, adj. troublesome, in the way, annoying, inconvenient

Gencive, sf. (*etym. L.* gingiva), gum

Gendarme, sm. (*etym.* gens, de, arme), gendarme, thief-catcher, man-at-arms, virago, flaw

se Gendarmer, vr. (*etym.* gendarme), to fire up

Gendarmerie, sf. (*etym.* gendarmer), gendarmery

Gendre, sm. (*etym. L.* generum, *acc. s. of* gener), son-in-law

Gêne, sf. (*contract. of* gehenne), rack, torture, tightness, uneasiness, inconvenience, trouble, annoyance, straitened circumstances. *Être sans* —, to make oneself at home

Généalogie, sf. (*etym. Gr.* γενεαλογία), genealogy, pedigree

§**Généalogique**, adj. (*etym.* généalogie), genealogical

Généalogiste, sm. (*etym.* généalogie), genealogist

Gêner, va. (*etym.* gêne), to hinder, to impede, to incommode, to be too tight, to squeeze, to straiten; *se* —, vr. to put oneself to inconvenience, to stand upon ceremony, to squeeze

Généralat, sm. (*etym.* général), generalship

Générale, sf. (*etym.* général), the general

Généralisation, sf. (*etym.* généraliser), generalization, generalizing

Généraliser, va. (*etym.* général), to generalize

Généralissime, sm. (*etym. L.* generalissimus), generalissimo

Généralité, sf. (*etym. L.* generalitatem), generality, generalship

Générateur, trice, adj. (*etym. L.* generatorem), generating

Génératif, ve, adj. (*etym. L.* generare), generative

Généreux, se, adj. (*etym. L.* generosus), generous, noble, munificent, handsome

Générique, adj. (*etym. L.* genus), generic, generical

Générosité, sf. (*etym. L.* generositatem), generosity, bounteousness

Génèse, sf. (*etym. Gr.* γένεσις), Genesis

Genêt, sm. (*etym. L.* genista), broom; (*etym. Sp.* gineto, *light horseman*), jennet

Genévrier, sm. (*etym.* genièvre), juniper, juniper-tree

Génie, sm. (*etym. L.* genius), genius, engineering, engineers. *Suivre son* —, to follow one's bent

Genièvre, sm. (*etym. L.* juniperus), juniper-tree, juniper

Génisse, sf. (*etym. L.* junicem), heifer

Génitif, sm. (*etym. L.* genitivus [casus]), genitive, genitive case

***Géniture**, sf. (*etym. L.* genitura), offspring, progeny

Genou, sm. (*etym. L.* geniculum, *dimin. of* genu, *knee*), knee

Genouillère, sf. (*etym.* genou), knee-piece, knee-cap

***Génovéfain**, sm. (*etym. L.* Genovefa, *Lat. name of* Geneviève), monk of St. Genevieve

Genre, sm. (*etym. L.* genere, *abl. of* genus), genus, kind, species, description, style, gender. *Le bon* —, fashionable manners

Gens, sm. f. plur. (*etym. L.* gens), people, persons, servants. *Le droit des* —, the law of nations

***Gent**, sf. (*etym. L.* gentem), race, gentry, tribe

Gentiane, sf. (*etym. L.* gentiana), gentian, feldwort, baldmony

Gentil, sm. (*etym. L.* gentilis), gentile. —, —*ille*, adj. nice, pretty

‡**Gentilhomme**, sm. nobleman, lord, noble

‡**Gentilhommière**, sf. poor mansion

‡**Gentillâtre**, sm. lordling, country squire

‡**Gentillesse**, sf. prettiness, gracefulness. ‡ *Faire une* — *à*, to do an act of politeness to

Gentiment, adv. (*etym.* gentil), prettily, nicely

Génuflexion, sf. (*etym. L.* genuflexionem), genuflection

Géodésie, sf. (*etym. Gr.* γεωδαισία), geodesy

Géographe, sm. (*etym. Gr.* γεωγράφος), geographer, surveying engineer

Géographie, sf. (*etym. Gr.* γεωγραφία), geography

‡**Géographique**, adj. (*etym. L.* geographicus), geographical

Geôle, sf. (*etym. L.* cavea, *cage*), gaol, jail, prison

Geôlier, sm. (*etym.* geôle), gaoler, gaol-keeper, turnkey

Geôlière, sf. gaoler's wife

Géologie, sf. (*etym. Gr.* γῆ, *earth*, λόγος, *doctrine*), geology

‡**Géologique**, adj. (*etym.* géologie), geological

Géologue, sm. geologist

‡**Géométral, e**, adj. geometrical, geometral

Géomètre, sm. (*etym. Gr.* γεωμέτρης), geometrician, mathematician. *Arpenteur* —, land-surveyor

Géométrie, sf. (*etym. Gr.* γεωμετρία), geometry

Géométrique, adj. (*etym. Gr.* γεωμετρικός), geometrical, geometric

Gérant, sm. (*etym.* gérer), manager, director, editor

Gerbe, sf. (*etym. O.H.G.* garba), sheaf. *Lier, mettre en* —*s*, to bind up into sheaves

Gercer, va., *se* —, vr. (*etym. L.L.* gersa), to chap, to crack, to cranny

Gerçure, sf. chap, crack

Gérer, va. (*etym. L.* gerere), to manage, to administer. — *une tutelle*, to administer the estate of a ward

Germain, e, adj. (*etym. L.* germanus), german, first *Cousin* —, first cousin. *Cousin issu de* —*s*, cousin once removed, second cousin

Germanisme, sm. (*etym.* germain), germanism

Germe, sm. (*etym. L.* germen), germ, sprout, shoot, cause, principle

Germer, vn. to shoot, to sprout, to germinate, to spring up

Gérondif, sm. (*etym. L.* gerundivus [modus]), gerund

Gésier, sm. (*etym. L.* gigeria), gizzard

***Gésir**, vn. (*etym. L.* jacere), to lie. *Ci-gît*, here lies

Geste, sm. (*etym. L.* gestus), gesture, action

Gestes, sm. plur. (*etym. L.* gesta), exploits, achievements

Gesticulateur, sm. (*etym. L.* gesticulatorem), gesticulator

Gesticuler, vn. (*etym. L.* gesticulare), to gesticulate

Gestion, sf. (*etym. L.* gestionem), management, administration

Gibbeux, se, adj. (*etym. L.* gibbosus), gibbous

Gibbosité, sf. gibbousness, gibbosity

Gibecière, sf. (*etym.* gibier), game-bag, juggler's-bag

Gibelin, sm. (*etym.* [Conrad von] Weibelingen), Ghibelline

Gibelotte, sf. (*etym. O.F.* gibelet), stewed rabbit

Giberne, sf. (*etym. L.L.* giba, *a bale*), pouch, cartridge-box

Gibet, sm. (*etym. I.* giubbetto), gibbet, gallows

Gibier, sm. (*etym. O.F.* gibeer = giboyer), game. — *à plume, à poil*, wild fowl, venison. *Gros* —, *menu* —, large game, small game. — *de potence*, gallows-bird

Giboulée, sf. (*etym. O.F.* gibe, *charge*), shower, hail-shower

Giboyer, vn. (*etym. L.L.* gibicare), to go a hunting

Giboyeux, se, adj. (*etym.* giboyer), abounding in game

‡**Gifle**, sf. (*etym.* ?), cheek, box on the ears

‡**Gifler**, va. (*etym.* gifle), to give a box on the ears

‡**Gigantesque**, adj. (*etym. I.* gigantesco), gigantic, huge

Gigot, sm. (*etym.* gigue), leg of mutton

‡**Gigotter**, vn. (*etym.* gigot), to fidget, to kick about

Gigue, sf. (*etym.* ?), leg; (*etym. O.H.G.* gige, *a violin*), jig

Gilet, sm. (*etym. prop. name* Gille ?), waistcoat

Gille, sm. (*etym. prop. name*), clown, ninny

***Gindre**, sm. (*etym. L.* junior), baker's man

Gingembre, sm. (*etym. L.* zinziberis), ginger

Girafe, sf. (*etym. Ar.* zurâfet), giraffe

Girofle, sm. (*etym. Gr.* καρυόφυλλον), clove. *Clou de* —, clove

Giroflée, sf. (*etym.* girofle), gilly-flower, stock. — *jaune*, wall-flower

Giroflier, sm. (*etym.* girofle), clove-tree

Giron, sm. (*etym. M.H.G.* gêre, *edge of a dress*), lap, bosom, pale, (*archit.*) tread

Girouette, sf. (*etym. L.* gyrare, *to turn*), weathercock, vane

Gisement, sm. (*etym.* gésir), bearing

Gîte, sm. (*etym.* gésir), home, lodging, halting-place, form, seat, deposit, locality, nether millstone

‡**Gîter**, vn., *se* —, vr. (*etym.* gîte), to lodge, to perch

Givre, sm. (*etym. L.* gelicidium), rime, hoar-frost

Glaçant, e, adj. icy, freezing

Glace, sf. (*etym. L.* glacies), ice, freezing-point, coldness, plate-glass, looking-glass, mirror, coach-window, flaw

Glacé, e, past part. adj. frozen, icy, cold, glazed

Glacer, va. (*etym.* glace), to freeze, to chill, to glaze, to ice

Glacial, e, adj. (*etym. L.* glacialis), icy, freezing, frigid, chilly

Glacier, sm. (*etym.* glace), glacier, confectioner

Glacière, sf. (*etym.* glacier), glacier, ice-house

Glacis, sm. (*etym.* glace), sloping bank, glacis, glazing

Glaçon, sm. (*etym.* glace), block of ice

Gladiateur, sm. (*etym. L.* gladiatorem), gladiator

Glaïeul, sm. (*etym. L.* gladiolus), iris, gladiole, cornflag

Glaire, sf. (*etym. L.L.* clara ovi, *white of an egg*), glair

Glaireux, se, adj. (*etym.* glaire), glaireous, mucous

Glaise, sf. (*etym. L.L.* glis, *thick earth*), clay, loam

Glaiser, va. to loam

Glaiseux, se, adj. loamy

Glaisière, sf. clay-pit

Glaive, sm. (*etym. L.* gladius), sword, falchion, blade, brand

Gland, sm. (*etym. L.* glandem), acorn, tassel

Glande, sf. (*etym. L.* glans), gland, kernel. *Avoir des* — *au cou*, to have the mumps

Glaner, va. (*etym. L.L.* gelima, gelina, *handful*), to glean

Glaneur, se, s. gleaner

Glapir, vn. (*etym. O.H.G.* klaffôn, *to bark*), to yelp, to squeak, to scream

Glapissant, e, adj. yelping, squeaking

Glapissement, sm. yelp, yelping, squeaking

Glas, sm. (*etym. L.* classicum, *signal made with the trumpet*), knell

Glauque, adj. (*etym. L.* glaucus), sea-green

Glèbe, sf. (*etym. L.* gleba), glebe, soil, clod, sod

Glissade, sf. (*etym.* glisser), slip, sliding, slide

Glissant, e, adj. slippery

Glisser, vn. (*etym. O.* glitschen), to slip, to slide, to glide, to touch lightly; — va. to slip, to insinuate; *se* —, vr. to slip, to glide, to steal, to creep

Glisseur, sm. slider

Glissoire, sf. slide

Globulaire, adj. globular, globose

Globuleux, se, adj. (*etym.* globule), globulous, globose

Gloire, sf. (*etym. L.* gloria), glory, halo, halo of glory. *Se faire* — *de*, to glory in

‡**Gloria**, sm. cup of coffee mixed with brandy

‡**Glorieux, se**, adj. (*etym. L.* gloriosus), glorious, glorified, conceited. — s. boaster, braggart. *Faire le* —, to play the braggart

Glorifier, va. (*etym. L.* glorificare), to glorify, to give glory to; *se* —, vr. to glory

Gloriole, sf. (*etym. L.* gloriola), vain-glory, empty pride

Glose, sf. (*etym. Gr.* γλῶσσα, *tongue*), gloss, glossology, parody, (*fig.*) comment, reflection

Gloser, va.n. to gloss, to expound, to comment, to carp at

Glossaire, sm. (*etym. L.* glossarium), glossary

Glossateur, sm. (*etym. L.* glossa), commentator

†**Glouglou,** sm. (*onomat.*), gurgling, gurgle

Gloussement, sm. (*etym.* glousser), clucking

Glousser, vn. (*etym. L.* glocire), to cluck, to gobble

Glouteron, sm. (*etym. O.F.* gletteron, *from* gletton), burdock

‖**Glouton, ne,** s. adj. (*etym. L.* glutonem), glutton, gluttonous, greedy

Gloutonnerie, sf. gluttony, greediness

Glu, sf. (*etym. L.* glutem), bird-lime, glue

Gluant, e, adj. (*etym.* glu), limy, slimy, sticky

Gluau, sm. lime-twig

Gluer, va. (*etym.* glu), to lime, to make sticky or slimy

Glutineux, se, adj. (*etym. L.* glutinosus), glutinous

Glyconique, *also* **Glyconien,** adj. m. (*etym. Gr.* Γλύκων, *prop. name*)

Glyptique, sf. (*etym. Gr.* γλυπτός, *engraved*), the art of engraving on precious stones

Gnostique, sm. (*etym. Gr.* γνωστικός), Gnostic

‡**Go (tout de),** loc. adv. (*etym.* gober), freely, without hindrance

Gobelet, sm. (*etym. L.L.* gubellus, *small cup*), goblet, mug, cup, buttery. *Joueur de —s,* juggler, (*fig.*) trickster

Gobelins, sm. plur. (*etym. prop. name of a family*), the Paris manufactory of tapestry

†**Gobelotter,** vn. (*etym.* gobelet), to drink

Gobe-mouches, sm. fly-catcher, ninny

Gober, va. (*etym. Gaël.* gob, gab, *mouth*), to swallow down, to gulp down. *— des mouches, du vent,* to stand idly gaping

†**se Goberger,** vr. (*etym. ?*), to laugh heartily at, to enjoy oneself

Godelureau, sm. (*etym. ?*), spark, coxcomb

Goder, vn. (*etym.* godet), to pucker

Godet, sm. (*etym. L.* guttus, *a drinking cup*), cup, mug, saucer, trough, drip-receiver, bowl

Godiveau, sm. (*etym. ?*), force-meat-pie

Goëland, sm. (*etym. Bret.* gwela, *to moan*), sea-gull, gull

Goëlette, sf. (*etym.* goëland), schooner

Goëmon, sm. (*etym. ?*), sea-weed

†**Gogo (à),** loc. adv. (*etym. ?*), in plenty

Goguenard, e, adj. (*etym. O.F.* gogue, *joke, jest*), bantering, jeering

Goguenarder, va. (*etym.* goguenard), to banter, to jeer

†**Goguettes,** sf. plur. (*etym. O.F.* gogue), merry stories. *Être en —,* to be in a merry mood

†**Goinfre,** sm. (*etym.* gouffre? gonfler ?), gormandizer, guzzler

†**Goinfrer,** vn. to guzzle

†**Goinfrerie,** sf. the act of guzzling

Goître, sm. (*etym. L.* guttur), wen

Goîtreux, se, adj. (*etym.* goître), wenny. *Un —,* wen-necked person

Golfe, sm. (*etym. L. Gr.* κόλφος, *gulf*), gulf, bay

Gomme, sf. (*etym. L.* gummi), gum. *— élastique,* India-rubber. *— adragante,* gum-dragon. *— gutte,* gamboge

Gommer, va. to gum

Gommeux, se, adj. gummy

Gommier, sm. gum-tree

Gond, sm. (*etym. L.L.* gumphus, *a nail*), hinge. *Mettre quelqu'un hors des —s,* quite to exasperate a person

Gondole, sf. (*etym. L. Gr.* κόνδυ, *a drinking cup*), gondola

Gonflement, sm. swelling, inflation, distension

Gonfler, va. (*etym. L.* conflare), to swell, to inflate, to distend ; *se —,* vr. to be swollen up

Gorge, sf. (*etym. L.* gurges), throat, gullet, gorge, breast, orifice, pass, strait, groove, roller. *Mal de —,* sore throat. *A pleine —,* at the top of one's lungs. *Faire rendre — à quelqu'un,* to make disgorge. *Faire — chaude de,* to feast upon, to jeer at. *Sous- —,* throat-lash. *—-de-pigeon,* shot-colour

Gorgée, sf. (*etym.* gorge), draught, mouthful

Gorger, va. (*etym.* gorge), to gorge, to glut ; *se —,* vr. to gorge or glut oneself

Gorgerette, sf. (*etym.* gorge), a kind of tippet

Gorgone, sf. (*etym. Gr.* Γοργώ), Gorgon

Gosier, sm. (*etym. ?*), throat, voice. ‡ *Avoir le — sec,* to be quite thirsty. *Coup de —,* breath

Gothique, adj. sm. (*etym. L.* gothicus), Gothic. *En caractères —s,* in black-letter

Gouache, sf. (*etym. I.* guazzo), water-colours

†§**Gouailler,** va. (*etym. ?*), to jeer, to banter

†§**Gouailleur, se,** s. a banterer

Goudron, sm. (*etym. Ar.* kattrân), pitch, tar

Goudronner, va. (*etym.* goudron), to tar, (*nav.*) to pay. *Toile goudronnée,* tarpaulin

Gouffre, sm. (*etym. see* GOLFE), gulf, abyss, whirlpool

Goujat, sm. (*etym. ?*), soldier's servant, hodman, vulgar fellow

Goujon, sm. (*etym. L.* gobionem), gudgeon, iron pin

Goulet, sm. (*etym. O.F.* goule = gueule), narrow entrance of a harbour

Goulot, sm. (*etym.* goule), neck

‡**Goulu, e,** adj. (*etym.* goule), gluttonous, greedy

§**Goupille,** sf. (*etym. O.F.* goupil = *fox*), pin

§**Goupillon,** sm. (*etym.* goupil), holy-water sprinkler, brush

°**Gourd, e,** adj. (*etym. L.* gurdus), benumbed

Gourde, sf. (*etym. O.F.* gourdi, *swollen*), gourd, piastre

Gourdin, sm. (*etym.* gourd), cudgel, club, thick stick

Gourmade, sf. (*etym.* gourmer), blow in the face. *En venir aux —s,* to come to fisticuffs

Gourmand, e, adj. s. (*etym. ?*), greedy, gluttonous, glutton, gourmand, sucker. *Branches —s,* off-shoots, suckers

Gourmander, va. to chide, to rebuke sharply, to curb, to check

Gourmandise, sf. greediness, gluttony

Gourme, sf. (*etym. ?*), strangles, bad humours. *Jeter sa —,* to sow one's wild oats

Gourmer, va. (*etym.* gourme ?), to put the curb-chain on, to pommel, to cuff. *Être gourmé,* to be stiff and starched, to be solemn ; *se —,* vr. to pommel each other

Gourmet, sm. (*etym. D.* grom, *a lad*), judge of wine, epicure

Gourmette, sf. (*etym.* gourmer), curb-chain, curb

Gousse, sf. (*etym. ?*), shell, husk, cod. *— d'ail,* clove of garlic

Gousset, sm. (*etym. dimin. of* gousse), arm-pit, gusset, pocket, fob, bracket. ‡ *Avoir le — bien garni,* to have one's pocket well lined

Goût, sm. (*etym. L.* gustus), taste, relish, flavour, savour. *Mettre en —,* to whet one's appetite

Goûter, va. to taste, to relish, to try, to approve of, to like ; — vn. to lunch ; *se —,* vr. to like each other. — sm. luncheon, lunch

Goutte, sf. (*etym. L.* gutta), drop, sup, water-drop, the gout. *Ne voir —,* not to see at all

Gouttelette, sf. (*etym.* goutte), little drop

Goutteux, se, adj. (*etym.* goutte), gouty

Gouttière, sf. (*etym.* goutte), gutter, spout, fore-edge, groove

§**Gouvernail,** sm. (*etym. L.* gubernaculum), rudder, helm. *Barre de —,* tiller. *— de fortune,* jury-rudder

Gouvernante, sf. governor's wife, governess, housekeeper

Gouvernants, sm. plur. rulers, those who govern

Gouverne, sf. (*etym.* gouverner), guide, guidance. *Pour votre —,* for your guidance

Gouvernement, sm. (*etym.* gouverner), direction, management, government

°**Gouvernemental, e,** adj. (*etym.* gouverner), pertaining to government

Gouverner, va. (*etym. L.* gubernare), to steer, to manage, to rule, to govern ; — vn. to answer the helm, to steer. *Ne pas —,* to have no steerage room. *Se —,* vr. to govern oneself, to act, to be governed

Gouverneur, sm. (*etym. L.* gubernatorem), governor, tutor, steersman

Grabat, sm. (*etym. Gr.* κράβατος), pallet, truckle-bed. *Être sur le —,* to be wretchedly poor

‡**Grabuge,** sm. (*etym. G.* graben, *to dig*), quarrel

Grâce, sf. (*etym. L.* gratia), favour, grace, thanks, mercy, forgiveness, gracefulness

Gracier, va. to pardon

Gracieuseté, sf. (*etym.* gracieux), graciousness

‖**Gracieux, se,** adj. (*etym. L.* gratiosus), graceful, gracious, pleasant, engaging

Grade, sm. (*etym. L* gradus), rank, degree

Gradé, adj. m. *Militaire —,* non-commissioned officer

Gradin, sm. (*etym.* grade), shelf, benches, seats

‖**Graduel, le,** adj. (*etym. L.* gradus), gradual. — sm. gradual

Graduer, va. (*etym. L.* gradus), to graduate

§**Graillon,** sm. (*etym. O.F.* graille = gril), broken victuals, burnt grease

Grain, sm. (*etym. L.* granum), grain, berry, bead, squall. *— de beauté,* mole, beauty-spot

Graine, sf. (*etym.* grain), seed, eggs, set, breed. *Monter en —,* to run to seed. ‡ *C'est de la — de niais,* it is only fit to catch fools with

Grainier, ère, smf. (*etym.* grain), seedsman, seedswoman

Graissage, sm. (*etym.* graisse), greasing, grease

Graisse, sf. (*etym.* gras), fat, grease, dripping, kitchen-stuff

‡**Graisser,** va. to grease. ‡ *— le marteau,* to fee the porter. ‡ *— la patte à,* to grease the fist of. *— les épaules à,* to thwack the shoulders of. — vn. to get oily

Graisseux, se, adj. (*etym.* graisse), greasy, oily, fat

Graminée, sf. adj. f. (*etym. L.* gramen), gramineous plant, gramineous, grassy

Grammaire, sf. (*etym. L.L.* gramma), grammar

Grammairien, sm. (*etym.* grammaire), grammarian

§**Grand, e,** adj. (*etym. L.* grandis), great, large, big, wide, spacious, high, tall, lofty. ‡ *A la —e*, grandly. — sm. great man, magnate, grandee

Grandesse, sf. (*etym.* grand), rank of a grandee

Grandeur, sf. (*etym.* grand), greatness, magnitude, size, largeness, height

Grandiose, adj. (*etym. I.* grandioso), grand, imposing

Grandir, vn. (*etym. L.* grandire), to grow, to increase in size; *se* —, vr. to make oneself taller or greater

Grandissime, adj. (*etym. L.* grandissimus), very great

Grand'maman, sf. grandmamma

Grand'mère, sf. grandmother

Grand-oncle, sm. great uncle

Grand-père, sm. grandfather, grandsire

Grand'tante, sf. greataunt

Grange, sf. (*etym. L.L.* granica), barn. *Aire de* —, barn-floor. *Mettre en* —, to house

Granit, sm. (*etym. L.L.* granitum), granite

Granitique, adj. (*etym.* granit), granite, granitic

Granivore, adj. (*etym. L.* granum, vorare), granivorous. *Les —s*, granivorous birds

Granuleux, se, adj. (*etym. L.* granulum, *dimin. of* granum), granulous, granular

Graphique, adj. (*etym. Gr.* γραφικός), graphical

Grappe, sf. (*etym. L.L.* grappa), cluster, bunch, grape-shot, grape. ‡ *Mordre à la* —, (*fig.*) to jump at the proposal

§**Grappiller,** va.n. (*etym.* grappe), to glean in the vines, (†) to make one's little profits

§**Grappilleur, se,** smf. (*etym.* grappiller), a grape gleaner

§**Grappillon,** sm. small cluster, small bunch

Grappin, sm. (*etym. see* Grappe), grappling-iron, grapnel

§**Gras, Grasse,** adj. (*etym.* grassus), fat, corpulent, rich, fleshy, heavy, greasy, slippery, smutty. *Les jours* —, shrove-tide. — sm. fat, meat, flesh. — *-fondu*, sm. *or* — *-fondure*, sf. molten grease. — adv. thick. *Peindre à* —, to touch up a picture when the colours are still wet

Gras-double, sm. tripe

Grasseyement, sm. (*etm.* gras), lisp, lisping

Grasseyer, vn. to lisp, to speak thick

§**Grassouillet, te,** adj. (*etym.* gras), plump, fatty

Gratification, sf. (*etym. L.* gratificationem), gratuity, extra pay

Gratifier, va. (*etym. L.* gratificare), to bestow on, to favour

Gratin, sm. (*etym.* gratter), burned part

Gratte-papier, sm. quill-driver; *plur.* des gratte-papier

Gratter, va.n. (*etym. L.L.* cratare), to scrape, to scratch, to scoop out, to dig. † — *du papier*, to put black upon white; *se* —, vr. to scratch oneself, (†) to caress each other

Grattoir, sm. (*etym.* gratter), scraper, scratching-knife

§**Gratuit, e,** adj. (*etym. L.* gratuitus), gratuitous

Gratuité, sf. (*etym.* gratuit), gratuitousness

§**Grave,** adj. (*etym. L.* gravis), heavy, grave, sedate, demure, weighty, serious, deep, low

Graveleux, se, adj. (*etym.* gravelle), gravelly, gritty, affected with gravel, smutty

Gravelle, sf. (*etym.* grave = grève), gravel

Gravelure, sf. (*etym. see* Graveleux), loose talk

Graver, va. (*etym. G.* graben, *to hollow*), to engrave, to grave, to impress on; *se* —, vr. to be engraved, to impress oneself

Graveur, sm. (*etym.* graver), engraver. — *sur bois*, wood-engraver. — *à l'eau forte*, etcher

Gravier, sm. (*etym.* grave = grève), gravel, grit

Gravir, va.n. (*etym.* ?), to climb up, to ascend

Gravité, sf. (*etym. L.* gravitatem), gravity, graveness, sedateness, demureness, momentousness, deepness

Graviter, vn. (*etym. L.* gravis, *heavy*), to gravitate

Gravois, Gravats, sm. plur. (*etym. see* Gravier), rubbish

Gravure, sf. (*etym.* graver), engraving, cut, print. — *à l'eau forte*, etching

Gré, sm. (*etym. L.* gratum), will, pleasure, mind, taste, agreement. *Savoir bon* — *à quelqu'un de quelque chose*, to be thankful to a person for a thing. *De — ou de force*, by fair means or foul. *Bon —, mal —*, willingly or unwillingly. *De — à —*, by mutual agreement

Grec, sm. adj. Greek, Grecian, blackleg, usurer

Gréciser, va. (*etym.* Grec), to grecize

Grecque, sf. adj. (*etm.* Grec), Grecian lady, (*arch.*) fret-work, (*bookbind.*) saw

Gredin, sm. (*etym. Scand.* gråd, *hunger*), scamp, scoundrel, rascal, lap-dog

Gredinerie, sf. (*etym.* gredin), rascality, villany

Gréement, Grément, sm. (*etym.* gréer), rigging

Gréer, va (*etym. G.* gereiten, *to prepare*), to rig, to fit out

Gréeur, sm. (*etym.* gréer), rigger

Greffe, sm. (*etym. O.F.* grefe, *a style for writing*; *Gr.* γραφεῖον), clerk's office, record office. — sf. graft, grafting

Greffer, va. (*etym.* greffe), to graft, to whipgraft; *se* —, vr. to be grafted

Greffier, sm. (*etym.* greffe), clerk of the court, registrar

Greffoir, sm. (*etym.* greffe), grafting-knife

Grège, adj. f. (*etym. I.* greggio, grezzo, *raw*). *Soie* —, raw silk

***Grégeois,** adj. m. (*etym. L.* Graecensis). *Feu* —, Greek fire

Grégorien, ne, adj. (*etym. proper name* Gregorius), Gregorian

***Grègues,** sf. plur. (*etym. I.* grechesco, *after the Greek fashion*), breeches, galligaskins. † *Tirer ses* —, to scamper off

Grêle, adj. (*etym. L.* gracilis), slender, lank, puny, shrill. — sf. (*etym. see* Grésil), hail, a hail-storm

Grêler, v. imp. to hail; — va. to ravage with hail, to ruin

Grelin, sm. (*etym. G.* greling), cablet, line

Grêlon, sm. (*etym.* grêle, *subst.*), hail-stone

Grelot, sm. (*etym. L.* crotalum, *small bell*), bell, small bell

Grelotter, va. (*etym.* grelot), to shiver with cold

Grenade, sf. (*etym. L.* (malum) granatum, *an apple full of grains*), pomegranate, grenade, hand-grenade

Grenadier, sm. (*etym.* grenade), pomegranate-tree, grenadier

§**Grenaille,** sf. (*etym.* grain), metal in grains, small shot

Grenat, sm. (*etym. L.* granatum), garnet, crimson

Greneler, va. (*etym.* grain), to shagreen, to rough-grain

Grener, vn. (*etym.* grain), to seed; — va. to reduce into grains

Grèneterie, sf. (*etym.* grènetier), seed-trade

Grènetier, ère, s. (*etym.* grain), corn-chandler, seedsman

Grenier, sm. (*etym. L.* granarium), loft, granary, garret, attic

§**Grenouille,** sf. (*etym. L.* ranunculus *or* ranuncula, *dimin. of* rana, *frog*), frog

§**Grenouillère,** sf. (*etym.* grenouille), marsh, fen

Grenu, e, adj. (*etym.* grain), full of grain, rough-grained, clotted

Grès, sm. (*etym. O.H.G.* griez, grioz, *sand*), sandstone

Grésil, sm. (*etym.* grès ?), sleet

§**Grésiller,** v. imp. (*etym.* grésil), to sleet; — va. to shrivel up

Grève, sf. (*etym. a root* grav *or* grau), sands, strand, sandy beach, strike. *Faire —, se mettre en —*, to strike

Grever, va. (*etym. L.* gravari, *to be burdensome*), to injure, to burden, to encumber

§**Gribouillage,** sm. (*etym.* gribouiller), daub, scrawl

§**Gribouiller,** vn. (*etym. D.* krabbelen, *to scribble*), to daub, to scrawl

§***Grief, ève,** adj. (*etym. L.* gravis), grievous

***Grief,** sm. grievance

***Grièveté,** sf. (*etm. L.* gravitatem), gravity, grievous nature

Griffe, sf. (*etym. G.* griff, *act of seizing*), claw, fang, pounce, signature, music pen

Griffer, va. (*etym. G.* greifen, *to seize*), to claw, to scratch

Griffon, sm. (*etym. Gr.* γρύψ, *griffin*), griffon, griffin

Griffonnage, sm. (*etym.* griffonner), scrawl

Griffonner, va. (*etym.* griffon), to scrawl, to scribble

§**Grignoter,** va. (*etym. O.F.* grigner, *to show one's teeth*), to nibble

§**Grigou,** sm. (*etym.* ?), curmudgeon

Gril, sm. (*etym. masc. form of* grille), gridiron

§**Grillade,** sf. (*etym.* griller), broiling, toast

§**Grillage,** sm. (*etym.* griller), wirework, grating, roasting, frame

§**Grille,** sf. (*etym. L.L.* craticula), bars, grating, railing, iron gate, grated parlour, the nuns

§**Griller,** va. (*etym.* gril), to broil, to grill, to toast, to scorch. † — *dans sa peau*, to burn with impatience; *se* —, vr. to be broiled, to roast or scorch oneself, to be burnt; va. (*etym.* grille), to grate, to rail in

§**Grillon,** sm. (*etym. L.* gryllus), cricket

Grimaçant, e, adj. grinning, grimacing, full of creases

Grimace, sf. (*etym. O.H.G.* grim, *fierce*), grimace, wry face, sham, pincushion wafer-box

Grimacer, vn. (*etym.* grimace), to grin, to grimace, to be full of creases

Grimacier, ère, adj. (*etym.* grimace), grinning, fond of making wry faces, simpering, dissembling

Grimaud, sm. (*etym.* grime), urchin, scribbler

Grime, sm. (*etym. I.* grimo, *wrinkled*), urchin, (*theat.*) dotard

se Grimer, vr. (*etym.* grime), to paint one's face

Grimoire, sm. (*etym. Gr.* γράμμα, *letter*), magic scroll, dark discourse, scrawl

Grimpant, e, adj. climbing

Grimper, vn. (*etym. D.* grippen, *to seize*), to climb, to creep

Grimpeurs, sm. plur. (*etym.* grimper), climbers

Grincement, sm. (*etym.* grincer), gnashing of teeth

Grincer, va.n. (*etym. O.H.G.* gremizôn, *to grind one's teeth*), to gnash, to grind. — *des dents*, to gnash one's teeth

†**Gringalet**, sm. (*etym.* ?), a weak, insignificant man

Grippe, sf. (*etym. see* Gripper), whim, the influenza. ‡ *Prendre en* —, *se prendre de* — *contre*, to take a dislike to

Grippeminaud, sm. (*etym.* gripper, minaud), grimalkin

Gripper, va. (*etym. Goth.* greipan, *to seize*), to pounce upon, to catch hold of, to nab. *Être grippé*, to have an attack of the influenza; *se* —, vr. to shrivel, to shrink, to be given to whimsics

†**Grippe-sou**, sm. rent-gatherer; *plur.* des grippe-sous

Gris, e, adj. (*etym. O.S.* gris, *grey-haired*), grey or gray, brown, dull, raw, tipsy. *Vin* —, pale wine. *Il fait* —, it is dull weather. — sm. grey. *Petit-* —, minever

§**Grisaille**, sf. (*etym.* gris), painting in which only black and white are used

Grisâtre, adj. (*etym.* gris), greyish

Griser, va. (*etym.* gris), to make tipsy, giddy; *se* —, vr. to get tipsy

Grisette, sf. (*etym.* gris), a girl or woman of the lower class

Grison, ne, adj. (*etym.* gris), greyish, grey-haired, grizzled. — sm. grey-beard, spy, grizzle, donkey, purbeck-stone

Grisonner, vn. to grow grey

Grisou, sm. (*etym.* gris), fire-damp

Grive, sf. (*etym.* ?), thrush

Grivois, e, adj. (*etym.* grivoise, *tobacco-grater*), jolly

§**Grognard, e**, adj. (*etym.* grogner), grumbling, growling. *Un vieux* —, an old soldier

§**Grognement**, sm. (*etym.* grogner), grunt, grunting

§**Grogner**, vn. (*etym. L.* grunnire), to grunt, to growl

§**Grogneur, se**, adj. (*etym.* grogner), grunting, grumbling

§**Grognon**, adj. grumbling

Groin, sm. (*etym.* grogner), snout

Grommeler, vn. (*etym. O.H.G.* grummeln, *to grumble*), to grumble, to mutter, to growl

Grondement, sm. (*etym.* gronder), rumbling, roar

Gronder, vn. (*etym. L.* grundire = grunnire, *to grunt*), to grumble, to mutter, to growl, to roar; — va. to scold, to chide

Gronderie, sf. (*etym.* gronder), scolding, chiding

Grondeur, se, adj. scolding, grumbling. — sm. scolding man. — sf. scold

§**Gros, Grosse**, adj. (*etym. L.L.* grossus), big, large, bulky, gruff, deep, swollen, pregnant, with child, stormy, rough, coarse, thick. *Par un* — *temps*, by a heavy gale of wind. — sm. body, bulk, thickest part, main body, drachm, large hand. — adv. a great deal, much. *En* —, wholesale, in a summary way

Gros-bec, sm. gross-beak

§**Groseille**, sf. (*etym. H.G.* kräusbeere, kräuselbeere), currant. — *à maquereau*, gooseberry

§**Groseillier**, sm. (*etym.* groseille), currant-bush, gooseberry-bush

Grosse, sf. (*etym.* gros), gross, large text, engrossed text, bottomry. *Contrat à la* —, bottomry-bond. *Prêter à la* —, to lend upon bottomry

Grossesse, sf. pregnancy

Grosseur, sf. (*etym.* gros), size, bigness, bulk, swelling

§**Grossier, ère**, adj. (*etym.* gros), gross, thick, coarse, plain, homely

Grossièreté, sf. rudeness, clumsiness, coarseness

Grossir, va. to make bigger, to enlarge, to increase; — vn., *se* —, vr. to become bigger, to increase, to swell

Grossissant, e, adj. magnifying

Grossissement, sm. magnifying

Grossoyer, va. (*etym.* gros), to engross

Grotte, sf. (*etym. L.L.* crupta, grupta), grotto

§**Grouillant**, adj. alive, crawling

§**Grouiller**, vn. (*etym. see* Crouler), to stir, to move, to shake, to be all alive, to swarm

Group, sm. (*etym.* ?), bag of money

Groupe, sm. (*etym. see* Croupe), group, knot

Grouper, va. to group; *se* —, vr. to gather, to cluster, to crowd

Gruau, sm. (*etym. O.F.* gru; *Ang.-Sax.* grut), oatmeal, groats, gruel

Grue, sf. (*etym. L.* grus), crane, a fool. ‡ *Faire le pied de* —, to stand kicking one's heels

Gruger, va. (*etym. L.G.* grusen, *to crush*), to crunch, to eat up

Grume, sf. (*etym.* ?), bark. *En* —, unbarked

Grumeau, sm. (*etym. L.* grumellus, *dimin. of* grumus, *a little heap*), clot, clod, lump

se Grumeler, vr. (*etym.* grumeau), to clot

Grumeleux, se, adj. (*etym.* grumeau), clotted

Gué, sm. (*etym. L.* vadum), ford

Gué! interj. (*same word as* gai), gay!

Guéable, adj. (*etym.* guéer), fordable

Guèbre, sm. (*etym. Pers.* Ghebar, *fire-worshipper*), Gheber, fire-worshipper

Guède, sf. (*etym. O.H.G.* weit), woad

Guéer, va. (*etym.* gué), to ford, to wash

Guelfe, sm. (*etym. G. prop. name* Welf), Guelph

§**Guenille**, sf. (*etym.* ?), rag, (*plur.*) tattered clothes

Guenon, Guenuche, sf. (*etym.* ?), ape, monе, fright

Guêpe, sf. (*etym. L.* vespa), wasp

Guêpier, sm. (*etym.* guêpe), wasps' nest. *Tomber dans un* —, to fall into a nest of hornets

Guère, Guères, adv. (*etym.* ?), little, but little, not much, hardly any one, hardly anything but

Guéret, sm. (*etym. L.* vervactum, *fallow ground*), ploughed land, fields

Guéridon, sm. (*etym.* ?), round table

Guérir, va. (*etym. O.H.G.* werjan, *to protect*), to heal, to cure; — vn. to get well again, to recover; *se* —, vr. to be cured, to get cured, to be getting well

Guérison, sf. (*etym.* guérir), cure, recovery

Guérissable, adj. which may be cured

Guérisseur, sm. doctor, healer

Guérite, sf. (*etym.* guérir), sentry-box, watch-tower

Guerre, sf. (*etym. O.H.G.* werra, *quarrel*), war, hostilities, variance, dissension. *Petite* —, desultory war, mimic warfare. *C'est de bonne* —, it is all fair. *Nom de* —, nickname. ‡ *De* — *lasse*, for quietness' sake. *A la* — *comme à la* —, one must take things as they come

Guerrier, ère, adj. s. (*etym.* guerre), warlike, martial, warrior, captain

Guerroyer, vn. (*etym.* guerre), to make war, to war

Guerroyeur, sm. (*etym.* guerroyer), warrior

Guet, sm. (*etym. O.H.G.* wahta, *watch*), watch. *Être au* —, to be on the watch

Guet-apens, sm. (*etym.* guet, à, penser), snare, ambuscade, treacherous scheme, felony

Guêtres, sf. plur (*etym.* ?), gaiters, spatterdashes

Guetter, va. to watch, to wait for, to waylay

Guetteur, sm. (*etym.* guet), look-out, signal-man

Gueule, sf. (*etym. L.* gula), mouth. † *N'avoir que de la* —, to be all talk. *Être fort en* —, to be a brawler, to be foul-mouthed

Gueules, sm. plur. (*etym. L.L.* gulæ), (*her.*) gules

†**Gueuleton**, sm. (*etym.* gueule), a feast

†**Gueuletonner**, va. (*etym.* gueuleton), to feast, to guzzle

†**Gueusard**, sm (*etym.* gueux), beggar, blackguard

Gueuse, sf. (*etym. G.* guss, *cast-iron*), pig-iron, sow

Gueuser, va.n. to beg

Gueuserie, sf. (*etym.* gueuser), beggery, misery

Gueux, se, adj. s. (*etym. see* Queux), beggarly, poor, needy, beggar, ragamuffin, scoundrel

Gui, sm. (*etym. L.* viscus), mistletoe, (*nau.*) main-boom

Guichet, sm. (*etym. Scand.* vik, *a nook*), wicket, gate

Guichetier, sm. (*etym.* guichet), turnkey, door-keeper

Guide, sm. (*etym. L.L.* guido), guide. — sf. rein. *Conduire à grandes* —*s*, to drive four in hand

Guider, va. to guide, to lead, to actuate; *se* —, vr. to be guided

Guidon, sm. small flag, ensign, cornet, broad pendant

§**Guigne**, sf. (*etym. L.L.* guindolum), cherry

§**Guigner**, vn. (*etym.* ?), to peep. — *de l'œil*, to peer out from under one's eyelids, to peep at, to glance at, to have an eye on

§**Guignon**, sm. (*etym.* guigner), bad luck, unlucky chance

§**Guillemets**, sm. plur. (*etym. prop. name* Guillemet), inverted commas

§**Guilleret, te**, adj. (*etym.* ?), brisk, sprightly, alert, merry

§**Guilleri**, sm. (*onomatop.*) chirp

§**Guillocher**, va. (*etym. prop. name* Guillot), to guilloche, to engine-turn

§**Guillochis**, sm. guilloche, engine-turning

¶§**Guillotine**, sf. (*etym. prop. name* Guillotin), guillotine

¶§**Guillotiner**, va. to guillotine

Guimauve, sf. (*etym. L.* ibiscum, malva), marsh-mallow

Guimbarde, sf. (*etym.* ?), van, jew's harp

Guimpe, sf. (*etym. O.H.G.* wimpal, *summer-dress*), wimple, stomacher

Guindage, sm. hoisting, swaying up

Guindé, e, past part. stiff and starched, high-flown

Guinder, va. (*etym. O.H.G.* windan = *Eng. to wind*), to hoist up, to sway up, to strain, to force; *se* —, vr. to sway *or* hoist oneself up, to be strained, to fall into bombast

Guinée, sf. guinea, blue cloth

Guingan, sm. (*etym. prop. name* Guingamp, *a town in Brittany*), gingham

Guingois, sm. (*etym.* ?), crookedness, something awry

Guinguette, sf. (*etym. O.F.* guinguet, *a kind of poor*

wine), country public-house with gardens

Guirlande, sf. (*etym.* ?), wreath, garland, chaplet

¶**Guirlander,** va. to adorn with garlands

Guisarme, sf. (*etym.* ?) a kind of double-edged battle-axe

Guise, sf. (*etym.* O.H.G. wisa = *Eng.* wise), way, guise, manner, fancy, liking

Guitare, sf. (*etym.* L. cithara), guitar

!**Guitarerie,** sf. a set of people playing on the guitar

!**Guitariser,** vn. to strum on the guitar

Guitariste, sm. guitar-player, guitarist

Guivre, *also* **Givre,** sf. (*etym.* L. vipera), a serpent, in heraldry

Gymnase, sm. (*etym.* Gr. γυμνάσιον), gymnasium

Gymnaste, sm. (*etym.* Gr. γυμναστής), gymnast

Gymnastique, sf. (*etym.* Gr. γυμναστικός), gymnastics. — adj. gymnastic

Gymnique, adj. sf. (*etym.* Gr. γυμνικός), gymnic, gymnastics

Gymnopédie, sf. (*etym.* Gr. γυμνοπαιδία, *from* γυμνός, *naked,* παῖς, *child*), gymnopædia

Gymnosophiste, sm. (*etym.* Gr. γυμνοσοφιστής), gymnosophist

Gynécée, sm. (*etym.* Gr. γυναικεῖον), gynæceum

Gypse, sm. (*etym.* Gr. γύψος), gypsum, plaster of Paris

H

H, sf. h

***Ha!** interj. ha!

‖**Habile,** adj. (*etym.* L. habilis), clever, talented, able, skilful, artful, knowing

Habileté, sf. (*etym.* L. habilitatem), ability, cleverness, skill

Habilité, sf. (*etym.* see HABILETÉ), competency

§**Habillement,** sm. (*etym.* habiller), clothing, clothes, raiment, habiliment

§**Habiller,** va. (*etym.* habile *in the sense of convenient*), to dress, to clothe, to be one's tailor, to fit, to become. *Un habit habillé,* a dress coat; *s'*—, vr. to dress, to put on one's clothes, to find oneself in clothes, (!) to abuse each other

Habit, sm. (*etym.* L. habitum), clothes, garb, attire, coat. *Prendre l'*—, to become a monk. *Prise d'*—, taking of one's vows. *L'— ne fait pas le moine,* it is not the cowl that makes the friar

Habitable, adj. (*etym.* L. habitabilis), inhabitable

Habitacle, sm. (*etym.* L. habitaculum), abode, bittacle, binnacle

Habitant, e, s. inhabitant, dweller, resident

Habitation, sf. (*etym.* L. habitationem), habitation, stay, abode

Habiter, va.n. (*etym.* L. habitare), to inhabit, to live in, to tenant

Habitude, sf. (*etym.* L. habitudinem), habit, custom, practice, use, constitution. *Avoir — auprès de, en,* to frequent

Habitué, e, s. frequenter, regular customer, friend

‖**Habituel, le,** adj. (*etym.* L. habitualis), customary, habitual, usual, wonted

Habituer, va. (*etym.* L. habituare), to accustom, to use, to inure: *s'*—, vr. to get used, to accustom oneself

***Hâbler,** va. (*etym.* Sp. hablar, *to speak*), to draw the long bow, to boast, to brag

***Hâblerie,** sf. boasting, bragging

***Hâbleur,** sm. great talker, boaster

***Hache,** sf. (*etym.* G. hacke), axe, hatchet. *Fait à coups de —,* (*fig.*) clumsily made

***Hache-paille,** sm. chaff-cutter

***Hacher,** va. (*etym.* hache), to chop, to hew, to hash, to mince, to mangle, to cut up, to hatch

***Hachette,** sf. (*etym.* hache), hatchet

***Hachis,** sm. (*etym.* hacher), hash, mince-meat

***Hachure,** sf. (*etym.* hacher), hatching

***Hagard, e,** adj. (*etym.* O.E. hauke = hawk), haggard, wild

***Haie,** sf. (*etym.* O.H.G. haga, *hedge*), hedge, fence, line, row, beam. — *vive,* quick-set hedge. *Course de —s,* hurdle-race

***Haie!** interj. (*onomatop.*), gee-ho!

§***Haillon,** sm. (*etym.* O.H.G. hadil, *rag*), rag, tatter

***Haine,** sf. (*etym.* Wall. haime), hate, hatred, loathing

!***Haineux, se,** adj. (*etym.* haine), hateful, malevolent, malignant

***Haïr,** va. (*etym.* Goth. hatan, *to hate*), to hate, to loathe, to dislike; *se —,* vr. to hate *or* loathe oneself, to hate each other

***Haire,** sf. (*etym.* O.H.G. hârn, *hair-cloth*), hair-shirt

***Haïssable,** adj. (*etym.* haïr), hateful, odious

***Halage,** sm. (*etym.* haler), towage, towing. *Chemin de —,* towing-path

***Halbran,** sm. (*etym.* G. halbente, [*lit.*] *half a duck*), teal, young wild duck

***Hâle,** sm. (*etym.* see HÂLER), sun, sunburning

***Hâlé, e,** adj. sun-burnt, tanned by the sun, swarthy

***Haleine,** sf. (*etym.* L. halare), breath, strength of breath, wind. *Avoir beaucoup d'—,* to be long-winded. *Hors d'—,* out of breath. *Tout d'une —,* in the same breath. *Courir à perte d'—,* to run oneself out of breath, to run till quite out of breath. *Ouvrage de longue —,* work of time. *Être en —,* to be in the right mood. *Remettre en —,* (*fig.*) to keep in practice

***Haler,** va. (*etym.* O.H.G. halôn, *to pull*), to haul in, to tow

***Hâler,** va. (*etym.* Flem. hael, *dry*), to tan, to brown, to burn; *se —,* vr. to become tanned, to be sunburnt

***Haletant, e,** adj. panting for breath, panting

***Haleter,** vn. (*etym.* L. halitare), to pant

***Halle,** sf. (*etym.* O.H.G. halla, *temple*), market-place. *Fort de la —,* market-porter

***Hallebarde,** sf. (*etym.* O.H.G. helmbarte, *a kind of hatchet*), halberd. *Il pleut des —s,* it rains cats and dogs

Hallebardier, sm. halberdier, pike-man

***Hallier,** sm. (*etym.* L.L. hasla, *branch*), thicket, dense brushwood

***Halte,** sf. (*etym.* G. halten, *to stop*), halt, stop, halting-place. —! interj. halt! —*là!* stand! hold!

***Hamac,** sm. (*etym.* G. hangematte), hammock, cot

Hamadryade, sf. (*etym.* Gr. ἁμαδρυάς), Hamadryad

***Hameau,** sm. (*etym.* O.H.G. cham, *home*), hamlet

***Hameçon,** sm. (*etym.* L. hamus), fish-hook, hook

***Hampe,** sm. (*etym.* G. handhabe, *handle*), staff, stem, handle

***Hanche,** sf. (*etym.* O.H.G. ancha, *leg*), hip, haunch

***Hangar,** sm. (*etym.* L.L. angarium, *place for shoeing horses*), shed, cart-shed, out-house

***Hanneton,** sm. (*etym.* G. hahn), cockchafer

***Hanse,** sf. (*etym.* O.H.G. hansa, *troop*), the Hanse-towns

***Hanséatique,** adj. (*etym.* Hanse), hanseatic

***Hanter,** va. (*etym.* L. habitare ?), to haunt, to frequent

***Hantise,** sf. familiar intercourse

***Happer,** va. (*etym.* D. happen, *to bite*), to snap up, to snatch at

***Haquenée,** sf. (*etym.* Engl. hackney), ambling nag

***Haquet,** sm. (*dimin. of* O.F. haque, *horse*), dray

!***Haquetier,** sm. drayman

***Harangue,** sf. (*etym.* O.H.G. hring, *assembly, circle*), harangue, address

***Haranguer,** va.n. to harangue, to address

***Harangueur,** sm. haranguer, speech-maker, orator

***Haras,** sm. (*etym.* L.L. haracium), paddocks, grazing grounds and stables

***Harasser,** va. (*etym.* ?), to harass, to tire out

***Harceler,** va. (*etym.* O.F. harce, *dimin. of* hart, *a stick*), to worry, to annoy

***Harde,** sf. (*etym.* ?), herd, leash

***Hardes,** sf. plur. (*etym.* O.F. fardes = fardeau), wearing apparel

!***Hardi, e,** adj. (*etym. past part. of O.F.* hardir = enhardir), bold, daring, hardy, impudent. — *comme un page,* as bold as brass. —*!* interj. courage!

***Hardiesse,** sf. boldness, hardihood, fearlessness

***Hareng,** sm. (*etym.* O.H.G. harinc), herring. — *saur,* red-herring. *La caque sent toujours le —,* (*prov.*) a bad education goes through life

***Harenguison,** sf. (*etym.* hareng), herring-season

***Harengère,** sf. fish-woman, coarse woman

§***Hargneux, se,** adj. (*etym.* O.F. hargne, *bad temper*), surly, cross-grained, crabbed, snappish, snarling

***Haricot,** sm. (*etym.* ?), kidney-bean, stew. —*s verts,* French beans. —*s blancs,* white kidney-beans. —*s d'Espagne,* scarlet runners

***Haridelle,** sf. (*etym.* ?), sorry jade

Harmonie, sf. (*etym.* Gr. ἁρμονία, *arrangement*), harmony. *Table d'—,* sound-board

(**Harmonieux, se,** adj. harmonious, tuneful

‖**Harmonique,** adj. (*etym.* Gr. ἁρμονικός), harmonic

Harmoniste, sm. (*etym.* harmonie), harmonist

***Harnachement,** sm. (*etym.* harnacher), harnessing, harness, trappings

***Harnacher,** va. (*etym.* harnais), to harness

***Harnais** or **Harnois**, sm. (*etym. Celt.* harnez, *iron*), harness, armour, tackle. ‡ *Blanchir sous le* —, to grow grey in armour

****Haro**, sm. (*etym.* !), hue and cry. *Faire clameur de* —, to raise the hue and cry

Harpagon, sm. (*etym. Gr.* ἅρπαξ, *thief*), miser

***Harpe**, sf. (*etym. Scan.* harpa), harp, (*mason.*) toothing

***Harpie**, sf. (*etym. Gr.* ἅρπυια), harpy

***Harpiste**, sm. (*etym.* harpe), harpist, harper

***Harpon**, sm. (*etym. O.H.G.* harfan, *to seize*), harpoon, spear

***Harponner**, va. to harpoon, to spear

***Harponneur**, sm. harpooneer

***Hart**, sf. (*etym.* !), withe, halter, rope

***Hasard**, sm. (*etym. Arab.* al-sár, *game of dice*), chance, accident, hazard, risk, danger. *Jeu de* —, game of chance. *Au — de*, at the risk of. *A tout* —, at all hazards. *Au* —, at random. *Marchandises de* —, second-hand goods

***Hasarder**, va. to risk, to venture, to hazard. *Expression hasardée*, bold expression. *Se* —, vr. to venture, to hazard oneself

***Hasardeux, se**, adj. venturesome, hazardous, slippery

Hastaire, sm. (*etym. L.* hastarius, *from* hasta, *spear*), hastarius, spearman

***Hâte**, sf. (*etym. O.Scan.* hasta), haste, speed, hurry, eagerness. *A la* —, hastily, in haste, in a hurry

***Hâter**, va. (*etym.* hâte), to hasten, to urge on, to quicken, to hurry; *se* —, vr. to hasten, to haste

‖***Hâtif, ve**, adj. (*etym.* hâte), precocious, forward

***Hauban**, sm. (*etym. Fl.* hobant = hoofband, *band for the head*), (*nav.*) shroud. — *du grand mât*, — *de misaine*, main shroud, fore shroud

***Hausse**, sf. (*etym.* hausser), lift, piece, rise, overlay. *Les fonds sont en* —, stocks are rising. *Jouer à la* —, to speculate on a rise

***Hausse-col**, sm. gorget

***Haussement**, sm. (*etym.* hausser), raising. — *d'épaules*, shrug

***Hausser**, va. n. *etym. L.L.* altiare), to raise, to raise up, to rise, to shrug, to increase; *se* —, vr. to rise, to be raised, to clear up

***Haussière**, sf. (*etym. Engl.*), hawser. — *de touage*, tow-line

‖***Haut, e**, adj. (*etym. L.* altus), high, lofty, tall, upper, elevated, proud, haughty. ‡ *Tenir la bride —e à*, to keep a tight hand over. *Le prendre sur un ton très-* —, to talk very arrogantly. — sm. height, top, summit, high notes, haughtiness. ‡ *Tomber de son* —, to fall down on the ground, (*fig.*) to stagger with astonishment. *Traiter quelqu'un du — en bas*, to treat a person with disdain. — adv. high, high up, loud, aloud, haughtily. ‡ *Être pendu — et court*, to be strung up short and quick. — *le pied!* let us be gone! — *la main*, with a high hand, off-hand. *Traiter de* —, to treat arrogantly. *Le prendre très-* —, to talk very big. *Portez-le moins* —, be less proud. *En* —, above, upstairs

‖***Hautain, e**, adj. (*etym.* haut), haughty, proud, lofty, overbearing

***Hautbois**, sm. hautboy, performer on the hautboy

***Haut-de-chausses**, sm. breeches

***Hautesse**, sf. (*etym.* haut), Highness. *Sa* —, His Highness

***Hauteur**, sf. (*etym.* haut), height, altitude, hill, rising ground, firmness, loftiness, haughtiness, pride

***Haut-fond**, sm. shoal, shallow

***Hâve**, adj. (*etym. Ang.-Sax.* hasva, *dried up, pale*), wan, emaciated

***Havre**, sm. (*etym. O.Scan.* höfn, *haven*), harbour, haven, port

***Havre-sac**, sm. (*etym. G.* haber, *oats*, sack), knapsack, wallet

***Hé!** interj. hoy! why! egad! hey!

***Heaume**, sm. (*etym. O.Scan.* hiälmer, *helmet*), helm, helmet, head-piece

***Hebdomadaire**, adj (*etym. Gr.* ἑβδομάς, *week*), weekly

Héberger, va (*etym. O.H.G.* heriberga, *military encampment*), to lodge, to entertain

Hébété, e, s. (*etym.* hébéter), blockhead, dolt, dullard

Hébéter, va. (*etym. L.* hebetare, *from* hebes, *blunt*), to stultify, to dull, to besot

Hébraïque, adj. (*etym. Gr.* ἑβραϊκός, *Hebrew*), Hebrew

Hébraïsant, sm. (*etym. Gr.* ἑβραΐζειν, *to talk Hebrew*), hebraist

Hébraïsme, sm. (*etym.* hébraïsant), hebraism

Hébreu, sm. adj. (*etym. Gr.* ἑβραῖος), Hebrew

Hécatombe, sf. (*etym. Gr.* ἑκατόμβη, *from* ἑκατόν, *hundred*, βοῦς, *ox*), a hecatomb

Hectare, sm. (*etym.* hect . . . . *prefix*, are), a measure of 2 acres, 1 rood, 35 perches

Hectique, adj. (*etym. Gr.* ἑκτικός, *which consumes*), hectic

Hectogramme, sm. (*etym.* hecto . . . . *prefix*, gramme), 3 oz. 4/7

Hectolitre, sm. (*etym.* hecto . . . . *prefix*, litre), about 22 gallons 1/9, about 2 bushels 3/4

Hectomètre, sm. (*etym.* hecto . . . . *prefix*, mètre), about 109 yards, 1 foot, and 1 inch

Hégire, sf. (*etym. Arab.* hejirett, *flight*), Hegira

***Hein!** interj. eh! what?

Hélas! interj. alas! *Faire de grands* —, to sigh most piteously

***Héler**, va. (*etym. Engl.*), to hail, to speak

Hélice, sf. (*etym. Gr.* ἕλιξ), screw, helix. *Navire à* —, screw-ship

Héliotrope, sm. (*etym.* hélio . . . *Gr.* τροπή, *turning*), heliotrope, sun-flower

Hellénique, adj. (*etym. Gr.* ἑλληνικός), Grecian, Greek, Hellenic

Hellénisme, sm. (*etym. Gr.* ἑλληνισμός), Hellenism, Greek idiom

Helléniste, sm. (*etym.* ἑλληνιστής), Hellenist

Hémistiche, sm. (*etym. Gr.* ἡμιστίχιον, *half a line*), hemistich

Hémorragie, sf. (*etym. Gr.* αἱμοῤῥαγία), hæmorrhage

Hémorroïdes, sf. plur. (*etym. Gr.* αἱμοῤῥοΐς, *flow of blood*), hæmorrhoids, piles

Hendécagone, sm. adj. (*Gr.* ἕνδεκα, *eleven*, γωνος, *angle*), hendecagon, hendecagonal

Hendécasyllabe, adj. (*etym. Gr.* ἕνδεκα, syllabe), hendecasyllabic

***Henné**, sm. (*Arab. word*), henna

***Hennir**, vn. (*etym. L.* hinnire), to neigh

***Hennissement**, sm. neigh, neighing

Hépatique, adj. sf. (*etym. Gr.* ἡπατικός, *from* ἧπαρ, *liver*), hepatical, belonging to the liver, hepatica

Heptagone, sm. (*etym. Gr.* ἑπτά, *seven*, γωνος), heptagon

Heptarchie, sf. (*etym. Gr.* ἑπτά, ἀρχή), heptarchy

Héraldique, adj. (*etym.* héraut), heraldic

***Héraut**, sm. (*etym. L.L.* heraldus, *from* !), herald, precursor

Herbacé, e, adj. (*etym. L.* herbaceus), herbaceous

Herbage, sm. (*etym. L.L.* herbaticum, *from* herba), herbage, pasture, meadow

Herbe, sf. (*etym. L.* herba), herb, grass. —*s potagères*, pot-herbs. *Mauvaises* —*s*, weeds. ‡ *Sur quelle — a-t-il marché ce matin?* what can be the matter with him this morning?

Herbette, sf. sward, grass

Herbeux, se, adj. (*etym. L.* herbosus), grassy

Herbier, sm (*etym. L.* herbarium), herbal

Herbivore, adj. (*etym. L.* herba, vorare), herbivorous

Herborisation, sf. (*etym.* herboriser), herborization, arboriz…

Herboriser, v… borize

Herboriste, sm… HERBE), herbalist,

Herbu, e, adj. …

Herculéen, … (*etym.* Hercule, *pr*… herculean

****Hère**, sm. (… wretch. *Pauvre* … devil

‖**Héréditaire**, … *L.* hereditarius), h…

Hérédité, sf. … hereditatem), heir… ditary right

Hérésiarque, … (*Gr.* αἱρεσιάρχης, … sect), arch-hereti… arch

Hérésie, sf. (… αἵρεσις), heresy

Hérétique, adj … hæreticus), heretic… a heretic

***Hérissé, e**, adj … bristly, shaggy, ere… bristling, thickse… with, full of

***Hérisser**, va. … HÉRISSON), to bristl… up, to arm; *se* … bristle up, to star… be armed, (*fig.*) to …

***Hérisson**, sm. … hericius, ericius, … hedgehog, spro… (*fortif.*) herisson, sea-urchin

Héritage, sm. … inheritance, legac…

Hériter, vn. (*et*… ditare), to inheri… into, to be heir to

Héritier, sm. … hereditarius), heir

Héritière, sf. …

‖**Hermétique**, … Hermès), hermet… tical

Hermine, sf. … Armenius, *Armu*… mius

***Herniaire**, … hernie), hernial, truss

***Hernie**, sf. … hernia), hernia, …

Héroï-comi… heroi-comic, mock…

‖**Héroïque**, ad… heroicus = *Gr.* ἡρω… heroical

Héroïsme, … héros), heroism

Héron, sm. (*et*… heigro), heron

***Héros**, sm. … ἥρως), hero. *En* —

***Herse**, sf. (*etym*… *kind of harrow*), … cullis, triangular …

***Herser**, va. to …

Hésiter, va. … hæsitare), to … falter

Hétéroclite, … *Gr.* ἑτερόκλιτος, … *regularly*), heter… roclitical, queer,

Hétérodoxe, … *Gr.* ἑτερόδοξος, …

opinion), heterodox, unorthodox

Hétérogène, adj. (*etym.* ἑτερογενής, *of another kind*), heterogeneous, dissimilar

Hétérogénéité, sf. heterogeneousness

'**Hêtre**, sm. (*etym. Flem.* heester, *a shrub*), beech, beech-tree

Heur, sm. (*etym. L.* augurium), chance, luck

Heure, sf. (*etym. L.* hora), hour, o'clock, time, prayer-book, hours. *A l'—*, by the hour. *Être à l'—*, to be employed by the hour. *Prendre l'—, mettre sa montre à l'—*, to set one's watch right. *Sur les deux —s*, about two o'clock. *Il ne fait rien qu'à ses —s*, he chooses his own time for everything. *L'— du berger*, the propitious hour. *De bonne —*, early. *A la bonne —*, that's right. *Tout à l'—*, just now, presently. *Sur l'—*, directly. *Pour l'—*, for the present

|**Heureux, se**, adj. (*etym.* heur), happy, blissful, fortunate, lucky, pleasing, prepossessing

'**Heurt**, sm. shock, knock, bruise

'**Heurté, e**, adj. harsh, rough

'**Heurter**, va.n. (*etym.* ?), to strike against, to shock, to offend, to run counter to; *se —*, vr. to strike, to hit, to knock, to run counter to

Hexaèdre, adj. sm. (*etym.* hexa, *Gr.* ἕδρα, *face, side*), hexahedral, hexahedron

Hexagone, adj. sm. (*etym.* hexa, *Gr.* γωνία), hexagonal, hexagon

Hexamètre, adj. sm. (*etym. Gr.* ἑξάμετρος), hexameter

'**Hibou**, sm. (*etym. onomatop.* ?), owl

|'**Hic**, sm. (*L.*), rub

|**Hideux, se**, adj. (*etym. O.F.* hideur, *from* hide, *fright*), hideous, frightful, horrible

'**Hie**, sf. (*etym. Flem.* hei), (*mech.*) beetle, ram, monkey

Hier, am. (*etym. L.* heri), yesterday

'**Hiérarchie**, sf. (*etym. L.* hierarchia), hierarchy

|**Hiérarchique**, adj. (*etym.* hiérarchie), hierarchical

Hiéroglyphe, sm. (*etym. Gr.* ἱερός, *sacred*, γλύφω, *I engrave*), hieroglyphic, hieroglyph

Hiéroglyphique, adj. (*etym.* hiéroglyphe), hieroglyphical

Hiérophante, sm. (*etym. Gr.* ἱεροφάντης, *he who shows sacred things*), hierophant

Hilarité, sf. (*etym. L.* hilaritatem), hilarity, cheerfulness, merriment

Hippopotame, sm. (*etym. Gr.* ἵππος, *horse*, ποταμός, *river*), hippopotamus

Hirondelle, sf. (*etym. L.* hirundo), swallow

'**Hisser**, va. (*etym. G.* hissen, *to hoist*), to hoist; *se —*, vr. to hoist or raise oneself

Histoire, sf. (*etym. L.* historia), history, story, tale. *C'est une tout autre —*, that is quite another story. ¦ *Voilà bien des —s!* what a fuss about nothing!

Historien, sm. (*etym.* histoire), historian

Historier, va. (*etym.* histoire), to embellish

Historiette, sf. (*etym.* histoire), little story, short tale, anecdote

Historiographe, sm. (*etym. Gr.* ἱστοριογράφος), historiographer

|**Historique**, adj. (*etym. L.* historicus), historical, historic. *C'est —*, 'tis a fact. — sm. history

Histrion, sm. (*etym. L.* histrionem), common player, stage-player

Hiver, sm. (*O.F.* ivern; *etym. L.* hibernus), winter, the winter season

Hivernage, sm. (*etym. L.L.* hibernaticum), winter-season, winter-harbour, winter-fallowing

Hivernal, e, adj. (*etym. L.* hibernalis), wintry, hibernal

Hiverner, vn.a. (*etym. L.* hibernare), to winter, to winter-fallow; *s'—*, vr. to get used to winter

'**Ho!** interj. ho! hoy! holla!

'**Hobereau**, sm. (*etym. O.F.* hobe, *a small bird of prey*), hobby, country-squire

'**Hoche**, sf. (*etym.* ?), notch

'**Hochement**, sm. (*etym.* hocher), nod, shake, wag, toss

'**Hochequeue**, sm. wagtail

'**Hocher**, va. (*etym. Flem.* hotsen, *to shake*), to shake or wag, to toss; — vn. to shake the bit

'**Hochet**, sm. (*etym.* hocher), coral, rattle, toy, bauble

Hoir, sm. (*etym. L.* heres), heir

Hoirie, sf. (*etym.* hoir), inheritance, heritage

Holà! interj. holla! hallo! *Mettre le —*, to put a stop to a quarrel

Holocauste, sm. (*etym. Gr.* ὁλόκαυστον, *entirely consumed*), burnt-offering, holocaust

'**Hom!** interj. hem!

'**Homard**, sm. (*etym. Dan.* hommer), lobster

Hombre, sm. (*Span.*), ombre

Homélie, sf. (*etym. Gr.* ὁμιλία, *conversation*), homily

Homérique, adj. (*etym. proper name* Homer), homeric

Hommage, sm. (*etym. L.L.* hominaticum), homage. *See* RENDRE

|**Hommasse**, adj. having the appearance of an ugly man

Homme, sm. (*etym. L.* hominem), man, mankind, (*pop.*) good man, old man, husband

Homœopathe, sm. adj. (*etym. Gr.* ὅμοιος, *similar*, πάθος, *affection*), homœopathist, homœopathic

Homœopathie, sf. (*etym.* homœopathe), homœopathy

Homœopathique, adj. (*etym.* homœopathie), homœopathic

|**Homogène**, adj. (*etym. Gr.* ὁμογενής, *of the same kind*), homogeneous

Homogénéité, sf. homogeneousness

Homologation, sf. (*etym.* homologue), confirmation

Homologue, adj. (*etym. Gr.* ὁμόλογος, *analogous*), homologous, like

Homologuer, va. to confirm, to homologate

Homonyme, adj. (*etym. Gr.* ὁμώνυμος, *having the same name*), homonymous. — sm. homonym, namesake

Homonymie, sf. homonymy

'**Hongre**, adj. (*etym. O.F.* Hongre = Hongrois, *Hungarian*), gelded. *Cheval —*, a gelding

|**Honnête**, adj. (*etym. L.* honestus), honest, upright, good, virtuous, respectable, praiseworthy, proper, fair, seemly. — sm. honesty

Honnêteté, sf. (*etym.* honnête), honesty, integrity, rectitude, honour, virtue, respectability, propriety, decency, civility, politeness. *Faire mille —s à*, to be extremely polite to

Honneur, sm. (*etym. L.* honor), honour, rectitude, credit, repute, (*pl.*) honours, preferments. *En tout bien tout —*, with the most honourable intentions. *Être à l'— de*, to redound to the credit of. *Tenir à — de*, to deem it a point of honour to. *Avoir trois —s, quatre d'—s*, to be two by honours, four by honours

'**Honnir**, va. (*etym. O.H.G.* honjan), to scoff at, to revile, to disgrace

|**Honorable**, adj. (*etym. L.* honorabilis), honourable, reputable, respectable

Honoraire, adj. (*etym. L.* honorarius), honorary

Honoraires, sm. plur. (*etym. L.* honorarium), fee, salary

Honoré, e, adj. honourable

Honorer, va. (*etym. L.* honorare), to honour, to be an honour to; *s'—*, vr. to honour oneself, to win honour

Honorifique, adj. (*etym. L.* honorificus), honorary

'**Honte**, sf. (*etym. O.Sax.* honda, *disgrace*), disgrace, shame, scandal, discredit. *Faire — à, causer de la —*, to shame, to disgrace, to make a person ashamed of

|'**Honteux, se**, adj. (*etym.* honte), ashamed, abashed, disgraceful, scandalous, shy, bashful. ¦ *Pauvres —*, poor people who are ashamed to beg

Hôpital, sm. (*etym. L.* hospitale), hospital

'**Hoquet**, sm. (*onomatop.*) hiccup, hiccough

'**Hoqueton**, sm. (*etym. Arab.* al-qôton, *wadded stuff*), a coat or jacket

Horaire, adj. (*etym. L.* horarius), horary

'**Horde**, sf. (*etym. Slav.* hord, *the king's court*), horde, band, crew, the hordes of the north

'**Horion**, sm. (*etymol.* ?), thump, thwack

Horizon, sm. horizon

|**Horizontal, e**, adj. (*etym.* horizon), horizontal

Horloge, sm. (*etym. L.* horologium), clock

Horloger, sm. watch and clock maker

Horlogerie, sf. watch and clock making, clocks and watches

'**Hormis**, prep. (*etym.* hors, mis), except, excepting

Horoscope, sm. (*etym. L.* horoscopus), horoscope, nativity. *Faire l'— de*, to cast the nativity of

Horreur, sf. (*etym. L.* horrorem), horror, dread, detestation, awe, fright. *Dire des —s*, to say shocking things

Horriblement, adv. (*etym.* horrible = *L.* horribilis), horridly, horribly

'**Hors**, '**Hors de**, prep. (*etym. L.* foris), out of, without, outside, except, save. *Être — de combat*, to be disabled

'**Hors-d'œuvre**, sm. (*etym.* hors, œuvre), outwork, digression, excrescency, side dish

Horticulteur, sm. (*etym. L.* hortus, *garden*, cultor, *cultivator*), horticulturist, gardener

Horticulture, sf. (*etym. L.* hortus, cultura), horticulture, gardening

Hospice, sm. (*etym. L.* hospitium), convent, guests' house, alms-house

|**Hospitalier, ère**, adj. (*etym. L.L.* hospitalarius), hospitable. — sm. hospitaller, knight

Hospitalité, sf. (*etym. L.* hospitalitatem), hospitality

Hostie, sf. (*etym. L.* hostia), victim, host, wafer

|**Hostile**, adj. (*etym. L.* hostilis), hostile

Hostilité, sf. (*etym. L.* hostilitatem), hostility, enmity

Hôte, sm. (*etym. L.* hospitem), landlord, host, innkeeper, guest. *Table d'—*, ordinary

Hôtel, sm. (*etym. L.* hospitale), mansion, hotel, inn. *Maître d'—*, house-steward. *— de ville*, town-hall

Hôtellerie, sf. (*etym.* hôtel), inn

Hôtelier, ère, s. (*etym.* hôtel), inn-keeper

Hôtesse, sf. (*etym.* hôte), landlady, lady of the house

***Hotte,** sf. (*etym. G.* hotze, *basket*), basket, chimney funnel

***Hottée,** sf. basketful

***Houblon,** sm. (*etym. a root* houble, *from the L.L.* hupulus), hop, hop plant. *Perche à* —, hop-pole

***Houblonnière,** sf. hop-garden

***Houe,** sf. (*etym. M.H.G.* howe; *Engl.* hoe), hoe

§***Houille,** sf. (*etym.* ?), coal, pit-coal

§***Houiller, ère,** adj. coal

§***Houillère,** sf. coal mine, coal pit

***Houle,** sf. (*etym. Celt.* houl), swell of the sea

***Houlette,** sf. (*etym. L.* sagolum), shepherd's crook, gardener's trowel

***Houleux, se,** adj. rough, billowy

***Houppe,** sf. (*etym. see* HUPPE), tuft

***Houppé, e,** adj. tufted, crested

***Houppelande,** sf. (*etym.* ?), great coat, upper coat

***Hourra,** sm. (*etym. Slav.* hu-raj, *in Paradise*), hurrah, huzza, outcry

§***Houspiller,** va. (*etym.* ?), to bemaul, to worry, to rate sharply

***Housse,** sf. (*etym. O.H.G.* hulst, *covering*), housing, horse-cloth, saddle-cloth, hammer-cloth, cover

***Houssine,** sf. (*etym.* houx), switch

***Houx,** sm. (*etym. O.H.G.* hûliz, *thorny shrub*), holly, holm-tree

***Hoyau,** sm. (*etym.* houe), mattock, grubbing axe

***Huche,** sf. (*etym. L.L.* hutica), hutch, bin

***Hucher,** va. (*etym. L.L.* huccus, *a kind of call*), to call

***Hue!** interj. (*onomat.*), gee! gee-ho! ‡ *L'un tire à* —, *l'autre à dia*, one pulls one way, and t'other t'other

***Huée,** sf. whoop, hooting, hoot

***Huer,** va. to whoop after, to hoot

Huile, sf. (*etym. L.* oleum), oil. — *à brûler*, lamp-oil. — *de poisson*, train-oil. *Commerce des* —*s*, the oil-trade. *Couleurs à l'*—, oil-colours. *Peindre à l'*—, to paint in oil-colours

Huiler, va. to oil, to anoint *or* smear with oil

Huilerie, sf. oil-mill

Huileux, se, adj. oily, greasy

Huilier, sm. cruet-stand

***Huis,** sm. (*etym. L.* ostium), door. *A — clos*, private, with closed doors. ‡ *Demander le — clos*, to demand the exclusion of the public

Huisserie, sf. door-frame

Huissier, sm. usher, sheriff's officer

***Huit,** adj. sm. (*etym. L.* octo; *O.F.* oit), eight, eighth. *Dans — jours*, in a week's time. *Tous les — jours*, once a week

***Huitain,** sm. stanza of eight verses

***Huitaine,** sf. week, eight days. *Dans la* —, in the course of the week, within the week. *Remis à* —, adjourned till this day week

***Huitième,** adj. sm. (*etym. L.* octesimus), eighth, eighth part

Huître, sf. (*etym. L.* ostrea, *O.F.* uistre, oistre), oyster

Hulotte, sf. (*etym. a root* hule, *from the L.* ulula), owl

‖**Humain, e,** adj. (*etym. L.* humanus), human, humane. *Le genre* —, mankind, the human kind

Humains, sm. plur. human beings, mankind

Humaniser, va. to humanize, to soften; *s'*—, vr. to become humanized, to soften down, to mingle and converse familiarly

Humaniste, sm. humanist

Humanité, sf. (*etym. L.* humanitatem), humanity, human nature, mankind, the humanities

‖**Humble,** adj. (*etym. L.* humilis), humble, lowly. *Faire de très —s remerciments à*, to offer one's most humble thanks. *Votre très — serviteur*, your most humble servant

Humectation, sf. (*etym. L.* humectationem), refreshing, moistening

Humecter, va. (*etym. L.* humectare), to moisten, to bedew, to wet; *s'*—, vr. to become moist, to be bedewed, to refresh oneself

***Humer,** va. (*etym.* ?), to suck down, to suck in, to inhale, to take in

Humeur, sf. (*etym. L.* humorem), humour, temper, disposition, inclination, ill-temper, ill-humour. —*s froides*, scrofula. *D'— difficile*, hard to please. *De mauvaise* —, ill-tempered. *Être d'— à*, to be of a temper to. *Être en — de*, to be inclined to. *Avoir un accès d'*—, to be in a pet. *Prendre de l'*—, to grow cross

Humide, adj. (*etym. L.* humidus), watery, humid, damp. — sm. moisture, humidity, moist

Humidité, sf. (*etym. L.* humiditatem), humidity, moisture, dampness

Humiliant, e, adj. humiliating, mortifying

Humiliation, sf. (*etym. L.* humiliationem), humiliation, mortification, abasement

Humilier, va. (*etym. L.* humiliare), to humble, to cast down, to abase, to mortify, to humiliate; *s'*—, vr. to humble oneself, to stoop

Humilité, sf. (*etym. L.* humilitatem), humility, humbleness, submissiveness. *En toute* —, with all due humility

Humoriste, adj. sm. (*etym. L.* humor), peevish, cross, humorist

Humoristique, adj. humorous, comical

Humus, sm. (*etym. L.* humus), soil

***Hune,** sf. (*etym. Ang.-Sax.* hun), (*nav.*) top, bell-support. *Grande* —, main-top. *Petite* —, foretop. *Mât de* —, top-mast. *Petit mât de* —, fore-top mast. *Voile d'étai de* —, main-top stay-sail

***Hunier,** sm. top-sail. *Déborde les* —*s*, let go the top-sail sheets. *Vergue de grand* —, main-top-sail yard. *Petit* —, fore-top-sail. *Vergue de bonnette de* —, top-mast studding-sail yard

***Huppe** sf. (*etym. L.* upupa), lapwing, hoopoo, tuft, crest

***Huppé, e,** adj. tufted, crested, high, tip-top

***Hure,** sf. (*etym.* ?) head, jowl. — *de sanglier*, boars' head

***Hurlement,** sm. (*etym.* *hurler), howling, howl, yell, yelling

***Hurler,** vn. (*etym. L.* ululare; *O.F.* uller), to howl, to shriek, to bellow

‡**Hurluberlu,** sm. (*etym.* ?), a giddy person

***Hussard,** sm. (*etym. Hung.* huszar), hussar

****Hutin,** adj. (*etym. O.F.* hustin, *quarrel*), headstrong, stubborn

***Hutte,** sf. (*etym. G.* hütte), hut, cabin

Hyacinthe, sf. (*etym. L.* hyacinthus), hyacinth

Hyades, sf. plur. (*etym. L.* Hyades), Hyads

Hybride, adj. (*etym.* hybrida), hybrid, mongrel

Hydraté, adj. (*etym. Gr.* ὕδωρ, *water*), hydrated

Hydraulique, sf. adj. (*etym. L.* hydraulicus), hydraulics, hydraulical. *Bélier* —, water-ram

Hydre, sf. (*etym. L.* hydra), hydra

Hydrocéphale, sf. (*etym. Gr.* ὑδροκέφαλον), hydrocephalus

Hydrochlorique, adj. (*etym.* hydro . . . chlorique), hydrochloric

Hydrodynamique, sf. (*etym. Gr.* ὕδωρ, δύναμις, *power*), hydrodynamics

Hydrogène, sm. adj. (*etym. Gr.* ὕδωρ, γένος, *birth*), hydrogen

Hydrogéné, e, adj. hydrogenized, hydrogenate

Hydrographe, sm. (*etym. Gr.* ὕδωρ, γράφειν, *to write*), hydrographer

Hydrographie, sf. hydrography

Hydrographique, adj. hydrographical

Hydromètre, sm. (*etym. Gr.* ὕδωρ, μέτρον, *measure*), hydrometer

Hydrométrie, sf. hydrometry

Hydrophobe, s. adj. (*etym. L.* hydrophobus), person affected with hydrophobia

Hydrophobie, sf. hydrophobia

Hydropique, adj. (*etym. L.* hydropicus), dropsical, hydropical

Hydropisie, sf. (*etym. L.* hydropisis), dropsy

Hydrostatique, sf. adj. (*etym.* hydro . . . statique), hydrostatics, hydrostatical

Hydrosulfate *or* **Hydrosulfure,** sm. (*etym.* hydro . . . sulfate, sulfure), hydrosulphate, hydrosulphuret

Hydrosulfurique, adj. hydrosulphuric

Hydrure, sm. (*etym.* hydr . . . *for* hydrogène, *and the chemical syllable* ure), hydruret

Hyémal, e, *or* **Hiémal, e,** adj. (*etym. L.* hiemalis), hyemal, wintry

Hyène, sf. (*etym. Gr.* ὕαινα), hyena

Hygiénique, adj. (*etym.* hygiène), hygienic

Hygromètre, sm. (*etym.* ὑγρός, *damp*, μέτρον, *measure*), hygrometer

Hygrométrie, sf. hygrometry

Hygrométrique, adj. hygrometrical

Hyménoptère, adj. sm. (*etym. Gr.* ὑμήν, *membrane*, πτερόν, *wing*), hymenopteral, hymenopter, bee

Hymne, smf. (*etym. L.* hymnus), hymn

Hyperbole, sf. (*etym. L.* hyperbola), hyperbole, hyperbola

‖**Hyperbolique,** adj. hyperbolical

Hyperborée, *or* **Hyperboréen, ne,** adj. (*etym. L.* hyperboreus), hyperborean

Hypercritique, adj. (*etym.* hyper . . . critique), hypercritic

Hypnotique, adj. (*etym. Gr.* ὑπνωτικός), which produces sleep

Hypnotisme, sm. hypnotism

Hypocondre, sm. (*etym. L.* hypocondria), hypochondrium, hypochondriac

Hypocondriaque, adj. hypochondriacal

Hypocondrie, sf. hypochondriasis, hypochondria

Hypocrisie, sf. (*etym. L.* hypocrisis), hypocrisy

‖**Hypocrite,** adj. s. (*etym. L.* hypocrita), hypocritical, dissembling, hypocrite, dissembler

Hypogastre, sm. (*etym. Gr.* ὑπογάστριον), hypogastrium

Hypogastrique, adj. hypogastric

Hypogée, sm. (*etym. L.* hypogeum), hypogeum

Hypostase, sf. (*etym. L.* hypostasis), hypostasis

Hypothécaire, adj. (*etym. L.* hypothecarius), on mortgage, of mortgage. *Créancier* —, mortgagee

Hypothèque, sf. (*etym. L.* hypotheca), mortgage. *Bureau des* —*s*, mortgage office. *Créancier, débiteur sur* —, mortgagee, mortgager

Hypothéquer, va. to mortgage

Hypothèse, sf. (*etym. L.* hypothesis), hypothesis, supposition

Hypothétique, adj (*etym. L.* hypotheticus), hypothetical, supposed, conditional

Hysope, sf. (*etym. L.* hyssopum), hyssop

Hystérie, sf. (*etym. L.* hysteria), hysteria, hysterics

Hystérique, adj. (*etym. L* hystericus), hysterical

Hystérologie, sf. (*etym. Gr* ὕστερον, *last*, λόγος, *discourse*), hysterology, inverted order

Hystérotomie, sf. (*etym. Gr.* ὑστέρα, *womb*, τομή, *section*), hysterotomy, Cæsarean operation

Hystriciens, sm pl (*etym. Gr.* ὕστριξ, *porcupine*), hystricians, an order of quadrupeds

I

I, sm. I, i. *Mettre les points sur les i*, to dot the I's, (i) to be very particular. *Droit comme un I*, straight as an arrow

Iambe, sm. (*etym. L.* iambus), iambus, iambic

Iambe, Iambique, adj. (*etym. L.* iambicus), iambic

Icelui, Icelle, pron. (*etym. see* CE), this, the said

Ichthyologie, sf. (*etym. Gr.* ἰχθυολογία, *discourse about fishes*), ichthyology

Ichthyophage, adj. (*etym. Gr.* ἰχθυοφάγος, *fish-eater*), ichthyophagous

Ici, adv. (*etym. see* CE), here, hither, now, to-day. — *et là*, here and there. — *près*, hard by, close at hand. *Par* —, this way, through here. *D'* — *là*, from here to there, between this and then. *Jusqu'*—, hitherto, until now, down to there

Iconoclaste, sm. (*etym. Gr.* εἰκονοκλάστης, *image-breaker*), iconoclast, image-breaker

Iconographie, sf. (*etym. L.* iconographia), iconography

Iconologie, sf. (*etym. Gr.* εἰκονολογία, *explanation of images*), iconology

Icosaèdre, sm. (*etym. Gr* εἴκοσι, *twenty*, ἕδρα, *basis*), icosahedron

Idéal, e, adj. sm. (*etym. L.* idealis), ideal

Idéaliser, va. to idealise

Idéalisme, sm. idealism

Idéaliste, smf. idealist

Idée, sf. (*etym. L.* idea), idea, notion, thought, recollection, outline, idle fancy, crotchet. *Ce sont des* —*s*, those are idle fancies. *Se mettre dans l'*— to take it into one's head. *Avoir dans l'*— *que*, to have a notion that

Identifier, va. (*etym. L.* idem), to identify; *s'*—, vr. to identify oneself, to be identified

Identique, adj. (*etym. L.* identicus), identical, the same

Identité, sf. (*etym. L.* identitatem), identity

Idéologie, sf. (*etym. Gr.* ἰδέα, λόγος), ideology

Idéologique, adj. ideological

Idéologue, Idéologiste, sm. ideologist, dreamer

Idiomatique, adj. idiomatical

Idiome, sm. (*etym. L.* idioma), idiom

Idiot, e, adj. s. (*etym. L.* idiota), idiotical, foolish, senseless, idiot, born fool

Idiotie, sf. idiocy, imbecility

Idiotisme, sm. (*etym. L.* idiotismus), idiocy, idiotism, idiom

Idolâtre, adj s. (*etym. L.* idolatra), idolatrous, fond to idolatry, idolater, heathen

Idolâtrer, va.n. to idolise, to worship idols; *s'*—, vr to idolize oneself, to idolize each other

Idolâtrie, sf. (*etym. L.* idolatria), idolatry

Idole, sf. (*etym. L.* idolum), idol

Idylle, sf. (*etym. L.* idyllium), idyl

If, sm. (*etym. O.H.G.* iwa), yew-tree, illumination lamp-stand

Igname, sf. (*etym. Port.* inhame), yam

§**Ignare,** adj. (*etym. L.* ignarus), ignorant. *Un* —, a dunce

Igné, e, adj. (*etym. L.* igneus), igneous

§**Ignominie,** sf. (*etym. L.* ignominia), ignominy, shame

§**Ignominieux, se,** adj. (*etym. L.* ignominiosus), ignominious, shameful, disgraceful

§**Ignorantin,** sm. (*etym.* ignorant), Ignorantine friar

§**Ignoré, e,** adj. unknown, secret, private

§**Ignorer,** va. (*etym. L.* ignorare), not to know, to be unacquainted with, to be ignorant of; *s'*—, vr. not to know oneself

Il, pron. m. (*etym. L.* ille), he, it. — *est arrivé trois lettres*, three letters have arrived

Île, sf. (*etym. L.* insula), island, isle

Iliade, sf. (*etym. Gr.* Ἰλιάς), the Iliad

Illégalité, sf. (*etym.* illégal), illegality, unlawfulness

§**Illégitime,** adj. (*etym. L.* illegitimus), illegitimate, unlawful, spurious

Illégitimité, sf. illegitimacy

Illettré, e, adj. (*etym. L.* illiteratus), illiterate, unlettered

§**Illicite,** adj. (*etym. L.* illicitus), illicit, unlawful

Illimité, e, adj (*etym. see* LIMITÉ), unlimited, unbounded, boundless

§**Illisible,** adj. (*etym. see* LISIBLE), illegible, unreadable

Illuminé, sm. illuminate, illuminati

Illuminer, va. (*etym. L* illuminare), to light up, to illuminate, to enlighten

Illuminisme, sm fanciful opinions of the illuminati

Illusion, sf. (*etym. L.* illusionem), illusion, delusion. *Faire* —, to delude

§**Illusoire,** adj. (*etym. L.* illusorius), delusive, illusive, illusory

Illustre, adj. (*etym. L.* illustris), illustrious

Illustrer, va. (*etym. L.* illustrare), to shed a lustre over, to illustrate; *s'*—, vr to render oneself illustrious

Illustrissime, adj. (*etym. L.* illustrissimus), most illustrious

Îlot, sm. (*etym. see* ÎLE), islet

Ilote, sm. (*etym. L.* Ilota), helot

Ilotisme, sm. helotism

Image, sm. (*etym. L.* imaginem), image, picture, resemblance, coloured cut

Imaginaire, adj. (*etym. L.* imaginarius), imaginary, fancied

Imaginatif, ve, adj. (*etym. L.* imaginativus), imaginative, full of imagination

Imaginer, va. (*etym. L.* imaginari), to imagine, to contrive, to frame, *s'*—, vr to imagine oneself, to imagine, to fancy

Imbécillité, sf. (*etym. L* imbecillitatem), imbecility, stupidity

Imberbe, adj. (*etym. L* imberbis), beardless

Imbiber, va. (*etym. L.* imbibere), to imbibe, to soak; *s'*—, vr. to imbibe, to drink in, to soak

Imbu, e, adj. (*etym. L.* imbutus), imbued

Imitateur, trice, adj. s. (*etym. L.* imitatorem), imitative, follower, imitator

Imitatif, ve, adj (*etym. L.* imitativus), imitative, mimic

Imiter, va. (*etym. L.* imitari), to imitate, to copy, to mimic

Immaculé, e, adj (*etym. L.* immaculatus), unblemished, immaculate

§**Immanquable,** adj. (*etym. see* MANQUABLE), infallible, sure

Immatérialité, sf. (*etym. see* IMMATÉRIEL), immateriality

Immatériel, le, adj. (*etym. L.* immaterialis), immaterial

Immatriculation, sf. matriculation

Immatricule, sf. (*etym.* im. *for* in, matricule), matriculation

Immatriculer, va. to matriculate

§**Immédiat, e,** adj. (*etym. L.* immediatus), immediate

Immensément, adv. (*etym.* immense), immensely, immeasurably

Immensité, sf. (*etym. L* immensitatem), immensity

Immerger, va. (*etym. L.* immergere), to immerge, to immerse

Immeuble, adj. real. — sm. (*etym. L.* immobilis), real estate, house

Immigrer, va. (*etym. L.* immigrare), to immigrate

s'Immiscer, vr. (*etym. L.* immiscere), to intermeddle, to interfere, (*law*) to enter upon

Immixtion, sf. (*etym. L.* immixtionem), interference, meddling

§**Immobile,** adj. (*etym. L.* immobilis), motionless, immoveable

Immobilier, ère, adj. real, of real estate

Immobilisation, sf. conversion of moveable property into real

Immobiliser, va. to convert moveable property into real; *s'*—, vr. to remain unimproved

Immobilité, sf. (*etym. L.* immobilitatem), immoveableness, supineness

Immodéré, e, adj. (*etym. L.* immoderatus), immoderate, intemperate

‖**Immodeste,** adj. (*etym. L.* immodestus), immodest
Immodestie, sf. (*etym. L.* immodestia), immodesty
Immoler, va. (*etym. L.* immolare), to sacrifice, to immolate, to offer up; *s'—*, vr. to sacrifice or immolate oneself, to yield, to give up
Immonde, adj. (*etym. L.* immundus), filthy, unclean
Immondice, sf. (*etym. L.* immunditia), filth, uncleanness
Immoralité, sf. (*etym.* immoral), immorality
Immortaliser, va. (*etym. see* IMMORTEL), to immortalize· *s'—*, vr. to immortalize oneself
Immortalité, sf. (*etym. L.* immortalitatem), immortality
Immortel, le, adj. s. (*etym. L.* immortalis), immortal, deathless. *—le*, sf. everlasting, immortal-herb
‖**Immuable,** adj. (*etym. L.* immutabilis), unalterable, immutable, unchangeable
Immunité, sf. (*etym. L.* immunitatem), immunity
Immutabilité, sf. (*etym. L.* immutabilitatem), immutability
Impair, e, adj. (*etym. see* PAIR), odd, uneven
Impalpabilité, sf. (*etym.* impalpable), impalpability
Impardonnable, adj. (*etym. see* PARDONNABLE), unpardonable, not to be forgiven
‖**Imparfait, e,** adj. sm. (*etym. see* PARFAIT), imperfect, incomplete, imperfection
Imparisyllabique, adj. (*etym. see* PARISYLLABIQUE), imparisyllabic
‖**Impartial, e,** adj. (*etym. see* PARTIAL), impartial, unbiassed
Impartialité, sf. impartiality
Impasse, sf. (*etym. see* PASSE), no thoroughfare, inextricable difficulty
Impassibilité, sf. (*etym. L.* impassibilitatem), impassibility
Impatientant, e, adj. provoking, tiresome
Impatienter, va. (*etym.* impatient), to put out of patience, to provoke; *s'—*, vr. to grow impatient, to be fretful
s'Impatroniser, vr. (*etym. see* PATRON), to play the master
Impayable, adj. (*etym.* payer), priceless, worth any money
Impeccabilité, sf. (*etym. L.* impeccabilitatem), sinlessness
Impeccable, adj. (*etym. L.* impeccabilis), sinless
Impénétrabilité, sf. (*etym.* impénétrable), impenetrability
‖**Impératif, ve,** adj. sm. (*etym. L.* imperativus), commanding, imperative, of command

Impératrice, sf. (*etym. L.* imperatricem), empress
‖**Impérial, e,** adj. (*etym. L.* imperialis), imperial. *Les Impériaux*, the Imperialists
Impériale, sf. roof, top, outside of a coach, (*cards*) all-fours
‖**Impérieux, se,** adj. (*etym. L.* imperiosus), imperious, lordly, dictatorial
‖**Impérissable,** adj. (*etym. see* PÉRISSABLE), imperishable
Impéritie, sf. (*etym. L.* imperitia, *pronounce* impéricie), unskilfulness, incapacity
Imperméabilité, sf. (*etym. see* PERMÉABILITÉ), imperviousness
Imperméable, adj. (*etym. see* PERMÉABLE), impervious, water-proof, air-tight
‖**Impersonnel, le,** adj. (*etym. L.* impersonalis), impersonal
Impertinence, sf. impertinence, extravagance, pert thing. *Dire des —s*, to speak impertinently
‖**Impertinent, e,** adj. s. (*etym. L.* impertinentem), impertinent, wretched, extravagant, impertinent creature
Imperturbabilité, sf. imperturbability
‖**Imperturbable,** adj. (*etym. L.* imperturbabilis), imperturbable, unshaken
Impétrant, e, s. (*etym.* impétrer), grantee, candidate
‖**Impétueux, se,** adj. (*etym. L.* impetuosus), impetuous, wild, boisterous, fierce
Impétuosité, sf. (*etym. L.* impetuositatem), impetuosity, impetuousness
Impie, adj. s. (*etym. L.* impius), impious, godless, ungodly
Impiété, sf. (*etym. L.* impietatem), impiety, impiousness, ungodliness
‖**Impitoyable,** adj. (*etym. see* PITOYABLE), ruthless, unmerciful, pitiless, unpitying
s'Implanter, vr. (*etym. see* PLANTER), to be planted, to be lodged
Implexe, adj. (*etym. L.* implexus), implex, complicated
‖**Implicite,** adj. (*etym. L.* implicitus), implicit
Impliquer, va. (*etym. L.* implicare), to implicate, to involve
Implorer, va. (*etym. L.* implorare), to implore, to cry to, to beseech
§**Impoli, e,** adj. (*etym. L.* impolitus), uncivil, unpolite, rude
Impolitesse, sf. (*etym. see* POLITESSE), incivility, unpoliteness
§**Impolitique,** adj. (*etym. see* POLITIQUE), impolitic
¶**Impopulaire,** adj. (*etym. see* POPULAIRE), unpopular
¶**Impopularité,** sf. (*etym. see* POPULARITÉ), unpopularity

Importance, sf. (*etym. see* IMPORTER), importance, consequence, moment, consequentialness. ‡ *Faire l'homme d'—, se donner des airs d'—*, to set up for a man of importance. *D'un ton d'—*, in a consequential tone
Important, e, adj. important, material, weighty, momentous. — sm. the important part, the main point, man of importance. ‡ *Faire l'—*, to assume a consequential look
Importer, va. (*etym. L.* importare), to import; — vn. to import, to be of importance, to matter, to signify, to care for. ‡ *Peu importe*, it matters little. *N'importe!* never mind
Importun, e, adj. (*etym. L.* importunus), troublesome, importunate, tiresome, irksome. — sm. a troublesome person
Importunément, adv. in a troublesome manner
Importuner, va. to trouble, to importune, to molest
Importunité, sf. (*etym. L.* importunitatem), importunity
Imposable, adj. liable to taxation
Imposant, e, adj. imposing, commanding, striking, awful
Imposer, va. n. (*etym. see* POSER), to lay hands on, to impose, to prescribe, to tax, to assess, to obtrude, to awe. *Les plus imposés*, the highest tax-payers. *— du respect à*, — *à*, to awe, to overawe. *En — à*, to impose upon. *S'—*, vr. to lay down to, to obtrude oneself
Imposition, sf. (*etym. L.* impositionem), imposition, laying on, infliction, tax, duty, (*print.*) imposing
Impossibilité, sf. (*etym. L.* impossibilitatem), impossibility
‖**Impossible,** adj. sm. (*etym. L.* impossibilis), impossible, impossibilities. ‡ *Faire, tenter l'—*, to do, to try impossibilities. ‡ *A l'— nul n'est tenu*, there is no doing impossibilities. *Par —*, against all possibility
Imposte, sf. (*etym. I.* imposta), (*archit.*) impost
Imposteur, sm. (*etym. L.* impostor), impostor
Impôt, sm. (*etym. L.* impositus), tax. *Frapper d'un —*, to tax
§**Imprégner,** va. (*etym. L.* impregnare), to impregnate, to imbue, to taint; *s'—*, vr. to become impregnated
Imprenable, adj. (*etym. see* PRENABLE), impregnable
Imprescriptibilité, sf. indefeasibility
Imprescriptible, adj. (*etym. see* PRESCRIPTIBLE), indefeasible, imprescriptible

Impression, sf. (*etym. L.* impressionem), impression, stamping, print, edition. *Faute d'—*, error of the press. *Frais d'—*, printing expenses
¶**Impressionnable,** adj. sensitive, easily moved, easily affected
¶**Impressionner,** va. to affect, to move; *s'—*, vr to be affected, to be sensitive
Imprévoyance, sf. want of foresight, improvidence, thoughtlessness
Imprévoyant, e, adj. (*etym. see* PRÉVOYANT), improvident
Imprévu, e, adj. (*etym. see* PRÉVU), unforeseen, unlooked for
Imprimé, sm. printed papers
Imprimer, va. (*etym. L.* imprimere), to imprint, to stamp, to print, to impress, (*paint*) to prime, to stain; *s'—*, vr. to be imprinted or impressed, to be printed
Imprimerie, sf. printing, printing-house, printer's tools
Imprimeur, sm. printer
Improbateur, trice, s. adj. (*etym. L.* improbatorem), disapprover, of disapprobation
Improbation, sf. (*etym. L.* improbationem), disapprobation, disapproval
Improbité, sf. (*etym. L.* improbitatem), dishonesty, improbity
‖**Improductif, ve,** adj. (*etym. see* PRODUCTIF), unproductive, barren
Impromptu, sm. adj. (*etym. L.* in . . . promptu), extempore, extemporary
‖**Impropre,** adj. (*etym. L.* improprius), improper, wrong
Impropriété, sf. impropriety
Improuver, va. (*etym. see* PROUVER), to disapprove
Improvisateur, trice, s. improvisator, improvisatress, extemporary speaker
Improvisation, sf. extempore speech, improvisation, prompt getting up of
Improvisé, e, adj. extempore, unpremeditated, got up at a moment's notice
Improviser, va. (*etym. L.* improvisare), to extemporize, to get up a party &c. at a moment's notice
Improviste (à l'), loc. adv. (*etym. I.* improvvisto), unawares, unexpectedly
Impudeur, sf. (*etym. see* PUDEUR), immodesty, indecency, unblushing impudence
Impudicité, sf. (*etym. see* PUDICITÉ), lewdness
‖**Impudique,** adj. (*etym. L.* impudicus), lewd, unchaste
Impuissance, sf. powerlessness, impotency, inability
Impuissant, e, adj. (*etym. see* PUISSANT), powerless, impotent

Impulsion, sf. (*etym. L.* impulsionem), impulse, impetus

Impunément, adv. (*etym.* impuni), with impunity

Impuni, e, adj. (*etym. L.* impunitus), unpunished

Impunité, sf. (*etym. L.* impunitatem), impunity

Impur, e, adj. (*etym. L.* impurus), impure, unchaste, unclean

Impureté, sf. (*etym. L.* impuritatem), impurity, foulness

Imputer, va. (*etym. L.* imputare), to impute, to ascribe, to deduct; *s'—*, vr. to ascribe to oneself, to accuse oneself of

Inabordable, adj. (*etym. see* ABORDABLE), unapproachable, inaccessible

Inacceptable, adj. (*etym. see* ACCEPTABLE), unacceptable

Inaccordable, adj. (*etym. see* ACCORDABLE), irreconcilable, not to be granted

Inaccoutumé, e, adj. (*etym. see* ACCOUTUMÉ), unwonted, unaccustomed, unusual

Inachevé, e, adj. (*etym. see* ACHEVÉ), unachieved, unfinished, incomplete

Inactif, ve, adj. (*etym. see* ACTIF), inactive, sluggish

Inactivité, sf. (*etym. see* ACTIF), inactivity

Inadmissibilité, sf. (*etym.* admissible), inadmissibility

Inadvertance, sf. (*etym. L.L.* inadvertentia), inadvertence, oversight

Inaliénabilité, sf. unalienableness

Inaliénable, adj. (*etym.* aliéner), unalienable

Inaltérable, adj. (*etym.* altérer), unalterable, unchanging, never-failing

Inamovibilité, sf. irremovability

Inamovible, adj. (*etym.* amovible), for life

Inanimé, e, adj. (*etym. L.* inanimatus), inanimate, lifeless, vapid

Inanité, sf. (*etym. L.* inanitatem), emptiness, inanity

Inaperçu, e, adj. (*etym.* aperçu), unseen, unperceived

Inappliqué, e, adj. (*etym.* appliqué), indolent, inattentive

Inarticulé, e, adj. (*etym.* articulé), inarticulate

Inattaquable, adj. (*etym.* attaquable), inexpugnable, unassailable, unobjectionable

Inattendu, e, adj. (*etym.* attendu), unexpected, unforeseen

Inattentif, ve, adj. (*etym.* attentif), inattentive, unmindful

Inaugurer, va. (*etym. L.* inaugurare), to inaugurate

Incapacité, sf. (*etym. L.* in, capacitatem), incapacity, incapability

Incarcérer, va. (*etym. L.* incarcerare), to incarcerate, to imprison

Incarnat, e, adj. (*etym. I.* incarnato), flesh-coloured. — sm. carnation

Incarné, e, adj. (*etym. L.* incarnatus), incarnate

s'Incarner, vr. (*etym. L.* incarnare), to become incarnate

Incartade, sf. (*etym. Sp.* encartada, *the action of taking a bad card*), insult, (*pl.*) freaks, pranks

Incendiaire, sm. adj. (*etym. L.* incendiarius), incendiary

Incendie, sm. (*etym. L.* incendium), fire, conflagration

Incendier, va. to set fire to

Incertain, e, adj. (*etym. see* CERTAIN), uncertain, questionable, unsettled. — sm. the uncertain, uncertainty

Incertitude, sf. (*etym. L.* incertitudinem), uncertainty, unsettled character

Incessant, e, adj. (*etym. L.* incessantem), unceasing, incessant, ceaseless

Incessible, adj. (*etym.* céder), untransferable

Inceste, sm. (*etym. L.* incestus), incest, incestuous person

Incestueux, se, adj. incestuous

Incident, e, adj. (*etym. L.* incidentem), incidental, incident

Incirconcis, e, adj. (*etym.* circoncis), uncircumcised

Incirconcision, sf. uncircumcision

Incise, sf. (*etym. L.* incisus) incidental phrase

Inciser, va. (*etym. L.* incisare), to make an incision in, to tap, to incise

Incisif, ve, adj. incisive

Incitant, e, adj. inciting

Inciter, va. (*etym. L.* incitare), to incite, to urge on

Incivil, e, adj. (*etym. L.* incivilis), uncivil, rude

Incivilité, sf. (*etym. L.* incivilitatem), incivility, rudeness

Incivique, adj. (*etym.* civique), incivic, unpatriotic

Incivisme, sm. (*etym.* civisme), incivism

Inclémence, sf. (*etym. L.* inclementia), inclemency

Inclinaison, sf. (*etym. L.* inclinationem), inclination, (*mines*) dip, dipping

Incliner, va. (*etym. L.* inclinare), to incline, to bow, to bend, to feel inclined *or* disposed, to dip; *s'—*, vr. to incline, to lean, to bow, to hang down

Inclus, e, adj. (*etym. L.* inclusus), enclosed. *Ci —*, herein enclosed

Inclusivement, adv. inclusively

Incohérence, sf. (*etym.* incohérent), incoherency

Incolore, adj. (*etym. L.* incolor), colourless

Incombustibilité, sf. (*etym.* incombustible), incombustibility

Incommensurabilité, sf. (*etym.* incommensurable), incommensurability

Incommode, adj. (*etym. L.* incommodus), incommodious, inconvenient, clumsy, troublesome, tiresome

Incommoder, va. (*etym. L.* incommodare), to inconvenience, to incommode, to disturb, to disagree with; *s'—*, vr. to put oneself to inconvenience, to be in each other's way

Incommodité, sf. (*etym. L.* incommoditatem), inconvenience, incommodiousness, ailment, distress

Incompatibilité, sf. (*etym.* incompatible), incompatibility

Incompétence, sf. (*etym.* compétence), incompetency

Incomplet, e, adj. (*etym.* complet), incomplete

Incomplexe, adj. (*etym. L.* incomplexus), incomplex, simple

Incompressibilité, sf. (*etym.* incompressible), incompressibility

Incompris, e, adj. (*etym.* compris), not understood

Inconcevable, adj. (*etym.* concevable), inconceivable

Inconciliable, adj (*etym.* conciliable), irreconcilable

Inconduite, sf. (*etym.* conduite), misconduct, bad behaviour

Incongru, e, adj. (*etym. L.* incongruus), incongruous, unseemly

Incongruité, sf. (*etym. L.* incongruitatem), impropriety, incongruity

Inconnu, e, adj. s. (*etym.* connu), unknown, stranger, unknown person, the unknown

Inconséquence, sf. (*etym. L.* inconsequentia), inconsistency

Inconséquent, e, adj. (*etym. L.* inconsequentem), inconsistent, incautious, forgetful of propriety

Inconsidéré, e, adj. (*etym. L.* inconsideratus), inconsiderate, heedless, unwise

Inconstance, sf. (*etym. L.* inconstantia), inconstancy, unsteadiness, unstableness

Inconstitutionnel, le, adj. (*etym.* constituer), unconstitutional

Incontesté, e, adj. (*etym.* contester), uncontested

Incontinent, adv. (*etym. L.* in, continenti), forthwith

Inconvenance, sf. impropriety, unbecomingness

Inconvenant, e, adj (*etym.* convenir), improper, unbecoming

Inconvénient, sm. (*etym. L.* inconvenientem), inconvenience

Incorporel, le, adj. (*etym. L.* incorporalis), incorporeal

Incorporer, va. (*etym. L.* incorporare), to incorporate, to embody; *s'—*, vr to incorporate, to become embodied

Incorrection, sf. (*etym.* incorrect), incorrectness, inaccuracy

Incorrigibilité, sf. (*etym.* incorrigible), incorrigibleness

Incorruptibilité, sf. (*etym. L.* incorruptibilitatem), incorruptibility

Incrédibilité, sf. (*etym. L.* incredibilitatem), incredibility

Incrédule, adj. s. (*etym. L.* incredulus), incredulous, slow of belief, unbeliever, disbeliever

Incrédulité, sf. (*etym. L.* incredulitatem), incredulousness, unbelief

Incréé, e, adj. (*etym. L.* increatus), uncreated, increate

Incriminer, va. (*etym. L.* incriminari), to criminate, to incriminate

Incroyable, adj. sm. (*etym.* croyable), incredible, beyond all belief, the incredible, something incredible, (!) a dandy

Incruster, va. (*etym. L.* incrustare), to inlay, to incrustate; *s'—*, vr. to become incrusted

Inculpation, sf. (*etym. L.* inculpationem), crimination, accusing

Inculpé, e, smf. the accused

Inculper, va. (*etym. L.* inculpare), to criminate, to accuse; *s'—*, vr to criminate oneself, to criminate each other

Inculquer, va. (*etym. L.* inculcare), to inculcate, to impress; *s'—*, vr. to be inculcated

Inculte, adj. (*etym. L.* incultus), uncultivated, waste, untilled, wild, uneducated, unpolished

Incurie, sf. (*etym. L.* incuria), carelessness, heedlessness

Incuriosité, sf. (*etym.* curiosité), listlessness of mind, incuriosity

Indécence, sf. (*etym. L.* indecentia), indecency, indecorum

Indéchiffrable, adj. (*etym.* déchiffrer), undecipherable, illegible, unintelligible

Indécis, e, adj. (*etym. L.* indecisus), undecided, doubtful, wavering, irresolute

Indécrottable, adj (*etym.* décrotter), impossible to clean, (!) clownish, untractable

Indéfini, e, adj. (*etym. L.* indefinitus), indefinite

Indéfinissable, adj. (*etym.* définir), undefinable

Indélébile, adj. indelible

Indélicat, e, adj. (*etym.* délicat), indelicate, unhandsome

Indélicatesse, sf. indelicacy, unhandsome action

Indemniser, va. (*etym. L.* indemnis), to indemnify, to make good; *s'—*, vr. to indemnify oneself

Indemnité, sf. (*etym. L.* indemnitatem), indemnity

Indépendance, sf. independence, freedom

‖**Indépendant, e**, adj. (*etym.* dépendant), independent

Indestructibilité, sf. (*etym.* indestructible), indestructibility

Indéterminé, e, adj. (*etym.* déterminé), indeterminate, irresolute

Indicatif, ve, adj. sm. (*etym.* L. indicativus), indicative mood

Indice, sm. (*etym.* L. indicium), indication, token, sign, mark, proof

‖**Indicible**, adj. (*etym.* L. dicibilis), unutterable, unspeakable

Indienne, sf. (*etym.* Inde), printed calico, chintz

Indigène, adj. s. (*etym.* L. indigena), indigenous, native

Indigeste, adj. (*etym.* L. indigestus), indigestible, undigested, crude

§‖**Indigne**, adj. (*etym.* L. indignus), unworthy, undeserving

§**Indigner**, va. (*etym.* L. indignari), to rouse the indignation of; *s'*—, vr. to be indignant, to wax wroth

§**Indignité**, sf. (*etym.* L. indignitatem), unworthiness, undeservingness, indignity, baseness

Indigotier, sm. (*etym.* indigo), indigo plant

Indiquer, va. (*etym.* L. indicare), to point out, to indicate, to show

Indiscipliné, e, adj. (*etym.* L. indisciplinatus), undisciplined

‖**Indiscret, ète**, adj. (*etm.* L. indiscretus), indiscreet, inconsiderate, injudicious, prying, inquisitive

¶**Indiscutable**, adj. (*etym.* discuter), which does not allow of discussion

Indisposé, e, adj. indisposed, unwell, poorly

Indisposer, va. (*etym.* disposer), to disorder, to indispose, to set

Indissolubilité, sf. (*etm.* dissoluble), indissolubility

Individu, sm. (*etym.* L. individuus), individual, fellow. † *Soigner son* —, to take care of number one

Individualiser, va. to individualise

¶**Individualisme**, sm. individualism

Individualité, sf. individuality

‖**Individuel, le**, adj. (*etym.* individu), individual

Indivis, e, adj. (*etym.* L. indivisus), undivided

Indivisibilité, sf. (*etym.* indivisible), indivisibility

In-dix-huit, sm. adj. decimo octavo, 18mo

Indocilité, sf. (*etym.* indocile), indocility, waywardness, untractableness

‖**Indomptable**, adj. (*etym.* dompter), indomitable, untameable, uncontrollable

Indompté, e, adj. (*etym.* dompter), untamed, wild

In-douze, adj. sm. duodecimo, 12mo

‖**Indu, e**, adj. (*etym.* dû), undue, unseasonable, late

Induire, va. (*etym.* L. inducere), to induce, to lead, to infer

Industrie, sf. (*etym.* L. industria), ingenuity, trade, business. ‡ *Vivre d'*—, to live by one's wits. *Chevalier d'*—, swindler

‖**Industriel, le**, adj. manufacturing, mechanical. — sm. manufacturer

‖**Industrieux, se**, adj. (*etym.* L. industriosus), ingenious, clever

‖**Inébranlable**, adj. (*etm.* ébranler), immoveable, unshaken, resolute

Inédit, e, adj. (*etym.* L. ineditus), unpublished, inedited

Ineffabilité, sf. (*etym.* ineffable), ineffableness

‖**Ineffaçable**, adj. (*etym.* effacer), indelible

‖**Inefficace**, adj. (*etym.* L. inefficacem), inefficacious, ineffectual, inefficient

‖**Inefficacité**, sf. inefficacy, inefficiency

‖**Inégal, e**, adj. (*etym.* L. inaequalis), unequal, uneven, irregular

Inégalité, sf. (*etym.* L. inaequalitatem), inequality, unevenness, irregularity

¶**Inéligibilité**, sf. (*etym.* inéligible), ineligibility

Inepte, adj. (*etym.* L. ineptus), unfit, unapt, unsuitable, stupid, foolish

Ineptie, sf. (*etym.* L. ineptia, *pronounce* inepcie), folly, absurdity

Inépuisable, adj. (*etym.* épuiser), inexhaustible, exhaustless

Inerte, adj. (*etym.* L. inertem), inert, sluggish

Inertie, sf. (*etym.* L. inertia, *pronounce* inercie), inertia, state of rest, inertness, sluggishness

‖**Inespéré, e**, adj. (*etym.* espérer), unhoped for

Inexactitude, sf. (*etym.* exactitude), inaccuracy, incorrectness, inexactness

Inexécutable, adj. (*etym.* exécuter), impracticable

Inexercé, e, adj. (*etym.* exercer), unexercised

Inexigible, adj. (*etym.* exiger), that cannot be required

Inexpérimenté, e, adj. (*etym.* expérimenter), unpractised, inexperienced, inexpert

Inexplosible, adj. (*etym.* explosible), inexplosive

Inexprimable, adj. (*etm.* exprimer), unutterable, inexpressible

Inextinguible, adj. (*etm.* L. inextinguibilis), unquenchable, inextinguishable, irrepressible

§‖**Infaillibilité**, sf. infallibility

§‖**Infaillible**, adj. (*etym.* faillir), infallible, unerring

Infamant, e, adj. ignominious

Infâme, adj. (*etym.* L. infamis), infamous, squalid, filthy

Infamie, sf. (*etym.* L. infamia), infamy. ‡ *Dire des* —*s*, to say all manner of horrid things

Infant, e, s. (*etym.* Sp. infante), Infante, Infanta

Infanterie, sf. (*etym.* I. infanteria), infantry, foot-soldiers

‖**Infatigable**, adj. (*etym.* L. infatigabilis), unwearied, untiring, indefatigable

Infatuer, va. (*etym.* L. infatuare), to infatuate, to bewitch; *s'*—, vr. to become infatuated

Infécond, e, adj. (*etym.* L. infecundus), unfruitful, barren

Infécondité, sf. (*etym.* L. infecunditatem), unfruitfulness, barrenness

Infect, e, adj. (*etym.* L. infectus), foul, stinking, tainted, infectious

Infecter, va. to infect, to taint

Inféoder, va. (*etym.* L.L. infeodare), to infeoff

Inférer, va. (*etym.* L. inferre), to infer, to conclude

‖**Inférieur, e**, adj. (*etym.* L. inferiorem), lower, inferior, nether. — sm. subaltern, underling, understrapper

Infériorité, sf. inferiority

‖**Infernal, e**, adj. (*etym.* L. infernalis), hellish, infernal, of hell. *Pierre* —*e*, caustic

‖**Infertile**, adj. (*etym.* L. infertilis), unfertile, barren

Infertilité, sf. infertility, barrenness

Infester, va. (*etym.* L. infestare), to infest, to haunt

‖**Infidèle**, adj. s. (*etym.* L. infidelis), faithless, false, unfaithful, untrue, infidel, unbeliever

Infidélité, sf. (*etym.* L. infidelitatem), faithlessness, untruth, dishonesty, unbelief

s'**Infiltrer**, vr. (*etym.* filtre), to infiltrate, to glide, to creep in

Infime, adj. (*etym.* L. infimus), meanest, lowest

‖**Infini, e**, adj. (*etym.* L. infinitus), infinite, unbounded, boundless, endless. — sm. infinity, the infinite

Infinité, sf. (*etym.* L. infinitatem), infinity, infiniteness, infinitude

Infinitif, sm. adj. (*etym.* infinitivus), infinitive mood, infinitive

Infirmatif, ve, adj. (*etym.* L. infirmativus), of invalidation

Infirme, adj. (*etym.* L. infirmus), infirm, feeble

Infirmer, va. (*etym.* L. infirmare), to invalidate, to reverse

Infirmerie, sf. sick-ward, infirmary

Infirmier, sm. attendant on the sick

Infirmière, sf. nurse, sick-nurse

Infirmité, sf. (*etym.* L. infirmitatem), infirmity, failing

Inflammatoire, adj. (*etym.* inflammation), inflammatory

s'**Infléchir**, vr. (*etym.* L. inflectere), to bend, to be inflected

Inflexibilité, sf. (*etym.* inflexible), inflexibility

Inflexion, sf. (*etym.* L. inflexionem), inflection

Infliger, va. (*etym.* L. infligere), to inflict, to impose; *s'*—, vr. to inflict upon oneself

Influencer, va. (*etym.* influence), to influence, to bias

Influent, e, adj. influential

Influer, vn. (*etym.* L. influere), to influence

In-folio, sm. adj. folio

Informe, adj. (*etym.* L. informis), shapeless, ill-shapen, unformed, crude, imperfect

Informer, va. (*etym.* L. informare), to inform, to apprise, to acquaint; — vn. to institute an inquiry; *s'*—, vr. to inquire

Infortune, sf. (*etym.* L. infortunium), misfortune

Infortuné, e, adj. (*etym.* L. infortunatus), unfortunate, ill-fated, wretched

Infréquenté, e, adj. (*etm.* fréquenter), unfrequented

‖**Infructueux, se**, adj. (*etym.* L. infructuosus), unfruitful, unavailing

Infus, e, adj. (*etym.* L. infusus, *poured upon*), intuitive

Infuser, va. to infuse, to steep

Infusoire, adj. infusory

Infusoires, sm. plur. infusoria

Ingambe, adj. (*etym.* I. ingambo, *nimble*), nimble, brisk

s'**Ingénier**, vr. (*etym.* L. ingeniari), to tax one's ingenuity, to contrive

Ingénieur, sm. (*etym.* L.L. ingeniatorem), engineer

‖**Ingénieux, se**, adj (*etym.* L. ingeniosus), ingenious, clever, witty

‖**Ingénu, e**, adj. s. (*etym.* L. ingenuus), artless, guileless, without guile, ingenuous-hearted person. *Faire l'*—, to affect simplicity. *Jouer les* —*es*, to play the parts of artless girls

Ingénuité, sf. (*etym.* L. ingenuitatem), artlessness, simplicity, ingenuousness, character of artless girls

s'**Ingérer**, vr. (*etym.* L. ingerere), to meddle, to dabble, to take upon oneself

‖**Ingrat, e**, adj. (*etym.* L. ingratus), ungrateful, thankless, unprofitable, unpleasant, unpromising. — s. ungrateful person

Inguérissable, adj. (*etym.* guérir), incurable

‖**Inhabile**, adj. (*etym.* *L.* inhabilis), inexpert, unskilled, awkward, incompetent

Inhabileté, sf. inability, inexpertness

Inhabitable, adj. (*etym.* *L.* inhabitabilis), uninhabitable

Inhabité, e, adj. (*etym.* habiter), uninhabited, untenanted

‖**Inhospitalier**, ère, adj. inhospitable

Inhospitalité, sf. (*etym.* *L.* inhospitalitatem), inhospitality

‖**Inhumain**, e, adj. (*etym.* *L.* inhumanus), inhuman

Inhumanité, sf. (*etym.* *L.* inhumanitatem), inhumanity

Inhumation, sf. burial, interment

Inhumer, va. (*etym.* *L.* inhumare), to entomb, to inhume

Inimaginable, adj. (*etym.* imaginable), unimaginable

Inimitié, sf. (*etym.* *L.* inimicitatem, *pronounce* inimicié), enmity, ill-will, hatred

Inintelligible, adj. (*etym.* intelligible), unintelligible

Inique, adj. (*etym.* *L.* iniquus), iniquitous, unrighteous

Iniquité, sf. (*etym.* *L.* iniquitatem), iniquity, evil-doing, piece of iniquity

Initié, e, s. (*pron.* inicié), the initiated

Initier, va. (*etym.* *L.* initiare, *pron.* inicier), to initiate

Injecter, va. (*etym.* *L.* injectare), to inject; *s'*—, vr. to make injections, to become injected

Injonction, sf. (*etym.* *L.* injunctionem), injunction, behest

Injure, sf. (*etym.* *L.* injuria), wrong, injury, insult, taunt, (*plur.*) abusive language

Injurier, va. (*etym.* *L.* injuriari), to revile, to abuse; *s'*—, vr. to abuse each other

‖**Injurieux**, se, adj. (*etym.* *L.* injuriosus), insulting, abusive, outrageous, injurious

‖**Injuste**, adj. (*etym.* *L.* injustus), unjust, wrongful, wrong. — sm. the unjust man, the wrong-doer, what is unjust

Inné, e, adj. (*etym.* *L.* innatus), inborn, innate

Innocenter, va. (*etym.* innocent), to acquit

Innocuité, sf. (*etym.* *L.* innocuitatem), harmlessness, innocuousness

‖**Innombrable**, adj. (*etym.* *L.* innumerabilis), countless, innumerable

Innovateur, sm. innovator

Innover, va.n. (*etym.* *L.* innovare), to innovate, to make innovations

Inobservation, sf. (*etym.* observation), inobservance, breach

Inoccupé, e, adj. (*etym.* occuper), unoccupied, unemployed

In-octavo, sm.adj. octavo, 8vo

Inoculateur, trice, s. (*etym.* *L.* inoculatorem), inoculator

Inoculer, va. (*etym.* *L.* inoculare), to inoculate, to ingraft; *s'*—, vr. to be inoculated, to be ingrafted

Inodore, adj. (*etym.* *L.* inodorus), inodorous, scentless

‖**Inoffensif**, ve, adj. (*etym.* offensif), inoffensive, harmless

Inondation, sf. (*etym.* *L.* inundationem), inundation, flood

Inonder, va. (*etym.* *L.* inundare), to overflood, to overflow, to deluge

Inopiné, e, adj. (*etym.* *L.* inopinatus), unexpected, unlooked for

Inopportun, e, adj. (*etym.* *L.* inopportunus), unseasonable, inopportune

Inopportunément, adv. inopportunely

Inopportunité, sf. (*etym.* *L.* inopportunitatem), unseasonableness, inopportuneness

Inorganique, adj. (*etym.* organique), inorganic

Inouï, e, adj. (*etym.* ouïr), unheard of, most wonderful

¶**Inqualifiable**, adj. (*etym.* qualifiable), without a name

In-quarto, sm.adj. quarto, 4to

‖**Inquiet**, ète, adj. (*etym.* *L.* inquietus), disquieted, anxious, uneasy

Inquiétant, e, adj. alarming, disquieting

Inquiéter, va. (*etym.* *L.* inquietare), to disquiet, to make uneasy, to alarm; *s'*—, vr. to make oneself uneasy, to concern oneself, to care for or about

Inquiétude, sf. (*etym.* *L.* inquietudinem), disquiet, uneasiness, anxiety, restlessness

Inquisiteur, sm. (*etym.* *L.* inquisitorem), inquisitor

‖**Insaisissable**, adj. (*etym.* saisir), not liable to distrainment, undiscernible, imperceptible

‖**Insalubre**, adj. (*etym.* *L.* insalubris), insalubrious, unwholesome, unhealthy

Insalubrité, sf. (*etym.* *L.* insalubritatem), insalubrity, unhealthiness, unwholesomeness

Insatiabilité, sf. (*etym.* *L.* insatiabilitatem), insatiableness

Inscription, sf. (*etym.* *L.* inscriptionem), inscription, term, allegation, plea. *Prendre ses* —*s*, to enter for the term. *Former une* — *de faux*, to allege forgery

Inscrire, va. (*etym.* *L.* inscribere), to put down, to enter, to inscribe. *Se faire* —, to have one's name put down. *S'*—, vr. to write down one's name. *S'*— *en faux*, to plead the falsity of, completely to deny

‖**Insensé**, e, adj. s. (*etym.* *L.* insensatus), mad, insane, foolish, rash, maniac, insane person, fool

Insensibilité, sf. (*etym.* *L.* insensibilitatem), insensibility, insensibleness, unconcern

Insérer, va. (*etym.* *L.* inserere), to insert, to put

¶**Insermenté**, e, adj. (*etym.* serment), unsworn

‖**Insidieux**, se, adj. (*etym.* *L.* insidiosus), insidious

§**Insigne**, adj. (*etym.* *L.* insignis), signal, egregious. — sm. insignia, badge, sign

Insignifiance, sf. unmeaningness, insignificance

Insignifiant, e, adj. (*etym.* signifier), unmeaning, insignificant

Insinuant, e, adj. insinuating

Insinuer, va. (*etym.* *L.* insinuare), to insinuate, to hint; *s'*—, vr. to insinuate oneself

‖**Insipide**, adj. (*etym.* *L.* insipidus), insipid, tasteless, dull

Insipidité, sf. insipidity, dulness

Insistance, sf. persistence, insisting

Insister, vn. (*etym.* *L.* insistere), to persist, to insist, to urge, to dwell upon

Insociabilité, sf. unsociableness

‖**Insociable**, adj. (*etym.* *L.* insociabilis), unsociable, sullen

Insolite, adj. (*etym.* *L.* insolitus), unusual, unwonted, unprecedented

Insolubilité, sf. (*etym.* *L.* insolubilitatem), insolubility, insolvability

Insolvabilité, sf. insolvency

Insolvable, adj. (*etym.* solvable), insolvent

Insomnie, sf. (*etym.* *L.* insomnia), sleeplessness

Insouciance, sf. carelessness, heedlessness

Insouciant, e, adj. (*etym.* soucier), careless, heedless, unmindful

Insoumis, e, adj. (*etym.* soumettre), unsubdued

‖**Insoutenable**, adj. (*etym.* soutenable), untenable, insupportable

Inspecter, va. (*etym.* *L.* inspectare), to inspect, to survey

Inspecteur, sm. (*etym.* *L.* inspectorem), inspector

Inspirateur, trice, adj. (*etym.* *L.* inspiratorem), inspiring, inspiratory

Inspiré, e, s. a person inspired

Inspirer, va. (*etym.* *L.* inspirare), to inspire, to breathe into, to prompt, to impel

Instabilité, sf. (*etym.* *L.* instabilitatem), instability, unstableness

Installer, va. (*etym.* stalle), to instal; *s'*—, vr. to instal oneself

Instance, sf. (*etym.* *L.* instantia), entreaty, instance

‖**Instant**, e, adj. (*etym.* *L.* instantem), earnest, urgent, instant. — sm. moment, instant

‖**Instantané**, e, adj. instantaneous

Instar (**à l'**), loc. prep. (*etym.* *L.* instar), in imitation of, like

Instigateur, trice, s. (*etym.* *L.* instigatorem), instigator

Instiller, va. to instil

‖**Instinctif**, ve, adj. (*etym.* instinct), instinctive

Instituer, va. (*etym.* *L.* instituere), to institute, to establish, to appoint

Institut, sm. (*etym.* *L.* institutum), institution, order, institute

Instituteur, sm. (*etym.* *L.* institutorem), institutor, tutor, teacher

Institutrice, sf. institutress, governess, schoolmistress

Instructeur, sm.adj. (*etym.* *L.* instructorem), instructer, instructing. *Capitaine* —, drill-captain. *Juge* —, examining magistrate

Instructif, ve, adj. (*etym.* *L.* instructivus), instructive

Instruction, sf. (*etym.* *L.* instructionem), instruction, education attainments, direction, examination. *Juge d'*—, examining magistrate

Instruire, va. (*etym.* *L.* instruere), to instruct, to educate, to inform, to examine; *s'*—, vr. to acquire instruction, to be under examination

Instruit, e, past part. adj. acquainted with, well-informed, well-educated

Instrumentaire, adj. (*etym.* instrument), to a deed

Instrumentation, sf. composition of the instrumental part

Instrumenter, vn.a. (*etym.* instrument), to draw up a deed, to compose the instrumental part

Insu, sm. (*etym.* see Savoir), without the knowledge. *A l'*— *de*, unknown to. *A mon* —, unknown to me

Insubordonné, e, adj. (*etym.* subordonner), insubordinate

Insuffisance, sf. (*etym.* *L.* insufficentia), insufficiency

‖**Insuffisant**, e, adj. (*etym.* *L.* insufficientem), insufficient, inadequate

Insulaire, adj. sm. (*etym.* *L.* insularis), insular, islander

Insultant, e, adj. insulting

Insulte, sf. (*etym. L.* insultus), insult, affront, taunt

Insulter, va.n. (*etym. L.* insultare), to insult, to affront, to taunt

Insurgé, e, s.adj. insurgent

s'Insurger, vr. (*etym. L.* insurgere), to rise in insurrection

‖**Insurmontable,** adj. (*etym.* surmonter), insurmountable, impuperable

¶**Insurrectionnel, le,** adj. (*etym.* insurrection), insurrectionary

Intact, e, adj. (*etym. L.* intactus), untouched, inviolate, undamaged

‖**Intarissable,** adj. (*etym.* tarir), never-failing, inexhaustible, exhaustless

Intégralité, sf. (*etym.* intégral), wholeness, entireness

Intégrant, e, adj. integral. *Partie —e de*, part and parcel of

‖**Intègre,** adj. (*etym. L.* integer), upright, just, of integrity

Intégrer, va. (*etym. L.* integrare), to integrate

Intégrité, sf. (*etym. L.* integritatem), integrity

‖**Intellectuel, le,** adj. (*etym. L.* intellectualis), intellectual

Intelligence, sf. (*etym. L.* intelligentia), intelligence, understanding, ability, harmony, compact. *Entretenir des —s avec quelqu'un*, to keep up a correspondence with a person

Intempérie, sf. (*etym. L.* intemperies), intemperateness, inclemency

‖**Intempestif, ve,** adj. (*etym. L.* intempestivus), ill-timed, mistimed, unseasonable

Intendance, sf. superintendence, management, stewardship, commissariat, intendant's house or office

Intendant, sm. (*etym. L.* intendentem), steward, agent, intendant, surveyor. — *militaire*, commissary of stores. — *en chef*, chief commissary

Intensité, sf. (*etym.* intense), intensity

Intenter, va. (*etym. L.* intentare), to enter, to bring

Intentionné, e, adj. (*etym.* intention), intentioned, meaning

‖**Intentionnel, le,** adj. intentional

Intercalaire, adj. (*etym. L.* intercalaris), intercalary

Intercaler, va. (*etym. L.* intercalare), to intercalate, to interpolate

Intercéder, vn. (*etym. L.* intercedere), to intercede

Intercepter, va. (*etym. L.* interceptare), to intercept, to stop

Intercesseur, sm. (*etym. L.* intercessorem), intercessor

Interdire, va. (*etym. L.* interdicere), to forbid, to interdict, to suspend, to stupefy. ‡ *Faire — quelqu'un*, to obtain an act of lunacy against a person

Interdit, sm. (*etym. L.* interdictum), interdict

Intéressant, e, adj. interesting

Intéressé, e, past part. adj. concerned, interested

Intéresser, va. (*etym. L.* interesse), to interest, to give an interest, to gain over, to injure; *s'—*, vr. to interest oneself in

Intérêt, sm. (*etym. L.* interest), interest, self-interest, selfishness. *Les —s des —s*, compound interest

‖**Intérieur, e,** adj. (*etym. L.* interiorem), inward, inner, interior. — sm. inside, interior, inner part, the home, home department

¶**Intérimaire,** adj. (*etym. L.* interim), ad interim, temporary

Interjection, sf. (*etym. L.* interjectionem), interjection. — *d'appel*, lodging of an appeal

Interjeter, va. (*etym. L.* interjectare), to lodge an appeal

§**Interligne,** sm. (*etym. L.* inter, ligne), space between two lines. — sf. lead, spaceline

§**Interligner,** va. to lead

Interlinéaire, adj. interlinear

Interlocuteur, trice, s. (*etym. L.* interlocutorem), speaker, interlocutor, opponent

Interlocutoire, sm.adj. interlocutory judgment, interlocutory

¶**Interlope,** sm.adj. (*etym. Engl.* interlope), interloper, interloping

Interloquer, va. (*etym. L.* interloqui), to grant an interlocutory, (†) to nonplus

Intermède, sm. (*etym. L.* intermedius), interlude, intermediate

Intermédiaire, adj. intermediate, intervening. — sm. intermedium, intermediate agent, middle-man

Intermédiat, e, adj. intermediate

Intermittence, sf. (*etym.* intermittent), intermission

Internat, sm. boarding-school, a house-surgeon's employment

Interne, adj. (*etym. L.* internus), internal, interior, (*anat.*) mesial. — sm. boarder, house-surgeon

Internonce, sm. (*etym. L.* internuntius), internuncio

Interpeller, va. (*etym. L.* interpellare), to call upon, to challenge, to apostrophize

Interpolateur, sm. (*etym.* interpoler), interpolator

Interpoler, va. (*etym. L.* interpolare), to interpolate

Interposer, va., *s'—*, vr. (*etym. L.* inter, poser), to interpose

Interprète, sm. (*etym. L.* interpretem), interpreter, expounder

Interpréter, va. (*etym. L.* interpretari), to interpret, to expound, to explain; *s'—*, vr. to be interpreted

Interrègne, sm. (*etym. L.* interregnum), interregnum

Interrogateur, trice, s. (*etym. L.* interrogatorem), questioner, interrogator

Interrogatif, ve, adj. (*etym. L.* interrogativus), interrogative

Interrogatoire, sm. examination, interrogatory

Interroger, va. to question, to interrogate; *s'—*, vr. to examine oneself, to question each other

Interrompre, va. (*etym. L.* interrumpere), to interrupt, to break off, to put a stop to; *s'—*, vr. to break off, to interrupt oneself

Interrupteur, trice, s. (*etym. L.* interruptorem), interrupter

Intervalle, sm. (*etym. L.* intervallum), interval

Intervenant, e, adj. intervening

Intervenir, vn. (*etym. L.* intervenire), to interfere, to intervene

Interversion, sf. (*etym.* interversionem), inversion

Intervertir, va. (*etym. L.* intervertere), to invert, to reverse, to change

Intestat, adj. sm. (*etym. L.* intestatus), intestate. *Ab —*, intestate

Intestin, e, adj. (*etym. L.* intestinus), intestine, civil, domestic. — sm. intestine, bowel

‖**Intime,** smf. adj. (*etym. L.* intimus), intimate, inmost

Intimé, e, s. appellee, defendant

Intimer, va. (*etym. L.* intimare), to notify, to give notice of

Intimider, va. (*etym.* timide), to intimidate; *s'—*, vr. to feel intimidated

Intimité, sf. closeness, close connection, intimacy

Intitulé, sm. title

Intituler, va (*etym. L.* intitulare), to entitle, to call, to name; *s'—*, vr. to call oneself, to take the title of

Intraduisible, adj. (*etym.* traduire), untranslatable

Intraitable, adj. (*etym.* traiter), overbearing, uncivil, unmanageable, untractable

‖**Intrépide,** adj. (*etym. L.* intrepidus), intrepid, fearless

Intrépidité, sf. intrepidity, fearlessness

Intrigant, e, adj. intriguing. — s. intriguer, adventurer

Intriguer, va. (*etym.* intrigue = *I.* intrigo), to perplex, to puzzle, to put a great deal of plot into; — vn., *s'—*, vr. to intrigue

Intrinsèque, adj. (*etym. L.* intrinsecus), intrinsic, intrinsical

Introducteur, trice, s. (*etym. L.* introductorem), introducer

Introduire, va. (*etym. L.* introducere), to introduce, to show in, to lead; *s'—*, vr. to get in, to find one's way in

Intronisation, sf. throning

Introniser, va. (*etym. L.L.* inthronizare), to throne; *s'—*, vr. to be throned

Introuvable, adj. (*etym.* trouver), undiscoverable, not to be found

Intrus, e, adj. s. (*etym. L.* intrusum), intruding, intruder

‖**Intuitif, ve,** adj. (*etym. L.* intuitivus), intuitive

Inusité, e, adj. (*etym. L.* inusitatus), unwonted, not in use

‖**Inutile,** adj. (*etym. L.* inutilis), useless, needless, unnecessary

Inutilité, sf. (*etym. L.* inutilitatem), uselessness, needlessness

Invaincu, e, adj. (*etym.* vaincu), unconquered, unvanquished

Invalide, adj. smf. (*etym. L.* invalidus), infirm, invalid

Invalider, va. to invalidate

Invalidité, sf. invalidity, nullity

Invariabilité, sf. (*etym.* invariable), invariableness, unchangeableness

Invectiver, va. (*etym.* invective = *L.* invectiva), to rail at *or* against, to revile

Invendable, adj. (*etym.* vendable), unsaleable

Invendu, e, adj. (*etym.* vendu), unsold

Inventaire, sm. (*etym. L.* inventorium), inventory. ‡ *Sous bénéfice d'—*, without liability to debts beyond the assets descended

Inventer, va. (*etym. L.* inventare), to invent, to contrive, to find out

Inventeur, trice, s. (*etym. L.* inventorem), inventor, contriver

Inventif, ve, adj. (*etym.* inventer), inventive, quick, ingenious

Inventorier, va. (*etym.* inventaire), to inventory

¶**Inversable,** adj. (*etym.* verser), which cannot be upset

Invertébré, adj. (*etym.* vertébré), invertebrate

Inverti, e, past part. (*etym. L.* invertere), reversed

Investigateur, trice, s. (*etym. L.* investigatorem), investigator. — adj. searching, prying, inquisitive

Investir, va. (*etym. L.* investire), to invest

Investissement, sm. investment

Invétérer, vn., *s'—*, vr. (*etym. L.* inveterare), to grow inveterate

Inviolabilité, sf. (*etym.* inviolable = *L.* inviolabilis), inviolability

Invisibilité, sf. (*etym. L.* invisibilitatem), invisibility

Invité, e, smf. person invited

Inviter, va. (*etym. L.* invitare), to invite, to bid; *s'*—, vr. to invite oneself

‖**Involontaire**, adj. (*etym. L.* involuntarius), involuntary

Involution, sf. (*etm. L.* involutionem), involvement

Invoquer, va. (*etym. L.* invocare), to call upon, to invoke

‖**Invraisemblable**, adj. (*etym.* vraisemblable), unlikely, improbable

Invraisemblance, sf. (*etym.* vraisemblance), unlikelihood, improbability

Iode, sm. (*etym. Gr.* ἰώδης, *of a violet colour*), iodine

Iodure, sm. ioduret

Ionien, ne, adj. (*etym. proper name* Ἴων), Ionian, Ionic

Ionique, adj. Ionic

Irascibilité, sf. (*etym.* irascible = *L.* irascibilis), irascibility

s'Iriser, vr. (*etym.* iris), to take all the hues of the rainbow

Ironie, sf. (*etym. L.* ironia), irony

‖**Ironique**, adj. ironical, ironic

‖**Irraisonnable**, adj. (*etym.* raisonnable), irrational, void of reason

‖**Irrationnel, le**, adj. (*etym. L.* irrationalis), irrational

‖**Irrécusable**, adj. (*etym. L.* irrecusabilis), unimpeachable

Irréductibilité, sf. irreducibleness

Irréductible, adj. (*etym.* réduire), irreducible

Irréfléchi, e, adj. (*etym.* réfléchir), unguarded, inconsiderate

Irréflexion, sf. (*etym.* réflexion), thoughtlessness, want of reflection

Irrégularité, sf. (*etym.* régularité), irregularity

‖**Irrégulier, ère**, adj. (*etym.* régulier), irregular

‖**Irréligieux, se**, adj. (*etym. L.* irreligiosus), irreligious

‖**Irrémédiable**, adj. (*etm. L.* irremediabilis), past recovery, irretrievable, irremediable

‖**Irréprochable**, adj. (*etym.* réprochable), irreproachable, blameless

‖**Irrésolu, e**, adj. (*etym.* résolu), irresolute, unsteady

‖**Irrespectueux, se**, adj. (*etym.* respectueux), disrespectful

Irrévérencieux, se, adj. (*etym.* révérencieux), irreverent

Irrévocabilité, sf. (*etym.* irrévocable = *L.* irrevocabilis), irrevocableness

Irritabilité, sf. (*etym. L.* irritabilitatem), irritability

Irritant, e, adj. irritating

Irriter, va. (*etym. L.* irritare), to irritate, to anger, to provoke; *s'*—, vr. to grow angry, to become provoked *or* exasperated

Isabelle, adj. (*etym. ? see* Littré), light yellow, isabella, dove-coloured, light bay

Islamisme, sm. (*etym. Ar.* islam, *submission*), Islamism

Isocèle, adj. (*etym. Gr.* ἰσοσκελής, *with equal legs*), isosceles

Isochrone, adj. (*etym. Gr.* ἰσόχρονος, *having equal duration*), isochronal, isochronous

Isochronisme, sm. isochronism

‖**Isolé, e**, adj. insulated, isolated, detached, lonely

Isolement, sm. insulation, loneliness

Isoler, va. (*etm. L.* insulatus), to insulate, to isolate, to detach; *s'*—, vr. to live lonely, to be detached

Isoloir, sm. insolator

Issu, e, adj. (*past part. of the O.F.* issir = *L.* exire), sprung from, born

Isthme, sm. (*etym. L.* isthmus), isthmus

Isthmique, adj. Isthmian

Italique, sm. adj. (*etym. L.* Italicus), italic

‖**Itératif, ve**, adj. (*etym. L.* iterativus), iterative, repeated

Itinéraire, sm. adj. (*etym. L.* itinerarius), itinerary

Ivoire, sm. (*etym. L.* eboreus, *belonging to ivory*), ivory

Ivraie, sf. (*etym. L.* ebriaca, *from* ebrius, *intoxicated*), tares

Ivre, adj. (*etym. L.* ebrius), intoxicated, drunk, transported

Ivresse, sf. intoxication, drunkenness, rapture

§**Ivrogne**, sm. adj. drunkard, drunken

§**Ivrognerie**, sf. drunkenness

§**Ivrognesse**, sf. drunken woman

J

J, sm. the tenth letter of the alphabet, J

Jabot, sm. (*etym. ?*), crop, maw, frill, shirt-frill

‡**Jaboter**, vn. to jabber, to prate

‡**Jacasser**, va. (*etym.* Jacques, *name given to the magpie*), to chatter, to jabber

Jachère, sf. (*etym. L.L.* gascaria; *O.F.* jaschière, gaschière), fallow land

Jacinthe, sf. (*etym. L.* hyacinthus), hyacinth. — *des prés*, blue-bell, hare-bell

Jacobin, sm. (*etym. L.* Jacobus), Jacobin monk, Jacobin

Jaconas, sm. (*etym. ?*), jaconet

Jacquot, sm. (*fam. for* Jacques = *James*), Poll, poll-parrot

Jactance, sf. (*etym. L.* jactantia), boasting

Jaculatoire, adj. (*etym. L.* jaculatorius), ejaculatory

Jadis, adv. (*etym. O.F.* jà = *L.* jam; dis = *L.* dies), once, formerly

§**Jaillir**, vn. (*etym. O.F.* jailler = *L.* jaculare, *to dart*), to gush out, to leap up

§**Jaillissant, e**, adj. gushing

§**Jaillissement**, sm. gushing

Jais, sm. (*etym. O.F.* jayet = *L.* gagates, *jet*), jet

Jalon, sm. (*etym. ?*), stake, landmark

Jalonner, vn.a. to stake out, to place landmarks

Jalouser, va. to be jealous of; *se* —, vr. to be jealous of each other

Jalousie, sf. jealousy, umbrage, Venetian blinds

‖**Jaloux, se**, adj. (*etym. L.* zelosus), jealous, anxious. — s. jealous person

Jamais, adv. (*etym. O.F.* jà = *L.* jam; mais = *L.* magis), never, not ever, ever. *A* —, *pour* —, for ever. *A tout* —, for ever and ever

Jambage, sm. jamb, downstroke

Jambe, sf. (*etym. L.* gamba, *thigh*), leg, foot, jamb. *Courir à toutes* —*s*, to run as hard as one can. *Jouer des* —*s*, to take to one's heels. † *Cela vous fait une belle* —, a vast deal of good that does you. *Par-dessous* —, cleverly

Jambon, sm. ham

Jambonneau, sm. knuckle of ham

Janissaire, sm. (*etym. T.* jenitcheri), Janizary

Jansénisme, sm. Jansenism

Janséniste, sm. (*etym. proper name* Jansenius), Jansenist

Jante, sf. (*etym. L.L.* camitem), rim

Janvier, sm. (*etym. L.* Januarius), January

Jappement, sm. yelping, yelp

Japper, vn. (*onomatop.*), to yelp

Jaquette, sf. (*etym.* jaque, *a jacket*), jacket

Jardin, sm. (*etym. G.* garten), garden

Jardinage, sm. gardening, garden

Jardiner, vn. to garden

Jardinier, sm. gardener

Jardinière, sf. gardener's wife, gardener, flower-stand, dish of vegetables, low ruffle

Jargon, sm. (*etym. ?*), jargon, gibberish

Jargonner, vn.a. to talk jargon

Jarre, sf. (*etym. Sp.* jarra), jar

Jarret, sm. (*etym. O.F.* garret, *from a root* garre), ham, hough, (*arch.*) unevenness

Jarretière, sf. garter

Jars, sm. (*etym. ?*), gander

Jaser, vn. (*etym. Prov.* gasar, *to chat*), to chatter, to gossip

Jaseur, se, s. chatterer

Jasmin, sm. (*etym. Sp.* jasmin), jessamine

Jaspe, sm. (*etym. L.* iaspis), jasper

Jasper, va. to marble, to vein

Jatte, sf. (*etym. O.F.* gatte, *L.* gatta, *bowl*), bowl, porringer

Jattée, sf. bowlful

Jauge, sf. gauge, gauging-rod, burden, tonnage

Jaugeage, sm. gauging

Jauger, va. (*etym. ?*), to gauge

Jaugeur, sm. gauger

Jaunâtre, adj. yellowish

‖**Jaune**, adj. (*etym. O.F.* jalne = *L.* galbinus, *yellow*), yellow, sallow. — sm. yellowness, sallowness. *Un* — *d'œuf*, the yolk of an egg

Jaunet, sm. buttercup, (†) yellow boy, sovereign

Jaunir, va. to colour yellow, to gild. — vn. to grow yellow, to turn yellow

Jaunissant, e, adj. turning yellow

Jaunisse, sf. jaundice

Javeline, sf. (*etym. I.* giavelina), javelin, spear

Javelle, sf. (*etym. O.F.* gavelle; *I.* gavella), bundle of corn. *Eau de* —, bleaching-liquid

Javelot, sm. (*etym. ?*), javelin

Je, pron. (*etym. L.* ego; *O.F.* jo, io, eo), I

Jérémiade, sf. wailing, complaint

Jésuite, sm. (*etym.* Jésus; *O.F.* Jesuiste), Jesuit. — *de robe courte*, lay Jesuit

Jésuitique, adj. jesuitical

Jésuitisme, sm. jesuitism

Jet, sm. (*etym. see* JETER), throwing, cast, haul, jet, gush, sudden ray, casting, young swarm, jess

Jetée, sf. jetty, pier, breakwater

Jeter, va. (*etym. I.* gettare = *L.* jactare), to throw, to fling, to hurl, to drop, to lay, to bend, to heave, to suppurate, to swarm, to shoot, to strike; *se* —, vr. to throw oneself, to rush, to pounce, to fall

Jeton, sm. (*etym.* jeter), counter. † *Faux comme un* —, as false as a brass shilling

Jeu, sm. (*etym. L.* jocus; *Prov.* joc), play, sport, fun, joke, freak, frolic. —*x innocents*, forfeits. —*x d'esprit*, witticisms. *Tenir un* —, to keep a gaming-table. ‡ *Mettre quelqu'un en* —, to mix a person up in an affair. *De bon* —, all fair. *A — découvert*, cards above board. *Donner beau* —, to give good cards, to give every advantage. *Faire le* —, to lay down the stakes. *Son honneur était en* —, his honour was at stake. *Être à deux de* —, to be even

Jeudi, sm. (*etym. I.* Giovedi), Thursday

Jeun, loc. adv. (*etym. L.* jejunus), fasting

Jeune, adj. (*etym. L.* juvenis), young, youthful

Jeûne, sm. (*etym. L.* jejunium), fasting, fast

Jeûner, vn. (*etym. L.* jejunare), to fast

Jeunesse, sf. (*etym.* jeune), youth. *Il faut que — se passe*, youth must have its time

§**Joaillerie,** sf. (*etym. see* JOYAU), jewellery, jeweller's business

§**Joaillier, ère,** s. jeweller

¶†**Jobard,** sm. (*etym.* ?), simpleton, ninny

Jocrisse, sm. (*etym.* ?), silly fellow

Joie, sf. (*etym. L.* gaudia; *plur. of* gaudium), joy, gladness, happiness

§**Joignant, e,** adj. prep. adjoining

Joindre, va. (*etym. L.* jungere), to join, to unite; — vn. to join; *se* —, vr. to join, to associate, to be joined, to adjoin, to be superadded

Joint, e, past part. (*etym. L.* junctus), joined, etc.

Joint, sm. joint, seam

Jointé, e, adj. jointed

Jointure, sf. (*etym. L.* junctura), joint

‖**Joli, e,** adj. (*etym. O.Sc.* jul, *joy*), pretty, nice, comfortable

Jonc, sm. (*etym. L.* juncus), rush, bulrush, cane, guard. — *d'Espagne*, rush-broom

Joncher, va. (*etym.* jonc), to strew, to heap

Jonchets, sm. plur. spellicans

Jonction, sf. (*etym. L.* junctionem), junction, joining

Jongler, vn. (*etym. L.* joculari, *to joke*), to juggle

Jonglerie, sf. trickery, juggling

Jongleur, sm. juggler, trickster

Jonque, sf. (*Eastern word*), junk

§**Jonquille,** sf. (*etym. Sp.* junquillo), the jonquil

Joubarbe, sf. (*etym. L.* Jovis barba), houseleek, white stonecross

Joue, sf. (*etym. L.L.* gauta, *cheek*), cheek. *En —!* present! *Coucher, mettre en* —, to level one's musket at, (*fig.*) to have one's eye on

Jouer, vn. (*etym. L.* jocari), to play, to sport, to gambol, to gamble, to speculate, to run the risk of, to trifle, to handle. — *de bonheur*, to be in luck. — va. to play, to stake, to venture, to deceive. *C'est un jeu joué*, it is a got-up thing. — *le velours*, to imitate velvet. *Se* —, vr. to sport, to frolic, to play with, to laugh at, to baffle

Jouet, sm. (*etym. dimin. of* jeu), plaything, laughing-stock, sport

Joueur, se, s. player, gambler, stock-jobber. — *à la baisse*, a bear. — *à la hausse*, a bull

Joufflu, e, adj. (*etym.* joue), chubby

Joug, sm. (*etym. L.* jugum), yoke, sway

Jouir, vn. (*etym. L.* gaudere), to enjoy

Jouissance, sf. enjoyment, possession

Joujou, sm. (*etym.* jeu), plaything, toy

Jour, sm. (*etym. L.* diurnus), day-time, day, daylight, light, aperture, opening, way. *Donner le bon — à*, to wish a good morning. *Être dans son bon* —, to be in a good humour. *Être à* —, to be in order. *Vivre au — le* —, to live from hand to mouth. *Tous les deux —s, de deux —s l'un*, every other day. *Demi-* —, imperfect light. *Au petit* —, at peep of day. *A* —, open. *Bas à* —, open-worked stockings. *Percé à* —, bored through. *Mettre à* —, to lay open. *Se faire* —, to force one's way, to come to light. *Voir — à*, to see any way of

Journal, sm. (*etym. L.* diurnale), diary, journal, newspaper, day-book

Journalier, ère, adj. daily, variable. — sm. journeyman

¶**Journalisme,** sm. journalism

Journaliste, sm. journalist

Journée, sf. day, day-time, day's work, day's wages, day's journey, battle. *Femme de* —, charwoman. *Aller en* —, to go out to work by the day, to char. *Marcher à grandes —s, à petites —s*, to travel by long stages, by short stages

Journellement, adv. daily, every day

Joute, sf. tilt, tilting, joust, strife

Jouter, vn. (*etym. L.L.* juxtare, *to draw near*), to tilt, to joust, to cope with

Jouteur, sm. champion

***Jouvence,** sf. (*etym. L.L.* juventia), youth

***Jouvenceau,** sm. (*etym. L.L.* juvenicellus), stripling, youth

***Jouvencelle,** sf. damsel, maiden

Joyau, sm. (*etym. L.L.* jocale, *jewel*), jewel

‖**Joyeux, se,** adj. (*etym. L.* gaudiosus), joyful, blithe, blithesome, joyous

Jubé, sm. (*thus called because the prayer* jube, domine, dicere . . . *was formerly sung from that place*), rood-loft. † *Venir à* —, to come to terms

Jubilation, sf. (*etym. L.* jubilationem), merriment, festivity

Jubilé, sm. (*etym. L.* jubilæus), jubilee

Jucher, vn. (*etym.* ?), to roost, to perch; *se* —, vr. to go to roost, to perch oneself up

Juchoir, sm. roosting-place, perch

Judaïque, adj. (*etym. L.* judaicus), Jewish, Judaical

Judaïsme, sm. (*etym. L.* judaismus), Judaism

Judas, sm. Judas, traitor, peep-hole

‖**Judiciaire,** adj. (*etym. L.* judiciarius), judicial, judiciary. — sf. judgment

‖**Judicieux, se,** adj. (*etym. L.* judiciosus), judicious, sensible

Juge, sm. (*etym. L.* judicem), judge, magistrate, justice. — *assesseur*, recorder

Jugement, sm. (*etym.* juger), judgment, trial, sentence, opinion, view

Juger, va.n. (*etym. L.* judicare), to judge, to try, to pass sentence; *se* — vr. to judge oneself, to judge one another

Jugulaire, sf. adj. (*etym. L.* jugulum, *throat*), jugular vein, strap

Juif, ve, s. adj. (*etym. L.* Judæus), Jew, Jewess, Jewish, Hebrew

§**Juillet,** sm. (*etym. L.* Julius), July

Juin, sm. (*etym. L.* Junius), June

Juiverie, sf. Jewry

Jujubier, sm. (*etym.* jujube = *L.* zizyphum), jujube, lote-tree

Julienne, sf. (*etym.* ?), dame's violet, rocket, vegetable soup

Jumeau, elle, s. adj. (*etym. L.* gemellus), twin, double

Jumelles, sf. plur. double opera-glass, (*mechan.*) cheeks

Jument, sf. (*etym. L.* jumentum), mare

Junte, sf. (*etym. L.* junctus), junta

Jupe, sf. (*etym. Ar.* jubbet, *underclothing*), skirt, petticoat

Jupon, sm. petticoat

Jurande, sf. (*etym.* juret), wardenship of trade corporations

Juré, e, adj. sworn. — sm. juryman, member of the jury

Jurement, sm. oath, curse

Jurer, va. (*etym. L.* jurare), to swear, to blaspheme; — vn. to swear, to take an oath, to jar, to clash, not to harmonize; *se* —, vr. to swear to oneself, to swear to each other

Juridiction, sf. (*etym. L.* jurisdictionem), jurisdiction, department, line

‖**Juridique,** adj. (*etym. L.* juridicus), judicial, legal

Jurisconsulte, sm. (*etym. L.* jurisconsultus), jurisconsult, lawyer

Juriste, sm. (*etym. L.* juris), jurist

Juron, sm. oath

Jus, sm. (*etym. L.* jus), juice, gravy

Jusant, sm. (*O.F.* jus; *etym. L.L.* jusum, *down*), ebb-tide, ebb. *Flot et* —, ebb and flow

Jusque, Jusqu'à, Jusques à, prep. (*etm. L.* usque), even, to, till, until, up to

Jusquiame, sf. (*etym. L.* jusquiamus), henbane

Justaucorps, sm. (*etym.* juste, au, corps), jerkin

‖**Juste,** adj. (*etym. L.* justus), just, rightful, fair, accurate, exact, appropriate, true, tight. — sm. the upright man, what is just. — adv. accurately, rightly, just, tight, scantily, in tune. *Au* —, *au plus* —, *tout au* —, exactly

Justesse, sf. (*etym. L.* justitia), justness, accuracy, precision, truth

Justice, sf. (*etym. L.* justitia), justice, goodness, the judges, the law, gallows. *Faire, rendre — à*, to do justice to. *Faire — de*, to treat as it deserves. ‡ *Se brouiller avec la* —, to fall out with the law

Justiciable, adj. sm. amenable to, under the jurisdiction of

Justicier, va. to execute, to hang. — sm. lover of justice, justiciary

Justificatif, ve, adj. justificative. *Pièces —ves*, proofs and illustrations

Justifier, va.n. (*etym. L.* justificare), to justify, to clear, to vindicate; *se* —, vr. to justify oneself, to be justified

Juteux, se, adj. (*etym.* jus), juicy

§**Juveigneur,** sm. (*etym. L.* juveniorem), (*feud. law*) a younger son endowed with an appanage

¶**Juvénilité,** sf. (*etym.* juvénile), the character of being juvenile

Juxtaposer, va. (*etym. L.* juxta, *near*, poser), to place in juxtaposition

K

K, sm. k
Kabbale, sf. kabbala
Kakatoes, sm. (*onomat.*) cockatoo
Kan, sm. (*etym. Pers.* khân), khan
Képi, sm. (*etym. ?*), a kind of military cap
Kermès, sm. (*etym. Sans.* karmi, *worm*), kermes
Ketmie, sf. (*etym. Arab.* kathmiyy, *mallow*), ketmia, Syrian mallow
Kilo, or **Kilogramme**, sm. (*etym. Gr.* χίλιοι, *thousand*, γράμμα), kilogram, 2 lb. 3 oz. 4 2/3 drams avoirdupois weight; 2 lb. 8 oz. 3 dwt. 2 gr. troy weight
Kilolitre, sm. (*etym. see* Litre), about 220 imperial gallons, 1 pint (*liquids*); 3 quarters, 3 bushels, 1 gallon 3/5 (*dry measure*)
Kilomètre, sm. (*etym. see* Mètre), kilometre (about 1093 yards, 1 foot, 10 inches)
Kiosque, sm. (*etym. Turk.* kienchk, *a gallery*), kiosk
Kyrielle, sf. (*etym. Gr.* Κύριε ἐλέησον), litany, string of nonsense

L

L, sfm. l, L, fifty
La, **L'**, art. f. (*etym. L.* illa), the
La, **L'**, pron. pers. her, it
Là, adv. (*etym. L.* illac), there, thither
Là, **Là**! interj. there! there now!
La, sm. (*mus.*), A
Labeur, sm. (*etym. L.* laborem), toil, labour, bookwork
Labié, **e**, adj. (*etym. L.* labium, *lip*), labiate, labiated
Laboratoire, sm. (*etym. L.* laboratorium), laboratory
‖**Laborieux**, **se**, adj. (*etym. L.* laboriosus), industrious, hardworking, laborious
Labour, sm. (*etym.* labourer), tillage, ploughing. *Terres en* —, ploughed lands
Labourable, adj. arable
Labourage, sm. husbandry, tillage
Labourer, va. (*etym. L.* laborare), to plough, to till, to dig, to rip up; — vn. to toil
Laboureur, sm. husbandman, ploughman
Labyrinthe, sm. (*etym. L.* labyrinthus), maze, labyrinth
Lac, sm. (*etym. L.* lacus), lake, loch
Lacer, va. (*etym.* lacs), to lace; *se* — vr. to lace oneself
Lacérer, va. (*etym. L.* lacerare), to lacerate, to tear
Lacet, sm. lace, springe, snare, noose, winding. — *de corset*, stay-lace. *Mouvement de* —, (*locom.*) oscillation
‖**Lâche**, adj. (*etym. L.* lascus, *transpos. for* laxus), loose, slack, lax, close, sluggish, cowardly, poor-spirited. — sm. coward, lazy hound
Lâcher, va. (*etym. L.* laxare), to loosen, to slacken, to unbend, to let go, to release, to let slip. — *l'eau*, to open the water, to make water. — *une bordée*, to let fly. — *un coup*, to let fly. ‡ — *son argent*, to come down with. — *la main à*, to hold a slacker hand over. ‡ — *la main*, to lower one's pretensions. — *pied*, to give way. — *le mot*, to speak the word. — vn. to slacken, to grow loose, to slip; *se* —, vr. to slacken, to grow loose
Lâcheté, sf. (*etym. L.* laxitatem), sloth, remissness, cowardice
‖**Laconique**, adj. (*etym. L.* Laconicus), laconic, brief
Laconisme, sm. laconism, brevity
Lacrymal, **e**, adj. (*etym. L.* lacrymalis), lachrymal
Lacrymatoire, sm. lachrymatory
Lacs, sm. (*etym.* laqueus), string, springe, snare
Lacté, **e**, adj. (*etym. L.* lacteus), lacteous, lacteal. *Voie* —*e*, the Milky Way
Lacune, sf. (*etym. L.* lacuna), gap, blank
Ladre, adj. (*etym. L.* Lazarus), leprous, measly, stingy, mean. — sm. leper, niggard
Ladrerie, sf. leprosy, lazar-house, stinginess
Lagune, sf. (*etym. I.* laguna), lagoon
Lai, **e**, adj. (*etym. L.* laicus), lay; — sm. (*etym. Celt.* llais, *melody*), lay
Laid, **e**, adj.s. (*etym. O.H.G.* laid, *odious*), ugly, ill-favoured, ugliness
Laideron, sm. ugly creature
Laideur, sf. ugliness, plainness
Laie, sf. (*etym. ?*), wild sow; (*etym. L.L.* lecta, *a path*), forest-path
Lainage, sm. woollens, fleece, wool, teasling
Laine, sf. (*etym. L.* lana), wool, worsted. ‡ *Se laisser manger la* — *sur le dos*, to suffer oneself to be eaten out of house and home
Laineux, **se**, adj. (*etym. L.* lanosus), woolly, fleecy
Laïque, adj. (*etym. L.* laicus), lay, laical
Laisse, sf. (*etym. L.L.* laxa), string, leash. *Passer une* — *à*, to tie a string round
Laisser, va. (*etym. L.* laxare), to leave, to part with. *C'est à prendre ou à* —, you must take it or leave it. ‡ *Laissez donc*, nonsense! *Ne pas laisser de*, nevertheless, all the same, for all that, not to cease to be. *Cela ne laisse pas d'être*, it nevertheless exists. *Se* — vr. to allow oneself to. *Se* — *mener*, to allow oneself to be led. *Se* — *aller à*, to allow oneself to be borne along by. *Laissez-vous faire*, only keep quiet. *Se* — *manger*, to be eatable enough
Laisser-aller, sm. unconstraint, freedom, listlessness
Laisser-passer, sm. pass
Lait, sm. (*etym. L.* lactem), milk, white. *Petit* —, whey. ‡ *S'emporter comme une soupe au* —, to fire up in an instant. — *de poule*, mulled egg. — *de chaux*, whiting
Laitage, sm. milk diet
Laitance, **Laite**, sf. (*etym. L.* lactes), soft roe, milt
Laité, **e**, adj. soft-roed
Laiterie, sf. dairy
Laiteux, **se**, adj. milky
Laitier, sm. slag, dross
Laitier, **ère**, smf. milkman, milkwoman
Laitière, adj. having much milk, milch
Laiton, sm. (*etym. ?*), brass, wire
Laitue, sf. (*etym. L.* lactuca), lettuce
Lamaneur, sm. (*etym. O.F.* laman), coasting pilot
Lambeau, sm. (*etym. ?*), shred, strip, rag, tatter, bit of flesh
Lambin, **e**, s. (*etym. prop. name of a celebrated scholar*), dawdler
Lambiner, vn. to dawdle
Lambris, sm. (*etym. O.F.* lambre), wainscot, lining, roof, ceiling
Lambrissage, sm. wainscoting
Lambrisser, va. to wainscot
Lame, sf. (*etym. L.* lamina), thin and narrow plate, slip, blade, swordsman, cunning jade, billow, wave, surge, gold wire, silver wire, foil, scale, lamina
Lamé, **e**, adj. worked with gold wire or silver wire
Lamenter, va. (*etym. L.* lamentari), to bewail, to mourn, to lament. — *une chanson*, to sing a doleful ditty. *Se* —, vr. to bewail, to lament, to mourn over
Lamentin, *also* **Lamantin**, sm. (*etym. ?*), sea-cow, lamentine
Lamie, sf. (*etym. L.* lamia), white shark, lamia
Laminage, sm. laminating, rolling
Laminer, va. (*etym. L.* laminare), to laminate, to flatten, to roll
Laminoir, sm. mill, flatting-mill, rolling-mill
Lampe, sf. (*etym. L.* lampas), lamp
Lampion, sm. illumination lamp
Lampiste, sm. lamp-maker, lamp-lighter
Lamproie, sf. (*etym. L.* lampetra), lamprey
Lance, sf. (*etym. L.* lancea), lance, spear, staff
Lancer, va. to hurl, to fling, to throw, to pour in, to dart, to issue, to send forth, to toss, to launch. ‡ *Jeune homme lancé*, fast young man. *Se* —, vr. to rush, to fly, to dart, to launch out, to be a little wild
Lancette, sf. lancet
Lancier, sm. lancer
Lancinant, **e**, adj. (*etym. L.* lancinantem), sharp, throbbing
Lande, sf. (*etym. G.* lande), moor, sandy plains, barren parts
Langage, sm. (*etym. see* Langue), language
Lange, sm. (*etym. L.* lanea), swaddling-band, swaddling clothes
‖**Langoureux**, **se**, adj. (*etym.* langueur), languishing, languid
Langouste, sf. (*etym. L.* locusta), lobster
Langue, sf. (*etym. L.* lingua), language, tongue. — *de terre*, narrow strip of land, neck of land. — *de bœuf*, ox-tongue.

Tirer la —, to put out one's tongue. *A la — dorée*, honey-tongued. ‡ *Avoir la — bien pendue, affilée*, to have the gift of the gab. *Coup de* —, reflection, backbiting, taunt

Languette, sf. tongue, partition, (*mus.*) key, index of a pair of scales, slide-rail

Langueur, sf. (*etym. L.* languorem), languor, languidness

Languir, vn. (*etym. L.* languere), to languish, to pine away, to flag

‖**Languissant, e**, adj. languid, languishing, flat

Lanière, sf. (*etym. L.* lanaria, *from* lana, *wool*), thong

Lanterne, sf. (*etym. L.* lanterna), lantern, skylight, trundle. — *sourde*, dark lantern. ¶ *Mettre à la* —, to hang up at the lamp-post

Laper, va. (*etym. G.* lappen, *to lap*), to lap up, to lap

Lapereau, sm. (*etym. see* LAPIN), young rabbit

Lapidaire, sm. adj. (*etym. L.* lapidarius), lapidary

Lapider, va. (*etym. L.* lapidare), to stone

Lapin, e, s. (*etym. the root* lap), rabbit

Laps, sm. (*etym. L.* lapsus), lapse

Laquais, sm. (*etym. Sp.* lacayo), footman, lackey

Laque, sf. (*etym. I.* lacca), lake. — sm. lacker

Larcin, sm. (*etym. L.* latrocinium), theft, pilfering, larceny

Lard, sm. (*etym. L.* lardum), bacon. † *Gras à* —, as fat as a pig. † *Faire du* —, to sleep oneself fat

Larder, va. to lard

Lardoire, sf. larding-pin

Lardon, sm. bit of pig's fat, gibe, taunt

‖**Large**, adj. (*etym. L.* largus), broad, wide, bountiful, liberal, bold, grand. — sm. breadth, width, the open sea, the offing. *En long et en —, de long en* —, backwards and forwards. † *Du long et du* —, of all sorts. *Être au* —, to have elbow room, to be in the offing. *Passez au — ! Au — !* keep off! *Pousser au* —, to sheer off. *Courir au —, prendre, gagner le* —, to stand out to sea *or* for the offing, to sheer off

Largesse, sf. (*etym. L.* largitia), bounty, largesse

Largeur, sf. breadth, width, amplitude

Larguer, va. (*etym. I.* largo), to let go, to loosen a sail, to strain violently

Larme, sf. (*etym. L.* lacryma), tear, the least drop

Larmier, sm. drip, eye-vein

Larmoiement, sm. wateriness of the eyes

Larmoyant, e, adj. rueful, weeping, in tears

Larmoyer, va. to cry, to shed tears

Larron, sm. (*etym. L.* latronem), thief, dog's ear in a book

Larve, sf. (*etym. L.* larva, *mark*), larva

Las, Lasse, adj. (*etym. L.* lassus), weary, tired

‖**Lascif, ve**, adj. (*etym. L.* lascivus), lascivious, lewd, lustful

Lascivetè, sf. (*etym. L.* lascivitatem), lasciviousness, lewdness

Lassant, e, adj. wearisome, tiring

Lasser, va. (*etym. L.* lassare), to tire out; *se* —, vr. to tire oneself, to be weary

Last, Laste, sm. (*etym. G.* last), last

Latanier, sm. (*etym.* ?), palm-tree, macaw-tree

Latin, sm. (*etym. L.* Latinus), Latin. ‡ *Être au bout de son* —, to be at a stick-fast

Latiniser, va. to latinize

Latinisme, sm. latinism

Latiniste, sm. latinist

Latinité, sf. (*etym. L.* latinitatem), latinity

Latrines, sf. plur. (*etym. L.* latrina), privy

Latte, sf. (*etym. G.* latte, latte), lath, broadsword

Latter, va. to lath

Lattis, sm. lathing, laths

Laudatif, ve, adj. (*etym. L.* laudativus), laudatory

Laudes, sf. plur. (*Latin word*), lauds

Lauréat, adj. sm. (*etym. L.* laureatus), laureate

Laurier, sm. (*etym. L.* laurarius), laurel, bay-tree

Lavabo, sm. (*Latin word*), linen, wash-hand stand

Lavage, sm. (*etym.* laver), washing, slops

Lavande, sf. (*etym. I.* lavanda), lavender

Lavandière, sf. washerwoman, wag-tail

Lave, sf. (*etym. I.* lava), lava

Lavement, sm. washing, clyster

Laver, va. to wash, to bathe, to lave, to wash out, to steep in alum. *A — la tête d'un âne on perd sa lessive*, it is washing a blackamoor white. † — *la tête à quelqu'un*, to scold. *Se* —, vr. to wash oneself

Laveur, se, s. washer, scourer. —*se d'assiettes*, scullion

Lavis, sm. (*drawing*), wash

Lavoir, sm. wash-house, scullery

Lavure, sf. dishwater, hog's-wash, scouring

Laxatif, ve, adj. (*etym. L.* laxativus), laxative, opening

Layetier, sm. packing-case maker, trunk-maker

Layette, sf. (*etym. O.F.* laye, *box*), a set of baby-linen

Lazaret, sm. (*etym. I.* lazaretto), quarantine hospital, lazaretto

Lazzi, sm. (*Ital. word*), buffoonery, jest

Le, L', art. m. (*etym. L.* illum), the. — pron. m. him, it

Lé, sm. (*etym. L.* latus), breadth

Lèchefrite, sf. (*etym.* ?), dripping-pan

Lécher, va. (*etym. G.* lecken), to lick, to labour. † *A lèche-doigts*, just enough to taste; *se* —, vr. to lick oneself

Leçon, sf. (*etym. L.* lectionem), lesson, lecture, warning, reading

Lecteur, trice, sm f. (*etym. L.* lectorem), reader, lecturer

Lecture, sf. (*etym. L.* lectura), reading, perusal

Légaliser, va. (*etym.* légal), to legalize

Légalité, sf. (*etym. L.* legalitatem), legality

Légat, sm. (*etym. L.* legatus), legate

Légataire, sm. (*etym. L.* legatarius), legatee

Légendaire, adj. legendary

Légende, sf. (*etym. L.* legenda), legend

‖**Léger, ère**, adj. (*etym. L.L.* leviarius), light, thin, flimsy, nimble, swift. *A la légère*, loc. adv. lightly, inconsiderately. *De* —, unthinkingly, thoughtlessly

Légèreté, sf. lightness, buoyancy, flimsiness, nimbleness, swiftness, fleetness, levity, unsteadiness

Légionnaire, sm. (*etym. L.* legionarius), legionary, knight of the Legion of Honour

Législateur, trice, s. adj. lawgiver, legislator, legislating

Législatif, ve, adj. (*etym. L.* legislativus), legislative

Légiste, sm. (*etym. L.L.* legista), legist

‖**Légitime**, adj. (*etym. L.* legitimus), lawful, legitimate, rightful. — sf. property, portion

Légitimer, va. (*etym.* légitime), to legitimate, to recognize

¶**Légitimiste**, sm. legitimist

Légitimité, sf. legitimacy, lawfulness

Legs, sm. legacy, bequest

Léguer, va. (*etym. L.* legare), to leave, to bequeath

Légume, sm. (*etym. L.* legumen), vegetable, legumen

Légumineux, se, adj. leguminous

Lemme, sm. (*etym. L.* lemma), lemma

Lendemain, sm. (*etym.* le, en, demain), the next day, the morrow

Lénitif, ve, adj. (*etym. L.L.* lenitivus), lenitive, emollient. — sm. lenitive

‖**Lent, e**, adj. (*etym. L.* lentus), slow, sluggish, dull, low

Lente, sf. (*etym. L.* lendem), nit

Lenteur, sf. (*etym. L.* lentorem), slowness, sluggishness, slackness, dulness

Lenticulaire, Le culé, adj. (*etym. L.* ... cularis), lenticular

§**Lentille**, sf. (*etym. L.* ... cula), lentil, lens, pendu... bob, freckles. — *d'eau*, ... weed

Lentisque, sm. (*ety*... lentiscus), lentisk, masti...

Léonin, e, adj. (*ety*... leoninus), leonine, lion-l...

Lépidoptère, sm. (*etym.* lépido ... *Gr.* ... *wing*), lepidopter, lep... terous

Lèpre, sf. (*etym. L.* l... leprosy

Lépreux, se, adj. s. (... *L.* leprosus), leprous, lep...

Lequel, Laquelle, Lesquels, Lesquel... pron. rel. who, that, w... which

Les, art. plur. the. — ... pers. (*etym. L.* illos), the...

Lèse, adj. (*etym. L.* la... high treason against. -*majesté*, high treason

Léser, va. to wrong, injure, to aggrieve

Lésine, sf. (*etym. I.* le... stinginess

Lésiner, vn. to be sti...

Lésinerie, sf. stingy t... stinginess

Lésion, sf. (*etym.* ... sionem), wrong, inj... wound

Lessive, sf. (*etym. L.* lix... the wash, lye-wash, linen, lixivium, (†) ... play. *Jour de* —, wa... day

Lessiver, va. to wash

Lest, sm. (*etym. G.* last... last

Lestage, sm. ballastin...

‖**Leste**, adj. (*etym. I.* ... brisk, nimble, smart, ... free

Lester, va. to ballast; ... vr. to take in ballast, store one's stomach

Léthargie, sf. (*et*... lethargia), lethargy

Léthargique, ad... thargic

Léthifère, adj. (*ety*... lethifer), lethiferous, d...

Lettre, sf. (*etym. L.* ... letter. *En toutes —s*, ... length, plainly. ‡ ... *trois —s*, a downrigh... *A la —, au pied de la* ..., rally

Lettré, adj. (*etym.* ... teratus), lettered

Leude, sm. (*etym* ... leudes), vassal, leud

Leur, pron. pers. plur. ... *L.* illorum), to them, ... — adj. poss. their

Leurre, sm. (*etym* ... luoder, *deceit*), lure

Leurrer, va. to lur... lure; *se* —, vr. to deceive

Levain, sm. (*etym.* ... vamen), leaven

Levant, sm. the E... rising sun, the Leva... adj. rising

Levée, sf. raising, ... up, removal, (*cards*) embankment, levy

ever, va. (*etym.* *L.* levare), o raise, to lift up, to remove, o levy; — vn. to come up, to ise. *Faire — un lièvre*, to tart a hare. *Se* —, vr. to get p, to arise. — sm. getting p, levee. ¦ *Un — de rideau*, *heat.*) a small play

evier, sm. lever, crowbar, eam of a pair of scales, handpike. — *de déclanchement*, e *renversement*, handgear, eversing lever

évitique, sm. (*etym.* *L.* eviticus), the Book of Leviticus

evraut, sm. (*etym.* lièvre), evret

èvre, sf. (*etym.* *L.* labrum), p. ¦ *Avoir le cœur sur les —s*, be a true-hearted person

evrette, sf. (*etym.* lièvre), eyhound, greyhound bitch

évrier, sm. greyhound, arrier

evûre, sf. (*etym.* lever), east, barm

exicographe, sm. lexicographer

exique, sm. (*etym.* *Gr.* ικόν), lexicon

ézard, sm. (*etym.* *L.* lacers), lizard

ézarde, sf. crack, crevice

ézardé, e, adj. full of acks, cracked

Lézarder, vr. to crack, crevice

ais, sm. (*etym.* ?), lias

aison, sf. (*etym.* *L.* ligaem), binding, joining, upoke, thickening

ane, sf. (*etym.* lier), Spanish odbine

ant, e, adj. easy, pliant, mplying

ard, sm. (*etym.* ?), farng

arder, vn. to contribute mall sum, (?) to be stingy

asse, sf. (*etym.* lier), file, odle

alle, sf. (*etym.* *L.* libellus), el

ibéralisme, sm. (*etym.* éral), liberalism

béralité, sf. (*etym.* *L.* eralitatem), liberality, municence

bérateur, trice, smf. ym. *L.* liberator), deliverer, erator

bération, sf. (*etym.* *L.* rationem), deliverance, disrge

érer, va. (*etym.* *L.* rare), to discharge, to liate; *se* —, vr. to clear one, to pay off

erté, sf. (*etym.* *L.* liberm), liberty, freedom, ease

berticide, adj. (*etym.* *L.* rtus, cædere, *to kill*), deractive of liberty

ertin, e, adj. s. (*etym.* libertinus), licentious, litine, free-thinking

ertinage, sm. libersm, dissolute life, irgion

idineux, se, adj. ym. *L.* libidinosus), libidis

raire, sm. (*etym.* *L.* librarius), bookseller. — *éditeur*, bookseller and publisher

Librairie, sf. (*etym.* *L.* libraria), book-trade, bookselling, bookseller's shop

‖**Libre,** adj. (*etym.* *L.* liber), free. *Papier* —, unstamped paper. *Propos —s*, licentious talk. *Vers —s*, verses of unequal metre

Lice, sf. (*etym.* ?), lists; (*etym.* *L.* lycisca, *bitch*), bitch-hound

Licence, sf. (*etym.* *L.* licentia), licence, leave, liberty, licentiousness, licentiate's degree

Licencié, sm. licentiate

Licenciement, sm. disbanding

Licencier, va. to disband, to dismiss

‖**Licencieux, se,** adj. (*etym.* *L.* licentiosus), licentious, dissolute

Licitation, sf. (*etym.* *L.* licitationem), public auction

‖**Licite,** adj. (*etym.* *L.* licitus), lawful, licit, allowable

Licorne, sf. (*etym.* *I.* licorno), unicorn

Licou *or* **Licol,** sm. (*etym.* lier, col), halter

Licteur, sm. (*etym.* *L.* lictorem), lictor

Lie, sf. (*etym.* ?), dregs, lees

***Lie,** adj. (*etym.* *L.* læta), jolly. *Faire chère* —, to feed well

Liége, sm. (*etym.* *L.* levis), cork-tree, cork

Lien, sm. (*etym.* *L.* ligamen), withe, band, (*plur.*) bonds, fetters

Lier, va. (*etym.* *L.* ligare), to tie, to bind, to fasten, to join, (*notes*) to slur, to enter into, to thicken. *Jouer en partie liée*, to play a rubber. *Se* —, vr. to be fastened *or* bound, to form a league, to become acquainted, to bind oneself, to thicken, to bind

Lierre, sm. (*etym.* *L.* hedera; *O.F.* lerre, hierre), the ivy

***Liesse,** sf. (*etym.* *L.* lætitia), jollity

Lieu, sm. (*etym.* *L.* locus), place, spot, scene, (*plur.*) premises, stead, lieu, room, turn, place, estate, extraction, reason, cause. *—x d'aisance*, privy. — *à l'anglaise*, water-closet

Lieue, sf. (*etym.* *L.* leuca), league

Lieutenance, sf. (*etym.* tenir, lieu), lieutenancy

Lièvre, sm. (*etym.* leporem), hare

Ligature, sf. (*etym.* *L.* ligatura), ligature

***Lige,** adj. (*etym.* ?), liege

§**Lignage,** sm. (*etym.* *L.L.* lineaticum), lineage

§**Ligne,** sf. (*etym.* *L.* linea), line, path, way. *Hors* —, in the margin. *Être hors de* —, to be quite superior

§**Lignée,** sf. (*etym.* ligne), issue, progeny, offspring

§**Ligneux, se,** adj. (*etym.* *L.* lignosus), ligneous

Ligue, sf. league, confederacy

Liguer, va. (*etym.* *L.* ligare, *to bind*), to unite in a league; *se* —, vr. to league together

Ligueur, sm. leaguer

Lilas, sm. (*etym.* *I.* lilac), lilac-bush, lilac. — adj. lilac-coloured

Liliacé, e, adj. (*etym.* *L.* liliaceus), liliaceous

Limace, sf. (*etym.* *L.* limacem), slug, Archimedes' screw

Limaçon, sm. snail, cochlea. — *de mer*, periwinkle. *Escalier en* —, winding staircase

§**Limaille,** sf. (*etym.* limer), filings

Limande, sf. (*etym.* limer), dab

Limbe, sm. (*etym.* *L.* limbus), limb. —*s*, sm. pl. limbo

Lime, sf. (*etym.* *L.* lima), file. — *sourde*, dead-file, hypocrite. *Passer la — sur*, to polish

Limer, va. (*etym.* *L.* limare), to file, to polish

Limier, sm. (*etym.* *O.F.* liemier, *from O.F.* liem, *a leash* — *L.* ligamen), bloodhound. — *de police*, police spy

Limite, sf. (*etym.* *L.* limitem), boundary, bound, limit

Limiter, va. (*etym.* *L.* limitare), to limit, to fix the bounds of, to restrain

Limitrophe, adj. (*etym.* *L.* limitrophus), bordering, adjacent

Limon, sm. (*etym.* *L.* limus), slime, mud, clay, dust; (*etym.* ?), shaft of a cart, string-board; (*etym.* *I.* limon), lime, lemon

Limonade, sf. (*etym.* limon), lemonade. — *gazeuse*, effervescing lemonade

Limonadier, ère, s. coffee-house keeper

Limoneux, se, adj. slimy, muddy

Limonier, sm. shaft-horse, lemon-tree

Limonière, sf. shaft, four-wheeled vehicle

Limousine, sf. (*prop. name* Limousin, *a province of France*), carter's coat

Limpide, adj. (*etym.* *L.* limpidus), limpid, clear

Limpidité, sf. (*etym.* *L.* limpiditatem), limpidity, clearness

Limure, sf. filing, polish

Lin, sm. (*etym.* *L.* linum), flax, linen. *Farine de graine de* —, linseed meal

Linaire, sf. toad-flax

Linceul, sm. (*etym.* *L.* linteolum), winding-sheet, shroud

Linéaire, adj. (*etym.* *L.* linearis), linear

Linge, sm. (*etym.* *L.* lineum), linen

Linger, ère, smf. linen-draper

Lingère, sf. sempstress

Lingot, sm. (*etym.* ?), ingot, wedge, slug

Lingotière, sf. ingot-mould

Linguiste, sm. (*etym.* *L.* lingua), linguist

Linguistique, sf. linguistics

Linière, sf. field of flax

Linon, sm. lawn

Linot, sm., **Linotte,** sf. (*etym.* *L.* lin), linnet. ¦ *Tête de* —, giddy pate

Linteau, sm. (*etym.* *L.L.* limitellus), lintel

Lionne, sf. (*etym.* lion), lioness

Lionceau, sm. lion's cub *or* whelp, cub

Lippe, sf. (*etym.* *G.* lippe), thick lip

Lippée, sf. mouthful

Lippu, e, adj. thick-lipped

Liquéfier, va., *se* —, vr. (*etym.* *L.* liquefacere), to liquefy, to melt

Liqueur, sf. (*etym.* *L.* liquorem), liquor, cordial, liqueur. —*s fortes*, spirits. *Vins de* —, sweet wines

Liquidateur, sm. liquidator

Liquide, adj. (*etym.* *L.* liquidus), liquid, clear. — sm. liquid

Liquider, va. to liquidate, to pay off; *se* —, vr. to clear off one's debts

Liquoreux, se, adj. luscious, sweet

Liquoriste, sm. spirit-dealer

Lire, va. (*etym.* *L.* legere), to read, to peruse

Lis, sm. (*etym.* *L.* lilius, *for* lilium), lily, lys

Liséré, sm. (*etym.* *O.F.* liserer, *to edge, to border*), piping, border

Liseron, sm. (*etym.* lis), convolvulus, bindweed

Liseur, se, s. reader

‖**Lisible,** adj. legible, readable

Lisière, sf. (*etym.* liste), list, leading-strings, skirt, verge

Lisse, adj. (*etym.* *I.* liscio, *smooth*), smooth, sleek, glossy

Lisse, sf. (*etym.* *L.* licium, *warp*), warp, (*nav.*) riband, rail

Lisser, va. to smooth, to polish

Liste, sf. (*etym.* *O.H.G.* lista, *border*), list, roll

Lit, sm. (*etym.* *L.* lectum), bed. *Bois de* —, bedstead. *N'être pas du même* —, not to be by the same mother. *Le — du vent*, the wind's eye

Litanie, sf. (*etym.* *Gr.* λιτανεία, *supplication*), litany

Liteau, sm. (*etym.* *see* LISTE), stripe, lair

Literie, sf. bedding

Lithographe, sm. lithographer

Lithographie, sf. (*etym.* *Gr.* λίθος, *stone*, γράφειν, *write*), lithography, lithograph, lithographic printing-office

Lithographié, e, adj. past part. lithographed

Lithographier, va. to lithograph
Lithographique, adj. lithographic
Lithotomie, sf. (*etym. Gr.* λίθος, τέμνειν, *to cut*), lithotomy
Lithotritie, sf. (*etym. Gr.* λίθος, *L.* tritus, *pounded, bruised*), lithotrity
Litière, sf. (*etym. L.L.* lectariam), litter
Litige, sf. (*etym. L.* litigium), litigation
Litigieux, se, adj. (*etym. L.* litigiosus), litigious
Litre, sm. (*etym. Gr.* λίτρα), about 1 pint 3 gills 1/5
Littéraire, adj. (*etym. L.* litterarius), literary
‖**Littéral, e**, adj. (*etym. L.* litteralis), literal, exact
Littérateur, sm. (*etym. L.* litteratorem), man of letters
Littérature, sf. (*etym. L.* litteratura), literature
Littoral, e, sm. adj. (*etym. L.* littoralis), coast, of the sea-shore
Liturgie, sf. (*etym. Gr.* λειτουργία), liturgy
Liturgique, adj. liturgical
Livide, adj. (*etym. L.* lividus), livid
Lividité, sf. lividness
Livraison, sf. (*etym. L.* liberationem), delivery, number, part. *Par* —, in numbers or parts
Livre, sm. (*etym. L.* librum), book, account book. *A — ouvert*, right off. *Grand-* —, the ledger
Livre, sf. (*etym. L.* libra), pound, livre, franc
Livrée, sf. (*etym.* livrer), livery
Livrer, va. (*etym. L.* liberare), to deliver, to hand over, to give; *se* —, vr. to give oneself up, to indulge, to yield
Livret, sm. little book
Local, sm. (*etym. L.* localis), place, premises, the locality
Localiser, va. to localize
Localité, sf. (*etym. L.* localitatem), locality, place
Locataire, sm. (*etym. L.* locatarius), tenant, lodger. — *à bail*, leaseholder
Locatif, ve, adj (*etym. L.* locativus), tenantable, tenant's, in rent
Location, sf. (*etym. L.* locationem), letting out, hiring, renting. *Bureau de* —, box-office
Loch, sm. (*etym. Engl.* log), log. *Filer, jeter le* —, to heave the log
Locomotif, ve, adj. (*etym. L.* loco, *abl. of* locus, *L.L.* motivus), locomotive
Logarithme, sm. (*etym. Gr.* λόγος, ἀριθμός), logarithm
Logarithmique, adj. sf. logarithmical, logarithmical curve
Loge, sf. (*etym. I.* loggia — *L.L.* laubia), hut, log-house, lodge, cell, den, (*theat.*) box, (*arch.*) loggia

Logeable, adj. inhabitable
Logement, sm. lodging, house-room
Loger, va.n. to lodge, to harbour; *se* —, vr. to take lodgings, lodge
Logeur, se, s. lodging-house keeper
Logicien, sm. logician
‖**Logique**, sf. adj. (*etym. L.* logica), logic, logical
Logis, sm. house, habitation. *Corps de* —, part of the building. ‡ *La folle du* —, our fancy
Logogriphe, sm. (*etym. Gr.* λόγος, γρῖφος), logogriph
Logomachie, sf. (*etym. Gr.* λογομαχία wordy war, wrangling
Loi, sf. (*etym. L.* legem), the law, statute, dominion, standard. *Hors la* —, outlawed. *Avoir force de* —, to be law
Loin, adv. (*etym. L.* longe), far
Lointain, e, adj. (*etym. L.L.* longitanus), far-distant, remote. — sm. distance
Loir, sm. (*etym. L.* glirem), dormouse
Loisible, adj. allowed
Loisir, sm. (*etym. L.* licere), leisure
Lombes, sm. plur. (*etym. L.* lumbus), loins, lumbar region
‖**Long, ue**, adj. (*etym. L.* longus), long, slow. *A la longue*, in the long run. *De longue main*, of old, long since. — sm. length. — adv. a great deal. *En savoir* —, to know all about it
Longanimité, sf. (*etym. L.* longanimitatem), longanimity, forbearance
Longe, sf. tether, loin
Longer, va. to follow, to go along, to skirt
Longévité, sf. (*etym. L.* longævitatem), longevity
Longtemps, adv. long, a long time
Longueur, sf. length, prolixity, slowness. *Traîner, tirer une affaire en* —, to spin out a thing
Lopin, sm. (*etym.* ?), smack, bit. — *de terre*, patch of ground
Loquace, adj. (*etym. L.* loquacem), loquacious, talkative
Loquacité, sf. (*etym. L.* loquacitatem), loquacity, talkativeness
Loque, sf. (*etym. O.H.G.* loc, *a hanging thing*), rag, tatter
Loquet, sm. (*etym. O.F.* loc, *latch*), latch
§**Lorgner**, va. (*etym. Sw. G.* loren, *to look*), to eye, to cast a glance at, to ogle
§**Lorgnette**, sf. spy-glass, opera-glass
§**Lorgnon**, sm. eye-glass, quizzing-glass
Loriot, sm. (*etym. L.* aureolus; *O.F.* oriol), gold-hammer, goldfinch
Lors, adv. (*etym. O.F.* lores) then

Lorsque, conj. when
Losange, sm. (*etym.* ?), lozenge
Lot, sm. (*Engl. word*), lot, fate, prize
Loterie, sf. lottery, raffle
Lotir, va. to portion off
Lotissement, sm. portioning off
Lotte, sf. (*etym.* ?), eel-pout
‖**Louable**, adj. praiseworthy, laudable
Louage, sm. letting out, hire
Louange, sf. (*etym. L.L.* laudemia), praise, commendation
Louanger, va. to bepraise
Louangeur, se, s. adj. fulsome praiser, laudatory
Louche, adj. (*etym. L.* luscus), squinting, suspicious, muddy. — sm. something suspicious, ambiguity
Loucher, vn. to squint, to have a cast in one's eye
Louchet, sm. (*etym.* ?), spad
Louer, va. (*etym. L.* locare), to let out, to hire, to rent; *se* —, vr. to hire oneself, to be let, to be hired. — va. (*etym. L.* laudare), to praise, to laud, to commend; *se* —, vr. to praise oneself, to praise each other, to be well pleased
Loueur, se, s. letter out, bepraiser
Lougre, sm. (*from the English*), lugger
Louis, sm. (*proper name*), louis, twenty-four franc piece, 19 shillings
Loup, sm. (*etym. L.* lupus), wolf, cat-fish, velvet mask. — *-cervier*, lynx. ‡ *Un froid de* —, bitter cold. *A pas de* —, with stealthy steps. — *de mer*, weather-beaten tar
Loupe, sf. (*etym.* loup), wen, knob, magnifying-glass
Loup-garou, sm. (*etym.* loup; *Swed.* varulf = var, *man*, ulf, *wolf*), were-wolf, bugbear, surly fellow
‖**Lourd, e**, adj. (*etym. L.* luridus, *dirty*), heavy, expensive, dull-witted, clumsy, sultry, oppressive
Lourdaud, sm. blockhead
Lourdeur, sf. heaviness, weight, clumsiness, tediousness
Loustic, sm. (*etym. G.* lustig, *joyful*), wag
Loutre, sf. (*etym. L.* lutra), otter, otter-fur
Louve, sf. (*etym.* loup), she-wolf, sling
Louveteau, sm. wolf's cub, cub
Louveterie, sf. wolf-hunting train
Louvoyer, vn. (*etym. O.F.* lovoyer, *from* lof = *Engl.* loof), to tack, to tack about
Loyauté, sf. (*etym. L.* legalitatem), fairness, honesty, loyalty
Loyer, sm. (*etym. L.L.* locarium), rent, reward
‡**Lubie**, sf. (*etym. L.* lubere), whim, crotchet
Lubricité, sf. lubricity, lechery

‖**Lubrique**, adj. (*etym. L.* lubricus), lecherous, lewd
Lucarne, sf. (*etym. L.L.* lucarna = lucerna), garret window, little window
‖**Lucide**, adj. (*etym. L.* lucidus), lucid
Lucidité, sf. (*etym. L.* luciditatem), lucidity
‖**Lucratif, ve**, adj. (*etym. L.* lucrativus), lucrative
Luette, sf. (*O.F.* l'uette; *L.* uva), uvula
Lueur, sf. (*etym. L.L.* lucorem), glimmer, glimpse
‖**Lugubre**, adj. (*etym. L.* lugubris), dismal, mournful, lugubrious, doleful
Lui, pron. pers. (*see* Le), he, it. — *-même*, himself, itself
Luire, vn. (*etym. L.* lucere), to shine, to dawn, to glitter, to gleam
Luisant, e, adj. shining, glittering, glossy. — sm. gloss
Lumière, sf. (*etym. L.* luminaria), light, knowledge, intellect, abilities
§**Lumignon**, sm. (*etym. L.L.* luminionem), snuff of a candle, candle-end
Luminaire, sm. (*etym. L.* luminare), light, luminary
‖**Lumineux, se**, adj. (*etym. L.* luminosus), luminous
Lunaire, adj. lunar, lunary
Lunaison, sf. lunation
Lunatique, adj. (*etym. L.* lunaticus), lunatic, moon-struck, fantastical
Lundi, sm. (*etym. L.* lunæ dies), Monday. — *gras*, Shrove Monday
Lune, sf. (*etym. L.* luna), moon, month. — *rousse*, April moon. † *Faire un trou à la* —, to disappoint one's creditors
Lunette, sf. telescope, (*pl.*) spectacles, glasses, merry-thought, lunette
Lupercales, sf. plur. Lupercalia
Lupin, sm. (*etym. L.* lupinus), lupine
‡**Luron**, sm. (*etym.* ?), a jolly fellow
‡**Luronne**, sf. a buxom woman
Lustrer, va. (*etym. L.* lustrare), to give a gloss to, to glaze
Lustrine, sf. lutestring
Luth, sm. (*etym. I.* liuto), lute
Luthéranisme, sm. (*etym. prop. name* Luther), Lutheranism
Luthérien, ne, adj. s. Lutheran
Luthier, sm. musical instrument maker
Lutin, sm. (*etym.* ?), elf, sprite, goblin, imp, urchin. — *e*, adj. roguish, sprightly
Lutiner, va. to tease, to plague; — vn. to be doing mischief
Lutrin, sm. (*O.F.* letrin, *from L.L.* lectrinum), music desk, the choristers

Lutte, sf. (*etym. L.* lucta), wrestling, scuffle, struggle, contest

Lutter, vn. to wrestle, to scuffle, to struggle, to contend

Lutteur, sm. wrestler, champion

Luxe, sm. (*etym. L.* luxus), luxury, profuseness, exuberance

Luxer, va. (*etym. L.* luxare), to lux, to luxate

Luxure, sf. (*etym. L.* luxuria), lewdness

§**Luxurieux, se**, adj. (*etym. L.* luxuriosus), lewd

Luzerne, sf. (*etym.* ?), lucerne

Luzin, sm. house-line

Lycée, sm. (*etym. Gr.* λύκειον), Lyceum, grammar school

Lycéen, sm. Lycean, school-boy

Lycopode, sm. (*etym. Gr.* λύκος, *wolf*, ποὺς, *foot*), lycopodium, club-moss

Lymphatique, adj. (*etym. L.* lymphaticus), lymphatic

Lymphe, sm. (*etym. L.* lympha), lymph, sap

Lyre, sf. (*etym. L.* lyra), lyre, Lyra

Lyrique, adj. (*etym. L.* lyricus), lyric

Lyz, sm. see Lis

M

M, sfm. m, M, one thousand

§**Macadamiser**, va. (*etym.* Macadam), to macadamize

Macaron, sm. (*etym. I.* maccherone), macaroon

Macaronique, adj. (*etym. I.* maccheronico), macaronic

Macédoine, sf. (*etym.* ?), medley

Macérer, va. (*etym. L.* macerare), to macerate; *se* —, vr. to be macerated, to macerate one's body

Mâche, sf. (*etym.* ?), corn-salad

Mâchefer, sm. (*etym.* ?), scoria, hammerslag

Mâchelière, sf. jaw-tooth

Mâcher, va. (*etym. L.* masticare), to chew, to masticate, to mumble. — *à vide*, to move one's jaws up and down to no purpose, to feed upon hope. ‡ — *la besogne à*, to cut out the work for. † *Ne pas — ce qu'on a sur le cœur*, not to mince the matter

Mâcheur, sm. chewer

Machiavélique, adj. (*prop. name* Machiavel), machiavelian

Machiavélisme, sm. machiavelism

Machicoulis, sm. (*etym.* ?), a piece of ancient fortification

§**Machinal, e**, adj. (*etym. L.* machinalis), mechanical

Machinateur, sm. (*etym. L.* machinatorem), contriver, plotter

Machine, sf. (*etym. L.* machina), machina, engine, machination, contrivance, machinery

Machiner, va. (*etym. L.* machinari), to plan, to plot, to machinate

Machiniste, sm. machinist, scene-shifter

Mâchoire, sf. (*etym.* mâcher), jaw, jawbone, (†) blockhead

Mâchonner, va. to mumble

Macis, sm. (*Latin word*), mace

Maçon, sm. (*etym. L.L.* macionem), mason, bricklayer

Maçonner, va. to do the masonry of, to wall up, (‡) to bungle

Maçonnerie, sf. masonry

Maçonnique, adj. masonic

Macreuse, sf. (*etym.* ?), widgeon, sea-duck

Macule, sf. (*etym. L.* macula), spot

Maculer, va. to maculate

Madone, sf. (*etym. I.* madona), madonna

Madré, e, adj. (*etym. O.F.* madre), speckled, crafty, sly

Madrier, sm. (*etym. L.L.* materiarius), thick oaken plank, (*fortif.*) madrier

Magasin, sm. (*etym. Ar.* machâzin, *stores*), storehouse, warehouse, magazine, shop, boot of a carriage. *Mettre en* —, to warehouse. *Marchandises en* —, stock in hand. *Garçon de* —, warehouseman, porter. *Dame, demoiselle de* —, shopwoman, shop-girl

Magasinage, sm. warehousing

Mage, sm. (*etym. L.* magus), magian

Magicien, ne, s. magician

Magie, sf. (*etym. L.* magia), magic

Magique, adj. magic, magical

Magister, sm. (*Latin word*), village schoolmaster

§**Magistral, e**, adj. (*etym. L.* magistralis), magisterial, principal, according to prescription

Magistrat, sm. (*etym. L.* magistratus), magistrate, justice

Magistrature, sf. magistracy, the bench

§**Magnanerie**, sf. silkworm nursery

§**Magnanier, ère**, s. silkworm breeder

§**Magnanime**, adj. (*etym. L.* magnanimus), high-minded, magnanimous

§**Magnanimité**, sf. (*etym. L.* magnanimitatem), high-mindedness, magnanimity

Magnat, sm. (*etym. L.* magnatus), magnate, lord

§**Magnésie**, sf. (*etym. L.* magnes), magnesia

§**Magnétique**, adj. (*etym. L.* magneticus), magnetic

§**Magnétiser**, va. (*etym.* magnétique), to magnetize

§**Magnétiseur**, sm. magnetizer

§**Magnétisme**, sm. magnetism

§**Magnifier**, va. (*etym. L.* magnificare), to magnify

§**Magnifique**, adj. (*etym. L.* magnificus), magnificent

§**Magnolier**, **Magnolia**, sm. (*etym. proper name* Magnol, *a botanist*), magnolia

Magot, sm. (*etym.* ?), baboon, grotesque figure, (*) hoard

Mahométisme, sm. Mahometanism

Mai, sm. (*etym. L.L.* madius = maius), May, May-pole

§**Maigre**, adj. sm. (*etym. L.* macrum), lean, meagre, gaunt, food other than meat. *Soupe* —, vegetable soup. *Jours* —*s*, days of abstinence

Maigrelet, te, adj. thin

Maigreur, sf. (*etym. L.* macrorem), leanness, meagreness, spareness

Maigrir, vn. to grow lean, to fall away

§**Mail**, sm. (*etym. L.* malleum), mall

§**Maille**, sf. (*etym. L.* macula), stitch, mesh, link of mail, speckle, web; (*etym. L.* metallea), small coin. — *tombée*, loose stitch. ‡ *Avoir — à partir ensemble*, to have a crow to pluck together

§**Maillet**, sm. (*etym.* mail), mallet

§**Mailloche**, sf. beetle, heavy mallet

§**Maillot**, sm. (*etym.* maille), swaddling-bands *or* clothes

Main, sf. (*etym. L.* manus), hand, handwriting, quire of paper, paw, deal, lead, trick, hand-shovel, tirrbus, clasper, hook. ‡ *Savoir de bonne* —, to know from good authority. *Acheter de la première* —, to buy from the manufacturer. *N'y pas aller de — morte*, to strike hard. *Avoir la — heureuse*, to be lucky. *Avoir le cœur sur la* —, to be open-hearted. *Être aux* —*s*, to be fighting. *Faire sa* —, to make a good thing of it. *Faire la — à, se faire la* —, to get one's hand in. *Jouer à la — chaude*, to play at hot cockles. *J'en mettrais la — au feu*, I would stake my life on it. *Tenir la — à, à ce que*, to see. *Avoir une belle* —, to have a good handwriting

Main-d'œuvre, sf. workmanship, handicraft

Main-forte, sf. assistance

Main-levée, sf. withdrawal, replevin

Mainmorte, sf. mortmain

Maint, e, adj. (*etym. O.H.G.* manag = many), many a, a great many

Maintenant, adv. now

Maintenir, va. (*etym.* main, tenir), to uphold, to sustain, to bear up, to maintain; *se* —, vr. to keep up, to remain

Maintien, sm. maintenance, upholding, keeping up, carriage, deportment

Maire, sm. (*etym. L.* major), mayor

Mairie, sf. mayoralty, town-hall

Mais, conj. adv. (*etym. L.* magis), but

Maïs, sm. (*etym. Sp.* mahiz) maize, Indian wheat

Maison, sf. (*etym. L.* mansionem), house, the premises, home, house affairs, household, firm. — *de détention*, jail. *Les petites* —*s*, a madhouse

Maisonnée, sf. whole house

Maisonnette, sf. cottage

Maître, sm. (*etym. L.* magister), ruler, master, lord, owner, teacher, head, upper, chief. *Fait de main de* —, done in a masterly style. *Un — homme*, a clever one. *Être passé — en*, to be deeply skilled in

Maîtresse, sf. mistress, ruler, lady, owner, teacher, governess. — *femme*, superior woman

Maîtrise, sf. trade's corporation, freedom, mastership

Maîtriser, va. to rule, to lord it over, to master, to keep down; *se* —, vr. to control oneself

Majesté, sf. (*etym. L.* majestatem), majesty

Majestueux, se, adj. majestic, stately, majestical

Majeur, e, adj. (*etym. L.* majorem), major, greater. *Sauf les cas de force* —, except in the case of impossibilities

Majordome, sm. (*etym. L.* major, domus), major-domo, steward

Majorité, sf. (*etym. L.* majorem), majority

Majuscule, adj. sf. (*etym. L.* majusculus), capital, big

Mal, sm. (*etym. L.* malum), evil, ill, wrong, mischief, pain, ache, sore, complaint, sickness, trouble, toil. *Tomber du haut* —, to have the falling sickness. *Avoir le — de mer*, to be sea-sick. *Être en — d'enfant*, to be in labour. *Avoir bien du* —, to have hard work of it. — adv. (*etym. L.* male), badly, ill, amiss, wrong. *Se trouver* —, to faint. *Mettre quelqu'un — avec*, to set a person at variance with

Malade, adj. (*etym. L.* male, aptus; *O.F.* malabde; *Prov.* malapte), ill, sick, unwell, diseased. — s. invalid, sick person, patient

Maladie, sf. illness, sickness, disease, malady

Maladif, ve, adj. sickly, unhealthy

Maladrerie, sf. (*etym.* malade, ladrerie), leper's hospital

Maladresse, sf. (*etym. see* ADRESSE), awkwardness, clumsiness

§**Maladroit, e,** adj. (*etym. see* ADROIT), awkward, clumsy, bungling

Malaise, sm. (*etym. see* AISE), uncomfortableness, uneasiness, straitened circumstances

§**Malaisé, e,** adj. difficult, hard, in straitened circumstances

Malavisé, e, adj. ill-judged

Mâle, sm. adj. (*etym. L.* masclus = masculus), male, manly, masculine, virile

Maléfice, sm. (*etym. L.* maleficium), witchcraft

§**Malencontreux, se,** adj. (*etym.* mal, encontre), untoward, unlucky

Malentendu, sm. misunderstanding

Malepeste, interj. (*etym.* male = mauvaise, peste), plague take it!

Malfaisant, e, adj. mischievous, spiteful, malevolent

Malfaiteur, sm. (*etym. L.* malefactorem), evil-doer, malefactor

Malgré, prep. (*etym.* mal = mauvais, gré), in spite of, despite of, notwithstanding. — *que j'en aie*, in spite of myself

§**Malhabile,** adj. unskilful

Malheur, sm. unhappiness, woe, misery, misfortune. *A quelque chose — est bon*, 'tis an ill wind that blows nobody good

§**Malheureux, se,** s. adj. wretch, unhappy, wretched, woful, unfortunate

§**Malhonnête,** adj. dishonest, rude, unmannerly, indecent

Malhonnêteté, sf. rudeness, incivility, rude thing

Malice, sf. (*etym. L.* malitia), malice, spite, love of mischief, roguishness, archness, piece of waggery, sly thing. ‡ *Ne pas entendre — à quelque chose*, to mean no mischief. *Entendre — à quelque chose*, to find a sly meaning in a thing. *Ne pas y entendre* —, to mean nothing by it

§**Malicieux, se,** adj. malicious, spiteful, mischievous, roguish

§**Malignité,** sf. (*etym. L.* malignitatem), malignity, malice

Malin, Maligne, adj. (*etym. L.* malignus), malicious, mischievous, malignant, waggish, sly

Malines, sf. (*prop. name of a town*), Mechlin lace

Malingre, adj. (*etym.* mal; *O.F.* haingre, = *L.* ægrum), sickly, puny, weakly

Malintentionné, e, adj. ill-designing, evil-minded

Malitorne, adj. (*etym.* mal? torné = tourné?), ungainly, awkward

Malle, sf. trunk, pedlar's box, mail

Malléabilité, sf. (*etym.* malléable), malleability

Malmener, va. to bemaul, to abuse

Malotru, sm. (*etym. L.* male; *L.L.* astrutus, *under the influence of a star*), ill-bred fellow

§**Malpropre,** adj. slovenly, dirty, unfit

Malpropreté, sf. dirtiness, slovenliness

Malsain, e, adj. unhealthy, unwholesome

Malséant, e, adj. unseemly, unbecoming

Malsonnant, e, adj. ill-sounding

Maltôte, sf. (*etym.* mal; *O.F.* tolte = *L.L.* tolta, *tax*), oppressive tax

Maltôtier, sm. tax-gatherer

Maltraiter, va. to ill-use, to ill-treat, to maltreat

§**Malveillance,** sf. malevolence, ill-will

§**Malveillant, e,** adj. (*etym. see* BIENVEILLANT), malevolent, ill-natured

Malvoisie, sm. (*etym. L.L.* Malvaxia, Malvagia, *proper name*), malmsey

Maman, sf. (*onomatop.*), mamma. *Bonne* —, grandmamma. *Une grosse* —, a portly dame

Mamelle, sf. (*etym. L.* mamilla), breast, udder

Mamelon, sm. nipple, dug, hill, eminence

Mammifère, adj. (*etym. L.* mamma, ferre), mammiferous

Mammouth, sm. (*etym.?*), the mammoth

Manant, sm. (*etym. L.* manentem, *remaining*), countryman, churl

§**Mancenillier,** sm. (*etym. Sp.* manzanilla, *small apple*), manchineel-tree

Manche, sm. (*etym. L.* manica), handle. — sf. sleeve, hose, channel, canal

Manchette, sf. ruffle

Manchon, sm. muff, casing

Manchot, e, adj. s. (*etym. O.F.* manc = *L.L.* mancus), one-handed, one-armed, one-armed person

Mancie, sf. (*etym. Gr.* μαντεία), suffix meaning divination by

Mandant, sm. employer, principal

Mandat, sm. (*etym. L.* mandatum), mandate, order, check, warrant, writ

Mandataire, sm. proxy, mandatory

Mandement, sm. mandate, charge, order

Mander, va. (*etym. L.* mandare), to send word, to write, to send for. *Contre-* —, to countermand

Mandibulaire, adj. mandibular

Mandibule, sf. (*etym. L.* mandibula), mandible

Mandoline, sf. (*etym. I.* mandolino), mandoline

Mandragore, sf. (*etym. L.* mandragora), mandrake

Manége, sm. (*etym. I.* maneggio), training, horsemanship, riding-school, manœuvre

§**Mangeaille,** sf. food, eating

Mangeoire, sf. manger, crib

Manger, va.n. (*etym. L.* manducare), to eat, to squander, to eat up; *se* —, vr. to be eaten, to prey upon each other, to be cut off. ‡ *Se — des yeux*, to look ready to devour each other. — sm. food, eating

Mange-tout, sm. spendthrift

Mangeur, sm. eater, spendthrift

Mangle, Manglier, sm. mangrove

Manguier, sm. mango-tree

Maniable, adj. easy to be handled, easily worked, manageable

Maniaque, adj. (*etym. L.* maniacus), maniac

Manichéen, sm. (*etym. prop. name* Manès), manichean

Manie, sf. (*etym. L.* mania), mania, passion

Maniement, sm. handling, management

Manier, va. (*etym. L.* manicare), to handle, to touch, to manage, to govern

Manière, sf. (*etym. L.L.* maneria), way, manner, kind, sort, style, mannerism

Maniéré, e, adj. finical, affected

Manieur, sm. handler. —*s d'argent*, money-dealers

§**Manifeste,** adj. (*etym. L.* manifestus), manifest, plain. — sm. manifesto, manifest

Manifester, va. to manifest; *se* —, vr. to manifest oneself, to become manifest

†**Manigance,** sf. (*etym. L.* manus), manœuvre

Manipulateur, sm. (*etym.* manipuler), manipulator

Manipuler, va. (*etym. L.* manipulus), to manipulate

Maniveau, sm. (*etym.?*), basket

Manivelle, sf. (*etym.?*), handle, crank, winch

Manne, sf. (*etym. L.* manna), manna; (*etym. G.* manne), hamper, wicker-cradle

Mannequin, sm. (*etym. G.* manne), hamper, basket; (*etym. D.* manneken), manikin, puppet

Manœuvre, sf. (*etym. L.L.* manu-opera), working, rope, rigging, manœuvre, drill. — sm. common workman, bungler, artful fellow

Manœuvrer, vn.a. to work the ship, to work, to manœuvre, to drill

Manœuvrier, sm. clever seaman, tactician

Manoir, sm. (*etym. L.L.* manerium), manor-house, abode

Manomètre, sm. (*etym. Gr.* μανός, *not dense*, μέτρον, *measure*), gauge, manometer

Manouvrier, sm. day-labourer

Manque, sm. want

Manqué, e, adj. lame, imperfect, defective. ‡ *Avocat* —, bit of a lawyer

Manquement, sm. oversight, shortcomings, failure, want

Manquer, vn.a. (*etym. L.L.* mancare), to err, to fail, to miss fire, to be wanting in, to be short of, to miss; *se* —, vr. to miss oneself, to miss each other, to forget what is due to oneself

Mansarde, sm. (*etym. prop. name of* Mansard, *the architect*), garret, attic. *Chambre en* —, *or mansardée*, room with sloping ceilings

Mante, sf. (*etym. L.L.* mantum, *cloak*), mantle

Manteau, sm. cloak, mantle. *Sous le* —, under the rose

Mantelet, sm. short cloak, canopy-front, mantlet

§**Mantille,** sf. (*etym. Sp.* mantilla), mantilla

Manuel, le, adj. (*etym. L.* manualis), manual

Manuel, sm. manual, hand-book

Manufacturer, va. (*etym.* manufacture), to manufacture

Manufacturier, sm. manufacturer

Manufacturier, ère, adj. manufacturing

Manuscrit, e, adj. (*etym. L.* manu, scriptum), manuscript. — sm. manuscript, copy

Manutention, sf. (*etym.* maintenir), management, maintenance, army bake-house

Mappemonde, sf. (*etym. L.* mappa, mundi), map of the world

Maquereau, sm. (*etym.?*), mackerel

§**Maquignon,** sm. (*etym*

Flem. maeken, *to traffic*), horse-dealer, horse-jockey

§**Maquignonnage,** sm. horse-jobbing, manœuvring

Marabout, sm. (*etym. Ar.* marabath, *devoted to God*), marabout, ugly fellow, big-bellied kettle, marabou, urgil, marabou feathers

Maraîcher, sm. market-gardener

Marais, sm. (*etym. L.L.* mariscus, *marsh*), marsh, morass, swamp, moor, market-gardener's ground. — *salant*, salt marsh. *Oiseaux de* —, moor-fowl

Marasme, sm. (*etym. Gr.* μαρασμός, *consumption*), marasmus, consumption

Marâtre, sf. (*etym. L.L.* matraster, *step-mother*), step-mother. — adj. most unkind

Maraud, sm. (*etym.* ?), knave, scoundrel

Maraude, sf. marauding

Marauder, vn. to go marauding

Maraudeur, sm. marauder

Maravédis, sm. (*etym. Sp.* maravedi), maravedi

Marbre, sm. (*etym. L.* marmoreum), marble, slab of marble, (*plur.*) marble statues

Marbrer, va. to marble

Marbrerie, sf. marble-cutting, marble-yard

Marbrier, sm. marble-cutter

Marbrière, sf. marble quarry

Marbrure, sf. marbling

Marc, sm. (*etym. O.H.G.* marc, *sign*), mark; (*etym.* ?), residue

Marcassin, sm. (*etym.* ?), young wild boar

Marchand, e, s. (*etym. L.L.* mercatantem, *selling*), dealer, tradesman, shopkeeper, merchant. —*e*, adj. wholesale, trading, commercial, mercantile, good for trade

Marchandage, sm. task-work

Marchander, va. to ask the price of, to bargain, (*fig.*) to spare; — vn. to stand haggling

Marchandise, sf. merchandise, commodity, goods

Marche, sf (*etym.* marcher), walk, walking, gait, step, course, march, marching, stair, treadles

Marché, sm. (*etym. L.* mercatum), market, mart, bargain, agreement. *A bon* —, cheap, cheaply. *Avoir bon — de*, easily to get the upper hand of. *Faire bon — de*, to care but little for. *Faire — pour*, to strike a bargain for

Marchepied, sm. steps, footstool, stepping-stone

Marcher, vn. (*etym. L.L.* marcare), to walk, to walk up, to go, to step, to march, to sail, to proceed. — sm. walk, gait

Marcheur, sm. walker, pedestrian. *Bon* —, capital sailer

Marcotte, sf. (*etym. L.* mergus), (*bot.*) a layer

Marcotter, va. (*bot.*) to layer

Mardi, sm. (*etym. L.* martis, dies), Tuesday. *Faire le — gras*, to keep Shrove Tuesday

Mare, sf. (*etym. L.L.* mara, *pond*), pool, pond, puddle

Marécage, sm. (*etym. see* Marais), marsh, bog, fen, swamp

Marécageux, se, adj. marshy, boggy, fenny

Maréchal, sm. (*etym. L.L.* mariscalcus, *he who attends to the king's horses*), farrier, Marshal. — *expert*, sworn farrier. — *de camp*, Major-General

Maréchale, sf. marshal's lady

Maréchaussée, sf. (*etym. L.L.* marescalciata), Marshalsea

Marée, sf. (*etym. L.* mare), tide, salt-water fish

Marelle, sf. (*etym. see* Mérelle), hopscotch

Marge, sf. (*etym. L.* marginem), margin. ¦ *Avoir de la* —, to have time enough. *Donner, laisser de la* —, to leave room enough

Margelle, sf. kerb, brink

Margraviat, sm. (*etym. L.* margrave), margraviate

Marguerite, sf. (*etym. L.* margarita, *pearl*), daisy *Reine* —, China aster

§**Marguillerie,** sf. church-wardenship

§**Marguillier,** sm. (*etym. L.L.* matricularius, *registrar*), churchwarden

Mari, sm. (*etym. L.* maritus), husband, spouse

Mariable, adj. marriageable

Mariage, sm. (*etym. L.L.* maritaticum), marriage, wedlock

Marié, e, s. married man, married woman

Marier, va. (*etym. L.L.* maritare), to marry, to ally, to pair, to match; *se* —, vr. to marry, to get married, to pair, to match

Marieur, se, s. match-maker

Marin, e, adj. (*etym. L.* marinus), sea, marine, nautical. *Avoir le pied* —, to be a good sailor. — sm. seaman, sailor, mariner

Marine, sf. navigation, navy, the sea, sea-view, sea-piece, the Admiralty

Mariner, va. to pickle, to cure

Marinier, sm. bargeman

Marionnette, sf. (*etym. O.F.* mariolette, *small images of the Virgin Mary*), puppet

Maritorne, sf. (Maritorna, *name of a servant in Don Quixote*), a clumsy servant girl

Marivaudage, sm. (*etym. prop. name of* Marivaux, *a writer*), affected style

Marjolaine, sf. (*etym. L.L.* majoraca, *from the Gr.* 'Αμάρακος), sweet marjoram

§**Marmaille,** sf. (*etym. see* Marmot), little brats

Marmelade, sf. (*etym. Sp.* mermelada), marmalade

Marmite, sf. (*etym.* ?), pot, copper. — *de Papin*, Papin's digester

Marmiton, sm. scullion

Marmot, sm. (*etym. a root* marm . . . *of which the origin is unknown*), marmoset, (?) brat. ¦ *Croquer le* —, to kick one's heels about (to wait)

Marmotte, sf. (*etym. I.* marmotta), marmot, kerchief round one's head

Marmotter, va. to mutter, to purr

Marmouset, sm. (*etym.* ?), grotesque figure, little chit, andiron

Marnage, sm. marling

Marne, sf. (*etym. O.F.* marle; *L.* margula, *marl*), marl

Marner, va. to marl

Marneux, se, adj. marly

Marnière, sf. marl-pit

Maroquin, sm. (*etym. prop. name* Maroc, *Morocco*), Morocco, Morocco leather

Maroquiner, va. to dress like Morocco

Marotique, adj. (*etym. prop. name* Marot, *a poet*), in the style of Marot

Marotte, sf. (*etym. see* Marionnette), fool's bauble, hobby. ¦ *Caresser sa* —, to ride one's hobby

Maroufle, sm. (*etym.* ?), scoundrel

Marquant, e, adj. of note, striking

Marque, sm. (*etym. G.* mark), mark, token, proof, instance, brand, mole, pit, marker, badge

Marqué, e, past part. marked. *Papier* —, stamped paper. *Traits* —*s*, strong features

Marquer, va. to mark, to stamp, to brand, to appoint, to state, to testify, to score; — vn. to mark, to be remarkable

Marqueter, va. (*etym.* marquer), to speckle, to checker, to inlay; *se* —, vr. to tattoo oneself

Marqueterie, sf. inlaid work, patch-work

Marqueur, sm. marker, scorer

Marquisat, sm. (*etym.* Marquis = *L.L.* marchensis, *warden of the marches*), marquisate

Marquise, sf. marchioness, marquee, awning

Marraine, sf. (*etym. L.L.* matrina), god-mother, god-mamma

***Marri, e,** adj. (*O.F.* marrir), concerned, sorry

Marron, sm. (*etym. I.* marrone), chestnut, cracker, mark. — *d'Inde*, horse chestnut

Marron, ne, adj. chestnut-coloured; (*etym. Sp.* cimarron, *wild*), *nègre* —, runaway slave. *courtier* —, unlicensed broker

Marronnage, sm. running away of slaves

Marronnier, sm. chestnut-tree. — *d'Inde*, horse-chestnut-tree

Marsouin, sm. (*etym. O.H.G.* mëri-suin, *porpoise*), porpoise

Marteau, sm. hammer, knocker

***Martel,** sm. (*etym. L.L.* martellus = martulus, *hammer*), hammer. ¦ *Avoir, se mettre — en tête*, to be sorely tormented

Marteler, va. to hammer, to torment

Martinet, sm. (*etym. prop. name* Martin), marten; (*etym. L.L.* martus, *hammer*), tilt hammer, cat o' nine tails

Martingale, sf. (*etym. prop. name* Martigues, *a town in Provence*), martingal, double *or* quits

Martin-pêcheur, sm. kingfisher

Martre, sm. (*etym. L.L.* martulus), martin, sable

Martyre, sm. (*etym. Gr.* μάρτυρ), martyrdom

Martyriser, va. to martyrize

Martyrologe, sm. (*etym. Gr.* μάρτυρ, λόγος), martyrology

Mascarade, sf. (*etym.* . mascherata), masquerade

Mascaron, sm. (*etym. I.* mascherone), mask

Masculin, e, adj. (*etym. L.* masculinum), male, masculine

Masque, sm. (*etym. I.* maschera), mask, masker. — sf. witch

Masquer, va. to mask, to cloak, to disguise; *se* —, vr. to put on a mask, to disguise oneself

Massacrante, adj. f. horribly cross. *D'une humeur* —, as cross as can be

Massacre, sm. massacre, slaughter, spoiling, bungler, (*hum.*) head

Massacrer, va (*etym. L.G.* matsken, *to kill*), to massacre, to spoil, to botch up

Masse, sf. (*etym. L.* massa), mass, lump, bulk, mob, block, heap, stock, capital; (*etym. L.L.* mateola, *a hammer*), sledge-hammer, mace

Massepain, sm. (*etym. I.* marzapane; *O.F.* marcepaine), marchpane

Masser, va. to dispose in masses, to shampoo

Massier, sm. mace-bearer

Massif, ve, adj. massive, clumsy. — sm. clump, solid mass, wall

Massue, sf. (*etym. L.L.* maxuca, *club*), club

Mastic, sm. (*etym. L.* mastiche), mastic, putty, cement

Mastiquer, va. to putty, to cement

Mastodonte, sm. (*etym. Gr. ὀδούς, tooth, μαστός, breast*), mastodon

Masure, sf. (*etym. L.L.* mansura, *dwelling*), ruins, hovel

Mat, e, adj. (*etym. G.* matt, *weak*), dead, dull, unpolished

Mat, sm. (*etym. Pers.* mat, *dead*), (*chess*) mate. *Être —*, to be checkmated

Mât, sm. (*etym. G.* mast), mast, spar, pole. *— de perroquet, de grand perroquet, de petit perroquet,* mizen-top mast, main-top-gallant mast, fore-top-gallant mast. *— de pavillon,* flag-staff. *— de rechange,* spare mast. *Aller à —s et à cordes,* to sail under bare poles. *Fixer un —,* to step a mast. *— de fortune,* jury-mast

Matamore, sm. (*etym. Sp.* matamoros, *killer of Moors*), bully, hector

Matelas, sm. (*etym. Ar.* al matrah, *mattress*), mattress, cushion

Matelasser, va. to line with cushions

Matelassier, ère, s. mattress-maker

Matelot, sm. (*etym.* ?), sailor, seaman. *Logement des —s,* the steerage

Matelote, sf. stewed fish

Mater, va. to checkmate, to bring down

Mâter, va. to mast

Matérialiser, va. (*etym.* matériel), to materialize

Matérialisme, sm. materialism

Matérialiste, sm. materialist

Matériaux, sm. plur. (*etm. O.F.* matérial), materials

‖**Matériel, le,** adj. material, coarse, heavy. — sm. stock, stores, fittings

‖**Maternel, le,** adj. (*etym. L.* maternalis), motherly, of a mother, maternal

Maternité, sf. (*etym. L.* maternitatem), maternity

Mathématicien, ne, s. mathematician

‖**Mathématique,** adj. (*etym. L.* mathematica), mathematical

Matière, sf. (*etym. L.* materia), matter, material, subject-matter, topic, cause, reason, grounds. *—s premières,* raw materials

Matin, sm. (*etym. L.* matutinum), morning. *De bon, de grand —,* early in the morning. — adv. early

Mâtin, sm. (*etym. L.L.* mansatinus, *house-dog*), cur, mastiff

‖**Matinal, e,** s. adj. early riser, early

Matinée, sf. morning, forenoon. *Dormir la grasse —,* to lie abed late

Matines, sf. plur. matins

Matineux, se, adj. early riser, early

Matir, va. to deaden

‖**Matois, e,** adj. (*etym.* ?), sharp, shrewd, cunning. — s. a cunning dog

Matou, sm. (*etym.* ?), tom-cat

Matras, sm. (*etym.* ?), matrass

Matrice, sf. (*etym. L.* matricem), matrix, matrice, standard, weight *or* measure

Matricule, sf. (*etym. L.* matricula), matriculation

Matrone, sf. (*etym. L.* matrona), matron, dame

Mâture, sf. masts, spars, masting, mast-store, mast-yard

Maturité, sf. (*etym. L.* maturitatem), maturity, ripeness

Maudire, va. (*etym. L.* maledicere), to curse

Maudit, e, adj. past part. confounded, cursed

Maugréer, vn.a. (*etym.* mal, gré), to curse and swear

Mausolée, sm. (*etym. L.* mausoleum), mausoleum

‖**Maussade,** adj. (*etym.* mal; *O.F.* sade, *of a pleasant taste* = *L.* sapidus), sulky, sullen, dull, unpleasant

Maussaderie, sf. sulkiness, sullenness

Mauvais, e, adj. (*etym.* ?), bad, ill, naughty, mischievous. — adv. badly, ill

Mauve, sf. (*etym. L.* malva), mallow, marsh-mallow, gull

Mauviette, sf. (*etym. O.F.* mauvis, *a black bird*), field-lark

§**Maxillaire,** adj. (*etym. L.* maxillaris), maxillary

Maxime, sf. (*etym. L.* maxima [sententia]), maxim

Mazette, sf. (*etym.* ?), bad horse, milksop, butter-fingers

Méandre, sm. (*etym. proper name: the river* Meander), maze, meander, winding

Mécanicien, sm. mechanician, engine-builder, engine-man

‖**Mécanique,** sf. (*etym. L.* mechanica), (*science*) mechanics, machinery. — adj. mechanical

Mécanisme, sm. mechanism

Méchanceté, sf. wickedness, wicked deed, spite

‖**Méchant, e,** adj. (*etym. O.F.* mescheant, *unlucky*), wicked, bad, spiteful, paltry, wretched. — sm. the wicked man, the evil-doer

Mèche, sf. (*etym. L.* myxus, *wick*), wick, match, linstock, screw, lash, lock of hair, tassel. *— anglaise,* centre-bit

Mécompte, sm. misreckoning, mistake, disappointment

se Mécompter, vr. to misreckon, to fall into a mistake

Méconnaissable, adj. not to be recognized

Méconnaissance, sf. unthankfulness, misappreciation

Méconnaissant, e, adj. unthankful, unmindful

Méconnaître, va. (*etym.* mes . . . . connaître), not to recognize, to disown, to slight; *se —,* vr. to forget oneself

Mécontent, e, adj. s. displeased, discontented, dissatisfied, malcontent

Mécontentement, sm. discontent, dissatisfaction

Mécontenter, va. to discontent, to displease

Mécréant, sm. (*etym.* mes . . . créant = croyant), disbeliever, unbeliever

§**Médaille,** sf. (*etym. I.* medaglia), medal

§**Médaillier,** sm. cabinet of medals

§**Médailliste,** sm. medallist

§**Médaillon,** sm. medallion

Médecin, sm. (*etym. L.* medicinus), physician, doctor

Médecine, sf. (*etym. L.* medicina), physic, medicine

Médeciner, va. to physic, to doctor; *se —,* vr. to physic oneself

‖**Médiat, e,** adj. (*etym. L.* mediatus), mediate

Médiateur, trice, s. (*etym. L.L.* mediator), mediator, mediatrix

Médiatiser, va. to mediatize

Médicament, sm. (*etym. L.* medicamentum), medicine

Médicamenter, va. to physic

‖**Médiocre,** adj. (*etym. L.* mediocrem), middling, moderate, poor. — sm. mediocrity

Médiocrité, sf. (*etym. L.* mediocritatem), mediocrity

Médire, vn. (*etym.* mes . . . dire), to speak ill of, to slander

Médisance, sf. slander, scandal

Médisant, e, adj. slanderous. — s. slanderer

Méditatif, ve, adj. (*etym. L.* meditativus), meditative, musing

Méditer, va.n. (*etym. L.* meditare), to contemplate, to meditate

Méditerrané, e, adj. (*etym. L.* mediterraneus), inland

Méfait, sm. (*etym.* mes . . . fait), misdeed, misdoing

Méfiance, sf. distrust, mistrust

Méfiant, e, adj. distrustful, mistrustful

se Méfier, vr. (*etym.* mes . . . fier), to distrust, to suspect

Mégarde, loc. adv. (*etym. O.F.* mesgarder, *not to keep carefully*), unawares

Mégère, sf. (*etym. L.* Megæra, *one of the Furies*), Megera, vixen, scold

Mégisserie, sf. leather-dressing, tawing

Mégissier, sm. (*etym. O.F.* megis, *a preparation of ashes and alum*), leather-dresser, tawer

§**Meilleur, e,** adj. (*etym. L.* meliorem), better, best — sm. best, cream

Mélancolie, sf. (*etym. L.* melancholia), melancholy, sadness

‖**Mélancolique,** adj. (*etm. L.* melancholicus), melancholy, gloomy, cheerless

Mélange, sm. (*etym.* mêler), mixture, medley, miscellany, mixing, blending. *Règle des —s,* (*arithm.*) alligation

Mélanger, va., *se —,* vr. to mix, to mingle, to blend

Mélasse, sf. (*etym. Sp.* melaza, *molasses*), molasses, treacle

Mêlée, sf. conflict, close fight, scuffle, fray, squabble

Mêler, va. (*etym. L.L.* misculare, *to mix*), to mix, to mix up, to mingle, to join, to jumble, to entangle, to implicate, to shuffle; *se —,* vr. to mix, to mingle, to blend, to take a concern in, to interfere

Mélèze, sm. (*etym.* ?), larch, larch-tree

Mélisse, sf. (*etym. Gr.* μέλισσα, *bee*), balm-mint

Mélodie, sf. (*etym. Gr.* μελῳδία), melody

‖**Mélodieux, se,** adj. melodious, tuneful, dulcet

Mélodramatique, adj. melodramatic

Mélodrame, sm. (*etym. Gr.* μέλος, *music,* δρᾶμα), melodrama

Mélomane, s. adj. (*etym. Gr.* μέλος, μανία), music-mad

Mélopée, sf. (*etym. Gr.* μελοποιία, *rules for the composition of songs*), melopœia

Membraneux, se, adj. (*etym.* membrane), membraneous

Membre, sm. (*etym. L.* membrum), limb, member

Membré, e, adj. limbed, membered

Membrure, sf. panel-frame, timbers

Même, adj. (*etym. L.* metipsissimus), same, very, self-same. — adv. even. *Être à — de,* to be within reach of or able to. *Mordre à —,* to bite off. *Mettre à —,* to enable. *De —,* in the same way, likewise. *Tout de —,* the same way

Mémoire, sf. (*etym. L.* memoria), memory remembrance, recollection. — sm. memorandum, memorial, bill, memoir

Menaçant, e, adj. threatening

Menacer, va. (*etym. L.* minacia), to threaten, to menace; *se —,* vr. to threaten each other

Ménage, sm. (*etym. L.L.* mansionaticum, *expenses of a house*), housekeeping, household, family, couple, set of furniture. *Vivre de —,* to live thriftily. *Entrer en —,* to begin housekeeping. *Faire bon —, mauvais —,* to live happily, unhappily together. *Faire des —s*, to go out a charring. *Femme de —*, housewife, charwoman. *Pain de —*, home-made bread

Ménagement, sm. caution, regard, consideration

Ménager, va. to husband, to save, to spare, to manage, to treat with regard, to prepare, to bring about; *se —*, vr. to be careful of oneself, to walk warily, to treat one another with regard

Ménager, ère, s. thrifty person. — adj. thrifty, sparing

Ménagerie, sf. menagerie

Mendiant, e, s. beggar, mendicant. *Les quatre —s*, the four orders of Mendicant Friars, (*fruit.*) figs, nuts, almonds and raisins

¶**Mendicité**, sf. (*etym. L.* mendicitatem), beggary, mendicity, vagrancy

Mendier, va. (*etym. L.* mendicare), to beg, to implore

Menée, sf. intrigue, underhand practices, track

Mener, va. (*etym. L.* minare, *to lead*), to lead, to drag, to carry, to drive, to convey

Ménestrel, sm. (*etym. L.L.* ministrale), minstrel

Ménétrier, sm. (*etym. L.L.* ministerarius), fiddler

Meneur, sm. leader

Menin, sm. (*etym. Sp.* menino, *a young man of good birth*), gentleman (to the dauphin)

Ménisque, sm. (*etym. Gr.* μηνίσκος), meniscus

Menotte, sf. (*etym.* main), tiny hand, handcuffs, manacles

Mensonge, sm. (*etym.* mentir), falsehood, lie, fiction

Mensonger, ère, adj. untrue, deceitful

‖**Mensuel, le**, adj. (*etym. L.* mensis, *month*), monthly

‖**Mental, e**, adj. (*etym. L.* mentalis), mental

Menterie, sf. fib, story

Menteur, se, s. adj. liar, story-teller, lying, delusive

Menthe, sf. (*etym. L.* mentha), mint

Mentionner, va. (*etym.* mention), to mention

Mentir, va. (*etym. L.* mentiri), to lie, to tell a falsehood. ‡ *A beau — qui vient de loin*, travellers see strange things

Menton, sm. (*etym. L.* mentonem), chin

Mentonnière, sf. chin-piece, bandage

Menu, e, adj. (*etym. L.* minutus), slender, small, minor. *—s plaisirs*, pocket-money. *—s propos*, small talk. — sm. minute, detail), bill of fare. — adv. small

Menuet, sm. (*etym.* menu), minuet

Menuiserie, sf. (*etym.* menu), joiner's work, carpentry

Menuisier, sm. carpenter and joiner

Méphitique, adj. (*etym. L.* mephiticus), mephitic, noxious

se Méprendre, vr. (*etym.* mes . . . prendre), to be mistaken, to mistake

‖**Mépris**, sm. (*etym.* mépriser), contempt, scorn

Méprisable, adj. contemptible, despicable

Méprisant, e, adj. scornful, contemptuous

Méprise, sf. (*etym.* méprendre), mistake, oversight, error

Mépriser, va. to despise, to scorn; *se —*, vr. to despise oneself, to despise each other

Mer, sf. (*etym. L.* mare), the sea. *La haute —, la pleine —*, the high sea, the open sea. *A la —*, overboard

Mercenaire, adj. s. (*etym. L.* mercenarius), mercenary, hireling

Mercerie, sf. (*etym.* mercier), haberdashery, mercery

Merci, sf. (*etym. L.* mercedem), mercy. *— de ma vie!* Gad's life! — sm. thanks, thank you

Mercier, ère, s. (*etym. L.L.* mercerius, *mercer*), haberdasher, mercer

Mercredi, sm. (*etym. L.* Mercurii dies), Wednesday

Mercure, sm. (*etym. L.* mercurius), mercury, quicksilver

Mercuriale, sf. lecture, market-prices

Mercuriel, le, adj. mercurial

Mère, sf. (*etym. L.* matrem), mother, dam

Mérelle, sf. (*etym. L.L.* matrella, *a kind of game*), hopscotch

Méridien, ne, sm. adj. (*etym. L.* meridianus), meridian

Méridienne, sf. meridian line, mid-day nap

Meringue, sf. (*etym.* ?), sort of cake full of whipped cream

Mérinos, sm. (*etym. Sp.* merino), Spanish wool, merino, merino sheep

Merise, sf. (*etym.* ?), wild cherry

Merisier, sm. wild cherry-tree

Méritant, e, adj. deserving

Mérite, sm. (*etym. L.* meritum), merit, worth, desert, due

Mériter, va.n. to deserve, to merit, to earn

‖**Méritoire**, adj. meritorious, deserving

Merlan, sm. (*etym.* ?), whiting

Merle, sm. (*etym. L.* merula), blackbird

Merlin, sm. (*etym. L.L.* marculinus, *hammer*), axe; (*etym. Engl.* marline), marline

Merluche, sf. (*etym. L.* mare, lucius, *pike*), salt-cod

§**Merveille**, sf. (*etym. L.* mirabilia), wonder, marvel

§**Merveilleux, se**, adj. wonderful, marvellous. — sm. (*lit.*) the machinery, the marvellous. —, se, s. coxcomb, an affected lady

Mésalliance, sf. misalliance, bad match

Mésallier, va. (*etym.* mes . . . allier), to marry below one's rank; *se —*, vr. to make a misalliance, to demean oneself

Mésange, sf. (*etym. Ang.-Sax.* mâse, *tom-tit*), tom-tit, titmouse

Mésaventure, sf. misadventure, mishap

Mésestimer, va. to have no esteem for, to underrate

Mésintelligence, sf. misunderstanding

*****Mesmérisme**, sm. (*etym. proper name* Mesmer), mesmerism

‖**Mesquin, e**, adj. (*etym. Sp.* mezquino, *slave*), paltry, mean

Mesquinerie, sf. shabbiness, meanness

Messager, ère, s. (*etym.* message), messenger, carrier

Messagerie, sf. stage-coach, coach-office

Messe, sf. (*etym. L.* missa), mass

Messéant, e, adj. unbecoming, unseemly

Messeoir, vn. (*etym.* mes . . . seoir), to be unbecoming

Messie, sm. (*etym. L.* Messias), the Messiah

Messier, sm. (*etym. L.* messarius, *from* messis, *harvest*), watcher in harvest-time

Messire, sm. ***Messer**, sm. (*etym. O.F.* mes = mon, sire), sir, master

Mesure, sf. (*etym. L.* mensura), measure, measurement, size, bounds, propriety, decorum, (*mus.*) bar, time. *Garder des —s*, to be cautious. *Être en — de*, to be in a situation to

Mesuré, e, adj. past part. prudent, circumspect, wary, moderate

Mesurer, va. (*etym. L.* mensurare), to measure, to mete out, to proportion, to calculate; *se —*, vr. to be measured, to be proportioned, to measure swords, to try one's strength

Mesureur, sm. measurer, meter

Mésuser, vn. to misuse, to abuse

Métacarpe, sm. (*etym. Gr.* μετακάρπιον), metacarpus

Métairie, sf. (*O.F.* métayerie; *see* MÉTAYER), farm

Métallique, adj. (*etym. L.* metallicus), metallic

Métallurgie, sf. (*etym. Gr.* μεταλλουργία), metallurgy

Métallurgique, adj. metallurgic

Métallurgiste, sm. metallurgist

Métamorphose, sf. (*etym. Gr.* μεταμόρφωσις), metamorphosis, change, transformation

Métamorphoser, va. to metamorphose, to transform, to change; *se —*, vr. to metamorphose oneself, to be metamorphosed

Métaphore, sm. (*etym. Gr.* μεταφορά), metaphor

‖**Métaphorique**, adj. metaphorical

Métaphysicien, ne, s. metaphysician

‖**Métaphysique**, sf. (*etym. Gr.* μετά, *after*, φυσικά, *natural things*), metaphysics. — adj. metaphysical

Métayer, ère, s. (*etym. L.L.* medietarius, *he who pays his rent in kind*), farmer

Métempsycose, sf. (*etym. Gr.* μετεμψύχωσις), metempsychosis

Météore, sm. (*etym. Gr.* μετέωρος, *which takes place in the air*), meteor

Météorique, adj. meteoric

Météorologie, sm. (*etym. Gr.* μετέωρος, λόγος), meteorology

Météorologique, adj. meteorological

Météorologiste, sm. meteorologist

Méthode, sf. (*etym. Gr.* μέθοδος), method, way, habit. *Avec plus de —*, more methodically

‖**Méthodique**, adj. methodical

*****Méthodisme**, sm. methodism

*****Méthodiste**, sm. methodist

‖**Méticuleux, se**, adj. (*etym. L.* meticulosus), particular

Métier, sm. (*etym. L.* ministerium), trade, handicraft, business, loom, frame, stocks. *Corps de —*, corporation, guild. *Jouer un tour, servir un plat de son — à*, to play one of one's trick on. *Faire en —*, to weave. *— mécanique*, power-loom

Métis, se, s. adj. (*etym. L.L.* mixtitius, *mixed*; *O.F.* mestis), half-breed, mongrel, hybrid

Métonymie, sf. (*etym. Gr.* μετωνυμία), metonymy

Métope, sm. (*etym. Gr.* μετόπη), metope

Mètre, sm. (*etym. Gr.* μέτρον), metre, 1 yard 3 1/3 inches

Métrique, adj. (*etym. Gr.* μετρικός), metrical

Métromane, sm. metromaniac

Métromanie, sf. (*etym. Gr.* μέτρον, μανία), metromania

Métropole, sf. (*etym. Gr.* μητρόπολις), metropolis

Métropolitain, e, adj. sm. metropolitan

Mets, sm. (*etym. L.* missum, *what is sent or helped*), dish, viand, mess

Mettable, adj. wearable

Metteur, sm. mounter, setter, clicker, maker up

Mettre, va. (*etym. L.* mittere), to put, to lay, to set, to place, to put on, to dress, to invest, to set about, to bestow. — *bas*, to put off, to doff, to bring forth. *Je les mets à faire pis*, I defy them to do worse. *Se* —, vr. to put oneself, to place oneself, to begin, to set about, to dress. *Se — en haleine*, to get used to it. *Se — bien, mal*, to ingratiate oneself with, to get out of favour with. *S'y* —, to begin, to fall to

Meuble, adj. (*etym. L.* mobilis), loose, moveable. — sm. furniture, household furniture. *Être dans ses —s*, to have furniture of one's own. *Des —s meublants*, household furniture

Meubler, va.n. to furnish, to stock, to be handsome; *se* —, vr. to be furnished, to furnish one's lodgings

Meule, sf. (*etym. L.* mola), millstone, grindstone, (*etym. L.L.* metula, *from* meta, *a stack*), stack, rick. *Mettre en* —, to stack

Meulière, sf. millstone, millstone quarry

Meunier, sm. (*etym. L.L.* molinarius), miller, miller's thumb

Meunière, sf. mistress of a mill, miller's wife

Meurtre, sm. (*etym. L.L.* mordrum, *murder*), murder, sin, shame

Meurtri, e, past part. bruised, murdered, spotted

Meurtrier, ère, s. adj. murderer, murderess, murderous

Meurtrière, sf. loophole

Meurtrir, va. to bruise; *se* —, vr. to bruise oneself

Meurtrissure, sf. bruise

Meute, sf. (*etym. L.L.* mota, *a troop raised for an expedition*), pack (of hounds)

Mi, part. (*etym. L.* medius), half, mid. — sm. (*mus.*) E, mi

Miasme, sm. (*etym. Gr.* μίασμα), miasma, noxious effluvium

Miaulement, sm. mewing

Miauler, vn. (*onomatop.*) to mew

Micacé, e, adj. (*etym. L.* micare, *to shine*), micaceous

Miche, sf. (*etym. Flem.* micke), loaf

‡**Micmac,** sm. (*etym. G.* mischmasch), foul play

Microcosme, sm. (*etym. Gr.* μικρόκοσμος, *small world*), microcosm

Microscopique, adj. (*etym.* microscope, *from the Gr.* μικρός, *small*, σκοπεῖν, *to observe*), microscopical

Midi, sm. (*etym.* mi; *L.* diem), noon, midday, meridian, the south. ‡ *Chercher — à quatorze heures*, to look for a knot in a bulrush

Mie, sf. (*etym. L.* mica, *crumb*), crumb. * — adv. *pas*, not any

Miel, sm (*etym. L.* mel), honey. *Mouche à* —, bee

‖**Mielleux, se,** adj. honeyed

Mien, ne, pron. (*etym. see* Mon), mine

Miette, sf. (*etym.* mie), crumb

Mieux, adj. adv. (*etym. L.* melius), better. *A qui — —*, in emulation of each other. — sm. improvement

Mièvre, adj. (*etym.* ?), arch, roguish

Mièvrerie, Mièvreté, sf. archness, roguery

§‖**Mignard, e,** adj. (*etym. O.H.G.* minnia, *love*), mincing, pretty

§**Mignarder,** va. to pet, to fondle, to affect quaintness in anything; *se* —, vr. to nurse oneself

§**Mignardise,** sf. delicacy, prettiness, mincing manner, feathered pink

§‖**Mignon, ne,** adj. s. pretty, delicate, tiny, darling, minion

Migraine, sf. (*etym. L.* hemicranium), a sick headache, megrim

Mijaurée, sf. (*etym.* ?), conceited creature

Mijoter, vn. (*etym.* ?), to let to simmer. — va. to nurse up

Mil, adj. num. (*etym. see* Mille), one thousand

Mil, or **Millet,** sm. (*etym. L.* milium), millet

Milan, sm. (*etym. Sp.* milano), kite

Miliaire, adj. (*etym. L.* miliarius), miliary

Milice, sf. (*etym. L.* militia), militia

Milicien, sm. militiaman

Milieu, sm. (*etym.* mi, lieu), middle, midst, mean, medium, society

‖**Militaire,** adj. (*etym. L.* militaris), military, soldier-like. — sm. soldier, military man

Militer, vn. (*etym. L.* militare), to militate

Mille, adj. num. (*etym. L.* mille), one thousand. — sm. mile

Mille-feuilles, sf. yarrow, milfoil

Millénaire, adj. sm. (*etym. L.* millenarius), millenary, millennium, millenarian

Mille-pieds, sm. wood-louse, millepede

Millésime, sm. (*etym. L.* millesimus), date (of coins, &c.)

Milliaire, adj. (*etym. L.* milliarius), miliary

Milliard, sm. a thousand millions

Millième, adj. sm. (*etym. L.* millesimus), thousandth

Millier, sm. (*etym. L.* milliarium), a thousand, ten cwt.

Milligramme, sm. milligramme

Millimètre, sm. millimetre (1/25 of an inch)

Millionième, adj. sm. millionth

Millionnaire, sm. worth a million

Mimique, adj. (*etym. L.* mimicus), mimic

Minauder, va. (*etym.* mine), to simper

Minauderie, sf. mincing air, simpering

Minaudier, ère, s. affected creature

Mince, adj. (*etym.* ?), thin, slender, inconsiderable

Mine, sf. (*etym. I.* mina), look, mien, bearing, wry face. ‡ *Payer de* —, to have a fair outside. *Faire bonne, mauvaise, froide — à*, to look sweet, sour, coldly upon. *Faire la* —, to sulk. *Faire — de*, to feign

Mine, sf. (*etym. see* Miner), mine, ore, stone. *Crayon de — de plomb*, black-lead pencil; (*etym. L.* mina), mina

Miner, va. (*etym. L.* minare, *to lead*), to undermine, to wear away

Minerai, sm. ore

Minéraliser, va. (*etym.* minéral), to mineralize

Minéralogie, sf. mineralogy

Minéralogique, adj. mineralogical

Minéralogiste, sm. mineralogist

Minet, te, s. (*etym.* ?), puss

Mineur, e, s. adj. (*etym. L.* minorem), under age, a minor

Miniature, sf. (*etym. L.* miniatura), miniature

Minière, sf. earth, &c., containing ore

Minime, adj. sm. inconsiderable, very slight, minim (monk)

Ministère, sm. (*etym. L.* ministerium), office, ministry, ministration, medium, agency, minister's offices. *Le — public*, the prosecuting magistrate

Ministériel, le, adj ministerial

Ministre, sm. (*etym. L.* minister), minister

Minois, sm. (*etym.* mine), face

Minorité, sf. (*etym. L.* minoritatem), minority

Minotaure, sm. (*etym. L. prop. name* Minos, taurus), Minotaur

Minuit, sm. midnight

Minuscule, adj. sf. (*etym. L.* minusculus), small, little letter

Minute, sf. (*etym. L.* minuta), minute, first draught

Minuter, va. to minute down, to contemplate

Minutie, sf. (*etym. L.* minutia; *pronounce* minucie), trifle, trifling matter

‖**Minutieux, se** (*pronounce* minucieux, minucieuse), adj. minute, circumstantial

‡**Mioche,** sm. (*etym.* mie), a brat, a small person

Mirabelle, sf. (*etym. Sp.* mirabel), mirabelle plum

‖**Miraculeux, se,** adj. (*etym. L.* miraculosus), miraculous

Mirage, sm. (*etym. see* Mirer), mirage, looming

Mire, sf. sight. *Point de* —, aim

Mirer, va. (*etym. L.* mirari), to take one's aim at, to have in view. — *des œufs*, to hold eggs up to the light. *Se* —, vr. to contemplate oneself, to see oneself

‡**Mirliflor,** sm. (*etym.* ?), coxcomb

Mirliton, sm. (*etym.* ?), reed-pipe

Miroir, sm. (*etym.* mirer), mirror, looking-glass

Miroiter, vn. to shine, to glisten

Miroitier, sm. looking-glass maker

Mis, e, adj. dressed, clad, accoutred

Misaine, sf. (*etym. I.* mezzana, *mizen*), foremast

Misanthropie, sf. (*etym. Gr.* μισανθρωπία), misanthropy

Misanthropique, adj. misanthropical

Mise, sf. (*etym. see* Mettre), share, stake, bidding, circulation, fashion, dress. — *en scène*, getting up. — *en page, en train*, (*print.*) making up, making ready. — *en accusation*, indictment. ‡ *Être de* —, to be presentable

‖**Misérable,** s. adj. (*etym. L.* miserabilis), wretch, villain, wretched, miserable

Misère, sf. (*etym. L.* miseria), misery, poverty, wretchedness, mere nothing. *Crier* —, to complain of poverty

Miséricorde, sf. (*etym. L.* misericordia), mercy. *A tout péché* —, we must not desire the death of the sinner. — ! interj. mercy on us!

‖**Miséricordieux, se,** adj. merciful

Missel, sm. (*etym. L.* missale), missal, mass-book

Missionnaire, sm. (*etym.* mission), missionary

Mitaine, sf. (*etym. O.H.G.* mittamo, *half*), mitten

Mitiger, va. (*etym. L.* mitigare), to mitigate, to qualify

Mitonner, vn. (*etym.* ?), to stew; — va. to cuddle, to humour, to prepare quietly; *se* —, vr. to stew, to cuddle oneself

Mitoyen, ne, adj. (*etym. L.* medietanus, *middle*), party

Mitoyenneté, sf. joint property

§**Mitraillade,** sf. discharge of grape-shot

§**Mitraille,** sf. (*O.F.* mitaille; *etym. O.F.* mite, *small copper coin*), old iron, coppers, grape-shot

§**Mitrailler,** vn.a. to fire grape-shot

Mitre, sf. (*etym. L.* mitra), mitre, chimney-pot

Mitré, adj. m. mitred

Mitron, sm. (*etym.* mitre), baker's man

Mixte, sm. adj. (*etym. L.* mixtus), mixed, compound, mixed body
Mnémonique, adj. (*etym. Gr.* μνημονική [τέχνη]), mnemonic; *also* **Mnémotechnie,** sf. mnemonics
Mobile, adj. (*etym. L.* mobilis), moveable, moving, marching, unsettled, versatile. — sm. body in motion, mover, motive
Mobilier, ère, adj. personal, of personal property. — sm. furniture
Mobilisation, sf. mobilization, liberation, converting into moveables
Mobiliser, va. to mobilize, to liberate, to convert into moveables
Mobilité, sf. (*etym. L.* mobilitatem), mobility
Mode, sf. (*etym. L.* modus), fashion, mode, manner. *A la* —, fashionable. *Magasin, marchande de* —*s*, milliner's shop, milliner. — sm. mode, mood
Modelage, sm. modelling
Modèle, sm. (*etym. I.* modello), model, pattern, copy
Modelé, sm. model
Modeler, va. to model, to mould; *se* —, vr. to take pattern from
Modérateur, trice, s. adj. (*etym. L.* moderatorem), moderator, moderating
Modéré, e, adj. moderate
Modérer, va. (*etym. L.* moderari), to moderate, to restrain, to slacken, to retrench; *se* —, vr. to abate, to grow moderate, to restrain oneself
Moderne, adj. s. (*etym. L.* modernus), modern, modern style
§Modeste, adj. (*etym. L.* modestus), modest, unassuming, moderate
Modestie, sf. (*etym. L.* modestia), modesty, moderation
Modicité, sf. (*etym. L.* modicitatem), smallness
Modificatif, ve, adj. modifying
Modifier, va. (*etym. L.* modificare), to modify; *se* —, vr. to become modified
§Modillon, sm. (*etym. I.* modiglione), modillion
Modique, adj. (*etym. L.* modicus), moderate, small
Modiste, s. milliner
Moduler, va.n. (*etym. L.* modulari), to modulate, to warble
Moelle, sf. (*etym. L.* medulla), marrow, pith
Moelleux, se, adj. marrowy, pithy, racy, mellow, soft. — sm. mellowness, softness
Moellon, sm. (*etym. ?*), rough stone, ashlar
Mœurs, sf. plur. (*etym. L.* mores), morals, morality, habits, manners
Moi, pron. pers. (*etym. L.* mi, *contract. for* mihi), me, to me
§Moignon, sm. (*etym. ?*), stump
Moindre, adj. comp. (*etym. L.* minor; *O.F.* mendre), less, smaller
Moine, sm. (*etym. L.L.* monius = *Gr.* μόνος, *alone*), monk, friar
Moineau, sm. (*O.F.* moisnel, *contract. for* moissonel, *from O.F.* moisson = *L.L.* muscionem, *small bird*), sparrow. — *franc*, house-sparrow
Moins, adv. (*etym. L.* minus), less, fewer, but, except, minus. *A* —, for less, with less. *A* — *de*, for less than, under, unless, without. — sm. minus, (*print.*) rule
Moire, sf. (*etym. Engl.* mohair), watering, clouding, watered silk
Moirer, va. to water silk
Mois, sm. (*etym. L.* mensis), month, month's salary or wages
Moisi, sm. mouldiness, mouldy part. —*e*, adj. rusty, mouldy, musty
Moisir, va. (*etym. L.* mucere; *O.F.* muisir), to make mouldy; *se* —, vr. to grow mouldy
Moisson, sf. (*etym. L.* messionem), harvest
Moissonner, va. to reap, to gather in, to mow down
Moissonneur, se, s. reaper
Moite, adj. (*etym. L.L.* mustens, *juicy*, *O.F.* moiste), moist, damp
Moiteur, sf. moisture
Moitié, sf. adv. (*etym. L.* medietatem), half. *Être de* —, to go halves
Molaire, adj. (*etym. L.* molaris), molar, grinder
Molester, va. (*etym. L.* molestare), to molest, to annoy
Molette, sf. (*etym. L.* mola), grindstone, rowel
Mollasse, adj. (*etym.* mou), flabby, flimsy
Mollesse, sf. (*etym. L.L.* mollitia), softness, mildness, delicacy, effeminacy
Mollet, te, adj. (*etym.* mole), soft. *Pain* —, roll. — sm. calf (of the leg)
Molleton, sm. swanskin, quilting
Mollifier, va. to mollify
Mollir, vn. (*etym. L.* mollire), to soften, to flag, to give way
Mollusque, sm. (*etym. L.* mollusca), mollusk, shell-fish
Moment, sm. (*etym. L.* momentum), moment, time, momentum, leverage
Momentané, e, adj. (*etym. L.* momentaneus), momentary
Momerie, sf. (*etym. O.F.* momer, *to mask*), mummery
Momie, sf. (*etym. I.* mummia), mummy
Mon, Ma, Mes, adj. poss. (*etym. L.* meus), my
Monacal, e, adj. (*etym. L.* monachus), monkish, monachal
Monade, sf. (*etym. L.* monadem), monad
Monarchie, sf. (*etym. Gr.* μοναρχία), monarchy
§Monarchique, adj. monarchical
§Monarchiste, sm. monarchist
Monarque, sm. (*etym. Gr.* μονάρχης), monarch
Monastère, sm. (*etym. L.* monasterium), convent, monastery
Monastique, adj. (*etym. L.* monasticus), monastic, monastical
Monceau, sm. (*etym. L.L.* monticellum), heap
Mondain, e, adj. s. (*etym. L.* mundanus), worldly, worldly-minded, worldling
Monde, sm. (*etym. L.* mundus), world, people, crowd, company, society, some one. *Le beau* —, the fashionable world. *Le grand* —, high life. *Savoir le* —, *avoir du* —, to know the world
Monder, va. (*etym. L.* mundare), to hull
Monétaire, adj. (*etym. L.* monetarius), monetary, money
Moniteur, trice, s. (*etym. L.* monitorem), monitor, monitress
Monnaie, sf. (*etym. L.* moneta), coin, money, change, the Mint. *De la petite* —, small change. — *blanche*, silver. ‡ *Donner à quelqu'un la* — *de sa pièce*, to give a Roland for an Oliver. *Payer en* — *de singe*, only to laugh at
Monnayage, sm. coinage, coining
Monnayer, va. to coin
Monnayeur, sm. coiner. *Faux* —, forger
Monogramme, sm. (*etym. Gr.* μονογράμματον), monogram
Monographie, sf. (*etym. Gr.* μονογραφία), monography
Monolithe, sm. (*etym. Gr.* μονόλιθος), monolith
Monomane, adj. s. monomaniac
Monomanie, sf. (*etym. Gr.* μόνος, μανία), monomania
Monopole, sm. (*etym. Gr.* μονοπωλία), monopoly
Monopoleur, sm. monopolist
Monopoliser, va. to monopolize
Monosyllabe, sm. (*etym. Gr.* μονοσύλλαβος), monosyllable
Monosyllabique, Monosyllabe, adj. monosyllabic
Monotone, adj. (*etym. Gr.* μονότονος), monotonous
Monotonie, sf. monotony, sameness
§Monseigneur, sm. my lord, your lordship, crowbar
Monsieur, sm. sir, gentleman. *Un vilain* —, a despicable fellow. ‡ *Faire le* —, to play the man of consequence
Monstre, sm. (*etym. L.* monstrum), monster
§Monstrueux, se, adj. (*etym. L.* monstruosus), monstrous
Monstruosité, sf. monstrosity
Mont, sm. (*etym. L.* montem), mount, mountain. *Par* —*s et par vaux*, over hill and dale. ‡ —*s et merveilles*, no end of wonders
Mont-de-Piété, sm. Government Pawnbroking Establishment
Montage, sm. carrying up, setting, mounting
§Montagnard, e, adj. s. mountain, mountaineer
§Montagne, sf. (*etym. L.L.* montanea), mountain
§Montagneux, se, adj. mountainous
Montant, sm. upright, post, amount, sum total, high flavour, height. —, *e*, adj. rising, uphill, stand-up, relieving
Monté, e, past part. mounted, raised, stocked, supplied. ‡ *Être bien, mal* —, (*fig.*) to be in a good, bad humour
Montée, sf. ascent, acclivity, step, height
Monter, va. (*etym.* mont), to ascend, to go up, to mount, to carry up, to take up, to raise, to tune, to set, to stock, to wind up. ‡ *Un coup monté*, a got-up thing. — *la tête à* (*exciter*), to work up. — vn. to go up, to ascend, to mount, to amount, to spring up. *Se* —, vr. to amount, to rise, to provide oneself, to get excited
§Montgolfière, sf. (*etym. prop. name* Montgolfier), fire-balloon
Monticule, sm. (*etym. L.* monticulus), hillock, mound
Montoir, sm. horse-block
Montre, sf. (*etym. see* MONTRER), watch, sample, shop-window, show-glass, show
Montrer, va. (*etym. L.* monstrare), to show, to point out, to prove, to teach; *se* —, vr. to show oneself, to prove
Montueux, se, adj. (*etym. L.* montuosus), hilly
Monture, sf. beast, nag, mounting, setting, frame, stock of a gun
se Moquer, vr. (*etym. ?*), to laugh at, to quiz, to make game of, not to care, to jest
Moquerie, sf. mockery, jeering, scoff
Moquette, sf. (*etym. ?*), Wilton carpet
Moqueur, se, adj. s. mocking, scornful, scoffing, scoffer
Moraine, sf. moraine, border
§Moral, sm. (*etym. L.* moralis), the mind, mental or moral faculties. —, *e*, adj. moral
Morale, sf. morality, ethics, moral
Moralisateur, Moraliste, sm. moralist

Moraliser, va.n. to moralize, to read a lecture to

Moralité, sf. (*etym. L.* moralitatem), morality, moral reflection

Morbide, adj. (*etym. L.* morbidus), morbid

¶**Morbidesse,** sf. morbidezza

Morbifique, adj. morbific

Morbleu! interj. (*euphemism for* mort-Dieu), zounds!

Morceau, sm. (*etym. L.L.* morsellum), bit, piece, morsel, passage. *Par —x*, piecemeal. † *Un — sur le pouce*, a snack. *Mettre les —x doubles*, to eat double quick time

Morceler, va. to parcel out

Morcellement, sm. parcelling out

Mordacité, sf. (*etym. L.* mordacitatem), mordacity, bitterness

Mordant, e, adj. biting. — sm. mordant, thrilling sound, point, poignancy

†**Mordicus,** adv. (*Latin adjective*), stoutly

§**Mordiller,** va. (*etym.* mordre), to nibble

Mordoré, e, adj. sm. (*etym. O.F.* more; *L.L.* maurus, *black*, doré), reddish brown

Mordre, va. (*etym. L.* mordere), to bite, to eat away, to take an effect, to make an impression, to sew lower down, to catch. *Faire mine de —*, to snap at. *Se —*, vr. to bite oneself, to bite each other

More, sm. Moor, blackamoor

Moresque, adj. sf. (*etym.* More), Moorish, morris-dance, Moorish dance

Morfondre, va. (*etym.* morve, fondre), quite to chill, to make one shiver; *se —*, vr. to shiver with cold, to be quite chilled

Morganatique, adj. morganatic

Morgue, sf. (*etm. ?*), stately look, haughtiness, conceit, inspection-room, the Morgue

Morguer, va. to browbeat

Moribond, e, adj. (*etym. L.* moribundus), dying

†**Moricaud, e,** s. adj. (*etm.* More), blackamoor, blackish

Morigéner, va. (*etym. L.* morigerari), to form the morals of, to tutor

§**Morille,** sf. (*etym. O.H.G.* morhila), moril

Morne, adj. (*etym. O.H.G.* mornen, *to be sad*), gloomy, dismal, dull. — sm. (*etym. Sp.* morron, *hillock*), bluff

Morosité, sf. (*etym. L.* morositatem), moroseness, surliness

Morphine, sf. (*etym. Gr.* Μορφεύς, *the God of sleep*), morphia

Mors, sm. (*etym. L.* morsus), bit. *Prendre le — aux dents*, to run away, to sit down earnestly to work, to give a free course to one's passions

Morse, sm. (*etym. ?*), walrus, morse, sea-horse

Morsure, sf. (*etym. L.L.* morsura), bite, sting

Mort, sf. (*etym. L.* mortem), death. ‡ *Mourir de sa belle —*, to die a natural death. — e, adj. past part. a. dead, pale, lifeless, dull, dead man *or* woman, corpse. *Faire le —*, to pretend to be dead

Mortaise, sf. (*etym. ?*), mortise

Mortalité, sf. (*etym. L.* mortalitatem), mortality

Morte-eau, sf. neap tide

‖**Mortel, le,** adj. s. (*etym. L.* mortalis), deadly, mortal

Mortier, sm. (*etym. L.L.* mortarium), mortar

Mortifère, adj. (*etym. L.* mortiferus), mortiferous

Mortifiant, e, adj. mortifying

Mortifier, va. (*etym. L.* mortificare), to mortify; *se —*, vr. to grow tender, to mortify one's body

Mortuaire, adj. (*etym. L.* mortuarius), burial. *Drap —*, pall

Morue, sf. (*etym. ?*), cod, cod-fish

Morve, sf. (*etym. L.* morbum), snot, the glanders

Morveux, se, adj. snotty, glandered

Mosaïque, adj. (*etym. L.* mosaicus), Mosaic. — sf. (*etm. I.* musaico), piece of mosaic work, tesselated pavement

Mosquée, sf. (*etym. Ar.* mesgid), mosque

Mot, sm. (*etym. L.* muttum), word, saying, sentence, meaning, motto. *De gros —s*, oaths, high words. *— pour rire*, joke. *Je vous prends au —*, I take you at your word. *— d'ordre*, watchword. *Se donner le —*, to agree together

Moteur, sm. (*etym. L.* motorem), contriver, mover, motor. —, *trice*, adj. motive, moving

Motif, sm. (*etym. L.L.* motivus), motive, incentive, subject

Motiver, va. to state the grounds of, to be the motive of

Motte, sf. (*etym. ?*), clod, ball of earth. *— à brûler*, peat, turf

‡**Motus!** interj. (*etym. ?*), not a word!

Mou, *or* **Mol, le,** adj. (*etym. L.* mollis), soft, mellow, weak. — sm. lights of animals

Mouchard, sm. (*etym.* mouche), informer, police-spy

Mouche, sf. (*etym. L.* musca), fly, patch, lou, spy, button of a foil. *— bleue*, blue-bottle fly. *— à viande*, blow-fly. *Tache de —*, fly-blow. ‡ *Quelle — le pique!* what whim has he got into his head now? *Prendre la —*, to be easily offended. *Pieds, pattes de —*, (*fig.*) a scrawl. *Fine —*, a sly person

Moucher, va. (*etym. L.* muccare), to blow the nose of, to snuff; *se —*, vr. to blow one's nose. ‡ *Ne pas se — du pied*, to be no fool

Moucheron, sm. gnat, midge

Moucheté, e, adj. spotted, speckled, blunted

Moucheter, va. to spot, to speckle, to blunt

Mouchettes, sf. plur. snuffers

Moucheture, sf. spot, speckle

Moucheur, sm. candle-snuffer

Mouchoir, sm. handkerchief

Mouchure, sf. candle-snuff

Moudre, va. (*etym. L.* molere; *O.F.* molre, moldre), to grind. *Être moulu de coups*, to be bruised all over

Moue, sf. (*etym. Dutch* mowe), pouting

Mouette, sf. (*dimin. of the O.F.* moue), sea-gull, sea-mew

Moufle, sf. (*etym. ?*), tackle, block and fall; (*etym. L.L.* muffula, *glove*), muffler. — sm. muffle

Mouflon, sm. (*etym. ?*), muflon, musmon

§**Mouillage,** sm. anchorage, anchoring-ground

§**Mouiller,** va. (*etym. L.L.* molliare, *to soften*), to wet, to moisten, to water, to pronounce with a liquid sound, to drop the anchor; *se —*, vr. to get wet, to be drenched, to wet one's lips, to grow moist

§**Mouillette,** sf. sippet with eggs

Moulage, sm. moulding

Moule, sf. (*etym. L.* musculus), mussel, muscle. — sm. mould, cast

Moulé, e, adj. printed, which looks like print

Mouler, va. to mould, to cast; *se —*, vr. to model oneself

Mouleur, sm. moulder

Moulin, sm. (*etym. L.L.* molinus), mill. *— à bras*, *à vent*, handmill, windmill. ‡ *— à paroles*, chatterbox

Mouliner, va. to throw, to grind

Moulinet, sm. drum, mill. *Faire le —*, to flourish one's stick

Moulure, sf. moulding

Mourant, e, adj. s. dying, expiring, deathlike, dying person

Mourir, vn. (*etym. L.* moriri, *archaism for* mori), to die, to expire; *se —*, vr. to be dying, to die away

Mouron, sm. (*etym. ?*), chickweed

Mousquet, sm. (*etym. I.* moschetto), musket

Mousquetaire, sm. musketeer

Mousqueterie, sf. musketry, volley of musketry

Mousqueton, sm. blunderbuss, musketoon

Mousse, sm. (*etym. I.* mozzo, *young boy*), cabin-boy, ship-boy. — sf. (*et* mos, *moss*), moss, f lather. — adj. mots, *blunt*), blun

Mousseline, *prop. name of town*), muslin

Mousser, vn. t foam, to sparkle, ‡ *Faire —*, (*fig.*) t

Mousseron, room

Mousseux, se, foaming, sparklin

Mousson, sm. (mousão, *monsoon*) trade wind

Moussu, e, a moss-grown

Moustache, s mostaccio), moust kers. ‡ *Une vieill grise*, an old cam

§**Moustille,** sf. mustum, *must*), a light sparkling

Moustiquaire quito-net

Moustique, *Sp.* mosquito), m

Moût, sm. (*etym.* must

‡¶**Moutard,** sm brat, urchin

Moutarde, moût), mustard

Moutardier, s pot, mustard-ma *croire le premier* to think no sm oneself

Mouton, sm. sheep, wether, mu leather, prison-sp mer, beetle, be white-crested wav *à nos —s*, to re subject

Moutonné, e,

Moutonner,

Moutonnier, sheep-like

Mouture, sf. molitura), grind fee, meslin. *Ti deux —s*, to ge profit out of a t

Mouvance, sf.

Mouvant, e, ing, shifting, *Sable —*, quicks

Mouvement, *L.* movimentum) movement, bust tion, disturbanc sensation, life, works. *— de va* and fro motion

Mouvoir, va. movere), to mov start; *se —*, vr. stir

Moyen, ne, s medianus), mid sized, average, m means, way, power, medium parts

Moyennant, means of

Moyenne, s mean, medium

Moyenner, moyen), to contri

Moyeu, sm. (*etym.* *L.* modiolus), nave of a wheel
Muable, adj. (*etym.* *L.* mutabilis), mutable
Mucilagineux, se, adj (*etym.* mucilage), mucilaginous
Mucosité, sf. (*etym.* *L* mucosus), mucus
Mue, sf. (*etym.* muer), moulting, moulting-time, mew, coop
Muer, vn. (*etym.* *L.* mutare, *to change*), to moult, to break (voice)
Muet, te, adj. s. (*etym.* *L.* mutus), dumb, speechless, mute
Mufle, sm. (*etym.* ?), muzzle, snout
Mugir, vn. (*etym.* *L.* mugire), to bellow, to roar
Mugissant, e, adj. bellowing, lowing, roaring
Mugissement, sm. bellowing, lowing, roaring
Muguet, sm. (*etym.* *L.L.* musquettus, *dimin. of* muscus, *musk*), lily of the valley, ‡ young spark, coxcomb
Muid, sm. (*etym.* *L.* modius), hogshead
Mulâtre, tresse, adj. s. (*etym.* *Sp.* mulato), mulatto
Mule, sf. (*etym.* *L.* mula), mule, she-mule, slipper
Mulet, sm. (*etym.* *L.* mulus), mule; (*etym.* *L.* mulla), mullet
Muletier, sm. muleteer, mule-driver
Mulot, sm. (*etym.* *D.* mol, *mole*), field-mouse, wood-mouse
Multiflore, adj. (*etym.* *L.* multiflorus), multiflorous
Multiforme, adj (*etym.* *L.* multiformis), multiform
Multiplicande, sm. (*etym.* *L.* multiplicandus), multiplicand
Multiplicateur, sm. (*etym.* *L.* multiplicator), multiplier
Multiplicité, sf. (*etym.* *L.* multiplicitatem), multiplicity, multifariousness
Multiplié, e, past part. adj. multiplied, manifold
Multiplier, va.n. (*etym.* *L.* multiplicare), to multiply; *se* —, vr. to multiply, to be multiplied, to be renewed
Municipalement, adv. (*etym.* municipal), by a corporation
Municipalité, sf. municipality
Municipe, sm. (*etym.* *L.* municipium), municipal officer
Munir, va. (*etym.* *L.* munire), to provide, to arm, to strengthen; *se* —, vr. to provide oneself, to arm oneself
Munition, sf. ammunition, provisions, stores. *Pain de* —, soldier's bread
Muqueux, se, adj. (*etym.* *L.* mucosus), mucous
Mûr, adj. (*etym.* *L.* maturus), ripe, mature, serious
Mur, sm. (*etym.* *L.* murus), wall. *Mettre au pied du* —, to bring to a standstill
§**Muraille,** sf. wall
Mûre, sf. (*etym.* *L.* mora), mulberry. — *sauvage*, blackberry
Murène, sf. (*etym.* *L.* muræna), muræna, sea-eel
Murer, va. to wall in, to wall up
Muriatique, adj. (*etym.* *L.* muria, *salt*), muriatic
Mûrier, sm. mulberry-tree. — *sauvage*, blackberry-bush
Mûrir, va.n. to ripen, to mature
Murmure, sm. (*etym.* *L.* murmur), murmur, grumbling, repining, hum, whispering
Murmurer, vn.a. (*etym.* *L.* murmurare), to murmur, to grumble, to repine, to mutter, to whisper; *se* —, vr. to be whispered about
Musard, e, adj. s. (*etym.* muser), loiterer, trifler
Muse, sm. (*etym.* *L.* muscum), musk
Muscade, sf. (*etym.* *L.L.* muscata), nutmeg. *Fleur de* —, mace
Muscadier, sm. nutmeg-tree
Muscadin, sm. dandy
Muscat, adj. sm. (*etym.* *L.L.* muscatus), muscadine, muscadel, muscadine grape, musk-pear
Musculaire, adj. (*etym.* *L.* muscularis), muscular
Musculeux, se, adj. (*etym.* *L.* musculosus), muscular, brawny
Museau, sm. (*etym.* *O.F.* muse = museau), snout, nose, muzzle
Musée, Muséum, sm. (*etym.* *L.* museum), museum
Museler, va. to muzzle, to gag
Muselière, sf. muzzle
Muser, vn. (*etym.* ?), to dawdle. *Qui refuse, muse*, he that will not when be may, when he fain would, shall have nay
Musette, sf. (*etym.* ?), bagpipe
Musicien, ne, s. (*etym.* musique), musician
Musique, (*etym.* *L.* musica), music, band. *Faire de la* —, to play music. *Mettre en* —, to set to music
Musquer, va. (*etym.* musc), to scent with musk. *Rat musqué*, musk-rat. ‡ *Paroles musquées*, soft words. *Écrivain musqué*, affected writer
Mutabilité, sf. (*etym.* *L.* mutabilitatem), mutability
Mutiler, va. (*etym.* *L.* mutilare), to mutilate, to maim, to mangle; *se* —, vr. to maim oneself
Mutin, e, adj. s. (*etym.* *see* MEUTE), headstrong, froward, mutinous, mutineer
se ‡**Mutiner,** vr. to be headstrong, to be refractory, to mutiny
Mutinerie, sf. frowardness, mutiny
Mutisme, sm. (*etym.* *L.* mutus), silence, dumbness
‡**Mutuel, le,** adj. (*etym.* *L.* mutualis), mutual
Mutule, sf. (*etym.* *L.* mutulus, *shell*), (*arch.*) corbel, bracket
Myagrum, sm. (*Latin word*), (*bot.*) myagrum, gold of pleasure
Myope, adj. s. (*etym.* *Gr.* μυωψ), short-sighted, short-sighted person
Myopie, sf. near *or* short sightedness
Myriade, sf. (*etym.* *Gr.* μύριοι, 10,000), myriad
Myriagramme, sm. (*etym.* *Gr.* μυρίοι, γράμμα), myriagramme (about 22 lbs. 1.23)
Myriamètre, sm. (*etym.* *Gr.* μύριοι, μέτρον), myriametre (6 miles, 1 furlong, 28 poles)
Myrrhe, sf. (*etym.* *L.* myrrha), myrrh
Myrte, sm. (*etym.* *L.* myrtus), myrtle
Mystère, sm. (*etym.* *L.* mysterium), mystery
‡**Mystérieux, se,** adj. mysterious
Mysticisme, sm., **Mysticité,** sf. (*etym.* *L.* mysticitatem), mysticism
Mystificateur, sm. hoaxer
Mystifier, va. (*etym.* *L.L.* mystificare), to hoax, to mystify
‡**Mystique,** adj. (*etym.* *L.* mysticus), mystic, mystical
Mythe, sm. (*etym.* *Gr.* μῦθος), myth
Mythologie, sf. (*etym.* *Gr.* μυθολογία), mythology
Mythologique, adj. mythological
Mythologue, sm. mythologist

N

N, smf. N, n
Nabab, sm. (*etym.* *Ar.* nâbab, *lieutenant*), nabob
Nacelle, sf. (*etym.* *L.L.* navicella), skiff, wherry, bark, (*arch.*) scotia
Nacre, sm. (*etym.* *Pers.* nakar, *pearl*), mother of pearl
Nacré, e, adj. pearly
Nage, sf. rowlocks, perspiration, sweat. *A la* —, by swimming. *Être en* —, to sweat
Nageoire, sf. fin, corks, bladders
Nager, vn. (*etym.* *L.* navigare), to swim, to welter, to float, to be buoyed up. — *entre deux eaux*, to swim under water, (*fig.*) to trim one's sail
Nageur, se, s. swimmer, oarsman
Naguère, adv. (*etym.* ne, a, guères), but lately, not long ago
Naïade, sf. (*etym.* *L.* naiadem), naiad
‡**Naïf, ve,** adj. (*etym.* *L.* nativus), artless, ingenuous, silly
Nain, e, s. adj. (*etym.* *L.* nanus), dwarf. *Le — jaune*, Pope Joan
Naissance, sf. (*etym.* *L.* nascentia), extraction, rise, birth, spandrel
Naissant, e, adj. infant, new-born, rising, dawning
Naître, vn. (*etym.* *L.L.* nascere = nasci), to be born, to spring. *Mort-né*, still-born
Naïveté, sf. artlessness, ingenuousness, simplicity, silly thing
Nanan, sm. (*onomatop.*), something nice, lollipop
Nankin, sm. (*prop. name of a town*), nankeen
Nantir, va. (*etym.* *O.F.* nam, *pledge*), to give a security to; *se* —, vr. to seize, to secure, to line one's nest
Nantissement, sm. pledge, security
Naphte, sm. (*etym.* *L.* naphtha), naphtha
Nappe, sf. (*etym.* *L.* mappa), table-cloth, cloth. — *d'eau*, sheet of water
Narcisse, sm. (*etym.* *L.* *prop. name* Narcissus), narcissus, daffodil
Narcotique, adj. sm. (*etym.* *Gr.* ναρκωτικός), narcotic, opiate
Nard, sm. (*etym.* *L.* nardus), nard, spikenard
Nargue, sf disdain, scorn. — *à* ... a fig for ... !
Narguer, va. (*etym.* *L.L.* naricare, *to turn up one's nose*), to snap one's fingers at, to set at defiance
Narine, sf. (*etym.* *L.L.* naricula, *from* naris, *nostril*), nostril
Narquois, e, adj. (*etym.* narguer), mocking
Narrateur, sm. (*etym.* *L.* narratorem), narrator
Narratif, ve, adj. (*etym.* *L.* narrativus), narrative
Narré, sm. narration

Narrer, va. (*etym. L.* narrare), to narrate, to relate, to tell a story
Nasarde, sf. (*etym. L.* nasus, *nose*), fillip
Naseau, sm. (*etym. L.* nasellus, *from* nasus), nostril
§**Nasillard, e,** adj. s. (*etym.* nasiller), snuffling, snuffler
§**Nasillement,** sm. snuffling
§**Nasiller,** vn. to speak through one's nose, to snuffle
Nasse, sf. (*etym. L.* nassa), weir, bow-net
Natation, sf. (*etym. L.* natationem), swimming
Natatoire, adj. (*etym. L.* natatorius), swimming, natatory
Natif, ve, adj. s. (*etym. L.* nativus), native
Nationalité, sf. (*etym.* national), nationality
Nativité, sf. (*etym. L.* nativitatem), nativity
Natte, sf. (*etym. L.* matta), mat, matting, plait, straw-mat, rush-mat
Natter, va. to mat, to plait
Naturaliser, va. (*etym.* naturel), to naturalize
Naturaliste, sm. naturalist
Naturalité, sf. quality of a native
Nature, sf. (*etym. L.* natura), nature, description. *Payer en* —, to pay in kind
‡**Naturel, le,** adj. (*etym. L.* naturalis), natural, native, untaught, plain, ingenuous. — sm. native, nature, property, disposition. *Au* —, to the life, simply cooked
Naufrage, sm. (*etym. L.* naufragium), wreck, shipwreck
Naufragé, e, adj. wrecked, shipwrecked
Naumachie, sf. (*etym. L.* naumachia), mock sea-fight
Nauséabond, e, adj. (*etym. L.* nauseabundus), loathsome, nauseous
Nausée, sf. (*etym. L.* nausea), qualmishness, nausea
Nautile, sm. (*etym. L.* nautilus), nautilus
Nautique, adj. (*etym. L.* nauticus), nautical
Nautonier, sm. (*etym. O.F.* noton, *sailor*), sailor, mariner
Navet, sm. (*etym. L.L.* nappettus, *dimin. of* napus, *turnip*), turnip
Navette, sf. (*etym.* navet), rape, rape-seed; (*etym. L.* navis, *boat*), incense-box, weaver's shuttle. *Faire la* —, to go backwards and forwards
Navigateur, sm. adj. (*etym. L.* navigatorem), navigator, voyager, seafaring
Naviguer, vn. (*etym. L.* navigare), to navigate, to sail
Navire, sm. (*etym. L.L.* navirium), ship
Navrant, e, adj. heart-breaking
Navrer, va. (*etym. Scand.* nafar, *sharp instrument*), to grieve most deeply, to wound
‡**Ne,** adv. (*etym. L.* non; *O.F.* nen), no, not
Néanmoins, conj. nevertheless, however
Néant, sm. (*etym. L.L.* necentem, *not being*), nothing, nothingness, no
Nébuleux, se, adj. (*etym. L.* nebulosus), cloudy, gloomy, lowering, nebulous
Nébuleuse, sf. nebula
‡**Nécessaire,** adj. (*etym. L.* necessarius), necessary, needful. — sm. necessaries, the needful, work-box, dressing-case. ‡ *Faire le* —, to bustle about as a person of importance
Nécessité, sf. (*etym. L.* necessitatem), need, necessity. *Faire de — vertu*, to make a virtue of necessity
Nécessiter, va. to necessitate, to bind down
Nécessiteux, se, adj. needy, necessitous
Nécrologe, sm. (*etym. Gr.* νεκρός, *dead*, λόγος, *discourse*), obituary
Nécrologie, sf. necrology
Nécromancie, sf. (*etym. Gr* νεκρός, μαντεία, *divination*), necromancy
Nécromancien, ne, s., *also* **Nécromant,** sm. necromancer
Nécropole, sf. (*etym. Gr.* νεκρόπολις), necropolis, burial-ground
Nef, sf. (*etym. L.* navem), ship, nave. — *latérale*, lateral aisle
Néfaste, adj. (*etym. L.* nefastus), solemn, unlucky, inauspicious
Nèfle, sf. (*etym. L.* mespilum, *medlar*), medlar
Néflier, sm. medlar-tree
‡**Négatif, ve,** adj. (*etym. L.* negativus), negative
Négligé, sm. dishabille, undress, negligence
Négligemment, adv. (*etym.* négligent), negligently
Négligence, sf. (*etym. L.* negligentia), neglect, negligence, remissness
Négliger, va. (*etym. L.* negligere), to neglect; *se* —, vr. to take no care of oneself, to grow careless, to commit negligences
Négoce, sm. (*etym. L.* negotium), trade, business
Négociable, adj. negotiable
Négociant, sm. merchant
Négociateur, trice, s. (*etym. L.* negotiator), negotiator
Négocier, va.n. (*etym. L.* negotiari), to negotiate; *se* —, vr. to be negotiating
Nègre, sm. (*etym. Sp.* negro), negro
Négresse, sf. negress
Négrier, adj. sm. slave. *Bâtiment* —, slave-ship. *Capitaine* —, captain of a slave-ship
§**Négrillon, ne,** s. negro-boy, negro-girl
Neige, sf. (*etym. L.* nivea), snow. ‡ *Faire la boule de* —, to increase rapidly
Neiger, vn. impers. to snow
Neigeux, se, adj. snowy
Nenni, adv. (*etym. L.* non, illud), no, not at all
Nénufar, sm. (*etym. Pers.* noûfer, *water-lily*; *O.F.* neufar), nenuphar, water-lily
Néologie, sf. (*etym. Gr* νέος, *new*, λόγος), neology
Néologisme, sm. neologism
Néphrétique, adj. (*etym. Gr.* νεφριτικός), nephretic
Népotisme, sm. (*etym. L.* nepotem), nepotism
Néréide, sf. (*etym. L.* nereidem), nereid, sea-nymph
Nerf, sm. (*etym. L.* nervus), nerve, band, slip, cord. *Une attaque de* —*s*, hysterics. — *de bœuf*, a bull's pizzle. *Donner du — à*, to give strength to
Nerveux, se, adj. (*etym. L.* nervosus), nervous, vigorous
Nervure, sf. nerves
‡**Net, te,** adj. (*etym. L.* nitidus), clean, clear, fair, frank, net. ‡ *En avoir le cœur* —, to know all about something. *Faire maison* —, to clear one's house (of one's servants)
Netteté, sf. cleanness, clearness
Nettoiement, Nettoyage, sm. cleaning, clearing
Nettoyer, va. to clean, to scour, to clear; *se* —, vr. to clean oneself, one's hands, &c., to be cleaned
Neuf, adj s. (*etym. L.* novem), nine. —, *ve*, adj (*etym. L.* novus), new, fresh, raw, inexperienced. *A* —, anew
Neutralement, adv. neutrally
Neutraliser, va. (*etym. L.* neutralis), to neutralize: *se* —, vr. to neutralize each other
Neutralité, sf. (*etym. L.L.* neutralitatem), neutrality
Neutre, adj. sm. (*etym. L.* neutrum), neutral, neuter
Neuvaine, sf. (*etym. L.L.* novena), novena
‡**Neuvième,** adj. sm. (*etym. L.L.* novesimus), ninth
Neveu, sm. (*etym. L.* nepotem), nephew. *Petit*- —, grand-nephew. — *à la mode de Bretagne*, cousin once removed
Névralgie, sf. (*etym. Gr.* νεῦρον, *nerve*, ἄλγος, *pain*), neuralgia
Névralgique, adj. neuralgic
Névrose, sf. (*etym. Gr* νεῦρον), nervous affection
Nez, sm. (*etym. L.* nasus), nose, smell, scent, prow
Ni, conj. (*etym. L.* nec), nor
Niable, adj. (*etym.* nier), deniable
‡**Niais, e,** adj. s. (*etym. L.L.* nidacem, *unfledged*), silly, foolish, simple, eyas, nias, simpleton
Niaiser, va. to dawdle, to say silly things
Niaiserie, sf. s... nonsense, trifle, si...
Niche, sf. (*etym.* ... niche, kennel; ... Nique), trick. *Fa...* to play tricks
Nichée, sf. nest,
Nicher, vn. (*ety...* care), to have it... nestle; — va. to p... to lodge; *se* —, ... its nest, to cree... lodge
Nid, sm. (*etym.* ... nest, berth
Nielle, sf. (*etym.* ... *black*), wild fenn... blight, mildew; (*e...* gellum), black ena...
Nieller, va. to ... blight
Nier, va. to deny
Nigaud, e, adj. ... silly, noodle, booby
Nimbe, sm. (*ety...* bus), glory, nimbu...
Nippe, sf. (*etym. I...* *clothes*), article ... (*plur.*) clothes, th...
Nipper, va. to fit... vr. to fit oneself ou...
Nique, sf. (*et...* nyck, *trick*), sign o... *Faire la — à*, to l...
‡**Nitouche** [sa... (*etym.* n'y touche... looking person
Nitreux, se, ... nitre), nitrous
Nitrique, adj. ...
Niveau, sm (*e...* bella, *level*; *O.I...* level
Niveler, va. t... make even; *se* —... levelled
Niveleur, sm.
Nivellement, ... ling
Nobiliaire, adj ... *L.* nobiliaris), pa... of the nobility
Noblesse, sf. ... nobilitis), nobility ... *La petite* —, the g... *oblige*, nobility ... quires nobleness o...
Noce, sf. (*etym.* ... wedding, nuptial... feast, the wedd... *Être de la* —, *ê...* go to the wedding... ding. ‡ *N'être p...* (*fig.*) to be in no... tuation. *Faire* ... to revel and feast
Nocher, sm. (... nocchiere), pilot
Nocturne, adj ... *L.* nocturnus), ni... turnal, nocturn
Noël, sm. (*etym.* ... *birthday*), Christ... mas carol. *Bûche* ... log
Nœud, sm. (*etym* ... knot, bow, tie, k... node
Noir, e, adj. (*e...* grum), black, da... dismal, base, hei... *nière* —*e*, mezzoti... black. — *animal*, ... — *de fumée*, lamp...

Noirâtre, adj. blackish
Noirceur, sf. blackness, baseness, heinousness, foul deed, foul aspersion
Noircir, va. to blacken, to tan, to throw a gloom over, to asperse; — vn. to blacken, to grow black; *se* —, vr. to blacken one's hair, &c., to grow black or dark
Noire, sf. (*mus.*) crotchet
Noise, sf. (*etym. L.* nausea), quarrel. *Chercher* — *à*, to pick a quarrel with
Noisetier, sm. nut-tree, hazel-tree
Noisette, sf. (*etym.* noix), nut, hazel-nut
Noix, sf. (*etym. L.* nucem), walnut, nut, knee, cap, kernel, cone, box of a gun
Nolis, Nolissement, sm. freighting
Noliser, va. (*etym. I.* noleggiare), to freight, to charter
Nom, sm. (*etym. L.* nomen), name, renown, noun
Nomade, adj. (*etym. L.* nomadem), wandering, nomad
Nombre, sm. (*etym. L.* numerus), number, a great many, multifariousness, harmony. — *nombrant*, abstract number
Nombrer, va. (*etym. L.* numerare), to number, to reckon
Nombreux, se, adj. (*etym. L.* numerosus), numerous, multifarious, harmonious
Nombril, sm. (*etym. L.L.* umbiliculus), navel, (*bot.*) eye
Nomenclateur, sm. (*etym. L.* nomenclator), nomenclator
Nominatif, ve, sm. adj. (*etym. L.* nominativus), nominative case, of names, of the names
Nominaux, sm. pl. (*etym. L.* nominalis), nominalists
Nommé, e, adj. past part. named, by name, appointed
Nommer, va. (*etym. L.* nominare), to call, to name, to mention, to elect; *se* —, vr. to tell one's name, to be called
Non, adv. (*etym. L.* non), no, not, nem
Nonagénaire, adj. (*etym. L.* nonagenarius), ninety years of age
Nonante, adj. (*etym. L.* nonaginta), ninety
Nonce, sm. (*etym. I.* nunzio), Pope's nuncio
Nonchalance, sf. listlessness, carelessness
Nonchalant, e, adj. (*etym.* non; *O.F.* chaloir), listless, careless
Nonciature, sf. (*etym. I.* nunziatura), nunciature
Non-lieu, sm. not sufficient cause
Nonne, Nonnain, sf. (*etym. L.L.* nonna), nun
Nonnette, sf. young nun, (*confect.*) gingerbread nuts
Nonobstant, prep. conj. (*etym. L.* non, obstante), notwithstanding
Non-sens, sm. nonsense
Nord, sm. (*etym. G.* nord), the north, the north wind
Nord-est, sm. north-east
Nord-ouest, sm. north-west
Nosographie, Nosologie, sf. (*etym. Gr.* νόσος, *illness*, λόγος, γραφία), nosology
Nostalgie, sf. (*etym. Gr.* νόστος, *return*, ἄλγος, *pain*), nostalgia, home-sickness
Nota, sm. note
Notabilité, sf. (*etym. L.* notabilis), respectability, (*pl.*) principal persons
Notaire, sm. (*etym. L.* notarius), notary public
Notamment, adv. more particularly
Notariat, sm. notary's functions
Notarié, e, adj. notarial
Note, sf. (*etym. L.* nota), note, bill, account
Noter, va. (*etym. L.* notare), to note, to remark, to bear in mind
Notifier, va. (*etym. L.* notificare), to notify
Notoire, adj. (*etym. L.* notorius), well-known, manifest
Notoriété, sf. notoriety
Notre, Nos, adj. (*etym. L.* nostrum), our
Notre-Dame, sf. Our Lady
Nouer, va. (*etym. L.* nodare), to tie in a knot, to tie up, to concert, to enter into, (*hort.*) to be knotted; *se* —, vr. (*hort.*) to knot, to become rickety
Noueux, se, adj. (*etym. L.* nodosus), knotty, gnarled
Nourrice, sf. (*etym. L.* nutricem), nurse. *Mettre en* —, to put out to nurse
Nourricier, sm. foster-father, fosterer. —, *ère*, adj. nutritious, nutritive. *Père* —, foster-father
Nourri, e, adj. fed, nourished, full, strong, rich, sharp
Nourrir, va. (*etym. L.* nutrire), to nourish, to feed, to nurture, to maintain, to board, to suckle, to foster, (*in games*) to keep on doubling; *se* —, vr. to feed, to live, to board oneself, to feed oneself
Nourrissage, sm. rearing of cattle
Nourrissant, e, adj. nutritious, nutritive
Nourrisseur, sm. cow-keeper
Nourrisson, sm. (*etym. L.* nutritionem), nursling, foster-child
Nourriture, sf. (*etym. L.* nutritura), nourishment, food, nutrition, board, provender, suckling, nurture, education
Nous, pron. pers. (*etym. L.* nos), we, us. *Ce que c'est que de* —*!* what poor creatures we are!
Nouveau, Nouvel, le, adj. (*etym. L.* novellus), new, recent, novel. — adv. newly, new. *A* —, in a new account
Nouveauté, sf. (*etym. L.L.* novellitatem), novelty, newness, fancy articles, new publication. *Marchand de* —*s*, linendraper. *Magasin de* —*s*, linendraper's shop
Nouvelle, sf. (*etym. L.L.* novella), news, intelligence, tale. *Donnez-nous de vos* —*s*, let us hear from you. *Je sais de vos* —*s*, I have heard of your goings on
Nouvelliste, sm. newsmonger, quidnunc, tale-writer
Novateur, sm. (*etym. L.* novator), innovator
Novembre, sm. (*etym. L.* november), November
Noviciat, sm. (*etym.* novice), novitiate
Noyade, sf. drowning
Noyau, sm. (*etym. L.* nucalis), stone, nucleus, core, newel
Noyer, sm. (*etym. L.L.* nucarius), walnut-tree
Noyer, va. to drown, to immerge; *se* —, vr. (*etym. L.* necare), to be drowned, to drown oneself
Nu, e, adj. (*etym. L.* nudus), naked, bare, plain, unadorned. *Va-—pieds*, a vagabond. *A* —, laid bare, naked
Nuage, sm. cloud, gloom
Nuageux, se, adj. cloudy
Nuance, sf. (*etym.* nue), shade
Nuancer, va. to shade, to vary
Nubile, adj. (*etym. L.* nubilis), marriageable
Nudité, sf. (*etym. L.* nuditatem), nakedness, nudity
Nue, sf. (*etym. L.* nubem), cloud
Nuée, sf. cloud, swarm, flight
Nuer, va. to shade
Nuire, vn. (*etym. L.* nocere), to injure, to harm, to stand in one's way; *se* —, vr. to injure oneself, to injure each other
Nuisible, adj. (*etym. L.* nocibilis), hurtful, prejudicial, detrimental
Nuit, sf. (*etym. L.* noctem; *O.F.* noit), night, darkness
Nuitamment, adv. in the night, by night
Nul, le, adj. pron. (*etym. L.* nullus), no, not one, null and void, of no importance. *Homme* —, cypher
Nullité, sf. nullity, incapacity, cypher
Numéraire, adj. sm. (*etym. L.* numerarius), legal, specie
Numérateur, sm. (*etym. L.* numerator), numerator
Numérique, adj. (*etym. L.* numericus), numerical
Numéro, sm. (*etym. I.* numero), number
Numérotage, sm. numbering
Numéroter, va. to number
Numismate, sm. (*etym. Gr.* νόμισμα, *coin*), numismatologist
Numismatique, adj. sf. (*etym. Gr.* νομισματικός), numismatic, numismatics
Nuncupatif, ve, adj. (*etym. L.L.* nuncupativus, *designated*), nuncupative
Nuque, sf. (*etym. D.* nocke, *the spine*), nape of the neck
Nutritif, ve, adj (*etym. L.L.* nutritivus), nutritive
Nymphe, sf. (*etym. L.* nympha), nymph

O

O, sm. O, o
O! interj. O! oh!
Obéir, vn. (*etym. L.* obedire), to obey, to yield, to be pliant
Obéissance, sf. obedience, allegiance, dominion, pliancy
Obéissant, e, adj. obedient, dutiful, pliant
Obélisque, sm. (*etym. Gr.* ὀβελίσκος), obelisk
Obérer, va. (*etym. L.* obaerare), to involve in debt: *s'*—, vr. to involve oneself in debt
Obésité, sf. (*etym. L.* obesitatem), obesity
Objecter, va. (*etym. L.* objectare), to object, to upbraid with
Objectif, ve, adj. (*etym. L.* objectivus), object, objective. — sm. object-glass, objective
Obligatoire, adj. (*etym. L.* obligatorius), obligatory
Obligeance, sf. (*etym.* obliger), obligingness
Obligeant, e, adj. obliging
Obligé, e, past part. adj. s. obliged, necessary, debtor
Obliger, va. (*etym. L.* obligare), to oblige
s'Obliger, vr. to oblige oneself, to oblige each other
Obliquer, vn. (*etym.* oblique), to oblique
Obliquité, sf. (*etym. L.* obliquitatem), obliquity, obliqueness
Oblitérer, va. (*etym. L.* obliterare), to obliterate; *s'*—, vr. to become obliterated

Obscénité, sf. (*etym. L.* obscenitatem), obscenity, obsceneness

Obscur, e, adj. (*etym. L.* obscurus), dark, obscure, gloomy

Obscurcir, va. to darken, to obscure, to dim; *s'*—, vr. to grow dark, to be obscured

Obscurcissement, sm. darkening

Obscurément, adv. obscurely, darkly

Obscurité, sf. (*etym. L.* obscuritatem), darkness, obscurity

Obséder, va. (*etym. L.* obsidere, *to besiege*), to beset, to possess

Obsèques, sf. plur. (*etym. L.* obsequiæ), obsequies

‖**Obséquieux, se**, adj. (*etym. L.* obsequiosus), obsequious

Observateur, trice, s. adj. (*etym. L.* observator), of observation, observant

Observatoire, sm. (*etym. L.* observatus), observatory

Observer, va. (*etym. L.* observare), to observe; *s'*—, vr. to be upon one's guard, to observe each other

Obstination, sf. (*etym. L.* obstinationem), obstinacy, self-will

‖**Obstiné, e**, adj. (*etym. L.* obstinatus), obstinate, self-willed, wilful

Obstiner, va. (*etym. L.* obstinare), to make obstinate; *s'*—, vr. to persist, to be bent upon

Obstruer, va. (*etym. L.* obstruere), to stop up, to obstruct

Obtempérer, va. (*etym. L.* obtemperare), to comply with, to obey

Obtenir, va. (*etym. L.* obtinere), to prevail upon, to obtain; *s'*—, vr. to be obtained

Obtention, sf. (*etym. L.* obtentionem), obtaining

‖**Obtus, e**, adj. (*etym. L.* obtusus), obtuse, dull, blunt

Obtusangle, adj. obtuse-angled

Obus, sm. (*etym. Sp.* obuz), shell, howitzer-shell

Obusier, sm. howitzer

Obvier, vn. (*etym. L.* obviare), to obviate

Occasion, sf. (*etym. L.* occasionem), occasion, opportunity. *Par* —, accidentally, by private hand. *D'* —, second-hand

‖**Occasionnel, le**, adj. occasional

Occasionner, va. to occasion

Occident, sm. (*etym. L.* occidentem), west

***Occire**, va. (*etym. L.* occidere), to kill, to slay

‖**Occulte**, adj. (*etym. L.* occultus), occult

Occupé, e, adj. past part. taken up, occupied, engaged, busy

Occuper, va. (*etym. L.* occupare), to occupy, to take up, to busy; *s'*—, vr. to occupy oneself, to apply oneself

Ocre, sm. (*etym. Gr.* ὤχρα, *yellow earth*), ochre

Octaèdre, sm. (*etym. Gr.* ὀκτάεδρος, *a solid with eight sides*), octahedron

Octobre, sm. (*etym. L.* October), October

Octogénaire, adj. s. (*etym. L.* octogenarius), octogenarian

Octogone, adj. sm. (*etym. Gr.* ὀκτώ, γῶνος, *angle*), octagonal, octagon

***Octroi**, sm. grant, city toll, toll-house

***Octroyer**, va. (*etym. L.L.* auctoricare, *to grant*), to grant

Oculaire, adj. sm. (*etym.* ocularius), ocular, eye-glass

Oculiste, sm. (*etym. L.* oculus), oculist

Odalisque, sf. (*etym. Turk.* odalik), odalisk

Odeur, sf. (*etym. L.* odorem), smell, odour, fragrancy

‖**Odieux, se**, adj. (*etym. L.* odiosus), hateful, odious, hated

Odorant, e, adj. (*etym. L.* odorantem), fragrant, odoriferous, sweet-smelling

Odorat, sm. (*etym. L.* odoratus), smell, the sense of smell

Odoriférant, e, adj. (*etm. L.* odorem, ferentem), odoriferous, sweet-scented

Odyssée, sf. (*etym. Gr.* 'Οδυσσεία), Odyssey

Œcuménique, adj. (*etym. Gr.* οἰκουμενικός, *universal*), œcumenical

Œil, sm. (*etym. L.* oculus), the eye, the sight, hole (in cheese, bread, &c.), (*plur.* œils), gloss, fire, (*print.*) face. ‡ *Entre deux yeux*, full in the face. *Donner dans les yeux à*, to dazzle one's eyes. *Faire les yeux doux à*, to look lovingly at. *Voir d'un bon, d'un mauvais* —, to see with pleasure, displeasure. *Coup d'*—, glance, peep, prospect. — *-de-bœuf*, bull's eye; (*plur.* des œils-de-bœuf)

§**Œillade**, sf. glance, leer

§**Œillère**, sf. eye-tooth, winker, blinker

§**Œillet**, sm. eyelet, eyelet-hole, pink, carnation. — *de poète*, sweet William

Œsophage, sm. (*etym. Gr.* οἰσοφάγος), œsophagus, gullet

Œuf, sm. (*etym. L.* ovum), egg, spawn, roe

Œuvé, e, adj. hard-roed

Œuvre, sf. (*etym. L.* opera), work, deed, act. *Fils de ses* —*s*, a self-made man. *Mettre en* —, to work up, to set. *Mettre tout en* —, to leave no stone unturned. *Maître des hautes* —*s*, the executioner. — sm. work. *Travailler au grand* —, to seek the philosopher's stone. *Dans* —, (*arch.*) in the clear. *A pied d'*—, in the neighbourhood. *Travail sous* —, *en sous-'*—, underpinning. *Reprendre en sous-* —, to underpin, to begin all over again on another plan

Offensant, e, adj. offensive

Offense, sf. offence, transgression

Offensé, e, s. the offended party

Offenser, va. (*etym. L.* offensare), to offend, to sin against, to transgress, to injure; *s'*—, vr. to take exception, to take offence

Offenseur, sm. offender

‖**Offensif, ve**, adj. offensive

Offerte, sf., **Offertoire**, sm. (*etym.* offrir), offertory

Office, sm. (*etym. L.* officium), office, duty, service, divine service, church-time, household. *D'*—, in virtue of his office. — sf. pantry, servants' hall

Officiant, e, adj. s. officiating, the officiating priest

‖**Officiel, le**, adj. (*etym. L.* officialis), official

Officier, vn. to officiate — sm. officer. *Sous-* —, non-commissioned officer

‖**Officieux, se**, adj. officious, obliging

Offrande, sf. (*etym. L.* offerenda), offering, offer

Offrant, sm. bidder

Offre, sf. offer, tender

Offrir, va. (*etym. L.L.* offerere, *from L.* offerre), to offer, to bid, to give; *s'*—, vr. to offer oneself, to offer each other

Offusquer, va. (*etym. L.* offuscare), to cloud, to obscure, to dazzle, to give offence to; *s'*—, vr. to take exception

Ogival, e, adj. (*etym.* ogive, *from the L.L.* augiva), pointed

Ogre, sse, s. (*etym. L.* Orcus, *the God of hell*), ogre, ogress

Oie, sf. (*etym. L.L.* auca = *L.* anser), goose

§**Oignon, Ognon**, sm. (*etym. L.* unionem), onion, bulb, bulbous root, bunnion

Oindre, va. (*etym. L.* ungere), to anoint

Oiseau, sm. (*etym. L.L.* aucellus, *small bird*), bird, hod. *L'*— *-mouche*, the humming-bird. *A vol d'*—, as a crow flies. *Plan à vue d'*—, a bird's-eye view of

Oiseleur, sm. fowler, bird-catcher

Oiselier, sm. bird-fancier

‖**Oiseux, se**, adj. (*etym. L.* otiosus), idle

‖**Oisif, ve**, adj. s. (*etym. L.* otium), idle, unoccupied, idler

§**Oisillon**, sm. young bird

Oisiveté, sf. idleness

Oison, sm. gosling

Oléagineux, se, adj. (*etym. L.L.* oleaginosus), oily, oleaginous

***Olibrius**, sm. (*etym. prop. name* Olybrius), giddy-pated boaster

Oligarchie, sf. (
ὀλιγαρχία), oligarchy

Oligarchique,
garchical

Olivâtre, adj. (*et*
olive-coloured

Olivier, sm. olive

Olographe,
Holographe,
(*etym. Gr.* ὁλόγραφ
graph

Olympe, sm. (
Olympus), Olympu

Olympiade, sf.
Olympiadem), Olym

Olympien, ne,
pian

Olympique, ad
L. Olympicus), Olym

Ombilical, e, s
ombilic; *L.* umbil
bilical

Ombrage, sm.
umbraticum), sha
brage

Ombrager, va. (

‖**Ombrageux**,
skittish, shy, umb

Ombre, sf. (*etym*
shade, shadow, b
umbrage, umber.
under pretence th
— *à*, to throw into
to give umbrage to
noises, transparenc
d'—, umber

Ombrelle, sf.
ombrella), parasol

Ombrer, va. (*et*
brare), to shade

‖**Ombreux, se**,
L. umbrosus), sha

Omettre, va.
omittere), to omit
out, to pass over

Omnivore, adj.
omnivorus), omniv

On, L'on, pron. h
L. homo), one, w
a man, you, they

On-dit, sm. mer

Onagre, sm.
onagrus), wild ass,

***Onc, Oncqu**
(*etym. L.* unquam

Once, sf. (*etym.*
[*for the measur*
youz [*for the*
ounce

Oncial, e, adj.
uncialis), uncial

Oncle, sm. (*etym*
culus; *Prov.* avonc

Onction, sf.
unctionem), anoin
tion, grace

‖**Onctueux, se**,
L.L. onctuosus),
oily, impressive

Onde, sf. (*etym.*
wave, surge, strea

Ondée, sf. showe

Ondin, e, s. w
Undine

Ondoiement,
ondoyer), private
waving motion

Ondoyant, e,
dulating, waving,

Ondoyer, va. (*et*
to baptize private
to float, to wave, t

Ondulation, s
tion, wavy motion

Ondulatoire, adj. undulating

Onduler, vn. (*etym. L.* undulare), to undulate, to flow gently

Onéreux, se, adj. (*etym. L.* onerosus), burdensome, onerous. *A titre —*, burdened with certain conditions

Ongle, sm. (*etym. L.* ungula), nail, claw, hoof. *Rogner les —s*, (*fig.*) to clip a person's wings. *Coup d'—*, scratch

Onglée, sf. numbness of the fingers

Onglet, sm. (*bind.*) guard, (*print.*) one-leaf cancel

Onguent, sm. (*etym. L.* unguentum), ointment, salve, unguent

Onomatopée, sf. (*etym. Gr.* ὀνοματοποιία), onomatopoeia

Onze, adj. sm. (*etym. L.* undecim), eleventh, eleven

Onzième, adj. eleventh

Oolithe, sm. (*etym. Gr.* ὠόν, *egg*, λίθος, *stone*), oolite, roe-stone

Oolithique, adj. oolitic

Opale, sf. (*etym. L.* opalus), opal

Opérateur, sm. (*etym. L.* operatorem), operator

Opérer, va.n. (*etym. L.* operari), to work out, to operate, to effect, to tell. *Se faire —*, to undergo an operation. *S'—*, vr. to be wrought or operated

Ophicléide, sm. (*etym. Gr.* ὄφις, *serpent*, κλείς, *key*), ophicleid

Ophthalmie, sf. (*etym. Gr.* ὀφθαλμία), ophthalmia, ophthalmy

Ophthalmique, adj. ophthalmic

Opiacé, e, adj. (*etym.* opium), opiate

Opiat, sm., **Opiate,** sf. (*etym. Gr.* ὄπιον, *poppy-juice*), opiate

Opime, adj. (*etym. L.* opimus). *Dépouilles —s*, spolia opima

Opinant, sm. speaker

Opiner, vn. (*etym. L.* opinari), to give one's opinion, to speak

Opiniâtre, adj. (*etym.* opiner), obstinate, stubborn, persevering

Opiniâtrément, adv. obstinately

Opiniâtrer, vr. to remain obstinate, to struggle obstinately

Opiniâtreté, sf. obstinacy, stubbornness, perseverance

Opportun, e, adj. (*etym. L.* opportunus), well-timed, timely, opportune

Opportunément, adv. opportunely

Opportunité, sf. (*etym. L.* opportunitatem), opportuneness, expediency, opportunity

Opposant, e, adj. sm. opposing, opponent

Opposé, e, adj. past part. opposite, facing, opposed

Opposer, va. (*etym. see* Poser), to oppose; *s'—*, vr. to be opposed, to oppose, to object (to)

Oppresser, va. (*etym. see* Presser), to oppress

Oppresseur, sm. adj. (*etym. L.* oppressor), oppressor, oppressive

Oppressif, ve, adj. oppressive

Opprimer, va. (*etym. L.* opprimere), to oppress, to crush down

Opprobre, sm. (*etym. L.* opprobrium), disgrace, opprobrium, shame

Optatif, ve, adj. sm. (*etym. L.* optativus), optative

Opter, vn. (*etym. L.* optare), to choose

Opticien, sm. optician

Optimisme, sm. (*etym. L.* optimus), optimism

Optimiste, sm. adj. optimist

Optique, sf. (*etym. Gr.* ὀπτικός), optics, show-box. — adj. optical, optic

Opuscule, sm. (*etym. L.* opusculum), tract, short treatise

Or, conj. (*etym. L.* hora), now. —, — çà, now then. — sm. (*etym. L.* aurum), gold. *Au poids de l'—*, for its weight in gold. ¦ *Parler d'—*, to speak like an angel. — *moulu*, ormolu

Orage, sm. (*etym. L.L.* auraticum, *from* aura, *breeze*), storm, tempest

Orageux, se, adj. stormy, tempestuous

Oraison, sf. (*etym. L.* orationem), oration, speech, prayer. *L'— dominicale*, the Lord's prayer

Orangé, e, adj. sm. (*etym.* orange = *Arab.* nâranj), orange-colour, orange

Orangeat, sm. candied orange-peel

Oranger, sm. orange-tree

Orangerie, sf. orange-grove, orange-conservatory

Orateur, sm. (*etym. L.* oratorem), orator, speaker

¦**Oratoire,** adj. sm. (*etym. L.* oratorium), oratorical, oratory

Orbe, sm. adj. (*etym. L.* orbis), orb, bruising

Orbiculaire, adj. (*etym. L.* orbicularis), orbicular

Orbite, sf. (*etym. L.* orbita, *revolution*), orbit, socket

Orchestration, sf. scoring

Orchestre, sm. (*etym. Gr.* ὀρχήστρα, *part of the stage in the Greek theatre*), orchestra, band. *Chef d'—*, leader of the band. *A grand —*, with a full band

Ordalie, sf. (*etym. L.L.* ordalium = *Ang.-Sax.* ordâl, *judgment of God*), ordeal

¦**Ordinaire,** adj. (*etym. L.* ordinarius), usual, common, ordinary, in ordinary, vulgar, plain. *Bon —*, (*com.*) middling. — sm. wont, usual practice, commons

Ordonnance, sf. order, ordering, regulation, prescription. *Compagnie d'—*, unattached troop. *Habit d'—*, regimentals. *D'—*, orderly

Ordonnancement, sm. payment

Ordonnancer, va. to sign for payment

Ordonnateur, sm. orderer, regulator

¦**Ordonné, e,** adj. ordered, regulated

Ordonner, va. (*etym. L.* ordinare), to order, to enjoin, to appoint

Ordre, sm. (*etym. L.* ordinem), order, command, behest. *Mettre — à, en —, de l'— à*, to set in order. *En sous-—*, subordinately, under another. *Avance à l'—*, (*milit.*) advance and give the pass-word

Ordure, sf. (*etym. O.F.* ord = *L.* horridus), excrements, filth, dirt, ribaldry

Ordurier, ère, adj. ribald, filthy

§**Oreille,** sf. (*etym. L.* auricula, *dimin. of* auris, *ear*), ear, fluke, kevel. *Avoir de l'—*, to have a correct ear. *Faire la sourde —*, to turn a deaf ear. ¦ *Dormir sur les deux —s*, to sleep quietly. *Se faire tirer l'—*, to be unwilling. *Montrer le bout de l'—*, (*fig.*) to show oneself as one is. — *d'ours*, auricula

§**Oreiller,** sm. pillow, cross chock

§**Oreillette,** sf. auricle

§**Oreillons,** sm. plur. the mumps

Orfèvre, sm. (*etym. L.* aurifabrum), gold and silversmith. *Vous êtes —, monsieur*, (*fig.*) you are in the trade, sir

Orfèvrerie, sf. goldsmith's art, gold or silver wares

Orfraie, sf. (*etym. L.* ossifraga), osprey

Organe, sm. (*etym. L.* organum), organ, voice, spokesman

¦**Organique,** adj. organic, organical

Organisateur, trice, adj. organizing

Organisation, sf. organization

Organiser, va. to organize; *s'—*, vr. to be organized

Organisme, sm. organism

Organiste, sm. organist

Organsin, sm. (*etym.* ?), organzine silk

Orge, sf. (*etym. L.* hordeum), barley. — *mondé*, — *perlé*, (*m.*) peeled barley, pearl barley

Orgue, smf. (*etym. L.* organon), organ, organ-loft, portcullis, tub. — *de Barbarie*, street-organ, barrel-organ. *Jeu d'—*, organ-stop

Orgueil, sm. (*etym. G.* orgel, *proud*), pride, arrogance

§**Orgueilleux, se,** adj. proud, arrogant, haughty

Orientaliste, sm. (*etym.* orient), orientalist

Orienter, va. to set towards the east, to set rightly, to trim, to close haul; *s'—*, vr. to turn towards the east, to find one's way

¦**Originaire,** adj. (*etym. L.* originarius), originally come from, a native, indigenous

¦**Original,** sm., —, —e, adj. (*etym. L.* originalis), humorist, original, eccentric

Originalité, sf. originality, eccentricity

Origine, sf. (*etym. L.* originem), origin

¦**Originel, le,** adj. original

Orin, sm. (*etym.* ?), buoy-rope

Oripeau, sm. (*etym. L.L.* auri pellem, *gold-leaf*), tinsel, (*plur.*) rags

Orme, sm. (*etym. L.* ulmus; *Prov.* olm), elm

Ormeau, sm. elm, young elm

Orne, sm. (*etym. L.* ornus), wild ash

Ornement, sm. (*etym. L.* ornamentum), ornament

Orner, va. (*etym. L.* ornare), to adorn, to decorate

Ornière, sf. (*etym. L.L.* orbitaria, *from* orbita, *rut*), cart-rut, beaten track

Ornithologie, sf. (*etym.* ὄρνις, *bird*, λόγος), ornithology

Orphelin, e, s. (*etym. L.L.* orphaninus; *O.F.* orphanin, orphenin), orphan

Orphelinat, sm. orphan's institute

Ort, sm. (*etym.* ?), gross, gross-weight

Orteil, sm. (*etym. L.* articulus; *O.F.* arteil), toe

¦**Orthodoxe,** adj. sm. (*etym. Gr.* ὀρθόδοξος), orthodox

Orthodoxie, sf. orthodoxy

Orthographe, sf. (*etym. Gr.* ὀρθογραφία), orthography, spelling

Orthographier, va. to spell

¦**Orthographique,** adj. orthographical

Orthopédie, sf. (*etym. Gr.* ὀρθός, *right*, παιδεία, *education*), orthopedy

Orthopédique, adj. orthopedic

Orthopédiste, sm. orthopedist

Ortie, sf. (*etym. L.* urtica), nettle, rowel

Os, sm. (*etym. L.* os), bone

Oscillatoire, adj. oscillatory

Osciller, vn. (*etym. L.* oscillare), to oscillate

Osé, e, adj. bold, daring

§**Oseille,** sf. (*etym. L.* oxalis), sorrel

Oser, vn.a. (*etym. L.L.* ausare), to dare, to venture

Osier, sm. (*etym. Gr.* οἶσος, *wicker*), water-willow, osier

Osselet, sm. small bone, knuckle-bones

Ossement, sm. bone

Osseux, se, adj. (*etym. L.L.* ossuosus), bony

Ossifier, va. (*etym. L.L.*

ossificare), to ossify ; *s'*—, vr. to become ossified
Ossuaire, sm. (*etym. L.* ossuarium), ossuary
Ostensiblement, adv. ostensibly
Ostensoir, sm. (*etym. L.L.* ostensorium), monstrance
Ostéologie, sf. (*etym. Gr.* ὀστεολογία), osteology
Ostracisme, sm. (*etym. Gr.* ὀστρακισμός), ostracism
Otage, sm. (*etym. L.L.* obsidaticum), hostage
Oter, va. (*etym. L.* haustare, *frequent. of* haurire, *to draw out*), to take away, to remove ; *s'*—, vr. to get out, to take away from oneself, to rid oneself of
Ottomane, sf. (*etym. prop. name* Ottoman), ottoman
Ou, conj. (*etym. L.* aut), or
Où, adv. (*etym. L.* ubi), whither, where, when
§**Ouailles,** sf. plur. (*etym. L.* ovicula, *from* ovis), flock, sheep
Ouais! interj. (*onomat.*), hey-day !
Ouate, sf. (*etym. ?*), wadding, padding
Ouater, va. to wad, to pad
Oubli, sm. (*etym. L.* oblitus, *forgotten*), forgetfulness, oblivion, oversight
Oublie, sf. (*etym. L.* oblata, *offered up*), wafer
Oublier, va. (*etym. L.L.* oblitare = oblivisci, *to forget*), to forget, to neglect ; *s'*—, vr. to forget oneself, to be forgotten
Oubliettes, sf. plur. oubliette
Ouest, sm. (*etym. G.* west), the west
Ouf! interj. (*onomat.*), oh !
Oui, adv. sm. (*etym. L.* hoc illud ; *O.F.* oil), yes, ay. —*-da !* ay indeed !
Oui-dire, sm. hearsay, rumour
Ouïe, sm. hearing, gills, hole
Ouïr, va. (*etym. L.* audire), to hear
Ouragan, sm. (*etym. Sp.* huracan), hurricane
Ourdir, va. (*etym. L.* ordiri), to warp, to hatch, to plot
Ourler, va. (*etym. L.* orulare, *to border*), to hem
Ourlet, sm. hem
Ours, sm. (*etym. L.* ursus), bear
Ourse, sf. (*etym. L.* ursa), she-bear, Ursa, the furthest Pole, mizen bowline
Oursin, sm. sea-urchin, seahedgehog
Ourson, sm. bear's cub, cub, bear-skin cap
Outarde, sf. (*etym. L.* avistarda), bustard
Outil, sm. (*etym. L.L.* usitellum, *tool*), tool, implement
§**Outillage,** sm. stock of tools
§**Outiller,** va. to supply with tools
Outrageant, e, adj. outrageous
Outrager, va. (*etym. see* OUTRER), to outrage
‖**Outrageux, se,** adj. outrageous
Outrance, adv. to excess, to the utmost, unrelentingly. *Guerre à* —, war to the knife
Outre, sf. (*etym. L.* utrem), skin, goat's skin. — adv. prep. (*etym. L.* ultra), further, beyond. *D'— en* —, through and through. *En* —, besides. *Passer* —, to go on
Outrecuidance, sf. (*etym.* outre ; *O.F.* cuidance, *from O.F.* cuider = *L.* cogitare), presumption, audacity
Outremer (bleu d'), sm. ultra-marine
Outre-passer, va. to overstep
Outrer, va. (*etym. L.* ultra), to overstrain, to exaggerate, to overtask, to incense. *Je suis outré,* I am out of all patience. *S'*—, vr. to overtask oneself
‖**Ouvert, e,** adj. open, unfortified, apt, ready. *A bureau* —, on presentation
Ouverture, sf. (*etym.* ouvrir), opening, aperture, chasm, overture, aptness
Ouvrable, adj. (*etym. O.F.* ouvrer, *to work*), working. *Jours* —*s*, work-days
Ouvrage, sm. work, piece, workmanship. *Avoir le cœur à l'*—, to work with a will
Ouvragé, e, adj. wrought
Ouvré, e, adj. wrought, diapered (linen)
Ouvreur, se, s. (*etym.* ouvrir), opener
Ouvrier, ère, s.adj. workman, workwoman, working
Ouvrir, va.n. (*etym. L.* aperire ; *O.F.* avrir), to open. — *un avis,* to start an opinion. *S'*—, vr. to open oneself
Ouvroir, sm. (*etym.* ouvrer), work-room
Ovaire, sm. (*etym. L.* ovum), ovary
Ovale, sm. adj. (*etym. L.* ovalis), oval
Ove, sm. (*etym. L.* ovum), (*archit.*) egg, ovolo
Ovipare, adj. sm. (*etym. L.* oviparus), oviparous, oviparous animal
Oxyder, va., *s'*—, vr. (*etym.* oxyde), to oxydize
Oxygène, sm. adj. (*etym. Gr.* ὀξύς, *acid,* γίνος, *birth*), oxygen
Oxygéner, va. to oxygenate

P

P, sm. P, p
Pacage, sm. (*etym. L.L.* pascuaticum), pasture-ground, pasturage
Pachyderme, adj. sm. (*etym. Gr.* παχύς, *thick,* δέρμα, *skin*), pachydermatous, pachydermatous animal
Pacificateur, sm. (*etym. L.* pacificator), pacificator, pacifier. —, —*trice,* adj. peace-making, pacifying
Pacifier, va. (*etym. L.* pacificare), to pacify
‖**Pacifique,** adj. (*etym. L.* pacificus), pacific, mild, gentle
§**Pacotille,** sf. (*etym. see* PAQUET), venture, small stock. *Marchandises de* —, private goods, trumpery ware
Pacte, sm. (*etym. L.* pactum), compact, covenant, pact
Pactiser, va. to make a covenant, to compound
Pagaie, sf. (*etym. ?*), paddle
Paganisme, sm. paganism
Pagayer, vn. to paddle
Page, sf. (*etym. L.* paginem), page. *Mettre en* —, to make up. — sm. (*etym. ?*), page. *Être hors de* —, to be no longer a boy. ‡ *Tour de* —, schoolboy's trick
Pagination, sf. paging
Paginer, va. (*etym. L.L.* paginare), to page
§**Pagne,** sm. (*etym. Sp.* paño), piece of cotton (worn by the savages round the waist)
Pagode, sf. (*etym. Pers.* butkhoda, *house of idols*), pagoda
Païen, ne, adj. s. (*etym. L.* paganus), heathen, pagan
§**Paillasse,** sf. (*etym.* paille), straw-mattress. — sm. clown
§**Paillasson,** sm. mat, matting
§**Paille,** sf. (*etym. L.* palea), straw, flaw, mote, long pin. ‡ *Rompre la* —, to fall out. *Tirer à la courte* —, to draw lots. — *-en-queue,* tropic-bird
§**Paillette,** sf. spangle
Pain, sm. (*etym. L.* panis), bread, loaf, cake
Pair, adj. sm. (*etym. L.* par), equal, even, peer. — *ou non,* odd or even. *De* —, on a par. ‡ *Traiter de — à compagnon,* to be hail fellow well met with
Paire, sf. pair, brace
Pairesse, sf. peeress
Pairie, sf. peerage
‖**Paisible,** adj. (*etym.* paix), peaceful, peaceable, quiet
Paître, va.n. (*etym. L.L.* pascere, *from* pasci), to graze, to feed ; *se* —, vr. to feed
Paix, sf. (*etym. L.* pacem), peace, quiet. — interj. peace ! hush !
Pal, sm. (*etym. L.* palus), pale
Palais, sm. (*etym. L.* palatium), palace, court, the Bar, the law, palate
Palan, sm. (*etym. I.* palanco), tackle. — *de côté,* gun-tackle
Palanquin, sm. (*etym. Sansc.* palangka), palankeen, rudder-tackle. — *de ris,* reeltackle
Palatin, e, adj. s. (*etym. L.* palatinus), Palatine
Palefrenier, sm. (*etym.* palefroi), groom, ostler
Palefroi, sm. (*etym. L.L.* paraveredus, *post-horse*), palfrey
Paléographe, sm. paleograph
Paléographie, sf. (*etym. Gr.* παλαιός, *old,* γράφειν), paleography
Palet, sm. (*etym. L.* pala), disk, quoit
Palette, sf. bat, paddlewheel
Palétuvier, sm. (*etym. ?*), mangrove-tree
Pâleur, sf. (*etym. L.* pallorem), paleness
Palier, sm. (*etym. O.F.* paillier, *from* paille), landing, stair-head
Palimpseste, sm. (*etym. Gr.* παλίμψηστος, *erased over again*), palimpsest
Palinodie, sf. (*etym. Gr.* παλινῳδία, *recantation*), palinody. *Chanter la* —, to recant
Pâlir, va.n. (*etym.* pâle), to turn pale, to make turn pale
Palis, sm. (*etym. L.L.* palicium), pale, paling
Palissader, va. (*etym.* palissade), to palisade, to pale in
Palissandre, sm. (*etym. ?*), violet ebony wood
Pâlissant, e, adj. turning pale, pallid
Palisser, va. to pale up
Palliatif, ve, adj. sm. palliative
Pallier, va. (*etym. L.* palliare), to palliate
Palme, sf. (*etym. L.* palma), palm-branch, palm. — sm. (*etym. L.* palmus), palm, hand
Palmé, e, adj. handed, fin-toed, webbed
Palmier, sm. (*etym. L.* palmarius), palm-tree, palm
Palmipède, sm. adj. (*etym. L.* palmipedem), web-footed animal, web-footed
Palmiste, sm. cabbagetree
Palombe, sf. (*etym. L.* palumba), ring-dove
Palper, va. (*etym. L.* palpare), to feel, to finger
Palpitant, e, adj. panting, gasping, palpitating
Palpiter, vn. (*etym. L.* palpitare), to pant, to palpitate,

Paltoquet, sm. (*etym.* paletot, *O.F.* paletoc = *D.* paltsrock, *a coarse woollen gown*), lout, lubber

Pâmer, vn., *se* —, vr. (*etym. L.* spasmare), to swoon, to faint away

Pâmoison, sf. swoon, fainting fit

Pamphlétaire, sm. (*etm.* pamphlet), pamphleteer

Pamplemousse, sf. (*etm.* Tamil, bambolmas), shaddock

Pampre, sm. (*etym. L* pampinus), vine-branch

Pan, sm. (*etym. L.* pannus), skirt, lappet, piece, side, (*nav.*) flat front. — *coupé*, cant. *A —s coupés*, cantwise

Pan! interj. (*onomatop.*), flick! rap!

Panacée, sf. (*etym. L.* panacea), panacea, nostrum

Panache, sm. (*etym. I.* pennachio), plume, top, panache

Panaché, e, adj. streaked, plumed

Panacher, vn., *se* —, vr. to break into streaks, to streak

Panade, sf. (*etym. I.* panata), panada, panado

Panais, sm. (*etym. L.* panacem), parsnip

Panaris, sm. (*etym. L.* panaricium), whitlow

Pancarte, sf. (*etym. L.L.* panchartа), bill, placard

Pandectes, sf. plur. (*etym. L* pandectæ), pandects

Panégyrique, sm. (*etym. Gr* πανηγυρικός, [λόγος]), panegyric

Panégyriste, sm. panegyrist, eulogist

Paner, va. (*etym.* pain), to cover with bread-crumbs. *Eau panée*, toast and water

Paneterie, sf. pantry, buttery

Panetier, sm. pantler

Panier, sm. (*etym. L.* panarium, *bread-basket*), basket, hamper, pannier, hoop-petticoat. ¦ *Un — percé*, (*fig.*) a spendthrift

Panique, adj. (*etym. Gr.* πανικόν, [δεῖμα], *panic fear*), panic

Panne, sf. (*etym. L.L.* panna), plush, fat, (*nav.*) lying to, porling, the small end. *Être, rester en* —, to be lying to. *Mettre en* —, to heave to

Panneau, sm. (*etym.* pan), pannel, snare, (*nav.*) hatch

Panonceau, sm. (*etym.* pennon), scutcheon

Panse, sf. (*etym. L.* panticem, *belly*), paunch, belly

Pansement, sm. dressing, grooming, rubbing down

Panser, va. (*etym. O.F.* penser; *L.* pensare, *to take care of*), to dress, to groom

Pantalon, sm. (*Italian word*), trowsers, pantaloons, pantaloon

Pantalonnade, sf. pantaloon's dance, buffoonery

Pantelant, e, adj. (*etym.* pantois), gasping, panting

Panthéisme, sm. (*etym. Gr.* πᾶς, *all*, θεός, *God*), pantheism

Panthère, sf. (*etym. L.* panthera), panther

Pantin, sm. (*etym.* ?), dancing-jack, puppet

Pantois, e, adj. (*etym. Celt.* pant, *oppression*), dumbfounded

Pantoufle, sf. (*etym. I.* pantofola), slipper

Paon, sm. (*etym. L.* pavonem), peacock, emperor moth

Paonne, sf. pea-hen

Papas, sm. (*etym. L.L.* pappa), Pope in the Greek church

Papauté, sf. papal see, papacy, popedom

Pape, sm. Pope

Papelard, e, adj. s. (*etym.* ?), canting, hypocrite

Paperasse, sf. (*etym.* papier), old paper

Paperasser, va. to turn over old papers, to scribble

Paperassier, ère, sm. adj. scribbler, scribbling

Papeterie, sf. paper-manufactory, paper-making, stationery

Papetier, sm. paper-manufacturer, stationer

Papier, sm. (*etym. L.L.* papyrius), paper, bills. — *de Chine*, India paper. ¦ *Figure de — mâché*, a face as white as a turnip. —*s peints*, paper-hangings, stained paper. *Être bien, mal dans les —s de quelqu'un*, to be in, out of (a person's) books

§**Papillon,** sm. (*etym. L.* papilionem), butterfly. — *de nuit*, moth

§**Papillonner,** vn. to flutter about from one to another

§**Papillotage,** sm. blinking, dazzling, (*print.*) slurring

§**Papillote,** sf. (*etym. L.* papillon), curl-paper, paper, sweetmeat (in paper)

§**Papilloter,** vn. to blink, to dazzle, to slur

Papisme, sm. papistry, popery

Papiste, sm. papist

Pâque, *or* **Pâques,** smf. (*etym. L.* pascha), the Passover, Easter. —*s fleuries*, Palm Sunday. *Faire ses —s*, to receive the Sacrament at Easter

Paquebot, sm. (*English word*), packet-boat. — *à vapeur*, steam-packet

Pâquerette, sf. (*etym. O.F.* pasquier, *pasturage*), daisy

Paquet, sm. (*etym. L.L.* paccus, *parcel*), parcel, bundle, package, (*print.*) slip. ¦ *Donner son — à*, to give a scolding to. † *Risquer le —*, to run the risk

Par, prep. (*etym. L.* per), by, through, out of, from, in, for the sake of. *De* —, in the name of. *De — le roi*, in the king's name

Parabole, sf. (*etym. L.* parabola), parable; (*etym. Gr.* παραβολή), parabola

¦**Parabolique,** adj. parabolic

Parachever, va. to complete

Paraclet, sm. (*etym. Gr.* παράκλητος, *one who is invoked*), Comforter, Paraclete

Parade, sf. (*etym. Sp.* parada, *abrupt movement of the horse*), parade, show, display, parrying. *Lit de* —, bed of state

Parader, va. to show off

Paradis, sm. (*etym. L.* paradisus), Paradise, upper gallery

Paradoxe, sm. (*etym. Gr.* παράδοξος), paradox

Parafe, *or* **Paraphe,** sm. (*etym. L.* paragraphus), flourish in writing

Parafer, *or* **Parapher,** va. to put one's initials and flourish to

Parage, sm. (*etym. L.L.* paraticum), degree, birth; (*etym.* ?), quarter, parts

Paragraphe, sm. paragraph

Paraître, vn. (*etym. L.L.* parescere = parere, *to appear*), to appear, to stand forth

Parallactique, adj. parallactic

Parallaxe, sm. (*etym. Gr.* παράλλαξις, *change*), parallax

¦**Parallèle,** adj. smf. (*etym. Gr.* παράλληλος), parallel

Parallélipipède, sm. (*etym. Gr.* παραλληλεπίπεδον), parallelopipede

Parallélisme, sm. (*etym.* parallele), parallelism

Parallélogramme, sm. (*etym. Gr.* παραλληλόγραμμον), parallelogram

Paralogisme, sm. (*etym. Gr.* παραλογισμός), paralogism

Paralyser, va. to paralyze

Paralysie, sf. (*etym. Gr.* παράλυσις), palsy, paralysis

Paralytique, adj. s. paralytic, palsied, paralytic

Parangon, sm. (*etym. Sp.* paragon), paragon. *Gros* —, *petit* —, (*print.*) double pica, paragon

Paraphraser, va. (*etym.* paraphrase), to paraphrase

Parapluie, sm. (*etym.* parer, à, pluie), umbrella

Paratonnerre, sm. (*etm.* parer, à, tonnerre), conductor, lightning-rod

Paravent, sm. (*etym.* parer, à, vent), folding-screen, screen

Parbleu! interj. (*for* par Dieu), egad! forsooth!

Parc, sm. (*etym. L.L.* parcus), park, fold, pen. — *d'huîtres*, artificial oyster-bed

Parcelle, sf. (*etym. L.L.* particella), part, particle

Parce que, conj. because

Parchemin, sm. (*etym. L.L.* pergamena), parchment

Parcheminerie, sf. parchment-making, parchment-manufactory

Parcimonie, sf. (*etym. L.* parcimonia), parsimony

¦**Parcimonieux, se,** adj. parsimonious

Parcourir, va. (*etym. L.* percurrere), to travel over *or* through, to go over, to survey, to glance over

Parcours, sm. (*etym. L.L.* percursus), course, commonage, length

Pardessus, sm. great-coat

Pardieu! Pardi! interj. to be sure!

¦**Pardonnable,** adj. pardonable

Pardonner, vn. (*etym. L.L.* perdonare), to forgive, to pardon; *se* —, vr. to be pardoned, to pardon oneself, to forgive each other

¦**Pareil, le,** adj. (*etym. L.L.* pariculus, *from* par, *equal*), alike, the same

Parement, sm. ornament, facings, cuff, big sticks, kerbstone

Parenté, sf. (*etym.* parent), relationship, kindred

Parenthèse, sf. parenthesis

Parer, va. (*etym. L.* parare), to adorn, to set off, to deck, to ward off, to parry, (*nav.*) to see ready, to weather. — vn. to guard, to get ready. *Se* —, vr. to adorn oneself, to boast, to ward off

Paresse, sf. (*etym. L.* pigritia), idleness, sloth, laziness, indolence

¦**Paresseux, se,** adj. s. idle, slothful, lazy, sluggard. — sm. sloth

Parfaire, va. to complete

¦**Parfait, e,** adj. perfect, complete. ¦ *C'est* —, capital! — sm. perfection, perfect tense

Parfiler, va. to undo thread by thread

Parfois, adv. sometimes, now and then

Parfum, sm. (*etym.* parfumer), perfume, scent

Parfumer, va. to perfume, to scent; *se* —, vr. to perfume one's person

Parfumerie, sf. perfumery

Parfumeur, se, s. perfumer

Parhélie, Parélie, sm. (*etym. Gr* παρήλιος), parhelion

Pari, sm. bet, wager

Parier, va. (*etym. L.* pariare, *to balance an account*), to bet, to wager, to lay. *Il y a gros à — que*, I'd wager anything that

Pariétaire, sf. (*etym. L.* parietaria), parietary, pellitory

Parieur, sm. better

Parisien, -ne, adj. s. Parisian

Parité, sf. (*etym. L.* paritatem), parity, comparison

Parjure, sm. (*etym. L.* perjurus), perjury, perjurer. — adj. perjured, forsworn

se **Parjurer,** vr. (*etym. L.* perjurare), to perjure oneself

Parlant, e, adj. speaking, talkative

Parlement, sm. parliament

Parlementaire, adj. parliamentary. — sm. flag of truce, parliamentarian

Parlementer, vn. to parley, to come to terms

Parler, va.n. (*etym. L.L.* parabolare, *to speak*), to speak, to talk; *se* —, vr. to be spoken, to talk to oneself, to talk to each other. — sm. way of speaking, accent

Parleur, se, s. talker

Parloir, sm. parlour

Parmi, prep. (*etym. L.* permedium), among, amongst, amid, amidst

Parnasse, sm. (*etym. L.* parnassus), Parnassus

Parodie, sf. (*etym. Gr.* παρῳδία), parody

Parodier, va. to parody, to mimic

Parol, sf. (*etym. L.* parietem), wall, side

Paroisse, sf. (*etym. L.* parœcia), parish

Paroissial, e, adj. parish, parochial

Paroissien, ne, s. parishioner. — sm. prayer-book

Parole, sf. (*etym. L.* parabola), word, speech, utterance. *Avoir, demander, donner la* —, to have, to request, to give leave or permission to speak. *Céder la* —, to decline speaking. *Prendre la* —, to begin to speak. *Porter la* —, to be the spokesman. *Un homme de* —, a man of his word. *Perdre sur* —, to lose upon trust

Paroxysme, sm. (*etym. Gr.* παροξυσμός, *irritation*), paroxysm

Parque, sf. (*etym. L.* parca), Fate

Parquer, va. (*etym.* parc), to pen, to park, to bed (oysters); — vn. to be folded; *se* —, vr. (*artill.*) to lodge

Parquet, sm. bar, magistrate's office, prosecuting magistrate, stockbroker's station, floor, orchestra, chimney-frame

Parqueter, va. to floor

Parrain, sm. (*etym. L.L.* patrinus), godfather, sponsor

Parsemer, va. to strew, to stud, to spangle

Parsi, sm. (*etym.* Perse), Parsee

Part, sf. (*etym. L.* partem), share, part, concern. *Faire la — du feu*, to sacrifice something. *Billet, lettre de faire* —, circular. *De —, en* —, through and through, right through. *A — moi*, to myself

Partage, sm. (*etym.* partir = *L.* partiri, *to share*), sharing, division, share, part

Partageant, sm. sharer, partaker

Partager, va. to divide, to share, to part; *se* —, vr. to share, to divide, to be divided, to part

Partance, sf. (*etym.* partant), sailing. *Coup de* —, sailing-gun. *En* —, ready to sail

Partant, adv. and therefore

Partenaire, s. (*from the English*), partner

Parterre, sm. flower-bed, flower-garden, pit of a theatre

Parti, sm. (*etym.* partir), party, part, decision, method, terms, good use, match. ‡*Faire un mauvais — à quelqu'un*, to play a person some ugly trick. *Épouser un bon* —, to make a good match

Partiaire, adj. (*etym. L.L.* partiarius), produce-sharing

Partialité, sf. (*etym.* partial), partiality

Participant, e, adj. participating

Participe, sm. participle

Participer, vn. (*etym. L.L.* participare), to partake, to participate in

Particulariser, va. (*etym. L.* particularis), to particularize

Particularité, sf. (*etym. L.* particularitatem), particular

Particule, sf. (*etym. L.* particula), particle

‖**Particulier, ère,** adj. (*etym. L.* particularis), particular, private. — sm. private person, individual. *Un simple* —, a private individual

Partie, sf. (*etym.* partir), part, lot, parcel, account, line of business, game, party, suitor in law. ‡ — *nulle*, drawn game. *Coup de* — decisive move. *Se porter — civile*, to appear as prosecutor. *Prendre à* —, to sue, to lay blame on

‖**Partiel, le,** adj. (*etym. L.L.* partialis), partial

Partir, vn. (*etym. L.* partiri), to set out, to set off, to start, to go off, to proceed. — *d'un éclat de rire*, to burst out into a fit of laughter

‖**Partitif, ve,** adj. partitive

Partout, adv. everywhere

Parure, sf. (*etym.* parer), dress, ornament, attire

Parvenir, vn. (*etym. L.* pervenire), to reach, to get to, to arrive at, to succeed in

Parvenu, e, s. upstart, self-made man

Parvis, sm. (*etym. L.* paradisus), open space before a church, court

Pas, sm. (*etym. L.* passus), pace, step, rate, pacing, trouble, footprint, precedency, passage, scrape, step. — *de vis*, furrow. — *de fusée*, turn. *Au — de charge, au — de course*, double-quick time. *Faire un faux* —, to slip, to take a false step. ‡*Franchir, sauter, le* —, to take the leap, to die. *Prendre le* —, to slacken to a foot pace. — adv. not

Pas, adv. not, no

Pascal, e, adj. (*etym. L.* paschalis), Paschal

Passablement, adv. (*etym.* passable), tolerably

Passade, sf. (*etym. I.* passata), very short stay

‖**Passager, ère,** adj. s. (*etym.* passage), of passage, passing, transient, transitory, passenger. — adv. transiently

Passant, e, adj. frequented, public. — sm. passer-by

Passavant, sm. gangway permit

Passe, sf. passage, pass, situation, channel. — *de chapeau*, front of a bonnet

Passé, sm. the past, past times. —, —*e*, adj. past, bygone, last, out of use, faded

Passe-debout, sm. permit (for transit); *plur.* des passe-debouts

Passe-droit, sm. favour, injustice; *plur.* des passe-droits

Passe-lacet, sm. bodkin; *plur.* des passe-lacets

Passementerie, sf. (*etym.* passer), lace-making, lace-trade

Passementier, ère, s. lace-maker

Passe-partout, sm. master-key, latch-key, a kind of frame for pictures, (*print.*) factotum; *plur.* des passe-partouts

Passe-passe, sm. sleight of hand. *Faire des tours de* —, to play sleight of hand tricks

Passe-poil, sm. braid for edging; *plur.* des passe-poils

Passe-port, sm. passport, recommendation; *plur.* des passe-ports

Passer, vn. (*etym. L.L.* passare), to pass, to go, to call on a person, to overlook, to pass muster, to be handed down, to cease, to fade; — va. to pass, to cross, to carry, to slip on, to leave out, to spend, to while away, to outstrip. — *un contrat*, to draw up a deed. — *une envie*, to gratify a wish. *Se* —, vr. to pass from one to another, to forgive each other, to pass away, to fade, to happen, to be satisfied, to gratify, to dispense with

Passereau, sm. (*etym. L.* passerellus), sparrow

Passerelle, sf. narrow foot-bridge

Passe-temps, sm. pastime, sport

Passeur, sm. ferryman

‖**Passif, ve,** adj. sm. (*etym. L.* passivus), passive, liabilities, debts, passive voice

‖**Passionné, e,** adj. (*etym.* passion), impassioned, passionate, passionately fond, deeply prejudiced

Passionner, va. to impassion, to prepossess; *se* —, vr. to give way to passion, to be smitten with, to become madly fond of

Passoire, sf. strainer, cullender

Pastèque, sf. (*etym. Sp.* pateca), water-melon

Pasteur, sm. (*etym. L.* pastorem), shepherd, pastor, clergyman

Pastiche, sf. (*etym. Ital.* pasticcio), pasticcio, imitation

Pastoureau, le, s. (*etym. L.L.* pastorellus), shepherd-boy, shepherd-lass

Patache, sf. (*etym. Sp.* patache, *a cart*), lugger, stage-cart

Patate, sf. (*etym. Sp.* patata), Spanish potato

Patatras! interj. (*onomatop.*), crack, bump!

Pataud, sm. (*etym.* patte), thick-pawed dog. —, —*e*, adj. s. clumsy creature

Patauger, vn. (*etym.* patte), to dabble, to flounder about

Pâte, sf. (*etym. L.L.* pasta), paste, dough, constitution, sort

Pâté, sm. pie, pasty, blot, block of buildings

Pâtée, sf. paste, mess

Patelin, e, adj. (*name of a character in an old play*), smirking, smooth-tongued

Patelinage, sm. wheedling

Patène, sf. (*etym. L.* patena), patine

Patenôtre, sf. (*etym. L.* pater, noster), paternoster

Patent, e, adj. (*etym. L.* patentem), obvious, evident

Patente, sf. licence, bill of health

Patenté, e, adj. s. licensed, licensed dealer

Patère, sf. (*etym. L.* patera), patera, clothes-peg, curtain-screw

‖**Paterne,** adj. (*etym. L.* paternus), paternal

‖**Paternel, le,** adj. (*etym. L.L.* paternalis), fatherly, paternal, by the father's side

Paternité, sf. (*etym. L.* paternitatem), paternity

Pâteux, se, adj. sticky, pasty, clammy

‖**Pathétique,** adj. sm. (*etym. Gr.* παθητικός), pathetic, moving, true pathos, the pathetic

Pathologie, sf. (*etym. Gr.* πάθος, *illness*, λόγος, *discourse*), pathology

‖**Pathologique,** adj. pathological

Patibulaire, adj. (*etym. L.* patibulum, *the gallows*), of the gallows. *Fourches* —*s*, the gallows. *Mine* —, hang-dog look

Patienter, vn. (*etym.* patient), to take patience

Patin, sm. (*etym.* patte), high-heeled shoe, clog, patten, skate, sill

Patiner, vn. to skate

Patineur, sm. skater

Pâtir, vn. (*etym. L.L.* patiri, *from* pati, *to suffer*), to suffer

Pâtisserie, sf. pastry, pastry-cook's business

Pâtissier, ère, s. (*etym. I.* pasticciere, *pastry-cook*), pastry-cook

Patois, sm. (*etym. ?*), jargon, brogue, dialect

†**Patraque,** sf. (*etym. ?*), rubbishing thing, feeble creature

Pâtre, sm. (*etym. L.* pastor), herdsman, shepherd

‖**Patriarcal, e,** adj. patriarchal

Patriarcat, sm. patriarchate

Patriarche, sm. (*etym. Gr.* πατριάρχης, *chief of a family*), patriarch

Patrice, sm. (*etym. L.* patricius), patrician

Patriciat, sm. order of patricians, patriciate

Patricien, ne, adj. s. patrician

Patrie, sf. (*etym. L.* patria), native country, home, birthplace

Patrimoine, sm. (*etym. L.* patrimonium), patrimony, inheritance

Patriote, sm. (*etym. Gr.* πατριώτης), patriot

‖**Patriotique,** adj. patriotic

Patriotisme, sm. patriotism

Patron, sm. (*etym. L.* patronus), patron, patron saint, employer, master, skipper, coxswain, pattern

Patronne, sf. patroness

Patronner, va. to patronize

Patronymique, adj. (*etym. Gr.* πατρωνυμικός), patronymic

§**Patrouille,** sf. (*etym. I.* pattuglia, *patrol*), patrol. — *grise*, night patrol

Patte, sf. (*etym. ?*), paw, foot, leg, fluke, flap, root. *Donner un coup de* — *à*, (*fig.*) to make a person feel one's claw. *Faire* — *de velours*, to draw in one's claws, to be all smirks and smiles

Patte-d'oie, sf. goose's foot, place where several roads meet, crow's foot

Pâturage, sm. pasture, pasture-land

Pâture, sf. (*etym. L.* pastura), food, pasture. *Vaine* —, common

Pâturer, vn. to graze, to pasture

Pâturon, sm. pastern

Paucité, sf. (*etym. L.* paucitatem), paucity

Paume, sf. (*etym. L.* palma), palm, hand, tennis

Paumer, va. to punch

Paupérisme, sm. (*etym. L.* pauperus, *archaism for pauper*), pauperism

Paupière, sf. (*etym. L.* palpebra), eyelid, eyes

‖**Pauvre,** adj. sm. (*etym. L.* pauperus), poor, sorry, wretched, poor man, pauper, beggar

Pauvresse, sf. beggar-woman

Pauvret, te, s. poor little thing

Pauvreté, sf. (*etym. L.* paupertatem), wretchedness, poverty, wretched production

Pavage, sm. (*etym. see* Paver), paving, pavement

se **Pavaner,** vr. (*etym. Sp.* pavana, *a kind of dance*), to strut, to strut about

Pavé, sm. paving-stone, pavement. *Le* — *du roi*, the king's high road. *Le haut du* —, the wall. ‡ *Tenir le haut du* —, to be the cock of the walk. *Tâter le* —, to step cautiously along. *Être sur le* —, to be houseless

Paver, va. (*etym. L.L.* pavare), to pave

Paveur, sm. paviour

§**Pavillon,** sm. (*etym. L.* papilionem, *tent*), pavilion, tent, veil, bell of a musical instrument, flag, colours, marker

Pavois, sm. (*etym. Ital.* pavese, *shield*), shield, armour

Pavoiser, va. to deck with flags

Pavot, sm. (*etym. L.* papaver), poppy

Payant, e, s. adj. payer, one who pays, paying. *Billet* —, paid ticket

Paye, Paie, sf. pay, paymaster. *Haute* —, extra pay

Payement, Paiement, sm. payment

Payer, va. (*etym. L.* pacare, *to appease*), to pay, to discharge, to requite, to atone for; *se* —, vr. to pay oneself, to be paid

Payeur, sm. paymaster

Pays, sm. (*etym. L.* [ager] pagensis), country, land, birth-place, fellow-countryman. ‡ *Battre le* —, *du* —, to roam about the country. † *Faire voir du* — *à*, to lead a dance. *Gagner du* —, to gain ground. *Avoir le mal du* —, to be homesick

Paysage, sm. landscape, scenery

Paysagiste, sm. landscape painter

Paysan, ne, s. countryman, countrywoman. *A la* —*ne*, country-fashioned

Péage, sm. (*etym. L.L.* pedaticum, *toll*), toll, toll-house

Péager, sm. publican, receiver of tolls

Peau, sf. (*etym. L.* pellem), skin, life. ‡ *Crever dans sa* —, to burst with spite. *Être dans la* — *de*, to be in a person's shoes

Peaussier, sm. adj. (*etym. L.L.* pelliciarius, *dealer in skins*), skinner, cutaneous

§**Peccadille,** sf. (*etym. I.* peccadiglio), peccadillo

Pêche, sf. (*etym. L.* persicum), peach

Pêche, sf. (*etym. see* Pêcher), fishing, fishery, right of fishery, fish. — *à la ligne*, angling. *Garde-* —, water-bailiff

Péché, sm. sin

Pécher, vn. (*etym. L.* peccare), to sin, to offend

Pêcher, sm. peach-tree. — va. (*etym. L.* piscare), to fish. — *à la ligne*, to angle

Pêcherie, sf. fishery

Pécheur, eresse, s. (*etym. L.* peccatorem, peccatricem), sinner

Pêcheur, sm. fisherman, fisher. *Bateau* —, fishing boat, smack

Pécore, sf. (*etym. I.* pecora), animal, fool, goose

Péculat, sm. (*etym. L.* peculatus), peculation

Pécule, sm. (*etym. L.* peculium), store, board, money

Pécune, sf. (*etym. L.* pecunia), money

‖**Pécuniaire,** adj. pecuniary

Pédagogie, sf. (*etym. Gr.* παιδαγωγία), pedagogy

‖**Pédagogique,** adj. pedagogical

Pédale, sf. (*etym. L.* pedalis), pedal

Pédant, e, adj. s. (*etym. I.* pedante), pedantic, pedant

Pédanterie, sf., **Pédantisme,** sm. (*etym. I.* pedanteria), pedantry

‖**Pédantesque,** adj. (*etym. I.* pedantesco), pedantic

‖**Pédestre,** adj. (*etym. L.* pedestris), pedestrian

Pédiculaire, adj. (*etym. L.* pedicula, *louse*), pedicular

Pédoncule, Pédicule, sm. (*etym. L.* pedunculus, pediculus), pedicle, stalk

§**Peigne,** sm. (*etym. L.* pectinem), comb. — *fin*, small-toothed comb

§**Peigner,** va. (*etym. L.* pectinare), to comb, to thrash. *Style bien peigné*, elaborate style. *Se* —, vr. to comb one's hair

§**Peignoir,** sm. dressing-gown

Peindre, va. (*etym. L.* pingere), to paint, to pourtray. ‡ *Fait à* —, strikingly handsome. *Se* —, vr. to paint oneself, to paint one's hair, &c., to be reflected in

Peine, sf. (*etym. L.* poena), penalty, punishment, pain, trouble. *Faire de la* — *à*, to vex, to distress. ‡ *Se mettre en* — *de*, to trouble oneself about. ‡ *Homme de* —, porter. *Mourir à la* —, to perish in the attempt. *En être pour sa* —, to lose one's labour. *A* —, loc. adv. hardly, scarcely, barely

Peiner, va. to give trouble, to labour at, to grieve. *Style peiné*, elaborate style. — vn. to toil hard, to be loth. *Se* —, vr. to toil hard

Peintre, sm. (*etym. L.L.* pinctor, *from L.* pictor), painter

Peinture, sf. (*etym. L.L.* pinctura, *from L.* pictura), painting, picture, paint

Pelage, sm. (*etym. L.L.* pilaticum, *from L.* pilus), colour of the hair, hair

Pelé, e, adj. bare, bald-headed

Pêle-mêle, adv. sm. (*etym.* pelle, mêler), pell-mell, confused jumble

Peler, va. (*etym.* peau), to peel, to strip off. — *la terre*, to take the turf off. — vn., *se* —, vr. to peel off, to come off

Pèlerin, e, s. (*etym. L.* peregrinus), pilgrim, dissembler

Pèlerinage, sm. pilgrimage

Pèlerine, sf. tippet

Pelle, sf. (*etym. L.* pala), shovel

Pelletée, sf. shovelful

Pelleterie, sf. (*etym. O.F.* pel = peau), peltry, furriery

Pellicule, sf. (*etym. L.* pellicula), pellicle

Pelote, sf. (*etym. L.* pila, *ball*), ball, pin-cushion. *Faire sa* —, to feather one's nest

Peloton, sm. ball, tennis-ball, cluster, platoon

Pelotonner, va. to wind, to gather together; *se* —, vr. to roll oneself *or* itself up, to form a cluster

Pelouse, sf. (*etym. Prov.* palos, *thick*), greensward

Pelu, e, adj. (*etym. L.L.* pilutus), hairy

Peluche, sf. (*etym. L.L.* piluccius, *from* pilus), plush, shag

Pelure, sf. (*etym.* peler), peel, paring

Pénalité, sf. (*etym.* pénal), body of penal law

Penaud, e, adj. (*etym.* peine), abashed, sheepish

Penchant, e, adj. inclined, inclining, tottering. — sm. declivity, slope, brink, inclination

Pencher, va. (*etym. L.L.* pendicare), to incline, to lean, to bend, to stoop; *se* —, vr. to bend, to lean, to stoop

Pendable, adj. (*etym.* pendre), hanging, abominable

Pendaison, sf. hanging

Pendant, e, adj. hanging, pendent, pending, aweigh. — sm. pendant, ear-drop, counterpart, fellow. — prep. during, for

Pendard, sm. hangdog, rogue

Pendeloque, sf. (*etym.* pendre, loque), ear-drop, drop of a chandelier, shred

Pendentif, sm. pendentive

Pendre, va. (*etym. L.* pendere), to hang up. ‡ *Dire pis que* — *de*, to say everything that's bad of. — vn. to hang, to dangle. *Se* —, vr. to hang oneself up, to cling

Pendu, e, past part. adj. s. hanging, hung up, clinging. *Avoir de la corde de* —, (*fig.*) to have the devil's own luck

Pendule, sm. (*etym. L.L.* pendulus), pendulum. — sf. clock, time-piece

Pène, sm. (*etym. L.* pessulum; *O.F.* pesle), bolt

Pénétrabilité, sf. (*etym.* pénétrable), penetrability

Pénétrant, e, adj. penetrating, piercing, acute, impressive

Pénétré, e, adj. past part. penetrated, affected, grateful

Pénétrer, va.n. (*etym. L.* penetrare), to penetrate, to go through, to impress deeply

se Pénétrer, vr. to be deeply impressed, to impress one's mind

‖**Pénible,** adj. (*etm.* peine), painful, toilsome

Péniche, sf. (*etym. from the English*), pinnace

Péninsule, sf. peninsula

Pénitencier, sm., *also* **Pénitentiaire,** adj. sm. (*etym.* penitence), penitentiary

Pénombre, sf. (*etym. L.* pæne, *nearly*, umbra), penumbra

Pensée, sf. thought, opinion, mind, idea, meaning, heart's-ease, pansy

Penser, vn.a. (*etym. L.* pensare, *to weigh*), to think, to deem, to judge, to consider. ‡ *Laisser à* —, to look suspicious

Penseur, sm. thinker

Pensif, ve, adj. pensive, thoughtful

Pension, sf. (*etym. L.* pensionem), board, boarding-house, boarding-school, academy

Pensionnaire, sm. pensioner, boarder

Pensionnat, sm. school, school-house

Pensionner, va. to pension

Pensum, sm. (*Lat. word*), imposition, task

Pentagone, sm. adj. (*etym. Gr.* πεντάγωνος), pentagon, pentagonal, five-cornered

Pentamètre, sm. adj. (*etym. Gr.* πεντάμετρος [στίχος], *line having five feet*), pentameter

Pentateuque, sm. (*etym. Gr.* πεντάτευχος [βίβλος], *a work divided into five books*), Pentateuch

Pente, sf. (*etym.* pendre), slope, declivity, bent, valance, gradient

Pentecôte, sf. (*etym. Gr.* πεντηκοστή [ἡμέρα], *fiftieth day*), Pentecost, Whitsuntide

Pénultième, adj. sf. (*etym. L.* penultimus), penultimate, penult

Pénurie, sf. (*etym. L.* penuria), penury

Pépie, sf. (*etym. L.* pituita), pip

Pépin, sm. (*etym. ?*), pip, kernel, grapestone

Pépinière, sf. nursery

Pépiniériste, sm. nursery-gardener

Pépite, sf. (*etym. Sp.* pepita, *grain*), nugget

Péquin, sm. (*etym. ?*), a slang word used by soldiers to mean a civilian

Percale, sf. (*etym. ?*), cambric muslin

Percaline, sf. glazed cotton lining

Perçant, e, adj. (*etym.* percer), piercing, sharp, keen, quick, shrill

Perce, loc. adv. tapped. *Mettre en* —, to broach, to tap

Percée, sf. opening, vista

Percement, sm. piercing, opening

Perce-neige, sf. snowdrop; *plur.* des perce-neiges

§**Perce-oreille,** sm. earwig; *plur.* des perce-oreilles

Percepteur, sm. (*etym. L.* perceptorem), tax-collector

Perception, sf. (*etym. L.* perceptionem), perception, collecting, collector's post

Percer, va. (*etym. ?*), to pierce, to bore, to drill, to broach, to tap, to open; — vn. to break, to enter, to pierce, to break out, to transpire, to rise into notice; *se* —, vr. to pierce oneself

Percevoir, va. (*etym. L.* percipere), to gather in, to perceive

Perche, sf. (*etym. L.* perca [*fish*], pertica [*pole*]), perch, rod, pole, antlers

Percher, vn., *se* —, vr. to perch, to roost

Perchoir, sm. perch

Perclus, e, adj. (*etym. L.* perclusus), crippled

Perdant, sm. adj. loser, losing

Perdre, va. (*etym. L.* perdere), to lose, to waste, to lead astray, to defame, to ruin; *se* —, vr. to be cast away, to be lost, to fall into disuse, to go to ruin

Perdreau, sm. young partridge

Perdrix, sf. (*etym. L.* perdicem), partridge. *Œil-de-* —, corn between the toes, pale-coloured wine

Perdu, e, past part. lost, out of the way, uninhabited, ruined. *A coups* —*s*, at random. *Fonds* —*s*, annuity. *Sentinelle* —*e*, advanced sentry

Père, sm. (*etym. L.* patrem), father. *Jouer les* —*s nobles*, (*theat.*) to play the parts of fathers

‖**Péremptoire,** adj. (*etym. L.* peremptorius), peremptory

¶**Perfectibilité,** sf. (*etym.* perfectible), perfectibility

Perfectionnement, sm. (*etm.* perfection), improvement, improving

Perfectionner, va. to perfect, to improve; *se* —, vr. to improve, to become more perfect

‖**Perfide,** adj. (*etym. L.* perfidus), perfidious, hollow, false

Perfidie, sf. (*etym. L.* perfidia), perfidiousness, perfidy, guile

Perforer, va. (*etym. L.* perforare), to bore, to perforate

Péricliter, vn. (*etym. L.* periclitari), to be in jeopardy

Périgée, sm. (*etym. Gr.* περίγειον), perigeum

Périhélie, sm. (*etym. Gr.* περί, *around*, ἥλιος, *sun*), perihelium

§**Périlleux, se,** adj. (*etym. L.* periculosus), perilous, hazardous

¶**Périmer,** va.n. (*etym. L.* perimere), to bar by limitation, to have fallen into disuse

Périmètre, sm. (*etym. Gr.* περίμετρος), perimeter

Période, sf. period. — sm. period, stage, pitch

Périodicité, sf. periodicity

‖**Périodique,** adj. (*etym. L.* periodicus), periodic, periodical

Péripatéticien, ne, sm. adj. (*etym. Gr.* περιπατητικός), peripatetic

Péripétie, sf. (*etym. Gr.* περιπέτεια, *unforeseen conclusion*), catastrophe, peripeteia

Périr, vn. (*etym. L.* perire), to perish, to decay

Périssable, adj. perishable

Perle, sf. (*etym. L.* pirula, *from* pirum, *pear*), pearl, bead

Perlé, e, past part. adj. finished, brilliant, pearl (barley)

Perler, vn. to bead

Perméabilité, sf. (*etym.* perméable), perviousness

Perméable, adj. (*etym. L.* permeabilis), pervious

Permettre, va. (*etym. L.* permittere), to allow, to permit; *se* —, vr. to allow oneself, to indulge in

Permis, e, adj allowed, lawful. — sm. permission, permit

Permuter, va. (*etym. L.* permutare), to exchange, to permute

‖**Pernicieux, se,** adj. (*etym. L.* perniciosus), pernicious, hurtful

Péronnelle, sf. (*etym. L. prop. name* Petronilla), silly jade

Péroraison, sf. (*etym. L.* perorationem), peroration

Pérorer, vn. (*etym. L.* perorare), to speechify, to spout

Peroxyde, sm. peroxide

‖**Perpendiculaire,** adj sf. (*etym. L.* perpendicularis), perpendicular

Perpétrer, va. (*etym. L.* perpetrare), to perpetrate

‖**Perpétuel, le,** adj. perpetual, endless

Perpétuer, va. (*etym. L.* perpetuare), to perpetuate; *se* —, vr. to be perpetuated

Perpétuité, sf. (*etym. L.* perpetuitatem), perpetuity

Perplexe, adj. (*etym. L.* perplexus), perplexed, perplexing

Perplexité, sf. (*etym. L.* perplexitatem), perplexity

Perquisition, sf. (*etym. L.* perquisitionem), search, perquisition. *Mandat de* —, search-warrant

Perron, sm. (*etym. see* PIERRE), flight of steps

Perroquet, sm. (*etym. I.* perrochetto), parrot, (*nav.*) gallant, gallant-sail

Perruche, sf. (*etym.* perroquet), female parrot

Perruque, sf. (*etym. I.* perruca), wig, periwig, peruke. — *à marteaux*, bob-wig

Perruquier, ère, s. hair-dresser, wig-maker

Pers, e, adj. (*etym. L* persicum, *peach*), bluish

Perse, sf. (*etym. prop. name* Perse, *Persia*), chintz

Persécuter, va. (*etym. L.* persecutari), to persecute; *se* —, vr. to persecute each other

Persécuteur, trice, s. adj. persecutor, persecuting

Persévérant, e, adj. steady, industrious, persevering

Persévérer, vn. (*etym. L.* perseverare), to persevere

Persienne, sf. (*etym. see* PERSE), outer window-blind

Persiflage, sm. quizzing

Persifler, va. (*etym.* per = par, siffler), to quiz

Persifleur, sm. quiz

Persil, sm. (*etym. L.* petroselinum), parsley

Persistance, sf. persistence

Persister, vn. (*etym. L.* persistere), to persist

Personnage, sm. personage, character, part

Personnalité, sf. personality, selfishness

Personne, sf. (*etym. L.* persona), person. *Payer de sa* —, to expose one's life, to bestir oneself. — indef. pron. some one, any one

‖**Personnel, le,** adj. (*etym. L.* personalis), personal, selfish. — sm. officers, clerks

Personnification, sf. personification

Personnifier, va. to personify, to impersonate; *se* —, vr. to be personified

¶**Perspicace,** adj. (*etym. L.* perspicacem), perspicacious

Perspicacité, sf. perspicacity

Perspicuité, sf. (*etym. L.* perspicuitatem), perspicuity

Persuader, va. (*etym. L.* persuadere), to persuade, to induce; *se* —, vr. to persuade oneself

‖**Persuasif, ve,** adj. (*etym.* persuasion), persuasive

Perte, sf. (*etym. see* PERDRE), loss, waste. *A* — *de vue*, out of sight

‖**Pertinent, e,** adj. (*etym. L.* pertinentem), pertinent, apposite

Pertuis, sm. (*etym. L.* pertusus, *pierced*), straits, pass

Pertuisane, sf. (*etym. I.* partigiana), partisan, halberd

Perturbateur, trice, s. adj. (*etym. L.* perturbator), disturber, disturbing

Pervenche, sf. (*etym. L.* pervinca), periwinkle

‖**Pervers, e,** adj. (*etym. L.* perversus), perverse, froward

Perversité, sf. (*etym. L.* perversitatem), perverseness, perversity
Pervertir, va. (*etym. L.* pervertere), to pervert; *se* —, vr. to be perverted
Pesage, sm. weighing
‖**Pesant, e,** adj. heavy, ponderous, weighty, burdensome
Pesanteur, sf. heaviness, weight, ponderousness, force of gravity, sluggishness
Pesée, sf. weighing, weight
¶**Pèse-lettre,** sm. letter-weigher; *plur.* des pèse-lettres
Pèse-liqueur, sm. hydrometer, water-poise; *plur.* des pèse-liqueurs
Peser, va. (*etym. L.* pensare), to weigh, to ponder; — vn. to weigh, to lie heavy, to lay a stress; *se* —, vr. to be weighed, to weigh oneself
Peseur, sm. weigher
Peson, sm. steelyard
¶**Pessimiste,** sm. (*etym. L.* pessimus), pessimist
Peste, sf. (*etym. L.* pestis), plague, bane. — interj. bless me! the deuce!
Pester, vn. to inveigh, to fret and fume
Pestiféré, e, adj. s. pestiferous, infected, plague-stricken
Pestilentiel, le, adj. (*etym.* pestilence), pestilential
Pétale, sm. (*etym. Gr.* πέταλον, *leaf*), petal
Pétarade, sf. (*etym.* pet), farting, insulting noise
‡**Pétaud,** sm. *La cour du roi* —, all speakers and no hearers
‡**Pétaudière,** sf. bear-garden
Péter, vn. to crack, to snap, to explode, to fart
§**Pétillant, e,** adj. crackling, sparkling
§**Pétillement,** sm. crackling, sparkling
§**Pétiller,** vn. to crackle, to sparkle, to boil with, to be full of, to long
‖**Petit, e,** adj. (*etym. I*), small, little, diminutive, petty, shabby. — *à* —, little by little. — s. little boy, little girl, young one, little one. — adv. not much, poorly, shabbily, meanly
Petitesse, sf. smallness, littleness
Pétition, sf. (*etym. L.* petitionem), petition. — *de principe*, begging the question
¶**Pétitionnaire,** s. petitioner
Pétitionner, va. to petition
Petit-maître, sm. coxcomb, dandy
Petite-maîtresse, sf. foppish woman
Pétrifiant, e, adj. petrifactive, petrifying
Pétrification, sf. petrification
Pétrifier, va. (*etym. L.L.* petrificare), to petrify; *se* —, vr. to petrify, to be petrified
Pétrin, sm. (*etym. L.* pistrinum), kneading-trough. ‡ *Être dans le* —, to be in trouble
Pétrir, va. (*etym. L.L.* pisturire), to knead, to make, to form; *se* —, vr. to be kneaded
Pétrissage, sm. kneading
Peu, adv. sm. (*etym. Prov.* pauc; *L.* paucus), little, few. *Tant soit* —, ever so little. *Pour* — *que*, if . . . if ever so little. *Quelque* — *que, si* — *que*, however little, how little soever. *Si* — *que rien*, a mere nothing
Peuplade, sf. people, tribe
Peuple, sm. (*etym. L.* populus), people, nation. — adj. vulgar
Peupler, va. to people, to stock *se* —, vr. to be peopled, to become populous
Peuplier, sm. (*etym. L.* populus), poplar
Peur, sf. (*etym. L.* pavorem), fear, fright, dread
‖**Peureux, se,** adj. s. timorous, fearful, shy, coward
Peut-être, adv. loc. perhaps
Phalange, sf. (*etym. L.* phalangem), phalanx
Phalène, sf. (*etym. Gr.* φάλαινα, *moth*), true moth, moth
Pharaon, sm. faro
Phare, sm. (*etym. Gr.* φάρος), light-house, beacon
Pharisaïque, adj. pharisaical
Pharisaïsme, sm. pharisaism
Pharisien, sm. (*etym. L.* Pharisæus), pharisee
Pharmaceutique, adj. sf. (*etym. Gr.* φαρμακευτικός), pharmaceutic, pharmaceutics
Pharmacie, sf. (*etym. Gr.* φαρμακεία), pharmacy, apothecary's trade, dispensary, medicine chest
Pharmacien, sm. chemist and druggist
Pharmacopée, sf. (*etym. Gr.* φαρμακοποιία), pharmacopœia
Phase, sf. (*etym. Gr.* φάσις), phasis, stage, turn, aspect
Phénomène, sm. (*etym. Gr.* φαινόμενον), phenomenon
Philanthrope, sm. (*etym. Gr.* φιλάνθρωπος), philanthropist
Philanthropie, sf. philanthropy
Philanthropique, adj. philanthropical
Philharmonique, adj. (*etym. Gr.* φίλος, *friend*, ἁρμονία, *harmony*), philharmonic
Philippique, sf. (*etym. Gr.* φιλιππικός [λόγος], *speech relating to Philip*), philippic
Philologie, sf. (*etym. Gr.* φιλολογία), philology
Philologue, sm. philologist
Philosophale, adj. f. *La pierre* —, the philosopher's stone
Philosophe, sm. philosopher
Philosopher, vn. to philosophize
Philosophie, sf. (*etym. Gr.* φιλοσοφία), philosophy, (*print.*) small pica
‖**Philosophique,** adj. philosophical
Philotechnique, adj. (*etym. Gr.* φιλότεχνος), philotechnic
Philtre, sm. (*etym. Gr.* φίλτρον), philter, love-charm
Phoque, sm. (*etym. Gr.* φώκη), seal
Phosphore, sm. (*etym. Gr.* φωσφόρος), phosphorus
Phosphoreux, adj. phosphorous
Phosphorique, adj. phosphoric
Phosphure, sm. phosphuret
¶**Photographie,** sf. (*etym. Gr.* φῶς, γράφω), photography
¶**Photographique,** adj. photographic
Phraséologie, sf. (*etym. Gr.* φρασεολογία), phraseology
Phraser, vn. a. (*etym.* phrase), to phrase
¶**Phrénologie,** sf. (*etym. Gr.* φρήν, *mind*, λόγος, *discourse*), phrenology
¶**Phrénologique,** adj. phrenological
¶**Phrénologiste,** sm. phrenologist
Phthisie, sf. (*etym. Gr.* φθίσις), consumption, phthisis, decline
Phthisique, adj. s. consumptive
Phylactère, sm. (*etym. Gr.* φυλακτήριον, *talisman*), phylactery
Physicien, sm. natural philosopher
Physiologie, sf. (*etym. Gr.* φυσιολογία), physiology
‖**Physiologique,** adj. physiological
Physiologiste, sm. physiologist
Physionomie, sf. (*etym. Gr.* φυσιογνωμονία), physiognomy, face, look. *N'avoir pas de* —, to want expression
Physionomiste, sm. physiognomist
‖**Physique,** sf. (*etym. Gr.* φυσική [τέχνη], *study of natural things*), natural philosophy, physics. — adj. physical, bodily. — sm. natural constitution, the body
Piaffer, vn. (*etym. I*), to paw the ground
§**Piailler,** vn. (*onomatop.*), to bawl, to squall
§**Piailleur, se,** s. bawler
Pianiste, s. pianist, piano-player
Piano, sm. (*Italian word*), piano, piano-forte. — *droit, à queue*, upright, grand piano. *Tenir le* —, to accompany on the piano
Piastre, sf. (*etym. I.* piastra), piaster
Piauler, vn. (*onomatop.*), to pule, to whine
Pic, sm. (*etym. Celt.* pic), pick-axe, peak; (*etym. L.* picus), wood-pecker, pique. *A* —, perpendicular, precipitous. *Faire* —, *repic et capot*, to piquer, repiquer and capote
Picorée, sf. (*etym. Sp.* picorea, *plunder*), marauding, booty
Picotement, sm. tingling, prickling
Picoter, va. (*etym. see* PIQUER), to prick, to cause to tingle, to peck; *se* —, vr. to peck at each other
Picotin, sm. peck, peck of oats
Pie, sf. (*etym. L.* pica), magpie. — *-grièche*, a speckled magpie, (*fig.*) shrew. ‡ *Trouver la* — *au nid*, to make a great discovery. — adj. piebald; (*etym. L.* pia), pious, good
Pièce, sf. (*etym. L.L.* petium, *a plot of land*), piece, bit, patch, puncheon, cask, head, room. *Tout d'une* —, all of one piece. ‡ *Jouer une* —, *faire* — *à quelqu'un*, to play a trick. *Bonne* —, *méchante* —, sly jade, malicious creature. *Donner la* —, to give something. *Près de ses* —*s*, low in cash
Pied, sm. (*etym. L.* pedem), foot, leg, footing. *Au petit* —, (*fig.*) on a small scale. — *plat*, splay foot, pitiful fellow. ‡ *Le coup de* — *de l'âne*, the unkindest cut of all. — *-à-terre*, small lodging. *Mettre* — *à terre*, to alight. *Aller de son* — *léger*, to foot it lightly along. *Récolte sur* —, standing crop. *Avoir, faire un* — *de nez*, to be disappointed, to take a sight at. *Pied-de-chèvre*, handspike
Piédestal, sm. (*etym. I.* piedestallo), pedestal
Piége, sm. (*etym. L.* pedica), snare, trap
Pierre, sf. (*etym. L.* petra), stone. — *d'attente*, toothing-stone. — *à briquet*, flint. — *à laver*, sink. ‡ *Jeter des* —*s dans le jardin de*, to throw out innuendoes against
Pierreries, sf. plur. precious stones, gems
Pierreux, se, adj. (*etym. L.* petrosus), stony
Pierrier, sm. stone drain, swivel-gun
Pierrot, sm. (*etym. prop. name* Pierre), sparrow, clown
Piété, sf. (*etym. L.* pietatem), piety
Piétinement, sm. trampling, stamping, pawing
Piétiner, vn. (*etym. O.F.* piétin, *dimin. of* pied), to trample, to stamp, to paw the ground
¶**Piétiste,** sm. pietist
Piéton, sm. (*etym. L.L.* peditorem), foot-passenger, pedestrian
Piètre, adj. (*etym. L.* pedestris), paltry, beggarly, sorry

‖**Pieu**, sm. (*etym. L.* palus; *O.F.* pel), stake

Pieux, se, adj. (*etym. L.* pius), godly

•**Piffre**, adj. (*etym. I.* piféro, *flute-player*), fat

Pigeonneau, sm. (*etym.* pigeon), young pigeon

Pigeonnier, sm. pigeon-house, dove-cot

§**Pignon**, sm. (*etym. I.* pignone), gable, kernel of a fir-cone. *Avoir — sur rue*, to have a house of one's own

Pilastre, sm. (*etym. I.* pilastro), pilaster

Pile, sf. (*etym. L.* pila), pile, pier, pounding stone, (*numism.*) reverse, tail, thrashing. — *ou face*, head or tail

Piler, va. (*etym. L.* pilare), to pound

Pilier, sm. (*etym.* pile), pillar, column, post

§**Pillard**, sm. plunderer

§**Piller**, va. (*etym. I.* pigliare, *to take*), to plunder, to pillage, to seize. *Pille! pille!* seize him! seize him!

Pilon, sm. pestle, (*poultry*) drumstick

Pilori, sm. (*etym.* ?), pillory, stocks

Pilotage, sm. piloting, piling

Pilote, sm. (*etym. I.* pilota), pilot

Piloter, va.n. to pilot, to pile, to drive in piles

Pilotin, sm. pilot-boy

Pilotis, sm. pile

Pilule, sf. (*etym. L.* pilula), pill

Piment, sm. (*etym. L.* pigmentum), pimento, all-spice

Pimpant, e, adj. (*etym.* ?), smart, spruce

Pimprenelle, sf. (*etym. I.* pimpinella), pimpernel, burnet. — *d'Afrique*, honey-flower

Pin, sm. (*etym. L.* pinus), pine, pine-tree, Scotch fir

Pinacle, sm. (*etym. I.* pinacolo), pinnacle

Pinasse, sf. (*etym. I.* pinaccia), pinnace

Pince, sf. pincer, claw, plait, (*pl.*) nippers, tweezers, sugar-tongs, pinch, gripe, crowbar

Pinceau, sm. (*etym. L.* penicillum), brush, pencil

Pincé, e, adj. stiff, pinched

Pincée, sf. pinch

§‡**Pince-maille**, sm. skin-flint

Pincement, sm. pinching

Pincer, va. (*etym. D.* pitsen, *to pinch*), to pinch, to nip hard, to catch, (*mus.*) to lay on, to nip off, (*nav.*) to hug. *Se faire* —, to get caught. *Se* —, vr. to pinch oneself

‡**Pince-sans-rire**, sm. dry joker

Pincettes, sf. plur. tongs, pincers, nippers, tweezers

Pindarique, adj. (*etym. prop. name* Pindar), pindaric

Pingouin, Pinguin, sm. (*etym. from the English*), penguin

Pinson, sm. (*etym. Celt.* pinc, *goldfinch*) chaffinch, finch

Pintade, sf. (*etym. Sp.* pintada), guinea-fowl

Pinte, sf. (*from the Engl.*), pint

Pioche, sf. (*etym.* pic), pick-axe, mattock

Piocher, va. to dig; ‡— vn. to fag hard

‡**Piocheur**, sm. industrious fellow

Pion, sm. (*etym. L.L.* pedonem, *a foot passenger*), pawn, man, (†) usher in a school

Pionnier, sm. pioneer

°†**Pion-piou**, sm. (*etym.* ?), foot-soldier

Pipeau, sm. (*etym.* pipe), reed-pipe, bird-call, lime-twigs

Pipée, sf. bird-catching

Piper, va. to snare, to take in, to cog the dice, to prepare the cards

Piquant, e, adj. (*etym.* piquer), pointed, prickly, sharp-pointed, stinging, pungent, piquant, smart. — sm. prickle, quill, piquancy, zest

Pique, sf. (*etym.* piquer), pike, pike-length, (*fig.*) degrees, pique. — sm. (*cards*) spade

Piqué, sm. quilling

Pique-nique, sm. pic-nic

Piquer, va.n. (*etym.* pic), to prick, to sting, to bite, to goad, to spur, to quilt, to stitch, to pink, to indent, to lard, to be piquant to, not to be fresh. *Piqué des vers*, worm-eaten. — *des deux*, to set spurs to one's horse. *Se* —, vr. to prick oneself, to sting oneself, to take a pique, to plume oneself, to be worm-eaten, to be spotted

Piquet, sm. peg, stake, picket, (*game*) piquet. *Planter, lever le* —, to pitch, to strike one's tent

Piquette, sf. sour wine

Piqueur, sm. whipper-in, huntsman, outrider, overseer, stud-groom

Piqueuse, sf. stitcher

Piqûre, sf. prick, sting, puncture, bite, worm-hole, fly-blow, quilting, stitching, pinking

Pirater, vn. (*etym.* pirate), to commit piracy

Piraterie, sf. piracy, extortion

Pire, adj. worse, the worst. *De — en* —, worse and worse

Pirouette, sf. (*etym.* ?), whirligig, pirouette, subterfuge. *Faire une* —, to turn on one's heel

Pirouetter, vn. to turn on one's heel, to turn round, (*fig.*) to beat the bush

Pis, adv. (*etym. L.* pejus), worse, the worst. *De — en* —, worse and worse. *De mal en* —, from bad to worse. *Tant* —, so much the worse. — sm. (*etym. L.* pectus), udder

Pis-aller, sm. the worst, last resource, makeshift

Piscine, sf. (*etym. L.* piscina), fish-pond, pool, piscina

Pisé, sm. (*etym. L.* pisare, *to pound*), pisé

Pissenlit, sm. (*etym.* pisser, en, lit), dandelion, pissabed

Pistache, sf. (*etym. L.* pistacium), pistachio, pistachio-nut

Pistachier, sm. pistachio-tree

Piste, sf. (*etym. L.* pistus, *pounded*), track, scent, trail. *Suivre à la* —, to track

Pistolet, sm. (*etym. I.* pistola), pistol

Piston, sm. (*etym. L.L.* pistonem), sucker, piston, forcer. *Course du —, jeu du* —, length of stroke of the piston. *Fusil à* —, percussion-gun

Pitance, sf. (*etym. L.L.* pistantia, *monk's repast*), pittance, allowance

‖**Piteux, se**, adj. (*etym. L.L.* pietosus, *merciful*), piteous, pitiful, woful

Pitié, sf. (*etym. L.* pietatem), pity. *Par* —, out of pity, for pity's sake. ‡*Prendre en* —, to look with an eye of pity on. *Faire — à*, to move one's pity. *C'est à faire* —, it is pitiful

Piton, sm. (*etym.* ?), screw-ring, peak

‖**Pitoyable**, adj. (*etym.* pitié), pitiful

Pittoresque, adj (*etym. I.* pittoresco), picturesque

Pivert, sm. (*etym.* pic), green woodpecker

Pivoine, sf. (*etym. L.* pæonia; *O.F.* pioine), peony. — sm. bullfinch

Pivotant, e, adj. tap-rooted, tap

Pivoter, vn. (*etym.* pivot), to pivot, to turn, (*bot.*) to tap, (*nav.*) to slue the ship round

Placage, sm. (*etym.* plaquer), veneering, plating, patch-work

Placard, sm. placard, cup-board, bill, (*print.*) slip

Placarder, va. to post up, to post, to stick up a libel against

Place, sf. (*etym. L.* platea), place, room, seat, stead, post, office, square, coach-stand, market, change, the merchants. *Faire — à*, to make room for. *Faire faire* —, to clear the way before. *En* —, to your places. *Les gens en* —, men in office. *La — d'armes*, the Parade. ‡*Faire la* —, to be out-door clerk. *Vendre sur* —, to sell on the premises. — *de guerre*, fortified town

Placement, sm. investment, sale, placing

Placer, va. to place, to put, to set, to invest, to put out, to dispose of. — *un mot*, to edge in a word. *Se* —, vr. to place oneself, to take one's place, to obtain a situation or place, to be invested, to sell. — sm. diggings

Placet, sm. (*etym. L.* placet), petition, stool

Placeur, se, s. register office keeper

Plafond, sm. (*etym.* plat, fond), ceiling

Plafonner, va. to do the ceiling-work

Plage, sf. (*etym. L.* plaga), shore, beach, flat and low shore

Plagiaire, sm. adj. (*etym. L.* plagiarius), plagiary, plagiarist; piratical

Plagiat, sm. (*etym. L.L.* plagiatus), plagiarism

Plaid, sm. (*etym. L.L.* placitum), plea, court, sitting

Plaidant, e, adj. litigant. *Avocat* —, barrister. *Les parties —es*, the litigants

Plaider, vn. to go to law, to plead; *se* —, vr. to be pleaded, to come on

Plaideur, se, s. litigant, litigious person

Plaidoirie, sf. pleading, speech. *Entendre les —s*, to hear the trial

Plaidoyer, sm. speech, harangue, discussion

Plaie, sf. (*etym. L.* plaga), sore, wound, plague, evil ‡*Ne demander que — et bosse*, to think the more mischief the better sport

§**Plaignant, e**, s. plaintiff

Plain, e, adj. (*etym. L.* planus), level, flat. ‡*De — pied*, on a level, (*fig.*) abruptly. *Pièces de — pied*, rooms on the same floor

Plaindre, va. (*etym. L.* plangere), to pity, to grudge; *se* —, vr. to complain, to expostulate, to grudge oneself

Plaine, sf. plain

Plainte, sf. complaint, groaning, whining. *Porter* —, to lodge a complaint

‖**Plaintif, ve**, adj plaintive, mournful, querulous

Plaire, vn. (*etym. L.* placere), to please, to be pleasant. *Cela vous plaît à dire*, you are pleased to say so. *Se — à ...* to delight in ...

Plaisance, sf. pleasure. *Maison de* —, pleasure-house

Plaisant, e, adj. pleasant, humorous, laughable, diverting, waggish. — sm. wag, joker, the ludicrous. ‡*Faire le* —, to play the wag. *Un mauvais* —, a mischievous wag

Plaisanter, vn.a. to jest, to joke, to trifle

Plaisanterie, sf. jocoseness, humour, pleasantry, joking, waggish trick, practical joke. ‡*Entendre la* —, to know how to take a joke. *Faire une —, des —s sur*, to cut jokes on. *Faire une — à*, to play a practical joke. *Prêter à la* —, to be ludicrous. *Tourner en* —, to jeer at

Plaisir, sm. (*etym. L.* placere), pleasure, diversion, sport, kindness, wafer. ‡*A* —, carefully, designedly, wantonly. *Conte fait à* —, made-up story

Plaît (il), v. imp. to be pleased, to please, to choose. ‡*Comme il vous plaira*, as you please. *Plaise au roi,* may it please his Majesty. *A Dieu ne plaise!* God forbid! *Plaît-il?* what did you say? *S'il vous plaît,* if you please. *Se* —, vr. to please oneself, to please each other, to delight

Plan, e, adj. (*etym. L.* planus), even, level, plane. — sm. plane, plan, groundwork. *La levée des* —*s*, surveying. *Premier* —, foreground. *Arrière-* —, *second* —, background

Planche, sf. (*etym. L.* planca), board, plank, shelf, plate, bed

Planchéier, va. to plank, to board. *Une chambre planchéiée*, a room with a wooden floor

Plancher, sm. floor, ceiling. ‡ *Vous me feriez sauter au* —, it is enough to drive one mad. † *Le* — *des vaches,* the dry land

Planchette, sf. little plank, circumferentor

Plane, sm. (*etym. L.* platanus), plane-tree. — sf. plane

Planer, vn. to hover, to soar, to look down on: — va. to plane, to trim, to shave, to planish

Planétaire, adj. planetary. — sm. orrery

Planète, sf. (*etym. L.* planeta), planet

Plant, sm. (*etym.* planter), slip, sapling, plantation of young trees

Plante, sf. plant, sole of the foot. — *grasse*, crassula. —*s marines*, sea-weed

Planté, e, part. adj. erect, settled, planted

Planter, va (*etym. L.* plantare), to plant, to drive in, to set, to place, (†) to give the slip, (†) to leave in the lurch, to lay the foundation of. ‡ *Arrive qui plante!* come what may! *Se* —, vr. to be planted, to set oneself

Planteur, sm. planter

Plantoir, sm. dibble

Planton, sm. orderly soldier

Plantureux, se, adj. (*etym. L.* plenus), plentiful, fertile

Plaque, sf. (*etym. Fl.* placke, *piece of wood*), plate, sheet, slab, back, ticket, star. — *tournante*, turn-plate, turn-table

Plaqué, sm. plated metal, veneered. *En* —, plated

Plaquer, va. to plate, to veneer

Plastron, sm. (*etym. I.* plastrone), breast-plate, plastroon, (*fig.*) butt, drill-plate

Plat, e, adj. (*etym. G.* platt, *flat*), flat, level, straight, regular, vapid, dull. *Calme* —, dead calm. — sm. flat, flat part, dish, mess, scale

Platane, sm. (*etym. L.* platanus), plane-tree

Plat-bord, sm. gunwale

Plateau, sm. scale, tray, table-land

Plate-bande, sf. plat-band, (*nav.*) rails, cap squares, clamps

Platée, sf. dishful, foundation

Plate-forme, sf. platform

Platine, sm. (*etym. Sp.* platino), platina. — sf. (*etym.* plat), screw-plate, pillar-plate, platine, plate

Platitude, sf. flatness, vapidness, nonsense

Platonicien, ne, adj. s. (*etym. proper name* Plato), platonic, platonist

Platonique, adj. platonic

Plâtrage, sm. plastering, plaster-work, flimsy work

Plâtras, sm. rubbish

Plâtre, sm. (*etym. L.L.* plastrum), plaster, plaster figure, paint

Plâtré, e, adj. past part. plastered, patched up, white-washed

Plâtrer, va. to plaster over; *se* —, vr. to bedaub oneself

Plâtreux, se, adj. chalky

Plâtrier, sm. plasterer

Plâtrière, sf. plaster-kiln, plaster-quarry

Plausibilité, sf. plausibility

Plausiblement, adv. (*etym.* plausible), plausibly

Plèbe, sf. (*etym. L.* plebem), lower orders

Plébéien, ne, s. adj. plebeian

Pléiades, sf. plur. (*etym. Gr.* πλειάδες), Pleiads

‡**Plein, e,** adj. (*etym. L.* plenus), full, filled, fraught, whole, entire, stout, solid, thorough, (*anim.*) with young. — prep. full. — sm. full, plenum, thick stroke, down stroke

Plénière, adj. f. (*etym. L.L.* plenarius), plenary

Plénipotentiaire, sm. (*etym. L.* plenus, potentia), plenipotentiary

Pléonasme, sm. (*etym. Gr.* πλεονασμός, *superabundance*), pleonasm

Pléthore, sf. (*etym. Gr.* πληθώρη, *plenitude*), plethora

Pléthorique, adj. plethoric

Pleur, sm. tear

‡**Pleurard, e,** s. whimperer

Pleurer, vn.a. (*etym. L.* plorare), to weep, to cry, to bewail, (*vine*) to bleed

Pleurésie, sf. (*etym. Gr.* πλευρῖτις [νόσος], *disease in the side*), pleurisy

Pleureur, se, s. whimperer, mute, hired mourner, (*pl.*) weepers

‡**Pleurnicher,** vn. to whine, to whimper

‡**Pleurnicheur, se,** s. whimperer

†**Pleutre,** sm. (*etym.* ?), contemptible fellow

Pleuvoir, vn. (*etym. L.* pluere), to rain, to pour down, to shower down. — *à verse*, to rain hard

Pli, sm. (*etym.* plier), fold, plait, crease, cover, bend, bent, wrinkle. — *de terrain*, undulation of ground

Pliage, sm. folding

Pliant, sm. camp-stool, folding-chair

Plié, sm. bend

Plier, va.n. (*etym. L.* plicare, *to fold*), to fold, to furl, to bend, to bow; *se* —, vr. to be folded, to bend, to comply with

Plieur, se, s. folder

Plinthe, sf. (*etym. L.* plinthus), plinth, skirt

Plissement, sm. plaiting, folding, puckering

Plisser, va. (*etym. L.L.* plictiare, *from L.* plicare), to plait, to crease, to pucker, to wrinkle; — vn., *se* —, vr. to catch creases, to pucker, to corrugate

Plissure, sf. plaiting, plait, fold

Plomb, sm. (*etym. L.* plumbum), lead, bullet, shot, leaden stamp, plummet, sink, plumb-line

Plombage, sm. lead-work, leading

Plombagine, sf. plumbago, graphite

Plombé, e, adj. leaden, leaden-hued

Plomber, va. to plumb, to glaze, to stop, to fill, to lead, to beat

Plomberie, sf. lead-making, lead-works

Plombier, sm. plumber

Plongeant, e, adj. plunging, downward

Plongeon, sm. the diver. *Faire le* —, to plunge in, (*fig.*) to back out

Plonger, va.n. (*etym. L.L.* plumbicare, *to fall heavily*), to plunge, to immerge, to dip, to dive; *se* —, vr. to plunge, to dive, to revel in

Plongeur, sm. plunger, diver

Ployer, va.n. (*etym. L.* plicare), to bend, to fold up; *se* —, vr. to bend

Pluie, sf. (*etym. L.* pluvia), rain, shower

Plumassier, sm. dealer in feathers

Plume, sf. (*etym. L.* pluma), feather, (*plur.*) feathers, pen, plume, quill, (*fig.*) writer

Plumeau, sm. feather-broom

Plumer, va. to pluck, to plume, to fleece

Plumet, sm. feather, plume of feathers

Plumetis, sm. needle-embroidery

Plupart (la), sf. (*etym.* plus, part), most, the generality, the greatest part

Pluralité, sf plurality

Pluriel, le, adj. sm. (*etym. L.* pluralis), plural

Plus, adv. (*etym. L.* plus), more

Plusieurs, adj. sm. plur. (*etym. L.L.* pluriores), several, many, several people

Plus-que-parfait, sm. pluperfect

Plutôt, adv. (*etym.* plus tôt), rather

Pluvial, e, adj. (*etym. L.* pluvialis), of rain, water

Pluvier, sm. (*etym. L.* pluvia), plover

Pluvieux, se, adj. (*etym. L.* pluviosus), rainy, showery

Pneumatique, sf. (*etym. Gr.* πνευματικός, *relating to the air*), pneumatics. — adj. pneumatic. *La machine* —, the air-pump

Pneumonie, sf. (*etym. Gr.* πνευμονία, *inflammation of the lungs*), pneumony

Pochade, sf. rough sketch

Poche, sf. (*etym. Ang.-Sax.* pocca, *pocket*), pocket, pouch, bag, crop, pucker

Pocher, va. to give a pair of black eyes, to poach (*eggs*)

Pochette, sf. fob, purse-net, kit, pocket-violin

Podagre, sf. (*etym. L.* podagra), the gout. — adj gouty

Poêle, sm. (*etym. L.L.* petalum, *a sheet of gold placed over the head of the Pope*), pall, canopy; (*etym. L.* pensile, *suspended*), stove. — sf. (*etym. L.* patella, *dish*), frying-pan

Poêlée, sf. panful

Poêlier, sm. stove-builder

Poêlon, sm. saucepan

Poëme, sm. (*etym. L.* poema), poem

Poésie, sf. (*etym. L.* poesis), poetry

Poëte, sm. (*etym. L.* poeta), poet, poetess

‡**Poétique,** adj. (*etym. L.* poeticus), poetic, poetical. — sf. poetics, poetry

Poétiser, vn. to versify; — va. to poetize

Poids, sm. (*etym. L.* pensum, *weight*), weight, burden, gravity

§**Poignard,** sm. (*etym.* poing), dagger, poniard

§**Poignarder,** va. to stab with a dagger; *se* —, vr. to stab oneself

§**Poignée,** sf. handle, handful, hilt, holder. *Une* — *de main*, a shake of the hands

§**Poignet,** sm. wrist, wrist-band

Poil, sm. hair, nap, shag, bristle, wool. ‡ *A contre-* —, against the grain. *Monter à* —, to ride bare-back

Poilu, e, adj. hairy

Poinçon, sm. (*etym. L.* punctionem), bodkin, stamp, puncheon, punch, post

Poindre, vn. (*etym. L.* pungere, *to prick*), to appear, to dawn, to break; — va. to sting, to prick

Poing, sm. (*etym. L.* pugnus), fist

Point, adv. not, no. — sm. (*etym. L.* punctum), point, speck, dot, full-stop, mark, hole, ship's place, day's reckoning, clue, tack. — *de couture*, stitch. ‡ — *de côté*, pain in the side. *A* — *nommé*, in the nick of time. *Tout à* —, the right mo-

ment. *A* —, to a nicety. *Deux* —*s*, a colon. — *et virgule*, semi-colon. — *d'orgue*, pause. *De — en* —, punctually. *De tout* —, *en tout* —, in every sense. *Faire le* —, to work out the day's reckoning
Pointage, sm. pointing, aiming
Pointe, sf. point, tip, etching, needle, tack, headland, foreland, smack, dash, touch, pun, fight. ‡ *Être en — de vin*, to be a little flustered *Pousser une* —, *en* —, to make a sudden attack, to pursue one's point
Pointer, va. to point, to stab, to prick off, to register; — vn. to soar, to rear, to sprout
Pointeur, sm. gunner
§**Pointiller,** vn. to dot, to cavil, to tease; *se* —, vr. to bicker
§**Pointilleux, se,** adj. punctilious
Pointu, e, adj. pointed, sharp
Poire, sf. (*etym. L.* pirum), pear. — *à poudre*, powder-horn, powder-flask. ‡ *Garder une — pour la soif*, to lay by something for a rainy day
Poiré, sm. perry
Poireau, *or* **Porreau,** sm. (*etym. L.L.* porrellus), leek, wart
Poirier, sm. pear-tree
Pois, sm. (*etym. L.* pisum), pea. — *cassés*, split peas. — *chiches*, chick-peas
Poissarde, sf. fishwoman, fishing
Poisser, va. (*etym.* poix), to pitch, to make sticky
Poisson, sm. (*etym. L.* piscis), fish, quartern. —*s rouges*, gold fish
Poissonnerie, sf. fish-market
Poissonneux, se, adj. abounding in fish
Poissonnière, sf. fish-kettle
Poitrail, sm. (*etym. L.L.* pectoraculum), chest, breast-harness, breast-summer
Poitrinaire, s. adj. consumptive, in a decline
Poitrine, sf. (*etym. L.L.* pectorina), chest, bosom, breast, lungs, brisket
Poivrade, sf. pepper-sauce
Poivre, sm. (*etym. L.* piperem), pepper. — *d'Inde*, cayenne
Poivrer, va. to pepper
Poivrier, sm. pepper-plant, pepper-box
Poivrière, sf. pepper-caster, pepper-box
Poix, sf. (*etym. L.* picem), pitch
Polaire, adj. (*etym.* pôle), polar
Polarisation, sf. polarization
Polariser, va. to polarize
Polarité, sf. polarity
Polémique, adj. sf. (*etym. Gr.* πολεμικός, *belonging to battle*), polemical, polemics

‖**Poli, e,** past part. adj. polished, bright, sleek, polite. — sm. polish
Police, sf. (*etym. L.* politia), police, police regulations; (*etym. I.* polizza, *contract*) policy. *Agent de* —, policeman. *Faire la* —, to maintain order. *Salle de* —, guard-room
Policé, e, adj. past part. polished, civilized
Policer, va. to polish, to refine; *se* —, vr. to become refined
Polichinelle, sm. (*etym. L.* pulcinella), punch, buffoon, puppet
Polir, va. (*etym. L.* polire), to polish; *se* —, vr. to acquire a polish
Polisseur, se, s. polisher
Polissoir, sm. polisher
Polisson, sm. (*etym. ?*), scapegrace, blackguard
Polissonner, vn. to play the fool
Polissonnerie, sf. roguish trick, (*plur.*) loose talking
Politesse, sf. (*etym. I.* pulitezza), politeness, civility
‖**Politique,** adj. (*etym. L.* politicus), political, shrewd, — sm. politician. — sf. politics, policy, polity
¶**Polker,** vn. to dance the polka
Polluer, va. (*etym. L.* polluere), to pollute, to defile
Poltron, ne, adj. n. cowardly, craven, coward, poltroon
Poltronnerie, sf cowardice, poltroonery
Polyèdre, sm (*etym. Gr.* πολύεδρος, *which has many bases*), polyhedron
Polygame, sm. adj. polygamist, polygamous
Polygamie, sf. (*etym. Gr.* πολυγαμία), polygamy
Polyglotte, s. adj. (*etym. Gr.* πολύγλωττος), polyglot
Polygone, sm. (*etym. Gr.* πολύγωνος, *having many angles*), polygon, ordnance-yard
Polype, sm. (*etym. L.* polypus), polypus
Polysyllabe, adj sm. (*etm. Gr.* πολυσύλλαβος), polysyllabic, polysyllable
Polytechnique, adj. (*etym. Gr.* πολύτεχνος, *skilled in many arts*), polytechnic
Polythéisme, sm. (*etym. Gr.* πολύς, *many*, θεός, *god*), polytheism
Pommade, sf. (*etym. I.* pommata), pomatum
Pommader, va. to pomatum
Pomme, sf. (*etym. L.* pomum), apple, knob, ball, head, (*nav.*) acorn, truck. — *de pin*, fir-cone. — *de terre*, potato
Pommeau, sm. pummel
se Pommeler, vr. to become dappled
Pommette, sf. cheek-bone, knob, pommel
Pommier, sm. apple-tree
Pompe, sf. (*etym. L.* pompa), pomp; (*etym. ?*), pump. — *à incendie*, fire engine. — *à feu*, steam pump. — *foulante*, forcing pump. — *aspirante et foulante*, lift and force pump. *Corps de* —, barrel of a pump
Pomper, va.n. to pump up
Pompeux, se, adj. pompous, stately
Pompier, sm. pump-maker, fireman
Pompon, sm. top-knot, tuft
†**Pomponner,** va. to bedizen, to trick out; *se* —, vr. to bedizen oneself
Ponce, sf. (*etym. L.* pumicem), pounce, pumice
Ponceau, sm. (*etym. L.L.* ponticellus, *from L.* pons), culvert — sm. adj. (*etym. L.* puniceus, *bright red*), corn-poppy, poppy-colour, flame-colour
Ponction, sf. (*etym. L.* punctionem), punction, tapping
Ponctualité, sf. punctuality
Ponctuation, sf. punctuation
‖**Ponctuel, le,** adj. (*etym. L.L.* punctualis), punctual
Ponctuer, va. (*etym. L.* punctum), to punctuate, to stop
Pondre, va.n. (*etym. L.* ponere), to lay eggs
Pont, sm. (*etym. L.* pons), bridge, deck. —*-levis*, drawbridge. — *suspendu*, suspension-bridge. — *tournant*, swing-bridge. *École des —s et chaussées*, school for civil engineers. *Faux-* —, lower deck. *Premier* —, lower deck. — *volant*, hanging stage
Ponte, sm. (*etym. Span.* punto, *point*), punto, punter. — sf. (*etym.* pondre), laying eggs, eggs
Ponter, va. (*nav.*) to deck, to punt
Pontife, sm. (*etym. L.* pontifex), pontiff
Pontificat, sm. (*etym. L.* pontificatus), pontificate
Pont-neuf, sm. popular song
Ponton, sm. (*etym. L.* pontonem, *ferry boat*), pontoon-bridge, pontoon, prison-ship
Pontonnier, sm. pontoon-soldier
Popeline, sf. poplin
Populaire, adj (*etym. L.* popularis), popular
Populariser, va. to popularize; *se* —, vr. to make oneself popular
Popularité, sf. (*etym. L.* popularitatem), popularity
Populeux, se, adj. (*etym. L.* populosus), populous
Porc, sm. (*etym. L.* porcus), pig, hog, pork
Porcelaine, sf. (*etym. I.* porcellana), china, porcelain, cowry
Porc-épic, sm. (*etym.* porc, épic; *O.F.* espic = *L.* spicus), porcupine
Porche, sm. (*etym. L.* porticus), porch, gateway

Porcher, sm. swineherd, pig-driver
Poreux, se, adj. (*etym.* pore), porous
Porosité, sf. porosity
Porphyre, sm. (*etym. L.* porphyrites), porphyry
Port, sm. (*etym. L.* portus), harbour, port, wharf, seaport. *Officier du* —, harbour master. ‡ *Arriver à bon* —, to arrive safe. — (*etym.* porter), burden, tonnage, carriage, postage. *Être au — d'arme*, to shoulder arms
Portage, sm. carriage, (*nav.*) chafing
Portail, sm. (*etym. L.L.* portaculum), porch, portal
Portant, e, adj. in . . . . health, close
Portatif, ve, adj. (*etym. L.L.* portativus), portable
Porte, sf. (*etym. L.* porta), door, gate, entrance, eye. *La grande* —, *la — cochère*, the gate. ‡ *Demeurer à la — de*, to live close by. *Conduire à la* —, to see out. *Jeter, mettre à la* —, to kick out of doors. *Gagner, prendre la* —, to slip out
Porte- . . . , s. . . . bearer, . . . stand, . . . box, . . . holder
Porté, e, adj. inclined, disposed, projected
Porteballe, sm. pedlar
Porte-clefs, sm. turnkey, (*mus.*) key-board
Porte-crayon, sm. pencil-case
Porte-drapeau, sm. ensign
Portée, sf. brood, litter, reach, range, ability, import, (*arch.*) pitch, bearing, (*mus.*) stave, (*plur.*) traces
Portefaix, sm. porter, street-porter
§**Portefeuille,** sm. pocket-book, portfolio. ‡ *Ministre sans* —, minister without a department. *Effets en* —, bills and acceptances
Portemanteau, sm. portmanteau, clothes-peg
Porte-monnaie, sm. flat purse
Porter, va. (*etym. L.* portare), to bear, to carry, to wear, to have on, to deal, to cast, to entertain, to enact. ‡ *L'un portant l'autre*, one with the other. — *le nez au vent*, to snuff the air. — vn. to bear, to rest, to lie, to carry, to tell, to strike, to go with young. *Se* —, vr. to repair, to go, to proceed, to resort, to incline, to be, to be worn
Porte-respect, sm. life preserver, insignia of one's rank, awe-inspiring person
Porteur, se, adj. bearer. near horse
Porte-voix, sm. speaking-trumpet
Portier, sm. (*etym.* porte), porter, doorkeeper
Portière, sf. portress, coach-door, falling curtain. — adj. of an age to bear

Portique, sm. (*etym. L.* porticus), portico, porch

Portrait, sm. (*etym. L.* pro, trahere), picture, likeness, portrait. — *en pied*, full-length portrait

Pose, sf. laying, putting up, posture

Posé, e, adj. sedate, staid, steady

Poser, va. (*etym. L.* pausare), to lay, to set, to put, to put up; — vn. to lie, to sit for one's likeness, to assume an attitude; *se* —, vr. to perch, to tread, to obtain a position, to assume an attitude

Poseur, sm. layer, hanger, one who assumes consequential airs

;**Positif, ve**, adj. (*etym. L.* positivus), positive. — sm. the positive, reality, (*mus.*) choir-organ

Possédé, e, s. person possessed

Posséder, va. (*etym. L.* possidere), to possess, to own, to have; *se* —, vr. to be master of oneself

Possesseur, sm. (*etym. L.* possessorem), owner, possessor

Possessif, ve, adj. (*etym L.* possessivus), possessive

Possibilité, sf. (*etym L.* possibilitatem), possibility, practicability

Postdater, va. to post-date, to afterdate

Poste, sf. (*etym. L.* posita), post, post-house, stage, post-office, swan-shot. — sm. (*etym. I.* posto), post, guard-house, station. *A — fixe*, resident

Poster, va. to post, to station; *se* —, vr. to post oneself

‖**Postérieur, e**, adj. (*etym. L.* posterior), subsequent, posterior

Postérité, sf. (*etym. L.* posteritatem), posterity, issue

Posthume, adj. (*etym. L.* posthumus), posthumous

Postiche, adj. (*etym. I.* posticcio), superadded, false

§**Postillon**, sm. (*etym. I.* postiglione), postillon, post-boy

Postuler, va. (*etym. L.* postulare), to solicit

Pot, sm. (*etym. L.* potus), pot, jug. — *-au-feu*, boiled beef and broth. ⁏ *Être à — et à rôt*, to have one's knife and fork laid. *Tourner autour du* —, to beat about the bush. — *pourri*, hotch-potch. *Le — au roses*, the secret. — *-de-vin*, goodwill. — *à feu*, (*artil.*) stink-pot

Potage, sm. soup. ⁏ *Pour tout* —, in all

Potager, sm. kitchen-garden, stove, soup-can

Potager, ère, adj. vegetable

Potasse, sf. (*etym. G.* pot-asche), potash

Poteau, sm. (*etym. L.L.* postellus, *a small post*), post

Potée, sf. potful. — *d'émeri*, emery-dust, moulding loam. — *d'étain*, pewter

Potelé, e, adj. (*etym.* ?), plump

Potence, sf. (*etym. L.L.* potentia, *crutch*), potence, gallows, (*tailor.*) standard, crutch. *Formé en* —, shaped like a T

Potentat, sm. (*etym. L.L.* potentatus), potentate

Poterie, sf. earthenware, pottery, waste-pipe

Poterne, sf. (*etym. Ital.* postierla, *hidden gallery*), postern

Potier, sm. potter. — *d'étain*, pewterer

Potiron, sm. (*etym.* ?), pumpkin

Pou, sm. (*etym. L.* pediculus), louse

Pouah! interj. (*onomat.*), baugh!

Pouce, sm. (*etym. L* pollicem), thumb, inch. ⁏ *Serrer les —s à*, to force to it. *Mettre les —s*, to knuckle down. *Se mordre les —s de*, to rue bitterly

Poucet, sm. *Petit* —, Hop-o'-my-thumb

Poucettes, sf. plur. hand-cuffs, manacles

Pou-de-soie, sm. (*from the English*), paduasoy

Poudingue, sm. (*from the English*), pudding-stone

Poudre, sf. (*etym. L.* pulverem), powder, dust. *Œil de* —, sprinkling of powder. ⁏ *Jeter sa — aux moineaux*, to waste one's powder and shot. *Mettre le feu aux —s*, to put all in a blaze

Poudrer, va. to powder

Poudrette, sf. desiccated night-soil

Poudreux, se, adj. dusty, covered with dust

Poudrier, sm. dealer in gunpowder, sand-box

Poudrière, sf. powder-mill, powder-magazine, powder-box

Pouf! interj. (*onomatop.*), plump!

Pouffer, vn. — *de rire*, to burst out laughing

§**Pouilles**, sf. plur. (*etym.* pou). *Chanter —s à*, to abuse

§**Pouilleux, se**, adj. lousy

§**Poulailler**, sm. (*etym.* poule), hen-roost, poultry-house, poulterer, egg-cart

Poulain, sm. (*etym. L.L.* pullanus), colt, foal

Poularde, sf. fat pullet

Poule, sf. (*etym. L.* pulla), hen, pool. — *d'eau*, moor-hen. — *d'Inde*, turkey-hen. ⁏— *mouillée*, chicken-hearted fellow

Poulet, sm. chicken, billet-doux, note-paper

Pouliche, sf. (*etym.* poulain), filly

Poulie, sf. (*etym. Ang.-Sax.* pullian, *to pull*), pulley, (*nav.*) block

Poulinière, adj.f. s. brood, brood-mare, breeder

Pouls, sm. (*etym. L.* pulsus), pulse

Poumon, sm. (*etym. L.* pulmonem), lung

Poupard, sm. (*etym. see* Poupée), baby, doll

Poupe, sf. (*etym. L.* puppis), stern, poop. ⁏ *Avoir le vent en* —, to sail before the wind, to be prosperous

Poupée, sf. (*etym. L.* pupa, *little girl*), doll, puppet. *Enter en* —, to cleft-graft

Poupon, ne, s. chubby-faced boy, girl, baby

Pour, prep. (*etym. L.* pro), for, on account of, as, as to, in order to

Pour que, loc. conj. that, in order that

Pour lors, adv. therefore, then

Pour-boire, sm. something to drink

Pourceau, sm. hog, pig. — *de mer*, porpoise

Pourchasser, va. to chase, to pursue

Pourfendeur, sm. swaggerer

Pourfendre, va. to cleave in twain

Pourparler, sm. parley

Pourpier, sm. (*etym. L.* pullipedem), purslain

Pourpoint, sm. (*etym. O.F.* pourpoindre, *to embroider*), doublet, jerkin

Pourpre, smf. adj. (*etym. L.* purpura), purples, purple fever, purple

Pourpré, e, adj. purple

Pourquoi, conj. adv. sm. why, wherefore, the reason why

Pourri, e, adj. sm. rotten, rottenness

Pourrir, va.n. (*etym. L* putrere), to rot

Pourriture, sf. rottenness, rot

Poursuite, sf. pursuit, prosecution

Poursuivant, sm. applicant, suitor, plaintiff

Poursuivre, va. (*etym. L.* prosequi), to pursue, to follow after, to persecute, to proceed, to prosecute

Pourtant, adv. however, yet, still

Pourtour, sm. circumference

Pourvoi, sm. appeal

Pourvoir, vn.a. (*etym. L.* providere), to provide, to supply, to make an appointment; *se* —, vr. to provide oneself, to sue, to petition

Pourvoyeur, sm. purveyor

Pourvu que, loc. conj. provided

Pousse, sf. shoot, sprout, broken wind

Poussée, sf. pushing, push, (*arch.*) thrust

Pousser, va. (*etym. L* pulsare), to push, to thrust, to urge on; — vn. to shoot, to sprout, to grow, to bulge, to push on, to be broken-winded; *se* —, vr. to push each other, to push forward

Poussier, sm. coal-dust, charcoal-dust

Poussière, sf. (*etym. L.* pulvis), dust, spray

Poussif, ve, adj. sm. (*etym.* pousser), pursy, short-breathed, broken-winded, pursy fellow

Poussin, sm. (*etym. L.* pullicenus), chicken, chick

Poutre, sf. (*etym. L.L.* pulletrum, *a foal*), beam, rafter

Poutrelle, sf. stop-plank, small beam

Pouvoir, vn. (*etym. L.L.* potere), to be able. *Ne pas* —, to be unable. ⁏ *Il n'en peut mais*, it is not his fault. *N'en — plus*, to be quite exhausted. — va. to be able to do. *Se* —, vr. to be possible, to be likely. — sm. power

Pragmatique, adj. pragmatic. — sf. pragmatic sanction

Prairie, sf. (*etym. L.L.* prataria, *meadow*), meadow, prairie

Praline, sf. (*etym. proper name* the Marshal de Praslin), burnt almond

Praliner, va. to bake in sugar

Praticable, adj. practicable, feasible

Praticien, sm. ⁏ practitioner

Pratique, sf. (*etym. L.* practicus), practice, dealings, observances, custom, customer, squeaker. — adj. practical

Pratiquer, va. to practise, to associate with, to bribe, to procure, to make; *se* —, vr. to be customary, to be done

Pré, sm. (*etym. L.* pratum), meadow, mead

‖**Préalable**, adj. (*etym.* pré, aller), previous. — sm. preliminary

Préambule, sm. (*etym. L.* præambulus, *who precedes*), preamble

Préau, sm. (*etym. L.L.* pratellum), paddock, yard

Prébende, sf. (*etym. L.L.* præbenda), prebend

‖**Précaire**, adj. (*etym. L.* precarius), precarious

Précautionné, e, adj. guarded, wary

se Précautionner, vr. (*etym.* précaution), to provide

‖**Précédent, e**, adj. sm. preceding, precedent

Précéder, va. (*etym. L.* præcedere), to precede, to go before

Précepte, sm. (*etym. L.* præceptum), precept

Précepteur, sm. tutor, teacher

Préceptorat, sm. tutorship, preceptory

Prêche, sm. preaching, meeting-house

Prêcher, va. (*etym. L.* prædicare), to preach, to laud. — *d'exemple*, to practise what one preaches

Prêcheur, sm. preacher. —, —se, adj. preaching

Précieuse, sf. affected lady

‖**Précieux, se,** adj. (*etym. L.* pretiosus), precious, valuable, affected, finical

Précipitamment, adv. precipitately

Précipité, e, adj. hurried, hasty, precipitate, precipitous

Précipiter, va. (*etym. L.* præcipitare), to fling headlong, to hurl, to precipitate, to hurry; *se* —, vr. to fling oneself headlong, to rush down

Précis, e, adj. (*etym. L.* præcisus), precise. — sm. abstract

Précisément, adv. precisely

Préciser, va. to specify, to state

Précité, e, adj. (*etym. L.* præ, *and* cité), aforementioned

Précoce, adj. (*etym. L.* præcocem), precocious, early

Précocité, sf. precocity

Préconiser, va. (*etym. L.* præconisare), to preconize, to extol

Précurseur, sm. (*etym. L.* præcursor), forerunner, precursor, harbinger. — adj. precursory

Prédécesseur, sm. (*etym. L.* prædecessor), predecessor

Prédestiner, va. (*etym. L.* prædestinare), to predestinate

Prédicateur, sm. (*etym. L.* prædicator), preacher

Prédication, sf. (*etym. L.* prædicationem), preaching, sermon

Prédire, va. (*etym. L.* prædicere), to foretell, to predict

Prédominer, vn (*etym. L.* præ, *and* dominer), to predominate, to prevail

Préexistant, e, adj. (*etym. L.* præ, *and* existant), preexistent

Préférablement, adv. (*etym.* préférable), preferably

Préférer, va. (*etym. L.* præferre), to prefer

Préfet, sm. (*etym. L.* præfectus), prefect

Préfix, e, sm. adj. (*etym. L.* præfixus), prefix, fixed beforehand

Préjudiciable, adj. (*etm.* préjudice), injurious, prejudicial

Préjudiciel, le, adj. (*etym. L.* præjudicialis), interlocutory

Préjudicier, vn. (*etym.* préjudice), to be prejudicial

Préjugé, sm. (*etym.* préjuger), precedent, appearance, prejudice

Préjuger, va. (*etym. L.* præ, *and* juger), to prejudge

se **Prélasser,** vr. (*etym.* prélat), to strut along, to loll

Prélat, sm. (*etym. L.* prælatus), prelate

Prélèvement, sm. previous deduction

Prélever, va. (*etym. L.* præ, *and* lever), previously to deduct

Préliminaire, adj. sm. (*etym. L.* præ, liminaris, *initial*), preliminary

Préluder, vn. (*etym. L.* præludere), to prelude

‖**Prématuré, e,** adj. (*etm. L.L.* præmaturatus), untimely, premature

Prématurité, sf. prematureness, prematurity

Prémédité, e, past part. premeditated

Préméditer, va. (*etym. L.* præmeditari), to premeditate

Prémices, sf. plur. (*etym. L.* primitiæ), first-fruits, firstlings

‖**Premier, ère,** adj. (*etym. L.* primarius), first, former. — sm. first, foremost, first floor. ‡ *Jouer les jeunes —s,* to act lovers' parts. *Un — Paris,* a leading article

Prémunir, va. (*etym. L.* præmunire), to forewarn; *se* —, vr. to provide

Prenable, adj. pregnable, to be won

Prenant, e, adj. taking. *Les —s, les parties —es,* the sharers. *A queue —e,* with a prehensile tail

Prendre, va. (*etym. L.* prendere), to take, to take up, to snatch, to grasp, to capture, to borrow, to catch. ‡ *— de l'âge,* to be growing old. *— son doigt dans une porte,* to jam one's finger in a door. *— l'eau,* to let in water. *A tout —,* upon the whole, in the main. *En venir au fait et au —,* to come to the scratch. *Prenez que,* suppose that. *Une taille bien prise,* a well-formed shape. — vn. to take, to take root, to be frozen, to thicken, to be taken with. *Bien, mal lui a pris,* it was well for him, it fared ill for him. *Se —,* vr. to be taken, to be caught, to grasp, to come upon, to impute to, to freeze, to thicken

Preneur, se, s. taker, lessee

Prénom, sm. (*etym. L.* prænomen), Christian name

Préoccuper, va. (*etym. L.* præoccupare), to pre-occupy, to disturb, to prepossess; *se* —, vr. to be pre-occupied

Préopinant, e, s. (*etym.* préopiner), the previous speaker

Préopiner, vn. (*etym. L.* præ *and* opiner), to vote before

Préparatif, sm. preparation, preparative, disposition

Préparatoire, adj. preparatory

Préparer, va. (*etym. L.* præparare), to prepare, to dispose; *se* —, vr. to prepare, to prepare oneself

Prépondérant, e, adj. (*etym. L.* præponderantem), preponderating

Préposé, sm. officer

Préposer, va. to establish, to set

Prépositif, ve, adj. prepositive

Près, Près de, prep. (*etym. L.* pressus, *close*), near, close to, on the point of, in comparison to. *A cela —,* this excepted. *A beaucoup —,* not nearly. *A peu —,* nearly, almost

Présager, va. (*etym. L.* præsagium), to forebode, to presage

Pré-salé, sm. salt meadow mutton

Presbyte, adj. (*etym. Gr* πρεσβύτης, *old*), far-sighted. *Un —,* a presbyope

Presbytère, sm. (*etym. Gr.* πρεσβυτέριον), parsonage, vicarage

Presbytérien, ne, s. adj. presbyterian

Prescrire, va.n. (*etym. L.* præscribere), to prescribe; *se* —, vr. to prescribe to oneself, to be lost by prescription

Préséance, sf. (*etym. L.* præsidentia), precedency

Présentement, adv. (*etym.* présent), immediately

Présenter, va. to present; *se* —, vr. to present oneself, to call, to come forward, to occur. *Se — bien, mal,* to have a good address, a bad address, to promise well, not to look well

Préservateur, trice, adj. s. (*etym.* préserver), preservative, preserver

Préservatif, ve, adj. sm. preservative

Préserver, va. to preserve; *se* —, vr. to preserve oneself

Présidence, sf. (*etym.* président), presidency, presidentship

Présider, va.n. (*etym. L.* præsidere), to preside

Présomptif, ve, adj. (*etym. L.* præsumptivus), presumptive

Présomption, sf. (*etym. L.* præsumptionem), presumption

‖**Présomptueux, se,** adj. (*etym. L.* præsumptuosus), presumptuous, presuming

Presque, adv. (*etym.* près, que), almost, nearly, scarcely

Presqu'île, sf. peninsula

Pressant, e, adj. urgent, earnest

Presse, sf. (*etym.* presser), throng, press, hurry. ‡ *Faire la —,* to impress seamen. *— à copier,* copying-machine. *Sous —,* in the press

Pressentiment, sm. presentiment, misgivings

Pressentir, va. (*etym. L.* præsentire), to have a presentiment of, to have a glimpse of, to ascertain, to sound

Pressé, e, adj. pressed, squeezed, closely linked, urgent, busy, concise. ‡ *— d'argent,* straitened for money

Presser, vn. (*etym. L.* pressare), to be urgent; — va. to press, to squeeze, to tread down, to crush, to entreat, to urge. *— son style,* to avoid diffusion. *Se —,* vr. to squeeze, to press, to throng, to be quick

Pressier, sm. pressman

Pression, sf. (*etym. L.* pressionem), pressure

Pressoir, sm. (*etym. L.L.* pressorium), wine-press

Pressurer, va. (*etym. L.* pressura, *the action of pressing*), to press, to grind down, to make a sponge of

Prestance, sf. (*etym. L.* præstantia), an imposing deportment

‖**Preste,** adj. (*etym. Ital.* presto), nimble, quick

Prestesse, sf. (*etym. I.* prestezza), nimbleness

Prestidigitateur, sm. (*etym.* preste; *L.* digitus, *finger*), conjuror, juggler

Prestidigitation, sf. sleight of hand, legerdemain

Prestige, sm. (*etym. L.* præstigia), magic spell, fascination, prestige

Prestigieux, se, adj. enchanting

Présumer, va.n. (*etym. L.* præsumere), to presume

Présupposer, va. to presuppose

Présure, sf. (*etym. Ital.* presura), rennet, runnet

Prêt, sm. (*etym.* prêter), loan

Prêt, e, adj. (*etym. L.L.* præstus, *ready*), ready

†**Pretantaine,** sf. (*etym.* ?). *Courir la —,* to gad about

Prétendant, e, s. claimant, pretender, suitor

Prétendre, va.n. (*etym. L.* prætendere), to pretend to, to claim, to maintain, to mean

Prétendu, e, adj. s. so-called, fictitious, sham, self-styled, intended husband *or* wife

Prête-nom, sm. person that lends his name

Prétentieux, se, adj. conceited, affected

Prétention, sf. (*etym. L.* prætentionem), pretension, claim, affectation

Prêter, va. (*etym. L.* præstare), to lend, to ascribe. ‡ *Prêté rendu,* a Roland for an Oliver. — vn. to stretch, to be fertile, to give rise. *Se —,* vr. to yield, to give way, to countenance, to be lent

Prétérit, sm. (*etym. L.* præteritum), preterite, perfect

Prêteur, se, s. lender. *— sur gages,* pawnbroker, lender on deposits

Préteur, sm. (*etym. L.* prætor), prætor

Prétexte, sf. (*etym. L.* prætexta), prætexta. — sm. (*etym. L.* prætextus), pretext, pretence

Prétexter, va. to feign, to pretend, to allege

†**Pretintailles,** sf. plur. (*etym.* ?), women's trinkets

Prétoire, sm. (*etym. L.* prætorium), prætorium

Prétorien, ne, adj. (*etym. L.* prætorianus), prætorian

Prêtre, sm. (*etym. L.* presbyter), priest

Prêtresse, sf. priestess

Prêtrise, sf. priesthood

Préture, sf. (*etym. L.* prætura), prætorship

Preuve, sf. (*etym. L.* proba), proof, token, testimony

Preux, adj. m. (*etym. ?*), doughty, valiant. — sm. doughty warrior

Prévaloir, vn. (*etym. L.* prævalere), to prevail; *se* —, vr. to avail oneself of

Prévaricateur, sm. adj. (*etym. L.* prævaricator), prevaricator, prevaricating

Prévariquer, vn. (*etym. L.* prævaricari), to prevaricate

Prévenance, sf. obligingness, kind attentions. ¦ *Faire des* —*s* à, to show attention to

Prévenant, e, adj. complaisant, prepossessing

Prévenir, va. (*etym. L.* prævenire), to precede, to forestall, to prevent, to anticipate, to prepossess, to bias, to apprise; *se* —, vr. to be prepossessed

Préventif, ve, adj. preventive, before trial

Prévention, sf. (*etym. L.* præventionem), prepossession, prevention, preventing, accusation

Prévenu, e, past part. adj. s. preceded, anticipated, prevented, prepossessed, forewarned, proud, accused, sent for

Prévoir, va. (*etym. L.* prævidere), to foresee; *se* —, vr. to be foreseen

Prévôt, sm. (*etym. L.* præpositus), provost. *Grand* —, provost-marshal

Prévoyance, sf. foresight

Prévoyant, e, adj. provident, prudent

Prie-dieu, sm. prayer-stool

Prier, va. (*etym. L.* precare), to pray, to beseech, to entreat. ¦ *Dîner prié*, grand dinner

Prière, sf. (*etym. L.L.* precaria), prayer, request

Prieur, e, s. (*etym. L.* priorem), prior, prioress

Prieuré, sm. priory

Primaire, adj. (*etym. L.* primarius), elementary, primary

Primat, sm. (*etym. L.* primatem), primate

Primauté, sf. (*etym. L.L.* primalitatem), primacy, priority

Prime, sf. (*etym. L.* primus), prime, primero, premium, prize, pebble, prime wool

Prime abord (de), loc. adv. at first

Primer, vn.a. to take the lead, to overtop

Prime-saut (de), loc. adv. off-hand

Prime-sautier, ère, adj. impulsive

Primeur, sf. early season, (*plur.*) early fruit, early vegetables, (*fig.*) earliest communication

Primevère, sf. (*etym. L.* primum, ver), primrose, cowslip

¦**Primitif, ve**, adj. (*etym. L.* primitivus), primitive

Princesse, sf. (*etym.* prince), princess

Princier, ère, adj. (*etym.* prince), princely

Principalement, adv. (*etym.* principal), chiefly, principally

Principauté, sf. (*etym. L.* principalitatem), principality

Principe, sm. principle. *Dans le* —, in the beginning, primitively. *Par* —, on principle. *Avoir des* —*s*, to be a man of principle

Printanier, ère, adj. (*etym.* printemps), spring, vernal

Printemps, sm. (*etym. L.* primum tempus), springtide, spring

Priorité, sf. (*etym. L.L.* prioritatem), priority

Prise, sf. (*etym. L.* prehensio), taking, prize, capture, hold, influence, quarrel, dose, pinch of snuff. ¦ *Être en* —, to be in danger of capture. *Part de* —, prize-money. *Être de bonne* —, to be a lawful prize. — *de corps*, arrest. — *d'eau*, canal for irrigation, right of irrigation. *En être aux* —*s*, to be at it. *En venir aux* —*s*, to come to words, to grapple with each other

Priser, va. (*etym. L.L.* pretiare), to appraise, to value, to prize; — vn. to take snuff

Priseur, se, s. snuff-taker. *See* COMMISSAIRE

Prismatique, adj. prismatic

Prisme, sm. (*etym. Gr.* πρίσμα), prism

Prisonnier, ère, s. (*etym.* prison), prisoner, captive

¦**Privatif, ve**, adj. (*etym. L.* privativus), privative

Privauté, sf. (*etym. L.L.* privatitatem), familiarity

¦**Privé, e**, adj. (*etym. L.* privatus), private, tame

Priver, va. (*etym. L.* privare), to deprive, to take, to debar, to tame; *se* —, vr. to deprive *or* debar oneself

Privilége, sm. (*etym. L.* privilegium), previous claim, privilege

Privilégié, e, adj. privileged

Prix, sm. (*etym. L.* pretium), price, cost, rate, expense, reward, value, prize, (*plur.*) stakes. ¦ — *pour* —, on a fair comparison. — *fait*, regular price. *Mise à* —, upset price. *Au plus juste* —, at the lowest possible price. *A vil* —, under price

Probabilité, sf. (*etym. L.* probabilitatem), likelihood, probability

Probablement, adv. (*etym.* probable), likely, probably

Probant, e, adj. (*etym. L.* probantem), genuine, convincing, authentic

Probe, adj. (*etym. L.* probus), honest, upright

Probité, sf. (*etym. L.* probitatem), integrity, honesty

¦**Problématique**, adj. (*etym. Gr.* προβληματικός), doubtful, problematical

Problème, sm. (*etym. Gr.* πρόβλημα), problem

Procédé, sm. proceeding, behaviour, process. ¦ *Avoir des* —*s*, to act handsomely. *Manquer aux* —*s*, to act unhandsomely

Procéder, vn. (*etym. L.* procedere), to proceed, to behave

Procédure, sf. proceedings. *Frais de* —, law-expenses

Procès, sm. (*etym. L.* processus), lawsuit, trial. *Être en* —, to be at law. *Faire un* — à, to bring an action against, to pick a quarrel with

Processif, ve, adj. litigious

Processionnellement, adv. (*etym.* procession), in procession

¦**Prochain, e**, adj. next, nearest, coming. — sm. neighbour

Proche, adj. adv. prep. near, nigh. —*s*, sm. plur. kindred, near relations

Proclamer, va. (*etym. L.* proclamare), to proclaim; *se* —, vr. to proclaim oneself, to be proclaimed

Proconsulaire, adj. (*etym. L.* proconsularis), proconsular

Proconsulat, sm. (*etym. L.* proconsulatus), proconsulship

Procréer, va. (*etym. L.* procreare), to beget

Procurer, va. (*etym. L.* procurare), to procure, to get; *se* —, vr. to procure, to get for oneself, to come by

Procureur, sm. (*etym. L.* procuratorem), proxy, attorney

Prodigalité, sf. (*etym. L.* prodigalitatem), prodigality, extravagance

Prodige, sm. (*etym. L.* prodigium), wonder, prodigy

¦**Prodigieux, se**, adj. (*etym. L.* prodigiosus), prodigious, stupendous

Prodigue, adj. sm. (*etym. L.* prodigus), prodigal, lavish, wasteful, spendthrift

Prodiguer, va. to lavish, to be prodigal of, to squander; *se* —, vr. to be lavished with profusion, to call every man one's friend

Producteur, trice, adj. s. (*etym. L.* productor), productive, producer

Productible, adj. (*etym. L.L.* productibilis), producible

Productif, ve, adj. (*etym. L.L.* productivus), productive

Produire, va. (*etym. L.* producere), to produce, to beget, to bear, to yield; *se* —, vr. to come forward, to make oneself known

Produit, sm. (*etym. L.* productus), produce, production, proceeds, product

Proéminence, sf. prominence, protuberance

Proéminent, e, adj. (*etym. L.* proeminentem), prominent

Profanateur, trice, s. (*etym. L.* profanator), profaner

Profaner, va. (*etym. L.* profanare), to profane

Proférer, va. (*etym. L.* proferre), to utter

Profès, se, adj. (*etym. L.* professus), professed

Professer, va. to profess, to exercise, to teach

Professeur, sm. (*etym. L.* professor), professor, teacher

Professoral, e, adj. (*etym. L.L.* professoralis), professorial

Professorat, sm. (*etym. L.L.* professoratus), professorship

Profil, sm. (*etym. I.* profilo), profile

Profiter, vn. (*etym.* profit), to profit, to improve, to be profitable

Profond, e, adj. (*etym. L.* profundus), deep, low, profound, consummate

Profondément, adv. profoundly, deeply

Profondeur, sf. depth, profundity

Profusément, adv. (*etym. L.* profusus), profusely

Progéniture, sf. (*etym. L.L.* progenitura), progeny, offspring

Progrès, sm. (*etym. L.* progressus), progress, march, course

¦**Progressif, ve**, adj. progressive, forward

Prohiber, va. (*etym. L.* prohibere), to prohibit, to forbid

Proie, sf. (*etym. L.* præda), prey. *En* — à, a prey to

Projet, sm. (*etym. L.* projectus), project, scheme, design, draught. — *de loi*, bill

Projeter, va. to project, to contemplate, to purpose; *se* —, vr. to stand out, to project

Prolégomènes, sm. pl. (*etym. Gr.* προλεγόμενα, *things said before*), prolegomena

Prolétaire, sm. (*etym. L.* proletarius), proletary

Prolifique, adj. (*etym. L.* prolificus), prolific

¦**Prolixe**, adj. (*etym. L.* prolixus), prolix, long-winded

Prolixité, sf. (*etym. L.* prolixitatem), prolixity

Prolonge, sf. binding-rope, ammunition-waggon

Prolongement, sm. extension, lengthening, continuation

Prolonger, va. (*etym. L.* prolongare), to prolong, to protract, to spin out, to bring alongside; *se* —, vr. to be prolonged, to extend, to stretch out

Promener, va. (*etym. L.L.* prominare, *to lead*), to take about, to take out for a walk, to turn, to befool; *se* —, vr. to walk, to take a walk, a drive, a ride. ‡*Allez vous* —, go about your business

Promeneur, se, s. walker

Promenoir, sm. covered walk

Promesse, sf. (*etym. L.* promissa), promise, promissory note

Promettre, va.n. (*etym. L.* promittere), to promise, to be hopeful, to look promising; *se* —, vr. to promise oneself, to promise each other

Promiscuité, sf. (*etym. L.* promiscuitatem), promiscuousness

Promise, sf. betrothed

Promission, sf. (*etym. L.* promissionem), promise

Promontoire, sm. (*etym. L.* promontorium), promontory, headland

Promoteur, sm. (*etym. L.L.* promotor), promoter

Promouvoir, va. (*etym. L.* promovere), to promote

Promptement, adv. (*etm.* prompt), promptly

Promulguer, va. (*etym. L.* promulgare), to promulgate

Prône, sm. (*etym. L.* præconium, *announcement*), sermon

Prôner, va.n. to preach, to extol, to prose; *se* —, vr. to preach up oneself, to preach one another up

Prôneur, se, s. praiser, proser

Pronom, sm. (*etym. L.* pronomen), pronoun

Prononcé, e, adj. prominent, decided

Prononcer, va.n. (*etym. L.* pronuntiare), to utter, to pronounce; *se* —, vr. to be pronounced, to declare oneself

Prononciation, sf. (*etm. L.* pronuntiationem), pronunciation, utterance, pronouncing

Pronostic, sm. (*etym. Gr.* *προγνωστικόν*), prognostic

Pronostiquer, va. to prognosticate

Propagande, sf. (*etym. L.* propagare), propaganda. *Faire de la* —, to make proselytes

Propager, va. to propagate, to diffuse; *se* —, vr. to be propagated, to spread

Prophète, sm. (*etym. L.* propheta), prophet, seer

Prophétesse, sf. (*etym. L.* prophetissa), prophetess

Prophétie, sf. (*etym. L.* prophetia), prophecy

‖**Prophétique,** adj. (*etym. L.* propheticus), prophetic

Prophétiser, va. (*etym. L.L.* prophetizare), to prophesy

Propice, adj. (*etym. L.* propitius), favourable, propitious

‖**Proportionnel, le,** adj. (*etym. L.* proportionalis), proportional

Proportionner, va. (*etm.* proportion), to proportion; *se* —, vr. to accommodate oneself

Propos, sm. (*etym. L.* propositum), purpose, discourse, talk, remark. *A* —, loc. adv. at the proper time, opportunely, to the purpose. *A* —, now I think of it. *A* —, adj. proper, right. *A*-—, sm. seasonableness

Proposable, adj. suitable

Proposer, va. (*etym. L.* pro, poser), to propose, to proffer, to propound, to move, to bid; *se* —, vr. to propose oneself, to propose to oneself, to purpose

Proposition, sf. (*etym. L.* propositionem), proposal, proposition. *Pain de* —, shewbread

‖**Propre,** adj. (*etym. L.* proprius), own, very, selfsame, proper, peculiar, fit, clean, neat, tidy. — sm. characteristic, proper meaning, real property, proper prayers

Propret, te, adj. spruce, neat, tidy

Propreté, sf. cleanliness, tidiness

Propriétaire, s. (*etym. L.L.* proprietarius), owner, proprietor, landlord, landlady. *Nu*-—, bare owner

Propriété, sf. (*etym. L.* proprietatem), ownership, property, estate, propriety. *Nue* —, bare ownership

Propylée, sm. (*etym. Gr.* *προπύλαιος, vestibule*), propylæum

Prorata (au), loc. adv. (*etym. L.* pro rata [parte], *according to the fixed part*), in proportion

Proroger, va. (*etym. L.* prorogare), to prorogue

Prosaïque, adj. (*etym. L.* prosaicus), prosaic

Prosateur, sm. (*etym.* prose), prose-writer

Proscrire, va. (*etym. L.* proscribere), to proscribe, to outlaw

Proscrit, e, s. (*etym. L.* proscriptus), proscribed person, outlaw

Prosélytisme, sm. (*etym.* prosélyte), proselytism

Prosodie, sf. (*etym. Gr.* *προσῳδία*), prosody

Prosodique, adj. prosodical

Prosopopée, sf. (*etym. Gr.* *προσωποποιία, impersonation*), prosopopœia

Prospère, adj. thriving, prosperous

Prospérer, va. (*etym. L.* prosperare), to prosper, to thrive

Prospérité, sf. (*etym. L.* prosperitatem), prosperity

Prosterné, e, adj. prostrate

se **Prosterner,** vr. (*etym. L.* prosternere), to prostrate oneself

Prostituer, va. (*etym. L.* prostituere), to prostitute

Prote, sm. (*etym. Gr.* *πρῶτος, first*), (printer's) overseer

Protecteur, trice, adj. s. (*etym. L.* protector), patronizing, sheltering, protector, protectress

Protectorat, sm. protectorate

Protée, sm. (*etym. L.* Proteus), Proteus

Protégé, e, s. dependant

Protéger, va. (*etym. L.* protegere), to protect, to shield, to patronize

Protestantisme, sm. (*etym.* protestant), Protestantism

Protester, va.n. (*etym. L.* protestari), to protest

Protêt, sm. (*etym.* protester), protest. *Faire faire le* —, to have the bill protested

Protocole, sm. (*etym. Gr.* *πρωτόκολλον, the first leaf of a book*), protocol

•**Prou,** adv. (*etym. L.* probe), much

Proue, sf. (*etym. Sp.* proa, *prow*), stem, prow, head

Prouesse, sf. (*etym.* preux), prowess

Prouver, va. (*etym. L.* probare), to substantiate, to prove

Provenance, sf. production

Provende, sf. (*etym. L.* præbenda), provender

Provenir, vn. (*etym. L.* provenire), to proceed, to arise

Proverbe, sm. (*etym. L.* proverbium), proverb, adage

Proverbialement, adv. (*etym.* proverbial), proverbially

Provin, sm. (*etym. L.* propaginem), layer

Proviseur, sm. (*etym. L.* provisor), head-master

Provision, sf. (*etym. L.* provisionem), stock, supply, provision, assets. *Par* —, provisionally

‖**Provisionnel, le,** adj. provisional

Provisoire, adj. sm. (*etym. L.L.* provisorius), provisional, provisional state

Provocateur, trice, adj. (*etym.* provocator), provocatory. *Agent* —, hired disturber of the peace. — s. provoker, instigator, aggressor

Provoquer, va. (*etym. L.* provocare), to provoke, to elicit, to promote

Proximité, sf. (*etym. L.* proximitatem), proximity, near relationship. *A* — *de*, in the neighbourhood of

Prude, adj. sf. (*etym. L.* prudens), prudish, prude

Prudemment, adv. (*etm.* prudent), prudently

Pruderie, sf. prudishness, prudery

Prud'homme, sm. good and true man, skilful handicraftsman, arbitrator, umpire

Prune, sf. (*etym. L.* prunum), plum. — *de Damas*, damson. — *de Monsieur*, Orleans plum. † *Pour des* —*s*, (*fig.*) for nothing

Pruneau, sm. French plum, prune

Prunelle, sf. sloe, eyeball, prunello

Prunier, sm. plum-tree

Prussique, adj. (*etym. prop. name* Prusse), prussic

Prytanée, sm. (*etym. Gr.* *πρυτανεῖον*), prytaneum, public school

Psalmiste, sm. (*etym. L.* psalmista), psalmist

Psalmodie, sf. (*etym. L.* psalmodia), psalmody

Psalmodier, va. to chant psalms, to drone out

Psaume, sm. (*etym. L.* psalmus), psalm

Psautier, sm. (*etym. L.* psalterium), psalter, psalm-book

Pseudonyme, adj. sm. (*etym. Gr.* *ψευδώνυμος*), pseudonymous, fictitious name

Psyché, sf. (*etym. Gr.* *ψυχή, soul*), cheval-glass

Psychologie, sf. (*etym. Gr.* *ψυχή, λόγος*), psychology

Psychologique, adj. psychological

Puant, e, adj. (*etym.* puer), stinking

Puanteur, sf. stench, stink

Puberté, sf. (*etym. L.* pubertatem), puberty

Publicain, sm. (*etym. L.* publicanus), publican

Publiciste, sm. (*etym.* public), publicist

Publicité, sf. publicity

Publier, va. (*etym. L.* publicare), to publish

Publiquement, adv. (*etym.* public), publicly

Puce, sf. (*etym. L.* pulicem), flea. ‡ *Mettre la* — *à l'oreille de*, to make uneasy. — adj. puce-coloured

Pucelle, sf. (*etym. L.L.* pulicella, *from* puella), maid

Puceron, sm. plant-louse

Pudeur, sf. (*etym. L.* pudor), modesty, shame, bashfulness

Pudibond, e, adj. (*etym. L.* pudibundus), bashful

Pudicité, sf. (*etym. L.* pudicitatem), pudicity

‖**Pudique,** adj. (*etym. L.* pudicus), chaste, modest

Puer, vn.a. (*etym. L.* putere), to smell of, to stink

‖**Puéril, e,** adj. (*etym. L.* puerilis), childish, puerile

Puérilité, sf. (*etym. L.* puerilitatem), childishness

Pugilat, sm. (*etym. L.* pugilatus), pugilism, boxing

Puiné, e, adj. s. (*etym. L.* post, natus), younger; younger brother, younger sister

Puis, adv (*etym. L.* post), then, next, afterwards
Puisage, sm. (*etym.* puits), drawing up
Puisard, sm. cesspool, (*min.*) sump
Puiser, va. to draw, to fetch, to take
Puisque, conj since, as
Puissance, sf. power, might, cogency
‡**Puissant, e**, adj (*etym. L.L.* possentem), powerful, mighty, cogent, wealthy. fat
Puits, sm. (*etym. L.* puteus), well, shaft, pit. ¦ *Foncer un* —, to sink a shaft
Pulluler, vn. (*etym. L.* pullulare), to multiply, to swarm
Pulmonaire, adj. (*etym. L.* pulmonarius), pulmonary. — sf. lungwort
Pulmonie, sf. disease of the lungs
Pulpe, sf. (*etym. L.* pulpa), pulp
Pulpeux, se, adj (*etym. L.* pulposus), pulpy, pulpous
Pulvériser, va. (*etym. L.* pulverisare), to grind to dust, to pulverise
Punais, e, adj. (*etym. O.F.* put, *fœtid, and suffix* nais — *L.* inaceus), one who has a stinking nose
Punaise, sf. bug
Punique, adj. (*etym. L.* Punicus), Punic
Punir, va. (*etym. L.* punire), to punish, *se* —, vr. to punish oneself
Punissable, adj. punishable
Punisseur, adj. m avenging. — sm. avenger
Punition, sf. (*etym. L.* punitionem), punishment
Pupille, s. (*etym. L.* pupilla) ward, pupil. — sf. pupil of the eye
Pupitre, sm. (*etym. L.* pulpitum), desk
‡**Pur, e**, adj (*etym. L.* purus), pure, unmingled, unalloyed, genuine
Purée, sf. (*etym. L.L.* piperata, *seasoned with pepper*), soup
Pureté, sf. (*etym. L.* puritatem), purity, pureness, spotlessness
Purgatif, ve, sm. adj (*etym. L.* purgativus), purgative
Purgatoire, sm (*etym.* purgatorius), purgatory
Purger, va.n. (*etym. L.* purgare), to purge, to cleanse; *se* —, vr to purge oneself
Purifier, va (*etym. L.* purificare), to purify; *se* —, vr to become purified, to purify oneself
Purisme, sm. purism
Puriste, sm. purist
Puritain, e, s. adj (*etym. from the English*), Puritan
Puritanisme, sm. Puritanism
Purpurin, e, adj. (*etym. L.* purpurinus), purple-hued
Pus, sm (*etym. L.* pus), matter
Pusillanime, adj (*etym. L.* pusillanimis), chicken-hearted, pusillanimous
Pusillanimité, sf. (*etym. L.* pusillanimitatem), pusillanimity
Pustuleux, se, adj. (*etym. L.* pustulosus), covered with pustules
Putatif, ve, adj. (*etym. L.* putativus, *supposed*), reputed, putative
Putois, sm. (*etym. L.* putidus, *stinking*), polecat
Putréfier, va., *se* —, vr. (*etym. L.L.* putreficare), to putrefy, to rot
Putride, adj. (*etym. L.* putridus), putrid
Pygmée, sm. (*etym. Gr* πυγμαῖος, *one cubit high*), pygmy
Pylore, sm (*etym. Gr.* πυλωρός, *porter*), pylorus
Pyramide, sf. (*etym. L.* pyramidem), pyramid
Pyramider, vn. to form a pyramid
Pyriteux, se, adj. (*etym.* pyrite), pyritous
Pyroligneux, se, adj. (*etym. Gr.* πῦρ, *fire*, ligneux), pyroligneous
Pyromètre, sm. (*etym. Gr.* πῦρ, μέτρον), pyrometer
Pyrotechnie, sf. (*etym. Gr.* πῦρ, τέχνη), pyrotechnics
Pyrotechnique, adj. pyrotechnical
Pyrrhique, sf. Pyrrhic dance. — sm. (*etym. Gr.* πυρρίχη), Pyrrhic foot
Pyrrhonien, ne, s. adj. (*etym. prop. name* Pyrrhon), pyrrhonian
Pythagoricien, sm. (*etm. Gr.* πυθαγορικός), Pythagorean
Pythique, adj. (*etym. Gr. prop. name* Πυθία), Pythian
Pythonisse, sf. (*etym. Gr.* πυθώνισσα, *prophetess*), pythoness, prophetess. *La — d'Endor*, the witch of Endor

Q

Q, sm. the seventeenth letter of the alphabet, Q, q
Quadragésime, sf. (*etym. L.* quadragesima), first Sunday in Lent
Quadrangulaire, adj. (*etm. L.* quadrangulus), quadrangular
Quadrige, sm. (*etym. L.* quadrigæ), quadriga
Quadrilatère, sm. adj. (*etym. L.* quadrilaterus), quadrilateral
Quadrumane, adj. sm. (*etm. L.* quadrumanus), quadrumanous, quadruman
Quadrupède, sm. adj. (*etym. L.* quadrupedus), quadruped, four-footed
Quadrupler, va.n. (*etym.* quadruple), to quadruple, to increase fourfold
Quai, sm. (*etym. Bret.* kaë), quay, wharf
Qualificatif, ve, adj. (*etym. L.L.* qualificativus), qualifying
Qualifié, e, adj. of quality, indictable
Qualifier, va. (*etym. L.* qualificare), to qualify, to style; *se* —, vr. to style oneself
Qualité, sf. (*etym. L.* qualitatem), quality, rank, qualification
Quand, adv. (*etym. L.* quando), when. — conj. though, even. — *même*, even though, even if
Quant à, prep. (*etym. L.* quantum), as for, as to. ¦ *Se tenir sur son — à soi*, to keep up one's dignity
Quantième, sm. day of the month
Quantité, sf. (*etym. L.* quantitatem), quantity, a deal, many
Quarantaine, sf. two score, about forty, quarantine. *Faire* —, to perform quarantine
Quarante, adj. sm. (*etym. L.* quadraginta), forty. *Les* —, the forty members of the French Academy
Quarantième, adj. fortieth
Quart, sm. (*etym. L.* quartus), quarter, fourth, (*nav.*) watch, point
Quartaut, sm. quarter-cask
Quarte, adj. sf. quartan, quart, fourth, quarte
Quarteron, sm. quarter of a lb., two dozen. —, —*ne*, s. quadroon
Quartier, sm. (*etym. L.* quartarius), quarter, piece, quarter's rent, quarter's income, ward, barracks
Quartier-maître, sm. quarter-master
Quasi, adv. (*Latin word*), almost
Quaterne, sm. (*etym. L.* quaternus), quaternary
Quatorze, adj. sm. (*etym. L.* quatuordecim), fourteen, fourteenth
Quatorzième, adj. sm. fourteenth
Quatre, adj. sm. (*etym. L.* quatuor), four, fourth. ¦ *Se mettre en — pour*, to do one's utmost
Quatre-temps, sm. the Ember-days
Quatre-vingtième, adj. eightieth
Quatre-vingts, adj. eighty, fourscore
Quatrième, adj. sm. fourth, fourth floor
Que, pron. rel. (*etym. L.* quem), whom, that, which, what? — conj. (*etym. L.* quod), that, than. — adv. how? how much? why? wherefore?
Quel, le, adj. (*etym. L.* qualis), what, who, which
Quelconque, adj. (*etym. L.* qualecunque), whatever, whatsoever
Quelque, adj. some, any, a few, whatever. — adv. however, howsoever, some, about
Quelquefois, adv sometimes
Quelqu'un, e, pron. ind. some one, somebody, any one, anybody
Quémander, va. (*etym.* ?), to beg
Quémandeur, sm. beggar
Qu'en-dira-t-on, sm. what people say
†**Quenotte**, sf. (*etym. O.F.* quenne, *tooth*), tooth
§**Quenouille**, sf. (*etym. L.* colucula, *from* colus, *distaff*), distaff. ¦ *Tomber en* —, to fall into the hands of females
Querelle, sf. (*etym. L.* querela), quarrel, strife, feud, brawl, cause
Quereller, va. to quarrel with, to scold; *se* —, vr. to wrangle, to quarrel
Querelleur, se, adj. s. quarrelsome, wrangler
Quérir, va. (*etym. L.* quærere), to fetch
Questeur, sm. (*etym. L.* quæstorem), quæstor
Questionnaire, sm. (*etm.* question), executioner, book of questions
Questionner, va. to question
Questionneur, se, s. questioner, querist
Questure, sf. (*etym. L.* quæstura), quæstorship
Quête, sf. (*etym.* quérir), search, quest, collection
Quêter, va. to seek for, to collect
Quêteur, se, s. alms-collector
Queue, sf. (*etym. L.* cauda), tail, fag-end, stalk, handle, train, pig-tail, billiard-cue; (*etym.* ?), cask, file. ¦ *Tirer le diable par la* —, to be hard put to it. — *de rat*, round file. *Tenir la — de la poêle*, (*fig.*) to be at the helm. *Faire fausse* —, to miss the cue. *Prendre la* —, to fall in the rear. *Faire* —, to wait one's turn. *A la* —, *en* —, behind the others

***Queux**, sm. (*etym. L.* coquus), cook. — sf. (*etym. L.* cotem), a hone

Qui, pron. rel. (*etym. L.* qui), who, whom, that, whoever, which, what

Quiconque, pron. ind. (*etym. L.* quicumque), whosoever, whomsoever, whichever

Quidam, sm. (*Latin word*), certain person, individual

Quiétisme, sm. (*etym. L.* quietus), quietism

§**Quille**, sf. (*etym. Sp.* quilla, *keel*), keel, bottom; (*etym. O.H.G.* kegil, *skittle*), skittle, ninepin

§**Quincaillerie**, sf. (*etym. O.F.* clincaille, *iron goods*), ironmongery, hardware, the hardware-trade

§**Quincaillier**, sm. ironmonger, hardwareman

Quinconce, sm. (*etym. L.* quincunce), quincunx

Quine, sm. (*etym. L.* quini), five winning numbers

Quinquagésime, sf. (*etym. L.* quinquagesima), Quinquagesima Sunday

Quinquet, sm. (*proper name of the inventor*), lamp

Quinquina, sm. (*etym. Peruv.* kina-kina), bark, cinchona

Quint, adj. (*etym. L.* quinta), fifth

Quintal, sm. (*etym. Arab.* quintâr, *a hundredweight*), hundredweight

Quinte, sf. fifth, tenor, violin, quint, fit of coughing, vagary, crotchet

Quintessencier, va. (*etym.* quintessence), to extract the quintessence from, to subtilize

Quinteux, se, adj. whimsical, capricious

Quintuple, adj. (*etym. L.* quintuplex), fivefold

Quintupler, va. to increase fivefold

Quinzaine, sf. fifteen, fortnight

Quinze, adj. sm. (*etym. L* quindecim), fifteen, fifteenth

Quinzième, adj. fifteenth

Quittance, sf. (*etym. L.L* quietantia), receipt, discharge

Quitte, adj. (*etym L.* quietus), quits, free, clear. — *à perdre mon procès*, even should I lose my lawsuit

Quitter, va. to leave, to quit, to part from, to forsake, *se* —, vr. to part from each other, to leave each other

Quitus, sm receipt in full

Qui va là? sm. who goes there? ‡ *Avoir toujours réponse à* —, to have an answer always ready

Qui-vive, sm. who goes there? challenge. ‡ *Être sur le* —, to be on the alert

Quoi, pron. rel. (*etym. L.* quid), which, that, what? *De* —, wherewith. *Avoir de* —, to want for nothing. *Il n'y a pas de* —, don't mention it. — *que*, whatever. — interj. what! how!

Quoique, conj though, although

Quolibet, sm. (*otm. L* quod libet, *what pleases*), jest, pun

Quote-part, sf. (*etym. L.* quota, pars), share, quota

Quotidien, ne, adj. (*etym. L.* quotidianus), daily, quotidian

Quotité, sf. (*etym. L* quotus), quota, part, share

R

R, sm. R, r, (*pronounce* arr)

Rabâchage, sm. (*etym. ?*), eternal repetition, idle twaddle

Rabâcher, va.n. to repeat eternally (the same thing), to twaddle

Rabâcheur, se, s. twaddler

Rabais, sm. reduction in price, abatement. *Au* —, at reduced prices, by contract. ‡ *Mettre au* —, (*fig.*) to talk slightingly of

Rabaisser, va. (*etym.* re, abaisser), to lower, to bring down, to abate; *se* —, vr. to abase oneself

Rabau, sm. (*nav.*) rope-band

Rabat, sm band, beating-up, roof-end (*at skittles*), tipping

Rabat-joie, sm. spoil-sport damper

Rabattre, va. (*etym.* re, abattre), to beat down, to lower, to quell, to lessen, to beat up (game). *Épée rabattue*, blunt sword. *Se* —, vr. to fall, to fall down, to alight, to turn off, to limit oneself

Rabbin, sm. (*etym. Heb.* rabbi), rabbi

Râble, sm. (*etym. ?*), back of an animal; (*etym. L.L* rutabulum, *poker*), rake, stirrer

Rabonnir, va n. (*etym.* re, bon), to improve, to better

Rabot, sm. plane, plaster-beater, paving-stone

Raboter, va. (*etym.* re; *O.F.* bouter = heurter), to plane, to polish

Raboteux, se, adj. knotty, rugged

Rabougri, e, adj. (*etym. ?*), stunted

Rabougrir, vn. to be stunted; *se* —, vr. to grow stunted

Rabrouer, va. (*etym. ?*), to snub, to snap at

§**Racaille**, sf. (*etym. O.E.* rack, *dog*), rabble, rascals, rubbish

Raccommodage, sm. mending, repairing

Raccommodement, sm. reconciliation

Raccommoder, va. (*etym.* re, accommoder), to mend, to patch, to piece, to set to rights, to reconcile; *se* —, vr. to mend one's clothes, to be reconciled

Raccommodeur, se, s. mender

Raccord, sm. joining, accord

Raccordement, sm. joining, levelling

Raccorder, va. (*etym.* re, accorder), to join, to unite

Raccourci, sm. foreshortening, abridgment

Raccourcir, va. (*etym.* re, accourcir), to shorten, to curtail, to foreshorten ‡ *A bras raccourci*, with might and main. *Taille raccourcie*, stunted stature. — vn. to grow shorter. *Se* —, vr. to contract, to shrink

Raccourcissement, sm. shortening

se Raccoutumer, vr (*etym.* re, accoutumer), to get used again

Raccroc, sm. (*etym.* raccrocher), lucky hit. *Par un coup de* —, by a lucky hit. ‡ *Roi de* —, chance-made king

Raccrocher, va. (*etym.* re, accrocher), to hook on again, to hang up; *se* —, vr. to be hooked on again, to be hung up, to cling to, to fall back on, to recover one's losses

Race, sf. (*etym. I.* razza, *race*), race, seed, breed, stock. *Cheval de* —, thoroughbred horse

Rachat, sm. (*etym.* see RACHETER), redemption

Rachetable, adj. redeemable

Racheter, va. (*etym.* re, acheter), to buy back, to redeem, to atone for; *se* —, vr. to buy one's freedom, to be atoned for, to be ralcemed

Rachitique, adj. (*etym. Gr.* ῥάχις, *the spine*), rickety

Rachitis, Rachitisme, sm. the rickets

Racine, sf. (*etym. L.L.* radicina), root

Racler, va. (*etym. L.L.* rasiculare, *to scrape*), to scrape

Racloir, Racle, sm. scraper

Raclure, sf. scraping

Racoler, va. (*etym.* col), to entice into enlistment

Racoleur, sm. hired enlister, crimp

Raconter, va. (*etym.* re, conter), to relate, to tell, to recount

Racornir, va. (*etym.* re, corne), to make as hard as horn, to shrivel up; *se* —, vr. to grow hard, to shrivel up

Racornissement, sm. hardening, shrivelling up

se Racquitter, vr. (*etym.* re, acquitter), to win back one's losses

Rade, sf. (*etym. I.* rada), road, roadstead

Radeau, sm. (*etym. L.L.* radellus), raft

Radiation, sf. (*etym. L.* radiationem), striking out, erasure, radiation

Radicalement, adv. (*etm.* radical), radically

Radié, e, adj. (*etym. L.* radiatus), radiated

‖**Radieux, se**, adj. (*etym. L.* radiosus), beaming, radiant, blazing

Radis, sm. (*etym. L.* radicem, *root*), radish

Radotage, sm., **Radoterie**, sf. dotage, foolish talk

Radoter, vn. (*etym.* re, *O.F.* doter = *Engl.* to dote), to be in one's dotage, to twaddle

Radoteur, se, s. dotard, twaddler

Radoub, sm. repair, refitting. *En* —, under repairs

Radouber, va, *se* —, vr. (*etym.* re, *O.F.* doub; *comp. Engl.* to dub), to refit, to repair

Radoucir, va. (*etym.* re, adoucir), to soften, to soften down, to pacify, to allay; *se* —, vr. to soften, to grow milder, to relent, to subside

Radoucissement, sm. softening, getting milder, relenting

Rafale, sf. (*etym. ?*), squall, gust of wind

Raffermir, va. (*etym.* re, affermir), to harden, to fasten, to confirm, to buoy up; *se* —, vr. to grow harder, to be fastened, to gather strength

Raffermissement, sm. hardening, fastening, securing, confirmation

Raffinage, sm. refining

Raffinement, sm. refinement

Raffiner, vn. (*etym.* re, affiner), to refine, to be critical; *se* —, vr. to become more refined

Raffinerie, sf. refinery

Raffineur, sm. refiner

Raffoler, vn. (*etym.* re, affoler), to dote

Rafle, sf. grape-stalk, (*game*) pair royal. *Faire* — *de tout*, to sweep away everything

Rafler, va. (*etym. Dan.* rafle, *to carry off*), to sweep away

Rafraîchir, va. (*etym.* re, fraîchir), to cool, to refresh, to renew, to repair, to rub up, to trim, to crop; — vn., *se* —, vr. to become cool, to refresh oneself, to rest, to freshen

Rafraîchissant, e, adj. cooling, refreshing. — sm. cooling draught

Rafraîchissement, sm. refreshment, fresh provisions

§**Ragaillardir,** va. (*etym.* re, gaillard), to cheer up

Rage, sf. (*etym. L.* rabies), madness, violent pain, rage, fury, mania. ‡ — *de dent*, violent tooth-ache. *Avec* —, madly. *Avoir la — de*, to be mad for. *Aimer à la* —, to love to distraction. *Dire — de*, to say all imaginable evil of. *Faire* —, to set everything topsy-turvy, to do wonders

‡**Ragot,** sm. (*etym.* ?), a short, stumpy man

Ragoût, sm. stew, pleasure, relish

Ragoûtant, e, adj. savoury, pleasing

Ragoûter, va. (*etym.* re, goûter), to revive one's stomach, to quicken, to stir up

Ragrandir, va. (*etym.* re, agrandir), to enlarge; *se* —, vr. to grow larger

Raide, *see* Roide

Raie, sf. (*etym. L.* radius), line, stroke, streak, stripe, weal, furrow, parting; (*etym. L.* raia), skate, ray, thornback

Raifort, sm. (*etym. O.F.* rai = *Lat.* radix, fort), horse-radish

§**Railler,** va.n., *se* —, vr. (*etym. L.L.* radiculare = radere, *to raze*), to twit, to banter, to laugh at, to mock, to jest

§**Raillerie,** sf. raillery, bantering, jeering. ‡ *Entendre* —, to know how to take a joke. *Ne pas entendre* —, not to be trifled with

§**Railleur, se,** adj. given to jesting, taunting, scoffing. — s. joker, banterer, jeerer

Rainette, sf. (*etym. L.* rana), green frog; (*etym.* reine), a kind of apple

Rainure, sf. (*etym.* ?), groove

Raiponce, sf. (*Sp. word*), rampion

Raisin, sm. (*etym. L.* racemus), grapes. *Un grain de* —, a grape. — *de Corinthe*, dried currants. —*s secs*, raisins. — *d'ours*, bear's whortleberry

Raisiné, sm. raisiné (grape jam)

Raison, sf. (*etym. L.* rationem), reason, sense, judiciousness, satisfaction, proof, account, reason, firm, share, ratio. ‡ *Être de* —, imaginary being. *Mettre à la* —, to bring to one's senses. *Age de* —, years of discretion. *Mariage de* —, sensible match. *Comme de* —, of course. *Plus que de* —, more than is reasonable. *Entendre* —, to listen to reason. *A telle fin que de* —, to serve in case of need. *Avoir — de*, to get the mastery over. *Donner — à*, to decide in favour of. *Se faire* —, to right oneself. *Demander, tirer — de*, to demand, to obtain satisfaction from. *Faire — à*, to give satisfaction, to pledge. *Rendre — de*, to account for

‡**Raisonnable,** adj. (*etym. L.* rationabilis), rational, reasonable, sensible, judicious

Raisonné, e, past part. adj. rational, in accordance with the dictates of reason, supported by proofs, analytical

Raisonnement, sm. reasoning, answer

Raisonner, vn. to reason, to argue; — va. to consider; *se* —, vr. to reason with oneself

Raisonneur, se, s. reasoner, answerer, dialectician. *Faire le* —, to stand arguing the question. — adj. that gives answers

Rajeunir, va. (*etym.* re, jeune), to restore to youth, to give a young look to; — vn. to grow young again; *se* —, vr. to make oneself look young again, to revive

Rajeunissement, sm. making *or* growing young again

Rajustement, sm. re-adjustment

Rajuster, va. (*etym.* re, ajuster), to re-adjust, to set to rights, to reconcile; *se* —, vr. to be re-adjusted, to put oneself to rights

Râle, sm. rattling, rattle in the throat, (*bird*) crake, rail

Râlement, sm. rattle

Ralentir, va., *se* —, vr. (*etym. see* Lent), to slacken, to lessen, to abate, to flag

Ralentissement, sm. slackening

Râler, vn. (*etym.* ?), to rattle in one's throat

Ralinguer, va. to set the bolt-ropes on; — vn. to fly loose to the wind, to shiver

Ralingues, sf. plur. (*etym. G.* raaleik), bolt-ropes of a sail

Ralliement, sm. rallying

Rallier, va. (*etym.* allier), to rally, to haul; *se* —, vr. to rally, to join the party, (*nav.*) to hug

Rallonge, sf. eking-piece, leaf of a table

Rallongement, sm. lengthening

Rallonger, va. (*etym.* allonger), to lengthen

Rallumer, va. (*etym.* allumer), to light again, to rekindle; *se* —, vr. to be lighted again, to break out again, to revive

Ramage, sm. (*etym. L.L.* ramaticum, *from* ramus), warbling, singing, chirping, prattle, flowers in a pattern. *A* —, flowered

Ramas, sm. heap, set, band

Ramasser, va. (*etym.* amasser), to gather up, to scrape together, to pick up; *se* —, vr. to collect, to be scraped together, to get up again, to gather oneself up

Ramassé, e, adj. thick-set, squat, clustered

Ramassis, sm. heap, collection

Rame, sf. (*etym. L.* remus, *oar*), oar, stick; (*etym. Ar.* rizma, *a bale of paper*), ream

Ramé, e, adj. growing on sticks. *Balles* —*es*, *boulets* —*es*, bar (shot)

Rameau, sm. (*etym. L.L.* ramellus), bough, branch. *Le dimanche des* —*x*, Palm Sunday

Ramée, sf. (*etym. L.L.* ramata, *from* ramus), green boughs, green arbour

Ramener, va. (*etym.* re, amener), to bring back, to take back, to bring over, to pacify, to reclaim, to pull, to draw, (*nav.*) to lower the head of

Ramer, vn. (*etym.* rame), to row, to pull. — va. (*hort.*) to prop

Rameur, sm. rower, oarsman. *Banc de* —*s*, rowers' benches

Rameux, se, adj. (*etym.* ramée), branching

Ramier, sm. (*etym.* ramée), wood-pigeon, ring-dove

se Ramifier, vr. (*etym. L.L.* ramificare), to branch out, to ramify

Ramollir, va. (*etym.* re, amollir), to soften, to enervate, to unman; *se* —, vr. to grow soft, to soften

Ramonage, sm. (*etym. O.F.* ramon, *a small broom*), chimney-sweeping

Ramoner, va. to sweep chimneys

Ramoneur, sm. chimney-sweeper

Rampant, e, adj. crawling, creeping, cringing, grovelling, low, rampant. *Lierre* —, ground ivy

Rampe, sf. flight of stairs, banisters, slope, inclined plane, (*theat.*) foot-lights

Rampement, sm. crawling, creeping

Ramper, vn. (*etym. L.G.* rapen, *to cling to*), to crawl, to creep, to be low, to cringe and crouch, to fawn

Ramure, sf. (*etm. L.* ramus), branching, hunting attire

Rance, adj. (*etym. L.* rancidus), rancid, rank

Rancir, vn. to grow rancid

Rançon, sf. (*etym. L.* redemptionem), ransom

Rançonnement, sm. ransoming, fleecing, extortion

Rançonner, va. to set a ransom on, to fleece, to overcharge

Rancune, sf. (*etym. O.F.* rancure; *L.L.* rancura), spite, malice, ill-will, rancour. ‡ *Avoir* —, to have a spite. *Garder* —, to bear a grudge. *Sans* —! no malice, I hope!

Rancunier, ère, adj. spiteful, rancorous

Rang, sm. (*etym. O.H.G.* hring, *circle*), row, range, tier, rank, station, degree, (*nav.*) rate. *Être en* —, to be drawn up. *Sur trente de* —, thirty abreast. *Se mettre en* —, *former les* —*s*, to fall in

Rangé, e, adj. pitched (*battle*), steady, sedate, sober

Rangée, sf. row, range, tier

Ranger, va. to put in order, to arrange, to array, to rank, to put aside, to bring back, (*nav.*) to range along, to sail close to; *se* —, vr. to place oneself, to draw up, to fall back, to step aside, to reform, to amend, to veer

Ranimer, va. (*etym.* animer), to restore to life again, to recover, to re-animate, to inspirit, to cheer up, to brighten; *se* —, vr. to come to life again, to revive

Rapace, adj. (*etym. L.* rapacem), rapacious

Rapacité, sf. (*etym. L.* rapacitatem), rapacity, rapaciousness

Rapatriement, Rapatriage, sm. reconciliation, sending back to one's country

Rapatrier, va. (*etym.* re, à, patrie), to reconcile, to send back to one's country; *se* —, vr. to become friends again

Râpe, sf. rasp, grater

Râpé, e, adj. grated, threadbare

Râper, va. (*etym. O.H.G.* raspôn, *to grate*), to rasp, to grate

Rapetisser, va. (*etym.* petit), to lessen, to shorten; — vn., *se* —, vr. to grow less, to shrink

‡**Rapide,** adj. (*etym. L.* rapidus), swift, rapid, fleet, speedy, steep. — sm. rapid

Rapidité, sf. (*etym. L.* rapiditatem), swiftness, fleetness, rapidity, speed

Rapiécer, va. (*etym.* pièce), to patch, to piece

Rapiécetage, sm. patching, patchwork

Rapiéceter, va. to piece all over, to patch

Rapière, sf. (*etym.* ?), rapier

Rappareiller, va. (*etym.* re, pareil), **Rapparier,** va. (*etym.* re, apparier), to match

Rappel, sm. recall, call, distribution, roll-call, recheat. *Battre le* —, to beat to arms

Rappeler, va. (*etym.* re, appeler), to call again, to call off, to recall; *se* —, vr. to recollect

Rapport, sm. revenue, produce, bearing, account, statement, report, evidence, tale, affinity, resemblance, agreement, relation, reference, intercourse, ratio, refunding.

‡ *Être d'un bon —, d'un faible —*, to be very productive, to be unproductive. *En plein —*, in full bearing. *Faire des —s*, to tell tales. *Par — à*, with respect to. *Terres de —*, artificial soil. *Pièces de —*, inlaid work, patchwork

Rapporter, va. (*etym.* re, apporter), to bring back, to refund, to repeal, to yield, to relate, to report, to tell tales, to quote, to refer, to ascribe, to trace, (*book-keeping*) to post. *Se —*, vr. to agree, to tally, to relate, to refer, to be akin to. *S'en —*, vr. to refer the matter to, to trust to, to give credit to

Rapporteur, sm. reporter, judge-advocate, (*math.*) protractor

Rapporteur, se, s. tale-bearer, tell-tale

Rapprendre, va. (*etym.* re, apprendre), to learn over again

Rapprochement, sm. bringing nearer, reconciliation, comparing. *Faire des —s*, to make comparisons

Rapprocher, va. (*etym.* re, approcher), to draw near again, to bring together, to compare; *se —*, vr. to draw near again, to become friends again, to begin to agree

Rapsode, sm. (*etym.* Gr. *ῥαψῳδός, one who tacks songs together*), rhapsodist

Rapsodie, sf. rhapsody

Rapt, sm. (*etym.* L. raptus), rape, carrying off, abduction

Raquette, sf. (*etym.* ?), racket, battledore, snow-shoe, Indian fig-tree, prickly pear-tree

‖**Rare**, adj. (*etym.* L. rarus), uncommon, rare, unusual, thin, scanty, slow ‡ *Devenir —*, to grow quite a stranger *Être — comme les beaux jours*, to be quite a stranger

Raréfier, va. (*etym.* L.L. rareficare), to rarefy; *se —*, vr. to become rarefied

Rareté, sf. (*etym.* L. raritatem), scarcity, rarity, uncommonness, novelty, thinness. ‡ *Pour la — du fait*, for the novelty of the thing

Ras, e, adj. (*etym.* L. rasus), close-shaven, smooth, shorn, open, strickle. ‡ *Couper —*, to cut close off. *A poil —*, short-haired. *A — de bord*, up to the brim. *Au — de l'eau, à — l'eau*, close to the water

Ras de marée, sm. (*etym.* L.Br. *raz, a violent current*), race

Rasade, sf. (*etym.* raser), bumper

Rasant, e, adj. (*fortif.*) razant

Raser, va. (*etym.* ras), to shave, to raze to the ground, to cut down, to skim along, (*nav.*) to hug

Rasoir, sm. razor

Rassasiement, sm. satiety, surfeit

Rassasier, va. (*etym.* re; *O.F.* assasier, *to satisfy*), to satisfy, to satiate, to sate, to load; *se —*, vr. to take one's fill

Rassemblement, sm. gathering, collection, mob

Rassembler, va. (*etym.* re, assembler), to reassemble, to collect, to call together; *se —*, vr. to reassemble, to meet, to flock, to gather

Rasseoir, va. (*etym.* re, asseoir), to reseat, to replace, to calm, to settle; *se —*, vr. to sit down again, to calm down, to settle

Rasséréner, va. (*etym.* re, *O.F.* asserener), to clear up, to restore serenity to; *se —*, vr. to clear up, to recover one's serenity

Rassis, e, adj. (*etym.* re, assis), stale, calm, settled, sedate

Rassoter, va. (*etym.* re, *O.F.* assoter), to infatuate

Rassurant, e, adj. tranquillizing, encouraging

Rassurer, va. (*etym.* re, assurer), to consolidate, to strengthen, to reassure; *se —*, vr. to take heart again, to grow more tranquil, to be reassured

Rat, sm. (*etym.* O.H.G. rato, *a rat*), rat, crotchet. ‡ *Mort aux —s*, rats' bane. *Nid à —s*, (*fig.*) dismal hole. *— de cave*, exciseman, taper. *Prendre un —*, to miss fire, to miss one's blow

Ratatiné, e, adj shrivelled, shrunken

se Ratatiner, vr (*etym.* ?), to shrink, to shrivel up

Rate, sf. (*etym.* D. rate, *honeycomb*), spleen

Râteau, sm. (*etym.* L. rastellum, *rake*), rake. *Passer au —*, to rake

Râtelier, sm. rack, set of teeth

Rater, vn. (*etym.* rat), to miss fire, to flash in the pan; —va. to miss

Ratière, sf. rat-trap

Ratifier, va. (*etym.* L.L. ratificare), to ratify

Rationalisme, sm. rationalism

‖**Rationnel, le**, adj. (*etym.* L. rationalis), rational

Rationner, va. (*etym.* ration), to put on short allowance, to stint

Ratisser, va. (*etym.* rature), to scrape, to rake

Ratissoire, sf. scraper

Raton, sm. little rat, racoon

Rattacher, va. (*etym.* attacher), to fasten up again, to tie up again, to connect; *se —*, vr. to be fastened, to be tied, to become again attached, to be connected

Ratteindre, va. (*etym.* atteindre), to retake, to overtake

Rattraper, va. (*etym.* attraper), to catch again, to retake, to overtake, to recover

Rature, sf. (*etym.* O F rater, *to erase*), word scratched out, erasure

Raturer, va. to scratch out, to erase

Rauque, adj. (*etym.* L. raucus), rough, hoarse

Ravager, va. (*etym.* ravir), to ravage, to lay waste, to plunder

Ravageur, sm. ravager, mudlark

Ravalement, sm. disparagement, rough-casting

Ravaler, va. (*etym.* avaler), to swallow again, to pull down, to disparage, to rough-cast; *se —*, vr. to debase oneself

Ravaudage, sm. mending, darning, botching

Ravauder, va. (*etym.* O.F. avander, *to strengthen*), to mend, to darn

Ravaudeuse, sf. mender of stockings

Rave, sf. (*etym.* L. rapa, *radish*), radish

†**Ravigoter**, va. (*etym.* L. vigorem; *O.F.* ravigorer), to strengthen

Ravilir, va. (*etym.* re, avilir), to debase; *se —*, vr to debase oneself

Ravin, sm., *or* **Ravine**, sf. (*etym.* L. rapina), ravine, deep hollow, torrent

Ravir, va. (*etym.* L. rapere), to ravish, to carry off, to snatch away, to enrapture, to delight. ‡ *A —*, delightfully. *Fait à —*, admirably made or shaped

se Raviser, vr. (*etym.* aviser), to alter one's mind

Ravissant, e, adj ravenous, rapacious, charming, delightful, ravishing

Ravissement, sm. rape, rapture, ravishment, ecstasy

Ravisseur, sm. ravisher, spoiler

§**Ravitaillement**, sm. revictualling

§**Ravitailler**, va. (*etym.* O.F. avitailler, *to provision*), to revictual

Raviver, va. (*etym.* aviver), to revive

Ravoir, va. to get back

Rayé, e, adj striped, rifled, streaked

Rayer, va. (*etym.* L. radiare), to stripe, to streak, to scratch, to scratch out, to rifle

Rayon, sm. (*etym.* L. radius), ray, beam, radius, circumference, spoke, furrow, shelf, honeycomb

Rayonnant, e, adj. beaming, radiant, radiating

Rayonnement, sm. radiancy, radiance, radiation

Rayonner, vn. to irradiate, to beam, to radiate

Rayure, sf. streak, stripe, rifling, groove

Réactif, ve, adj. (*etym.* L.L. reactivus), reacting, reactive. — sm. reagent

Réactionnaire, adj. (*etym.* réaction), reacting. — sm. reactionist

Réagir, vn. (*etym.* agir), to react

Réalisation, sf. realization, realizing

Réaliser, va. (*etym.* r[...]alis), to realize; *se —*, v[...] be realized

Réaliste, sm. realist

Réalité, sf. (*etym.* realitatem), reality

Réapparition, sf. (*e*[...] re, apparition), reappear[...]

Rébarbatif, ve, (*etym.* re, barbe), surly, s[...] looking

Rebâtir, va. (*etym.* bâtir), to rebuild

Rebattre, va. (*etym.* battre), to beat again, to [...] over and over again

Rebelle, adj. (*etym.* L. bellis), rebellious, stubb[...] ill-adapted. — sm. rebel

se Rebeller, vr. (*et*[...] L. rebellare), to rebel

se Rebiffer, vr. (*etym.* [...]) to kick against the pricks

Reboundi, e, adj. plu[...] chubby

Rebondir, vn. (*etym.* bondir), to rebound

Rebondissement, rebounding, rebound

Rebord, sm. (*etym.* border), ledge, brim, bor[...] hem. *— de fenêtre*, wind[...] sill

Reboucher, va. (*e*[...] re, boucher), to stop or [...] up again; *se —*, vr. t[...] stopped up again

Rebours, sm. (*etym.* [...] reburrus, *bristling*), w[...] way, wrong side, reve[...] contrary. ‡ *A —, au — de*, wrong way. *Prendre [...] au —*, to misconstrue ev[...]thing. *Les esprits à —*, cr[...]grained wits. *—, —e*, cross-grained

Rebouteur, sm. (*e*[...] re, bouter), bone-setter

Rebrousse-poil, loc. [...] against the grain

Rebrousser, va.n. (*e*[...] see Brosse; *O.F.* rebros[...] to turn back, to turn [...] *— chemin, — en arrière*, go back

Rebrunir, va. (*etym* [...] brunir), to burnish agai[...]

Rebuffade, sf. (*etym.* [...] rabbuffo, *rebuff*), rebuff, [re]pulse

Rebut, sm. (*etym.* rebu[...] rebuff, refusal, refuse, [rub]bish. ‡ *Mettre au —*, to th[row] aside. *Mettre une lettre au —*, to send a letter to dead-letter office

Rebutant, e, adj re[pul]sive, displeasing

Rebuter, va. (*etym.* buter), to repel, to rebu[ff] refuse, to dishearten; *s*[...] vr. to be disheartened

Recacheter, va. (*e*[...] re, cacheter), to reseal, t[...] wafer

Récalcitrant, e, (*etym.* L. recalcitrantem [re]fractory, froward

Récalcitrer, vn. (*e*[...] L. recalcitrare), to kick

Récapituler, va. (*e*[...] L.L. recapitulare), to re[capi]tulate

Recarder, va. to card [...]

el, sm. receiving of stolen
élement, sm. conceal-
éler, va. (*etym.* re,), to receive stolen goods, bezzle, to conceal
éleur, se, s. receiver len goods
ensement, sm. cen- return, statement, verifi- n
enser, va. (*etym.* re, r), to take the census of
rent, e, adj. (*etym.* *L.* tem), recent, new, fresh,
épissé, sm. (*L. word*), pt
ette, sf. (*etym.* *L.* re-), receipt, receivership, er's office, recipe
evable, adj. receiv- admissible
ceveur, sm. receiver
cevoir, va. (*etym.* *L.* are), to receive, to ac- to admit, to harbour
change, sm. (*etym.* re, er), a change, spare , spare stores, re-ex- e. *Habits de* —, a change thes
chapper, va. (*etym.* re, per), to escape, to re- ¦ *Un réchappé de po-* a gallows-bird
chargement, sm. re- ng, reloading
charger, va. (*etym.* re, er), to reload, to charge
chaud, sm. (*etym.* re, er), chafing-dish
chauffé, sm. warmed ish *or* dinner, a mere tion
chauffer, va. (*etym.* chauffer), to warm, to again, to give new life e —, vr. to warm one- o grow warm again
che, adj. (*etym.* *G.* , *rough*), rough, sour
cherche, sf. search, , pursuit, (*plur.*) re- es, inquiries, wooing, courtship, studied ele- , refinement
cherché, e, adj. choice, d, affected, far-fetched, ously elegant, in great st
chercher, va. (*etym.* chercher), to seek again, ok again for, to search to investigate, to seek to court, to finish off; , vr. to seek each other's any
chigné, e, adj. sour- , surly-looking, sulky
chigner, va. (*etym.*), to look surly, to sulk
chute, sf. (*etym.* re-), second fall, relapse. *e une* —, to have a re-
cidive, sf. (*etym.* *L.* re- us), relapse, second of- . *Il y a* —, this is not first offence
cidiver, vn. to repeat offence

Récif, Rescif, sm. (*etym.* *Port.* recife), reef *or* ridge of rocks
Récipé, sm. (*Latin word*), recipe
Récipiendaire, sm. (*etym.* *L.L.* recipiendarius), new member
Récipient, sm. (*etym.* *L.* recipientem), recipient, receiver, well, cistern
Réciprocité, sf. (*etym.* *L.* reciprocitatem), reciprocity
Réciproque, adj. (*etym.* *L.* reciprocus), reciprocal, mutual. — sm. the same thing. — sf. converse, reciprocal
Récit, sm. recital, narration, relation, story, recitative
Récitant, e, adj. (*mus.*) solo
Récitatif, sm. recitative, recitativo
Réciter, va. (*etym.* *L.* recitare), to recite, to rehearse, to repeat, to relate, to sing *or* play a recitative
Réclamation, sf. (*etym.* *L.* reclamationem), demand, claim, objection, complaint
Réclame, sf. catch-word, puff, advertisement. — sm. call (of birds)
Réclamer, va. (*etym.* *L.* reclamare), to entreat, to implore, to claim, to claim back, to call; — vn. to object, to complain; *se* —, vr. to make use of one's name
Reclus, e, adj. s. (*etym.* *L.* reclusus), sequestered, shut up, recluse
Réclusion, sf. confinement, reclusion. *A la peine de la* —, to solitary confinement
Recoin, sm. (*etym.* re, coin), nook, corner
Recoller, va. (*etym.* re, coller), to paste again, to glue again
Récollet, sm. (*etym.* *L.* recollectus), Franciscan
Récolte, sf. (*etym.* *I.* raccolta), crop, harvest
Récolter, va. to reap, to gather in
Recommandable, adj. respectable, commendable
Recommandation, sf. recommendation, reference, detainer. ¦ *Avoir en* —, to hold in high esteem
Recommander, va. (*etym.* re, commander), to recommend, to commend, to request, to beg, to lodge a detainer against; *se* —, vr. to recommend oneself, to implore the protection
Recommencer, va.n. (*etym.* re, commencer), to begin again, to recommence
Récompense, sf. reward, requital, recompense, compensation
Récompenser, va. (*etym.* re, compenser), to reward, to requite, to recompense, to make amends; *se* —, vr. to make up for it
Recomposer, va. (*etym.* re, composer), to recompose

Recompter, va. (*etym.* re, compter), to count over again
Réconciliable, adj. reconcilable
Réconcilier, va. (*etym.* *L.* reconciliare), to reconcile; *se* —, vr. to be reconciled
Reconduire, va. (*etym.* re, conduire), to reconduct, to take again, to take back, to go back with
Réconforter, va. (*etym.* re, conforter), to refresh, to exhilarate, to comfort; *se* —, vr. to take some refreshment
Reconnaissable, adj. recognizable
Reconnaissance, sf. recognition, discovery, review, examination, reconnoitring, acknowledgment, gratitude, recognizance. ¦ *Aller en* —, *faire une* —, to go out reconnoitring. *Envoyer en* —, to send out a reconnoitring party
Reconnaissant, e, adj. grateful, thankful
Reconnaître, va. (*etym.* re, connaître), to recognize, to know again, to discover, to acknowledge, to explore, to visit, to reconnoitre, to challenge, to be grateful for
Reconquérir, va. (*etym.* re, conquérir), to reconquer
Reconstituer, va. (*etym.* re, constituer), to reconstitute
Reconstruction, sf. (*etym.* re, construction), rebuilding
Reconstruire, va. (*etym.* re, construire), to build up again, to rebuild
Reconvention, sf. (*etym.* re, convention), cross demand
Recopier, va. (*etym.* re, copier), to copy out again, to recopy
Recorder, va. (*etym.* *L.* recordari), to rehearse; *se* —, vr. to rehearse to oneself, to concert
Recors, sm. (*etym.* recorder), bailiff's man
Recoucher, va. (*etym.* re, coucher), to put to bed again, to lay down again; *se* —, vr. to go to bed again
Recoupe, sf. stone-chips, pollen
Recouper, va.n. (*etym.* re, couper), to cut again
Recourber, va. (*etym.* re, courber), to bend, to bend round; *se* —, vr. to be curved *or* bent
Recourir, vn. (*etym.* re, courir), to run again, to run back again, to have recourse, to take refuge
Recours, sm. recourse, resource, relief, refuge, appeal. ¦ — *en cassation*, appeal to the supreme court. — *en grâces*, petition for mercy
Recouvrable, adj. recoverable
Recouvrance, sf. recovery
Recouvrement, sm. recovery, getting back, outstanding debts, lap, cap. *A* —, capped
Recouvrer, va. (*etym.* *L.* recuperare), to recover
Recouvrir, va. (*etym.* re, couvrir), to cover up again, to cover over, to cloak, to mask
Récréance, sf. provisional possession. *Lettres de* —, letters of recall
Récréatif, ve, adj. recreative
Récréation, sf. recreation, refreshment, play, play-time. *Cour de* —, play-ground. *En* —, at play. *Pendant la* —, during play-hours
Recréer, va. (*etym.* re, créer), to recreate, to create anew
Récréer, va. (*etym.* *L.* recreare), to divert, to refresh, to recreate, to exhilarate, to gladden; *se* —, vr. to take some diversion, to find some refreshment
Recrépir, va. (*etym.* re, crépir), to plaster over
se Récrier, vr. (*etym.* re, écrier), to cry out loudly, to express one's admiration
Récriminatoire, adj. recriminating
Récriminer, vn. (*etym.* re; *L.* criminari), to recriminate
Récrire, va. (*etym.* re, écrire), to write again
§**se Recroqueviller,** vr. (*etym.* ?), *also* **se Recoquiller,** vr. (*etym.* re, coquille), to curl up, to shrivel up
Recru, e, adj. (*etym.* *O.F.* recroire), tired out, knocked up
Recrue, sf. (*etym.* recroître), addition, recruit
Recrutement, sm. recruiting
Recruter, va. (*etym.* recrue), to recruit; *se* —, vr. to recruit
Recruteur, sm. recruiter, recruiting officer
Rectangle, adj. (*etym.* *L.L.* rectiangulus), rectangular, right-angled. — sm. rectangle
Rectangulaire, adj. rectangular
Recteur, sm. (*etym.* *L.* rector), rector
Rectifier, va. (*etym.* *L.* rectificare), to rectify
§**Rectiligne,** adj. (*etym.* *L.* rectilineus), rectilineal, rectilinear
Recto, sm. (*Latin word*), first page, right side
Rectorat, sm. rectorship
Reçu, e, adj. customary, usual, in use, allowed. — sm. receipt. *Au — de*, on receipt of
§**Recueil,** sm. collection
§**Recueillement,** sm. collectedness, serious thought, meditation
§**Recueillir,** va. (*etym.* *L.* recolligere), to collect, to gather in, to reap, to acquire, to receive, to listen to; *se* —, vr. to collect one's thoughts, to reflect, to commune with oneself

Recuire, va.n. (*etym.* re, cuire), to cook over again

Recuit, sm., **Recuite**, sf. annealing, rebeating, baking

Recul, sm. recoil

Reculade, sf. backing, retreat, falling back

Reculé, e, adj. remote, far-distant, backward

Reculer, va. (*etym.* cul), to move back, to draw back, to back; — vn. to fall back, to go back, to recede, to start back, to recoil, to shrink; *se* —, vr. to go back, to fall back, to go further back

Reculons (à), adv. backwards

Récupérer, va. (*etym. L.* recuperare), to recover, to retrieve; *se* —, vr. to retrieve one's losses

Récurer, va. (*etym.* re, écurer), to scour over again

Récusable, adj. (*etym. L.* recusabilis), exceptionable, liable to challenge

Récusation, sf. (*etym. L.* recusationem), challenge, exception

Récuser, va. (*etym. L.* recusare), to challenge, to except to; *se* —, vr. to excuse oneself, to decline pronouncing, judging, voting, &c., to draw off

Rédacteur, sm. (*etym. L.L.* redactor), writer, author, editor. — *en chef*, chief editor

Rédaction, sf. (*etym. L.L.* redactionem), drawing up, wording, editorship, the editors, editor's office

Reddition, sf. (*etym. L.* redditionem), surrender, giving in

Redemander, va. (*etym.* re, demander), to ask again

Rédempteur, sm. (*etym. L.* redemptor), Redeemer

Redescendre, va.n. (*etym.* re, descendre), to come down again, to bring down again

Redevable, adj. (*etym.* redevoir), in the debt of, indebted

Redevance, sf. rent, fine, tenure

Redevenir, vn. (*etym.* re, devenir), to become again

Redevoir, va. (*etym.* re, devoir), to owe still

Rédhibitoire, adj. (*etym. L.* redhibitorius), redhibitory

Rédiger, va. (*etym. L.* redigere), to draw up, to edit, to word, to write

Redimer, va. (*etym. L.* redimere), to redeem

Redingote, sf. (*etym. E.* riding, coat), frock-coat, surtout

Redire, va. (*etym.* re, dire), to repeat, to say again, to tell again, to find fault. ‡ *Trouver à* —, to find fault

Redite, sf. repetition

Redondance, sf. (*etym. L.* redundantia), redundancy

Redondant, e, adj. (*etym. L.* redundare), redundant

Redonner, va. (*etym.* re, donner), to give again, to restore; — vn. to charge again, to begin again, to fall again; *se* —, vr. to return

Redoublé, e, adj. redoubled, increased, repeated, double quick

Redoublement, sm. increase, reduplication, paroxysm

Redoubler, va.n. (*etym.* re, doubler), to redouble, to increase, to new-line

Redoute, sf. (*etym. I.* ridotto), redoubt

Redouter, va. (*etym.* re, douter), to dread, to fear

Redressement, sm. redress, straightening, righting

Redresser, va. (*etym.* re, dresser), to straighten, to make straight, to set upright, to right, to redress, to correct; *se* —, vr. to become straight again, to stand erect, to sit up again, to draw oneself up, to be redressed

Redresseur, sm. redresser, righter

Réductible, adj. (*etym. L.L.* reductibilis), reducible

Réduire, va. (*etym. L.* reducere), to reduce, to convert, to grind, to boil down, to compel; *se* —, vr. to be reduced, to dwindle away, to amount, to be summed up, to confine oneself, to be brought under

Réduit, sm. habitation, retreat, nook

Réduplicatif, ve, adj. am. (*etym. L.L.* reduplicativus), reduplicative

§**Réel, le**, adj. (*etym. L.L.* realis), real, genuine

Réélire, va. (*etym.* re, élire), to re-elect

Refaire, va. (*etym.* re, faire), to do again, to make again, to do up, to have a new deal, to revive; *se* —, vr. to recruit one's strength, to retrieve one's losses

Réfection, sf. (*etym. L.* refectionem), repairs, refection

Réfectoire, sm. (*etym. L.L.* refectorium), dining-hall, refectory

Référé, sm. plea of urgency

Référendaire, sm. (*etym. L.L.* referendarius), referendary

Référer, va. (*etym. L.* referre), to refer, to ascribe; (*en*) — vn. to refer; — (*à*), to report; *se* —, vr. to refer, to relate, to trust

Refermer, va. (*etym.* re, fermer), to shut again; *se* —, vr. to close again, to be closed

Réfléchi, e, past part. adj. reflected, deliberate, well-pondered, thinking, guarded

Réfléchir, va. (*etym. L.* reflectere), to reflect back, to reflect, to throw back; — vn. to be reflected, to reflect, to ponder, to think; *se* —, vr. to be reflected

Réfléchissement, sm. reflection

Réflecteur, sm. (*etym. L.* reflectorem), reflector. — adj. reflective

Reflet, sm. reflection, reflex

Refléter, va.n. (*etym. L.* reflectere), to reflect; *se* —, vr. to be reflected back

Refleurir, vn. (*etym.* re, fleurir), to flower anew, to blossom again, to flourish again

Réflexibilité, sf. reflexibility

Réflexion, sf. (*etym. L.* reflexionem), reflection, consideration, thought. ‡ *Toute* — *faite*, all things considered

Refluer, vn. (*etym. L.* refluere), to ebb, to flow back

Reflux, sm. (*etym.* re, flux), ebb

Refondre, va. (*etym.* re, fondre), to melt down, to cast again, to remould, to recoin; *se* —, vr. to reform

Refonte, sf. recasting, remoulding, recoining

Réformateur, sm. (*etym. L.* reformator), reformer

Réforme, sf. reform, reduction, half-pay, invaliding. *Traitement de* —, half-pay. *Congé de* —, invaliding

Réformé, e, adj. reformed. *Les* —*s*, the Protestants

Reformer, vn., *se* —, vr. (*etym. L.* reformare), to form again

Réformer, va. to reform, to put on half-pay, to invalid, to sell off, to restamp, to reverse; *se* —, vr. to reform, to amend

¶**Réformiste**, sm. reformist

Refoulement, sm. driving back

Refouler, va. (*etym.* re, fouler), to drive back, to force back, to ram. *La mer refoule*, the tide ebbs

Refouloir, sm. rammer, gun-stick

Réfractaire, adj. (*etym. L.* refractarius), refractory, stubborn. — sm. runaway conscript

Réfracter, va. (*etym. L.L.* refractare), to refract, to break; *se* —, vr. to be refracted

Réfractif, ve, adj. (*etym. L.* refractivus), refractive

Refrain, sm. (*etym. O.F.* refraindre, *to break*), chorus, burden

Réfrangibilité, sf. (*etym.* réfrangible), refrangibility

Refréner, va. (*etym. L.* refrenare), to curb, to bridle

Réfringent, e, adj. (*etym. L.* refringentem), refracting

§**Refrogné, e, Renfrogné, e**, adj. frowning, surly, scowling

§**Refrognement, Renfrognement**, sm. frowning, frown, scowl

§**se Refrogner, se Renfrogner**, vr. (*etym.* ?), to frown, to knit one's brows, to scowl

Refroidir, va. (*etym.* re, froid), to cool, to chill, to make cold; — vn., *se* —, vr. to grow cool, to cool, to grow chilly, to catch cold

Refroidissement, sm. cooling, chilliness, refrigeration, cold

Réfugié, sm. refugee

se Réfugier, vr. (*etym.* refuge), to take refuge, to seek a shelter

Refus, sm. refusal, denial, thing refused, (*hunt.*) three-year-old

Refuser, va. (*etym. L.L.* refutiare), to refuse, to deny; *se* —, vr. to deny oneself, to grudge oneself, to object

Réfuter, va. (*etym. L.* refutare), to refute, to confute

§**Regagner**, va. (*etym.* re, gagner), to recover, to regain, to win back, (*nav.*) to get the weathergauge, to get back to, to reach

Regain, sm. (*etym.* re; *O.F.* gain = grass), aftermath; (*etym.* regagner), revival

Régal, sm. feast, treat, entertainment

Régalant, e, adj. pleasant

Régale, sf. (*etym. L.* regalis), royal privilege (of appropriating the revenues of vacant bishoprics). — adj. *L. Eau* —, aqua regalis

Régaler, va. (*etym. Sp.* regalar), to treat; *se* —, vr. to treat oneself, to feast, to enjoy oneself

Regard, sm. look, glance, frown, (*plur.*) eyes, attention, notice, aspect, draught-hole. *En* —, opposite

Regardant, sm. looker-on, beholder. ‡ — e, adj. particular, stingy, saving

Regarder, va. (*etym.* re, garder), to look at, to look on, to consider, to face, to front, to look out upon, to concern; — vn. to look, to mind. ‡ — *de près*, to look narrowly to a thing, to be very particular about a thing. ‡ *Y* — *à deux fois*, to look twice at a thing. *Se* —, vr. to look at oneself, to look at each other, to look upon oneself, to be looked at, to face each other

Régate, sf. (*etym. I.* regatta), regatta

Régence, sf. (*etym. L.* rego), regency

Régénérateur, trice, s. adj. (*etym. L.L.* regenerator), regenerator, regenerating

Régénérer, va. (*etym. L.* regenerare), to regenerate; *se* —, vr. to be regenerated

Régenter, va. (*etym.* régent), to govern, to lord it over

Régie, sf. (*etym.* régir), administration, excise, excise-office. *Employé de la* —, clerk of the excise

Regimber, vn. (*etym.* ?), to kick

Régime, sm. (*etym. L.* regimen), regimen, government, diet, system, rules, object

‡ *Se mettre au* —, to observe a regimen. *Être au* —, to be on low diet

Régimentaire, adj. (*etym.* régiment), regimental

Régir, va. (*etym. L.* regere), to rule, to govern, to manage

Régisseur, sm. (*etym.* régir), steward, manager, stage-director

Registre, sm. (*etym. L.L.* registrum, regestrum = regestum, *a journal*), register, account-books, damper, register-stove, valve. *Tenir* — *de*, to keep an account of

Règle, sf. (*etym. L.* regula), ruler, rule, regularity, pattern, guide, sum. — *mobile*, sliding rule. ‡ *Repas en* —, well-ordered repast. *En* —, in right order, regular, in due form

§**Réglé, e,** adj. regular, punctual

Règlement, sm. regulations, settlement, settling

Réglementaire, adj. concerning regulations

Réglementer, va. to make regulations

Régler, va. (*etym. L.* regulare), to rule, to regulate, to order, to settle; *se* —, vr. to be regulated, to take pattern, to be guided

Réglisse, sf. (*etym. Sp.* regaliz, *liquorice*), liquorice. *Jus de* —, Spanish liquorice

§**Régnant, e,** adj. prevailing, reigning, prevalent

§**Règne,** sm. (*etym. L.* regnum), reign, prevalence

§**Régner,** vn. (*etym. L.* regnare), to reign, to rule, to be prevalent, to reach, to extend

§**Régnicole,** sm. (*etym. L.* regnicola), native

Regonfler, va.n. (*etym.* re, gonfler), to swell, to rise

Regorgement, sm. overflowing

Regorger, vn. (*etym.* re, gorge), to overflow, to wallow, to be plentiful

Regrat, sm. huckstering, huckster's wares, retail licence for salt

Regratter, va.n. (*etym.* re, gratter), to scratch *or* scrape again, to bargain

Regrattier, ère, s. huckster, salesman, saleswoman

Regrettable, adj. much to be regretted

Regretter, va. (*etym. O.F.* regreter; *etym.* re, greter, *to pity*), to regret, to be sorry

Régularisation, sf. putting in order, setting right, regularity

Régulariser, va. (*etym. L.* regularis), to make regular, to set right

Régularité, sf. (*etym. L.* regularitatem), regularity

Régularisateur, trice, *or* **Régulateur, trice,** s. standard, regulator

§**Régulier, ère,** adj. (*etym. L.* regularis), regular, agreeable to rule, right

Réhabiliter, va. (*etym.* re, habiliter), to rehabilitate, to reverse, to reinstate; *se* —, vr. to rise again

Rehaussement, sm. raising, increased value

Rehausser, va. (*etym.* re, hausser), to raise, to raise higher, to relieve, to set off, to enhance, to extol; *se* —, vr. to raise oneself in public esteem

Réimporter, va. (*etym.* re, importer), to re-import

Réimposer, va. (*etym.* re, imposer), to impose *or* assess again

Réimposition, sf. further assessment, re-imposition

Réimpression, sf. (*etym.* re, impression), reprint, reprinting

Réimprimer, va. (*etym.* re, imprimer), to reprint

Rein, sm. (*etym. L.* ren), kidney, the loins. ‡ *La chûte des* —*s*, the small of the back. *A force de* —*s*, by main strength

Reine, sf. (*etym. L.* regina), queen. *Un port de* —, a queenly bearing

Reine-Claude, sf. greengage (plum)

Reinette, sf. pippin, rennet

Réintégration, sf. (*etym. L.* redintegrationem), reinstating

Réintégrer, va. (*etym. L.* redintegrare), to reinstate

Réitérer, va. (*etym. L.* reiterare), to reiterate

Reître, sm. (*etym. G.* reiter, *horseman*), German trooper, fox

§**Rejaillir,** vn. (*etym.* re, jaillir), to gush out, to spring up, to flash, to fly off, to be reflected

§**Rejaillissement,** sm. gushing, spirting, breaking, flashing, rebounding, reflection

Rejet, sm. rejection, carrying, running into the next verse, shoot of a tree

Rejeter, va. (*etym. L.* rejectare), to throw again, to throw back, to throw away, to throw out, to shoot, to reject, to refuse; *se* —, vr. to fall back

Rejeton, sm. shoot, sprout, scion

Rejoindre, va. (*etym.* re, joindre), to rejoin, to overtake; *se* —, vr. to reunite, to be joined, to join each other, to meet again

Rejointoyer, va. (*etym.* re, joint), to rejoint, to point the joints of

Réjoui, e, adj. s. jovial, cheerful, jovial fellow, buxom dame, bouncing lass

Réjouir, va. (*etym.* re, jouir), to gladden, to cheer, to rejoice, to divert; *se* —, vr. to rejoice, to be delighted, to enjoy oneself

Réjouissance, sf. rejoicing, (†) makeweight (bones), coarse meat

Réjouissant, e, adj. diverting

Relâche, sm. respite, relaxation, intermission, rest, (*theat.*) no performance. — sf. stay, harbour

Relâché, e, adj. loose, lax, remiss

Relâchement, sm. slackening, loosening, looseness, mildness, remissness, relaxation

Relâcher, va. (*etym. L.* relaxare), to slacken, to loosen, to relax, to release, to enlarge, to forego a part, (*nav.*) to put into, to make a stay at; *se* —, vr. to grow loose, to slacken, to grow milder, to grow remiss, to take some rest, to make some abatement

Relais, sm. (*etym. see* RELAYER), relay, fresh horses, stage, derelict land

Relancer, va. (*etym.* re, lancer), to start anew, to follow, to beset, to snub

Relaps, e, adj. (*etym. L.* relapsus), relapsed

Relater, va. (*etym. L.L.* relatare), to relate

§**Relatif, ve,** adj. (*etym. L.* relativus), relative

Relaxer, va. (*etym. L.* relaxare), to relax, to enlarge, to release

Relayer, va.n. (*etym.* re; *O.F.* layer = to cease, to stop), to relieve, to change horses; *se* —, vr. to relieve one another

Reléguer, va. (*etym. L.* relegare), to banish, to confine, to send off, to consign; *se* —, vr. to shut oneself up, to confine oneself, to be consigned

§**Relevailles,** sf. plur. (*etym.* relever), churching. *Faire ses* —*s*, to be churched

Relevé, e, adj. exalted, high, lofty, pungent. — sm. statement, return, abstract. *Faire le* — *de*, to draw up an account of

Relevée, sf. afternoon

Relèvement, sm. raising, account, abstract, (*nav.*) bearing

Relever, va. to raise up again, to set up again, to pick up, to set afloat, to weigh again, to take the bearings of, to draw up, to give a relish to, to set off, to relieve, to point out, to criticise, to take up, (*nav.*) to set, to recover (the scent); — vn. to turn up, to raise one's feet, to be held, to depend, to be amenable, to recover. — *de couches*, to have just been confined. *Se* —, vr. to rise again, to stand up, to right, to get over, to retrieve, to relieve each other

Relief, sm. (*etym.* relever), relief, relievo, embossment, lustre, consideration, (*plur.*) fragments, remnants. *Donner du* — à, to serve as a foil to, to give lustre *or* consideration to

Relier, va. (*etym. L.* religare), to bind anew, to bind, to hoop

Relieur, sm. binder, bookbinder

§**Religieux, se,** adj. (*etym. L.* religiosus), religious, strict, scrupulous. — s. friar, monk nun

Religion, sf. (*etym. L.* religionem), religion. ‡ *Entrer en* —, to take the cowl *or* the veil. *Mettre en* —, to make a nun. *Ceux de la* — (*réformée*), the Protestants. *Surprendre la* — *de*, to deceive

Religionnaire, sm. Protestant

Reliquaire, sm. (*etym.* relique), reliquary

Reliquat, sm. (*etym. L.* reliquatum), balance, remains

Relique, sf. (*etym. L.* reliquiae), relic

Relire, va. (*etym.* re, lire), to read again

Reliure, sf. binding

Reluire, vn. (*etym. L.* relucere), to shine, to glitter, to gleam

Reluisant, e, adj. glittering, shining

‡**Reluquer,** va. (*etym.* ?), to ogle, to leer at, to have an eye upon

Remaniement, sm. doing over again, handling again, altering, alterations, (*print.*) over-running

Remanier, va. (*etym.* re, manier), to handle anew, to do over again, to mend, to repair, (*print.*) to over-run

Remarier, va. (*etym.* re, marier), to marry again; *se* —, vr. to marry again, to get married again

§**Remarquable,** adj. remarkable, worthy of note

Remarque, sf. remark

Remarquer, va. (*etym.* re, marquer), to remark, to notice, to note; *se* —, vr. to be remarked

Remballer, va. (*etym.* re, emballer), to pack up again

Rembarquement, sm. re-embarkation

Rembarquer, va. (*etym.* re, embarquer), to re-embark; *se* —, vr. to re-embark

Rembarrer, va. (*etym.* re, *O.F.* embarrer = *F.* barrer), to snub, to repel

Remblai, sm. filling up, embankment, bank. *Terre de* —, earth brought from other places

Remblayer, va. (*etym.* re, *O.F.* emblayer), to fill up, to embank

Remboîter, va. (*etym.* re, emboîter), to fit in again, to set

Rembourrer, va. (*etym.* bourre), to stuff

Remboursable, adj. payable

Remboursement, sm. reimbursement. *Faire suivre en* —, to charge forward

Rembourser, va. (*etym.* re, bourse), to reimburse, to pocket ; *se* —, vr. to reimburse oneself

Rembruni, e, adj. gloomy

Rembrunir, va. (*etym.* brun), to make browner, to cast a gloom over, to darken ; *se* —, vr. to grow browner, gloomy, to darken, to begin to lower

Remède, sm. (*etym. L.* remedium), remedy, cure, clyster

Remédier, vn. (*etym. L.* remediare), to remedy, to cure, to repair

se Remémorer, vr. (*etm. L.* rememorari), to remember

Remercier, va. (*etym.* merci), to thank, to give thanks, to decline the offer of, to desire to be excused, to dismiss

Remerciement, Remercîment, sm. thanks

Réméré, sm. (*etym. ?*), redemption. *A* —, with faculty of redemption

Remettre, va. (*etym.* re, mettre), to put back, to put up again, to put down again, to restore, to set, to recover, to bring round again, to soothe, to calm, to deliver, to give, to send, to remit, to resign, to defer, to reconcile, to recollect ; *se* —, vr. to go back, to sit down again, to begin to, to apply oneself again, to recollect, to be reconciled, to recover, to surrender, to commit oneself

Remise, sf. (*etym.* remettre), delivery, remittance, release, remission, commission, discount, delay, fine, coach-house, shelter, lighting-place. *Faire une* —, to allow a commission, a discount. ‡ *Voiture de* —, job-carriage. *Loueur de voitures de* —, keeper of livery stables. — sm. hired carriage

Remiser, va. to put in the coach-house

Remonte, sf. (*etym.* remonter), remounting. *Chevaux de* —, new horses

Remonter, vn. (*etym.* re, monter), to reascend, to go up again, to get up again, to go back, to rise ; — va. to reascend, to go up again, to toil up again, to take up again, to raise, to new-stock, to remount, to new-mount, to wind up, to revive ; *se* —, vr. to be wound up, to take in a fresh supply (of)

Remontrance, sf. remonstrance

Remontrer, va. (*etym.* re, montrer), to show again ; — vn. to teach. ‡ *En* — *à*, to show a trick to. *Se* —, vr. to show one's face again

Remords, sm. (*etym.* re, mordre), remorse, compunction

Remorquage, sm. towing, dragging

Remorque, sf. (*O.F.* remolque ; *etym. L.* remulcum, towing-cable), towing, dragging, tow-rope. *Câble de* —, tow-rope. *A la* —, in tow

Remorquer, va. to tow, to drag along

Remorqueur, sm. tug tow-boat, steam-tug

Remoudre, va. (*etym.* re, moudre), to grind again

Remoulade, sf. remoulade-sauce

Remouleur, sm. (*etym.* remoudre), knife-grinder

Remous, sm. (*etym.* remoudre), eddy, eddy-water

§**Rempailler**, va. (*etym.* paille), to new-bottom

§**Rempailleur, se**, s. chair-mender

Rempart, sm. (*etym.* remparer), rampart, bulwark

Remplaçant, sm. substitute

Remplacement, sm. supplying the place, substitution, reinvestment

Remplacer, va. (*etym.* re, placer), to supply the place of, to succeed, to reinvest ; *se* —, vr. to succeed each other, to take in a new stock

Remplir, va. (*etym.* re, emplir), to replenish, to fill again, to stock, to furnish, to complete, to make up, to crowd, to throng, to fill, to hold, to fulfil, to perform, to refund ; *se* —, vr. to fill, to be filled, to be thronged, to fill oneself

Rempli, e, adj. filled, full, fraught, fulfilled

Remplissage, sm. filling, filling in, rubbish, middle harmony

Remplisseuse, sf. filler in

Remplumer, va. (*etym.* plume), to new-feather ; *se* —, vr. to get new feathers, to get stout again, to get rich again

Remporter, va. to take back, to carry back, to carry away, to bear, to gain, to win

Remuant, e, adj. stirring, bustling, active, fidgety, restless

Remue-ménage, sm. rummage, stir, disturbance

Remuement, sm. stir, stirring, movement

Remuer, va.n. (*etym.* re, muer), to move, to stir, to shake, to rummage ; *se* —, vr. to move, to stir, to bustle about

Rémunérateur, trice, s. adj. (*etym. L.* remunerator), remunerator, remunerating

Rémunérer, va. (*etym. L.* remunerare), to remunerate

Renâcler, vn. (*etym. ?*), to snort, to turn up one's nose at

Renaissance, sf. new birth, regeneration, revival

Renaissant, e, adj. reviving, springing up afresh, returning

Renaître, vn. (*etym.* re, naître), to be born again, to grow again, to revive, to be restored

Renard, sm. (*etym. G.* reginhart, *cunning, cruel*), fox

Renardeau, sm. fox's cub

Renchéri, e, adj. dainty, particular. ‡ *Faire le* —, to give oneself airs

Renchérir, va. (*etym.* re, enchérir), to raise the price of ; — vn. to rise in price, to improve on

Renchérissement, sm. rise in price

Rencontre, sf. meeting, clash, shock, rencounter, encounter, chance. ‡ *Marchandises de* —, second-hand goods. *Roue de* —, balance-wheel

Rencontrer, va. (*etym.* re, *O.F.* encoutrer), to meet, to encounter, to find, to stumble on ; *se* —, vr. to meet each other, to agree, to coincide, to be found. ‡ *Les beaux esprits se rencontrent*, wits jump together

Rendement, sm. (*etym.* rendre), produce

Rendez-vous, sm. appointment, rendezvous, time of meeting, place of meeting, meet. ‡ *Donner un* — *à*, to make an appointment with. *Se donner* —, *prendre* —, to make an appointment

Rendormir, va. (*etym.* re, endormir), to lull to sleep again ; *se* —, vr. to go to sleep again

Rendre, va. (*etym. L.L.* rendere = reddere) to make, to render, to return, to restore, to deliver, to yield, to bear, to be lucrative, to evacuate, to eject, to express, to reproduce, to give, to issue ; — vn to lead ; *se* —, vr. to go, to repair, to come, to resort, to lead to, to render oneself, to become, to yield, to surrender

Rendu, e, past part. adj. delivered, roughly spent, arrived

Rêne, sf. (*etym. I.* redina, *rein*), rein

Renégat, sm. (*etym. I.* rinnegato), renegade

Renfermé, sm. close smell, musty smell. ‡ *Sentir le* —, to smell close

Renfermer, va. (*etym.* re, enfermer), to shut up, to immure, to confine, to include, to contain, to hold ; *se* —, vr. to shut, to be shut again, to shut oneself up again, to confine oneself, to retire

Renflé, e, adj. swelling, inflated

Renflement, sm. swelling

Renfler, vn. (*etym.* re, enfler), to swell, to swell again

Renfoncement, sm. knock, hollow, cavity, recess, background

Renfoncer, va. (*etym.* re, enfoncer), to knock, (*print.*) to indent

Renforcement, sm. reinforcement, strengthening

Renforcer, va. (*etym.* force), to strengthen, to reinforce ; *se* —, vr. to gather strength, to be reinforced

Renfort, sm. reinforcement, help. *Cheval de* —, additional horse

Rengagement, sm. re-engagement, reenlistment

Rengager, va., *se* —, vr. (*etym.* re, engager), to reengage, to reenlist

Rengainer, va. (*etym.* re, engainer), to sheathe, to put up, to pocket

se Rengorger, vr. (*etym.* re, engorger), to bridle up, to carry it high

Reniable, adj. deniable

Reniement, sm. denial

Renier, va. (*etym.* re, nier) to deny, to disown, to blaspheme. ‡ *Un renié*, a recreant

Reniflement, sm. snivel, sniffing

Renifler, vn. (*etym.* re, *O.F.* nifler, *from L.G.* nif, *nose*), to snivel, to sniff, to turn up one's nose at

Renne, sm. (*etym. Swed.* ren, *reindeer*), reindeer

Renom, sm. renown

Renommé, e, adj. renowned, famous

Renommée, sf. renown, fame, public rumour

Renommer, va. (*etym.* re, nommer), to rename, to reelect, to reappoint, to celebrate ; *se* —, vr. to make use of the name

Renonce, sf. (having) no card of the colour, revoke. ‡ *Faire une* —, to revoke

Renoncement, sm. renouncement

Renoncer, va.n. (*etym. L.* renunciare), to renounce, to give up, to disclaim, to disown

Renonciation, sf. (*etym. L.* renunciationem), renunciation

Renoncule, sf. (*etym. L.* ranunculus), ranunculus, crowfoot

Renouer, va. (*etym.* re, nouer), to tie again, to put together, to renew, to resume ; *se* —, vr. to be renewed

Renouveler, va. (*etym. L.L.* renovellare), to renovate, to renew, to revive ; *se* —, vr. to be renewed, to be revived, to change

Renouvellement, sm. renewal, revival

§**Renseignement**, sm. information, intelligence, reference. ‡ *A titre de* —, merely for information' sake. *Aller aux* —*s*, *prendre des* —*s*, to make inquiries

§**Renseigner**, va. (*etym.* re, enseigner), to teach anew to give information, to direct ; *se* —, vr. to make inquiries

Rente, sf. (*etym.* rendre), income, annuity, funds, profit. ‡ *Vivre de ses* —*s*, to have an independent income. *Faire une* — *à*, to allow a pension to

Renter, va. to endow

Rentier, ère, s. independent person

Rentoiler, va. (*etym.* re toile), to put new linen to, to new-canvas

Rentrant, pres.part.m. reentering. — sm. new player

Rentrée, sf. reentrance, reentering, reopening, reappearance, return, gathering in, housing

Rentrer, vn. (*etym.* re, entrer), to reenter, to go in again, to come in again, to go home, to return, to resume, to reopen, to reappear; — va. to house, to take *or* carry in, to gather in, to garner, to indent

Renverse (à la), loc. adv. on one's back, backwards

Renversé, e, past part. adj. overthrown, upset, blown down, inverted, reversed. ¦ *Figure* —*e*, discomposed features

Renversement, sm. upsetting, throwing down, overthrow, derangement, inversion, reversion

Renverser, va. (*etym.* re, envers), to throw down, to overthrow, to upset, to knock down, to invert, to reverse, to shift; *se* —, vr. to fall back, to throw oneself back, to throw each other down, to fall down, to be overthrown

Renvoi, sm. return, sending back, reverberation, dismissal, referring, adjournment, reference

Renvoyer, va. (*etym.* re, envoyer), to send again, to return, to dismiss, to refer, to adjourn, to reject, to refuse; *se* —, vr. to bandy, to exchange

Réorganisation, sf. reorganization

Réorganiser, va. (*etym.* re, organiser), to reorganize

Réouverture, sf. (*etym.* re, ouverture), reopening

Repaire, sm. (*etym.* O.F. repairer, *to go home*), den, lair, haunt, dung

Repaître, va.n. (*etym.* re, paître), to feed, to feast. ¦ *Être repu*, to be full. *Se* —, vr. to feed, to feast, to glut oneself

Répandre, va. (*etym.* re, épandre), to pour out, to pour, to sprinkle, to shed, to scatter, to lavish, to strew, to spread; *se* —, vr. to be poured out, to be spilt, to flow, to be shed, to be scattered, to break out, to launch out, to go into society

Répandu, e, past part. adj. poured out, spilt, spread, who sees a great deal of company, prevailing

Reparaître, vn. (*etym.* re, paraître) o reappear, to appear again

Réparateur, sm. (*etym.* L. reparator), repairer, righter. —, —*trice*, adj. invigorating, refreshing

Réparation, sf. (*etym.* L. reparationem), repair, reparation, compensation. ¦ *En* —, under repair. *Les grosses* —*s*, the heavy repairs

Réparé, e, adj. repaired

Réparer, va. (*etym.* L. reparare), to repair, to mend, to restore. — *le temps perdu*, to make up for lost time. *Se* —, vr. to be repaired

Reparler, vn. (*etym.* re, parler), to speak again

Repartie, sf. repartee reply, rejoinder. ¦ *Avoir la — prompte*, to be quick at repartee

Repartir, va.n. (*etym.* re, partir), to reply, to answer, to go away again

Répartir, va. (*etym.* ré, part), to distribute, to share, to assess

Répartiteur, sm. distributer, assessor

Répartition, sf. distribution, assessment

Repas, sm. (*etym.* L.L. repastus), meal, repast

Repassage, sm. setting, grinding, ironing

Repasser, vn. (*etym.* re, passer), to repass, to pass again, to return; — va. to repass, to set, to whet, to iron out, to revolve, to rehearse, to read over again

Repasseur, sm. knife-grinder

Repasseuse, sf. ironer

Repêcher, va. (*etym.* re, pêcher), to fish out *or* up again

Repeindre, va. (*etym.* re, peindre), to paint anew

Repentant, e, adj. sorry, repentant

se Repentir, vr. (*etym.* re, O.F. pentir = to repent), to repent, to rue

Repentir, sm. repentance, alteration

Répercussion, sf. (*etym.* L. repercussionem), reverberation

Répercuter, va. (*etym.* L. repercutere), to reverberate; *se* —, vr. to be reverberated

Reperdre, va. (*etym.* re, perdre), to lose again

Repère, sm. (*etym.* L. reperire), bench-mark, mark. *Point de* —, guiding-mark

Répertoire, sm. (*etym.* L. repertorium), index, repertory, chronicle, stock plays

Répéter, va. (*etym.* L. repetere), to repeat, to say again, to rehearse, to give private lessons, to claim back, to repeat over and again; *se* —, vr. to be repeated, to be renewed, to say over and over again the same thing

Répétiteur, sm. private teacher, professor, (*nav.*) repeater ship

Répétition, sf. (*etym.* L. repetitionem), repetition, private lesson, rehearsal, claim. ¦ *Montre à* —, repeater

Repeupler, va. (*etym.* re, peupler), to repeople, to new-stock; *se* —, vr. to be repeopled, to be new-stocked

Répit, sm. (*etym.* L. respectus), respite, delay

Replacer, va. (*etym.* re, placer), to replace; *se* —, vr. to replace oneself

Replâtrage, sm. new-plastering, patched-up reconciliation

Replâtrer, va. (*etym.* re, plâtre), to new-plaster, to patch up

Replet, ète, adj. (*etym.* L. repletus), stout, obese, lusty

Repli, sm. coil, fold, winding, recess

Replier, va. (*etym.* re, plier), to fold up, to bend up, to coil up; *se* —, vr. to coil oneself up, to wind, to bend, to fall back

Réplique, sf. answer, reply, rejoinder, cue

Répliquer, va. (*etym.* L. replicare), to reply, to rejoin

Replonger, va. (*etym.* re, plonger), to plunge again, to immerge anew; — vn., *se* —, vr. to dive again, to be immersed again

Répondant, sm. respondent, bail, surety

Répondre, va. (*etym.* L. respondere), to answer, to reply; — vn. to answer, to come up, to lead, to be felt, to be security, to be answerable, to warrant. ¦ — *en Normand*, to give a canny Scot's answer. *Qui répond paye*, go bail and you'll pay. *Se* —, vr. to answer oneself, to answer each other, to correspond

Répons, sm. response

Réponse, sf. answer, reply, written answer, rejoinder

Report, sm. carrying forward, sum brought over

Reporter, va. (*etym.* L. reportare), to carry back, to carry forward, to carry over; *se* —, vr. to go back

Repos, sm. rest, repose, stillness, pause, landing-place. ¦ *Être en* —, to be at half-cock

Reposer, va. (*etym.* re, poser), to lay back again, to rest, to relieve, to freshen, to repose. ¦ — *les armes*, to ground (arms). *A tête reposée*, more at leisure. — vn. to rest, to repose, to lie down, to lean, to dwell, to settle. *Se* —, vr. to place oneself again, to rest, to lie down, to rely

Reposoir, sm. temporary altar

Repoussant, e, adj. forbidding, repulsive, repelling

Repousser, va. (*etym.* re, pousser), to push again, to thrust back, to spurn away, to beat off, to resent, to repel, to ward off, to shoot out again; — vn. to spring again, to grow again, to kick, to be quite repulsive

Repoussoir, sm. driving-bolt, set-off, punch

Reprendre, va. (*etym.* re, prendre), to retake, to resume, to acquire, to return to, to repair, to reprove, to rebuke; — vn. to reply, to rejoin, to resume, to revive, to close up again; *se* —, vr. to be retaken, to correct oneself, to close again

§**Représaille,** sf. (*etym.* I. represaglia), reprisal

Représentant, sm. representative

Représentatif, ve, adj. (*etym.* L.L. repræsentativus), representative

Représentation, sf. (*etym.* L. repræsentationem), representation, display, appearances

Représenter, va. (*etym.* L. repræsentare), to represent, to typify; — vn. to have an imposing appearance, to receive a great deal of company, to set forth; *se* —, vr. to present oneself again, to occur again, to picture to oneself, to fancy

Répressif, ve, adj. (*etym.* L.L. repressivus), repressive

Répréhensible, adj. repressible

Réprimande, sf. (*etym.* L. reprimenda), reprimand, reproof, rebuke

Réprimander, va. to reprimand, to chide

Réprimer, va. (*etym.* L. reprimere), to repress, to restrain, to quell

Repris, sm. (*etym.* re, pris), returned convict

Reprise, sf. (*etym.* re, prise), resumption, retaking, recovery, renewal, return, revival, (*song*) burden, (*mus.*) repetition, error, (*plur.*) reprisals, claims, underpinning, fine-drawing. ¦ *A plusieurs* —*s*, several times, over and over again. — *perdue*, place fine-drawn. *Faire des* —*s à*, to darn

Repriser, va. to mend, to darn

Réprobateur, trice, adj. (*etym.* L. reprobator), reproachful

Reproche, sm. reproach, upbraiding, objection. ¦ *Soit dit sans* —, without intending the slightest reproach

Reprocher, va. (*etym.* L.L. repropiare, *to bring near*), to reproach, to object, to grudge; *se* —, vr. to reproach oneself with, to upbraid one another with, to begrudge oneself

Reproducteur, trice, adj. (*etym.* re, producteur), reproductive

Reproductible, adj. (*etym.* re, productible), reproducible

Reproduire, va. (*etym.* re, produire), to reproduce, to bring forward again; *se* —, vr. to be reproduced, to reappear again, to occur again

Réprouvé, e, s. reprobate

Réprouver, va. (*etym.* re, prouver), to disallow, to disapprove of

Républicain, e, adj. s. republican

¶**Républicanisme,** sm. republicanism

République, sf. (*etym.* L. res, publica), republic, commonwealth

Répudier, va. (*etym.* L. repudiare), to put away, to repudiate, to renounce

§**Répugner,** vn. (*etym. L.* repugnare), to be repugnant, to be contradictory, to feel repugnance

Répulsif, ve, adj. (*etym. L.L.* repulsivus), repulsive

Réputer, va. (*etym. L.* reputare), to repute, to hold, to account, to deem

Requérant, e, adj. applying. *Le* —, the applicant

Requérir, va. (*etym. L.* requirere), to request, to require, to call upon, to claim

Requête, sf. (*etym. L.* requisita), request, petition

Requin, sm. (*etym. ?*), shark

‡**se Requinquer,** vr. (*etym. ?*), to bedizen oneself

Réquisitoire, sm. (*etym. L.L.* requisitorium), address to the court. *Faire son* —, to address the court

Rescinder, va. (*etym. L.* rescindere), to rescind

Rescision, sf. (*etym. L.* rescisionem), rescission

°**Rescousse, Recousse,** sf. (*etym. L.L.* excussa, *a thing shaken*), rescue

Rescription, sf. (*etym. L.* rescriptionem), order

Rescrit, sm. (*etym. L.* rescriptum), rescript

Réseau, sm. (*etym. L.L.* retiolum, *a net*), net, network, wire-work, (*anatom.*) system, tracery

Réséda, sm. (*Latin word*), mignonette

Réserve, sf. reserve, caution, shyness

Réservé, e, past part. adj. reserved, guarded, cautious, shy

Réserver, va. (*etym. L.* reservare), to reserve, to keep back, to lay by; *se* —, vr. to reserve for oneself, to reserve oneself

Réservoir, sm. tank, reservoir, well. — *d'air*, air-box. — *de la vapeur*, steam-chamber

Résidant, e, adj. resident

Résidence, sf. residence, abode, residentship

Résider, vn. (*etym. L.* residere), to reside, to live, to lie

Résidu, sm. (*etym. L.* residuum), residue, residuum, waste

§**Résigner,** va. (*etym. L.* resignare), to resign; *se* —, vr. to be resigned, to resign, to submit

Résiliation, sf. cancelling

Résilier, va. (*etym. L.* resilire), to cancel

§**Résille,** sf. network, head-dress

Résine, sf. (*etym. L.* resina), resin, rosin. *Poix* —, white resin

Résineux, se, adj. (*etym. L.* resinosus), resinous

Résistance, sf. résistance. ‡ *Pièce de* —, solid joint

Résister, vn. (*etym. L.* resistere), to resist, to withstand, to undergo

‖**Résolu, e,** past part. adj. (*etym. L.* resolutus), decided, resolved, resolute. ‡ *Faire le* —, to put on a look of resolution

Résoluble, adj. (*etym. L.* resolubilis), resolvable

Résolution, sf. (*etym. L.* resolutionem), abrogation, resolution

Résonnant, e, adj. sounding

Résonner, vn. (*etym. L.* resonare), to resound, to echo

Résoudre, va. (*etym. L.* resolvere), to resolve, to melt, to solve, to unriddle, to cancel; *se* —, vr. to resolve, to melt

Respect, sm. (*etym. L.* respectus), respect, regard. ‡ *Le* — *humain*, fear of the world's opinion

Respecter, va. to respect; *se* —, vr. to respect oneself

‖**Respectif, ve,** adj. (*etym. L.L.* respectivus), respective

‖**Respectueux, se,** adj. (*etym. L.L.* respectuosus), respectful, deferential

Respirable, adj. breathable

Respiratoire, adj. respiratory, of breathing. *Les voies* —*s*, the windpipe

Respirer, va.n. (*etym. L.* respirare), to breathe, to long for

Resplendir, vn. (*etym. L.* resplendere), to be resplendent

Resplendissant, e, adj. resplendent

Responsabilité, sf. responsibility

Responsable, adj. (*etym. L.L.* responsabilis), responsible, answerable, accountable

Ressac, sm. (*etym. ?*), surf

Ressaisir, va. (*etym.* re, saisir), to seize again; *se* —, vr. to seize again

Ressasser, va. (*etym.* re, sasser), to sift carefully. ‡ — *toujours les mêmes choses*, to be always dinning your ears with the same things

Ressaut, sm. projection

Ressemblance, sf. likeness, resemblance, similarity

Ressemblant, e, adj. like, resembling

Ressembler, vn. (*etym.* re, sembler), to be like, to resemble, to seem like; *se* —, vr. to be like each other, to resemble one another. ‡ *Qui se ressemble s'assemble*, birds of a feather flock together

Ressemelage, sm. new-soling

Ressemeler, va. (*etym.* re, semelle), to new-sole, to new-foot

Ressenti, e, adj. strongly expressed

Ressentiment, sm. return, touch, resentment, gratitude

Ressentir, va. (*etym.* re, sentir), to feel, to resent, to betoken; *se* —, vr. to feel the effects of, to resent, to be grateful

Resserrement, sm. contraction, tightening, scarcity, narrowing, heaviness

Resserrer, va. (*etym.* re, serrer), to tighten, to narrow, to contract, to bind, to depress, to confine, to coop up, closely to invest, to condense; *se* —, vr. to contract, to be contracted, to grow narrower, to be drawn closer, to shrink, to retrench one's expenses, to confine oneself. ‡ *L'argent se resserre*, capital holds back

Ressort, sm. spring, elasticity, buoyancy. *A* —, with a spring. ‡ *Le grand* —, the main spring. *Faire jouer tous les* —*s*, to put every spring in motion

Ressort, sm. jurisdiction, department, province. ‡ *En dernier* —, without appeal

Ressortir, vn. (*etym.* re, sortir), to go out again, to come out again, to stand out, to set off by, to be implied, to spring, to be in jurisdiction, to be amenable

Ressortissant, e, adj. appealable

Ressouder, va. (*etym.* re, souder), to new-solder

Ressource, sf. (*etym.* re, source), resource, expedient, shift. *Faire* — *de tout*, to sell off everything

se Ressouvenir, vr. (*etym.* re, souvenir), to remember, to recollect. *Faire* —, to remind

Ressouvenir, sm. recollection, remembrance, twinge

Ressusciter, va.n. (*etym. L.* resuscitare), to raise from the dead, to bring to life again, to rise from the dead

Ressuyer, va., *se* —, vr. (*etym.* re, essuyer), to dry

Restant, e, adj. remaining, left. — sm. remainder, residue

Restaurant, e, adj. restorative. — sm. restorative, dining-rooms

Restaurateur, trice, s. restorer, eating-house keeper

Restauration, sf. (*etym. L.* restaurationem), restoration

Restaurer, va. (*etym. L.* restaurare), to restore, to revive; *se* —, vr. to refresh oneself

Reste, sm. remainder, rest, remnant, last stake, change. ‡ *Je fais mon* —, I stake all I have before me. *Jouer de son* —, to play one's last stake, to make a last push, to make the most of the thing. *Être en* — *avec*, to be in arrears. *Au* —, *du* —, besides, withal

Rester, vn. (*etym. L.* restare), to remain, to be left, to be remaining, to stay. ‡ *En* — *là*, to stop there

Restituable, adj. may be restored, payable

Restituer, va. (*etym. L.* restituere), to restore, to give back

Restreindre, va. (*etym. L.* restringere), to restrict; *se* —, vr. to restrict oneself, to retrench

Restrictif, ve, adj. (*etym. L.L.* restrictivus), restrictive

Résultant, sm. result

Résultante, sf. resultant

Résulter, vn. (*etym. L.* resultare, *to spring back*), to result, to arise, to follow

Résumé, sm. recapitulation, summing up, summary. *Au* —, *en* —, upon the whole, after all

Résumer, va. (*etym. L.* resumere), to sum up, to give a summary of; *se* —, vr. to sum up, to be condensed

Retable, sm. (*etym. ?*), altar-screen

Rétablir, va. (*etym.* re, établir), to re-establish, to restore, to repair, to retrieve; *se* —, vr. to recover, to be restored, to look better

Rétablissement, sm. re-establishment, restoration, thorough repair, retrieving

Retaper, va. (*etym.* re, taper), to comb the hair the wrong way, to do up hats

Retard, Retardement, sm. delay, slowness

Retardataire, sm. loiterer, one in arrears, straggler

Retarder, va. (*etym. L.* retardare), to retard, to delay, to put back; — vn. to be slow, to lose, to come later

Retenir, va. (*etym. L.* retinere), to hold again, to withhold, to keep back, to deduct, (*arith.*) to carry, to engage, to bespeak; *se* —, vr. to hold on, to cling to, to keep for oneself, to check oneself, to remember

Rétention, sf. (*etym. L.* retentionem), reservation, retention

Retentir, vn. (*etym.* re, *O.F.* tentir = *L.* tinnitare, *to ring*), to ring, to resound, to echo

Retentissant, e, adj. sounding, echoing, resounding, loud

Retentissement, sm. sound, echo. *Avoir du* —, to make a great noise, to be spread abroad, to be repeated

Retenu, e, adj. reserved, cautious, wary

Retenue, sf. reserve, caution, stoppage, pupils kept in, fixture

Rétif, ve, adj. (*etym. L.L.* restivus), restive, stubborn, impatient

Rétine, sf. (*etym. L.L.* retina), retina

Retiré, e, adj. retired, secluded, sequestered

Retirer, va. (*etym.* re, tirer), to draw again, to withdraw, to pull back, to draw in, to withhold, to retract, to rescue, to derive, to reap, to redeem, to harbour, to dismiss; — vn. to be ebbing; *se* —, vr. to retire, to withdraw, to draw back, to retreat, to contract, to subside, to ebb

Retomber, vn. (*etym.* re, tomber), to fall again, to have a relapse

Retordre, va. (*etym.* re, tordre), to twist

Retorquer, va. (*etym. L.* retorquere), to retort

Retors, sm. (*etym. L.* retortus), crafty, wily, artful

Retorte, sf. (*etym. L.* retorta), retort

Retouche, sf. after-touch

Retoucher, va.n. (*etym.* re, toucher), to touch again, to retouch

Retour, sm. (*etym.* re, tour), return, coming back, reverse, winding, artifice, reversion. ¦ *Payer de* —, to return, to requite. *Être sur le* —, to be on the wane. *Beauté sur le* —, antiquated beauty. *Faire* — *à*, to return to. *En* —, *en* — *d'équerre*, (*archit.*) at right angles with

Retourne, sf. turned-up card, trump

Retourner, vn. (*etym.* re, tourner), to return, to go back, to be turned up, to be going on. ¦ *De quoi il retourne*, what is going on. — va. to turn. *Se* —, vr. to turn round, to turn oneself round, to turn about. *S'en* —, vr. to return, to go back

Retracer, va. (*etym.* re, tracer), to trace again, to resent; *se* —, vr. to recall to mind, to recur

Rétracter, va., *se* —, vr. to retract, to unsay, to recant

Retraire, va. (*etym. L.* retrahere), (*law*) to take out, to redeem

Retrait, sm. (*etym.* retraire), repurchase, withdrawal

Retraite, sf. retreat, retiring, seclusion, den, shelter, resort, superannuation, retiring pension, (*archit.*) set-back, shrinking, redraft. ¦ *En* —, superannuated. *Mettre à la* —, to superannuate. *Caisse des* —*s*, superannuation fund

Retraité, e, adj. superannuated

Retranchement, sm. curtailment, retrenchment, recess, intrenchment

Retrancher, va. (*etym.* re, trancher), to curtail, to retrench, to cut off, to intrench, to subtract; *se* —, vr. to restrain oneself, to retrench, to intrench, to plead

Rétréci, e, adj. narrow, shrunken, cramped, limited. ¦ *A tête* —*e*, shallow-brained

Rétrécir, va.n. (*etym.* re, *O.F.* trécir), to narrow, to contract, to straiten, to take, to cramp, to shrink; *se* —, vr. to grow narrow, to shrink

Rétrécissement, sm. narrowing, shrinking, cramping

Retremper, va. (*etym.* re, tremper), to temper again, to strengthen, to temper; *se* —, vr. to be strengthened, to acquire new vigour

Rétribuer, va. (*etym. L.* retribuere), to remunerate

¦ **Rétroactif, ve,** adj. (*etym. L.* retro, activus), retroactive

Rétroactivité, sf. retroactive effect

Rétrograder, vn. (*etym. L.* retrogradare), to march back

¦ **Rétrospectif, ve,** adj. retrospective

Retroussé, e, adj. turned up, hollow. *Au nez* —, snub-nosed

Retrousser, va. (*etym.* re, trousser), to turn up, to tuck up; *se* —, vr. to tuck up one's gown

Retroussis, sm. cock of a hat, facing of a coat. *Bottes à* —, top-boots

Retrouver, va. (*etym.* re, trouver), to find again, to recover, to recognise; *se* —, vr. to find oneself, to be oneself, to find one's way, to meet again

Rets, sm. (*etym. L.* retis), net, snare

Réunir, va. (*etym.* re, unir), to reunite, to rejoin, to reannex, to bring together again, to summon; *se* —, vr. to assemble again, to reunite, to meet, to combine

Réussir, va.n. (*etym.* re, *O.F.* ussir = *L.* exire), to succeed, to prosper, to carry out

Réussite, sf. success

Revaloir, va. (*etym.* re, valoir), to be even with

Revanche, sf. revenge, turn. *En* —, in return.

Revancher, va. (*etym.* re, *L.* vindicare), to stand up for; *se* —, vr. to defend oneself, to have one's turn

Rêvasser, vn. (*etym.* rêve), to have troubled dreams, to dream idly.

Rêvasserie, sf. troubled dream, (*plur.*) idle dreams

Rêvasseur, sm. dreamer

Rêve, sm. (*etym.* ?), dream

Revêche, adj. (*etym. I.* reveschio, crabbed), rough, harsh, crabbed, peevish

§ **Réveil,** sm. awaking, waking, alarum, (*milit.*) reveille. ¦ *Avoir un fâcheux* —, to be cruelly disappointed

§ **Réveille-matin,** sm. alarum-clock, Chanticleer, disturber of one's rest, intelligence

§ **Réveiller,** va. (*etym.* re, éveiller), to awake; to call up, to quicken, to revive, to rouse; *se* —, vr. to awake, to wake up, to be roused, to be revived

§ **Réveillon,** sm. midnight supper, (*paint.*) strong stroke of light. *Faire* —, to have a midnight supper

Révélateur, trice, s. (*etym. L.* revelator), revealer, discloser, informer

Révéler, va. (*etym. L.* revelare), to reveal, to disclose, to discover; *se* —, vr. to reveal oneself, to be revealed

Revenant, sm. ghost

Revenant-bon, sm. emoluments, perquisites

Revendeur, se, s. huckster, petty dealer. ¦ —*se à la toilette*, second-hand clothes-dealer

Revendication, sf. (*etym. L.* re, vindicationem), claiming, claim

Revendiquer, va. (*etym. L.* re, vindicare), to claim back, to claim

Revendre, va. (*etym.* re, vendre), to sell again. ¦ *En avoir à* —, to have enough and to spare

Revenir, vn. (*etym.* re, venir), to come back, to return, to appear, to haunt, to grow again, to recur, to begin again, to come round, to adopt, to retract, to be appeased, to suit, to be congenial, to amount, to cost, to accrue. ¦ *Faire* —, to call back, to recover, to revive, to parboil. *Il est revenu de loin*, he has had a narrow escape. *Je n'en reviens pas*, I can't get over my surprise. *Sa figure me revient assez*, I don't dislike his appearance. *Prix de revient*, cost price. *Il me revient que*, I hear that . . . *S'en* —, vr. to come back

Revenu, sm. revenue, income

Rêver, va.n. to dream, to rave, to think

Réverbère, sm. reflector, street-lamp. *A* —, reverberatory

Réverbérer, va.n. (*etym. L.* reverberare), to reverberate

Reverdir, vn. (*etym.* re, verdir), to grow green again, to bloom again

Révéremment, adv. (*etym.* révérend), reverently

Révérence, sf. reverence, bow, courtesy. ¦ *Faire la* —, *tirer sa* —, to bow, to courtesy

Révérenciel, le, adj. reverential

¦ **Révérencieux, se,** adj. reverent, reverential

Révérendissime, adj. right or most reverend

Révérer, va. (*etym. L.* revereri), to revere, to reverence, to stand in awe of

Rêverie, sf. revery, musing, thought, idle dream, raving

Revers, sm. (*etym. L.* reversus), back, reverse, opposite side, counterpart, facing, top, hollow

Réversible, adj. (*etym.* re, verser), revertible

Revêtement, sm. (*arch.*) casing, facing, lining

Revêtir, va. (*etym.* re, vêtir), to clothe, to array, to adorn, to invest, to buckle on, to assume, (*archit.*) to line, to face, to coat. ¦ *Acte revêtu de la forme prescrite*, act drawn up with every necessary formality. *Se* —, vr. to clothe oneself, to don, to assume

Rêveur, se, adj. dreaming, thoughtful. — sm. dreamer

Revirement, sm. tacking, transfer, sudden change

Revirer, vn. (*etym.* re, virer), to tack about again

Reviser, va. (*etym. L.* revisere), to revise, to review

Révision, sf. (*etym. L.* revisionem), revision, revisal, review. ¦ *Conseil de* —, board of examination for recruits

Révivifier, va. (*etym. L.* revivicare), to revivify

Revivre, vn. (*etym. L.* revivere), to live again, to revive

Révocable, adj. (*etym. L.* revocabilis), revokable

Revoici, adv. here . . . . is again

Revoilà, adv. there . . . is again

Revoir, va. (*etym.* re, voir), to see again, to look at again, to review, to revise; *se* —, vr. to behold oneself, to meet again, to be seen again

Revoler, vn. (*etym.* re, voler), to fly again

Révoltant, e, adj. revolting, shocking, disgusting

Révolte, sf. (*etym. L.* rivolta), revolt, rebellion

Révolter, va. to urge to revolt, to stir up, to be revolting to, to disgust; *se* —, vr. to rebel, to revolt, to mutiny

Révolu, e, adj. (*etym. L.* revolutus), revolved, accomplished, elapsed

¶ **Révolutionnaire,** adj. sm. revolutionary, revolutionist

¶ **Révolutionner,** va. to revolutionise

Revomir, va. (*etym. L.* revomere), to vomit again, to throw up again

Révoquer, va. (*etym. L.* revocare), to dismiss, to recall, to revoke, to reverse

Revue, sf. (*etym.* revoir), review. *Passer la* —, *en* —, to pass a review, to be passed in review, to muster up

Révulsif, ve, adj. sm. (*etym.* révulsion), revulsive

Rez, prep. (*etym. L.* rasus), on a level with

Rez-de-chaussée, sm. ground-level, ground-floor

Rhéteur, sm. (*etym. L.* rhetor), orator

Rhétoricien, sm. rhetorician

Rhétorique, sf. (*etym. L.* rhetorica), rhetoric, oratory

Rhombe, sm. (*etym. L.* rhombus), rhomb, rhombus

Rhomboïdal, e, adj. rhomboidal

Rhomboïde, sm. (*etym. L.* rhomboides), rhomboid

Rhubarbe, sf. (*etym. L.* rheubarbarum), rhubarb

Rhum, sm. (*from the English*) rum

Rhumatismal, e, adj. rheumatic

Rhumatisme, sm. (*etym. L.* rheumatismus), rheumatism

Rhume, sm. (*etym. L.* rheuma), cold. — *de cerveau*, cold in the head

Rhythme, sm. (*etym. L.* rhythmus), rhythm

Rhythmique, adj. (*etym. L.* rhythmicus), rhythmical

Riant, e, adj. (*etym. L.* ridentem), smiling, cheerful, pleasant

†**Ribambelle,** sf. (*etym.* ?), lot, string

†**Ribote,** sf. (*etym.* ?), debauch, intoxication, carouse

†**Riboter,** vn., *also* **être en ribote,** to be drunk, to carouse

†**Riboteur, se,** s. a debauchee, a drunkard

Ricanement, sm. sneer

Ricaner, vn. (*etym.* ?), to sneer

Ricanerie, sf. sneer

Ricaneur, se, s. adj. sneerer, sneering

‖**Riche,** adj. (*etym. G.* reich), rich, wealthy, costly, precious, copious, full. — sm. a rich man

Richesse, sf. riches, wealth, opulence, richness, costliness, copiousness, fulness

†**Richissime,** adj. extravagantly

Ricin, sm. (*etym. L.* ricinus), castor-oil plant. *Huile de* —, castor-oil

Ricocher, vn. (*etym.* ?), to rebound

Ricochet, sm. duck and drake, ricochet, rebound, repeating-bird, chain. *Par* —, indirectly, by accident. *Coup de* —, chance stroke

Ride, sf. (*etym.* rider), ripple, wrinkle, laniard

Ridé, e, adj. wrinkled

Rideau, sm. (*etym.* ride), curtain, screen

Rider, va. (*etym. M.H.G.* riden, *to wrinkle*), to wrinkle, to contract, to ripple; *se* —, vr. to wrinkle, to be wrinkled, to frown, to contract, to ripple

‖**Ridicule,** adj. (*etym. L.* ridiculum), ridiculous. — sm. ridiculousness, ridicule, folly

Ridiculiser, va. to ridicule

Ridiculité, sf. ridiculousness, ridicule

Rien, sm. (*etym. L.* rem), nothing, not anything, anything, nought. ‡*En moins de* —, *en un* — *de temps*, in no time, in a trice

Rieur, se, s. (*etym.* rire), laugher, merry person. — adj. laughing

‖**Rigide,** adj. (*etym. L.* rigidus), rigid, strict, severe

Rigidité, sf. (*etym. L.* rigiditatem), rigidity, stiffness

Rigodon, sm. (*onomat.*) rigadoon

Rigole, sf. (*etym. I.* rigoro), trench, channel, gutter

Rigorisme, sm. (*etym. L.* rigor), austerity, strictness

Rigoriste, sm. precisian, puritan

‖**Rigoureux, se,** adj. (*etym. L.* rigorosus), rigorous, strict, inclement, sharp

Rigueur, sf. (*etym. L.* rigorem), rigour, strictness, severity. ‡*Il me tint* — *longtemps*, he was long obdurate. *Cela est de* —, that is indispensable. *Jouer de* —, to play the strict rule. *A la* —, rigorously, strictly

§**Rimailler,** vn. to rhyme, to make sorry verses

§**Rimailleur,** sm. rhymester

Rime, sf. (*etym. L.* rhythmus), rhyme

Rimer, va.n. to rhyme, to make verses, to put into rhyme

Rimeur, sm. rhymester, rhymer

Rinceau, sm. (*etym. L.L.* ramicellus, *from* ramus, *bough*), (*arch.*) bough, foliage

Rincer, va. (*etym. Scand.* hreinsa, *to clean*), to rinse, to wash; *se* —, vr. to be rinsed. *Se* — *la bouche*, to wash one's mouth

Rinçure, sf. rinsing, (*pl.*) slops

†§**Ripaille,** sf. (*etym.* ?), feast. *Faire* —, to have a feast, to feast

†**Ripopée,** sf. (*etym.* ?), slop

Riposte, sf. (*etym. L.* riposta), reply, parry and thrust

Riposter, vn. to reply, to parry and thrust

Rire, vn. (*etym. L.* ridere), to laugh, to smile, to bear a smiling aspect, to jest, to joke, to scoff, to make game of. ‡ — *aux éclats*, to burst out a laughing. *Il n'y a pas de quoi* —, there is nothing to laugh at. *Rira bien qui rira le dernier*, they are best off who laugh last. — *jaune*, to laugh at the wrong side of one's mouth. *C'est pour* —, it's in fun. *Histoire de* —, for the fun of the thing. *Apprêter à* —, to make oneself a laughing-stock. *Se* —, vr. to laugh. — sm. laughter, laughing, laugh. *Un gros* —, a horse laugh, a loud laugh. *Un bon gros* —, a hearty laugh

Ris, sm. (*etym. L.* risus), laugh, laughter. — sm. reef. *Prendre un* —, to take in a reef, to reef in. *Au bas* —, close-reefed

Ris, sm. (*etym.* ride), sweetbread

Risée, sf. laugh, laughter, derision, laughing-stock, puff of wind

Risibilité, sf. risibility

‖**Risible,** adj. (*etym. L.* risibilis), risible, laughable, funny

Risquable, adj. may be risked

Risque, sm. (*etym. Span.* risco, *a rock at sea*), risk, hazard. ‡*A tout* —, at every risk. *A ses* —*s et périls*, at your risk and peril

Risquer, va. to venture, to risk. ‡*Qui ne risque rien n'a rien*, nothing venture, nothing have. — *le tout pour le tout*, to risk all to win all. *Se* —, vr. to risk oneself, to risk

Rissoler, va. (*etym. Dan.* riste, *to roast*), to brown. *Du rissolé*, a bit of brown

Rit, Rite, sm. (*etym. L.* ritus), rite

Ritournelle, sf. (*etym. I.* ritornello), flourish, burden of a song

Rituel, sm. (*etym. L.* ritualis), ritual

Rivage, sm. (*etym. L.L.* ripaticum), shore, beach, bank, strand

Rivaliser, vn. (*etym.* rival), to rival, to vie

Rivalité, sf. (*etym. L.* rivalitatem), rivalry

Rive, sf. (*etym. L.* ripa), bank, shore, margin, strand, skirt, border

River, va. (*etym. Dan.* rive, *to flatten*), to rivet, to clench. *Fer à* —, bolt iron

Riverain, sm. borderer. —, —*e*, adj. bordering, neighbouring

Rivière, sf. (*etym. L.L.* riparia), river

Rixdale, sf. (*etym. G.* reichsthaler), rixdollar

Rixe, sf. (*etym. L.* rixa), scuffle, affray, brawl

Riz, sm. (*etym. I.* riso), rice. — *au lait*, rice-milk. *Gâteau au* —, rice-pudding

Rizière, sf. rice-plantation

Rob, Robre, sm. (*etym. Engl.* rubber), rubber (of whist). *Faire un* —, to play a rubber

Robe, sf. (*etym. L.L.* rauba, *garment*), gown, dress, frock, robe, magistracy, the law, coat (of an animal), skin, husk. ‡ — *de ville*, walking out dress. — *de chambre*, morning gown. —*s de cérémonie*, state-robes. *Gens de* —, gentlemen of the long robe. *La* — *et l'épée*, the law and the army. *Porter la* —, to be a magistrate

Robinet, sm. (*etym. prop. name* Robin), cock, tap, plug, pipe

‖**Robuste,** adj. (*etym. L.* robustus), sturdy, robust, athletic, hardy, strong

Roc, sm. (*etym. L.* rupes), rock

§**Rocaille,** sf. rock-work, pebbles

§**Rocailleux, se,** adj. pebbly, stony, rugged, rocky

Roche, sf. (*etym. Gael.* roc), rock. *Eau de* —, clear water. ‡*De la vieille* —, (*fig.*) of the old school

Rocher, sm. rock

Rocheux, se, adj. rocky

Rôder, vn. (*etym. Prov.* rodar), to prowl, to roam

Rôdeur, sm. prowler, stroller

Rodomont, sm. (*etym. I.* rodomonte), blusterer, braggart

Rodomontade, sf. rhodomontade, blustering

Rogation, sm. (*etym.* ?) broken-meat, scrap, lumber

Rogations, sf. (*etym. L.* rogationem), Rogation-week, Rogation-days

Rogatoire, adj. (*etym. L.L.* rogatorius), of inquiry

§**Rogne,** sf. (*etym. L.* robiginem, *rust*), inveterate itch, mange

§**Rogner,** va. (*etym. O.F.* roond = rond, *round*), to cut off, to pare, to clip

§**Rognon,** sm. (*etym. L.L.* renionem, *from* ren, *loin*), kidney

§**Rognure,** sf. remnant, shred, paring, clipping

Rogue, adj. (*etym. Icel.* hrok *arrogant*), supercilious

Roi, sm. (*etym. L.* regem), king. *Le* — *d'armes*, king at arms. *Le jour des* —*s*, Twelfth-night. *Faire les* —*s*, to keep Twelfth-night

‖**Roide, Raide,** adj. (*etym. L.* rigidus), stiff, tight, steep, pertinacious, stubborn, harsh. ‡*Être tué* — *sur le coup*, to fall stone dead. — adv. quick

Roideur, Raideur, sf. stiffness, tightness, steepness, strength, stubbornness, harshness

Roidir, Raidir, va.n. to stiffen, to stretch, to tighten; *se* —, vr. to stiffen, to battle hard, to bear up

Roitelet, sm. wren, petty king

Rôle, sm. (*etym. L.* rotulus), roll, list, part, character. — *d'équipage*, muster-roll

Rôlet, sm. bit of a part

Romain, sm. (*etym. L.* romanus), (*print.*) primer, Roman

Romaine, sf. steel-yard, cos lettuce

Roman, sm. novel, romance. — *de mœurs*, novel. *Un héros de* —, a hero of romance. *Tenir du* —, to be like a romance. *Aventure de* —, romantic adventure

Romance, sf. romance, romaunt, ballad

Romancier, sm. novel-writer, novelist

Romanesque, adj. romantic

Romarin, sm. (*etym. L.* rosmarinus), rosemary

Rominagrobis, sm. (*etym.* ?), Grimalkin

Rompre, va. (*etym. L.* rumpere), to break to snap, to rout, to draw back, to divert, to turn off, to deaden, to inure, to train up. ‡ — *les chiens*, to call off the dogs. — *son ban*, to break one's bounds. — vn. to break, to snap, to fall out. *Se* —, vr. to break, to snap, to inure oneself, to get inured

Rompu, e, past part. adj. broken, used, inured, trained, fractionary

Ronce, sf. (*etym. L.L.* runcalis, *covered with briars*), bramble, briar

‖**Rond, e,** adj. (*etym. L.* rotundus), round, rounded,

full, plump, jolly, frank, even (sum), coarse (thread). — sm. round, ring. *En* —, round, in a ring. *Quart de* —, ovolo, quarter round

Rondache, sf. (*etym.* rond), round shield

Ronde, sf. round, stakes, roundelay, (*mus.*) semi-breve, round-hand. ¦ *Faire la* —, *sa* —, to go the round. *A la* —, all around, round about

Rondeau, sm. rondeau, rondo

Rondelet, te, adj. plump, coarse (silk)

Rondelle, sf. round, rundle, round nose chisel, small round shield

Rondeur, sf. roundness, fulness, openness, plain dealing. ¦ *Avoir de la* —, to be a plain-dealing man

Rondin, sm. round bit of wood, cudgel

Rond-point, sm. apsis

Ronflant, e, adj. high-sounding

Ronflement, sm. snore, snoring, snorting, rumbling, roaring, pealing, peal, humming

Ronfler, vn. (*etym. f*), to snore, to snort, to rumble, to roar, to peal, to hum. ¦ *Faire — les vers*, to spout verses

Ronfleur, se, s. snorer

Ronger, va. (*etym. L.L.* rumigare, *to ruminate*), to gnaw, to nibble, to pick, to bite, to eat away, to prey upon

Rongeur, adj. gnawing, cankering, heart-consuming. *Les —s*, (*nat. hist.*) the gnawers. *Le ver* — (*le remords*), the never-dying worm

Ron-ron, sm. (*onomat.*) purring. *Faire* —, to pur

Roquet, sm. (*etym. prop. name* Saint-Roche), pug-dog, insignificant fellow

Rosace, sf. (*etym. L.* rosacea), rose, rose-window

Rosacées, sf. plur. (*etym. L.* rosacea), rose tribe

Rosaire, sm. (*etym. L.* rosarius), rosary

Rosat, adj. (*etym. I.* rosato), of roses, roseate

Rose, sf. (*etym. L.* rosa), rose, rose-window. —*-pivoine*, peony-rose

Rosé, e, adj. rosy, roseate

Roseau, sm. (*etym. Goth.* raus, *reed*), reed

Rose-croix, sm. Rosicrucian

Rosée, sf. (*etym. O.F.* roser = *L.* rosare, *to fall as the dew*), dew

Rosette, sf. rosette, red ink, red chalk, rose-copper

Rosier, sm. (*etym. L.* rosarium), rose-tree, rose-bush

Rosière, sf. girl that gains the rose given as a prize for good conduct

Rosse, sf. (*etym. G.* ross, *horse*), jade

Rosser, va. to thrash, to lick

§**Rossignol,** sm. (*etym. L.* lusciniola), nightingale, pick-lock, (*argot*) pi...

Rostres, sm. plur. (*etym. L.* rostra), rostrum

Rot, sm. (*etym. L.* ructus), belch

Rôt, sm. roast meat

Rotatoire, adj. (*etym. L.* rotatorius), rotatory

Rote, sf. (*etym. I.* rota), rota

Roter, vn. to belch

Rôti, sm. roast joint. —, —*e*, adj. roast, roasted

Rôtie, sf. slice of toast. —*s au beurre*, buttered toast

Rotin, sm. rattan

Rôtir, va.n. (*etym. O.H.G.* rostjan, *to roast*), to roast, to toast, to parch; *se* —, vr. to be roasted, to roast oneself, to burn

Rôtisseur, se, s. master, mistress of a cook-shop. *De chez le* —, from the cook-shop

Rôtissoire, sf. Dutch-oven

Rotonde, sf. (*etym. I.* rotonda), rotunda

Rotondité, sf. (*etym. L.* rotunditatem), plumpness, rotundity

Rotule, sf. (*etym. L.* rotula), knee-pan

Roture, sf. (*etym. L.* ruptura), plebeian state, commonalty

Roturier, ère, s. adj. commoner, plebeian

Rouage, sm. (*etym.* roue), wheel-work, wheels, movement, machinery. *Bois de* —, wheelwright's timber

Rouan, adj. (*etym. I.* roano), roan (horse)

Roucoulement, sm. cooing

Roucouler, va.n. (*onom.*) to coo, to warble out

Roue, sf. (*etym. L.* rota), wheel. ¦ — *motrice*, driving-wheel. — *mue en dessus, en dessous*, overshot wheel, undershot wheel. *Bande de* —, tire of a wheel. *Écrou de* —, linch-pin. *Condamner à la* —, to sentence to be broken on the wheel. *Faire la* —, to turn on one's hands and feet like a wheel, to spread out its tail, to strut about

Roué, sm. rake, sly one

Rouennerie, sf. (*etym. proper name* Rouen), coarse printed cotton

Rouer, va. to break on the wheel, to coil up

Rouerie, sf. trick

Rouet, sm. wheel, spinning-wheel

Rouge, adj. (*etym. L.* rubeus), red, red-hot, blood-shot. — sm. red, red colour, redness, flush, blush, rouge, red-haired fellow, red republican, shoveller. *Se mettre du* —, to rouge

Rougeâtre, adj. reddish

Rougeaud, e, adj. ruddy, red-faced

Rouge-gorge, sm. robin redbreast

Rougeole, sm. the measles

Rouget, sm. red mullet

Rougeur, sf. redness, flush, blush colour, rosy-drop

Rougir, va. to redden. *De l'eau rougie*, wine and water. — vn. to redden, to flush, to colour up, to blush

§**Rouille,** sf. (*etym. L.L.* rubigula), rust, blight, mildew

§**Rouillé, e,** adj. rusty

§**Rouiller,** va., *se* —, vr. to grow rusty, to rust

Rouir, va.n. (*etym. Dutch* roten, *to ret*), to ret, to be retted

Rouissage, sm. retting

Roulade, sf. rolling, roll, trill, quaver

Roulage, sm. rolling, land-carriage, carriage by waggons. *Maison, bureau de* —, waggon-office. *Voiture de* —, waggon

Roulant, e, adj. rolling, easy moving, in activity. ¦ *Faire un feu* —, to keep up a running fire

Rouleau, sm. (*etym. L.L.* rotulellum, *a small roll*), roll, coil, phial, roller, rolling-pin. *Mettre en* —, to roll up

Roulement, sm. rolling, roll, rumbling, rattle, rotation. *Fonds de* —, cash in hand

Rouler, va. (*etym. L.L.* rotulare, *to roll*), to roll, to roll up, to wheel, to revolve; — vn. to roll, to roll along, to rattle, to rumble along, to revolve, to turn, to ramble. *Roulez! cocher*, all right, coachman. — *sur l'or*, to roll in wealth. *Se* —, vr. to roll, to roll oneself, to wind, to wallow

Roulette, sf. small wheel, castor, roller, bath chair, roulette. ¦ *Aller comme sur des —s*, (*fig.*) to run along quite smoothly

Roulier, sm. waggoner, carter

Roulis, sm. rolling

Roupie, sf. (*etym. f*), drop, rupee

Roussâtre, adj. (*etym.* roux), reddish, russet

Rousseur, sf. freckle, redness. *Taches de* —, freckles

Roussi, sm. Russia leather, burnt smell. *Sentir le* —, to have a burnt smell

Roussin, sm. (*etym. see* Roux), cob. — *d'Arcadie*, ass

Roussir, va.n. to redden, to singe, to scorch

Route, sf. (*etym. L.* rupta [via], *a broken-up path*), road, way, route, course, track. ¦ *Se mettre en* —, to set out, to start. *Faire la — à pied*, to walk it. *Faire — pour*, to make for, to sail to. *Faire fausse* —, to take a wrong course, to take a wrong step. *La — estimée*, (*nav.*) the dead reckoning

Routier, sm. track-chart, stager. —, —*ère*, adj. road, of roads

Routiner, va. to accustom

Routinier, ère, s. adj. one who acts by routine, of routine

Rouverin, adj. hot, brittle

Rouvrir, va., *se* —, vr. to open again

Roux, Rousse, adj. (*etym. L.* russus, *red*), red, reddish, sandy, red-haired, brown, nipping. — sm. red, sandy hue, brown sauce. *D'un — ardent*, of a fiery red

Royalement, adv. (*etym.* royal), royally

¶**Royalisme,** sm. royalism

¶**Royaliste,** s. adj. royalist

Royaume, sm. (*etym. L.L.* regalimen, *realm*), kingdom, realm

Royauté, sf. sovereignty, royalty

Ruade, sf. (*etym.* ruer), kick. *Lâcher des —s*, to kick out

Ruban, sm. (*etym. f*), ribbon, riband, stripe. — *de fil ou coton*, tape. *Ouvrier en —s*, ribbon-weaver

Rubanerie, sf. ribbon-weaving, ribbon-trade

Rubicond, e, adj. (*etym. L.* rubicundus), rubicund

Rubis, sm. (*etym. Sp.* rubi), ruby. *Monté sur* —, jewelled. ¦ *Boire — sur l'ongle*, to drink to the last drop. *Payer — sur l'ongle*, to pay down in cash

Rubrique, sf. (*etym. L.* rubrica), rubric, method, trick, ruddle, red chalk

Ruche, sf. (*etym. Bret.* rusken, *hive*), hive, bee-hive, quilling

¦**Rude,** adj. (*etym. L.* rudis), rough, harsh, rugged, uneven, hard-featured, difficult, rude, unpolished, uncouth

Rudesse, sf. roughness, harshness, churlishness, rudeness, ungentle words or actions

Rudoyer, va. (*etym.* rude), to use roughly

Rue, sf. (*etym. L.* ruga, *furrow*), street, (*plant*) rue

Ruelle, sf. lane, bed-side

Ruer, va. (*etym. L.* ruere, *to rush*), to hurl, to deal; — vn. (*anim.*) to kick; *se* —, vr. to rush

Rugir, vn. (*etym. L.* rugire), to roar

Rugissement, sm. roar, roaring

Rugosité, sf. (*etym. L.* rugositatem), rugosity, wrinkle

Rugueux, se, adj. (*etym. L.* rugosus), wrinkled

Ruine, sf. (*etym. L.* ruina), ruin, decay

Ruiner, va.n. to ruin, to destroy, to overthrow, to undo, to be ruinous

Ruineux, se, adj. ruinous

Ruisseau, sm. (*etym. L.L.* rivicellus), stream, brook, rivulet, gutter

Ruisseler, vn. to stream, to gush, to run down, to trickle

Rumeur, sf. (*etym. L.* rumor), rumour, report, uproar, noise, murmur, stir

Ruminant, e, adj. ruminant, chewing the cud

Ruminer, va.n. (*etym. L.* ruminare), to ruminate, to muse

Ruse, sf. artifice, cunning, craft, trick

Rusé, e, adj. artful, cunning, crafty, sly

Ruser, vn. to use artifice, to shift, (*hunt.*) to double

Rustaud, e, adj. s. boorish, boor

Rusticité, sf. rusticity, boorishness

Rustique, adj. rustic, rural, rude, coarse, boorish

Rustiquer, va. to jag out, to rough-cast

Rustre, adj. boorish, clownish

Rustre, sm. boor, clown

S

S, smf. S, s

Sabbat, sm. (*etym. L.* Sabbatum), Sabbath, revels, uproar, racket, caterwauling

Sable, sm. (*etym. L.* sabulum), sand, gravel. — *argileux*, loam-sand

Sabler, va. to sand, to gravel, to quaff

Sableux, se, adj. sandy, gritty

Sablière, sf. sand-pit, gravel-pit, (*carp.*) raising-piece

Sablon, sm. small sand, grit

Sablonneux, se, adj. sandy

Sabord, sm. (*etym.* ?), port-hole, port

Sabot, sm. (*etym.* ?), wooden shoe, hoof, whipping-top, slipper-bath, shoe of a wheel

Sabotier, sm. maker of wooden shoes

Sabre, sm. (*etym. G.* säbel, *sabre*), sabre, sword, broad-sword, cutlass

Sabrer, va. to cut down, to botch

Sabretache, sm. (*etym. G.* säbeltasche, *pocket of the sword*), sabretash

Sabreur, sm. a hotspur

Sac, sm. (*etym. L.* saccus), sack, bag, knapsack, carpet-bag, sackcloth, pouch, hammock. ‡— *de nuit*, carpet-bag. — *à ouvrage*, work-bag. — *à terre*, earth-sack. — *à vin*, drunken sot. — (*etym. O.F.* sacquer, *to sack*), sacking, plunder. *Mettre à* —, to sack

Saccade, sf. (*etym. I.* staccato), jerk, shake, rating. ‡ *Parler par* —*s*, to jerk out one's words

Saccadé, e, adj. jerking, by jerks, abrupt

Saccagement, sm. sacking, plunder

Saccager, va. (*etym. I.* sacchoggiare, *to plunder*), to ransack

Sacerdoce, sm. (*etym. L.* sacerdotium), priesthood

Sachée, sf. sackful

Sachet, sm. sachet, bag

Sacoche, sf. (*etym. I.* saccocia), saddle-bag, money-bag, leathern purse

§**Sacramental, e; Sacramentel, le,** adj. (*etym. L.* sacramentalis), sacramental

Sacre, sm. (*etym. L.* sacrum), coronation, anointing, consecration

Sacré, e, adj. (*etym. L.* sacratus), sacred, holy, cursed, confounded. — sm. the sacred, sacred things

Sacrement, sm. (*etym. L.* sacramentum), sacrament. *S'approcher des* —*s*, to receive the Sacraments

Sacrer, va. (*etym. L.* sacrare), to anoint, to crown, to consecrate, to curse and swear

Sacrificateur, sm. (*etym. L.* sacrificator), sacrificer

Sacrifier, va. (*etym. L.* sacrificare), to sacrifice, to devote; *se* —, vr. to sacrifice oneself

Sacrilège, sm. (*etym. L.* sacrilegium), sacrilege, sacrilegious man. — adj. sacrilegious

Sacripant, sm. (*etym. I. prop. name* Sacripante), rascal, braggart

Sacristain, sm. (*etym. L.L.* sacristanus), vestry-clerk, sexton

Sacristie, sf. (*etym. L.L.* sacristia), vestry-room

Saducéen, sm. Sadducee

Safran, sm. (*etym. I.* zafferano), saffron, crocus

Sagace, adj. (*etym. L.* sagacem), sagacious, acute, shrewd

Sagacité, sf. (*etym. L.* sagacitatem), sagacity, acuteness

§**Sage,** adj. (*etym. L.L.* sapius), wise, sensible, judicious, discreet, steady, sober, prudent, gentle. — sm. wise man

Sage-femme, sf. midwife

Sagesse, sf. wisdom, good sense, judiciousness, prudence, discretion

Sagittaire, sm. (*etym. L.* sagittarius), archer, (*bot.*) arrow-head

Sagou, sm. (*from the Eng.*), sago. *Palmier* —, sago-tree

†**Sagouin,** sm. (*etym.* ?), a slovenly person

§**Saignant, e,** adj. bleeding, very underdone

§**Saignée,** sf. bleeding, blood-letting, small of the arm, drain. ‡ *Pratiquer une* —, to breathe a vein, to cut a drain, to drain

§**Saignement,** sm. bleeding

§**Saigner,** va. n. (*etym. L.L.* sanguinare), to bleed, to kill, to drain. *Se faire* —, to be bled. *Se* —, vr. to bleed oneself, to drain oneself

§**Saillant, e,** adj. jutting, projecting, salient, striking, forcible

§**Saillie,** sf. gush, spurt, start, fit of passion, flash of wit, sally, prominence, projection, (*locom.*) spindle. ‡ *Faire* —, to project, to jut out

§**Saillir,** vn. (*etym. L.* salire), to gush out, to jut out, to project. *Faire* —, to bring out, to render conspicuous

§**Sain, e,** adj. (*etym. L.* sanus), healthy, hale, sound, wholesome. — *et sauf*, safe and sound

Saindoux, sm. (*etym. L.L.* sagimen, *fat*), lard

Sainfoin, sm. (*etym.* sain, foin), sainfoin, French grass

§**Saint, e,** adj. (*etym. L.* sanctus), godly, holy, sainted, saintly, sacred. — sm. saint. *Le — du jour*, the idol of the day. *La* — *-Michel*, Michaelmas day. *A la* — *-Jean d'été*, on Midsummer's day

Sainte, sf. saint

Sainteté, sf. (*etym. L.* sanctitatem), holiness, sanctity, sacredness

Saisi, e, past part. seized, apprehended, struck, shocked, startled, distrained, in possession

Saisie, sf. seizure, distress, execution. ‡ — *-arrêt*, attachment. *Faire pratiquer une* —, to put in an execution

Saisir, va. (*etym. L.L.* sacire, *to seize*), to lay hold of, to seize, to grasp, to clutch, to catch at, to apprehend, to discern, to startle, to distrain, to vest in, to bring before. — *au corps*, to seize by the body, to apprehend. *Se* —, vr. to seize, to lay hold, to secure

Saisissable, adj. liable to seizure

Saisissant, e, adj. chilling, striking, startling, distraining

Saisissement, sm. chill, shock

Saison, sf. (*etym. L.* sationem, *sowing-time*), season. *La nouvelle* —, spring

Salade, sf. (*etym. L.* salata), salad; (*etym. L.* celata), sallet

Saladier, sm. salad-bowl

Salaire, sm. (*etym. L.* salarium), salary, pay, hire, wages. ‡ *Toute peine mérite* —, the labourer is worthy of his hire

Salaison, sf. (*etym. L.L.* salationem), salting, salt provisions

Salamandre, sf. (*etym. L.* salamandra), salamander

Salarié, e, adj. sm. hired, paid; one who receives a salary

Salarier, va. to pay

§**Sale,** adj. (*etym. O.H.G.* salo, *dim*), dirty, filthy. *Tout* —, quite dirty

Salé, e, adj. salt, briny, pointed, keen, smutty. — sm. salt meat. *Petit* —, salt pork

Saler, va. (*etym. L.L.* salare), to salt

Saleté, sf. dirtiness, filthiness, dirty trick, filthy words

Saliens, adj. sm. plur. (*etym. L.* Salii), Salii

Salière, sf. salt-cellar, hollow

Salin, e, adj. (*etym. L.* salinus), saline

Saline, sf. salt works, salt pit, salt rock

Salique, adj. (*etym. L.* salicus), Salic

Salir, va. to dirty, to soil, to sully, to taint; *se* —, vr. to dirty oneself, to be soiled, to get dirty, to be sullied

Salissant, e, adj. dirty, easily soiled

Salive, sf. (*etym. L.* saliva), spittle, saliva

Saliver, vn. to salivate

Salle, sf. (*etym. L.L.* sala, *abode*), room, hall, house, play-house, ward, bower. — *basse*, ground-floor room. — *à manger*, dining-room. — *des domestiques, du commun*, servants' hall. — *de spectacle*, play-house

Salmigondis, sm. (*etym.* ?), salmagundi

Salon, sm. drawing-room, saloon, the fashionable circles, exhibition. ‡ *Petit* —, parlour. *Homme de* —, man of fashion

†**Saloperie,** sf. (*etym.* ?), dirt

Salpêtrier, sm. (*etym.* salpêtre), saltpetre maker

Salpêtrière, sf. saltpetre works

§**Salsepareille,** sf. (*etym. I.* salsapariglia), sarsaparilla

Salsifis, sm. (*etym. I.* sassefrica), salsify, (*bot.*) goat's beard

Saltimbanque, sm. (*etym. I.* saltimbanco), mountebank

Salubre, adj. (*etym. L.* saluber), salubrious, wholesome

Salubrité, sf. (*etym. L.* salubritatem), healthfulness, salubrity, health. ‡ *Conseil de* —, board of health

Saluer, va. (*etym. L.* salutare), to salute, to greet, to bow to, to curtsey to, to fire a salute, to cheer, to hail; *se* —, vr. to exchange salutes, to salute each other

Salure, sf. saltness

Salut, sm. (*etym. L.* salutem), safety, salvation, salute, bow, greeting, cheers, evening prayers to the Virgin. ‡ *Faire*

son —, to work out one's salvation

Salutaire, adj. (*etym. L.* salutaris), salutary, wholesome, beneficial

Salve, sf. (*etym. L.* salva), volley, salute, round. *Faire, tirer une — de cent coups de canon*, to fire a salute of a hundred guns

Samedi, sm. (*etym. L.* Sabbati dies), Saturday. — *saint*, Easter-eve

Sanctifiant, e, adj. sanctifying

Sanctifier, va. (*etym. L.* sanctificare), to sanctify, to hallow; *se* —, vr. to sanctify oneself

Sanctionner, va. (*etym.* sanction), to sanction

Sanctuaire, sm. (*etym. L.* sanctuarium), sanctuary, chancel

Sandal, Santal, sm. (*etym. Sansc.* tchandana), sandal-wood

Sandale, sf. (*etym. L.* sandalium), sandal

Sandaraque, sf. (*etym. L.* sandaraca), sandarach, pounce

Sang, sm. (*etym. L.* sanguis), blood, race, extraction, relationship, parentage. ¦ *Coup de* —, apoplectic fit. *Se battre au premier* —, to fight till blood is drawn. *Faire faire du mauvais* —, to vex, to annoy. *Avoir le — chaud, vif*, to be hot-blooded, passionate. *De — rassis*, dispassionate. *Un pur — (cheval)*, a thorough-bred horse

Sang-froid, sm. coolness, composure, presence of mind

Sanglant, e, adj. (*etym. L.L.* sanguilentus), bloody, bleeding, cutting, deadly, outrageous, blood-coloured

Sangle, sf. (*etym. L.* cingula, *a girth*), strap, band, saddle-girth. ¦ *Lit de* —, folding-bed

Sangler, va. to girth, to deal. *Trop sanglé*, laced too tight. — *avec un fouet*, to horsewhip. *Se* —, vr. to lace oneself too tight

Sanglier, sm. (*etym. L.* (porcus) singularis), wild boar, boar, boar-fish

Sanglot, sm. sobbing, sob

Sangloter, vn. (*etym. L.* singultare), to sob

Sangsue, sf. (*etym. L.* sanguisuga), leech, blood-sucker

Sanguin, e, adj. (*etym. L.* sanguineus), sanguine. *Vaisseau* —, blood-vessel

Sanguinaire, adj. (*etym. L.* sanguinarius), sanguinary, bloody

Sanguine, sf. red chalk, blood-stone

Sanguinolent, e, adj. (*etym. L.* sanguinolentus), sanguineous, bleeding

Sanhédrin, sm. (*etym. Gr.* συνέδριον, *council*), sanhedrim

Sanie, sf. (*etym. L.* saniem), sanies

Sanitaire, adj. (*from the English*), sanitary

Sans, prep. (*etym. L.* sine), without, but, for, besides

Sans-gêne, sm. free and easy manners, liberty. ¦ *C'est d'un — étonnant*, it is marvellously cool

Sansonnet, sm. (*etym. proper name* Sanson), starling

Santé, sf. (*etym. L.* sanitatem), health, constitution. ¦ *Officier de* —, apothecary. *Bureau de* —, board of health. *Maison de* —, private hospital. *Porter la — de*, to propose the health of

Sapajou, sm. (*etym. Braz.* cayouvassou), sapajo, ugly monkey

Sape, sf. (*etym. L.L.* sappa), sap

Saper, va. to sap, to undermine

Sapeur, sm. sapper. — *-pompier*, fireman

Saphique, adj. (*etym. pr. name* Sappho), Sapphic

Saphir, sm. (*etym. L.* sapphirus), sapphire

Sapide, adj. (*etym. L.* sapidus), sapid, palatable

Sapin, sm. (*etym. L.* sappinus), fir-tree, fir, hackney-coach

Saponaire, sf. (*etym. L.L.* saponarius), soap-wort

Sarabande, sf. (*etym. Sp.* zarabanda), saraband

Sarbacane, sf. (*etym. L.* sarbacane), pea-shooter, air-cane

Sarcasme, sm. (*etym. L.* sarcasmus), sarcasm, taunt

Sarcastique, adj. (*etym.* σαρκαστικός), sarcastic, taunting

Sarcelle, sf. (*etym. L.* querquedula) widgeon, teal

Sarclage, sm. weeding

Sarcler, va. (*etym. L.* sarculare), to weed, to hoe

Sarcophage, sm. (*etym. Gr.* σαρκοφάγος), sarcophagus

Sardine, sf. (*etym. L.* sardina), pilchard

Sardoine, sf. (*etym. L.* sardonyx), sardonyx

Sardonique, Sardonien, adj m. (*etym. Gr.* σαρδάνιος [γέλως], *convulsive laughter*), sardonic

Sarigue, sf. (*etym. Braz.* Carigueia), opossum, didelphis

Sarment, sm. (*etym. L.* sarmentum), vine-branch

Sarmenteux, se, adj. (*etym. L.* sarmentosus), sarmentous, full of twigs

Sarrasin, adj. sm. (*etym. prop. n.* Sarrasin, *Saracen*), *blé* —, buck-wheat

Sarrau, sm. (*etym.* ?), smock-frock

Sas, sm. (*etym. L.* setaceum, *made of horse-hair*), sieve. — *mobile*, cradle. *Passer au* —, *au gros* —, to sift, to sift carelessly

Sasser, va. to sift

Satanique, adj. (*etym.* Satan), satanic, satanical

Satiété, sf. (*etym. L.* satietatem), satiety

Satinade, sf. (*etym.* satin), satinet

Satinage, sm. satining, hot-pressing

Satiné, e, past part. adj. satin, hot-pressed. *Peau* —*e*, skin as soft as velvet

Satiner, va. to satin, to hot-press; — vn. to be as white as satin

Satirique, adj. sm. (*etym.* satire), satirical, satiric, satirist

Satisfaire, va.n. (*etym. L.* satisfacere), to satisfy, to gratify, to give satisfaction to, to fulfil; *se* —, vr. to satisfy oneself, to gratify oneself

Satisfaisant, e, adj. satisfactory

Satisfait, e, adj. past part. satisfied, gratified

Satrape, sm. (*etym. L.* satrapa), satrap

Satrapie, sf. satrapy

Saturer, va. (*etym. L.* saturare), to saturate

Saturnales, sf.pl. (*etym. L.* Saturnalia), saturnalia

Saturne, sm. (*etym. L.* Saturnus), Saturn

Satyre, sm. (*etym. L.* satyrus), satyr

Saucer, va. (*etym.* sauce), to sop, to souse, to scold

Saucière, sf. sauce-boat

Saucisse, sf. (*etym. L.L.* salsitia, *sausage*), sausage

Saucisson, sm. sausage

Sauf, ve, adj. (*etym. L.* salvus), safe. — prep. save, saving, excepting, reserving

Sauf-conduit, sm. safe-conduct

Sauge, sf. (*etym. L.* salvia), sage

Saugrenu, e, adj. (*etym. O.F.* saigrenu, *coarse salt*), absurd, ridiculous

Saule, sm. (*etym. O.H.G.* sala, *willow*), willow. — *pleureur*, weeping willow. — *étêté*, pollard willow

Saumâtre, adj. (*etym. L.L.* salmastrum, *briny*), brackish, briny

Saumon, sm. (*etym. L.* salmonem), salmon, (*metal.*) pig. — *de fonte*, pig-iron

Saumoné, e, adj. salmon

Saumure, sf. (*etym. L.* sal, *salt*, muria, *pickle*), pickle, brine

Saunage, sm. (*etym.* sauner), salt trade. *Faux* —, contraband

Sauner, vn. (*etym. L.* salinare), to make salt

Saunerie, sf. salt works

Saunier, sm. (*etym. L.* salinarius), salter, salt maker. *Faux* —, contraband

Saupoudrer, va. (*etym.* sau *for* sel, poudrer), to sprinkle, to intersperse, to interlard

Saur, adj.m. (*etym. Dutch* soor, *dried up*), smoked (fish), dried up

Saure, adj. sorrel

Sauriens, sm. (*etym. Gr.* σαῦρος, *lizard*), lizard-tribe, saurians

Saussaie, sf. (*etym. L.L.* salicetum), willow plantation

Saut, sm. (*etym. L.* saltus), leap, jump, skip, fall, waterfall. ¦ *D'un* —, at a leap. *De plein* —, all at once. *Faire un* —, *le* —, to take a leap. *Faire faire le — à quelqu'un*, to oust a person out of his place. *Au — du lit*, the first thing in the morning. — *de loup*, ha-ha. — *périlleux*, summersault

Saute, sf. (*nav.*) shift (of wind)

Sauter, vn. (*etym. L.* saltare), to jump, to leap, to skip, to blow up, (*nav.*) to pitch and send, to jump round, to shift. ¦ *Faire — l'escalier à*, to kick down stairs. *Faire — quelqu'un de son emploi*, to oust a person out of his place. *Faire — la coupe*, to shift the cut. — va. to leap, to leap over, to skip

Sauté, e, adj. stewed

Saute-mouton, sm. leap-frog

Sauterelle, sf. locust, grasshopper, shifting bevel

Saute-ruisseau, sm. skip-kennel, outdoor clerk

Sauteur, se, a leaper, jumper, tumbler, mountebank, weathercock

Sautillement, sm. skipping, skip, hop

Sautiller, vn. to skip, to hop

Sautoir, sm. St. Andrew's cross, saltire

Sauvage, adj. (*etym. L.L.* salvaticus, *for* silvaticus), wild, savage, inhuman, unsociable, shy. — s. savage, unsociable fellow

Sauvageon, sm. wild stock

Sauvagerie, sf. unsociableness

Sauvegarde, sf. safeguard, (*nav., pl.*) rudder pendant

Sauvegarder, va. to watch over, to secure

Sauver, va. (*etym. L.* salvare), to save, to rescue, to deliver. ¦ — *les dehors, les apparences*, to keep up appearances. *Se* —, vr. to escape, to break away, to run away, to flee, to work out one's salvation, to indemnify oneself. *Sauve qui peut!* every man for himself! *Se — à toutes jambes*, to take to one's heels

Sauvetage, sm. salvage, rescue, rescuing. *Appareil de* —, life-preserver, fire-escape. *Bateau de* —, life-boat

Sauveur, sm. (*etym. L.* salvatorem), saver, deliverer, Saviour

Savane, sf. (*etym. Sp.* savana), savannah

Savant, e, adj. (*etym.* savoir), learned, well-informed, masterly, knowing, wise. — s. scholar, learned person, scientific man

‡**Savantasse,** sm. a man who pretends to be learned

Savate, sf. (*etym. I.* ciabatta, *slipper*), old shoe, hunt the slipper, French boxing. ‡ *Trainer la* —, to go ragged

Savetier, sm. cobbler

Saveur, sf. (*etym. L.* saporem), savour, zest, flavour

Savoir, va. (*etym. L.* sapere), to know, to be aware of, to be apprised of, to be acquainted with. ‡ — *de bonne part*, to have from good authority. *Que je sache*, for all I know. — *faisons*, we hereby give notice. *C'est à* —, *à* —, —, to wit, namely. *Se* —, vr. to be known

Savoir, sm. science, learning

Savoir-faire, sm. management, dexterity

Savoir-vivre, sm. good breeding

Savon, sm. (*etym. L.* saponem), soap. *Eau de* —, soapsuds. *Pain de* —, cake of soap

Savonnage, sm. washing

Savonner, va. to soap, to wash, to lather; *se* —, vr. to wash, to lather

Savonnerie, sf. soap-manufactory

Savonnette, sf. wash-ball

Savonneux, se, adj. soapy

Savourer, va. (*etym.* saveur), to savour, to relish

‖**Savoureux,** se, adj. savoury

Sayon, sm. (*etym.* saie, *L.L.* saga), sagum

Sbire, sm. (*etym. I.* sbirro), sbirro, myrmidon

Scabieuse, sf. (*etym. L.* scabiosa), scabious

Scabreux, se, adj. (*etym. L.* scabrosus, *rough*), rugged, slippery, ticklish, dangerous

Scalène, adj. (*etym. Gr.* σκαληνός, *unequal*), scalene

Scalper, va. (*from the English*), to scalp

Scandale, sm. (*etym. L.* scandalum), scandal, exposure, noise, shameful act. *Pierre de* —, stumbling-block

§**Scandaleux,** se, adj. scandalous

Scandaliser, va. (*etym. L.L.* scandalizare), to scandalize; *se* —, vr. to be scandalized

Scander, va. (*etym. L.* scandere), to scan

Scapulaire, sm.adj. (*etym. L.L.* scapularis), scapular, scapulary

Scarabée, sm. (*etym. L.* scarabæus), beetle

Scarificateur, sm. (*etym.* scarifier), scarificator

Scarifier, va. (*etym. L.* scarificare), to scarify

Scarlatine, sf. (*etym. I.* scarlatina), scarlatina. — adj. f. scarlet

Sceau, Seel, sm. (*etym. L.* sigillum), seal

Scélérat, e, adj. (*etym. L.* sceleratus), villanous, rascally, wicked, nefarious. — sm. miscreant, villain, wretch

Scélératesse, sf. villany

Scellé, sm. seal. ‡ *Faire apposer les* —*s*, *mettre les* —*s*, to affix the seals. *Sous le* —, under seal. *Bris de* —, breaking of the seal

Scellement, sm. fastening, sealing

Sceller, va. to seal up, to seal, to fasten

Scène, sf. (*etym. L.* scena), stage, scene, scenery. ‡ *Entrer en* —, to come on the stage. *On entre en* —, the play begins. *Mettre en* —, to get up for the stage. *Faire une* — *à*, to upbraid outrageously. *Pas de* — ! no noise !

Scénique, adj. (*etym. L.* scenicus), theatrical, scenic

Scepticisme, sm. scepticism

Sceptique, sm. adj. (*etym. L.* scepticus), sceptic, sceptical

Schabraque, or **Chabraque,** sf. (*etym. G.* schabrake), shabrack

Schelling, sm. (*from the English*), shilling

Schismatique, adj. sm. (*etym. L.L.* schismaticus), schismatical, schismatic

Schisme, sm. (*etym. L.L.* schisma), schism

Schiste, sm. (*etym. L.* schistos), slate, schist, clay-slate, shale

Schlague, sf. (*etym. G.* schlag, *a blow*), a flogging, cat o' nine tails

Sciage, sm. (*etym.* scier), sawing

Sciatique, sf.adj. (*etym. L.* ischiadicus), sciatica, sciatic

Scie, sf. saw, saw-fish, bore. — *à main*, hand-saw. — *de scieur de long*, pit-saw

Sciemment, adv. (*etym. L.* scientem), knowingly, wittingly

‖**Scientifique,** adj. (*etym.* science), scientific, scientifical

Scier, va. (*etym. L.* secare), to saw, to reap, to cut down, (*nav.*) to back astern. ‡ — *le dos à quelqu'un*, to bore some one to death

Scierie, sf. saw-mill

Scieur, sm. sawyer, reaper. — *de long*, sawyer, pit-sawyer

Scinder, va. (*etym. L.* scindere), to divide

§**Scintillant, e,** adj. scintillating, twinkling

§**Scintiller,** vn. (*etym. L.* scintillare), to twinkle, to scintillate

Scissionnaire, sm. seceder

Sciure, sf. sawdust

Scolaire, adj. (*etym. L.* scholaris), school

§**Scolastique,** adj. sm. (*etm. L.* scholasticus), scholastic, schoolman. — sf. scholastic philosophy

Scoliaste, sm. (*etym. Gr.* σχολιάστης), scholiast

Scolie, smf. (*etym. Gr.* σχόλιον, *a note*), scholium

Scorbut, sm. (*etym. Dutch* scheurbuk), scurvy

Scorbutique, adj. s. scorbutic

Scorie, sf. (*etym. L.* scoria), scoria, dross, slag

Scorifier, va. to scorify

Scrofules, sf. plur. (*etym. L.* scrofulæ), scrofula

Scrofuleux, se, adj. scrofulous

Scrupule, sm. (*etym. L.* scrupulus), scruple, scrupulousness

‖**Scrupuleux,** se, adj. (*etym. L.* scrupulosus), scrupulous

Scrutateur, sm. (*etym. L.* scrutator), searcher, scrutator. — adj. searching, scrutinizing

Scruter, va. (*etym. L.* scrutari), to search, to scrutinize

Scrutin, sm. (*etym. L.* scrutinium), ballot. ‡ *Au* — *secret*, with vote by ballot. — *de liste*, ballot for a list

Sculpter, va. (*etym. L.L.* sculptare), to carve

Sculpteur, sm. (*etym. L.* sculptor), sculptor, carver

Sculpture, sf. (*etym. L.* sculptura), sculpture, carving

Se, pron. (*etym. L.* se), himself, herself, itself, themselves, oneself

Séance, sf. (*etym.* séant), seat, sitting, meeting. ‡ *Tenir* —, to hold a sitting. — *tenante*, forthwith, before separating. *La* — *est levée*, the meeting is closed. *Faire une longue* —, to sit a long while

Séant, e, part. adj. (*etym. L.* sedentem), sitting, becoming, seemly. — sm. sitting part. ‡ *Être sur son* —, to be sitting up. *Mettre quelqu'un sur son* —, to help to sit up

Seau, sm. (*etym. L.L.* sitellum, *a vase*), pail, bucket. — *à charbon*, coal-scuttle. — *à incendie*, fire-bucket. *Pleuvoir à* —*x*, to rain in torrents

Sébile, sf. (*etym.* ?), wooden bowl

‖**Sec, Sèche,** adj. (*etym. L.* siccus), dry, gaunt, spare, threadbare, hard, barren, plain, unfeeling. ‡ *Froid* —, sharp cold. *A pied* —, dry-footed. *Coup* —, quick blow. *Bruit* —, sharp noise. *Argent* —, hard cash. — adv. drily. *Répondre tout* —, to answer drily. *Tout* —, nothing but. *Faire* —, to he dry weather. *A* —, dry, drained, (*nav.*) high and dry (on the shore), under bare poles. *Mettre à* —, to drain, to dry up. *Être à* —, to be hard up, to be out of cash, to he empty. — sm. dryness, dry fodder

Sécante, sf. (*etym. L.* secantem), secant

Sèche, Seiche, sf. (*etym. L.* sepia), cuttle-fish

Sécher, va.n. (*etym. L.* siccare), to dry, to dry up, to wither, to pine away; *se* —, vr. to dry oneself

Sécheresse, sf. drought, dryness, sharpness, aridity, stiffness

Séchoir, sm. drying room, drying place

‖**Secondaire,** adj. (*etym. L.* secundarius), secondary. *Enseignement* —, classical tuition

Seconde, sf. the second form, second, (*fencing*) segoon

Seconder, va. (*etym. L.* secundare), to second, to help, to back

Secouer, va. (*etym. L.L.* succutare), to shake, to jog, to jolt, to throw off; *se* —, vr. to shake oneself, to move about, to be up and doing

Secourable, adj. helpful, helping, charitable, relievable

Secourir, va. (*etym. L.* succurere), to help, to succour, to relieve; *se* —, vr. to help one another

Secours, sm. help, succour, relief

Secousse, sf. (*etym. L.L.* succussa), shock, shake, jog, jolt, jolting

‖**Secret, ète,** adj. (*etym. L.* secretus), secret, who can keep counsel

Secret, sm. (*etym. L.* secretum), secret, secrecy, secret spring, secret drawer

Secrétaire, sm. (*etym.* secret), secretary, desk

Secrétairerie, sf. secretary's office

Secrétariat, sm. secretaryship, secretary's office

Secrète, sf. secret prayer

Sécréter, va. (*etym. L.L.* secretare), to secrete

Sectaire, sm. sectarian, sectary

Sectateur, sm. (*etym. L.* sectator), votary

Secte, sf. (*etym. L.* secta), sect

Secteur, sm. (*etym. L.* sector), sector

Séculaire, adj. (*etym. L.* secularis), secular, ancient, reverend

Sécularisation, sf. secularization

Séculariser, va. to secularize

Sécularité, sf. secular jurisdiction

Séculier, ère, adj. sm. (*etym. L.* secularis), secular

Sécurité, sf. (*etym. L.* securitatem), security

Sédatif, ve, adj. sm. (*etym. L.L.* sedativus), sedative

‖**Sédentaire,** adj. (*etym. L.* sedentarius), sedentary

‖**Séditieux, se,** adj. (*etym. L.* seditiosus), seditious

Séducteur, trice, s. adj. (*etym. L.* seductor), seducer, deluder; seducing, deluding

Séduction, sf. (*etym. L.* seductionem), seduction, allurement, subornation

Séduire, va. (*etym. L.* seducere), to seduce, to insnare, to captivate, to bribe

Séduisant, e, adj. seductive, alluring, winning, captivating

Segment, sm. (*etym. L.* segmentum), segment

Séide, sm. (*etym. prop. n. of a character in one of Voltaire's tragedies*), fanatical supporter

§**Seigle,** sm. (*etym. L.* secale), rye

§**Seigneur,** sm. (*etym. L.* seniorem), lord

§**Seigneurial, e,** adj. lordly, seignorial

§**Seigneurie,** sf. seignory, manor, lordship

Sein, sm. (*etym. L.* sinus), bosom, breast, womb, midst

Seine, sf. (*etym. L.* sagena), drag-net, sein

Seing, sm. (*etym. L.* signum), signature, sign manual. *Acte sous — privé*, private deed

Seize, adj. s. (*etym. L.* sedecim), sixteen, sixteenth

Seizième, adj. s. sixteenth, 16th

Séjour, sm. stay, sojourn, continuance, abode

Séjourner, va. (*etym. L.L.* subdiurnare), to stay, to remain, to stop

Sel, sm. (*etym. L.* sal), salt, poignancy, wit

Selle, sf. (*etym. L.* sella), saddle, stool. *— pour dame*, side-saddle. *Bois de —*, saddle-tree. ‡*Être bien en —*, to sit well in one's saddle. *Se mettre en —*, to mount. *Sauter en —*, to vault into the saddle

Seller, va. to saddle

Sellerie, sf. saddlery, saddle-room

Sellette, sf. stool, settle, collar, pillow, shoeblack's box. ‡*Tenir sur la —*, to cross-question

Sellier, sm. saddle and harness maker

Selon, prep. (*etym. L.* sublongum), according to, agreeably to, pursuant to

Semailles, sf. pl. (*etym. L.* seminalia), sowing seed, seed, sowing time. *Faire les —s*, to sow seed

Semaine, sf. (*etym. L.* septimana), week, week's time, week's labour, week's earnings, weekly allowance

Semainier, ère, s. person on duty for the week

Sémaphore, sm. (*etym. Gr.* σῆμα, *sign*, φορός, *bearing*), coast signal-mast

Semblable, adj. similar, alike, like. — sm. fellow-creature, fellow-man

Semblant, sm. seeming, appearance, show

Sembler, vn. (*etym. L.* simulare), to seem, to appear

Semelle, sf. (*etym. ?*), sole, foot, shoe, step, sleeper. *Battre la —*, to warm one's feet

Semence, sf. (*etym. L.L.* sementia), seed, cause, fine sprigs

Semer, va. (*etym. L.* seminare), to sow, to strew, to scatter, to sprinkle; *se —*, vr. to be sown

Semestre, sm. (*etym. L.* semestris), half, half-year, half-yearly income, furlough

Semestriel, le, adj. half-yearly

Semeur, sm. sower

§**Sémillant, e,** adj. (*etym. Celt.* sim, *light, active*), brisk, lively

Séminaire, sm. (*etym. L.* seminarium), seminary (for priests)

Séminariste, sm. seminarist

Semis, sm. seed-bed, seed-plot

Sémitique, adj. (*etym. prop. name* Shem), Semitic

Semonce, sf. (*etym.* semondre), rebuke, lecture, invitation. *Faire une — à*, to rebuke

Semoncer, va. to rebuke, to lecture

***Semondre,** va. (*etym. L.* submonere), to invite (to a ceremony

Semoule, sf. (*etym. I.* semola), semolina

Sempiternel, le, adj. (*etym. L.L.* sempiternalis), everlasting

Sénat, sm. (*etym. L.* senatus), senate, senate-house

Sénateur, sm. (*etym. L.* senator), senator

Sénatorerie, sf. senator's rank

Sénatorien, ne, adj. senatorian

Sénatus-consulte, sm. (*etym. L.* senatûs consultum), senatus-consultum

Séné, sm. (*etym. Ar.* sana, *arrow*), senna

Sénéchal, e, s. (*etym. L.* seniscalcus, *overseer*), seneschal, seneschal's lady

Sénéchaussée, sf. seneschal's jurisdiction, seneschal's court

Séneçon, sm. (*etym. L.* senecionem), groundsel

Sénevé, sm. (*etym. L.* sinapi), mustard-seed

Sens, sm. (*etym. L.* sensus), sense, the senses, judgment, purport, construction, interpretation, side, way, direction. ‡*Donner dans le — de*, to agree with, to chime in with

‖**Sensé, e,** adj. (*etym. L.* sensatus), sensible, judicious

Sensibilité, sf. (*etym. L.* sensibilitatem), sensibility, sensitiveness

‖**Sensible,** adj. (*etym. L.* sensibilis), sensible, tender, lively, acute, sensitive

Sensiblerie, sf. sentimentality

‖**Sensitif, ve,** adj. (*etym.* sens), sentient, sensitive

Sensitive, sf. sensitive plant

Sensualité, sf. (*etym. L.* sensualitatem), sensuality

‖**Sensuel, le,** adj. (*etym. L.* sensualis), sensual, voluptuous

Sentencieux, se, adj. (*etym. L.* sententiosus), sententious

Senteur, sf. (*etym.* sentir), smell, scent, perfume. ‡*Eau de —*, scented water. *Pois de —*, sweet peas

Sentier, sm. (*etym. L.L.* semitarius), path, footpath, pathway

Sentiment, sm. (*etym.* sentir), sensation, feeling, sentiment, sense, intuitive perception, opinion, scent

Sentine, sf. (*etym. L.* sentina), sink

Sentinelle, sf. (*etym. I.* sentinella), sentry, sentinel. *— perdue*, forlorn sentry

Senti, e, past part. felt, well expressed

Sentir, va.n. (*etym. L.* sentire), to feel, to be sensible of, to foresee, to smell, to taste of, to perceive, to bear; *se —*, vr. to feel, to know oneself, to feel in oneself, to be felt

Seoir, vn. (*etym. L.* sedere), to be seated, to sit down, to become, to be becoming

Séparation, sf. (*etym. L.* separationem), separation, parting, severing

‖**Séparé, e,** adj. separate, apart

Séparer, va. (*etym. L.* separare), to separate, to divide, to distinguish, to divorce; *se —*, vr. to separate, to fall off, to part, to break up

Sept, sm. adj. (*etym. L.* septem), seven

Septante, adj. (*etym. L.* septuaginta), seventy. *Les —*, the Septuagint

Septembre, sm. September

***Septembriseur,** sm. Septembrist

Septennal, e, adj. septennial

Septentrion, sm. (*etym. L.* septentrionem), the North

Septentrional, e, adj. (*etym. L.* septentrionalis), northern

‖**Septième,** adj. sm. seventh

Septuagénaire, adj. sm. (*etym. L.* septuagenarius), seventy years old, a person seventy years of age

Septuagésime, sf. (*etym. L.* septuagesimus), Septuagesima Sunday

Septuple, sm. adj. (*etym. L.* septuplus), sevenfold

Sépulcral, e, adj. (*etym. L.* sepulcralis), sepulchral

Sépulcre, sm. (*etym. L.* sepulcrum), sepulchre

*†**Séquelle,** sf. (*etym. L.* sequela), set, tag-rag and bob-tail

Séquestre, sm. (*etym. L.* sequester), sequestration, sequestrator, depositary, deposit

Séquestrer, va. (*etym. L.* sequestrare), to sequester, to sequestrate; *se —*, vr. to sequester oneself

§**Sérail,** sm. (*etym. Turk.* seral, *palace*), seraglio

Séraphin, sm. (*etym. Heb.* saraph, *fiery*), seraph

Séraphique, adj. seraphic

Serein, e, adj. (*etym. L.* serenus), serene, placid, undisturbed, happy. — sm. night dew, evening damp

Sérénissime, adj. serene

Sérénité, sf. (*etym. L.* serenitatem), serenity, placidity, cheerfulness

Séreux, se, adj. (*etym. L.* serosus), serous

Serf, ve, s. adj. (*etym. L.* servus), serf, thrall; servile

Sergent, sm. (*etym. L.* servientem), bailiff, serjeant, (*joiner.*) cramp, (*nav.*) hold-fast

Séricole, Séricicole, adj. (*etym. L.* serica, *silk stuff*), silk, of silk

Série, sf. (*etym. L.* seriem), series

‖**Sérieux, se,** adj. (*etym. L.L.* seriosus), serious, grave, thoughtful, earnest, real, bona fide. — sm. seriousness, gravity serious look, serious character. ‡*Garder son —*, to keep one's countenance

Serin, sm. (*etym. L.* citrinus, *lemon-colour*), canary bird, canary

Serine, sf. hen canary, canary bird

Seriner, va. to play on the bird-organ, to teach, to repeat over and over again

Serinette, sf. bird-organ

Seringa, Syringa, sm. (*etym. L.* syrinx, *reed*), syringa

Seringue, sf. (*etym. L.* syringa), squirt, clyster-pipe

Seringuer, va. to syringe, to squirt, (*nav.*) to rake, to enfilade

Serment, sm. (*etym. L.* sacramentum), oath

Sermonnaire, sm. collection of sermons, author of sermons

Sermonner, va. (*etym.* sermon), to lecture

Sermonneur, sm. proser, lecturer

Sérosité, sf. (*etym. L.L.* serositatem), serosity

Serpe, sf. (*etym. L.* sarpere, *to cut*), pruning bill, hedge bill

Serpent, sm. (*etym. L.* serpentem), serpent, snake, serpent player

Serpentaire, sf. (*etym. L.* serpentaria), snake-root, serpentaria

Serpenteau, sm. young serpent, squib

Serpenter, vn. to meander, to wind. *— doucement*, to steal its way

Serpentin, e, adj. serpentine. — sm. (*chem.*) worm

Serpentine, sf. serpentine, grass plantain

Serpette, sf. pruning knife

§**Serpillière,** sf. (*etym. ?*), packing cloth, mole-cricket

Serpolet, sm (*etym. L.* serpullum), wild thyme

Serre, sf. greenhouse, conservatory, talon, pressure, squeezing

Serré, e, past part. tight, clasped, pressed, concise, close-fisted. — adv. a great deal, hard. ‡*Jouer —*, to play cautiously, to mind what one is about

Serre-file, sm. (*milit.*) bringer-up, (*nav.*) sternmost ship; *plur.* des serre-file. *En* —, as bringer-up

Serrement, sm. pressing, squeezing. *Avec un — de cœur*, with a shrinking of the heart

Serre-papiers, sm. paper-holder, paper-weight

Serrer, va. (*etym. L.L. serare, to lock up*), to tighten, to strain, to fasten, to press, to squeeze, to clasp, to lock, to hug, to fit, to clench, to condense, to pursue, to haul close to, to put by or away, to lock up, to house; *se* —, vr. to press close, to crowd, to grow tighter

Serre-tête, sm. headband; *plur.* des serre-tête

Serrure, sf. lock. — *de sûreté*, safety lock

Serrurerie, sf. locksmith's business, locksmith's work, ironmongery

Serrurier, sm. locksmith

Servage, sm. (*etym. serf*), villeinage, thraldom

Servant, adj.m. serving, in waiting, lay (brother). — sm. servant, gunner

Servante, sf. maid-servant, maid, dumb-waiter

Serviable, adj. obliging, serviceable

Service, sm. (*etym. L. servitium*), service, attendance, duty, course, set. ¦*Être au* —, to be in the army *or* navy. *Être de* —, to be on duty. *Officier de* —, attendant, officer on duty. — *de table*, dinner-service. — *à thé*, set of tea-things

Serviette, sf. napkin, towel

Servilement, adv. (*etym. servile*), servilely, slavishly

Servilité, sf. servility

Servir, va. (*etym. L. servire*), to serve, to be a servant to, to attend, to wait upon, to help, to pay, to supply, to work; — vn. to serve *as or* for, to act as, to perform the office of, to stand in lieu of; *se* —, vr. to serve oneself, to wait upon oneself, to make use of, to avail oneself, to be served up

Serviteur, sm. (*etym. L. servitor*), servant

Ses, adj. poss. *see* Son

Sésame, sm. (*etym. L. sesamum*), sesame, sesamum

Setier, sm. (*etym. L. sextarius*), twelve bushels, two gallons

Séton, sm. (*etym. I. setone*), seton, rowel

§**Seuil,** sm. (*etym. L. soleum*), threshold, door-sill

¦**Seul, e,** adj. (*etym. L. solus*), only, sole, alone

Sève, sf. (*etym. L. sapa*), sap, strength, pith, vigour

¦**Sévère,** adj. (*etym. L. severus*), severe, stern, strict, austere. — sm. the severe style

Sévérité, sf. (*etym. L. severitatem*), severity, sternness, strictness

Sévices, sm.plur. (*etym. L. sævitiæ*), cruelty

Sévir, vn. to act with vigour, to ill-treat

Sevrage, sm. weaning. *En* —, being weaned

Sevrer, va. (*etym. L. separare*), to wean, to estrange, to deprive; *se* —, vr. to estrange oneself

Sexagénaire, adj.s. (*etym. L. sexagenarius*), sixty years old. *Un* —, a sexagenarian

Sexe, sm. (*etym. L. sexus*), sex

Sextupler, va. (*etym. sextuple*), to increase sixfold, to multiply by six

Sexuel, le, adj. (*etym. L. sexualis*), sexual

Shako, sm. (*Hungar. word*), a military hat

Shérif, sm. (*English word*), sheriff

Si, conj. (*etym. L. si*), adv. (*etym. L. sic*), if, so, whether, how much, yes, yet, however. *Que* —, if, but if. — sm. if, (*mus.*) B, si

Sibylle, sf. (*etym. L. sibylla*), sibyl

Sibyllin, adj.m. (*etym. L. sibyllinus*), sibylline

Sicaire, sm. (*etym. L. sicarius*), hired assassin

Siccatif, ve, adj.sm. (*etym. L. siccativus*), siccative

Siècle, sm. (*etym. L. sæculum*), century, age

Siége, sm. (*etym. siéger*), seat, coachman's box, rumble, dickey, bench, judgment-seat, see, siege

Siéger, vn. (*etym. L.L. sediare*), to sit, to be seated, to lie

Sien, Sienne (le, la), Siens, Siennes (les), pron. poss. (*etym. see* Son), his, his own, her, her own, its own, one's own

Sieste, sf. (*etym. Sp. siesta*), siesta. *Faire la* —, to take one's siesta

Sieur, sm. (*corruption of seigneur*), Mr. *Un — Paul*, a certain Mr. Paul

Sifflant, e, adj. sibilant

Sifflement, sm. hissing, whistling

Siffler, va.n. (*etym. L.L. sifilare*), to hiss, to whistle, to wheeze, to whizz, (*nav.*) to pipe

Sifflet, sm. whistle, cat-call, call

Siffleur, se, s. whistler, hisser, wood-wren. — adj. whistling, wheezing

Sigisbée, sm. (*etym. I. cicisbeo*), cicisbeo

§**Signalé, e,** adj. (*etym. signal*), signal

§**Signalement,** sm. description

§**Signaler,** va. to give the description of, to point out, to mark out, to make signals of, to signalize; *se* —, vr. to signalize oneself

§**Signaliste,** sm. signal-man

§**Signataire,** sm. signer, subscriber

§**Signe,** sm. (*etym. L. signum*), sign, nod, beck

§**Signer,** va.n. (*etym. L. signare*), to sign, to subscribe, to witness; *se* —, vr. to cross oneself

§**Signet,** sm. marker

§**Significatif, ve,** adj. (*etym. L. significativus*), significant, significative, meaning

§**Signification,** sf. (*etym. L. significationem*), signification, meaning, import, legal notice

§**Signifier,** va. (*etym. L. significare*), to signify, to mean, to import, to intimate, to serve a notice

¦**Silencieux, se,** adj. (*etym. L. silentiosus*), silent, still

Silhouette, sf. (*prop. n. of a French statesman*), silhouette

Silice, sf. (*etym. L. silicem*), flint, silica

Siliceux, se, adj. silicious, flinty

§**Sillage,** sm. (*etym. Scand. sila, to furrow*), track, wake, ship's way, steerage-way, rate of sailing

§**Sillon,** sm. furrow, plains, field, trail, train, track, groove. *Tracer des —s dans*, to plough

§**Sillonné, e,** past part. adj. furrowed, intersected, sulcated

§**Sillonner,** va. to plough, to furrow, to flash through, to intersect, to cross in every direction

Silo, sm. (*Spanish word*), pit (for preserving corn, &c.)

Simagrée, sf. (*etym. si m'agrée, thus it pleases me*), grimace, affectation. *Faire des —s*, to make grimaces. *Faire la — de*, to make pretence to

Simarre, sf. (*etym. I. zimarra*), judge's gown, simar

Similaire, adj. (*etym. L. similaris*), similar

Similor, sm. (*etym. L. simili*), pinchbeck

Simonie, sf. (*etym. L.L. simonia*), simony

Simplement, adv. (*etym. simple*), merely, simply, with simplicity

Simplesse, sf. simpleness

Simplicité, sf. (*etym. L. simplicitatem*), simplicity, simpleness

Simplifier, va. to simplify; *se* —, vr. to be simplified

Simulacre, sm. (*etym. L. simulacrum*), image, shadow, sham

Simulation, sf. (*etym. L. simulationem*), feigning

Simuler, va. (*etym. L. simulare*), to feign, to counterfeit, to simulate

Simultané, e, adj. (*etym. L.L. simultaneus*), simultaneous

Simultanéité, sf. simultaneousness

Sinapisé, e, adj. with flower of mustard

Sinapisme, sm. (*etym. L.L. sinapismus*), mustard poultice

Sincèrement, adv. (*etym. sincère*), sincerely, unfeignedly

Sincérité, sf. (*etym. L. sinceritatem*), sincerity, sincereness, ingenuousness

Singe, sm. (*etym. L. simius*), monkey, ape, mimic, pantograph, windlass. — adj. aping

Singer, va. to ape, to mimic

Singeresse, adj.f. aping

Singerie, sf. grimace, antic, apish trick, mimicry

Singulariser, va. (*etym. L. singularis*), to render singular; *se* —, vr. to render oneself singular, to affect singularity

Singularité, sf. (*etym. L. singularitatem*), singularity, peculiarity, oddness

¦**Singulier, ère,** adj. (*etym. L. singularis*), singular, peculiar, queer, odd, single. — sm. singular, singular number

¦**Sinistre,** adj. (*etym. L. sinister*), sinister, inauspicious, ill-favoured. — sm. disaster, casualty, shipwreck

Sinon, conj. otherwise, or else, if not, unless it be

Sinueux, se, adj. (*etym. L. sinuosus*), winding, meandering, sinuous

Sinuosité, sf. (*etym. L.L. sinuositatem*), sinuosity, winding

Sinus, sm. (*Latin word*), sine, sinus

Sire, sm. (*see* Seigneur), sire, sir, lord. ¦*Un pauvre* —, a poor devil

Sirène, sf. (*etym. L. siren*), mermaid, syren

Siroc, Sirocco, sm. (*etym. I. scirocco, S.E. wind*), sirocco

Sirop, sm. (*etym. I. siroppo*), syrup

Siroter, va.n. (*etym. ?*), to sip (one's wine)

Sis, e, past part. (*etym. L. situs*), situated

Sitôt, adv. so soon, as soon

Situé, adj. (*etym. site*), situated

Sixain, sm. (*etym. six*), stanza of six verses, six packs of cards

Sixième, adj. sm. sixth

Sixte, sf. (*etym. L. sextus*), sixth

Sobre, adj. (*etym. L. sobrius*), abstemious, sober

Sobriété, sf. (*etym. L. sobrietatem*), abstemiousness, sobriety

Sobriquet, sm. (*etym. ?*), nickname

Soc, sm. (*etym. L. soccus*), ploughshare

Sociabilité, sf. (*etym. L.L. sociabilitatem*), sociability, sociableness

Social, e, adj. (*etym. L. socialis*), social, (*comm.*) belonging to a firm. ¦*Sous la raison —e de*, under the firm of

¶**Socialisme,** sm. socialism

¶**Socialiste,** sm. adj. socialist

Sociétaire, smf. member, associate, partner, shareholder

Société, sf. (*etym. L.* societatem), society, company, fellowship. ‡*Faire, tenir* — *à*, to bear *or* keep company. *Entrer en* —, to enter into partnership

Socinianisme, sm. (*etym. prop. n.* Socin), Socinianism

Socinien, ne, s. adj. Socinian

Socle, sm. (*etym. I.* zoccolo), pedestal

Socque, sm. (*etym. L.* soccus), clog, patten, sock

Socratique, adj. (*etym. prop. name* Socrates), Socratic

Sœur, sf. (*etym. L.* soror), sister, (*pharm.*) sisterhood. — *de lait*, foster-sister

Soi, Soi-même, pron. indef. (*etym. L.* sibi), oneself, himself, herself, self, itself

Soi-disant, adj. indef. self-styled, would be, self-dubbed

Soie, sf. (*etym. L.* seta), silk

Soierie, sf. silk, silk goods, silk warehouse, silk manufactory, silk trade. *Marchand de* —*s*, silk mercer

Soif, sf. (*etym. L.* sitim), thirst

§**Soigné, e,** adj. elaborate, carefully done

§**Soigner,** va (*etym.* soin), to take care of, to be mindful of, to nurse, to attend; *se* —, vr. to take care of oneself, to nurse oneself

§**Soigneux, se,** adj. careful, mindful, regardful, tidy

Soin, sm. (*etym.* ?), care, attendance, duty, task

Soir, sm. (*etym. L.* serum, *evening*), evening, even, eve, afternoon

Soirée, sf. evening, evening party

Soit, adv. be it so, say. ‡ — *encore*, I grant that too. — conj. either, whether

Soixantaine, sf. sixty, sixty years of age. *Une* — *de*, about sixty

Soixante, adj. sm. (*etym. L.* sexaginta), sixty, threescore, the sixtieth

Soixanter, va. to count sixty

§**Soixantième,** adj. sixtieth

Sol, sm. (*etym. L.* solum), ground, soil, (*mas.*) wall, (*mus.*) G, sol

Solaire, adj. (*etym. L.* solaris), solar, sun, of the sun

Soldat, sm. (*etym. I.* soldato), soldier

Soldatesque, sf. (*etym. I.* soldatesca), soldiery

Solde, sf. (*etym. I.* soldo), pay. — sm. balance, settling, discharge

Solder, va. (*etym. I.* soldare), to pay, to settle, to balance; *se* —, vr. to be balanced

Sole, sf. (*etym. L.* solea), sole; (*etym. L.* solum), (*agric.*) break

Solécisme, sm. (*etym. Gr.* σολοικισμός), solecism

§**Soleil,** sm. (*etym. L.L.* soliculus), the sun, sunshine, sun-flower

§**Solennel, le,** adj. (*etym. L.L.* solennalis), solemn

Solennisation, sf. solemnization

Solenniser, va. to solemnize

Solennité, sf. (*etym. L.* solemnitatem), solemnity

Solfège, sm. (*etym. I.* solfeggio), solfeggio

Solfier, va. (*etym. I.* solfa), to solfa

§**Solidaire,** adj. (*etym.* solide), binding upon every one, jointly and severally liable

Solidarité, sf. responsibility of each and all together

§**Solide,** adj. sm. (*etym. L.* solidus), solid, well grounded, standing; reality

Solidifier, va., *se* —, vr. to solidify

Solidité, sf. (*etym. L.* soliditatem), solidity

Soliloque, sm. (*etym. L.* soliloquium), soliloquy

Solipède, adj. sm. (*etym. L.* solum, pedem), soliped

§**Solitaire,** adj. (*etym. L.L.* solitarius), solitary, lonesome, lonely. — sm. hermit, solitary

Solive, sf. (*etym. L.* sublevare), joist

Soliveau, sm. small joist, log of wood

Sollicitation, sf. (*etym. L.* sollicitationem), solicitation, entreaty

Solliciter, va. (*etym. L.* sollicitare), to invite, to solicit, to beg for

Solliciteur, se, s. solicitor, solicitress

Sollicitude, sf. solicitude, care

Solubilité, sf. (*etym. L.L.* solubilitatem), solubility

Solvabilité, sf. (*etym. L.L.* solvabilitatem), solvency

Solvable, adj. (*etym. L.L.* solvabilis), solvent

Sombre, adj. (*etym. Span.* sombra), gloomy, dark, dismal, overcast, dull, sombre

Sombrer, vn. (*etym. L.L.* subumbrare), to founder, to go down

§**Sommaire,** adj. sm. (*etym. L.* summarium), summary, abstract, sum

Sommation, sf. summons, summing up

Somme, sf. (*etym. L.* summa), sum, compendium; (*etym. L.L.* salma, *burden*), burden. — *toute, en* —, in sum, in the main. *Bête de* —, beast of burden

Somme, sm. (*etym. L.* somnus), nap, sleep. *Faire un* —, to take a nap

§**Sommeil,** sm. (*etym.* somme, sm.), sleep, slumber

§**Sommeiller,** vn. to doze, to slumber

Sommelier, sm. (*etym. L.L.* saumalarius, *from* salma *or* sauma, *burden*), butler

Sommellerie, sf. butler's office, buttery, pantry

Sommer, va. (*etym. L.L.* summare), to summon, to call upon, to sum up

Sommet, sm. (*etym. L.* summum), summit, height, top, (*arch.*) crown, pinnacle, vertex

Sommier, sm. pack-horse, sumpter-horse, sumpter-mule, mattress, sound-board, (*arch.*) summer, (*print.*) winter

Sommité, sf. (*etym. L.* summitatem), top, summit, prominent part, extremity. ‡*Les* —*s sociales*, the influential people

Somnambule, s. (*etym. L.* somnus, ambulare), somnambulist

Somnambulisme, sm. somnambulism

Somnifère, adj. sm. (*etym. L.* somnifer), somniferous; narcotic, opiate

Somptuaire, adj. (*etym. L.* sumptuarius), sumptuary

§**Somptueux, se,** adj. (*etym. L.* sumptuosus), sumptuous, costly

Somptuosité, sf. (*etym. L.* sumptuositatem), sumptuosity, sumptuousness

Son, Sa, Ses, adj. (*etym. L.* suum), his, her, its, one's

Son, sm. (*etym. L.* sonum), bran; (*etym. L.* sonum), sound, strain, beat, roll, blast, chink

Sonate, sf. (*etym. I.* sonata), sonata

Sondage, sm. sounding, (*min.*) boring

Sonde, sf. (*nav.*) lead, sounding lead, fathom line, probe

Sonder, va. (*etym. L.* subundare), to sound, to probe, to fathom

Songe, sm. (*etym. L.* somnium), dream

Songe-creux, sm. visionary, dreamer

Songer, vn. to dream, to muse, to think, to bear in mind

Songerie, sf. dreaming, musing

Songeur, se, s. dreamer

Sonnant, e, adj. sounding, which strikes the hours. ‡*En espèces* —*es*, in hard cash, money down. *A l'heure* —*e*, punctual to the hour

Sonner, va. n. (*etym. L.* sonare), to sound, to ring, to toll, to blow

Sonnerie, sf. ring, ringing the bells, the striking part

Sonnette, sf. bell, (*mech.*) pile-driver

Sonneur, sm. bell-ringer

Sonore, adj. (*etym. L.* sonorus), sonorous, sounding

Sonorité, sf. (*etym. L.L.* sonoritatem), sonorousness

Sophisme, sm. (*etym. L.* sophisma), sophism

Sophiste, sm. (*etym. L.* sophista), sophist

Sophistique, adj. (*etym. L.* sophisticus), sophistical

Sophistiquer, va. to use sophistry in, to sophisticate

Soporifique, adj. sm. (*etym. L.L.* soporificus), soporific

Sorbet, sm. (*etym. I.* sorbetto), sherbet

Sorbier, sm. (*etym. L.* sorbum), sorb, service-tree

Sorcellerie, sf. (*etym.* sorcier), witchcraft, sorcery

Sorcier, sm. (*etym. L.L.* sortiarius), wizard, sorcerer, conjurer

Sorcière, sf. witch, sorceress

§**Sordide,** adj. (*etym. L.* sordidus), sordid, stingy

Sorite, sm. (*etym. L.* sorites), sorites

Sornettes, sf. plur. (*etym. Celt.* sorn, *trifles*), idle tales, nonsense

Sort, sm. (*etym. L.* sortem), fate, lot, condition, state, spell, charm

Sortable, adj. suitable

Sortant, adj. sm. coming out, leaving office; comer out, goer out

Sorte, sf. (*etym. I.* sorta ?), kind, sort, species, manner

Sortie, sf. going out, coming out, exit, holiday, exportation, outlet, issue, sally, tirade

Sortilège, sm. (*etym. L.L.* sortilegium), charm, witchcraft

Sortir, vn. (*etym. L.* sortiri), to go out, to walk out, to leave, to stand out, to come up, to spring up, to escape, to gush out, to descend, to swerve, to recover. — (*faire*), *also* — va. to bring out, to send out, to pull out, to call out, to fetch out

Sot, te, adj. s. (*etym.* ?), foolish, silly, senseless; fool, blockhead, silly creature

Sotie, sf. farce

Sottise, sf. foolishness, silliness, folly, insult, abuse. *Dire des* —*s à*, to abuse

Sou, Sol, sm. (*etym. L.* solidus), sou, halfpenny

Soubassement, sm. (*etym.* sous, *I.* basamento), basement, base

Soubresaut, sm. (*etym. Sp.* sobresalto), start, jump, leap

Soubrette, sf. (*etym.* ?), abigail

Souche, sf. (*etym.* ?), stock, stump, stem, block, counterpart, chimney-stack. ‡*Faire* — *de*, to found a line of

Souci, sm. (*etym. L.L.* solsequium), marigold; (*etym.* soucier), care, anxiety, solicitude. ‡*C'est là le moindre, le cadet de mes* —*s*, that is the least of my concerns. *Sans* —, careless

Soucier, va. to disturb, to trouble; *se* —, vr. (*etym. L.* sollicitare), to care, to be concerned, to reck

Soucieux, se, adj. anxious, gloomy, full of care

Soucoupe, sf. (*etym.* sous, coupe), saucer, salver

Soudain, e, adj. (*etym. L.L.* subitanus), sudden, unexpected

Soudaineté, sf. suddenness
Soudan, sm. (etym. L.L. soldanus), sultan (of Egypt)
Soudard, Soudart, sm. (etym. I. soldardo), old soldier
Soude, sf. (etym. L. solida), kali, glass-wort, kelp
Souder, va. (etym. L.L. solidare), to solder, to weld; se —, vr. to join, to unite
Soudoyer, va. (etym. L.L. soldicare), to keep in one's pay
Soudure, sf. solder, soldering
Soufflage, sm. glass-blowing, (nav.) sheathing, spindle
Souffle, sm. breath, puff, inspiration
Souffler, vn. (etym. L. sufflare), to blow, to breathe, to pant to open one's mouth. ‡ *Machine soufflante*, blast engine, bellows. — va. to blow, to inflate, to prompt, to huff, to chouse
Soufflet, sm. bellows, head of a coach, box on the ear, cuff, affront
Souffleter, va. to box (a person's) ears, to insult
Souffleur, se, s. blower, prompter
Soufflure, sf. flaw, swelling
Souffrance, sf. suffering, permission, suspense. ‡ *Jour de* —, permitted light. *En* —, standing over, unliquidated
Souffrant, e, adj. suffering, in pain, diseased
Souffre-douleur, sm. drudge, butt
Souffreteux, se, adj. (etym. O. F. souffraite, distress), needy, sickly, ailing, poorly
Souffrir, vn.a. (etym. L.L. sufferrere), to suffer, to be in pain, to labour under; se —, vr. to bear each other
Soufre, sm. (etym. L. sulfur), brimstone, sulphur
Soufrer, va. to do over with brimstone
Souhait, sm. wish, desire, longing
Souhaitable, adj. desirable
Souhaiter, va. (etym. sous, O.F. haiter, to desire), to wish. ‡ — *la bienvenue à*, to wish welcome. *Il serait à — qu'il le fît*, it is to be wished he would do it
Souiller, va. (etym. L.L. suculare, to wallow like a pig [L.L. suculus]), to soil, to dirty, to sully; se —, vr. to soil or dirty oneself, to disgrace oneself
§Souillon, s. sloven, slut, kitchen-wench
§Souillure, sf. stain, spot, dirt, contamination
Soûl, e, adj. (etym. L.L. satullus, satiated), glutted, drunk, surfeited. — sm. fill
Soulagement, sm. relief, alleviation
Soulager, va. (etym. L.L. subleviare), to relieve, to ease, to lighten, to assuage; se —, vr. to relieve oneself, to assist each other, to be relieved
Soûler, va. to glut, to surfeit, to make drunk; se —, vr. to glut oneself, to get drunk
Soulèvement, sm. heaving, swelling, rising, insurrection, burst of indignation
Soulever, va. (etym. L. sublevare), to raise, to lift up, to heave, to bear up, to stir up; se —, vr. to raise oneself, to heave, to swell, to revolt, to be indignant
Soulier, sm. (etym. L.L. solarium, from L. solea, sandal), shoe. —*s ferrés*, hobnail shoes
§Souligner, va. to underline
Soumettre, va. (etym. L. submittere), to subject, to subdue, to submit, to refer; se —, vr. to submit, to yield, to consent, to engage
Soumis, e, past part. adj. (etym. L. submissus), subject, submissive
Soumission, sf. (etym. L. submissionem), submission, yielding, obedience, submissiveness, marks of respect, tender, contract. ‡ —*s cachetées*, sealed tenders
Soumissionnaire, sm. party tendering
Soumissionner, va. to tender for
Soupape, sf. (etym. ?), valve, plug. ‡ *A* —, with a valve. — *d'arrêt*, stop-valve. — *dormante*, fixed valve. — *mobile*, moveable safety valve. — *renversée*, reverse valve. — *pour purger le condensateur*, upper blow-through valve
Soupçon, sm. (etym. O.F. souspeçon), suspicion, distrust, surmise, touch, smack, taste
Soupçonner, va. to suspect, to have a suspicion of, to surmise, to think. *Faire — à quelqu'un*, to make one suspicious, to bring into suspicion, to raise a suspicion
Soupçonneux, se, adj. suspicious, distrustful
Soupe, sf. (etym. G. suppe), soup
Soupente, sf. (etym. sous, pendre), main-braces, strap, loft
Souper, vn. to sup, to eat supper
Souper, Soupé, sm. supper
Soupeser, va. (etym. sous, peser), to weigh (in one's hand)
Soupeur, sm. supper-eater
Soupière, sf. soup-tureen
Soupir, sm. sigh, breath, gasp, (mus.) crotchet. ‡ *Jeter, pousser un gros —, un profond* —, to heave a deep sigh. *Rendre le dernier* —, to breathe one's last. *Recevoir les derniers —s de quelqu'un*, to receive a person's last breath. *Demi-* —, quaver. *Quart de* —, demi-quaver
§Soupirail, sm. (etym. L.L. suspiraculum), air-hole, vent-hole
Soupirant, sm. suitor, wooer
Soupirer, vn.a. (etym. L. suspirare), to sigh, to gasp, to breathe
Souple, adj. (etym. L. supplex), pliant, supple, tough, yielding
Souplesse, sf suppleness, toughness, pliancy, versatility. ‡ *Esprit plein de* —, versatile mind
§Souquenille, sf. (etym. ?), smock-frock
Source, sf. (etym. sourdre), spring, source, rise, authority
Sourcil, sm. (etym. L. supercilium), eyebrow
§Sourciller, vn. to knit one's brows. *Sans* —, without wincing
§Sourcilleux, se, adj. careworn, unquiet, haughty, cloud-capped, lofty
Sourd, e, adj. (etym. L. surdus), deaf, dead, hollow, rumbling, dull, underhand, surd. ‡ — *comme un pot*, as deaf as a post. *Faire la —e oreille*, to turn a deaf ear. — s. deaf person. *Il n'y a de pire — que celui qui ne veut pas entendre*, none so deaf as those who won't hear. » *Frapper comme un* —, to beat unmercifully
Sourdine, sf. sourdine, (music) mute. *A la* —, secretly
Sourd-muet, sm., **Sourde-muette**, sf. deaf and dumb man or woman
Sourdre, vn. (etym. L. surgere), to bubble up, to arise
Souriceau, sm. little mouse
Souricière, sf. mouse-trap, trap
Souriquois, e, adj. micy, belonging to mice
Sourire, vn (etym. L. subridere), to smile, to please, to delight
Sourire, Souris, sm. smile
Souris, sf. (etym. L. soricem), mouse. *Gris de* —, mouse colour
Sournois, e, adj. (etym. ?), underhand, sneaking, sullen. — s. sneak
Sournoiserie, sf. underhand trick
Sous, prep. (etym. L. subtus), under, beneath, below, on; (in compound words) sub, under, deputy, subaltern
Sous-affermer, va. to under-let, to under-rent
Sous-aide, sm. under-assistant
Sous-amendement, sm. second amendment
Sous-chef, sm. deputy head-clerk
Souscripteur, sm. subscriber
Souscription, sf. subscription
Souscrire, va. (etym. L. subscribere), to subscribe
Sous-entendre, va. to understand; se —, vr. to be understood
Sous-entendu, sm. th understood
Sous-entente, sf. men reservation
Sous-gouvernante, under-governess
Sous-intendant, sm. puty-commissary
Sous-lieutenance, sub-lieutenancy, ensigncy
Sous-lieutenant, sub-lieutenant, ensign
Sous-locataire, under-tenant
Sous-location, sf. unc letting, under-tenancy
Sous-louer, va. to und let, to under-hire, to unc rent
Sous-marin, e, adj. s-marine
Sous-ordre, sm. subdis bution, subordinate
Sous-pied, sm. str trouser-strap
Sous-sel, sm. subsalt
§Soussigné, sm. the un signed
Sous-sol, sm. subsoil, s stratum
Sous-tendante, sf. tense
Sous-tendre, va. to tend
Soustraction, sf. subt tion, taking away, purl ing
Soustraire, va. (et sous, traire), to subtract take, to abstract, to purl to screen, to shelter; se vr. to escape, to flee, to e
Sous-traitant, sm. un farmer, sub-contractor
Sous-traité, sm. sub-tract
Sous-traiter, vn. under-farm, to sub-contr
Sous-ventrière, sf. b band
Soutache, sf. (etym. braid
Soutacher, va. to brai
Soutane, sf. (etym. I. tana), cassock. ‡ *Prendre* —, to become a priest
Soute, sf. (etym. I. so low), (nav.) store-room. *aux poudres*, powder-ma zine. — *au charbon*, c hole
Soutenable, adj. sust able, bearable, tenable
Soutènement, sm. (*bui* support, written explanat
Soutenir, va. (etym. L. s tinere), to hold up, to sust to uphold, to support, abide by, to abet, to maint to afford; se —, vr. to st up, to hold oneself up, to up, to be borne up, to m tain oneself, to be firm, resist, to hold good, to s port each other
Soutenu, e, past part. a unremitting, steady, consta lofty, well kept up, unfl ging
Souterrain, e, adj. (et L. subterraneus), subter

...n, underground. — sm. ...it, cave, tunnel

...tien, sm. (*etym.* sou-...ir), support, prop, stay, holder

...tirer, va. (*etym.* sous, ...er), to draw off, to rack, to ...

...venance, sf. remembrance

Souvenir, vr. (*etym. L.* ...bvenire), to remember, to collect, to bear in mind. *Il s'en souvient*, I remember

...uvenir, sm. recollection, ...membrance, memory, me...orial, keepsake, remem...rancer, fond recollections. *Rappelez-moi à son bon* —, ...member me kindly to him, her

...vent, adv. (*etym. L.* ...bende), often, frequently

...ouverain, e, adj. s. (*etym. L.* superanus, *chief*), sove...ign

...uveraineté, sf. sove...ignty, dominion

...yeux, se, adj. silky, ...ken

...pacieux, se, adj. (*etym.* ...spatiosus), spacious, roomy

...dassin, sm. (*etym. I.* adaccino), bravo

...arte, sm. (*etym. L.* spar...m, *kind of reed*), esparto, ...atweed, broom

...arterie, sf. esparto ma...facture, esparto articles

...asme, sm. (*etym. L.* ...sma), spasm

...asmodique, adj. (*etym.* ...r. σπασμώδης), spasmodic

...ath, sm. (*German word*), ...par

...atule, sf. (*etym. L.* spa...la), slice, spatula, spoonbill

...pécial, e, adj. (*etym. L.* ...ecialis), special, especial, ...articular, peculiar, profes...onal

...écialité, sf. (*etym. L.* ...ecialitatem), speciality, de...artment, line, branch

...écieux, se, adj. (*etym.* ...speciosus), specious

...écifier, va. (*etym. L.L.* ...ecificare), to specify

...pécifique, adj. sm. spe...fic

...ectacle, sm. (*etym. L.* ...ectaculum), sight, spectacle, ...how, theatre, play-house, ...erformance, magnificence. — *forain*, raree-show. *Pièce* ...*grand* —, play got up with ...eat magnificence

...ectateur, trice, s. ...*tym. L.* spectator), spectator, ...ker-on, beholder

...pectre, sm. (*etym. L.* ...ectrum), spectre, spectrum

...éculaire, adj. (*etym. L.* specularius), specular

...éculateur, trice, s. ...*ym. L.* speculator), specula...r

...éculatif, ve, adj. ...*ym. L.* speculativus), specu...ive. — sm. speculative ...rson

...éculer, va. (*etym. L.* ...eculari), to observe; — vn. speculate

Sphéricité, sf. sphericity

Sphérique, adj. (*etym. L.* sphæricus), spheric, spherical

Sphéroïde, sm. (*etym. L.* sphæroides), spheroid

Spirale, sf. (*etym. L.* spira), spiral. *En* —, winding, spiral. *Aller en* —, to wind. *Se rouler en* —, to wind round

Spiritualiser, va. (*etym. L.* spiritualis), to spiritualize

Spiritualisme, sm. spiritualism

Spiritualiste, adj. s. spiritualist

Spiritualité, sf. spirituality

Spirituel, le, adj. spiritual, clever, witty, intelligent. — sm. the spiritual, spiritual power

Spiritueux, se, adj. (*from the English*), spirituous. — sm. spirits. *Débit de* —, spirit-vaults

Splendeur, sf. (*etym. L.* splendor), splendour, refulgence

Splendide, adj. (*etym. L.* splendidus), splendid, refulgent, glorious

Spoliateur, trice, s. (*etym. L.* spoliator), spoiler, despoiler. — adj. of spoliation

Spolier, va. (*etym. L.* spoliare), to despoil, to rob

Spondaïque, adj. sm. (*etym. L.* spondaicus), spondaic

Spondée, sm. (*etym. L.* spondæus), spondee

Spongieux, se, adj. (*etym. L.* spongiosus), spongy

Spontané, e, adj. (*etym. L.* spontaneus), spontaneous, voluntary

Spontanéité, sf. spontaneousness

Sporadique, adj. (*etym. Gr.* σποραδικός, *scattered*), sporadical

Squale, sm. (*etym. L.* squalus), dog-fish

Squelette, sm. (*etym. Gr.* σκελετός, *dried up*), skeleton

Squille, sf. (*etym. Gr.* σκίλλα, *sea-onion*), sea-onion

Squirre, sm. (*etym. Gr* σκίρρος, *hard tumour*), scirrhus, scirrhosity

St! st! interj. Pst! Pst!

Stabilité, sf. (*etym. L.* stabilitatem), stability

Stade, sm. (*etym. Gr.* στάδιον), stadium, (*med.*) stage

Stage, sm. (*etym. L.* stare), residence, terms. *Faire son* —, to keep one's terms

Stagiaire, adj. attending terms. — sm. young licentiate (in law)

Stalle, sf. (*etym. L.L.* stallum, *stall*), stall

Stance, sf. (*etym. I.* stanza), stanza

Stathouder, sm. (*Dutch word*), stadtholder

Stathoudérat, sm. stadtholdership

Station, sf. (*etym. L.* stationem), station, coach-stand. *Chef de* —, station-master. *Être en* —, (*nav.*) to be on one's cruising ground

Stationnaire, adj. stationary. — sm. guard-ship

Stationnement, sm. stopping, standing

Stationner, vn. to stand, to stop

Statique, sf. (*etym. Gr.* στατική [ἐπιστήμη], *knowledge of equilibrium*), statics

Statisticien, sm. statistician

Statistique, sf. (*etym. Gr.* στατίζειν, *to establish*), statistics

Statuaire, sm. f. adj. (*etym. L.* statuarius), statuary

Statuer, va. n. (*etym. L.* statuere), to decide, to enact

Statuette, sf. small statue

Statut, sm. (*etym. L.* statutum), rule, regulation, statute

Stellionat, sm. (*etym. L.L.* stellionatus), stellionate

Sténographe, sm. (*etym. Gr.* γράφω, *I write*, στενός, *narrow*), shorthand writer, stenographer. *Rédacteur* —, reporter

Sténographie, sf. shorthand, stenography

Sténographier, va. to take down in shorthand

Sténographique, adj. shorthand

Steppe, sm. (*Russian word*), steppe

Stère, sm. (*etym. Gr.* στερεός, *solid*), (cubic metre)

Stéréographie, sf. (*etym. Gr.* στερεός, γράφω), stereography

Stéréométrie, sf. (*etym. Gr.* στερεός, μέτρον), stereometry

Stéréotomie, sf. (*etym. Gr.* στερεός, τομή, *action of cutting*), stereotomy

Stéréotypage, sm. (*etym. Gr.* στερεός, τύπος, *impression*), stereotyping

Stéréotyper, va. to stereotype

Stérilité, sf. (*etym. L.* sterilitatem), barrenness, sterility. *Frapper de* —, to render barren

Sternutatoire, adj. s. (*etym. L.* sternutare, *to sneeze often*), sternutative

Stibié, e, adj. (*etym. L.L.* stibiatus), stibial

Stigmate, sm. (*etym. L.* stigmatis), mark, brand, blot, stigma

Stigmatiser, va. to stigmatize

Stillation, sf. (*etym. L.* stillationem), falling drop by drop

Stimulant, e, adj. stimulating. — sm. stimulus, spur, stimulant

Stimuler, va. (*etym. L.* stimulare), to stimulate, to spur on, to rouse up

Stipendiaire, adj. (*etym. L.* stipendiarius), stipendiary

Stipendier, va. (*etym. L.* stipendiare), to hire

Stipuler, va. (*etym. L.* stipulari), to stipulate, to covenant

Stoïcien, ne, adj. stoic, stoical. — sm. stoic

Stoïcisme, sm. stoicism

Stoïque, adj. (*etym. L.* stoicus), stoical, stoic

Stomacal, e, adj. (*etym. L.* stomachus), good for the stomach

Stomachique, adj. sm. stomachic

Stopper, va. (*nav.*) to stop

Store, sm. (*etym. L.* storea, *a matting made of reeds*), blind, roller-blind

Strabisme, sm. (*etym. Gr.* στραβισμός, *action of squinting*), squinting, strabismus

Strapontin, sm. (*etym.* ?), bracket-seat

Stratagème, sm. (*etym. L.* strategema), stratagem

Stratégie, sf. (*etym. L.* strategia), strategy

Stratégique, adj. strategical

Stratégiste, sm. strategist

Stratifier, va. (*etym. L.L.* stratificare), to stratify

Strictement, adv. (*etym.* strict), strictly

Strident, e, adj. harsh, screaking

Strié, e, adj. (*etym. L.* striatus), striate, striated, streaked

Stries, sf. plur. (*etym. L.* stria), striæ, (*arch.*) strigæ

Strychnine, sf. (*etym. L.* strychnus), strychnia

Stuc, sm. (*etym. I.* stucco), stucco

Studieux, se, adj. (*etym. L.* studiosus), studious

Stupéfait, e, adj. (*etym. L.* stupefactus), stupefied

Stupéfiant, e, adj. sm. stupefactive

Stupéfier, va. (*etym. L.* stupefieri), to stupefy

Stupeur, sf. (*etym. L.* stupor), stupor

Stupide, adj. s. (*etym. L.* stupidus), stupid, dull; stupidity, what is stupid, stupid creature, blockhead

Stupidité, sf. (*etym. L.* stupiditatem), stupidity, dulness

Styler, va. (*etym.* style), to train

Stylet, sm. (*etym. I.* stiletto), stiletto

Su, sm. knowledge, privity

Suaire, sm. (*etym. L.* sudarium), shroud, winding-sheet, grave-clothes

Suave, adj. (*etym. L.* suavis), sweet, pleasant

Suavité, sf. (*etym. L.* suavitatem), suavity, sweetness

Subalterne, adj. s. (*etym. L.L.* subalternus), subaltern, inferior

Subdélégation, sf. subdelegation

Subdélégué, sm. subdelegate

Subdiviser, va. to subdivide; *se* —, vr. *to be subdivided*

Subir, va. (*etym. L.* subire), to undergo, to suffer, to endure

Subit, e, adj. (*etym. L.* subitus), sudden

Subito, adv. (*ablat. of the L.* subitus), all of a sudden

‖**Subjectif, ve,** adj. (*etym. L.* subjectivus), subjective
Subjonctif, adj.sm. (*etym. L.* subjunctivus), subjunctive, subjunctive mood
Subjuguer, va. (*etym. L.* subjugare), to subjugate, to overcome, to overpower
Sublimé, sm. sublimate
Sublimer, va. (*etym. L.* sublimare), to sublimate
Sublimité, sf. (*etym. L.* sublimitatem), sublimity, sublimeness
Sublunaire, adj. sublunary
Submerger, va. (*etym. L.* submergere), to submerge, to drown
Subordonné, e, adj.s. subordinate
Subordonner, va. to subordinate, to make subordinate
Suborner, va. (*etym. L.* subornare), to suborn, to bribe
Suborneur, sm. suborner. —, —*se*, adj. of subornation, persuasive
Subrécargue, sm. (*etym. Sp.* sobrecargo), supercargo
‖**Subreptice,** adj. (*etym. L.* surrepticius), surreptitious
Subroger, va. (*etym. L.* subrogare), to surrogate, to substitute. ¦ *Subrogé tuteur*, surrogate guardian
Subséquemment, adv. (*etym.* subséquent), subsequently
Subside, sm. (*etym. L.* subsidium), subsidy
‖**Subsidiaire,** adj. (*etym. L.* subsidiarius), subsidiary
Subsistance, sf. (*etym. L.* subsistentia), subsistence, sustenance, maintenance, (*pl.*) provisions
Subsister, vn. (*etym. L.* subsistere), to subsist, to be extant
‖**Substantiel, le,** adj. (*etym. L.* substantialis), substantial
Substantif, adj.sm. (*etym. L.* substantivus), substantive, noun substantive
Substantivement, adv. substantively
Substituer, va. (*etym. L.* substituere), to substitute, to appoint
Substitut, sm. (*etym. L.* substitutus), substitute, deputy
Substitution, sf. (*etym. L.* substitutionem), substitution, entail
‖**Subtil, e,** adj. (*etym. L.* subtilis), subtile, acute, artful, finespun
Subtiliser, va.n. to subtilise, to deceive
Subtilité, sf. (*etym. L.* subtilitatem), subtility, acuteness
Subvenir, vn. (*etym. L.* subvenire), to relieve, to provide
Subvention, sf. (*etym. L.L.* subventionem), relief, subsidy, grant
Subversif, ve, adj. (*etym. L.L.* subversivus), subversive

Subvertir, va. (*etym. L.* subvertere), to overthrow, to subvert
Suc, sm. (*etym. L.* succus), juice, substance, quintessence
Succéder, vn. (*etym. L.* succedere), to succeed, to follow; *se* —, vr. to succeed each other
Succès, sm. (*etym. L.* successus), success. ¦ — *d'estime, de vogue, fou*, quiet success, fashionable success, tremendous success
Successeur, sm. (*etym. L.* successor), successor
‖**Successif, ve,** adj. (*etym. L.L.* successivus), successive
Succin, sm. (*etym. L.* succinum), yellow amber
Succinctement, adv. (*etym.* succinct), succinctly, concisely, briefly
Succion, sf. (*etym. L.L.* suctionem), suction
Succomber, vn. (*etym. L.* succumbere), to sink, to faint, to succumb, to fail, to die
Succursale, sf. (*etym. L.L.* succursalis), branch establishment, branch office, chapel of ease
Sucer, va. (*etym. L.L.* suctiare, *from L.* sugere), to suck, to imbibe
Suçoir, sm. sucker
Sucre, sm. (*etym. L.* saccharum), sugar. — *de canne*, colonial sugar. — *brut*, brown sugar, raw sugar. *Morceau de* —, lump of sugar
Sucré, e, past part. adj. sugared, sweetened, demure
Sucrer, va. to sugar, to sweeten
Sucrerie, sf. sugar-mill, sugar-refinery, sweetmeat, comfit
Sucrier, sm. sugar-basin
Sud, sm. (*etym. Ang-Sax.* sudh), the south. —*-est-quart-est*, south-east by east. — adj. south
Sudorifique, adj.sm. sudorific
Suer, vn.a. (*etym. L.* sudare), to perspire, to sweat, to toil ¦ — *à grosses gouttes*, to be in a profuse perspiration
Suette, sf. the sweating sickness
Sueur, sf. (*etym. L.* sudorem), perspiration, sweat
Suffire, vn. (*etym. L.* sufficere), to suffice, to be sufficient, to be adequate; ¦ *se* —, vr. to provide for oneself
Suffisance, sf. sufficiency, enough, capacity, consequence, sufficient property, self-conceit. *Avec* —, self-conceitedly
‖**Suffisant, e,** adj. s. sufficient, enough, self-conceited. ¦ *Un* —, a coxcomb. *Faire le* —, to give oneself airs
Suffixe, sm. (*etym. L.* sub, figere), suffix
Suffocant, e, adj. stifling, suffocating
Suffoquer, va. (*etym. L.* suffocare), to suffocate, to stifle, to choke; — vn. to choke, to be choked

Suffragant, adj.sm. (*etym. L.* suffragantem), suffragan
Suggérer, va. (*etym. L.* suggerere), to suggest, to hint
se Suicider, vr. (*etym.* suicide), to commit suicide or self-murder
Suie, sf. (*etym.* ?), soot
Suif, sm. (*etym. L.* sevum), tallow
Suint, sm. grease
Suintement, sm. oozing, leakage
Suinter, vn. (*etym. Engl.* to sweat), to ooze out, to leak, to sweat (*of a wall*)
Suisse, sm. porter, beadle
Suite, sf. the others, the rest retinue, train, sequel, continuation, concatenation, set, consequence, coherency, series. ¦ *Par* — *de*, in consequence of, in pursuance of. *Des propos sans* —, incoherent or unconnected talk. *Avoir peu de* — *dans les idées*, to have no method in one's ideas
Suivant, e, adj. following, next, in attendance. — sm. the next, follower. —*e*, sf. waiting-maid. — prep. according to, in proportion to
Suivant que, loc. conj. according as, as
Suivi, e, past part. adj. followed, popular, in vogue, regular, well connected
Suivre, va.n. (*etym. L.* sequi), to follow, to keep up with, to watch, to attend to, to frequent, to wait upon. ¦ — *de près*, to follow close upon. — *de loin*, to follow from afar. *Comme il suit*, as follows. *A faire* —, to be forwarded. *Se* —, vr. to follow each other, to be well connected
Sujet, te, adj. (*etym. L.* subjectus), subject, liable, inclined. — sm. subject, cause motive, subject-matter, fellow, stock. ¦ *Bon* —, steady young fellow. *Mauvais* —, worthless fellow
Sujétion, sf. (*etym. L.* subjectionem), subjection, thraldom
Sujette, sf. subject, female subject
Sulfate, sm. sulphate
Sulfite, sm. sulphite
Sulfure, sm. (*etym. L.* sulfur), sulphuret
Sulfureux, se, adj. sulphurous, sulphureous
Sulfurique, adj. sulphuric
Sultane, sf. (*etym.* sultan), sultana, sultaness
Superbe, sf. (*etym. L.* superbus), pride, vainglory. ¦ — adj. proud, vainglorious, haughty, gorgeous, superb, boastful. — sm. proud man
Supercherie, sf. (*etym. I.* soperchieria, *deceit*), deceit, fraud
Superfétation, sf. (*etym. L.L.* superfetationem), redundancy, excrescency
Superficie, sf. (*etym. L.* superficies), surface, superficies, area

‖**Superficiel, le,** adj. (*etym. L.* superficialis), superficial, shallow
Superfin, e, adj.sm. superfine, superfine quality
Superflu, e, adj. (*etym. L.* superfluus), superfluous, needless. — sm. superfluity, superfluousness
Superfluité, sf. (*etym. L.* superfluitatem), superfluity, overabundance
‖**Supérieur, e,** adj.s. (*etym. L.* superior), upper, superior
Supériorité, sf. (*etym. L.L.* superioritatem), superiority
‖**Superlatif, ve,** adj. sm. (*etym. L.* superlativus), superlatively, superlative
Superposer, va. to superpose
‖**Superstitieux, se,** adj. (*etym. L.* superstitiosus), superstitious
Supin, sm. (*etym. L.* supinum), supine
Supplanter, va. (*etym. L.* supplantare), to supplant; *se* —, vr. to supplant one another
Suppléant, e, s. substitute. — adj. deputy, assistant
Suppléer, va. (*etym L.* supplere), to make good, to supply, to fill up; — vn. to supply the place, to supply the deficiency
Supplémentaire, adj. (*etym.* supplément), supplementary, extra
Supplétif, ve, adj. (*etym. L.L.* suppletivus), suppletory
Supplice, sm. (*etym. L.* supplicium), punishment, torture, torment. ¦ *Condamner au dernier* —, to sentence to death. *Être au* —, to be on the rack
Supplicié, e, s. executed criminal
Supplicier, va. to execute
Supplier, va. (*etym. L.* supplicare), to entreat, to beseech, to beg, to supplicate, to implore
Supplique, sf. (*etym. I.* supplica), petition, prayer
Support, sm. prop, support, pillar, fulcrum
Supporter, va. (*etym. L.* supportare), to support, to bear up, to prop, to put up with; *se* —, vr. to bear each other, to be supported
Supposé, e, adj. supposititious
Supposer, va. (*etym. L.L.* suppausare), to suppose, to imply, to infer. *Supposé que*, suppose
Suppôt, sm. (*etym. L* suppositus), member, abettor, agent. ¦ — *de justice*, hireling of the law. — *de Satan*, limb of Satan
Supprimer, va. (*etym. L.* supprimere), to suppress, to quell, to hold back
Suppuratif, ve, adj. (*etym. L.L.* suppurativus), suppurative
Suppurer, vn. (*etym. L.* suppurare), to suppurate

Supputer, va. (*etym. L.* supputare), to suppute, to compute

Suprématie, sf. (*etym.* suprême), supremacy

Sûr, e, adj. (*etym. L.* securus), sure, certain, trustworthy, safe, settled

Sur, e, adj. (*O.H.G. word*), sour

Sur, prep. (*etym. L.* super), on, upon, over, above, into, to, in, on board, about, out of, of, for. — partic. over . . ., super . . ., extra . . .

Surabondance, sf. superabundance

‡**Surabondant, e,** adj. superabundant

Surabonder, vn. to superabound, to be overabundant

Suranné, e, adj. (*etym.* sur, an), expired, obsolete, antiquated

Surbaissé, e, adj. surbased

Surcharge, sf. additional burden, excess, surplus, exuberance, word written over another

Surcharger, va. to overload, to overburden, to surcharge, to write over, to overstock; *se* —, vr. to overburden oneself

Surcroît, sm. increase, surplus, addition

Surcroître, va. to increase excessively

Surdité, sf. (*etym. L.* surditatem), deafness

Sureau, sm. (*etym. L.* sabucus), elder, elder-tree — *des marais*, guelder-rose

Surenchère, sf. higher bid

Surenchérir, vn. to overbid

Surérogation, sf. (*etym.* sur, rogation), supererogation

Surérogatoire, adj. supererogatory

Suret, ette, adj. sourish

Sûreté, sf. safety, security, surety, precaution, steadiness, sureness

Surévaluation, sf. overvaluation

Surévaluer, va. to overestimate

Surexcitation, sf. excessive excitation

Surexciter, va. to overexcite

Surfaire, va.n. to overrate

Surgir, vn. (*etym. L.* surgere), to land, to spring up, to arise

Surhaussement, sm. raising

Surhausser, va. (*archit.*) to raise, excessively to raise

Surhumain, e, adj. superhuman

Surintendance, sf. superintendence

Surintendant, sm. superintendent

Surintendante, sf. superintendent, superintendent's lady

Surjet, sm. whip, overcasting

Surlendemain, sm. third day

Surmener, va. to overdrive, to jade

Surmontable, adj. surmountable

Surmonter, vn. to rise above, to overcome, to surmount, to master, to surpass; *se* —, vr. to overcome oneself

Surnager, vn. to swim, to survive, to float

‡**Surnaturel, le,** adj. supernatural

Surnom, sm. surname

Surnommer, va. to surname

Surnuméraire, adj. sm. supernumerary

Surnumérariat, sm. the time one is a supernumerary

Surpasser, va. to rise above, to be higher than, to exceed, to excel, to surpass, to amaze; *se* —, vr. to surpass oneself

Surplis, sm. (*etym. L.* super, *L.L.* pellicium), surplice

Surplomber, va.n. to overhang, to hang over, to slope

Surplus, sm. overplus, surplus, remainder. ¦*Au* —, besides, after all

Surprenant, e, adj. surprising, amazing, wonderful

Surprendre, va. to detect, to surprise, to overtake, to deceive, to obtain by undue means, to intercept; *se* —, vr. to surprise oneself, to catch oneself

Surprise, sf. surprise, mistake, deceit, abuse. *Faire des* —*s à*, to abuse

Sursaut, sm. start. *En* —, with a start

Surseoir, va.n. to suspend, to put off

Sursis, sm. delay, reprieve

Surtaxe, sf. additional tax, overtaxation

Surtaxer, va. to overtax

Surtout, adv. above all, chiefly. — sm. great-coat, upper benjamin, epergne, basket-cart

§**Surveillance,** sf. inspection, superintendence, watchfulness, guardianship

§**Surveillant,** sm. overseer, superintendent, surveyor, guardian

§**Surveillante,** sf. superintendent

§**Surveille,** sf. two days before

§**Surveiller,** vn. to keep a watchful eye; — va. to watch over

Survenant, sm. chance comer

Survendre, va. to overcharge

Survenir, vn. to come on, to occur, to befall, to come up, to drop in

Survie, sf. survival, survivorship

Survivance, sf. reversion, survivorship

Survivant, e, adj. survivor

Survivre, vn. to outlive, to survive; *se* —, vr. to outlive one's faculties, to live over again

Sus à, loc. prep. (*etym. L.* sursum), upon. ¦*Courir* — *à*, to fall upon

Sus (en), adv. over and above, to boot. *Le tiers en* —, the third more

Sus! Sus donc! interj. courage! come!

Susceptibilité, sf. (*etym. L.L.* susceptibilitatem), susceptibility, delicacy, feelings, irritability

Susceptible, adj. (*etym. L.L.* susceptibilis), susceptible, that can admit of, irritable, easily offended

Susciter, va. (*etym. L.* suscitare), to raise up, to create, to stir up, to bring on

Suscription, sf. (*etym. L.* subscriptionem), superscription

Susdit, e, adj. aforesaid, said

Suspect, e, adj. (*etym. L.* suspectus), suspicious, suspected. ¦*Tenir pour* —, to look upon as suspicious. *La loi des* —*s*, the law against suspicious persons

Suspecter, va. (*etym. L.* suspectare), to suspect

Suspendre, va. (*etym. L.* suspendere), to hang up, to suspend, to stay, to intermit; *se* —, vr. to hang, to suspend oneself

Suspendu, e, adj. hanging, hung up, suspended, dangling

Suspens, adj. m. suspended. *En* —, in suspense, undecided, outstanding

Suspensif, ve, adj. (*etym.* suspens), of suspension, suspensive

Suspensoir, sm. suspensory bandage

Sustenter, va. (*etym. L.* sustentare), to sustain, to feed; *se* —, vr. to sustain oneself, to keep body and soul together

Suzerain, e, adj. (*etym. F.*), paramount. — s. lord (lady) paramount

Suzeraineté, sf. suzerainty

Svelte, adj. (*etym. I.* svelto, *light*), slender, slim

Sycomore, sm. (*etym. L.L.* sycomorus), sycamore, maple

Sycophante, sm. (*etym. L.* sycophanta), sycophant, fawning rogue

Syllabaire, sm. spelling-book

Syllabe, sf. (*etym. L.* syllaba), syllable

Syllabique, adj. syllabic, syllabical

Syllepse, sf. (*etym. L.L.* syllepsis), syllepsis

Syllogisme, sm. (*etym. L.* syllogismum), syllogism, a judging of things brought together

Syllogistique, adj. (*etym. L.* syllogisticus), syllogistical

Sylphe, sm. (*etym.* ?), sylph

Sylphide, sf. sylph, sylphid

Sylvestre, adj. (*etym. L.* silvestris), woodland, sylvan

Sylviculture, sf. (*etym. L.* silva, *wood*, colo, *I till*), forestry

Symbole, sm. (*etym. Gr.* σύμβολον), symbol, creed

Symbolique, adj. symbolical

Symétrie, sf. (*etym. L.* symmetria), symmetry. *Faire* —, to be in symmetry. *Faire de la* —, to introduce symmetry

‡**Symétrique,** adj. symmetrical

Sympathie, sf. (*etym. Gr.* συμπάθεια), sympathy, fellow-feeling

Sympathique, adj. sympathetic, engaging, sympathising

Sympathiser, vn. to sympathise

Symphonie, sf. (*etym. L.* symphonia), symphony

Symptôme, sm. (*etym. Gr.* σύμπτωμα), symptom, token, sign

Synallagmatique, adj. (*Gr.* συναλλαγματικός, *relating to contracts*), reciprocal

Synchrone, adj. synchronous

Synchronisme, sm. (*etym. Gr.* συγχρονισμός, *coincidence*), synchronism

Syncope, sm. (*etym. Gr.* συγκοπή), syncope, swoon. *Tomber en* —, to faint away

Syndic, sm. (*etym. L.* syndicus), syndic. — *de faillite*, assignee

Syndical, e, adj. of a syndic. *La Chambre* —*e*, (*polit.*) the Syndics

Syndicat, sm. syndicate

Synérèse, sf. (*etym. Gr.* συναίρεσις, *contraction*), synæresis

Synode, sm. (*etym. Gr.* σύνοδος, *meeting*), synod

Synodique, adj. synodic, synodal

Synonyme, adj. (*etym. Gr.* συνώνυμος), synonymous. — sm. synonym

Synonymie, sf. synonymy

Synonymique, adj. synonymous

Synoptique, adj. (*etym. Gr.* συνοπτικός), synoptical, synoptic

Syntaxe, sf. (*etym. Gr.* σύνταξις), syntax

Syntaxique, adj. syntaxical

Synthèse, sf. (*etym. Gr.* σύνθεσις), synthesis

Synthétique, adj. (*etym. Gr.* συνθετικός), synthetical

Systématique, adj. systematical, systematic

Système, sm. (*etym. Gr.* σύστημα), system

Syzygie, sf. (*etym. Gr.* συζυγία, *conjunction*), syzygy

T

T, sm. T, t

Tabac, sm. (*etym. Sp.* tabaco), tobacco, snuff. *Marchand, débitant de —*, tobacconist. *Débit de —*, tobacconist's shop. *Prendre du —*, to take snuff

·**Tabagie,** sf. tap-room, tobacco-box

Tabatière, sf. snuff-box

***Tabellion,** sm. (*etym. L.L.* tabellionem), scrivener

Tabis, sm. (*etym. ?*), tabby

Tabiser, va. to tabby

Tablature, sf. tablature. ‡*Donner de la —*, to create an embarrassment

Table, sf. (*etym. L.* tabula), table, mess, meal, food, board

Tableau, sm. (*etym. L.L.* tabulellum), picture, painting, description, list, catalogue, panel, board, (*nav.*) aft-board, breastwork

Tabletier, ère, s. (*etym.* tablette), dealer in toys

Tablette, sf. shelf, tablet, cake, lozenge, memorandum-book, (*nav.*) rising-staff

Tabletterie, sf. toy-trade

Tablier, sm. apron, pinafore, platform, flooring, backgammon-board

Tabouret, sm. (*etym. see* TAMBOUR), stool, settle. ‡*Avoir — à la cour*, to be entitled to sit in the royal presence

Tac, sm. (*etym. ?*), the rot

Tache, sf. (*etym. ?*), spot, stain, speck, blemish

Tâche, sf. (*etym. L.L.* tasca, *property-tax*), task, job

Tacher, va. to spot, to stain, to sully; *se —*, vr. to stain one's clothes, to dirty oneself, to be sullied

Tâcher, vn. to endeavour, to strive, to try

Tâcheron, sm. task-master

Tacheté, e, adj. spotted, speckled

Tacheter, va. to spot, to speckle

§**Tacite,** adj. (*etym. L.* tacitus), tacit, implied

Taciturne, adj. (*etym. L.* taciturnus), taciturn, of few words

Taciturnité, sf. taciturnity

Tact, sm. (*etym. L.* tactus), touch, tact, judgment

Tacticien, sm. tactician

Tactique, sf. (*etym. Gr.* τακτική [τέχνη], *the art of marshalling troops*), tactics

Taffetas, sm. (*etym. Pers.* tafteh), taffeta, light silk. *— d'Angleterre*, court-plaster

Tafia, sm. (*etym. ?*), taffia, rum arrack

Taïaut, sm. (*onomatop.*), tally-ho. *Crier —*, to halloo

Taie, sf. (*etym. L.* theca, *a sheath*), pillow-case, speck, film

§**Taillable,** adj. liable to be taxed. ‡*—s et corvéables à merci*, taxable and workable at their lord's discretion

§**Taillade,** sf. (*etym. I.* tagliata, *slash*), slash, cut, gash

§**Taillader,** va. to slash, to cut

§**Taillandier,** sm. edge-tool maker

§**Taillant,** sm. edge

§**Taille,** sf. cutting, cut, fashion, pruning, dressing, coppice, cutting for the stone, edge, stature, size, height, waist, shape, tally, tax, poll-tax, deal (in a game), tenor part

§**Taille-crayon,** sm. pencil-pointer

§**Taille-mer,** sm. (*nav.*) cutwater

§**Taille-plume,** sm. pen-cutter

§**Tailler,** va. (*etym. L.L.* taleare, *to cut*), to cut, to hew, to prune, to dress, to carve, to cut for the stone, to deal. *— en pièces*, to cut to pieces

§**Tailleur,** sm. tailor, cutter, dealer

§**Taillis,** sm. copsewood, coppice, underwood

Tain, sm. (*corrupt. from* étain), tin-foil, tin-leaf

Taire, va.n. (*etym. L.* tacere), not to say, to suppress. *Faire — quelqu'un*, to make one hold one's tongue, to silence. *Se —*, vr. to hold one's tongue, to keep silence, to be kept secret

Talion, sm. (*etym. L.* talionem), retaliation, tit for tat

Talismanique, adj. (*etm.* talisman), talismanic

Talmouse, sf. (*etym. ?*), cheese-cake

Taloche, sf. (*etym. ?*), cuff. *Donner des —s à*, to cuff

Talon, sm. (*etym. L.* talus), heel, stock. ‡*Montrer (tourner) les —s*, to take to one's heels. *Les —s rouges*, the nobility

Talonner, va. to follow close at the heels of, to urge, to press, to dun; — vn. to touch, to strike

Talus, sm. (*etym. L.* talus), slope, embankment. *En —*, aslope, slopingly

Tamarin, Tamarinier, sm. (*etym. I.* tamarindo), tamarind-tree, tamarind, tamarin

Tamaris, Tamarisc, sm. (*etym. L.* tamarix), tamarisk

Tambour, sm. (*etym. Pers.* tambûr, *O.F.* tabour), drum, drummer, tambour, embroidery frame, (*mechan.*) barrel. ‡*Battre le —, du —*, to beat the drum, to beat a tattoo. *— voilé, couvert de crêpe*, muffled drum. *— de basque*, tabour

Tambourin, sm. tabour, timbrel, tambourine

Tambouriner, vn. to drum; — va. to cry (something lost, by beat of drum)

Tamis, sm. (*etym. Dutch* tems, *sieve*), sieve, bolt. *Passer par le —*, to sift, to be sifted

Tamisage, sm. sifting

Tamiser, va. to sift, to bolt

Tampon, sm. (*etym. see* TAPER), stopper, plug, bung, tampion, buffer

Tamponner, va. to plug, to stop up

Tancer, va. (*etym. L.L.* tentiare, *to contend*), to rate, to chide

Tanche, sf. (*etym. L.* tinca), tench

Tandis que, conj. (*etym. L.* tam, diu), while, whilst

Tangage, sm. pitching, pitching and sending

Tangence, sf. (*etym. L.L.* tengentia), contact

Tangente, sf. tangent. ‡*S'échapper par la —*, to go off at a tangent

Tanguer, va. (*etym. ?*), to pitch, to pitch and send, to heave and set

Tanière, sf. (*etym. O.F.* taisson), den

Tanin, sm. (*etym.* tan), tannin

Tannage, sm. tanning

Tanné, e, adj. tawny, tan-coloured

Tanner, va. to tan, (†) to provoke, to annoy

Tannerie, sf. tan-yard, tannery

Tanneur, sm. tanner

Tant, adj. (*etym. L.* tantum), so much, such, both, as well as, so long, as far, so far, odd. ‡*— plus que moins*, more or less. *— et —, — et plus*, a vast number. *— mieux, — pis*, so much the better, so much the worse. *En — que*, in so far as. *— il y a que*, however. *Si — est que*, if so be that

Tante, sf. (*etym. L.* amita, *O.F.* ante), aunt

‡**Tantet, Tantinet,** sm. a very little

Tantôt, adv. (*etym.* tant, tôt), by and by, presently, just now, a little while ago, almost

Taon, sm. (*etym. L.* tabanus), gad-fly, breeze. *— marin*, sea-breeze

Tapage, sm. racket, uproar, noise, dust

Tapageur, sm. noisy fellow, blusterer. —, —se, adj. riotous, noisy

Tape, sf. smack, slap, tap, rap

Tapé, e, adj. (*fruit*) dried

Taper, va.n. (*etym. ?*), to smack, to slap, to hit, to stamp, to strum. † *Réponse bien tapée*, smart answer

Tapinois (en), loc. adv. (*etym.* tapir), stealthily, slily

se Tapir, vr. (*etym. ?*), to crouch, to squat

Tapis, sm. (*etym. L.* tapete), carpet, rug

Tapisser, va. to hang with tapestry, to paper, to carpet, to embroider, to bedeck; *se —*, vr. to be embroidered

Tapisserie, sf. tapestry, upholstery. *Faire de la —*, to make tapestry. ‡*Faire —*, to line the walls

Tapissier, ère, s. upholsterer

Tapissière, sf. spring-van

Tapoter, va. (*etym.* taper), to pat, to strum

Taquer, va. to plane down

Taquin, e, adj. (*etym. Sp.* tacaño, *tease*), teasing, tiresome. — s. tease, plague

Taquiner, va. to tease, to plague; *se —*, vr. to tease each other

Taquinerie, sf. teasing

Tarabuster, va. (*etym. ?*), to plague, to huff, to snub, to push

Tarare! interj. (*etym. ?*), fiddlestick!

Taraud, sm. (*etym. L.L.* tarare, *to bore*), screw-tap, tap

Tard, adv. (*etym. L.* tardus), late

Tarder, vn. to delay, to linger, to loiter, to dally, to long

§**Tardif, ve,** adj. tardy, late, slow

Tare, sf. (*etym. I.* tara), waste, blemish, tare and tret

Taré, e, adj. damaged, ill-famed, of ill repute

Tarentelle, sf. (*etym. I.* tarentella), tarentella

Tarentule, sf. (*etym. I.* tarentola), tarentula

Tarer, va. to damage, to injure, to tare

Targette, sf. (*etym.* targe), flat bolt

se Targuer, vr. (*etym.* targe), to brag, to boast

Tarière, sf. (*etym. L.L.* taratrum), auger, wimble, borer, terebra

Tarif, sm. (*etym. I.* tariffa), tariff, rate

Tarifer, va. to rate, to tariff

Tarir, va.n. (*etym. O.H.G.* tharjian, *to dry up*), to dry up, to exhaust; *se* —, vr. to dry up

Tarissable, adj. exhaustible

Tarissement, sm. drying up

Tarlatane, sf. tarlatan

Tarot, sm. (*etym. I.* tarocho), spotted card

Tartane, sf. (*etym. I.* tartana), tartan

Tarte, sf. (*etym. ?*), tart

Tartelette, sf. tartlet

Tartine, sf. slice of bread and butter, jam, &c., (†) article in a newspaper

Tartre, sm. (*etym. L.L.* tartarum), tartar

Tartrique, Tartarique, adj. tartaric

Tartufe, sm. (*prop. name*), hypocrite

Tartuferie, sf. hypocrisy

Tas, sm. (*Dutch word*), heap, lot, set, hand anvil. *Se mettre en* —, to crowd together

Tasse, sf. (*etym. I.* tazza), cup, mug. † *La grande* —, (*fig.*) the deep sea

Tasseau, sm. (*etym. L.* taxellus), bracket, ledge

Tassement, sm. sinking, subsiding

Tasser, va. to heap up; — vn. to grow thick; *se* —, vr. to sink, to subside, to squeeze a little

Tâter, va.n. (*etym. L.L.* taxitare), to feel, to try, to taste; *se* —, vr. to feel oneself, to feel one's way with each other, to nurse oneself

§**Tatillon, ne,** s. busybody, fidgety person

§**Tatillonner,** vn. to be fidgeting *or* meddling

Tâtonnement, sm. feeling, fumbling, groping

Tâtonner, vn. to feel one's way, to grope one's way, to fumble

Tâtons (à), loc. adv. groping in the dark

Tatouage, sm. tattooing, tattoo

Tatouer, va. (*from the English*), to tattoo; *se* —, vr. to tattoo oneself

Taudis, sm. (*etym. O.F.* taudir, *to cover*), wretched lodging, hole

Taupe, sf. (*etym. L.* talpa), mole

Taupier, sm. mole-catcher

Taupière, sf. mole-trap

Taupinière, Taupinée, sf. mole-hill

Taureau, sm. (*etym. L.* taurus), bull

Tautologie, sf. (*etym. Gr.* ταυτολογία), tautology

Taux, sm. (*etym. L.* taxare), rate, price

Taveler, va. (*etym. L.L.* tabella), to speckle, to spot; *se* —, vr. to grow speckled

Tavelure, sf. speckles

Taverne, sf. (*etym. L.* taberna), tavern

Tavernier, ère, s. tavern-keeper

Taxe, sf. (*etym. L.* taxare), tax, toll, taxation, fixing, price fixed

Taxer, va. to tax, to fix, to assess, to charge; *se* —, vr. to tax oneself, to tax one another

Te, pron.m.f. (*Latin word*), thee, to thee

Technique, adj. (*etym. Gr.* τεχνικός), technical

Technologie, sf. (*etym. Gr.* τεχνολογία), technology

Technologique, adj. technological

§**Teigne,** sf. (*etym. L.* tinea), scurf, scald-head, scald, moth, thrush

§**Teigneux, se,** adj. scurvy

Teindre, va. (*etym. L.* tingere), to dye, to tinge, to stain; *se* —, vr. to be dyed, to be tinged, to be stained, to dye one's hair

Teint, sm. dye, tincture, colour, complexion. *Faux* —, fugitive dye

Teinte, sf. tint, tincture, tinge. — *plate*, uniform tint. *Demi-* —, mezzo-tinto

Teinter, va. to tint

Teinture, sf. dye, dyeing, tincture, hue. *Bois de* —, dye-wood

Teinturier, ère, s. dyer

¶**Tel, le,** adj. (*etym. L.* talis), such, like. — pron. indef. such a one, so and so. — *qui*, many a one

¶**Télégraphe,** sm. (*etym. Gr.* γράφω, *I write*, τῆλε, *far*), telegraph

¶**Télégraphique,** adj. telegraphic

¶**Téméraire,** adj. s. (*etym. L.* temerarius), rash, inconsiderate, headlong; rash man *or* woman

Témérité, sf. (*etym. L.* temeritatem), temerity, rashness

§**Témoignage,** sm. witness, testimony, evidence, token, mark, testimonial, certificate

§**Témoigner,** va.n. to testify, to witness, to show

Témoin, sm. (*etym. L.* testimonium), witness, second, token, sign. ¦ *Prendre à* —, to take to witness. *Prendre pour* —, to take as a witness. —*s à décharge*, evidence for the prisoner

Tempe, sf. (*etym. L.* tempora), temple

Tempérament, sm. constitution, temper, middle course, temperament. *Par* —, constitutionally

Tempérant, e, adj. temperate

Tempéré, e, adj. temperate, middle. — sm. middle style

Tempérer, va. (*etym. L.* temperare), to temper, to allay; *se* —, vr. to calm oneself, to grow temperate

Tempête, sf. (*etym. L.* tempestatem), tempest, storm

Tempêter, vn. to storm

Tempêtueux, se, adj. stormy

Templier, sm. (*etym.* temple), knight templar

¶**Temporaire,** adj. (*etym. L.* temporarius), temporary

Temporalité, sf. (*etym.* temporal), temporality

¶**Temporel, le,** adj. (*etym. L.* temporalis), temporal. — sm. temporality, temporal power

Temporiser, vn. (*etym. L.* tempus), to temporize

Temporiseur, sm. temporizer

Temps, sm. (*etym. L.* tempus), time, while, season, opportunity, hour, weather, tense. ¦ *Avec le* —, in time. *Être à* —, to be in time. *De* — *en* —, *de* — *à autre*, from time to time, now and then. *Avoir fait son* —, to have served one's time. *Se donner du bon* —, to pass one's time merrily. *En* — *et lieu*, in the proper time and place

Tenace, adj. (*etym. L.* tenacem), tenacious

Ténacité, sf. (*etym. L.* tenacitatem), tenaciousness, tenacity

§**Tenaille,** sf. (*etym. L.* tenacula), tenaille

§**Tenailler,** va. to tear off the flesh with red-hot pincers, to torture

§**Tenailles,** sf. plur. pincers, nippers, tongs

Tenancier, ère, s. tenant. *Franc* —, freeholder

Tenant, sm. (*etym.* tenir), challenger, defendant, champion, master. ¦ *Les* —*s et aboutissants*, the parts adjacent, the ins and outs. *Tout en un* —, *tout d'un* —, in a ring-fence

Tendance, sf. tendency

Tendant, e, adj. tending

Tendeur, sm. layer of snares

Tendre, adj. (*etym. L.* tenerum), tender, soft, new, fond, loving. — sm. liking

Tendre, va. (*etym. L.* tendere), to stretch, to strain, to bend, to pitch, to spread, to lay, to hang up, to throw out; — vn. to lead, to go, to tend, to conduce; *se* —, vr. to be stretched out

Tendresse, sf. tenderness, fondness, marks of kindness, love

Tendron, sm. tender shoot, tender maiden, gristle

Tendu, e, past part. adj. tight, held out, bent, stiff

Ténèbres, sf. plur. (*etym. L.* tenebræ), darkness, gloom, shades, tenebræ

Ténébreux, se, adj. darksome, dark, gloomy, dark-minded

Teneur, sf. (*etym.* tenir), tenor, purport, percentage

Tenir, va. (*etym. L.* tenere), to hold, to have hold of, to owe, to keep, to detain, to pursue, to follow, to side with. ¦ — *à quatre*, to bind hand and foot. *Faire* — *à*, to forward, to convey. — vn. to take, to resemble, to hold fast, to adhere, to be attached, to be connected, to be contiguous, to proceed from, to be held, to hold, to side with, to withstand, (*nav.*) to sail close to the wind. *Il a de quoi* —, he is a chip of the old block. *Tenez bon, tenez ferme*, persevere, (*nav.*) avast. *En* —, vn. to be in for it, to be caught, to be hit, to be smitten, to be fuddled. *Y* —, vn. to care about it, to wish it, to stand. *Il tient*, v.imp. to depend upon, to rest with, to be in the power of. *Qu'à cela ne tienne*, never mind that. *Il n'y a homme qui tienne, chose qui tienne*, no matter what happens. *Se* —, vr. to hold each other, to hold together, to cling, to stand, to stand by, to be satisfied, to keep, to remain. *S'en* —, vr. to stop, to stand to, to abide by

Tenon, sm. tenon, bolt, nut of an anchor. *Assemblage, assembler à* —*s et à mortaises*, cocking, to cock

Tentacule, sm. (*etym. L.* tentacula), tentacle, feeler, horn

Tentant, e, adj. tempting, enticing

Tentateur, trice, s. tempter

Tentation, sf. (*etym. L.* tentationem), trial, temptation

Tentative, sf. attempt, trial, endeavour

Tente, sf. (*etym. L.L.* tenta), tent, pavilion, awning, lint-tent

Tenter, va. (*etym. L.* tentare), to attempt, to try, to tempt

Tenture, sf. (*etym. L.L.* tentura), hangings, tapestry

Ténu, e, adj. (*etym. L.* tenuis), slender, tenuous

Tenue, sf. (*etym.* tenir), session, holding, seat, bearing, behaviour, dress, uniform, appearance, steadiness, (*mus.*) holding-note, holding-ground. ¦ *Tout d'une* —, all of a piece. *N'avoir pas de* —, to be awkward-looking, to be untidy, not to know one's own mind. *En grande, petite* —, in full dress or uniform, in undress

Ténuité, sf. (*etym. L.* tenuitatem), tenuity, insignificance

Tenure, sf. tenure

Tercet, sm. (*etym. L.* tertius), triplet, tiercet

Térébenthe, sm. (*etym. L.* terebinthus), turpentine-tree

Térébenthine, sf. turpentine

Tergiverser, vn. (*etym. L.* tergiversari), to tergiversate, to shuffle

Terme, sm. (*etym. L.* terminus), term, end, boundary, bound, time, quarter, quarter's rent, expression, word,

‡ *A court* —, *long* —, for a short, long time

Terminaison, sf. (*etym. L.* terminationem), termination

Terminer, va. (*etym. L.* terminare), to bound, to terminate, to end, to conclude. ‡ *Traits terminés,* marked features. *Se* —, vr. to end, to be bounded

Terminologie, sf. terminology

Ternaire, adj. (*etym. L.* ternarius), ternary

Terne, adj. (*etym. O.H.G.* tarni, *veiled*), dull, wan, lack-lustre, tame, spiritless. — sm. (*lottery*) trey, prize, two threes

Ternir, va. to tarnish, to dull, to dim; *se* —, vr. to be tarnished or dimmed

Terrain, sm. (*etym. L.* terrenum), piece of ground, land, soil, rock. ‡ *Aller sur le* — (*en duel*), to go out. *Ménager le* —, to proceed cautiously. *Être sur son* —, to be in one's element

Terrasse, sf. (*etym. I.* terracia), terrace, earthwork, foreground

Terrassement, sm. earthwork

Terrasser, va. to embank, to throw to the ground, to strike with dismay, to floor, to nonplus

Terrassier, sm. navvy

Terre, sf. (*etym. L.* terra), the earth, land, ground, soil, territory. ‡ *Prendre* —, to land, to go ashore. *Dans les* —*s*, inland, up the country

Terreau, sm. vegetable mould, compost

Terre-neuvier, sm. Newfoundland fisherman, Newfoundland vessel

Terre-plein, sm. platform

se Terrer, vr. to go to earth, to throw up an earthwork

Terrestre, adj. (*etym. L.* terrestris), earthly, terrestrial

Terreur, sf. (*etym. L.* terrorem), terror, dismay, awe

Terreux, se, adj. (*etym. L.* terrosus), earthy, dirty, dull, cadaverous

Terriblement, adv. (*etm.* terrible), dreadfully, terribly

Terrien, sm. landholder

Terrier, sm. hole, burrow, earth

Terrifier, va. (*etym.* terreur), to terrify, to affright

Terrine, sf. earthen pan

Territoire, sm. territory, dominions

Terroir, sm. soil, land. ‡ *Un goût de* —, racy taste. *Sentir le* —, *avoir un goût de* —, to smack of its soil

§**Terroriser,** va. (*etym.* terreur), to terrorize

§**Terroriste,** sm. terrorist

Tertiaire, adj. (*etym. L.* tertiarius), tertiary

Tertre, sm. (*etym.* ?), knoll, mound, hillock

Tes, adj. poss. plur. *see* Ton

Tesson, sm. (*etym. L.L.* testonem), bit of broken glass, (*plur.*) potsherds

Testacé, e, adj. (*etym. L.* testaceus), testaceous

Testamentaire, adj. (*etym.* testament), testamentary, by will

Testateur, trice, s. (*etym. L.* testator), testator, testatrix

Tester, vn. (*etym. L.* testari), to make one's will

Testimonial, e, adj. (*etym. L.* testimonialis), testifying, testimonial

Têtard, sm. (*etym.* tête), tadpole

Tête, sf. (*etym. L.* testa, *skull*), head, top, head of hair, wits, senses, brains, resolution. ‡ *Faire, tenir* — *à*, to make head against, to cope with. *Se jeter à la* — *des gens*, to make oneself cheap. — *à* —, alone together, face to face. *Avoir de la* —, to be a person of strong mind. *Homme de* —, a man of sense, a man of resolution. *En* — *et en queue*, front and rear

Tête-à-tête, sm. private conversation, interview

Teter, va. (*etym. Ang.-Sax.* tita, *teat*), to suck. *Donner à* —, to suckle

Tétraèdre, sm. (*etym. Gr.* *τέτταρες, four, ἕδρα, base*), tetrahedron

Tétrarque, sm. (*etym. Gr.* *τέτραρχος*), tetrarch

Têtu, e, adj. stubborn, wrong-headed

Texte, sm. (*etym. L.* textus), text, (*print.*) brevier

‖**Textuel, le,** adj. textual

Thé, sm. (*etym. Chin.* té), tea. ‡ *Donner un* —, to give a tea-party

Théâtral, e, adj. theatrical

Théâtre, sm. (*etym. L.* theatrum), theatre, play-house

Théière, sf. teapot

Théisme, sm. (*etym. Gr.* *θεός, god*), theism

Théiste, sm. theist

Thème, sm. (*etym. Gr.* *θέμα, subject*), theme, topic, exercise

Théocratie, sf. (*etym. Gr.* *θεοκρατία*), theocracy

Théocratique, adj. theocratical

Théodicée, sf. (*etym. Gr.* *θεός, δίκη, justice*), theodicy

Théogonie, sf. (*etym. Gr.* *θεογονία, generation of the gods*), theogony

Théologale, adj. f. theological

Théologie, sf. (*etym. Gr.* *θεολογία*), theology

Théologien, sm. divine, theologian

‖**Théologique,** adj. theological

Théorème, sm. (*etym. Gr.* *θεώρημα*), theorem

Théoricien, sm. theorist

Théorie, sf. (*etym. Gr.* *θεωρία*), theory, speculation

‖**Théorique,** adj. (*etym. Gr.* *θεωρικός*), theoretic

Thérapeutique, sf. (*etm. Gr.* *θεραπευτικός*), therapeutics

Thermes, sm. plur. (*etym. L.* thermæ), baths, thermæ

Thermomètre, sm. (*etym. Gr.* *θερμός, μέτρον*), thermometer

Thésauriser, va. (*etym. L.* thesaurizare), to hoard up money

Thésauriseur, sm. hoarder up of money

Thèse, sf. (*etym. L.* thesis), thesis, question, argument

Thibaude, sf. (*etym. prop name* Thibaud), coarse drugget, hair-cloth

Thon, sm. (*etym. L.* thunnus), tunny

Thuriféraire, sm. (*etym. L.* thurifer), incense-bearer

Thym, sm. (*etym. L.* thymum), thyme

Thyrse, sm. (*etym. L.* thyrsus), thyrsus

Tiare, sf. (*etym. L.* tiara), tiara, tiar

Tic, sm. (*onomatop.*), tic, habit

Tic-tac, sm. (*onomat.*), tick-tack

‖**Tiède,** adj. (*etym. L.* tepidus), lukewarm, tepid

Tiédeur, sf. lukewarmness, tepidity, sloth

Tiédir, vn.a. to cool, to grow cool

Tien (le), Tienne (la), pron. (*etym.* ton), thine

Tiens, sm. (*etym.* tenir), what one has

Tierce, sf. (*etym. L.* tertia), third, tierce, press revise

Tiers, Tierce, adj. (*etym. L.* tertius), third. *Fièvre* —, tertian ague. — sm. third person, stranger, third part. ‡ *Le* — *et le quart*, no matter who

Tige, sf. (*etym. L.* tibia), stalk, stem, trunk, stock, shaft, (*mechan.*) rod

Tigre, Tigresse, s. (*etym. L.* tigris), tiger, tigress

Tigré, e, Tigre, adj. spotted, speckled

§**Tillac,** sm. (*etym. O.Scan.* thilia, *floor*), deck

§**Tilleul,** sm. (*etym. L.L.* tiliolus), lime-tree, linden-tree

Timbale, sf. (*etym. I.* timballo), kettle-drum, tymbal, mug, cup, leather-covered battledore

Timbalier, sm. kettle-drummer

Timbre, sm. (*etym. L.* tympanum), bell, clock-bell, sound, tone, cord, stamp, post-mark, stamp-office, stamp-duty, brains. — *-poste*, postage stamp

Timbré, e, adj. stamped, cracked, crack-brained

Timbrer, va. to stamp

‖**Timide,** adj. (*etym. L.* timidus), timid, timorous, fearful, faint-hearted

Timidité, sf. (*etym. L.* timiditatem), timidity, faint-heartedness, shyness

Timon, sm. (*etym. L.* temonem), pole, carriage-pole, shaft, (*nav.*) tiller, helm

Timonerie, sf. steerage. *En* —, steerage

Timonier, sm. wheeler, wheel-horse, thill-horse, steersman, helmsman

Timoré, e, adj. (*etym. L.L.* timoratus), timorous

Tinctorial, e, adj. (*etym. L.* tinctorius), dye, for dyeing

Tintamarre, sm. (*etym.* ?), clatter, hubbub

Tintement, sm. tinkling, tolling, knell, jingling

Tinter, va. (*etym. L.* tinnitare), to ring, to toll, (*nav.*) to support with blocks of wood; — vn. to tinkle, to toll

Tintouin, sm. ringing in the ears, anxiety

Tique, sf. (*from the Engl.*), tick

Tir, sm. shooting, archery, archery grounds, archery meeting, firing, shooting gallery, shooting match, rifle match, range

Tirade, sf. passage, tirade, long speech

Tirage, sm. draught, drawing, tow-path, striking off, working, winding off

§**Tiraillement,** sm. tug, pull, pulling about, twinge, pain, trouble

§**Tirailler,** va. to pull about, to plague; — vn. to shoot away to no purpose, to skirmish; *se* —, vr. to pull each other about, to thwart each other

§**Tirailleur,** sm. sharp-shooter, skirmisher

Tirant, sm. string, strap. — *d'eau*, draught of water, ship's gauge

Tire (tout d'une), loc. adv. at a stretch

Tire-balle, sm. worm-screw

Tire-botte, sm. boot-jack, boot-hook

Tire-bouchon, sm. cork-screw

Tire-bourre, sm. wad-hook, worm-screw

Tire-bouton, sm. button-hook

Tire d'aile, sm. jerk of the wing

Tire-larigot, loc. adv. (*etym.* ?). *Boire à* —, to drink hard

§**Tire-ligne,** sm. line-drawing pen

Tirelire, sf. money-box

Tire-pied, sm. shoemaker's stirrup

Tiré, e, past part. adj. haggard, wan

Tirer, va. (*etym. D.* tërer, *to pull*), to draw, to pull, to drag, to lug, to haul, to tug, to extract; — vn. to draw, to shoot, to fence; *se* —, vr. to extricate oneself, to recover

Tiret, sm. slip of parchment, hyphen

Tiretaine, sf. linsey-woolsey

Tireur, sm. drawer, marksman, shot, gamekeeper. *Fin* —, capital shot

Tireuse de cartes, sf. fortune-teller (by cards)

Tiroir, sm. drawer, second rank, slide, slide-valve

Tisane, sf. (*etym.* *L.* ptisana), cooling draught, ptisane

Tison, sm. (*etym.* *L.* titionem), brand, firebrand, (*plur.*) the embers

Tisonner, vn. to stir the fire

Tisonnier, sm. poker, fire-iron

Tissage, sm. weaving. — *mécanique*, power-loom weaving

Tisser, va. (*etym.* *L.* texere), to weave

Tisserand, sm. weaver

Tissu, past part. woven. — sm. texture, tissue, web

Titiller, va. (*etym.* *L.* titillare), to titillate, to tickle

Titre, sm. (*etym.* *L.* titulus), title, title-page, head, right, claim

Titrer, va. to give a title to

Titulaire, adj. sm. titular

Tocsin, sm. (*etym.* toquer, *O.F.* sin = *L.* signum), alarm-bell

Toge, sf. (*etym.* *L.* toga), toga, gown, robe

Tohu-bohu, sm. (*etym.* *Hebr.* tohoo-vabohoo, *confusion*), hurly-burly

Toi, pers. pron. (*etym.* *L.* tibi), thou, thee, you

Toile, sf. (*etym.* *L.* tela), linen, linen cloth, canvas, duck

Toilerie, sf. linendrapery

Toilette, sf. (*etym.* toile), toilet-cloth, toilet, dressing-table, toilet-glass, dressing, dress

Toilier, ère, s. dealer in linen cloths, linen-cloth maker

Toise, sf (*etym.* *L.L.* tensa, *fathom*), two yards, six feet, fathom, two yard measure, stature

Toisé, sm. measuring, mensuration

Toiser, va. to eye, to scan, to measure

Toiseur, sm. measurer, surveyor

Toison, sf. (*etym.* *L.* tonsionem, *the action of fleecing*), fleece

Toit, sm. (*etym.* *L.* tectum), roof, top of the house, house

Toiture, sf. roof, roofing

Tôle, sf. (*etym.* *L.* tabula, *O.F.* taule), sheet-iron. — *étamée*, tin-plates

Tolérablement, adv. tolerably

Tolérance, sf. toleration, sufferance, allowance

Tolérer, va. (*etym.* *L.* tolerare), to tolerate, to suffer

Tollé, sm. (*etym.* *L.* tolle), an outcry. ¦ *Crier — sur*, to raise a hue and cry against

Tomate, sf. (*Span. word*), love-apple, tomato

Tombant, e, adj. falling, flowing

Tombe, sf. (*etym.* *L.* tumba), tomb, grave, tombstone

Tombeau, sm. (*etym.* *L.L.* tumbellus), tomb, grave

Tomber, vn. (*etym.* *Scand.* tumba, *to fall*), to fall, to drop, to tumble, to sink. — (*faire*), loc. verb, to make fall, to shake down, to overthrow, to shower down, to bring

Tombereau, sm. cart, tumbril

Ton, Ta, Tes, adj. (*etym.* *L.* tuum), thy

Ton, sm. (*etym.* *L.* tonus), tone, tune, accent, sound. *Le bon —*, the fashion, ton

Tondaison, sf. (*etym.* tondre), sheep-shearing

Tondeur, se, s. sheep-shearer

Tondre, va. (*etym.* *L.* tondere), to shear, to clip, to graze

Tonique, adj. sm. (*etym.* ton), tonic

Tonnant, e, adj. thundering

Tonne, sf. (*etym.* *f*), tun, ton

Tonneau, sm. cask, ton. *Petit —*, keg

Tonnelier, sm. cooper

Tonnelle, sf. arbour, tunnel-net

Tonnellerie, sf. cooperage

Tonner, vn. (*etym.* *L.* tonare), to thunder

Tonnerre, sm. thunder, thunderclap, chamber of a fire-arm

Tonsurer, va. (*etym.* tonsure), to shave (the crown)

Tonte, sf. sheep-shearing

Tontinier, ère, s. (*etym.* tontine), annuitant of a tontine

Topaze, sf. (*etym.* *L.* topazion), topaz

Toper, vn. (*etym.* *I.* toppare), to agree. *Tope là! topez là!* agreed! done!

Topinambour, sm. Jerusalem artichoke

Topique, adj. (*etym.* *Gr.* τοπικός, *local*), topical. — sm. topic

Topographie, sf. (*etym.* *Gr.* τοπογραφία), topography

†**Topographique,** adj. topographical

Toque, sf. (*etym.* *I.* tocca), bonnet, cap

Toquer, va. (*etym.* *L.L.* toccare), to touch

Torche, sf. torch, link

†**Torcher,** va. (*etym.* *L.L.* tortiare), to wipe with a wisp of straw

Torchis, sm. mud-plaster

Torchon, sm. duster, dish-clout. — *de paille*, wisp of straw

Tordage, sm. twisting

Tordre, va. (*etym.* *L.* torquere, *to twist*), to wring, to twist

Tore, sm. (*etym.* *L.* torus), torus

Toréador, sm. (*Spanish word*), taureador, bull-fighter

Torpeur, sf. (*etym.* *L.* torporem), torpor, numbness

§**Torpille,** sf. (*etym.* *L.* torpere), torpedo

Torréfier, va. (*etym.* *L.L.* torrefacare), to torrefy

Torrentueux, se, Torrentiel, le, adj. (*etym.* torrent), torrent, ravined, drenching

Torride, adj. (*etym.* *L.* torridus), torrid, burning

Tors, e, or **Torte,** adj. (*etym.* *L.* tortus, *twisted*), twisted, wry

Torsade, sf. twisted fringe, bullion

Torse, sm. (*etym.* *I.* torso), torso, body

Torsion, sf. twisting

Tort, sm. (*etym.* *L.* tortus), wrong, fault, injury, harm. *A —*, wrongfully

§**Tortiller,** va. n. (*etym.* *L.L.* torticulare, *to twist*), to twist about, to waddle, to shuffle

Tortu, e, adj. crooked, twisted, wry

Tortue, sf. (*etym.* *L.L.* tortuca), tortoise, turtle, testudo

†**Tortueux, se,** adj (*etym.* *L.* tortuosus), winding, tortuous, crafty

Torturer, va. (*etym.* torture), to torture, to wrest

Tôt, adv. (*etym.* *L.* tot, cito), soon, quickly

Totalement, adv. (*etym.* total), totally, wholly, entirely

Totalité, sf. totality, whole

Toton, sm. (*onomatop.*), teetotum

Touage, sm. (*etym.* touer), towage, towing

Touchant, e, adj. affecting, moving, touching

Touche, sf. key, stop, touch, assay, stroke, pen, (*print.*) inking

Toucher, va.n. (*etym.* *f*), to touch, to feel, to hit, to offend, to affect, to concern to assay, to ink, to whip on, to receive, to play on, to express; *se —*, vr. to touch one another, to be adjoining to each other. — sm. touch, feeling

Toue, sf. ferry-boat

Touée, sf. towline, warp

Touer, va. (*etym.* *Engl.* to tow), to tow, to warp; *se —*, vr. to haul oneself ahead

Touffe, sf. (*etym.* *L.G.* topp, *tuft*), tuft, clump

Touffu, e, adj. tufted, bushy, spreading

Toujours, adv. (*etym.* tout, jour), always, ever, still, all the same, in the meanwhile, however

Toupet, sm. (*etym.* *O.F.* toupe, *tuft of hair*), tuft of hair, (†) impudence

Toupie, sf. (*etym.* *English* top, *O.F.* topie), top, peg-top, spinning-top

Tour, sf. (*etym.* *L.* turrim), tower, castle

Tour, sm. (*etym.* tourner), turn, turning, revolution, winding, round, compass, excursion, trip, trick, feat, wile, mould

Tourbe, sf. (*etym.* *L.* turba), rabble, mob, herd, peat, turf

Tourbière, sf. bog, bog-water, turf-pit

§**Tourbillon,** sm. (*etym.* *L.L.* turbicula), whirlwind, cloud, whirlpool, vortex, eddy

§**Tourbillonnant, e,** adj whirling, eddying

§**Tourbillonner,** vn. to whirl, to eddy

Tourelle, sf. (*etym.* tour), turret

Tourière, sf. portress

§**Tourillon,** sm. axle, trunnion

Touriste, sm. tourist

Tourment, sm. (*etym.* *L.* tormentum), torment, pang, anguish

Tourmentant, e, adj. troublesome, tormenting

Tourmente, sf. storm, tempest

Tourmenter, va. to torment, to torture, to distress, to molest, to jolt; *se —*, vr. to torment oneself, to fret, to be uneasy, to toss about, to warp, to strain

Tournant, sm. turning, turn, eddy, whirlpool, shift, wheel

Tournebride, sm. inn, public-house

Tournebroche, sm. turnspit, jack

Tournée, sf. round, circuit, tour of inspection. *Être en —*, to be on one's round

Tourner, va.n. (*etym.* *L.* tornare), to turn, to turn round, to wind, to outflank, to construe, to revolve, to turn sour; *se —*, vr. to turn round, to become

Tournesol, sm. sunflower, turnsol

Tourneur, sm. turner

Tournevis, sm. screw-driver, turnscrew

Tourniquet, sm. turnstile, turnpike, screw-jack, sash-pulley

Tournoi, sm. (*etym.* tournoyer), tournament

Tournoiement, sm. turning, wheeling, eddying, dizziness

Tournoyer, vn. (*etym.* *L.L.* tornicare), to turn round and round, to eddy, to beat about the bush

Tournure, sf. turn, figure, shape

Tourte, sf. (*etym.* *L.L.* torta, *cake*), tart, pie

Tourteau, sm. oil-cake, . . .-cake

Tourtereau, sm. (*etym.* *L.L.* turterellus), young turtle-dove

Tourterelle, sf. turtle-dove

Toussaint (la), sf. (*etym.* tout, saint), All-Saints' day

Tousser, vn. (*etym.* toux), to cough

Tousseur, se, s. cougher

Tout, Toute, (*pl.*) **Tous, Toutes,** adj. (*etym.* *L.* totus), all, whole. — sm. everything, all, the whole, the main point. *Tous, Toutes*, s. plur. all, everybody. — adv. wholly, entirely, thoroughly, all

Toutefois, adv. however, nevertheless, still, yet

⁑**Touton**, sm. (*onomatop.*), dog

Toux, sf. (*etym. L.* tussis), cough

Toxicologie, sf. toxicology

Toxique, sm. (*etym. Gr.* τοξικόν, *poison*), poison

Tracas, sm. worry, bustle, stir, noise

Tracasser, vn. (*etym.* traquer), to fidget, to bustle about; —va. to worry; *se* —, vr. to worry oneself

Tracasserie, sf. worry, worrying, vexation, bickering

Trace, sf. trace, track, step, footstep

Tracé, sm. outline, sketch, laying out, direction. *Faire le — de*, to sketch, to lay out

Tracer, va. (*etym. L.L.* tractiare, *to trace*), to trace, to draw, to lay out; — vn. to run out (roots)

Trachée-artère, sf. (*etym. L.* trachia), trachea, windpipe

Trachéotomie, sf. (*etym. Gr.* τραχεῖα, *rough*, τέμνω, *I cut*), tracheotomy

¦**Traditionnel, le**, adj. (*etym.* tradition), traditional

Traducteur, sm. translator

Traduction, sf. (*etym. L.* traductionem), translation

Traduire, va. (*etym. L.* traducere), to translate, to explain, to transfer, to arraign, to indict; *se* —, vr. to be construed

Traduisible, adj. translatable

Trafic, sm. (*etym. I.* traffico), traffic, trade, dealings

Trafiquant, sm. trader, dealer

Trafiquer, vn. (*etym. I.* trafficare), to traffic, to deal, to trade

Tragédie, sf. (*etym. L.* tragœdia), tragedy

Tragédien, ne, s. tragedian

¦**Tragique**, adj. (*etym. L.* tragicus), tragic, tragical — sm. tragedy, tragic author

Trahir, va. (*etym. L.* tradere), to betray, to be false to; *se* —, vr. to be false to oneself, to be false to each other, to betray oneself

Trahison, sf. treachery, treason

Train, sm. (*etym.* traire), pace, rate, quarters, carriage, train

Traînage, sm. sledging

Traînant, e, adj. trailing, languid, dull, drawling, shuffling

Traînard, sm. loiterer, lagger, laggard

Traîneau, sm. sledge, sleigh, drag-net

Traînée, sf. trail, train, track

Traîner, va. (*etym.* train), to drag, to draw, to haul, to track, to drawl out; — vn. to trail, to draggle, to linger, to droop, to flag; *se* —, vr. to crawl along, to crawl

Traîneur, sm. fellow that carries a sword, poacher

Traire, va. (*etym. L.* trahere), to milk

Trait, e, adj. (*etym. L.* tractus), wiredrawn. — sm. shaft, arrow, dart, stroke, trait, traces, leash, turn of the scale, feature

Traitable, adj. tractable, docile, malleable, ductile

Traitant, sm. farmer of the revenue

Traite, sf. distance, journey, stage, transport, exportation, trade, draught

Traité, sm. (*etym. L.* tractatus), treatise, treaty

Traitement, sm. treatment, usage, salary, honours

Traiter, va.n. (*etym. L.* tractare), to treat, to use, to deal, to execute, to negotiate, to be on a treaty for; *se* —, vr. to be treated, to make (good, bad) cheer, to be one's own doctor

Traiteur, sm. eating-house keeper

Traître, Traîtresse, adj. (*etym. L.* traditor), treacherous, traitorous, false, faithless. — s. traitor, traitress. *Prendre en* —, to fall treacherously upon

Traîtreusement, adv. treacherously

Trajectoire, sf. (*etym. L.L.* trajectoria), trajectory

Trajet, sm. (*etym. L.* trajectus), passage, way, interval

Trame, sf. (*etym. L.* trama), woof, thread, course

Tramer, va. to weave, to plot, to hatch; *se* —, vr. to be hatched *or* laid

Tramontane, sf. (*etym. I.* tramontana, *polar star*), the tramontane wind

Tranchant, e, adj. sharp, edge, peremptory, glaring. — sm. edge

Tranche, sf. (*etym.* trancher), slice, edge, series, period

Tranchée, sf. trench, cholic

Tranchefile, sf. head-band

Tranchelard, sm. cook's knife

Tranche-montagne, sm. swaggerer

Trancher, va. (*etym. I*), to cut, to solve, to decide, to curtail; — vn. to cut, to decide, to set up for, to contrast

Tranchet, sm. shoemaker's knife

¦**Tranquille**, adj. (*etym. L.* tranquillus), smooth, still, quiet, peaceful

Tranquillisant, e, adj. tranquillizing

Tranquilliser, va. to tranquillize, to quiet; *se* —, vr. to make oneself easy

Tranquillité, sf. (*etym. L.* tranquillitatem), tranquillity, stillness, quiet

Transaction, sf. (*etym. L.* transactionem), transaction, compromise

Transalpin, e, adj. transalpine

Transatlantique, adj. transatlantic

Transbordement, sm. transshipment

Transborder, va. to tranship

Transcendance, sf. transcendency

Transcendant, e, adj. (*etym. L.* transcendentem), transcendent

Transcrire, va. to transcribe

Transe, sf. (*etym.* transir), fright

Transférer, va. (*etym. L.* transferre), to transfer; *se* —, vr. to pass, to be transferred

Transfert, sm. transfer

se Transfigurer, vr. to be transfigured

Transformer, va. to transform; *se* —, vr. to be transformed, to transform oneself

Transfuge, sm. (*etym. L.* transfuga), deserter, fugitive

Transfuser, va. (*etym. L.L.* transfusare), to transfuse

Transgresser, va. (*etym. L.L.* transgressare), to transgress

Transgresseur, sm. transgressor

Transiger, vn. (*etym. L.* transigere), to compound

Transir, va.n. (*etym. L.* transire, *to die*), to chill, to freeze

¦**Transitif, ve**, adj. (*etym. L.* transitivus), transitive

¦**Transitoire**, adj. (*etym. L.* transitorius), transient, transitory

Transmettre, va. to transfer, to make over, to transmit; *se* —, vr to be transmitted, to be handed down

Transmuable, adj. transmutable

Transmuer, va. (*etym. L.* transmutare), to transmute

Transparence, sf. transparency

Transparent, sm. (*etym. L.L.* transparentem), transparency

Transpercer, va to pierce through and through, to transpierce; *se* —, vr. to run oneself through

Transpiration, sf. transpiration, perspiration, exhalation

Transpirer, vn. (*etym. L.L.* transpirare), to perspire, to transpire

Transplanter, va. (*etym. L.L.* transplantare), to transplant; *se* —, vr. to be transplanted, to transplant oneself

Transport, sm. conveyance, carriage, transport, transfer

Transporter, va. (*etym. L.* transportare), to convey, to transport, to remove, to transfer; *se* —, vr. to repair, to go, to transport oneself

Transposer, va. to transpose

Transsuder, vn. (*etym. L.L.* transsudere), to transude

Transvaser, va. (*etym. L.* trans, *F.* vase), to decant, to transfuse

Transversalement, adv. (*etym.* transversal), transversally, crosswise

Trapèze, sm. (*etym. Gr.* τράπεζα, *table*), trapezium

Trapézoïde, sm. trapezoid

Trappe, sf. (*etym. L.L.* trappa), trap-door, trap, pitfall

Trappiste, sm. (*etym. prop. name* La Trappe), Trappist

Trapu, e, adj. (*etym. ?*), thickset, squat

Traquenard, sm. trap, snare

Traquer, va. (*etym. Dutch* trekken, *to draw*), to beat up, to encircle, to hunt out

Traquet, sm. trap, mill-clapper, stone-chat

Traqueur, sm. huntsman, hunter

§**Travail**, sm. (*etym. L.* trabem, *beam*), labour, work, toil, pains, trouble, trave

§**Travaillé**, past part. wrought, worked, elaborate, labouring, overworked

§**Travailler**, vn. to labour, to work, to toil; — va to work, to labour at, to work at; *se* —, vr. to be wrought or worked, to labour hard, to fret oneself

§**Travailleur**, sm. labourer, operative, workman, hard worker. —, —*se*, adj. hard-working, painstaking

§**Travailleuse**, sf. workwoman

Travée, sf. (*etym. L.L.* trabata, *from L.* trabem, *beam*), bay of joists, balustrade, upper gallery

Travers, sm. (*etym. L.* traversus), breadth, irregularity, eccentricity, oddity, ridicule, freak, whim, (*nav.*) beam, broadside. *Au — de, à —*, loc.prep. through, athwart. *De —, en —*, loc. adv. crosswise, across, awry, askance, wrong

Traverse, sf. cross-bar, cross-piece, sleeper, traverse, cross-road, untoward accident

Traversée, sf. passage, voyage

Traverser, va. to cross, to go through, to traverse

Traversin, sm. bolster, (*nav.*) cross-tree, cross-bit, stretcher

Travestir, va. (*etym. I.* travestire), to travesty, to misinterpret. *Bal travesti*, fancy ball. *Se* —, vr. to disguise oneself

Travestissement, sm. disguise

Trayon, sm. (*etym.* traire), teat, dug

Trébuchant, e, adj. stumbling, of full weight

Trébucher, vn. (*etym. L.L.* transbuccare, *to fall backwards*), to stumble, to trip, to fall

Trébuchet, sm. gin, trap, snare, money-scales

Trèfle, sm. (*etym. L.* trifolium), clover, trefoil, (*cards*) club

§**Treillage**, sm. trellis, trellis-work, lattice-work

§**Treillageur**, sm. trellis-maker

§**Treille**, sf. (*etym. L.* trichila, *trellis*), vine-arbour, vine

§**Treillis**, sm. lattice, trellis, trellis-work

§**Treillisser**, va. to trellis, to lattice

Treize, adj. sm. (*etym. L.* tredecim), thirteen, thirteenth

|**Treizième**, adj. sm. thirteenth

Tréma, sm. (*etym. Gr.* τρῆμα, *hole*), diæresis

Tremblaie, sf. aspen-grove

Tremblant, e, adj. trembling

Tremble, sm. (*etym. L.* tremula), aspen

Tremblé, e, adj. trembling

Tremblement, sm. trembling, shaking, quaking, shivering

Trembler, vn. (*etym. L.L.* tremulare), to tremble, to shake, to quake, to shiver

Trembleur, se, s. trembler, quaker

Tremblotant, e, adj. trembling, tremulous, shivering

Trembloter, vn. to tremble, to quiver

Trémie, sf. (*etym. L.* tres, modia, *bushels; O.F.* tremuie), mill-hopper

Trémière, adj. f. (*etym. ?*). *Rose* —, hollyhock, rose-mallow

se Trémousser, vr. to frisk about, to move about, to bestir oneself

Trempe, sf. temper, tempering, steeping, stamp, cast, cast of character, constitution, paper-wetting

Tremper, va. (*etym. L.* temperare), to soak, to steep, to dip; — vn. to soak, to steep, to be imbrued, to be implicated

Tremplin, sm. (*etym. I.* trempellino), spring-board

Trentaine, sf. about thirty (. . .), a score and a half

Trente, adj. sm. (*etym. L.* triginta), thirty, thirtieth

Trentième, adj. sm. thirtieth

Trépan, sm. (*etym. I.* trepano), trepan, trepanning

Trépaner, va. to trepan

Trépas, sm. (*etym.* trépasser), death. ¦ *Aller de vie à* —, to pass from life to death

Trépassé, e, s. dead person

Trépasser, vn. (*etym. L.L.* transpassare, *to go beyond*), to die, to depart this life

Trépied, sm. (*etym. L.* tripedem), tripod, trivet

§**Trépignement**, sm. stamping, transport of joy

§**Trépigner**, vn. (*etym. O.F.* treper, *to stamp*), to stamp, to leap, to paw

Très, adv. (*etym. L.* trans), very, much, very much

Trésor, sm. (*etym. L.* thesaurus), treasure, treasury

Trésorerie, sf. treasury

Trésorier, ère, s. treasurer

§**Tressaillement**, sm. start, thrill, bound

§**Tressaillir**, vn. (*etym. L.L.* transsalire, *to jump much*), to start, to feel a thrill of

Tresse, sf. tress, plait, braid

Tresser, va. (*etym. L.L.* triciare, *to plait*), to plait, to weave, to tress, to braid

Tréteau, sm. (*etym. L.* transtrum), trestle, boards of a booth, booth

§**Treuil**, sm. (*etym. L.* torculum, *press*), windlass, hand winch, wheel and axle

Trêve, sf. (*etym. Goth.* triggua, *security*), truce, rest

Tri, sm. (*etym.* trier), sorting

Triade, sf. (*etym. L.* tres), triad

Triage, sm. choice, sorting, picking and choosing, winnowing

|**Triangulaire**, adj. (*etym. L.* triangularis), triangular

Tribord, sm. starboard

Tribraque, sm. tribrach

Tribu, sf. (*etym. L.* tribus), tribe

Tribun, sm. (*etym. L.* tribunus), tribune

Tribune, sf. (*etym. I.* tribuna), pulpit, rostrum, tribune, gallery, stand

Tribunitien, ne, adj. tribunitian

Tribut, sm. (*etym. L.* tributum), tribute

Tributaire, adj. sm. (*etym. L.* tributarius), tributary

Tricher, va. (*etym. O.H.G.* trechen, *to hurl a dart*), to cheat, to trick

Tricherie, sf. cheating, trickery

Tricheur, se, s. cheat, trickster

Tricolore, adj. (*etym. L.L.* tricolor), tricoloured

Tricot, sm. knitting

Tricotage, sm. knitting

Tricoter, va. and vn. (*etm. ?*), to knit

Tricoteur, se, s. knitter

Trictrac, sm. (*onomatop.; O.F.* tic-tac), backgammon, backgammon board

Triennal, e, adj. (*etym. L.L.* triennalis), triennial

Trier, va. to sort, to choose, to winnow

Trieur, se, s. sorter

Triglyphe, sm. (*etym. Gr.* τρίγλυφος, *thrice slit*), triglyph

Trigonométrie, sf. (*etm. Gr.* τρίγωνον, *triangle*, μέτρον), trigonometry

§**Trille**, sm. (*etym. I.* trillo), quaver, trill, shake

Trilogie, sf. (*etym. Gr.* τριλογία), trilogy

†**Trimbaler**, va. (*etym. ?*), to drag about

†**Trimer**, vn. (*etym. ?*), to run about, to tire oneself

Trimestre, sm. (*etym. L.* trimestris), quarter, quarter's pay, quarter's income

Trimestriel, le, adj. quarterly

Tringle, sf. (*etym. ?*), curtain rod, tringle, rod

Trinité, sf. (*etym. L.* trinitatem), Trinity, Trinity-Sunday

Trinôme, sm. (*etym. Gr.* τρεῖς, *three*, νόμος, *rule*), trinomial

Trinquer, vn. (*etym. G.* trinken, *to drink*), to touch glasses

|**Triomphal, e**, adj. triumphal

Triomphant, e, adj. triomphant

Triomphateur, sm. (*etm. L.* triumphator), triumpher, conqueror

Triomphe, sm. (*etym. L.* triumphus), triumph

Triompher, vn. to triumph, to be triumphant

Triperie, sf. (*etym.* tripe), tripe-stall

Tripier, Tripière, s. tripe-seller

|**Triple**, adj. sm. (*etym. L.* triplus), treble, triple, threefold

Tripler, vn. to treble, to triple

Tripot, sm. (*etm. O.F.* triper, *to dance*), gambling-house, bad set (of people)

Tripotage, sm. jumble, medley, low intriguing, jobbing

Tripoter, vn. (*etm.* tripot), to jumble together, to intrigue. — va. to handle, to job

Tripotier, ère, s. low intriguer

Trique, sf. (*etym. ?*), cudgel

Trisaïeul, e, s. (*etym. Lat.* tres, *F.* aïeul), great great-grandfather, great-great-grandmother

Trisme, sm. lock-jaw

|**Triste**, adj. (*etym. L.* tristis), sad, mournful, sorrowful, melancholy, dull, gloomy, pitiful

Tristesse, sf. (*etym. L.* tristitia), sadness, mournfulness, sorrowfulness, sorrow, melancholy

Triturer, va. (*etym. L.* triturare), to triturate

Triumvirat, sm. (*etym.* triumvir), triumvirate

Trivialement, adv. (*etym.* trivial), trivially, vulgarly

Trivialité, sf. triviality, trivialness, vulgarity

Troc, sm. (*etym.* troquer), barter, exchange, truck

Trochaïque, adj. sm. (*etm. Gr.* τροχαϊκός), trochaic

Troëne, sm. (*etym. ?*), privet

§†**Trogne**, sf. (*etym. ?*), phiz, face

§**Trognon**, sm. (*etym. ?*), core

Trois, adj. sm. (*etym. L.* tres), three, third

|**Troisième**, adj. sm. f. third; third story, third class

Trois-mâts, sm. three-masted ship

Trombe, sf. (*etym. L.* turbo), waterspout

Tromblon, sm. (*etym. I.* tromba, *fire-arm*), blunderbuss

Trompe, sf. (*etym. ?*), trumpet, horn, trunk, proboscis

Tromper, va. to deceive, to delude, to beguile, to cheat, to elude, to disappoint; *se* —, vr. to be mistaken, to deceive oneself, to err, to deceive one another

Tromperie, sf. deceit, cheat, imposture

Trompeter, va. to summon *or* to proclaim by sound of trumpet; — vn. to scream (*of the eagle*)

Trompette, sf. trumpet. — sm. trumpeter, trumpet-shell

Trompeur, se, adj. s. deceitful, delusive; deceiver, cheat, impostor

Tronc, sm. (*etym. L.* truncus), trunk

Tronchet, sm. block

Tronçon, sm. fragment, broken piece, stump, piece, section

Trône, sm. (*etym. L.* thronus), throne

Tronquer, va. (*etym. L.* truncare), to mutilate, to maim

Trop, adv. (*etym. ?*), too much, too many, over, too long, too. — sm. too much, too great, excess, exuberance

Trophée, sm. (*etym. L.* tropæum), trophy

Tropique, adj. (*etym. L.* tropicus), tropical. — sm. tropic

Trop-plein, sm. overflow, overplus

Troquer, va. (*etym. Sp.* trocar), to barter, to exchange, to truck

Trotte, sf. trot

Trotte-menu, adj. wee-footed

Trotter, vn. (*etym. L.L.* tolutare, *to trot*), to trot, to run about, to go on

Trotteur, sm. trotter

Trottiner, vn. to amble along

Trottoir, sm. foot-pavement, foot-path

Trou, sm. hole, gap, orifice

Trouble, adj. (*etym. L.L.* turbulus, *that which is in disorder*), turbid, muddy, thick, sour, foggy, overcast. — sm. confusion, disturbance, perplexity, uneasiness

Trouble-fête, sm. mar-sport

Troubler, va. (*etym. L.L.* turbulare, *to disturb*), to muddy, to disturb, to make turbid, to thicken, to sour, to trouble, to bring discord into; *se* —, vr. to grow turbid, muddy, thick, to be overcast, to grow dim, to become unsettled

Trouée, sf. gap

Trouer, va. to make a hole in, to bore

Trou-madame, sm. pigeon-hole (*game*)

Troupe, sf. (*etym. L.L.* troppus, *herd*), troop, band, knot, set, gang, company, herd, drove, flight

Troupier, sm. soldier

Trousse, sf. truss, bundle, quiver, surgeon's case, razor-case

Troussé, e, adj. *Bien* —, gallantly curled up, dapper, neat, well-turned

Trousseau, sm. bunch (of keys), marriage outfit, kit

Trousser, va. (*etym. L.L.* tortiare, *to bind together*), to tuck up, to truss, to toss up, to despatch, to carry off; *se* —, vr. to tuck up one's clothes

§**Trouvaille,** sf. prize, finding

Trouver, va. (*etym. L.* turbare, *to move*), to find, to meet with, to chance upon, to get, to seek out; *se* —, vr. to be found, to be met with, to find in oneself, for oneself

Truand, sm. (*etym. L.L.* trutannus, *vagabond*), vagrant

Truchement, sm. (*etym. Sp.* trucheman), interpreter, spokesman

Truelle, sf. (*etym. L.* trua, *a kind of spoon*), trowel, fish-slice

Truffe, sf. (*etym.* ?), truffle

Truie, sf. (*etym. L.L.* troia, *sow*), sow

Truite, sf. (*etym. L.* tructa), trout. — *saumonée*, salmon-trout

Truité, adj. mottled, red-speckled

Trumeau, sm. (*etym.* ?), pier, pier-glass, leg of beef

Tu, pron. (*Lat. word*), thou. ‡ *Ils sont déjà à — et à toi*, they are already hand and glove together

Tuant, e, adj. killing, wearisome

Tubercule, sm. (*etym. L.* tuberculum), tubercle

Tuberculeux, se, adj. tubercular

Tubéreuse, adj. (*etym. L.* tuberosa), tuberous. — sf. tuberose

Tudesque, adj. sm. (*etym. L.L.* teutiscus, theotiscus, *German*), old Teutonic, Gothic

Tudieu! interj. (*abbrev. of* vertu-Dieu), odsfish

Tuer, va. (*etym. L.* tutari, *to protect*), to slay, to kill, to slaughter; *se* —, vr. to kill oneself, to kill each other

Tuerie, sf. butchery, slaughter, slaughter-house

Tueur, sm. killer

Tuile, sf. (*etym. L.* tegula, *tile*), tile, pantile

Tuilerie, sf. tile-kiln

Tuilier, sm. tiler, tile-maker

Tulipe, sf. (*etym. Span.* tulipa), tulip

Tulipier, sm. tulip-tree

Tuméfier, va., *se* —, vr. (*etym. L.L.* tumeficare, *to swell*), to tumefy

Tumeur, sf. (*etym. L.* tumorem), tumour, swelling

Tumulaire, adj. (*etym. L.L.* tumularis), of a grave. *Pierre* —, tombstone

Tumulte, sm. (*etym. L.* tumultus), tumult, uproar

Tunique, sf. (*etym. L.* tunica), tunic

Turgescence, sf. (*etym. L.* turgescere, *to swell*), turgescency, turgidity

Turlupin, sm. (*prop. name of a French actor*), sorry punster, scurvy jester

Tutélaire, adj. (*etym. L.* tutelaris), tutelar, tutelary

Tutelle, sf. (*etym. L* tutela), guardianship, tutelage, protection

Tuteur, trice, s. (*etym. L.* tutor), guardian, prop

Tutoiement, sm. thee-thouing

Tutoyer, va. (*etym.* tu, toi), to thee-thou; *se* —, vr. to thee-thou one another

Tuyau, sm. (*etym. L.* tubulus, *a small tube*), pipe, engine-hose, organ-pipe, chimney-flue, shaft, shank, nozzle, barrel of a pen

Tuyauter, va. to flute, to gauffer

Tuyère, sf. blast-pipe

Tympan, sm. (*etym. L.* tympanum), drum, tympanum

Tympaniser, va. to cry down

Tympanon, sm. dulcimer

Type, sm. (*etym. L.* typus, *model*), type, standard, plan

Typhoïde, adj. (*etym. Gr.* τυφώδης, *connected with fever*), typhoid

Typhon, sm. (*etym. Gr.* τυφῶς, *storm*), typhoon, water-spout

Typique, adj. typical

Typographe, sm. printer, typographer

Typographie, sf. (*etym. Gr.* τύπος, γράφω), typography, letterpress printing, printing-office

Tyran, sm. (*etym. L.* tyrannus), tyrant

Tyrannie, sf. tyranny

‖**Tyrannique,** adj. tyrannical, tyrannous

Tyranniser, va. to tyrannize over

U

U, sm. U, u

Ubiquité, sf. (*etym. L.* ubique, *everywhere*), ubiquity

Udomètre, sm. (*etym. Gr.* ὕδωρ, *water*, μέτρον, *measure*), rain-gauge

Uhlan, sm. (*German word*), uhlan

Ulcère, sm. (*etym. L.* ulceris), ulcer

Ulcéré, e, past part. ulcerated, ulcerous. *Cœur* —, embittered heart

Ulcérer, va. to ulcerate, to embitter; *s'*—, vr. to ulcerate, to grow embittered

Ulcéreux, se, adj. ulcerous

Uliginaire, adj. (*etym. L.* uligo), growing in uliginous places

Uligineux, se, adj. uliginous

‖**Ultérieur, e,** adj. (*etym. L.* ulterior), subsequent, ulterior

Ultramontain, e, adj. sm. (*etym. I.* oltramontano), ultramontane

Un, e, adj.s. (*etym. L.* unus), one. *L'— dans l'autre, l'— portant l'autre*, one with another. † *N'en faire ni —e ni deux*, to decide at once

‖**Unanime,** adj. (*etym. L.* unanimus), unanimous

Unanimité, sf. unanimity, unanimousness. *A l'—*, unanimously

‖**Uni, e,** past part. adj. (*etym.* unir), united, smooth, level, even, plain, uniform, frank

Unième, adj. first

Uniflore, adj. uniflorous

Uniforme, adj. sm. (*etym. L.* uniformis), uniform. ‡ *En grand* —, in full uniform

Uniformément, adv. uniformly

Uniformité, sf. uniformity

Unilatéral, e, adj. (*etym. L.* unum, latus), unilateral, bearing flowers only on one side

Unipersonnel, adj. m. impersonal

‖**Unique,** adj. (*etym. L.* unicus), only, sole, unrivalled, unequalled

Unir, va. (*etym. L.* unire), to unite, to join, to link together, to smooth, to level; *s'*—, vr. to unite, to join, to be united

Unisson, sm. (*etym. L.L.* unisonus), unison. ‡ *A l'*—, in unison. *Se mettre à l'— de*, to suit oneself to the tone

Unitaire, sm. Unitarian

Unité, sf. (*etym. L.* unitatem), unity, unit

Univers, sm. (*etym. L.* universum), the universe

Universalité, sf. (*etym. L.L.* universalitatem), universality

‖**Universel, le,** adj. (*etym. L.* universalis), universal

Universitaire, adj. sm. of the university, member of the university

Université, sf. (*etym. L.* universitatem) university

Univoque, adj. univocal

Urbain, e, adj. (*etym. L.* urbanus), urban

Urbanité, sf. urbanity

Urcéolé, e, adj. (*etym. L.* urceus, *pitcher*), having the shape of a small bottle

Ure, sm. (*etym. Gr.* οὖρος), wild bull, aurochs

Urgence, sf. (*etym.* urgent), urgency, pressure

Uriner, vn. (*etym.* urine), to urine, to make water

Urne, sf. (*etym. L.* urna), urn. — *électorale, du scrutin*, ballot-box

Urticaire, sf. (*etym. L.* urtica, *nettle*), nettle-rash, urticaria

***Us,** sm. plur. (*etym. L.* usus), uses

Usage, sm. custom, usage, use. *Avoir de l'*—, to know the habits of society. *D'*—, in use, usual

Usé, e, past part. adj. worn out, threadbare

User, vn. (*etym. L.L.* usare = *L.* uti, *to use*), to use, to make use, to enjoy; — va. to use, to use up, to wear out. ‡ *En* —, vn. to act, to behave, to treat, to deal. *S'*—, vr. to wear out, to wear away, to be spent, to decay. — sm. wear, use. *Être d'un bon* —, to wear well

Usine, sf. (*etym. L.L.* usina, *the use of water-courses*), manufacture, works

Usité, e, adj. (*etym. L.* usitari), used, in use

Ustensile, sm. (*etym. L.* utensilia), utensil, implement, tool, kitchen utensils

‖**Usuel, le,** adj. (*etym. L.* usualis), usual, customary

Usufruit, sm. (*etym. L.* ususfructus), usufruct, use

Usufruitier, ère, adj. usufructuary

‖**Usuraire,** adj. usurious

Usure, sf. (*etym. L.* usura), usury, wear and tear

Usurier, ère, s. usurer

Usurpateur, trice, s. adj. usurper, usurping

Usurper, va.n. (*etym. L.* usurpare), to usurp, to encroach

Utérin, e, adj. (*etym. L.* uterinus), by the mother's side, uterine

‖**Utile,** adj. (*etym. L.* utilis), useful, serviceable, expedient. ‡ *En temps* —, in due time. — sm. utility, what is useful

Utiliser, va. to turn to good use, to make use of, to utilize; *s'*—, vr. to make oneself useful, to be turned to good use

Utilité, sf. utility, usefulness, use, (*theat.*) useful men, utilities

Utopie, sf. (*etym. Gr.* οὐ, τόπος, *no place*), Utopia

Utopiste, sm. Utopist

V

V, sm. V, v, five
Va! interj. go! believe me! done!
Vacance, sf. vacancy, holidays, recess
Vacant, e, adj. (*etym. L.* vacantem), vacant, empty, untenanted, unclaimed
Vacarme, sm. (*etym. D.* wacharmer, *woe to thee!*), uproar, hubbub
Vacation, sf. (*etym. L.* vacationem), sitting, day's time, day's sale, fee, (*pl.*) vacation, recess, (*nav.*) voyage money
Vaccin, sm. (*etym. L.* vaccinus), vaccine matter
Vaccine, sf. cow-pox, vaccination
Vacciner, va. to vaccinate
Vache, sf. (*etym. L.* vacca), cow, neat-leather, boot of a carriage. — *à lait, laitière,* milch-cow, dairy-cow. *Pis de* —, udder. ‡ *Qu'il mange un peu de — enragée,* let him rough it a little
Vacher, ère, s. cowherd, neatherd
Vacherie, sf. cow-house
§**Vacillant, e,** adj. unsteady, vacillating, flickering
§**Vaciller,** vn. (*etym. L.* vacillare), to vacillate, to be unsteady, to stagger, to flicker
Vacuité, sf. (*etym. L.* vacuitatem), vacuity, emptiness
Va-et-vient, sm. traversing gear, to and fro motion, ferry-boat, (*nav.*) pass-rope. ‡ *Établir un* —, to fix a pass-rope
Vagabond, e, adj (*etym. L.* vagabundus), roving, vagrant, wandering. — s. vagrant, vagabond, trespasser
Vagabondage, sm. vagrancy
Vagabonder, vn. to be a vagabond, to rove about, to roam
Vagir, vn. (*etym. L.* vagire), to wail, to cry
Vagissement, sm. cry, crying
Vague, sf. (*etym. O.H.G.* wâc, *wave*), wave, billow, sea, surge. — adj. (*etym. L.* vagus, *wandering*), vague, empty, rambling, loose. — sm. vacuum, vagueness, emptiness
Vaguemestre, sm. (*etym. G.* wagenmeister, *master of the equipages*), (*milit.*) baggage-master, postman
Vaguer, va. (*etym. L.* vagari), to stray
§**Vaillance,** sf. (*etym. L.L.* valentia), valour
§**Vaillant, e,** adj. (*etym. L.* valentem), valiant, valorous, stalwart. — sm. all one is worth. — adv., *Sans un sou* —, without a penny in the world
§**Vaillantise,** sf. high deed
‖**Vain, e,** adj. (*etym. L.* vanus), vain, fruitless, ineffectual, empty, idle, foolish. ‡ *Terres —es et vagues,* waste lands
Vaincre, va. (*etym. L.* vincere), to overcome, to vanquish, to conquer, to worst; *se* —, vr. to conquer oneself, to conquer each other
Vaincu, sm. vanquished man
Vainqueur, sm. conqueror, victor, vanquisher
Vairon, adj. (*etym. O.F.* vair = *L.* varius), wall-eyed
Vaisseau, sm. (*etym. L.* vascellum, *dimin. of* vas), vessel, vase, ship, shipping, structure, duct
Vaisselle, sf. plates and dishes
Val, sm. (*etym. L.* vallis), vale, valley, dale
‖**Valable,** adj. (*etym.* valoir), valid, good
Valériane, sf. (*prop. n.*), valerian
Valet, sm. (*etym. L.L.* vassaletus, *from* vassalis), footman, valet, man-servant, menial, (*cards*) knave, door-weight, holdfast, claw, wad. ‡ *Âme de* —, cringing soul
§**Valetaille,** sf. valets, menials
Valétudinaire, adj. sm. (*etym. L.* valetudinarius), valetudinarian, invalid
Valeur, sf. (*etym. L.L.* valorem), value, price, worth, weight, bills, valour, gallantry. *Des non-* —*s,* bills of no value, bad debts
‖**Valeureux, se,** adj. valorous, valiant, gallant
‖**Valide,** adj. (*etym. L.* validus), valid, able-bodied, healthy
Valider, va. to render valid
Validité, sf. validity
Valise, sf. (*etym. I.* valigia), portmanteau, cloak-bag
Vallée, sf. valley, vale
Vallon, sm. vale, dale, dell
Valoir, vn. (*etym. L.* valere), to be worth; — va. to bring in, to yield, to be worth, to procure. ‡ *À* —, on account. *Vaille que vaille,* come what may. — *mieux,* vn. to be better. — (*faire*), loc. verb, to turn to account, to improve, to urge, to enhance, to make the most of, to command. — (*se faire*), vr. to keep up one's dignity *or* importance, to win distinction
§**Valse,** sf. (*etym. G.* walzen), waltz, waltzing. *Faire un tour de* —, to waltz a little
Valser, vn. to waltz
Valseur, se, s. waltzer
Van, sm. (*etym. L.* vannus), fan
Vandalisme, sm. (*etym. prop. name* Vandale), Vandalism
§**Vanille,** sf. (*etym. Sp.* vainilla), vanilla
§**Vanillier,** sm. vanilla-tree
Vanité, sf. (*etym. L.* vanitatem), vanity, emptiness, self-conceit
Vaniteux, se, adj. vain, vainglorious. — sm. vain man
Vanne, sf. sluice, water-gate
Vanneau, sm. lapwing, peewit
Vanner, va. to winnow
Vannerie, sf. basket-work, basket-making
Vanneur, sm. winnower
Vannier, sm. basket-maker
§**Vantail,** sm. (*etym.* vent), leaf of a door; *plur.* vantaux
Vantard, adj. boastful, boasting. — sm. boaster, braggart
Vanter, va. (*etym. L.L.* vanitare, *to boast*), to praise, to vaunt, to cry up; *se* —, vr to praise up oneself, to boast, to brag
Vanterie, sf. boast, vaunt, boasting, vaunting
Va-nu-pieds, sm. beggar, ragamuffin
Vapeur, sf. (*etym. L.* vaporem), vapour, steam, fume. — sm. steamer, steam-vessel. — *à hélice,* screw steam-vessel
Vaporeux, se, adj. vapory, vaporous, vaporish
Vaporisation, sf. vaporization
Vaporiser, va., *se* —, vr. to vaporize
Vaquer, vn. (*etym. L.* vacare), to be vacant, not to sit, to have a holiday, to attend
Varech, sm. (*etym. Ang.-Sax.* vrâc, *wreck*), sea-weed, sea-wrack, foundered vessel
Vareuse, sf. (*etym.* ?), stuff-jacket, sail-cloth
Variabilité, sf. (*etym.* variable), variableness, variability
Variant, e, adj. fickle, varying
Variante, sf. different reading
Varice, sf. (*etym. L.* varicem), varix
Varicelle, sf. varicella
Varicocèle, sf. varicocele
Varié, e, adj. varied, variegated
Varier, va.n. (*etym. L.* variare), to vary, to change, to variegate, to differ
Variété, sf. (*etym. L.* varietatem), variety
Variole, sf. (*etym. L.L.* variola), small-pox, variola
Varioloïde, sf. chicken-pox, varioloid
Varlope, sf. (*etym.* ?), jointing-plane, jointer
Vase, sm. (*etym. L.* vasum), vase, vessel, bell. — sf. (*Ang.-Sax. word*), slime, mud, mire, ooze
Vaseux, se, adj. slimy, muddy, oozy
Vasistas, sm. (*etym.* ?), casement window
Vasselage, sm. (*etym.* vassal), vassalage
Vaste, adj (*etym. L.* vastus), vast, immense, wide, spacious, capacious
Va-tout, sm. one's all. *Faire son* —, to stake one's all
Vaudevilliste, sm. (*etym.* vaudeville, *from* vau-de-vire = *valley of the* [*river*] *Vire*), writer of vaudevilles
Vau l'eau (*à*), loc. adv. (*etym.* aval-l'eau = *down the stream*), down the river. ‡ *Aller à* —, to go to rack and ruin
Vaurien, sm. (*etym.* vaut, rien; *comp.* fainéant = fait, néant), good-for-nothing fellow, scamp
Vautour, sm. (*etym. L.* vulturius), vulture
se Vautrer, vr. (*etym. L.L.* voltulare, *O.F.* voltrer), to wallow, to loll
Veau, sm. (*etym. L.* vitellus), calf, veal, calfskin. — *marin,* seal
Vedette, sf. (*etym. I.* vedetta), (*milit.*) vedette, horse-sentry, scout, watch-tower, a line by itself
Végétal, sm. (*etym. L.L.* vegetalis), vegetable, plant. —, —*e,* adj. vegetable. *Terre —e,* mould
Végétant, e, adj. vegetative
Végéter, vn. (*etym. L.* vegetare), to vegetate
Véhémence, sf. vehemence, vehemency
Véhément, e, adj (*etym. L.* vehementem), vehement
Véhémentement, adv. vehemently
Véhicule, sm. (*etym. L.* vehiculum), vehicle
§**Veille,** sf. watch, vigil, sleeplessness, wakefulness, eve
§**Veillée,** sf. vigil, evening work, working-party, night attendance
§**Veiller,** vn. (*etym. L.* vigilare), to sit up, to stay up, to keep awake, to watch, to look, to take care; — va. to sit up by, to watch by

§**Veilleur**, sm. watchman, watcher

§**Veilleuse**, night lamp, float-light

Veine, sf. (*etym. L.* vena), vein, seam. ‡ *Ouvrir une* —, to breathe a vein. — *couchée*, flat vein. — *droite*, — *perpendiculaire*, rake vein

Veiné, e, adj. veined, veiny

Veineux, se, adj. veined, veiny, venous

Velche, sm. (*prop. name* Welsh), ignoramus

Vêler, vn. (*etym.* veau), to calve

Vélin, sm. (*etym.* veau), vellum

Velléité, sf. (*etym. L.* velle), slight desire, slight notion

Véloce, adj. (*etym. L.* velocem), swift

Vélocité, sf. velocity, speed, swiftness

Velours, sm. (*etym. L.* villosus, *hairy*, *O.F.* velous), velvet. ‡ — *épinglé*, Terry velvet. — *de coton*, velveteen

Velouté, e, adj. velvet, velveted, fine-flavoured dark red (wine). — sm. velvet lace

Velu, e, adj. (*etym. L.* villosus), hairy, shaggy, villous

Venaison, sf. (*etym. L.* venationem), venison. *Être en* —, to be in season, to be fat

Vénalité, sf. (*etym.* vénal), venality

Venant, adj.m. thriving, regularly forthcoming. — sm. comer. *A tout* —, to the first comer

Vendable, adj. saleable, marketable

Vendange, sf. vintage

Vendanger, vn.a. (*etym. L.* vindemiare), to gather the grapes, to sweep away, to devastate

Vendangeur, se, s. grape-gatherer

Vendeur, se, s. seller, dealer, vendor

Vendre, va. (*etym. L.* vendere), to sell, to vend. *A* —, for sale. *Se* —, vr. to be sold, to sell, to sell oneself, to betray oneself

Vendredi, sm. (*etym. L.* Veneris dies), Friday. — *saint*, Good Friday

Venelle, sf. (*etym.* veine), small street. ‡ *Enfiler la* —, to run away

Vénéneux, se, adj. (*etym. L.* venenosus), poisonous, venomous

Vénérer, va. (*etym. L.* venerari), to venerate, to revere, to reverence

Vénerie, sf. (*etym. L.* venari), hunting, hunt, hunting-train, kennel

Veneur, sm. huntsman

Venger, va. (*etym. L.* vindicare), to avenge, to revenge; *se* —, vr. to be revenged, to revenge oneself

Vengeur, eresse, s. adj. avenger; avenging, revengeful

Véniel, le, adj. (*etym. L.* venialis), venial

Venimeux, se, adj. venomous, poisonous, baneful, spiteful

Venin, sm. (*etym. L.* venenum), venom, virulency, spite

Venir, vn. (*etym. L.* venire), to come, to occur, to happen, to chance, to fall, to grow, to thrive. *En* —, vn. to come, to proceed, to have recourse, to be reduced, to come off. — (*faire*), loc. verb, to send for, to call in, to grow, to raise. — (*laisser*), loc. verb, to let come, to wait a little, to let things take their course. — (*voir*), loc. verb, to see a thing come, to see what one is aiming at

Vent, sm. (*etym. L.* ventus), wind, breeze, gale, scent, emptiness, windage. ‡ — *arrière*, stern wind. *Au* —, to windward. *Sous le* —, to leeward. — *frais*, stiff breeze. *Prendre* —, to snuff the wind

Vente, sf. (*etym.* vendre), sale, selling. *En* —, for sale. *Lettre, livre de* —*s*, bill of sales, sales-book

Venter, vn. to blow. ‡ *Il ventait bon frais*, there was a brisk breeze

Venteux, se, adj. windy, gusty

Ventilateur, sm. (*etym. L.* ventilator), ventilator, fan, air-trap, bellows, (*nav.*) wind-sail

Ventiler, va. (*etym. L.* ventilare, *to fan, to set in motion*), to ventilate

Ventouse, sf. (*etym. L.L.* ventosa), cupping-glass, cupping, vent, air-hole

Ventouser, va. to cup

Ventre, sm. (*etym. L.* ventrem), belly, stomach, paunch, womb. *Bas-* —, abdomen. *Courir* — *à terre*, to go full speed

Ventrebleu! Ventre-saint-gris! interj. gadzooks! odsbud!

Ventricule, sf. (*etym. L.* ventriculus), ventricle

Ventriloque, adj.sm. (*etym. L.* ventriloquus), ventriloquous, ventriloquist

Ventriloquie, sf. ventriloquy

Ventru, e, adj. tun-bellied, big-bellied

Venu, e, past part. come, a (good, bad) impression, received. — s. comer

Venue, sf. coming, growth. ‡ *Tout d'une* —, all of a size

Vêpres, sf. plur. (*etym. L.* vesper, *evening*), vespers

Ver, sm. (*etym. L.* vermis), worm, maggot, mite, moth. ‡ — *blanc*, maggot. — *luisant*, glow-worm, fire-fly. — *à soie*, silk-worm. — *solitaire*, tænia, tape-worm. *Mangé, piqué, rongé par les* —*s*, worm-eaten. *Tirer les* —*s du nez à quelqu'un*, to pump a person

Véracité, sf. (*etym. L.L.* veracitatem), veracity, truthfulness

§**Verbal, e**, adj. (*etym. L.* verbalis), verbal. *Procès-* —, official report, report. *Faire un procès-* —, to draw up an official report

Verbaliser, vn. to state the facts, to draw up an official report

Verbe, sm. (*etym. L.* verbum), verb, tone of voice. ‡ *Avoir le* — *haut*, to speak authoritatively

Verbeux, se, adj. (*etym. L.* verbosus), wordy, verbose

Verbosité, sf. (*etym. L.* verbositatem), verbosity

Ver-coquin, sm. maggot

Verdâtre, adj. (*etym.* vert), greenish

Verdelet, te, adj. greenish, tart, hale and hearty

Verdeur, sf. sap, briskness, tartness

Verdier, sm. greenfinch

Verdir, va.n. to paint green, to grow green

Verdoyant, e, adj. verdant, green

Verdoyer, vn. to grow green, to be green

Verdure, sf. verdure, greenness, pot-herbs

Véreux, se, adj. (*etym.* ver), rotten, suspicious

Verge, sf. (*etym. L.* virga), rod, wand, mace, switch, twig, birch, (*nav.*) shank, shaft, spear

Vergé, e, adj. streaky, (*paper*) laid

Verger, sm. (*etym. L.* viridarium), orchard

Vergette, sf. brush, bundle of rods

Verglas, sm. (*etym.* verre, glace), glazed frost, ice

§**Vergogne**, sf. (*etym. L.* verecundia, *shame*), shame

Vergue, sf. (*etym. L.* virga), yard, boom. ‡ *La grande* —, the main-yard. — *du grand perroquet*, main top-gallant yard. *Bout de* —, yard-arm. *Sur les* —*s!* man the yards!

Véridicité, sf. truthfulness, veracity

Véridique, adj. (*etym. L.* veridicus), truth-speaking, veracious

Vérificateur, sm. examiner, (*customs*) land-waiter

Vérifier, va. (*etym. L.L.* verificare), to verify, to examine, to confirm; *se* —, vr. to be verified

§**Véritable**, adj. (*etym.* vérité), true, genuine, veritable

Vérité, sf. (*etym. L.* veritatem), truth

Verjus, sm. (*etym.* vert, jus), verjuice, sour grapes

§**Vermeil, le**, adj. (*etym. L.L.* vermiculus, *scarlet*), vermillion, ruddy, rosy. — sm. silver-gilt

Vermicelle, sm. (*etym. I.* vermicelli), vermicelli

Vermiculaire, adj. vermicular

§**Vermillon**, sm. vermillion

Vermine, sf. (*etym. L.* vermis), vermin

Vermisseau, sm. (*etym. L.L.* vermicellus), worm, small worm

Vermoulu, e, adj. (*etym.* ver, moudre), worm-eaten

Vermout, sm. (*etym. G.*), bitters

Vernir, Vernisser, va. (*etym. L.L.* vitrinire, *to make as brilliant as glass*), to varnish, to glaze; *se* —, vr. to be varnished

Vernis, sm. varnish, gloss, polish, glazing

Vernisseur, sm. varnisher

Vérole (petite), sf. (*etym. L.L.* variola), small-pox

Véronique, sf. (*etym. L.* veronica), speedwell, veronica

Verrat, sm. (*etym. L.* verres), boar, boar-pig

Verre, sm. (*etym. L.* vitrum), glass

Verrerie, sf. glass-works, glass-house, glass-making, glass wares

Verrier, sm. glass-founder, glassman, glass basket

Verrière, Verrine, sf. glass case, glass frame

Verroterie, sf. small glass ware, glass trinkets

Verrou, sm. (*etym. L.* veruculum), bolt

§**Verrouiller**, va. to bolt; *se* —, vr. to bolt oneself in

Verrue, sf. (*etym. L.* verruca), wart

Vers, sm. (*etym. L.* versus), verse, line. — prep. towards, about

Versant, sm. side, slope, watershed

Versatilité, sf. versatility

Verse (à), loc. adv. fast, hard. *Pleuvoir à* —, to rain in torrents

Versé, e, adj. versed, conversant, skilled. *Peu* — *dans*, unversed in

Verseau (le), sm. (*etym.* verser, eau), Aquarius, the water-bearer

Versement, sm. payment, deposit

Verser, va. (*etym. L.* versare), to pour, to spill, to discharge, to empty, to shed, to pay in, to upset; — vn. to pour out, to break down, to overturn

Verset, sm. verse

Versificateur, sm. versifier

Versifier, vn.a. to versify, to make verses, to turn into verse

Verso, sm. (*Latin word*) reverse, back

Verste, sf. (*Russian word*), verst

Vert, e, adj. (*etym. L.* viridis), green, grassy, verdant, brisk; hale, hearty, undried, tart. ‡ *Il n'est feu que de bois* —, (*fig.*) sprightliness belongs to youth alone. — sm. green, grass, tartness. *Gros* —, cabbage green. — *de vessie*, sap-green. *Mettre au* —, to put (a horse) out to grass. *Em-*

ployer le — et le sec, to go through thick and thin. *Prendre sans* —, to take one unprepared

Vert-de-gris, sm. verdigris

Vertébral, e, adj. vertebral. *Colonne —e*, spinal column, backbone

Vertèbre, sf. (*etym. L.* vertebra), vertebra

Vertébré, e, adj. vertebrated, backboned

Verticalement, adv. (*etym.* vertical), vertically

Vertige, sf. (*etym. L.* vertigo), giddiness, dizziness

Vertigineux, se, adj. (*etym. L.* vertiginosus), dizzy, giddy

Vertigo, sm. whim, dizziness

Vertu, sf. (*etym. L.* virtutem), virtue, property

Vertueux, se, adj. virtuous

Vertugadin, sm. (*etym.* vertu, garde), farthingale

Verve, sf. (*etym. L.L.* verva, *a sculptured ram's head*), animation, spirit, freak

Verveine, sf. (*etym. L.* verbenæ), verbena, vervain

Vesce, sf. (*etym. L.* vicia), vetch

Vésicatoire, adj. sm. (*etym. L.* vesica), blistering, blister

Vésicule, sf. (*etym. L.* vesicula), vesicle, bladder

Vessie, sf. (*etym. L.* vesica), bladder

Vestale, sf. (*etym. L.* Vestalis), Vestal

Veste, sf. (*etym. L.* vestis), vest, jacket

Vestiaire, sm. (*etym. L.* vestiarium), vestiary

Vêtement, sm. (*etym. L.* vestimentum), garment, vestment, piece of clothing

Vétérance, sf. (*etym. L.* veteranus), quality of a veteran

Vétérinaire, adj. (*etym. L.* veterinarius), veterinary, horse. — sm. veterinary surgeon, horse-doctor

§**Vétillard, e**, s. trifler

§**Vétille**, sf. (*etym. Piedm.* vetilla, *trifle*), trifle

§**Vétiller**, vn. to trifle, to stand upon trifles

§**Vétilleur, se**, s. trifler, person who stands upon trifles

§**Vétilleux, se**, adj. requiring minute attention, caring about trifles

Vêtir, va. (*etym. L.* vestire), to clothe, to robe, to array, to put on; *se* —, vr. to dress, to clothe oneself

Vêture, sf. ceremony of taking the habit *or* the veil

Vétusté, sf. (*etym. L.* vetustatem), old age, antiquity, oldness

Veuf, ve, adj. s. (*etym. L.* viduus), widowed, bereft, shorn; a widower, a widow

Veule, adj. (*etym.* ?), light, soft

Veuvage, sm. widowhood, bereavement

Vexatoire, adj. vexatious

Vexer, va. (*etym. L.* vexare), to molest, to vex

Viabilité, sf. likelihood of living

Viable, adj. (*etym.* vie), likely to live

Viaduc, sm. (*etym. L.* via, ductus), viaduct

Viager, ère, adj. (*etym. L.L.* vitaticarius), for life. *Rentes —ères*, life annuity. — sm. life interest

Viande, sf. (*etym. L.L.* vivanda), meat. *Basse* —, coarse meat. *Grosse* —, butcher's meat. — *creuse*, meagre diet, empty delusions

Viatique, sm. (*etym. L.* viaticum), viaticum

Vibord, sm. (*etym.* ?), (*nav.*) waist

Vibrant, e, adj. vibratory, vibrating

Vibrer, vn. (*etym. L.* vibrare), to vibrate

Vicaire, sm. (*etym. L.* vicarius), vicar, curate

Vicariat, sm. vicariate, vicegerency, curacy, vicarage

Vice-gérant, sm. deputy-manager

Vice-roi, sm. viceroy

Vice-royauté, sf. vice-royalty

Vicié, e, adj. tainted, corrupt

Vicier, va. (*etym. L.* vitiare), to vitiate, to taint, to corrupt

‡**Vicieux, se**, adj. (*etym. L.* vitiosus), vicious

Vicinal, e, adj. (*etym. L.* vicinalis), parochial, parish

Vicomte, sm. (*etym. L.* vice, comitem), viscount

Vicomté, sf. viscounty

Vicomtesse, sf. viscountess

Victime, sf. (*etym. L.* victima), victim

Victimer, va. to devote, to victimize

Victoire, sf. (*etym. L.* victoria), victory

‡**Victorieux, se**, adj. (*etym. L.* victoriosus), victorious

§**Victuaille**, sf. (*etym. L.L.* victualia), food, victuals, provisions

Vidange, sm. (*etym.* vider), emptying, clearance, privy-emptying

Vide, adj. (*etym. L.* viduus), empty, vacant, void, destitute. — sm. void, emptiness, gap, chasm, hole, blank, vacuum

§**Vide-bouteille**, sm. country-box, arbour

Vider, va. to empty, to draw off, to bore, to hollow out, to gut, to leave, to vacate, to settle, to decide. — *les lieux*, to vacate the premises. *Se* —, vr. to empty oneself, to be emptied, to be settled

Viduité, sf. (*etym. L.* viduitatem), widowhood

Vie, sf. (*etym. L.* vita), life, heart's blood, lifetime, days, livelihood, living, racket, noise

Vieil *or* **Vieux, Vieille**, adj. (*etym. L.L.* veclus, vetlus, *for L.* vetulus), old, aged, in years

§**Vieillard**, sm. old man, elder, patriarch

§**Vieillerie**, sf. piece of old lumber

§**Vieillesse**, sf. old age, age, oldness

§**Vieillir**, vn. to grow old, to grow in years, to grow out of date; — va. to make old, to make look old; *se* —, vr. to make oneself look old, to exaggerate one's years

§**Vieillot, te**, s. old man, old woman

Vielle, sf. (*etym. L.L.* vitella), hurdy-gurdy, vielle

Vielleur, se, s. hurdy-gurdy player

Vierge, sf. (*etym. L.* virgo), virgin, maiden. *Fil de la* —, gossamer thread. — adj. virginal, virgin

Vieux, Vieille, smf. old man, old woman, old hag. ‡ *Allons la* —, come, old lady

‡**Vif, ve**, adj. (*etym. L.* vivus), alive, living, quick, lively, spirited, hasty, passionate, sharp, bright. ‡ *Eau —ve*, running water. *—ves eaux*, (*nav.*) spring-tides. — sm. quick, living person. *Donation entre —s*, deed of gift between living people. *Le mort saisit le* —, the heir at law inherits of course

Vif-argent, sm. quicksilver

Vigie, sf. (*etym. L.* vigil), look-out man, lurking rock. *Être en* —, to be on the look-out

Vigile, sf. vigil, eve. *Faire* —, to keep vigil

§**Vigne**, sf. (*etym. L.* vinea), vine, vineyard. — *-vierge*, ivy grape. ‡ *Être dans les —s*, to be tipsy

§**Vigneron, ne**, s. vine-dresser

§**Vignoble**, sm. (*etym. L.* vini, opulens), vineyard. *Pays* —, wine-country. *Propriétaire de —s*, vine-grower

§**Vigogne**, sf. (*etym. Span.* vicuña), alpaca

‡**Vigoureux, se**, adj. vigorous, sturdy, stout

Vigueur, sf. (*etym. L.* vigorem), vigour, strength

Viguier, sm. (*etym. L.* vicarius), royal provost

Vil, e, adj. (*etym. L.* vilis), vile, despicable, base, low

Vilain, sm. (*etym. L.L.* villanus, *tenant of a farm*), villein, thrall, bondman, scurvy fellow, curmudgeon, nasty fellow. —, —e, adj. ugly, unsightly, unpleasant, nasty, villanous, scurvy

Vilebrequin, sm. (*etym.* virer, brequin, *O.F.* berquin, *from the Dutch* boreken, *a gimlet*), wimble, centre-bit wimble

Vilenie, sf. nastiness, scurviness

Vileté, sf. low price, worthlessness

Vilipender, va. (*etym. L.* vilipendere), to cry down, to vilify

Villageois, sm., —, —e, adj. (*etym.* village), villager, cottager, cotter, countryman; of a village, village

Ville, sf. (*etym. L.* villa), town, city. *En* —, in town, out. ‡ *Dîner en* —, to dine out

Vin, sm. (*etym. L.* vinum), wine. ‡ *Gros* —, heavy wine. — *chaud*, mulled wine. *Avoir le — bon, mauvais, gai, triste*, to be amiable, unamiable, merry, dull in one's cups. *Être entre deux —s*, to be half seas over. *Pris de* —, tipsy

Vinaigre, sm. vinegar, vinegar salts

Vinaigrer, va. to season with vinegar

Vinaigrette, sf. vinegar sauce, Bath-chair, cab

Vinaigrier, sm. vinegar-maker, vinegar-cruet

Vindas, sm. (*etym. O.H.G.* windan, *to wind*), windlass

Vindicatif, ve, adj. (*etym. L.L.* vindicativus), revengeful, vindictive

Vindicte, sf. (*etym. L.* vindicta), vengeance

Vinée, sf. vintage

Vineux, se, adj. strong-bodied, strong, wine-producing, wine-coloured, vinous. — sm. wine colour

Vingt, adj. sm. (*etym. L.* viginti), twenty. *Six-—s*, six score

Vingtaine, sf. a score, about twenty

‡**Vingtième**, adj. sm. twentieth

Vinicole, adj. wine-growing

Viol, sm. (*etym.* violer), rape, ravishment

Violacé, e, adj. (*etym.* violet), violet-hued

Violacées, sf. plur. violet-tribe

Violat, adj.m. of violet

Violateur, trice, s. violator, transgressor

Viole, sf. (*etym. I.* viola), viol

Violence, sf. violence, stress, fury

‡**Violent, e**, adj. violent, strong, pelting, boisterous, passionate

Violenter, va. to do violence to

Violer, va. (*etym. L.* violare), to violate, to transgress, to ravish

Violette, sf. (*etym.* violet), violet. ‡ *A la première* —, when the violet blooms

Violier, sm. wall-flower

Violon, sm. (*etym. I.* violone), violin, fiddle, cage, (*plur.*) bees. ‡ *Râcler du* —, to scrape a fiddle. *Donner les —s*, to give a serenade. *Payer les —s*, to pay the piper

Violoncelle, sm. (*etym. I.* violoncello), violoncello

Violoniste, sm. violinist, violin-player

Viorne, sm. (*etym. L.* viburnum), viburnum

Vipère, sf. (*etym. L.* vipera), viper, adder

Virelai, sm. (*etym.* virer, lai), virelay

Virement, sm. veering about, clearing, transfer. ‡ — *d'eau*, turn of the tide. — *de parties*, clearing of accounts

Virer, vn a. (*etym. O.F.* vire, *circle, ring*), to turn, to twist, to tack, to veer, to heave up, to hoist away. — *de bord*, to tack about. — *devant*, to tack

Virginité, sf. (*etym. L.* virginitatem), virginity, maidenhood

Virgule, sf. (*etym. L.* virgula), comma

§**Viril, e,** adj. (*etym. L.* virilis), virile, man's

Virilité, sf. manhood, manliness

Virole, sf. (*etym.* virer), ferrule

Virtualité, sf. (*etym. L.* virtus), power

§**Virtuel, le,** adj. virtual

Virtuose, sm. (*etym. I.* virtuoso), virtuoso

Vis, sf. (*etym. L.* vitis, *tendril of the vine*), screw. *Pas de* —, furrow of a screw. *Fermer à* —, to screw down

Visage, sm. (*O.F.* vis, *etym. L.* visus), face, countenance, look, visage, aspect. ‡ *Avoir bon* —, to look hearty. *Trouver — de bois*, to find nothing but the door-post. *Faire bon* —, to receive kindly

Vis-à-vis, prep. adv. sm. opposite, over against, towards; opposite neighbour

Viscères, sm. plur. (*etym. L.* viscera), viscera

Visée, sf. aim, end, design

Viser, vn.a. (*etym. L.L.* visare), to aim, to take aim

Visibilité, sf. (*etym.* visible), visibility

Visiblement, adv. obviously, visibly

Visière, sf. (*etym. O.F.* vis), beaver, visor, shade, sight. ‡ *Rompre en — à*, to come to an open quarrel with

Visionnaire, adj.s. (*etym.* vision), visionary, fanciful; dreamer

Visir, Vizir, sm. (*Turkish word*), vizier

Visirat, Vizirat, sm. viziership

Visite, sf. visit, call, review, search, visitation. *Aller en* —, to go upon a visit

Visiter, va.n. (*etym. L.* visitare), to visit, to inspect, to review; *se* —, vr. to visit each other

Visiteur, sm. visitor, visitant, searcher

Visqueux, se, adj. (*etym. L.* viscosus), slimy, sticky, clammy, viscous

Visser, va. to screw; *se* —, vr. to be screwed down

Visuel, le, adj. (*etym. L.L.* visualis), visual

Vitalité, sf. (*etym.* vital), vitality

Vite, adj. (*etym.* ?), quick, swift, fleet, speedy. — adv. quickly

Vitelotte, sf. (*etym.* ?), kidney potato

Vitesse, sf. swiftness, speed, fleetness, quickness. *A toute* —, *à grande* —, at full speed

Vitrage, sm. glass windows, glass partition, glazing

§**Vitrail,** sm. church window; *plur.* vitraux

Vitre, sf. (*etym. L.* vitrum, *glass*), pane of glass, glass. *Casser les* —*s*, to break the windows, (*fig.*) to speak out

Vitré, e, adj. glass, vitreous

Vitrer, va. to glaze, to glass

Vitrerie, sf. glazier's business

Vitreux, se, adj. vitreous, glassy

Vitrier, sm. glazier

Vitrifier, va., *se* —, vr. to vitrify

Vitriolique, adj. (*etym.* vitriol), vitriolic

Vivace, adj. (*etym. L.* vivacem), long-lived, vivacious, tenacious, perennial

Vivacité, sf. (*etym. L.* vivacitatem), vivacity, sprightliness, liveliness, fire, mettle, acuteness, sallies of wrath

Vivandier, ère, s. (*etym. I.* vivandiere), sutler

Vivant, e, adj. living, alive. — sm. living man, person alive. ‡ *Un bon* —, a jolly fellow. *Un* —, a resolute man. *Du — de mon père*, while my father lived

Vivat, interj. sm. huzza! hurrah!

Vive! Vivent! interj. long live! God save! hurrah for!

Viveur, sm. high-liver, debauchee

Vivier, sm. (*etym. L.* vivarium), fish-pond

Vivifiant, e, adj. vivifying, quickening

Vivifier, va. (*etym. L.* vivificare), to vivify, to quicken, to enliven

Vivipare, adj. (*etym. L.* viviparus), viviparous

Vivoter, vn. to live poorly, to make shift to live

Vivre, vn. (*etym. L.* vivere), to live, to subsist. ‡ *Le bien-vivre*, an easy life. *Savoir* —, to be well-bred. — sm. food, (*pl.*) victuals, provisions, stores, victualling department

Vocabulaire, sm. (*etym. L.L.* vocabularium), vocabulary

Vocalisation, sf. vocalization

Vocaliser, vn. (*etym.* vocal), to vocalize

Vocatif, sm. (*etym. L.* vocativus), vocative, vocative case

Vociférer, vn.a. (*etym. L.* vociferari), to vociferate, to cry out

Vœu, sm. (*etym. L.* votum), vow, wish, prayer, desire, vote

Vogue, sf. rowing, vogue, repute, credit, fashion

Voguer, vn. (*etym. I.* vogare, *to float*), to move forward, to row, to sail

Voici, prep. (*etym.* vois, ci), behold! lo! here is, here are

Voie, sf. (*etym. L.* via), way, road, line, path, course, carriage track, trail, conveyance, duct, channel, load (of wood), two pailfuls of water, chaldron, leak. ‡ — *de droit*, due course of law. —*s de fait*, violence, assault and battery

Voilà, adv. (*etym.* vois, là), behold! lo! there is, there are

Voile, sm. (*etym. L.* velum), veil, cloak, cover

Voilé, e, adj. past part. clouded, rigged

Voiler, va. to veil, to shroud, to hide, to cover, (*nav.*) to set sails on

Voilerie, sf. sail-loft, sail-yard

Voilier, sm. sail-maker, sailor

Voilure, sf. the sails, a set of sails, trim of sails

Voir, va. (*etym. L.* videre), to see, to behold, to descry, to perceive, to look out upon, to examine; *se* —, vr. to see oneself, to see one another, to meet, to visit one another, to be seen

Voire, adv. (*etym. L.* vere), indeed

Voirie, sf. (*etym.* voyer), public streets and roads commissioners, common sewer, offal. *Jeter à la* —, to bury in a ditch

Voisin, e, adj. s. (*etym. L.* vicinus), neighbouring, near, adjacent; neighbour

Voisinage, sm. neighbourhood

Voisiner, vn. to be neighbourly, to visit one's neighbours

Voiture, sf. (*etym. L.* vectura), vehicle, carriage, coach, cart, fare, coachful. *Lettre de* —, way-bill

Voiturer, va. to convey, to carry

Voiturier, sm. carrier, carter, waggoner

Voix, sf. (*etym. L.* vocem), voice, vote. *Aller aux* —, to come to the vote. *Mettre aux* —, to put to the vote

Vol, sm. (*etym.* voler), flight, hawking, largest width, game, theft, robbery, stealing

Volable, adj. easily stolen, to be robbed

Volage, adj. (*etym. L.* volaticum), fickle, inconstant, unsteady, volatile. — s. fickle one, inconstant

§**Volaille,** sf. (*etym. L.* volatilia), poultry, fowls

Volant, e, adj. flying. *Feuille* —*e*, fly-leaf, loose leaf, pamphlet. — sm. shuttlecock, fly-wheel, flounce

Volatil, e, adj. (*etym. L.* volatilis), volatile

Volatile, sm. adj. fowl, bird

Volatiliser, va. to volatilize

Volatilité, sf. volatility

Vol-au-vent, sm. a kind of pie

Volcan, sm. (*etym. I.* volcano), volcano

Volcanique, Volcanisé, e, adj. volcanic

Vole, sf. vole. *Faire la* —, to win the vole

Volée, sf. flight, flock, brood, troop, bevy, rank, volley, discharge, full peal, splinter-bar. ‡ *A la* —, flying, quickly, unadvisedly, broadcast. *Prendre sa* —, to take wing. *Personne de la haute* —, *de la première* —, a person of high rank. *Tirer à toute* —, to fire off full volleys, to shoot at random. *Donner une — de coups de bâton*, to give a sound cudgelling. *Sonner à toute* —, to ring a full peal. *Cheval de* —, leader

Voler, vn. (*etym. L.* volare), to fly, to soar; — va. to steal, to rob, to filch, to usurp. *Il ne l'a pas volé*, (*fig.*) it serves him right

Volet, sm. shutter, dove-cot

Voleter, vn. to flutter

Voleur, sm. thief, robber. *Au —! au —!* thieves! stop thief! — *de grand chemin*, highwayman. † *Être fait comme un* —, to have one's dress in disorder

Voleuse, sf. thief, female thief

Volière, sf. aviary, large bird-cage

Volige, sf. thin plank

Volontaire, adj. (*etym. L.* voluntarius), voluntary, willing, wilful, wayward, headstrong. — sm. volunteer, self-willed person

Volonté, sf. (*etym. L.* voluntatem), will, (*pl.*) whims, caprices. *Arme à —!* slope arms! *Voiture à* —, omnibus for hire

Volontiers, adv. (*etym. L.* voluntariò), willingly, readily, usually, easily

Voltaïque, adj. (*etym. prop. name* Volta), voltaic

Volte, sf. (*etym. I.* volta), volt

Voltige, sf. slack rope, tumbling, vaulting

Voltigeant, e, adj. fluttering, hovering

Voltiger, vn. (*etym. I.* volteggiare), to flutter about, to hover, to tumble, to vault

Voltigeur, sm. vaulter, tumbler, light infantry soldier

Volubilis, sm. (*Lat. word*), convolvulus

Volubilité, sf. (*etym. L.* volubilitatem), volubility

Volumineux, se, adj. (*etym.* volume), bulky, large-sized

Volupté, sf. (*etym. L.* voluptatem), voluptuousness

§**Voluptueux, se,** adj. (*etym. L.* voluptuosus), voluptuous. — sm. voluptuary

Vomique, adj. (*etym. L.* vomica). *Noix* —, nux vomica

Vomir, va. (*etym. L.* vomere), to throw up, to vomit, to pour forth

Vomissement, sm. vomiting

Vomitif, ve, adj. vomitive. — sm. emetic

Vomitoire, sm. vomitory

Vorace, adj. (*etym. L.* voracem), voracious, ravenous

Voracité, sf. (*etym. L.* voracitatem), voracity, voraciousness

Votant, sm. voter. —, —*e*, adj. voting, having a vote

Voter, va.n. (*etym.* vote, *L.* votum), to vote

Votif, ve, adj. (*etym. L.* votivus), votive

Votre, adj. poss. (*etym. L.* vostrum = vestrum), your; *plur.* vos

Vôtre (le, la), Vôtres (les), pron. poss. yours, your own

Vouer, va. (*etym. L.L.* votare), to devote, to dedicate, to consecrate, to vow; *se* —, vr. to devote oneself. *Ne savoir à quel saint se* —, not to know what saint to pray to

Vouloir, va.n. (*etym. L.L.* volere = *L.* velle), to will, to order, to require, to wish, to intend, to mean, to have a mind. ¦ — *du bien*, to wish well. — *du mal*, to wish evil or harm. *Se faire bien, mal* — *de quelqu'un*, to win (a person's) affection, to get disliked by. *En* —, vn. to have a grudge, to have a longing. *S'en* —, vr. to be angry with oneself

Voulu, e, adj. required, requisite. *Bien* — *de*, loved by. *Mal* — *de*, disliked by

Vous, pron. pers. (*etym. L.* vos), you

Voussoir, sm. (*etym. L.L.* volutiare, *to bend*), archstone, wedge

Voussure, sf. coving

Voûte, sf. (*etym. L.L.* voluta), arch, vault, archway, roof, canopy. — *d'arête*, groined vault

Voyage, sm. (*etym. L.* viaticum), travelling, journeying, travels, voyage

Voyager, vn. to travel, to journey

Voyageur, se, s. traveller, voyager, passenger

Voyant, e, adj. (*etym.* voir), showy, glaring, gaudy. — sm. seer, prophet

Voyelle, sf. (*etym. L.* vocalis), vowel. *Demi-* —, semivowel

Voyer, sm. (*etym. L.L.* viarius, *having reference to roads*), road-surveyor

¦**Vrai, e,** adj. (*etym. L.L.* veracum, *true*), true, genuine, truth-speaking, truly, right, downright. — sm. truth, what is true, reality

¦**Vraisemblable,** adj. sm. likely, probable; probability, likelihood

Vraisemblance, sf. probability, likelihood

§**Vrille,** sf. (*etym. L.L.* vericula, *from* vericum, *a spit*), gimlet, tendril

Vu, e, past part. (*etym.* voir), seen, looked upon, duly examined, duly considered. ¦ *Bien* —, *mal* —, liked, disliked

Vu, sm. examination, inspection, sight. ¦ *Au* — *et su de tout le monde*, in the sight and with the knowledge of the whole world

Vu que, loc. conj. seeing that

Vue, sf. sight, eyesight, view, window, light, design. ¦ *Donner dans la* — *de*, to please the eye of. *Garder à* —, not to let out of one's sight. *Longue-* —, *lunette de longue-* —, telescope. *Être en* —, (*nav.*) to heave in sight. *À* — *de pays*, at a cursory glance, by guess. *À* —, at sight

¦**Vulgaire,** adj. (*etym. L.* vulgaris), vulgar, every day, low. — sm. the vulgar, the common herd

Vulgariser, va. to vulgarize; *se* —, vr. to become vulgarized

Vulgarité, sf. vulgarity

Vulnéraire, adj. (*etym. L.* vulnerarius), vulnerary

X

X, sm. X, x, ten

Xérès, sm. (*proper name of a town*), sherry wine, sherry, Xeres

Y

Y, sm. Y, y

Y, adv. (*etym. L.* ibi), there, thither, here, hither, at home, within. — pron. it, them, him, her

Yatagan, sm. (*Turkish word*), yataghan

Yeuse, sf. (*etym. L.* ilicem), evergreen oak, holme

Yole, sf. (*from the English*), yawl, captain's gig

Z

Z, sm. Z, z

Zain, adj. m. (*etym. I.* zaino), whole-coloured, zain

Zèbre, sm. (*word of African origin*), zebra

Zébré, e, adj. striped

Zélateur, trice, s. person zealous, zealot

Zèle, sm. (*etym. L.* zelus), zeal, warmth

Zélé, e, adj. zealous

Zéphire, Zéphyr, sm. (*etym. L.* Zephyrus), zephyr, Zephyrus

Zéro, sm. (*etym. Ar.* cifrun, *cipher*), nought, cipher, zero

Zest, sm. (*etym. L.* schistos, *separated*). *Être entre le zist et le* —, to hang between, to be neither one nor the other. — interj. fiddlestick! quick!

Zeste, sm. zest, straw

Zézayement, sm. lisping

Zézayer, vn. (*onomat.*), to lisp

Zibeline, sf. (*etym. I.* zibellino), sable

Zingueur, sm. (*etym.* zinc), zinc-worker

Zizanie, sf. (*etym. L.* zizania), tares, dissension. *En* —, at variance

Zodiaque, sm. (*etym. L.* zodiacus), the zodiac

Zoolithe, sm. (*etym. Gr.* ζῷον, λίθος), zoolite

Zoologie, sf. (*etym. Gr.* ζῷον, λόγος), zoology

Zoologique, adj. zoological

Zoologue, sm. zoologist

Zootomie, sf. (*etym. Gr.* ζῷον, τέμνω), zootomy

DICTIONNAIRE GÉOGRAPHIQUE,

CONTENANT LES NOMS DES NATIONS, VILLES, PROVINCES, FLEUVES MONTAGNES, ETC. QUI S'ÉCRIVENT DIFFÉREMMENT DANS LES DEUX LANGUES.

A

Abdère, s. Abdera
Abruzze (l'), sf. Abruzzo (*plur.* the Abruzzi)
Abyssinie (l'), sf. Abyssinia
Abyssinien, ne, adj. s. Abyssinian
Acadie (l'), sf. Acadia
Acarnanie (l'), sf. Acarnania
Achaïe (l'), sf. Achaia
Achéen, ne, adj. s. Achæan
Achéron (l'), sm. the Acheron
Açores (les), sf. the Azores
Adriatique (l'), sf. the Adriatic
Adriatique, adj. Adriatic
Africain, e, adj. s. African
Afrique (l'), sf. Africa
Agrigente, sm. Agrigentum
Albain, e, adj. s. Alban
Albanais, e, adj. s. Albanese
Albanie (l'), sf. Albania
Albe, sf. Alba
Albigeois (les), s. the Albigenses
Albion (la Nouvelle-), sf. New Albion
Aléoutiennes (les îles), sf. the Aleutian Islands
Alep, sm. Aleppo
Alexandrette, sf. Alexandretta
Alexandrie, sf. Alexandria
Algarves (les), sf. Algarva
Alger, sm. Algiers
Algérie (l'), sf. Algeria
Algérien, ne, adj. s. Algerian
Alicante, s. Alicant
Allemagne (l'), sf. Germany
Allemand, e, s. German
Alpes (les), sf. the Alps
Alphée (l'), sm. the Alpheus
Alsace (l'), sf. Alsatia
Alsacien, ne, s. Alsatian
Amalécite, adj. s. Amalekite
Amazone (l'), sm. the Amazon
Amazones (le pays des), sf. Amazonia
Amboine, sf. Amboyna
Américain, e, adj s. American
Amérique (l'), sf. America. *L'— Centrale*, Central America. *L'— Méridionale, du Sud*, South America. *L'— du Nord*, North America. *Les États-Unis d'—*, the United States of America
Amirauté (les îles de l'), sf. the Admiralty Islands
Amis (les îles des), sf. plur. the Friendly Islands
Anatolie (l'), sf. Anatolia, Natolia
Ancône, sf. Ancona
Andalousie (l'), sf. Andalusia
Andaloux, se, adj. s. Andalusian
Andorre (le val d'), s. the Valley of Andorra
Angers, s. Angiers
Angevin, e, adj. s. of Angiers, native of Angiers
Anglais, e, adj. s. English
Angleterre (l'), sf. England. *La Nouvelle-* —, New England
Anséatiques (les villes), adj. plur. the Hanse towns
Antigoa, Antigue, sf. Antigua
§**Antilles** (les), sf.pl. the West Indies, the Antilles. *Les Grandes* —, the Greater Antilles. *Les Petites* —, the Lesser Antilles. *La mer des* —, the Caribbean Sea
Antioche, sf. Antioch
Anvers, sm. Antwerp
Apennins (les), sm.pl. the Apennines
Apulie (l'), sf. Apulia
Aquilée, sf. Aquileia
Aquitaine (l'), sf. Aquitaine
Arabe, adj s. Arab
Arabie (l'), sf. Arabia. *L'— Déserte*, Arabia Deserta. *L'— Heureuse*, Arabia Felix. *L'— Pétrée*, Arabia Petræa, Stony Arabia
Arabique (le golfe), sm. the Arabian Gulf
Arbèles, sf. Arbela
Arcadie (l'), sf. Arcadia
Arcadien, adj. sm. Arcadian
Archipel (l'), sm. the Archipelago
Argien, adj. sm. Argive
Argolide (l'), sf. Argolis, Argia
Arménie (l'), sf. Armenia
Arménien, ne, adj. s. Armenian
Armorique (l'), sf. Armorica
Asie (l'), sf. Asia. *L'— Mineure*, Asia Minor, Lesser Asia. *La Haute* —, Upper Asia
Asiatique, adj. s. Asiatic
Asphaltite (le lac), sm. the Dead Sea
Assyrie (l'), sf. Assyria
Assyrien, ne, adj. s. Assyrian
Asturies (les), sf. plur. the Asturias
Athènes, sf. Athens
Athénien, ne, adj. s. Athenian
Athos, sm. Athos. *Le mont* —, Mount Athos
Atlantide (l'), sf. Atlantis
Atlantique (l'), adj. sm. the Atlantic, the Atlantic Ocean
Atlas, sm. Atlas. *Le mont* —, Mount Atlas
Attique (l'), sf. Attica
Attique, adj. Attic
Augsbourg, sm. Augsburg
Aulide (l'), sf. Aulis
§**Aurigny**, sm. Alderney
Australie (l'), sf. Australia
Australasie (l'), sf. Australasia
Autriche (l'), sf. Austria
Autrichien, ne, adj. s. Austrian
Aventin (l'), sm. the Aventine hill
Averne (l'), sm. the Avernus, the Averno
Azincourt, sm. Agincourt
Azof, Azov, sm. Azof. *La mer d'* —, the sea of Azof

B

Babylone, sf. Babylon
Babylonien, ne, adj. Babylonian
Bactre, sf. Bactria
Bactriane (la), sf. Bactriana
Bactrien, ne, adj. s. Bactrian
Bade, sm. Baden
Baffin (baie, mer d
sf. Baffin's Bay
Bâle, sm. Basle
Baléares (les), sf. pl
the Balearic Islands
Baltique (la), sf. the B
tic. *La mer* —, the Baltic
Barbade (la), sf. B
badoes
Barbaresques (
états), sm. plur. the B
bary States
Barbarie (la), sf. B
bary
Barboude (la), sf. B
buda
Barcelone, sf. Barcelo
Basan, sm. Bashan, Ba
Basque, adj. s. Biscay
Batavie (la), sf. Bata
Bavarois, e, adj. s.
varian
Bavière (la), sf. Bava
Belgique (la), sf. Belg
Belge, sm. Belgian
Bénévent, sm. Benev
Bengalais, e, adj. s. B
galese
Bengale, sm. Bengal.
golfe du —, the Bay of Be
Béotie (la), sf. Bœotia
Béotien, ne, adj. s. B
tian
Bergame, sm. Bergam
Berg-op-Zoom, sm. B
gen-op-Zoom
Bermudes (les île
sf. plur. the Bermudas,
Bermuda Islands
Berne, sf. Berne
Bersabée, sf. Beer-she
Bessarabie (la), sf. B
arabia
Béthanie, sf. Bethany
Bethléem, sm. Bethle
Bétique (la), sf. Betı
Birman (l'empire),
the Birman Empire, the B
man Empire
Biscaye (la), sf. Bis
Le golfe de —, the Bay
Biscay
Bithynie (la), sf. Bithy
Bohême (la), sf. Bohe
Bohémien, ne, adj. s.
hemian
§**Bologne**, sf. Bologna
Bolonais (les), sm.
the Bolognese
Bordelais, e, adj. s.
Bordeaux, native of Borde
Borysthène (le), sm.
Borysthenes

osniaque, adj. Bosnian
osnie (la), sf. Bosnia
osphore (le), sm. the Bosphorus. *Le — de Thrace,* the Straits of Constantinople
othnie (la), sf. Bothnia
ougie, sf. Bugia
Bourgogne (la), sf. Burgundy
Bourguignon, ne, adj. Burgundian
ragance, sf. Braganza
rahmapoutre (le), sm. the Brahmapootra
randebourg, sm. Brandenburg
rême, sm. Bremen
résil (le), sm. Brazil
résilien, ne, adj. s. Brazilian
Bretagne (la), sf. Britain, Britannia; (*une*) Brittany (*France*). *La Grande-* —, Great Britain. *La Nouvelle-* —, New Britain
reton, ne, s. Briton
reton, ne, adj. of Brittany
rindes, sm. Brindisi
ritannique, adj. Britannic, British
ritanniques (les îles), sf. plur. the British Islands
rousse, sf. Bursa
ruxelles, sm. Brussels
ucharie (la), sf. Bucharia
ude, sf. Buda
ulgare, adj. s. Bulgarian
ulgarie (la), sf. Bulgaria
yzance, sf. Byzantium
yzantin, e, adj. Byzantine

C

achemire, sm. Cashmere
adix, sm. Cadiz
afrérie (la), sf. Caffraria
aire (le), sm. Cairo. *Le Grand* —, Grand Cairo
alabre (la), sf. Calabria
alabrais, e, adj. s. Calabrian
alcédoine, sf. Chalcedon
alédonie (la), sf. Caledonia. *La Nouvelle-* —, New Caledonia
alédonien, ne, adj. s Caledonian
alifornie (la), sf. California. *La Basse, la Vieille-* —, Lower, Old California. *La Haute, la Nouvelle-* —, Upper, New California. *Le golfe de* —, the Gulf of California, the Vermilion Sea
almouck, sm. adj. Calmuck
Campagne de Rome (la), sf. the Campagna di Roma
ampanie (la), sf. Campania
anadien, ne, adj. s Canadian
ananéen, ne, s. Canaanite
anarie, sf. Canary. *Les* —*s,* the Canaries. *Les îles* —*s,* the Canary Islands
Candie (l'île de), sf. Candia
Canée (la), sf. Canea
Cannes, sm. Cannæ (*Italy*), Cannes (*France*)
Cantorbéry, sm. Canterbury
Cap, sm. Cape. *Le — Vert,* Cape Verd. *Les îles du — Vert,* the Verd Islands. *Le — de Bonne-Espérance,* the Cape of Good Hope. *Le* —, *la ville du* —, Cape Town. *La colonie du* —, Cape Colony
Capharnaum, sm. Capernaum
Capoue, sf. Capua
Cappadoce (la), sf. Cappadocia
Cappadocien, ne, adj s. Cappadocian
Caraïbes (les îles), sf. plur the Caribbee Islands
Carie (la), sf. Caria
Carinthie (la), sf. Carinthia
Carnatique (le), sm. the Carnatic
Caroline (la), sf. Carolina. *La — du Sud,* South Carolina. *La — du Nord,* North Carolina
Carpathes, Krapacks (les monts), sm. plur. the Carpathian Mountains
Carthagène, sf. Carthagena
Carthaginois, e, adj. s. Carthaginian
Caspienne (la mer), sf the Caspian Sea
§**Castillan, e,** adj. s. Castilian
§**Castille (la),** sf. Castile. *La Nouvelle-* —, New Castile. *La Vieille-* —, Old Castile
Catalan, e, adj. s. Catalonian
§**Catalogne (la),** sf. Catalonia
Catane, sf. Catana
Caucase (le), Caucasus. *Le mont* —, Mount Caucasus. *Du* —, Caucasian
Caucasien, ne, adj. s. Caucasian
Célésyrie, sf. Cœlesyria, Cœlosyria
Celte, sm. Celt
Celtibérie, sf. Celtiberia
Celtique, adj. Celtic
Césarée, sf. Cæsarea
Ceylan, sf. Ceylon. *Les natifs de* —, the Singhalese
Chaldée (la), sf. Chaldea
Chaldéen, ne, adj. s. Chaldean
Chéronée, sf. Chæronea
Chersonèse (la), sf. Chersonesus. *La — Cimbrique,* Chersonesus Cimbrica. *La — Taurique,* Chersonesus Taurica. *La — de Thrace,* Thracian Chersonesus
Chine (la), sf. China
Chinois, e, adj. s. Chinese. *Les* —, the Chinese
Christophe (Saint-), sm. Saint Kitt's
Chypre, sf. Cyprus
Cilicie (la), sf. Cilicia
Cimbre, sm. Cimbrian. *Les* —*s,* the Cimbri
Circassie (la), sf. Circassia
Circassien, ne, adj. s. Circassian
Cithéron (le), sm. Mount Cithæron
Cochinchine (la), sf. Cochin-China
Cochinchinois, e, adj. s. Cochin-Chinese. *Les* —, the Cochin-Chinese
Cocyte (le), sm. the Cocytus
Coïmbre, sf. Coimbra
Colchide (la), sf. Colchis
Colombie (la), sf. Columbia
Compostelle, sm. Compostella. *Saint Jacques de* —, Saint Iago of Compostella
Copenhague, sm. Copenhagen
§**Cordillères (les),** sf. pl. the Cordilleras
Cordoue, sf. Cordova
Corée (la), sf. Corea
Corfou, sm. Corfu
Corinthe, sm. Corinth. *L'isthme de* —, the Isthmus of Corinth
Corinthien, ne, adj. s. Corinthian
§**Cornouailles (le),** sm. Cornwall. *La pointe de* —, Land's End
§**Corogne (la),** sf. Corunna
Corse (la), sf. Corsica
Corse, adj. s Corsican
Cosaque, adj. sm. Cossack
Côte d'Or (la), sf. the Gold Coast
Courlande (la), sf. Courland
Cracovie, sf. Cracow
Crémone, sf Cremona
Crétois, e, adj. s. Cretan
Crimée (la), sf. the Crimea
Croate, adj. s. Croatian
Croatie (la), sf. Croatia
Cume, sf. Cuma
Cumes, sf. plur. Cumæ
Cyrénaïque (la), sf. Cyrenaica
Cyrénéen, ne, adj s. Cyrenean
Cythère, sf. Cythera

D

Dace, adj s. Dacian
Dacie (la), sf Dacia
Dalécarlie (la), sf. Dalecarlia
Dalécarlien, ne, adj. s Dalecarlian
Dalmate, adj. s. Dalmatian
Dalmatie (la), sf. Dalmatia
Damas, sm. Damascus
Damiette, sf. Damietta
Danemark, sm. Denmark
Danois, e, s. Dane, Danish woman
Danois, e, adj. Danish
Dardanie (la), sf. Dardania
Dauphiné (le), sm. Dauphiny
Davis (le détroit de), sm. Davis's Straits
Dékhan (le), sm. Deccan
Delphes, sm. Delphi, Delphos
Dents (la côte des), sf. the Ivory Coast
Diémen (la terre de Van), sf. Van Diemen's Land, Tasmania
Djéhoun (le), sm. the Jihon
Domingue (Saint-), sm. San Domingo, Hayti
Dominique (la), sf. Dominica
Doride (la), sf. Doris
Dorien, ne, adj. s. Dorian
Douvres, sm. Dover
Dresde, sm. Dresden
Dunkerque, sm. Dunkirk

E

Èbre (l'), sm. the Ebro
Ecbatane, sm. Ecbatana
Écossais, e, adj. s Scotch, Scot. *Un* —, a Scotchman. *Une* —*e,* a Scotchwoman. *Les* —, the Scotch, the Scots
Écosse (l'), sf. Scotland. *La Nouvelle-* —, Nova Scotia
Édesse, sf. Edessa
Édimbourg, sm. Edinburgh
Égée (la mer), sf. the Ægean Sea
Église (les États de l'), sm. plur. the States of the Church
Égypte (l'), sf. Egypt. *La Basse-* —, Lower Egypt. *La Haute-* —, Upper Egypt. *La Moyenne-* —, Middle Egypt
Égyptien, ne, adj. s. Egyptian
Elbe (l'île d'), sf. the Island of Elba
Élide (l'), sf. Elis
Elseneur, sm Elsinore
Émathie (l'), sf. Emathia. *Les champs de l'* —, the Emathian fields
Éphèse, sf. Ephesus
Éphésien, ne, adj. s. Ephesian
Épices (les îles aux), sf. plur. the Spice Islands
Épidaure, sm. Epidaurus
Épire, sf. Epirus
Érié (le lac), sm. Lake Erie
Escaut (l'), sm. the Scheldt
Esclaves (la côte des), sf. the Slave Coast
Esclavonie (l'), sf. Sclavonia
§**Espagne (l'),** sf. Spain. *La Nouvelle-* —, New Spain
§**Espagnol, e,** adj. s. Spanish; Spaniard, Spanish woman. *Les* —*s,* the Spaniards
Estramadure (l'), sf. Estramadura, Estremadura
États-Unis (les), sm. pl. the United States
Éthiopie (l'), sf. Ethiopia
Éthiopien, ne, adj s. Ethiopian
Etna (l'), sm. Etna. *Le mont* —, Mount Etna
Étrurie (l'), sf. Etruria
Étrusque, adj. sm. Etrurian

Eubée, sf. Eubœa
Euphrate (l'), sm. the Euphrates
Europe (l'), sf. Europe
Européen, ne, adj. s. European

F

Fer (île de), sf. Ferro
Féroé (les îles), sf. pl. the Faroe Islands
Ferrare, sf. Ferrara
Figuières, sf. plur. Figueras
Finistère (Cap), sm. Land's End (*England*), Cape Finisterra (*Spain*), Cape Finisterre (*France*)
Finlande (la), sf. Finland
Finlandais, e, Finnois, e, s. Finlander
Flandre (la), sf. Flanders
Flessingue, sm. Flushing
Floride (la), sf. Florida
Fontarabie, sf. Fontarabia
Forêt-Noire (la), sf. the Black Forest
Formose, sf. Formosa
Forth (le golfe du), sm. the Frith of Forth
Français, e, adj. s. French
Francfort, sm. Frankfort. *— -sur-le-Main*, Frankfort-on-the-Maine. *— -sur-l'Oder*, Frankfort-on-the-Oder
Franconie (la), sf. Franconia
Fribourg, s. Friburg, Freyburg
Frioul (le), sm. Friuli
Frise (la), sf. Friesland
§**Frontignan,** s. Frontigniac

G

Gaélique, adj. Gaelic, Celtic
Gaëte, sf. Gaeta
Galaad, sm. Gilead
Galatie (la), sf. Galatia
Galice (la), sf. Gallicia
Galles (le pays de), sf. Wales. *La Nouvelle- — du Sud*, New South Wales
Gallois, e, adj. s. Welsh. *Les —*, the Welsh
Gambie (la), sf. Gambia
Gand, sm. Ghent
Gange (le), sm. the Ganges
§**Gascogne (la),** sf. Gascony. *Le golfe de —*, the Bay of Biscay
Gaule (la), sf. Gaul
Gaulois, e, adj. s. Gaul. *Les —*, the Gauls
Gênes, sf. Genoa
Génois, e, adj. s. Genoese. *Les —*, the Genoese
Genève, sf. Geneva
Genevois, e, adj. s. Genevese. *Les —*, the Genevese
George (le canal de Saint-), sm. St. George's Channel
Géorgie (la), sf. Georgia
Géorgien, ne, adj. s. Georgian

Germain, e, adj. sm. German
Germanie (la), sf. Germany
Gessen, sm. Goshen
Ghattes (les), sf. the Ghauts
Gœttingue, sf. Göttingen
Golconde, sf. Golconda
Goth, sm. Goth. *Les —s*, the Goths
Gothie (la), sf. Gothland
Goudjérate, sm. Guzerat
Graines (côte des), sf. Grain Coast
Grampiens (les monts), sm. the Grampian Mountains
Granique (le), sm. the Granicus
Grèce (la), sf. Greece
Grec, Grecque, adj. s. Greek
Grenade, sf. Granada (*town*)
Grenade (la), sf. Granada. *La Nouvelle- —*, New Granada
Groenland (le), sm. Greenland
Groenlandais, e, s. Greenlander
Guadeloupe (la), sf. Guadaloupe
Gueldre (la), sf. Gueldera
Guernesey, s. Guernsey
Guinée (la), sf. Guinea. *La Nouvelle- —*, New Guinea, Papua
Guyane (la), sf. Guiana

H

Hainaut (le), sm. Hainault
Haïti, sm. Hayti
Halicarnasse, sm. Halicarnassus
Hambourg, sm. Hamburg
Hanovre (le), sm. Hanover. *Le Nouvel- —*, New Hanover
Hanovrien, ne, adj. s. Hanoverian
Hanséatiques, sf. plur. see Anséatiques
Hapsbourg, sm. Hapsburg
Havane (la), sf. Havannah. *De —*, adj. Havannah
Hawaii, sf. Owhyhee
Haye (la), sf. the Hague
Hélène (Sainte-), sf. St. Helena
Helvétie (l'), sf. Helvetia
Héraclée, sf. Heraclea
Hespérie (l'), sf. Hesperia
Hessois, e, adj. s. Hessian
Hibernie (l'), sf. Hibernia
Hindoustan (l'), sm. Hindostan
Hindou, e, adj. s. Hindoo. *Les —s*, the Hindoos
Hollandais, e, adj. s. Dutch. *Un —*, a Dutchman. *Les —*, the Dutch
Hollande (la), sf. Holland. *La Nouvelle- —*, New Holland
Hombourg, sm. Homburg

Hongrie (la), sf. Hungary
Hongrois, e, adj. s. Hungarian
Hudson (la baie de), sf. Hudson's Bay
Hydaspe (l'), sm. the Hydaspes
Hyperboréens (les monts), sm. plur. the Riphean Mountains
Hyrcanie (l'), sf. Hyrcania

I

Ibérie (l'), sf. Iberia
Icarie (l'), sf. Icaria
Icarienne (la mer), sf. the Icarian Sea
Idalie (l'), sf. Idalia
Idumée (l'), sf. Idumæa
Île-de-France (l'), sf. the Isle of France
Illyrie (l'), sf. Illyria
Illyrien, ne, adj. s. Illyrian
Inde (l'), sf. India. *Les —s*, the Indies. *Les Grandes- —s, les —s orientales*, the East Indies. *Les —s occidentales*, the West Indies. *L'— en deçà du Gange*, India within the Ganges
Indien, ne, adj. s. Indian
Indo-Chine (l'), sf. Indo-China, Chin-India, Further India
Indostan (l'), sm. see Hindoustan
Ionie (l'), sf. Ionia
Ionien, ne, adj. s. Ionian. *Les îles —nes*, the Ionian Islands
Irlande (l'), sf. Ireland. *La mer d'—*, the Irish Sea
Irlandais (les), adj. s. Irish. *Un —*, an Irishman
Islande (l'), sf. Iceland
Islandais, e, s. Icelander
Istrie (l'), sf. Istria
Ismaélite, adj. s. Ishmaelite
Isthmique, adj. Isthmian
Italie (l'), sf. Italy
Italien, ne, adj. s. Italian
Ithaque, sf. Ithaca
Ivoire (la côte d'), sf. the Ivory Coast

J

Jamaïque (la), sf. Jamaica
Japon (le), sm. Japan
Japonais, e, adj. s. Japanese. *Les —*, the Japanese
Jourdain (le), sm. the Jordan
Javanais, e, s. Javanese
Judée (la), sf. Judæa
Juif, ve, adj. s. Jew, Jewess

K

Krapacks (les monts), sm. plur. the Carpathian Mountains

L

Labrador (le), sm. Labrador
Lacédémone, sf. Lacedæmon, Sparta
Lacédémonien, ne, adj. s. Lacedæmonian
Laconie (la), sf. Laconia
Lampsaque, sm. Lampsacus
Lancastre, sm. Lancaster
Laodicée, sf. Laodicea
Lapithes (les), sm. plur. the Lapithæ
Lapon, ne, s. Laplander
Laponie (la), sf. Lapland
Laquedives (les îles), sf. pl. the Laccadives
Larisse, sf. Larissa
Larrons (les îles des), sf. pl. the Ladrone Islands
Lépante (le golfe de), sm. the Gulf of Lepanto
Lerne, s. Lerna. *L'hydre de —*, the Lernæan hydra
Lestrigons (les), sm. pl. the Lestrygones
Leuctres, sf. Leuctra
Levant (le), sm. the Levant
Levantin, e, adj. Levantine
Leyde, sf. Leyden
Liban (le), sm. Lebanon. *Le mont —*, Mount Lebanon
Libye (la), sf. Libya
Libyen, ne, adj. Libyan
Ligure, sm. Ligurian
Ligurie (la), sf. Liguria
Lisbonne, sf. Lisbon
Lithuanie (la), sf. Lithuania
Livonie (la), sf. Livonia
Livourne, sf. Leghorn
Locride (la), sf. Locris
Lombardie (la), sf. Lombardy
Londres, sm. London. *Les habitants de —*, the Londoners
Lorette, sf. Loretto
Louisiane (la), sf. Louisiana
Lucayes (les îles), sf. pl. the Bahama Islands, the Lucaya Islands
Lucques, sf. Lucca
Lusace (la), sf. Lusatia
Lusitanie (la), sf. Lusitania
Lycie (la), sf. Lycia
Lycien, ne, adj. s. Lycian
Lydie (la), sf. Lydia
Lydien, ne, adj. s. Lydian
Lyon, sm. Lyons
Lyonnais, sm. Lyonnese

M

Macédoine (la), sf. Macedonia, Macedon
Madère, sf. Madeira
Magellan (le détroit de), sm. the Straits of Magellan
Mahrattes (les), sm. pl. the Mahrattas
Majorque, sf. Majorca

Malais, adj. sm. Malay. *Les* —, the Malays
Malaisie (la), sf. Malaysia
Malines, sf. Mechlin
Malouines (les îles), sf. pl. the Falkland Islands
Maltais, se, adj. s. Maltese. *Les* —, the Maltese
Malte, sf. Malta
Manche (la), sf. the British Channel, the Channel, La Mancha (*Spain*). *Les îles de la* —, the Channel Islands
§**Manille,** sf. Manilla
Mantinée, sf. Mantinea
Mantoue, sf. Mantua
Marmara (la mer de), sf. the Sea of Marmora
Maroc (le), sm. Morocco
Marocain, e, s. Moor
Marquises (les îles), sf. the Marquesas Islands
§**Marseillais, e,** s. inhabitant of Marseilles
§**Marseille,** sf. Marseilles
Martinique (la), sf. Martinico
Maure, sm. adj. Moor, Moorish
Mauresque, sf. Moorish woman, Mooress
Maurice (l'île), sf. Mauritius
Mauritanie (la), sf. Mauritania
Mecque (la), sf. Mecca
Mède, sm. Mede
Médie (la), sf. Media
Médine, sf. Medina
Méditerranée (la), sf. the Mediterranean. *La mer* —, the Mediterranean Sea
Mégare, sf. Megara
Méonie, sf. Mæonia. *De* —, Mæonian
Mer (la), sf. the sea. *La — Morte*, the Dead Sea. *La — Blanche*, the White Sea. *La — Jaune*, the Yellow Sea. *La — Rouge*, the Red Sea. *La — d'Allemagne, du Nord*, the German Ocean, the North Sea
Mésie (la), sf. Mœsia
Mésopotamie (la), sf. Mesopotamia
Messénie (la), sf. Messenia
Messénien, ne, adj. s. Messenian
Messine, sf. Messina
Mexicain, e, adj. s. Mexican
Mexique (le), sm. Mexico
Milanais (les), sm. the Milanese
Milet, s. Miletus
Mingrélie (la), sf. Mingrelia
Minorque, sf. Minorca
Minturnes, sf. Minturna
Modénais (les), sm. the Modenese
Modène, sf. Modena
Mogol, sm. Mogul. *Le Grand* —, the Great Mogul
Moldave, adj. s. Moldavian
Moldavie (la), sf. Moldavia
Moluques (les îles), sf. plur. the Molucca Islands
Morave, adj. sm. Moravian
Moravie (la), sf. Moravia
Morée (la), sf. the Morea
Moscou, sm. Moscow
Moscovie (la), sf. Muscovy
Murcie (la), sf. Murcia
Mycènes, sf. Mycenæ
Mysie (la), sf. Mysia

N

Napolitain, e, adj. s. Neapolitan
Nauplie (la), sf. Nauplia
Navarin, sm. Navarino
Navigateurs (l'archipel des), sm. the Navigator Islands
Naxos, sf. Naxos
Négrepont, sf. Negropont
Némée, sf. Nemea. *Le lion de* —, the Nemean lion
Neustrie (la), sf. Neustria
Neustrien, sm. Neustrian
Nicomédie, sf. Nicomedia
Nigritie (la), sf. Negroland, Nigritia
Nil (le), sm. the Nile
Nimègue, sm. Nimeguen
Ninive, sf. Nineveh
Normand, e, adj. s. Norman. *Les —s*, the Normans
Normandie (la), sf. Normandy
Norvége (la), sf. Norway
Norvégien, ne, adj. s. Norwegian
Nouvelle-Zemble (la), sf. Nova Zembla
Nubie (la), sf. Nubia
Nubien, ne, adj. s. Nubian
Numance, sf. Numantia

O

Océanie (l'), sf. the South Sea Islands (*plur.*), Oceania
Olympe (l'), sm. Olympus. *Le mont* —, Mount Olympus
Olynthe, s. Olynthus
Olynthien, ne, adj. s. Olynthian
Orcades (les), sf. the Orkneys, the Orkney Islands
Orénoque (l'), sm. the Orinoco
Orléans (la Nouvelle-), sf. New Orleans
Ostende, sf. Ostend
Ostie, sf. Ostia
Otahiti, sf. Otaheite
Otrante, sf. Otranto
Ouessant, sm. Ushant
Oural (l'), sm. the Ural
Ourals (les monts), sm. plur. the Ural Mountains

P

Pactole (le), sm. the Pactolus
Padoue, sf. Padua
Palatinat (le), sm. the Palatinate
Palerme, sm. Palermo
Palmyre, sf. Palmyra
Palos (les îles), sf. plur. the Pellew Islands
Palus Méotides, sf. pl. the Palus Mæotis
Pampelune, sf. Pampeluna
Pamphylie (la), sf. Pamphylia
Pannonie (la), sf. Pannonia
Paphlagonie (la), sf. Paphlagonia
Papous (la terre des), sf. Papua
Parnasse (le), sm. Parnassus. *Le mont* —, Mount Parnassus
Parthe, sm. Parthian
Parthie (la), sf. Parthia
Patagon, sm. Patagonian
Patagonie (la), sf. Patagonia
Pausilippe (le), sm. Pausilippo
Pavie, sf. Pavia
Pays-Bas (les), sm. plur. the Netherlands, the Low Countries
Pélasges, sm. plur. Pelasgians *or* Pelasgi
Péloponnèse (le), sm. the Peloponnesus
Pensylvanie (la), sf. Pennsylvania
Pergame, sm. Pergamus
Pérou (le), sm. Peru
Persan, e, adj. s. Persian
Perse (la), sf. Persia
Perse, s. Persian
Persique (le golfe), sm. the Persian Gulf
Péruvien, ne, adj. s. Peruvian
Pétersbourg (Saint-), sm. St. Petersburg
Pharsale, sf. Pharsalia
Phase (le), sm. the Phasis
Phénicie (la), sf. Phœnicia
Phénicien, ne, adj. s. Phœnician
Philadelphie (la), sf. Philadelphia
Philippes, sm. Philippi
Philippines (les îles), sf. plur. the Philippine Islands
Philipsbourg, sm. Philipsburg
Philistin, e, adj. s. Philistine
Phocée, sf. Phocæa
Phocéen, ne, adj. s. Phocæan
Phocide (la), sf. Phocis
Phrygie (la), sf. Phrygia
Phrygien, ne, adj. s. Phrygian
Picard, e, adj. s. native of Picardy
Picardie (la), sf. Picardy
Piémont (le), sm. Piedmont
Piémontais, e, adj. s. Piedmontese
Pinde (le), sm. Pindus
Pirée (le), sm. Piræus
Pise, sf. Pisa
Plaisance, sf. Placentia, Placentia
Platée, sf. Platæa
§**Pologne (la),** sf. Poland
Polonais, e, adj. s. Polish, Pole
Polynésie (la), sf. Polynesia
Poméranie (la), sf. Pomerania
Pont (le), sm. Pontus
Pont-Euxin (le), sm. the Euxine
Pontins (les marais), sm. pl. the Pontine Marshes
Porto, sm. Oporto. *Vin de* —, Port wine
Portugais, e, adj. s. Portuguese. *Les* —, the Portuguese
Potidée, sf. Potidæa
§**Pouille (la),** sf. Apulia
Poyas (les monts), sm. pl. the Ural Mountains, Poyas Mountains
Propontide (la), sf. Propontis
Prusse (la), sf. Prussia
Prussien, ne, adj. s. Prussian
Pyrénées (les), sf. pl. the Pyrenees, the Pyrenean Mountains

R

Raguse, sf. Ragusa
Ratisbonne, sf. Ratisbon
Ravenne, sf. Ravenna
Rhétie (la), sf. Rhetia
Rhin (le), sm. the Rhine. *Le Bas-* —, the Lower Rhine. *Le Haut-* —, the Upper Rhine
Riphées (les monts), sm plur. the Riphean Mountains
§**Romagne (la),** sf. Romagna
Romain, e, adj. s. Roman. *Les —s*, the Romans
Romélie (la), sf. Roumelia
Rosette, sf. Rosetta
Royaume-Uni (le), sm. the United Kingdom
Russe, adj. s. Russian
Russie (la), sf. Russia. *La — Américaine*, Russian America. *La — Blanche*, White Russia. *La Grande* —, Great Russia. *La — Noire*, Black Russia. *La Nouvelle-* —, New Russia. *La Petite-* —, Little Russia. *La — Rouge*, Red Russia. *La — d'Asie*, Asiatic Russia, Russian Asia. *La — d'Europe*, Russia in Europe

S

Saba, sf. Sheba
Sabin, e, adj. s. Sabine
Sabine (la), sf. Sabina
Sagonte, sf. Saguntum
Saint-Jean, sm. St. John. — *d'Acre*, Acre
Saint-Laurent (le), sm. the St. Lawrence
Sainte-Lucie (la), sf St. Lucia
Salamanque, sf. Salamanca
Salamine, sf. Salamis
Salé, sm. Sallee. *Vieux* —, Sallee
Salente, sf. Salentum
Salerne, sf. Salerno
Salonique, sf. Salonica
Samarie (la), sf. Samaria

Samaritain, e, adj. s. Samaritan
Samothrace (la), sf. Samothracia, Samothrace
Samoyèdes (les), sf.pl. Samoides
Saragosse, sf. Saragossa
§**Sardaigne (la),** sf. Sardinia
Sarde, adj. s. Sardinian
Sardes (les états), sm. pl. the Sardinian States
Sardes, sf. Sardis
Sarmate, adj. s Sarmatian
Sarmatie (la), sf. Sarmatia
Saverne (la), sf. the Severn
Savoie (la), sf. Savoy
Savoisien, ne, adj. s native of Savoy
Saxe (la), sf. Saxony
Saxon, ne, adj. s. Saxon
Scamandre (le), sm. the Scamander
Scandinave, adj. s. Scandinavian
Scandinavie (la), sf. Scandinavia
Scanie (la), sf. Scania
Schaffouse, sf. Schaffhausen
Scythe, adj. s. Scythian
Scythie (la), sf. Scythia
Ségovie, sf. Segovia
Séleucide (la), sf Seleucis
Sénégambie (la), sf. Senegambia
Servie (la), sf. Servia
Séville, sf. Seville
Siamois, e, adj s. Siamese. *Les —*, the Siamese
Sibérie (la), sf. Siberia
Sichem, sm Shechem
Sicile (la), sf. Sicily
Siciles (les Deux-), sf. pl. the Two Sicilies
Sicilien, ne, adj. s. Sicilian
Sicyone, sf. Sicyon
Sienne, sf. Sienna
Silésie (la), sf. Silesia
Siloé, sm. Siloa
Siloh, sm. Shiloh
Sind (le), sm. Scinde
Smyrne, sf. Smyrna
Société (les îles de la), sf.pl. the Society Islands *or* Isles
Sodome, sf. Sodom

Sogdiane (la), sf. Sogdiana
Solway (le golfe de), sm. the Solway Frith
Solyme, sf. Solyma
Sonde (l'archipel de la), sm. the Sunda Isles
Sorlingues (les îles), sf. pl. the Scilly Isles
Souabe (la), sf. Suabia
Sparte, sf. Sparta
Spartiate, adj. s. Spartan
Spitzberg (le), sm. Spitzbergen
Stagyre, sf. Stagyra
Steinkerque, sm. Steenkirk
Strasbourg, sm Strasburg
Stuttgart, sm. Stuttgard, Stuttgart
Styrie (la), sf. Styria
Suède (la), sf. Sweden
Suédois, e, adj.s. Swedish. Swede
Suisse (la), sf. Switzerland. — adj. s. Swiss. *Les —s*, the Swiss. *Une Suissesse*, a Swiss woman
Sund (le), sm. the Sound
Supérieur (le lac), sm. Lake Superior
Surate, sf. Surat
Suse, sf. Susa
Susiane (la), sf. Susiana
Syrie (la), sf. Syria
Syrien, ne, adj. s. Syrian

T

Table (la baie de la), sf. Table Bay
Table (le mont de la), sm. Table Mountain
Tage (le), sm. the Tagus
Taiti, sm. Otaheite
Tamise (la), sf. the Thames
Tanger, sm. Tangiers
Tarse, sm. Tarsus
Tartare, adj. s. Tartar
Tartarie (la), sf. Tartary
Tauride (la), sf. Tauris, Tabriz
Ténare (le), sm. Tænarus
Terceire, sf. Terceira
Terracine, sf. Terracina
Terre de Feu (la), sf. Terra del Fuego

Terre-Ferme (la), sf. Terra-Firma
Terre-Neuve, sf. Newfoundland
Terre Sainte (la), sf. the Holy Land
Thébaïde (la), sf. Thebais
Thébain, e, adj.s. Theban
Thermopyles (les), sf. plur. Thermopylæ
Thessalie (la), sf. Thessaly
Thessalien, ne, adj. s. Thessalian
Thessalonien, ne, adj s Thessalonian
Thessalonique, sf. Thessalonica
Thurgovie (la), sf. Thurgovia
Thuringe (la), sf. Thuringia
Tibre (le), sm. the Tiber
Tigre (le), sm. the Tigris
Tolède, sf. Toledo
Tortose, sf. Tortosa
Toscan, e, adj. s. Tuscan
Toscane (la), sf. Tuscany
Transylvanie (la), sf. Transylvania
Trasimène (le), sm. Lake Trasimenus
Trebie (la), sf. the Trebia
Trébizonde, sf. Trebizond
Trente, sf. Trent
Trincomale, Trinquemale, sm Trincomalee
Trinité (la), sf. Trinidad. *L'île de la —*, Trinidad
Troade (la), sf. Troas
Troie, sf. Troy
Turc, Turque, adj. s Turkish, Turk, Turkish woman. *A la turque*, in the Turkish fashion
Turcomanie (la), sf. Turcomania
Turquie (la), sf. Turkey. *La — d'Asie*, Asiatic Turkey, Turkey in Asia. *La — d'Europe*, European Turkey, Turkey in Europe
Tyr, sf. Tyre
Tyrien, ne, adj. s. Tyrian

U

Utique, sf. Utica

V

Valachie (la), sf. Wallachia
Valaque, adj. Wallachian
Valette (la), sf. Valetta
Valteline (la), sf. the Valtelina
Varsovie (la), sf. Warsaw
Varsovien, ne, adj. s. Warsovian
Vénétie (la), sf. Venetia
Venise, sf. Venice
Vénitien, ne, adj. s. Venetian
§**Vermeille (la mer),** sf. the Vermilion Sea, the Gulf of California
Vérone, sf. Verona
Vésuve (le), sm. Vesuvius
Vicence, sf. Vicenza
Vienne, sf. (*Austria*) Vienna, (*France*) Vienne
Vierges (les îles), sf. pl. the Virgin Islands
Virginie (la), sf. Virginia
Visapour, sm. Visapore
Vistule (la), sf. the Vistula
Volsque, sm. Volscian

W

Westphalie (la), sf. Westphalia
Westphalien, ne, adj. s. Westphalian
Wurtzbourg, sm. Wurtzburg
Wurtembergeois, e, adj. s. Wurtemburger

X

Xanthe (le), sm. the Xanthus

Z

Zélande (la), sf. Zealand. *La Nouvelle- —*, New Zealand
Zurich, sm. Zurich
Zuiderzée (le), sm. the Zuyder-see

DICTIONNAIRE

DES NOMS PROPRES MYTHOLOGIQUES ET HISTORIQUES

DONT L'ORTHOGRAPHE VARIE DANS LES DEUX LANGUES.

A

Abdolonyme, sm. Abdolonymus
Abdias, sm. Obadiah
Absalon, sm. Absalom
Aceste, sm. Acestes
Achab, sm. Ahab
Achate, sm. Achates
Achille, sm. Achilles
Actéon, sm. Actæon
Admète, sm. Admetus
Adraste, sm. Adrastus
Adrien, sm. Adrian, Hadrian
Agar, sf. Hagar
Agathocle, sm. Agathocles
Agésilas, sm. Agesilaus
Aggée, sm. Haggai
Agrippine, sf. Agrippina
Albane (l'), sm. Albano
Alcée, sm. Alcæus
Alcibiade, sm. Alcibiades
Alcide, sm. Alcides
Alcmène, sf. Alcmena
Alexandre, sm. Alexander
Alcuin, sm. Alwin
Amalec, sm. Amalek
Amalthée, sf. Amalthea
Aman, sm. Haman
Améric Vespuce, sm. Americus Vespucius
Amilcar, sm. Hamilcar
Ammien, sm. Ammianus
Amurat, sm. Amurath
Anaxagore, sm. Anaxagoras
Anchise, sm. Anchises
Andromaque, sf. Andromache
Andromède, sf. Andromeda
Annibal, sm. Hannibal, Annibal
Antée, sm. Antæus
Antigone, sm. Antigonus
Antigone, sf. Antigone
Antiochus, sm. Antiochus. — *Epiphane,* Antiochus Epiphanes
Antisthène, sm. Antisthenes
Antonin, sm. Antoninus — *le Pieux,* Antoninus Pius
Apollodore, sm. Apollodorus
Apollon, sm. Apollo
Appien, adj. sm. Appian. *La voie —nne,* the Appian Way
Apulée, sm. Apuleius
Aquin, sm. Aquinas
Archimède, sm. Archimedes
Argonautes (les), sm. plur. the Argonauts
Aréthuse, sf. Arethusa
Ariane, sf. Ariadne
Arioste (l'), sm. Ariosto
Arioviste, sm. Ariovistus
Aristarque, sm. Aristarchus
Aristée, sm. Aristæus
Aristide, sm. Aristides
Aristophane, sm. Aristophanes
Aristote, sm. Aristotle
Aroun, sm. see Haroun
Arsace, sm. Arsaces
Artaxerxès, sm. Artaxerxes. — *Longue-Main,* Artaxerxes Longimanus
Artémise, sf. Artemisia
Ascagne, sm. Ascanius
Asmodée, sm. Asmodeus
Aspasie, sf. Aspasia
Assuérus, sm. Ahasuerus
Astrée, sf. Astrea
Astyage, sm. Astyages
Atalante, sf. Atalanta
Athalie, sf. Athalia
Atrée, sm. Atreus
Atride, sm. Atrides
Augias, sm. Augeas, Augias
Auguste, sm. Augustus
Augustule, sm. Augustulus
Aulu-Gelle, sm. Aulus Gellius
Aurèle, sm. Aurelius. *Marc —,* Marcus Aurelius
Aurélien, sm. Aurelian
Averne (l'), sm. the Avernus

B

Bajazet, sm. Bajazeth
Balthazar, sm. Balthazar
Barberousse, sm. Barbarossa
Bède, sm. Bede
Bélisaire, sm. Belisarius
Bellone, sf. Bellona
Belshazzar, sm. Belshazzar
Belzébuth, sm. Beelzebub
Bethsabé, sf. Bathsheba
Boèce, sm. Boethius
Boccace, sm. Boccaccio
Borée, sm. Boreas
Booz, sm. Boaz
Briarée, sm. Briareus

C

Caïn, sm. Cain
Caïphe, sm. Caiaphas
Calcas, Calchas, sm. Calchas
Callicrate, sm. Callicrates
Candaule, sm. Candaules
Canut, sm. Canute
Capitolin, sm. Capitolinus
Cassandre, sm. Cassander
Cassandre, sf. Cassandra
Caton, sm. Cato. — *l'Ancien,* Cato the Elder. — *d'Utique,* Cato of Utica
Catulle, sm. Catullus
Celse, sm. Celsus
Céphale, sm. Cephalus
Cerbère, sm. Cerberus
Cérès, sf. Ceres
César, sm. Cæsar
Cham, sm. Ham
Charles, sm. Charles. — *le Bel,* Charles the Fair. — *le Gros,* Charles the Fat. — *Martel,* Charles the Hammerer. — *Quint,* Charles the Fifth (Emperor of Germany). — *le Téméraire,* Charles the Bold
Claude, sm. Claudius
Cicéron, sm. Cicero, Tully
Cléopâtre, sf. Cleopatra
Clytemnestre, sf. Clytemnestra
Collatin, sm. Collatinus
Colomb, sm. Columbus
Côme, sm. Cosmo
Commode, sm. Commodus
Comnène, sm. Comnenus
Comnène, sf. Comnena *Anne —,* Anna Comnena
Constance, sm. Constantius
Constantin, sm. Constantine
Copernic, sm. Copernicus
Corinne, sf. Corinna
Coriolan, sm. Coriolanus
Cornélie, sf. Cornelia
Crésus, sm. Crœsus
Créuse, sf. Creusa
Cupidon, sm. Cupid
Curiaces (les), sm. plur the Curiatii
Cyaxare, sm. Cyaxares
Cybèle, sf. Cybela, Cybele
Cyclope, sm. Cyclop
Cythérée, sf. Cytheræa

D

Danaïdes, sf. plur. Danaids
Dédale, sm. Dædalus
Déjanire, sf. Dejanira
Démocrate, sm. Democrates
Démosthène, sm. Demosthenes
Denis, sm. Dionysius. — *l'Ancien,* Dionysius the Elder. — *le Jeune,* Dionysius the Younger
Diane, sf. Diana, Dian
Didon, sf. Dido
Dioclétien, sm. Diocletian, Dioclesian
Diodore, sm Diodorus
Diogène, sm. Diogenes
Diomède, sm. Diomedes
Dominiquin (le), sm. the Domenichino, Zampieri
Domitien, sm. Domitian
Dracon, sm. Draco

E

Éaque, sm. Æacus
Égée, sm. Ægeus
Égérie, sf. Egeria
Égésippe, sm. Hegesippus
Égisthe, sm. Ægisthus
Électre, sf. Electra
Élie, sm. Elijah
Élisée, sm. Elisha
Énée, sm. Æneas
Éole, sm. Æolus
Épaminondas, sm. Epaminondas
Épictète, sm. Epictetus
Épicure, sm. Epicurus
Épigones (les), sm. plur. the Epigoni
Épiménide, sm. Epimenides
Érasme, sm. Erasmus
Éraste, sm. Erastus
Ératosthène, sm. Eratosthenes

Ératosthène, sm. Eratosthenes
Érèbe (l'), sm. Erebus
Eschine, sm. Æschines
Eschyle, sm. Æschylus
Esculape, sm. Æsculapius
Ésope, sm. Æsop
Euclide, sm. Euclid
Eumée, sm. Eumæus
Eumène, sm. Eumenes
Euripide, sm. Euripides
Europe, sf. Europa
Euryale, sm. Euryalus
Eurysthée, sm. Eurystheus
Eusèbe, sm. Eusebius
Évandre, sm. Evander
Ézéchias, sm. Hezekiah
Ézéchiel, sm. Ezekiel

F

Faust, sm. Faustus
Faustine, sf. Faustina
Flavien, sm. Flavian
Flore, sf. Flora
Fulvie, sf. Fulvia

G

Galathée, sf. Galathea
Galilée, sm. Galileo
Gédéon, sm. Gideon
Gordien, sm. Gordian
Gracques (les), sm.plur. the Gracchi

H

Habacuc, sm. Habakkuk
Aggée, sm. Haggai
Harpocrate, sm. Harpocrates
Hébé, sf. Hebe
Hécate, sf. Hecate
Hécube, sf. Hecuba
Hélène, sf. Helen
Héliodore, sm. Heliodorus
Héliogabale, sm. Heliogabalus
Hénoch, sm. Enoch
Hercule, sm. Hercules
Hérode, sm. Herod
Hérodote, sm. Herodotus
Hésiode, sm. Hesiod
Hespérus, sm. Hesperus
Hiéron, sm. Hiero
Hippocrate, sm. Hippocrates
Hippolyte, sm. Hippolytus
Hippolyte, sf. Hippolyta
Hippomène, sm. Hippomenes
Homère, sm. Homer
Horaces (les), sm.pl. the Horatii
Hystaspe, sm. Hystaspes

I

Idoménée, sm. Idomeneus
Iphigénie, sf. Iphigenia
Isaïe, sm. Isaiah
Ismaël, sm. Ishmael
Isocrate, sm. Isocrates
Israël, sm. Israel

J

Jeanne d'Arc, sf. Joan of Arc
Jephté, sm. Jephthah
Jérémie, sm. Jeremiah
Jocaste, sf. Jocasta
Joïada, sm. Jehoiada
Jonas, sm. Jonah, Jonas
Josaphat, sm. Jehoshaphat
Josèphe (Flavius), sm. Josephus (Flavius)
Josias, sm. Josiah
Josué, sm. Joshua
Juda, sm. Judah
Judas Iscariote, sm. Judas Iscariot
Junon, sf. Juno
Jupiter, sm. Jupiter. — *Olympien*, Olympian Jove. — *Férétrien*, Jupiter Feretrius
Justinien, sm. Justinian

L

Lactance, sm. Lactantius
Laërce, sm. Laertius
Laërte, sm. Laertes
Lapithes, sm.pl. Lapithæ
Latone, sf. Latona
Lazare, sm. Lazarus
Léandre, sm. Leander
Léonidas, sm. Leonidas
Lépide, sm. Lepidus
Lévi, sm. Levi
Linnée, sm. Linnæus
Longin, sm. Longinus
Louis, sm. Louis. — *le Bègue*, Louis the Stammerer. — *le Gros*, Louis the Fat. — *le Hutin*, Louis the Headstrong
Lucain, sm. Lucan
Lucrèce, sm. Lucretius
Lucrèce, sf. Lucretia
Lycurgue, sm. Lycurgus
Lysandre, sm. Lysander
Lysimaque, sm. Lysimachus
Lysippe, sm. Lysippus

M

Machabée, sm. Maccabeus
Machabées (les), sm.pl. the Maccabees
Macrobe, sm. Macrobius
Mahomet, sm. Mahomet, Mahommed
Manassé, sm. Manasseh
Marc-Antoine, sm. Mark Antony
Marc-Aurèle, sm. Marcus Aurelius
Mardochée, sm. Mordecai
Mathusalem, sm. Methuselah
Mausole, sm. Mausolus
Maximien, sm. Maximian
Maximilien, sm. Maximilian
Mécène, sm. Mæcenas
Médée, sf. Medea
Méduse, sf. Medusa
Melchisédech, sm. Melchizedek
Ménélas, sm. Menelaus
Mercure, sm. Mercury
Messaline, sf. Messalina
Métastase, sm. Metastasio
Michée, sm. Micah
Michel-Ange, sm. Michael Angelo
Milon, sm. Milo
Miltiade, sm. Miltiades
Minerve, sf. Minerva
Mithridate, sm. Mithridates
Moïse, sm. Moses
Morphée, sm. Morpheus
Morus (Thomas), sm. Sir Thomas More
Musée, sm. Musæus

N

Nabuchodonosor, sm. Nebuchadnezzar
Narcisse, sm. Narcissus
Nazareth, sm. Nazarite
Néhémie, sm. Nehemiah
Néméen, ne, adj. Nemean
Néoptolème, sm. Neoptolemus
Nérée, sm. Nereus
Néron, sm. Nero
Niobé, sf. Niobe
Noé, sm. Noah
Noémi, sf. Naomi

O

Océan, sm. Oceanus
Octave César, sm. Octavius Cæsar
Octavie, sf. Octavia
Octavien, sm. Octavianus
Odin, sm. Odin, Woden
Odoacre, sm. Odoacer
Œdipe, sm. Œdipus
Oreste, sm. Orestes
Origène, sm. Origen
Orphée, sm. Orpheus
Osée, sm. Hosea
Othon, sm. Otho
Ovide, sm. Ovid

P

Paléologue, sm. Palæologus
Pandore, sf. Pandora
Parménion, sm. Parmenio
Patrocle, sm. Patroclus
Paul-Émile, sm. Paulus Æmilius
Pégase, sm. Pegasus
Pélage, sm. Pelagius
Pélée, sm. Peleus
Pénélope, sf. Penelope
Penthésilée, sf. Penthesilea
Périclès, sm. Pericles
Perse, sm. Persius
Persée, sm. Perseus
Pétrarque, sm. Petrarch
Pétrone, sm. Petronius
Pharaon, sm. Pharaoh
Phébus, sm. Phœbus
Phèdre, sm. Phædrus
Phèdre, sf. Phædra
Philippe, sm. Philip. — *le Beau*, Philip the Handsome (of Spain). — *le Bel*, Philip the Fair (of France)
Philoctète, sm. Philoctetes
Philomèle, sf. Philomela
Phinée, sm. Phinehas
Pie, sm. Pius
Polybe, sm. Polybius
Polycrate, sm. Polycrates
Ponce-Pilate, sm. Pontius Pilate
Pindare, sm. Pindar
Pisistrate, sm. Pisistratus
Platon, sm. Plato
Plaute, sm. Plautus
Pline, sm. Pliny. — *l'Ancien*, Pliny the Elder. — *le Jeune*, Pliny the Younger
Plutarque, sm. Plutarch
Pluton, sm. Pluto
Polymnie, sf. Polymnia
Polyphème, sm. Polyphemus
Pomone, sf. Pomona
Pompée, sm. Pompey
Praxitèle, sm. Praxiteles
Prométhée, sm. Prometheus
Protée, sm. Proteus
Protésilas, sm. Protesilaus
Psyché, sf. Psyche
Ptolémée, sm. Ptolemy. *Les —s*, the Ptolemies
Putiphar, sm. Potiphar
Pylade, sm. Pylades
Pyrame, sm. Pyramus
Pythagore, sm. Pythagoras

Q

Quichotte (Don), sm. (Don) Quixote
Quinte-Curce, sm. Quintus Curtius
Quintilien, sm. Quintilian

R

Rémus, sm. Remus
Rhadamante, sm. Rhadamanthus
Rhéa, sf. Rhea

S

Salluste, sm. Sallust
Salomon, sm. Solomon
Samson, sm. Samson
Sardanapale, sm. Sardanapalus
Sapho, sf. Sappho
Saturne, sm. Saturn
Saturnin, sm. Saturninus
Saül, sm. Saul
Scipion, sm. Scipio. — *l'Africain*, Scipio Africanus. — *l'Asiatique*, Scipio Asiaticus
Séjan, sm. Sejanus
Sem, sm. Shem
Sénèque, sm. Seneca
Septime, sm. Septimus. — *Sévère*, Septimus Severus
Sforce, sm. Sforza

Sigismond, sm. Sigismund
Silène, sm. Silenus
Simonide, sm. Simonides
Sisyphe, sm. Sisyphus
Sixte, sm. Sixtus. — *Quint*, Sixtus the Fifth
Sminthée, sm. Smintheus
Socrate, sm. Socrates
Sophocle, sm. Sophocles
Stace, sm. Statius
Stilicon, sm. Stilicho
Strabon, sm. Strabo
Suétone, sm. Suetonius
Symmaque, sm. Symmachus

T

Tacite, sm. Tacitus
Tamerlan, sm. Tamerlane
Tantale, sm. Tantalus
Tarquin, sm. Tarquin. — *l'Ancien*, Tarquinius Priscus. — *le Superbe*, Tarquin the Proud
Tartare (le), sm. Tartarus
Tasse (le), sm. Tasso
Télémaque, sm. Telemachus
Térée, sm. Tereus
Tertullien, sm. Tertullian
Thalie, sf. Thalia
Thémistocle, sm. Themistocles
Théocrite, sm. Theocritus
Théodose, sm. Theodosius
Théophraste, sm. Theophrastus
Thersite, sm. Thersites
Thésée, sm. Theseus
Thétis, sf. Thetis
Thucydide, sm. Thucydides
Thyeste, sm. Thyestes
Tibère, sm. Tiberius
Tite-Live, sm. Livy, Titus Livius
Tithon, sm. Tithonus
Titien (le), sm. Titian
Tobie, sm. Toby, Tobias
Triptolème, sm. Triptolemus
Tullie, sf. Tullia
Tydée, sm. Tydeus
Tyndare, sm. Tyndarus
Tyrtée, sm. Tyrtaeus

U

Ulysse, sm. Ulysses
Uranie, sf. Urania

V

Valentinien, sm. Valentinian
Valère, sm. Valerius. — *Maxime*, Valerius Maximus
Valérien, sm. Valerian
Valkyries (les), sf.pl. the Valkyriur
Varron, sm. Varro
Vénus, sf. Venus
Vertumne, sm. Vertumnus
Vespasien, sm. Vespasian
Virgile, sm. Virgil
Vitruve, sm. Vitruvius
Vulcain, sm. Vulcan

X

Xantippe, sm. Xantippus
Xantippe, sf. Xantippe
Xénocrate, sm. Xenocrates
Xénophon, sm. Xenophon
Xercès, Xerxès, sm. Xerxes

Z

Zacharie, sm. Zachariah
Zénobie, sf. Zenobia
Zénon, sm. Zeno
Zéphire, sm. Zephyrus
Zoïle, sm. Zoilus
Zoroastre, sm. Zoroaster

DICTIONNAIRE

DES NOMS DE BAPTÊME D'HOMME ET DE FEMME

DONT L'ORTHOGRAPHE VARIE DANS LES DEUX LANGUES.

A

Abigail, sf. Abigail
Ada, sf. Adah
Adélaïde, sf. Adelaide
Adolphe, sm. Adolphus
Agathe, sf. Agatha
Agnès, sf. Agnes
Aimée, sf. Amy
Alain, sm. Allen
Alphonse, sm. Alphonso
Ambroise, sm. Ambrose
Amédée, sm. Amadeus
Amélie, sf. Amelia
Anastase (Saint), sm. St. Anastasius
André, sm. Andrew
Ange, sm. Angelo
Anne, sf. Ann, Anna, Anne
Annette, sf. Annette, (*fam.*) Nancy
Anselme, sm. Anselm, Anselmo
Antoine, sm. Anthony, (*fam.*) Tony
Arabelle, sf. Arabella
Athanase (Saint), sm. St. Athanasius
Auguste, sm. Augustus
Augustin (Saint), sm. St. Augustine, St. Austin
Aurélie, sf. Aurelia
Aurélien, sm. Aurelian
Aurore, sf. Aurora

B

Babet, sf. Betsy
Barbe, sf. Barbara
Barnabé (Saint), sm. St. Barnabas
Barthélemy (Saint), sm. St. Bartholomew
Basile, sm. Basil
Baudouin, sm. Baldwin
Béatrix, sf. Beatrice
Benjamin, sm. Benjamin, (*fam.*) Ben
Benoît (Saint), sm. St. Benedict
Berthe, sf. Bertha
Bertrand, sm. Bertram
Blanche, sf. Blanche, Bianca
Brigitte, sf. Bridget, (*fam.*) Biddy

C

Camille, sf. Camilla
Catherine, sf. Catherine, (*fam.*) Kate, Kitty, Katie
Cécile, sf. Cecilia, (*fam.*) Cecily, Cicely
Célestin, sm. Celestine
Célie, sf. Celia
Charlot, sm. (*fam.*) Charley
Chrétien, sm. Christian
Christine, sf. Christina
Christophe, sm. Christopher, (*fam.*) Kitt
Chrysostôme (Saint), sm. St. Chrysostom
Clarisse, sf. Clarissa
Claudie, sf. Claudia
Cléanthe, sm. Cleanthes
Clélie, sf. Clelia
Clémentine, sf. Clementina
Clotilde, sf. Clotilda
Cordélie, sf. Cordelia
Crépin (Saint), sm. St. Crispin
Cyprien, sm. Cyprian

D

Daniel, sm. Daniel, (*fam.*) Dan
Débora, sf. Deborah
Délie, sf. Delia
Dominique (Saint), sm. St. Dominic
Dorothée, sf. Dorothea, Dorothy, (*fam.*) Dolly, Dot, Dorrit

E

Edmond, sm. Edmund. — *Côte de fer*, Edmund Ironside
Édouard, sm. Edward, (*fam.*) Ned, Neddy
Éléonore, sf. Eleanor, (*fam.*) Nelly, Nell
Elisa, Élise, sf. Eliza, (*fam.*) Lizzy, Lizzie
Élisabeth, sf. Elizabeth, (*fam.*) Betsy, Betty, Bess
Émilie, sf. Emily
Esther, sf. Esther, (*fam.*) Hetty
Eudoxie, sf. Eudoxia
Eugène, sm. Eugene, Eugenius
Eugénie, sf. Eugenia

F

Fabien, sm. Fabian
Fanchon, Fanchette, sf. Fanny, (*fam.*) Fan
Félicité, sf. Felicity
Flore, sf. Flora
François, sm. Francis
Françoise, sf. Frances, Fanny
Frédéric, sm. Frederick, (*fam.*) Fred

G

Gauthier, sm. Walter, (*fam.*) Wat

Geoffroy, sm. Geoffrey
Georges, sm. George
Gervais (Saint), sm. St. Gervase
Gilles, sm. Giles
Godefroy, sm. Godfrey
Gratien, sm. Gratian
Grégoire, sm. Gregory
§**Guillaume**, sm. William, (*fam.*) Bill, Billy, Will. — *le Conquérant*, William the Conqueror. — *le Roux*, William Rufus. — *Longue Épée*, William Longsword
Gustave, sm. Gustavus

H

Hélène, sf. Helen, Helena
Héloïse, sf. Eloisa
Henri, sm. Henry, (*fam.*) Harry, Hal
Henriette, sf. Henrietta, Harriet
Hilaire (Saint), sm. St. Hilary
Hugues, sm. Hugh
Hyacinthe, sm. Hyacinthus

I

Ignace (Saint), sm. St. Ignatius
Isabeau, Isabelle, sf. Isabella, Isabel, (*fam.*) Bella

J

Jacques, sm. James, (*fam.*) Jem, Jemmy
Jean, sm. John, (*fam.*) Jack, Johnnie. — *sans Terre*, John Lackland
Jeanne, sf. Jane, (*fam.*) Jenny, Joan
Jeannette, sf. Janet, Jenny
Jonathas, sm. Jonathan
Joseph, sm. Joseph, (*fam.*) Joe, Joey
Jules, sm. Julius
Julie, sf. Julia
Julien, sm. Julian
Julienne, sf. Juliana
Juliette, sf. Juliet
Junie, sf. Junia
Justine, sf. Justina

L

Lancelot, sm. Launcelot
Laure, sf. Laura
Laurent, sm. Laurence
Lavinie, sf. Lavinia
Lisette, sf. Lizzy
Livie, sf. Livia
Lothaire, sm. Lothario, Lotharius
Louis, sm. Lewis
Louise, sf. Louisa, (*fam.*) Loo
Luc, sm. Luke
Lucie, sf. Lucy
Lucien, sm. Lucian
Lydie, sf. Lydia

M

Madeleine, sf. Magdalen
Madelon, sf. Maud, Maudlin
Marc, sm. Mark
Marcellin, sm. Marcellinus
Margot, sf. Margery, Meg, Madge
Marguerite, sf. Margaret, (*fam.*) Madge, Meg
Marie, sf. Mary, (*fam.*) Poll, Polly, Moll, Molly
Marthe, sf. Martha, (*fam.*) Patty
Mathilde, sf. Matilda, Maud
Matthieu, sm. Matthew, (*fam.*) Mat
Mélisse, sf. Melissa
Michaud, sm. Mike
Michée, sm. Micah, (*fam.*) Mike
Michel, sm. Michael
Montaigu, sm. Montague

N

Nannette, sf. Nancy, Nanny
Nathaniel, sm. Nathaniel, (*fam.*) Nat, Natty
Nicodème, sm. Nicodemus
Nicolas, sm. Nicholas, (*fam.*) Nick
Ninon, sf. Nino

O

Olivie, sf. Olivia
Olivier, sm. Oliver, (*fam.*) Noll
Olympe, sf. Olympia
Onésime, sm. Onesimus
Ophélie, sf. Ophelia

P

Patrice, sm. Patrick, (*fam.*) Pat
Pierre, sm. Peter
Polydore, sm. Polydorus
Porcie, sf. Portia, Porcia
Priscille, sf. Priscilla
Properce, sm. Propertius
Pulchérie, sf. Pulcheria
Pylade, sm. Pylades

R

Randolphe, sm. Randolph, Randal
Raoul, sm. Ralph
Richard, sm. Richard, (*fam.*) Dick, Dickey. — *Cœur-de-Lion*, Richard the Lion-hearted
Robert, sm. Robert, (*fam.*) Bob, Robin
Rodolphe, sm. Rodolph
Roland, sm. Rowland
Rosamonde, sf. Rosamond
Roxane, sf. Roxana
Ruben, sm. Reuben

S

Sabine, sf. Sabina
Samuel, sm. Samuel, (*fam.*) Sam
Sara, sf. Sarah, (*fam.*) Sally, Sal
Silvestre (Saint), sm. St. Silvester
Sophie, sf. Sophia, (*fam.*) Sophy
Sophonisbe, sf. Sophonisba
Sulpice, sm. Sulpitius
Susanne, sf. Susan, Susannah, (*fam.*) Sukey, Sue
Sylvain, sm. Sylvan, Sylvanus

T

Théophile, sm. Theophilus
Thérèse, sf. Theresa
Thomas, sm. Thomas, (*fam.*) Tom, Tommy
Timothée, sm. Timothy, (*fam.*) Tim

U

Urbain, sm. Urban
Ursule, sf. Ursula

V

Valentin, sm. Valentine
Valérie, sf. Valeria
Véronique (Sainte), sf. St. Veronica
Virginie, sf. Virginia
Vivien, sm. Vivian

W

Wilhelmine, sf. Wilhelmina

AN ENGLISH-FRENCH DICTIONARY.

AN ENGLISH-FRENCH

DICTIONARY.

A, s. A, a, (*mus.*) la. *A big A*, un A majuscule

A, **An**, art. indef. un, une

Aback, adv. en arrière, sur le mât, déconcerté

Abacus, s. buffet, *m.*, console, *f.*, (*archit.*) tailloir, *m.*, abaque, *m.*

Abaft, adv. à l'arrière, en arrière

Abandon, va. abandonner, délaisser, se désister de

Abandon, **Abandoning**, **Abandonment**, s. abandon, *m.*, abandonnement, *m.*

Abandoned, past part. adj. abandonné, livré, réprouvé

Abandoner, s. celui, celle qui abandonne, *m.f.*

Abase, va. abaisser, humilier, rabattre, avilir

Abasement, **Abasing**, s. abaissement, *m.*, humiliation, *f*, avilissement, *m.*

Abash, va. décontenancer, déconcerter, confondre

Abate, va. diminuer, rabattre, rabaisser, remettre, faire remise (de), affaiblir ; — vn. diminuer, baisser, s'apaiser, devenir nul

Abatement, s. diminution, *f*, adoucissement, *m.*, soulagement, *m.*, rabais, *m.*, cessation, *f.*, annulation, *f*, (*herald.*) abattement, *m.* *Plea of* —, exception dilatoire

Abbacy, s. dignité abbatiale, *f.*, droits abbatiaux, *m.plur.*, abbaye, *f.*, abbatial, *m*

Abbatial, adj. abbatial (*plur* abbatiaux)

Abbess, s. abbesse, *f.*

Abbey, s. abbaye, *f.* — *-lubber*, moine fainéant, *m*

Abbot, *also* **Abbé**, sm. abbé

Abbreviate, va. abréger, raccourcir, réduire

Abbreviation, s. abréviation, *f.*

Abbreviator, s. abréviateur, *m.*

A B C, s. A B C. — *book*, abécédaire, *m.*

Abdicate, va n. abdiquer, se démettre de

Abdication, s. abdication, *f.*, renonciation, *f.*

Abdomen, s. abdomen, *m.*, bas-ventre, *m.*

Abdominal, **Abdominous**, adj. abdominal, ventru

Abduction, s. écartement, *m.*, abduction, *f.*, enlèvement, *m.*

Aberrant, adj. qui s'écarte

Aberration, s. aberration, *f.*, égarement, *m.*

Abet, va. soutenir, encourager, exciter

Abetment, s. aide, *f.*, appui, *m.*

Abetter, **Abettor**, s. aide, *m.*, soutien, *m.*, fauteur, instigateur, *m.*

Abeyance, s. vacance, *f.*, attente, *f.*, suspens, *m.*

Abhor, va. abhorrer, avoir en horreur

Abhorrence, s. horreur, *f*, aversion extrême, *f.*

Abhorrent, adj. saisi d'horreur, opposé, répugnant

Abhorrer, s. ennemi juré, *m.*

Abhorring, s. haine, *f.*, objet d'horreur, *m.*

Abide, vn. demeurer, rester, séjourner, soutenir, supporter, souffrir, s'en rapporter. *To — by a promise*, rester fidèle à une promesse. — va. attendre de pied ferme, résister (à), endurer, supporter, soutenir, payer

Abiding, adj. constant, ferme, durable. — s. séjour *m.*, persévérance, *f.*, permanence, *f.*, stabilité, *f.*

Abigail, s. soubrette, *f.*, suivante, *f.*

Ability, s. faculté, *f.*, pouvoir, *m.*, capacité, *f.*; *—ies*, (*plur*) talents. *To the best of his —ies*, de son mieux

Abject, adj. abject, méprisable. — s. être abject

Abjectedness, **Abjectness**, **Abjection**, s. abjection, *f.*, bassesse, *f.*

Abjectly, adv. d'une manière abjecte

Abjuration, s. abjuration, *f.*

Abjure, va. abjurer, renoncer (à)

Abjurer, s. personne qui abjure

Ablative, adj. s. ablatif, *m.*

Able, adj. capable, à même, en état, robuste, expérimenté, habile. — *-bodied*, adj. robuste, vigoureux

Ableness, s. habileté, *f.*, vigueur, *f.*

Ablution, s. ablution, *f.*

Ably, adv. habilement, avec talent

Abnegation, s. abnégation, *f.*

Abnormal, adj. anormal, irrégulier, difforme

Aboard, adv. à bord. *To fall — of*, aborder, heurter. — prep. à bord de

Abode, s. séjour, *m.*, demeure, *f.*

Abolish, va. abolir, détruire

Abolishment, **Abolition**, s. abolissement, *m.*, abolition, *f.*

Abolitionism, s. abolitionisme, *m.*

Abolitionist, s. abolitioniste, *m.f.*

Abominable, adj. abominable, impur

Abominableness, s. nature abominable, *f.*, odieux, *m.*

Abominably, adv. abominablement

Abominate, va. avoir en abomination, abhorrer

Abomination, s. abomination, *f.*

Aboriginal, adj. primitif. — s. un des aborigènes, *m.*, naturel, *m.*

Aborigines, s.plur. aborigènes, *m pl.*

Abortion, **Abortment**, s. avortement, *m.*, avorton, *m*

Abortive, adj. abortif, infécond, avorté. — s. avorton, *m.*, (*med.*) remède abortif, *m.*

Abortively, adv. avant terme, prématurément

Abortiveness, s. avortement, *m.*, insuccès, *m.*

Abound, vn. abonder (en), être abondant (en), regorger (de)

About, prep autour de, près de, vers, sur, environ, touchant, au sujet de, à l'égard de, (être) à faire, occupé à, en train de faire, après, dans, par, à travers. *To be — a thing*, être à faire une chose. — adv. tout autour, alentour, à la ronde, à peu près, environ, sur le point, près, en virant. *All the country round* —, tout le pays d'alentour. *To wander* —, errer çà et là. *He went a mile* —, il fit un détour d'un mille

Above, prep. au-dessus de, par-dessus, (*speaking of a river*) en amont de. — *-board*, adv. à jeu découvert, cartes sur table, loyalement. — *-deck*, sur le pont, (*fig.*) loyalement. — *-ground*, de ce monde, en vie, sur la terre. — adv. en haut, au-dessus de nous, par-dessus, ci-dessus

Abreast, adv. de front, sur la même ligne, (*nav.*) par le travers (de), vis-à-vis

Abridge, va. abréger, restreindre, réduire, rogner, dépouiller

Abridger, s. abréviateur, *m.*

Abridgment, s. abrégé, *m.*, diminution, *f*, privation, *f.*

Abroach, adv. en perce, débouché

Abroad, adv. au loin, dehors, absent. *To be all* —, n'avoir pas la tête à quelque chose. *What news* —? quelles nouvelles y a-t-il en ville? *To go* —, aller à l'étranger

Abrogate, va. abroger

Abrogation, s. abrogation, *f.*

Abrupt, adj. abrupt, escarpé, raboteux, brusque. — s. abîme, *m.*

Abruptly, adv. brusquement

Abruptness, s. roideur, *f.*, aspérité, *f.*, brusquerie, *f.*, vivacité, *f.*, décousu, *m.*

Abscess, s. abcès, *m.*

Abscond, vn. se soustraire (à), se cacher (à), s'échapper furtivement

Absence, s. absence, *f.*, éloignement, *m.*, (*mind*) distraction, *f.*

Absent, adj. absent, éloigné, distrait

Absent oneself, vr. s'absenter

Absentee, s. absent, *m.*, propriétaire qui ne réside pas sur ses terres

Absenteeism, s. absentéisme, *m.*

Absolute, adj. absolu, illimité, pur et simple, (*downright*) fieffé, franc, franche

Absolutely, adv. absolument, véritablement, complètement

Absoluteness, s. nature absolue, *f.*, pouvoir absolu, *m.*, l'absolu, *m.*

Absolution, s. absolution, *f.* *A general* —, l'absoute

Absolutism, s. absolutisme, *m.*

Absolutist, s. absolutiste, *m.*
Absolve, va. absoudre, délier, dégager, affranchir, résoudre
Absorb, va. absorber, engloutir
Absorbent, s. absorbant *m.*
Absorption, s. absorption, *f.*
Abstain, vn. s'abstenir; — va. empêcher
Abstemious, adj. sobre, abstème, d'abstinence
Abstemiously, adv. sobrement
Abstemiousness, s. sobriété, *f.*, abstinence, *f.*
Abstention, s. abstention, *f.*
Abstinence, s. abstinence, *f.*
Abstinent, adj. sobre, abstinent
Abstract, va. détacher, abstraire, faire abstraction de, soustraire (de, à), résumer, abréger, extraire; — vn. faire abstraction d'idées
Abstract, adj. abstrait, pur. — s. abrégé, *m.*, précis, *m.*, résumé, *m.*, abstraction, *f.* *In the* —, d'une manière abstraite, par abstraction
Abstracted, past part. adj. séparé, détaché, purifié, abstrait, distrait
Abstractedly, adv. abstractivement, d'une manière distraite
Abstractedness, s. nature abstraite, *f.*
Abstraction, s. abstraction, *f.*, distraction, *f.*, détachement du monde, *m.*, vol, *m.*, enlèvement, *m.*
Abstractively, adv. abstractivement
Abstractly, adv. d'une manière abstraite, par abstraction
Abstractness, s. nature abstraite, *f.*, caractère abstrait, *m.*
Abstruse, adj. caché, abstrus, obscur
Abstrusely, adv. obscurément, d'une manière abstruite
Abstruseness, s. nature abstruse, *f.*, obscurité, *f.*
Absurd, adj. absurde
Absurdity, Absurdness, s. absurdité, *f.*
Absurdly, adv. absurdement
Abundance, s. abondance, *f.*, foule, *f.*
Abundant, adj. abondant
Abundantly, adv. abondamment
Abuse, va. abuser (de), faire un mauvais usage (de), maltraiter, injurier, médire (de), tromper, séduire
Abuse, s. abus, *m.*, injures, *f.pl.*, invectives, *f pl.*
Abuser, s. qui abuse de, personne qui insulte, trompeur, *m.*
Abusive, adj. abusif, injurieux, mensonger
Abusively, adv. abusivement, injurieusement

Abusiveness, s. langage injurieux, *m.*, outrages, *m.pl.*
Abut, vn. aboutir (à)
Abutment, s. (*bridge*) culée, *f.*, (*edifice*) arc-boutant, *m.*, (*carp.*) about, *m.*
Abyss, Abysm, s. abîme, *m.*, gouffre, *m.*
Acacia, s. acacia, *m.*
Academic, s. académicien, *m.*, étudiant, *m.*
Academical, adj. académique, universitaire
Academicals, s. plur. costume universitaire, robe
Academically, adv. académiquement
Academician, s. académicien, *m.*, membre d'une académie, *m.*
Academy, s. académie, *f.*, école, *f.*, pension, *f.*
Acanthus, s. acanthe, *f.*
Accede, vn. accéder
Accelerate, va. accélérer, précipiter. *Accelerating force*, force accélératrice
Acceleration, s. accélération, *f.*
Accelerative, Acceleratory, adj. accélérateur, -trice
Accension, s. inflammation, *f.*
Accent, s. accent, *m.*, parole, *f.*, langage, *m.*
Accent, Accentuate, va. accentuer
Accentuation, s. accentuation, *f.*
Accept, va. accepter, donner son consentement (à), faire acception (de), entendre
Acceptable, adj. acceptable, agréable
Acceptableness, Acceptability, s. mérite, *m.*, admissibilité, *f.*
Acceptably, adv. d'une manière agréable
Acceptance, s. acceptation, *f.*, réception, *f.*, approbation, *f.*, acception, *f.*
Acceptation, s. acceptation, *f.*, accueil, *m.*, réception, *f.*, approbation, *f.*, (*of a word*) acception, *f.*
Accepter, Acceptor, s. celui, celle qui accepte
Access, s. accès, *m.*, approche, *f.*, abord, *m.*, surcroît, *m.*
Accessary, *see* ACCESSORY
Accessible, adj. accessible
Accession, s. augmentation, *f.*, acquisition, *f.*, avènement, *m.*, accession, *f.*, adhésion, *f.*, accès, *m.*
Accessorial, adj. de complicité
Accessorily, adv. accessoirement
Accessory, adj. s. accessoire, participant (à), complice (de)
Accidence, s. rudiment *m.*
Accident, s. accident, *m.*, hasard, *m.*, incident, *m.*, malheur, *m.*, sinistre, *m.*
Accidental, adj. fortuit, accidentel, de hasard. — s. accessoire, *m.*, propriété accidentelle, *f.*, accident, *m.*

Accidentally, adv. fortuitement, accidentellement
Acclaim, va. acclamer
Acclaim, Acclamation, s. acclamation, *f.*
Acclamatory, adj. bruyant, d'acclamation
Acclimate, Acclimatize, va. acclimater
Acclimation, Acclimatization, s. acclimatement, *m.*
Acclivity, s. montée, *f.*, pente, *f.*, rampe, *f.*
Accommodate, va accommoder, conformer, mettre d'accord, donner, loger, obliger (par); — vn. s'accommoder
Accommodating, adj. commode, accommodant, obligeant
Accommodation, s accommodement, *m.*, ajustement, *m.*, commodité, *f.*, bien-être, *m.*, logement, *m.*, prêt d'argent, *m.*, service, *m.* — *-bill*, — *-note*, — *-paper*, billet de complaisance
Accommodative, adj. *see* ACCOMMODATING
Accommodator, s. celui, celle qui accommode
Accompaniment, s. accompagnement, *m.*
Accompanist, s. accompagnateur, *m.*, accompagnatrice, *f.*
Accompany, va. accompagner, suivre
Accomplice, s. complice, *m.f.*
Accomplish, va. accomplir
Accomplished, adj. accompli, parfait, distingué
Accomplishment, s. accomplissement *m.*, talent, *m.*, (*plur.*) les arts d'agrément, *m.*
Accompt, Accomptant, s. *see* ACCOUNT
Accord, s. accord, *m.*, gré, *m.*, consentement, *m.* *With one* —, d'un commun accord. *Of one's own* —, de son plein gré
Accord, va. accorder, faire accorder; — vn. s'accorder, être d'accord
Accordance, s. accord, *m.*, rapport, *m.*
Accordant, adj. conforme (à), d'accord (avec), à l'unisson
According, adj. conforme, harmonieux, -se. — *as*, selon que. — *to*, suivant
Accordingly, adv. en conséquence
Accordion, s. accordéon, *m.*
Accost, va. accoster, aborder, parler à
Accostable, adj. abordable. — *nature*, caractère affable
Accoucheur, s. accoucheur, *m.*
Account, s. compte, *m.*, mémoire, *m.*, le calcul, la tenue des livres, liste, *f.*, raison, *f.*, considération, *f.*, importance, *f.*, profit, *m.*, récit, *m.*, rapport, *m.*, nouvelles, *pl.f.* *To call a person to* —, demander compte à quelqu'un de sa conduite. *On no* —, pour rien au monde. *On* — *of*, à cause de. *To take into* —, faire entrer en ligne de compte. *To make no* — *of*, ne faire aucun cas de. *To make* — *that*, compter que
Account, va. regarder (comme), compter; — vn. rendre compte, être responsable, expliquer, s'expliquer
Accountable, adj. comptable, responsable
Accountability, Accountableness, s. responsabilité, *f.*
Accountant, s. comptable, *m.*, agent comptable, *m.* *The* —*'s office*, le bureau de comptabilité. — adj. responsable
Accountantship, s. charge d'agent comptable, *f.*
Accouple, va. accoupler
Accouplement, s. accouplement, *m.*
Accoutre, va. accoutrer, équiper
Accoutrement, s. habillement, *m.*, accoutrement, *m.*
Accredit, va. accréditer
Accretion, s. accroissement, *m.*, (*med.*) accrétion, *f.*
Accretive, adj. de croissance
Accrue, vn. en résulter (pour), s'ensuivre (pour)
Accubation, s. posture à demi couchée, *f.*
Accumbent, adj. à demi couché, appuyé, accoudé
Accumulate, va. accumuler, entasser, amonceler
Accumulation, s. accumulation, *f.*, amas, *m.*, monceau, *m.*
Accumulative, adj. qui accumule
Accumulator, s celui, celle qui accumule
Accuracy, s. exactitude, *f.*, justesse, *f.*, soin, *m.*
Accurate, adj. exact, juste, soigné
Accurately, adv. avec exactitude, avec justesse, avec soin
Accurse, va. maudire, frapper d'anathème
Accusable, adj. accusable
Accusal, Accuse, s. accusation, *f.*
Accusation, s. accusation, *f.*
Accusative, adj. s. accusateur, accusatif, *m*
Accusatory, adj. accusateur, d'accusation
Accuse, va. accuser
Accuser, s. accusateur *m.*, accusatrice, *f.*
Accusing, adj. accusateur -trice
Accustom, va. accoutumer, habituer. *To* — *oneself*, s'habituer, s'accoutumer. *To get* —*ed*, se faire (à)
Accustomable, adj. habituel, ordinaire
Accustomably, adv habituellement, selon la coutume
Accustomary, *see* CUSTOMARY

Accustomed, past part., adj. accoutumé, habitué, habituel
Ace, s. as, m., rien, m. *Within an — of his ruin*, à deux doigts de sa perte
Acerb, adj. acerbe, âpre
Acerbity, s. acerbité, *f.*
Acervose, adj. plein de monticules
Acescency, s. acidité, *f.*
Acescent, adj. acide
Acetate, s. acétate, *m.*
Acetic, adj. acétique
Acetite, s. acétite, *m.*
Acetose, adj. acéteux
Ache, s. douleur, *f.*, mal, *m.*
Ache, vn. faire mal à, être douloureux, souffrir
Achievable, adj. exécutable, praticable
Achieve, va. accomplir, achever
Achievement, s. exécution, *f.*, exploit, *m.*, acquisition, *f.*, *(herald.)* écusson, *m.*
Achiever, s. auteur, *m.* celui qui accomplit
Aching, adj. douloureux, endolori, affligé. — s. douleur, *f.*, souffrance, *f.*
Achromatic, adj. achromatique
Acid, adj. s. acide, *m.*
Acidify, va. acidifier
Acidity, s. acidité, *f.*
Acidulate, va. aciduler
Acidulous, adj. acidule
Acknowledge, va. reconnaître, avouer, accuser (*réception d'une lettre*), se montrer reconnaissant de
Acknowledgment, s. reconnaissance, *f.*, aveu, *m.*, témoignage de reconnaissance, *m.*, accusé de réception (*d'une lettre*)
Acme, s. comble, *m.*, le plus haut point, *m.*, crise, *f.*
Acolyte, s. acolyte, *m.*
Aconite, s. aconit, *m.*
Acorn, s. gland, *m.*
Acorn, vn. ramasser des glands. *Full- —ed*, nourri de glands, chargé de glands
Acotyledon, s. acotylédone, *f.*
Acoustic, adj. acoustique
Acoustics, s. plur. l'acoustique, *sing. f.*, instruments d'acoustique, *pl. m.*
Acquaint, va. faire connaître, faire savoir, instruire
Acquainted with (to be), connaître, se connaître, être au fait de
Acquaint oneself, vr. apprendre, se mettre au courant (de)
Acquaintance, s. connaissance, *f.*, personne, *f.*, de connaissance
Acquaintanceship, s. connaissance, *f.*, liaison, *f.*
Acquainted, past part. connu, familier
Acquest, s. acquisition, *f.*, acquêt, *m.*
Acquiesce, vn. acquiescer, consentir
Acquiescence, s. acquiescement, *m.*, consentement, *m.*
Acquiescent, adj. consentant, facile, accommodant
Acquirable, adj. qui peut s'acquérir
Acquire, va. acquérir, s'acquérir
Acquirement, s. acquisition, *f.*, talent, *m.*, connaissances, *f. pl.*
Acquirer, s. acquéreur, *m.*
Acquiring, s. acquisition, *f.*
Acquisition, s. acquisition, *f.*
Acquisitive, adj. porté à acquérir
Acquisitiveness, s. penchant pour acquérir
Acquit, va. acquitter, s'acquitter de, absoudre, tenir quitte
Acquitment, Acquittal, s. acquittement, *m.*, décharge, *f.*
Acquittance, s. quittance, *f.*
Acre, s. arpent, *m.*, acre, *m.* (*French measure 40 ares 46·71*), champ, *m.*
Acreage, s. contenance, *f.*, arpentage, *m.*
Acred, adj. possesseur d'arpents de terre, *m.* *Long- — men, many- — men*, de riches propriétaires fonciers
Acrid, adj. âcre, aigre
Acridity, Acridness, s. âcreté, *f.*
Acrimonious, adj. acrimonieux, aigre
Acrimoniously, adv. avec acrimonie
Acrimoniousness, **Acrimony**, s. acrimonie, *f.*, âcreté, *f.*
Acrobat, s. acrobate, *m.*
Across, prep. à travers, au travers de, par, sur, dans, contre. *To come — one*, donner de la tête contre quelqu'un. — adv. en travers, en croix, croisé
Acrostic, s. acrostiche, *m.*
Act, vn. agir, faire, se comporter, (*theat.*) jouer un rôle; — va. exécuter, commettre, jouer, jouer le rôle (de), contrefaire, remplir les fonctions
Act, s. acte, *m.*, fait, *m.*, action, *f.*, pièce, *f.*, titre, *m.*
Acting, s. action, *f.*, jeu, *m.*, feinte, *f.* — adj. qui agit, faisant fonctions (de), gérant, de service, (*mechan.*) à effet
Action, s. action, *f.*, fait, *m.*, acte, *m.*, procès, *m.* *To bring an — against*, intenter un procès (à)
Actionable, adj. sujet à procès
Activate, va. activer
Active, adj. actif, laborieux, leste
Actively, adv. activement
Activeness, Activity, s. activité, *f.*
Actor, s. acteur, *m.*, comédien, *m.*, (*law*) plaignant, *m.*
Actress, s. actrice, *f.*, comédienne, *f.*
Actual, adj. actuel, réel, effectif
Actuality, Actualness, s. actualité, *f.*
Actualize, va. réaliser
Actually, adv. réellement
Actuary, s. secrétaire, *m.*, gérant, *m.*
Actuate, va. porter, agir, influencer, pousser
Acumen, s. pénétration, *f.*, jugement, *m.*
Acuminate, vn. s'élever en cône; — va. aiguiser, former en pointe
Acute, adj. aigu, fin, violent, subtil, perçant
Acutely, adv. en pointe, vivement, subtilement
Acuteness, s. pointe, *f.*, tranchant, *m.*, vivacité, *f.*, finesse, *f.*, âpreté, *f.*
Adage, s. adage, *m.*, proverbe, *m.*
Adagio, s. adv. adagio, *m.*
Adamant, s. diamant, *m.*
Adamantine, adj. adamantin, de diamant
Adamic, adj. d'Adam, adamique
Adapt, va. adapter, approprier, ajuster, proportionner
Adaptable, adj. applicable
Adaptation, Adaption, s. adaptation, *f.*
Adapter, s. qui adapte
Adaptness, s. conformité, *f.*, juste rapport, *m.*
Add, va. ajouter, joindre, additionner; — vn. ajouter (à), accroître
Adder, s. couleuvre, *f.*, vipère, *f.* — *-fly*, demoiselle, *f.* *—'s tongue*, (*bot.*) langue-de-serpent, *f.* *—'s wort*, (*bot.*) bistorte, *f.*, vipérine, *f.*
Addibility, s. faculté de pouvoir être ajouté, *f.*
Addible, adj. qu'on peut ajouter
Addice, s. doloire, *f.*
Addict oneself, vr. s'adonner, être adonné
Addictedness, Addiction, s. goût (pour), *m.*, penchant (à), *m.*
Additament, s. addition, *f.*, ajoutage, *m.*
Addition, s. addition, *f.*, surcroît, *m.*, acquisition, *f.*, titre, *m.*
Additional, adj. additionnel
Additionally, adv. par addition, en sus
Addle, adj. (*egg*) clair, stérile, infécond
Addle, va. corrompre. *—ed eggs*, œufs pourris. — vn. croître, gagner
Address, va. préparer, se préparer, s'adresser à, accoster, haranguer, faire sa cour à, adresser
Address, s. adresse, *f.*, pétition, *f.*, discours, *m.*, épître dédicatoire, *m.*, manières, *f. pl.*, hommages, *m. pl.*
Addresser, s. celui qui s'adresse à, pétitionnaire, *m.*
Adduce, va. avancer, produire, citer
Adducer, s. qui avance, qui produit
Adducible, adj. qu'on peut avancer
Adduction, s. adduction, *f.*, production, *f.*, citation, *f.*
Adept, s. adepte, *m. f.*, initié, *m.*, initiée, *f.* — adj. savant, versé
Adequacy, s. juste proportion, *f.*, rapport, *m.*
Adequate, adj. juste, proportionné, équivalent, complet, compétent, adéquat
Adequately, adv. en juste proportion
Adequateness, s. juste proportion, *f.*, rapport, *m.*
Adhere, vn. adhérer, être attaché, être favorable
Adherence, Adherency, s. adhérence, *f.*, adhésion, *f.*, attachement, *m.*
Adherent, adj. adhérent, attaché. — s. adhérent, *m.*, qualité, *f.*
Adherer, s. adhérent, *m.*
Adhesion, s. adhésion, *f.*
Adhesive, adj. adhérent, qui tient, visqueux. — *envelopes*, enveloppes gommées
Adhesiveness, s. propriété d'adhérer, *f.*, viscosité, *f.*
Adieu, s. adv. adieu, *m.*
Adipose, Adipous, adj. adipeux
Adit, s. passage souterrain, *m.*, galerie, *f.*
Adjacence, Adjacency, s. contiguïté, *f.*, voisinage, *m.*
Adjacent, adj. adjacent, avoisinant, contigu. — s. voisin, *m.*
Adject, va. ajouter
Adjection, s. addition, *f.*
Adjectival, adj. comme adjectif
Adjective, s. adj. adjectif, *m.* *To —*, va. changer en adjectif
Adjectively, adv. adjectivement
Adjoin, va. adjoindre, joindre; — vn. être contigu, toucher
Adjoining, adj. adjacent, contigu, avoisinant
Adjourn, va. ajourner, remettre; — vn. s'ajourner, se retirer
Adjournment, s. ajournement, *m.*, remise, *f.*
Adjudge, va. adjuger, juger, condamner
Adjudicate, va.n. adjuger, juger
Adjudication, s. adjudication, *f.*, jugement, *m.*
Adjudicator, s. juge, *m.*, adjudicateur, *m.*
Adjunct, s. accessoire, *m.*, qualité, *f.*, adjoint, *m.* — adj. joint, adjoint
Adjunction, s. adjonction, *f.*
Adjunctive, adj. s. qui joint, addition, *f.*
Adjuration, s. adjuration, *f.*
Adjure, va. adjurer
Adjust, va. ajuster, arranger, régler, rendre conforme
Adjuster, s. celui qui ajuste, qui règle
Adjustment, s. ajustement, *m.*, arrangement, *m.*, règlement, *m.*

Adjutancy, s. fonctions d'adjudant, *f.pl.*, agencement, *m.*
Adjutant, s. adjudant, *m.*, secours, *m.*
Adjuvant, adj. secourable. — s. aide
Admeasurement, s. mesurage, *m.*, mesures, *f.pl.*, (*law*) partage, *m.*
Administer, va. administrer, gouverner, donner, appliquer, rendre; — vn. contribuer, subvenir, gérer
Administration, s. administration, *f.*, gouvernement, *m.*
Administrative, adj. administratif
Administrator, s. administrateur, *m.*
Administratorship, s. fonctions d'administrateur, *f. pl.*
Admirable, adj. admirable
Admirableness, s. nature admirable, *f.*, beauté, *f.*
Admirably, adv. admirablement, à ravir, fait à ravir
Admiral, s. amiral, *m.*, vaisseau amiral, *m.* *Rear*- —, contre-amiral. *Port*- —, amiral commandant dans le port, préfet maritime
Admiralship, s. amirauté, *f.*, grade d'amiral, *m.*
Admiralty, s. amirauté, *f.*, ministère de la marine, *m.*
Admiration, s. admiration, *f.*, étonnement, *m.*
Admire, va.n. admirer, s'étonner de
Admirer, s. admirateur, -trice
Admiring, adj. d'admiration, admiratif, qui admire
Admiringly, adv. avec admiration
Admissibility, s. admissibilité, *f.*
Admissible, adj. admissible
Admission, **Admittance**, s. admission, *f.*, entrée, *f.*, concession, *f.*, aveu, *m.*
Admit, va. admettre, laisser entrer, recevoir, souffrir
Admixtion, **Admixture**, s. mélange, *m.*
Admonish, va. reprendre doucement, conseiller, exhorter, prémunir, admonester, admonéter
Admonisher, s. mentor, *m.*
Admonishment, **Admonition**, s. réprimande, *f.*, avertissement, *m.*, admonition, *f.*
Admonitive, **Admonitory**, adj. sage, d'avertissement
Ado, s. peine, *f.*, difficulté, *f.*, bruit, *m.*, cérémonie, *f.* *I made no more* —, *but*, je ne fis ni une ni deux, mais
Adolescence, s. adolescence, *f.*
Adolescent, s. adj. adolescent, *m.*, adolescente, *f.*

Adonis, s. Adonis, *m.*
Adonize, vn. s'adoniser
Adopt, va. adopter
Adopted, adj. adoptif, d'adoption
Adoptedly, adv. par adoption
Adopter, s. celui, celle qui adopte, adoptant, *m.*, (*chem.*) récipient, *m.*
Adoption, s. adoption, *f.*
Adorable, adj. adorable
Adorableness, s. nature adorable, *f.*
Adorably, adv. adorablement
Adoration, s. adoration, *f.*
Adore, va. adorer
Adorer, s. adorateur, -trice
Adoringly, adv. avec adoration
Adorn, va. orner, parer
Adornment, s. ornement, *m.*, parure, *f.*
Adown, prep. le long de, vers la terre. — adv. en bas, à terre
Adrift, adv. en dérive, à l'abandon, à l'aventure. *To run* —, s'égarer
Adroit, adj. adroit
Adroitly, adv. adroitement
Adroitness, s. adresse, *f.*
Adulation, s. adulation, *f.*
Adulator, s. adulateur, *m.*
Adulatory, adj. adulateur, trice
Adult, adj. s. adulte
Adulterate, vn. commettre un adultère; — va. altérer, falsifier, frelater, adultérer
Adulterate, adj. altéré, falsifié, frelaté, corrompu, adultère
Adulterateness, **Adulteration**, s. altération, *f.*
Adulterer, s. adultère, *m.*
Adulteress, s. femme adultère, *f.*
Adulterine, s. adj. adultérin
Adulterous, adj. adultère, altéré, corrompu
Adultery, s. adultère, *m.*
Adumbrate, va. offrir une image de, représenter imparfaitement
Adust, **Adusted**, adj. aduste, brûlé, brûlant
Adustion, s. adustion, *f.*
Advance, va. avancer, faire avancer, porter en avant, ennoblir, élever. *To* — *large sums*, faire de grandes avances. — vn. avancer, s'avancer, monter
Advance, **Advancement**, s. avance, *f.*, marche, *f.*, progrès, *m.*, perfectionnement, *m.*, hausse, *f.*
Advancer, s. qui avance
Advantage, **Advantageousness**, s. avantage, *m.*, utilité, *f.*, intérêt, *m.* *To* —, avantageusement. *To take* — *of*, profiter, mettre à profit. *To take an unfair* — *of*, abuser de
Advantage, va. avantager, favoriser

Advantageous, ad[j.] avantageux
Advantageously, ad[v.] avantageusement
Advent, s. venue, *f.*, l'Ave[nt] *m.*
Adventitious, adj. a[d]ventice
Adventitiously, ad[v.] fortuitement
Adventure, s. aventu[re] *f.*, hasard, *m.*, accident, *m.* incident, *m.*, (*com.*) pacotil[le] *f.*
Adventure, vn. s'ave[n]turer; — va. aventurer, h[a]sarder
Adventurer, s. ave[n]turier, *m.*, aventurière, *f.*
Adventurous, adj. ave[n]tureux, audacieux
Adventurously, ad[v.] audacieusement
Adventurousness, hardiesse, *f.*
Adverb, s. adverbe, *m.*
Adverbial, adj. adverbi[al]
Adverbially, adv. a[d]verbialement
Adversary, s. adversair[e] *m.*
Adverse, adj. contrair[e] opposé (à), ennemi (de), ma[l]heureux
Adversely, adv. malhe[u]reusement
Adverseness, s. hostilit[é] *f.*, opposition, *f.*
Adversity, s. l'adversité,
Advert, vn. faire attentio[n] faire allusion (à), parler (de)
Advertency, s. attentio[n] *f.*
Advertent, adj. attentif
Advertise, va. averti[r] informer, faire annonce (*newspapers*), afficher
Advertisement, s. avi[s] *m.*, avertissement, *m.*, an[]nonce, *f.*, affiche, *f.*
Advertiser, s. celui qu[i] fait annoncer, *m.*, feuill[e] d'annonces, *f.*
Advice, s. conseil, *m.*, avi[s] *m.*, prudence, *f.*, nouvelles, *f.* *A piece of* —, un conseil. *T[o] take* — *of*, demander des con[]seils (à), suivre les conseils (de) *As per* — *from*, suivant avi[s] de. — *-boat*, s. aviso, *m.*
Advisable, adj judicieux sage, convenable, docile au[x] avis
Advisableness, s. sa[]gesse, *f.*, convenance, *f.*, do[ci]lité aux avis, *f.*
Advise, va. conseiller, re[]commander, prévenir; — vn réfléchir, consulter, se con[]seiller, délibérer
Advised, adj. avisé, judi[]cieux. *Ill*- —, mal avisé peu judicieux
Advisedly, adv. avec ré[]flexion
Advisedness, s. délibéra[]tion, *f.*
Adviser, s. conseiller, *m.*, conseillère, *f.*
Advocacy, s. défense, *f.*
Advocate, va. défendre, soutenir, plaider
Advocate, s. avocat, *m.*, intercesseur, *m.*

Affirmer, Affirmant, s. (*law*) celui qui affirme
Affix, va. attacher, ajouter, apposer
Affix, s. affixe, *f.*
Afflict, va. affliger
Affliction, s. affliction, *f.*
Afflictive, adj. affligeant
Affluence, s. affluence, *f.*, concours, *m.*, richesses, *f. pl.*
Affluent, adj. riche, opulent, affluant. — s. affluent, *m.*
Afflux, s. afflux, *m.*, affluence, *f.*
Afford, va. donner, offrir, être assez riche pour, avoir les moyens de
Afforest, va. convertir en forêt
Affranchise, va. affranchir
Affray, s. rixe, *f.*, querelle, *f.*
Affreight, va. affréter
Affright, va. épouvanter, effrayer
Affright, s. effroi, *m.*, épouvante, *f.*
Affrightedly, adv. avec épouvante
Affront, va. faire un affront à, offenser, insulter
Affront, s. affront, *m.*, offense, *f.*, outrage, *m.* *To give, to offer an — to, to put an — on,* faire un affront à. *To pocket an —,* boire un affront
Affronter, s. qui affronte
Affrontive, adj. offensant
Afield, adv. aux champs, en campagne
Afloat, adv. à flot, (*fig.*) sur pied, lancé, en train, répandu. *To set —,* mettre à flot. *There is a rumour —,* un bruit court
Afoot, adv. à pied, en marche, debout
Afore, prep. avant, devant. — adv. précédemment, pardevant
Aforesaid, adj. susdit
Afraid, adj. effrayé, ayant peur, craignant
Afresh, adv. de nouveau, de plus belle
Afront, adv. de front
Aft, adv. à l'arrière
After, prep. adv. après, à la suite de, ensuite de, d'après, suivant. — *all,* après tout, aussi bien
After-eye, va. suivre du regard
After-math, s. regain, *m.*
Aftermost, adj. le plus en arrière
Afternoon, s. après-midi, *f.*
After-part, s. partie postérieure, *f.*, arrière, *m.*
After-piece, s. petite pièce, *f.*
After-taste, s. arrière-goût, *m.*, déboire, *m.*
After-thought, s. arrière-pensée, *f.*, réflexion après coup, *f.*
Afterward, Afterwards, adv. ensuite, après
After-wit, s. esprit après coup, *m.*

Aga, s. aga, *m.*, seigneur, *m.*
Again, adv. de nouveau, encore une fois, une seconde fois, encore
Against, prep. contre, à l'encontre de, en face de, vis-à-vis de, pour. *Be ready — I come back,* tenez-vous prêt pour le moment de mon arrivée
Agape, s. agape, *f.*
Agape, adj. la bouche béante. *To set —,* ébahir
Agate, s. agate, *f.*
Agaze, va. frapper d'étonnement
Age, s. âge, *m.*, génération, *f.*, temps, *m.*, siècle, *m.*, vieillesse, *f.* *To be of —,* être majeur. *To be under —,* être mineur. *To come of —,* arriver à sa majorité. —*-worn,* usé par la vieillesse
Aged, adj. âgé, vieux
Agency, s. action, *f.*, intermédiaire, *m.*, agence, *f.*
Agenda, s. agenda, *m.*
Agent, s. agent, *m.*, homme d'affaires, *m.*, facteur, *m.*
Agglomerate, vn. s'agglomérer; — va. agglomérer
Agglomeration, s. agglomération, *f.*
Agglutinate, va.n. agglutiner, s'agglutiner
Agglutination, s. agglutination, *f.*
Aggrandize, va.n. agrandir, s'agrandir
Aggrandizement, s. agrandissement, *m.*
Aggravate, va. aggraver, augmenter, vexer
Aggravation, s. aggravation, *f.*
Aggregate, va. rassembler
Aggregate, adj. réuni. — s. assemblage, *m.*, somme, *f.*, agrégat, *m.*
Aggregately, adv. collectivement, dans l'ensemble
Aggregation, s. agrégation, *f.*, assemblage, *m.*
Aggress, va. être l'agresseur
Aggression, s. agression, *f.*
Aggressive, adj. agressif
Aggressiveness, s. caractère agressif, *m.*
Aggressor, s. agresseur, *m.*
Aggrieve, va. chagriner, molester
Aggroup, va. grouper
Aghast, adj. frappé de terreur, consterné
Agile, adj. agile
Agileness, Agility, s. agilité, *f.*
Agio, s. agio, *m.*
Agitate, va. agiter, troubler, méditer (*un projet, etc.*)
Agitation, s. agitation, *f.*, mouvement, *m.*, délibération, *f.*
Agitator, s. agitateur, *m.*
Agnail, s. mal d'aventure, *m.*
Agnate, s. adj. agnat, *m.* — *words,* des mots de même famille
Agnize, va. (*law*) reconnaître

Agnus, s. agnus Dei, *m.*
Ago, adv. il y a, passé. *Long —,* il y a longtemps
Agog, adj. impatient, désireux. *All — to,* tous impatients de
A-going, pres. part. allant, en mouvement. *To set —,* mettre en train (*a person*), faire aller (*a thing*)
Agonistes, s. athlète, *m.*
Agonize, vn. être à l'agonie, souffrir horriblement; — va. mettre au supplice, torturer
Agony, s. agonie, *f.*
Agouti, s. agouti, *m.*
Agrarian, adj. agraire
Agree, vn. s'accorder, être d'accord, consentir (à), accorder, demeurer d'accord (sur), convenir, être bon (pour); — va. réconcilier
Agreeable, adj. conforme, conformément, agréable. *I am —,* (*fam.*) je le veux bien
Agreeably, adv. conformément, agréablement
Agreement, s. accord, *m.*, harmonie, *f.*, rapport, *m.*, ressemblance, *f.*, consentement, *m.*, agrément, *m.*, convention, *f.*, marché, *m.*, contrat, *m.*
Agricultural, adj. agricole
Agriculture, s. agriculture, *f.*
Agriculturist, s. agriculteur, *m.*, agronome, *m.*
Aground, adv. échoué, arrêté. *To run —,* échouer, faire échouer
Ague, s. fièvre intermittente, *f.*, fièvre, *f.* —*-fit,* accès de fièvre, *m.* —*-proof,* à l'épreuve de la fièvre. —*-powder,* fébrifuge, *m.* —*-drops,* gouttes fébrifuges. —*-struck,* fiévreux. —*-tree,* sassafras, *m.*
Aguish, adj. fiévreux
Ah! interj. ah!
Aha! Aha! interj. ah ah! ah ah!
Ahead, adj. en avant, en tête. *To get — of, to shoot — of,* dépasser, devancer. *Go —!* allez de l'avant!
Ahem! interj. hem!
Ahold, adv. près du vent. *Lay her —!* serrez le vent!
Ahoy! interj. ho! holà! *Ship —!* ohé du navire!
Ahull, adv. à sec de voiles
Aid, va. aider, assister, secourir
Aid, s. aide, *f.*, secours, *m.*, assistance, *f.*, subside, *m.*
Aide-de-camp, s. aide-de-camp, *m.*
Aider, s. aide, *m.*
Aidless, adj. sans aide
Aigret, s. aigrette, *f.*
Ail, va. être souffrant; — va. faire mal à. *What —s him?* qu'est-ce qu'il a?
Ailment, Ail, s. mal, *m.*, maladie, *f.*, indisposition, *f.*
Aim, vn. viser (à), tendre; — va. diriger, lancer, ajuster
Aim, s. but, *m.*, visée, *f.*, point de mire, *m.*, objet, *m.*, coup, *m.*, conjecture, *f.*

Aimless, adj., **Aimlessly,** adv. sans but, sans objet
Air, s. air, *m.*, vent, *m.*, vapeur, *f.*, publicité, *f.*, renseignements, *pl. m.*, apparence, *f.*, manière affectée, *f.* *In the open —,* en plein air, à la belle étoile. *To let some —,* donner de l'air. *To take —,* transpirer, s'éventer. *To show —s, to put on —s,* se donner des airs, prendre des airs. *With something of an —,* avec un certain air
Air- . . ., d'air, de l'air, fait d'air, par l'air. —*-balloon,* aérostat, *m.* —*-bed,* matelas rempli d'air, *m.* —*-blown,* porté par les airs. —*-built castles,* châteaux en Espagne. —*-cell,* —*-chamber,* trachée, *f.* —*-drawn,* imaginaire. —*-embraced,* entouré d'air. —*-escape,* soupape à l'air, *f.* —*-gun,* fusil à vent, *m.* —*-holder,* tube à l'air, *m.* —*-hole,* soupirail, *m.*, évent, *m.* —*-jacket,* appareil de sauvetage, *m.* —*-pipe,* ventilateur, *m.* —*-pump,* machine pneumatique, *f.* —*-shaft,* puits d'aérage, *m.* —*-tight,* imperméable à l'air. —*-trap,* ventilateur, *m.* —*-vessel,* réservoir d'air, trachée
Air, va. donner de l'air à, aérer, éventer, sécher. *To — oneself,* prendre l'air. *Well —ed linen,* du linge bien sec
Airily, adv. allègrement
Airiness, s. exposition ouverte, *f.*, situation aérée, *f.*, vivacité, *f.*
Airing, s. promenade, *f.*, aérage, *m.*, ventilation, *f.*, exposition au feu (*of linen*), *f.* *To give an — to,* faire prendre l'air à. *To take an —,* aller prendre l'air
Airless, adj. sans air
Airy, adj. aérien, d'air, aéré, exposé à l'air, léger, délicat, vain, gai, allègre
Aisle, s. aile, *f.*, nef latérale, *f.*, bas-côté, *m.*
Aisled, past part. ayant des bas-côtés
Ajar, adv. entre-bâillé
Akimbo, adv. sur les hanches
Akin, adj. parent (de), allié (à)
Alabaster, s. albâtre, *m.* — adj. d'albâtre
Alack! interj. hélas!
Alacrity, s. allégresse, *f.*, ardeur, *f.*, empressement, *m.*
Alamode, adj. à la mode
Alarm, s. alarme, *f.*, frayeur, *f.*, réveil, *m.* *To take — at,* s'alarmer de. —*-bell,* cloche d'alarme, *f.*, tocsin, *m.* —*-clock,* réveille-matin, *m.*
Alarm, va. alarmer, donner l'alarme à
Alarmingly, adv. d'une manière alarmante
Alarmist, s. alarmiste, *m.*
Alarum, see ALARM
Alas! interj. hélas!
Alb, s. aube, *f.*
Albatross, s. albatros, *m.*

Albeit, conj. quoique
Albescent, adj. blanchissant
Albinos, s. albinos, *m.*
Albugineous, adj. albugineux
Album, s. album, *m.*
Albumen, s. albumine, *f.*
Alcaic, adj. alcaïque
Alcaid, Alcaide, s. alcade, *m.*
Alchymic, adj. alchimique
Alchymist, s. alchimiste, *m.*
Alcohol, s. alcool, *m.*
Alcoholic, adj. alcoolique
Alcoholize, va. alcooliser
Alcoholmeter, s. alcoomètre, *m.*
Alcoran, s. Coran, Alcoran, *m.*
Alcove, s. alcove, *f.*, niche, *f.*
Alcyon, s. adj. see HALCYON
Alder, s. aune, *m.* — *-plot*, aunaie, *f.*
Alderman, s. alderman, *m*
Aldermanry, s. dignité d'alderman, *f.*
Aldern, adj. de bois d'aune
Ale, s. ale, *f.*, bière forte, *f.* — *-bench*, banc de cabaret. — *-conner*, vérificateur des mesures pour la bière, *m.* — *-hoof*, lierre terrestre, *m.* — *-house*, cabaret, *m.* — *-house keeper*, cabaretier, *m.* — *-wife*, cabaretière, *f.* *Low* — *-house*, cabaret borgne, *m.*, bouchon, *m.*
Aleatory, adj. aléatoire
Alee, adv. sous le vent
Alembic, s. alambic, *m.*
Alert, adj. alerte, leste, agile, vif. — *s.* alerte, *f.*, alarme, *f.*
Alertness, s. vigilance, *f.*, agilité, *f.*
Alexandrine, s. adj. alexandrin, *m.*
Algebra, s. algèbre, *f.*
Algebraic, Algebraical, adj. algébrique
Algebraically, adv. algébriquement
Algebraist, s. algébriste, *m.*
Alguazil, s. alguazil, *m.*
Alias, adv. autrement nommé. — s. autre nom, *m.*
Alibi, s. alibi, *m.*
Alidade, s. alidade, *f.*
Alien, adj. étranger, opposé (à), éloigné (de). — s. étranger, étrangère
Alienability, s. qualité d'être aliénable
Alienable, adj. aliénable
Alienate, va. aliéner, détacher, s'aliéner
Alienate, adj. étranger (à), éloigné (de). — s. étranger, *m.*, étrangère, *f.*
Alienation, s. aliénation, *f.*, éloignement, *m.*, folie, *f.*
Alight, adj. allumé
Alight, vn. descendre, mettre pied à terre, s'abattre, tomber
Alike, adv. également, pareillement, de la même manière. — adj. semblable, pareil, indifférent (à), la même chose (pour)
Aliment, s. aliment, *m.*
Alimental, adj. nutritif
Alimentary, adj. alimentaire
Alimentation, s. alimentation, *f.*
Alimony, s. pension alimentaire, *f.*
Aliquant, adj. aliquante
Aliquot, adj. aliquote
Alive, adj. en vie, vivant, vif, sensible (à), animé, en train. — *to praise*, sensible à la louange. *The proudest man* —, l'homme du monde le plus orgueilleux
Alkalescent, adj. alcalescent
Alkali, s. alcali, *m.*
Alkaline, adj. alcalin
Alkalize, va. alcaliser
All, adj. tout, *m.*, toute, *f.* (*plur.* tous, toutes), entier. *We are three* — (*game*), nous sommes trois à trois. *For — that*, malgré cela. *For — she is a woman*, toute femme qu'elle est. — adv. tout, entièrement. *Not at* —, pas du tout. — *but*, excepté. — s. tous, *m.*, toutes, *f.* *Our — is at stake*, il s'agit de notre fortune tout entière. *He was — in — for me*, il était tout pour moi. —'s *well*, tout va bien, (*milit.*) sentinelles, prenez garde à vous! (*nav.*) bon quart!
All-, tout, tout à fait. — *-dreaded*, redouté de tous
Allah, s. Allah, *m.*
Allay, va. apaiser, calmer, allier; — vn. s'apaiser
Allay, s. see ALLOY
Allayer, s. personne qui adoucit, qui apaise
Allayment, s. apaisement, *m.*, allégement, *m.*
Allegation, s. allégation, *f.*
Allege, va. alléguer
Allegeable, adj. qu'on peut alléguer
Allegiance, s. allégeance, *f.*, obéissance, *f.*
Allegoric, Allegorical, adj. allégorique
Allegorically, adv. allégoriquement
Allegoricalness, s. nature allégorique, *f.*
Allegorist, s. allégoriste, *m.*
Allegorize, va. allégoriser
Allegory, s. allégorie, *f.*
Allegro, s. allegro, *m.*
Allelujah, s. alléluia, *m.*
Alleviate, va. alléger, adoucir, atténuer
Alleviation, s. allégement, *m.*, atténuation, *f.*
Alley, s. allée, *f.*, ruelle, *f.*, passage, *m.*, bille, *f.* *Side*-—, contre-allée, *f.* *Blind* —, impasse, *f.*, cul-de-sac, *m.*
All-Fools'-day, s. le 1er avril
All-fours, s. à quatre pattes, sorte de jeu de cartes
All-good, s. source de tout bien, *f.*
All-Hallows-day, s. la Toussaint
All-Hallowmas, All-Hallow-tide, s. le temps de la Toussaint, *m.*
Alliance, s. alliance, *f.*
Alligation, s. (*arith.*) alliage, *m.*, règle des mélanges, *f.* — *medial, alternate*, règle d'alliage simple, composée
Alligator, s. alligator, *m.*
Allision, s. choc, *m.*
Alliteration, s. allitération, *f.*
Alliterative, adj. d'allitération, plein d'allitération
Allocation, s. allocation, *f.*
Allocution, s. allocution, *f.*
Allodial, adj. allodial
Allonge, s. allonge, *f.*, (*for a horse*) longe, *f.*, (*fenc.*) botte, *f.*
Allonge, vn. allonger une botte
Allopathic, adj. allopathique
Allopathist, s. médecin allopathe, *m.*
Allopathy, s. allopathie, *f.*
Allot, va. distribuer, assigner, départir
Allotment, s. distribution, *f.*, lot, *m.*
Allow, va. admettre, reconnaître, avouer, permettre, souffrir, autoriser, accorder, allouer, déduire; — vn. tenir compte (de), avoir égard (à), excuser
Allowable, adj. admissible, permis
Allowableness, s. nature licite, *f.*
Allowably, adv. légitimement
Allowance, s. admission, *f.*, reconnaissance, *f.*, aveu, *m.*, permission, *f.*, pension, *f.*, argent de poche, *m.*, ration, *f.*, remise, *f.*, excuse, *f.* *To be on short* —, être rationné. *On half* —, à la demi-ration. *To make — for*, avoir égard à
Allowance, va. rationner
Alloy, s. alliage, *m.*, mélange, *m.*
Alloy, va. allier, corrompre, altérer
All-Saints'-day, s. la Toussaint
All-Souls'-day, s. le jour des Morts
All-spice, s. piment, *m.*
All-to, adv. complètement
Allude, vn. faire allusion
Allure, va. attirer, leurrer, allécher, engager
Allurement, s. attrait, *m.*, charme, *m.*
Allurer, s. tentateur, *m.*
Alluring, adj. attrayant, séduisant
Alluringly, adv. d'une manière attrayante
Alluringness, s. charme, *m.*, attrait, *m.*, séduction, *f.*
Allusion, s. allusion, *f.* *In — to*, par allusion à
Allusive, Allusory, adj. qui fait allusion, plein d'allusions
Allusively, adv. par allusion
Alluvial, Alluvious, adj. alluvial, d'alluvion
Alluvion, Alluvium, s. alluvion, *f.* —*via*, pl. terres d'alluvion, *f. pl.*
Ally, s. allié, *m.*
Ally, va. allier
Almanack, s. almanach, *m.*
Almightiness, s. toute-puissance, *f.*
Almighty, adj. s. tout-puissant
Almond, s. amande, *f.* — *-tree*, amandier, *m.* — *-furnace*, fourneau d'affineur, *m.* — *-willow*, saule blanc, *m.*
Almoner, s. aumônier, *m.*
Almonry, s. aumônerie, *f.*
Almost, adv. presque
Alms, s. l'aumône, *f.*, la charité, *f.* *To give* —, faire l'aumône. — *-deed*, œuvre de charité, *f.* — *-giving*, l'aumône. — *-houses*, maisons de charité, *f.* — *-man*, homme qui vit d'aumône, homme qui fait l'aumône
Aloe, *pl.* **Aloes,** s. aloès, *m.*
Aloft, adv. en haut, en l'air
Alone, adj. adv. seul, tout seul. *To let* or *leave* —, laisser tranquille, ne pas toucher à. *Let well* —, le mieux est l'ennemi du bien. *Let — his hasty temper*, à part sa vivacité
Along, adv. au long, en avant. *Get — with you*, allez-vous-en. *Come* —, venez donc. — *with*, avec. — prep le long de. — *-shore*, le long du rivage
Alongside, adv. (*nav.*) à côté de. *To come — of*, accoster. *Come — !* accoste!
Aloof, adv. à distance, à l'écart. *To stand* or *keep* —, se tenir à distance
Aloofness, s. distance, *f.*
Alopecy, s. l'alopécie, *f.*
Aloud, adv. à haute voix, haut
Alp, s. montagne, *f.* *The* —*s*, les Alpes, *f. pl.*
Alpaca, s. alpaca, *m.*, alpaga, *m.*
Alpha, s. alpha, *m.*
Alphabet, s. alphabet, *m.*
Alphabetic, Alphabetical, adj. alphabétique
Alphabetically, adv. alphabétiquement
Alpine, adj. alpestre, des Alpes
Already, adv. déjà
Also, adv. conj. aussi, de plus
Altar, s. autel, *m.* *High* —, maître-autel, *m.* — *-cloth*, nappe d'autel, *f.* — *-piece*, tableau d'autel, *m.* — *-screen*, retable, *m.*
Alter, va. changer, altérer, corriger; — vn. changer, se changer, se corriger
Alterable, adj. qu'on peut changer, variable
Alterant, adj. causant du changement
Alteration, s. changement, *m.*, altération, *f.*

Altercate, vn. avoir une altercation

Altercation, s. altercation, *f.*

Altern, adj. alterne

Alternacy, s. succession, *f.*, alternat, *m.*

Alternant, adj. alternant

Alternate, adj. alternatif, réciproque. — *rhyme*, rimes croisées. — adv. tour à tour

Alternate, va. faire alternativement, faire succéder; — vn. alterner, se succéder

Alternately, adv. tour à tour

Alternation, s. alternative, *f.*, alternation, *f.*

Alternative, adj. alternatif, successif. — s. alternative, *f.*

Alternatively, adv. alternativement

Although, conj. quoique, bien que

Altitude, s. altitude, *f.*, hauteur, *f.*

Alto, s. alto, *m.*

Altogether, adv. tout à fait, tout ensemble

Alum, s. alun, *m.* — *-pit*, alunière, *f.* — *-slate*, schiste alumineux, *m.* — *-stone*, alun de roche, *m.* — *-water*, eau alumineuse, *f.*

Alumina, Alumine, s. alumine, *f.*

Aluminous, adj. alumineux

Aluminium, s. aluminium, *m.*

Alumite, s. alun de roche, *m.*

Alveolar, adj. alvéolé

Alveolus, s. alvéole, *m.*

Always, adv. toujours

Amability, s. amabilité, *f.*

Amain, adv. avec force, (*nav.*) tout, tout ensemble

Amalgam, s. amalgame, *m.*

Amalgamate, va. amalgamer; — vn. s'amalgamer

Amalgamation, s. amalgamation, *f.*

Amanuensis, s. secrétaire, *m.*, copiste, *m.*

Amaranth, s. amarante, *f.*

Amaranthine, adj. amarante, d'amarante, impérissable

Amaryllis, s. amaryllis, *f.*

Amass, va. amasser

Amateur, s. amateur, *m.*

Amateurship, s. qualité d'amateur, *f.*

Amatory, adj. d'amour

Amaurosis, s. amaurose, *f.*

Amaze, va. étonner, surprendre, confondre

Amazedly, adv. dans la stupeur

Amazement, s. grand étonnement, *m.*, stupéfaction, *f.*, épouvante, *f.*

Amazing, adj. étonnant, terrifiant

Amazingly, adv. étonnamment, étrangement

Ambages, s.pl. ambages, *f.pl.*, détour, *m.*

Ambassade, s. ambassade, *f.*

Ambassador, s. ambassadeur, *m.*

Ambassadress, s. ambassadrice, *f.*

Amber, s. ambre, *m.* — *-dropping.* — *-weeping*, qui distille l'ambre. — adj. d'ambre

Amber, va. ambrer

Ambergris, s. ambre gris, *m.*

Ambidexter, s. ambidextre, *m.*, fripon, *m.*

Ambidextrous, adj. ambidextre, fourbe

Ambidextrousness, Ambidexterity, s. ambidextérité, *f.*, duplicité, *f.*

Ambient, adj. ambiant

Ambigu, s. ambigu, *m.*

Ambiguity, s. ambiguïté, *f.*

Ambiguous, adj. ambigu

Ambiguously, adv. ambigument, obscurément

Ambiguousness, s. ambiguïté, *f.*

Ambit, s. tour, contour, *m.*

Ambition, s. ambition, *f.*

Ambition, va. ambitionner

Ambitionless, adj. peu ambitieux

Ambitious, adj. ambitieux

Ambitiously, adv. ambitieusement

Ambitiousness, s. nature ambitieuse, *f.*, ambition, *f.*

Amble, vn. aller l'amble, trottiner

Amble, s. amble, *m.*

Ambler, s. cheval qui va l'amble, *m.*, haquenée, *f.*

Ambling, s. amble, *m.*

Amblingly, adv. à l'amble

Ambo, Ambon, s. (*arch.*) jubé, *m.*, ambon, *m.*

Ambrosia, s. ambroisie, *f.*

Ambrosial, adj. d'ambroisie, délicieux

Ambrosian, adj. d'ambroisie, ambroisien

Ambsace, s. ambesas, *m.*

Ambulance, s. ambulance, *f.*

Ambulant, adj. ambulant

Ambulatory, adj. ambulatoire

Ambuscade, s. embuscade, *f.*

Ambuscaded (to be), v. pass. s'embusquer, être embusqué

Ambush, s. embuscade, *f.*, embûche, *f.*, piége, *m.*

Ambush, va. embusquer; — vn. s'embusquer

Ameer, Amir, s. émir, *m.*

Ameliorate, va.n. améliorer, s'améliorer

Amelioration, s. amélioration, *f.*

Amen, adv. s. amen, *m.*

Amenability, Amenableness, s. responsabilité, *f.*

Amenable, adj. comptable, responsable, justiciable

Amend, va. amender, corriger, arranger; — vn. s'amender, se corriger

Amendable, adj. susceptible d'amendement, amendable

Amendatory, adj. qui corrige

Amender, s. réformateur, *m.*

Amendment, s. amendement, *m.*, réforme, *f.*, amélioration, *f.*

Amends, s. compensation, *f.*, dédommagement, *m.*

Amenity, s. aménité, *f.*

Amerce, va. condamner à une amende, punir, priver

Amercement, s. amende, *f.*, privation, *f.*

Americanism, s. américanisme, *m.*

Americanize, va. naturaliser Américain

Amess, s. aumusse, *f.*

Amethyst, s. améthyste, *f.*

Amethystine, adj. d'améthyste

Amiability, Amiableness, s. amabilité, *f.*

Amiable, adj. aimable

Amiably, adv. d'une manière aimable

Amianthus, s. amiante, *m.*

Amicable, adj. amical, bon

Amicableness, s. nature amicale, *f.*

Amicably, adv. amicalement

Amice, s. amict, *m.*

Amid, Amidst, adv. au milieu de, parmi

Amidships, adv. (*nav.*) au milieu du navire

Amiss, adj. adv. mal, mauvais, en mal, déplacé, indisposé. *To construe* —, interpréter en mal. *To speak* — *of*, parler mal de. *Nothing comes* — *to her*, elle s'arrange de tout

Amity, s. amitié, *f.*

Ammonia, s. ammoniaque, *f.*

Ammoniac, s. gomme ammoniaque, *f.*

Ammoniacal, adj. ammoniacal. — *salts*, sel ammoniac, *m.*

Ammonite, s. corne d'Ammon, *f.*, ammonite, *f.*

Ammunition, s. adj. munitions (de guerre), *f.pl.*, de munition

Amnesty, s. amnistie, *f.*

Among, Amongst, prep. parmi, entre, chez. *From* —, du milieu de

Amorous, adj. amoureux

Amorously, adv. amoureusement

Amorousness, s. amour, *m.*, tempérament amoureux, *m.*

Amount, vn. s'élever, se monter, monter

Amount, s. montant, *m.*, total, *m.*, somme, *f.* *To the* — *of*, jusqu'à concurrence de

Amour, s. amours, *f.pl.*

Amphibian, s. amphibie, *m.*

Amphibious, adj. amphibie

Amphibiousness, s. nature amphibie, *f.*

Amphibological, adj. amphibologique

Amphibologically, adv. amphibologiquement

Amphibology, s. amphibologie, *f.*

Amphibrach, s. amphibraque, *m.*

Amphictyonic, adj. amphictyonique

Amphictyony, s. Amphictyonie, *f.*

Amphictyons, s.pl. Amphyctions, *m.pl.*

Amphitheatre, s. amphithéâtre, *m.*

Amphitheatrical, adj. d'amphithéâtre

Amphora, s. amphore, *f.*

Ample, adj. spacieux, vaste, ample, copieux

Ampleness, s. étendue, *f.*, grandeur, *f.*, ampleur, *f.*

Ampliation, s. amplification, *f.*, accroissement, *m.*

Amplification, s. amplification, *f.*, accroissement, *m.*

Amplify, va. amplifier, exagerer; — vn. s'étendre

Amplitude, s. étendue, *f.*, ampleur, *f.*, grandeur, *f.*, amplitude, *f.*

Ampul, Ampulla, s. ampoule, *f.*

Amputate, va. amputer

Amputation, s. amputation, *f.*

Amulet, s. amulette, *m.*

Amusable, adj. amusable

Amuse, va. amuser, divertir

Amusement, s. amusement, *m.*, divertissement, *m.*, jeu, *m.*

Amuser, s. personne qui amuse

Amusing, adj. amusant

Amusingly, adv. d'une manière amusante

An, conj. si, comme si

Ana, s. ana, *m.*

Anabaptism, s. doctrine des Anabaptistes, *f.*

Anabaptist, s. Anabaptiste, *m.*

Anabaptistical, adj. d'anabaptiste

Anachronism, s. anachronisme, *m.*

Anaconda, s. Anaconda, *m.*

Anacreontic, adj. anacréontique. — s. pièce de vers anacréontique, *f.*

Anæsthesia, s. anesthésie, *f.*

Anæsthetic, s. adj. anesthésique, *m.*

Anagogy, s. anagogie, *f.*

Anagogical, adj. anagogique

Anagogics, s.pl. interprétations anagogiques, *f.pl.*

Anagram, s. anagramme, *m.*

Anagrammatic, adj. anagrammatique

Anagrammatist, s. anagrammatiste, *m.*

Anagrammatize, vn. anagrammatiser, faire des anagrammes

Analecta, s. pl. analectes, *m.pl.*

Analogical, adj. analogique

Analogically, adv. analogiquement

Analogize, va. expliquer analogiquement

Analogous, adj. analogue (à)

Analogy, s. analogie, *f.*, rapport, *m.*

Analysis, s. analyse, *f.*

Analyst, s. analyste, *m.*

Analytical, adj. analytique

Analytically, adv. analytiquement

Analytics, s. l'analytique, *f.*

Analyzable, adj. analysable

Analyzation, s. analyse, *f.*

Analyze, va. analyser

Analyzer, s. analyste, *m.*, dissolvant, *m.*

Ananas, s. ananas, *m.*

Anapæst, s. anapeste, *m.*

Anapæstic, adj. s. anapestique, pièce en vers anapestiques, *f.*

Anarchical, adj. anarchique

Anarchist, s. anarchiste, *m.*

Anarchy, Anarchism, s. anarchie, *f.*

Anathema, s. anathème, *m.*

Anathematism, Anathematization, s. déclaration d'anathème, *f.*

Anathematize, va. anathématiser

Anathematizer, s. celui, celle qui frappe d'anathème

Anatomic, Anatomical, adj. anatomique

Anatomically, adv. anatomiquement

Anatomist, s. anatomiste, *m.*

Anatomization, s. dissection, *f.*

Anatomize, va. anatomiser, disséquer, analyser

Anatomy, s. anatomie, *f.*, dissection, *f.*, analyse, *f.*, squelette, *m.*

Ancestor, s. ancêtre, *m.*, aïeul, *m.*

Ancestorial, Ancestral, adj. héréditaire, de ses ancêtres

Ancestress, s. aïeule, *f.*

Ancestry, s. suite d'ancêtres, *f.*, haute extraction, *f.*

Anchor, s. ancre, *f.* *To be, to lie, to ride at* —, être à l'ancre. *To come to an* —, mouiller l'ancre. *To cast, to drop* —, jeter l'ancre, mouiller, ancrer. *To weigh the* —, lever l'ancre. — *-ground*, mouillage, *m.* — *-stock*, jas d'ancre, *m.* *Sheet* —, maîtresse ancre, ancre de salut. *Bower* —, ancre d'affourche. *Flood* —, ancre de flot. *Ebb* —, ancre de jusant. *Shore* —, ancre de terre. *Sea* —, ancre du large. *Kedge* —, ancre à jet. *Spare* —, ancre de rechange

Anchor, vn. jeter l'ancre, s'ancrer; — va. mouiller l'ancre

Anchorage, s. mouillage, *m.*, les ancres, *f.pl.*, droit d'ancrage, *m.*

Anchored, past part. ancré

Anchorite, Anchoret, s. anachorète, *m.*

Anchovy, s. anchois, *m.*

Anchylosis, s. ankylose, *f.*

Ancient, adj. s. ancien, antique

Anciently, adv. anciennement

Ancientness, s. ancienneté, *f.*

Ancientry, s. ancienneté, *f.*, vieillerie, *f.*

And, conj. et, de...en. *Coffee — milk*, café au lait, *m.* *Coach — six*, voiture à six chevaux *f.*

Andante, adj. s. andante, *m.*

Andantino, adj. andantino

Andiron, s. chenet, *m.* *Small* —, chevrette, *f.*

Androgynous, adj. androgyne

Anecdote, s. anecdote, *f.*

Anecdotical, adj. anecdotique

Anecdotist, s. conteur d'anecdotes, *m.*

Anemometer, s. anémomètre, *m.*

Anemone, Anemony, s. anémone, *f.*

Anent, prep. vis-à-vis, touchant, sur

Aneurism, s. anévrisme, *m.*

Aneurismal, adj. anévrismal

Anew, adj. de nouveau, encore

Anfractuous, adj. anfractueux

Anfractuosity, s. anfractuosité, *f.*

Angel, s. ange, *m.*, messager, *m.*

Angel-fish, s. ange, *m.*

Angel-shot, s. boulet ramé, *m.*

Angel, Angelic, Angelical, adj. angélique, d'ange

Angelica, s. angélique, *f.*

Angelically, adv. d'une manière angélique

Angelicalness, s. nature angélique

Angelus, s. angelus, *m.*

Anger, s. colère, *f.*, courroux, *m.*

Anger, va. irriter, fâcher

Angina, s. angine, *f.*

Angle, s. angle, *m.*, coin, *m.*, (*fishing*) ligne, *f.* — *-rod*, canne à pêcher, *f.*

Angle, vn. pêcher à la ligne, (*fig.*) tâcher d'attirer; — va. captiver (*the hearts*)

Angled, adj. à angles

Angler, s. pêcheur à la ligne, *m.*

Anglican, s. adj. Anglican, *m.*, Anglicane, *f.*

Anglicism, s. anglicisme, *m.*

Anglicize, va. angliciser

Angling, s. la pêche à la ligne

Anglomania, s. anglomanie, *f.*

Anglo-Norman, s. adj. Anglo-normand, *m.*, Anglo-normande, *f.*

Anglo-Saxon, s. adj. Anglo-saxon, *m.*, Anglo-saxonne, *f.*

Angrily, adv. avec colère

Angry, adj. en colère, fâché, courroucé, porté à la colère. *To be — with*, être fâché, se fâcher contre. *To get or grow* —, se fâcher, se mettre en colère

Anguish, s. angoisse, *f.*, tourment, *m.*

Angular, adj. angulaire

Angularly, adv. angulairement

Angularity, s. forme angulaire, *f.*

Anile, adj. débile

Animadversion, s. observation, *f.*, animadversion, *f.*, reproche, *m.*

Animadvert, vn. observer, censurer, blâmer

Animadverter, s. observateur, *m.*, frondeur, *m.*, critique, *m.*

Animal, s. adj. animal, *m.*, d'animal

Animalcule, s. animalcule, *m.*

Animalism, s. nature animale, *f.*, doctrine de l'animalité, *f.*

Animality, s. animalité *f.*

Animalization, s. animalisation, *f.*

Animalize, va. animaliser

Animate, va. animer

Animate, adj. animé

Animated, adj. animé

Animating, adj. qui anime, encourageant

Animation, s. animation, *f.*

Animative, adj. qui anime

Animator, s. personne, chose qui anime

Animosity, s. animosité, *f.*

Anise, s. anis, *m.* — *-seed* or *aniseed*, graine d'anis, *f.*

Anker, s. quartaut

Ankle, s. cheville du pied, *f.* — *-deep*, jusqu'à la cheville

Anklet, s. anneau, *m.*

Annalist, s. annaliste, *m.*

Annals, s. plur. annales, *f.plur.*

Annats, s. plur. annates, *f.plur.*

Anneal, va. recuire, éprouver

Annealing, s. recuit, *m.*, recuite, *f.*

Annex, va. annexer, joindre, attacher

Annex, s. annexe, *f.*

Annexation, Annexion, Annexment, s. annexion, *f.*

Annihilate, va. anéantir, annihiler

Annihilate, adj. annihilé

Annihilation, s. anéantissement, *m.*, annihilation, *f.*

Annihilator, s. destructeur, *m.*

Anniversary, adj. s. anniversaire, jour anniversaire, *m.*

Annotate, va. annoter

Annotation, s. annotation, *f.*, note, *f.*

Annotator, s. annotateur, *m.*

Announce, va. annoncer, proclamer

Announcement, s. annonce, *f.*, proclamation, *f.*, affiche, *f.*

Announcer, s. celui qui annonce

Annoy, va. ennuyer, tourmenter, importuner, contrarier

Annoyance, s. ennui, *m.*, tourment, *m.*, contrariété, *f.*

Annoying, adj. ennuyeux, contrariant, gênant

Annual, adj. annuel, -le. — s. annuaire, *m.*, plante annuelle, *f.*

Annually, adv. annuellement, tous les ans

Annuitant, s. détenteur d'annuités, *m.*

Annuity, s. annuité, *f.* *Life* —, rente viagère, *f.*

Annul, va. annuler, effacer

Annular, Annulary, adj. annulaire

Annulment, s. annulation, *f.*

Annunciation, s. annonciation, *f.*, proclamation, *f.*, annonce, *f.*

Anodyne, s. adj. anodin, *m.*, calmant

Anoint, va. oindre, frotter

Anointing, Anointment, s. onction, *f.*

Anointer, s. celui qui oint

Anomalous, adj. anormal, irrégulier

Anomalously, adv. d'une manière anormale

Anomaly, Anomalism, s. anomalie, *f.*

Anon, adv. tout à l'heure, parfois. *Ever and* —, de temps à autre

Anonymous, adj. anonyme

Anonymously, adv. sous le voile de l'anonyme

Anonymousness, s. caractère anonyme, *m.*

Anormal, *also* **Abnormal,** adj. anormal

Another, adj. pron. un autre, une autre. *Just such* —, un tout pareil

Answer, vn. répondre, faire réponse, garantir, se porter garant (de), correspondre (à), suffire, faire le raisonneur (*fem.* la raisonneuse); — va. répondre (à), résoudre, satisfaire (à), payer, expier

Answer, s. réponse, *f.*, réfutation, *f.*, solution, *f.*

Answerable, adj. auquel on peut répondre, responsable, correspondant (à), équivalent

Answerably, adv. conformément

Answerer, s. personne qui répond, raisonneur, *m.*, raisonneuse, *f.*

Answering, adj. sympathique

Answerless, adj. sans réponse, sans réplique

Ant, s. fourmi, *f.* — *-bear,* fourmilier, *m.* — *-eater,* fourmi-lion, *m.* — *-hill,* — *-hillock,* fourmilière, *f.*

Antagonism, s. antagonisme, *m.*

Antagonist, s. antagoniste, *m.*

Antarctic, adj. antarctique

Antecede, va. précéder

Antecedence, s. antériorité, *f.*, (*astron.*) antécédence, *f.*

Antecedent, adj. s. antécédent, *m.*

Antecedently, adv. antérieurement

Antechamber, s. antichambre, *f.*

Antedate, va. antidater, anticiper sur

Antedate, s. antidate, *f.*

Antediluvian, adj. s. antédiluvien, *m.*

Antelope, s. antilope, *f.*

Antemeridian, adj. avant midi

Antenna, s. antenne, *f.*

Antepenult, Antepenultimate, adj. s. antépénultième, *m.*

Anterior, adj. antérieur

Anteriority, s. antériorité, *f.*

Anteroom, s. antichambre, *f.*

Anthem, s. antienne, *f.*, hymne, *m.*

Anther, s. anthère, *f.*

Anthology, s. anthologie, *f.*

Anthracite, s. anthracite, *m.*

Anthrax, s. anthrax, *m.*, charbon, *m.*

Anthropologist, s. professeur d'anthropologie, *m.*

Anthropology, s. anthropologie, *f.*

Anthropomorphism, s. anthropomorphisme, *m.*

Anthropophagous, adj. anthropophage

Anthropophagus, s. anthropophage, *m.*

Anthropophagy, s. anthropophagie, *f.*

Antibilious, adj. antibilieux, -se

Antic, adj. bouffon, grotesque, antique. — s. tour, *m.*, singerie, *f.*, bouffonnerie, *f.*, bouffon, *m.*, figure grotesque, *f.* *To play —s,* faire des tours, faire des gambades

Antichrist, s. Antechrist, *m.*

Antichristian, adj. antichrétien, -ne

Anticipant, adj. qui prévoit, qui prévient, etc.

Anticipate, va. anticiper, prévenir, aller au-devant de, prévoir, goûter par avance

Anticipation, s. anticipation, *f.*, prévision, *f.*, pressentiment, *m.*

Antidotal, adj. préservatif

Antidote, s. antidote, *m.*

Antilogy, s. antilogie, *f.*

Antimacassar, s. dossier de fauteuil, de canapé, *m.* (*ouvrage au crochet, m.*)

Antimonarchical, adj. antimonarchique

Antimonial, adj. antimonial

Antimony, s. antimoine, *m.*

Antinomy, s. antinomie, *f.*

Antipapal, adj. hostile à la papauté

Antipathetic, adj. antipathique

Antipathy, s. antipathie, *f.*

Antiphonal, Antiphonar, Antiphonary, s. antiphonaire, *m.*, antiphonier, *m.*

Antiphony, s. antiphonie, *f.*

Antiphrasis, s. antiphrase, *f.*

Antipode, s. antipode, *m.*

Antipope, s. antipape, *m.*

Antiquarian, adj. d'antiquaire

Antiquary, s. antiquaire, *m.*

Antiquarianism, s. goût d'antiquaire, *m.*

Antiquated, past part. suranné, vieilli, qui n'est plus de mode

Antique, adj. antique, ancien, à l'antique

Antiquely, adv. à l'antique

Antiquity, s. antiquité, *f.*, ancienneté, *f.*

Antiscorbutic, adj. s. antiscorbutique, *m.*

Antiseptic, adj. s. antiseptique, *m.*

Antislavery, adj. abolitioniste

Antisocial, adj. antisocial

Antispasmodic, adj. s. antispasmodique, *m.*

Antistrophe, s. antistrophe, *f.*

Antithesis, s. antithèse, *f.*

Antithetical, adj. antithétique

Antithetically, adv. par antithèse

Antitype, s. antitype, *m.*

Antler, s. (*horns*) bois, *m.*, andouiller, *m.*, cornes, *f.* *The brow —,* le maître andouiller

Antlered, past part. à la tête surmontée d'un bois

Antonomasia, s. antonomase, *f.*

Anvil, s. enclume, *f.* *To be on the —,* (*fig.*) être sur le chantier

Anxiety, s. inquiétude, *f.*, anxiété, *f.*, désir, *m.*

Anxious, adj. inquiet, soucieux, plein d'anxiété, désireux

Anxiously, adv. avec anxiété

Anxiousness, s. anxiété, *f.*

Any, pron. adj. aucun, quelque, du, de la, des, quelqu'un, quelques-uns, en, tout, quelconque, n'importe lequel. — *one,* — *body,* quelqu'un, quelques-uns, qui que ce soit. — ... *but,* tout autre ... que. — *man who,* tout homme qui. *Come at — time,* venez quand il vous plaira

Anyhow, adv. n'importe comment, dans tous les cas

Anything, pron. quelque chose, rien, tout ce que. — *but useful,* rien moins qu'utile

Anywhere, adv. n'importe où, quelque part

Anywise, adv. n'importe comment

Aorist, s. aoriste, *m.*

Aorta, s. aorte, *f.*

Apace, adv. vite, à vue d'œil

Apart, adv. à part, à l'écart, séparé. *To pull —,* séparer

Apartment, s. chambre, *f.*, appartement, *m.*

Apathetic, Apathetical, adj. apathique

Apathy, s. apathie, *f.*

Ape, s. singe, *m.*, guenon, *f.*

Ape, va. singer

Apeak, adv. à pic

Aper, s. imitateur, *m.*

Aperient, Aperitive, adj. apéritif

Aperture, s. ouverture, *f.*, croisée, *f.*

Apex, s. pointe, *f.*, sommet, *m.*

Aphæresis, s. aphérèse, *f.*

Aphelion, s. aphélie, *f.*

Aphorism, s. aphorisme, *m.*

Aphoristical, adj. aphoristique

Aphoristically, adv. par aphorisme

Aphthæ, s. plur. aphthes, *m.pl.*

Apiary, s. rucher, *m.*

Apiece, adv. pièce, la pièce, chacun, par tête

Apish, adj. singe, de singe, plein de fatuité. — *trick,* singerie, *f.*

Apishly, adv. comme un singe, avec fatuité

Apishness, s. singerie, *f.*, esprit d'imitation, *m.*, fatuité, *f.*

Apocalypse, s. apocalypse, *f.*

Apocalyptical, adj. apocalyptique

Apocope, s. apocope, *f.*

Apocrypha, s. pl. les livres apocryphes, *m.pl.*

Apocryphal, adj. apocryphe

Apogee, Apogæon, Apogeum, s. apogée, *m.*

Apologetic, Apologetical, adj. apologétique

Apologetically, adv. en excuse, d'un ton d'excuse

Apologist, Apologizer, s. apologiste, *m.*

Apologize, vn. s'excuser, faire des excuses

Apologue, s. apologue, *m.*

Apology, s. défense, *f.*, apologie, *f.*, excuse, *f.*

Apophthegm, also **Apothegm,** s. apophthegme, *m.*

Apoplectic, Apoplectical, adj. apoplectique. — *stroke,* attaque d'apoplexie, *f.*

Apoplexy, s. apoplexie, *f.*

Apostasy, s. apostasie, *f.*

Apostate, s. adj. apostat, *m.*

Apostatize, vn. apostasier

Aposteme, s. apostème, *m.*

Apostle, s. apôtre, *m.*

Apostleship, Apostolate, s. apostolat, *m.*

Apostolic, Apostolical, adj. apostolique

Apostrophe, s. apostrophe, *f.*

Apostrophize, va. apostropher

Apothecary, s. pharmacien, *m.*, apothicaire, *m.*

Apothegmatical, adj. sentencieux

Apotheosis, s. apothéose, *f.*

Appal, va. épouvanter

Appalling, adj. épouvantable, effrayant

Appallingly, adv. d'une manière effrayante

Appanage, s. apanage, *m.*

Apparatus, s. appareil, *m.*

Apparel, s. vêtements, *m. pl.*, habits, *m.pl.*, mise, *f.*, parure, *f.* *Wearing —,* habits, *m.*

Apparel, va. vêtir, parer, (*nav.*) équiper

Apparent, adj. visible, évident. *Heir —,* héritier présomptif, *m.*

Apparently, adv. apparemment, évidemment

Apparition, s. apparition, *f.*

Apparitor, s. appariteur, *m.*

Appeal, vn. en appeler (à), prendre à témoin, avoir recours (à)

Appeal, s. appel, *m.*, recours, *m.*

Appealing, adj. suppliant

Appear, vn. paraître, se montrer, apparaître, (*law*) comparaître

Appearance, s. apparition, *f.*, (*law*) comparution, *f.*, apparence, *f.*, air, *m.*, mine, *f.*, semblant, *m.*, probabilité, *f.* *First —,* début, *m.* *For — sake,* pour les apparences

Appearing, s. apparition, *f.*, air, *m.*

Appease, va. apaiser, calmer

Appeasement, s. apaisement, *m.*

Appeaser, s. personne qui apaise, *f.*

Appellant, s. appelant, -e

Appellation, s. nom, *m.*, appellation, *f.*

Appellative, s. nom commun, *m.*, nom, *m.*

Append, va. appendre, ajouter

Appendage, s. accessoire, *m.*, dépendance, *f.*, appendice, *m.*

Appendant, adj. accessoire, ajouté

Appendix, s. appendice, *m.*

Appertain, vn. appartenir

Appetence, Appetency, s. appétit, *m.*, appétence, *f.*

Appetite, s. appétit, *m.*, soif, *f.*, désir, *m.*

Appetize, va. donner de l'appétit (à)

Appetizer, s. chose qui donne de l'appétit

Applaud, va. applaudir

Applauder, s. celui, celle qui applaudit

Applause, s. applaudissement, *m.*

Applausive, adj. d'applaudissement

Apple, s. pomme, *f.*, prunelle (*of the eye*), *f.* *Crab-* —, pomme sauvage. — *-tart*, — *-pie*, tourte aux pommes. *In* — *-pie order*, rangé avec le plus grand soin. — *-tree*, pommier, *m.*

Appliable, Applicable, adj. applicable

Appliance, s. remède, *m.*, moyen, *m.*, instrument, *m.*, appareil, *m.*

Applicableness, Applicability, s. possibilité d'appliquer, *f.*

Applicant, s. solliciteur, *m.*, pétitionnaire, *m.*, postulant, *m.*, (*law*) demandeur, *m.*, demanderesse, *f.*

Application, s. application, *f.*, remède, *m.*, demande, *f.*, démarche, *f.*

Applicatory, adj. facile à appliquer

Apply, va. appliquer, porter, mettre, adresser; — vn. s'appliquer, avoir rapport, s'adresser (à), solliciter

Appoint, va. fixer, donner, désigner, prescrire, équiper (*troops*); — vn. décider, ordonner

Appointment, s. fixation, *f.*, désignation, *f.*, choix, *m.*, rendez-vous, *m.*, ordre, *m.*, emploi, *m.*, charge, *f.*, nomination, *f.*, équipement, *m.* *To make an* —, prendre rendez-vous, donner un rendez-vous (à)

Apportion, va. répartir, assigner

Apportionment, s. répartition, *f.*

Apposite, adj. à propos, juste, qui convient

Appositely, adv. à propos

Appositeness, s. à-propos, *m.*, justesse, *f.*, convenance, *f.*

Apposition, s. apposition, *f.*

Appraise, va. estimer, évaluer, priser

Appraisement, s. estimation, *f.*, évaluation, *f.*, appréciation, *f.*

Appraiser, s. commissaire-priseur, *m.*, estimateur, *m.*, expert, *m.*

Appreciable, adj. appréciable

Appreciate, va. apprécier

Appreciation, s. appréciation, *f.*

Appreciative, adj. appréciatif

Apprehend, va.n. saisir, prendre, appréhender au corps, imaginer, concevoir, craindre

Apprehensible, adj. concevable, imaginable

Apprehension, s. arrestation, *f.*, intelligence, *f.*, pensée, *f.*, appréhension, *f.*, crainte, *f.*

Apprehensive, adj. appréhensif, intelligent, craintif, inquiet

Apprehensively, adv. avec crainte

Apprehensiveness, s. vivacité de conception, *f.*, crainte, *f.*

Apprentice, s. apprenti, *m.*, apprentie, *f.*, (*of lawyers*) clerc, *m.*, novice, *m.* *To bind* — *to*, mettre en apprentissage chez

Apprentice, va. mettre en apprentissage

Apprenticeship, s. apprentissage, *m.*, noviciat, *m.* *To serve one's* —, faire son noviciat

Apprise, va. informer, avertir

Approach, vn.a. s'approcher, approcher, (*hortic.*) greffer en approche

Approach, s. approche, *f.*, accès, *m.*, avenue, *f.*, ressemblance, *f.*, (*math.*) approximation, *f.*

Approachable, adj. abordable, accessible

Approaching, adj. qui s'approche, prochain

Approachless, adj. inabordable

Approbation, s. approbation, *f.*, noviciat, *m.*

Approbatory, adj. approbateur, -trice; approbatif, -ve

Appropriate, va. s'approprier, s'appliquer, se rendre propre, approprier, affecter, destiner

Appropriate, adj. propre, approprié, juste

Appropriately, adv. convenablement, avec justesse, à juste titre

Appropriateness, s. convenance, *f.*, justesse, *f.*

Appropriation, s. appropriation, *f.*, application, *f.*, emploi, *m.*, chose allouée (*money, &c.*), *f.*

Appropriator, s. qui s'approprie, propriétaire, *m.*

Approvable, adj. digne d'approbation

Approval, Approvement, s. (*law*) dénonciation, *f.*

Approve, va. approuver, rendre digne d'approbation, essayer, dénoncer

Approved, adj. approuvé, éprouvé

Approver, s. approbateur, -trice, (*law*) dénonciateur, *m.*

Approving, adj. d'approbation, approbatif

Approvingly, adv. avec approbation

Approximate, adj. approximatif, approchant

Approximate, va.n. approcher, s'approcher

Approximately, adv. approximativement

Approximation, s. approximation, *f.*, rapprochement, *m.*

Approximative, adj. approximatif

Approximatively, adv. approximativement

Appurtenance, s. dépendance, *f.*, accessoire, *m.*

Apricot, s. abricot, *m.* — *-tree*, abricotier, *m.*

April, s. avril, *m.* — *fool*, poisson d'avril

Apron, s. tablier, *m.*, rebord (*of a window*), *m.*, platine, *f.*, (*nav., arch.*) contre-étrave, *f.*

Aproned, adj. à tablier

Apt, adj. propre, apte, porté, sujet, exposé, intelligent, prompt

Aptitude, s. aptitude, *f.*, talent naturel, *m.*, penchant, *m.*

Aptly, adv. convenablement, à propos, avec facilité

Aptness, s. convenance, *f.*, justesse, *f.*, aptitude, *f.*, penchant, *m.*, vivacité d'intelligence, *f.*

Aqua, s. eau, *f.* — *-fortis*, eau-forte, *f.*

Aquarius, s. le Verseau

Aquatic, Aquatical, adj. aquatique

Aqueduct, s. aqueduc, *m.*

Aqueous, adj. aqueux

Aquiline, adj. d'aigle, aquilin

Arab, s. adj. Arabe, *m.*, la langue arabe

Arabesque, s. adj. arabesque, *f.*

Arabian, adj. arabe, d'Arabie. *The — Nights*, les Mille et Une Nuits

Arabic, adj. arabe, arabique

Arable, adj. arable, labourable

Arbiter, s. arbitre, *m.*

Arbitrable, adj. arbitraire, qu'on peut décider

Arbitrament, s. arbitre, *m.*

Arbitrarily, adv. arbitrairement

Arbitrariness, s. l'arbitraire, *m.*

Arbitrary, adj. arbitraire, absolu

Arbitrate, vn. juger en arbitre. *To — upon*, décider de. — va. arbitrer

Arbitration, s. arbitrage, *m.* *By* —, arbitral, arbitralement

Arbitrator, s. arbitre, *m.*

Arbour, s. berceau, *m.* — *-vine*, vigne vierge, *f.*

Arboriculture, s. arboriculture, *f.*

Arborization, s. arborisation, *f.*

Arbute, — *-tree*, s. arbousier, *m.* — *-berry*, arbouse, *f.*

Arc, s. arc, *m.*

Arcade, s. arcade, *f.*

Arcanum, s. arcane, *m.*, secret, *m.*

Arch, s. voûte, *f.*, arche, *f.*, arc, *m.*, cintre, *m.* — *-stone*, voussoir, *m.*

Arch, va.n. faire la voûte, construire des voûtes, voûter, cintrer, arrondir. —*ed brow*, sourcils arqués, *m.pl.*

Arch, adj. grand, principal, archi. . ., arch. . ., insigne, espiègle. — *enemy*, grand ennemi, *m.* — *saying*, espièglerie, *f.*

Archaism, s. archaïsme, *m.*

Archangel, s. archange, *m.*

Archangelic, adj. d'archange

Archbishop, s. archevêque, *m.*

Archbishopric, s. archevêché, *m.*

Archchancellor, s. archichancelier, *m.*

Archdeacon, s. archidiacre, *m.*

Archdeaconry, s. archidiaconat, *m.*, archidiaconé, *m.*

Archdeaconship, s. archidiaconat, *m.*

Archducal, adj. archiducal

Archduchess, s. archiduchesse, *f.*

Archduchy, Archdukedom, s. archiduché, *m.*

Archduke, s. archiduc, *m.*

Archæologian, Archæologist, s. archéologue, *m.*

Archæological, adj. archéologique

Archæology, s. archéologie, *f.*

Archer, s. archer, *m.*

Archeress, s. tireuse à l'arc, *f.*

Archery, s. science de l'arc, *f.*, tir à l'arc, *m.*

Archetypal, adj. original

Archetype, s. archétype, *m.*

Archfiend, s. chef des démons, *m.*

Archidiaconal, adj. d'archidiacre

Archiepiscopacy, s. archiépiscopat, *m.*

Archiepiscopal, adj. archiépiscopal

Archimandrite, s. archimandrite, *m.*

Archipelago, s. archipel, *m.*

Architect, s. architecte, *m.*

Architectonic, adj. architectonique. —*s*, l'architectonique, *f.*

Architectural, adj. d'architecture, *f.*

Architecture, s. architecture, *f.*

Architrave, s. architrave *f.*

Archives, s. pl. archives, *f.pl.*
Archivist, s. archiviste, *m.*
Archivolt, s. archivolte, *f.*
Archlike, adj. en forme de voûte
Archly, adv. avec espièglerie, finement
Archness, s. espièglerie, *f.*, finesse, *f.*
Archon, s. archonte, *m.*
Archonship, s. archontat, *m.*
Archpriest, s. archiprêtre, *m.*
Archway, s. passage voûté, *m.*, arche, *f.*
Archwise, adv. en voûte, en cintre
Arctic, adj. arctique
Ardent, adj. ardent
Ardently, adv. avec ardeur
Ardour, s. ardeur, *f.*, chaleur, *f.*
Arduous, adj. ardu, escarpé, rude, difficile
Arduousness, s. difficulté, *f.*, caractère ardu, *m.*
Area, s. aire, *f.*, surface, *f.*, espace, *m.*, arène, *f.*, enceinte, *f.*, cour (*of a house*), *f.*, parvis (*of a temple*), *m.*
Arena, s. arène, *f.*
Arenaceous, adj. sablonneux
Areometer, s. aréomètre, *m.*
Areopagite, s. Aréopagite, *m.*
Areopagus, s. Aréopage, *m.*
Argentiferous, adj. argentifère
Argentine, adj. argentin
Argil, s. argile, *f.*
Argillaceous, adj. argileux
Argilliferous, adj. argilifère
Argonaut, s. Argonaute, *m.*
Argonautic, adj. des Argonautes
Argosy, s. navire, *m.*
Argue, vn. argumenter (contre), discuter (avec), raisonner, répondre. *It —s well for*, c'est un bon signe pour. — va. plaider, attester, convaincre
Arguer, s. dialecticien, *m.*, argumentateur, *m.*, raisonneur, *m.*
Arguing, s. raisonnement, *m.*, discussion, *f.*
Argument, s. argument, *m.*, discussion, *f.*, preuve, *f.*, motif, *m.*
Argumental, adj. du raisonnement
Argumentation, s. argumentation, *f.*
Argumentative, adj. démonstratif, raisonné, qui prouve, argumentateur
Argumentatively, adv. démonstrativement
Argus, s. Argus, *m.*
Arian, s. adj. Arien, -ne
Arianism, s. Arianisme, *m.*
Arid, adj. aride
Aridity, s. aridité, *f.*
Aries, s. (*astron.*) le Bélier
Arietta, s. ariette, *f.*
Arise, vn. s'élever, monter, se lever, se soulever, surgir, provenir
Aristarch, s. Aristarque, *m.*
Aristocracy, s. l'aristocratie, *f.*
Aristocrat, s. aristocrate, *m.*
Aristocratic, Aristocratical, adj. aristocrate, aristocratique
Aristocratically, adv. aristocratiquement
Aristotelian, adj. s. Aristotélicien, -ne
Arithmetic, s. l'arithmétique, *f.*
Arithmetical, adj. arithmétique, d'arithmétique
Arithmetically, adv. arithmétiquement
Arithmetician, s. arithméticien, *m.*
Ark, s. arche, *f.*
Arm, s. bras, *m.*, branche (*of a tree*), *f.*, arme, *f.*, armature, *f.*
Arm, va. armer, munir, garnir; — vn. s'armer, prendre les armes
Armadillo, s. tatou, *m.*
Armament, s. armement, *m.*
Armature, s. armure, *f.*, armature, *f.*
Arm-chair, s. fauteuil, *m.*
Armful, s. brassée, *f.*
Armhole, s. aisselle, *f.*
Armillary, adj. armillaire
Arming, s. armement, *m.*
Arminian, s. adj. Arminien, -ne
Armistice, s. armistice, *m.*
Armless, adj. sans armes
Armorial, adj. armorial. *— bearings*, armoiries, *f.pl.*
Armory, s. arsenal, *m.*, salle d'armes, *f.*, musée d'armes, *m.*, fabrique d'armes, *f.*
Armour, s. armure, *f.* *—-bearer*, écuyer. *Top- —*, (*nav.*) pavois, *m.*
Armpit, s. aisselle, *f.*
Arms, s.plur. armes, *f.pl.*, la guerre, *f.*, armement, *m.*, armoiries, *f.pl.*, (*mech.*) bras, *m.* *In —*, les armes à la main. *Man at —*, homme d'armes. *To take up —*, prendre les armes. *Carry, present, ground —!* portez, présentez, reposez armes! *Support —!* armes au bras! *Shoulder —!* portez armes! *A coat of —*, armoiries, *f.pl.*
Army, s. armée, *f.*, le service des armes, *m.*
Arnica, s. arnica, *m.*
Aroma, s. arome, *m.*
Aromatic, Aromatical, adj. aromatique
Aromatize, va. aromatiser
Around, adv. prep. autour, alentour. *All —*, tout autour, à la ronde
Arouse, va. réveiller, exciter, stimuler
Arquebuse, s. arquebuse, *f.*
Arquebusier, s. arquebusier, *m.*
Arrack, s. arrack, *m.*, rack, *m.*
Arraign, va. mettre en accusation, préparer (*a case*)
Arraigns, s.pl. mise en accusation, *f.*
Arrange, va. arranger, ranger; — vn. s'arranger
Arrangement, s. arrangement, *m.*
Arrant, adj. franc, fieffé, insigne
Arrantly, adv. notoirement
Arras, s. tentures, *f.plur.*, tapisseries à personnages, *f.plur.*
Array, s. ordre, *m.*, rang, *m.*, appareil, *m.*, étalage, *m.*, cortége, *m.*, ajustements, *m.plur.*, splendeur, *f.*, tableau (*of the jury*), *m.*, les jurés, *m.plur.*
Array, va. ranger, déployer, parer, envelopper, faire l'appel nominal
Arrear, s. arriéré, *m.*, arrérages, *m.pl.*, arrière-garde, *f.*
Arrearage, s. arrérages, *m.plur.*
Arrest, va. arrêter, fixer, saisir, suspendre (*a judgment*)
Arrest, s. arrêt, *m.*, arrestation, *f.*, les arrêts, *m.plur.*, suspension (*of a judgment*), *f.* *To put under —*, envoyer aux arrêts
Arrestation, s. arrestation, *f.*
Arris, s. (*arch.*) arête, *f.*
Arrival, s. arrivée, *f.*, (*nav., com.*) arrivage, *m.*
Arrive, vn. arriver, parvenir
Arrogance, Arrogancy, s. arrogance, *f.*
Arrogant, adj. arrogant
Arrogantly, adv. arrogamment
Arrogate, vn. s'arroger
Arrogation, s. prétention, *f.*, (*law*) adoption publique, *f.*
Arrow, s. flèche, *f.*, trait, *m.*
Arsenic, s. arsenic, *m.*
Arsenical, adj. arsenical, d'arsenic
Arson, s. crime d'incendie, *m.*
Art, s. art, *m.*, habileté, *f.* *The black —*, la magie, *f.*
Arterial, adj. artériel
Artery, s. artère, *f.*
Artesian, adj. d'Artois, artésien. *— well*, puits artésien, *m.*
Artful, adj. fait avec art, habile
Artfully, adv. avec art
Artfulness, s. art, *m.*, habileté, *f.*, artifice, *m.*, caractère rusé, *m.*
Artichoke, s. artichaut, *m.* *The bottom of an —*, un cul d'artichaut, *m.* *Jerusalem —*, topinambour, *m.*
Article, s. article, *m.*, conditions, *f.plur.*, clause, *f.*, moment, *m.* *The —s of war*, les règlements militaires, de marine, *m.pl.* *Leading —*, article de fond, *m.*
Article, va. articuler, accuser, mettre en apprentissage. *—d clerk*, clerc, *m.* *—d pupil*, élève en pharmacie, *m.*, élève institutrice, *f.* — vn. stipuler
Articular, adj. articulaire
Articulate, adj. articulé, distinct, exposé article par article
Articulate, va.n. articuler, prononcer, faire une convention
Articulately, adv. distinctement, article par article
Articulation, s. articulation, *f.*
Artifice, s. artifice, *m.*, ruse, *f.*
Artificer, s. fabricant, *m.*, artisan, *m.*
Artificial, adj. artificiel, factice, fictif
Artificially, adv. artificiellement
Artificialness, s. nature artificielle, *f.*
Artillery, s. artillerie, *f.* *Field —, flying —*, artillerie de campagne, légère. *Heavy —*, grosse artillerie, *f.*
Artisan, s. artisan, *m.*
Artist, s. artiste, *m.*
Artistic, adj. artistique
Artistically, adv. avec art, artistement
Artless, adj. peu habile (dans), ignorant (de), naïf, simple, innocent, candide. *— girl*, (*theat.*) ingénuité, *f.*, rôle d'ingénuité, *m.*
Artlessly, adv. naïvement, simplement, innocemment
Artlessness, s. naïveté, *f.*, simplicité, *f.*, innocence, *f.*, candeur, *f.*
As, s. as, *m.*
As, adv. comme, tel que, en, pour, en tant que, en qualité de. — . . . —, aussi . . . que. *— if, — though*, comme si, comme. *— it were*, pour ainsi dire. *— for, — to*, quant à, pour. — conj. comme, pendant que, puisque, suivant que
Asbestos, s. asbeste, *m.*
Ascend, vn.a. monter, s'élever, atteindre
Ascendant, s. ascendant, *m.*
Ascendency, s. ascendant, *m.*, empire, *m.*, influence, *f.*, supériorité, *f.*, le dessus, *m.*
Ascending, adj. ascendant
Ascension, s. ascension, *f.*
Ascensional, adj. ascensionnel
Ascent, s. ascension, *f.*, montée, *f.*
Ascertain, va. s'assurer de, savoir, constater, vérifier, fixer
Ascertainable, adj. dont on peut s'assurer

Ascertainment, s. règle certaine, *f.*, certitude, *f.*, assurance, *f.*
Ascetic, s. adj. ascète, *m.*, ascétique
Asceticism, s. ascétisme, *m.*
Asclepiad, s. asclépiade, *m.*
Ascribable, adj. qu'on peut attribuer, imputable
Ascribe, va. attribuer
Ash, s. frêne, *m.*, bois de frêne, *m.* *Mountain* —, le frêne sauvage
Ashamed, part. honteux, confus. *To be* —, avoir honte, rougir (de). *To be quite* —, être tout honteux. *You make me* —, vous me faites rougir
Ashelf, adv. échoué
Ashen, adj. en bois de frêne, de couleur cendrée
Ashlar, s. moellon, *m.* —*work*, maçonnerie de moellon, *f.*
Ashore, adv. à terre, échoué. *To get* —, prendre terre. *To set* —, débarquer. *To run* —, échouer
Ashy, adj. cendré, de cendres, pâle
Aside, adv. de côté, à l'écart, à part. — prep. à côté de
Asinine, adj. d'âne
Ask, vn.a. demander, chercher, s'informer, interroger, prier, inviter, publier les bans (*of marriage*)
Askance, adv. de côté, de travers. *To look — at, to eye* —, regarder de travers
Asker, s. demandeur, *m.*, solliciteur, *m.*, (*anim.*) lézard d'eau, *m.*
Askew, adv. de travers, de biais
Aslant, adv. prep. obliquement, de biais, en travers de
Asleep, adv. adj. endormi. *To be fast —, sound* —, être profondément endormi
Aslope, adv. de biais, obliquement, en talus
Asp, s. aspic, *m.*
Asparagus, s. asperges, *f.pl.* *A bundle of* —, une botte d'asperges
Aspect, s. aspect, *m.*, air, *m.*
Aspen, s. tremble, *m.* — adj. de tremble, tremblant. —*-tree*, tremble, *m.*
Asperity, s. aspérité, *f.*, rudesse, *f.*
Asperse, va. asperger, calomnier, diffamer
Asperser, s. calomniateur, *m.*, -trice, *f.*
Aspersion, s. aspersion, *f.*, (*fig.*) pluie, *f.*, calomnie, *f.*, diffamation, *f.*
Aspersive, adj. calomnieux
Aspersively, adv. calomnieusement
Asphalt, Asphaltum, s. asphalte, *m.*
Asphaltic, adj. asphaltique
Asphodel, s. asphodèle, *m.*
Asphyxia, s. asphyxie, *f.* *To put an end to oneself by* —, s'asphyxier
Aspic, s. aspic, *m.*
Aspirant, s. aspirant (à), *m.*, candidat (pour), *m.* — adj. ambitieux
Aspirate, va.n. aspirer, prendre l'aspiration
Aspirate, s. esprit rude, *m.*
Aspiration, s. aspiration, *f.*, élan, *m.* *Soft* —, esprit doux
Aspire, vn. aspirer (à), ambitionner, s'élever
Aspiring, s. aspiration, *f.*, élan, *m.* — adj. ambitieux
Aspiringly, adv. ambitieusement
Asquint, adv. de travers, en louchant
Ass, s. âne, *m.*, sot, *m.* *A wild* —, un onagre. *She-* —, ânesse, *f.*
Assafœtida, s. assa-fœtida, *f.*
Assail, va. attaquer, assaillir, critiquer vivement
Assailable, adj. attaquable
Assailant, Assailer, s. assaillant, *m.*, agresseur, *m.*
Assassin, s. assassin, *m.*
Assassinate, va.n. assassiner
Assassination, s. assassinat, *m.*
Assault, s. assaut, *m.*, attaque, *f.* — *and battery*, voies de fait
Assault, va. attaquer, frapper (*the ears*)
Assay, s. essai, *m.*, épreuve, *f.*
Assay, va. essayer, mettre à l'essai
Assayer, s. essayeur, *m.*
Assemblage, s. assemblage, *m.*
Assemble, va. assembler, réunir; — vn. s'assembler, se réunir
Assembler, s. qui assemble
Assembling, s. réunion, *f.*, rassemblement, *m.*
Assembly, s. assemblée, *f.*, réunion, *f.* —*-room*, salon, *m.*
Assent, s. assentiment, *m.* *To nod* —, faire un signe d'assentiment
Assent, vn. donner son assentiment, consentir, reconnaître
Assert, va. affirmer, assurer
Assertion, s. assertion, *f.*, soutien, *m.*, revendication, *f.*
Assertor, s. défenseur, *m.*
Assess, va. imposer, répartir (*taxes*), taxer, fixer. —*ed taxes*, impôts directs
Assessment, s. imposition, *f.*, répartition, *f.*, assiette (*of taxes*), *f.*, taxe, *f.*, fixation, *f.*
Assessor, s. assesseur, *m.*, aide, *m.*, répartiteur (*of taxes*), *m.*
Assets, s. actif, *m.*, dettes actives, *f.pl.*
Asseverate, va. affirmer solennellement
Asseveration, s. affirmation, *f.*, protestation, *f.*
Assiduity, s. assiduité, *f.*
Assiduous, adj. assidu
Assiduously, adv. assidûment
Assiduousness, s. assiduité, *f.*
Assign, va. assigner, désigner, fixer, (*law*) céder, transférer
Assignable, adj. assignable, qu'on peut constater
Assignation, s. désignation, *f.*, rendez-vous, *m.*, (*law*) cession, *f.*, transfert, *m.*
Assignee, s. ayant cause, *m.*, cessionnaire, *m.*, (*bankruptcy*) syndic, *m.*
Assignment, s. nomination, *f.*, assignation, *f.*, transfert (*of property*), *m.*
Assigns, s.pl. ayant-causes, *m.pl.*
Assimilable, adj. qu'on peut assimiler
Assimilate, vn.a. s'assimiler, assimiler
Assimilation, s. assimilation, *f.*
Assimilative, adj. d'assimilation
Assist, vn.a. aider, assister
Assistance, s. aide, *f.*, secours, *m.*, assistance, *f.*
Assistant, adj. qui aide, auxiliaire. — s. aide, *m.*, assistant, *m.*
Assize, s. session, *f.*, assises, *f.pl.*, taxe (*of provisions*), *f.*
Assizer, s. vérificateur, *m.*
Associate, vn. s'associer, fréquenter, hanter; — va. associer, combiner
Associate, adj. s. confédéré, allié, adjoint, associé, -e
Association, s. association, *f.*
Assort, va.n. assortir, convenir
Assortment, s. assortiment, *m.*
Assuage, va. apaiser, calmer, modérer, soulager; — vn. diminuer, s'apaiser
Assuagement, s. soulagement, *m.*, adoucissement, *m.*
Assuasive, adj. touchant
Assume, va. prendre, se donner, revêtir, s'attribuer, affecter, supposer; — vn. présumer trop de soi-même, s'en faire accroire
Assuming, adj. arrogant
Assumption, s. action de prendre, de revêtir, *f.*, supposition, *f.*, Assomption, *f.*
Assurance, s. assurance, *f.*
Assure, va. assurer, rassurer, enhardir
Assured, adj. certain, assuré
Assuredly, adv. assurément
Assuredness, s. assurance, *f.*
Assurer, s. personne qui assure
Aster, s. aster, *m.* *China* —, reine Marguerite, *f.*
Asterisk, s. astérisque, *m.*
Astern, adv. à l'arrière, derrière
Asteroid, s. astéroïde, *m.*
Asthma, s. asthme, *m.*
Asthmatic, adj. asthmatique
Astir, adv. debout, en émoi
Astonish, va. étonner, surprendre
Astonishing, adj. étonnant
Astonishingly, adv. étonnamment
Astonishment, s. étonnement, *m.*
Astound, va. étonner, frapper de stupeur, étourdir, effrayer
Astraddle, adv. à califourchon
Astragal, s. astragale, *m.*
Astral, adj. astral
Astray, adv. du droit chemin
Astride, adv. à califourchon
Astringent, adj. astringent
Astrolabe, s. astrolabe, *m.*
Astrologer, s. astrologue, *m.*
Astrologic, Astrological, adj. astrologique
Astrologically, adv. par l'astrologie
Astrology, s. astrologie, *f.*
Astronomer, s. astronome, *m.*
Astronomic, Astronomical, adj. astronomique
Astronomically, adv. astronomiquement
Astronomy, s. astronomie, *f.*
Astute, adj. astucieux
Astuteness, s. astuce, *f.*
Asunder, adv. en deux, séparément, à part
Asylum, s. asile, *m.*, hospice, *m.*
Asymptote, s. asymptote, *f.*
At, prep. à, auprès de, chez, en, contre
Atheism, s. l'athéisme, *m.*
Atheist, s. adj. athée, *m.*
Atheistic, Atheistical, adj. athée, d'athée
Atheistically, adv. en athée
Athenæum, s. athénée, *m.*
Athlete, s. athlète, *m.*
Athletic, adj. athlétique, d'athlète
Athwart, prep. adv. à travers, (*nav.*) par le travers (de)
Atilt, adv. la lance en arrêt
Atlas, s. atlas, *m.*
Atmosphere, s. atmosphère, *f.*
Atmospheric, Atmospherical, adj. atmosphérique
Atom, s. atome, *m.*
Atomic, Atomical, adj.

des atomes, atomique, corpusculaire

Atone, vn. s'accorder, être d'accord

Atonement, s. réconciliation, *f.*, expiation, *f.*, compensation, *f.*

Atony, s. atonie, *f.*

Atrabilarian, Atrabilarious, adj. atrabilaire

Atrocious, adj. atroce

Atrociously, adv. atrocement

Atrociousness, Atrocity, s. atrocité, *f.*

Atrophied, adj. atrophid

Atrophy, s. atrophie, *f.*

Attach, va. attacher, arrêter

Attaché, s. attaché (*of an embassy*), *m.*

Attachment, s. attachement, *m.*, affection, *f.*, (*law*) saisie-arrêt, *f.*

Attack, va. attaquer, s'attaquer (à)

Attack, s. attaque, *f.*

Attain, va.n. parvenir (à), atteindre (à)

Attainable, adj. qu'on peut atteindre

Attainder, s. atteinte, *f.*, tache, *f.*, condamnation, *f.*

Attainment, s. portée, *f.*, atteinte, *f.*, acquisition, *f.*, talent, *m.*, connaissances, *f. plur.*

Attaint, va. porter atteinte (à), flétrir, corrompre, condamner

Attaint, s. atteinte, *f.*, tache, *f.*, flétrissure, *f.*, condamnation, *f.*

Attempt, va. tenter, essayer

Attempt, s. tentative, *f.*, essai, *m.*, attaque (contre), *f.*, attentat (*criminal*), *m.*

Attend, va. faire attention (à), écouter, se rendre (à) (*to one's duty*), obéir (à), suivre, accompagner, donner des leçons (à); — vn. faire attention, prendre garde, écouter, soigner, s'occuper (de)

Attendance, s. service, *m.*, assistance, *f.*, présence, *f.*, attention, *f.*

Attendant, adj. qui accompagne, qui suit, dépendant (de) — s. serviteur, *m.*, compagnon, *m.*

Attention, Attentiveness, s. attention, *f.*, soin, *m.*

Attentive, adj. attentif, appliqué, plein d'attention, assidu

Attentively, adv. attentivement

Attenuate, va. atténuer, diminuer

Attenuation, s. atténuation, *f.*

Attest, va. attester

Attestation, s. attestation, *f.*

Attester, Attestor, s. témoin, *m.*

Attic, s. mansarde, *f.*, attique, *m.*

Attic, adj. attique

Atticism, s. Atticisme, *m.*

Attire, va. parer, vêtir, habiller

Attire, Attiring, s. vêtements, *m.pl.*, appareil, *m.*, ajustements, *m.plur.*, atours, *m.plur.*

Attitude, s. attitude, *f.*

Attorney, s. avoué, *m.*, procureur, *m.*

Attorneyship, s. charge de procureur, d'avoué, *f.*, procuration, *f.*

Attract, va. attirer

Attractability, s. obéissance aux lois de l'attraction, *f.*

Attraction, s. attraction, *f.*, attrait, *m.*, charme, *m.*

Attractive, adj. attractif, attrayant

Attractively, adv. par attraction, d'une manière attrayante

Attractiveness, s. attraction, *f.*, attrait, *m.*, séduction, *f.*

Attractor, s. agent qui attire, *m.*

Attributable, adj. qu'on peut attribuer

Attribute, va. attribuer

Attribute, s. attribut, *m.*

Attribution, s. attribution, *f.*

Attributive, adj. s. attributif, attribut, *m.*

Attrition, s. attrition, *f.*

Attune, va. mettre à l'unisson, accorder

Auburn, adj. châtain, châtain clair

Auction, s. vente aux enchères, *f.*

Auctioneer, s. commissaire-priseur, *m.*

Audacious, adj. audacieux

Audaciously, adv. audacieusement

Audaciousness, Audacity, s. audace, *f.*

Audible, adj. facile à entendre

Audibly, adv. à haute voix, intelligiblement, distinctement

Audience, s. action d'écouter, *f.*, audience, *f.*, auditoire, *m.*

Audit, va.n. apurer, vérifier (*accounts*)

Audit, s. audition, *f.*, apurement, *m.*

Auditor, s. auditeur, censeur, *m.*

Auditorship, s. charge d'auditeur, *f.*

Auditory, s. auditoire, *m.*, salle du tribunal, *f.*

Auditory, Auditorial, adj. auditif

Auger, s. tarière, *f.*

Aught, pron. quelque chose

Augment, va.n. augmenter, s'augmenter

Augment, s. accroissement, *m.*, augment, *m.*

Augmentation, s. augmentation, *f.*, accroissement, *m.*

Augmentative, adj. s. augmentatif

Augur, s. augure, *m.*, devin, *m.*, devineresse, *f.*

Augur, vn.a. augurer, conjecturer

Auguration, s. divination, *f.*

Augurer, s. augure, *m.*

Augury, s. augure, *m.*

August, s. août, *m.* — adj. auguste

Augustine, adj. s. de l'ordre de saint Augustin

Augustly, adv. majestueusement

Augustness, s. majesté, *f.*

Aulic, adj. aulique

Aumnce, s. aumusse, *f.*

Aunt, s. tante, *f.*

Aureate, adj. doré

Auricle, s. oreillette, *f.*

Auricula, s. oreille d'ours, *f.*

Auricular, adj. auriculaire

Auriferous, adj. aurifère

Aurochs, s. urus, auroch, *m.*

Aurora, s. aurore, *f.* — *Borealis*, aurore boréale, *f.*

Auscultation, s. auscultation, *f.*

Auspice, s. auspices, *m.pl.*

Auspicious, adj. heureux, propice, d'un bon augure

Auspiciously, adv. sous d'heureux auspices, favorablement

Austere, adj. austère

Austerely, adv. avec austérité

Austereness, Austerity, s. austérité, *f.*

Austral, adj. austral

Authentic, Authentical, adj. authentique

Authentically, adv. authentiquement

Authenticate, va. prouver l'authenticité (de)

Authentication, s. preuve authentique, *f.*, attestation légale, *f.*, légalisation, *f.*

Author, s. auteur, *m.*, cause, *f.*

Authoress, s. femme auteur, *f.*

Authoritative, adj. d'autorité

Authoritatively, adv. avec autorité

Authoritativeness, s. autorité, *f.*

Authority, s. autorité, *f.*, influence, *f.*

Authorization, s. autorisation, *f.*

Authorize, va. autoriser, sanctionner

Authorship, s. qualité d'auteur, *f.*

Autobiography, s. autobiographie, *f.*

Autochthone, s. autochthone, *m.*

Autocracy, s. autocratie, *f.*

Autocrat, s. autocrate, *m.*, autocratrice, *f.*

Autograph, s. autographe, *m.*

Autographic, Autographical, adj. autographique

Autography, s., autographie, *f.*

Automatic, Automatical, Automatous, adj. automatique, d'automate

Automatism, s. automatisme, *m.*

Automaton, s. automate, *m.*

Autonomy, s. autonomie, *f.*

Autumn, s. automne, *m.*

Auxiliar, Auxiliary, adj. s. auxiliaire, aide, *m.*

Avail, va.n. profiter (à), servir, favoriser. *To — oneself*, vr. mettre à profit, profiter (de), se servir (de)

Availability, Availableness, s. efficacité, *f.*, validité, *f.*

Available, adj. valable, profitable

Avalanche, s. avalanche, *f.*

Avarice, s. avarice, *f.*

Avaricious, adj. avare

Avariciously, adv. en avare, avec avarice

Avariciousness, s. avarice, *f.*

Ave, Ave-Mary, Ave-Maria, s. avé, *m.*, avé maria, *m.*

Avenge, va. venger, faire justice, tirer vengeance de

Avenger, s., **Avenging,** adj. vengeur, *m.*, vengeresse, *f.*

Aventurine, s. aventurine, *f.*

Avenue, s. avenue, *f.*

Aver, va. affirmer

Average, s. moyenne, *f.*, (*nav.*) avarie, *f.*

Average, va. prendre la moyenne (de), répartir également; — vn. revenir terme moyen (à), former une moyenne (de)

Averment, s. affirmation, *f.*, attestation, *f.*

Averse, adj. qui a de l'éloignement

Averseness, Aversion, s. aversion, *f.*, éloignement, *m.*, répugnance, *f.*

Avert, va. détourner, écarter, éloigner

Avidity, s. avidité, *f.*

Avocation, s. occupation, *f.*

Avoid, va. éviter, évacuer, annuler; — vn. se retirer, devenir nul

Avoidable, adj. facile à éviter

Avoidance, s. fuite, *f.*, épuisement, *m.*

Avouch, va. affirmer, déclarer, avouer

Avow, va. avouer

Avowal, s. aveu, *m.*

Avowedly, adv. de son propre aveu, ouvertement

Avowry, s. défense (*law*)

Avuncular, adj. d'oncle

Await, vn. attendre

Awake, va. éveiller, réveiller; — vn. s'éveiller, se réveiller

Awakening, s. réveil, *m.* — adj. qui réveille, d'alarme

Award, va. adjuger, décerner

Award, s. sentence, *f.*, sentence arbitrale, *f.*
Awarder, s. arbitre, *m.*
Aware, adj. observateur, instruit (de), qui sait, au fait (de)
Away, adv. au loin, absent, dehors, en route
Awe, s. crainte respectueuse, *f.*, terreur, *f.*
Awe, va. imposer (à), faire trembler
Awful, adj. imposant, majestueux, terrible
Awfully, adv. avec une frayeur respectueuse
Awhile, adv. un moment, pendant quelque temps
Awkward, adj. gauche, maladroit
Awkwardly, adv. gauchement, maladroitement
Awl, s. alène, *f.*
Awning, s. petite tente, *f.*, auvent, *m.*
Awry, adj. de travers
Axe, s. hache, *f.*, cognée, *f.*
Axiom, s. axiome, *m.*
Axis, s. axe, *m.*
Axle, s. essieu, *m.*, axe, *m.*, tourillon, *m.*
Aye, **Ay**, s. oui. — adv. toujours
Azalea, s. azalée, *f.*
Azimuth, s. azimut, *m.* — adj. d'azimut, azimutal
Azote, s. azote, *m.*
Azure, adj. azuré. — s. azur, *m.*
Azyme, s. adj. azyme, *m.*

B

B, s. B, b, *m.*, (*mus.*) si, *m.* — *natural*, bécarre, *m.* — *flat*, bémol, *m.*
Baa, **Baaing**, s. bêlement, *m.*
Baa, vn. bêler
Babble, vn.a. * babiller, jaser, gazouiller
Babble, s. babil, *m.*
Babbler, s. babillard, *m.*, babillarde, *f.*
Babbling, s. babil, *m.*, babillement, *m.*, babillage, *m.*, murmure, *m.*
Babe, s. enfant, *m.*, petit innocent, *m.*
Baboon, s. babouin, *m.*
Baby, s. enfant, *m.*, bébé, *m.*, poupée, *f.* — *-linen*, — *-things*, —*'s clothes*, layette, *f.* — *-house*, maison de poupée, *f.*
Babyish, adj. enfantin
Baccalaureate, s. baccalauréat
Bacchanalia, **Bacchanals**, s.pl. bacchanales, *f.pl.*
Bacchanalian, s.adj. bachique
Bacchante, s. bacchante, *f.*
Bachelor, s. garçon, *m.*, célibataire, *m.* —*'s button*, bluet (*flower*), *m.* —*'s degree*, diplôme de bachelier. — *of arts*, bachelier ès arts
Bachelorship, s. célibat, *m.*
Back, s. dos, *m.*, derrière, *m.*, revers (*hand*), *m.*, dossier (*of a chair*), *m.*, fond (*of a carriage, chimney, &c.*), *m.*, râble (*of a hare, rabbit, &c.*), *m.*, (*milit.*) arrière-garde, *f.* *At the* — *of*, derrière. — adj. de derrière, arrière . . ., éloigné. — *stairs*, — *pair of stairs*, escalier dérobé, escalier de service, *m.* — *door*, porte de derrière, *f.* — *parlour*, petit salon, *m.* — *seat*, siége de derrière, *m.*, fond, *m.* — *stroke*, coup d'arrière, *m.* — *-hander*, d'un coup du revers de la main. — *-ground*, fond, *m.*, arrière-plan, *m.* — adv. arrière, en arrière, derrière, de retour
Back, va.n. enfourcher, monter (sur), appuyer, seconder, parier (pour), faire reculer, mettre au dos (à), écrire sur le dos (de), contre-signer. *To — out of*, sortir à reculons de, se retirer de. *To — the sails*, masquer les voiles
Backed, adj. au dos . . ., qui a le dos . . . *Broad-* —, aux larges épaules
Backbite, va. médire (de)
Backbiter, s. médisant, *m.*
Backbiting, s. médisance, *f.*
Backbone, s. épine du dos, *f.*
Backer, s. soutien, *m.*, ami, *m.*, parieur, *m.*
Backgammon, s. trictrac, *m.* — *-board*, trictrac, *m.*
Backhanded, adj. donné avec le revers de la main, déloyal
Backing, s. mouvement en arrière, *m.*, reculade, *f.*, recul, *m.*
Backside, s. derrière, *m.*
Backslide, vn. apostasier
Backslider, s. apostat, *m.*
Backsliding, s. apostasie, *f.*
Backstay, s. galhauban, *m.*
Backstitch, s. arrière-point, *m.*
Backsword, s. espadon, *m.*
Backward, **Backwards**, adv. en arrière, à la renverse, à reculons, rétrogradant, à rebours
Backward, adj. peu disposé à, tardif, lent, d'une conception lente, en retard
Backwardly, adv. à contre-cœur, mal
Backwardness, s. lenteur, *f.*, répugnance, *f.*, peu de disposition, *m.*
Backwoodsman, s. habitant des bois, *m.*
Bacon, s. lard, *m.* — *-fed*, nourri de lard. *To save one's* —, se tirer d'affaire sain et sauf
Bad, adj. mauvais, méchant, malade, mal, nuisible (à), triste
Badge, s. insignes, *m.pl.*, marque, *f.*, médaille, *f.*, signe, *m.*, symbole, *m.*
Badger, s. blaireau, *m.* —*'s hair*, poil de blaireau, *m.*
Badger, va. harceler, tourmenter
Badly, adv. mal. — *off*, pauvre, malheureux
Badness, s. mauvaise qualité, *f.*, mauvais état, *m.*, méchanceté, *f.*
Baffle, va. échapper (à), se dérober (à), déconcerter
Baffler, s. celui *or* celle qui déjoue
Bag, s. sac, *m.*, bissac, *m.* *Money-* —, sacoche, *f.* — *-net*, filet, *m.*
Bag, va. mettre dans des sacs, mettre dans sa gibecière, (*billiards*) mettre dans la blouse; — vn. enfler, s'enfler
Bagatelle, s. bagatelle, *f.*, petite table de billard, *f.*
Baggage, s. bagage, *m.*, friponne, *f.*
Bagging, s. toile à sac, *f.*, mise en sacs, *f.*
Bagpipe, s. cornemuse, *f.*, musette, *f.*
Bagpiper, s. joueur de cornemuse, *m.*
Bail, s. caution, *f.*, garant, *m.*
Bail, va. mettre en liberté sous caution, cautionner
Bailable, adj. qu'on peut admettre à caution
Bailiff, s. bailli (*law officer*), *m.*, garde de commerce, *m.*, inspecteur, *m.* —*'s man*, garnisaire, recors, *m.*
Bailiwick, s. bailliage, *m.*
Bait, va. amorcer, appâter, donner à manger (à), faire reposer, harceler *Bull-* —*ing*, combat de taureaux, *m.* — vn. s'arrêter pour se rafraîchir
Bait, s. appât, *m.*, amorce, *f.*, rafraîchissement (*on a journey*), *m.*
Baize, s. serge, *f.*
Bake, va.n. sécher, calciner, faire cuire, se calciner
Bakehouse, s. boulangerie, *f.*, four, *m.*, raffinerie (*for sugar*), *f.*
Baker, s. boulanger, *m.*, boulangère, *f.* —*'s man*, garçon boulanger, *m.*, mitron, *m.*
Baking, s. cuisson, *f.*, cuite (*of bricks, &c.*), *f.*, boulangerie, *f.*, fournée (*of bread*), *f.*
Balance, s. balance, *f.*, équilibre, *m.*, balancier (*of a watch*), *m.* — *-maker*, balancier, *m.* — *-pole*, balancier, *m.* — *-weight*, contrepoids, *m.* — *-knife*, couteau à bascule, *m.* *To lose one's* —, perdre l'équilibre. *To strike a* —, faire la balance. — *-sheet*, bilan, *m.* — *-wheel*, balancier, *m.*
Balance, va. peser, balancer; — vn. balancer, hésiter
Balancing, s. balancement, *m.*
Balcony, s. balcon, *m.*
Bald, adj. chauve, pelé, nu, méprisable
Balderdash, s. balivernes, *f.pl.*
Baldly, adv. pauvrement
Baldness, s. calvitie, *f.*, sécheresse, *f.*
Baldric, s. baudrier, *m.*
Bale, s. ballot, *m.*
Bale, va. mettre en ballot, vider l'eau
Baleful, adj. funeste, dangereux
Balefully, adv. d'une manière funeste
Balk, s. poutre, *f.*, (*agric.*) billon, *m.*, déception, *f.*
Balk, va. tromper l'attente (de), frustrer, déjouer
Ball, s. boule, *f.*, globe, *m.*, balle, *f.*, ballon, *m.*, pelote (*of silk, &c.*), *f.*, peloton, *m.*, bille (*of billiards*), *f.*, prunelle (*of the eye*), *f.*, boulette (*of meat*), *f.*, bol (*pill*), *m.*, bal, *m.*
Ballad, s. ballade, *f.*, romance, *f.*
Ballast, s. lest, *m.*, sable (*roads*), *m.* *To sail in* —, partir sur lest. *Shingle* —, lest en pierre, *m.* — *-lighter*, bateau délesteur, *m.*
Ballast, va. lester, empierrer (*roads*)
Ballastage, s. droit de lestage, *m.*
Ballasting, s. lestage, *m.*, lest, *m.*, empierrement, *m.*
Ballet, s. ballet, *m.* — *-master*, directeur des ballets, *m.*
Ballista, s. baliste, *f.*
Ballistic, adj. de balistique
Ballistics, s. plur. la balistique
Balloon, s. ballon, *m.*, aérostat, *m.*
Ballot, s. scrutin, *m.*, vote au scrutin, *m.* — *-box*, urne du scrutin, *f.*
Ballot, vn. élire au scrutin
Balloting, s. vote au scrutin, *m.*
Balm, s. baume, *m.*, mélisse, *f.*
Balm, va. oindre, baigner, rafraîchir
Balmily, adv. doucement
Balminess, s. douceur, *f.*

Balmy, adj. balsamique, qui produit le baume, embaumé, doux, rafraîchissant
Balsam, s. baume, m., balsamine, f.
Balsamic, Balsamical, adj. balsamique
Baluster, s. balustre, m.; —s, rampe (*of a staircase*), f.sing.
Balustered, past part. à balustres
Balustrade, s. balustrade, f.
Bamboo, s. bambou, m.
Bamboozle, va. attraper, duper
Ban, s. ban, m., malédiction, f., défense, f.
Ban, va. maudire, interdire
Banana, s. bananier, m., (*fruit*) banane, f.
Banco, s. banco, m.
Band, s. bande, f., lien, m., fers, m.pl., bandage, m., bandeau, m., cordon (*hat*), m., rabat, m., musique, f., orchestre, m. *With a full* —, à grand orchestre
Band, vn. se réunir en troupe, se liguer
Bandage, s. bandage, m., bandeau, m.
Bandanna, s. foulard, m.
Bandbox, s. carton, m. —*-maker*, cartonnier, m.
Bandelet, s. bandelette, f.
Bandit, s. brigand, m., bandit, m.
Bandog, s. chien de garde, m.
Bandy, va. envoyer, se renvoyer, échanger; — vn. se disputer
Bandy-leg, s. jambe torte, f.
Bandy-legged, adj. bancal
Bane, s. poison, m., malheur, m., ruine, f.
Baneful, adj. venimeux, empoisonné, funeste
Banefulness, s. nature funeste, f.
Bang, va. battre, maltraiter, fermer (*a door*) avec bruit
Bang, s. coup, m., bruit (*of a door*), m. —! interj. pan!
Banian, s. figuier d'Inde, m.
Banish, va. bannir, exiler
Banishment, s. bannissement, m., exil, m.
Banister, s. *see* BALUSTER
Bank, s. banc (*grass, flowers*), m., remblai (*of earth*), m., terrasse, f., bord, m., rivage, m., (*mar.*) banc, m., banque, f., maison de banque, f. —*-bill*, —*-note*, billet de banque, m. —*-post bill*, mandat de la banque, m. —*-stock*, —*securities*, actions de la banque, f.pl.
Bank, va. remblayer, encaisser; — vn. avoir pour banquier
Banker, s. banquier, m., (*mar.*) terre-neuvier, m.
Banking, s.adj. banque, f., de banque
Bankrupt, adj. en faillite, en banqueroute, ruiné. — s. failli, m., banqueroutier, m. —*'s certificate*, concordat, m. *To become a* —, faire faillite
Bankruptcy, s. faillite, f., banqueroute, f. *Court of* —, cour des faillites, f.
Banner, s. bannière, f., étendard, m.
Bannered, adj. avec des bannières
Banneret, s. (*a knight*) banneret, m., petite bannière, f.
Bannock, s. gâteau d'avoine, m.
Banquet, s. banquet, m., festin, m.
Banquet, va. donner des banquets (à), fêter; — vn. festiner
Banter, va. railler, plaisanter
Banter, Bantering, s. raillerie, moquerie, f.
Banterer, s. railleur, m., railleuse, f., goguenard, m.
Bantering, adj. railleur, goguenard
Bantling, s. bambin, m., marmot, m.
Baobab, s. baobab, m.
Baptism, s. baptême, m.
Baptismal, adj. baptismal
Baptist, s. Baptiste, m., Anabaptiste, m.
Baptistery, s. baptistère, m.
Baptize, va. baptiser. *To — privately*, ondoyer
Bar, s. barre, f., barreau, m., barrière, f., obstacle, m., comptoir (*public-house*), m., petite salle, f. —*-iron*, fer en barre, m. —*-post*, poteau de barrière, m. —*-maid*, fille de comptoir, f.
Bar, va. barrer, empêcher, défendre, éloigner, excepter, (*law*) prescrire. *To — out*, barrer la porte contre
Barb, s. barbe, f., pointe (*arrows, &c.*), f., cheval barbe, m.
Barb, va. armer (*an arrow*)
Barbarian, s. adj. barbare, m.f.
Barbarism, s. barbarie, f., barbarisme, m.
Barbarity, s. barbarie, f., cruauté, f.
Barbarous, adj. barbare
Barbarously, adv. d'une manière barbare
Barbarousness, s. barbarie, f.
Barbary, s. cheval barbe, m.
Barbecue, s. bœuf, cochon, etc., rôti tout entier
Barbecue, va. rôtir tout entier
Barbed, adj. barbelé (*arrow, &c.*), armé, acéré (*horse*), bardé de fer
Barbel, s. barbeau, m., barbillon, m.
Barber, s. barbier, m.
Barberry, s. épine-vinette, f.
Barbican, s. barbacane, f.
Barcarolle, s. barcarolle, f.
Bard, s. barde, m.
Bard, va. barder (*a horse, &c.*)
Bardic, adj. des bardes
Bare, adj. nu, découvert, (*tree*) dépouillé, simple, seul. — s. (*arts*) le nu
Bare, va. mettre à nu, découvrir, dépouiller
Barebone, s. squelette, m.
Areboned, adj. décharné
Barefaced, adj. à visage découvert, effronté, impudent
Barefacedly, adv. ouvertement, impudemment
Barefoot, Barefooted, adj. pieds nus, nu-pieds. —*friar* or *Carmelite*, Carme déchaussé
Barege, s. barége, m.
Bareheaded, adj. tête nue, chapeau bas
Barelegged, adj. les jambes nues, nu-jambes
Barely, adv. pauvrement, à peine
Barenecked, adj. le cou nu
Bareness, s. nudité, f., maigreur, f., dénûment, m.
Barepicked, adj. rongé de près
Bareworn, adj. usé jusqu'à la corde, (*field*) brouté de près
Bargain, s. marché, m., occasion, f., bonne affaire, f.
Bargain, vn. marchander, convenir
Barge, s. barque, f., chaloupe, f., chaland, m.
Bargeman, s. batelier, m.
Bark, s. écorce, f., quinquina, m., (*mar.*) barque, f., (*dogs*) aboiement, m. —*-pit*, fosse de tanneur
Bark, va. écorcer; — vn. aboyer
Barker, s. aboyeur, m.
Barking, s. aboiement, m., décortication (*of a tree*), f.
Barley, s. orge, f. *Peeled* —, orge mondé, m. *Pearl* —, orge perlé, m. —*-water*, tisane d'orge, f.
Barn, s. grange, f. —*-door fowls*, poules et poulets
Barn, va. engranger
Barnacle, s. (*shell*) anatife, m., (*bird*) barnache, f.; *plur.* besicles, f.pl.
Barometer, s. baromètre, m.
Barometrical, adj. barométrique
Barometrically, adv. au moyen du baromètre
Baron, s. baron, m.
Baronage, s. l'assemblée des barons, f.
Baroness, s. baronne, f.
Baronet, s. baronnet, m.
Baronetcy, s. rang de baronnet, m.
Baronial, adj. de baron
Barony, s. baronnie, f.
Barouche, s. barouche, f.
Barrack, s. caserne, f., baraque, f., hutte, f. —*-master*, quartier-maître
Barratry, s. baraterie, f.
Barrel, s. baril (*guns, &c.*), m., canon, m., caisse (*drum*), f., tuyau (*quill*), m., barillet (*watch*), m., cylindre (*organ*), m. —*-organ*, orgue de Barbarie, f.
Barrel, va. mettre en baril, encaquer, bomber, faire bomber (*a road*). *Double-barrelled gun*, fusil à deux coups, m.
Barren, adj. stérile, aride, dénué (de), sans intelligence
Barrenness, s. stérilité, f.
Barricade, s. barricade, f., barrière, f.
Barricade, va. barricader, barrer
Barrier, s. barrière, f.
Barrister, s. avocat, m.
Barrow, s. brouette, f., tumulus, m., tertre, m., verrat (*pig*), m. *A hand-* —, un brancard, une civière
Barter, va. échanger, troquer; — vn. trafiquer, faire un échange
Barter, s. échange, m., troc, m., (*arith.*) règle des échanges
Baryta, s. baryte, f.
Barytone, s.adj. baryton, m.
Basalt, s. basalte, m.
Basaltic, adj. basaltique
Base, adj. bas, inférieur, illégitime, indigne, ignoble, vil. — s. base, f., fondement, m., piédestal, m., barrière, f., (*play*) barres, f.pl., (*mus.*) basse, f. —*-clef*, clef de fa, f. *Thorough* —, basse continue. *Double* —, contrebasse, f.
Base, va. baser
Baseless, adj. sans base, chimérique
Basely, adv. bassement
Basement, s. (*arch.*) soubassement, m., rez-de-chaussée, m.
Baseness, s. bassesse, f., peu de valeur, m., gravité (*of sound*), f.
Bashaw, s. pacha, m.
Bashful, adj. timide, honteux
Bashfully, adv. timidement, modestement, avec pudeur
Bashfulness, s. timidité, f., mauvaise honte, f., modestie, f.
Basil, s. (*botan.*) basilic, m., (*leather*) basane, f.
Basilica, s. basilique, f.
Basilisk, s. basilic, m.
Basin, s. bassin, m., cuvette, f.
Basis, s. base, f., fondement, m.
Bask, vn. se chauffer, s'étendre, se coucher; — va. chauffer, exposer
Basket, s. panier, m., corbeille, f., bourriche (*for fish, game, &c.*), f., hotte, f., (*arch.*) corbeille, f. —*-maker*, vannier, m. —*-making*, —*-work*, vannerie, f. —*-hilted sword*, épée à poignée en coquille, f.
Bas-relief, s. bas-relief, m.
Bass, s. tilleul d'Amérique, m., écorce de tilleul, f. —

-mat, natte d'écorce, *f.*, paillasson, *m.*
Bass, s. adj. (*mus.*) *see* BASE
Bassoon, s. basson, *m.*
Bassoonist, s. basson, *m.*
Bastard, s.adj. bâtard, *m.*, bâtarde, *f.*, illégitime
Bastardize, va. déclarer illégitime
Baste, va. battre, bâtonner, arroser (*meat*), bâtir, faufiler (*needle-work*)
Bastinado, s. bastonnade, *f.*
Bastinado, va. donner la bastonnade (à), bâtonner
Bastion, s. bastion, *m.*
Bastioned, adj. bastionné
Bat, s. batte, *f.*, battoir, *m.*, crosse, *f.*, morceau, *m.*, chauve-souris, *f.*
Batch, s. fournée, *f.*
Bate, va. rabattre, diminuer, retrancher
Bath, s. bain, *m.* — *sent home*, bain à domicile. *Sitting —*, bain de siége
Bathe, va. baigner, arroser, bassiner (*a wound*); — vn. se baigner
Bather, s. baigneur, *m.*, baigneuse, *f.*
Bathing, s. bains, *m.pl.* — *gown*, peignoir, *m.* — *tub*, baignoire, *f.*
Bathos, s. pathos, *m.*, galimatias, *m.*
Bating, prep. hormis
Battalion, s. bataillon, *m.*
Batten, va. engraisser; — vn. s'engraisser
Batten, s. volige, *f.*
Batter, s. pâte, *f.*
Batter, va. battre, battre en brèche, délabrer, bossuer. *To — down*, renverser. *—ing-piece*, pièce de siége, *f.* *—ing-train*, artillerie de siége, *f.* *—ing-ram*, bélier, *m.*
Battery, s. batterie, *f.*, (*law*) voies de fait, *f.pl.*
Battle, s. bataille, *f.* — *piece*, tableau de bataille, *m.*, bataille, *f.*
Battle, vn. combattre, batailler
Battledoor, s. raquette, *f.*
Battlement, s. créneau, *m.*
Battlemented, adj. crénelé
Battling, s. combat, *m.*
Bauble, *see* BAWBLE
Baulk, *see* BALK
Bavin, s. cotret, *m.*
Bawble, s. marotte (*of a fool*), *m.*, babiole, *f.*, bagatelle, *f.*
Bawl, vn. crier, brailler, criailler
Bawler, s. braillard, *m.*
Bawling, s. cris, *m.pl.*, criaillerie, *f.*
Bay, adj. s. bai, *m.*, baie, *f.*, golfe, *m.* — *salt*, sel gris, *m.* — *of joists*, travée, *f.* — *-window*, fenêtre en saillie, *f.* — *-tree*, laurier, *m.* *At —*, aux abois. *To bring to —*, acculer
Bay, vn.a. aboyer, poursuivre, cerner
Baying, s. aboiement, *m.*
Bayonet, s. baïonnette, *f.*
Bayonet, va. percer de coups de baïonnette
Bazaar, s. bazar, *m.*
Be, vn. être, exister, consister; (with *there*), il y a, il est, il existe; avoir (*hungry, thirsty, &c.*), faire (*fine, bad, &c.*), se porter, aller (*well, ill, &c.*), devoir, falloir. *It is with . . . as with . . .*, il en est de . . . comme de. *How are you?* comment allez-vous? *We are to set off*, nous devons partir. *What is that to me?* qu'est-ce que cela me fait?
Beach, s. rivage, *m.*, plage, *f.* *Sandy —*, grève, *f.*
Beached, adj. plein de galets, échoué
Beachy, adj. de rivages
Beacon, s. feu, *m.*, signal (*of alarm*), *m.*, (*nav.*) fanal, *m.*, (*nav.*) balise, *f.*
Bead, s. grain, *m.*, perle, *f.*, chapelet, *m.*, goutte, *f.* *Glass —s*, perles en verre, verroterie, *f.* *String of —s*, collier, *m.*, chapelet, *m.* *To say over one's —s*, dire son chapelet
Beadle, s. bedeau, *m.*, appariteur, *m.*
Beadroll, s. liste, *f.*
Beagle, s. chien courant, *m.*
Beak, s. bec, *m.*, avant (*of a ship*), *m.* *—full*, becquée
Beaked, adj. à bec, à pic
Beaker, s. gobelet, *m.*, coupe, *f.*
Beam, s. poutre, *f.*, (*nav.*) bau, *m.*, (*scales*) fléau, *m.*, (*carriage*) timon, *m.*, (*bell*) mouton, *m.*, (*weaver*) ensouple, *m.*, (*machine*) balancier, *m.*, (*light*) rayon, *m.*, éclat, *m.* *Small —*, poutrelle, *f.* *Abaft the —*, un peu par l'arrière. *—tree*, alisier, *m.*
Beam, vn. rayonner, briller; — va. darder, faire rayonner
Beamless, adj. morne, sans éclat
Beamy, adj. radieux, massif, (*stag*) aux bois élevés
Bean, s. fève, *f.*, haricot, *m.* *Common —*, *garden —*, fève de marais. *Horse —*, féverole, *f.* *French —s*, haricots verts. *White kidney —s*, haricots blancs
Bear, va. porter, supporter, transporter, avoir, comporter, admettre, enfanter. *There is no —ing you*, vous êtes insupportable. *To — hard*, en vouloir à. *To — oneself*, se comporter. *To — along, to — away*, emporter, entraîner, emmener, remporter. *To — back*, remporter, repousser. *To — down*, accabler. *To — on*, exciter, encourager. *To — off*, emporter, emmener. *To — out*, soutenir, défendre. *To — through*, porter, à travers, soutenir, justifier. *To — up*, supporter, soulever. *To — with*, avoir patience avec, être indulgent pour. — vn. endurer, supporter. *To — upon*, avoir trait (à), (*nav.*) porter, se diriger (vers). *To — away, off*, (*nav.*) s'éloigner. *To — back*, reculer. *To — down upon*, (*nav.*) porter, s'approcher de. *To — hard upon*, traiter durement. *To — onward*, se porter en avant. *To — out*, (*wall*) faire saillie, résister. *To — up*, tenir bon
Bear, s. ours, *m.*, ourse, *f.*, (*exchange*) baissier, *m.* — *-whelp*, ourson, *m.* *—baiting*, combat d'ours, *m.* — *-garden*, lieu pour les combats d'ours, lieu bruyant, *m.*
Bearable, adj. supportable
Beard, s. barbe, *f.*, pointe, *f.*
Beard, va. prendre par la barbe, braver
Bearded, adj. barbu, (*arrow*) barbelé
Beardless, adj. imberbe
Bearer, s. porteur, *m.*, porteuse, *f.*, (*archit.*) support, *m.* *Cross —*, porte-croix, *m.*
Bearing, s. mise au monde, *f.*, rapport, *m.*, port, *m.*, maintien, *m.*, mine, *f.*, conduite, *f.*, aspect, *m.*, (*nav.*) gisement, *m.*, hauteur, *f.*, support, *m.*, (*herald.*) armoiries, *f.pl.* — *-surface*, point d'appui, *m.*
Bearish, **Bearlike**, adj. d'ours, grossier
Beast, s. bête, *f.*, animal, *m.*, brute, *f.*
Beastlike, adj. bestial
Beastliness, s. bestialité, *f.*, saleté, *f.*
Beastly, adj. bestial, sale, vilain
Beat, va. battre, se frapper, broyer, piler, se briser contre, surpasser. *To — back*, repousser. *To — down*, renverser, rabattre. *To — in*, enfoncer, défoncer. *To — into*, faire entrer. *To — off*, repousser. *To — up*, battre, réveiller. — vn. battre, se briser contre, (*nav.*) louvoyer. *To — about*, chercher partout, (*nav.*) louvoyer, réfléchir à
Beat, s. coup, *m.*, battement, *m.*, (*policemen*) ronde, *f.*, station, *f.*, (*mus.*) mesure, *f.*
Beaten, adj. battu, frayé, rebattu
Beater, s. batteur, *m.*, batte, *f.*
Beatific, adj. béatifique
Beatification, s. béatification, *f.*
Beatify, va. béatifier
Beating, s. coups, *m.pl.*, correction, *f.*, battement (*of the heart, &c.*), *m.*
Beatitude, s. béatitude, *f.*
Beau, s. élégant, *m.*, petit-maître, *m.*
Beauteous, adj. beau, *m.*, belle, *f.*, ravissant
Beauteously, adv. d'une manière ravissante
Beauteousness, s. beauté, *f.*
Beautifier, s. celui, celle qui embellit, ce qui embellit
Beautiful, adj. beau, *m.*, belle, *f.*
Beautifully, adv. admirablement, supérieurement
Beautifulness, s. beauté, *f.*
Beautify, va. embellir, rendre beau, orner; — vn. s'embellir
Beautifying, s. embellissement, *m.*
Beauty, s. beauté, *f.*, (*fam.*) belle, *f.* — *spot*, grain de beauté, *m.*, mouche, *f.*
Beaver, s. castor, *m.*, visière, *f.*, casque, *m.*
Beccafico, s. bec-figue, *m.*
Becalm, va. calmer, tranquilliser, (*nav.*) abriter
Becalming, s. calme, *m.*
Because, adv. parce que, de ce que
Bechance, va.n. arriver (à)
Bechance, adv. par hasard
Beck, s. signe de tête, *m.*, signe de doigt, *m.*, ordre, *m.*, ruisseau, *m.* *To be at the — and call of*, être aux ordres de
Beckon, vn.a. faire signe, faire signe à
Become, vn. devenir; — va. convenir (à), seoir (à), aller (à)
Becoming, adj. convenable, bienséant, gracieux, qui sied à
Becomingly, adv. convenablement, avec grâce
Becomingness, s. bienséance, *f.*, grâce, *f.*
Bed, s. lit, *m.*, coucher, *m.*, (*hortic.*) parterre, *m.*, (*vegetables*) couche, *f.*, (*road*) encaissement, *m.*, (*mechan.*) fondation, *f.*, (*artil.*) coussin de mire, *m.* *Four-post —*, lit à colonnes. *To be in —*, être au lit. *To go to —*, se coucher. *To get into —*, se mettre au lit. *To put to —*, coucher. *To take to one's —*, s'aliter. *To be brought to — of*, accoucher de. *—chamber*, *—room*, chambre à coucher, *f.* — *clothes*, les draps et les couvertures. — *hangings*, rideaux de lit. — *linen*, draps de lit, *m.pl.* — *maker*, garçon (*servant*), *m.*, chambrière, *f.* — *post*, colonne de lit, *f.* — *side*, côté du lit. *From — and board*, (*law*) de corps et de biens
Bed, vn.a. (*hortic.*) planter, semer, (*mason.*) sceller
Bedded, adj. à . . . lit, couché. *Single- —*, *double- — room*, chambre à un lit, à deux lits, *f.*
Bedding, s. literie, *f.*, lit, *m.*
Bedeck *or* **Bedizen**, va. parer, orner, attifer
Bedesman, s. pauvre, *m.*
Bedevil, va. maltraiter, faire endiabler, gâter
Bedew, va. arroser, baigner
Bedstead, s. couchette, *f.*, bois de lit, *m.*
Bee, s. abeille, *f.* *Humble —*, bourdon, *m.* — *-eater*,

guêpier, *m.* —*-flower*, orchis, *m.* — *-hive*, ruche, *f.* — *-house*, rucher, *m.* — *-master*, éleveur d'abeilles, *m.*

Beech, *s.* hêtre, *m.* — *-tree*, hêtre. — *-mast*, — *-nut*, faîne, *f.*

Beechen, adj. de hêtre

Beef, *s.* bœuf, *m.* —*-steak*, bifteck, *m.* *Boiled* —, bouilli, *m.*, bœuf bouilli. *Roast* —, rosbif, *m.*, bœuf rôti. — *-eater*, hallebardier (*yeoman of the Queen's guard*)

Beer, *s.* bière, *f.* *He thinks no small — of himself*, il se croit le premier moutardier du Pape. —*-shop*, cabaret, *m.*, débit de bière, *m.*

Beet, **Beetroot**, *s.* betterave, *f.*, bette, *f.*

Beetle, *s.* maillet, *m.*, mailloche, *f.*, (*paving*) demoiselle, *f.*, hie, *f.*, (*piling*) mouton, *m.*, scarabée, *m.*, escarbot, *m.* — *brows*, épais sourcils

Beetle, vn. surplomber, avancer

Befall, vn. arriver (à)

Befit, va. convenir (à)

Befitting, adj. convenable

Befool, va. se moquer (de), tromper

Before, prep. adv. avant, devant, en avant, auparavant

Beforehand, adv. d'avance

Befriend, va. être l'ami (de), aider

Beg, vn.a. mendier, vivre d'aumône, prier, faire une pétition. *To — leave*, demander la permission, (*in letters*) avoir l'honneur de . . .

Beget, va. engendrer

Beggar, *s.* mendiant, *m.*, mendiante, *f.*, pauvre, *m.*, gueux, *m.*, gueuse, *f.*

Beggar, va. réduire à la mendicité, appauvrir

Beggarly, adj. de mendiant, pauvre, chétif. — adv. misérablement

Beggary, *s.* mendicité, *f.*, misère, *f.*

Begin, va.n. commencer

Beginner, *s.* commençant, *m.*, commençante, *f.*

Beginning, *s.* commencement, *m.*, début, *m.*

Begird, va. ceindre, assiéger

Begone! interj. va-t'en! allez-vous-en!

Begrime, va. barbouiller

Beguile, va. tromper, séduire, échapper (à), charmer, passer (*the time*)

Beguiler, *s.* trompeur, *m.*

Behalf or **Behoof**, *s.* avantage, *m.*, profit, *m.*, faveur, *f.* *On, in — of*, en faveur de, pour, au profit de

Behave, vn., **Behave oneself**, vr. se conduire, se comporter, agir

Behaviour, *s.* conduite, *f.*, manière d'agir, *f.*, tenue, *f.*

Behead, va. décapiter

Beheading, *s.* décapitation, *f.*

Behest, *s.* ordre, *m.*, commandement, *m.*

Behind, prep. derrière, après, après la mort de, inférieur à. *To be — time*, être en retard, retarder. — adv. par derrière, en arrière, en retard

Behindhand, adv. adj. retard, en arrière; arriéré

Behold, va. voir, apercevoir. —! interj. voilà que . . .! voilà! voici!

Beholden, past part. redevable, obligé

Beholder, *s.* spectateur, *m.*, spectatrice, *f.*, témoin, *m.*

Beholding, *s.* vue, *f.*, regards, *m.pl.*

Behove, v. imp. il convient, il est convenable

Being, *s.* l'être, *m.*, l'existence, *f.*

Belabour, va. travailler, excéder de coups, battre

Belch, vn.a. roter, vomir

Belch, *s.* rot, *m.*, éructation, *f.*

Beldam, *s.* vieille femme, *f.*, vieille sorcière, *f.*

Beleaguer, va. assiéger

Beleaguerer, *s.* assiégeant, *m.*

Belfrey, *s.* beffroi, *m.*, clocher, *m.*

Belie, va. calomnier, démentir, mentir (à)

Belief, *s.* croyance, *f.*, foi, *f.*, symbole, *m.* *Hard of* —, peu crédule. *Past all* —, incroyable

Believe, va.n. croire, croire (à), ajouter foi (à)

Believer, *s.* personne qui croit, fidèle, *m.f.*

Believing, *s.* croyance, *f.*

Bell, *s.* cloche, *f.*, sonnette, *f.*, grelot, *m.*, clochette, *f.*, (*bot.*) calice, *m.*, (*archit.*) campane, *f.*, (*of trumpets, &c.*) pavillon, *m.* — *-ringer*, sonneur, *m.* — *-founder*, fondeur de cloches, *m.* — *-tower*, clocher, *m.*, beffroi, *m.* *A house* —, une sonnette, *f.* *A hand* —, une sonnette, *f.* — *-hanging*, la pose des sonnettes. — *-rope*, — *-pull*, cordon de sonnette, *m.* *Clock* —, timbre, *m.* — *-bearer*, porte-grelot, *m.* — *-fashioned*, — *-shaped*, en forme de cloche. — *-mouthed*, évasé. — *-flower*, clochette, *f.*, campanule, *f.*

Bell, vn.a. fleurir en forme de cloche, (*of a stag*) bramer, attacher le grelot (à)

Belladonna, *s.* belladone, *f.*

. . . . **Bellied**, adj. au ventre

Belligerent, adj. *s.* belligérant, *m.*

Bellman, *s.* crieur public, *m.*

Bellow, vn. mugir, beugler, brailler

Bellowing, *s.* mugissement, *m.*, beuglement, *m.*

Bellows, *s.* soufflet, *m.* — *-mender*, raccommodeur de soufflets, *m.*

Belly, *s.* ventre, *m.*, panse, *f.* — *-ache*, colique, *f.*, mal au ventre, *m.* — *-band*, sous-ventrière, *f.*

Bellyful, *s.* soûl, *m.*, le ventre plein

Belong, vn. appartenir, regarder, concerner

Belonging, pres. part. ce qu'on possède. —*s*, *s.pl.* parents, *m.*, proches, *m.*

Beloved, adj. aimé, chéri

Below, prep. adv. au-dessous de, sous, ici-bas, en enfer

Belt, *s.* ceinture, *f.*, baudrier, *m.*, courroie, *f.* *Shoulder* —, bandoulière, *m.*

Belt, va. ceindre, entourer

Belvidere, *s.* belvédère, *m.*

Bemaul, va. maltraiter

Bemoan, va. pleurer, lamenter, gémir de

Bemock, va. se moquer (de), railler

Bemol, *s.* bémol, *m.*

Bench, *s.* banc, *m.*, banquette, *f.*, siége, *m.*, tribunal, *m.*, (*carpenter*) établi, *m.*, berme, *f.*, (*road*) point de repère, *m.*

Bench, va. garnir de bancs, (*to promote*) avancer; — vn. siéger

Bencher, *s.* ancien, *m.*, juge, *m.*

Bend, va. courber, ployer, plier, fléchir, (*a bow*) bander, (*out of shape*) fausser, soumettre, (*nav.*) étalinguer. *To — round, backward*, recourber. *Bent double*, tout courbé. *To be bent on*, être résolu à. — vn. se courber, fléchir, se fléchir, se pencher, s'incliner, faire saillie, se fausser, (*road, &c.*) faire le coude. *To — down*, se pencher

Bend, **Bending**, *s.* courbure, *f.*, courbe, *f.*, flexion, *f.*, inclinaison, *f.*, (*road*) détour, *m.*, coude, *m.*, (*nav.*) nœud, *m.*, (*herald.*) bande, *f.*

Beneath, prep. adv. sous, au-dessous de, en bas

Benedict, *s.* Benoît, (*fig.*) un homme marié

Benedictine, adj. des Bénédictins. — *s.* Bénédictin, -e

Benediction, *s.* bénédiction, *f.*

Benefaction, *s.* bienfait, *m.*

Benefactor, *s.* bienfaiteur, *m.*

Benefactress, *s.* bienfaitrice, *f.*

Benefice, *s.* bénéfice, *m.*

Beneficed, adj. pourvu d'un bénéfice

Beneficence, *s.* bienfaisance, *f.*

Beneficent, adj. bienfaisant, généreux

Beneficently, adv. libéralement

Beneficial, adj. avantageux, utile. — *owner*, usufruitier, *m.*

Beneficially, adv. profitablement, utilement

Beneficiary, adj. feudataire, bénéficial. — *s.* bénéficier, *m.*

Benefit, *s.* bienfait, *m.*, bien, *m.*, avantage, *m.*, bénéfice, *m.*, (*theat.*) représentation à bénéfice, *f.* — *-night*, représentation à bénéfice, *f.* *For the — of*, au bénéfice de

Benefit, va. faire du bien (à), profiter (à); — vn. profiter, retirer un profit

Benevolence, *s.* bienveillance, *f.*, don gratuit, *m.*

Benevolent, adj. bienveillant, bon, bienfaisant

Benevolently, adv. avec bienveillance

Bengal-lights, *s.* plur. feu, feux de Bengale, *m.*

Benight, va. couvrir de ténèbres, obscurcir

Benighted, adj. plongé dans les ténèbres, surpris par la nuit

Benign, adj. bienveillant, bénin, favorable

Benignant, adj. bienveillant, doux

Benignity, **Benignness**, *s.* bénignité, *f.*, douceur, *f.*

Benignly, **Benignantly**, adv. avec bienveillance, avec bénignité

Benison, *s.* bénédiction, *f.*

Bent, *s.* courbure, *f.*, flexion, *f.*, courbe, *f.*, force, *f.*, élan, *m.*, pli, *m.*, penchant, *m.*

Benumb, va. engourdir

Benumbedness, *s.* engourdissement, *m.*

Benzine, *s.* benzine, *f.*

Benzoin, *s.* benjoin, *m.*

Bepraise, va. accabler d'éloges

Bequeath, va. léguer, laisser

Bequest, *s.* legs, *m.*

Bereave, va. priver (de), enlever

Bereavement, *s.* privation, *f.*, perte, *f.*

Bergamot, *s.* bergamote, *f.*

Berry, *s.* baie, *f.*, grain, *m.*

Berth, *s.* mouillage, *m.*, hamac, *m.*, (*fig.*) poste, *m.*, emploi, *m.* *To give a wide — to*, se garder d'approcher de

Beryl, *s.* béryl, *m.*

Beseech, va. supplier, implorer

Beseechingly, adv. d'un air suppliant

Beseem, va. convenir à

Beseemingly, adv. convenablement

Beset, va. cerner, serrer de près, entourer, assaillir

Beside, **Besides**, prep. à côté de, auprès de, excepté, sans, en dehors de. — adv. d'ailleurs, en outre, le reste

Besiege, va. assiéger

Besieger, *s.* assiégeant, *m.*

Besmear, va. barbouiller

Besmut, va. noircir

Besot, va. hébéter, abrutir, infatuer

Bespatter, va. éclabousser, crotter, calomnier

Bespeak, va. commander, retenir, annoncer

Besprinkle, va. arroser, asperger

Best, adj. le meilleur, la meilleure, les meilleurs, les meilleures, le mieux. *At —*, au mieux. *To be —*, valoir mieux. — adv. le mieux, de la meilleure manière. — s. ce qu'il y a de mieux, le dessus. *At the —, in the —*, au mieux. *To make the — of a thing*, tirer le meilleur parti d'une chose. *To the — of my power*, de mon mieux. *To do one's —*, faire de son mieux. *To have the — of it*, avoir le dessus

Bestial, adj. bestial

Bestiality, s. brutalité, *f.*, bestialité, *f.*

Bestir, va. mettre en mouvement, exercer

Bestow, va. mettre, placer, appliquer, accorder

Bestowal, Bestowment, s. disposition, *f.*, dispensation, *f.*, don, *m.*

Bestower, s. dispensateur, *m.*, dispensatrice, *f.*

Bestride, va. enjamber, enfourcher

Bestud, va. garnir, parsemer

Bet, s. pari, *m.*, gageure, *f.* *To lay a —*, faire un pari

Bet, va. parier, gager

Betake oneself, vr. se rendre (à), se diriger (vers), s'adonner, avoir recours à

Bethink oneself, vr. s'aviser (de), songer (à)

Betide, va. arriver (à)

Betimes, adv. de bonne heure, à temps

Betoken, va. annoncer, dénoter

Betokening, s. présage, *m.*

Betray, va. trahir, dénoncer, entraîner

Betrayer, s. traître, *m.*, traîtresse (envers), *f.*, dénonciateur, *m.*, dénonciatrice, *f.*, indice, *m.*

Betroth, va. fiancer. *The —ed*, le fiancé, la fiancée, les fiancés

Betrothal, Betrothment, Betrothing, s. fiançailles, *f.pl.*

Better, s. parieur, *m.*, supérieur, *m.* — adj. meilleur, mieux. *For —, for worse*, dans le bien comme dans le mal. *To make —*, améliorer. *To grow —*, aller mieux, s'améliorer. *To look —*, avoir meilleur visage, prendre un meilleur aspect. *All the —*, tant mieux. *It will be — for him*, il y gagnera. — adv. mieux, plus. — *off*, plus riche, plus avancé. *One had — believe*, on ferait mieux de croire

Better, va. améliorer; — vn. s'améliorer

Bettering, s. amélioration, *f.*

Betting, s. pari, *m.*

Between, Betwixt, prep. entre

Bevel, s. biseau, *m.* — adj. de biais. — *gear*, engrenage conique, *m.*

Bevel, va. tailler en biseau, couper en biais; — vn. être en biseau, aller de biais

Beverage, s. boisson, *f.*, breuvage, *m.*

Bevy, s. volée, *f.*, (*fig.*) réunion, *f.*

Bewail, va. gémir sur, se déplorer

Beware of, vn. se garder de, prendre garde de

Bewilder, va. égarer, dépayser, effarer

Bewilderment, s. perplexité, *f.*

Bewitch, va. ensorceler, charmer

Bewitching, adj. enchanteur, -teresse

Bewitchingly, adv. d'une façon enchanteresse

Bewray, va. trahir

Bey, s. bey, *m.*

Beyond, prep. au-delà de, plus loin que, qui dépasse, excepté. — adv. là-bas

Bezel, s. chaton, *m.*

Bias, s. force, *f.*, poids, *m.*, direction, *f.*, pente, *f.*, goût, *m.*

Bias, va. incliner, faire biaiser, influencer

Bib, s. bavette, *f.*

Bible, s. Bible, *f.*

Biblical, adj. biblique

Bibliographer, s. bibliographe, *m.*

Bibliographical, adj. bibliographique

Bibliography, s. bibliographie, *f.*

Bibliomania, s. bibliomanie, *f.*

Bibliomaniac, s. bibliomane, *m.*

Biceps, s. biceps, *m.*

Bicker, va. se quereller, se chamailler

Bickering, s. querelle, *f.*, bisbille, *f.*

Bickern, s. bigorne, *f.*

Bid, va. ordonner, commander, dire, souhaiter, inviter, offrir un prix, enchérir. *To — for*, enchérir. *To — fair for*, faire espérer, promettre

Bid, s. enchère, *f.*, offre, *f.*

Bidder, s. enchérisseur, *m.*, offrant, *m.*

Bidding, s. ordre, *m.*, commandement, *m.*, invitation, *f.*, enchère, *f.* *Do my —*, faites ce que je vous dis

Bide, va. endurer, attendre

Biennial, adj. biennal

Bier, s. bière, *f.*, cercueil, *m.*

Biffin, s. pomme tapée, *f.*

Bifurcated, adj. bifurqué

Bifurcation, s. bifurcation, *f.*

Big, adj. gros, grand, épais, (*anim.*) pleine, fier. *To look —*, prendre de grands airs. — *-wig*, (*fig.*) gros bonnet, *m.*

Bigamist, s. bigame, *m.f.*

Bigamy, s. bigamie, *f.*

Bight, s. balant de cordage, *m.*, crique, *f.*

Bigness, s. grosseur, *f.*

Bigot, s. bigot, -e, fanatique

Bigoted, adj. bigot, fanatique

Bigotry, s. bigoterie, *f.*, attachement fanatique, *m.*

Bilateral, adj. bilatéral

Bilberry, s. airelle, *f.*

Bile, s. bile, *f.*

Bilge, s. (*nav.*) largeur, *f.* — *-water*, eau dans la cale, *f.*, eau sale, *f.*

Bilge, vn. crever, défoncer

Bilious, adj. bilieux

Bilk, va. filouter, frustrer

Bill, s. (*birds, anchor*) bec, (*garden*) serpe, *f.*, croissant, *m.*, hache d'armes, *f.* (*com.*) mémoire, *m.*, note, *f.*, compte, *m.*, billet, *m.*, effet, *m.*, (*eating-house*) addition, *f.*, carte, *f.*, (*play*) affiche, *f.*, programme, *m.*, (*lodgings*) écriteau, *m.*, (*law*) requête, *f.*, projet de loi, *m.* — *-hook*, serpe, *f.* *—s payable, receivable*, effets à payer, à recevoir. *—s and acceptances*, effets en portefeuille. — *-book*, carnet d'échéances, *m.* — *-broker*, agent de change, *m.* — *of exchange*, lettre de change, *f.* — *of sale*, compte de vente, *m.* — *of lading*, connaissement, *m.* — *of parcels*, facture, *f.* — *-sticker*, colleur d'affiches. *To find a true — against*, prononcer le renvoi en jugement de. — *of indictment*, acte d'accusation, *m.* — *of fare*, menu, *m.* — *of health*, patente de santé, *f.* — *of mortality*, registre mortuaire

Bill, vn. se becqueter, se caresser

. . . -Billed, adj. au . . . bec, au bec . . .

Billet, s. billet de logement, *m.*, (*wood*) bûche, *f.*, (*herald.*) billette, *f.*

Billet, va. loger

Billiard, adj. de billard. — *marker*, garçon de billard, *m.* — *stick*, queue de billard, *f.* — *-table*, billard, *m.*, table de billard, *f.*

Billiards, s. le billard

Billingsgate, s. langage de la halle, *m.*

Billion, s. billion, *m.*

Billow, s. flot, *m.*, vague, *f.*, houle, *f.*

Billow, vn. s'agiter, s'enfler

Billowy, adj. houleux, agité

Bin, s. coffre, *m.*, huche, *f.*

Bind, va. attacher, garrotter, enchaîner, (*a wound*) bander, lier, obliger, engager, (*hem*) border, (*of the body*) rendre constipé, relier. *To — in*, enchaîner, enfermer. *To — out*, mettre en apprentissage. *To — up*, lier, attacher. *To — oneself*, se lier, s'obliger. *To be bound for*, s'engager pour. *I'll be bound*, je parierais. *To — over*, obliger de comparaître. *To — down*, obliger

Bind, s. tige de houblon, *f.*, (*mus.*) liaison, *f.*, (*mines*) schiste, *m.*

Binder, s. relieur, *m.*, lieur, *m.*, ligature, *f.*

Binding, s. bandage, *m.*, reliure, *f.*, (*clothes*) bordure, *f.* — *note*, (*mus.*) liaison, *f.*

Bindweed, s. liseron, *m.*

Binnacle, s. habitacle, *m.*

Binocle, s. binocle, *m.*

Binocular, adj. binoculaire

Binomial, adj. s. binôme, *m.*

Biographer, s. biographe, *m.*

Biographic, Biographical, adj. biographique

Biography, s. biographie, *f.*

Biped, s. bipède, *m.*

Birch, s. bouleau, *m.*, les verges, *f.pl.* — *-tree*, bouleau, *m.* — *broom*, balai de bouleau, *m.*

Birch, Birchen, adj. de bouleau

Bird, s. oiseau, *m.* *A — in the hand is worth two in the bush*, un tiens vaut mieux que deux tu l'auras. *To kill two —s with one stone*, faire d'une pierre deux coups. — *-call*, appeau, *m.*, pipeau, *m.* — *-catcher*, — *-man*, oiseleur, *m.* — *-catching*, la chasse aux oiseaux, *f.* *—'s-eye view*, à vue d'oiseau. — *-fancier*, oiselier, *m.* — *-lime*, glu, *f.* — *-organ*, serinette, *f.* *—'s nest*, nid d'oiseau, *m.*

Birth, s. naissance, *f.*, (*child-bed*) couche, *f.*, portée, *f.*, enfant, *m.*, produit, *m.*, production, *f.* *By —*, de naissance. *A man of no —*, un homme de rien. — *-day*, jour de naissance, *m.* — *-place*, lieu natal, *m.* — *-right*, droit d'aînesse, *m.* *At a —*, d'une couche, d'une portée

Biscuit, s. biscuit, *m.*

Bisect, va. couper en deux

Bishop, s. évêque, *m.*, (*chess*) fou, *m.*, (*liquor*) bishop, *m.*, bischof, *m.*

Bishopric, s. évêché, *m.*

Bismuth, s. bismuth, *m.*

Bison, s. bison, *m.*

Bissextile, s. année bissextile, *f.*

Bistre, s. bistre, *m.*

Bit, va. brider

Bit, s. mors, *m.*, frein, *m.*, (*food*) morceau, *m.*, peu, *m.*, (*auger, &c.*) mèche, *f.* *To shake the —*, hocher. *Not a — of it*, pas le moins du monde. *Centre —*, mèche anglaise, *f.*

Bitch, s. chienne, *f.*

Bite, va.n. mordre, donner un coup de dent à, cuire, faire mal. *To — off*, enlever d'un coup de dent

Bite, s. coup de dent, *m.*, morsure, *f.*, piqûre, *f.*, bouchée, *f.*, fourberie, *f.*

Biter, s. celui, celle qui mord, trompeur, -se

Biting, s. morsure, *f.* — adj. âpre, piquant, mordant

Bitingly, adv. d'une manière mordante *or* caustique

Bittacle, s. habitacle, *m.*

Bitter, adj. amer, âpre, aigre, (*fig.*) acharné, cruel, fâcheux. — s. l'amer, *m.*, amertume, *f.*, (*nav.*) tour de bitte, *m.*; *—s*, l'absinthe, *f.* — *end*, bitture, *f.*

Bitterly, adv. amèrement, (*fig.*) cruellement, durement

Bittern, s. butor, *m.*

Bitterness, s. amertume, *f.*, âpreté, *f.*, causticité, *f.*, aigreur, *f.*

Bitume, **Bitumen**, s. bitume, *m.*, asphalte, *m.*

Bituminate, va. bitumer

Bituminous, adj. bitumineux

Bivalve, adj. bivalve

Bivouac, s. bivouac, bivac, *m.*

Bivouac, vn. bivouaquer, bivaquer

Blab, vn. jaser, bavarder; — va. divulguer, trahir, redire

Blab, s. bavard, -e

Black, adj. noir, obscurci, sombre. *To be all — and blue*, être tout meurtri. *A — eye*, un œil poché. *To give a — eye to*, pocher l'œil (à). *To look — upon*, regarder d'un air de menace. *— -board*, tableau noir, *m.* *— -friar*, frère prêcheur, *m.* *— -jack*, broc de cuir, *m.* *— -lead*, s. adj. mine de plomb, *f.* *— -letter*, s. adj. caractères gothiques, *m. plur.* *— -mail*, tribut illicite, *m.* *— -pudding*, boudin, *m.* *— -rust*, rouille, *f.* *— -thorn*, prunellier, *m.* — s. obscurité, *f.*, ténèbres, *f. pl.*, noir, *m.*

Black, va. noircir, cirer (*boots, shoes*)

Blackamoor, s. adj. noir, -e

Blackball, s. boule noire (*vote*), *f.*

Blackball, va. rejeter

Blackberry, s. mûre sauvage, *f.* *— -bush*, mûrier sauvage, *m.*, ronce, *f.*

Blackbird, s. merle, *m.*

Blacken, va. noircir, (*a pipe*) culotter, (*fig.*) diffamer; — vn. noircir, se noircir

Blackey, s. noiraud, *m.*

Blackguard, s. adj. goujat, *m.*, drôle, *m.*, polisson, *m.*, ignoble

Blacking, s. cirage, *m.*

Blackish, adj. noirâtre

Blackleg, s. brebis aux pattes noires, *f.*, grec, *m.*

Blackly, adv. en noir, avec noirceur

Blackness, s. couleur noire, *f.*, noirceur, *f.*, obscurité, *f.*

Blacksmith, s. forgeron, *m.*

Bladder, s. vessie, *f.* *— -nut-tree*, baguenaudier, *m.*

Blade, s. (*grass*) brin, *m.*, (*sword, &c.*) lame, *f.*, épée, *f.*, (*anat.*) omoplate, *f.*, (*oar*) plat, *m.*, (*pers.*) gaillard, *m.*, luron, *m.* *— -bone*, omoplate, *f.* *A jolly —*, un joyeux compagnon

Bladed, adj. en tige, à lame. *Single- —, two- — knife*, couteau à une lame, à deux lames

Blain, s. pustule, *f.*

Blamable, adj. blâmable

Blamableness, s. caractère blâmable

Blamably, adv. d'une façon blâmable

Blame, va. blâmer, reprendre, censurer

Blame, s. blâme, *m.*, faute, *f.*, reproche, *m.*

Blameful, adj. blâmable

Blamefully, adv. d'une manière blâmable

Blameless, adj. irréprochable, exempt de blâme

Blamelessly, adv. d'une manière irréprochable

Blamelessness, s. innocence, *f.*

Blanch, va. blanchir, faire pâlir, (*peel*) peler

Blanching, s. blanchiment, *m.*

Blanc-mange, s. blanc-manger, *m.*

Bland, adj. doux, caressant

Blandishment, s. flatterie, *f.*

Blandness, s. douceur, *f.*

Blank, adj. blanc, en blanc, pâle, (*archit.*) fausse (*door, window*), (*cartridges*) sans balle

Blank, s. blanc, *m.*, lacune, *f.*, vide, *m.*, (*lottery*) billet blanc, *m.*

Blanket, s. couverture, *f.*, (*print.*) blanchet, *m.*, (*pear*) blanquette, *f.* *To toss in a —*, berner

Blanketing, s. couvertures, *f. plur.*

Blarney, s. blague, *f.*, flatteries, *f. pl.*

Blaspheme, va.n. blasphémer

Blasphemer, s. blasphémateur, *m.*

Blaspheming, s. les blasphèmes, *m. pl.*

Blaspheming, **Blasphemous**, adj. blasphématoire, impie

Blasphemously, adv. en blasphémant

Blasphemy, s. blasphème, *m.*

Blast, s. vent, *m.*, rafale, *f.*, (*trumpet, &c.*) son, *m.*, (*mine*) explosion, *f.*, (*agric.*) nielle, *f.* *— -engine*, machine soufflante, *f.* *— -furnace*, haut fourneau, *m.* *— -pipe*, tuyère, *f.*

Blast, va. foudroyer, frapper, flétrir, dessécher, ruiner

Blasting, s. destruction, *f.*, (*mine*) explosion, *f.*

Blatant, adj. beuglant

Blaze, s. flamme, *f.*, lumière, *f.*

Blaze, vn. flamber, flamboyer, briller; — va. publier, marquer (*trees*). *To — forth*, proclamer

Blazon, va. blasonner, parer, louer

Blazoning, s. blason, *m.*, proclamation, *f.*

Bleach, va.n. blanchir. *—ing field, house*, blanchisserie, *f.*

Bleacher, s. blanchisseur, *m.*

Bleaching, s. blanchiment, *m.*

Bleak, adj. nu, glacial, (*fig.*), morne, désolant. — s. able, *m.*

Bleakness, s. exposition découverte, *f.*, froid, *m.*, aspect morne, *m.*

Blear, adj. chassieux, (*fig.*) trompeur. *— -eyed*, chassieux

Blear, va. rendre (*the eyes*) chassieux, (*fig.*) troubler (*sight*)

Blearedness, s. chassie, *f.*

Bleat, vn. bêler

Bleat, **Bleating**, s. bêlement, *m.*

Bleed, vn. saigner, donner son sang, mourir, (*fig.*) tomber goutte à goutte; — va. saigner, tirer du sang à

Bleeding, s. saignée, *f.*, saignement (*of the nose*), *m.*

Blemish, va. défigurer, gâter, ternir

Blemish, s. défaut, *m.*, tache, *f.*

Blench, vn. reculer

Blend, va. mêler, confondre, marier, nuancer; — vn. se mêler, se confondre, se marier

Blending, s. mélange, *m.*

Bless, va. bénir, rendre heureux, accorder. — *my stars!* bon Dieu! *To be —ed with*, jouir de, être doué de

Blessed, adj. béni, bienheureux, heureux, saint

Blessedness, s. félicité, *f.*, béatitude, *f.*

Blessing, s. bénédiction, *f.*, grâce, *f.*, faveur, *f.*, bienfait, *m.*

Blight, s. (*agric., bot.*) nielle, *f.*, rouille, *f.*, brouissures, *f. plur.*, (*fig.*) flétrissure, *f.*, tache, *f.*

Blight, va. (*agric., bot.*) nieller, rouiller, brouir, (*fig.*) flétrir

Blind, adj. aveugle, insensible (à), obscur. *A — man*, un aveugle. *A man born —*, un aveugle-né. *— of one eye*, borgne. *— -man's-buff*, colin-maillard, *m.* *— side*, côté faible, *m.* — s. tout ce qui intercepte la vue, store, *m.*, petit rideau, *m.*, jalousie, *f.*, (*fig.*) masque, *m.*, leurre, *m.*, œillère (*of a horse*), *f.* *Venetian —s*, jalousies, *f. plur.*

Blind, va. aveugler, éblouir, obscurcir

Blindage, s. blindage, *m.*

Blindfold, adj. les yeux bandés

Blindfold, va. bander les yeux (à)

Blindly, adv. aveuglément

Blindness, s. cécité, *f.*, aveuglement, *m.*

Blink, vn. clignoter, cligner (*the eye*)

Blink, s. coup d'œil, *m.*

Blinker, s. personne qui clignote

Blink-eyed, adj. à la vue faible

Blinking, s. clignotement, *m.*

Bliss, **Blissfulness**, s. félicité, *f.*, bonheur, *m.*

Blissful, adj. bienheureux, heureux

Blissfully, adv. heureusement

Blister, s. ampoule, *f.*, cloche, *f.*, vésicatoire, *m.* *— -fly*, mouche cantharide, *f.*

Blister, vn. s'élever en ampoules; — va. couvrir d'ampoules, brûler (*the tongue*), appliquer un vésicatoire

Blistering, s. application de vésicatoires, *f.*

Blithe, **Blitheful**, **Blithesome**, adj. joyeux, gai

Blithely, adv. gaiement

Blitheness, **Blithesomeness**, s. gaieté, *f.*, allégresse, *f.*

Bloat, va. enfler, gonfler, bouffir; — vn. s'enfler, grossir

Bloated, adj. enflé, gonflé

Bloatedness, s. enflure, *f.*

Bloater, s. hareng saur, *m.*

Block, s. bloc, quartier (*of stone*), *m.*, bûche (*of wood*), *f.*, (*for chopping*) billot, *m.*, (*fig., pers.*) lourdaud, *m.*, (*houses*) pâté, *m.*, obstacle, *m.*, (*mechan.*) poulie, *f.* *Hatter's —*, forme, *f.* *— -tin*, étain sans alliage, *m.* *— and fall*, moufle, *f.* *— -machine*, machine pour faire des poulies, *f.* *— -maker*, fabricant de poulies, *m.*

Block, **Block up**, va. bloquer, obstruer

Blockade, va. bloquer, faire le blocus de

Blockade, s. blocus, *m.*

Blockhead, s. imbécile, *m.*, lourdaud, *m.*

Blockhouse, s. blockhaus, *m.*

Blond, **Blond-lace**, s. blonde, *f.*

Blood, s. sang, *m.*, naissance, *f.*, (*pers.*) élégant, *m.*, jus (*of the vine, &c.*), *m.* *To let —*, saigner. *In cold —*, de sang-froid. *To breed ill —*, faire du mauvais sang, (*fig.*) engendrer de l'animosité. *— -flower*, hémanthe, *f.* *— -horse*, pur sang, cheval de race, *m.* *— -hound*, limier, *m.* *— -root*, *— -wort*, salicaire, *f.* *— -stone*, sanguine, *f.* *— -sucker*, sangsue, *f.*, vampire, *m.*

Blood, va. ensanglanter, acharner, habituer au sang

. . . -Blooded, adj. à sang . . .

Bloodily, adv. cruellement, d'une manière sanglante

Bloodiness, s. état sanglant, *m.*, disposition sanguinaire, *f.*

Bloodless, adj. inanimé, mort, d'une pâleur mortelle, sans effusion de sang, lâche

Bloodlessly, adv. sans effusion de sang

Bloodshed, s. effusion de sang, *f.*

Bloodshot, adj. injecté de sang, enflammé

Bloody, adj. sanglant, ensanglanté, sanguinaire. — -*minded*, sanguinaire

Bloom, s. fleur, *f.*, floraison, *f.*, (*fruits, &c.*) velouté, *m.* *In full* —, tout épanoui

Bloom, vn. fleurir, s'épanouir

Blooming, adj. fleuri, épanoui, en fleur

Bloomy, adj. *see* BLOOMING

Blossom, s. fleur, *f.*

Blossom, vn. fleurir, être en fleur

Blot, va. effacer, faire des pâtés (*of ink*) sur, tacher, ternir

Blot, s. rature, *f.*, pâté, *m.*, tache, *f.*

Blotch, s. pustule, *f.*

Blotch, va. couvrir de pustules

Blotting, s. barbouillage, *m.* —-*book*, —-*case*, buvard, *m.* —-*paper*, papier buvard, *m.*

Blow, s. coup, *m.*, atteinte, *f.*, piqûre (*of a fly*), *f.*, (*nav.*) brise, *f.*, (*trumpet*) son, *m.* *At one* —, en un coup. —-*fly*, mouche à viande, *f.* *In* —, en fleur

Blow, vn. souffler, venter, être essoufflé, sonner (*the horn*), fleurir, s'épanouir. *To — over*, passer, se dissiper. *To — up*, faire explosion, sauter en l'air. *Full blown*, épanoui. — va. (*wind*) pousser, conduire, (*pers.*) souffler, sonner de (*the horn, &c.*), enfler, faire fleurir, (*flies*) piquer, gâter. —*ing engine*, machine soufflante, *f.* — *your nose*, mouchez-vous. *To — away*, emporter, chasser. *To — down*, renverser. *To — off*, faire tomber

Blower, s. souffleur, *m.*, (*chimneys*) plaque, *f.*

Blow-hole, s. évent, *m.*

Blowing, s. action de souffler, *f.*, souffle, *m.*, son, *m.*

Blow-pipe, s. chalumeau, *m.*

Blowze, s. rougeaude, *f.*

Blowzed, adj. rougeaud, brûlé (*by the sun*)

Blubber, s. graisse de baleine, *f.*

Blubber, vn. pleurer comme un veau; — va. gonfler

Blubbering, adj. pleurard

Bludgeon, s. gourdin, *m.*

Blue, s. adj. bleu, *m.*, noir (*sadness*), *m.*, azuré, livide, déconcerté, triste. *The* —*s*, maladie noire. — *ribbon*, ruban bleu. *To look* —, avoir l'air déconcerté, broyer du noir. — -*bonnet*, (*bot.*) centaurée, *f.* — -*bottle*, mouche bleue, *f.*, (*bot.*) bluet, *m.* *The — devils*, le spleen. — -*peter*, (*nav.*) signal de départ, *m.* — *ruin*, les spiritueux, *m.pl.*

Blue, va. bleuir, teindre en bleu, passer au bleu

Bluebeard, s. la Barbe bleue

Bluebell, s. campanule, *f.*

Bluff, adj. gros, brusque, (*point*) émoussée, (*hill*) escarpé. — s. morne, *f.*, cap à pic, *m.*

Bluffness, s. brusquerie, *f.*

Bluish, Bluey, adj. bleuâtre

Bluishness, s. teinte bleuâtre, *f.*

Blunder, vn. faire des bévues. *To — into*, se jeter étourdiment dans. *To — out*, bredouiller (*a compliment, &c.*)

Blunder, s. bévue, *f.*, balourdise, *f.*, faute, *f.*

Blunderbuss, s. espingole, *f.*, tromblon, *m.*

Blunderer, s. brouillon, *m.*

Blunderhead, s. balourd, *m.*

Blundering, adj. étourdi

Blunt, va. émousser

Blunt, adj. émoussé, (*fig.*) obtus

Bluntly, adv. brusquement

Bluntness, s. état émoussé, *m.*, (*fig.*) brusquerie, *f.*

Blur, s. tache, *f.*

Blur, va. tacher, défigurer

Blurt out, va. dire brusquement

Blush, vn. rougir

Blush, Blushing, s. rougeur, *f.* *To put to the* —, faire rougir, faire honte à

Blushing, adj. rougissant, qui fait rougir

Bluster, vn. mugir, (*fig.*) tempêter

Bluster, Blustering, s. tempête, *f.*, orage, *m.*, tapage, *m.*

Blusterer, s. tapageur, *m.*

Boa, s. boa, *m.*

Boar, s. verrat, *m.* *Wild* —, sanglier, *m.* *Young wild* —, marcassin, *m.* —'*s head*, hure de sanglier, *f.* — -*spear*, épieu, *m.*

Board, s. planche, *f.*, ais, *m.*, tableau (*for writing, &c.*), *m.*, (*food*) la table, la pension, conseil, *m.*, administration, *f.*, (*binding*) carton, *m.*, cartonnage, *m.*, (*nav.*) bordée, *f.* *Council* —, table du conseil, *f.* — *and lodging*, la table et le logement. *To be on* — -*wages*, avoir tant pour se nourrir. — -*day*, jour de conseil, *m.* — -*room*, salle de conseil, *f.* *In* —*s*, cartonné. *To put in* —*s*, cartonner. *On* —, à bord. *To go by the* —, tomber à la mer

Board, va. couvrir de planches, planchéier, (*nav.*) aborder, prendre à l'abordage, prendre, mettre en pension. *To be* —*ed*, avoir la table. — vn. manger, être en pension

Boarder, s. pensionnaire, *m.f.*, (*school*) interne, *m.*, (*nav.*) matelot d'abordage, *m.* *Day* —, demi-pensionnaire

Boarding, s. abordage, *m.* — -*netting*, filets de bastingage, *m.*

Boarding-house, s. pension bourgeoise, *f.*

Boarding-school, s. pension, *f.*, pensionnat, *m.*

Boast, vn. se vanter, se glorifier; — va. vanter, échaucher

Boast, s. vanterie, *f.*, fanfaronnade, *f.* *To make a — of*, se vanter de. *To make it one's* —, se faire gloire

Boaster, s. fanfaron, *m.*, vantard, *m.*

Boastful, Boasting, adj. plein de jactance, fanfaron

Boastfulness, s. caractère fanfaron, *m.*

Boasting, s. jactance, *f.*, fanfaronnade, *f.*, (*sculp.*) ébauche, *f.*

Boastingly, adv. avec jactance

Boat, s. bateau, *m.*, chaloupe, *f.*, barque, *f.* — -*builder*, constructeur de bateaux. — -*hook*, gaffe, *f.* — -*timber*, bois de bateau, *m.*

Boat, va.n. transporter en bateau, aller en bateau. *To — up the river*, remonter le fleuve en bateau

Boatman, s. batelier, *m.*

Boatswain, s. maître d'équipage, *m.* —'*s mate*, contre-maître, *m.*

Bob, va. lever, baisser vivement (*the head*), battre, duper, escamoter; — vn. se balancer, pendiller

Bob, s. pendant d'oreille, *m.*, gland, *m.*, tape, *f.*, mouvement rapide (*of the head*), *m.*, (*song*) refrain, *m.*, perruque ronde, *f.*, carillon, *m.*, asticot, *m.*, (*clock*) lentille, *f.* — *wig*, perruque ronde, *f.*

Bobbin, s. bobine, *f.*, fuseau, *m.*

Bode, va. présager, annoncer

Bodeful, adj. plein de présages

Bodice, s. corsage, *m.*

...-**Bodied**, adj. au corps ...

Bodiless, adj. sans corps

Bodily, adj. du corps, physique. — adv. corporellement

Boding, s. présage, *m.*, pressentiment, *m.*

Boding, adj. plein de (tristes) pressentiments

Bodkin, s. poinçon, *m.*, passe-lacet, *m.*

Body, s. corps, *m.*, le physique, *m.*, personne, *f.*, masse, *f.* — *corporate*, corporation, *f.* *A* —, une personne, on. *The main* —, le gros de l'armée. — -*guard*, garde du corps

Bog, s. tourbière, *f.*, marécage, *m.* — -*iron ore*, — -*earth*, minerai de fer des marais, *m.* — -*water*, tourbière, *f.*

Boggle, vn. hésiter

Boggy, adj. marécageux

Bogle, s. revenant, *m.*, spectre, *m.*

Bogy, s. croquemitaine, *m.*

Boil, vn. bouillir, bouillonner. *To — away*, se réduire à rien. *To — over*, s'en aller dans le feu. — va. faire bouillir, cuire à l'eau. *Over* — trop cuit

Boil, s. clou, *m.*, furoncle, *m.*

Boiler, s. qui fait bouillir, chaudron, *m.* — -*man*, chaudronnier, *m.* — -*factory*, chaudronnerie. — -*plates*, plaques de fer de chaudière

Boiling, s. ébullition, bouillonnement, *m.*

Boisterous, adj. furieux, impétueux, violent, turbulent, bruyant

Boisterously, adv. furieusement

Boisterousness, violence, *f.*, turbulence, *f.*

Bold, adj. hardi, audacieux, (*fam.*) crâne, effronté, (*rocks, &c.*) escarpé, abrupt. *To put a — face on the matter*, payer d'audace. *To make — to*, prendre la liberté de

Boldly, adv. hardiment, audacieusement, effrontément

Boldness, s. hardiesse, *f.*, audace, *f.*

Boll, vn. monter en graine

Bolster, s. traversin, *m.*, chevet, *m.*, coussin (*of a saddle*), *m.*, (*med.*) compresse, *f.*

Bolster, va. mettre un traversin sous

Bolstering, s. soutien, *m.*

Bolt, s. (*dart*) trait, *m.*, carreau (*of a cross bow*), *m.*, (*thunder*) foudre, *f.*, (*door*) verrou, *m.*, (*lock*) pêne, *m.*, (*pin*) boulon, *m.*, cheville, *f.*, (*sieve*) blutoir, *m.*, tamis, *m.* — -*iron*, fer à river, *m.* *Bed* —, vis de lit, *f.* — adj. — *upright*, tout droit

Bolt, va. verrouiller, fermer au verrou, enchaîner, avaler, bluter, tamiser, cheviller, boulonner. *To — a person in*, enfermer quelqu'un au verrou. — vn. s'élancer, prendre la clef des champs, (*polit.*) apostasier

Bolter, s. blutoir, *m.*, tamis, *m.*

Bolting, s. blutage, *m.* — -*cloth*, étamine, *f.* — *machine*, blutoir, *m.*

Bolus, s. bol, *m.*

Bomb, s. bombe, *f.* — -*ketch*, — -*vessel*, galiote à bombes, *f.*, bombarde, *f.* — -*shell*, bombe, *f.*

Bombard, s. bombarde, *f.*, tonneau, *m.*

Bombard, va. bombarder

Bombardier, s. artilleur, *m.*

Bombardment, s. bombardement, *m.*

Bombast, s. boursouflage, *m.* *To write* —, écrire avec enflure

Bombast, Bombastic, adj. boursouflé, ampoulé

Bombazine, s. bombasin, *m.*

Bona-fide, adj. adv. de bonne foi, sérieux, loyal

Bond, s. lien, *m.*, la prison, attache, *f.*, nœud, *m.*, devoir,

..., obligation, *m.*, pacte, *m.*, (*treasury*) bon, *m.*, (*custom-house*) entrepôt, *m.* —*-holder*, porteur d'obligations, de bons du trésor, *m.* *In* —, entreposé. *To put in* —, entreposer. — adj. esclave

...d, va. entreposer. —*ed*, entrepôt. —*ed* or —*ing house*, entrepôt, *m.*

...dage, s. les fers, la captivité, *f.*, esclavage, *m.*, asservissement, *m.*

...ndman, Bondmaid, Bondwoman, s. esclave, *m.f.*

Bondsman, s. esclave, *m.*, caution, *f.*

Bone, s. os, *m.*, ossements, *m.pl.*, (*of a fish*) arête, *f.*, (*stays*) busc, *m.*, baleine, *f.* —*-black*, noir animal, *m.* *A* — *of contention*, une pomme de discorde, *f.*

Bone, va. désosser, mettre des baleines à

Boneless, adj. sans os

Bonesetter, s. rebouteur, *m.*

Bonfire, s. feu de joie, *m.*

Bonnet, s. chapeau, *m.*, (*fortif.*, *nav.*) bonnette, *f.* —*-maker*, modiste, *f.*

Bonny, adj. joli, joyeux

Bonus, s. boni, *m.*, prime, *f.*, pot-de-vin, *m.*

Bony, adj. osseux, décharné. — *arm*, bras décharné

Bonze, s. bonze, *m.*

Booby, s. nigaud, -e. — adj. niais

Book, s. livre, *m.*, livre de comptes, *m.*, registre, *m.*, (*savings' bank*) livret, *m.*, cahier, *m.*, (*races* livre de paris, *m.* *Old* —, bouquin, *m.* *To be in, out of a person's* —*s*, être bien, mal dans les papiers de quelqu'un. —*-binder*, relieur, *m.* —*-binding*, reliure, *f.* —*-case*, bibliothèque, *f.* —*-keeper*, teneur de livres, *m.* —*-learned*, érudit, *m.* —*-louse*, mite, *f.* —*-oath*, serment prêté sur la Bible, *m.* —*-shop*, —*-store*, librairie, *f.* —*-stall*, étalage, *m.*, boutique (*of second-hand books*), *f.* *Keeper of a* —*-stall*, bouquiniste, *m.* —*-stand*, bibliothèque portative (*furniture*), *f.*

Book, va. inscrire, enregistrer, retenir. —*ing office*, bureau de voitures publiques, *m.*

Bookish, adj. studieux

Bookishness, s. passion pour l'étude, *f.*

Bookseller, s. libraire, *m.* — *and publisher*, libraire-éditeur, *m.* *Second-hand* —, bouquiniste, *m.*

Bookselling, s. la librairie, *f.*

Bookworm, s. mite, *f.*, (*fig.*) personne qui pâlit sur les livres, *f.*

Boom, s. (*nav.*) bout dehors, *m.*, (*harbour*) chaîne, *f.*, grondement (*of the waves, artillery, &c.*), *m.*

Boom, vn. gronder

Booming, s. grondement, *m.*

Boon, s. don, *m.*, faveur, *f.* — adj. joyeux, bon

Boor, s. cultivateur, *m.*, rustre, *m.*

Boorish, adj. rustre, grossier

Boorishly, adv. en rustre

Boorishness, s. rusticité, *f.*

Boot, s. botte, *f.*, brodequin, *m.*, (*carriage*) coffre, *m.* *Half-* —, bottine, *f.*, brodequin, *m.* *Dress* —*s*, bottes vernies, *f.* *Jack* —*s*, bottes fortes, *f.* *Riding* —*s*, bottes à l'écuyère, *f.* *Top* —*s*, bottes à revers, *f.* *To pull off one's* —*s*, se débotter. —*-jack*, —*-hook*, tire-botte, *m.* —*-last*, —*-tree*, embauchoir, *m.* —*-maker*, bottier, *m.*

Boot, s. profit, *m.*, avantage, *m.* *To* —, par-dessus le marché

Boot, va. botter; — vn. servir à, profiter à

Bootes, s. le Bouvier

Booth, s. baraque, *f.*, tente, *f.*

Bootless, adj. infructueux, vain

Boots, s. commissionnaire, *m.*, décrotteur (*in an inn*), *m.*

Booty, s. butin, *m.*

Boozy, Bousy, adj. gris

Bopeep, s. coucou, *m.*

Borage, s. bourrache, *f.*

Borax, s. borax, *m.*

Border, s. bordure, *f.*, bord, *m.*, frontière, *f.*, limite, *f.*

Border, vn. avoisiner, confiner

Borderer, s. riverain, *m.*, habitant des frontières, *m.*, voisin, *m.*

Bordering, adj. avoisinant, contigu, adjacent

Bore, va. percer, forer, (*well, mine*) sonder, (*to weary*) ennuyer

Bore, s. trou, *m.*, perforation, *f.*, (*mines, &c.*) trou de sonde, *m.*, (*cannon, &c.*) calibre, *m.*, (*gimlet*) tarière, *f.*, foret, *m.*, (*pers.*) ennuyeux, fâcheux, *m.*, ennui, *m.*

Boreal, adj. boréal

Boreas, s. Borée, *m.*

Borer, s. qui perce, tarière, *f.*

Boring, s. forage, *m.*, sondage, *m.*

Born, past part. né. *To be* —, naître. — *a poet*, né poëte. *A* — *foe to*, ennemi-né de. *In all my* — *days*, de toute ma vie. *Low-* —, de basse naissance. *First-* —, premier-né. *New-* — *child, baby*, nouveau-né

Borough, s. bourg, *m.*

Borrow, va. emprunter

Borrowed, adj. emprunté, d'emprunt

Borrower, s. emprunteur, *m.*, emprunteuse, *f.*

Borrowing, adj. d'emprunter

Bosom, s. sein, *m.* — adj. intime, du cœur

Boss, s. bosse, *f.*

Botanic, Botanical, adj. botanique

Botanist, s. botaniste, *m.*

Botanize, vn. faire de la botanique, herboriser

Botany, s. botanique, *f.*

Botch, s. bouton, *m.*, pustule, *f.*, défaut, *m.*, raccommodage grossier, *m.*

Botch, va. raccommoder grossièrement, ravauder, bâcler, couvrir de pustules. *To* — *up*, brocher

Botcher, s. ravaudeur, *m.*, gâcheur, *m.*

Both, adj. les deux, tous deux. — pron. tous les deux, l'un et l'autre. — conj. et, tant, à la fois

Bother, va. embarrasser, (*fam.*) assommer

Bother, s. ennui, *m.*

Botheration! interj. que le diable l'emporte!

Bottle, s. bouteille, *f.*, (*hay*) botte, *f.* *To treat a person to a* —, payer bouteille à. *Wine-* —, bouteille à vin. —*-case*, cantine, *f.* —*-nose*, gros nez, *m.* —*-rack*, planche à bouteilles, *f.*

Bottle, va. mettre en bouteille, (*hay*) botteler

Bottled, adj. mis en bouteille, en forme de bouteille

Bottling, s. mise en bouteille, *f.*

Bottom, s. (*lowest part*) bas, *m.*, (*deepest part*) fond, *m.*, fondement, *m.*, base, *f.*, le derrière, le postérieur, (*dregs*) lie, *f.* *A horse of good* —, un cheval qui a du fond. —*-glade*, vallon, *m.* *In one* —, sur un seul navire. *In neutral* —*s*, sous pavillon neutre

Bottom, va. mettre un fond à, fonder. *To new-* — *chairs*, rempailler des chaises. — vn. se fonder, se baser

Bottomed, adj. au fond . . ., à fond de. *Double-* —, à double fond

Bottomless, adj. sans fond

Bottomry, s. la grosse, la grosse aventure. —*-bond*, contrat à la grosse, *m.* *On* —, à la grosse

Bough, s. rameau, *m.*, branche, *f.*

Boulder, s. roche arrondie, *f.*, galet, *m.*

Bounce, vn. bondir, s'élancer, sauter, faire le fanfaron. *To* — *out*, sortir avec fracas

Bounce, s. bond, *m.*, coup, *m.*, fracas, *m.*, mensonge, *m.*, fanfaronnade, *f.*

Bouncer, s. vantard, *m.*, hâbleur, *m.*

Bouncing, adj. vigoureux

Bound, s. borne, *f.*, limite, *f.*, bond, *m.*, élan, *m.* *At a* (*single*) —, d'un (seul) bond

Bound (to), past part. adj. (*nav.*) en partance (pour), à destination (de)

Bound, va. borner, limiter; — vn. bondir, sauter

Boundary, s. borne, *f.*, limite, *f.* —*-line*, ligne de démarcation, *f.*

Bounden, adj. obligé

Boundless, adj. sans bornes, illimité

Boundlessness, s. infinité, *f.*, immensité, *f.*

Bounteous, Bountiful, adj. bon, généreux, libéral

Bounteously, adv. généreusement

Bounteousness, s. bonté, *f.*, munificence, *f.*

Bounty, s. bonté, *f.*, générosité, *f.*, don, *m.*, prime d'encouragement, *f.*

Bouquet, s. bouquet, *m.*

Bourn, s. ruisseau, *m.*, borne, *f.*, limite, *f.*

Bout, s. essai, *m.*, assaut, *m.*, partie, *f.* *To have a* — *with*, s'essayer avec

Bovine, adj. bovine

Bow, va. courber, arquer, fléchir, incliner, faire plier; — vn. se courber, fléchir le genou, s'incliner. *To* — *out*, reconduire avec force saluts

Bow, s. salut, *m.*, (*nav.*) avant, *m.* —*-piece*, canon de chasse, *m.* *On the* —, par le travers

Bow, s. arc, *m.*, (*knot*) nœud, *m.*, boucle, *f.*, (*saddle*) arçon, *m.*, (*fiddle*) archet, *m.* —*-legged*, aux jambes arquées. —*-window*, fenêtre en saillie, *f.*

Bowels, s. plur. entrailles, *f.plur.*

Bower, s. berceau (*of a garden*), *m.*, retraite ombragée, *f.*, boudoir, *m.*

Bowie-knife, s. couteau, *m.*, poignard, *m.*, catalan, *m.*

Bowl, s. bol, *m.*, jatte, *f.*, vase, *m.*, (*of a pipe*) fourneau, *m.*, boule, *f.* *Jack in the* —, cul-de-jatte, *m.* *To play at* —*s*, jouer aux boules

Bowl, va. envoyer, lancer, rouler; — vn. jouer aux boules, servir la balle. *To* — *off*, (*fig.*) quitter la partie

Bowler, s. joueur à la boule, *m.*, celui qui sert la balle

Bowlful, s. jattée, *f.*

Bowling-green, s. (lieu pour) le jeu de boules, *m.*, boulingrin, *m.*

Bowman, s. archer, *m.*

Bowsprit, s. beaupré, *m.*

Bowstring, s. corde, *f.*

Bow-wow, s. aboiement, *m.*, toutou, *m.* *To say* —, japper

Bowyer, s. archer, *m.*, fabricant d'arcs, *m.*

Box, s. (*botan.*) buis, *m.* —*-tree*, buis, *m.* —*-wood*, bois de buis, *m.*

Box, s. boîte, *f.*, caisse, *f.*, malle, *f.*, cassette, *f.*, (*coach*) siége, *m.*, (*theat.*) loge, *f.*, (*stable*) stalle, *f.*, (*house*) maisonnette, *f.*, (*pump*) corps, *m.*, (*present*) cadeau, *m.* —*-coat*, pardessus, *m.* —*-keeper*, ouvreuse de loges, *f.* —*-ticket*, coupon de loge, *m.* *To be in the wrong* —, s'être fourvoyé

Box, s. coup, *m.* *A — on the ear*, un soufflet
Box, va. renfermer, frapper, (*tree*) inciser. *To — a person's ears*, souffleter. — vn. boxer
Boxer, s. boxeur, *m.*
Boxing, s. la boxe. *A — -match*, une partie de boxe
Boy, s. garçon, *m.*, enfant, *m.*, fils, *m.* *Old —*, mon vieux
Boyar, s. boyard, *m.*
Boyhood, s. enfance, *f.*
Boyish, adj. d'enfant, puéril
Boyishly, adv. en enfant
Boyishness, s. manières d'enfant, *f.pl.*, enfantillage, *m.*, puérilité, *f.*
Brace, va. comprimer, serrer, (*rope*) tendre, (*drum*) bander, (*to strengthen*) fortifier, donner du ton à
Brace, s. bandage, *m.*, bretelle, *f.*, (*drum*) tirant, *m.*, (*coach*) soupente, *f.*, couple, *f.*, paire, *f.*, (*print.*) accolade, *f.*
Bracelet, s. bracelet, *m.*
Bracing, adj. fortifiant, sain
Bracket, s. tasseau, *m.*, gousset, *m.*, (*print.*) crochet, *m.*, accolade, *f.*
Brackish, adj. saumâtre
Brad, s. pointe, *f.* — *-awl*, poinçon, *m.*
Brag, vn. se vanter, se glorifier. *To — and bluster*, faire le crâne
Brag, s. vanterie, *f.*, hâblerie, *f.* *To make a great — of*, vanter beaucoup
Braggadocio, s. bravache, *m.*
Braggart, Bragger, s. rodomont, *m.*, vantard, *m.*, hâbleur, *m.* *To play the —*, faire le crâne
Bragging, s. vanterie, *f.*, rodomontades, *f.pl.*
Brahmin, s. Brahmine, Brahmane, *m.*
Braid, va. tresser, entrelacer, (*milliner*) soutacher, border de passe-poil
Braid, s. tresse, *f.*, (*milliner*) soutache, *f.*, passe-poil, *m.*
Brain, s. cerveau, *m.*, cervelle, *f.*, tête, *f.*, esprit, *m.* — *fever*, fièvre cérébrale, *f.* — *-pan*, crâne, *m.* *The craftiest —*, la tête la plus rusée
Brain, va. casser la tête (à)
Brained, adj. au cerveau . . ., qui a un cerveau
Brainless, adj. sans cervelle
Brake, s. (*hemp*) brisoir, *m.*, (*agric.*) herse, *f.*, (*horses*) travail, *m.*, voiture d'entraînage, *f.*, (*bridle*) bridon, *m.*, (*coach*) enrayure, *f.*, (*railway*) frein, *m.*, (*pump*) brimbale, *f.*, (*baker*) huche, *f.*, (*artil.*) levier, *m.*, fougère, *f.*, fourré, *m.*
Brakesman, s. garde-frein, *m.*
Bramble, s. ronce, *f.* — *-berry*, mûre sauvage, *f.* — *-bush*, buisson de ronces, *m.*
Brambled, Brambly, adj. couvert or plein de ronces
Bran, s. son, *m.*
Branch, s. branche, *f.*, partie, *f.*, (*railway*) embranchement, *m.*, succursale, *f.* — *-coach*, voiture de correspondance, *f.* — *line*, — *-road*, embranchement, *m.*, — *-bank*, — *-establishment*, — *-office*, succursale, *f.*
Branch, vn. pousser des branches, se ramifier, se bifurquer, s'étendre, se lancer dans des digressions
Branching, adj. qui s'étend en branches
Branching, s. ramification, *f.*, embranchement, *m.* — *off*, bifurcation, *f.*
Branchless, adj. sans branches, nu
Branchy, adj. branchu
Brand, s. brandon, *m.*, tison, *m.*, flambeau, *m.*, (*mark*) marque, *f.*, flétrissure, *f.*, (*sword*) glaive, *m.* — *-iron*, fer à marquer, *m.*
Brand, va. marquer, stigmatiser
Brandish, va. brandir
Brand-new, Bran-new, adj. tout battant neuf
Brandy, s. eau-de-vie, *f.*
Brass, s. cuivre jaune, *m.*, laiton, *m.*, airain, *m.*, (*impudence*) affronterie, *f.* — adj. de cuivre, jaune, de laiton, d'airain. — *-wire*, fil de laiton, *m.* — *-work*, ouvrage en cuivre, *m.*
Brassy, adj. d'airain, effronté
Brat, s. marmot, *m.*, moutard, *m.*
Bravado, s. bravade, *f.*, rodomontade, *f.*
Brave, adj. brave, vaillant
Brave, va. braver
Bravely, adv. bravement
Bravery, s. bravoure, *f.*
Bravo, s. interj. bravo, *m.*
Brawl, vn. se chamailler, brailler
Brawl, s. querelle, *f.*, brouille, *f.*
Brawler, s. querelleur, *m.*
Brawn, s. chair de porc, *f.*, muscle, *m.*, (*body*) partie charnue, *f.*
Brawny, adj. musculeux, charnu
Bray, va. broyer; — vn. braire
Bray, Braying, s. braiment, *m.*
Braze, va. souder
Brazen, adj. d'airain, effronté
Brazier, s. chaudronnier, *m.*, brasier, *m.*
Breach, s. rupture, *f.*, brèche, *f.*, ouverture, *f.*, manque (*of promise*), *m.*, (*law*) infraction, *f.*
Bread, s. pain, *m.* — *-chipper*, mitron, *m.* — *-fruit*, fruit à pain. — *-tree*, arbre à pain. — *-room*, (*nav.*) soute au pain, *f.*
Breadless, adj. sans pain
Breadth, s. largeur, *f.*, (*gown, &c.*) lé, *m.*
Break, va. briser, casser, rompre, (*passage*) se frayer, forcer, se faire, (*health, &c.*) ruiner, (*horse, &c.*) dompter, réprimer, (*com.*) faire faillite, casser aux gages, congédier, (*word*) manquer, (*law*) enfreindre, violer, (*fall*) amortir, (*business*) entamer, (*bank*) faire sauter, (*habits*) corriger, guérir. *To — in pieces*, mettre en pièces. *To — one's neck*, se casser le cou. *To — the ranks*, rompre les rangs. *To — down*, renverser, abattre. *To — in (a door)*, enfoncer, défoncer, (*work*) rompre, (*horse*) dresser. *To — off*, casser, rompre, cesser. *To — open*, ouvrir de force, briser, décacheter. *To — through*, se frayer un chemin à travers, (*hedge*) franchir, (*difficulties*) surmonter, (*law*) violer, enfreindre. *To — up*, mettre en morceaux, casser, (*ice*) débâcler, (*meeting*) lever, dissoudre, congédier. — vn. se casser, casser, se briser, éclater, (*abscess*) percer, crever, (*day*) poindre, (*com.*) faire faillite, (*army*) se débander, (*health*) se casser, décliner, (*voice*) muer. *To — away*, se dégager (de), s'arracher (à). *To — down*, se casser, décliner, verser, (*horse*) s'abattre, échouer, manquer. *To — in, into*, entrer de force. *To — in upon*, interrompre, troubler, fondre sur. *To — out*, (*fever, &c.*) éclater, se déclarer, (*person*) se laisser aller (à), (*eruption*) sortir. *To — forth*, éclater. *To — off*, s'interrompre, se retirer (de). *To — up*, se séparer, entrer en vacances, (*weather*) s'éclaircir. *To — with*, rompre avec, s'expliquer avec (*quelqu'un*)
Break, s. rupture, *f.*, brèche, *f.*, ouverture, *f.*, pause, *f.*, interruption, *f.*, lacune, *f.* — *of day*, point du jour, *m.*
Breakage, s. casse, *f.*
Breaker, s. personne qui brise, dompteur, *m.*, violateur, *m.*, qui enfreint, (*nav.*) brisant, *m.*
Breakfast, va. déjeuner
Breakfast, s. déjeuner, *m.* *Meat —*, déjeuner à la fourchette. *A — -service*, un déjeuner
Breaking, s. action de briser, *f.*, fracture, *f.*, bris, *m.*, (*com.*) faillite, *f.* — *down*, accident de voiture. — *in*, irruption, *f.*, (*horses*) entraînage, *m.* — *into*, — *open*, effraction, *f.* — *out*, éruption, *f.*, action d'éclater. — *up*, labourage, *m.*, (*meeting*) levée, *f.*, entrée en vacances, *f.*, (*ice*) débâcle, *f.*
Breakneck, s. casse-cou, *m.*
Breakwater, s. jetée, *f.*
Bream, s. brème, *f.*
Bream, va. (*nav.*) chauffer,
Breast, s. sein, *m.*, poitrine, *f.*, poitrail, *m.*, estomac, *m.*, mamelle, *f.*, (*fig.*) conscience, *f.* — *-bone*, sternum, *m.* — *-deep*, jusqu'à la poitrine. — *-high*, à hauteur d'appui
Breast, va. opposer sa poitrine à, lutter contre
Breasted, adj. *Broad- —*, à la large poitrine. *Double- —*, croisé. *Single- —*, droit
Breastplate, s. cuirasse, *f.*
Breastwork, s. parapet, *m.*
Breath, s. haleine, *f.*, respiration, *f.*, soupir, *m.*, (*fig.*) souffle, *m.* *To draw a long —*, respirer avec force. *Out of —*, hors d'haleine. *Under one's —*, à voix basse. *In the same —*, au même instant
Breathe, vn-a. respirer, vivre, souffler, soupirer, (*horses, &c.*) tenir en haleine, exercer, (*med.*) ouvrir. *To — forth*, exhaler
Breathing, s. respiration *f.*, aspiration, *f.*, repos, *m.* — adj. qui respire, vivant, pour respirer. — *-hole*, soupirail, *m.* — *-place*, halte, *f.*, pause, *f.* — *-time*, temps pour respirer, *m.*, répit, *m.*
Breathless, adj. hors d'haleine, essoufflé, inanimé, paisible
Breech, s. derrière, *m.*, (*fire-arms*) culasse, *f.*
Breech, va. culotter, (*artil.*) mettre une culasse
Breeches, s.pl. culotte, *f.* — *-maker*, culottier, *m.*
Breed, va. élever, destiner (à), engendrer, procréer, produire; — vn. se multiplier, naître
Breed, s. race, *f.*, espèce, *f.*, couvée, *f.*, portée, *f.* *Half- —*, métis, métisse
Breeder, s. éleveur, *m.*, (*hen*) bonne couveuse, *f.*, (*mare*) poulinière, *f.* *Horse —*, *cattle —*, éleveur, *m.*
Breeding, s. nourriture, *f.*, éducation, *f.*, savoir-vivre, *m.*, (*animals*) élevage, *m.* *Good- —*, politesse, *f.*, savoir-vivre, *m.* *Ill- —*, manque d'usage, *m.*
Breeze, s. brise, *f.*, (*cinders*) fraisil, *m.*, (*fly*) taon, *m.* *Stiff —*, vent frais
Breezy, adj. exposé au vent, frais
Brevet, s. brevet, *m.* — adj. à brevet
Brevet, va. nommer à brevet
Breviary, s. bréviaire, *m.*
Brevity, s. brièveté, *f.*
Brew, va. brasser, mélanger, (*treason*) tramer; — vn. faire de la bière, se préparer, se tramer
Brew, Brewage, s. mélange, *m.*
Brewer, s. brasseur, *m.*
Brewery, Brew-house, s. brasserie, *f.*
Brewing, s. brassin, *m.*
Briar, s. ronce, *f.*, églantier

m. *Sweet, wild* —, églantier odorant, sauvage

Bribe, s. présent, *m.*, moyen de corruption, *m.*

Bribe, va. corrompre, acheter, suborner

Briber, s. suborneur, *m.*, séducteur, *m.*

Bribery, s. corruption, *f.*, achat de votes, *m.*

Bribing, s. corruption, *f.*

Brick, s. brique, *f.*, de brique, à briques, excellent garçon, *m.*, brave homme, *m.* —*-bat*, morceau de brique, *m.* —*-clay*, —*-earth*, terre à brique, *f.* —*-dust*, poussière de brique, *f.* —*-field*, —*-kiln*, four à briques, *m.*, briqueterie, *f.* —*-maker*, briquetier, *m.* —*-making*, briqueterie, *f.*

Brick, va. garnir en briques. *To — over*, voûter en briques

Bricklayer, s. maçon, *m.*

Brickwork, s. briquetage, *m.*

Bridal, s. adj. noce, *f.*; nuptial, de noces

Bride, s. épouse, *f.*, mariée, *f.*, fiancée, *f.* *The — and bridegroom*, les (nouveaux) mariés. —*-cake*, gâteau de noces, *m.* —*-chamber*, chambre nuptiale, *f.*

Bridegroom, s. époux, *m.*, marié, *m.*, fiancé, *m.*

Bridesmaid, s. demoiselle d'honneur, *f.*

Bridesman, s. garçon d'honneur, *m.*

Bridewell, s. maison de correction, maison de force, *f.*

Bridge, s. pont, *m.*, (*nose*) dos, *m.*, chevalet, *m.* *Above, below* —, en amont, en aval

Bridge, va. jeter un pont sur

Bridle, s. bride, *f.*, frein, *m.*, (*nav.*) branches, *f.pl.* —*hand*, main gauche *f.* —*path*, petit chemin, *m.*

Bridle, va. brider, tenir en bride, contenir. — (*up*), vn. se rengorger

Brief, adj. bref, concis, court, éphémère. — s. abrégé, *m.*, (*barrister*) dossier, *m.*, cause, *f.*, (*of the Pope*) bref, *m.*, (*mus.*) brève, *f.*

Briefless, adj. sans cause

Briefly, adv. brièvement

Briefness, s. brièveté, *f.*

Brig, s. brick, *m.*

Brigade, s. brigade, *f.* —*-major*, chef d'état-major, *m.*

Brigadier, s. général de brigade, *m.*

Brigand, s. brigand, *m.*

Brigantine, s. brigantin, *m.*

Bright, adj. brillant, resplendissant, clair, intelligent, épanoui

Brighten, va. faire briller, éclaircir, animer; — vn. devenir brillant, s'éclaircir, s'animer, s'épanouir

Brightly, adv. brillamment, avec éclat

Brightness, s. éclat, *m.*, splendeur, *f.*, brillant, *m.*, clarté, *f.*, (*looks*) épanouissement, *m.*, (*mind*) vivacité, *f.*

Brill, s. barbue, *f.*

Brilliancy, s. éclat, *m.*, brillant, *m.*

Brilliantly, adv. brillamment, d'une manière brillante

Brim, s. bord, *m.*

Brimful, adj. rempli jusqu'aux bords

Brimless, adj. sans bords

Brimmer, s. rasade, *f.*

Brimstone, s. soufre, *m.*

Brinded, Brindled, adj. tacheté, tavelé

Brine, s. saumure, *f.*, eau salée, *f.*, la mer

Brine, va. tremper dans la saumure

Bring, va. apporter, amener, conduire, attirer, porter, ramener, (*profit*) valoir, rapporter, procurer, réduire. *To — about*, amener, déterminer, exécuter, faire. *To — again*, rapporter, ramener. *To — away*, emporter, emmener. *To — along*, apporter, amener. *To — back*, rapporter, ramener, faire revenir. *To — down*, descendre, faire descendre, (*pride*) abaisser, (*prices*) réduire, faire baisser. *To — forth*, produire, donner naissance à. *To — forward*, (*proofs*) produire, faire avancer, (*proposition*) mettre en avant, (*com.*) reporter. *To — in*, introduire, (*candidate*) nommer, faire nommer, proposer, alléguer, rendre un verdict de, (*profit*) rapporter, valoir. *To — into*, mettre dans, engager dans. *To — low*, abattre, affaiblir, abaisser. *To — on*, faire avancer, amener, faire naître. *To — off*, ramener, dégager (*prize*) remporter, faire acquitter. *To — out*, faire sortir, produire. *To — over*, apporter, gagner, (*to an opinion*) convertir. *To — through*, faire traverser. *To — to*, (*nav.*) mettre en panne, arrêter. *To — together*, réunir, rassembler. *To — to pass*, amener, faire arriver. *To — under*, soumettre (à), réduire. *To — up*, monter, apporter en haut, rapporter, (*child*) élever, (*vomit*) vomir

Brinish, Briny, adj. saumâtre

Brink, s. bord, *m.*, penchant, *m.*

Brisk, adj. vif, éveillé, animé, ingambe, (*com.*) actif, (*wine*) piquant

Brisket, s. poitrine, *f.*

Briskly, adv. vivement

Briskness, s. vivacité, *f.*, activité, *f.*

Bristle, s. (*hogs*) soie, *f.*, (*bot.*) poil, *m.*

Bristle, va. hérisser. *To — up*, hérisser. — vn. se hérisser. *To — up*, se hérisser

Bristly, adj. hérissé, aux poils hérissés, (*bot.*) poilu

British, adj. anglais, britannique

Brittle, adj. cassant, fragile

Brittleness, s. fragilité, *f.*

Britzska, s. britzka, *m.*

Broach, va. embrocher, mettre en perce, (*fig.*) ouvrir, entamer, (*doctrine*) émettre, communiquer

Broacher, s. auteur, *m.*

Broad, adj. large, grand, vaste, bien prononcé (*words*), grossier

Broadcast, adj. adv. (*sowing*) à la volée, au loin

Broadcloth, s. drap fin, *m.*

Broaden, va.n. élargir, s'élargir

Broadly, adv. largement, clairement

Broadness, s. largeur, *f.*

Broadside, s. (*nav.*) bordée, *f.*, flanc, *m.*, (*print.*) placard, *m.*, feuille imprimée, *f.*

Broadsword, s. sabre, *m.*

Broadwise, adv. dans le sens de la largeur

Brocade, s. brocart, *m.*

Brocaded, adj. de brocart, broché

Broccoli, s. brocoli, *m.*

Brogue, s. soulier, *m.*, accent, *m.*, prononciation, *f.*, patois, *m.*

Broil, s. rixe, *f.*, dissension, *f.*

Broil, va. griller, faire cuire sur le gril; — vn. se griller

Broiler, s. brouillon, *m.*, brandon de discorde, *m.*, gril, *m.*

Broken, adj. cassé, brisé, rompu, navré, (*sleep*) interrompu, (*style*) coupé, (*country*) accidenté, (*road*) défoncé, (*language*) mauvais. —*down*, décrépit, (*horse*) fourbu, (*strength*) abattu. —*meat*, —*victuals*, restes, *m.pl.*, débris, *m.pl.* —*-kneed horse*, cheval couronné, *m.* — *steps*, pas chancelants, *m.pl.* —*-winded*, poussif. — *language*, baragouin, *m.*

Broker, s. courtier, *m.* *Bill-* —, *change* —, courtier de change, *m.* *Furniture* —, marchand de meubles, *m.*, brocanteur, *m.* *Ship* —, courtier de navires, *m.* *Stock* —, agent de change, *m.* *Unlicensed* —, courtier marron, *m.*

Brokerage, s. courtage, *m.*

Brome, s. brome, *m.*

Bronchia, s. bronches, *f.pl.*

Bronchial, adj. bronchique, des bronches

Bronchitis, s. bronchite, *f.*

Bronze, s. bronze, *m.* — adj. de bronze

Bronze, va. bronzer, couvrir, endurcir

Bronzing, s. art de bronzer, *m.*

Brooch, s. broche, *f.*, épingle, *f.*

Brood, vn. couver (*of eggs*), féconder, (*a plan*) faire mûrir. *To — over*, songer à, méditer sur

Brood, s. couvée, *f.*, race, *f.*, engeance, *f.*, (*fig.*) produit, *m.*, action de couver, *f.* —*hen*, poule couveuse, *f.* —*mare*, jument poulinière, *f.*

Brook, s. ruisseau, *m.*

Brook, va. souffrir, supporter

Brooklet, s. petit ruisseau, *m.*

Broom, s. (*bot.*) genêt, *m.*, balai, *m.* *Rush* —, genêt d'Espagne. *Hair* —, *house* —, balai de crin. —*-stick*, manche à balai, *m.* *To pass the — over*, donner un coup de balai à

Broomy, adj. couvert de genêts

Broth, s. bouillon, *m.*

Brother, s. frère, *m.*, confrère, *m.* —*-in-law*, beau-frère, *m.*

Brotherhood, s. fraternité, *f.*

Brotherless, adj. sans frère

Brotherly, adj. adv. fraternel, en frère

Brougham, s. coupé, *m.*

Brow, s. sourcil, *m.*, front, *m.*, visage, *m.*, (*hill*) cime, *f.*, (*precipice*) bord, *m.*

Browbeat, va. intimider, traiter avec dédain

Browbeating, s. essais d'intimidation, *m.pl.*, ton impérieux, *m.*

Brown, adj. brun, (*bread*) bis, (*paper*) d'emballage, goudronné, (*fig.*) sombre, profond, (*cookery*) rissolé. *To make* —, brunir. *To turn* —, brunir, se rembrunir

Brown, s. brun, *m.*

Brown, va.n. brunir

Browning, s. brunissage, *m.*, (*cook.*) sauce brune, *f.*, gratinage, *m.*

Brownish, Browny, adj. brunâtre

Brownness, s. teinte brune, *f.*

Browse, va.n. brouter

Browse, Browse-wood, Browsing, s. branchage, *m.*

Bruise, va. meurtrir, faire une contusion (à), se faire une contusion (à), bossuer, écraser

Bruise, s. meurtrissure, *f.*, contusion, *f.*

Bruit about, va. ébruiter

Brunt, s. choc, *m.*, élan, *m.*

Brush, s. brosse, *f.*, pinceau, *m.*, (*fox*) queue, *f.*, (*attack*) affaire, *f.*, rencontre, *f.* —*-wood*, fourré, *m.*, broussailles, *f.pl.* —*-trade*, —*-manufactory*, brosserie, *f.*

Brush, va. brosser, (*graze*) effleurer, raser. *To — up*, donner un coup de brosse à, polir. *To — away*, *to — off*, balayer, enlever, essuyer. *To — over*, passer rapidement. *To — off*, vn. décamper

Brutal, adj. brutal

Brutality, s. brutalité, *f.*

Brutalize, vn.a. s'abrutir, abrutir

Brutally, adv. brutalement

Brute, adj. brut, brutal. — s. bête brute, *f.*

Brutify, va. abrutir

Brutish, adj. de bête, brutal, grossier, ignorant
Brutishly, adv. brutalement
Brutishness, s. brutalité, *f.*
Bubble, s. bulle d'air, *f.*, (*fig.*) chimère, *f.*, (*com.*) duperie, *f.*
Bubble, vn. bouillonner, couler en murmurant
Buccaneer, s. boucanier, *m.*
Bucentaur, s. Bucentaure, *m.*
Bucephalus, s. Bucéphale, *m.*
Buck, s. (*anim.*) daim, *m.*, chevreuil, *m.*, mâle, *m.*, (*pers.*) élégant, *m.*, (*linen*) la lessive, *f.* — *-basket*, panier au linge, *m.* — *-washing*, lessivage, *m.*
Bucket, s. seau, *m.*
Bucketful, s. seau, *m.*
Buckle, s. boucle, *f.*
Buckle, va. boucler, s'apprêter. *To — under*, plier
Buckler, s. bouclier, *m.*
Buckram, s. bougran, *m.*
Buckskin, s. adj. (en) peau de daim, *f.*
Buckwheat, s. sarrasin, *m.*
Bucolic, s. bucoliques, *f. pl.*, poète bucolique, *m.* — adj. bucolique
Bud, s. bourgeon, *m.*, bouton, *m.*, germe, *m.* *To put forth —s*, bourgeonner
Bud, vn. bourgeonner, éclore, pousser; — va. greffer en écusson
Buddhism, s. le Bouddhisme
Buddhist, s. Bouddhiste, *m. f.*
Budge, vn. bouger
Budget, s. petit sac, *m.*, budget, *m.*
Buff, s. buffle, *m.*, peau de buffle, *f.*, (*med.*) couenne, *f.* — adj. de peau de buffle, de cuir, couleur chamois
Buffalo, s. buffle, *m.*
Buffer, s. tampon, *m.*, boudin, *m.* — *-head*, tampon, *m.*
Buffet, s. coup, *m.*, buffet, *m.*
Buffet, va. battre, frapper
Buffing, adj. — *apparatus*, appareil de ressorts à boudins, *m.*
Buffoon, s. adj. bouffon, *m.* *To play the —*, faire le bouffon
Buffoon, va.n. bafouer, faire le bouffon
Buffoonery, **Buffooning**, s. bouffonnerie, *f.*
Buffy, adj. couenneux
Bug, s. punaise, *f.*, épouvantail, *m.*
Bugbear, s. épouvantail, *m.*, loup-garou, *m.*
Buggy, s. boghei, *m.*
Bugle, s. cor de chasse, *m.*, clairon, *m.*
Build, va.n. bâtir, construire, fonder, baser. *To — up*, bâtir, murer
Build, s. construction, *f.*, forme, *f.*

Builder, s. constructeur, *m.*, celui qui bâtit, entrepreneur de bâtiments, *m.*
Building, s. construction, *f.*, bâtiment, *m.*
Bulb, s. bulbe, *m.*, (*thermometer*) cuvette, *f.*
Bulbous, adj. bulbeux
Bulge, vn. (*nav.*) crever, faire saillie
Bulk, s. volume, *m.*, grosseur, *f.*, corpulence, *f.*, la masse, saillie, *f.*, (*nav.*) chargement, *m.*, tonnage, *m.* *To break —*, commencer à décharger. *Goods in —*, chargement en grenier, *m.*
Bulkhead, s. cloison, *f.*
Bulkiness, s. grosseur, *f.*, volume, *m.*
Bulky, adj. gros, volumineux, corpulent
Bull, s. taureau, *m.*, (*stock-jobbing*) joueur à la hausse, *m.*, bulle, *f.*, (*blunder*) bêtise, *f.*, naïveté, *f.* — *-calf*, veau, *m.*, (*fig.*) benêt, *m.* — *-fight*, combat de taureaux, *m.* — *-fly*, taon, *m.* — *-frog*, grosse grenouille, *f.* — *-head*, lourdaud, *m.*, (*fish*) meunier, *m.*, chabot, *m.* — *-hide*, peau de bœuf, *f.* —*'s eye*, œil de bœuf, *m.*, (*artil.*) centre, *m.*
Bulldog, s. bouledogue, *m.*
Bullet, s. balle, *f.*
Bulletin, s. bulletin, *m.*
Bullfinch, s. bouvreuil, *m.*
Bullion, s. or, argent en lingot, *m.*
Bullock, s. bœuf, *m.*
Bully, s. bravache, *m.*, matamore, *m.*
Bully, va. intimider, tyranniser; — vn. faire le bravache
Bullying, s. airs de bravache, *m. plur.*, tyrannie, *f.*
Bulrush, s. jonc, *m.*
Bulwark, s. rempart, *m.*, boulevard, *m.*
Bumboat, s. bâteau à provisions, *m.*
Bump, s. coup, *m.*, choc, *m.*, (*head*) bosse, *f.*
Bump, va. cogner; — vn. retentir
Bumper, s. rasade, *f.*, rouge bord, *m.*
Bumpkin, s. rustre, lourdaud, *m.*
Bumptious, adj. présomptueux
Bun, s. brioche, *m.*
Bunch, s. bosse, *f.*, (*grapes*) grappe, *f.*, (*vegetables*) botte, *f.*, (*keys*) trousseau, *m.*, (*knot*) nœud, *m.*, (*hair*) touffe, *f.* *A small —*, grappillon, *m.*, bottillon, *m.*
Bunchy, adj. en grappes, en touffes
Bundle, s. paquet, *m.*, ballot, *m.*, (*arrows*) faisceau, *m.*, (*hay, &c.*) botte, *f.*, (*papers*) liasse, *f.*, poignée, *f.* — *of wood*, fagot, *m.*
Bundle, va. empaqueter. *To — in*, faire entrer. *To — off*, plier bagage
Bung, s. bonde, *f.* — *-hole*, bonde, *f.*

Bung, va. mettre une bonde à
Bungle, vn. travailler grossièrement (à), se prendre gauchement. *To — up*, mal faire, brocher
Bungle, s. mauvaise besogne, bévue, *f.*
Bungler, s. maladroit, *m.*, manœuvre, *m.*
Bungling, adj. maladroit, mauvais, mal fait
Bunglingly, adv. gauchement
Bunion, **Bunyon**, s. oignon, *m.*
Bunting, s. étamine, *f.*
Buoy, s. bouée, *f.* *Life- —*, bouée de sauvetage, *f.* — *-rope*, orin, *m.*
Buoy (up), va. faire flotter, soutenir, raffermir; — vn. flotter, percer
Buoyancy, s légèreté, *f.*, élasticité, *f.*, vivacité, *f.*
Buoyant, adj. léger, flottant, (*fig.*) élastique, énergique
Buoyantly, adv. légèrement
Burden, s. fardeau, *m.*, charge, *f.*, (*ship*) tonnage, *m.*, (*song*) refrain, *m.*
Burden, va. charger, peser sur
Burdensome, adj. à charge, pesant, incommode
Burdensomeness, s. fardeau, *m.*
Burdock, **Bur**, s. bardane, *f.*
Bureau, s. bureau, *m.*
Burgess, s. bourgeois, *m.*, membre du parlement, *m.*, maire, *m.*
Burgher, s. bourgeois, *m.*
Burghership, s. droit de bourgeoisie, *m.*
Burglar, s. voleur, *m.*
Burglarious, adj. de nuit avec effraction
Burglariously, adv. la nuit avec effraction
Burglary, s. vol la nuit avec effraction, *m.*
Burgomaster, s. bourgmestre, *m.*
Burgonet, s. bourguignote, *f.*
Burgrave, s. burgrave, *m.*
Burgundy, s. adj. vin de Bourgogne, *m.*
Burial, s. enterrement, *m.*, sépulture, *f.*, inhumation, *f.* — *-fees*, la sépulture. — *-ground*, cimetière, *m.* — *-place*, lieu de sépulture, *m.* — *-service*, office des morts, *m.* — *-vault*, caveau, *m.*
Burier, s. qui enterre
Burk, va. assassiner, étouffer
Burker, s. étouffeur, *m.*
Burlesque, s. adj. burlesque, *m.*
Burlesque, va. travestir, parodier
Burly, adj. grand et gros, gros
Burn, va.n. brûler, cuire, calciner, s'échauffer
Burn, s. brûlure, *f.*
Burner, s. celui qui brûle, qui met le feu à, bec (*lamp*), *m.*

Burning, s. embrasement, *m.*, incendie, *m.*, cuisson, *f.*, cuite, *f.*, ardeur, *f.* *To smell of —*, sentir le brûlé, le roussi. — adj. brûlant, ardent, extrême. — *glass*, lentille, *f.*
Burnish, va. brunir, polir, rendre brillant; — vn. briller
Burnish, s. poli, *m.*, éclat, *m.*
Burnisher, s. brunisseur, *m.*, brunisseuse, *f.*, brunissoir, *m.*
Burnishing, s. brunissage, *m.*
Burnous, s. burnous, *m.*
Burrow, s. terrier, *m.*, trou, *m.*, clapier, *m.*
Burrow, vn. se faire un terrier, se terrer, (*fig.*) se cacher
Bursar, s. économe, *m.*, dépensier, *m.*, (*exhibitioner*) boursier, *m.*
Burst, vn. éclater, faire explosion, crever, (*heart*) se fendre, (*person*) s'emporter, (*tears*) fondre, se précipiter, (*water*) jaillir. *To — asunder*, se briser. *To — forth*, éclater, se précipiter. *To — out a-laughing*, éclater de rire. *To — through*, se faire jour à travers. — va. faire éclater, faire faire explosion à, rompre, briser
Burst, s. éclat, *m.*, explosion, *f.*, (*fig.*) transport, *m.*, mouvement, *m.* — *of laughter*, éclat de rire
Bursting, s. explosion, *f.*
Bury, va. enterrer, ensevelir, inhumer, (*dagger*) plonger
Bus, s. omnibus, *m.*
Bush, s. buisson, *m.*, (*ale-house*) bouchon, *m.* *To beat about the —*, tourner autour du pot, biaiser. *Good wine needs no —*, à bon vin point d'enseigne
Bush, vn. venir en touffes. *—ing*, touffu
Bushel, s. boisseau, *m.*
Bushman, s. Boscheman, *m.*
Bushy, adj. couvert de buissons, (*hair*) touffu, épais
Busily, adv. activement
Business, s. occupation, *f.*, travail, *m.*, besogne, *f.*, affaire, *f.*, profession, *f.*, métier, *m.*, clientèle, *f.*, fonds de commerce, *m.* *Mind your own —*, mêlez-vous de vos affaires. *You have no — here*, vous n'avez que faire ici. *Go about your —*, allez vous promener. *To send about one's —*, envoyer se promener. *To do — with*, être en relation d'affaires avec. — *-like*, pratique, régulier, fait dans les règles. *In my line of —*, dans ma partie
Busk, s. busc, *m.*
Buskin, s. bottine, *f.*, brodequin, *m.*
Buskined, adj. chaussé de brodequins
Buss, va. embrasser
Buss, s. baiser, *m.*
Bust, **Busto**, s. buste, *m.*
Bustard, s. outarde, *f.*

Bustle, vn. se remuer, se donner du mouvement. *To — through*, passer vivement à travers
Bustle, s. mouvement, m., tracas, m., remue-ménage, m.
Bustler, s. personne active, f.
Bustling, adj. remuant, affairé
Busy, adj. occupé, affairé, pressé, actif. *— streets*, rues encombrées, f. *—-body*, tatillon, m., officieux, m.
Busy, va. occuper. *To — oneself*, s'occuper
But, conj. mais, si ce n'est que, si, *si* . . . ne pas. — prep. excepté, hormis. *— for*, sans, si ce n'eût été. — adv. ne . . . que, seulement. *All —*, presque. *— now*, tout à l'heure
Butcher, s. boucher, m. *—'s boy*, garçon boucher, m. *—'s shop*, boucherie, f. *—-bird*, oiseau boucher, m., pie-grièche, f.
Butcher, va. égorger, tuer
Butchery, s. boucherie, f., tuerie, f., carnage, m.
Butler, s. sommelier, m., majordome (*principal servant*), m.
Butt, s. but, m., point de mire, m., cible, f., (*pers.*) plastron, m., jouet, m., risée, f., (*of rams*) coup de tête, m., (*fencing*) botte, f., (*measure*) muid, m. *—-end*, bout, gros bout, m. *To run full — at*, courir tête baissée sur
Butt, va.n. frapper de la tête
Butter, s. beurre, m. *Best —*, beurre fin. *—-cup*, *—-flower*, bouton d'or, m. *—-dealer*, marchand de beurre, m. *—-dish*, beurrier, m. *—-fingers*, *—-fingered*, mazette, f. *—-milk*, petit-lait, m. *—-pear*, beurré, m. *—-sauce*, sauce blanche, f. *—-wife*, *—-woman*, marchande de beurre
Butter, va. beurrer
Butterfly, s. papillon, m.
Buttery, s. office, f., (*univ.*) dépense, f.
Buttock, s. croupe, f., derrière, m.
Button, s. bouton, m. *To put a — on*, mettre un bouton à. *I don't care a — for it*, je m'en soucie comme de cela. *—-hole*, boutonnière, f. *—-hook*, tire-bouton, m. *—-maker*, fabricant de boutons, m. *—-wood*, platane d'Amérique, m.
Button, va. boutonner. *Buttoned up*, (*fig.*) réservé
Buttress, s. arc-boutant, m., contre-fort, m. *Flying —*, arc-boutant, m.
Buttress, va. arc-bouter
Buxom, adj. avenant, réjouissant, gai
Buxomness, s. air avenant, m.
Buy, va.n. acheter. *To — of*, acheter à. *To — in*, acheter à. *To — off*, racheter. *To — up*, acheter en masse, accaparer, racheter
Buyer, s. acheteur, -euse
Buzz, vn. bourdonner, chuchoter. *To — abroad*, répandre
Buzz, Buzzing, s. bourdonnement, m.
Buzzard, s. buse, f. *Bald —*, balbusard, m.
By, prep. par, de, en, d'après, à, auprès de, à côté de, (*nav.*) quart, par devers, (*measure*) à, sur. — adv. auprès, près, retiré, écarté, accessoire, secondaire. *—-blow*, coup de hasard, m. *—-corner*, renfoncement, m. *—-gone*, passé, suranné. *Let —-gones be —-gones*, oublions le passé. *—-lane*, ruelle déserte. *—-law*, loi locale, f. *—-name*, sobriquet, m. *—-path*, sentier écarté. *—-play*, jeu muet, à-parté, m. *—-profits*, le tour du bâton. *—-road*, chemin de traverse, écarté, m. *—-speech*, digression, f. *—-stander*, assistant, m., spectateur, m. *—-street*, rue écartée. *—-stroke*, botte secrète, f., coup de Jarnac, m. *—-turning*, petit chemin, m. *—-wash*, tuyau de dérive, m. *—-way*, chemin de traverse, m. *—-word*, proverbe, m., dicton, m., la fable, la risée
By and by, loc. adv. tout à l'heure, tantôt
Bye, s. *By the —*, par parenthèse, à propos. *Good- —*, adieu, au revoir

C

C, s. C, c, m., (*mus.*) ut, m., do, m.
Cab, s. cabriolet, m. *—-stand*, station de fiacres, f.
Cabal, s. cabale, f.
Cabal, vn. cabaler
Cabalistic, Cabalistical, adj. cabalistique
Caballer, s. cabaleur, m.
Cabbage, s. chou, m., (*tailor*) gratte, f. *White-headed —*, chou pommé, chou cabus, m. *Savoy —*, chou frisé, chou de Milan. *—-lettuce*, laitue pommée, f. *—-plant*, plant de chou, m. *—-stump*, trognon de chou, m. *—-palm*, chou-palmiste, m.
Cabbage, vn.a. pommer
Cabin, s. cabane, f., case, f., hutte, f., (*nav.*) chambre, f. *—-boy*, mousse, m.
Cabinet, s. cabinet, m. *—-council*, conseil des ministres, m.
Cable, s. câble, m. *Chain —*, câble-chaîne, m. *At (half) a —'s length from*, à une (demi-) encâblure de
Cable, va. attacher par un câble
Cabman, Cabby, s. cocher, m.
Caboose, s. (*nav.*) cuisine, f.
Cabriolet, s. cabriolet, m.
Cacao, s. cacao, m., cacaotier, m.
Cacique, s. cacique, m.
Cackle, vn. (*hen*) caqueter, glousser, (*goose*) crier, (*fig.*) caqueter, ricaner
Cackle, Cackling, s. gloussement, m., cri, m., caquet, m., caquetage, m.
Cactus, s. cactus, cactier, m.
Cad, s. conducteur (*of an omnibus*), m., petit commissionnaire, m., (*vulgar fellow*) gamin, m.
Cadaverous, adj. cadavéreux
Caddy, s. boîte (*for tea*), f.
Cade, s. caque, f., baril, m.
Cadence, s. cadence, f.
Cadence, va. cadencer
Cadet, s. cadet, m., (*in the army*) sous-lieutenant
Cadetship, s. brevet de "cadet," m., sous-lieutenance, f.
Cadi, s. cadi, m.
Caduceus, s. caducée, m.
Cæsura, s. césure, f.
Cage, s. cage, f.
Cage, va. mettre en cage, emprisonner
Caitiff, s. adj. misérable, félon
Cajole, va. cajoler
Cajoler, s. cajoleur, -euse
Cajolery, s. cajolerie, f.
Cake, s. gâteau, m., pain (*wax, colours, &c.*), m., tablette, f., (*agric.*) tourteau, m.
Cake, vn. se prendre, se durcir, former une croûte, (*blood*) se cailler
Calabash, s. calebasse, f. *—-tree*, calebassier, m.
Calamine, s. calamine, f.
Calamitous, adj. calamiteux, funeste, infortuné
Calamity, s. calamité, f.
Calcareous, adj. calcaire
Calcination, s. calcination, f.
Calcine, va.n. calciner, se calciner
Calculable, adj. calculable
Calculate, va. calculer, tirer (*a horoscope*), (*fig.*) adapter, faire
Calculating, adj. calculateur, de calcul
Calculation, s. calcul, m.
Calculator, s. calculateur, m.
Calculus, s. calcul, m.
Caldron, s. chaudron, m.
Calendar, s. calendrier, m., liste, f.
Calendar, adj. *— month*, mois, mois solaire, m.
Calendar, va. enregistrer
Calender, va. calendrer
Calender, s. calandre, f., calandreur, m.
Calenderer, s. calandreur, m.
Calends, s. calendes, f. pl.
Calf, s. veau, m., (*fig.*) nigaud, m., (*of the leg*) mollet, m. *Cow with —*, vache pleine. *—-skin*, veau, cuir de veau, m.
Calibre, s. calibre, m. *—-compasses or calipers*, compas de calibre, d'épaisseur, m. sing.
Calico, s. calicot, m. — adj. de calicot. *Printed —*, indienne, f., toile peinte, f.
Caligraphy, s. calligraphie, f.
Caliph, s. calife, m.
Caliphate, s. califat, m.
Calk, va. (*nav.*) calfater
Calker, s. calfat, m.
Calkin, s. crampon, m.
Calking, s. calfatage, m. *—-iron*, bigorne, f.
Call, va. appeler, nommer, convoquer, assembler, sommer, réveiller, (*send for*) faire venir, en appeler à, invoquer, (*to name*) annoncer, proclamer, accuser. *To — again*, rappeler, appeler de nouveau. *To — to mind*, se rappeler. *To — by name*, faire l'appel nominal. *To — aside*, prendre à part. *To — away*, appeler, faire sortir, détourner. *To — back*, faire revenir, révoquer. *To — down*, faire descendre. *To — for*, aller demander, prendre, faire venir, faire avancer. *To — forth*, faire sortir, produire. *To — in*, faire entrer, prier d'entrer, faire venir, faire rentrer, exiger le payement de, (*of the circulation*) retirer. *To — off*, rappeler, détourner, (*of dogs*) rompre. *To — out*, crier, faire sortir, appeler en duel, faire prendre les armes à. *To — over*, faire l'appel. *To — together*, convoquer. *To — up*, faire monter, évoquer. — vn. appeler, aller voir, se présenter. *To — to*, *to — after*, *to — out to*, crier à, appeler à haute voix. *To — in*, entrer un instant. *To — on, upon*, aller voir, faire une visite à, (*God*) invoquer
Call, s. appel, m., ordre, m., nécessité, f., devoir, m., demande, f., invitation, f., vocation, f., visite, f., appel nominal, m., (*milit.*) rappel, m., (*instr.*) sifflet, m., appeau, m. *Be within —*, tenez-vous à la portée de ma

voix. — *-boy*, (*theat.*) avertisseur, *m.* *Give us a* —, venez nous voir. — *-bird*, chanterelle, *f.*

Calling, s. appel, *m.*, cri, *m.*, vocation, *f.*, profession, *f.*, état, *m.*

Callosity, s. callosité, *f.*

Callous, adj. calleux, endurci, insensible

Callousness, s. callosité, *f.*, endurcissement, *m.*, insensibilité, *f.*

Callow, adj. sans plumes

Calm, adj. calme. — s. calme, *m.* *Dead* —, calme plat

Calm, va. calmer, apaiser

Calmer, s. celui, celle qui calme, qui apaise

Calming, adj. qui calme, qui apaise. *A — draught*, un calmant

Calmly, adv. avec calme, tranquillement

Calmness, s. calme, *m.*

Calomel, s. calomel, *m.*

Caloric, s. calorique, *m.*

Caltrop, s. chausse-trappe, *f.*

Calumet, s. calumet, *m.*

Calumniate, va.n. calomnier

Calumniation, s. diffamation, *f.*

Calumniator, s. calomniateur, *m.*

Calumnious, adj. calomnieux

Calumniously, adv. calomnieusement

Calumniousness, s. nature calomnieuse, *f.*

Calumny, s. calomnie, *f.*

Calvary, s. Calvaire, *m.*

Calve, va. véler

Calvinism, s. Calvinisme, *m.*

Calvinist, s. Calviniste

Calvinistic, adj. des Calvinistes, de Calvin

Calyx, s. calice, *m.*

Cambric, s. batiste, *f.* — adj. de batiste

Camel, s. chameau, *m.* *She* —, chamelle, *f.* — *-backed*, bossu. — *-driver*, chamelier, *m.*

Camellia, s. camélia, *m.*

Cameo, s. camée, *m.*

Camera obscura, s. chambre obscure, *f.*

Camlet, s. camelot, *m.*

Camomile, s. camomille, *f.*

Camp, s. camp, *m.* — *-bedstead*, lit de camp, *m.* — *-boy*, goujat, *m.* — *-meeting*, prêche, *m.*, assemblée religieuse en plein air, *f.* — *-gear*, effets de campement, *m.pl.* — *-stool*, pliant, *m.*

Camp, va.n. camper, faire camper, se camper

Campaign, s. campagne, *f.*

Campaign, vn. faire la campagne

Campaigner, s. vieux soldat, *m.*

Campanile, s. campanile, *m.*

Campanula, s. campanule, *f.*

Camphor, s. camphrier, *m.*

Camphor, Camphorate, va. camphrer

Camphorated, adj. camphré

Camping, s. campement, *m.*

Can, s. canette, *f.*, pot, *m.*, bidon, *m.*

Canal, s. canal, *m.*

Canalization, s. canalisation, *f.*

Canalize, va. canaliser

Canary, s. serin, *m.*, vin des Canaries, *m.* — *-bird*, serin, *m.*, canari, *m.* *Hen-* —, serine, *f.*

Cancel, va. annuler, (*erase*) biffer, supprimer, (*deed*) résilier

Cancel, s. (*print.*) carton, *m.*

Cancelling, s. annulation, *f.*, résiliation, *f.*

Cancer, s. cancer, *m.*

Cancerate, vn. se changer en cancer

Cancerous, adj. cancéreux

Candelabrum, s. candélabre, *m.*

Candid, adj. candide, ingénu, impartial

Candidate, s. candidat, aspirant. *To stand — for*, se porter candidat pour

Candidateship, s. candidature, *f.*

Candidly, adv. avec candeur

Candidness, s. candeur, *f.*

Candle, s. chandelle, *f.*, lumignon, *m.* *Tallow* —, chandelle, *f.* *Between daylight and — -light*, entre chien et loup. — *-end*, bout de chandelle, *m.* — *-mine*, amas de suif, *m.* — *-snuffer*, moucheur de chandelles, *m.* — *-stick*, chandelier, flambeau, *m.* *Chamber, flat — -stick*, bougeoir, *m.* — *-stuff*, suif, *m.*

Candlemas, s. la Chandeleur.

Candour, s. candeur, *f.*

Candy, va.n. candir, glacer, se candir

Cane, s. canne, *f.*, roseau, *m.* *Air-* —, sarbacane, *f.* — *-bottomed chair*, chaise de canne, *f.* — *-mill*, usine à sucre, *f.*

Cane, va. donner des coups de canne

Canicular, adj. caniculaire

Canine, adj. de chien, canin

Caning, s. des coups de canne, *m.pl.*

Canister, s. corbeille, *f.*, boîte à thé, *f.* — *-shot*, mitraille, *f.*

Canker, s. chancre, *m.*, plaie, *f.*, rosier sauvage, *m.* — *-bloom*, *-blossom*, fleur d'églantier, *f.* — *-worm*, ver rongeur, *m.*

Canker, vn. se corrompre, (*metal*) s'oxyder; — va. corroder, ronger, corrompre

Cankered, adj. malfaisant, méchant, corrompu. — *conscience*, conscience ulcérée, *f.*

Cankering, Cankerous, adj. rongeur, qui ronge

Cannibal, s. adj. cannibale, *m.*, anthropophage, *m.*

Cannibalism, s. anthropophagie, *f.*

Cannon, s. canon, *m.*, canons, *m.pl.*, artillerie, *f.*, (*billiards*) carambolage, *m.*, carambole, *f.* — *-ball*, boulet de canon, *m.* — *-shot*, boulet de canon, *m.*, coup de canon, *m.*, portée de canon, *f.* *Within — -shot*, à portée de canon. *To make a* —, caramboler

Cannonade, s. canonnade, *f.*

Cannonade, va.n. canonner, se canonner

Cannoneer, s. canonnier, *m.*

Canny, adj. fin, avisé, prudent

Canoe, s. canot, *m.*, pirogue, *f.*

Canon, s. canon, *m.*, chanoine, *m.* — *-law*, droit canon, *m.*

Canoness, s. chanoinesse, *f.*

Canonical, adj. canonique

Canonicals, s. pl. grand costume, *m.*

Canonicate, Canonry, Canonship, s. canonicat, *m.*

Canonization, s. canonisation, *f.*

Canonize, va. canoniser

Canopy, s. dais, *m.*, (*archit.*) baldaquin, *m.*, voûte, *f.*

Canopy, va. couvrir d'un dais, (*fig.*) couvrir

Cant, s. air hypocrite, *m.*, hypocrisie de langage, *f.*, jargon, *m.*, argot, *m.*, (*arch.*) pan coupé, *m.* —*wise*, à pans coupés

Cant, adj. d'argot, du métier, (*nav.*) dévoyé. —*phrase*, mot du métier, *m.*

Cant, vn. parler avec affectation, faire l'hypocrite; — va. pousser

Cantankerous, adj. chagrin, acariâtre

Cantata, s. cantate, *f.*

Canteen, s. cantine, *f.*

Canter, s. hypocrite, *m.*, cafard, *m.*, (*riding*) petit galop, *m.*

Canter, vn. aller au petit galop

Cantharis, s. cantharide, *f.*

Canticle, s. cantique, *m.*

Canting, adj. hypocrite, cafard, (*voice*) nasillard, (*herald.*) parlantes

Canto, s. chant, *m.*

Canton, s. canton, *m.*

Canton, va. diviser, cantonner

Cantonment, s. cantonnement, *m.*

Canvas, Canvass, s. toile de chanvre, *f.*, canevas, *m.*, toile, *f.*, (*nav.*) les voiles, *f.pl.*; examen, *m.*, discussion, *f.*, brigue, *f.*

Canvas, adj. de toile

Canvass, va. examiner, débattre, solliciter des votes

Canvasser, s. solliciteur de votes, *m.*

Cap, s. bonnet, *m.*, coiffe, *f.*, casquette, *f.*, (*college*) toque, *f.*, (*cardinal*) barrette, *f.*, (*archit.*) couronnement, *m.*, (*fire-arms*) capsule, *f.*, (*artil.*) plaque, *f.*, (*watches*) cuvette, *f.*, (*mech.*) chapeau, *m.*, chape, *f.* *To set one's — at*, chercher à captiver. — *in hand*, le bonnet à la main. *Fool's* —, bonnet d'âne. *To wear the fool's — and bells*, porter la marotte

Cap, va. recouvrir, (*bottle*) coiffer, (*fig.*) couronner, passer, dépasser. *Capped*, (*watch*) à recouvrement. — vn. se découvrir

Capability, s. capacité, *f.*

Capable, adj. capable, susceptible (de)

Capacious, adj. vaste, spacieux, étendu

Capaciousness, s. capacité, *f.*, contenance, *f.*, étendue, *f.*

Capacitate, va. rendre capable (de), mettre en état (de)

Capacity, s. capacité, *f.*, contenance, *f.*, talent, *m.*, moyens, *m.pl.*

Cap-a-pee, adv. de pied en cap

Caparison, s. caparaçon, *m.*

Caparison, va. caparaçonner

Cape, s. cap, *m.*, (*of a cloak*) collet, *m.*, (*for ladies*) pèlerine, *f.*

Caper, s. cabriole, *f.*, entrechat, *m.*, (*fig.*) folie, *f.*, (*bot.*) câpre, *f.* *To cut —s*, faire des entrechats, faire des cabrioles. — *-bush*, — *-tree*, câprier, *m.* — *-sauce*, sauce aux câpres, *f.*

Caper, vn. cabrioler, danser

Capillaire, s. capillaire, *m.*

Capillarity, s. capillarité, *f.*

Capillary, adj. capillaire. — s. tube capillaire, *m.*

Capital, adj. capital, (*city*) capitale, (*letter*) capitale, majuscule, (*fig.*) grand, excellent, parfait

Capital, s. (*archit.*) chapiteau, *m.*, (*geogr.*) capitale, *f.*, (*com.*) capital, *m.*, (*gram.*) capitale, *f.*, majuscule, *f.*

Capitalist, s. capitaliste, *m.*

Capitalize, va. capitaliser

Capitally, adv. comme coupable de crime capital; admirablement

Capitation, s. capitation, *f.*

Capitol, s. Capitole, *m.*

Capitular, adj. capitulaire

Capitular, Capitulary, s. capitulaire, *m.*, membre, *m.*

Capitulate, vn. capituler

Capitulation, s. capitulation, *f.*

Capon, s. chapon, *m.*

Capot, s. capot, *m.*

Capot, va. faire capot

Capote, s. capote, *f.*

Caprice, s. caprice, *m.*

Capricious, adj. capricieux

Capriciously, adv. capricieusement

Capriciousness, s. nature capricieuse, *f.*, caractère capricieux, *m.*

Capricorn, s. Capricorne, *m.*

Capsize, va.n. chavirer, faire chavirer

Capstan, Capstern, s. cabestan, *m.* *To man the* —, armer le cabestan

Capsular, adj. capsulaire

Capsule, s. capsule, *f.*

Captain, s. capitaine, *m.*, chef d'ouvriers, *m.* *Post* —, capitaine de vaisseau. — *of a merchant vessel*, capitaine d'un navire marchand, capitaine au long cours. — *of a gun*, chef de pièce

Captaincy, s. grade de capitaine, *m.*

Captainship, s. grade de capitaine, *m.*, capitainerie, *f.*

Captious, adj. chicaneur, (*argument*) captieux, insidieux

Captiously, adv. captieusement

Captiousness, s. nature captieuse, *f.*

Captivate, va. faire captif, (*fig.*) captiver, séduire

Captivating, adj. séduisant, attrayant

Captive, s. adj. captif, *m.*, captive, *f.*

Captivity, s. captivité, *f.*

Captor, s. vainqueur, *m.*, celui qui prend, (*nav.*) vaisseau prenant, *m.*

Capture, s. capture, *f.*, prise, *f.*

Capture, va. prendre, (*nav.*) capturer

Capuchin, s. Capucin, *m.*

Car, s. char, *m.*, chariot, *m.*, charrette, *f.*

Carack, s. caraque, *f.*

Caracole, s. caracole, *f.*

Caracole, vn. caracoler

Caramel, s. caramel, *m.*

Carapace, s. carapace, *f.*

Carat, s. carat, *m.*

Caravan, s. caravane, *f.*

Caravansary, s. caravansérail, *m.*

Caraway, s. carvi, *m.* — *-comfit*, bonbon à graine de carvi, *m.*

Carbine, s. carabine, *f.*

Carbineer, s. carabinier, *m.*

Carbon, s. carbone, *m.*

Carbonate, s. carbonate, *m.*

Carbonated, adj. carboné

Carbonic, adj. carbonique

Carboniferous, adj. carbonifère

Carbonization, s. carbonisation, *f.*

Carbonize, va. carboniser

Carbuncle, s. escarboucle, *f.*, (*med.*) charbon, *m.*

Carbuncled, adj. orné d'escarboucles

Carburet, s. carbure, *f.*

Carburetted, adj. carburé

Carcanet, s. carcan, *m.*

Carcase, s. carcasse, *f.*

Card, s. carte, *f.*, (*direction*) adresse, *f.*, (*nav.*) rose des vents, *f.*, (*wool*) peigne, *m.* — *-board*, carton, *m.* *Visiting* —, carte de visite. — *-case*, porte-cartes, *m.*, étui, *m.* — *-rack*, porte-cartes, *m.* *Playing* —*s*, cartes à jouer. *Court* —, figure, *f.*, carte peinte, *f.* *Small* —, basse carte, *f.* *Odd* —, fausse carte, *f.* — *-party*, réunion pour jouer aux cartes, *f.* — *-room*, salle de jeu, *f.* — *-table*, table de jeu, *f.*

Card, va. carder (*wool, &c.*)

Carder, s. cardeur, cardeuse, (*mechan.*) carde mécanique, *f.*

Cardinal, adj. s. cardinal, *m.*

Cardinalate, s. cardinalat, *m.*

Carding, s. cardage, *m.*

Carding, adj. à carder

Cardoon, s. cardon, *m.*

Care, s. souci, *m.*, inquiétude, *f.*, douleur, *f.*, soin, *m.*, diligence, *f.*, attention, *f.*, garde (*protection*), *f.* *Full of* —, soucieux, inquiet. — *-worn*, rongé de soucis. *To take* — (*of*), avoir soin (de), prendre garde (à). *To take* — *not to*, avoir soin de ne pas, se garder de, n'avoir garde de

Care, va.n. se mettre en peine, s'inquiéter, s'occuper

Careen, va. caréner; — vn. donner à la bande

Careening, s. carénage, *m.*

Career, s. carrière, *f.*, course, *f.*

Career, vn. parcourir

Careful, adj. inquiet, soucieux, soigneux, diligent

Carefully, adv. avec inquiétude, avec sollicitude, soigneusement

Carefulness, s. inquiétude, *f.*, sollicitude, *f.*, soin, *m.*

Careless, s. sans souci, insouciant, peu soigneux, négligent, nonchalant

Carelessly, adv. sans soin, négligemment, nonchalamment

Carelessness, s. insouciance, *f.*, indifférence, *f.*, négligence, *f.*, inexactitude, *f.*

Caress, va. caresser

Caress, s. caresse, *f.*

Caressing, adj. caressant, tendre

Caressingly, adv. d'un ton caressant

Caret, s. signe d'omission, *m.*

Cargo, s. cargaison, *f.*, chargement, *m.*, charge, *f.* *To be taking in her* —, être en charge

Caricature, s. caricature, *f.*, charge, *f.*

Caricature, va. caricaturer, tourner en ridicule

Caricaturist, s. caricaturiste

Caries, s. carie, *f.*

Carman, s. charretier, *m.*, voiturier, *m.*

Carmelite, s. Carme, *m.*, Carmélite, *f.*

Carmine, s. carmin, *m.*

Carnage, s. carnage, *m.*

Carnal, adj. charnel

Carnality, s. sensualité, *f.*

Carnally, adv. charnellement

Carnation, s. carnation, *f.*, (*bot.*) œillet (*red*), *m.*

Carnival, s. carnaval, *m.*

Carnivorous, adj. carnivore, carnassier

Carob-tree, s. caroubier, *m.*

Carol, s. chant, *m.*, hymne, *m.* *A Christmas* —, un noël

Carol, vn.a. chanter

Carolling, s. chant, *m.*

Carousal, s. banquet, *m.*, festin, *m.*

Carouse, vn.a. boire, riboter

Carouse, s. ripaille, *f.*, orgie, *f.*

Carouser, s. buveur, *m.*

Carp, s. carpe, *f.* *Young* —, carpeau, *m.*, carpillon, *m.*

Carp, vn.a. critiquer, chicaner

Carpenter, s. charpentier, *m.* — *and joiner*, menuisier, *m.* *Ship* —, charpentier de marine. —*'s mate*, aide-charpentier, *m.* —*'s trade*, la charpenterie

Carpentering, Carpentry, s. charpenterie, *f.*

Carper, s. critique, frondeur, *m.*

Carpet, s. tapis, *m.* *Wilton* —, moquette, *f.* — *-bag*, sac de nuit, *m.*

Carpet, va. couvrir de tapis

Carpeting, s. étoffe à tapis, *f.*, tapis, *m.pl.*

Carping, adj. frondeur, chagrin

Carping, s. critique vétilleuse, *f.*, chicanes, *f.pl.*

Carriage, s. port, *m.*, transport, *m.*, (*vehicle*) voiture, *f.*, carrosse, *m.*, (*gun*) affût, *m.*, (*print.*) train, *m.*, (*deportment*) maintien, *m.*, port, *m.*, démarche, *f.* *Land* —, *water* —, transport par terre, roulage, transport par eau. — *paid*, port payé. *T' keep one's* —, avoir voiture rouler carrosse. — *and four*, voiture à quatre chevaux. *One horse* —, voiture à un cheval, demi-fortune, *f.* *Close* —, voiture fermée. *Open* —, voiture découverte. *Travelling* —, voiture de voyage. — adj. de voiture, pour voiture. — *-horse*, cheval de carrosse, *m.* — *-maker*, carrossier, *m.* — *-road*, route carrossable, *f.*, grande avenue, *f.* — *-window*, portière, *f.*

Carrier, s. porteur, *m.*, qui porte, messager, *m.*, voiturier, *m.*, commissionnaire de roulage, *m.* *Canal-* —, commissionnaire chargeur, *m.* — *-pigeon*, pigeon voyageur, *m.*

Carrion, s. charogne, *f.* — adj. de charogne. — *-crow*, corbeau, *m.*

Carronade, s. caronade, *f.*

Carrot, s. carotte, *f.*

Carroty, adj. couleur de carotte, roux (*hair*). — *-headed*, à la tête rousse

Carry, va. (*goods, travellers*) porter, transporter, voiturer, (*earth, sand*) charrier, mener, (*to incite*) pousser, présenter, communiquer, transmettre, (*a consequence*) impliquer, entraîner, (*a victory*) remporter, gagner, obtenir, (*business*) conduire, (*milit.*) emporter d'assaut, enlever, s'emparer de, (*arith.*) retenir, (*com.*) porter, passer. *To* — *the day* (*against*), remporter la victoire (sur). *To* — *it*, l'emporter. *To* — *it high*, affecter de grands airs. *To* — *about*, colporter, mener partout. *To* — *about oneself*, avoir sur soi. *To* — *along*, emporter, entraîner. *To* — *away*, emporter, emmener. *To* — *back*, remporter, faire remonter. *To* — *down*, descendre. *To* — *forward*, reporter. *To* — *off*, emporter, emmener. *To* — *it off*, s'en tirer. *To* — *on*, poursuivre, continuer, pousser, (*trade*) faire, continuer, (*correspondence*) avoir, entretenir. *To* — *out*, porter au dehors, exécuter, accomplir, mettre en pratique. *To* — *over*, faire passer, reporter. *To* — *through*, exécuter, mener à bonne fin, faire réussir. *To* — *oneself through*, se tirer d'affaire. *To* — *up*, monter, porter en haut

Cart, s. charrette, *f.*, (*with boards all round*) tombereau, *m.*, (*mil.*) fourgon, *m.* *The* — *before the horse*, la charrue devant les bœufs. — *-horse*, cheval de trait, *m.* — *-house*, hangar, *m.* — *-load*, charretée, *f.* — *-way*, chemin de charroi, *m.*

Cart, va. charrier. — *away*, emporter

Cartage, s. charroi, charriage, *m.*

Cartel, s. cartel, *m.*

Carter, s. charretier, *m.*

Carthusian, s. Chartreux, *m.*

Cartilage, s. cartilage, *m.*

Carting, s. charriage, *m.*

Cartoon, s. carton, *m.*

Cartouch, Cartridge, s. cartouche, *f.* — *-box*, — *-pouch*, (*mil.*) giberne, *f.*, cartouchière, *f.*

Carve, va.n. sculpter, ciseler, tailler, (*at table*) découper

Carver, s. sculpteur, *m.* ciseleur, *m.*, (*of meat*) découpeur, *m.*, écuyer tranchant, *m.*, (*knife*) couteau à découper, *m.*, (*for fish*) truelle *f.*

Carving, s. sculpture, *f.*, ciselure, *f.*, (*at table*) découpage, *m.* — *-knife*, couteau à découper, *m.*
Cascade, s. cascade, *f.*
Case, s. (*sheath*) étui, *m.*, gaîne, *f.*, fourreau, *m.*, (*box*) boîte, *f.*, (*packing*) caisse, *f.*, (*needles*, &c.) étui, *m.*, (*jewels*) écrin, *m.*, (*clock*) boîte, *f.*, (*for a book*) étui, *m.*, (*piano*) caisse, *f.*, (*organ*) buffet, *m.*, (*stair*, *bells*) cage, *f.*, (*door*) chambranle, *m.*, (*print.*) casse, *f.*, (*event*) cas, *m.*, (*state*) état, *m.*, condition, *f.*, (*question*) question, *f.*, chose, *f.*, (*instance*) exemple, *m.*, (*law*) cause, *f.*, matière à procès, *f.* *That is the* —, il en est ainsi. *If I were in your* —, si j'étais à votre place. — *-maker*, gainier, *m.* — *-shot*, mitraille, *f.*
Case, va. serrer, enfermer, recouvrir, (*arch.*) revêtir
Cased, adj. *Armour-* —, *iron-* —, (*nav.*) cuirassé
Casemate, s. casemate, *f.*
Casement, s. fenêtre, croisée, *f.*, (*compartment*) vasistas, *m.*
Cash, s. argent, *m.*, espèces, *f.pl.*, numéraire, *m.*, (*bookkeeping*) caisse, *f.* *Hard* —, espèces sonnantes. *Loose* —, monnaie, *f.* *To sell for* —, vendre au comptant. — *-book*, livre de caisse, *m.* — *-box*, caisse, cassette, *f.* — *down*, argent comptant
Cash, va. payer, changer, (*discount*) escompter
Cashew-nut, s. noix d'acajou, *f.*
Cashier, s. caissier, *m.*
Cashier, va. destituer, (*mil.*) dégrader
Cashmere, s. cachemire, *m.*
Cashoo, s. cachou, *m.*
Casing, s. (*arch.*) revêtement, *m.*, (*machines*) enveloppe, *f.*, (*covering*) couverture, *f.*
Cask, s. tonneau, baril, *m.*, fût, *m.* — *-stand*, chantier, porte-fût, *m.*
Cask, va. mettre en baril *or* en tonneau
Casket, s. cassette, *f.*, écrin, *m.*
Cassia, s. casse, *f.*
Cassock, s. casaque, *f.*, soutane, *f.*
Cast, va. (*throw*) jeter, lancer, (*sow*) semer, répandre, (*change*) changer, (*weigh down*), faire pencher (*la balance*, &c.), (*metals*) fondre, (*print.*) clicher, (*mould*) mouler, couler, (*reckon*) compter, calculer, (*consider*) examiner, (*decide*) tirer au sort, (*theat.*) distribuer; — vn. (*think*) songer, (*wood*) se déjeter. — *away*, jeter, prodiguer, (*nav.*) jeter à la côte. — *by*, rejeter. — *down*, jeter par terre, (*fig.*) abattre, (*eyes*) baisser. — *forth*, jeter, pousser. — *off*, rejeter, mettre au rebut, (*shake off*) secouer, — *out*, rejeter, chasser. — *up*, vomir, rendre, additionner, (*eyes*) lever
Cast, s. (*throw*) coup, *m.*, (*distance*) jet, *m.*, (*metals*) fonte, *f.*, (*fig.*) trempe, *f.*, caractère, *m.*, expression, *f.*, (*shape*) forme, *f.*, tournure, *f.*, (*mould*) moule, *m.*, (*image*) statuette, *f.*, buste, *m.*, bronze, *m.*, plâtre, *m.*, (*shade*) nuance, *f.*, (*sowing*) volée, *f.*, (*theat.*) distribution, *f.*, rôles, acteurs, *m.pl.*
Castanet, s. castagnette, *f.*
Castaway, s. réprouvé, *m.*
Caste, s. caste, *f.* *To lose* —, se rabaisser, s'encanailler
Castellan, s. châtelain, *m.*
Castellated, adj. encastré, (*embattled*) crénelé
Caster, s. calculateur, *m.*, (*of furniture*) roulette, *f.*
Castigate, va. châtier
Castigation, s. châtiment, *m.*
Casting, s. fonte, *f.*, (*print.*) clichage, *m.*, (*moulding*) moulage, *m.*, (*reckoning*) calcul, *m.* — *-vote*, voix prépondérante, *f.*
Castle, s. château, *m.*, (*chess*) tour, *f.*, (*nav.*) gaillard, *m.* —*s in the air*, des châteaux en Espagne
Castled, adj. couronné d'un château
Castor, s. castor, *m.* — *-oil*, huile de ricin, *f.*
Castrate, va. châtrer
Castration, s. castration, *f.*
Casual, adj. accidentel, fortuit, de passage
Casually, adv. fortuitement
Casualty, s. cas fortuit, *m.*, accident, *m.*, (*of fire*, *shipwreck*) sinistre, *m.*, (*mil.*) perte, *f.*
Casuist, s. casuiste, *m.*
Casuistical, adj. de casuiste
Cat, s. chat, *m.*, chatte, *f.*, (*whip*) fouet, *m.*, (*game*) bâtonnet, *m.* *To let the* — *out of the bag*, éventer la mèche. *To rain* —*s and dogs*, pleuvoir des hallebardes. — *o'-nine tails*, martinet, *m.* — *-call*, — *-pipe*, sifflet, *m.* — *-gut*, corde à boyau, *f.* — *-head*, bossoir, *m.* — *-hole*, chatière, *f.* — *-mint*, herbe aux chats, cataire, *f.* —*'s paw*, (*fig.*) dupe, *f.*, instrument, *m.*
Cataclysm, s. cataclysme, *m.*
Catacomb, s. catacombe, *f.*
Catalepsy, s. catalepsie, *f.*
Cataleptic, adj. cataleptique
Catalogue, s. catalogue, *m.*
Catalogue, va. cataloguer
Catalpa, s. catalpa, *m.*
Cataract, s. cataracte, *f.*
Catarrh, s. catarrhe, *m.*
Catarrhal, adj. catarrhal
Catastrophe, s. catastrophe, *f.*, (*conclusion*) dénoûment, *m.*
Catch, va. attraper, saisir, retenir, (*surprise*) prendre, surprendre, (*a train*) arriver à temps pour, (*fire*) prendre, (*the sight*) frapper, attirer, (*gain*) gagner; — vn. s'accrocher (à), se prendre (à), se communiquer. *To* — *it*, (*be scolded or punished*) en recevoir. — *at*, s'accrocher à, saisir. — *up*, saisir, (*overtake*) rattraper, (*notice*) relever
Catch, s. prise, capture, *f.*, profit, *m.*, affaire, *f.*, (*trick*) attrape, *f.*, (*mus.*) reprise, *f.*, (*of locks*, &c.) crampon, cliquet, *m.* — *-penny*, attrape-nigaude, *m.* — adj. de réclame, de boutique. — *-question*, question embarrassante, *f.* — *-word*, (*theat.*) réplique, *f.*
Catcher, s. attrapeur, *m.*, -euse, *f.*
Catching, adj. contagieux, séduisant
Catchup, s. *see* CATSUP
Catechism, s. catéchisme, *m.*
Catechist, s. catéchiste, *m.*
Catechize, va. catéchiser
Catechumen, s. catéchumène, *m.f.*
Categorical, adj. catégorique
Categorically, adv. catégoriquement
Category, s. catégorie, *f.*
Cater, vn. pourvoir (à)
Caterer, s. pourvoyeur, *m.*
Caterpillar, s. chenille, *f.*
Caterwaul, vn. crier, (*fig.*) faire du tintamarre
Caterwauling, s. sabbat, *m.*, (*any noise*) tintamarre, *m.*
Cathedral, s. adj. cathédrale, *f.*
Catholic, adj. s. catholique
Catholicism, s. catholicisme, *m.*
Catholicity, s. catholicité, *f.*
Catkin, s. chaton, *m.*
Catlike, adj. de chat
Catsup, s. sauce piquante, *f.*
Cattle, s. bétail, *m.sing.*, bestiaux, *m.pl.* — *-market*, marché aux bestiaux, *m.* — *-plague*, peste bovine, *f.*, typhus du gros bétail, *m.* — *-shed*, — *-house*, étable, *f.* — *-show*, exposition de bétail, *f.*
Caul, s. coiffe, *f.*
Cauliflower, s. chou-fleur, *m.*
Cause, s. cause, *f.*, raison, *f.*
Cause, va. causer
Causeless, adj. non fondé, sans raison
Causelessly, adv. sans cause, sans raison
Causeway, s. chaussée, *f.*
Caustic, s. adj. caustique, *m.*
Causticity, s. causticité, *f.*
Cauterism, **Cauterization**, **Cauterizing**, s. cautérisation, *f.*
Cauterize, va. cautériser
Cautery, s. cautère, *m.*
Caution, s. prudence, précaution, *f.*, (*notice*) avis, avertissement, *m.*
Caution, va. mettre en garde, prémunir (contre), prévenir (de), avertir (de)
Cautionary, adj. d'avertissement
Cautious, adj. prudent, circonspect, précautionné, (*of*) en garde (contre)
Cautiously, adv. avec précaution *or* circonspection
Cautiousness, s. prudence, *f.*
Cavalcade, s. cavalcade, *f.*
Cavalry, s. cavalerie, *f.*
Cave, s. caverne, *f.*, souterrain, antre, *m.*
Caveat, s. opposition, *f.*
Cavern, s. caverne, *f.*
Cavernous, adj. caverneux
Caviare, s. caviar, *m.*
Cavil, vn. ergoter, chicaner
Cavil, *or* **Cavilling**, s. pointillerie, ergoterie, chicane, *f.*
Caviller, s. chicanier, ergoteur, *m.*
Cavilling, adj. pointilleux
Cavity, s. cavité, *f.*
Cayman, s. caïman, *m.*
Cease, va.n. cesser
Ceaseless, adj. continuel
Ceaselessly, adv. sans cesse
Ceasing, s. cessation, *f.*
Cedar, s. cèdre, *m.*
Cedar, adj. de cèdre
Cede, va.n. céder
Cedilla, s. cédille, *f.*
Cedrat, s. cédrat, *m.*
Ceil, va. plafonner
Ceiling, s. plafond, *m.*
Celandine, s. chélidoine, *f.*
Celebrant, s. célébrant, *m.*
Celebrate, va. célébrer
Celebrated, adj. célèbre
Celebration, s. célébration, *f.*
Celebrity, s. célébrité, *f.*
Celerity, s. célérité, *f.*
Celery, s. céleri, *m.*
Celestial, adj. céleste. — s. esprit céleste, *m.*
Celestin, s. célestin, *m.*
Celibacy, s. célibat, *m.*
Cell, s. cellule, *f.*, (*compartment*) case, *f.*, (*bees*) alvéole, *f.*, (*mil.*) cachot, *m.*
Cellar, s. cave, *f.*, cellier, *m.*, (*small*) caveau, *m.* — *-man* (*butler*), sommelier, *m.*
Cellarage, s. caves, *f.pl.*
Cellaret, s. cave, *f.*
Cellular, adj. cellulaire
Celtic, adj. celtique
Cement, s. ciment, *m.*
Cement, va. cimenter; — vn. se cimenter
Cemetery, s. cimetière, *m.*
Cenobite, s. cénobite, *m.*
Cenobitic, adj. cénobitique
Cenotaph, s. cénotaphe, *m.*

Censer, s. encensoir, *m.*
Censor, s. censeur, *m.*
Censorial, adj. de censeur
Censorious, adj. critique, hargneux
Censoriously, adv. en censeur
Censoriousness, s. disposition à la critique, *f.*
Censorship, s. censure, *f.*
Censurable, adj. censurable, blâmable
Censurably, adv. d'une manière blâmable
Censure, s. censure, *f.*, blâme, *m.*
Censure, va. censurer, critiquer, blâmer
Censurer, s. censeur, critique, *m.*
Census, s. recensement, *m.*
Cent, s. *Per* —, pour cent
Centenarian, s. adj. centenaire, *m.f.*
Centenary, adj. centenaire
Centenary, s. centaine, *f.*, centième anniversaire, *m.*
Centennial, adj. séculaire
Centesimal, adj. centésimal
Centesimal, s. chiffre centésimal, *m.*
Centigrade, adj. centigrade
Centiped, s. scolopendre, *f.*
Central, adj. central
Centralization, s. centralisation, *f.*
Centralize, va. centraliser
Centrally, adv. d'une manière centrale
Centre, s. centre, milieu, *m.*, (*archit.*) cintre, *m.* — *-bit*, tarière, *f.*
Centre, va. placer au centre, (*fig.*) concentrer; — vn. être placé au centre, (*fut out*) faire centre, (*fig.*) se concentrer
Centreing, s. concentration, *f.*, (*archit.*) cintre, *m.*, (*fig.*) centre, *m.*
Centrifugal, adj. centrifuge
Centripetal, adj. centripète
Centuple, adj. s. centuple, *m.*
Centuple, va. centupler
Centurion, s. centurion, *m.*, (*in Scripture*) centenier, *m.*
Century, s. siècle, *m.*, centurie, *f.*
Ceramic, adj. céramique
Cereal, adj. s. céréale, *f.*
Cerebral, adj. cérébral
Cerecloth, s. toile gommée, toile d'embaumement, *f.*
Ceremonial, adj. de cérémonie. — s. cérémonial, *m.*, étiquette, *f.*
Ceremonious, adj. cérémonieux
Ceremoniously, adv. avec cérémonie
Ceremoniousness, s. formalisme, *m.*
Ceremony, s. cérémonie, *f.*, cérémonies, façons, *f.pl.*
Certain, adj. s. certain, *m.* *For* —, pour sûr
Certainly, adv. certainement, (*at least*) au moins, du moins
Certainty, s. certitude, *f.*, chose certaine, *f.* *To a* —, pour sûr, à coup sûr
Certificate, s. certificat, *m.*, diplôme, *m.*, (*birth, marriage, death*) acte, *m.*, (*copy of ditto*) extrait, *m.*, (*baptism*) extrait, *m.*, (*bankrupts*) concordat, *m.*
Certificated, adj. diplômé
Certify, va. certifier, notifier
Cerulean, adj. bleu, azuré
Cesarian, adj. césarienne
Cessation, s. cessation, *f.*
Cession, s. cession, *f.*
Cesspool, s. puisard, *m.*, (*closets*) fosse d'aisance, *f.*
Cestus, s. ceste, *m.*
Cetacean, s. cétacé, *m.*
Chafe, va. chauffer, réchauffer, (*fig.*) irriter; — vn. s'échauffer, s'irriter, être irrité, (*rubbing*) frotter, s'écorcher
Chafer, s. hanneton, *m.*
Chaff, s. menue paille, *f.*, (*jeer*) gausserie, plaisanterie, *f.* — *-cutter*, hachepaille, *m.*
Chaff, va. se gausser de, gouailler, berner
Chaffer, va. marchander, barguigner
Chaffinch, s. pinson, *m.*
Chaffy, adj. de paille, plein de paille
Chain, s. chaine, *f.*, (*for keys*) châtelaine, *f.* *Albert* —, chaine de gilet. — *-pier*, jetée suspendue, *f.* — *-shot*, boulet ramé, *m.*
Chain, va. enchainer, fermer par une chaine
Chair, s. (*seat*) chaise, *f.*, fauteuil, *m.*, (*professors*) chaire, *f.*, (*president*) fauteuil, *m.*, (*fig.*) président, *m.*, (*rail.*) coussinet, *m.* *Bath* —, vinaigrette, *f.* *Easy* —, fauteuil, *m.* *Elizabethan* —, *low-seat* —, chauffeuse, *f.* *To be in the* —, tenir or occuper le fauteuil. — *!* — *!* à l'ordre! à l'ordre! — *-bottomer*, empailleur, *m.* — *-cover*, housse, *f.* — *-mender*, rempailleur, *m.*
Chair, va. porter en triomphe
Chairman, s. président, *m.*, (*of a Bath chair*) traîneur de vinaigrette, *m.*
Chaise, s. chaise, *f.*
Chalcedony, s. calcédoine, *f.*
Chalice, s. calice, *m.*, coupe, *f.*
Chalk, s. craie, *f.*, crayon, *m.* — *-pit*, carrière de craie, *f.* — *-stone*, pierre de chaux, *f.*
Chalk, va. marquer avec de la craie, crayonner, tracer, (*agric.*) marner. — *out*, tracer
Chalky, adj. crayeux
Challenge, s. cartel, défi, *m.*, prétention, demande, *f.*, (*law*) récusation, *f.*, (*mil.*) qui-vive, *m.*
Challenge, va. défier, provoquer, appeler en duel, (*rights*) reclamer, (*law*) récuser, (*mil.*) crier qui-vive
Challenger, s. provocateur, agresseur, *m.*
Chalybeate, adj. ferrugineux. — s. source d'eau ferrugineuse, *f.*
Chamber, s. chambre, *f.*, (*office*) bureau, *m.*, cabinet, *m.*; —*s*, pl. bureaux, *m.pl.*, (*solicitors*) étude, *f.*, appartement de garçon, *m.* *In* —*s*, (*judges*) en référé. — *-counsel*, avocat consultant, *m.* — *-maid*, fille de chambre, *f.*
Chambered, adj. à . . . coups. *Six-* — *revolver*, revolver à six coups
Chamberlain, s. chambellan, *m.*
Chameleon, s. caméléon, *m.*
Chamois, s. chamois, *m.*
Champ, va.n. ronger, mâcher
Champaign, s. adj. campagne, plaine, *f.*; de campagne, plat, ouvert
Champion, s. champion, *m.*
Chance, s. chance, *f.*, hasard, *m.* *To take one's* —, courir la chance
Chance, adj. accidentel, de hasard, imprévu
Chance, vn. arriver, se rencontrer. *To* — *it*, risquer le paquet
Chancel, s. sanctuaire, *m.*
Chancellor, s. chancelier, *m.* *Lord* —, ministre de la justice, *m.* — *of the Exchequer*, ministre des finances, *m.*
Chancellorship, s. dignité de chancelier, *f.*
Chancery, s. chancellerie, *f.*
Chandelier, s. lustre, *m.*
Chandler, s. fabricant or marchand de chandelles, *m.*, marchand (de . . .), fournisseur, *m.*
Change, va.n. changer, se changer (en), (*the moon*) se renouveler
Change, s. changement, *m.*, vicissitude, *f.*, (*money*) monnaie, *f.*, (*exchange*) bourse, *f.*, (*the moon*) phase, *f.*
Changeable, adj. changeant
Changeableness, s. caractère changeant, *m.*, mobilité, *f.*
Changeably, adv. avec inconstance
Changeless, adj. invariable
Changeling, s. enfant substitué, *m.*
Changer, s. changeur, *m.*
Channel, s. canal, *m.*, (*fig.*) voie, *f.*, (*rivers*) lit, *m.*, (*harbours*) passe, *f.*, (*roads*) rigole, *f.*, (*naut.*) détroit, *m.*, (*arch.*) cannelure, *f.* *The* (*British*) —, la Manche, *f.*
Channel, va. creuser, sillonner, (*arch.*) canneler
Chant, va.n. chanter
Chant, s. chant, *m.*
Chanter, s. chantre, *m.*
Chanticleer, s. le réveille-matin, le coq, *m.*
Chaos, s. chaos, *m.*
Chaotic, adj. de chaos, confus
Chap, va.n. gercer, se gercer
Chap, s. gerçure, *f.*, (*jaw*) mâchoire, *f.*, (*pig*) bajoue, *f.*, (*fellow*) garçon, *m.*, gaillard, *m.*
Chapel, s. chapelle, *f.* — *of ease*, succursale, *f.*
Chaperone, s. chaperon, *m.*
Chaperone, va. chaperonner
Chaplain, s. chapelain, *m.*
Chaplaincy, s. chapellenie, *f.*
Chaplet, s. chapelet, *m.*, (*peacock*) aigrette, *f.*
Chapman, s. marchand, *m.*
Chapter, s. chapitre, *m.*
Char, s. ouvrage à la journée, *m.*, tâche, *f.* — *-woman*, femme de journée, *f.*
Char, va. carboniser, purifier; — vn. se charbonner, (*work*) aller en journée
Character, s. caractère, *m.*, (*state*) rang, *m.*, (*part*) rôle, *m.*, (*person*) personnage, *m.*, (*odd man*) original, *m.*, (*description*) portrait, *m.*, réputation, *f.*, honneur, *m.*, (*morality*) moralité, *f.*, (*sort*) genre, *m.*, nature, *f.*, (*servants*) certificat, *m.*, renseignements, *m.pl.* *Bad* —, mauvais sujet, *m.*
Characteristic, adj. caractéristique
Characteristic, s. trait caractéristique, propre, *m.*
Characteristically, adv. d'une manière caractéristique
Characterize, va. caractériser
Charade, s. charade, *f.*
Charcoal, s. charbon de bois, charbon, *m.* *Animal* —, noir animal, *m.* — *-burner*, charbonnier, *m.*
Charge, va.n. charger (*price, fee*) prendre, demander, (*on a bill*) compter, (*admin.*) taxer, percevoir, (*order*) ordonner (à), (*accuse*) accuser, (*impute*) imputer (à), (*book-keep.*) porter (à)
Charge, s. charge, *f.*, soin, *m.*, garde, *f.*, dépôt, *m.*, ordre, *m.*, accusation, *f.*, (*judge*) réquisitoire, *m.*, résumé, *m.*, (*bishop*) mandement, *m.*, (*expenses*) frais, dépens, *m.pl.*, (*price*) prix, *m.*, (*admin.*) taxe, *f.* *To bring a* — *against*, accuser. *To give in* —, faire arrêter. *To take* — *of*, se charger de, avoir soin de. — *-sheet*, (*police*) livre de consignation, *m.*

Chargeable, adj. à charge (à), à la charge (de), imputable (à), accusable (de), imposable

Charger, s. cheval de bataille, *m.*

Chariot, s. chariot, char, *m.*

Charioteer, s. conducteur, *m.*

Charitable, adj. charitable, de charité, de bienfaisance

Charitableness, s. charité, *f.*

Charitably, adv. charitablement

Charity, s. charité, *f.*, bienfaisance, *f.* — *begins at home*, charité bien ordonnée commence par soi-même

Charlock, s. (*bot.*) sénevé, *m.*

Charm, s. charme, *m.*, (*trinket*) breloque, *f.*

Charm, va.n. charmer

Charmer, s. enchanteur, *m.*, -teresse, *f.*

Charmingly, adv. d'une manière charmante

Charmless, adj. sans charme

Charnel, **Charnel-house**, s. charnier, *m.*

Chart, s. carte, *f.*

Charter, s. chartre, charte, *f.*, (*law*) acte, *m.*

Charter, va. fréter, noliser

Chartered, adj. institué par une charte, (*nav.*) frété

Chary, adj. soigneux, circonspect

Chase, va. chasser, donner la chasse (à), poursuivre, (*metals*) ciseler

Chase, s. chasse, poursuite, *f.*

Chaser, s. chasseur, *m.*, (*metals*) ciseleur, *m.*

Chasing, s. ciselure, *f.*

Chasm, s. ouverture, *f.*, vide, creux, *m.*, abîme, *m.*

Chaste, adj. chaste, pudique, pur

Chastely, adv. chastement, purement

Chasten, va. purifier, châtier

Chasteness, s. pureté, *f.*

Chastise, va. châtier, punir

Chastisement, s. châtiment, *m.*

Chastiser, s. personne qui châtie, *f.*

Chastity, s. chasteté, *f.*, pureté, *f.*

Chasuble, s. chasuble, *f.*

Chat, vn. causer, jaser

Chat, s. causerie, *f.* *To have a —*, causer, jaser

Chattels, s. biens, *m.pl.*, effets, *m.pl.*

Chatter, vn. jaser, babiller, jacasser, (*teeth*) claquer

Chatter, s. jaserie, *f.*, caquetage, *m.* — *-box*, moulin à paroles, *m.*, jacasse, *f.*

Chatterer, s. jaseur, *m.*, -euse, *f.*, babillard, *m.*, -e, *f.*

Chattering, s. jaserie, *f.*, caquetage, *m.*, (*teeth*) claquement, *m.*

Chatty, adj. causeur

Cheap, adj. à bon marché, de peu de valeur. *Dirt-* —, à vil prix, pour rien

Cheapen, va. marchander

Cheapener, s. marchandeur, *m.*

Cheaply, adv. à bon marché, à peu de frais

Cheapness, s. bon marché, bas prix, *m.*

Cheat, va.n. tromper, filouter, tricher

Cheat, s. tromperie, fourberie, tricherie, *f.*, (*pers.*) trompeur, fourbe, filou, *m.*, tricheur, *m.*

Check, va. réprimer, arrêter, reprendre, blâmer, vérifier, (*names on a list*) pointer

Check, s. échec, *m.*, obstacle, *m.*, réprimande, *f.*, (*blow*) coup, *m.*, (*curb*) frein, *m.*, (*on stuffs*) carreau, *m.*, (*stuff*) étoffe à carreaux, *f.* *With —s, checked*, à carreaux — *-mate*, échec et mat. — *-mate*, va. mater, faire échec et mat

Checker, **Chequer**, va. marqueter, (*stuffs*) diaprer, (*variegate*) bigarrer, nuancer, (*mix*) mélanger

Checker, s. — *-board*, damier, *m.* — *-work*, marqueterie, *f.*

Checkered, **Chequered**, adj. (*fig.*) varié, plein d'accidents

Cheek, s. joue, *f.*, (*pigs*) bajoue, *f.*, (*door*) feuillure, *f.*, (*press*) jumelle, *f.*, impudence, *f.*, front, *m.* — *by jowl*, côte à côte. — *-bone*, pommette, *f.* — *-tooth*, dent molaire, *f.*

Cheeked, adj. aux joues . . .

Cheeky, adj. impudent, peu gêné

Cheer, va. réjouir, égayer, animer, encourager, consoler, applaudir; — vn. se réjouir, pousser des acclamations. — *up*, se dérider, prendre courage

Cheer, s. chère, *f.*, gaieté, *f.*, courage, *m.*, acclamation, *f.*, applaudissement, *m.*

Cheerful, adj. gai, joyeux

Cheerfully, adv. gaiment, joyeusement, de bon cœur

Cheerfulness, s. gaieté, joie, *f.*

Cheerily, adv. gaiment

Cheering, s. acclamations, *f.pl.*, applaudissements, *m.pl.*

Cheerless, adj. triste, sombre

Cheese, s. fromage, *m.* — *-cake*, talmouse, *f.* — *-curds*, lait caillé, *m.* — *-scoop*, couteau à fromage, *m.* — *-stand*, jatte à fromage, *f.* — *-taster*, sonde à fromage, *f.* — *-dish*, plat à fromage, *m.* — *-vat*, éclisse, *f.*

Cheesy, adj. fromageux, comme il faut

Cheffonier, s. chiffonnier, *m.*

Chemical, adj. chimique, de chimie

Chemical, s. produit chimique, *m.* — *-works*, fabrique de produits chimiques, *f.*

Chemically, adv. chimiquement

Chemise, s. chemise (*de femme*), *f.*

Chemisette, s chemisette, *f.*

Chemist, s. chimiste, *m.*, (*apothecary*) pharmacien, *m.* —*'s shop*, pharmacie, *f.*

Chemistry, s. chimie, *f.*

Cheque, s. mandat, bon, *m.*, chèque, *m.*, (*ticket*) contremarque, *f.*, (*omnibuses*) bulletin de correspondance, *m.*, correspondance, *f.* — *-book*, cahier de chèques, *m.* — *-taker*, donneur de contremarques, *m.*

Cherish, va. chérir, protéger, soigner

Cheroot, s. bout coupé, *m.* *Manilla* —, manille à bout coupé, *m.*

Cherry, s. cerise, *f.*, (*wood*) merisier, cerisier, *m.* — *-cheeked*, aux joues vermeilles. — *-laurel*, laurier-cerise, *m.* — *-orchard*, cerisaie, *f.* — *-pie*, tourte aux cerises, *f.* — *-tree*, cerisier, *m.*

Cherry, adj. cerise, vermeil

Cherub, s. chérubin, *m.*

Cherubic, adj. de chérubin

Chervil, s. cerfeuil, *m.*

Cheshire cheese, s. fromage de Chester, *m.*

Chess, s. échecs, *m.pl.* — *-board*, échiquier, *m.* — *-man*, pion, *m.*

Chest, s. (*box*) coffre, *m.*, caisse, boîte, *f.*, (*small*) coffret, *m.*, (*pers.*) poitrine, *f.*, torse, *m.*, (*horses*) poitrail, *m.* — *of drawers*, commode, *f.*

Chested, adj. à poitrine

Chestnut, s. châtaigne, *f.*, marron, *m.* — *-colour*, châtain, *m.* — *-plantation*, châtaigneraie, *f.* — *-tree*, châtaignier, *m.*, marronnier, *m.*

Chestnut, adj. châtain, (*horses*) alezan

Cheval-glass, s. psyché, *f.*

Cheval-screen, s. écran de cheminée, *m.*

Chew, va.n. mâcher, (*tobacco*) chiquer, (*fig.*) ruminer, méditer

Chewing, s. mastication, *f.*

Chicane, **Chicanery**, s. chicane, *f.*

Chick, s. poussin, *m.*, (*pers.*) poulet, *m.*, poulette, *f.* — *-pea*, pois chiche, *m.* — *-weed*, mouron, *m.*

Chicken, s. poulet, *m.* — *-hearted*, adj. timide

Chickling, s. poussin, *m.*

Chicory, s. chicorée, *f.*

Chide, va.n. réprimander, blâmer

Chider, s. grondeur, *m.*, -euse, *f.*

Chiding, adj. grondeur

Chiding, s. gronderie, *f.*

Chief, s. chef, *m.* — adj. premier, principal, (*leading*) en chef

Chiefly, adv. principalement, surtout

Chieftain, s. chef, *m.*

Chilblain, s. engelure, *f.*

Child, s. enfant, *m.f.* *From a* —, dès l'enfance. *With* —, enceinte, grosse. — *-bearing*, travail d'enfant, *m.* — *-bed*, couches, *f.pl.* — *-birth*, enfantement, *m.* — *-murder*, infanticide, *m.*

Childermas-day, s. fête des saints Innocents, *f.*

Childhood, s. enfance, *f.*

Childish, adj. enfant, (*things*) enfantin, d'enfant, (*trifling*) puéril

Childishly, adv. puérilement

Childishness, s. enfantillage, *m.*, puérilité, *f.*

Childless, adj. sans enfant

Childlike, adj. d'enfant

Chill, s. froid, *m.*, refroidissement, *m.*, frisson, *m.*, sentiment de tristesse, *m.* *To take the — off*, faire dégourdir

Chill, adj. froid, glacé

Chill, va. refroidir, glacer, geler, faire frissonner

Chilliness, s. frisson, frissonnement, *m.*

Chilly, adj. (*pers.*) frileux, (*things*) un peu froid

Chilness, s. froid, *m.*, frisson, *m.*

Chime, s. accord, *m.*, harmonie, *f.*, (*bells*) carillon, *m.*

Chime, vn. (*bells*) carillonner, (*agree*) s'accorder (avec); — va. mettre en mouvement

Chimera, s. chimère, *f.*

Chimerical, adj. chimérique

Chimerically, adv. chimériquement

Chimney, s. cheminée, *f.* — *on fire*, feu de cheminée, *m.* — *-corner*, coin du feu, *m.* — *-cowl*, tabourin, *m.* — *-flue*, tuyau de cheminée, *m.* — *-piece*, cheminée, *f.*, chambranle, *m.* — *-pot*, mitre, *f.* — *-sweeper*, ramoneur, *m.*

Chin, s. menton, *m.*

China, s. (*ware*) porcelaine, porcelaine de Chine, *f.* — *-man*, Chinois, *m.* — *-ware*, porcelaine, *f.*

Chinchilla, s. chinchilla, *m.*

Chine, s. échine, échinée, *f.*

Chinese, adj. — *bells*, chapeau chinois, *m.*

Chink, s. fente, crevasse, *f.*, (*sounds*) tintement, son, *m.*

Chink, va. crevasser, (*jingle*) faire sonner; — vn. se crevasser, sonner

Chinky, adj. crevassé

Chinned, adj. à menton

Chintz, s. perse, cretonne, *f.*

Chip, va. couper, hacher; — vn. s'éclater, (*china*) s'écailler

Chip, s. (*wood*) copeau, *m.*, (*stone*) éclat, *m.* *A — in porridge*, un cautère sur une jambe de bois. *To be a — of the old block*, chasser de race.

— *-axe*, doloire, *f.* — *-hat*, chapeau brésilien, *m.*
Chiromancer, s. chiromancien, *m.*, -ne, *f.*
Chiromancy, s. chiromancie, *f.*
Chiropodist, s. pédicure, *m.*
Chirp, Chirrup, vn. gazouiller, chanter, grisoller, (*insects*) crier, chanter
Chirp, Chirping, Chirrup, s. gazouillement, ramage, *m.*, chant, *m.*, (*insects*) cri, *m.*
Chisel, s. ciseau, *m.*
Chisel, va. ciseler, (*cheat*) flouter
Chit, s. germe, *m.*, (*child*) bambin, marmot, *m.*
Chit-chat, s. causerie, *f.*, babil, caquet, *m.*
Chitterlings, s. andouille, *f.*
Chivalrous, adj. chevaleresque
Chivalry, s. chevalerie, *f.*
Chives, s. ciboulette, civette, *f.*
Chlorate, s. chlorate, *m.*
Chloride, s. chlorure, *m.*
Chlorine, s. chlore, *m.*
Chloroform, s. chloroforme, *m.* *To administer — to*, chloroformer
Chocolate, s. chocolat, *m.* — *-almonds*, chocolat praliné. — *-custard*, crème au chocolat, *f.* — *-dealer*, chocolatier, *m.* — *-drop*, pastille de chocolat, *f.* — *-pot*, chocolatière, *f.*
Choice, s. choix, *m.*, (*pers.*) élite, *f.*
Choice, adj. choisi, de choix, exquis, (*wine*) fin, (*pers.*) d'élite, scrupuleux dans le choix
Choicely, adv. avec choix, avec goût
Choiceness, s. choix, *m.*, excellence, supériorité, *f.*
Choir, s. chœur, *m.*
Choke, va.n. suffoquer, étouffer, étrangler. — *up*, engorger, boucher
Choke, s. foin, *m.*
Choke-damp, s. mofette, *f.*
Choker, s. cravate, *f.*
Choking, s. suffocation, *f.*
Choky, adj. suffocant, étouffant
Cholera, s. choléra, *m.*
Choleric, adj. cholérique, bilieux
Choose, va. choisir, élire; — vn. préférer
Chooser, s. personne qui choisit, *f.*
Choosing, s. choix, *m.*
Chop, va.n. hacher, couper, fendre, (*wind*) changer, tourner, (*sea*) clapoter. — *and change*, troquer, échanger, changer. — *off*, trancher, couper. — *up*, hacher, dévorer
Chop, s. côtelette, *f.*, (*mouth*) gueule, *f.*, (*vice*) mâchoire, *f.* — *and change*, troc, *m.*, veine et déveine, *f.*, vicissitude, *f.* — *-fallen*, adj. penaud. — *-house*, restaurant, *m.* — *-stick*, aiguille, baguette, *f.*
Chopper, s. couperet, *m.*
Chopping, s. coupe, *f.*, (*nav.*) clapotage, *m.* — *-board*, hachoir, *m.*, (*butchers*) ais, *m.* — *-block*, billot, *m.* — *-knife*, couperet, *m.*
Chopping, adj. (*sea*) clapoteux, (*wind*) variable
Choral, adj. de chœur, en chœur
Chorally, adv. en chœur
Chord, s. corde, *f.*
Chorist, s. choriste, *m.*
Chorister, s. chantre, *m.*
Chorus, s. chœur, *m.*, (*fig.*) concert, *m.*
Chouse, va. attraper, carotter
Chrism, s. chrême, *m.*
Christen, va. baptiser
Christendom, s. chrétienté, *f.*
Christening, s. baptême, *m.*
Christian, s.adj. chrétien, *m.*, -ne, *f.*
Christianity, s. christianisme, *m.*
Christianize, va. christianiser
Christianlike, Christianly, adj. chrétien, de chrétien, en chrétien
Christianly, adv. chrétiennement
Christmas, s. Noël, *m.* — *-box*, étrennes, *f.pl.* — *-day*, jour de Noël, *m.*
Chrome, s. chrôme, *m.*
Chronic, adj. chronique
Chronicle, s. chronique, *f.*; —s, pl. Paralipomènes, *m.pl.*
Chronicle, va. enregistrer
Chronicler, s. chroniqueur, *m.*
Chronological, adj. chronologique
Chronology, s. chronologie, *f.*
Chronometer, s. chronomètre, *m.*
Chrysalis, s. chrysalide, *f.*
Chrysanthemum, s. chrysanthème, *m.*
Chrysolite, s. chrysolithe, *f.*
Chub, s. chabot, meunier, *m.* — *-cheeked*, *-faced*, adj. joufflu
Chubby, adj. joufflu
Chuck, vn.a. (*hens*) glousser, appeler; caresser
Chuck, s. gloussement, *m.*, (*gentle blow*) petite tape sous le menton, *f.* — *-farthing*, fossette, *f.*
Chuckle, vn. rire tout bas (de)
Chuckle, s. rire étouffé, *m.*
Chum, s. camarade, *m.*, intime, *m.*
Chump, Chunk, s. tronçon, *m.*
Church, s. église, *f.*, (*Protestant*) temple, *m.*, (*profession*) état ecclésiastique, *m.* — *of England*, Eglise anglicane. — *-lands*, biens d'église, *m.pl.* — *-mouse*, rat d'église, *m.* — *-plate*, argenterie, *f.* — *-rate*, taxe pour l'entretien de l'église, *f.* — *-time*, office divin, *m.* — *-warden*, marguillier, *m.* — *-yard*, cimetière, *m.*
Churching, s. relevailles, *f.pl.*
Churchman, s. ecclésiastique, *m.*, anglican, *m.*
Churl, s. rustre, manant, *m.*
Churlish, adj. grossier, brutal
Churlishly, adv. grossièrement, brutalement
Churlishness, s. grossiereté, brutalité, *f.*
Churn, s. baratte, *f.* — *-staff*, batte à beurre, *f.*
Churn, va. baratter, (*beat*) battre, agiter
Chyle, s. chyle, *m.*
Ciceronian, adj. cicéronien
Cider, s. cidre, *m.* — *-mill*, pressoir à pommes, *m.*
Cigar, s. cigare, *m.* *Foreign* —, havane, *m.* — *-case*, porte-cigares, *m.* — *-divan*, fumoir, *m.* — *-holder*, *-tube*, brûle-cigare, porte-cigare, *m.* — *-shop*, bureau *or* débit de tabac, *m.*
Cigarette, s. cigarette, *f.* — *-paper*, papier à cigarettes, *m.*
Cincture, s. ceinture, *f.*
Cinder, s. cendre, *f.*, (*coals*) escarbille, *f.* — *-pail*, *-sifter*, tamiseur, étouffoir, *m.*
Cinderella, s. Cendrillon, *f.*
Cinerary, adj. cinéraire
Cinnabar, s. cinabre, *m.*
Cinnamon, s. cannelle, *f.* — *-tree*, cannellier, *m.*
Cinque, s. cinq, *m.*
Cipher, s. zéro, *m.*, chiffre, *m.*
Cipher, vn. chiffrer, calculer
Ciphering, s. calcul, *m.*
Circle, s. cercle, *m.*
Circle, va. entourer, environner; — vn. former un cercle, faire le tour, revenir
Circlet, s. anneau, cercle, *m.*
Circuit, s. circuit, tour, *m.*, rotation, *f.*, (*enclosure*) enceinte, *f.*, (*judges*) tournée, *f.*
Circuitous, adj. détourné
Circuitously, adv. d'une manière détournée
Circuity, s. circuits, détours, *m.pl.*
Circulable, adj. qui peut être mis en circulation
Circular, adj. s. circulaire, *f.*, bulletin, *m.*
Circularly, adv. circulairement
Circulate, vn. circuler; — va. mettre en circulation
Circulating-library, s. cabinet de lecture, *m.*
Circulation, s. circulation, *f.*
Circulatory, adj circulatoire
Circumcise, va. circoncire
Circumcision, s. circoncision, *f.*
Circumference, s. circonférence, *f.*
Circumflex, adj. s. circonflexe, *m.*
Circumjacent, adj. circonvoisin
Circumlocution, s. circonlocution, *f.*
Circumlocutory, adj. indirect, verbeux
Circumnavigate, va. naviguer autour de, contourner
Circumnavigation, s. circumnavigation, *f.*
Circumscribe, va. circonscrire
Circumscription, s. circonscription, *f.*
Circumspect, adj. circonspect
Circumspection, s. circonspection, *f.*
Circumstance, s. circonstance, *f.*; —s, pl. état, *m.*, cas, *m.*, moyens, *m.pl.* *To be in bad —s*, être mal dans ses affaires
Circumstance, va. fournir d'incidents
Circumstanced, adj. dans une position
Circumstantial, adj. accessoire, circonstancié, détaillé, (*evidence*) indirect, par induction
Circumstantially, adv. par les circonstances, minutieusement
Circumstantiate, va. détailler
Circumvallation, s. circonvallation, *f.*
Circumvent, va. circonvenir
Circumvolution, s. circonvolution, *f.*
Circus, s. cirque, *m.*
Cistern, s. citerne, *f.*, fontaine, *f.*, (*pumps*) réservoir, *m.*
Cit, s. badaud, *m.*
Citadel, s. citadelle, *f.*
Citation, s. citation, *f.*
Cite, va. citer
Citer, s. citateur, *m.*, -trice, *f.*
Citizen, s. citoyen, *m.*, bourgeois, *m.*, habitant, *m.*
Citizenship, s. droit de cité, *m.*
Citrate, s. citrate, *m.*
Citric, adj. citrique
Citrine, adj. citrin
City, s. ville, *f.*, cité, *f.* — *-article*, (*newspapers*) bulletin de la Bourse, *m.*
Civet, — *-cat*, s. civette, *f.*
Civic, adj. civique
Civil, adj. civil, poli
Civilian, s. légiste, *m.*, bourgeois, *m.*
Civility, s. civilité, politesse, *f.*
Civilization, s. civilisation, *f.*
Civilize, va. civiliser
Civilly, adv. civilement
Clack, s. claquet. — *-valve*, clapet, *m.*
Clack, vn. cliqueter
Clacker, s. claquet, *m.*
Clad, adj. habillé, vêtu (de). *Iron-* —, (*ship*) cuirassé
Claim, va. réclamer, exiger, prétendre à

Claim, s. demande, *f.*, droit, *m.*, prétention, *f.*, (*law*) réclamation, *f.*

Claimant, s. prétendant, *m.*

Clam, s. mollusque, *m.*

Clam, va. engluer

Clamber, vn. grimper

Clamminess, s. viscosité, *f.*

Clammy, adj. gluant, pâteux

Clamorous, adj. bruyant, criard

Clamorously, adv. bruyamment, à grands cris

Clamour, s. clameur, *f.*, cri, *m.*

Clamour, vn. crier, vociférer, (*for*) demander à grands cris

Clamourer, s. criard, *m.*, -e, *f.*

Clamp, s. crampon, *m.*, (*wood*) emboîture, *f.*, (*bricks*) tas de briques, *m.*

Clamp, va. fixer

Clan, s. clan, *m.*, (*association*) clique, coterie, *f.*

Clandestine, adj. clandestin

Clandestinely, adv. clandestinement

Clang, vn. résonner; — va. faire résonner

Clang, Clangour, s. bruit, son aigu, *m.*, (*arms*) cliquetis, *m.*

Clangorous, adj. résonnant

Clap, va. frapper, (*hands*) claquer, applaudir, (*throw*) jeter, flanquer, fourrer, appliquer, (*doors*) fermer. — *up*, bâcler, claquemurer

Clap, s. coup, *m.*, (*hands*) battement, claquement, *m.*, (*slap*) claque, *f.* — *-board*, douve, *f.* — *-net*, filet, *m.*, nappe, *f.* — *-trap*, coup de théâtre, *m.*, blague, *f.* — adj. à effet, captieux

Clapper, s. claqueur, *m.*, (*bells*) battant, *m.*, (*mills*) claquet, *m.*, (*pumps*) clapet, *m.*, (*snap*) cliquette, *f.*

Clapping, s. battements, *m.pl.*, applaudissements, *m. pl.*

Clare-obscure, s. clair-obscur, *m.*

Claret, s. vin de Bordeaux, *m.*

Clarification, s. clarification, *f.*

Clarify, va.n. clarifier, se clarifier

Clarinet, s. clarinette, *f.*

Clarion, s. clairon, *m.*

Clash, vn. résonner, s'entre-choquer, se contrarier, être en opposition; — va. faire résonner

Clash, Clashing, s. fracas, *m.*, choc, *m.*, opposition, *f.*

Clashing, adj. résonnant, opposé

Clasp, s. agrafe, *f.*, fermoir, *m.*, étreinte, *f.* — *-knife*, couteau de poche, *m.*

Clasp, va. agrafer, étreindre, embrasser, (*hands*) joindre

Class, s. classe, *f.*, (*course*) cours, *m.* — *-fellow*, camarade de classe, *m.* — *-room*, classe, *f.*

Class, va. classer

Classic, Classical, adj. classique

Classic, s. classique, *m.*

Classification, s. classification, *f.*

Classify, va. classifier

Classing, s. classement, *m.*

Clatter, s. bruit, fracas, *m.*

Clatter, vn. faire du bruit, retentir

Clattering, s. bruit, *m.*

Clause, s. clause, *f.*, membre de phrase, *m.*

Claustral, adj. claustral

Claw, s. griffe, *f.*, (*lobsters*) pince, *f.*

Claw, va. griffer, déchirer. — *away*, *off*, déchirer

Clawed, adj. onguiculé

Clay, s. argile, terre glaise, *f.*, (*mud*) boue, *f.*, (*earth*) terre, *f.*

Clayey, Clayish, adj. argileux

Clean, adj. propre, net, pur, (*dexterous*) adroit, (*linen*) blanc, (*boots*) ciré

Clean, adv. entièrement, tout à fait, adroitement

Clean, va. nettoyer, (*pick out*) éplucher, (*with sand*) écurer, (*boots*) décrotter, cirer, (*wells*, &c.) curer, (*wool*) dégraisser

Cleaning, s. nettoyage, *m.*, curage, *m.*, dégraissage, *m.*

Cleanliness, s. propreté, *f.*

Cleanly, adj. propre, pur. — adv. proprement

Cleanness, s. propreté, *f.*, pureté, innocence, *f.*

Cleanse, va. nettoyer, laver, purifier, (*wells*, &c.) curer

Cleanser, s. chose qui nettoie, *f.*

Cleansing, s. nettoyage, *m.*, (*fig.*) purification, *f.*, curage, *m.*

Clear, adj. clair, certain, pur, net, (*whole*) plein, (*free*) libre (de), innocent (de). *To get* —, se tirer d'affaire. *To keep — of*, éviter. — *-sighted*, clairvoyant. — *-sightedness*, clairvoyance, *f.* — *-starch*, blanchir à neuf. — *-starcher*, blanchisseuse de fin, *f.*

Clear, adv. clairement, entièrement

Clear, va. éclaircir, clarifier, dégager, débarrasser, faire évacuer, (*leap over*) franchir, (*gain*) gagner, avoir un bénéfice net de, (*acquit*, &c.) acquitter, libérer, justifier, (*goods*) acquitter les droits, (*lands*) défricher, (*nav.*) doubler, (*mil.*) balayer. — *the table*, desservir. — *away*, — *off*, débarrasser, desservir, (*rubbish*) déblayer. — *off one's arrears*, se mettre au courant

Clearance, s. acquit, *m.*, (*com.*) débarras, *m.*

Clearing, s. justification, *f.*, acquittement, *m.*, (*lands*) défrichement, *m.*

Clearly, adv. clairement, évidemment

Clearness, s. clarté, *f.*, netteté, pureté, *f.*

Cleave, va. fendre; — vn. se fendre, (*stick*) se coller (à), (*fig.*) s'attacher (à)

Cleaver, s. couperet, *m.*, (*wood*) merlin, *m.*, (*pers.*) fendeur, *m.*

Cleft, s. fente, ouverture, *f.*

Clematis, s. clématite, *f.*

Clemency, s. clémence, *f.*, (*weather*) douceur, *f.*

Clement, adj. clément, doux

Clemently, adv. avec clémence

Cleptomania, s. cleptomanie, *f.*

Clergy, s. clergé, *m.*

Clergyman, s. ecclésiastique, *m.*, (*Protestant*) ministre, *m.*, pasteur, *m.*, (*Catholic*) prêtre, abbé, *m.*

Clerical, adj. clérical

Clerically, adv. cléricalement

Clerk, s. clerc, *m.*, ecclésiastique, *m.*, secrétaire, *m.*, (*law courts*) greffier, *m.*, (com.) commis, *m.* *Junior* —, (*lawyers*) petit clerc, *m.*

Clerkship, s. place de clerc, place de commis, *f.*

Clever, adj. habile, adroit, intelligent, d'esprit, ingénieux, (*well done*) bien fait

Cleverly, adv. habilement, adroitement, bien

Cleverness, s. habileté, adresse, *f.*, intelligence, *f.*, moyens, *m.pl.*

Click, vn. faire tic-tac

Click, s. cliquet, *m.*

Clicker, s. coupeur cordonnier, *m.*

Clicking, s. tic-tac, *m.*

Client, s. client, *m.*

Cliff, s. falaise, *f.*, rocher, *m.*, (*hill*) colline, *f.*

Cliffy, adj. rocailleux

Climacteric, adj. climatérique; —*s*, pl. année climatérique, *f.*

Climate, s. climat, *m.*

Climatic, adj. de climat

Climax, s. gradation, *f.*

Climb, va.n. grimper, gravir, monter, escalader, (*fig.*) s'élever

Climber, s. personne qui grimpe, *f.*, (*bot.*) plante grimpante, *f.*

Clime, s. climat, *m.*

Clinch, va. tenir à poing fermé, (*the fist*) fermer, serrer, (*nails*) river, (*log.*) établir

Clinch, Clincher, s. crampon, *m.*, mot sans réplique, *m.* *To give one a* —, river à quelqu'un son clou, mettre quelqu'un à sa place

Cling, vn. se cramponner, se coller (à), s'attacher (à)

Clinical, adj. clinique

Clink, vn. tinter, résonner; — va. faire résonner

Clink, s. tintement, *m.*

Clinker, s. mâchefer, *m.*

Clip, va. couper, rogner, (*horses*) tondre, (*words*) estropier

Clipper, s. rogneur, *m.*, tondeur, *m.*, (*ship*) clipper, *m.*

Clipping, s. rognure, *f.*

Cloak, s. manteau, *m.*, capote, *f.*, (*fig.*) masque, *m.* — *-bag*, valise, *f.* — *-room*, vestiaire, *m.*, dépôt de bagages, *m.*

Cloak, va. couvrir d'un manteau, (*fig.*) masquer

Clock, s. horloge, *m.*, (*apartments*) pendule, *f.* *O'clock*, heure, *f.sing.*, heures, *f.pl.* — *-maker*, horloger, *m.* — *-making*, horlogerie, *f.* — *-tower*, tour d'horloge, *f.* — *-work*, sonnerie, *f.*, mouvement, *m.* *As regular as — -work*, réglé comme un papier de musique

Clod, s. motte (de terre), *f.*, morceau, *m.*, (*pers.*) lourdaud, *m.*, -e, *f.* — *-crusher*, brise-mottes, *m.*

Cloddy, adj. de mottes, en mottes

Clodhopper, s. rustre, *m.*

Clodpated, adj. sot, lourdaud

Clog, va. embarrasser, arrêter, charger; — vn. s'embarrasser, s'attacher (à)

Clog, s. billot, *m.*, (*horses*) entraves, *f.pl.*, (*overshoe*) socque, *m.*, galoche, *f.*, (*wooden shoe*) sabot, *m.*

Cloggy, adj. embarrassant

Cloister, s. cloître, *m.*

Cloistered, adj. (*pers.*) cloîtré, (*things*) claustral

Close, va. clore, fermer, terminer, conclure, (*to stop*) boucher, (*mil.*) serrer; — vn. se fermer, se terminer, finir, (*settle*) convenir (de), (*agree*) s'accorder (avec), (*mil.*) en venir aux mains

Close, s. clos, enclos, *m.*, (*cathedrals*) cloître, *m.*, (*end*) fin, clôture, *f.* *To bring to a* —, terminer. *To draw to a* —, tirer à sa fin

Close, adj. clos, fermé, (*narrow*) étroit, (*dense*) serré, (*air*) renfermé, (*weather*) lourd, (*prisoners*) au secret, (*fights*) corps à corps, (*elections*) bien contesté, (*near*) près, proche, (*close-cut*) ras, (*style*) concis, (*study*, &c.) appliqué, assidu, suivi, exact

Close, adv. de près, près, serré, économiquement, (*shutting*) bien, tout à fait. — *by*, tout près. — *together*, tout près l'un de l'autre (*or* les uns des autres). — *to the ground*, à fleur de terre. — *-set*, adj. dru

Closely, adv. de près, attentivement, intimement, exactement, étroitement, serré, (*shutting*) bien

Closeness, s. étroitesse, *f.*, solidité, *f.*, solitude, *f.*, avarice, *f.*, vigueur, *f.*, discrétion, *f.*, intimité, *f.*, scrupule, *m.*, exactitude, *f.*, concision, *f.*, logique serrée, *f.*, (*air*) manque d'air, *m.*, (*weather*) état lourd, *m.*

Closet, s. cabinet, m., (*clothes*) garde-robe, armoire, f.

Closet, va. enfermer dans un cabinet

Closing, adj. dernier

Closing, s. clôture, fin, f., fermeture, f.

Clot, s. grumeau, caillot, m.

Clot, vn. se cailler

Cloth, s. drap, m., (*linen*) toile, f., (*piece*) linge, m., (*meals*) nappe, f., (*tables*) tapis, m., (*duster*) torchon, m., (*clergy*) habit, m. *Long* —, percale, f., madapolam, m. *To lay the* —, mettre le couvert. *To remove the* —, desservir. —*-shearer*, tondeur de drap, m.

Clothe, va. habiller, vêtir

Clothes, s. habits, vêtements, m.pl., (*fam.*) hardes, nippes, f.pl., costume, m., (*bed*) couverture, f., (*linen*) linge, m. *Long* —, maillot, m. *Plain* —, habit bourgeois, m., habit de ville, m. *Short* —, jaquette, f. *Suit of* —, habillement complet, m. —*-basket*, panier au linge sale, m. —*-brush*, brosse à habits, f. —*-horse*, séchoir, m. —*-lines*, étendage, m. —*-peg*, portemanteau, m. *Old* — *man*, fripier, marchand d'habits, m.

Clothier, s. fabricant de draps, m., marchand de draps, m. *Army*- —, fabricant d'équipements militaires, m.

Clothing, s. habillement, m.

Cloud, s. nuage, m., nue, f., nuée, f. —*-capped*, qui se perd dans les nues

Cloud, va. couvrir de nuages, (*fig.*) obscurcir, (*sorrow*) assombrir, rembrunir ; — vn. se couvrir, s'obscurcir

Cloudily, adv. obscurément

Cloudiness, s. état nuageux, m., (*fig.*) obscurité, f., (*sadness*) tristesse, f.

Cloudless, adj. sans nuage

Cloudy, adj. nuageux, (*fig.*) sombre, obscur, terne, (*liquids*) trouble. *It is* —, le temps est couvert. *It is getting* —, le temps se couvre

Clout, s. torchon, m., (*mending*) pièce, f., (*blow*) tape, f., (*nail*) clou à tête plate, m.

Clout, va. rapiécer, (*with nails*) garnir de clous

Clove, s. clou de girofle, m., (*garlick*) gousse, f. —*-tree*, giroflier, m.

Cloven, adj. fendu, fourchu. —*-foot*, pied fourchu, m. —*-footed*, —*-hoofed*, qui a le pied fourchu

Clover, s. trèfle, m. *To live in* —, vivre dans l'abondance

Clown, s. paillasse, clown, m.

Clownish, adj. grossier

Clownishness, s. grossièreté, f.

Cloy, va. affadir, rassasier

Cloying, s. affadissement, m., satiété, f.

Club, s. bâton, m., gourdin, m., massue, f., (*society*) cercle, m., club, m., (*share*) part, f., (*cards*) trèfle, m. —*-foot*, —*-footed*, pied bot. —*-house*, cercle, m. —*-law*, loi du plus fort, f. —*-room*, salle d'assemblée, f.

Club, vn. se réunir, se cotiser

Cluck, vn. glousser

Clucking, s. gloussement, m.

Clue, s. fil, m., indice, m.

Clump, s. block, m., masse, f., (*trees*) bouquet, m., (*boots*) patin, m. —*-soles*, semelles à patins, f.pl.

Clumsily, adv. grossièrement, maladroitement, gauchement

Clumsiness, s. maladresse, gaucherie, f.

Clumsy, adj. grossier, maladroit, gauche, lourd, disgracieux

Cluster, s. groupe, m., (*fruits*) grappe, f., (*cherries*) bouquet, m., (*nuts*) paquet, m., (*trees*) bouquet, m., (*mob*) amas, m., (*bees*) essaim, m., (*diamonds*) attache, f.

Cluster, vn. croître en grappes, se grouper

Clutch, va. empoigner, saisir

Clutch, s. griffe, f.

Clyster-pump, s. clysopompe, m.

Co., s. (*com.*) Cie. (compagnie), f.

Coach, s. voiture, f., (*tutor*) préparateur, m. *Slow* —, lambin, m., -e, f., clampin, m., -e, f., esprit lourd, m. —*-house*, remise, f. —*-maker*, —*-builder*, carrossier, m. —*-office*, bureau des voitures, m. —*-smith*, ferreur en voitures, m.

Coach, va. — *up*, (*fig.*) préparer, pousser

Coachman, s. cocher, m.

Coadjutor, s. collaborateur, m., collègue, m., coadjuteur, m.

Coagulate, vn. se coaguler

Coagulation, s. coagulation, f.

Coal, s. charbon (de terre), m., houille, f. *To carry* —*s to Newcastle*, porter de l'eau à la rivière. —*-black*, noir comme du charbon. —*-box*, boîte à charbon, f. —*-cellar*, —*-hole*, —*-house*, charbonnier, m. —*-dust*, poussier de charbon, m., fraisil, m. —*-heaver*, —*-man*, charbonnier, m. —*-master*, exploitant de houillière, m. —*-merchant*, marchand de charbon, m. —*-mine*, mine de houille, f. —*-miner*, houilleur, m. —*-pit*, houillière, f. —*-scuttle*, seau à charbon, m. —*-wharf*, quai à houille, m. —*-whipper*, déchargeur de houille, m. —*-work*, houillère, f.

Coalesce, vn. s'unir, se fondre

Coalescence, s. union, f.

Coalition, s. coalition, f., fusion, f.

Coaly, adj. houilleux

Coarse, adj. gros, grossier, (*metals*) brut

Coarsely, adv. grossièrement

Coarseness, s. grossièreté, f.

Coast, s. côte, f., rivage, m., littoral m. —*-guard*, gardecôtes, m. —*-pilot*, pilot côtier, lamaneur, m. —*-wise*, vers la côte, en suivant la côte

Coast, vn. ranger la côte, (*nav.*) caboter ; — va. côtoyer

Coaster, s. caboteur, m.

Coasting, s. cabotage, m. —*-pilot*, pilote côtier, m. —*-ship*, —*-vessel*, cabotier, m. —*-trade*, cabotage, m.

Coat, s. habit, m., (*animals*) robe, f., poil, m., fourrure, f., (*birds*) plumage, m., (*sheep*) toison, f., (*skin*) peau, f., (*paint*) couche, f., (*anat.*) paroi, tunique, f. — *of arms*, cotte d'armes, f., armes, armoiries, f.pl., écusson, m. — *of mail*, cotte de mailles, f. *Dress* —, habit, m. *Great* —, *over* —, paletot, m., pardessus, m., (*mil.*) capote, f. —*-stand*, portemanteau, m.

Coat, va. revêtir, couvrir (de), enduire (de)

Coated, adj. *Iron*- —, (*ship*) cuirassé

Coating, s. étoffe pour habits, f., (*paint*) couche, f.

Coax, va. amadouer, cajoler

Coaxer, s. cajoleur, m., enjôleur, m.

Coaxing, s. cajolerie, f.

Cob, s. (*bird*) mouette, f., (*horse*) double poney, m.

Cobalt, s. cobalt, m.

Cobble, va. saveter

Cobbler, s. savetier, m.

Cobweb, s. toile d'araignée, f.

Cochineal, s. cochenille, f.

Cock, s. coq, m., (*male*) mâle, m., (*weathercock*) girouette, f., (*spout*) robinet, m., (*arrows*) coche, f., (*gun*) chien, m., (*hay*) tas, m., (*balancer, dials*) aiguille, f. *Black* —, coq de bruyère, m. *At full* —, armé. *At half*- —, au repos. — *and a bull story*, coq-à-l'âne, m. —*-boat*, coquet, petit bateau, m. —*-brained*, étourdi, écervelé. —*-chafer*, hanneton, m. —*-crow*, chant du coq, m. —*-fight*, combat de coqs, m. —*-horse*, dada, m. —*-loft*, grenier, m.

Cock, va. (*erect*) relever, redresser, (*turn up*) retrousser, (*fire-arms*) armer, (*hay*) mettre en tas

Cockade, s. cocarde, f.

Cockaded, adj. à cocarde

Cockatoo, s. kakatoès, m.

Cockatrice, s. basilic, m.

Cocked, adj. à cornes

Cocker, va. choyer, dorloter

Cocket, s. sceau de la douane, m.

Cockle, s. (*bot.*) nielle, f., (*shell*) coque, palourde, f.

Cockle, va. recoquiller ; — vn. se recoquiller, (*the sea*) moutonner

Cockney, s. badaud, m.

Cockpit, s. arène, f., (*nav.*) poste des malades, m.

Cockroach, s. blatte, f.

Cockswain, s. patron de chaloupe, m.

Cocktail, s. adj. métis, m.

Coco, s. coco, m. —*-nut*, coco, m., noix de coco, f. —*-nut tree*, cocotier, m.

Cocoa, s. cacao, m., (*tree*) cacaoyer, m. —*-nibs*, cacao en grains

Cocoon, s. cocon, m.

Cod, s. (*fish*) morue, f., (*husk*) cosse, f. —*-liver oil*, huile de foie de morue, f.

Coddle, va. bouillir, (*pers.*) dorloter

Code, s. code, m.

Codger, s. bonhomme, m.

Codicil, s. codicille, m.

Codification, s. codification, f.

Codify, va. codifier

Codling, s. pomme à cuire, f.

Coerce, va. contraindre, réprimer

Coercion, s. coercition, f.

Coercive, adj. coercitif

Coeval, adj. contemporain

Coexist, vn. coexister

Coffee, s. café, m. —*-berry*, fève de café, f. —*-cup*, tasse à café, f. —*-filter*, filtre à café, m. —*-house*, café, m. —*-house keeper*, cafetier, limonadier, m. —*-mill*, moulin à café, m. —*-pot*, cafetière, f. —*-roaster*, brûleur à café, m. —*-room*, salon, café, m. —*-tree*, caféier, cafier, m. —*-urn*, fontaine à café, f.

Coffer, s. coffre, m., caisse, f., cassette, f., (*arch.*) caisson, m. —*-dam*, batardeau, m.

Coffin, s. cercueil, m., bière, f.

Coffin, va. enfermer dans un cercueil

Cog, va. cajoler, enjôler, (*dice*) piper, (*wheels*) garnir de dents

Cog, s. dent, f., cran, m. —*-wheel*, roue dentée, f.

Cogency, s. force, puissance, f.

Cogent, adj. fort, puissant

Cogently, adv. fortement, irrésistiblement

Cogged, adj. à dents, à crans

Cognate, adj. de la même famille, analogue

Cognizable, adj. du ressort

Cognizance, s. connaissance, f.

Cognizant, adj. instruit, (*law*) compétent

Cohabit, vn. cohabiter

Cohabitation, s. cohabitation, f.

Coheir, s. cohéritier, m.

Coheiress, s. cohéritière, f.

Cohere, vn. adhérer (à), s'accorder (avec)

Coherence, s. cohésion, *f.*, (*fig.*) cohérence, *f.*

Coherent, adj. adhérent, (*connected*) cohérent, (*consistent*) conséquent

Coherently, adv. avec cohérence

Cohesion, s. cohésion, *f.*, (*connection*) cohérence, *f.*, rapport, *m.*

Cohort, s. cohorte, *f.*

Coif, s. calotte, *f.*

Coif, va. coiffer

Coil, va. replier, rouler, enrouler

Coil, s. rouleau, *m.*, tour, *m.*, (*serpents*) repli, *m.*

Coin, s. monnaie, *f.* *To pay one back in his own* —, rendre à quelqu'un la monnaie de sa pièce

Coin, va. monnayer, frapper, inventer. *To — money*, battre monnaie

Coinage, s. monnayage, *m.*, monnaie, *f.*, invention, *f.*

Coincide, vn. coïncider, (*agree*) s'accorder

Coincidence, s. coïncidence, *f.*, rencontre, *f.*, hasard, *m.*

Coincident, adj. coïncident, (*agreeing*) d'accord

Coiner, s. monnayeur, *m.*, faiseur, *m.*, inventeur, *m.* — *of bad money*, faux-monnayeur

Coining, s. *see* Coinage

Coke, s. coke, *m.*

Colander, s. passoire, *f.*

Cold, adj. froid. — *-blooded*, (*fig.*) de sang-froid, prémédité, délibéré

Cold, s. froid, *m.*, froidure, *f.*, rhume, *m.* — *in the head*, rhume de cerveau. — *on the chest*, rhume de poitrine. *To catch —, to get a —*, attraper un rhume, s'enrhumer. *To give a —*, enrhumer. *To have a —*, être enrhumé. *To have a bad —*, avoir un gros rhume. *To have a — in the head*, être enrhumé du cerveau

Cold, adj. froid

Coldish, adj. un peu froid, frais

Coldly, adv. froidement

Coldness, s. froid, *m.*, froideur, *f.*

Cole, s. chou, *m.* — *-wort*, chou vert, *m.*

Colic, s. colique, *f.*

Collapse, vn. tomber l'un sur l'autre, s'affaisser, s'écrouler

Collapse, s. rapprochement, *m.*, affaissement, *m.*, écroulement, *m.*

Collar, s. collier, *m.*, (*horse*) bricole, *f.*, (*coats, &c.*) collet, *m.*, (*shirts*) col, *m.*, (*tucker*) collerette, *f.*, (*butch.*) rouleau, *m.* *Against the —*, avec désavantage, à perte, à contre-cœur. — *-bone*, clavicule, *f.*

Collar, va. colleter, prendre au collet, (*to put a collar on*) mettre un collier à, (*butch.*) rouler

Collate, va. collationner, (*appoint*) nommer

Collateral, adj. collatéral, parallèle, additionnel

Collaterally, adv. en ligne collatérale, à côté l'un de l'autre, indirectement

Collation, s. collation, *f.*, (*gift*) don, présent, *m.*

Collator, s. personne qui collationne, *f.*, (*livings*) collateur, *m.*

Colleague, s. collègue, *m.*

Collect, va. recueillir, rassembler, ramasser, (*taxes*) percevoir, (*debts*) recouvrer, faire le recouvrement de, (*alms*) quêter, (*letters*) faire la levée de ; — vn. s'amasser. — *oneself*, se recueillir

Collect, s. collecte, *f.*

Collected, adj. réuni, rassemblé

Collectedness, s. recueillement, *m.*, calme, *m.*

Collection, s. collection, *f.*, recueil, *m.*, amas, assemblage, *m.*, (*pers.*) rassemblement, *m.*, (*taxes*) perception, *f.*, (*debts, rents*) recouvrement, *m.*, (*alms*) quête, *f.*, (*post*) levée des boîtes, *f.*

Collective, adj. collectif

Collectively, adv. collectivement

Collector, s. collecteur, *m.*, (*works of art, &c.*) collectionneur, *m.*, (*taxes*) percepteur, receveur, *m.*, (*church*) quêteur, *m.*, -euse, *f.*

Collectorship, s. place de percepteur, *f.*

College, s. collége, lycée, *m.*, (*med.*) faculté, *f.*

Collegian, s. collégien, *m.*

Collegiate, adj. de collége, collégial

Collier, s. houilleur, *m.*, (*nav.*) charbonnier, *m.*

Colliery, s. houillère, *f.*

Collision, s. collision, *f.*, choc, *m.*

Collodion, s. collodion, *m.*

Collop, s. escalope, *f.*, tranche, *f.*

Colloquial, adj. de la conversation, du langage de la conversation, qui ne s'emploie que dans la conversation, familier

Colloquially, adv. dans la conversation, familièrement

Colloquy, s. entretien, *m.*, colloque, *m.*

Collusion, s. collusion, *f.*, connivence, *f.*, intelligence, *f.*, compérage, *m.*

Collusive, adj. collusoire

Collusively, adv. collusoirement

Colocynth, s. coloquinte, *f.*

Colon, s. deux points, *m.pl.*

Colonel, s. colonel, *m.*

Colonelcy, s. grade de colonel, *m.*

Colonial, adj. colonial

Colonist, s. colon, *m.*

Colonization, s. colonisation, *f.*

Colonize, va. coloniser

Colonnade, s. colonnade, *f.*

Colony, s. colonie, *f.*

Colossal, adj. colossal

Colosseum, s. colisée, *m.*

Colossus, s. colosse, *m.*

Colour, s. couleur, *f.*, prétexte, *m.*, ombre, *f.*, (*mil.*) —*s*, pl., drapeau, *m.*, (*nav.*) pavillon, *m.* *With flying —s*, enseignes déployées. — *-sergeant*, porte-drapeau, *m.*

Colour, va. colorer, colorier, enluminer, (*a pipe*) culotter ; — vn. (*pers.*) rougir, (*things*) se colorer, (*pipes*) se culotter

Colourable, adj. plausible

Colourably, adv. d'une manière plausible

Coloured, adj. de couleur

Colourer, s. coloriste, *m.*

Colouring, s. couleur, *f.*, coloris, *m.*

Colourist, s. coloriste, *m.*

Colourless, adj. sans couleur

Colt, s. poulain, *m.*, (*pers.*) étourdi, *m.*, novice, *m.* —*'s-foot*, pas d'âne, *m.* —*'s-tooth*, dent de lait, *f.*

Colter, s. coutre, *m.*

Columbine, adj. de pigeon, (*colour*) gorge-de-pigeon

Columbine, s. (*bot.*) ancolie, *f.*

Column, s. colonne, *f.*

Columnar, adj. de colonne, en colonne

Columned, adj. à colonnes

Colza, s. colza, *m.*

Comb, s. peigne, *m.*, (*cocks*) crête, *f.*, (*honey*) rayon, *m.* *Large-tooth —*, démêloir, *m.* *Small-tooth —*, peigne fin, *m.* — *-brush*, brosse à peignes, *f.* — *-case*, porte-peigne, *m.*

Comb, va. peigner, (*horses*) étriller

Combat, va.n. combattre

Combat, s. combat, *m.*

Combatant, s. combattant, *m.*

Comber, s. peigneur, *m.*, (*machine*) peigneuse, *f.*

Combination, s. combinaison, *f.*, ligue *f.*, coalition, *f.*

Combine, va. combiner, réunir, coaliser ; — vn. se combiner, se réunir, se coaliser

Combing, s. peignage, *m.*

Combustible, adj. s. combustible

Combustion, s. combustion, *f.*

Come, vn. venir, arriver, se présenter, avancer, (*happen*) se faire, (*amount*) revenir (à), se monter (à), (*be reduced*) se réduire, (*pers.*) être réduit, en venir (à), (*end in*) aboutir (à), résulter (de), (*be about to*) aller. *To — to the same*, revenir au même. *To — to oneself*, revenir à soi. *To — to* (*a person*), venir à, venir trouver. *To — and see, — and play, &c.*, venir voir, venir jouer, etc. — *! — along ! — on !* allons ! venez ! venez donc ! *To —*, (*future*) à venir, futur. — *what may* (or *will*), arrive que pourra. — *about*, arriver, changer, tourner. — *across*, donner de la tête contre, (*fall upon*) tomber sur, (*meet*) rencontrer. — *after*, suivre, venir après. — *again*, revenir. — *along*, s'en venir. — *at*, (*reach*) atteindre, (*succeed*) parvenir à. — *away*, s'en venir, s'en aller. — *back*, revenir. — *back again*, s'en retourner. — *by*, passer par, obtenir, acquérir, se procurer, (*succeed*) parvenir à. — *down*, descendre, (*fall suddenly*) tomber, baisser, (*pay*) financer, dégainer, (— *from town*) venir. — *for*, venir chercher. — *forward*, s'avancer, se présenter. — *in*, entrer, arriver, rentrer, (*tide*) monter. — *in for*, (*property*) acquérir, hériter de. — *in and out*, aller et venir. — *into*, entrer dans *or* en, consentir à, approuver. — *next*, suivre. — *of*, résulter de, venir de *or* de ce que. — *off*, tomber, se détacher, (*spots*) s'enlever, (*to end*) se terminer, (*get out of*) se tirer d'affaire, en être quitte (pour), (*take place*) arriver, avoir lieu, (*mil.*) descendre. — *on*, s'avancer (*happen*) arriver, survenir. — *out*, sortir, (*appear*) se montrer, paraître, (*in society*) débuter, se lancer, (*declare*) se déclarer, (*to be found out*) se découvrir, (*spots*) s'effacer. — *over*, traverser, passer, (*seize*) s'emparer de. — *round*, faire le tour de, venir, revenir, (*recover*) se rétablir, se remettre, (*yield*) céder, (*wheedle*) circonvenir. — *to*, hériter de, consentir à, (*recover*) se remettre. — *together*, venir ensemble, se réunir. — *under*, être compris sous, être soumis à. — *up*, monter, s'élever, (*get*) arriver, (*grow*) pousser, (— *to town*) venir. — *up to*, (*a person*) venir à, venir trouver, (*reach*) atteindre, (*near*) approcher de, (*correspond*) répondre à, satisfaire. — *up with*, atteindre. — *upon*, s'avancer sur, (*fall upon*) tomber sur, (*seize*) attaquer, s'emparer de. — *upon* (*one*) *for* . . ., s'en prendre à, s'adresser à (quelqu'un) pour . . .

Comedian, s. comédien, *m.*, -ne, *f.*, comique, *m.*

Comedy, s. comédie, *f.*

Comeliness, s. beauté, *f.*, grâce, *f.*, dignité, *f.*

Comely, adj. beau, gracieux, avenant, (*becoming*) convenable, digne

Comer, s. venant, *m.*, (*first —*), premier, *m.*, -ère, *f.*, venu, *m.*, -e, *f.*

Comet, s. comète, *f.*

Comfit, s. dragée, *f.*

Comfort, va. reconforter, consoler, (*relieve*) soulager

Comfort, s. bien-être, *m.*, aisance, *f.*, consolation, *f.*, soulagement, *m.*, (*convenience*) agrément, *m.*

Comfortable, adj. confortable, commode, agréable,

consolant, suffisant, convenable, (*pers.*) à son aise, bien. *To make oneself* —, se mettre à son aise, se donner toutes ses aises

Comfortableness, s. bonheur, *m.*, jouissance, *f.*

Comfortably, adv. commodément, confortablement, à son aise, bien, agréablement

Comforter, s. consolateur, *m.*, -trice, *f.*, (*scarf*) cachenez, *m.*

Comfortless, adj. désagréable, sans consolation, (*pers.*) inconsolable

Comic, Comical, adj. comique

Comically, adv. comiquement

Comicalness, s. caractère comique, *m.*, comique, *m.*

Coming, adj. qui vient, prochain, (*future*) à venir. —*! I am* —*!* j'y vais! on y va! voilà!

Coming, s. venue *f.*, arrivée, *f.*, approche, *f.*, (*Christ*) avènement, *m.* — *back*, retour, *m.* — *in*, entrée, *f.* — *out*, sortie, *f.* — *in and out*, allées et venues, *f.pl.*

Comma, s. virgule, *f.* *Inverted* —, guillemet, *m.*

Command, va. commander, avoir à sa disposition, (*overlook*) dominer. *To — a view of*, dominer

Command, s. commandement, *m.*, ordres, *m.pl.*, pouvoir, *m.*, empire, *m.*, (*knowledge*) connaissance, *f.*, (*fluency*) facilité, *f.*

Commander, s. commandant, *m.*, général, *m.*, commandeur, *m.*

Commandery, s. commanderie, *f.*

Commanding, adj. imposant

Commandment, s. commandement, *m.*, précepte, *m.*

Commemorate, va. rappeler, célébrer

Commemoration, s. commémoration, *f.*, souvenir, *m.*, mémoire, *f.*, célébration, *f.*

Commemorative, adj. commémoratif

Commence, va. commencer, devenir

Commend, va. recommander, (*praise*) louer, (*trust*) confier (à), (*set off*) faire valoir

Commendable, adj. recommandable, louable

Commendably, adv. d'une manière louable

Commendation, s. éloge, *m.*, louange, *f.*, qualité, *f.*

Commendatory, adj. d'éloges

Commender, s. panégyriste, *m.*

Commensurable, adj. commensurable

Commensurate, adj. proportionné (à)

Comment, va.n. commenter

Comment, Commentary, s. commentaire, *m.*

Commentator, s. commentateur, *m.*

Commerce, s. commerce, *m.*

Commercial, adj. commercial, de commerce, (*countries, towns*) commerçant. — *undertaking*, entreprise commerciale. — *house, traveller, broker, treaty*, maison, voyageur, courtier, traité de commerce. — *directory*, almanach du commerce. — *man*, commerçant, *m.* — *navigation*, commerce maritime, *m.*

Commercially, adv. commercialement

Comminatory, adj. menaçant, (*law*) comminatoire

Commingle, vn. se mêler

Commiserate, va. avoir compassion de

Commiseration, s. commisération, *f.*

Commissariat, s. intendance militaire, *f.*

Commissary, s. commissaire, *m.*, (*mil.*) intendant militaire, *m.*

Commissaryship, s. commissariat, *m.*

Commission, s. commission, *f.*, ordre, *m.*, perpétration, *f.*, (*officers*) brevet, *m.* *On* —, à commission. — *-agent*, commissionnaire en marchandises, *m.*, expéditeur, *m.*

Commission, va. commissionner, déléguer, charger (de)

Commissioner, s. commissaire, *m.* *Chief — of police*, préfet de police, *m.*

Commit, va. commettre, confier (à), envoyer en prison, compromettre, engager, (*parl.*) renvoyer à une commission

Committal, Commitment, s. emprisonnement, *m.*

Committee, s. comité, *m.*, (*parlm.*) commission, *f.*

Commode, s. *Night-* —, chaise percée, *f.*

Commodious, adj. commode

Commodiously, adv. commodément

Commodiousness, s. commodité, *f.*

Commodity, s. marchandise, *f.*, (*polit. econ.*) produit, *m.*

Commodore, s. chef de division, *m.*, chef d'escadre, *m.*

Common, adj. commun, vulgaire, ordinaire, public, (*soldier*) simple, (*people*) bas. — *-council*, — *-councillor*, s. see *Town-council, &c.* — *-law*, s. droit commun, *m.*, droit coutumier, *m.* — *-place*, s.adj. lieu commun, *m.*, banal, terre à terre. — *-place-book*, s. cahier de notes, *m.* — *sense*, s.adj. sens commun, *m.*, du sens commun, sensé, raisonnable

Common, s. plaine, *f.*, terre inculte, *f.*, bruyère, *f.*, landes, *f.pl.*, communaux, *m.pl.*, vaine pâture, *f.*

Commonage, s. usage, *m.*, (*law*) droit de vaine pâture, *m.*

Commonalty, s. bourgeoisie, *f.*

Commoner, s. bourgeois, *m.*

Commonly, adv. communément, ordinairement

Commons, s. bourgeoisie, *f.*, (*House of* —) Chambre des Communes, *f.*, (*in France*) Corps législatif, *m.*, Chambre des députés, *f.*, (*food*) ordinaire, *m.*, chère, *f.*

Commonwealth, s. république, *f.*, état, *m.*

Commotion, s. commotion, *f.*

Commune, vn. conférer, converser

Communicable, adj. communicable

Communicant, s. communiant, *m.*, -e, *f.*

Communicate, va.n. communiquer, (*sacraments*) communier

Communicating, adj. de communication

Communication, s. communication, *f.*

Communicative, adj. communicatif

Communicativeness, s. caractère communicatif, *m.*

Communion, s. communication, *f.*, relations, *f.pl.*, (*sacrament*) communion, *f.* — *-table*, sainte table, *f.*

Communism, s. communisme, *m.*

Communist, s. communiste, *m.*

Communistic, adj. communiste

Community, s. communauté, *f.*, société, *f.*, public, *m.*, état, *m.*

Commutable, adj. commuable

Commutation, s. commutation, *f.*

Commutative, adj. commutatif

Commute, va. commuer

Compact, adj. compacte, (*close*) serré

Compact, s. pacte, *m.*, contrat, *m.*

Compactly, adv. d'une manière compacte, avec concision

Compactness, s. compacité, *f.*, densité, *f.*

Companion, s. compagnon, *m.*, compagne, *f.*, camarade, *m.f.*, (*ladies*) demoiselle *or* dame de compagnie, *f.*, (*pictures, &c.*) pendant, *m.*

Companionable, adj. sociable

Companionship, s. camaraderie, *f.*, (*company*) société, *f.*

Company, s. compagnie, *f.*, (*actors*) troupe, *f.*, (*troop*) bande, *f.*, (*guild*) corporation, *f.*, (*associates*) entourage, *m.*, (*nav.*) équipage, *m.* *To keep* —, tenir compagnie à, (*receive*) voir du monde. *To keep — with*, fréquenter

Comparable, adj. comparable

Comparably, adv. à beaucoup près

Comparative, adj. comparatif, relatif, comparé

Comparative, s. comparatif, *m.*

Comparatively, adv. comparativement, relativement

Compare, va. comparer. —*d with*, en comparaison de

Comparison, s. comparaison, *f.* *In — of* or *with*, en comparaison de

Compartment, s. compartiment, *m.*

Compass, s. cercle, *m.*, tour, *m.*, étendue, *f.*, espace, *m.*, sphère, *f.*, limites, *f.pl.*, bornes, *f.pl.*, (*enclosure*) enceinte, *f.*, (*reach*) portée, *f.*, (*nav.*) boussole, *f.* *Pair of* —*es*, compas, *m.* — *-card*, rose des vents, *f.*

Compass, va. environner, embrasser, traquer, assiéger, bloquer, accomplir, comploter

Compassion, s. compassion, *f.*, pitié, *f.*

Compassionate, adj. compatissant

Compassionate, va. compatir à, avoir compassion de

Compatibility, s. compatibilité, *f.*

Compatible, adj. compatible

Compatriot, s. compatriote, *m.*

Compeer, s. compagnon, *m.*, (*accomplice*) compère, *m.*

Compel, va. forcer, obliger

Compendious, adj. abrégé

Compendiously, adv. en abrégé

Compendiousness, s. brièveté, *f.*, concision, *f.*

Compendium, s. abrégé, *m.*

Compensate, va.n. compenser, dédommager; — vn. se compenser

Compensation, s. compensation, *f.* — *-balance*, compensateur, *m.*

Compete, vn. concourir, faire concurrence (à)

Competence, Competency, s. capacité, *f.*, (*fortune*) aisance, *f.*, compétence, *f.* *To have a* —, avoir de quoi vivre

Competent, adj. convenable, suffisant, compétent

Competently, adv. convenablement

Competition, s. concurrence, *f.*, (*prize, a place, &c.*) concours, *m.*

Competitive, adj. de *or* de la concurrence. — *examination*, concours, *m.*

Competitor, s. compétiteur, *m.*, concurrent, *m.*

Compilation, s. compilation, *f.*

Compile, va. compiler

Compiler, s. compilateur, *m.*

Complacency, s. complaisance, *f.*, satisfaction, *f.*

Complacent, adj. de complaisance

Complacently, adv. avec complaisance

Complain, vn. se plaindre

Complainant, s. plaignant, m., -e, f.

Complainer, s. personne qui se plaint, f.

Complaint, s. plainte, f., grief, m., maladie, f., mal, m.

Complement, s. complément, m., (height) comble, m., (mil., nav.) complet, m.

Complete, adj. complet, achevé, (at the height) au comble

Complete, va. compléter, achever, consommer, combler, mettre le comble à

Completely, adv. complètement

Completion, s. achèvement, m., perfection, f., accomplissement, m., (utmost height) comble, m., (mil., nav.) complètement, m.

Complex, adj. complexe

Complexion, s. (face) teint, m., (constitution) complexion, f., tempérament, m.

Complexioned, adj. de teint

Complexity, s. complexité, f., complication, f.

Compliance, s. condescendance, f., acquiescement, m., complaisance, f. *In — with*, conformément à, suivant

Compliant, adj. complaisant, (things) soumis (à)

Complicate, va. compliquer

Complication, s. complication, f.

Complicity, s. complicité, f.

Compliment, s. compliment, m. *—s of the season, (at Christmas)* compliments de bonne année, m.pl. *Best —s*, compliments empressés, m.pl.

Compliment, va. complimenter, féliciter

Complimentary, adj. complimenteur, flatteur

Compline, s. complies, f.plur.

Comply, vn. condescendre (à), se conformer (à), se rendre (à), satisfaire (à), observer

Component, adj. constituant

Comport, vn. s'accorder (avec), convenir (à)

Compose, va. composer, écrire, rédiger, calmer, apaiser, tranquilliser. *To — oneself*, se calmer

Composed, adj. sérieux, calme

Composer, s. auteur, m., (mus., print.) compositeur, m.

Composing, s. composition, f. *—-stick*, composteur, m.

Composite, s. adj. composé, (arch.) composite

Composition, s. composition, f., nature, f., (bankrupt) concordat, m., atermoiement, m.

Compositor, s. compositeur, m.

Compost, s. compost, m.

Composure, s. calme, m., tranquillité, f., sang-froid, m.

Compound, va. composer, combiner, arranger; — vn. s'arranger, transiger, s'atermoyer

Compound, adj. composé, (alg.) complexe

Compound, s. composé, m.

Compounder, s. arbitre, m.

Comprehend, va. comprendre

Comprehensible, adj. compréhensible, intelligible

Comprehension, s. compréhension, f.

Comprehensive, adj. vaste, étendu, compréhensif, d'une grande intelligence

Comprehensively, adv. largement

Comprehensiveness, s. étendue, f.

Compress, va. comprimer, (fig.) resserrer

Compress, s. compresse, f.

Compressibility, s. compressibilité, f.

Compressible, adj. compressible

Compression, s. compression, f., concision, f.

Comprise, va. comprendre, renfermer

Compromise, s. compromis, m.

Compromise, va. compromettre, arranger; — vn. transiger

Compulsion, s. contrainte, f.

Compulsive, Compulsory, adj. obligatoire

Compulsively, Compulsorily, adv. par force

Compunction, s. remords, m., componction, f.

Computable, adj. calculable

Computation, s. supputation, f., calcul, m., (chronology) computation, f.

Compute, va. supputer, calculer, évaluer

Computer, s. calculateur, m.

Comrade, s. camarade, m.

Con, prep. contre

Con, va. étudier, repasser

Concatenation, s. enchaînement, m.

Concave, adj. concave

Concavity, s. concavité, f.

Conceal, va. cacher, receler

Concealer, s. receleur, m.

Concealment, s. action de cacher, f., secret, m., retraite, f., (law) recèlement, m.

Concede, va. accorder, admettre

Conceit, s. imagination, f., vanité, f., suffisance, f. *Out of — with*, dégoûté de

Conceited, adj. vain, suffisant

Conceitedly, adv. avec vanité

Conceitedness, s. vanité, f., suffisance, f.

Conceivable, adj. concevable

Conceive, va. concevoir, imaginer

Concentrate, va. concentrer

Concentration, s. concentration, f.

Concentre, vn. se concentrer; — va. concentrer

Concentric, adj. concentrique

Conception, s. conception, f.

Concern, va. concerner, regarder, intéresser, affliger, peiner, importer (de), inquiéter. *— oneself*, se mêler (de), s'intéresser (à), s'inquiéter (de)

Concern, s. affaire, f., intérêt, m., importance, f., affection, f., chagrin, m., (care) soin, m., (com.) entreprise, f., (fest.) boutique, f.

Concerning, prep. concernant, touchant, sur

Concert, va. concerter; — vn. se concerter

Concert, s. concert, m. *In —*, de concert

Concertina, s. concertina, m.

Concerto, s. concerto, m.

Concession, s. concession, f.

Conch, s. conque, f.

Conciliate, va. concilier, se concilier

Conciliation, s. conciliation, f.

Conciliator, s. conciliateur, m., -trice, f.

Conciliatory, adj. conciliant

Concise, adj. concis

Concisely, adv. avec concision

Conciseness, s. concision, f.

Conclave, s. conclave, m.

Conclude, va.n. conclure, (finish) terminer, finir

Concluding, adj. final, dernier

Conclusion, s. conclusion, f., décision, f., (end) fin, f.

Conclusive, adj. concluant, décisif, final

Conclusively, adv. d'une manière concluante or décisive

Concoct, va. digérer, (ripen) mûrir, (to plot) machiner, tramer

Concomitance, s. concours, m.

Concomitant, adj. qui accompagne

Concomitant, s. compagnon, m., compagne, f., accessoire, m.

Concord, s. concorde, f., accord, m., harmonie, f., (gram.) concordance, f.

Concordance, s. concordance, f.

Concordant, adj. d'accord

Concordat, s. concordat, m.

Concourse, s. concours, m.

Concrete, adj. s. concret

Concrete, vn. se solidifier

Concretion, s. concrétion, f.

Concubinage, s. concubinage, m.

Concubine, s. concubine, f.

Concupiscence, s. concupiscence, f.

Concur, vn. concourir, s'accorder, être d'accord

Concurrence, s. concours, m., consentement, m.

Concurrent, Concurring, adj. qui concourt (à), (agreeing) qui s'accorde (avec), (united) réuni

Concurrently, adv. concurremment

Concussion, s. ébranlement, m., (shock) secousse, f.

Condemn, va. condamner, blâmer, (theat.) siffler

Condemnable, adj. condamnable

Condemnation, s. condamnation, f.

Condensable, adj. condensable

Condensation, s. condensation, f.

Condense, va. condenser, (fig.) resserrer; — vn. se condenser, (fig.) se resserrer

Condenser, s. condensateur, m.

Condescend, vn. condescendre (à), se soumettre (à)

Condescendence, s. condescendance, f.

Condescendingly, adv. par condescendance

Condescension, s. condescendance, f.

Condign, adj. mérité, juste

Condignly, adv. justement

Condiment, s. assaisonnement, m.

Condition, s. condition, f., (state) état, m. *In a — to*, en état de. *On or upon —*, à condition. *Out of —*, en mauvais état

Conditional, adj. conditionnel

Conditionally, adv. conditionnellement

Conditioned, adj. conditionné

Condole, vn. prendre part à la douleur (de), faire ses compliments de condoléance (à)

Condolence, s. condoléance, f., compliments de condoléance, m.pl.

Condonation, s. pardon, m.

Condone, va. pardonner

Condor, s. condor, m.

Conduce, vn. contribuer (à), servir (à)

Conducive, adj. qui contribue or sert (à). *To be —*, contribuer, servir (à)

Conduct, va. conduire

Conduct, s. conduite, f., direction, f., démarches, f.pl.

Conducting, adj. conducteur

Conductor, s. conducteur, m., guide, m., (lightning) paratonnerre, m.

Conductress, s. conductrice, *f.*
Conduit, s. conduit, *m.*
Cone, s. cône, *m.*
Coney, s. lapin, *m.*
Confection, s. composition, *f.*, (*pharm.*) opiat, *m.*
Confectioner, s. confiseur, *m.*
Confectionery, s. confiserie, *f.*, sucreries, *f.pl.*, bonbons, *m.pl.*
Confederacy, s. confédération, *f.*, ligue, *f.*, (*cheating*) compérage, *m.*
Confederate, va. confédérer; — vn. se confédérer, se liguer
Confederate, s. confédéré, allié, *m.*, (*cheating*) compère, *m.*
Confederation, s. confédération, *f.*
Confer, va.n. conférer
Conference, s. conférence, *f.*
Confess, va. confesser, avouer, reconnaître; — vn. se confesser
Confessedly, adv. de son aveu
Confession, s. confession, *f.*, aveu, *m.* *To go to —*, aller à confesse
Confessional, s. confessionnal, *m.*
Confessor, s. confesseur, *m.*
Confidant, s. confident, *m.*, -e, *f.*
Confide, va. confier; — vn. se confier (à), avoir confiance (en, dans)
Confidence, s. confiance, *f.*, (*secrets*) confidence, *f.*
Confident, adj. confiant, certain, sûr, hardi
Confidential, adj. (*pers.*) sûr de confiance, (*things*) confidentiel
Confidentially, adv. confidentiellement
Confidently, adv avec confiance, positivement, bien
Configuration, s. configuration, *f.*
Confine, s. confins, *m.pl.*, limite, *f.*
Confine, vn. confiner, toucher (à); — va. confiner, reléguer, enfermer, (*in bed*) retenir, (*limit*) borner, (*restrain*) restreindre, (*bind down*) assujettir, (*med.*) resserrer. *To be —d*, faire ses couches, être accouchée, accoucher
Confinement, s. détention, *f.*, emprisonnement, *m.*, réclusion, *f*, prison, *f.*, contrainte, *f.*, assujettissement, *m.*, (*women*) couches, *f.pl.*, (*mil.*) arrêts, *m.pl.*
Confirm, va. confirmer, (*strengthen*) fortifier, affermir
Confirmation, s. confirmation, *f.*, (*strengthening*) affermissement, *m.*
Confirmative, Confirmatory, adj. confirmatif, qui confirme, à l'appui (de)
Confirmed, adj. enraciné, invétéré, bien décidé, déterminé, endurci, incorrigible

Confiscate, va. confisquer
Confiscation, s. confiscation, *f.*
Conflagration, s. conflagration, *f.*, embrasement, *m.*, (*fire*) incendie, *m.*
Conflict, s. conflit, *m.*, lutte, *f.*
Conflict, vn. se heurter, (*fig.*) lutter
Conflicting, adj. qui se heurte, (*fig.*) en conflit, opposé, contraire, contradictoire
Confluence, s. confluent, *m.*
Conform, va. conformer; — vn. se conformer
Conformable, adj. conforme (à)
Conformably, adv. conformément
Conformation, s. conformation, *f.*
Conformist, s. conformiste, *m.*
Conformity, s. conformité, *f.* *In — with*, conformément à
Confound, va. confondre, déconcerter
Confounded, adj. maudit, sacré, enragé
Confoundedly, adv. terriblement, furieusement, diablement
Confraternity, s. confrérie, *f.*
Confront, va. confronter
Confrontation, s. confrontation, *f.*
Confuse, va. mettre en désordre, (*perplex*) troubler, embrouiller
Confused, adj. confus, troublé
Confusedly, adv. confusément
Confusion, s. confusion, *f.*, désordre, *m.*, trouble, *m.*
Confute, va. réfuter
Congeal, va. congeler, glacer; — vn. se congeler
Congealable, adj. congelable
Congelation, s. congélation, *f.*
Congenial, adj. homogène, naturel, sympathique (à), favorable (à), analogue (à)
Congeniality, s. affinité, *f.*, conformité, *f.*
Conger, s. congre, *m.*
Congestion, s. congestion, *f.*
Congratulate, va. féliciter (de)
Congratulation, s. félicitation, *f.*, compliment, *m.*
Congratulatory, adj. de félicitation
Congregate, va. rassembler; — vn. se rassembler
Congregation, s. amas, *m.*, (*pers.*) congrégation, *f.*, (*church*) assemblée, *f.*, fidèles, *m.pl.*, paroissiens, *m.pl.*, auditoire, *m.*
Congress, s. congrès, *m.*
Congruity, s. convenance, *f.*, conformité, *f.*

Congruous, adj. convenable (à), conforme (à)
Congruously, adv. convenablement
Conic, Conical, adj. conique
Conics, s sections coniques, *f.pl.*
Conifer, s. conifère, *m.*
Conjectural, adj. conjectural
Conjecturally, adv. conjecturalement
Conjecture, s. conjecture, *f.*
Conjecture, va. conjecturer
Conjecturer, s. faiseur de conjectures, *m.*
Conjoin, va. unir, conjoindre, adjoindre; — vn. se joindre
Conjoint, adj. uni, lié
Conjointly, adv. conjointement, d'accord, de concert
Conjugal, adj. conjugal
Conjugally, adv. conjugalement
Conjugate, va. conjuguer
Conjugation, s. conjugaison, *f.*
Conjunction, s. conjonction, *f.*, union, *f*
Conjuncture, s concours, *m.*, (*crisis*) conjoncture, *f.*
Conjuration, s. évocation, *f.*, (*sorcery*) sorcellerie, *f.*
Conjure, va. conjurer, ensorceler, (*spirits*) évoquer, (*juggle*) escamoter; — vn. faire de la sorcellerie
Conjurer, s. sorcier, *m.*, -ière, *f.*, magicien, *m.*, -ne, *f.*, (*juggler*) prestidigitateur, physicien, *m.*
Conjuring, s. sorcellerie, *f.*, (*juggling*) prestidigitation, *f.* — *-book*, grimoire, *m.*
Connect, va. joindre, lier, unir, rattacher (à), allier (à)
Connected, adj. continu, en rapport
Connection, s. connexion, *f.*, (*relation*) rapport, *m.*, liaison, *f.*, (*coherence*) suite, *f.*, (*intercourse*) relations, *f.pl.*, (*family —*) parent, *m.*, (*business*) clientèle, *f.*
Connivance, s. connivence, *f.*
Connive, vn. conniver
Conniving, adj. de connivence
Connoisseur, s. connaisseur, *m.*
Connubial, adj. conjugal
Conquer, va. vaincre, conquérir
Conqueror, s. vainqueur, *m.*, conquérant, *m.*
Conquest, s. conquête, *f.*, victoire, *f.*
Consanguinity, s. consanguinité, *f.*
Conscience, s. conscience, *f.*
Conscientious, adj. consciencieux
Conscientiously, adv. consciencieusement
Conscientiousness, s. conscience, *f.*

Conscious, adj. qui a la conscience (de), (*aware*) instruit (de), (*things*) dont on a la conscience. *To be — of*, avoir la conscience de
Consciously, adv. en parfaite connaissance
Consciousness, s. conscience, *f.*
Conscript, adj. s. conscrit, *m.*
Conscription, s. conscription, *f.*
Consecrate, va. consacrer, bénir, (*bishops, kings*) sacrer. *—d ground*, terre sainte, *f.*
Consecration, s. consécration, *f.*, (*bishops, kings*) sacre, *m.*
Consecrator, s. consécrateur, *m.*
Consecutive, adj. consécutif
Consecutively, adv. consécutivement, de suite
Consent, vn. consentir (à)
Consent, s. consentement, *m.*, accord, *m.*
Consentient, adj. consentant, d'accord, unanime
Consequence, s. conséquence, suite, *f.*, effet, *m.*, importance, *f.* *The — is that ...*, il résulte de là que ..., il en résulte que ..., il s'ensuit que ...
Consequent, adj. *— upon*, qui est la conséquence de, qui suit, par suite de, en conséquence de
Consequential, adj. important, suffisant
Consequentially, adv. avec importance
Consequently, adv. conséquemment, par conséquent, en conséquence
Conservancy, Conservation, s. conservation, *f.*
Conservative, adj. s. conservateur, *m.*
Conservator, s. conservateur, *m.*, -trice, *f.*
Conservatory, s. conservatoire, *m.*, (*garden*) serre, *f.*
Consider, va. considérer, estimer, regarder comme, tenir pour; — vn. considérer, examiner, (*think*) réfléchir, faire attention, (*deem*) être d'avis, juger
Considerable, adj. considérable, important
Considerableness, s. importance, *f.*
Considerably, adv. considérablement
Considerate, adj. réfléchi, prudent, attentionné, attentif
Considerately, adv. avec réflexion, avec prudence, avec modération, avec attention
Considerateness, s. prudence, *f*
Consideration, s. considération, *f.*, examen, *m.*, réflexion, *f*, compensation, *f.*, dédommagement, *m.*, récompense, *f.*, équivalent, *m.*
Considering, prep. considérant, attendu vu, eu égard à

Consign, va. livrer (à), (*trust*) confier (à), (*com.*) consigner (à)
Consignee, s. consignataire, *m.*
Consigner, s. consignateur, *m.*, -trice, *f.*
Consignment, s. consignation, *f.*
Consist, vn. consister, (*of*) se composer (de), (*agree*) s'accorder (avec)
Consistency, s. consistance, *f.*, constance, *f.*
Consistent, adj. solide, ferme, conséquent, compatible (avec)
Consistently, adv. conséquemment, (*agreeably*) conformément
Consistorial, adj. consistorial
Consistory, s. consistoire, *m.*
Consolable, adj. consolable
Consolation, s. consolation, *f.*, dédommagement, *m.*
Consolatory, adj. consolant
Console, s. console, *f.* —-*table*, console, *f.*
Console, va. consoler
Consoler, s. consolateur, *m.*, -trice, *f.*
Consolidate, va. consolider; — vn. se consolider
Consolidation, s. consolidation, *f.*
Consols, s. consolidés, *m. plur.*
Consonance, s. consonance, *f.*, (*fig.*) accord, *m.*, conformité, *f.*
Consonant, adj. consonant, (*fig.*) conforme (à)
Consonant, s. consonne, *f.*
Consort, s. compagnon, *m.*, compagne, *f.*, époux, *m.*, épouse, *f.*, (*ship*) conserve, *f.*
Consort, vn. s'associer (à)
Conspicuous, adj. visible, en évidence, (*striking*) frappant, (*eminent*) marquant, remarquable, grand
Conspicuously, adv. en évidence, éminemment
Conspicuousness, s. visibilité, *f.*, distinction, *f.*, célébrité, *f.*, réputation, *f.*
Conspiracy, s. conspiration, *f.*, conjuration, *f.*
Conspirator, s. conspirateur, *m.*, conjuré, *m.*
Conspire, vn. conspirer
Conspiring, adj. conjuré
Constable, s. connétable, *m.*, officier de paix, *m.* *Chief* —, commissaire de police, *m.*
Constabulary, s. police, *f.*, gendarmerie, *f.*
Constancy, s. stabilité, *f.*, constance, *f.*
Constant, adj. stable, constant, continuel
Constantly, adv. constamment
Constellation, s. constellation, *f.*
Consternation, s. consternation, *f.*
Constipate, va. constiper

Constipation, s. constipation, *f.*
Constituency, s. circonscription électorale, *f.*, collége électoral, *m.*, commettants, *m.pl.*
Constituent, adj. constituant
Constituent, s. commettant, *m.*
Constitute, va. constituer
Constitution, s. constitution, *f.*
Constitutional, adj. constitutionnel
Constitutional, s. (*fest.*) promenade pour la santé, *f.*
Constitutionalist, s. constitutionnel, *m.*
Constitutionally, adv. constitutionnellement
Constitutive, adj. constitutif
Constrain, va. contraindre, forcer, retenir, gêner
Constrainable, adj. contraignable
Constrainedly, adv. par contrainte
Constraint, s. contrainte, *f.*
Constrictor, s. constricteur, *m.*
Construct, va. construire
Constructer, s. constructeur, *m.*
Construction, s. construction, *f.*, (*fig.*) interprétation, *f.*, sens, *m.* *To put a good — on*, interpréter en bonne part
Constructively, adv. par interprétation, implicitement, censément
Construe, va. construire, interpréter, traduire, expliquer
Consul, s. consul, *m.*
Consular, adj. consulaire
Consulate, s. consulat, *m.*
Consulship, s. consulat, *m.*
Consult, va. consulter; — vn. se consulter
Consultation, s. consultation, *f.* —-*room*, cabinet, *m.*
Consumable, adj. consumable, consommable
Consume, va. consumer, dévorer, (*to use*) consommer; — vn. se consumer
Consumer, s. consommateur, *m.*
Consummate, va. consommer
Consummate, adj. consommé, achevé, fini
Consummation, s. consommation, *f.*, accomplissement, *m.*, (*end*) fin, *f.*
Consumption, s. consomption, *f.*, (*use*) consommation, *f.*, (*med.*) maladie de poitrine, *f.*, phthisie, *f.*
Consumptive, adj. (*pers.*) poitrinaire, phthisique, (*connected with the lungs*) pulmonaire
Contact, s. contact, *m.*
Contagion, s. contagion, *f.*
Contagious, adj. contagieux

Contagiousness, s. caractère contagieux, *m.*
Contain, va. contenir
Container, s. contenant, *m.*
Contaminate, va. souiller
Contaminate, adj. souillé
Contamination, s. souillure, *f.*
Contemn, va. mépriser
Contemner, s. contempteur, *m.*
Contemplate, va.n. contempler, méditer, projeter
Contemplation, s. contemplation, *f.*, (*thought*) pensée, *f.*, (*purpose*) projet, *m.*, (*view*) vue, *f.*
Contemplative, adj. contemplatif
Contemplatively, adv. en contemplation
Contemplator, s. contemplateur, *m.*, -trice, *f.*
Contemporaneity, s. contemporanéité, *f.*
Contemporaneous, adj. contemporain
Contemporary, adj. s. contemporain, *m.*, -e, *f.*
Contempt, s. mépris, *m.*, dédain, *m.*, (— *of court*) offense, *f.*, désobéissance, *f.*, refus de comparaître, *m.*, contumace, *f.* *In* —, par mépris. *In — of*, au mépris de
Contemptible, adj. méprisable
Contemptibleness, s. caractère méprisable, *m.*
Contemptibly, adv. d'une manière méprisable
Contemptuous, adj. méprisant, dédaigneux
Contemptuously, adv. avec mépris
Contemptuousness, s. mépris, *m.*
Contend, vn. combattre, lutter, contester, (*for*) se disputer, (*affirm*) soutenir, prétendre
Contending, adj. rival, opposé
Content, adj. content, satisfait. *To be* —, (*to consent*) consentir (à), vouloir bien
Content, va. contenter, satisfaire
Content, s. contentement, *m.*, (*parliam.*) voix pour, *f.* *Not* —, voix contre, *f.* —*s*, pl. contenu, *m.* *Table of* —*s*, table des matières, *f.*
Contented, adj. content (de), satisfait (de)
Contentedly, adv. content
Contentedness, s. contentement, *m.*
Contention, s. contention, *f.*, débat, *m.*, (*strife*) lutte, *f.*
Contentious, adj. disputeur, querelleur
Contentiousness, s. humeur querelleuse, *f.*
Contentment, s. contentement, *m.*
Contest, va.n. contester, lutter, rivaliser (de)
Contest, s. contestation, *f.*, débat, *m.*, (*strife*) lutte, *f.*, combat, *m.*

Contestable, adj. contestable
Context, s. contexte, *m.*, sens, *m.*
Contexture, s. contexture, *f.*, tissu, *m.*, (*series*) enchaînement, *m.*
Contiguity, s. contiguïté, *f.*
Contiguous, adj. contigu
Continence, s. continence, *f.*, retenue, *f.*, modération, *f.*
Continent, adj continent, retenu, modéré
Continent, s. continent, *m.*
Continental, adj. continental
Continently, adv. avec continence, (*moderately*) avec retenue
Contingency, s. contingence, *f.*, éventualité, *f.*, hasard, *m.*, cas fortuit, *m.*
Contingent, adj contingent, éventuel, incertain
Contingent, s. événement fortuit, *m.*, (*troops*) contingent, *m*
Contingently, adv. fortuitement
Continual, adj. continuel
Continually, adv. continuellement
Continuance, s. continuation, *f.*, continuité, *f.*, persévérance, *f.*, durée, *f.*, (*abode*) séjour, *m.*
Continuation, s. continuation, *f.*, suite, *f.*, durée, *f.*
Continuator, s. continuateur, *m.*
Continue, vn. continuer, persévérer, (*remain*) rester, demeurer; — va. continuer, poursuivre, prolonger, conserver, perpétuer
Continued, adj. continu, prolongé, (*fig.*) soutenu, suivi
Continuedly, adv. sans interruption
Continuer, s. continuateur, *m.*
Continuity, s. continuité, *f.*
Continuous, adj. continu
Contortion, s. contorsion, *f.*
Contraband, s. contrebande, *f.*
Contraband, adj. de contrebande
Contrabandist, s. contrebandier, *m.*
Contract, va. contracter, resserrer, rétrécir, (*brow*) rider, (*abridge*) abréger; — vn. se contracter, se resserrer, rétrécir, se rider, (*bargain*) traiter, s'engager (à), entreprendre
Contract, s. contrat, *m.*, (*public works, supplies*) soumission, *f.*, adjudication, *f.*, entreprise, *f.* *By* —, (*com.*) à forfait, par entreprise
Contraction, s. contraction, *f.*, (*shortening*) raccourcissement, *m.*
Contractor, s. contractant, *m.*, (*farmer*) fermier, *m.*, (*works*) entrepreneur, *m.*

(*the army*) fournisseur, *m.*, (*admin.*) adjudicataire, *m.*

Contradict, va. contredire

Contradicter, s. contradicteur, *m.*

Contradiction, s. contradiction, *f.*

Contradictorily, adv. contradictoirement

Contradictory, adj. contradictoire

Contradistinction, s. *In — to*, par opposition à

Contradistinguish, va. distinguer

Contralto, s. contralto, *m.*

ontrariety, s. contrariété, *f.*

ontrarily, adv. contrairement, différemment

ontrary, adj. contraire (à). — *to*, (adv. prep.) contrairement à, au contraire de, ontre

ontrary, s. contraire, *m.* *In the —*, au contraire. *To the —*, en sens contraire, ontre

ontrast, s. contraste, *m.*, (à, avec)

ontrast, va. contraster, mettre en contraste; — vn. ontraster

ontravallation, s. contrevallation, *f.*

ontravene, va. contrevenir à

ontravention, s. contravention, *f.*

ontribute, va. payer, urnir, donner; — vn. contribuer (à), concourir (à)

ontribution, s. contribution, *f.*, (*writing*) article,

ontributive, Contributory, adj. qui contribue

ontributor, s. personne i contribue (à), *f.*, (*journal*) llaborateur, *m.*, -trice, *f.*, lacteur, *m.*, correspondant,

ntrite, adj. contrit

ntritely, adv. avec contion

ntrition, s. contrition,

ntrivance, s. invenn, *f.*, combinaison, *f.*, idée, projet, *m.*, artifice, *m.*, chine, *f.*

ntrive, va. inventer, ouver, imaginer, concevoir, nbiner, (*manage*) arranger, tiquer; — vn. s'arranger ur), trouver moyen (de), (*about*) s'y prendre, faire ur), (*succeed*) parvenir (à), ir à bout (de)

ntriver, s. inventeur, , auteur, *m.*

ntrol, s. contrôle, *m.*, pire, *m.*, autorité, *f.*, inence, *f.*, contrainte, *f.*, *eck*) frein, *m.*

ntrol, va. contrôler, avoir l'empire sur, réprimer, verner, régler

ntrollable, adj. sous à l'autorité (de)

ntroller, s. contrôleur,

Controllership, s. emploi de contrôleur, *m.*

Controversial, adj. de controverse

Controversialist, s. controversiste, *m.*

Controversy, s. controverse, *f.*, dispute, *f.*

Controvert, va. controverser, agiter

Controvertible, adj. sujet à controverse

Contumacious, adj. obstiné, opiniâtre, rebelle, pervers, (*law*) contumace

Contumaciously, adv. avec opiniâtreté

Contumacy, s. obstination, *f.*, opiniâtreté, *f.*, (*law*) contumace, *f.*

Contumelious, adj. injurieux, outrageant, (*contemptuous*) méprisant

Contumeliously, adv. injurieusement

Contumely, s. outrage, *m.*, insulte, *f.*, (*contempt*) mépris, *m.*, dédain, *m.*

Contuse, va. contusionner

Contusion, s. contusion, *f.*

Conundrum, s. jeu de mots, *m.*

Convalescence, s. convalescence, *f.*

Convalescent, adj. convalescent

Convene, va. convoquer, réunir

Convenience, s. commodité, *f.*, convenance, *f.*, aise, *f.* *At your —*, à votre convenance. *At your earliest —*, aussitôt que vous le pourrez. *To meet the — of*, arranger

Convenient, adj. commode. *If it is — to you*, si cela ne vous gêne pas. *If you could make it — to be there*, si vous pouviez vous arranger de manière à vous y trouver

Conveniently, adv. commodément, à son aise, sans se gêner, bien

Convent, s. couvent, *m.*

Conventicle, s. conventicule, *m.*

Convention, s. convention, *f.*

Conventional, adj. conventionnel, de convention

Conventionalism, Conventionality, s. phrase, *f.*, affaire, *f.*, de convention, *f.*

Conventionalist, s. (*hist.*) conventionnel, *m.*

Conventionally, adv. conventionnellement

Conventual, adj. conventuel

Converge, vn. converger

Convergence, s. convergence, *f.*

Convergent, Converging, adj. convergent

Conversable, adj. sociable

Conversant, adj. familier, (*skilled*) versé (dans)

Conversation, s. conversation, *f.*, commerce, *m.*

Conversational, adj. de conversation. *A person of great — powers*, une personne qui cause très bien

Conversationally, adv. par *or* pour la conversation

Conversazione, s. réunion, *f.*, cercle, *m.*, conférence, *f.*

Converse, vn. converser, causer, s'entretenir

Converse, s. réciproque, *f.*

Conversely, adv. réciproquement

Conversion, s. conversion, *f.*

Convert, va. convertir, approprier, appliquer; — vn. se convertir

Convert, s. converti, *m.* *To become a —*, se convertir

Convertibility, s. convertibilité, *f.*

Convertible, adj. convertible

Convex, adj. convexe, bombé

Convexity, s. convexité, *f.*, bombement, *m.*

Convey, va. porter, transporter, transmettre, communiquer, donner, exprimer, transférer

Conveyance, s. transport, *m.*, moyen de transport, *m.*, voiture, *f.*, (*way*) voie, *f.*, transmission, *f.*, (*law*) transfert, *m.* *Deed of —*, acte de cession, *m.*

Conveyancer, s. notaire, *m.*

Convict, va. convaincre, condamner

Convict, s. condamné, *m.*, -e, *f.*, forçat, *m.*, détenu, *m.*, -e, *f.* *Returned —*, forçat libéré. *— -establishment*, colonie pénitentiaire, *f.*

Conviction, s. conviction, *f.*, condamnation, *f.*

Convince, va. convaincre

Convincing, adj. convaincant; — part. convainquant

Convincingly, adv. d'une manière convaincante

Convivial, adj. de festin, (*pers.*) joyeux, jovial

Conviviality, s. gaieté franche, *f.*, joyeuse réunion, *f.*

Convocation, s. convocation, *f.*, assemblée, *f.*

Convoke, va. convoquer

Convolvulus, s. convolvulus, *m.*, volubilis, *m.*

Convoy, va. convoyer

Convoy, s. convoi, *m.*, (*mil.*) escorte, *f.*

Convulse, va. donner des convulsions à, agiter, ébranler, bouleverser

Convulsed, adj. en convulsions, agité, tremblant, crispé

Convulsion, s. convulsion, *f.*

Convulsive, adj. convulsif

Convulsively, adv. convulsivement

Coo, vn. roucouler

Cooing, s. roucoulement, *m.*

Cook, va. cuire, faire cuire, apprêter; — vn. faire la cuisine

Cook, s. cuisinier, *m.*, -ière, *f.* *— -maid*, cuisinière, *f.* *— -shop*, rôtisserie, *f.* *— -shop keeper*, rôtisseur, *m.*, traiteur, *m.*

Cookery, s. cuisine, *f.* *— -book*, livre de cuisine, *f.*

Cooking, s. cuisine, *f.*, (*doing*) cuisson, *f.* — adj. de cuisine

Cool, adj. frais, tiède, (*pers.*) calme, tranquille, (*fam.*) impudent, hardi, sans gêne

Cool, s. frais, *m.*

Cool, va.n. rafraîchir, (*fig.*) refroidir, calmer, se refroidir, se calmer

Cooler, s. rafraîchissoir, *m.*, (*med.*) rafraîchissant, *m.*

Coolly, adv. fraîchement, (*fig.*) froidement, de sang-froid

Coolness, s. fraîcheur, *f.*, frais, *m.*, (*indifference*) froideur, *f.*, (*composure*) sang-froid, *m.*, (*fam.*) impudence, *f.*, sans-gêne, *m.*

Coom, s. cambouis, *m.*

Coop, s. poulailler, *m.*, mue, *f.*

Coop, va. enfermer, emprisonner

Cooper, s. tonnelier, *m.*, boisselier, *m.*

Cooperage, s. tonnellerie, *f.*

Cooperate, vn. coopérer (à), concourir (à)

Cooperation, s. coopération, *f.*, concours, *m.*

Cooperative, adj. coopérant

Cooperator, s. coopérateur, *m.*

Copaiva, s. copahu, *m.*

Copal, s. copal, *m.*

Copartner, s. associé, *m.*, -e, *f.*

Copartnership, s. association, *f.*

Cope, s. coiffe, *f.*, (*heaven, &c.*) voûte, *f.*, (*church*) chape, *f.*

Cope, vn. lutter, rivaliser

Copier, s. copiste, *m.*

Coping, s. chape, *f.*

Copious, adj. copieux, abondant, riche

Copiously, adv. copieusement, abondamment

Copiousness, s. abondance, *f.*

Copper, s. cuivre, *m.*, (*boiler*) chaudière, *f.*, cuve, *f.*, (*coin*) monnaie de cuivre, *f.*, sous, *m.pl.* *— -bottomed*, à fond de cuivre. *— -colour*, cuivré. *— -nose*, nez couperosé, *m.* *— -plate*, taille-douce, *f.* *— -smith*, chaudronnier, *m.* *— -works*, usine de cuivre, *f.*

Copper, adj. de *or* en cuivre

Copper, va. cuivrer, doubler en cuivre

Copperas, s. couperose, *f.*

Coppery, adj. cuivreux

Coppice, Copse, s. taillis, *m.*

Copy, s. copie, *f.*, exemplaire, *m.*, (*newspapers*) numéro, *m.*, (*model*) exemple, *m.* *A true* —, pour copie conforme. *Rough* —, brouillon, *m.* *To make or write a fair* — *of*, mettre au net. —*-book*, cahier, *m.* —*-right*, propriété littéraire, *f.*, droit d'auteur, *m.*

Copy, va.n. copier, transcrire

Copying-clerk, s. expéditionnaire, *m.* — *-press*, presse à copier, *f.*

Copyist, s. copiste, *m.*

Coquetry, s. coquetterie, *f.*

Coquettish, adj. coquet

Coral, s. corail, *m.*, (*child's*) hochet, *m.*

Coral, adj. de corail

Coralline, s. coralline, *f.*

Cord, s. corde, *f.*, cordon, *m.*, (*trimming*) ganse, *f.* —*-maker*, cordier, *m.*

Cord, va. corder

Cordage, s. cordage, *m.*

Corded, adj. cordé, (*stuffs*) à côtes

Cordelier, s. cordelier, *m.*

Cordial, adj. s. cordial, *m.*

Cordiality, s. cordialité, *f.*

Cordially, adv. cordialement

Cordon, s. cordon, *m.*

Corduroy, s. velours à côtes, *m.*

Core, s. cœur, *m.*, (*cabbage, apple, &c.*) trognon, *m.*, cœur, *m.*, (*abscess*) fond, *m.*, bourbillon, *m.*

Co-religionist, s. coreligionnaire, *m.f.*

Co-respondent, s. complice, *m.*

Coriander, s. coriandre, *f.*

Cork, s. liége, *m.*, (*stopper*) bouchon, *m.*, (*float*) nageoire, *f.* —*-cutter*, bouchonnier, *m.* —*-screw*, tire-bouchon, *m.* —*-screw staircase*, escalier en limaçon, *m.* —*-tree*, chêne-liége, *m.*

Cork, va. boucher

Cormorant, s. cormoran, *m.*

Corn, s. blé, *m.*, (*in general*) grain, *m.*, grains, *m.pl.*, céréales, *f.pl.*, (*feet*) cor, *m.* *Indian* —, blé de Turquie, *m.*, maïs, *m.* —*-chandler*, marchand de blé, *m.*, grainetier, *m.* —*-cutter*, pédicure, *m.* —*-drill*, semoir, *m.* —*-exchange*, —*-market*, halle au blé, *f.* —*-field*, champ de blé, *m.* —*-flag*, glaïeul, *m.* —*-flower*, bluet, *m.* —*-laws*, lois sur les céréales, *f.pl.* —*-pipe*, chalumeau, *m.* —*-plant*, céréale, *f.* —*-poppy*, —*-rose*, coquelicot, *m.* —*-salad*, mâche, doucette, *f.* —*-trade*, commerce des grains, *m.*

Corn, va. grener, (*salt*) saler

Cornea, s. cornée, *f.*

Cornel-tree, s. cornouiller, *m.*

Cornelian, s. — *-stone*, cornaline, *f.* —*-tree*, cornouiller, *m.*

Corner, s. coin, *m.*, encoignure, *f.*, angle, *m.*, réduit, *m.*, recoin, *m.* *Puss in the* —, (*game*) les quatre coins, *m.pl.* —*-house*, maison du coin, *f.*, maison qui fait le coin, *f.* —*-stone*, pierre angulaire, *f.*

Cornered, adj. à . . . coins, à angles . . .

Cornet, s. cornet, *m.*, (*mil.*) sous-lieutenant de cavalerie, *m.*

Cornetcy, s. sous-lieutenance, *f.*

Cornice, s. corniche, *f.*, (*curtains*) galerie de croisée, *f.*

Cornish, adj. de Cornouailles

Cornist, s. corniste, *m.*

Cornopean, s. cornet à pistons, *m.*

Cornopeist, s. piston, *m.*

Cornucopia, s. corne d'abondance, *f.*

Corolla, s. corolle, *f.*

Corollary, s. corollaire, *m.*

Coronation, s. couronnement, *m.*, sacre, *m.*

Coronet, s. couronne, *f.*

Corporal, s. caporal, *m.*, (*cavalry*) brigadier, *m.*

Corporal, Corporeal, adj. corporel, matériel

Corporate, adj. érigé en corporation

Corporation, s. corporation, *f.*, communauté, *f.*, société, *f.*, municipalité, *f.*, (*corpulence*) bedaine, *f.*, (du) ventre, *m.*

Corps, s. corps, *m.*

Corpse, s. cadavre, *m.*, corps mort, *m.*, corps, *m.*

Corpulence, s. corpulence, *f.*, embonpoint, *m.*

Corpulent, adj. corpulent

Corpus-Christi, s. la Fête-Dieu, *f.*

Corpuscle, s. corpuscule, *m.*

Corpuscular, adj. corpusculaire

Correct, adj. correct, exact, juste

Correct, va. corriger, (*a person speaking*) reprendre. *To stand corrected*, reconnaître son erreur

Correction, s. correction, *f.*

Corrective, adj. s. correctif, *m.*

Correctly, adv. correctement

Correctness, s. correction, *f.*, exactitude, *f.*

Corrector, s. correcteur, *m.* — *of the press*, correcteur d'imprimerie

Correlation, s. corrélation, *f.*

Correlative, adj. corrélatif

Correspond, vn. correspondre

Correspondence, s. correspondance, *f.*, relation, *f.*

Correspondent, adj. correspondant, qui se rapporte (à)

Correspondent, s. correspondant, *m.*

Corrigible, adj. corrigible, punissable

Corroborate, va. corroborer

Corroboration, s. corroboration, *f.*

Corroborative, adj. corroboratif, qui confirme

Corrode, va. corroder, (*fig.*) ronger

Corroding, adj. corrodant, (*fig.*) rongeur

Corrosion, s. corrosion, *f.*

Corrosive, adj. s. corrosif, *m.*

Corrosiveness, s. mordacité, *f.*

Corrupt, va. corrompre; — vn. se corrompre

Corrupt, adj. corrompu

Corrupter, s. corrupteur, *m.*

Corruptibility, s. corruptibilité, *f.*

Corruptible, adj. corruptible

Corrupting, adj. corrupteur

Corruption, s. corruption, *f.*

Corruptive, adj. qui corrompt

Corruptly, adv. d'une manière corrompue, (*by bribery*) par corruption

Corruptress, s. corruptrice, *f.*

Corsair, s. corsaire, *m.*, forban, *m.*

Corselet, s. corselet, *m.*

Corvette, s. corvette, *f.*

Coryphеus, s. coryphée, *m.*

Cosily, adv. à l'aise, commodément

Cosmetic, adj. s. cosmétique, *m.*

Cosmographical, adj. cosmographique

Cosmography, s. cosmographie, *f.*

Cosmopolitan, adj. cosmopolite

Cosmopolite, s. cosmopolite, *m.*

Cossack, s. cosaque, *m.*

Cost, vn.a. coûter. — *what it will* or *may*, coûte que coûte

Cost, s. prix, *m.* —*s*, pl. (*law*) dépens, *m.pl.* *At any* —, à tout prix, coûte que coûte

Costermonger, s. marchand des quatre saisons, *m.*

Costive, adj. constipé

Costiveness, s. constipation, *f.*

Costliness, s. grande dépense, *f.*, somptuosité, *f.*

Costly, adj. coûteux, précieux, somptueux

Costume, s. costume, *m.*

Cosy, adj. à l'aise, commode, confortable

Cot, s. cabane, *f.*, (*sheep*) parc, *m.*, (*infants*) lit d'enfant, *m.*, barcelonnette, *f.*, (*nav.*) cadre, *m.*, hamac, *m.*

Co-trustee, s. curateur, *m.*

Cottage, s. cabane, *f.*, chaumière, *f.*, petite maison, *f.*, villa, *f.*

Cottager, s. paysan, *m.*, -ne, *f.*

Cotton, s. coton, *m.* *Darning* —, coton plat, *m.* *Printed* —, indienne, *f.*, rouennerie, *f.* *Sewing* —, fil d'Écosse, *m.* —*-cloth*, toile de coton, *f.*, cotonnade, *f.* —*-manufactory*, —*-mill*, filature de coton, *f.* —*-plant*, —*-shrub*, —*-tree*, cotonnier, *m.* —*-wool*, ouate de coton, *f.*, ouate, *f.* —*-yarn*, fil de coton, *m.*

Cotton, adj. de coton, cotonnier

Cotton, vn. se cotonner

Cottony, adj. cotonneux

Couch, vn. se coucher, (*stoop*) se baisser; — va. coucher, (*spread*) étendre, (*in writing*) rédiger, (*spears*) tenir en arrêt, (*an eye*) abaisser

Couch, s. couche, *f.*, (*lounge*) chaise longue, *f.*, (*formerly*) lit de repos, *m.* —*-grass*, chiendent, *m.*

Couching, s. courbette, *f.*, (*surg.*) abaissement de la cataracte, *m.*

Cough, s. toux, *f.* —*-lozenges*, pastilles contre la toux, *f.pl.*

Cough, vn. tousser; — va. expectorer

Cougher, s. tousseur, *m.*, -euse, *f.*

Coughing, s. toux, *f.*

Could. *I* —, (*was able*) je pouvais, je pus, (*should be able*) je pourrais, (*have been able*) j'ai pu, (*after a verb, conj., &c. governing the subjunctive mood*) je pusse

Coulter, s. coutre, *m.*

Council, s. conseil, *m.*, (*eccles.*) concile, *m.* —*-board*, conseil, *m.* —*-man*, conseiller municipal, *m.*

Councillor, s. conseiller, *m.*

Counsel, s. conseil, *m.*, secret, *m.*, (*barrister*) avocat, *m.*, défenseur, *m.*

Counsel, va. conseiller

Counsellor, s. conseiller, *m.*, (*lawyer*) avocat, *m.*

Count, va.n. compter

Count, s. compte, *m.*, (*law*) charge, *f.*, chef, *m.*, (*pers.*) comte, *m.*

Countenance, s. contenance, *f.*, visage, *m.*, physionomie, *f.*, air, *m.*, mine, *f.*, appui, *m.*, protection, *f.*, encouragement, *m.*, approbation, *f.* *Out of* —, décontenancé. *To keep one's* —, faire bonne contenance, (*not to laugh*) garder son sérieux. *To put out of* —, décontenancer

Countenance, va. appuyer, soutenir, défendre, protéger encourager, approuver, être en faveur de

Counter, s. comptoir, *m.*, (*play*) jeton, *m.*, (*mus.*) haute-contre, *f.*, (*instrument*) compteur, *m.*, (*boots*) contre-fort, *m.* *Over the* —, au comptant

Counter, adv. contre, contraire, (*the wrong way*) à l'encontre (de). — *buff*, contre-coup, *m.* — *-check*, va. contre-carrer; — s. opposition, *f.*, réprimande, *f.* — *-evidence*, s. déposition contradictoire, *f.* — *-seal*, va. contre-sceller. — *-signature*, s. contre-seing, *m.* — *-tenor*, s. haute-contre, *f.* — *-work*, va. déjouer, confondre

Counteract, va. contrarier, déjouer, neutraliser, détruire

Counteraction, s. opposition, *f.*

Counterbalance, va. contre-balancer

Counterbalance, s. contre-poids, *m.*

Counterfeit, va. contrefaire, (*fig.*) imiter

Counterfeit, adj. contrefait, imité, feint, (*coin*) faux

Counterfeit, s. contrefaçon, *f.*, (*bad money*) fausse monnaie, *f.*, (*fig.*) imitation, *f.*, (*pers.*) imposteur, *m.*

Counterfeiter, s. faussaire, *m.*, contrefacteur, *m.*, faux-monnayeur, *m.*

Counterfoil, s. souche, *f.*

Countermand, va. contre-mander, décommander

Counterpane, s. couvre-pieds, *m.*

Counterpart, s. contre-partie, *f.*, (*fellow*) pendant, *m.*, (*law*) double, *m.*

Counterplot, s. contre-ruse, *f.*

Counterpoise, va. contre-balancer

Counterscarp, s. contre-scarpe, *f.*

Countersign, va. contre-signer

Countersign, s. contre-seing, *m.*, (*mil.*) mot de ralliement, *m.*

Countervail, va. contre-balancer, compenser

Countess, s. comtesse, *f.*

Counting-house, s. bureau, *m.*, comptoir, *m.*

Countless, adj. innombrable

Countrified, adj. rustique, campagnard

Country, s. pays, *m.*, (*region*) contrée, *f.*, (*native land*) patrie, *f.*, (*not a town*) campagne, *f.*, (*not the capital*) départements, *m.pl.*, province, *f.* *In* or *into the* —, à la campagne, dans la campagne, dans les champs, dans les départements, en province. — *-house*, maison de campagne, *f.* — *-life*, (*rural*) vie champêtre, *f.*, (*in the* —) vie de province, *f.* — *-parson*, curé de campagne, *m.*, curé de village, *m.* — *-seat*, maison de campagne, *f.*, château, *m.*

Countryman, Countrywoman, compatriote, *m.f.*, (*peasant*) paysan, *m.*, -ne, *f.*, campagnard, *m.*, -e, *f.*

County, s. comté, *m.*, (*in France*) département, *m.* — *-court*, tribunal de première instance, *m.* — *-town*, chef-lieu, *m.*

County, adj. départemental

Couple, s. couple, *m.f.*

Couple, va. coupler, accoupler, (*fig.*) joindre; — vn. s'accoupler

Couplet, s. distique, *m.*, (*songs*) couplet, *m.*, strophe, *f.*

Coupling, s. accouplement, *m.*

Courage, s. courage, *m.*

Courageous, adj. courageux

Courageously, adv. courageusement

Courier, s. courrier, *m.* — *-bag*, gibecière, *f.*

Course, s. cours, *m.*, progrès, *m.pl.*, (*race*) course, *f.*, carrière, *f.*, courant, *m.*, (*means*) marche, *f.*, conduite, *f.*, moyen, *m.*, parti, *m.*, (*order*) ordre, *m.*, (*succession*) suite, *f.*, (*of life*) genre, *m.*, train, *m.*, (*table*) service, *m.*, (*stones*) assise, *f.*, (*of a ship*) route, *f.* *In* — *of*, en voie de. *Of* —, naturellement, bien entendu, cela va sans dire, (*law*) de droit. *Matter of* —, chose qui va sans dire, *f.*

Course, va.n. chasser, courir, poursuivre, faire courir, parcourir

Courser, s. coursier, *m.*

Coursing, s. chasse (à courre), *f.*

Court, s. cour, *f.*, tribunal, *m.*, (*meeting*) assemblée, *f.*, (*street*) passage, *m.*, (*no thoroughfare*) impasse, *f.* — *-card*, figure, *f.* — *-day*, jour d'audience, jour de palais, *m.* — *-fool*, fou du roi *or* de la reine, *m.*, bouffon, *m.* — *-martial*, conseil de guerre, *m.* — *-plaster*, taffetas d'Angleterre, *m.* — *-yard*, cour, *f.*

Court, va. faire la cour à, courtiser, rechercher, briguer

Courteous, adj. poli, courtois

Courteously, adv. poliment

Courtesan, s. courtisane, *f.*

Courtesy, s. courtoisie, *f.*, politesse, *f.*, (*bow*) révérence, *f.*

Courtesy, vn. faire une révérence

Courtier, s. homme de *or* de la cour, *m.*, courtisan, *m.*

Courtliness, s. élégance, *f.*

Courtly, Courtlike, adj. de cour, poli, du grand monde, élégant

Courtship, s. cour, *f.*

Cousin, s. cousin, *m.*, -e, *f.* *First* —, cousin germain

Cove, s. anse, *f.*, (*pers.*) gaillard, *m.*, particulier, *m.*

Cove, va. voûter

Covenant, s. convention, *f.*, contrat, *m.*

Covenant, vn. convenir (de), (*law*) s'engager (à); — va. stipuler

Covenanter, s. partie contractante, *f.*

Cover, va. couvrir, recouvrir, (*hide*) cacher, déguiser, (*the step*) emboîter, (*birds*) couver. — *over*, recouvrir

Cover, s. couverture, *f.*, (*letters*) enveloppe, *f.*, (*a lid*) couvercle, *m.*, (*dishes, &c.*) cloche, *f.*, couvre-plat, *m.*, (*chairs, &c.*) housse, *f.*, (*tables*) tapis, *m.*, (*disguise*) voile, *m.*, masque, *m.*, (*shelter*) abri, *m.*, (*requisites for eating*) couvert, *m.*, (*hiding-place*) couvert, *m.* *Under* —, (*letters, &c.*) sous enveloppe, (*mil.*) sous la protection (de), (*fig.*) à la faveur (de)

Covering, s. couverture, *f.*, enveloppe, *f.*, (*lid*) couvercle, *m.*, (*clothing*) habits, *m.pl.*

Coverlet, s. couvre-pieds, *m.*, couvre-lit, *m.*

Covert, s. (*shelter*) couvert, *m.*, abri, *m.*, (*hiding-place*) fort, *m.*, gîte, *m.*

Covert, adj. couvert, (*fig.*) caché, secret, (*women*) en puissance de mari

Covertly, adv. secrètement

Coverture, s. (*shelter*) abri, *m.*, (*law*) puissance de mari, *f.*

Covert-way, s. chemin couvert, *m.*

Covet, va.n. convoiter, désirer ardemment

Coveting, s. convoitise, *f.*

Covetous, adj. avide, cupide, avare

Covetously, adv. avidement, sordidement

Covetousness, s. convoitise, *f.*, cupidité, *f.*

Covey, s. couvée, *f.*, volée, *f.*, (*of game*) compagnie, *f.*

Cow, s. vache, *f.* — *-hair*, bourre de vache, *f.* — *-herd*, vacher, *m.* — *-house*, *-shed*, étable à vaches, *f.*, vacherie, *f.* — *-keeper*, nourrisseur, *m.*

Cow, va. dompter, intimider

Coward, s. poltron, *m.*, -ne, *f.*, lâche, *m.*

Cowardice, s. poltronnerie, *f.*, lâcheté, *f.*

Cowardly, adj. poltron, lâche; — adv. en poltron, en lâche, lâchement

Cower, — *down*, vn. se blottir, s'accroupir

Cowl, s. capuchon, *m.*, (*of chimneys*) tabourin, *m.*

Cowslip, s. coucou, *m.*

Coxcomb, s. fat, petit-maître, *m.*, (*bot.*) passe-velours, *m.*

Coxswain, *see* Cockswain

Coy, adj. modeste, timide, réservé

Coyly, adv. modestement, timidement, avec réserve

Coyness, s. modestie, *f.*, timidité, *f.*, réserve, *f.*

Cozen, va. tromper, duper

Cozenage, s. fourberie, *f.*

Cozener, s. fourbe, *m.*

Crab, s. crabe, *m.*, cancre, *m.*, (*apple*) pomme sauvage, *f.*, (*of men*) loup-garou, *m.*, (*of women*) pie-grièche, *f.*, (*astr.*) écrevisse, *f.*, cancer, *m.* — *-tree*, pommier sauvage, *m.*

Crabbed, adj. acariâtre, bourru, (*rough*) dur, (*stiff*) rude

Crabbedly, adv. durement

Crabbedness, s. âcreté, *f.*, (*pers.*) humeur acariâtre, *f.*, (*things*) difficulté, *f.*

Crack, va. fendre, (*brittle things*) fêler, (*on the surface*) gercer, (*nuts, &c.*) casser, (*fig.*) rompre, briser, (*the brain*) fêler, (*a joke*) faire, dire, lâcher, (*a whip*) faire claquer, (*a bottle*) faire sauter, décoiffer, (*swallow*) avaler; — vn. se fendre, se fêler, se gercer, (*sound*) craquer, (*whips*) claquer, (*boast*) se vanter

Crack, s. fente, *f.*, crevasse, *f.*, (*brittle things*) fêlure, *f.*, (*noise*) craquement, *m.*, (*an instant*) instant, *m.*, clin d'œil, *m.*, (*pers.*) fou, *m.*, (*boaster*) craqueur, *m.*, (*boast*) craquerie, *f.* — *-brained*, timbré, fou

Crack, adj. fameux, de première force, le plus fort, de haute volée

Cracked, adj. (*pers.*) timbré, fêlé, (*walls*) lézardé

Cracker, s. (*firework*) pétard, *m.*, (*sweetmeat*) diablotin, *m.*, (*boaster*) vantard, *m.*

Cracking, s. craquement, *m.*, (*of a whip*) claquement, *m.*

Crackle, vn. craqueter, pétiller

Crackling, s. pétillement, *m.*, (*roast pork*) rissolé, *m.*, (*browned dishes*) gratin, *m.* —*s*, pl. (*cakes*) pains de cretons, cretons, *m.pl.*

Cracknel, s. craquelin, *m.*, échaudé, *m.*

Cradle, s. berceau, *m.*

Craft, s. ruse, *f.*, art, *m.* métier, *m.*, (*nav.*) embarcations, *f.pl.*, bâtiments, *m.pl.*

Craftily, adv. artificieusement

Craftiness, s. astuce, *f.*

Craftsman, s. artisan, *m.*

Craftsmaster, s. maître, *m.*

Crafty, adj. rusé, astucieux

Crag, s. roc, *m.*, rocher escarpé, *m.*

Cragged, Craggy, adj. rocailleux

Cragginess, s. état rocailleux, *m.*

Crake, s. râle, *m.*

Cram, va. (*fill*) remplir (de), farcir (de), bourrer, gorger (de), entasser, (*poultry*) empâter, (*to coach students*) seriner, préparer spécialement

Crambo, s. jeu de bouts rimés, *m.*

Crammer, s. préparateur, *m.*, répétiteur, *m.*

Cramming, s. études indigestes, *f.*

Cramp, s. crampe, *f.*, crampon, *m.*

Cramp, adj. biscornu

Cramp, va. donner la crampe à, courbaturer, engourdir, (*squeeze*) serrer, (*confine*) gêner, entraver, resserrer, forcer, (*fasten*) cramponner

Cranberry, s. canneberge, *f.*, airelle, *f.*

Crane, s. grue, *f.*, siphon, *m.*

Crank, s. (*winding*) détour, *m.*, (*machine*) manivelle, *f.*

Crannied, adj. crevassé

Cranny, s. crevasse, *f.*

Crape, s. crêpe, *m.*

Crash, vn. faire un grand fracas

Crash, s. fracas, *m.*

Crater, s. cratère, *m.*

Craunch, or **Cranch**, va. croquer

Cravat, s. cravate, *f.*

Crave, va. demander, implorer, solliciter

Craven, s. lâche, *m.*, poltron, *m.*

Craven, va. intimider

Craving, s. désir ardent, *m.*

Craving, adj. insatiable

Cravingly, adv. avec instance, d'un ton suppliant

Crawfish, *see* CRAYFISH

Crawl, vn. ramper, (*fig.*) se traîner, (*steal in*) se glisser, s'insinuer. — *in*, entrer. — *up*, grimper

Crawler, s. reptile, *m.*

Crayfish, s. écrevisse, *f.*

Crayon, s. crayon, *m.*, pastel, *m.*

Crayon, va. crayonner, tracer

Craze, va. briser, écraser, (*the mind*) affaiblir, rendre fou

Craziness, s. caducité, *f.*, (*of the mind*) démence, *f.*

Crazy, adj. caduc, (*of the mind*) faible, (*mad*) fou

Creak, vn. crier, craquer

Creaking, s. cri, *m.*, craquement, *m.*

Creaking, adj. qui crie, qui craque

Cream, s. crème, *f.* *Cold* —, cold-cream, *m.*, cérat, *m.* — *-cheese*, fromage à la crème, *m.* — *-coloured*, couleur café au lait. — *-faced*, pâle. — *-laid*, vergé blanc. — *-pot*, pot à crème, *m.* — *-sauce*, béchamel, *f.*

Cream, va. écrémer; — vn. crémer

Creamy, adj. de crème, crémeux

Crease, s. pli, *m.*, faux-pli, *m.*

Crease, va. faire des plis *or* des faux-plis à

Create, va. créer, produire, engendrer, causer, constituer, (*make*) faire

Creation, s. création, *f.*

Creative, adj. créateur

Creator, s. créateur, *m.*

Creature, s. créature, *f.*, animal, *m.*, personne, *f.*, (*fellow*) être, *m.*, (*drink*) consolation, *f.*, bouteille, *f.* — *-comforts*, vivres, *m.pl.*, mangeaille, *f.*

Credence, s. créance, *f.*, foi, *f.*

Credentials, s. lettres de créance, *f.pl.*

Credibility, s. crédibilité, *f.*

Credible, adj. croyable, (*pers.*) digne de foi

Credibly, adv. d'une manière digne de foi

Credit, s. crédit, *m.*, honneur, *m.*, (*belief*) croyance, *f.*, foi, *f.* *On* —, à crédit. *To give — to*, ajouter foi (à), (*com.*) faire crédit (à)

Credit, va. croire (à), ajouter foi (à), (*com.*) donner à crédit, (*book-keep.*) porter au crédit (de)

Creditable, adj. honorable

Creditableness, s. estime, *f.*

Creditably, adv. honorablement

Creditor, s. créancier, *m.*, (*book-keep.*) créditeur, *m.*, avoir, *m.* — *-side*, crédit, *m.*, avoir, *m.*

Credulity, s. crédulité, *f.*

Credulous, adj. crédule

Credulously, adv. avec crédulité

Creed, s. symbole, *m.*, (*belief*) croyance, *f.*, (*fig.*) profession de foi, *f.*

Creek, s. anse, *f*, crique, *f.*

Creep, vn. ramper, se traîner. — *in*, se glisser, s'insinuer, se faufiler, avancer. — *on*, s'avancer, (*seize*) s'emparer (de). — *out*, sortir, (*steal away*) s'esquiver. — *up*, grimper. — *-hole*, trou, *m.*, (*fig.*) échappatoire, *f.*

Creeper, s. reptile, *m.*, plante grimpante, *f.*, (*bird*) grimpereau, *m.*

Creeping, s. (*sensation*) fourmillement, *m.*

Crenelle, s. créneau, *m.*

Crenellated, adj. crénelé

Creole, s. créole, *m.f*

Creosote, s. créosote, *f.*

Crepuscular, adj. crépusculaire

Crescent, s. croissant, *m.*, (*place*) demi-lune, *f.*

Cress, s. cresson, *m.* — *-bed*, cressonnière, *f.*

Crest, s. (*cocks*) crête, *f.*, (*helmets*) cimier, *m.*, (*her.*) écusson, *m.*, (*birds*) huppe, *f.*, (*peacocks*) aigrette, *f.*, (*pride*) orgueil, *m.* — *-fallen*, abattu, penaud

Crested, adj. crêté, huppé, orné d'un cimier

Cretinism, s. crétinisme, *m.*

Crevice, s. crevasse, *f.*, lézarde, *f.*

Creviced, adj. crevassé, lézardé, *f.*

Crew, s. troupe, *f.*, bande, *f.*, clique, *f.*, (*nav.*) équipage, *m.*

Crib, s. crèche, *f.*, (*horses*) mangeoire, *f.*, (*cottage*) chaumière, *f.*, (*for infants*) lit d'enfant, *m.* — *-biting*, tic, *m.*

Crib, va. prendre, chiper, copier

Crick, s. crampe, *f*

Cricket, s. (*insect*) grillon, *m.*

Crier, s. crieur, huissier, *m.*

Crime, s. crime, *m.*

Criminal, adj. s. criminel

Criminality, s. culpabilité, *f.*, criminalité, *f.*

Criminally, adv. criminellement

Criminate, va. incriminer, faire le procès (à)

Crimination, s. incrimination, *f.*

Crimp, va. friser, gaufrer

Crimp, s. commissionnaire, *m.*, (*mil.*) racoleur, *m.*

Crimson, adj. s. cramoisi, *m.*

Cringe, vn. faire le chien couchant, ramper

Cringing, s. basse servilité, *f.*

Crinoline, s. crinoline, *f.*

Cripple, adj. s. estropié, perclus, boiteux

Cripple, va. estropier, (*to disable*) mettre hors de combat, (*fig.*) paralyser

Crisis, s. crise, *f.*

Crisp, adj. frisé, (*brittle*) cassant, friable, (*pastry*) croquant

Crisp, va.n. friser, (*stuffs*) crêper

Crisped, adj. crépu, crispé

Crisping, s. frisure, *f.*

Criterion, s. critérium, *m.*

Critic, s. critique, *m.*, frondeur, *m.*

Critical, adj. critique, délicat, difficile

Critically, adv. d'une manière critique, (*exactly*) rigoureusement

Criticism, s. critique, *f.*

Criticize, va.n. critiquer

Criticizer, s. critiqueur, *m.*

Croak, vn. (*ravens*) croasser, (*frogs*) coasser, (*grumble*) grogner, marronner

Croak, **Croaking**, s. croassement, *m.*, coassement, *m.*

Croaker, s. grognon, *m.*

Crockery, s. faïence, *f.*, vaisselle, *f.* — *-ware*, faïence, *f.*

Crocodile, s. crocodile, *m.*

Crocus, s. crocus, *m.*, safran, *m.*

Croft, s. petit clos, *m.*

Crone, s. vieille femme, vieille, *f.*

Crony, s. vieille connaissance, *f.*, vieux camarade, *m.*, compère, *m.*, commère, *f.*

Crook, s. courbure, *f.*, (*shepherds*) houlette, *f.* — *-back*, bossu, *m.*, -e, *f.* — *-backed*, bossu. — *-kneed*, cagneux. — *-legged*, qui a les jambes tortues

Crook, va. courber, tortuer, pervertir

Crooked, adj. courbe, crochu, (*twisted*) tortu, (*winding*) tortueux, (*pers.*) contrefait, (*oblique*) de travers, (*perverse*) pervers, (*adverb.*) de travers

Crookedly, adv. tortueusement, (*fig.*) de travers

Crookedness, s. courbure, *f.*, tortuosité, *f.*, difformité, *f.*, perversité, *f.*

Crop, s. (*harvest*) récolte, *f.*, moisson, *f.*, (*of fruits*) cueillette, *f.*, (*hair cut off, jest.*) tonte, *f.*, (*birds*) jabot, *m.* *Second* —, regain, *m.* — *-ful*, s. jabot, *m.*, plein, *m.*, (adj.) plein jusqu'au gosier

Crop, va. couper, (*harvest*) moissonner, (*fruit*) cueillir, (*animals*) tondre, (*the tail or ears*) écourter, (*browse*) brouter. — *-eared*, bretaudé

Crosier, s. crosse, *f.*

Crosiered, adj. crossé

Cross, s. croix, *f.*, affliction, *f.*, (*obstacle*) traverse, *f.*, contrariété, *f.*, (*intersection*) croisée, *f.*, carrefour, *m.*

Cross, adj. transversal, en travers, oblique, de travers, contraire (à), (*vexatious*) contrariant, (*unfortunate*) malheureux, (*peevish*) de mauvaise humeur, maussade. — *-bar*, traverse, *f.* — *-bar-shot*, boulet ramé, *m.* — *-beam*, traverse, *f.*, (*steam-engine*) balancier, *m.* — *-bearer*, porte-croix, *m.* — *-bow*, arbalète, *f.* — *-bowman*, arbalétrier, *m.* — *-breed*, race croisée, *f.* — *-examination*, contre-interrogatoire, *m.* — *-examine*, va. faire subir un contre-interrogatoire à. — *-examined*, part. adj. interrogé par l'avocat adverse or par la partie adverse. — *-grained*, dont le fil se croise, (*fig.*) revêche. — *-legged*, les jambes croisées. — *-like*, en forme de croix. — *-line*, (*rail.*) de croix. — *-piece*, traverse, *f.*, (*nav.*) traversin, *m.* — *-post*, service de correspondance, *m.* — *-purposes*, propos interrompus, (*fig.*) contradiction, *f.* — *-path*, — *-road*, — *-way*, chemin de traverse, *m.* — *-sill*, coussinet, *m.* — *-tie*, traverse, *f.*

Cross, prep. à travers, de l'autre côté de, par-dessus

Cross, va. croiser, mettre en travers, traverser, franchir, passer, marquer d'une croix, biffer, barrer, (*fig.*) se présenter, s'offrir, venir, traverser, contrarier, contrecarrer. *To — oneself*, faire un signe de croix, se signer. — vn. être posé en croix, être mis en travers, se croiser, passer, faire la traversée

Crossing, s. traversée, *f.*, croisement, *m.*, signe de croix, *m.*, passage pour traverser, *m.*, changement de voie, *m.*

Crossly, adv. de travers, (*fig.*) avec humeur

Crossness, s. intersection, *f.*, (*fig.*) mauvaise humeur, *f.*, esprit de contrariété, *m.*, désagrément, *m.*

Crotchet, s. (*mus.*) noire, *f.*, (*archit.*) étai, *m.*, (*fig.*) lubie, *f.*, quinte, *f.*, billevesée, *f.*, caprice, *m.*

Crotchety, adj. quinteux, sujet aux lubies, capricieux
Crouch, vn. ramper, se tapir, se blottir
Croup, s. croupe, *f.*, (*med.*) croupe, *m.*
Crow, vn. chanter, (*fig.*) chanter victoire
Crow, s. corbeau, *m.*, corneille, *f.*, (*of cocks*) chant, *m.*, (*lever*) pince, *f.* *As a — flies*, à vol d'oiseau. *To pluck or pull a —*, disputer sur des vétilles. *—-keeper*, épouvantail, *m.* *—-foot*, *—'s-foot*, patte d'oie, *f.*, (*mil.*) chausse-trape, *f.*, (*bot.*) renoncule, *f.* *—-bar*, pince, *f.*
Crowd, s. foule, *f.*, (*mob*) cohue, *f.*, multitude, *f.*, vulgaire, *m.*
Crowd, va. remplir, encombrer, presser, faire entrer en pressant, se presser autour de; — vn. se presser en foule, se presser, se serrer
Crown, s. couronne, *f.*, tête, *f.*, sommet de la tête, *m.*, (*eccles.*) tonsure, *f.*, sommet, *m.*, cime, *f.*, (*money*) écu, *m.*, (*fig.*) comble, *m.* *—-office*, *—-side*, parquet, *m.* *—-saw*, scie circulaire, *f.* *—-wheel*, roue de rencontre, *f.*
Crown, va. couronner, (*fig.*) combler, mettre le comble à
Crowning, s. couronnement, *m.*
Crownless, adj. sans couronne
Crucible, s. creuset, *m.*
Crucifix, s. crucifix, *m.*, Christ, *m.*
Crucifixion, s. crucifiement, *m.*
Crucify, va. crucifier, mettre en croix
Crude, adj. cru, âpre, peu mûr, non mûr, (*fig.*) grossier, imparfait
Crudely, adv. dans un état de crudité, d'une façon indigeste
Crudeness, Crudity, s. crudité, *f.*
Cruel, adj. cruel, inhumain
Cruelly, adv. cruellement, avec cruauté
Cruelty, Cruelness, s. cruauté, *f.*, (*law*) sévices, *m.pl.*
Cruet, s. burette, *f.* *—-stand*, huilier, *m.*
Cruise, s. flacon, *m.*
Cruise, s. croisière, *f.*, (*privateer*) course, *f.* *On a —*, en croisière
Cruise, vn. croiser. *—ing station*, s. croisière, *f.*
Cruiser, s. croiseur, *m.*
Crum, Crumb, va. émietter
Crumb, s. miette, *f.*, (*bread*) mie, *f.*
Crumble, va. émietter, réduire en poussière, faire écrouler, briser; — vn. s'émietter, se briser, s'écrouler, s'en aller en poussière
Crummy, adj. de mie
Crumple, va. plisser, friper, chiffonner, froisser; — vn. se contracter, se ratatiner, se friper
Crunch, va. broyer, écraser
Crupper, s. croupe, *f.*, croupière, *f.*
Crusade, s. croisade, *f.*
Crusader, s. croisé, *m.*
Crush, va. écraser, briser, broyer, serrer; — vn. s'écraser
Crushing, s. broiement, *m.*
Crust, s. croûte, *f.*
Crust, va. couvrir d'une croûte, encroûter, envelopper; — vn. se couvrir d'une croûte
Crustaceau, Crustaceous, adj. s. crustacé
Crustily, adv. d'un ton bourru
Crustiness, s. nature croustillante, *f.*, (*fig.*) humeur bourrue, *f.*
Crusty, adj. ayant beaucoup de croûte, croustillant, (*fig.*) bourru
Crutch, s. béquille, *f.*
Cry, vn. crier, s'écrier, dire, pleurer. *— for*, implorer, demander à grands cris. *— out*, vociférer, s'écrier, se récrier, clabauder. — va. pleurer, crier. *— down*, décrier. *— up*, vanter, louer
Cry, s. cri, *m.*, pleurs, *m.pl.*, voix, *f.*
Crying, s. cris, *m.pl.*, pleurs, *m.pl.*
Crypt, s. crypte, *f.*
Cryptogam, s. cryptogame, *m.*
Cryptogamic, Cryptogamous, adj. cryptogame
Crystal, s. cristal, *m.* *Rock —*, cristal de roche, *m.*
Crystal, adj. (*fig.*) de cristal, cristallin, clair
Crystalline, adj. cristallin. *The — humour*, le cristallin
Crystallization, s. cristallisation, *f.*
Crystallize, va. cristalliser; — vn. se cristalliser
Cub, s. (*of an animal*) petit, *m.*
Cub, va.n. mettre bas
Cubature, s. cubage, *m.*, cubature, *f.*
Cube, s. cube, *m.* *—-root*, racine cubique, *f.*
Cube, va.n. cuber
Cubic, Cubical, adj. cubique, cube
Cubit, s. coudée, *f.*
Cubless, adj. privé de ses petits
Cuckoo, s. coucou, *m.* *—-bud*, coucou, *m.*, bouton d'or, *m.* *—-flower*, cardamine, *f.*
Cucumber, s. concombre, *m.* *As cool as —*, avec un sang-froid imperturbable
Cucurbit, s. cucurbite, *f.*
Cucurbitaceous, adj. cucurbitacé
Cud, s. bol alimentaire, *m.*, premier estomac, *m.*, chique, *f.* *To chew the —*, (*fig.*) ruminer, méditer
Cuddle, vn. se tapir; — va. dorloter, bercer
Cudgel, s. bâton, *m.*, trique, *f.*, gourdin, *m.* *—-player*, bâtonniste, *m.* *To cross the —s*, (*fig.*) déposer les armes. *To take up the —s*, entrer en lice, prendre le parti
Cudgel, va. bâtonner, donner des coups de bâton à. *To — one's brains*, se casser la tête
Cudgelling, s. coups de bâton, *m.pl.*, bastonnade, *f.*
Cue, s. queue, *f.*, (*theat.*) réplique, *f.*, rôle, *m.*, mot d'ordre, *m.*
Cuff, s. coup de poing, *m.*, coup, *m.*, (*sleeve*) parement, *m.*
Cuff, vn. se battre à coups de poing; — va. battre, donner des coups de poing (à)
Cuirass, s. cuirasse, *f.*
Cuirassier, s. cuirassier, *m.*
Cuiss, s. cuissard, *m.*
Culinary, adj. culinaire
Cull, va. cueillir, (*fig.*) choisir
Cullender, s. passoire, *f.*
Cullis, s. coulis, *m.*, (*arch.*) coulisse, *f.*, gouttière, *f.*
Culminant, Culminating, adj. culminant, au méridien
Culminate, vn. culminer, passer au méridien
Culmination, s. culmination, *f.*
Culpability, Culpableness, s. culpabilité, *f.*
Culpable, adj. coupable
Culpably, adv. d'une manière coupable
Culpatory, adj. de blâme
Culprit, s. prévenu, *m.*, accusé, *m.*, coupable, *m.f.*
Cultivable, adj. cultivable
Cultivate, Culture, va. cultiver
Cultivation, Culture, s. culture, *f.*
Cultivator, s. cultivateur, *m.*
Culverin, s. coulevrine, *f.*
Cumber, va. embarrasser, encombrer, gêner
Cumbersome, Cumbrous, adj. embarrassant, gênant
Cumbersomeness, Cumbrousness, s. embarras, *m.*, nature gênante, *f.*
Cumbrance, s. embarras, *m.*, fardeau, *m.*
Cumbrously, adv. d'une manière embarrassante *or* gênante
Cummin, s. cumin, *m.*
Cumulative, adj. cumulatif
Cuneal, Cuneated, Cuneiform, Cuniform, adj. cunéiforme
Cunning, adj. rusé, fin, artificieux, astucieux, adroit
Cunning, s. ruse, *f.*, finesse, *f.*, artifice, *m.*, astuce, *f.*, adresse, *f.*
Cunningly, adv. avec ruse, avec finesse, artificieusement, adroitement, habilement
Cunningness, s. ruse, *f.*, finesse, *f.*
Cup, s. coupe, *f.*, gobelet, *m.*, tasse, *f.*, calice, *m.*, (*med.*) ventouse, *f.* *—-bearer*, échanson. *The parting —*, le coup de l'étrier. *There's many a slip 'twixt the — and the lip*, de la main à la bouche se perd souvent la soupe. *A man in his —s*, un homme qui a bu. *— and ball*, bilboquet, *m.*
Cup, va. donner à boire à, appliquer des ventouses à, ventouser
Cupboard, s. armoire, *f.*, placard, *m.*, buffet, *m.*
Cupboard, va. renfermer, (*fig.*) entasser
Cupel, s. coupelle, *f.*
Cupful, s. tasse, *f.*
Cupid, s. Cupidon, *m.*, l'Amour, *m.*
Cupidity, s. cupidité, *f.*, désir, *m.*
Cupola, s. coupole, *f.*, dôme, *m.*
Cupped, past part. (*med.*) en forme de coupe
Cupper, s. chirurgien, *m.*
Cupping, s. les ventouses, *f.pl.* *—-glass*, ventouse, *f.*
Cur, s. mâtin, *m.*, chien, *m.*, chien hargneux, *m.*
Curable, adj. curable
Curaçoa, s. curaçao, *m.*
Curacy, s. cure, *f.*, vicariat, *m.*
Curate, s. vicaire, *m.*, desservant, *m.*
Curative, adj. curatif
Curator, s. curateur, *m.*
Curb, s. gourmette, *f.*, frein, *m.*, (*of a well*) margelle, *f.*; (*pavement*) bord, *m.* *—-chain*, gourmette, *f.*
Curb, va. mettre la gourmette (à), retenir, mettre un frein (à), mettre une margelle (à)
Curbing, s. frein, *m.*
Curd, Curds, s. lait caillé, *m.*
Curd, va. cailler
Curdle, va. cailler, caillebotter, (*fig.*) figer, glacer; — vn. se cailler, se coaguler, se figer, se glacer
Curdy, adj. caillé
Cure, s. cure, *f.*, remède, *m.*, guérison, *f.*
Cure, va. guérir, corriger, (*fig.*) remédier (à); (*to salt*) saler, sécher, fumer, mariner; — vn. guérir, se guérir
Cureless, adj. incurable
Curer, s. guérisseur, *m.*
Curfew, s. couvre-feu, *m.*
Curing, s. guérison, *f.*, salaison, *f.*
Curiosity, s. curiosité, *f.*, recherche, *f.*, soin excessif, *m.*
Curious, adj. curieux, recherché, soigneux, (*work*) délicat, artistement fait
Curiously, adv. curieusement, avec curiosité, avec soin, artistement, bizarrement
Curl, s. (*of hair*) boucle, *f.*, courbe, *f.*, pli, *m.*, ondulation, *f.*, bouffée, *f.*, (*of the lip*) mouvement dédaigneux, *m.* *—-paper*, papillotte, *f.*
Curl, va. friser, boucler, enrouler, plisser, (*lips*) fair

en mouvement dédaigneux ; — vn. friser, s'enrouler, s'entrelacer, s'élever en spirales

Curlew, s. courlis, m., courlieu, m.

Curling, adj. bouclé, qui frise. — *-irons*, — *-tongs*, fer à friser

Curly, adj. bouclé, frisé

Curmudgeon, s. ladre, m., grippe-sou, m., avare, m.

Currant, s. raisin de Corinthe, m., groseille, f. — adj. de groseilles. *Dried —s*, raisins de Corinthe. — *-bush*, — *-tree*, groseillier, m. *Black —s*, du cassis

Currency, s. cours, m., continuité, f., facilité, f., abondance, f., autorité, f., réputation, f., crédit, m., monnaie légale, f., agent de circulation, m.

Current, adj. rapide, courant, généralement reçu, général, commun, en vogue, à la mode

Current, s. (*air, water*) courant, m., fil de l'eau, m., cours d'eau, m., fleuve, m., (*fig.*) cours, m.

Currently, adv. d'une manière continue, généralement

Currentness, s. libre cours, m., (*of speaking*) facilité, f.

Curricle, s. coupé ouvert, m., carosse coupé, m.

Currier, s. corroyeur, m.

Currish, adj. hargneux

Currishly, adv. d'une manière hargneuse

Currishness, s. caractère hargneux, m.

Curry, va. corroyer, étriller

Curry, s. "curry," m.

Curse, va. maudire, (*fig.*) (*with*) affliger (de); — vn. jurer, blasphémer, maugréer

Curse, Cursing, s. malédiction, f., imprécation, f., jurement, m.

Cursed, adj. maudit, abominable

Cursedly, adv. furieusement, abominablement

Cursedness, s. malédiction, f.

Curser, s. celui, celle qui maudit, blasphémateur, m., -trice, f.

Cursive, adj. cursive

Cursorily, adv. rapidement, fait en courant, superficiellement

Cursoriness, s. rapidité, f., caractère superficiel, m.

Cursory, adj. rapide, fait à la hâte, précipité, superficiel, général

Curt, adj. court. — *-hose*, Courte-Heuse

Curtail, va. raccourcir, abréger, écourter, (*fig.*) retrancher, diminuer, rogner

Curtailing, Curtailment, s. raccourcissement, m., retranchement, f., diminution, f.

Curtain, s. rideau, m., (*theat.*) toile, f., (*fortif.*) courtine, f. — *-lecture*, semonce conjugale, f. — *-rod*, tringle, f.

Curtain, vn. entourer, garnir de rideaux, (*fig.*) envelopper

Curtainless, adj. sans rideaux

Curtness, s. brièveté, f.

Curule, adj. curule. — *chair*, chaise curule, f.

Curvature, s. courbure, f.

Curve, Curved, adj. courbe, courbé, en courbe. — s. courbe, f.

Curve, va. courber

Curvedness, s. courbe, f.

Curvilineal, Curvilinear, adj. curviligne

Cushat, s. palombe, f.

Cushion, s. coussin, m., carreau, m., (*techn.*) coussinet, m., matelas, m., (*billiard*) bande, f.

Cushion, va. garnir de coussins, faire asseoir sur des coussins

Cusp, s. corne, f., pointe, f.

Custard, s. crème, f., flan, m.

Custodian, s. gardien, m.

Custody, s. garde, f., captivité, f., emprisonnement, m.

Custom, s. coutume, f., usage, m., mœurs, f. plur., habitude, f., (*shop*) clientèle, f., achalandage, m., (*dues*) droit de douane, m., taxe, f., (*law*) droit coutumier, m. *The — -house*, douane, f.

Customable, adj. soumis à un droit

Customarily, adv. habituellement

Customariness, s. habitude, f.

Customary, adj. habituel, ordinaire, d'usage

Customer, s. chaland, m., pratique, f., acheteur, m., client, m.

Cut, va. couper, tailler, trancher, (*teeth*) faire, (*the air*) fendre, (*to avoid*) éviter, méconnaître. — *and dry*, tout fait. *To — one's stick*, (*pop.*) décamper. *To — the concern*, abandonner l'affaire. — *away*, couper, élaguer, retrancher. — *down*, couper, abattre, renverser, (*nav.*) raser. — *off*, couper, enlever, retrancher, abattre, amputer. *To — off with a shilling*, déshériter. — *out*, tailler, découper, exclure, retrancher, évincer, surpasser, éclipser. — *short*, couper court à, abréger, interrompre. — *up*, couper en morceaux, découper, hacher, disséquer. — vn. couper, percer, tailler. — *along*, filer vite. *To — and run*, décamper, filer. — *in*, couper pour savoir qui doit jouer

Cut, s. coupe, f., coupure, f., coup, m., blessure, f., (*stuff*) coupon, m., (*engrav.*) bois, m., planche, f., taille, f., gravure, f., estampe, f. — *purse*, coupeur de bourse, m., filou, m. — *-toothed*, déchiqueté. — *-throat*, coupe-jarret, m. — *-throat place*, coupe-gorge, m. *Deep —*, entaille, balafre. — *with a whip*, un coup de fouet. *A short —*, un chemin de traverse. *To shift the —*, faire sauter la coupe

Cutaneous, adj. cutané

Cuticle, s. (*anat.*) cuticule, f., (*bot.*) pellicule, f.

Cuticular, adj. cutanée

Cutlass, s. coutelas, m.

Cutler, s. coutelier, m.

Cutlery, s. coutellerie, f.

Cutlet, s. côtelette, f.

Cutter, s. coupeur, m., (*teeth*) (dent) incisive, f., (*nav.*) cutter, m., cotre, m.

Cutting, s. coupe, f., taille, f., entaille, f., rognure, f., (*hort.*) bouture, f., tranchée, f., excavation, f., (*play*) coupe, f., courbette, f. — *of teeth*, la dentition. — *-off*, amputation, f.

Cutting, adj. tranchant, (*fig.*) piquant, mordant

Cuttingly, adv. d'une manière piquante

Cuttle, s. sèche, f., seiche, f.

Cutty-stool, s. sellette, f.

Cycle, s. cycle, m.

Cyclic, Cyclical, adj. cyclique

Cycloid, s. cycloïde, f.

Cyclone, s. cyclone, m., trombe, f., ouragan, m.

Cyclop, s. cyclope, m.

Cyclopædia, s. encyclopédie, f.

Cyclopean, Cyclopic, adj. cyclopéen

Cygnet, s. jeune cygne, m.

Cylinder, s. cylindre, m. *Steam — and jacket*, cylindre à vapeur et son enveloppe

Cylindric, Cylindrical, adj. cylindrique

Cyma, s. (*bot.*) cyme, f. (*archit.*) cymaise, f.

Cymbal, s. cymbale, f.

Cynic, Cynical, adj. cynique

Cynically, adv. d'une façon cynique

Cynicalness, Cynicism, s. cynicisme, m.

Cynosure, s. cynosure, f., petite Ourse, f., (*fig.*) point de mire, m., centre, m.

Cypress, s. cyprès, m. — adj. de cyprès

Cypsele, s. cérumen, m., cire des oreilles, f.

Cyst, s. kyste, m.

Cytisus, s. cytise, f.

Czar, s. czar, m.

Czarina, s. czarine, f.

Czarish, adj. czarien

Czarowitz, s. czarowitz, m.

D

D, s. D, d, m., (*mus.*) re, m.

Dab, va. éponger, étuver, frapper

Dab, s. léger coup, (*lump*) petit morceau, m., (*liquid*) flaquée, f., éclaboussure, f., (*expert*) maître, m., (*fish*) limande, f.

Dabble, va. barbouiller, éclabousser, mouiller ; — vn. barboter, patauger, se mêler (de)

Dabbler, s. personne qui barbote, f., barbouilleur, faiseur, m.

Dace, s. vandoise, f., dard, m.

Daddy, s. papa, m. — *-longlegs*, faucheux, m.

Daffodil, s. asphodèle, m.

Dagger, s. poignard, m., (*print.*) croix, f. *At —s drawn*, à couteaux tirés. — *-knife*, couteau-poignard, m.

Daguerreotype, s. daguerréotype, m.

Dahlia, s. dahlia, m.

Daily, adj. journalier, quotidien, (*astr.*) diurne. — adv. journellement, tous les jours

Daintily, adv. délicatement

Daintiness, s. délicatesse, f.

Dainty, adj. friand, délicat

Dainty, s. friandise, f.

Dairy, s. laiterie, f. — *-house*, *-room*, laiterie, f. — *-maid*, *-woman*, fille de laiterie, f., crémière, laitière, f. — *-man*, garçon de laiterie, m., crémier, m., laitier, m.

Daisy, s. marguerite, f., pâquerette, f.

Dale, s. vallon, m., vallée, f.

Dalliance, s. caresses, f. pl., (*play*) badinage, m.

Dallier, s. personne légère, f.

Dally, vn. tarder, (*trifle*) s'amuser, perdre son temps, (*play*) badiner

Dalmatic, s. dalmatique, f.

Dam, s. (*animals*) mère, f., (*mole*) digue, f., (*rivers*) barrage, m., batardeau, m.

Dam, va. diguer, contenir, arrêter

Damage, s. dommage, m., dégât, m.

Damage, va. endommager, faire tort à, avarier; — vn. s'endommager

Damageable, adj. susceptible de s'endommager

Damaging, adj. pernicieux

Damask, s. damas, m. — -*worker*, damasseur, m.

Damask, adj. damassé

Damask, va. damasser

Damaskeen, va. damasquiner

Damaskeening, s. damasquinerie, f.

Damasking, s. damassure, f.

Dame, s. dame, f.

Damn, va. damner, condamner, (*theat.*) siffler

Damnable, adj. damnable, maudit

Damnably, adv. damnablement, diablement

Damnation, s. damnation, f., (*of a play*) chûte, f., fiasco, m.

Damned, adj. damné, sacré, (*things*) de damné, sacré

Damning, adj. qui condamne

Damp, s. humidité, f., vapeur, f., exhalaison, f., (*fig.*) nuage, m., tristesse, f., froid, m.

Damp, adj. humide

Damp, va. humecter, rendre humide, (*spirits*) abattre, refroidir, glacer, attrister, (*stifle*) étouffer

Damper, s. (*mus.*) étouffoir, m., sourdine, f., (*fig.*) éteignoir, m., rabat-joie, m., trouble-fête, m.

Dampish, adj. un peu humide

Dampness, s. humidité, f.

Damsel, s. jeune fille, f., (*attendant*) suivante, f.

Damson, s prune de damas, f.

Dance, va.n. danser

Dance, s. danse, f.

Dancer, s. danseur, m., -euse, f., cavalier, m., dame, f.

Dancing, s. danse, f. — -*master*, maître de danse, m. — -*room*, salle de danse, f. — -*school* or *academy*, école de danse, f. — -*party*, soirée dansante, f.

Dandelion, s. dent-de-lion, f., pissenlit, m.

Dandle, va. bercer, (*fondle*) dorloter

Dandriff, s. crasse (de la tête), f., pellicules, f.pl.

Dandy, s. gandin, m.

Danewort, s. hièble, f.

Danger, s. danger, m., péril, m.

Dangerous, adj. dangereux

Dangerously, adv. dangereusement

Dangle, vn. pendiller, (*after*) être pendu (après); — va. laisser pendre

Dangler, s. godelureau, m., parasite, m.

Dank, adj. see DAMP

Dapper, adj. leste, vif, fringant

Dapple, adj. pommelé, truité, (*of the bay colour*) miroité

Dapple, va. tacheter; — vn. se pommeler

Dappled, adj. pommelé

Dare, vn. oser; — va. oser, affronter, défier, braver, intimider. *I — say*, je crois bien (que), il est probable (que), sans doute (que), je parie (que)

Daring, adj. audacieux, hardi, brave

Daring, s. audace, f.

Daringly, adv. audacieusement

Dark, adj. noir, obscur, sombre, ténébreux, nuit, (*colours*) foncé, (*complexion*) brun, (*secret*) sourd, (*lantern*) sourde. *To see only the — side of things*, voir tout en noir

Dark, s. obscurité, f., ténèbres, f.pl., ignorance, f., (*night*) nuit, f.

Darken, va. obscurcir, assombrir, brunir, (*disturb*) troubler; — vn. s'obscurcir

Darkening, s. obscurcissement, m.

Darkish, adj. noirâtre, un peu sombre, (*complexion*) un peu brun

Darkly, adv. dans les ténèbres, (*fig.*) obscurément, (*secretly*) sourdement

Darkness, s. obscurité, f., ténèbres, f.pl., (*colours*) teinte foncée, f., (*complexion*) couleur brune, f.

Darksome, adj. sombre

Darling, adj. chéri, favori, mignon

Darling, s. favori, m., -te, f., mignon, m., -ne, f., (*child*) ange, m., (*fam.*) chou, m.

Darn, va. repriser

Darnel, s. ivraie, f.

Darner, s. ravaudeuse, f.

Darning, s. reprise, f.

Dart, s dard, m., trait, m.

Dart, va. darder, (*at*) lancer (contre); — vn. (*upon*) fondre (sur), s'élancer (sur)

Darting, adj. qui darde or lance

Dash, va. jeter, précipiter, briser, heurter, choquer, (*fig.*) renverser, troubler, abattre, confondre, mouiller, tremper. *To — off*, essuyer vivement (des larmes), faire en un clin d'œil. *To — out*, faire sauter, barrer, raturer. — vn. se précipiter, s'élancer, bondir, esquisser à grands traits

Dash, s. choc, m., coup, m., attaque subite, f., peu, m., figure, f., brillant, m., (*gram.*) barre [—], (*mus.*) [']. *To make a — at*, fondre sur. — -*board* or *dasher*, garde-crotte, m. *To cut a —*, faire figure

Dashing, adj. audacieux, qui veut faire figure, brillant

Dastard, s. adj. lâche, poltron

Dastardliness, s. lâcheté, f.

Dastardly, adj. lâche, poltron

Date, s. (*fruit*) datte, f.; date, f., fin, f. — (*of coins, &c.*) millésime, m. *Out of —*, suranné, passé de mode

Date, va.n. dater, assigner une date à. *Short-dated*, *long-dated*, à courte échéance, à longue échéance

Dateless, adj. sans date

Dative, s. adj. datif, m.

Daub, va. barbouiller, enduire, surcharger, (*fig.*) couvrir, déguiser

Daub, **Daubing**, s. barbouillage, m., croûte, f.

Dauber, s. barbouilleur, m., (*print.*) rouleau, m.

Daughter, s. fille, f. — -*in-law*, belle-fille, f.

Daunt, va. intimider, décourager

Dauntless, adj. intrépide, indomptable

Dauntlessness, s. intrépidité, f.

Dauphin, s. dauphin, m.

Dauphiness, s. dauphine, f.

Daw, s. choucas, m., corneille des clochers, f.

Dawdle, vn. flâner, muser

Dawdler, s. flâneur, m., -euse, f., musard, m., -e, f.

Dawn, vn. poindre, paraître, luire, naître, (*fig.*) (*upon*) commencer à paraître (à), se faire jour (dans, en)

Dawn, **Dawning**, s. aube du jour, f., aurore, f., naissance, f., commencement, m.

Day, s. jour, m., journée, f., temps, m., victoire, f., bataille, f. *A —*, un jour, par jour. *The — after*, le lendemain. *The third — after*, le surlendemain de. *The — before*, la veille. *Two —s before*, deux jours avant, l'avant-veille de. *By —*, pendant le jour. — *by —*, jour à jour, jour par jour, tous les jours, au jour le jour. *From — to —*, de jour en jour, d'un jour à l'autre. *This — week*, d'aujourd'hui en huit. *Every —*, tous les jours, chaque jour, de tous les jours, ordinaire, journellement. *Every other —*, tous les deux jours, de deux jours l'un. — -*book*, livre journal, m., journal, m. — -*dream*, rêve d'un homme éveillé, m., rêverie, f. — -*fly*, éphémère, m. — -*lily*, asphodèle, m. — -*scholar*, externe. — -*spring*, aurore, f., aube, f. — -*time*, le jour, la journée

Daybreak, s. point du jour, m., aube, f., aurore, f.

Daylight, s. jour, m., clarté du jour, f. *In broad —*, au grand jour, en plein jour

Dazzle, vn. éblouir

Dazzle, **Dazzling**, s. éblouissement, m.

Dead, adj. mort, (*fig.*) de mort, profond, (*place*) désolé, vide, (*sound*) sourd, (*colour*) mat, terne, (*liquid*) éventé, (*letter*) au rebut. *To send to the — -letter office*, mettre au rebut. — -*beat*, battu à plates coutures. — -*born*, mort-né. — -*drunk*, ivre-mort. — -*lift*, masse inerte. — -*march*, marche funèbre. — -*set*, complot, (*at*) charge à fond de train (sur)

Dead, s. repos profond, m. *In the — of night, of winter*, dans le silence de la nuit, au cœur de l'hiver

Deaden, va. amortir, affaiblir, (*fig.*) endurcir, rendre insensible, (*colour*) amortir, (*liquids*) éventer

Deadliness, s. nature mortelle, f., mortalité, f., danger, m., acharnement, m.

Deadly, adj. mortel, funeste, acharné, implacable

Deadly, adv. mortellement, à mort. — *pale*, pâle comme la mort

Deadness, s. mort, f., (*fig.*) langueur, f., apathie, f., engourdissement, m., torpeur, f., (*business*) stagnation, f., (*liquids*) évent, m.

Deaf, adj. sourd, assourdi. *To turn a — ear*, faire la sourde oreille

Deafen, va. assourdir étourdir

Deafness, s. surdité, f.

Deal, s. quantité, f., (*cards*) donne, f., (*wood*) bois blanc, m., sapin, m.

Deal, va. donner, distribuer, dispenser, (*blows*) asséner, porter, (*of cards*) donner, faire. — *out*, distribuer, frapper. — vn. agir (envers), se comporter (envers), en user (avec), (*com.*) faire le commerce, trafiquer, (*with*) faire affaire (avec), (*fig.*) s'occuper, se mêler, avoir affaire

Dealer, s. marchand, -e, m.f., trafiquant, m. *Plain —*, un homme de bonne foi. *False —*, homme de mauvaise foi

Dealing, s. action, f., conduite, f., traitement, m., procédés, m.pl., commerce, m., (*fig.*) relations, f.pl.

Dean, s. doyen, m.

Deanery, **Deanship**, s. décanat, m., doyenné, m.

Dear, adj. cher, coûteux, bien-aimé, chéri

Dear, s. cher, m., chère, f.

Dear! interj. mon Dieu! hélas! — *me!* mon Dieu! *Oh —!* oh là!

Dear, **Dearly**, adv. chèrement, cher, tendrement

Dearness, s. cherté, f., grand prix, m., tendresse, f.

Dearth, s. disette, f.

Death, s. mort, f., trépas, m. *To be the — of*, donner la mort à. *To die a natural —*, mourir de sa belle mort. *To beat to —*, faire mourir sous le bâton. — -*struggles*, l'agonie, f. — -*token*, signe de mort, m. — -*warrant*, ordre d'exécution, m. — -*watch*, horloge de la mort, f., perce-bois, m.

Deathlike, adj. de mort

Debar, va. priver (de), exclure (de), interdire

Debase, va. avilir, ravaler, dégrader, (*coinage*) altérer,

— *oneself*, s'avilir, se dégrader, se ravaler

Debasement, s. avilissement, *m.*, dégradation, *f.*, altération, *f.*

Debatable, adj. contestable, sujet à controverse

Debate, s. débat, *m.*, discussion, *f.*

Debate, va. débattre, discuter, agiter

Debater, s. argumentateur, *m.*, orateur, *m.*

Debauch, va. débaucher, corrompre; — vn. se débaucher

Debauch, s. débauche, *f.*

Debauchee, s. débauché, *m.*

Debaucher, s. débaucheur, *m.*

Debauchery, s. débauche, *f.*, dérèglement de mœurs, *m.*

Debenture, s. bon, *m.*, obligation, *f.*

Debilitate, va. débiliter

Debilitation, s. débilitation, *f.*

Debility, s. débilité, *f.*

Debit, s. débit, *m.*, débet, *m.*

Debit, va. débiter

Debt, s. dette, *f.* *To be in* —, avoir des dettes, être endetté. *To run into* —, faire des dettes. *To be out of* —, n'avoir plus de dettes

Debtor, s. débiteur, *m.*, débitrice, *f.*, (*book-keeping*) Doit

Decagon, s. décagone, *m.*

Decalogue, s. décalogue, *m.*

Decamp, vn. décamper

Decampment, s. décampement, *m.*

Decant, va. transvaser, décanter

Decanter, s. carafe, *f.* *Small* —, carafon, *m.*

Decay, vn. dépérir, périr, décliner, s'affaiblir, défaillir, s'en aller, (*health*) se délabrer, (*meat*) se gâter, (*fruit*) pourrir, (*teeth*) se gâter, se carier

Decay, s. décadence, *f.*, dépérissement, *m.*, déclin, *m.*, affaiblissement, *m.*, ruine, *f.*, (*states*) déclin, *m.*, (*fortune*) délabrement, *m.*, perte, *f.*, ruine, *f.*, désastre, *m.*, (*after death*) corruption, *f.*

Decease, s. décès, *m.*, mort, *f.*

Deceased, adj. défunt, décédé

Deceit, s. supercherie, *f.*, tromperie, *f.*, déception, *f.*, fraude, *f.*, fourberie, *f.*, fourbe, *f.*, illusion, *f.*

Deceitful, adj. trompeur, faux, décevant, mensonger

Deceitfully, adv. faussement, perfidement

Deceitfulness, s. fausseté, *f.*, perfidie, *f.*

Deceivable, adj. facile à tromper, sujet à se tromper

Deceive, va. tromper, abuser, décevoir, en imposer (à), surprendre la religion (de)

Deceiver, s. trompeur, *m.*, -euse, *f.*

December, s. Décembre, *m.*

Decency, s. convenances, *f.pl.*, bienséance, *f.*, décence, *f.*, modestie, *f.*

Decennial, adj. décennal

Decent, adj. décent, convenable, bienséant, honnête, passable

Decently, adv. décemment, convenablement, avec bienséance, honnêtement, passablement

Deception, s. déception, *f.*

Deceptive, adj. trompeur, mensonger, illusoire

Decide, va.n. décider, statuer, se décider

Decided, adj. décidé, résolu, positif, décisif, péremptoire

Decidedly, adv. décidément, positivement

Decider, s. arbitre, *m.*

Decimal, adj. décimal

Decimate, va. lever la dîme, décimer

Decimation, s. décimation, *f.*

Decipher, va. déchiffrer

Decipherer, s. déchiffreur, *m.*, déchiffreuse, *f.*

Deciphering, s. déchiffrement, *m.*

Decision, s. décision, *f.*, résolution, *f.*, fermeté, *f.*

Decisive, adj. décisif, qui décide

Decisively, adv. d'une manière décisive

Decisiveness, s. caractère décisif, *m.*, ton tranchant, *m.*

Deck, va. recouvrir, parer, orner, (*ship*) ponter

Deck, s. pont, *m.*, tillac, *m.* *Middle* —, deuxième pont. *Spare* —, faux pont

Decker, s. qui pare, (*ship*) vaisseau à . . . ponts

Decking, s. embellissement, *m.*

Declaim, va. déclamer, débiter

Declaimer, s. déclamateur, *m.*

Declamation, s. déclamation, *f.*

Declamatory, adj. déclamatoire, déclamateur

Declaration, s. déclaration, *f.*

Declaratory, adj. qui déclare, qui énonce, (*law*) déclaratoire

Declare, va. déclarer, affirmer, proclamer; — vn. se déclarer. — *off*, renoncer, n'en être plus

Declension, s. déclinaison, *f.*, déclivité, *f.*, pente, *f.*, déclin, *m.*, décadence, *f.*

Declinable, adj. déclinable

Declination, s. déclinaison, *f.*, descente, *f.*, (*fig.*) décadence, *f.*, déclin, *m.*

Decline, va.n. incliner, pencher, s'écarter, dévier, éviter, éluder, refuser, décliner, baisser

Decline, s. déclin, *m.*, décadence, *f.*, maladie de langueur, *f.*, phthisie, *f.*

Declivitous, Declivous, adj. escarpé, rapide

Declivity, s. pente, *f.* déclivité, *f.*

Decoction, s. décoction, *f*

Decollation, s. décollation, *f.*

Decompose, va. décomposer; — vn. se décomposer

Decomposition, s. décomposition, *f.*

Decorate, va. décorer, orner, embellir

Decoration, s. décoration, *f.*, ornement, *m.*, embellissement, *m.*, (*archit.*) décor, *m.*

Decorator, s. décorateur, *m.*

Decorous, adj. décent, convenable, bienséant

Decorously, adv. décemment, convenablement, avec bienséance

Decorum, s. décorum, *m.*, les convenances, *f.pl.*, bienséance, *f.*, décence, *f.*

Decoy, va. leurrer, attirer

Decoy, s. leurre, *m.*, appât, *m.*, piège, *m.* — *-bird*, appeau, appelant

Decrease, va.n. décroître

Decrease, s. décroissement, *m.*, décroissance, *f.*, (*waters*) décrue, *f.*

Decree, va.n. décréter, ordonner, arrêter

Decree, s. décret, *m.*, édit, *m.*

Decrepit, adj. décrépit, caduc

Decrepitude, s. décrépitude, *f.*, caducité, *f.*

Decrial, s. clameurs, *f.pl.*

Decrier, s. qui décrie

Decry, va. décrier

Decuple, adj. s. décuple, *m.*

Decuple, va. décupler

Dedicate, va. dédier, consacrer, vouer

Dedication, s. dédicace, *f.*, consécration, *f.*

Dedicatory, adj. dédicatoire

Deduce, va. déduire

Deducible, adj. qu'on peut déduire

Deduct, va. déduire, retrancher

Deduction, s. déduction, *f.*

Deed, s. fait, *m.*, action, *f.*, acte, *m.*, coup, *m.*, exploit, *m.*, (*law*) acte, *m.*, contrat, *m.* *Private* —, acte sous seing privé

Deem, va.n. penser, juger, estimer, croire, regarder comme

Deep, adj. profond, creux, difficile à pénétrer, caché, (*person*) malin, fin, rusé, (*in*, dans) plongé, enfoncé, absorbé, (*edge*) large, (*colour*) foncé, gros, (*sound*) bas, grave, creux, (*milit.*) de profondeur

Deep, s. (*sea*) abîme, *m.*, profondeur, *f.*

Deep, adv. profondément. *To go, to strike, to run* — (*into*), pénétrer bien avant (dans)

Deepen, va. creuser, rendre plus profond, approfondir, augmenter, rehausser, épaissir, assombrir, (*colour*) foncer, (*sound*) renforcer, rendre plus grave; — vn. devenir plus profond, augmenter, s'épaissir, devenir plus foncé, plus grave

Deeply, adv. profondément, sérieusement, extrêmement

Deer, s. daim, *m.*, daine, *f.*, bête fauve, *f.* *Fallow* —, les bêtes fauves. *Red* —, cerf, *m.* — *-stalker*, chasseur de daims, *m.* — *-stalking*, chasse aux daims, *f.*

Deface, va. défigurer, dégrader, mutiler, effacer. *A defaced medal*, médaille fruste, *f.*

Defacement, s. dégradation, *f.*, mutilation, *f.*

Defalcate, va. défalquer

Defalcation, s. défalcation, *f.*, détournement, *m.*

Defamation, s. diffamation, *f.*

Defamatory, adj. diffamatoire, diffamant

Defamer, s. diffamateur, *m.*

Default, s. défaut, *m.*, (*law*) contumace, *f.* *In — of*, à défaut de

Defaulter, s. auteur d'un détournement, *m.*, (*law*) défaillant, -e, *m.f.*, délinquant, *m.*

Defeat, s. défaite, *f.*, déroute, *f.*, (*fig.*) renversement, *m.*

Defeat, va. défaire, battre, mettre en déroute, (*plans*) déjouer, faire échouer, frustrer

Defect, s. défaut, *m.*, erreur, *f.*, insuffisance, *f.*

Defection, s. défection, *f.*

Defective, adj. défectueux, imparfait, défectif

Defectively, adv. défectueusement

Defectiveness, s. imperfection, *f.*

Defence, s. défense, *f.*

Defenceless, adj. sans défense

Defend, va. (*from, against*, de, contre) défendre

Defendant, s. défenseur, *m.*, (*law*) défendeur, *m.*, -eresse, *f.*

Defender, s. défenseur, *m.*, appui, *m.*, soutien, *m.*

Defensible, adj. qui peut être défendu, tenable, justifiable

Defensive, adj. défensif, -ve

Defensive, s. défensive, *f.*

Defensively, adv. sur la défensive

Defer, va.n. déférer, avoir égard, (*to put off*) différer

Deference, s. déférence, *f.*, égards, *m.pl.* *In or out of — to*, par déférence pour

Deferential, adj. de déférence, plein de déférence

Deferentially, adv. avec déférence

Defiance, s. défi, *m.*, mépris, *m.* *To bid, breathe* — *to*, défier, lancer un défi à, braver, narguer. *In* — *of*, au mépris de

Defiant, adj. de défi, hardi

Defiantly, adv. d'un ton de défi, avec assurance

Deficiency, s. manque, *m.*, défaut, *m.*, insuffisance, *f.*, imperfection, *f.*, faiblesse, *f.*, lacune, *f.*, déficit, *m.*

Deficient, adj. qui manque, pauvre, dépourvu, défectueux, faible, insuffisant

Deficiently, adv. imparfaitement

Deficit, s. déficit, *m.*, découvert, *m.*

Defile, va. souiller; — vn. défiler

Defile, s. défilé, *m.*

Defilement, s. souillure, *f.*

Defiler, s. corrupteur, *m.*

Define, va. définir, limiter

Definer, s. personne qui définit, *m.*

Definite, adj. défini

Definitely, adv. d'une manière déterminée

Definiteness, s. caractère défini, *m.*

Definition, s. définition, *f.*, description, *f.*

Definitive, adj. s. définitif, -ve

Definitively, adv. définitivement

Deflect, vn. dévier, décliner; — va. détourner

Deflection, s. déviation, *f.*, écart, *m.*, (*needle*) déclinaison, *f.*, (*light*) déflexion, *f.*

Deflour, Deflower, va. déflorer, défleurir

Deform, va. rendre difforme, déformer, défigurer, enlaidir

Deformation, s. déformation, *f.*

Deformed, adj. difforme, contrefait

Deformity, s. difformité, *f.*, laideur, *f.*

Defraud, va. frauder, faire du tort (à), frustrer

Defrauder, s. fraudeur, *m.*, trompeur, *m.*

Defray, va. défrayer, payer, couvrir

Defunct, adj. s. défunt, *m.*, -e, *f.*

Defy, va. défier, mettre au défi, braver, narguer

Degeneracy, s. abâtardissement, *m.*, dégénération, *f.*, dégénérescence, *f.*

Degenerate, vn. dégénérer, s'abâtardir

Deglutition, s. déglutition, *f.*

Degradation, s. dégradation, *f.*, avilissement, *m.*

Degrade, va. dégrader, (*geog.*) réduire

Degree, s. degré, *m.*, marche, *f.*, rang, *m.*, condition, *f.*, (*univ.*) grade, *m.* *By* —*s*, peu à peu, par degrés, graduellement

Deification, s. déification, *f.*

Deify, va. diviniser, déifier

Deign, vn. daigner

Deism, s. déisme, *m.*

Deist, s. déiste, *m.*

Deistical, adj. déiste, de déiste

Deity, s. Divinité, *f.*, Dieu, *m.*

Deject, va. abattre, décourager

Dejection, s. abattement, *m.*, tristesse, *f.*, (*med.*) déjection, *f.*

Delation, s. transmission, *f.*, délation, *f.*

Delay, va.n. remettre (à), différer (de), tarder (à), retarder

Delay, s. retard, *m.*, délai, *m.*, remise, *f.*

Delectable, adj. délectable, délicieux, charmant

Delectably, adv. délicieusement

Delegate, va. déléguer

Delegate, s. adj. délégué, *m.*, -e, *f.*

Delegation, s. délégation, *f.*, députation, *f.*

Deleterious, adj. délétère, pernicieux

Deliberate, vn. délibérer (sur), mettre . . . en délibération

Deliberate, adj. avisé, circonspect, mûrement réfléchi, lent

Deliberately, adv. de propos délibéré, avec réflexion

Deliberateness, s. circonspection, *f.*

Deliberation, s. délibération, *f.*

Deliberative, adj. délibérant, délibératif

Deliberatively, adv. après réflexion

Delicacy, s. délicatesse, *f.*, morceau délicat, *m.*, friandise, *f.*

Delicate, adj. délicat

Delicately, adv. délicatement

Delicateness, s. délicatesse, *f.*

Delicious, adj. délicieux

Deliciously, adv. délicieusement

Deliciousness, s. goût délicieux, *m.*, délices, *f.pl.*

Delight, s. délices, *f.pl.*, charme, *m.*, plaisir, *m.*

Delight, va. charmer, enchanter, ravir; — vn. se plaire (à), prendre plaisir (à), se faire un plaisir (de), aimer (à)

Delightful, adj. délicieux, charmant, délectable, enchanteur, ravissant

Delightfully, adv. délicieusement, à ravir

Delightfulness, s. enchantement, *m.*, charme, *m.*

Delineate, va. dessiner, esquisser, tracer

Delineation, s. délinéation, *f.*, esquisse, *f.*, description, *f.*

Delinquency, s. délit, *m.*, faute, *f.*

Delinquent, s. délinquant, *m.*, -e, *f.*

Delirious, adj. en délire, du délire, délirant

Delirium, Deliriousness, s. délire, *m.*

Deliver, va. délivrer, sauver, (*goods*) remettre, livrer, (*letters*) distribuer, (*speeches*) débiter, prononcer, (*a message*) faire, (*childbirth*) accoucher. *Stand and* — ! la bourse ou la vie ! *Goods to be delivered*, marchandises livrables

Deliverable, adj. livrable, à livrer

Deliverance, s. délivrance, *f.*, (*speech*) débit, *m.*, diction, *f.*

Deliverer, s. sauveur, *m.*, libérateur, -trice, *m.f.*

Delivery, s. délivrance, *f.*, liberté, *f.*, (*goods*) remise, *f.*, livraison, *f.*; distribution, *f.*, débit, *m.*, diction, *f.*, expression, *f.*, énonciation, *f.*, (*commission*) exécution, *f.*, (*med.*) délivrance, *f.*

Dell, s. vallon, *m.*, creux, *m.*

Delta, s. delta, *m.*

Delude, va. tromper, abuser, faire illusion

Deluder, s. trompeur, *m.*

Deluding, Delusive, Delusory, adj. mensonger, décevant, illusoire, trompeur

Deluge, s. déluge, *m.*, inondation, *f.*

Deluge, va. inonder, submerger

Delusion, s. déception, *f.*, illusion, *f.*, erreur, *f.*, mensonge, *m.*

Delusively, adv. illusoirement

Delusiveness, s. caractère illusoire, *m.*

Demagogue, s. démagogue, *m.*

Demagogy, s. démagogie, *f.*

Demand, va. demander

Demand, s. demande, *f.*, réclamation, *f.* *On* —, (*com.*) à présentation. *In great* —, fort recherché, fort demandé

Demandant, s. demandeur, *m.*, -eresse, *f.*

Demarcation, s. démarcation, *f.*

Demean oneself, vn. se comporter, se conduire, s'abaisser, s'avilir

Demeanour, s. maintien, *m.*, contenance, *f.*, air, *m.*

Demerit, s. démérite, *m.*

Demesne, s. domaine, *m.*, terre, *f.*

Demi-, adj. demi, à demi

Demise, s. transmission, *f.*, (*death*) décès, *m.*

Demise, va. transmettre, donner à bail, léguer par testament

Democracy, s. démocratie, *f.*

Democrat, s. démocrate, *m.*

Democratic, Democratical, adj. démocratique

Democratically, adv. démocratiquement

Demolish, va. démolir

Demolisher, s. démolisseur, *m.*

Demolition, s. démolition, *f.*

Demon, s. démon, *m.*, génie, *m.*, esprit, *m.*

Demoniac, s. démoniaque, *m.f.*

Demoniac, Demoniacal, adj. démoniaque, diabolique

Demonology, s. démonologie, *f.*

Demonstrability, s. facilité de démonstration, *f.*

Demonstrable, adj. démontrable

Demonstrably, adv. incontestablement

Demonstrate, va. démontrer

Demonstration, s. démonstration, *f.*

Demonstrative, adj. démonstratif

Demonstratively, adv. démonstrativement

Demonstrator, s. démonstrateur, *m.*

Demoralization, s. démoralisation, *f.*

Demoralize, va. démoraliser

Demoralizing, adj. démoralisateur, -trice

Demur, vn. hésiter (à), balancer (pour), soulever des difficultés, temporiser, (*law*) produire une exception (à)

Demur, s. hésitation, *f.*, doute, *m.*

Demure, adj. modeste, réservé, grave, prude

Demurely, adv. modestement, solennellement, avec pruderie

Demureness, s. air modeste, *m.*, décence, *f.*, gravité, *f.*, pruderie, *f.*

Demurrer, s. qui hésite sans cesse, *m.f.*, (*law*) exception, *f.*

Demy, s. papier coquille, *m.*

Den, s. tanière, *f.*, repaire, *m.*, antre, *m.*, caverne, *f.*, (*menagerie*) loge, *f.*

Deniable, adj. niable

Denial, s. dénégation, *f.*, refus, *m.*, (*law*) déni, *m.*, reniement, *m.* — *of oneself*, abnégation, *f.*

Denizen, s. citoyen, *m.*, habitant, *m.*, (*law*) étranger qui a reçu les petites lettres de naturalisation, *m.*

Denominate, va. nommer, appeler, (*law*) dénommer

Denomination, s. dénomination, *f.*

Denominative, adj. dénominatif

Denominator, s. dénominateur, *m.*

Denote, va. dénoter, indiquer, montrer

Denounce, va. annoncer, dénoncer, déclarer, accuser

Denouncer, s. celui qui annonce, *m.*

Dense, adj. épais

Density, Denseness, s. épaisseur, *f.*, densité, *f.*

Dent, s. marque, *f.*, bosse, *f.*, renfoncement, *m.*
Dent, va. laisser une marque (sur), bosser
Dental, adj. dental. — s. dentale, *f.*
Dentifrice, s. dentifrice, *m.*
Dentist, s. dentiste, *m.*
Denude, va. dénuder, mettre à nu
Denunciation, s. déclaration, *f.*, dénonciation, *f.*, délation, *f.*
Denunciator, s. celui qui déclare, dénonciateur, *m.*, délateur, *m.*
Deny, va. nier, disconvenir de, démentir, refuser, rejeter, renoncer à, abjurer. *To — oneself*, renoncer à soi-même, se refuser, faire défendre sa porte, fermer sa porte, dire qu'on n'y est pas
Deodorize, va. désinfecter
Deodorizer, s. désinfectant
Deodorizing, s. désinfection, *f.*
Depart, vn. partir, s'en aller, se retirer, s'éloigner, (*die*) trépasser, mourir. *The —ed*, les trépassés
Department, s. département, *m.*, service, *m.*, ressort, *m.*, partie, *f.*
Departure, s. départ, *m.*, trépas, *m.*, mort, *f.*, (*fig.*) éloignement, *m.*, abandon, *m.*
Depend, vn. dépendre, pendre, être suspendu, compter (sur), se fier (à)
Dependant, s. celui, celle qui dépend, *m.f.*, client, *m.*, subordonné, *m.*, serviteur, *m.*
Dependence, Dependency, s. suspension, *f.*, chose suspendue, *f.*, dépendance, *f.*, confiance, *f.*, colonie, *f.*, accessoire, *m.*
Dependent, adj. dépendant, de dépendance, soumis, esclave
Depict, va. peindre, dépeindre
Depilate, va. épiler
Depilatory, s. dépilatoire, *m.* — adj. dépilatif
Deplorable, adj. déplorable
Deplorableness, s. état *or* caractère déplorable
Deplorably, adv. lamentablement
Deploration, Deploring, s. lamentation, *f.*, regrets, *m.pl.*
Deplore, va. déplorer, pleurer
Deploringly, adv. en pleurant, avec regret
Deploy, va. déployer; — vn. se déployer
Deploy, Deployment, s. déploiement, *m.*
Deponent, s. déposant, *m.*, témoin, *m.*, (*verb*) déponent, *m.*
Depopulate, va. dépeupler
Depopulation, s. dépopulation, *f.*, dépeuplement, *m.*

Deportment, s. maintien, *m.*, tenue, *f.*, conduite, *f.*
Depose, va. déposer
Deposit, s. dépôt, *m.*
Deposit, va. déposer
Depositary, s. dépositaire, *m.*
Deposition, Deposing, s. déposition, *f.*, dépôt, *m.*
Depositor, s. déposant, *m.*, -e, *f.* —'*s book*, livret de caisse d'épargne, *m.*
Depository, s. (lieu de) dépôt, *m.*
Depravation, s. dépravation, *f.*
Deprave, va. dépraver
Depravedly, adv. d'une manière dépravée
Depravedness, Depravity, s. dépravation, *f.*
Depraver, s. corrupteur, *m.*, -trice, *f.*
Deprecate, va. conjurer, détourner par la prière, faire des vœux contre
Deprecation, s. prière *f.*, vœu contre, *m.*, supplication, *f.*
Deprecative, Deprecatory, adj. destiné à détourner, de prière, suppliant
Depreciate, va. déprécier; — vn. se déprécier
Depreciation, s. dépréciation, *f.*
Depreciator, s. qui déprécie, *m.*
Depredate, va. piller, ravager, saccager
Depredation, s. déprédation, *f.*, ravage, *m.*
Depredator, s. déprédateur, *m.*, maraudeur, *m.*
Depress, va. abaisser, baisser, déprimer, (*fig.*) humilier, décourager, attrister, (*trade*) faire languir, (*prices*) faire baisser
Depression, s. abaissement, *m.*, affaissement, *m.*, humiliation, *f.*, abattement, *m.*, (*trade*) stagnation, *f.*, (*prices*) baisse, *f.*
Deprivation, s. privation, *f.*
Deprive, va. priver, dépouiller
Depth, s. profondeur, *f.*, hauteur, *f.*, abîme, *m.*, (*winter*) cœur, *m.*, (*colour*) vigueur, *f.*, (*print.*) corps, *m.*
Depurate, va. épurer
Depuration, s. dépuration, *f.*
Deputation, s. députation, *f.*, délégation, *f.*
Depute, va. députer, envoyer
Deputy, s. député, *m.*, envoyé, *m.*, représentant, *m.*, suppléant, *m.*, adjoint, *m.*, sous- . . ., vice- . . ., *m.*
Derange, va. déranger
Derangement, s. dérangement, *m.*
Dereliction, s. abandon, *m.*
Deride, va. railler, tourner en dérision
Derider, s. railleur, *m.*, moqueur, *m.*

Derision, s. dérision, *f.*, moquerie, *f.*, raillerie, *f.*, risée, *f.*
Derisive, Derisory, adj. moqueur, dérisoire
Derisively, adv. par dérision
Derivable, adj. qu'on peut retirer, qui descend, qu'on peut déduire
Derivation, s. dérivation, *f.*
Derivative, s. adj. (*med.*) dérivatif, *m.*; dérivé
Derive, va. dériver, faire dériver, (*fruit*) retirer, tirer, recueillir; — vn. venir, dériver
Derogate, vn. déroger (à)
Derogate, adj. dégénéré
Derogation, s. dérogation, *f.*
Derogatory, adj. dérogatoire
Dervish, s. derviche, *m.*
Descant, va. disserter, discourir
Descend, va.n. descendre, tomber, (*fig.*) s'abaisser (à)
Descendant, s. descendant, *m.*, -e, *f.*
Descent, s. descente, *f.*, chûte, *f.*, dégradation, *f.*, pente, *f.*, descendance, *f.*, naissance, *f.*
Describable, adj. qu'on peut décrire
Describe, va. décrire, dépeindre
Describer, s. auteur de la description
Description, s. description, *f.*, (*law*) signalement, *m.*, (*kind*) sorte, *f.*, classe, *f.*, espèce, *f.*, genre, *m.*
Descriptive, adj. descriptif
Descry, va. discerner, découvrir, distinguer
Desecrate, va. souiller, profaner
Desecration, s. profanation, *f.*
Desert, adj. désert, -e
Desert, s. désert, *m.*, solitude, *f.*, (*what one deserves*) mérite, *m.*, dû, *m.*
Desert, va. déserter, délaisser, abandonner; — vn. déserter
Deserter, s. déserteur, *m.*, transfuge, *m.*
Desertion, s. désertion, *f.*, abandon, *m.*, délaissement, *m.*
Deserve, va.n. mériter, être digne (de)
Deservedly, Deservingly, adv. à juste titre, à bon droit
Deserving, adj. méritant, de mérite, méritoire
Desideratum, s. chose qui manque, *f.*, lacune, *f.*
Design, va. désigner, décrire, (*draw*) dessiner; projeter
Design, s. dessein, *m.*, projet, *m.*, intention, *f.*, but, *m.*, (*drawing*) dessin, *m.*, plan, *m.*
Designate, va. désigner
Designation, s. désignation, *f.*, signification, *f.*

Designedly, adv. à dessein, avec intention
Designer, s. auteur, *m.*, intrigant, *m.*, dessinateur, *m.*
Designing, adj. artificieux, intrigant
Desirable, adj. désirable, à désirer, souhaitable, avantageux
Desire, s. désir, *m.*, envie, *f.*, souhait, *m.*
Desire, va. désirer, souhaiter, vouloir, prier, donner l'ordre (à)
Desirer, s. celui, celle qui désire
Desirous, adj. désireux
Desist, vn. se désister (de), renoncer (à)
Desk, s. pupitre, *m.*, bureau, *m.*, (*schoolmaster's*) chaire, *f.*, (*lectern*) lutrin, *m.*
Desolate, adj. désert, inhabité, seul, délaissé, en ruines, triste, au désespoir
Desolate, va. désoler
Desolation, s. désolation, *f.*
Despair, s. désespoir, *m.*
Despair, vn. désespérer, se désespérer
Despairingly, adj. avec désespoir
Despatch, va. expédier, dépêcher, en finir (de)
Despatch, s. envoi, *m.*, dépêche, *f.*, télégramme, *m.*, (*business*) expédition, *f.*; activité, *f.*, promptitude, *f.* — *box*, buvard, *m.*
Desperado, s. forcené, *m.*, désespéré, *m.*
Desperate, adj. qui désespère, sans espoir, désespéré, terrible, furieux
Desperately, adv. en désespéré, furieusement, terriblement, extrêmement, à l'excès
Desperation, s. acharnement, *m.*, désespoir, *m.*, fureur, *f.*
Despicable, adj. méprisable
Despicableness, s. nature méprisable, *f.*, bassesse, *f.*
Despicably, adj. d'une manière méprisable
Despise, va. mépriser, dédaigner
Despiser, s. contempteur, *m.*
Despite, s. dépit, *m.* *In — of*, — *of*, —, en dépit de, malgré
Despoil, va. dépouiller
Despond, vn. se décourager, se laisser abattre
Despondence, Despondency, s. abattement, *m.*, découragement, *m.*, désespoir, *m.*
Despondent, adj. découragé, abattu
Despondently, Despondingly, adv. avec abattement, tristement
Despot, s. despote, *m.*
Despotic, Despotical, adj. despotique
Despotically, adv. despotiquement

Despotism, s. despotisme, *m.*
Dessert, s. dessert, *m.*
Destination, s. destination, *f.*
Destine, va. destiner, fixer
Destiny, s. destinée, *f.*, destin, *m.*, sort, *m.*
Destitute, adj. dénué, dépourvu, privé, destitué, indigent
Destituteness, s. dénûment, *m.*
Destitution, s. dénûment, *m.*, indigence, *f.*, abandon, *m.*
Destroy, va. détruire
Destroyer, s. **Destroying**, adj. destructeur, *m.*, -trice, *f.*, exterminateur, *m.*, -trice, *f.*
Destructible, adj. qui peut être détruit, périssable
Destruction, s. destruction, *f.*, perte, *f.*, ruine, *f.*, perdition, *f.*
Destructive, adj. destructif
Destructively, adv. dangereusement
Destructiveness, s. puissance de destruction, *f.*
Desultorily, adv. d'une manière décousue, à bâtons rompus, sans suite
Desultoriness, s. décousu, *m.*
Desultory, adj. irrégulier, décousu, à bâtons rompus, sans suite
Detach, va. détacher
Detachment, s. détachement, *m.*
Detail, va. détailler, raconter en détail, (*milit.*) détacher
Detail, s. détail, *m.*, (*mil.*) détachement, *m.*
Detain, va. retenir, détenir, arrêter, retarder
Detainer, s. détenteur, *m.*
Detect, va. découvrir
Detection, s. découverte, *f.*, conviction, *f.*, preuve de fait, *f.*
Detective, s. agent de la police de sûreté, *m.*
Detention, s. détention, *f.*, retard, *m.*
Deter, va. détourner, empêcher
Deteriorate, va.n. détériorer, se détériorer
Deterioration, s. détérioration, *f.*, dégradation, *f.*
Determinable, adj. qu'on peut déterminer
Determinate, adj. déterminé, décisif, définitif, résolu
Determinately, adv résolûment, définitivement
Determination, s. détermination, *f.*
Determine, va. borner, limiter, déterminer, décider, fixer; — vn. se déterminer, résoudre, se décider
Detersion, s. détersion, *f.*
Detest, va. détester
Detestable, adj. détestable
Detestably, adv. détestablement
Detestation, s. détestation, *f.*, haine, *f.*, horreur, *f.*
Dethrone, va. détrôner
Dethronement, s. déposition, *f.*
Detonate, vn. détoner
Detonation, s. détonation, *f.*
Detract, va. enlever, dénigrer, diffamer
Detraction, s. enlèvement, *m.*, (*fig.*) détraction, *f.*
Detractive, **Detractory**, adj. diffamatoire
Detractor, s. détracteur, *m.*
Detriment, s. détriment, *m.*, préjudice, *m.*, désavantage, *m.*
Detrimental, adj. préjudiciable, désavantageux
Deuce, s. (*play*) deux, *m.*; diable, *m.*, diantre, *m.* *The — is in him!* il a le diable au corps!
Deuced, adj. diablement
Deucedly, adv. diablement
Deuteronomy, s. deutéronome, *m.*
Devastate, va. dévaster, ravager
Devastation, s. dévastation, *f.*
Develop, va. développer
Development, s. développement, *m.*
Deviate, vn. dévier, s'écarter
Deviation, s. déviation, *f*
Device, s. stratagème, *m.*, invention, *f.*, ruse, *f.*, (*emblem*) devise, *f.*
Devil, s. diable, *m.* *The — upon two sticks*, le diable boiteux. *She- —*, diablesse, *f.* *— may care*, adj. gaillard d'une complète insouciance. *Printer's —*, apprenti imprimeur, *m.*
Devilish, adj. diabolique, de diable
Devilishly, adv. *see* DEUCEDLY
Devilry, s. diablerie, *f.*
Devious, adj. détourné, écarté, de traverse
Deviously, adv. en déviant, hors du droit chemin, à tort
Devisable, adj. imaginable, (*law*) qu'on peut léguer
Devise, va. imaginer, inventer, préparer, (*law*) léguer; — vn. songer, chercher moyen
Deviser, s. auteur, *m.*, inventeur, *m.*
Devoid, adj. vide, dénué, dépourvu, privé
Devolve, va. rouler en bas, précipiter, remettre, transmettre; — vn. rouler en bas, échoir, descendre, revenir
Devote, va. dévouer, vouer, consacrer
Devoted, past part. adj. dévoué, voué, consacré, maudit, malheureux
Devotedly, adv. avec dévouement, avec respect
Devotedness, s. dévouement, *m.*
Devotee, s. dévot, *m.*, -e, *f.*
Devotion, s. dévotion, *f.*, dévouement, *m.*, empressement, *m.*
Devotional, adj. de dévotion, de piété, religieux
Devour, va. dévorer
Devourer, s. dévorateur, *m.*, -trice, *f.*
Devouring, adj. dévorateur, dévorant
Devout, adj. pieux, dévot, dévoué
Devoutly, adv. pieusement, dévotement, avec dévotion, sincèrement
Dew, s. rosée, *f.* *— -bent*, chargé de rosée. *— -berry*, baie de ronce, *f.* *— -drop*, goutte de rosée, *f.* *— -lap*, fanon, *m.* *— -worm*, ver de terre, *m.*
Dewy, adj. de rosée, humide de rosée
Dexterity, **Dexterousness**, s. dextérité, *f.*, adresse, *f.*
Dexterous, adj. adroit
Dexterously, adv. avec dextérité, adroitement
Dey, s. dey, *m.*
Diabetes, s diabète, *m.*
Diabolic, **Diabolical**, adj. diabolique, infernal
Diabolically, adv. diaboliquement
Diachylon, s. diachylon, *m.*
Diadem, s. diadème, *m.*
Diæresis, s. diérèse, *f.*, tréma, *m.*
Diagnosis, s. diagnostic, *m.*
Diagnostic, adj. diagnostique
Diagonal, adj. diagonal, -e
Diagonal, s. diagonale, *f.*
Diagonally, adv. en diagonale
Diagram, s. diagramme, *m.*
Dial, s. cadran, *m.*, cadran solaire, *m.*
Dialect, s. dialecte, *m.*, langage, *m.*
Dialectic, **Dialectical**, adj. de dialecte, idiomatique, dialectique
Dialogue, s. dialogue, *m.*
Diameter, s. diamètre, *m.*
Diametrical, adj. diamétral
Diametrically, adv. diamétralement
Diamond, s. diamant, *m.*, (*cards*) carreau, *m.* *— -cutter*, lapidaire, *m.*
Diamond, adj. de diamant, en losange
Diapason, s. diapason, *m.*
Diaper, s. linge ouvré, *f.*
Diaper, va. ouvrer, diaprer
Diaphanous, adj. diaphane
Diaphragm, s. diaphragme, *m.*
Diarrhœa, s. diarrhée, *f.*
Diary, s. journal, *m.*
Diatribe, s. diatribe, *f.*
Dibble, s. plantoir, *m.*
Dibble, va. planter
Dice-box, s. cornet, *m.*
Dickey, s. siége de derrière, *m.*
Dictate, va.n. dicter, prescrire, commander
Dictate, s. ordre, *m.*, règle, *f.*
Dictation, s. dictée, *f.*
Dictator, s. dictateur, *m.*
Dictatorial, **Dictatory**, adj. dictatorial
Dictatorially, adv. en maître
Dictatorship, s. dictature, *f.*
Diction, s. diction, *f.*, débit, *m.*
Dictionary, s. dictionnaire, *m.*
Didactic, adj. didactique
Didactically, adv. d'une manière didactique
Diddle, vn. chanceler, muser; — va. duper
Die, s. dé, *m.*, (*stamp*) coin, *m.* *The — is cast*, le sort en est jeté
Die, vn. mourir, périr, se perdre, cesser. *Never say —!* il ne faut jamais désespérer. *— away*, mourir, se mourir, s'éteindre. *— off*, s'éteindre, tomber dans l'oubli
Diet, s. nourriture, *f.*, diète, *f.*, régime, *m.*
Diet, va. nourrir, mettre à la diète; — vn. se repaître, se mettre à la diète
Dietary, adj. de diète, de régime
Dietary, s. régime, *m.*
Differ, vn. différer, n'être pas d'accord
Difference, s. différence, *f.*, différend, *m.*, dissidence, *f.*, divergence, *f.* *To make no —*, ne faire rien. *To make up a —*, ajuster un différend
Different, adj. différent, divers
Differential, adj. différentiel
Differently, adv. différemment, diversement
Difficult, adj. difficile, malaisé, gêné, embarrassé
Difficulty, s. difficulté, *f.*, peine, *f.*, gêne, *f.*, embarras, *m.*
Diffidence, s. défiance de soi-même, *f.*, timidité, *f.*
Diffident, adj. défiant, qui se défie
Diffidently, adv. avec défiance, timidement, avec modestie
Diffuse, va. répandre, propager, étendre
Diffuse, adj. répandu au loin, diffus, prolixe
Diffusely, adv. diffusément
Diffuseness, s. diffusion, *f.*
Diffusion, s. diffusion, *f.*, dissémination, *f.*, propagation, *f.*
Diffusive, adj. expansif, qui se répand, abondant

Dig, va.n. creuser, fouiller, bêcher, plocher. *To — out, up*, retirer, déterrer. *To — through*, percer
Digest, s. digeste, *m.*
Digest, va. digérer, mûrir
Digestible, adj. facile à digérer
Digestion, s. digestion, *f.*
Digestive, adj. digestif, -ve
Digestive, s. digestif, *m.*
Digger, s. celui qui creuse, *m.*, qui bêche, *m.*, ouvrier mineur, *m.*
Digging, s. creusement, *m.*, excavation, *f.*, fouille, *f.* *—s*, mines, *f.pl.*, placers, *m.pl.*
Digit, s. doigt, *m.*, chiffre, *m.*
Digital, adj. digital
Digitalis, s. digitale, *f.*
Dignified, adj. plein de dignité, digne, noble, fier
Dignify, va. revêtir de *or* élever à une dignité, honorer, décorer
Dignitary, s. dignitaire, *m.*
Dignity, s. dignité, *f.*
Digress, vn. s'écarter, s'éloigner, faire des digressions
Digression, s. digression, *f.*
Dike, s. fossé, *m.*, digue, *f.*
Dike, va. endiguer
Dilapidate, va. délabrer, (*revenues*) dilapider; — vn. se délabrer
Dilapidation, s. délabrement, *m.*, (*finances*) dilapidation, *f*
Dilatation, s. dilatation, *f.*
Dilate, va. dilater, (*fig.*) raconter en détail, (*fig.*) développer; — vn. se dilater, (*fig.*) s'étendre
Dilation, s. délai, *m.*
Dilatorily, adv. tardivement, lentement
Dilatoriness, s. lenteur, *f.*
Dilatory, adj. lent, tardif, en retard, (*law*) dilatoire
Dilemma, s. dilemme, *m.*, alternative, *f.*
Diligence, s. diligence, *f.*, application, *f.*, soin, *m.*
Diligent, adj. appliqué, diligent, assidu
Diligently, adv. diligemment
Dill, s. aneth, *m.*
Dilly-Dally, vn. flâner, lanterner
Dilute, va. (*liquids*) couper, étendre d'eau, (*lime, &c.*) délayer, détremper, (*colour*) affaiblir
Diluted, adj. past part. coupé, étendu d'eau, trempé, affaibli
Dilution, s. action d'étendre d'eau, *m.*, délayement, *m.*, affaiblissement, *m.*
Diluvial, adj. diluvien
Dim, adj. faible, trouble, obscur, obscurci, (*colour*) terne. *—-sighted*, qui a la vue faible *or* trouble
Dim, va. obscurcir, rendre trouble, affaiblir, offusquer, assombrir, ternir

Dimension, s. dimension, *f.*
Dimensioned, adj. à … dimensions
Diminish, va. diminuer, amoindrir; — vn. diminuer
Diminution, s. diminution, *f.*, amoindrissement, *m.*
Diminutive, adj. petit, chétif, diminutif
Diminutive, s. diminutif, *m.*, nain, *m.*
Diminutively, adv. en petit
Diminutiveness, s. petitesse, *f.*, exiguïté, *f.*
Dimissory, adj. *— letters*, lettres dimissoriales, *f.*, dimissoire, *m.*
Dimity, s. basin, *m.*
Dimly, adv. faiblement, peu, obscurément
Dimness, s. faible lueur, *f.*, faiblesse, *f.*, obscurité, *f.*, manque d'éclat, *m.*
Dimple, s. fossette, *f.*
Dimple, vn. se former en fossettes, se rider doucement
Din, s. fracas, *m.*, tapage, *m.*, bruit, *m.*
Din, va. étourdir, assourdir, (*repeat*) corner
Dine, vn. dîner. *— out*, dîner en ville. *— with Duke Humphrey*, dîner par cœur. *Dining-hall*, réfectoire, *m.* *Dining-room*, salle à manger, *f.*, réfectoire, *m.* *Dining-rooms*, restaurant, *m.*
Diner-out, s. qui dîne souvent en ville, *m.*
Dinginess, s. obscurité, *f.*, couleur sombre *or* terne, *f.*, teinte sale, *f.*
Dingy, adj. sombre, terne, sale
Dinner, s. dîner, *m.* *A doll's —*, dînette, *f.* *—-bell*, cloche du dîner. *—-service*, service de table, *m.* *—-table*, table de salle à manger. *—-hour*, *—-time*, l'heure du dîner
Dint, s. pouvoir, *m.*, force, *f.*, coup, *m.* *By — of*, à force de
Diocesan, adj. diocésain
Diocesan, s. (évêque) diocésain, *m.*
Diocese, s. diocèse, *m.*
Diorama, s. diorama, *m.*
Dip, va. plonger, tremper, mouiller, (*fig.*) engager, baptiser; — vn. plonger, pénétrer, prendre part (à), tremper (dans), (*book*) parcourir, effleurer, incliner
Dip, Dipping, s. immersion, *f.*, (*pop.*) bain, *m.*, plongeon, *m.*, (*magnet., geol.*) inclinaison, *f.*, (*candle*) chandelle, *f.*
Diphtheria, s. angine couenneuse, *f.*, diphthérite, *f*
Diphthong, s. diphthongue, *f.*
Diploma, s. diplôme, *m.*
Diplomacy, s. diplomatie, *f.*
Diplomatic, adj. diplomatique
Diplomatically, adv. diplomatiquement

Diplomatics, s.pl. diplomatique, *f.*
Diplomatist, s. diplomate, *m.*
Dipper, s. plongeur, *m.*, (*ladle*) cuiller à pot, *f.*
Dire, adj. affreux, terrible, sinistre, cruel
Direct, adj. direct, droit, formel, positif
Direct, va. diriger, indiquer *or* montrer (le chemin), (*letters*) adresser, (*order*) charger, dire (à), enjoindre (à), prescrire (à)
Direction, s. direction, *f.*, sens, *m.*, côté, *m.*, (*road*) tracé, *m.*, (*letters*) adresse, *f.*, (*orders*) instructions, *f.pl.*, ordre, *m.*
Directly, adv. directement, sur-le-champ, tout de suite, dès que
Directness, s. mouvement en ligne directe, *m.*, rectitude, *f.*
Director, s. directeur, *m.*, guide, *m.*
Directorship, s. direction, *f.*
Directory, s. almanach du commerce, *m.*, annuaire, *m.*, direction, *f.*, administration, *f.*, Directoire, *m.*, livre de règles, *m.*
Directress, s. directrice, *f.*
Direful, adj. terrible, horrible, cruel, affreux
Direfully, adv. terriblement, affreusement
Direfulness, s. horreur, *f.*
Dirge, s. chant funèbre, *m.*, chant de mort, *m.*
Dirk, s. poignard, *m.*
Dirt, s. saleté, *f.*, malpropreté, *f.*, crasse, *f.*, boue, *f.*, crotte, *f.*, ordures, *f.pl.*, (*fig.*) bassesse, *f.*
Dirtily, adv. salement, (*fig.*) bassement
Dirtiness, s. malpropreté, *f.*, saleté, *f.*, (*fig.*) bassesse, *f.*
Dirty, adj. malpropre, sale, crasseux, crotté, (*colour*) terne, (*fig.*) bas, sordide
Dirty, va. salir, crotter, souiller
Disability, s. incapacité, *f.*
Disable, va. rendre incapable, mettre hors d'état, rendre infirme, mettre hors de combat, (*nav.*) désemparer
Disabuse, va. désabuser
Disaccustom, va. désaccoutumer
Disadvantage, s. désavantage, *m.*
Disadvantageous, adj. désavantageux
Disadvantageously, adv. désavantageusement
Disaffect, va. désaffectionner, déranger
Disaffected, adj. mal disposé
Disaffectedly, adv. avec mécontentement
Disaffection, s. désaffection, *f.*
Disagree, vn. différer, ne pas s'accorder, se quereller, se brouiller, ne pas agréer, faire mal (à), incommoder ne pas convenir (à)
Disagreeable, adj. désagréable, en désaccord
Disagreeableness, s. désagrément, *m.*, nature désagréable, *f.*
Disagreeably, adv. désagréablement
Disagreement, s. différence, *f.*, désaccord, *m.*, dissidence, *f.*, brouille, *f.*, disconvenance, *f.*
Disallow, va. désapprouver, défendre, ne pas permettre
Disappear, vn. disparaître
Disappearance, s. disparition, *f.*
Disappoint, va. tromper *or* décevoir dans son attente, désappointer, frustrer, priver, manquer de parole (à), faire faux bond (à), déjouer, faire échouer, contrarier, déranger
Disappointment, s. attente *or* espérance déçue, *f.*, désappointement, *m.*, désillusion, *f.*, contrariété, *f.*, contre-temps, *m.*
Disapprobation, Disapproval, s. désapprobation, *f.*
Disapprove, va. désapprouver, trouver mauvais
Disapprovingly, adv. avec désapprobation
Disarm, va.n. désarmer
Disarmament, Disarming, s. désarmement, *m.*
Disarrange, va. déranger
Disarrangement, s. dérangement, *m.*
Disarray, va. mettre en désarroi *or* en désordre
Disarray, s. désarroi, *m.*, désordre, *m.*
Disaster, s. désastre, *m.*
Disastrous, adj. désastreux, funeste, malheureux
Disavow, va. désavouer
Disavowal, s. désaveu, *m.*
Disband, va. congédier, licencier; — vn. être licencié, se débander, aller à la débandade, se désorganiser
Disbar, va. rayer du tableau des avocats
Disbelief, s. incrédulité, *f.*, refus de croire, *m.*
Disbelieve, va. ne pas croire
Disbeliever, s. incrédule, *m.*, mécréant, *m.*, infidèle, *m.*
Disburden, va. décharger, débarrasser, soulager
Disburse, va. débourser, payer
Disbursement, s. payement, *m.*, déboursés, *m.pl.*, débours, *m.pl.*
Discard, va. écarter, congédier, renvoyer, repousser
Discern, va. distinguer, discerner
Discerner, s. qui discerne, *m.f.*, juge, *m.*, connaisseur, *m.*

Discernible, adj. perceptible

Discernibly, adv. visiblement

Discerning, adj. sagace, judicieux

Discerningly, adv. avec discernement

Discernment, s. discernement, *m.*

Discharge, va.n. décharger, débarrasser, délivrer, (*guns*) tirer, (*arrows*) lancer, décocher, (*debts*) s'acquitter (de), (*creditor*) satisfaire, payer, donner quittance (à), (*dismiss*) congédier, renvoyer, donner son congé, (*prisoner*) élargir, mettre en liberté, absoudre

Discharge, s. déchargement, *m.*, émission, *f.*, flot, *m.*, (*guns*) décharge, *f.*, (*matter*) écoulement, *m.*, suppuration, *f.*, (*duty*) accomplissement, *m.*, (*debt*) décharge, *f.*, payement, *m.*, (*dismissal*) congé, *m.*, renvoi, *m.*, (*obligation*) libération, *f.*, pardon, *m.*, quittance, *f.*, (*from prison*) élargissement, *m.*, mise en liberté, *f.*

Disciple, s. disciple, *m.*

Disciplinarian, s. homme fort sur la discipline, *m.*, officier sévère, *m.*

Disciplinarian, Disciplinary, adj. disciplinaire

Discipline, s. discipline, *f.*

Discipline, va. discipliner, instruire, châtier

Disclaim, va. désavouer, renier, abjurer, renoncer (à)

Disclaimer, s. désaveu, *m.*

Disclose, va. découvrir, exposer, montrer, déceler, mettre au jour, divulguer

Discloser, s. révélateur, *m.*

Disclosure, s. découverte, *f.*, révélation, *f.*, exposition, *f.*

Discoloration, s. décoloration, *f.*

Discolour, va. décolorer, altérer

Discomfit, va. mettre en déconfiture, déconfire

Discomfiture, s. déconfiture, *f.*, défaite, *f.*

Discomfort, s. chagrin, *m.*, inquiétude, *f.*, malaise, *m.*, inconvénient, *m.*, désagrément, *m.*

Discompose, va. déranger, mettre en désordre, troubler, agiter, altérer, décomposer

Discomposure, s. dérangement, *m.*, trouble, *m.*, agitation, *f.*, altération, *f.*, décomposition, *f.*

Disconcert, va. déconcerter, troubler

Disconnect, va. séparer, désunir

Disconnection, s. séparation, *f.*, désunion, *f.*

Disconsolate, adj. désolé, inconsolable

Disconsolately, adv. avec désolation, tristement, inconsolablement

Disconsolateness, s. désolation, *f.*, affliction, *f.*

Discontent, s. mécontentement, *m.*

Discontent, Discontented, adj. mécontent, chagrin

Discontent, va. mécontenter

Discontentedly, adv. avec mécontentement

Discontentedness, Discontentment, s. mécontentement, *m.*

Discontinuance, Discontinuation, s. discontinuation, *f.*, interruption, *f.*

Discontinue, va. discontinuer, interrompre, cesser

Discontinuity, s. discontinuité, *f.*, solution de continuité, *f.*

Discontinuous, adj. discontinu

Discord, s. discorde, *f.*, discordance, *f.*

Discordance, s. discordance, *f.*

Discordant, adj. discordant, en désaccord

Discordantly, adv. d'une manière discordante, sans accord

Discount, s. escompte, *m.*, décompte, *m.*, rabais, *m.*, (*arithmet.*) règle d'escompte, *f.*

Discount, va. faire un escompte, décompter, rabattre, escompter

Discountenance, va. décontenancer, déconcerter, décourager

Discounter, s. escompteur, *m.*

Discourage, va. décourager, rebuter, repousser, dissuader, détourner

Discouragement, s. découragement, *m.*

Discourager, s. qui décourage, *m.*

Discourse, s. discours, *m.*, conversation, *f.*, entretien, *m.*

Discourse, vn. raisonner, discourir, s'entretenir

Discourser, s. discoureur, *m.*, orateur, *m.*

Discoursive, adj. logique, discursif, dialogué, (*pers.*) communicatif

Discourteous, adj. discourtois

Discourteously, adv. d'une manière peu courtoise

Discourteousness, Discourtesy, s. incivilité, *f.*, manque de courtoisie, *m.*

Discover, va. découvrir, montrer, faire voir, faire preuve de

Discoverable, adj. qu'on peut découvrir, visible, apparent

Discoverer, s. personne qui découvre, *m.*, auteur d'une découverte, *m.*

Discovery, s. découverte, *f.*

Discredit, s. discrédit, *m.*, déconsidération, *f.*

Discredit, va. refuser de croire à, décréditer, déconsidérer

Discreditable, adj. déshonorant, honteux

Discreditably, adv. d'une manière déshonorante

Discreet, adj. discret, prudent

Discreetly, adv. discrètement, avec discrétion *or* prudence

Discreetness, s. discrétion, *f.*

Discrepancy, s. différence, *f.*

Discrepant, adj. différent

Discretion, s. discrétion, *f.*, sagesse, *f.*, volonté, *f.*

Discretional, Discretionary, adj. discrétionnaire

Discriminate, va.n. distinguer, faire des distinctions

Discriminately, Discriminatively, adv. avec discernement

Discriminating, Discriminative, adj. distinctif, sagace, judicieux

Discrimination, s. distinction, *f.*, jugement, *m.*, discernement, *m.*

Discrown, va. ôter la couronne à, détrôner

Discuss, va. agiter, discuter

Discussion, s. discussion, *f.*

Disdain, va. dédaigner, mépriser

Disdain, s. dédain, *m.*, mépris, *m.*

Disdainful, adj. de dédain, dédaigneux

Disdainfully, adv. dédaigneusement, avec dédain

Disease, s. maladie, *f.*, mal, *m.*

Diseased, adj. malade

Disembark, va.n. débarquer

Disembarkation, Disembarkment, s. débarquement, *m.*

Disembarrass, va. débarrasser

Disembody, va. priver de corps, désincorporer

Disembogue, va. décharger; — vn. se jeter, tomber, déboucher, se décharger, débouquer

Disemboguement, s. débouchement, *m.*, décharge, *f.*

Disembroil, va. débrouiller

Disenchant, va. désenchanter

Disencumber, va. débarrasser

Disencumbrance, s. débarras, *m.*, absence de tout ennui, *f.*

Disengage, va. dégager, débarrasser, délivrer

Disengagement, s. dégagement, *m.*, liberté, *f.*, loisir, *m.*

Disentangle, va. débrouiller, démêler, dégager, délivrer, affranchir, tirer d'embarras

Disenthral, va. affranchir

Disenthrone, va. détrôner

Disentitle, va. faire perdre son droit

Disentrance, va. réveiller

Disespouse, va. ne pas épouser

Disesteem, Disestimation, s. mésestime, *f.*, déconsidération, *f.*

Disesteem, va. mésestimer

Disfavour, s. défaveur, *f.*, disgrâce, *f.*, mauvais office, *m.*

Disfavour, va. décourager, voir avec défaveur

Disfiguration, Disfigurement, s. enlaidissement, *m.*, difformité, *f.*

Disfigure, va. défigurer, déparer

Disfranchise, va. priver de ses franchises, priver du droit électoral

Disfranchisement, s. privation de ses franchises, *f.*, privation du droit électoral, *f.*

Disgorge, va. vomir, dégorger, rejeter, rendre; — vn. rendre gorge

Disgrace, s. disgrâce, *f.*, défaveur, *f.*, honte, *f.*, opprobre, *m.*, déshonneur, *m.*

Disgrace, va. disgracier, couvrir de honte, déshonorer, avilir

Disgraceful, adj. honteux, déshonorant

Disgracefully, adv. honteusement

Disgracefulness, s. déshonneur, *m.*

Disguise, va. déguiser

Disguise, s. déguisement, *m.*, travestissement, *m.*

Disgust, s. dégoût, *m.*

Disgust, va. dégoûter

Disgusting, adj. dégoûtant, nauséabond, repoussant

Disgustingly, adv. d'une manière repoussante

Dish, s. plat, *m.*, mets, *m.*, (*agric.*) creux, *m.*, (*mines*) auge, *f.* — *-cloth*, — *-clout*, torchon, *m.* — *-cover*, cloche, *f.* — *-water*, eau de vaisselle, *f.*, lavure, *f.*

Dish, va. servir, creuser

Dishearten, va. abattre, décourager

Dishevel, va. décheveler; — vn. flotter en désordre

Dishful, s. platée, *f.*

Dishonest, adj. malhonnête, sans probité, déloyal, déshonorant

Dishonestly, adv. malhonnêtement, sans probité, déloyalement

Dishonesty, s. improbité, *f.*, malhonnêteté, *f.*, action malhonnête, *f.*

Dishonour, s. déshonneur, *m.*

Dishonour, va. déshonorer, (*bills*) laisser protester

Dishonourable, adj. déshonorant, peu honorable, sans honneur

Dishonourably, adv. d'une manière déshonorante, peu honorablement

Disinclination, s. aversion, *f.*, éloignement, *m.*
Disincline, va. éloigner (de)
Disincorporate, va. désincorporer
Disinfect, va. désinfecter
Disinfection, s. désinfection, *f.*
Disingenuous, adj. faux, tortueux, peu sincère, sans franchise, de mauvaise foi
Disingenuously, adv. sans franchise, sans sincérité, faussement
Disingenuousness, s. manque de franchise *or* de sincérité, *m.*, fausseté, *f.*
Disinherit, va. déshériter
Disinter, va. exhumer, déterrer, mettre au jour, révéler
Disinterested, adj. désintéressé
Disinterestedly, adv. avec désintéressement
Disinterestedness, s. désintéressement, *m.*
Disinterment, s. exhumation, *f.*
Disjoin, va. déjoindre, disjoindre, (*fig.*) désunir, séparer
Disjoint, va. disloquer, démettre, déboîter, (*take to pieces*) démonter, disjoindre, (*divide*) démembrer
Disjunction, s. séparation, *f.*
Disk, s. disque, *m.*, (*coin*) flan, *m.*
Dislike, s. antipathie, *f.*, aversion, *f.*, répugnance, *f.*, éloignement, *m.*, dégoût, *m.* *To take a — to*, prendre en aversion, prendre en grippe
Dislike, va. ne pas aimer, avoir de l'aversion *or* de l'éloignement pour
Dislocate, va. démettre, disloquer, déboîter
Dislocation, s. dislocation, *f.*
Dislodge, va.n. déloger, (*a stag*) débucher
Disloyal, adj. traître, rebelle, désaffectionné, déloyal
Disloyally, adv. traîtreusement, déloyalement, infidèlement
Disloyalty, s. trahison, *f.*, défection, *f.*, déloyauté, *f.*, infidélité, *f.*
Dismal, adj. lugubre, triste, sombre, morne, horrible, funeste
Dismally, adv. lugubrement, tristement, horriblement
Dismalness, s. tristesse, *f.*, aspect sombre, *m.*, horreur, *f.*
Dismantle, va. dépouiller, démantibuler, (*a fortress*) démanteler, (*nav.*) dégréer, désarmer
Dismast, va. démâter
Dismay, va. épouvanter, consterner, décourager
Dismay, s. épouvante, *f.*, consternation, *f.*, terreur, *f.*, effroi, *m.*
Dismember, va. démembrer
Dismemberment, s. démembrement, *m.*
Dismiss, va. renvoyer, congédier, laisser partir, (*a thought*) chasser, (*a public servant*) destituer
Dismissal, **Dismission**, s. renvoi, *m.*, congé, *m.*, destitution, *f.*, radiation, *f.*
Dismount, va. démonter, désarçonner; — vn. descendre de cheval, mettre pied à terre, baisser, descendre
Disobedience, s. désobéissance, *f.*
Disobedient, adj. désobéissant
Disobey, va. désobéir (à)
Disoblige, va. désobliger
Disobliging, adj. désobligeant
Disobligingly, adv. désobligeamment
Disobligingness, s. désobligeance, *f.*
Disorder, s. désordre, *m.*, dérangement, *m.*, maladie, *f.*, indisposition, *f.*
Disorder, va. mettre en désordre, troubler, déranger
Disordered, adj. désordonné, déréglé, irrégulier, malade
Disorderly, adj. sans ordre, en désordre, (*fig.*) désordonné, déréglé, tumultueux, turbulent
Disorderly, adv. sans ordre, en désordre
Disorganization, s. désorganisation, *f.*
Disorganize, va. désorganiser
Disown, va. désavouer, renier, renoncer
Disparage, va. dénigrer, (*an action*) déprécier, ravaler; déparer, gâter
Disparagement, s. dénigrement, *m.*, dépréciation, *f.*, déshonneur, *m.*, tort, *m.*
Disparagingly, adv. par dénigrement, d'un ton méprisant
Disparity, s. disparité, *f.*
Dispassionate, adj. impassible, calme, froid, rassis, de sens rassis
Dispassionately, adv. avec calme
Dispatch, s. *see* DESPATCH
Dispel, va. chasser, dissiper, disperser, écarter
Dispensary, s. dispensaire, *m.*, pharmacie, *f.*
Dispensation, s. dispensation, *f.*, volonté, *f.*, loi, *f.*, dispense, *f.*, pardon, *m.*
Dispensatory, s. dispensaire, *m.*
Dispensatory, adj. qui peut accorder des dispenses
Dispense, va. dispenser, départir, répandre, distribuer, (*justice*) administrer; — vn. dispenser, excuser, se dispenser, se passer
Disperse, va. disperser, dissiper, chasser, écarter; — vn. se disperser
Dispersion, s. dispersion, *f.*
Dispirit, va. décourager, abattre
Dispirited, adj. abattu, découragé
Dispiritedness, s. découragement, *m.*
Displace, va. déplacer, destituer, renverser
Displacing, s. déplacement, *m.*
Displant, va. déplanter, transplanter
Display, va. déployer, (*goods*) étaler, (*troops*) déployer; faire paraître, montrer, faire parade de; — vn. faire de l'étalage
Display, s. déploiement, *m.*, étalage, *m.*, spectacle, *m.*, parade, *f.*
Displease, va. déplaire (à), mécontenter, fâcher
Displeasing, adj. déplaisant
Displeasure, s. déplaisir, *m.*, mécontentement, *m.*, disgrâce, *f.*, courroux, *m.*
Disport, vn. — *oneself*, s'ébattre, folâtrer, se jouer
Disposable, adj. disponible
Disposal, s. disposition, *f.*, manière de disposer, *f.*, contrôle, *m.*
Dispose, va. disposer, arranger, distribuer, préparer, (*incline*) diriger, faire tourner. — *of*, vn. disposer de, vendre, se défaire de, se débarrasser de, employer, (*tickets*) placer
Disposer, s. dispensateur, *m.*, -trice, *f.*, maître, *m.*, arbitre, *m.*
Disposition, s. disposition, *f.*, arrangement, *m.*, distribution, *f.*, préparatif, *m.*, humeur, *f.*, naturel, *m.*, caractère, *m.*
Dispossess, va. déposséder, priver, (*law*) exproprier
Dispossession, s. dépossession, *f.*, (*law*) expropriation, *f.* — *for public purposes*, (*law*) expropriation pour cause d'utilité publique
Disproof, s. réfutation, *f.*
Disproportion, s. disproportion, *f.*
Disproportionate, adj. disproportionné
Disproportionately, adv. d'une manière disproportionnée, hors de toute proportion
Disprove, va. réfuter
Disputable, adj. disputable, contestable
Disputant, s. disputant, *m.*
Disputation, s. dispute, *f.*, argumentation, *f.*
Disputatious, adj. disputeur, chicaneur
Dispute, va.n. disputer
Dispute, s. dispute, *f.*, discussion, *f.*
Disqualification, s. incapacité (à), *f.*, inhabileté (à), *f.*
Disqualify, va. rendre incapable (de), rendre inhabile (à)
Disquiet, **Disquietness**, **Disquietude**, s. inquiétude, *f.*, trouble, *m.*
Disquiet, va. inquiéter
Disquisition, s. recherches, *f.pl.*, dissertation, *f.*
Disregard, s. négligence, *f.*, mépris, *m.*
Disregard, va. n'avoir pas égard (à), dédaigner, négliger, mépriser, faire peu de cas de
Disregardful, adj. négligent
Disrelish, s. dégoût, *m.*, déboire, *m.*
Disrelish, va. ne pas aimer, perdre le goût de
Disreputable, adj. de mauvaise réputation, décrié, peu honorable, honteux
Disreputably, adv. d'une manière peu honorable
Disrepute, **Disreputation**, s. mauvaise réputation, *f.*, discrédit, *m.*, déshonneur, *m.*
Disrespect, s. manque de respect, *m.*, insolence, *f.*, manque d'égards, *m.*, mépris, *m.*
Disrespectful, adj. peu respectueux, irrespectueux, sans respect, insolent
Disrespectfully, adv. sans respect, peu respectueusement
Disrobe, va. dépouiller
Disruption, s. rupture, *f.*
Dissatisfaction, s. mécontentement, *m.*, déplaisir, *m.*
Dissatisfactory, adj. peu satisfaisant
Dissatisfied, past part. peu satisfait, mécontent
Dissatisfy, va. mécontenter
Dissect, va. disséquer
Dissection, s. dissection, *f.*
Dissector, s. dissecteur, *m.*, anatomiste, *m.*
Dissemble, va.n. dissimuler, déguiser, feindre
Dissembler, s. fourbe, *m.*, dissimulé, *m.*, -e, *f.*, dissimulateur, *m.*
Dissembling, adj. dissimulé, de dissimulation
Dissemblingly, adv. en dissimulant
Disseminate, va. disséminer
Dissemination, s. dissémination, *f.*
Dissension, s. dissension, *f.*, zizanie, *f.*
Dissent, vn. différer d'opinion, être en dissentiment
Dissent, s. dissentiment, *m.*, dissidence, *f.*
Dissenter, s. dissident, *m.*, -e, *f.*
Dissentient, adj dissident, opposant
Dissertation, s. dissertation, *f.*
Dissever, va. séparer
Dissidence, s. dissidence, *f.*
Dissident, s.adj. dissident, -e
Dissimilar, adj. dissemblable (à), différent (de), dissimilaire

Dissimilarity, Dissimilitude, s. dissemblance, *f.*, dissimilitude, *f.*
Dissimulation, s. dissimulation, *f.*
Dissipate, va. dissiper ; — vn. se dissiper
Dissipation, s. dissipation, *f.*, distraction, *f.*
Dissoluble, Dissolvable, adj. dissoluble, soluble
Dissolute, adj. dissolu
Dissolutely, adv. dissolument
Dissoluteness, s. dissolution, *f.*
Dissolution, s. dissolution, *f.*, mort, *f.*
Dissolve, va. dissoudre, fondre, désunir, séparer ; — vn. se dissoudre, mourir, périr
Dissolvent, adj. s. dissolvant
Dissonance, s. dissonance, *f.*, discordance, *f.*
Dissonant, adj. dissonant, discordant, peu d'accord (avec), éloigné (de)
Dissuade, va. dissuader, déconseiller
Dissuasion, s. dissuasion, *f.*
Dissuasive, adj. s. qui dissuade, motif pour détourner, *m.*
Distaff, s. quenouille, *f.*
Distance, s. distance, *f.*, éloignement, *m.*, lointain, *m.*, réserve, *f.*, respect, *m.*, (*mus.*) intervalle, *m.* *In the* —, dans l'éloignement, dans le lointain
Distance, va. distancer, dépasser, éloigner
Distant, adj. éloigné, lointain, distant, (*fig.*) réservé, froid, hautain
Distantly, adv. à distance, de loin, (*fig.*) avec réserve, avec hauteur
Distaste, s. dégoût, *m.*
Distasteful, adj. désagréable, déplaisant. *To be — to,* déplaire à
Distastefulness, s. goût désagréable, *m.*, désagrément, *m.*
Distemper, s. maladie, *f.*, désordre, *m.*, dépravation, *f.*, (*paint.*) détrempe, *f.*
Distemper, va. altérer, troubler, (*paint.*) détremper
Distend, va. étendre, élargir, dilater, gonfler, enfler
Distention, s. distension, *f.*
Distich, s. distique, *m.*
Distil, vn. distiller, tomber goutte à goutte ; — va. distiller
Distillation, s. distillation, *f.*
Distiller, s. distillateur, *m.*
Distillery, s. distillation, *f.*, distillerie, *f.*
Distinct, adj distinct, distingué, marqué
Distinction, s. distinction, *f.*, division, *f.*, discernement, *m.*
Distinctive, adj. distinctif, doué de discernement
Distinctly, adv. distinctement
Distinctness, s. nature distincte, *f.*, netteté, *f.*, clarté, *f.*
Distinguish, va. diviser, distinguer
Distinguishable, adj. qu'on peut distinguer *or* reconnaître, reconnaissable
Distinguishing, adj. distinctif, servant à distinguer
Distort, va. contourner, tordre, défigurer, décomposer, altérer, (*facts*) dénaturer, torturer
Distortion, s. contorsion, *f.*, altération, *f.*, décomposition, *f.*, (*facts*) action de dénaturer
Distract, va. distraire, séparer, détourner l'attention de, tourmenter, troubler, rendre fou
Distracted, past part. adj. tourmenté, tiraillé, harcelé, éperdu, bouleversé, fou
Distractedly, adv. follement, à la folie, éperdûment
Distractedness, s. trouble, *m.*, folie, *f.*
Distraction, s. distraction, *f.*, tiraillement, *m.*, dissension, *f.*, trouble d'esprit, *m.*, désespoir, *m.*, folie, *f.*
Distracting, adj. capable de faire perdre l'esprit
Distrain, va. saisir
Distraint, s. saisie, *f.*
Distress, s. détresse, *f.*, désolation, *f.*, douleur, *f.*, affliction, *f.*, misère, *f.*, gêne, *f.*, (*law*) saisie, *f.*
Distress, va. affliger, désoler, embarrasser, (*law*) saisir
Distressed, past part. adj. dans la détresse, affligé, malheureux
Distribute, va. distribuer, répartir
Distributer, s. distributeur, *m.*, -trice, *f.*, répartiteur, *m.*
Distribution, s. distribution, *f.*, répartition, *f.*
Distributive, adj. distributif
District, s. district, *m.*, arrondissement, *m.*, région, *f.*
District, adj. de district
Distrust, va. se défier de, se méfier de, douter de
Distrust, s. défiance, *f.*, méfiance, *f.*, doute, *m.*, soupçon, *m.*
Distrustful, adj. défiant, méfiant, soupçonneux
Distrustfully, adv. avec défiance
Disturb, va. troubler, agiter, bouleverser, déranger
Disturbance, s. trouble, *m.*, agitation, *f.*, perturbation, *f.*, désordre, *m.*, émeute, *f.*, inquiétude, *f.*
Disturber, s. perturbateur, *m.*, -trice, *f.*
Disunion, s. désunion, *f.*
Disunite, va. désunir ; — vn. se désunir
Disuse, s. désuétude, *f.*
Disuse, va. cesser de se servir de, déshabituer
Ditch, s. fossé, *m.*
Ditch, vn. creuser un fossé ; — va. entourer d'un fossé
Ditto, s. adv. idem, *m.*, dit, *m.*, dite, *f.*, dits, *m.pl.*, dites, *f.pl.*
Ditty, s. chanson, *f.*, ballade, *f.*, lai, *m.*, chansonnette, *f.*
Diuretic, adj. diurétique
Diurnal, adj. journalier, quotidien, diurne
Divan, s. divan, *m.*
Dive, vn. plonger, se plonger, pénétrer, approfondir
Diver, s. plongeur, *m.*, (*bird*) plongeon, *m.*
Diverge, vn. diverger
Divergence, s. divergence, *f.*
Divergent, adj. divergent
Diverse, adj. divers
Diversely, adv. différemment, dans différentes directions
Diversification, s. diversité, *f.*, changement, *m.*
Diversify, va. diversifier, distinguer, (*colour*) nuancer
Diversion, s. diversion, *f.*, divertissement, *m.*, distraction, *f.*
Diversity, s. diversité, *f.*, variété, *f.*
Divert, va. divertir, détourner, distraire, écarter
Diverting, adj. divertissant
Divertingly, adv. d'une manière amusante
Divertisement, s. divertissement, *m.*
Divest, va. dépouiller
Divide, va. diviser, partager, séparer, (*fig.*) brouiller ; — vn. se partager, se diviser, se séparer, (*on a vote*) aller aux voix
Dividend, s. dividende, *m.*
Divider, s. celui, celle, ce qui divise, partage, etc. —*s*, pl. compas, *m.*
Divination, s. divination, *f.*
Divine, adj. divin
Divine, s. ecclésiastique, *m.*, théologien, *m.*
Divine, va.n. deviner, prédire, pressentir
Divinely, adv. divinement
Diviner, s. devin, *m.*, devineresse, *f.*, habile à deviner, *m.f.*, devineur, *m.*, -euse, *f.*
Diving, s. art, *m.*, métier du plongeur, *m.* — *-apparatus,* appareil de plongeur, *m.* — *-bell,* cloche de plongeur, *f.*
Divinity, s. divinité, *f.*, théologie, *f.*
Divisibility, Divisibleness, s. divisibilité, *f.*
Divisible, adj. divisible
Division, s. division, *f.* *Upon a —,* en allant aux voix
Divisor, s. diviseur, *m.*
Divorce, s. divorce, *m.*
Divorce, va.n. prononcer le divorce, se séparer (de), (*fig.*) séparer, arracher
Divulge, va. divulguer, proclamer
Dizziness, s. étourdissement, *m.*, vertiges, *m pl.*
Dizzy, adj. étourdi, vertigineux, qui donne des vertiges
Do, va. faire, finir, achever, (*service, &c.*) rendre, (*cook*) cuire, faire cuire. — *away* (*with*), enlever, éloigner, supprimer, détruire. — *for,* achever, (*pop.*) enfoncer, couler, faire son affaire (à), (*things*) faire l'affaire (de), aller (à). — *on,* mettre, endosser. — *over,* enduire. — *up,* refaire, réparer, (*parcels*) faire, empaqueter, emballer. — vn. faire, agir, se conduire, (*with,* avec) finir, en finir, se porter, aller, faire l'affaire, être, aller bien, être convenable, suffire, passer. — *by,* faire à, en agir avec. *To have to — with,* avoir affaire à. *To have done with,* en avoir fini avec, avoir rompu avec. *How — you —?* comment vous portez-vous ? — *without,* se passer de. *Help me, —,* aidez-moi, je vous en prie
Docile, adj. docile
Docility, s. docilité, *f.*
Dock, s. bassin, *m.*, (*court*) banc des prévenus, *m.*, (*bot.*) patience, *f.*, (*of the tail*) partie charnue, *f.* — *-master,* directeur de l'arsenal, *m.* — *-yard,* arsenal de marine, *m.* *Graving —, dry —,* bassin de construction. *Wet —,* darse, *f.* *Floating —,* bassin à flot, *m.*
Dock, va. (*to lop off*) écourter, rogner, introduire dans le bassin
Docket, s. abrégé, *m.*, étiquette, *f.*, (*law*) rôle des causes, *m.*
Docket, va. étiqueter, enregistrer sommairement
Doctor, s. docteur, *m.*, médecin, *m.*
Doctor, va. (*med.*) soigner, médicamenter, (*pop.*) droguer
Doctoral, adj. doctoral, de docteur
Doctrinal, adj. doctrinal, de doctrine
Doctrine, s. doctrine, *f.*, enseignement, *m.*, science, *f.*
Document, s. document, *m.*, pièce, *f.*, écrit, *m.*
Dodge, vn. faire des tours et des détours, s'esquiver, user d'artifice, biaiser ; — va. esquiver, suivre à la piste, épier
Dodge, s. détour, *m.*, tour, *m.*
Dodger, s. rusé, *m.*, biaiseur, *m.*
Doe, s. daine, *f.* — *-rabbit,* lapine, *f.*
Doer, s. auteur, *m.*, acteur, *m.*
Doff, va. ôter, se dépouiller (de)
Dog, s. chien, *m.*, (*person*) coquin, *m.*, gaillard, *m.*, farceur, *m.*, (*andiron*) chenet, *m.* *To go to the —s,* se perdre, s'en aller au diable.

Sad —*s*, mauvais sujets. —*-briar*, —*-rose*, églantier. —*-cheap*, pour rien. —*-day*, jour caniculaire. *In the* —*-days*, dans la canicule. —*'s-ear*, corne, *f.* *To* —*'s-ear*, faire des cornes à. —*'s-fennel*, —*'s-grass*, —*'s-wheat*, chiendent. —*-fancier*, marchand de chiens. —*-latin*, latin de cuisine. —*'s-meat*, viande de rebut

Dog, va. suivre, guetter

Doge, s. doge, *m.*

Dogged, adj. bourru, revêche, hargneux, opiniâtre

Doggedly, adj. d'un ton bourru, opiniâtrément

Doggedness, s. nature revêche, *f.*, ton bourru, *m.*, opiniâtreté, *f.*

Doggish, adj. de chien

Doggrel, adj. s. irrégulier, -ère, sans mesure

Dogma, s. dogme, *m.*

Dogmatic, Dogmatical, adj. dogmatique

Dogmatically, adv. dogmatiquement

Dogmatism, s. caractère *or* ton dogmatique, *m.*

Dogmatist, Dogmatizer, s. dogmatiste, *m.*

Dogmatize, vn. dogmatiser

Doily, s. nappe de toilette, *f.*, petite nappe, *f.*, dessous de lampe, de vase, etc., *m.*

Doing, s. action, *f.*, fait, *m.* —*s*, faits et gestes, *m.pl.*

Dole, s. distribution, *f.*, partage, *m.*, aumône, *f.*

Dole (out), va. distribuer avec parcimonie

Doleful, Dolesome, adj. piteux, triste, plaintif, lugubre, affligé

Dolefully, adv. piteusement, tristement

Dolefulness, s. air piteux, *m.*, tristesse, *f.*, ton plaintif, *m.*

Doll, s. poupée, *f.* *A* —*'s dinner*, dînette, *f.*

Dollar, s. dollar, *m.*

Dolphin, s. dauphin, *m.*

Dolt, s. butor, *m.*, sot, *m.*

Doltish, adj. stupide, sot

Domain, s. domaine, *m.*, empire, *m.*

Dome, s. dôme, *m.*, coupole, *f.*

Domestic, adj. domestique, de famille, (*pers.*) casanier, (*administ.*) intérieur

Domestic, s. domestique, *m.f.*

Domesticate, va. rendre casanier, (*animals*) apprivoiser

Domestication, s. vie de famille, *f.*, (*animals*) action d'apprivoiser, *f.*

Domicile, s. domicile, *m.*

Domiciliary, adj. domiciliaire

Dominant, adj. dominant, dominateur. — s. (*music*) dominante, *f.*

Domination, s. domination, *f.*

Domineer, va. dominer

Domineering, adj. tyrannique, impérieux

Dominical, adj. dominical

Dominican, s. dominicain, *m.*

Dominion, s. empire, *m.*, pouvoir, *m.*, autorité, *f.*, États, *m.pl.*

Domino, s. domino, *m.*

Don, s. seigneur, *m.*, (*pop.*) gros bonnet, *m.*

Don, va. mettre, se revêtir de

Donation, s. donation, *f.*, don, *m.*

Done, past part. of Do. —*brown*, (*fam.*) refait. —*for*, ruiné, perdu

Done! interj. tope là!

Donkey, s. âne, *m.*, baudet, *m.*

Donor, s. donateur, *m.*, -trice, *f.*

Doom, va. condamner, destiner

Doom, s. condamnation, *f.*, sentence, *f.*, jugement, *m.*, arrêt, *m.*, sort, *m.*, destin, *m.*

Doomsday, s. le jour du jugement. —*-book*, livre du cadastre d'Angleterre, *m.*

Door, s. porte, *f.* *With closed* —*s*, à portes closes, (*law*) à huis clos. *In* —, dans la maison, interne. *Out* —, hors de la maison, externe. *Out-* —*clerk*, commis qui fait la place. *To kick, to turn out of* —*s*, jeter, mettre à la porte. *To keep within* —*s*, garder la maison. *To see, to show to the* —, reconduire, conduire à la porte. *To lay a thing at the* — *of*, (*fig.*) imputer quelque chose à. —*-case*, —*-frame*, châssis de porte. —*-keeper*, portier, *m.*, concierge, *m.*, gardien, *m.* —*-nail*, clou de marteau, *m.* —*-post*, jambage, *m.*, montant, dormant de porte, *m.* —*-sill*, seuil de la porte, *m.* —*-stead*, baie de porte, *f.* —*-stone*, pas de la porte, *m.* —*-way*, porte, entrée de la porte, *f.*

Doric, adj. dorique

Dormant, adj. dormant, endormi, qui dort, tombé en désuétude, commanditaire. *To lie* —, dormir, sommeiller, être tombé en désuétude

Dormer. —*-window*, lucarne, *f.*

Dormitory, s. dortoir, *m.*

Dormouse, s. loir, *m.*

Dorsal, adj. dorsal

Dose, s. dose, *f.*, drogue, *f.*

Dose, va. diviser en doses, (*fig.*) droguer

Dot, s. point, *m.*

Dot, va.n. mettre un point *or* des points sur, tacheter, nuancer, (*art*) pointer, pointiller

Dotage, s. seconde enfance, *f.*, radotage, *m.*, engouement, *m.*

Dotard, s. vieillard en enfance, *m.*, vieux radoteur, *m.*

Dotation, s. dotation, *f.*

Dote, vn. radoter, raffoler (de), aimer éperdûment, être engoué (de)

Dotingly, adv. éperdûment

Double, adj. adv. double (de), deux fois autant (que), (*fig.*) perfide. — *or quits*, quitte ou double. — *quick time*, (au) pas redoublé *or* accéléré. —*-barrelled gun*, fusil à deux coups. —*-bottomed*, à deux fonds. —*-breasted*, croisé. *To* —*-lock*, fermer à double tour

Double, s. double, *m.*, pendant, *m.*

Double, va. doubler, porter au double, être le double de, plier; — vn. doubler, s'augmenter du double, faire des détours, (*fig.*) user d'artifice

Doubloon, s. doublon, *m.*

Doubly, adv. doublement, deux fois, (*fig.*) avec duplicité

Doubt, vn. douter, hésiter, soupçonner fort; — va. se méfier de, douter de, ne pas croire

Doubt, s. doute, *m.*, soupçon, *m.*, méfiance, *f.*, crainte, *f.* *No* —, sans doute. *No* — *but that*, sans doute que

Doubtful, adj. douteux, incertain, indécis

Doubtfully, adv. avec doute, d'une manière douteuse, avec crainte, obscurément

Doubtfulness, s. doute, *m.*, ambiguïté, *f.*

Doubtless, adj. indubitable, sans crainte. — adv. sans doute, indubitablement

Douceur, s. douceur, *f.*

Dough, s. pâte, *f.*

Doughty, adj. preux, vaillant

Doughy, adj. pâteux, mou

Douse, va. plonger, (*nav.*) larguer tout

Dove, s. colombe, *f.*, pigeon, *m.* —*-coloured*, couleur gorge-de-pigeon, isabelle. —*-cot*, —*-house*, colombier, *m.*

Dovetail, s. queue d'aronde, *f.*

Dovetail, va. assembler en queue d'aronde

Dowager, s. adj. douairière, *f.*

Dowdy, s. adj. femme gauche et mise sans goût. *To look quite* —, être mal fagotée

Dower, s. don, *m.*, dot, *f.*, douaire, *m.*

Down, s. duvet, *m.*, coton, *m.*, poil follet, *m.* —*-bed*, lit de plume. —*s*, pl. dunes, *f.pl.*; bas, *m.*

Down, prep. en bas de, vers le bas de. — *to*, jusqu'à. — *the stream*, en aval

Down, adv. en bas, vers le bas, à terre, (*fig.*) comptant, en espèces sonnantes, (*astron.*) couché, sous l'horizon, (*clock*) pas monté. — *below*, en bas. —*-stroke*, descente, *f.*

Down! interj. — *with* . . . ! à bas . . . !

Down, va. couvrir *or* garnir de duvet

Downcast, adj. baissé vers la terre, abattu

Downfall, s. chûte, *f.*, ruine, *f.*, décadence, *f.*

Downright, adj. véritable, vrai, complet, franc, fieffé, sincère, droit

Downright, adv. tout droit, complètement, franchement, tout de bon

Downward, adj. vers le bas, de haut en bas, qui descend, descendant, incliné

Downward, Downwards, adv. vers le bas, en bas, vers la terre, (*nav.*) en aval

Downy, adj. de duvet, convert de duvet, cotonneux, (*fig.*) fin, léger

Dowry, s. *see* Dower

Doze, vn. dormir, sommeiller, s'assoupir, être assoupi

Doze, s. somme, *m.*, assoupissement, *m.*

Dozen, s. douzaine, *m.* *A round* —, treize à la douzaine

Doziness, s. assoupissement, *m.*

Drab, s. souillon, *f.*, coureuse, *f.*, (*colour*) brun

Drachm, s. drachme, *f.*

Draft, s. (*com.*) traite, *f.*, (*mil.*) détachement, *m.*

Draft, va. (*mil.*) détacher, expédier, (*fig.*) faire sortir, (*writing*) rédiger, (*drawing*) dessiner

Drag, va. traîner, tirer, (*locom.*) remorquer, (*water*) draguer, (*fishing*) pêcher à la drague; — vn traîner à terre, se traîner, tirer la drague, (*nav.*) chasser

Drag, s. (*net*) drague, *f.*, traîneau, *m.*, croc, *m.*, crochet, *m.*, (*carriage*) diable, *m.*, (*for carriages*) sabot, *m.*, chaîne, *f.*, enrayure, *f.*, (*railway*) frein, *m.*, (*agric.*) herse, *f.* —*-net*, seine, *f.* —*-hook*, croc, *m.* *To put the* — *on*, enrayer. —*-bar*, —*-bolt*, barre, boulon d'attelage

Draggle, va. traîner à terre; — vn. se crotter

Dragoman, s. dragoman, *m.*

Dragon, s. dragon, *m.* —*-fly*, demoiselle, *f.*, libellule, *f.*

Dragoon, s. dragon, *m.*

Drain, va. faire écouler, faire égoutter, vider, (*exhaust*) épuiser, (*land*) saigner, (*mines*) assécher, (*agric.*) drainer; — vn. égoutter, s'égoutter, s'écouler

Drain, s. égout, *m.*, canal, *m.*, rigole, *f.*, tranchée, *f.*, fossé d'écoulement, *m.*

Drainage, s. épuisement, *m.*, écoulement, *m.*, dessèchement, *m.*, drainage, *m.*

Drake, s. canard, *m.*

Dram, s. drachme, *f.*, gros, *m.*, goutte, *f.*, liqueur forte, *f.*, spiritueux, *m.pl.*

Drama, s. drame, *m.*, pièce de théâtre, *f.*, littérature dramatique, *f.*

Dramatic, adj. dramatique

Dramatically, adv. d'une manière dramatique

Dramatist, s. poète or auteur dramatique, *m.*

Dramatize, va. arranger pour la scène

Draper, s. drapier, *m.*

Drapery, s. draperie, *f.*

Draught, s. tirage, *m.*, trait, *m.*, action de tirer, *m.*, (*drink*) breuvage, *m.*, boisson, *f.*, (*med.*) potion, *f.*, (*of wind*) courant d'air, *m.*, deux airs, *m.pl.*, vent coulis, *m.*, (*drawing*) plan, *m.*, dessin, *m.*, tracé, *m.*, esquisse, *f.*, (*letters*) brouillon, *m.*, projet, *m.*, (*fishing*) coup de filet, *m.*, (*game*) jeu de dames, *m.*, (*chimney*) tirage, *m.* — *-engine*, pompe d'épuisement, *f.* — *-horse*, cheval de trait. — *-net*, seine, *f.* — *-board*, damier, *m.*

Draughtsman, s. dessinateur, *m.*

Draw, va. tirer, traîner, attirer, entraîner, (*sword*) dégainer, (*air*) respirer, aspirer, humer, (*take out*) retirer, sortir, extraire, (*water*) puiser, (*prize*) gagner, (*extend*) allonger, étirer, (*sketch*) dessiner, tracer, représenter, dépeindre, (*comparison*) faire, (*law*) rédiger, dresser, (*com.*) tirer, faire *or* fournir, (*poultry*) vider. *To — about*, entraîner çà et là. *To — along*, tirer, traîner. *To — aside*, tirer à l'écart, prendre à part. *To — away*, retirer, entraîner, emmener. *To — back*, retirer, tirer en arrière. *To — down*, baisser, tirer, faire descendre. *To — forth*, faire avancer, produire, susciter. *To — in*, faire entrer, rentrer, se contracter, se rétrécir, aspirer, humer. *To — near*, approcher, s'approcher de. *To — off*, retirer, tirer, ôter, enlever, éloigner, (*liquids*) tirer à clair. *To — on*, tirer, mettre, faire avancer. *To — out*, faire sortir, tirer dehors, produire, tirer, traîner en longueur, étirer, étendre. *To — over*, attirer, gagner. *To — round*, attirer autour de, s'assembler autour de. *To — up*, élever, faire monter, (*a bill, &c.*) rédiger, dresser, (*carriages*) arrêter. *To — oneself up*, se redresser de toute sa hauteur. — vn. tirer, se contracter, se rétrécir, dégainer, dessiner, (*med.*) suppurer, (*tea, &c.*) infuser, (*com.*) tirer. *To — back*, reculer, hésiter. *To — near or nigh*, s'approcher. *To — off*, se retirer, battre en retraite. *To — on*, s'avancer, arriver, approcher. *To — together*, s'assembler, se réunir, s'accorder. *To — up*, s'approcher, (*carriage*) s'arrêter, (*mil.*) se ranger en bataille

Drawback, s. désavantage, *m.*, mécompte, *m.*, contre-temps, *m.*

Drawbridge, s. pont-levis, *m.*, pont tournant, *m.*

Drawer, s. tireur, *m.*, tiroir, *m.* —*s*, caleçon, *m.* *A pair of flannel —s*, un caleçon de flanelle

Drawing, s. tirage, *m.*, action de tirer, *m.*, dessin, *m.*, (*hunt*) battue, *f.* *Chalk —*, pastel, *m.* — *-pen*, tire-ligne, *m.* — *-up*, rédaction, *f.*

Drawing-room, s. salon, *m.*, (*at court*) réception, *f.* *To hold a —*, recevoir

Drawl, vn. parler d'une voix traînante; — va. dire d'une voix traînante

Drawling, adj. traînant, prolixe

Drawn, adj. égal, nul. — *-battle*, bataille indécise. — *-game*, partie nulle

Draw-net, s. seine, *f.*

Draw-plate, s. filière, *f.*

Dray, s. — *-cart*, camion, *m.*, haquet, *m.*

Drayman, s. camionneur, *m.*, haquetier, *m.*

Dread, s. terreur, *f.*, effroi, *m.*, épouvante, *f.* — adj. redoutable

Dread, va.n. redouter, craindre

Dreadful, adj. terrible, épouvantable

Dreadfully, adv. terriblement

Dreadfulness, s. nature terrible, *f.*

Dreadnought, s. drap fort, *m.*, paletot-pilote, *m.*

Dream, s. rêve, *m.*, songe, *m.*, chimère, *f.*

Dream, vn.a. rêver, songer (à), imaginer

Dreamer, s. rêveur, *m.*, songeur, *m.*, songe-creux, *m.*, visionnaire, *m.f.*

Dreaminess, s. rêverie, *f.*

Dreamingly, adv. comme dans un rêve

Dreamy, adj. rêveur, songeur, rempli de rêves

Dreary, adj. triste, morne, lugubre, sombre

Drearily, adv. tristement

Dreariness, s. tristesse, *f.*, aspect morne, *m.*

Dredge, s. drague, *f.*

Dredge, va. draguer, (*with flour, sugar, &c.*) saupoudrer. *Dredging-machine*, drague, *f.*, dragueur, *m.* — *for*, pêcher à la drague. — *out*, retirer

Dredger, s. dragueur, *m.*

Dregs, s.pl. lie, *f.sing.*

Drench, va. tremper, mouiller

Dress, va. soigner, mettre en ordre, (*vine*) tailler, (*field*) donner une façon à, (*wound*) panser, (*cook*) apprêter, accommoder, (*salad*) assaisonner, (*stuffs*) apprêter, habiller, vêtir, revêtir, (*hair*) coiffer, (*ship*) pavoiser, (*mil.*) aligner. —*ed*, en toilette. *Full- —ed*, en grande toilette, en grande tenue. — vn. s'habiller, se mettre, faire de la toilette, (*mil.*) s'aligner

Dress, s. toilette, *f.*, mise, *f.*, parure, *f.*, habits, *m.pl.*, vêtements, *m.pl.*, costume, *m.*, tenue, *f.*, uniforme, *f.* — *-maker*, couturière en robes. *A high —*, une robe montante. *A low —*, une robe décolletée. *In full —*, en grande toilette, (*mil.*) en grande tenue, en grand costume

Dresser, s. habilleur, *m.*, -euse, *f.*, (*stuff*) apprêteur, *m.*, (*side-board*) dressoir, *m.*, buffet, *f.*

Dressing, s. habillement, *m.*, toilette, *f.*, apprêt, *m.*, assaisonnement, *m.*, (*wounds*) pansement, *m.*, appareil, *m.*, (*agric.*) façon, *f.* — *-case*, nécessaire de toilette, *m.* — *-gown*, peignoir, *m.* — *-glass*, — *-table*, miroir, *m.*, table de toilette, *f.*

Dressy, adj. luxueux dans sa mise, coquette

Dribble, vn. tomber goutte à goutte; — va. laisser tomber goutte à goutte

Dribbling, adj. petit, faible, chétif

Driblet, s. bribe, *f.*, petite somme, *f.*

Drift, s. (*snow*) monceau, *m.*, (*floating*) objet flottant, *m.*, (*impetus*) force, *f.*, violence, *f.*, cours, *m.*, direction, *f.*, impulsion, *f.*, (*fig.*) but, *m.*, tendance, *f.*, (*mines*) galerie, *f.*, (*nav.*) dérive, *f.*, (*geol.*) dépôt de diluvion, *m.* *What is the — of all this?* où aboutit tout cela?

Drift, adj. mobile, flottant. — *-way*, accotement, *m.*, passage pour le bétail, *m.*, (*nav.*) dérive, *f.*, (*mines*) galerie, *f.* — *-wind*, vent violent, *m.* — *-wood*, bois flottant, *m.*

Drift, va. pousser, chasser, amonceler; — vn. voguer, flotter être poussé, (*nav.*) dériver

Driftless, adj. sans but

Drill, va. percer, forer, (*mil.*) exercer, faire manœuvrer, (*to teach*) dresser, instruire, former, (*agric.*) semer par sillons; — vn. être à l'exercice, semer par sillons, manœuvrer

Drill, s. foret, *m.*, mèche, *f.*, (*mil.*) exercice, *m.*, manœuvre, *f.*, (*agric.*) sillon, *m.*, semoir, *m.*, (*cloth*) coutil, *m.* — *-bow*, archet, *m.* — *-plate*, plastron, *m.* — *-sergeant*, sergent instructeur, *m.* — *-plough*, semoir, *m.*

Drilling, s. forage, *m.*, (*mil.*) exercice, *m.*, semis par sillons, *m.*, grosse cotonnade, *f.*

Drink, vn.a. s'abreuver, boire. *To — deep, hard*, boire sec, dur. *To — like a piper*, boire comme un trou

Drink, s. boisson, *f.*, breuvage, *m.* — *-money*, un pourboire. — *-offering*, libation, *f.*

Drinkable, adj. potable, buvable

Drinker, s. buveur, *m.* *Hard —*, buveur intrépide

Drinking, adj. de boire, buveur. — *-bout*, partie de débauche, *f.* — *-house*, cabaret, *m.* — *-song*, chanson à boire

Drip, vn. tomber goutte à goutte, dégoutter

Drip, s. goutte, *f.* — or — *-stone*, larmier, *m.*

Dripping, s. eau qui tombe, *m.*, goutte, *f.*, graisse, *f.* — *-pan*, lèchefrite, *f.*

Drive, va. pousser, chasser, (*a nail*) enfoncer, (*from*) chasser (de), éloigner, (*a carriage*) conduire, mener, forcer, contraindre, (*mad*) rendre, (*bargain*) faire, (*nav.*) chasser, pousser à la dérive. — *about*, — *along*, chasser, pousser, conduire, parcourir. — *away*, chasser, disperser, écarter. — *back*, repousser, refouler, faire reculer, reconduire. — *by*, passer. — *down*, faire descendre. — *in*, enfoncer, planter, refouler. — *off*, chasser, repousser. — *on*, pousser, entraîner. — *out*, mener promener. — *over*, passer sur le corps de, renverser. — *through*, enfoncer, chasser, traverser. — vn. s'avancer, être poussé *or* chassé, courir (sur, à), aller (à), conduire, en vouloir venir

Drive, s. promenade, *f.*, course, *f.*, grande avenue, *f.*

Drivel, vn. baver, (*fig.*) radoter

Drivel, s. bave, *f.*, (*fig.*) radoteur, *m.*

Driveller, s. radoteur, *m.*, idiot, *m.*

Drivelling, adj. baveux, idiot, qui radote

Driver, s. celui, celle qui conduit, cocher, *m.*, voiturier, *m.*, charretier, *m.*, conducteur, *m.*, surveillant, *m.*, (*mech.*) moteur, *m.*, force motrice, *f.*

Driving, adj. moteur, -trice

Drizzle, vn. bruiner, brouillasser, distiller. *Drizzling rain*, bruine, *f.*

Drizzle, s. bruine, *f.*, pluie fine, *f.*

Drizzly, adj. de bruine, humide, qui tombe en pluie fine

Droll, s. adj. bouffon, *m.*, comique

Drollery, s. drôlerie, *f.*, bouffonnerie, *f.*

Dromedary, s. dromadaire, *m.*

Drone, s. (*insect*) bourdon, *m.*, frélon, *m.*, (*idler*) fainéant, *m.*, (*noise*) bourdonnement, *m.*, (*mus.*) bourdon, *m.*

Drone, va. bourdonner, (*fig.*) fainéanter, lire d'une voix endormante

Droning, s. bourdonnement, *m.*

Droop, vn. languir, se pencher, se faner, s'affaisser, se décourager

Drooping, s. affaissement, *m.*, langueur, *f.*

Droopingly, adv. langu[illegible]samment

Drop, s. goutte, *f.*, (*earring*) pendant, *m.*, pendeloque, *f.*, boucle d'oreille, *f.*, (*scaffold*) trappe, *f.*, (*sweet*) pastille, *f.* — *-scene*, rideau d'entr'acte, *m.*

Drop, va. laisser tomber, lâcher, laisser échapper, (*tears*) verser, (*anchor*) jeter, (*curtain*) baisser, abandonner, renoncer à, cesser. *Let us — the subject, pray*, brisons-là, s'il vous plaît. *— in*, (*action*) glisser, introduire. — vn. tomber, se laisser tomber, tomber goutte à goutte. *To — down*, se laisser tomber or glisser. *To — in*, (*person*) entrer pour un instant, (*upon*) venir surprendre. *To — off*, tomber, disparaître, s'en aller

Droplet, s. gouttelette, *f.*

Dropping, s. goutte, *f.*, eau qui tombe, *f.*

Dropsical, adj. hydropique

Dropsy, s. hydropisie, *f.*

Dross, s. scorie, *f.*, rouille, *f.*, rebut, *m.*

Drought, s. sécheresse, *f.*, aridité, *f.*

Drove, s. troupeau, *m.*

Drover, s. bouvier, *m.*, conducteur de bestiaux, *m.*

Drown, va. noyer, submerger, (*fig.*) couvrir, étouffer, dominer, éclipser; — vn. se noyer

Drowning, s. l'action de se noyer, *f.*

Drowsily, adv. comme endormi

Drowsiness, s. assoupissement, *m.*, sommeil, *m.*, envie de dormir, *f.*

Drowsy, adj. assoupi, endormi, endormant, soporifique

Drubbing, s. volée, *f.*

Drudge, vn. travailler péniblement, se fatiguer

Drudge, s. esclave, *m.*, souffre-douleur, *m.*

Drudgery, s. gros ouvrages, *m.pl.*, travaux pénibles, *m.pl.*, corvée, *f.*

Drug, s. drogue, *f.*, (*com.*) marchandise de rebut, *f.*

Drug, va. droguer, médicamenter

Drugget, s. droguet, *m.*

Druggist, s. droguiste, *m.*

Druid, s. druide, *m.*

Druidess, s. druidesse, *f.*

Druidical, adj. druidique, des druides

Druidism, s. druidisme, *m.*

Drum, s. tambour, *m.*, caisse, *f.*, tympan, *m.* *To cry by beat of —*, tambouriner. *—-stick*, baguette de tambour, *f.*, (*in fowls*) pilon, *m.*

Drum, vn. battre du tambour, tambouriner

Drummer, s. tambour, *m.*

Drunk, adj. ivre. *Dead —*, ivre mort

Drunkard, s. ivrogne, *m.*

Drunkenness, s. ivresse, *f.*, ivrognerie, *f.*

Dry, adj. sec, à sec, desséché, altéré, aride. *—-salter*, marchand de produits chimiques

Dry, va. sécher, faire sécher, dessécher; — vn. se sécher, se dessécher

Dryad, s. dryade, *f.*

Drying, s. action de sécher, *f.*, dessication, *f.* *—-room, —-place, —-ground*, séchoir, *m.*

Dryly, adv. sèchement

Dryness, s. sécheresse, *f.*, aridité, *f.*

Dual, adj. s. duel, *m.*

Dub, va. armer, qualifier; — vn. battre

Dub, s. coup, *m.*

Dubious, adj. incertain, indécis, douteux

Dubiously, adv. avec doute

Dubiousness, s. incertitude, *f.*

Ducal, adj. ducal, de duc

Ducat, s. ducat, *m.*

Duchess, s. duchesse, *f.*

Duchy, s. duché, *m.*

Duck, s. canard, *m.*, cane, *f.*, (*bow*) mouvement de tête, *m.*, courbette, *f.*, (*endearment*) chou, *m.*, bichon, *m.*, poulet, *m.*, (*linen*) toile, *f.*, coutil, *m.*, pantalon blanc, *m.sing.* *Young —*, caneton, *m.* *—s and drakes*, (*fig.*) ricochets. *—-gun*, canardière, *f.* *—-legged*, qui marche comme une cane

Duck, vn. plonger, s'enfoncer, faire une courbette; — va. plonger, faire faire le plongeon (à)

Ducking, s. plongeon, *m.*, bain, *m.*, (*bow*) courbette, *f.*

Duckling, s. caneton, *m.*

Ductileness, Ductility, s. ductilité, *f.*

Dudgeon, s. colère, *f.* *To be in high —*, être fort en colère

Due, adj. dû, qu'on doit, mérité, juste, qui doit être arrivé, voulu, exact, occasionné (par), causé (par). *With all — deference*, sauf le respect que je vous dois. *To be —, to become —, to fall —*, échoir. *When —*, à l'échéance

Due, s. dû, *m.*, ce qu'on doit à, *m.*, impôt, *m.*

Duel, s. duel, *m.*

Duelling, s. duel, *m.* — adj. de duel

Duellist, s. duelliste, *m.*

Duenna, s. duègne, *f.*

Duet, s. duo, *m.*

Duffer, s. imbécile, *m.*

Dug, s. mamelle, *f.*, sein, *f.*, (*cow*) pis, *m.*

Duke, s. duc, *m.*

Dukedom, s. duché, *m.*

Dulcet, s. doux, suave

Dull, adj. stupide, lourd, lent, hébété, (*senses*) émoussé, (*hearing*) dur, (*colour*) terne, peu brillant, (*sound*) sourd, (*sad*) triste, ennuyeux, ennuyé, (*com.*) calme, plat, mort

Dull, va. hébéter, émousser, lasser, amortir, ternir, attrister

Dullard, s. lourdaud, *m.*, lourd, sans intelligence

Dully, adv. sottement, sourdement

Dulness, s. stupidité, *f.*, lenteur, *f.*, sottise, *f.*, difficulté, *m.*, fil émoussé, *m.*, peu d'éclat, *m.*, tristesse, *f.*, ennui, *m.*, assoupissement, *m.*

Duly, adv. dûment, exactement, convenablement

Dumb, adj. muet, -te. *—show*, scène muette, pantomime. *—-waiter*, (*table*) servante, *f.*

Dumbness, s. mutisme, *m.*, silence, *m.*

Dumfound, va. confondre, abasourdir

Dummy, s. muet, *m.*, (*whist*) le mort. *To play —*, faire le mort

Dump, s. tristesse, *f.* *To be in the —s*, être triste comme un bonnet de nuit

Dumpish, adj. triste

Dumpishness, s. tristesse, *f.*

Dumpy, adj. triste, courtaud, -e, trapu, gros et court

Dun, adj. brun, de couleur foncée, (*horse*) bai

Dun, s. créancier, *m.*, réclamation, *f.*

Dun, va. importuner, (*fish*) saler

Dunce, s. âne, *m.*, cancre, *m.*, sot, *m.* *—'s cap*, bonnet d'âne, *m.*

Duncery, s. bêtise, *f.*

Dunderhead, s. buse, *f.*, imbécile, *m.*

Dung, s. fumier, *m.*, crotte, *f.*, (*horse*) crottin, *m.* *—-cart*, tombereau, *m.* *—-fork*, fourche, *f.* *—-yard*, cour de ferme, *f.*

Dung, va. fumer

Dungeon, s. cachot, *m.*

Dunghill, s. fumier, *m.*

Dunning, s. importunité, *f.*

Duo, s. duo, *m.*

Duodecimal, s. adj. duodécimal

Duodecimo, s. in-12, *m.*

Dupe, s. dupe, *m.*

Dupe, va. duper

Dupery, s. duperie, *f.*

Duplicate, s. double, *m.*, duplicata, *m.*, (*pawn-broker*) reconnaissance, *f.*

Duplication, s. duplication, *f.*, pli, *m.*

Duplicity, s. duplicité, *f.*

Durability, s. durée, *f.*, solidité, *f.*

Durably, adv. d'une manière durable

Durance, s. captivité, *f.* *In — vile*, dans un vil cachot

Duration, s. durée, *f.*

During, prep pendant, dans, durant

Dusk, adj. obscur, sombre

Dusk, s. crépuscule, *m.*, brune, *f.*, obscurité, *f.*

Duskiness, s. obscurité, *f.*, couleur sombre, *f.*

Duskish, adj. sombre, foncé, tirant sur le noir

Duskishly, adv. obscurément

Dusky, adj. sombre

Dust, s. poussière, *f.*, poudre, *f.* *—-cart*, tombereau, *m.* *—-brush*, vergette, *f.* *—-hole*, trou aux ordures, *m.* *—-pan*, seau aux ordures, *m.* *To beat the — out of*, épousseter

Dust, va. épousseter, essuyer

Duster, s. torch[...] *horses*) épousset[...]

Dustiness, s. [...] état poudreux, *m*[...]

Dustman, s. b[...]

Dusty, adj. couv[...] sière, poudreux. [...] ramasser de la [...] couvrir de poussi[...]

Duteousness [...] FULNESS

Dutied, adj. [...] droits et impositi[...]

Dutiful, Dut[...] obéissant, soum[...] tueux

Dutifully, ad[...] mission

Dutifulness, [...] sance, *f.*, soumis[...] férence, *f.*, (*thin*[...] respectueux, *m.*

Duty, s. devoir, [...] *m.pl.*, hommages, [...] *m.*, garde, *f.* *I*[...] respect pour. *T*[...] de service, être [...] (*eccles.*) officier. [...] *off —*, être, n'[...] service or de gar[...] *one's — to*, prése[...] mages à. *To ret*[...] —, rentrer dan[...] *As in — bound*, [...] —, comme c'est d[...] *— free*, sans dro[...]

Duumvir, s. [...]

Duumvirate [...] virat, *m.*

Dwale, s. (*her*[...] noire, *f.*, bellado[...]

Dwarf, adj. [...] naine, *f.*

Dwarf, va. rab[...] tisser

Dwarfish, a[...] nain, petit, rabo[...]

Dwarfishly, [...]

Dwarfishne[...] tesse, *f.*, taille [...]

Dwell, vn. d[...] sider, habiter, ([...] tendre, appuyer, [...]

Dweller, s. h[...] -e, *f.*

Dwelling, s. [...] *f.*, demeure, *f.*, [...] *—-house*, mai[...] *-place*, lieu de d[...]

Dwindle, vn. [...] moindrir, se réd[...]

Dye, s. teintur[...] tinctoriale, *f.*, t[...] leur, *f.*, nuance, [...] teint solide. *Gol*[...] doré. *—-house* [...] teinturerie, *f.* — [...] tinctoriale, *f.* [...] de teinture, *m.*

Dye, va. teindr[...]

Dyeing, s. tei[...]

Dyer, s. teintu[...]

Dynamic, [...]cal, adj. dyna[...]

Dynamics, [...] mique, *f.*

Dynastic, ad[...]

Dynasty, s. d[...]

Dysenteric, [...] terique, (*pers.*) dyssenterie

Dysentery, s [...] *f.*

Dyspepsia, s [...]

E

E, E, e, (*mus.*) mi, *m.*
Each, adj. pron. chaque, chacun, *m.*, chacune, *f.* — *other*, l'un l'autre
Eager, adj. ardent, empressé, impatient, avide, fort désireux
Eagerly, adv. ardemment, avec empressement, vivement, avec impatience
Eagerness, s. ardeur, *f.*, empressement, *m.*, vivacité, *f.*, impatience, *f.*
Eagle, s. aigle, *m.* *Young* —, aiglon, *m.* — *-eyed*, — *-sighted*, aux yeux d'aigle
Eaglet, s. aiglon, *m.*
Ear, s. oreille, *f.*, (*handle*) anse, *f.*, (*corn*) épi. *To set people by the —s*, brouiller les gens. — *-wax*, cire des oreilles, *f.*, cérumen, *m.* — *-witness*, témoin auriculaire, *m.* — *-lap*, lobe de l'oreille, *m.* — *-ring*, boucle d'oreilles, *f.* — *-trumpet*, cornet acoustique, *m.*
Ear, vn. épier, monter en épi
. . . **-Eared,** past part. aux . . . oreilles
Earl, s. comte, *m.*
Earldom, s. comté, *m.*
Earless, adj. sans oreille
Earliness, s. diligence, *f.*, état avancé, *m.*
Early, adj. premier, ancien, précoce, hâtif, prématuré, de bonne heure, matinal, matineux. — *-rising*, action de se lever matin, *f.*
Early, adv. de bonne heure, matin
Earn, va. gagner, mériter
Earnest, adj. ardent, empressé, chaleureux, sérieux, sincère, attentif
Earnest, s. sérieux, *m.*, tout de bon, *m.*, gage, *m.*, (*money*) arrhes, *m.pl.*, denier à Dieu, *m.*, (*foretaste*) avant-goût, *m.*
Earnestly, adv. avec ardeur, instamment, sérieusement, fixement
Earnestness, s. ardeur, *f.*, empressement, *m.*, chaleur, *f.*
Earning, s. action de gagner, *f.*; —*s*, pl. gages, *m.pl.*, salaire, *m.*, gains, *m.pl.*
Earth, s. terre, *f.*, sol, *m.*, enveloppe, *f.*, (*fox-hole*) terrier, *m.* — *-bank*, tertre, *m.* — *-born*, vil, de basse naissance. — *-slip*, éboulement, *m.* — *-work*, terrassement, *m.*, travaux de terrassement, *m.pl.* — *-worm*, ver de terre, *m.*, (*miser*) grippe-sou, *m.*
Earth, va. enfouir, enterrer, couvrir de terre; — vn. se terrer
Earthen, adj. de terre, en terre
Earthenware, s. poterie, *f.*, faïence, *f.*
Earthiness, s. nature terrestre, *f.*, grossièreté, *f.*
Earthly, adj. terrestre, d'ici-bas, mondain, grossier, matériel
Earthquake, s. tremblement de terre, *m.*
Earthward, adj. vers la terre
Earthy, adj. terreux, terrestre
Earwig, s. perce-oreille, *m.*
Ease, s. aise, *f.*, aisance, *f.*, bien-être, *m.*, commodité, *f.*, paix, *f.*
Ease, va. alléger, délivrer, soulager, apaiser
Easel, s. chevalet, *m.*
Easily, adv. facilement, aisément
Easiness, s. facilité, *f.*, aisance, *f.*, douceur, *f.*
East, s. est, *m.*, orient, *m.*, levant, *m.*
East, adj. d'est, oriental
Easter, s. Pâques, *m.* — *Monday*, le lundi de Pâques
Easterly, adj. est, de l'est, d'est
Easterly, Eastward, adv. à l'est, vers l'est, vers l'Orient
Eastern, adj. oriental, d'Orient, est, d'est
Easy, adj. facile, aisé, tranquille, en repos, commode, accommodant, dans l'aisance, à l'aise. *To take things* —, ne s'embarrasser de rien. *In — circumstances*, dans l'aisance
Eat, va.n. manger, ronger, dévorer, (*one's words*) rétracter
Eatable, adj. mangeable, comestible
Eatable, s. comestible, *m.*, provisions de bouche, *f.pl.*
Eater, s. mangeur, *m.*, -euse, *f.*
Eating, s. manger, *m.* — *-house*, — *-rooms*, restaurant, *m.*, traiteur, *m.* — *-house-keeper*, restaurateur, *m.*, traiteur, *m.*
Eaves, s pl. bord du toit, *m.*, toit, *m.* — *-drop*, (*fig.*) écouter aux portes. — *-dropper*, écouteur aux portes, *m.*
Ebb, s. reflux, *m.*, (*nav.*) jusant, *m.*, (*fig.*) déclin, *f.*, décadence, *f.*
Ebb, vn. refluer, descendre, décliner, baisser
Ebony, s. ébène, *m.*, bois d'ébène, *m.*
Ebony, adj. d'ébène
Ebullition, s. ébullition, *f.*, débordement, *m.*
Eccentric, adj. excentrique, opposé, original
Eccentric, s. cercle excentrique, *m.*, (*person*) original, *m.* — *rods*, tirants, *m.* — *-gear*, appareil de l'excentrique, *m.* — *-wheel*, excentrique, *f.*
Eccentricity, s. excentricité, *f.*
Ecclesiastic, Ecclesiastical, adj. ecclésiastique
Echo, s. écho, *m.*, Écho, *f.*
Echo, vn. retentir, résonner, être répété, être réfléchi; — va. répéter
Eclectic, adj. éclectique
Eclecticism, s. éclectisme, *m.*
Eclipse, s. éclipse, *f.*
Eclipse, va.n. éclipser, s'éclipser
Ecliptic, s. adj. écliptique
Eclogue, s. éclogue, *m.*
Economic, Economical, adj. économique, économe, dirigé avec économie
Economically, adv. économiquement
Economist, s. économiste, *m.*
Economize, va.n. économiser
Economy, s. économie, *f.*
Ecstasy, s. extase, *f.*, ravissement, *m.*, transport, *m.*
Ecstatic, Ecstatical, adj. extatique, d'extase
Ecstatically, adv. avec extase
Eddy, s. remous, *m.*, tourbillon, *m.*, tournant, *m.* — *-water*, remous, *m.* — *-wind*, revolin, *m.*
Eddy, adj. tourbillonnant
Eddy, vn. tourbillonner
Eden, s. Éden, *m.*
Edge, s. fil, *m.*, tranchant, *m.*, coupant, *m.*, taillant, *m.*, (*wit*) vivacité, *f.*; force, *f.*, pointe, *f.*, bordure, *f.*, lisière, *f.*, (*a book*) tranche, *m.*, (*coin*) cordon, *m.* *To give an — to*, donner le fil (à). *To set one's teeth on* —, agacer les dents. — *-tool-maker*, taillandier, *m.* — *-rail*, bande feuillante, *f.*
Edge, va. aiguiser, exciter, stimuler, border
Edged, adj. affilé, bordé, à tranches. *Sharp-* —, tranchant, coupant
Edgeless, adj. émoussé, sans pointe
Edgewise, adj. de côté, de champ
Edging, s. bordure, *f.*, garniture, *f.* *Braid for* —, passepoil, *m.*
Edible, adj. bon à manger
Edict, s. édit, *m.*
Edification, Edifying, s. édification, *f.*
Edifice, s. édifice, *m.*
Edify, va. édifier
Edifyingly, adv. d'une manière édifiante
Edile, s. édile, *m.*
Edileship, s. édilité, *f.*
Edit, va. rédiger, éditer, préparer
Edition, s. édition, *f.*
Editor, s. (*newspaper*) rédacteur, *m.*, gérant, *m.*, (*publisher*) éditeur, *m.*
Editorial, adj. du rédacteur en chef, d'éditeur
Editorship, s. emploi de rédacteur, *m.*
Educate, va. faire l'éducation de, élever, instruire
Education, s. éducation, *f.*
Educational, adj. d'éducation
Educator, s. maître, *m.*
Educe, va. tirer
Eel, s. anguille, *f.* — *-pie*, pâté aux anguilles, *m.*
Efface, va. effacer
Effect, s. effet, *m.* *Of no* —, inutile, (*law*) non avenu
Effect, va. effectuer, faire, accomplir, exécuter
Effective, adj. effectif, efficace
Effectively, adv. efficacement
Effectiveness, s. bon effet
Effectual, adj. efficace
Effectually, adv. efficacement
Effeminacy, s. mollesse, *f.*, nature efféminée, *f.*
Effeminate, adj. efféminé
Effeminate, va. amollir, rendre efféminé; — vn. s'amollir
Effeminately, adv. d'une manière efféminée, avec mollesse
Effervesce, vn. être *or* entrer en effervescence
Effervescence, s. effervescence, *f.*
Effervescent, adj. effervescent, (*drinks*) gazeux
Effete, adj. stérile, épuisé, infécond
Efficacious, adj. efficace
Efficaciously, adv. efficacement, avec efficacité
Efficacy, Efficiency, s. efficacité, *f.*, bonne condition, *f.*, bon état, *m.*
Efficient, adj. efficace, effectif
Efficiently, adv. efficacement
Effigy, s. effigie, *f.*
Effluvium, s. exhalaison, *f.*, miasme, *m.*
Effort, s. effort, *m.*

Effrontery, s. effronterie, *f.*
Effulgence, s. éclat, *m.*
Effulgent, adj. resplendissant
Effusion, s. effusion, *f.*, épanchement, *m.*
Eft, s. salamandre, *f.*
Egg, s. œuf, *m.*, (*arch.*) ove, *m.* *Boiled —*, œuf à la coque. *Buttered —s*, des œufs brouillés. *— -cup*, coquetier, *m.* *— -flip*, lait de poule, *m.* *— shell*, coquille d'œuf, *f.*, coque, *f.* *— -merchant*, coquetier, *m.*
Eglantine, s. églantier, *m.*
Egoism, Egotism, s. manie de parler de soi, *f.*, égoïsme, *m.*
Egoist, Egotist, s. égoïste, *m.*
Egotistical, adj. égoïste
Egotistically, adv. avec égoïsme
Egregious, adj. insigne, parfait, achevé
Egregiously, adv. d'une manière insigne
Egress, s. sortie, *f.*, issue, *f.*
Eh! interj. eh! hé! hein!
Eider, — *-duck*, s. eider, *m.* *— -down*, édredon, *m.*
Eight, adj. s. huit, *m.*
Eighteen, adj. dix-huit
Eighteenth, adj. s. dix-huitième, dix-huit
Eighth, adj. s. huitième
Eighthly, adv. huitièmement
Eightieth, adj. quatre-vingtième
Eighty, adj. s. quatre-vingts
Either, adj. pron. l'un ou l'autre, l'une ou l'autre, chacun, chacune, chaque
Either, conj. ou, soit, (*negative*) non plus
Ejaculate, va. éjaculer, pousser, s'écrier
Ejaculation, s. éjaculation, *f.*, prière fervente, *f.*
Ejaculatory, adj. éjaculateur, -trice
Eject, va. rejeter, chasser, expulser, évincer
Ejection, s. déjection, *f.*, expulsion, *f.*
Eke, va. allonger. *An eking-piece*, une allonge. *To — out*, augmenter, prolonger, suppléer à
Elaborate, va. élaborer, travailler avec soin, perfectionner
Elaborate, adj. travaillé avec soin, soigné
Elaborately, adv. avec soin, laborieusement
Elaborateness, s. pénible travail, *m.*, soin, *m.*, perfection, *f.*
Elaboration, s. élaboration, *f.*
Elapse, vn. s'écouler, se passer
Elastic, adj. élastique
Elasticity, s. élasticité, *m.*
Elate, adj. exalté, transporté

Elate, va. exalter, transporter, enorgueillir
Elation, s. transport, *m.*, ivresse, *f.*, exaltation, *f.*, orgueil, *m.*
Elbow, s. coude, *m.* *Out at the —s*, percé au coude. *To have — -room*, avoir ses coudées franches
Elbow, va. coudoyer, pousser du coude
Elder, adj. aîné, ancien
Elder, s. ancien, *m.*, vieillard, *m.*, (*bot.*) sureau, *m.*
Elderly, adj. déjà âgé, d'un certain âge
Eldest, adj. aîné, âgé. *My — -born*, mon aîné
Elect, va. choisir, élire
Elect, adj. élu
Election, s. choix, *m.*, option, *f.*, élection, *f.*, distinction, *f.*
Electioneer, va. solliciter les suffrages, travailler les électeurs
Electioneering, s. sollicitation des votes, *f.*, manœuvres électorales, *f.pl.*
Elective, adj. électif, facultatif. *— franchise*, droit électoral
Elector, s. électeur, *m.*
Electoral, adj. électoral
Electorate, s. électorat, *m.*
Electress, s. électrice, *f.*
Electric, Electrical, adj. électrique. *— jar*, bouteille de Leyde
Electricity, s. électricité, *f.*
Electrify, va. électriser
Electro-magnetism, s. électro-magnétisme, *m.*
Electrometer, s. électromètre, *m.*
Electroplate, s. galvanoplastie, *f.*
Electrotype, va. électrotyper
Electuary, s. électuaire, *m.*
Eleemosynary, adj. de charité, charitable
Elegance, s. élégance, *f.*
Elegant, adj. élégant
Elegantly, adv. élégamment, avec élégance
Elegiac, adj. élégiaque
Elegiast, s. auteur d'élégies, *m.*
Elegy, s. élégie, *f.*
Element, s. élément, *m.*
Elemental, Elementary, adj. élémentaire
Elephant, s. éléphant, *m.* *— -driver*, cornac, *m.* *— -beetle*, gros scarabée, *m.*
Elevate, va. élever, exciter, animer
Elevation, s. élévation, *f.*
Eleven, s. adj. onze
Eleventh, s. adj. onzième, onze
Elf, s. fée, *f.*, lutin, *m.*, esprit follet, *m.*, nain, *m.*
Elfin, Elfish, adj. de lutin, malicieux, de nain
Elicit, va. faire jaillir, faire sortir, tirer, découvrir
Eligibility, Eligibleness, s. éligibilité, *f.*, avantage, *m.*, agrément, *m.*

Eligible, adj. éligible, avantageux, désirable
Eligibly, adv. avantageusement
Eliminate, va. éliminer, faire évanouir, exclure
Elimination, s. élimination, *f.*
Elision, s. élision, *f.*
Elixir, s. élixir, *m.*
Elk, s. élan, *m.*
Ell, s. aune, *f.*
Ellipse, Ellipsis, s. ellipse, *f.*
Ellipsoid, s. ellipsoïde, *f.*
Elliptic, Elliptical, adj. elliptique. *— curve*, coronoïde
Elliptically, adv. elliptiquement
Elm, s. orme, *m.*, ormeau, *m.*
Elocution, s. élocution, *f.*, débit, *f.*
Elongate, va. allonger, éloigner
Elope, vn. s'enfuir
Elopement, s. fuite, *f.*
Eloquence, s. éloquence, *f.*
Eloquent, adj. éloquent
Eloquently, adv. éloquemment
Else, pron. adj. autre, antre chose. *Any body —*, tout autre. *Nor any body —*, ni aucun autre. *Nothing —*, rien autre chose, personne autre. *What — ?* quelle autre chose?
Else, adv. autrement, ou autrement, ailleurs, autre part
Elucidate, va. éclaircir
Elucidation, s. éclaircissement, *m.*, illustration, *f.*
Elude, va. éviter, échapper à, éluder, tromper
Elysian, adj. élyséen, -ne, (*fig.*) de délices. *The — fields*, les champs Élysées
Emaciate, va. amaigrir; — vn. maigrir, s'amaigrir
Emaciated, adj. amaigri, (*anim.*) étique
Emaciation, s. amaigrissement, *m.*, maigreur, *f.*
Emanate, vn. émaner
Emanation, s. émanation, *f.*
Emancipate, va. émanciper, affranchir
Emancipate, adj. affranchi
Emancipation, s. émancipation, *f.*, affranchissement, *m.*
Emasculate, va. châtrer, (*fig.*) énerver, amollir
Embalm, va. embaumer
Embalmer, s. embaumeur, *m.*
Embalming, Embalmment, s. embaumement, *m.*
Embank, va. faire une levée contre, (*a river*) endiguer, (*a railway*) remblayer
Embankment, s. remblai, *m.*, talus, *m.*
Embargo, s. embargo, *m.*
Embargo, va. mettre un embargo sur, interrompre
Embark, va. n. embarquer
Embarkation, Embarkment, s. embarquement, *m.*
Embarrass, va. embarrasser
Embarrassment, s. embarras, *m.*
Embassy, s. ambassade, *f.*
Embattle, va. ranger en bataille; — vn. se ranger en bataille
Embed, va. coucher, incruster, (*build.*) sceller
Embellish, va. embellir, orner
Embellishment, s. embellissement, *m.*, ornement, *m.*
Embers, s. plur. cendres, *f.pl.*, étincelle, *f.* *Live —*, charbons ardents, *m.plur.*, braise, *f.*
Embezzle, va. détourner, s'approprier
Embezzlement, s. détournement, *m.*, somme détournée
Embezzler, s. homme coupable de détournement
Embitter, va. rendre amer, remplir d'amertume, (*pleasures*) empoisonner, (*heart*) ulcérer
Emblazon, va. blasonner, exalter, porter aux nues, proclamer
Emblem, s. emblème, *m.*
Emblematic, Emblematical, adj. emblématique
Emblematically, adv. d'une manière emblématique
Embody, va. revêtir d'un corps, personnifier, (*mil.*) incorporer
Embolden, va. enhardir
Emboss, va. couvrir de bosses, bosseler, relever en bosse, (*sculpt.*) travailler en bosse
Embossment, s. bosselure, *f.*, relief, *m.*, éminence, *f.*
Embrace, va. embrasser, saisir, adopter, comprendre, renfermer; — vn. embrasser, s'embrasser
Embrace, s. étreinte, *f.*, embrassement, *m.*, embrassade, *f.*
Embrasure, s. embrasure, *f.*
Embroider, va. broder, faire de la broderie
Embroiderer, s. brodeur, *m.*, -euse, *f.*
Embroidery, s. broderie, *f.*
Embroil, va. embrouiller, bouleverser
Embroilment, s. embrouillement, *m.*, confusion, *f.*
Embryo, s. embryon, *m.*, germe, *m.*
Emendation, s. correction, *f.*
Emerald, s. émeraude, *f.* — adj. d'émeraude
Emerge, vn. émerger, sortir, surgir
Emergency, s. action de surgir, *f.*, hasard, *m.*, conjoncture, *f.*, circonstance critique, *f.*

Emery, s. émeri, *m.*
Emigrate, vn. émigrer
Emigration, s. émigration, *f.*
Eminence, s. éminence, *f.*, colline, *f.*, monticule, *m.*, position éminente, *f.*, grandeur, *f.*, distinction, *f.*
Eminent, adj. éminent (en), distingué (par)
Eminently, adv. éminemment
Emir, s. émir, *m.*
Emissary, s. émissaire, *m.*
Emission, s. émission, *f.*
Emit, va. émettre, exhaler, dégager
Emmet, s. fourmi, *m.*
Emmew, va. claquemurer
Emollient, adj. s. émollient, -e
Emolument, s. émolument, *m.*
Emotion, s. émotion, *f.*
Emperor, s. empereur, *m.*
Emphasis, s. force, *f.*, accent, *m.*, emphase, *f.*
Emphasize, va. accentuer fortement, appuyer sur
Emphatic, adj. emphatique, fortement accentué
Emphatically, adv. emphatiquement, avec force, expressément, absolument
Empire, s. empire, *m.*
Empiric, adj. s. empirique
Empirically, adv. empiriquement
Empiricism, s. empirisme, *m.*
Employ, va. employer, occuper, faire usage de
Employ, s. emploi, *m.*
Employer, s. patron, *m.*, maître, *m.*, maîtresse, *f.*
Employment, s. travail, *m.*, occupation, *f.*, emploi, *m.*
Emporium, s. marché, *m.*, entrepôt, *m.*
Empower, va. autoriser (à), donner plein pouvoir (de), donner procuration
Empress, s. impératrice, *f.*
Emptiness, s. vide, *m.*, creux, *m.*, (*fig.*) ignorance, *f.*
Empty, adj vide, à jeun, vain, creux
Empty, va. vider; — vn. se vider, se décharger
Empyrean, s. Empirée, *m.*
Emulate, va. tâcher d'égaler, rivaliser
Emulation, s. émulation, *f.*, lutte, *f.*, rivalité, *f.*
Emulous, adj. rival, avide, désireux
Emulously, adv. avec émulation, à l'envi
Emulsion, s. émulsion, *f.*
Enable, va. rendre capable, mettre à même
Enact, va. décréter, ordonner, rendre, porter, (*law*) faire
Enactment, s. loi, *f.*, ordonnance, *f.*, décret, *m.*
Enamel, va. émailler; — vn. peindre en émail
Enamel, s. émail, *m.* — adj. en émail
Enameller, s. émailleur, *m.*
Enamelling, s. émaillure, *f.*
Enamour, va. rendre amoureux, (*fig.*) charmer. *To become —ed of*, s'amouracher de
Encamp, vn. camper, se camper; — va. camper, faire camper
Encampment, **Encamping**, s. campement, *m.*
Encaustic, s. encaustique, *f.* — adj. encaustique, à l'encaustique
Enchant, va. enchanter, charmer, ravir
Enchanter, s. enchanteur, *m.*
Enchanting, adj. enchanteur, ravissant
Enchantingly, adv. à ravir, d'une manière enchanteresse
Enchantment, s. enchantement, *m.*, charme, *m.*
Enchantress, s. enchanteresse, *f.*
Enchase, va. enchâsser
Enchasing, s. monture, *f.*
Encircle, va. entourer
Enclose, va. clore, enclore, entourer, fermer, envelopper, joindre (à), mettre sous enveloppe
Enclosure, s. action de clore, *f.*, clôture, *f.*, enceinte, *f.*, enclos, *m.*, (*letters*) contenu, *m.*
Encomiast, s. panégyriste, *m.*
Encomium, s. éloge, *m.*
Encompass, va. entourer, environner, ceindre, investir, embrasser, renfermer
Encore! interj. bis!
Encore, va. bisser, redemander
Encounter, s. rencontre, *f.*, choc, *m.*, combat, *m.*
Encounter, va. rencontrer, aller au-devant de, affronter, aborder de front, combattre, attaquer
Encourage, va. encourager
Encouragement, s. encouragement, *m.*
Encourager, s. qui encourage, protecteur, *m.*
Encouragingly, adv. de manière à encourager
Encroach, vn. empiéter, entreprendre, usurper, abuser
Encroacher, s. usurpateur, *m.*
Encroachment, s. empiètement, *m.*
Encumber, va. encombrer, embarrasser, (*with debts*) charger, grever
Encumbrance, s. encombrement, *m.*, embarras, *m.*, (*family*) charge, *f.*
Encyclical, adj. encyclique
End, s. bout, *m.*, extrémité, *f.*, fin, *f.*, mort, *f.*, issue, *f.* *To make both —s meet*, joindre les deux bouts. *On —*, debout, droit. *To be at an —*, cesser. *To make an — of, to put an — to*, mettre fin à, finir, terminer. *To come to a bad —*, finir mal
End, va.n. finir, achever, terminer
Endanger, va mettre en danger *or* en péril, exposer, compromettre, risquer, hasarder
Endear, va. faire aimer, faire chérir, rendre cher, attacher
Endearing, adj. caressant, tendre, affectueux
Endearment, s. caresse, *f.*, agrément, *m.*, affection, *f.*
Endeavour, s. effort, *m.*, tentative, *f.*
Endeavour, vn. s'efforcer (de), chercher (à), tâcher (de), travailler (à)
Endemic, adj. endémique
Ending, s. fin, *f.*, terminaison, *f.*, désinence, *f.*
Endive, s. chicorée, *f.*
Endless, adj. sans fin, infini, éternel, perpétuel, interminable
Endlessly, adv. sans fin, perpétuellement
Endorse, va. endosser
Endorsement, s. endossement, *m.*, endos, *m.*
Endorser, s. endosseur, *m.*
Endow, va. douer, doter
Endowment, s. dot, *f.*, dotation, *f.*, talent, *m.*, avantage, *m.*
Endurable, adj. supportable
Endurance, s. patience, *f.*, action de supporter, *f.*, durée, *f.*
Endure, va.n. endurer, supporter, souffrir, pâtir, durer
Enduring, adj. patient, durable, qui dure
Endways, **Endwise**, adv. debout, de champ
Enemy, s. ennemi, *m.*, -e, *f.*
Energetic, adj. énergique
Energetically, adv. énergiquement
Energy, s. énergie, *f.*
Enervate, va.n. énerver, s'énerver
Enfeeble, va. affaiblir
Enfeeblement, s. affaiblissement, *m.*, faiblesse, *f.*
Enfilade, s. enfilade, *f.*
Enforce, va. appuyer, confirmer, corroborer, faire valoir, mettre en vigueur *or* en force, faire exécuter
Enforcement, s. force, *f.*, violence, *f.*, contrainte, *f.*, sanction, *f.*, mise en vigueur, *f.*
Enfranchise, va. affranchir, naturaliser
Enfranchisement, s. affranchissement, *m.*
Engage, va. engager, enrôler, arrêter, (*servants*) retenir, attirer, (*the mind*) occuper; promettre en mariage. — vn. s'engager, engager le combat, en venir aux mains
Engaged, adj. engagé, promis
Engagement, s. engagement, *m.*, invitation, *f.*, promesse de mariage, *f.*, combat, *m.*, action, *f.*
Engaging, adj. engageant
Engagingly, adv. d'une manière engageante
Engender, va. engendrer, faire naître; — vn. s'engendrer
Engine, s. machine, *f.*, locomotive, *f.*, machine à vapeur, *f.*, pompe à incendie, *f.*, instrument, *m.*, machine, *f.*, engin, *m.* —*-driver*, —*-man*, mécanicien. —*-house*, dépôt de pompes à incendie
Engineer, s. ingénieur, *m.*, (*railways*) mécanicien, *m.* *Civil —*, ingénieur des ponts et chaussées. *The — corps*, le génie
Engineering, s. l'art de l'ingénieur, *m.*, le génie, *m.*
English, s. Anglais, *m.pl.*, l'anglais, *m.*, la langue anglaise, *f.* *Old —*, (*print. black letter*) gothique
Engrave, va. graver, imprimer
Engraver, s. graveur, *m.* *Wood —*, graveur sur bois, *m.*
Engraving, s. gravure, *f.*, estampe, *f.*
Engross, va. accaparer, absorber, occuper complètement, (*law*) grossoyer
Engrosser, s. accapareur, *m.*, -euse, *f.*, (*law*) copiste d'actes, *m.*
Engrossment, s. accaparement, *m.*, (*law*) écriture à la grosse, *f.*
Enhance, va. enchérir, rehausser, relever
Enhancement, s. renchérissement, *m.*, hausse, *f.*, embellissement, *m.*, augmentation, *f.*
Enigma, s. énigme, *m.*
Enigmatic, **Enigmatical**, adj. énigmatique
Enigmatically, adv. énigmatiquement, par énigme
Enjoin, va. enjoindre (à), prescrire (à)
Enjoy, va. jouir de, goûter, posséder. *To — oneself*, s'amuser, se divertir
Enjoyment, s. jouissance, *f.*, plaisir, *m.*
Enlarge, va. agrandir, élargir, étendre, développer, (*the mind*) élever, (*to set free*) mettre en liberté; — vn. s'agrandir, s'augmenter, s'élargir, s'étendre (sur), développer (...)
Enlargement, s. agrandissement, *m.*, accroissement, *m.*, développement, *m.*, mise en liberté, *f.*
Enlighten, va. éclairer, illuminer, éclaircir
Enlightenment, s. lumières, *f.pl.*
Enlist, va. enrôler, engager; — vn. s'engager, s'enrôler, se ranger sous la bannière de
Enlistment, s. engagement, *m.*, enrôlement, *m.*
Enliven, va. animer, vivifier
Enmity, s. inimitié, *f.*, hostilité, *f.*

Ennoble, va. anoblir, ennoblir, illustrer
Ennoblement, s. anoblissement, *m.*, noblesse, *f.*, grandeur, *f.*, élévation, *f.*
Enormity, s. énormité, *f.*
Enormous, adj. énorme, monstrueux, anomal, irrégulier
Enormously, adv. énormément
Enough, s. adj. adv. assez *Large* —, assez grand. *Be kind* — *to*, soyez assez bon pour
Enrage, va. exaspérer, irriter, rendre furieux, mettre en fureur
Enrapture, va. ravir, transporter
Enrich, va. enrichir, rendre riche, (*soil*) fertiliser
Enrichment, s. enrichissement, *m.*
Enroll, va. enrôler, inscrire, écrire, enregistrer
Enrolment, s. enrôlement, *m.*, inscription, *f.*, registre, *m.*
Ensconce, va. cacher, retrancher
Enshrine, va. enchâsser, ouvrir un sanctuaire à, renfermer précieusement
Ensign, s. drapeau, *m.*, enseigne, *f.*, (*nav.*) pavillon, *m.*, (*fig.*) signal, *m.*, (*mil.*) sous-lieutenant, *m.* — *-bearer*, porte-drapeau, *m.*
Ensigncy, s. grade de sous-lieutenant, *m.*
Enslave, va. asservir, rendre esclave, réduire à l'esclavage
Enslavement, s. esclavage, *m.*
Enslaver, s. celui, celle qui asservit, tyran, *m.*
Ensnare, *see* INSNARE
Ensue, vn. s'ensuivre
Ensuing, adj. suivant, prochain
Entablature, Entablement, s. entablement, *m.*
Entail, s. substitution, *f.*, bien substitué, *m.*
Entail, va. substituer, léguer, transmettre, (*fig.*) imposer
Entangle, va. embarrasser, empêtrer, embrouiller, enchevêtrer
Entanglement, s. embarras, *m.*, confusion, *f.*
Enter, va. entrer, débuter (dans), être admis (dans), admettre, inscrire, faire inscrire, (*account*) porter, (*law*) intenter. — vn. entrer, débuter, pénétrer, entamer, commencer, s'engager
Entering, s. entrée, *f.*
Enterprise, s. entreprise, *f.*, aventure, *f.*, esprit entreprenant, *m.*
Enterpriser, s. esprit entreprenant, *m.*
Enterprising, adj. entreprenant
Entertain, va. recevoir, accueillir, régaler, traiter, (*proposition*) admettre, (*ideas*) concevoir, (*hopes*) entretenir; amuser, divertir
Entertainer, s. amphitryon, *m.*, hôte, *m.*, hôtesse, *f.*
Entertaining, adj. amusant, divertissant, charmant
Entertainment, s. hospitalité, *f.*, réception, *f.*, festin, *m.*, repas, *m.*, grand dîner, *m.*, amusement, *m.*, divertissement, *m.*
Enthrone, va. mettre sur un trône, (*bishops*) introniser
Enthusiasm, s. enthousiasme, *m.*
Enthusiast, s. enthousiaste, *m.*
Enthusiastic, adj. enthousiaste, plein d'enthousiasme
Enthusiastically, adv. avec enthousiasme
Entice, va. entraîner, (*to evil*) exciter, attirer, séduire
Enticement, s. tentation, *f.*, entraînement, *m.*, instigation, *f.*, attrait, *m.*, charme, *m.*
Enticer, s. tentateur, *m.*
Enticing, adj. tentant, attrayant
Enticingly, adv. d'une manière séduisante *or* attrayante
Entire, adj. entier, complet, plein, intégral
Entirely, adv. entièrement, tout entier, complètement, intégralement
Entireness, s. totalité, *f.*, le tout, *m.*, intégralité, *f.*
Entitle, va. intituler, donner pour titre, nommer, qualifier de, avoir pour titre, donner droit
Entity, s. entité, *f.*, être, *m.*
Entomb, va. mettre dans la tombe, ensevelir, enterrer
Entombment, s. sépulture, *f.*
Entomology, s. entomologie, *f.*
Entrails, s. pl. entrailles, *f. pl.*
Entrance, s. entrée, *f.*, initiation, *f.*, début, *m.*, commencement, *m.*, embouchure, *f.* — *-hall*, vestibule, *m.* — *-fee*, — *-money*, entrée, *f.*, prix d'entrée, *m.*
Entrance, va. plonger dans un sommeil léthargique, transporter, enchanter
Entrancement, s. sommeil léthargique, *m.*, extase, *f.*
Entrap, va. prendre dans un piége, attraper
Entreat, va. supplier, prier, implorer
Entreaty, s. instance, *f.*, prière, *f.*, supplication, *f.*, sollicitation, *f.*
Entry, s. entrée, *f.*, embouchure, *f.*, passage, *m.*, avenue, *f.*, (*accounts*) écriture, *f.*, article, *m.*, partie, *f.*, (*law*) déclaration, *f.*, prise de possession, *f.*, entrée en jouissance, *f.* *To make an* — *of*, passer écriture de. *By single* —, *by double* —, en partie simple, en partie double
Entwine, va. entrelacer, enlacer
Enumerate, va. énumérer
Enumeration, s. énumération, *f.*
Enunciate, va. énoncer, déclarer; — vn. articuler
Enunciation, s. énonciation, *f.*, (*of a problem*) énoncé, *m.*
Envelope, va. envelopper
Envelope, s. enveloppe, *f.*
Envenom, va. envenimer, rendre odieux
Enviable, adj. digne d'envie, désirable
Envier, s. envieux, *m.*, jaloux, *m.*
Envious, adj. envieux, jaloux, qui porte envie à
Enviously, adv. avec envie
Envoy, s. envoyé, *m.*, envoi, *m.*
Envy, va. envier, porter envie à
Envy, s. envie, *f.*, jalousie, *f.*
Epaulet, s. épaulette, *f.*
Epergne, s. surtout de table, *m.*
Ephemera, s. éphémère, *m.*
Ephemeral, adj. éphémère
Epic, adj. épique. — s. poëme épique, *m.*
Epicure, s. épicurien, *m.*, -ne, *f.*, gourmet, *m.*
Epicurean, s. adj. épicurien, d'Épicure
Epicureanism, Epicurism, s. épicurisme, *m.*
Epidemic, s. épidémie, *f.*
Epidemic, Epidemical, adj. épidémique
Epidermis, s. épiderme, *m.*
Epigram, s. épigramme, *f.*
Epigrammatic, Epigrammatical, adj. épigrammatique
Epigraph, s. épigraphe, *f.*
Epilepsy, s. épilepsie, *f.*
Epileptic, Epileptical, adj. épileptique
Epilogue, s. épilogue, *m.*
Epiphany, s. Épiphanie, *f.*, jour des rois, *m.*
Episcopacy, s. épiscopat, *m.*
Episcopal, Episcopalian, adj. épiscopal
Episode, s. épisode, *m.*
Episodic, adj. épisodique
Epistle, s. épître, *f.*, lettre, *f.*
Epistolary, adj. épistolaire
Epitaph, s. épitaphe, *f.*
Epithet, s. épithète, *f.*
Epitome, s. épitomé, *m.*, abrégé, *m.*, précis, *m.*
Epitomize, va. abréger
Epoch, s. époque, *f.*
Equal, adj. égal, juste, impartial, proportionné, de force
Equal, s. égal, *m.*, -e, *f.*, pair, *m.*, pareil, *m.*, pareille, *f.*, égalité, *f.*
Equal, va. égaler, être égal à
Equality, s. égalité, *f.*
Equalization, s. égalisation, *f.*
Equalize, va. égaliser
Equally, adv. également, avec justice
Equanimity, s. égalité d'âme, *f.*
Equation, s. équation, *f.*
Equator, s. équateur, *m.*
Equatorial, adj. équatorial, de l'équateur
Equerry, s. écuyer, *m.*
Equestrian, adj. équestre
Equilibrate, va. équilibrer
Equilibrium, s. équilibre, *m.*
Equinoctial, adj. équinoxial, d'équinoxe
Equinox, s. équinoxe, *m.*, vent d'équinoxe, *m.*
Equip, va. équiper, accoutrer
Equipage, s. équipement, *m.*, appareil, *m.*, équipage, *m.*
Equipment, s. équipement, *m.*
Equipoise, s. équilibre, *m.*
Equitable, adj. équitable
Equitably, adv. équitablement
Equivalence, s. égalité de valeur, *f.*
Equivalent, adj. s. équivalent, -e
Equivocal, adj. équivoque
Equivocally, adv. d'une manière équivoque
Equivocate, vn. équivoquer, user d'équivoque
Equivocation, s. équivoque, *f.*
Equivocator, s. homme qui use d'équivoques, *m.*
Era, s. ère, *f.*
Eradicate, va. extirper, déraciner
Eradication, s. extirpation, *f.*
Erase, va. effacer, oblitérer, raturer
Erasure, s. rature, *f.*
Ere, conj. avant que, plutôt que. — prep. avant
Erect, va. dresser, élever, ériger, (*fig.*) fonder, instituer, établir
Erect, adj. droit, debout, ferme
Erection, s. érection, *f.*, élévation, *f.*, établissement, *m.*
Ermine, s. hermine, *f.*
Ermined, adj. fourré d'hermine, revêtu d'hermine
Erotic, adj. érotique
Err, vn. errer, s'égarer, s'écarter
Errand, s. commission, *f.*, visite, *f.* — *-boy*, petit commissionnaire
Errant, adj. errant
Errantry, s. courses vagabondes, *f. pl.*
Erratic, adj. errant, erratique
Erratum, s. erratum, *m.*; *plur.* errata
Erring, adj. égaré, faillible, exposé à se tromper

Erroneous, adj. erroné, faux, égaré
Erroneously, adv. d'une manière erronée
Erroneousness, s. erreur, *f.*
Error, s. erreur, *f.*, faute, *f.*
Eructation, s. éructation, *f.*
Erudite, adj. érudit
Erudition, s. érudition, *f.*
Eruption, s. éruption, *f.*
Eruptive, adj. éruptif
Erysipelas, s. érysipèle, *m.*
Escape, va. échapper (à); — vn. s'échapper (de), échapper (à), s'évader
Escape, s. évasion, *f.*, fuite, *f.*, action d'échapper, *f.*, salut, *m.*, délivrance, *f.*, (*of gas, &c.*) fuite, *f.*, dégagement, *m.*, (*blunder*) bévue, *f.*, (*clocks*) échappement, *m.* *To have a narrow* —, l'échapper belle. *What an* —*!* je l'ai échappé belle!
Escapement, s. échappement, *m.*
Escarpment, s. escarpement, *m.*
Escheat, s. bien en deshérence, *m.*, biens confisqués, *m.pl.*
Eschew, va. éviter, fuir, renoncer (à)
Escort, s. escorte, *f.*
Escort, va. escorter
Esculent, adj. s. bon à manger, nourrissant, comestible
Escutcheon, s. écusson, *m.*, écu, *m.*
Escutcheoned, adj. orné d'écussons
Especially, adv. spécialement, surtout, principalement
Esplanade, s. esplanade, *f.*
Espousal, s. mariage, *m.*, accordailles, *f.pl.*
Espouse, va. épouser, marier, fiancer, embrasser, adopter
Espy, va. voir, découvrir, épier
Essay, va. essayer
Essay, s. effort, *m.*, tentation, *f.*, essai, *m.*, épreuve, *f.*
Essayist, s. auteur d'essais, *m.*
Essence, s. essence, *f.*
Essential, adj. s. essentiel
Essentially, adv. essentiellement
Establish, va. établir, confirmer, affermir
Establishment, s. établissement, *m.*, ratification, *f.*, confirmation, *f.*, état de maison, *m.*, maison montée, *f.*
Estate, s. terre, *f.*, propriété, *f.*, domaine, *m.*, bien, *m.*, bien-fonds, *m.* — *agent*, agent d'affaires
Esteem, va. estimer, évaluer, penser
Esteem, s. estime, *f.*, estimation, *f.*, opinion, *f.*
Esteemer, s. estimateur, *m.*, appréciateur, *m.*
Estimable, adj. estimable, digne d'estime
Estimate, va. estimer, évaluer, apprécier
Estimate, s. estimation, *f.*, évaluation, *f.*, devis, *m.*, état estimatif, *m.*
Estimation, s. estimation, *f.*, valeur, *f.*, opinion, *f.*, estime, *f.*
Estimator, s. estimateur, *m.*
Estrange, va. aliéner, retirer, éloigner
Estrangement, s. aversion, *f.*, éloignement, *m.*
Estuary, s. bras de mer, *m.*, embouchure de fleuve, *f.*
Etch, va. graver à l'eau-forte, tracer
Etcher, s. graveur à l'eau-forte, *m.*
Etching, s. gravure à l'eau-forte, *f.*
Eternal, adj. éternel
Eternal, s. Éternel, *m.*, choses éternelles, *f.pl.*
Eternally, adv. éternellement
Eternity, s. éternité, *f.*
Eternize, va. éterniser
Ether, s. éther, *m.*
Ethereal, adj. éthéré, céleste
Ethics, s. pl. éthique, *f.*, morale, *f.*
Ethnographical, adj. ethnographique
Ethnography, s. ethnographie, *f.*
Etiolate, va. étioler
Etiolation, s. étiolement, *m.*
Etiquette, s. étiquette, *f.*, cérémonial, *m.*
Etymological, adj. étymologique
Etymology, s. étymologie, *f.*
Eucharist, s. Eucharistie, *f.*
Eucharistic, Eucharistical, adj. eucharistique
Eulogist, s. panégyriste, *m.*
Eulogistic, Eulogistical, adj. d'éloge, de louanges
Eulogistically, adv. avec éloges
Eulogize, va. faire l'éloge de, louer
Eulogy, s. éloge, *m.*, panégyrique, *m.*
Eunuch, s. eunuque, *m.*
Euphemism, s. euphémisme, *m.*
Euphonic, Euphonious, adj. euphonique
Euphony, s. euphonie, *f.*
Evacuate, va. évacuer, faire évacuer
Evacuation, s. évacuation, *f.*
Evade, va. échapper (à), éviter, esquiver, éluder; — vn. user de moyens évasifs
Evanescent, adj. éphémère, passager
Evangelical, adj. évangélique
Evangelist, s. évangéliste, *m.*
Evangelize, va. évangéliser
Evaporate, vn. s'évaporer; — va. évaporer
Evaporation, s. évaporation, *f.*
Evasion, s. évasion, *f.*, défaite, *f.*, subterfuge, *m.*
Evasive, adj. évasif
Evasively, adv. d'une manière évasive
Eve, s. soir, *m.*, veille, *f.*
Even, s. soir, *m.*
Even, adj. uni, égal, plat, aplani, de niveau (avec), à fleur (de), (*owing nothing*) quitte, (*number*) pair, (*sum*) rond
Even, adv. même, précisément, justement. — *now*, à l'instant même. — *then*, même alors. — *though*, — *if*, quand même. — *so*, précisément
Even, va. égaler, unir, niveler, aplanir
Evening, s. soir, *m.*, soirée, *f.*, déclin, *m.*
Evening, adj. du soir. — *-party*, soirée, *f.* — *-tide*, soir
Evenly, adv. également, uniment, de niveau, impartialement
Evenness, s. égalité, *f.*
Event, s. événement, *m.*, issue, *f.*, dénoûment, *m.* *At all* —*s*, dans tous les cas, en tout cas
Eventful, adj. plein d'événements, bien rempli
Eventual, adj. éventuel, final, définitif
Eventually, adv. éventuellement, définitivement
Ever, adj. jamais, toujours, sans cesse, quelque ... que. *For* —, à jamais, pour jamais, pour toujours. *For* — *and* —, à tout jamais. — *after*, depuis ce temps-là, depuis lors. — *since*, depuis, depuis que. *Be it* — *so good*, quelque bon que ce soit. *If* ... — *so little*, pour peu que ... — *so many*, je ne sais combien
Evergreen, adj. toujours vert. — s. arbre vert
Everlasting, adj. éternel, perpétuel, immortel
Everlasting, s. l'éternité, *f.*
Everlastingly, adv. éternellement
Evermore, adv. toujours, éternellement
Every, adj. chaque, tout, toute, tous les, toutes les. — *day*, tous les jours. — *third day*, de trois jours l'un. — *week*, tous les huit jours, toutes les semaines. — *body*, — *one*, tout le monde
Evict, va. évincer
Eviction, s. éviction, *f.*
Evidence, s. évidence, *f.*, témoignage, *m.*, déposition, *f.* *To give* —, déposer
Evidence, va. prouver, montrer
Evident, adj. évident
Evidently, adv. évidemment
Evil, adj. mauvais, méchant, pervers, malheureux
Evil, s. mal, *m.*
Evil, adv. mal. — *-doer*, méchant, pervers. — *-speaking*, médisance. — *-minded*, malintentionné, malveillant
Evince, va. montrer, témoigner
Evocation, s. évocation, *f.*
Evoke, va. évoquer
Evolution, s. évolution, *f.*, développement, *m.*
Evolve, va. développer, déployer, débrouiller, (*chem.*) dégager
Ewe, s. brebis, *f.*
Ewer, s. aiguière, *f.*
Exact, adj. exact, précis
Exact, va. exiger; — vn. commettre des exactions
Exacter, s. exacteur, *m.*, celui qui exige
Exaction, s. exaction, *f.*, exigence, *f.*
Exactly, adv. exactement, juste, de point en point
Exactness, s. exactitude, *f.*
Exaggerate, va. exagérer
Exaggeration, s. exagération, *f.*
Exalt, va. exalter, louer, vanter
Exaltation, s. exaltation, *f.*, élévation, *f.*, transport, *m.*
Examination, s. visite, *f.*, (*goods*) inspection, *f.*, vérification, *f.*, examen, *m.*, (*witness*) interrogatoire, *m.* *Post-mortem* —, autopsie, *f.* *Board of* —, jury d'examen, *m.*
Examine, va. examiner, visiter, inspecter, vérifier, interroger. *Examining judge*, juge d'instruction
Examiner, s. vérificateur, *m.*, observateur, *m.*, examinateur, *m.*, juge d'instruction, *m.*
Examinership, s. poste or emploi d'examinateur, *m.*
Example, s. exemple, *m.* *For* —, par exemple
Exasperate, va. irriter, exaspérer, aigrir
Exasperation, s. exaspération, *f.*, aggravation, *f.*
Excavate, va. creuser
Excavation, s. excavation, *f.*, fouilles, *f.pl.*, tranchée, *f.*, grotte, *f.*
Exceed, va. excéder, dépasser, outrepasser, surpasser, l'emporter sur
Exceedingly, adv. excessivement, extrêmement
Excel, va.n. exceller, surpasser, l'emporter sur, dépasser
Excellence, Excellency, s. excellence, *f.*, supériorité, *f.*, qualité, *f.*, mérite, *m.*
Excellent, adj. excellent, éminent, très-grand
Excellently, adv. parfaitement, supérieurement, éminemment
Except, va. excepter; — vn. faire des objections, s'opposer, (*law*) récuser (...), exciper (de)

Except, Excepting, prep. excepté, à l'exception de, hormis, sauf. — conj. à moins que
Exception, s. exception, *f.*, objection, *f.*, offense, *f.* *With this, that* —, à cette exception près, à cela près *To take — to* or *at*, faire des objections à, se formaliser de, s'offenser de
Exceptionable, adj. blâmable, à critiquer
Exceptional, adj. exceptionnel
Exceptionally, adv. exceptionnellement
Excess, s. excès, *m.*, excédant, *m.*
Excessive, adj. excessif, extrême
Excessively, adv. excessivement, à l'excès
Exchange, va. échanger, troquer, changer
Exchange, s. échange, *m.*, troc, *m.*, (*com.*) change, *m.*, (*public building*) la Bourse, *f.* — *-office*, change de monnaies, *m.* — *-broker*, courtier de change, *m.*
Exchangeable, adj. qu'on peut échanger
Exchequer, s. échiquier, *m.*, ministère des finances, *m.*, trésor, *m.* — *-bill*, bon du trésor, *m.*
Excisable, adj. sujet aux droits
Excise, s. contributions indirectes, *f.pl.*, régie, *f.* — *-office*, la régie
Exciseman, s. préposé or employé de la régie, *m.*
Excitable, adj. excitable, nerveux, irritable
Excitation, s. excitation, *f.*
Excite, va. exciter, animer, échauffer, émouvoir, porter
Excitement, s. excitation, *f.*, émotion, *f.*, motif (pour), *m.*, stimulant (à), *m.*
Exciter, s. excitateur, *m.*
Exclaim, vn. s'écrier, crier, se récrier
Exclamation, s. exclamation, *f.*, cri, *m.* *Note of* —, point d'exclamation
Exclude, va. exclure (de), rejeter (hors de)
Exclusion, s. exclusion, *f.*
Exclusive, adj. exclusif
Exclusively, adv. exclusivement. — *of*, non compris, à l'exclusion de
Exclusiveness, s. nature exclusive, *f.*, caractère peu libéral, *m.*
Excommunicate, va. excommunier
Excommunication, s. excommunication, *f.*
Excoriation, s. excoriation, *f.*, écorchure, *f.*
Excrement, s. excrément, *m.*
Excrescence, s. excroissance, *f.*, hors-d'œuvre, *m.*
Excrescent, adj. formant excroissance
Excretion, s. excrétion, *f.*
Excruciate, va. torturer, mettre à la torture, tourmenter
Excruciation, s. torture, *f.*, tourment, *m.*
Exculpate, va. disculper
Exculpation, s. justification, *f.*, défense, *f.*
Exculpatory, adj. apologétique, justificatif
Excursion, s. excursion, *f.*, course, *f.*, petit voyage, *m.* — *-train*, train de plaisir, *m.*
Excursive, adj. vagabond
Excusable, adj. excusable
Excuse, va. excuser, dispenser. — *me!* pardon! pardonnez-moi!
Excuse, s. excuse, *f.*, apologie, *f.*, prétexte, *m.*
Execrable, adj. exécrable
Execrably, adv. exécrablement
Execrate, va. exécrer
Execration, s. exécration, *f.*
Executable, adj. exécutable, praticable
Execute, va. exécuter, accomplir, effectuer
Execution, s. exécution, *f.*, mise à exécution, *f.*, accomplissement, *m.*, (*law*) saisie-exécution, *f.* *Writ of* —, exécutoire, *m.*
Executioner, s. exécuteur, *m.*, -trice, *f.*, bourreau, *m.*
Executive, adj. exécutif
Executor, s. exécuteur testamentaire, *m.*
Executorship, s. office d'exécuteur
Executrix, s. exécutrice, *f.*
Exegesis, s. exégèse, *f.*
Exemplar, s. modèle, *m.*
Exemplary, adj exemplaire
Exemplification, s. illustration, *f.*, (*law*) ampliation, *f.*
Exemplify, va. illustrer par un exemple, donner l'exemple de
Exempt, va. exempter, affranchir, délivrer
Exempt, adj. exempt, libre, affranchi, délivré
Exemption, s. exemption, *f.*
Exercise, s. exercice, *m.*, (*school-boy's*) devoir, *m.*, thème, *m.*
Exercise, va. exercer, faire prendre de l'exercice à, (*mil.*) faire faire l'exercice à; — vn prendre de l'exercice, (*mil.*) faire l'exercice
Exert, va. déployer, exercer, mettre en jeu, faire usage de
Exertion, s. effort, *m.*, activité, *f.*, exercice, *m.*
Exfoliate, vn. s'exfolier
Exfoliation, s. exfoliation, *f.*
Exhalation, s. exhalation, *f.*, exhalaison, *f.*
Exhale, va. exhaler, émettre; — vn. s'exhaler
Exhaust, va. épuiser, absorber
Exhaustible, adj. qui peut être épuisé
Exhaustion, s. épuisement, *m.*, aspiration, *f.*
Exhaustive, adj. qui épuise
Exhaustless, adj. inépuisable
Exhibit, va. montrer, faire voir, exposer, faire l'exposition de, (*law*) exhiber, produire; — vn. (*theat.*) donner des représentations (de)
Exhibiter, s. exposant, *m.*, montreur, *m.*
Exhibition, s. action de montrer, *f.*, spectacle, *m.*, (*pictures*) exposition, *f.* (*univ.*) bourse, *f.*, pension, *f.*
Exhibitioner, s. boursier, *m.*
Exhilarate, va. égayer, réjouir
Exhilarating, adj. divertissant
Exhilaration, s. hilarité, *f.*, gaîté, *f.*
Exhort, va. exhorter, encourager
Exhortation, s. exhortation, *f.*
Exhumation, s. exhumation, *f.*
Exhume, va. exhumer
Exigency, s. exigence, *f.*, besoin, *m.*, conjoncture, *f.*
Exile, s. exil, *m.*, bannissement, *m.*, exilé, *m.*, -e, *f.*, banni, *m.*
Exist, vn. exister, être
Existence, s. existence, *f.*
Existent, Existing, adj. qui existe, existant
Exit, s. sortie, *f.*
Exonerate, va. décharger, dispenser
Exoneration, s. décharge, *f.*
Exorbitance, s. extravagance, *f.*, excès, *m.*
Exorbitant, adj. exorbitant, excessif
Exorcise, va. exorciser
Exorcism, s. exorcisme, *m.*
Exordium, s. exorde, *m.*
Exotic, adj. exotique
Expand, va. étendre, déployer, développer, (*flowers*) épanouir, faire épanouir, (*the heart*) dilater; — vn. s'épanouir, s'ouvrir, s'étendre, se développer, se dilater
Expanse, s. étendue, *f.*, surface, *f.*
Expansion, s. déploiement, *m.*, extension, *f.*, épanouissement, *m.*, dilatation, *f.*
Expansive, adj. expansif
Expatiate, vn. s'étendre, discourir, disserter
Expatriate, va. expatrier
Expatriation, s. expatriation, *f.*
Expect, va.n. attendre, s'attendre à, espérer, compter
Expectancy, s. attente, *f.*, expectative, *f.*
Expectant, adj. expectant, dans l'expectative
Expectation, s. attente, *f.*, espérance, *f.*, espoir, *m.*, prétention, *f.*, demande, *f.*
Expectorate, va. expectorer
Expectoration, s. expectoration, *f.*
Expediency, s. convenance, *f.*, à-propos, *m.*, avantage, *m.*, utilité, *f.*
Expedient, adj. expédient, convenable, à propos, avantageux, utile. — s. expédient, *m.*, moyen, *m.*
Expediently, adv. convenablement, à propos
Expedite, va. expédier, hâter, faciliter
Expedition, s. expédition, *f.*, diligence, *f.*
Expeditionary, adj. d'expédition
Expeditious, adj. expéditif, diligent, prompt
Expeditiously, adv. avec diligence, promptement
Expeditiousness, s. expédition, *f.*, diligence, *f.*
Expel, va. expulser, chasser
Expend, va. dépenser, employer
Expenditure, s. dépense, *f.*
Expense, s. frais, *m.pl.*, dépense, *f.*, dépens, *m.pl.* *At the — of*, aux frais de, aux dépens de. *To put to* —, induire en frais
Expensive, adj. (*pers.*) dépensier, dispendieux, coûteux
Expensively, adv. à grands frais, d'une manière dispendieuse
Expensiveness, s. goûts dispendieux, *m.*, prodigalité, *f.*, frais, *m.pl.*
Experience, s. expérience *f.*
Experience, va. éprouver, faire l'expérience de, connaître, expérimenter
Experienced, adj. habile, expérimenté, exercé
Experiment, s. expérience, *f.*
Experiment, va. éprouver, expérimenter
Experimental, adj. expérimental
Experimentally, adv. par expérience
Expert, adj. habile (dans), adroit (en), expert (en)
Expertly, adv. habilement
Expertness, s. habileté, *f.*, adresse, *f.*
Expiable, adj. qu'on peut expier
Expiate, va. expier, réparer
Expiation, s. expiation, *f.*
Expiatory, adj. expiatoire
Expiration, s. expiration, *f.*, fin, *f.*, terme, *m.*
Expire, vn. expirer, mourir
Expire, va. expirer, exhaler
Explain, va. expliquer
Explainer, s. interprète, *m.*, explicateur, *m.*
Explanation, s. explication, *f.*
Explanatory, adj. explicatif
Expletive, adj. explétif. — s. mot explétif, *m.*

Explicable, adj. explicable
Explication, s. explication, *f.*
Explicit, adj. explicite, formel, clair
Explicitly, adv. explicitement
Explode, vn. faire explosion, éclater; — va. désapprouver fort, décrier, faire tomber en désuétude
Exploit, s. exploit, *m.*
Exploration, s. exploration, *f.*
Explore, va. explorer, reconnaître
Explorer, s. explorateur, *m.*
Explosion, s. explosion, *f.*
Explosive, adj. qui fait explosion, fulminant
Exponent, s. exposant, *m.*, représentant, *m.*
Export, va. exporter
Export, s. exportation, *f.* — adj. d'exportation. — *trade*, le commerce d'exportation
Exportation, s. exportation, *f.*, sortie, *f.*
Exporter, s. exportateur, *m.*
Expose, va. exposer, démasquer, dévoiler, ridiculiser
Exposer, s. exposant, *m.*
Exposition, s. exposition, *f.*, explication, *f.*
Expositor, s. interprète, *m.*
Expostulate, *see* REMONSTRATE
Expostulation, s. remonstrance, *f.*, reproche, *m.*, plainte, *f.*
Expostulatory, adj. de remonstrance
Exposure, s. exposition, *f.*, action de démasquer, de dévoiler, *f.*, éclat, *m.*, scandale, *m.*
Expound, va. exposer, expliquer
Expounder, s. interprète, *m.*
Express, va. exprimer, énoncer, dire
Express, adj. exprès, explicite, formel, clair
Express, s. exprès, *m.*, estafette, *f.*, courrier, *m.*, train express, *m.*
Expressible, adj. exprimable
Expression, s. expression, *f.*
Expressive, adj. expressif
Expressively, adv. d'une manière expressive
Expressiveness, s. expression, *f.*
Expressly, adv. expressément
Expropriate, va. exproprier
Expropriation, s. expropriation, *f.*
Expulsion, s. expulsion, *f.*
Expunge, va. effacer
Expurgate, va. purger, corriger
Expurgation, s. correction, *f.*
Exquisite, adj. exquis, parfait, excessif
Exquisite, s. élégant, *m.*, -e, *f.*
Exquisitely, adv. d'une manière exquise, excessivement
Exquisiteness, s. nature exquise, *f.*, violence, *f.*
Extant, adj. existant, qui existe
Extemporaneous, **Extemporary**, adj. improvisé, impromptu
Extemporize, va. improviser
Extemporizer, s. improvisateur, *m.*
Extend, va. étendre, allonger, prolonger; — vn. s'étendre
Extensibility, s. extensibilité, *f.*
Extensible, adj. extensible
Extension, s. extension, *f.*, prolongement, *m.*
Extensive, adj. étendu, vaste, spacieux
Extensively, adv. d'une manière étendue, avec étendue
Extensiveness, s. étendue, *f.*
Extent, s. étendue, *f.*, longueur, *f.*, (*law*) estimation, *f.* *To a certain* —, jusqu'à un certain point
Extenuate, va. exténuer, diminuer, amaigrir. *Extenuating circumstances*, circonstances atténuantes
Extenuation, s. exténuation, *f.*, (*mitigation*) atténuation, *f.*, adoucissement, *m.*
Exterior, adj. s. extérieur
Exterminate, va. exterminer, éliminer
Extermination, s. extermination, *f.*
Exterminator, s. exterminateur, *m.*
External, adj. externe, extérieur
Externally, adv. extérieurement, à l'extérieur
Extinct, adj. éteint. *To become* —, s'éteindre
Extinction, s. extinction, *f.*
Extinguish, va. éteindre, détruire
Extinguisher, s. éteignoir, *m.*
Extirpate, va. extirper, exterminer
Extirpation, s. extirpation, *f.*
Extol, va. exalter, célébrer, porter aux nues, vanter
Extolment, s. louange, *f.*
Extort, va. extorquer, arracher
Extortion, s. extorsion, *f.*
Extortioner, s. auteur d'extorsions, *m.*, concussionnaire, *m.*
Extra, adj. extraordinaire, supplémentaire, en sus
Extract, va. extraire, tirer, retirer, arracher
Extract, s. extrait, *m.*, extraction, *f.*
Extracter, s. celui, celle qui extrait, (*surg.*) forceps, *m.*
Extradition, s. extradition, *f.*
Extrajudicial, adj. extrajudiciaire
Extrajudicially, adv. extrajudiciairement
Extraneous, adj. étranger (à), en dehors (de)
Extraordinarily, adv. extraordinairement
Extraordinariness, s. caractère extraordinaire, *m.*, rareté, *f.*
Extraordinary, adj. extraordinaire
Extravagance, s. extravagance, *f.*, prodigalité, *f.*, folles dépenses, *f.pl.*
Extravagant, adj. extravagant, déraisonnable, dépensier, prodigue
Extravagantly, adv. d'une manière extravagante, follement
Extravasate, adj. extravasé
Extravasation, s. extravasation, *f.*
Extreme, adj. extrême
Extreme, s. extrême, *m.*, extrémité, *f.*, excès, *m.*, comble, *m.*
Extricate, va. dégager, débarrasser, retirer, tirer
Extrication, s. délivrance, *f.*
Extrinsic, **Extrinsical**, adj. extrinsèque
Extrude, va. expulser, repousser
Extrusion, s. expulsion, *f.*
Exuberance, s. exubérance, *f.*, surabondance, *f.*
Exuberant, adj. exubérant
Exuberantly, adv. avec exubérance, surabondamment
Exudation, s. exsudation, *f.*
Exude, vn. exsuder, faire exsuder
Exult, vn. se réjouir, triompher
Exultation, s. allégresse, *f.*, joie, *f.*, triomphe, *m.*
Exulting, adj. joyeux, triomphant
Exultingly, adv. avec joie, d'un ton *or* d'un air de triomphe
Exuviae, s. dépouilles, *f.pl.*, (*geol.*) débris, *m.pl.*
Eyas, s. niais, *m.*, jeune faucon, *m.*
Eye, s. œil, *m.*, regard, *m.*, aspect, *m.*, face, *f.*, (*of a needle*) trou, *m.* —*ball*, prunelle de l'œil, *f.* —*bone*, arcade sourcilière, *f.* —*brow*, sourcil, *m.* —*-flap*, œillère (de cheval), *f.* —*-glance*, coup d'œil, *m.*, œillade, *f.* —*glass*, lorgnon, *m.* *Double —glass*, binocle, *m.*, pince-nez, *m.* —*lash*, cil, *m.* —*lid*, paupière, *f.* —*-pit*, orbite de l'œil, *m.* —*sight*, vue, *f.* —*sore*, bête noire, *f.*, objet d'aversion, *m.*
Eye, va. regarder, observer, lorgner
. . . -Eyed, adj. . . . aux yeux . . . *Blue-* —, aux yeux bleus. *One-* —, borgne
Eyeless, adj. aveugle
Eyelet, s. œillet, *m.*
Eyre, s. tournée, *f.* *Justice in* —, juge en tournée

F

F, s. F, f, *m.*, (*mus.*) fa, *m.*
Fa, s. fa, *m.*, clef de fa, *f.*
Fable, s. fable, *f.*
Fable, vn. feindre, prétendre; — va. imaginer, inventer
Fabled, adj. fabuleux, de la fable
Fabric, s. édifice, *m.*, construction, *f.*, tissu, *m.*, étoffe, *f.*
Fabricate, va. fabriquer
Fabrication, s. fabrication, *f.*, construction, *f.*
Fabricator, s. architecte, *m.*, constructeur, *m.*, fabricateur, *m.*
Fabulist, s. fabuliste, *m.*
Fabulous, adj. fabuleux, de la fable
Fabulously, adv. fabuleusement
Fabulousness, s. nature fabuleuse, *f.*
Face, s. face, *f.*, surface, *f.*, visage, *m.*, figure, *f.*, mine, *f.*, maintien, *m.*, grimace, *f.*, aspect, *m.*, apparence, *f.*, assurance, *f.*, audace, *f.*, impudence, *f.*, (*diamonds*) facette, *f.*, (*print.*) œil, *m.* *Before the — of*, sous les yeux de, en présence de. —*-ache*, tic douloureux, *m.*, névralgie faciale, *f.* *To put a good — on the matter*, faire

bonne contenance. *He had the — to*, il eut le front de

Face, va. faire face à, affronter, braver en face, (*a wall*) revêtir, (*a coat*) mettre un revers à. *To — down*, confondre par son effronterie. *To — out*, braver en face, braver. *To — it out*, payer d'effronterie. *—d with red*, à revers rouges. — vn. dissimuler, (*mil.*) faire front. *To — about*, faire volte-face

. . . **-Faced**, adj. à . . . visage, à figure . . .

Facet, s. facette, *f.*

Facetious, adj. facétieux

Facetiously, adv. facétieusement

Facetiousness, s. caractère facétieux, *m.*, facétie, *f.*, gaîté, *f.*

Facial, adj. facial

Facilitate, va. faciliter

Facilitation, s. facilité, *f.*

Facing, s. (*of a wall*) revêtement, *m.*, parement, *m.*, (*of a coat*) revers, *m.*, (*of a uniform*) retroussis, *m.*, (*mil.*) front, *m.*

Fac-simile, s. fac-simile, *m.*

Fact, s. fait, *m.* *In —*, de fait, en effet. *In point of —*, à vrai dire, au fait

Faction, s. faction, *f.*

Factious, adj. factieux

Factiously, adv. d'une manière factieuse

Factiousness, s. caractère or esprit factieux, *m.*

Factitious, adj. factice

Factor, s. facteur, *m.*, agent, *m.*

Factorage, s. droit de commission, *m.*

Factory, s. comptoir, *m.*, factorerie, *f.*, fabrique, *f.*, manufacture, *f.*, filature, *f.*

Factotum, s. factotum, *m.*

Faculty, s. faculté, *f.*, talent, *m.*

Fade, vn. disparaître, s'évanouir, s'effacer, (*flower*) se faner, se flétrir, (*colour*) se passer, passer, ternir, (*fig.*) périr

Fading, adj. qui se flétrit, se fane, etc.; qui périt, qui se passe

Fading, s. disparition, *f.*, flétrissure, *f.*, dépérissement, *m.*

Fag, vn. se fatiguer, travailler, (*fam.*) piocher

Fag, s. "fag," *m.* —-*end*, bout, *m.*, lisière, *f.*

Fagging, s. coups, *m.pl.*, le système de "fagging," *m.*, travail, *m.*

Fagot, Faggot, s. fagot, *m.*, cotret, *m.*, bourrée, *f.*, (*mil.*) fascine, *f.*

Fail, vn. manquer, faillir, faiblir, défaillir, s'affaiblir, périr, succomber, (*promises*) ne pas s'accomplir, (*plans*) échouer, manquer, avorter, (*business*) faire faillite, manquer, faillir; — va. manquer à, faire défaut à, faire faute à, trahir, abandonner

Fail, s. faute, *f.*, mauvais succès, *m.*, mort, *f.* *Without —*, sans faute

Failing, s. défaillance, *f.*, affaiblissement, *m.*, manque, *m.*, défaut, *m.*

Failure, s. manque, *m.*, défaut, *m.*, manquement, *m.*, mauvaise réussite, *f.*, mauvais succès, *m.*, échec, *m.*, coup manqué, *m.*, projet manqué, *m.*, (*theat.*) chute, *f.*, (*com.*) faillite, *f.*

Fain, adj. content, heureux, aise, obligé (de), réduit (à), désireux. *I was — to do it*, j'étais obligé de le faire

Fain, adv. volontiers. *I would — know*, je voudrais bien savoir

Faint, vn. s'évanouir, disparaître, se trouver mal, tomber en faiblesse, perdre connaissance, se pâmer, être épuisé, devenir faible. *To — away*, s'évanouir

Faint, adj. faible, affaibli, épuisé, (*colours, sound*) faible, léger, (*timide*) timide, pusillanime, abattu. — -*hearted*, pusillanime, faible de cœur, découragé. — -*heartedly*, avec pusillanimité, timidement. — -*heartedness*, faiblesse de cœur, *f.*, pusillanimité, *f.*

Fainting, s. défaillance, *f.*, évanouissement, *m.* — -*fit*, évanouissement, *m.*, syncope, *f.*, pâmoison, *f.*

Faintish, adj. un peu faible, défaillant

Faintishness, s. faiblesse, *f.*

Faintly, adv. faiblement, d'une voix éteinte, timidement, mollement, imparfaitement

Faintness, s. faiblesse, *f.*, défaillance, *f.*, pusillanimité, *f.*, mollesse, *f.*

Fair, adj. beau, (*weather*) bon, favorable, propice, (*complexion*) blanc, (*hair*) blond pur, net, sans tache, en vue, loyal, juste, de bonne foi, équitable, impartial, bon, légitime, permis, (*writing*) nette, bien lisible, bonne, passable. *At set —*, au beau fixe. — -*complexioned*, à la peau blanche, blond. — *fame*, réputation sans tache. *To be in a — way*, être en bonne voie. *To stand — for*, être en bonne position pour, être en passe pour. — -*dealing*, bonne foi, procédé loyal. — -*play*, franc jeu, bonne foi, justice. *A — offer*, offre raisonnable. — *statement*, exposé impartial. *A — profit*, un honnête profit. *By — means*, par des moyens honorables, par la douceur. — *hand*, une belle écriture. *A — business*, d'assez bonnes affaires. *Good —*, bon courant

Fair, adv. bien, en bons rapports, doucement. *To carry it —*, avoir belle apparence. *To keep — with*, être bien avec, ménager

Fair, s. belle, *f.*, beauté, *f.*, foire, *f.*, fête, *f.*

Fairing, s. cadeau acheté à la foire, *m.*

Fairish, adj. assez beau

Fairly, adv. bien, agréablement, loyalement, de bonne foi, honnêtement, avec impartialité, nettement, proprement

Fairness, s. beauté, *f.*, blancheur, *f.*, couleur blonde, *f.*, pureté, *f.*, netteté, *f.*, clarté, *f.*, loyauté, *f.*, bonne foi, *f.*, honnêteté, *f.*, impartialité, *f.*, justice, *f.*, franchise, *f.*

Fairy, s. fée, *f.*

Fairy, adj. de fée, des fées, féerique

Faith, s. foi, *f.* *Of easy —*, assez crédule. *To be true to one's —*, garder sa foi. *To break one's —*, manquer à sa foi. *To place, to put — in*, avoir foi en. *Breach of —*, manque de foi

Faithful, adj. fidèle, digne de foi

Faithfully, adv. fidèlement, avec fidélité

Faithfulness, s. fidélité, *f.*

Faithless, adj. infidèle (à), sans foi, déloyal, perfide, traître

Faithlessly, adv. infidèlement, sans foi, déloyalement

Faithlessness, s. infidélité, *f.*, déloyauté, *f.*

Fakir, s. fakir, *m.*

Falchion, s. glaive, *m.*

Falcon, s. faucon, *m.*

Falconer, s. fauconnier, *m.*

Falconet, s. fauconneau, *m.*

Falconry, s. fauconnerie, *f.*

Faldstool, s. pliant, *m.*, prie-Dieu, *m.*

Fall, vn. tomber, choir, s'abattre, succomber, périr, baisser, descendre, (*river*) se jeter, se décharger, (*prices*) baisser, tomber, (*features*) s'allonger, s'attrister, (*events*) arriver, advenir, (*lot*) échoir, revenir, descendre, (*bills*) échoir, (*words*) échapper, tomber. — *again*, retomber, tomber de nouveau. —*away*, tomber, maigrir, dépérir, s'éloigner (de), abandonner (. . .), s'écarter, se départir. *To — back*, tomber en arrière, se renverser, se rejeter en arrière, reculer, se rabattre. *To — behind*, rester en arrière. *To — down*, tomber. *To — in*, s'écrouler, s'affaisser, se mettre en rangs. *To — in with*, rencontrer par hasard, être d'accord, cadrer avec, rencontrer. *To — off*, tomber, se détacher, (*from*) se détacher (de), abandonner. *To — on* or *upon*, tomber sur, se jeter sur, s'abattre, fondre sur, trouver (par hasard). *To — over*, tomber par-dessus. *To — out*, tomber, arriver, se brouiller, rompre. *To — short*, manquer, être or se trouver à court, être au-dessous de, ne pas répondre à. *To — to*, se mettre à, commencer à. *To — under*, tomber sous, être compris dans, se ranger dans, être conçu par

Fall, s. chute, *f.*, (*fam.*) culbute, *f.*, (*water*) chute, *f.*, cascade, *f.*, avalanche, *f.*, (*of the year*) automne, *m.*, (*decay*) décadence, *f.*, ruine, *f.*, (*of a glass*) abaissement, *m.*, (*prices*) baisse, *f.*, (*river*) débouchement, *m.*, décharge, *f.*, (*ground*) pente, *f.*, (*trees*) abatage, *m.*, abatis, *m.*, coupe, *f.*

Fallacious, adj. fallacieux, mensonger, trompeur

Fallaciously, adv. fallacieusement

Fallacy, s. fausseté, *f.*, mensonge, *m.*, illusion, *f.*, erreur, *f.*, sophisme, *m.*

Fallen, adj. tombé, déchu

Fallibility, s. faillibilité, *f.*

Fallible, adj. faillible

Falling, s. chute, *f.* — *away*, amaigrissement, *m.*, ruine, *f.*, défection, *f.*, apostasie, *f.* — *in*, écroulement, *m.* — *off*, chute, *f.*, abandon, *m.*, diminution, *f.* — -*sickness*, le haut mal, mal caduc, *m.*, épilepsie, *f.* — *star*, étoile filante

Fallow, adj. (*colour*) fauve, (*agric.*) en jachère, en friche sans culture

False, adj. faux, perfide, déloyal, traître, feint, prétendu, mauvais, illégal. — *bottom*, double fond, *m.*

False, Falsely, adv. faussement, faux

Falsehood, s. fausseté, *f.*, mensonge, *m.*, fraude, *f.*

Falseness, s. fausseté, *f.*

Falsification, s. falsification, *f.*

Falsifier, s. falsificateur, *m.*, menteur, *m.*

Falsify, va. falsifier, dénaturer, fausser

Falsity, s. fausseté, *f.*

Falter, vn. hésiter, être interdit, se troubler, chanceler, trembler, défaillir

Faltering, adj. hésitant, tremblant, mal assuré, chancelant

Faltering, s. hésitation, *f.*, tremblement, *m.*

Falteringly, adv. en hésitant, avec hésitation, en tremblant

Fame, s. bruit public, *m.*, renommée, *f.*, renom, *m.*, gloire, *f.*, célébrité, *f.*

Famed, adj. renommé, célèbre, fameux, connu

Familiar, adj. de famille, domestique, familier, intime. *To be — with*, connaître familièrement

Familiarity, s. familiarité, *f.*

Familiarize, va. familiariser

Familiarly, adv. familièrement

Family, s. famille, *f.* — adj. de famille. *In the — way*, enceinte

Famine, s. famine, *f.*
Famish, va. affamer, faire mourir de faim, priver; — vn. mourir de faim, être affamé
Famous, adj. célèbre, fameux
Famously, adv. avec une grande renommée, (*fam.*) furieusement, extrêmement
Fan, s. éventail, *m.*, (*bellows*) soufflet, *m.*, machine soufflante, *f.*, (*agric.*) van, *m.* — *-seller*, éventailliste, *m.f.* — *-light*, ventilateur, *m.*
Fan, va. éventer, rafraîchir, frapper, agiter, exciter, aviver, (*agric.*) vanner
Fanatic, Fanatical, adj. fanatique
Fanatically, adv. avec fanatisme, en fanatique
Fanaticism, s. fanatisme, *m.*
Fanaticize, va. fanatiser
Fancier, s. amateur, *m.*, (*dealer*) marchand (de), *m.*
Fanciful, adj. doué or plein d'imagination, romanesque, fantastique, visionnaire, fantasque, capricieux, (*things*) chimérique
Fancifully, adv. avec imagination, d'une manière fantastique, bizarrement
Fancifulness, s. nature fantastique, caractère chimérique
Fancy, s. imagination, *f.*, fantaisie, *f.*, idée, *f.*, envie, *f.*, guise, *f.*, (*fam.*) l'art de la boxe, *f.*
Fancy, adj. de fantaisie. — *article*, objet de fantaisie, *m.* — *-ball*, bal costumé, *m.* — *biscuits*, petits fours, *m.pl.*
Fancy, vn. s'imaginer, se figurer, croire; — va. s'imaginer, se figurer, croire, aimer, avoir du goût pour, avoir envie de
Fang, s. (*dogs*) croc, *m.*, (*wild boar*) défense, *f.*, (*reptiles*) crochet, *m.*, (*birds*) griffe, *f.*, serre, *f.*
Fanged, adj. armé de crocs, de défenses, de dents, etc.
Fangled, adj. inventé, sot. *New-* —, de nouvelle invention, d'un nouveau genre
Fantastic, adj. fantastique, imaginaire, bizarre, fantasque, capricieux
Fantastically, adv. d'une manière fantastique, bizarrement, d'une manière fantasque
Fantasticalness, s. bizarrerie, *f.*, naturel fantasque, *m.*
Far, adv. loin, au loin, (*much*) bien, de beaucoup, beaucoup. *How* —*!* combien de distance? jusqu'où? *As* — *as*, aussi loin que, jusqu'à, en tant que. *So* —, si loin, aussi loin, tellement, jusqu'au point. *So* —, *so good*, c'est très-bien jusqu'ici. *So* — *as*, aussi loin que, jusqu'à, autant que. *Thus* —, jusqu'ici, jusque-là, jusqu'à ce point. — *from*, loin de, loin que. — *and wide*, au loin, de tous côtés. — *off*, au loin. *By* —, de beaucoup. — *-fetched*, apporté de loin, tiré par les cheveux
Far, adj. éloigné, lointain, reculé
Farce, s. farce, *f.*
Farcical, adj. burlesque
Farcy, s. farcin, *m.*
Fare, vn. aller, passer, voyager, se trouver, être, se porter, se nourrir, manger. *To* — *alike*, partager le même sort. *You might go further and* — *worse*, vous pourriez tomber de mal en pis. — *you well*, adieu! je vous souhaite une bonne santé. *It* —*d ill with them*, les choses allèrent mal pour eux
Fare, s. (*drive*) course, *f.*, prix de la course, *m.*, place, *f.*, voyageur, *m.*, (*eating*) chère, *f.*, nourriture, *f.*, menu, *m.*
Farewell, interj. s. adieu. — adj. d'adieu
Farinaceous, adj. farineux, (*bot.*) farinacé
Farm, s. ferme, *f.*, métairie, *f.*, bail à ferme, *m.*, patente, *f.* — *-house*, ferme, *f.* — *-yard*, cour de la ferme, *f.*, basse-cour, *f.*
Farm, va. affermer, donner à ferme, prendre à ferme, exploiter, faire valoir. *To* — *out*, affermer
Farmer, s. fermier, *m.*, colon, *m.*, cultivateur, *m.*, (*of the taxes*) traitant, *m.*
Farming, s. agriculture, *f.*, culture, *f.*, exploitation, *f.*, culture à bail, *f.*, (*taxes*) ferme, *f.*
Farrago, s. mélange, *m.*, confus, *m.*
Farrier, s. maréchal ferrant, *m.*
Farriery, s. maréchalerie, *f.*
Farrow, s. portée, *f.*
Farrow, adj. stérile
Farrow, va.n. mettre bas
Farther, adv. plus loin (que), au delà (de), en outre, davantage
Farther, adj. plus éloigné, plus loin, encore
Farthing, s. liard, *m.*
Fascinate, va. fasciner, charmer
Fascinating, adj. charmant
Fascination, s. fascination, *f.*, charme, *m.*
Fascine, s. fascine, *f.*
Fashion, s. façon, *f.*, forme, *f.*, (*of coats*) coupe, *f.*, (*taste*) mode, *f.*, goût, *m.*, style, *m.*, genre, *m.*, (*high life*) beau monde, *m.* *In* —, *quite the* —, à la mode, à la dernière mode. *To be, to go out of* —, passer de mode. *To bring into* —, mettre à la mode
Fashion, va. façonner, former, faire, adapter, accommoder
Fashionable, adj. à la mode, fashionable, distingué, beau
Fashionable, s. élégant, *m.*, fashionable, *m.*
Fashionably, adv. à la mode, élégamment
Fast, vn. jeûner
Fast, s. jeûne, *m.*, jour de jeûne, *m.*
Fast, adj. ferme, solide, attaché, fixé, (*friend*) fidèle, attaché, (*colour*) solide, (*knot*) serré, (*sleep*) profond, (*quick*) rapide, vite, (*man*) lancé, dissipé, dissolu, dépensier. *To stand* —, se tenir ferme. *To set* —, affermir. — *-handed*, serré, dur à la détente. — *and loose*, inconstant
Fast, adv. ferme, fortement, solidement, bien, vite, rapidement, (*watch*) en avance, (*sleep*) profondément. — *by*, — *beside*, tout auprès de. *To live* —, *too* —, mener grand train la vie, faire la vie
Fasten, va. attacher, fixer, assujettir, (*nav.*) amarrer, (*doors*) fermer, barrer, (*dress*) agrafer; — vn. s'attacher, s'acharner
Fastening, s. attache, *f.*, fermeture, *f.*, chevillage, *m.*
Faster, s. jeûneur, *m.*, -euse, *f.*
Fastidious, adj. dédaigneux, altier, difficile, délicat, dégoûté, vétilleux
Fastidiously, adv. dédaigneusement
Fastidiousness, s. dédain, *m.*, goût *or* caractère difficile, *m.*
Fasting, s. jeûne, *m.*
Fastly, adv. fermement
Fastness, s. force, *f.*, solidité, *f.*, (*stronghold*) forteresse, *f.*, retraite, *f.*
Fat, adj. gras, gros, fertile
Fat, s. gras, *m.*, graisse, *f.*, (*fig.*) le meilleur, *m.*
Fat, va. nourrir, engraisser; — vn. s'engraisser. *To turn out to* —, mettre à l'engrais
Fatal, adj. fatal, inévitable, funeste, mortel
Fatalism, s. fatalisme, *m.*
Fatalist, s. fataliste, *m.*
Fatality, s. fatalité, *f.*
Fatally, adv. fatalement
Fate, s. destin, *m.*, sort, *m.*, trépas, *m.*, mort, *f.*
Fated, adj. destiné
Father, s. père, *m.* — *-in-law*, beau-père, *m.* — *-land*, patrie, *f.*, pays natal, *m.*
Father, va. servir de père à, adopter, s'approprier, se dire l'auteur de
Fatherhood, s. paternité, *f.*
Fatherless, adj. sans père, orphelin
Fatherly, adj. paternel, de père
Fathom, s. toise, *f.*, (*nav.*) brasse, *f.*, (*fig.*) intelligence, *f.*, portée, *f.* — *-line*, sonde, *f.*
Fathom, va. sonder, approfondir
Fathomless, adj. sans fond
Fatigue, s. fatigue, *f.*, lassitude, *f.*, (*mil.*) corvée, *f.*
Fatigue, va. fatiguer, lasser
Fatling, s. brebis grasse, *f.*
Fatness, s. graisse, *f.*, embonpoint, *m.*, fertilité, *f.*
Fatten, va. engraisser, s'engraisser
Fatty, adj. grassouillet, gras
Fatuity, s. impertinence, *f.*
Fault, s. faute, *f.*, défaut, *m.*, (*mines*) faille, *f.* *To be at* —, *at a* —, être, se trouver en défaut. *To find* — *with a thing*, trouver à redire à, épiloguer sur, blâmer. — *-finder*, épilogueur, censeur. *To make good a* —, relever un défaut
Faultily, adv. d'une manière fautive
Faultiness, s. imperfection, *f.*, culpabilité, *f.*
Faultless, adj. parfait, sans faute, sans défaut
Faulty, adj. en faute, fautif, à blâmer, imparfait, défectueux
Faun, s. faune, *m.*
Favour, s. faveur, *f.*, bonnes grâces, *f.pl.*, protection, *f.*, plaisir, *m.*, (*com.*) estimée, *f.*, estimée lettre, *f.*, (*ribbon*) faveur, *f.*, couleurs, *f.pl.* *Under* — *of the night*, à la faveur de la nuit
Favour, va. favoriser, protéger, gratifier, faire l'honneur *or* le plaisir de
Favourable, adj. favorable, propice
Favourableness, s. caractère favorable, *m.*, bienveillance, *f.*
Favourably, adv. avec faveur, favorablement
Favoured, adj. favorisé. *Ill-* —, de mauvaise mine, laid, disgracié. *Well-* —, de bonne mine, beau
Favourer, s. protecteur, *m.*, -trice, *f.*, partisan, *m.*
Favourite, adj. s. favori, -te, bien-aimé, -e, chéri, -e
Favouritism, s. favoritisme, *m.*
Fawn, s. faon, *m.*
Fawn, va.n. faonner, mettre bas, caresser, flatter bassement
Fawner, s. sycophante, *m.*, adulateur, *m.*, flatteur, *m.*
Fawning, s. caresses, *f.pl.*, basse flatterie, *f.*, adulation, *f.*
Fawning, adj. caressant, bassement flatteur
Fawningly, adv. d'une manière caressante, en flattant bassement
Fealty, s. foi, *f.*
Fear, s. crainte, *f.*, peur, *f.*, frayeur, *f.*, effroi, *m.* *Out of* —, *through* —, par crainte, *f.* *For* — *of*, de peur de. *For* — . . . *should*, de peur que . . . ne
Fear, va.n. craindre, avoir peur de, redouter
Fearful, adj. craintif, peureux, timide, terrible, effrayant
Fearfully, adv. craintivement, timidement, terriblement, d'une manière effrayante

Fearfulness, s. timidité, *f.*, crainte, *f.*, terreur, *f.*
Fearless, adj. intrépide, sans crainte, sans peur
Fearlessly, adv. intrépidement, sans crainte
Fearlessness, s. intrépidité, *f.*
Feasibility, Feasibleness, s. praticabilité, *f.*, possibilité, *f.*
Feasible, adj. praticable, faisable
Feast, s. festin, *m.*, banquet, *m.*, régal, *m.*, fête, *f.*, solennité, *f.*
Feast, vn. faire festin, festoyer, se régaler ; — va. traiter, festoyer, régaler, charmer, réjouir
Feaster, s. viveur, *m.*, amateur de bonne chère, *m.*, amphitryon, *m.*
Feastful, adj. joyeux, de fête
Feat, s. haut fait, *m.*, exploit, *m.*, action, *f.*
Feather, s. plume, *f.*, plumage, *m.*, (*fig.*) espèce, *f.*, farine, *f.*, (*mil.*) plumet, *m.*, (*horses*) épi, *m.* — *-seller*, plumassier, *m.* *To be in high* —, en excellente condition. *To show the white* —, reculer. *Birds of a* —, (*fig.*) gens de même farine. *Birds of a — flock together*, qui se ressemble s'assemble. *It is a — in his cap*, il peut en être fier
Feather, va. habiller de plumes, orner d'une plume, (*fig.*) enrichir, élever. *To — one's nest*, mettre du foin dans ses bottes, faire sa pelote. *To — oneself*, s'enrichir
Feathered, adj. à plumes, couvert de plumes, emplumé, (*fig.*) ailé, rapide
Feathery, adj. garni de plumes, plumeux, léger
Feature, s. trait, *m.*, visage, *m.*, caractère, *m.*, point, *m.* —*s*, traits, *m.pl.*
Featured, adj. ayant des traits, au visage . . . ., aux traits . . .
Febrifuge, adj. s. fébrifuge
Febrile, adj. fébrile
February, s. février, *m.*
Fecula, s. fécule, *f.*
Fecundate, va. féconder
Fecundation, s. fécondation, *f.*
Fecundity, s. fécondité, *f.*
Federal, adj. fédéral
Federalism, s. fédéralisme, *m.*
Federalist, s. fédéraliste, *m.*
Federate, adj. fédéré
Federation, s. fédération, *f.*
Federative, adj. fédératif
Fee, s. honoraires, *m.pl.*, émoluments, *m.pl.*, salaire, *m.*, droits, *m.pl.*, (*law*) fief, *m.*, propriété héréditaire, *f.*
Fee, va. payer des honoraires (à), (*counsel*) retenir, acheter, corrompre
Feeble, adj. faible, débile

Feebleness, s. faiblesse, *f.*
Feebly, adv. faiblement
Feed, va. nourrir, donner à manger à, faire paître, (*fig.*) alimenter, entretenir ; — vn. se nourrir (de), manger, s'alimenter, paître, se repaître
Feed, s. manger, *m.*, pâturage, *m.*, repas, *m.*, aliment, *m.*, pâture, *f.* — *-pipe*, tuyau d'alimentation, *m.*
Feeder, s. qui nourrit, qui donne à manger (à), pourvoyeur (de), nourrisseur, *m.*, éleveur, *m.*, (*fig.*) fauteur, *m.*, convive, *m.*, canal d'alimentation, *m.*
Feeding, s. nourriture, *f.*, alimentation, *f.*
Feel, vn. sentir, s'émouvoir, être ému *or* touché, se sentir, se trouver, être. *To — after* or *for*, chercher à tâtons. *To — for*, compatir à, prendre intérêt à. — va. tâter, toucher, sentir, ressentir, éprouver, tâter le pouls à. *To — the ground*, tâter le terrain. *To — one's way with*, tâter
Feel, s. toucher, *m.*, tact, *m.*
Feeler, s. antenne, *f.*, tentacule, *m.*, pierre d'essai, *f.*
Feeling, adj. touchant, plein de sentiment, sensible, vif
Feeling, s. tact, *m.*, toucher, *m.*, tâtonnement, *m.*, sensation, *f.*, sentiment, *m.*, sensibilité, *f.*, compassion, *f.*
Feelingly, adv. avec sentiment, avec âme, d'une manière touchante
Feign, va.n. inventer, imaginer, feindre, simuler, contrefaire
Feignedly, Feigningly, adv. avec feinte, fictivement
Feint, s. feinte, *f.*
Felicitate, va. féliciter
Felicitation, s. félicitation, *f.*
Felicitous, adj. heureux
Felicity, s. félicité, *f.*, bonheur, *m.*
Feline, adj. de chat, félin
Fell, adj. cruel, féroce
Fell, s. peau, *f.*, colline, *f.*, montagne, *f.* — *-monger*, marchand de peaux
Fell, va. abattre, renverser, terrasser
Feller, s. celui qui abat, bûcheron, *m.*
Felling, s. abatage, *m.*, abatis, *m.*, coupe, *f.*
Fellow, s. compagnon, *m.*, camarade, *m.*, semblable, *m.*, pair, *m.*, égal, *m.*, collègue, *m.*, confrère, *m.*, pareil, *m.*, pendant, *m.*, (*univ.*) agrégé, *m.* ; homme, *m.*, garçon, *m.*, personnage, *m.*, gaillard, *m.*, compère, *m.*, sujet, *m.*, homme du commun, *m.*, diable, *m.* *A good* —, un bon garçon. *A little* —, un petit bon homme. *Old* —, vieux bonhomme, (*fam.*) mon vieux. *A pretty* —, un joli garçon. *Poor* — ! pauvre garçon ! pauvre diable ! *A steady young* —, un bon sujet. *A good-for-nothing* —, un mauvais garnement. *Young* —, jeune homme. *A sad* —, un mauvais sujet. *Idle* —, paresseux. *Drunken* —, ivrogne. — *-adventurer*, camarade d'aventures. — *-being*, — *-creature*, — *-man*, semblable, *m.* — *-citizen*, — *-townsman*, concitoyen, *m.* — *-counsellor*, collègue au conseil, *m.* — *-countryman*, compatriote, *m.* — *-feeling*, sympathie, *f.* — *-heir*, cohéritier, *m.* — *-labourer*, — *-worker*, compagnon de travail, *m.*, collaborateur, *m.* — *-helper*, aide, *m.* — *-member*, collègue, *m.*, confrère, *m.* — *-scholar*, — *-student*, camarade de collége, *m.*, camarade d'études, *m.*, condisciple, *m.* — *-traveller*, compagnon, *m.*, compagne de voyage, *f.*
Fellowship, s. société, *f.*, rapports, *m.pl.*, relations, *f. pl.*, sociabilité, *f.*, association, *f.*, communauté, *f.*, (*univ.*) agrégation, *f.*, place, *f.*, rang d'agrégé, *m.* *To hold — with*, avoir des relations avec. *Good* —, sociabilité, *f.*, joyeuse humeur, *f.*
Felly, s. jante, *f.*
Felo-de-se, s. suicide, *m.*
Felon, s. criminel, *m.*
Felonious, adj. criminel, méchant, perfide, scélérat
Feloniously, adv. criminellement, traîtreusement
Felony, s. crime, *m.*, crime capital, *m.*, félonie, *f.*
Felt, s. feutre, *m.*, (chapeau de) feutre, *m.*
Felucca, s. felouque, *f.*
Female, s. femme, *f.*, (*anim.*) personne, *f.*, jeune personne, *f.*, femelle, *f.*
Female, adj. de femme, féminin, femelle
Feminine, adj. féminin, de femme, fin, délicat, efféminé
Feminine, s. féminin, *m.*
Fen, s. marais, *m.*, marécage, *m.*, fondrière, *f.*
Fence, s. défense, *f.*, barrière, *f.*, clôture, *f.*, enceinte, *f.*, haie, *f.*, palissade, *f.*
Fence, va. défendre, clore, garder, entourer, clôturer. *To — in*, défendre, protéger, clore, entourer. *To — up*, barrer. *Fenced cities*, villes fortifiées. — vn. se défendre (contre), s'abriter (de), faire des armes, tirer les armes
Fenceless, adj. ouvert
Fencer, s. maître d'armes, *m.*, tireur d'armes, *m.*, tireur, *m.*
Fencing, s. escrime, *f.*, manière de faire des armes, *f.*, clôture, *f.* — *-master*, maître d'armes, *m.*, maître d'escrime, *m.* — *-match*, assaut d'armes, *m.* — *-school*, salle d'escrime, *f.*
Fend, va. abriter contre, se garder de, (*a flock*) parquer. *To — off*, parer
Fender, s. garde-feu, *m.*

Fennel, s. fenouil, *m.*
Fenny, adj. marécageux
Ferment, vn. fermenter; — va. faire fermenter
Ferment, s. ferment, *m.*, fermentation, *f.*
Fermentation, Fermenting, s. fermentation, *f.*
Fern, s. fougère, *f.* — *-plot*, fougeraie, *f.*
Ferny, adj. couvert de fougère
Ferocious, adj. féroce
Ferociously, adv. avec férocité
Ferociousness, Ferocity, s. férocité, *f.*
Ferret, s. furet, *m.*
Ferret, va. fureter. — *out*, dépister, dénicher
Ferreter, s. fureteur, *m.*
Ferruginous, adj. ferrugineux
Ferrule, s. virole, *f.*, bout, *m.*
Ferry, s. bac, *m.* — *-boat*, bac, *m.* — *-man*, passeur, *m.*, batelier, *m.*
Ferry, va.n. passer
Fertile, adj. fécond, fertile
Fertility, s. fertilité, *f.*
Fertilization, s. fertilisation, *f.*
Fertilize, va. fertiliser
Fervency, s. ferveur, *f.*, ardeur, *f.*, chaleur, *f.*
Fervent, s. fervent, *m.* — adj. fervent, brûlant, ardent, vif
Fervently, adv. avec ferveur, avec ardeur
Fervid, adj. ardent
Fervour, s. ferveur, *f.*, chaleur, *f.*, ardeur, *f.*
Fescue, s. baguette, *f.*, touche, *f.*
Fester, vn. se corrompre, s'envenimer
Fester, s. pustule, *f.*
Festival, adj. de fête, solennel, joyeux
Festival, s. fête, *f.* *High* —, fête solennelle
Festive, adj. de fête, joyeux, gai. — *-board*, table du festin
Festivity, s. gaieté, *f.*, joie, *f.*, allégresse, *f.*
Festoon, s. feston, *m.*
Festoon, va. festonner, orner de festons
Fetch, va. chercher, aller chercher, aller prendre, apporter, amener, (*dogs*) rapporter, (*breath*) prendre, (*a sigh*) pousser, tirer, (*blow*) porter, frapper, (*price*) rapporter, valoir, (*pumps*) charger, amorcer. *To send to* —, envoyer chercher. *To — and carry*, rapporter. *To — away*, emporter, emmener. *To — back*, rapporter, ramener. *To — in*, faire entrer. *To — out*, faire sortir. *To — over*, apporter, amener de l'autre côté. *To — up*, monter, élever, faire monter
Fetid, adj. fétide
Fetidness, s. fétidité, *f.*
Fetish, s. adj. fétiche, *m.*
Fetishism, s. fétichisme, *m.*

Fetlock, s. fanon, *m.* — *-joint* boulet, *m.*

Fetter, va. entraver, mettre dans les fers, enchaîner

Fetters, s.pl. entraves, *f.pl.*, fers, *m.pl.*, chaînes, *f.pl.*

Feud, s. querelle, *f.*, haine, *f.*

Feudal, adj. féodal

Feudalism, s. féodalité, *f.*

Feudatory, s. feudataire, *m.*

Fever, s. fièvre, *f.*

Feverish, adj. fiévreux, agité par la fièvre, (*fig.*) fébrile, capricieux, brûlant

Few, adj. peu de, peu nombreux, peu de gens, peu de personnes. *A — books*, quelques livres

Fewer, adj. moins

Fib, s. mensonge, *m.*, menterie, *f.*, conte, *m.*

Fib, vn. mentir, dire des menteries

Fibre, s. fibre, *f.*

Fibrous, adj. fibreux

Fickle, adj. volage, changeant

Fickleness, s. humeur changeante, *f.*, inconstance, *f.*

Fiction, s. fiction, *f.*

Fictitious, adj. fictif, faux

Fictitiously, adv. fictivement

Fiddle, s. violon, *m.*, (*fam.*) crin-crin, *m.* — *-faddle*, fadaises, *f.pl.*, sornettes, *f.pl.*, niaiseries, *f.pl.*, balivernes, *f.pl.* *To — -faddle, to talk — -faddle*, s'amuser à des riens, baguenauder, dire des fadaises. — *-stick*, archet, *m.* — *-de-dee!* interj. allons donc! — *-string*, corde de violon, *f.* — *-wood*, bois de guitare, *m.*

Fiddle, vn. jouer du violon, (*fig.*) s'amuser à des riens, niaiser

Fiddler, s. joueur de violon, *m.*, ménétrier, *m.*, (*fam.*) crin-crin, *m.*

Fiddling, s. action de jouer du violon, *f.*, (*fig.*) niaiseries, *f.pl.*

Fiddling, adj. qui s'amuse à des riens

Fidelity, s. fidélité, *f.*

Fidget, vn. s'agiter, se remuer, se tourmenter, tatillonner

Fidget, s. agitation, *f.*, inquiétudes, *f.pl.*, impatiences, *f.pl.*, crispations, *f.pl.*, (*pers.*) tatillon, *m.*, tatillonne, *f.*

Fidgety, adj. remuant, inquiet

Fie! interj. fi! fi donc! — *for shame!* fi! l'horreur!

Fief, s. fief, *m.*

Field, s. champ, *m.*, (*mil.*) campagne, *f.*, bataille, *f.* *To take the —*, entrer or se mettre en campagne, ouvrir la campagne. — *-day*, jour de revue, *m.* — *-fare*, litorne, *f.* — *-marshal*, maréchal, *m.* — *-mouse*, mulot, *m.* — *-officer*, officier supérieur, *m.* — *-sports*, les exercices au grand air (la chasse, les courses, la pêche, etc.). — *-works*, travaux, ouvrages, *m.pl.*

Fiend, s. démon, *m.*

Fiendish, adj. de démon, infernal

Fierce, adj. cruel, féroce, sauvage, farouche

Fiercely, adv. avec férocité, cruellement, impétueusement, excessivement

Fierceness, s. férocité, *f.*, violence, *f.*, impétuosité, *f.*

Fieriness, s. chaleur, *f.*, (*fig.*) fougue, *f.*, ardeur, *f.*

Fiery, adj. de feu, de flamme, (*fig.*) fougueux, impétueux, irascible, emporté

Fife, s. fifre, *m.*

Fifer, s. fifre, *m.*

Fifteen, s. adj. quinze

Fifteenth, s. adj. quinzième, *m.*, quinze

Fifth, s. cinquième, *m.*, quinte, *f.* — adj. cinq. *Charles the — of Spain and Germany*, Charles-Quint

Fifthly, adv. cinquièmement

Fiftieth, adj. cinquantième

Fifty, adj. s. cinquante

Fig, s. figue, *f.* *A — for*, loin de, fi de, nargue de. *I don't care a — for it*, je m'en soucie comme de cela

Fight, va.n. se battre, combattre. *To — it through, out*, combattre jusqu'au bout. *To — one's way through*, se frayer un chemin de vive force

Fight, s. combat, *m.*, bataille, *f.*, rixe, *f.*, lutte, *f.* *To have a —*, se battre. *Close —*, combat de près, *m.*, mêlée, *f.*

Fighter, s. combattant, *m.*, (*contempt.*) batailleur, *m.*, ferrailleur, *m.*

Fighting, s. combat, *m.*, coups, *m.pl.*, rixe, *f.*, batterie, *f.*

Figment, s. fiction, *f.*

Figurant, s. figurant, *m.*, -e, *f.*, comparse, *m.f.*

Figurative, adj. figuratif, symbolique

Figuratively, adv. figurativement, en langage or style figuré

Figure, s. figure, *f.*, (*appearance*) forme, *f.*, tournure, *f.*, (*rank*) rang, *m.*, splendeur, *f.*, (*arithmet.*) chiffre, *m.*, (*com.*) prix, *m.* *To make a — in the world*, briller dans le monde

Figure, va. figurer, donner une forme à, façonner, tailler, orner, ouvrager; — vn. figurer, jouer un rôle

Filament, s. filament, *m.*

Filbert, s. aveline, *f.*

Filch, va. filouter, escamoter, dérober

File, s. lime, *f.*, (*fig. pers.*) finaud, *m.*, -e, *f.*, matois, *m.*, -e, *f.*, (*letters, bills*) porte-factures, *m.*, liasse, *f.*, dossier, *m.*, (*papers*) collection, *f.*, liste, *f.*, catalogue, *m.*, (*mil.*) file, *f.*, rang, *m.*, (*carriages*) queue, *f.* *Dead —*, lime sourde. *Round —*, queue-de-rat, *f.* — *-cutter*, tailleur de limes. *Cunning old —*, vieux finaud. — *-leader*, chef de file, *m.* *Right —*, par file à droite. *To stand in a —*, faire queue

File, va. limer, (*fig.*) affiler, aiguiser, (*bills*) mettre or garder en liasse, (*law*) enregistrer, produire. *To — off*, enlever avec la lime. — vn. (*mil.*) défiler, marcher à la file. *To — in, out*, entrer, sortir à la file. *To — off*, défiler

Filial, adj. filial

Filially, adv. filialement

Filiation, s. filiation, *f.*

Filibuster, s. flibustier, *m.*

Filigree, s. filigrane, *m.*

Filings, s.pl. limaille, *f.*

Fill, va. remplir, emplir, garnir, (*satisfy*) rassasier, combler, (*to appoint*) nommer à. *To — in*, remplir, remblayer. *To — out*, verser, étendre. *To — up*, remplir, combler, compléter. — vn. remplir son verre, sa coupe, etc., se remplir

Fill, s. suffisance, *f.*, soûl, *m.*

Fillet, s. bandelette, *f.*, bandeau, *m.*, (*veal*) rouelle, *f.*, (*beef*) filet, *m.*

Filling, s. action de remplir. — *in*, remplissage, *m.* — *up*, remblai, *m.*

Fillip, va. donner une chiquenaude à

Fillip, s. chiquenaude, *f.*

Filly, s. pouliche, *f.*

Film, s. pellicule, *f.*, membrane, *f.*, (*anat.*) tunique, *f.*, (*eye*) taie, *m.*, fil de la Vierge, *m.*

Filmy, adj. membraneux

Filter, s. filtre, *m.*

Filter, va.n. filtrer, se filtrer

Filtering, s. filtration, *f.*

Filth, s. ordures, *f.pl.*, saletés, *f.pl.*, immondices, *f.pl.*

Filthily, adv. salement

Filthiness, s. saleté, *f.*, malpropreté, *f.*

Filthy, adj. sale, malpropre, ordurier, immonde

Filtration, s. filtration, *f.*

Fin, s. nageoire, *f.*, (*whales*) fanon, *m.* — *-footed*, palmipède

Finable, adj. passible d'amende

Final, adj. final, dernier définitif, décisif

Finale, s. finale, *m.f.*

Finally, adv. enfin, finalement, définitivement, en définitive

Finances, s. finances, *f.pl.*

Financial, adj. financier, de finances

Financier, s. financier, *m.*

Finch, s. pinson, *m.*

Find, va. trouver, découvrir, voir, surprendre, (*supply*) donner, fournir, pourvoir, (*law*) déclarer, (*verdict*) prononcer, rendre, (*damages*) adjuger, accorder. — *-fault*, censeur, épilogueur

Finder, s. personne qui trouve, *m.*, inventeur, *m.*

Finding, s. découverte, *f.*, trouvaille, *f.*, (*law*) verdict, *m.*

Fine, adj. beau, fin, (*sharp*) affilé, (*slender*) délié, menu, (*weather*) beau, (*elegant*) élégant. — *-draw*, faire une reprise perdue à. — *-drawing*, reprises perdues. — *-spun*, filé fin, (*fig.*) subtil, recherché

Fine, s. amende, *f.* *Liable to a —*, passible d'amende

Fine, va. affiner, (*wine*) clarifier, coller, (*punishment*) mettre à l'amende

Finely, adv. fin, menu, finement, subtilement, vivement, élégamment, bien, délicatement

Fineness, s. finesse, *f.*, pureté, *f.*, délicatesse, *f.*, beauté, *f.*, élégance, *f.*

Finery, s. parure, *f.*, ornement, *m.*, colifichets, *m.pl.*, (*iron.*) étalage, *m.*

Finesse, vn. jouer au fin, user de finesse, finasser

Finessing, s. artifice, *m.*

Finger, s. doigt, *m.*, (*mus.*) souplesse, *f.*, exécution, *f.*, doigté, *m.* *To have a — in the pie*, en être, être mêlé à. — *-board*, (*violin*) manche, *m.*, (*piano*) clavier, *m.* — *-bowl*, — *-glass*, bol, *m.* — *-plate*, plaque, *f.* — *-post*, poteau indicateur, *m.* — *-stall*, doigtier, *m.*

Finger, va. toucher, manier; — vn. doigter

Fingering, s. maniement, *m.*, (*mus.*) doigté, *m.*

Finical, Finikin, adj. maniéré, affecté, précieux, apprêté, fastidieux

Finically, adv. avec afféterie

Finicalness, s. afféterie, *f.*

Fining, s. affinage, *m.* —*s*, (*wines*) collage, *m.*

Finish, va. finir, achever, terminer, mettre fin à. *A —ed gentleman*, un homme accompli. *To — off*, mettre la dernière main à. — vn. finir, s'achever

Finish, s. fini, *m.*

Finite, adj. fini

Finny, Finned, adj. pourvu de nageoires. *The — tribe*, les habitants des eaux

Fir, s. sapin, *m.* — *-apple*, pomme de pin, *f.*

Fire, s. feu, *m.*, incendie, *m.*, (*fig.*) fougue, *f.*, ardeur, *f.*, vivacité, *f.* *Ball of —*, globe de feu, *m.* *To go through — and water for*, se jeter au feu pour. *Greek —*, feu grégeois. — *!* — *!* au feu! au feu! *To catch —*, prendre feu. *On —*, en feu, embrasé. *To be on —*, être en feu, brûler. *To set — to, to set on —*, mettre le feu à, incendier. *He will never set the Thames on —*, il n'a pas inventé la poudre. — *-arms*, armes à feu, *f.pl.* — *-ball*, grenade, *f.*, ballon d'artifice, *m.* — *-balloon*, montgolfière, *f.* —

-*bars*, grille, *f.* — -*basket*, fourneau portatif, *m.* — -*blast*, (*agric.*) rouille, *f.* — -*board*, plaque de cheminée, *f.* — -*brigade*, corps de pompiers, *m.* — -*broom*, petit balai, *m.* — -*bucket*, seau à incendie, *m.* — -*damp*, feu grisou. — -*dog*, chenet, *m.* — -*eater*, mangeur de feu, *m.*, fanfaron, *m.* — -*engine*, pompe à incendie, *f.* — -*escape*, appareil de sauvetage, *m.* — -*fly*, ver luisant, *m.*, mouche luisante, *f.*, luciole, *f.* — -*grate*, grille, *f.* — -*irons*, — -*set*, garniture de feu, *f.* — -*kiln*, four, *m.* — -*master*, (*mil.*) chef des artificiers, *m.* — -*plug*, robinet à incendie, *m.* — -*proof*, à l'épreuve du feu. — -*ship*, brûlot, *m.* — -*works*, feu d'artifice, *m.* — -*wood*, bois à brûler, *m.*

Fire, va. mettre le feu à, mettre en feu, incendier, embraser, (*a gun*) tirer, décharger ; — vn. prendre feu, s'enflammer, s'emporter, (*mil.*) faire feu, tirer

Fire! interj. feu !

Firebrand, s. tison, *m.*, (*fig.*) incendiaire, *m.*, boutefeu, *m.*

Firelock, s. fusil, *m.*, mousquet, *m.*

Fireman, s. pompier, *m.*, chauffeur, *m.*

Fireplace, s. cheminée, *f.*, âtre, *m.*, foyer, *m.*

Fireside, s. foyer, *m.*, foyer domestique, *m.*

Fireside, adj. du coin du feu, intime, familier

Firing, s. action de mettre le feu à, incendie, *m.*, décharge, *f.*, (*mil.*) feu, *m.*, fusillade, *f.*, canonnade, *f.*, tir, *m.*, chauffage, *m.*, combustibles, *m.pl.* — -*practice*, l'exercice du tir, *m.*

Firkin, s. quartaut, *m.*

Firm, s. (*com.*) maison, *f.*, raison sociale, *f.*

Firm, adj. ferme, solide, assuré, dévoué

Firmament, s. firmament, *m.*

Firmly, adv. fermement, avec fermeté

Firmness, s. fermeté, *f.*, solidité, *f.*, stabilité, *f.*, fidélité, *f.*

First, adj. s. premier unième, le plus grand, le premier. — -*rate*, de premier rang, éminent, de premier force, (*com.*) de choix, de première qualité

First, adv. premièrement, d'abord, auparavant. — *of all*, — *and foremost*, tout d'abord, avant tout

Firstly, adv. premièrement, 1°.

Firstling, s. prémices, *f. pl.*, premier-né, *m.*

Firth, s. *see* Frith

Fiscal, adj. s. fiscal, *m.*, -e, *f.*

Fish, s. poisson, *m.*, (*cards*) fiche, *f.* *A queer* —, (*person*) un drôle de corps. *Fresh-water* —, *salt-water* —, poisson de rivière, poisson de mer, *m.*, marée, *f.* — -*bone*, arête, *f.* — -*carver*, — -*knife*, — -*slice*, truelle à poisson, *f.* — -*block*, jumelle, *f.* — -*day*, jour maigre, *m.* — -*fag*, — -*wife*, — -*woman*, poissarde, *f.*, marchande de poisson, *f.* — -*hook*, hameçon, *m.* — -*kettle*, poissonnière, *f.* — -*market*, poissonnerie, *f.* — -*pond*, — -*pool*, vivier, *m.*, étang, *m.*

Fish, vn.a. pêcher, jeter le hameçon à, (*fig.*) rechercher, quêter. *To* — *out*, découvrir, surprendre

Fisher, Fisherman, s. pêcheur, *m.*

Fishery, s. pêche, *f.*, poissonnerie, *f.*

Fishing, s. pêche, *f.*

Fishing, adj. de pêche. — -*boat*, bateau pêcheur. — -*hook*, hameçon, *m.* — -*line*, — -*rod*, ligne à pêcher, *f.* — -*gear*, — -*tackle*, attirail de pêche, *m.*

Fishy, adj. de poisson, poissonneux

Fissure, s. fissure, *f.*

Fist, s. poing, *m.*

Fisted, *see* Close

Fisticuff, s. coup de poing, *m.*

Fistula, s. fistule, *m.*

Fit, s. accès, *m.*, attaque, *f.*, convulsions, *f.pl.*, intervalle, *m.*, humeur, *m.*, disposition *f.*, (*clothes*) ajustement. *By* —*s and starts*, par sauts et par bonds, à bâtons rompus

Fit, adj. propre à, fait (pour), qui convient (à), digne (de), capable (de), commode, aisé à supporter, (*clothes*) qui va bien

Fit, va. ajuster, adapter, accommoder, convenir à, aller à, (*boots*) chausser, (*tailors*) habiller. *To* — *into*, ajuster. *To* — *out*, monter, équiper, donner un trousseau à. *To* — *up*, arranger, monter, meubler. — vn. s'ajuster, s'adapter, convenir, servir à, aller, chausser. *To* — *into*, entrer dans, s'adapter à

Fitful, adj. agité, changeant, irrégulier

Fitly, adv. convenablement, bien, commodément

Fitness, s. convenance, *f.*, à-propos, *m.*, aptitude, *f.*

Fitter, s. ajusteur, *m.*

Fitting, s. ajustement, *m.*, garniture, *f.*, assemblage, *m.*, agencement, *m.*, meubles, *m. pl.* — *out*, équipement, *m.*, trousseau, *m.* — *up*, arrangement, *m.*, ameublement, *m.*

Five, s. adj. cinq. — -*fold*, quintuple

Fives, s. pl. balle au mur, *f.* — *court*, jeu de balle, *m.*

Fix, va. fixer, attacher, arrêter, établir ; — vn. se fixer, devenir fixé *or* fixe. *To* — *on or upon*, faire choix de, s'arrêter à, adopter

Fix, s. difficulté, *f.*, embarras, *m.*

Fixed, adj. fixe

Fixedly, adv. fixement

Fixedness, s. fixité, *f.*

Fixture, s. position, *f.*, fixité, *f.*, meuble, *m.*, a demeure, *m.*

Fizz, Fizzle, vn. siffler

Flabbiness, s. flaccidité, *f.*

Flabby, adj. flasque, mollasse

Flaccid, adj. flasque

Flaccidity, s. flaccidité, *f.*

Flag, vn. pendre mollement, (*nav.*) battre contre le mât, (*slacken*) se ralentir, languir, faiblir, traîner, s'affaisser ; — va. daller, paver de dalles

Flag, s. (*bot.*) iris, *m.*, glaïeul, *m.*, (*stone*) dalle, *f.*, drapeau, *m.*, (*nav.*) pavillon, *m.* *A white* —, *a* — *of truce*, (*mil.*) un drapeau blanc, (*nav.*) un bâtiment parlementaire. *To deck with* —*s*, pavoiser. — -*officer*, chef d'escadre, *m.* — -*ship*, vaisseau pavillon, *m.* — -*staff*, mât de pavillon, *m.*

Flagellate, va. flageller

Flagellation, s. flagellation, *f.*

Flageolet, s. flageolet, *m.*

Flagitious, adj. scélérat, de scélératesse, infâme

Flagitiously, adv. d'une manière scélérate

Flagitiousness, s. scélératesse, *f.*

Flagon, s. flacon, *m.*, broc, *m.*, (*church*) burette, *f.*

Flagrancy, s. feu, *m.*, ardeur, *f.*, énormité, *f.*

Flagrant, adj. flagrant, ardent, patent

Flagrantly, adv. d'une manière flagrante

Flail, s. fléau, *m.*

Flake, s. (*snow*) flocon, *m.* — *of fire*, flammèche, *f.* — -*white*, blanc de céruse, *m.*

Flake, va. former en flocons, écailler ; — vn. s'écailler

Flaky, adj. floconneux, écaillé

Flam, s. conte, *m.*, sornette, *f.*

Flame, s. flamme, *f.*, feu, *m.*, flambeau, *m.*, (*pers.*) passion, *f.*

Flame, vn. briller, flamboyer, flamber, (*fig.*) s'enflammer, éclater

Flameless, adj. sans flammes

Flamingo, s. flamant, *m.*

Flamy, adj. de flamme, étincelant

Flank, s. flanc, *m.*, (*build.*) aile, *f.*

Flank, va.n. flanquer, prendre en flanc

Flannel, s. flanelle, *f.* — adj. de flanelle

Flap, s. partie, *f.*, bout qui tombe, *m.*, (*table*) battant, *m.*, (*flapper*) clapet, *m.*, (*coat*) pan, *m.*, (*bonnet*) bord, *m.*, rebord, *m.*, (*pocket*) patte, *f.*, (*shirt*) flanquet, *m.*, (*blow*) coup, *m.*, tape, *f.*, (*of a wing*) coup d'aile, *m.*, (*of the ear*) bout, *m.*

Flap, va. frapper, (*wings*) battre. *To* — *away*, *off*, chasser, écarter. *To* — *over* rabattre. — vn. battre, se rabattre

Flare, vn. briller, vaciller, jeter un éclat passager, flamboyer, éblouir. — *up*, (*fig.*) s'enflammer

Flash, s. éclair, *m.*, flamme subite, *f.*, lueur soudaine, *f.*, jet de lumière, *m.*, (*wit*) trait, *m.*, (*hope*) lueur, *f.*, transport, *m.*, (*iron.*) élégance, *f.*

Flash, adj. (*iron.*) beau, magnifique. — *language*, argot, *m.* — *man*, voleur, *m.*, escroc, *m.* — *money*, fausse monnaie, *f.* — -*house*, demeure de voleurs, *f*

Flash, vn. briller, étinceler, luire, flamboyer, venir *or* paraître rapide comme un éclair, éclater, s'élancer. *To* — *in the pan*, rater. — va. lancer, faire jaillir, faire éclater, rendre éclatant

Flashy, adj. éblouissant, brillant, éclatant, (*iron.*) élégant, vain, vide, (*quick*) prompt, emporté

Flask, s. flacon, *m.*, bouteille, *f.*, (*powder*) poire, *f.*

Flasket, s. corbeille, *f.*

Flat, adj. plat, uni, plane, tout de son long, étendu, (*nose*) épaté, (*tasteless*) plat, éventé, insipide, (*sad*) abattu, attristé, (*com.*) plat, languissant, (*certain*) positif, net, (*mus.*) bémol. *Quite* —, tout à plat

Flat, s. surface unie *or* plane, *f.*, terrain plat, *m.*, plat, *m.*, (*nav.*) bas-fond, *m.*, (*of a house*) étage, *m.*, (*mus.*) bémol, *m.*, (*pers.*) nigaud, *m.*, niais, *m.*, dupe, *m.*

Flatly, adv. à plat, de niveau, platement, (*fig.*) nettement, positivement

Flatness, s. égalité, *f.*, nature plate, *f.*, (*taste*) platitude, *f.*, évent, *m.*

Flatten, va. aplatir, aplanir, (*wine*) éventer, (*colour*) amortir, (*metals*) laminer, abattre, attrister, émousser, (*mus.*) rendre grave. — vn. s'aplatir, s'aplanir, s'éventer, s'émousser

Flatter, va. flatter, encenser

Flatterer, s. flatteur, *m.*, -euse, *f.*

Flattering, adj. flatteur, -euse

Flattery, s. flatterie, *f.*, encens, *m.*

Flatting, s. aplatissement, *m.*, (*metals*) laminage, *m.* — -*mill*, laminoir, *m.*

Flattish, adj. plat

Flatulency, s. flatuosité, *f.*, vide, *m.*

Flatulent, adj. flatueux, (*fig.*) vaniteux, vide, (*style*) ampoulé

Flaunt, vn. se pavaner, faire de l'étalage, avoir l'air insolent

Flaunt, s. étalage, *m.*, magnificence, *f.*

Flaunting, adj. superbe, éclatant

Flauntingly, adv. magnifiquement, insolemment
Flaveur, s. odeur, *f.*, senteur, *f.*, goût, *m.*, saveur, *f.*, (*meat*) fumet, *m.*, (*wine*) bouquet, *m.*, fumet, *m.*, (*tea, &c.*) arome, *m.*
Flavour, va. donner du goût, un bouquet, un arome. *To — of*, sentir
Flaw, s. fragment, *m.*, morceau, *m.*, défaut, *m.*, (*break*) écornure, *f.*, (*crack*) fente, *f.*, fêlure, *f.*, crevasse, *f.*, paille, *f.*, (*law*) vice, *m.*, nullité, *f.*
Flawless, adj. sans défaut
Flax, s. lin, *m.*
Flaxen, Flaxy, adj. de lin, blond
Flay, va. écorcher, enlever
Flayer, s. écorcheur, *m.*
Flea, s. puce, *f.* — *-bite*, morsure de puce, *f.*, (*colour*) moucheté, *m.*, tacheté, *m.*, (*horses*) étourneau, *m.*
Fleck, va. tacheter
Fledge, va. couvrir de plumes, garnir
Fledged, adj. en état de voler
Flee, vn.a. fuir, s'enfuir, prendre la fuite
Fleece, s. toison, *f.*
Fleece, va. tondre, (*fig.*) écorcher, rançonner, escroquer
Fleecy, adj. chargé de toisons, laineux, (*fig.*) blanchissant, blanc
Fleer, va.n. se moquer (de), railler, ricaner
Fleer, s. moquerie, *f.*, raillerie, *f.*, ricanement, *m.*
Fleet, s. flotte, *f.*
Fleet, adj. rapide, (*agric.*) léger
Fleeting, adj. rapide, fugitif, éphémère, passager
Fleetness, s. rapidité, *f.*
Flesh, s. chair, *f.*, viande, *f.* *Proud* —, chair baveuse. — *-brush*, brosse à friction, *f.* — *-day*, jour gras, *m.*
Flesh, va. acharner, engraisser, rassasier, assouvir, (*try*) essayer
Fleshless, adj. décharné
Fleshly, adj. de chair, (*fig.*) charnel
Fleshy, adj. charnu, bien en chair
Flexibility, s. flexibilité, *f.*
Flexible, adj. flexible, souple
Flexion, s. flexion, *f.*, pli, *m.*
Flicker, vn. s'agiter, trembloter, vaciller, (*birds*) battre de l'aile, se trémousser
Flickering, s. mouvement rapide, *m.*, vacillation, *f.*
Flier, s. fuyard, *m.*, fugitif, *m.*, (*mechan.*) volant, *m.*, balancier, *m.*
Flight, s. vol, *m.*, essor, *m.*, (*birds*) volée, *f.*, troupe, *f.*, bande, *f.*, (*escape*) fuite, *f.*, évasion, *f.*, (*fancy*) élan, *m.*, transport, *m.*, (*stairs*) escalier, *m.*, perron, *m.*
Flighty, adj. léger, inconsidéré, étourdi, volage, capricieux

Flimsily, adv. à la légère, légèrement
Flimsiness, s. légèreté, *f.*, manque de consistance, *m.*, faiblesse, *f.*
Flimsy, adj. sans consistance, peu solide, léger, mollasse, frivole, pauvre, insignifiant
Flinch, vn. reculer, broncher, s'écarter (de), hésiter, sourciller
Fling, va. jeter, lancer, rejeter, repousser, renverser à terre. — *away*, jeter, rejeter loin de soi, renoncer (à) — *down*, jeter à terre, abattre — *off*, rejeter loin de soi, dérouter, priver. — *out*, jeter dehors, lancer (des mots). — *open*, ouvrir vivement. — *up*, jeter en l'air, (*fig.*) renoncer à, abandonner. — vn. ruer, lâcher des ruades, regimber, s'emporter
Fling, s. jet, *m.*, coup, *m.*, (*fig.*) mot, *m.*, sarcasme, *m.*, coup de patte, *m.*
Flint, s. silex, *m.*, pierre à fusil, *f.*, caillou, *m.* — *-glass*, crystal, *m.* — *-lock*, fusil à pierre, *m.*
Flinty, adj. siliceux, pierreux, caillouteux, (*fig.*) dur, de pierre
Flippancy, s. faconde, *f.*, pétulance, *f.*, impertinence, *f.*
Flippant, adj. bavard, (*tongue*) bien pendue, affilée, (*person*) dégagé, leste, cavalier
Flippantly, adv. avec volubilité, avec pétulance, d'un air leste, cavalièrement
Flirt, vn. folâtrer, batifoler, faire des coquetteries (à), coqueter (avec)
Flirt, s. coquette, *f.*
Flirtation, s. coquetterie, *f.* *To carry on a — with*, faire la coquette avec
Flit, vn. passer *or* se glisser rapidement
Flitch, s. flèche, *f.*
Float, vn. flotter, surnager. *To — down*, descendre. — va. mettre à flot, faire flotter
Float, s. flux, *m.*, flot, *m.*, (*of wood*) radeau, *m.*, train, *m.*, (*angling*) flotte, *f.* — *board*, palette, *f.*, aube, *f.*
Floating, adj. flottant, bateau de sauvetage
Floating, s. mise à flot, *f.*
Flock, s. troupeau, *m.*, (*birds*) troupe, *f.*, bande, *f.*, (*eccles.*) ouailles, *f.pl.*, (*crowd*) foule, *f.*, troupe, *f.*, (*wool*) flocon, *m.*, (*coarse wool*) bourre, *f.* — *-bed*, — *-mattress*, matelas en bourre de laine. — *-paper*, papier velouté
Flock, vn. aller par troupeau, aller par bandes, accourir, courir en foule, s'attrouper, s'empresser, s'assembler
Flocky, adj. floconneux
Floe, s. banquise, *f.*
Flog, va. fouetter, fustiger
Flogging, s. fouet, *m.*, verges, *f.pl.*

Flood, s. déluge, *m.*, inondation, *f.*, torrent, *m.*, (*tide*) flot, *m.*, flux, *m.*, marée haute, *f.*
Flood, va. inonder, submerger
Flooding, s. inondation, *f.*, débordement, *m.*
Floor, s. plancher, *m.*, parquet, *m.*, (*story*) étage, *m.*, (*barn*) aire, *f.*, (*bridge*) tablier, *m.* *On the* —, à terre, par terre. — *-cloth*, toile cirée. *Basement* —, sous-sol, *m.* *On the same* —, sur le même palier, de plain-pied
Floor, va. planchéier, parqueter, (*to knock down*) renverser, terrasser
Flooring, s. parquet, *m.*, plancher, *m.*
Floral, adj. floral
Florid, adj. fleuri
Floridity, Floridness, s. fraîcheur, *f.*, éclat, *m.*, style fleuri, *m.*
Floridly, adv. en style fleuri
Florin, s. florin, *m.*
Florist, s. fleuriste, *m.*
Floss, s. bourre de soie, *f.*, filoselle, *f.*, soie plate, *f.*
Flotilla, s. flottille, *f.*
Flounce, vn. se démener, se débattre; — va. garnir de volants
Flounce, s. mouvement vif, *m.*, (*of a gown*) volant, *m.*
Flounder, s. carrelet, *m.*
Flounder, vn. patauger, se débattre
Flour, s. farine, *f.*, fleur de farine, *f.* — *-dredge*, boîte à farine, *f.* — *-mill*, moulin, *m.*, minoterie, *f.* — *-merchant*, marchand de farine, *m.*
Flourish, va.n. fleurir, venir bien, prospérer, (*fig.*) faire des floritures, (*mus.*) sonner une fanfare, (*writing*) faire des traits de plume, (*a stick*) faire le moulinet, (*a sword*) brandir
Flourish, s. prospérité, *f.*, éclat, *m.*, beauté, *f.*, fleur de rhétorique, *f.*, floriture, *f.*, (*writing*) trait de plume, *m.*, paraphe *or* parafe, *m.*, (*mus.*) fanfare, *f.*, (*stick*) moulinet, *m.*, action de faire tourner en l'air, *f.*
Flourishing, adj. florissant
Floury, adj. farineux
Flout, va.n. (*at*) se moquer de, railler, insulter à, braver
Flow, vn. couler, s'écouler, se répandre, (*result*) découler, provenir, venir, (*tide*) monter, (*dress*) flotter, ondoyer
Flow, s. flux, *m.*, marée montante, *f.*, courant, *m.*, épanchement, *m.*
Flower, s. fleur, *f.*, élite, *f.*, fleuron, *m.*, ornement, *m.* — *-bed*, parterre, *m.* — *-de-luce*, fleur-de-lis, *f.* — *-pot*, pot à fleurs, *m.* — *-garden*, parterres, *m.pl.*, jardin, *m.* — *-gardener*, fleuriste, *m.* — *-show*, exposition de fleurs, *f.* — *-stand*, jardinière, *f.* — *-silks*, brocart à fleurs, *m.*

Flower, vn. fleurir, être en fleurs, s'épanouir; — va. orner de fleurs
Floweret, s. fleurette, *f.*, petite fleur, *f.*
Flowery, adj. fleuri, à fleurs
Fluctuate, vn. flotter, ondoyer, hésiter, rester indécis, varier
Fluctuation, s. fluctuation, *f.*, variation, *f.*
Flue, s. tuyau de cheminée, *m.*, cheminée, *f.*, (*down*) duvet, *m.*
Fluency, s. facilité, *f.*
Fluent, adj. coulant, facile, (*pers.*) à la parole facile, disert
Fluently, adv. couramment, facilement
Fluff, s. duvet, *m.*, poussière, *f.*
Fluffy, adj. (plein) de duvet
Fluid, adj. s. fluide, *m.*
Fluidity, s. fluidité, *f.*
Fluke, s. (*anchor*) patte, *f.*, oreille, *f.*, (*fish*) carrelet, *m.*, (*luck*) raccroc, *m.*
Flummery, s. fromentée, *f.*, bouillie, *f.*, (*fig.*) flagornerie, *f.*, blague, *f.*
Flunky, s. laquais, *m.*, (*fig.*) pied-plat, *m.*
Flurry, s. agitation, *f.*, émoi, *m.*
Flurry, va. ahurir, agiter
Flush, vn. se précipiter, monter, accourir, rougir; — va. rougir, colorer, enluminer, transporter, (*hunt.*) faire lever, (*cleansing*) laver à grande eau
Flush, adj. frais, vigoureux, bien pourvu, prodigue
Flush, s. rougeur, *f.*, fleur, *f.*, éclat, *m.*, transport, *m.*, (*cards*) flux, *m.*
Flushing, s. rougeur, *f.*, nettoiement, *m.*
Fluster, va. étourdir, ahurir, agiter; — vn. être ahuri, se démener
Fluster, s. agitation, *f.*
Flute, s. flûte, *f.*, (*archit.*) cannelure, *f.*, (*frills*) tuyau, *m.* — *-player*, joueur de flûte, *m.* *Three-holed* —, galoubet, *m.* — *-stop*, jeu de flûte, *m.*
Flute, va. canneler, tuyauter
Flutist, s. joueur de flûte, *m.*
Flutter, vn. battre de l'aile, se débattre, s'agiter, voltiger, voler, (*pulse*) battre irrégulièrement; — va. faire flotter, agiter, effaroucher, (*fans*) jouer (de)
Flutter, Fluttering, s. battement d'ailes, *m.*, mouvement rapide, *m.*, agitation, *f.*, émoi, *m.*, confusion, *f.*, trouble, *m.*
Fluvial, adj. fluvial
Flux, s. courant, *m.*, cours, *m.*, flux, *m.*
Fly, vn. s'envoler, voler, fuir, s'enfuir, (*rumour*) passer, se répandre. *To — in the face of*, braver, contrecarrer. *To let* —, lâcher, laisser s'envoler, lancer. — *about*, voler

ça et là, voltiger. — *at*, s'élancer sur, se jeter sur, sauter à. — *away*, s'envoler, s'enfuir. — *back*, revoler, retourner, faire ressort. — *down*, s'abattre, descendre rapidement. — *in* or *into*, entrer. — *off*, s'envoler, s'effaroucher, déserter. — *out*, s'envoler, sortir, s'élancer dehors, (*anger*) s'emporter, éclater. — *open*, s'ouvrir soudain. — *over*, passer sur *or* par-dessus. — *up* or *upwards*, monter, s'élever. — va. fuir, éviter, (*a kite*) faire voler, (*a hawk*) chasser au faucon

Fly, s. mouche, *f.*, (*mech.*) volant, *m.*, balancier, *m.*, (*vehicle*) cabriolet, *m.*, voiture de remise, *f.* *The — on the coach wheel*, la mouche du coche. — *-blow*, œuf de mouche, *f.* — *-blown*, piqué de mouches, corrompu. — *-boat*, flibot, *m.* — *-case*, carapace, *f.* — *-catcher*, gobe-mouche, *m.* — *-flap*, — *-net*, chasse-mouches, *m.* — *-leaf*, feuille volante, *f.* — *-speck*, tache de mouche, *f.* — *-wheel*, volant, *m.*, balancier, *m.*

Foal, s. poulain, *m.*, pouliche, *f.*

Foal, va.n. mettre bas, pouliner

Foam, s. écume, *f.*

Foam, vn. écumer, baver, (*the sea*) moutonner

Foamy, adj. écumeux

Fob, s. gousset, *m.*

Focus, s. foyer, *m.*

Fodder, s. fourrage, *m.*

Foe, s. ennemi, *m.*, -e, *f.*

Fog, s. brouillard, *m.*, brume, *f.*

Foggy, adj. plein de brouillards, brumeux, (*fig.*) vieil imbécile

Fogy, Fogey, s. *Old —*, vieille, bête

Foible, s. faible, *m.*, côté faible, *m.*

Foil, va. déjouer, faire échouer, émousser, (*hunt.*) dépister

Foil, s. échec, *m.*, (*fencing*) fleuret, *m.*, (*metal*) feuille de métal, *f.*, (*tin*) tain, *m.*, (*contrast*) repoussoir, *m.*, contraste, *m.* *Sharp —s*, fleurets démouchetés

Foist, va. glisser, interposer, faire passer, imposer

Fold, s. parc, *m.*, bercail, *m.*, troupeau, *m.*, (*door*) battant, *m.*, (*of a dress, &c.*) repli, *m.*, (*arith.*) fois, *f.*

Fold, va. plier, ployer, envelopper, (*the arms*) se croiser, (*the hands*) joindre, (*sheep*) parquer

Folder, s. (*pers.*) plieur, *m.*, plieuse, *f.*, (*things*) plioir, *m.*

Folding, adj. qui se replie. — *-bed*, lit de sangle, *m.* — *-chair*, pliant, *m.* — *-doors*, portes à deux battants. — *-screen*, paravent, *m.*

Folding, s. pliage, *m.*, (*of sheep*) parcage, *m.*

Foliage, s. feuillage, *m.*

Folio, s. in-folio, *m.* — adj. folio

Follot, s. esprit follet, *m.*

Folk, Folks, s. pl. gens, *m.f.*, personnes, *f.pl.*

Follow, va. suivre, poursuivre, relancer, rechercher, (*profession*) exercer. — *close upon*, suivre de près. — *up*, suivre de près, poursuivre. — *after*, poursuivre. — vn. suivre, s'ensuivre, résulter. *As follows*, comme suit, ainsi qu'il suit

Follower, s. celui, celle qui suit, suivant, *m.*, -e, *f.*, serviteur, *m.*, gens, *m.*, disciple, *m.*, sectateur, *m.*, amoureux, *m.*

Following, adj. suivant, qui suit, ensuite

Folly, s. folie, *f.*, vice, *m.*, crime, *m.*

Foment, va. fomenter

Fomentation, s. fomentation, *f.*

Fomenter, s. personne qui fomente, (*fig.*) fauteur, *m.*

Fond, adj. fou, insensé, tendre, aimant, indulgent, faible, amateur (de), qui a du goût (pour), (*hopes*) vain, frivole. *To be — (of)*, aimer

Fondle, va. caresser, dorloter, choyer

Fondling, s. enfant gâté, *m.*

Fondly, adv. avec amour, avec ardeur, ardemment

Fondness, s. folie, *f.*, tendresse, *f.*, affection, *f.*, faiblesse, *f.*, indulgence, *f.*, penchant, *m.*, engouement, *m.*

Font, s. source, *f.*, fontaine, *f.*, fonts baptismaux, *m.pl.*, (*print.*) fonte, *f.*

Food, s. nourriture, *f.*, aliment, *m.*, vivres, *m.pl.*, (*animals*) pâture, *f.*

Fool, s. sot, *m.*, sotte, *f.*, imbécile, *m.*, bête, *f.*, (*court-jester*) fou, *m.*, bouffon, *m.* *To make a — of*, se jouer de. *To make a — of oneself*, se faire moquer de soi

Fool, vn. faire la bête. — va. duper, escroquer, gaspiller

Foolery, s. bêtises, *f.pl.*, folie, *f.*, niaiserie, *f.*

Foolish, adj. sot, insensé, imbécile, niais, bête, absurde, ridicule. *A — thing*, une folie, une sottise

Foolishly, adv. sottement, follement, d'une manière insensée *or* absurde, niaisement, bêtement

Foolishness, s. folie, *f.*, sottise, *f.*

Foot, s. pied, *m.*, (*claw*) patte, *f.*, (*table*) pied, *m.*, (*mil.*) infanterie, *f.*, fantassins, *m.pl.*, (*compasses*) jambe, *f.* *On —*, à pied, pédestrement, sur pied, debout. *To set on —*, mettre en train, entamer. *To put one's — in it*, mettre le pied dans le plat, s'embourber. — *-ball*, ballon, *m.* — *-board*, marche-pied, *m.*, pédale, *f.* — *-boy*, petit laquais, *m.* — *-bridge*, passerelle, *f.* — *-cloth*, tapis de pied, *m.*, housse, *f.* — *-lights*, rampe, *f.* — *-match*, course à pied, *f.*, lutte à la course, *f.* — *-mark*, empreinte d'un pied, *f.* — *-passenger*, piéton, *m.* — *-path*, — *-way*, sentier, *m.*, trottoir, *m.*, bord du chemin, *m.* — *-pavement*, trottoir, *m.* — *-print*, empreinte de pas, *f.* — *-stool*, tabouret, *m.*, marchepied, *m.* — *-warmer*, chaufferette, *f.* — *-way*, trottoir, *m.*

Foot, va.n. aller à pied, marcher, aborder, danser, fouler, frapper avec le pied

Footed, adj. avec des pieds, ayant des pieds, à pieds

Footing, s. pas, *m.*, (*ground*) terrain, *m.*, (*support*) point d'appui, *m.*, soutien, *m.*, (*state*) condition, *f.*, (*entrance*) entrée, *f.*, admission, *f.*, établissement, *m.*, droit de cité, *m.*, (*boots*) remontage, *m.*, (*arch.*) base, *f.* *To gain, to get a —*, prendre pied. *To find a —*, avoir son entrée. *To pay one's —*, payer sa bienvenue

Footman, s. valet, *m.*, laquais, *m.*, domestique, *m.*

Footmanship, s. service, *m.*

Footstep, s. pas, *m.*, trace, *f.*

Fop, s. fat, *m.*, petit-maître, *m.*, dameret, *m.*

Foppery, s. fatuité, *f.*, folie, *f.*, frivolité, *f.*

Foppish, adj. fat

Foppishly, adv. en fat

Foppishness, s. fatuité, *f.*

For, prep. pour, à cause de, pour l'amour de, par, en place de, en lieu de, vers, malgré, pendant, comme, comme étant, pour que

For, conj. car

Forage, s. fourrage, *m.*

Forage, vn. (*mil.*) aller au fourrage, fourrager, parcourir le pays. *Foraging cap*, bonnet de police, *m.* — va. fourrager, donner du fourrage à

Forager, s. fourrageur, *m.*

Forasmuch, conj. puisque. — *as*, d'autant que

Foray, s. incursion, *f.*

Forbear, va.n. éviter, s'abstenir, s'empêcher, se garder, supporter, avoir de l'indulgence pour, épargner

Forbearance, Forbearing, s. abstention, *f.*, patience, *f.*, douceur, *f.*, indulgence, *f.*

Forbearingly, adv. avec patience, avec indulgence

Forbid, va. défendre, interdire, interdire l'entrée de, empêcher

Forbidding, adj. repoussant, rebutant. — s. défense, *f.*

Force, s. force, *f.*, effort, *m.*, troupes, *f.pl.*, forces, *f.pl.* *By main —*, de vive force. *In —*, en vigueur. *Put in —*, mettre en force. — *-meat*, viande farcie, *f.* — *-meat-ball*, boulette de viande hachée, *f.* — *-pump*, pompe foulante, *f.*

Force, va. forcer, contraindre, exercer sa force, prendre de force, arracher, extorquer, chasser, (*meat*) farcir. *To — one's way*, s'ouvrir un passage de vive force. — *back*, repousser. — *down*, faire descendre de force. — *in* or *into*, faire entrer de force, enfoncer. — *open*, forcer, briser, enfoncer. — *out*, pousser dehors

Forced, adj. forcé

Forcedly, adv. forcément

Forcedness, s. caractère forcé

Forceful, adj. puissant

Forcefully, adv. puissamment

Forceps, s. pince, *f.*, forceps, *m.*

Forcible, adj. fort, puissant, énergique, pressant, à force ouverte, contraint

Forcibly, adv. avec force, fortement, forcément, de force

Forcing, s. contrainte, *f.* — *-pump*, pompe foulante, *f.* — *-house*, serre chaude, *f.* — *-pit*, couche, *f.*

Ford, s. gué, *m.*

Ford, va. passer à gué

Fordable, adj. guéable

Fore, adj. antérieur, de devant, premier. — s. avant, *m.*

Fore, adv. avant, (*in comp.*) d'avance, avant. — *and aft*, de l'avant à l'arrière

Forearm, va. armer d'avance, prémunir

Forebode, va. présager, prédire

Foreboding, adj. prophétique

Foreboding, s. présage, *m.*, pressentiment, *m.*

Forecast, va.n. calculer d'avance, projeter, préméditer, prévoir

Forecast, s. plan préconçu, *m.*, prévoyance, *f.*

Forecastle, s. gaillard d'avant, *m.*

Foreclose, va. forclore, empêcher

Foreclusion, s. forclusion, *f.*

Foreconceive, va. concevoir d'avance

Foredate, va. antidater

Foredeck, s. avant, *m.*

Foredesign, va. préméditer

Foredetermine, va. déterminer d'avance

Foredoom, va. prédestiner, condamner d'avance

Forefather, s. ancêtre, *m.*, aïeul, *m.*, devancier, *m.*; —*s*, pl. aïeux

Forefend, va. détourner, défendre, préserver

Forefinger, s. index, *m.*

Forego, va. renoncer à, s'abstenir de, se refuser, sacrifier

Foregoing, adj. précédent

Foregone, adj. passé, anticipé. — *conclusion*, opinion préconçue

Foreground, s. premier plan, *m.*, devant, *m.*

Forehead, s. front, *m.*, face, *f.*

Foreign, adj. étranger. *The — office.* le ministère des affaires étrangères

Foreigner, s. étranger, *m.*, étrangere, *f.*

Foreknowledge, s. préscience, *f.*, connaissance acquise, *f.*

Foreland, s. cap, *m.*, pointe, *f.*

Forelock, s. cheveux sur le devant *or* sur le front. *To take time by the —*, prendre l'occasion aux cheveux

Foreman, s. (*jury*) chef, *m.*, (*workshop*) contre-maître, *m.*, chef d'atelier, *m.*

Foremast, s. mât de misaine, *m.*

Forementioned, adj. *see* ABOVE

Foremost, adj. s. premier, plus avancé, au premier rang, en tête

Forenoon, s. matinée, *f.*

Forensic, adj. du barreau, du palais. *— medicine*, la médecine légale

Fore-part, s. devant, *m.*, avant, *m.*, avant-corps, *m.*, (*nav.*) proue, *f.*, avant, *m.*

Forepassed, adj. passé

Foreplan, va. projeter d'avance

Forepossessed, adj. déjà dans la possession, (*pers.*) prévenu

Foreprize, va. estimer d'avance

Forepromised, adj. déjà promis

Forequoted, adj. déjà cité

Fore-rank, s. premier rang, *m.*

Forereach, va.n. (*upon*) gagner (sur)

Forerecited, past part. déjà cité

Foreright, adj. s. droit en avant, rapide

Forerun, va. devancer, annoncer

Forerunner, s. avant-coureur, *m.*, précurseur, *m.*, ancêtre, *m.*

Foresaid, adj. susdit

Foresee, va. prévoir, pourvoir

Foreshadow, va. figurer d'avance

Foreshorten, va. raccourcir

Foreshortening, s. raccourci, *m.*

Foreside, s. devant, *m.*, façade, *f.*

Foresight, s. prévoyance, *f.*, sagacité, *f.*

Forest, s. forêt, *f.*, bois, *m.*

Forest, adj. des forêts, des bois, champêtre, forestier

Forestall, va. anticiper sur, prévenir, devancer, (*law*) accaparer, faire hausser les prix

Forester, s. garde forestier, *m.*, habitant d'une forêt, *m.*, (*tree*) arbre de haute futaie, *m.*

Foretaste, s. avant-goût, *m.*

Foretell, va n. prédire, annoncer

Foreteller, s. prophète, *m.*, prophétesse, *f.*, avant-coureur, *m.*

Forethought, s. prévoyance, *f.*, prudence, *f.*, prévision, *f.*

Foretop, s. tour, *m.*, toupet, *m.*

Forewarn, va. avertir d'avance, prévenir, prémunir. *Forewarned, forearmed*, un averti en vaut deux

Forewarning, s. avis, *m.*, avertissement, *m.*

Forewoman, s. première ouvrière, *f.*

Forfeit, s. forfaiture, *f.*, perte, *f.*, confiscation, *f.*, amende, *f.*, (*bargain*) dédit, *m.*, forfait, *m.*, (*play*) gage, *m.*

Forfeit, va. forfaire, perdre, déchoir (de), confisquer, avoir à payer un dédit *or* une amende de

Forfeiture, s. forfaiture, *f.*, confiscation, *f.*, objet confisqué, *m.*, déchéance, *f.*

Forge, s. forge, *f.*, action de forger, *f.*

Forge, va. forger, inventer, fabriquer, (*coin, bills*) contrefaire

Forger, s. forgeron, *m.*, (*of false news*) forgeur, *m.*, (*of goods, writings, &c.*) contrefacteur, *m.*, faussaire, *m.*, (*coiner*) faux monnayeur, *m.*

Forgery, s. supposition, *f.*, contrefaçon, *f.*, fabrication de fausse monnaie, *f.*, faux, *m.*

Forget, va. oublier, mettre en oubli

Forget-me-not, s. myosotis, *m.*, ne m'oubliez pas, *m.*

Forgetful, adj. oublieux, oubliant

Forgetfully, adv. par oubli, négligemment

Forgetfulness, s. oubli, *m.*, manque de mémoire, *m.*, négligence, *f.*

Forgive, va. pardonner, (*a debt*) remettre, faire remise de, faire grâce de

Forgiveness, s. pardon, *m.*, grâce, *f.*, rémission, *f.*, remise, *f.*

Forgiving, adj. prompt à pardonner, clément, indulgent

Fork, s. fourche, *f.*, fourchette, *f.*, (*roads*) bifurcation, *f.*

Fork, vn. (*trees*) fourcher, se fourcher, (*roads*) se bifurquer, faire la fourche ; — va. remuer *or* enlever avec une fourche. *To — out*, (*money*) allonger

Forked, adj. fourchu, en fourche

Forlorn, adj. privé, désolé, malheureux, triste, perdu, petit

Forlornness, s. désolation, *f.*, tristesse, *f.*, état désespéré, *m.*

Form, s. forme, *f.*, figure, *f.*, (*beauty*) beauté, *f.*, (*formula*) formule, *f.*, (*bench*) banc, *m.*, banquette, *f.*, (*class*) classe, *f.*

Form, va. former, faire, se former, se faire, façonner ; — vn. se former, prendre forme, se façonner

Formal, adj. formel, de forme, pour la forme, en forme, dans les formes, régulier, cérémonieux, (*pers.*) formaliste, façonnier, grave

Formalism, s. formalisme, *m.*

Formalist, s. formaliste, *m.*

Formality, s. formalité, *f.*, formes, *f.pl.*, étiquette, *f.*

Formally, adv. formellement, dans les formes, cérémonieusement

Formation, s. formation, *f.*

Former, adj. s. premier, ancien, d'autrefois, passé, celui-là, celle-là, etc. ; l'un, les uns, etc.

Formerly, adv. autrefois, anciennement, dans l'ancien temps

Formidable, adj. formidable, redoutable, terrible

Formidably, adv. d'une manière redoutable

Formula, s. formule, *f.*

Formulary, s. formulaire, *m.*

Forsake, va. abandonner, délaisser, s'écarter de, quitter

Forsaking, s. abandon, *m.*

Forsooth! interj. vraiment ! en vérité ! parbleu !

Forswear, vn. se parjurer, jurer faussement ; — va. jurer de renoncer à, abjurer

Fort, s. fort, *m.*

Forth, adv. en avant, au dehors, dehors, hors, au grand jour. *— -coming*, prêt à paraître

Forthwith, adv. sur-le-champ, tout de suite, aussitôt, incontinent

Fortieth, adj. quarantième

Fortification, s. fortification, *f.*

Fortify, va. fortifier

Fortitude, s. force d'âme, *f.*, fermeté, *f.*, courage, *m.*

Fortnight, s. quinzaine, *f.*, quinze jours, *m.pl.* *This day —*, (*to come*) d'aujourd'hui en quinze, (*past*) il y a quinze jours aujourd'hui

Fortress, s. forteresse, *f.*

Fortuitous, adj. fortuit

Fortuitously, adv. fortuitement

Fortuitousness, s. caractère fortuit

Fortunate, adj. heureux, fortuné, propice

Fortunately, adv. heureusement

Fortune, s. fortune, *f.*, (*destiny*) la bonne aventure, *f.* *— -hunter*, coureur de dots, aventurier. *— -hunting*, la chasse aux héritières. *— -teller*, diseur, diseuse de bonne aventure. *To tell one's —*, dire la bonne aventure à

Forty, adj. s. quarante

Forum, s. forum, *m.*

Forward, Forwards, adv. en avant. *From that time —*, depuis ce jour-là

Forward, adj. avancé, en avant, en tête, empressé, présomptueux, avantageux, tranchant

Forward, va. avancer, assister, aider à, seconder, activer, hâter, faire parvenir, envoyer, expédier, (*expenses*) faire suivre

Forwarder, s. promoteur, *m.*, qui expédie, *m.*

Forwardly, adv. avec empressement

Forwardness, s. état avancé, *m.*, empressement, *m.*, ardeur, *f.*, présomption, *f.*, (*studies*) progrès, *m.pl.*

Fossil, adj. s. fossile

Foster, va. nourrir, élever, protéger, favoriser, créer, développer

Foster, adj. nourricier. *— -child*, nourrisson, *m.* *— -brother*, frère de lait. *— -father*, père nourricier. *— -mother*, mère nourricière

Foul, adj. sale, malpropre, impur, immonde, (*water*) trouble, (*breath*) infecte, fétide, (*tongue*) chargée, (*crime*) noir, odieux, (*sedition*) déloyal, perfide, (*language*) obscène, injurieux, insultant, (*proof*) chargée, (*weather*) mauvais, gros

Foul, va. souiller, salir

Foully, adv. salement, impurement, odieusement, honteusement, cruellement, déloyalement

Foulness, s. malpropreté, *f.*, impureté, *f.*, mauvaise odeur, *f.*, fétidité, *f.*, état chargé, *f.*, noirceur, *f.*, laideur, *f.*

Found, va. fonder, baser, (*metals*) fondre

Foundation, s. fondation, *f.*, fondement, *m.*, base, *f.*, création, *f.*

Founder, s. fondateur, *m.*, fondatrice, *f.*, (*metals*) fondeur, *m.*

Founder, va. rendre fourbu ; — vn. (*nav.*) sombrer, couler à fond

Foundering, s. courbature, *f.*, foulure, *f.*, (*nav.*) action de sombrer, *f.*

Founding, s. fondation, *f.*, fonderie, *f.*, fonte, *f.*

Foundling, s. enfant trouvé, *m.*, hospice des enfants trouvés, *m.*

Foundress, s. fondatrice, *f.*

Fount, s. source, *f.*, fontaine, *f.*, (*printing*) fonte, *f.*

Fountain, s. fontaine, *f.*, source, *f.*, jet d'eau, *m.* *— -head*, source, *f.*

Four, adj. s. quatre. *On all —s*, à quatre pattes. *— -in-hand*, à grandes guides

Fourfold, adj. s. quadruple, quatre fois autant

Fourscore, s. quatre-vingts

Fourteen, s. adj. quatorze

Fourteenth, adj. s. quatorzième, quatorze

Fourth, adj. quatrième
Fourth, s. quart, *m.*, (*mus.*) quarte, *f.*
Fourthly, adv. quatrièmement
Fowl, s. oiseau, *m.*, volatile, *m.*, oiseau de basse-cour, *m.*
Fowler, s. oiseleur, *m.*
Fowling, s. chasse aux oiseaux sauvages, *f.* — *-piece*, fusil de chasse, *m.*
Fox, s. renard, *m.*, (*fig.*) matois, *m.*
Fraction, s. fraction, *f.*
Fractional, adj. fractionnaire
Fractious, adj. hargneux
Fractiousness, s. nature hargneuse, *f.*
Fracture, s. fracture, *f.*, cassure, *f.*
Fracture, va. fracturer, casser
Fragile, adj. fragile
Fragility, s. fragilité, *f.*
Fragment, s. fragment, *m.*
Fragrance, s. doux parfum, *m.*, suave odeur, *f.*
Fragrant, adj odorant, odoriférant, parfumé
Fragrantly, adj. avec un doux parfum
Frail, adj. frêle, fragile, faible
Frailty, s. fragilité, *f.*, faiblesse, *f.*
Frame, va. former, créer, construire, disposer, imaginer, inventer, (*forge*) fabriquer, forger, (*a plan*) ourdir, (*a picture*) encadrer
Frame, s. cadre, *m.*, encadrement, *m.*, (*window*) châssis, *f.*, (*door*) chambranle, *m.*, (*umbrella*) monture, *f.*, (*embroidery*) métier, *m.*, (*body*) corps, *m.*, charpente, *f.*, (*system*) système, *m.*, ordre réglé, *m.*, *mind*) disposition, *f.*
Framer, s. auteur, *m.*, créateur, *m.*, encadreur, *m.*
Framework, s. encadrement, *m.*, cadre, *m.*, charpente, *f.*, carcasse, *f.*, métier, *m.*
Franchise, s. franchise, *f.*, immunité, *f.*, droit électoral, *m.*
Frank, adj. franc, généreux
Frank, s. contre-seing, *m.*, lettre contre-signée, *f.*, lettre affranchie, *f.*, (*coin*) franc, *m.*
Frank, va. contre-signer, affranchir
Frankincense, s. encens, *m.*
Frankly, adv. franchement
Frankness, s. franchise, *f.*, libéralité, *f.*
Frantic, adj. frénétique, fou, forcené, furieux
Frantically, adv. avec frénésie, en fou
Fraternal, adj. fraternel
Fraternally, adv. fraternellement, en frère
Fraternity, s. fraternité, *f.*, confrérie, *f.*

Fraternize, vn. fraterniser; — va. faire fraterniser
Fratricide, s. fratricide, *m.*
Fraud, Fraudulence, Fraudulency, s. fraude, *f.*, supercherie, *f.*
Fraudulent, adj. (*pers.*) de mauvaise foi, frauduleux, acquis par la fraude
Fraudulently, adv. frauduleusement, par fraude
Fraught, adj. chargé, rempli, plein
Fray, s. éraillure, *f.*, (*fight*) bataille, *f.*, combat, *m.*, rixe, *f.*
Fray, va. érailler, frayer; — vn. s'érailler
Freak, s. caprice, *m.*, boutade, *f.*
Freakish, adj. capricieux
Freckle, s. tache de rousseur, *f.*, rousseur, *f.*
Freckle, va. donner des taches de rousseur à, couvrir de taches de rousseur; — vn. se couvrir de rousseurs
Free, adj. libre, à l'état libre, délivré, dégagé, débarrassé, exempt, franc, sincère, libéral, généreux, large, prodigue, volontaire, dégagé, sans gêne
Free, va. mettre en liberté, délivrer, affranchir, libérer, débarrasser, dégager, ouvrir
Freebooter, s. maraudeur, *m.*, flibustier, *m.*
Freebooting, s. pillage, *m.*, maraude, *f.*
Freedman, s. affranchi, *m.*
Freedom, s. liberté, *f.*, franchise, *f.*, droit de cité, *m.*, (*of a corporation*) maîtrise, *f.*, (*manners*) sans gêne, *m.*, (*theatre*) entrée libre, *f.*
Freehold, s. franc-alleu, *m.*, propriété en biens-fonds, *f.*
Freeholder, s. franc tenancier, *m.*, propriétaire foncier, *m.*
Freely, adv. librement, franchement, généreusement, gratuitement, abondamment, volontairement
Freeman, s. homme libre, *m.*
Freeze, vn. geler, se geler, glacer, se glacer; — va. geler, glacer
Freezing, adj. glacial
Freezing, s. glace, *f.*, congélation, *f.* — *mixture*, mélange réfrigérant
Freight, va. affréter, noliser, charger
Freight, s. fret, *m.*, chargement, *m.*
Freighter, s. affréteur, *m.*
French, s français, *m.* — adj. français. *To take — leave*, partir sans prendre congé
Frenchify, va. franciser, arranger à la française
Frenzied, adj. forcené
Frenzy, s. frénésie, *f.*, délire, *m.*
Frequency, s. fréquence, *f.*, répétition fréquente, *f.*, affluence, *f.*

Frequent, adj. fréquent, nombreux
Frequent, va. fréquenter, hanter
Frequentation, s. fréquentation, *f.*
Frequentative, adj. s. fréquentatif
Frequenter, s. habitué, *m.*
Frequently, adv. fréquemment
Fresco, s. fresque, *m.* *In* —, à fresque
Fresh, adj. frais, nouveau, novice, (*water*) douce, (*tipsy*) en train
Fresh, adv. fraîchement, frais, nouvellement, récemment
Fresh, s. courant d'eau douce, *m.*
Freshen, vn. a. fraîchir, rafraîchir, se rafraîchir, (*nav.*) changer
Freshly, adv. fraîchement, frais, récemment, nouvellement, vigoureusement, vivement
Freshman, s. étudiant de première année, *m.*, novice, *m.*
Freshness, s. fraîcheur, *f.*, nouveauté, *f.*, frais, *m.*, vigueur, *f.*, force, *f.*
Fret, va. user par le frottement, érailler, ronger, écorcher, (*tease*) irriter, chagriner, tourmenter, (*emboss*) sculpter, ciseler, relever en bosse; — vn. s'user par le frottement, s'érailler, se frayer, être rongé, s'agiter, se tourmenter, se chagriner
Fret, s. agitation, *f.*, bouillonnement, *m.*, fermentation, *f.*, mauvaise humeur, *f.*, irritation, *f.*
Fretful, adj. irritable, chagrin, de mauvaise humeur
Fretfully, adv. de mauvaise humeur
Fretfulness, s. humeur chagrine, *f.*
Fretwork, s. ouvrage en bosse, *m.*
Friability, s. friabilité, *f.*
Friable, adj. friable
Friar, s. moine, *m.*, frère, *m.*, religieux, *m.*
Friary, s. monastère, *m.*, couvent, *m.*
Fribble, vn. niaiser, chanceler
Fribble, s. homme *or* femme frivole
Fribble, adj. frivole
Friction, s. friction, *f.*, frottement, *m.* — *-wheel*, roue conductrice, *f.*
Friday, s. vendredi, *m.* *Good* —, vendredi saint
Friend, s. ami, *m.*, -e, *f.*, partisan, *m.* —*s*, pl. famille, *f.*, parents, *m.pl.*
Friendless, adj. sans amis, abandonné
Friendliness, s. nature amicale, *f.*, bienveillance, *f.*
Friendly, adj. d'ami, amical, bien disposé (pour), bienveillant, propice, favorable
Friendly, adv. amicalement

Friendship, s. amitié, *f.*
Frieze, s frise, *f.*
Frigate, s. frégate, *f*
Fright, s. frayeur, *f.*, effroi, *m.*, peur, *f.*, épouvante, *f.*, épouvantail, *m.*
Frighten, va. effrayer, épouvanter, faire peur. — *away*, effrayer, chasser
Frightful, adj effrayant, effroyable, affreux, épouvantable
Frightfully, adv affreusement, effroyablement, à faire peur
Frigid, adj. froid, glacial
Frill, s. collerette, *f.*, jabot, *m.*
Fringe, s. frange, *f.*, crépine, *f.*, bord, *m.* — *-maker*, frangier, *m.*
Fringe, va. franger, border
Frippery, s. friperie, *f.*
Frisk, va. folâtrer, s'ébattre, prendre ses ébats, gambader, bondir
Frisk, s. gambade, *f.*, fredaine, *f.*
Friskiness, s. folâtrerie, *f.*, vivacité, *f.*, gaieté, *f.*
Frisky, adj. folâtre, enjoué, frétillant
Frith, s. détroit, *m.*, embouchure, *f.*
Fritter, s. beignet, *m.*
Fritter, va. couper en tranches, briser, morceler. — *away*, réduire à rien, gaspiller
Frivolity, s. frivolité, *f.*
Frivolous, adj. frivole
Frivolously, adv. avec frivolité
Frizz, Frizzle, va. friser, crêper
Frizz, Frizzle, s. boucle de cheveux crépus, *f.*
Fro, adv. en revenant. *To and* —, çà et là
Frock, s. blouse, *f.*, (*child's*) robe, *f.*, (*monk's*) froc, *m.* — *-coat*, redingote, *f.*
Frog, s. grenouille, *f.*, (*horse*) fourchette, *f.*
Frolic, s. jeu, *m.*, ébats, *m. pl.*, gambade *f.*, fredaine, *f.* *To have a* —, s'amuser
Frolic, vn. folâtrer, s'ébattre, gambader, faire des fredaines
Frolicsome, adj. folâtre, enjoué, gai, joyeux, badin, espiègle
Frolicsomeness, s. gaieté, *f.*, folâtrerie, *f.*
From, prep. de, loin de, depuis, dès, à partir de, (*motive*) par, (*on the part of*) de la part de, de chez, dans, avec, contraire à
Front, s. front, *m.*, (*shop*) devant, *m.*, (*building*) façade, *f.*, (*milit.*) front, *m.*, étendue, *f.*, (*perspective*) élévation, *f.*, (*bridge*) tête, *f.*, (*bonnet*) passe, *f.*
Front, adj. de devant, de face. — *-box*, loge de face, *f* — *-line*, premier rang, *m.* — *-room*, chambre sur le devant, *f.*
Front, va. faire face à, tenir tête à, attaquer, mettre aux prises. *To new* —, remonter.

— vn. se tenir au premier rang, faire face, être en face, être vis-à-vis
Frontal, s. bandeau, m., bandelette, f., (arch.) fronton, m.
Frontier, s. frontière, f. — adj. frontière, placé sur la frontière
Fronting, pr. part. faisant face à, en face de, vis-à-vis
Frontispiece, s. frontispice, m.
Frontlet, s. bandelette, f., fronteau, m.
Frost, s. gelée, f., frimas, m pl., givre, m.
Frost, va. glacer
Frosty, adj. glacial, de gelée, froid
roth, s. écume, f., mousse, f., (fig.) frivolité, f., crème fouettée, f.
roth, vn. écumer, mousser; — va. faire écumer, faire mousser
Frothiness, s. écume, f., mousse, f.
rothy, adj. écumant, écumeux, mousseux, (fig.) frivole, futile, vide
roward, adj. indocile, volontaire, entêté, revêche
rowardly, adv. avec indocilité
rowardness, s. indocilité, f., humeur revêche,
rown, vn. froncer le sourcil, se refrogner, prendre un air sévère. To — at or upon, regarder d'un air menaçant, (things) être contraire à
rown, s. froncement de sourcil, m., regard sévère or courroucé, m., (fig.) rigueurs, pl.
rozen, adj. gelé, glacé, froid. — in, retenu par les glaces. — out, privé d'ouvrage par la glace. — over, pris, gelé
ugal, adj. frugal, sobre, économe
ugality, s. frugalité, f., sobriété, f.
ugally, adv. avec frugalité
ugivorous, adj. frugivore
uit, s. fruit, m. First —s, prémices, f.pl.
uit, adj. à fruit, fruitier, arbre fruitier
uiterer, s. fruitier, m., fruitière, f.
uitful, adj. fertile, fécond, fructueux
uitfully, adv. avec fertilité, fructueusement, avec fruit
uitfulness, s. fertilité, fécondité, f.
uition, s. jouissance,
uitless, adj. stérile, inutile, vain
uitlessly, adv. sans fruit, infructueusement, inutilement
uitlessness, s. stérilité, inutilité, f., vanité, f.
ump, s. vieille grognon,
Frumpish, adj. grognon
Frustrate, va. déjouer, rendre inutile, annuler
Frustration, s. ruine, f., défaite, f., échec, m., désappointement, m.
Fry, s. fretin, m., frai, m., petits poissons, m.pl. Small —, menu fretin
Fry, va. faire frire, frire; — vn. frire
Frying-pan, s. poêle, f. To fall out of the — into the fire, tomber de fièvre en chaud mal
Fuchsia, s. fuchsia, m.
Fuddle, va. griser; — va. se griser
Fudge, s. bourde, f.
Fudge! interj. bah!
Fuel, s. combustible, m., chauffage, m., (fig.) aliment, m.
Fugacity, s. brièveté, f.
Fugitive, s. (mil.) fuyard, m., fugitif, m., réfugié, m.
Fugitive, adj. fugitif, passager, éphémère
Fugue, s. fugue, m.
Fulcrum, s. appui, m., point d'appui, m.
Fulfil, va. accomplir, réaliser, exécuter
Fulfilment, s. accomplissement, m.
Full, adj. plein, rempli, comble, repu, rassasié, (fat) gras, replet, rebondi, (complete) entier, complet, tout, grand, (clothes) ample, bouffant, (sound) plein, sonore
Full, s. plein, mesure complète, f., plus haut point, m., comble, m., suffisance, f., satiété, f., soûl, m.
Full, adv. tout, tout à fait, complètement, bien
Fuller, s. foulon, m. —'s mill, fullery, moulin à foulon
Fully, adv. pleinement, complètement, tout à fait, bien, amplement
Fulminant, **Fulminating**, adj. fulminant
Fulminate, va. fulminer, tonner
Fulmination, s. fulmination, f.
Fulness, s. état de ce qui est plein, m., état complet, m., perfection, f., comble, m., abondance, f., (clothes) ampleur, f.
Fulsome, adj. nauséabond, dégoûtant, grossier
Fulsomeness, s. caractère nauséabond, m., grossièreté, f.
Fumble, vn. tâtonner, toucher, (for . . .) fouiller dans . . . pour trouver, chercher; — va. arranger
Fumbler, s. maladroit, m., -e, f.
Fumblingly, adv. gauchement
Fume, s. fumée, f., vapeur, f., idée vaine, f., colère, f. To get into a —, se mettre en colère
Fume, vn. fumer, émettre or envoyer des fumées, entrer en colère, (fam.) fumer; — va. fumer, parfumer, encenser
Fumigate, va. faire des fumigations dans
Fumigating, adj. fumigatoire
Fumigation, s. fumigation, f.
Fumy, adj. fumeux
Fun, s. amusement, m., divertissement, m., farce, f. In —, for —, pour rire, pour m'amuser. For the — of the thing, histoire de rire. To make — of, se moquer de
Function, s. exercice, m., fonction, f., devoir, m.
Functionary, s. fonctionnaire, m.
Fund, s. fonds, m., capital, m.
Fund, va. placer, consolider, inscrire sur le grand-livre. The funded debt, la dette consolidée. Funded property, rentes sur l'État, argent dans les fonds publics
Fundamental, adj. s. principe fondamental
Fundamentally, adv. fondamentalement
Funeral, s. funérailles, f. pl., enterrement, m., convoi, m.
Funeral, **Funereal**, adj des funérailles, funéraire, (fig.) funèbre
Fungosity, s. fongosité, f.
Fungous, adj. fongueux
Fungus, s. champignon, m., (med.) fongus, m., excroissance, f.
Funk, s. venette, f., puanteur, f. To be, to get in a —, avoir, donner la venette à
Funk, vn. avoir la venette
Funnel, s. entonnoir, m., tuyau, m., (chimney) cheminée, f.
Funny, adj. drôle, amusant, plaisant, comique, bouffon
Fur, s. fourrure, f., peau, f.
Fur, adj. de fourrure
Fur, va. fourrer, garnir or doubler de fourrures, (the tongue) charger; — vn. (boiler) s'incruster, s'encrasser
Furbish, va. fourbir, donner un nouvel éclat à
Furbisher, s. fourbisseur, m.
Furious, adj. furieux, en fureur, furibond, impétueux
Furiously, adv. avec furie, avec fureur, furieusement
Furiousness, s. furie, f., fureur, f., impétuosité, f.
Furl, va. ferler
Furlough, s. (mil.) congé, m.
Furnace, s. fournaise, f.
Furnish, va. fournir, pourvoir, (fit up) équiper, (house) meubler, garnir
Furniture, s. meubles, m. pl., ameublement, m., mobilier, m., (ornament) garniture, f., (fitting out) équipement, m., équipage, m.
Furrier, s. fourreur, m., pelletier, m.
Furriery, s. commerce des fourrures or des pelleteries, m.
Furring, s. (arch.) renflement, m.
Furrow, s. sillon, m., trace, f., marque, f., (groove) rainure, f.
Furrow, va. sillonner, creuser
Furrowed, adj. sillonné, à rainures
Furry, adj. fourré, de fourrure
Further, adj. plus éloigné, plus lointain, ultérieur, encore un autre, nouveau
Further, adv. plus loin, au delà, outre, de plus
Further, va. avancer, favoriser, seconder, aider à, appuyer
Furtherance, s. avancement, m., progrès, m., aide, m., secours, m., appui, m
Furtherer, s. promoteur, m.
Furthermore, adv. de plus, en outre
Furthermost, **Furthest**, adj. (le) plus éloigné or lointain or reculé. — adv. à la distance la plus éloignée, à l'époque la plus reculée or éloignée, le plus loin
Furtive, adj. furtif
Furtively, adv. furtivement
Furuncle, s. furoncle, m., clou, m.
Furuncular, adj. furonculaire
Fury, s. furie, f., fureur, f., délire, m.
Furze, s. genêt épineux, m., ajonc, m.
Furzy, adj. couvert de genêts
Fuscous, adj. terne
Fuse, va. fondre, liquéfier; — vn. se fondre
Fusee, s. fusée, f., allumette, f.
Fusibility, s. fusibilité, f.
Fusible, adj fusible
Fusiform, adj. fusiforme
Fusileer, s. fusilier, m.
Fusion, s. fusion, f.
Fuss, s. embarras, m., façon, f., bruit, m., fracas, m., histoires, f.pl.
Fuss, va. faire des embarras, faire du bruit, faire sonner bien haut (quelque chose)
Fussiness, s. air, m., ton d'importance, m.
Fust, vn. sentir mauvais, sentir le renfermé, moisir
Fustian, s. futaine, f., (fig.) boursouflure, f., galimatias, m.
Fustiness, s. moisi, m., odeur de moisi, f.
Futile, adj. futile
Futility, s. futilité, f.
Future, adj. futur, à venir, à naître
Future, s. futur, m., avenir, m.
Futurity, s. l'avenir, m., chose future, f.
Fuzzle, va. griser

G

G, s. G, g, (*mus.*) sol, *m.*, clef de sol, *f.*

Gab, vn. bavarder, mentir

Gab, s. langue, *f.*, loquacité, *f.*, faconde, *f.* *To have the gift of the —*, avoir la langue bien pendue

Gabble, va. caqueter

Gabble, Gabbling, s. caquetage, *m.*

Gabbler, s. babillard, *m.*

Gabion, s. gabion, *m.*

Gable, s. pignon, *m.* — *-end*, pignon

Gaby, s. bêta, *m.*

Gad, vn. courir, courir çà et là, vagabonder

Gadfly, s. taon, *m.*

Gaffer, s. compère, *m.*, vieux, *m.*, père, *m.*

Gag, va. bâillonner, mettre un bâillon à

Gag, s. bâillon, *m.*

Gaggle, vn. caqueter

Gaiety, s. gaieté, *f.*, gaîté, *f.*

Gaily, adv. gaiement, avec gaieté

Gain, s. gain, *m.*, profit, *m.*, bénéfice, *m.*

Gain, va. gagner, obtenir, acquérir, se faire. — *over to*, gagner à, attirer à, amener à. — *on* or *upon*, gagner sur. — vn. (*clocks, watches*) avancer

Gainer, s. gagnant, *m.* *To be a — by it*, y gagner

Gainful, adj. lucratif, profitable

Gainings, s.pl. gains, *m.pl.*

Gainless, adj. stérile

Gainsay, va. contredire, démentir

Gainsayer, s. contradicteur, *m.*

Gait, s. marche, *f.*, allure, *f.*, démarche, *f.*, maintien, *m.*

Gaiter, s. guêtre, *f.*

Gala, s. gala, *m.*

Galaxy, s. voie lactée, *f.*, (*fig.*) réunion brillante, *f.*

Gale, s. coup de vent, *m.*, tempête, *f.*, brise, *f.*

Galiot, s. galiote, *f.*

Gall, s. fiel, *m.*, bile, *f.*, (*scratch*) écorchure, *f.* — *-nut*, noix de galle, *f.*

Gall, va. érailler, frayer, écorcher, blesser, froisser, piquer, tourmenter. *A galling —*, un feu bien nourri

Gallant, adj. s. brave, vaillant, hardi, courageux, élégant, beau, galant

Gallantly, adv. vaillamment, magnifiquement, avec galanterie, galamment, élégamment

Gallantry, s. bravoure, *f.*, valeur, *f.*, vaillance, *f.*, esprit chevaleresque, *m.*, galanterie, *f.*

Galleon, s. gallion, *m.*

Gallery, s. galerie, *f.*

Galley, s. galère, *f.* — *-slave*, galérien, *m.*

Gallic, adj. Gallique, Gaulois

Gallican, adj. Gallican

Gallicism, s. Gallicisme, *m.*

Gallon, s. gallon, *m.*

Gallop, vn. galoper, aller au galop. *To — after, away* or *off, back, by, down, over* or *through*, suivre, partir, retourner, passer, descendre, traverser au galop

Gallop, s. galop, *m.*, galopade, *f.*

Gallows, s. potence, *f.*, gibet, *m.*, échafaud, *m.*

Galvanic, adj. galvanique

Galvanism, s. galvanisme, *m.*

Galvanize, va. galvaniser

Gamble, vn. jouer. *To — away*, jouer, perdre au jeu

Gambler, s. joueur, *m.*, -euse, *f.*

Gambling, s. jeu, *m.*, passion du jeu, *f.* — *-house*, maison de jeu, *f.*

Gamboge, s. gomme-gutte, *f.*

Gambol, vn. gambader, folâtrer, s'ébattre

Gambol, s. gambade, *f.*, ébats, *m.pl.*

Game, s. jeu, *m.*, partie, *f.*, (*fig.*) jeu, *m.*, dessein *m.*, (*hunt.*) chasse, *f.*, gibier, *m.* *To make — of*, se moquer de, se jouer de. — *-bag*, — *-pouch*, gibecière, *f.*, carnassière, *f.* — *-cock*, coq de combat, *m.* — *-keeper*, garde-chasse, *m.*, garde, *m.* — *-leg*, pied boiteux

Game, vn. jouer

Gamesome, adj. enjoué

Gamester, s. joueur, *m.*

Gaming, see GAMBLING

Gammon, s. jambonneau, *m.*, (*game*) trictrac, *m.*, (*deceit*) blague, *f.*

Gammon, vn. (*bacon*) fumer, (*deceive*) mettre dedans, (*nav.*) tier

Gamut, s. gamme, *f.*

Gander, s. jars, *m.*

Gang, s. bande, *f.*, troupe, *f.*, (*workmen*) brigade, *f.*, (*in contempt*) clique, *f.*

Ganger, s. chef de brigade, *m.*

Gangway, s. passavant, *m.*

Gantlet, s. (*nav.*) peine de la bouline, *f.*, gantelet, *m.* *To run the —*, courir la bouline

Gaol, see JAIL

Gaoler, s. geôlier, *m.*

Gap, s. brèche, *f.*, trou, *m.*, ouverture, *f.*, lacune, *f.*, trouée, *f.*, (*hiatus*) bâillement, *m.* — *-toothed*, brèche-dents, *m.*

Gape, vn. bâiller, bayer, rester la bouche béante, s'ouvrir, s'entr'ouvrir, être béant. *To — at*, regarder la bouche béante. *To — for*, ouvrir la bouche pour recevoir, bayer après

Gape, s. bâillement, *m.*

Gaper, s. bâilleur, *m.*, -euse, *f.*

Gaping, s. bâillement, *m.*

Garb, s. habit, *m.*, vêtement, *m.*, costume, *m.*, appareil, *m.*, (*fig.*) dehors, *m.pl.*

Garbage, s. entrailles, *f. pl.*, rebut, *m.*, refus, *m.*

Garble, va. éplucher, (*fig.*) tronquer, mutiler

Garden, s. jardin, *m.* — adj. de jardin. — *-mould*, terreau, *m.*, terre de bruyère, *f.* — *-stuff*, — *-ware*, jardinage, *m.*

Garden, va.n. jardiner, tracer un jardin

Gardener, s. jardinier, *m.*, horticulteur, *m.* *Head- —*, jardinier en chef. *Under- —*, aide-jardinier

Gardening, s. jardinage, *m.*, horticulture, *f.*

Gargle, s. gargarisme, *m.*

Gargle, va.n. (se) gargariser, gazouiller

Gargling, s. gargarisme, *m.*

Garish, adj. brillant, trop éclatant, voyant, fastueux

Garland, s. guirlande, *f.*

Garlic, s. ail, *m.*; (*pl.*) ails or aulx

Garment, s. vêtement, *m.*, habillement, *m.*

Garner, s. grenier, *m.*

Garner, va. mettre en grenier, rentrer, amonceler, amasser

Garnet, s. grenat, *m.*

Garnish, va. garnir, orner

Garot, va. étrangler

Garotter, s. étrangleur, *m.*

Garret, s. grenier, *m.*, mansarde, *f.*, galetas, *m.*

Garrison, s. garnison, *f.*, place de guerre, *f.* — *-town*, ville de garnison, *f.*

Garrison, va. mettre en garnison dans, défendre

Garrulity, Garrulousness, s. loquacité, *f.*

Garrulous, adj. loquace

Garter, s. jarretière, *f.*

Gas, s. gaz, *m.* — *-burner*, bec de gaz, *m.* — *-fitter*, ajusteur de gaz, *m.* — *-holder*, gazomètre, *m.* — *-lamp*, — *-light*, bec de gaz, *m.* — *-lighting*, éclairage au gaz, *m.* — *-main*, conduit principal de gaz, *m.* — *-meter*, compteur à gaz, *m.* — *-pipe*, tuyau à gaz, *m.* — *-stove*, fourneau chauffé au gaz, *m.* — *-tar*, goudron de gaz, *m.* — *-tight*, imperméable au gaz. — *-works*, usine à gaz, *f.*

Gaselier, s. lustre à gaz, *m.*

Gash, va. entailler, balafrer, taillader

Gash, s. large blessure, *f.*, balafre, *f.*, entaille, *f.*, estafilade, *f.*

Gasometer, s. gazomètre, *m.*

Gasp, vn.a. haleter, être haletant, respirer avec peine

Gasp, Gasping, s. respiration haletante, *f.*, soupir convulsif, *m.*

Gastric, adj. gastrique

Gastritis, s. gastrite, *f.*

Gastronomic, Gastronomical, adj. gastronomique

Gastronomist, s. gastronome, *m.*

Gastronomy, s. gastronomie, *f.*

Gate, s. porte, *f.*, grande porte, *f.*, porte cochère, *f.*, (*road*) barrière, *f.*, passage *m.*, (*on canals*) porte d'écluse, *f.* — *-house*, loge de parc, *f.*, maison de l'éclusier *f.* — *-keeper*, — *-man*, portier, *m.*, garde-barrière, *m.* — *-way*, porte cochère, *f.*, porte, *f.*, porche, *m.*, vestibule, *m.*

Gather, va. assembler, rassembler, réunir, ramasser (*flowers*) cueillir, réunir (*alms*) quêter, (*taxes*) percevoir, (*to infer*) conclure, inférer, comprendre, (*pucker*) froncer. *To — in*, recueillir rentrer, récolter, percevoir *To — together*, rassembler, réunir, ramasser. *To — up*, ramasser, réunir. — vn. se rassembler, s'assembler, se réunir, s'amasser, (*med.*) former un abcès

Gather, s. fronce, *f.*

Gatherer, s. personne qui assemble, qui recueille, qui perçoit, etc.

Gathering, s. rassemblement, *m.*, réunion, *f.*, assemblée, *f.*, (*taxes*) perception, *f.* (*fruits*) cueillette, *f.*, récolte *f.*

Gaudily, adv. fastueusement

ment, pompeusement, avec des couleurs voyantes

Gaudiness, s. faste, m., ostentation, f., pompe, f., faux brillant, m., clinquant, m.

Gaudy, adj. fastueux, pompeux, éclatant, voyant

Gauffer, va. gaufrer

Gauge, va. jauger, mesurer

Gauge, s. jauge, f., mesure, f., (*phys.*) manomètre, m., (*mar.*) tirant d'eau, m., (*mil.*) largeur, f. — -*cock*, robinet de jauge, m.

Gauger, s. jaugeur, m.

Gauging, s. jaugeage, m. — -*rod*, jauge, f.

Gaunt, adj. maigre, décharné

Gauntlet, s. gantelet, m., gant, m.

Gauze, s. gaze, f.

Gawky, adj s. grand dégingandé, grand nigaud

Gay, adj. gai, joyeux, fastueux, beau, magnifique, brillant

Gaze, vn a. regarder, considérer, contempler, s'ébahir

Gaze, s. regard, m

Gazelle, s. gazelle, f.

Gazer, s. spectateur, m., -trice, f.

Gazette, s gazette, f.

Gazette, va. mettre or publier dans la Gazette officielle

Gazetteer, s. journaliste, m., gazetier, m., dictionnaire de géographie, m.

Gear, s. appareil, m., habillement, m., vêtements, m. pl., accoutrement, m., harnais, m., (*mech.*) engrenage, m. *To put in* —, engrener

Gelatine, s. gélatine, f.

Gelatinous, adj gélatineux

Geld, va. châtrer, mutiler

Gelding, s. cheval hongre, m., castration, f.

Gem, s. pierre précieuse, f., pierrerie, f., joyau, m., fleuron, m., (*bot.*) bourgeon, m., (*hort.*) écusson, m.

Gem, va. orner de pierreries, rendre étincelant, (*bot.*) faire pousser les bourgeons de; — vn. bourgeonner

Gender, s. genre, m.

Gender, va. engendrer; — vn. s'unir

Genealogical, adj. généalogique, de généalogie

Genealogist, s. généalogiste, m.

Genealogy, s. généalogie, f.

General, adj. général, commun, du public

General, s. généralité, f., général, m.

Generality, s. généralité, f.

Generalization, s. généralisation, f.

Generalize, vn. généraliser

Generally, adv. généralement, en général

Generalship, s. généralat, m., talent de général, m., tactique, f.

Generate, va. engendrer, produire

Generating, adj. générateur

Generation, s. génération, f.

Generic, Generical, adj. générique

Generosity, s. générosité, f.

Generous, adj. généreux, vaillant, noble

Generously, adv. généreusement, avec générosité, noblement

Genesis, s. Genèse, f.

Genial, adj. vivifiant, fécondant, générateur, propice, naturel, bienfaisant, joyeux, animé

Geniality, Genialness, s. puissance vivifiante, f., naturel, m., gaieté, f.

Genitive, adj. s. génitif, du génitif, au génitif

Genius, s. génie, m., dispositions, f. pl.

Genteel, adj. poli, bien élevé, plein d'urbanité, comme il faut, de bon goût

Genteelly, adv. d'une manière distinguée, avec distinction, élégamment

Gentian, s. gentiane, f.

Gentile, s. adj. gentil, m., des gentils

Gentility, s. naissance distinguée, f., bon goût, m., manières distinguées, f. pl., urbanité, f.

Gentle, adj. noble, bien né, doux, tranquille, paisible

Gentle, s. asticot, m.

Gentlefolks, s. gens de distinction, m. pl.

Gentleman, s. gentilhomme, m., homme de condition, m., homme d'honneur, m., galant homme, m., homme du monde, m., (*partner*) cavalier, m., homme, m. *Gentlemen*, Messieurs. — *commoner*, étudiant de famille, m. — -*pensioner*, garde du roi, de la reine, m. — -*usher*, huissier du palais, m.

Gentlemanlike, Gentlemanly, adj. honorable, noble, délicat, distingué, comme il faut, bien élevé

Gentleness, s. douceur, f., bienveillance, f.

Gentlewoman, s. femme de condition, f., dame, f., femme de distinction, f.

Gently, adv. doucement, paisiblement, tranquillement

Gentry, s. personnes de distinction, f. pl., familles distinguées, f., bourgeoisie, f. pl.

Genuflection, s. génuflexion, f.

Genuine, adj. pur, vrai, véritable, authentique, sincère

Genuineness, s. pureté, f., vérité, f., authenticité, f., sincérité, f.

Genus, s. genre, m.

Geographer, s. géographe, m.

Geographical, Geographic, adj. géographique, de géographie

Geography, s. géographie, f.

Geologer, Geologist, s. géologue, m.

Geological, adj. géologique

Geology, s. géologie, f.

Geomancy, s. géomancie, f.

Geometer, s. géomètre, m.

Geometric, Geometrical, adj. géométrique, géométral

Geometrically, adv. géométriquement, géométralement

Geometrician, s. géomètre, m.

Geometry, s. géométrie, f.

Geranium, s. géranium, m.

Gerfalcon, s. gerfaut, m.

Germ, s. germe, m.

Germinate, vn. germer; — va faire germer

Germination, s germination, f.

Gesticulate, vn. gesticuler, faire des gestes

Gesticulation, s. gesticulation, f.

Gesture, s. geste, m.

Get, va.n. obtenir, se procurer, acquérir, trouver, recevoir, avoir, procurer, aller chercher, gagner, attraper, (*from*) arracher (à), enlever (à), (*to learn by heart*, &c.) apprendre par cœur, (*to*) arriver, parvenir, atteindre. *To — one's part*, apprendre son rôle *To — a thing done* or *made*, faire faire une chose. *To — oneself dressed*, se faire habiller. *To — before*, se mettre devant, devancer, prendre la place de. *To — asleep, drunk, beloved*, s'endormir, s'enivrer, se faire aimer. *To — better*, se rétablir. *To — above*, s'élever, se mettre au-dessus de *To — about*, entourer, obtenir environ. *To — along*, s'avancer, cheminer. *To — among*, s'introduire parmi. *To — at*, arriver (à), atteindre (à). *To — away*, échapper (à), se sauver. *To — back*, être de retour, revenir, faire revenir, se faire rendre. *To — by*, passer, faire passer, gagner à. *To — down*, descendre faire descendre, avaler. *To — from*, s'échapper de. *To — in*, entrer, faire entrer, (*money*) faire rentrer. *To — into*, entrer dans, s'introduire dans, faire entrer dans, se mettre dans, s'embarrasser dans, (*habit*) acquérir. *To — forward*, s'avancer, avancer, faire avancer, faire faire des progrès à. *To — off*, descendre de, ôter, retirer, se tirer d'affaire, s'échapper de, tirer. *To — on with*, avancer dans, marcher d'accord avec. *To — out*, sortir, faire sortir, se tirer d'affaire, arracher, obtenir. *To — over*, passer, traverser, faire passer, franchir, escalader; (*difficulties*) surmonter, vaincre; (*illness*) se remettre de. *To — together*, se rassembler, réunir, ramasser. *To — through*, traverser, parcourir, faire traverser, achever, venir à bout de. *To — under*, arriver, se placer, se mettre dessous, maîtriser, se rendre maître de. *To — up*, monter, faire monter, se lever, arriver, arranger, (*a book*) publier, (*a play*, &c.) monter, (*a story*) fabriquer. *To — up again*, remonter, se relever. *To — upon*, monter sur. *To — well*, se rétablir, guérir. *To — within*, s'introduire dans

Getter, s. personne qui obtient, f.

Getting, s. acquisition, f., gain, m.

Gewgaw, s. babiole, f., brimborion, m., colifichet, m.

Ghastliness, s. aspect effrayant, m., pâleur, f.

Ghastly, adj. affreux, effrayant, hideux, horrible, pâle

Gherkin, s. cornichon, m.

Ghost, s. esprit, m., âme, f., ombre, f., revenant, m., fantôme, m., apparition, f.

Ghostliness, s. spiritualité, f.

Ghostly, adj. spirituel, pieux, de spectre, lugubre

Giantess, s. géante, f.

Gibberish, s. jargon, m., baragouin, m., baragouinage, m.

Gibbet, s. gibet, m., potence, f.

Gibbet, va. attacher au gibet

Gibe, va.n. se moquer de, railler

Gibe, s. raillerie, f., sarcasme, m.

Gibing, adj. railleur, moqueur

Giblets, s. pl. abatis, m. pl.

Giddily, adj. étourdiment, à l'étourdie

Giddiness, s. étourdissement, m., vertige, m., (*heedlessness*) étourderie, f.

Giddy, adj. étourdi, pris de vertiges or d'étourdissements, vertigineux, qui donne le vertige, rapide, tournant, (*fig.*) étourdi

Gift, s. don, m., cadeau, f., présent, m., offrande, f., donation, f., (*fig.*) talent, m. *New year's* —, étrennes, f. pl. *In the — of*, à la nomination de

Gift, va. (*with*) douer (de), doter (de)

Gig, s. (*mar.*) yole, f., canot, m.; cabriolet, m. — -*mill*, laineuse mécanique, f.

Gigantic, adj. gigantesque

Giggle, Giggling, s. petit rire, m., rire étouffé, m., ricanement, m.

Giggle, vn. rire tout bas, ricaner

Gild, va. dorer, (*fig.*) jaunir, embellir

Gilder, s. doreur, m.

Gilding, s. dorure, m.

Gill, s. (*fish*) ouïe, *f.*, jabot, *m.*, (*measure*) treize centilitres, *f.*
Gillyflower, s. giroflée, *f.*
Gimcrack, s. babiole, *f.*, patraque, *f.*
Gimlet, s. vrille, *f.*
Gin, s. (*drink*) genièvre, *m.*, (*mech.*) machine, *f.*, grue, *f.*, (*snare*) trébuchet, *m.*, piége, *m.*
Gin, va. (*cotton*) égrener, prendre au trébuchet
Ginger, s. gingembre, *m.* — -*beer*, — -*pop*, bière au gingembre, *f.* — -*bread*, pain d'épice, *m.*
Gingerly, adv. délicatement
Gingham, s. guingan, *m.*
Ginging, s. revêtement, *m.*
Gipsy, s. bohémien, *m.*, -ne, *f.*
Gipsy, adj. des bohémiens
Giraffe, s. girafe, *f.*
Girandole, s. girandole, *f.*
Gird, Girdle, va. ceindre, entourer, environner, (*horses*) sangler
Girder, s. traverse, *f.*
Girdle, s. ceinture, *f.*, ceinturon, *m.*, enceinte, *f.*, cercle, *m.*
Girl, s. jeune fille, *f.*, fille, *f.*, demoiselle, *f.*
Girlhood, s. jeunesse, *f.*
Girlish, adj. de jeune fille, enfantin
Girlishness, s. manières, *f.*, caractère de jeune fille, *m.*, puérilité, *f.*
Girt, va. sangler
Girt, s. sangle, *f.*
Girth, s. contour, *m.*, circonférence, *f.*
Gist, s. point principal, *m.*
Give, va. donner, rendre, livrer, accorder, permettre, (*a decree*) prononcer, rendre, décider, (*a blow*) porter. *To — him as good as he brings*, lui rendre la monnaie de sa pièce. — *and take*, donnant, donnant
Giver, s. donneur, *m.*, donneuse, *f.*, dispensateur, *m.*, dispensatrice, *f.*
Giving, s. don, *m.*, donation, *f.*, (*weather*) adoucissement, *m.*
Gizzard, s. gésier, *m.*
Glacier, s. glacier, *m.*
Glad, adj. aise, bien aise, heureux, content, joyeux
Gladden, va. égayer, réjouir
Glade, s. clairière, *f.*, percée, *f.*
Gladiator, s. gladiateur, *m.*
Gladiole, s. glaïeul, *m.*
Gladly, adv. avec plaisir, volontiers, de bon cœur
Gladness, s. allégresse, *f.*, joie, *f.*
Gladsome, adj. joyeux, d'allégresse
Glance, s. éclair, *m.*, trait de lumière, *m.*, flamme rapide, *f.*
Glance, vn. (*to shine*) briller, étinceler, luire, (*to look*) porter ses regards (*sur*), regarder, jeter un coup d'œil (*sur*), (*to start off*) glisser, obliquer, se détourner
Gland, s. glande, *f.*
Glandered, adj. atteint de la morve
Glanders, s.pl. morve, *f.*
Glare, vn. briller (*to look*) lancer des regards enflammés, regarder d'un air farouche
Glare, s. flamme, *f.*, lumière, *f.*, clarté, *f.*, lueur, *f.*, regard, *m.*
Glaring, adj. brillant, éblouissant, (*colour*) voyant, éclatant, tranché, (*crime*) manifeste, monstrueux
Glass, s. verre, *m.*, cristal, *m.*, miroir, *m.*, glace, *f.*, (*for windows*) vitre, *f.*, (*hour-glass*) sablier, *m.*, (*eye-glass*) lorgnon, *m.*, lunettes, *f.pl.*, baromètre, *m.* *Field-* —, lunette de poche, *f.*
Glass, adj. de verre, en verre, vitré
Glassful, s. verre, *m.*
Glassy, adj. vitreux, de cristal, cristallin, limpide, transparent
Glaze, va. mettre des vitres à, vitrer, (*varnish*) vernir, vernisser, (*metals*) polir, (*gloves*) glacer, (*cloth*) lustrer —*d frost*, du verglas. —*d hat*, chapeau ciré, *m.*
Glaze, s. vernis, *m.*
Glazier, s. vitrier, *m.*
Glazing, s. vitrage, *m.*, vitrerie, *f.*, vernis, *m.*, glacé, *m.*, (*cloth*) catissage, *m.*
Gleam, Gleaming, s. lueur, *f.*, trait, *m.*, rayon, *m.*
Gleam, vn. luire, briller, jeter une faible lueur
Gleaming, Gleamy, adj. brillant, étincelant
Glean, va.n. glaner, grappiller, ramasser, (*fig.*) recueillir
Gleaner, s. glaneur, *m.*, -euse, *f.*
Gleaning, s. glanage, *m.*, glanure, *f.*, épis glanés, *m.pl.*
Glebe, s. glèbe, *f.*, sol, *m.*, terre, *f.*
Glee, s. gaîté, *f.*, joie, *f.*, (*song*) chanson à reprises *f.*
Gleeful, adj. joyeux
Glen, s. vallon, *m.*, gorge, *f.*
Glib, adj. glissant, coulant, facile, délié
Glibly, adv. doucement, facilement, avec faconde
Glide, vn. glisser, se glisser, couler
Glimmer, vn. luire, jeter une faible lueur, briller faiblement
Glimmer, s. lueur, *f.*, faible clarté, *f.*
Glimpse, s. lueur, *f.*, éclat passager, *m.*, trait de lumière, *m.*, vue rapide, *f.*, coup d'œil, *m.* *To catch, to get, to have a* (*slight*) — *of*, entrevoir, pressentir
Glisten, vn. briller, étinceler
Glitter, vn. étinceler, briller, reluire. *All that —s is not gold*, tout ce qui reluit n'est pas or
Glitter, s. brillant, *m.*, éclat, *m.*
Glittering, adj. brillant, étincelant
Gloat, vn. dévorer or couver des yeux
Globe, s. globe, *m.*, cercle, *m.*
Globular, adj. globuleux, sphérique, en globe
Gloom, s. obscurité, *f.*, ténèbres, *f.pl.*, aspect sombre, *m.*
Gloomily, adv. obscurément, tristement
Gloominess, s. obscurité, *f.*, tristesse, *f.*, air sombre, *m.*
Gloomy, adj. sombre, obscur, morne, triste
Glorification, s. glorification, *f.*
Glorify, va. glorifier
Glorious, adj. glorieux, resplendissant, superbe
Gloriously, adv. glorieusement, splendidement, admirablement
Glory, s. gloire, *f.*, splendeur, *f.*, magnificence, *f.*, merveille, *f.*
Glory, vn. se glorifier, se faire gloire
Gloss, s. glose, *f.*, commentaire, *m.*, (*of stuffs*) lustre, *m.*, brillant, *m.*, apprêt, *m.*, éclat, *m.*, nouveauté, *f.*
Gloss, va a. faire une glose, gloser
Glossary, s. glossaire, *m.*
Glossiness, s. lustre, *m.*, apprêt, *m.*, brillant, *m.*, fraîcheur, *f.*
Glossy, adj. brillant
Glove, s. gant, *m.* — -*stretcher*, baguette à gants, *f.* — -*trade*, ganterie, *f.*
Glover, s. gantier, *m.*
Glow, vn. briller, brûler, (*get animated*) s'animer, s'enflammer, s'échauffer
Glow, s. chaleur, *f.*, flamme, *f.*, éclat, *m.*, splendeur, *f.*, teint animé, *m.*, rougeur, *f.* *To be in a* —, brûler
Glowing, adj. brillant, brûlant, animé, chaleureux
Glowworm, s. ver luisant, *m.*
Gloze, vn. flatter, pallier
Glue, s. colle forte, *f.*, glu, *f.*
Glue, va. coller
Gluey, adj. gluant
Glum, adj. triste comme un bonnet de nuit, refrogné, maussade
Glut, va. gorger, assouvir, repaître, rassasier, dégoûter
Glut, s. assouvissement, *m.*, excès, *m.*, surabondance, *f.*, encombrement, *m.*
Gluten, s. gluten, *m.*
Glutinous, adj. glutineux
Glutton, s. glouton, *m.*, -ne, *f.*, gourmand, *m.*, -e, *f.*, (*vulg.*) goulu, *m.*, -e, *f.*
Glutton, Gluttonous, adj. glouton, gourmand, vorace
Gluttonously, adv. gloutonnement
Gluttony, s. gloutonnerie, *f.*, gourmandise, *f.*, intempérance, *f.*
Glycerine, s. glycérine, *f.*
Gnarled, adj. noueux
Gnash, va.n. grincer des dents
Gnashing, s. grincement, *m.*
Gnat, s. moucheron, *m.*, cousin, *m.*
Gnaw, va.n. ronger, mordre
Gnawer, s. rongeur, *m.*, -euse, *f.*
Gnawing, adj. rongeur
Gnawing, s. action de ronger, *f.*, tiraillement, *m.*
Gnome, s. gnome, *m.*
Gnomic, Gnomical, adj. gnomique
Go, vn. aller, se rendre, aller trouver, marcher, faire partir, s'en aller, disparaître, (*time*) passer, s'écouler, (*contribute*) contribuer. *To — by*, passer, passer là, passer devant, (*time*) s'écouler, (*a rule*) suivre, (*a name*) être connu sous. *To — down*, descendre, (*waters*) baisser, (*the sun*) se coucher
Go, s. mode, *f.*, coup, *m.*, amusement, *m.* *To be all the* —, faire fureur. *It's no* —, cela ne passe pas
Go-between, s. intermédiaire, *m.*, entremetteur, *m.*, -euse, *f.*
Go-by, s. évasion, *f.*, négligence, *f.*
Goad, s. aiguillon, *m.*
Goad, va. aiguillonner, piquer, exciter, stimuler, (*remorse*) bourreler
Goal, s. but, *m.*, terme, *m.*, barrière, *f.*
Goat, s. bouc, *m.*, chèvre, *f.*, bique, *f.* *She-* —, chèvre, *f.*, bique, *f.*
Goatish, adj. de bouc
Gobble, va.n. engloutir, gober
Gobbler, s. goulu, *m.*, dindon, *m.*
Goblet, s. gobelet, *m.*, coupe, *f.*
Goblin, s. démon, *m.*, lutin, *m.*
God, s. Dieu, *m.* — -*child*, filleul, *m.*, -e, *f.* — -*daughter*, filleule, *f.* — -*father*, parrain, *m.* — -*mother*, marraine, *f.* *To stand* — -*father* or — -*mother to*, tenir sur les fonts
Goddess, s. déesse, *f.*
Godhead, s. divinité, *f.*
Godless, adj. impie
Godlike, adj. divin, semblable à un dieu
Godliness, s. piété, *f.*
Godly, adj. pieux, dévot, juste
Godly, adv. pieusement
Goer, s. allant, *m.*, marcheur, *m.*, coureur, *m.* *Sure* —, au pied sûr
Goggle, s. roulement d'yeux, *m.*, (*of a horse*) œillère, *f.*, (*spectacles*) lunettes vertes, *f.pl.* — -*eyes*, — -*eyed*, (*ayant*) de gros yeux à fleur de tête
Goggle, vn. rouler de gros yeux
Going, s. allée, *f.*, départ, *m.*, marche, *f.* —*s and com-*

ings, allées et venues. —*s on*, faits et gestes, belles choses
Gold, s. or, *m.* — adj. d'or. *It is as good as* —, c'est de l'or en barre
Golden, adj. d'or, en or, doré ; (*fig.*) brillant, resplendissant, précieux
Goldfinch, s. chardonneret, *m.*
Goldhammer, s. loriot, *m.*
Goldsmith, s. orfèvre, *m.*
Gondola, s. gondole, *f.*
Gondolier, s. gondolier, *m.*
Gone, past part. (*time*) passé, écoulé, (*stale*) avancé, (*auction*) vendu, (*dead*) mort, (*drunk*) ivre
Gong, s. gong, *m.*
Good, adj. bon, de bien, brave, sage, (*solvent*) solvable, solide, (*worth*) valable, (*clever*) habile
Good, s. bien, *m.*, bon, *m.*, bons, *m.pl.*, gens de bien, *m.pl.*, (*things*) biens, *m.pl.*, effets, *m.pl.*, marchandises, *f.pl.*
Good! interj. bon! bien cela!
Goodliness, s. beauté, *f.*
Goodly, adj. beau, heureux
Goodness, s. bonté, *f.*, bien, *m.*, bienfait, *m.*
Goody, s. commère, *f.*, mère, *f.*, madame, *f.*
Goose, s. oie, *f.*, sot, *m.*, sotte, *m.*, (*tailor's*) carreau, *m.*
Gooseberry, s. grosse groseille, *f.*, groseille à maquereau, *f.* — *-bush*, groseillier, *m.*
Gordian, adj. gordien. *To cut the — knot*, trancher le nœud gordien
Gore, s. sang, *m.*, (*needle*) pointe, *f.*
Gore, va. donner des coups de corne à, frapper, percer
Gorge, s. gorge, *f.*, gosier, *m.*
Gorge, va. gorger, rassasier; — vn. se gorger
Gorgeous, adj. somptueux, magnifique, splendide, fastueux
Gorgeously, adv. somptueusement
Gorgeousness, s. somptuosité, *f.*, magnificence, *f.*, pompe, *f.*
Gorget, s. gorgerin, *m.*, hausse-col, *m.*
Gorgon, s. Gorgone, *f.*
Gorilla, s. gorille, *m.*
Gormandize, vn. bâfrer
Gormandizer, s. gourmand, *m.*, glouton, *m.*, gros mangeur, *m.*
Gorse, s. genêt épineux, *m.*, ajonc, *m.*
Gorsy, adj. couvert d'ajoncs
Gory, adj. sanglant, ensanglanté
Go-hawk, s. autour, *m.*
Gosling, s. oison, *m.*
Gospel, s. Évangile, *m.*
Gospel, adj. de l'Évangile
Gossamer, s. fil de la Vierge, *m.*, fil léger, *m.*
Gossamer, adj. léger, aérien
Gossip, s. compère, *m.*, commère, *f.*, (*tatler*) cancanier, *m.*, cancanière, *f.*, (*chat*) causerie, *f.*, (*in a bad sense*) commérages, *m.pl.*, cancans, *m.pl.*
Gossip, vn. causer, bavarder, faire des cancans *or* commérages
Goth, s. Goth, *m.*, Ostrogoth, *m.*
Gothic, adj. & s. gothique
Gouge, s. gouge, *f.*
Gouge, va. gouger, crever l'œil
Gourd, s. calebassier, *m.*, courge, *f.*, (*fruit*) gourde, *f.*, calebasse, *f.*
Gout, s. goutte, *f.* *A fit of the* —, un accès de goutte
Goutiness, s. état goutteux, *m.*
Gouty, adj. goutteux, podagre
Govern, va. gouverner, diriger, régir, commander à ; — vn. se gouverner
Governable, adj. docile, maniable
Governess, s. souveraine, *f.*, maîtresse, *f.*, (*teacher*) institutrice, *f.*, gouvernante, *f.*, (*in a school*) sous-maîtresse, *f.*
Government, s. gouvernement, *m.*, régime, *m.*, direction, *f.*, maniement, *m.*
Governmental, adj. gouvernemental
Governor, s. maître, *m.*, souverain, *m.*, gouvernant, *m.*, gouverneur, *m.*, régulateur, *m.*, précepteur, *m.*, (*fam.*) père, *m.*
Governorship, s. gouvernement, *m.*
Gown, s. robe, *f.*, toge, *f.* *Bed-* —, *night-* —, chemise de nuit, *f.* *Morning* —, robe de chambre, *f.*
Gowned, adj. à robe, en robe, en toge
Gownsman, s. homme de robe, *m.*, étudiant, *m.*
Grace, s. grâce, *f.*, faveur, *f.*, pardon, *m.*, agrément, *m.*, (*before meat*) bénédicité, *m.*, (*aft. meat*) grâces, *f.pl.*, (*univ.*) décret, *m.*, (*mus.*) agrément, *m.*, roulade, *f.* *To do a thing with good* —, *with ill* —, faire une chose de bonne grâce, de mauvaise grâce. *To do — to*, honorer
Grace, va. donner de la grâce, de l'agrément à, parer, embellir, honorer, favoriser
Graceful, adj. gracieux, plein de grâce
Gracefully, adv. avec grâce
Gracefulness, s. grâce, *f.*
Graceless, adj. abandonné
Gracelessness, s. perversité, *f.*
Gracious, adj. gracieux, doué de la grâce. *Good —! goodness —!* bon Dieu ! bonté divine !
Graciously, adv. gracieusement, avec bonté
Graciousness, s. condescendance, *f.*, gracieuseté, *f.*, bonté, *f.*, grâce, *f.*
Gradation, s. gradation, *f.*
Grade, s. grade, *m.*, degré, *m.*
Gradient, s. rampe, *f.*, plan incliné, *m.* — adj. en pente
Gradual, adj. graduel
Gradually, adv. graduellement, peu à peu
Graduate, s. gradué, *m.*
Graduate, va. graduer; — vn. prendre ses grades
Graduation, s. graduation, *f.*
Graft, s. greffe, *f.*, (*fig.*) germe, *m.*
Graft, va.n. greffer, enter
Grafting, s. greffe, *f.* — *-knife*, greffoir, *m.*
Grain, s. grain, *m.*, (*brewery*) drêche, *f.*, (*metal*) grain, *m.*, fil, *m.*, (*wood*) fibres, *f.pl.*
Grain, va. grener, greneler, veiner
Grained, adj. grené, grenelé, (*bot.*) grenu
Grainy, adj. plein de grains
Grammar, s. grammaire, *f.* — *-school*, lycée, collège, *m.*
Grammarian, s. grammairien, *m.*
Grammatical, adj. grammatical, de grammaire
Grammatically, adv. grammaticalement
Grampus, s. épaulard, *m.*
Granary, s. grenier, *m.*
Grand, adj. grand, sublime, grandiose
Grandee, s. grand, *m.* *Rank of a* —, grandesse, *f.*
Grandeur, s. grandeur, *f.*, élévation, *f.*, noblesse, *f.*
Grandiloquent, adj. au langage pompeux, beau parleur
Grandly, adv. grandement, en grand, noblement, avec grandeur
Grange, s. grange, *f.*, ferme isolée, *f.*
Granite, s. granit, *m.* — adj. de granit
Granivorous, adj. granivore
Granny, s. grand'mère, *f.*, bonne maman, *f.*
Grant, va. accorder, concéder, admettre, convenir de *or* que, supposer, exaucer, octroyer. —*ed!* d'accord ! soit ! *To take for* —*ed*, être persuadé, croire, penser, regarder comme convenu. *God — it!* Dieu le veuille !
Grant, s. don, *m.*, concession, *f.*, cession, *f.*
Grantee, s. concessionnaire, *m.*
Granter, s. qui accorde
Granulate, va. granuler; — vn. se granuler
Grape, s. grain de raisin, *m.*, vigne, *f.*, (*artil.*) mitraille, *f.* —*s*, pl. du raisin, raisins
Graphic, adj. graphique, (*fig.*) pittoresque
Graphically, adv. graphiquement, d'une manière pittoresque
Grapnel, s. grappin, *m.*
Grapple, vn. être aux prises (avec), lutter (contre), (*a subject*) manier ; — va. saisir à bras le corps, étreindre, prendre, accrocher
Grasp, va. étreindre, se saisir de, saisir, empoigner, embrasser. — *all, lose all*, qui trop embrasse mal étreint. — vn. vouloir se saisir (de), s'efforcer de saisir
Grasp, s. étreinte, *f.*, prise, *f.*, main, *f.*, possession, *f.*, portée, *f.*, puissance, *f.*, pouvoir, *m.*
Grasping, adj. avide, cupide
Grass, s. herbe, *f.*, gazon, *m.* *To turn a horse out to* —, mettre un cheval au vert
Grasshopper, s. sauterelle, *f.*
Grassy, adj. de gazon, couvert de gazon, verdoyant, vert, herbeux, herbu
Grate, s. grille, *f.*
Grate, va. râper, (*rub*) frotter, (*teeth*) grincer, (*ears*) écorcher, (*fig.*) blesser, froisser, offenser, (*to enclose*) griller. *A grated door*, une porte grillée. — vn. frapper d'un son discordant, (*teeth*) agacer, (*ears*) écorcher, (*to wound*) blesser, offenser, choquer, déplaire à
Grateful, adj. reconnaissant, plein de reconnaissance, (*pleasant*) agréable, doux, délicieux
Gratefully, adv. avec reconnaissance, agréablement
Gratefulness, s. see GRATITUDE
Grater, s. râpe, *f.*
Gratification, s. contentement, *m.*, satisfaction, *f.*, plaisir, *m.*, jouissance, *f.*, gratification, *f.*
Gratify, va. contenter, satisfaire à, satisfaire, plaire à, charmer, enchanter, flatter
Gratifying, adj. agréable, doux, flatteur
Grating, s. action de râper, *f.*, son *or* bruit discordant, *m.*, grillage, *m.*, grille, *f.*, barres, *f.pl.*
Grating, adj. rude, dur, discordant, désagréable, déplaisant, choquant
Gratis, adv. gratis
Gratitude, s. reconnaissance, *f.*, gratitude, *f.*
Gratuitous, adj. gratuit, bénévole
Gratuitously, adv. gratuitement
Gratuitousness, s. gratuité, *f.*
Gratuity, s. gratification, *f.*, don gratuit, *m.*
Gratulate, va. féliciter, complimenter
Gratulation, s. félicitation, *f.*
Grave, va.n. creuser, graver, buriner, ciseler

Grave, s. tombeau, *m.*, tombe, *f.*, fosse, *f.*
Grave, adj. grave, sérieux, sévère d'aspect
Gravel, s. gravier, *m.*, sable, *m.*, (*med.*) gravelle, *f.*, pierre, *f.* — *-pit*, sablière, *f.*, sablonnière, *f.* — *-stone*, gravier, *m.* — *-walk*, allée sablée, *f.*
Gravel, va. couvrir de gravier, sabler, ensabler, embarrasser
Graveless, adj. sans sépulture
Gravelly, adv. de sable, plein de sable *or* de gravier, graveleux
Gravely, adv. gravement, sérieusement
Gravitate, vn. graviter
Gravitation, s. gravitation, *f.*
Gravity, s. gravité, *f.*, pesanteur, *f.*, poids, *m.*, sérieux, *m.*, importance, *f.*
Gravy, s. jus, *m.*, sauce, *f.*
Gray, *see* Grey
Graze, vn. paître, manger l'herbe, brouter, (*to touch*) effleurer, raser, friser, frôler; — va. faire paître, mener paître, effleurer, raser, friser, frôler, (*skin*) écorcher
Grazier, s. éleveur, *m.*
Grazing, s. action de paître, *f.*, élève, *m.*, touche légère, *f.*
Grease, s. graisse, *f.*, malandre, *f.* *Cart-* —, vieux oing, *m.*
Grease, va. graisser, (*fig.*) acheter
Greasily, adv. avec de la graisse, (*fig.*) gras, salement
Greasiness, s. état graisseux, *m.*
Greasy, adj. graisseux, gras, huileux, de graisse, couvert de graisse
Great, adj. grand, magnanime, important, somptueux, familier
Greatly, adv. grandement, beaucoup, fort, extrêmement, noblement, glorieusement, vaillamment
Greatness, s. grandeur, *f.*, force, *f.*
Greave, s. jambière, *f.*
Greed, s. avidité, *f.*
Greedily, adv. avidement, avec voracité
Greediness, s. avidité, *f.*, gloutonnerie, *f.*
Greedy, adj. avide, vorace, glouton, affamé
Green, adj. vert, nouveau, récent, frais, (*fig.*) jeune, novice, inexpérimenté, (*pale*) blême, livide
Green, s. vert, *m.*, (*sward*) pelouse, *f.*, tapis vert, *m.*, gazon, *m.*, prairie, *f.*, verdure, *f.* —*s*, pl. (*vegetables*) légumes verts, *m.pl.*, choux, *m.pl.*
Greenish, adj. verdâtre
Greenly, adv. en vert, nouvellement
Greenness, s. couleur verte, *f.*, verdeur, *f.*, verdure, *f.*, caractère récent, *m.*, simplicité, *f.*

Greet, va. saluer, féliciter, complimenter, aller au-devant de
Greeting, s. salutation, *f.*, salut, *m.*, félicitation, *f.*
Gregarious, adj. vivant par troupes, par bandes
Gregorian, adj. grégorien
Grenade, s. grenade, *f.*
Grenadier, s. grenadier, *m.*
Grey, adj. gris. *To get, grow, or turn* —, grisonner, blanchir
Grey, s. gris, *m.*, couleur grise, *f.*
Greyhound, s. lévrier, *m.*, levrette, *f.*
Greyish, adj. grisâtre, tirant sur le gris
Gridiron, s. gril, *m.*
Grief, s. chagrin, *m.*, douleur, *f.*, peine, *f.*, affliction, *f.*
Grievance, s. grief, *m.*, tort, *m.*, abus, *m.*
Grieve, va. affliger, peiner, chagriner, attrister; — vn. s'affliger, se chagriner, s'attrister
Grievous, adj. affligeant, cruel, douloureux, triste, pénible
Grievously, adv. cruellement, douloureusement, péniblement, grièvement
Grievousness, s. dureté, *f.*, poids accablant, *m.*, malheurs, *m.pl.*, gravité, *f.*, grièveté, *f.*
Griffin, s. griffon, *m.*
Grig, s. anguille, *f.*, (*merry*) égrillard, *m.*, -e, *f.* *As merry as a* —, gai comme pinson
Grill, va. griller
Grim, adj. farouche, menaçant, hideux
Grimace, s. grimace, *f.*
Grimalkin, s. Rominagrobis, *m.*
Grime, s. saleté, *f.*, noir, *m.*
Grime, va. barbouiller
Grimly, adv. d'un air farouche, d'une manière effrayante, horriblement
Grimness, s. air *or* expression farouche, *m.*, aspect effrayant, *m.*, laideur affreuse, *f.*
Grimy, adj. noir, barbouillé
Grin, vn. montrer les dents, grimacer, faire des grimaces, ricaner
Grin, s. grimace, *f.*, rire, *m.*, ricanement, *m.*
Grind, va. moudre, broyer, réduire en poudre, écraser, pressurer, (*teeth*) grincer, (*knives*) aiguiser, repasser, polir
Grinder, s. celui qui moud *or* qui broie, rémouleur, *m.*, (*teeth*) molaire, *f.*, (*tutor*) répétiteur, *m.*
Grindstone, s. meule, *f.*
Grinner, s. qui montre les dents, qui fait des grimaces
Grinning, s. rire, *m.*, ricanement, *m.*
Gripe, s. étreinte, *f.*, serre, *f.*, main, *f.*, prise, *f.*, colique, *f.*

Gripe, va.n. saisir, empoigner, étreindre, agripper, s'agripper à, donner la colique à
Griping, s. étreinte, *f.*, prise, *f.*, colique, *f.*, peines, *f.pl.*
Griskin, s. échine, *f.*
Grisly, adj. affreux, menaçant, effrayant
Grist, s. blé, *m.*, grain, *m.* *To bring — to the mill*, faire venir l'eau au moulin
Gristle, s. cartilage, *m.*
Gristly, adj. cartilagineux
Grit, s. gruau, *m.*, (*sand*) gravier, *m.*, grès, *m.* — *-stone*, grès dur
Gritty, adj. plein de gravier
Grizzle, s. grison, *m.*, baudet, *m.*
Grizzled, adj. gris, grisonnant
Groan, vn. grogner, gémir
Groan, s. gémissement, *m.*, grognement, *m.*
Groaning, s. gémissement, *m.*
Groat, s. (*fig.*) obole, *f.*, sou, *m.* *Not to be worth a* —, n'avoir ni sou ni maille
Groats, s.pl. gruau d'avoine, *m.*
Grocer, s. épicier, *m.*
Grocery, s. épiceries, *f.pl.*, magasin, *m.*, boutique d'épicier, *f.*
Grog, s. grog, *m.* — *-blossom*, bourgeon, *m.*
Groggy, adj. gris
Groin, s. aine, *f.*, (*archit.*) nervure, *f.*, arête, *f.*, (*breakwater*) brise-lame, *m.*
Groined, adj. d'arête
Groom, s. valet d'écurie, *m.*, palefrenier, *m.*, gentilhomme de la chambre, *m.*, marié, *m.*, époux, *m.* — *in waiting*, gentilhomme de service. — *of the stole*, premier gentilhomme de la chambre
Groom, va. avoir soin de, panser
Groomsman, s. garçon d'honneur, *m.*
Groove, va. canneler, faire une rainure à
Groove, s. cannelure, *f.*, rainure, *f.*
Grooved, adj. cannelé, à rainures
Grope, vn. marcher à tâtons, chercher à tâtons *or* en tâtonnant. *To — in, out*, entrer, sortir à tâtons
Gropingly, adv. à tâtons
Gross, adj. gros, grossier, épais
Gross, s. gros, *m.*, masse, *f.*, somme totale, *f.*, (*com.*) grosse, *f.* *In the —, by the* —, en bloc, en masse, en somme
Grossly, adv. grossièrement
Grossness, s. grosseur, *f.*, grossièreté, *f.*, épaisseur, *f.*
Grotesque, adj. s. grotesque
Grotto, s. grotte, *f.* — *-work*, rocaille, *f.*
Ground, s. terre, *f.*, terrain, *m.*, sol, *m.*, territoire, *m.*, jardins, *m.pl.*, (*fig.*) fondement, *m.*, base, *f.*, principe, *m.*, sujet, *m.*, motif, *m.*, cause, *f.*, (*in a stuff*) fond, *m.*, (*dregs*) lie, *f.*, sédiment, *m.*, marc, *m.*

Ground, va. poser à terre, établir, asseoir, fixer, fonder, baser, motiver, justifier, apprendre à fond à; — vn. échouer, toucher. — *arms!* reposez armes!
Groundless, adj. sans fondement, sans cause, sans motif, sans raison, frivole
Groundlessness, s. manque de fondement, *m.*, frivolité, *f.*
Groundsel, s. seuil, *m.*, (*constr.*) semelle, *f.*, (*bot.*) jacobée, *f.*, séneçon, *m.*
Groundwork, s. fondement, *m.*, base, *f.*, fond, *m.*, principe, *m.*, plan, *m.*, canevas, *m.*
Group, s. groupe, *m.*
Group, va. grouper
Grouping, s. l'art de grouper, *m.*
Grouse, s. coq de bruyère, *m.*
Grove, s. bocage, *m.*, bosquet, *m.*, charmilles, *f.pl.*
Grovel, vn. ramper, se vautrer
Grow, vn. croître, grandir, pousser, venir, s'avancer, devenir, provenir, naître
Grow, va. cultiver, faire pousser, produire
Grower, s. cultivateur, *m.*, producteur, *m.*
Growing, s. croissance, *f.*, augmentation, *f.*, progrès, *m.*, culture, *f.*
Growing, adj. qui grandit, qui pousse, croissant
Growl, va. grogner, gronder
Growl, Growling, s. grognement, *m.*, grondement, *m.*
Growler, s. chien qui gronde, (*person*) grognard, *m.*
Growth, s. croissance, *f.*, crue, *f.*, venue, *f.*, taille, *f.*, récolte, *f.*, fruit, *m.*, produit, *m.*, cru, *m.*, terroir, *m.*, (*fig.*) origine, *f.*, production, *f.*, création, *f.*, développement, *m.*
Grub, vn.a. creuser, travailler péniblement, fouir, bêcher, (*pop.*) manger
Grub, s. ver, *m.*, ver de terre, *m.*, (*pop.*) mangeaille, *f.*
Grubber, s. qui creuse, qui arrache, (*agric.*) hoyau, *m.*
Grudge, va.n. donner *or* recevoir à contre-cœur, plaindre, permettre à contre-cœur, envier à, regarder avec envie, porter envie à
Grudge, s. répugnance, *f.*, mauvaise volonté, *f.*, inimitié, *f.*, rancune, *f.*, ressentiment, *m.* *To bear or owe anyone a — for*, en vouloir à quelqu'un de, garder du ressentiment à quelqu'un de
Grudgingly, adv. à con-

tre-cœur, en rechignant, avec rancune
Gruel, s. gruau, m.
Gruff, adj. brusque, rude, bourru, renfrogné, rechigné
Gruffly, adv. d'un ton bourru, brusquement, rudement, d'un air renfrogné
Gruffness, s. brusquerie, f., rudesse, f.
Grumble, vn. se plaindre (de), murmurer (contre), grommeler, grogner, gronder, bougonner
Grumbler, s. mécontent, m., -e, f., grognard, m., grognon, m.
Grumbling, s. plainte, f., murmure, m., grondement, m.
Grumbling, adj s. grondeur, -euse, mécontent, -e
Grunt, vn. grogner
Grunt, Grunting, s. grognement, m.
Grunter, s. cochon, m., grogneur, m., -euse, f.
Gruntingly, adv. en grognant
Guano, s. guano, m.
Guarantee, s. garantie, f., caution, f., gage, m., garant, m.
Guarantee, va. garantir
Guard, va. garder (de), défendre (de), protéger (contre), veiller (sur); — vn se garder, se tenir *or* se mettre sur ses gardes, prendre ses précautions
Guard, s. garde, f., défense, f., protection, f., sauvegarde, f., (*railway*) conducteur, m., (*of a watch*) chaîne longue, f.
Guarded, adj. gardé, protégé, réservé, circonspect
Guardedly, adv. avec réserve, avec circonspection
Guardedness, s. réserve, f., circonspection, f.
Guardian, s. gardien, m., défenseur, m., garde, m., (*law*) tuteur, m., (*of poor-rates*) administrateur, m. *Joint* —, cotuteur. *Deputy* —, subrogé tuteur
Guardian, adj tutélaire, gardien
Guardianship, s. protection, f
Guardsman, s. garde, m., factionnaire, m.
Guava, s. goyavier, m., goyave, f.
Gudgeon, s. goujon, m., dupe, f.
Gudgeon, va. duper
Guess, va.n. deviner, conjecturer, croire, penser
Guess, s. conjecture, f. *To make a — at*, essayer de deviner. *A good —, a bad —*, bien deviné, mal deviné. *At one —*, du premier coup. *By —*, conjecturalement
Guesser, s. qui devine
Guest, s. invité, m., hôte, m., convive, m.
Guidance, s. conduite, f., direction, f.
Guide, va. guider, conduire, diriger
Guide, s. guide, m., conducteur, m. *—-post*, poteau indicateur, m., (*fig.*) point de repère, m.
Guideless, adj. sans guide
Guild, s. corporation, f., corps de métier, m.
Guildhall, s. hôtel de ville, m.
Guile, s. artifice, m., astuce, f.
Guileful, adj. artificieux, astucieux, perfide
Guileless, adj. franc, sincère, innocent, pur
Guillotine, s. guillotine, f
Guillotine, va. guillotiner
Guilt, s. culpabilité, f., forfait, m., crime, m.
Guiltily, adv. d'une manière coupable, criminellement
Guiltiness, s. culpabilité, f.
Guiltless, adj. innocent, pur
Guiltlessly, adv. innocemment
Guiltlessness, s. innocence, f.
Guilty, adj. coupable, criminel
Guinea, s. guinée, f.
Guise, s. air, m., maintien, m., habitude, f., apparence, f.
Guitar, s. guitare, f.
Gules, s. (*herald*) gueules, m.
Gulf, s. golfe, m., baie, f., (*fig.*) abîme, m., gouffre, m.
Gull, va. duper
Gull, s. duperie, f., dupe, f., gobe-mouches, m., (*bird*) mouette, f.
Guller, s. fourbe, m.
Gullet, s. gosier, m.
Gullibility, s. crédulité, f.
Gullible, adj. facile à duper
Gully, s. ravin, m., rigole, f.
Gulp, va. engloutir, avaler, gober
Gulp, s. gorgée, f., coup, m., trait, m.
Gum, s. (*teeth*) gencive, f., gomme, f., gommier, m.
Gum, va. gommer; — vn. distiller de la gomme
Gumboil, s. abcès aux gencives, m.
Gumminess, s. viscosité, f., abondance de gomme, f.
Gummy, adj. gommeux, riche en gomme
Gumption, s. savoir, m., tête, f., esprit, m., sagacité, f.
Gun, s. fusil, m., carabine, f., canon, m., pièce d'artillerie, f. *—s*, pl. artillerie, f., canons, m.pl. *Morning —*, diane, f. *—-boat*, canonnière, f., chaloupe canonnière, f. *—-cotton*, poudre-coton, f. *—-deck*, franc tillac, m., batterie, f. *—-lock*, platine de fusil, f. *—-powder*, poudre à canon, f. *—-powder plot*, la conspiration des poudres. *—-shot*, coup de feu, m., portée de fusil *or* de canon, f. *—-smith*, armurier, m., arquebusier, m. *—-stick*, baguette, f., (*artil.*) refouloir, m.
Gunnel, s. plat-bord, m.
Gunner, s. artilleur, m., canonnier, m.
Gunnery, s. artillerie, f., tir, m., exercice du tir, m.
Gurgle, vn. faire glou-glou, murmurer
Gurgle, Gurgling, s. glou-glou, m., (*of a stream*) murmure, m.
Gurnet, s. rouget, m.
Gush, vn. jaillir. *To — forth, to — out*, jaillir, sortir, couler avec abondance
Gush, Gushing, s. jaillissement, m., jet, m., (*fig.*) effusion, f.
Gusset, s. gousset, m.
Gust, s. coup de vent, m., rafale, f., bouffée, f., (*fig.*) accès, m., transport, m.
Gusty, adj. orageux
Gut, s.pl. intestins, m.pl., boyaux, m.pl., entrailles, f. pl., ventre, m., panse, f.
Gut, va. vider, (*fig.*) saccager
Gutta, s. goutte, f *—-percha*, gutta-percha, m.
Gutter, s. gouttière, f., (*street*) ruisseau, m., (*hollow*) sillon, m., rigole, f
Gutter, va. garnir de gouttières *or* de ruisseaux, sillonner; — vn (*to run*) couler
Guttural, adj. guttural. — s. gutturale, f.
Guy, s. (*nav*) gui, m., (*person*) caricature, f., pantin, m.
Guzzle, va.n. boire
Guzzler, s. sac à vin, m.
Gymnasium, s. gymnase, m.
Gymnast, s. gymnaste, m.
Gymnastic, adj. gymnastique
Gymnastically, adv. en athlète
Gymnastics, s.pl. gymnastique, f.
Gypsum, s. gypse, m., plâtre, m
Gyration, s. tournoiement, m.

H

H, s. H, h, m.f. *Don't drop your h's*, faites donc sentir l'aspiration
Haberdasher, s. mercier, m., -ère, f.
Haberdashery, s. mercerie, f
Habiliment, s. habillement, m., costume, m., vêtements, m.pl.
Habit, s. tempérament, m., habitude, f., coutume, f., mœurs, f.pl., usages, m.pl., (*dress*) habit, m. *From —, by —, out of —*, par habitude. *To be in the — (of)*, avoir pour habitude (de). *To get into the —, out of —*, contracter *or* prendre l'habitude, perdre l'habitude. *To break oneself of a —*, se défaire d'une habitude
Habitable, adj. habitable
Habitation, s. habitation, f.
Habitual, adj. habituel
Habitually, adv. habituellement, d'habitude
Habituate, va. habituer
Hack, va. hacher, tailler en pièces, (*notch*) ébrécher, (*a language*) massacrer
Hack, s. coup, m., entaille, f., marque, f., cheval de louage, m. *Literary —*, manœuvre littéraire, m.
Hackle, va. déchirer, sérancer
Hackle, s. sérançoir, m., soie *or* laine écrue, f.
Hackney, adj. de louage, (*fig*) banal, rebattu. *—-coach*, fiacre, m.
Hackneyed, adj. rebattu, banal
Haddock, s. merluche, f.
Haft, s. manche, m., poignée, f.
Haft, va. emmancher
Hag, va. tourmenter
Hag, s. sorcière, f., vieille, f., mégère, f., furie, f.
Haggard, adj. sauvage, farouche, hagard, égaré
Haggle, va.n. marchander, débattre le prix, barguigner
Haggler, s. celui, celle qui marchande, barguigneur, m., -euse, f.
Ha-ha, s. saut de loup, m.
Hail, s. grêle, f., appel, m. *—-shot*, petite mitraille, f. *—-stone*, grêlon, m. *—-storm*, grêle, f.
Hail! interj. salut! *All —!* salut!
Hail, vn tomber de la grêle, grêler, tomber comme (la) grêle; — va. faire pleuvoir comme de la grêle, (*to salute*) saluer, (*nav.*) héler
Hair, s. cheveu, m., chevelure, f., (*of the body*) poil, m., (*horses*) crin, m., (*boars*) soies, f pl.

. . -**Haired,** adj. aux cheveux, aux poils
Hairiness, s. nature velue *or* poilue, *f.*
Hairless, adj. chauve, sans poils
Hairy, adj. poilu, velu, chevelu
Halberd, s. hallebarde, *f.*, pertuisane, *f.*
Halberdier, s. hallebardier, *m.*
Halcyon, s. alcyon, *m.*
Halcyon, adj. paisible, heureux, serein
Hale, adj. vigoureux, bien portant, dispos
Half, s. moitié, *f.*, demie, *f.* *By* —, de moitié. *By halves,* à moitié, à demi. *In* —, par la moitié. *To go halves,* se mettre de moitié, être de moitié dans. *My better* —, ma moitié. *Next* —, au semestre prochain
Half, adj. demi
Half, adv. à moitié, à demi, (*in comp.*) demi, mi- . . . semi
Hall, s. grande salle, *f.*, salle, *f.*, (*entrance*) vestibule, *m.*, entrée, *f.*, (*residence*) château, *m.*, manoir, *m.*, demeure, *f.*, collége, *m.*, (*for dining*) réfectoire, *m.* —*-mark,* (*mint*) contrôle, *m.*
Hallelujah, s. alléluia, *m.*
Hallo! interj. holà!
Halloo, vn. crier, (*to laugh at*) huer, se moquer; — va. encourager, exciter, appeler, huer
Halloo, Hallooing, s. cri, *m.*, huée, *f*
Hallow, va. consacrer, sanctifier
Hallowed, adj. sanctifié, saint, vénéré
Hallucination, s. illusion, *f.*, erreur, *f.*, hallucination, *f.*
Hallucinatory, adj. illusoire, trompeur
Halo, s. halo, *m.*, cercle lumineux, *m.*, (*fig.*) auréole, *f.*, (*paint.*) gloire, *f.*, nimbe, *m.*
Halo, vn. former une auréole
Halser, see Hawser
Halt, vn. s'arrêter, faire halte, (*to walk lame*) boiter, être boiteux, clocher, (*fig.*) hésiter, flotter. —! halte! halte-là!
Halt, va. arrêter, (*mil.*) faire halte à
Halt, adj. boiteux, estropié
Halt, s. halte, *f.*, pause, *f.*, arrêt, *m.*, action de boiter, *f.*, clochement, *m.* *To make a* —, *a dead* —, faire halte, s'arrêter tout court
Halter, s. corde, *f.*, (*for horses*) licou, *m.*, licol, *m.*, (*pers.*) boiteux, *m.*, boiteuse, *f.*
Halter, va. mettre la corde au cou à, mettre le licou à
Halting, s. halte, *f.*, (*fig.*) pause, *f.*, hésitation, *f.*, infirmité, *f.*, clochement, *m.*
Halve, va. partager

Ham, s. jarret, *m.*, jambon, *m.*
Hamadryad, s. hamadryade, *f.*
Hamlet, s. hameau, *m.*
Hammer, s. marteau, *m.*, (*auction*) encan, *m.*, enchères, *f.pl.*, (*gun*) batterie, *f.* *To bring or come to the* —, faire vendre, être vendu à l'encan
Hammer, va. battre avec le marteau, travailler au marteau, marteler, forger. *To* — *into,* faire entrer à coups de marteau, (*fig.*) faire entrer dans la tête. *To* — *out,* étendre sous le marteau, (*fig.*) faire avec peine. —*ed steel,* acier martelé. — vn. donner des coups de marteau, travailler avec le marteau, (*fig.*) se casser la tête
Hammerer, s. marteleur, *m.*
Hammering, s. coups *or* bruit de marteau, *m.*
Hammock, s. hamac, *m.*, branle, *m.*
Hamper, s. panier, *m.*, manne, *f.*, bourriche, *f.*
Hamper, va. empêtrer, embarrasser
Hamstring, s. tendon du jarret, *m.*
Hamstring, va. couper le jarret à
Hand, s. main, *f.*, paume, *m.*, côté, *m.*, part, *f.*, autorité, *f.*, ouvrage, *m.*, travail, *m.*, (*fig.*) adresse, *f.*, savoir-faire, *m.*, talent, *m.*, méthode, *f.*, discipline, *f.*, contrôle, *m.*, (*play*) jeu, *m.*, partie, *f.*, (*means*) entremise, *f.*, moyen, *m.*, intermédiaire, *m.*, (*workmen*) ouvrier, *m.*, -ère, *f.*, homme, *m.*, personne, *f.*, (*of a watch*) aiguille, *f.*, index, *m.*, (*writing*) écriture, *f.*, (*seal*) seing, *m.* —*s off!* à bas les mains! *To be* — *and glove together,* être comme les deux doigts de la main, être à tu et à toi. *With both* —*s,* à deux mains, des deux mains. *Into his own* —*s,* en main propre. *In good* —*s,* en mains sûres. *At* —, tout près, sous la main, à portée, là. *By* —, à la main, par la main, avec la main. *To bring up by* —, (*an infant*) au biberon, (*a lamb*) à la cuillère, (*a bird*) à la brochette. — *to* —, corps à corps. *From* — *to* —, de main en main. *To live from* — *to mouth,* vivre au jour le jour. *In* —, en main, en train, en préparation, (*com.*) en caisse, en portefeuille, en magasin. — *in* —, la main dans la main, (*fig.*) d'accord, de concert. *On* —, en main. *To have on or upon one's* —*s,* avoir à sa charge. *Out of* —, sur-le-champ, sans hésiter, fait, fini. *To one's* — *or* —*s,* sous la main, prêt à servir. *To change* —*s,* changer de main, changer de propriétaire. *To come to* —, tomber sous la main, (*letters*) se présenter, parvenir à destination. *To have a* — *in,* prendre part à, participer à. *To lay* —*s on,* mettre la main sur, faire main basse sur. *To lay violent* —*s on oneself,* se donner la mort, se tuer. *To lend a helping* —, donner un coup de main, aider. *To take from all* —*s,* prendre à toutes mains. *At the* — *of,* de la part de. *To be a capital* — *at, the worst* — *in the world at,* s'entendre parfaitement à, être l'homme le plus maladroit du monde pour. *To be no* — *at,* ne pas s'entendre à, n'être pas adroit à. *To get one's* — *in,* se faire la main. *My* — *is in,* je suis en train *or* en veine. *To treat with a high* —, mener haut la main, mener tambour battant. *To have a good* —, avoir beau jeu. *To take a* — *at cards,* faire une partie. *Large* —, écriture en gros, *f.* *Small* —, écriture en fin, *f.* *Round* —, écriture moyenne, *f.* *Running* —, courante, *f.*
Hand, adj. (*in comp.*) à la main, de la main, dont se sert la main
Hand, va. passer de main en main, passer, donner, donner la main, conduire, guider. *To* — *about,* faire passer de main en main, conduire partout. *To* — *down,* faire passer, aider à descendre, transmettre. *To* — *down to dinner,* donner le bras (à une dame). *To* — *in, out, up,* donner la main pour entrer, pour sortir, pour monter, (*things*) faire passer. *To* — *over,* donner la main pour traverser, remettre. *To* — *round,* faire passer, faire circuler
Handcuff, s. menotte, *m.*
Handcuff, va. mettre les menottes à
Handed, adj. (*in comp.*) à mains, aux mains, à la main
Handful, s. poignée, *f.*, brassée, *f*
Handicraft, s. métier, *m.*, art mécanique, *m.*
Handicraftsman, s. ouvrier, *m.*, artisan, *m.*
Handily, adv. adroitement, facilement, à point nommé, commodément
Handiness, s. adresse, *f.*, commodité, *f.*
Handiwork, s. ouvrage, *m.*, travail, *m.*
Handkerchief, s. mouchoir, *m.* *Silk* —, foulard, *m.*
Handle, va. toucher à, manier, traiter. *Easily* —*d,* facile à manier, maniable. *Roughly to* —, maltraiter fort
Handle, s. manche, *m.*, (*of a cup*) anse, *f.*, poignée, *f.*, manivelle, *f.*, (*pump*) brimbale, *f.*, (*engine*) mannette, *f.*, (*door*) bouton, *m.*, (*frying-pan*) queue, *f.*, bras, *m.*, (*hilt*) garde, *f.*, poignée, *f.*, (*fig.*) prise, *f.*

Handless, adj. sans mains
Handling, s. maniement, *m.*, usage, *m.*, traitement, *m.*, (*arts*) manière, *f.*, style, *m.*
Handmaid, Handmaiden, s. servante, *f.*, (*fig.*) aide, *f.*, compagne, *f.*
Handsome, adj. beau, élégant, gracieux, généreux, flatteur, convenable. *To grow* —, s'embellir. *I have done the* —, j'ai fait les choses comme il faut
Handsomely, adv. bien, élégamment, généreusement, délicatement, comme il faut, galamment
Handsomeness, s. beauté, *f.*, grâce, *f.*, élégance, *f.*, générosité, *f.*, délicatesse, *f.*, noblesse, *f.*
Handspike, s. anspect, *m.*
Handy, adj. fait avec la main, de la main, adroit, habile, commode, à la portée de la main
Hang, va. pendre, suspendre, accrocher, (*fig.*) s'attacher, se pendre, laisser pendre, pencher, baisser, traîner, (*door, bell*) poser, (*paper*) tendre, tapisser, garnir. *To* — *up,* suspendre. *To* — *out,* mettre à la fenêtre, déployer, arborer. — vn. pendre, être suspendu, être *or* demeurer suspendu, tomber, prendre, flotter, s'attacher, s'accrocher, (*mil.*) harceler, (*to lean*) s'incliner, être en pente, (*fig.*) dépendre, reposer, rester fixé *or* attentif, être à charge, peser
Hangdog, s. pendard, *m.* *A* — *look,* une mine patibulaire
Hanger, s. qui pend *or* qui fait pendre, (*executioner*) bourreau, *m.*, (*a hook*) croc, *m.*, crochet, *m.*, (*cutlass*) couteau de chasse, *m.*, coutelas, *m.*, (*writing*) jambage, *m.* — *on,* dépendant, *m.*, parasite, *m.*, habitué, *m.*, flâneur, *m.*, fâcheux, *m.*
Hanging, s. chose suspendue, *f.*, suspension, *f.*, pendaison, *f.*, corde, *f.*, gibet, *m.*, tentures, *f.pl.*, tapisseries, *f.pl.*, chose accessoire, *f.*, appendice, *m*
Hanging, adj. suspendu, pendant, patibulaire, (*deed*) pendable
Hangman, s. bourreau, *m*
Hangnail, s. envie, *f*
Hank, s. poignée d'écheveaux, *f.*, frein, *m.*
Hanker, vn. désirer avidement, soupirer (après)
Hansom, s. cabriolet, *m.*
Hap, s. hasard, *m.*, accident, *m.*, malheur, *m.* —*-hazard, by* —*-hazard,* au hasard
Hapless, adj. infortuné
Haply, adv. peut-être, par hasard
Happen, vn. arriver, se passer, advenir, venir, se trouver. *If I* —*ed to say,* s'il

m'arrivait de dire. *Do you — to know!* connaissez-vous par hasard? *Should it so —*, le cas échéant

Happily, adv. heureusement, par bonheur

Happiness, s. bonheur, *m.*

Happy, adj. heureux, content, charmé

Harangue, s. harangue, *f.*

Harangue, va. haranguer; — vn. prononcer une harangue

Harass, va. harasser, harceler, tourmenter

Harbinger, s. précurseur, *m.*, avant-coureur, *m.*, avant-courrière, *f.*

Harbour, s. port, *m.*, havre, *m.*, gîte, *m.*, asile, *m.* — *-master*, capitaine de port, *m.* *Inner* —, arrière-port, *m.* — *dues*, droit de mouillage, *m.*

Harbour, va. accueillir, donner asile à, recevoir chez soi, (*fig.*) nourrir, entretenir; — vn. loger, séjourner, trouver un asile

Harbourage, s. refuge, *m.*, hospitalité, *f.*

Harbourer, s. qui donne asile à, hôte, *m.*

Hard, adj. dur, difficile, malaisé, pénible, rude, ardu, (*taste*) âpre, (*weather*) rigoureux. — *to do*, difficile à faire. — *earnings*, pénibles gains. *To say — things to, to call — names*, dire des duretés à. *To be — upon*, traiter durement, être exigeant pour. *He is too — for you*, vous n'êtes pas de force avec lui. — *times*, des temps difficiles

Hard, adv. près, auprès, de près, laborieusement, fort, ferme, difficilement, avec peine, durement, cruellement, avec force, (*rain*) à verse, (*frost*) dur, (*drinking*) sec. — *by*, tout contre, tout auprès. — *-pressed*, serré de près, poussé vivement. *To be — put to it*, avoir beaucoup de peine, (*fam.*) tirer le diable par la queue. *To be — up*, être très-gêné, être à sec. *To be — set*, être serré de près. *To be — at it, at work*, travailler ferme. *To go — (with)*, tourner *or* aller mal (pour), être malheureux. *To ride —*, aller grand train. — *-besetting*, pressant. — *-earned*, péniblement gagné. — *-favoured*, — *-featured*, au visage dur, aux traits durs. — *-fought*, acharné. — *-got*, acquis avec peine. — *-handed*, aux mains calleuses, tyrannique. — *-hearted*, inhumain, cruel, inexorable. — *-heartedly*, avec cruauté. — *-heartedness*, dureté de cœur, *f.* — *-nibbed*, au bec dur. — *-won*, gagné difficilement

Harden, va. durcir, rendre dur, donner de la trempe à, affermir, endurcir (à); — vn. durcir, se durcir, (*fig.*) s'endurcir

Hardening, s. durcissement, *m.*, endurcissement, *m.*

Hardihood, **Hardiness**, s. hardiesse, *f.*, intrépidité, *f.*

Hardily, adv. hardiment

Hardly, adv. difficilement, avec peine, à peine, ne ... guère, durement. — *ever*, presque jamais

Hardness, s. dureté, *f.*, difficulté, *f.*, sévérité, *f.*, (*season*) rigueur, *f.*

Hardship, s. peine, *f.*, fatigue, *f.*, privation, *f.*, souffrance, *f.*

Hardware, s. quincaillerie, *f.* — *-man*, quincaillier, *m.*

Hardy, adj. hardi, intrépide, brave, dur, endurci, (*plants*) vigoureux, robuste

Hare, s. lièvre, *m.* *To run with the — and hold with the hounds*, ménager la chèvre et le chou. — *-bell*, campanule, *f.* — *-brained*, écervelé. — *-lip*, bec-de-lièvre, *m.* *To be — -lipped*, avoir un bec-de-lièvre

Harem, s. harem, *m.*

Hark, vn. écouter

Harlequin, s. Arlequin, *m.* —*'s trick*, arlequinade, *f.*

Harlot, s. courtisane, *f.* — adj. de courtisane, comme une courtisane

Harm, s. mal, *m.*, (*wrong*) tort, *m.* *Out of —'s way*, en sûreté

Harm, va. faire du mal à, faire du tort à, nuire à

Harmful, adj. nuisible (à), malfaisant, mauvais (pour)

Harmfully, adv. d'une manière nuisible

Harmfulness, s. mal, *m.*, nature nuisible, *f.*

Harmless, adj. inoffensif, innocent

Harmlessly, adv. innocemment, sans faire mal

Harmonic, adj. harmonique

Harmonica, s. harmonica, *m.*

Harmonics, s.pl. harmonie, *f.*

Harmonious, adj. harmonieux, (*fig.*) en harmonie

Harmoniously, adv. harmonieusement, (*fig.*) en bon accord

Harmonist, s. harmoniste, *m.*

Harmonium, s. harmonium, *m.*

Harmonize, va. rendre harmonieux, mettre en harmonie, faire accorder; — vn. s'harmoniser, être en harmonie

Harmony, s. harmonie, *f.*, accord, *m.*, (*of texts*) concordance, *f.*

Harness, s. harnais, *m.*, harnois, *m.* — *-maker*, bourrelier, *m.* *To put in —*, atteler

Harness, va. mettre le harnais à, harnacher

Harp, s. harpe, *f.* — *-case*, étui de harpe, *m.* *Jew's —*, guimbarde, *f.*

Harp, vn. jouer de la harpe, (*fig.*) (*on*) revenir (sur), répéter sans cesse, rabâcher

Harpist, s. harpiste, *m.f.*

Harpoon, s. harpon, *m.*

Harpoon, va. harponner

Harpsichord, s. clavecin, *m.*

Harpy, s. harpie, *f.*

Harridan, s. haridelle, *f.*

Harrier, s. chien courant, *m.*, lévrier, *m.*

Harrow, s. herse, *f.*

Harrow, va. herser, (*fig.*) déchirer

Harsh, adj. (*of taste*) âpre, (*of touch*) dur, rude, (*to the ear*) discordant, (*features*) dur, rude, (*character*) sévère, rigide. — *measures*, voies de rigueur, *f.*

Harshly, adv. durement, rudement, avec dureté, désagréablement

Harshness, s. âpreté, *f.*, dureté, *f.*, rudesse, *f.*, son discordant, *m.*, discordance, *f.*

Hart, s. cerf, *m.*

Hartshorn, s. corne de cerf, *f.*

Harum-scarum, adj. (*person*) écervelé, braque, (*things*) étourdi, en l'air, à l'étourdie

Harvest, s. moisson, *f.*, temps de la moisson, *m.*, récolte, *f.*

Harvest, va. moissonner, rentrer

Harvester, s. moissonneur, *m.*

Hash, va. hacher menu, réchauffer

Hash, s. hachis, *m.*

Hasp, s. moraillon, *m.*, fuseau, *m.*

Hassock, s. coussin, *m.*, natte, *f.*

Haste, s. hâte, *f.*, célérité, *f.*, diligence, *f.*, promptitude, *f.*, emportement, *m.*, vivacité, *f.* *To make —*, se dépêcher, faire hâte, suivre promptement

Haste, **Hasten**, vn. se hâter, se dépêcher, se presser, s'empresser, (*to*) se rendre en toute hâte, accourir. *To — on*, presser le pas. — va. hâter, presser, accélérer, précipiter

Hastily, adv. en hâte, à la hâte, vite, précipitamment, inconsidérément, brusquement

Hastiness, s. hâte, *f.*, précipitation, *f.*, emportement, *m.*, vivacité, *f.*, brusquerie, *f.*

Hasty, adj. précipité, rapide, pressé, inconsidéré, irréfléchi, emporté, brusque, vif

Hat, s. chapeau, *m.*, (*cardinal's*) barrette, *f.* — *-band*, bourdalou, *m.*, cordon de chapeau, *m.* — *-box*, — *-case*, carton *or* étui de chapeau, *m.* — *-brush*, brosse à chapeau, *f.* — *-maker*, chapelier, *m.* — *-manufactory*, — *-trade*, chapellerie, *f.* — *in hand*, chapeau bas. —*s off!* chapeaux bas!

Hatch, va. couver, faire éclore, (*fig.*) nourrir, (*a plot*) machiner, tramer, ourdir, (*drawing*) hacher. *Hatching-strokes*, hachure, *f.* — vn. éclore, (*fig.*) se préparer, se tramer

Hatch, s. couvée, *f.*, éclosion, *f.*, (*of a plot*) découverte, *f.*, (*a door*) porte coupée, *f.*, (*nav.*) écoutille, *f.*

Hatchet, s. hache, *f.*, hachette, *f.*

Hatching, s. incubation, *f.*, éclosion, *f.*, (*drawings*) hachure, *f.* — *-stroke*, hachure, *f.*

Hatchment, s. écusson, *m.*, armoiries, *f.pl.*

Hatchway, s. écoutille, *f.* *Main —*, grande écoutille. *Small —*, écoutillon, *m.*

Hate, va. haïr, avoir en haine, avoir de la haine pour

Hate, s. haine, *f.*

Hateful, adj. haineux, haïssable, odieux

Hatefully, adv. odieusement

Hatefulness, s. caractère odieux, *m.*, nature odieuse, *f.*, odieux, *m.*

Hater, s. qui hait, *m.*, ennemi, *m.*

Hatred, s. haine, *f.*, inimitié, *f.*

Hatter, s. chapelier, *m.*

Haughtily, adv. avec hauteur *or* arrogance

Haughtiness, s. hauteur, *f.*, arrogance, *f.*

Haughty, adj. hautain, arrogant, superbe, dédaigneux

Haul, va. traîner, tirer, (*nav.*) haler. *To — about*, tirailler, tirer de côté et d'autre. — *up*, hisser

Haul, s. tirage, *m.*, traction, *f.*

Haunch, s. hanche, *f.*, quartier *or* cuissot, *m.*

Haunt, va. visiter, fréquenter, se plaire dans, hanter, poursuivre, vivre dans la mémoire

Haunt, s. lieu fréquenté, *m.*, séjour, *m.*, retraite, *f.*, repaire, *m.*

Haunter, s. qui hante, qui visite, qui fréquente, habitué, *m.*, -e, *f.*, (*in a bad sense*) pilier, *m.*

Hautboy, s. hautbois, *m.*

Have, va. avoir, tenir, posséder, (*to consider*) regarder, considérer, (*a meal, &c.*) faire, (*a night*) passer. *I — you fast*, je vous tiens. *I would not — it thought*, je ne voudrais pas que l'on pensât. *He will — (it) that I am mistaken*, il soutient que je me trompe. *I will — you know*, je veux que vous sachiez. — *him arrested*, faites-le arrêter. — *back*, faire revenir, faire rendre. — *on*, avoir, porter. — *down, up, in, out*, faire descendre, faire monter, faire entrer, faire sortir. —

him out, faites-le sortir, appelez-le en duel. *To — it out with*, s'expliquer avec. *— with you!* je suis des vôtres!

Haven, s. port, *m.*, havre, *m.*, (*fig.*) asile, *m.*, retraite, *f.*

Haversac, s. havre-sac, *m.*

Havoc, s. carnage, *m.*, dévastation, *f.*, ravage, *m.* *To make — of*, ravager

Haw, s. cenelle, *f.* *—-haw*, saut-de-loup, *m.*

Haw, vn. ânonner. *See* Hum

Hawk, s. faucon, *m.*, épervier, *m.*

Hawk, va.n. chasser au faucon, voler, s'élever, colporter

Hawker, s. fauconnier, *m.*, (*com.*) colporteur, *m.*, marchand ambulant, *m.*

Hawking, s. fauconnerie, *f.*, vol au faucon, *m.*, (*com.*) colportage, *m.*

Hawser, s. haussière, *f.*, câble, *m.*

Hawthorn, s. aubépine, *f.*, épine blanche, *f.* *—-bush*, buisson d'aubépine, *m.*

Hay, s. foin, *m.* *To make —*, faire les foins, faner. *—-cock*, meule de foin, *f.*, veillotte, *f.* *—-loft*, grenier à foin, *m.* *—-maker*, faneur, *m.*, -euse, *f.* *—-making*, fenaison, *f.* *—-market*, marché aux foins, *m.* *—-mow*, *—-rick*, *—-stack*, meule de foin, *f.* *—-time*, fenaison, *f.*

Hazard, s. hasard, *m.*, chance, *f.*, risque, *m.*, péril, *m.*

Hazard, va. hasarder, risquer, aventurer; — vn. se hasarder

Hazardous, adj. hasardeux, chanceux

Hazardously, adv. d'une manière hasardeuse

Haze, s. brume, *f.*, brouillard, *m.*

Hazel, s. (*tree*) coudrier, *m.*, noisetier, *m.* *—-copse*, petit bois de coudriers, *m.* *—-switch*, baguette de coudrier, *f.* *—-nut*, noisette, *f.*

Haziness, s. état brumeux, *m.*

Hazy, adj. brumeux

He, pron. il, lui, celui, celui-là, (*of animals*) mâle

Head, s. tête, *f.*, chef, *m.*, (*wild boar*) hure, *f.*, (*coin*) tête, *f.*, face, *f.*, (*ship*) avant, *m.*, proue, *f.*, figure, *f.*, (*bed*) chevet, *m.*, tête, *f.*, (*table*) haut bout, *m.*, haut, *m.*, (*cabbage*) pomme, *f.*, (*spear*) fer, *m.*, (*arrow*) pointe, *f.*, (*cask*) fond, *m.*, (*river*) source, *f.*, (*bag*) ouverture, *f.*, (*newspaper*) rubrique, *f.*, (*chapter*) tête, *f.*, (*speech*) point principal, *m.*, (*chief*) chef, *m.*, principal, *m.*, directeur, *m.* *So much per —, a —*, tant par tête. *From — to foot*, de pied en cap. *Over — and ears*, par-dessus les oreilles. *— over heels*, en faisant la culbute. *To give the —*, lâcher la bride. *To make — against*, tenir tête à. *— or tail*, pile ou face. *To have in one's —*, avoir en tête. *To take it into one's —*, s'aviser (de). *To get into one's —*, monter à la tête. *To be out of one's —*, être un peu timbré. *Of his own —*, de son chef. *To go out of one's —*, sortir de l'idée

Head-..., adj. chef, principal, en chef, de la tête, à la tête, en tête. *—-ache*, migraine. *—-attire*, *—-tire*, *—-dress*, coiffure, *f.* *—-work*, travail de tête, *m.*

Head, va. conduire, être à la tête de, commander, (*letter, &c.*) mettre *or* faire une tête à. *—ed by*, ayant en tête, conduit *or* commandé par. *To — down trees*, étêter des arbres. — vn. se former une tête

...-Headed, adj. à la tête, à tête

Header, s. chef, *m.*, tonnelier, *m.* *To take a —*, piquer une tête

Headful, s. tête pleine, *m.*

Headily, adv. précipitamment

Headiness, s. précipitation, *f.*, entêtement, *m.*, (*wines*) nature capiteuse, *f.*

Heading, s. en-tête, *m.*, tête, *f.*, titre, *m.*

Headland, s. cap, *m.*, promontoire, *m.*

Headless, adj. sans tête, décapité, (*fig.*) étourdi, inconsidéré

Headlong, adj. escarpé, soudain, précipité, impétueux, (*fig.*) aveugle, inconsidéré

Headlong, adv. tête baissée, à corps perdu, précipitamment, inconsidérément, de gaieté de cœur

Headmost, adj. de tête, en tête, à la tête, en avant, premier

Headship, s. direction, *f.*

Headsman, s. bourreau, *m.*

Headstrong, adj. volontaire, têtu, indocile

Heady, adj. (*wine*) capiteux

Heal, va. guérir, (*a wound*) cicatriser, fermer, (*quarrels*) apaiser; — vn. guérir, se guérir

Healer, s. qui guérit

Healing, adj. qui guérit, sain, curatif, doux, calmant

Healing, s. guérison, *f.*, santé, *f.*

Health, s. santé, *f.*, bonne santé, *f.*, salubrité, *f.* *Board of —*, conseil de salubrité, *m.* *To propose, to drink the — of*, porter la santé de. *Here's your —!* à votre santé!

Healthful, Healthy, adj. (*pers.*) bien portant, plein de santé, en santé, sain, (*face*) qui respire la santé, (*things*) sain, salubre, salutaire, de santé

Healthfully, Healthily, adv. sainement

Healthfulness, **Healthiness**, s. santé, *f.*, salubrité, *f.*

Heap, s. monceau, *m.*, amas, *m.*, tas, *m.*

Heap, va. (*up*) amasser, amonceler, entasser, accumuler, empiler

Heaping, s. entassement, *m.*, accumulation, *f.*

Hear, va. entendre, apprendre (de), entendre dire (à *or* par), (*a lesson*) faire répéter, (*a prayer*) exaucer, écouter. (*a trial*) entendre, juger. *To make oneself —d*, se faire entendre. *To — it said*, entendre dire, ouïr dire. — vn. entendre, entendre parler, (*from*) recevoir des nouvelles

Hearer, s. celui, celle qui écoute, auditeur, *m.*, auditoire, *m.*

Hearing, s. l'ouïe, *f.*, l'oreille, *f.*, audition, *f.*, audience, *f.*, attention, *f.*, portée de la voix, *f.* *Hard of —*, dur d'oreille. *To be quick of —*, avoir l'oreille *or* l'ouïe fine. *To give a — to*, donner audience à, prêter l'oreille à. *To be within —, out of —*, être, n'être pas à la portée de la voix. *In my —*, devant moi or en ma présence

Hearken, va.n. écouter, prêter l'oreille à

Hearsay, s. ouï-dire, *m.*

Hearse, s. char mortuaire, *m.*, corbillard, *m.*, bière, *f.* *—-cloth*, drap mortuaire, *m.*

Heart, s. cœur, *m.*, vie, *f.*, énergie, *f.*, courage, *m.*, affection, *f.*, amour, *m.*, conscience, *f.*, (*chief point*) cœur, *m.*, centre, *m.*, fond, *m.* *With all my —*, de tout (mon) cœur, du meilleur de (mon) cœur. *Bless my —! Bless my — alive!* bon Dieu! *To your —'s delight, content*, au gré de vos désirs, à souhait, à cœur joie. *To get or learn by —*, apprendre par cœur. *To have set one's — on*, avoir à cœur de, désirer fortement. *To be, to put out of —*, perdre courage, faire perdre courage. *To find the — to*, avoir le cœur de

Heart-..., (*in compos.*) *The —-ache, —-aching*, les peines du cœur, le chagrin. *—-break*, vrai chagrin, *m.*, crève-cœur, *m.* *—-breaker*, accroche-cœur, *m.* *—-breaking*, s. déchirement de cœur, *m.* — adj. navrant, déchirant. *—-burn*, aigreurs, *f.pl.*, (*med.*) cardialgie, *f.* *—-burning*, cardialgie, *f.*, (*fig.*) animosité, *f.*, haine, *f.* *—-ease*, *—'s ease*, la paix du cœur, (*bot.*) pensée, *f.* *—-felt*, profondément senti. *—-searching*, qui sonde les cœurs. *—-shaped*, en forme de cœur. *—-sick*, profondément affligé. *—-sickening*, à soulever le cœur, navrant. *—-sore*, crève-cœur, *m.* *—-stricken*, frappé au cœur

Hearth, s. âtre, *m.*, foyer, *m.*, cheminée, *f.* *—-broom*, petit balai, *m.* *—-stone*, foyer, *m.*, pierre-ponce, *f.* *—-rug*, tapis de cheminée, *m.*

Heartily, adv. de cœur, cordialement, du fond du cœur, avec appétit, bien (portant)

Heartiness, s. cordialité, *f.*, ardeur, *f.*

Heartless, adj. sans cœur, timide, insensible, cruel, sans pitié

Heartlessly, adv. sans cœur, cruellement, sans pitié

Heartlessness, s. insensibilité, *f.*, brutalité, *f.*, cruauté, *f.*

Hearty, adj. cordial, de cœur, sincère, chaud, zélé, vigoureux, bien portant, qui a bon appétit, (*meal*) abondant, (*blow*) rude, vigoureux. *A — laugh*, un gros rire

Heat, s. chaleur, *f.*, (*phys.*) calorique, *m.*, ardeur, *f.*, effervescence, *f.*, excitation, *f.*, coup, *m.*, effort, *m.*, (*racing*) épreuve, *f.*, (*in the face*) rougeurs, *f.pl.* *At a —*, d'un coup

Heat, va.n. chauffer, échauffer, enflammer, animer

Heater, s. chauffeur, *m.*

Heath, s. bruyère, *f.*, lande, *f.*

Heathen, s. païen, *m.*, -ne, *f.*

Heathenish, adj. païen, -ne, barbare

Heathenism, s. paganisme, *m.*, barbarie, *f.*

Heather, s. bruyère, *f.* *—-bell*, fleur de bruyère, *f.*

Heating, s. chauffe, *f.*, (*fig.*) échauffement, *m.*

Heating, adj. échauffant

Heave, va. soulever, lever, élever, (*a sigh*) pousser, (*nav.*) virer, hisser, (*to throw*) jeter. *To — up*, soulever, lever, (*nav.*) hisser. *To — down*, abattre en carène. — vn. haleter, palpiter, se soulever, hausser et baisser, s'agiter, (*the heart*) battre, (*by sickness*) se soulever. *To — to*, mettre en panne

Heave, Heaving, s. effort, *m.*, soulèvement, *m.*, secousse, *f.*, (*waves, &c.*) agitation, *f.*, (*heart*) soulèvement, *m.*

Heaven, s. le ciel, *m.*, les cieux, *m.pl.*, le sublime.

Heavenly, adj. céleste, du ciel, divin, angélique

Heaver, s. portefaix, *m.*, débardeur, *m.*, (*tool*) levier, *m.*

Heavily, adv. pesamment, lourdement, difficilement, péniblement, tristement, avec ennui

Heaviness, s. pesanteur, *f.*, lourdeur, *f.*, poids, *m.*, appesantissement, *m.*, accablement, *m.*, assoupissement, *m.*, ennui, *m.*, tristesse, *f.*, (*of the land*) nature grasse, *f.*

Heavy, adj. lourd, pesant, grave, gros, grand, (*misfor-*

tune) accablant, (*tedious*) pénible, ennuyeux, lent, à charge, (*with*) appesanti (par), accablé (de), (*roads*) pénible, difficile, (*land*) gras, (*sea, &c.*) gros. *To be, to lie, to hang — on*, s'appesantir (sur), être à charge (à), (*time*) peser à. — *debts*, de grosses dettes

Hebraic, adj. hébraique

Hebraist, s. hébraisant, *m.*

Hebrew, s. adj. Hébreu, *m.*, des Hébreux, la langue hébraique

Hecatomb, s. hécatombe, *f.*

Hectic, adj. hectique, étique. — *fever, flush*, fièvre, rougeur hectique

Hector, s. fanfaron, *m.*, bravache, *m.*, matamore, *m.*

Hedge, s. haie, *f.*, des haies, *f.pl.*

Hedge, va. entourer *or* clore d'une haie, protéger, entourer. *To — in*, enfermer, introduire. *To — off*, séparer par une haie. *To — out*, empêcher d'entrer. *To — up*, obstruer, fermer

Hedgehog, s. hérisson, *m.*

Hedger, s. faiseur de haies, *m.*

Hedging, s. action de planter des haies, *f.*, taille des haies *f.* — *-bill*, serpe, *f.*, croissant, *m.*

Heed, va. n. faire attention à, prendre garde à, écouter

Heed, s. attention, *f.*, garde, *f.*, soin, *m.* *To take (good) — of*, prendre garde à, faire attention à, se garder de

Heedful, adj. attentif (à), soigneux (de)

Heedfully, adv. avec attention, soigneusement

Heedfulness, s. attention, *f.*, soin, *m.*, vigilance, *f.*, circonspection, *f.*

Heedless, adj. étourdi, léger, irréfléchi, insouciant

Heedlessly, adv. étourdiment

Heedlessness, s. étourderie, *f.*, inattention, *f.*, négligence, *f.*

Heel, s. talon, *m.*, (*spur*) éperon, *m.*

Heel, va. mettre un talon à

Hegira, s. hégire, *f.*

Heifer, s. génisse, *f.*

Height, s. hauteur, *f.*, haut, *m.*, élévation, *f.*, (*persons*) taille, *f.*, stature, *f.*, (*glory*) comble, *m.*, apogée, *m.*, faîte, *m.*

Heighten, va. rehausser, relever, augmenter, accroître

Heightening, s. accroissement, *m.*, aggravation, *f.*, embellissement, *m.*, perfectionnement, *m.*

Heinous, adj. atroce, noir, odieux, détestable

Heinously, adv. odieusement

Heinousness, s. atrocité, *f.*, énormité, *f.*, odieux, *m.*

Heir, s. héritier, *m.* — *at law*, héritier naturel. — *under a will*, héritier testamentaire

Heiress, s. héritière, *f.*

Heirless, adj. sans héritier

Heirloom, s. meuble de famille, *m.*, bijoux transmis par héritage dans la même famille, *m.pl.*

Heirship, s. hérédité, *f.*

Heliotrope, s. héliotrope, *m.*

Helix, s. hélice, *f.*

Hell, s. enfer, *m.*, les enfers, *m.pl.*, maison de jeu, *f.* *Of —*, d'enfer, des enfers, infernal

Hellebore, s. ellébore, *m.*

Hellenic, adj. hellénique

Hellenism, s. hellénisme, *m.*

Hellenist, s. helléniste, *m.*

Hellish, adj. infernal, d'enfer

Helm, s. gouvernail, *m.*, timon, *m.*, barre, *f.*

Helmet, s. casque, *m.*, heaume, *m.*

Helmsman, s. timonier, *m.*

Helot, s. ilote, *m.*

Helotism, s. ilotisme, *m.*

Help, va. aider, aider à, assister, secourir, être utile à, (*at table*) servir, offrir, (*forbear*) s'empêcher de, éviter. *To — oneself, one another*, s'aider, s'entr'aider. *To — in, out, on, up, down, over*, aider à entrer, à sortir, à monter, à descendre, à surmonter. — vn. aider, servir, contribuer. *To — out*, venir en aide

Help, s. aide, *f.*, secours, *m.*, assistance, *f.*, (*pers.*) aide, *f.*, soutien, *m.* *With the — of*, à l'aide de. *To cry out for —*, crier au secours

Helper, s. aide, *m.*, auxiliaire, *m.*

Helpful, adj. secourable

Helpless, adj. faible, impuissant, sans appui, délaissé, sans remède

Helplessly, adv. faiblement, sans secours

Helplessness, s. faiblesse, *f.*, impuissance, *f.*, abandon, *m.*, délaissement, *m.*

Helpmate, s. compagnon, *m.*, compagne, *f.*, moitié, *f.*

Helter-skelter, adv. pêle-mêle, en confusion, à la débandade

Hem, s. ourlet, *m.*, bord, *m.*

Hem! interj. hem! hom!

Hem, va. ourler, border — *in, about, around*, enfermer, renfermer, cerner, entourer

Hemisphere, s. hémisphère, *m.*

Hemistich, s. hémistiche, *m.*

Hemlock, s. ciguë, *f.*

Hemorrhage, s. hémorragie, *f.*

Hemp, s. chanvre, *m.*, étoupe, *f.* — *-field*, chènevière, *f.* — *-seed*, chènevis, *m.*

Hempen, adj. de chanvre

Hen, s. poule, *f.*, (*female*) femelle, *f.*

Henbane, s. jusquiame, *f.*

Hence, adv. d'ici, à partir d'aujourd'hui

Henceforth, adv. désormais, dorénavant, à l'avenir

Heptarchy, s. heptarchie, *f.*

Her, pron. elle, la, lui, à elle. — adj. poss. son, sa, ses

Herald, s. héraut, *m.*, messager, *m.*, messagère, *f.*, avant-courrier, *m.*, -ère, *f.*

Herald, va. introduire

Heraldic, adj. héraldique

Heraldry, s. la science héraldique, le blason. *Book of —*, armorial, *m.*

Herb, s. herbe, *f.* — *-shop*, boutique d'herboriste, *f.*, herboristerie, *f.* — *-woman*, marchande de légumes, *f.*

Herbaceous, adj. herbacé, (*animal*) herbivore

Herbage, s. herbage, *m.*

Herbal, s. herbier, *m.*

Herbalist, s. botaniste, *m.*, herboriste, *m.*

Herbivorous, adj. herbivore

Herbless, adj. sans herbes

Herborize, vn. herboriser

Herculean, adj. herculéen, d'Hercule

Herd, s. troupeau, *m.*, troupe, *f.*

Herd, vn. aller *or* vivre en troupeau, par troupes, (*fig.*) s'associer (à); — va. réunir *or* assembler en troupeaux, associer

Herdsman, s. pâtre, *m.*

Here, adv. ici, ici-bas, voici, que voici. — *is*, — *are*, voici. — *I am*, me voici. —*'s to*, je bois à la santé de

Here! interj. tiens! tenez!

Hereabout, Hereabouts, adv. près d'ici, à peu près ici, par ici

Hereafter, adv. plus tard, par la suite, à l'avenir, dans la vie à venir

Hereat, adv. à ceci, de ceci

Hereby, adv. par là, (*by this letter*) par ces présentes, tout près d'ici

Hereditament, s. bien, *m.*

Hereditarily, adv. héréditairement

Hereditary, adj. héréditaire

Herein, adv. en cela, ci-inclus, sous ce pli

Hereof, adv. de cela, d'où

Heresiarch, s. hérésiarque, *m.*

Heresy, s. hérésie, *f.*

Heretic, s. hérétique, *m.*

Heretical, adj. hérétique, entaché d'hérésie

Heretofore, adv. jadis, jusqu'ici

Hereupon, adv. là-dessus

Herewith, adv. avec ceci

Heritage, s. héritage, *m.*

Hermaphrodite, s. adj. hermaphrodite

Hermetically, adv. hermétiquement

Hermit, s. ermite, *m.*

Hermitage, s. ermitage, *m.*

Hermitical, adj. d'ermite

Hernia, s. hernie, *f.*

Hero, s. héros, *m.*

Heroic, Heroical, adj. héroïque

Heroically, adv. héroïquement, avec héroïsme

Heroine, s. héroïne, *f.*

Heroism, s. héroïsme, *m.*

Heron, s. héron, *m.*

Heronry, s. héronnière, *f.*

Herring, s. hareng, *m.* *Red —*, hareng saur. — *-season*, la harengaison

Hers, pron. à elle, le sien, la sienne, les siens, les siennes. *A friend of —*, un de ses amis

Herself, pron. se, elle-même, elle

Hesitate, vn. hésiter

Hesitatingly, adv. en hésitant, avec hésitation

Hesitation, s. hésitation, *f.*

Heterodox, adj. hétérodoxe

Heterodoxy, s. hétérodoxie, *f.*

Hew, va. tailler, couper, hacher

Hey! interj. hé! hein!

Heyday, s. ardeur, *f.*, apogée, *m.* *In the — of life*, au printemps de la vie

Hiatus, s. abîme, *m.*, lacune, *f.*, brèche, *f.*

Hiccough, Hiccup, s. hoquet, *m.*

Hiccough, Hiccup, vn. avoir le hoquet

Hickory, s. noyer d'Amérique, *m.*

Hide, va. cacher, dissimuler, recéler, (*pop.*) rosser; — vn. se cacher

Hide, s. peau, *f.*, cuir, *m.* *Dressed —*, cuir, *m.*

Hideous, adj. hideux, affreux, horrible

Hideously, adv. hideusement

Hideousness, s. aspect hideux, *m.*, caractère hideux, *m.*

Hider, s. qui cache, qui se cache

Hiding, s. (*pop.*) roulée, *f.*

Hierarchy, s. hiérarchie, *f.*

Hieroglyph, s. hiéroglyphe, *m.*

Hieroglyphic, Hieroglyphical, adj. hiéroglyphique

Higgle, va. colporter, marchander; — vn. liarder, lésiner

Higgledy-piggledy, adv. pêle-mêle

Higgler, s. colporteur, *m.*, marchandeur, *m.*, -euse, *f.*

Higgling, s. barguignage, *m.*

High, adj. haut, élevé, grand, relevé, (*proud*) altier, hautain, superbe, haut, (*threatening*) menaçant, sévère, fort, violent, (*colours*) haut, vif, tranché, (*sea*) haute, grosse, (*opinion*) haut, flatteur, (*game*) avancé, (*taste*) relevé, (*dress*) montant. *To be six feet* —, avoir six pieds de haut *or* de hauteur. *Words ran* —, la dispute s'échauffait. *It is — time*, il est grand temps

High, adv. haut, en haut, à haute voix, fort, fortement, avec hauteur, profondément, (*at play*) gros jeu. *On* —, en haut, en l'air. *To stand* —, être haut *or* élevé. — *-bred*, d'une éducation distinguée. — *-coloured*, (*face*) haut en couleur, d'une couleur éclatante. — *-crowned*, haut de forme. — *-fed*, bien nourri. — *-feeding*, nourriture substantielle. — *-flown*, orgueilleux, (*style*) ampoulé. — *-flavoured*, (d'un goût) relevé. — *-flying*, au vol élevé, (*fig.*) ambitieux. — *-handed*, arbitraire, tyrannique. — *-lows*, souliers à recouvrement. — *-minded*, magnanime, orgueilleux. — *-principled*, loyal. — *-road*, grande route, *f.* — *-seasoned*, fortement épicé. — *-spirited*, plein de force *or* d'audace, hautain. — *-water*, la haute marée, *f.*, les hautes eaux, *f.pl.* — *-water-mark*, ligne, *f.*, *or* niveau des hautes eaux

Highlander, s. montagnard, *m.*

Highlands, s. pl. montagnes, *f.*, pays montagneux, *m.*

Highly, adv. en haut lieu, en haut, fort, infiniment, ambitieusement, avec hauteur, avantageusement, d'une manière flatteuse. *To think — of*, faire grand cas de

Highness, s. hauteur, *f.*, élévation, *f.*

Highway, s. grand chemin, *m.*, grande route, *f.* — *-man*, — *-robbery*, voleur, vol de grand chemin

Hilarity, s. hilarité, *f.*

Hill, s. colline, *f.*, montagne, *f.*, hauteur, *f.*, coteau, *m.* *Over — and dale*, par monts et par vaux. — *-slope*, déclivité, *f.*, pente, *f.* — *-top*, sommet de la colline, *m.*

Hillock, s. monticule, *m.*

Hilly, adj. montueux, montagneux

Hilt, s. poignée, *f.*, garde, *f.*

Him, pron. le, lui, celui

Himself, pron. se, lui-même, lui

Hind, s. biche, *f.*, (*pers.*) rustre, *m.*, paysan, *m.*

Hind, adj. de derrière, postérieur, arrière

Hinder, va.n. empêcher, arrêter, gêner

Hindermost, **Hindmost**, adj. dernier, plus en arrière, de derrière

Hindrance, s. empêchement, *m.*, obstacle, *m.*, (*fam.*) anicroche, *m.*

Hinge, s. gond, *m.*, charnière, *f.*, (*fig.*) pivot, *m.*, point principal, *m.* *Off its —s*, hors des gonds

Hint, va.n. faire allusion à, désigner, donner à entendre, insinuer

Hint, s. allusion, *f.*, demi-mot, *m.*, intimation, *f.*, avis, *m.*, suggestion, *f.*, insinuation, *f.*, aperçu, *m.*, idée, *f.* *To throw out a* —, donner à entendre, laisser entendre

Hip, s. hanche, *f.*, (*bot.*) gratte-cul, *m.* — *-gout*, sciatique, *f.* — *-shot*, déhanché, *m.*, *-e*, *f.*

Hippodrome, s. hippodrome, *m.*

Hippopotamus, s. hippopotame, *m.*

Hire, va. louer, prendre à louage *or* en location, (*soldiers*) soudoyer

Hire, s. location, *f.*, louage, *m.*

Hireling, s. adj. mercenaire

Hirer, s. qui loue

Hirsute, adj. velu, hérissé de poils, hérissé d'épines

His, pron. son, sa, ses, à lui, le sien, la sienne, les siens, les siennes

Hiss, va.n. siffler

Hiss, **Hissing**, s. sifflement, *m.*, sifflet, *m.*, coup de sifflet, *m.*

Historian, s. historien, *m.*

Historic, **Historical**, adj. historique

Historically, adv. historiquement

Historiographer, s. historiographe, *m.*

History, s. histoire, *f.*

Histrionic, adj. histrionique

Hit, va. frapper, heurter, cogner, (*fencing*) toucher, (*a mark*) attraper, saisir, toucher, (*to guess*) trouver, deviner. *To — hard*, frapper fort. *To — out*, lancer des coups de poing. *To — off*, rencontrer, représenter exactement. *To — the right nail on the head*, mettre le doigt dessus

Hit, vn. (se) heurter, aller frapper *or* heurter, (se) trouver, (se) bien rencontrer, tomber juste, s'accorder, être d'accord

Hit, s. coup, *m.*, hasard, *m.*, coup de hasard, *m.*, rencontre, *f.*, coup heureux, *m.*, réussite, *f.*

Hitch, vn. clocher, s'embarrasser, sautiller, s'entretailler

Hitch, s. anicroche, *f.*, embarras, *m.*, temps d'arrêt, *m.*, hésitation, *f.*, lacune, *f.*

Hither, s. adj. ici, y. — *and thither*, çà et là

Hitherto, adv. jusqu'ici

Hive, s. ruche, *f.*, essaim, *m.*

Hive, va. mettre dans une ruche, amonceler; — vn. vivre ensemble

Hoar, **Hoary**, adj. blanc, gris, blanchi par l'âge, chenu, vénérable, vieux, blanc, blanchâtre, gris, couvert de givre

Hoard, s. trésor, *m.*, richesses amassées, *f.pl.*

Hoard (up), va. amasser, entasser; — vn. thésauriser, amasser

Hoarder, s. thésauriseur, *m.*

Hoarding, s. accumulation, *f.*, (*fence*) clôture de planches, *f.*

Hoariness, s. blancheur, *f.*

Hoarse, adj. enroué, à la voix rauque. *To grow* —, s'enrouer

Hoarsely, adv. d'une voix enrouée

Hoarseness, s. enrouement, *m.*, voix rauque, *f.*, son rauque, *m.*

Hoax, va. mystifier

Hoax, s. mystification, *f.*

Hob, s. manant, *m.*, (*elf*) farfadet, *m.*, (*in chimneys*) plaque, *f.*

Hobble, vn. aller clopin-clopant, clocher, chanceler. *To — along*, aller clopin-clopant; — va. embarrasser, entraver

Hobble, s. clochement, *m.*, hésitation, *f.*, embarras, *m.*, difficulté, *f.*

Hobby, s. (*whim*) marotte, *f.*, folie, *f.* *To ride one's* —, caresser sa marotte. — *horse*, cheval de bois, *m.*

Hobgoblin, s. lutin, *m.*, farfadet, *m.*, esprit, *m.*

Hobnail, s. clou à grosse tête, *m.*, caboche, *f.*, (*fig.*) manant, *m.*

Hobnailed, adj. garni de gros clous

Hock, s. jarret, *m.*, vin du Rhin, *m.*

Hock, **Hockle**, va. couper le jarret à

Hockey, s. jeu de la crosse, *m.*

Hocus, va. filouter

Hocus-pocus, s. tour de passe-passe, *m.*, jonglerie, *f.*

Hodgepodge, s. salmigondis, *m.*

Hodman, s. gâcheur, *m.*, goujat, *m.*

Hoe, s. houe, *f.*

Hoe, va. travailler avec la houe

Hog, s. porc, *m.*, cochon, *m.*, pourceau, *m.*

Hoggish, adj. brute, bestial

Hoggishly, adv. en porc

Hoggishness, s. nature bestiale, *f.*, cochonnerie, *f.*

Hogshead, s. muid, *m.*, demi-pièce, *f.*

Hoiden, s. fille mal-apprise, *f.*, garçonnière, *f.*

Hoidenish, adj. rustique, grossier

Hoist (up), va. hisser, arborer, élever

Hold, va. tenir, retenir, contenir, maintenir, attacher, suspendre, arrêter, avoir, occuper, poursuivre, continuer, (*a discussion*) soutenir, (*an opinion*) s'attacher à, (— *to*) tenir (à), obliger (de), contraindre (de), (— *as*) tenir (pour), regarder (comme), estimer, croire, (*a feast*) célébrer, (*a meeting*) présider à, convoquer; — vn. tenir, se tenir, s'attacher, se maintenir, se soutenir, demeurer, continuer, s'abstenir, adhérer, ne pas se démentir

Hold! interj. arrêtez! attention! halte-là!

Hold, s. prise, *f.*, main, *f.*, étreinte, *f.*, soutien, *m.*, appui, *m.*, point d'appui, *m.*, influence, *f.*, (*dungeon*) prison, *f.*, (*castle*) forteresse, *f.*, (*den*) tanière, *f.*

Holder, s. qui tient, tenancier, *m.*, occupant, *m.*, détenteur, *m.*, possesseur, *m.*, (*things*) porte- . . ., poignée, *f.*, anse, *f.*, manche, *m.* — *-forth*, péroreur, *m.*

Holdfast, s. crampon, *m.*, main de fer, *f.*, appui, *m.*

Holding, s. tenure, *f.*, prise, *f.*, possession, *f.*, influence, *f.*

Hole, s. trou, *m.*, creux, *m.*, caverne, *f.*, antre, *m.* *To find, to pick a hole in one's coat*, trouver par où l'empoigner, critiquer quelqu'un

Hole, vn. se terrer, entrer dans un trou, (*billiard*) faire (la bille)

Holiday, s. fête, *f.*, jour de fête, *m.*, jour férié, *m.*, congé, *m.* —*s*, pl. vacances, *f.pl.*

Holily, adv. saintement

Holiness, s. sainteté, *f.*

Holla, **Hollo**, **Holloa**, *see* HALLOO

Holland, s. toile de Hollande, *f.* —*s*, pl. genièvre de Hollande, *m.* *Brown* —, toile écrue, *f.*

Hollow, adj. creux, (*sound*) sourd, caverneux, (*fig.*) perfide, faux, trompeur. *To grow* —, creuser, se creuser

Hollow, s. creux, *m.*, cavité, *f.*, excavation, *f.*, gouffre, *m.*

Hollow, adv. creux, complètement. *To beat* —, battre à plate couture

Hollow (out), va. creuser, évider; — vn. creuser, se creuser

Hollowness, s. creux, *m.*, cavité, *f.*, (*fig.*) fausseté, *f.*

Holly, s. houx, *m.* — *-tree*, houx, *m.* — *-grove*, houssaie, *f.*

Hollyhock, s. rose trémière, *f.*

Holocaust, s. holocauste, *m.*

Holograph, s. testament olographe, *m.*

Holster, s. fonte, *f.*, arçon, *m.*

Holy, adj. saint, sacré, béni. — *Ghost*, le Saint-Esprit. — *-rood*, la sainte croix. — *-stone*, pierre ponce, *f.* — *Thursday*, le jour de l'Ascension. — *-water font*, bénitier, *m.* — *-week*, la semaine sainte. — *Writ*, les saintes Écritures

Homage, s. hommage, *m.*

Home, s. chez moi, chez soi, chez nous, etc., maison, *f.*, logis, *m.*, demeure, *f.*, foyers, *m.pl.* *A — of my own, of one's own*, un chez moi, au chez soi. *At* —, à la maison, chez lui, etc., à l'intérieur, visible, qui reçoit, à son aise, dans son élément, au fait de . . . *Make yourself at* —, faites comme chez vous. *To feel at* —, être à son aise, être dans son élément. *From* —, sorti, pas à la maison, en voyage

Home, adj. de ménage, domestique, de la maison, d'intérieur, indigène, de l'intérieur, (*fig.*) direct, à brûle-pourpoint

Home, adv. à la maison, chez soi, en famille ; à, vers, *or* dans sa patrie *or* son pays ; directement, droit au but, nettement. *We must go* —, il faut rentrer, il faut retourner chez nous. *To come* —, revenir chez soi, rentrer, toucher de près, toucher au vif. *To bring* —, amener *or* apporter à la maison, prouver. *To strike* —, frapper fort, (*fig.*) porter coup. — *-born*, — *-bred*, naturel, indigène, intestin. — *-brewed*, (bière) brassée à la maison. — *-department*, ministère de l'intérieur. — *-driven*, bien frappé *or* bien enfoncé. — *-keeping*, casanier. — *-felt*, profondément senti, intime. — *-made*, de ménage, fait à la maison, de fabrique indigène. — *-secretary*, secrétaire d'État pour le département de l'intérieur. — *-speaking*, énergique. — *-sick*, qui a le mal du pays. — *-sickness*, s. mal du pays, *m.*, nostalgie, *f.*

Homeless, adj. sans toit, sans asile

Homeliness, s. soins du ménage, *m.pl.*, simplicité, *f.*, air commun, *m.*, grossièreté, *f.*

Homely, adj. du ménage, simple, rude, rustique, grossier

Homestead, s. château, *m.*, ferme, *f.*

Homeward, Homewards, adv. vers la maison, vers la patrie, vers son pays. — *-bound*, qui retourne au pays. — *-cargo*, cargaison or fret de retour

Homicidal, adj. homicide

Homicide, s homicide, *m.*

Homily, s. homélie, *f*

Homœopathic, adj. homœopathique, homœopathe

Homœopathist, s. (médecin) homœopathe, *m.*

Homœopathy, s. homœopathie, *f.*

Homogeneous, adj. homogène

Homonym, s. homonyme, *m.*

Hone, s. pierre (à rasoir), *f.*

Honest, adj. honnête, honorable, probe, loyal, de bonne foi

Honestly, adv. honnêtement, honorablement, avec probité, loyalement

Honesty, s. honnêteté, *f.*, probité, *f.*, loyauté, *f.*, sincérité, *f.*, chasteté, *f.*, vertu, *f.*

Honey, s. miel, *m.*, douceur, *f.*, (*person*) cœur, *m.*, ange, *m.*, chéri, *m.*, chérie, *f.* — *-bee*, mouche à miel, *f.* — *-comb*, rayon de miel, *m.* — *-dew*, miélat, *m.* — *-moon*, lune de miel, *f.*

Honeyed, adj. emmiellé, doux, mielleux

Honeysuckle, s. chèvrefeuille, *m.*

Honorary, adj. (*without pay*) honoraire, honorifique

Honour, s. honneur, *f.*, dignité, *f* *To be two by* —*s*, (*cards*) avoir deux d'honneurs

Honour, va honorer, (*com.*) faire honneur à

Honourable, adj. honorable, d'honneur, honnête

Honourableness, s. caractère honorable, *m.*, nature honorable, *f.*

Honourably, adv. honorablement, avec honneur

Hood, s. capuchon, *m.*, chaperon, *m.*, coiffe, *f.*, (*of a coach*) capote, *f.*, (*chimney*) chapeau, *m.*

Hood, va. encapuchonner, mettre un capuchon à, bander les yeux à

Hoodwink, va. chaperonner, bander les yeux à, tromper, aveugler

Hoof, s. sabot, *m.*, ongle, *m.* — *-bound*, encastelé

Hoofed, adj ferré, à sabots

Hook, s. (*fish*) crochet, *m.*, croc, *m.*, hameçon, *m.*, (*dress*) agrafe, *f.*, (*for cutting*) faucille, *f.*, (*boat*) gaffe, *f.*, (*fig.*) amorce, *f.*, bonne affaire, *f.*, profit, *m.* *By* — *or by crook*, d'une manière ou d'une autre. *Off the* —*s*, déconcerté, démonté. — *and eye*, agrafe et porte. *On one's own* —, pour son propre compte

Hook, va. accrocher, saisir avec un croc, attraper, mettre le grappin sur, prendre à l'hameçon, agrafer ; — vn. se courber. *To* — *it*, filer

Hookah, s. pipe à la turque, *f*

Hooked, adj crochu, recourbé

Hoop, s cercle, *m.*, cerceau, *m.*, anneau, *m.*, (*wheels*) jante, *f.*, (*dresses*) vertugadin, *m.*, panier, *m.*, (*noise*) cri, *m.*

Hoop, va. cercler, garnir de cercles, garnir de jantes ; — vn. crier, vociférer

Hooper, s. tonnelier, *m.*

Hooping-cough, s. coqueluche, *f.*

Hoopoo, s. (*bird*) huppe, *f.*

Hoot, va.n. huer, poursuivre de huées

Hoot, Hooting, s. huée, *f*

Hop, vn. danser, sauter, sautiller, sauter à cloche-pied

Hop, s. danse, *f.*, (*fam.*) sauterie, *f.*, bal, *m.*, saut à cloche-pied, *m.*, (*plant*) houblon, *m.* — *-scotch*, la marelle, *f.* — *-bag*, — *-pocket*, sac à houblon, *m.* — *-bind*, tige de houblon, *f.* — *-garden*, — *-ground*, — *-yard*, houblonnière, *f.* — *-gathering*, la cueillette du houblon

Hope, s. espérance, *f.*, attente, *f.*, espoir, *m.*

Hope, vn.a. espérer, mettre son espoir

Hopeful, adj. plein d'espoir *or* d'espérance, (*fig.*) plein d'avenir, de grande espérance, qui promet beaucoup, (*things*) heureux, riant

Hopefully, adv. avec bon espoir, de manière à encourager

Hopefulness, s. bon espoir, *m.*, confiance, *f.*, élasticité, *f.*

Hopeless, adj. sans espoir, désespéré, désespérant

Hopelessly, adv. sans espoir, avec désespoir, sans retour

Hopelessness, s. désespoir, *m.*, état *or* caractère désespéré

Hopingly, adv. avec espoir

Hopper, s. sauteur, *m.*, (*mill*) trémie, *f.*

Hopping, s. sautillement, *m.*, danse, *f.*, sauterie, *f.*, cueillette de houblon, *f.*

Horary, adj. horaire

Horde, s. horde, *f.*

Horizon, s. horizon, *m.*

Horizontal, adj. de l'horizon, horizontal

Horizontally, adv. horizontalement

Horn, s. corne, *f.*, (*antlers*) bois, *m.*, (*insects*) antenne, *f.*, (*cup*) coupe, *f.*, gobelet, *m.*, (*mus.*) cor, *m.*, cornet, *m.*

Horned, adj. cornu, à cornes, en croissant

Hornet, s. frelon, *m.* *A* —*'s nest*, un guêpier

Hornpipe, s. cornemuse, *f.*

Horny, adj. de corne, cornu, comme la corne, (*hands*) calleuses

Horoscope, s. horoscope, *m.*

Horrible, adj. horrible, affreux, effroyable

Horribly, adv. horriblement, affreusement

Horrid, adj. hérissé, horrible, affreux

Horridly, adv. horriblement

Horridness, s. horreur, *f.*

Horrific, adj horrible

Horrify, va. épouvanter

Horror, s. horreur, *f.*

Horse, s. cheval, *m.*, cavalerie, *f.*, (*frame*) chevalet, *m.* *To change* —*s*, changer de chevaux, relayer. *A thousand* —, mille hommes de cavalerie, mille chevaux. — *-barracks*, quartier de cavalerie, *m.* — *-bean*, féverole, *f.* — *-block*, montoir, *m.* — *-box*, box, *m.*, case, *f.*, wagon pour les chevaux, *m.* — *-breaker*, écuyer qui dresse les chevaux, *m.* — *-chestnut*, marronnier d'Inde, *m.*, (*fruit*) marron d'Inde, *m.* — *-cloth*, couverture de cheval, *f.*, housse, *f.* — *-dealer*, marchand de chevaux, *m.*, maquignon, *m.* — *-doctor*, vétérinaire, *m.* — *-fair*, foire aux chevaux, *f.* — *-fly*, taon, *m.* — *-guard*, garde à cheval, *m.*, gardes du corps, *m.* — *-guards*, plur. bureau de la guerre, *m.* — *-hair*, crin de cheval, *m.* — *-jockey*, maquignon, *m.* — *-laugh*, gros rire, *m.* — *-leech*, grosse sangsue, *m.*, (*doctor*) vétérinaire, *m.* — *-play*, jeu brutal, *m.*, jeu de mains, *m.* — *-pond*, abreuvoir, *m.* — *-power*, force de. . . chevaux, *m.* — *-race*, course de chevaux, *f.* — *-radish*, raifort, *m.* — *-road*, — *-way*, chemin de halage, *m.*, sentier pour les chevaux, *m.* — *-shoe*, fer de cheval, *m.* — *-whip*, cravache, *f.* — *-woman*, cavalière, *f.*, écuyère, *f.*

Horse, va. fournir un cheval, monter

Horseback, s. dos de cheval, *m.* *To be on* —, être à cheval. *To get on* —, monter à cheval

Horseman, s. cavalier, *m.*, écuyer, *m.*

Horsemanship, s. équitation, *f.*, manége, *m.*

Horticultural, adj. horticultural, d'horticulture

Horticulture, s. horticulture, *f.*

Horticulturist, s. horticulteur, *m.*

Hose, s. bas, *m.*, (*pipe*) tuyau, *m.*, (*mar.*) manche, *f.*

Hosier, s. bonnetier, *m.*

Hosiery, s. bonneterie, *f.*

Hospitable, adj. hospitalier

Hospitably, adv. avec hospitalité

Hospital, s. hôpital, *m.*, hospice, *m.*

Hospitality, s. hospitalité, *f.*

Host, s. hôte, *m.*, maître de maison, *m.*, amphitryon, *m.*, (*inn-keeper*) aubergiste, *m.*, (*army*) armée, *f.*, (*fig.*) foule, *f.*, multitude, *f.*, (*Cathol. rel.*) hostie, *f.*, Saint Sacrement, *m.*

Hostage, s. otage, *m.*, gage, *m.*

Hostess, s. hôtesse, *f.*, maîtresse de maison, *f.*

Hostile, adj. hostile, ennemi

Hostilely, adv. en ennemi

Hostility, s. hostilité, *f.*

Hot, adj. chaud, échauffé, ardent, (*fig.*) bouillant, violent, fougueux, emporté, vif, (*to taste*) piquant, épicé. *All* —, tout chaud. — *-headed*, à tête chaude, fougueux, emporté, violent. — *-house*, s. serre chaude, *f.* — *-press*, s. calandre, *f.* *To* — *-press*, va. (*paper*) satiner, calandrer, (*cloth*) catir à chaud

Hotel, s. hôtel, *m.*

Hotly, adv. chaudement,

ardemment, vivement, vigoureusement, de près

Hotness, s. chaleur, *f.*

Hough, s. jarret, *m.*

Hound, s. chien de chasse, *m.*, chien courant, *m.* *The master of the —s*, le grand veneur. *Bitch- —*, lice, *f.* *Wolf- —*, chien pour le loup, *m.*

Hound, va. chasser, poursuivre

Hour, s. heure, *f.*, temps, *m.*, moment, *m.* *By the —*, à l'heure. *To keep good —s, bad —s, late —s*, rentrer *or* se retirer *or* se coucher de bonne heure, à des heures irrégulières, fort tard. *— -glass*, sablier, *m.* *— -hand*, petite aiguille, *f.* *— -plate*, cadran, *m.*

Hourly, adj. de chaque heure, de toutes les heures, continuel, incessant

Hourly, adv. à toute heure, d'heure en heure, d'un moment à l'autre

House, s. maison, *f.*, logis, *m.*, corps de logis, *m.*, bâtiment, *m.*, famille, *f.*, état de maison, *m.*, table, *f.*, (*polit.*) Chambre, *f.*, Parlement, *m.*, (*theatre*) salle, *f.* *At or to my —, his —, your father's —*, chez moi, chez lui, chez votre père. *To begin — -keeping*, entrer en ménage. *To keep —*, tenir maison. *A good —, a miserable —, open —*, bonne table, un pauvre état de maison, table ouverte

House, adj. de la maison, du ménage, domestique. *— -boat*, s. bateau couvert, *m.* *— -breaker*, s., *— -breaking*, s. voleur, vol avec effraction, *m.* *— -cricket*, s. grillon, *m.* *— -dog*, s. chien de garde, *m.* *— -gear*, s. meubles, *m. pl.* *— -keeper*, s. ménagère, *f.*, gouvernante, *f.*, femme de charge, *f.* *— -keeping*, s. ménage, *m.*, conduite d'une maison, *f.*, l'entretien d'une maison, état de maison. *— -maid*, s. bonne, *f.*, servante, *f.*, fille de service, *f.* *— -rent*, s. loyer, *m.* *— -painter*, s. peintre en bâtiments, *m.* *— -room*, s. place, *f.*, logement, *m.* *— -rule*, s. autorité, *f.* *— -steward*, s. majordome, *m.* *— -top*, s. toit, *m.* *To give a — -warming*, pendre la crémaillère

House, va. héberger, loger, forcer de se réfugier, (*cattle*) faire rentrer, mettre à couvert, abriter

Houseful, s. maisonnée, *f.*

Household, s. maison, *f.*, ménage, *m.*, famille, *f.*, gens de service, *m.pl.*, domestiques, *m.pl.*, serviteurs, *m.pl.*

Household, adj. de ménage, domestique, familier, de tous les jours, connu de tous. *— troops*, maison du roi, *f.* *— words*, mots familier, s. *m. pl.*

Householder, s. chef de famille, *m.*

Houseless, adj. sans abri

Housewife, s. maîtresse de maison, *f.*, ménagère, *f.*

Housewifery, s. conduite d'une maison, *f.*, devoirs d'une bonne ménagère, *m.pl*

Housing, s. (*horses*) housse, *f.*, rentrée, *f.*, magasinage, *m.*

Hovel, s. hutte, *f.*, cabane, *f.*, (*contempt*) bicoque, *f.*

Hover, vn. voler, voltiger, planer, (*fig.*) se balancer, rester en suspens

How, adv. comment, (*exclamation*) combien, comme, que. *— long, — far*, see Far, Long. *— so!* comment cela? *— is it that!* comment se fait-il que? d'où vient que? *— now!* comment!

Howbeit, adv. néanmoins, cependant

However, adv. de quelque façon *or* manière que, à quelque degré que, en quelque état que, quelque ... que, tout ... que. *— mild our remonstrances*, quelque douces que soient nos remontrances. *— unhappy you may be*, quelque malheureux que vous soyez, tout malheureux que vous êtes

However, conj. cependant, toutefois, pourtant, néanmoins, du reste, d'ailleurs

Howitzer, s. obusier, *m.*

Howl, vn. hurler, rugir, (*wind*) mugir

Howl, Howling, s. hurlement, *m.*, cri, *m.*

Hubbub, s. vacarme, *m.*, brouhaha, *m.*, tumulte, *m.*, désordre, *m.*

Huckaback, s. grosse toile ouvrée, *f.*

Huckle, s. hanche, *f.* *— -bone*, os de la hanche, *m.*

Huckster, s. revendeur, *m.*, porte-balle, *m.*

Huddle, va. jeter pêle-mêle, entasser confusément, brouiller, confondre. *— in*, faire entrer pêle-mêle. *— on*, s'affubler de, mettre à la hâte. *— together*, jeter pêle-mêle. *— up*, faire à la hâte. — vn. venir pêle-mêle, se presser confusément, agir précipitamment. *Huddled work*, travail broché *or* fait sans soin

Huddle, s. confusion, *f.*, désordre, *m.*, tohu-bohu, *m.*, ramas, *m.*

Hue, s. couleur, *f.*, teinte, *f.*, huée, *f.*, cri, *m.* *— and cry*, clameur, *f.*

Huff, s. accès subit, *m.*, colère, *f.* *In a —*, en colère

Huff, va. brusquer, malmener, tancer, pester contre, (*at play*) souffler; — vn. faire le bravache, pester. *— and puff*, souffler, haleter

Hug, va. serrer, étreindre, presser, (*fig.*) chérir, s'attacher à, (*nav.*) serrer, pincer

Hug, s. étreinde, *f.*, embrassement, *m.*

Huge, adj. énorme, grand, gros, immense, vaste

Hugely, adv. énormément

Hugeness, s. volume énorme, *m.*, grandeur, *f.*, grosseur, *f.*, immensité, *f.*

Huguenot, s. huguenot, *m.*, -e, *f.*

Hulk, s. navire, *m.*, ponton, *m.*, carcasse, *f.*

Hull, s. (*of a ship*) coque, *f.*, corps, *m.*, cosse, *f.*, gousse, *f.*, enveloppe, *f.*

Hull, va. percer la coque, peler, écosser, écaler, (*barley*) monder

Hum, vn.a bourdonner, murmurer, (*pers.*) fredonner, chantonner, (*top*) ronfler, (*to hesitate*) ânonner

Hum, s. bourdonnement, *m.*, bruit, *m.*, murmure, *m.*, (*hoax*) attrape, *f.*

Hum! interj. hom! hem!

Human, adj. humain, de l'homme

Humane, adj. humain, bon, bienfaisant, compatissant

Humanely, adv. avec humanité

Humanist, s. humaniste, *m.*

Humanitarian, s. humanitaire, *m.*

Humanity, s. humanité, *f.*, genre humain, *m.*

Humanize, va. humaniser, adoucir

Humankind, s. genre humain, *m.*, hommes, *m.pl.*

Humanly, adv. humainement

Humble, adj. humble

Humble, va. humilier, abaisser, abattre

Humbleness, s. humilité, *f.*

Humbly, adv. humblement, pauvrement

Humbug, s. mystification, *f.*, blague, *f.*, farce, *f.*, (*pers.*) hâbleur, *m.*, farceur, *m.*, blagueur, *m.*

Humbug, va. attraper

Humdrum, adj. endormant, assommant, ennuyeux, stupide

Humdrum, s. pronotoire, *f.*, scie, *f.*

Humid, adj. humide

Humidity, s. humidité, *f.*

Humiliate, va. humilier

Humiliation, s. humiliation, *f.*

Humility, s. humilité, *f.*

Humming, s. bourdonnement, *m.*, (*of a tune*) fredonnement, *m.* *— -bird*, colibri, *m.*, oiseau-mouche, *m.* *— -top*, toupie d'Allemagne, *f.*

Humorist, s. original, *m.*, esprit fantasque, *m.*, esprit badin, *m.*

Humorous, adj. capricieux, fantasque, plaisant, comique, enjoué

Humorously, adv capricieusement, plaisamment

Humour, s. humeur, *f.*, caractère, *m.*, disposition, *f.*, penchant, *m.*, caprice, *m.*, (*wit*) badinage, *m.*, esprit, *m.*, enjouement, *m.*, comique, *m.* *In a — for*, en humeur de. *Good —*, bonne humeur. *Ill —*, mauvaise humeur. *Out of —, (with)* de mauvaise humeur, mécontent (de). *Dry —*, badinage piquant. *Broad —*, grosse gaieté

Humour, va. se prêter aux caprices *or* aux désirs de, complaire à, mener en cajolant

Humoured, adj. de ... humeur. *Good- —*, de bonne humeur, bon, enjoué

Humouredly, adv. de ... humeur

Hump, s. bosse, *f.*

Humped, adj. qui a une bosse

Hunch, s. coup de coude *or* de poing, *m.*, bosse, *f.*, (*lump*) grosse tranche, *f.* *— -back, — -backed*, see Hump

Hundred, adj. cent. *— -fold*, centuple. *A — -weight*, s. un quintal

Hundred, s. centaine, *f.*, cent, *m.*

Hundredth, adj. centième

Hung-beef, s. bœuf fumé, *m.*

Hunger, s. faim, *f.*

Hunger, vn. avoir faim, (*fig.*) avoir soif (de), désirer ardemment

Hungrily, adv. avec faim, avec voracité, de faim

Hungry, adj. ayant faim, qui a faim, affamé. *To be or feel —*, avoir faim

Hunks, s. ladre, *m.*, grippe-sou, *m.*

Hunt, va. chasser, (*stag*) courre, (*fig.*) chercher, être à la recherche de. *To — down*, forcer, accabler. *To — out*, chercher, trouver, dénicher. *— the slipper*, (*game*) la savate. — vn. chasser, faire la chasse, être à la recherche (de), chercher

Hunt, s. chasse, *f.*, équipage de chasse, *m.*, vénerie, *f.*, meute, *f.*

Hunter, s. chasseur, *m.*, cheval de chasse, *m.*

Hunting, s. chasse, *f.*, (*after*) poursuite (de), *f.*, recherche (de), *f.*

Huntress, s. chasseresse, *f.*

Huntsman, s. chasseur, *m.*, piqueur, *m.*, veneur, *m.*

Hurdle, s. claie, *f.*, ouvrage à claire voie, *m.*, barrière, *f.*

Hurdy-gurdy, s. vielle, *f.*

Hurl, va. lancer, jeter, précipiter

Hurl, s. action de jeter, *f.*, jet, *m.*

Hurly-burly, s. brouhaha, *m.*, vacarme, *m.*, tohu-bohu, *m.*

Hurrah, s. interj. hourra! vivat!

Hurricane, s. ouragan, *m.*

Hurried, adj. précipité, pressé, fait *or* dit à la hâte

Hurriedly, adv. précipitamment, à la hâte, rapidement

Hurry, va. presser, hâter, pousser, accélérer, précipiter. *To — away, off*, faire partir précipitamment, entraîner, emmener, enlever. — vn. se presser, se hâter, se dépêcher

Hurry, s. précipitation, *f.*, hâte, *f.*, presse, *f.*, confusion, *f.*, tumulte, *f.*

Hurt, va. faire mal à, blesser, endommager, gâter, choquer, offenser. *To — oneself, each other*, se faire du mal

Hurt, s. blessure, *f.*, mal, *m.*, coup, *m.*, (*wrong*) préjudice, *f.*, détriment, *m.*, dommage, *m.*

Hurter, s. auteur d'un mal, *m.*, d'une blessure, d'un tort, d'un dommage

Hurtful, adj. nuisible, préjudiciable, pernicieux

Hurtfully, adv. d'une manière nuisible

Hurtfulness, s. tort, *m.*, préjudice, *m.*

Hurtle, vn. se presser, se mouvoir, s'agiter

Hurtless, adj. innocent, qui ne fait point de mal, qui n'éprouve point de mal, intact

Husband, s. mari, *m.*, époux, *m.*

Husband, va. ménager, cultiver

Husbandage, s. commission allouée à l'armateur gérant à bord, *f.*

Husbandless, adj. sans mari

Husbandman, s. cultivateur, *m.*, agriculteur, *m.*, laboureur, *m.*

Husbandry, s. agriculture, *f.*, labourage, *m.*, économie, *f.*

Hush, va. faire taire, imposer silence à, calmer, assoupir, apaiser. *To — up*, étouffer, assoupir. — vn. se taire

Hush! interj. chut!

Hush, s. silence, *m.*

Hush-money, s. prix du silence, *m.*, argent donné pour acheter le silence, *m.*

Husk, s. enveloppe, *f.*, balle, *f.*, (*peas, &c.*) cosse, *f.*, gousse, *f.*

Husk, va. ôter l'enveloppe de, vanner, écosser, éplucher

Husked, adj. (*grains*) vanné, (*fruits and veget.*) écossé, à cosse, cossu

Huskiness, s. état d'avoir une enveloppe, *m.*, une cosse, *m.*, (*voice*) son rauque, *m.*, enrouement, *m.*

Husky, adj. cossu, enveloppé, (*voice*) rauque, enroué, rude

Hussar, s. hussard, *m.*

Hussy, s. friponne, *f.*, coquine, *f.*, gueuse, *f.*

Hustings, s.pl. estrade, *f.*, élections, *f.pl.*

Hustle, va.n. pousser, se pousser

Huswife, s. ménagère, *f.*

Hut, s. hutte, *f.*, cabane, *f.*, baraque, *f.*

Hut, va. loger dans des baraques; — vn. se hutter, se baraquer

Hutch, s. coffre, *m.*, huche, *f.*, (*rabbits*) clapier, *m.*, (*rats*) ratière, *f.*

Hyacinth, s. jacinthe, *f.*

Hybrid, s. adj. hybride

Hydra, s. hydre, *f.*

Hydraulic, adj. hydraulique

Hydraulics, s. hydraulique, *f.*

Hydrogen, s. hydrogène, *m.*

Hydrographer, s. hydrographe, *m.*

Hydrography, s. hydrographie, *f.*

Hydromel, s. hydromel, *m.*

Hydropathic, adj. hydropathique

Hydropathist, s. hydropathe, *m.*

Hydropathy, s. hydropathie, *f.*

Hydrophobia, s. hydrophobie, *f.*

Hydrostatics, s. hydrostatique, *f.*

Hyemal, adj. hyémal

Hyemation, s. hivernation, *f.*

Hyena, s. hyène, *f.*

Hygiene, s. hygiène, *f.*

Hygienic, adj. hygiénique

Hygrometer, s. hygromètre, *m.*

Hygrometric, Hygrometrical, adj. hygrométrique

Hymen, s. hymen, *m.*, hyménée, *m.*

Hymeneal, adj. de l'hymen

Hymn, s. hymne, *m.f.*

Hymn, va.n. célébrer, chanter par des hymnes, chanter des hymnes

Hyperbole, s. hyperbole, *f.*

Hypercritic, s. hypercritique, *m.*

Hypercritical, adj. critique à l'excès

Hypercriticism, s. critique exagérée *or* outrée, *f.*

Hyphen, s. trait d'union, *m.*

Hypnotic, adj. hypnotique

Hypochondria, s. hypocondrie, *f.*

Hypocrisy, s. hypocrisie, *f.*

Hypocrite, s. hypocrite, *m.f.*

Hypocritical, adj. hypocrite

Hypocritically, adv. hypocritement, avec hypocrisie

Hypothesis, s. hypothèse, *f.*

Hypothetical, adj. hypothétique

Hyssop, s. hysope, *f.*

Hysteria, s. hystérie, *f.*

Hysteric, Hysterical, adj. hystérique

Hysterics, s.pl. hystérie, *f.*, attaque de nerfs, *f.* *To fall into —*, avoir une attaque de nerfs

I

I, i, s. I, i, *m.*

I, pron. je, moi

Iambic, adj. iambique

Ice, s. glace, *f.* *Bay —*, glace nouvellement formée. *Brash —*, glaçons détachés. *Field of —*, banc de glace, *m.*, banquise, *f.*

Ice, adj. de glace. *— -bound*, retenu par les glaces, enfermé *or* pris dans les glaces. *— -house*, glacière, *f.* *— -water*, eau à la glace, *f.* *— -work*, (construction en) glace, *f.*

Ice, va. glacer, (*wine*) frapper

Iceberg, s. montagne de glace, *f.*, banc de glace, *m.*

Icicle, s. glaçon, *m.*

Iciness, s. froid glacial, *m.*

Icy, adj. de glace, glacial, glacé

Idea, s. idée, *f.* *Adventitious, definite, fixed —*, idée acquise, distincte, fixe. *The —!* par exemple! voilà qui est fort!

Ideal, s. adj. idéal

Identical, adj. identique

Identically, adv. identiquement

Identification, s. identification, *f.*

Identify, va. constater l'identité de, reconnaître

Identity, s. identité, *f.*

Idiocy, s. idiotisme, *m.*, imbécillité, *f.*

Idiom, s. idiotisme, *m.*, génie, *m.*, caractère propre, *m.*, (*dialect*) idiome, *m.*, dialecte, *m.*

Idiomatic, Idiomatical, adj. qui forme *or* qui renferme un idiotisme, idiomatique

Idiomatically, adv. conformément au génie d'une langue

Idiot, s. idiot, *m.*, -e, *f.*, imbécile, *m.f.*

Idiotic, Idiotical, adj. idiot, imbécile

Idle, adj. oisif, désœuvré, inoccupé, paresseux, fainéant, (*time*) d'oisiveté, de loisir, perdu, (*vain*) vain, inutile, impuissant, fou, folle. *— talk, tales*, paroles, contes en l'air

Idle, vn. passer son temps dans l'oisiveté, perdre son temps, ne rien faire; — va. (*away*) perdre, gaspiller

Idleness, s. oisiveté, *f.*, désœuvrement, *m.*, paresse, *f.*, indolence, *f.*, (*fig.*) vanité, *f.*, inutilité, *f.*, folie, *f.*

Idler, s. oisif, *m.*, fainéant, *m.*, désœuvré, *m.*, paresseux, *m.*

Idly, adv. dans l'oisiveté, paresseusement, inutilement, vainement

Idol, s. idole, *f.*

Idolater, s. idolâtre, *m.*

Idolatrous, adj. idolâtre, des idoles

Idolatry, s. idolâtrie, *f.*

Idolize, va. idolâtrer

Idyl, s. idylle, *f.*

If, conj. si, quand même, lors même que, n'était que, ne fût-ce que. *— not, no*, sinon, non

Igneous, adj. igné, de formation ignée

Ignis fatuus, s. feu follet, *m.*

Ignite, va. mettre en feu, enflammer; — vn. prendre feu, s'enflammer

Ignition, s. ignition, *f.*

Ignoble, adj. de basse naissance, (*fig.*) ignoble, vil, sans valeur

Ignobly, adv. ignoblement, honteusement

Ignominious, adj. ignominieux, ignoble, infamant

Ignominiously, adv. ignominieusement

Ignominy, s. ignominie, *f.*

Ignoramus, s. ignorant, *m.*

Ignorance, s. ignorance, *f.*

Ignorant, adj. ignorant, étranger (à). *To be — of*, ignorer

Ignorantly, adv. dans l'ignorance, par ignorance, sans le savoir

Ignore, vn. prononcer un verdict de non-lieu, ignorer

Iliac, Iliacal, adj. iliaque

Iliad, s. Iliade, *f.*

Ill, adj. mauvais, malade, mal portant, souffrant

Ill, s. mal, *m.*

Ill, adv. mal, difficilement. *But —*, mal, imparfaitement. *— -bred, — -mannered*, adj. mal élevé, malappris. *— -faced*, adj. de mauvaise mine, laid. *— -judged*, adj. malavisé, peu sage. *— -starred*, adj. malencontreux, malheureux. *— -treat*, va. maltraiter. *— -trained*, adj. mal discipliné, mal élevé. *— -used*, adj. maltraité, malmené. *— -will*, s. mauvais vouloir, *m.*, inimitié, *f.*

Illegal, adj. illégal

Illegality, s. illégalité, *f.*

Illegally, adv. illégalement

Illegible, adj. illisible

Illegibly, adv. d'une manière illisible

Illegitimacy, s. illégitimité, *f.*

Illegitimate, adj. illégitime

Illegitimately, adv. illégitimement
Illiberal, adj. mesquin, peu généreux, (*mind*) étroit, illibéral, peu libéral
Illiberality, s. mesquinerie, *f.*, petitesse, *f.*, intolérance, *f.*
Illiberally, adv. mesquinement, avec peu de générosité, avec un esprit peu libéral, étroit *or* exclusif
Illicit, adj. illicite
Illimitable, adj. illimitable
Illiterate, adj. illettré, ignorant
Illness, s. maladie, *f.*, méchanceté, *f.*
Illogical, adj. illogique
Illuminate, va. éclairer, illuminer, (*painting*) enluminer
Illumination, s. illumination, *f.*, splendeur, *f.*, (*painting*) enluminure, *f.*
Illumine, va. éclairer, illuminer, embellir
Illusion, s. illusion, *f.*
Illusive, Illusory, adj. illusoire, trompeur, mensonger
Illusively, adv. illusoirement
Illustrate, va. illuminer, éclairer, (*fig.*) illustrer, rendre illustre, (*fig.*) éclaircir, expliquer
Illustration, s. illustration, *f.*, célébrité, *f.*, éclaircissement, *m.*, explication, *f.*, comparaison, *f.*
Illustrative, adj. explicatif, qui rend illustre
Illustrious, adj. illustre
Illustriously, adv. avec éclat, d'une manière illustre
Illustriousness, s. nature illustre, *f.*, éclat, *m.*
Image, s. image, *f.*, portrait, *m.*, idole, *f.*
Image, va. représenter par une image, (*fig.*) s'imaginer, se figurer
Imagery, s. figures, *f.pl.*, statues, *f.pl.*, sculpture, *f.*, images, *f.pl.*
Imaginable, adj. imaginable, qu'on peut imaginer
Imaginary, adj. imaginaire
Imagination, s. imagination, *f.*, idée, *f.*, conception, *f.*
Imaginative, adj. imaginatif
Imagine, va.n. imaginer, s'imaginer, se figurer, se faire une idée (de)
Imbecile, adj. s. faible, imbécile, (*things*) vain, impuissant
Imbecility, s. imbécillité, *f.*
Imbibe, va. absorber, s'imbiber de, boire, être imbu de, se pénétrer de
Imbue, va. tremper; — va. imprégner (de), teindre (en), (*fig.*) (*with*) inculquer à
Imitable, adj. imitable, à imiter
Imitate, va. imiter, (*com.*) contrefaire

Imitation, s. imitation, *f.*, pastiche, *m.*, (*com.*) contrefaçon, *f.*
Imitative, adj. imitatif, imitateur, d'imitation
Imitator, s. imitateur, *m.*, imitatrice, *f.*, contrefacteur, *m.*
Immaculate, adj. immaculé, pur, sans tache
Immaterial, adj. immatériel, (*fig.*) de peu d'importance, peu important, indifférent
Immeasurable, adj. qu'on ne saurait mesurer, vaste, immense, infini
Immeasurably, adv. démesurément, outre mesure, sans limites
Immediate, adj. immédiat, direct, prompt, urgent
Immediately, adv. immédiatement, sur-le-champ, tout de suite
Immemorial, adj. immémorial, de temps immémorial
Immense, adj. immense
Immensely, adv. immensément, énormément
Immensity, s. immensité, *f.*
Immerge, Immerse, va. plonger, submerger, encher
Immersion, s. immersion, *f.*
Imminence, s. imminence, *f.*
Imminent, adj. imminent
Immobility, s. immobilité, *f.*
Immoderate, adj. immodéré, excessif
Immoderately, adv. immodérément, à l'excès, sans modération
Immoderateness, Immoderation, s. peu de modération, *m.*, nature excessive, *f.*
Immodest, adj. immodeste, déshonnête, impudique
Immodestly, adv. immodestement, sans modestie, déshonnêtement
Immodesty, s. immodestie, *f.*, impudeur, *f.*
Immolate, va. immoler
Immolation, s. immolation, *f.*
Immoral, adj. immoral
Immorality, s. immoralité, *f.*
Immorally, adv. d'une manière immorale
Immortal, adj. s. immortel, -elle
Immortality, s. immortalité, *f.*
Immortalize, va. rendre immortel, immortaliser
Immortally, adv. éternellement
Immovable, adj. inébranlable, immuable, immobile, (*law*) immeuble
Immovables, s.pl. immeubles, *m.pl.*
Immovably, adv. inébranlablement, immuablement

Immunity, s. immunité, *f.*
Immure, va. entourer, renfermer, emprisonner
Immutability, Immutableness, s. immutabilité, *f.*
Immutable, adj. immutable
Imp, s. diablotin, *m.*, lutin, *m.*, farfadet, *m.*, démon, *m.*, (*child*) gamin, *m.*
Impair, va. affaiblir, altérer, détériorer, endommager, délabrer
Impale, *see* Empale
Impalpable, adj. impalpable
Impart, va. donner en partage, communiquer, faire part, faire savoir, faire connaître
Impartial, adj. impartial
Impartiality, s. impartialité, *f.*
Impartially, adv. impartialement
Impassable, adj. infranchissable, impraticable
Impassibility, s. impassibilité, *f.*
Impassible, adj. impassible
Impassion, va. passionner
Impassive, adj. impassible, insensible
Impatience, s. impatience, *f.*
Impatient, adj. impatient, indocile (à), furieux (de). *To get* or *grow* —, devenir impatient, s'impatienter
Impatiently, adv. impatiemment, avec impatience
Impeach, va. mettre en accusation, accuser
Impeachable, adj. qu'on peut mettre en accusation, etc., attaquable, blâmable
Impeachment, s. accusation, *f.*, mise en accusation, *f.*, attaque, *f.*, censure, *f.*
Impede, va. empêcher, retarder
Impediment, s. empêchement, *m.*, obstacle, *m.*, embarras, *m.*
Impel, va. pousser, engager, entraîner
Impend, vn. menacer, être suspendu (sur)
Impending, adj. penché, suspendu; imminent, menaçant
Impenetrability, s. impénétrabilité, *f.*
Impenetrable, adj. impénétrable, insensible
Impenetrably, adv. impénétrablement
Impenitence, s. impénitence, *f.*
Impenitent, adj. impénitent
Impenitently, adv. dans l'impénitence
Imperative, s. adj. impératif, impérieux
Imperatively, adv. impérativement, d'un ton impératif
Imperceptible, adj. imperceptible

Imperceptibly, adv. imperceptiblement
Imperfect, adj. imparfait, inachevé, défectueux
Imperfection, s. imperfection, *f.*
Imperfectly, adv. imparfaitement
Imperial, adj. impérial
Imperialist, s. impérialiste, *m.*
Imperil, va. mettre en péril *or* en danger, exposer, hasarder
Imperious, adj. impérieux, hautain, arrogant, tyrannique
Imperiously, adv. impérieusement, en maître
Imperiousness, s. ton *or* air impérieux, *m.*, hauteur, *f.*, arrogance, *f.*
Imperishable, adj. impérissable
Imperishably, adv. d'une manière impérissable
Impermeability, s. imperméabilité, *f.*
Impermeable, adj. imperméable
Impersonal, adj. impersonnel
Impersonality, s. impersonnalité, *f.*
Impersonally, adv. impersonnellement
Impersonate, va. personnifier
Impertinence, s. défaut de rapport *or* de liaison, *m.*, impertinence, *f.*, malhonnêteté, *f.*, inconvenance, *f.*
Impertinent, adj. extravagant, impertinent, malhonnête, inconvenant
Impertinently, adv. impertinemment, hors de propos, malhonnêtement, d'une manière inconvenante
Imperturbability, s. imperturbabilité, *f.*
Imperturbable, adj. imperturbable
Imperturbably, adv. imperturbablement
Impervious, adj. imperméable, impénétrable
Imperviousness, s. imperméabilité, *f.*, impénétrabilité, *f.*
Impetuosity, Impetuousness, s. impétuosité, *f.*
Impetuously, adv. impétueusement
Impetus, s. force d'impulsion, *f.*, force impulsive, *f.*
Impiety, s. impiété, *f.*
Impious, adj. impie
Impiously, adv. en impie, avec impiété
Implacability, s. nature implacable, *f.*
Implacable, adj. implacable
Implacably, adv. impitoyablement
Implant, va. implanter, imprimer, graver
Implement, s. ustensile, *m.*, outil, *m.*, attirail, *m.*
Implicate, va. entremêler, impliquer
Implication, s. enche-

vêtrement, *m.*, (*fig.*) induction, *f.*
Implicit, adj. implicite, (*fig.*) aveugle
Implicitly, adv. implicitement, aveuglément
Implore, va. implorer
Imploringly, adv. d'un air *or* d'un ton de supplication
Imply, va. impliquer, faire supposer, signifier
Impolicy, s. imprudence, *f.*, inopportunité, *f.*
Impolite, adj. impoli, malhonnête
Impolitely, adv. impoliment, avec impolitesse
Impoliteness, s. impolitesse, *f.*
Impolitic, adj. imprudent, impolitique
Import, va. importer, introduire, signifier, indiquer, impliquer
Import, s. (*of goods*) importation, *f.*, (*words*) signification, *f.*, sens, *m.*, portée, *f.* — *-duty*, droit d'importation, *m.*
Importance, s. importance, *f.*, valeur, *f.*, portée, *f.*
Important, adj. important, qui importe
Importation, s. importation, *f.*
Importer, s. importateur, *m.*
Importunate, adj. importun, incommode
Importunately, adv. avec importunité, avec instance
Importune, va. importuner
Importunity, s. importunité, *f.*
Impose, va. imposer. *To — on* or *upon*, vn. en imposer à, tromper, abuser, en faire accroire
Imposition, s. imposition, *f.*, (*tax*) impôt, *m.*, (*punishment*) pensum, *m.*, (*cheat*) supercherie, *f.*, fraude, *f.*, tromperie, *f.*
Impossibility, s. impossibilité, *f.*, chose impossible, *f.*
Impossible, adj. impossible
Impost, s. impôt, *m.*, (*arch.*) imposte, *f.*
Impostor, s. imposteur, *m.*
Imposture, s. imposture, *f.*
Impotence, s. impuissance, *f.*, faiblesse, *f.*
Impotent, adj. impuissant, (*crippled*) impotent, perclus
Impotently, adv. sans force
Impound, va. mettre en fourrière, enfermer
Impoverish, va. appauvrir
Impoverishment, s. appauvrissement, *m.*
Impracticability, s. impraticabilité, *f.*, impossibilité, *f.*

Impracticable, adj. impraticable, (*pers.*) intraitable
Imprecate, va. maudire
Imprecation, s. imprécation, *f.*
Impregnable, adj. imprenable, inébranlable
Impregnate, va. imprégner, féconder
Impregnation, s. imprégnation, *f.*
Imprescriptible, adj. imprescriptible
Impress, va. imprimer, empreindre, faire une empreinte
Impress, s. empreinte, *f.*, impression, *f.*, emblème, *m.*
Impression, s. impression, *f.*, empreinte, *f.*, idée, *f.*
Impressive, adj. impressif, frappant, sérieux, touchant, émouvant
Impressively, adv. de manière à faire impression, d'un air sérieux, d'une manière touchante
Imprint, va. imprimer, empreindre, marquer
Imprison, va. emprisonner
Imprisonment, s. emprisonnement, *m.*
Improbability, s. invraisemblance, *f.*
Improbable, adj. peu probable, invraisemblable
Improbably, adv. d'une manière peu probable
Improbity, s. improbité, *f.*
Impromptu, s. adj. impromptu, *m.*
Improper, adj. peu convenable, malséant, inconvenant
Improperly, adv. d'une manière peu convenable, improprement, d'une manière inconvenante
Impropriety, s. impropriété, *f.*, inconvenance, *f.*
Improvable, adj. susceptible d'amélioration
Improve, va. améliorer, faire faire des progrès à, (*land, wine*) bonifier, perfectionner, (*mind*) cultiver, (*money, &c.*) faire valoir, mettre en valeur, (*land*) exploiter ; — vn. s'améliorer, gagner, se bonifier, faire des progrès, s'instruire, s'embellir, renchérir, être en hausse. *To — on acquaintance*, gagner à être connu. *To — on* or *upon*, perfectionner, surpasser
Improvement, s. amélioration, *f.*, mieux, *m.*, embellissement, *m.*, perfectionnement, *m.*, progrès, *m.pl.*, culture, *f.*, emploi profitable, *m.*
Improver, s. celui, celle, ce qui améliore, qui perfectionne, etc.
Improvidence, s. imprévoyance, *f.*
Improvident, adj. imprévoyant
Improvidently, adv. avec imprévoyance
Improvisation, s. improvisation, *f.*

Improvise, va.n. improviser
Imprudence, s. imprudence, *f.*
Imprudent, adj. imprudent
Imprudently, adv. imprudemment, avec imprudence
Impudence, s. impudence, *f.*
Impudent, adj. impudent, effronté
Impudently, adv. impudemment, effrontément
Impugn, va. attaquer, contester
Impulse, **Impulsion**, s. impulsion, *f.*, mouvement, *m.*, motif, *m.*, choc, *m.*
Impulsive, adj. impulsif
Impulsively, adv. par impulsion, par un mouvement involontaire
Impunity, s. impunité, *f.*
Impure, adj. impur
Impurely, adv. avec impureté
Impurity, s. impureté, *f.*
Imputable, adj. qui doit être imputé *or* attribué
Imputation, s. imputation, *f.*, accusation, *f.*, prévention, *f.*
Impute, va. imputer, attribuer
In, prep. dans, en, (*out of*) sur, selon, par, sous, avec, chez, (*for*) pour, à propos de, touchant
In, adv. s. dedans, au dedans, entré, rentré, tout près, (*law*) en possession, au pouvoir. *To be — for*, être pris, y être. *The —s and outs*, les tenants et les aboutissants
Inability, s. incapacité, *f.*, inhabileté, *f.*, impuissance, *f.*
Inaccessible, adj. inaccessible, inabordable
Inaccuracy, s. inexactitude, *f.*, incorrection, *f.*
Inaccurate, adj. inexact, incorrect
Inaccurately, adv. inexactement
Inaction, s. inaction, *f.*
Inactive, adj. inactif, inerte
Inactivity, s. inactivité, *f.*
Inadequacy, s. insuffisance, *f.*, imperfection, *f.*
Inadequate, adj. insuffisant, imparfait, disproportionné (à)
Inadequately, adv. insuffisamment, imparfaitement, d'une manière disproportionnée
Inadmissible, adj. inadmissible
Inadvertence, **Inadvertency**, s. inadvertance, *f.*
Inadvertent, adj. négligent, inattentif
Inadvertently, adv. par inadvertance
Inalienable, adj. inaliénable
Inamorata, s. inamorata, *f.*

Inane, adj. vide, vain, futile, inutile
Inanimate, adj. inanimé
Inanition, s. inanition, *f.*
Inapplicable, adj. inapplicable
Inapposite, adj. fait mal à propos, qui ne convient pas
Inappreciable, adj. inappréciable
Inaptitude, s. inaptitude, *f.*
Inarticulate, adj. inarticulé
Inarticulately, adv. d'une manière inarticulée
Inasmuch as, loc. adv. vu que, attendu que, puisque, d'autant que
Inattention, s. inattention, *f.*, négligence, *f.*, insouciance, *f.*
Inattentive, adj. inattentif, distrait, négligent, insouciant
Inaudible, adj. qu'on ne peut entendre
Inaugurate, va. inaugurer
Inauguration, s. inauguration, *f.*
Inauspicious, adj. peu propice, défavorable
Inauspiciously, adv. défavorablement, sous de mauvais auspices
Inborn, **Inbred**, adj. inné, naturel
Incalculable, adj incalculable
Incantation, s. incantation, *f.*, charme, *m.*
Incapability, **Incapableness**, s. incapacité, *f.*
Incapable, adj. incapable, peu susceptible
Incapacitate, va. rendre incapable, mettre hors d'état
Incapacity, s. incapacité, *f.*
Incarcerate, va. incarcérer, emprisonner
Incarceration, s. incarcération, *f.*
Incarnate, adj. incarné
Incarnation, s. incarnation, *f.*
Incautious, adj. imprudent, imprévoyant
Incendiarism, s. crime d'incendie, *m.*
Incendiary, adj. s. incendiaire
Incense, va. irriter, exaspérer
Incense, s. encens, *m.*
Incentive, s. encouragement, *m.*, stimulant, *m.*, aiguillon, *m.*, mobile, *m.*
Incessant, adj. incessant
Incessantly, adv. incessamment
Incest, s. inceste, *m.*
Incestuous, adj. incestueux
Incestuously, adv. incestueusement
Inch, s. pouce, *f.* *By —es*, peu à peu. *— by —*, pied à pied. *Within an — of ruin*, à deux doigts de sa ruine
Incidence, s. incidence, *f.*

Incident, s. incident, m., événement, m.
Incident, adj. qui arrive, qui appartient, qui tient
Incidental, adj. fortuit, accidentel, accessoire, incident
Incidentally, adv. fortuitement
Incipient, adj. qui commence, naissant
Incise, va. inciser, graver
Incision, s. incision, f.
Incisive, adj. incisif
Incite, va. inciter, exciter, pousser
Incitement, s. encouragement, m., incitation, f.
Inciter, s. instigateur, m.
Incivility, s. incivilité, f., impolitesse, f.
Inclemency, s. inclémence, f., rigueur, f.
Inclement, adj. inclément, rigoureux
Inclination, s. inclination, f., (declivity) inclinaison, f., (fig.) penchant, m., goût, m., envie, f.
Incline, vn. incliner, s'incliner, pencher, être porté, être disposé, (colours) tirer (sur); — va. incliner, faire pencher, pencher, porter, disposer
Include, va. renfermer, contenir, comprendre
Inclusive, adj. qui entoure, y compris, inclusivement
Inclusively, adv. inclusivement
Incognito, adj. adv. incognito
Incoherence, **Incoherency**, s. incohérence, f.
Incoherent, adj. incohérent
Incoherently, adv d'une manière incohérente
Incombustibility, s. incombustibilité, f.
Incombustible, adj. incombustible
Income, s. revenu, m., rentes, f.pl. — -tax, impôt sur le revenu, m.
Incomer, s. nouveau propriétaire, m.
Incoming, s. entrée, f., revenu, m.
Incommensurability, s. incommensurabilité, f.
Incommensurable, adj. incommensurable
Incommensurate, adj. pas en proportion, disproportionné
Incommensurately, adv. sans proportion
Incommode, va. incommoder
Incommodious, adj. incommode, gênant
Incommodiously, adv. d'une manière incommode or gênante
Incomparable, adj. incomparable
Incomparably, adv. incomparablement, sans comparaison
Incompatibility, s. incompatibilité, f.
Incompatible, adj. incompatible
Incompatibly, adv. d'une manière incompatible
Incompetence, **Incompetency**, s. incapacité, f., insuffisance, f., (law) incompétence, f.
Incompetent, adj. incapable, insuffisant, incompétent
Incompetently, adv. incompétemment
Incomplete, adj. incomplet
Incompletely, adv. d'une manière incomplète
Incompleteness, **Incompletion**, s. état incomplet, m.
Incomprehensibility, s. incompréhensibilité, f.
Incomprehensible, adj. incompréhensible
Inconceivable, adj. inconcevable
Inconceivably, adv. inconcevablement
Inconclusive, adj. peu concluant, qui n'est pas concluant
Inconclusively, adv. d'une manière peu concluante, sans conclure
Incongruity, s. défaut de rapport, m., incongruité, f., absurdité, f.
Incongruous, adj. qui n'est pas en rapport (avec), incongru, inconvenant
Incongruously, adv. sans convenance, sans rapport, incongrûment
Inconsiderable, adj. peu considérable, insignifiant
Inconsiderableness, s. nature insignifiante, f.
Inconsiderate, adj. inconsidéré
Inconsiderately, adv. inconsidérément
Inconsiderateness, s. irréflexion, f., imprudence, f.
Inconsistency, s. inconséquence, f., contradiction, f.
Inconsistent, adj incompatible, inconséquent, contradictoire
Inconsistently, adv. d'une manière incompatible or inconséquente or contradictoire
Inconsolable, adj. inconsolable
Inconstancy, s. inconstance, f.
Inconstant, adj. inconstant
Incontestable, adj. incontestable
Incontestably, adv. incontestablement
Incontinence, s. incontinence, f.
Incontinent, adj. incontinent
Incontinently, adv. avec incontinence
Inconvenience, s. incommodité, f., gêne, f., embarras, m.
Inconvenience, va. incommoder, gêner, déranger
Inconvenient, adj. incommode, gênant. If it is not — to you, si cela ne vous dérange pas
Inconveniently, adv. incommodément, mal
Inconvertible, adj. non-convertible
Incorporate, adj. incorporé
Incorporate, va. incorporer, constituer en corps politique; — vn. s'incorporer
Incorporation, s. incorporation, f., constitution, f., établissement, m.
Incorporeal, adj. incorporel
Incorrect, adj. incorrect, inexact
Incorrectly, adv. inexactement, incorrectement
Incorrectness, s. inexactitude, f., incorrection, f.
Incorrigible, adj. incorrigible
Incorrupt, adj. qui n'est pas corrompu, sain, pur
Incorruptible, adj. incorruptible
Incorruptness, s. pureté, f., absence de corruption, f.
Increase, va.n. s'accroître, s'augmenter, se développer, grandir, se multiplier, grossir, augmenter
Increase, s. augmentation, f., accroissement, m., surcroît, m., agrandissement, m., profit m., produit, m., fruit, m., (waters) crue, f.
Increasing, adj. croissant
Incredibility, s. nature incroyable, f., incrédibilité, f.
Incredible, adj. incroyable
Incredibly, adv. incroyablement
Incredulity, s. incrédulité, f.
Incredulous, adj. incrédule
Incredulously, adv. avec incrédulité
Incriminate, va. incriminer
Incrust, va. incruster, couvrir d'une couche
Incrustation, s. incrustation, f.
Incubate, vn couver
Incubation, s. incubation, f.
Incubus, s. incube, m., cauchemar, m.
Inculcate, va. inculquer
Inculcation, s. inculcation, f.
Incumbency, s. action de se coucher, f., position couchée, f., (eccles.) possession, f.
Incumbent, adj. qui pèse, pesant, couché, qui se repose, (on) du devoir (de), obligatoire (pour), enjoint (à)
Incumbent, s. titulaire, m., possesseur, m.
Incur, va. encourir, s'attirer, s'exposer à, (debts, &c.) contracter
Incurability, s. incurabilité, f.
Incurable, s. adj. incurable, inguérissable
Incurably, adv. sans remède
Incursion, s. incursion, f.
Incurvation, s. incurvation, f.
Indebted, adj. débiteur, endetté, redevable
Indecency, s. indécence, f.
Indecent, adj. indécent
Indecently, adv. indécemment
Indecision, s. indécision, f., irrésolution, f.
Indecisive, adj. indécis, peu décisif, qui ne décide pas
Indecisively, adv. d'une manière indécise
Indeclinable, adj. indéclinable
Indecorous, adj. indécent, malséant, inconvenant
Indecorously, adv. d'une manière inconvenante
Indeed, adv. en effet, à vrai dire, en vérité, je vous l'assure, et même
Indeed! interj. vraiment!
Indefatigable, adj. infatigable
Indefatigably, adv. sans se lasser
Indefeasible, adj. inattaquable, irrévocable
Indefensible, adj insoutenable, inexcusable
Indefinite, adj. indéfini
Indefinitely, adv. indéfiniment
Indelible, adj indélébile, ineffaçable
Indelibly, adv. d'une manière indélébile
Indelicacy, s. indélicatesse, f., grossièreté, f., inconvenance, f.
Indelicate, adj. indélicat, grossier, inconvenant
Indemnification, s. indemnité, f., réparation, f., dédommagement, m.
Indemnify, va. indemniser
Indemnity, s. indemnité, f., garantie, f., assurance, f.
Indent, va denteler, (a tool, &c.) ébrécher, échancrer, découper, (a deed) obliger, mettre en apprentissage; — vn. faire des détours, être dentelé, ébréché, etc., dresser un contrat
Indent, s. entaille, f., dentelure, f., brèche, f.
Indentation, s. entaille, f., brèche, f., dentelure, f., découpure, f.
Indenture, s. contrat, m. —s, pl. brevet d'apprentissage, m.
Independence, s. indépendance, f.
Independent, adj. indépendant, libre, qui vit de ses rentes
Independently, adv. indépendamment, sans tenir compte
Indescribable, adj. indescriptible

Indestructible, *adj.* indestructible
Indeterminable, *adj.* qu'on ne saurait déterminer
Indeterminate, *adj.* indéterminé
Indeterminately, *adv.* d'une manière indéterminée, vaguement
Index, *s.* signe indicateur, *m.*, poteau indicateur, *m.*, index, *m.*, (*dial*) aiguille, *f.*, (*book*) table de matières, *f.*, (*algebr.*, *arithm.*) exposant, *m.* —-*hand*, aiguille de cadran, *f.*
India-rubber, *s.* gomme élastique, *f.*, caoutchouc, *m.*
Indicate, *va.* indiquer
Indication, *s.* indication, *f.*, indice, *m.*, signe, *m.*
Indicative, *adj.* *s.* indicatif (de), qui indique
Indicator, *s.* celui qui indique, indicateur, *m.*
Indict, *va.* mettre en accusation, poursuivre, traduire en justice
Indictable, *adj.* passible de poursuites, (*things*) qualifié
Indictment, *s.* acte d'accusation, *m.*, accusation, *f.* *To find an* —, renvoyer devant le jury
Indifference, *s.* indifférence, *f.*, impartialité, *f.*
Indifferent, *adj.* indifférent, impartial, médiocre, assez mauvais, passable
Indifferently, *adv.* indifféremment, sans faire de différence, sans distinction, avec impartialité, médiocrement, passablement, tant bien que mal, d'une manière telle quelle
Indigence, *s.* indigence, *f.*
Indigenous, *adj.* indigène, natif
Indigent, *adj.* indigent
Indigestible, *adj.* indigeste
Indigestion, *s.* indigestion, *f.*
Indignant, *adj.* indigné, en courroux, courroucé
Indignantly, *adv.* avec indignation
Indignation, *s.* indignation, *f.*, courroux, *m.*
Indignity, *s.* indignité, *f.*
Indigo, *s.* indigo, *m.*, indigotier, *m.*
Indirect, *adj.* indirect, détourné
Indirectly, *adv.* indirectement, d'une voie détournée
Indiscreet, *adj.* indiscret, imprudent
Indiscreetly, *adv.* indiscrètement, sans discrétion, imprudemment
Indiscretion, *s.* indiscrétion, *f.*, imprudence, *f.*
Indiscriminate, *adj.* qui ne sait pas faire une distinction, aveugle, confus, indifférent, indistinct
Indiscriminately, *adv.* sans distinction, à tort et à travers
Indispensable, *adj.* indispensable
Indispensably, *adv.* indispensablement
Indispose, *va.* déranger, éloigner, détourner, indisposer, prévenir
Indisposition, *s.* dérangement, *m.*, éloignement, *m.*, aversion, *f.*, indisposition, *f.*
Indisputable, *adj.* incontestable
Indisputably, *adv.* incontestablement
Indissolubility, *s.* indissolubilité, *f.*
Indissoluble, *adj.* indissoluble
Indissolubly, *adv.* indissolublement
Indistinct, *adj.* indistinct
Indistinctly, *adv.* indistinctement
Indite, *va.* rédiger, composer
Individual, *adj.* individuel
Individual, *s.* individu, *m.*
Individuality, *s.* individualité, *f.*
Individually, *adv.* individuellement, isolément
Indivisibility, *s.* indivisibilité, *f.*
Indivisible, *adj.* indivisible
Indocile, *adj.* indocile
Indocility, *s.* indocilité, *f.*
Indolence, *s.* indolence, *f.*
Indolent, *adj.* indolent
Indolently, *adv.* indolemment
Indomitable, *adj.* indomptable
Indubitable, *adj.* indubitable
Indubitably, *adv.* indubitablement
Induce, *va.* porter, engager, amener, persuader, exciter, pousser, induire, produire, causer, faire naître
Inducement, *s.* motif, *m.*, mobile, *m.*, encouragement, *m.*, incitation, *f.*
Indue, *va.* revêtir (de), (*endow*) douer (de)
Indulge, *va.* avoir de l'indulgence pour, être indulgent pour, écouter trop, flatter, satisfaire, contenter, (*with*, *in*) se livrer (à), s'abandonner (à), se permettre, se donner, se régaler, se choyer ; — *vn.* être indulgent, (*in*) se livrer (à), s'abandonner, se choyer, chercher ses aises
Indulgence, *s.* indulgence, *f.*, faiblesse, *f.*, faveur, *f.*, satisfaction, *f.*, plaisir, *m.*
Indulgent, *adj.* indulgent, complaisant, facile, généreux, libéral
Indulgently, *adv.* avec indulgence, avec complaisance
Induration, *s.* durcissement, *m.*, endurcissement, *m.*
Industrial, *adj.* industriel
Industrious, *adj.* laborieux, diligent, assidu, persévérant
Industriously, *adv.* laborieusement, diligemment, avec assiduité, avec zèle
Industry, *s.* habitudes laborieuses, *f.pl.*, travail, *m.*, diligence, *f.*, persévérance, *f.*, assiduité, *f.*
Ineffable, *adj.* ineffable
Ineffective, **Ineffectual**, *adj.* inefficace, vain
Ineffectiveness, *s.* inefficacité, *f.*
Ineffectually, *adv.* sans effet
Inefficaciousness, **Inefficacy**, **Inefficiency**, *s.* inefficacité, *f.*
Inefficient, *adj.* inefficace, incapable
Inelegance, *s.* inélégance, *f.*, manque d'élégance, *m.*
Inelegant, *adj.* inélégant, peu élégant, de mauvais ton
Ineligible, *adj.* inéligible, peu désirable, peu avantageux
Inept, *adj.* qui n'est pas propre (à), inepte, sot
Inequality, *s.* inégalité, *f.*, insuffisance, *f.*
Inert, *adj.* inerte
Inertly, *adv.* avec inertie
Inertness, *s.* inertie, *f.*
Inestimable, *adj.* inestimable, incalculable
Inevitable, *adj.* inévitable
Inexcusable, *adj.* inexcusable
Inexcusably, *adv.* d'une manière inexcusable
Inexhaustible, **Inexhaustive**, *adj.* inépuisable
Inexorable, *adj* inexorable, inflexible
Inexorably, *adv.* inexorablement
Inexpediency, *s.* défaut d'à-propos, *m.*, inopportunité, *f.*
Inexpedient, *adj.* hors de propos, inopportun
Inexpediently, *adv.* inopportunément
Inexperience, *s.* inexpérience, *f.*
Inexperienced, *adj.* inexpérimenté
Inexpert, *adj.* inexpérimenté, maladroit
Inexpiable, *adj.* inexpiable
Inexplicable, *adj.* inexplicable
Inexpressible, *adj.* inexprimable, indicible
Inexpressive, *adj.* peu expressif, dénué d'expression, insignifiant
Inexpugnable, *adj.* inexpugnable
Inextinguishable, *adj.* inextinguible
Inextricable, *adj.* inextricable
Infallibility, *s.* infaillibilité, *f.*
Infallible, *adj.* infaillible
Infallibly, *adv.* infailliblement
Infamous, *adj.* infâme, exécrable, affreux, (*law*) infamant
Infamously, *adv.* d'une manière infâme, avec infamie
Infamy, *s.* infamie, *f.*
Infancy, *s.* enfance, *f.*, (*law*) minorité, *f.*
Infant, *s.* petit enfant, *m.*, (*law*) mineur, *m.*, mineure, *f.* — *school*, salle d'asile, *f.*
Infant, *adj.* jeune, petit, enfantin, naissant
Infante, *s.* infant, *m.*
Infanta, *s.* infante, *f.*
Infanticide, *s.* infanticide, *m.*
Infantine, *adj.* enfantin
Infantry, *s.* infanterie, *f.*
Infatuate, *va.* faire perdre l'esprit de, faire tomber en démence, (*fig.*) engouer, infatuer
Infatuate, *adj.* infatué
Infatuation, *s.* infatuation, *f.*, engouement, *m.*, démence, *f.*
Infect, *va.* infecter, corrompre, (*law*) entacher d'illégalité
Infection, *s.* infection, *f.*, contagion, *f.*
Infectious, *adj.* infect, infecté, contagieux, pestilentiel
Infectiously, *adv.* par infection
Infectiousness, *s.* nature contagieuse, *f.*, contagion, *f.*
Infer, *va.* inférer, conclure, déduire, supposer
Inference, *s.* conséquence, *f.*
Inferior, *adj.* inférieur
Inferiority, *s.* infériorité, *f.*
Infernal, *adj.* infernal, de l'enfer
Infernally, *adv.* d'une manière infernale
Infertility, *s.* infertilité, *f.*
Infest, *va.* infester, tourmenter
Infidel, *adj.* *s.* infidèle, incrédule
Infidelity, *s.* infidélité, *f.*, incrédulité, *f.*
Infiltrate, *vn.* s'infiltrer
Infiltration, *s.* infiltration, *f.*
Infinite, *adj.* infini
Infinitely, *adv.* infiniment
Infinitesimal, *adj.* infinitésimal
Infinitive, *adj.* infinitif
Infinitude, **Infinity**, *s.* infinité, *f.*
Infirm, *adj.* faible, infirme
Infirmary, *s.* infirmerie, *f.*, hospice, *m.*
Infirmity, *s.* infirmité, *f.*, faiblesse, *f.*
Infix, *va.* fixer, planter, (*fig.*) inculquer
Inflame, *va.* enflammer, exciter, allumer
Inflammable, *adj.* inflammable
Inflammation, *s.* inflammation, *f.* — *of the chest or lungs*, fluxion de poitrine, *f.*
Inflammatory, *adj.* inflammatoire

Inflate, va. gonfler, enfler
Inflation, s. gonflement, *m.*, (*fig.*) orgueil, *m.*, vanité, *f.*
Inflect, va. fléchir, (*voice*) moduler
Inflection, s. inflexion, *f.*
Inflexibility, Inflexibleness, s. inflexibilité, *f.*
Inflexible, adj. inflexible
Inflexibly, adv. inflexiblement
Inflict, va. infliger, imposer
Infliction, s. action d'infliger, *f.*, châtiment, *m.*
Influence, s. influence, *f.*
Influence, va. influencer, (*things*) influer sur
Influential, adj. influent
Influenza, s. grippe, *f.*
Influx, s. entrée, *f.*, introduction, *f.*, (*abundance*) affluence, *f.*
Infold, va. envelopper
Inform, va. donner une forme à, informer (de), instruire (de), faire savoir, faire part (de), avertir (de), annoncer, instruire; — vn. (*against*) dénoncer
Informal, adj. irrégulier, informe
Informality, s. défaut de formalité, *f.*, vice de forme, *m.*
Informally, adv. irrégulièrement
Informant, s. celui *or* celle qui informe, auteur, *m.*, autorité, *f.*, (*law*) dénonciateur, *m.*
Information, s. renseignements, *m.pl.*, nouvelle, *f.*, avis, *m.*, connaissances, *f. pl.*, savoir, *m.*, (*law*) accusation, *f.*, dénonciation, *f.*
Informer, s. celui qui renseigne, etc., (*law*) délateur, *m.*, dénonciateur, *m.*, (*fam.*) mouchard, *m.*
Infraction, s. infraction, *f.*, transgression, *f.*
Infringe, va. enfreindre, violer, transgresser, (*com.*) contrefaire. *To — upon*, empiéter sur, contrefaire
Infringement, s. infraction (à, de), *f.*, transgression (à), *f.*, violation (de), *f.*, (*com.*) contrefaçon, *f.*
Infringer, s. contrefacteur, *m.*
Infuriate, va. rendre furieux
Infuse, va. verser, introduire, inculquer (à), inspirer (à), (*with*) pénétrer (de), infuser, faire infuser
Infusible, adj. infusible
Infusion, s. action de verser, *f.*, inspiration, *f.*, suggestion, *f.*, infusion, *f.*
Ingathering, s. moisson, *f.*
Ingenious, adj. ingénieux, plein de savoir
Ingeniously, adv. d'une manière ingénieuse, spirituellement
Ingeniousness, Ingenuity, s. caractère *or* esprit ingénieux, *m.*, habileté, *f.*, industrie, *f.*, génie, *m.*, esprit, *m.*, talent, *m.*
Ingenuous, adj. ingénu, franc, candide
Ingenuously, adv. ingénument
Ingenuousness, s. ingénuité, *f.*
Inglorious, adj. sans gloire, déshonorant, ignominieux
Ingloriously, adv. sans gloire
Ingot, s. lingot, *m.*
Ingraft, va. greffer, enter
Ingrained, adj. enraciné, invétéré
Ingratiate (oneself), vr. se concilier la faveur, s'insinuer dans les bonnes grâces *or* dans la faveur
Ingratitude, s. ingratitude, *f.*
Ingredient, s. ingrédient, *m.*
Ingress, s. entrée, *f.*
Ingulf, va. engouffrer, (*fig.*) engloutir
Inhabit, va. habiter
Inhabitable, adj. habitable
Inhabitant, s. habitant, *m.*, -e, *f.*
Inhale, va. aspirer, respirer, humer
Inharmonious, adj. peu harmonieux, discordant
Inherent, adj. inhérent, naturel
Inherit, va. hériter, hériter de
Inheritance, s. héritage, *m.*, succession, *f.*
Inheritor, s. héritier, *m.*
Inhospitable, adj. inhospitalier
Inhospitably, adv. d'une manière inhospitalière
Inhospitality, s. inhospitalité, *f.*
Inhuman, adj. inhumain, barbare
Inhumanity, s. inhumanité, *f.*
Inhumanly, adv. inhumainement
Inhume, va. inhumer
Inimical, adj. ennemi, défavorable, hostile
Inimitable, adj. inimitable
Inimitably, adv. d'une manière inimitable
Iniquitous, adj. inique
Iniquity, s. iniquité, *f.*
Initial, adj. premier, initial
Initial, s. initiale, *f.*
Initiate, va. initier, commencer, entreprendre
Initiation, s. initiation, *f.*
Initiative, s. initiative, *f.* — adj. initiatif
Inject, va. jeter dans, (*med.*) injecter
Injection, s. injection, *f.*
Injudicious, adj. peu judicieux
Injudiciously, adv. peu judicieusement
Injunction, s. injonction, *f.*, ordre, *m.*, instructions, *f. pl.*, (*law*) arrêt de sursis, *m.*
Injure, va. nuire à, faire du tort *or* du mal à, léser, endommager, gâter, détériorer, (*com.*) avarier, (*health*) altérer, (*wound*) blesser
Injurer, s. personne qui nuit, qui fait du tort
Injurious, adj. nuisible, préjudiciable, mauvais, insultant, outrageant
Injuriously, adv. mal, avec préjudice, à tort, injurieusement, outrageusement
Injury, s. tort, *m.*, mal, *m.*, préjudice, *m.*, dommage, *m.*, détriment, *m.*, dégât, *m.*, (*com.*) avaries, *f.pl.*
Injustice, s. injustice, *f.*
Ink, s. encre, *f.* *Indian —*, encre de Chine. *Marking —*, encre à marquer le linge
Ink, va. noircir, barbouiller d'encre *or* imprégner d'encre
Inkling, s. avis, *m.*, vent, *m.*, idée, *f.*
Inkstand, s. encrier, *m.*
Inky, adj. d'encre, comme l'encre, taché d'encre, noir
Inland, adj. intérieur, dans l'intérieur, de l'intérieur
Inlay, va. travailler en marqueterie, incruster. *Inlaid work*, ouvrage en marqueterie, *m.*, marqueterie, *f.*
Inlayer, s. marqueteur, *m.*
Inlaying, s. incrustation, *f.*
Inlet, s. entrée, *f.*, passage, *m.*, voie, *f.*, canal, *m.*
Inmate, s. habitant, *m.*, -e, *f.*, locataire, *m.*, pensionnaire, *m.*
Inmost, adj. intérieur, plus retiré, intime, secret
Inn, s. auberge, *f.*, hôtel, *m.*, (*of law*) école de droit, *f.* —*-keeper*, hôte, *m.*, aubergiste, *m.*, hôtelier, *m.*
Innate, adj. inné
Innavigable, adj. qui n'est pas navigable, innavigable
Inner, adj. intérieur, de l'intérieur, arrière
Inning, s. rentrée de la récolte, *f.*, moisson, *f.*, (*at cricket*) tour, *m.*
Innocence, s. innocence, *f.*
Innocent, adj. innocent
Innocently, adv. innocemment, avec innocence
Innocuity, Innocuousness, s. innocuité, *f.*
Innocuous, adj. innocent, inoffensif
Innocuously, adv. sans faire de mal
Innovate, va.n. innover, faire des innovations
Innovation, s. innovation, *f.*
Innovator, s. novateur, *m.*
Innoxious, see INNOCUOUS
Innuendo, s. allusion, *f.*, insinuation, *f.*, mot couvert, *m.*
Innumerable, adj. innombrable, sans nombre
Innumerably, adv. sans nombre
Inoculate, va. greffer par écusson, (*med.*) inoculer
Inoculation, s. greffe par écusson, *f.*, (*med.*) inoculation, *f.*
Inodorous, adj. inodore, sans odeur
Inoffensive, adj. inoffensif, innocent
Inoffensively, adv. d'une manière inoffensive
Inoffensiveness, s. caractère inoffensif, *m.*
Inopportune, adj. inopportun
Inopportunely, adv. inopportunément, mal à propos
Inordinate, adj. désordonné, déréglé, excessif
Inordinately, adv. à l'excès, démesurément
Inorganic, adj. inorganique
Inquest, s. enquête, *f.*, recherche, *f.*
Inquire, va. demander (à), s'informer (à, auprès de), s'adresser, s'enquérir, prendre des informations (sur), demander, rechercher, approfondir, examiner
Inquiry, s. demande, *f.*, question, *f.*, interrogation, *f.*, recherches *f.pl.*, investigation, *f.*, examen (de), *m.*, renseignements, *m.plur.*, enquête, *f.* *Upon —*, en allant aux informations. *To make — after*, s'informer de, aller aux informations
Inquisition, s. perquisition, *f.*, enquête, *f.*, recherche, *f.*, examen, *m.*, inquisition, *f.*
Inquisitive, adj. curieux. *An — mind*, un esprit avide de savoir
Inquisitively, adv. curieusement
Inquisitiveness, s. curiosité, *f.*
Inquisitor, s. juge, *m.*, inquisiteur, *m.*
Inquisitorial, adj inquisitorial
Inroad, s. incursion, *f.*, irruption, *f.*, empiètement, *m.*
Insalubrious, adj. insalubre
Insane, adj. aliéné, fou, en démence
Insanity, s. folie, *f.*, démence, *f.*, aliénation mentale, *f.*
Insatiable, adj. insatiable
Insatiableness, s. insatiabilité, *f.*
Insatiably, adv. insatiablement
Inscribe, va. inscrire, graver, imprimer, (*dedicate*) dédier
Inscription, s. inscription, *f.*, (*title*) titre, *m.*, dédicace, *f.*
Inscrutable, adj. inscrutable
Inscrutableness, Inscrutability, s. impénétrabilité, *f.*
Insect, s. insecte, *m.* — adj. d'insecte

Insectivorous, adj. insectivore
Insecure, adj. incertain, peu assuré
Insecurity, s. incertitude, *f.*, défaut de sûreté, *m.*, danger, *m.*
Insensibility, s. insensibilité, *f.*, indifférence, *f.*
Insensible, adj. insensible, imperceptible, indifférent (à), qui méconnait
Insensibly, adv. insensiblement
Inseparable, adj. inséparable
Inseparably, adv. inséparablement
Insert, va. insérer, faire insérer
Insertion, s. insertion, *f.*
Inside, s. intérieur, *m.*, dedans, *m.* *To turn — out*, mettre à l'envers
Inside, adj. intérieur, d'intérieur
Inside, adv. à l'intérieur, au dedans, en dedans
Insidious, adj. insidieux, perfide
Insidiously, adv. insidieusement
Insidiousness, s. caractère insidieux, *m.*, perfidie, *f.*
Insight, s. connaissance, *f.*, éclaircissement, *m.*
Insignia, s. insignes, *m.pl.*
Insignificance, s. manque de sens, *m.*, absurdité, *f.*, insignifiance, *f.*, peu de valeur, *m.*
Insignificant, adj. vide de sens, insignifiant, de peu de valeur
Insignificantly, adv. d'une manière insignifiante
Insincere, adj. peu sincère, dissimulé, illusoire, faux
Insincerely, adv. sans sincérité
Insincerity, s. manque de sincérité, *m.*, fausseté, *f.*
Insinuate, va. insinuer, glisser
Insinuation, s. insinuation *f.*
Insipid, adj. insipide, fade
Insipidity, s. insipidité, *f.*, fadeur, *f.*
Insipidly, adv. insipidement
Insist, vn. porter, poser, insister, persister, exiger, maintenir
Insnare, va. prendre, attirer *or* faire tomber, séduire, tromper
Insolence, s. insolence, *f.*
Insolent, adj. insolent
Insolently, adv. insolemment
Insolubility, s. insolubilité, *f.*
Insoluble, adj. insoluble
Insolvable, adj. indissoluble
Insolvency, s. insolvabilité, *f.*, faillite, *f.*
Insolvent, adj. insolvable, qui a fait faillite
Insomuch, adv. tellement, au point, à un tel point, si bien

Inspect, va. examiner, inspecter, visiter
Inspection, s. examen, *m.*, inspection, *f.*, surveillance, *f.*
Inspector, s. inspecteur, *m.*, surveillant, *m.*, vérificateur, *m.*
Inspectorship, s. inspection, *f.*
Inspiration, s. inspiration, *f.*
Inspire, va. respirer, insuffler, inspirer
Inspirit, va. encourager, inspirer, enflammer
Instability, s. instabilité, *f.*, inconstance, *f.*
Install, va. installer
Installation, s. installation, *f.*
Instalment, s. installation, *f.*, siège, *m.*, (*money*) à-compte, *m.*, versement, *m.*
Instance, s. demande, *f.*, sollicitation, *f.*, instances, *f. pl.*, exemple, *m.* *For —*, par exemple *In the first —*, en premier lieu
Instance, vn. citer un exemple
Instant, adj. pressant, instant, ardent, fervent, immédiat, (*date*) courant
Instant, s. instant, *m.*, moment, *m.*
Instantaneous, adj. instantané
Instantaneously, adv. instantanément
Instantaneousness, s. instantanéité, *f.*
Instantly, adv. sur l'heure, sur-le-champ, à l'instant, aussitôt, tout de suite, immédiatement
Instauration, s. instauration, *f.*
Instead, adv. à la place. *— of*, au lieu de, à la place de. *To be — of, to stand — of*, tenir lieu de
Instep, s. cou-de-pied, *m.*
Instigate, va. exciter, pousser
Instigation, s. instigation, *f.*
Instigator, s. instigateur, *m.*, -trice, *f.*
Instil, va. instiller, inculquer
Instillation, s. instillation, *f.*, infusion, *f.*
Instinct, s. instinct, *m.*
Instinctive, adj. instinctif
Instinctively, adv. instinctivement
Institute, va. instituer, fonder, établir, (*law*) intenter
Institute, s. loi, *f.*, précepte, *m.*, principe, *m.*, institut, *m.*
Institution, s. institution, *f.*, instruction, *f.*
Institutor, s. instituteur, *m.*, -trice, *f.*
Instruct, va. instruire, enseigner, apprendre, donner des instructions
Instruction, s. instruction, *f.*, enseignement, *m.*, leçons, *f.pl.*, ordres, *m.pl.*

Instructive, adj. instructif
Instructor, s. maître, *m.*, instituteur, *m.*, précepteur, *m.*
Instrument, s. instrument, *m.*, moyen, *m.*
Instrumental, adj. instrumental, qui contribue *or* sert, utile
Instrumentalist, s. instrumentiste, *m.*
Instrumentality, s. action, *f.*, concours, *m.*, moyen, *m.*
Insubordinate, adj. insubordonné
Insubordination, s. insubordination, *f.*
Insufferable, adj. insupportable
Insufferably, adv. insupportablement
Insufficiency, s. insuffisance, *f.*
Insufficient, adj. insuffisant
Insufficiently, adv. insuffisamment
Insular, adj. insulaire
Insulate, va. isoler
Insult, s. insulte, *f.*, affront, *f.*, outrage, *m.*
Insult, va. insulter, outrager, injurier
Insulter, s. insulteur, *m.*, auteur d'une insulte, *m.*
Insulting, adj insultant
Insultingly, adv. d'une façon insultante, avec insulte
Insuperable, adj. insurmontable
Insuperably, adv. d'une manière insurmontable
Insupportable, adj. insupportable
Insupportably, adv. insupportablement
Insurance, s. assurance, *f.* *Fire and Life — Company*, Compagnie d'assurances contre l'incendie et sur la vie. *— office*, bureaux d'une Compagnie d'assurances
Insure, va n. assurer
Insurer, s. assureur, *m.*
Insurgent, s. adj. insurgé
Insurmountable, adj. insurmontable, infranchissable
Insurrection, s. insurrection, *f.*, soulèvement, *m.*
Insurrectionary, adv. insurrectionnel, d'insurrection
Intact, adj. intact
Intaglio, s. entaille, *f.*
Integer, s. nombre entier, *m.*
Integral, adj. entier, intégral
Integral, s. totalité, *f.*
Integrally, adv. intégralement
Integrity, s. intégrité, *f.*, probité, *f.*
Intellect, s intelligence, *f.*, entendement, *m.*, intellect, *m.*
Intellectual, adj. intellectuel
Intelligence, s. intelligence, *f.*, nouvelle, *f.*, avis, *m.*, renseignement, *m.* *— office*, bureau de renseignements

Intelligencer, s. nouvelliste, *m.*
Intelligent, adj. intelligent
Intelligently, adv. intelligemment, avec intelligence
Intelligible, adj. intelligible
Intelligibly, adv. intelligiblement, clairement
Intemperance, s. intempérance, *f.*, excès, *m.*
Intemperate, adj. intempérant, excessif, démesuré, immodéré, (*climate*) rigoureux
Intemperately, adv. à l'excès, avec intempérance, immodérément
Intend, va n. avoir l'intention (de), vouloir, compter, prétendre, entendre, se proposer, avoir en vue destiner (à). *I — nothing of the kind*, telle n'est pas mon intention
Intended, adj. projeté, proposé, intentionnel, fait à dessein, prémédité. (*future wife or husband*) prétendu, -e, futur, -e
Intense, adj. intense, fort, vif, violent, excessif, profond
Intensely, adv. avec intensité, vivement, fortement, profondément
Intensity, s. intensité, *f.*, force, *f.*, violence, *f.*, vigueur, *f.*, véhémence, *f.*, (*of mind*) contention, *f.*
Intent, adj. très attentif, très appliqué
Intent, Intention, s. intention, *f.*, dessein, but, *m.* *To all —s and purposes*, à tous égards
Intentional, adj. intentionnel, avec intention
Intentionally, adv. à dessein
Intently, adv. très attentivement, avec ardeur
Intentness, s. application sérieuse, *f.*
Inter, va. enterrer
Intercalary, adj. intercalaire
Intercalation, s. intercalation, *f.*
Intercede, vn. intercéder
Interceder, s. intercesseur, *m.*
Interceding, s. intercession, *f.*
Intercept, va. intercepter, arrêter
Intercession, s. intercession, *f.*
Intercessor, s. intercesseur, *m.*
Interchange, va. échanger
Interchange, s. échange, *m.*
Interchangeable, adj. réciproque
Interchangeably, adv. réciproquement
Intercourse, s. commerce, *m.*, relations, *f.pl.*, rapports, *m.pl.*, (*exchange*) échange, *m.*
Interdict, va. interdire
Interdict, s. interdit, *m.*
Interdiction, s. interdiction, *f.*

Interdictory, adj. d'interdiction
Interest, v.a. intéresser. *To be —ed in,* (*com.*) être intéressé dans, (*fig.*) s'intéresser à
Interest, s. intérêt, *m.*, (*right*) droit, *m.*, part, *f.*, (*influence*) crédit, *m.*
Interesting, adj. intéressant
Interfere, vn. intervenir, s'interposer, se mêler (de), s'immiscer (dans), contrarier, empêcher, nuire (à)
Interference, s. intervention, *f.*, entrave, *f.*, choc, *m.*, conflit, *m.*
Interim, s. intérim, *m.*, intervalle, *m.*, temps, *m.*
Interior, adj. intérieur. — s. intérieur, *m.*
Interjection, s. interjection, *f.*
Interlace, va. entremêler, entrelacer
Interlard, va. entrelarder, entremêler
Interleave, va. encarter, interfolier
Interline, va. écrire *or* imprimer entre les lignes
Interlinear, adj. interlinéaire
Interlineation, s. interlinéation, *f.*
Interlink, va. lier ensemble, unir au moyen de chaînons
Interlocutor, s. interlocuteur, *m.*, -trice, *f.*
Interlope, vn. faire le commerce interlope, (*fig.*) s'ingérer
Interloper, s. navire interlope, *m.*, contrebandier, *m.*
Interlude, s. intermède, *m.*
Intermarriage, s. mariage entre parents, *m.*
Intermarry, vn. se marier
Intermeddle, vn. s'immiscer (dans), se mêler (de), intervenir, s'interposer
Intermeddler, s. officieux, *m.*, -euse, *f.*, importun, *m.*, e, *f.*, brouillon, *m.*
Intermediate, adj. intermédiaire
Interment, s. enterrement, *m.*
Interminable, adj. interminable, infini
Intermingle, va. entremêler; — vn. s'entremêler
Intermission, s. entremise, *f.*, intermission, *f.*, relâche, *m.*, cesse, *f.*, intervalle, *m.*
Intermit, va.n. cesser, discontinuer
Intermittent, Intermitting, adj. intermittent
Intermix, va. *see* INTERMINGLE
Intermixture, s. mélange, *m.*
Internal, adj. interne, véritable, essentiel
Internally, adv. intérieurement
International, adj. international
Interpolate, va. interpoler, intercaler
Interpolation, s. interpolation, *f.*, intercalation, *f.*
Interpose, va. interposer, placer entre, offrir; — vn. s'interposer, s'entremettre, intervenir
Interposer, s. médiateur, *m.*, -trice, *f.*
Interposition, s. interposition, *f.*, intervention, *f.*, entremise, *f.*
Interpret, va. interpréter, expliquer
Interpretation, s. interprétation, *f.*
Interpretative, adj. interprétatif
Interpreter, s. interprète, *m.*
Interregnum, s. interrègne, *m.*
Interrogate, va.n. interroger, questionner
Interrogation, s. interrogation, *f.*, question, *f.*, (*law*) interrogatoire, *m.*
Interrogative, adj. interrogatif
Interrogatively, adv. par forme d'interrogation
Interrogator, s. interrogateur, *m.*, -trice, *f.*
Interrogatory, adj. interrogatif
Interrupt, va. interrompre
Interruptedly, adv. avec des interruptions
Interrupter, s. interrupteur, *m.*
Interruption, s. interruption, *f.*, intermission, *f.*
Intersect, va.n. couper, interrompre, faire intersection, se couper
Intersection, s. intersection, *f.*
Intersperse, va. parsemer, semer, répandre, diversifier, varier
Interstice, s. interstice, *m.*
Intertwine, va. entrelacer; — vn. s'entrelacer
Interval, s. intervalle, *m.*
Intervene, vn. intervenir, s'interposer, être *or* se trouver (entre), (*time*) s'écouler, (*happen*) survenir, arriver
Intervening, adj. intervenant
Intervention, s. intervention, *f.*, interposition, *f.*
Interview, s. entrevue, *f.*
Interweave, va. tisser ensemble, entrelacer, entremêler
Intestate, adj. s. intestat, *m.*
Intestinal, adj. intestinal
Intestine, s. intestin, *m.*
Intestine, adj. intestin, domestique
Inthral, vn. asservir, rendre esclave
Inthralment, s. esclavage, *m.*, servitude, *f.*
Intimacy, s. intimité, *f.*
Intimate, adj. intime
Intimate, va. annoncer, signifier, déclarer, donner à entendre
Intimately, adv. intimement, à fond, parfaitement
Intimation, s. avis, *m.*, indice, *m.*
Intimidate, va. intimider
Intimidation, s. intimidation, *f.*
Into, prep. dans, en, à
Intolerable, adj. intolérable, insupportable
Intolerably, adv. insupportablement
Intolerance, s. intolérance, *f.*
Intolerant, adj. intolérant, d'intolérance
Intonation, s. intonation, *f.*
Intone, vn. chanter; — va. entonner
Intoxicate, va. enivrer, rendre ivre. —*d with,* ivre de
Intoxicating, adj. enivrant
Intoxication, s. ivresse, *f.*, enivrement, *m.*
Intractable, adj. indocile, intraitable
Intrench, vn. empiéter; — va. retrancher
Intrenchment, s. retranchement, *m.*
Intrepid, adj. intrépide
Intrepidity, s. intrépidité, *f.*
Intrepidly, adv. intrépidement, avec intrépidité
Intricacy, s. complication, *f.*, embrouillement, *m.*
Intricate, adj. compliqué, embrouillé, difficile, embarrassé
Intricately, adv. d'une manière compliquée *or* embrouillée
Intrigue, s. intrigue, *f.*
Intrigue, vn. intriguer
Intriguer, s. intrigant, *m.*, -e, *f.*
Intriguing, adj. intrigant. — part. intriguant
Intrinsic, adj. intrinsèque, intime
Intrinsically, adv. intrinsèquement, véritablement
Introduce, va. introduire, faire entrer, présenter, faire adopter
Introducer, s. introducteur, *m.*, -trice, *f.*
Introduction, s. introduction, *f.*, présentation, *f.*, initiation, *f.*
Introductive, Introductory, adj. qui sert *or* pour servir d'introduction, préliminaire
Intrude, va. faire entrer de force, pousser dedans, introduire, imposer. *To — oneself on a person,* importuner quelqu'un. — vn. faire intrusion, s'introduire sans qualité, se fourrer, se faufiler, importuner, déranger
Intruder, s. intrus, *m.*, -e, *f.*, importun, *m.*, -e, *f.*
Intrusion, s. importunité, *f.*, action de se mêler de, *f.*, intervention, *f.*, dérangement, *f.*, envahissement (de), *f.*, empiètement (sur), *f.*
Intrusive, adj. importun, indiscret
Intrust, va. confier, charger
Intuition, s. intuition, *f.*
Intuitive, adj. intuitif, d'intuition
Intuitively, adv. par intuition, intuitivement
Inundation, s. inondation, *f.*
Inure, va. habituer (à), accoutumer (à), aguerrir (à, contre), rompre (à)
Inurement, s. habitude, *f.*
Invade, va. envahir, attaquer
Invader, s. envahisseur, *m.*
Invading, adj. envahissant, d'invasion
Invalid, adj. invalide, (*fig.*) faible
Invalid, s. valétudinaire, *m.*, malade, *m.*, invalide, *m.f.*
Invalidate, va. invalider, infirmer
Invalidity, s. invalidité, *f.*, faiblesse, *f.*
Invaluable, adj. inestimable, inappréciable
Invariability, Invariableness, s. invariabilité, *f.*
Invariable, adj. invariable
Invariably, adv. invariablement
Invasion, s. invasion, *f.*, envahissement, *m.*, violation (de), *f.*, atteinte (à), *f.*
Invective, s. invective, *f.*
Inveigh, vn. se déchaîner (contre), invectiver
Inveigle, va. séduire, cajoler, leurrer, attirer
Inveigler, s. séducteur, *m.*, enjôleur, *m.*, trompeur, *m.*
Invent, va. inventer
Invention, s. invention, *f.*
Inventive, adj. inventif, plein d'invention
Inventor, s. inventeur, *m.*
Inventory, s. inventaire, *m.*
Inventress, s. inventrice, *f.*
Inverse, adj. inverse
Inversion, s. interversion, *f.*, renversement, *m.*, inversion, *f.*
Invert, va. renverser, faire une inversion de, intervertir
Invest, va. vêtir, revêtir, investir, (*money*) placer
Investigate, va. rechercher, examiner, faire une enquête sur
Investigating, adj. investigateur
Investigation, s. investigation, *f.*, recherche, *f.*
Investigator, s. investigateur, *m.*, -trice, *f.*
Investiture, s. investiture, *f.*
Investment, s. action de vêtir, *f.*, action d'investir, *f.*, action de revêtir, *f.*, (*money*) placement, *f.*, (*mil.*) investissement, *m.*
Inveterate, adj. invétéré, enraciné, acharné
Invidious, adj. odieux, peu agréable, irritant
Invidiously, adv. odieusement, d'une manière irritante
Invidiousness, s. nature odieuse, *f.*, nature irritante, *f.*
Invigorate, va. fortifier, donner de la vigueur à
Invincible, adj. invincible
Invincibly, adv. invinciblement
Inviolable, adj. inviolable

Inviolably, adv. inviolablement
Invisibility, Invisibleness, s. invisibilité, *f.*
Invisible, adj. invisible
Invisibly, adv. invisiblement
Invitation, s. invitation, *f.*
Invite, va. inviter (à), prier (de)
Inviting, adj. engageant, attrayant
Invitingly, adv. d'une manière engageante *or* attrayante
Invocation, s. invocation, *f.*, prière, *f.*, demande, *f.*
Invoice, s. facture, f.
Invoice, va. faire la facture de
Invoke, va. invoquer
Involuntarily, adv. involontairement
Involuntary, adv. involontaire
Involve, va. envelopper, couvrir, impliquer, entraîner, comprendre, lier, enchaîner, saisir
Invulnerable, adj. invulnérable
Inward, Inwards, adj. en dedans, à l'intérieur
Inwardly, adv. intérieurement, dans l'âme
Iodine, s. iode, *m.*
Ionic, adj. ionique, ionien
Iota, s. iota, *m.*
I.O.U., s. reconnaissance, *f.*
Ipecacuanha, s. ipécacuana, *m.*
Irascibility, s. irascibilité, *f.*
Irascible, adj. irascible
Ire, s. courroux, *m.*, colère, *f.*
Ireful, adj. courroucé, furieux
Irefully, adv. avec courroux, avec colère
Iris, s. iris, *m.* *German* —, glaïeul, *m.*
Irksome, adj. ennuyeux, fatigant, fastidieux
Irksomeness, s. ennui, *m.*, fatigue, *f.*, nature fastidieuse, *f.*

Iron, s. fer, *m.* *Old* —, vieille ferraille, *f.* *Pig* —, fer en saumons, *m.*, gueuse, *f.* *Small pig* —, gueuset, *m.* *Sheet* —, tôle, *f.* *Wrought* —, fer forgé, *f.* *Box* —, *flat* —, fer à repasser, *m.*
Iron, adj. de fer, en fer
Iron, va. (*linen*) repasser, mettre les fers à, charger de fers, garnir de fer
Ironical, adj. ironique
Ironically, adv. ironiquement
Ironing, s. repassage, *m.*, mise aux fers, *f.* — *-board*, planche à repasser, *f.*
Irony, s. ironie, *f.*
Irradiate, va.n. rayonner sur, illuminer, éclairer, vivifier, animer
Irrational, adj. irraisonnable, dépourvu de raison, déraisonnable, irrationnel
Irrationality, s. déraison, *f.*
Irreclaimable, adj. incorrigible, indomptable
Irreconcilable, adj. irréconciliable, (*things*) inconciliable
Irreconcilableness, s. impossibilité de réconciliation, *f.*, incompatibilité, *f.*
Irreconcilably, adv. de manière à ne jamais se réconcilier, d'une manière inconciliable
Irrecoverable, adj. irréparable, perdu, sans retour, irrémédiable
Irrecoverably, adv. irréparablement, sans retour, sans ressource
Irreducible, adj. irréductible
Irrefragable, adj. irréfragable
Irrefragably, adv. d'une manière irréfragable
Irrefutable, adj. irréfutable
Irregular, adj. irrégulier, (*life*) déréglé
Irregularity, s. irrégularité, *f.*, désordre, *m.*

Irregularly, adv. irrégulièrement
Irrelevant, adj. étranger (à), inapplicable (à), sans rapport (avec)
Irreligion, s. irréligion, *f.*, impiété, *f.*
Irreligious, adj. irréligieux
Irreligiously, adv. irréligieusement
Irremediable, adj. irrémédiable
Irremediably, adv. sans ressource, à un point irrémédiable
Irremissible, adj. irrémissible
Irremovable, adj. inébranlable, inamovible
Irremovably, adv. immuablement
Irreparable, adj. irréparable
Irreparably, adv. irréparablement
Irreprehensible, adj. irrépréhensible
Irreprehensibly, adv. d'une manière irrépréhensible
Irreproachable, adj. irréprochable, sans reproche
Irreproachably, adv. sans reproche, d'une manière irréprochable
Irreprovable, adj. irrépréhensible
Irresistible, adj. irrésistible
Irresistibly, adv. irrésistiblement
Irresolute, adj. irrésolu
Irresolutely, adv. irrésolument
Irresolution, s. irrésolution, *f.*
Irrespective, adj. indépendant, (*of*) sans égard (pour)
Irresponsibility, s. irresponsabilité, *f.*
Irresponsible, adj. irresponsable
Irretrievable, adj. irréparable, irrémédiable
Irretrievably, adv. irréparablement, sans retour, sans remède

Irreverence, s. irrévérence, *f.*
Irreverent, adj. irrévérent, irrespectueux
Irreverently, adv. avec irrévérence, irrespectueusement
Irreversible, Irrevocable, adj. irrévocable
Irrevocably, adv. irrévocablement
Irrigate, va. arroser
Irrigation, s. irrigation, *f.*, arrosement, *m.*
Irritability, s. irritabilité, *f.*
Irritable, adj. irritable
Irritate, va. irriter
Irritation, s. irritation, *f.*
Irruption, s. irruption, *f.*
Isinglass, s. colle de poisson, *f.*
Island, s. île, *f.*
Islander, s. insulaire
Isle, s. île, *f.*
Islet, s. îlot, *m.*
Isolated, adj. isolé
Issue, s. issue, *f.*, fin, *f.*, succès, *m.*, (*in the arm*) cautère, *m.*, (*offspring*) enfans, *m.* —*s*, plur. lignée, *f.*
Issue, va. provenir, sortir, publier, émaner
Issueless, adj. sans enfans
Isthmus, s. isthme, *m.*
It, pron. ce, il, elle, le, la, en, y, cela
Italic, adj. italique
Itch, s. gale, *f.*, (*desire*) démangeaison, *f.*, envie, *f.*
Itch, va. démanger
Itching, s. démangeaison, *f.*
Itchy, adj. galeux
Item, adj. item, de plus
Item, s. avis, m., article, *m.*
Iteration, s. répétition, *f.*
Iterative, adj. itératif
Itinerant, adj. ambulant, -e
Itinerary, s. itinéraire, *m.*
Its, pron. son, sa, ses, (*of it*) en
Ivied, adj. couvert de lierre
Ivory, s. ivoire, *m.*
Ivy, s. lierre, *m.* *Ground*-—, lierre rampant

J

J, s. J, j.
Jabber, vn. jaboter, jacasser; — va. bredouiller, baragouiner
Jabber, Jabbering, s. caquetage, *m.*, bavardage, *m.*, baragouinage, *m.*, baragouin, *m.*
Jabberer, s. bavard, *m.*, -e, *f.*, baragouineur, *m.*, -euse, *f.*, bredouilleur, *m.*, -euse, *f.*
Jacconet, s. jaconas, *m.*
Jack, s. (*boot*) tire-botte, *m.*, (*spit*) tournebroche, *m.*, (*pitcher*) broc, *m.*, (*bowls*) cochonnet *m.*, (*machine*) cric, *m.*, (*fish*) brochet, *m.* (*mus.*) sautereau, *m.*, (*nav.*) pavillon de beaupré, *m.* — *of all trades*, maître Jacques, *m.*, homme de tous les métiers, *m.* — *-in-the-box*, (*toy*) boîte à surprises, *f.* — *-tar*, (*nav.*) loup de mer, *m.*, marin, *m.*
Jackal, s. chacal, *m.*
Jackanapes, s. faquin, *m.*, fat, *m.*
Jackass, s. âne, *m.*, bourriquet, *m.*, baudet, *m.*, grison, *m.*
Jackdaw, s. choucas, *m.*, corneille des clochers, *f.*
Jacket, s. veste, *f.*, (*ladies*) jaquette, *f.*, camisole, *f.* *Blue* —, marin, *m.*
Jacobin, s. jacobin, *m.*, moine jacobin, *m.*
Jade, s. rosse, *f.*, haridelle *f.*, (*fig.*) coquine, *f.*, friponne, *f.*, (*stone*) jade, *m.*
Jade, va. surmener, excéder, fatiguer, user
Jag, va. déchiqueter, entailler, ébrécher
Jag, s. entaille, *f.*, brèche, *f.*, dent de scie, *f.*
Jagged, adj. irrégulier, ébréché
Jaguar, s. jaguar, *m.*
Jail, s. prison, *f.*, geôle, *f.*, cage, *f.* — *-bird*, gibier de potence, *m.* — *-book*, livre d'écrou, *m.*
Jailer, s. geôlier, *m.* —*'s wife*, geôlière, *f.*
Jam, s. confitures, *f.pl.*, conserves, *f.pl.* *Currant* —, confitures de groseilles
Jam, Jamb, va. serrer, presser
Jamb, s. (*archit.*) jambage, *m.*, jambe, *f.*
Jangle, vn. *see* WRANGLE
Janissary, s. janissaire, *m.*
January, s. janvier, *m.*
Japan, s. laque, *f.*
Japan, adj. de laque, en laque. — *-earth*, terre du Japon, *f.* — *-wares*, meubles *or* objets en laque *or* vernissés en laque
Japan, va. vernisser en laque, vernir
Japanning, s. vernissure à la laque, *f.*
Jar, vn. être discordant (à), rendre un son discordant, frapper désagréablement, (*to fight*) se quereller
Jar, s. son *or* bruit discordant, *m.*, discorde, *f.*, contestation, *f.*, choc, *m.*, (*vessel*) cruche, *f.*, jarre, *f.*, vase, *m.*, bouteille, *f.*
Jargon, s. jargon, *m.*
Jarring, adj. discordant, rude, dur, en désaccord, opposé, contraire

Jasmine, s. jasmin, *m.*
Jasper, s. jaspe, *m.*
Jaundice, s. jaunisse, *f.*
Jaundiced, adj. atteint de jaunisse, jaune, (*fig.*) prévenu, jaloux
Jaunt, vn. errer çà et là faire une excursion. *Jaunting car*, char-à-bancs
Jaunt, s. excursion, *f.*, promenade à la campagne, *f.*, (*wheel*) jante, *f.*
Jauntiness, s. gentillesse, *f.*, grâce, *f.*, légèreté, *f.*, affectation, *f.*, manières prétentieuses, *f.pl.*
Jaunty, adj. gentil, gracieux, léger, magnifique, prétentieux
Javelin, s. javelot, *m.*, javeline, *f.*
Jaw, s. mâchoire, *f.*, bouche, *f.*, gueule, *f.*, (*death*) étreinte, *f.*, (*hell*) gouffre béant, *m.*, (*scold*) crierie, *f.*, (*pop.*) langage grossier, *m.*
Jaw, va. crier après
Jay, s. geai, *m.*
Jealous, adj. jaloux, zélé, craintif, méfiant
Jealously, adv. avec jalousie, en jaloux
Jealousy, s. jalousie, *f.*, crainte, *f.*, méfiance, *f.*
Jeer, vn. a. (*at*) railler, se moquer de, bafouer, tourner en plaisanterie
Jeer, s. raillerie, *f.*, sarcasme, *m.*, brocard, *m.*
Jeerer, s. railleur, *m.*, -euse, *f.*
Jeering, s. raillerie, *f*
Jeering, adj. railleur
Jeeringly, adv. en raillant, avec raillerie d'un ton moqueur
Jejune, adj. vide, à jeun, (*fig.*) maigre, pauvre, stérile, sec
Jelly, s. gelée, *f.*, (*sauce*) coulis, *m.*, (*fig.*) compote, *f.*, marmelade, *f.*
Jemmy, s. (*tool*) monseigneur, *m.*
Jeopardize, va. mettre en danger, hasarder, exposer, risquer
Jeopardy, s. danger, *m.*, péril, *m.*
Jerk, va. secouer, donner une secousse, tirer vivement, lancer vivement. *To — out, one's words*, parler par saccades
Jerk, s. mouvement vif, *m.*, secousse, *f.*, saccade, *f.*, trait, *m.* *By —s*, par saccades
Jessamine, s. jasmine, *m.*
Jest, va. plaisanter, railler, badiner, rire (de)
Jest, s. plaisanterie, *f.*, raillerie, *f.*, bon mot, *m.*, facétie, *f.*, risée, *f.*, tour, *m.*, farce, *f.* *To make a — of*, tourner en raillerie. *In —*, en plaisantant, par plaisanterie, pour rire
Jester, s. plaisant, *m.*, railleur, *m.*, diseur de bon mots, *m.*, mauvais plaisant, *m.*, (*court-fool*) fou, *m.*, bouffon, *m.*
Jesting, s. plaisanterie, *f.*, badinage, *m.*, raillerie, *f.*
Jestingly, adv. en plaisantant
Jesuit, s. Jésuite, *m.*
Jesuitic, Jesuitical, adj. jésuitique, de jésuite
Jet, s. jais, *m.*, jayet, *m.*
Jetty, adj. de jais, noir comme du jais
Jetty, s. jetée, *f.* *—-head*, tête de jetée, *f.*
Jew, s. Juif, *m.*
Jewel, s. bijou, *m.*, joyau, *m.*
Jewel, va. orner *or* couvrir de bijoux, enrichir de pierreries, (*watch*) monter sur rubis
Jeweller, s. bijoutier, *m.*, -ere, *f.*, joaillier, *m.*, -ere, *f.*
Jewellery, s. bijouterie, *f.*, joaillerie, *f.*, pierreries, *f.pl.*
Jewish, adj. juif, israélite, des Juifs, des Israélites
Jewry, s. Juiverie, *f.*
Jib, s. foc, *m.* *—-boom*, bâton de foc, *m.*
Jib, va. reculer
Jig, s. gigue, *f.*
Jilt, s. coquette, *f.*
Jilt, va. n. tromper, faire la coquette
Jingle, vn. tinter, sonner, cliqueter, retentir, (*glasses*) s'entre-choquer, (*rhymes*) faire l'écho, rimer; — va. faire tinter, faire retentir, choquer
Jingle, s. tintement, *m.*, grelotte, *m.*, clochette, *f.*, cliquetis, *m.*, consonnance, *f.*
Job, s. tout ouvrage qui se présente, *m.*, besogne, *f.*, petit travail, *m.*, petite corvée, *f.*, (*contract*) forfait, *m.*, travail à la tâche, *m.*, à la pièce, *m.*, affaire, *m.*, (*unfair*) tripotage, *m.* *By the —*, à la tâche, à la pièce, à forfait
Job, vn. faire du petits ouvrages, de petites corvées, travailler à la tâche *or* à la pièce, (*fig.*) tripoter, agioter, spéculer, (*letting of horses*) louer des voitures *or* des chevaux
Jobber, s. tâcheron, *m.*, tripotier, *m.*, agioteur, *m.*
Jobbing, s. action de faire de petits travaux, de petites corvées, travail à la tâche *or* à la pièce, (*fig.*) tripotage, *m.*, agiotage, *m.*
Jockey, s. jockey, *m.*, maquignon, *m.*, marchand de chevaux, *m.*
Jockey, va. duper, beurrer
Jocose, adj. plaisant, badin, enjoué, jovial, facétieux
Jocosely, adv. en plaisantant, en badinant, facétieusement
Jocular, adj. plaisant, badin, risible, jovial
Jocularity, s. badinage, *m.*, plaisanterie, *f.*, humeur joviale, *f.*
Jocularly, adv. en plaisantant, en riant
Jog, vn. avancer doucement, se mettre en route. *To — along, on*, marcher *or* cheminer lentement, aller cahin-caha
Jog, s. légère secousse, *f.*, coup de coude, *m.*, obstacle, *m.*, inégalité, *f.*
Jog-trot, s. petit trot, *m.*, lente allure, *f.*
Join, va. joindre, unir réunir, rejoindre, allier, assembler, se joindre à, prendre part à, (*roads*) relier; — vn. se joindre, se toucher, toucher à, s'unir, prendre part, se rencontrer
Joiner, s. menuisier, *m.*
Joinery, s. menuiserie, *f.*
Joint, s. joint, *m.*, jointure, *f.*, articulation, *f.*, (*hinge*) charnière, *f.*, (*meat*) grosse pièce, *f.* *Out of —*, démis, disloqué, luxé, (*fig.*) en désordre
Joint, adj. commun à deux *or* à plusieurs, en commun, réuni, combiné
Joint, va. unir par des articulations, joindre, réunir, rapporter, couper *or* diviser dans les articulations
Jointly, adv. conjointement, de concert
Jointure, s. douaire, *m.*
Joist, s. solive, *f.*, madrier, *m.*
Joke, s. plaisanterie, *f.*, bon mot, *m.*, facétie, *f.*
Joke, vn. plaisanter, rire; — va. plaisanter, railler, se moquer de
Joker, s. plaisant, *m.*, rieur, *m.*, -euse, *f.* *Dry* or *cutting —*, pince-sans-rire
Joking, s. plaisanterie, *f.*
Joking, adj. badin
Jollification, s. noce, *f.* *To have a —*, faire la noce
Jollily, adv. gaiement, joyeusement, d'une façon gaillarde
Jolliness, Jollity, s. gaieté, *f.*, joie, *f.*, plaisir, *m.*
Jolly, adj. gai, joyeux, jovial, gaillard, réjoui, dispos, bien portant. *—fellow*, bon vivant, gaillard
Jolly-boat, s. petit canot, *m.*
Jolt, vn. faire des cahots, secouer; — va. cahoter, secouer
Jolting, s. cahots, *m.pl.*, cahotage, *m.*
Jonquil, s. jonquille, *f.*
Jostle, va. pousser, coudoyer
Jot, s. iota, *m.*, brin, *m.*
Jot (down), va. prendre note de
Jotting, s. note, *f.*, remarque, *f.*
Journal, s. journal, *m.*
Journalism, s. journalisme, *m.*, presse, *f.*
Journalist, s. journaliste, *m.*
Journey, s. voyage, *m.* *On a —*, en voyage. *A pleasant — to you!* bon voyage!
Journey, vn. voyager, aller
Journeyman, s. ouvrier, *m.*, journalier, *m.*, compagnon, *m.*
Joust, s. joute, *f.*
Joust, vn. jouter
Jovial, adj. jovial, gai, joyeux, enjoué, réjoui, gaillard
Joviality, s. gaieté, *f.*
Jovially, adv. joyeusement
Jowl, s. joue, *f.*
Joy, s. joie, *f.*, plaisir, *m.* *To give — to*, faire plaisir à, féliciter
Joyful, adj. joyeux, heureux
Joyfully, adv. joyeusement
Joyfulness, s. joie, *f.*, gaieté, *f.*, humeur joyeuse, *f.*
Joyless, adj. triste
Joyous, *see* Joyful
Jubilant, adj. triomphant, de joie
Jubilation, s. triomphe, *m.*, allégresse, *f.*
Jubilee, s. jubilé, *m.*, (*fig.*) allégresse, *f.*
Judaic, Judaical, adj. judaïque
Judaism, s. judaïsme, *m.*
Judge, s. juge, *m.*, appréciateur, *m.*, connaisseur, *m.* *To be a — of*, se connaître en *or* à
Judge, va. n. juger
Judgment, s. jugement, *m.*, avis, *m.*
Judicature, s. judicature, *f.*, justice, *f.*, cour de justice, *f.*
Judicial, adj. judiciaire, juridique
Judicially, adv. judiciairement, juridiquement
Judicious, adj. judicieux
Judiciously, adv. judicieusement
Judiciousness, s. nature judicieuse, *f.*, sagesse, *f.*
Jug, s. cruche, *f.*, cruchon, *m.*, aiguière, *f.*, pot à eau, *m.*
Juggle, vn. escamoter, faire des tours de passe-passe, (*fig.*) duper; — va. duper, jouer. *— away*, escamoter
Juggle, s. jonglerie, *f.*, tour de passe-passe *or* d'escamotage, *m.*, duperie, *f.*, jonglerie, *f.*
Juggler, s. jongleur, *m.*, escamoteur, *m.*, joueur de gobelets, *m.*, fourbe, *m.*
Jugular, adj. jugulaire
Jugular, s. jugulaire, *f.*
Juice, s. jus, *m.*, suc, *m.*
Juiceless, adj. sans jus, sans suc
Juiciness, s. nature juteuse, *f.*, abondance de jus, *f.*
Juicy, adj. juteux, plein de jus *or* de suc
Jujube, s. jujube, *m.* *—-tree*, jujubier
Julep, s. julep, *m.*
July, s. juillet, *m.*
Jumble (together), va. mêler *or* entasser confusément, jeter pêle-mêle, confondre, brouiller
Jumble, s. mélange confus, *m.*, pêle-mêle, *m.*, confusion, *f.*
Jump, vn. sauter, bondir, (*at*) saisir avec empressement, (*with*) s'accorder (avec), se rencontrer (avec)
Jump, s. saut, *m.*, bond, *m.*, (*fig.*) coup, *m.*, hasard, *m.*
Jumper, s. sauteur, *m.*, -euse, *f.*
Junction, s. jonction, *f.*
Juncture, s. jointure, *f.*, (*fig.*) union, *f.*, conjoncture, *f.*
June, s. juin, *m.*

Junior, adj. s. le plus jeune, cadet. *A — clerk*, un des plus jeunes commis

Junior, s. frère cadet, *m.*, sœur cadette, *f.*, personne plus jeune qu'une autre, celui qui est moins ancien

Juniper, s. genièvre, *m.* — *-berry*, baie de genévrier, *f.* — *-tree*, genévrier, *m.*

Junk, s. jonque, *f.*

Junket, s. partie fine, *f.*

Junket, vn. festiner, aller *or* être en partie fine

Junta, s. junte, *f.*

Juridical, adj. juridique

Juridically, adv. juridiquement

Jurisconsult, s. jurisconsulte, *m.*

Jurisdiction, s. juridiction, *f.*

Jurisprudence, s. jurisprudence, *f.*

Jurist, s. juriste, *m.*

Juror, s. juré, *m.*

Jury, s. jury, *m.*, jurés, *m. pl.* — *-box*, banc du jury

Juryman, s. juré, *m.*

Jurymast, s. mât de fortune, *m.*

Just, adj. juste, régulier, bien ordonné

Just, adv. juste, justement, précisément, (*almost*) juste, tout juste, sur le point de. — so, précisément. *To have — or but —*, venir de. — *now*, il n'y a qu'un instant, tout à l'heure. *But —*, à l'instant, à peine. — *come and see*, venez un peu voir. — *tell me*, dites-moi un peu

Justice, s. justice, *f.*, (*pers.*) juge, *m.*, magistrat, *m.* — *of the peace*, magistrat, *m.*, juge de paix, *m.*

Justifiable, adj. légitime, justifiable

Justifiably, adv. de manière à pouvoir se justifier

Justification, s. justification, *f.*

Justificative, adj. justificatif

Justifier, s. justificateur, *m.*, qui justifie, *m.*, défenseur, *m.*

Justify, va. justifier, autoriser, permettre, donner le droit

Justle, va. *see* JOSTLE

Justle, s. choc, *m.*

Justly, adv. justement, avec justice, avec raison

Justness, s. justice, *f.*, (*correctness*) justesse, *f.*, exactitude, *f.*, convenance, *f.*

Jut, vn. faire saillie, être en saillie, avancer, s'avancer, se projeter, sortir de l'alignement. *To — upon*, se projeter sur

Jut, s. saillie, *f.*

Jute, s. chanvre de l'Inde, *f.*

Jutting, adj. en saillie

Jutting, s. saillie, *f.*

Juvenile, adj. jeune, de jeunesse, juvénile

K

K, s. K, k, *m.*

Kale, s. chou, *m.* *Sea- —*, chou de mer, *m.*

Kaleidoscope, s. kaléidoscope, *m.*

Keel, s. quille, *f.*, carène, *f.*

Keen, adj. affilé, tranchant, acéré, bien aiguisé, (*fig.*) ardent, empressé, (*sharp*) vif, âpre, pénétrant, piquant, (*sight*) perçant, (*ear*) fine, (*speech*) caustique, mordant, piquant, amer, (*wit*) pénétrant, fin, vif, subtil, (*appetite*) vif

Keenly, adv. avec un fil acéré *or* tranchant, vivement, ardemment, rudement, âprement, finement, amèrement

Keenness, s. tranchant, *m.*, nature acérée, *f.*, vivacité, *f.*, ardeur, *f.*, âpreté, *f.*, (*cold*) intensité, *f.*, nature pénétrante *or* piquante, *f.*, (*wit*) finesse, *f.*, nature mordante, *f.*; amertume, *f.*, vivacité, *f.*, pénétration, *f.*, sagacité, *f.*

Keep, va. garder, tenir, retenir, conserver, réserver, enfermer, veiller sur, protéger, (*observe*) accomplir, garder, suivre, obéir à, pratiquer, (*a school*) tenir, avoir, (*to support*) nourrir, (*a festival*) célébrer; — vn. se tenir, se maintenir, rester, loger, demeurer, (*fruits*) se garder, se conserver

Keep, s. donjon, *m.*, garde, *f.*, état, *m.*, condition, *f.*, (*board*) entretien, *m.*, nourriture, *f.*

Keeper, s. garde, *m.*, gardien, *m.*, garde-chasse, *m.*, (*museum*) conservateur, *m.*

Keeping, s. garde, *f.*, surveillance, *f.*, conservation, *f.*, entretien, *m.*, nourriture, *f.*, pension, *f.*, (*agreement*) accord, *m.*, unisson, *m.* *In — with*, en harmonie avec, à l'unisson de

Keepsake, s. souvenir, *m.*, gage d'amitié, *m.*

Keg, s. caque, *f.*, petit baril, *m.*

Ken, s. vue, *f.*, portée de la vue, *f.*

Kennel, s. chenil, *m.*, niche, *f.*, (*fox*) terrier, *m.*

Kept, past part. adj. entretenu

Kerb, s. — *-stone*, bord du trottoir, *m.*, parement, *m.*, (*of a well*) margelle, *f.*

Kerchief, s. coiffe, *f.*, fichu, *m.*, foulard, *m.*

Kermes, s. kermès, *m.*

Kernel, s. amande, *f.*, noyau, *m.*, (*of apples*) pepin, *m.*, (*of meat*) noix, *f.*, (*seed*) grain, *m.*

Kerseymere, s. casimir, *m.*

Ketch, s. quaiche, *f.*

Ketchup, s. *see* CATSUP

Kettle, s. bouilloire, bouillotte, *f.*, chaudière, *f.*, chaudron, *m.* *The — boils*, l'eau bout. — *-drum*, timbale, *f.* — *-drummer*, timbalier, *m.*

Key, s. clef, *f.*, (*of a piano*) touche, *f.*, (*embankment*) quai, *m.* — *-board*, clavier, *m.*

Keyed, past part. muni de sa clef

Kick, s. coup de pied, *m.*, (*of a horse*) ruade, *f.*, (*of a gun*) recul, *m.*

Kick, va. donner des coups de pied à, frapper avec le pied, lancer des ruades à; — vn. donner des coups de pied, ruer, regimber, reculer, repousser

Kid, s. chevreau, *m.*, chair de chevreau, *f.*, peau de chevreau, *f.*

Kidnap, va. enlever, voler

Kidnapper, s. auteur d'enlèvement, *m.*, voleur, *m.*

Kidnapping, s. enlèvement, *m.*

Kidney, s. rognon, *m.*, rein, *m.*, (*fig.*) acabit, *m.*, trempe, *f.* — *-bean*, haricot, *m.* — *-potato*, vitelotte, *f.*

Kilderkin, s. baril, *m.*

Kill, va. tuer, faire mourir, (*animals*) abattre

Killer, s. tueur, *m.*, meurtrier, *m.*, abatteur, *m.*

Kiln, s. four, *m.*

Kiln-dry, va. sécher au four

Kimbo, adj. courbé. *See* AKIMBO

Kin, s. parenté, *f.*, famille, *f.*, les proches, *m.pl.*, allié, *m.*, -ée, *f.*

Kin, adj. parent (de), allié (à), (*fig.*) analogue (à), qui tient (de)

Kind, adj. bon, aimable, bienveillant, obligeant, complaisant, tendre

Kind, s. race, *f.*, espèce, *f.*, genre, *m.*, sorte, *f.*, nature, *f.*, façon, *f.* *To pay in —*, payer en nature

Kindle, va. allumer, enflammer, embraser, exciter, irriter, éveiller, réveiller, vivifier; — vn. s'allumer, s'enflammer, prendre feu, brûler

Kindliness, s. bonté, *f.*, bienveillance, *f.*, bienfaisance, *f.*

Kindly, adj. bon, bienveillant, doux, (*things*) généreux

Kindly, adv. avec bonté, avec bienveillance, avec complaisance

Kindness, s. bonté, bienveillance, *f.*, amabilité, *f.*, indulgence, *f.*, service, *m.*

Kindred, s. parenté, *f.*, alliance, *f.*, parents, *m.pl.*, proches, *m.pl.*, espèce, *f.*, affinité, *f.*

Kindred, adj. de même famille, du même ordre, de même espèce, analogue, semblable, (*fig.*) sympathique

King, s. roi, *m.*, (*draughts*) dame, *f.* — *-post*, poinçon de comble, *m.*

Kingdom, s. royaume, *m.*, empire, *m.*, (*nat. hist.*) règne, *m.*

Kingfisher, s. martin-pêcheur, *m.*

Kingliness, s. air de roi, *m.*, caractère royal, *m.*

Kingly, adj. royal, de roi, comme un roi. — adv. royalement

Kinsman, s. parent, *m.*, allié, *m.*

Kinswoman, s. parente, *f.*, alliée, *f.*

Kiosk, s. kiosque, *m.*

Kiss, va. embrasser, baiser, (*fig.*) chérir, (*things*) caresser, effleurer

Kiss, s. baiser, *m.*, caresse, *f.* *A hearty —*, un gros baiser

Kissing, s. baiser, *m.* — *the Pope's foot*, baisement, *m.* *Hand- —*, baisemain, *m.* — *-crust*, baisure, *f.*

Kit, s. trousseau, *m.*, (*mus.*) pochette, *f.*, (*soldiers*) effets, *m.pl.*, (*tub*) bocal, *m.*, seau, *m.*, baquet, *m.*

Kitchen, s. cuisine, *f.* — *-garden*, jardin potager, *m.* — *-grate*, — *-range*, cuisine anglaise, *f.* — *-maid*, fille de cuisine, *f.*, laveuse de vaisselle, *f.* — *-stuff*, graisses, *f.pl.*

Kite, s. milan, *m.*, (*toy*) cerf volant, *m.*

Kitten, s. petit chat, *m.*, chaton, *m.*, petite chatte, *f.*

Kitten, vn. avoir des petits

Knack, s. babiole, *f.*, brimborion, *m.*, (*skill*) talent, *m.*, génie, *m.*, adresse, *f.*, tic, *m.*, chic, *m.*

Knacker, s. équarrisseur, *m.*

Knapsack, s. havresac, *m.*

Knave, s. (*cards*) valet, *m.*; fripon, *m.*, coquin, *m.*, drôle, *m.*

Knavery, Knavishness, s. fourberie, *f.*, friponnerie, *f.*

Knavish, adj. fourbe, (*fig.*) malin, fripon. — *trick*, fourberie, *f.*

Knavishly, adv. en fourbe

Knead, va. pétrir

Kneading, s. pétrissage, *m.* — *-trough*, pétrin, *m.*, huche à farine, *f.*

Knee, s. genou, *m.*, (*machines*) courbe, *f.*, coude, *m.* *On my —s, with bended —s*, à deux genoux. — *-cap*, — *-piece*, genouillère, *f.*

Kneed, adj qui a les genoux, aux genoux, (*techn.*) coudé. *Knock- —*, cagneux

Kneel (down), vn. s'agenouiller, se mettre à genoux

Kneeling, adj. à genoux

Kneeling, s. génuflexions, *f.pl.*

Knell, s. glas, *m.*

Knick-knack, s. babiole, *f.*, brimborion, *m.*, chinoiserie, *f.*

Knickerbockers, s. culotte bretonne, *f.*
Knife, s. couteau, *m.* *Dessert- —*, couteau à dessert, *m.* *Garden- —*, serpette, *f.* *Bring a — and fork*, apportez un couvert
Knight, s. chevalier, *m.*, (*chess*) cavalier, *m.*
Knight, va. faire *or* recevoir chevalier, décorer
Knighthood, s. chevalerie, *f.*
Knightly, adj. digne d'un chevalier, chevaleresque. — adv en chevalier, d'une manière chevaleresque
Knit, va. attacher, nouer, tricoter, tresser, joindre, (*brow*) froncer ; — vn. tricoter, se réunir, se rejoindre
Knitting, s. tricot, *m.*, (*fig.*) union étroite, *f.*
Knitting, adj. à tricoter, de tricot. — *-needle*, aiguille à tricoter, *f.*
Knob, s. bosse, *f.*, protubérance, *f.*, (*door*) bouton, *m.*, (*of a cane*) pomme, *f.*, (*of wood*) nœud, *m.*
Knobbed, Knobby, adj. plein de bosses, noueux
Knock, s. coup, *m.*
Knock, vn. frapper, heurter, cogner, se heurter, se cogner. *To — under*, céder, se soumettre. — va. frapper, cogner, heurter. *To — hard*, cogner ferme. *To — about*, frapper de tous côtés. *To — down*, terrasser, renverser, assommer, (*to*) adjuger (à). *To — in*, enfoncer, faire entrer. *To — off*, faire tomber, faire sauter, briser, (*work*) finir. *To — out*, faire sortir, faire tomber, (*an eye*) crever, (*the brains*) faire sauter *To — up*, réveiller, faire lever, (*to tire*) fatiguer, épuiser, éreinter
Knocker, s. marteau, *m.*
Knocking, s. coups, *m.pl.* *A loud —*, de grands coups
Knoll, s. tertre, *m.*, monticule, *m.*
Knot, s. nœud, *m.*, liens, *m.pl.*, (*puzzle*) difficulté, *f.*, (*plot*) intrigue, *f.*, (*crowd*) groupe, *m.*, cercle, *m.*, coterie, *f.*, (*shoulder*) épaulette, *f.*, aiguillette, *f.*
Knot, va. nouer, lier, unir, embrouiller ; — vn. faire des nœuds, se nouer
Knotted, adj. noué, noueux, plein de nœuds
Knotty, adj. noueux, plein de nœuds, (*fig.*) dur, difficile, épineux, embrouillé
Know, va. savoir, connaître, apprendre, reconnaître, s'entendre à, distinguer, avoir l'entente de ; — vn. savoir, ne pas ignorer, connaître, examiner, s'informer de. *For all I —*, que je sache. *I will let you —*, je vous le ferai savoir. *He —s better than . . .*, il est trop fin. *You must — best*, vous en êtes le meilleur juge. *Not that I — of*, pas que je sache
Knower, s. connaisseur, *m.*
Knowing, adj. instruit, intelligent, fin, habile, rusé. *A — look*, un air fin
Knowingly, adv. savamment, sciemment, avec connaissance de cause, finement, d'un air rusé
Knowledge, s. connaissance, *f.*, science, *f.*, savoir, *m.* *To my —*, à ma connaissance. *To the best of my —*, que je sache. *Without my —*, à mon insu
Knuckle, s. jointure, *f.*, articulation, *f.*, (*hinge*) charnière, *f.* — *-bone*, osselet, *m.* — *of ham*, jambonneau, *m.* — *of veal*, un jarret de veau, *m.*
Knuckle, va. battre. *To — under*, se soumettre, mettre les pouces
Koran, s. Coran, *m.*

L

L, s. L, l, *f.*
La! interj. allons! la! voyez donc! tiens! tenez!
La, s. (*mus.*) la, *m.*
Label, s. étiquette, *f.*, écriteau, *m.*
Label, va. étiqueter
Labial, adj. labial
Laboratory, s. laboratoire, *m.*
Laborious, adj. laborieux, travailleur, pénible
Laboriously, adv. laborieusement, péniblement
Laboriousness, s. caractère laborieux, *m.*, travail, *m.*, labeur, *m.*, difficulté, *f.*
Labour, s. travail, *m.*, labeur, *m.*, peine, *f.*, (*med.*) travail, *m.*, mal d'enfant, *m.* *Hard —*, travaux forcés
Labour, vn.a. travailler (à), se donner de la peine pour, peiner (à), (*fig.*) chercher (à), marcher péniblement, souffrir, (*med.*) être en mal d'enfant. *To — under*, souffrir de, être tourmenté de, être affligé de *or* par
Labourer, s. cultivateur, *m.*, laboureur, *m.*, ouvrier, *m.*, travailleur, *m.*, journalier, *m.*
Laburnum, s. cytise-aubour, *m.*, faux ébénier, *m.*
Labyrinth, s. labyrinthe, *m.*
Lac, s. laque, *f.*
Lace, s. dentelle, *f.*, point, *m.*, galon, *m.*, passementerie, *f.*, (*stays*) lacet, *m.* *French —*, point d'Alençon, *m.*
Lace, va. garnir de dentelles, galonner, lacer
Lacerate, va. déchirer, mutiler
Laceration, s. déchirement, *m.*, déchirure, *f.*, lacération, *f.*
Lachrymal, adj. lacrymal
Lachrymatory, s. lacrymatoire, *m.*
Lachrymose, adj. larmoyant, pitoyable
Lack, va. avoir besoin de, manquer de, n'avoir pas; — vn. manquer, être dans le besoin
Lack, s. besoin, *m.*, manque, *m.*, défaut, *m.*, absence, *f.*, (*in comp.*) qui manque de. *For — of*, faute de. *To be in — of*, manquer de. — *-brain*, tête sans cervelle, *f.* — *-land*, sans terre. — *-lustre*, terne, morne
Lackadaisical, adj. minaudier, larmoyant, sentimental
Lackaday! interj. hélas!
Lackey, s. laquais, *m.*, valet de pied, *m.*
Lackey, vn. suivre en laquais ; — va. servir, faire le valet auprès de
Laconic, Laconical, adj. laconique
Laconically, adv. laconiquement, avec laconisme
Laconism, s. laconisme, *m.*
Lacquer, s. vernisseur en laque, *m.*
Lacquer, va. vernisser en laque, vernir
Lad, s. jeune homme, *m.*, garçon, *m.*, enfant, *m.*, gaillard, *m.* *An honest —*, un brave garçon
Ladder, s. échelle, *f.*, escalier, *m.*
Lade, va. charger ; — vn. prendre son chargement, être en charge
Lading, s. chargement, *m.*
Ladle, s. cuiller à pot, *f.*, cuiller à potage, *f.*, louche, *f.*
Ladle (out), va. vider, puiser
Ladleful, s. cuillerée, *f.*
Lady, s. dame, *f.*, lady, *f.*, milady, *f.*, madame la . . ., maîtresse, *f.*, souveraine, *f.*, femme, *f.*, épouse, *f.* *Ladies and gentlemen*, messieurs et mesdames. *Young —*, demoiselle. — *-bird*, — *-bug*, — *-cow*, — *-fly*, coccinelle, *f.*, bête à bon Dieu, *f.* — *-day*, l'Annonciation, *f.* — *-killer*, homme à bonnes fortunes, *m.*, séducteur, *m.* — *-like*, distingué, de dame, comme il faut, élégant, délicat, féminin. *My — -love*, la dame de mes pensées
Ladyship, s. seigneurie, *f.*, madame la . . .
Lag, adj. tard, tardif, lent, dernier
Lag, vn. tarder, traîner, rester en arrière, marcher lentement, flâner
Laggard, Lagger, s. traînard, *m.*, lambin, *m.*
Lagoon, s. lagune, *f.*
Laic, Laical, adj. laïque
Laid, adj. posé, (*paper*) vergé. — *up*, alité
Lair, s. repaire, *m.*, tanière, *f.*, bauge, *f.*, lieu de repos, *m.*
Laity, s. laïques, *m.pl.*
Lake, s. lac, *m.*, (*colour*) laque, *f.*
Lama, s. lama, *m.*
Lamb, s. agneau, *m.*
Lamb, vn. agneler
Lambkin, s. petit agneau, *m.*, agnelet, *m.*
Lame, adj. boiteux, infirme, estropié, (*fig.*) imparfait, qui cloche. *To walk —*, boiter, clocher
Lame, va. rendre boiteux *or* boiteuse, estropier
Lamely, adv. en boitant, (*fig.*) imparfaitement, mal
Lameness, s. état d'être boiteux, *m.*, infirmité, *f.*, (*fig.*) imperfection, *f.*, défauts, *m.pl.*
Lament, vn. se lamenter, gémir ; — va. pleurer, déplorer
Lament, s. lamentation, *f.*, complainte, *f.*
Lamentable, adj. lamentable, déplorable
Lamentation, s. lamentation, *f.*
Lamp, s. lampe, *f.*, quinquet, *m.*, réverbère, *m.* *Argand —*, lampe d'Argand, *f.*, quinquet, *m.* *Foot —*, rampe, *f.* *Illumination —*, lampion, *m.* *Safety —*, lampe de sûreté, *f.* *Spirit —*, lampe d'esprit-de-vin, *f.* *Street —*, réverbère, *m.* — *-black*, s. adj. (de) noir de fumée, *m.* — *-lighter*, lampiste, *m.*, allumeur, *m.* — *-maker*, lampiste, *m.* — *-post*, candélabre à gaz, *m.* — *-stand*, dessous de lampe, *m.*
Lampoon, s. pasquinade, *f.*, satire personnelle, *f.*, libelle, *m.*
Lampoon, va. écrire une satire *or* une pasquinade sur, faire la satire de
Lampooner, s. auteur de pasquinades, *m.*
Lamprey, s. lamproie, *f.*
Lance, s. lance, *f.* — *-head*, tête de lance, *f.*
Lance, va. lancer, darder, percer, donner un coup de lancette à
Lancer, s. lancier, *m.*
Lancet, s. lancette, *f.* — *windows*, fenêtre en ogive, *f.*
Land, s. terre, *f.*, patrie, *f.*, pays, *m.*, bien-fonds, *m.*, propriété, *f.* *The dry —*, la terre ferme. *On —*, à terre

Land-...., adj. de terre, foncier. —*-ice*, s banc de glace qui tient au rivage, *m.* —*-wind*, s. vent de terre, *m.* —*-estate*, s. propriété foncière, *f.* —*-jobber*, s. spéculateur en terres, *m.* —*-lubber*, s. marin d'eau douce, *m.* —*-mark*, s. limite, *f.*, borne, *f.* —*-office*, s. bureau de cadastre, *m.* —*-owner*, s. propriétaire foncier, *m.* —*-rent*, s. rente foncière, *f.*, fermage, *m.* —*-steward*, s. intendant, *m.* —*-measuring*, —*-surveying*, s. arpentage, *m.* —*-surveyor*, s. arpenteur, *m.*, employé du cadastre, *m.* —*-tax*, s. impôt foncier, *m.*

Land, va.n. mettre à terre, débarquer, aborder

Landau, s. landau, *m.*

Landed, adj. foncier, en terre. *The — interest*, les propriétaires fonciers. —*men*, propriétaires fonciers. —*security*, hypothèque, *f.*

Landholder, s. propriétaire foncier, *m.*

Landing, s. débarquement, *m.*, atterrage, *m.*, (*archit.*) palier, *m.*, carré, *m.*, (*railway*) plate-forme, *f.*, gare, *f.*, (*quay*) débarcadère, *m.*

Landlady, s. propriétaire, *f.*, hôtesse, *f.*, femme d'aubergiste, *f.*, hôtellière, *f.*

Landlord, s propriétaire, *m.*, maître, *m.*, hôte, *m.*, aubergiste, *m.*, hôtellier, *m.*

Landrail, s. râle de genêt, *m.*

Landscape, s. paysage, *m.*, vue, *f.* —*-painter*, paysagiste, *m.*

Landslip, s. éboulement, *m.*

Landward, adv. vers la terre, du côté de la terre

Lane, s. ruelle, *f.*, (*in the country*) sentier, *m.*, chemin étroit, *m.*

Language, s. langage, *m.*, langue, *f.*, style, *m.*

Languid, adj. languissant

Languidly, adv. languissamment, langoureusement

Languidness, s. langueur, *f.*, lenteur, *f.*

Languish, vn. languir, regarder d'un air langoureux

Languishing, adj. languissant, langoureux

Languishingly, adv. languissamment, langoureusement

Lank, Lanky, adj. maigre, grêle, long, efflanqué, décharné, mou, flasque

Lankness, s. maigreur, *f.*, état flasque, *m.*

Lansquenet, s. lansquenet, *m.*

Lantern, s. lanterne, *f.*, falot, *m.*, (*nav.*) fanal, *m.*, phare, *m.* *Dark* —, lanterne sourde

Lap, s. pan, *m.*, giron, *m.*, tablier, *m.*, (*knees*) genoux, *m.pl.*, (*bosom*) sein, *m.*, (*arch.*) recouvrement, *m.*

Lap, va. plier, envelopper, rouler, mettre autour. (*water*) laper; — vn. se replier, retomber, recouvrir, laper. *To — over*, être à recouvrement, (*waistcoat*) croiser

Lapdog, s. petit chien, *m.*, bichon, *m.*

Lapful, s. plein les genoux *or* le tablier, *m.*

Lapidary, s. lapidaire, *m.*

Lappet, s. pan, *m.*, (*head-dress*) barbe, *f.*

Lapse, s. cours, *m.*, marche, *f.*, laps, *m.*, intervalle, *m.*, (*fault*) manquement, *m.*, faute, *f.*, écart, *m.*, (*law*) dévolution, *f.*

Lapse, vn. s'écouler, couler, tomber, se laisser aller (à), déchoir, manquer (à), (*law*) tomber en dévolu; — va. laisser tomber en dévolu

Lapwing, s. vanneau, *m.*

Larboard, s. bâbord, *m.* — adj. de bâbord

Larceny, s. vol, *m.*, larcin, *m.*

Larch, s. mélèze, *m.*

Lard, s. saindoux, *m.*, lard, *m.*

Lard, va. larder, graisser, engraisser, piquer

Larder, s. office, *f.*, dépense, *f.*

Larding-needle, Larding-pin, s. lardoire, *f.*

Large, adj. grand, gros, large, vaste, fort, nombreux, considérable. (*nav.*) largue. *At* —, en liberté, librement, en détail, en masse, en général

Largely, adv. grandement, largement, amplement

Largeness, s. grandeur, *f.*, grosseur, *f.*, étendue, *f.*, abondance, *f.*, ampleur, *f.*, libéralité, *f.*, générosité, *f.*

Largess, s. largesse, *f.*

Lark, s. alouette, *f.*, mauviette, *f.*, (*joke*) farce, *f.*, escapade, *f.*, (*pers.*) farceur, *m.* *Blithe as a* —, gai comme pinson. —*-spur*, —*'s-heel*, pied-d'alouette, *m.* *To have a* —, faire des farces, s'amuser

Larva, s. larve, *f.*

Larynx, s. larynx, *m.*

Lascivious, adj. lascif

Lasciviously, adv. lascivement

Lasciviousness, s. lasciveté, *f.*

Lash, s. laisse, *f.*, corde, *f.*, (*of a whip*) mèche, *f.*, fouet, *m.*, coup de fouet, *m.*, (*nav.*) coup de garcette, *m.*, (*fig.*) trait de satire, *m.*, sarcasme, *m.*, critique, *f.*

Lash, va.n. attacher, lier, (*nav.*) amarrer, (*whip*) fouetter, frapper, cingler, (*fig.*) flageller houspiller

Lashing, s. amarrage, *m.*, amarre, *f.*

Lass, s. jeune fille, *f.*, fillette, *f.*, fille, *f.*

Lassitude, s. lassitude, *f.*

Last, s. forme, *f.*

Last, adj. dernier, extrême, le plus haut. *The — but one*, l'avant-dernier. — *week*, la semaine dernière. — *night*, cette nuit, la nuit dernière. *For the — ten days*, depuis dix jours. *At* —, *at the* —, enfin, à la fin. *To the (very)* —, jusqu'à la fin, jusqu'au bout

Last, adv. la dernière fois, le dernier, en dernier lieu, enfin, dernièrement

Last, vn. durer. *To — out*, survivre à. — va. mettre sur la forme

Lasting, adj. durable, permanent

Lasting, s. durée, *f.*, (*shoemaker*) mise en forme, *f.*

Lastingly, adv. d'une manière durable, solidement

Lastly, adv. enfin, finalement, en dernier lieu

Latch, va. fermer au loquet

Latch, s. piége, *m.*, loquet, *m.* —*-key*, passe-partout, *m.*

Late, adj. tardif, en retard, (*hour*) avancé, (*former*) ancien, ex..., (*dead*) feu, défunt, décédé depuis peu, récent, dernier. *At a — hour*, une heure avancée. *The — queen*, feu la reine, la feue reine

Late, adv. tard, en retard, récemment, hier encore, naguère. *To get, to grow* —, se faire tard. *Don't be* —, ne venez par en retard. *Too — by five minutes*, en retard de cinq minutes. *Of* —, depuis peu

Lately, adv. récemment, dernièrement, il y a peu de temps, depuis peu

Lateness, s. heure avancée, *f.*, époque avancée, *f.*, retard, *m.*

Latent, adj. caché, secret, latent

Lateral, adj. latéral, de côté

Laterally, adv. latéralement

Latest, adj. *At the* —, au plus tard. *The — intelligence*, les dernières nouvelles

Lath, s. latte, *f.* —*-work*, lattis, *m.*

Lath, va. latter

Lathe, s. tour, *m.*

Lather, s. mousse de savon, *f.*, savon, *m.*, écume, *f.*

Lather, va. mousser, écumer; — vn. savonner, faire écumer

Latin, adj. latin, -e

Latin, s. latin, *m.*, la langue latine, *f.*

Latinism, s. latinisme, *m.*

Latinist, s. latiniste, *m.*

Latinity, s. latinité, *f.*

Latinize, va. latiniser

Latitude, s. latitude, *f.*, largeur, *f.*, étendue, *f.*

Latitudinarian, adj. s. latitudinaire

Latten, s. fer-blanc, *m.*, laiton, *m.* — *brass*, cuivre laminé, *m.*

Latter, adj. dernier, -ère, celui-ci, celle-ci, ceux-ci, celles-ci

Latterly, adv. dernièrement, récemment, depuis peu

Lattice, s. treillis, *m.*, treillage, *m.* —*-work*, treillis, *m.*, treillage, *m.*

Lattice, va. treillisser

Laudable, adj. louable

Laudably, adv. d'une manière louable

Laudanum, s. laudanum, *m.*

Laudative, Laudatory, adj. louangeur, laudatif

Laugh, vn. rire, sourire. *To — the other or the wrong side of one's mouth*, rire jaune. *To — in one's sleeve*, rire dans sa barbe *or* sous cape. — va. rire de

Laugh, s. rire, *m.*, risée, *f.* *To have the — of*, rire aux dépens de

Laughable, adj. risible

Laugher, s. rieur, *m.*, rieuse, *f.*

Laughing, adj. riant, rieur, plein de gaieté, risible. —*-stock*, jouet, *m.*, risée, *f.*, plastron, *m*

Laughingly, adv. en riant

Laughter, s. rire, *m.*, hilarité, *f.* *Fit of* —, accès de rire, *m.*

Launch, va. lancer, darder, mettre à la mer; — vn. lancer un navire, (*fig.*) se lancer, se jeter

Launch, s. mise à l'eau, *f.*, chaloupe, *f.*

Laundress, s. blanchisseuse, *f.*

Laundry, s. buanderie, *f.*, blanchissage, *m.*

Laureate, adj. lauréat

Laurel, s. laurier, *m.*

Laurel, adj. de laurier

Laurelled, adj. couronné de lauriers

Laurustine, s. laurier sauvage, *m.*, laurier-tin, *m.*

Lava, s. lave, *f.*

Lavender, s. lavande, *f.*

Lavish, adj. prodigue

Lavish, va. prodiguer

Lavisher, s. prodigue, *m.*

Lavishly, adv. avec prodigalité

Lavishness, s. prodigalité, *f.*

Law, s. loi, *f.*, règle, *f.*, règlement, *m.*, droit, *m.*, jurisprudence, *f.*, justice, *f.*, robe, *f.*, les gens de robe, *f. pl.*, barreau, *m.* *To be* —, faire loi, avoir force de loi. *To be at* —, être en procès. *To go to* —, poursuivre en justice. *To take the — into one's own hands*, se faire justice soi-même. *The — of nations*, le droit des gens *To study* —, faire son droit. —*-expenses*, frais de procédure, *m.* —*-giver*, —*-maker*, législateur, *m.* —*-officer*, officier de justice, *m.* —*-suit*, procès, *m.*, action, *f.* —*-term*, terme de palais, *m.*

Lawful, adj. légal, légitime, permis

Lawfully, adv. légalement, légitimement

Lawfulness, s. légalité, *f.*, légitimité, *f.*

Lawless, adj. illégal, arbitraire, (*fig.*) effréné, déréglé, désordonné

Lawlessly, adv. illégale-

ment, sans loi, arbitrairement, sans frein
Lawlessness, s. illégalité, *f.*, dérèglement, *m.*, licence, *f.*
Lawn, s. pelouse, *f.*, (*linen*) batiste, *f.*, linon, *m.*, (*bishop*) robe, *f.*, l'épiscopat, *m.*
Lawyer, s. homme de loi, *m.*, jurisconsulte, *m.*, avocat, *m.*
Lawyerly, adj. d'avocat, judiciaire
Lax, adj. lâche, flasque, mou, (*morals*) relâché
Laxative, adj. s. laxatif, *m.*
Laxity, s. peu de tension, *m.*, peu de consistance, *m.*, relâchement, *m.*, peu d'exactitude, *m.*
Lay, va. poser, mettre, placer, coucher, étendre, (*agric.*) marcotter, (*eggs*) pondre, (*com.*) verser, (*grass*) coucher, (*to strike*) abattre, (*dust*) abattre, (*to calm*) apaiser, calmer, (*to punish*) infliger, (*ascribe*) imputer, attribuer, (*nets*) tendre, (*bets*) parier. *To — across*, mettre en travers de, placer en croix. *To — along*, étendre le long de, étendre de toute sa longueur. *To — away*, ôter, quitter. *To — before*, soumettre à, mettre sous les yeux de, représenter à. *To — by*, serrer, déposer, mettre de côté, congédier, économiser. *To — down*, poser à terre, déposer, donner, quitter, renoncer à, établir. *To — forth*, étendre, ensevelir. *To — in*, faire provision de, amasser. *To — on*, appliquer, imposer, surfaire, écorcher. *To — out*, étendre, déployer, disposer, ensevelir, dépenser, (*grounds*) tracer, dessiner, planter. *To — over*, s'étendre sur, couvrir de. *To — up*, serrer, amasser, mettre de côté, aliter, (*agric.*) laisser reposer; — vn. pondre. *To — about*, frapper à droite et à gauche, frapper de tous côtés. *To — at*, vouloir percer. *To — on*, frapper fort, battre. *To — out* (*for* . . .), chercher, se proposer, dépenser
Lay, s. lai, *m.*, chant, *m.*
Lay, adj. laïque
Layer, s. qui pose, etc., poule qui pond, *f.*, (*geol.*) couche, *f.*, lit, *m.*, assise, *f.*, (*agric.*) marcotte, *f.*
Laying, s. mise, *f.*, pose, *f.*, ponte, *f.* *The — on of hands*, l'imposition des mains
Layman, s. laïque, *m.*
Laystall, s. fumier, *m.*, vacherie, *f.*
Lazaretto, s. lazaret, *m.*, hôpital, *m.*
Lazily, adv. paresseusement, dans la paresse
Laziness, s. paresse, *f.*, fainéantise, *f.*, indolence, *f.*
Lazy, adj. paresseux, lent, fainéant, indolent
Lead, s. plomb, *m.*, (*nav.*) sonde, *f.*, (*roof*) toiture, *f.*, (*pencil*) mine de plomb, *f.*, (*print.*) interligne, *f.*
Lead, adj. de plomb
Lead, va. plomber, couvrir *or* garnir de plomb, (*print.*) interligner
Lead, va.n. mener, conduire, guider, diriger, amener, engager, porter, faire, induire. *To — along*, conduire, mener. *To — away or off*, emmener, entraîner. *To — back*, ramener, reconduire. *To — down*, conduire, faire descendre. *To — forth or out*, conduire dehors, mener, amener, faire sortir. *To — on*, conduire, entraîner. *To — up*, conduire, faire monter *or* avancer, précéder
Lead, s. devants, *m.pl.*, conduite, *f.*, commandement, *m.*, direction, *f.*, influence, *f.*, préséance, *f.*, pas, *m.*, (*cards*) la main, *f.* *To take the —*, marcher le premier *or* en tête, présider
Leaden, adj. de plomb, en plomb, (*fig.*) lourd, accablant
Leader, s. guide, *m.*, conducteur, *m.*, conductrice, *f.*, chef, *m.*, commandant, *m.*, premier, *m.*, -ère, *f.*, meneur, *m.*, (*mus.*) chef, *m.*, (*news*) premier Londres, *m.*, premier Paris, *m.*, article principal, *m.*, (*horse*) cheval de volée, *m.*
Leadership, s. conduite, *f.*, direction, *f.*
Leading, adj. qui conduit, principal, premier. *— man*, chef, homme important. *— strings*, lisière, *f.* *— article*, article de fond, *m.*
Leading, s. conduite, *f.*, direction, *f.*
Leaf, s. feuille, *f.*, feuillage, *m.*, (*book*) feuillet, *m.*, (*door*) battant, *m.*, (*table*) rallonge, *f.* *To turn down a —*, faire une corne à un feuillet. *To turn over a new —*, (*fig.*) changer de conduite
Leafless, adj. sans feuilles, dépourvu de feuilles, nu, effeuillé
Leafy, adj. couvert de feuilles, feuillu
League, s. ligue, *f.*, (*distance*) lieue, *f.*
League, vn. se liguer
Leaguer, s. ligueur, *m.*, ligueuse, *f.*
Leak, s. fuite, *f.*, filtration, *f.*, perte d'eau, *f.*, voie d'eau, *f.* *To spring a —*, faire eau
Leak, vn. couler, fuir, (*nav.*) faire eau
Leakage, s. fuite, *f.*, perte, *f.*, filtration, *f.*, voie d'eau, *f.*
Leaky, adj. qui fuit, qui coule, qui prend l'eau
Lean, vn. pencher, se pencher, incliner, s'incliner, s'appuyer
Lean, adj. maigre, décharné, amaigri, mesquin. *To grow —*, maigrir, s'amaigrir
Lean, s. maigre, *m.*, du maigre, *m.*
Leaning, adj. penché, qui soutient
Leaning, s. action de pencher, *m.*, penchant, *m.*, tendance, *f.*
Leanness, s. maigreur, *f.*
Leap, vn. sauter, bondir, s'élancer, se précipiter
Leap, s. saut, *m.*, bond, *m.* *— -frog*, saute-mouton, *m.* *— -year*, année bissextile, *f.*
Learn, va.n. apprendre, s'instruire, prendre des leçons
Learned, adj. savant, instruit, docte, (*in*) versé (dans), habile (dans), expérimenté (dans)
Learnedly, adv. savamment, doctement
Learner, s. celui, celle qui apprend, commençant, commençante, élève, *m.f.*, écolier, *m.*, -ère, *f.*
Learning, s. savoir, *m.*, science, *f.*, connaissances, *f.pl.*, instruction, *f.*
Lease, s. bail, *m.*, terme, *m.*, durée, *f.*
Lease, va. louer à bail, affermer
Leasehold, s. tenure à bail, *f.* — adj. tenu à bail
Leaseholder, s. locataire à bail, *m.*
Leash, s. laisse, *f.*
Least, adj. s. le moindre, le plus petit. — adv. s. (le) moins. *At —*, au moins, du moins, pour le moins. *Not in the —*, pas le moins du monde
Leather, s. cuir, *m.*, peaux, *f.pl.* *Upper —*, empeigne, *f.* *— -dresser*, corroyeur, *m.*, mégissier, *m.* *— -seller*, marchand de cuirs, *m.* *— trade*, commerce des cuirs, *m.*
Leather, adj. de cuir, de peau
Leathery, adj. comme le cuir
Leave, s. permission, *f.*, adieu, *m.*, congé, *m.*
Leave, va. laisser, quitter, partir de, cesser, (*to*) s'en remettre (à), laisser faire (à). *To be left till called for*, poste restante, bureau restant. *To — about*, laisser traîner. *To — off*, cesser de, quitter, cesser de porter, renoncer à, abandonner. *To — short*, laisser inachevé. *To — out*, omettre, oublier, supprimer. — vn. cesser, quitter, partir
Leaved, adj. aux feuilles . . ., (*door*) à . . . battants, (*table*) à . . . rallonges
Leaven, s. levain, *m.*, levûre, *f.*
Leaven, va. faire lever, (*fig.*) aigrir, corrompre
Leavening, s. levain, *m.*, fermentation, *f.*
Leavings, s.pl. restes, *m.pl.*, débris, *m.pl.*
Lecher, s. libertin, *m.*
Lecherous, adj. lascif, débauché
Lectern, s. lutrin, *m.*
Lecture, s. leçon, *f.*, (*sermon*) sermon, *m.*, prêche, *f.*, prône, *f.*, (*scolding*) mercuriale, *f.*, réprimande, *f.*, (*fam.*) semonce, *f.* *To give a course of —s on* . . ., faire un cours de . . . *— -room*, salle de cours, *f.* *To read a — to*, faire une semonce à, morigéner
Lecture, va.n. faire un cours (à), chapitrer, faire une morale (à)
Lecturer, s. professeur, *m.*, orateur, *m.*, prédicateur, *m.*
Lectureship, s. chaire, *f.*
Lecturing, s. cours public, *m.*, leçons publiques, *f.pl.*, semonce, *f.*
Ledge, s. rebord, *m.*, bord, *m.*, (*archit.*) filet, *m.*, (*rocks*) banc, *m.*, écueil, *m.*, récif, *m.*
Ledger, s. grand-livre, *m.*, registre, *m.*
Lee, s. côté sous le vent, *m.*, lie, *f.*
Lee, adj. sous le vent. *— -way*, dérive, *f.*
Leech, s. sangsue, *f.*
Leek, s. poireau, *m.*, porreau, *m.*
Leer, s. œillade, *f.*, regard, *m.*
Leer, vn. (*at, on, upon*) regarder de côté, lancer des œillades à
Lees, s.pl. lie, *f.*
Leeward, s. adj. sous le vent
Left, adj. s. gauche, reste. *— -handed*, gaucher. *— off*, de rebut
Leg, s. jambe, *f.*, (*animals*) patte, *f.*, (*table*) pied, *m.*, (*fowl*) cuisse, *f.*, (*mutton*) gigot, *m.*, (*beef*) trumeau, *m.*, (*boots*) tige, *f.* *Black —*, (*fig.*) grec, *m.*, escroc, *m.*
Legacy, s. legs, *m.* *Contingent —*, legs éventuel
Legal, adj légal, juridique
Legality, s. légalité, *f.*
Legalization, s. légalisation, *f.*
Legalize, va. rendre légal, régulariser, légitimer
Legally, adv. légalement
Legate, s. légat, *m.*
Legatee, s. légataire, *m.*
Legation, s. légation, *f.*
Legend, s. légende, *f.*, vieille chronique, *f.*
Legendary, adj. légendaire, de légende, fabuleux, romanesque
Legerdemain, s. tour de passe-passe, *m.*, tour d'adresse, *m.*
Legged, adj. à jambes . . ., à pieds . . .
Legging, s. guêtre, *f.*
Leghorn, s. paille d'Italie, *f.*
Legibility, Legibleness, s. caractère lisible, *m.*, d'un caractère facile à lire
Legible, adj. lisible, qui se lit
Legibly, adv. lisiblement
Legion, s. légion, *f.*
Legislate, va. faire des lois
Legislation, s. législation, *f.*
Legislative, adj. législatif
Legislator, s. législateur, *m.*
Legislature, s. législature, *f.*

Legitimacy, s. légitimité, *f.*
Legitimate, adj. légitime
Legitimate, va. légitimer
Legitimately, adv. légitimement
Legitimation, s. légitimation, *f.*
Legitimist, s. légitimiste, *m.*
Leguminous, adj. légumineux
Leisure, s. loisir, *m.*, liberté, *f.*, temps, *m.* *At —*, à loisir. *To be at —*, avoir du loisir, avoir le temps
Leisure, adj. de loisir. *— hours*, moments perdus
Leisurely, adv. à loisir. — adj. fait à loisir
Lemon, s. citronnier, *m.*, (*fruit.*) citron, *m.*, limon, *m.*
Lemonade, s. limonade, *f.*
Lend, va. prêter, louer
Lender, s. prêteur, *m.*, -euse, *f.*
Lending, s. prêt, *m.*
Length, s. longueur, *f.*, longue durée, *f.*, étendue, *f.*, point, *m.*, degré, *m.*, carrière, *f.* *To be six feet in —*, avoir six pieds de long *or* de longueur. *At —*, tout au long, enfin, à la fin, à la longue *At full —*, tout au long, dans toute sa longueur. *A full —*, *a whole — portrait*, un portrait en pied. *At great —*, fort au long. *At some —*, assez longuement. *More at —*, plus au long
Lengthen, va. rallonger, allonger, étendre ; — vn. s'allonger, se rallonger, se prolonger, s'étendre
Lengthiness, s. longueurs, *f.pl.*
Lengthy, adj. long, assez long
Lenience, Leniency, see LENITY
Lenient, adj. doux, clément, indulgent, (*med.*) lénitif
Leniently, adv. avec douceur, avec indulgence
Lenitive, adj *s* lénitif, *m.*
Lenity, s. douceur, *m.*, clémence, *f.*, indulgence. *f.*
Lens, s. lentille, *f.*, verre lenticulaire, *m.*
Lent, s. carême, *m.* *To keep —*, faire carême
Lenticular, adj. lenticulaire
Lentil, s. lentille, *f.*
Lentisk, s. lentisque, *m.*
Leonine, adj. de lion, léonin
Leopard, s. léopard, *m.*
Leper, s. lépreux, *m.*, lépreuse, *f.*, ladre, *m.*
Leprosy, s. lèpre, *f.*
Leprous, adj. lépreux
Less, adj. moindre, plus petit, inférieur
Less, adv. moins. *— and —*, de moins en moins. *The —*, moins, d'autant moins. *For — than*, à moins de. *With —*, avec moins, à moins
Lessee, s. locataire à bail, *m.*
Lessen, vn.a. amoindrir, diminuer
Lesson, s. leçon, *f.*, semonce, *f.* *Private —*, leçon particulière, *f.*, répétition, *f.*
Lessor, s. bailleur, *m.*, -eresse, *f.*
Lest, conj. de peur que . . . ne, de crainte que . . . ne, de peur de
Let, va. laisser, permettre à, souffrir, louer. *To — a person have*, donner à quelqu'un. *To be —*, à louer. *To — out coaches*, louer des voitures. *— alone*, à part, sans compter, encore bien moins. *To — be*, laisser tranquille, ne pas se mêler de. *To — down*, laisser descendre, descendre, faire descendre, baisser, rabaisser, rabattre, (*mar.*) lâcher, (*prices*) réduire. *To — oneself down*, descendre, se laisser couler. *To — forth*, faire sortir. *To — in*, admettre, laisser entrer, ouvrir la porte à. *To — off*, relâcher, laisser partir, faire grâce à, faire partir, (*fireworks, &c.*) tirer. *To — out*, laisser sortir, faire sortir, laisser partir, (*a secret*) laisser échapper, (*extend*) élargir, (*on hire*) louer. *To — (a person) up*, laisser monter
Let, s. empêchement, *m.*
Lethargic, adj. léthargique
Lethargy, s. léthargie, *f.*
Letter, s. lettre, *f.*, caractère, *m.*, lettres, *f.pl.*, belles-lettres, *f.pl.* *— -case*, (*print.*) casse, *f.* *— -press*, impression typographique, *f.*
Lettered, adj. lettré, littéraire, (*books*) avec couverture imprimée
Lettering, s. titre, *m.*
Lettuce, s. laitue, *f.* *Cos —*, romaine, *f.*
Levee, s. lever, *m.*, réception, *f.* *To hold a —*, recevoir
Level, adj. au niveau (de), de niveau (avec), à fleur (de), horizontal, uni, plat
Level, s. niveau, *m.*, surface unie, *f.*, (*fig.*) plan, *m.*, règle, *f.* *On a — with the water*, à fleur d'eau. *Dead —*, niveau parfait, *m.*
Level, va.n. niveler, mettre de niveau avec, unir, aplanir, (*aim*) darder, lancer, (*a blow*) diriger, porter, (*gun*) pointer. *To — with the dust*, renverser jusqu'à terre, raser. *To — a gun (at)*, coucher en joue
Leveller, s. niveleur, *m.*
Levelling, s. nivellement, *m.*, aplanissement, *m.*, pointage, *m.*
Lever, s. levier, *m.*
Leveret, s. levraut, *m.*
Leviathan, s. léviathan, *m.*
Levite, s. lévite, *m.*
Levitical, adj. lévitique, des lévites
Leviticus, s. Lévitique, *m.*
Levity, s. légèreté, *f.*
Levy, va. lever, (*taxes*) imposer
Levy, s. levée, *f.*
Lewd, adj. impudique, abandonné, dissolu, libertin
Lewdly, adv. impudiquement
Lewdness, s. libertinage, *m.*, luxure, *f.*
Lexicographer, s. lexicographe, *m.*
Lexicographic, adj. lexicographique
Lexicography, s. lexicographie, *f.*
Lexicology, s. lexicologie, *f.*
Lexicon, s. lexique, *m.*, dictionnaire, *m.*
Liability, s. responsabilité, *f.*, danger (de), *m.*, (*to*) état d'être passible, *m.*, (*com.*) engagements, *m.pl.*, passif, *m.*
Liable, adj. responsable, exposé, sujet
Liar, s. menteur, *m.*, -euse, *f.*
Libation, s. libation, *f.*
Libel, s. libelle, *m.*, (*law*) diffamation par écrit, *f.*
Libel, va. faire un libelle contre, diffamer
Libeller, s. libelliste, *m.*, diffamateur, *m.*
Libellous, adj. diffamatoire
Liberal, adj. libéral, large, libre, copieux, abondant
Liberalism, s. libéralisme, *m.*
Liberality, s. libéralité, *f.*, candeur, *f.*
Liberally, adv. libéralement, avec un esprit libéral, largement
Liberate, va. mettre en liberté, élargir, délivrer, libérer
Liberation, s. élargissement, *m.*, délivrance, *f.*, affranchissement, *m.*, libération, *f.*
Liberator, s. libérateur, *m.*
Libertine, s. adj. libertin, *m.*, -e, *f.*
Libertinism, s. libertinage, *m.*
Liberty, s. liberté, *f.*, permission, *f.*, familiarité, *f.* *At —*, en liberté, libre. *To take liberties with*, se permettre des licences avec
Librarian, s. bibliothécaire, *m.*
Library, s. bibliothèque, *f.*
Licence, s. licence, *f.*, permission, *f.*, (*tradesmen*) patente, *f.*, brevet, *m.*, (*marriage*) dispense, *f.* *— to shoot*, port d'armes, *m.* *Shooting —*, permis de chasse, *m.*
License, va. autoriser, accorder un permis, une patente, un brevet, etc.
Licentiate, s. licencié, *m.*
Licentious, adj. licencieux, déréglé
Licentiously, adv. licencieusement
Licentiousness, s. licence, *f.*, dérèglement, *m.*
Lichen, s. lichen, *m.*
Lick, va. lécher, (*thrash*) rosser. *To — the dust*, mordre la poussière. *To — up*, lécher, dévorer
Licking, s. action de lécher, *f.*, (*thrashing*) volée de coups, *f.*, raclée, *f.*
Lictor, s. licteur, *m.*
Lid, s. couvercle, *m.* *Eye —*, paupière, *f.*
Lie, s. mensonge, *m.*, fausseté, *f.*, fiction, *f.* *To give the — to*, donner le démenti à, démentir
Lie, vn. mentir, (*to — stretched out*) être couché *or* étendu, être posé *or* couché, se reposer, (*to lean*) s'appuyer, (*to be*) être, se trouver, être placé *or* situé, exister, (*ships*) être mouillé, (*to depend*) dépendre (de), consister. *Here —s*, ci-gît, ici repose. *To — hid*, rester caché. *As much as in us —s*, autant qu'il est en nous. *To — about*, être posé çà et là, traîner partout. *To — by*, se reposer, rester sans emploi, être tenu en réserve. *To — down*, se coucher, se reposer, être couché. *To — in*, accoucher, faire ses couches. *To — over*, être remis, rester en suspens, n'être pas payé à l'échéance. *To — to*, (*mar.*) être, rester, mettre en panne. *To — under*, être sujet *or* exposé à, avoir à supporter de, être sous le coup
Lien, s. droit de retenir comme gage, *m.*
Lieu, s. lieu, *m.* *In — of*, au lieu de
Lieutenancy, s. grade de lieutenant, *m.*, lieutenance, *f.*
Lieutenant, s. lieutenant, *m.*
Lieve, adv. volontiers
Life, s. vie, *f.*, vivacité, *f.*, animation, *f.*, âme, *f.*, (*paint.*) nature, *f.*, (*pers.*) personne, *f.*, (*society*) monde, *m.*, société, *f.* *Appointed for —*, nommé à vie, inamovible. *For —*, (*law*) à perpétuité. *For the — of me*, quand il s'agirait de ma vie, pour rien au monde. *Larger than —*, plus grand que nature. *To the —*, d'une ressemblance parfaite. *Three —s were lost*, trois personnes périrent. *High —*, le grand monde. *— -boat*, s. *— -buoy*, s. bateau de sauvetage, *m.*, bouée de sauvetage, *f.* *— -estate*, s. bien viager, *m.* *— -giving*, adj. vivifiant. *— -guard*, s. garde du corps, *m.* *— -interest*, s. *— -rent*, s. usufruit, *m.*, rente viagère, *f.* *— -like*, adj comme la vie, animé. *— -line*, s. garde-fou, *m.*, garde-corps, *m.* *— -preserver*, s. appareil de sauvetage, *m.*, (*a weapon*) casse-tête, *m.*, assommoir, *m.*
Lifeless, adj. sans vie, inanimé
Lift, va. lever, soulever, hausser, enlever, dresser, relever, (*fig.*) exalter, enorgueillir, (*to rob*) piller, voler
Lift, s. action de lever, *f.*, de soulever, *f.*, coup de main,

m., coup d'épaule, *m.*, (*nav.*) balancine, *f.* *To give a* —, donner un coup d'épaule à, prendre dans sa voiture. — *-lock*, s. écluse, *f.*
Lifter, s. qui lève, *m.*, voleur, *m.*, voleuse, *f.*
Ligament, s. ligament, *m.*
Ligature, s. ligature, *f.*, liaison, *f.*
Light, s. lumière, *f.*, luminaire, *m.*, flambeau, *m.*, clarté, *f.*, lueur, *f.*, jour, *m.*, aspect, *m.*, face, *f.*, point, *m.*, (*nav.*) phare, *m.*, fanal, *m.* *To strike a* —, battre le briquet. *Blue* —*s*, feux de Bengale, *m.pl.* *Northern* —*s*, aurore boréale, *f.* *To give a* — *to*, donner de la lumière à, éclairer. *To be* —, faire jour. *To bring to* —, amener, produire, mettre au jour. *To come to* —, se faire jour, se savoir, se découvrir. *To stand in one's own* —, être dans son jour, (*fig.*) faire du tort *or* se nuire à soi-même. *Would you oblige me with a* —? (*smoking*) voulez-vous être assez bon pour me donner du feu? — *-house*, s. phare, *m.* — *-ship*, s. phare flottant, *m.*
Light, adj. clair, éclairé, (*hair*) blond, (*humour*) léger, facile, gai. — *of cash*, léger d'argent. *A* — *guinea*, une guinée qui n'a pas le poids, faible. *To be* — *-headed*, être étourdi, (*med.*) battre la campagne. — *-hearted*, heureux, gai. — *-horse*, cavalerie légère, chevau-léger
Light, adv. légèrement, à la légère. *To make* — *of*, traiter légèrement, faire peu de cas de, dédaigner
Light, va. allumer, (*a fire*) faire, (*to give light, &c.*) éclairer, illuminer. *To* — *up*, illuminer, éclairer, (*features, &c.*) animer. — vn. s'allumer, brûler, s'animer, s'enflammer, (*on*) tomber (sur), trouver par hasard, rencontrer, (*birds, &c.*) s'abattre, se poser. *To* — *down, off*, descendre (de)
Lighten, vn. éclairer, faire des éclairs, étinceler, (*weather*) s'éclaircir. *To* — *up*, s'animer. — va. éclairer, illuminer, (*burden*) alléger, décharger, soulager
Lighter, s. allumeur, *f.*, (*boat*) allége, *f.*
Lighterman, s. gabarier, *m.*
Lightly, adv. légèrement, de son pied léger, galment, allégrement. *To think* — *of*, faire peu de cas de
Lightness, s. légèreté, *f.*, facilité, *f.*, galeté, *f.*
Lightning, s. éclair, *m.*, foudre, *f.* — pl. éclairs, *m.pl.* — *-conductor*, — *-rod*, paratonnerre, *m.*
Lights, s.pl. mou, *m.*, poumons, *m.pl.*
Lightsome, adj. éclairé, clair, riant, enjoué, gai
Ligneous, adj. ligneux
Like, adj. semblable à, pareil, comme, égal, même, (*portraits*) ressemblant, vraisemblable. *To be very much* —, ressembler à, ressembler beaucoup à. *It or that is just* — *him*, c'est digne de lui. *That is something* —! à la bonne heure! — *father*, — *son*, tel père, tel fils
Like, adv. comme, semblablement à, ainsi que, de la même manière que, pareillement, probablement
Like, s. pareil, *m.*, pareille, *f.*, chose pareille *or* semblable, *f.*, goût, *m.*, préférence, *f.*, sympathie, *f.*, probabilité, *f.* *To do the* —, en faire autant. *And the* —, et d'autres choses *or* personnes semblables. *To have* — *to*, penser, faillir, manquer de
Like, va. aimer, désirer, vouloir, trouver. *To* — *best*, aimer mieux. — vn. vouloir, il plait à, juger convenable, aimer
Likelihood, s. probabilité, *f.*, apparence, *f.*, vraisemblance, *f.*
Likely, adj. probable, vraisemblable, (*capable*) dans le cas (de), de nature (à). *He is not* — *to do it*, il n'est pas probable qu'il le fasse
Likely, adv. probablement, vraisemblablement
Liken, va. comparer
Likeness, s. apparence, *f.*, image, *f.*, forme, *f.*, ressemblance, *f.*, portrait, *m.*
Likewise, adv. aussi, pareillement, de même
Liking, s. goût, *m.*, préférence, *f.*, sympathie, *f.*
Lilac, s. adj. lilas, *m.* — *-bush*, — *-tree*, lilas, *m.*
Lilliputian, s. adj. lilliputien, *m.*, -ne, *f.*
Lily, s. lis, *m.* — *of the valley*, *May* —, muguet, *m.*
Limb, s. membre, *m.*, (*tree*) branche, *f.*
Limbed, adj. membré, proportionné
Limber, adj. souple, flexible
Limber, s. (*artil.*) avant-train, *m.*
Limbo, s. limbes, *m.pl.*
Lime, s. (*for birds, &c.*) glu, *f.*, (*for building, &c.*) chaux, *f.*, (*bot.*) tilleul, *m.*, (*fruit*) limon, *m.* — *-burner*, chaufournier, *m.* — *-juice*, jus de citron *or* de limon, *m.* — *-kiln*, four à chaux, *m.* — *-pit*, carrière à chaux, *f.* — *-stone*, pierre calcaire, *f.* — *-tree*, tilleul, *m.* — *-twig*, gluau, *m.* — *-water*, eau de chaux, *f.*
Lime, va. engluer, tendre des gluaux à, (*manure*) chauler
Limehound, s. limier, *m.*
Limit, s. limite, *f.*, borne, *f.*
Limit, va. limiter, borner, fixer, assigner
Limitation, s. limitation, *f.*, restriction, *f.*, (*law*) prescription, *f.*
Limited, adj. limité, borné, restreint
Limn, va. peindre, enluminer
Limner, s. peintre, *m.*, artiste, *m.*
Limp, adj. flexible, mou, flasque
Limp, s. clochement, *m.*
Limp, vn. boiter, clocher
Limpid, adj. limpide
Limpidity, s. limpidité, *f.*
Limpingly, adv. en boitant
Limy, adj. gluant, calcaire
Linchpin, s. clavette, *f.*
Linden, s. tilleul, *m.*
Line, s. ligne, *f.*, trait, *m.*, contour, *m.*, esquisse, *f.*, borne, *f.*, limite, *f.*, équateur, *m.*, (*string*) cordeau, *m.*, (*soldier*) haie, *f.*, (*poetry*) vers, *m.*, (*family*) race, *f.*, famille, *f.*, lignée, *f.*, (*business*) partie, *f.*, spécialité, *f.*, profession, *f.*, métier, *m.*, ressort, *m.*, (*packets, &c.*) ligne, *m.*, (*railway*) voie, *f.*, ligne, *f.*
Line, va. doubler, garnir, (*milit.*) border, faire la haie, (*masonry*) revêtir
Lineage, s. race, *f.*, famille, *f.*, maison, *f.*, lignée, *f.*
Lineal, adj. linéal, direct, linéaire
Lineament, s. trait, *m.*, linéament, *m.*
Linear, adj. linéaire
Linen, s. toile de lin, *f.*, lin, *m.*, linge, *m.* *Coarse* —, grosse toile. *Fine* —, toile fine. — *-cloth*, toile de Hollande, *f.* — *-draper*, marchand de nouveautés, *m.*, marchand de toiles, *m.*, linger, *m.*, lingère, *f.* — *-draper's shop*, magasin de nouveautés, *m.*, magasin de blanc, *m.* — *-press*, armoire à linge, *f.* — *rag*, petit linge, *m.* — *shirt*, chemise de toile, *f.* — *yarn*, fil de lin, *m.*
Linger, vn. tarder, rester longtemps, trainer
Lingerer, s. trainard, *m.*, retardataire, *m.*
Lingering, adj. qui tarde, dernier, lent, long, prolongé, qui traine, hésitant
Lingeringly, adv. avec hésitation, lentement, languissamment
Lingo, s. jargon, *m.*
Linguist, s. linguiste, *m.*
Liniment, s. liniment, *m.*
Lining, s. doublure, *f.*, garniture, *f.*, paroi, *f.*, (*of a hat*) coiffe, *f.*
Link, s. anneau, *m.*, chaînon, *m.*, (*iron*) maille, *f.*, (*fig.*) attache, *f.*, lien, *m.*, enchaînement, *m.*, (*light*) torche, *f.*
Link, va. lier, attacher, enchaîner, unir
Linnæan, adj. de Linnée
Linnet, s. linotte, *f.*, linot, *m.*
Linseed, s. graine de lin, *f.* — *-cake*, tourteau de lin, *m.* — *-meal*, farine de graine de lin, *f.* — *-oil*, huile de lin, *f.*
Linsey-woolsey, s. tiretaine, *f.*
Lint, s. charpie, *f.*
Lintel, s. linteau, *m.*
Lion, s. lion, *m.*, (*fig.*) chose curieuse, *f.*, (*pers.*) célébrité, *f.*
Lioness, s. lionne, *f.*
Lionize, va.n. faire une célébrité de, montrer les choses curieuses à, visiter les choses curieuses
Lip, s. lèvre, *f.*, (*edge*) bord, *m.*, (*of some beasts*) babine, *f.* *Thick* —, lippe, *f.*, grosse lèvre, *f.* — *-salve*, pommade pour les lèvres, *f.*
Lipped, adj. (*in compounds*) aux lèvres . . ., aux rebords . . .
Liquefaction, s. liquéfaction, *f.*
Liquefy, va. liquéfier; — vn. se liquéfier
Liquid, adj. liquide, (*the letter l*) mouillée, (*fig.*) doux, harmonieux, coulant
Liquid, s. liquide, *m.*
Liquidate, va. liquider, acquitter, solder
Liquidation, s. liquidation, *f.*
Liquor, s. liqueur, *f.* *To be in* —, être gris
Liquorice, s. réglisse, *f.* — *-stick*, réglisse en bâton, *f.* *Spanish* —, jus de réglisse, *m.*
Lisp, vn.a. zézayer, balbutier, bégayer
Lisp, Lisping, s. zézayement, *m.*, balbutiement, *m.*, bégayement, *m.*
Lisper, s. qui zézaye, qui balbutie, qui bégaye
List, s. liste, *f.*, rôle, *m.*, état, *m.*, contrôle, *m.*, tableau, *m.*, (*limit*) borne, *f.*, limite, *f.*, (*arena*) lice, *f.*, arène, *f.*, (*cloth*) lisière, *f.*, (*archit.*) listel, *m.*
List, va. (*adorn*) calfeutrer, garnir de lisière; — vn. vouloir, avoir envie, s'enrôler, s'engager
Listen, vn. écouter, entendre
Listener, s. celui, celle qui écoute, auditeur, *m.*, écouteur, *m.*, -euse, *f.*
Listening, s. action d'écouter, *f.*
Listless, adj. nonchalant, indifférent, insouciant, distrait, inattentif
Listlessly, adv. nonchalamment, avec indifférence, avec insouciance
Listlessness, s. nonchalance, *f.*, indifférence, *f.*, insouciance, *f.*
Litany, s. litanie, *f.*
Literal, adj. de lettres, au moyen de lettres, littéral
Literally, adv. littéralement, à la lettre, au pied de la lettre
Literary, adj. littéraire, (*pers.*) de lettres, lettré
Literature, s. littérature, *f.*
Litharge, s. litharge, *f.*

Lithograph, va. lithographier

Lithograph, s. lithographie, *f.*

Lithographer, s. lithographe, *m.*

Lithographic, adj. lithographique

Lithography, s. lithographie, *f.*

Litigant, s. plaideur, *m.*, -euse, *f.*

Litigate, va.n. mettre en litige, defendre, être en procès

Litigation, s. litige, *m.*

Litigious, adj. litigieux, contentieux, (*pers.*) processif

Litter, s. litière, *f.*, (*for invalids*) civière, *f.*, (*confusion*) désordre, *m.*, fouillis, *m.*, (*cats, pigs*) portée, *f.*

Litter, va. faire la litière à, étendre de la paille dans, coucher, mettre en désordre, (*beasts*) mettre bas

Little, adj. petit, exigu, peu de, mesquin. — *ones*, petits enfants, (*of animals*) petits. — *-go*, examen préliminaire d'admissibilité, *m.*

Little, adv. peu, peu de, ne ... guère. — *by* —, *by* — *and* —, peu à peu, petit à petit. *Ever so* —, tant soit peu, si peu que ce soit

Little, s. peu, *m.*, peu de chose, *m.*

Littleness, s. petitesse, *f.*

Liturgy, s. liturgie, *f.*

Live, vn. vivre, demeurer, habiter, se perpétuer. — *on*, continuer de vivre. *To* — *out one's day*, fournir sa carrière. *To* — *up to*, vivre conformément à. *To* — *up to the height of one's fortune*, dépenser tous ses revenus. *To* — *again*, *to* — *over again*, revivre. *What does he* — *upon?* de quoi vit-il?

Live, adj. vivant, (*coals*) ardent. — *-stock*, bétail, *m.*, bestiaux, *m.pl.*

Livelihood, s. vie, *f.*, existence, *f.*, moyens d'existence, *m.pl.*

Liveliness, s. vivacité, *f.*, animation, *f.*, vie, *f.*

Livelong, adj. durable, long. *The* — *day*, tout le long du jour

Lively, adj. vif, animé, vivant, éveillé, gai, plaisant

Liver, s. foie, *m.*, (*pers.*) qui vit, vivant, *m.* *A high* —, viveur. *A fast* —, qui mène grand train la vie. — *-colour*, rouge foncé.

Livery, s. (*law*) remise d'héritage, *f.*, émancipation, *f.*, (*horses*) pension, *f.*, (*servants*) livrée, *f.*, (*of the city of London*) corporation, *f.* — *-stables*, établissement de loueur de chevaux, *m.* — *-stable keeper*, loueur de chevaux, *m.*

Livid, adj. livide

Lividness, s. lividité, *f.*

Living, adj. vivant, vif

Living, s. action de vivre, *f.*, vie, *f.*, existence, *f.*, (*church*) cure, *f.*, bénéfice, *m.*, (*pers.*) vivants, *m.pl.* *Good* —, bonne chère, *f.*

Lizard, s. lézard, *m.*

Lo! interj. voilà! voilà que! voici! voyez! tenez!

Loach, s. loche, *f.*

Load, s. charge, *f.*, fardeau, *m.*, chargement, *m.*, poids, *m.*

Load, va. charger, combler, accabler, (*a stick*) plomber. (*dice*) piper

Loader, s. qui charge

Loading, s. chargement, *m.*, charge, *f.* *Breech*- —, qui se charge par la culasse

Loadstar, s. étoile polaire, *f.*

Loadstone, s. aimant, *m.*, pierre aimantée, *f.* *To cap a* —, armer un aimant

Loaf, s. pain, *m.* *A* — *of bread*, un pain. — *-sugar*, sucre blanc

Loam, s. compost, *m.* glaise, *f.*, terre, *f.*

Loamy, adj. glaiseux

Loan, s. (*lending*) prêt, *m.*, (*borrowing*) emprunt, *m.*

Loath, adj. à contre-cœur, ne voulant pas, à qui il répugne. *To be* — *to*, ne vouloir pas, avoir de la répugnance à

Loathe, va. avoir du dégoût *or* de l'aversion pour, prendre en dégoût

Loathing, s. dégoût, *m.*, aversion, *f.*

Loathly, adv. avec répugnance

Loathness, s. répugnance, *f.*

Loathsome, adj. dégoûtant, odieux

Lobby, s. couloir, *m.*, (*theatre*) foyer, *m.*, salle d'attente, *f.*

Lobe, s. lobe, *m.*

Lobster, s. homard, *m.*

Local, adj. local

Locality, s. localité, *f.*

Localize, va. localiser

Locally, adv. localement

Loch, s. lac, *m.*, (*med.*) looch, *m.*

Lock, s. serrure, *f.*, (*fire-arms*) platine, *f.*, (*embrace*) étreinte, *f.*, (*canals*) écluse, *f.* *Safety* —, serrure de sûreté, *f.* — *-up*, violon, *m.*, corps de garde, *m.*, chambre de sûreté, *f.* *Under* — *and key*, sous clef. — *-keeper*, éclusier, *m.* — *of hair*, boucle, *f.*, mèche, *f.* — *-s*, pl. cheveux, *m.pl.*, chevelure, *f.*

Lock, va. fermer à clef, mettre sous clef, joindre, unir, enlacer, serrer. *To* — *in*, enfermer à clef. *To* — *out*, fermer la porte à clef sur. *To* — *up*, mettre sous clef, serrer. — vn. se fermer, fermer

Lockage, s. construction d'écluse, *f.*, écluse, *f.*, (*dues*) péage, *m.*

Lock-jaw, s. trismus, *m.*

Locker, s. coffre, *m.*, armoire, *f.*

Locket, s. fermoir, *m.*, médaillon, *m.*

Locksmith, s. serrurier, *m.*

Locomotion, s. locomotion, *f.*

Locomotive, adj. locomotif

Locomotive, s. locomotive, *f.*

Locust, s. sauterelle, *f.*, (*bot.*) caroube, *f.*, carouge, *f.*

Locution, s. locution, *f.*, discours, *m.*

Lode, s. filon, *m.*

Lodge, s. loge, *f.*, cabane, *f.*

Lodge, va. mettre, placer, déposer, lancer, envoyer, enfoncer, fixer, planter, loger, donner un logement *or* un gîte à, (*a complaint*) déposer, (*appeal*) interjeter; — vn. se loger, habiter, (*beasts*) gîter, se gîter

Lodger, s. locataire, *m.f.*, habitant, *m.*, -e, *f.*

Lodging, s. logement, *m.*, appartement, *m.*, gîte, *m.*, abri, *m.* — *-house*, hôtel garni, *m.*

Lodgment, s. logement, *m.*, (*money*) dépôt, *m.*, consignation, *f.*

Loft, s. grenier, *m.*, mansarde, *f.*, soupente, *f.*, étage, *m.*

Loftily, adv. en haut, avec élévation, noblement, avec hauteur

Loftiness, s. hauteur, *f.*, élévation, *f.*, noblesse, *f.*, orgueil, *m.*, dignité, *f.*

Lofty, adj. élevé, grand, orgueilleux, hautain, plein de dignité

Log, s. bûche, *f.*, soliveau, *m.*, bloc de bois, *m.*, (*nav.*) loch, *m.* — *-cabin*, — *-house*, — *-hut*, cabane *or* hutte bâtie avec des troncs d'arbres. — *-board*, table de loch, *f.* — *-book*, livre de loch, *m.* — *-chip*, loch, *m.* — *-line*, ligne de loch, *m.*

Logarithm, s. logarithme, *m.*

Loggerhead, s. lourdaud, *m.*, bêta, *m.* *To fall* or *go to* — *-s*, en venir aux mains

Logic, s. logique, *f.*

Logical, adj. logique, de la logique

Logically, adv. logiquement

Logician, s. logicien, *m.*

Logwood, s. bois de Campêche, *m.*

Loin, s. reins, *m.pl.*, dos, *m.*, (*of meat*) longe, *f.*

Loiter, vn. flâner, s'amuser, traîner

Loiterer, s. flâneur, *m.*, flâneuse, *f.*, traînard, *m.*, musard, *m.*, -e, *f.*

Loitering, s. flânerie, *f.*, paresse, *f.*

Loll, vn. se traîner, se dandiner, se coucher, s'étendre, s'étaler, s'appuyer, se pencher, (*the tongue*) pendre; — va. tirer, laisser pendre

Lollipop, s. sucre d'orge, *m.*

Loneliness, s. solitude, *f.*, isolement, *m.*

Lonely, adj. solitaire, seul, isolé

Long, adj. long, lent, étendu. *To be six feet* —, avoir six pieds de long. *To grow* — *-er*, s'allonger. *In the* — *run*, à la longue. *For a* — *while* or *time past*, depuis bien longtemps

Long, s. long, *m.*, syllabe longue, *f.*

Long, adv. fort, au loin, longtemps, pendant longtemps, depuis longtemps. *No longer*, ne ... plus, ne ... pas plus longtemps. *As* — *as*, *so* — *as*, tant que. *It is* — *since*, il y a longtemps que ... ne. *Not* — *since* or *ago*, il n'y a pas longtemps, naguère. *How* —*?* que de temps? jusqu'à quand? jusques à quand? combien de temps? depuis quand? combien de temps y a-t-il que ...? — *-boat*, s. chaloupe, *f.* — *-drawn*, adj. long, prolongé. — *-headed*, adj. sagace. — *-leg*, s. (*insect*) faucheur, *m.* — *-sighted*, adj. s. presbyte, (*fig.*) sagace. — *-spun*, adj. long, verbeux. — *-sufferance*, s. longanimité, *f.*, patience, *f.* — *-suffering*, adj. patient. — *-winded*, adj. à longue haleine, (*fig.*) interminable, ennuyeux

Long, vn. désirer fortement, avoir grande envie. *To* — *for* or *after*, avoir grande envie de, désirer vivement

Longevity, s. longévité, *f*

Longing, s. vif désir, *m.*, grande envie, *f.*

Longingly, adv. avec désir

Longitude, s. longitude, *f.*

Longitudinal, adj. longitudinal

Longitudinally, adv. longitudinalement

Loo, s. (*cards*) mouche, *f.*

Looby, s. dadais, *m.*, niais, *m.*

Look, vn. regarder, (*that*) faire attention (que), veiller (à ce que), paraître, sembler. — ! — ! regardez! regardez! *To* — *at*, regarder. *To* — *about*, regarder de tous côtés. *To* — *about oneself*, être sur ses gardes. *To* — *abroad*, regarder au loin. *To* — *after*, suivre du regard, veiller à, surveiller. *To* — *away*, détourner ses regards. *To* — *back*, regarder en arrière, faire un retour. *To* — *down*, regarder en bas *or* au-dessous de soi, baisser les yeux, (*com.*) tendre à la baisse. *To* — *down upon*, regarder avec mépris. *To* — *for*, chercher, rechercher, s'attendre à, prévoir. *To* — *forward*, regarder en avant, (*fig.*) s'attendre à, prévoir, anticiper. *To* — *in* (*on*), entrer un instant (chez), dire un petit bonjour (à). *To* — *into*, regarder dans, près, examiner, prendre connaissance de, s'informer de, (*windows*) avoir vue sur. *To* — *on* or *upon*, regarder, jeter les yeux sur, considérer. *To* — *out*, regarder au dehors, être sur ses gardes, (*into windows*) donner sur, avoir vue sur, (*milit.*) être en observation. *To — out sharp*, avoir l'œil ouvert. *To — out for*, chercher, s'attendre à. *To — over*, regarder par-dessus, fermer les yeux sur, compulser, vérifier, examiner, parcourir. *To — sharp*, se dépêcher. *To — sharp after*, surveiller de près, avoir l'œil ouvert sur. *To — to*, veiller à, avoir l'œil à, surveiller, soigner, s'adresser à, avoir recours à. *To — towards*, regarder vers *or* du côté de. *To — up*, regarder en l'air, lever les yeux, chercher, (*com.*) tendre à la hausse. *To — up to*, respecter, considérer, mettre son espoir en. *To — like*, avoir l'air de, avoir la mine de, paraître comme. *To — well*, (*pers.*) avoir bon visage *or* bonne mine, (*things*) avoir bonne apparence. *To — ill*, avoir mauvaise mine, (*things*) prendre une mauvaise tournure

Look, s. regard, *m.*, coup d'œil, *m.*, air, *m.*, mine, *f.*, aspect, *m.*, apparence, *f.*, extérieur, *m.* *—-in*, petite visite, *f.* *—-out*, guet, *m.*, vigie, *f.* *—-out man*, vigie, *f.* *To be on the —-out*, avoir l'œil au guet, être sur ses gardes. *That's my —-out*, c'est mon affaire

Looker, s. qui regarde. *—-on*, spectateur, *m.*, spectatrice, *f.*

Looking, adj. qui a ... mine *or* visage, à la mine... *Good-—*, de bonne mine

Looking, s. (*for*) attente (de), *f.*

Looking-glass, s. miroir, *m.*, glace, *f.* *—-maker*, s. miroitier, *m.*

Loom, s. métier, *m.*

Loom, vn. se montrer, paraître (indistinctement)

Looming, s. apparence indistincte, *f.*, (*nav.*) mirage, *m.*

Loop, s. boucle, *f.*, bride, *f.*, (*hat*) ganse, *f.*, (*archit.*) meurtrière, *f.*, (*fig.*) échappatoire, *f.*, défaite, *f.*

Loop, va. agrafer. *To — up*, relever

Loose, va. délier, détacher, lâcher, desserrer, délivrer, dégager

Loose, adj. (*free*) délié, détaché, dégagé, libre, (*not tight*) lâche, desserré, mal assemblé, flottant, large, (*shaking*) qui ne tient pas, peu solide, branlant, (*morals*) relâché, libertin, licencieux. *To break — from*, se dégager de, s'évader de, s'échapper de, (*things*) se déchaîner, se détacher. *To come —, to get —*, se défaire, se desserrer. *To hang —*, flotter librement. *To let —*, déchaîner, détacher, lâcher. *To set — from*, délier de, dégager de, affranchir de. *To stand — of*, être délié de

Loosely, adv. librement, lâche, peu serré, avec peu d'ordre, avec peu de solidité, vaguement, sans suite, licencieusement

Loosen, va. délier, détacher, desserrer, ébranler, relâcher

Looseness, s. état de ce qui n'est pas serré, état de ce qui est défait *or* délié, peu de tension, *m.*, relâchement, *m.*, (*of bowels*) dévoiement, *m.*, (*of morals*) licence, *f.*, libertinage, *m.*

Lop, va. élaguer, couper, ébrancher. *—-sided*, qui penche trop d'un côté

Loquacious, adj. loquace, babillard

Loquaciousness, Loquacity, s. loquacité, *f.*

Lord, s. Seigneur, *m.*, maître, *m.*, propriétaire, *m.*, époux, *m.* *My —*, Monseigneur, Milord. *The —'s day*, le jour du Seigneur. *The —'s Supper*, la Cène

Lord, vn. dominer, tyranniser

Lordlike, adj. en seigneur

Lordliness, s. dignité, *f.*, rang élevé, *m.*, hauteur, *f.*, orgueil, *m.*

Lordling, s. hobereau, *m.*, gentillâtre, *m.*

Lordly, adj. seigneurial, de seigneur, altier, impérieux

Lordly, adv. en seigneur, avec hauteur

Lordship, s. seigneurie, *f.*, autorité, *f.*, empire, *m.* *Your —*, votre Seigneurie, *f.*, Monseigneur, *m.*

Lore, s. science, *f.*, savoir, *m.*, doctrine, *f.*

Lose, va.n. perdre, gaspiller, manquer, faire perdre à, priver de, (*clocks, watches, &c.*) retarder

Loser, s. celui, celle qui perd, perdant, *m.*

Loss, s. perte, *f.*, préjudice, *m.*, destruction, *f.*, ruine, *f.*, embarras, *m.* *A dead —*, une perte sèche. *To sell at a —*, vendre à perte. *To be at a —*, être embarrassé, ne pas savoir, (*for*) manquer (de)

Lot, s. sort, *m.*, portion, *f.*, partage, *m.*, destin, *m.*, (*com.*) lot, *m.*, partie, *f.*, (*fig.*) quantité, *f.*, grand nombre, *m.*, (*pop.*) tas, *m.* *To be the — of*, arriver à. *By —*, au sort. *To cast* or *draw —s*, tirer au sort, (*at play*) tirer à la courte paille. *—s of money*, un argent fou. *A bad —*, un tas de polissons

Lotion, s. lotion, *f.*

Lotos, Lotus, s. lotus, *m.*

Lottery, s. loterie, *f.*

Loud, adj. grand, fort, haut, bruyant, retentissant, éclatant

Loud, Loudly, adv. haut, à voix haute, fort, hautement, bruyamment, avec grand bruit

Loudness, s. bruit, *m.*

Lounge, vn. flâner; — va. passer en flânant. *To — about*, flâner à droite et à gauche

Lounge, s. flânerie, *f.*, tour de promenade, *m.*, promenade publique, *f.*, sofa, *m.*

Lounger, s. flâneur, *m.*, oisif, *m.*

Lounging, adj. flâneur

Louse, s. pou, *m.*

Lousy, adj. pouilleux, (*fig.*) vil, ignoble

Lout, s. lourdaud, *m.*, butor, *m.*

Loutish, adj. lourd, sot

Love, va. aimer

Love, s. amour, *m.*, affection, *f.*, tendresse, *f.*, sympathie, *f.*, ange, *m.*, ami, *m.*, -e, *f.* *To be in — with*, être épris *or* amoureux de. *To fall in — with*, s'éprendre de, devenir amoureux de, s'amouracher de. *To make — to*, courtiser, faire la cour à, (*pop.*) conter fleurette à. *Give* or *send my — to*, faites mes amitiés à. — (*in compounds*) d'amour. *—-charm*, s. philtre, *m.* *—-day*, s. jour des amis, *m.* *—-feast*, s. agapes, *f.pl.* *—-knot*, s. lacs d'amour, *m.pl.*, nœud, *m.* *—-letter*, s. billet doux, *m.* *—-lock*, s. accroche-cœur, *m.* *—-making*, s. cour, *f.* *—-match*, s. mariage d'inclination, *m.* *—-sick*, adj. malade d'amour

Loveliness, s. beauté, *f.*, charmes, *m.pl.*

Lovely, adj. aimable, charmant, séduisant, beau, ravissant, gracieux

Lovely, adv. d'une manière charmante

Lover, s. amant, *m.*, -e, *f.*, adorateur, *m.*, prétendant, *m.*, -e, *f.*

Loving, adj. aimant, affectueux, affectionné, tendre

Lovingly, adv. tendrement, amoureusement

Low, adj. bas, peu élevé, petit, (*feeble*) faible, abattu, (*sad, &c.*) triste, découragé, (*of birth, &c.*) de basse naissance, humble, peu important, (*dress*) décolleté, (*hats*) bas de forme. *To become, get* or *grow — or lower*, baisser. *— water*, marée basse, *f.* *To feel —*, se sentir tout triste. *A — dog*, un homme de rien

Low, adv. bas, à voix basse, à bas prix. *—-bred*, mal élevé. *—-built*, peu élevé, (*nav.*) de bas bord. *—-priced*, à bas prix, pas cher, bon marché. *—-spirited*, triste, abattu, sans énergie, vil, bas

Low, va. abaisser; — vn. mugir

Lower, adj. plus bas (que), inférieur (à)

Lower, va.n. baisser, abaisser, descendre, (*nav.*) amener, (*weather*) s'obscurcir, s'assombrir, se couvrir de nuages, (*upon*) regarder de travers, menacer du regard

Lowering, adj. sombre, menaçant. *—* s. abaissement, *m.*, baisse, *f.*

Loweringly, adv. sombre, d'un air renfrogné *or* menaçant

Lowermost, adj. adv. le plus bas, le plus en dessous

Lowing, s. mugissement, *m.*

Lowing, adj. mugissant

Lowlands, s.pl. basses terres

Lowly, adj. bas, peu élevé, humble

Lowly, adv. bas, humblement

Lowness, s. position peu élevée, *f.*, abaissement, *m.*, (*sound*) gravité, *f.*, (*voice*) ton bas, *m.*, (*dejection*) tristesse, *f.*, abattement, *m.*, humilité, *f.*, (*prices*) bas prix, *m.*, modicité, *f.*

Loyal, adj. fidèle, loyal

Loyally, adv. fidèlement, loyalement

Loyalty, s. loyauté, *f.*, fidélité, *f.*

Lozenge, s. losange, *m.*, (*cake*) pastille, *f.*, tablette, *f.*

Lubber, s. lourdaud, *m.*, gros paresseux, *m.*

Lubberly, adj. lourd, gros

Lubberly, adv. lourdement, gauchement

Lucerne, s. luzerne, *f.*

Lucid, adj. lumineux, brillant, limpide, transparent, lucide

Lucidity, s. éclat, *m.*, limpidité, *f.*, clarté, *f.*, lucidité, *f.*

Lucifer, s. lucifer, *m.*, allumette, *f.* *—-match*, allumette chimique, *f.*

Luck, s. bonheur, *m.*, chance, *f.*, bonne fortune, *f.* *Good —*, bonheur, *m.*, heureuse fortune, *f.* *Bad —, ill —*, mauvaise chance, *f.*, guignon, *m.* *To be in —, in —'s way*, avoir du bonheur, jouer de bonheur. *To bring good — to, bad — to*, porter bonheur à, malheur à

Luckily, adv. heureusement, par bonheur

Luckiness, s. bonheur, *m.*

Luckless, adj. malencontreux, malheureux, qui a du guignon. *A — hour*, une heure fatale

Lucky, adj. heureux, qui a de la chance, propice

Lucrative, adj. lucratif

Lucre, s. lucre, *m.*

Lucubration, s. élucubration, *f.*

Ludicrous, adj. risible, plaisant

Ludicrously, adv. risiblement, plaisamment

Ludicrousness, s. comique, *m.*, plaisant, *m.*, nature risible, *f.*

Luff, vn. lofer

Lug, va. traîner, tirer

Luggage, s. bagages, *m.pl.* *—-ticket*, bulletin de bagages, *m.* *—-train*, train de marchandises, *m.*

Lugger, s. lougre, *m.*, chasse-marée, *m.*

Lugubrious, adj. lugubre

Lugubriously, adv. lugubrement

Lukewarm, adj. tiède

Lukewarmly, adv. tièdement

Lukewarmness, s. tiédeur, *f.*, attiédissement, *m.*

Lull, va. bercer, endormir, (*into*) plonger (dans), inspirer, assoupir; — vn. se calmer, s'apaiser

Lull, s. doux murmure, *m.*, moment de calme, *m.*

Lullaby, s. berceuse, *f.*, chanson pour bercer, *f.* *To sing — to*, bercer

Lumbago, s. lumbago, *m.*, courbature, *f.*

Lumber, s. débarras, *m.*, rebut, *m.*, fatras, *m.* — *-room*, chambre de débarras, *f.*

Luminary, s. corps lumineux, *m.*, astre, *m.*, flambeau, *m.*

Luminous, adj. lumineux, brillant

Lump, s. masse, *f.*, tas, *m.*, (*com.*) bloc, *m.* *In the —*, en bloc. — *-sugar*, sucre blanc

Lump, va. mettre *or* prendre en bloc *or* en masse

Lumpish, adj. lourd, pesant

Lumpy, adj. en masse

Lunacy, s. aliénation mentale, *f.*, folie, *f.*, démence, *f.*

Lunar, adj. lunaire, de la lune

Lunatic, adj. lunatique, d'aliénés, de fous

Lunatic, s. aliéné, *m.*, -e, *f.*, fou, *m.*, folle, *f.*

Lunation, s. lunaison, *f.*

Lunch, Luncheon, s. collation, *f.*, second déjeuner, *m.*

Lunch, vn. déjeuner

Lunette, s. lunette, *f.*

Lung, s. poumon, *m.*, (*calf's*) mou, *m.* *To tire one's —s*, s'époumoner

Lunge, s. botte, *f.*

Lupine, s. lupin, *m.*

Lurch, s. embarras, *m.*, abandon, *m.*

Lurcher, s. (sorte de) chien d'arrêt, *m.*

Lure, s. leurre, *m.*, attrait, *m.*

Lure, va. leurrer, attirer

Lurid, adj. sombre, lugubre, livide, blafard

Lurk, vn. tendre des piéges, se mettre aux aguets, se cacher

Lurker, s. personne aux aguets, en embuscade, *f.*, personne cachée, *f.*

Lurking, adj. des aguets, d'embuscade

Lurking-hole *or* **-place**, s. cachette, *f.*, retraite, *f.*

Luscious, adj. délicieux, très-doux

Lusciously, adv. délicieusement

Lusciousness, s. goût délicieux, *m.*, fadeur, *f.*

Lusory, adj. amusant, d'amusement, de jeu

Lust, s. convoitise, *f.*, soif, *f.*, (*sinful desire*) impureté, *f.*, luxure, *f.*, concupiscence, *f.*

Lust, vn. convoiter, avoir un mauvais désir de

Lustful, adj. impur, plein de luxure, sensuel

Lustfully, adv. avec convoitise, impudiquement

Lustfulness, s. *see* LUST

Lustily, adv. vigoureusement

Lustiness, s. vigueur, *f.*, embonpoint, *m.*

Lustral, adj. lustral

Lustrate, va. purifier par la lustration, purifier

Lustration, s. lustration, *f.*, purification, *f.*

Lustre, s. éclat, *m.*, splendeur, *f.*, lustre, *m.*

Lustring, s. lustrine, *f.*

Lusty, adj. vigoureux, gros, corpulent

Lute, s. luth, *m.*, (*chem.*) lut, *m.*

Lute, va. (*chem.*) luter

Lutheran, adj. s. luthérien, *m.*, -enne, *f.*

Lutheranism, s. luthéranisme, *m.*

Lutist, s. joueur, *m.*, joueuse de luth, *f.*

Luxate, va. luxer. *To become —d*, se luxer

Luxation, s. luxation, *f.*

Luxuriance, s. exubérance, *f.*, surabondance, *f.*, luxuriance, *f.*

Luxuriant, adj. vigoureux, exubérant, luxuriant

Luxuriate, vn. croître en abondance *or* avec vigueur, vivre dans le luxe, (*in*) se livrer tout entier (à)

Luxurious, adj. vigoureux, (*things*) somptueux, (*pers.*) adonné au luxe

Luxuriously, adv. somptueusement, avec luxe, voluptueusement

Luxuriousness, s. luxe, *m.*, somptuosité, *f.*, volupté, *f.*

Luxury, s. luxe, *m.*, volupté, *f.*, objet de luxe, *m.*, régal, *m.*

Lyceum, s. lycée, *m.*

Lye, s. lessive, *f.*

Lying, adj. menteur, -euse, mensonger, -ère. — s. mensonge, *m.*

Lying-in, adj. en couches. — *-hospital*, hospice pour les femmes en couches, *m.*

Lymph, s. lymphe, *f.*

Lymphatic, adj. lymphatique

Lynch, va. juger et exécuter sommairement. — *-law*, la loi de Lynch

Lynx, s. lynx, *m.*

Lyre, s. lyre, *f.*

Lyric, Lyrical, adj. lyrique

M

M, s. M, m, *m.*, mille, *m.*

Macadam, s. macadam, *m.* — *road*, route macadamisée, *f.*

Macadamize, va. macadamiser

Macaroni, s. macaroni, *m.*

Macaroon, s. macaron, *m.*

Mace, s. masse d'armes, *f.*, massue, *f.*, (*spice*) macis, *m.* — *-bearer*, massier, *m.*

Macerate, va. macérer, amaigrir

Maceration, s. macération, *f.*

Machinate, va. machiner

Machination, s. machination, *f.*

Machine, s. machine, *f.* *A bathing —*, voiture, *f.*

Machinery, s. mécanique, *f.*, mécanisme, *m.*, machines, *f.pl.*, (*in poems*) merveilleux, *m.*

Machinist, s. mécanicien, *m.*, machiniste, *m.f.*

Mackerel, s. maquereau, *m.*

Mackintosh, s. mackintosh, *m.*, manteau en caoutchouc, *m.*

Mad, adj. fou, insensé, en démence, aliéné, furieux, furibond, (*hydroph.*) enragé. *To go —, to run —*, devenir fou, tomber en démence. *To drive —, to make —*, rendre fou, faire perdre la tête à, exaspérer. *Like —*, comme un perdu, en désespéré. *To drive like —*, conduire ventre à terre. — *-cap*, s. adj. fou, *m.*, folle, *f.*, écervelé, *m.*, -e, *f.*, (*pop.*) tête fêlée, *f.* — *-house*, maison de fous, *f.*

Madam, s. madame, *f.*

Madden, va. rendre fou *or* furieux, désespérer, faire enrager

Maddening, adj. qui rend fou *or* furieux, (*pop.*) enrageant, démontant

Madder, s. garance, *f.* *Field of —*, garancière, *f.*

Made, past part. fait, confectionné. — *dishes*, entremets, *m.* — *up*, artificiel, (*strong*) conte fait à plaisir

Madeira, s. vin de Madère, *m.*

Madly, adv. follement, furieusement

Madman, s. fou, *m.*, aliéné, *m.*, forcené, *m.*

Madness, s. folie, *f.*, démence, *f.*, rage, *f.*

Madonna, s. Madone, *f.*

Madrepore, s. madrépore, *m.*

Madrigal, s. madrigal, *m.*

Madwoman, s. folle, *f.*, insensée, *f.*

Magazine, s. entrepôt, *m.*, magasin, *m.*, (*nav.*) soute aux poudres, *f.*, (*journal*) revue, *f.*, magasin, *m.*

Maggot, s. ver blanc, *m.*, larve, *f.*, (*whim*) lubie, *f.*, caprice, *m.*

Maggoty, adj. plein de vers, plein de lubies

Magic, s. magie, *f.*

Magic, adj. magique

Magically, adv. par magie, d'une manière magique

Magician, s. magicien, *m.*, magicienne, *f.*

Magisterial, adj. de maître, magistral

Magisterially, adv. magistralement, d'un ton magistral

Magistracy, s. magistrature, *f.*

Magistrate, s. magistrat, *m.*, juge de paix, *m.*

Magnanimity, s. magnanimité, *f.*, grandeur d'âme, *f.*

Magnanimous, adj. magnanime, grand

Magnanimously, adv. magnanimement, avec magnanimité

Magnate, s. magnat, *m.*, grand personnage, *m.*

Magnesia, s. magnésie, *f.*

Magnet, s. aimant, *m.*

Magnetic, adj. magnétique, aimanté

Magnetism, s. magnétisme, *m.*

Magnetize, va. aimanter, magnétiser

Magnificence, s. magnificence, *f.*

Magnificent, adj. magnifique

Magnificently, adv. magnifiquement

Magnifier, s. qui grossit, verre grossissant, *m.*, panégyriste, *m.*, qui exalte

Magnify, va. grossir, magnifier, louer, exalter. —*ing glass*, verre grossissant, *m.*

Magnitude, s. grandeur, *f.*, importance, *f.*

Magnolia, s. magnolia, *m.*, magnolier, *m.*

Magpie, s. pie, *f.*

Mahogany, s. acajou, *m.* — adj. d'acajou

Mahomedan, Mahometan, s. adj. mahométan, *m.*, -e, *f.*

Mahometanism, s. mahométisme, *m.*

Maid, s. jeune fille, *f.*, fille, *f.*, vierge, *f.*, servante, *f.*, domestique, *f.*, bonne, *f.*

Maiden, s. jeune fille, *f.*, vierge, *f.*

Maiden, adj. de jeune fille, de vierge, (*new*) frais, neuf, premier. — *name*, nom de demoiselle. — *-hair*, capillaire, *m.* — *speech*, discours de début, *m.* — *sword*, épée qui n'a jamais été tirée

Maidenhood, s. virginité, *f.*
Maidenly, adj. de jeune fille, virginal, modeste
Mail, s. (*coat*) maille, *f.*, (*despatches*) dépêches, *f.pl.*, malle, *f.*, malle-poste, *f.*, courrier, *m.* *A link of* —, une maille. —*-bag*, s. sac de dépêches, *m.* —*-boat*, s. —*-packet*, s. paquebot-poste, *m.* —*-coach*, s. malle-poste, *f.* —*-guard*, s., —*-muster*, s. courrier de la malle, *m.* —*-train*, s. train malle-poste, *m.*
Maim, va. mutiler, estropier, tronquer, paralyser
Maim, s. blessure, *f.*, mutilation, *f.*
Main, adj. principal, grand, premier, important, essentiel. —*-land*, s. continent, *m.*, terre ferme, *f.* —*-mast*, s. grand mât, *m.* *By — strength*, de haute lutte, de vive force
Main, s. gros, *m.*, masse, *f.*, plus grande partie, *f.*, majeure partie, *f.*, mer, *f.*, océan, *m.*, (*pipe*) grand conduit *or* tuyau, *m.* *In the —, for the* —, en général, pour la plupart, au fond
Mainly, adv. principalement, grandement
Maintain, va.n. maintenir, soutenir, (*to feed*) entretenir, nourrir
Maintainer, s. qui maintient, qui soutient, qui entretient
Maintenance, s. maintien, *m.*, soutien, *m.*, conservation, *f.*, entretien, *m.*, nourriture, *f.*
Maize, s. maïs, *m.*, blé de Turquie, *m.*
Majestic, adj. majestueux
Majestically, adv. majestueusement, avec majesté
Majesty, s. majesté, *f.*
Major, adj. majeur, (*milit.*) major
Major, s. majeur, *m.*, fille majeure, *f.*, (*cavalry*) chef d'escadron, *m.*, commandant, *m.*, (*infantry*) chef de bataillon, *m.*, (*mus.*) majeure, *f.*
Majority, s. majorité, *f.*, grade de major, *m.*
Make, va. faire, (*render*) rendre, (*clothes*) confectionner, (*pens*) tailler, (*compel*) forcer, contraindre, (*money*) gagner, (*nav.*) faire, arriver en vue de, gagner, arriver à. *To — against*, être contraire à, contrarier le dire de. *To — away*, faire disparaître, transférer, céder. *To — believe*, faire semblant. *To — for*, gagner, se diriger vers, (*things*) être en faveur de, profiter à. *To — from*, s'éloigner de. *To — much of*, faire cas de, estimer, aimer, tirer parti de. *To — out*, saisir, comprendre, trouver le sens de, déchiffrer, établir, produire, présenter, rédiger, composer, (*a bill*) établir, compléter, arranger. *To — over*, (*to*) transférer (à), céder (à). *To — up*, faire, confectionner, (*with*) faire la paix (avec), se réconcilier (avec), se raccommoder, (*a dispute*) arranger, (*a deficit*) combler, (*an error*) compenser, réparer, dédommager de, indemniser de, (*accounts*) régler. — vn. se diriger (vers), s'élancer (sur), faire semblant (de), faire (comme si). *To — after*, suivre, courir après. *To — away*, s'éloigner. *To — away with*, faire disparaître, se défaire de, tuer. *To — forth*, avancer. *To — off*, partir, s'en aller, décamper. *To — out*, (*to*) parvenir (à). *To — up to*, s'avancer vers, aller à, faire des avances à, faire la cour à. *To — up for*, compenser, tenir lieu de, réparer. *To — with*, marcher de concert avec, s'accorder avec
Make, s. forme, *f.*, façon, *f.*, coupe, *f.*, structure, *f.*, tournure, *f.*, taille, *f.*, nature, *f.*, genre, *m.*
Makepeace, s. pacificateur, *m.*, pacificatrice, *f.*
Maker, s. Créateur, *m.*, fabricant, *m.*, -e, *f.*, faiseur, *m.*, -euse, *f.*
Makeshift, s. expédient, *m.*, pis-aller, *m.*
Makeweight, s. complément de poids, *m.* *As a* —, pour faire le poids
Making, s. action de faire, *f.*, création, *f.*, fabrication, *f.*, confection, *f.*, figure, *f.*, taille, *f.*
Malachite, s. malachite, *f.*
Maladministration, s. mauvaise administration, *f.*
Malady, s. maladie, *f.*
Malapert, adj. s. malappris, insolent, impertinent
Malaria, s. malaria, *f.*
Malcontent, adj. s. mécontent
Male, adj. s. mâle, *m.*
Malediction, s. malédiction, *f.*
Malefactor, s. malfaiteur, *m.*
Malevolence, s. malveillance, *f.*, malice, *f.*
Malevolent, adj. malveillant, malicieux, ennemi
Malevolently, adv. avec malveillance
Malice, s. malice, *m.*, méchanceté, *f.*, rancune, *f.*
Malicious, adj. méchant, malveillant, malicieux
Maliciously, adv. méchamment, malicieusement
Maliciousness, s. méchanceté, *f.*, malignité, *f.*, malveillance, *f.*
Malign, **Malignant**, adj. malin, méchant, contraire, ennemi
Malign, va. maltraiter, diffamer, noircir
Malignancy, **Malignity**, s. malignité, *f.*, méchanceté, *f.*
Malignantly, **Malignly**, adv. méchamment, avec malignité
Malleability, **Malleableness**, s. malléabilité, *f.*
Malleable, adj. malléable
Mallet, s. maillet, *m.*, mailloche, *f.*
Mallow, s. mauve, *f.* —*-tea*, tisane de mauve, *f.*
Malmsey, s. malvoisie, *f.*
Malpractice, s. malversation, *f.*, méfait, *m.*
Malt, s. drêche, *f.* —*-drink*, s. —*-liquor*, s. bière, *f.*, boisson d'orge brassée, *f.* —*-house*, s. germoir, *m.* —*-kiln*, s. touraille, *f.*
Malting, s. maltage, *m.*
Maltreat, va. maltraiter
Maltster, s. malteur, *m.*
Malversation, s. malversation, *f.*
Mamma, s. maman, *f.*, petite mère, *f.*
Mammifer, s. adj. mammifère
Man, s. homme, *m.*, mari, *m.*, (*servant*) domestique, *m.*, valet, *m.*, serviteur, *m.*, (*pop.*) mon brave, *m.*, mon vieux, *m.*, mon cher, *m.*, (*ship*) navire, *m.*, vaisseau, *m.*, (*chess*) pièce, *f.*, (*draughts*) pion, *m.* *To come to —'s estate*, parvenir à l'âge d'homme. *To a* —, jusqu'au dernier. *Every — of them*, tous sans exception. — *and wife*, mari et femme. —*-eater*, s. anthropophage, *m.*, cannibale, *m.* —*-hater*, s. misanthrope, *m.* —*-hating*, s. la misanthropie. —*-killing*, s. meurtre, *m.*, homicide, *m.* —*-of-war*, s. vaisseau de guerre, *m.* —*-pleaser*, s. flatteur, *m.*, courtisan, *m.* —*-ropes*, s. tireveilles, *f.pl.* —*-servant*, s. domestique, *m.* —*-slaughter*, s. homicide sans préméditation, *m.* —*-slayer*, s. homicide, *m.*
Man, va. garnir d'hommes, garnir de monde *or* de troupes, (*nav.*) équiper, mettre du monde sur. — *the yards!* du monde sur les vergues!
Manacle, s. menotte, *f.*, fers, *m.pl.*
Manacle, va. mettre les menottes à, enchaîner, garotter
Manage, va. diriger, conduire, manier, mener, (*business*) administrer, gérer, gouverner, (*property*) régir, (*to tame*) venir à bout de, mener, dompter, (*it*) s'y prendre, s'arranger, (*weapons*) manier, ménager, user de ménagements avec, (*a horse*) dresser; — vn. diriger les affaires, agir, venir à bout de, trouver moyen de, parvenir à, s'y prendre
Manageable, adj. docile, traitable, dont on vient facilement à bout, (*things*) facile à manier
Manageableness, s. docilité, *f.*, maniement facile, *m.*
Management, s. direction, *f.*, conduite, *f.*, maniement, *m.*, administration, *f.*, gestion, *f.*, gouvernement, *m.*, emploi, *m.*
Manager, s. directeur, *m.*, administrateur, *m.*, gérant, *m.*, régisseur, *m.*
Mandarin, s. mandarin, *m.*
Mandatary, s. mandataire, *m.*
Mandate, s. ordre, *m.*, mandement, *m.*, (*law*) mandat, *m.*
Mandolin, s. mandoline, *f.*
Mandrake, s. mandragore, *f.*
Mane, s. crinière *f.*
Maned, adj. à la . . . crinière
Manes, s.pl. mânes, *m.pl.*
Manful, adj. mâle, viril, digne d'un homme, vaillant, hardi, intrépide
Manfully, adv. en homme, hardiment, avec courage, noblement
Manganese, s. manganèse, *m.*
Mange, s. gale, *f.*
Mangel-wurzel, s. betterave, *f.*
Manger, s. mangeoire, *f.*, (*for cattle*) crèche, *f.*
Mangle, va. mutiler, déchirer, (*linen*) calandrer
Mangle, s. calandre, *f.*
Mangler, s. qui mutile, qui déchire, calandreur, *m.*
Mangling, s. mutilation, *f.*, calandrage, *m.*
Mango, s. mangue, *f.* —*-tree*, manguier, *m.*
Mangy, adj. galeux
Manhood, s. nature humaine, *f.*, âge d'homme, *m.*, âge viril, *m.*, virilité, *f.*
Mania, s. folie, *f.*, manie, *f.*
Maniac, adj. s. fou, furieux
Manifest, adj. manifeste, visible, clair, évident
Manifest, s. manifeste, *m.*
Manifest, va. manifester, témoigner
Manifestation, s. manifestation, *f.*
Manifestly, adv. manifestement
Manifesto, s. manifeste, *m.*
Manifold, adj. multiple, nombreux, multiplié. —*-writer*, s. machine à copier des lettres, *f.*
Manikin, s. bout d'homme, *m.*
Manipulate, va. manipuler
Manipulation, s. manipulation, *f.*
Mankind, s. genre humain, *m.*, hommes, *m.pl.*, humanité, *f.*
Manlike, adj. semblable à un homme
Manliness, s. noblesse, *f.*, air mâle, *m.*, caractère mâle, *m.*, courage, *m.*, bravoure, *f.*
Manly, adj. *see* MANFULLY
Manna, s. manne, *f.*
Manner, s. manière, *f.*, façon, *f.*, mode, *f.*, maintien, *m.*, tenue, *f.*, politesse, *f.*, espèce, *f.*, sorte, *f.* —*s*, pl. mœurs, *f.pl.*, manières, *f.pl.*, coutumes, *f.pl.*, les belles manières, *f.pl.* *In this* —, de cette manière *or* façon. *In like* —, de la même manière.

In the same — as, ainsi que. *After the — of*, à la manière de. *In a —*, en quelque sorte, pour ainsi dire. *Good —s*, la politesse, les belles manières. *Forbidding —s*, manières disgracieuses. *For —' sake*, par politesse
. . . -**Mannered**, adj. aux manières . . .
Mannerism, s. air maniéré, m., affectation, f.
Mannerist, s. maniériste, m.
Mannerly, adj. poli. — adv. poliment
Manœuvre, s. manœuvre, f.
Manœuvre, va. manœuvrer, faire manœuvrer
Manor, s. manoir, m., seigneurie, f. *—-house*, manoir, m., château, m.
Mansion, s. maison, f., demeure, f., habitation, f., château, m., (*in town*) hôtel, m. *—-house*, mairie, f.
Mantilla, s. mantille, f.
Mantle, s. manteau, m. *—-piece*, *—-shelf*, manteau de cheminée, dessus de cheminée
Mantle, va. couvrir, envelopper; — vn. s'étendre, étendre ses branches, (*wine*) écumer
Manual, adj. s. manuel, m.
Manufactory, s. fabrique, f., manufacture, f., usine, f.
Manufacture, s. manufacture, f., fabrication, f.
Manufacture, va. manufacturer, fabriquer, mettre en œuvre; — vn. être manufacturier *or* industriel
Manufacturer, s. industriel, m., fabricant, m., manufacturier, m.
Manure, va. engraisser, fertiliser
Manure, s. engrais, m.
Manuscript, s. manuscrit, m.
Many, adj. beaucoup de, bien des, nombreux, (*with a sing.*) plus d'un, maint, -e. *A good —, a great — people*, bien des gens. *— and — a time*, mainte et mainte fois. *As —*, autant, autant de. *So —*, tant de, tant, si nombreux. *Not so —*, pas autant, etc. *How —*, combien, combien de, (*exclam.*) que de. *Too —*, trop de, trop nombreux, en trop grande quantité
Many, s. vulgaire, m., multitude, f., foule, f.
Map, s. carte, f. *The — of the world*, la mappemonde
Map, va. dessiner la carte de
Maple, s. érable, m.
Mappery, **Mapping**, s. cartographie, f.
Mar, va. gâter, faire du tort à, endommager, (*joy*) troubler, (*to deform*) défigurer
Maraschino, s. marasquin, m.
Marauder, s. maraudeur, m.
Marauding, s. maraude, f.
Marble, s. marbre, m., (*for playing*) bille, f.
Marble, adj. de marbre, marbré. *—-cutter*, s. marbrier, m. *—-cutting*, s. *—-works*, s. *—-yard*, s. marbrerie, f. *—-quarry*, s. carrière de marbre, f. *—-edged*, aux tranches marbrées
Marble, va. marbrer
Marbling, s. marbrure, f.
March, s. (*month*) mars, m.; marche, f., progrès, m. *—-past*, s. défilé, m.
March, vn. marcher, se mettre en marche. *To — in*, entrer. *To — out*, sortir. *To — off*, partir, s'en aller, (*pop.*) décamper. *To — on*, avancer past, défiler. — va. faire marcher, mettre en marche
Marching, s. marche, f. *—-past*, s. défilé, m.
Marchioness, s. marquise, f.
Mare, s. jument, f., cavale, f. *A —'s-nest*, mystification, f. *To look for a —'s-nest*, chercher midi à quatorze heures
Margin, s. bord, m., rive, f., (*of books*) marge, f. *In the —*, en marge
Margin, va. border, mettre une marge à
Marginal, adj. marginal
Marigold, s. souci, m.
Marine, adj. marin, de mer, naval, maritime. *—-stores*, bric-à-brac, m.
Marine, s. marine, f., soldat de marine, m.
Mariner, s. marin, m. *—'s card*, la rose des vents. *—'s compass*, boussole, f.
Marital, adj. marital
Maritime, adj. maritime
Marjoram, s. origan, m. *Sweet —*, marjolaine, f.
Mark, s. marque, f., signe, m., empreinte, f., trace, f., vestige, m., importance, f., (*aim*) but, m., blanc, m., cible, f., (*money*) croix, f. *You are not far from the —*, vous n'êtes pas loin de la vérité
Mark, va. n. marquer, remarquer, observer. *To — out*, marquer, désigner, choisir
Marker, s. marqueur, m., (*book*) signet, m., (*counter*) jeton, m.
Market, s. marché, m., halle, f., place, f., (*sale*) débouché, m., (*prices*) taux, m., prix, m. *In the —*, sur la place. *—-crier*, s. crieur, m. *—-day*, s. jour de marché, m. *—-gardener*, s. maraîcher, m. *—-place*, s. place du marché, f. *—-price*, s. *—-rate*, s. prix courant, m. *—-town*, s. ville où se tient un marché, f. *Money —*, s. bourse, f., bulletin financier, m.
Marketable, adj. d'un débit facile, courant
Marking, adj. à marquer
Marksman, s. habile tireur, m.
Marl, s. marne, f. *—-pit*, s. marnière, f. *—-stone*, s. marne dure, f.
Marl, va. marner
Marly, adj. marneux
Marmalade, s. marmelade, f.
Marmoset, s. petit singe, m., marmouset, m.
Marmot, s. marmotte, f.
Maroon, s. nègre marron, m.
Marquee, s. marquise, f.
Marquetry, s. marqueterie, f.
Marquis, s. marquis, m.
Marquisate, s. marquisat, m.
Marriage, s. mariage, m., noces, f.pl.
Marriageable, adj. en âge de se marier, nubile
Married, adj. marié, de mariage
Marrow, s. moelle, f. *—-bone*, os à moelle, m.
Marrowy, adj. moelleux
Marry, va. (*to unite*) marier, (*for oneself*) épouser, prendre pour femme, se marier avec; — vn. se marier. *To — into*, se marier dans, s'allier à. *To — below one's rank*, se mésallier
Marrying, s. mariage, m.
Marsh, s. marais, m., marécage, m.
Marshal, s. maréchal, m.
Marshal, va. ranger, mener
Marshy, adj. marécageux, de marais
Mart, s. entrepôt, m., marché, m., débouché, m.
Marten, **Martin**, s. martre, f., (*bird*) martinet, m.
Martial, adj. martial, guerrier, belliqueux. *— law*, code militaire, m., état de siége, m.
Martially, adv. vaillamment
Martingale, s. martingale, f.
Martinmas, s. Saint-Martin, f.
Martyr, s. martyr, m., -e, f.
Martyrdom, s. martyre, m.
Martyrology, s. martyrologe, m.
Marvel, s. merveille, f., chose merveilleuse, f.
Marvel, vn. s'émerveiller, s'étonner
Marvellous, adj. merveilleux
Marvellously, adv. merveilleusement, à merveille
Masculine, adj. mâle, masculin, viril, (*of women*) hommasse
Mash, s. mélange, m., pâte, f.
Mash, va. écraser, mélanger, (*to brew*) brasser. *Mashed potatoes*, purée de pommes de terre, f.
Mask, s. masque, m., voile, m. *Woman's —*, loup, m.
Mask, va. masquer, déguiser, cacher; — vn. se masquer
Masker, s. masque, m., personne masquée, f.
Mason, s. maçon, m.
Masonic, adj. maçonnique
Masonry, s. maçonnerie, f.
Masquerade, **Masquerading**, s. mascarade, f., bal masqué, m.
Masquerader, s. masque, m., coureur de bals masqués, m.
Mass, s. masse, f., amas, m., (*Cath. rel.*) messe, f. *High —*, la grand'messe. *—-book*, s. livre de messe, m.
Massacre, va. massacrer
Massacre, s. massacre, m.
Massive, adj. massif
Mast, s. mât, m., (*fruit*) faînes, f.pl., (*oak*) glands, m.pl., (*chestnut*) châtaignes, f.pl.
Mast, va. mâter
Master, s. maître, m., possesseur, m., propriétaire, m., (*nav.*) patron, m., capitaine, m., (*of workmen*) maître, m., patron, m., entrepreneur, m.; (*of a gentleman*) monsieur, m., (*law*) maître, m., conseiller, m. *As a —*, en maître. *Like —, like man*, tel maître, tel valet. *To be — of*, être maître de, (*to know*) connaître. *— of the horse*, Grand Écuyer, m. *— of the Mint*, Directeur de la Monnaie, m. *—-key*, s. passe-partout, m. *—-lode*, s. filon principal, m. *—-minds*, s. grandes âmes, f.pl. *—-piece*, s. chef-d'œuvre, m. *—-stroke*, s. *—-touch*, s. coup de maître, m.
Master, va. être le maître de, maîtriser, dominer, (*a difficulty*) surmonter, venir à bout de, bien connaître, apprendre à fond
Masterly, adj. de maître, fait de main de maître, excellent, parfait
Mastership, s. direction, f., (*in a college*) chaire, f.
Mastery, s. autorité, f., empire, m., possession, f., supériorité, f., victoire, f., dessus, m., connaissance parfaite, f.
Mastic, s. mastic, m., (*tree*) lentisque, m.
Masticate, va. mâcher
Mastication, s. mastication, f.
Mastiff, s. dogue, m., mâtin, m., chien, m.
Mat, s. natte, f., paillasson, m. *Rush —*, natte de jonc, f., (*for dishes, &c.*) dessous, m.
Mat, va. natter, couvrir de nattes or de paillassons, (*twist*) mêler, emmêler, (*stick*) aplatir, coller
Match, s. mèche, f., (*lucifer*) allumette, f., (*equal*) pareil, m., (*marriage*) mariage, m., union, f., (*pers.*) parti, m., (*agreement*) convention, f., (*game*) partie, f., (*wrestling*) lutte, f., (*fencing*) assaut, m.,

(*running*) course, *f.*, (*sailing*) joute, *f.*, (*shooting*) tir, *m.* — *-box*, s. porte-allumettes, *m.* — *-lock*, s. fusil à mèche, *m.* — *-maker*, s. fabricant d'allumettes, *m.* *He has not his* —, il n'a pas son pareil. *He is no — for him*, il n'est pas de force à lutter avec lui. *To meet with one's* —, trouver son maître, trouver à qui parler. *To be a good* —, *a bad* —, être bien, mal assorti, aller bien, mal ensemble. *Love-* —, s. mariage d'inclination, *m.* — *-maker*, s. faiseur de mariages, *m.*

Match, va. égaler, rivaliser avec, s'élever aussi haut que, proportionner, tenir tête à, lutter contre, se mesurer avec, assortir, appareiller, (*gloves, &c.*) apparier; — vn. se marier (dans), s'allier (à), s'assortir, se marier

Matchless, adj. incomparable, sans pareil, sans égal

Mate, s. époux, *m.*, épouse, *f.*, compagnon, *m.*, compagne, *f.*, camarade, *m.f.*, mâle, *m.*, femelle, *f.*, collègue, *m.*, commensal, *m.*, (*nav.*) second, *m.*, (*chess*) mat, *m.* *Master's* —, s. contre-maître, *m.* *Surgeon's* —, s. aide-major, *m.*

Mate, va. see Match

Material, adj. matériel, important, essentiel

Material, s. matière, *f.*, substance, *f.* —*s*. pl. matériaux, *m.pl.* *The raw* —*s*, les matières premières

Materialism, s. matérialisme, *m.*

Materialist, s. matérialiste, *m.*

Materiality, s. matérialité, *f.*

Materially, adv. matériellement, essentiellement, d'une manière importante

Maternal, adj. maternel

Maternally, adv. maternellement

Maternity, s. maternité, *f.*

Mathematical, adj. mathématique, des mathématiques

Mathematically, adv. mathématiquement

Mathematician, s. mathématicien, *m.*

Mathematics, s.pl. mathématiques, *f.pl.*

Matins, s.pl. matines, *f. plur.*

Matricide, s. matricide, *f.*

Matriculate, va. immatriculer

Matriculation, s. matricule, *f.*, immatriculation, *f.*, (*students*) inscription, *f.*

Matrimonial, adj. matrimonial, conjugal

Matrimonially, adv. conjugalement

Matrimony, s. mariage, *m.*

Matron, s. matrone, *f.*, (*of a hospital*) surveillante, *f.*

Matronly, adj. de femme, grave, respectable, d'âge mûr

Matter, s. matière, *f.*, matériaux, *m.pl.*, sujet, *m.*, question, *f.*, fait, *m.*, point, *m.*, fond, *m.*, affaire, *f.*, chose, *f.*, importance, *f.*, espace, *m.*, distance, *f.*, (*med.*) pus, *m.* *To speak to the* —, parler fort bien. *What is the* —? de quoi s'agit-il? qu'y a-t-il? qu'est-ce qu'il y a? *What is the — with you?* qu'avez-vous? *For the — of*, pour ce qui est de. — *of course*, chose toute naturelle. *Something, nothing is the — with the child*, l'enfant a quelque chose, n'a rien. *No* —, *it is no* —, n'importe. *It is no great* —, ce n'est pas une affaire

Matter, vn. importer, avoir de l'importance, (*med.*) suppurer. *It —s not*, il n'importe. *It —s little*, peu importe. *What —s it that* or *whether . . .?* qu'importe que or si . . .?

Matting, s. paillasson, *m.*

Mattock, s. pioche, *f.*, hoyau, *m.*

Mattress, s. matelas, *m.*, sommier, *m.* — *-maker*, s. matelassier, *m.*, -ère, *f.*

Mature, adj. mûr

Mature, va.n. mûrir, faire mûrir

Maturely, adv. mûrement

Maturity, s. maturité, *f.*, (*of a bill*) échéance, *f.*

Maudlin, adj. larmoyant, pleureur, (*tipsy*) gris, à moitié ivre

Maul, s. maillet, *m.*

Maul, va. malmener, battre

Maul-stick, s. appui-main, *m.*

Maundy-Thursday, s. le Jeudi saint

Mausoleum, s. mausolée, *m.*

Maw, s. estomac, *m.*, panse, *f.*, (*of birds*) jabot, *m.*

Mawkish, adj. fade, insipide

Mawkishly, adv. avec fadeur

Mawkishness, s. fadeur, *f.*

Maxim, s. maxime, *f.*

Maximum, s. maximum, *m.*

May, s. mai, *m.*, mois de mai, *m.*, (*bot.*) aubépine, *f.* — *-beetle*, s. — *-bug*, s. hanneton, *m.* — *-bloom*, s. aubépine, *f.* — *-day*, s. premier mai

May, va. pouvoir, être permis or libre. — *I go out?* puis-je sortir? *That — be*, *it — be so*, cela se peut. — *I die rather!* puissé-je mourir plutôt! — vn. cueillir des fleurs au printemps

Mayor, s. maire, *m.*

Mayoralty, s. mairie, *f.*

Mayoress, s. femme du maire, *f.*

Maze, s. dédale, *m.*, labyrinthe, *m.*

Mazy, adj. plein de détours, inextricable

Me, pron. me, moi, à moi

Mead, s. pré, *m.*, prairie, *f.*, (*drink*) hydromel, *m.*

Meadow, s. prairie, *f.*, pré, *m.*

Meagre, adj. maigre, décharné, amaigri, pauvre

Meagrely, adv. maigrement

Meagreness, s. maigreur, *f.*

Meal, s. repas, *m.*, (*flour*) farine, *f.*

Mealy, adj. farineux, poudreux, (*fig.*) doucereux, cotonneux

Mean, adj. bas, vil, méprisable, abject, sordide, ladre, avare, mesquin, humble, simple, (*middle*) moyen, intermédiaire. *In the —time* or *—while*, see Meantime

Mean, s. milieu, *m.*, moyen terme, *m.*, (*math.*) moyenne, *f.*, moyen, *m.*, médiocrité, *f.* —*s*, s.pl. moyen, *m.*, voie, *f.*, cause, *f.*, moyens, *m.pl.*, facultés, *f.pl.*, fortune, *f.* —*s of*, au moyen de, par le moyen de. *By all —s*, certainement, par tous les moyens possibles. *By any —s*, en aucune façon. *By no —s*, *by no manner of —s*, nullement, aucunement, en aucune façon. *By some —s or other*, de manière ou d'autre

Mean, va.n. (*to*) vouloir (. . .), avoir l'intention (de), se proposer (de), prétendre, vouloir dire, signifier, (*for*) destiner (à). *I — to say*, je veux dire. *What is meant by?* ce que veut dire, que signifie?

Meander, s. méandre, *m.*, détour, *m.*, dédale, *m.*, labyrinthe, *m.*

Meander, vn. serpenter; — va. faire serpenter

Meaning, s. intention, *f.*, dessein, *m.*, pensée, *f.*, idée, *f.*, sens, *m.*, signification, *f.* *What is the — of this word?* que veut dire ce mot?

Meanly, adv. bassement, d'une manière méprisable, vile or abjecte, médiocrement, mesquinement, humblement

Meanness, s. bassesse, *f.*, nature méprisable, vile, or abjecte, *f.*, lésinerie, *f.*, ladrerie, *f.*, médiocrité, *f.*

Meantime, Meanwhile, conj. pendant ce temps, sur ces entrefaites, dans l'intervalle, cependant, en attendant

Measles, s.pl. rougeole, *f.*, (*of pigs*) ladrerie, *f.*

Measurable, adj. qu'on peut mesurer

Measure, s. mesure, *f.*, (*geol.*) assise, *f.* *This is hard* —, voilà qui est bien dur. *Beyond all* —, outre mesure. *In a great* —, en grande partie. *In some* —, jusqu'à un certain point

Measure, va. mesurer, (*land*) arpenter, (*masonry*) toiser, (*for clothes*) prendre mesure à. *To — out*, mesurer. — vn. mesurer, avoir.

Measurement, s. action de mesurer, de prendre mesure à, *f.*, mesurage, *m.*, arpentage, *m.*, toisé, *m.*

Measurer, s. mesureur, *m.*, arpenteur, *m.*, toiseur, *m.*

Meat, s. (*flesh*) viande, *f.*, (*food*) nourriture, *f.*, manger, *m.*

Mechanic, s. artisan, *m.*, ouvrier, *m.*

Mechanical, adj. mécanique, machinal

Mechanically, adv. mécaniquement, machinalement

Mechanician, s. mécanicien, *m.*

Mechanics, s.pl. la mécanique

Mechanism, s. mécanisme, *m.*

Mechanist, s. machiniste, *m.*

Medal, s. médaille, *f.*

Medallion, s. médaillon, *m.*

Medallist, s. médailliste, *m.*, (*rewarded*) médaillé, *m.*

Meddle, vn. (*with*) se mêler (de), toucher (à), s'immiscer (dans), s'ingérer (dans)

Meddler, s. officieux, *m.*, -euse, *f.*, brouillon, *m.*, -ne, *f.*, importun, *m.*, -e, *f.*

Meddlesome, adj. officieux, brouillon, importun, qui aime à se mêler des affaires des autres

Mediæval, adj. du moyen âge

Mediate, vn. intervenir, intercéder, s'interposer

Mediation, s. médiation, *f.*, intercession, *f.*, intermédiaire, *m.*, entremise, *f.*

Mediator, s. médiateur, *m.*

Mediatrix, s. médiatrice, *f.*

Medical, adj. médical, de médecin. — *attendant*, médecin, *m.* — *attendance*, les soins d'un médecin. *The — man*, l'homme de l'art, *m.* médecin, *m.*

Medically, adv. au point de vue de la médecine

Medicament, s. médicament, *m.*

Medicate, va. traiter, guérir, donner des propriétés médicales à, (*wine*) droguer, frelater

Medicinal, adj. médicinal

Medicine, s. médecine, *f.* — *-chest*, pharmacie portative, *f.*

Mediocrity, s. médiocrité, *f.*

Meditate, vn. méditer (sur); — va. méditer

Meditation, s. méditation, *f.*

Meditative, adj. méditatif

Medium, s. milieu, *m.*, (*expedient*) moyen, *m.*, agent, *m.*, (*log.*) moyen terme, *m.*

Medlar, s. néflier, *m.*, nèfle, *f.*

Medley, s. mélange confus, *m.*, pêle-mêle, *m.*, (*lit.*) macédoine, *f.*

Medley, adj. mêlé, confus
Meed, s. récompense, *f.*
Meek, adj. doux, humble de cœur, débonnaire
Meekly, adv. avec douceur, humblement
Meekness, s. douceur, *f.*, humilité, *f.*
Meerschaum, s. écume de mer, *f.*, pipe d'écume de mer, *f.*
Meet, adj convenable, bon, digne, qui sied, propre
Meet, s. rendez-vous de chasse, *m.*
Meet, va. rencontrer, faire la rencontre de, (*to fight*) se battre avec, (*to see*) voir, (*to find*) trouver, (*look*) frapper, se présenter devant, (*to undergo*) subir, (*danger*) affronter, (*expenses*) faire face, (*engagements*) faire honneur, remplir. *To come to —, to go to —*, venir, aller au-devant de. — vn. se rencontrer, se voir, s'assembler, se réunir, (*things*) se joindre, se réunir. *To — again*, se revoir, se réunir de nouveau. *To — with*, rencontrer, se trouver avec, voir, (*things*) ramasser, découvrir, (*reception*) recevoir, (*disappointment*) éprouver, essayer, subir
Meeting, s. rencontre, *f.*, entrevue, *f.*, rendez-vous, *m.*, réunion, *f.*, assemblée publique, *f.*, séance, *f.*, (*dissenters*) office, *m.*, service, *m.*, (*rivers*) confluent, *m.*
Meetness, s. convenance, *f.*
Melancholy, s. mélancolie, *f.*
Melancholy, adj. mélancolique, triste, douloureux, affligeant
Mellow, adj. mûr, (*pear*) blette, douce, (*sound*) mélodieux, (*touch*) mou, mol, doux, moelleux, (*pers.*) entre deux vins, en train, gai
Mellow, va. mûrir, faire mûrir, rendre mélodieux, adoucir, (*agric.*) ameublir; — vn. mûrir, devenir mélodieux, s'adoucir, (*land*) devenir meuble
Mellowness, s. maturité, *f.*, mélodie, *f.*, douceur, *f.*, moelleux, *m.*
Melodious, adj. mélodieux
Melodiously, adv. mélodieusement
Melodiousness, s. mélodie, *f.*
Melodrama, s. mélodrame, *m.*
Melody, s. mélodie, *f.*
Melon, s. melon, *m.* — *-bed*, melonnière, *f.*
Melt, va. fondre, faire fondre, dissoudre, (*fig.*) attendrir, fléchir, adoucir; — vn. fondre, se fondre, se dissoudre, (*fig.*) s'attendrir
Melter, s. fondeur, *m.*
Melting, adj. fondant, qui fait fondre, (*fig.*) touchant, pathétique, (*weather*) étouffant
Melting, s. fonte, *f.*, fusion, *f.*, (*fig.*) attendrissement, *m.*
Member, s. membre, *m.*

Membrane, s. membrane, *f.*
Memento, s. mémento, *m.*, souvenir, *m.*
Memoir, s. mémoire, *m.*
Memorable, adj. mémorable
Memorably, adv. d'une manière mémorable
Memorandum, s. note, *f.*, (*com.*) bordereau, *m.* — *-book*, agenda, *m.*, calepin, *m.* *To make a — of*, prendre note de
Memorial, s. mémorial, *m.*, souvenir, *m.*, monument, *m.*, demande, *f.*, pétition, *f.*, (*report*) mémoire, *m.*
Memorial, adj. commémoratif
Memorialist, s. pétitionnaire, *m.f.*
Memorialize, va. pétitionner, adresser un mémoire à
Memory, s. mémoire, *f.*, (*remembrance*) souvenir, *m.*
Menace, s. menace, *f.*
Menace, va. menacer
Menagerie, s. ménagerie, *f.*
Mend, va. raccommoder, réparer, (*a pen*) tailler, (*fig.*) amender, corriger, réformer, améliorer, (*abuses*) redresser, (*one's step*) hâter, presser; — vn. se corriger, se réformer, s'améliorer, se rétablir
Mendacious, adj. mensonger
Mendacity, s. penchant au mensonge, *m.*, mensonge, *m.*
Mender, s. raccommodeur, *m.*, -euse, *f.*
Mendicancy, **Mendicity**, s. mendicité, *f.*
Mendicant, adj. s. mendiant, -e
Mending, s. raccommodage, *m.*, réparation, *f.*, (*of a pen*) taille, *f.* *Past —*, sans remède
Menial, adj. de domestique, vil
Menial, s. valet, *m.*, laquais, *m.*, domestique, *m.*
Mensuration, s. mesurage, *m.*, mesure, *f.*
Mental, adj. mental, intérieur
Mentally, adv. mentalement
Mention, s. mention, *f.*, allusion, *f.*
Mention, va. parler de, mentionner, prononcer. *Not to —*, sans compter. *Don't — it*, cela ne vaut pas la peine d'en parler
Mephitic, adj. méphitique
Mercantile, adj. mercantile, commercial, commerçant, de commerce
Mercenary, adj. s. mercenaire
Mercer, s. mercier, *m.*, -ère, *f.*
Mercery, s. mercerie, *f.*
Merchandise, s. marchandise, *f.*, négoce, *m.*, commerce, *m.*
Merchant, s. négociant, *m.*, commerçant, *m.*

Merchant, adj. marchand, commerçant. — *-man*, s. — *-ship*, s. bâtiment marchand, *m.*, navire marchand, *m.* — *service*, s. marine marchande, *f.*
Merciful, adj. miséricordieux, clément, compatissant, indulgent
Mercifully, adv. miséricordieusement, avec clémence, avec miséricorde
Mercifulness, s. miséricorde, *f.*, clémence, *f.*, compassion, *f.*
Merciless, adj. inhumain, cruel, sans miséricorde, impitoyable
Mercilessly, adv. sans miséricorde, cruellement, impitoyablement
Mercurial, adj. mercuriel, (*temper*) vif, ardent
Mercury, s. mercure, *m.*, vif-argent, *m.*
Mercy, s. miséricorde, *f.*, clémence, *f.*, merci, *f.*, compassion, *f.*, grâce, *f.* — *-seat*, s. propitiatoire, *m.*, trône de grâce, *m.* *For —'s sake*, par pitié. *To lie, to be at the — of*, être à la merci de
Mere, adj. simple, pur, seul, rien que
Merely, adv. simplement, purement, tout bonnement
Meretricious, adj. recherché, d'emprunt, faux
Merge, va. plonger, perdre, fondre, éteindre; — vn. se perdre
Meridian, s. méridien, *m.*, midi, *m.*, (*fig.*) apogée, *m.*
Meridional, adj. du méridien, méridional, du sud, midi
Merino, s. mérinos, *m.*
Merit, s. mérite, *m.*
Merit, va. mériter, être digne de
Meritorious, adj. méritoire
Meritoriously, adv. méritoirement
Meritoriousness, s. mérite, *m.*
Mermaid, s. sirène, *f.*
Merrily, adv. gaiment, joyeusement
Merriment, s. gaieté, *f.*, jeux, *m.pl.*, divertissements, *m.pl.*, amusements, *m.pl.*
Merry, adj. gai, joyeux, plaisant
Mesh, s. maille, *f.*
Mesh, va. prendre au filet
Meshy, adj. plein de mailles
Meslin, s. méteil, *m.*
Mesmerism, s. mesmérisme, *m.*
Mesmerize, va. magnétiser
Mess, s. mets, *m.*, plat, *m.*, (*officer's*) table, *f.*, pension, *f.*, (*soldiers*) gamelle, *f.*, (*confusion*) fouillis, *m.*, gâchis, *m.*, désordre, *m.*, (*scrape*) embarras, *m.*, difficulté, *f.* — *-room*, salle à manger, *f.* *To make a —*, faire du gâchis, mettre tout en désordre. *To be in a nice —*, être dans un joli état, être dans de beaux draps
Mess, vn. manger. *To — together*, prendre ses repas ensemble, (*private soldiers*) manger à la gamelle. — va. gâcher, salir
Message, s. message, *m.*, commission, *f.*, (*telegram*) dépêche, *f.*
Messenger, s. messager, *m.*, messagère, *f.*, (*fig.*) avant-coureur, *m.*, avant-courrière, *f.*
Messmate, s. commensal, *m.*, camarade, *m.*
Messuage, s. maison et dependances, *f.pl.*
Metage, s. mesurage, *m.*
Metal, s. métal, *m.*, rail, *m.*
Metal, va. (*roads*) ferrer, empierrer
Metallic, adj. métallique
Metallurgic, adj. métallurgique
Metallurgist, s. métallurgiste, *m.*
Metallurgy, s. métallurgie, *f.*
Metamorphose, va. métamorphoser
Metamorphosis, s. métamorphose, *f.*
Metaphor, s. métaphore, *f.*
Metaphoric, adj. métaphorique
Metaphorically, adv. métaphoriquement
Metaphysical, adj. métaphysique
Metaphysically, adv. métaphysiquement
Metaphysician, s. métaphysicien, *m.*
Metaphysics, s.pl. métaphysique, *f.*
Metastasis, s. métastase, *f.*
Mete, va. mesurer
Metempsychosis, s. métempsycose, *f.*
Meteor, s. météore, *m.*
Meteoric, **Meteorical**, **Meteorous**, adj. météorique
Meteorological, adj. météorologique
Meteorology, s. météorologie, *f.*
Meter, s. mesureur, *m.*, (*gas*) compteur, *m.*
Methinks, v.imp. il me semble
Method, s. méthode, *f.*, manière, *f.*, moyen, *m.*
Methodical, adj. méthodique
Methodically, adv. méthodiquement
Methodism, s. méthodisme, *m.*
Methodist, s. méthodiste, *m.*
Methodize, va. ordonner, mettre de la méthode dans
Methought, v.imp. il me semblait
Metonymy, s. métonymie, *f.*
Metre, s. mesure, *f.*, vers, *m.*, mètre, *m.*
Metrical, adj. métrique, en vers
Metropolis, s. capitale, *f.*, métropole, *f.*

Metropolitan, s. adj. métropolitain, *m.*
Mettle, s. ardeur, *f.*, fougue, *f.*, feu, *m.*, courage, *m.*
Mettled, adj. plein de cœur, courageux, (*horse*) fougueux
Mettlesome, adj. ardent, fougueux
Mew, s. (*bird*) mouette, *f.*, (*cage*) mue, *f.*, cage, *f.*, prison, *f.*, lieu de sûreté, *f.* —*s*, pl. écuries, *f.pl.*
Mew, va. enfermer; — vn. (*birds*) muer, se transformer, (*cats*) miauler
Mewing, s. (*birds*) mue, *f.*, (*cats*) miaulement, *m.*
Mewl, vn. vagir
Mewling, s. vagissement, *m.*
Miasm, s. miasme, *m.*
Mica, s. mica, *m.*
Michaelmas, s. Saint-Michel
Mickle, s. beaucoup. *Many a little makes a —*, les petits ruisseaux font les grandes rivières
Microscope, s. microscope, *m.*
Microscopic, Microscopical, adj. microscopique
Mid, adj. du milieu, mi-. — *-course*, s. milieu de la carrière, *m.* — *-day*, s. midi, *m.* *In — -winter*, au cœur de l'hiver
Middle, s. milieu, *m.*, centre, *m.*, (*waist*) ceinture, *f.*
Middle, adj. du milieu, central, (*fig.*) moyen, intermédiaire
Middling, adj. moyen, passable, médiocre, (*com.*) bon ordinaire, (*health*) tout doucement
Midge, s. moucheron, *m.*
Midland, s. adj. dans l'intérieur des terres, de l'intérieur
Midnight, s. minuit, *m.*
Midnight, adj. de minuit, de nuit
Midriff, s. diaphragme, *m.*
Midship, s. milieu du navire, *m.*
Midshipman, s. aspirant de marine, *m.*
Midst, s. milieu, *m.*, fort, *m.*
Midsummer, s. le cœur de l'été. — *holidays*, grandes vacances. — *-day*, Saint-Jean d'été, *f.*
Midwife, s. sage-femme, *f.*
Midwifery, s. l'art des accouchements, *m.*
Mien, s. mine, *f.*, air, *m.*
Might. *I told him he —*, je lui dis qu'il le pouvait. *One — think*, on pourrait croire. *That he — know*, afin qu'il sût
Might, s. pouvoir, *m.*, force, *f.*, puissance, *f.* *With — and main*, de toute sa force, de vive force
Mightily, adv. puissamment, fort, extrêmement
Mightiness, s. puissance, *f.*, grandeur, *f.*
Mighty, adj. puissant, fort, grand, violent

Mighty, adv. fort, extrêmement
Mignonette, s. réséda, *m.*
Migrate, vn. émigrer, passer
Migration, s. migration, *f.*
Migratory, adj. nomade, qui émigre, (*birds*) de passage
Milch, adj. laitière
Mild, adj. doux
Mildew, s. rouille, *f.*, nielle, *f.*, tache d'humidité, *f.*
Mildew, va. nieller, faire périr par la rouille, brouir, (*fig.*) tacher, souiller
Mildly, adv. doucement, modérément
Mildness, s. douceur, *f.*
Mile, s. mille, *m.* — *-post*, s. — *-stone*, s. borne milliaire, *f.*
Mileage, s. prix du mille, *m.*, allocation par mille pour frais de voyage, *f.*
Milfoil, s. millefeuille, *f.*
Miliary, adj. miliaire
Militant, adj. militant, combattant
Militarily, adv. militairement
Military, adj. militaire. *A — man*, un militaire. *The —*, s. la force armée
Militate, vn. militer
Militia, s. milice, *f.* — *-man*, soldat de la milice, *m.*
Milk, s. lait, *m.* *Bread and —*, — *-porridge*, soupe au lait, *f.* — *and water*, du lait coupé. — *-diet*, le laitage. — *-fever*, s. fièvre de lait, *f.* — *-maid*, s. laitière, *f.* — *-man*, s. laitier, *m.* — *-pail*, s. seau, *m.* — *-pan*, s. terrine à lait, *f.*, jatte à lait, *f.* — *-sop*, s. (*fig.*) poule mouillée, *f.* — *-tooth*, s. dent de lait, *f.* — *walk*, s. clientèle de laitier, *f.* — *-woman*, s. laitière, *f.*
Milk, va. traire
Milky, adj. de lait, à lait, laiteux, (*astron.*) lacté. *The — way*, la voie lactée
Mill, s. moulin, *m.*, moulin à . . ., manufacture, *f.*, fabrique, *f.*, filature, *f.*, (*coins*) moulinet, *m.*, (*pop.*) combat de boxe, *m.* *To turn the —*, faire tourner la meule. — *-board*, s. fort carton, *m.* — — *-course*, — *-race*, s. canal or courant de moulin, *m.*, biez, *m.*, bief, *m.* *-dam*, s. barrage de moulin, *m.* — *-gearing*, s. appareil de rouages, *m.* — *-hand*, s. ouvrier de filature, *m.* — *-head*, s. courant, *m.* — *-hopper*, s. trémie, *f.* — *-horse*, s. cheval de moulin, *m.* — *-owner*, s. propriétaire de moulin, *m.*, filateur, *m.*, chef de fabrique, *m.* — *-pond*, s. — *-pool*, s. réservoir de moulin, *m.* — *-stone*, s. meule, *f.*, pierre meulière, *f.* — *-tooth*, s. molaire, *f.* — *-wright*, s. constructeur de moulins, *m.*
Mill, va. moudre, fabriquer au moulinet, (*cloth*) fouler, (*chocolate*) faire mousser, (*to knock*) frapper à coups de poing. *Milled edge*, cordon, *m.*, cordonnet, *m.*
Milled, adj. (*cloth*) foulé. *Double- —*, croisé. *Double- — cloth*, s. cuir de laine, *m.*
Millenarian, adj. s. millénaire
Millenary, s. espace de mille ans, *m.*, millénaire, *m.*
Millennium, s. règne millénaire, *m.*
Milleped, s. mille-pieds, *m.*
Miller, s. meunier, *m.*, -ère, *f.*
Millesimal, adj. de millième
Millet, s. mil, *m.*, millet, *m.*
Milliner, s. modiste, *f.*, marchande de modes, *f.* —*'s shop*, magasin de modes, *m.*
Millinery, s. modes, *f.pl.*
Million, s. million, *m.* *Worth a —*, millionnaire
Millionth, adj. millionième
Milt, s. rate, *f.*, (*fish*) laite, *f.*, laitance, *f.*
Milt, va. féconder
Mime, s. mime, *m.*
Mimic, adj. mimique, imitateur, -trice
Mimic, s. mime, *m.*, imitateur, *m.*, -trice, *f.*
Mimic, va. imiter, contrefaire
Mimicry, s. mimique, *f.*, imitation, *f.*
Minaret, s. minaret, *m.*
Mince, va. hacher menu, (*fig.*) adoucir, atténuer, (*words*) manger. *Not to — matters*, parler net, ne pas mâcher ce qu'on a sur le cœur. — vn. marcher à petits pas, en minaudant, parler avec une délicatesse affectée
Mince, adj. haché. — *-meat*, s. hachis, *m.*, émincé, *m.*
Mincing, adj. minaudier, affecté. — *-knife*, — *-machine*, s. hachoir, *m.*
Mincingly, adv. en minaudant
Mind, s. esprit, *m.*, âme, *f.*, intelligence, *f.*, bon sens, *m.*, raison, *f.*, tête, *f.*, (*wish*) envie, *f.*, désir, *m.*, idée, *f.*, intention, *f.*, dessein, *m.*, parti, *m.*, (*opinion*) avis, *m.*, sentiment, *m.*, opinion, *f.*, pensée, *f.* *To call to —*, se représenter, se rappeler. *To have something on one's —*, avoir l'esprit préoccupé de quelque chose. *A man of strong —*, un homme de tête. *To be in one's —*, avoir sa raison. *To be out of one's —*, avoir perdu la raison or la tête, être hors de son bon sens. *To go out of one's —*, perdre la raison. *I have a —, a great —, half a —*, j'ai envie, bien envie, presque envie. *After one's —, to one's —*, à son gré, à son goût, à son idée. *To bring one's — to*, se résoudre à, s'habituer à. *Not to know one's own —*, ne pas savoir ce qu'on veut. *To make up one's —*, prendre son parti. *To be of the same — (as)*, être du même avis. *To break one's — to*, s'ouvrir à. *To speak one's —*, dire ce qu'on pense. *Time out of —*, de temps immémorial. *To bear in —*, se rappeler. *To recall to —*, se rappeler. *Put me in —*, faites-moi penser
Mind, va. faire attention à, avoir soin de, s'occuper (de), songer (à), (*to watch, &c.*) garder, veiller sur, surveiller, (*to care*) s'inquiéter de, regarder à, (*listen*) écouter, avoir égard à, faire attention à, prendre garde à, (*fear*) avoir peur de. — *your business*, appliquez-vous à vos affaires. *Never — !* n'y faites pas attention ! *I don't — what he says*, je ne m'inquiète pas de ce qu'il dit. *Not to — expense*, ne pas regarder à la dépense. *You don't — my cigar!* mon cigare ne vous gêne pas? *Do you — going!* tenez-vous à y aller? — vn. avoir envie, être d'humeur à
Minded, adj. à l'esprit, à l'âme, qui a l'esprit . . ., (*in compounds*) d'un avis . . ., d'humeur, disposé
Mindedness, s. disposition, *f.*, humeur, *f.*
Mindful, adj. attentif (à), soigneux (de), appliqué (à), (*of*) qui se souvient (de)
Mindfully, adv. avec soin, attentivement
Minding, s. attention, *f.*
Mindless, adj. sans esprit, sans intelligence, oublieux (de), inattentif (à), sans égard (pour)
Mine, poss. pron. le mien, la mienne, les miens, les miennes, à moi, mon, ma, mes. *This book is —*, ce livre est à moi or m'appartient. *A friend of —*, un de mes amis, un mien ami. *It is no fault of —*, ce n'est pas ma faute
Mine, s. mine, *f.*, minerai, *m.* *To work a —*, exploiter une mine
Mine, va.n. miner, creuser, saper
Miner, s. mineur, *m.*
Mineral, adj. s. minéral, *m.*
Mineralization, s. minéralisation, *f.*
Mineralize, va. minéraliser
Mineralizer, s. minéralisateur, *m.*
Mineralogic, Mineralogical, adj. minéralogique
Mineralogically, adv. en minéralogie
Mineralogist, s. minéralogiste, *m.*
Mineralogy, s. minéralogie, *f.*
Minever, s. petit-gris, *m.*
Mingle, va. mêler, mélanger, confondre; — vn. se mêler, se mélanger
Miniature, s. miniature, *f.*, portrait en miniature, *m.*

— *-painter*, peintre en miniature, *m.*
Minim, s. nain, *m.*, pygmée, *m.*, (*mus.*) blanche, *f.*
Minimum, s. minimum, *m.*
Mining, s. travail dans les mines, *m.*, exploitation des mines, *f.*
Minion, s. favori, *m.*, -ite, *f.*, mignon, *m.*, -ne, *f.*
Minister, s. ministre, *m.*
Minister, va.n. administrer, (*religion*) dispenser, donner, (*to do duty*) officier
Ministerial, adj. ministériel
Ministration, s. ministère, *m.*, entremise, *f.*, service, *m.*
Ministry, s. ministère, *m.*, entremise, *f.*, service, *m.*
Minium, s. minium, *m.*
Mink, s. loutre, *f.*
Minnow, s. goujon, *m.*, véron, *m.*
Minor, adj. moindre, plus petit, inférieur, léger, peu important, mineur
Minor, s. mineur, *m.*, mineure, *f.*
Minority, s. minorité, *f.*
Minster, s. cathédrale, *f.*
Minstrel, s. ménestrel, *m.*, barde, *m.*
Mint, s. monnaie, *f.*, hôtel de la Monnaie, *m.*, (*fig.*) fabrique, *f.*, (*bot.*) menthe, *f.*
Mint, va. monnayer, frapper, (*fig.*) fabriquer, forger
Mintage, s. sommes monnayées, *f.pl.*, droit de monnayage, *m.*
Minuet, s. menuet, *m.*
Minus, s. moins, *m.*
Minute, adj. menu, très petit, minutieux
Minute, s. minute, *f.*, moment, *m.* —*s*, pl. procès verbal, *m.* —*-gun*, s. coup de canon de minute en minute, *m.* —*-glass*, s. sablier d'une minute, *m.* —*-hand*, s. grande aiguille, *f.* *To take* or *make* —*s*, prendre des notes. —*-book*, s. agenda, *m.*, carnet, *m.*
Minute, va. prendre note de
Minutely, adj. adv. de chaque instant, à chaque instant, minutieusement
Minuteness, s. petitesse, *f.*, exiguïté, *f.*, finesse, *f.*
Minutiæ, s. minuties, *f. plur.*
Minx, s. friponne, *f.*, coquine, *f.*
Miracle, s. miracle, *m.*
Miraculous, adj. miraculeux
Miraculously, adv. miraculeusement
Mirage, s. mirage, *m.*
Mire, s. fange, *f.*, bourbe, *f.*, boue, *f.*, vase, *f.* *To stick (fast) in the* —, s'embourber
Mirror, s. miroir, *m.*
Mirth, s. gaieté, *f.*, joie, *f.*, hilarité, *f.*
Mirthful, adj. gai, joyeux, de gaieté, divertissant
Miry, adj. fangeux, bourbeux, boueux
Mis- . . . , (*in compounds*) mal . . . , més . . . , mé . . . , qui déteste, à tort, à faux
Misadventure, s. mésaventure, *f.*
Misalliance, s. mauvaise alliance, *f.*, mésalliance, *f.*
Misanthrope, Misanthropist, s. misanthrope, *m.*
Misanthropic, Misanthropical, adj. misanthrope, misanthropique
Misanthropy, s. misanthropie, *f.*
Misapplication, s. mauvaise application, *f.*
Misapply, va. appliquer mal, employer mal
Misapprehend, va. comprendre mal, entendre mal, se méprendre sur
Misapprehension, s. méprise, *f.*, idée fausse, *f.*
Misappropriate, va. détourner, distraire
Misappropriation, s. détournement, *m.*
Misbehave, vn. se conduire mal, se comporter mal, agir mal
Misbehaviour, s. mauvaise conduite, *f.*
Misbelief, s. fausse croyance, *f.*, incrédulité, *f.*
Misbeliever, s. mécréant, *m.*, infidèle, *m.*
Miscalculate, va. calculer mal, compter mal
Miscalculation, s. calcul erroné, *m.*, mécompte, *m.*
Miscarriage, s. insuccès, *m.*, mauvais succès, *m.*, échec, *m.*, coup manqué, *m.*, (*med.*) fausse couche, *f.*
Miscarry, vn. échouer, manquer, ne pas réussir, ne pas arriver à destination, s'égarer, (*med.*) faire une fausse couche, avorter
Miscellaneous, adj. varié, mêlé, mélangé
Miscellany, s. mélange, *m.*, (*lit.*) mélanges, *m.pl.*, miscellanées, *f.pl.*
Mischance, s. mauvaise chance, *f.*, malheur, *m.*, mésaventure, *f.*, accident fâcheux, *m.*
Mischief, s. malheur, *m.*, mal, *m.*, dommage, *m.*, tort, *m.*, (*wickedness*) méchanceté, *f.*
Mischievous, adj. méchant, malicieux, malfaisant, (*things*) nuisible
Mischievously, adv. méchamment, malicieusement, d'une manière nuisible
Mischievousness, s. malice, *f.*, méchanceté, *f.*
Misconceive, va.n. concevoir mal, juger mal
Misconception, s. fausse notion, *f.*
Misconduct, s. inconduite, *f.*
Misconduct, va. conduire mal
Misconstruction, s. interprétation fausse, *f.*, contresens, *m.*
Misconstrue, va. interpréter mal, traduire mal, (*fig.*) dénaturer
Miscount, va. faire une erreur de compte (de)
Miscreant, s. mécréant, *m.*, infidèle, *m.*, scélérat, *m.*
Misdeed, s. méfait, *m.*
Misdemean (oneself), vn. (se) comporter mal
Misdemeanour, s. délit, *m.*, offense, *f.* *High* —, grave délit, *m.*
Misdirect, va. diriger mal, renseigner mal, adresser mal
Miser, s. avare, *m.*
Miserable, adj. malheureux, misérable
Miserably, adv. malheureusement, misérablement
Miserly, adj. avare, d'avare
Misery, s. misère, *f.*, avarice, *f.*, (*torment*) supplice, *m.*
Misfit, s. vêtement manqué, *m.*, (*boots*) chaussure manquée, *f.*
Misfortune, s. malheur, *m.*, infortune, *f.*
Misgive, va. faire craindre à, inspirer des craintes à, faire pressentir
Misgiving, s. doute, *m.*, crainte, *f.*, appréhension, *f.*, pressentiment, *m.*
Misgovern, va. gouverner mal
Misgovernment, s. mauvaise administration, *f.*, mauvaise gestion, *f.*
Misguidance, s. fausse direction, *f.*, mauvais conseil, *m.*
Misguide, va. égarer, diriger mal
Misguided, adj. aveugle, égaré, qui s'abuse
Mishap, s. malheur, *m.*, mésaventure, *f.*, mauvaise chance, *f.*, contre-temps, *m.*
Misinform, va. informer mal, renseigner mal, dénoncer faussement
Misinterpret, va. interpréter mal, traduire mal, (*fig.*) dénaturer
Misinterpretation, s. fausse interprétation, *f.*, contre-sens, *m.*
Misjudge, va. juger mal, se tromper sur
Mislay, va. placer mal, (*to lose*) égarer, perdre
Mislead, va. égarer, fourvoyer, tromper, induire en erreur
Mismanage, va. diriger mal, conduire mal, administrer mal
Mismanagement, s. mauvaise direction, *f.*, mauvaise gestion, *f.*
Misname, va. nommer mal
Misnomer, s. erreur de nom, *f.*, faux nom, *m.*
Misplace, va. placer mal, déplacer
Misprint, va. imprimer mal *or* incorrectement
Misprint, s. faute d'impression, *f.*
Misquotation, s. fausse citation, *f.*
Misquote, va. citer mal *or* à faux
Misreckon, va. calculer mal
Misrepresent, va. dénaturer, représenter sous un faux jour
Misrepresentation, s. action de dénaturer, *f.*, faux rapport, *m.*, faux exposé, *m.*
Misrule, s. tyrannie, *f.*, désordre, *m.*, confusion, *f.*
Miss, va.n. manquer, (*lose*) ne pas trouver, perdre, (*leave out*) omettre, passer, sauter, (*to report*) s'apercevoir de l'absence de, (*billiards*) manquer de toucher. *To* — *fire*, rater
Miss, s. manque, *m.*, perte, *f.*, regret, *m.*, erreur, *f.*, omission, *f.*, mademoiselle, *f.*, demoiselle, *f.*
Missal, s. missel, *m.*
Misshape, va. former mal, difformer, défigurer
Misshapen, adj difforme
Missile, adj. de jet, de trait
Missile, s. projectile, *m.*, dard, *m.*, trait, *m.*
Mission, s. mission, *f.*
Missionary, s. missionnaire, *m.*
Missionary, adj. des missions, de missionnaire
Missive, s. adj. missive, *f.*
Misspell, va. épeler mal, écrire mal
Misspend, va. dépenser mal à propos, gaspiller, employer mal
Misstate, va. exposer incorrectement, rapporter inexactement
Misstatement, s. exposé *or* rapport inexact, *m.*, compte rendu erroné, *m.*
Mist, s. brume, *f.*, brouillard, *m.*, vapeur, *f.*
Mistakable, adj. qui prête à erreur
Mistake, va.n. comprendre mal, se tromper sur *or* de, se méprendre sur, (*for*) confondre (avec), prendre (pour). *To be mistaken*, se tromper, se méprendre
Mistake, s. erreur, *f.*, méprise, *f.*, faute, *f.*, bévue, *f.* *And no* —, c'est positif
Mistaken, past part. adj. (*things*) erroné, faux, mal entendu
Mistimed, adj. inopportun, mal à propos, déplacé
Mistletoe, s. gui, *m.*
Mistranslate, va. traduire incorrectement
Mistranslation, s. traduction inexacte, *f.*, contresens, *m.*
Mistress, s. maîtresse, *f.*, (*governess*) institutrice, *f.*, maîtresse, *f.* *My* — *is at home*, madame est chez elle
Mistrust, s. défiance, *f.*, méfiance, *f.*, doute, *m.*, soupçon, *m.*
Mistrust, va. se méfier de, se défier de, soupçonner, pressentir
Mistrustful, adj. méfiant, défiant, soupçonneux
Mistrustfully, adv. avec méfiance, avec défiance
Misty, adj. brumeux, couvert de brouillards, (*fig.*) obscur, ténébreux

Misunderstand, va. comprendre mal, entendre mal, se méprendre sur
Misunderstanding, s. mal-entendu, m., mésintelligence, f., désaccord, m.
Misusage, Misuse, s. mauvais usage, m., mauvais emploi, m.
Misuse, va. faire un mauvais usage *or* emploi de, mésuser de, maltraiter, malmener
Mite, s. (*insect*) mite, f., (*trifle*) denier, m., rien, m., petite portion, f.
Mitigate, va. adoucir, modérer, tempérer, mitiger
Mitigation, s. adoucissement, m., mitigation, f.
Mitre, s. mitre, f.
Mitred, adj. mitré
Mitten, Mite, s. mitaine, f.
Mix, va. mêler, mélanger, composer, (*salad*) retourner; — vn. se mêler, se mélanger, fréquenter
Mixed, adj. mêlé, mélangé, mixte
Mixture, s. mélange, m., (*pharmac.*) potion, f., mixture, f.
Mizzen, s. artimon, m.
Mizzen, adj d'artimon
Mizzle, vn. bruiner, (*fam.*) décamper
Mnemonic, adj. mnémonique
Mnemonics, Mnemotechny, s. mnémonique, f., mnémotechnie, f.
Moan, vn. gémir, se lamenter, geindre; — va. gémir de
Moan, s. gémissement, m., plainte, f., lamentation, f.
Moanful, adj. plaintif, lamentable, gémissant
Moanfully, adv. en gémissant
Moat, s. fossé, m.
Moat, va. entourer d'un fossé
Mob, s. rassemblement, m., attroupement, m., populace, f., tourbe, f., (*rabble*) canaille, f., cohue, f.
Mob, va. attaquer, houspiller
Mobility, s. mobilité, f., (*rabble*) populace, f., canaille, f.
Mobilization, s. mobilisation, f.
Mobilize, va. mobiliser
Mock, va.n. imiter, contrefaire, singer, se moquer de, tromper
Mock, s. moquerie, f., dérision, f.
Mock, adj. dérisoire, faux, feint, contrefait, burlesque. —*-turtle soup*, s. tête de veau à la tortue, f. —*-tortoise-shell*, s. imitation d'écaille, f. —*-epic*, s. —*-heroic* s. (*poems*) héroï-comique, f.
Mocker, s. moqueur, m., -euse, f., railleur, m., -euse, f.
Mockery, s. moquerie, f., raillerie, f., dérision, f.
Mocking, s. moquerie, f., raillerie, f. —*-bird*, s. oiseau moqueur, m. —*-stock*, s. jouet, m.
Mode, s. mode, m., forme, f., manière d'être, f., manière, f.
Model, s. adj. modèle, m.
Model, va. former, tracer, dessiner
Modeller, s. qui forme, qui façonne, dessinateur, m., modeleur, m.
Modelling, s. modelage, m.
Moderate, adj. modéré, (*value*) modique, raisonnable, (*polit. opin.*) modéré, (*talent*) ordinaire, passable
Moderate, va. modérer, tempérer; — vn. se modérer
Moderately, adv. modérément, passablement, médiocrement
Moderation, s. modération, f., mesure, f.
Moderator, s. modérateur, m., -trice, f., (*of an assembly*) président, m.
Modern, adj. moderne
Modernize, va. moderniser
Modest, adj. modeste
Modestly, adv. modestement, avec modestie
Modesty, s. modestie, f.
Modification, s. modification, f.
Modify, va. modifier
Modishness, s. conformité à la mode du jour, f., élégance affectée, f.
Modulate, va. moduler
Modulation, s. modulation, f., mélodie, f.
Mohair, s. poil de chèvre d'Angora, m.
Moiety, s. moitié, f., part, f., portion, f., partie, f.
Moil, vn. peiner, se fatiguer, travailler dur
Moire, s. moire, f.
Moist, adj. humide, mouillé, moite
Moisten, va. mouiller légèrement, rendre humide, humecter
Moisture, s. humidité, f., moiteur, f.
Molar, adj. s. molaire, f., dent molaire, f.
Molasses, s.pl. mélasse, f.
Mole, s. môle, m., jetée, f., digue, f., (*spot*) grain de beauté, m., verrue, f., (*anim.*) taupe, f. —*-cast*, s. —*-hill*, s. taupinière, f., taupinée, f. *-catcher*, s. taupier, m. —*-cricket*, s. taupe-grillon, f. —*-track*, s. traînée de taupe, f., galerie, f. —*-trap*, s. taupière, f.
Molecule, s. molécule, f.
Molest, va. molester, tourmenter, vexer, inquiéter
Molestation, s. tourment, m.
Mollify, va. amollir, adoucir, apaiser
Mollusk, s. mollusque, m.
Molten, adj. fondu
Moment, s. moment, m., instant, m., (*fig.*) force, f., importance, f., poids, m. *This very* —, à chaque instant, à tout instant, à l'instant
Momentarily, adv. à tout moment, momentanément
Momentariness, s. brièveté, f.
Momentary, adj. momentané, rapide, peu durable
Momentous, adj. important
Monarch, s. monarque, m., roi, m.
Monarchical, adj. monarchique
Monarchy, s. monarchie, f.
Monastery, s. monastère, m., couvent, m.
Monastic, Monastical, adj. monastique, du cloître
Monday, s. lundi, m.
Monetary, adj. monétaire
Money, s. argent, m., monnaie, f., écus, m.pl., numéraire, m., espèces, f.pl., (*price*) prix, m. —*s*, pl. propriété, f. *Public* —, deniers publics, m.pl. —*-box*, s. tirelire, f., caisse, f. —*-broker*, s., —*-dealer*, s. courtier de change, m. —*-changer*, s. changeur, m. —*-down*, argent comptant. —*-lender*, s. prêteur d'argent, m. —*-market*, s. place, f., bulletin financier, m. —*-order*, s. mandat de poste, m.
Moneyed, adj. qui a de l'argent, en argent. — *men*, capitalistes, m.pl.
Moneyless, adj. sans argent
Monger, s. (*in compounds*) marchand (de), m., vendeur (de), m., faiseur (de), m.
Mongrel, adj. s. métis, m., -isse, f., mélangé, m., hybride
Monition, s. avertissement, m.
Monitor, s. mentor, m., conseiller, m., (*at school*) moniteur, m.
Monitory, adj. d'avertissement
Monk, s. moine, m., religieux, m.
Monkey, s. singe, m., guenon, f.
Monkish, adj. monacal, de moine
Monogram, s. monogramme, m.
Monologue, s. monologue, m.
Monomania, s. monomanie, f.
Monomaniac, s. adj. monomane
Monopolist, s. monopoleur, m., accapareur, m.
Monopolize, va. accaparer, (*fig.*) monopoliser
Monopoly, s. monopole, m., accaparement, m.
Monosyllabic, Monosyllabical, adj. monosyllabique
Monosyllable, s. monosyllabe, m.
Monotonous, adj. monotone
Monotony, s. n f.
Monsoon, s. mo
Monster, s. mon
Monstrosity, strousness, s. sité, f.
Monstrous, strueux
Monstrously, strueusement, énor
Month, s. mois, m. *salary* or *wages*, m
Monthly, adj. tous les mois, (*by* au mois
Monthly, adv. mois
Monument, s. m m.
Monumental, mental, commémor
Mood, s. humeu position, f., (*gram* m.
Moodily, adv. pensivement
Moodiness, s. mauvaise humeur,
Moody, adj. triste, chagrin, sif
Moon, s. lune, f. lune rousse. — rayon de la lune, m s. monstre, m., idi *-struck*, adj. lunati
Moonlight, s. cla m.
Moonlight, adj de lune
Moonshine, s. lune, m., (*fig.*) bag vétille, f.
Moor, s. bruyère, f., (*marsh*) maréca *-cock*, s. —*-fowl*, s. coq de bruyère, m. poule d'eau, f.
Moor, va. amarr s'amarrer
Mooring, s. ama amarre, f.
Moot, va. agiter, débattre
Mop, s. balai à lave mace, f., (*head of* nière, f.
Mop, va.n. nettoy
Mope, vn. être t nuyer
Mope, s. reclus, imbécile, m.f.
Moral, adj. mor rale
Moral, s. moral pl. moralité, f., mo
Moralist, s. mor
Morality, s. n moralité, f
Moralize, vn.a.
Moralizer, s. qu
Morally, adv. moralement
Morass, s. marai récage, m.
Morbid, adj. mal sain, morbide
Morbidness, s. bide, m.
Mordant, s. mor
More, adj. plus plus nombreux, plus, encore. *Fire*

cinq pièces de plus. *A glass* —, encore un verre. *One* —, encore un

More, adv. plus, davantage, encore. — *and* —, de plus en plus. *No* —, ne . . . plus, rien de plus. *No* — *than*, pas plus que. *The* —, *all the* —, d'autant plus. *Any* —? jamais? de nouveau? (*with a negation*) plus jamais, jamais plus, pas plus, pas davantage

Moreen, s. damas de laine, *m.*

Morel, s. morille, *f.*

Moreover, adv. de plus, en outre, d'ailleurs

Morning, s. matin, *m.*, (*whole morning*) matinée, *f.* *Every* —, tous les matins

Morning, adj. du matin, de matin. — *-gown*, s. robe de chambre, *f.*

Morocco, s. adj. maroquin, *m.*, en maroquin

Morose, adj. morose, chagrin

Morosely, adv. d'un air morose, avec chagrin

Moroseness, s. caractère morose, *m.*, morosité, *f.*

Morris, s. danse moresque, *f.* — *-dance*, s. danse moresque *f.*

Morrow, s. demain, *m.*, lendemain, *m.* *To* —, demain. *The day after to* —, après-demain. *To* — *week*, demain en huit

Morse, s. morse, *m.*

Morsel, s. morceau, *m.*

Mortal, adj. s. mortel

Mortality, s. mortalité, *f.*

Mortally, adv. mortellement, à mort, à la mort

Mortar, s. mortier, *m.*

Mortgage, s. hypothèque, *f.* *On* —, *of* —, hypothécaire. *To pay off a* —, purger une hypothèque. — *-deed*, contrat hypothécaire, *m.*

Mortgage, va. hypothéquer

Mortgagee, s. créancier hypothécaire, *m.*

Mortgager, s. débiteur sur hypothèque, *m.*

Mortification, s. mortification, *f.*, (*med.*) gangrène, *f.*

Mortify, va. mortifier, déterminer la gangrène dans; — vn. se mortifier, se gangréner

Mortise, s. mortaise, *f.*

Mortise, va. mortaiser, assembler à mortaise

Mortmain, s. mainmorte, *f.*, biens de mainmorte, *m.pl.*

Mortuary, s. droit mortuaire, *m.*

Mortuary, adj. mortuaire

Mosaic, s. mosaïque, *f.*

Mosaic, **Mosaical**, adj. de mosaïque, en mosaïque

Mosque, s. mosquée, *f.*

Mosquito, s. moustique, *m.* — *-net*, s. moustiquaire, *f.*

Moss, s. mousse, *f.* — *-berry*, s. airelle, *f.* — *-clad*, adj., — *-covered*, adj., — *-grown*, adj. couvert de mousse, moussu. — *-rose*, s. rose mousseuse, *f.*

Mossy, adj. moussu, de mousse, couvert de mousse

Most, adj. plus de, (la) plupart de, plus grand

Most, adv. plus, surtout, très, fort, bien

Most, s. (la) plupart, *f.*, (le) plus grand nombre, *m.*, (la) plus grande partie, *f.*

Mostly, adv. pour la plupart, en plus grande partie, surtout

Mote, s. atome, *m.*, fétu, *m.*, paille, *f.*

Moth, s. papillon de nuit, *m.*, phalène *f.*, teigne, *f.*

Mother, s. mère, *f.* — *-in-law*, belle-mère, *f.* — *-of-pearl*, nacre, *f.*, (*adj.*) de nacre. — *Goose*, la mère l'Oie

Mother, adj. mère, maternel, naturel. — *-country*, s. la mère patrie, *f.*, la métropole, *f.* — *-tongue*, s. — *-language*, s. langue maternelle, *f.*

Motherhood, s. maternité, *f.*

Motherless, adj. orphelin, -e, sans mère

Motherly, adj. maternel, de mère

Motion, s. mouvement, *m.*, signe, *m.*, geste, *m.* (*proposal*) motion, *f.*, proposition, *f.*, (*med.*) selle, *f.*

Motion, vn.a. faire signe à, proposer

Motionless, adj. sans mouvement, immobile

Motive, adj. moteur, qui fait mouvoir, mobile

Motive, s. motif, *m.*, mobile, *m.*, raison, *f.*

Motley, adj. bigarré, mélangé, mêlé, divers, varié

Mottled, adj. pommelé, saumoné, truité, bigarré

Motto, s. devise, *f.* mot, *m.*

Mould, s. terre végétale, *f.*, terreau, *m.*, terre, *f.*, (*mustiness*) moisissure, *f.*, moisi, *m.*, (*shape*) moule, *m.*, (*fig.*) espèce, *m.*

Mould, vn. moisir, se moisir; — va. mouler, former, façonner, (*to knead*) pétrir

Moulder, s. mouleur, *m.*

Moulder, vn. tomber or s'en aller en poussière, crouler, dépérir; — va. réduire en poussière

Mouldiness, s. moisissure, *f.*

Moulding, s. action de mouler, *f.*, action de façonner, *f.*, moulure, *f.*

Mouldy, adj. moisi. *To grow* —, se moisir

Moult, vn. muer

Moult, **Moulting**, s. mue, *f.*

Mound, s. monticule, *m.*, tertre, *m.*, remblai, *m.*, digue, *f.*

Mount, s. mont, *m.*, montagne, *f.*, tertre, *m.*

Mount, vn.a. monter, s'élever, monter à cheval, monter sur, élever, hisser

Mountain, s. montagne, *f.*, monceau, *m.* *To make* —*s of mole-hills*, faire d'une mouche un éléphant. *The waves ran* —*s high*, les vagues s'élevaient hautes comme des montagnes

Mountain, adj. de montagne, des montagnes, montagnard

Mountaineer, s. montagnard, *m.*, montagnarde, *f.*

Mountainous, adj. montagneux, de montagnes

Mountebank, s. charlatan, *m.*, saltimbanque, *m.*, bateleur, *m.*

Mounter, s. qui monte, monteur, *m.*

Mounting, s. ascension, *f.*, action de monter, *f.*, (*action*) montage, *m.*, (*result*) monture, *f.*

Mourn, vn.a. pleurer, s'affliger, être affligé, porter le deuil

Mourner, s. personne affligée, *f.*, personne en deuil, *f.*, qui pleure la perte de, *f.*, (*at funerals*) personne qui suit le convoi, *f.*, (*hired*) pleureur, *m.*, -euse, *f.* *To be chief* —, mener le deuil

Mournful, adj. triste, lugubre, déplorable

Mournfully, adv. tristement, d'un ton *or* d'un air triste, lugubrement

Mournfulness, s. tristesse, *f.*, air triste *or* lugubre, *m.*

Mourning, s. deuil, *m.*, affliction, *f.*, (*dress*) habits de deuil, *m.pl.* *To be in* —, porter le deuil. *To go into* — (*for*), prendre le deuil (de). *To go out of* —, quitter le deuil. *Deep* —, *light* —, grand deuil, petit deuil

Mourning, adj. déploré, affligé, triste, de deuil

Mouse, s. souris, *f.* — *-hole*, s. trou de souris, *m.* — *-trap*, s. souricière, *f.*

Mouse, vn. prendre des souris, chasser les souris

Mouser, s. preneur de souris, *m.*

Mouth, s. bouche, *f.*, (*of carnivorous beasts, &c.*) gueule, *f.*, (*birds*) bec, *m.*, (*opening*) ouverture, *f.*, entrée, *f.*, (*vases*) orifice, *m.*, gorge, *f.*, (*pistol*) gueule, *f.*, (*rivers, &c.*) embouchure, *f.*, (*bottles, &c.*) trou, *m.*, (*furnace*) gueule *or* gueulard, *m.* — *-friend*, s. faux ami *m.* — *-piece*, s. (*things*) embouchure, *f.*; (*pers.*) truchement, *m.*, orateur, *m.* *To make* —*s at*, faire des grimaces à. *Down in the* —, déconcerté, triste

Mouth, vn.a. brailler, crier, hurler

Mouthed, adj. à la bouche . . . *Foul* —, mal embouché

Mouthful, s. bouchée, *f.*

Mouthing, s. déclamation, *f.*, ton arrogant, *m.*

Movable, adj. mobile, meuble

Movables, s. meubles, *m.pl.*, biens meubles, *m.pl.*, effets mobiliers, *m.pl.*

Move, vn. se mouvoir, faire un mouvement, bouger, se branler, s'agiter, (*change house*) déménager, (*in a meeting*) faire une motion. *To* — *away*, s'en aller, s'éloigner. — *back*, reculer. — *by*, passer. — *down*, baisser, descendre. — *forward*, s'avancer, avancer, marcher. — *in*, entrer, emménager. — *off*, s'éloigner, se retirer, (*fam.*) filer. — *on*, avancer, s'avancer, (*police*) circulez, avancez. — *out*, sortir, déménager. — *up*, monter, avancer, s'avancer. — va. mouvoir, faire mouvoir, mettre en mouvement, éloigner, (*to shake*) remuer, ébranler, (*excite*) exciter, porter, engager, persuader, (*touch*) émouvoir, toucher, attendrir, ébranler, (*propose*) proposer, présenter *or* faire la motion de, (*law*) demander, (*play*) jouer

Move, s. mouvement, *m.*, (*chess, &c.*) coup, *m.*, (*turn*) tour, *m.* *It is your* —, c'est à vous à jouer

Movement, s. mouvement, *m.*

Mover, s. moteur, *m.*, motrice, *f.*, force motrice, *f.*, mobile, *m.*, auteur d'une motion, *m.* *Prime* —, *master* —, cheville ouvrière, *f.*

Moving, adj. qui se meut, (*fig.*) émouvant, touchant

Moving, s. mouvement, *m.*

Movingly, adv. d'une manière émouvante *or* touchante, pathétiquement

Mow, s. meule, *f.*, tas, *m.*

Mow, va n. mettre en meule *or* en grange, faucher, couper, moissonner. *To* — *down*, moissonner

Mower, s. faucheur, *m.*

Mowing, s. fauchage, *m.*

Mr., s. monsieur, *m.*, sieur, *m.*

Mrs., s. madame, *f.*

Much, adj. beaucoup de

Much, adv. beaucoup. ne . . . guère, à peu près, quel . . . que, très, fort, bien. *As* — *as*, autant que, tant que, assez pour, jusque-là. *So* — *as*, autant que, tant que, même. *So* — *the better*, tant mieux. *So* — *the more*, d'autant plus

Much, s. beaucoup. *To make* — *of*, faire mille caresses *or* amitiés à, caresser, montrer beaucoup d'attention, vanter, faire grand cas de

Mucilage, s. mucilage, *m.*

Mucilaginous, adj. mucilagineux

Muck, s. fumier, *m.*, saleté, *f.*, boue, *f.*, fange, *f.* — *-heap*, — *-hill*, s. tas de fumier, *m.* — *-worm*, s. ver, *m.*, (*fig.*) avare, *m.*, pingre, *m.*

Mucky, adj. sale

Mucosity, s. mucosité, *f.*

Mucous, adj. muqueux

Mucus, s. mucus, *m.*, mucosité, *f.*

Mud, s. boue, *f.*, crotte, *f.*, vase, *f.*, fange, *f.* — *cart*, s. tombereau, *m.* — *-fish*, s. loche, *f.* — *-wall*, s. mur de boue, *m.*, mur en torchis, *m.*

Muddle, va. troubler, hébéter; — vn. se troubler, barboter, patauger

Muddy, adj. fangeux, boueux, bourbeux, vaseux, crotté, (*wine*) trouble

Muff, s. manchon, *m.*, (*pers.*) bêta, *m.*, cornichon, *m.*, imbécile, *m.*

Muffle, va. envelopper, couvrir, affubler, (*pop.*) emmitoufler, (*blindfold*) couvrir d'un bandeau, bander, (*drum*) voiler

Muffler, s. coiffe, *f.*, mentonnière, *f.*, bandeau, *m.*, (*face*) cache-nez, *m.*

Mug, s. tasse, *f.*, pot, *m.*, timbale, *f.*, gobelet, *m.*, (*face*) visage, *m.*

Muggy, adj. humide, lourd

Mulatto, s. mulâtre, *m.* — *woman*, mulâtresse, *f.*

Mulberry, s. mûre, *f.*, mûrier, *m.*

Mulct, va. punir d'une amende

Mule, s. mulet, *m.*, mule, *f.* — *-driver*, muletier, *m.*

Muleteer, s. muletier, *m.*

Mulish, adj. de mulet

Mull, s. (*geog.*) cap, *m.*, (*snuff-box*) tabatière de corne, *f.*, (*blunder*) faute, *f.*

Mull, va. faire chauffer et épicer

Mullet, s. muge, *m.*, mulet de mer, *m.* *Grey* —, surmulet, *m.*

Mullion, s. meneau, *m.*

Mullion, va. former en meneaux

Multifarious, adj. nombreux, multiplié, fort varié, d'une grande diversité

Multiple, adj. s. multiple, *m.*

Multiplicand, s. multiplicande, *m.*

Multiplication, s. multiplication, *f.*

Multiplicator, s. multiplicateur, *m.*

Multiplicity, s multiplicité, *f.*

Multiplier, s. qui multiplie, (*arithm.*) multiplicateur, *m.*

Multiply, va multiplier; — vn. multiplier, se multiplier

Multitude, s. multitude, *f.*

Multitudinous, adj de la multitude, nombreux, multiple

Mum, adj. silencieux, muet

Mum! interj. motus! silence! bouche close!

Mumble, va.n. marmotter, murmurer entre ses dents, mâchonner

Mumbler, s. qui marmotte, qui mâchonne

Mummery, s. mascarade, *f.*, momerie, *f.*

Mummy, s. momie, *f.* *To beat to a* —, battre comme plâtre

Mump, vn. mordiller, grignoter, marmotter

Mumps, s.pl. mauvaise humeur, *f.*, humeur maussade, *f.*, (*med.*) oreillons, *m.pl.*

Munch, va.n. mâcher

Mundane, adj. du monde, terrestre

Municipal, adj. municipal

Municipality, s. municipalité, *f.*

Munificence, s. munificence, *f.*

Munificent, adj. libéral, magnifique

Munificently, adv. magnifiquement, libéralement

Muniment, s. fortification, *f.*, aide, *f.*, (*law*) titre, *m.*, charte, *f.*, archives, *f.pl.*

Munition, s. fort, *m.*, munition, *f.*

Mural, adj. mural

Murder, s meurtre, *m.*, assassinat, *m.* *Wilful* —, meurtre avec préméditation, *m.* —! à l'assassin! au meurtre!

Murder, va. assassiner, tuer, (*language*) massacrer, estropier

Murderer, s. meurtrier, *m.*, assassin, *m.*

Murderess, s. meurtrière, *f.*

Murderous, adj. meurtrier, assassin, homicide, (*fig.*) sanguinaire

Murderously, adv. par le meurtre, par l'assassinat, en meurtrier, d'une manière meurtrière

Muriatic, adj. muriatique

Murkiness, s. ténèbres, *f.pl.*, obscurité, *f*

Murky, adj. noir, obscur, sombre

Murmur, s. murmure, *m.*

Murmur, vn.a. murmurer

Murmurer, s. qui murmure

Murmuringly, adv. en murmurant

Murrain, s. épizootie, *f.* *With a — to . . .! the — take . . .!* la peste soit de . . .!

Muscatel, s. muscat, *m.*

Muscle, s. muscle, *m.*

Muscular, adj. musculaire, musculeux

Muse, s. muse, *f.*, rêverie, *f.*, méditation, *f.*

Muse, vn. méditer, penser, rêver

Muser, s. rêveur, *m.*, rêveuse, *f.*, distrait, *m.*, -e, *f.*

Museum, s. musée, *m.*

Mushroom, s. champignon, *m.* — *-bed*, s. couche de champignons, *f.*, champignonnière, *f.* — *-house*, s. serre à champignons, *f.*

Music, s. musique, *f.* *To set to* —, mettre en musique. — *-book*, s. livre de musique, *m.* — *-folio*, s. carton de musique *m.* — *-licence*, s. autorisation de salle de concert, *f.*, de café-concert, *f.* — *-stand*, s. pupitre à musique, *m.* — *-stool*, s. tabouret de piano, *m.*

Music, adj. de musique

Musical, adj. musical, de musique, à musique, harmonieux. — *-glasses*, pl. harmonica, *m.*

Musically, adv. musicalement, harmonieusement, avec mélodie

Musicalness, s harmonie, *f.*, mélodie, *f.*

Musician, s. musicien, *m.*, musicienne, *f.*

Musing, s. méditation, *f.*, rêverie, *f.*

Musk, s. musc, *m.*, (*in compounds*) musqué

Musket, s. fusil, *m.*, (*old*) mousquet, *m.*

Musketeer, s. mousquetaire, *m.*

Musketoon, s. mousqueton, *m.*

Musketry, s. mousqueterie, *f.*

Musky, adj. parfumé de musc

Muslin, s. mousseline, *f.* *Book* —, organdi, *m.* *Cambric* —, linon, *m.*, batiste, *m.*

Mussel, s. moule, *f.*

Mussulman, s. adj. musulman, *m.*, musulmane, *f.*

Must, vn. imp. falloir, devoir. *One — do one's duty*, il faut faire son devoir. *I — learn*, il faut que j'apprenne, il me faut apprendre. *These plants — have water*, il faut de l'eau à ces plantes. *It — be cold in your country*, il doit faire froid dans votre pays. *She — have said it in a passion*, elle a dû le dire en colère

Must, s. moût, *m.*, moisi, *m.*

Mustard, s. moutarde, *f.*, sénevé, *m.* — *-pot*, moutardier, *m.* — *-seed*, graine de moutarde, *f.*

Muster, va. rassembler, réunir, (*troops*) passer en revue, faire l'appel de; — vn. s'assembler, se réunir, faire l'appel, passer la revue, (*amount*) s'élever au nombre de

Muster, s. appel, *m.*, revue, *f.*, réunion, *f.*, rassemblement, *m.*, (*lists*) états, *m.pl.*, contrôles, *m.pl.* *To pass* —, passer à l'appel, (*fig.*) passer. — *-book*, s., — *-file*, s., — *-roll*, s. rôle, *m.*, états, *m.pl.*, contrôles, *m.pl.* — *-master*, s. inspecteur des contrôles, *m.*, officier d'appel, *m.*

Mustily, adv. avec un goût moisi, avec un goût de renfermé

Mustiness, s. moisi, *m.*, renfermé, *m.*, aigreur, *f.*

Musty, adj. moisi, sentant le renfermé, aigre, (*fig.*) suranné, vieux. *To have a — smell*, sentir le moisi, le renfermé

Mutability, Mutableness, s. mutabilité, *f.*, inconstance, *f.*, instabilité, *f.*

Mutable, adj. sujet au changement, inconstant

Mutation, s. changement, *m.*, mutation, *f.*, révolution, *f.*

Mute, adj. muet, silencieux. *To sit* —, être assis en silence, garder le silence. *To stand* —, se tenir silencieux, refuser de répondre

Mute, s. muet, *m.*, muette, *f.*, (*at funerals*) pleureur, *m.*, (*mus.*) sourdine, *f.*, (*gramm.*) muette, *f.*, lettre muette, *f.*

Mutely, adv. en muet, silencieusement

Muteness, s. silence, *m.*

Mutilate, va. mutiler, tronquer, écourter *A mutilated curtsey*, une révérence écourtée, une demi-révérence

Mutilation, s. mutilation, *f.*

Mutilator, s. mutilateur, *m.*, -trice, *f.*

Mutineer, s. mutin, *m.*, séditieux, *m.*, insurgé, *m.*, révolté, *m.*, rebelle, *m.*

Mutinous, adj. mutin, mutiné, révolté, en révolte

Mutinously, adv. en mutin, en séditieux, en rebelle

Mutinousness, s. état mutin, *m.*, état séditieux, *m.*

Mutiny, s. mutinerie, *f.*, révolte, *f.*, insurrection, *f.*

Mutiny, vn. se mutiner, se révolter

Mutter, va. marmotter, marronner, murmurer

Mutter, s. murmure, *m.*

Mutterer, s. personne qui marmotte, marronne, murmure, *f.*

Mutteringly, adv. en marmottant, en marronnant, en murmurant

Mutton, s. mouton, *m.* — *-chop*, s., — *-cutlet*, s. côtelette de mouton, *f.* *Shoulder of* —, s. épaule de mouton, *f.*, éclanche, *f.*

Mutual, adj. mutuel, réciproque, commun

Mutuality, s. échange mutuel, *m.*, réciprocité, *f.*

Mutually, adv. mutuellement, réciproquement

Muzzle, s. museau, *m.*, muselière, *f.*, (*of a cannon*) bouche, *f.*, (*of bellows*) tuyau, *m.*

Muzzle, va. museler, retenir

My, adj. mon, ma, mes. *It is — own*, c'est le mien, c'est à moi

Myography, s. myographie, *f.*

Myology, s. myologie, *f.*

Myriad, s. myriade, *f.*

Myrmidon, s. myrmidon *m.*

Myrrh, s. myrrhe, *f.*

Myrtle, s. myrte, *m.*

Myself, pron. moi-même

Mysterious, adj. mystérieux

Mysteriously, adv. mystérieusement

Mysteriousness, s. nature mystérieuse, *f.*

Mystery, s. mystère, *m.*

Mystic, Mystical, adj. mystique

Mystically, adv. mystiquement, d'une manière mystique

Mystification, s. mystification, *f.*

Mystify, va. mystifier

Myth, s. mythe, *m.*

Mythologic, Mythological, adj. mythologique

Mythologically, adv. par la mythologie, d'une manière mythologique

Mythology, s mythologie *f.*

N

N, s. N, n, *f.*

Nab, va. happer, saisir

Nabob, s. nabab, *m.*

Nacarat, s. nacarat, *m.*

Nag, s. bidet, *m.*, petit cheval, *m.*, cheval de route, *m.*

Naiad, s. naiade, *f.*

Nail, s. ongle, *m.*, (*animals*) griffe, *f.*; clou, *m.* *On the* —, (*fig.*) rubis sur l'ongle. —*-brush*, s. brosse à ongles, *f.* —*-maker*, s., —*-seller*, s. cloutier, *m.* —*-scissors*, s. ciseaux à ongles, *m.pl.* —*-trade*, s. clouterie, *f.*

Nail, va. clouer. *I* —*ed him there*, je lui ai rivé son clou

Nailer, s. cloutier, *m.*

Nailery, s. clouterie, *f.*

Naive, adj. naif

Naively, adv. naivement

Naked, adj. nu, à nu, à découvert, sans armes, sans défense

Nakedly, adv. sans vêtements, à nu, sans défense, simplement

Nakedness, s. nudité, *f.*, faiblesse, *f.*

Namby-pamby, adj. maniéré, affecté. — s. être ridicule, *m.*

Name, s. nom, *m.*, (*pers.*) renommée, *f.*, réputation, *f.*, distinction, *f.*, injures, *f.pl.*, sottises, *f.pl.* *By* —, par son (leur, etc.) nom, nominalement, du nom de. *In* —, de nom. *In the* — *of*, au nom de. *In my* —, en mon nom. *What is his* —? comment se nomme-t-il? comment s'appelle-t-il? *To get a* —, *to win oneself a* —, *an ill* —, se faire un nom, se faire une mauvaise réputation. *He called me* —*s*, il me dit des injures

Name, va. nommer, appeler, dire le nom de, dire, fixer, convenir de, parler de, faire mention de. *To be* —*d*, se nommer, s'appeler. *To be* —*d after*, porter *or* recevoir le nom de. *Don't* — *it, I beg*, cela ne vaut pas la peine d'en parler

Nameless, adj. sans nom, qui n'a pas de nom, inconnu

Namely, adv. c'est-à-dire, à savoir, nommément

Namesake, s. homonyme, *m.*

Nankeen, s. nankin, *m.* *My* —*s*, mon pantalon de nankin

Nap, s. (*sleep*) somme, *m.*, (*of hats, &c.*) poil, *m.*, (*bot.*, *&c.*) duvet, *m.* *Afternoon* —, sieste, *f.* *To take a* —, faire un somme

Nap, vn. faire un somme, sommeiller, dormir, (*fig.*) s'endormir

Nape, s. nuque, *f.*

Naphtha, s. naphte, *m.*

Napkin, s. serviette, *f.* mouchoir, *m.* —*-ring*, rond de serviette, *m.*

Napless, adj. ras, sans poil

Narcissus, s. narcisse, *m.*

Narcotic, s. adj. narcotique, *m.*

Narrate, va. raconter, narrer, conter

Narration, s. narration, *f.*

Narrative, s. récit, *m.*, narration, *f.*

Narrative, adj. narratif

Narrator, s. narrateur, *m.*, conteur, *m.*, -euse, *f.*

Narrow, adj. étroit, (*fig.*) petit, resserré, rétréci, (*sparing*) mesquin, exact, rigoureux, attentif

Narrow, va. resserrer, rétrécir, rendre étroit, (*fig.*) réduire; — vn. devenir étroit, se resserrer, se rétrécir

Narrowing, s. (*fig.*) resserrement, *m.*, rétrécissement, *m.*

Narrowly, adv. étroitement, à l'étroit, (*fig.*) petitement, mesquinement, attentivement, rigoureusement, avec soin, à fond, (*nearly*) de près

Narrowness, s. étroitesse, *f.*, peu de largeur, *m.*, (*fig.*) petitesse, *f.*, peu d'élévation, *m.*, mesquinerie, *f.*

Nasal, adj. nasal, par le nez, du nez

Nastily, adv. salement, désagréablement

Nastiness, s. saleté, *f.*, malpropreté, *f.*

Nasturtium, s. capucine, *f.*

Nasty, adj. vilain, mauvais, sale, malpropre, ordurier, obscène

Natal, adj. natal

Nation, s. nation, *f.*

National, adj. national, public

Nationality, s. nationalité, *f.*, esprit national, *m.*

Nationalize, va. nationaliser

Nationally, adv. nationalement

Native, adj. natal, indigène, du pays, (*law*) regnicole, originaire. — *language*, s. langue maternelle, *f.* *The* — *inhabitants*, les indigènes

Native, s. natif, *m.*, -ive, *f.*, indigène, *m.* *f.*, naturel, *m.*, (*law*) national, *m.*, regnicole, *m.* *The* —*s*, les natifs, *m.pl.*, (*savages*) les naturels, *m.pl.*, (*law*) les nationaux, *m.pl.*, les regnicoles, *m.pl.*

Nativity, s. naissance, *f.*, (*theol.*) nativité, *f.*

Natty, adj. pimpant, propret

Natural, adj. naturel, naif, réel, (*mus.*) bécarre

Natural, s. idiot, *m.*, -e, *f.*, (*mus.*) bécarre, *m.*

Naturalism, s. naturalisme, *m.*

Naturalist, s. naturaliste, *m.*

Naturalization, s. naturalisation, *f.*

Naturalize, va. naturaliser, (*fig.*) rendre naturel

Naturally, adj. naturellement, de sa nature, de nature, au naturel

Naturalness, s. caractère naturel, *m.*, naturel, *m.*, naiveté, *f.*

Nature, s. nature, *f.*, (*fig.*) naturel, *m.*, caractère, *m.*, esprit, *m.* *Good-* —, s. bon naturel, *m.*, bonté, *f.*, bonhomie, *f.* *Ill-* —, s. mauvais naturel, *m.*, méchanceté, *f.*

Natured, adj. d'un naturel. *Good-* —, d'un bon naturel. *Ill-* —, d'un mauvais naturel, méchant

Naturedly, adv. *Good-* —, avec bonté. *Ill-* —, méchamment

Naught, s. rien, *m.*, (*fig.*) zéro, *m.* *It is* —, cela ne vaut rien. *To set at* —, braver, défier

Naughtily, adv. méchamment, mal

Naughtiness, s. méchanceté, *f.*, iniquité, *f.*

Naughty, adj. méchant, mauvais

Nausea, s. nausées, *f.pl.*, envie de vomir, *f.*

Nauseate, vn. éprouver du dégoût, avoir des nausées; — va. repousser avec dégoût, inspirer du dégoût à

Nauseous, adj. nauséabond

Nauseously, adv. d'une manière nauséabonde

Nauseousness, s. nature nauséabonde, *f.*, goût nauséabond, *m.*

Nautical, adj. nautique, marin, de marine

Nautilus, s. nautile, *m.*, argonaute, *m.*

Naval, adj. naval, maritime, de marine

Nave, s. (*wheels, &c.*) moyeu, *m.*, (*churches, &c.*) nef, *f.* —*-box*, moyeu, *m.*

Navel, s. nombril, *m.*, (*fig.*) cœur, *m.*, centre, *m.* —*-string*, s. cordon ombilical, *m.*

Navigable, adj. navigable

Navigate, vn. naviguer, aller sur mer; — va. gouverner

Navigation, s. navigation, *f.*

Navigator, s. navigateur, *m.*, nautonnier, *m.*

Navvy, s. terrassier, *m.*

Navy, s. flotte, *f.*, la marine, *f.* — *agency*, s. agence pour la marine, *f.* —*-board*, s. conseil d'amirauté, *m.* —*-yard*, s. arsenal de marine, *m.*

Nay, adv. non, et même, bien plus, que dis-je?

Neap-tide, s. morte-eau, *f.*

Near, adj. près, proche, voisin, rapproché, intime, (*stingy*) près, regardant, parcimonieux, (*side, &c.*) gauche, de gauche. *The* — *or* —*-side horse*, s. le cheval de gauche, sous la main. *The* —*-side of a horse*, le côté du montoir

Near, adv. prep. près, auprès, de près, presque, à peu près, (*nav.*) près du vent. *To come or draw* —, s'approcher de. *To come* —*er and* —*er*, s'approcher de plus en plus. *To bring* — *or nearer*, rapprocher. — *at hand*, sous la main, à sa portée, tout près

Near, va. s'approcher de

Nearly, adv. près, auprès, proche, (*fig.*) intimement, étroitement, à peu près, à peu de chose près, presque, (*miserly*) avec parcimonie. *They were not* — *so many*, ils n'étaient pas à beaucoup près autant. *He was* — *ruined*, il faillit être ruiné, il fut presque ruiné

Nearness, s. proximité, *f.*, voisinage, *m.*, peu de distance, *m.*, proche parenté, *f.*, intimité, *f.*, union étroite, *f.*, parcimonie, *f.*, avarice, *f.*

Neat, s. bétail *m.*, bestiaux, *m.pl.* —*'s tongue*, s. langue de bœuf, *f.* —*'s foot oil*, s. huile de pied de bœuf, *f.* —*-herd*, s. bouvier, *m.*, vacher, *m.*

Neat, adj. propre, net, gentil, bien tenu, bien rangé, (*dress, &c.*) propre, simple et convenable, (*pure*) pur

Neatly, adv. proprement, avec propreté, avec une simplicité élégante, élégamment, adroitement

Neatness, s. propreté, *f.*, netteté, *f.*, simplicité, *f.*, simplicité élégante, *f.*, adresse, *f.*

Nebulous, adj. nébuleux

Necessaries, s.pl. nécessaire, *m.*, choses nécessaires, *f.pl.*

Necessarily, adv. nécessairement, de toute nécessité

Necessary, adj. nécessaire, inévitable

Necessitous, adj. nécessiteux, indigent

Necessity, s. nécessité, *f.*, besoin, *m.*, dénûment, *m.*

Neck, s. cou, *m.*, col, *m.*, (*bottles, &c.*) goulot, *m.*, (*of a violin*) manche, *m* —*-beef*, s. collet de bœuf, *m.* —*-cloth*, s. —*-tie*, s. cravate, *f.*, col, *m.* — *or nothing*, tout ou rien. *A stiff-* —, un torticolis

Necked, adj. à cou, au cou, à goulot . . . , à col . . .

Neckerchief, s. cravate, *f.*, fichu, *m.*

Necklace, s. collier, *m.*

Necrology, s. nécrologie, *f.*

Necromancer, s. nécromancien, *m.*, -enne, *f.*

Necromancy, s. nécromancie, *f.*

Nectar, s. nectar, *m.*

Nectarine, s. brugnon, *m.*

Need, s. besoin, *m.*, nécessité, *f.* *If — be*, s'il le faut, si c'est nécessaire. *To be or stand in —, in great — of*, avoir besoin, avoir grand besoin de. *To supply the —s of*, pourvoir aux besoins de

Need, va. avoir besoin de, il faut à, être nécessaire. exiger ; — vn. avoir besoin, être nécessaire, devoir, avoir à

Needful, adj. nécessaire, de grand besoin

Needful, s. (*money*) le *or* du quibus

Needfully, adv. nécessairement

Needily, adv. dans le besoin, nécessairement

Neediness, s. indigence, *f.*, besoin, *m.*

Needle, s. aiguille, *f.*, (*mariner's compass*) aiguille aimantée, *f.*, boussole, *f.* —*-case*, s. étui à aiguilles, *m.* —*-fish*, s. aiguillat, *m.* —*-maker*, s. fabricant d'aiguilles, *m.* —*-woman*, s. couturière, *f.*, ouvrière à l'aiguille, *f.* —*-work*, s. ouvrage à l'aiguille, *m.* *To do —-work*, travailler à l'aiguille, faire de la couture. *Dipping* —, s. aiguille d'inclinaison, *f.*

Needleful, s. aiguillée, *f.*

Needless, adj. inutile, sans besoin

Needlessly, adv. inutilement, sans nécessité

Needlessness, s. inutilité, *f.*

Needs, adv. nécessairement, absolument

Needy, adj. nécessiteux, malheureux

Nefarious, adj. scélérat, méchant, abominable

Nefariousness, s. scélératesse, *f.*

Negation, s. négation, *f.*

Negative, adj. négatif

Negative, s. négative, *f.*, proposition négative, *f.*, (*pol.*) véto, *m.*, refus, *m.*

Negative, va. rejeter, réfuter

Negatively, adv. négativement, avec négation

Neglect, va. négliger, empêcher

Neglect, Negligence, s. négligence, *f.*, manque d'égards *or* d'attention, *m.*, froideur, *f.*, oubli, *m.*, désuétude, *f.*

Neglectful, Negligent, adj. négligent, qui néglige

Neglectfully, Negligently, adv. négligemment, avec négligence

Negotiable, adj. négociable

Negotiate, vn.a. négocier, faire le négoce

Negotiation, s. négociation, *f.*

Negotiator, s. négociateur, *m.*, -trice, *f.*

Negress, s. négresse, *f.*

Negro, s. nègre, *m.*, noir, *m.* —*-boy*, s. —*-child*, s. négrillon, *m.*, petit nègre, *m.*

Negus, s. vin chaud épicé, *m.*

Neigh, vn. hennir

Neigh, s. hennissement, *m.*

Neighbour, s. voisin, *m.*, voisine, *f.*

Neighbour, va. avoisiner, rapprocher, rendre familier

Neighbourhood, s. voisinage, *m.*, les voisins, *m.pl.*, alentours, *m.pl.*

Neighbouring, adj. voisin, d'alentour

Neighbourly, adv. de (bon) voisin, en (bon) voisin

Neighing, s. hennissement, *m.*

Neither, conj. ne . . ., ni, non plus

Neither, pron. adj. ni l'un ni l'autre, ni l'une ni l'autre, aucun, pas un

Neologism, s. néologisme, *m.*

Neologist, s. néologiste, *m.*

Neology, s. néologie, *f.*

Neophyte, s. néophyte, *m.f.*

Nephew, s. neveu, *m.*

Nepotism, s. népotisme, *m.*

Nereid, s. néréide, *f.*

Nerve, s. nerf, *m.*, (*fig.*) vigueur, *f.*, force, *f.*

Nerve, va. donner du nerf à, donner de la force à

Nerveless, adj. sans nerf, faible, énervé, sans vigueur

Nervous, adj. nerveux, des nerfs, qui a les nerfs malades, timide, que la moindre chose effraye, inquiet

Nervousness, s. vigueur, *f.*, force, *f.*, agitation des nerfs, *f.*

Nest, s. nid, *m.*, (*brood*) nichée, *f.*, (*fig.*) repaire, *m.*

Nestle, vn.a. nicher, faire son nid

Net, s. filet, *m.*, rets, *m.*, piége, *m.*, réseau, *m.*, (*for dress*) tulle, *m.*, tricot, *m.* — adj. de tricot, net, nette

Net, vn.a. faire du filet, tricoter, (*to bring in*) produire or rapporter net

Nether, adj. inférieur, bas, placé au-dessous

Nethermost, adj. le plus bas, le plus profond

Netting, s. filet, *m.*, réseau, *m.* —*-needle*, s. navette, *f.* —*-pin*, s. moule, *m.*

Nettle, s. ortie, *f.* —*-rash*, urticaire, *f.*

Nettle, va. piquer, blesser, irriter

Neuralgia, s. névralgie, *f.*

Neuralgic, adj. névralgique

Neuter, adj. s. neutre

Neutral, adj. neutre

Neutrality, s. neutralité, *f.*

Neutralization, s. neutralisation, *f.*

Neutralize, va. rendre neutre

Neutrally, adv. neutralement

Never, adv. ne . . . jamais, jamais . . . ne, ne . . . plus, ne . . . pas, ne . . . point, quelque . . . que, quelque . . . que ce soit. —*-fading*, adj. impérissable

Nevertheless, adv. néanmoins, toutefois, pourtant, cependant

New, adj. neuf, nouveau, nouvel, récent, renouvelé, (*bread*) tendre, frais, (*in compounds*) nouveau . . ., nouvellement, fraîchement, récemment. *To do up like* —, remettre à neuf. *To — create*, créer de nouveau. —*-fashioned*, fait à la mode du jour, nouveau. —*-laid egg*, œuf frais. —*-made*, qui vient d'être fait, récent. *To —-model*, faire d'après un nouveau modèle. —*-year's day*, s. le jour de l'an, *m.* —*-year's gift*, s. des étrennes. *To wish (a person) a happy — year*, souhaiter la bonne année à

Newish, adj. assez nouveau

Newly, adv. nouvellement, fraîchement, récemment

Newness, s. nouveauté, *f.*

News, s. nouvelle, *f.*, nouvelles, *f.pl* *A piece of —s*, une nouvelle. *To tell a piece of —s*, dire une nouvelle. *No — is good* —, point de nouvelles, bonnes nouvelles. *What — !* quoi de nouveau ? —*-man*, s., —*-vendor*, s. vendeur *or* colporteur de journaux, *m.* —*-monger*, s. nouvelliste, *m.*, colporteur de nouvelles, *m.*

Newspaper, s journal, *m.*, gazette, *f.*, feuille, *f.* *Daily* —, journal quotidien, *m.* *Weekly* —, journal hebdomadaire, *m.* —*-writer*, s. journaliste, *m.*

Newt, s. lézard, *m.*

Next, adj. le plus proche, le plus rapproché de, le plus près, le plus voisin, prochain, qui vient après, le plus cher à. *The — house*, la maison à côté. *The — in kin*, le plus proche parent. *The — chapter*, le chapitre suivant. *This life and the* —, cette vie et celle à venir

Next, adv. ensuite, après. *Well! and what — !* eh bien ! et ensuite — *to*, après, le premier après, à peu près

Nib, s. bec, *m.*

Nibbed, adj. à . . . bec

Nibble, va. grignoter, mordiller, mordre, ronger, (*the grass, &c.*) brouter, (*a bait, &c.*) mordre à ; — vn. mordre, (*fig.*) gloser (sur), chicaner

Nice, adj. bon, agréable, délicat, friand, (*pleasing*) gentil, joli, charmant, (*particular*) scrupuleux, difficile, exigeant, méticuleux, (*correct*) correct, précis, exact, (*difficult*) délicat, difficile, (*ingenious*) ingénieux, minutieux, (*careful*) soigneux, recherché, (*taste*) délicat. *A — bit*, un morceau délicat. *How — !* que c'est charmant ! *Such a — young man*, un si charmant jeune homme. — *weather*, un temps agréable. *It was — cold weather*, (*iron.*) il faisait un joli petit froid. *Be — and chaste*, sois pure et chaste. *To make — of*, avoir des scrupules sur, hésiter sur. *Over* —, par trop difficile

Nicely, adv. bien, gentiment, agréablement, d'une manière charmante, délicatement, avec délicatesse, exactement, scrupuleusement

Niceness, s. goût agréable, *m.*, gentillesse, *f.*, charme, *m.*, nature agréable, *f.*, (*dress*) recherche, *f.*, délicatesse, *f.*, (*exactness*) exactitude, *f.*, caractère scrupuleux, *m.*, subtilité, *f.*

Nicety, s friandise, *f.*, mets friand, *m.*, (*language*) délicatesse, *f.*, finesse, *f.*, exactitude, *f.*, justesse, *f.*, délicatesse, *f.*, soins scrupuleux, *m.pl.*, raffinement, *m.*, subtilité, *f.*

Niche, s. niche, *f.*

Nick, s. point, *m.*, moment précis, *m.* *To come just in the — (of time)*, venir à point nommé *or* fort à propos

Nick, va. (*fig.*) saisir à propos, rencontrer juste

Nicknack, s. see KNICK-KNACK

Nickname, s. sobriquet, m.

Nickname, va. donner un sobriquet à

Niece, s. nièce, f.

Niggard, s. ladre, m., avare, m.

Niggardliness, s. parcimonie, f.

Niggardly, adj. adv. avare, ladre, avec parcimonie, avec avarice

Nigger, s. nègre, m.

Nigh, adj. (*fig.*) proche, rapproché, près, près de

Nigh, prep. près de

Nigh, adv. à proximité, près, de près, presque

Night, s. nuit, f., obscurité, f., soir, m., (*theat.*) représentation, f., (*in compos.*) de nuit, nocturne. *To be* —, (*fig.*) faire nuit. *By* —, *in the* —, de nuit, nuitamment, pendant la nuit. *To stay out all* —, découcher. *Over* —, tard dans la nuit, pendant la nuit, la veille. —*'s lodging*, logement *or* gîte pour la nuit. *Good* —, bonsoir, bonne nuit. — *-bell*, s. sonnette de nuit, f. — *-brawler*, s. tapageur nocturne, m. — *-breeze*, s. brise de nuit, f. — *-cap*, s. bonnet de nuit, m. — *-cart*, s. voiture de vidange, f. — *-dress*, s. toilette de nuit, f. — *-fall*, la tombée de la nuit. — *-gown*, s. — *-shirt*, s. chemise de nuit, f. — *-lamp*, s. veilleuse, f. — *-man*, s. vidangeur, m. — *-mare*, s. cauchemar, m. — *-soil*, s. vidanges, f.pl. *Desiccated* — *-soil*, poudrette, f. — *-time*, s. nuit, f. — *-walker*, s. rôdeur de nuit, m., somnambule, m.f. — *-watch*, s. veilleur de nuit, m., garde de nuit, f. — *-watcher*, s. veilleur de nuit, m.

Nightingale, s. rossignol, m.

Nightly, adj. adv. de nuit, nocturne, de la nuit

Nightshade, s. morelle, f. *Deadly* —, belladone, f.

Nill, s. bluette, f., étincelle, f.

Nimble, adj. agile, leste, actif, léger, alerte, dispos, preste

Nimbleness, s. agilité, f., activité, f., légèreté, f., prestesse, f.

Nimbly, adv. agilement, avec agilité, prestement, avec prestesse

Nimbus, s. nimbe, m.

Nine, adj. s. neuf. — *-holes*, s. la balle au pot

Ninefold, adj. neuf fois autant

Ninepins, s.pl. quilles, f. *plur.*

Nineteen, adj. s. dix-neuf

Nineteenth, adj. s. dix-neuvième, dix-neuf

Ninetieth, adj. s. quatre-vingt-dixième

Ninety, adj. s. quatre-vingt-dix

Ninny, s. niais, m., -e, f., nigaud, m., -e, f.

Ninth, adj. s. neuvième, neuf

Ninthly, adv. neuvièmement

Nip, va. pincer, couper, mordre, (*blast, &c.*) brûler, détruire, (*jeer*) railler. *To* — *off*, couper, enlever, enlever le bout de

Nippers, s. pinces, f.pl., pincettes, f.pl.

Nipping, adj. piquant, qui pince

Nipple, s. mamelon, m., bout de sein, m., (*fire-arms*) cheminée, f.

Nit, s. lente, f.

Nitrate, s. nitrate, m.

Nitre, s. nitre, m.

Nitric, adj. nitrique

Nitrous, adj. nitreux

No, adv. non, ne . . . pas

No, adj. ne pas . . . de, ne point . . . de, il n'y a pas de, nul, ne . . . aucun, pas un, ne . . . pas, ne . . . point. *He has* — *friends*, il n'a pas d'amis. *It is* — *great matter*, ce n'est pas d'une grande importance. *There is* — *escaping*, il n'y a pas moyen de s'échapper

No, s. non, m. *The noes have it*, la majorité est contre

Nob, s. tête, f. *The big* —*s*, les gros bonnets

Nobility, s. noblesse, f.

Noble, adj. (*fig.*) noble, plein de noblesse, illustre, grand, élevé, sublime, libéral, magnifique. *To make* —, anoblir

Nobleman, s. noble, m., gentilhomme, m., seigneur, m.

Nobleness, s. noblesse, f., élévation, f.

Nobly, adv. noblement, avec noblesse, magnifiquement

Nobody, pron. ne . . . personne, personne ne . . . , nul, pas un. *To be* —, n'être personne, ne pas compter

Nocturnal, adj. nocturne, de nuit, de la nuit

Nod, vn. se pencher, s'incliner, incliner la tête, faire un signe de tête, faire un léger salut, (*to be drowsy*) sommeiller, s'assoupir

Nod, s. inclination, f., signe de tête, m.

Noddle, s. tête, f.

Noddy, s. nigaud, m., nigaude, f.

Node, s. nœud, m.

Noise, s. bruit, m., fracas, m., tapage, m., tintamarre, m. *To make a* —, faire du bruit

Noise, vn. faire du bruit, retentir ; — va. répandre, divulguer

Noiseless, adj. sans bruit, silencieux

Noiselessly, adv. sans bruit, silencieusement

Noisily, adv. bruyamment, avec bruit, à grand bruit, avec fracas

Noisiness, s. bruit, m.

Noisome, adj. nuisible, pernicieux, malfaisant, délétère, (*disgusting, &c.*) fétide, infect

Noisomeness, s. nature désagréable *or* infecte, f., fétidité, f.

Noisy, adj. bruyant, (*a person*) turbulent

Nomad, s. nomade, m.

Nomadic, adj. nomade

Nomarch, s. nomarque, m.

Nombles, s. nombles, m.pl.

Nome, s. nome, m.

Nomenclator, s. nomenclateur, m.

Nomenclature, s. nomenclature, f.

Nomial, s. nome, m.

Nominal, adj. nominal

Nominalist, s. nominal, m.

Nominally, adv. de nom, nominalement

Nominate, va. appeler, nommer (à), proposer, présenter

Nomination, s. nomination, f., présentation, f. *To have the* — *of*, nommer

Nominative, adj. s. nominatif. *In the* — *case*, au nominatif

Nominator, s. personne qui nomme, personne qui présente *or* propose

Nominee, s. personne dénommée, f., candidat, m., nominataire, m.

Non, adv. adj. qui n'est pas, non, défaut de, refus de, absence de. — *-ability*, s. incapacité, f., (*law*) inhabilité, f. — *-acceptance*, s. refus d'accepter, m., (*com.*) refus d'acceptation, m. — *-acquiescence*, s. refus de consentement, m. — *-admission*, s. refus d'admettre, m. — *-appearance*, s. état de ne pas paraître, m., (*law*) défaut de comparution, m. — *-appointment*, s. défaut de nomination, m. — *-attendance*, s. absence, f. — *-committal*, s. absence d'engagement politique, f. — *-compliance*, s. refus d'acquiescement, m. — *-compos-mentis*, s. atteint d'aliénation mentale, m., idiot, m., -e, f. — *-conducting*, adj. non-conducteur. — *-condensing*, adj. à haute pression. — *-delivery*, s. négligence *or* refus de livrer. — *-elect*, s. (*fig.*) qui ne sont pas au nombre des élus. — *-juring*, — *-juror*, s. (celui) qui refuse de prendre serment de fidélité. — *-observance*, s. inobservation, f. — *-payment*, s. refus *or* défaut de payer, m. — *-professional*, s. qui n'est pas du métier. — *-resistance*, s. obéissance passive, f.

Nonage, s. minorité, f.

Nonagenarian, s. nonagénaire, m.

Nonce, s. occasion, f., dessein, m. *For the* —, pour cette fois

Nondescript, adj. s. (objet) qu'on n'a pas décrit, (objet) impossible à décrire, (objet) indéfinissable

None, adj. pron. nul, aucun, pas un, personne ne . . . , (*things*) n'en . . . pas, ne . . . aucun, (*of*) ne . . . point (de). — *but*, nul autre que, seuls, seulement, il n'y a que . . . qui. *I have* —, je n'en ai pas. *I'll* — *of it*, je n'en veux point, je n'en ai que faire

Nonentity, s. non-existence, f., néant, m.

Nonesuch, s. qui n'a pas son pareil, incomparable, nonpareille

Nonplus, s. embarras extrême, m., (*fam.*) quia, m. *To be at a* —, être à bout, être à quia, ne savoir plus que dire

Nonplus, va. déconcerter, confondre, démonter, interdire, mettre au pied du mur, mettre à quia

Nonsense, s. nonsens, m., absurdité, f., sottise, f., bêtise, f., fadaises, f.pl., balivernes, f.pl. — *verses*, vers à retourner. — *!* allons donc ! *To talk* —, extravaguer, dire des sottises, des bêtises, des balivernes. *Come! none of your* — *!* allons ! point d'insolence !

Nonsensical, adj. absurde, vide de sens, sot, bête. *What* — *stuff!* quelles balivernes !

Nonsensically, adv. absurdement, sottement, contre le bon sens

Nonsuit, s. désistement, m., hors de cour, m.

Nonsuit, va. mettre hors de cour

Noodle, s. nigaud, m., -e, f.

Nook, s. recoin, m., coin, m., angle, m., renfoncement, m.

Noon, s. midi, m.

Noonday, s. midi, m. *As clear as* —, clair comme le jour

Noontide, s. see NOONDAY

Noose, s. nœud coulant, m., nasse, f.

Nopal, s. nopal, m.

Nor, conj. ni . . . ne, (*with reference to a preceding clause*) et ne . . . pas, pas . . . non plus

Normal, adj. normal. — *-school*, s. école normale, f. — *-line*, s. normale, f.

North, s. nord, m., septentrion, m. — adj. du nord. — *-east by* —, nord nord-est. — *-pole*, s. pôle arctique, m. — *-star*, s. étoile du nord, f.

Northerly, adj. du nord, septentrional, arctique

Northern, s. habitant du Nord, m.

Northernmost, adj. plus au nord

Northward, adj. du côté du nord, vers le nord, au nord, septentrional

Northward, Northwards, Northwardly, adv. du côté du nord, vers le nord, au nord, septentrional

Nose, s. nez, m., (*of animals*) museau, m., (*of bellows*) tuyau, m., canon, m. *Roman* —, nez aquilin, m. *Beneath*

his very —, à son nez et à sa barbe. *To allow oneself to be led by the* —, se laisser mener par le bout du nez. *To put anyone's — out of joint*, casser le nez à, (*fig.*) supplanter. *His — is out of joint*, il n'est plus en faveur. *To speak through the* . —, parler du nez, nasiller

Nosed, adj. qui a le nez . . . au nez . . . *Bottle-* —, au gros nez

Nosegay, s. bouquet, *m.*

Noseless, adj. sans nez

Nostril, s. narine, *f.*, (*of animal*) naseau, *m.*

Nostrum, s. remède secret, *m.*, remède, *m.*

Not, adv. ne . . . pas, ne . . . point, non, pas, non pas

Notability, s. notabilité, *f.*

Notable, adj. notable, remarquable, évident, manifeste, notoire

Notableness, s. caractère remarquable, *m.*, nature remarquable, *f.*

Notably, adv. d'une façon remarquable, remarquablement

Notary, s. notaire, *m.*

Notarial, adj. fait devant notaire, de notaire

Notation, s. notation, *f.*, (*math.*) numération écrite, *f.*

Notch, s. coche, *f.*, entaille, *f.*, (*edge-tools*) brèche, *f.*, (*machine*) cran, *m.*, échancrure, *f.* *To raise a — higher, to put a — lower*, hausser, baisser d'un cran

Notch, va. faire des entailles dans, ébrécher

Note, s. marque, *f.*, signe, *m.*, (*gram.*) point, *m.*, note, *f.*, commentaire, *m.*, (*small letter*) billet, *m.*, (*dipl.*) note, *f.*, (*com.*) billet, *m.*, bordereau, *m.*, (*attention*) attention, *f.*, garde, *f.*, (*celebrity*) marque, *f.*, distinction, *f.*, (*voice*) chant, *m.*, accent, *m.*, ton, *m.* *To make a — of*, prendre note de. — *-book*, s. cahier de notes, *m.*, agenda, *m.*, (*com.*) carnet, *m.* — *-paper*, s. petit papier à lettre, *m.* — *of hand*, s. billet à ordre, *m.* — *payable at sight*, billet à vue, *m.* *To take no — of*, ne pas faire attention à, ne pas prendre note de. — *-worthy*, adj. digne de remarque. *To change one's* —, changer de gamme. *Foot-* —, note au bas de la page. *Shoulder-* —, note en marge

Note, va. noter, prendre note de, prendre bonne note de, inscrire, remarquer, observer, dénoter

Noted, adj. connu, célèbre, remarquable, éminent, fameux, (*unfavourably*) fameux, insigne, franc, fieffé

Nothing, s. ne . . . rien, rien . . . ne, néant, *m.* *Good-for-* —, bon à rien, vaurien, *m.* — *good*, — *new*, rien de bon, rien de nouveau. *To do — of the kind*, n'en rien faire. *That is — to me*, cela ne me fait rien, à moi. *He is — to me*, il ne m'est de rien. — *whatever*, rien de rien, (*fig.*) rien du tout. *About* —, pour rien, (*fam.*) à propos de bottes, de rien. *Next to* —, moins que rien. *To amount to* —, n'aboutir à rien, ne pas aboutir, ne signifier rien. *To make — of*, ne tirer aucun profit de, ne faire aucun cas de, (*fig.*) ne trouver rien de difficile à, ne pas hésiter un instant, (*fam.*) ne faire ni une ni deux, n'y rien comprendre

Nothingness, s. néant, *m.*, rien, *m.*

Notice, s. observation, *f.*, connaissance, *f.*, attention, *f.*, avis, *m.*, information, *f.*, avertissement, *m.*, (*law*) notification, *f.*, (*to quit*) congé, *m.*, (*lit.*) notice, *f.*, (*engraving*) légende, *f.*, (*politeness*) attentions, *f.pl.*, égards, *m.*, politesse, *f.* *To take — of*, observer, faire attention à, prendre note de. *To take (but) little — of*, faire peu d'attention à. *To take no — of*, ne pas remarquer, ne pas faire attention à. *To bring into* —, faire connaître, faire valoir. *To come or rise into* —, (*pers.*) se faire remarquer *or* connaître, percer, (*things*) attirer l'attention. *It is beneath your* —, cela ne vaut pas la peine que vous y fassiez attention. *We hereby give* —, savoir faisons par ces présentes. *At a moment's* —, à la minute. *Without a moment's* —, sans un mot d'avertissement, en un clin d'œil. *At short* —, à court délai. *To give* —, faire savoir, donner avis, avertir, prévenir. *To give — to quit*, donner congé. *To give six months'* —, avertir six mois à l'avance. *To take great — of*, être plein d'attention pour, (*fig.*) s'occuper de

Notice, va. remarquer, observer, faire attention à, prendre garde à, faire connaître à, (*review*) parler de, s'occuper de, (*to show attention*) avoir des égards pour, avoir des attentions pour

Noticeable, adj. digne de remarque, digne d'attention, perceptible

Notification, s. notification, *f.*

Notify, va. faire connaître, faire savoir

Notion, s. notion, *f.*, idée, *f.*, opinion, *f.*, sentiment, *m.* *To have no — of*, n'avoir pas d'idée de, ne pas vouloir. *I have a — that*, j'ai dans l'idée que

Notoriety, **Notoriousness**, s. notoriété, *f.*

Notorious, adj. notoire, connu de tout le monde, reconnu, (*unfavourably*) bien connu

Notoriously, adv. notoirement, publiquement

Notwithstanding, prep. malgré, nonobstant

Notwithstanding, conj. néanmoins, malgré que

Nought, s. rien . . . ne, ne . . . rien, (*arith.*) 0, zéro

Noun, s. nom, *m.*

Nourish, va. nourrir, entretenir, (*discord*, &c.) fomenter, élever

Nourishing, adj. *see* NUTRITIOUS

Nourishment, s. nourriture, *f.*

Novel, adj. nouveau, nouvel, neuf

Novel, s. (*book*) roman, *m.* — *-writer*, s. romancier, *m.*

Novelist, s. romancier, *m.*, auteur de romans, *m.*

Novelty, s. nouveauté, *f.*

November, s. novembre, *m.*

Novice, s. novice, *m.f.*

Novitiate, s. noviciat, *m.*

Now, adv. maintenant, à présent, actuellement, tout à l'heure, naguère, alors. — *-a-days*, de nos jours, (*fig.*) par le temps qui court. — *and then, every — and then*, de temps en temps, de temps à autre. *Till* —, jusqu'ici, jusqu'à nos jours. *But* —, tout à l'heure, il n'y a qu'un instant. — . . . , — . . . , tantôt . . . , tantôt . . .

Now! interj. voyons!

Nowhere, adv. nulle part

Nowise, adv. nullement, en aucune façon, aucunement

Noxious, adj. malfaisant, nuisible, pernicieux

Noxiously, adv. d'une manière nuisible

Noxiousness, s. nature pernicieuse, *f.*, caractère nuisible, *m.*

Nozzle, s. nez, *m.*, museau, *m.*, bec, *m.*, bout, *m.*, (*of bellows*) canon, *m.*, tuyau, *m.*

Nubile, adj. nubile

Nucleus, s. noyau, *m.*

Nude, adj. nu

Nudge, va. pousser du coude

Nudge, s. petit coup de coude, *m.*

Nudity, s. nudité, *f.*

Nugatory, adj. frivole, futile, inefficace

Nugget, s. pépite, *f.*

Nuisance, s. plaie, *f.*, peste, *f.*, fléau, *m.*, (*things*, &c.) incommodité, *f.*, (*law*) dommage, *m.*, ordures, *f.pl.* *What a —!* quel ennui!

Null, adj. nul. — *and void*, nul et non avenu

Nullity, s. nullité, *f.*

Numb, adj. engourdi, transi

Numb, va. engourdir, (*fig.*) faire transir

Number, s. nombre, *m.*, chiffre, *m.*, grand nombre, *m.*, quantité, *f.*, numéro, *m.*, (*part of a work*) livraison, *f.* —*s*, pl., nombre, *m.*, harmonie, *f.* *To make up a* —, compléter un nombre, faire nombre. *To take care of — one*, soigner sa petite personne. *In —s*, par livraisons

Number, va. compter, supputer, nombrer, (*houses*, &c.) numéroter, (*to reckon*) mettre au nombre (de), compter (parmi)

Numberless, adj. innombrable, sans nombre

Numbness, s. engourdissement, *m.*, torpeur, *f.*

Numerable, adj. qu'on peut compter, pouvant se compter

Numeral, adj. numéral

Numeral, s. lettre numérale, *f.*, signe numéral, *m.*, chiffre, *m.*

Numerary, adj. numéraire

Numerate, va. compter, énumérer

Numeration, s. numération, *f.*, dénombrement, *m.*

Numerator, s. numérateur, *m.*

Numerical, adj. numérique

Numerically, adv. numériquement

Numerous, adj. nombreux

Numerously, adv. en grand nombre, avec un grand nombre de personnes

Numerousness, s. nombre, *m.*, grand nombre, *m.*

Numismatic, **Numismatical**, adj. numismatique

Numismatics, s.pl. numismatique, *f.*

Numismatologist, s. numismate, *m.*

Numskull, s. bêta, *m.*, idiot, *m.*

Nun, s. religieuse, *f.*, nonne, *f.* *To make a — of*, mettre en religion. *To become a* —, se faire religieuse

Nuncio, s. nonce, *m.*, messager, *m.*

Nunnery, s. couvent, *m.*

Nuptial, adj. nuptial, de noces, conjugal

Nuptials, s.pl. noces, *f.pl.*, épousailles, *f.pl.*

Nurse, s. bonne d'enfant, *f.*, nourrice, *f.*, (*fig.*) mère, *f.*, institutrice, *f.*, (*invalids*, &c.) garde malade, *m.f.*, infirmier, *m.*, infirmière, *f.* — *-maid*, s. bonne d'enfant, *f.* *To put out to* —, mettre en nourrice. *Wet* —, s. nourrice, *f.*

Nurse, va. soigner, garder, (*babies*) allaiter, nourrir, (*to rock*) bercer, dorloter, (*to bring up*) élever, (*fig.*) nourrir, alimenter

Nursery, s. (*children*) chambre des enfants, *f.*, (*trees*) pépinière, *f.*, (*asylum*, &c.) asile, *m.*, (*silk-worm*) magnanerie, *f.*, soins, *m.* — *-maid*, s. bonne d'enfant, *f.* — *-garden*, s. jardin pépiniériste, *m.* — *-gardener*, s. — *-man*, s. pépiniériste, *m.*

Nursing, s. soins, *m.pl.*

Nursling, s. nourrisson, *m.*, (*fig.*) mignon, *m.*, mignonne, *f.*

Nurture, s. nourriture, *f.*, (*fig.*) éducation, *f.*, discipline, *f.*

Nurture, va. nourrir, élever, instruire, discipliner

Nut, s. noisette, *f.*, (*tree*) noisetier, *m.*, (*mechan.*) écrou, *m.* *It's a hard — to crack*, cela nous (*or* vous, lui, etc.) donnera du fil à retordre. — *-brown*, adj. châtain. — *-crackers*, s. casse-noisettes, *m.* — *-frame*, s. fût, *m.* — *-gall*, s noix de galle, *f.* — *-hook*, s. crochet au linge, *m.* — *-shell*, s. coquille de noix, *f.*, (*fig.*) peu de chose, *m.* — *-tree*, s. noisetier, *m.*

Nut, vn. cueillir des noisettes. *To go a-nutting*, (*fig.*) aller cueillir des noisettes

Nutation, s. nutation, *f.*

Nutmeg, s. muscade, *f.*, noix muscade, *f.* *Oil of —*, s. beurre de muscade, *m.* — *-shell*, s. brou de muscade, *m.* — *-tree*, s. muscadier, *m.*

Nutrient, adj. nourrissant, nutritif, alimentaire

Nutriment, s. nourriture, *f.*, aliments, *m.pl.*

Nutrimental, adj. succulent

Nutrition, s. nutrition, *f.*, nourriture, *f.*

Nutritious, **Nutritive**, adj. nourrissant, nutritif, succulent, nourricier, (*med.*) alimenteux

Nutritiousness, s. propriétés nutritives, *f.pl.*

Nutty, adj. de noisette, qui a un goût de noisette

Nux vomica, s. noix vomique, *f.*

Nuzzle, va. nourrir, élever. (*to conceal*) nicher, cacher; — vn. cacher sa tête, se cacher. *To — along*, aller le nez bas

Nyctalops, s. nyctalope, *m.f.*

Nyctalopy, s. nyctalopie, *f.*

Nye, s. troupe (de faisans), *f.*

Nymph, s. nymphe, *f.* *Sea —*, nymphe de la mer, de l'océan

Nymphean, adj. consacré aux nymphes

Nymphlike, adj. de nymphe, comme une nymphe

Nympholepsy, s. transport, *m.*

O

O, s. O, o, *m.* —, (*circle*) cercle, *m.*, rond, *m.*, zéro, *m.*

O! interj. ô! oh!

Oak, s. chêne, *m.*, bois de chêne, *m.* — *-apple*, s. galle de chêne, *f.* — *-bark*, s. écorce de chêne, *f.*, (*tech.*) tan, *m.* — *-evergreen*, s. chêne vert, *m.*, yeuse, *f.* — *-gall*, s. noix de galle, *f.*

Oak, **Oaken**, adj. de chêne

Oakling, s. jeune chêne, *m.*

Oakum, s. étoupe, *f.* *To pick —*, faire de l'étoupe. — *-boy*, s. mousse de calfat, *m.*

Oar, s. rame, *f.*, aviron, *m.* *To be, to tug at the —*, tirer la rame. *Set of —s*, jeu d'avirons, *m.* *Stroke of the —*, coup d'aviron, *m.* *Stroke —*, premier rameur, *m.* *To back one's —s*, scier. *To boat the —s*, rentrer les avirons. *First —s*, premier bateau, *m.*, premier batelier, *m.*

Oar, va.n. ramer

Oared, adj. à . . . rames

Oarsman, s. rameur, *m.*

Oasis, s. oasis, *f.*

Oat, adj. d'avoine. — *-straw*, paille d'avoine, *f.* — *-cake*, galette d'avoine, *f.*

Oaten, adj. d'avoine

Oath, s. serment, *m.*, (*contempt.*) juron, *m.*, jurement, *m.*, imprécation, *f.* *Upon —*, sous serment, sous la foi du serment. — *-breaking*, parjure, *m.* *To take an —*, faire serment. *To take the — of fidelity*, prêter serment de fidélité. *To break one's —*, violer, rompre, fausser son serment. *To let fly a volley of —s*, lâcher une bordée de jurons

Oatmeal, s. farine d'avoine. *f.*

Oats, s.pl. avoine, *f.*

Obduracy, s. endurcissement, *m.*, impénitence, *f.*, (*obstinacy*) entêtement, *m.*

Obdurate, adj. endurci, dur, impénitent, opiniâtre, obstiné

Obdurately, adv. avec impénitence, avec endurcissement de cœur, obstinément, inexorablement

Obedience, s. obéissance, *f.*, soumission, *f.* *In — to*, par obéissance à. *To compel — from*, se faire obéir de

Obedient, adj. obéissant, soumis, docile

Obediently, adv. avec obéissance, avec soumission

Obeisance, s. révérence, *f.*, salut, *m.*

Obelisk, s. obélisque, *m.*

Obesity, s. obésité, *f.*

Obey, va. obéir à, obtempérer à

Obeyer, s. qui obéit

Obit, s. obit, *m.*, mort, *f.*, décès, *m.*

Obituary, s. obituaire, *m.*, nécrologie, *f.*

Object, va. opposer, interposer, objecter, reprocher; — vn. (*to, against*) s'opposer (à), faire des objections, objecter (à)

Object, s. objet, *m.*, chose, *f.*, but, *m.*, objet affreux, *m.*, horreur, *f.* (*gram.*) régime, *m.*, complément, *m.* — *-glass*, s. verre objectif, *m.*, objectif, *m.*

Objection, s. objection, *f.*, charge, *f.* *To make, to raise —s to*, faire des objections à. *I have no —*, je le veux bien, je ne m'y oppose pas

Objectionable, adj. blâmable, répréhensible, inadmissible

Objective, s. adj objectif *m.*

Objectively, adv. objectivement

Objurgation, s. objurgation, *f.*, vif reproche, *m.*

Objurgatory, adj. de reproche

Oblate, adj. aplati

Oblation, s. oblation, *f.*, offrande, *f.*, aumône, *f.*

Obligation, s. obligation, *f.*, engagement, *m.* *To lie under an — to a person for*, avoir des obligations à quelqu'un de. *To lay oneself or a person under an —*, accepter un service, rendre un service *or* obliger

Obligatory, adj. obligatoire

Oblige, va. obliger (à *or* de), astreindre (à), falloir (. .), faire le plaisir (de)

Obliging, adj. obligeant, complaisant, officieux

Obligingly, adv. obligeamment

Obligingness, s. obligeance, *f.*

Oblique, adj. oblique, indirect, détourné

Obliquely, adv. obliquement

Obliquity, s. obliquité, *f.*

Obliterate, va. effacer, (*writing*) biffer, oblitérer

Obliteration, s. rature, *f.*, oblitération, *f.*

Oblivion, s. oubli, *m.*

Oblivious, adj. d'oubli, de l'oubli, oublieux

Obliviousness, s. oubli, *m.*

Oblong, adj. oblong

Oblong, s. figure oblongue, *f.*

Obloquy, s. reproche, *m.*, blâme, *m.*, honte, *f.*

Obnoxious, adj. coupable, blâmable, digne de châtiment, sujet, exposé, odieux, offensant

Obnoxiously, adv. d'une manière blâmable, odieusement, d'une manière désagréable *or* offensante

Obscene, adj. obscène, déshonnête, immonde

Obscenely, adv. d'une manière obscène

Obscenity, s. obscénité, *f.*

Obscure, adj. obscur

Obscure, va. obscurcir, éclipser, cacher

Obscurely, adv. obscurément

Obscureness, **Obscurity**, s. obscurité, *f.*

Obsequies, s.pl. obsèques, *f.pl.*

Obsequious, adj. obséquieux, obéissant

Obsequiously, adv. obséquieusement, avec obéissance

Obsequiousness, s. soumission obséquieuse, *f.*, servilité, *f.*

Observable, adj. sensible, remarquable

Observance, s. observation, *f.*, pratique, *f.*, accomplissement, *m.*, (*relig.*) observance, *f.*, pratique, *f.*

Observant, adj. observateur, attentif

Observation, s. observation, *f.*, attention, *f.*

Observatory, s. observatoire, *m.*

Observe, va. observer, remarquer, apercevoir, faire observer

Observer, s. observateur, *m.*, observatrice, *f.*, curieux, *m.*

Observing, adj. observateur, attentif

Observingly, adv. attentivement

Obsolete, adj. tombé en désuétude, vieilli, hors d'usage

Obstacle, s. obstacle, *m.*, empêchement, *m.*

Obstinacy, s. obstination, *f.*, opiniâtreté, *f.*, entêtement, *m.*

Obstinate, adj. obstiné, entêté, acharné

Obstinately, adv. obstinément, opiniâtrément

Obstreperous, adj. bruyant, étourdissant, (*pers.*) turbulent, tapageur

U

Obstreperously, adv. bruyamment
Obstreperousness, s. bruit, *m.*, tapage, *m.*
Obstruct, va. obstruer, boucher, fermer, barrer, faire obstacle à
Obstruction, s. obstruction, *f.*, empêchement, *m.*, obstacle, *m.*
Obtain, va. obtenir, recevoir, tirer, procurer; — vn. s'établir, prévaloir, exister, régner
Obtainable, adj. qu'on peut obtenir, qu'on peut se procurer
Obtrude, *see* INTRUDE
Obtruder, s. personne qui impose, qui introduit de force
Obtrusion, s. (*upon*) action d'imposer (à), la chose imposée (à)
Obtrusive, adj. importun, qui veut s'imposer (à), indiscret
Obtrusively, adv. avec importunité
Obtund, va. émousser
Obturator, s. obturateur, *m.*
Obtuse, adj. obtus, (*blunt*) émoussé
Obtusely, adv. d'une manière obtuse
Obtuseness, s. état obtus, *m.*
Obviate, va. obvier à, prévenir
Obvious, adj. sensible, facile à saisir *or* à comprendre, clair, visible
Obviously, adv. sensiblement, évidemment, clairement
Obviousness, s. évidence, *f.*, clarté, *f.*
Occasion, s. occasion, *f.*, conjoncture, *f.*, rencontre, *f.*, sujet, *m.*, motif, *m.*, besoin, *m.* *To have — for*, avoir besoin de. *There is no — for* or *to*, il n'y a pas besoin de
Occasion, va. occasionner, causer, produire
Occasional, adj. fait par occasion *or* dans l'occasion, de circonstance, accidentel, occasionnel
Occasionally, adv. occasionnellement, de temps en temps, parfois
Occidental, adj. occidental, d'occident
Occult, adj. occulte
Occupancy, s. occupation, *f.*
Occupant, Occupier, s. occupant, *m.*, habitant, *m.*, locataire, *m.*, possesseur, *m.*
Occupation, s. occupation, *f.*, possession, *f.*, travail, *m.*, état, *m.*, métier, *m.*
Occupy, va. occuper, employer
Occur, vn. (*fig.*) se présenter à l'esprit, s'offrir, venir, venir à l'idée de, se rencontrer, se trouver, (*happen*) arriver, survenir, (*with*, avec) rencontrer, (*to*, à) opposer. *The idea —ed to me to see*, l'idée me vint de voir. *It —ed to me that*, il me vint à l'idée que. *This is said to have —ed*, cela, dit-on, est arrivé
Occurrence, s. événement, *m.*, incident, *m.*, occurrence, *f.*, rencontre, *f.*
Ocean, s. océan, *m.*, immensité, *f.*
Oceanic, adj. océanique
Ochre, s. ocre, *m.*
Octagon, s. octogone, *m.*
Octagonal, adj. octogone
Octave, s. octave, *f.*
Octavo, s. in-octavo, *m.*
October, s. octobre, *m.*, le mois d'octobre, *m.*
Octogenarian, s. octogénaire, *m.f.*
Ocular, adj. oculaire
Oculist, s. oculiste, *m.*
Odd, adj. (*not even*) impair, (*unmatched*) dépareillé, déparié, (*remaining*) de surplus, de plus, du reste, (*com.*) d'appoint, (*singular*) bizarre, singulier, étrange, drôle, baroque, (*time*) de loisir. *— or even*, pair ou impair. *An — volume*, un volume dépareillé. *— gloves*, des gants dépariés. *The — trick*, (*at whist*) la levée. *— money*, appoint, *m.* *Twenty and — years*, vingt et quelques années. *See* JOB. *— fancy*, drôle d'idée. *An — person*, une personne bizarre. *The club of — fellows*, club des excentriques *or* des originaux. *An — fish*, un drôle de corps. *— -looking*, à l'air bizarre. *— -shaped*, de forme bizarre. *— -like*, étrange. *I felt all — -like*, je me sentis tout chose
Oddity, s. bizarrerie, *f.*, singularité, *f.*, chose singulière, *f.*, (*person*) original, *m.*, -e, *f.*, drôle de corps, *m.*
Oddly, adv. en nombre impair, bizarrement, singulièrement, étrangement
Oddness, s. bizarrerie, *f.*, singularité, *f.*, nature singulière, *f.*
Odds, s.pl. inégalité, *f.*, différence, *f.*, avantage, *m.*, supériorité, *f.*, chances, *f.pl.*, pari, *m.*, querelle, *f.*, discorde, *f.*, guerre, *f.*, petites choses, pièces, *f.pl.* *It makes no —*, cela ne fait pas de différence. *What's the —?* qu'est-ce que cela fait? *It is — but*, (*fig.*) il y a gros à parier que . . . ne. *To be at —*, être mal ensemble. *To live at —*, vivre dans l'inimitié. *— and ends*, choses de rebut, *f.pl.*, pièces et morceaux
Ode, s. ode, *f.*
Odious, adj. odieux, détestable
Odiously, adv. odieusement
Odiousness, s. nature odieuse, *f.*, odieux, *m.*
Odium, s. haine, *f.*, odieux, *m.*
Odorant, adj. odorant
Odorousness, s. nature odoriférante, *f.*, parfum, *m.*
Odour, s. odeur, *f.*, parfum, *m.*
Odyssey, s. odyssée, *f.*
Œcumenical, adj. œcuménique
Of, prep. de, (*among*) d'entre, plus que. *A brother — mine*, un frère à moi. *I should like it — all things*, je l'aimerais par-dessus tout
Off, adv. de dessus, (*far*) au loin, loin, éloigné, (*cessation*) terminé, rompu, fini. *— and on*, à bâtons rompus, par boutades. *— with it*, enlevez-le, ôtez-le. *With one shoe —*, un pied déchaussé. *— -handed, — -hand*, brusque, prompt. *To be well —*, être à son aise, être dans l'aisance. *— with you, be —*, partez, filez
Off, prep. de dessus, non sur, loin de, éloigné de. *To dine — a leg of mutton*, dîner d'un gigot de mouton
Off, adj. hors de la main, le plus éloigné. *The — -side horse*, le cheval sous la main *or* de droite. *— -side*, côté hors montoir
Offal, s. issues, *f.pl.*, restes, *m.pl.*, débris, *m.pl.*
Offence, s. offense, *f.*, mécontentement, *m.*, déplaisir, *m.*, colère, *f.*, outrage, *m.*, injure, *f.*, injustice, *f.*, tort, *m.*, (*law*) contravention, *f.*, délit, *m.* *To give —*, faire ombrage à, blesser. *To take — (at, de)*, s'offenser, se trouver blessé, se fâcher. *Second —*, récidive, *f.* *This is not the first —*, il y a récidive. *To repeat the —*, récidiver
Offend, va. offenser, blesser, irriter, choquer
Offender, s. offenseur, *m.*, coupable, *m.*, criminel, *m.*, malfaiteur, *m.*, (*law*) délinquant, *m.*, -e, *f.*, contrevenant, *m.*, -e, *f.* *An old —*, un récidiviste, un repris de justice
Offensive, adj. offensif, offensant, blessant, injurieux, choquant, désagréable
Offensive, s. offensive, *f.*
Offensively, adv. offensivement, d'une manière offensante, désagréablement
Offensiveness, s. nature offensante, *f.*, blessante, *f.*, choquante, *f.*, désagréable, *f.*
Offer, va. offrir (à), proposer, présenter; — vn. s'offrir (à), faire l'offre, s'offrir, se présenter, essayer (de), tenter (de), vouloir
Offer, s. offre, *f.*, demande en mariage, *f.*
Offering, s. offrande, *f.*, sacrifice, *m.*
Offertory, s. offertoire, *m.*
Office, s. office, *m.*, charge, *f.*, fonctions, *f.pl.*, emploi, *m.*, ministère, *m.*, (*turn*) service, *m.*, (*room*) bureau, *m.*, cabinet, *m.*, (*lawyer's*) étude, *f.*, (*liturg.*) office, *m.* *— -hours*, s.pl. heures des bureaux. *— -keeper*, s. buraliste, *m.* *— -lead*, s. serre-papier, *m.* *The Government —s*, s.pl. les ministères
Officer, va. donner pour officier (à), pourvoir d'officiers. *Well officered*, bien commandé
Officer, s. officier, *m.*, fonctionnaire, *m.*, dignitaire, *m.*, (*justice, police*) agent, *m.*, huissier, *m.*
Official, adj. officiel, public
Official, s. official, *m.*, fonctionnaire, *m.*, employé, *m.*
Officially, adv. officiellement
Officiate, vn. (*church*) officier, desservir, exercer, exercer ses fonctions
Officiating, adj. officiant, desservant, qui exerce ses fonctions
Officious, adj. officieux, bienveillant, serviable
Officiously, adv. officieusement, avec empressement
Officiousness, s. empressement officieux, *m.*
Offing, s. large, *m.* *In the —*, au large. *To stand for the —*, courir au large
Offscouring, s. rebut, *m.*
Offset, s. rejeton, *m.*
Offshoot, s. rejeton, *m.*
Offspring, s. enfant, *m.*, enfants, *m.pl.*, descendant, *m.*, descendants, *m.pl.*, race, *f.*, postérité, *f.*, (*fig.*) fruit, *m.*, produit, *m.*
Oft, Often, adv. souvent, fréquemment. *We — see him*, nous le voyons souvent. *Very —*, bien souvent. *As — as*, aussi souvent que, autant de fois que, toutes les fois que. *How —?* combien de fois? *How —!* que de fois! combien de fois! *Too —*, trop souvent, trop de fois. *Once too —*, une fois de trop. *— -times*, souvent
Ogive, s. ogive, *f.*
Ogle, va. lorgner, regarder du coin de l'œil, lancer des œillades à
Ogle, s. œillade, *f.*, coup d'œil, *m.*
Ogler, s. lorgneur, *m.*
Ogling, s. œillades, *f.pl.*, action de lorgner, *f.*
Ogre, s. ogre, *m.*
Ogress, s. ogresse, *f.*
Oh! interj. oh!
Oil, s. huile, *f.* *Lamp- —* huile à brûler. *— -cake*, s. tourteau, *m.* *— -cloth*, s. toile cirée, *f.* *— -colours*, s.pl. couleurs à l'huile, *f.pl.* *— mill*, s. huilerie, *f.* *— -nut*, s. noix de ben, de coco, etc., *f.* *— -painting*, s. peinture *or* tableau à l'huile. *— -plant*, s. plante oléagineuse, *f.* *— -skin*, s. toile cirée *or* vernie, *f.* *— -trade*, s. commerce des huiles, *m.* *— -tree*, s. ricin, *m.*, palma-christi, *m.*
Oil, va. huiler
Oiliness, s. nature huileuse, *f.*, onctuosité, *f.*
Oilman, s. marchand d'huiles, *m.*
Oily, adj. huileux, graisseux, onctueux, oléagineux
Ointment, s. onguent, *m.*
Old, adj. vieux, vieil, âgé,

ancien, antique. — *people*, les vieilles gens, les vieillards, les vieux. *To get, to grow* —, vieillir, se faire *or* devenir vieux. *How — are you!* quel âge avez-vous? *I am forty years* —, j'ai quarante ans. — *fellow*, mon vieux. *Established of* —, établi depuis longtemps. *I know him of* —, je le connais de vieille date. — *-faced*, — *-looking*, à l'air vieux. — *-fashioned*, à l'ancienne mode, antique. — *-wife*, s. vieille femme, *f.*, vieille commère, *f.*

Olden, adj. ancien, vieux. *In the — time*, dans le temps jadis

Oldish, adj. un peu vieux

Oldness, s. vieillesse, *f.*, vétusté, *f.*, ancienneté, *f.*, antiquité, *f.*

Oleaginous, adj. oléagineux

Oleander, s. laurier-rose, *m.*

Olfactory, adj. olfactif

Oligarchy, s. oligarchie, *f.*

Olio, s. olla podrida, *f.*, macédoine, *f.*, recueil, *m.*

Olive, s. olivier, *m.*, (*fruit*) olive, *f.*, couleur olive, *f.* — *-branch*, s. branche d'olivier, *f.* — *-coloured*, adj. couleur olive, d'un teint olivâtre, olivâtre. — *-oil*, s. huile d'olive, *f.* — *-yard*, s. plants d'oliviers, *m.pl.*

Olympiad, s. olympiade, *f.*

Olympic, adj. olympique

Ombre, s. hombre, *m.*, ombre, *m.*

Omelet, s. omelette, *f.*

Omen, s. présage, *m.*, augure, *m.*, pronostic, *m.*

Omened, adj. d'un ... présage

Ominous, adj. de mauvais augure, de funeste présage

Ominously, adv. de mauvais augure

Omission, s. omission, *f.*

Omit, va. omettre, négliger, manquer, laisser échapper

Omnibus, s. omnibus, *m.*

Omnipotence, s. omnipotence, *f.*, toute-puissance, *f.*

Omnivorous, adj. omnivore

On, prep. sur, dessus, (*of, from*) de, (*in, while*) en, (*at, about*) à. — *each side*, de chaque côté. *To play — the violin*, jouer du violon. — *his arrival*, à son arrivée. *To have a ring — one's finger*, avoir une bague au doigt. — *Tuesday*, mardi. — *the 15th ult.*, le 15 du mois dernier. — *pain of death*, sous peine de la vie

On, adv. dessus, (*clothes*) sur soi, (*forward*) en avant, toujours, de suite, avant, avancé. *Sleep* —, continuez de dormir. *And so* —, et ainsi de suite. *Far — in the night*, bien avant dans la nuit. *To be neither — nor off*, être irrésolu, (*things*) n'être pas encore décidé

On! interj. en avant!

Once, adj. une fois, (*formerly*) autrefois, jadis. *At* —, à la fois, en même temps, sur-le-champ, tout de suite. *All at* —, tout *or* tous à la fois, tout à coup. — *upon a time*, une fois, il y avait une fois...

One, adj. s. un, une, quelqu'un, un certain, un nommé. *To be — of*, faire partie de, être au nombre de. *It's all* —, peu importe. *It's all — to me*, cela m'est égal. *All's — for that*, cela n'y fait rien, peu m'importe. — *by* —, un à un. — *and all*, tous sans exception. *At* —, d'accord. — *-sided*, adj. à une face, (*fig.*) partial. — *-sidedness*, s. partialité, *f.*

One, pron. on, se, soi, en ... un, en ... une. *The* —, celui, celui que, la personne (que). —*'s*, de soi, son, sa, ses. — *-self*, se, soi-même. *By — -self*, de soi-même, tout seul. — *another*, l'un l'autre, les uns les autres. — *with the other*, l'un avec l'autre, (*things*) l'un portant l'autre. *I have a very good* —, *very good —s*, j'en ai un très-bon, j'en ai de très-bons. *It is as difficult to form a great king as to be* —, il est aussi difficile de former un grand roi que de l'être. *The — you recommended*, celui que vous avez recommandé. *The — whom I spoke to*, celui à qui j'ai parlé. *The — we love*, la personne que nous aimons. *Everything has two handles, beware of the wrong* —, toute chose a deux anses, gare la mauvaise

Oneness, s. unité, *f.*

Onerous, adj. onéreux

Onion, s. oignon, *m.*, ognon, *m.* — *-peel*, s. pelure d'oignon, *f.* — *-sauce*, s. sauce Soubise, *f.*

Only, adj. seul, unique

Only, adv. seulement, ne ... que, simplement, uniquement. — *fancy*, imaginez un peu. — *taste*, goûte-le donc. *If* —, pour peu que

Onset, s. attaque, *f.*, assaut, *m.*, charge, *f.*

Onslaught, s. attaque, *f.*, assaut, *m.*

Onward, adv. en avant, plus loin, progressivement

Onward, adj. en avant, dirigé en avant

Onyx, s. onyx, *m.*

Oolite, s. oolithe, *m.*

Oolitic, adj. oolithique

Oology, s. oologie, *f.*

Ooze, s. vase, *f.*, bourbe, *f.*

Ooze, vn. suinter, couler doucement, filtrer, passer à travers, (*out of*) s'échapper (par), (*to become known*) s'ébruiter

Oozing, s. suintement, *m.*

Oozy, adj. vaseux, bourbeux

Opacity, s. opacité, *f.*, ténèbres, *f.pl.*

Opal, s. opale, *f.*

Opaque, adj. opaque

Open, va. ouvrir, (*a way*) frayer, (*a bottle*) déboucher, (*a letter*) ouvrir, décacheter, (*to begin*) commencer, entamer, (*uncover, expose*) découvrir, dévoiler, épancher, exposer, expliquer. *To — again*, rouvrir. *To half-* —, entr'ouvrir, entre-bâiller. *To — one's heart*, ouvrir son cœur, épancher son cœur, s'épancher. — vn. s'ouvrir, s'entr'ouvrir, (*into*) donner (sur, dans), avoir vue (sur), communiquer (avec), commencer, (*days*) donner de la voix, aboyer. *To — again*, se rouvrir. *To half-* —, s'entr'ouvrir

Open, adj. ouvert, (*fig.*) manifeste, évident, visible, franc, sincère, public, au grand jour, à ciel ouvert, (*country*) exposé, découvert, (*enemy*) déclaré, (*liberal*) libéral, (*weather*) doux. *Half-* —, entr'ouvert, (*fig.*) entre-bâillé. *With — force*, de vive force. *To blow* —, ouvrir. *The door flew wide* —, la porte s'ouvrit toute grande. *To pull* —, *to push* —, *to tear* —, *to throw* —, ouvrir vivement, (*fig.*) ouvrir. *To lie* —, être ouvert, être libre. *To stand* —, rester ouvert. *In — court*, en plein tribunal. *An — trial*, un jugement public. *The law is* —, on tient audience. *To lay* —, exposer, mettre à découvert, dévoiler. *To lay oneself — to*, s'exposer à. — *-handed*, adj. à la main ouverte, généreux. — *-hearted*, adj. au cœur ouvert, franc, généreux. — *-heartedly*, adv. à cœur ouvert, franchement, ouvertement. — *-heartedness*, s. franchise, *f.*, sincérité, *f.*, générosité, *f.* — *-work*, s. filigrane, *f.*, ouvrage découpé à jour, *m.* — *-worked stockings*, s. bas à jour, *m.*

Opener, s. ouvreur, *m.*, ouvreuse, *f.*, interprète, *m.*

Opening, s. ouverture, *f.*, jour, *m.*, entrée, *f.*, commencement, *m.*, chance de succès, *f.*, occasion, *f.*, (*com.*) débouché, *m.*

Openly, adv. ouvertement, publiquement, franchement

Openness, s. franchise, *f.*, sincérité, *f.*, ouverture de cœur, *f.*, abandon, *m.*, laisser-aller, *m.*

Opera, s. opéra, *m.* — *-glass*, s. lorgnette, *f.* — *-hat*, s. claque, *m.*

Operate, vn.a. opérer, agir, avoir de l'effet

Operatic, adj. d'opéra, lyrique

Operating, adj. qui opère

Operation, s. opération, *f.*, action, *f.*, effet, *m.*

Operative, adj. actif, efficace, manuel, pratique, ouvrier, -ère, des ouvriers, des artisans

Operative, s. ouvrier, *m.*, artisan, *m.* —*s*, pl. ouvriers, *m.pl.*, travailleurs, *m.pl.*

Operator, s. personne *or* chose qui opère, *f.*, agent, *m.*, opérateur, *m.*

Ophicleide, s. ophicléide, *m.*

Ophthalmic, adj. ophthalmique

Ophthalmia, Ophthalmy, s. ophthalmie, *f.*

Opiate, s. opiacé, *m.*, narcotique, *m.*

Opiate, adj. opiacé, narcotique

Opine, vn. être d'avis, penser, croire

Opinion, s. opinion, *f.*, avis, *m.*, sentiment, *m.*, jugement, *m.*, sens, *m.*, pensée, *f.*, idée, *f.*, consultation, *f.* *In my* —, à mon avis. *To be of the — of*, être de l'avis de, (*fig.*) abonder dans le sens de. *Matter of* —, affaire d'opinion

Opinionated, Opinionative, adj. opiniâtre, obstiné, entêté, suffisant

Opium, s. opium, *m.*

Opium, adj. d'opium

Opponent, adj. opposé, contraire

Opponent, s. adversaire, *m.*, antagoniste, *m.f.*, ennemi, *m.*, -e, *f.*

Opportune, adj. opportun, à propos, convenable

Opportunely, adv. à propos, en temps opportun, à point nommé

Opportunity, s. occasion, *f.*, opportunité, *f.*

Oppose, va.n. opposer, s'opposer à, résister à, combattre, empêcher, arrêter

Opposer, s. adversaire, *m.*

Opposite, s. opposé, *m.*, opposite, *m.*, contraire, *m.*

Opposite, adj. opposé, vis-à-vis, en face, à l'opposite, contraire, opposé

Oppositely, adv. en face, (*contrarily*) en sens opposé

Opposition, s. situation vis-à-vis, *f.*, opposition, *f.*, obstacle, *m.*, résistance, *f.*, concurrence, *f.* *Out of* —, par esprit d'opposition. *To be in — to*, être en opposition à. *In — to*, en opposition à, contrairement à, par opposition à. *Her Majesty's* —, l'opposition de Sa Majesté. *The — benches*, les bancs de l'opposition. *To be in the* —, être membre de l'opposition. *To set up an* —, entrer en concurrence. — *coach*, s. voiture faisant concurrence, *f.*

Oppress, va. opprimer, accabler, écraser, éclipser

Oppression, s. oppression, *f.*, malheur, *m.*, accablement, *m.*

Oppressive, adj. oppressif, accablant

Oppressor, s. oppresseur, *m.*

Opprobrious, adj. injurieux, outrageant, infamant

Opprobriously, adv. d'une manière outrageante, avec opprobre

Opprobrium, s. opprobre, *m.*

Optic, Optical, adj. optique, d'optique, qui traite de l'optique

Optician, s. opticien, *m.*

Optics, s.pl. l'optique, *f.*

Optimism, s. optimisme, *m.*

Optimist, s. optimiste, *m.*

Option, s. option, *f.*, choix, *m.*

Optional, adj. facultatif

Opulence, s. opulence, *f.*

Opulent, adj. opulent

Opulently, adv. avec opulence

Or, conj. ou, soit, (*neg.*) ni. — *else*, ou bien, ou, autrement

Oracle, s. oracle, *m.*

Oracular, adj. en style d'oracle, qui rend des oracles

Oral, adj. oral

Orally, adv. oralement

Orange, s. (*fruit*) orange, *f.*, (*colour*) orangé, *m.*, couleur orange, *f.* — *-blossom*, s., — *-blossom water*, s. fleur d'oranger, *f.* — *-colour*, adj., — *-coloured*, adj. couleur orange, orangé. — *-conservatory*, s. orangerie, *f.* — *-girl*, s., — *-woman*, s., — *-wife*, s. marchande d'oranges, *f.* — *-grove*, s. bois d'orangers, *m.* — *-peel*, s. écorce d'orange, *f.* — *-tawny*, adj. fauve. — *-tree*, s. oranger, *m.*

Orangery, s. orangerie, *f.*

Orang-outang, s. orang-outang, *m.*

Oration, s. discours, *m.*, harangue, *f.*

Orator, s. orateur, *m.*

Oratorially, Oratorically, adv. oratoirement, d'une façon oratoire

Oratorical, adj. oratoire

Oratorio, s. oratorio, *m.*

Oratory, s. art oratoire, *m.*, éloquence, *f.*, (*chapel*) oratoire, *m.*

Orb, s. globe, *m.*, (*astron.*) orbe, *m.*, orbite, *f.* — *-like*, adj. sphérique

Orbit, s. orbite, *f.*

Orchard, s. verger, *m.*, jardin fruitier, *m.*

Orchestra, s. orchestre, *m.*

Orchestral, adj. d'orchestre, de l'orchestre

Ordain, va. ordonner, décréter, prescrire, instituer, établir, destiner, préparer

Ordainer, s. ordonnateur, *m.*, (*eccles.*) ordinant, *m.*

Ordeal, s. épreuve, *f.*

Order, s. ordre, *m.*, (*rule*) règle, *f.*, règlement, *m.*, instructions, *f.pl.*, (*decree*) arrêté, *m.*, ordonnance, *f.*, (*com.*) demande, *f.*, commande, *f.*, (*money*) mandat, *m.*, (*for the play*) billet donné, *m.*, entrée de faveur, *f.* *In — to*, afin de, (*fig.*) en vue de. *In — that*, afin que. *To be out of —*, être dérangé. *To put out of —*, déranger, mettre en désordre. *— ! — !* à l'ordre ! *To call to —*, rappeler à l'ordre. *To rise to —*, se lever pour demander le rappel à l'ordre. *Breach of —*, infraction au règlement, *f.* *To obey —s*, obéir aux ordres. *Till further —s*, jusqu'à nouvel ordre. *To give a large —*, faire une forte commande. *To my —*, à mon ordre. *The lower —s*, les classes inférieures. *And other people of the lower —s*, et d'autre menu peuple. *To be in —s*, *to take —s*, être, entrer dans les ordres. — *-book*, s. livre des commandes, *m.*, (*milit.*) livre d'ordres, *m.*

Order, va. ordonner, disposer, mettre en ordre, arranger, régler, conduire, diriger, gouverner. *To — about*, envoyer à droite et à gauche. *To — away*, or *off*, dire de s'en aller, faire emporter, faire emmener. *To — back*, dire de s'en retourner, renvoyer, faire remmener. *To — down*, dire de descendre, faire descendre. *To — in*, dire d'entrer, faire entrer, faire apporter. *To — out*, faire sortir, (*a carriage*) faire atteler, appeler, (*troops*) faire sortir. *To — up*, faire monter, dire de monter

Orderer, s. ordonnateur, *m.*, régulateur, *m.*, -trice, *f.*

Ordering, s. ordonnance, *f.*, disposition, *f.* ordre, *m.*

Orderliness, s. ordre, *m.*, méthode, *f.*, régularité, *f.*, bon ordre, *m.*, tranquillité, *f.*, bonne conduite, *f.*

Orderly, adj. régulier, méthodique, (*pers.*) tranquille, raisonnable, rangé, (*milit.*) d'ordonnance. — *book*, s. livre d'ordres, *m.*

Orderly, adv. en ordre, dans l'ordre

Orderly, s. (*milit.*) ordonnance, *f.* — *sergeant*, s. sergent d'ordonnance, *m.*

Ordinal, adj. s. ordinal

Ordinance, s. ordonnance, *f.*, règlement, *m.*, décret, *m.*

Ordinarily, adv. ordinairement, pour l'ordinaire, d'ordinaire

Ordinary, adj. ordinaire, du commun, commun

Ordinary, s. (*eccles.*) ordinaire, *m.*, (*prison-chaplain*) aumônier, *m.*, (*custom*) habitude, *f.*, (*of hotels, &c.*) table d'hôte, *f.*

Ordination, s. ordination, *f.*

Ordnance, s. artillerie, *f.*, canons, *m.pl.* — *-office*, s. bureau de l'artillerie, *m.* *Board of —*, s. comité de l'artillerie, *m.* *Master of —*, s. directeur de l'artillerie, *m.*

Ore, s. minerai, *m.*, mine, *f.*, métal, *m.*

Organ, s. organe, *m.*, (*mus.*) orgue, *m.f.* — *-blower*, s. souffleur d'orgues, *m.* — *-builder*, s. facteur d'orgues, *m.* — *-loft*, s. tribune d'orgue, *f.* — *-pipe*, s. tuyau d'orgue, *m.* — *-player*, s. organiste, *m.* — *-stop*, s. jeu d'orgues, *m.*

Organic, adj. organique

Organism, s. organisme, *m.*

Organist, s. organiste, *m.*

Organization, s. organisation, *f.*

Organize, va. organiser

Orgy, s. orgie, *f.*

Oriel, s. fenêtre en ogive, *f.*

Oriental, adj. oriental, de l'Orient

Orientalist, s. orientaliste, *m.*

Orifice, s. orifice, *m.*

Origin, s. origine, *f.*

Original, adj. premier, originel, original

Original, s. origine, *f.*, principe, *m.*

Originality, s. originalité, *f.*

Originally, adv. originairement, dans l'origine

Originate, va. produire, créer, donner naissance à ; — vn. avoir son origine, tirer son origine (de), venir (de), provenir (de)

Origination, s. origine, *f.*, génération, *f.*, mode de production, *f.*

Originator, s. auteur, *m.*, cause première, *f.*, mobile, *m.*

Orillon, s. orillon, *m.*

Oriole, s. loriot, *m.*

Orison, s. oraison, *f.*

Ormolu, s. or moulu, *m.*

Ornament, s. ornement, *m.*

Ornament, va. orner, décorer

Ornamental, adj. d'ornement, qui sert d'ornement,

Ornamentally, adv. par manière d'ornement, pour servir d'ornement

Ornamentation, s. décoration, *f.*, embellissement, *m.*

Ornate, adj. orné, élégant

Ornately, adv. élégamment

Ornateness, s. élégance, *f.*

Ornithologic, Ornithological, adj. ornithologique

Ornithologist, s. ornithologiste, *m.*, ornithologue, *m.*

Ornithology, s. ornithologie, *f.*

Orological, adj. orologique, orographique

Orology, s. orologie, *f.*, orographie, *f.*

Orphan, s. adj. orphelin, *m.*, orpheline, *f.* — *institute* or *asylum*, orphelinat, *m.*

Orphanhood, Orphanage, s. état d'être orphelin or orpheline, *m.*

Orpiment, s. orpiment, *m.*

Orrery, s. planétaire, *m.*

Orthodox, adj. orthodoxe

Orthodoxy, s. orthodoxie, *f.*

Orthographical, adj. orthographique, d'orthographe

Orthography, s. orthographe, *f.*

Orthopedic, adj. orthopédique

Orthopedy, s. orthopédie, *f.*

Ortolan, s. ortolan, *m.*

Oscillate, vn. osciller, (*fig.*) balancer, hésiter

Oscillation, s. oscillation, *f.*

Oscillatory, adj. oscillatoire

Osier, s. adj. osier, *m.*, d'osier. — *-ground*, s., — *-holt*, s. oseraie, *f.*

Osprey, s. orfraie, *f.*, balbusard, *m.*

Ossification, s. ossification, *f.*

Ossify, va. ossifier ; — vn. s'ossifier

Ossuary, s. charnier, *m.*, ossuaire, *m.*

Ostensible, adj. ostensible

Ostensibly, adv. ostensiblement

Ostentation, s. ostentation, *f.*, faste, *m.*, étalage, *m.*

Ostentatious, adj. fastueux, plein de faste or d'ostentation

Ostentatiously, adv. avec ostentation, avec faste, fastueusement

Osteology, s. ostéologie, *f.*

Ostler, s. valet or garçon d'écurie, *m.*

Ostracism, s. ostracisme, *m.*

Ostrich, s. autruche, *f.*

Other, adj. pron. autre. —*s*, pl., autres, d'autres, autrui, l'autre, autre chose, autre. *Any —*, tout autre, quelque autre, aucun autre. *One with the —*, l'un avec l'autre, l'un portant l'autre. *No —*, personne autre, aucun autre. *All the —s*, tous les autres. *—s will come*, d'autres viendront. *For the good of —s*, pour l'avantage d'autrui. *The friend of all —s on whose devotion we could rely*, de tous nos amis celui sur le dévouement duquel nous pouvions surtout compter. *Every — day*, tous les deux jours, de deux jours l'un

Otherwise, adv. autrement, d'ailleurs, à d'autres égards

Otter, s. loutre, *f.*

Ottoman, s. (*pers.*) Ottoman, *m.*, (*seat*) ottomane, *f.*, divan, *m.*

Ought, vn. dois, devais, devrais. *You — to write*, vous devriez écrire. *I — to have*, j'aurais dû. *You — to have written*, vous auriez dû écrire

Ounce, s. once, *f.*

Our, pron. notre, nos. — *own*, notre, notre propre, à nous, le nôtre, la nôtre, les nôtres

Ours, pron. le nôtre, la nôtre, les nôtres, à nous. *These books are —*, ces livres sont à nous

Ourself, pron. nous-même

Ourselves, pron. plur. nous-mêmes, nous. *We — might find*, nous-mêmes nous pourrions trouver. *We think*

— *clever*, nous nous croyons habiles. *Is he one of —?* est-il des nôtres? *By —*, tout seuls

Oust, va. ôter, (*law*) évincer, déposséder; débusquer, mettre dehors

Out, adv. dehors, au dehors, sorti, absent, (*servant*) allé en course, (*secret, &c.*) public, découvert, connu, (*book*) publié, paru, (*fire*) éteint, (*ended*) épuisé, fini, (*lease*) expiré, fini, (*no longer in office*) qui n'est pas au pouvoir, sorti d'office, (*completely*) complètement, tout à fait, (*in error*) en faute, dans l'erreur, (*confused*) embarrassé, qui reste court, à quia, (*torn*) déchiré, troué, percé, (*loser*) en perte, (*exposed*) bien en vue, au dehors, (*sail*) dehors, déployé, (*troops*) sur pied, en mouvement. *To lock —*, renvoyer ses ouvriers. —, —, *I say*, hors d'ici, je vous dis. — *with him!* mettez-le dehors! à la porte! emmenez-le! — *with it*, dites-le donc, (*pop.*) achève donc, accouchez donc. *To be — with*, être brouillé avec. *My patience is —*, ma patience est à bout. — *and —*, complètement, tout à fait, à plate couture. — adj. complet, véritable, (*in bad part*) insigne, fieffé. — *at heel*, les souliers troués, (*fig.*) dans la gêne

Out of, prep. hors de, au dehors de, sorti de, loin de, dans, en, avec, parmi, sur, par, n'ayant pas de, à bout de. — *of the house*, hors de la maison. *As I was — of my time*, comme j'étais majeur, comme j'avais fini mon temps. — *of the way*, adj. bizarre, peu ordinaire. *Once — of the harbour of life*, une fois sorti du port de la vie. *To save us — of his hand*, nous sauver de sa main. — *of evil to bring forth good*, du mal faire sortir le bien. — *of sight*, — *of mind*, loin des yeux, loin du cœur. *Nine times — of ten*, neuf fois sur dix. — *of necessity*, par nécessité. — *of health, spirits, and money*, malade, triste et sans argent. — *of place*, sans emploi. *I am — of soap*, je n'ai plus de savon. — *of patience*, à bout de patience

Out! interj. dehors! hors d'ici! hélas

Out-and-Outer, s. qui n'a pas son pareil

Outact, va. surpasser, dépasser

Outargue, va. réduire au silence

Outbabble, va. caqueter plus que

Outbalance, va. l'emporter sur

Outbar, va. fermer, empêcher d'entrer

Outbeg, va. demander *or* crier plus ardemment que

Outbellow, vn. mugir *or* crier plus fort que

Outbid, va. surenchérir, enchérir sur

Outbidder, s. surenchérisseur, m.

Outbound, adj. en destination pour l'étranger

Outbrave, va. braver, défier, surpasser en bravoure *or* en effronterie, *or* en magnificence

Outbreak, s. **Outbreaking**, s. explosion, *f.*, débordement, m., déchaînement, m.

Outbuilding, s. dépendance, *f.*

Outburst, s. (*see* OUTBREAK)

Outcast, s. adj. proscrit, -e, exilé, -ée, réprouvé, -ée, abandonné, -ée

Outclearance, s. départ d'un port, m.

Outcrier, s. crieur des ventes, m.

Outcrop, s. affleurement, m.

Outcry, s. clameur, *f.*, grand cri, m., cri de détresse, m. *To raise an —*, pousser des clameurs, jeter les hauts cris

Outdo, va. surpasser, dépasser, l'emporter sur, enchérir sur. *To — Tiberius in cruelty*, enchérir sur la cruauté de Tibère, surpasser Tibère en cruauté

Outdoor, adj. du dehors, au grand air. — *work*, les travaux extérieurs

Outer, adj. extérieur, externe. *The — door*, la porte de la rue

Outermost, adj. extérieur, à l'extrême limite, le plus à l'extrémité

Outface, va. braver, affronter, faire baisser les yeux à, déconcerter, regarder fixement

Outfall, s. chute d'eau, *f.*, (*engin.*) embouchure, *f.*, (*quarrel*) brouille, *f.*

Outfit, s. (*of ships*) armement, m., (*persons*) équipement, m., trousseau, m., (*expenses*) frais de départ, m.

Outfitter, s. fournisseur d'objets d'équipement, d'un trousseau, m.

Outflank, va. déborder, tourner

Outflow, vn. s'écouler

Outflow, s. sortie, *f.*, émigration, *f.*

Out-gate, s. porte de sortie, *f.*

Outgeneral, va. surpasser en talent militaire, (*fig.*) l'emporter sur

Outgo, va. dépasser, surpasser, circonvenir

Outgoer, s. sortant, m.

Outgoing, s. sortie, *f.*, (*money*) avance de fonds, *f.*, (*limits*) frontière, *f.*, limite, *f.*

Outgrow, va. croître plus que *or* plus vite que, surpasser en croissance, devenir trop grand pour, se défaire avec l'âge de. *The nation had outgrown its institutions*, ses institutions n'allaient plus à la nation qui avait grandi

Outhouse, s. dépendance, *f.*, grange, *f.*, remise, *f.*, écurie, *f.*

Outlandish, adj. étranger, d'un autre pays, (*strange*) bizarre, étrange

Outlast, va. survivre, durer plus longtemps que

Outlaw, s. proscrit, m., brigand, m., voleur, m.

Outlaw, va. mettre hors la loi, proscrire, bannir

Outlawing, **Outlawry**, s. mise hors la loi, *f.*, proscription, *f.*

Outlay, va. exposer, étendre, (*spend*) débourser, dépenser

Outlay, s. frais, *m.pl.*, déboursés, *m.pl.*, somme dépensée, *f.*, somme à dépenser, *f.*, prix, m.

Outlet, s. issue, *f.*, sortie, *f.*, voie d'écoulement, *f.*, porte de dégagement, *f.*, (*fig.*) débouché, m.

Outlier, s. (*pers.*) non résident, (*geol.*) morceau détaché, m.

Outline, s. contour, m., esquisse, *f.*, ébauche, *f.*, (*fig.*) aperçu, m.

Outline, adj. fait au trait, (*map*) muette

Outlive, va. survivre à, vivre plus longtemps que

Outliver, s. survivant, m., -e, *f.*

Outlook, va. faire baisser les yeux à, intimider

Outlying, adj. frontière, sur les limites *or* frontières

Outmarch, va. devancer

Outnumber, va. surpasser en nombre, être plus nombreux que

Outpace, va. dépasser, devancer

Outpatient, s. malade du dehors, m.

Outporch, s. portique extérieur, m.

Outport, s. petit port, m.

Outpost, s. poste avancé, m.

Outpour, va. épancher, verser à flots

Outpouring, s. effusion, *f.*, épanchement, m.

Outrage, s. outrage, m., (*law*) atteinte, *f.*

Outrage, va. outrager, faire un outrage à, (*persons*) insulter, (*things*) insulter à, maltraiter

Outrageous, adj. violent, furieux, dépassant toutes les bornes, (*noisy*) tumultueux, turbulent, (*insulting*) outrageux, outrageant, outré, exagéré

Outrageously, adv. violemment, avec fureur, avec tumulte, d'une manière outrageante, avec exagération, d'une manière outrée, énormément

Outrageousness, s. violence, *f.*, fureur, *f.*, turbulence, *f.*, tumulte, m., nature outrageante, *f.*, énormité, *f.*

Outreach, va. dépasser, circonvenir, tromper, jouer

Outreason, va. l'emporter par ses arguments, dissuader

Outreckon, va. surpasser dans ses calculs

Outrider, s. piqueur, m., (*law*) porteur de contraintes, m. — *behind*, s. chasseur, m.

Outright, adv. sur-le-champ, tout de suite, complètement, entièrement, net, franchement, en termes clairs et nets, sans ménagement

Outrival, va. l'emporter sur

Outrun, va. courir plus vite que, dépasser à la course, (*fig.*) dépasser, excéder

Outsell, va. vendre *or* se vendre plus cher que, (*to surpass*) surpasser

Outsentry, s. sentinelle avancée, *f.*

Outset, s. début, m., commencement, m., principe, m.

Outshine, va. briller plus que, surpasser en éclat, surpasser, éclipser

Outside, s. extérieur, m., dehors, m., (*coach*) impériale, *f.*, banquette, *f.* —*s of bacon*, couennes de lard, *f.pl.*

Outside, adj. adv. extérieur, en dehors, au dehors, sur l'impériale, sur la banquette. *Inside and —*, à l'intérieur et sur l'impériale

Outsider, s. qui ne fait pas partie d'une association, d'un parti, etc., (*horses*) cheval qui n'est pas classé. *He is only an —*, il n'est pas du métier

Outskirt, s. (*town*) faubourg, m., (*wood*) lisière, *f.*, limite, *f.*, bord, m., extrémité, *f.*

Outsleep, va. dormir au delà de

Outspoken, adj. franc, clair, explicite

Outstand, va. résister à, dépasser, rester au delà de

Outstanding, adj. dû, non payé, en souffrance, non rentré, à percevoir, en suspens, en saillie

Outstare, va. faire baisser les yeux à, déconcerter

Outstep, va. dépasser

Outstretch, va. étendre, déployer

Outstrip, va. gagner de vitesse, dépasser

Outswear, va. jurer plus fort que

Outtalk, va. parler plus que, réduire au silence

Outvie, va. surpasser, l'emporter sur

Outvote, va. l'emporter sur

Outwalk, va. marcher plus vite *or* plus longtemps que, devancer

Outwall, s. mur extérieur, m., (*fig.*) dehors, m., apparence extérieure, *f.*, extérieur, m.

Outward, adj. extérieur, du dehors

Outward, s. extérieur, m.

Outward, **Outwards**, adv. vers le dehors, au dehors, à l'extérieur, (*nav.*) pour l'étranger. — *-bound*, en partance pour *or* à destination de *or* en route pour les pays d'outre-mer

Outwardly, adv. extérieurement, à l'extérieur, au dehors

Outweigh, va. peser plus que, l'emporter sur, surpasser

Outwit, va. duper, surpasser en finesse

Outwork, s. ouvrage extérieur, *m.*

Oval, adj. ovale

Oval, s. ovale, *m.*

Ovary, s. ovaire, *m.*

Ovation, s. ovation, *f.*

Oven, s. four, *m.* *Dutch* —, rôtissoire, *f.*, cuisinière, *f.*

Over, prep. (*on*) sur, par-dessus, au-dessus de, sur, (*on the other side*) de l'autre côté, au delà de, d'un côté à l'autre, de l'autre, (*through*) par, dans, (*more*) plus de, (*during*) pendant, durant. *To reign* —, régner sur. *To be — head and ears in love with*, être éperdument amoureux de. *From — the seas*, de par delà les mers. — *hill and — dale*, par monts et par vaux. *To sit up — night*, veiller tard *or* bien avant dans la nuit

Over, adv. par-dessus, par-dessus les bords, au-dessus, de l'un à l'autre, de large, en diamètre, (*surplus*) de plus, de reste, de l'autre côté, (*bookkeeping, &c.*) à reporter, (*throughout, &c.*) partout, sur la surface, d'un bout à l'autre, complètement, (*entirely*) excessivement, trop, par trop. *To run* —, déborder. — *and above*, de plus, en outre, en sus, par-dessus le marché. — *and* —, à plusieurs reprises, plusieurs fois, à différentes fois. — *again*, encore une fois. — *against*, vis-à-vis de. *All the world* —, dans le monde entier. *To feel a pain all* —, souffrir de partout. *All — dust*, couvert de poussière. *To argue* —, passer en revue dans sa discussion. *To read* —, lire

Over, adj. fini, passé, fait, supérieur. *It is all — with him*, c'en est fait de lui, tout est fini pour lui

Overact, va.n. exagérer, charger

Overall, s. pardessus, *m.*, (*smock-frock*) blouse, *f.* —*s*, pl. pantalon de voyage, *m.*

Over-anxiety, s. trop d'anxiété, *m.*

Over-anxious, adj. trop inquiet

Overawe, va. imposer à, imposer le respect à, intimider

Overbalance, va. l'emporter sur

Overbalance, s. excédant, *m.*, surplus, *m.*, (*fig.*) prépondérance, *f.*

Overbear, subjuguer, soumettre, dompter, (*to crush*) accabler, écraser, déborder sur

Overbearing, adj. accablant, écrasant, impérieux, arrogant, dominateur

Overbid, va. enchérir sur, offrir trop pour

Overboard, adv. par-dessus le bord, à la mer. *A man* — *!* un homme à la mer !

Overburden, va. surcharger

Overcast, va. obscurcir, couvrir, (*prices*) estimer trop haut, (*needle*) faire un surjet à. *To be* or *become* —, se couvrir de nuages

Overcasting, s. surjet, *m.*

Over-cautious, adj. par trop prudent

Overcharge, va. surcharger, (*prices*) demander trop cher, faire payer trop cher, rançonner

Overcharge, s. charge excessive, *f.*, prix excessif, *m.*, (*taxes*) surtaxe, *f.*

Overcloud, va. couvrir de nuages, assombrir, obscurcir

Overcoat, s. pardessus, *m.*

Overcold, adj. trop froid, glacé

Overcold, s. froid excessif, *m.*

Overcolour, va. surcharger de couleur, (*fig.*) représenter sous des couleurs trop vives, charger, exagérer

Overcome, va. vaincre, triompher de, soumettre, surmonter, dompter ; — vn. triompher, vaincre

Over-confidence, s. confiance excessive, *f.*, trop d'assurance, *f.*

Over-confident, adj. trop confiant, trop assuré, présomptueux, trop sûr de soi

Overcount, va. estimer trop

Overcover, va. couvrir entièrement

Over-daring, adj. trop audacieux

Overdate, va. postdater

Overdo, va. surcharger, charger, outrer, exagérer, (*cooking*) faire cuire trop. *Overdone meat*, de la viande trop cuite

Overdraw, va. (*bank*) excéder, dépasser le montant de son crédit, (*exaggerate*) exagérer, charger

Overdress, va. habiller trop, surcharger de parure

Overdrive, va. (*horse*) surmener, (*fig.*) pousser trop loin

Overdue, adj. en retard

Overdye, va. teindre d'une couleur trop foncée

Over-eager, adj. ardent, trop empressé

Over-eagerly, adv. trop ardemment

Over-earnest, adj. trop sérieux, en colère. *To be — with*, s'emporter contre

Overeat, va. manger trop

Overestimate, va. évaluer trop haut, estimer trop, présumer trop de

Over-excite, va. surexciter

Over-excitement, s. surexcitation, *f.*

Over-exquisite, adj. trop fastidieux

Over-eye, va. surveiller, observer

Overfall, s. chute d'eau, *f.*, (*nav.*) écueil, *m.*

Overfar, adv. trop loin

Overfatigue, va. fatiguer trop, excéder

Overfloat, va. inonder

Overflourish, va. orner superficiellement

Overflow, va. déborder, se déborder, couler par-dessus les bords, (*expand*) déborder, s'épancher ; — va. inonder, faire déborder, se répandre sur

Overflow, s. débordement, *m.*, inondation, *f.*, transport, *m.*, épanchement, *m.*, surabondance, *f.*, trop-plein, *m.*

Overflowing, s. débordement, *m.*, transport, *m.*, épanchement, *m.*, effusion, *f.*

Overflowing, adj. qui déborde, surabondant

Overflush, va. colorer trop, faire rougir trop, exalter trop

Over-fond, adj. qui aime trop, trop tendre, indulgent

Over-fondly, adv. avec trop de tendresse

Over-forward, adj. trop empressé, trop présomptueux, outrecuidant

Over-forwardness, s. trop grand empressement, *m.*, trop de présomption, *f.*, outrecuidance, *f.*

Over-free, adj. trop libre

Over-freely, adv. trop librement

Overfreight, va. charger trop, surcharger

Over-full, adj. trop plein

Over-glad, adj trop heureux, trop content

Overgrow, va. grandir plus que, grandir trop pour, (*cover*) couvrir, recouvrir, tapisser ; — vn. grandir *or* croître trop, se développer trop, devenir trop grand

Overgrown, adj. énorme, très gros, d'une taille démesurée

Overgrowth, s. croissance excessive, *f.*, accroissement excessif, *m.*

Overhang, va. être suspendu au-dessus de, surplomber, s'avancer au-dessus de, menacer

Over-haste, Over-hastiness, s. précipitation, *f.*

Over-hastily, adv. avec trop de précipitation

Over-hasty, adj. trop précipité, trop vif, trop emporté

Overhaul, va. (*nav.*) gagner de vitesse, examiner, étendre sur

Overhead, adv. au-dessus de la tête, en haut, en l'air

Overhear, va. entendre, surprendre

Overheat, va. chauffer trop, échauffer trop, (*techn.*) surchauffer

Overjoy, va. combler de joie, ravir, transporter

Overjoy, s. ravissement, *m.*, ivresse, *f.*

Over-kind, adj. trop bon

Over-kindness, s. excès de bonté, *m.*

Overlabour, va. harasser de travail, excéder, travailler avec trop de soin

Overlade, va. surcharger

Overland, adj. par voie de terre

Overlay, va. jeter sur, placer sur, recouvrir, (*cloud*) obscurcir, cacher, (*overwhelm*) surcharger

Overleap, va. franchir, dépasser

Overload, va. surcharger, trop charger, accabler

Overlook, va. voir *or* regarder d'en haut, planer sur, avoir vue sur, dominer, commander, (*examine*) examiner avec soin, revoir, reviser, (*tolerate*) fermer les yeux sur, tolérer, (*neglect*) négliger, laisser de côté, ne pas remarquer, ne pas prendre garde à, (*despise*) dédaigner

Overlooker, s. surveillant, *m.*, inspecteur, *m.*, (*in a workshop*) contre-maître, *m.*

Overlooking, s. surveillance, *f.*

Overmatch, va. être trop fort *or* trop forte partie pour, être supérieur à, vaincre

Overmatch, s. (*for*) trop forte partie (pour), supérieur (à)

Overmeasure, va. mesurer trop largement, estimer trop haut

Overmeasure, s. surplus, *m.*

Over-modest, adj. trop *or* par trop modeste

Over-moist, adj. trop humide

Over-moisture, s. excès d'humidité, *m.*

Overmount, va. s'élever au-dessus de

Overmuch, adv. trop, par trop, excessivement

Overmuch, s. excès, *m.*

Overmuch, adj. excessif

Overmultitude, va. surpasser en nombre

Overpass, va. traverser, (*fig.*) passer, subir, éprouver

Overpay, va. payer trop, récompenser trop largement

Overplus, s. surplus, *m.*, excédant, *m.*

Overpoise, s. contrepoids, *m.*

Overpoise, va. (*see* OVERWEIGH)

Overpower, va. être trop fort pour, vaincre, subjuguer, accabler, écraser, excéder de fatigue

Overpowering, adj. accablant, écrasant

Overpoweringly, adv. irrésistiblement

Overpraising, s. éloges excessifs, *m.pl.*

Overpress, va. presser vivement, (*with*) accabler (par), insister trop avec, vaincre par des instances

Overprize, va. tenir trop à, faire trop grand cas de, estimer trop

Overproportion, va. ne pas faire dans les proportions voulues

Over-provident, adj. trop économe

Overrate, va. estimer trop haut, exagérer

Overreach, va. dépasser, aller au delà de, (*to deceive*) duper, avoir l'avantage de. — *oneself*, se trahir soi-même

Override, va. passer sur le corps de, (*a horse*) surmener, (*to get beyond*) dépasser

Over-ripen, va. trop mûrir

Overrule, va. gouverner, diriger, contrôler, dominer, maîtriser, (*law*) rejeter

Overrun, va. parcourir, se répandre sur *or* dans, envahir, infester (de), (*print.*) chasser; — vn. déborder, regorger

Oversee, va. veiller sur, surveiller, avoir l'œil sur

Overseer, s. surveillant, m., inspecteur, m., administrateur de la taxe des pauvres, m., (*of fabrics*) contremaître, m., (*print*) prote, m.

Overset, va. renverser, bouleverser, (*a carriage*) verser, (*a boat*) faire chavirer

Overshade, Overshadow, va. ombrager, couvrir d'ombre, protéger, abriter, jeter dans l'ombre, éclipser, obscurcir

Overshoe, s. claque, f., soulier en caoutchouc, m.

Overshoot, vn. dépasser le but, porter trop loin; — va. dépasser, porter au delà de, franchir, traverser rapidement

Oversight, s. surveillance, f., inspection, f., (*mistake*) inadvertance, f., méprise, f., bévue, f., (*neglect*) négligence, f., omission, f.

Oversleep oneself, vr. s'éveiller trop tard, dormir trop longtemps, dormir au delà de l'heure fixée

Overslip, va. laisser échapper

Oversnow, va. couvrir de neige, (*fig.*) répandre ses neiges sur, blanchir

Overspent, adj. épuisé (de), accablé (par), éreinté

Overspread, va. se répandre sur, s'étendre sur, couvrir, envahir

Overstate, va. exagérer

Overstep, va. outrepasser, dépasser

Overstock, va. remplir trop, encombrer

Overstrain, vn. s'efforcer trop, s'excéder; — va. pousser trop loin, étendre trop, outrer, faire faire de trop violents efforts à

Over-strong, adj. trop fort

Over-sure, adj. trop certain, trop confiant

Overswell, va. déborder sur, s'élever au-dessus de

Overt, adj. patent, évident

Overtake, va. atteindre, attraper, rejoindre, surprendre

Overtask, va. surcharger de travail, faire trop travailler, exiger trop de

Overtax, va. surcharger d'impôts, surtaxer

Overthrow, va. renverser, bouleverser, vaincre, mettre en déroute

Overthrow, Overthrowing, s. renversement, m., (*fig.*) ruine, f., destruction, f., défaite, f.

Overtly, adv. ouvertement

Overtop, va. s'élever plus haut que, surpasser, être supérieur à

Overture, s. ouverture, f., proposition, f., offre, f.

Overturn, va. (see Overset)

Overvalue, va. estimer trop, exagérer la valeur de, avoir une trop haute opinion de

Overweening, adj. présomptueux, outrecuidant

Overweigh, va. (see Outweigh)

Overweight, s. excédant de poids, m.

Overwhelm, va. engloutir, submerger, accabler, écraser, combler

Overwhelmingly, adv. d'une manière accablante

Overwork, va. surcharger de travail, excéder de fatigue, (*a horse*) surmener

Overwork, s. travail excessif, travail en sus *or* extra

Ovine, adj. ovine

Oviparous, adj. ovipare

Owe, va. devoir

Owing, adj. dû, qu'il faut attribuer, par suite (de), à cause (de), imputable. *A hundred pounds — to him*, cent livres qui lui étaient dues. *Strength of nature in youth passeth over many excesses which are — a man till his old age*, la force de la nature dans la jeunesse permet bien des excès que l'homme ne paye que dans sa vieillesse. *Perhaps it might be — to a feeling of fear*, peut-être fallait-il l'attribuer à un sentiment de crainte. *His misery is — to his carelessness*, sa pauvreté provient de sa négligence. — *perhaps to the fatigue which*, par suite peut-être de la fatigue qui

Owl, s. hibou, m. *Barn* —, s. chouette, f. *Horned* —, s. grand duc, m.

Owlet, s. chouette, f., hulotte, f.

Own, adj. propre. *My* —, le mien, etc., mon, ma, mes. *His* —, le sien, etc., son, sa, ses. *Its* —, le sien, etc. *My — child*, mon enfant chéri. *It is not my* —, il n'est pas à moi. *My — self*, moi-même. *A house of my* —, une maison à moi. *Motives of his* —, des raisons particulières, des raisons à lui connues. *To come into one's* —, entrer en possession de sa fortune, hériter. *Hold one's* —, tenir sa place

Own, va. posséder, être propriétaire de, avoir en propre, (*to claim*) réclamer comme sien, (*to acknowledge*) reconnaître (pour), avouer, convenir (de), convenir (que), confesser

Owner, s. propriétaire, m., maître, m., maîtresse, f., possesseur, m.

Ownership, s. propriété, f., droit de propriété, m.

Ox, s. bœuf, m. — *-driver*, s. bouvier, m. — *-fly*, s. taon, m. — *-hide*, s. peau de bœuf, f. — *-lip*, s. primevère, f.

Oxalic, adj. oxalique

Oxidate, va. oxyder

Oxidation, s. oxydation, f.

Oxide, s. oxyde, m.

Oxonian, adj. étudiant de l'université d'Oxford

Oxygen, s. oxygène, m.

Oxygenated, adj. oxygéné

Oxygenation, s. oxygénation, f.

Oxygenize, va. oxygéner

Oxygenous, adj. d'oxygène

Oxygon, s. triangle oxygone, m.

Oxygonal, adj. oxygone

Oxymel, s. oxymel, m.

Oyster, s. huître, f. *Basket of —s*, cloyère *or* bourriche d'huîtres, f. *To bed —s*, parquer des huîtres. — *-bed*, s. banc d'huîtres, m. — *-patty*, s. petit pâté aux huîtres, m. — *-rooms*, s.pl. salon d'un marchand d'huîtres, m. — *-shell*, s. écaille d'huître, f. — *-wench*, s. — *-wife*, s. — *-woman*, s. écaillère, f., marchande d'huîtres, f.

Ozone, s. ozône, m.

P

P, s. P, p, m. *I must mind my —'s and Q's*, il faut me mettre sur mon bien-dire, il faut que je mette les points sur les i

Pace, pas, m., (*of a horse*) allure, f. *To hold or keep — with*, tenir pied à, suivre. *To put through his —s*, faire faire ses allures à. *To keep always one's* —, aller toujours le même train. *Quick* —, pas de charge. *To mend one's* —, hâter le pas

Pace, vn. aller au pas, marcher (lentement). *To — along* or *on*, s'avancer (lentement *or* à pas mesurés); — va. parcourir, arpenter, mesurer. *To — the room*, parcourir à grands pas la chambre

Paced, adj. au pas . . . , qui a le pas . . . , à l'allure . . . , (*trained*) dressé, exercé

Pacer, s. qui marche bien

Pacha, s. pacha, m.

Pacific, adj. pacifique, paisible

Pacification, s. pacification, f.

Pacificatory, adj. pacificateur

Pacifier, s. pacificateur, m.

Pacify, va. pacifier, apaiser

Pack, s. ballot, m., paquet, m., fardeau, m., charge, f., (*cards*) jeu, m., (*hounds*) meute, f., (*fig.*) bande, f., troupe, f., tas, m. — *-cloth*, s. — *-sheet*, s. toile d'emballage, f. — *-horse*, s. bête de somme, f., cheval de bât, m. — *-ice*, s. masse de glace flottante, f. — *-saddle*, s. bât, m. — *-thread*, s. fil d'emballage, m.

Pack, va. emballer, empaqueter, encaisser, (*fig.*) entasser, accumuler, (*meat*) embariller, (*herrings*) encaquer, (*cards*) trier subrepticement, (*a jury, &c.*) composer d'hommes à soi. *To — up one's things*, faire sa malle. — vn. emballer, faire des emballages, (*to be off*) décamper, partir. *To — up*, faire sa malle *or* ses malles. *To send —ing*, envoyer promener. *To — off* or *away*, plier bagage, partir

Package, s. colis, m., emballage, m., encaissement, m.

Packer, s. emballeur, *m.*

Packet, s. paquet, *m.*, (*nav.*) paquebot, *m.*

Packing, s. emballage, *m.*, encaissement, *m.*, garniture, *f.*, (*fig.*) collusion, *f.*, tromperie, *f.* —*-case*, s. caisse à emballage, *m.* —*-needle*, s. aiguille à emballage, *f.* —*-plate*, s. plateau de garniture, *m*

Pact, s. pacte, *m.*

Pad, s. bidet, *m.*, cheval de selle, *m.*, (*cushion*) bourrelet, *m.*, coussinet, *m.*, (*of rags*) tampon, *m.*, (*fencing*) plastron, *m.*

Pad, va. ouater, bourrer, mettre des bourrelets

Paddle, vn. jouer avec l'eau, battre l'eau, barboter, pagayer, ramer ; — va. toucher légèrement, (*nav.*) pagayer

Paddle, s. pagaye, *f.*, aviron, *m.*, (*wheels*) palette, *f.*, aube, *f.* —*-board*, s. palette, *f.*, aube, *f.* —*-box*, s. tambour de roue, *m.* —*-door*, s. vanne, *f.* —*-shaft*, s. arbre de roue, *m.* —*-wheel*, s. roue à aubes, *f.*

Paddock, s. enclos, *m.*, pâturage, *m.*, pré, *m.*

Paddy, s. riz, *m.*, (*fam.*) Patrick, *m.*, Irlandais, *m.*

Padlock, s. cadenas, *m.*

Padlock, va. cadenasser, fermer au cadenas, mettre des entraves à

Pagan, adj. s. païen, -enne

Paganism, s. paganisme, *m.*

Page, s. page, *f.*, (*boy*) page, *m.*

Page, va. paginer

Pageant, Pageantry, s. spectacle, *m.*, parade, *f.*, décoration, *f.*, pompe, *f.*, apparat, *m.*

Paging, s. pagination, *f.*

Pagoda, s. pagode, *f.*

Pail, Pailful, s. seau, *m.*

Pain, s. peine, *f.*, douleur, *f.*, souffrance, *f.*, mal, *m.*, inquiétude, *f.*, fatigue, *f.*, travail, *m.* *On — of death*, sous peine de la mort. *To give great — to*, faire beaucoup souffrir, (*fig.*) faire de la peine à

Pain, va. faire du mal à, faire souffrir, (*fig.*) affliger, faire de la peine à, attrister, tourmenter. *It —s one to see it*, cela fait peine à voir

Painful, adj. douloureux, affligeant, triste, pénible, difficile, laborieux, soigneux

Painfully, adv. douloureusement, péniblement, laborieusement, avec soin, avec peine

Painfulness, s. douleur, *f.*, nature douloureuse, *f.*, peine, *f.*, inquiétude, *f.*, fatigue, *f.*, travail, *m.*, labeur, *m.*

Pains, s. plur. peine, *f.*, fatigue, *f.*, soin, *m.*, travail, *m.* *To be at the —, at some — (to)*, se donner de la peine (pour). *To be at no — (to)*, ne pas se donner de la peine (de). *To bestow great — on*, apporter tous ses soins à. *To take —, great — with*, se donner de la peine, beaucoup de peine avec. *To require great —*, demander beaucoup de soin. —*-taker*, s. personne diligente, *f.*, travailleur, *m.*, (*pop.*) plocheur, *m.* —*-taking*, adj. diligent, appliqué, laborieux. —*-taking*, s. peine, *f.*, diligence, *f.*

Paint, va.n. peindre, (*the face*) farder, se farder, (*to describe*) peindre, dépeindre

Paint, s. couleur, *f.*, (*for the face*) fard, *m.*, rouge, *m.* —*-brush*, s. pinceau, *m.*

Painter, s. peintre, *m.*

Painting, s. peinture, *f.*, tableau, *m.*, (*fig.*) peinture, *f.*, description, *f.*

Pair, s. paire, *f.*, deux, *f.*, couple, *m.*, deux chevaux, *m.pl.*, (*stairs*) étage, *m.* *A chaise and —*, une chaise de poste avec deux chevaux. *Up three — of stairs*, au troisième étage

Pair, vn. s'accoupler, s'apparier, se marier, (*fig.*) s'assortir, s'accorder. —*ing-time*, s. saison de l'appariement, *f.* — *off*, (*parl.*) convenir avec un membre du parti opposé de s'absenter simultanément, pour maintenir la proportion des votes. — va. unir, accoupler, apparier, assortir. —*ing-off*, s. absence simultanée, *f.*

Palace, s. palais, *m.*

Paladin, s. paladin, *m.*

Palanquin, s. palanquin, *m.*

Palatable, adj. agréable au goût, (*fig.*) du goût de

Palatableness, s. goût agréable, *m.*

Palate, s. palais, *m.*, (*fig.*) goût, *m.*

Palatial, adj. du palais

Palatine, adj. s. palatin

Palaver, s. flagornerie, *f.*, blague, *f.*, conférence, *f.*

Palaver, va.n. flagorner

Pale, adj. pâle, blême, (*colour*) blafard, (*ale*) blanc, (*wine*) paillet

Pale, s. pal, *m.*, palis, *m.*, palissade, *f.*, (*enclosure*) clôture, *f.*, enceinte, *f.*, (*bosom*) sein, *m.*, giron, *m.*

Pale, va. palissader, clôturer

Paleness, s. pâleur, *f.*

Palfrey, s. palefroi, *m.*

Paling, s. palissade, *f.*

Palisade, va. palissader

Palish, adj. un peu pâle, pâlot, (*colour*) blafard

Pall, s. manteau, *m.*, (*for funerals*) poêle, *m.*, drap mortuaire, *m.* —*-bearer*, s. personne qui porte un coin du poêle

Pall, vn. s'éventer, s'affadir, devenir fade *or* insipide ; — va. affadir, rendre insipide, émousser, blaser, rassasier, (*cover*) couvrir, envelopper

Palladium, s. palladium, *m.*

Pallet, s. grabat, *m.*, lit, *m.*, (*for painting*) palette, *f.*

Palliate, va. pallier

Palliation, s. palliation, *f.*

Palliative, adj. palliatif

Palliative, s. palliatif, *m.*

Pallid, adj. pâle

Palm, s. paume, *f.*, (*tree*) palmier, *m.*, palme, *f.* *Common —, date —*, dattier, *m.* *Bourbon —*, latanier, *m.* —*-branch*, s. palme *f.* —*-colour*, adj. bai. —*-leaf*, s. feuille de palmier, *f.*, palmette, *f.* —*-oil*, s. huile de palme, *f.* —*-Sunday*, le dimanche des Rameaux, Pâques fleuries. —*-tree*, s. palmier, *m.*, palme, *f.* *The —-tribe*, les palmiers, *m.* —*-wine*, s. vin de palmier, *m.* *To bear (off) the — alone*, remporter seul la palme

Palm, va. escamoter, faire passer, imposer, manier, toucher. *You may — upon us new for old*, vous pourrez nous faire passer des neufs pour des vieux

Palmated, adj. palmé

Palmer, s. pèlerin, *m.*, (*swindler*) tricheur, *m.*, grec, *m.* —*-worm*, s. chenille, *f.*

Palmistry, s. chiromancie, *f.*, (*fig.*) tour de main, *m.*, escamotage, *m.*

Palmy, adj. de palmiers, (*fig.*) beau, glorieux, victorieux

Palpable, adj. palpable, manifeste

Palpably, adj. d'une manière palpable

Palpitate, vn. palpiter

Palpitation, s. palpitation, *f.*

Palsied, adj. frappé de paralysie, paralytique

Palsy, s. paralysie, *f.*

Palter, vn. tergiverser (avec), se jouer (de)

Paltriness, s. mesquinerie, *f.*, petitesse, *f.*

Paltry, adj. chétif, mesquin, méprisable, méchant

Pamper, va. trop nourrir, engraisser, rassasier, (*indulge*) flatter, caresser

Pamphlet, s. brochure, *f.*, pamphlet, *m.*

Pamphleteer, s. auteur de brochures, *m.*, pamphlétaire, *m.*

Pan, s. (*frying*) poêle, *f.*, (*stew*) casserole, *f.*, (*earthenware*) terrine, *f.*, (*of a gun*) bassinet, *m.* *To flash in the —*, faire long feu, rater

Panacea, s. panacée, *f.*

Pancake, s. crêpe, *f.*

Pander, s. complaisant, *m.*, -e, *f.*, entremetteur, *m.*, -euse, *f.*

Pander, vn. servir de complaisant *or* de ministre complaisant, aider à

Pane, s. carreau, *m.*, vitre, *f.*

Panegyric, s. panégyrique, *m.*

Panegyric, Panegyrical, adj. de panégyrique

Panegyrist, s. panégyriste, *m.*

Panegyrize, va. faire le panégyrique de, faire des panégyriques

Panel, s. panneau, *m.*, (*law*) liste, *f.*

Panel, va. diviser par panneaux, (*law*) dresser une liste de jurés, former un jury

Pang, s. vive douleur, *f.*, souffrance, *f.*, mal cuisant, *m.*, angoisse, *f.*

Panic, s. adj. panique, *f.*, terreur panique, *f.*

Pannel, s. bât, *m.*

Pannier, s. panier, *m.*

Panoply, s. panoplie, *f.*, armure complète, *f.*, trophée d'armes, *m.*

Panorama, s. panorama, *m.*

Panoramic, adj. de panorama

Pansy, s. pensée, *f.*

Pant, vn. battre, palpiter, se soulever, haleter, (*fig.*) soupirer (pour, après), désirer. *To — for breath*, être tout haletant. *To come —ing up*, accourir tout haletant. *To sit and —*, se poser haletant. *To — to*, voler tout haletant vers

Pant, s. battement du cœur, *m.*, palpitation, *f.*, souffle haletant, *m.*

Pantaloon, s. pantalon, *m.* *My —s*, mon pantalon. *A pair of —s*, un pantalon

Pantheon, s. panthéon, *m.*

Panther, s. panthère, *f.*

Pantile, s. tuile, *f.*, tuile faîtière, *f.*, faîtière, *f.*, tuile flamande, *f.*

Panting, s. palpitation, *f.*, souffle haletant, *m.*

Pantomime, s. pantomime, (*m. pers.*, *f. play*)

Pantry, s. office, *f.*, garde-manger, *m.*

Pap, s. mamelle, *f.*, *food*) bouillie, *f.*, (*of fruit*) pulpe, *f.*

Papa, s. papa, *m.*

Papacy, s. papauté, *f.*

Papal, adj. papal, du pape

Paper, s. papier, *m.*, feuille de papier, *f.*, (*document*) pièce, *f.*, document, *m.*, (*in contempt*) paperasse, *f.*, (*newspaper*) journal, *m.*, gazette, *f.*, article, *m.*, mémoire, *m.*, (*com.*) valeurs, *f.pl.*, papier, *m.*, billets, *m.pl.*, papier-monnaie, *m.* *Brown —*, s. papier goudronné, *m.*, papier d'emballage, *m.*, papier gris, *m.* *Laid —*, papier vergé. . . . —, papier à . . . *Letter —*, papier à lettre. *To put in —*, empaqueter, (*hair*) mettre en papillotes

Paper, adj. de papier, (*fig.*) mince, léger. —*-case*, s., —*-holder*, s. serre-papier, *m.*, papeterie, *f.* —*-credit*, s. crédit sur effets, *m.*, papier-monnaie, *m.* —*-currency*, s. billets de banque, *m.pl.*, papier-monnaie, *m.* —*-cutter*, s., —*-knife*, s. couteau à papier, *m.* —*-folder*, s. plioir, *m.* —*-hanger*, s. colleur de papier, *m.* —*-hanging*, s. papier-tenture, *m.*, papierpeint, *m.* — *-kite*, s. cerf-volant, *m.* — *-maker*, s. fabricant de papier, *m.* — *-making*, s. fabrication du papier, *m.*, papeterie, *f.* — *-mill*, s. fabrique de papier, *f.*, papeterie, *f.* — *-stainer*, s. fabricant de papier peint, *m.* — *-weight*, s. serre-papiers, *m.*

Paper, va. tapisser. *Prettily —ed*, tapissé d'un joli papier

Papilionaceous, adj. papilionacé

Papist, s. papiste, *m.f.*

Pappy, adj. mou

Par, s. pair, *m.* *On a —*, de pair *or* sur un pied d'égalité avec. *To be at —, above —*, être au pair, au-dessus du pair

Parable, s. parabole, *f.*

Parable, vn. représenter par une parabole

Parabola, s. parabole, *f.*

Parabolic, adj. en paraboles, (*geom.*) parabolique

Parabolically, adv. paraboliquement

Parachute, s. parachute, *m.*

Parade, s. parade, *f.*, étalage, *m.*, (*walk*) esplanade, *f.* *On —*, à la parade

Parade, vn. faire la parade, défiler, marcher en procession; — va. faire parade de, (*milit.*) faire faire la parade de

Paradigm, s. paradigme, *m.*

Paradise, s. paradis, *m.*

Paradox, s. paradoxe, *m.*

Paradoxical, adj. paradoxal

Paradoxically, adv. d'une manière paradoxale

Paradoxicalness, s. caractère paradoxal, *m.*, nature paradoxale, *f.*

Paragon, s. modèle parfait, *m.*

Paragram, s. jeu de mots, *m.*, calembour, *m.*

Paragrammatist, s. faiseur de calembours, *m.*

Paragraph, s. paragraphe, *m.*, (*new line*) alinéa, *m.*, (*newspaper*) article, *m.*, entrefilets, *m.*

Paragraph, va. diviser en alinéas, écrire un article sur *or* contre

Paralipomena, s. paralipomènes, *m.pl.*

Parallel, adj. parallèle, (*fig.*) semblable, pareil

Parallel, s. parallèle, *f.*, ligne parallèle, *f.*, (*fig.*) comparaison, *f.*, ressemblance, *f.*

Parallel, va. mettre parallèlement *or* dans une ligne parallèle à, (*fig.*) conformer, rendre conforme, égaler, répondre à, mettre en parallèle, comparer

Parallelism, s. parallélisme, *m.*, ressemblance, *f.*

Parallelogram, s. parallélogramme, *m.*

Parallelopiped, s. parallélipipède, *m.*

Paralysis, s. paralysie, *f.*

Paralytic, Paralytical, adj. paralytique

Paralyze, va. paralyser

Paramount, adj. principal, souverain, supérieur, suprême

Paramount, s. souverain, *m.*, chef, *m.*

Paramour, s. amant, *m.*, -e, *f.*

Parapet, s. parapet, *m.* *Earthen —*, (*fortif.*) cavalier, *m.*

Paraphernalia, s. pl. paraphernaux, *m.pl.*, (*fig.*) ornements, *m.pl.*, accessoires, *m.pl.*, appareil, *m.*

Paraphrase, s. paraphrase, *f.*

Paraphrase, va.n. paraphraser

Parasite, s. parasite, (*person*) écornifleur, *m.*

Parasitic, Parasitical, adj. de parasite, (*bot.*) parasite

Parasol, s. ombrelle, *f.*

Parboil, va. faire bouillir, *or* bouillir à demi, cuire à moitié

Parcel, s. partie, *f.*, portion, *f.*, parcelle, *f.*, fragment, *m.*, (*packet*) paquet, *m.*, (*set*) tas, *m.* *—s Delivery Company*, compagnie de factage, *m.*

Parcel, va. morceler, diviser, partager, distribuer par petites portions. *To — out*, morceler, diviser

Parch, va. brûler, dessécher, rôtir, griller

Parchment, s. parchemin, *m.* — *-making*, s., — *manufactory*, s., — *-trade*, s. parcheminerie, *f.* — *-maker*, s. parcheminier, *m.*

Pardon, va. pardonner à, pardonner, faire grâce *or* remise de, gracier

Pardon, s. pardon, *m.*, (*law*) grâce, *f.* *To beg —*, demander pardon de. *I beg your —*, je vous demande pardon, (*fam.*) je vous fais excuse

Pardonable, adj. pardonnable, excusable, (*law*) graciable

Pare, va. (*nails*) se couper, se rogner, (*fruits*) peler, (*paper*) ébarber, (*fig.*) rogner

Parent, s. père, *m.*, mère, *f.* *—s*, pl. parents, *m.pl.*

Parentage, s. naissance, *f.*

Parental, adj. paternel, du père, de la mère, maternel, du père et de la mère

Parenthesis, s. parenthèse, *f.*

Parenthetical, adj. par parenthèse

Paring, s. rognures, *f.pl.*, pelure, *f.*, épluchures, *f.pl.*

Parish, s. paroisse, *f.*, commune, *f.*

Parish, adj. de la paroisse, paroissial

Parishioner, s. paroissien, *m.*

Parisian, s. adj. parisien, *m.*, -ne, *f.*

Parisyllabic, Parisyllabical, adj. parisyllabique

Parity, s. parité, *f.*

Park, s. parc, *m.* — *-keeper*, s. gardien, *m.*

Park, va. enclaver, parquer

Parlance, s. conversation, *f.*, langage, *m.*

Parley, s. pourparler, *m.* *To break —*, entamer la conversation. *To beat, to sound a —*, battre, sonner la chamade

Parley, vn. être en pourparler, discuter, parlementer

Parliament, s. parlement, *m.*, (*in France*) chambres, *f.pl.*, (*in the French Republic*) assemblée nationale, *f.*

Parliamentary, adj. du parlement, parlementaire

Parlour, s. salon, *m.*, petit salon, *m.*, (*school*) parloir, *m.* — *-boarder*, élève en chambre

Parochial, adj. paroissial, de la paroisse

Parody, s. parodie, *f.*

Parody, va. parodier

Parole, s. parole, *f.* *Upon —*, sur parole

Paronomasia, s. paronomase, *f.*

Paronymous, adj. paronyme

Paroquet, s. perruche, *f.*

Paroxysm, s. paroxysme, *m.*

Parricidal, adj. parricide

Parricide, s. parricide, *m.*

Parrot, s. perroquet, *m.* *Female —*, s. perruche, *f.* *Poll —*, s. jacquot, *m.*

Parry, va.n. éluder, parer

Parse, va. analyser

Parsimonious, adj. parcimonieux

Parsimoniously, adv. avec parcimonie

Parsimoniousness, s., **Parsimony,** s. parcimonie, *f.*

Parsing, s. analyse, *f.*

Parsley, s. persil, *m.*

Parsnip, s. panais, *m.*

Parson, s. curé, *m.*

Parsonage, s. cure, *f.*, presbytère, *m.* — *-house*, s. presbytère, *m.*

Part, s. partie, *f.*, (*body, gown, work*) endroit, *m.*, (*share*) part, *m.*, portion, *f.*, parti, *m.*, (*theat.*) rôle, *m.*, personnage, *m.*, talent, *m.*, moyens, *m.pl.*, esprit, *m.*, intelligence, *f.*, facultés, *f.pl.*, (*country*) pays, *m.*, (*nav.*) parages, *m.pl.* *—s of speech*, parties du discours. *— and parcel of*, partie intégrante de. *For my (own) —*, pour ma part, pour moi, quant à moi. *To take in good —, in ill —*, prendre en bonne part, en mauvaise part. *A man of —s*, un homme de beaucoup d'esprit. *To play* or *sing one's —*, (*mus.*) faire sa partie. — *music*, s. morceau d'ensemble, *m.*

Part, adv. en partie, partie

Part, va. partager, diviser, répartir, séparer; — vn. se quitter, se séparer (de), se dessaisir, renoncer (à), se défaire (de)

Partake, vn.a. prendre part (à), participer (à), prendre sa part (de), partager

Partaker, s. qui prend part, qui participe, qui partage, complice, *m.*

Parted, adj. séparé, divisé

Partial, adj. partial, qui aime, qui a du goût (pour), (*fam.*) flatteur, (*not general*) partiel, particulier. *To be — to*, avoir une prédilection, un faible pour

Partiality, s. partialité, *f.*, prédilection, *f.*, tendresse, *f.*, goût, *m.*

Partially, adv. avec partialité, (*by parts*) partiellement, en partie

Participant, adj. s. participant, *m.*, -e, *f.*

Participate, vn. participer (à), prendre part (à), partager

Participation, s. participation (à), *f.*, part (de), *f.*

Participle, s. participe, *m.*

Particle, s. particule, *f.*, molécule, *f.*, fragment, *m.*

Particular, adj. particulier, spécial, déterminé, individuel, pris à part, (*odd*) extraordinaire, singulier, (*careful*) exact, soigneux, (*fastidious*) difficile, exigeant, fastidieux, délicat, susceptible, pointilleux, (*story*) circonstancié, détaillé. *— hair*, chaque cheveu de la tête. *— care*, un soin particulier. *I have been — in examining*, j'ai examiné avec un soin tout particulier. *Be — not to offend him*, ayez soin de ne pas l'offenser. *I shall be — in having*, j'aurai grand soin d'avoir. *Be — in having everything ready*, veillez bien à ce que tout soit prêt. *He was very — in having his household at church*, il tenait beaucoup à voir toute sa maison présente aux offices. *To be — in one's diet or dress*, être difficile sur la nourriture, être recherché dans sa mise

Particular, s. détail, *m.*, circonstance, *f.*, point, *m.*, particularité, *f.* *—s*, pl. renseignements, *m.pl.* *For further —s apply to*, s'adresser pour de plus amples renseignements chez *or* à. *In my own —*, pour ma part, quant à moi personnellement

Particularity, s. particularité, *f.*, détail, *m.*

Particularize, va. particulariser, détailler minutieusement

Particularly, adv. particulièrement, individuellement

Parting, s. partage, *m.*, séparation, *f.*, adieux (à), *m.pl.*

Parting, adj. d'adieu, de séparation, dernier, qui finit, sur son déclin, qui part

Partisan, s. partisan, *m.*, (*weapon*) pertuisane, *f.*

Partition, s. séparation, *f.*, division, *f.*, (*of rooms*) cloison, *f.*, (*property*) partage, *m.*

Partition, va. séparer par une cloison *or* par des cloisons, partager, diviser

Partitive, adj. partitif

Partly, adv. en partie

Partner, s. qui prend part (à), qui partage, compagnon (de), *m.*, compagne (de), *f.*, (*com.*) associé, *m.*, -ée, *f.* sociétaire, *m.*, (*dance*) cavalier, *m.*, danseur, *m.*, partenaire, *m. f.*, danseuse, *f.* *Sleeping* —, see DORMANT. *Managing* —, associé gérant. *Senior* —, associé principal

Partnership, s. association, *f.*, société, *f.* *To take into* —, s'associer

Partridge, s. perdrix, *f.* *Young* —, s. perdreau, *m.* *Common* —, s. perdrix grise, *f.* *Red-legged* —, s. perdrix rouge, *f.*

Party, s. parti, *m.*, (*recreation*) partie, *f.*, (*meeting*) société, *f.*, réunion, *f.*, soirée, *f.*, du monde, (*pers.*) partie (de), partie intéressée (dans), (*law*) partie, *f.*, (*milit.*) parti, *m.*, troupe, *f.*, bande, *f.* *To embrace a* —, se jeter dans un parti. *To get up, to go on a* — *of pleasure*, faire une partie de plaisir. *A hunting* —, une partie de chasse. *To join the* —, se mettre de la partie. *To make one of the* —, être de la partie. *To have a* —, recevoir *or* inviter du monde, donner une soirée (*see* DINNER). *To be a* — *in the injury*, être pour quelque chose, être de complicité dans cet attentat. *To be no* — *to*, n'être pour rien dans. *I made him a* — *to the secret*, je lui fis part du secret. *Straggling parties*, des bandes de traînards, des troupes isolées. *A* — *of men-at-arms*, un parti d'hommes d'armes. *Fatigue parties*, hommes de corvée

Party, adj. de parti, en partie. —*-coloured*, bigarré. —*-fence*, —*-wall*, s. mur mitoyen, *m.*

Paschal, adj. pascal, de Pâques

Pasquinade, s. pasquinade, *f.*

Pass, vn. (*time*) passer, s'écouler, (*to die*) mourir, trépasser, (*to occur*) se passer, avoir lieu, arriver, (*fencing*) faire une passe *or* des passes, (*law*) passer, être transmis. *To let* —, laisser passer. *To bring to* —, amener, faire arriver, effectuer, réaliser (*see* COME). *To* — *away*, passer, disparaître, (*time*) passer, s'écouler. *To* — *backwards and forwards*, passer et repasser. *To* — *by*, passer, passer devant *or* auprès, passer par là. *To* — *in and out*, entrer et sortir. *To* — *on*, (*pers.*) passer son chemin, poursuivre son chemin, (*things*) suivre son cours, continuer. *To* — *over*, passer par-dessus, passer, finir, se dissiper. — va. passer, passer par *or* devant, faire passer, transporter, (*beyond*) dépasser, passer, surpasser, (*sentence, &c.*) prononcer, (*criticism*) faire, (*trial*) passer par, subir, (*time*) passer, employer, (*omit*) passer sous silence, négliger, omettre, (*accounts*) approuver, (*law*) tendre, (*resolution*) adopter, (*fencing*) faire une passe sur, (*to make believe*) faire accroire. *He* —*ed me, my house*, il passa devant moi, devant chez moi. *To* — *each other*, se croiser. *To* — *a river*, passer une rivière. *To* — *troops*, faire passer des troupes. *To* — *the bottle*, passer la bouteille. *To* — *a bill*, (*com.*) passer un effet. *To* — *censure on*, censurer, critiquer. —*ed midshipman*, aspirant qui a passé son examen de lieutenant. *To* — *the winter*, passer l'hiver. *To* — *a word*, passer un mot. *To* — *oneself for*, se faire passer pour. *To* — *along*, passer le long de, suivre, passer. *To* — *away*, passer. *To* — *by*, passer devant, passer à côté de, (*neglect*) ne pas faire attention à, ne pas prendre garde à, (*forgive*) pardonner à, excuser. *To* — *over*, passer par-dessus, passer sur, parcourir, (*neglect*) laisser passer, négliger, ne pas s'occuper de, ne pas faire attention à. *To* — *round*, faire circuler

Pass, s. passage, *m.*, passe, *f.*, voie, *f.*, défilé, *m.*, gorge, *f.*, (*permit*) laissez-passer, *m.*, passe, *f.*, (*nav.*) lettres de mer, *f. pl.*, (*theatre*) entrée libre, *f.*, (*milit.*) permission, *f.*, (*fencing*) passe, *f.*, botte, *f.*, (*state*) point, *m.*, état, *m.*, condition, *f.* —*-key*, s. passe-partout, *m.* —*-word*, s. mot de passe, *m.*, consigne, *f.* —*-rope*, s. va-et-vient, *m.* *To fix a* —*-rope*, établir un va-et-vient. *Are things come to this* —? les choses en sont-elles venues là? *Before coming to that* —, avant d'en venir là. *Things were carried to such a* — *that*, les choses en vinrent au point que. *To make the* —, faire sauter la coupe

Passable, adj. (*roads*) praticable, (*rivers*) navigable, (*that will do*) qui peut passer

Passably, adv. passablement

Passage, s. passage, *m.*, voie, *f.*, route, *f.*, (*archit.*) couloir, *m.*, corridor, *m.*, (*crossing by sea*) traversée, *f.*, trajet, *m.*, (*event*) événement, *m.* *Birds of* —, oiseaux de passage, oiseaux passagers. *Those of* —, ceux qui sont passagers. *In* —, en passant. *A law amended in its* — *through the House*, une loi modifiée pendant la discussion. *To force a* —, se frayer un chemin. *Air* —*s*, voies aériennes. *A rough* —, une mauvaise traversée. *Direct* —, trajet direct. *To perform the* —, faire le trajet, la traversée. —*-boat*, s. bateau de passage, *m.*, bac, *m.* —*-money*, s. (prix du) passage, *m.*

Pass-book, s. livre de comptes particuliers, *m.*

Passenger, s. voyageur, *m.*, -euse, *f.*, passager, *m.*, -ère, *f.*, (*in the street*) passant, *m.* —*-train*, s. train de voyageurs, *m.* *Cabin* —, s. voyageur de première classe, *m.*

Passer, s. passant, *m.* —*-by*, s. passant, *m.*

Passing, adj. passager, rapide, fugitif, (*surpassing*) éminent, suprême, extraordinaire, grand. —*-bell*, glas de mort *or* des trépassés, *m.*

Passing, adv. extraordinairement, bien, fort, au suprême degré, suprêmement, étonnamment

Passing, s. passage, *m.*, (*of a law*) adoption, *f.*, (*of a sentence*) prononcé, *m.* *The* — *in and out*, les entrées et les sorties. *A constant* — *and repassing of people*, des gens qui passaient et repassaient constamment

Passion, s. passion, *f.*, amour, *m.*, flamme, *f.*, (*zeal*) ardeur, *f.*, zèle, *m.*, (*anger*) colère, *f.*, courroux, *m.*, emportement, *m.* —*-flower*, s. passiflore, *f.* —*-week*, la semaine sainte. *Ode to the* —*s*, ode aux Passions. *To give way to one's* —*s*, se laisser aller à *or* écouter ses passions, se passionner. —*-tossed*, adj. agité par ses passions. *To have a* — *for glory*, avoir la passion de la gloire, se passionner pour la gloire. *Fits of* —, accès de colère, emportements, *m. pl.* *In a* —, en colère. *To fall or get or fly or put oneself into a* —, s'emporter, se mettre en colère. *To put in a* —, mettre en colère

Passionate, adj. passionné, ardent, vif, chaleureux, irascible, emporté

Passionately, adv. avec passion, passionnément, ardemment, avec colère, avec emportement

Passionateness, s. caractère passionné, *m.*, nature emportée, *f.*

Passionless, adj. sans passion, peu passionné, impassible, calme

Passive, adj. s. passif

Passively, adv. passivement, d'une manière passive

Passiveness, s. nature passive, *f.*

Pass-key, s. passe-partout, *m.*

Passover, s. Pâque, *f.*

Passport, s. passe-port, *m.*

Past, adj. passé, dernier

Past, s. passé, *m.*

Past, prep. (ö… delà de, au-dessus … (*without*) sans, (*ne*… de. *Ten minutes* … heures dix. *He* … *forty*, il doit avoi… ans. — *shame*, dé… *is, that is* — *pray*… est fait de lui, c'es… pour demander c… — *enduring*, ne p… être enduré. — *e*… *cellence*, au-dessu… périorité d'une f… *all parallel*, hors … raison. — *cure*, — … remède

Paste, adj. s. pât… de farine, *f.*, (*jew*… stras. *Genoese* … d'Italie, *f.*

Paste, va. coller, … coller, afficher

Pasteboard, … *m.*, (*statuary*) car… *m.* —*-box*, s. boîte … *f.* —*-maker*, s. … *m.*

Pasteboard … carton

Pastel, s. pastel, …

Pastern, s. patu…

Pasticcio, s. pa…

Pastil, Pastill… tille, *f.*

Pastime, s. pa… *m.*

Pastor, s. pasteu…

Pastoral, adj. p… *poems*, poésies past…

Pastoral, s. pa… poème pastoral, *m*… —*s*, les églogues de …

Pastorally, a… quement, en pâtre, … toralement

Pastorlike, Pa… adj. (*fig.*) de pasteu…

Pastry, s. pâtiss… *-cook*, s. pâtissier, … sière, *f.* —*-cook's* … s. pâtisserie, *f.*, bo… pâtisserie, *f.*

Pasturage, s. … *m.*

Pasture, s. pâtu… turage, *m.*, herbag… *take to* —, mener … *-land*, s. pâturage … *drive from* —, ram… champs

Pasture, va. fai… mener paître; — v… pâturer

Pasty, s. pâté, *m.*

Pat, adj. à point (… convient on ne pe… (à)

Pat, adv. à point, … juste, on ne peut m… *come* — *to my pu*… venir bien à propos …

Pat, s. tape, *f.*, pet… — *of butter*, mo… beurre, *m.*

Pat, va. taper, tap…

Patch, s. pièce… ceau, *m.*, (*land*) mo… (*for the face*) m… —*-work*, pièces de … *f. pl.*, assemblage de … de morceaux, *m.*, ra… *m.*, (*fig.*) mosaïque, …

Patch, va. mettre une pièce *or* des pièces à, rapiécer, rapiéceter, raccommoder, réparer, plâtrer, mettre une mouche *or* des mouches à, (*fig.*) bâcler. *A —ed-up peace*, une paix fourrée

Pate, s. tête, *f.*, (*pop.*) caboche, *f.*, boule, *f.*

Pated, adj. à tête . . .

Paten, s. patène, *f.*

Patent, adj. patent, (*invention*) breveté

Patent, s. lettres patentes, *f.pl.*, lettres, *f.pl.*, privilége, *m.*, brevet, *m.*, brevet d'invention, *m.* *To grant a — to*, breveter. *To take out a — for*, faire breveter, obtenir un brevet pour. *— -leather*, s. cuir verni, *m.* *— -office*, s. bureau des brevets, *m.*

Patent, va. accorder des lettres patentes à, concéder un privilége à, breveter

Patentee, s. breveté, *m.*, -ée, *f.*

Paternal, adj. paternel

Paternally, adv. paternellement

Paternity, s. paternité, *f.*

Path, s. sentier, *m.*, chemin, *m.*, route, *f.*, voie, *f.* *In my —*, sur mon chemin. *Attendant —*, banquette, *f.* *The —s of glory*, les sentiers de la gloire. *The — to repentance*, le chemin du repentir

Pathetic, adj. pathétique

Pathetically, adv. pathétiquement, d'une manière pathétique

Pathless, adj. sans chemin frayé, sans sentier

Pathologic, adj. pathologique

Pathology, s. pathologie, *f.*

Pathos, s. pathétique, *m.*

Pathway, s. sentier, *m.*, chemin, *m.*

Patience, s. patience, *f.* *— brings all things about*, tout vient à point à qui sait attendre. *To bear with —*, prendre en patience, supporter avec patience. *To take —, to have —*, avoir de la patience, prendre patience, patienter, se donner patience. *To put a person quite out of —, (by, with, par)* impatienter, faire perdre la patience à, pousser la patience de quelqu'un à bout

Patient, adj. patient, qui supporte patiemment. *Be —*, soyez patient, ayez de la patience. *Be — in suffering*, souffrez patiemment

Patient, s. malade, *m.f.*, patient, *m.*

Patiently, adv. patiemment, avec patience

Patly, adv. bien, à propos, à point

Patriarch, s. patriarche, *m.*

Patriarchal, adj. patriarcal

Patriarchate, s. patriarcat, *m.*

Patrician, adj. s. patricien, *m.*, patricienne, *f.*

Patrimonial, adj. patrimonial

Patrimonially, adv. en patrimoine

Patrimony, s. patrimoine, *m.*

Patriot, s. patriote, *m.*

Patriotic, adj. patriotique, patriote, de patriote

Patriotically, adv. patriotiquement, en patriote

Patriotism, s. patriotisme, *m.*

Patrol, vn. faire la patrouille, faire patrouille

Patrol, s. patrouille, *f.*

Patron, s. patron, *m.* *— saint's day*, fête patronale, *f.*

Patronage, s. patronage, *m.*

Patronage, va. protéger

Patroness, s. patronne, *f.*, (*fig.*) protectrice, *f.*

Patronize, va. (*persons*) protéger, appuyer, (*things*) seconder, favoriser

Patronizing, adj. de protecteur, (*air*) de protection

Patronymic, adj. patronymique

Patten, s. socque à l'anglaise, *m.*

Patter, vn. frapper, tomber. *The —ing rain*, la pluie qui tombe avec bruit, le bruit de la pluie qui tombe

Patter, Pattering, s. petit bruit, *m.*, (*talk*) caquet, *m.*

Pattern, s. modèle, *m.*, échantillon, *m.*, (*design*) dessin, *m.*, patron, *m.* *— -card*, s., *— -book*, s. carte d'échantillons, *f.*, livre d'échantillons, *m.* *— -drawer*, s. dessinateur, *m.*

Patty, s. petit pâté, *m.*

Paucity, s. petit nombre, *m.*, petite quantité, *f.*

Paunch, s. panse, *f.*, bedaine, *f.*, ventre, *m.*

Pauper, s. pauvre, *m.*, pauvresse, *f.*

Pauperism, s. paupérisme, *m.*

Pauperize, va. réduire à la pauvreté

Pause, s. pause, *f.*, suspension, *f.*, temps d'arrêt, *m.*, intervalle, *m.*, (*mus.*) point d'orgue, *m.*

Pause, va. faire une pause, s'arrêter, attendre, réfléchir

Pave, va. paver. *To — the way for*, frayer un chemin à *or* le chemin de

Pavement, s. les pavés, *m.pl.*, pavé, *m.*, pavage, *m.*, dallage, *m.*, (*path*) trottoir, *m.*

Pavier, s. paveur, *m.*

Pavilion, s. tente, *f.*, pavillon, *m.*

Paving, s. pavage, *m.*, les pavés, *m.pl.*

Paw, s. patte, *f.*

Paw, va. frapper du pied, piétiner, (*scratch*) donner des coups de griffe à, (*ill-use*) malmener, (*caress*) caresser, faire patte de velours à. *To — the ground*, piétiner

Pawing, s. piétinement, *m.*

Pawn, s. gage, *m.*, nantissement, *m.*, (*chess*) pion, *m.* *To put in —*, engager. *To take out of —*, dégager. *— -broker*, s. prêteur sur gages, *m.*, commissionnaire du mont-de-piété, *m.*

Pawn, va. engager, mettre en gage

Pawner, s. qui met en gage, emprunteur, *m.*, -euse, *f.*

Pawning, s. engagement, *m.*

Pay, va. payer, acquitter, s'acquitter, (*troops*) solder, (*court, &c.*) faire, (*visit*) rendre, faire, (*homage*) avoir, témoigner, (*attention*) faire, (*to beat*) donner son compte à. *— yourself*, payez-vous. *To get paid*, se faire payer. *I promise to —*, je payerai. *— this first . . .*, il vous plaira payer cette première . . . *To put paid on*, mettre son acquit sur. *I will make him — dearly for it*, je le lui ferai payer cher. *To — a person for his trouble*, payer quelqu'un de sa peine. *To — back*, rendre, restituer. *To — down*, compter, payer. *To — for (with, de)*, payer. *To — in*, verser. *To — into*, verser à *or* chez. *To — off*, payer, solder, acquitter, (*dismiss*) congédier, (*nav.*) désarmer. *To — on*, continuer de payer. *To — out (cable)*, filer. *— vn (benefit)* payer, rapporter. *To — off, (nav.)* faire une abatée. *It —s well*, cela rapporte assez, on y gagne bien, c'est une bonne affaire. *It does not —*, on n'y gagne pas, c'est une mauvaise affaire

Pay, s. paye, paie, *f.*, solde, *f.*, gages, *m.pl.* *Extra —*, une haute paye. *Fatigue —*, supplément de solde. *On half —*, à demi-solde. *In my —*, à ma solde. *— -bill*, s., *— -list*, s., *— -roll*, s. état de solde, *m.*, (*financ.*) feuille d'émargement, *f.* *— -day*, s. jour de paye, *m.* *— -master*, s. payeur, *m.*, trésorier, *m.* *— -master-general*, s. payeur général, *m.* *— -office*, s. caisse, *f.*

Payable, adj. payable, dont on peut s'acquitter. *To make a bill — to*, faire *or* passer un effet à l'ordre de

Payment, s. payement, *m.*, (*financ.*) versement, *m.* *To make a heavy —*, faire un fort payement. *To defer the —*, différer le payement, atermoyer. *To obtain —*, se faire payer. *To stop —*, cesser ses payements

Pea, s. pois, *m.* *Green —s*, pois verts, petits pois. *Split —s*, pois cassés. *Sweet —s*, pois de senteur. *Stick —s*, pois ramés. *— -jacket*, s. veste de pilote, *f.* *— -shooter*, sarbacane, *f.* *— -soup*, s. purée aux pois, *m.*

Peace, s. paix, *f.* *To hold one's —*, se taire, garder le silence. *To keep the —*, garder la paix, ne pas troubler l'ordre public, veiller à l'ordre public. *— -offering*, s. offrande de paix, *f.* *— -officer*, s. officier de paix, *m.*, officier de police, *m.*

Peaceable, Peaceful, adj. paisible, tranquille, pacifique, calme

Peaceableness, Peacefulness, s. caractère paisible, *m.*, nature paisible, *f.*, tranquillité, *f.*

Peaceably, Peacefully, adv. paisiblement, en paix, tranquillement

Peach, s. pêche, *f.* *— -blossom*, s. fleur de pêcher, *f.* *— -stone*, s. noyau de pêche, *m.* *— -tree*, s. pêcher, *m.*

Peachick, s. petit paon, *m.*

Peacock, s. paon, *m.* *—'s train or tail*, s. queue de paon, *f.*

Peahen, s. paonne, *f.*

Peak, s. pic, *m.*, cime, *f.*, sommet, *m.*, pointe, *f.*

Peal, s. bruit *m.*, (*bells*) carillon, *m.*, volée, *f.*, son, *m.*, coup, *m.*, bruit, *m.*, (*thunder*) éclat, *m.*, (*cannon*) bruit, *m.*, grondement, *m.*, coups, *m.*, (*artillery*) salve, *f.*, (*organ*) son retentissant, *m.*, (*laughter*) éclat, *m.*

Peal, vn. retentir, gronder; — va. assourdir, étourdir, frapper, faire retentir

Pear, s. poire, *f.* *— -tree*, s. poirier, *m.* *Prickly — -tree*, s. raquette, *f.*

Pearl, s. perle, *f.* *— -ash*, s. perlasse, *f.*

Pearled, adj. de perles

Pearly, adj. de perle, semblable à des perles

Peasant, s. adj. paysan, *m.*, -ne, *f.*, campagnard, *m.*, -e, *f.*

Peasantry, s. les paysans, *m.pl.*, gens de campagne, *m.*

Peat, s. tourbe, *f.* *— -bog*, s. tourbière, *f.*, tourbe, *f.* *— -moss*, s. tourbe, *f.*, dépôt tourbeux, *m.* *— -pit*, s. tourbière, *f.*

Pebble, s. caillou, *m.* *— -work*, s. cailloutage, *m.*

Pebbled, Pebbly, adj. caillouteux, rempli de cailloux

Peccadillo, s. peccadille, *f.*

Peck, s. peck, *m.*, (*of oats*) picotin, *m.*, (*blow*) coup de bec, *m.*

Peck, va. becqueter, donner des coups de bec à. *To — up*, ramasser

Pecker, s. pivert, *m.*

Peckish, adj. en appétit

Pectoral, adj. pectoral

Peculate, vn. se rendre coupable de péculat *or* de concussion

Peculation, s. péculat, *m.*, concussion, *f.*

Peculator, s. concussionnaire, *m.*

Peculiar, adj. particulier, propre, singulier, remarquable

Peculiarity, s. qualité

or propriété particulière, *f.*, manie, *f.*
Peculiarly, adv. particulièrement
Pecuniary, adj. pécuniaire
Pedagogue, s. pédagogue, *m.*
Pedal, s. pédale, *f.*
Pedant, s. pédant, *m.*, -e, *f.*
Pedantic, adj. pédant, pédantesque
Pedantically, adv. d'une manière pédantesque, pédantesquement
Pedantry, s. pédantisme, *m.*
Peddle, va. colporter; — vn. niaiser
Peddling, adj. futile
Pedestal, s. piédestal, *m.*
Pedestrian, s. piéton, *m.*, coureur, *m.*
Pedestrian, adj. pédestre, à pied
Pedestrianism, s. course à pied, *f.*
Pedigree, s. généalogie, *f.*, arbre généalogique, *m.*
Pediment, s. fronton, *m.*, tympan, *m.*
Pedlar, s. colporteur, *m.* —*'s trade*, s., *pedlary*, s. colportage, *m.*
Peel (off), va. peler, dépouiller, écorcher, (*flax*) teiller, (*barley*) monder; — vn. se peler
Peel, s. pelure, *f.*, écorce, *f.*, (*tower*) fort, *m.*, tour, *f.* —*-house*, s. tour ronde, *f.*
Peeled, adj. pelé, nu
Peeling, s. pelure, *f.*, peau, *f.*
Peep, vn. regarder, (*day*) poindre, (*flowers*) percer, surgir
Peep, s. regard. *m.*, coup d'œil, *m.*, vue rapide, *f.*, action d'entrevoir, *f.*, (*of day*) pointe, *f.* —*-hole*, s., *peeping-hole*, s. cachette, *f.*, trou, *m.*
Peeper, s. curieux, *m.*, jeune oiseau *or* poussin qui crie, *m.*
Peer, s. pair, *m.*, pareil, *m.*, -le, *f.*, égal, *m.*, -e, *f.*, compagnon, *m.*, compagne, *f.*
Peer, vn. paraître, (*day*) poindre, regarder curieusement
Peerage, s. pairie, *f.*, (*book*) armorial, *m.*
Peeress, s. pairesse, *f.*, femme de pair, *f.*
Peerless, adj. incomparable, sans égal, sans pareil
Peerlessly, adv. sans pareil, sans égal, incomparablement
Peerlessness, s. supériorité incomparable, *f.*
Peevish, adj. revêche, chagrin, acariâtre, hargneux, bourru, maussade
Peevishly, adv. d'une manière hargneuse *or* bourrue
Peevishness, s. humeur chagrine *or* hargneuse, *f.*, maussaderie, *f.*, caractère grognon, *m.*
Peg, s. cheville, *f.*, (*of a cask*) fausset, *m.*, (*for hanging*) patère, *f.*, portemanteau, *m.*, champignon, *m.*, (*mus.*) cheville, *f.*, (*degree*) cran, *m.*, point, *m.*, degré, *m.* *To take down a* —, abaisser d'un cran, rabattre le caquet à *To come down a* —, baisser d'un cran —*-top*, s. toupie, *f.*
Pelf, s. richesses, *f.pl.*, argent, *m.*
Pelican, s. pélican, *m.*
Pelisse, s. pelisse, *f.*
Pellet, s. boulette, *f.*, pelote, *f.*
Pellicle, s. pellicule, *f.*
Pell-mell, adv. pêle-mêle
Pellucid, adj. transparent, limpide, (*phys.*) pellucide, (*fig.*) clair, lucide
Pellucidity, Pellucidness, s. transparence, *f.*
Pelt, s. peau, *f.*, coup, *m.*, bouclier, *m.* —*-monger*, s. peaussier, *m.* —*-rot*, s. pourriture, *f.*
Pelt, va. assaillir, frapper, battre (à coups de . .), lancer, jeter
Pelting, adj. violent, remuant
Peltry, s. pelleterie, *f*
Pen, s. plume, *f.*, (*for cattle*) parc, *m.*, (*coop*) poulailler, *m.* *Music* —, s. griffe, *f.* *Steel* —, s. plume de fer, *f.* *Feather of a* —, s. barbe de plume, *f.* —*-case*, s. étui à plumes, *m.* —*-holder*, s. porte-plume, *m.* —*-rack*, s. porte-plumes *m.* —*-wiper*, s. essuie-plume, *m.*
Pen, va. écrire, parquer, enfermer. *To* — *up*, parquer
Penal, adj. pénal
Penalty, s. peine, *f.*, amende, *f.*, châtiment, *m.*
Penance, s. pénitence *f.*
Pencil, s. crayon, *m.*, (*paint.*) pinceau, *m.*, (*opt.*) faisceau, *m.* *In* —, au crayon. —*-case*, s. porte-crayon, *m.* —*-pointer*, s. taille-crayon, *m.*
Pencil, va. marquer, dessiner *or* écrire, crayonner, peindre
Pendant, s. pendant d'oreille, *m.*, pendeloque, *f.*, ornement, *m.*, (*nav.*) flamme, *f.*, guidon, *m.*, cornette, *f.*, banderole, *f.*
Pendent, adj. suspendu, pendant, qui surplombe, en saillie
Pendentive, s. pendentif, *m.*
Pending, adj. prep. pendant
Pendulum, s. pendule, *m.*, balancier, *m.* *Gridiron*—, pendule compensateur, *m.*
Penetrability, Penetrableness, s. pénétrabilité, *f.*
Penetrable, adj. pénétrable
Penetrate, va. pénétrer
Penetration, s. pénétration, *f.*
Penguin, s. pingouin, *m.*, manchot, *m*
Peninsula, s. péninsule, *f.*, presqu'île, *f.*
Peninsular, adj. péninsulaire
Penitence, s. pénitence, *f.*, repentir, *m.*
Penitent, adj. s. pénitent, *m.*, -e, *f.*
Penitential, adj. de pénitence
Penitentiary, adj. pénitentiaire
Penitentiary, s. pénitencier, *m.*, maison pénitentiaire, *f.*
Penitently, adv. avec pénitence, avec repentir
Penknife, s. canif, *m.*
Penman, s. calligraphe, *m.*, écrivain, *m.*
Penmanship, s. écriture, *f.*
Pennant, s. *see* Pendant
Penniless, adj. sans le sou, pauvre, misérable
Penny, s. deux sous, *m.pl.*, décime, *m.* *Two pence*, vingt centimes. *Peter's pence*, le denier de saint Pierre. *To turn an honest* —, faire un profit légitime. —*-a-line invention*, canard, *m.*, invention de journaliste, *f.* —*-a-liner*, s. rédacteur à deux sous la ligne, *m.* *To be* —*-wise and pound-foolish*, être ménager de bouts de chandelles et dépenser sottement de fortes sommes
Pennyworth, s. valeur de deux sous, *f.*, (*bargain*) marché, *m.* *A* — *of*, pour deux sous de
Pension, s. pension, *f.*, rente, *f.*, (*officers'*), retraite, *f.* *Retiring* —, pension de retraite. *To retire on a* —, prendre sa retraite
Pension, va. pensionner. *To* — *off*, mettre à la retraite
Pensionary, adj pensionné
Pensionary, s. pensionnaire, *m.*
Pensioner, s. pensionnaire, *m.f.*, (*soldier*) invalide, *m.*
Pensioning, s. mise à la retraite avec une pension, *f.*
Pensive, adj. pensif, rêveur, triste
Pensively, adv. d'une manière pensive, d'un air pensif, tristement
Pensiveness, s. air pensif, *m.*, tristesse, *f.*
Pentateuch, s. pentateuque, *m.*
Pentecost, s. Pentecôte, *f.*
Penthouse, s. appentis, *m.*, hangar, *m.*
Penultimate, s. adj. pénultième, *f.*
Penumbra, s. pénombre, *f.*
Penurious, adj. avare, sordide, parcimonieux
Penury, s. pénurie, *f.*, ladrerie, *f.*
Peony, s. pivoine, *f.*
People, s. peuple, *m.*, nation, *f.*, (*individuals*) gens, *m.f.pl.*, personnes, *f.pl.*, du monde, *m.*, on, *m.* *So* — *say*, on le dit. *What will* — *think?* que pensera-t-on?
People, va. peupler
Pepper, s. poivre, *m.*, (*bot.*) poivrier, *m.* *Cayenne* —, poivre de Cayenne, *m.* *Black* —, poivre ordinaire, *m.* *Red* —, poivre rouge, *m.* —*-box*, s., —*-caster*, s. poivrier, *m.*, -ère, *f.* —*-corn*, s. grain de poivre, *m.* —*-plant*, s. poivrier, *m.* —*-sauce*, s. poivrade, *f.* —*-vine*, s vigne vierge, *f.*
Pepper, va. poivrer, (*fig.*) (*with shot, &c.*) cribler
Peppermint, s. menthe, *f.*, menthe poivrée, *f.* —*-lozenges*, s., —*-drops*, s. pastilles de menthe, *f.pl.*
Peppery, adj. de poivre, (*fig.*) violent, ardent
Per, prep. par
Perambulate, va. parcourir, visiter
Perambulation, s. parcours, *m.*, inspection, *f.*
Perambulator, s. qui parcourt, compteur, *m.*, odomètre, *m.*, (*carriage*) voiture d'enfants, *f.*
Perceivable, adj. perceptible, visible, apercevable
Perceivably, adv. d'une manière perceptible, sensiblement
Perceive, va.n. apercevoir, voir, s'apercevoir de
Percentage, s. tant pour cent, droit de commission, *m.*, remise, *f.*, commission, *f.*
Perceptibility, s. perceptibilité, *f.*
Perceptible, *see* Perceivable
Perceptibly, *see* Perceivably
Perception, s. perception, *f.*
Perch, s. perche, *f.*, (*for birds*) perchoir, *m.*
Perch, va.n. percher, se percher
Perchance, adv. par hasard, par aventure
Percolate, va.n. filtrer, passer
Percolation, s. filtration, *f.*
Percussion, s. percussion, *f.*, choc, *m.* —*-cap*, s. capsule, *f.* —*-gun*, s. fusil à piston, *m.*
Perdition, s. perte (totale), *f.*, ruine, *f.*, destruction, *f.*, perdition, *f.*
Peregrination, *see* Travel
Peremptorily, adv. péremptoirement, d'un ton tranchant
Peremptoriness, s. caractère péremptoire, *m.*, ton tranchant, *m.*
Peremptory, adj. péremptoire, tranchant
Perennial, adj. qui dure une année, perpétuel
Perfect, adj. parfait, accompli, consommé, (*in, dans*) passé maître
Perfect, va. rendre parfait, perfectionner, achever, accomplir, compléter. *To* — *oneself*, devenir, parfait,

(*in*) se perfectionner (dans), approfondir . . .
Perfectibility, s. perfectibilité, *f.*
Perfection, s. perfection, *f.* To —, à la perfection, dans la perfection, à ravir
Perfectly, adv. parfaitement
Perfidious, adj. perfide
Perfidiously, adv. perfidement
Perfidy, s. perfidie, *f.*
Perforate, va. percer, perforer
Perforation, s. percement, *m.*, perforation, *f.*, (*hole*) trou, *m.*
Perform, va.n. faire, accomplir, exécuter, s'acquitter de, remplir, (*play*) jouer, représenter
Performance, s. actions, *f.pl.*, faits, *m.pl.*, gestes, *m. pl.*, (*of*) accomplissement (de), *m.*, exécution, *f.*, (*play*) représentation, *f.*, jeu, *m.*, (*mus.*) exécution, *f.*, (*work*) œuvre, *f.*, ouvrage, *m.* No —, relâche
Performer, s. celui, celle qui accomplit, qui fait, qui exécute, (*theat.*) comédien, *m.*, comédienne, *f.*, acteur, *m.*, actrice, *f.*, sujet, *m.*, (*mus.*) exécutant, *m.*, artiste, *m.f.* — *on the piano*, pianiste, *m.f.*
Perfume, s. parfum, *m.*
Perfume, va. parfumer, embaumer
Perfumer, s. parfumeur, *m.*, -euse, *f.*
Perfumery, s. parfumerie, *f.*
Perfunctorily, adv. négligemment, par manière d'acquit
Perfunctoriness, s. négligence, *f.*
Perfunctory, adj. négligent, léger, fait par manière d'acquit
Perhaps, adv. peut-être
Peri, s. Péri, *f.*
Perianth, s. périanthe, *m.*
Periapt, s. amulette, *f.*, périapte, *m.*
Pericardium, s. péricarde, *m.*
Pericarp, s. péricarpe, *m.*
Perigee, s. périgée, *m.*
Perihelion, s. périhélie, *m.*
Peril, s. péril, *m.*, danger, *m.* *At your* —, à vos risques et périls, si vous l'osez
Peril, va. mettre en danger ; — vn. être en danger
Perilous, adj. périlleux
Perilously, adv. périlleusement
Period, s. période, *f.*, (*time*) période, *m.*, temps, *m.*, espace de temps, *m.*, durée, *f.*, époque, *f.*
Periodic, Periodical, adj. périodique
Periodical, s. publication périodique, *f.*, recueil périodique, *m.*, magasin, *m.*
Periodically, adv. périodiquement
Periodicity, s. périodicité, *f.*
Peripatetic, adj. s. péripatéticien
Peripateticism, s. péripatétisme, *m.*
Periphrase, s. périphrase, *f.*, circonlocution, *f.*
Periphrastic, Periphrastical, adj. de périphrase
Periphrastically, adv. par périphrase
Peripneumonia, s. péripneumonie, *f.*
Periscopic, Periscopical, adj. périscopique
Perish, vn. périr
Perishable, adj. périssable, (*goods*) sujet à s'avarier
Perishableness, s. nature périssable, *f.*
Peristyle, s. péristyle, *m.*
Periwig, s. perruque, *f.*
Periwinkle, s. (*bot.*) pervenche, *f.*, (*shellfish*) vignot, *m.*, bigorneau, *m.*
Perjure, va. *To — oneself*, se parjurer
Perjury, s. parjure, *m.*, faux témoignage, *m.*
Permanence, Permanency, s. permanence, *f.*
Permanent, adj. permanent, en permanence
Permanently, adv. d'une manière permanente
Permeability, s. perméabilité, *f.*
Permeable, adj. perméable
Permeate, va. pénétrer
Permissible, adj. qu'on peut permettre, permis, permissible
Permission, s. permission, *f.*
Permissive, adj. qui permet *or* autorise, permis, toléré
Permissively, adv. avec permission, par tolérance
Permit, va. permettre
Permit, s. permis, *m.*, passe, *f.*, pas-avant, *m.*, congé, *m.*, acquit-à-caution, *m.*
Permutation, s. permutation, *f.*
Pernicious, adj. pernicieux
Perniciously, adv. pernicieusement
Perniciousness, s. nature pernicieuse, *f.*
Peroration, s. péroraison, *f.*
Peroxide, s. peroxyde, *m.*
Perpend, va. peser, considérer
Perpendicular, adj. perpendiculaire
Perpendicular, s. perpendiculaire, *f.*, ligne perpendiculaire, *f.*
Perpendicularity, s. perpendicularité, *f.*
Perpendicularly, adv. perpendiculairement
Perpetrate, va. commettre, exécuter
Perpetration, s. action de commettre, *f.*, exécution, *f.*
Perpetrator, s. auteur, *m.*, coupable, *m.*
Perpetual, adj. perpétuel, continuel, sans fin, constant, incessant
Perpetually, adv. perpétuellement
Perpetuate, va. perpétuer
Perpetuation, s. perpétuation, *f.*
Perpetuity, s. perpétuité, *f.*
Perplex, va. embrouiller, embarrasser, mettre *or* jeter dans la perplexité
Perplexing, adj. embarrassant, perplexe
Perplexity, s. confusion, *f.*, embrouillement, *m.*, perplexité, *f.*, embarras, *m.*
Perquisite, s. gratification, *f.*, casuel, *m.*, éventuel, *m.*, revenants-bons, *m.pl.*, pourboire, *m.*
Perquisition, s. perquisition, *f.*
Perry, s. poiré, *m.*
Persecute, va. persécuter, poursuivre, harceler
Persecution, s. persécution, *f.*
Persecutor, s. persécuteur, *m.*, -trice, *f.*
Perseverance, s. persévérance, *f.*
Persevere, vn. persévérer, s'opiniâtrer
Persevering, adj. persévérant, opiniâtre
Perseveringly, adv. avec persévérance, opiniâtrément
Persist, vn. persister, persévérer, s'opiniâtrer, rester, demeurer
Persistence, Persistency, s. persistance, *f.*, obstination, *f.*
Persistent, adj. persistant
Persistingly, adv. avec persistance
Person, s. personne, *f.*, individu, *m.* —*s*, pl. personnes, *f.pl.*, gens, *m.f.pl.*
Personage, s. personnage, *m.*
Personal, adj. personnel
Personality, s. personnalité, *f.*
Personally, adv. personnellement, en personne
Personalty, s. biens personnels, *m.pl.*
Personate, va. jouer le rôle de, jouer le personnage de, passer pour
Personation, s. action de passer pour *or* de représenter
Personification, s. personnification, *f.*
Personify, va. personnifier
Perspective, s. perspective, *f.*, vue, *f.*
Perspective, adj. perspectif, en *or* de perspective, d'optique
Perspicacious, adj. à la vue perçante, pénétrant, perspicace
Perspicaciousness,
Perspicacity, s. perspicacité, *f.*, pénétration, *f.*
Perspicuity, s. clarté, *f.*, netteté, *f.*
Perspicuous, adj. clair, net
Perspicuously, adv. avec clarté, avec netteté
Perspiration, s. transpiration, *f.*, sueur, *f.*
Perspire, vn. transpirer; — va. évacuer par les pores
Persuade, va. persuader, convaincre, faire croire, décider (à), déterminer (à)
Persuasion, s. persuasion, *f.*, croyance, *f.*, opinion, *f.*, (*religious*) communion, *f.*, secte, *f.*
Persuasive, adj. persuasif
Persuasively, adv. d'une manière persuasive
Persuasiveness, s. force persuasive, *f.*, persuasion, *f.*
Pert, adj. éveillé, inconvenant, impertinent, malappris
Pertain, vn. appartenir, être, se rapporter
Pertinacious, adj. obstiné, opiniâtre, persévérant
Pertinaciously, adv. opiniâtrément, obstinément
Pertinacity, s. opiniâtreté, *f.*, entêtement, *m.*, constance, *f.*
Pertinency, s. à-propos, *m.*, justesse, *f.*, convenance, *f.*
Pertinent, adj. pertinent, juste, à propos, approprié, qui convient
Pertinently, adv. pertinemment, à propos, avec justesse
Pertly, adv. avec vivacité, avec pétulance, d'une manière inconvenante, d'un ton leste
Pertness, s. vivacité, *f.*, pétulance, *f.*, insolence, *f.*, impertinence, *f.*, ton leste, *m.*
Perturbation, s. agitation, *f.*, trouble, *m.*, bouleversement, *m.*, perturbation, *f.*
Peruke, *see* PERIWIG
Perusal, s. lecture, *f.*, examen, *m.*
Peruse, va. lire attentivement, examiner, étudier
Peruser, s. lecteur, *m.*, lectrice, *f.*, observateur, *m.*, observatrice, *f.*
Pervade, va. passer à travers, pénétrer dans, se répandre dans *or* sur, régner dans, (*to seize*) s'emparer de
Perverse, adj. perverti, pervers, méchant, contrariant
Perversely, adv. d'une manière perverse, méchamment
Perverseness, Perversity, s. perversité, *f.*, méchanceté, *f.*, humeur contrariante, *f.*
Perversion, s. perversion, *f.*
Pervert, va. pervertir, fausser, altérer, dénaturer
Pervert, s. perverti, *m.*, -e, *f.*
Perverter, s. qui pervertit, corrupteur, *m.*, -trice, *f.*

Pervious, adj. perméable, pénétrable
Pest, s. peste, *f.*, fléau, *m.* — *-house*, hôpital des pestiférés, *m.*, lazaret, *m.*
Pester, va. importuner, harceler, tourmenter
Pestiferous, adj. pestilentiel, pestiféré
Pestilence, s. pestilence, *f.*, peste, *f.*, épidémie, *f.*
Pestilent, Pestilential, adj. pestilentiel, (*fig.*) malfaisant, pernicieux
Pestilently, adv. d'une manière funeste, pernicieusement
Pestle, s. pilon, *m.*
Pet, adj. favori
Pet, s. favori, *m.*, -te, *f.*, mignon, *m.*, -ne, *f.*, enfant gâté, *m.*, (*fit of temper*) accès de mauvaise humeur, *m.*, mouvement de dépit *or* d'impatience, *m.* *To get into a —*, se mettre en colère
Pet, va. choyer, dorloter, mignarder, gâter
Petal, s. pétale, *m.*
Petard, s. pétard, *m.*
Petition, s. prière, *f.*, demande, *f.*, pétition, *f.*, supplique, *f.*, (*law*) requête, *f.*
Petition, va. prier, implorer, pétitionner, faire une pétition à, demander
Petitioner, s. suppliant, *m.*, suppliante, *f.*, pétitionnaire, *m.*
Petrifaction, s. pétrification, *f.*
Petrify, va. pétrifier; vn. se pétrifier
Petroleum, s. huile de pétrole, *f.*
Petticoat, s. jupon, *m.*, jupe, *f.*, cotillon, *m.* *To be under — government*, être mené par sa femme, être sous le régime du cotillon
Pettifogger, s. avoué de bas étage, *m.*
Pettifogging, s. chicane, *f.*
Pettiness, s. petitesse, *f.*
Pettish, adj. colère, qui a des accès d'humeur, irritable
Pettishly, adv. avec colère, avec dépit, avec humeur
Pettishness, s. impatience, *f.*, humeur chagrine, *f.*
Pettitoes, s.pl. pieds de cochon, *m.*, (*fig.*) pieds, *m.*
Petty, adj. petit, minime, mesquin, chétif, insignifiant. — *jury*, s. juré ordinaire, *m.* — *larceny*, s. vol minime, *m.*
Petulance, s. pétulance, *f.*, impertinence, *f.*
Petulant, adj. pétulant, impertinent
Petulantly, adv. avec pétulance, avec impertinence
Pew, s. banc d'église, *m.* *Churchwarden's —*, s. banc d'œuvre, *m.*
Pewet, s. vanneau, *m.*, huppe, *f.*
Pewter, s. étain, *m.*
Pewterer, s. potier d'étain, *m.*
Phaeton, s. phaéton, *m.*
Phalanx, s. phalange, *f.*
Phantasm, s. fantôme, *m.*
Phantasmagoria, s. fantasmagorie, *f.*
Phantasmagoric, adj. fantasmagorique
Phantom, s. fantôme, *m.*
Pharisaic, Pharisaical, adj. pharisaïque
Pharisee, s. pharisien, *m.*, -enne, *f.*
Pharmaceutic, Pharmaceutical, adj. pharmaceutique
Pharmacy, s. pharmacie, *f.*
Phase, s. phase, *f.*
Pheasant, s. faisan, *m.* *Young —*, faisandeau, *m.*
Pheasantry, s. faisanderie, *f.*
Phenomenon, s. phénomène, *m.*
Phial, s. fiole, *f.*
Philanthropic, adj. philanthropique
Philanthropist, s. philanthrope, *m.*
Philanthropy, s. philanthropie, *f.*
Philharmonic, adj. philharmonique
Philippic, s. philippique, *f.*
Philologic, Philological, adj. philologique
Philologist, s. philologue, *m.*, linguiste, *m.*
Philology, s. philologie, *f.*, linguistique, *f.*
Philosopher, s. philosophe, *m.*
Philosophic, Philosophical, adj. philosophique
Philosophically, adv. philosophiquement
Philosophize, va. philosopher
Philosophy, s. philosophie, *f.*
Philotechnic, adj. philotechnique
Philter, s. philtre, *m.*
Phiz, s. visage, *m.*, face, *f.*, (*pop.*) trogne, *f.*
Phlegm, s. phlegme, *m.*, flegme, *m.*
Phlegmatic, adj. phlegmatique
Phlegmatically, adv. avec flegme
Phœnix, s. phénix, *m.*
Phosphate, s. phosphate, *m.*
Phosphoric, adj. phosphorique
Phosphorous, adj. phosphoreux, phosphorescent
Phosphorus, s. phosphore, *m.*
Phosphuret, s. phosphure, *m.*
Phosphuretted, adj. phosphuré
Photograph, s. photographe, *m.*
Photograph, va. photographier
Photographer, s. photographe, *m.*
Photographic, adj. photographique
Photography, s. photographie, *f.*
Phrase, s. phrase, *f.*, locution, *f.*, style, *m.*, langage, *m.*
Phrase, va. exprimer, nommer, appeler, (*mus.*) phraser
Phraseology, s. phraséologie, *f.*
Phrenological, adj. phrénologique
Phrenologist, s. phrénologiste, *m.*
Phrenology, s. phrénologie, *f.*
Phthisis, s. phthisie, *f.*
Physic, s. médecine, *f.*, médicament, *m.*
Physic, va. faire prendre de la médecine à, médicamenter, droguer
Physical, adj. physique, médicinal
Physically, adv. physiquement
Physician, s. médecin, *m.*
Physics, s.pl. physique, *f.*
Physiognomic, Physiognomical, adj. physiognomonique
Physiognomy, s. physionomie, *f.*
Physiologer, s. physiologiste, *m.*
Physiology, s. physiologie, *f.*
Pianist, s. pianiste, *m.f.*
Piano, Pianoforte, s. piano, *m.*, pianoforte, *m.* *Grand —*, s. piano à queue, *m.* *Upright —*, s. piano droit, *m.* *To accompany on the —*, tenir le piano. — *-maker*, s. facteur de pianos, *m.*
Piaster, s. piastre, *f.*
Picaroon, s. forban, *m.*
Pick, va. (*to pick*) piquer, picoter, (*fig.*) becqueter, (*locks*) crocheter, (*flowers*) cueillir, (*to take away*) enlever, ôter, (*bones*) ronger, (*teeth, &c.*) se curer, se nettoyer, (*salad*) éplucher, (*choose*) prendre, choisir, trier, (*quarrel*) chercher, (*steal*) voler, prendre dans, vider. *To — off*, cueillir, enlever, choisir. *To — out*, arracher (à), choisir, trier, gagner péniblement. *To — up*, ramasser, prendre, relever. — vn. éplucher, grignoter. *To — up again*, se remettre
Pick, s. pioche, *f.*, pic, *m.*, (*techn.*) marteau à piquer, *m.*, fourchette, *f.*, piquant, *m.*, (*choice*) choix, *m.*, (*print.*) ordure, *f.*
Pickaxe, s. pioche, *f.*, pic, *m.*
Picked, adj. pointu, en pointe, (*soldiers*) d'élite
Picker, s. qui pique, qui choisit
Picket, s. piquet, *m.* — *fence*, s. clôture de piquets, *f.* *Out-lying —*, garde avancée, *f.*, premier piquet, *m.* *To play a game of —*, faire un cent de piquet
Picking, s. action de piquer, *f.*, action de becqueter, *f.*, action de crocheter, *f.*, action de cueillir, *f.*, action d'enlever, *f.*, action de ronger, *f.* —*s*, pl. restes, *m.pl.*, action de se curer, *f.*, action de se nettoyer, *f.*, action de se mettre les doigts dans, *f.*, épluchage, *m.*, choix, *m.*, triage, *m.*, vol, *m.*
Pickle, s. saumure, *f.*, marinade, *f.*, conserve au vinaigre, *f.*, (*state*) piteux état, *m.*, piteuse condition, *f.* *A pretty — you are in!* (*fig.*) vous voilà dans de beaux draps!
Pickle, va. mariner, conserver, saler
Picklock, s. crochet, *m.*, rossignol, *m.*, (*pers.*) crocheteur, *m.*
Pickpocket, s. filou, *m.*, voleur, *m.*
Pickpurse, s. filou, *m.*
Picnic, s. pique-nique, *m.*
Pictorial, adj. de peintre, de la peinture, illustré
Pictorially, adv. en peintre, par la peinture, avec des gravures
Picture, s. tableau, *m.*, peinture, *f.*, toile, *f.*, portrait, *m.*, image, *f.*, gravure, *f.* *To make a —*, faire un tableau. *Historical —*, tableau d'histoire. — *-drawer*, s. peintre, *m.*, peintre de portraits, *m.* — *-cards*, s. figures, *f.pl.* — *-cleaner*, s., — *-restorer*, s. restaurateur de tableaux, *m.* — *-frame*, s. cadre, *m.* — *-gallery*, galerie de tableaux, *f.* — *-like*, adj. comme un tableau. *My mother's —*, le portrait de ma mère. *He is the very — of*, il est le portrait de, la vivante image de. *A — -book*, un livre d'images. *To be but as —s*, n'être que des images. *The — of nature*, le tableau de la nature. *To draw a faithful — of*, faire *or* tracer un fidèle portrait *or* tableau de
Picture, va. peindre, représenter, dépeindre
Picturesque, adj. pittoresque
Pie, s. pâté, *m.*, (*fruit*) tarte, *f.*, tourte, *f.* *To have a finger in the —*, être mêlé dans l'affaire. *To eat humble —*, filer doux
Piebald, adj. pie
Piece, s. pièce, *f.*, morceau, *m.*, (*of land*) lopin, *m.*, bout, *m.*, brin, *m.*, fragment, *m.*, éclat, *m.*, (*artil.*) bouche à feu, *m.*, (*each*) chacun, *m.*, chacune, *f.*, l'un, *m.*, l'une, *f.*, (*picture*) tableau, *m.*, peinture, *f.*, scène, *f.*, toile, *f.*, (*from a book*) passage, *m.*, morceau, *m.*, fragment, *m.*, (*an act*), action, *f.*, acte, *m.*, trait, *m.* *Broken —*, morceau cassé, *m.*, fragment, *m.*, tronçon, *m.*, tesson, *m.* *Of a —*, uniforme, d'accord (avec), à l'avenant (de). *To take to —s*, démonter. *A two shilling —*, une pièce de deux schellings, un florin. — *-goods*, marchandises à la pièce, *f.pl.* — *-work*, travail

à la pièce, *m.* *A nice — of work you have done there!* vous avez fait là un beau chef-d'œuvre!

Piece, va. rapiécer, (*fig.*) mettre une pièce à. *To — up,* raccommoder, plâtrer

Piecemeal, adv. adj. en pièces, par morceaux, pièce à pièce, par pièces

Pied, adj. bariolé, bigarré, (*horse*) pie

Pier, s. pile, *f.*, jetée, *f.*, embarcadère, *m.*, (*archit.*) trumeau, *m.* — *-glass,* s. trumeau, *m.* — *-table,* s. console, *f.*

Pierage, s. droit de jetée, *m.*

Pierce, va.n. percer, pénétrer, émouvoir

Piercer, s. personne qui perce, *f.*, (*things*) perçoir, *m.*, poinçon, *m.*

Piercing, adj. (*sound*) perçant, aigu, (*look*) pénétrant, (*cold*) perçant, pénétrant

Piercingly, adv. d'une manière perçante

Piety, s. piété, *f.*

Pig, s. cochon, *m.*, porc, *m.*, pourceau, *m.*, (*iron*) saumon, *m.* — *-headed,* adj. stupide. — *-driver,* s. porcher, *m.* — *-sty,* s. toit à porcs, *m.*, étable à porcs, *f.* — *-tail,* s. (*of horses*) queue, *f.*, (*tobacco*) tabac en corde, *m.* *To buy a — in a poke,* acheter chat en poche

Pig, vn. mettre bas, cochonner

Pigeon, s. pigeon, *m.* *Wood —,* s. pigeon ramier, *m.* — *-hole,* s. boulin, *m.*, case, *f.*, casier, *m.* — *-house,* s. pigeonnier, *m.*, colombier, *m.*

Piggery, s. étable à porcs, *f.*

Piggish, adj. de porc, (*fig.*) glouton

Pigment, s. couleur, *f.*, cosmétique, *m.*, pigment, *m.*

Pike, s. (*fish*) brochet, *m.*, (*weapon*) pique, *f.*, (*tool*) pic, *m.*, pointe, *f.* *Young —,* s. brocheton, *m.* — *-headed,* adj. à tête de pique. — *-length,* s. pique, *f.* — *-man,* s. piquier, *m.*, hallebardier, *m.*, garde-barrière, *m.* — *-staff,* s. bois de pique, *m.*, bâton à fer pointu, *m.* *Short —,* s. demi-pique, *f.*

Piked, adj. pointu

Pilaster, s. pilastre, *m.*

Pilau, s. pilau, *m.*

Pilchard, s. sardine, *f.*

Pile, s. amas, *m.*, monceau, *m.*, entassement, *m.*, masse, *f.*, pile, *f.*, (*funeral*) bûcher, *m.*, (*buildings*) édifice, *m.*, construction, *f.*, bâtiment, *m.*, (*of arms*) faisceau, *m.*, (*stake*) pieu, *m.*, (*for buildings*) pilot, *m.*, pilotis, *m.*, (*of stuffs*) poil, *m.*

Pile, va. empiler, mettre en tas, amonceler, entasser, (*mil.*) mettre en faisceaux

Piles, s.pl. hémorroïdes, *f. pl.*

Pilfer, va.n. voler, soustraire, dérober, escamoter

Pilferer, s. voleur, *m.*, voleuse, *f.*, auteur d'un larcin, *m.*, escamoteur, *m.*

Pilfering, s. larcin, *m.*, vol, *m.*

Pilgrim, s. pèlerin, *m.*, pèlerine, *f.*

Pilgrim, adj. de pèlerin

Pilgrimage, s. pèlerinage, *m.*

Piling, s. action d'empiler, *f.*, action d'entasser, *f.*, entassement, *m.*, (*build.*) pilotage, *m.*

Pill, s. pilule, *f.*

Pillage, s. pillage, *m.*, butin, *m.*

Pillage, va. piller, saccager

Pillager, s. pillard, *m.*

Pillar, s. colonne, *f.*, pilier, *m.*, soutien, *m.*

Pillared, adj. soutenu par des colonnes

Pillion, s. selle, *f.*, coussinet, *m.*

Pillory, s. pilori, *m.*

Pillow, s. oreiller, *m.* — *-case,* — *-slip,* s. taie d'oreiller, *f.*

Pillowy, adv. comme un oreiller, doux

Pilot, s. pilote, *m.* *Coasting —,* s. lamaneur, *m.*, pilote côtier, *m.* — *-boat,* s. bateau pilote, *m.* — *-coat,* s. paletot pilote, *m.* — *-engine,* s. remorqueur, *m.*

Pilot, va. piloter, servir de pilote à, gouverner, diriger

Pilotage, Piloting, s. pilotage, *m.*

Pimento, s. piment, *m.*

Pimp, s. entremetteur, *m.*, -euse, *f.*

Pimpernel, s. pimprenelle, *f.*

Pimple, s. bouton, *m.*, pustule, *f.*, bourgeon, *m.* *All over —s,* tout couvert de boutons

Pimpled, adj. bourgeonné, pustuleux

Pin, s. épingle, *f.*, (*peg*) cheville, *f.*, (*wheels*) clavette, *f.*, (*watches*) goupille, *f.*, (*pop.*) jambe, *f.* *Larding —,* s. lardoire, *see* NISERISA. — *-case,* s. étui à épingles, *m.* — *-cushion,* s. pelote, *f.* — *-maker,* s. épinglier, *m.*, fabricant d'épingles, *m.* — *-money,* s. épingles, *f.pl.*, menus-plaisirs, *m.pl.*

Pin, va. attacher *or* clouer avec une épingle, épingler, cheviller. *To — down,* attacher, clouer. *To — up,* relever

Pinafore, s. tablier, *m.*, blouse d'enfant, *f.*, (*pers.*) moutard, *m.*

Pincers, s.pl. pince, *f.*, tenailles, *f.pl.*

Pinch, va.n. pincer, (*shoes*) serrer, blesser, (*straiten*) mettre à l'étroit, gêner, faire souffrir, (*save*) priver, épargner sur, refuser à, (*irritate*) piquer, irriter, blesser. *I know where the shoe —es him,* je sais où le bât le blesse. *To be —ed for means,* se trouver dans la gêne. *To — oneself,* se refuser le nécessaire

Pinch, s. pinçon, *m.*, (*quantity*) pincée, *f.*, (*snuff*) prise, *f.*, (*difficulty*) gêne, *f.*, (*anguish*) détresse, *f.*, douleur, *f.* *At a —,* (*fig.*) dans un moment de gêne, au besoin

Pinchbeck, s. similor, *m.*

Pinching, adj. qui pince, (*cold*) piquant, (*fig.*) dur, cruel, (*urgent*) pressant, urgent

Pindaric, adj. pindarique

Pine, s. (*tree*) pin, *m.*, (*fruit*) ananas, *m.* — *-apple,* s. ananas, *m.*

Pine, vn. languir. *To — away,* languir, dépérir. *To — for,* soupirer après, désirer ardemment

Pinery, s. serre à ananas, *f.*, culture d'ananas, *f.*

Pinion, s. aileron, *m.*, bout d'aile, *m.*, plume, *f.*, (*poet.*) ailes, *f.pl.*, (*for the arms*) lien, *m.*, (*wheels*) pignon, *m.*

Pinion, va. lier les ailes à, (*persons*) attacher, garrotter, (*fig.*) enchaîner, lier. *To — down,* attacher, enchaîner, lier

Pink, s. (*flower*) œillet, *m.*, (*colour, &c.*) couleur rose, *f.*, (*fig.*) fine fleur, *f.*, fleur, *f.*, élite, *f.*, (*nav.*) pinque, *f.*

Pink, adj. couleur rose, rose

Pink, va. faire des œillets à, faire de petits trous à, travailler à jour, (*to cut*) découper

Pinnace, s. pinasse, *f.*

Pinnacle, s. tourelle, *f.*, (*fig.*) faîte, *m.*, pinacle, *m.*, sommet, *m.*

Pint, s. pinte, *f.*, chopine, *f.*

Pioneer, s. pionnier, *m.*

Pioneer, va.n. frayer le chemin (à)

Pious, adj. pieux. — *-minded,* pieux, d'une âme pieuse

Piously, adv. pieusement

Pip, s. pépin, *m.*, (*birds*) pépie, *f.*, (*cards*) point, *m.*

Pip, vn. crier

Pipe, s. (*mus.*) pipeau, *m.*, chalumeau, *m.*, flûte, *f.*, (*water, gas, &c.*) tuyau, *m.*, conduit, *m.*, (*smoking*) pipe *f.*, (*a short clay*) brûle-gueule, *m.*, (*of enemas*) canule, *f.*, (*nav.*) sifflet, *m.* — *-layer,* s. poseur de conduits, *m.* — *-laying,* s. pose de conduits, *f.* *Delivery- —,* s. conduit de distribution, *m.* — *-clay,* s. terre de pipe, *f.* *To — -clay,* va. astiquer

Pipe, va.n. jouer, (*birds*) siffler

Piper, s. flûteur, *m.* *To pay the —,* payer les violons

Piping, adj. maladif, (*voice*) chevrotante, (*hot*) bouillant. *In these weak — times of peace,* dans ces ébats efféminés de la paix. — *hot,* tout chaud

Piping, s. cordonnet, *m.*

Pipkin, s. pot de terre, *m.*

Pippin, s. reinette, *f.*, pomme, *f.*

Piquancy, s. goût piquant, *m.*, (*fig.*) piquant, *m.*, pointe, *f.*

Piquant, adj. piquant

Piquantly, adv. d'une manière piquante

Pique, s. pique, *f.*, brouillerie, *f.*, (*of honour*) point, *m.*

Pique, va. piquer, piquer d'honneur, offenser

Piquet, s. piquet, *m.*

Piracy, s. piraterie, *f.*, (*of books*) contrefaçon, *f.*, plagiat, *m.* *To commit —,* faire acte de piraterie, faire la contrefaçon

Pirate, s. pirate, *m.*, forban, *m.*, corsaire, *m.*, écumeur de mer, *m.*, contrefacteur, *m.*, plagiaire, *m.*

Pirate, va.n. voler, contrefaire

Piratical, adj. de pirate, de contrefaçon, plagiaire

Pirogue, s. pirogue, *f.*

Pirouette, s. pirouette, *f.*

Pish! interj. bah!

Pismire, s. fourmi, *f.*

Pistachio, s. pistache, *f.* — *-tree,* s. pistachier, *m.*

Pistil, s. pistil, *m.*

Pistol, s. pistolet, *m.* *Horse —s,* pistolets d'arçon. — *-shot,* s. coup de pistolet, *m.*, (*distance*) portée de pistolet, *f.* *Within — -shot,* à portée de pistolet. *With —s,* à coups de pistolet. *To fight with —s,* se battre au pistolet. *To fire off a —,* tirer un coup de pistolet

Piston, s. piston, *m.* — *-rod,* s. tige de piston, *f.* — *-stroke,* s. coup de piston, *m.* *Length of stroke of the —,* course *or* jeu du piston. *Solid —,* piston plein

Pit, s. fosse, *f.*, abîme, *m.*, gouffre, *m.*, tombe, *f.*, (*mines*) puits, *m.*, (*for cock-fighting*) arène, *f.*, (*theatr.*) parterre, *m.*, (*hollow*) creux, *m.*, cavité, *f.*, (*mark*) marque, *f.*, (*arm*) aisselle, *f.*, (*stomach*) creux, *m.* — *-coal,* s. charbon de terre, *m.*, houille, *f.* — *-man,* s. mineur, *m.* — *-saw,* s. longue scie, *f.*

Pit, va. mettre dans une fosse, creuser, marquer. *A face —ted with the small-pox,* un visage marqué de la petite vérole, un visage grêlé

Pitapat, adv. en battant, en palpitant

Pitch, s. poix, *f.*, goudron, *m.* *Burgundy —, white —,* s. poix de Bourgogne, *f.* — *-plaster,* emplâtre de poix de Bourgogne, *m.* *Jews' —,* asphalte de Judée, *m.* *To be — -black, — -dark,* faire noir comme dans un four, faire nuit noire

Pitch, s. degré, *m.*, point, *m.*, élévation, *f.*, hauteur, *f.*, (*archit.*) portée, *f.*, (*slope*) pente, *f.*, penchant, *m.*, (*mines*) compartiment, *m.*, lot, *m.*, (*mus.*) ton, *m.*, diapason, *m.* *The highest —,* (*fig.*) le plus haut point, le comble, le faîte. *The lowest* —, le point le plus bas, les profondeurs. *At the highest — of his lungs*, de toute la force de ses poumons. *The game reached a most exciting* —, le jeu devint d'un entraînement irrésistible. — *-work*, s. travail par compartiments, *m.* — *-pipe*, s. diapason, *m.* — *-wheels*, s. engrenage, *m.*

Pitch, va. enduire de poix, goudronner, (*to throw*) jeter, lancer, précipiter, plonger, (*to fix*), jeter, fixer, établir, (*a camp*) établir, asseoir, (*a tent*) dresser, (*a net*) tendre, (*mus.*) donner le ton à, poser, paver; —vn. (*to fall*) s'abattre, tomber, se jeter, (*to choose*) s'arrêter (à), faire choix (de), choisir, (*to encamp*) camper, dresser ses tentes, (*nav.*) tanguer, plonger. *To — and send*, tanguer. *To — deep, hard*, canarder, tanguer durement

Pitched, adj. rangé

Pitcher, s. cruche, *f.*

Pitchfork, s. fourche, *f.*

Pitching, s. (*nav.*) tangage, *m.*, plongement, *m.*

Pitching, adj. plongeant, en pente

Pitchy, adj. enduit de poix, poissé, (*fig.*) noir, sombre

Piteous, adj. de pitié, de compassion, compatissant, digne de pitié, (*worthless*) pitoyable, pauvre, mesquin

Piteously, adv. avec pitié, piteusement, tristement, pitoyablement

Piteousness, s. pitié, *f.*, compassion, *f.*, tendresse, *f.*

Pitfall, s. piége, *m.*, trappe, *f.*

Pitfall, vn. attirer dans un piége

Pith, s. (*of plants*, &c.) moelle, *f.*, (*fig.*) sève, *f.*, vigueur, *f.*, force, *f.*, énergie, *f.*, poids, *m.*, (*fig.*) moelle, *f.*, essence, *f.*, âme, *f.*

Pith, va. ôter la moelle à

Pithily, adv. avec force, vigoureusement

Pithiness, s. vigueur, *f.*

Pithless, adj. sans moelle, (*fig.*) sans sève, sans vigueur, sans force

Pithy, adj. moelleux, (*fig.*) plein de sève, plein de vigueur

Pitiable, adj. digne de pitié, pitoyable

Pitiableness, s. état pitoyable, *m.*

Pitiful, *see* Piteous

Pitifully, *see* Piteously

Pitifulness, *see* Piteousness

Pitiless, adj. sans pitié, impitoyable

Pitilessly, adv. sans pitié, impitoyablement

Pittance, s. pitance, *f.*, portion, *f.*

Pitted, adj. grêlé, marqué

Pituitous, adj. pituiteux

Pity, s. pitié, *f.*, compassion, *f.*, dommage, *m.* *What a —!* quel dommage! *'Tis a —, 'tis a thousand pities*, c'est dommage *or* c'est fâcheux *or* il est à regretter, c'est grand dommage *or* c'est grand pitié *or* c'est bien fâcheux

Pity, va. avoir pitié de, plaindre, prendre en pitié

Pitying, adj. compatissant, de pitié

Pityingly, adv. avec pitié

Pivot, s. pivot, *m.* *To turn upon a* —, tourner sur un pivot, pivoter. — *-bolt*, s. cheville ouvrière, *f.* — *-gun*, s. canon qui tourne sur un pivot, *m.* — *-hole*, s. trou, *m.*

Pix, s. saint ciboire, *m.*

Placard, s. placard, *m.*, affiche, *f.*

Placard, va. placarder, afficher

Place, s. lieu, *m.*, endroit, *m.*, place, *f.*, (*habitation*) séjour, *m.*, résidence, *f.*, demeure, *f.*, (*for a house*) emplacement, *m.*, (*in a book*) passage, *m.*, endroit, *m.*, lieu, *m.*, (*rank*) rang, *m.*, position, *f.*, condition, *f.*, (*office*) emploi, *m.*, poste, *m.*, office, *m.*, fonction, *f.*, (*of*) lieu (de), motif (pour), *m.*, (*square*) place, *m.* *To take* —, avoir lieu, arriver. *To your —s*, en place. *In — of*, au lieu de. *In the first* —, en premier lieu, tout d'abord. *In the next* —, ensuite, puis. *To give* —, faire place à, céder la place. *To hold a* —, (*fig.*) occuper un rang. *Out of* —, sans place. — *-holders*, gens en place, fonctionnaires publics. *To take the — of* or *before*, prendre le pas, la préséance sur

Place, va. placer, mettre

Placer, s. qui place

Placid, adj. paisible, calme, doux, tranquille

Placidly, adv. paisiblement, avec calme, avec douceur

Plagiarism, s. plagiat, *m.*

Plagiarist, **Plagiary**, s. plagiaire, *m.*

Plagiarize, va.n. commettre un plagiat (sur)

Plague, s. peste, *f.*, plaie, *f.*, douleur, *f.*, détresse, *f.*, (*worrier*) fléau, *m.*, tourment, *m.* *The — broke out in the army*, la peste se mit dans l'armée. — *on*, peste soit de, foin de. *A — on all cowards!* peste soit de tous les poltrons! *A — -stricken man, woman, a person infected with the* —, un pestiféré, une pestiférée. — *-mark*, s. — *-spot*, — *-token*, s. signe de la peste, *m.* — *-sore*, s. plaie de peste, *f.* *Red* —, érésipèle, *m.* *The — of my life*, le fléau de ma vie. *What a — you are!* quel tourment vous faites! que vous êtes tourmentant!

Plague, va. frapper *or* infecter de la peste, tourmenter, importuner

Plaguily, adv. furieusement, affreusement

Plaguy, adj. maudit, affreux. — adv. furieusement

Plaice, s. carrelet, *m.*

Plaid, s. adj. plaid, *m.*

Plain, adj. uni, plat, égal, aplani, (*free*) libre, franc, (*sincere*) sincère, vrai, (*arrant*) fieffé, (*easy*) facile, sans recherche, (*dress*) simple, (*ugly*) laid, commun. — *-chant*, s., — *-song*, s. plain-chant, *m.* — *-dealer*, s. homme franc, *m.*, homme tout rond, *m.* — *-dealing*, adj. s. franc, franchise, rondeur, *f.* — *-speaking*, s. franc-parler, *m.* — *-spoken*, adj. franc, tout rond

Plain, adv. clairement, distinctement, franchement, nettement

Plain, s. plaine, *f.*, campagne, *f.*, pays plat, *m.*

Plainly, adv. clairement, distinctement, franchement, ouvertement, simplement, sans recherche

Plainness, s. surface plane, *f.*, égalité, *f.*, nature plate, *f.*, (*simplicity*) simplicité, *f.*, franchise, *f.*, netteté, *f.*, (*evidence*) clarté, *f.*, évidence, *f.*

Plaintiff, s. plaignant, *m.*, -e, *f.*

Plaintive, adj. plaintif

Plaintively, adv. plaintivement

Plaintiveness, s. ton plaintif, *m.*, tristesse, *f.*

Plait, s. (*of hair*) pli, *m.*, repli, *m.*, tresse, *f.*, natte, *f.*

Plait, va. plier, plisser, tresser, natter. *Large —ed*, à grands plis. *Small —ed*, à petits plis. *—ed shirt*, chemise plissée, *f.* *—ed tress*, natte, *f.* *—ed cunning*, les replis où se cache l'artifice

Plan, s. plan, *m.*, projet, *m.*, dessein, *m.* *To raise, to take a* —, lever un plan

Plan, va. faire *or* tracer le plan de, dessiner, (*fig.*) projeter, se proposer

Plane, s. plan, *m.*, surface plane, *f.*, rabot, *m.*, plane, *f.*, (*bot.*) platane, *m.* *Directing* —, plan de tableau, *m.* *Self-acting* —, automoteur, *m.* *Steep* —, pente rapide, *f.* — *-irons*, s. fer de rabot, *m.* — *-tree*, s. platane, *m.*

Plane, adj. plan, *m.*, -e, *f.* — *-table*, s. planchette, *f.*

Plane, va. raboter, aplanir. *Planing machine*, s. machine à raboter, *f.*

Planer, s. raboteur, *m.*, (*print.*) taquoir, *m.*

Planet, s. planète, *f.*

Planetary, adj. planétaire

Plank, s. planche, *f.*, madrier, *m.*, (*nav.*) bordage, *m.*

Plank, va. planchéier, couvrir de planches, (*nav.*) border

Plant, s. plante, *f.*, plant, *m.*, matériel, *m.*, appareil, *m.*

Plant, va. planter, établir, fixer

Plantain, s. plantain, *m.*

Plantation, s. plantation, *f.*, colonie, *f.*, établissement, *m.*

Planter, s. planteur, *m.*, colon, *m.*

Planting, s. plantation, *f.*

Plash, s. mare, *f.*, flaque d'eau, *f.*

Plash, va. patauger

Plashy, adj. boueux, bourbeux

Plaster, s. plâtre, *m.*, (*for wounds*) emplâtre, *m.* — *-kiln*, s. four à plâtre, *m.*, plâtrière, *f.* — *-stone*, s. gypse, *m.*

Plaster, va. plâtrer, mettre un emplâtre à

Plasterer, s. plâtrier, *m.*, mouleur en plâtre, *m.*

Plastic, adj. plastique

Plat, va. tresser, natter

Plat, s. (*land*) pièce de terre, *f.*, (*garden*) plate-bande, *f.*, (*hair*) tresse, *f.*

Plate, s. plaque, *f.*, (*dish*) assiette, *f.*, (*silver*) vaisselle plate, *f.*, vaisselle d'or *or* d'argent, *f.*, (*engrav.*) planche, *f.*, (*print.*) cliché, *m.*, (*prize*) prix, *m.*, (*mechan.*) platine, *f.* *Piece of* —, pièce d'argenterie. *—s and dishes*, la vaisselle. — *-armour*, s. armure de plaques de fer, *f.* — *-basket*, s. panier aux assiettes, *m.* — *-carrier*, s. plateau, *m.*, tour, *m.* — *-glass*, s. glace, *f.* — *-layer*, s. poseur de rails, *m.* — *-leather*, s. peau, *f.* — *-rack*, s. égoutte-assiette, *m.* — *-rolling*, s. laminage de tôle, *m.* — *-rolling mill*, s. cylindre à tôle, *m.* — *-room*, s. office, *f.* — *-warmer*, s. chauffe-assiette, *m.*

Plate, va. plaquer, revêtir d'armure, cuirasser, orner de plaques, réduire en plaques *or* en lames, (*mirrors*) étamer. *—d*, adj. plaqué, en plaqué. — *-metal*, s., — *articles*, s. du plaqué

Plateful, s. assiettée, *f.*

Platform, s. plateforme, *f.*, (*railways*) quai, *m.*, gare, *f.*

Platina, **Platinum**, s. platine, *m.*

Plating, s. placage, *m.*

Platonic, adj. platonicien, platonique

Platonism, s. doctrine de Platon, *f.*

Platoon, s. peloton, *m.*

Platter, s. personne qui tresse *or* tisse, (*dish*) plat de terre *or* de bois, *m.*, (*milit.*) gamelle, *f.*

Platting, s. action de tresser, de natter, *f.*

Plaudit, s. applaudissement, *m.*, bravo, *m.*

Plausibility, **Plausibleness**, s. caractère, *m.*, *or* nature plausible, *f.*, plausibilité, *f.*

Plausible, adj. plausible

Plausibly, adv. plausiblement

Play, vn.a. jouer, folâtrer, (*music*) jouer (de), toucher (de), (*harp*) pincer, jouer, (*machine*) jouer, agir, fonctionner, (*a part*) jouer le rôle de, (*colour in stuffs*) chatoyer. *To — false*, tricher. *To — high* or *deep*, jouer gros jeu. *To — low*, jouer petit jeu. *To — into the hands of*, donner beau jeu à, aider dans son jeu. *To — it out*, jouer jusqu'au bout

Play, s. jeu, *m.*, récréation, *f.*, badinage, *m.*, (*drama*) pièce de théâtre, *f.*, pièce, *f.*, comédie, *f.*, tragédie, *f.*, (*theatre*) spectacle, *m.*, théâtre, *m.*, comédie, *f.* (*cards*) jeu, *m.*, (*action*) jeu, mouvement, *m.*, fonctions, *f.pl.*, exécution, *f.*, (*discussion, &c.*) agitation, *f.*, discussion, *f.* *To be fond of —*, aimer le jeu. *To be at —*, être au jeu, être en récréation. *Rough — is bear's —*, jeu de main, jeu de vilain. *A — upon words*, un jeu de mots. *Out of mere —*, par pur badinage. *To bring into —*, faire jouer, mettre en jeu. *To give full — to*, donner libre cours *or* donner carrière à. *—-bill*, s. affiche de théâtre, *f.*, programme de spectacle, *m.* *—-goer*, s. coureur de théâtre, personne qui va souvent au spectacle. *—-going*, s. habitude d'aller au spectacle, *f.* *—-ground*, s. cour de récréation, *f.* *—-hours*, *—-time*, heures de récréation, *f.pl.* *—-house*, s. salle de spectacle, *f.*, théâtre, *m.* *—-room*, s. salle de récréation, *f.*, chambre des enfants, *f.* *—-wright*, s. auteur dramatique, *m.*

Player, s. joueur, *m.*, joueuse, *f.*, (*theat.*) acteur, *m.*, actrice, *f.*, artiste, *m.f.*, comédien, *m.*, comédienne, *f.*

Playfellow, Playmate, s. camarade de jeu, *m.*, compagnon de jeu, *m.*, compagne, *f.*

Playful, adj. enjoué, folâtre, badin, joyeux

Playfully, adv. avec enjouement, en badinant, en folâtrant

Playfulness, s. enjouement, *m.*, humeur enjouée, *f.*, badinage, *m.*

Plaything, s. jouet, *m.*, joujou, *m.*

Plea, s. procès, *m.*, cause, *f.*, poursuite, *f.* (*law*) allégation, *f.*, moyen, *m.*, exception, *f.*, défense, *f.*, excuse, *f.*, justification, *f.* *— of exception*, *dilatory —*, fin de non-recevoir, *f.* *— of the crown*, poursuite du ministère public

Plead, vn.a. plaider, alléguer, déclarer, faire valoir, intervenir, intercéder, s'avouer, se dire

Pleadable, adj. qui peut s'alléguer

Pleader, s. avocat plaidant, *m.*, avocat, *m.*, (*fig.*) intercesseur, *m.* *Special —*, s. avocat consultant, *m.*

Pleading, s. plaidoirie, *f.* *—s*, pl. plaidoiries, *f.pl.*, débats, *m.pl.*, allégation, *f.*, moyen de défense, *m.*, argument, *m.*, (*fig.*) prières, *f.pl.*, excuse, *f.*, justification, *f.*

Pleasant, adj. agréable (à), charmant (pour), aimable (à), doux (à), gai, (*things*) riant

Pleasantly, adv. agréablement, d'une manière charmante, gaiement, avec enjouement

Pleasantness, s. agréments, *m.pl.*, nature agréable, *f.*, gaieté, *f.*, enjouement, *m.*

Pleasantry, s. gaité, *f.*, enjouement, *m.*, plaisanterie, *f.*, mot plaisant, *m.*

Please, va.n. plaire à, faire plaisir à, charmer, complaire, agréer, contenter, satisfaire. *To — oneself*, se plaire, se faire plaisir. *— yourself*, faites comme bon vous semblera, à votre gré. *Those whom follies —*, ceux qui trouvent un plaisir dans la folie. *It has —ed God* (*to* de), il a plu à Dieu. *— God!* plaise à Dieu! s'il plaît à Dieu. *May it — your Majesty*, (*to*, de) plaise à votre Majesté. *What —ed me most*, ce qui me charma le plus. *To be —ed* (*with*, de) être charmé, (*to condescend*) vouloir, vouloir bien, daigner. *The king has been —ed to order*, il a plu au roi de commander, le roi a daigné commander. *You are —ed to say so*, cela vous plaît à dire. *If my offer —es you*, si mon offre vous agrée. *All his masters are —ed with him*, tous ses maîtres sont contents de lui. *Highly —ed with his dear self*, fort satisfait de sa petite personne. *Will you — to be seated*, veuillez vous asseoir. *If you —*, s'il vous plaît. *Show it to me, —*, montrez-le-moi, s'il vous plaît. *Spirits assume what shapes they —*, les esprits revêtent les formes qu'il leur plaît. *My desire that he would — give me my liberty*, mon désir qu'il lui plût de me donner la liberté. *Do as you —*, faites comme vous voudrez *or* comme bon vous semblera. *— to walk in*, veuillez entrer

Pleased, adj. content, satisfait, heureux. *Well —, the world you'll leave*, vous quitterez le monde, sans vous plaindre

Pleasing, (*see* PLEASANT)

Pleasurable, adj. agréable, charmant

Pleasurableness, s. agrément, *m.*, charme, *m.*

Pleasurably, adv. agréablement

Pleasure, s. plaisir, *m.*, agrément, *m.*, volonté, *f.*, gré, *m.* *It is a — to*, il y a plaisir. *For the — of the thing*, par plaisir. *To afford*, *to do*, *to give a —*, *much — to*, faire plaisir, grand plaisir à. *I esteem it a — to oblige you in this*, je me fais un plaisir de vous rendre ce service. *To feel*, *to have*, *to take a — in*, prendre plaisir à, se plaire à, se faire un plaisir de. *The — one feels in giving — to others*, le plaisir qu'on sent à en faire aux autres. *To be out upon —*, être en partie de plaisir. *The —s of a country life*, (*fig.*) les agréments de la vie à la campagne. *—-boat*, s. bateau d'agrément, *m.* *—-grounds*, s. parc, *m.*, jardins d'agrément, *m.pl.* *—-house*, s. maison de plaisance, *f.* *—-trip*, s. voyage d'agrément, *m.* *—-van*, char-à-bancs, *m.* *—-walk*, s. promenade, *f.* *At —*, *at one's —*, à volonté, à gré. *During the king's good —*, sous le bon plaisir du roi. *To do the — of*, faire la volonté de. *Use your —*, *do your —*, faites comme bon vous semblera. *What is your —?* qu'y a-t-il pour votre service?

Plebeian, adj. s. plébéien, -ienne, roturier, -ère

Pledge, s. gage, *m.*, nantissement, *m.*, (*surety*) garantie, *f.*, garant, *m.*, (*temperance*) vœu de tempérance, *m.*

Pledge, va. engager, mettre en gage (*answer for*) garantir, se porter garant de, (*toast*) faire raison, boire à. *To — oneself for*, se porter garant de

Plenary, adj. s. plein, complet, entier, (*indulgence*) plénière, *f.*

Plenipotentiary, adj. s. plénipotentiaire, *m.*

Plenitude, s. plénitude, *f.*

Plenteous, adj. abondant

Plenteously, adv. abondamment

Plenteousness, s. abondance, *f.*

Plentiful, adj. abondant, copieux

Plentifully, Plentifulness, *see* PLENTEOUSLY

Plenty, s. abondance, *f.* *Horn of —*, corne d'abondance. *We have — of time*, nous avons bien assez de temps. *— of everything*, tout en abondance

Plenty, adj. adv. abondant, en abondance

Pleonasm, s. pléonasme, *m.*

Plethora, s. pléthore, *f.*

Plethoric, adj. pléthorique

Pleurisy, s. pleurésie, *f.*

Pliability, Pliableness, Pliancy, s. flexibilité, *f.*

Pliable, adj. pliant, flexible, docile

Pliant, adj. pliant, souple, flexible, docile

Plight, va. engager, jurer

Plight, s. état, *m.*, condition, *f.*

Plod, vn. marcher péniblement, (*fig.*) piocher, travailler assidûment

Plodder, s. piocheur, *m.*

Plodding, adj. laborieux, piocheur

Plodding, s. travail lent et assidu

Plot, s. pièce, *f.*, terrain, *m.*, (*surveying*) plan, *m.*, (*conspiracy*) complot, *m.*, trame, *f.*, (*in novels*) intrigue, *f.* *To lay a —*, tramer un complot. *A — is being laid*, il se trame un complot. *—s have I laid*, j'ai ourdi des trames. *— and counter- —*, mine et contre-mine. *—-proof*, à l'épreuve des complots

Plot, vn.a. comploter, projeter, former le plan

Plotter, s. auteur de complots, *m.*, conspirateur, *m.*, machinateur, *m.*, intrigant, *m.*

Plough, s. charrue, *f.* *To drive the —*, conduire la charrue. *Fit for the —*, propre au labourage. *—-oxen*, s. bœufs de labour, *m.pl.* *To return to the —*, (*fig.*) reprendre le collier de misère. *—-boy*, s. garçon de charrue, valet de charrue, *m.* *—-iron*, s. fer de charrue, *m.* *—-land*, s. terre de labour, *f.*, terre en culture, *f.* *—-man*, s. laboureur, garçon de charrue, *m.*, rustre, *m.* *—-share*, s. soc de charrue, *m.*

Plough, va.n. labourer, faire passer la charrue, (*fig.*) sillonner, tracer des sillons dans, (*examine*) refuser (*see* PLUCK). *To — out*, *to — up*, labourer, déterrer, sillonner

Plougher, s. laboureur, *m.*

Ploughing, s. labourage, *m.*

Plover, s. pluvier, *m.*

Pluck, va. cueillir, arracher, enlever, tirer, (*poultry*) plumer (*exam.*) refuser. *To — asunder*, séparer en deux, détacher. *To — away*, arracher. *To — off*, *to — out*, arracher. *To — up*, arracher, enlever, déraciner, (*fig.*) (*courage*) reprendre. *To be —ed*, être fruit sec, être refusé

Pluck, s. action de tirer, d'arracher, de plumer, *f.*, (*of animals*) fressure, *f.*, (*spirit*) du cœur, *m.*, courage, *m.*, courage opiniâtre, *m.*

Plucky, adj. plein de cœur, courageux

Plug, s. tampon, *m.*, (*fountain*) robinet, *m.*, (*peg*) cheville, *f.* *—-beam*, s. tampon, *m.* *Hawse- —*, s. tape, *f.*, tampon, *m.* *Screw- —*, cheville visée, *f.*

Plug, va. tamponner

Plum, s. prune, *f.*, (*raisin*) raisin sec, *m.* *French —*, s. pruneau, *m.* *Orleans —*, s. prune de Monsieur, *f.* *—-tree*, s. prunier, *m.*

Plumage, s. plumage, *m.*

Plumb, s. plomb, *m.*, fil à plomb, *m.* *—-line*, s., *—-rule*, s. fil à plomb, *m.*, ligne de sonde, *f.*

Plumb, adv. à plomb, d'aplomb

Plumb, va. plomber, (*nav., mines*) souder

Plumbago, s. plombagine, *f.*

Plumber, s. plombier, *m.*

Plumbery, s. plomberie, *f.*

Plumbing, s. action de plomber, *f.*, (*nav.*) sondage, *m.*

Plume, s. plume, *f.*, panache, *m.*, (*soldiers*) plumet, *m.*, (*honour*) palme, *f.* — *of feathers*, s. panache, plumet, *m.*

Plume, va. orner, garnir de plumes, empanacher (*clean*) nettoyer, arranger, (*pluck*) plumer, ôter, arracher les plumes à. *Black-—d, white-—d*, au panache noir, au panache blanc. *On his crest sat horror—d*, sur son casque se tenait l'horreur. *To — oneself upon*, se glorifier de, se piquer de, être fier de

Plummet, s. plomb, *m.*, (*weight*) contre-poids, *m.* —*-line*, s. fil à plomb, *m.* *Ignorance is a — o'er me*, l'ignorance même me foule aux pieds

Plump, adj. dodu, potelé, gras

Plump, adv. interj. tout d'un coup, pouf!

Plump, va. rendre dodu, engraisser, gonfler, enfler. *To — up, — out*, engraisser, gonfler. *To — for*, voter en masse pour. — vn. tomber pesamment, s'engraisser

Plumper, s. vote donné à un seul candidat, *m.*, bourde, *f.*

Plumpness, s. état dodu, *m.*, rondeur, *f.*, embonpoint, *m.*

Plumy, adj. emplumé, empanaché

Plunder, va. piller, mettre au pillage, voler

Plunder, s. pillage, *m.*, butin, *m.*, vols, *m.pl.* *To give up to —*, livrer au pillage. —*-fed*, vivant de pillage

Plunderer, s. pillard, *m.*

Plunge, va.n. plonger, précipiter, se plonger, se précipiter, se jeter

Plunge, Plunging, s. action de plonger, *f.*, plongeon, *m.*

Plunger, s. plongeur, *m.*

Pluperfect, s. plus-que-parfait, *m.*

Plural, adj. s. pluriel

Pluralist, s. possesseur de plusieurs bénéfices, *m.*

Plurality, s. pluralité, *f.*, cumul, *m.*

Plus, s. plus, *m.*

Plush, s.adj. peluche, *f.*, de peluche

Ply, va. attaquer, serrer de près (*work*) exercer activement, travailler assidûment à, poursuivre activement, faire, exécuter, importuner, accabler, tourmenter. *To — with artillery, with stones, with axes*, attaquer à coups de canon, avec des pierres, à coups de hache. *To — the oar*, se courber sur les avirons, faire force de rames. *To — the needle*, travailler à l'aiguille. *To — the whip*, faire usage du fouet. *To — the distaff*, filer la quenouille. *The hyena plies his carnage*, l'hyène s'acharne à sa proie. *To — with questions*, accabler de questions. *Being plied with several glasses*, quand on lui eut versé plusieurs verres. — vn. travailler, courir, se rendre en toute hâte, (*coaches, &c.*) faire le service, faire le trajet, aller, (*nav.*) louvoyer

P.M., adj. de l'après-midi, du soir

Poach, va.n. (*eggs*) pocher, (*game*) braconner, (*upon*) piller

Poacher, s. braconnier, *m.*

Poaching, s. braconnage, *m.*

Pock, s. pustule, *f.* —*-fretted*, adj., —*-marked*, adj., —*-pitted*, adj. grêlé, marqué de la petite vérole

Pocket, s. poche *f.*, (*billiard*) blouse, *f.*, (*hops*) sac, *m.* —*-book*, s. portefeuille, *m.* —*-comb*, s. petit peigne, *m.* —*-compass*, s. petite boussole, *f.* —*-glass*, s. lunette de voyage, *f.* —*-handkerchief*, s. mouchoir de poche, *m.* —*-money*, s. argent de poche, *m.*, menus plaisirs, *m.pl.*, (*at school*) semaines, *f.pl.* —*-picking*, s. filouterie, *f.* *To be five pounds in — by, out of — by*, gagner, perdre cinq livres à. *Watch-—*, s. gousset, *f.*

Pocket, adj. de poche

Pocket, va. empocher, mettre dans sa poche, (*an affront*) avaler, digérer

Pod, s. cosse, *f.*, gousse, *f.*

Podagra, s. podagre, *f.*

Poem, s. poëme, *m.*

Poesy, s. poésie, *f.*

Poet, s. poëte, *m.* *To be a —*, être poëte. *To be born a —*, être né poëte. *As —s tell*, selon les poëtes. *Like a —, —-like*, en poëte, de poëte. *Minor —*, poëtes de second ordre

Poetaster, s. méchant poëte, *m.*, rimeur de balle, *m.*

Poetess, s. poëte, *m.*

Poet, Poetical, adj. poétique

Poetically, adv. poétiquement

Poetics, s.pl. poétique, *f.*

Poetize, vn. poétiser; — va. poétiser, prêter de la poésie à

Poetry, s. poésie, *f.*, vers, *m.*

Poignancy, s. vivacité *f.*, nature poignante *or* cuisante, *f.*, (*wit*) piquant, *m.*, pointe, *f.*

Poignant, adj. poignant, vif, amer, (*wit*) piquant, mordant, acéré

Poignantly, adv. vivement, d'une manière piquante *or* mordante

Point, s. (*short end*) pointe, *f.*, (*wit*) piquant, *m.*, (*spear*) fer, *m.*, pointe, *f.*, (*coins*) angle, *m.*, coin, *m.*, (*ragged point*) aiguillettes, *f.*, (*rails*) aiguille, *f.*, (*small space*) point, *m.*, (*time*) moment, instant, *m.*, (*fact*) fait, *m.*, (*quality*) qualité, *f.*, côté, *m.*, (*aim*) rapport, *m.*, but, *m.*, (*lace, cards*) point, *m.*, (*compass*) aire, *f.* *Ending in a —*, terminé en pointe. *At the sword's —*, à la pointe de l'épée. *Self-acting —*, aiguille à contre-poids. *What a — your falcon made*, votre faucon a bien poussé sa pointe. *A — of land*, un coin de terre. *Meeting-—*, s. point de jonction, *m.* *Starting-—*, s. point de départ, *m.* *At all —s*, de tout point, sur tous les points. *Armed at all —s*, armé de toutes pièces. *From every —*, de point en point, de tous côtés. *In every —*, de tout point, en tous points, de point en point. *At the — of death*, sur le point de mourir, à l'heure de la mort. *In this — of view*, sous ce point de vue. *I give up this —*, je n'insiste pas sur ce point. *It is a great —, a — of some consequence*, c'est un grand point, un point important. *A doubtful —*, un point douteux. *—s of controversy*, sujets de controverse, *m.pl.* *— of honour*, point d'honneur. *Come to the —*, venez au fait. *To speak to the —*, aller au fait. *Strange — and new*, question étrange et neuve. *She has her good —s*, elle a ses bons côtés. *In every —*, sous tous les rapports. *A case in —*, un cas analogue. *The story is in —*, l'histoire est à propos. *This is not in —, not to the —*, tout cela est étranger à (*or* sans rapport à) l'affaire dont il s'agit. *To gain one's —*, en venir à ses fins. *To make a — of* or *to*, regarder comme un devoir de, avoir soin de. *To deem, to make it a — of duty to, of honour to*, regarder comme un devoir de, tenir à honneur de

Point-blank, adj. adv. de but en blanc, en plein

Point, va. aiguiser, faire *or* mettre une pointe à, (*pencil*) tailler, (*artil.*) pointer, (*— at*) montrer le doigt, montrer du doigt, (*direct*) montrer, indiquer, (*grammar*) ponctuer, (*books*) pointer, (*name*) nommer. *He —ed his gun at me*, il me coucha en joue. *To — one's finger at*, montrer au doigt. *To be, to get —ed at*, être montré au doigt, se faire montrer au doigt. *To — out*, montrer, indiquer, montrer du doigt. — vn. se diriger, se tourner, montrer du doigt, désigner, indiquer, (*dogs*) arrêter

Pointed, adj. pointu, en pointe, aiguisé, piquant, mordant

Pointedly, adv. en pointe, d'une manière piquante, nettement, d'une manière significative

Pointedness, s. (*fig.*) état pointu, *m.*, pointe, *f.*, piquant, *m.*, caractère net, *m.*

Pointer, s. indicateur, *m.*, (*dial, rails*) aiguille, *f.*, (*dog*) chien d'arrêt, *m.*

Pointing, s. action d'aiguiser, *f.*, (*grammar*) ponctuation, *f.*

Pointless, adj. sans pointe, émoussé

Pointsman, s. aiguilleur, *m.*

Poise, s. poids, *m.*, balance, *f.*, équilibre, *m.*

Poise, va. balancer, mettre en équilibre, peser

Poison, s. poison, *m.*, venin, *m.* *To take —*, s'empoisonner, prendre du poison

Poison, va. empoisonner

Poisoner, s. empoisonneur, *m.*, -euse, *f.*

Poisoning, s. empoisonnement, *m.*

Poisonous, adj. empoisonné, vénéneux

Poisonously, adv. avec venin, avec du poison

Poisonousness, s. nature vénéneuse, *f.*, (*fig.*) poison, *m.*

Poke, s. poche, *f.*, (*push*) poussée, *f.* *To give a — to*, pousser

Poke, va.n. mettre, fourrer, pousser en avant, (*fire*) tisonner, attiser, fourgonner, (*to seek for*) chercher à tâtons

Poker, s. tisonnier, *m.*, fourgon, *m.*

Polar, adj. polaire, des pôles

Polarity, s. polarité, *f.*

Pole, s. pôle, *m.*, (*staff*) perche, *f.*, bâton, *m.*, (*for hops*) échalas, *m.*, (*rope-dancer*) balancier, *m.*, (*stable*) barre, *m.*, (*carriage*) timon, *m.*, (*agr.*) perche, *f.* *Greased —*, mât de cocagne, *m.* —*-axe*, s. hache d'armes, *f.*

Polecat, s. putois, *m.*

Polemic, Polemical, adj. s. (écrivain) polémique

Polemics, s. pl. polémique, *f.*

Polemist, s. écrivain polémique, *m.*

Police, s. police, *f.* —*-court*, s. tribunal de simple police, *m.* —*-magistrate*, s. tribunal de police correctionnelle, *m.* —*-office*, s. tribunal de police, *m.* —*-officer*, s. agent de police, *m.*, sergent de ville, *m.* —*-station*, s. poste, *m.*

Policeman, s. agent de police, *m.*, sergent de ville, *m.*

Policy, s. politique, *f.*, gouvernement, *m.*, conduite, *f.*, (*financ.*) titre de placement, *m.*, (*insurance*) police, *f.*

Polish, va. polir, donner du poli à, (*pers.*) dégourdir, façonner, (*a nation*) policer, (*colours*) aviver, (*boots*) cirer, (*furniture*) vernir; — vn. se polir, prendre un poli, se façonner

Polish, s. poli, m., vernis, m., élégance, f.
Polisher, s. (pers.) polisseur, m., -euse, f., (things) polissoir, m.
Polishing, s. polissure, f., polissage, m., poli, m., vernis, m. —-brush, s. brosse à polir, f. —-iron, s. polissoir, m.
Polite, adj. poli, honnête. — learning, les belles-lettres, f.pl.
Politely, adv. poliment, avec politesse, honnêtement
Politeness, s. politesse, f.
Politic, Political, adj. politique
Politically, adv. politiquement
Politician, s. politique, m., homme d'État, m. To be too good a —, être trop bon politique
Politicly, adv. politiquement
Politics, s.pl. politique, f. To study, to talk —, étudier la politique, parler politique
Polity, s. politique, f., constitution politique, f. The English —, la politique anglaise
Polka, s. polka, f.
Poll, s. tête, f., individu, m., liste, f., liste électorale, f., élection, f., (voting) scrutin, m., vote, m., (fish) meunier, m., chabot, m., (parrot) jacquot, m.
Poll, va. (trees) étêter, élaguer, (shear) raser, tondre, (vote) voter, aller au vote, faire inscrire
Pollard, s. saule étêté, m., têtard, m.
Pollen, s. pollen, m., recoupe, f.
Polling, s. taxation, f., action de voter or d'enregistrer les votes, f., élection, f., —-booth, s. bureau du scrutin, m.
Pollute, va. souiller, rendre impur, polluer, corrompre, profaner
Polluter, s. personne qui souille, qui profane
Pollution, s. pollution, f., souillure, f., profanation, f.
Poltroon, s. poltron, m.
Poltroonery, s. poltronnerie, f.
Polyandria, s. polyandrie, f.
Polygamist, s. polygamiste, m.
Polygamy, s. polygamie, f.
Polyglot, s. adj. polyglotte
Polygon, s. polygone, m.
Polygraph, s. polygraphe, m.
Polyhedral, adj. à plusieurs faces
Polymathy, s. polymathie, f.
Polynomial, s. polynôme, m.
Polynomial, adj. de plusieurs termes
Polype, Polypus, s. polype, m.
Polysyllabic, Polysyllabical, adj. polysyllabique
Polysyllable, s. polysyllabe, m.
Polytechnic, adj. polytechnique
Polytheism, s. polythéisme, m.
Polytheist, s. polythéiste, m.
Polytheistic, Polytheistical, adj. du polythéisme
Pomatum, s. pommade, f.
Pomegranate, s. (fruit) grenade, f. —-tree, s. grenadier, m.
Pommel, s. pommette, f., (sword, saddle, &c.) pommeau, m.
Pommel, va. gourmer, malmener, battre, frotter
Pommelled, adj. à pommeau
Pomp, s. pompe, f., éclat, m., faste, m.
Pompion, see Pumpkin
Pomposity, s. pompe, f., emphase, f.
Pompous, adj. pompeux
Pompously, adv. pompeusement
Pond, s. étang, m., mare, f., vivier, m.
Ponder, va.n. peser, considérer, réfléchir à, méditer
Ponderability, s. pondérabilité, f.
Ponderable, adj. pondérable
Ponderous, adj. pesant, lourd, massif
Ponderously, adv. pesamment
Ponderousness, s. poids, m., pesanteur, f.
Poniard, s. poignard, m.
Poniard, va. poignarder
Pontiff, s. Pontife, m.
Pontifical, adj. pontifical, des pontifes
Pontifically, adv pontificalement, en pontife
Pontificate, s. pontificat, m.
Pontifice, s. pont, m., structure d'un pont, m.
Pontoon, s. ponton, m. —-bridge, s. ponton, m. —-soldier, s. pontonnier, m. —-train, s. équipage de pont, m.
Pony, s. poney, m.
Poodle, s. caniche, m., barbet, m.
Pooh! interj. bah!
Pool, s. mare, f., étang, m., (play) poule, f.
Poop, s. poupe, f., dunette, f.
Poor, adj. pauvre, indigent, malheureux, (bad) mesquin, triste, mauvais. — people, pauvres gens. To be —, être pauvre. To grow —, devenir pauvre, s'appauvrir. As — as a church rat, gueux comme un rat d'église. A — man, un homme pauvre, un pauvre. As — as Job, pauvre comme Job. A — soil, un sol pauvre. — in spirit, pauvre d'esprit. —-box, s. tronc des pauvres, m. —-house, s. hospice, m., maison de retraite des pauvres, f. —-law, s. loi des pauvres, f. —-rate, s. taxe des pauvres, f.
Poorly, adv. pauvrement, tristement, mal
Poorly, adj. indisposé, souffrant
Poorness, s. pauvreté, f., peu de valeur, m., mauvais état, m.
Pop, s. petit bruit sec et vif, m. —-gun, s. canonnière, f.
Pop, vn. agir or se mouvoir vivement et soudainement, survenir or se montrer subitement, aller précipitamment, (at) tirer (sur). To — down, descendre subitement. To — in, entrer subitement, entrer pour un instant. To — off, partir subitement, disparaître. To — out, sortir subitement, se montrer subitement. To — up, se montrer, se lever subitement. — va. mettre vivement, passer. To — in, fourrer dans. To — out, (a word) lâcher. To — up, relever, montrer. Did you — the question? lui avez-vous demandé d'être votre femme?
Pop! interj. crac!
Pope, s. pape, m. — Joan, le nain jaune. —'s eye, s. noix, f. —'s head, s. loup, m.
Popedom, s. papauté, f.
Popery, s. papisme, m.
Popinjay, s. papegai, m., (fop) freluquet, m.
Popish, adj. papiste, de papiste
Popishly, adv. en papiste
Poplar, s. peuplier, m.
Poplar, adj. de peuplier
Poplin, s. popeline, f.
Poplin, adj. de popeline
Poppy, s. pavot, m., coquelicot, m. —-oil, s. huile d'œillette, f.
Populace, s. populace, f.
Popular, adj. populaire. To make oneself —, se rendre populaire, se populariser. To become —, se rendre populaire, se populariser
Popularity, s popularité, f.
Popularize, va. populariser
Popularly, adv. populairement
Populate, va. peupler; — vn. se peupler, multiplier
Population, s. population, f.
Populous, adj. populeux
Populously, adv. avec une nombreuse population
Populousness, s. nombreuse population, f.
Porcelain, s. porcelaine, f.
Porch, s. portique, m., porche, m., portail, m., vestibule, m.
Porcupine, s. porc-épic, m.
Pore, s. pore, m.
Pore, vn. regarder attentivement, étudier, lire. To — on or upon or over, regarder attentivement, avoir les yeux fixés sur
Pork, s. porc, m. —-butcher, s. charcutier, m. —-chop, s. côtelette de porc frais. —-pie, s. pâté de porc, m.
Porker, s. porc, m., pourceau, m., cochon, m.
Porosity, s. porosité, f.
Porous, adj. poreux
Porphyry, s. porphyre, m.
Porpoise, s. marsouin, m.
Porridge, s. soupe, f., potage, m.
Porringer, s écuelle, f.
Port, s. port, m., port de mer, m., (nav.) sabord, m., vin d'Oporto, m.
Portability, Portableness, s. nature portative, f.
Portable, adj. portatif, (fig.) supportable
Portal, s. portail, m., porte, f.
Portcullis, s. herse, f.
Portend, va. présager
Portent, s. présage, m.
Portentous, adj. d'augure étrange, plein de tristes présages, funeste, monstrueux
Portentously, adv. de mauvais augure
Porter, s. portier, m., suisse, m., concierge, m., portefaix, m., commissionnaire, m., (shop) garçon, m., (railway) facteur, m., (beer) bière brune, f. —'s lodge, s. loge du concierge, f.
Porterage, s. port, m., factage, m.
Portfolio, s. portefeuille, m.
Portico, s. portique, m.
Portion, s. portion, f., part, f., partie, f., (marriage) dot, m.
Portion, va. distribuer, répartir, partager, doter. To — out, distribuer, répartir
Portionless, adj. sans dot
Portliness, s. port or maintien noble, m., corpulence, f.
Portly, adj. majestueux, noble, corpulent, gros. Like a — gentleman, comme un noble cavalier
Portmanteau, s. portemanteau, m.
Portrait, Portraiture, s. portrait, m.
Portray, va. peindre, dessiner, dépeindre
Portrayer, s peintre, m.
Portress, s. portière, f.
Pose, va. embarrasser, fermer la bouche à
Poser, s. personne qui embarrasse or qui adresse des questions embarrassantes, question embarrassante, f.
Posing, adj. embarrassant
Position, s. position, f., proposition, f., principe mis en avant, m.

Positive, adj. positif, absolu, (*order, &c.*) formel, positif, exprès, (*convinced*) certain, assuré, convaincu, (*obstinate*) tranchant, entêté, opiniâtre, dogmatique

Positive, s. chose réelle, *f.*, (*gram.*) positif

Positively, adv. positivement, absolument, formellement, péremptoirement, d'un ton tranchant

Positiveness, s. nature positive, *f.*, réalité, *f.*, précision, *f.*, caractère péremptoire, *m.*, assurance, *f.*, ton tranchant, *m.*, opiniâtreté, *f.*

Positivism, s. positivisme, *m.*

Possess, va. posséder, avoir, être possesseur de, se rendre maître de, s'emparer de, occuper. *To — oneself of*, se rendre maître de

Possession, s. possession, *f.*, jouissance, *f.* *To come into —, to enter upon — of*, entrer en possession de, en jouissance de. *To gain — of, to get — of, to take — of*, se mettre en possession de, s'emparer de, entrer en jouissance de

Possessive, adj. possessif

Possessor, s. possesseur, *m.*

Possibility, s. possibilité, *f.*, chose possible, *f.*

Possible, adj. possible

Possibly, adv. avec possibilité, peut-être. *Can he — be guilty?* se peut-il qu'il soit coupable? *It — may be so*, cela se peut

Post, s. poteau, *m.*, pilier, *m.*, borne, *f.*, (*door*) jambage, *m.*, (*station, &c.*) poste, *m.*, emploi, *m.*, charge, *f.*, (*letter*) poste, *f.*, courrier, *m.*, malle-poste, *f.*, (*stage*) étape, *f.*, relais, *m.* *Street —*, s. borne, *f.* *— of trust*, poste de confiance, *m.* *To put a letter in the —*, mettre une lettre à la poste. *To write one's letters for the —*, faire son courrier. *By this day's —*, par le courrier d'aujourd'hui. *By return of —*, par le retour du courrier, courrier par courrier. *— -bag*, s. sac des dépêches, *m.*, les dépêches, *f. pl.*, la malle, *f.* *— -bill*, s. feuille de route du courrier, *f.* *— -boy*, s. courrier, *m.*, postillon, *m.* *— -chaise*, s. chaise de poste, *f.* *— -day*, s. jour de courrier, *m.* *— -free*, adj. franc de port. *General — -office*, s. grande poste, *f.* *— -horn*, s. cor du courrier, *m.* *— -house*, s. bureau de poste, *m.*, poste aux chevaux, *f.* *— -mark*, s. timbre de la poste, *m.* *— -master*, s. directeur d'un bureau de poste, *m.*, maître de poste, *m.* *— -note*, s. mandat de la Banque, *m.* *— -office*, s. poste aux lettres, *f.*, bureau de poste, *m.* *— -paid*, adj. affranchi, port payé. *— -paper*, s. papier à lettre, *m.* *— -town*, s. ville où il y a un bureau de poste, *f.*, ville où il y a une poste aux chevaux, *f.* *To ride* or *travel —*, voyager en poste, courir la poste, *m.*

Post, va. poster, stationner, placer, (*bills*) afficher, placarder, (*accounts*) porter au grand livre, enregistrer, (*letters*) mettre à la poste. *To — off*, remettre, renvoyer. *To — up*, afficher. — vn. courir la poste, voyager en poste. *To — away, to — off*, s'en aller en toute hâte

Postage, s. port, *m.*, port de lettre, *m.* *Extra —*, port en sus. *To pay the — of*, payer le port de, affranchir. *Payment of —*, affranchissement, *m.* *— -stamp*, s. timbre-poste

Postdate, va. postdater

Poster, s. voyageur en poste, *m.*, courrier, *m.*, cheval de poste, *m.*, (*bill*) affiche, *f.*, placard, *m.*

Posterior, adj. postérieur

Posteriority, s. postériorité, *f.*

Posterity, s. postérité, *f.*

Postern, s. poterne, *f.*, (*archit.*) porte de derrière, *f.*, porte dérobée, *f.*

Posthumous, adj. posthume

Posthumously, adv. après la mort

Postilion, s. postillon, *m.*

Posting, s. voyage en poste, *m.*, louage de chevaux de poste, *m.*, mise à la poste, *f.*, (*accounts*) inscription au grand livre, *f.*, (*bills*) affichage, *m.* *— -house*, s. la poste aux chevaux, *f.*

Postman, s. facteur, *m.*

Postpone, va. remettre, ajourner, (*to subordinate, &c.*) placer après, mettre au second rang

Postponement, s. ajournement, *m.*, remise, *f.*, retard, *m.*

Postponer, s. qui remet, qui ajourne

Postscript, s. post-scriptum, *m.*

Postulant, s. postulant, *m.*, -e, *f.*

Postulate, va. avancer sans preuve, solliciter, postuler, réclamer

Postulate, s. postulat, *m.*

Postulation, s. postulat, *m.*, (*jurispr. eccles.*) postulation, *f.*

Postulatory, adj. hypothétique

Posture, s. posture, *f.*, pose, *f.*, attitude, *f.*, position, *f.*

Posy, s. devise, *f.*, bouquet, *m.*

Pot, s. pot, *m.*, marmite, *f.* *To put the — on*, mettre le pot-au-feu. *To keep the — boiling*, faire bouillir la marmite. *— -bellied*, adj. ventru, pansu. *— -belly*, s. ventre, *m.*, panse, *f.* *— -boy*, s. garçon de cabaret, *m.* *Chimney —*, s. cheminée, *f.* *— companion*, s. camarade de bouteille, *m.* *— -hanger*, s. crémaillère, *f.* *— -herb*, s. plante potagère, *f.* *— -house*, s. cabaret, *m.* *— -man*, s. camarade de bouteille, *m.*, garçon de cabaret, *m.* *— -valiant*, brave le verre en main

Pot, va. empoter, mettre en pot

Potable, adj. potable

Potash, s. potasse, *f.*

Potation, s. partie à boire, *f.*, libation, *f.*, boisson, *f.*

Potato, s. pomme de terre, *f.* *Kidney —*, s. vitelotte, *f.*

Potency, s. puissance, *f.*, force, *f.*, vigueur, *f.*

Potent, adj. puissant

Potentate, s. potentat, *m.*

Potential, adj. virtuel, potentiel

Potentiality, s. virtualité, *f.*

Potentially, adv. virtuellement

Potently, adv. puissamment

Potentness, s. puissance, *f.*, efficacité, *f.*

Pother, s. bruit, *m.*, vacarme, *m.*, tapage, *m.*, embarras, *m.*

Pothook, s. crémaillère, *f.*, (*writing*) jambage, *m.* *—s and hangers*, jambages, *m. pl.*

Potion, s. potion, *f.*, breuvage, *m.*

Potluck, s. (à) la fortune du pot

Potsherd, s. morceau d'un pot de terre, *m.*, tesson, *m.*

Pottage, s. potage, *m.*

Potter, s. potier, *m.*

Pottery, s. poterie, *f.*

Potting, s. mise en pots, *f.*

Pottle, s. mesure de deux litres, *f.*, (*strawberries*) panier, *m.*

Pouch, s. poche, *f.*, petit sac, *m.*

Pouldron, s armure, *f.*

Poulp, s. pulpe, *f.*, poulpe, *m.*

Poulterer, s. marchand de volailles, *m.*, poulailler, *m.*

Poultice, s. cataplasme, *m.* *Mustard —*, s. sinapisme, *m.*

Poultice, va. mettre un cataplasme

Poultry, s. volaille, *f.* *— -house*, s. poulailler, *m.* *— -yard*, s. basse-cour, *f.*

Pounce, s. serre, *f.*, griffe, *f.*, (*for paper*) poudre de sandaraque, *f.*, sandaraque, *f.*, (*for drawings*) ponce, *f.* *— -box*, s. poudrier, *m.*, -rière, *f.*

Pounce, vn. (*on*) fondre (sur); — va. poudrer, poncer

Pound, s. (*weight*) livre, *f.*, (*coin*) livre sterling, *f.*, (*enclosure*) fourrière, *f.* *To put in the —*, mettre en fourrière

Pound, va. mettre en fourrière, battre, broyer, piler, concasser

Poundage, s. droit, *m.*, commission de tant par livre, *f.*

Pounder, s. pilon, *m.* *Twenty-four —*, s. pièce de canon de vingt-quatre, *f.*

Pour, va. verser, répandre, faire tomber, exhaler, émettre. *To — down*, faire pleuvoir, verser, répandre, épancher. *To — forth*, verser, répandre, envoyer dehors, faire sortir, exhaler, émettre. *To — in*, verser, verser à flots, verser dedans, lancer. *To — out*, verser, répandre, épancher, débiter, lâcher, envoyer. — vn. (*rain*) tomber à verse, pleuvoir à verse, (*torrent*) se précipiter, (*to rush*) fondre, se précipiter, (*to flow*) couler

Pout, vn. faire la moue, bouder

Pouting, s. moue, *f.*, bouderie, *f.*

Poutingly, adv. en faisant la moue

Poverty, s. pauvreté, *f.* *In —*, dans la pauvreté, pauvrement. *To come to great —*, être réduit à une grande pauvreté. *To plead —*, alléguer sa pauvreté

Powder, s. poudre, *f.*, poussière, *f.* *Tooth —*, s. poudre dentifrice, *f.* *— -box*, s. boîte à poudre, *f.* *— -puff*, s. houppe à poudrer, *f.* *A sprinkling of —*, un œil de poudre. *— -cart*, s. caisson, *m.* *— -flask*, s., *— -horn*, s. poire à poudre, *f.*, corne d'amorce, *f.* *— -magazine*, s. poudrière, *f.*, (*nav.*) soute aux poudres, *f.* *— -mill*, s. poudrière, *f.* *— -monkey*, s. mousse, *m.* *— -room*, s. la Sainte-Barbe, *f.*, soute aux poudres, *f.*

Powder, va. réduire en poudre, pulvériser, (*hair*) poudrer, (*to sprinkle*) saupoudrer

Powdering, s. pulvérisation, *f.*, (*salting*) salaison, *f.* *— -tub*, s. saloir, *m.*

Powdery, adj. friable, poudreux

Power, s. pouvoir, *m.*, puissance, *f.*, force, *f.*, faculté, *f.*, (*ability*) talent, *m.*, pouvoir, *m.*, puissance, *f.*, (*pop.*) force, *m.*, grand nombre, *m.* *—s*, pl. moyens, *m. pl.* *To come into —*, arriver au pouvoir

Powerful, adj. puissant, fort

Powerfully, adv. puissamment

Powerless, adj. impuissant, sans puissance, sans pouvoir

Powerlessness, s. impuissance, *f.*, faiblesse, *f.*, inefficacité, *f.*

Pox, s. maladie contagieuse, *f.* *Cow- —*, s. vaccine, *f.* *Small- —*, s. petite vérole, *f.*

Practicability, Practicableness, s. praticabilité, *f.*, possibilité, *f.*, nature praticable, *f.*

Practicable, adj. praticable

Practicably, adv. d'une manière praticable

Practical, adj. pratique. — *joke*, s. mauvaise plaisanterie, *f.*, mauvais tour, *m.*

Practically, adv. en pratique, réellement

Practice, s. pratique, *f.*, exercice, *m.*, habitude, *f.*, usage, *m.*, adresse, *f.*, (*artifice, &c.*) intrigue, *f.*, menée, *f.*, (*lawyer*) clientèle, *f.*, (*milit.*) exercice, *m.*, tir, *m.*, (*on the piano*) étude, *f.* *The — of speaking in public*, l'habitude de parler en public. *To know by —*, connaître à la pratique, par pratique. *To put in —, into —*, mettre en pratique *or* en œuvre, pratiquer. *To reduce to —*, (*fig.*) mettre en pratique. *To make it one's — to*, se faire une habitude de . . . *To be out of —*, avoir perdu l'habitude. *Evil —s*, de mauvaises habitudes. *Words in —*, des mots en usage. *Active —*, agilité, *f.* *This disease is beyond my —*, cette maladie est au-dessus de mon art. *Clandestine —s*, de sourdes menées. *With a thriving —*, avec une nombreuse clientèle

Practice, va. pratiquer, mettre en pratique, exercer, user de, employer, (*on the piano*) étudier. *To — deceit on*, user de supercherie envers. *To — shooting*, s'exercer au tir. *To — the city into an address to the queen*, amener, sous main, la ville à présenter une adresse à la reine. — vn. (*on, with*) s'exercer (sur, à), s'étudier (à), se faire une habitude (de), (*on the piano, &c.*) étudier, travailler, (*as a surgeon, etc.*) exercer (la profession de), être établi (comme), (*with*, avec) avoir des intelligences, (*upon*) agir par artifice (sur), user de supercherie (envers), tromper. *To — with the rifle*, s'exercer à la carabine. *To — an hour*, étudier son piano pendant une heure. *His fears were —ed upon*, on exploita ses terreurs

Practitioner, s. praticien, *m.*, médecin praticien, *m.*

Pragmatic, Pragmatical, adj. pragmatique, suffisant, officieux

Pragmatically, adv. avec suffisance, officieusement

Prairie, s. prairie, *f.*

Praise, s. louange, *f.*, éloge, *m.* *To sing the —es of*, chanter les louanges de. *To speak (highly) in — of*, faire l'éloge de, faire de grands éloges de. *To sound one's own —s*, faire soi-même son éloge. *In — of*, à la louange de, à l'éloge de

Praise, va. louer, faire l'éloge de, célébrer, chanter, prôner

Praiser, s. prôneur, *m.*, approbateur, *m.*, admirateur, *m.*

Praiseworthy, adj. louable, digne d'éloges

Prance, vn. se cabrer, (*fig.*) chevaucher fièrement, se pavaner

Prancing, adj. fringant, qui se cabre

Prank, s. escapade, *f.*, espièglerie, *f.*, malice, *f.*, tour, *m.*, niche, *f.* *To play one's —s*, faire des siennes. *To play —s on*, jouer des tours à

Prate, va. babiller, bavarder, jaser, jacasser, caqueter

Prater, s. babillard, *m.*, -e, *f.*, bavard, *m.*, -e, *f.*, caqueteur, *m.*, -euse, *f.*, jaseur, *m.*, -euse, *f.*

Prating, s. babil, *m.*, bavardage, *m.*, caquetage, *m.*

Prating, adj. babillard, bavard, jaseur

Prattle, see PRATE

Prattle, s. babil, *m.*, caquet, *m.*

Prawn, s. crevette, *f.*, salicoque, *f.*

Pray, vn.a. (*to*) prier, (*for*) demander, implorer. — *tell me*, dites-moi, je vous prie. — *be seated*, veuillez donc vous asseoir

Prayer, s. prière, *f.*, demande, *f.* — *-book*, s. livre de prières, *m.*, liturgie, *f.*, rituel, *m.* *They said their —s*, ils dirent *or* firent leur prière. *At —s*, à prier, en prière. *Famed for —*, renommé pour sa piété. — *-meeting*, réunion pour prier

Preach, va. n. prêcher, (*fig.*) prôner, recommander, conseiller. *To — a sermon*, faire un sermon. *To practise what one —es*, prêcher d'exemple. *To — up*, prêcher, prôner, vanter

Preacher, s. prédicateur, *m.*

Preaching, s. prédication, *f.*, sermon, *m.*

Preamble, s. préambule, *m.*

Prebend, s. prébende, *f.*, (*pers.*) chanoine, *m.*, prébendier, *m.*

Prebendary, s. chanoine, *m.*, prébendier, *m.*

Precarious, adj. précaire, incertain

Precariously, adv. d'une manière précaire

Precariousness, s. état précaire, *m.*, nature précaire, *f.*

Precaution, s. précaution, *f.* *By way of —*, par précaution. *Too much —, too little —*, le trop, le trop peu de précaution. *To take one's —s*, prendre ses précautions, se précautionner

Precautionary, adj. de précaution

Precede, va. précéder, devancer, avoir le pas sur, avoir la préséance de

Precedence, s. préséance, *f.*, pas, *m.*, priorité, *f.* *To contend for — with*, disputer le pas à, se disputer la préséance. *To have — of*, avoir la préséance de, avoir le pas sur. *To take — of*, prendre le pas sur, précéder. *To give — to*, céder le pas à. *The good —*, le bien qui précédait

Precedent, s. précédent, *m.*, indice, *m.* *To become or to be taken as a —*, être regardé comme un précédent, tirer à conséquence

Preceding, adj. précédent

Precentor, s. chantre, *m.*

Precept, s. précepte, *m.*, (*law*) mandat, *m.*

Preceptor, s. précepteur, *m.*

Preceptorial, adj. de précepteur, preceptoral

Preceptory, Preceptorship, s. préceptorerie, *f.*, préceptorat, *m.*

Preceptress, s. gouvernante, *f.*, institutrice, *f.*

Precinct, s. limite, *f.*, borne, *f.*, enceinte, *f.*, territoire, *m.*, jurisdiction, *f.*

Precious, adj. précieux, (*pop.*) fameux, fier

Preciously, adv. précieusement, fameusement, fièrement

Preciousness, s. grand prix, *m.*

Precipice, s. précipice, *m.*

Precipitate, va. précipiter, accélérer

Precipitate, adj. précipité

Precipitately, adv. précipitamment, avec précipitation

Precipitation, s. précipitation, *f.*

Precipitous, adj. précipité, à pic

Precise, adj. précis, exact, pointilleux

Precisely, adv. précisément, exactement, au juste. *At six —*, à six heures précises. — *so*, précisément

Preciseness, s. précision, *f.*

Preclude, va. exclure, empêcher, prévenir. *To — all possibility of*, rendre impossible. *To — all, every objection*, écarter *or* prévenir toute objection. *To be —d from a free choice of*, être empêché de choisir en toute liberté. *To be —d from an opportunity of*, être privé de l'occasion de

Precocious, adj. précoce

Precociously, adv. avec précocité

Precociousness, Precocity, s. précocité, *f.*

Preconceive, va. se figurer, se former d'avance une opinion

Precursor, s. précurseur, *m.*, avant-coureur, *m.*

Precursory, adj. précurseur, qui précède

Predatory, adj. de rapine, de pillage

Predecessor, s. prédécesseur, *m.*, devancier, *m.*, -ière, *f.*

Predestinate, va. prédestiner

Predicament, s. catégorie, *f.*, position, *f.*, état, *m.*, situation difficile, *f.*

Predicate, va. n. affirmer

Predicate, s. attribut, *m.*

Predication, s. affirmation, *f.*

Predict, va. prédire

Prediction, s. prédiction, *f.*

Predilection, s. prédilection, *f.* *To feel, to have a — for*, avoir de la prédilection pour. *To show a — for*, marquer de la prédilection pour

Predispose, va. prédisposer, disposer d'avance

Predisposition, s. prédisposition, *f.*

Predominance, Predominancy, s. ascendant, *m.*, prépondérance, *f.*, (*med.*) prédominance, *f.*

Predominant, adj. dominant, prédominant

Predominate, vn. prédominer, dominer, prendre le dessus

Preelect, va. élire d'avance

Preeminence, s. prééminence, *f.*, supériorité, *f.*

Preeminent, adj. prééminent

Preeminently, adv. d'une manière prééminente

Preemption, s. préemption, *f.*

Preengage, va. engager *or* lier d'avance *or* antérieurement *or* préalablement

Preengagement, s. engagement antérieur

Preestablish, va. préétablir

Preexamination, s. examen préalable, *m.*

Preexist, vn. préexister

Preexistence, s. préexistence, *f.*

Preface, s. préface, *f.*, avant-propos, *m.*

Preface, va. faire précéder, préluder à

Prefatory, adj. servant d'avant-propos, préliminaire

Prefect, s. préfet, *m.*

Prefecture, s. préfecture, *f.*

Prefer, va. préférer, aimer mieux, (*offer*) présenter, offrir, adresser, (*promote*) avancer, élever. *To — dancing to singing*, aimer mieux danser que chanter. *Jeanie Deans —ed death to falsehood*, Jeanie Deans aimait mieux perdre la vie que de mentir. *To — poetry to music*, préférer la poésie à la musique, aimer mieux la poésie que la musique

Preferable, adj. (*to*, à) préférable

Preferableness, s. nature préférable, *f.*

Preferably, adv. préférablement, de préférence

Preference, s. préférence, *f.* *In — to*, de préférence à. — *share*, s. obligation, *f.*

Preferment, s. avancement, *m.*, promotion, *f.*

Prefiguration, s. symbole, *m.*, type, *m.*

Prefigurative, adj. symbolique

Prefigure, va. figurer d'avance

Prefix, va. mettre en tête (de), faire précéder

Prefix, s. préfixe, *m.*

Pregnancy, s. grossesse, *f.*, fécondité, *f.*

Pregnant, adj. enceinte, grosse, (*fig.*) fécond, fertile, important

Pregnantly, adv. avec fécondité

Prehensile, adj. préhensile

Prehension, s. préhension, *f.*

Prehistoric, adj. antérieur aux époques historiques

Prejudge, va. prejuger, condamner d'avance

Prejudgment, s. jugement d'avance, *m.*

Prejudicate, adj. préjugé, prévenu, qui a des préjugés

Prejudicative, adj. qui juge *or* qui condamne sans examen

Prejudice, s. préjugé, *m.*, prévention, *f.*, (*injury*) tort, *m.*, dommage, *m.* *To entertain a strong — to*, avoir un violent préjugé contre. *Without — to*, sans préjudice de. *To do a — to*, causer du préjudice, faire du tort à

Prejudice, va. prévenir, donner des préjugés *or* des préventions à, faire du tort *or* du dommage à, préjudicier

Prejudiced, adj. prévenu, plein de préjugés, à préjugés

Prejudicial, adj. préjudiciable, nuisible, dommageable. *To be — to*, être préjudiciable à, porter préjudice *or* dommage à, faire du tort à, nuire à

Prejudicially, adv. d'une manière préjudiciable

Prejudicialness, s. nature préjudiciable

Prelacy, s. épiscopat, *m.*

Prelate, s. prélat, *m.*

Prelateship, s. prélature, *f.*

Prelatical, adj. de prélat, des prélats

Preliminary, adj. préliminaire

Prelude, s. prélude, *m.*

Prelude, vn. préluder

Premature, adj. prématuré

Prematurely, adv. prématurément

Prematureness, s. prématureté, *f.*

Premeditate, va.n. préméditer, méditer d'avance, méditer par avance

Premeditation, s. préméditation, *f.*

Premier, s. premier ministre, *m.*, président du conseil des ministres, *m.*

Premiership, s. fonctions *or* dignité de premier ministre, *f.*, présidence du conseil, *f.*

Premise, va. déclarer d'avance, expliquer d'avance; — vn. commencer (par), faire remarquer

Premise, s. prémisse, *f.*, (*law*) déclaration antérieure, *f.*, intitulé d'acte, *m.*, déclaration faite dans un acte, *f.* —*s*, pl. (*place*) lieux, *m.pl.*, local, *m.*, dépendances, *f.pl.*, établissement, *m.* *To visit the —s*, pour visiter les lieux. *To be drunk on the —s*, pour être bu dans l'établissement. *The —s will be sold*, la propriété sera vendue

Premium, s. prime, *f.*, prix, *m.*, récompense, *f.* *Their shares are at a —*, leurs actions se vendent à prime. *High —*, forte prime

Premonitory, adj. qui avertit d'avance, indicateur

Prenominate, va. nommer d'avance

Prenominated, adj. susnommé

Prenote, va. noter d'avance

Prenotion, s. prénotion, *f.*, prescience, *f.*

Preoccupation, s. prise de possession antérieure, *f.*, préoccupation, *f.*, anticipation, *f.*

Preoccupy, va. occuper, (*prepossess*) préoccuper, prévenir, donner des préventions à

Preordain, va. ordonner, régler, arrêter, disposer d'avance

Preordinance, s. première résolution, *f.*

Preordination, s. détermination antérieure, *f.*, prédétermination, *f.*

Prepaid, past part. affranchi

Preparation, s. préparation, *f.*, apprêts, *m.pl.*, appareil, *m.*

Preparatory, adj. préparatoire, qui prépare. *All this was — to*, tout cela était pour préparer, tout cela servait d'introduction à

Prepare, va. préparer, apprêter. *To — oneself for*, se préparer à. *Nothing was —d for his reception*, on n'avait rien préparé pour le recevoir. *He was not —d for it*, il n'y était pas préparé. — vn. se préparer, s'apprêter, se disposer. *To — for action*, se préparer au combat. *Bid them to — for dinner*, dites-leur de préparer le dîner. *Great events are preparing*, il se prépare de grands événements

Preparer, s. celui, celle qui prépare, qui apprête, préparateur, *m.*

Prepay, va. payer d'avance, affranchir

Prepayment, s. payement d'avance, *m.*, affranchissement, *m.*

Prepense, adj. & prémédité. *With malice —*, avec préméditation

Preponderance, Preponderancy, s. prépondérance, *f.*

Preponderant, adj. prépondérant

Preponderate, va.n. peser plus que, l'emporter sur, méditer

Preposition, s. préposition, *f.*

Prepositor, s. moniteur, *m.*

Prepossess, va. occuper, s'emparer de, (*mind*) prévenir, préoccuper. *To be highly —ed in favour of*, être fortement prévenu en faveur de. *You are easily —ed*, vous vous prévenez aisément

Prepossessing, adj. prévenant, engageant. *Of a most — appearance*, de l'aspect le plus engageant. *His look was far from —*, son apparence ne prévenait pas en sa faveur

Prepossession, s. occupation antérieure, *f.*, prévention, *f.*

Preposterous, adj. contraire à l'ordre, (*fig.*) absurde, déraisonnable

Preposterously, adv. absurdement

Preposterousness, s. absurdité, *f.*

Prerogative, s. prérogative, *f.* — *-court*, s. cour de la prérogative, *f.* — *-office*, s. bureau d'enregistrement de la cour de la prérogative, *m.*

Presage, va. présager

Presage, s. présage, *m.*

Presbyterian, s. & adj. presbytérien, *m.*, -enne, *f.*

Presbyterianism, s. presbytérianisme, *m.*

Presbytery, s. presbytère, *m.*

Prescience, s. prescience, *f.*

Prescient, adj. doué de prescience

Prescribe, va.n. prescrire, ordonner, (*medic.*) faire une ordonnance, soigner

Prescription, s. précepte, *m.*, ordre, *m.*, (*medicine*) ordonnance, *f.*, prescription, *f.* *To plead —*, opposer la prescription. *To be lost by —*, se prescrire

Presence, s. présence, *f.*, assistance, *f.*, (*appearance*) prestance, *f.*, mine, *f.*, air, *m.* — *-chamber*, s., — *-room*, s. grand salon de réception, *m.*, salle du trône, *f.* *In — of*, en présence de, devant, à la face de. *In each other's —*, en présence. *Discountenanced with such unwonted —*, embarrassé en se trouvant en si auguste présence. *In such a —*, devant une telle réunion. *No man in the —*, aucun des assistants. *With great — of mind*, avec une grande présence d'esprit, avec beaucoup de sang-froid. *The sovereign —*, la souveraine présence

Present, adj. présent, actuel, (*month*) courant, attentif (à). *All —*, tous ceux qui étaient présents, tous les assistants. *To be — at*, être présent à, assister à. *The — time, the — tense*, le temps présent, le présent. *At the — time*, au moment actuel, actuellement, encore aujourd'hui. *The — owner*, le propriétaire actuel. *To have a — wit*, avoir l'esprit présent

Present, s. présent, *m.*, temps présent, *m.*, (*gift*) présent *m.*, cadeau *m.*, don, *m.* *The —*, le présent. *At —*, à present, maintenant, aujourd'hui, au moment actuel, actuellement. *In the —*, au présent. *To make a — to*, faire un présent, un cadeau à. *I made him a — of it*, je lui en fis cadeau. *As a — to*, en présent à, en cadeau à. *By these —s*, par ces présentes. *Know all men by these —s*, à tous ceux qui ces présentes verront. *To all to whom these —s shall come, greeting!* à tous présents et à venir, salut!

Present, va. présenter, offrir, faire hommage de, faire cadeau à, donner en present. *To — a person with a thing*, faire présent de quelque chose à quelqu'un. — *arms!* présentez armes! — *! fire!* en joue! feu! — vn. se présenter, nommer

Presentable, adj. présentable. *Ideas not — but by language*, des idées qui ne peuvent être représentées qu'à l'aide de la parole

Presentation, s. présentation, *f.*, représentation, *f.* *On —*, à présentation, à bureau ouvert. — *copy*, s. exemplaire dont l'auteur fait hommage, *m.*

Presentiment, s. pressentiment, *m.*

Presently, adv. tout à l'heure, bientôt

Preservation, s. action de préserver, *f.*, conservation, *f.*, salut, *m.*

Preservative, s. préservatif, *m.*

Preservative, adj. préservateur, -trice, conservateur, -trice

Preserve, va. préserver (de), garantir (de), protéger (contre), conserver, garder, faire des conserves de. *To — oneself from*, se préserver de. *God — me from*, Dieu me préserve de. *He —d my life*, il m'a sauvé la vie. *To — one's health, one's life*, conserver la santé, la vie. —*d meats*, s. conserves, *f.pl.*

Preserve, s. confiture, *f.*, (*for game*) chasse réservée, *f.*

Preserver, s. sauveur, *m.*, conservateur, *m.*, -trice, *f.*, personne qui fait des confitures

Preside, vn. présider (à)

Presidency, s. présidence, *f.*

President, s. président, *m.*, -e, *f.*

Presidential, adj. de président, présidentiel

Presidentship, s. présidence, *f.*

Presiding, adj. qui préside, tutélaire

Press, va. presser, serrer, pressurer, écraser, tourmenter, harceler, (*insist*) insister sur, (*inculcate*) faire valoir, faire sentir, faire comprendre, (*paper*) satiner. *To — down*, comprimer, appuyer fortement sur, accabler. *To — out*, exprimer. *To — hard*, presser fort, serrer fort, (*fig.*) serrer de près. *To — close*, (*fig.*) serrer. *To — forward*, pousser en avant, hâter. — vn. s'avancer, accourir, se presser, se hâter, (*on*) empiéter (sur), envahir, (*upon*) se presser, se serrer, serrer. *To — forward again*, s'avancer de nouveau. *To — on*, avancer, poursuivre son chemin. *To — up to*, se presser contre, se frayer un chemin vers

Press, s. pressoir, *m.*, (*printing*) presse, *f.*, (*crowd*) presse, *f.*, foule, *f.*, confusion, *f.*, (*hurry*) urgence, *f.*, (*cupboard*) armoire, *f.*, (*mar.*) force, *f.* *To put in —*, mettre en presse. *Ready to go* or *to send to —*, prêt à mettre sous presse. *In the —*, sous presse. *Error of the —*, faute d'impression. *To correct for the —*, corriger des épreuves. *To carry a — of sail*, forcer de voiles. *Under a — of sail*, faisant force de voiles. *—-room*, s. atelier des presses, *m.* *—-work*, s. tirage, *m.* *—-bed*, lit en forme d'armoire, *m.*

Pressing, s. action de presser, *f.*, serrement, *m.*, (*entreaty*) prières *f.pl.*, insistance, *f.*, (*paper*) pressage, *m.* *To require no —*, ne pas se faire prier

Pressingly, adv. d'une manière pressante, avec insistance

Pressman, s. pressier, *m.*

Pressure, s. pression, *f.*, empreinte, *f.*, impression, *f.*, (*fig.*) malheur, *m.*, oppression, *f.*, urgence, *f.*

Prest, s. adj. prêt, *m.*

Prestation, s. prestation, *f.*

Prester, s. prêtre, *m.*

Prestige, s. prestige, *m.*

Presto, adv. presto

Presumable, adj. présumable

Presumably, adv. d'une manière présumable

Presume, va. présumer. *It is to be —d*, il est à présumer, il est présumable. *Every man is to be —d innocent till* ..., tout homme doit être présumé innocent, jusqu'à ce que ... — vn. oser, prendre la liberté (de), se permettre (de), (*upon*) présumer (de), abuser (de), (*on of*) compter (sur), faire fond (sur)

Presumer, s. adj. personne qui présume

Presuming, adj. présomptueux

Presumption, s. présomption, *f.*, confiance, *f.*, assurance, *f.*

Presumptive, adj. présumé, présomptif, (*fig.*) présomptueux

Presumptively, adv. par présomption

Presumptuous, s. présomptueux

Presumptuously, adv. présomptueusement

Presumptuousness, s. présomption, *f.*

Presuppose, va. présupposer

Presurmise, s. soupçon, *m.*

Pretence, s. faux semblant, *m.*, apparence, *f.*, feinte, *f.*, prétexte, *m.*, prétention, *f.*

Pretenceless, adj. sans feinte, sans prétexte, sans prétention

Pretend, va.n. prétexter, prendre pour prétexte, alléguer, (*feign*) feindre, faire semblant, faire mine, affecter, (*maintain*) prétendre, affirmer, soutenir, (*claim*) prétendre à, demander

Pretended, adj. prétendu, feint, faux, simulé

Pretendedly, adv. faussement

Pretender, s. qui prétend à, prétendant, *m.*

Pretendingly, adv. présomptueusement

Pretension, s. prétention, *f.*

Pretentious, adj. prétentieux

Preterhuman, adj. surhumain

Preterite, s. prétérit, *m.*, parfait, *m.*

Preterition, s. prétérition, *f.*

Pretermission, s. omission, *f.*, (*rhet.*) prétérition, *f.*

Pretermit, va. omettre

Preternatural, adj. surnaturel

Preternaturally, adv. surnaturellement, contre nature

Preternaturalness, s. état surnaturel, *m.*, état contre nature, *m.*

Pretext, s. prétexte, *m.* *To be a — for*, servir de prétexte à

Pretor, s. préteur, *m.*

Pretorial, adj. des préteurs

Pretorian, adj. d'un préteur, des préteurs, prétorien. *The — bands* or *cohorts*, la garde prétorienne, les prétoriens, les cohortes prétoriennes

Pretorship, s. préture, *f.*

Prettily, adv. gentiment, joliment, agréablement, avec grâce

Prettiness, s. jolie figure, *f.*, gentillesse, *f.*

Pretty, adj. joli, gentil, mignon, plaisant. *Oh! how —!* oh! que c'est joli! *A — fellow*, un joli garçon, un gentil garçon. *— girl*, jolie fille. *The prettiest part*, le joli. *The child's — ways*, les gentillesses, les manières mignonnes, les mignardises de l'enfant. *— thoughts*, des gentillesses. *To play — tricks*, faire des gentillesses. *The trick is a — one*, le tour est joli. *You cut a — figure in this business*, vous faites là un gentil personnage

Pretty, adv. assez, passablement, à peu près, gentiment. *— much* or *— near the same thing*, à peu près la même chose

Prevail, vn. prévaloir (sur), l'emporter (sur), triompher (de), avoir l'avantage (sur), réussir, triompher, (*persuade*) persuader, gagner, amener, décider. *He was —ed upon to yield*, on lui persuada de céder

Prevailing, **Prevalent**, adj. dominant, prédominant, influent, puissant, efficace, régnant, répandu

Prevalence, **Prevalency**, s. influence, *f.*, ascendant, *m.*, empire, *m.*, pouvoir, *m.*, efficacité, *f.*

Prevaricate, vn. prévariquer, tergiverser, user d'équivoque

Prevarication, s. prévarication, *f.*, tergiversation, *f.*, équivoque, *f.*

Prevaricator, s. prévaricateur, *m.*, qui tergiverse, qui use d'équivoques

Prevent, va. devancer, prévenir, empêcher. *If the rain —s us from walking out* or *—s our walking out*, si la pluie nous empêche de nous promener *or* empêche qu'on se promène

Preventable, adj. qu'on peut empêcher

Prevention, s. action de devancer, *f.*, empêchement, *m.*, préjugé, *m.*, prévention, *f.*

Preventive, adj. qui empêche, préservatif (contre). *The — service*, le service des garde-côtes

Preventive, s. préservatif, *m.*

Preventively, adv. pour prévenir, pour empêcher

Previous, adj. antérieur à, avant, qui précède, précédent, préalable. *— to my marriage*, avant *or* antérieur à mon mariage. *Sound — to the storm*, bruit précurseur de l'orage. *His — success*, ses succès antérieurs. *Without — notice*, sans avertissement préalable. *— intimation*, avis préalable. *— understanding*, entente préalable. *The — question*, la question préalable.

Previously, adv. précédemment, auparavant, d'abord, antérieurement

Prevision, s. prévision, *f.*

Prey, s. proie, *f.*, butin, *m.* *To be a — to*, être la proie de, (*fig.*) être en proie à. *To fall an easy — to*, devenir une proie facile pour. *To give up a — to*, livrer en proie à

Prey, vn. faire sa proie (de), dévorer, piller, (*fig.*) miner, ronger.

Preyer, s. spoliateur, *m.*, -trice, *f.*

Price, s. prix, *m.*, récompense, *f.* *—-current*, s. prix courant, *m.* *The — of corn*, le prix du blé. *At the — of*, au prix de. *At half —*, à moitié prix, (*theat.*) à la moitié de la représentation. *At a fair —*, à juste prix. *At the lowest possible —*, au plus juste prix. *At a high —*, à une prix élevé. *At any —*, à quelque prix que ce soit, coûte que coûte. *Regular —*, prix ordinaire, prix fait. *Under —*, à vil prix, au-dessous du cours, au rabais. *Above all —*, sans prix. *Beyond all —*, hors de prix, inestimable. *To set a — on the head of*, mettre à prix la tête de. *Take it at your own —*, mettez le prix vous-même

Priceless, adj. inestimable, sans prix

Prick, va. piquer, (*ears*) dresser, (*fix*) enfoncer, ficher, fixer, (*mark*) pointer, piquer, marquer, désigner, (*stir*) aiguillonner, exciter, pousser, (*with remorse*) toucher de componction, piquer de remords, piquer au vif, (*mus.*) pointer. *She —ed her finger*, elle se piqua le doigt. *To — up one's ears*, dresser les oreilles. *To — down* or *off*, pointer, piquer. *To — out*, désigner, choisir. *His courage —ed him forth to wed*, son courage le poussa à se marier. — vn. piquer, piquer des deux, s'avancer, viser, se piquer, se parer. *Before each van — forth the aery knights*, les chevaliers aériens s'avancent devant chaque front d'armée. *— wine*, piquette

Prick, s. piqûre, *f.*, chose pointue, *f.*, pointe, *f.*, piquant, *m.*, aiguillon, *m.*, (*of a hare*) trace, *f.*

Pricker, s. poinçon, *m.*, pointe, *f.*, piquant, *m.*, (*milit.*) épinglette, *f.*

Pricking, s. action de piquer, *f.*, picotement, *m.*

Prickle, s. piquant, *m.*, épine, *f.*

Prickly, adj. piquant, armé de piquants, (*bot.*) épineux

Pride, s. orgueil, *m.*, fierté, *f.*, hauteur, *f.*, insolence, *f.*, (*pomp*) faste, *m.*, pompe, *f.*, éclat, *m.*, splendeur, *f.* *— is hateful*, l'orgueil est odieux. *To be the — of*, or *to*, faire l'orgueil de. *To take a — in*, mettre son orgueil à, être fier de. *To take no — in*, ne pas tirer vanité de, n'être pas fier de. *The — of the village green*, l'orgueil de la place du village. *A noble —*, une noble fierté. *Empty —*, vain orgueil, gloriole. *To relieve the wretched was his —*, il mettait sa gloire à soulager les malheureux. *Summer's —*, la pompe de l'été. *In all the — of youth*, dans tout l'éclat de la jeunesse

Pride, vn. s'enorgueillir. *To — oneself upon*, s'enorgueillir de, tirer vanité de

Prier, s. curieux, *m.*, -euse, *f.*

Priest, s. prêtre, *m.* — *-ridden*, adj. mené par les prêtres

Priestcraft, s. intrigues de prêtres, *f.pl.*

Priestess, s. prêtresse, *f.*

Priesthood, s. sacerdoce, *m.*, prêtrise, *f.*, clergé, *m.*

Priestly, adj. de prêtre, sacerdotal. *The — office*, s. le sacerdoce, *m.*

Prig, va.n. filouter, voler

Prig, s. fat, *m.*, faquin, *m.*

Priggish, adj. fat, suffisant

Prim, adj. affecté, précieux, minaudier, tiré à quatre épingles

Primacy, s. primatie, *f.*, primauté, *f.*, (*fig.*) prééminence, *f.*

Primarily, adv. primitivement, dans le principe, d'abord

Primary, adj. primitif, principal, premier, (*education*) primaire

Primate, s. primat, *m.*

Prime, adj. premier, primitif, principal, de première qualité, excellent, (*math.*) premier. — *-minister*, s. premier ministre, *m.* — *-wool*, s. prime, *f.*

Prime, s. aube, *f.*, point du jour, *m.*, matin, *m.*, premiers jours, *m.pl.*, commencement, *m.*, (*spring*) printemps, *m.*, (*of life*) printemps, *m.*, fleur, *f.*, tout l'éclat, *m.*, (*best*) élite, *f.*, choix, *m.*, meilleur, *m.*, (*goods*) marchandises de choix, *f.pl.* *Nature in her —*, la nature aux premiers jours. *To be in one's —*, (*pers.*) être à la fleur de l'âge, être dans tout l'éclat de sa beauté, (*fam.*) battre son plein, être dans toute sa fleur, dans toute sa beauté, (*flowers, &c.*) être en pleine saison. *In the — of youth*, dans la fleur de la jeunesse

Prime, va. amorcer, (*paint.*) préparer

Primely, adv. dans le principe, parfaitement, à merveille

Primer, s. (*education*) premier livre de lecture, *m.*, abécédaire, *m.*, (*artil.*) épinglette, *f.* *Great —*, (*print.*) gros-romain. *Long —*, petit-romain

Primeval, adj. primitif, premier, des premiers siècles

Priming, s. amorce, *f.*, (*print.*) impression, *f.* — *-wire*, s. épinglette, *f.* — *-pan*, s. bassinet, *m.*

Primitive, adj. primitif

Primitively, adv. primitivement

Primitiveness, s. caractère primitif, *m.*

Primly, adv. avec afféterie

Primness, s. afféterie, *f.*

Primogenial, adj. primordial, premier, élémentaire

Primogenitor, s. premier père, *m.*

Primogeniture, s. primogéniture, *f.*

Primordial, adj. primordial

Primrose, s. primevère, *f.* *Common —*, s. coucou, *m.*, brayette, *f.* — *-bed*, s. banc de primevères, *m.* — *path*, s. sentier fleuri, *m.*

Prince, s. prince, *m.*

Princeliness, s. air de prince, *m.*, majesté, *f.*, noblesse, *f.*

Princely, adj. princier, de prince, (*fig.*) noble, magnifique

Princely, adv. en prince, en princesse

Princess, s. princesse, *f.*

Principal, adj. principal

Principal, s. partie principale, *f.*, chef, *m.*, acteur principal, *m.*, (*schools*) proviseur, *m.*, principal, *m.*, (*head of a house*) patron, *m.*, (*com.*) commettant, *m.*

Principality, s. principauté, *f.*

Principally, adv. principalement

Principle, s. principe, *m.* *On —*, par principe. *To hold as a —*, poser en principe. *To lay down as a —*, poser en principe

Principled, adj. à principes. *Ill- —*, adj. qui a de mauvais principes. *Well- —*, adj. qui a des principes, de bons principes

Print, va. imprimer; faire une empreinte sur, marquer d'une empreinte. *To — off*, tirer

Print, s. empreinte, *f.*, impression, *f.*, marque, *f.*, trace, *f.*, (*stamp*) moule, *m.*, (*of a book*) impression, *f.*, caractère, *m.*, (*a sheet*) imprimé, *m.*, journal, *m.*, gazette, *f.*, (*engraving*) estampe, *f.*, gravure, *f.*, (*calico*) indienne, *f.* *In —*, imprimé. *Out of —*, épuisé. *The public —s*, les journaux. — *-seller*, s. marchand d'estampes. — *-shop*, magasin d'estampes. — *-works*, s. imprimerie pour étoffes, *f.*

Printer, s. imprimeur, *m.*, typographe, *m.* — *and publisher*, s. imprimeur-éditeur, *m.*

Printing, s. impression, *f.*, imprimerie, *f.* — *expenses*, s. frais d'impression, *m.* — *-house*, s. — *-office*, s. imprimerie, *f.* — *-press*, s. presse, *f.*

Prior, adj. antérieur (à) avant

Prior, s. prieur, *m.*

Prioress, s. prieure, *f.*

Priority, s priorité, *f.*

Priory, s. prieuré, *f.*

Prism, s. prisme, *m.*

Prismatic, **Prismatical**, adj. prismatique

Prison, s. prison, *f* *Breach of —*, évasion de prison, *f.*, bris de prison, *m.* *To be in —*, être en prison. *To put into —*, mettre en prison. *To send to —*, faire mettre en prison. *To get put into —*, se faire mettre en prison. *Out of —*, sorti de prison, libre. — *-bars*, s. barres, *f.pl.* — *-van*, s. voiture cellulaire, *f.* — *-house*, s. prison, *f.* — *-yard*, s. préau, *m.*

Prisoner, s. prisonnier, *m.*, prévenu, *m.*, -e, *f.*, accusé, *m.*, -e, *f.* — *'s base*, s. barres, *f.pl.*

Pristine, adj. primitif, premier, ancien

Privacy, s. secret, *m.*, silence, *m.*, retraite, *f.*, solitude, *f.* *To live in —*, vivre dans la retraite. *To disturb our —*, nous troubler dans notre retraite, dans notre intérieur. *To secure —*, pour nous protéger contre les importuns. *In his most retired —ies*, dans ses plus secrètes retraites

Private, adj. particulier, (*not public*) personnel, privé, (*secret*) secret, confidentiel, (*retired*) retiré, caché, (*soldier*) simple, (*clothes*) bourgeois, (*law*) à huis clos. *They wish to be —*, ils veulent être seuls. *Of his own — authority*, de son autorité privée. *A — gentleman*, un simple particulier. *In — clothes*, en habits bourgeois. *Case heard in —*, cause jugée à huis clos

Private, s. simple soldat, *m.*

Privateer, s. corsaire, *m.*, vaisseau armé en course, *m.*

Privateer, vn. faire la course

Privately, adv. en particulier, secrètement

Privation, s. privation, *f.*, perte, *f.*, absence, *f.*

Privet, s. troëne, *m.*

Privilege, s. privilége, *m.*

Privilege, va. privilégier, exempter

Privily, adv. secrètement

Privity, s. connaissance, *f.* *With the — of*, au su de. *Without the — of*, à l'insu de

Privy, adj. privé, secret, retiré, caché, dérobé, (*knowing*) instruit, qui a connaissance. *The — council*, le conseil privé. *The — seal*, le petit sceau

Privy, s. lieux, *m.pl.*, lieux d'aisances, *m.pl.*

Prize, s. prix, *m.*, (*lottery*) lot, *m.*, (*capture*) prise, *f.*, butin, *m.*, proie, *f.* *The highest —*, le gros lot. — *-fighter*, s. boxeur, *m.* — *-fighting*, s. la boxe, *f.* — *-man*, s. qui remporte des prix, *m.*, lauréat, *m.* — *-master*, s. officier commandant la prise, *m.* — *-money*, s. part de prise, *f.*

Prize, va. priser, estimer, faire cas de, tenir à. *Life I — not a straw*, je ne fais pas plus de cas de la vie que d'un fétu. *You know how much I —d them*, tu sais combien j'y tenais. *Highly —d*, fort estimé

Pro, s. pour, *m.*

Probability, s. probabilité, *f.*, vraisemblance, *f.*

Probable, adj probable

Probably, adv. probablement

Probate, s. acte probatif de la sincérité et de la validité d'un testament, *m.* *Court of —*, cour pour l'enregistrement et l'examen des testaments. — *-duty*, s. droit de succession par testament, *f.*

Probation, s. preuve, *f.*, épreuve, *f.*, examen, *m.*, noviciat, *m.*

Probational, **Probationary**, adj. d'épreuve, de probation

Probationer, s. candidat, *m.*, aspirant *m.*, novice, *m.*

Probe, s. sonde, *f.*

Probe, va. sonder, scruter, approfondir, éprouver

Probity, s. probité, *f.*

Problem, s. problème, *m.*

Problematic, **Problematical**, adj. problématique

Problematically, adv. problématiquement

Proboscis, s. trompe, *f.*

Procedure, s. procédé, *m.*, conduite, *f.*, (*law*) procédure, *f.*

Proceed, vn. s'avancer, marcher, faire des progrès, se rendre, se porter, aller, (*to continue*) poursuivre, continuer, (*to begin*) se mettre (à), se mettre en devoir (de), commencer (de), se porter (à), (*come from*) provenir, procéder, tirer son origine, partir, émaner, (*to act*) procéder, agir, se comporter, faire, s'y prendre, (*take place*) se passer, se faire, avoir lieu. *How does the trial — ?* comment marche le procès? *To — forward*, continuer sa route. *Before we — any further*, avant d'aller plus loin. *To — directly to London*, se rendre, aller sur-le-champ à Londres. *To — with*, poursuivre, continuer, donner suite à. *—ing from place to place*, passant d'un endroit à un autre. *Let us — to business*, passons aux affaires, commençons. *To — to action*, se mettre en devoir d'agir. *To — out of*, sortir de, provenir de. *To — against*, poursuivre, procéder contre

Proceeder, s. qui avance

Proceeding, s. procédé, *m.*, manière d'agir, *f.*, ce qui se fait or se passe, événement, *m.*, fait, *m.*, acte, *m.*, (*of assemblies*) procès-verbal, *m.* —*s*, pl. (*law*) procédure, *f.*, poursuites, *f.pl.* *To institute* —*s*, (*law*) intenter des poursuites
Proceeds, s.pl. produit, *m.*, rapport, *m.*, revenu, *m.*, *Net* —, produit net
Process, s. cours, *m.*, suite, *f.*, marche, *f.*, progrès, *m.*, acte, *m.*, (*science*) procédé, *m.*, méthode, *f.*, (*law*) procès, *m.*, sommation, *f.* *To be in the* — *of*, être à, être dans l'acte de. *The* — *of burning and breathing*, les opérations de la combustion et de la respiration. *Chemical* —, procédé chimique. *To* — *by*, agir par des voies légales
Procession, s. procession, *f.*, cortége, *m.* *In* —, en procession
Processional, adj. de procession
Proclaim, va. proclamer, publier, déclarer
Proclamation, s. proclamation, *f.*, publication, *f.*, ordonnance, *f.*
Proclivity, s. penchant, *m.*, propension, *f.*, inclination, *f.*
Proconsul, s. proconsul, *m.*
Proconsular, adj. proconsulaire
Proconsulship, s. proconsulat, *m.*
Procrastinate, va.n. différer, remettre, user de délai
Procrastination, s. délai, *m.*, retards, *m.pl.*, temporisation, *f.*
Procrastinator, s. personne qui remet toujours au lendemain
Procreate, va. procréer
Procreation, s. procréation, *f.*, (*fig.*) production, *f.*
Procreative, adj. de procréation, (*fig.*) de production
Procreativeness, s. faculté de procréer, *f.*
Procrustean, adj. de procruste
Proctor, s. avoué, *m.*, (*univ.*) censeur, *m.*
Procurable, adj. qu'on peut se procurer
Procuration, s. action de (se) procurer, *f.*, (*law*) procuration, *f.* *By* —, par procuration
Procurator, s. procurateur, *m.*
Procure, va. procurer, faire avoir, obtenir, se procurer, amener, causer
Procurement, s. acquisition, *f.*, obtention, *f.*, entremise, *f.*
Procurer, s. celui, celle, ce qui procure, fait avoir, entremetteur, *m.*
Procuress, s. entremetteuse, *f.*
Prodigal, adj. s. prodigue. *The* — *son*, l'enfant prodigue
Prodigality, s. prodigalité, *f.* *Act of* —, prodigalité
Prodigally, adv. d'une manière prodigue
Prodigious, adj. prodigieux. *To be* —, être prodigieux, tenir du prodige
Prodigiously, adv. prodigieusement
Prodigiousness, s. nature prodigieuse, *f.*, énormité, *f.*
Prodigy, s. prodige, *m.*
Proditor, s. traître, *m.*
Proditory, adj. traître
Produce, va. produire, prolonger
Produce, s. produit, *m.*
Producer, s. producteur, *m.*, -trice, *f.*, qui produit
Producibility, s. productibilité, *f.*
Producible, adj. qu'on peut produire, productible
Producing, s. production, *f.*, prolongement, *m.*
Product, s. produit, *m.*
Production, s. production, *f.*, produit, *m.*, origine, *f.*
Productive, adj. qui produit, fécond, productif, d'un bon rapport
Productively, adv. profitablement
Productiveness, s. bon rapport, *m.*
Profanation, s. profanation, *f.*
Profane, adj. profane, licencieux
Profane, va. profaner
Profanely, adv. avec profanation
Profaneness, Profanity, s. caractère profane, *m.*, conduite profane, *f.*, langage profane, *m.*
Profaner, s. profanateur, *m.*, -trice, *f.*
Profess, va. professer, faire profession de, déclarer, dire, avouer, exercer, indiquer, dénoter, (*to boast*) prétendre à, faire parade de. *To* — *oneself a* . . ., se déclarer, se dire . . . — vn. faire profession, faire des protestations d'amitié
Professed, adj déclaré, (*relig.*) profès, -esse. — *gambler*, s. joueur de profession, *m.*
Professedly, adv. de profession, publiquement, ouvertement, par son propre aveu
Profession, s. profession, *f.* *To make* — *of*, —*s of*, faire profession de. *By his* —, de profession, par état, par son propre aveu
Professional, adj. de la profession, du métier. *Some* — *man*, quelque homme du métier
Professionally, adv. de profession, par profession, par état
Professor, s. qui fait profession (de), qui professe, professeur, *m.*
Professorial, adj. professoral
Professorship, s. professorat, *m.*
Proffer, va. offrir, proposer
Proffer, s. offre, *f.*, tentative, *f.*
Profferer, s. qui offre or propose
Proficiency, s. progrès, *m.pl.*, force, *f.*, talent, *m.*, habileté, *f.*
Proficient, adj. fort, avancé, versé dans
Profile, s. profil, *m.* *In* —, de profil, en profil
Profile, va. profiler
Profit, s. profit, *m.*, bénéfice, *m.*, gain, *m.*, rapport, *m.*, revenu, *m.*, utilité, *f.*, avantage, *m.*, bien, *m.* — *and loss*, profits et pertes. *To yield a good* —, donner de gros bénéfices. *Gross* —, *net* —, bénéfice brut, net. *To make a* — *by*, bénéficier sur, gagner sur. *To derive* or *reap* — *from*, retirer du profit, du bénéfice de
Profit, va. profiter à, faire du bien à, avantager, avancer; — vn. profiter, bénéficier, tirer du profit, gagner, faire des progrès
Profitable, adj. profitable, utile, avantageux, lucratif
Profitableness, s. nature profitable or avantageuse, *f.*, utilité, *f.*, profit, *m.*
Profitably, adv. profitablement, utilement, avantageusement
Profiting, s. profit, *m.*
Profitless, adj. sans profit
Profligacy, s. dérèglement, *m.*, libertinage, *m.*, dissolution, *f.*, dépravation, *f.*
Profligate, adj. abandonné, déréglé, libertin, dissolu
Profligate, s. abandonné, *m.*, homme dissolu, *m.*, homme dépravé, *m.*
Profligately, adv. dans le dérèglement, sans mœurs
Profligation, s. déroute, *f.*
Profound, adj. profond
Profoundly, adv. profondément
Profoundness, Profoundity, s. profondeur, *f.*
Profuse, adj. prodigue, extravagant, excessif, en profusion. *To be* — *in*, prodiguer
Profusely, adv. profusément, avec profusion, avec prodigalité
Profuseness, Profusion, s. profusion, *f.* *In* —, à profusion
Progenitor, s. ancêtre, *m.*, aïeul, *m.*, premier père, *m.*
Progeny, s. postérité, *f.*, race, *f.*, lignée, *f.*, famille, *f.*
Prognostic, adj. prognostique
Prognostic, s. prognostic, *m.*
Prognosticate, va. pronostiquer, (*things, &c.*) présager
Prognostication, s. prédiction, *f.*
Prognosticator, s. augure, *m.*
Program, Programme, s. programme, *m.*
Progress, s. marche, *f.*, avance, *f.*, route, *f.*, course, *f.*, (*journey*) voyage, *m.*, tournée, *f.* *To make great* —, faire de grands progrès. *In* —, en état de progrès, en cours d'exécution. *To report* —, faire un rapport sur l'état de la question
Progress, vn. s'avancer, faire des progrès
Progression, s. progression, *f.*
Progressional, adj. en état de progrès, croissant
Progressionist, s. progressiste, *m.*
Progressive, adj. progressif
Progressively, adv. progressivement
Progressiveness, s. marche progressive, *f.*
Prohibit, va. défendre (à), interdire (à), empêcher, (*law*) prohiber
Prohibiter, s. celui qui défend, qui interdit
Prohibition, s. défense, *f.*, interdiction, *f.*, (*law*) prohibition, *f.*
Prohibitive, Prohibitory, adj. qui défend, d'interdiction, (*law*) prohibitif
Project, va. projeter, jeter en avant, tracer, former le dessein de; — vn. saillir, être en saillie, avancer
Project, s. projet, *m.* *To form* —*s*, faire des projets
Projectile, adj. s. projectile, *m.*
Projection, s. projection, *f.*
Projector, s. faiseur de projets, *m.*, homme à projets, *m.*
Prolate, adj. prolongé
Prolegomena, s. prolégomènes, *m.pl.*
Proletarian, adj. de prolétaire
Proletary, s. adj. prolétaire, *m.*
Prolific, Prolifical, adj. prolifique, vivifiant, fécondant
Prolix, adj. prolixe, fatigant
Prolixity, Prolixness, s. prolixité, *f.*
Prolocutor, s. président, *m.*
Prologue, s. prologue, *m.*
Prologue, va. introduire par un prologue
Prolong, va. prolonger, allonger, retarder, différer. *If his life is prolonged*, si sa vie se prolonge

Prolongation, s. prolongation, *f.*

Promenade, s. promenade, *f.*

Promenade, va.n. se promener (dans)

Prominence, Prominency, s. proéminence, *f.*, éminence, *f.*, distinction, *f.*

Prominent, adj. proéminent, (*jutting out*) en saillie, qui sort, (*conspicuous*) accentué, prononcé, éminent, remarquable. — *features*, des traits accentués

Prominently, adv. d'une manière proéminente, en saillie, en relief, éminemment, remarquablement

Promiscuity, Promiscuousness, s. mélange, *m.*, confusion, *f.*, promiscuité, *f.*

Promiscuous, adj. mêlé, confus, sans ordre, sans distinction

Promiscuously, adv. confusément

Promise, s. promesse, *f.*, (*hopes*) espérances, *f.pl.* *To make a* —, faire une promesse. *Of greater — than performance*, qui promet plus qu'il ne tient. *Land of* —, terre promise. *Of great* —, qui donne de grandes espérances, qui promet beaucoup

Promise, va.n. promettre, annoncer, s'annoncer, se présenter. *To — oneself*, se promettre. *To — each other*, se promettre. *I — you*, je vous le promets. *The —d land*, la terre promise. *He —d my father*, il promit à mon père. *It is one thing to — and another to perform*, promettre et tenir sont deux. *To — fair*, (*pers.*) faire de belles promesses, donner de belles espérances. *The thing —s well, —s nothing good*, l'affaire s'annonce *or* se présente bien, l'affaire ne promet rien de bon *or* s'annonce mal

Promiser, s. prometteur, *m.*, -euse, *f.*

Promising, adj. qui promet, qui donne des espérances. *A — youth*, un jeune homme qui donne de belles espérances. *To look* —, promettre

Promissory, adj. qui contient des promesses. — -*note*, s. promesse, *f.*, billet à ordre, *m.*

Promontory, s. promontoire, *m.*

Promote, va. favoriser, encourager, protéger, (*raise*) avancer, donner de l'avancement à, promouvoir, élever. *To be —d*, recevoir de l'avancement

Promoter, s. personne qui encourage, promoteur, *m.*, protecteur, *m.*

Promotion, s. encouragement, *m.*, protection, *f.*, avancement, *m.*, promotion, *f.*

Prompt, adj. prompt, empressé

Prompt, va. inspirer, exciter, pousser, conseiller, (*an actor*) souffler. — -*book*, s. exemplaire du souffleur, *m.*

Prompter, s. conseiller, *m.*, (*of actors, &c.*) souffleur, *m.*

Promptitude, s., **Promptness,** s. promptitude, *f.*

Promptly, adv. promptement, avec promptitude

Promulgate, va. promulguer

Promulgation, s. promulgation, *f.*

Promulgator, s. qui promulgue

Prone, adj. (*sloping*) incliné, penché en avant, (*disposed*) porté, enclin, disposé

Proneness, s. inclination, *f.*, posture couchée, *f.*, disposition, *f.*

Prong, s. fourchon, *m.*, dent, *f.*

Pronged, adj. à fourchons

Pronominal, adj. pronominal

Pronominally, adv. pronominalement

Pronoun, s. pronom, *m.*

Pronounce, va. prononcer, déclarer. *To — oneself*, se prononcer, se déclarer. *How is this word —d?* comment ce mot se prononce-t-il? comment prononce-t-on ce mot? *To — one's will*, déclarer sa volonté. *It was —d to be*, on déclara que c'était

Pronunciation, s. prononciation, *f.*

Proof, s. preuve, *f.*, épreuve, *f.*, (*spirits*) degré, *m.*, (*print.*) épreuve, *f.* *As a* —, en preuve. *In* —, pour preuve. *Without any* —, sans preuve. *To make good a* —, faire la preuve. *To give —s of*, donner des preuves de, faire preuve de, faire ses preuves de. *To bring in —s of*, produire des preuves de. *'Tis a common — that*, c'est une vérité d'expérience que. *To be . . . -* —, *to be — against*, être à l'épreuve de. — *against all temptation*, à l'épreuve des tentations. *To put to the* —, mettre à l'épreuve. *Armour of* —, armure éprouvée. *Above* —, *beyond* —, *over* —, au-dessus de l'épreuve. — -*sheet*, s. épreuve, *f.*

Proofless, adj. sans preuve, dénué de preuves

Prop, va. étayer, soutenir, (*vines*) échalasser, (*trees*) mettre un tuteur. *To — up*, étayer, soutenir, appuyer

Prop, s. étai, *m.*, étançon, *m.*, soutien, *m.*, appui, *m.*, (*vine*) échalas, *m.*, (*tree*) tuteur, *m.*

Propagandism, s. esprit de propagande, *m.*

Propagandist, s. propagandiste, *m.*

Propagate, va. propager, répandre; — vn. se propager

Propagation, s. propagation, *f.*, extension, *f.*

Propagator, s. propagateur, *m.*

Propel, va. pousser en avant, mettre en mouvement, (*throw*) lancer

Propeller, s. moteur, *m.*, propulseur, *m.* *Screw* —, hélice, *f.*, (*steamer*) navire à hélice, *m.*

Propensity, s. propension, *f.*, penchant, *m.*, inclination, *f.* *Evil —ies*, de mauvais penchants, des propensions au mal

Proper, adj. propre, particulier, naturel, (*becoming*) convenable. — *conduct*, conduite convenable. *Is it — for you to act thus?* est-il convenable, convient-il, est-il bien, est-il à propos que vous agissiez ainsi, d'agir ainsi? *At the — time*, au moment convenable, à propos. *To deem it — to*, juger convenable de. *The — meaning*, le sens propre. *The — word*, le mot propre. *A marvellous — man*, un homme singulièrement bien tourné. — *youth*, beau jeune homme

Properly, adv. proprement, convenablement

Property, s. propriété, *f.*, propre, *m.*, biens, *m.pl.*, (*theat.*) accessoire, *m.* *Real* —, biens immeubles, *m.pl.* *A man of* —, homme qui a du bien. — -*tax*, s. impôt sur les propriétés, *m.* — -*man*, s. (*theat.*) costumier, *m.*

Prophecy, s. prophétie, *f.*

Prophesier, s. prophète, *m.*

Prophesy, va.n. prophétiser, prédire

Prophesying, s. prophétie, *f.*

Prophet, s. prophète, *m.* *The lesser —s*, les petits prophètes. — *of evil*, prophète de malheur. *False* —, faux prophète. — -*like*, adj. comme un prophète

Prophetess, s. prophétesse, *f.*

Prophetic, Prophetical, adj. prophétique

Prophetically, adv. prophétiquement

Propitiate, va. rendre propice *or* favorable

Propitiation, s. apaisement, *m.*, expiation, *f.*, propitiation, *f.*

Propitiatory, adj. propitiatoire, de propitiation

Propitious, adj. propice, favorable

Propitiously, adv. d'une manière propice, favorablement

Propitiousness, s. disposition propice *or* favorable, *f.*, nature propice, *f*

Proponent, s. auteur d'une proposition, *m.*

Proportion, s. proportion, *f.* *In — as*, à proportion que. *In — to*, en proportion de, à proportion de

Proportion, va. proportionner, former

Proportionable, adj. qu'on peut proportionner, en proportion (avec), proportionné (à)

Proportionably, *see* PROPORTIONATELY

Proportional, adj. proportionnel, en proportion (avec), proportionné (à). *Mean* —, moyenne proportionnelle

Proportionality, s. proportionnalité, *f.*

Proportionally, *see* PROPORTIONATELY

Proportionate, adj. proportionné

Proportionately, adv. en proportion, proportionnément

Proportionless, adj. sans proportion

Proposal, s. proposition, *f.* *To make —s for*, faire des propositions à, demander, offrir sa main à

Propose, va. proposer, se proposer; — vn. se proposer de, avoir l'intention de, offrir sa main, faire sa demande

Proposer, s. auteur d'une proposition, *m.*, personne qui propose

Proposition, s. proposition, *f.*

Propound, va. proposer, avancer

Proprietary, s. propriétaire, *m.*

Proprietary, adj. de propriétaire

Proprietor, s. propriétaire, *m.*

Proprietorship, s. propriété, *f*

Proprietress, s. propriétaire, *f.*

Propriety, s. propriété, *f.*, convenance, *f.*, bienséance, *f.*

Propulsion, s. propulsion, *f.*

Propulsive, adj. qui pousse en avant

Prorata, adv. en proportion de, au prorata

Probe, s. proue, *f.*

Prorogation, s. prorogation, *f.*

Prorogue, va. proroger

Proruption, s. éruption, *f.*

Prosaic, Prosaical, adj. prosaïque

Prosaically, adv. prosaïquement

Proscribe, va. proscrire

Proscriber, s. proscripteur, *m.*

Proscript, s. proscrit, *m.*

Proscription, s. proscription, *f.*

Proscriptive, adj. de proscription

Prose, s. prose

Prose, adj. en prose

Prose, vn. écrire *or* raconter longuement, fastidieusement

Prosecutable, adj. pouvant être poursuivi
Prosecute, va. poursuivre, continuer, (*law*) poursuivre, diriger des poursuites contre, faire valoir
Prosecuting, adj. chargé des poursuites
Prosecution, s. action de poursuivre, *f.*, (*law*) poursuites, *f.pl.* *To carry on a* —, diriger des poursuites
Prosecutor, s. celui qui poursuit, qui continue, (*law*) plaignant, poursuivant
Prosecutrix, s. plaignante, *f.*
Proselyte, s. prosélyte, *m.f.*
Proselytism, s. prosélytisme, *m.*
Prosily, adv. ennuyeusement
Prosiness, s. ennui, *m.*, longueurs, *f.pl.*
Prosing, s. longs discours, *m.pl.*
Prosody, s. prosodie, *f.*
Prospect, s. vue, *f.*, point de vue, *m.*, perspective, *f.*, paysage, *m.*, aspect, *m.*, (*hopes*) perspective, *f.*, espérance, *f.*, avenir, *m.*, carrière, *f.*
Prospective, adj. de l'avenir, qui regarde l'avenir, en perspective. — *glass*, s. verre de longue-vue, *m.*
Prospective, s. perspective, *f.*, verre de longue-vue, *m.*
Prospectively, adv. en perspective
Prospectus, s. prospectus, *m.*
Prosper, va. faire prospérer, faire réussir; — vn. prospérer, réussir
Prosperity, **Prosperousness**, s. prospérité, *f.*
Prosperous, adj. prospère
Prosperously, adv. heureusement
Prostitute, va. prostituer
Prostitute, adj. prostitué
Prostitute, s. prostituée, *f.*
Prostitution, s. prostitution, *f.*
Prostrate, adj. étendu, couché, la face contre terre, prosterné. *To fall* —, tomber de tout son long
Prostrate, va. coucher, prosterner, abattre, détruire. *To — oneself*, se prosterner
Prostration, s. action de coucher à plat, prosternation, *f.*, renversement, *m.*, destruction, *f.*
Prosy, adj. ennuyeux
Protect, va. protéger, défendre, garantir, mettre à l'abri
Protecting, adj. protecteur
Protectingly, adv. de manière à protéger, pour protéger, d'un ton, d'un air protecteur
Protection, s. défense, *f.*, garantie, *f.*, protection, *f.*, abri, *m.*
Protectionist, s. protectionniste, *m.*
Protective, adj. protecteur
Protector, s. protecteur, *m.*
Protectorate, **Protectorship**, s. protectorat, *m.*
Protectress, s. protectrice, *f.*
Protest, vn.a. protester, attester, affirmer
Protest, s. protestation, *f.*, (*com.*) protêt, *m.*
Protestant, s. adj. protestant, -e
Protestantism, s. protestantisme, *m.*
Protestation, s. protestation, *f.*
Protester, s. celui, celle qui proteste
Protocol, s. protocole, *m.*
Prototype, s. prototype, *m.*
Protract, va. prolonger, traîner *or* tirer en longueur
Protractor, s. qui prolonge, rapporteur, *m.*
Protrude, va. avancer, pousser en avant; — vn. s'avancer, faire saillie, être en saillie
Protrusion, s. action d'avancer, de pousser en avant, *f.*, saillie, *f.*, projection, *f.*
Protuberance, s. protubérance, *f.*
Protuberant, adj. formant saillie
Proud, adj. orgueilleux, fier, superbe, altier, hautain, (*med.*) spongieux, baveux. — *of his name*, fier de son nom. *Don't be so* —, ne faites pas le fier, portez-le moins haut. *The — man, the — woman*, l'orgueilleux, l'orgueilleuse. *The* —, les orgueilleux. *She is* —, elle est orgueilleuse, c'est une orgueilleuse. —*-hearted*, —*-minded*, adj. orgueilleux. *A — steed*, un fier coursier. *A — palace*, un palais superbe. *The opposing armies ranged in — array*, les deux armées rangées dans un ordre magnifique. *The —est day of my life*, le plus beau jour de ma vie. — *flesh*, chair baveuse
Proudly, adv. fièrement, orgueilleusement
Prove, va. prouver, (*show*) démontrer, (*experience*) éprouver, faire l'épreuve de, (*try*) essayer, éprouver, (*law*) homologuer, (*arithm.*) faire la preuve de. *To — my story true*, pour prouver que mon histoire est vraie. *To — the truth of*, démontrer la vérité de. *I will — it to you*, je vais vous le prouver. *Can you — his presence, his being present?* pouvez-vous prouver sa présence, qu'il était présent? *To — oneself worthy*, se montrer digne, montrer qu'on est digne. — *all things*, examinez, éprouvez toutes choses. *To — masteries*, voir *or* essayer qui est le plus fort.
— vn. se montrer, montrer qu'on est, se trouver, être, se trouver être. *He will — worthy of his fortune*, il se montrera digne de sa fortune. *Hoping they should immortal —*, espérant qu'ils seraient immortels. *Lest his sheaves — chaff*, de peur que ses gerbes ne soient que de la paille. *To — to be*, se trouver, être
Provender, s. fourrage, *m.*
Proverb, s. proverbe, *m.* *To become a* —, passer en proverbe
Proverbial, adj. proverbial
Proverbially, adv. proverbialement
Provide, va. préparer (pour), procurer (à), pourvoir, munir, fournir, garnir, (*foresee*) stipuler, prévoir. *To — against*, se pourvoir contre. *To — for*, pourvoir à. *This had been —d for*, on y avait pourvu. *His children are —d for*, ses enfants sont pourvus. *He had —d him with masters*, il lui avait procuré des maîtres
Providence, s. Providence, *f.*, prévoyance, *f.*, prudence, *f.*
Provident, adj. prévoyant, prudent
Providential, adj. providentiel
Providentially, adv. providentiellement, par la Providence
Providently, adv. avec prévoyance, d'une manière prévoyante
Provider, s. pourvoyeur, *m.*, -euse, *f.*
Province, s. province, *f.*, (*fig.*) ressort, *m.*, département, *m.*, compétence, *f.* *It is the — of the court to judge . . .*, c'est du ressort de la cour de juger . . .
Provincial, adj. s. provincial, de province
Provincialism, s. provincialisme, *m.*
Provision, s. action de pourvoir à, *f.*, prévoyance (de), *f.*, préparatifs (pour), *m.*, provision, *f.*, (*to eat*) vivres, *m.pl.*, comestibles, *m.pl.*, munitions de bouche, *f.pl.*, approvisionnements, *m.pl.*, (*law*) dispositif, *m.* *To make — for*, pourvoir à, faire provision pour, faire des préparatifs pour. *To make a — for*, pourvoir aux besoins de, pourvoir à. —*-dealer*, s., —*-warehouse*, s. marchand, *m.*, magasin de comestibles, *m.*
Provision, va. approvisionner
Provisional, adj. provisoire, (*law*) provisionnel
Provisionally, adv. provisoirement, provisionnellement
Provisionary, adj. du dispositif. *The — part*, le dispositif
Proviso, s. clause conditionnelle, *f.* *With a — that*, sous condition que, pourvu que
Provisory, adj. conditionnel, provisoire
Provocation, s. provocation, *f.*, stimulant, *m.*, invitation, *f.*, colère, *f.*, irritation, *f.*
Provocative, adj. qui provoque, qui excite; — s. stimulant, *m.*
Provocativeness, s. nature excitante, *f.*
Provoke, va. provoquer, (*challenge*) défier, exciter, inciter, inviter, irriter, fâcher, impatienter, contrarier, agacer. *What —s me most is, . . .*, ce qui m'irrite le plus c'est que . . .
Provoker, s. provocateur, *m.*, -trice, *f.*
Provoking, adj. irritant, impatientant, contrariant
Provokingly, adv. d'une manière irritante, contrariante, impatientante. *He was so — polite*, (tant) sa politesse me donnait sur les nerfs
Provost, s. prévôt, *m.*, (*univ.*) proviseur, *m.* — *marshal*, s. grand prévôt, *m.*
Provostship, s. prévôté, *f.*, provisorat, *m.*
Prow, s. proue, *f.*
Prowess, s. prouesse, *f.*, vaillance, *f.* *Acts of* —, s. actes de prouesse, *m.pl.*, prouesses, *f.pl.*
Prowl, vn. rôder. *To — about*, rôder dans, rôder partout. —*ing animal*, s. bête de proie, *f.*
Prowl, s. action de rôder, *f.* *To be ever on the* —, être toujours à rôder
Prowler, s. rôdeur, *m.*
Proximate, adj. prochain, immédiat
Proximately, adv. immédiatement
Proximity, s. proximité, *f.*
Proxy, s. procuration, *f.*, délégation, *f.*, (*pers.*) mandataire, *m.*, délégué, *m.*, fondé de pouvoirs, *m.* *By* —, par procuration
Prude, s. prude, *f.*
Prudence, s. prudence, *f.*, sagesse, *f.*
Prudent, adj. prudent, sage. *To be* —, être prudent, avoir de la prudence
Prudential, adj. de prudence, dicté par la prudence
Prudentially, *see* PRUDENTLY
Prudentials, s.pl. maximes de prudence, *f.pl.*
Prudently, adv. avec prudence, prudemment, sagement
Prudery, s. pruderie, *f.*
Prudish, adj. prude
Prudishly, adv. avec pruderie
Prune, va. élaguer, émonder, tailler
Prune, s. pruneau, *m.* *French* —, s. pruneaux, *m.pl.*, pruneaux de Tours, *m.pl.*

Prunello, s. prunelle, *f.*
Pruner, s. élagueur, *m.*
Pruning, s. élagage, *m.*, taille, *f.* — *-hook*, s. — *-bill*, s. serpe, *f.* — *-knife*, s. serpette, *f.* — *-shears*, s. sécateur, *m.*
Pruriency, s. démangeaison, *f.*, désir immodéré, *m.*
Prurient, adj. qui démange, (*fig.*) ardent, brûlant
Prussic, adj. prussique
Pry, vn. fouiller, mettre le nez, fourrer son nez (dans), se mêler (de)
Prying, adj. curieux, inquisiteur, indiscret. *His — temper*, sa curiosité, son indiscrétion
Pryingly, adv. curieusement, avec curiosité
Psalm, s. psaume, *m.* — *-book*, s. psautier, *m.* *To sing —s*, psalmodier, chanter des psaumes
Psalmist, s. psalmiste, *m.*
Psalmodize, vn. psalmodier
Psalmody, s. psalmodie, *f.*
Psalter, s. psautier, *m.*
Pseudo, adj. pseudo- . . . , faux
Pseudonym, s. pseudonyme, *m.*
Pseudonymous, adj. pseudonyme
Pshaw! interj. bah! fi donc!
Psychologic, Psychological, adj. psychologique
Psychologically, adv. d'après la psychologie
Psychologist, s. psychologue, *m.*, psychologiste, *m.*
Psychology, s. psychologie, *f.*
Puberty, s. puberté, *f.*
Pubescence, s. âge de puberté, *f.*
Pubescent, adj. arrivé à l'âge de puberté, pubère
Public, adj. public. — *-house*, s. cabaret, *m.*, auberge, *f.*
Publican, s. (*hist.*) publicain, *m.*, cabaretier, *m.*, aubergiste, *m.*
Publication, s. publication, *f.*
Publicist, s. publiciste, *m.*
Publicity, s. publicité, *f.*
Publicly, adv. publiquement
Publish, va. publier, éditer
Publisher, s. éditeur, *m.*
Puce, adj. puce
Puck, s. lutin, *m.*
Pucker, va. rider, (*clothes*) froncer, plisser. *To — up one's eyebrows*, froncer les sourcils
Pucker, s. ride, *f.*, pli, *m.*, poche, *f.*
Pudding, s. (*black*) boudin, *m.* *Apple —*, s. pudding aux pommes, *m.* *Black —*, s. boudin noir, *m.* *Hasty —*, s. bouillie, *f.*
Puddle, s. mare d'eau, *f.*, flaque d'eau, *f.*, (*constr.*) corroi, *m.* *A storm in a —*, une tempête dans un verre d'eau
Puddle, va. rendre trouble *or* bourbeux, (*constr.*) corroyer, (*metal*) puddler
Puddler, s. puddleur, *m.*
Puddling, s. puddlage, *m.* — *furnace*, four à puddler
Puerile, adj. puéril
Puerility, s. puérilité, *f.*
Puff, s. (*breath*) souffle, *m.*, (*wind*) bouffée, *f.*, rafale, *f.*, (*smoke*) bouffée, *f.*, (*cake*) gâteau léger, *m.*, chou, *m.*, (*powder*) houppe à poudrer, *f.*, (*of a dress*) bouillon, *m.*, (*advertisement*) pouf, *m.*, puff, *m.* — *-paste*, s. pâte feuilletée, *f.*
Puff, vn.a. (*blow*) souffler, (*cheeks*) gonfler ses joues, (*pant*) haleter, (*boast*) faire ses embarras, faire de l'étalage, (*advertise*) se faire mousser, faire l'article. *To — away*, s'en aller soufflant, lancer des bouffées. *—ing and blowing*, tout essoufflé, tout haletant. *To — up with*, bouffer de, bouffir de
Puffiness, s. bouffissure, *f.*, boursouflure, *f.*, enflure, *f.*
Puffing, s. action de souffler, *f.*, pouf, *m.*
Puffingly, adv. avec enflure, avec boursouflure, en haletant
Puffy, adv. enflé, bouffi, boursouflé
Pug, s. (*dog*) roquet, *m.*, carlin, *m.*, bichon, *m.* — *-faced*, adj. à figure de singe. — *-nose*, s. nez épaté, *f.*, museau épaté, *f.*
Pugilism, s. pugilat, *m.*
Pugilist, s. pugiliste, *m.*, boxeur, *m.*
Pugnacious, adj. batailleur, d'humeur batailleuse
Pugnacity, s. humeur batailleuse, *f.*, disposition querelleuse, *f.*, pugnacité, *f.*
Puisne, adj. inférieur
Puissance, s. puissance, *f.*
Puissant, adj. puissant
Puke, vn. vomir, baver
Pule, vn. piauler
Puling, adj. piauleur, -euse, piaulard, -e
Puling, s. piaulement, *m.*
Pull, va.n. tirer, traîner, faire tomber, (*gather*) cueillir, (*tear*) arracher (à), déchirer. *To — into pieces*, mettre en pièces, déchirer. *To — the door*, tirer la porte. *He'll — your ear for you*, il vous tirera les oreilles. *To — the oars*, manier les avirons. *To — a stroke*, donner un coup de rame. *To — about*, tirailler, tirer, traîner çà et là. *To — apart*, séparer. *To — along*, traîner après soi, entraîner. *To — away*, arracher, entraîner. *To — back*, tirer en arrière, faire reculer. *To — down*, tirer en bas, abaisser, descendre, démolir, renverser. *To — off*, (*boots*) ôter, (*to tear*) arracher de, enlever de, faire descendre, (*print.*) tirer. *To — on*, tirer, mettre, entraîner. *To — out*, tirer, faire sortir, produire, montrer. *To — together*, s'entendre. *To — to*, (*the door*) fermer, tirer. *To — up*, tirer en haut, faire monter, arracher, déraciner, extirper, (*scold*) gronder
Pull, s. action de tirer, *f.*, secousse, *f.*, tiraillement, *m.*, (*bell, &c.*) coup, *m.*, (*oars*) action de ramer, *f.* *Give him a —*, tirez-le. *To give a violent — at the bell*, donner un grand coup de sonnette. *To have a good —*, faire une bonne partie de canot
Pull-back, s. obstacle, *m.*, mécompte, *m.*
Puller, s. personne qui tire
Pullet, s. poulette, *f.* *Fat —*, s. poularde, *f.*
Pulley, s. poulie, *f.*
Pulmonary, adj. pulmonaire
Pulmonic, adj. (*things*) pulmonique, (*pers.*) phtisique
Pulp, s. pulpe, *f.*, (*for paper*) pâte, *f.*
Pulpit, s. chaire, *f.*, tribune, *f.* *In the —*, en chaire. *To go up into the —*, monter en chaire. — *eloquence*, s. — *oratory*, s. l'éloquence de la chaire, *f.* — *orator*, s. orateur sacré, *m.*, prédicateur, *m.*
Pulpous, Pulpy, adj. pulpeux
Pulsation, s. pulsation, *f.*
Pulse, s. pouls, *m.*, pulsation, *f.*, légume, *m.*, (*bot.*) plante légumineuse, *f.*
Pulverization, s. pulvérisation, *f.*
Pulverize, va. pulvériser
Pumice, s. ponce, *f.*, pierre ponce, *f.*
Pumice, va. poncer
Pump, s. pompe, *f.*, (*shoe*) escarpin, *m.* *Barrel of a —*, s. corps de pompe, *m.* *Lift and force —*, pompe aspirante et foulante (*see* Forcing). — *-gear*, s. garniture de pompe, *f.*
Pump, va. pomper, (*question*) sonder, tirer les vers du nez de. *To — out*, pomper. *To — the water out of a mine*, épuiser l'eau d'une mine. *To — dry*, tirer (de quelqu'un) tout ce qu'il sait
Pumpion, Pumpkin, s. potiron, *m.*, citrouille, *f.*, courge, *f.*
Pun, s. calembour, *m.*, pointe, *f.* *To make —s*, faire des calembours
Pun, vn. faire des calembours
Punch, va. percer, (*to strike*) cogner, donner un coup de poing à. *To — out*, briser
Punch, s. poinçon, *m.*, emporte-pièce, *m.*, (*blow*) coup de poing, *m.*, (*drink*) punch, *m.*, (*show*) Polichinelle, *m.*
Puncheon, s. (*measure*) tonneau, *m.*, (*instrument*) poinçon, *m.*
Punchinello, s. polichinelle, *m.*
Punctilio, s. formalité, *f.*, forme, *f.*, vétille, *f.*
Punctilious, adj. pointilleux, susceptible
Punctiliously, adv. scrupuleusement, minutieusement
Punctiliousness, s. caractère pointilleux, *f.*, attention minutieuse, *f.*
Punctual, adj. ponctuel, exact
Punctuality, s. ponctualité, *f.*, exactitude, *f.*
Punctually, adv. ponctuellement
Punctuate, va. ponctuer
Punctuation, s. ponctuation, *f.*
Puncture, s. piqûre, *f.*, (*surgery*) ponction, *f.*
Pungence, Pungency, s. âcreté, *f.*, goût piquant *or* fort, *m.*, (*fig.*) piquant, *m.*
Pungent, adj. piquant, (*grief*) poignant, cuisant
Pungently, adv. d'une manière piquante
Punic, adj. punique
Puniness, s. nature chétive, *f.*
Punish, va. punir, châtier. *To — oneself*, se punir. *To have a boy —ed*, faire punir un enfant. *To get —ed*, se faire punir, faire punir
Punishable, adj. punissable
Punisher, s. personne qui punit, vengeur, *m.*
Punishment, s. punition, *f.*, châtiment, *m.*, peine, *f.* *Capital —*, s. peine de mort, *f.*
Punster, s. faiseur de calembours, *m.*
Punt, s. ras, *m.*, bateau plat, *m.*
Punt, vn. (*play*) ponter
Punter, s. ponte, *m.*
Puny, adj. chétif, faible
Pup, vn. mettre bas
Pup, s. jeune chien *or* chienne, *m.f.*
Pupil, s. (*eye*) pupille, *f.*, (*scholar*) élève, *m.f.*, écolier, *m.*, -ère, *f.*, (*law*) pupille, *m.f.*
Pupilage, s. état d'élève, *m.*, (*law*) minorité, *f.*
Pupillary, adj. pupillaire
Puppet, s. poupée, *f.*, marionnette, *f.* — *-master*, s. maître d'un spectacle de marionnettes, *m.* — *-play*, s. comédie de marionnettes, *f.* — *-player*, s. joueur de marionnettes, *m.* — *-show*, s. spectacle de marionnettes, *f.*
Puppy, s. jeune chien *or* chienne, *m.f.*, (*person*) freluquet, *m.*, faquin, *m.*, fat, *m.*
Puppyism, s. fatuité, *f.*
Pur *or* **Purr,** vn. faire ron-ron, filer

Pur, s. ron-ron, *m.*, rouet, *m.*

Purblind, adj. ayant la vue basse, myope

Purchase, va. acheter, faire l'achat de, acquérir. *To — out*, racheter

Purchase, s. achat, *m.*, emplette, *f.*, acquisition, *f.* *— -money*, s. prix d'achat, *m.* *— -deed*, s. contrat d'achat, *m.*

Purchaser, s. acheteur, *m.*, acquéreur, *m.*

Pure, adj. pur, franc

Purely, adv. purement, avec pureté, simplement

Pureness, s. pureté, *f.*

Purgation, s. purgation, *f.*, purification, *f.*

Purgative, adj. purgatif

Purgative, s. purgatif, *m.*, purgation, *f.*

Purgatory, s. purgatoire, *m.*

Purge, va. purger, épurer, purifier, nettoyer, débarrasser; — vn. se purger

Purge, Purging, s. purgation, *f.*

Purification, s. purification, *f.*

Purifier, s. qui purifie, purificateur, *m.*

Purify, va. purifier, épurer, (*a liquid*) clarifier; — vn. se purifier, s'épurer, se clarifier

Purism, s. purisme, *m.*

Purist, s. puriste, *m.f.*

Puritan, s. adj. puritain, -e

Puritanical, adj. de puritain

Puritanism, s. puritanisme, *m.*

Purity, s. pureté, *f.*

Purl, s. murmure, *m.*, (*drink*) ale épicée et mêlée de genièvre, *f.*

Purl, vn. murmurer, onduler

Purlieus, s. limites, *f.pl.*, alentours, *m.pl.*

Purling, s. murmure, *m.*

Purloin, va.n. voler, dérober, soustraire

Purloining, s. vol, *m.*

Purple, s. pourpre, *f.*

Purple, adj. de pourpre, pourpre, rouge, (*med.*) pourpré

Purple, va. teindre en pourpre, empourprer

Purport, s. but, *m.*, objet, *m.*, sens, *m.*, valeur, *f.*, portée, *f.* *The — of your visit*, le but de votre visite. *And other words to the same —*, et d'autres mots dans le même sens

Purport, va. signifier, vouloir dire, tendre à montrer, paraître. *A bill —ing to be drawn at London*, un effet qui, d'après sa teneur, paraît avoir été tiré à Londres

Purpose, s. but, *m.*, objet, *m.*, fin, *f.*, intention, *f.*, dessein, *m.*, avantage, *m.*, (*want*) besoin, *m.* usage, *m.* *A fixed —*, un dessein bien arrêté. *His — was to leave him there*, il se proposait de l'y laisser. *And much more to the same —*, et beaucoup d'autres choses qui revenaient au même. *For the —*, dans ce but, à cet effet. *On —, of —*, exprès, exprès (pour), dans le but (de). *To speak to the —*, parler utilement, parler sans ambages. *To answer the —*, faire l'affaire. *Nothing to the —*, rien d'utile, rien à propos. *To no —*, en pure perte. *To what —?* à quoi bon? à quoi sert? *To (some) —*, efficacement, utilement

Purpose, va.n. se proposer, avoir l'intention, avoir le dessein, avoir en vue

Purposedly, Purposely, adv. à dessein, exprès, de propos délibéré

Purposeless, adj. sans but, inutile

Purse, s. bourse, *f.* *A silk —*, une bourse de soie. *An empty —, a well-lined —*, une bourse plate, bien garnie. *To have the same —, one —*, faire bourse commune. *To hold, to draw the — -strings*, tenir, serrer les cordons de la bourse. *— -bearer*, s. porte-bourse, *m.* *— -proud*, adj. fier de son argent

Purse (up), va. mettre dans sa bourse, embourser, (*to pucker*) plisser, froncer

Purser, s. agent comptable, *m.*

Purslain, s. pourpier, *m.* *— -tree*, s. portulacaire, *f.*

Pursuance, s. poursuite, *f.*, conséquence, *f.*, effet, *m.* *In — of*, conformément à, en vertu de

Pursuant, adj. (*to*) en conséquence (de), conformément (à), en vertu (de)

Pursue, va.n. poursuivre, suivre, continuer, (*to seek*) rechercher

Pursuit, s. poursuite, *f.*, recherche, *f.*, quête, *f.*, (*business*) emploi, *m.* *—s*, pl. carrière, *f.*, occupation, *f.*, travaux, *m.pl.* *To send, to set out in — of*, mettre, se mettre à la poursuite de. *To carry on, to follow up the —*, continuer la poursuite. *In the — of*, à la poursuite de, à la recherche de. *In his — after knowledge*, dans ses efforts pour s'instruire. *Commercial —s*, la carrière commerciale. *To engage in scientific —*, embrasser la carrière des sciences. *His literary —s*, ses travaux littéraires. *He followed up all these —s at the same time*, il menait de front tous ces travaux. *A very pleasant —*, une occupation des plus agréables

Pursy, adj. qui à l'haleine courte, gros et poussif. *A — fellow*, un gros poussif

Purtenance, s. intestins, *m.pl.*, fressure, *f.*

Purulence, Purulency, s. purulence, *f.*

Purulent, adj. purulent

Purvey, va. pourvoir, se procurer, obtenir

Purveyance, s. approvisionnement, *m.*, provisions, *f.pl.*

Purveyor, s. pourvoyeur, *m.*, -euse, *f.*

Pus, s. pus, *m.*

Push, va.n. pousser, repousser, (*to strike*) frapper, (*to carry*) porter. *To — hard*, pousser ferme. *To — us from our chairs*, pour nous repousser de nos chaises. *To — one's fortunes*, se pousser, pousser sa fortune. *To — the interests of*, avancer les intérêts de. *To — an objection too far*, pousser une objection trop loin. *Ambition —es the soul to great actions*, l'ambition porte l'âme à faire de grandes actions. *We are —ed for an answer*, on nous presse de répondre. *To — away*, repousser, éloigner. *To — back*, repousser, faire reculer. *To — down*, renverser, faire tomber. *To — forward*, pousser en avant, avancer. *To — oneself forward*, se pousser, faire son chemin. *To — in or into*, faire entrer (dans). *To — on*, pousser, faire avancer rapidement, hâter

Push, s. poussée, *f.*, coup, *m.*, impulsion, *f.* attaque, *f.*, effort, *m.*, moment difficile, *m.*, circonstance critique, *f.*, besoin, *m.* *To give a — to*, pousser. *At one —*, d'un seul coup. *— of pike*, coup de pique, *m.* *At a —, in a —*, dans une extrémité, à l'heure du besoin, au moment critique. *When it comes to the —*, quand on vient au fait et au prendre

Pushing, adj. entreprenant, énergique

Pusillanimity, s. pusillanimité, *f.*

Pusillanimous, adj. pusillanime

Pusillanimously, adv. avec pusillanimité

Puss, Pussy, s. minet, *m.*, minette, *f.*, chat, *m.*, chatte, *f.*, (*hare*) lièvre, *m.* *To play at — in the corner*, jouer aux quatre coins

Pustule, s. pustule, *f.*

Pustulous, adj. pustuleux

Put, va.n. mettre, poser, placer, appliquer, employer, demander, faire, (*question, &c.*) poser, mettre en avant, proposer, exprimer, (*to compel*) forcer, pousser, contraindre, porter, engager. *And there he — the man whom he had formed*, et c'est là qu'il mit l'homme qu'il avait formé. *To — a person to work*, mettre une personne à travailler. *— him his task*, donnez-lui sa tâche. *To — linen to dry*, mettre sécher du linge. *To — in doubt*, mettre en doute, faire douter. *To — oneself*, se mettre. *— it far from you*, éloignez-le de vous. *— it on the table*, mettez-le, posez-le sur la table. *The use they — their faculties to*, l'usage qu'ils font de leurs facultés. *Now I — it to you whether ...* maintenant je vous demande si ... *We are not —ting cases of dishonest men*, nous ne supposons pas le cas d'hommes sans probité. *That is the way I should — it*, voilà comme, moi, je l'exprimerais. *You — things so pleasantly*, vous présentez les choses sous un aspect si agréable. *If I had been — to it*, si j'y avais été contraint, si l'on m'y avait poussé, si l'on m'en avait pressé. *I — the mare fairly at it*, j'y poussai vivement la jument. *To — about*, faire circuler, faire passer, faire déranger. *To — again*, remettre. *To — away*, (*lock up*) serrer, éloigner, (*send away*) renvoyer, répudier. *To — back*, remettre, reculer, (*nav.*) rentrer au port. *To — by*, mettre de côté, économiser, repousser, détourner, écarter, serrer. *To — down*, déposer, faire descendre, humilier, réprimer, (*answer*) confondre, réfuter, faire taire, (*writing*) mettre par écrit, inscrire. *To — forth*, (*fig.*) étendre, proposer, avancer, mettre en avant, (*leaves, &c.*) pousser, (*display*) déployer, montrer, exercer. *To — forward*, mettre en avant, avancer, pousser, presser. *To — in*, mettre dans or en, serrer, faire entrer, introduire, placer, (*nav.*) entrer au port, relâcher à, (*law*) donner, fournir. *To — in for*, offrir pour, se mettre sur les rangs. *To — off*, ôter, se dépouiller de, mettre de côté, quitter, renvoyer, remettre, différer, accréditer, (*nav.*) pousser au large. *To — on or upon*, mettre sur, revêtir, prendre, se donner, (*ascribe*) imputer à, attribuer à, mettre sur le compte de, imposer à. *To — upon*, (*fig.*) en imposer à, tromper, se jouer de. *To — out*, mettre dehors, mettre, expulser, (*money*) placer, (*fire*) éteindre, (*eyes*) crever, (*plants*) pousser, (*stretch*) étendre, avancer, alonger, (*display*) déployer, (*annoy*) gêner, déranger, déconcerter, mettre de mauvaise humeur, fâcher. *To — over*, mettre dessus de, faire passer par-dessus (*postpone*) différer, remettre. *To — to*, ajouter à, (*horses, &c.*) atteler à, (*puzzle, &c.*) embarrasser, gêner. *To — together*, joindre, mettre ensemble, réunir, (*machines*) remonter. *To — up*, lever, mettre en haut, fixer, mettre en place, (*prayers*) adresser, présenter, mettre (aux enchères), offrir, (*conceal*) cacher, serrer, mettre de côté, (*sword*) rengainer, (*pack up*) emballer, empaqueter. *To — a person up to a thing*, initier quelqu'un à quelque chose. *To — up* *with*, souffrir, supporter, endurer, pardonner, s'accommoder de, s'arranger de, se contenter de

Putative, adj. putatif

Putlog, s. boulin, *m.*

Put-off, s. excuse, *f.*, défaite, *f.*

Put-on, s. duperie, *f.*

Putrefaction, s. putréfaction, *f.*

Putrefactive, adj. putréfactif, de putréfaction

Putrefy, va. putréfier, corrompre, se putréfier

Putrescence, s. état de putréfaction, *m.*

Putrescent, adj. en état de putréfaction

Putrid, adj. putride

Putridity, s. putridité, *f.*

Putty, s. mastic, *m.*

Puzzle, va. embarrasser, embrouiller

Puzzle, s. embarras, *m.*, énigme, *f.*, jeu de patience, *m.*

Pygmy, s. pygmée, *m.*

Pyramid, s. pyramide, *f.*

Pyramidal, adj. pyramidal

Pyramidically, adv. en pyramide

Pyre, s. bûcher, *m.*

Pyrite, Pyrites, s. pyrite, *f.*

Pyrotechnic, Pyrotechnical, adj. pyrotechnique

Pyrotechnics, Pyrotechny, s. pyrotechnie, *f.*

Pyrotechnist, s. artificier, *m.*

Pyrrho, s. Pyrrhon, *m.*

Pyrrhonic, adj. pyrrhonien

Pyrrhonism, s. pyrrhonisme, *m.*

Pyrrhonist, s. pyrrhonien, *m.*, -enne, *f.*

Pythagorean, adj. pythagoricien, de Pythagore

Pythian, adj. pythien, -enne

Pythoness, s. pythonisse, *f.*

Pythonic, adj. de devin

Pythonist, s. devin, *m.*

Pyx, s. ciboire, *m.*

Q

Q, s. Q, q, *m.*

Quack, vn. nasiller

Quack, s. cri, *m.*, charlatan, *m.*, empirique, *m.*, vendeur d'orviétan, *m.*, hâbleur, *m.* — *-doctor*, s. charlatan, *m.*, empirique, *m.* — *-medicine*, s. remède de charlatan, *m.*

Quackery, s. charlatanisme, *m.*, charlatanerie, *f.*

Quadragesima, s. carême, *m.*, Quadragésime, *m.*

Quadrangle, s. quadrilatère, *m.*, carré, *m.*

Quadrant, s. quart de cercle, *m.*

Quadrature, s. quadrature, *f.*, carré, *m.* *The — of the circle*, la quadrature du cercle

Quadrilateral, adj. quadrilatère

Quadrilateral, s. quadrilatère, *m.*

Quadrille, s. quadrille, *m.*, contredanse, *f.*

Quadroon, s. quarteron, *m.*, -ne, *f.*

Quadruped, adj. quadrupède

Quadruple, va. quadrupler

Quaff, va. boire à grands traits, ingurgiter

Quaffer, s. buveur, *m.*

Quaggy, adj. marécageux

Quagmire, s. fondrière, *f.*, marécage, *m.*

Quail, vn. faiblir, perdre courage, se décourager

Quail, s. caille, *f.* *Young —*, s. cailleteau, *m.* — *-call*, — *-pipe*, s. courcaillet, appeau pour attirer les cailles, *m.* — *-fighting*, combat de cailles, *m.*

Quaint, adj. agréable, élégant, ingénieux, subtil, recherché, prétentieux, affecté, singulier, original, fantasque

Quaintly, adv. avec élégance, gentiment, avec exactitude, subtilement, bizarrement, fantasquement

Quaintness, s. élégance, *f.*, bizarrerie, *f.*, originalité, *f.*

Quake, vn. trembler, frémir, frissonner, chanceler

Quake, s. tremblement, *m.*, frisson, *m.*

Quaker, Quakeress, s. trembleur, *m.*, -euse, *f.*, (*relig.*) quaker, *m.*, quakeresse, *f.*

Quakerish, adj. de quaker

Quakerism, Quakery, s. la doctrine, la discipline des quakers, *f.*

Quaking, s. tremblement, *m.*, frémissement, *m.*, trépidation, *f.*, convulsion, *f.*

Quaking, adj. tremblant, mouvant. — *-bog*, s. fondrière, *f.*, tourbière, *f.* — *grass*, s. brize, *f.*

Quakingly, adv. tout tremblant

Qualifiable, adj. qu'on peut rendre propre *or* apte à, qui peut être mitigé, adouci, qu'on peut modifier

Qualification, s. préparation, *f.*, qualité, *f.*, condition, *f.*, aptitude, *f.*, talent, *m.*, capacité, *f.*, modification, *f.*, réduction, *f.*, diminution, *f.*

Qualify, va. rendre capable (de), rendre propre *or* apte (à), préparer (pour *or* à), (*law*) habiliter, donner pouvoir *or* qualité, mettre à même (de), mettre en état, modérer, atténuer, diminuer, restreindre, alléger, soulager, moduler, faire des variations. *With a view of —ing me for holy orders*, afin de me préparer à entrer dans les ordres. *To — them for the pleasures of that happy place*, pour les disposer à goûter le bonheur de cet heureux séjour. *To be qualified for* avoir les qualités requises pour, avoir tout ce qu'il faut pour. *Qualified approval*, approbation restreinte

Quality, s. qualité, *f.*, nature, *f.*, condition, *f.*

Qualm, s. nausée, *f.*, soulèvement de cœur, *m.*, malaise, *m.*, remords, *m.*, scrupule de conscience, *m.* *To feel some —s of conscience*, avoir des remords de conscience

Qualmish, adj. qui a envie de vomir, sujet aux nausées

Quandary, s. doute, *m.*, incertitude, *f.*, difficulté, *f.*, perplexité, *f.* *To be in a —*, être terriblement embarrassé

Quantitative, adj. appréciable, quantitatif

Quantity, s. quantité, *f.*, foule, *f.*, multitude, *f.*, abondance, *f.*, portion, *f.*, partie, *f.*

Quantum, s. total, *m.*, montant, *m.*

Quarantine, s. quarantaine, *f.*

Quarrel, s. querelle, *f.*, dispute, *f.*, altercation, *f.*, débat, *m.*, démêlé, *m.*, différend, *m.*, (*arrow*) carreau, *m.*, flèche, *f.* *They debate their —s*, ils agitent leurs différends. *In our last —*, lors de notre dernière querelle. *Their little —s*, leurs petites querelles, leurs bisbilles, leurs picoteries. *To rise to a —*, dégénérer en querelle. *To pick a — with*, chercher chicane *or* querelle à, chercher noise à, faire un procès à. *A man who hastens to pick a — with others that they may not have time to pick one with him*, un homme qui le premier fait un procès aux autres, afin qu'on n'ait pas le temps de lui faire le sien. *To come to a —*, en venir à une brouillerie. *Drunken —*, rixe d'ivrognes. *To remove all ground of —*, écarter tout motif de discorde. *To avenge a —*, venger une injure

Quarrel, vn. se quereller, se disputer, se chamailler, se chicaner, gronder, faire des reproches à, (*find fault*) trouver à redire (à), critiquer

Quarreller, s. querelleur, *m.*, -euse, *f.*

Quarrelling, s. querelle, *f.*, dispute, *f.*

Quarrelsome, adj. querelleur, batailleur, irascible, emporté. *Ill-natured and — when drunk, or in their drink*, méchants et querelleurs quand ils ont bu

Quarry, s. (*prey*) proie, *f.*, curée, *f.*, carrière, *f.* — *man*, s. ouvrier carrier, *m.*

Quart, s. quatrième partie, *f.*, (*measure*) litre, *m.*, (*cards*) quatrième, *f.*

Quartan, s. quart, *m.* — *ague*, or *a —*, fièvre quarte or quartaine, *f.*

Quarter, s. quart, *m.*, quatrième partie, *f.*, quartier, *m.*, (*year*) trimestre, *m.*, (*meat, shore, &c.*) quartier, *m.*, (*mil.*) quartier, *m.*, cantonnement, *m.*, garnison, *f.*, (*in battle*) merci, *f.* *In southern —s*, dans les régions du sud. *In what — is the wind?* de quel côté vient le vent? *The four —s of the globe*, les quatre parties du monde. *In that — of the town*, dans ce quartier *or* dans cette partie de la ville. *To come from all —s*, arriver de tous côtés. *You have nothing to fear from that —*, vous n'avez rien à craindre de ce côté. *From the same —*, du même côté, de la même part, de la même source. *To apply in the proper —*, s'adresser bien, s'adresser à qui de droit. *He was fearful of giving pain in any —*, il craignait de faire de la peine à qui que ce fût. *It was objected to in some very high moral —s*, on y trouva à redire dans de certaines régions où l'on se targue d'une haute moralité. *In high —*, en haut lieu, chez les grands. *Having sufficiently teased him in that —*, l'ayant assez tourmenté de ce côté. *To go into winter —s*, prendre ses quartiers d'hiver. *Pleasant —*, garnison agréable. *Free —s*, droit au logement. *All hands to —s*, chacun à son poste. *To beat to —s*, faire branle-bas. *They cannot but admit love, yet they make it keep —*, ils ne peuvent refuser d'admettre l'amour, mais ils se tiennent en garde contre lui. *To cry for —*, demander quartier. *To give no —*, ne point faire quartier. *Take —*, acceptez la vie. — *-day*, s. jour de terme, *m.*

— *deck*, s. gaillard d'arrière, *m.*, tillac, *m.* — *-face*, s. visage vu de profil. — *-master*, s. (*mil.*) quartier-maître, *m.*, maréchal des logis, *m.* —*'s rent*, s. —*'s pay*, s. terme, *m.*, quartier, *m.*, trimestre, *m.* — *-sessions*, s. cour trimestrielle de comté, *f.* — *staff*, s. bâton à deux bouts, *m.* — *-staff-player*, s. bâtoniste, *m.*

Quarter, va.n. diviser en quatre, diviser par quartiers, (*punishment*, &c.) écarteler, (*troops*) loger, mettre en quartier, (*herald*) écarteler

Quartering, s. division en quatre parties, *f.*, écartèlement, *m.*, logement, *m.*, cantonnement, *m.*, (*herald*) écartelure, *f.*

Quarterly, adj. contenant *or* qui est le quart de, trimestriel

Quarterly, adv. une fois tous les trois mois, par trimestre

Quartern, s. (*liquids*) quart, *m.*, (*pop.*) canon, *m.*, pain de quatre livres, *m.* *A half- — loaf*, un pain de deux livres

Quartet, s. quatuor, *m.*

Quarto, s. adj. in-quarto, *m.*

Quartz, s. quartz, *m.*

Quartz, adj. de quartz

Quash, va. écraser, aplatir, (*subdue*) dompter, subjuguer, (*law*) annuler, casser, faire cesser

Quatrain, s. quatrain, *m.*

Quaver, vn. chevroter, trembler, faire des roulades *or* des trilles

Quaver, **Quavering**, chevrotement, *m.*, roulade, *f.*, trille, *m.*, cadence, *f.*, (*mus.*) croche, *f.* — *-rest*, s. demi-soupir, *m.* *Demi — -rest*, s. quart de soupir, *m.*

Quay, s. quai, *m.*

Queasiness, s. nausées, *f.pl.*

Queasy, adj. ayant mal au cœur, malade, nauséabond, dégoûté, difficile, délicat

Queen, s. reine, *f.*, (*cards*) dame, *f.*

Queenly, adj. royal, digne d'une reine, de reine

Queenship, s. majesté, *f.*, dignité de reine, *f.*

Queer, adj. bizarre, étrange, baroque, singulier, capricieux, fantasque, (*ill*) tout je ne sais quoi. — *old town, drawbridged and walled*, vieille ville à l'aspect bizarre, avec pont-levis et murailles. *He was one of the —est-looking boys that I had ever seen*, ce garçon avait une des plus singulières tournures que j'eusse jamais vues. *A — fellow*, un original

Queerly, adv. d'une manière bizarre *or* singulière

Queerness, s. nature bizarre, *f.*, bizarrerie, *f.*, singularité, *f.*, humeur fantasque, *f.*

Quell, va. réprimer, étouffer, apaiser, calmer

Quench, va. éteindre, faire cesser, anéantir, (*thirst*) étancher, (*fig.*) apaiser, calmer, tempérer, amortir. *To — one's thirst*, étancher sa soif, se désalterer

Quenchless, adj. inextinguible

Querist, s. questionneur, *m.*

Querulous, adj. qui se plaint souvent, chagrin, gémissant, mécontent

Querulously, adv. en se plaignant, dolemment

Querulousness, s. disposition à se plaindre, *f.*, humeur chagrine, *f.*

Query, s. question, *f.*

Query, vn.a. faire des questions, s'informer, questionner

Quest, s. quête, *f.*, recherche, *f.*, poursuite, *f.* *In — of*, à la recherche de, en quête de, à la poursuite de

Question, s. question, *f.*, interrogation, *f.*, demande, *f.*, (*doubt*) doute, *m.*, controverse, *f.*, dispute, *f.*, (*law*) procès, *m.*, enquête, *f.*, (*supplice*) question, *f.*, torture, *f.* *He had the same —s put to him which he had been asked the evening before*, il se vit faire les mêmes questions que celles qui lui avaient été faites la veille au soir. *To ask —s*, faire des questions. *Book of —s*, questionnaire, *m.* *It is a — whether*, c'est à savoir si. *He that can only converse upon —s about which*, celui qui ne sait seulement parler que sur des matières que. *To call in —*, faire qu'on s'occupe de, faire qu'on pense à. *Out of —, beyond all —*, incontestable, hors de doute. *It is quite out of the —*, il ne saurait en être question. *To call into —*, mettre en doute, en question. *Though some necessary — of the play be then to be considered*, bien que quelque point essentiel de la pièce exige alors toute l'attention. *You paid me liberally for the lie in —*, vous m'avez largement payé pour le mensonge dont il s'agit

Question, vn.a. questionner, interroger, se demander, procéder par interrogations, arguments, mettre en doute, douter de, mettre en question, révoquer en doute

Questionable, adj. douteux, incertain, suspect

Questionableness, s. état douteux, *m.*, incertitude, *f.*, indécision, *f.*, état suspect, *m.*

Questionably, adv. avec doute, d'une manière incertaine

Questionary, adj. questionneur, investigateur. — s. colporteur de reliques, *m.*

Questioner, s. interrogateur, *m.*, questionneur, *m.*, interlocuteur, *m.*, examinateur, *m.*

Questor, s. questeur, *m.*

Questorship, s. questure, *f.*

Quibble, s. faux-fuyant, *m.*, moyen évasif, *m.*, argutie, *f.*, chicane, *f.*, (*pun*) quolibet, *m.*, calembour, *m.*, jeu de mots, *m.*

Quibble, vn. jouer sur les mots, chicaner, faire des pointes, des quolibets

Quibbler, s. ergoteur, *m.*, faiseur de quolibets, *m.*, de calembours, *m.*, de pointes, *m.*

Quibbling, *see* Quibble

Quibblingly, adv. d'une manière évasive, en jouant sur les mots

Quick, adj. vite, prompt, leste, rapide, agile, vif, fin, délié, diligent, expéditif, alerte, accéléré, bien portant. *Be — about it*, faites vite, dépêchez-vous. — *and violent motions*, mouvements forts et rapides. *The several generations which rise up and disappear in such — successions*, les nombreuses générations qui s'élèvent et disparaissent dans un cours si rapide. — *eye*, œil vif. — *affections kindling into flame at virtue's name*, ardeur des sentiments dont le nom de la vertu fait briller la flamme. — *pace*, pas accéléré. *The — and the dead*, les vivants et les morts. — *-sand*, sable mouvant. — *-lime*, chaux vive. — *-sighted*, à la vue prompte, pénétrant. — *-witted*, à l'esprit prompt

Quick, adv. vite, promptement, rapidement, avec célérité, lestement. *He walks rather too — for you, don't he?* il marche un peu trop vite pour vous, n'est-ce pas? *Give me a shawl here, —!* donnez-moi un châle, dépêchons!

Quick, s. vivant, vif, ce qui vit

Quicken, va. donner la vie à, donner l'existence à, faire revivre, ressusciter, (*hasten*) dépêcher, hâter, (*rouse*) exciter, stimuler. — *us now*, faites-nous vivre. *He —ed his pace into a kind of trot*, il hâta le pas et se mit à courir. *When his mind was —ed by competition*, lorsque son esprit était stimulé par la rivalité

Quickly, adv. vite, vitement, rapidement, (*soon*) bientôt

Quickness, s. vitesse, *f.*, rapidité, *f.*, vivacité, *f.*, promptitude, *f.*, pénétration, *f.*, sagacité, *f.*

Quickset, s. aubépine, *f.*, plante pour haie, *f.* — *-hedge*, s. haie vive, *f.*

Quicksilver, s. vif-argent, *m.*, mercure, *m.*

Quid, s. chique, *f.*

Quidnunc, s. curieux, *m.*, nouvelliste, *m.*

Quidproquo, s. quiproquo, *m.*

Quiesce, vn. (*letter*) être muette

Quiescence, s. absence de son, *f.*, repos, *m.*, tranquillité, *f.*

Quiescent, adj. en repos, immobile, tranquille, calme, muette

Quiet, adj. calme, paisible, en repos, tranquille, (*unostentatious*) modeste, sans éclat

Quiet, s. immobilité, *f.*, repos, *m.*, tranquillité, *f.*, calme, *m.*

Quiet, va. mettre au repos, apaiser, calmer, tranquilliser, pacifier

Quietism, s. quiétisme, *m.*

Quietist, s. quiétiste, *m.*

Quietly, adv. en repos, au repos, sans mouvement, tranquillement, paisiblement, avec calme

Quietness, s. repos, *m.*, calme, *m.*, tranquillité, *f.*

Quietude, s. repos, *m.*, quiétude, *f.*, tranquillité, *f.*

Quietus, s. coup de grâce, *m.*, coup mortel, *m.* *To make one's —*, se donner le repos. *To get a —*, se faire mettre à la retraite, se faire renvoyer, se faire tuer

Quill, s. plume, *f.*, plume d'oie, *f.*, (*porcupine*) piquant, *m.* *To carry a good —*, écrire bien. — *-pen*, s. plume d'oie, *f.* *Gray goose —*, s. plume d'oie en panache, *f.* — *driver*, s. gratte-papier, *m.* — *-nib*, s. bec de plume, *m.*

Quill, va. tuyauter, rucher

Quilt, s. courte-pointe, *f.*, couvre-pied, *m.*

Quilt, va. piquer

Quilting, s. piqué, *m.*

Quince, s. coing, *m.* — *-tree*, s. cognassier, *m.*

Quincunx, s. quinconce, *m.*

Quinine, s. quinine, *f.*

Quinquagesima, s. Quinquagésime, *f.*

Quinquennial, adj. quinquennal

Quinquina, s. quinquina, *m.*

Quinsy, s. esquinancie, *f.*

Quint, s. quinte, *f.*

Quintessence, s. quintessence, *f.*

Quintet, s. quintette, *m.*

Quintillion, s. quintillion, *m.*

Quintuple, adj. quintuple, de quinte

Quintuple, adj. quintupler

Quip, s. badinage, *f.*, raillerie, *f.*, sarcasme, *m.*, lardon, *m.*

Quip, va. brocarder, railler, accabler de sarcasmes, rétorquer; — vn. se moquer, se railler

Quire, s. main, *f.* *In —s*, en feuilles

Quirk, s. biais, *m.*, subterfuge, *m.*, faux-fuyant, *m.*, saillie, *f.*

Quit, va. quitter, laisser, se séparer de, renoncer à, acquitter, payer. — *my sight!* hors de ma vue! *To — sight of,* perdre de vue. *I insist on your —ting the room directly,* j'exige que vous vous retiriez à l'instant. — *-ting his conductor,* abandonnant son guide. *To — oneself of,* se débarrasser de. *To — you of this fear,* pour vous débarrasser de cette crainte. *To — oneself from,* se décharger, s'affranchir, s'acquitter, reconnaître, récompenser. *To — cost,* s'acquitter, se libérer

Quit, adj. quitte, débarrassé. *To get — of,* se débarrasser de. *To be —,* être quitte. *To be — with,* être quitte avec. *I'll be — with you for this,* vous me le payerez

Quite, adv. tout, tout à fait, entièrement, complètement, pleinement, excessivement, extrêmement. — *otherwise,* tout autrement. — *ready,* tout prêt. *I found myself — recovered,* je me trouvai complètement rétabli. *I am — out of the world,* je ne suis plus du tout de ce monde. — *young,* très-jeune, tout petit

Quits, adv. quitte

Quits! interj. nous voilà quittes!

Quittance, s. quittance, *f.,* libération, *f.,* récompense, *f.,* décharge, *f.,* acquit, *m.,* reçu, *m.,* paiement, *m.*

Quiver, s. carquois, *m.*

Quiver, vn. trembler, frémir, trembloter, frissonner

Quivered, adj. muni d'un carquois

Quivering, s. tremblement, *m.,* frémissement, *m.,* frissonnement, *m.*

Quixotic, adj. de don Quichotte, extravagant

Quixotisme, Quixotry, s. donquichotisme, *m.,* lubie, *f.,* extravagance, *f.*

Quiz, s. mystification, *f.,* plaisanterie, *f.,* (*pers.*) railleur, *m.,* -euse, *f.,* moqueur, *m.,* -euse, *f.*

Quiz, va. mystifier, persifler, dauber, (*to look, &c.*) lorgner

Quoit, s. disque, *m.,* palet, *m.*

Quondam, adj. d'autrefois, ancien, ci-devant

Quorum, s. nombre suffisant. *To form a —,* être en nombre

Quota, s. quote-part, *f.,* contingent, *m.*

Quotation, s. citation, *f.,* (*com.*) cote, *f.,* cours, *m.* *To make a — from,* citer

Quote, va. citer, alléguer, parler de, (*com.*) coter

Quoter, s. citateur, *m.,* qui cite

Quotidian, adj. quotidien

Quotidian, s. (fièvre) quotidienne, *f.*

Quotient, s. quotient, *m.*

R

R, s. R, r, *m.f.*

Rabbet, s. enchevauchure, *f.,* rainure, *f.*

Rabbi, s. rabbin, *f.* *Chief —,* grand rabbin, *m.*

Rabbinic, Rabbinical, adj. rabbinique

Rabbinism, s. rabbinisme, *m.*

Rabbinist, s. rabbiniste, *m.*

Rabbit, s. lapin, *m.* *Young —,* s. lapereau, *m.* *Welsh —,* s. rôtie au fromage, *f.* — *-warren,* s. garenne, *f.* —*'s nest,* s. rabouillère, *f.*

Rabble, s. cohue, *f.,* populace, *f.,* canaille, *f.*

Rabid, adj. enragé, atteint de la rage, furieux

Rabidness, s. rage, *f.*

Race, s. race, *f.,* (*running*) course, *f.,* carrière, *f.,* (*nav.*) ras, *m.,* ras de marée, *m.,* mascaret, *m.* *The Anglo-Saxon —,* la race anglo-saxonne. *A — of colts,* une course de jeunes étalons. — *-ginger,* racine de gingembre. *To begin his —,* commencer sa course. *To run one's —,* fournir sa carrière. *To run a —,* lutter à la course. *To win the —,* gagner le prix de la course (*see* HORSE, FOOT). — *-course,* s. terrain des courses, *m.,* hippodrome, *m.* — *-cup,* s. prix de course, *m.* — *-ground,* s. terrain des courses, *m.* — *-horse,* s. cheval de course, *m.,* coureur, *m.*

Race, vn. lutter à la course

Racer, s. coureur, *m.,* cheval de course, *m.*

Raciness, s. goût du terroir, *m.,* (*wine*) bouquet, *m.,* (*fig.*) caractère distinctif, *m.,* vigueur, *f.*

Racing, *see* RACE

Rack, s. (*torture*) roue, *f.,* chevalet, *m.,* torture, *f.,* tourment, *m.,* (*in compounds*) porte- . . . (*plates*) égoutte-assiettes, *m.,* (*tools, &c.*) râtelier, *m.,* (*liquor*) arack, *m.,* rack, *m.,* (*toothed*) crémaillère, *f.,* (*watches*) rochet, *m.* *To be on the —,* être soumis à la torture, être sur la roue. *To set on the —,* mettre à la torture. *Hat- —,* s. porte-chapeau, *m.* — *-rent,* s. rente égale au revenu, *f.* *To go to — and ruin,* aller à vau l'eau

Rack, va. rouer, mettre à la torture, torturer, tendre, porter au plus haut degré, (*wine*) soutirer. —*ed with deep despair,* abîmé dans le désespoir

Racket, s. raquette, *f.,* (*noise*) tintamarre, *m.,* tapage, *m.,* caquet, *m.*

Racket, vn. faire du tintamarre, faire du tapage

Racketing, s. tapage, *m.*

Rackety, adj. tapageur, bruyant

Racking, s. action de rouer, *f.,* de mettre à la torture, *f.,* tourments, *m.pl.,* (*wine*) soutirage, *m.*

Racy, adj. qui sent le terroir, qui a du bouquet, vigoureux

Radiance, s. rayonnement, *m.,* éclat, *m.,* splendeur, *f.*

Radiant, adj. rayonnant, radieux, radié

Radiate, vn. rayonner, (*med.*) irradier

Radiation, s. rayonnement, *m.,* radiation, *f.,* chaleur, *f.*

Radical, adj. radical

Radicalism, s. radicalisme, *m.*

Radically, adv. radicalement

Radish, s. radis, *m.* — *-bed,* s. ravière, *f.* — *-dish,* s. ravier, *m.,* rayon, *m.,* (*anat.*) radius, *m.*

Raffle, s. loterie, *f.* *To make a —,* faire une loterie

Raffle, vn. mettre en loterie, faire une loterie de, (*for,* pour) prendre des billets

Raft, s. radeau, *m.,* train de bois flottant, *m.* *To make a —,* construire un radeau

Rafter, s. poutre, *f.,* chevron, *m.*

Raftsman, s. flotteur, *m.*

Rag, s. chiffon, *m.,* lambeau, *m.,* (*garments*) haillons, *m.pl.* guenilles, *f.pl.,* loques, *f.pl.* *All in —s and patches,* tout en lambeaux et en pièces. *Woollen —,* chiffon de laine. *To be boiled to —s,* s'en aller en bouillie. — *-dealer,* s. marchand de chiffons, *m.* — *-gatherer,* s. chiffonnier, *m.* — *-fair,* s. marché aux vieux habits, *f.* — *-man,* s. marchand de chiffons, *m.* — *-stone,* s. pierre à aiguiser, *f.*

Ragamuffin, s. gueux, *m.,* goujat, *m.*

Rage, s. fureur, *f.,* rage, *f.,* furie, *f.,* emportement, *m.,* violence, *f.* *Mad with —,* fou de colère, furibond. *To break out into a fit of —,* éclater en fureur. *To be in a —,* être furieux. *To get into a —,* se mettre en fureur, en colère, entrer en furie. *To be all the —,* faire rage

Rage, vn. (*pers.*) être furieux, être en colère *or* en fureur, s'emporter, tempêter, (*wind*) être furieux, être déchaîné, (*passions*) être déchaîné, régner en maître, (*plague*) sévir. *Six days the storm had been raging,* depuis six jours la tempête était déchaînée

Ragged, adj. (*things*) déchiré, en lambeaux, (*pers.*) déguenillé, en guenilles, en haillons, (*rocks*) raboteux, déchiqueté, sauvage, âpre. — *-school,* s. école déguenillée

Raggedly, adv. en guenilles

Raggedness, s. état déguenillé, *m.,* guenilles, *f.pl.,* haillons, *m.pl.,* inégalité, *f.,* nature raboteuse, *f.,* âpreté, *f.*

Raging, adj furieux, déchaîné, en fureur, violent, impétueux, — *mad,* fou à lier. *The — sea,* la mer en fureur. *The — winds,* les vents déchaînés *or* furieux. — *fever,* fièvre ardente

Raging, s. fureur, *f.,* furie, *f.,* déchaînement, *m.,* violence, *f.,* impétuosité, *f.*

Raid, s. incursion, *f.,* irruption, *f.*

Rail, s. barre, *f.,* barreau, *m.* —*s,* pl. grille, *f.,* rampe, *f.,* garde-fou, *m.,* (*baluster*) rampe, (*railway*) chemin de fer, *m.,* (*archit.*) traverse, *f.,* (*bird*) râle, *m.* — *-fence,* s. barrière, *f.* *Guard- —,* s. contre-rail, *m.* — *-car,* s. wagon, *m.* *To run off the —s,* dérailler. *Running off the —s,* déraillement. *To go, to travel by —,* aller, voyager en chemin de fer. —*s of the upper works,* lisses d'accastillage. *Quarter and fore —s,* rails de rabattue. *Upper —s of the stern,* rails du couronnement. — *of the head,* rail d'éperon. *To set the —s,* lisser. *Little —,* listeau, *m.*

Rail, va. griller, fermer avec une grille, entourer d'une grille. *To — in*, fermer avec une grille. *To — off*, séparer par une grille. — vn. railler, se moquer (de), injurier, se déchaîner (contre)

. . . **-Railed.** adj. à . . . voie. *Single-* —, à une seule voie. *Double-* —, à deux voies

Railer, s. railleur, *m.*, -euse, *f.*

Railing, s. raillerie, *f.*, moquerie, *f.*, injures, *f.pl.*, invectives, *f.pl.*, (*enclosure*) grille, *f.*, (*for stairs*) rampe, *f.*, garde-fou, *m.*, parapet, *m.*

Raillery, s. raillerie, *f.* *The art of* —, l'art de la raillerie. *To have a good knack at* —, entendre la raillerie, savoir railler

Railroad, **Railway**, s. chemin de fer, *m.*, voie de fer, *f.*, voie ferrée, *f.* — *-share*, s., — *-bond*, s. action, *f.*, obligation de chemin de fer, *f.* — *-slide*, s., — *-turn-plate*, s. plaque tournante, *f.* — *-station*, s., — *-terminus*, s. station, *f.*, gare de chemin de fer, *f.* — *-guide*, s., — *tables*, s. indicateur des chemins de fer, *m.*

Raiment, s. vêtements, *m.pl.*

Rain, s. pluie, *f.* *We are going to have* —, le temps est à la pluie. *The — is falling*, il pleut, il tombe de la pluie. *To stay out, to stand in the* —, rester à la pluie. *We have had no — all the month*, il n'a pas plu de tout le mois. — *-gauge*, s. pluviomètre, *m.* — *-water*, s. eau de pluie, *f.*, eaux pluviales, *f.pl.*

Rain, vn. pleuvoir, tomber de la pluie, tomber. *The — it —ed every day*, la pluie tombait tous les jours. *It is likely to* —, le temps est à la pluie. *It is going to* —, il va pleuvoir, il va tomber de la pluie *or* de l'eau. *To — hard*, pleuvoir à verse *or* très-fort. *To — down*, pleuvoir. *To — in*, y pleuvoir. *It —ed in*, la pluie entrait. *The rain continued to — on*, la pluie continuait à tomber. *Standing patiently to be —ed on*, recevant patiemment la pluie sur le dos. *Tears —ed at their eyes*, les larmes coulaient de leurs yeux. —va. faire pleuvoir. *To — down*, faire pleuvoir, verser, faire tomber. *If it —ed cats and dogs*, quand même il pleuvrait des hallebardes

Rainbow, s. arc-en-ciel, *m.* *To take all the hues of the* —, s'iriser, prendre toutes les couleurs de l'arc en ciel. *Tinged with the hues of the* —, — *-tinted*, irisé

Rainy, adj. de pluie, pluvieux. *On a — day*, par un jour de pluie. *The — season*, la saison des pluies. — *-weather*, temps de pluie, *m.* — *climate*, climat pluvieux, *m.* *It is* —, *it looks* —, le temps est à la pluie. *The barometer pointed to — weather*, le baromètre était à la pluie

Raise, va. élever, lever, soulever, monter, (*to build*) élever, ériger, construire, (*a mast*) dresser, (*the ground*) exhausser, hausser, (*to excite*) exciter, animer, (*troubles*) susciter, (*questions*) soulever, (*a report*) faire courir, (*a storm*) faire naître, exciter, (*the dead*) ressusciter, (*prices*) hausser, faire monter, (*value*) rehausser, (*troops*) lever, assembler, (*taxes*) lever, (*money*) trouver, se procurer, battre, (*a cry*) pousser, faire entendre, (*cattle*) élever, (*corn, &c.*) cultiver, faire pousser, produire, (*paste*) faire lever, (*a siege*) lever. *To — the wind*, faire souffler le vent, (*fig.*) faire venir l'eau au moulin

Raisin, s. raisin sec. *Figs, nuts, almonds, and —s*, les quatre mendiants

Rake, s. râteau, *m.*, (*pers.*) roué, *m.*, libertin, *m.*, débauché, *m.*

Rake, va.n. ratisser, passer au râteau, racler, (*fig.*) ramasser, fouiller dans, (*mil.*) enfiler, (*the fire*) remuer, dégager. *To — out*, (*the fire*) éteindre. *To — up*, ramasser au râteau, râteler, (*fire*) couvrir, (*conjure up*) réveiller

Raker, s. qui ratisse, (*agric.*) râteleur, *m.* *A — of*, un fureteur de

Raking, s. ratissage, *m.*, raclage, *m.*, râtelage, *m.*, (*mil.*) enfilade, *f.*, (*course of life*) libertinage, *m.*, vie déréglée, *f.*

Raking, adj. qui ratisse, (*mil.*) d'enfilade. — *fire*, s. feu d'enfilade, *m.*, enfilade, *f.*

Rakish, adj. dissolu, débauché

Rakishness, s. mœurs déréglées, *f.pl.*

Rally, va. rallier, réunir, (*senses*) rappeler, (*courage*) reprendre, (*joke*) railler, se railler de, se moquer de; — vn. se rallier, se rassembler, se réunir, se remettre, reprendre ses esprits, ses forces, prendre le dessus, railler, se moquer. *To — back*, se rallier et revenir à la charge. *His constitution was unable to* —, sa constitution ne put prendre le dessus

Rally, **Rallying**, s. ralliement, *m.*, recouvrement, *m.*, raillerie, *f.*

Rallying, adj. de ralliement. — *point*, s., — *sign*, s., — *word*, s. point, *m.*, signe, *m.*, mot de ralliement, *m.*

Ram, s. bélier, *m.* *Water-* —, s. bélier hydraulique, *m.*

Ram, va. enfoncer, (*fire-arms*) bourrer, (*fig.*) bourrer, remplir. *To — in*, enfoncer. *To — down*, renfoncer, battre. *To — up*, fermer

Ramble, vn. errer, se promener, flâner, rôder, faire des courses, des excursions, (*fig.*) divaguer. *To — about*, errer çà et là. *To — over*, parcourir. *To — from the point*, divaguer

Ramble, s. promenade, *f.*, excursion, *f.*, course, *f.* *To take a* —, faire une promenade, se promener

Rambler, s. promeneur, *m.*, -euse, *f.*, voyageur, *m.*, (*fig.*) discoureur sans suite, *m.*

Rambling, s. excursions, *f.pl.*, courses, *f.pl.*, promenades, *f.pl.*, divagations, *f.pl.*

Rambling, adj. errant, vagabond, de voyage, plein de divagations, décousu. *My — propensities*, mon goût pour les voyages. — *thoughts*, pensées vagabondes. — *talk*, conversation décousue, de pures divagations

Ramblingly, adv. d'une manière vagabonde, en vagabond, d'une manière décousue

Ramification, s. ramification, *f.*

Ramify, vn. se ramifier; — va. diviser en ramifications

Rammer, s. (*gun*) baguette, (*artil.*) écouvillon, *m.*, (*paviour's*) hie, *f.*, (*machine*) mouton, *m.*

Ramp, vn. grimper, sauter

Ramp, s. élan, *m.*, saut, *m.*, (*mil.*) rampe, *f.*

Rampant, adj. vigoureux, exubérant, dominant, effréné, rampant

Rampart, s. rempart, *m.*

Rampion, s. raiponce, *f.*

Ramrod, s. baguette, *f.*

Rancid, adj. rance. *To grow, to get* —, rancir, devenir rance. *To smell* —, sentir le rance

Rancidity, **Rancidness**, s. rancidité, *f.*

Rancorous, adj. rancuneux, haineux

Rancorously, adv. avec rancune, avec haine, par haine

Rancour, s. rancune, *f.*, ressentiment, *m.*, haine, *f.* *To bear no* —, ne point garder rancune à. *Out of — to*, par haine pour

Random, s. hasard, *m.*, (*artil.*) portée à toute volée, *f.* *At* —, au hasard, à l'aventure, à tort et à travers

Random, adj. au hasard. — *shot*, s. coup perdu, *m.*

Range, s. rangée, *f.*, (*mountain*) chaîne, *f.*, (*ladder*) échelon, *m.*, (*kitchen*) fourneau, *f.*, (*travel*) voyage, *m.*, excursion, *f.*, (*extent*) étendue, *f.*, (*fire-arms*) portée, *f.* — *of beings*, ordre d'êtres. *To take a — over or of*, parcourir. *The — of thought*, l'étendue de la pensée, *f.* *Creation's ample* —, le vaste champ de la création. *My — of reading*, le cours de mes lectures. *To extend one's — of observation*, étendre le cercle de ses observations. *Within* —, à portée de canon, à portée de fusil. *To make a — of cable*, prendre une bitture de câble

Range, va. arranger, ranger, aligner, (*go over*) parcourir, errer librement dans. *To — oneself under*, se ranger sous. *To — the air, the forest*, parcourir, errer librement dans les airs, la forêt. *To — the world*, parcourir le monde. — vn. errer librement, vagabonder, être rangé, être au nombre de, s'étendre. *To — about*, errer çà et là, parcourir. *To — along the coast*, ranger la côte

Ranger, s. garde forestier, *m.*, (*soldier*) chasseur, *m.*

Rangership, s. emploi de garde forestier, *m.*

Ranging, s. vie errante, *f.*, courses, *f.pl.*, excursions, *f.pl.*, arrangement, *m.*, alignement, *m.*

Rank, adj. vigoureux, luxuriant, fort, (*smell*) sentant fort, rance, (*excessive*) excessif, violent, (*coarse*) grossier. — *grass*, s. herbe haute et touffue. *The rankest weeds*, les (mauvaises) herbes les plus vigoureuses. — *land*, sol riche. — *-smelling*, fort en odeur. — *idolatry*, une grossière idolâtrie. *Ha! so —!* ah! est-il si violent? *My offence is* —, mon crime est trop grand. *A — rate*, un plus grand profit

Rank, s. rangée, *f.*, rang, *m.* —*s*, pl. simples soldats, *m.pl.*, ordre, *m.*, classe, *f.*, (*mil.*) grade, *m.*, (*cabs*) place, *f.* *In the foremost* —, au premier rang. *In serried —s*, en rangs serrés. *To come out of the —s*, sortir des rangs. *Three hundred — and file*, trois cents hommes. *To fall into the —s*, se mettre en rang. *To reduce to the —s*, casser de son grade. *To rise from the —s*, sortir des rangs. *To take from the —s*, retirer des rangs. *A romance of the —s*, roman de la vie d'un soldat. *All —s of men*, toutes les classes d'hommes. *Of whatever* —, de quelque rang qu'on soit. *Of a meaner* —, d'un rang inférieur. *The — is but the guinea's stamp*, le rang n'est que l'empreinte sur la pièce d'or. *A man of* —, un homme de haut rang. *High* —, grade élevé. *Officers of high* —, des officiers supérieurs. *To rise from — to* —, s'élever de grade en grade. *To take* —, prendre rang. *To take — of*, avoir le pas sur

Rank, va. ranger, classer, mettre (au rang de); — vn. se ranger, être rangé *or* placé, avoir rang de, prendre rang avec. *To — next to*, prendre rang après. *To — high*, avoir *or* occuper un haut rang, un rang élevé

Rankle, va.n. s'envenimer, s'enflammer

Rankling, adj. envenimé,

enflammé, (*fig.*) irrité, violent

Rankling, s. inflammation, *f.*, (*fig.*) fureur, *f.*, violence, *f.*, venin, *m.*

Rankly, adv. vigoureusement, fortement, (*smell*) avec une odeur de rance, sentant fort, (*coarsely*) grossièrement. — *abused*, grossièrement abusé

Rankness, s. vigueur, *f.*, végétation luxuriante, *f.*, insolence, *f.*, odeur forte, *f.*, odeur de rance, *f.*, excès, *m.*, extravagance, *f.*

Ransack, va. fouiller, saccager, mettre à sac, piller

Ransom, s. rançon, *f.*, (*law*) composition, *f.*

Ransom, va. racheter

Rant, vn. faire l'énergumène, déclamer bruyamment

Rant, s. vaine déclamation, *f.*, discours d'énergumène, *m.pl.*

Ranter, s. énergumène, *m.*, déclamateur, *m.*

Rap, s. tape, *f.*, petit coup, *m.*, (*ever so little*) rouge liard, *m.*

Rap, va.n. frapper, ravir

Rapacious, adj. rapace, avide

Rapaciously, adv. avec rapacité

Rapaciousness, **Rapacity**, s. rapacité, *f.*

Rape, s. enlèvement, *m.*, rapt, *m.*, viol, *m.*, (*bot.*) colza, *m.*, navette, *f.* — *-oil*, s., — *-seed oil*, s. huile de colza, *f.* — *-root*, s., — *-seed*, colza, *m.*, graine de colza, *f.*, graine de navette, *f.*

Rapid, adj. rapide

Rapidity, s. rapidité, *f.*

Rapidly, adv. rapidement, avec rapidité

Rapier, s. rapière, *f.*

Rapine, s. rapine, *f.*

Rapper, s. qui frappe, *m.*, frappeur, *m.*, (*on a door*) marteau, *m.*

Rapping, s. action de frapper (*see* Spirit), *f.*, coups, *m. pl.*

Rapture, s. ravissement, *m.*, extase, *f.*, transport, *m.*, enthousiasme, *m.*, charme indicible, *m.* *To be in —s with*, s'extasier sur, être ravi or enchanté de. *To fall into —s* (*with, at*), s'enthousiasmer (de), s'extasier (sur), tomber en extases. *To throw into —s*, ravir, transporter, faire s'extasier

Raptured, *see* Enraptured

Rapturous, adj. ravissant, enthousiaste, frénétique

Rapturously, adv. avec ravissement

Rare, adj. rare, (*thin*) clairsemé, (*exquisite*) merveilleux, incomparable, excellent. *I am a — one to shake hands*, je suis une personne comme il y en a peu pour donner une poignée de mains. *To be in a — humour for*, être en belle humeur de, être bien disposé à

Raree-show, s. spectacle ambulant, *m.*, curiosité, *f.*

Rarefaction, s. raréfaction, *f.*

Rarefy, va.n. raréfier, se raréfier

Rarely, adv. rarement, merveilleusement

Rareness, s. rareté, *f.*

Rarity, s. rareté, *f.*

Rascal, s. fripon, *m.*, coquin, *m.*, misérable, *m.*, canaille, *f.*

Rascality, s. coquinerie, *f.*, friponnerie, *f.*

Rascallion, s. canaille, *f.*

Rascally, adj. fripon, coquin, misérable

Rase, va. raser, effacer, raturer

Rash, adj. téméraire, inconsidéré, irréfléchi. — *-headed*, téméraire, emporté

Rash, s. éruption, *f.*

Rash, va. tailler en pièces, taillader, abattre

Rasher, s. tranche de lard, *f.*

Rashly, adv. témérairement, inconsidérément

Rashness, s. témérité, *f.*, précipitation, *f.*, imprudence, *f.*

Rasp, s. râpe, *f.*

Rasp, va. râper, (*bread*) chapeler

Raspberry, s. framboise, *f.* — *-bush*, s. framboisier, *m.*

Raspings, s.pl. râpure, *f.*, (*of bread*) chapelure, *f.*

Rat, s. rat, *m.* — *-catcher*, s. preneur de rats, *m.* —*'s bane*, s. mort-aux-rats, *f.* — *-trap*, s. ratière, *f.* *To smell a —*, (*fig.*) flairer un piège, un danger

Rat, vn. faire défection, abandonner son parti

Ratable, adj. qu'on peut évaluer

Ratafia, s. ratafia, *m.*

Rate, s. taux, *m.*, cours, *m.*, prix, *m.*, raison, *f.*, proportion, *f.*, rang, *m.*, valeur, *f.*, mérite, *m.*, (*speed*) train, *m.*, pas, *m.*, allure, *f.*, (*taxes*) taxe, *f.*, impôt, *m.*, contributions, *f.pl.* *At the — of*, au taux de. *At a high —*, à un taux élevé. *At a cheap —*, à bon compte. *At that —*, à ce taux-là, sur ce pied-là, à ce compte-là. *At dear —s*, à grands frais. *A spirit of no common —*, un esprit d'une trempe peu ordinaire. *See* First. *At any —*, dans tous les cas, quoi qu'il en soit. *At the — he goes*, au train dont il va. *To live at a high —*, mener la vie grand train. *Parish —s*, taxes communales. *Poor —s*, taxe des pauvres, *f.* — *-payer*, s. contribuable, *m. f.*

Rate, va. estimer, apprécier, évaluer, classer, (*to scold*) tancer vertement, gourmander

Rather, adv. plutôt, de préférence, (*somewhat*) assez, un peu. *I would —*, *I had —*, j'aimerais mieux, je préfère. *I'd — not, thank you*, j'aime mieux en être dispensé, merci. — *better*, un peu mieux. *I — think*, je crois plutôt. *The — as, the — for*, d'autant plus que

Ratification, s. ratification, *f.*

Ratify, va. ratifier

Rating, s. semonce, *f.*, mercuriale, *f.*, réprimande, *f.*, répartition, *f.*

Ratio, s. raison, *f.*, rapport, *m.*

Ration, s. ration, *f.*

Rational, adj. raisonnable, conforme à la raison, doué de raison

Rationalism, s. rationalisme, *m.*

Rationally, adv. raisonnablement, rationnellement

Rattan, s. rotin, *m.*

Ratteen, s. ratine, *f.*

Rattle, vn.a. résonner, retentir, faire du bruit, (*talk*) caqueter, jacasser. *To — away, to — on*, parler tout du long de l'aune

Rattle, s. bruit, *m.*, (*of chains*) cliquetis, *m.*, (*talk*) caquet, *m.*, caquetage, *m.*, bavardage, *m.*, (*police*) crécelle, *f.*, (*toy*) hochet, *m.*, (*in the throat*) râle, *m.* — *-brained*, adj., — *-headed*, adj., — *-pated*, adj. écervelé, étourdi. *To spring a —*, agiter une crécelle

Rattlesnake, s. serpent à sonnettes, *m.*, crotale, *m.*

Rattling, adj. bruyant, qui fait du bruit

Rattling, s. bruit, *m.*

Ravage, va. ravager

Ravage, s. ravage, *m.*

Ravager, s. dévastateur, *m.*

Rave, vn. avoir le délire, être en délire, (*fam.*) battre la campagne, divaguer, extravaguer, (*at*) s'emporter (contre)

Ravel, va. embrouiller, emmêler, enchevêtrer; — vn. s'embrouiller

Raven, s. corbeau, *m.* *Young —*, s. corbillat, *m.*, corbillard, *m.*

Ravenous, adj. vorace, dévorant

Ravenously, adv. avec voracité, d'une manière vorace

Ravenousness, s. voracité, *f.*

Ravin, s. rapine, *f.*

Ravine, s. ravin, *m.*, -e, *f.*

Raving, adj. en délire, furieux, extravagant. — *mad*, fou à lier, fou furieux

Ravish, va. ravir, (*law*) enlever

Ravisher, s. ravisseur, *m.*

Ravishing, adj. ravissant

Ravishingly, adv. d'une manière ravissante, à ravir

Ravishment, s. ravissement, *m.*, enlèvement, *m.*

Raw, adj. écorché, (*uncooked*) cru, (*fruit*) vert, pas mûr, (*unskilled*) inexpérimenté, novice, (*weather*) froid et humide, âpre, (*textures*) brut, non apprêté, (*spirits*) pur. *They eat their meat —*, ils mangent leur viande crue. — *troops*, des troupes non aguerries. — *hands*, (*nar.*) novices. — *and young*, jeune et sans expérience. — *tricks*, de nouveaux tours. — *metal*, métal cru. — *hides*, peaux non apprêtées. — *silk*, soie grège, soie crue or brute. — *sugar*, sucre brut. — *water*, eau non distillée

Rawboned, adj. maigre, décharné

Rawhead, s. tête de mort, *f.*, loup garou, *m.*

Rawish, adj. gris, froid et humide

Rawly, adv. inhabilement, en novice, nouvellement

Rawness, s. crudité, *f.*, inexpérience, *f.*, (*weather*) froid humide, *f.*

Ray, s. rayon, *m.*

Razor, s. rasoir, *m.*

Razure, s. rature, *f.*

Reach, va.n. tendre, étendre, atteindre à, (*to give*) passer, donner, (*to come to*) arriver à, parvenir à. — *hither thy finger*, porte ici ton doigt. *To — out or forth*, tendre, avancer, présenter. *He shall — his branches*, il étendra ses branches. *To — the sky*, toucher au ciel, s'élever jusqu'aux nues, atteindre au ciel, (*poet.*) aller toucher les astres. *To — the bottom*, toucher le fond. *To — down*, descendre, atteindre. *To — the heart*, atteindre au cœur, (*fig.*) toucher le cœur. — *me a chair*, donnez-moi une chaise. *On —ing Paris*, en arrivant à Paris. *Before this letter —es your hands*, avant que cette lettre vous arrive entre les mains, vous parvienne. *The thing —ed the king's ears*, la chose parvint or vint aux oreilles du roi. *To — perfection*, atteindre à, parvenir à, arriver à la perfection. *As far as the eye can —*, aussi loin que porte le regard. *Boots —ing halfway up his legs*, des bottes qui lui montent à mi-jambes. —*ing to his heels*, descendant jusqu'à ses talons. *To — above our nature*, nous élever au-dessus de notre nature. *To — after, at or unto*, chercher à atteindre, arriver à, parvenir à

Reach, s. atteinte, *f.*, portée, *f.*, pénétration, *f.* *Beyond (the) — of, out of the — of*, hors de la portée de, à l'abri de, loin de. *Beyond —, out of —*, hors d'atteinte. *Within —*, à portée

Reachable, adj. qu'on peut atteindre, à portée

Reaching, s. effort pour atteindre à, *f.*, action d'étendre, *f.*, effort pour vomir, *m.*, vomissement, *m.*

Reaching, adj. qui s'étend

au loin. — *hands*, des mains qui s'etendent au loin, (*fam.*) le bras long

React, vn. réagir

Reaction, s. réaction, *f.*

Reactionary, adj. réactif, réactionnaire

Read, va. lire, étudier, expliquer, interpréter, deviner, (*lecture*) faire un cours de. *To spend an hour in —ing works of piety*, passer une heure à de pieuses lectures. *I'll get your brother to — it to me*, je me le ferai lire par votre frère. *The articles having been —*, lecture faite des articles. *To — to oneself*, lire tout bas. *To hear a book —*, entendre lire un livre. *You'll — yourself ill*, vous vous rendrez malade à force de lire. *To — again*, relire. *To — over*, lire, parcourir. *To — off*, lire de suite. *To — out*, lire en entier. *To — law*, étudier le droit; — vn. faire la lecture, étudier, (*passage*) être conçu. *Can your boy —?* votre enfant sait-il lire. *Whilst the play was —ing*, pendant la lecture de la pièce. *To — in the features, through the soul*, lire dans les traits, dans l'âme. *To — of*, dont les livres parlent, connaître par la lecture, apprendre que, lire que. *The heroes you — of in history*, les héros dont l'histoire vous parle. *I have — of an Eastern king who . . .* j'ai vu dans mes livres qu'un roi d'Orient . . . *To — on*, continuer de lire, continuer sa lecture. *To — out loud, to — up*, lire à haute voix. *To — out*, lire jusqu'au bout, lire en entier

Read, adj. *A well- — man*, un homme instruit, qui a beaucoup lu

Readable, adj. lisible, qu'on peut lire

Reader, s. lecteur, *m.*, -trice, *f.*, (*studious*) personne studieuse, liseur, *m.*, (*univ*) professeur, *m.*, (*print.*) correcteur, *m.* — *to the queen*, lectrice de la reine. *Gentle —*, ami lecteur. *Fair —*, belle lectrice. *Address to the —*, avis au lecteur

Readily, adv. promptement, sans hésiter, volontiers

Readiness, s. promptitude, *f.*, (*easy*) facilité, *f.*, (*wit*) vivacité, *f.* *Everything was in — to receive him*, tout était préparé pour le recevoir. *When he had got all in —*, quand il eut fait tous ses préparatifs

Reading, s. lecture, *f.*, (*professor*) leçon, *f.*, (*variation in a text*) leçon, *f.*, texte, *m.*, (*barometer*) hauteur, *f.* *To be fond of —*, aimer la lecture. *Light —*, la littérature legère. *To profit by one's —*, tirer du profit de ce qu'on lit *or* de ses lectures. *The right —*, la vraie leçon, le vrai texte

Reading, adj. studieux, travailleur, de lecture. — *man*, s. travailleur, *m.*, (*fam.*) piocheur, *m.* — *desk*, s. pupitre, (*lecture*) lutrin, *m.* — *-rooms*, s. cabinet de lecture, *m.*

Readjust, va. rajuster

Readmission, Readmittance, s. réadmission, *f.*

Readmit, va. réadmettre

Readopt, va. adopter de nouveau

Readorn, va. orner de nouveau

Readvance, vn. s'avancer de nouveau

Ready, adj. prêt, prompt, vif, facile, habile, (*to*) prêt, (à), empressé (de), (*near*) près, sur le point, proche, à sa portée, sous la main, (*money*) comptant. *To make —*, preparer, préparer tout. *Make — ! fire !* en joue ! feu ! *To get —*, préparer, se préparer. — *about !* (*nav.*) pare à virer ! *To be —*, être prêt, se tenir prêt. *His — sense*, son intelligence vive. *A — consent*, une prompte acquiescence. *The readiest way*, le moyen le plus facile, le plus expéditif. — *reckoner*, s. barême, *m.* *A — writer*, un écrivain habile. *For — money only*, (expressément) au comptant. *To pay — money*, payer comptant

Ready, adv. tout prêt, d'avance. — *made clothes*, des habits tout faits, (*com.*) habits confectionnés. — *-witted*, adj. à l'esprit prompt

Ready, s. argent comptant, espèces sonnantes

Real, adj. réel, véritable, vrai, (*property*) immobilier, immeuble

Reality, s. réalité, *f.*, réel, *m.*

Realization, s. réalisation, *f.*

Realize, va. réaliser, se faire une idée de, bien comprendre, concevoir, se figurer. *His hopes were —d*, ses espérances se réalisèrent

Really, adv. réellement, vraiment, véritablement

Realm, s. royaume, *m.*

Ream, s. rame, *f.*

Reanimate, va. ranimer

Reanimation, s. action de ranimer, nouvelle animation, *f.*

Reap, va.n. moissonner, récolter, recueillir

Reaper, s. moissonneur, *m.*, -euse, *f.*, (*mach.*) moissonneuse, *f.*

Reaping, s. moisson, *f.*, récolte, *f.* — *-hook*, s. faucille, *f.* — *-machine*, s. moissonneuse, *f.*

Reappear, vn. reparaître

Reappearance, s. réapparition, *f.*, (*of an actor*) rentrée, *f.* *On his —*, lorsqu'il reparut

Reapplication, s. nouvelle application, *f.*

Reappoint, va. nommer, instituer de nouveau

Reappointment, s. nouvelle nomination, *f.*

Rear, s. arrière-garde, *f.*, dernier rang, *m.*, queue, *f.* *To bring up the —*, fermer la marche

Rear, adj. à l'arrière garde, dernier, (*of meat*) cru

Rear, va. (*bring up*) élever, diriger

Reargue, va. discuter de nouveau

Reascend, va.n. remonter, gravir de nouveau

Reason, s. raison, *f.*, raisonnement, *m.* *Pure —*, la raison pure. *In —'s ear*, à l'oreille de la raison. *The — why*, la raison par laquelle, pourquoi. *By — of*, en raison de, pour cause de. *Without a —*, sans raison. *With good —*, à bon droit, pour cause. *With still greater —*, à plus forte raison. *So much the more — to do so*, raison de plus pour le faire. *For —s best known to myself*, pour des raisons à moi connues. *As in — (bound)*, comme de raison. *To listen to —*, entendre raison. *It stands to — that*, la raison *or* le simple bon sens veut que. *Out of all —*, contre toute raison. *I have, there is every — to believe*, j'ai, il y a tout lieu de croire

Reason, va.n. raisonner, parler, s'entretenir. *To — with oneself*, se raisonner. *And this is the way I —ed*, et voici le raisonnement que je me fis. *I was endeavouring to — with her*, j'essayais de lui faire entendre raison. *Men that will not be —ed into their senses, may be laughed into them*, la raillerie suffit quelquefois à faire écouter les leçons du sens commun à ceux qui ne veulent pas écouter la raison. *I —ed her out of her fears*, je réussis à dissiper ses craintes par mes raisons. *To — down*, vaincre

Reasonable, adj. raisonnable, doué de raison

Reasonableness, s. raison, *f.*, modération, *f.*

Reasonably, adv. raisonnablement

Reasoner, s. dialecticien, *m.*, -enne, *f.*

Reasoning, s. raisonnement, *m.*

Reassemble, va. rassembler; — vn. se rassembler

Reassert, va. affirmer derechef

Reassure, va. rassurer, (*com.*) réassurer

Reattach, va. rattacher

Reattempt, va. essayer de nouveau

Rebaptize, va. baptiser de nouveau

Rebel, s. rebelle, *m.*

Rebel, vn. se révolter, se soulever

Rebellion, s. rébellion, *f.*

Rebellious, adj. rebelle

Rebelliously, adv. en rebelle

Rebelliousness, s. caractère de rébellion, *m.*, rébellion, *f.*

Rebound, vn. rebondir, retentir

Rebound, s. rebondissement, *m.*, contre-coup, *m.*, rejaillissement, *m.*

Rebuff, s. répulsion, *f.*, échec, *m.*, rebuffade, *f.*

Rebuff, va. repousser

Rebuild, va. rebâtir, reconstruire

Rebuke, va. réprimander, reprendre, gronder, censurer

Rebuke, s. réprimande, *f.*, reproche, *m.* *To escape —*, échapper au blâme

Rebus, s. rébus, *m.*

Rebut, va. repousser

Recall, va. rappeler, révoquer, (*remember*) se rappeler

Recall, s. rappel, *m.*, révocation, *f.*

Recant, va. rétracter, désavouer; — vn. se rétracter, (*fam.*) chanter la palinodie

Recantation, s. rétractation, (*fam.*) palinodie, *f.* *To make a public — of*, désavouer *or* rétracter publiquement

Recapitulate, va. récapituler

Recapitulation, s. récapitulation, *f.*

Recapitulatory, adj. récapitulatif

Recapture, va. réprendre

Recast, va. jeter de nouveau, refondre

Recede, vn. se retirer, s'éloigner, se désister (de)

Receipt, s. réception, *f.*, reçu, *m.*, (*recipe*) recette, *f.*, (*money*) reçu, *m.*, quittance, *f.*, acquit, *m.* *On — of your letter*, au reçu de votre lettre. *His weekly —s*, sa recette hebdomadaire. *To put one's — to*, mettre son acquit sur, acquitter. — *-stamp*, s. timbre pour quittance, *m.* — *-book*, s. livre de ménage, *m.*

Receipt, va. acquitter, mettre son acquit sur, mettre pour acquit

Receivable, adj. recevable

Receive, va. recevoir, admettre, agréer, accepter. *To — a letter, visit*, recevoir une lettre, des visites. *Long —d custom*, usage reçu depuis longtemps. — *my best thanks*, agréez mes sincères remerciements

Received, adj. reçu, pour acquit

Receiver, s. celui, celle qui reçoit, *m.*, (*administr.*) receveur, *m.*, percepteur, *m.*, (*law*) recéleur, *m.*, -euse, *f.*, (*phys. and chem.*) récipient, *m.*, (*of letters*) destinataire, *s.*

Receiving, s. réception, *f.*, (*law*) recel, *m.* — *-house*, s. petite poste, *f.*, bureau de poste, *m.*

Recent, adj. récent, de date récente, frais, nouveau

Recently, adv. récemment

Receptacle, s. réceptacle, *m.*

Reception, s. réception, *f.*, accueil, *m.*

Recess, s. retraite, *f.*, (*vacation*) vacances, *f.pl.*, prorogation, *f.*, (*secret*) replis, *m. pl.*, (*in a wall*) niche, *f.*, enfoncement, *m.*, recoin, *m.*

Recession, s. retraite, *f.*, éloignement, *m.*, désistement, *m.*

Recipe, s. recette, *f.*

Recipient, s (*chem.*) récipient, *m.*, (*pers.*) recevant, *m.*, (*things*) réceptacle, *m.*, (*of a diploma*) impétrant, *m.*

Reciprocal, adj. réciproque

Reciprocally, adv. réciproquement

Reciprocalness, Reciprocality, s. réciprocité, *f.*

Reciprocate, vn. alterner, se succéder, rendre la pareille; — va. échanger, rendre, payer de retour. *To — civilities*, échanger des politesses. *—d duties*, devoirs réciproques

Reciprocating, adj. alternatif

Reciprocation, Reciprocity, s. échange, *f.*, retour réciproque, *m.*, réciprocité, *f.*

Recital, s. récitation, *f.*, (*tale*) récit, *m.*, narration, *f.*, (*law*) exposé d'acte, *m.* *To make a — of*, faire un récit de

Recitation, s. récitation, *f.*

Recitative, Recitativo, s. récitatif, *m.*

Recite, va. réciter, répéter, (*relate*) raconter, narrer, énumérer

Reciter, s. personne qui récite, narrateur, *m.*

Reck, va.n. se soucier de, tenir à, faire cas de. *Not —ing danger*, méprisant le danger. *Little he'll —*, il ne s'en souciera guère, peu lui importe, à lui. *He —ed not of the life he lost*, peu lui importait la vie qu'il perdait. *It —s me not of night*, peu m'importe la nuit

Reckless, adj. insouciant (de), indifférent (à), téméraire

Recklessness, s. insouciance, *f.*, indifférence, *f.*, témérité, *f.*

Reckon, va.n. compter, calculer, regarder comme, estimer. *To — up*, compter, additionner. *—ing from to-day*, à compter d'aujourd'hui

Reckoner, s calculateur, *m.*, chiffreur, *m.*

Reckoning, s. compte, *m.*, supputation, *f.*, (*at an inn*) écot, *m.*, compte, *m.*, carte à payer, *f.*, (*esteem*) égard, *m.*, (*nav.*) estime, *f.* *— up*, s. addition, *f.* *Short —s make long friends*, les bons comptes font les bons amis. *After- —*, comptes à rendre plus tard. *— -book*, s. livre de comptes, *m.* *— -day*, s. jour où se règlent les comptes, (*fig.*) d'expiation, *m.*

Reclaim, va. corriger, réformer, faire revenir, ramener

Reclaimable, adj. qu'on peut ramener au bien

Reclaimless, adj. qu'on ne saurait corriger, incorrigible

Reclamation, s. réforme, *f.*, amendement, *m.*, rentrée en possession, *f.*

Recline, va. incliner, pencher, appuyer, reposer; — vn. être couché, s'incliner, se pencher, s'appuyer. *Reclining on the grass*, couché sur l'herbe

Recliner, s. cadran réclinant, *m.*

Recluse, adj. s. reclus, *m.*, -e, *f.*

Reclusion, s. réclusion, *f.*

Reclusive, adj. solitaire

Recognition, s. reconnaissance, *f.*

Recognizance, s. (*law*) reconnaissance, *f.*, obligation, *f.* *To enter into —s*, donner caution, s'engager à comparaître

Recognize, va. reconnaître; — vn. s'engager à comparaître

Recoil, vn. reculer, rebondir, retomber

Recoil, Recoiling, s. recul, *m.*

Recoin, va. refondre

Recoinage, s. refonte, *f.*

Recollect, va. se rappeler, se souvenir de. *To — oneself*, recueillir *or* rassembler ses souvenirs, se recuillir

Recollection, s. souvenir, *m.*, mémoire, *f.* *To the best of my —*, autant que je puis m'en souvenir. *I have no — of it, of having said so*, je ne puis me le rappeler, je ne puis me rappeler de l'avoir dit. *Some — of*, un léger souvenir de. *I had no — of him*, je ne me souvenais pas de l'avoir vu, je ne me le rappelais pas

Recombine, va. combiner de nouveau

Recommence, va.n. recommencer

Recommencement, s. recommencement, *m.*

Recommend, va. recommander, rendre agréable, prévenir en faveur de, (*a petition*) apostiller une demande. *To — oneself to*, se rendre agréable à

Recommendable, adj. recommandable

Recommendation, s. recommandation, *f.*, apostille, *f.* *He is his own —*, il se recommande de lui-même. *Letter of —*, lettre de recommandation. *In — of*, pour recommander, à la louange de. *With him, misfortune was a powerful —*, pour lui, le malheur était un avocat puissant

Recommendatory, adj. de recommandation

Recommender, s. qui recommande

Recommit, va. commettre de nouveau, renvoyer en prison

Recommitment, Recommittal, s. renvoi en prison, *m.*

Recompense, va. récompenser, (*to compensate*) compenser, (*indemnify*) dédommager

Recompense, s. récompense, *f.*, dédommagement, *m.*, compensation, *f.*

Recompose, va. tranquilliser de nouveau, recomposer

Recomposition, s. recomposition, *f.*

Reconcilable, adj. réconciliable, (*things, &c.*) conciliable (avec), conforme (à)

Reconcilableness, s. possibilité de réconciliation, *f.*, conformité, *f.*, compatibilité, *f.*

Reconcile, va. réconcilier, (*things*) concilier, faire accorder. *To get, to grow, to become —d to a situation*, se faire à, s'habituer à une situation

Reconcilement, Reconciliation, s. réconciliation, *f.*, conciliation, *f.*, accord, *m.*, conformité, *f.*

Reconciler, s. réconciliateur, *m.*

Recondense, va. condenser de nouveau

Recondite, adj. caché, occulte, abstrus, abstrait

Reconduct, va. reconduire

Reconnoitre, va.n. (*mil.*) reconnaître, faire la reconnaissance de, faire une reconnaissance

Reconnoitring, s. reconnaissance, *f.* *To be, to go out —*, être en reconnaissance, aller en reconnaissance *or* faire une reconnaissance. *— party*, s. reconnaissance, *f.* *To send out — parties*, envoyer en reconnaissance

Reconquer, va. reconquérir

Reconsider, va. considérer de nouveau, revenir sur

Reconsideration, s. nouvelles réflexions, *f.*, nouvel examen, *m.*, action de revenir, *f.* *Upon —*, en réfléchissant de nouveau

Reconstruct, va. reconstruire

Reconstruction, s. reconstruction, *f.*

Reconvention, s. reconvention, *f.*

Reconvert, va. convertir de nouveau

Record, va. enregistrer, rapporter, écrire, inscrire, raconter, répéter, chanter

Record, s. registre, *m.*, rapport, *m.*, récit, *m.*, relation, *f.*, souvenir, *m.* *—s*, pl. archives, *f.pl.* *Keeper of the —s*, s. archiviste, *m.* *The — office*, s. le greffe, *m.*, les archives, *f.pl.* *To make a — of*, inscrire dans un registre enregistrer. *It is the most remarkable instance on —*, c'est l'exemple le plus remarquable rapporté dans l'histoire. *The — of past ages*, les annales des siècles passés. *Sweet —s*, de doux souvenirs. *A sure —*, monument, *m.*, récit infaillible, *m.* *The —s of his covenant*, monuments de son alliance

Recorder, s. greffier municipal, *m.*, archiviste, *m.*

Recordership, s. charge de greffier, *f.*, d'archiviste, *f.*

Recount, va. recompter, raconter, rapporter

Recoup, va. indemniser, dédommager (de). *To — oneself*, (*by*) se rattraper (sur)

Recourse, s. recours, *m.* *To have — to*, avoir recours à, recourir à

Recover, va. regagner, recouvrer, rentrer en possession de, retrouver, reprendre, reconquérir, (*time*) réparer, (*cure*) guérir, rappeler, à la vie, (*deliver*) dégager, délivrer, sauver. *To — one's senses, to — oneself*, reprendre ses sens, se remettre, revenir à soi; — vn. se rétablir, recouvrer la santé, guérir, relever, revenir à soi

Recoverable, adj. recouvrable, qu'on peut regagner

Recovery, s. recouvrement, *m.*, reprise, *f.*, conquête, *f.*, (*health*) guérison, *f.*, (*debts*) recouvrement, *m.* *Past —*, sans espoir de guérison, sans remède, désespéré, irrémédiable

Recreant, s. lâche, *m.*, poltron, *m.*, apostat, *m.*

Recreate, va. recréer

Recreation, s. récréation, *f.*, distraction, *f.*

Recreative, adj. récréatif

Recriminate, vn. (*on*) récriminer (contre)

Recrimination, s. récrimination, *f.*

Recrudescence, Recrudescency, s. recrudescence, *f.*

Recrudescent, adj. recrudescent

Recruit, va. ranimer, refaire, réparer, (*troops*) recruter. *To — one's strength*, réparer ses forces. — vn. (*milit.*) se recruter, (*fig.*) se refaire, se rétablir

Recruit, s. recrue, *f.*, jeune soldat, *m.*, renfort, *m.*, conscrit, *m.*

Recruiter, s. recruteur, *m.*

Recruiting, s. recrutement, *m.* *— officer*, s. recruteur, *m.*

Rectangle, s. rectangle, *m.*

Rectangular, adj. rectangle, rectangulaire

Rectification, s. rectification, *f.*

Rectify, va. rectifier, redresser

Rectitude, s. rectitude, *f.*, droiture, *f.*

Rector, s. (*univ.*) recteur, *m.*, principal, *m.*, (*church*) curé, *m.*

Rectorate, Rectorship, s. rectorat, *m.*, cure, *f.*

Rectory, s. rectorat, *m.*, cure, *f.*, (*house*) presbytère, *m.*

Recumbent, adj. couché, appuyé

Recur, vn. (*pers.*) retourner, avoir recours, recourir, revenir, s'offrir, se présenter. *To — to the mind*, revenir à l'esprit

Recurrence, Recurrency, s. retour, *m.*

Recurrent, adj. périodique

Recurring, adj. qui revient, périodique

Red, adj. rouge, (*hair*) roux, (*lips*) vermeille

Red . . . (*in compounds*). — *-breast*, s. rouge-gorge, *m.* — *-flecked*, adj. taché de rouge. — *-gum*, s. feu de dents, *m.* — *-lead*, s. minium, *m.* — *-letter day*, s. jour de fête, *m.*, jour férié, *m.* — *-pole*, s. linotte, *f.* — *-tapist*, s. bureaucrate, *m.* — *-tapism*, s. bureaucratie, *f.*

Redden, va. rougir; — vn. rougir, devenir rouge

Reddish, adj. rougeâtre

Reddish, s. roussâtre, *f.*

Redeem, va. racheter, délivrer, (*time*) bien employer, mettre à profit, réparer, (*pledge*) retirer, dégager, (*promise*) s'acquitter de

Redeemable, adj. rachetable

Redeemer, s. libérateur, *m.*, -trice, *f.*, Rédempteur, *m.*

Redemption, s. rachat, *m.*, rédemption, *f.* *With faculty of —*, avec faculté de rachat, réméré

Redistribution, s. nouvelle distribution

Redness, s. rougeur, *f.*, couleur rouge, *f.*

Redolence, s. parfum, *m.*

Redolent, adj. embaumé, odorant, parfumé

Redouble, va.n. redoubler

Redoubt, s. redoute, *f.*

Redoubtable, adj. redoutable

Redound, vn. rejaillir, retomber, revenir (à), contribuer, concourir, servir. *There will no small use — from them to that manufacture*, il en resultera d'assez grands avantages pour cette manufacture. *What —ed most to his honour*, ce qui était surtout à son honneur

Redress, va. redresser, arranger, mettre en ordre, corriger, (*help*) secourir, faire justice à

Redress, s. redressement, *m.*, réforme, *f.*, réparation, *f.*, secours, *m.*, soulagement, *m.*, justice, *f.*

Redresser, s. redresseur, *m.*

Reduce, va. réduire, (*degrade*) abaisser, dégrader, (*to bring back*) rameuer. *To — to nothing*, réduire à rien. *To — to the dust*, faire rentrer dans la poussière. *To — one's expenses*, réduire ses dépenses. *In —d circumstances*, dans la gêne. *He was greatly —d in circumstances*, il était alors dans un grand état de gêne, mal dans ses affaires. *To — to rules*, ramener or soumettre à des règles

Reducible, adj. réductible

Reduction, s. réduction, *f.*

Redundance, Redundancy, s. surabondance, *f.*, (*rhet.*) rédondance, *f.*

Redundant, adj. surabondant, rédondant

Redundantly, adv. surabondamment, d'une manière rédondante

Reduplicate, va. doubler

Reduplication, s. redoublement, *m.*, (*gram.*) réduplication, *f.*

Reduplicative, adj. double

Reecho, vn. retentir, résonner, répondre; — va. répéter, renvoyer, retentir de

Reed, s. roseau, *m.*, jonc, *m.*, ajonc, *m.*, (*pipe*) chalumeau, *m.*, pipeau, *m.*, (*mouth-piece*) anche, *f.* *Indian —*, s. bambou, *m.*, rotin, *m.* — *that bends*, roseau pliant. — *-buck*, s. antilope des marécages, *m.* — *-bunting*, s., — *-sparrow*, s. ortolan des marais, *m.* — *-crowned*, adj. couronné de roseaux. — *-grass*, s. roseau, *m.* — *-mace*, s. roseau des étangs, *m.* — *-organ*, s. harmonium, *m.* — *-pipe*, s. chalumeau, *m.*, pipeau, *m.* — *-stop*, s. jeu de flûtes, *m.*

Reedit, va. éditer de nouveau

Reedy, adj. abondant en roseaux

Reef, s. (*nav.*) ris, *m.*, (*rocks*) récif, *m.*, écueil, *m.*, banc de rochers, *m.* *To take in a —*, prendre un ris. *To let out a —*, larguer un ris. — *-band*, s. bande de ris, *f.* — *-line*, s. garcette de ris, *f.*

Reef (in), va. prendre un ris

Reek, s. fumée, *f.*, vapeur, *f.*

Reek, va. fumer, exhaler des vapeurs

Reeking, adj. fumant, qui exhale des vapeurs. *Her — hide*, sa peau fumante. — *odours*, les vapeurs de l'encens

Reeky, adj. enfumé, noir de fumée

Reel, s. dévidoir, *m.*, bobine, *f.*, (*dance*) branle, *m.*

Reel, va. dévider; — vn. (*pers.*) chanceler, vaciller, trébucher, (*th.*) tourner à. *To — from*, s'éloigner en chancelant. *My head —s*, la tête me tourne

Reelect, va. réélire

Reelection, s. réélection, *f.*

Reeligibility, s. rééligibilité, *f.*

Reeligible, adj. rééligible

Reembark, va. rembarquer; — vn. se rembarquer

Reembarcation, s. rembarquement, *m.*

Reenact, va. ordonner de nouveau, remettre en vigueur

Reengage, va. rengager

Reengagement, s. rengagement, *m.*

Reenlist, va. enrôler de nouveau; — vn. se rengager

Reenlistment, s. rengagement, *m.*

Reenter, va. rentrer dans, rentrer à

Reentering, adj. rentrant

Reenthrone, va. remettre sur le trône

Reestablish, va. rétablir

Reestablishment, s. rétablissement, *m.*, restauration, *f.*, réintégration, *f.*

Reexamine, va. examiner de nouveau, revoir

Reexport, va. réexporter

Reexportation, s. réexportation, *f.*

Refection, s. rafraîchissement, *m.*, collation, *f.*

Refectory, s. réfectoire, *m.*

Refer, va. rapporter, renvoyer, adresser, attribuer, faire honneur de. *To — the matter to*, s'en référer à, s'en rapporter à. *To — oneself*, s'adresser. — vn. (*th.*) se rapporter, avoir rapport or trait, se référer, en référer, (*pers.*) s'en référer, s'en rapporter, s'adresser (à), consulter, faire allusion

Referee, s. arbitre, *m.*

Reference, s. (*relation*) rapport, *m.*, égard, *m.*, (*quotation*) allusion, *f.*, mention, *f.*, (*to yourself*) action de consulter, *f.*, renseignements, *m. pl.*, (*person*) répondants, *m. pl.*, recommandations, *f. pl.*, (*com.*) références, *f. pl.*, (*law*) renvoi devant arbitre, *m.*, référé, *m.* *In — to*, à l'égard de, à propos de. *To have — to*, *no — to*, avoir rapport à, n'avoir aucun rapport à. *On — to*, en s'adressant à, en consultant. *To give — to*, renvoyer à, adresser à. *—s given and required*, l'on donnera et l'on demandera des renseignements

Refine, va. (*liquids*) épurer, (*metals*) affiner, (*sugar*) raffiner, (*fig.*) épurer, purifier, polir. *—d taste*, goût épuré. *—d mind*, esprit élégant. *—d wits*, des esprits délicats. *—d manners*, des mœurs polies. *—d writers*, des écrivains élégants. — vn. s'épurer, se purifier, perfectionner, faire mieux que

Refinedly, adv. avec raffinement

Refinement, s. épuration, *f.*, affinage, *m.*, raffinage, *m.*, (*fig.*) pureté, *f.*, politesse, *f.*, vernis, *m.*, élégance, *f.*

Refiner, s. affineur, *m.*, (*sugar*) raffineur, *m.*

Refinery, s. raffinerie, *f.*

Refit, va. réparer remettre en état, (*nav.*) radouber

Reflect, va. réfléchir, refléter, (*honours*) rapporter, procurer, valoir (à); — vn. réfléchir, se réfléchir, faire réflexion or des réflexions, (*fig.*) rejaillir, retomber, blâmer, critiquer, censurer

Reflecting, adj. (*phys.*) réflecteur, réfléchi

Reflectingly, adv. en réfléchissant, avec réflexion, en blâmant, avec censure

Reflection, s. réflexion, *f.*, reflet, *m.*, image, *f.*, (*blame*) blâme, *m.*, censure, *f.*, reproche, *m.* *On —*, *upon —*, en y réfléchissant, toute réflexion faite. *To make —s*, faire des réflexions. *To cast or convey a — on the honour of*, s'attaquer à l'honneur de. *To cast —s on*, déverser le blâme sur, censurer, fronder

Reflective, adj. qui réfléchit, réflecteur

Reflector, s. réflecteur, *m.*

Reform, va. reformer, former de nouveau, réformer; — vn. se reformer

Reform, s. réforme, *f.* — *bill*, s. bill de réforme, *m.* *To introduce great — into*, faire de grandes réformes dans

Reformation, s. réformation, *f.*, réforme, *f.*, nouvelle formation, *f.*

Reformative, Reformatory, adj. de réforme

Reformatory, s. maison de correction, *f.*, maison de jeunes détenus, *f.*

Reformer, s. réformateur, *m.*

Reformist, s. réformiste, *m.*

Refract, va. réfracter

Refracting, adj. réfringent, à réfraction

Refraction, s. réfraction, *f.*

Refractive, adj. réfractif

Refractoriness, s. indocilité, *f.*, nature réfractaire, *f.*

Refractory, adj. rebelle, indocile, récalcitrant, (*mil.*) réfractaire. *To be, to prove —*, faire le récalcitrant

Refrain, vn. s'abstenir de, s'empêcher de, (*pers.*) retenir, contenir. *To — from tears*, retenir ses larmes. *I could not — from questioning her*, je ne pus m'empêcher de l'interroger. *— from these men*, évitez ces hommes. — va. refréner, retenir, contenir. *To — oneself*, se contenir

Refresh, va. rafraîchir, délasser, (*rest*) reposer, refaire, remettre, (*cheer*) récréer. *Go and — yourself*, allez vous rafraîchir. *To feel quite —ed*, se sentir tout reposé, se sentir tout autre *or* bien mieux. *To — the mind* (*fig.*) récréer l'esprit

Refreshing, adj. rafraîchissant, qui ranime, qui délasse, qui repose. — *breeze*, fraîche brise. *It was — to hear*, cela faisait du bien d'entendre. — *sleep*, sommeil réparateur

Refreshingly, adv. de manière à rafraîchir

Refreshingness, s. caractère rafraîchissant, *m.*

Refrigerate, va. rafraîchir

Refrigeration, s. réfrigération, *f.*, refroidissement, *m.*

Refrigerator, s. réfrigérateur, *m.*, glacière, *f.*

Refuge, s. refuge, *m.*, abri, *m.*, asile, *m.* *To fly* or *flee for — to*, se réfugier auprès de. *To take — in* or *with*, *to seek a — in* or *with*, se réfugier dans *or* auprès de. *Place of —*, lieu d'asile. *I sought a — from their noise*, je cherchai à me soustraire à leur bruit. *I found a —*, je trouvai un abri. *Cities of —*, villes de refuge

Refugee, s. réfugié, *m.*

Refund, va. rembourser, rendre

Refurnish, va. meubler de nouveau

Refusal, s. refus, *m.*, (*option*) choix, *f.* *On his —*, sur son refus. *I gave a flat —*, je refusai net. *To meet with a flat —*, essuyer un refus net. *You shall have the —*, vous aurez le choix or l'option

Refuse, va.n. refuser, se refuser à, rejeter, rebuter. *To be —d*, être refusé, (*pers.*) se voir refuser (quelque chose), on refuse (quelque chose à quelqu'un). *This was —d him*, on le lui refusa. *We were —d admission*, on refusa de nous admettre. *To — oneself*, se refuser. *That is not to be —d*, cela n'est pas de refus. *Too good to be —d*, trop bon pour qu'on le refuse

Refuse, s. rebut, *m.*

Refuse, adj. de rebut, sans valeur

Refutable, adj. qu'on peut réfuter, qui peut être réfuté

Refutation, s. réfutation, *f.*

Refute, va. réfuter

Regain, va. regagner, recouvrer

Regal, adj. royal

Regale, vn. recevoir, régaler, festoyer

Regalia, s.pl. insignes de la royauté, *m.pl.*

Regally, adv. royalement

Regard, va. regarder, faire attention à, avoir rapport à, concerner, estimer, respecter

Regard, s. égard, *m.*, (*esteem*) considération, *f.*, (*relation*) rapport, *m.* *With — to*, à l'égard de, quant à. *My kindest —s to*, mille amitiés de ma part à

Regardful, adj. attentif (à), soigneux (de), qui a égard (à)

Regardfully, adv. avec soin, avec égard

Regarding, adv. à l'égard de, concernant

Regardless, adj. inattentif (à), peu soucieux (de), indifférent (à)

Regardlessly, adv. avec indifférence *or* insouciance, négligemment

Regardlessness, s. indifférence, *f.*, insouciance, *f.*, négligence, *f.*

Regatta, s. régate, *f.*

Regency, s. régence, *m.*, conseil de régence, *m.*

Regenerate, va. régénérer

Regenerate, adj. régénéré

Regeneration, s. régénération, *f.*

Regenerator, s. régénérateur, *m.*

Regent, s. régent, *m.*, -e, *f.*

Regicide, s. régicide, *m.*

Regimen, s. régime, *m.* *To observe, to keep a —*, se mettre au régime, suivre un régime, vivre de régime. *Under a —*, au régime

Regiment, s. régiment, *m.*

Regimental, adj. de régiment, du régiment

Regimentals, s.pl. uniforme, *m.* *In full —*, en grand uniforme

Region, s. région, *m.*

Register, s. registre, *m.* — *-office*, s. bureau de placement, *m.*

Register, va. enregistrer, (*fig.*) imprimer, graver, (*print.*) pointer, (*patterns*) déposer, (*letters*) charger

Registrar, s. teneur de registres, *m.*, (*of births, &c.*) officier d'état civil, *m.*, greffier, *m.*, (*law*) archiviste, *m.*

Registrarship, s. charge de greffier, *f.*

Registration, s. enregistrement, *m.*

Registry, s. enregistrement, *m.*, bureau d'enregistrement, *m.*

Reglet, s. (*archit.*) réglet, *m.*, (*print.*) réglette, *f.*

Regnant, adj. régnant, dominant

Regorge, va. vomir, revomir, (*of, with*) gorger (de), avaler

Regrant, va. concéder de nouveau

Regress, s. retour, *m.*, retraite, *f.*

Regress, va. s'en retourner

Regression, s. retour, *m.*

Regret, s. regret, *m.* *To my great —*, à mon grand regret. *With —*, avec regret, à regret. *Without —*, sans regret. *His — for the loss of*, ses regrets de la perte de. *His — at being denied admission*, son regret de ce qu'on lui refusât l'entrée. *To feel —*, éprouver *or* avoir du regret

Regret, va. regretter (de), avoir du regret (à), se repentir de. *To be regretted*, à regretter, regrettable. *An ever to be regretted death*, une mort à jamais regrettable

Regular, adj. régulier, réglé, véritable, vrai, (*downright*) franc, fieffé, (*in due form*) en règle. — *in small things*, régulier dans les petites choses. — *in coming*, exact à venir. *A — mode of living*, une vie réglée. *As — as clock-work*, réglé comme un papier de musique. *To make —*, régulariser

Regularity, s. régularité, *f.*

Regularize, va. régulariser

Regularly, adv. régulièrement, avec régularité, véritablement

Regulate, va. régler

Regulation, s. règlement, *m.*

Regulator, s. régulateur, *m.*, -trice, *f.*

Rehabilitate, va. réhabiliter

Rehabilitation, s. réhabilitation, *f.*

Rehear, va. entendre de nouveau

Rehearing, s. seconde audition, *f.*

Rehearsal, s. récitation, *f.*, déclamation, *f.*, (*narrative*) récit, *m.*, relation, *f.*, (*theat.*) répétition, *f.* *To be, to put in —*, être, mettre en répétition

Rehearse, va. réciter, raconter, (*theat.*) répéter

Reign, vn. régner

Reign, s. règne, *m.*, souveraineté, *f.*

Reigning, adj. régnant, dominant

Reimburse, va. rembourser

Reimbursement, s. remboursement, *m.*

Reimport, va. réimporter

Reimpose, va. imposer de nouveau

Reimpregnate, va. imprégner de nouveau

Reimpress, va. réimprimer, graver de nouveau

Reimpression, s. réimpression, *f.*

Reimprint, vn. réimprimer

Reimprison, va. remettre en prison

Reimprisonment, s. nouvel emprisonnement, *m.*, renvoi en prison, *m.*

Rein, s. rêne, *f.* *To hold the —s*, tenir les rênes, tenir la bride. *To slacken the —s of*, lâcher la bride à. *Give him the —*, lâchez-lui la bride. *To keep a tight — over*, tenir la bride serrée à. *To hold, to take the —s of State*, diriger, prendre les rênes de l'Etat

Rein, va. conduire à la bride, manier, (*fig.*) contenir, retenir

Reincorporate, va. incorporer de nouveau

Reincur, va. encourir de nouveau

Reindeer, s. renne, *m.*

Reinforce, va. renforcer, envoyer des renforts à. *Being —d*, ayant reçu des renforts, s'étant renforcé

Reinforcement, s. renforcement, *m.*, renfort, *m.*

Reinhabit, va. habiter de nouveau

Reinsert, va. insérer de nouveau

Reinsertion, s. nouvelle insertion, *f.*

Reinspection, s. nouvelle inspection, *f.*

Reinspire, va. inspirer de nouveau

Reinstall, va. réinstaller, rétablir

Reinstate, va. rétablir, réintégrer

Reinstatement, s. réintégration, *f.*, rétablissement, *m.*

Reinsurance, s. contre-assurance, *f.*

Reinsure, va. réassurer

Reintegrate, va. réintégrer, rétablir

Reintegration, s. réintégration, *f.*

Reinter, va. enterrer de nouveau

Reintroduce, va. introduire de nouveau

Reinvest, va. investir de nouveau

Reinvestment, s. nouvel investissement, *m.*, nouveau placement, *m.*

Reinvigorate, va. rendre de la vigueur à, ranimer, donner de nouvelles forces à

Reinvite, va. réinviter

Reissue, va. émettre de nouveau

Reissue, s. nouvelle émission, *f.*

Reiterate, va. réitérer

Reiteration, s. réitération, *f.*

Reject, va. rejeter

Rejection, s. rejet, *m.*

Rejoice, va. réjouir, égayer; — vn. se réjouir. — *at it*, je m'en réjouis. — *in the Lord*, soyez dans la joie en Notre-Seigneur. *To go on one's way rejoicing*, poursuivre son chemin avec joie

Rejoicing, s. réjouissance, *f.*, joie, *f.*, allégresse, *f.*, jubilation, *f.* *Great —s*, de grandes réjouissances

Rejoicingly, adv. avec joie

Rejoin, va. rejoindre; — vn. répliquer, répondre

Rejoinder, s. réplique, *f.*, réponse, *f.*

Rejoindure, s. embrassement, *m.*
Rejoint, va. rejoindre, rejointoyer
Rejudge, va. rejuger, juger à nouveau
Rekindle, va. rallumer
Relapse, vn. retomber, revenir
Relapse, s. rechute, *f.*
Relate, va. raconter, rapporter, réciter; — vn. avoir rapport, se rapporter
Related, adj. ayant rapport à, (*connected with*) allié (à), parent (de). *To be nearly — to*, être proche parent de, être allié de près à
Relater, s. narrateur, *m.*, conteur, *m.*
Relating, adj. ayant rapport (à), relatif
Relation, s. relation, *f.*, récit, *m.*, (*connection*) rapport, *m.*, (*kin*) parenté, *f.*, alliance, *f.*, (*pers.*) parent, *m.*, proche, *m.f.* *To make a — of*, faire le récit de. *In — to*, relativement à, par rapport à, sous le rapport de, concernant. *Friendly —s*, des relations d'amitié. *A — of ours*, un de nos parents, une de nos parentes. *— by marriage*, parent, parente par alliance
Relationship, s. parenté, *f.*, alliance, *f.*
Relative, adj. relatif
Relative, s. parent, *m.*, -e, *f.*
Relatively, adv. relativement
Relativeness, s. caractère relatif
Relax, va. relâcher, desserrer, détendre, reposer; — vn. se relâcher, prendre du relâche, (*fig.*) se dérider. *To — into a smile*, se dérider
Relax, adj. lâche
Relaxation, s. relâchement, *m.*, relâche, *m.*, repos, *m.*
Relay, s. relais, *m.*
Relay, va. poser de nouveau
Release, va. relâcher, élargir, (*deliver*) délivrer, décharger
Release, s. élargissement, *m.*, délivrance, *f.*, soulagement, *m.*, relâchement, *m.*, (*debt*) décharge, *f.*, (*taxes*) remise, *f.*
Relegate, va. bannir
Relent, vn. s'amollir, mollir, s'attendrir, se dissoudre, se fondre, (*yield*) s'attendrir, fléchir, se radoucir. *To cause to —*, attendrir, fléchir, toucher. *He would not —*, il demeura impitoyable. *Not to —*, ne pas se laisser toucher
Relenting, s. action de s'attendrir, *f.*, de fléchir, *f.*, attendrissement, *m.* *There was no — on his part*, il ne se laissa point toucher. *To show no signs of —*, ne pas se montrer touché *or* ému, demeurer implacable
Relentless, adj. implacable, impitoyable, inflexible, inexorable
Relentlessly, adv. impitoyablement, inexorablement
Relentlessness, s. nature implacable, *f.*
Relet, va. louer de nouveau, relouer
Relevancy, s. convenance, *f.*, relation, *f.*, rapport, *m.*
Relevant, adj. (*to*, à) applicable, qui a rapport à
Reliability, Reliableness, s. confiance, *f.*
Reliable, adj. digne de confiance. *The least —*, le moins digne de confiance
Reliance, s. confiance, *f.* *To place — on*, mettre sa confiance dans
Reliant, adj. (*on*, sur) comptant
Relic, s. relique, *f.* —s, pl. (*remains*) restes, *m.pl.*
Relict, s. veuve, *f.*
Relief, s. soulagement, *m.*, allégement, *m.*, adoucissement, *m.*, secours, *m.*, aide, *f.*, (*money*) subvention, *f.*, (*law*) redressement, *m.*, réparation, *f.*, justice, *f.*, (*mil.*) action de relever, *f.*, garde, *f.*, sentinelle qui en relève une autre, *f.*, (*artil.*) relief, *m.* *To feel some —*, éprouver un certain soulagement. *To give some —*, apporter quelque soulagement, soulager un peu. *Out-door —*, secours donnés à domicile. *He could get no —*, il ne put obtenir justice. *To pray —*, demander justice *or* réparation. *To stand out, to bring out in strong —*, ressortir, faire ressortir vigoureusement. *In —*, en relief. *High —*, haut relief, relief entier
Reliefless, adj. sans secours
Relier, s. (*on*, sur) qui compte
Relievable, adj. qu'on peut secourir
Relieve, va. soulager, alléger, adoucir, délivrer, secourir, aider, venir en aide à, assister, subvenir à, (*law*) redresser, faire justice à, (*sentries*) relever. *To feel somewhat —d*, se sentir un peu soulagé. *To — from pain*, soulager, apaiser la douleur de. *The eye was agreeably —d*, l'œil fut agréablement reposé. *Apply to me, and I will — you*, adressez-vous à moi, et je vous viendrai en aide. *To — each other*, se relever
Reliever, s. qui secourt
Relieving, adj. qui donne des secours, de retraite. *— officer*, s. commissaire des pauvres, *m.*
Relight, va. rallumer, éclairer de nouveau
Religion, s. religion, *f.*
Religious, adj. religieux, pieux. *— book*, s. livre de piété, *m.*
Religiously, adv. religieusement
Relinquish, va. abandonner, renoncer à, se désister d' (une prétention)
Relinquishment, s. abandon, *m.*
Reliquary, s. — adj. reliquaire
Relish, s. goût, *m.*, saveur, *f.*, (*fig.*) charme, *m.*, attrait, *m.*, (*cooking, &c.*) assaisonnement, *m.*, morceau friand, *m.* *To have a — for*, avoir le goût de. *To preserve some — of antiquity*, garder un certain parfum d'antiquité
Relish, va. donner du goût à, relever, goûter, savourer, aimer; — vn. avoir bon goût (à), plaire (à), sentir (de)
Relishing, adj. savoureux
Reload, va. recharger
Reluctance, Reluctancy, s. répugnance, *f.* *To show great — to*, se montrer peu empressé
Reluctant, adj. (*pers.*) qui ne veut pas, qui fait *or* agit avec répugnance *or* à contre-cœur, (*th.*) fait à contre-cœur. *I was or I felt — to*, j'avais *or* j'éprouvais de la répugnance à, il me répugnait de, je ne voulais pas, j'hésitais à, c'eût été à contre-cœur que j'eusse. *I gave a — consent*, j'y consentis bien à contre-cœur. *— witness*, témoin qui hésite. *— friends*, des amis peu empressés. *— obedience*, obéissance donnée à contre-cœur
Reluctantly, adv. à contre-cœur, malgré soi, avec répugnance
Rely, vn. compter, se reposer, faire fond (sur) (*see* DEPEND)
Remain, vn. rester, demeurer. *To — in friendship*, rester *or* demeurer amis. *To — alive, seated, doubtful*, demeurer vivant, rester assis, demeurer *or* rester indécis. *I —ed at home reading*, je restai à lire à la maison. *To — over one's time*, rester plus que son temps, (*fig.*) dépasser son heure. *I — yours truly*, je suis votre tout dévoué. *Nothing —s*, il ne reste rien. *All that —s of*, tout ce qui reste de. *While breath —s thee*, tant que la vie te restera. *What —s to be done*, ce qu'il reste à faire. *That —s to be proved*, voilà ce qui reste à prouver. *There —s, it still —s for me to thank you for*, il me reste à vous remercier de. *To — over*, rester en sus
Remainder, s. reste, *m.*, restant, *m.* *For the — of my days*, pendant tout le reste de ma vie
Remaining, adj. qui reste, de reste, restant. *My — days*, le reste de mes jours. *Some — vigour*, un reste de vigueur. *All I have —*, tout ce qui me reste
Remains, s.pl. restes, *m.pl.*, débris, *m.pl.*, dépouille mortelle, *f.* *Some —s of*, un reste de, quelques restes de
Remand, va. faire revenir, commander de revenir, (*law*) renvoyer à une autre audience, (*com.*) contremander
Remark, s. remarque, *f.* *To make a —, to pass —s*, faire une remarque, des remarques. *To elude —*, éviter l'observation
Remark, va.n. remarquer, observer. *Did you — it?* l'avez-vous remarqué? *To cause to be —ed*, faire remarquer. *To be —ed*, être remarqué, (*fig.*) se faire remarquer. *His manacles — him*, ses chaînes le font reconnaître. *He —ed to me that*, il me fit remarquer que. *He bade me — that*, il me fit remarquer que. *His conduct was —ed on with great severity*, sa conduite fut l'objet de remarques sévères
Remarkable, adj. remarquable
Remarkableness, s. nature remarquable, *f.*, singularité, *f.*
Remarkably, adv. remarquablement, d'une façon remarquable
Remarry, vn. se remarier; — va. (*to, with*) remarier (à)
Remeasure, va. mesurer de nouveau, retracer
Remediable, adj. à quoi on peut remédier, réparable
Remedial, adj. réparateur
Remediless, adj. sans remède, irrémédiable, irréparable
Remedy, s. remède, *m.* *Past —*, sans remède
Remedy, va. remédier à, apporter *or* porter remède à. *That may be remedied*, on peut y remédier. *That cannot be remedied*, on ne saurait y remédier *or* c'est sans remède
Remember, va. se souvenir de, se rappeler, se ressouvenir de, (*recognize*) reconnaître. *Who —s nothing*, qui ne se souvient de rien. *I — seeing it*, je me souviens, (*fig.*) il me souvient de l'avoir vu. *— I* souviens-toi! souvenez-vous. *If I — rightly*, si je m'en souviens bien, si j'ai bonne mémoire, si bien il m'en souvient. *Don't you — me?* est-ce que vous ne me reconnaissez pas? *— me kindly to him*, rappelez-moi à son bon souvenir, faites-lui mes amitiés. *Something to — me*, quelque chose pour qu'on se souvienne de moi. *He will — you in his will*, il ne vous oubliera pas dans son testament. *I have —ed you, waiter*, je vous ai donné, garçon. *Please to — us*, ne nous oubliez pas, s'il vous plaît
Remembrance, s. souvenir, *m.*, mémoire, *f.* *I have no — of it*, je n'en ai aucun souvenir. *To be in — ,* vivre dans nos souvenirs. *In — of*, en mémoire de. *To the best of my —*, autant que je m'en souvienne, autant que je puis m'en souvenir. *— wakes*, les souvenirs s'éveil-

lent. *Things are my —*, les choses qui ont eu lieu dans un temps trop reculé pour que j'en aie pu garder le souvenir. *Within man's —*, de mémoire d'homme. *Within my —, within the — of*, à une époque assez rapprochée pour que je puisse m'en souvenir, pour qu'on s'en souvienne. *Give my kind —s to him*, dites-lui bien des choses de ma part

Remembrancer, s. mémento, *m.*, souvenir, *m.*, secrétaire, *m.*, gardien des archives, *m.*

Remind, va. rappeler à, faire souvenir à, remettre dans la mémoire à, faire penser à. *— me of my promise*, rappelez-moi, faites-moi souvenir de ma promesse. *That —ed me how many good things*, cela me fit penser combien de bonnes choses. *Lest you should — him of us*, de peur que vous ne le fassiez penser à nous

Reminder, *see* REMEMBRANCER

Remindful, adj. remémoratif

Reminiscence, s. réminiscence, *f.*

Remiss, adj. négligent, inexact, lent, mou, peu zélé

Remission, s. adoucissement, *m.*, relâchement, *m.*, remise, *f.*, rémission, *f.*, (*med.*) rémission, *f.*, (*com.*) remise, *f.*

Remissly, adv. négligemment, avec négligence

Remissness, s. négligence, *f.*, inattention, *f.*

Remit, va. se relâcher de, (*forgive*) remettre, (*taxes, &c.*) remettre, faire remise, (*to give*) remettre, (*com.*) remettre, faire des remises de fonds; — vn. se relâcher, se ralentir, se calmer, diminuer d'intensité

Remittance, s. remise, *f.* *To make large —s*, faire de fortes remises

Remittent, adj. rémittent

Remitter, s. personne qui remet des fonds, qui envoie de l'argent, personne qui remet, (*law*) réintégration, *f.*

Remnant, s. reste, *m.*, restant, *m.*, débris, *m.*, (*stuffs*) coupon, *m.* *—s of wit*, bribes d'esprit, *f.*

Remodel, va. donner une nouvelle forme à, refondre

Remonstrance, s. remontrance, *f.* *To make strong —s to*, faire de fortes remontrances à

Remonstrate, vn. faire des remontrances. *He was —d out of his resolutions*, leurs remontrances le firent changer de résolutions

Remorse, s. remords, *m.* *To feel —*, avoir des remords. *Stung with —*, plein de remords. *To disjoin — from power*, faire taire chez les puissants la voix du remords.

Without any — of voice, sans baisser la voix

Remorseless, adj. sans remords, impitoyable

Remorselessly, adv. sans remords, sans pitié

Remorselessness, s. absence de remords *f.*, cruauté, *f.*

Remote, adj. éloigné, lointain, reculé, étranger. *— from cities*, loin des villes. *Not very —*, peu éloigné. *At no very — period*, à une époque assez récente. *A — idea*, une légère idée. *— resemblance*, faible ressemblance

Remotely, adv. loin, de loin, au loin, (*slightly*) faiblement, légèrement. *— related to*, un parent éloigné de, une parente éloignée de, qui n'a qu'un faible rapport à

Remoteness, s. éloignement, *m.*, distance, *f.*

Remount, va.n. remonter

Remount, Remounting, s. (*mil.*) remonte, *f.*

Removable, adj. qu'on peut déplacer, amovible

Removal, s. éloignement, *m.*, déplacement, *m.*, transport, *m.*, enlèvement, *m.*, (*of furniture*) déménagement, *m.*, (*dismissal*) destitution, *f.*, renvoi, *m.*, suppression, *f.* (*surg.*) levée, *f.* *For the — of*, pour retirer, pour ôter

Remove, va. éloigner, déplacer, transporter, retirer, ôter, enlever, écarter, lever, (*furniture*) déménager, (*discard*) destituer, renvoyer, redresser, supprimer, (*surg.*) lever; — vn. s'éloigner (de), quitter, (. . .), se retirer (de), déménager, se transporter. *To — from place to place*, changer sans cesse de place, de résidence. *To be always —ing*, être toujours à déménager. *To — into the country*, aller vivre à la campagne, en province

Remove, s. éloignement, *m.*, déplacement, *m.*, déménagement, *m.*, degré, *m.*, distance, *f.*, intervalle, *m.*, (*cookery*) entrée, *f.* *Three —s are as good as a burn*, trois déménagements valent un incendie. *To drag at each — a lengthening chain*, traîner une chaîne qui s'allonge à chaque pas. *Our cousins, even to the fortieth —*, nos cousins, même au quarantième degré

Removed, adj. éloigné, retiré, isolé, solitaire, au . . . degré. *A cousin seven times —*, un cousin au septième degré

Remunerate, va. rémunérer, récompenser, rétribuer

Remuneration, s. rémunération, *f.*

Remunerative, Remuneratory, adj. rémunératoire, rémunérateur

Rend, va. déchirer, fendre, briser. *To — asunder, in twain*, déchirer en deux, fendre en deux. *To — away, to — off*, arracher. *To — one's garments was a token of grief*, le déchirement des habits était une marque de douleurs. — vn. se déchirer, se fendre

Render, va. rendre. *To — evil for good*, rendre le mal pour le bien. *To — a service*, rendre un service. *To — death familiar*, rendre la mort familière. *To — back*, rendre, restituer. *To — what we have in charge*, dire ce dont nous sommes chargés. *To — oneself*, se rendre, se livrer. *To — up*, rendre, livrer, renoncer à, céder

Rendering, s. action de rendre, *f.*, traduction, *f.*

Rendezvous, vn. se donner rendez-vous, se réunir

Renegade, s. renégat, *m.*

Renew, va. renouveler, renouer

Renewable, adj. renouvelable

Renewal, Renewing, s. renouvellement, *m.*

Rennet, s. caillette, *f.*, présure, *f.*

Renounce, va. renoncer à, (*deny*) renier. *I — going thither*, je renonce à y aller

Renovate, va. renouveler, faire renaître

Renovation, s. rénovation, *f.*, renouvellement, *m.*

Renown, s. renommée, *f.*, renom, *m.*, célébrité, *f.* *To win —*, se faire un nom, acquérir de la renommée. *Of no —*, sans renommée

Renowned, adj. renommé, célèbre. *To be —*, avoir du renom

Rent, s. déchirure, *f.*, déchirement, *m.*, schisme, *m.*, (*cleft*) fissure, *f.*, (*of houses*) loyer, *m.*, (*lands*) fermage, *m.*, rente, *f.*, redevance, *f.* *Heavy —*, fort loyer. *—s are high*, les loyers sont élevés. *Quarter's —*, terme, *m.* *— -day*, le jour du terme. *— free*, exempt de loyer, sans payer de loyer. *— -charge*, s. rente annuelle. *— -roll*, s. état des revenus, *m.*, livre censier, *m.* *— -seck*, rente annuelle. *— service*, s. fermage avec corvée

Rent, va. louer, prendre à loyer, (*lands*) affermer, prendre à ferme, (*to rent out*) louer, donner à loyer, affermer, donner à ferme

Rentable, adj. qu'on peut louer

Rental, s. locataire, *m.*, fermier, *m.*

Renunciation, s. renonciation, *f.*, renoncement, *m.*

Reopen, va. rouvrir

Reopening, s. réouverture, *f.*

Reorganization, s. réorganisation, *f.*

Reorganize, va. réorganiser

Repaint, va. repeindre

Repair, va. réparer, (*clothes*) raccommoder, (*ship*) radouber, (*health*) rétablir. *To — a loss, a wrong*, réparer une perte, un tort. *To be —ed*, être réparé, se réparer. *The house is being —ed*, la maison est en réparation. — vn. se rendre, se transporter, aller. *To — back*, s'en retourner

Repair, s. réparation, *f.*, entretien, *m.*, état, *m.*, radoub, *m.* *To be under —*, être en réparation. *To make the —s*, faire les réparations. *To keep in —*, faire les réparations nécessaires, entretenir. *To undergo a thorough —*, être réparé de fond en comble. *The heavy —s*, les grosses réparations. *To cost a good deal for —s*, être d'un grand entretien. *In good —*, en bon état

Repairer, s. réparateur, *m.*, -trice, *f.*

Reparable, adj. réparable

Reparation, s. réparation, *f.*

Repartee, s. repartie, *f.*, riposte, *f.* *To be quick at —*, avoir la repartie prompte, être prompt à la riposte

Repartition, s. répartition, *f.*

Repass, va.n. repasser

Repast, s. repas, *m.*, nourriture, *f.*

Repasture, s. pâture, *f.*

Repay, va. rembourser, récompenser, payer, dédommager

Repayable, adj. remboursable

Repayment, s. remboursement, *m.*

Repeal, va. rappeler, (*law*) rapporter

Repeal, s. abrogation, *f.*, révocation, *f.*, rappel, *m.*

Repealer, s. qui abroge, (*polit.*) partisan du rappel, *m.*

Repeat, va. répéter, redire, (*by heart*) réciter. *To — over and over again*, répéter à plusieurs reprises, répéter sans cesse. *To make a person —*, faire répéter à quelqu'un. *To have a thing —ed*, faire répéter quelque chose. *It must not be —ed*, il ne faut pas que cela se répète

Repeatedly, adv. à plusieurs reprises, plusieurs fois

Repeater, s. qui répète, etc., (*watch*) montre à répétition, *f.*

Repeating, adj. qui répète, à répétition

Repel, va. repousser

Repent, vn. se repentir de

Repentance, s. repentir, *m.*, repentance, *f.*

Repentant, adj. repentant, -e

Repentant, s. celui, celle qui se repent

Repenting, adj. repentant

Repentingly, adv. avec repentir, en se repentant, d'un ton de repentir

Repeople, va. repeupler
Repeopling, s. repeuplement, *m.*
Repercussion, s. répercussion, *f.*
Repertory, s. répertoire, *m.*
Repetition, s. répétition, *f.*, récitation, *f.*
Repine, vn. murmurer (contre), se plaindre (de)
Repining, s. murmures, *m.pl.*, plaintes, *f.pl.*, regrets, *m.pl.* *Cease this* —, cessez ces murmures. *Without* —, sans regrets
Repiningly, adv. en murmurant
Replace, va. remettre en place, (*by substitution*) remplacer. *To — each other*, se remplacer
Replacement, s. remise en place, *f.*, remplacement, *m.*
Replant, va. replanter
Replantation, s. replantation, *f.*
Replenish, va. remplir
Replenishment, s. action de remplir, *f.*, approvisionnement, *m.*
Replete, adj. rempli, plein
Replier, s. qui répond
Reply, vn.a. répliquer, répondre
Reply, s. réponse, *f.*, réplique, *f.*
Repolish, va. repolir
Report, va. rapporter, raconter, dire, (*give an account*) faire le rapport de *or* sur, rendre compte de. *To — oneself*, se présenter, faire viser ses papiers
Report, s. (*statement*) rapport, *m.*, compte, *m.*, récit, *m.*, exposé, *m.*, compte-rendu, *m.*, procès-verbal, *m.*, (*rumour*) bruit, *m.*, bruit public, *m.*, rumeur, *f.*, renommée, *f.*, ouï-dire, *f.*, (*repute*) considération, *f.*, réputation, *f.*, (*of guns*) détonation, *f.* *To make a* —, rendre compte, faire un rapport. *To make a false — of*, rendre faussement compte de. *To make a —, an official* —, faire son rapport, dresser un procès-verbal, verbaliser, faire un compte-rendu. *There was a — that*, le bruit courait que. *Common* —, le bruit public, la commune renommée. *A current* —, un bruit qui court. *Of good* —, bien famé. *Through good or ill* —, quoi qu'on pût dire
Reporter, s. rapporteur, *m.*, sténographe, *m.*, journaliste, *m.*, correspondant, *m.* *The — of this fact*, celui qui rapporte ce fait. *Parliamentary* —, sténographe des chambres, *m.*
Reposal, s. confiance, *f.*, appui, *m.*
Repose, va. reposer, confier; — vn. se reposer, (*trust*) se reposer (sur)
Repose, s. repos, *m.*
Reposit, va. déposer
Repository, s. dépôt, *m.*, entrepôt, *m.*, magasin, *m.*
Repossess, va. posséder de nouveau, rentrer en possession de. *To — oneself*, se remettre en possession de, s'emparer de nouveau de
Repossession, s. rentrée en possession, *f.*
Reprehend, va. reprendre, réprimander
Reprehensible, adj. répréhensible
Reprehensibly, adv. d'une manière répréhensible
Reprehension, s. répréhension, *f.*
Reprehensive, **Reprehensory**, adj. de reproche
Represent, va. représenter
Representation, s. représentation, *f.*
Representative, adj. représentatif, -ive
Representative, s. député, *m.*, représentant, *m.*
Representatively, adv. par représentation
Repress, va. réprimer
Represser, s. qui réprime, dompteur, *m.*
Repression, s. répression, *f.*
Repressive adj. répressif
Reprieve, va. accorder un sursis à, surseoir à l'exécution de, (*fig.*) donner du répit à
Reprieve, s. sursis, *m.*, répit, *m.*
Reprimand, va. réprimander
Reprimand, s. réprimande, *f.*
Reprint, va. réimprimer
Reprint, s. réimpression, *f.*
Reprisal, s. représaille, *f.* *By way of* —, par représailles, par manière de représailles. *To make —s*, user de représailles
Reprise, s. reprise, *f.*
Reproach, va. faire des reproches à, blâmer, reprocher. *To — sharply*, faire de vifs reproches à. *To — oneself for* or *with*, se reprocher
Reproach, s. reproche, *m.*, opprobre, *m.* *I say this without intending the slightest* —, soit dit sans reproche. *To receive —es for*, recevoir des reproches de
Reproachable, adj. digne de reproche
Reproachful, adj. de reproche, outrageant, injurieux. *In a — tone*, d'un ton de reproche. — *words*, des mots injurieux
Reproachfully, adv. d'un ton de reproche, avec reproche, injurieusement, avec opprobre
Reprobate, adj. s. réprouvé, (*fam.*) vaurien, *m.*
Rebrobation, s. réprobation, *f.*
Reproduce, va. reproduire
Reproduction, s. reproduction, *f.*
Reproductive, **Reproductory**, adj. reproducteur, reproductif
Refroof, s. reproche, *m.*, réprimande, *f.* *To bear* —, souffrir, supporter les reproches
Reprovable, adj. répréhensible
Reproval, s. reproches, *m.pl.*
Reprove, va. blâmer (de), faire des reproches à, censurer, reprendre
Reprover, s. censeur, *m.*
Reptile, s. reptile, *m.*
Reptile, adj. reptile, rampant, bas
Republic, s. république, *f.*
Republican, adj. s. républicain, -e
Republicanism, s. républicanisme, *m.*
Republicanize, va. républicaniser
Republication, s. republication, *f.*, nouvelle édition, *f.*
Republish, va. republier
Repudiate, va. répudier
Repudiation, s. répudiation, *f.*
Repugnance, s. répugnance, *f.*, résistance, *f.*, contrariété, *f.* *To have* or *feel a — to*, avoir de la répugnance pour, répugner à
Repugnant, adj. répugnant, qui répugne, incompatible. *It is — to my feelings to*, il me répugne de. *To be — to*, répugner à
Repugnantly, adv. avec répugnance
Repulse, s. échec, *m.*, refus, *m.*, rebuffade, *f.* *To meet with a —, to know* —, essuyer un échec, un refus, être repoussé
Repulsion, s. répulsion, *f.*
Repulsive, adj. répulsif, repoussant
Repulsively, adv. d'une manière repoussante
Repulsiveness, s. caractère repoussant, *m.*
Repurchase, va. racheter
Repurchase, s. rachat, *m.*, nouvelle acquisition, *f.*
Reputable, adj. considéré, honorable
Reputableness, s. bonne réputation, *f.*, caractère honorable, *m.*
Reputably, adv. honorablement
Reputation, s. réputation, *f.* *To bring into* —, mettre en réputation. *To get* or *win a* —, se faire une réputation. *To ruin the — of*, perdre de réputation
Repute, va. réputer pour, regarder comme. *To be —d*, passer pour, être réputé
Repute, s. réputation, *f.*, bonne réputation, *f.* *To be in* —, avoir de la réputation, être en réputation. *Of good —, of ill* —, de bonne, de mauvaise réputation. *Of no* —, sans réputation. *Upheld by old* —, soutenu par une vieille réputation. *To bring into* —, mettre en réputation, mettre en vogue
Reputed, adj. censé, réputé
Request, s. demande, *f.*, prière, *f.*, requête, *f.*, recherche, *f.*, vogue, *f.*, honneur, *m.*, crédit, *m.* *To make a* —, faire une demande, présenter *or* faire une requête. *At his* —, sur sa demande. *At the — of*, à la demande de, à la requête de. *To comply with a* —, se rendre à une prière. *The court of —s*, la cour des requêtes, *f.* *To be in great —, in little* —, être fort recherché *or* demandé, être peu recherché *or* demandé, être en grand honneur, n'être guère en honneur
Request, va. demander, solliciter, prier (de), inviter (à). *To — a favour of*, demander une faveur à, solliciter une faveur de
Requiem, s. requiem, *m.*
Require, va. (*right*) demander (à), exiger (de), vouloir, requérir (de), (*must have*) falloir, (*need*) avoir besoin de. *This the law of God requireth at our hands*, la loi de Dieu l'exige de chacun de nous. *What is —d of us*, ce qu'on exige de nous. *He —s obedience*, il veut être obéi. *I am —d to send some one*, on veut que j'envoie quelqu'un, on m'invite à envoyer quelqu'un. *Faith is not all that is —d*, ce n'est pas tout que d'avoir la foi. *What our wants* —, ce qu'exigent nos besoins. *It —s great care to*, il faut de grands soins pour. *Requiring great care*, qui a besoin de grands soins. *The business —d my presence*, l'affaire demandait, exigeait, requérait ma présence
Requirement, s. exigence, *f.*, besoin, *m.*, nécessité, *f.*, qualité voulue, *f.*
Requisite, adj. requis, exigé, voulu
Requisite, s. qualité requise, *f.*, condition requise, *f.*, chose nécessaire, *f.*
Requisition, s. réquisition, *f.*, demande, *f.*, réclamation, *f.*, revendication, *f.* *To put into* —, mettre en réquisition
Requital, s. récompense, *f.*, retour, *m.* *In — of*, en retour de
Requite, va. récompenser, payer, reconnaître
Rescind, va. rescinder, abroger, annuler, casser
Rescript, s. rescrit, *m.*
Rescue, va. délivrer, sauver, arracher (à), (*things*) recouvrer
Rescue, s. rescousse, *f.*, secours, *m.*, délivrance, *f.*
Research, s. recherche, *f.*
Research, va. rechercher, chercher de nouveau

Researcher, s. auteur de recherches, investigateur, *m.*

Reseat, va. rasseoir, remettre sur son siége

Reseize, va. ressaisir

Reseizure, s. nouvelle saisie, *f.*

Resemblance, s. ressemblance, *f.*

Resemble, va. ressembler à

Resent, va. se ressentir. *He highly —ed it,* il en fut profondément irrité. *Have I not enough to —?* n'ai-je pas assez de motifs de ressentiment?

Resentful, adj. plein de ressentiment, rancunier, vindicatif, irritable. *In a — tone,* d'un ton de ressentiment. *His — temper,* son caractère rancunier

Resentfully, adv. avec ressentiment

Resentive, adj. irritable

Resentment, s. ressentiment, *m.*

Reservation, s. réserve, *f.*, restriction, *f.*, (*law*) réservation, *f.* *In heedful —,* avec soin et réserve. *Full of —s,* plein de restrictions. *Mental —,* restriction mentale. *With the — of his rights,* à la reserve de ses droits

Reserve, va. réserver, garder, conserver. *To — to oneself,* se réserver. *To be —d for,* être réservé pour, se réserver pour

Reserve, s. réserve, *f.*, restriction, *f.*, retenue, *f.*, discrétion, *f.* *To hold in —,* tenir en réserve. *Body of —,* corps de réserve, *m.*, réserve, *f.* *With —,* avec réserve. *Without any —,* sans réserve. *To plead for a —,* demander à être excepté. *To make —s,* faire des réserves. *Mental —,* restriction mentale. *To stand on the —,* se tenir sur la réserve

Reserved, adj. réservé, mis en réserve. *To pretend to be —,* faire le réservé

Reservedly, adv. avec réserve

Reservoir, s. réservoir, *m.*

Resettle, va. rétablir, reposer, replacer, indiquer de nouveau

Resettlement, s. rétablissement, *m.*, assurance, *f.*

Reship, va. rembarquer

Reside, vn. résider, demeurer

Residence, s. résidence, *f.*, séjour, *m.*, demeure, *f.*, (*law*) domicile, *m.* *To take up one's —,* faire sa résidence, se fixer

Resident, adj. s. résidant, qui réside, résident. *—-master,* s. maître interne, *m.*

Residentship, s. résidence, *f.*

Residuary, adj. restant, de résidu. *— legatee,* légataire universel

Residue, s. reste, *m.*, (*of a debt, &c.*) reliquat, *m.*

Residuum, s. résidu, *m.*, marc, *m.*

Resign, va. résigner (*office*) se démettre de, donner sa démission, céder, renoncer à. *To — the crown,* abdiquer. *To — oneself (up) to,* se résigner à, se soumettre. *To — one's soul to God,* résigner son âme à Dieu. *We must be resigned,* il faut nous résigner or être résignés. — vn. donner sa démission

Resignation, s. résignation, *f.*, démission, *f.*, abandon, *m.*, cession, *f.*, renonciation, *f.* *To give in one's —,* donner sa démission

Resignedly, adv. avec résignation

Resin, s. résine, *f.*, (*for violins*) colophane, *f.*

Resinous, adj. résineux

Resist, va.n. résister à, combattre

Resistance, s. résistance, *f.*

Resistant, adj. qui résiste, de résistance

Resistless, adj. irrésistible, sans défense

Resistlessly, adv. irrésistiblement

Resistlessness, s. force irrésistible, *f.*

Resolute, adj. résolu. *To be —,* être résolu, avoir de la résolution

Resolutely, adv. résolûment

Resoluteness, s. résolution, *f.*, fermeté, *f.*

Resolution, s. résolution, *f.*, décision, *f.*, fermeté, *f.*, proposition, *f.*, décision, *f.* *To come to a —, to set a —,* prendre une résolution. *A man of —,* un homme résolu. *To put on a look of —,* prendre un air résolu. *To move a —,* faire une proposition. *To adopt, to pass a —,* adopter une proposition

Resolvable, adj. résoluble, soluble

Resolve, va. résoudre, (*to melt*) dissoudre, fondre, (*difficulties*) expliquer, (*doubts*) éclaircir, lever. *—d in death, —d to die in arms,* résolu à la mort, résolu de mourir en combattant. *The House —d itself into a committee* la Chambre se forma en comité secret. — vn. se résoudre, se dissoudre, se décomposer, arrêter, décider. *On what have you —d?* à quoi vous êtes-vous décidé? *He —d on consulting him, to consult him,* il résolut de le consulter, il se décida à le consulter

Resolve, s. résolution, *f.*, décision, *f.*

Resonance, s. résonnance, *f.*

Resonant, adj. résonnant

Resort, vn. se rendre (à), aller (à), fréquenter, avoir recours

Resort, s. action d'aller, *f.*, fréquentation, *f.*, visite, *f.*, rendez-vous, *m.*, lieu fréquenté, *m.*, (*law*) ressort, *m.* *A great place of — for invalids,* un lieu très-fréquenté par les malades

Resound, vn. (*with,* de) résonner, retentir. *To — back,* revenir, retentir

Resource, s. ressource, *f.*

Resourceless, adj. sans ressources

Respect, va. respecter, regarder, considérer, avoir égard à, (*things*) avoir rapport à. *To make oneself —ed by,* se faire respecter de. *To — oneself, to — each other,* se respecter

Respect, s. respect, *m.*, égard, *m.*, acception, *f.* *—s,* pl. hommages, *m.pl.*, devoirs, *m.pl.* *To have, to feel a great — for,* avoir un grand respect pour. *Out of — to,* par respect pour, par égard pour. *With profound —,* avec un profond respect. *To impress with —, to create — in,* imprimer le respect dans. *To be wanting in — towards,* manquer de respect à. *To pay one's —s to,* rendre, présenter ses respects, ses hommages à. *With — to,* à l'égard de, pour ce qui est de, par rapport à. *In — of,* à l'égard de, pour ce qui est de. *In this —,* à cet égard, sous ce rapport. *In every —,* à tous égards, sous tous les rapports. *In no —,* sous aucun rapport. *In some —s,* à certains égards, sous quelques rapports. *In one —,* sous un rapport

Respectability, s. caractère respectable *or* honorable, *m.*, considération, *f.*, honnêteté, *f.*, décence, *f.* *The — of his character,* son caractère respectable. *To conduce to —,* donner de la considération

Respectable, adj. respectable, honorable, dans une position honorable, considéré, (*assemblies*) bien composé

Respectably, adv. respectablement, honorablement, dans la considération, passablement

Respectful, adj. respectueux. *To be — to,* avoir du respect pour, être respectueux de

Respectfully, adv. respectueusement, avec respect

Respectfulness, s. caractère respectueux, *m.*

Respecting, prep. touchant, relativement à, à l'égard de, quant à. *— you,* à votre égard

Respective, adj. respectif, relatif

Respectively, adv. respectivement, relativement

Respectless, adj. sans respect

Respirable, adj. respirable

Respiration, s. respiration, *f.*, repos, *m.*, intervalle, *m.*

Respirator, s. respirateur, *m.*

Respite, s. répit, *m.*, relâche, *m.*, (*law*) sursis, *m.*

Respite, va. donner du répit à, suspendre, (*law*) surseoir à

Resplendence, s. splendeur, *f.*, éclat, *m.*

Resplendent, adj. resplendissant. *To be —,* resplendir

Resplendently, adv. avec splendeur, avec éclat

Respond, vn. (*to*) répondre (à)

Respondent, s. répondant, *m.*, (*law*) défendeur, *m.*, -eresse, *f.*

Response, s. réponse, *f.*, réplique, *f.*, (*church*) répons, *m.*

Responsibility, s. responsabilité, *f.* *On my —,* sous ma responsabilité. *To assume the — of,* se rendre responsable de

Responsible, adj. responsable

Rest, s. repos, *m.*, paix, *f.*, (*for a lance*) arrêt, *m.*, (*prop*) appui, *m.*, support, *m.*, (*mus.*) pause, *f.*, (*poet.*) césure, *f.* *Place of —,* lieu de repos. *To be at —,* être en repos. *A bit of —,* un moment d'arrêt, un peu de repos. *—-harrow,* s. ononis, *m.* *—-house,* s. auberge, *f.* *To retire to —,* aller se reposer, aller prendre du repos, se coucher. *To take no —,* ne pas prendre de repos. *To have a good night's rest,* passer une bonne nuit. *I could get no —,* je ne pus dormir. *To put to —,* coucher, faire cesser. *To set at —,* faire cesser, éclaircir, décider. *Everlasting —,* le repos éternel. *Place of —,* champ de repos, *m.* *To fix one's lance in (its) —,* mettre sa lance en arrêt. *To set up one's — upon,* mettre toutes ses espérances dans

Rest, vn. se reposer, reposer, dormir, (*to trust*) se reposer (sur), se confier, se fier (à), compter (sur), (*to lean*) s'appuyer, reposer, être appuyé, se baser. *Go and —,* allez vous reposer. *Let him —,* laissez-le reposer. *Here —s,* ici repose. — va. reposer, faire reposer, donner le repos à, calmer, (*to support*) reposer, appuyer, poser, (*to establish*) baser, fonder, (*confidence*) mettre avoir

Resting, adj. de repos

Resting, s. *— -place,* s. lieu de repos, *m.*

Restitution, s. restitution, *f.*

Restive, adj. rétif, indocile

Restless, adj. sans repos, incessant, (*anxious*) inquiet, agité, (*noisy*) turbulent, remuant

Restlessly, adv. sans repos, incessamment, avec agitation, avec inquiétude, avec turbulence

Restlessness, s. mouvement incessant, *m.*, insomnie

f., agitation, *f.*, inquiétude, *f.*

Restorable, adj. qui peut être restitué *or* rendu, qui peut être restauré *or* rétabli

Restoration, s. restitution, *f.*, rétablissement, *m.*, restauration, *f.*

Restorative, adj. s. restaurant

Restore, va. rendre, remettre, restituer, rétablir, réintégrer, (*to health*) rendre, (*to life*) rappeler, (*repair*) restaurer. *To — to the throne*, rétablir, remettre sur le trône

Restorer, s. restaurateur, *m.*

Restrain, va. retenir, contenir, réprimer, (*hinder*) empêcher, (*to turn away*) détourner, éloigner, (*prohibit*) interdire à, défendre à

Restrainable, adj. qu'on peut retenir, contenir

Restraining, adj. restrictif

Restraint, s. contrainte, *f.*, gêne, *f.*, frein, *m.*, (*hindrance*) empêchement, *m.*, restriction, *f.*, défense, *f.*

Restrict, va. restreindre

Restriction, s. restriction, *f.*

Restrictive, adj. restrictif. *To be — of*, mettre, porter quelque restriction a

Restrictively, adv. avec restriction

Restringent, adj. astringent, -e

Result, vn. résulter. *No good will — from it*, il n'en résultera rien de bon

Result, s. résultat, *m.* *Which will give no —*, dont il ne résultera rien

Resume, va. reprendre, continuer

Resumption, s. reprise, *f.*, continuation, *f.*

Resurrection, s. résurrection, *f.*

Resurvey, va. examiner de nouveau, revoir, arpenter de nouveau

Resuscitate, va. ressusciter; — vn. ressusciter, revivre

Resuscitation, s. résurrection, *f.*, retour à la vie, *m.*, renaissance, *f.*, renouvellement, *m.*

Retail, va. détailler, vendre en détail

Retail, s. détail, *m.* — *-shopkeeper*, s. détaillant, *m.*, -e, *f.*

Retail, adj. en détail

Retailer, s. détaillant, *m.*, -e, *f.*

Retain, va. retenir, conserver, garder, prendre à son service, engager

Retainer, s. personne qui retient, dépendant, *m.*, partisan, *m.*, serviteur, *m.* —*s*, pl. gens, *m.pl.*, suite, *f.*, (*fees*) honoraires, *m.pl.*

Retaining, adj. de soutènement, (*law*) qui retient les services de

Retake, va. reprendre

Retaliate, va.n. rendre, payer de retour, se venger de, user de représailles

Retaliation, s. pareille, *f.*, talion, *m.*, représailles, *f. plur.*

Retard, va. retarder

Retardation, s. retardement, *m.*, retard, *m.*, retardation, *f.*

Retch, vn. faire des efforts pour vomir

Retention, s. conservation, *f.*, mémoire, *f.*, (*med.*) rétention, *f.*

Retentive, adj. qui retient, qui garde, qui conserve, (*memory*) fidèle, tenace, sûr

Retentiveness, s. fidélité, *f.*, ténacité, *f.*, sûreté, *f.*

Reticence, s. réticence, *f.*

Reticular, adj. réticulaire

Reticule, s. sac, *m.*, ridicule, *m.*

Retina, s. rétine, *f.*

Retinue, s. suite, *f.*, cortége, *m.* *Without a —*, sans suite

Retire, va. retirer; — vn. se retirer

Retired, adj. retiré, caché. *On the — list*, en retraite, à la retraite

Retiredly, adv. dans la retraite

Retirement, s. retraite, *f.*

Retiring, adj. qui se retire, (*bashful*) réservé, modeste, (*out of office*) sortant, (*pension*) de retraite

Retort, va. renvoyer, réfléchir; (*argument*) rétorquer; — vn. répliquer, riposter. — *on or upon*, rembarrer

Retort, s. réplique, *f.*, riposte, *f.*, (*chem.*) cornue, *f.*

Retouch, va. retoucher

Retouch, s. retouche, *f.*

Retrace, va. retracer, remonter à, revenir *or* retourner sur

Retract, va. retirer, rétracter; — vn. se rétracter, se dédire

Retraction, s. rétractation, *f.*

Retranslate, va. retraduire

Retreat, s. retraite, *f.* *To effect a —*, opérer sa retraite

Retreat, vn. se retirer, (*milit.*) battre en retraite, être en retraite

Retreating, adj. en retraite, qui bat en retraite, fuyant

Retrench, va. retrancher, restreindre; — vn. se retrancher

Retrenchment, s. retranchement, *m.*

Retribute, va. (*for*, de) rétribuer

Retribution, s. retour, *m.*, récompense, *f.*, rétribution, *f.*, (*punishment*) châtiment, *m.*

Retributive, **Retributory**, adj. qui récompense

Retrievable, adj. qu'on peut retrouver, réparer, rétablir

Retrieve, va. retrouver, réparer, racheter, rétablir, relever, (*reclaim*) arracher (à)

Retriever, s. épagneul écossais, *m.*

Retrim, va. arranger de nouveau

Retroaction, s. rétroaction, *f.*

Retroactive, adj. rétroactif

Retrograde, adj. rétrograde

Retrograde, vn. rétrograder

Retrogradingly, adv. en rétrogradant

Retrogression, s. mouvement rétrograde, *m.*

Retrogressive, adj. rétrograde

Retrospect, **Retrospection**, s. regard jeté en arrière (sur), *m.*, revue, *f.*, examen, *m.*

Retrospective, adj. rétrospectif

Retrospectively, adv. d'une manière rétrospective

Retting, s. rouissage, *m.*

Return, vn. (*go back*) retourner, s'en retourner, (*go home*) revenir, (*in doors*) rentrer, (*answer*) répondre, répliquer. *To — to England*, retourner en Angleterre. *To have —ed*, être de retour. *To be on the point of —ing*, être sur le retour. *To — unto dust*, retourner en poussière. *Never to —*, pour ne plus jamais revenir. *He —ed as he went*, il revint comme il était parti *or* avec sa courte honte. *To — to the charge, to one's subject*, revenir à la charge, à son sujet. *But to — to our subject*, mais revenons à nos moutons. — va. rendre, restituer, (*send back*) renvoyer, remporter, (*put back*) remettre, (*compliment*) rendre, (*answer*) rendre, (*account*) rendre compte de, faire un rapport de, (*administ.*) dresser l'état de, (*elect*) élire, nommer, envoyer, (*com.*) retourner

Return, s. retour, *m.*, rentrée, *f.*, restitution, *f.*, action de rendre, *f.*, (*sending back*) renvoi, *m.*, (*place*) remise, *f.*, (*fortune*) retour, *m.*, (*paying back*) remboursement, *m.*, (*recompense*) retour, *m.*, (*profit*) gain, *m.*, profit, *m.*, (*statement*) rapport, *m.*, compte rendu, *m.*, état, *m.*, relevé, *m.*, (*election*) nomination, *f.*, élection, *f.*, (*answer*) réponse, *f.*, réplique, *f.*, riposte, *f.*, repartie, *f.*, (*archit.*) retour, *m.*, (*bank account*) bilan, *m.* — *-ticket*, s. billet d'aller et retour, *m.*

Returnable, adj. restituable, (*law*) de renvoi

Reunion, s. réunion, *f.*

Reunite, va. réunir; — se réunir

Reveal, va. révéler

Revealer, s. révélateur, *m.*, -trice, *f.*

Reveille, s. réveil, *m.*, diane, *f.* *To beat the —*, battre le réveil

Revel, vn. se divertir, se réjouir, s'ébattre, festiner, banqueter

Revel, s. ébats, *m.pl.*, divertissements, *m.pl.*, réjouissances, *f.pl.*, festin, *m.*

Revelation, s. révélation, *f.*

Reveller, s. joyeux convive, *m.*, viveur, *m.*, buveur, *m.*

Revelling, **Revelry**, see Revel

Revenge, va. venger, se venger de. *To — oneself on, to be —d on*, se venger de. *To — oneself, to be —d of a thing on a person*, se venger de quelque chose sur quelqu'un, avoir, prendre, tirer vengeance de quelque chose sur quelqu'un

Revenge, s. vengeance, *f.*, (*in a mild sense*) revanche, *f.* *Out of — for*, en vengeance de, pour venger. *Out of mere —*, par pur esprit de vengeance. *Burning for —*, plein du désir de la vengeance, brûlant de se venger. *Eager for —*, avide de vengeance. *Prone to —*, porté à la vengeance. *Without —*, sans vengeance. *To take — for*, se venger de

Revengeful, adj. vindicatif, porté à la vengeance

Revengefully, adv. par vengeance, par esprit de vengeance

Revengefulness, s. caractère vindicatif *m.*, esprit de vengeance, *m.*

Revenger, s. vengeur, *m.*, -eresse, *f.*

Revenue, s. revenu, *m.* — *-cutter*, s. patache, *f.* — *-officer*, s. officier de la douane, *m.*

Reverberate, va. renvoyer, réfléchir, réverbérer, (*sound*) répercuter

Reverberation, s. réverbération, *f.*, réflexion, *f.*, répercussion, *f.*

Reverberatory, adj. à réverbère

Revere, va. révérer

Reverence, s. vénération, *f.*, révérence, *m.* *To hold in —*, révérer. *To do or to pay —*, rendre hommage. *Your —*, mon Révérend

Reverence, va. révérer, vénérer

Reverend, adj. vénérable, révérend

Reverential, adj. révérencieux, révérenciel, respectueux

Reverentially, **Reverently**, adv. avec vénération, révérencieusement, avec respect

Reversal, s. annulation, *f.*, cassation, *f.*, réhabilitation, *f.*

Reverse, va. renverser, révoquer

Reverse, adj. inverse

Reverse, s. revers, *m.*, (*opposite*) inverse, *f.*, opposé, *m.*, contre-pied, *m.*, (*fortune*) retour, *m.*, vicissitude, *f.*, revers, *m.*, (*medal*) revers, *m.*, (*page*) verso, *m.* *To do just the —*, faire justement l'inverse. *— of fate*, revers de fortune. *By a strange — of things*, par un bizarre retour des choses. *To meet with —s*, avoir des revers

Reversed, past part. renversé

Reverseless, adj. irrévocable

Reversely, adv. en sens inverse

Reversible, adj. révocable

Reversion, s. retour, *m.*, survivance, *f.*, réversion, *f.*

Reversionary, adj. faisant retour, réversible

Revert, vn. retourner, revenir

Revertible, adj. réversible

Revetement, s. revêtement, *m.*

Revictual, va. ravitailler

Review, va. revoir, (*book*) reviser, critiquer, rendre compte de, analyser, examiner, (*milit.*) passer en revue, passer la revue de

Review, s. revue, *f.*, révision, *f.*, (*book, &c.*) critique, *f.*, compte rendu, *m.*, analyse, *f.*, article, *m.*, (*mil.*) revue, *f.*, (*law*) révision, *f.* *To take a — of, to pass in —*, faire une revue de, faire la revue de. *The period under —*, l'époque que nous passons en revue

Reviewer, s. réviseur, *m.*, (*of books*) critique, *m.*

Revigorate, adj. doué d'une nouvelle vigueur

Revile, va. injurier, dire des injures à, insulter

Revise, va. revoir, réviser

Revise, s. révision, *f.*, seconde épreuve, *f.*

Reviser, s. qui revoit, réviseur, *m.*

Revision, s. révision, *f.*

Revisit, va. visiter de nouveau

Revival, s. retour à la vie, *m.*, (*of letters*) renaissance, *f.*, (*of strength*) rétablissement, *m.*

Revive, vn. revenir à la vie, revivre, ressusciter, se ranimer, reprendre; — va. faire revivre, rappeler *or* rendre à la vie, ressusciter, (*rouse*) ranimer, faire renaître, renouveler, raviver, (*a hat*) retaper, (*to put in use*) remettre en vigueur

Reviver, s. qui fait revivre, qui ranime, restaurateur, *m.*

Revivification, s. révivification, *f.*

Reviving, adj. qui ranime, qui se ranime, renaissant. *To be quite —*, ranimer les esprits, donner une nouvelle vie. *His — strength*, ses forces qui revenaient. *Ever — hope*, espoir toujours renaissant

Revocable, adj. révocable

Revocation, s. révocation, *f.*

Revoke, va. révoquer; — vn. (*at cards*) renoncer, faire une renonce

Revoke, s. renonce, *f.*

Revolt, vn. se révolter, se soulever; — va. révolter, soulever

Revolt, s. révolte, *f.* *In* en (état de) révolte. *To —, urge or rouse to —*, faire se révolter

Revolted, adj. révolté, en révolte, soulevé, rebelle

Revolter, s. révolté, *m.*

Revolting, adj. qui se révolte, révoltant. *A — sight*, un spectacle révoltant. *To be — to*, révolter

Revolution, s. révolution, *f.*, (*of a wheel, &c.*) tour, *m.*

Revolutionary, adj. révolutionnaire

Revolutionist, s. révolutionnaire, *m.*

Revolutionize, va. révolutionner

Revolve, vn.a. tourner, opérer *or* faire sa révolution, (*fig.*) rouler dans son esprit, penser à

Revolvency, s. mouvement de révolution, *m.*

Revolver, s. revolver, *m.*, pistolet revolver, *m.*

Revolving, adj. tournant, qui fait sa révolution, périodique

Revulsion, s. éloignement, *m.*, changement complet, *m.*

Reward, va. récompenser. *To be —ed with*, recevoir en récompense

Reward, s. récompense, *f.*, salaire, *m.*, prix, *m.* *As a — for*, en récompense de, pour récompense de. *Handsome —*, s. belle récompense, *f.* *Suitable —, handsome —*, s. récompense honnête, *f.* *A large —*, une forte récompense. *—s and punishments*, peines et récompenses

Rewarder, s. rémunérateur, *m.*, -trice, *f.*

Rewrite, va. récrire

Reynard, s. renard, *m.*, maître renard, *m.*

Rhapsodical, s. extravagant, de rapsodie

Rhapsodist, s. rapsodiste, *m.*

Rhapsody, s. rapsodie, *f.*

Rhenish, s. vin du Rhin, *m.*

Rhetoric, s. rhétorique, *f.*

Rhetorical, adj de rhétorique

Rhetorically, adv. suivant les règles de la rhétorique, en orateur, en rhéteur

Rhetorician, s. rhéteur, *m.*

Rheum, s. rhume, *m.*, catarrhe, *m.*

Rheumatic, adj. rhumatique, rhumatismal. *— disease*, s. affection rhumatismale

Rheumatisme, s. rhumatisme, *m.*

Rhinoceros, s. rhinocéros, *m.*

Rhodium, s. rhodium, *m.*

Rhododendron, s. laurier-rose, *m.*, rhododendron, *m.*

Rhomb, s. rhombe, *m.*

Rhomboid, s. rhomboïde, *m.*

Rhomboidal, adj. rhomboïdal

Rhubarb, s. rhubarbe, *f.*

Rhyme, s. rime, *f.*, vers, *m.*, poésie, *f.* *Without — or reason*, sans rime ni raison. *To put into —*, mettre en rime, rimer

Rhyme, vn.a. rimer, faire des vers, rimailler

Rhymer, Rhymester, s. rimeur, *m.*, rimailleur, *m.*

Rhythm, s. rhythme, *m.*

Rhythmical, adj. rhythmique

Rhythmically, adv. selon le rhythme, d'une manière rhythmique

Rib, s. côte, *f.*, (*build.*) ferme, *f.*

Ribald, adj. vil, bas, obscène

Ribaldry, s. langage licencieux, *m.*, obscénité, *f.*

Riband, see RIBBON

Ribbed, adj. à côtes. *— stockings*, s. bas à côtes. *Iron- —*, aux côtes de fer. *Thick- —*, aux côtes épaisses, épais

Ribbing, s. charpente, *f.*

Ribbon, s. ruban, *m.* *—s*, pl. (*fam.*) rênes, *f.pl.*, guides, *f.pl.* *—-trade*, s. rubanerie, *f.* *—-weaver*, s. ouvrier en rubans, *m.*, rubanier, *m.* *To handle the —s*, tenir les guides, conduire. *To tear into —s*, mettre en lambeaux

Ribless, adj. sans côtes

Rice, s. riz, *m.* *—-field*, s. rizière, *f.* *—-milk*, s. riz au lait, *m.* *—-paper*, s. papier de riz, *m.* *—-pudding*, s. gâteau de riz, *m.* *—-soup*, s. potage au riz, *m.* *—-water*, s. eau de riz, *f.*

Rich, adj. riche, somptueux, magnifique, exquis, libéral, succulent, (*dishes*) d'un goût relevé, savoureux. *— man*, un homme riche. *To pretend to be —*, faire le riche

Riches, s.pl. richesses, *f.pl.* *Immense —*, des riches immenses

Richly, adv. richement, dans l'opulence, somptueusement, amplement, largement, grandement

Richness, s. richesse, *f.*, nature succulente, *f.*, goût relevé, *m.*, haut goût, *m.*, (*of colour*) éclat, *m.* *The — of the furniture, of the soil*, la richesse de l'ameublement, du sol

Rick, s. meule, *f.* *—-yard*, s. cour de la ferme, *f.*

Rickets, s.pl. rachitis, *m.*, rachitisme, *m.*

Rickety, adj. rachitique, noué, (*furniture*) branlant, chancelant

Rid, va. délivrer, affranchir, purger, débarrasser. *To — oneself of, to get — of*, se débarrasser *or* se défaire de

Riddance, s. délivrance, *f.*, débarras, *m.* *Good —!* bon débarras!

Riddle, s. énigme, *f.* *To read a —*, deviner une énigme. *Answer to a —*, mot d'une énigme

Riddle, va. passer au crible, cribler

Riddler, s. qui parle par énigmes

Riddingly, adv. par énigmes

Ride, vn.a. monter, être monté, aller, faire, se promener, (*on the waters*) voguer, être porté, flotter, (*nav.*) être mouillé, être à l'ancre. *He made him to — in the second chariot*, il le fit monter dans le second char. *The chariots and those that — in them*, les chars et ceux qui les montent. *To — on a bay horse*, être monté sur *or* monter un cheval bai. *Let me — on your back*, portez-moi sur votre dos. *Skill to —*, le talent de monter à cheval, l'art de l'écuyer. *I rode for a long distance*, je fis une assez grande distance. *To — about*, aller, chevaucher çà et là. *To — along*, passer à cheval, en voiture, poursuivre sa route. *To — along the street, the ranks*, passer à cheval *or* en voiture dans la rue, parcourir les rangs à cheval or monté sur son cheval, chevaucher devant les rangs. *To — away*, partir, s'éloigner. *To — back*, s'en retourner, retourner sur ses pas. *To — behind*, suivre à cheval, monter en croupe, aller sur le siége derrière la voiture. *To — by*, passer devant. *To — off*, partir, s'éloigner. *To — over*, passer sur le corps de, (*fig.*) opprimer, primer

Ride, s. course, *f.*, promenade, *f.*, (*place*) promenade, *f.*

Rider, s. cavalier, *m.*, écuyer, *m.*, écuyère, *f.*, femme *or* jeune fille qui monte à cheval, *f.*, (*deeds*) codicille, *m.*, annexe, *f.*

Ridge, s. dos, *m.*, haut, *m.*, rangée de montagnes, *f.*, hauteur, *f.*, cime, *f.*, arête, *f.*, (*archit.*) faîte, *m.* *—-band*, s. dossière, *f.* *—-bone*, s. épine dorsale, *f.* *Along the —*, le long des hauteurs *or* de la montagne

Ridicule, s. ridicule, *m.* *To bring into —*, donner, prêter un *or* des ridicules à, faire rire de. *The — he brings upon himself*, le ridicule qu'il se donne. *To turn into —*, tourner en ridicule. *In — of*, pour ridiculiser

Ridicule, va. tourner en ridicule, ridiculiser

Ridiculer, s. railleur, m., -euse, f.

Ridiculous, adj. ridicule. *To be* —, être ridicule. *To have — ways about one*, avoir des ridicules. *To make oneself* —, se rendre ridicule

Ridiculously, adv. ridiculement, d'une manière ridicule

Ridiculousness, s. ridicule, m.

Riding, s. équitation, f., (*district*) canton, m. district, m. — *-cloak*, s. manteau (de voyage), m. — *-coat*, s. redingote, f. — *-habit*, s. amazone, f. — *-hood*, s. capuchon, m. — *-house*, s. manège, m. — *-master*, s. maître d'équitation, m. — *-whip*, s. cravache, f., houssine, f. *Little Red Riding-hood*, le petit Chaperon rouge

Rife, adj. abondant, dominant, (*rumour*) général, répandu, accrédité. *To be* —, être répandu, être accrédité, régner, se faire entendre distinctement

Riffraff, s. rebut, m., racaille, f.

Rifle, va. enlever, dérober, piller, dévaliser, (*a gun, &c.*) rayer, carabiner. *—d gun*, s. canon rayé, m., fusil rayé, m.

Rifle, s. carabine, f., fusil à canon rayé, m. *The — brigade, the —s*, les carabiniers à pied

Rifleman, s. carabinier à pied, m., chasseur à pied, m.

Rifler, s. pillard, m. — *of purses*, s. coupe-bourse, m.

Rig, s. tour, m., farce, f. *To carry on one's —s a little too far*, pousser ses tours un peu trop loin. *To run a — upon*, jouer un tour à

Rig, va. accoutrer, équiper, attifer, (*nav.*) gréer. *To — out*, accoutrer

Rigadoon, s. rigodon, m.

Rigger, s. gréeur, m.

Rigging, s. agrès, m.pl., gréement, m., manœuvres, f.pl., (*dress*) accoutrement, m.

Riggish, adj. amoureux

Right, adj. droit, direct, (*fig.*) juste, bon, convenable, qu'il faut, bien, en règle, comme il faut, vrai. *A — line*, une ligne droite. *It is* —, c'est bien, il est juste. *The inference is* —, la conclusion est juste. *It is — you should know*, il est bon que vous sachiez. *The — door*, la bonne porte, la vraie porte. *In the — place*, bien placé, dans l'endroit convenable. *That is —!* voilà qui est bien! à la bonne heure! vous avez raison. *To be* —, (*pers.*) avoir raison, (*th.*) être bon, juste, etc. *He was not far from* —, il n'avait pas tout à fait tort. — *or wrong*, à tort ou à raison, à tort et à travers. *To set* —, redresser, corriger rectifier, désabuser, mettre sur la voie. *All —!* c'est convenu! tout va bien! à la bonne heure! allez! roulez! quand il vous plaira. *Is your watch —?* votre montre va-t-elle bien? *On my — hand*, à ma droite. — *and left*, à droite et à gauche, à tort et à travers

Right! interj. c'est juste! vous avez raison! bien!

Right, adv. droit, en droite ligne, bien, justement, comme il faut, très, fort. — *down to*, tout droit à. *To go —, to be all* —, aller bien. *To hit —, to guess* —, frapper juste, deviner juste. — *away*, — *off*, sur-le-champ, à l'instant même

Right . . . . . (*in compounds*). — *-handed*, droitier, tournant de droite à gauche. — *-minded*, à l'âme droite, d'un esprit droit, honnête, bien disposé

Right, s. côté droit, m., droite, f., main droite, f., (*fig.*) bien, m., droit, m., justice, f., raison, f. *On my* —, à ma droite. *To turn to the* —, prendre à droite *or* sur sa droite. *To go, to send to the — -about*, faire, faire faire un demi-tour à droite. — *and wrong*, le bien et le mal. *To —s*, en droite ligne, en ordre. *To set to —s*, arranger, mettre en ordre. *By —, of* —, de plein droit, de droit. *Might overcame* —, la force primait le droit. *In her own* —, de son chef, en propre. *To have a — to*, avoir le droit de, être en droit de, avoir droit à. *Everybody has a — to live*, il faut que tout le monde vive. *To give a — to*, donner droit à, mettre en droit de. *To seek one's* —, réclamer ses droits. *To do — to*, faire justice à, faire raison à. *Bill of —s*, déclaration des droits

Right, va. rendre justice à, faire droit à, redresser, corriger

Righteous, adj. juste, droit

Righteously, adv. bien, avec droiture

Righteousness, s. droiture, f., justice, f.

Rightful, adj. légitime, juste

Rightfully, adv. légitimement, à juste titre

Rigid, adj. roide, raide, rigide

Rigidity, **Rigidness**, s. roideur, f., rigidité, f.

Rigidly, adv. avec roideur, rigidement

Rigmarole, s. rabâchage, m.

Rigorism, s. rigorisme, m.

Rigorous, adj. rigoureux

Rigorously, adv. rigoureusement, avec rigueur, en toute rigueur

Rigorousness, s. rigueur, f.

Rigour, s. roideur, f., dureté, f., (*fig.*) rigueur, f.

Rile, va. mettre en colère, faire rager

Rill, s. (petit) ruisseau, m.

Rim, s. bord, m., rebord, m., (*of a wheel*) jante, f.

Rime, s. frimas, m., givre, m., gelée blanche, f.

Rimous, adj. crevassé

Rimple, s. ride, f., pli, m.

Rimple, va. rider, plisser

Rimy, adj. couvert de givre

Rind, s. écorce, f., peau, f., pelure, f., (*of cheese*) croûte, f., (*of bacon*) couenne, f.

Ring, s. cercle, m., rond, m., (*finger*) bague, f., anneau m., (*ear*) boucle, m., (*game*) arène, f., enceinte de pesage, f., enceinte, f., (*persons*) les parieurs, m.pl., cercle autour des boxeurs, m., (*sound*) retentissement, m., bruit, m., son, m., (*peal*) sonnerie, f., carillon, m., (*housebell*) coup de sonnette, m. *To make a* —, faire un cercle. *In a* —, en cercle, en rond. *A —, a loud — was heard*, on entendit sonner, on entendit un grand coup de sonnette

Ring . . . . . (*in compounds*). — *-bolt*, cheville à boucle, f. — *-dove*, palombe, f., pigeon ramier, m. — *-fence*, enclos, m. *In a — -fence*, d'un seul tenant, tout d'un tenant. — *-finger*, (doigt) annulaire, m. — *-formed*, — *-shaped*, annulaire. — *-streaked*, annelé. — *-tail*, paille-en-queue, f. (*nav.*) tapecul, m. — *-tailed*, à voile de tapecul, m.

Ring, va.n. sonner, tirer, faire sonner, faire retentir, répéter. *To — in*, sonner la bienvenue à. *To — changes upon*, sonner des airs différents sur, (*fig.*) jouer sur les sens d'un mot. — *away*, carillonner. *To — for*, sonner. *My ears* —, les oreilles me tintent

Ringer, s. sonneur, m.

Ringing, s. action de sonner, f., (*noise*) son, m., bruit, m., tintement, m. *There came a loud* —, on sonna très-fort

Ringleader, s. meneur, m., chef, m.

Ringlet, s. cercle, m., rond, m., petit anneau, m., (*hair*) boucle, f. *To wear one's hair in —s*, porter les cheveux bouclés, porter des anglaises

Ringworm, s. impétigo, m., dartre, f.

Rinse, va. rincer. *To — one's mouth*, se rincer la bouche

Rinsing, s. rinçure, f.

Riot, s. tumulte, m., vacarme, m., émeute, f., rassemblement tumultueux, m., révolte, f., (*noisy frolic*) fêtes, f.pl., festins, m.pl., plaisirs bruyants, m.pl., orgies, f.pl., dissipation, f., excès, m., intempérance, f. — *-act*, s. loi contre les attroupements. *To run* —, se déchaîner, faire des excès

Riot, vn. faire du vacarme, faire une émeute, se livrer aux plaisirs, aux excès, être désordonné *or* déréglé. *To — among the good things*, se vautrer au milieu des friandises

Rioter, s. qui se livre aux plaisirs bruyants, émeutier, m.

Rioting, s. plaisirs bruyants, m., vacarme, m., émeute, f.

Riotous, adj. tumultueux, séditieux, déréglé, désordonné, intempérant. — *assembly*, s. attroupement séditieux, m.

Riotously, adv. tumultueusement, séditieusement, d'une manière désordonnée, avec excès

Riotousness, s. tumulte, m., vacarme, m., dérèglement, m., intempérance, f.

Rip, va. déchirer, fendre, ouvrir, arracher, découdre. *To — up, to — open*, éventrer

Ripe, adj. mûr, (*fig.*) accompli, parfait

Ripely, adv. mûrement, à temps

Ripen, vn. mûrir. *His greatness is a —ing*, sa grandeur marche vers la maturité

Ripeness, s. maturité, f.

Ripple, vn. se rider, onduler; — va. rider, faire rider

Ripple, s. ride, f.

Rise, vn. se lever, s'élever, monter, se relever, (*to a position*) parvenir, (*spring*) naître, se lever, prendre sa source, (*to occur*) se présenter, naître, (*prices*) monter, augmenter, (*revolt*) se soulever, (*meeting*) se séparer, (*paste*) lever. *To — up*, s'élever, se soulever. *To — into the air*, s'élever dans les airs. *The tide is rising*, la marée monte. *The funds are rising*, les fonds montent, sont en hausse. *His hopes rose high*, ses espérances se donnèrent carrière. *To — again*, ressusciter. *To — to opulence*, parvenir à l'opulence. *To — in the world*, faire son chemin, parvenir. *False prophets will* —, de faux prophètes se lèveront. *A thought rose in me*, une pensée me vint à l'esprit. *Tears rose in my eyes*, les larmes me vinrent aux yeux. *To cause to* —, faire venir. *The whole nation rose*, la nation tout entière se souleva

Rise, s. ascension, f., élévation, f., (*water*) crue, f., (*hill*) montée, f., (*the sun*) lever, m., (*promotion*) avancement, m., (*prices*) hausse, f., augmentation, f., renchérissement, m., (*origin*) source, f., origine, f., naissance, f., commencement, m. *A sudden* —

in the funds, une hausse subite de fonds. *To be on the —*, être en hausse, monter. *To take its —*, prendre sa source. *To give — to*, donner naissance à, faire naître, donner lieu à. *To have, to take its — (in)*, avoir sa source, prendre naissance (dans), provenir (de). *To get a — out of*, faire mettre en colère

Riser, s. qui se lève. *I was ever a late —, an early —*, j'ai toujours eu pour habitude de me lever tard, de me lever de bonne heure

Risibility, s. risibilité, *f.*

Risible, adj. risible

Rising, s. ascension, *f.*, élévation, *f.*, crue, *f.*, lever, *m.*, action de se lever, *f.*, action de se relever, *f.*, montée, *f.*, avancement, *m.*, levée, *f.*, clôture, *f.*, soulèvement, *m.*

Risk, s. risque, *m.*, péril, *m.*, hasard, *m.* *At the — of*, au risque de, au hasard de. *At every —, at all —s*, à tout risque, à tout hasard. *At your — and peril*, à vos risques et périls. *To run the — of, no —*, courir le risque de, ne courir aucun risque. *To stand the — of*, s'exposer au hasard de

Risk, va. risquer, hasarder, risquer de

Rite, s. rit, *m.*, rite, *m.*

Ritual, adj. du rit, du rite, des rites

Ritual, s. rituel, *m.*

Rival, s. rival, *m.*, -e, *f.*, émule, *m.*

Rival, adj. rival

Rival, va. rivaliser avec ; — vn. rivaliser

Rivalry, s. rivalité, *f.*, émulation, *f.*

Rive, va. fendre, briser, déchirer ; — vn. se fendre

River, s. rivière, *f*, fleuve, *m.*

Rivet, s. rivet, *m.*, rivure, *f.*, (*for china*) attache, *f.*

Rivet, va. river, clouer, (*fig.*) resserrer, consolider

Rivulet, s. ruisseau, *m.*

Roach, s. gardon, *m.*

Road, s. route, *f.*, chemin, *m.*, chaussée, *f.*, course, *f.*, (*nav.*) rade, *f.* *On the —*, sur la route, en route. *— -book*, s. guide du voyageur, *m.* *— -map*, s. carte routière, *f.* *— -way*, s. chaussée, *f.*, voie, *f.* *— -side*, s. bord de la route, *f.*

Roadstead, s. rade, *f.*

Roadster, s. cheval de fatigue, *m.*, bidet, *m.*

Roam, vn. errer, voyager, rôder

Roam, Roaming, s. course errante, *f.*, course vagabonde, *f.*

Roamer, s. voyageur, *m.*, vagabond, *m.*

Roan, adj. rouan

Roan, s. rouan, *m.*, basane marbrée, *f.*

Roar, vn. rugir, (*bulls*) mugir, (*thunder*) gronder, (*fire*) ronfler, (*pers.*) rugir, beugler, crier, jeter de hauts cris, vociférer, (*laughter*) éclater. *To — (out) for help*, crier au secours. *To — out in anger*, rugir de colère

Roar, s. rugissement, *m.*, mugissement, *m.*, grondement, *m.*, ronflement, *m.*, cris, *m.pl.*, hurlements, *m.pl.*, (*laughter*) éclat, *m.* *To set in a —*, faire éclater de rire

Roarer, s. cheval corneur, *m.*

Roaring, or **Roar**, s. (*veter.*) cornage, *m.*

Roaring, adj. rugissant, mugissant, qui gronde, ronflant, bruyant, d'une gaieté bruyante, (*veter.*) atteint de cornage

Roast, va. rôtir, faire rôtir, (*coffee*) brûler, torréfier, (*potatoes*) faire cuire ; — vn. rôtir, griller

Roast, adj. rôti

Roaster, s. rôtisseur, *m.*, (*th.*) rôtissoire, *f.*, (*for coffee*) brûloir, *m.*

Roasting, s. action de faire rôtir, *f.*, torréfaction, *f.*

Rob, va. dérober, voler, dévaliser, piller. *To — Peter to pay Paul*, emprunter à Pierre pour payer Paul. *He has been —ed*, on l'a volé. *He was —ed of his money*, on lui vola son argen

Robber, s. voleur, *m.*, -euse, *f.*

Robbery, s. vol, *m.*, brigandage, *m.*

Robe, s. robe, *f.*, costume, *m.* *—s*, pl. habits, *m.pl.* *In their —s*, en robes, en grand costume. *Gentlemen of the long —*, gens de robe. *State —s*, robes de cérémonie. *Clad in his royal —s*, vêtu de ses habits royaux. *Master of the —s*, intendant de la garde-robe

Robe, va. vêtir, revêtir ; — vn. mettre sa robe, se vêtir

Robin, s. rouge-gorge, *m.* *— -red-breast*, s. rouge-gorge, *m.*

Robust, adj. robuste, vigoureux

Robustness, s. nature robuste, *f.*

Rocambole, s. rocambole, *f.*

Rochet, s. rochet, *m.*

Rock, s. rocher, *m.*, roc, *m.*, roche, *f.* *— -crystal*, s. cristal de roche, *m.* *— -salt*, s. sel gemme, *m.* *— -work*, s. rocaille, *f.*

Rock, va. agiter, (*string*) balancer, ébranler, faire trembler, (*a child*) bercer. *To — to sleep*, bercer, endormir en berçant ; — vn. se balancer, chanceler, trembler

Rocker, s. berceuse, *f.*

Rocket, s. fusée, *f.*, (*bot.*) julienne, *f.*, roquette, *f.* *— -stick*, baguette de fusée, *f.*

Rockiness, s. nature rocailleuse, *f.*

Rocking, s. balancement, *m.*, agitation, *f.*, ébranlement, *m.*

Rocking, adj. qui balance, qui berce. *— -chair*, s. chaise à bascule, *f.* *— -horse*, s. cheval à bascule, *m.* *— -stone*, s. rocher branlant, *m.*

Rockless, adj. sans rochers

Rocky, adj. rocheux, rocailleux, (*fig.*) dur, de rocher, de roc, de roche

Rod, s. baguette, *f*, petite branche, *f.*, rameau, *m.*, verge, *f.*, (*to punish*) verges, *f.pl.*, fouet, *m.*, (*sway*) sceptre, *m.*, (*curtains*) tringle, *f.*, (*shepherd's*) houlette, *f.*, (*fishing*) ligne, *f.*, (*mechan.*) tige, *f.* *I have a — in pickle for him*, je la lui garde bonne. *Fishing —*, s. canne, *f.*

Rodomontade, s. rodomontade, *f.*

Roe, s. chevrette, *f.*, biche, *f.*, chevreuil, *m.*, (*of a fish*) œufs de poisson, *m.pl.* *Hard —*, s. œufs, *m.pl.* *Soft —*, s. laite, *f.*, laitance, *f.*

Roebuck, s. chevreuil, *m.*

Roed, adj. à frai, à laite. *Hard- —*, œuvé. *Soft- —*, laité

Rogation, s. rogation, *f.* *— -week*, *— -days*, s. semaine des rogations, *f.*, rogations, *f.pl.*

Rogue, s. coquin, *m.*, fripon, *m.*, fourbe, *m.*, coquine, *f.*, friponne, *f.*, fourbe, *f.*, (*in a joke*) espiègle, *m.*, fripon, *m.*, bandit, *m.*, drôle, *m.*

Roguery, s. friponnerie, *f.*, fourberie, *f.*, espièglerie, *f.*

Roguish, adj. coquin, fripon, de coquin, de fripon, vagabond, malin, espiègle. *— eye*, œil fripon. *An air of — good humour*, un air de malice et de bonne humeur. *— trick*, s. espièglerie, *f.*, malice, *f.*

Roguishly, adv. en fripon, avec malice *or* espièglerie

Roister, vn. faire le tapageur

Roisterer, s. tapageur, *m.*

Roll, va. rouler, faire rouler, mettre en rouleau, (*a walk*) passer au rouleau, (*metals*) laminer. *To — down*, rouler en bas. *To — in*, faire entrer en roulant. *To — out*, rouler dehors. *To — up*, rouler en haut, rouler, enrouler, envelopper. *To — oneself up*, s'enrouler, se pelotonner, s'envelopper. — vn. rouler, se rouler, faire sa révolution, (*time*) s'écouler, (*ship*) être ballotté, être le jouet de

Roll, s. rouleau, *m.*, écrit, *m.*, annales, *f.pl.*, (*list*) liste, *f.*, tableau, *m.*, (*mil.*) contrôle, *m.*, (*nav.*) rôle d'équipage, *m.*, (*bread*) petit pain, *m.*, flûte, *f.*, (*nav.*) roulis, *m.*, (*drum*) roulement, *m.* *To call the —*, faire l'appel. *To put on, to strike off the —s*, porter sur le tableau, rayer du tableau

Roller, s. rouleau, *m.*, (*metals*) cylindre, *m*, laminoir, *m* *Garden- —*, s. rouleau de jardin, *m.*

Rollicking, adj. joyeux

Rolling, adj. qui roule, roulant, qui s'écoule

Rolling, s. action de rouler, (*see* ROLL) *f.*, roulement, *m.*, révolution, *f.*, (*metal*) laminage, *m.*, (*nav.*) roulis, *m.* *— -mill*, s., *— -machine*, s. laminoir, *m.* *— -pin*, s. rouleau, *m.* *— -press*, s. presse à cylindre, *f.*

Roly-Poly, s. pudding aux confitures, *m.*

Romance, s. roman, *m.*, fiction, *f.* *— -writer*, s. romancier

Romance, va. faire des romans

Romancer, s. romancier, *m.*, (*fig.*) faiseur de romans, *m.*

Romanism, s. religion catholique romaine, *f.*

Romanist, s. catholique romain, *m.*, catholique romaine, *f.*

Romantic, adj. romantique, romanesque

Romantically, adv. d'une façon romanesque

Romish, adj. romain

Romp, s. gamine, *f.*, tapageuse, *f.*, (*play*) jeu bruyant et violent, *m.*

Romp, vn. jouer bruyamment

Romping, s. jeu bruyant, *m.*

Roof, s. toit, *m.*, toiture, *f.*, faîte, *m.*, (*fig.*) maison, *f.*, demeure, *f.*, (*mouth*) palais, *m.*, (*coaches*) impériale, *f.*

Roof, va. couvrir d'un toit, (*fig.*) accueillir, recevoir, abriter

Roofless, adj. sans toit, sans toiture, sans abri, sans asile

Roofy, adj. couvert d'un toit

Rook, s. freux, *m.*, corneille, *f.*, (*cheat*) fripon, *m*, (*at chess*) tour, *f.*

Rookery, s. colonie de corneilles, *f.*, colonie de freux, *f.*

Room, s. place, *f.*, espace, *m.*, champ, *m.*, (*occasion*) lieu, *m.*, matière, *f.*, (*in a house*) chambre, *f.*, salle, *f.*, appartement, *m.* *To take one's —*, prendre champ. *— on the ground-floor*, salle basse. *— with a fire-place*, chambre à feu

Roomful, s. chambre pleine, *f.*, chambrée, *f.*

Roominess, s. grandeur, *f.*, dimension spacieuse, *f.*

Roomy, adj. spacieux, vaste

Roost, s. juchoir, *m.*, perchoir, *m.*

Roost, vn. se jucher, percher

Rooster, s. coq, *m.*

Root, s. racine, *f.*, (*fig.*)

fondement, *m.*, source, *m.*, (*grown*) radical, *m.* *To strike deep — into*, jeter *or* pousser de profondes racines dans. *To take* —, prendre racine, s'enraciner. — *-bound*, enraciné, fixé

Root, vn. s'enraciner, prendre racine, (*as swine*) fouiller avec le groin; — va. enraciner, fixer, fouiller. *To — out, to — up*, déraciner, extirper, arracher

Rope, s. corde, *f.*, cordage, *m.*, (*nav.*) cordage, *m.*, manœuvre, *f.*, (*of onions*) glane, *f.*, (*of house-bell*) cordon, *m.*, (*room*) ses coudées franches, latitude, *f.* *To be (all) upon the high —s*, être monté sur ses grands chevaux. — *-dancer*, s. danseur, *m.*, danseuse de cordes, *f.* — *-ladder*, s. échelle de corde, *f.* — *-maker*, s. cordier, *m.* — *-making*, s. corderie, *f.* — *-walk*, s. corderie, *f.*

Rope, vn. filer

Ropy, adj. qui file, visqueux

Rose, s. rose, *f.*, (*ribbons*) rosette, *f.*, (*of a watering pot*) pomme, *f.*, (*of the winds*) rose des vents, *f.*, (*archit.*) rosette, *f.*

Rosary, s. rosaire, *m.*

Rose- . . . . adj. de rose, rose, rosé. — *-bud*, s. bouton de rose, *m.* — *-bush*, s. rosier, *m.* — *-mallow*, s. rose-trémière, *f.*, passe-rose, *f.* — *-rash*, s. rougeole boutonneuse, *f.* — *-tree*, s. rosier, *m.* — *-tribe*, s. rosacées, *f.pl.* — *-window*, s. rosace, *f.*

Roseate, adj. rosé, de rose, vermeil

Rosemary, s. romarin, *m.*

Rosette, s. rosette, *f.*

Rosewood, s. adj. palissandre, *m.*, en palissandre, de palissandre

Rosin, *see* Resin

Rosin, va. frotter de résine, de colophane

Rosiness, s. couleur rose, *f.*, roses, *f.pl.*

Rosy, adj. de rose, couleur de rose, rosé, rose, vermeil

Rot, vn. pourrir, se pourrir, se putréfier, tomber en putréfaction, se corrompre, (*teeth*) se carier; — va. pourrir, faire pourrir, putréfier, corrompre, (*teeth*) carier

Rot, s. pourriture, *f.*, putréfaction, *f.*, (*sheep*) clavelée, *f.*

Rota, s. rote, *f.*

Rotation, s. rotation, *f.*, roulement, *m.*, succession, *f.* *In* —, à tour de rôle

Rotatory, **Rotary**, adj. rotatoire, de rotation

Rote, s. routine, *f.*, répétition, *f.*

Rotten, adj. pourri (*see* To Rot), (*teeth, &c.*) carié, (*wood*) vermoulu, (*fig.*) corrompu, faux. — *-stone*, s. tripoli, *m.*

Rottenness, s. pourriture, *f.*, état pourri, *m.*, carie, *m.*,

Rotund, adj. rond

Rotunda, s. rotonde, *f.*

Rotundity, s. rotondité, *f.*

Rouge, vn. se mettre du rouge, se farder; — va. farder, mettre du rouge à

Rough, adj. rude, raboteux, inégal, (*coarse*) grossier, gros, (*unpolished*) brut, non poli, (*weather*) mauvais, (*taste*) rude, âpre, (*sound*) discordant, (*storm*) brusque, violent, dur, (*not exact*) approximatif, à peu près, à vue de pays, à première vue. — *road*, chemin raboteux. — *-clad*, grossièrement vêtu. — *coat*, gros pardessus. — *sea*, mer grosse, mer houleuse. — *copy*, — *draught*, brouillon, *m.*, (*paint.*) ébauche, *f.* — *sketch*, canevas, *m.*, ébauche, *f.* *At a — guess*, à vue de pays. — *-rider*, écuyer instructeur

Rough, s. polisson, *m.* —*s*, pl. canaille, *f.*

Rough, va. rendre rude, (*horses*) dresser, dompter. *To — it*, manger de la vache enragée, en voir de dures. *To — it out*, supporter jusqu'au bout

Roughcast, s. ébauche, *f.*, (*mason.*) crépi, *m.*

Roughcast, va. ébaucher, crépir

Roughdraw, va. ébaucher, dégrossir

Roughen, va. rendre rude, *To — down*, dégrossir

Roughhew, va. ébaucher, dégrossir

Roughish, adj. un peu rude

Roughly, adv. inégalement, d'une manière raboteuse, âprement, rude, durement, brusquement, violemment

Roughness, s. dureté, *f.*, inégalité, *f.*, nature raboteuse, *f.*, grossièreté, *f.*, rudesse, *f.*, âpreté, *f.*, sévérité *f.*, violence, *f.*

Roughshod, adj. ferré à glace. *To ride — over*, passer sur le corps à, (*fig.*) pressurer, opprimer

Roughwork, va. travailler grossièrement

Round, adj. rond, circulaire, (*sum*) bon, (*fig.*) rond, (*business*) franc, net, positif, coulant, facile. *A — price*, un bon prix. *At a — pace*, d'un bon pas

Round, s. rond, *m.*, cercle, *m.*, (*dance*) ronde, *f.*, (*mus.*) rondeau, *m.*, (*motion*) mouvement en rond, *m.*, cercle, *m.*, révolution, *f.*, (*walk*) tournée, *f.*, (*business*) occupation, *f.*, affaires de chaque jour, *f.pl.*, (*game*) tour, *m.*, (*applause*) salve, *f.*, (*ladder*) échelon, *m.*, degré, *m.*, (*milit.*) ronde, *f.*, (*cartridge*) cartouche, *f.*, (*volley*) décharge générale, *f.*, (*beef*) rouelle, *f.*, (*fencing*) assaut, *m.* *To fire a* —, faire une décharge générale

Round, adv. en rond, autour, à l'entour, tout autour, à la ronde, tour à tour. *To turn* —, se mouvoir en rond. *To bring* —, amener. *To come* —, (*fig.*) venir, arriver. *To go, to turn — and* —, tourner toujours. *To go* —, tourner, se retourner. *To move* —, tourner, se mouvoir en rond, se retourner. *All* —, tout autour. *Ten leagues* —, dix lieues à la ronde. *Glasses* —, des verres pour tout le monde

Round, prep. autour de. *To come, to get* —, circonvenir, entortiller

Round- . . . . (*in compounds*). — *-headed*, à la tête ronde. — *-backed*, — *-shouldered*, au dos rond *or* voûté. — *-house*, s. corps de garde, *m.*, violon, *m.* — *-robin*, écrit avec les signatures en cercle

Round, va. arrondir, (*go round*) entourer, environner, ceindre, (*to move*) faire le tour de. *To — off in*, s'arrondir en. *To — in, up*, haler, hisser. *To — oneself into a ball*, se pelotonner, se ramasser en boule; — vn. s'arrondir, faire la ronde

Roundabout, adj. détourné, indirect

Roundabout, s. jeu de bagues, *m.*

Rounders, s.pl. balle au camp, *f.*

Roundly, adv. en rond, (*fig.*) rondement

Roundness, s. rondeur, *f.*

Rouse, va. éveiller, réveiller, agiter, (*game*) faire lever, faire partir, lancer

Rout, s. cohue, *f.*, foule, *f.*, multitude, *f.*, réunion, *f.*, assemblée, *f.*, déroute, *f.* — *-cakes*, s.pl. petits fours, *m. pl.* *To put to the* —, mettre en déroute

Rout, va. mettre en déroute

Route, s. route, *f.*

Rove, vn. errer, voyager, courir

Rover, s. voyageur, *m.*, vagabond, *m.*, corsaire, *m.*, écumeur de mer, *m.*, pirate, *m.*

Roving, s. course, *f.*, course vagabonde, *f.*, voyage, *m.*

Roving, adj. qui aime à errer, voyageur, vagabond, inconstant

Row, s. rangée, *f.*, rang, *m.*, (*of figures*) colonne, *f.*, (*in a boat*) action de ramer, *f.*, promenade en bateau, *f.* *To set in a* —, mettre en rang. *To have a hard* —, ramer ferme, ramer en diable. *To kick up a* —, faire du tapage. *What's the* —? qu'y a-t-il? *To get into a* —, s'attirer une querelle, être mêlé dans une dispute. — *-boat*, s. bateau à rames, *m.* — *-port*, s. sabord à aviron, *m.* — *-lock*, s. tolletière, *f.*

Row, vn. ramer, mener en ramant, promener en bateau

Rowdy, s. tapageur, *m.*, homme turbulent, *m.*

Rowel, s. anneau, *m.*, (*of bits*) bossette, *f.*, (*of spurs*) molette, *f.*

Rower, s. rameur, *m.*

Rowland, s. Roland, *m.* *A — for an Oliver*, à bon chat, bon rat, prêté rendu. *I gave him a — for his Oliver*, je lui ai donné la monnaie de sa pièce

Royal, adj. royal, du roi

Royalism, s. royalisme *m.*

Royalist, s. royaliste, *m.*

Royally, adv. royalement, en roi

Royalty, s. royauté, *f.*

Rub, va. frotter, (*med.*) frictionner. *To — away*, effacer, enlever. *To — down*, (*a horse*) bouchonner, étriller. *To — off*, effacer, enlever, (*an old bill*) régler. *To — out*, effacer, enlever. *To — over*, polir, retoucher. *To — up*, frotter polir, (*memory*) dérouiller, rafraîchir

Rub, s. frottement, *m.*, friction, *f.*, coup de brosse, *m.*, action de bouchonner, *f.*, (*puzzle*) obstacle, *m.*, difficulté, *f.*, embarras, *m.*, (*fam.*) hic, *m.*, contrariété, *f.*, misère, *f.*, point difficile, *m.*, (*blame*) coup de langue, *m.*, reproche, *m.* *To come to the* —, en venir au fait et au prendre.

Rubadub, s. ran-tan-plan, *m.*, bruit du tambour, *m.*, bruit incessant, *m.*

Rubber, s. (*pers.*) frotteur, *m.*, chose qui sert à frotter, (*india* —) gomme élastique, *f.*, (*at play*) partie liée, *f.*, (*whist*) rub, *m.*, robre, *m.*, (*elect.*) frottoir, *m.*

Rubbing, s. frottement, *m.*, friction, *f.*, frottage *m.*

Rubbish, s. décombres, *m.pl.*, gravois, *m.pl.*, gravats, *m.pl.*, déblais, *m.pl.*, ordures, *f.pl.*, immondices, *f.pl.*, (*fig.*) (choses de) rebut, *m.*, vieilles hardes, *f.pl.* — *-cart*, s. tombereau, *m.* *Old* —, vieilleries, *f.pl.*

Rubbishy, adj. sans valeur

Rubble, s. moellon, *m.*, blocage, *m.*, (*mines*) fragments de roc, *m.* — *-stone*, s. moellon, *m.*

Rubicund, adj. rubicond

Rubric, s. rubrique, *f.*

Ruby, s. rubis, *m.*

Ruby, adj. de rubis, couleur de rubis, vermeil

Rudder, s. gouvernail, *m.*

Ruddiness, s. teint rouge *or* vermeil, *m.*, incarnat, *m.*, fraîcheur, *f.*

Ruddy, adj. vermeil, rouge de santé

Rude, adj. rude, grossier, ignorant, malhonnête, malappris, violent, sévère, rigoureux, fait sans art, informe

Rudely, adv. grossièrement, rudement, malhonnêtement, violemment, sévèrement

Rudeness, s. rudesse, *f.*, grossièreté, *f.*, malhonnêteté,

f., violence, f., turbulence, f., rigueur, f., sévérité, f.
Rudiment, s. rudiment, m. *In one's —s*, aux rudiments
Rudimental, Rudimentary, adj. rudimentaire, élémentaire
Rue, va. regretter, se repentir de, déplorer
Rue, s. rue, f., rhue, f.
Rueful, adj. triste, lamentable, lugubre
Ruefully, adv. lamentablement
Ruefulness, s. air or ton lamentable, m.
Ruff, s. fraise, f., plis, m. pl., chose plissée, f.
Ruffian, s. brigand, m., bandit, m., scélérat, m.
Ruffianly, adj. brutal
Ruffle, va. mettre en désordre, déranger, (*fam.*) ébouriffer, (*wrinkle*) chiffonner, froisser, (*trouble*) agiter, troubler, (*linen*) plisser, froncer. *To — it*, se pavaner, faire le bravache. — vn. s'agiter, (*wind*) se déchaîner, se hérisser, s'ébouriffer
Ruffle, s. manchette, f., jabot, m., fraise, f., agitation, f., trouble, m.
Rug, s. couverture de lit, f., (*carpet*) tapis de foyer, m., (*bed*) descente de lit, f., tapis, m., (*at the door*) natte, f.
Rugged, adj. raboteux, rude, âpre, (*temper*) rude, dur, brutal, violent, refrogné, (*hair*) hérissé, aux poils hérissés, poilu
Ruggedly, adv. rudement, durement
Ruggedness, s. aspérité, f., nature raboteuse, f., âpreté, f., rudesse, f.
Rugose, Rugous, adj. rugueux
Rugosity, s. rugosité, f.
Ruin, s. ruine, f., perte, f. *To fall* or *go to —*, tomber en ruine. *He will be your —*, il vous perdra
Ruin, va. ruiner; — vn. tomber en ruines, (*pers.*) se ruiner
Ruinous, adj. en ruines, ruineux
Ruinously, adv. d'une manière ruineuse
Rule, s. gouvernement, m., empire, m., autorité, f., (*instr.*) règle, f., conduite, f., (*print.*) filet, m., (*law*) ordonnance, f. *Sliding —*, s. règle mobile, f. *According to —*, selon les règles. *To lay down a —*, faire, poser une règle. *To be the —*, être de règle de or que. *To make it a — to*, avoir pour règle de, se faire une règle de. — vn. dominer, gouverner, être de règle
Ruler, s. maître, m., gouverneur, m., (*instr.*) règle, f.
Ruling, adj. dominant, souverain, maître
Rum, s. rhum, m., (*pers.*) drôle de corps, m.
Rum, adj. au rhum, (*odd*) drôle, original

Rumble, vn. gronder, rouler avec bruit
Rumble, s. siège de derrière, m.
Rumbler, s. qui gronde
Rumbling, s. grondement, m., (*carriage*) bruit, m., roulement, m.
Rumbling, adj. *An old — mansion*, une vieille maison toute prête à tomber
Rumblingly, adv. en grondant, avec bruit
Ruminant, adj. s. ruminant
Ruminate, vn. ruminer
Rumination, s. rumination, f., (*fig.*) réflexions, f. pl.
Rummage, va. n. fouiller, bouleverser
Rummage, s. remue-ménage, m., recherche, f.
Rumour, s. rumeur, f., bruit, m., renommée, f.
Rumour, va. répandre le bruit
Rump, s. croupe, f., croupion, m., culotte, f. *— steak*, s. rump-steak, m., bifteck, m.
Rumple, s. pli, m., faux pli, m.
Rumple, va. chiffonner, friper, froisser, plisser
Rumpus, s. bruit, m., tapage, m.
Run, vn. courir, (*to*, à) accourir, se jeter, se précipiter, se heurter, (*from*, de, entre; *to*, à, et) (*coach*) faire le service, (*road*) passer, (*ships*) courir, faire route, (*away*) fuir, s'enfuir, se sauver, (*liquids*) couler, s'écouler, (*vase*) fuir, (*abcess*) suppurer, (*melt*) fondre, se fondre, se liquéfier, devenir liquide, (*fig.*) s'attendrir, se fondre, (*nose*) couler, (*eyes*) pleurer, couler, (*watch*) marcher, aller, (*time*) passer, s'écouler, fuir, (*letter*) être conçu, s'exprimer, (*thought*) s'occuper, passer, trotter, (*rumour*) courir, circuler, (*book*) avoir la vogue, circuler, durer, se perpétuer, continuer, se transmettre, (*com.*) courir, (*bill*) avoir de date, (*tide*) monter, s'élever, (*law*) conserver son effet. *To — before the wind*, courir vent arrière. *To — for one's life*, chercher son salut dans la fuite. *To — about*, courir çà et là, courir dans. *To — across*, courir de l'autre côté, traverser en courant, s'étendre dans. *To — after*, courir après, poursuivre, suivre en courant. *To — at*, courir sur, fondre sur, se jeter sur, attaquer. *To — away* (*from*), s'enfuir (de, de chez de), s'échapper (de), échapper (à), (*horse*) s'emporter, prendre le mors aux dents, (*with*) emporter, (*time*) passer, s'enfuir. *To — back*, retourner, rebrousser chemin, (*river*) remonter vers sa source. *To — backwards*, courir en arrière, aller à reculons. *To — backwards and forwards*, aller et venir. *To — before*, précéder. *To — behind*, suivre en courant. *To — down*, courir en bas, descendre en courant, dégoutter, (*chain*) se dérouler. *To — in*, entrer en courant, (*upon*, *to*, sur) courir, (*to*, chez) courir, (*with*, avec) tomber d'accord, s'accorder. *To — into*, entrer en courant dans, (*a ship*) aborder, (*fig.*) se livrer à, se jeter or se précipiter dans, tomber dans, devenir, se changer en. *To — off*, s'éloigner, partir en courant, (*to*, à) passer. *To — on*, continuer sa course, courir en avant, (*time*) s'écouler, (*bill*) monter, (*tongue*) aller, marcher, (*pers.*) discourir, parler, (*conversation*, &c.) rouler sur, (*thought*) s'occuper de, s'arrêter sur, (*print.*) suivre, faire suivre. *To — out*, courir dehors, sortir en courant, (*fig.*) finir, expirer, tirer à sa fin, s'épuiser, se dissiper, (*pers.*) se ruiner, (*liquid*) couler, (*into*, en) s'étendre, (*land*) s'allonger, (*tide*) descendre, (*pers.*) (*into*) se livrer (à), se jeter (dans), se lancer (dans). *To — over*, déborder, (*milk*) monter, (*horse*, &c.) renverser, écraser, (*to*, à) courir, passer, s'en aller, (*fig.*) parcourir. *To — together*, courir ensemble, se confondre. *To — through*, parcourir, traverser en courant, passer par, (*fortune*) manger, dissiper, (*fig.*) parcourir. *To — round*, courir autour, (*gallery*) régner autour de, entourer. *To — up*, monter rapidement, (*to*, vers) accourir, courir, (*plants*) grimper, monter, s'élever, (*bill*) monter, s'élever. *To — up again*, remonter. *To — up and down*, courir çà et là, courir de côté et d'autre. *To — upon*, courir sur, marcher sur, rouler sur, aller sur. — va. courir, (*nav.*) filer, parcourir, fournir, poursuivre, suivre, (*risks*) courir, (*a coach*) faire courir, faire marcher, (*into*, dans) enfoncer, fourrer, pousser, (*metals*) fondre, faire fondre, couler, (*liquids*) verser, répandre, laisser couler. *To — a gun up, back*, (*artil.*) mettre une pièce en batterie, hors de batterie. *To be — hard for*, avoir grand besoin de
Run, s. course, f., excursion, f., promenade, f., (*water*) cours, m., (*poetry*) cadence, f., (*play*) veine, f., (*ordinary qualities*) qualités ordinaires, f., (*opinion*) vogue, f., durée, f., succès, m., cris, m. pl., clameur, f., (*pression*) demandes pressantes, f. pl., pression, f., (*water*) petit cours d'eau, m., (*nav.*) voyage, m., vitesse, f., (*hunt*) chasse, f. *Let us have a —*, courons un peu. *In the* or *at the long —*, à la longue. *Above* or *out of the common —*, au-dessus de l'ordinaire, hors ligne, à part. *A prodigious —*, un succès prodigieux
Runaway, s. fugitif, m., fugitive, f., fuyard, m., déserteur, m.
Rundle, s. échelon, m., roue, f., cercle, m.
Rundlet, s. barillet, m.
Runner, s. coureur, m., courrier, m., (*bot.*) rejeton, m. *Scarlet —*, s. haricot d'Espagne, m.
Running, s. course, f. action de courir, f., jeu, m., cours, m., écoulement, m., (*wound*) suppuration, f. *— away*, s. fuite, f. *Such —s up and down*, tant d'allées et de venues
Rupee, s. roupie, f.
Rupture, s. rupture, f., (*med.*) hernie, f., descente, f.
Rupture, va. rompre, causer une hernie; — vn. se rompre
Rural, adj. champêtre, rural
Rush, s. jonc, m., paille, f., (*fig.*) fétu, m., (*run*) course précipitée, f., mouvement précipité, m., charge à fond, f., élan, m., bond, m., attaque, f., foule qui se précipite, f., (*fig.*) émotion, f., transport violent, m., mouvement subit, choc, m. *— -bottomed*, adj. (à fond) de paille. *— -candle*, s., *— -light*, s. veilleuse, f. *— -like*, adj. comme un roseau. *— -mat*, s. natte de jonc, f. *To make a — at*, faire une charge à fond sur
Rush, vn. se précipiter, s'élancer, fondre, se jeter, courir, (*tears*) venir aux yeux, (*blood*) affluer, monter. *To — along*, se précipiter. *To — down the rocks*, descendre précipitamment les rochers. *To — forward*, on or *onward*, se précipiter en avant. *To — to battle*, courir à la bataille. *To — to meet*, se précipiter au-devant de. *To — into each other's arms*, se précipiter dans les bras l'un de l'autre
Rushed, adj. plein de joncs
Rushing, s. course précipitée, f., élan, m., impétuosité, f., charge, f.
Rushing, adj. impétueux
Rushy, adj. plein de joncs, de joncs
Rusk, s. biscotte, f.
Russet, adj. rouge, rouge grisâtre, (*coarse*) grossier, rustique, agreste
Russet, s. (*apple*) reinette grise, f., (*pear*) rousselet, m. *In — clad*, vêtu de bure
Rust, s. rouille, f., (*fig.*) impureté, f., (*fig.*) rusticité, f. *Black —*, s. nielle, f., charbon, m. *To rub off the — from*, ôter la rouille de, dérouiller
Rust, vn. se rouiller; — va. rouiller
Rustic, adj. rustique, champêtre, grossier

Rustic, s. rustre, *m.*, paysan, *m.*

Rustically, adj rustiquement, avec rusticité

Rusticate, va. reléguer à la campagne, habituer à la vie champêtre, (*univ.*) renvoyer; — vn. vivre à la campagne

Rustication, s. vie à campagne, *f.*, (*univ.*) expulsion, *f.*

Rusticity, s. rusticité, *f.*, rudesse, *f.*

Rustiness, s. état de rouille, *m.*

Rustle, vn. bruire, frémir, (*silk*) faire froufrou, (*pers.*) se pavaner

Rustle, Rustling, s. bruissement, *m.*, léger bruit, *m.*, frémissement, *m.*, froufrou, *m.*

Rusty, adj. rouillé, moisi. *To get, to grow* —, se rouiller

Rut, s. ornière, *f.*, (*of animals*) rut, *m.*

Ruth, s. pitié, *f.*, compassion, *f.*, chagrin, *m.*, douleur, *f.*

Ruthful, adj. compatissant

Ruthfully, adv. avec compassion

Ruthless, adj. cruel, inhumain, barbare, impitoyable, sans compassion, insensible

Ruthlessly, adv. sans pitié

Ruthlessness, s. cruauté, *f.*

Rutilant, adj. brillant, éclatant

Rutty, adj. coupé d'ornières

Rye, s. seigle, *m.* —*-grass*, s. ivraie, *f.*

S

S, s. S, s. *m.f.*

Sabbatarian, s. observateur du dimanche, *m.*

Sabbath, s. sabbat, *m.*, dimanche, *m.*, repos, *m.*

Sable, s. zibeline, *f.*, martre zibeline, *f.*, (*fig.*) deuil, *m.*, vêtements de deuil, *m.pl.*

Sable, adj. noir, sombre, (*herald*) sable, (*fig.*) de deuil

Sabre, s. sabre, *m.*

Sabre, va. sabrer

Sacerdotal, adj. sacerdotal

Sack, s. sac, *m.*, (*wine*) vin sec, *m.*, vin de Canaries, *m.*, vin de Xérès, *m.*

Sack, va. mettre en sacs, ensacher, (*to destroy*) saccager, mettre à sac

Sackcloth, s. toile à sac, *f.*, (*rel.*) cilice, *m.*, sac, *m.* *To wear* —, porter un cilice

Sackclothed, adj. vêtu d'un cilice

Sackful, s. sac plein, *m.*, sachée, *f.*

Sacking, s. saccagement, *m.*, sac, *m.*, toile à sac, *f.*

Sacrament, s. sacrement, *m.*, la sainte communion, la sainte table

Sacramental, adj. sacramentel

Sacred, adj. sacré, saint, consacré

Sacredly, adv. saintement, religieusement

Sacredness, s. nature sacrée, *f.*, caractère sacré, *m.*, sainteté, *f.*

Sacrifice, va.n. sacrifier, offrir en sacrifice, immoler

Sacrifice, s. sacrifice, *m.*

Sacrificer, s. sacrificateur, *m.*

Sacrilege, s. sacrilége, *m.* *To commit a* —, faire un sacrilége

Sacrilegious, adj. sacrilége

Sacrilegiously, adv. d'une manière sacrilége

Sad, adj. triste affligé, lugubre, sombre, grave, malheureux

Sadden, va. attrister, contrister, rendre triste, assombrir

Sadddle, s. selle, *f.* *To sit well in one's* —, être bien en selle. *To vault into the* —, sauter en selle. *To venture the* — *after losing the horse*, jeter le manche après la cognée. *To rise in the* —, se lever sur les étriers, monter à l'anglaise. —*-bags*, s. valise, *f.*, sacoche, *f.* —*-bow*, s. arçon, *m.* —*-cloth*, s. housse, *f.* —*-gall*, s. écorchure faite par la selle, *f.* —*-girth*, s. sangle, *f.* —*-horse*, s. cheval de selle, *m.* —*-maker*, s. sellier, *m.* —*-room*, s. sellerie, *f.* —*-shaped*, adj. en forme de selle, à dos d'âne

Saddle, va. seller, mettre la selle à, (*with*) charger (de), mettre sur le dos à

Saddler, s. sellier, *m.*

Saddlery, s. sellerie, *f.*, objets de sellerie, *m.pl.*, bourrelerie, *f.*

Sadly, adv. tristement, avec tristesse, sérieusement, (*fam.*) bien, beaucoup, fort

Sadness, s. tristesse, *f.*, sérieux, *m.*, air sérieux, *m.*

Safe, adj. en sûreté, à l'abri, en lieu sûr, sauf, de sûreté, (*pers.*) sûr, de confiance. — *bind*, — *find*, la défiance est mère de la sûreté. — *and sound*, sain et sauf. — *conduct*, s. sauf-conduit, *m.*, escorte, *f.*

Safe, s. lieu de sûreté, *m.*, coffre-fort, *m.*, caisse, *f.*, garde-manger, *m.*

Safeguard, s. sauvegarde, *f.*, protection, *f.*, escorte, *f.*, sauf-conduit, *m.*, (*rail*) chasse-pierres, *m.*

Safely, adv. en sûreté, sûrement, sain et sauf, sans danger, sans accident, en lieu sûr

Safety, s. sûreté, *f.*, salut, *m.* —*-buoy*, s. ceinture de sauvetage, *f.* —*-cock*, s. robinet de sûreté, *m.* —*-lamp*, s. lampe de sûreté, *f.* —*-plug*, s. bouchon fusible, *m.* —*-valve*, s. soupape de sûreté, *f.*

Safron, s. safran, *m.*

Safron, Safrony, adj. de safran, jaune safran. *Meadow* —, s. colchique d'automne, *m.*

Safron, va. teindre couleur de safran, safraner

Sagacious, adj. sagace

Sagaciously, adv. avec sagacité

Sagaciousness, Sagacity, s. sagacité, *f.*

Sage, s. (*bot.*) sauge, *f.*, (*pers.*) sage, *m.*

Sage, adj. sage, grave

Sagely, adv. sagement

Sago, s. sagou, *m.*

Sail, s. voile, *f.*, (*ship*) navire, *m.*, vaisseau, *m.*, (*excursion*) promenade à la voile, *f.*, (*fig.*) aile, *f.* *To get under* —, appareiller. *Getting under* —, appareillage, *m.* *With all* —*s set or out*, à pleines voiles, toutes voiles dehors. *The* —*s*, les voiles, la voilure. *A set of* —*s*, un jeu de voiles, une voilure. *To make* —, faire voile, faire de la voile. *To set* —, mettre à la voile. *To set all* —*s on*, voiler, couvrir de voiles. *To strike* —, amener les voiles, baisser pavillon. —*-cloth*, s. toile à voiles or à tentes. —*-loft*, s. voilerie, *f.* —*-maker*, s. voilier, *m.* —*-making*, s. voilerie, *f.* —*-room*, s. magasin à voiles, *m.* —*-yard*, s. vergue, *f.*

Sail, vn. voguer, naviguer, cingler, filer, mettre à la voile, appareiller, (*fish*) nager, (*fig.*) voguer, voler dans l'air, fendre. *To* — *along*, voguer. *To* — *about*, croiser, voguer çà et là, faire des promenades en mer, sur la rivière, etc. *To* — *before the wind*, voguer vent arrière, avoir le vent en poupe. *To* — *down, up a river*, descendre, monter un fleuve. *To* — *round the world*, faire le tour du monde. *To* — *through*, traverser. *To* — *into port*, entrer dans le port. — va. voguer sur, naviguer sur, fendre, diriger, guider

Sailer, s. voilier, *m.*, marcheur, *m.* *Swift* —, fin voilier

Sailing, s. navigation, *f.*, marche, *f.*

Sailor, s. matelot, *m.*, marin, *m.* —*-boy*, s. mousse, *m.*

Sainfoin, s. sainfoin, *m.*

Saint, s. saint, *m.*, -e, *f.*

Saintlike, Saintly, adj. saint, de saint, de sainteté

Sake, s. cause, *f.*, (*of*, pour, par) amour, *m.*, égard, *m.* *For glory's* —, pour la gloire. *For my own* —, dans mon propre intérêt. *For your* —, par égard pour vous

Salacious, adj. *see* Lascivious

Salad, s. salade, *f.* —*-bowl*, s. saladier, *m.* —*-oil*, s. huile à manger, *f.*

Salamander, s. salamandre, *f.*

Salaried, adj. salarié

Salary, s. appointements, *m.pl.*, traitement, *m.*, gages, *m.pl.*, salaire, *m.* *To receive a* — *of*, toucher un traitement

Sale, s. vente, *f.*, débit, *m.*, marché, *m.* *On* —, *for* —, en vente, à vendre. *To put up for* —, mettre en vente. *A ready* —, un prompt débit, une bonne vente. *For private* —, pour vendre à l'amiable

Salesman, s. marchand, *m.*, vendeur, *m.*, courtier de commerce, *m.*

Salic, adj. salique

Salient, adj. bondissant, qui saute

Saline, adj. s. salin, salé

Saliva, s. salive, *f.*

Salivate, va. faire saliver; — vn. saliver

Salivation, s. salivation, *f.*

Sallow, adj. jaune, blême

Sallowness, s. teint blême, *m.*, teint jaunâtre, *m.*

Sally, s. (*milit.*) sortie, *f.*, (*fig.*) excursion, *f.*, (*wit*) sortie, *f.*, saillie, *f.*, trait d'esprit, *m.*, boutade, *f.*

Sally, vn. (*milit.*) faire une sortie. *To* — *forth into*, sortir dans, s'élancer vivement dans

Salmagundi, s. salmigondis, *m.*

Salmon, s. saumon, *m.* —*-peal*, s. saumoneau, *m.* —*-pipe*, s. piége à saumon, *m.* —*-trout*, s. truite saumonée, *f.*

Z

Saloon, s. salon, *m.*
Salsify, s. salsifis, *m.*
Salt, s. sel, *m.*, salière, *f.* —*s*, pl. marais salants, *m.pl.*, sels, *m.pl.*, (*fam.*) marin, *m.* *He is not worth his* —, il ne vaut pas le pain qu'il mange
Salt, adj. salé, de sel, salant. —*-box*, s. boîte au sel, *f.* —*-cellar*, s. salière, *f.* —*-junk*, s. bœuf salé. —*-mine*, s. mine de sel, *f.* —*-pan*, s. —*-pit*, s. saline, *f.* —*-spring*, s. source d'eau salée, *f.* —*-works*, s. saline, *f.* —*-marshes*, s. marais salants, *m.pl.* —*tears*, s. larmes amères, *f.pl.*
Salt, va. saler; — vn. déposer du sel
Salter, s. saleur, *m.*
Salting, s. salaison, *f.*, marais salants, *m.pl.*
Saltish, adj. un peu salé, saumâtre
Saltless, adj. sans sel, insipide
Saltness, s. salure, *f.*
Saltpetre, s. salpêtre, *m.* —*-maker*, s. salpêtrier, *m.* —*-works*, s. salpêtrière, *f.*
Salubrious, adj. salubre, sain, bon pour la santé
Salubriously, adv. avec salubrité
Salubriousness, Salubrity, s. salubrité, *f.*
Salutarily, adv. d'une manière salutaire
Salutariness, s. nature salutaire, *f.*
Salutary, adj. salutaire
Salutation, s. salutation, *f.*, salut, *m.*
Salute, va. saluer
Salute, s. salut, *m.*, salutation, *f.*, embrassement, *m.*, (*mil.*) salve, *f.*
Salvage, s. sauvetage, *m.* —*-money*, s. prix de sauvetage, *m.*
Salvage, adj. sauvage
Salvation, s. salut, *m.* *To work out one's* —, faire son salut
Salve, s. onguent, *m.*, pommade, *f.*, (*fig.*) remède, *m.*, baume, *m.* *To have a — for every sore*, avoir un remède à tous maux
Salve, va. panser, mettre de l'onguent à, remédier à, guérir, sauver
Salver, s. plateau, *m.*
Salvo, s. salve, *f.*
Sal-volatile, s. sels, *m.pl.*
Same, adj. même, lui-même, elle-même, susdit, -e. *In the — way*, de la même façon, de même, tout de même. *To do the* —, faire de même, en faire autant. *One and the — thing*, une seule et même chose. *It is the — with me, with him*, il en est de même de moi, de lui. *It is all or quite the — to me*, cela m'est indifférent. *Much about the* —, à peu près de même. *Much the — as*, à peu près comme
Sameness, s. identité, *f.*, ressemblance, *f.*, uniformité, *f.*, monotonie, *f.*
Samphire, s. fenouil marin *m.*, salicorne, *f.*

Sample, s. échantillon, *m.*, exemple, *m.*
Sampler, s. travail de couture *or* de broderie, *m.*, canevas, *m.*
Sanative, Sanatory, adj. curatif
Sanctification, s. sanctification, *f.*
Sanctified, adj. sanctifié, saint, (*iron.*) béat, dévot
Sanctifier, s. sanctificateur, *m.*
Sanctify, va. sanctifier
Sanctimonious, adj. saint, (*iron.*) béat, dévot
Sanctimoniously, adv. saintement, avec un air de sainteté
Sanctimoniousness, Sanctimony, s. dévotion, *f.*, air de sainteté, *m.*
Sanction, s. sanction, *f.*, loi, *f.*
Sanction, va. sanctionner
Sanctity, s. sainteté, *f.*, saint, *m.*
Sanctuary, s. sanctuaire, *m.*, asile, *m.* *Right of* —, droit d'asile, *m.*
Sand, s. sable, *m.*, grain de sable, *m.*, (*sea shore*) grève, *f.*, bord de la mer, *m.* —*s*, pl. sables, *m.pl.*, banc de sable, *m.* —*-bank*, s. banc de sable, *m.*, ensablement, *m.* —*-blind*, adj. qui a la vue trouble. —*-box*, s. sablier, *m.*, poudrière, *f.* —*-drift*, s. amoncellement de sable, *m.* —*-flood*, s. sable mouvant, *m.* —*-fly*, s. moucheron, *m.* —*-glass*, s. sablier, *m.* —*-heat*, s. chaleur du bain de sable, *f.* —*-paper*, s. papier de verre, *m.* —*-piper*, s. (sorte de) pluvier, *m.* —*-pit*, s. sablière, *f.* —*-stone*, s. grès, *m.* *Grit —-stone*, s. grès dur, *m.* *To run on a —-bank*, ensabler. *To play on the —s*, jouer sur la grève
Sand, va. sabler, couvrir de sable, ensabler
Sandal, s. sandale, *f.*, (bois de) sandal, *m.*
Sandarack, s. sandaraque, *f.*
Sanded, adj. sablé, couvert de sable, sablonneux
Sandiness, s. nature sablonneuse, *f.*
Sandwich, s. sandwich, *m*
Sandy, adj. sablonneux, de sable
Sane, adj. sain
Saneness, s. état sain, *m.*
Sanguinary, adj. sanguinaire
Sanguine, adj. sanguin, (*fig.*) ardent, vif, plein d'espérance
Sanguinely, adj. ardemment, avec confiance
Sanguineness, s. état sanguin, *m.*, ardeur, *f.*, élasticité de caractère, *f.*, confiance, *f.*
Sanguineous, adj. sanguin
Sanitary, adj. sanitaire
Sanity, s. état sain
Sanscrit, s. sanscrit, *m.*

Sap, s. sève, *f.*, (*bot.*) aubier, *m.*, (*milit.*) sape, *f.*
Sap, va. saper; — vn. aller à la sape
Sapless, adj. sans sève, desséché
Sapling, s. jeune arbre, *m.*, plant, *m.*
Sapper, s. sapeur, *m.* *Royal —s and miners*, troupes du génie
Saphire, s. saphir, *m.*
Saphire, adj. de saphir
Saphirine, adj. de saphir
Sappiness, s. abondance de sève, *f.*
Sappy, adj. plein de sève, (*fig.*) tout jeune
Sarcasm, s. sarcasme, *m.*
Sarcastic, Sarcastical, adj. sarcastique
Sarcastically, adv. d'une manière, d'un ton sarcastique
Sarcenet, s. taffetas léger, *m.*, florence, *m.*
Sarcenet, adj. de taffetas
Sarcophagus, s. sarcophage, *m.*
Sardine, s. sardine, *f.*
Sardonic, adj. sardonique
Sardonix, s. sardonyx, *f.*
Sarsaparilla, s. salsepareille, *f.*
Sash, s. ceinture *f.*, (*of a window*) châssis, *m.* —*-frame*, s. châssis dormant. —*-window*, s. fenêtre à coulisses *or* à guillotine, *f.*
Satan, s. Satan
Satanic, adj. satanique, de satan
Satanically, adv. diaboliquement
Satchel, s. petit sac, *m.*
Sate, va. rassasier
Satellite, s. satellite, *m.*
Satiate, va. rassasier, assouvir, contenter
Satiation, s. satiété, *f.*
Satin, s. satin, *m.*
Satin, adj. de satin, satiné. —*-wood*, s. bois de citron, *m.*, citronnier, *m.*
Satinet, s. satinade, *f.*
Satire, s. satire, *f.* *To write a* —, faire une satire
Satiric, Satirical, adj. satirique
Satirically, adv. satiriquement
Satirist, s. satirique, *m.*
Satirize, va. satiriser
Satisfaction, s. satisfaction, *f.*, contentement, *m.*, réparation, *f.*, conviction, *f.*, confirmation, *f.*, (*law*) payement, *m.* *To give great — to*, donner de la satisfaction à, satisfaire, contenter. *A cause of* —, un motif de satisfaction. *To my own* —, à ma propre satisfaction. *To your entire* —, de manière à vous satisfaire complètement. *To demand — for an offence from a person*, demander raison à quelqu'un d'une offense. *To give — for*, rendre raison de. *To obtain — for*, tirer satisfaction *or* raison de. *For a — of my thought*, pour confirmer ma propre pensée. — *pistols*, pistolets de duel

Satisfactorily, adv. d'une manière satisfaisante
Satisfactory, adj. satisfaisant. *To be — in every respect, highly* —, ne laisser rien à désirer. *To be far from* —, laisser beaucoup à désirer
Satisfy, va.n. satisfaire, contenter, (*convince*) convaincre, assurer, (*with food*) rassasier. *These desires are not to be satisfied*, ces désirs ne sauraient être satisfaits. *I am satisfied that he was not there*, je suis convaincu qu'il n'y était pas. *I will — myelf of his sincerity*, je m'assurerai moi-même de sa sincérité
Satrap, s. satrape, *m.*
Saturate, va. saturer
Saturation, s. saturation, *f.*
Saturday, s. samedi, *m.*
Saturnalia, s.pl. saturnales, *f.pl.*
Saturnalian, adj. des saturnales
Saturnine, adj. sombre, taciturne, grave
Satyr, s. satyre, *m.*
Sauce, s. sauce, *f.*, (*pop.*) impertinence, *f.* *Onion* —, s. sauce aux oignons. —*-boat*, s. saucière, *f.*
Saucebox, s. impertinent, *m.f.*
Saucepan, s. casserole, *f.*
Saucer, s. soucoupe, *f.*, (*for colours*) godet, *m.*
Saucily, adv. insolemment
Sauciness, s. insolence, *f.*, impertinence, *f.*
Saucy, adj. impertinent, insolent
Saunter, vn. flâner, marcher lentement. *To — along*, flâner. *To — away*, va. perdre
Saunterer, s. flâneur, *m.*, -euse, *f.*
Sausage, s. saucisse, *f.*, (*large*) saucisson, *m.* *Pork* —, s. saucisse de porc, *f.* *Bologna* —, s. saucisson de Bologne, *f.*
Savage, adj. sauvage, agreste, cruel. *In a — state*, à l'état sauvage. —*-looking*, adj. d'un aspect sauvage
Savage, s. sauvage, *m.f.*
Savagely, adv. en sauvage, d'une manière sauvage
Savageness, s. nature sauvage, *f.*, férocité, *f.*, cruauté, *f.*
Savanna, s. savane, *f.*
Save, va. (*rescue*) sauver, délivrer, (*spare*) épargner, éviter, (*lay by*) mettre de côté, économiser, mettre en réserve, ménager, épargner, (*not to miss*) ne pas manquer, arriver à temps pour. *God — the queen!* vive la reine! *One that I —d from drowning*, un homme que j'ai tiré de l'eau. *You have —d my life, my honour*, vous m'avez sauvé la vie, l'honneur. *To — trouble*, pour s'épargner *or* pour éviter de la peine. *To — a lady's honour*, pour ménager la pudeur d'une dame.

To — my horse, pour ménager mon cheval. *Just saving the tide*, arrivant juste à temps pour profiter de la marée

Save, prep. excepté, hormis, sauf

Save, adv. excepté, si ce n'est

Saveall, s. brûle-tout, m.

Saveloy, s. cervelas, m.

Saver, s. sauveur, m., personne économe, f., ménager, -ère, f.

Saving, adj. économe, ménager

Saving, prep. sauf, hormis, excepté, si ce n'est que

Saving, s. économie, f., exception, f. *—s*, pl. économies, f.pl., épargne, f. *—s-bank*, s. caisse d'épargne, f.

Savingly, adv. avec économie

Saviour, s. sauveur, m. *The — of mankind*, le Sauveur des hommes

Savour, s. saveur, f., goût, m.

Savour, vn.a. avoir du goût, sentir, ressembler à, goûter, sentir, (*fig.*) aimer, rechercher

Savourily, adv. savoureusement

Savouriness, s. goût savoureux, f., odeur aromatique, f.

Savoury, adj. savoureux, suave

Savoy, s. chou frisé, m., chou de Milan, m.

Saw, s. scie, f., (*saying*) dicton, m., proverbe, m. *—-file*, s. lime à scie, f. *—-gin*, s. machine à égrener le coton, f. *—-like*, adj. dentelé. *—-mill*, s. scierie, f. *—-pit*, s. fosse de scieur de long, f. *—-set*, s., *—-wrest*, s. fer à scie, m. *—-toothed*, adj. dentelé. *—-yard*, s. scierie, f.

Saw, va. scier; — vn. se scier

Sawdust, s. sciure de bois, f.

Sawfish, s. scie, f.

Sawyer, s. scieur, m., scieur de long, m.

Say, va.n. dire, parler, (*lesson*) répéter, réciter, (*prayers*) faire, dire. *It is said that*, on dit que. *You don't — so*, vous plaisantez. *Least said is soonest mended*, trop parler nuit. *To — nothing of*, sans parler de. *Let us — no more about it*, n'en parlons plus. *—ing which*, en parlant ainsi. *It is not —ing much*, c'est peu dire. *Much might be said about that*, il y a bien à dire là-dessus. *It is —ing a great deal to . . .*, c'est beaucoup dire que de . . . *I — !* dites donc! eh! *That is to —*, c'est-à-dire. *As much as to —*, comme pour dire. *That is as much as to —*, autant dire que

Say, s. dire, m., discours, m. *Have thy —*, dis ton dire

Saying, s. mot, m., parole, f., remarque, f., maxime, f., sentence, f., dicton, m. *—s and doings*, faits et gestes.

As the — is or goes, comme on dit

Scab, s. croûte, f., escarre, f., gale, f., (*pers.*) gueux, m., gueuse, f.

Scabbard, s. fourreau, m., gaine, f.

Scabbed, Scabby, adj. couvert de croûtes, galeux, (*fig.*) gueux

Scabious, adj. galeux

Scabious, s. scabieuse, f.

Scaffold, s. échafaudage, m., échafaud, m., estrade, f. *To die on the —*, mourir sur l'échafaud

Scaffold, va. échafauder

Scaffolding, s. échafaudage, m.

Scald, va. échauder, brûler

Scalding, adj. bouillant. *— hot*, tout bouillant. *—-house*, s., *—-tub*, s. échaudoir, m.

Scale, s. (*of a balance*) plateau, m., balance, f., (*milit.*) escalade, f., (*ladder*) échelle, f., (*mus.*) gamme, f., (*of fish*) écaille, f., (*thin plate*) écaille, f., petite lame mince, f. *A pair of —s*, une balance. *— in hand*, la balance à la main. *In the — of beings*, sur l'échelle des êtres. *The — of society*, l'échelle sociale. *On a large —*, sur une grande échelle, en grand, sur un grand pied. *—-maker*, s. balancier, m.

Scale, va. escalader, monter à l'assaut de, (*weigh*) peser, mettre dans la balance, écailler. *To — the walls*, monter à l'escalade. *To attempt to — the walls*, tenter l'escalade. — vn. s'écailler, se détacher par écailles, s'élever, monter. *To — off*, s'écailler

Scaling, s. escalade, f. *—-ladder*, s. échelle de siège, f.

Scallion, s. ciboule, f.

Scallop, s. pétoncle, m., coquille, f., (*indentation*) feston, m., dentelure, f.

Scallop, va. denteler, (*cook*) faire cuire en coquille

Scalp, s. cuir chevelu, m., tête, f.

Scalp, va. scalper

Scalpel, s. scalpel, m.

Scaly, adj. écailleux, couvert d'écailles

Scamp, s. chenapan, m., mauvais garnement, m.

Scamper, va. décamper, s'enfuir. *To — away, off*, décamper lestement

Scamper, Scampering, s. course, f., fuite précipitée, f.

Scan, va. scander, (*fig.*) scruter, examiner, (*fam.*) éplucher

Scandal, s. scandale, m., éclat fâcheux, f., honte, f., opprobre, m., (*words*) médisance, f., diffamation, f. *The hill of —*, la montagne du scandale. *To the great — of*, au grand scandale de. *To avoid a —*, pour éviter le scandale. *To cause a —*, faire scandale, faire un scandale. *To seek for a —*, vouloir du scandale. *Free from —*, libre de honte. *The school for —*, l'École de la Médisance

Scandalize, va. scandaliser, médire de, calomnier, diffamer

Scandalous, adj. scandaleux, honteux, médisant, calomnieux

Scandalously, adv. scandaleusement, d'une manière scandaleuse, honteusement

Scandalousness, s. nature scandaleuse, f., scandale, m.

Scanning, Scansion, s. action de scander

Scantily, adv. étroitement, à l'étroit

Scantiness, s. rareté, f., disette, f., étroitesse, f., manque d'ampleur, m., pauvreté, f., modicité, f., peu, m.

Scantling, s. échantillon, m., portion, f., (*carp.*) volige, f.

Scanty, adj. resserré, étroit, limité, peu ample, étriqué, sans ampleur, pauvre, mesquin, faible, clair-semé, (*of*, de) chiche, avare

Scape, s. action de s'échapper, f., fuite, f., évasion, f., escapade, f., folie, f. *—-gallows*, s. pendard, m. *—-goat*, s. bouc émissaire, m.

Scapegrace, s. vaurien, m., mauvais garnement, m.

Scapement, s. échappement, m.

Scapular, Scapulary, adj. scapulaire. — s. scapulaire, m.

Scar, s. cicatrice, f., marque, f., balafre, f., brûlure, f.

Scar, va. laisser une marque, faire une cicatrice à, cicatriser, balafrer. *—red all over*, couvert de cicatrices, couturé

Scarce, adj. rare. *Make yourself —*, (*fam.*) filez, décampez

Scarcely, adv. à peine, avec peine. *— ever*, presque jamais, rarement

Scarcity, s. rareté, f., disette, f.

Scare, va. effrayer, faire peur à, effaroucher. *To — away*, faire fuir

Scarecrow, s. épouvantail, m.

Scarf, s. écharpe, f., cravate longue, f.

Scarification, s. scarification, f.

Scarifier, s. scarificateur, m.

Scarify, va. scarifier

Scarlatina, s. fièvre scarlatine, f., scarlatine, f.

Scarlet, s. écarlate, f.

Scarlet, adj. écarlate, rouge, vermeil. *—-beans*, s., *—-runners*, s. haricots d'Espagne, m. *—-fever*, s. fièvre scarlatine, f.

Scarp, s. escarpe, f.

Scatter, va. éparpiller, répandre, disperser, dissiper, joncher. *Thinly —ed*, adj. clairsemé. *To — about*, éparpiller, joncher. *To — abroad*, disperser, dissiper. *To — away*, dissiper. — vn. se disperser. *—-brain, —-brains*, étourneau, étourdi

Scattered, past part. dispersé, épars, jonché, éparpillé, répandu

Scavenger, s. boueur, m.

Scene, s. lieu, m., (*scenery*) scène, f., décor, m., décoration, f., (*of war*) théâtre, f. *—-shifter*, s. machiniste, m. *—-painter*, s. peintre en décors, m. *—-painting*, s. peinture des décors, f. *Behind the —s*, derrière les coulisses

Scenery, s. scène, f., vue, f., paysage, m., coup d'œil, m., point de vue, m., (*theatre*) décors, m.pl. *The — is most magnificent*, les décors sont magnifiques

Scenic, adj. scénique, théâtral

Scent, s. odeur, f., senteur, f., parfum, m., (*animals*) odorat, m., (*dogs*) nez, m., (*track*) piste, f. *—-bottle*, s. flacon d'odeur, m. *—-bag*, s., *—-cushion*, s. sachet d'odeurs, m. *To put on the right —*, mettre sur la (bonne) voie. *To put on the wrong —*, mettre en défaut, (*fig.*) donner, faire prendre le change à. *To throw off the —*, mettre en défaut. *To recover the —*, relever le défaut, retrouver la voie

Scent, va. sentir, parfumer

Scented, adj. parfumé, odorant, à odeur . . .

Scentless, adj. sans odeur

Sceptic, Sceptical, s. adj. sceptique

Scepticism, s. scepticisme, m.

Sceptre, s. sceptre, m.

Schedule, s. rouleau, m., annexe, f., inventaire, m., liste, f., (*of prices*) série, f., (*law*) bilan, m.

Scheme, s. système, m., plan, m., projet, m., dessein, m. *To form —s*, faire des projets

Scheme, va. projeter, faire le plan de; — vn. faire un projet, des projets, intriguer, comploter

Schemer, s. homme or femme à projets, m., (*jobber*) intrigant, m., -e, f.

Scheming, s. projets, m. pl., machinations, f.pl.

Scheming, adj. à projets, intrigant

Schism, s. schisme, m.

Schismatic, Schismatical, s. adj. schismatique

Scholar, s. élève, m.f., écolier, m., écolière, f., savant, m., érudit, m., personne instruite, f., (*on a foundation*) boursier, m., élève boursier, m. *A Greek —*, helléniste. *Latin —*, Latiniste. *To be a —*, être un savant, avoir fait ses études

Scholarly, adj. d'écolier, d'élève, d'érudit

Scholarly, adv. en écolier, en savant, en homme instruit

Scholarship, s. savoir, m., instruction, f., érudition, f., (*exhibition*) bourse, f.

Scholastic, adj. scolastique, des écoles. — *philosophy*, la scolastique

Scholastic, s. scolastique, m.

Scholastically, adv. à la manière scolastique *or* des écoles

Scholiast, s. scoliaste, m.

School, s. école, f., lycée, m., collége, m., pension, f., (*lesson*) classe, f. *To be at* —, être à l'école, au lycée, à la pension, etc., être en classe. *To go to* —, aller à l'école, au lycée, etc. *To send to* —, envoyer à l'école, mettre au lycée, au collége, en pension. *To come out of* —, sortir de classe. *To keep* —, *to teach a* —, tenir une école. *And in thine own heart let them first keep* —, et que tout d'abord ton cœur écoute leurs leçons. —*s of painting*, écoles de peinture. *A man of the old* —, un homme de la vieille roche, de l'ancienne école. *To be at the head of a* —, *to found a* —, faire école, fonder une école. *High* —, s. école supérieure. *Day-* —, s. externat, m. — *-divinity*, s. la scolastique, f. — *-assistant*, s. sous-maître, m. — *-book*, s. livre de classe, m., livre classique, m. — *bookseller*, s. librairie classique, f. — *-boy*, s. écolier, m., élève, m., lycéen, m., collégien, m., pensionnaire, m. — *-boy's trick*, s. malice d'écolier, f. — *-committee*, s. conseil de surveillance, m. — *-day*, s. jour de classe, m. — *-fellow*, s. camarade d'école, m.f., condisciple, m. — *-girl*, s. écolière, f., élève, f. — *-house*, s. école, maison d'école, f. — *-hours*, — *-time*, la classe, f., heures de la classe, f., le temps de la classe. — *-master*, s. maître d'école, m., instituteur, m., maître de pension, m. — *-mistress*, s. maîtresse d'école, f., institutrice, f., maîtresse de pension, f. — *-room*, s. classe, f.

School, va. instruire, enseigner, apprendre, former, réprimander

Schooling, s. instruction, f., enseignement, m., (*fees*) prix de l'école, m., prix de la pension, m.

Schoolman, s. scolastique, m.

Schooner, s. schooner, m., goëlette, f.

Sciatica, s. sciatique, f.

Science, s. science, f.

Scientific, Scientifical, adj. scientifique

Scientifically, adv. scientifiquement

Scimitar, s. cimeterre, m.

Scintillate, va. scintiller

Scintillation, s. scintillation, f.

Sciolist, s. demi-savant, m.

Scion, s. rejeton, m., scion, m.

Scioptic, adj. scioptique

Scission, s. action de couper, f., (*fig.*) scission, f. *To bring about a* —, faire une scission

Scissors, s.pl. ciseaux, m. pl., paire de ciseaux, f. — *-case*, s. étui à ciseaux, m.

Scoff, va.n. railler, se moquer de, bafouer, se railler de

Scoff, s. raillerie, f., moquerie, f.

Scoffer, s. railleur, m.

Scoffing, s. railleries, f.pl.

Scoffing, adj. railleur, moqueur

Scoffingly, adv. en raillant, par moquerie

Scold, va.n. gronder

Scold, s. grondeuse, f., criailleuse, f.

Scolding, adj. qui gronde sans cesse

Scolding, s. gronderie, f., reproches, m.pl. *Give him a good* —, grondez-le bien

Sconce, s. fort, m., (*head*) tête, f., (*fam.*) caboche, f., (*bracket*) bras, m., (*socket*) bobèche, f.

Scoop, s. grande cuiller, f., cuiller à pot, f., (*nav.*) escope, f., (*for cheese*) couteau, m.

Scoop, va. puiser, vider, (*hollow out*) creuser, (*nav.*) écoper. *To — out of*, creuser dans, déblayer dans

Scope, s. vue, f., étendue, f., portée, f., (*aim*) but, m., intention, f., dessein, m., espace, m., place, f., carrière, f., liberté, f., licence, f., (*import*) portée, f. *To give free* —, *full* — *to*, donner libre carrière à, laisser entière liberté à. *To have full* —, avoir ses coudées franches

Scorbutic, adj scorbutique

Scorch, va.n. brûler, griller, dessécher

Scorching, adj. brûlant

Score, s. (*notch*) entaille, f., coche, f., (*bill*) écot, m., compte, m., (*motive*) raison, f., cause, f., motif, m., (*twenty*) vingtaine, f., (*mus.*) partition, f. *To run up a* — (*with*), contracter une dette (avec). *On the — of my being an Englishman*, parce que je suis Anglais. *Half a — of*, une dizaine de. *Some —s of*, quelques vingtaines de. *Three —s*, soixante, la soixantaine

Score, va. entailler, graver, marquer, tracer, mettre *or* porter en compte, marquer, (*fig.*) attribuer, (*mus.*) orchestrer

Scorer, s. marqueur, m.

Scoria, s. scorie, f., mâchefer, m.

Scorn, va.n. dédaigner (de), ne pas s'abaisser (à), mépriser

Scorn, s. dédain, m., mépris, m., objet de mépris, m., objet de risée, m. *To look with — on*, regarder avec dédain, dédaigner. *Full of — for*, dédaigneux de, plein de dédain *or* de mépris pour

Scorner, s. dédaigneux, m., qui méprise, railleur, m., -euse, f.

Scornful, adj. dédaigneux, méprisant

Scornfully, adv. dédaigneusement, avec dédain, avec mépris

Scorpion, s. scorpion, m.

Scot, s. écot, m., quote-part, f., Écossais, m.

Scotch, va. (*to cut*) blesser, faire une entaille à, (*wheel*) enrayer

Scotch, s. entaille, f., coche, f.

Scoundrel, s. gueux, m., misérable, m., coquin, m., gredin, m. *Pack of —s*, tas de coquins

Scour, va.n. (*clean*) écurer, nettoyer, polir, (*linen*) lessiver, blanchir, (*cloth*) dégraisser, (*go over*) parcourir, (*pirate*) écumer, courir. *To — along the coast*, parcourir la côte. *To — away*, partir en courant, décamper

Scourer, s. écureur, m., écureuse, f., (*cloth*) dégraisseur, m., (*runner*) coureur, m.

Scourge, s. fouet, m., châtiment, m., fléau, m.

Scourge, va. flageller, fouetter, châtier

Scourging, s. flagellation, f., châtiment, m.

Scouring, s. écurage, m., nettoyage, m., dégraissage, m., course rapide, f.

Scout, s. (*milit.*) éclaireur, m., (*nav.*) vedette, f., (*univ.*) garçon, m.

Scout, vn. aller en éclaireurs, faire des reconnaissances, battre la campagne; — va. repousser avec mépris, tourner en dérision

Scowl, vn. regarder de travers, regarder avec haine *or* aversion, regarder d'un air de menace

Scowl, s. regard farouche, m., regard de travers, m., aspect menaçant, m.

Scowling, adj. farouche, menaçant, de haine

Scowlingly, adv. d'un regard *or* air farouche *or* menaçant

Scrag, s. bout saigneux, m., cou, m.

Scragged, Scraggy, adj. rude, raboteux, (*lean*) décharné

Scragginess, s. nature raboteuse *or* rude, f., inégalités, f.pl., (*leanness*) maigreur, f.

Scramble, vn. lutter, (*to fight for*) se battre, se disputer, (*up*) grimper, avancer à l'aide des pieds et des mains

Scramble, s. lutte, f., effort, m. *There was a — for*, on se disputa

Scrambling, s. lutte, f., dispute, f., efforts, m.pl.

Scrap, s. bribes, f.pl., fragment, m., bout, m., brin, m., petit morceau, m., chiffon, m. — *-book*, s. album, m. — *-iron*, s. ferraille, f.

Scrape, va.n. gratter, racler, (*clean*) ratisser, (*gather*) amasser. — *your shoes*, décrottez vos souliers. *To — together*, amasser sou à sou, péniblement. *To — off*, ôter, enlever en grattant. *To — acquaintance*, faire connaissance. — vn. grincer, gratter, racler, (*on a fiddle*) racler du violon, (*to drag along*) traîner le pied

Scrape, s. action de gratter, de racler, m., raclage, m., coup de racloir, m., (*noise*) bruit, m., (*difficulty*) embarras, m., difficulté, f., mauvaise affaire, f. *To get into a* —, s'attirer *or* se faire une mauvaise affaire. *To get out of a* —, (va.) tirer d'embarras, (vn.) se tirer d'embarras. *To lead into a* —, mettre dans l'embarras

Scraper, s. grattoir, m., racloir, m., ratissoire, f., (*for feet*) décrottoir, m., (*musician*) racleur de violon, m., (*miser*) grippe-sou, m.

Scraping, s. grattage, m., action de racler, f., (*ivory*) raclure, f., (*feet*) piétinement, m., (*noise*) bruit d'un mauvais violon, m. —*s*, (*savings*) pl. épargnes, f.pl.

Scratch, va. égratigner, griffer, donner un coup de griffe à, gratter, se gratter, se faire une égratignure à, (*write*) griffonner, (*mark*) rayer, (*erase*) effacer, biffer, (*horses*) retirer, payer forfait pour, (*dig*) creuser en grattant. *To — out*, arracher, biffer, effacer. *I will — out your eyes*, je vous arracherai les yeux. *To — the face of*, égratigner le visage à, dévisager

Scratch, s. égratignure, f., rayure, f., raie, f., (*writing*) pattes de mouche, f.pl. *To come to the* —, en venir au fait et au prendre, commencer

Scrawl, va. griffonner, gribouiller

Scrawl, s. griffonnage, m., pattes de mouche, f.pl., mauvaise écriture, f.

Scrawler, s. griffonneur, m., -euse, f.

Screak, Scream, vn. crier, pousser des cris. *To — out*, pousser un cri, des cris. *To — with pain*, pousser des cris de douleur

Scream, s. cri, m.

Screaming, s. cris, m.pl.

Screech, vn. crier, pousser un cri perçant *or* aigu

Screech, s. cri perçant, m., cri aigu, m. — *-owl*, s. chat-huant, m.

Screen, s. écran, m., paravent, m., (*fig.*) garde, f., défense, f., abri, m., (*sieve*) crible, m., (*archit.*) cloison, f.

Screen, va. abriter (de *or* contre), garantir (de), protéger (contre), préserver (de), (*from punish.*) soustraire, dérober, (*sift*) cribler, passer au crible

Screw, s. vis, *f.*, hélice, *f.*, (*pers.*) pince-maille, *m.*, grigou, *m.* *Archimedes'* —, s. vis d'Archimède, *f.* *Endless* —, s. vis sans fin, *f.* — *-jack*, s. cric, *m.* — *-nut*, s. écrou, *m.* *To put on* or *use the* —, serrer la vis, employer la force. *There's a* — *loose somewhere*, il y a quelque chose qui ne va pas. — *-ship*, s., — *-steamer*, s. navire à hélice, *m.*, vapeur à hélice, *m.* — *-shell*, s. hélice, *f.*

Screw, va. visser, fixer avec des vis, serrer, (*fig.*) amener de force, porter, élever. *To* — *down*, visser, pressurer, (*profits*) rogner les ongles. *To* — *down the corners of the lips*, plisser les coins des lèvres. *To* — *in*, visser, fixer, faire entrer de force. *To* — *out*, dévisser, (*fig.*) tirer, extorquer. *To* — *up*, serrer, fermer à vis, visser. *To* — *courage*, prendre son courage à deux mains

Scribble, va.n. griffonner, barbouiller. *To* — *on*, écrire rapidement

Scribbling, s. griffonnage, *m.*, barbouillage, *m.*

Scribbler, s. griffonneur, *m.*, -euse, *f.*, écrivailleur, *m.*, écrivassier, *m.*

Scribe, s. écrivain public, *m.*, officier ministériel, *m.*, clerc, *m.*, scribe, *m.*

Scrip, s. besace, *f.*, petit sac, *m.*, (*paper*) chiffon de papier, *m.*, écrit, *m.*, liste, *f.*, (*financ.*) actions, *f.pl.*, obligations, *f.pl.*, titre de rente, *m.* — *-holder*, s. porteur d'actions, *m.*

Scriptural, adj. de l'Écriture, biblique

Scripture, s. l'Écriture sainte, *f.*, saintes Écritures, *f.pl.*

Scrivener, s. notaire, *m.*, écrivain public, *m.*, courtier de change, *m.*

Scrofula, s. les scrofules, *f.pl.*, les écrouelles, *f.pl.*

Scrofulous, adj. scrofuleux

Scroll, s. rouleau, *m.*, écrit, *m.*, liste, *f.*

Scrub, va. frotter ferme, laver avec une brosse dure ; — vn. (*fig.*) travailler dur et vivre de peu

Scrub, s. être chétif, *m.*, être vil, *m.*, homme de peine, *m.*

Scrubby, adj. chétif, rabougri

Scrubbing-brush, s. brosse dure, *f.*

Scruple, s. scrupule, *m.*

Scruple, vn. se faire scrupule, hésiter

Scrupulosity, s. scrupules, *m.pl.*, nature scrupuleuse, *f.*

Scrupulous, adj. scrupuleux, qui a des scrupules, difficile, chicanier. *To be over-* —, avoir trop de scrupules

Scrupulously, adv. scrupuleusement

Scrupulousness, s. *see* SCRUPULOSITY

Scrutinize, va. scruter, examiner

Scrutinizer, s. scrutateur, *m.*

Scrutinizing, adj. scrutateur, inquisiteur, pénétrant

Scrutiny, s. examen, *m.*, recherche rigoureuse, *f.*

Scud, vn. fuir, s'enfuir, se sauver, courir, décamper, (*nav.*) courir

Scuffle, vn. lutter, se battre

Scuffle, s. rixe, *f.*, lutte, *f.*, querelle, *f.*, mêlée, *f.*, confusion, *f.*

Sculk, *see* SKULK

Scull, s. bateau, *m.*, batelet, *m.*

Scullery, s. arrière-cuisine, *f.* — *-maid*, s. aide de cuisine, *f.*, laveuse de vaisselle, *f.*

Scullion, s. marmiton, *m.*, laveur, *m.*, laveuse de vaisselle, *f.*

Sculptor, s. sculpteur, *m.*

Sculpture, s. sculpture, *f.*

Sculpture, va. sculpter. —*d vase*, vase ciselé

Scum, s. écume, *f.*, (*metal.*) crasse, *f.*, scorie, *f.*, (*fig.*) écume, *f.*, lie, *f.*, rebut, *m.*

Scum, va. écumer

Scurf, s. (*on the head*) pellicules, *f.pl.*, crasse, *f.*, (*on the skin*) croûte, *f.* *A glossy* —, une croûte luisante

Scurfy, adj. couvert de pellicules, couvert de crasse, teigneux

Scurrility, s. grossièreté, *f.*, langage grossier, *m.*

Scurrilous, adj. grossier, ignoble, injurieux

Scurvily, adj. bassement

Scurviness, s. état scorbutique, *m.*, bassesse, *f.*, mesquinerie, *f.*

Scurvy, s. scorbut, *m.*

Scurvy, adj. scorbutique, atteint du scorbut, (*fig.*) vil, méprisable, injurieux, grossier, mesquin. — *-grass*, cochléaria

Scutcheon, s. *see* ESCUTCHEON

Scuttle, s. panier, *m.*, seau à charbon, *m.*, (*nav.*) écoutille, *f.* — *-fish*, s. sèche, *f.* *With an easy* —, d'un pas leste *or* dégagé

Scuttle, va. saborder

Scythe, s. faux, *f.*

Scythe, va. faucher, armer de faux

Sea, s. mer, *f.*, lame, *f.*, vague, *f.*, coup de mer, *f.*, flots, *m.pl.*, déluge, *m.* *At* —, en mer. *To be at* —, être en mer. *Far out at* —, en pleine mer. *Over all the* —*s*, par toutes les mers. *By* — *and land*, par terre et par mer. *A heavy* —, une grosse mer, une mer houleuse, etc. *The high* —, la haute mer. *On the high* —*s*, sur la haute mer. *The open* —, la pleine mer. *The South* —, la mer du Sud. *To put to* —, mettre en mer, mettre à la mer. *To be mistress of the* —*s*, *to keep out at* —, tenir la mer. *To go to* —, aller en mer, prendre la mer, se faire marin. *To send to* —, embarquer, faire un marin de. — *-bar*, s. hirondelle de mer, *f.* — *-beach*, s. bord de la mer, *m.* — *-bear*, s. ours blanc, *m.* — *-beat*, adj., — *-beaten*, adj. battu par la mer. — *-bird*, s. oiseau de mer, *m.* — *-board*, adv. du côté de la mer ; — s. bord de la mer, *m.* ; — adj. qui avoisine la mer, maritime. — *-born*, adj. né de la mer, né sur la mer. — *-bound*, adj., — *-bounded*, adj. que borne la mer. — *-boy*, s. mousse, *m.* — *-breach*, s. irruption de la mer, *f.* — *-bream*, s. dorade, *f.* — *-bred*, adj. élevé pour être marin. — *-breeze*, s. brise de mer, *f.*, brise de large, *f.* — *-built*, adj. bâti sur la mer, qui se dresse sur la mer. — *-calf*, s. veau marin, *m.* — *-captain*, s. capitaine de navire, *m.*, patron de navire, *m.* — *-card*, s. rose des vents, *f.* — *-chart*, s. carte marine, *f.* — *-cliff*, s. falaise, *f.* — *-coal*, s. charbon de terre, *m.* — *-coast*, s. côte de la mer, *f.*, rivage, *m.* — *-compass*, s. boussole, *f.* — *-coot*, s. foulque, *f.* — *-cow*, s. morse, *m.* — *-crow*, s. goéland, *m.* — *-elephant*, s. phoque à trompe, *m.* — *-engagement*, s., — *-fight*, s. combat naval, *f.* — *-fish*, s. poisson de mer, *m.* — *-foam*, s., — *-froth*, s. écume de mer, *f.* — *-forces*, s. forces navales, *f.pl.* — *-fowl*, s. oiseau de mer, *m.* — *-gage*, s. tirant d'eau, *m.* — *-girt*, s. ceint par la mer, *f.* — *-green*, s. vert de mer, *m.* — *-gull*, s. mouette, *f.* — *-hog*, s. marsouin, *m.* — *-holm*, s. îlot inhabité. — *-horse*, s. morse, *m.*, cheval marin, *m.* — *-letter*, s. certificat de nationalité, *m.* — *-maid*, s. sirène, *f.* — *-mall*, s., — *-mew*, s., — *-mute*, s. mouette, *f.* — *-moss*, s. corail, *m.* — *-nursed*, adj. bercé par la mer. — *-piece*, s. marine, *f.* — *-pike*, s. aiguille de mer, *f.* — *-reed*, s. roseau marin, *m.* — *-risk*, s. risques de la mer, *m.pl.* — *-robber*, s. pirate, *m.* — *-robin*, s. rouget, *m.* — *-room*, s. eau à courir, *f.*, de l'espace, *m.* — *-rover*, s. corsaire, écumeur de mer, *m.* — *-service*, s. service sur mer, *m.*, la marine, *f.* — *-shark*, s. requin, *m.* — *-shell*, s. coquillage, *m.* — *-shore*, s., — *-side*, s. bord de la mer. — *-sick*, adj. qui a le mal de mer. — *-sickness*, s. mal de mer. — *-surgeon*, s. chirurgien de vaisseau, *m.* — *-tossed*, adj., — *-tost*, adj. ballotté sur les eaux. — *-turn*, s. brise de mer, *f.* — *-urchin*, s. oursin, *m.* — *-view*, s. vue de la mer, *f.*, marine, *f.* — *-voyage*, s. voyage sur mer, *m.* — *-wall*, s. digue, *f.* — *-worn*, adj. usé par la mer. — *-worthiness*, s. bon état, *m.* — *-worthy*, adj. en état. — *-wrack*, s. varech, *m.*

Seafarer, s. marin, *m.*, navigateur, *m.*, homme de mer, *m.*

Seafaring, adj. marin, navigateur, de mer. — *-life*, s. vie de marin, *f.*

Seal, s. phoque, *m.*, veau marin, *m.*, (*stamp*) sceau, *m.*, cachet, *m.* — *-skin*, s. peau de veau marin, *f.* — *-fisher*, s. pêcheur de phoques, *m.* *Broad* —, grand sceau. *The great* —, le grand sceau. *To affix* or *set one's* — *to*, *the seals on*, apposer son sceau à, faire apposer les scellés sur *or* mettre les scellés sur. *Under* —, sous le scellé. *Breaking of the* —, bris de scellé. *Under the hand and* — *of*, signé et scellé par. *A gold* —, un cachet d'or. *A flying* —, un cachet volant. *To break the* — (*of*), briser le cachet (de), décacheter. *Under the* — *of secrecy*, sous le sceau du secret. *The* — *of victory*, le sceau de la victoire

Seal, va. sceller, cacheter, (*ratify*) mettre le sceau à, confirmer, (*shoot*) fermer, clore, (*build*) sceller. *To* — *up*, sceller, cacheter, fermer, clore

Sealing, s. action de sceller, *f.*, apposition de sceau, *f.*, action de cacheter, *f.* — *-wax*, s. cire à cacheter, *f.*

Seam, s. couture, *f.*, suture, *f.*, cicatrice, *f.*, (*mines*) veine, *f.*, couche, *f.* — *-rent*, s. décousure, *f.*

Seam, va. coudre, couturer

Seaman, s. marin, *m.*, matelot, *m.*, homme de mer, *m.* — *-like*, adj. le marin, en bon marin

Seamanship, s. talent de marin, *m.*, connaissance de la mer, *f.*

Seamless, adj. sans couture

Seamstress, s. *see* SEMPSTRESS

Seamy, adj. qui montre la couture. *To turn the* — *side without*, mettre à l'envers

Seaport, s. port de mer, *m.*

Sear, va. dessécher, sécher, brûler, cautériser, flétrir, rendre insensible

Sear, adj. desséché, séché, fané. — *leaf*, s. feuille morte, *f.*

Search, va.n. explorer, visiter, examiner, chercher, fouiller, (*a person*) visiter, lire avec soin, étudier, rechercher, scruter, (*wound*) sonder. *His house was* —*ed*, on fouilla la maison, on fit chez lui une visite domici-

·llaire. *He was —ed*, on le fouilla. *Has your luggage been —ed?* a-t-on visité votre bagage? *They have —ed everywhere*, on a visité *or* fouillé partout

Search, s. recherche, *f.*, quête, *f.*, poursuite, *f.*, (*law*) perquisition, *f.*, visite domiciliaire, *f.*, descente de justice, *f.* *In — of*, à la recherche de, en quête de. *To make a —*, faire des recherches, visiter. *To issue a —-warrant*, lancer un mandat de perquisition. *Right of —*, s. droit de visite, *m.*

Searcher, s. qui recherche, investigateur, *m.*, (*custom*) officier de douane, *m.*, visiteur, *m.*

Searching, adj. scrutateur, pénétrant

Searching, s. recherches, *f.pl.*, examen, *m.*, investigation, *f.*, visite, *f.*, perquisition, *f.*

Searchingly, adv. d'un regard pénétrant *or* scrutateur, d'une manière pressante

Season, s. saison, *f.*, temps, *m.*, moment, *m.*, temps convenable, *m.* *The four —s*, les quatre saisons. *Dull —*, la morte saison. *In due —*, dans la saison, à temps convenable. *Out of —*, hors de saison, mal à propos

Season, va. acclimater, habituer, rompre, faire, endurcir, (*wood*) préparer, sécher; — vn. s'acclimater, (*wood*) se sécher

Seasonable, adj. opportun, à propos, de saison

Seasonableness, s. à propos, *m.*, opportunité, *f.*

Seasonably, adv. à propos, au moment opportun, bien à temps

Seasoning, s. assaisonnement, *m.*, piquant, *m.*, (*wood*) séchage, *m.*

Seat, s. siége, *m.*, chaise, *f.*, banc, *m.*, place, *f.*, (*coach*) banquette, *f.*, (*dwelling*) résidence, *f.*, demeure, *f.*, (*country-house*) maison de campagne, *f.*, château, *m.*, (*of war*) théâtre, *m.*, (*chairs, trousers*) fond, *m.* *To have a — in parliament*, être membre du parlement, siéger au parlement. *To give a — to*, donner une chaise à. *To keep a — for*, garder une place à. *To leave one's —*, quitter sa place. *To lose one's —*, perdre sa place, perdre son siége au parlement, (*in riding*) perdre la selle. *To take one's —*, prendre sa place, s'asseoir. *A nobleman's —*, un château de grand seigneur. *To have a good —*, se tenir bien en selle

Seat, va. faire asseoir, asseoir, établir, fixer, placer, donner un siége à, (*chairs*) mettre un fond à. *The guests were —ed*, les invités étaient assis. *To — oneself*, s'asseoir, se fixer, s'établir. *To remain —ed*, rester assis. *Pray, be —ed*, veuillez vous asseoir

Seated, adj. (*in compounds*) à . . . place

Seaward, adj. *and* adv. vers la mer

Sea-weed, s. algue, *f.*, plante marine, *f.*, varech, *m.*

Secant, s. adj. sécant, -e

Secede, vn. se séparer, faire sécession, faire scission

Seceder, s. sécessioniste, *m.*, dissident, *m.*, -e, *f.*, séparatiste, *m.f.*

Seceding, adj. sécessioniste, dissident

Secession, s. sécession, *f.*, scission, *f.*, dissidence, *f.*

Seclude, va. séparer, exclure, garantir contre, éloigner. *To — oneself*, se séparer, se tenir à l'écart de

Secluded, adj. retiré, dans la solitude

Seclusion, s. reclusion, *f.*, retraite, *f.*, séparation, *f.*

Second, adj. second, deux, deuxième, (*fig.*) inférieur. *— captain*, capitaine en second, *m.* *—-best*, qualité No. 2. *Every — day*, de deux en deux jours. *The — of March*, le deux mars. *— hand*, d'occasion, de seconde main. *—-rate*, de second rang, (*pers.*) de qualité inférieure, d'importance secondaire. *To be — to none*, ne le céder à personne

Second, s. soutien, *m.*, appui, *m.*, (*in a duel*) témoin, *m.*, second, *m.*, (*time*) seconde, *f.*, (*mus.*) seconde, *f.*, (*flour*) farine de deuxième qualité, *f.*

Second, va. seconder, appuyer, aider, favoriser

Secondarily, adv. secondairement, accessoirement

Secondary, adj. secondaire, de second ordre, subalterne, inférieur

Seconder, s. personne qui seconde, qui appuie

Secondly, adv. deuxièmement, en deuxième lieu

Secrecy, s. secret, *m.*, discrétion, *f.*, (*place*) retraite, *f.*, solitude, *f.* *In —*, en secret, sous le secret. *To observe, to promise —*, garder, promettre le secret. *With —*, en secret. *Committee of —*, comité secret. *To swear —*, jurer de garder le secret. *Art sworn to —?* as-tu juré de garder le secret?

Secret, adj. s. secret, caché, dérobé. *To keep —*, tenir secret. *Things which must be kept —*, des choses qui doivent se taire. *Can you be —?* êtes-vous discret?

Secretary, s. secrétaire, *m.* *Confidential — to the prince*, secrétaire intime du prince. *— to an or the embassy*, secrétaire d'ambassade. *—, under- — of state*, secrétaire, sous-secrétaire d'État. *— of War*, secrétaire d'État au departement de la guerre. *—'s office*, secrétariat, *m.*, secrétairerie, *f.* *— for Foreign affairs*, ministre des affaires étrangères, *m.*

Secretaryship, s. place *or* fonctions de secrétaire, *f.*, secrétariat, *m.*

Secrete, va. cacher, (*med.*) sécréter

Secretion, s. sécrétion, *f.*

Secretly, adv. secrètement, en secret, mystérieusement

Secretory, adj. sécrétoire

Sect, s. secte, *f.*

Sectarian, adj. de sectaire

Sectarian, s. sectaire, *m.*

Sectarianism, s. esprit de secte, *m.*

Section, s. action de couper, *f.*, division, *f.*, portion, *f.*, section, *f.*, (*archit.*) coupe, *f.*, (*print.*) paragraphe, *m.*

Sector, s. secteur, *m.*, compas de proportion, *m.*

Secular, adj. séculaire, séculier, temporel. *The — jurisdiction*, la juridiction séculière

Secular, s. séculier, *m.*, laïque, *m.*

Secularism, s. attachement aux choses de ce monde, *m.*, mondanité, *f.*

Secularization, s. sécularisation, *f.*

Secularize, va. séculariser

Secularly, adv. séculièrement, mondainement

Secure, adj. (*confident*) sans inquiétude, dans la sécurité, se croyant en sûreté, sans crainte, assuré, (*safe*) assuré, certain, à l'abri (de), en sûreté (contre), garanti (contre), à couvert (de)

Secure, va. assurer (contre), mettre en sûreté (contre), mettre à l'abri (de), garantir (de), protéger (contre), préserver (de), s'assurer (de), s'emparer (de), avoir, posséder sûrement, se rendre maître de, (*a place*) retenir, arrêter, assurer, raffermir, maintenir, (*a door*) fermer et barrer

Securely, adv. en sûreté, à l'abri, avec confiance, sans crainte

Security, s. sécurité, *f.*, sûreté, *f.*, (*pledge*) garantie, *f.*, nantissement, *m.*, (*pers.*) caution, *f.* *In —*, en sûreté. *The surest of all securities*, la plus sûre des valeurs

Sedan, s. chaise à porteurs, *f.* *—-chair*, s. chaise à porteurs, *f.*

Sedate, adj. calme, rassis, posé, tranquille

Sedately, adv. avec calme, posément

Sedateness, s. calme, *m.*, sérieux, *m.*

Sedative, adj. sédatif

Sedative, s. sédatif, *m.*

Sedentarily, adv. d'une manière sédentaire, d'une vie sédentaire

Sedentariness, s. état sédentaire, *m.*, vie sédentaire, *f.*

Sedentary, adj. sédentaire, lent, inactif

Sedge, s. glaïeul, *m.*, jonc, *m.*

Sedged, Sedgy, adj. de joncs

Sediment, s. sédiment, *m.*, dépôt, *m.*

Sedimentary, adj. sédimentaire

Sedition, s. sédition, *f.*, soulèvement, *m.*

Seditionary, adj. séditieux

Seditious, adj. séditieux. *— person*, s. séditieux, *m.*

Seditiously, adv. séditieusement

Seditiousness, s. caractère séditieux, *m.*, esprit séditieux, *m.*

Seduce, va. séduire, tenter, corrompre

Seducer, s. séducteur, *m.*, -trice, *f.*

Seducible, adj. qu'on peut séduire *or* corrompre, facile à séduire

Seducingly, adv. d'une manière séduisante

Seduction, s. séduction, *f.*

Seductive, adj. séduisant, attrayant

Sedulity, s. assiduité, *f.*

Sedulous, adj. appliqué, assidu, diligent

Sedulously, adv. assidûment, avec assiduité, diligemment

Sedulousness, s. assiduité, *f.*, application, *f.*, diligence, *f.*

See, s. siége episcopal, *m.*, évêché, *m.*, archevêché, *m.* *The holy —*, le saint-siége

See, interj. voyez! regardez!

See, va.n. voir, apercevoir, s'apercevoir de, (*visit*) fréquenter, recevoir, (*take care*) voir, veiller à ce, (*conduct*) conduire. *I saw him fall*, je le vis tomber. *Do you — any one coming?* voyez-vous venir quelqu'un? *I do not — him coming*, je ne le vois pas venir. *I — him coming*, je le vois qui vient. *I saw his house built*, j'ai vu bâtir cette maison. *Just — if*, voyez un peu si. *Let me — if*, voyons si. *He insists upon —ing everything with his own eyes*, il veut tout voir par lui-même. *I can't — at all*, je ne vois pas du tout, je ne vois goutte. *Not to — a jot*, n'y voir goutte. *I can't — my way*, je ne vois pas mon chemin, (*fig.*) je ne sais comment m'y prendre, je n'y vois goutte. *To — again*, revoir. *To — over and over again*, voir et revoir. *To — oneself in a glass*, se voir dans un miroir. *To be —n*, être vu, se voir. *Easily —n, easy to be —n*, facile à voir. *That is easily —n*, (*iron.*) il y paraît! *That remains to be —n*, c'est à voir. *To allow to be —n*, (*by*, à) laisser voir, laisser paraître. *To go to —, to go and —*, aller voir. *To improve by —ing men*, se perfectionner en fréquentant les hommes. *To — nobody, to — no company*, ne voir, ne recevoir personne. *He —s a great deal of com-*

pany, il reçoit beaucoup de monde, il est très-répandu. *To — a person home*, reconduire une personne chez elle. *To — about*, penser à, songer à, veiller à. *To — away, to — off*, voir partir, conduire au chemin de fer, à la voiture, etc. *To — out*, voir partir, reconduire, voir jusqu'au bout, voir comment cela finira. *To — through*, voir à travers, (*fig.*) pénétrer. *To — to*, veiller à, avoir soin de, penser à, prendre garde à ce que

Seed, s. semence, *f.*, graine, *f.*, semaille, *f.*, (*people*) race, *f.*, peuple, *m.* *To run to —*, monter en graine. *Sowing —*, semailles. — *-cake*, s. gâteau à graine d'anis, *m.* — *-coat*, s. épisperme, *m.* — *-plot*, s. semis, *m.* — *-time*, s. semailles, *f.pl.* — *-trade*, s. grèneterie, *f.*

Seed, vn. venir en graine

Seedling, s. sauvageon, *m.*

Seedsman, s. grènetier, *m.*

Seedy, adj. grenu, plein *or* chargé de graines, abondant en graines, (*clothes, pers.*) râpé

Seeing, adj. qui voit

Seeing, s. la vue, *f.*, vision, *f.*

Seeing, conj. vu que, puisque

Seek, va.n. chercher, rechercher, (*ask*) demander. — *and you will find*, cherchez et vous trouverez. *To — one's bread, revenge*, chercher son pain, chercher à se venger. *To — each other*, se chercher. *To — each other's company*, se rechercher. *To — to comfort*, chercher à consoler, vouloir consoler. *To — after, for*, chercher, rechercher, en vouloir à, chercher à, prendre

Seeker, s. chercheur, *m.*, -euse, *f.*

Seel, va. rouler fort

Seem, vn. sembler, paraître. *You — to think*, vous semblez croire, vous paraissez croire. *It —s, it would — that*, il semble que, il paraît que. *It would —*, ce semble. *It would — so*, à ce qu'il paraît *or* paraîtrait. *As it —s, as it would —*, à ce qu'il semble *or* paraît. *The thing —s true*, la chose paraît être vraie. *To — to be*, paraître être *or* qu'on est

Seeming, s. semblant, *m.*, apparence, *f.*, dehors, *m.pl.*

Seeming, adj. apparent, qui fait semblant, specieux. *He gave a — consent*, il parut consentir

Seemingly, adv. en apparence

Seemingness, s. apparence, *f.*, caractère spacieux, *m.*

Seemliness, s. bienséance, *f.*, convenance, *f.*

Seemly, adj. convenable, bienséant. *It is not —*, il ne sied pas, il n'est pas convenable

Seer, s. adj. qui voit, prophète, clairvoyant, -e. *All —*, qui voit tout

Seesaw, vn. faire un mouvement de bascule, aller et venir, (*play*) se balancer

Seesaw, s. bascule, *f.*, mouvement de va-et-vient, *m.*

Seesaw, adj. de bascule, de va-et-vient

Seethe, *see* To Boil

Segment, s. segment, *m.*, portion, *f.*

Seignior, s. seigneur, *m.*

Seigniorial, adj. seigneurial

Seine, s. seine, *f.*

Seizable, adj. saisissable

Seize, va.n. saisir, se saisir de. *To — on* or *upon*, saisir, se saisir de, s'emparer de

Seizer, s. qui saisit

Seizure, s. action de saisir, *f.*, prise, *f.*, prise de possession, *f.*, (*law*) saisie, *f.*, confiscation, *f.*

Seldom, adv. rarement

Select, va. choisir, trier

Select, adj. choisi, de choix, d'élite, meilleur. *A — collection*, un choix. — *committee*, commission d'enquête

Selection, s. choix, *m.*

Self, adj. pron. même, soi-même, soi, le moi, personne, *f.*, individu, *m.* *That — way*, dans la même direction. *His own —*, lui-même, sa propre personne. *To think of none but —*, ne penser qu'à soi. *My wretched —*, mon misérable individu. *Well pleased with one's own dear —*, content de sa petite personne. *For my own —*, pour ma part, en mon particulier

Self- (*in compounds*). — *-acting*, adj. automateur, agissant de soi-même. — *-admiration*, s. admiration de soi-même, *f.* — *-admiring*, adj. qui s'admire soi-même, admirateur de soi-même. — *-affairs*, s. ses propres affaires, *m.pl.* — *-affrighted*, adj. qui a peur de soi-même. — *-aggrandizement*, s. agrandissement de soi-même, *m.* — *-annihilated*, adj. anéanti par soi-même. — *-annihilation*, s. anéantissement de soi-même, *m.* — *-applause*, s. contentement de soi, *m.*, approbation de soi-même, *f.* — *-approbation*, s. approbation de soi-même, *f.* — *-approving*, adj. qui s'approuve. *One — -approving hour*, s. une heure d'approbation de soi-même. — *-assumed*, adj. pris de sa propre autorité. — *-assured*, adj. qui s'est assuré soi-même. — *-banished*, adj. qui s'exile volontairement. — *-begotten*, adj., — *-born*, adj. né de soi-même, conçu par soi-même. — *-beguiled*, adj. trompé *or* déçu par soi-même. — *-centred*, se servant de centre à soi-même, fixé sur son centre. — *-charity*, s. l'amour de soi-même. — *-command*, s. empire sur soi-même, sang-froid, *m.* — *-collected*, adj. recueilli en soi-même. — *-complacent*, adj. content de soi. — *-conceit*, s., — *-conceitedness*, s. amour-propre, *m.*, suffisance, *f.*, présomption, *f.* — *-conceited*, adj. rempli d'amour-propre, suffisant, présomptueux. — *-condemnation*, s. condamnation de soi-même, *f.* — *-confidence*, s. confiance en soi-même, *f.*, assurance, *f.* — *-confident*, adj., — *-confiding*, adj. plein de confiance en soi-même. — *-conscious*, adj. qui a la conscience de soi-même. — *-consciousness*, s. conscience de soi-même, *f.* — *-consuming*, adj. qui se consume soi-même. — *-contradiction*, s. contradiction avec soi-même, *f.* — *-contradictory*, adj. en contradiction avec soi-même, qui se contredit. — *-control*, s. empire sur soi-même, sang-froid, *m.* — *-convicted*, convaincu par ses propres paroles, condamné par soi-même. — *-conviction*, s. conviction par ses propres paroles, *f.* — *-created*, adj. créé par soi-même. — *-deceit*, s. illusion, *f.* — *-deceived*, adj. trompé par lui-même. — *-deceiving*, adj. qui se trompe soi-même. — *-defence*, s. défense personnelle. *In — -defence*, dans sa propre défense, à son corps défendant. — *-denial*, s. abnégation, *f.*, désintéressement, *m.*, oubli de soi-même, *m.*, renoncement à soi-même, *m.* — *-denying*, adj. d'abnégation, (*pers.*) qui se sacrifie. — *-dependent*, adj., — *-depending*, adj. indépendant. — *-destruction*, s. suicide, *m.* — *-determined*, adj. qui s'est déterminé soi-même. — *-devoted*, adj. personellement dévoué, qui se dévoue soi-même. — *-devotion*, s. dévouement de soi-même, *m.*, dévouement personnel, *m.* — *-devouring*, adj. qui se dévore soi-même. *-educated*, adj. qui ne doit son éducation qu'à soi-même, qui s'est instruit soi-même. — *-enjoyment*, s. contentement de soi, *m.*, satisfaction intérieure, *f.* — *-esteem*, s., — *-estimation*, s. sa propre estime, estime de soi-même, vanité, *f.* — *-evidence*, s. évidence de soi, en soi, *f.* — *-evident*, adj. évident de soi, qui parle de soi-même. — *-evidently*, adv. d'une manière évidente de soi. — *-examination*, s. examen de conscience, *m.* — *-fed*, adj. qui se nourrit soi-même, qui se repaît de soi-même. — *-flattering*, adj. flatteur, qui se flatte. — *-flattery*, s. flatterie de soi-même, *f.* — *-government*, s. empire sur soi-même, *m.*, (*polit.*) gouvernement du pays par le pays, *m.* — *-interest*, s. son intérêt personnel, *m.* — *-interested*, adj. intéressé, égoïste. — *-love*, s. l'amour de soi, *m.*, la personnalité, *f.* égoïsme, *m.* — *-made man*, s. fils de ses œuvres, *m.* — *-mastery*, s. empire sur soi-même, *m.* — *-possession*, s. empire sur soi-même, *m.*, calme, *m.*, sang-froid, *m.* — *-praise*, s. éloge de soi-même, *f.* — *-preservation*, s. conservation de soi-même, *f.* — *-reliance*, s. confiance en soi-même, *f.* — *-same*, s. le même, *m.*, exactement le même, *m.* — *-styled*, adj. soi-disant, prétendu. — *-taught*, adj. qui s'est instruit *or* formé soi-même. — *-will*, s. opiniâtreté, *f.* — *-willed*, adj. opiniâtre, volontaire, obstiné, têtu

Selfish, adj. égoïste, intéressé

Selfishly, adv. en égoïste, avec égoïsme

Selfishness, s. égoïsme, *m.*

Sell, va. vendre, (*pop.*) jouer, mettre dedans. *To — for nothing*, vendre pour rien. *To — off*, liquider, vendre en liquidation. *To — out*, vendre. *Sold again!* encore pris! encore joué! — vn. se vendre, se débiter. *To — well*, se vendre bien, être d'un bon débit. *To — out*, se liquider, vendre ses rentes, etc.

Seller, s. vendeur, *m.*, -euse, *f.*

Seltzer-water, s. eau de Seltz, *f.*

Selvage, **Selvedge**, s. bord façonné, *m.*, lisière, *f.*

Semaphore, s. sémaphore, *m.*

Semblance, s. ressemblance, *f.*, image, *f.*

Semi-, adj. semi-, demi-

Semi-annual, adj. semi-annuel, semestriel

Semi-barbarian, **Semi-barbarous**, adj. semi-barbare

Semi-barbarian, s. semi-barbare, *m.*

Semi-breve, s. semi-brève, *f.*

Semicircle, s. demi-cercle, *m.*, hémicycle, *m.*

Semicircular, adj. demi-circulaire

Semicolon, s. point-virgule, *m.*

Seminal, adj. séminal

Seminarist, s. séminariste, *m.*

Seminary, s. institution, *f.*, pension, *f.*, école, *f.*, (*eccles.*) séminaire, *m.*, (*pers.*) séminariste, *m.*

Semiquaver, s. double croche, *f.* *Demi-semi- —*, s. triple croche, *f.*

Semipheric, **Semipherical**, adj. en forme de demi-sphère

Semitone, s. demi-ton, *m.*

Semolina, s. semoule, *f.*

Sempstress, s. couturière, *f.*

Senate, s. sénat, *m.*

Senator, s. sénateur, *m.*

Senatorial, adj. sénatorial

Senatorship, s. sénatorerie, *f.*, rang de sénateur, *m.*

Senatus-consultum, s. sénatus-consulte, *m.*

Send, va.n. envoyer, (*things*) envoyer, expédier, (*before a judge*) renvoyer, (*spread*) répandre. *To — to ask how a person does*, envoyer demander des nouvelles de quelqu'un. *He —s me to say that ...*, il m'envoie dire que. *I sent a word to her*, je le lui fis dire, je lui envoyai un mot. *To — away*, renvoyer, congédier. *To — back*, renvoyer. *To — down*, envoyer en bas, faire descendre, répandre, faire pleuvoir. *To — for*, envoyer chercher, faire venir. *To — forth*, envoyer, lancer, (*shoot out*) pousser, montrer, faire paraître, (*odour, &c.*) exhaler, (*heat*) dégager, (*a law*) promulguer, publier. *To — in*, envoyer, faire entrer, introduire. *To — off*, renvoyer, faire partir, expédier. *To — out*, envoyer dehors, envoyer, faire sortir. *To — up*, monter, servir

Send, s. soulèvement, *m.*, tangage, *m.*

Sender, s. envoyeur, *m.*, -euse, *f.*, expéditeur, *m.*

Seneschal, s. sénéchal, *m.*

Senile, adj. sénile

Senior, adj. aîné, (*com.*) principal, (*univ.*) ancien, supérieur. *The — clerk*, le premier commis, le premier clerc. *The — captain*, le capitaine le plus ancien en grade. *My — -officer*, mon ancien, mon officier supérieur

Senior, s. aîné, *m.*, -e, *f.*, associé principal, *m.*, ancien en fonctions, *m.*, ancien, *m.*, doyen, *m.*

Seniority, s. supériorité d'âge, *f.*, priorité d'âge, *f.*, ancienneté de grade, *f.*

Senna, s. séné, *m.*

Sensation, s. sensation, *f.* *To make, to create a —, quite a —*, faire sensation, mettre tout en émoi

Sensational, adj. sensible, qui sent, des sens, (*fig.*) qui fait sensation, à sensation

Sense, s. sens, *m.*, sensation, *f.*, (*fig.*) bon sens, *m.*, sens commun, *m.*, esprit, *m.*, raison, *f.*, (*opinion*) sentiment, *m.*, avis, *m.*, conviction, *f.*, (*meaning*) sens, *m.*, signification, *f.* *The five —s*, les cinq sens. *A man of —, of great —*, homme de sens, homme de beaucoup d'esprit. *Good —*, bon sens. *Mere common —*, le simple sens commun. *With his good common —*, avec son gros bon sens. *To have good sound —*, avoir le sens droit. *He does not want —*, il ne manque pas d'esprit. *Are you in your —s, in your right — ?* êtes-vous dans votre bon sens? *To be out of one's —s*, être hors de son bon sens, avoir perdu la raison. *To drive out of one's —s*, faire perdre la raison, la tête à. *To recover one's —s*, reprendre ses sens, ses esprits. *To talk —*, parler raison. *To express one's — of*, dire ce qu'on pense de. *I can make no — of it*, je n'y puis rien comprendre. *To bring you to a proper — of your extravagance*, pour vous faire bien comprendre, pour bien vous pénétrer du sentiment de votre folie. *To have a deep — of*, ressentir vivement

Senseless, adj. insensible, sans connaissance, absurde, insensé

Senselessly, adv. d'une manière insensée, sottement, absurdement

Senselessness, s. insensibilité, *f.*, absurdité, *f.*, sottise, *f.*, stupidité, *f.*

Sensibility, s. sensibilité, *f.*, sentiment, *m.*

Sensible, adj. sensible, (*conscious*) convaincu, persuadé, qui a le sentiment de, (*reasonable*) sensé, en pleine connaissance. *To be — of*, sentir, avoir le sentiment de. *To make a person — of a thing*, faire sentir quelque chose à quelqu'un. *— man*, un homme de sens, un homme sensé

Sensibleness, s. sensibilité, *f.*, sens, *m.*, bon sens, *m.*, raison, *f.*

Sensibly, adv. sensiblement, (*wisely*) sensément

Sensitive, adj. sensitif, (*pers.*) sensible, (*touchy*) susceptible

Sensitiveness, s. nature sensitive, *f.*, sensibilité, *f.*, susceptibilité, *f.*

Sensual, adj. sensuel

Sensualism, s. sensualisme, *m.*

Sensualist, s. sensualiste, *m.*

Sensuality, s. sensualité, *f.*

Sensualize, va. rendre sensuel

Sensually, adv. sensuellement, avec sensualité

Sensuous, adj. qui affecte les sens

Sentence, s. sentence, *f.*, jugement, *m.*, (*grammat.*) phrase, *f.* *Under — of death*, sous sentence de mort. *To pass —*, passer condamnation, prononcer la sentence. *To undergo one's —*, subir son arrêt, sa condamnation. *Short —s*, des phrases coupées. *Well constructed —s*, des phrases bien coupées

Sentence, va. prononcer une sentence, un jugement sur *or* contre

Sententious, adj. sentencieux

Sententiously, adv. sentencieusement, d'un ton sentencieux

Sententiousness, s. ton sentencieux, *m.*, concision énergique, *f.*

Sentient, adj. sensible, doué de sens, qui sent

Sentiment, s. sentiment, *m.*, sensibilité, *f.*, (*opinion*) jugement, *m.*, avis, *m.*, (*thought*) pensée, *f.*

Sentimental, adj. sentimental, sensible

Sentimentality, s. sensiblerie, *f.*

Sentimentally, adj. d'une manière sentimentale

Sentinel, Sentry, s. sentinelle, *f.*, factionnaire, *m.*, faction, *f.*, garde, *f.* *To stand —*, être de faction *or* de garde, faire faction. *To keep — over*, veiller sur. *— -box*, s. guérite, *f.*

Separable, adj. séparable

Separably, adv. à part

Separate, va. séparer, désunir, isoler, éloigner: — vn. se séparer, se quitter, se disjoindre

Separate, adj. séparé, à part, distinct, disjoint, isolé

Separately, adv. séparément, à part

Separation, s. séparation, *f.*, (*law*) séparation de corps, *f.*, divorce, *m.*

Sepia, s. seiche, *f.*, (*paint.*) sépia, *f.*

Sepoy, s. cipaye, *m.*

September, s. septembre, *m.*

Septennial, adj. septennal

Septuagenarian, s. septuagénaire, *m.f.*

Sepulchral, adj. sépulcral

Sepulchre, s. sépulcre, *m.*, tombeau, *m.*

Sepulture, s. sépulture, *f.*

Sequel, s. suite, *f.*, conséquence, *f.*

Sequence, s. suite, *f.*, conséquence, *f.*, ordre, *m.*, succession, *f.*, (*mus.*) série, *f.*, (*cards*) séquence, *f.*

Sequester, va. séparer, écarter, séquestrer, retirer, éloigner

Sequestered, adj. retiré, écarté, (*law*) en séquestre

Sequestrate, va. séquestrer

Sequestration, s. isolement, *m.*, mise à l'écart, *f.*, (*law*) séquestration, *f.*

Sequestrator, s. séquestre, *m.*

Seraglio, s. sérail, *m.*

Seraph, s. séraphin, *m.*

Seraphic, Seraphical, adj. séraphique

Serenade, s. sérénade, *f.*

Serenade, va.n. donner une sérénade à

Serene, adj. serein, calme, paisible. *All — !* parfait!

Serenely, adv. avec sérénité

Serenity, s. sérénité, *f.*

Serf, s. serf, *m.*

Serfdom, Serfage, s. servage, *m.*, servitude, *f.*

Serge, s. serge, *f.*

Sergeant, Serjeant, s. (*infantry*) sergent, *m.*, (*caval.*) maréchal de logis, *m.*, (*law*) sergent, *m.* *— -major*, s. sergent-major, *m.*, maréchal des logis chef, *m.* *Pay- —*, s., *quartermaster —*, s. sergent fourrier, *m.*

Sergeantship, s. grade de sergent, *m.*

Serial, adj. d'une série

Serial, s. ouvrage qui paraît par livraisons, *m.*

Series, s. série, *f.*, suite, *f.*

Serio-comic, Serio-comical, adj. sério-comique

Serious, adj. sérieux, grave. *A — look*, un air grave. *A very — business*, une affaire très-sérieuse *or* grave. *The case is a — one*, le cas est grave. *Are you — ?* parlez-vous sérieusement? *To take a thing for —*, prendre une chose au sérieux

Seriously, adv. sérieusement, pour tout de bon

Seriousness, s. sérieux, *m.*, gravité, *f.*, air sérieux, *m.*

Sermon, s. sermon, *m.*

Sermonize, va. prêcher, (*fig.*) sermonner

Serous, adj. séreux

Serpent, s. serpent, *m.*, (*squib*) serpenteau, *m.* *Young —*, s. jeune serpent, *m.*, serpenteau, *m.* *— -eater*, s. oiseau serpentaire, secrétaire, *m.* *— -cucumber*, s. trichosanthe, *m.* *— -fish*, s. cépole rouge, *f.* *— -like*, adj. comme un serpent, de serpent. *—'s tongue*, (*bot.*) ophioglosse, *m.* *— -player*, s. serpent, *m.*

Serpentine, adj. serpentin, sinueux, qui serpente, tortueux. *— -form*, s. forme de serpent, *f.* *— -line*, s. ligne serpentine, *f.* *— tongue*, s. langue serpentine. *— -stone*, s. serpentine, *f.*, ophite, *m.* *— -worm*, s. (*chem.*) serpentin, *m.*

Serpentine, s. (*min. bot.*) serpentine, *f.*, serpentin, *m.*

Serried, adj. serré, compacte

Serum, s. serum, *m.*

Servant, s. serviteur, *m.*, servante, *f.*, domestique, *m.f.* *— -boy*, s., *— -girl*, s. jeune domestique, *m.f.* *— -maid*, domestique, *f.*, bonne, *f.*

Serve, va. servir, (*church*) desservir, (*to be of use*) servir à, être utile à, aider à, seconder, (*flatter*) flatter, se montrer complaisant envers, (*for*, de) servir à, tenir lieu à, (*to play a trick upon*) jouer, (*milit.*) servir, (*law*) signifier. *To — God, one's country, the public*, servir Dieu, sa patrie, le public. *—d in plate*, servi dans de la vaisselle plate. *To — in*, servir. *To — out*, distribuer, (*one's time*) faire, (*pop.*) payer. *To — up*, servir, (*pop.*) exposer au ridicule. *The dinner is —d up in this manner*, le dîner se sert, est servi de cette façon.

To — a battery, a pump, servir une batterie, une pompe. *To — an office*, remplir les fonctions d'une charge. *It can — another end*, cela pourra servir à une autre fin. *To — the time*, flatter le pouvoir. *To — as an excuse for something*, servir de prétexte à, pour quelque chose. *He —ed me ungratefully*, il a agi avec moi en ingrat. *It —s you, him right*, c'est bien fait (pour vous, pour lui), vous ne l'avez pas volé, il ne l'a pas volé. *You shall be —d in the same way*, on vous traitera de la même façon. *To — the king*, servir le roi. *To have —d thirty years*, avoir trente ans de service. *To — three campaigns*, faire trois campagnes. — vn. servir, suffire, être convenable, être favorable

Service, s. service, *m.*, (*respect*) respect, *m.*, hommage, *m.*, (*church*) service divin, *m.*, (*use*) utilité, *f.*, avantage, *m.*, (*law*) notification, *f.*, signification, *f.*, (*bot.*) sorbier domestique, *m.*, fruit du sorbier, *m.* *To be out of* —, n'avoir plus de place, avoir quitté sa place. *To go out to* —, entrer or se mettre en service. *To do —, a —, to render great —s*, rendre service, un service, de grands services. *To see* —, avoir du service. *Secret — -money*, s. (*polit.*) fonds secrets, *m.pl.* *With my* —, avec mes respects. *To be of — to*, être utile, rendre service à. — *-book*, s. livre d'offices, *m.*, rituel, *m.*

Serviceable, adj. utile, avantageux, profitable, serviable

Serviceableness, s. utilité, *f.*, avantage, *m.*, nature serviable, *f.*

Servile, adj. esclave, asservi, servile, abject

Servilely, adv. servilement

Servility, s. servilité, *f.*, servitude, *f.*

Serving, s. action de servir, *f.*, service, *m.*

Serving, adj. qui sert, servant

Servitude, s. servitude, *f.*, asservissement, *m.*, esclavage, *m.*

Session, s. session, *f.*, (*sittings*) séances, *f.pl.*, (*law*) assises, *f.pl.*

Set, va. poser, mettre, placer, (*seal*) apposer, (*task*) imposer, (*example*) donner, rendre, faire devenir, (*fix*) enfoncer, fixer, (*jewels*) monter, enchâsser, (*mare*) tendre, dresser, fixer, désigner, (*watch*) régler, (*garden*) planter, (*price*) charger, estimer, apprécier, faire cas de, (*annoy*) presser, embarrasser, tourmenter, (*price*) mettre à, (*to music*) mettre, (*razors*) repasser, (*limbs*) remettre, (*print.*) composer, (*nau.*) mettre, (*hunting*) arrêter, (*milk*) faire repuser, faire cailler. *To — one's foot on*, poser le pied sur. *To — a king over the people*, donner un roi au peuple. *Those whom he has — over us*, ceux à qui il a donné autorité sur nous. *To — one's affections on*, fixer ses affections sur, s'attacher à. *To — oneself a task*, s'imposer une tâche. *To — even*, égaliser, régler. *To — open*, ouvrir. *Eyes — in the head*, les yeux enfoncés dans leurs orbites. *A stone plain* —, une pierre simplement montée. *To — a-going*, mettre en mouvement, faire jouer, faire aller, mettre en train. *Not to — one's life at a pin's fee*, faire cas de la vie comme d'une épingle. *Who else —s me at defiance!* qui encore me défie? *I — my life upon a chance*, je joue ma vie sur un coup de dés. *To — about*, se mettre à, se mettre en devoir de, s'occuper de, se prendre, s'y prendre. *To — against* or *to — up against*, mettre près de, opposer à, comparer à, faire compensation à, servir d'équivalent à. *To — oneself against*, s'opposer à. *To — aside*, écarter, rejeter (*see* Aside, Apart). *To — by*, mettre de côté. *To — down*, (*carriages*) déposer, descendre, (*write*) écrire, inscrire, prendre en note, (*establish*) établir, (*to look upon as*) regarder comme. *To — forth*, mettre en avant, déployer, étaler, publier, exposer. *To — forward*, avancer (*see* To forward). *To — in*, mettre dans la bonne voie. *To — much by*, faire grand cas de. *To — off*, faire partir, rehausser, embellir, réserver, compenser. *To — on*, poser sur, mettre, servir, exciter, pousser, assaillir, fondre sur, attacher à. *To — out*, avancer, faire sortir, assigner, proclamer, (*adorn*) orner, parer, rehausser, (*table*) servir, montrer, étaler. *To — up*, élever, ériger, dresser, établir, fonder, (*cry*) pousser, faire entendre, (*doctrine*) mettre en avant, avancer, (*person*) faire valoir, faire la fortune de. — vn. (*the sun*) se coucher, descendre, (*teeth*) se serrer, (*fluids*) prendre, se fixer, (*fruit*) se nouer, (*from*, *de*) partir, mettre, (*hunt*) arrêter, chasser, (*garden*) planter, se diriger, porter, (*pers.*) se mettre. *To — about*, commencer, se mettre à, monter. *To — forth*, partir. *To — forward*, partir, se mettre en route. *To — off*, partir. *To — off again*, repartir. *To — out*, partir, commencer. *To — to*, se mettre à. *To — up*, s'établir, s'ériger, faire profession (de)

Set, adj. régulier, formel, apprêté, étudié, élégant, fixe, immobile, obstiné, opiniâtre, établi, (*battle*) rangé, régulier. *To be hard* —, être serré de près

Set, s. assortiment, *m.*, série, *f.*, collection, *f.*, assemblage, *m.*, (*tea*) service, *m.*, (*chimney*) garniture, *f.*, (*jewels*) parure, *f.*, (*persons*) classe, *f.*, groupe, *m.*, bande, *f.*, tas, *m.*, clique, *f.*, coterie, *f.*, (*dancers*) couple, *m.*, (*sun*) coucher, *m.*, (*honest*) arrêt, *m.*, (*garden*) plant, *m.* *A — of false teeth*, un râtelier, *m.* *To be at a dead* —, (*hunt.*) être bien en arrêt, (*fig.*) être dans un état de stagnation complète. *To make a dead — at*, arrêter net, comploter contre, fondre sur

Set-down, s. action de déposer, *m.*, (*fig.*) argument sans réplique, *m.*, (*fam.*) coup d'assommoir, *m.*

Set-off, s. compensation, *f.*, ornement, *m.*, parure, *f.*, relief, *m.*, qui rehausse, qui sert à faire valoir

Set-out, s. équipage, *m.*, chose qui fait de l'effet, *f.*, affaire, *f.*

Set-to, s. assaut, *m.*, combat, *m.*, (*fam.*) prise de bec, *f.*

Seton, s. séton, *m.*

Settee, s. canapé, *m.* — *-bed*, s. lit-canapé, *m.*

Setter, s. qui place, poseur, *m.*, (*hound*) chien couchant, *m.*, (*pers.*) agent, *m.*, embaucheur, *m.*, (*mus.*) compositeur, *m.* — *on*, s. instigateur, *m.*

Setting, s. pose, *f.*, mise, *f.*, action de placer, de poser, de mettre, *f.*, (*jewels*) monture, *f.*, montage, *m.*, (*sun*) coucher, *m.*, (*fig.*) déclin, *m.*, (*surgery*) remboîtement, *m.*, (*knives*) repassage, *m.*

Settle, va. établir, fixer, (*marry*) établir, pourvoir à, (*explain*) éclaircir, déterminer, (*doubts*) décider, raffermir, (*deed*) décider, déterminer, arrêter, (*the soil*) tasser, (*assign*) constituer, assigner, (*fix*) attacher (à), fixer (sur), (*quiet*) calmer, composer, rasseoir, (*dispute*) terminer, arranger, régler, (*punish*) arranger, mettre ordre à, (*fam.*) arranger, faire son affaire à, achever, (*a bill*) arrêter, régler, payer; — vn. (*liquids*) déposer, (*rest*) reposer, (*in life*) se fixer, s'établir, (*to marry*) se marier, (*pers.*) se ranger, devenir rangé, se mettre sérieusement à faire, (*wind*) se fixer, devenir fixe, (*birds*) se poser, (*th.*) s'attacher (à), s'abaisser, descendre, (*quiet*) se calmer, s'apaiser, (*upon*) se déterminer (à), se décider (de), s'arrêter (à), faire choix (de), (*with*, *avec*) s'arranger, prendre des arrangements, payer, (*soil*) tasser, se tasser

Settle, s. banc, *m.*, tabouret, *m.* — *-bed*, s. lit pliant, *m.*

Settlement, s. établissement, *m.*, fixation, *f.*, stabilité, *f.*, arrangement, *m.*, ajustement, *m.*, accommodement, *m.*, colonisation, *f.*, colonie, *f.*, établissement, *m.*, mise en possession, *f.*, (*bills*) règlement, *m.*, (*in life*) établissement, *m.*, (*of liquids*) sédiment, *m.*, lie, *f.*, résidu, *m.*, (*law*) constitution, *f.*, rente, *f.*, pension, *f.*, douaire, *m.*, domicile légal, *m.* *To make a — on*, constituer une rente à

Settler, s. colon, *m.*, immigrant, *m.*

Seven, adj. sept, *m.*

Seventeen, adj. dix-sept

Seventeenth, adj. dix-septième

Seventh, adj. septième, sept

Seventhly, adv. septièmement

Seventieth, adj. soixante-dixième

Seventy, adj. soixante-dix, (les) Septante

Sever, va. séparer; — vn. se séparer, s'entr'ouvrir

Several, adj. divers, différent, plusieurs, séparé, particulier, respectif

Severally, adv. séparément, à part, chacun à part, individuellement, diversement

Severe, adj. sévère, austère, violent, dur, rigoureux

Severely, adv. sévèrement, gravement, avec sévérité, rigoureusement, rudement, vivement

Severity, s. sévérité, *f.*, rigueur, *f.*, violence, *f.*

Sew, vn.a. coudre. *To — up*, coudre, recoudre

Sewage, s. eaux d'écoulement, *f.pl.*, système d'égouts, *m.*

Sewer, s. égout, *m.*, conduit, *m.*, cloaque, *m.*

Sewerage, s. construction d'égouts, *f.*, système d'égouts or de drainage, *m.*

Sewing, s. action de coudre, *f.*, couture, *f.* — *-machine*, s. machine à coudre, *f.* — *-press*, s. cousoir, *m.* — *-silk*, s. soie à coudre, *f.*

Sex, s. sexe, *m.* *The fair* —, le beau sexe, les dames

Sexagenarian, s. sexagénaire, *m.*

Sexagenary, adj. sexagénaire

Sexagesima, s. la Sexagésime, *f.*

Sexagesimal, adj. sexagésimal

Sextant, s. sextant, *m.*

Sexton, s. sacristain, *m.*, fossoyeur, *m.*

Sextuple, adj. sextuple

Sexual, adj. sexuel

Shabbily, adv. (*with clothes*) avec les habits râpés, (*stingily*) mesquinement, petitement

Shabbiness, s. état usé, *m.*, état râpé, *m.*, pauvreté, *f.*, (*fig.*) mesquinerie, *f.*, petitesse, *f.*, avarice sordide, *f.*, bassesse de sentiments, *f.*

Shabby, adj. (*clothes*) usé, râpé, qui montre la corde, (*dress*) pauvre, sordide, (*pers.*)

mal vêtu, râpé, mesquin, petit, méprisable, vile, sordide

Shackle, s. fers, *m.pl.*, chaines, *f.pl.*, entrave, *f.*, (*railway*) boucle d'accouplement, *f.* *Hand- —s*, s. menottes, *f.pl.*

Shackle, va. charger de fers, enchainer, (*carriages*) accoupler, (*fig.*) garrotter, entraver

Shad, s. alose, *f.*

Shaddock, s. pamplemousse, *f.*

Shade, s. ombre, *f.*, ombrage, *m.*, (*lamps*) garde-vue, *m.*, abat jour, *m.*, (*of a cap*) visière, *f.*, (*colour*) nuance, *f.*, teinte, *f.*, (*fig.*) abri, *m.*, protection, *f.*, (*ghost*) ombre, *f.*, mânes, *m.pl.*, (*small quantity*) brin, *m.*, (*wine*) caveau, *m.*, (*clock*) verre, *m.*, globe, *m.*, cylindre, *m.* *To throw into the —*, rejeter dans l'ombre

Shade, va. ombrager, couvrir d'ombre, (*fig.*) voiler, cacher, couvrir, abriter, protéger, (*paint.*) ombrer, nuancer

Shadiness, s. ombrage, *m.*

Shadow, s. ombre, *f.*

Shadow, va. ombrager, jeter son ombre sur, (*paint.*) ombrer, nuancer, esquisser, ébaucher, (*to figure*) représenter, figurer. *To — forth, to — out*, représenter, figurer, indiquer

Shadowness, s. obscurité, *f.*, nature ombragée, *f.*

Shadowless, adj. sans ombre

Shadowy, adj. ombrageux, plein d'ombre, obscur

Shady, adj. ombragé, ombreux

Shaft, s. trait, *m.*, flèche, *f.*, dard, *m.*, (*column*) fût, *m.*, (*chimney*) souche, *f.*, (*carriage*) brancard, *m.*, (*cart*) timon, *m.*, manche, *m.*, bois, *m.*, (*lance*) hampe, *f.*, (*well*) puits, *m.*, (*mines*) bure, *f.* *— -horse*, s. cheval de brancard, *m.*, limonier, *m.*, timonier, *m.*

Shag, s. poil rude, *m.*, poil *m.*, peluche, *f.*, (*tobacco*) tabac à fumer, *m.*, caporal, *m.*

Shaggy, Shagged, adj. poilu, aux poils hérissés, hérissé

Shagreen, s. peau de chagrin, *f.*

Shagreen, adj. en chagrin

Shake, va. secouer, agiter, remuer, branler, (*to make totter*) ébranler, faire trembler, bouleverser, (*frighten*) intimider, (*throw off*) rejeter, écarter, se défaire, (*mus.*) cadencer. *To — down*, faire tomber. *To — in*, faire entrer. *To — off*, secouer, faire tomber, ôter, se débarrasser de, se défaire de. *To — out*, faire tomber, faire sortir, arracher. *To — up*, remuer, secouer. — vn. s'agiter, branler, s'ébranler, chanceler, trembler

Shake, s. secousse, *f.*, (*of hands*) serrement, *m.*, (*of the head*) hochement, *m.*, (*mus.*) cadence, *f.* *No great —s*, pas grand'chose. *— -down*, s. lit improvisé, *m.*

Shaking, s. secousse, *f.*, tremblement, *m.*, agitation, *f.*

Shaky, adj. peu solide, infirme

Shall, vn. voulez-vous que . . . ? faut-il que . . . ? devoir. *— I open the window ?* voulez-vous que j'ouvre la fenêtre ?

Shallop, s. chaloupe, *f.*, barque, *f.*

Shallot, s. échalote, *f.*

Shallow, adj. peu profond, (*fig.*) superficiel, léger, futile, (*pers.*) faible d'esprit, borné, sot

Shallowness, s. peu de profondeur, *m.*, (*fig.*) futilité, *f.*, nature superficielle, *f.*

Sham, va. duper, tromper, faire accroire, feindre, faire, simuler

Sham, s. feinte, *f.*

Sham, adj. feint, simulé, faux, factice. *— fight*, s. petite guerre, *f.*

Shamble, vn. marcher en trainant les pieds, se trainer

Shambles, s. étaux de boucher, *m.pl.*, marché à la viande, *m.*

Shambling, adj. pas lourd et trainant

Shame, s. honte, *f.*, opprobre, *m.*, ignominie, *f.* *To put to —*, faire honte à, couvrir de honte. *To cry — !* crier à l'infamie. *For — !* fi donc ! quelle horreur !

Shame, va. couvrir de honte, faire honte à, déshonorer. *A —d life*, une vie de honte

Shamefaced, adj. honteux

Shameful, adj. honteux, déshonorant

Shamefully, adv. honteusement

Shameless, adj. déhonté, impudemment, effrontément

Shamelessness, s. impudence, *f.*, effronterie, *f.*

Shamoy, s. peau de chamois, *f.*

Shampoo, va. masser, frictionner, nettoyer

Shampooing, s. massage, *m.*, frictionnement, *m.*

Shamrock, s. trèfle, *m.*

Shank, s. jambe, *f.*, os de la jambe, *m.*, tibia, *m.*, (*shaft*) tige, *f.*, (*anchors*) tige, *f.*, verge, *f.*, (*chimney*) tuyau, *f.*

Shanked, adj. à jambes, à tige

Shanty, s. cabane, *f.*

Shape, va. former, façonner, faire, tourner, régler, diriger

Shape, s. forme, *f.*, figure, *f.*, taille, *f.*, tournure, *f.* *In the — of*, sous la forme de, en forme de

Shaped, past part. formé, façonné, en forme de, de forme à

Shapeless, adj. informe, difforme

Shapely, adj. beau, bien fait

Share, va.n. partager, se partager

Share, s. part, *f.*, portion, *f.*, (*com.*) action, *f.*, (*plough*) soc, *f.* *To go —s with, in*, partager avec, avoir part à. *To fall to the — of*, échoir en partage à. *— -broker*, s. agent de change, *m.*, courtier de bourse, *m.* *— -holder*, s. actionnaire, porteur d'actions, *m.*

Sharer, s. partageant, *m.*, -e, *f.* *Joint- —* s. copartageant, *m.*

Shark, s. requin, *m.*, (*fig.*) escroc, *m.*, fripon, *m.*

Sharp, adj. tranchant, affilé, qui coupe bien, acéré, aigu, (*pers.*) intelligent, fin, habile, (*child*) vif, éveillé, d'esprit, (*cunning*) rusé, malin, (*things*) vif, pénétrant, subtil, ingénieux, (*look*) vif, pénétrant, perçant, (*vigilant*) vigilant, alerte, sur le qui vive, (*light*) vif, (*sound*) aigu, perçant, âpre, (*taste*) piquant, âpre, acide, (*air*) vif, perçant, pénétrant, âpre, (*fig.*) acerbe, aigre, âpre, mordant, (*techn.*) dur, (*visage*) maigre, effilé, amaigri, (*mus.*) dièse. *Is your knife — ?* votre couteau coupe-t-il bien ? *To make —*, rendre intelligent, dégourdir. *— at a bargain*, qui sait faire un marché. *To keep a — eye on*, surveiller de près. *In a — tone*, d'un ton acerbe. *A — reproof*, une verte réprimande, de vifs reproches. *— law*, loi cruelle. *A —er life*, une vie moins douce. *— fight*, combat vif. *— desire*, vif désir. *— assault*, attaque furieuse. *— pain*, vive douleur. *— features*, traits amaigris. *— -cornered*, aux angles aigus. *— -pointed*, piquant, à la pointe acérée. *— -set*, affamé, vorace, (*fig.*) avide (de). *— shooter*, s. (*milit.*) tirailleur, *m.*, tireur, *m.* *— -sighted*, à la vue perçante, perspicace

Sharp, s. son aigu, *m.*, (*mus.*) dièse, *m.*

Sharpen, va. aiguiser, affiler, donner le fil à, (*appetite*) ouvrir, (*person*) dégourdir, rendre plus vif, (*mus.*) diéser ; — vn. devenir plus tranchant, plus acéré, plus vif

Sharper, s. chevalier d'industrie, *m.*, escroc, *m.*, filou, *m.*

Sharply, adv. à la pointe acérée, en pointe, (*wittily*) avec intelligence, finement, spirituellement, (*ingeniously*) ingénieusement, d'un coup d'œil vif *or* perçant, attentivement, avec soin, vivement, (*taste*) avec un goût piquant *or* acide, (*temper*) aigrement, avec acerbité, vertement, rigoureusement, avec violence

Sharpness, s. qualité de ce qui est tranchant *or* affilé, de ce qui coupe bien, pointe acérée, *f.*, pointe, *f.*, (*fig.*) intelligence, *f.*, esprit, *m.*, vivacité, *f.*, pénétration, *f.*, perspicacité, *f.*, sagacité, *f.*, finesse, *f.*, subtilité, *f.*, vigilance, *f.*, vivacité, *f.*, (*sound*) son aigu, *m.*, son discordant, *m.*, (*taste*) acidité, *f.*, goût piquant, *m.*, (*weather*) rudesse, *f.*, âpreté, *f.*, (*temper*) aigreur, *f.*, acerbité, *f.*, amertume, *f.*, (*pain*) vivacité, *f.*

Shatter, va. fracasser, briser en éclats *or* en morceaux, faire voler en éclats, (*health*) délabrer, (*brains*) déranger, détraquer ; — vn. se briser, se fracasser

Shatter, s. éclat, *m.*, fragment, *m.* *— -brained*, adj., *— -pated*, adj. écervelé

Shave, va. faire la barbe à, se raser, raser, tondre, couper ras, (*fig.*) raser, effleurer, (*carpent.*) planer, (*cheat*) rançonner, plumer. *To get —d*, se faire raser, faire faire sa barbe ; — vn. se raser, se faire la barbe, couper bien, (*fig.*) tondre sur un œuf

Shave, s. action de faire la barbe, *f.*, une barbe, *f.*, (*tool*) plane, *f.* *You have had a near — of it*, vous l'avez échappé belle

Shaver, s. barbier, *m.*

Shaving, s. action de faire la barbe *or* de raser, (*of wood*) copeau, *m.*, (*of paper*) rognure, *f.* *— -basin*, s. plat à barbe, *m.* *— -brush*, s. brosse à barbe, *f.*

Shawl, s. châle, *m.*

She, pron. elle, *f.*, femme, *f.*

She, adj. (*of animals*) femelle

Sheaf, s. gerbe, *f.*, javelle, *f.*, (*arrows*) faisceau, *m.*, paquet, *m.*

Sheaf, vn. engerber

Shear, va. tondre, couper ras, (*fig.*) dépouiller, priver, frustrer

Shearing, s. tonte, *f.*, tondaison, *f.* *— -time*, s. la tonte des brebis, *f.*

Shears, s. grands ciseaux, *m.pl.*, (*for metals*) cisailles, *f.pl.*

Sheath, s. (*scabbard*) fourreau, *m.*, gaine, *f.*, (*scissors*) étui, *m.*

Sheathe, va. mettre *or* remettre dans le fourreau, rengainer, enfermer dans l'étui, (*fig.*) renfermer, recouvrir

Sheathing, s. doublage, *m.*

Shed, va. répandre, verser, (*throw off*) laisser tomber, dépouiller, se dépouiller de, (*teeth*) perdre, (*horns*) jeter ; — vn. se dépouiller, (*reptiles*) muer

Shed, s. hangar, *m.*, appentis, *m.*

Shedding, s. action de répandre, de verser, *f.*, effusion, *f.*

Sheep, s. mouton *m.*, brebis, *f.*, (*relig.*) brebis, *f.pl.*

ouailles, *f.pl.*, (*binding*) basane, *f.* — -*cot*, s., — -*fold*, s., — -*pen*, s. bergerie, *f.*, bercail, *m.*, parc à moutons, *m.* — -*hook*, s. houlette, *f.* — -*pelt*, s. peau de mouton, *f.* —'s *eye*, s. œillade, *f.*, yeux doux, *m.pl.* — -*skin*, s. peau de mouton, *f.*, basane, *f.* — -*walk*, s. parcage, *m.* — -*track*, s. chemin frayé par les moutons, *m.* —'s-*trotters*, s. pieds de mouton, *m.pl.*

Sheepish, adj. penaud, interdit. — *look*, air penaud

Sheepishly, adv. timidement, niaisement

Sheepishness, s. timidité niaise, *f.*, air penaud, *m.*

Sheer, adj. pur, véritable, extrême

Sheer, vn. s'écarter, dévier, (*nav.*) faire des embardées. *To* — *off*, (*nav.*) fuir, prendre chasse, (*fig.*) s'éloigner, s'esquiver

Sheerly, adv. net, tout à fait, absolument, directement, droit

Sheet, s. drap, *m.*, (*paper*) feuille, *f.*, (*water*) nappe, *f.*, (*metal*) feuille, *f.*, (*nav.*) écoute, *f.* *A pair of* —*s*, une paire de draps

Sheeting, s. toile pour draps de lit, *f.*

Shelf, s. rayon, *m.*, planche, *f.*, tablette, *f.*, (*nav.*) récif, *m.*, écueil, *m.*, haut-fond, *m.* *To lay on the* —, mettre *or* poser sur la planche, (*fig.*) mettre de côté, négliger

Shelfy, adj. plein d'écueils *or* de récifs

Shell, s. coquille, *f.*, coquillage, *m.*, (*oyster*) écaille, *f.*, (*tortoise*) écaille, *f.*, carapace, *f.*, (*eggs*) coque, *f.*, coquille, *f.*, (*walnuts*) coquille, *f.*, (*seeds*) cosse, *f.*, (*house*) carcasse, *f.*, (*coffin*) cercueil, *m.*, (*artil.*) bombe, *f.*, obus, *m.* — -*fish*, s. coquillage, *m.*, mollusque, *m.*, crustacé, *m.* — -*work*, s. coquillage, *m.*

Shell, va. (*seeds*) écosser, égrener, (*walnuts*) écaler, (*a town*) bombarder, lancer des obus sur

Shelly, adj. de coquille, qui abonde en coquillages

Shelter, s. abri, *m.*, couvert, *m.*, asile, *m.*, protection, *f.*, refuge, *m.* *To take* —, se mettre à l'abri, s'abriter. *Under the* — *of*, à l'abri de. *To seek a* — *from*, chercher un abri contre

Shelter, va. abriter, protéger, recueillir

Shelterless, adj. sans abri

Shelve, vn. aller en pente, être en pente

Shelving, adj. en pente

Shepherd, s. berger, *m.*, pasteur, *m.*, pâtre, *m.*

Shepherdess, s. bergère, *f.*

Sherbet, s. sorbet, *m.*

Sheriff, s. shériff, *m.*, préfet, *m.*

Sherry, s. vin de Xérès, *m.*

Shield, s. bouclier, *m.*, écu, *m.*, (*myth.*) égide, *f.*, (*herald*) écu, *m.*, écusson, *m.* — -*bearer*, s. écuyer, *m.*

Shield, va. couvrir de son bouclier, (*fig.*) abriter (contre), mettre à l'abri (de), protéger (contre), garantir

Shift, vn.a. changer de place, changer, se modifier, changer de vêtements *or* de linge, etc., (*fig.*) se tirer d'affaire, trouver des expédients. *To* — *for oneself*, se tirer d'affaire, se retourner

Shift, s. changement, *m.*, expédient, *m.*, moyen, *m.*, ressource, *f.*, (*cunning*) ruse, *f.*, artifice, *m.*, subterfuge, *m.*, faux-fuyant, *m.*, (*shirt*) chemise, *f.* *To make a* — (*to*), trouver moyen (de), s'arranger (pour). *It was his last* —, c'était sa dernière ressource

Shifter, s. qui change, qui change de place (*see* SCENE), (*fig.*) madré, *m.*, homme retors, *m.*

Shifting, s. changement, *m.*

Shifting, adj. changeant

Shillelah, **Shilleleh**, s. gourdin, *m.*, bâton, *m.*

Shilling, s. schelling, *m.*

Shilly-shally, adv. en hésitant, indécis

Shilly-shally, vn. hésiter

Shin, s. os de la jambe, *m.*, tibia, *m.*

Shindy, s. querelle, *f.*, bataille, *f.*, tapage, *m.*

Shine, va. briller, reluire, luire. *To* — *forth* or *out*, éclater, se montrer

Shine, s. éclat, *m.*, brillant, *m.* *To take the* — *out of*, éclipser, rabattre le caquet à

Shingle, s. bardeau, *m.*, galet, *m.*, caillou roulé, *m.* —*s*, pl. (*med.*) zona, *m.*

Shingly, adj. plein de galets

Shining, s. éclat, *m.*, lumière, *f.*, splendeur, *f.*

Shining, **Shiny**, adj. brillant, luisant, éclatant, resplendissant

Ship, s. navire, *m.*, vaisseau, *m.*, bâtiment, *m.* — -*board*, adv. à bord. — -*boy*, s. mousse, *m.* — -*broker*, s., — -*agent*, s. courtier de navire, *m.* — -*builder*, s. constructeur de navires, *m.* — -*chandler*, s. fournisseur de la marine, *m.* — -*holder*, s., — -*owner*, s. armateur, *m.* — -*load*, s. chargement, *m.*, fret, *m.* — -*master*, s. patron de navire, *m.* — -*yard*, s. chantier de constructions navales, *m.*

Ship, va. embarquer, prendre à son bord, charger, expédier (*helm*) monter, (*oars*) border. *To* —, *to* — *off*, embarquer

Shipment, s. embarquement, *m.*, chargement, *m.*

Shipper, s. expéditeur, *m.*, affréteur, *m.*

Shipping, s. embarquement, *m.*, vaisseaux, *m.pl.*, marine marchande, *f.* — -*articles*, conditions, clauses d'embarquement, *f.pl.*

Shipwreck, s. naufrage, *m.*, sinistre, *m.*

Shipwreck, va.n. faire faire naufrage à

Shire, s. comté, *m.*

Shirk, vn. user de supercheries, finasser; — va. escroquer, écornifler, éviter

Shirk, s. écornifleur, *m.*, paresseux, *m.*

Shirt, s. chemise (d'homme), *f.* — -*collar*, s. col de chemise, *m.* — -*front*, s. devant de chemise, *m.*, chemisette, *f.* — -*maker*, s. chemisier, *m.* *In his* — -*sleeves*, en manches de chemise

Shirting, s. toile pour chemise, *f.*

Shirtless, adj. sans chemise

Shiver, va. briser en morceaux, en éclats, fracasser. — vn. se briser, voler en éclats, se fracasser, éclater, (*cold, fear*) grelotter, frissonner, trembler, trembloter. *To go* —*ing along*, marcher en grelottant. *To* — *all over*, frissonner par tout le corps, être dans les frissons. *You make me* —, vous me faites frissonner

Shiver, s. morceau, *m.*, éclat, *m.*, fragment, *m.*, fuseau, *m.*, (*cold*) frisson, *m.*, tremblement, *m.*, frissonnement, *m.* *To break into* —*s*, briser, se briser en éclats éclater. *A cold* — *ran through me*, il me prit un frisson

Shivering, s. frissonnement, *m.*, tremblement, *m.*, frisson, *m.*, action de briser *or* de se briser en éclats, *f.* *A* — *fit*, un accès de frisson

Shiveringly, adv. en grelottant, en frissonnant

Shivery, adj. cassant, tremblant, frissonnant

Shoal, adj. peu profond

Shoal, s. multitude, *f.*, foule, *f.*, (*fish*) banc, *m.*, (*nav.*) banc de sable, *m.*, hautfond, *m.*

Shoal, vn. s'attrouper, se réunir en foule, (*water*) diminuer de profondeur

Shoaly, adj. obstrué de bancs de sable

Shock, s. choc, *m.*, secousse, *f.*, coup, *m.*, assaut, *m.*, attaque, *f.*, (*of corn*) tas de gerbes, *m.* *A violent* —, une forte secousse. *It gave me quite a* —, cela me fit une secousse, cela m'impressionna d'une manière des plus désagréables. *A* — *of hair*, une épaisse chevelure

Shock, va. secouer, choquer, heurter, offenser, révolter, frapper d'horreur, mettre en tas, entasser. *To be* —*ed at*, être choqué de, se choquer de. *I was quite* —*ed*, j'en fus vivement affligé

Shocking, adj. choquant, révoltant, affreux, offensant. *A* — *sight*, un spectacle affreux

Shockingly, adv. affreusement, horriblement, d'une manière choquante *or* déplorable. *To look* —, avoir très mauvaise mine

Shoddy, s. effilochage, *m.*, effilode, *m.*

Shoe, s. soulier, *m.*, chaussure, *f.*, (*horse*) fer, *m.*, (*carriages*) sabot, *m.* *Put on, take off your* —*s*, mettez, ôtez vos souliers. *High* —*s*, souliers montants. *High-heeled* —*s*, souliers à hauts talons. *Low* —*s*, souliers découverts. *Wooden* —*s*, sabots. — -*black*, s. décrotteur, *m.* — -*brush*, s. brosse à souliers, *f.* — -*horn*, s. chausse-pied, *m.* — -*factor*, s. fabricant de chaussures en gros, *m.* — -*leather*, s. cuir de souliers, *m.* *To save* — -*leather*, pour épargner des souliers. — -*nail*, s. clou à souliers, *m.* — -*stone*, s. pierre à aiguiser, *f.* — -*strap*, s. dessous de pied, *m.*, cordon de cuir, *m.* — -*string*, s., — -*tie*, s. cordon de soulier, *m.* *With his* —*s down at heel*, les souliers éculés. *It's ill waiting for dead men's* —*s*, qui s'attend à l'écuelle d'autrui a souvent mal dîné. *I would not be in your* —*s*, je ne voudrais pas être à votre place, dans votre peau. *To step into, to wait for another man's* —*s*, prendre, attendre la place d'un autre. *To cast a* —, (*horse*) perdre un fer. *He has a* — *loose*, il va perdre un fer

Shoe, va. chausser, (*horses*) ferrer, mettre un fer à

Shoeing, s. action de chausser, *f.*, ferrage, *m.*

Shoeless, adj. sans souliers, pieds nus

Shoemaker, s. cordonnier, *m.*

Shoemaking, s. cordonnerie, *f.*

Shoot, va. (*arrows*) lancer, décocher, darder, (*fire-arms*) tirer, décharger, faire partir, (*gun*) lâcher un coup de, (*hunt*) tirer, chasser, (*hit*) frapper, atteindre, tirer sur, tuer, (*military punishment*) fusiller, passer par les armes, (*a look*) lancer, darder, décocher, (*to throw*) lancer, décharger, (*buds*) pousser, (*to go quickly*) traverser rapidement, franchir, (*bridge*) passer sous, descendre. *To* — *off*, tirer, faire partir, décharger. *To* — *through*, percer de part en part, transpercer. *He shot him dead*, il le tua roide. *To* — *forth* or *out*, pousser, lancer, darder. — vn. chasser, aller à la chasse, (*through*) passer à travers *or* rapidement, s'élancer, se précipiter, courir, (*fig.*) s'élancer, jaillir, (*plants*) pousser, (*to jut out*) avancer, faire saillie, (*pain*) élancer. *To* — *at*, tirer sur, tirer à. *To* — *along*, voler. *To* — *off*, partir *or* s'élancer comme un trait. *To* — *forth*, *to* — *out*, pousser. *To teach the young idea how to* —, apprendre à la jeune idée à se développer. *To — through*, percer de part en part

Shoot, s. pousse, *f.*, rejeton, *m.*, scion, *m.*

Shooter, s. tireur, *m.*

Shooting, s. action de tirer, *f.*, tir, *m.*, fusillade, *f.*, (*sport*) chasse, *f.*, (*pain*) élancement, *m.* *To practice —*, s'exercer au tir. *Pistol —*, tir au pistolet. *Rifle —*, tir à la carabine

Shooting, adj. qui tire, qui lance, (*pain*) lancinante. *—-gallery*, s, *—-grounds*, s. tir, *m.* *—-match*, s. partie de tir, *f.* *—-box*, s. rendez-vous de chasse, *m.* *—-jacket*, s. veste de chasse, *f.* *—-party*, s. partie de chasse, *f.* *—-star*, s. étoile filante, *f.*

Shop, s. boutique, *f.*, magasin, *m.*, (*workshop*) atelier, *m.* *—-board*, s. établi, *m.* *—-book*, s. main courante, *f.* *—-boy*, petit commis, *m.*, garçon de magasin, *m.* *—-front*, s. devanture, *f.* *—-girl*, s. fille de boutique, *f.*, demoiselle de magasin, *f.* *—-keeper*, s. boutiquier, *m.*, -ère, *f.* *—-lifter*, s. voleur, *m.*, -euse, *f.* *—-lifting*, s. vol dans les magasins, *m.* *—-man*, s. commis marchand, *m.*, garçon de boutique, *m.* *—-walker*, s. surveillant, *m.*

Shop, vn. faire des emplettes, courir les magasins. *To go, to have been a —-ping*, courir les magasins, aller faire des emplettes

Shore, s. rivage, *m.*, bord, *m.*, côte, *f.*, (*prop*) étai, *m.*, étançon, *m.* *To make for the —, to reach the —*, gagner le rivage. *To go on —*, débarquer

Shore, va. étayer, étançonner, (*fig.*) soutenir

Shoreless, adj. sans bords

Short, adj. court, petit, bref, passager, au-dessous (de), (*in want of*) à court, mal pourvu, (*prosod.*) bref, (*abrupt*) brusque. *To make —er*, raccourcir, (*fig.*) abréger. *To grow —er*, raccourcir, se raccourcir. *To make a long story —*, pour en finir, pour ne pas vous retenir trop longtemps. *A — life and a merry one*, une vie courte et bonne. *To go the —est way*, prendre par le plus court. *Too — in the waist*, trop court de taille. *— breath*, courte haleine. *To be rather — of memory*, avoir la mémoire un peu courte. *A — distance*, une petite distance. *A — man*, un petit homme. *Remember how — my time is*, souvenez-vous combien j'ai peu de temps. *A — stay*, un court séjour. *At a — notice*, au premier avis, à court délai. *At a — date*, à courte échéance. *To come —*, être insuffisant, manquer, (*of*, de) être au-dessous de. *To run —*, commencer à manquer, manquer. *Ten crowns —*, dix écus de manque. *— of my expectations*, au-dessous de mon attente. *To fall — of*, être au-dessous de, ne pas répondre à. *It would be little — of cruelty*, ce serait presque de la cruauté. *To be — of*, être à court de

Short, adv. court, brusquement, vivement, peu. *To stop —, to stop dead —*, s'arrêter tout court

Short, s. court, *m.* *In —*, bref, en un mot, enfin

Short-...., (*in compounds*). *—-armed*, adj. aux bras courts. *—-cake*, s. gâteau croustillant, *m.* *—-coming*, s. insuffisance, *f.* *—s*, pl. fautes, *f.pl.*, omissions, *f.pl.*, négligences, *f.pl.* *—-lived*, adj. dont la vie est courte éphémère. *—-nosed*, adj. au petit nez. *—-sighted*, adj. myope, qui a la vue basse. *—-sightedness*, s. myopie, *f.*, vue basse, *f.*, (*fig.*) imprévoyance, *f.* *—-winded*, adj. à l'haleine courte, poussif. *—-witted*, adj. d'un esprit borné, peu intelligent

Short-hand, s. sténographie, *f.* *— writer*, s. sténographe, *m.*

Short-hand, adj. sténographique. *To take down in —*, va. sténographier

Shorten, va. raccourcir, rapetisser, (*journey*) abréger, (*contract*) resserrer, (*ears, &c.*) écourter, couper; — vn. se raccourcir, rapetisser, diminuer

Shortening, s. raccourcissement, *m.*

Shortly, adv. bientôt, sous peu, (*briefly*) brièvement

Shortness, s. peu de longueur, *m.*, peu de distance, *m.*, (*stature*) petitesse, *f.*, brièveté, *f.*, peu de durée, *m.*, imperfection, *f.*

Shot, s. (*fire-arms*) coup, *m.*, (*arrow*) trait, *m.*, (*cannon*) boulet, *m.*, (*gun, pistol*) balle, *f.*, (*for sport*) plomb, *m.*, (*reach*) portée, *f.*, (*fig.*) décharge, *f.*, volée, *f.*, (*pers.*) tireur, *m.*, (*reckoning*) écot, *m.* *Small —*, petit plomb

Shotten, adj. (*of herrings*) gai

Should, v. def. and aux. or sign of conditional devrais, etc. *We — have liked to go*, nous aurions aimé y aller

Shoulder, s. épaule, *f.*, (*fort.*) épaulement, *m.* *To put one's — to the wheel*, pousser à la roue, mettre la main à la pâte. *To give the cold — to*, battre froid à. *Round —s*, dos rond *—-belt*, s. baudrier, *m.* *—-blade*, s. omoplate, *f.* *—-knot*, s. aiguillette, *f.* *—-strap*, s. bretelle, *f.*

Shoulder, va. pousser de l'épaule, prendre or charger sur ses épaules, (*milit.*) porter (armes)

Shouldered, adj. aux épaules

Shout, s. cri, *m.*, acclamation, *f.*, clameur, *f.*

Shout, vn. pousser or jeter un cri or des cris, crier

Shouter, s. celui qui crie

Shouting, s. cris, *m.pl.*, acclamations, *f.pl.*

Shove, va.n. pousser. *To — away*, repousser, éloigner, s'éloigner. *To — back*, faire reculer. *To — by*, passer brusquement, pousser de côté. *To — down*, faire tomber. *To — on*, s'avancer, pousser en avant. *To — out* pousser dehors

Shove, s. action de pousser, *f.*, secousse, *f.*

Shovel, s. pelle, *f.*

Shovel, va. prendre, jeter avec la pelle. *To — up*, ramasser

Shovelful, s. pelletée, *f.*

Show, va. montrer, faire voir, expliquer, faire connaître, (*into*, dans) introduire, faire entrer. *To — down*, reconduire en bas. *To — forth*, exposer, publier, manifester. *To — in*, faire entrer, introduire. *To — off*, faire montre, faire valoir, rehausser. *To — oneself off*, se donner des airs, poser. *To — out*, reconduire. *To — up* faire monter, conduire, (*fig.*) exposer, démasquer. — vn. paraître, avoir l'air

Show, s. action de montrer, *m.*, spectacle, *m.*, exposition, *f.*, concours, *m.*, (*display*) étalage, *m.*, faste, *m.*, (*pretence*) apparence, *f.*, semblant, *m.*, dehors, *m.*, jeu, *m.* *A — of hands*, la levée des mains. *To make a — of*, faire montre or parade de

Show-...., (*in compounds*). *—-bread*, s. pain de proposition, *m.* *—-bill*, s. pancarte, *f.*, grande affiche, *f.* *—-box*, s. montre, *f.*, optique, *f.* *—-card*, s. liste de prix, *f.* *—-case*, s. montre, *f.* *—-man*, s. directeur de spectacle forain, *m.* *—-room*, s. magasin, *m.*, salon, *m.*, salle d'exposition, *f.* *—-window*, s. étalage, *m.*, montre, *f.*

Shower, s. ondée, *f.*, averse, *f.*, pluie, *f.*, (*fig.*) grêle, *f.*, pluie, *f.* *—-bath*, s. douche, *f.*

Shower, vn. pleuvoir à verse, pleuvoir; — va. (*down*) faire pleuvoir sur, arroser, répandre

Showery, adj. pluvieux

Showily, adv. d'une manière voyante, fastueusement

Showiness, s. éclat, *m.*, couleurs voyantes, *f.pl.*, ostentation, *f.*

Showy, adj. brillant, qui fait de l'effet, (*gaudy*) voyant, (*pompous*) fastueux

Shred, va. couper en morceaux

Shred, s. lambeau, *m.* *—s and patches*, pièces et morceaux

Shrew, s. mégère, *f.*, femme acariâtre et criarde, *f.* *—-mouse*, s. musaraigne, *f.*

Shrewd, adj. fin, sagace, adroit, malin, (*things*) adroit

Shrewdly, adv. finement, avec sagacité, adroitement

Shrewdness, s. finesse, *f.*, sagacité, *f.*, pénétration, *f.*

Shrewish, adj. grondeur, acariâtre

Shrewishly, adv. en grondant

Shrewishness, s. humeur grondeuse, *f.*, caractère acariâtre, *m.*

Shriek, vn. pousser un cri perçant, crier

Shriek, s. cri perçant, *m.*, cri, *m.*

Shrill, adj. aigu, perçant, clair

Shrillness, s. son clair, *m.*

Shrimp, s. crevette, *f.*, (*pers.*) nain, *m.*, bout d'homme, *m.*

Shrine, s. châsse, *f.*, autel, *m.*

Shrink, vn. se rétrécir, se contracter, se raccourcir, se resserrer, se retirer, (*wrinkle*) se ratatiner, (*recoil*) reculer, trembler

Shrinkage, **Shrinking**, s. rétrécissement, *m.*, contraction, *f.*

Shrive, va.n. confesser

Shrivel (up), vn. se recroqueviller, se racornir, se ratatiner, se rider; — va. racornir, grésiller, dessécher, faire ratatiner or rider

Shroud, s. (*for the dead*) linceul, *m.*, suaire, *m.*, (*nav.*) hauban, *m.*

Shroud, va. couvrir, cacher, voiler, abriter, (*bury*) ensevelir, mettre dans un linceul or suaire; — vn. s'abriter

Shrovetide, s. carnaval, *m.*, carême-prenant, *m.*

Shrove-Tuesday, s. mardi gras, *m.*

Shrub, s. arbuste, *m.*, arbrisseau, *m.*

Shrubbery, s. plantation d'arbrisseaux, *f.*

Shrubby, adj. couvert d'arbrisseaux

Shrug, va. hausser les épaules

Shrug, **Shrugging**, s. haussement, *m.*

Shudder, vn. frissonner, frémir, trembler

Shudder, s. frisson, *m.*, frissonnement, *m.*, frémissement, *m.*

Shuffle, va.n. agiter, remuer, mélanger, confondre, (*cards*) battre, mêler, (*deceive*) tromper. *To — away*, éloigner secrètement, enlever adroitement, escamoter. *To — in or into*, introduire secrètement. *To — off*, rejeter, se débarrasser de, se dépouiller de. *To — up*, arranger à la hâte, bâcler

Shuffle, s. confusion, *f.*, mouvement désordonné, *m.*, (*trick*) tour, *m.*, artifice, *m.*, (*excuse*) évasion, *f.*, équivoque, *f.*

Shuffler, s. fourbe, *m.*

Shuffling, s. action de battre les cartes, mélange, *m.*, confusion, *f.*, subterfuge, *m.*, détours, *m.pl.*

Shuffling, adj. évasif, équivoque, (*pers.*) fourbe, qui biaise
Shufflingly, adv. évasivement, en biaisant
Shun, va. éviter, fuir
Shunt, s. voie d'évitement, *f.*
Shunt, vn. changer de ligne; — va. faire passer sur une autre ligne
Shut, va. fermer, enfermer. *To — in*, enfermer. *To — off*, intercepter. *To — out*, exclure, fermer la porte sur, interdire l'entrée à, intercepter. *To — up*, fermer, enfermer, renfermer, (*silence*) désarçonner. — vn. fermer, se fermer. *To — close, hard*, fermer bien, se fermer avec bruit
Shutter, s. volet, *m.*, jalousie, *f.*, (*for wounded*) brancard, *m.*
Shuttle, s. navette, *f.*
Shuttle-cock, s. volant, *m.*
Shy, adj. réservé, timide, circonspect, soupçonneux, (*horses*) ombrageux
Shy, s. coup, *m.* *To have, to take a — at*, jeter une pierre à
Shy, vn. être ombrageux, faire un écart; — va. éviter, lancer
Shyly, adv. avec réserve, timidement
Shyness, s. réserve, *f.*, timidité, *f.*, mauvaise honte, *f.*
Sibyl, s. sibylle, *f.*
Sibylline, adj. sibyllin
Siccative, adj. siccatif
Sick, adj. malade, qui a mal au cœur, (*of*, de) dégoûté, las. *To be — at heart*, avoir la mort dans le cœur. *To feel —*, avoir mal au cœur. *To make —*, faire mal au cœur à, soulever le cœur. *— -bed*, s. lit de douleur, *m.* *— -berth*, s. poste des malades, *m.* *— -list*, s. rôle des malades, *m.* *— -ward*, s. infirmerie, *f.*
Sicken, va. affaiblir, faire mal au cœur à, donner des nausées à, (*fig.*) dégoûter, faire mal au cœur à; — vn. tomber malade, languir, s'affaiblir, (*to be weary of*) se dégoûter (de)
Sickening, adj. nauséabond, dégoûtant, (*fig.*) triste, navrant
Sickle, s. faucille, *f.*
Sickliness, s. état malingre, *m.*, nature maladive, *f.*, insalubrité, *f.*
Sickly, adj. maladif, malingre, délicat, malade, faible, (*things*) malsain, insalubre
Sickness, s. maladie, *f.*, mal au cœur, *m.*, nausées, *f.pl.*
Side, s. côté, *m.*, flanc, *m.*, (*mountain*) bord, *m.*, versant, *m.*, (*wall*) paroi, *f.* *On this —*, de ce côté. *On* or *from all —s*, *on every —*, de tous côtés. *On both —s*, des deux côtés. *On neither —*, ni d'un côté ni de l'autre. *By his —*, à ses côtés. *— by —*, côte à côte. *To change —s*, changer de parti. *To take —s with*, prendre le parti de
Side, adj. de côté, latéral, oblique, de profil. *— -door*, s. porte latérale, *f.* *— -look*, s., *— -view*, s. vue de côté, *f.* *— -arms*, s. baïonnette, *f.*, armes blanches, *f.pl.* *— -box*, s. loge de côté, *f.*, avant-scène, *f.* *— -rails*, s. contre-rails, *m.* *— -saddle*, s. selle pour dame, *f.* *— -scene*, s. coulisse, *f.* *— -table*, s. buffet, *m.* *— -walk*, s. contre-allée, *f.*, trottoir, *m.* *— -way*, s. trottoir, *m.*
Side, vn. prendre le parti de, épouser la cause de
Sideboard, s. buffet, *m.*
Sided, (*in compounds*). *One- —*, qui n'a qu'un côté, qui ne voit qu'un côté
Sideral, Sidereal, adj. sidéral, des astres, des étoiles, étoilé
Siding, s. gare d'évitement, *f.*, voie de chargement et de déchargement, *f.*
Sidle, vn. marcher de côté, marcher doucement
Siege, s. siége, *m.* *To lay — to*, faire le siége de, mettre le siége devant, assiéger
Sieve, s. tamis, *m.*, sas, *m.*, crible, *m.*
Sift, va. tamiser, sasser, cribler, (*fig.*) examiner, éplucher, sonder. *To — carelessly*, passer au gros sas. *It must be carefully —ed*, il faut l'examiner à fond. *To — out*, tâcher de découvrir. *I'll — it out of him*, je saurai bien le lui faire dire
Sifting, s. tamisage, *m.*, (*fig.*) examen, *m.*, action de sonder, *m.*
Sigh, vn. soupirer, pousser des soupirs. *To — heavily*, soupirer profondément. *To — for*, soupirer pour *or* après, regretter, gémir. *To — over*, gémir sur, déplorer, lamenter. *To — most piteously*, soupirer piteusement, faire de grands hélas. *To — away*, exhaler dans un soupir, passer à soupirer, consumer dans les soupirs. *To — out*, soupirer
Sigh, s. soupir, *m.* *With a —*, en soupirant. *To give, heave* or *fetch a deep, a heavy —*, pousser un profond soupir, un gros soupir. *To give — for —*, répondre aux soupirs de
Sight, s. vue, *f.*, vision, *f.*, coup d'œil, *m.*, spectacle, *m.*, chose curieuse, *f.*, curiosité, *f.*, ouverture, *f.*, trou, *m.*, (*mathematical instrument*) lumière, *f.*, (*fire-arms*) mire, *f.*, (*pop.*) pied de nez, *m.* *At —*, (*com.*) à vue, à première vue, à livre ouvert. *At first —*, à première vue, du premier coup d'œil, du premier coup. *At three days' —*, *three days after —*, à trois jours de vue. *In —*, *full in —*, en vue, bien en vue. *To come in —*, apparaître, arriver en vue de, apercevoir. *Within —*, en vue, à la portée de la vue. *Out of —*, hors de la portée de la vue. *To get, catch*, or *gain — of*, apercevoir. *To know by —*, connaître de vue. *To lose — of*, perdre de vue. *— -seeing*, adj. curieux. *— -hole*, s. ouverture, *f.*, trou, *m.*, lumière, *f.* *To take —*, viser, (*artill.*) pointer. *To take a — at*, faire un pied de nez à
Sight, vn. viser; — va. apercevoir
. . . -Sighted, (*in compounds*) aux yeux de, à la vue. *Near- —*, qui a la vue basse, myope
Sightedness, s. vue, *f.* *Near- —, short- —*, vue basse, *f.*, myopie, *f.*
Sightless, adj. aveugle, privé de la vue
Sightly, adj. beau, agréable à voir, gracieux
Sign, s. signe, *m.*, (*shop*) enseigne, *f.*, (*omen*) présage, *m.*, (*signature*) seing, *m.*, signature, *f.* *As a — of*, en signe de. *A sure — that* or *of*, signe certain que *or* de. *To give —s of*, donner signe de. *To make —s*, or *a — to*, faire des signes à, faire signe. *To make the — of the cross*, faire le signe de la croix, se signer. *— -board*, s. enseigne, *f.* *— -painter*, s. peintre d'enseignes, *m.* *— -post*, s. poteau d'enseigne, *m.* (*see* MANUAL)
Sign, va. signer, (*show*) signifier, représenter, montrer; — vn. faire signe à
Signal, s. signal, *m.*, signe, *m.* *To give the — for* or *of*, signal de combat. *To look out for —s*, veiller aux signaux. *— for action*, (*nav.*) branle-bas de combat, *m.* *To give the — for mounting*, sonner le boute-selle. *Fog- —*, signal de brume, *m.* *Sailing —*, signal de partance, *— -chest*, s. coffre des signaux, *m.* *— -fire*, s. feu d'alarme, *m.* *— -gun*, s. coup de canon d'alarme, *m.* *— -man*, s. signaliste, *m.* *— -light*, s. fanal, *m.* *— -mast*, s., *— -post*, s., *— -staff*, s. sémaphore, *m.*
Signal, adj. signalé, remarquable
Signalize, va. signaler
Signally, adv. d'une manière signalée
Signature, s. signature, *f.*, seing, *m.*, (*stamp*) marque, *f.*, trace, *f.*, empreinte, *f.*
Signer, s. signataire, *m.*
Signet, s. sceau, *m.*, cachet, *m.* *— -ring*, s. sceau avec cachet, *m.*
Significance, s. sens, *m.*, signification, *f.*, force, *f.*, énergie, *f.*, importance, *f.*, portée, *f.*, gravité, *f.*
Significant, Significative, adj. significatif
Significantly, Significatively, adv. d'une manière significative
Signification, s. signification, *f.*, sens, *m.*
Signify, va. signifier, exprimer, faire savoir, faire connaître
Silence, s. silence, *m.*, taciturnité, *f.* *To keep —*, garder le silence, se taire. *To pass over in —*, passer sous silence. *To put to —*, faire taire, faire silence à, réduire au silence (*see* CONSENT)
Silence, va. faire taire, réduire au silence, imposer silence à, faire cesser, mettre fin à
Silent, adj. silencieux, taciturne, paisible, (*gramm.*) muet. *To be —, to remain —*, se taire, garder le silence, faire silence. *The law is — on that subject*, la loi est muette, ne dit rien à ce sujet. *— joy*, joie muette. *— partner*, associé commanditaire. *— night*, la nuit silencieuse
Silently, adv. en silence, silencieusement
Silex, Silica, s. silice, *f.*
Silk, s. soie, *f.* *—s*, pl. (*com.*) soieries, *f.pl.* *Shot —*, s. soie changeante, *f.*, taffetas, *m.*
Silk, adj. de soie, en soie. *— goods*, s. soieries, *f.* *— -district*, s. pays séricicole, *m.* *— -mercer*, *— -dealer*, s. marchand de soieries, *f.* *— -mill*, s. filature de soie, *f.*, fabrique de soieries, *f.* *— -reel*, s. dévidoir de soie, *m.* *— -spinning*, s. filature de soie, *f.* *— -spinner*, s. filateur de soie, *m.* *— -trade*, s. commerce de la soie, *m.*, soierie, *f.* *— -weaver*, s. canut, *m.*
Silken, Silky, adj. de soie, fait de soie, soyeux, (*fig.*) doux, tendre
Silkiness, s. nature soyeuse, *f.*, douceur, *f.*
Silkworm, s. ver à soie, *m.* *— -breeder*, s. magnanier, *m.* *— -nursery*, s. magnanerie, *f.*
Sill, s. seuil, *m.*, (*window*) rebord, *m.*
Sillily, adv. sottement
Silliness, s. niaiserie, *f.*, sottise, *f.*, simplicité, *f.*
Silly, adj. niais, nigaud, sot, simple
Silver, s. argent, *m.*, (*change*) argent blanc, *m.*
Silver, adj. d'argent, en argent, brillant comme l'argent (*sound*) argentin, mélodieux. *— coin*, s. monnaie d'argent, *f.* *— -gilt*, adj. argent doré. *— -ore*, s. minerai d'argent, *m.* *— -paper*, s. papier joseph, *m.* *— -beater*, s. batteur d'argent, *m.* *— -fish*, s. argentine, *f.* *— -grey*, adj. d'un gris argenté. *— -headed*, adj. aux cheveux blancs *or* argentés, (*stick*) à tête *or* à pomme d'argent. *— -mounted*, adj. monté en argent
Silver, va. argenter, (*glass*) étamer

Silvering, s. argenture, *f.*
Silversmith, s. orfèvre, *m.*
Silvery, adj. d'argent, argenté, blanc comme l'argent, (*voice*) argentin. — *wing*, s. aile d'argent, *f.* — *feet*, s. pieds blancs, *m.pl.*
Similar, adj. semblable, pareil
Similarity, s. similitude, *f.*, ressemblance, *f.*, similarité, *f.*
Similarly, adv. d'une manière semblable, pareillement
Simile, s. comparaison, *f.*
Similitude, s. ressemblance, *f.*, similitude, *f.*
Simitar, s. cimeterre, *m.*
Simmer, vn. bouillir doucement
Simoniacal, adj. simoniaque
Simony, s. simonie, *f.*
Simoom, Simoon, s. simoun, *m.*
Simper, vn. sourire niaisement *or* avec afféterie, mignarder
Simper, Simpering, s. sourire niais, *m.*, minauderie, *f.*
Simperingly, adv. avec un sourire affecté *or* niais, en mignardant
Simple, adj. simple. — *-hearted*, adj., — *-minded*, adj. simple, ingénu, franc. — *-mindedness*, s. simplicité, *f.*
Simple, s. simple, *m.*
Simpleness, s. simplicité, *f.*
Simpleton, s. nigaud, *m.*, -e, *f.*, niais, *m.*, -e, *f.* *What a — you are!* que vous êtes nigaud!
Simplicity, s. simplicité, *f.*
Simplification, s. simplification, *f.*
Simplify, va. simplifier
Simply, adv. simplement, purement et simplement, bonnement, niaisement
Simulate, feindre, simuler
Simulation, s. simulation, *f.*, feinte, *f.*, déguisement, *m.*
Simultaneous, adj. simultané
Simultaneously, adv. simultanément
Simultaneousness, s. simultanéité, *f.*
Sin, s. péché, *m.* — *-offering*, s. sacrifice expiatoire, *m.*
Sin, vn. pécher
Sinapism, s. sinapisme, *m.*
Since, conj. puisque, depuis que, que. *Ever — he went*, depuis qu'il est parti
Since, adv. il y a, passé, depuis, depuis lors. *He left me six weeks —*, il me quitta il y a six semaines
Since, prep. depuis
Sincere, adj. sincère
Sincerely, adv. sincèrement
Sincerity, s. sincérité, *f.*, bonne foi, *f.*
Sine, s. sinus, *m.*
Sinecure, s. sinécure, *f.*
Sinew, s. tendon, *m.*, nerf, *m.*
Sinewy, adj. nerveux, vigoureux
Sinful, adj. coupable de péché, pécheur, criminel
Sinfully, adv. criminellement
Sinfulness, s. culpabilité, *f.*
Sing, vn.a. chanter, retentir, (*wind*) siffler, (*ears*) tinter. *To — in tune, out of tune*, chanter juste, faux
Singe, va. roussir, flamber, passer par la flamme
Singeing, s. action de roussir, de brûler légèrement, etc.
Singer, s. chanteur, *m.*, -euse, *f.*, (*profess.*) cantatrice, *f.*
Singing, s. chant, *m.*
Singing, adj. de chant, chanteur, (*of cats*) ron-ron. — *boy*, s. enfant de chœur, *m.* — *-man*, s. chantre, *m.* — *-master*, s. maître de chant, *m.* — *-mistress*, s. maîtresse de chant, *f.* — *-school*, s. école de chant, *f.*
Single, adj. seul, simple, unique, particulier, individuel, isolé, (*unmarried*) non marié, (*combat*) singulier. *A — life*, un célibat. *A — man*, un célibataire, garçon. *To live —*, vivre dans le célibat. — *-handed*, adj. manchot, (*unaided*) seul, sans secours. — *-hearted*, adj. sincère. — *-heartedness*, s. simplicité, *f.* — *-minded*, adj. simple, sincère. — *-stick*, s. canne, *f.*
Single, va. choisir, isoler, distinguer. *To — out*, choisir, distinguer
Singleness, s. unité, *f.*, isolement, *m.*, simplicité, *f.*
Singly, adv. simplement, seulement, uniquement, séparément
Singsong, s. chant monotone
Singsong, adj. traînant, monotone
Singular, adj. seul, unique, simple, singulier, particulier, remarquable, (*queer*) étrange, bizarre
Singularity, s. singularité, *f.*, particularité, *f.*, propriété particulière, *f.* *To affect —*, se singulariser
Singularly, adv. singulièrement
Sinister, adj. sinistre, méchant, pervers
Sink, vn. s'enfoncer, enfoncer, tomber *or* aller au fond, (*ship*) sombrer, couler bas, (*into*, dans) s'enfoncer, entrer, pénétrer, (*sun*) descendre, disparaître, (*give way*) s'affaisser, succomber, (*in strength*) décliner, s'affaiblir, (*into*, dans) dégénérer, tomber, défaillir, être abattu, (*heart*) se serrer, (*prices*) diminuer de valeur, baisser, (*earth*) se tasser. *To — down into*, s'abîmer dans, s'engloutir dans. *To — in*, s'écrouler. *To — to sleep*, s'endormir. — va. enfoncer, faire aller *or* tomber au fond, (*ship*) couler bas, (*dig*) creuser, (*the well*) foncer, (*into*, dans) enfoncer, plonger, (*prices*) baisser, abaisser, faire baisser, diminuer, (*to suppress*) supprimer, faire disparaître, (*not to mention*) ne pas parler de, laisser de côté, (*fortune*) dissiper, (*financ.*) placer à fonds perdus, placer *or* mettre en viager, (*the public debt*) amortir
Sink, s. égout, *m.*, cloaque, *m.*, (*kitchen*) évier, *m.*, (*fig.*) sentine, *f.*, cloaque, *m.*, abîme, *m.*
Sinker, s. fonceur, *m.*
Sinking, s. action d'enfoncer, etc., (*well*) foncement, *m.*, (*soil, &c.*) tassement, *m.*, (*heart*) serrement, *m.*, (*courage, &c.*) affaissement, *m.*, (*strength*) affaiblissement, *m.*, déclin, *m.*, (*funds*) placement à fonds perdus *or* en viager, *m.*, amortissement, *m.* *The — -fund*, le fonds *or* la caisse d'amortissement
Sinless, adj. sans péché, innocent
Sinlessness, s. innocence, *f.*
Sinner, s. pécheur, *m.*, pécheresse, *f.*
Sinuosity, s. sinuosité, *f.*
Sinuous, adj. sinueux
Sip, va.n. boire à petits coups, siroter
Sip, s. gorgée, *f.*, petit trait, *m.*, petit coup, *m.*, goutte, *f.*
Siphon, s. siphon, *m.*
Sippet, s. morceau trempé, *m.*
Sir, s. monsieur, *m.*, (*English title*) sir, *m.* *Did you ring, —?* monsieur a-t-il sonné?
Sire, s. père, *m.* —*s*, pl. pères, *m.pl.*, aïeux, *m.pl.*
Siren, s. sirène, *f.*
Siren, adj. de sirène, enchanteur
Sirloin, s. aloyau, *m.*, surlonge de bœuf, *f.*
Sirocco, s. siroc, *m.*, siroco, *m.*
Sirrah, s. drôle, *m.*, coquin, *m.*, maraud, *m.*
Sirup, s. sirop, *m.*
Sirupy, adj. en sirop, sirupeux
Sister, s. sœur, *f.* *Like a —*, en sœur. — *-in-law*, s. belle-sœur, *f.* *Younger —*, s. sœur cadette, *f.*
Sister, adj. sœur, de même nature, de même espèce
Sisterhood, s. état d'être sœur, *m.*, communauté de sœurs, *f.*
Sisterly, adj. de sœur, d'une sœur. — *love*, affection de sœur, *f.*
Sit, vn. être assis, s'asseoir, (*court*) siéger, être, se tenir, (*birds*) percher, se poser, (*to brood*) couver, (*judge*) juger, (*on, at*, sur) (*to weigh*) peser, (*dress*) aller, s'ajuster, (*for a painting*) poser. *To — down*, s'asseoir, (*at table*) se mettre, (*milit.*) (*before*, devant) mettre le siége. *To — out*, être en dehors, être sans emploi, être hors du jeu. *To — up*, se mettre sur son séant, se tenir droit, se redresser, passer la nuit. *To — up with a sick person*, veiller un malade. *To — still*, rester assis. — *quiet*, tenez-vous tranquille. — va. asseoir, se tenir sur, (*a horse*) monter. *To — oneself down*, s'asseoir
Site, s. situation, *f.*, emplacement, *m.*
Sitting, adj. assis, (*bird*) perché
Sitting, s. action de s'asseoir, posture d'être assis, (*for portraits*) pose, (*church*) chaise, *f.*, place, *f.*, (*court*) séance, *f.*, (*parliament*) audience, *f.*, (*birds*) incubation, *f.* — *up*, veillée. *To hold a —*, tenir séance
Situate, Situated, adj. situé, en position
Situation, s. situation, *f.*, position, *f.*, (*office*) place, *f.*, emploi, *m.* *To be out of a —*, être sans place
Six, adj. s. six. *To be at —es and sevens*, être tout sens dessus dessous
Sixfold, adj. s. sextuple, *m.*
Sixpence, s. sixpence (60 centimes), *m.*
Sixteen, adj. s. seize
Sixteenth, adj. seizième, seize
Sixth, adj. s. sixième, six, (*mus.*) sixte, *f.*
Sixthly, adv. sixièmement
Sixtieth, adj. s. soixantième, *m.*
Sixty, adj. s. soixante
Sizar, s. étudiant boursier, *m.*
Sizarship, s. bourse d'étudiant, *f.*
Size, s. grandeur, *f.*, (*bulk*) dimension, *f.*, volume, *m.*, grosseur, *f.*, (*person*) taille, *f.*, grandeur, *f.*, (*book*) format, *m.*, (*artil.*) calibre, *m.*, (*measure*) mesure, *f.* *All of a —*, tout d'une venue
Size, va. coller
. . . -Sized, adj. de grandeur . . ., de grosseur . . ., de dimension . . ., de taille . . . *Common- —*, de grosseur ordinaire. *Full- —*, qui a atteint toute sa grandeur naturelle
Skate, s. patin, *m.*, (*fish*) raie, *f.*
Skate, vn. patiner
Skater, s. patineur, *m.*, -euse, *f.*
Skating, s. action de patiner
Skein, s. écheveau, *m.*
Skeleton, s. squelette, *m.*, (*fig.*) charpente, *f.* — *-key*, s. passe-partout
Sketch, s. esquisse, *f.*, croquis, *m.*, (*fig.*) ébauche, *f.*, aperçu, *m.*, canevas, *m.* —

-book, s. album, *m.*, cahier d'esquisses, *m.*
Sketch, va. esquisser, faire le croquis de
Skew, adj. oblique, en biais
Skewer, s. brochette, *f.*
Skewer, va. attacher avec des brochettes
Skid, s. chaîne, *f.* — *-pan*, s. sabot, *m.*
Skid, va. enrayer
Skiff, s. esquif, *m.*, barque, *f.*
Skilful, adj. habile, adroit
Skilfully, adv. habilement, adroitement
Skill, s. habileté, *f.*, adresse, *f.*, talent, *m.*, savoir-faire, *m.*
Skilled, adj. habile, versé, expert
Skillet, s. casserole, *f.*
Skim, va.n. (*milk*) écrémer, (*broth*) écumer, (*pass by*) raser, effleurer
Skimmer, s. écumoire, *f.*
Skimming, s. action d'écrémer, *m.*, écrémage, *m.*
Skin, s. peau, *f.*, (*hide*) cuir, *m.*, (*fig.*) écorce, *f.* *Wet to the* —, mouillé jusqu'aux os
Skin, va. écorcher, tondre, (*cover*) couvrir. *To — a flint*, tondre sur un œuf. — vn. se couvrir d'une peau
Skinflint, s. fesse-mathieu, *m.*, grigou, *m.*, pince-maille, *m.*, ladre, *m.*
Skinner, s. écorcheur, *m.*, (*dealer*) peaussier, *m.*, pelletier, *m.*, fourreur, *m.*
Skinny, adj. de peau, décharné
Skip, vn. sauter, sautiller, bondir, sauter à la corde; — va. (*to omit*) sauter, passer, omettre
Skip, s. saut, *m.*, sautillement, *m.*, bond, *m.* — *-jack*, s. taupin, *m.*
Skipper, s. sauteur, *m.*, -euse, *f.*, (*of a ship*) patron, *m.*, capitaine, *m.*
Skipping, adj. qui saute, bondissant
Skipping, s. action de sauter, *f.*, omission, *f.* — *-rope*, s. corde à sauter, *m.*
Skirmish, s. escarmouche, *f.*
Skirmish, vn. escarmoucher
Skirmisher, s. escarmoucheur, *m.*, tirailleur, *m.*
Skirmishing, s. escarmouches, *f.pl.*
Skirt, s. (*of a gown*) jupe, *f.*, jupon, *m.*, pan, *m.*, basque, *f.*, (*edge*) bord, *m.*, garniture, *f.*, (*town*) extrémité, *f.*, (*wood*) lisière, *f.*, (*anat.*) diaphragme, *m.*
Skirt, va. mettre une jupe à, mettre des basques à, border, garnir, longer
Skirting, s. bord, *m.*, bordure, *f.*
Skit, s. (*pers.*) coquette, *f.*, (*th.*) raillerie, *f.*
Skittish, adj. ombrageux, timide, capricieux, volage, folâtre
Skittishly, adv. timidement, capricieusement
Skittishness, s. caractère ombrageux, *m.*, nature capricieuse, *m.*
Skittle, s. quille, *f.* —*s*, pl. quilles *f.pl.*, jeu de quilles, *m.* — *-ball*, s. boule, *f.* — *-ground*, s. jeu de quilles, *m.*
Skulk, vn. se cacher, se tenir caché
Skull, s. crâne, *m.*, tête de mort, *f.* — *-cap*, s. calotte, *f.*
Sky, s. ciel, *m.*, nuages, *m. pl.* — *-blue colour*, s. bleu de ciel, *m.* — *-high*, adj. aussi haut que les nuages. — *-rocket*, s. fusée volante, *f.*
Skylark, s. alouette, *f.*
Sky-light, s. abat-jour, *m.*, lucarne, *f.*
Slab, s. plaque, *f.*, table, *f.*, dalle, *f.*
Slabber, vn. *see* Slobber
Slabbering, s. baveur, *m.*, -euse, *f.*
Slack, adj. lent, négligent, nonchalant, (*weak*) faible, mou, (*loose*) lâche, (*com.*) peu vif
Slack, adv. imparfaitement
Slack, va. (*lime*) éteindre. —*ed lime*, chaux éteinte
Slacken, vn. se ralentir, diminuer, se détendre, se relâcher, se desserrer; — va. ralentir, détendre, desserrer, (*fire*) diminuer, ralentir, amortir
Slackening, s. ralentissement, *m.*
Slackly, adv. lentement, mollement, nonchalamment
Slackness, s. lenteur, *f.*, négligence, *f.*, (*weakness*) mollesse, *f.*, faiblesse, *f.*
Slag, s. scorie, *f.*
Slake, va. (*lime*) éteindre
Slam, va.n. fermer violemment *or* avec bruit
Slander, va. diffamer, calomnier, médire de
Slander, s. calomnie, *f.*, médisance, *f.*, diffamation, *f.*
Slanderer, s. (*law*) calomniateur, *m.*, -trice, *f.*, médisant, *m.*, -e, *f.*, diffamateur, *m.*, -trice, *f.*
Slanderous, adj. calomnieux, calomniateur, diffamatoire
Slanderously, adv. calomnieusement, avec médisance
Slang, s. argot, *m.*, jargon, *m.*
Slang, **Slangy**, adj. trivial, d'argot
Slant, s. plan incliné, *m.*, pente, *f.*
Slant, vn. aller *or* être en pente, incliner, biaiser, être de biais
Slanting, adj. en pente, incliné, oblique, de biais
Slantingly, adv. en pente, obliquement, de biais
Slap, s. claque, *f.*, tape, *f.*, gifle, *f.* — *in the face*, soufflet
Slap, adv. droit, en plein. — *-dash*, tout d'un coup, droit, à tout hasard. — *-up*, fameux, soigné
Slap, va. frapper, claquer
Slash, va. taillader, déchiqueter, (*the face*) balafrer, (*criticise*) éreinter. —*ing articles*, articles de critique qui emportent la pièce
Slash, s. blessure, *f.*, taillade, *f.*, balafre, *f.*
Slate, s. ardoise, *f.* — *-coloured*, adj. couleur ardoisée, gris d'ardoise. — *-pencil*, s. crayon d'ardoise, *m.* — *-quarry*, s. ardoisière, *f.*
Slate, va. couvrir d'ardoises
Slater, s. couvreur (en ardoises), *m.*
Slating, s. toiture en ardoises, *f.*
Slattern, s. femme malpropre, *f.*, femme sans soin, *f.*, souillon, *f.*
Slattern, adj. malpropre, négligent
Slatternly, adj. adv. malpropre, négligent, malproprement
Slaty, adj. d'ardoise, de couleur d'ardoise, ardoisé
Slaughter, s. carnage, *m.*, (*of beasts*) tuerie, *f.*, boucherie, *f.*, abattage, *m.* — *-house*, s. abattoir, *m.*
Slaughter, va. massacrer, égorger, tuer, abattre
Slaughterer, s. qui égorge, qui massacre, tueur, *m.*, equarisseur, *m.*
Slave, vn. travailler comme un esclave
Slaver, s. bâtiment négrier, *m.*, bave, *f.*, salive, *f.*
Slaver, vn. baver, être couvert de bave; —va. couvrir de bave
Slavery, s. esclavage, *m.*, servitude, *f.*
Slavish, adj. d'esclave, servile
Slavishly, adv. en esclave, servilement
Slavishness, s. servilité, *f.*
Slay, va. tuer, faire mourir, égorger
Slayer, s. tueur, *m.*, meurtrier, *m.*
Sledge, s. traîneau, *m.* — *-hammer*, s. marteau de forgeron
Sleek, **Sleeky**, adj. luisant, poli, d'un beau poil, lisse, (*fig.*) doux. — *-headed*, aux cheveux gras, à la face luisante. — *-stone*, s. lissoir, *m.*
Sleek, va. rendre luisant, rendre lisse
Sleep, vn. dormir, s'endormir, (*to spend the night*) coucher. *To — again*, se rendormir. *To — on*, continuer de dormir. *To see if —ing on it would not change his determination*, voir si la nuit ne porterait pas conseil. *To — in the Lord, with God*, dormir dans le Seigneur, reposer dans le sein de Dieu. *To — like a top*, dormir comme un sabot *or* sur les deux oreilles. *Who —s in the second chamber?* qui couche, qui est couché dans la seconde chambre? *To — out, not to — at home*, découcher. *To — on the ground, on bare boards*, coucher sur la dure. *My foot —s*, j'ai le pied engourdi. *The matter —s*, on laisse dormir l'affaire. *To — away*, passer (son temps) à dormir. *To — off*, guérir par le sommeil
Sleep, s. sommeil, *m.* *To go to* —, s'endormir. *He went to — again*, il se rendormit. *I have had no* —, je n'ai pas fermé l'œil, je n'ai pas dormi du tout. *To be overcome with* —, tomber *or* être accablé de sommeil. — *-walker*, s. somnambule, *m.f.* — *-walking*, s. somnambulisme, *m.*
Sleeper, s. dormeur, *m.*, dormeuse, *f.*, personne endormie, *f.*, (*constr.*) traverse, *f.*, semelle, *f.* *To be a heavy* —, dormir d'un sommeil pesant, être difficile à éveiller
Sleepily, adv. comme endormi, d'un air endormi
Sleepiness, s. envie de dormir, *f.*, sommeil, *m.*, air endormi, *m.*, (*fig.*) pesanteur, *f.*
Sleeping, s. sommeil, *m.*, repos, *m.*, (*fig.*) assoupissement, *m.*
Sleeping, adj. de sommeil, de repos, endormi, (*com.*) commanditaire. — *-draught*, s. narcotique, *m.* — *-potion*, s. potion calmante. — *-room*, s. chambre à coucher, *m.*, dortoir, *m.*
Sleepless, adj. sans sommeil
Sleeplessness, s. insomnie, *f.*
Sleepy, adj. qui a sommeil, endormi, soporifique, (*fig.*) endormi, lourd. *To be* —, *to feel* —, avoir sommeil, avoir envie de dormir. *To look* —, avoir l'air tout endormi. *With a — look*, d'un air endormi. — *-looking*, adj. qui à l'air endormi. — *Morpheus*, Morphée ami du sommeil. — *pear*, poire blette. — *business*, affaire sur la quelle on peut s'endormir
Sleet, s. grésil, *m.*
Sleet, vn. grésiller
Sleety, adj. de grésil
Sleeve, s. manche, *f.* *Shirt —s*, s. manches de chemises, *f. pl.* — *-button*, s. bouton de manche, *m.*
Sleight, s. tour, *m.*, (*fig.*) tour de passe-passe, *m.*, artifice, *m.*, ruse, *f.* — *of hand tricks*, s. tours de passe-passe, *m.pl.*, prestidigitation, *f.*
Slender, adj. mince, ténu, grêle, frêle, (*waist*) svelte, élancé, mince, (*frail*) fragile, léger, (*weak*) faible, léger. — *waist*, s. taille svelte, *f.*, taille mince, *f.* — *frame*, s. corps frêle, *m.*, tempérament délicat, *m.* — *-limbed*, adj. au corps grêle. — *probabilities*, de légères proba-

bilités. *A lad of — parts*, un garçon de peu de moyens. *To have but a — wit*, avoir médiocrement d'esprit. *— meal*, repas exigu. *My — table*, mon modeste repas

Slenderness, s. état mince, *m.*, état grêle, *m.*, état svelte, *m.*, finesse, *f.*, fragilité, *f.*, faiblesse, *f.*

Slice, va. couper par tranches, diviser, partager

Slice, tranche, *f.*, (*of fowls*) aiguillette, *f.*, (*of bread and butter*) tartine, *f.*, (*spatula*) spatule, *f.* *A — of fowl*, un morceau de blanc. *A — of bread and butter, of bread and jam*, un tartine de pain et de beurre, une tartine de confitures

Slide, vn.a. glisser, se glisser, (*from*, de) s'éloigner doucement, s'écarter, sortir, (*into*) tomber insensiblement (dans). *To — on a pond*, glisser sur un étang. *To — along*, glisser, s'avancer. *To — away*, glisser, s'éloigner doucement, s'écouler, passer. *To — down*, glisser en bas de, descendre, se laisser glisser *or* couler. *To — into a room*, (*fig.*) entrer doucement dans une chambre

Slide, s. glissade, *f.*, glissoire, *f.*, (*groove*) coulisse, *f.*, (*purse*) coulant, *m.*, (*of earth*) éboulement, *m.*, (*mechan.*) tiroir, *m.*, (*mus.*) coulé, *m.*, (*magic lantern*) verre, *m.* *To have a —*, glisser. *To make a —*, faire une glissade. *Diamond —*, s. coulant, *m.* *— -groat*, s. jeu de galet, *m.* *— -rule*, s. échelle de proportion, *f.* *— -rails*, s. pl. languettes, *f.* *— -box*, s., *— -rod*, s., *— -valve*, s. boîte, tige, soupape des tiroirs, *f.* *— -valve spindles*, s. goujon, *m.* *— s and blocks*, s. guides des tiges des pistons, *f.pl.*

Slider, s. glisseur, *m.*, (*things*) coulisse, *f.*

Sliding, s. glissade, *f.*

Sliding, adj. glissant, coulant, à coulisse. *— -rule*, s. échelle de proportion, *f.* *— -scale*, s. échelle mobile, *f.* *— -door*, s. porte à coulisse, *f.*

Slight, adj. léger, faible, superficiel. *— is the subject*, ce sujet n'est pas important. *— effort*, effort léger. *— errors*, des fautes légères. *A dark — man*, un homme brun et maigre

Slight, s. manque d'égards, *m.*, dédain, *m.*, négligence, *f.* *To put a — upon*, manquer d'égards envers

Slight, va. négliger, faire peu de cas de, mépriser, dédaigner, manquer d'égards. *To — over*, faire à la légère

Slightingly, adv. négligemment, avec dédain

Slightly, adv. légèrement, à la légère. *— valued*, adj. traité sans égards

Slightness, s. légèreté, *f.*, faiblesse, *f.*

Slim, adj. (*weak*) faible, frivole, futile, élancé, svelte, grêle

Slime, s. limon, *m.*, vase, *f.*, (*of snails*) bave, *f.*

Sliminess, s. nature limoneuse, *f.*, viscosité, *f.*

Slimy, adj. limoneux, vaseux, visqueux, gluant

Sling, s. fronde, *f.*, (*bandage*) écharpe, *f.*, (*of a musket*) bretelle, *f.*, (*nav.*) élingue, *f.* *The — of the hailstones*, le choc *or* la chute violente de la grêle. *In a —*, en écharpe

Sling, va. lancer avec une fronde, (*over*, sur) suspendre, (*nav.*) élinguer

Slinger, s. frondeur, *m.*

Slink, va. se glisser furtivement, se retirer, s'esquiver. *To — in*, entrer honteusement *or* furtivement. *To — out*, s'esquiver, sortir furtivement. *The dog would — to his master's side*, l'oreille basse, le chien se serrait contre son maître. *With his tail slunk between his legs*, serrant la queue

Slip, vn. glisser, se glisser, (*escape*) couler, échapper, (*err*) faire un faux pas, faire une faute, faillir. *My foot —ped*, mon pied glissa, le pied me glissa. *What made me —!* ce qui me fit glisser? *He —ped into the room*, il se glissa, il se faufila dans la chambre. *Some mistakes may have —ped into it*, il a pu s'y glisser quelques erreurs. *To — away*, s'échapper, s'esquiver, (*time*) s'écouler. *To — down*, se laisser tomber, tomber. *To — in*, entrer à la dérobée *or* doucement, s'y glisser, s'y faufiler. *To — off*, (*from*, de) se laisser glisser *or* couler, tomber, s'échapper, s'esquiver. *To — out*, sortir doucement, s'échapper, s'esquiver. *It —ped through my fingers*, il me coula à travers les doigts. *— into him!* (*pop.*) tapez ferme! *That the water may — off*, (*fig.*) afin que l'eau en découle. *It —ped from me unawares*, cela m'a échappé. *To let —*, laisser échapper, lâcher. — va. glisser, faire glisser, introduire, (*occasion*) laisser échapper, perdre, (*hortic.*) couper pour boutures. *To — on*, (*dress*) mettre vivement, passer. *To — off*, ôter vivement, enlever, faire tomber, se dégager de

Slip, s. glissade, *f.*, faux pas, *m.*, action de s'échapper, *m.*, (*mistake*) faute, *f.*, erreur, *f.*, méprise, *f.*, (*hortic.*) bouture, *f.*, plant, *m.*, (*small piece*) bande étroite, *f.*, pièce étroite, *f.*, (*of dogs*) laisse, *f.*, (*theatre*) coulisse, *f.*, (*petticoat*) jupe, *f.*, (*earth*) éboulement, *m.*, (*print.*) placard, *m.* *— -not*, s. nœud coulant. *To give (a person) the —*, fausser compagnie à, planter là. *A — of the pen*, une erreur de la plume. *A — of my tongue*, une parole qui m'a échappé par mégarde. *—s of lead*, bandes étroites de plomb. *— of wood*, morceau de bois. *Land- —*, s. éboulement, *m.* *In —s*, en placards

Slipper, s. pantoufle, *f.*, savate, *f.*, (*the Pope's*) mule, *f.* *Hunt the —*, (*play*) la savate

Slipperiness, s. nature glissante, *f.*

Slippery, adj. glissant, difficile à tenir, sur qui on ne peut compter, incertain, (*delicate*) scabreux

Slipshod, adj. en savates, négligé

Slipslop, s. lavasse, *f.*, ripopée, *f.*

Slit, va. fendre, trancher

Slit, s. fente, *f.*

Slobber, va.n. baver. *— -chops*, s. baveux, *m.*, -euse, *f.*

Slobber, s. bave, *f.*, salive, *f.*

Slobberer, s. baveux, *m.*, -euse, *f.*

Sloe, s. prunelle, *f.*

Sloop, s. sloop, *m.*, corvette, *f.*

Slop, va. répandre, renverser

Slop, s. (*clothes*) confections, *f.pl.*, habits tout faits, *m.pl.*, (*poor drink*) ripopée, *f.* *—s*, pl. (*kitchen-washing*) rinçures, *f.pl.* *— -basin*, s., *— -bowl*, s. bol, *m.* *— -pail*, s. seau, *m.* *— -seller*, s. marchand de confections, *m.* *— -shop*, s. magasin de confections, *m.*

Slope, s. pente, *f.*, déclivité, *f.*, talus, *m.*, remblai, *m.*

Slope, va. pencher, incliner, couper en biais, faire aller en biais. *— arms*, armes à volonté. — vn. être en pente, incliner, être disposé en talus, aller en biais. *To — gently down to*, descendre par une pente douce à

Sloping, adj. en pente, en talus, de biais

Slopingly, adv. en pente, obliquement

Sloppy, adj. gâcheux, humide

Sloth, s. lenteur, *f.*, paresse, *f.*, fainéantise, *f.*, indolence, *f.*, (*anim.*) paresseux, *m.*

Slothful, adj. paresseux, indolent

Slothfully, adv. paresseusement, avec indolence

Slouch, vn. marcher lourdement, gauchement, et sans lever les yeux; — va. rabattre

Slouching, adj. lourd et gauche, rabattu

Slough, s. fondrière, *f.*, marécage, *m.*, bourbier, *m.*, (*serpent*) dépouille, *f.*, (*surg.*) escarre, *f.*, croûte, *f.*

Sloughy, adj. bourbeux

Sloven, adj. sans-soin, malpropre

Slovenliness, s. malpropreté, *f.*, négligence, *f.*

Slovenly, adj. malpropre, sans soin, négligent

Slovenly, adv. salement, sans soin

Slow, adj. lent, indolent, (*tedious*) ennuyeux, monotone, (*train*) de petite vitesse, (*fig.*) lourd, peu intelligent, de peu de moyens, (*watch*) en retard. *— to hear*, lent à entendre. *— to anger*, lent à s'irriter. *A — coach*, voiture qui va lentement, (*fig.*) un lambin, un garçon lourd. *— pulse*, un pouls faible. *By or over a — fire*, à petit feu. *My watch is five minutes —*, ma montre retarde de cinq minutes. *You are too —*, vous retardez

Slow, adv. lentement, (*watch*) en retard. *— -worm*, s. serpent de verre, *m.*, orvet, *m.*

Slowly, adv. lentement, tardivement

Slowness, s. lenteur, *f.*

Slug, s. (*zool.*) limace, *f.*, (*pers.*) paresseux, *m.*, -euse, *f.*, (*shot*) lingot, *m.*

Sluggard, s. adj. fainéant, -e, paresseux, -euse

Sluggish, adj. paresseux, indolent, apathique

Sluggishly, adv. paresseusement, avec indolence, lentement

Sluggishness, s. paresse, *f.*, indolence, *f.*, apathie, *f.*, lenteur, *f.*

Sluice, s. écluse, *f.*, vanne *f.*

Sluice, va. lâcher, inonder. *To — out*, faire couler

Slumber, vn. sommeiller, dormir

Slumber, s. sommeil, *m.*, repos, *m.*

Slumberer, s. dormeur, *m.*, -euse, *f.*

Slums, s. pl. quartiers mal famés, *m.pl.*

Slur, va. souiller, barbouiller, tacher, (*pass over*) passer légèrement sur, (*mus.*) couler

Slur, s. tache, *f.*, flétrissure, *f.*, barbouillage, *m.*, (*mus.*) liaison, *f.* *To put a — upon*, tacher, flétrir, dénigrer

Slush, s. boue, *f.*, neige fondue, *f.*

Slut, s. souillon, *f.*, malpropre, *f.*, péronnelle, *f.*, coquine, *f.*

Sly, adj. malin, rusé, en dessous, sournois. *Upon the —*, en cachette, en sournois. *— -boots*, finaud, fin matois, sournois

Slyness, s. artifice, *m.*, malice, *f.*, finesse, *f.*

Smack, vn. goûter (comme), avoir un goût (de), sentir (le), (*whip*, &c.) claquer, retentir. *To — of heresy*, sentir l'hérésie. *All ages — of this vice*, tous les âges ont plus ou moins ce vice. *To — of every sin*, abonder en tous les péchés. — va. faire claquer

Smack, s. goût, *m.*, saveur, *f.*, (*fig.*) teinte, *f.*, connaissance légère, *f.*, (*whip*) claquement, *m.*, (*kiss*) baiser retentissant, *m.*, (*ship*) bateau caboteur, *m.* *Fishing* —, s. barque de pêcheur, *f.*

Small, adj. petit, menu, fin, (*unimportant*) mince, chétif, pauvre. *Both — and great*, et les petits et les grands. *It was no — comfort*, ce n'était pas une petite consolation. — *talk*, s. conversation insignifiante sur la pluie et le beau temps, *f.*, banalités, *f.pl.* — *poets*, de petits poëtes. — *-arms*, s. armes portatives, *f.pl.* — *-beer*, s. petite bière, *f.* — *clothes*, s. culotte, *f.* — *-coal*, s. menu charbon, *m.* — *-craft*, s. petits bâtiments, *m.pl.*, petit bâtiment, *m.* — *-grained*, adj. à grain petit. — *-piece*, s. piécette, *f.* — *-pox*, s. petite vérole, *f.* — *-stuff*, s. (*nav.*) petits cordages, *m.pl.* — *-wares*, s. mercerie, *f.*

Small, s. partie mince, *f.* — *of the back*, chute des reins. — *of the leg*, bas de la jambe

Smallish, adj. un peu petit

Smallness, s. petitesse, *f.*, peu d'étendue, *m.*, peu de volume, *m.*

Smalt, s. smalt, *m.*

Smart, s. douleur cuisante, *f.*, vive douleur, *f.*, cuisson, *f.*

Smart, adj. cuisant, piquant, douloureux, vif, rude, vigoureux, (*witty*) spirituel, brillant, (*well dressed*) pimpant, élégant, bien mis, (*clever*) intelligent, adroit, (*active*) leste, actif. — *-money*, s. dommages-intérêts en sus, *m.*, (*mil.*) prix d'exonération, *m.*

Smart, vn. cuire, éprouver une vive douleur, souffrir, (*fam.*) en cuire à. *How it —s!* comme cela me cuit. *My eyes* —, les yeux me cuisent. *It made it* —, cela cuisait. *You may one day — for it!* il pourrait bien vous en cuire. *I will make you — for it*, je vous en ferai repentir

Smartly, adv. d'une manière cuisante, douloureusement, vivement, rudement, vigoureusement, spirituellement, d'une manière pimpante, bien, habilement, lestement

Smartness, s. vivacité, *f.*, cuisson, *f.*, vigueur, *f.*, (*fig.*) piquant, *m.*, esprit, *m.*, brillant, *m.*, élégance, *f.*, intelligence, *f.*, adresse, *f.*, activité, *f.*

Smash, va. écraser, briser

Smash, s. fracas, *m.*, action de briser en morceaux, *f.*, (*com.*) faillite, *f.*

Smatter, vn. n'avoir qu'une teinture (de), parler à tort et à travers

Smatter, Smattering, s. teinture, *f.*, connaissance légère, *f.*

Smatterer, s. qui n'a qu'une teinture (de), qui connait superficiellement

Smear, va. barbouiller, souiller

Smear, s. tache, *f.*, barbouillage, *m.*

Smell, va. sentir, (*fig.*) flairer. *To — out*, flairer, découvrir. *To — a rat*, se douter de quelque chose. — vn. sentir, avoir *or* exhaler une odeur

Smell, s. odorat, *m*, odeur, *f.*, (*of animals*) flair, *m.*, nez, *m.*

Smelling, s. action de sentir, *f.*, qui sent, d'odeurs. — *-bottle*, s. flacon d'odeurs, *m.* — *-salts*, s. sels, *m.pl.*

Smelt, s. éperlan, *m.*

Smelt, va. fondre

Smelter, s. fondeur, *m.*

Smelting, s. fonte, *f.* — *-house*, s. fonderie, *f.* — *-furnace*, s. haut fourneau, *m.*

Smile, vn. sourire

Smile, s. sourire, *m.*, souris, *m.* *He was all —s*, son visage s'épanouissait en sourires. *Dry* —, sourire sarcastique. *To draw a — from*, faire sourire. *With a* —, en souriant. *To provoke a — at*, faire sourire de

Smiling, adj. souriant, (*th.*) riant, agréable. *With a — face*, avec un visage souriant, le visage souriant

Smirk, vn. minauder, faire des minauderies

Smirk, s. sourire affecté, *m.* —*s*, pl. minauderie, *f.*

Smirking, adj. minaudier, de minauderie, affecté

Smite, va. frapper, (*with love*) rendre épris, engouer (de), passionner (pour)

Smith, s. forgeron, *m.*, artisan, *m.*

Smithery, Smithy, s. forge, *f.*

Smock, s. blouse, *f.* — *-frock*, s. blouse, *f.*, sarrau, *m.*

Smokable, adj. qu'on peut fumer

Smoke, s. fumée, *f.*, vapeur, *f.*, exhalaison, *f.* — *-consumer*, s. fumivore, *m.*

Smoke, vn. fumer, (*fig.*) s'irriter, s'enflammer; — va. fumer, sécher à la fumée, enfumer. *To — out*, fumer jusqu'au bout, enfumer. *To — -dry*, fumer

Smokeless, adj. sans fumée

Smoker, s. fumeur, *m.*

Smoking, s. action de fumer. *No — allowed*, défense de fumer. — *has become general*, presque tout le monde fume

Smoking, adj. qui fume, de fumeur, pour fumer. — *-room*, s. fumoir, *m.*, estaminet, *m.*, tabagie, *f.*

Smoky, adj. qui fume, (*full of smoke*) enfumé, (*fig.*) plein de fumée, (*smoke-like*) de fumée, noir sombre

Smooth, adj. uni, égal, (*glossy*) lisse, poli, (*fig.*) doux, paisible, d'un cours égal. — *bore*, (*pistols*) à canon lisse, (*artillery*) non rayé. — *-spoken*, adj., — *-tongued*, adj. aux paroles mielleuses, mielleux

Smooth, va. rendre uni *or* égal, aplanir, niveler, (*hair*) lisser, (*road*) frayer, aplanir, (*fault*) atténuer, pallier, (*difficulty*) apaiser, calmer, (*brow*) dérider. *To — the pillow of*, veiller sur la couche de, veiller sur. —*ing its feathers*, lissant ses plumes. *To — one's brow*, se dérider, dérider son front

Smoothly, adv. doucement, mollement, facilement

Smoothness, s. égalité, *f.*, douceur, *f.*

Smother, va. étouffer, suffoquer, asphyxier, (*fig.*) étouffer, cacher, (*fire*) éteindre; — vn. être étouffé, être suffoqué

Smother, s. poussière étouffante, *f.*, fumée, *f.*, étouffement, *m.*

Smoulder, vn. couver, brûler lentement. *To lie —ing*, couver (sous la cendre). —*ing ashes*, cendres mal éteintes. *A —ing fire*, un feu qui couve, un feu caché

Smudge, va. barbouiller

Smudge, s. saleté, *f.*, barbouillage, *m.*, tache, *f.*

Smug, adj. pimpant

Smuggle, vn. faire la contrebande, frauder, faire la fraude; — va. passer, faire passer en contrebande *or* en fraude (*fig.*) passer en cachette. *To — in*, entrer, passer en contrebande *or* en fraude. —*d goods*, marchandises de contrebande

Smuggler, s. contrebandier, *m.*, fraudeur, *m.*, vaisseau de contrebandier, *m.*

Smuggling, s. contrebande, *f.*, fraude, *f.*

Smut, s. noir, *m.*, tache, *f.*, (*agric.*) charbon, *m.*, (*talk*) propos graveleux, *m.*

Smut, va. noircir, barbouiller, souiller, ternir, (*agric.*) nieller

Smuttily, adv. salement

Smuttiness, s. noirceur, *f.*, (*language*) saleté, *f.*

Smutty, adj. noir, noirci, barbouillé de noir, enfumé, (*agric.*) niellé, (*speech*) graveleux, sale

Snack, s. morceau, *m.* *To take a* —, casser une croûte, prendre un morceau sur le pouce

Snaffle, s. bridon, *m.*, filet, *m.*

Snag, s. nœud, *m.*, (*tooth*) dent, *f.*, branche, *f.*

Snaggy, adj. noueux, plein de nœuds

Snail, s. colimaçon, *m.*, limaçon, *m.*, escargot, *m.* — *-like*, adj., — *-paced*, adj. à pas de tortue

Snake, s. serpent, *m.* *A — in the grass*, anguille sous roche

Snaky, adj. serpentant, sinueux, tortueux, de serpents

Snap, va. saisir vivement, happer, gober, (*break*) briser, casser, (*fingers*) faire claquer, (*scold*) reprendre. *To — up*, happer, gober, (*fig.*) reprendre aigrement. *To — off*, mordre. — vn. essayer de happer, faire mine de mordre, se jeter sur, (*at*, . . .) quereller aigrement, reprendre aigrement, (*break*) se casser net, se rompre, se briser. *To — off*, se casser net, se détacher net

Snap, s. coup de dent, *m.*, effort pour mordre, *m.*, cassure, *f.*, rupture, *f.*, bruit sec, *m.*, claquement, *m.*, (*of a bracelet, &c.*) fermoir, *m.*

Snappish, adj. hargneux, aigre, querelleur, acariâtre

Snappishly, adv. aigrement, d'un ton hargneux

Snappishness, s. aigreur, *f.*, ton hargneux, *m.*

Snare, s. piége, *m.*

Snarl, vn. grogner, gronder, montrer les dents (à)

Snarler, s. grognon, *m.f.*, personne hargneuse, *f.*

Snarling, adj. hargneux

Snarling, s. grognement, *m.*

Snatch, va. arracher, enlever. *To — at*, chercher à saisir, se jeter avidement sur. *To — away*, arracher, enlever. *To — up*, enlever, ramasser vivement

Snatch, s. effort pour saisir, *m.*, accès, *m.*, boutade, *f.*, bribe, *f.*, (*piece*) morceau, *m.*, fragment, *m.* *By —es*, à bâtons rompus

Sneak, vn. se glisser furtivement *or* honteusement, (*crowd*) ramper, faire le capon. *To — away, to — off*, s'esquiver, s'en aller l'oreille basse, s'enfuir. *To — up to*, s'approcher honteusement de

Sneak, s. capon, *m.*, sournois, *m.*, -e, *f.*, pied plat, *m.*

Sneaking, adj. sournois, capon, rampant

Sneakingly, adv. en sournois, bassement, d'une manière honteuse

Sneer, vn. ricaner, railler, se moquer (de)

Sneer, s. ricanement, *m.*, rire moqueur, *m.*, air méprisant, *m.*, raillerie, *f.*, sarcasme, *m.*

Sneerer, s. ricaneur, *m.*, -euse, *f.*, railleur, *m.*, -euse, *f.*

Sneering, adv. en ricanant, en raillant, en se moquant

Sneeze, vn. éternuer. *To — at*, (*fig.*) dédaigner

Sneeze, s. éternument, *m.*

Sniff, vn. renifler, humer l'air; — va. aspirer en reniflant

Sniff, s. reniflement, *m.*

Snip, va. couper

Snip, s. coup de ciseaux, *m.*, (*piece*) morceau, *m.*, fragment, *m.*, (*share*) part, *f.*

Snipe, s. bécassine, *f.*

Snivel, s. morve, *f.*, goutte au nez, *f.*
Snivel, vn. être morveux, couler, (*to cry*) pleurnicher
Sniveller, s. morveux, *m.*, -euse, *f.*, pleurnicheur, *m.*, -euse, *f.*
Snivelling, adj. morveux, pleurnicheur
Snivelling, s. piaillerie, *f.*, pleurnicherie, *f.*
Snob, s. parvenu, *m.*, poseur, *m.*
Snobbish, adj. commun, vulgaire
Snobbishness, s. sottise orgueilleuse, *f.m.*
Snobbism, s. sottise orgueilleuse, *f.*, les sots orgueilleux, *m.pl.*
Snooze, s. somme, *m.*
Snooze, vn. dormir, sommeiller
Snore, Snort, vn. ronfler
Snore, Snoring, s. ronflement, *m.*
Snorer, s. ronfleur, *m.*, -euse, *f.*
Snout, s. museau, *m.*, (*pig*) groin, *m.*, (*wild boar*) boutoir, *m.*, (*of bellows*) tuyau, *m.*, canon, *m.*
Snout, va. fournir d'un bout
Snow, s. neige, *f.* — *-ball*, s. boule de neige, *f.* *To* — *-ball*, va. lancer des boules de neige (à). — *-blind*, adj. frappé de cécité par la neige. — *-drift*, s. amas de neige, *m.* — *-drop*, s. perce-neige, *f.* — *-flake*, s. flocon de neige, *m.* — *-shoe*, s. raquette, *f.* — *-slip*, s. avalanche, *f.* — *-white*, adj. blanc comme la neige
Snow, vn. neiger, tomber de la neige
Snowy, Snowish, adj. de neige, neigeux, couvert de neige, blanc comme la neige
Snub, va. rabrouer, rudoyer, gourmander, relancer
Snub-nosed, adj. camus
Snuff, s. tabac à priser, *m.*, tabac en poudre, *m.*, (*of wicks*) lumignon, *m.*, mèche charbonnée, *f.* *To take* —, priser, prendre du tabac. — *-box*, s. tabatière, *f.* — *-taker*, s. priseur, *m.* *To be up to* —, (*pop.*) ne pas se moucher du pied
Snuff, va. aspirer, humer, (*candles*) moucher. *To* — *out*, éteindre
Snuffers, s.pl. mouchettes, *f.pl.* — *-stand*, s., — *-tray*, s. porte-mouchettes, *m.*
Snuffle, vn. nasiller, parler du nez
Snuffler, s. nasillard, *m.*, -e, *f.*
Snug, adj. serré (contre), tout auprès (de), où l'on est à l'aise
Snug, adv. commodément, bien, à l'aise
Snuggery, s. gentille petite chambre, *f.*
Snugly, adv. serré, tout auprès, chaudement, commodément, à l'aise

Snugness, s. commodité, *f.*, agrément, *m.*, gentillesse, *f.*
So, adv. aussi, (*as*, que) aussi, si, autant, tant, (*that*, que) si, tellement, au point (que), (*as*, pour) assez, (*that*) de sorte (que), de façon (que), si bien (que), de manière (que), (*as*) de manière (à), de façon (à, que), afin de, de même, de la même manière, tel, ainsi, comme cela, de cette façon, pour cela, à cause de cela, par cela même, soit, bon, c'est bien, puisse-t-il, à peu près, environ, passablement. — *very bright*, si brillant. *He is* — *prudent that everybody consults him*, il est si prudent que tout le monde le consulte. — *good a master*, un aussi bon maître. — *obstinate he was* tant il était entêté. — *wise are we grown*, tant nous sommes devenus sages. — *widely different*, tellement différent. *Why complain* — *bitterly*, pourquoi se plaindre avec tant d'amertume *or* si amèrement. — *much* — *that*, au point que, tellement que. *Be* — *kind as to inform me whether*, soyez assez bon pour me dire si. *No book was* — *bad but that he drew some profit from it*, il n'y avait pas de livre assez mauvais pour qu'il n'en tirât quelque profit *or* tellement mauvais qu'il n'en tirât quelque profit. — *that he was compelled to give in*, de sorte que, si bien, qu'il fut obligé de céder. — *as to make me believe*, de façon à me faire croire. *As the tree is*, — *is the fruit*, tel arbre, tel fruit. — *then*, ainsi donc. *But* — *it was*, mais il en était ainsi, quoi qu'il en soit. — *-called*, prétendu. — *forth*, — *on*, ainsi de suite, et cætera. *He says* —, il le dit. *Since you are pleased*, — *am I*, puisque vous êtes content, je le suis aussi. *Much more* —, bien plus encore. — *I shall ask her, eh!* aussi je vais l'inviter, n'est ce pas? *An intellectual creature, and* — *capable of dominion*, un être intelligent, et par cela même capable de gouverner. — *please your highness*, plaise à votre altesse. *A week or* —, environ une semaine. *A score or* —, une vingtaine ou à peu près *or* quelque chose d'approchant. — —, tout doucement, couci-couci, comme cela, assez bien, passablement
So, conj. pourvu que
Soak, va. tremper, faire tremper, mouiller. *To* — *the moisture in*, absorber, imbiber l'humidité. — vn. tremper, s'infiltrer, pénétrer, (*pop.*) boire comme une éponge
Soaker, s. action de tremper *or* d'être trempé

Soaking, adj. qui trempe, (*rain*) violente
Soap, s. savon, *m.* *Cake of* —, pain de savon. — *-ball*, s. savonnette, *f.* — *-boiler*, s., — *-maker*, s. fabricant de savon, *m.* — *-boiling*, s., — *-manufactory*, s. savonnerie, *f.* — *-bubble*, s. bulle de savon, *f.* — *-stone*, s. pierre de savon, *f.* — *-suds*, s. eau de savon, *f.* — *-wort*, s. saponaire, *f.*
Soapy, adj. savonneux, plein de savon
Soar, vn. s'élever, prendre son essor, planer
Soar, Soaring, s. essor, *m.*, vol élevé, *m.*
Soaring, adj. élevé, altier
Sob, vn. sangloter. *As if he would* — *his heart out*, comme si son cœur allait éclater (à force de sanglots)
Sob, Sobbing, s. sanglot, *m.*
Sober, adj. sobre, tempérant, qui n'a pas bu, sensé, modéré, sérieux, grave, posé, calme, rassis, de sang-froid. — *of praise*, sobre de louanges. *He was quite* —, *scarcely ever* —, il n'avait pas bu, il était presque toujours ivre. *When he is* —, *in a* — *state*, quand il n'a pas bu, quand il sera dégrisé. *To sleep oneself* —, cuver son vin. *A* — *writer*, un écrivain sobre. *With* — *pace*, à pas lents. *In* — *earnest*, sérieusement, sans plaisanterie. — *-looking*, adj. à l'air grave. — *-minded*, adj. sérieux, calme, sensé. — *-mindedness*, s. raison, *f.*, sagesse, *f.* *A* — *hour*, une heure sérieuse
Sober, va. rendre sobre or tempéré, dégriser, désenivrer, rendre sensé, calmer
Soberly, adv. sobrement, avec tempérance, modérément
Soberness, Sobriety, s. sobriété, *f.*, tempérance, *f.*, sagesse, *f.*, modération, *f.*, sang-froid, *m.*
Sociability, Sociableness, s. sociabilité, *f.*
Sociable, adj. sociable, aimable, affable
Sociably, adv. d'une manière sociable
Social, adj. social, sociable
Socialism, s. socialisme, *m.*
Socialist, s. socialiste, *m.f.*
Socially, adv. d'une manière sociale
Society, s. société, *f.* *Benefit* —, société de secours mutuels. *To go into* —, aller dans le monde
Sock, s. chaussette, *f.* (*inner sole*) semelle, *f.*
Socket, s. (*of candles*) bobèche, *f.*, (*teeth*) alvéole, *m.*, (*eye*) orbite, *f.*, (*bones*) emboîture, *f.*
Socle, s. socle, *m.*
Sod, s. motte de gazon, *f.*, gazon, *m.*
Soda, s. soude, *f.* — *-water*, s. eau de Seltz, *f.*

Sodden, adj. bouilli, trempé, amolli
Soever, conj. que ce soit. *What great thing* — *a man propose to do in his life*, . . . quelque grande chose qu'on se soit proposé de faire dans sa vie, . . .
Sofa, s. canapé, *m.*, sofa, *m.* — *-bed*, s. lit canapé, *m.*
Soft, adj. mou, mol, molle, mollet, doux, tendre, (*fig.*) doux, aimable, délicat, (*colour*) tendre, (*light*) doux, (*weak*) mou, faible, sans énergie, niais, simple, trop bon, faible, (*water*) douce. — *climate*, doux climat. *The* — *er sex*, le sexe aimable. *Her form more* —, sa figure plus délicate. — *words!* tout doux! — *fellows*, les niais. — *-headed*, adj. au cerveau faible. — *-hearted*, adj. qui a le cœur tendre, pusillanime — *-voiced*, adj., — *-spoken*, adj. à la voix douce. — *-sawder*, s., — *-soap*, s. eau bénite de cour, *f.*
Soften, va. amollir, adoucir, radoucir, attendrir, apaiser, calmer, pallier. *To* — *down*, adoucir, radoucir, etc., (*faults*) atténuer. — vn. s'amollir, se ramollir, se radoucir, s'attendrir, s'apaiser, se calmer
Softening, s. amollissement, *m.*, ramollissement, *m.*, radoucissement, *m.*
Softly, adv. mollement, doucement, délicatement
Softness, s. mollesse, *f.*, douceur, *f.*, nature efféminée, *f.*, pusillanimité, *f.*, timidité, *f.*, docilité, *f.*, faiblesse d'esprit, *f.*, crédulité, *f.*, niaiserie, *f.*
Soil, va. salir, souiller, tacher, ternir
Soil, s. (*stain*) tache, *f.*, souillure, *f.*, saleté, *f.*, (*earth*) sol, *m.*, terre, *f.* terrain, *m.*, (*dung*) immondices, *f.pl.* *Night-* —, s. poudrette, *f.*
Sojourn, vn. rester, séjourner
Sojourn, s. séjour, *m.*
Sojourner, s. hôte passager, *m.*, qui ne fait qu'un court séjour
Sojourning, s. séjour, *m.*
Solace, va. soulager, adoucir, consoler, égayer
Solar, adj. solaire, du soleil
Solder, va. souder
Solder, s. soudure, *f.*
Soldering, s. soudure, *f.*
Soldier, s. soldat, *m.* militaire, *m.* (*see* FOOT, HORSE, &c.)
Soldierlike, Soldierly, adj. de soldat, militaire, martial
Soldiery, s. soldats, *m.pl.*, (*contempt*) soldatesque, *f.*
Sole, s. (*foot*) plante, *f.*, (*shoes*) semelle, *f.*, (*fish*) sole, *f.*
Sole, adj. seul, unique
Sole, va. mettre une semelle à. *To new-* —, ressemeler. *New-soling*, s. ressemelage, *m.* *To half-* —, mettre des

demi-semelles. *Thick- —d*, adj. à semelles épaisses
Solecism, s. solécisme, *m.*
Solely, adv. uniquement
Solemn, adj. solennel, grave, sérieux
Solemnity, s. solennité, *f.*, gravité, *f.*
Solemnization, s. solennisation, *f.*
Solemnize, va. solenniser, célébrer
Solemnly, adv. solennellement
Solicit, va. solliciter, inviter
Solicitation, s. sollicitation, *f.*
Solicitor, s. solliciteur, *m.*, (*law*) avoué, *m.*, notaire, *m.* *—'s office*, s. étude d'avoué, *f.* *— -general*, s. avocat général, *m.*
Solicitous, see ANXIOUS
Solid, adj. solide, massif, (*measure*) de capacité. *In — gold*, en or massif
Solid, s. solide, *m.*
Solidarity, s. solidarité, *f.*
Solidify, va. solidifier ; — vn. se solidifier
Solidity, s. solidité, *f.*
Solidly, adv. solidement
Soliloquy, s. monologue, *m.*, soliloque, *m.*
Solitarily, adv. solitairement
Solitariness, s. isolement, *m.*, solitude, *f.*, état solitaire, *m.*
Solitary, adj. solitaire, isolé, retiré
Solitude, s. solitude, *f.*, isolement, *m.*
Solo, s. solo, *m.*
Solstice, s. solstice, *m.*
Soluble, adj. soluble
Solution, s. solution, *f.*, dissolution, *f.*
Solve, va. résoudre
Solvency, s. solvabilité, *f.*
Solvent, adj. dissolvant, (*com.*) solvable
Solvent, s. dissolvant, *m.*
Some, adj. quelque, en . . . de, certains, plusieurs, un, une, du, de la, des, un peu de. *— -one*, quelqu'un, quelqu'une. *I have — good ones*, j'en ai de bons, *— people think*, certaines personnes croient
Some, pron. indef. quelques-uns, quelques-unes, les uns, les unes, en, un peu, une portion. *— . . ., others . . .*, les uns . . ., les autres . . .
Somebody, s. quelqu'un, *m.*, quelqu'une, *f.*, quelque chose, un personnage, *m.* *— else*, s. quelque autre
Somehow, adv. de façon ou d'autre
Somerset, s. culbute, *f.*, saut périlleux, *m.*
Something, s. quelque chose, *m.* *— like*, quelque chose qui ressemble à. *That is — like*, voilà qui est bien. *— good*, quelque chose de bon
Something, adv. quelque peu

Sometime, adv. autrefois, jadis
Sometimes, adv. quelquefois, parfois, tantôt
Somewhat, adv. quelque peu, un peu
Somewhat, adj. un tant soit peu
Somewhere, adv. quelque part
Somnambule, **Somnambulist**, s. somnambule, *m.f.*
Somnambulism, s. somnambulisme, *m.*
Somniferous, adj. somnifère, soporifique
Somnolence, s. somnolence, *f.*
Somnolent, adj. somnolent
Son, s. fils, *m.*, enfant, *m.* *— -in-law*, s. gendre, *m.* *His father's own —*, le fils de son père. *The Son of God*, le Fils de Dieu. *He is no — of mine*, il n'est pas mon fils, je le renie pour mon fils
Sonata, s. sonate, *f.*
Song, s. chant, *m.*, chanson, *f.*, ballade, *f.*, vers, *m.* *War —*, chant de guerre. *—s of woe*, des chants de deuil. *No —, no supper*, point d'argent, point de suisse. *To sing —s, comic —s*, chanter des chansons, des chansonnettes or la chansonnette. *— -book*, s., *— -writer*, s. chansonnier, *m.* *To make —s on*, chansonner, faire des chansons sur. *The poet's —*, le chant du poëte. *— -ennobled*, adj. célébré par les poëtes. *The — of —s, the — of Solomon*, le cantique des cantiques. *—s of peace*, cantiques de paix. *To buy for an old —*, acheter pour presque rien, pour un morceau de pain. *He is not to be put off with an old —*, il ne se contentera pas de
Songster, s. chanteur, *m.*
Songstress, s. chanteuse, *f.*
Sonnet, s. sonnet, *m.* *— -writer*, s. auteur de sonnets, *m.*
Sonorous, adj. sonore, retentissant
Sonorously, adv. d'une manière sonore
Sonorousness, s. sonorité, *f.*, nature sonore, *f.*, son éclatant, *m.*
Soon, adv. bientôt, tôt, (*early*) de bonne heure. *As — as*, aussitôt que, dès que. *Too —*, trop tôt. *—er or later*, tôt ou tard. *At the —est*, au plus tôt. *No —er had he uttered the words*, il n'avait pas plus tôt prononcé ces paroles. *He no —er had it*, dès qu'il l'eut. *I had or I would as — die as . . .*, j'aimerais autant mourir que . . . *—er than see you want*, plutôt que de vous voir dans le besoin
Soot, s. suie, *f.*
Sooth, adj. vrai, doux, agréable
Sooth, s. vérité, *f.*, réalité, *f.*

Soothe, va. flatter, charmer, apaiser, calmer
Soothsayer, s. devin, *m.*, devineresse, *f.*
Soothsaying, s. prédiction, *f.*
Sooty, adj. qui produit de la suie, de suie, barbouillé de suie, (*fig.*) noir, sombre
Sop, s. morceau trempé, *m.*, pain trempé, *m.*, appât, *m.*, (*fig.*) os à ronger, *m.*
Sophism, s. sophisme, *m.*
Sophist, s. sophiste, *m.*
Sophistic, **Sophistical**, adj. sophistique
Sophisticate, va. sophistiquer, altérer, falsifier
Sophistication, s. sophistication, *f.*, falsification, *f.*, frelatage, *m.*
Sophistry, s. sophismes, *m.pl.*
Soporific, adj. s. soporifique
Sorb, s. sorbier, *m.*, fruit du sorbier, *m.* *— -apple*, s. fruit du sorbier, *m.* *— -tree*, s. sorbier, *m.*
Sorcerer, s. sorcier, *m.*
Sorceress, s. sorcière, *f.*
Sorcery, s. sorcellerie, *f.*
Sordid, adj. malpropre, sale, vil, bas, sordide, avare
Sordidly, adv. salement, sordidement
Sordidness, s. malpropreté, *f.*, avarice sordide, *f.*
Sore, s. plaie, *f.*, mal, *m.*
Sore, adj. malade, qui fait mal, endolori, sensible, douloureux, (*severe*) violent, rude. *I have a — throat*, j'ai mal à la gorge. *To have — eyes*, avoir les yeux malades. *My finger is —*, le doigt me fait mal. *Don't touch it, it is so —*, ne touchez pas, (*fig.*) c'est trop sensible. *My arm is — all over*, j'ai le bras tout endolori
Sorely, adv. douloureusement, cruellement, amèrement
Soreness, s. sensibilité, *f.*, douleur, *f.*, mal, *m.*
Sorrel, s. oseille, *f.*
Sorrel, adj. saure, (*horse*) alezan. *Burnt —, light —*, alezan brûlé, alezan clair
Sorrily, adv. pauvrement, misérablement, chétivement
Sorrow, s. douleur, *f.*, chagrin, *m.*, peine, *f.*, tristesse, *f.*, affliction, *f.*
Sorrow, vn. s'affliger
Sorrowful, adj. triste, affligé, dans l'affliction, chagriné, douloureux, (*things*) affligeant
Sorrowfully, adv. tristement, avec chagrin
Sorrowfulness, s. tristesse, *f.*, douleur, *f.*
Sorrowing, s. affliction, *f.*
Sorrowless, adj. sans chagrin
Sorry, adj. fâché, contrarié, peiné, (*sad*) triste, (*paltry*) méchant, pauvre, mesquin, misérable. *I am — I did not see him*, je regrette de ne l'avoir pas vu. *I am — for it on your account*, j'en suis fâché pour vous
Sort, s. sorte, *f.*, genre, *m.*, espèce, *f.*, manière, *f.*, façon, *f.*, classe, *f.* *A good — of fellow, of woman*, un brave garçon, une bonne pâte de femme. *Of the right —*, de la bonne espèce. *One of the right —*, un brave homme. *Very good — of people*, de fort braves gens. *And all that — of thing*, et le reste. *In some —*, en quelque sorte. *To be out of —s*, être triste, n'être pas dans son assiette. *To put out of —s*, détraquer
Sort, va. trier, classer, ranger, (*match*) assortir ; — vn. se joindre, se réunir, (*metals*) s'allier, s'accorder, cadrer, être en rapport
Sorter, s. trieur, *m.*, -euse, *f.*
Sorting, s. triage, *m.*, tri, *m.*
Sot, s. sot, *m.*, (*drunkard*) ivrogne, *m.*
Sottish, adj. sot, imbécile, ivrogne, ivre
Sottishly, adv. sottement, en ivrogne
Sottishness, s. sottise, *f.*, abrutissement de l'ivresse, *m.*
Soul, s. âme, *f.*, (*person*) créature, *f.*, (*life*) vie, *f.* *All —s' day*, jour des morts, *m.*
Sound, adj. sain, entier, bien portant, (*strong*) sain, bon, solide, (*sleep*) profond, doux
Sound, s. (*geog.*) détroit, *m.*, sund, *m.*, (*fish*) vessie, *f.*, (*surg.*) sonde, *f.*, (*noise*) son, *m.*, bruit, *m.* *— -board*, s. table d'harmonie, *f.*, sommier d'orgue, *m.*, (*pulpit*) abat-voix, *m.* *— -post*, s. âme (de violon), *f.*
Sound, vn. sonner, retentir, résonner, (*appear*) paraître, sembler, avoir l'air, (*nav.*) sonder, jeter la sonde, (*surg.*) sonder ; — va. sonner de, faire sonner, faire retentir, faire résonner, (*praise*) chanter, célébrer
Sounding, adj. retentissant, qui résonne, sonore, (*fig.*) ronflant, pompeux
Soundly, adj. sainement, bien, de la bonne manière, (*well*) vigoureusement, comme il faut, ferme, (*sleep*) profondément
Soundness, s. état sain, *m.*, bon état, *m.*, bonne condition, *f.*, santé, *f.*, vigueur, *f.*, force, *f.*, sûreté, *f.*
Soup, s. soupe, *f.*, potage, *m.* *Rice —*, s. potage au riz, *m.* *Gravy —*, s. bouillon gras, *m.*, consommé, *m.* *Portable —*, s. bouillon en tablette, *f.* *— -kitchen*, s. fourneau gratuit, *f.* *— -ladle*, s. cuiller à potage, *f.*, louche, *f.* *— -plate*, s. assiette à soupe, *f.* *— -ticket*, s. bon de soupe, *m.* *— -tureen*, s. soupière, *f.*
Sour, adj. sur, aigre, (*fruit*) vert, acide, (*temper*) aigre, revêche, acariâtre, morose, dur, acerbe, âpre. *Rather*

—, *somewhat* —, un peu aigre, aigrelet. *To turn* —, va. aigrir, vn. s'aigrir. — *-crout*, s., — *-krout*, s. choucroute, *f.*
Sour, va. aigrir, acidifier, faire fermenter; — vn. s'aigrir, devenir aigre, fermenter
Source, s. source, *f.*, principe, *m.*, berceau, *m.*
Sourish, adj. aigrelet, suret
Sourly, adv. aigrement
Sourness, s. aigreur, *f.*, acidité, *f.*
Souse, s. marinade, *f.*
Souse, va. mariner, plonger, (*to wet*) mouiller, tremper, s'abattre sur
South, s. sud, *m.*, midi, *m.*
South, **Southerly**, adj. au sud, sud, au midi, du midi, du sud, méridional
Southern, adj. du sud, du midi, méridional, austral
Southward, adv. vers le sud
Sovereign, s. souverain, *m.*, -raine, *f.*, (*coin*) souverain (25 fr. 20 c.)
Sovereign, adj. souverain, suprême
Sovereignly, adv. souverainement, suprêmement
Sovereignty, s. souveraineté, *f.*
Sow, s. (*animal*) truie, *f.*, (*of iron*) gueuse, *f.*, (*of lead*) saumon, *m.*
Sow, va.n. semer, ensemencer, (*spread*) parsemer, répandre
Sower, s. semeur, *m.*, qui sème
Sowing, s. ensemencement, *m.* — *season* s. les semailles, *f.pl.* — *seed*, s. semaille, *f.*
Space, s. espace, *m.*, étendue, *f.*, intervalle, *m.*
Space, va. espacer
Spacious, adj. spacieux, vaste, immense
Spaciously, adv. spacieusement
Spaciousness, s. espace, *m.*, vaste étendue, *f.*, grandeur, *f.*
Spade, s. bêche, *f.*, (*cards*) pique, *m.*
Spadeful, s. pelletée, *f.*
Span, s. empan, *m.*, main, *f.*, (*arch.*) largeur, portée, *f.*, (*wings*) envergure, *f.*, (*horses, oxen*) paire, *f.* *The stretching of a* —, la longueur de la main. — *-long*, adj. de la longueur de la main, de la durée d'un instant. *This* — *of life*, cette vie si courte. *Whose days are dwindled to the shortest* —, dont les jours sont arrivés à leur dernière limite. *A beam twenty feet clear* —, une poutre ayant vingt pieds de portée franche
Span, adv. — *new*, tout flambant neuf (*see* SPICK)
Span, va. mesurer, atteler, (*nav.*) brider
Spangle, s. paillette, *f.*
Spangle, va. pailleter, parsemer de paillettes
Spaniel, s. épagneul, *m.*, -e, *f.*
Spanish, adj. Espagnol, d'Espagne. — *fly*, s. mouche cantharide, *f.* — *liquorice*, s. jus de réglisse, *f.*
Spar, s. (*nav.*) espars, *m.pl.*, (*min.*) spath, *m.*
Spar, vn. boxer, se disputer, quereller
Spare, va. réserver, mettre de côté, (*give*) disposer de, donner, céder, (*save*) épargner, faire grâce, épargner à, (*do without*) se passer de, épargner, ménager, (*grant*) accorder, dispenser. *I cannot* — *time to do it*, je ne puis trouver *or* je n'ai pas le temps de le faire. *I cannot* — *it*, je ne puis (vous) le donner. *If you have any to* —, si vous en avez de trop. *To have enough and to* —, en avoir plus qu'il n'en faut, en avoir à revendre. *To* — *the aged*, épargner les vieillards. — *my sight this pain*, épargnez cette douleur à mes yeux. *You are* — *d this affliction*, cette douleur vous est épargnée. — *your politics*, faites-nous grâce de votre politique. *We cannot* — *him*, nous ne pouvons nous passer de lui. *Without sparing any expense*, sans épargner aucuns frais. *Not to* — *one's trouble*, ne pas s'épargner de peine. — *yourself that trouble*, épargnez-vous cette peine. *Don't* — *me*, ne m'épargnez pas, ne me ménagez pas. *To* — *one's health*, ménager sa santé — vn. économiser, être économe, s'abstenir, se faire scrupule
Spare, adj. frugal, sobre, (*thin*) maigre, (*not wanted*) de rechange, de reste, de trop, disponible, de réserve. *To have a few* — *hours*, pouvoir disposer de quelques heures
Sparing, adj. faible, insuffisant, maigre, économe, qui épargne, frugal, sobre
Sparingly, adv. peu, faiblement, frugalement, modérément, parcimonieusement
Sparingness, s. frugalité, *f.*, parcimonie, *f.*
Spark, s. étincelle, *f.*, bluette, *f.*, (*pers.*) petit maître, *m.*, élégant, *m.*
Sparkle, s. étincelle, *f.*, éclat, *m.*
Sparkle, vn. (*beverages*) étinceler, pétiller, mousser
Sparkling, adj. étincelant
Sparrow, s. moineau, *m.*, passereau, *m.*, pierrot, *m.* — *-hawk*, s. épervier, émouchet, *m.*
Sparse, adj. clair-semé, épars
Spasm, s. spasme, *m.*
Spasmodic, **Spasmodical**, adj. spasmodique
Spatter, va. *see* BESPATTER
Spatterdashes, s.pl. guêtres, *f.pl.*
Spatula, s. spatule, *f.*
Spavin, s. éparvin, *m.*
Spawn, s. frai, *m.*, (*pers.*) race, *f.*, engeance, *f.*
Spawn, va. engendrer, produire; — vn. frayer
Speak, vn.a. parler, (*with*, avec) s'entretenir, parler, causer. *So to* —, pour ainsi dire. *To* — *well, ill*, parler bien, mal, dire du bien de, médire de. *To* — *out, to* — *up*, parler haut, parler hardiment
Speaker, s. personne qui parle, *m.*, orateur, *m.*, (*parliamentary*) président, *m.*, *The last* —, le préopinant
Speakership, s. présidence, *f.*
Speaking, s. parole, *f.*, discours, *m.* — *-trumpet*, s. porte-voix, *m.*, cornet acoustique, *m.* — *-tube*, s. cordon acoustique, *m.*
Spear, s. lance, *f.*, (*fishing*) harpon, *m.*
Spear, va. percer de sa lance, harponner
Spearman, s. lancier, *m.*
Special, adj. particulier, spécial, extraordinaire
Speciality, s. spécialité, *f.*
Specially, adv. spécialement, particulièrement, principalement
Specialty, s. contrat sous seing privé, *m.*
Specie, s. espèces, *f.pl.*, numéraire, *m.*
Species, s. forme, *f.*, espèce, *f.*
Specific, **Specifical**, adj. spécifique
Specific, s. spécifique, *m.*, remède, *m.*
Specifically, adv. spécifiquement
Specification, s. spécification, *f.*
Specify, va. spécifier, déterminer
Specimen, s. spécimen, *m.*, échantillon, *m.*, modèle, *m.*
Specious, adj. spécieux, plausible
Speciously, adv. spécieusement
Speciousness, s. nature spécieuse, *f.*
Speck, s. tache, *f.*, point, *m.*
Speck, va. tacher
Speckle, s. tache, *f.*
Speckle, va. tacheter, moucheter. —*d stockings*, des bas chinés
Spectacle, s. spectacle, *m.* —*s*, pl. lunettes, *f.pl.*, besicles, *f.pl.*
Spectator, s. spectateur, *m.*, -trice, *f.*
Spectre, s. spectre, *m.*, fantôme, *m.*
Spectrum, s. spectre solaire, *m.*
Speculate, vn. spéculer, méditer, (*com.*) jouer à la bourse
Speculation, s. spéculation, *f.*, méditation, *f.*
Speculative, adj. spéculatif, (*com.*) spéculateur
Speculator, s. spéculateur, *m.*, joueur, *m.*
Speculum, s. miroir, *m.*, (*surg.*) spéculum, *m.*
Speech, s. parole, *f.*, discours, *m.*, langage, *m.*, propos, *m.pl.*, harangue, *f.*, oraison, *f.* *The parts of* —, les parties du discours
Speechify, vn. pérorer
Speechless, adj. sans parole, interdit
Speechlessness, s. mutisme, *m.*
Speed, vn. se hâter, accourir, (*to succeed*) réussir, être heureux; — va. expédier, envoyer *or* faire partir à la hâte, hâter, presser, favoriser, assister
Speed, s. diligence, *f.*, hâte, *f.*, célérité, *f.*, rapidité, *f.*, vitesse, *f.*, succès, *m.*, réussite, *f.* *With all* —, en toute hâte. *At full* —, *full* —, (*pers.*) de toute sa vitesse, à toutes jambes, (*horse*) au grand galop, ventre à terre, à toute bride, à fond de train, (*carriages*) à grande vitesse
Speedily, adv. promptement, vite, rapidement
Speediness, s. diligence, *f.*, promptitude, *f.*, célérité, *f.*
Speedy, adj. prompt, rapide
Spell, s. récit, *m.*, charme, *m.*, sort, *m.* — *-bound*, adj. charmé, sous le charme
Spell, va.n. (*to write*) écrire, orthographier, épeler, lire, déchiffrer, (*charm*) charmer
Spellicans, s. onchets, *m. pl.*
Spelling, s. orthographe, *f.*, épellation, *f.* — *-book*, s. syllabaire, *m.*
Spend, va.n. dépenser, épuiser, consumer, (*time*) passer, (*waste*) perdre, prodiguer, gaspiller, (*exhaust*) épuiser, fatiguer. *A spent ball*, une balle morte
Spendthrift, s. prodigue, *m.*, dissipateur, *m.*, panier percé, *m.*
Sperm, **Spermaceti**, s. spermaceti, *m.* — *-oil*, s. huile de cachalot, *f.*
Spew, va.n. vomir
Sphere, s. sphère, *f.*
Spherical, adj. sphérique
Spherically, adv. sphériquement
Sphinx, s. sphinx, *m.*
Spice, s. épice, *f.*, aromate, *m.*, (*fig.*) peu, *m.*, brin, *m.*, grain, *m.*
Spice, va. épicer
Spick, adj. — *and span new*, tout battant neuf
Spicy, adj. épicé, fertile en épices, aromatique, (*fam.*) excellent, fameux, gentil
Spider, s. araignée, *f.*
Spigot, s. fausset, *m.*
Spike, s. (*grain*) épi, *m.*, (*nail*) grand clou, *m.*, (*wooden*) cheville, *f.*, (*bot.*) épi, *m.*
Spike, va. clouer, armer de pointes, hérisser, (*cannon*) enclouer
Spikenard, s. nard, *m.*
Spill, va.n. répandre, renverser, verser
Spill, s. allumette, *f.*
Spin, va.n. (*unroll*) filer, dérouler, (*protract*) prolonger,

(*tops*) faire aller, (*turn*) faire tourner. *To — out*, prolonger, allonger, faire traîner en longueur

Spinach, s. épinards, *m. pl.*

Spinal, adj. spinal, vertébral. — *marrow*, s. moelle épinière, *f.*

Spindle, s. fuseau, *m.*, broche, *f.*, pivot, *m.*, (*compass*) aiguille, *f.*, (*mach.*) essieu, *m.*, axe, *m.* — *-legs*, s., — *-shanks*, s. jambes de fuseau, *f.*

Spine, s. épine du dos, *f.*

Spinner, s. fileur, *m.*, -euse, *f.*, (*mill-owner*) filateur, *m.*

Spinning, s. filage, *m.*, filature, *f.* — *-jenny*, s., — *-frame*, s., — *-machine*, s., — *-mill*, s. filature, *f.*, filateur, *m.* — *-wheel*, s. rouet, *m.*

Spinster, s. fileuse, *f.*, (*not married*) demoiselle, *f.*

Spiral, adj. spiral

Spiral, s. spirale, *f.*

Spire, s. spirale, *f.*, (*steeples*) aiguille, *f.*, flèche, *f.*, clocher, *m.*

Spirit, s. souffle, *m.*, esprit, *m.*, âme, *f.*, fantôme, *m.*, apparition, *f.*, génie, *m.*, fierté, *f.*, cœur, *m.*, courage, *m.*, force, *f.*, vigueur, *f.*, fougue, *f.*, empressement, *m.*, entrain, *m.*, essence, *f.*, nature, *f.*, caractère, *m.*, spiritueux, *m.pl.*, liqueurs spiritueuses *or* alcooliques, *f.pl.*, alcool, *m.* — *-stirring*, adj. qui réveille l'âme, le courage. *To be in —s, in high —s*, être gai, en train, en verve. *To be out of —s, in low —s*, être triste, être tout triste, être abattu. *To raise one's —s*, encourager, égayer. *To keep up one's —s*, ne pas perdre courage. *To put in —s*, mettre en train. *—s of wine*, esprit-de-vin, trois-six, *m.* *—s of turpentine*, s. essence de térébenthine, *f.* — *-lamp*, s. lampe à esprit-de-vin, *f.* — *-level*, s. niveau à bulle d'air, *m.*

Spirit, va. animer, encourager, exciter. *To — away*, enlever secrètement

Spirited, adj. animé, à caractère . . ., à disposition . . ., d'humeur . . ., plein de courage, (*horse*) fougueux, plein de feu, (*fig.*) entraînant, chaleureux, vigoureux

Spiritedly, adv. avec courage, chaleureusement, avec force

Spiritedness, s. cœur, *m.*, courage, *m.*, feu, *m.*, ardeur, *f.*, force, *f.*, vigueur, *f.*, verve, *f.*

Spiritless, adj. sans esprit, sans âme, sans courage, lâche, abattu, morne, triste

Spiritual, adj. spirituel

Spiritualism, s. spiritualisme, *m.*

Spirituality, s. spiritualité, *f.*, spirituel, *m.*

Spiritually, adv. spirituellement

Spirituous, adj. spiritueux

Spirt, vn. jaillir, rejaillir, s'élancer ; — va. faire jaillir

Spirt, s. jaillissement, *m.*, rejaillissement, *m.*

Spiry, adj. spiral, enroulé, élancé, en flèche

Spit, s. broche, *f.* *To put on the —*, mettre à la broche

Spit, va.n. embrocher, (*to expectorate*) cracher. *It is not to be — upon*, ce n'est pas de la petite bière

Spite, **Spitefulness**, s. dépit, *m.*, (*hatred*) rancune, *f.*, méchanceté, *f.* *In — of*, en dépit de, malgré. *Out of —*, par pur dépit. *To have, to owe, to bear a — to*, en vouloir à, avoir une dent contre

Spite, va. en vouloir à, blesser, offenser

Spiteful, adj. haineux, rancunier, méchant, malveillant, ennemi

Spitefully, adv. méchamment, par méchanceté

Spitting, s. crachement, *m.*

Spittle, s. salive, *f.*

Spittoon, s. crachoir, *m.*

Splash, vn.a. clapoter, éclabousser, patauger

Splash, s. éclaboussure, *f.*, chûte dans l'eau, *f.*, bruit, *m.*

Splashboard, s. garde-crotte, *m.*

Splay, va. étendre, déployer, faire obliquer, écarter, (*a horse*) épauler. — *-foot*, s. pied plat. — *-footed*, adj. au large pied, au pied plat

Spleen, s. rate, *f.*, bile, *f.*, (*anger*) colère, *f.*, mauvaise humeur, *f.*, (*temper*) humeur noire, *f.*, ennui, *m.*

Spleened, adj. dératé

Splendid, adj. resplendissant, éclatant, splendide, magnifique, somptueux

Splendidly, adv. avec éclat, d'une manière resplendissante, splendidement, magnifiquement

Splendour, s. splendeur, *f.*, éclat, *m.*, magnificence, *f.*

Splenetic, adj. atrabilaire

Splice, va. (*nav.*) épisser, (*fam.*) unir, marier

Splice, s. épissure, *f.*

Splinter, s. éclat, *m.*, (*bone*) esquille, *f.*, (*surg.*) éclisse, *f.*

Splinter va. briser en éclats, (*surg.*) éclisser

Split, va. fendre, diviser, partager, (*nav.*) crever, déchirer. *To — hairs*, épiloguer. — vn. se fendre, se briser, éclater, (*laughter*) crever

Split, s. fente, *f.*, crevasse, *f.*, (*fig.*) séparation, *f.*, querelle, *f.* — *-peas*, s. pois cassés, *m.pl.*

Splitter, s. fendeur, *m.*

Splutter, s. vacarme, *m.*

Splutter, vn. bredouiller, (*pen*) cracher, éclabousser. *To — out*, cracher, rejeter

Spoil, va. (*strip*) dépouiller, piller, spolier, voler, (*goods*) gâter, corrompre ; — vn. se gâter, se corrompre

Spoil, s. butin, *m.*, dépouilles, *f.pl.*, (*serpent*) dépouille, *f.*

Spoiler, s. spoliateur, *m.*, -trice, *f.*, pillard, *m.*, qui gâte, *m.*, corrupteur, *m.*, -trice, *f.*

Spoiling, s. action de dépouiller, de gâter, etc.

Spoke, s. rayon, *m.*, (*wheel*) rais, *m.pl.*

Spokesman, s. orateur, *m.*, organe, *m.*

Spoliate, va.n. spolier, piller

Spoliation, s. spoliation, *f.*

Sponge, s. éponge, *f.*, (*artil.*) écouvillon, *m.* — *-cake*, s. biscuit léger, *m.*

Sponge, va. éponger, nettoyer avec une éponge, passer l'éponge sur, (*artil.*) écouvillonner ; — vn. (*upon, on, . . .*) écornifler

Sponger, s. qui éponge, pique-assiette, *m.*

Sponginess, s. nature spongieuse, *f.*

Sponging-house, s. maison de garde de commerce, *f.*

Spongy, adj. spongieux

Sponsor, s. parrain, *m.*, marraine, *f.*, garant, *m.*

Spontaneity, s. spontanéité, *f.*

Spontaneous, adj. spontané

Spontaneously, adv. spontanément

Spoon, s. cuiller, *f.*, cuillère, *f.*, (*pop.*) nigaud, *m.* *To be born with a silver — in one's mouth*, être né coiffé

Spooney, s. nigaud, *m.*

Spooney, adj. langoureux

Spoonful, s. cuillerée, *f.*

Sporadic, adj. sporadique

Sport, s. jeu, *m.*, divertissement, *m.*, amusement, *m.*, plaisir, *m.*, ébats, *m.pl.*, (*toy*) jouet, *m.*, jeu, *m.*, (*fun*) moquerie, *f.*, raillerie, *f.*, (*in the country*) chasse, *f.*, pêche, *f.*, (*races*) courses, *f.pl.* *In —*, en riant, pour rire. *To make — at*, se divertir de

Sport, va. divertir, représenter, étaler, se pavaner dans. *To — one's oak*, montrer visage de bois. — vn. jouer, se divertir, s'amuser, s'ébattre, folâtrer, chasser, pêcher, etc., suivre les courses

Sportful, adj. joyeux, gai, folâtre

Sportfully, adv. joyeusement, avec enjouement, en plaisantant

Sportfulness, s. gaieté, *f.*, enjouement, *m.*, folâtrerie, *f.*

Sporting, s. chasse, *f.*, pêche, *f.*

Sportive, see SPORTFUL

Sportsman, s. chasseur, *m.*, pêcheur, *m.*

Spot, s. tache, *f.*, souillure, *f.*, (*speckle*) moucheture, *f.*, (*place*) endroit, *m.*, lieu, *m.*, place, *f.* *On* or *upon the —*, sur le lieu, à l'endroit même

Spot, va. tacher, souiller, (*speckle*) moucheter, marquer

Spotless, adj. sans tache, pur

Spotty, adj. see SPOTTED

Spouse, s. époux, *m.*, épouse, *f.*

Spout, s. tuyau, *m.*, (*of houses*) gouttière, *f.*, (*of vases*) bec, *m.*, bout, *m.*, (*water*) trompe, *f.*, typhon, *m.*

Spout, va. faire jaillir, lancer, (*fam.*) déclamer, débiter, cracher. *To — Latin*, cracher du Latin. — vn. jaillir, rejaillir, déclamer

Spouter, s. déclamateur, *m.*

Spouting, s. jaillissement, *m.*, déclamation, *f.*

Sprain, va. donner une entorse à, fouler

Sprain, s. entorse, *f.*, foulure, *f.*

Sprat, s. éperlan, *m.* *To give a — to catch a herring*, donner un œuf pour avoir un bœuf

Sprawl, vn. s'étendre, se prélasser, s'étaler, (*child*) se traîner à quatre pattes

Spray, s. (*twig*) branche, *f.*, brindille, *f.*, brin, *m.*, (*water*) écume, *f.*

Spread, va. étendre, déployer, (*scatter*) répandre, se répandre sur, épandre, (*sails*) ouvrir, étendre, (*table*) couvrir. *To — abroad*, étendre au loin, répandre au loin, propager, faire courir. *To — out*, étendre, étaler, répandre. — vn. s'étendre, se déployer, s'élargir, se dérouler

Spread, s. étendue, *f.*, expansion, *f.*, développement, *m.*, propagation, *f.* — *-eagle*, s. aigle éployée, *f.*

Spreader, s. propagateur, *m.*

Spreading, s. extension, *f.*, propagation, *f.*

Spree, s. farce, *f.*, bamboche, *f.*

Sprig, s. brin, *m.*, brindille, *f.*

Sprightliness, s. vivacité, *f.*, animation, *f.*, vie, *f.*, espièglerie, *f.*

Sprightly, adj. animé, vif, espiègle, éveillé, malin, enjoué, gai

Spring, vn. (*to grow*) naître, pousser, (*fig.*) naître, descendre, (*water, light*) jaillir, rejaillir, s'élancer, (*from*, de) naître, sortir, provenir, venir, découler, dériver, (*day*) poindre, naître, (*to bound*) s'élancer, bondir, sauter, se précipiter, faire ressort, (*wood, &c.*) déjeter. *To — away* s'éloigner d'un bond. *To — back*, sauter en arrière, reculer vivement, faire ressort. — va. (*game*) faire lever, (*a mine, a rattle, &c.*) faire jouer, (*to jump*) franchir, franchir d'un bond, s'élancer par-dessus, (*a leak*) faire

Spring, s. printemps, *m.*, (*water*) source, *f.*, fontaine, *f.*, (*mechan.*) ressort, *m.*, élasticité, *f.*, élan, *m.*, (*fig.*) source, *f.*, origine, *f.*, cause, *f.*, principe, *m.*, (*jump*) bond, élan, *m.*, saut, *m.*, (*nav.*) fente oblique, *f.*, voie d'eau, *m.* *To take a —*, prendre son élan, faire un bond, (*at*, sur) s'élancer

Spring, adj. du printemps, printanier, à ressort, élastique, (*carriages*) suspendu. — *-tide*, s. grande marée, *f.* — *-back*, dos brisé. — *-board*, s. tremplin, *m.* — *-carriage*, s. carrosse suspendu, *m.* — *-cart*, s. voiture suspendue, *f.* — *-mattress*, s. sommier élastique, *m.* — *-van*, s. tapissière, *f.*

Springe, s. lacet, *m.*, lacs, *m.*, collet, *m.*

Springiness, s. élasticité, *f.*

Springing, s. croissance, *f.*, (*water*) jaillissement, *m.*, crue, *f.*

Springy, adj. élastique, plein de sources

Sprinkle, va. répandre, jeter, (*liquids*) arroser, (*salt*) saupoudrer, (*holy water*) asperger

Sprinkler, s. aspersoir, *m.*, goupillon, *m.*

Sprinkling, s. action de répandre, *f.*, aspersion, *f.*, (*fig.*) petite quantité, *f.*, brin, *m.*

Sprite, s. esprit, *m.*, farfadet, *m.*, lutin, *m.*

Sprout, vn. germer, pousser, bourgeonner

Sprout, s. jet, *m.*, pousse, *f.*, germe, *m.*, (*cabbage*) chou vert, *m.* —*s*, pl. choux (de Bruxelles), *m.pl.*

Spruce, s. sapin, *m.*

Spruce, adj. pimpant, beau, bien mis, bien paré

Spruce, va. attifer, parer, habiller ; — vn. se parer, se requinquer

Spruceness, s. mise pimpante, *f.*

Spume, s. écume, *f.*

Spume, vn. écumer

Spur, s. éperon, *m.*, aiguillon, *m.*, stimulant, *m.*, mobile, *m.*, impulsion, *f.*, excitation, *f.*, (*of birds*) ergot, *m.*, éperon, *m.*, (*mountains*) contre-fort, *m.*, (*agric.*) ergot, *m.*, seigle ergoté, *m.* *To act upon the — of the moment*, agir sous l'impulsion du moment

Spur, va. donner de l'éperon à, (*fig.*) aiguillonner, stimuler, pousser, exciter ; — vn. courir à franc étrier, stimuler, exciter. *To — after, to — on*, suivre, courir de toute la vitesse de son cheval

Spurious, adj. bâtard, illégitime, (*drugs, &c.*) falsifié, (*writing*) apocryphe

Spuriousness, s. illégitimité, *f.*, nature falsifiée, *f.*, (*fig.*) fausseté, *f.*, (*books*) caractère apocryphe, *m.*

Spurn, va. repousser *or* rejeter avec dédain, traiter avec mépris

Spurred, adj. éperonné, ergoté

Sputter, vn. cracher, bredouiller, (*pens*) cracher, éclabousser

Sputterer, s. bredouilleur, *m.*, -euse, *f.*

Spy, s. espion, *m.* *To play the —*, faire l'espion. *For a —*, comme espion. — *-money*, s. salaire d'espion, *m.*, (*polit.*) fonds secrets, *m.pl.*

Spy, va.n. voir, apercevoir, découvrir, épier, espionner. *To — out*, découvrir, (*into*) scruter, examiner de près

Squab, s. canapé, *m.*, coussin, *m.*

Squabble, vn. se chamailler

Squabble, s. querelle, *f.*, bagarre, *f.*

Squabbler, s. querelleur, *m.*, qui chamaille

Squabby, adj. gros et court, corpulent, épais

Squad, s. (*milit.*) escouade, *f.*

Squadron, s. (*milit.*) escadron, *m.*, (*nav.*) escadre, *f.*

Squalid, adj. malpropre, sale, crasseux

Squalidity, Squalidness, s. malpropreté, *f.*, saleté, *f.*

Squall, vn. brailler, crier

Squall, s. cri, *m.*, (*wind*) grain, *m.*, rafale, *f.* *Look out for a —*, veillez au grain, gare la bombe

Squaller, s. braillard, *m.*, -e, *f.*

Squalling, adj. braillard

Squalling, s. braillerie, *f.*

Squally, adj. de rafale, d'orage

Squander, va. dissiper, gaspiller, manger

Squanderer, s. dissipateur, *m.*, prodigue, *m.f.*, gaspilleur, *m.*

Squandering, s. gaspillage, *m.*

Square, adj. carré, (*fig.*) vrai, juste, honnête, équitable, (*accounts*) égalisé, balancé. — *-built*, adj. aux épaules carrées. *To make —, all —*, égaliser, mettre tout en règle

Square, s. carré, *m.*, (*pattern*) carreau, *m.*, (*chess*) case, *m.*, (*place*) place, *f.*, (*instr.*) équerre, *m.*, (*honesty*) rectitude, *f.*, probité, *f.* *To form into —*, former en carré, se former en carré. *To break the —*, rompre le carré. *To stand upon a —*, être à une case. *To see how —s go*, voir comment va le jeu, comment il en est. *In the public —*, sur la place publique. *All 's —*, tout est en règle. *Ten feet in —*, dix pieds de côté. *To live upon the — with*, vivre sur un pied d'égalité avec. *To play upon the —*, jouer carrément

Square, va. carrer, régler, mesurer, accommoder, (*account*) égaliser, balancer, (*math.*) carrer, (*wood*) équarrir ; — vn. cadrer (avec), s'accorder (avec), se rapporter à

Squareness, s. forme carrée, *f.*

Squash, va. écraser, aplatir

Squash, s. écrasement, *m.*, aplatissement, *m.*, (*bot.*) courge, *f.*

Squat, vn. s'accroupir, se blottir, se tapir

Squat, adj. accroupi, blotti, (*short and thick*) ramassé, trapu

Squatter, s. colon, *m.*

Squeak, vn. crier, pousser un cri aigu

Squeak, s. cri, *m.*, cri aigu, *m.*

Squeaker, s. criard, *m.*

Squeaking, s. cris aigus, *m.pl.*, son aigre, *m.*

Squeaking, adj. criard

Squeal, vn. crier, brailler

Squeal, s. cri aigu, *m.*

Squeamish, adj. sujet aux nausées, facile à dégoûter, (*fig.*) fastidieux, difficile, qui fait le dégoûté

Squeamishness, s. disposition aux nausées, *f.*, (*fig.*) délicatesse exagérée, *f.*, goût difficile, *m.*

Squeeze, va.n. presser, serrer, comprimer, (*out, of*, de) faire sortir, exprimer, tirer, (*through*, à travers) forcer, (*fig.*) pressurer, opprimer. *He —d my hand*, il me serra la main. *We shall be —d to death*, on sera serré à étouffer. *To — in*, faire entrer, mettre en serrant beaucoup. *To — out*, exprimer, faire sortir. *To — oneself into*, entrer en se serrant beaucoup dans, se faufiler dans

Squeeze, Squeezing, s. compression, *f.*, (*of hands*) serrement, *m.*

Squib, s. pétard, *m.*, (*satire*) satire personnelle, *f.*, pasquinade, *f.*

Squint, adj. louche. — *-eyed*, adj. louche, au regard louche

Squint, s. regard louche, *m.*, coup d'œil, *m.*, regard de côté, *m.* *To give, to have a — at*, regarder de côté, regarder

Squint, vn.a. loucher

Squinting, s. strabisme, *m.*

Squire, s. écuyer, *m.*, (*gentleman*) propriétaire campagnard, *m.*, (*fig.*) chevalier, *m.*, cavalier, *m.*

Squirrel, s. écureuil, *m.*

Squirt, va. lancer, seringuer

Squirt, s. seringue, *f.*, (*water*) jet, *m.*

Stab, va. percer, frapper, poignarder

Stab, s. coup, *m.*, coup de poignard, *m.*, coup de couteau, *m.*

Stability, s. stabilité, *f.*, constance, *f.*, consistance, *f.*, permanence, *f.*, solidité, *f.*

Stable, adj. stable, fixe, arrêté, constant

Stable, s. écurie, *f.*, (*for cows, &c.*) étable, *f.* — *-boy*, s., — *-man*, s. garçon d'écurie, *m.* — *-keeper*, s. loueur de chevaux, *m.* — *-yard*, s. cour d'écurie, *f.*

Stable, va. loger, faire entrer dans une écurie *or* dans une étable

Stabling, s. écuries, *f.pl.*, étables, *f.pl.*

Stack, s. (*hay*) meule, *f.*, (*wood*) pile, *f.*, (*milit.*) faisceau, *m.*, (*chimney*) souche, *f.*

Stack, va. mettre en meule, ameulonner, empiler, mettre en faisceaux

Stadtholder, s. stathouder, *m.*

Stadtholdership, s. stathoudérat, *m.*

Staff, s. bâton, *m.*, soutien, *m.*, (*pilgrim*) bourdon, *m.*, (*of a lance*) bois, *m.*, hampe, *f.*, (*mus.*) portée, *f.*, (*milit.*) état-major, *m.* — *-officer*, s. officier d'état-major, *m.*, (*pers.*) corps, *m.*, personnel, *m.* *Editorial —*, s. rédaction, *f.*

Stag, s. cerf, *m.* — *-beetle*, s. cerf-volant, *m.* — *-hound*, s. chien courant, *m.*

Stage, s. estrade, *f.*, échafaud, *m.*, (*theatre*) scène, *f.*, (*degree*) période, *f.*, phase, *f.*, degré, *m.*, (*relay*) étape, *f.*, relais, *m.pl.*, (*coach*) diligence, *f.*, voiture publique, *f.* *To come* or *go on the —*, entrer en scène. *To represent upon the —*, mettre sur la scène. *To be all the time upon the —*, être toujours en scène. *To quit the —*, disparaître de la scène. — *-box*, s. loge d'avant-scène, *f.* — *-directions*, s.pl. indications scéniques, *f.pl.* — *-door*, s. entrée des artistes, *f.* — *-play*, s. pièce de théâtre, *f.* — *-player*, s. comédien, *m.*, -enne, *f.* — *-coach*, s. diligence, *f.*, voiture publique, *f.*

Stager, s. routier, *m.*

Stagger, vn. chanceler, hésiter ; — va. faire chanceler, faire hésiter, ébranler, frapper de stupeur

Staggering, s. action de chanceler, *f.*, hésitation, *f.*, faiblesse, *f.*

Staggers, s.pl. vertige, *m.*, délire, *m.*

Stagnancy, s. stagnation, *f.*

Stagnant, adj. stagnant, dans un état de stagnation, engourdi, inactif

Stagnate, vn. être *or* devenir *or* rester stagnant, (*business*) être dans un état de stagnation

Stagnation, s. stagnation, *f.*

Staid, adj. posé, sérieux, grave

Staidness, s. gravité, *f.*, sérieux, *m.*

Stain, va. tacher, entacher, souiller, (*glass, &c.*) peindre, (*stuffs*) teindre, (*paint*) peindre, imprimer

Stain, s. tache, *f.*, souillure, *f.*, opprobre, *m.*, honte, *f.*, couleur, *f.*, teinte, *f.* *To get out a —*, ôter, enlever une tache

Stained, adj. taché, souillé, terni, (*paper*) peint, teint, (*wood, &c.*) mis en couleur, imprimé. — *glass*, s. verre de couleur, *m.* — *glass-windows*, s.pl. vitraux peints, *m.pl.*

Stainer, s. teinturier, *m.*

Stainless, adj. sans tache, pur

Stair, s. marche, *f.*, degré, *m.* —*s*, pl. escalier, *m.* *Above —s, up —s*, en haut, dans le salon. *Below —s, down —s*, en bas, dans la cuisine. *To come or go up —s, down —s*, monter, descendre (l'escalier)

Staircase, s. escalier, *m.* *Private —*, s. escalier dérobé, *m.* *Principal —*, s. grand escalier, *m.*

Stake, s. pieu, *m.*, pal, *m.*, échalas, *m.*, jalon, *m.*, piquet, *m.*, (*pile*) bûcher, *m.*, (*at play*) enjeu, *m.*, jeu, *m.*, (*races*) prix, *m.* *His honour was at —*, son honneur était en jeu

Stake, va. garnir de pieux, (*play*) mettre au jeu, jouer. *To — out*, jalonner

Stalactite, s. stalactite, *f.*

Stale, adj. (*bread*) rassis, (*beer*) éventé, plat, (*old*) vieux, (*out of date*) suranné, usé

Stale, s. vieille urine, *f.*

Stale, vn. uriner

Staleness, s. (*of bread*) état rassis, *m.*, (*beer, &c.*) évent, *m.*, (*triteness*) état vieilli, *m.*, état suranné, *m.*

Stalk, vn. marcher doucement, (*hunt*) chasser à l'affût, (*to walk with pride*) marcher fièrement, d'un pas majestueux

Stalk, s. (*bot.*) tige, *f.*, pied, *m.*, (*flower*) pédoncule, *m.*, (*walk*) pas majestueux, *m.*, démarche fière, *f.*

Stalking-horse, s. cheval simulé, *m.*, (*fig.*) masque, *m.*, prétexte, *m.*

Stall, s. (*of stables*) stalle, *f.*, étable, *f.*, (*small shop*) étalage, *m.*, échoppe, *f.*, (*butcher's*) étal, *m.*, (*church, theatre*) stalle, *f.*

Stall, va. mettre dans une étable or dans une écurie

Stallage, s. étalage, *m.*

Stallion, s. étalon, *m.*

Stalwart, adj. robuste, vigoureux, athlétique

Stamen, s. (*bot.*) étamine, *f.*, constitution, *f.*, force vitale, *f.*, force, *f.*

Stammer, vn.a. bégayer, balbutier

Stammer, **Stammering**, s. bégaiement, *m.*, balbutiement, *m.*

Stammerer, s. bègue, *m.f.*

Stammering, adj. bègue

Stamp, va.n. (*with the foot*) frapper du pied, frapper, (*pound*) broyer, briser, (*ore*) bocarder, (*mark*) empreindre, imprimer, marquer, mettre l'empreinte à, (*fig.*) imprimer, graver, empreindre, (*coins*) monnayer, frapper, estamper, (*com.*) estampiller, estamper, (*letters*) timbrer, (*gold, silver*) contrôler, poinçonner. *To — on, upon*, frapper du pied, piétiner sur, fouler aux pieds. *To — out*, éteindre, (*fig.*) étouffer à coup de

Stamp, s. (*coin*) poinçon, *m.*, coin, *m.*, (*impression*) empreinte, *f.*, marque, *f.*, (*fig.*) sceau, *m.*, (*kind, fig.*) caractère, *m.*, ordre, *m.*, genre, *m.*, calibre, *m.*, trempe, *f.*, (*image*) image, *f.*, médaille, *f.*, (*cut*) estampe, *f.*, (*admin.*) timbre, *m.*, (*gold*) contrôle, *m.*, (*com.*) estampille, *f.*, (*metal*) bocard, *m.*, pilon, *m.* *With a —*, en frappant du pied. *To be of the right —*, être du bon coin, être de la bonne trempe. *To set the — to*, mettre le sceau. *One of his own —*, un homme du même calibre que lui, de sa trempe. —*-act*, s. loi du timbre, *f.* —*-collector*, s. percepteur du droit de timbre, *f.* —*-duty*, s. timbre, *m.*, impôt du timbre, *m.* —*-note*, s. estampille de douane, *f.* —*-office*, s. timbre, *m.*, bureau du timbre, *m.*

Stampede, s. fuite précipitée, *f.*

Stamper, s. qui timbre, etc., pilon, *m.*, bocard, *m.*

Stamping, s. action de frapper du pied, *f.*, trépignement, *m.*, piétinement, *m.*, action d'empreindre, de timbrer, *m.* —*-machine*, s. machine pour frapper la monnaie, *f.* —*-mill*, s. bocard, *m.*

Stanch, va. étancher, arrêter; — vn. s'arrêter

Stanch, adj. solide, fort, ferme, dévoué

Stanchion, s. étançon, *m.*

Stand, vn. être debout, se tenir debout, (*rise*) se dresser, s'élever, (*not to fall*) soutenir, (*not to move*) s'arrêter, rester, (*water*) être stagnante, (*last*) exister, durer, (*colours*) être bon teint, (*remain in force*) se maintenir, subsister, (*against*, contre) s'élever (*for*, pour) lutter, combattre, (*resist*) se défendre, tenir, attendre de pied ferme, (*fig.*) persister, persévérer, (*in an order*) se tenir, être, se trouver, (*for*) tenir lieu (de), remplacer, (*in*, de) consister, (*as a candidate*) se présenter, (*at cards*) s'y tenir. *I — corrected*, j'avoue que j'ai tort. *As matters —*, au point où en sont les affaires. — *and deliver!* la bourse ou la vie! *To — good*, être valable, se trouver vrai. *To — for the port*, se diriger vers le port. *To — away*, s'éloigner, s'écarter. *To — against*, se tenir contre, résister à. *To — back*, se tenir en arrière, reculer. *To — by*, être auprès (de), être présent, y être, être négligé, soutenir, défendre, s'en tenir à, s'en rapporter à. *To — for*, représenter, tenir lieu de, signifier, soutenir, (*candidate*) se présenter pour, se porter pour. *To — forth* or *forward*, se mettre en avant, s'offrir. *To — in*, être dans, être exposé à, persister dans. *To stand out*, sortir (*arts*) se détacher, ressortir, (*resist*) tenir bon, tenir ferme. *To — out to sea*, gagner le large. *To — to*, persister dans, soutenir, maintenir, appuyer, s'en tenir à, travailler à, (*arms*) prendre. *To — up against*, se lever contre, s'attaquer à, supporter. *To — up for*, défendre. *To — upon*, se tenir sur, être sur, se piquer de, être fier de. *To — with*, être conforme à, contester, disputer. — va. mettre debout, placer, poser, (*a siege*) soutenir, (*a position*) maintenir, résister à, endurer, supporter, (*a chance*) courir, (*fam.*) payer. *To — fire*, aller au feu, soutenir le feu. *To — the test*, résister à l'épreuve

Stand, s. place, *f.*, position, *f.*, halte, *f.*, pause, *f.*, arrêt, *m.*, interruption, *f.*, (*com.*) stagnation, *f.*, résistance, *f.*, difficulté, *f.*, position embarrassante, *f.*, (*support*) table, *f.*, dessous, *m.*, pied, *m.*, (*at races*) tribune, *f.*, (*stall*) comptoir, *m.*, (*market*) étal, *m.*, (*cabs*) place, *f.*, station, *f.*, (*fire-irons*) garniture, *f.* *To be at a —*, s'arrêter, être dans l'embarras. *To come to a —*, s'arrêter. *To make a —*, s'arrêter, faire halte. *Liquor- —*, s. porte-liqueurs, *m.* — *of arms*, fusil et accessoires, les armes, *f.pl.* — *of colours*, s. drapeau, *m.*

Stand-point, s. place, *f.*, point de vue, *m.*

Stand-still, s. action de s'arrêter, *f.* *To be at a —*, rester, demeurer, se trouver court. *To bring to a —*, arrêter court

Standard, s. étendard, *m.*, bannière, *f.*, drapeau, *m.*, (*nav.*) pavillon, *m.*, (*type*) étalon, *m.*, type, *m.*, (*fig.*) modèle, *m.*, (*of gold, &c.*) mesure, *f.*, règle, *f.*, (*tree*) arbre en plein vent, *m.*, (*prop*) support, *m.* —*-bearer*, s. porte-étendard, *m.*, porte-drapeau, *m.*

Standard, adj. qui sert d'étalon, de type, de modèle, (*author*) classique, (*money*) au titre, (*price*) régulateur, (*hort.*) de plein vent

Stander, s. qui se tient debout. —*-by*, s. spectateur, *m.*, assistant, *m.*

Standing, adj. (*com.*) sur pied, (*upright*) à pied, debout, (*fixed*) fixe, à demeure, permanent, invariable, de fondation, habituel, (*colour*) solide, durable, (*water*) dormant, stagnant. — *measure*, mesure type, *f.* — *army*, armée permanente, *f.* *A — dish*, plat de fondation, *m.* — *joke*, plaisanterie habituelle, *f.*

Standing, s. action de se tenir debout, *f.*, (*pers.*) pose, *f.*, place, *f.*, position, *f.*, (*duration*) durée, *f.*, date, *f.*, (*lawyer's*) stage, *m.*, (*shop*) boutique, *f.*, étalage, *m.* —*-still*, s. inaction, *f.*

Stannary, s. mine d'étain, *f.* — *rights*, droits royaux sur les mines d'étain, *m.pl.*

Stanza, s. stance, *f.*, strophe, *f.*

Staple, s. (*iron*) crampon, *m.*, piton, *m.*, (*of a lock*) gâche, *f.*, (*market*) entrepôt, *m.*, marché, *m.*, (*goods*) denrées, *f.pl.*, denrée principale, *f.*, produit principal, *m.*, (*fig.*) objet principal, *m.*, matière, *f.*, (*quality*) qualité, *f.*, propriété, *f.*, (*a small piece of silk, &c.*) fibre, *f.*, brin, *m.*

Staple, adj. d'entrepôt, de marché, (*settled*) établi, régulier, principal

Stapler, s. marchand, *m.*, -e, *f.*

Star, s. étoile, *f.*, astre, *m.*, (*badge*) décoration, *f.*, crachat, *m.*, (*print.*) astérisque, *m.*, étoile, *f.*

Star, va. étoiler, semer d'étoiles, (*fig. with*) semer (de), parsemer (de); — vn. briller, rayonner

Starboard, s. tribord, *m.*

Starboard, adj. de tribord

Starch, s. amidon, *m.*, empois, *m.*, (*fig.*) roideur, *f.*, manières empesées, *f.pl.* — *manufactory*, s. amidonnerie, *f.* —*-maker*, s. amidonnier, *m.*

Starch, va. empeser, amidonner

Starched, adj. empesé, amidonné, (*fig.*) empesé, roide, guindé

Starchedness, s. roideur, *f.*, manières empesées, *f.pl.*

Starcher, s. empeseur, *m.*, -euse, *f.*

Stare, vn.a. regarder fixement, fixer ses yeux sur, regarder effrontément, ouvrir de grands yeux (à), regarder avec étonnement

Stare, s. regard fixe, *m.*, regard effronté, *m.*

Starer, s. qui regarde

Staring, adj. grand ouvert, ébahi, (*colours*) voyant, grand, à grand dessin

Stark, adj. vigoureux, pur, vrai, véritable, franc

Starless, adj. sans étoiles

Starlight, s. lumière des étoiles, *f.*

Starlight, adj. étoilé, éclairé par les étoiles

Starling, s. sansonnet, *m.*, étourneau, *m.*

Starred, adj. étoilé, parsemé d'étoiles, né sous une (mauvaise) étoile

Starry, adj. étoilé, parsemé d'étoiles, étincelant

Start, vn. tressaillir, faire un mouvement subit, être étonné, s'étonner, (*rush*) s'élancer, (*from*, de) se lever vivement, (*to grow*) s'élever, surgir, naître, (*to go aside*) s'écarter, se jeter de côté, (*with*, avec) commencer, débuter, (*against*) en opposition à, (*for*, pour) se présenter, (*from*, *out of*, de) sortir, (*to wake*) s'éveiller en sursaut, (*wood*) se déjeter, (*boards*) se disjoindre, (*cask*) fuir. *To — with*, comme point de départ, pour commencer. *To — in life*, débuter dans la vie. *To — aside*, faire un écart. *To — away*, partir vivement. *To — back*, se jeter en arrière. *To — forth*, *to — out*, s'élancer dehors. *To — out of one's sleep*, s'éveiller en sursaut. *To — off*, partir précipitamment. — va. faire tressaillir, faire peur à, alarmer, effrayer, troubler, (*a stag*) lancer, faire lever, faire partir, (*races*) donner le signal du départ, (*an idea*) lancer, mettre en avant, mettre sur le tapis, (*question*) soulever, démettre, déboîter, (*boards*) disjoindre, (*wood*) faire déjeter, (*cask*) défoncer

Start, s. tressaillement, *m.*, mouvement subit, *m.*, saut, *m.*, élan, *m.*, départ, *m.*, début, *m.*, commencement, *m.*, avance, *f.* *By —s*, par boutades. *To have* or *get the — of*, devancer, prendre les devants sur

Starter, s. auteur, *m.*, inventeur, *m.*, qui met en avant, qui soulève, (*hunt.*) batteur, *m.*, chien qui fait lever le gibier

Starting, s. tressaillement, *m.*, mouvement subit, *m.*, (*from*, de) éloignement, *m.*, égarement, *m.*, départ, *m.*, sortie, *f.*, (*beginning*) commencement, *m.*, début, *m.*, mise en mouvement, *f.*, mise en train, *f.*

Startle, vn. tressaillir, frémir; — va. faire tressaillir, faire frémir, effrayer

Startle, s. tressaillement, *m.*, frémissement, *m.*, saisissement, *m.*

Startling, adj. saisissant, effrayant, étonnant

Starvation, s. faim, *f.*, inanition, *f.*, besoin, *m.*

Starve, vn. mourir de faim; — va. faire mourir de faim, affamer, vaincre par la faim. *To — out*, réduire *or* soumettre par la faim

Starveling, adj. s. meurt-de-faim, *m.*, famélique, *m.*

Starving, adj. mourant de faim, affamé

State, s. état, *m.*, condition, *f.*, ordre, *m.*, (*in society*) rang, *m.*, condition, *f.*, (*pomp*) majesté, *f.*, pompe, *f.*, apparat, *m.*, grandeur, *f.*, dignité, *f.* *To lie in —*, être exposé sur un lit de parade. *To keep —*, *to hold —*, présider à *or* tenir sa cour

State, adj. d'État, politique. — *-apartments*, grands appartements, *m.pl.* — *-barge*, s. barque d'honneur, *f.* — *-bed*, s. lit de parade, *m.* — *-carriage*, s. voiture de cérémonie, *f.* — *-craft*, s. diplomatie, *f.*, politique, *f.* — *-criminal*, s. criminel d'État, *m.* — *-house*, s. salle des états, *f.* — *-room*, s. salle d'apparat, *f.*, salle du trône, *f.* — *-trial*, s. procès politique, *m.*

State, va. établir, régler, fixer, (*explain*) exposer, déclarer, constater, dire

Stated, adj. fixe, réglé

Stateliness, s. majesté, *f.*, aspect imposant, *m.*, grandeur, *f.*, pompe, *f.*, faste, *m.*

Stately, adj. majestueux, imposant, grand, superbe, magnifique, plein de dignité

Stately, adv. majestueusement

Statement, s. exposition, *f.*, exposé, *m.*, rapport, *m.*, compte rendu, *m.*, relevé de comptes, *m.*, situation, *f.*

Statesman, s. homme d'État politique, *m.* — *-like*, adj. d'homme d'État, en homme d'État

Statesmanship, s. la science du gouvernement, *f.*

Statics, s. pl. la statique, *f.*

Station, s. station, *f.*, place, *f.*, poste, *m.*, position, *f.*, condition, *f.*, (*railway*) station, *f.*, gare, *f.*, débarcadère, *m.* *Police —*, s. corps de garde, *m.* — *-master*, s. chef de gare, *m.*

Station, va. placer, mettre, (*mil.*) poster, poser

Stationary, adj. fixe, stationnaire

Stationer, s. papetier, *m.* *—'s hall*, s. dépôt de la librairie. *Entered at —'s hall*, déposé

Stationery, s. papeterie, *f.*

Statistic, Statistical, adj. statistique, de statistique

Statistician, s. statisticien, *m.*

Statistics, s.pl. statistique, *f.*

Statuary, s. statuaire, *f.*, (*pers.*) statuaire, *m.*

Statue, s. statue, *f.* *Small —*, s. statuette, *f.*

Stature, s. stature, *f.*, taille, *f.*

Status quo, s. statu quo, *m.*

Statutable, adj. conforme au statuts, à la loi

Statute, s. statut, *m.*, loi, *f.* — *-book*, s. code, *m.* — *-labour*, s., — *-work*, s. corvée, *f.*, prestation, *f.*

Staunch, see Stanch

Stave, s. douve, *f.*, (*psalm*) verset, *m.*, (*mus.*) portée, *f.*

Stave, va. défoncer, briser. *To — in*, défoncer, briser. *To — off*, chasser à coups de bâton, (*fig.*) repousser, retarder

Stay, vn. rester, demeurer, (*wait*) attendre, (*stop*) s'arrêter, (*on*, *upon*, sur) s'appuyer, se reposer (sur), mettre sa confiance (en). *To — away*, s'absenter. *To — in*, rester à la maison. *To — out*, rester dehors. *To — up*, ne pas se coucher, veiller. — va. arrêter, contenir, réprimer, retenir, (*from*, de) empêcher, (*prop*) étayer, soutenir, (*hunger*) apaiser

Stay, s. séjour, *m.*, action de rester, de s'arrêter, permanence, *f.*, stabilité, *f.*, (*prop*) étai, *m.*, support, *m.*, appui, *m.*, soutien, *m.*, (*nav.*) étai, *m.*

Stays, s. pl. corset, *m.* *A pair of —*, un corset. — *-lace*, s. lacet de corset, *m.* — *-maker*, s. corsetière, *f.*

Stead, s. lieu, *m.*, place, *f.* *In my —*, à ma place. *To stand in great —*, être d'une grande utilité à

Steadfast, adj. stable, immobile, solide, ferme, constant

Steadfastly, adv. fermement

Steadfastness, s. stabilité, *f.*, solidité, *f.*, (*fig.*) fermeté, *f.*

Steadily, adv. sans chanceler, d'un pas ferme, fermement, avec persistance, assidûment, avec persévérance, avec sagesse

Steadiness, s. fermeté, *f.*, pas ferme, *m.*, persistance, *f.*, assurance, *f.*, assiduité, *f.*, persévérance, *f.*, conduite rangée, *f.*

Steady, adj. ferme, assuré, sûr, régulier, persistant, constant, assidu, posé, rangé, (*nav.*) fait

Steady! interj. comme ça! droit!

Steady, va. affermir, assurer, rendre plus sage

Steak, s. tranche, *f.*, (*beef*) bifteck, *m.*

Steal, va.n. voler, dérober, enlever, (*win*) gagner, séduire, surprendre, (*glance*) lancer, jeter à la dérobée, (*to slip*) se glisser furtivement, sortir furtivement *or* sans bruit. *To — away*, *to — off*, s'en aller, se retirer, s'éloigner furtivement *or* à la dérobée. *To — down*, descendre furtivement or sans bruit. *To — out*, sortir furtivement, se glisser dehors sans bruit. *To — in*, entrer sans bruit. *To — upon*, surprendre, s'emparer de

Stealer, s. voleur, *m.*, -euse, *f.*

Stealing, s. vol, *m.*

Stealingly, adv. par vol, à la dérobée, furtivement

Stealth, s. secret, *m.*, dérobée, *f.* *By —*, secrètement, à la dérobée, en tapinois

Stealthily, adv. see By Stealth

Stealthy, adj. furtif, secret, dérobé

Steam, s. vapeur, *f.* *With all its — up* or *on*, à toute vapeur. *To be getting up her* or *its —*, chauffer

Steam . . ., adj. de vapeur, à vapeur. — *-boat*, s. bateau à vapeur, *m.* — *-boiler*, s. chaudière à vapeur, *f.* — *-carriage*, s. voiture à vapeur, *f.* — *-chest*, s. boîte à vapeur, *f.* — *-engine*, s. machine à vapeur, *f.*, locomotive, *f.* — *-gauge*, s. manomètre, *m.*, éprouvette, *f.* — *-power*, s. force de la vapeur, *f.* — *-tight*, adj. imperméable à la vapeur, étanche

Steam, vn. jeter de la vapeur, (*smoke*) fumer, s'évaporer, (*navigate*) naviguer *or* marcher à la vapeur. *To — away*, s'évaporer, s'éloigner à toute vapeur. *To — it*, aller, venir en bateau à vapeur. *To — into* or *out of harbour*, entrer dans le port, sortir du port. — va. faire évaporer, faire cuire à la vapeur

Steamer, s. bateau à vapeur, *m.*, bâtiment à vapeur, *m.*

Steamy, adj. plein de vapeur

Stearic, adj. stéarique

Stearine, s. stéarine, *f.*

Steed, s. coursier, *m.*

Steel, s. acier, *m.*, (*fig.*) fer, *m.*, épée, *f.*, lame, *f.*, (*for striking a light*) briquet, *m.*, (*butcher's*) fusil, *m.*, (*med.*) ferrugineux, *m.pl.* *Cast —*, s. acier fondu, *m.* *Shear —*, acier raffiné, *m.* — *-plated*, adj. cuirassé. — *-wine*, s. vin ferré, *m.* — *-works*, s.pl. aciérie, *f.*

Steel, va. acérer, cuirasser, (*harden*) endurcir, armer, fortifier

Steelyard, s. romaine, *f.*, peson, *m.*

Steep, adj. escarpé, rapide, roide, à pic

Steep, s. escarpement, *m.*, précipice, *m.*

Steep, va. tremper, faire infuser, plonger

Steeple, s. clocher, *m.* — *-chase*, s. course au clocher, *f.*

Steepled, adj. surmonté de clocher

Steepness, s. nature escarpée, *f.*, pente roide, *f.*, roideur, *f.*

Steer, s. (jeune) bœuf, (jeune) taureau, *m.*

Steer, va.n. diriger, gouverner, (*fig.*) se gouverner, se diriger

Steerage, s. timonerie, *f.*, logement des matelots, *m.*, logement des voyageurs de seconde classe, *m.*, (*fig.*) gouvernement, *m.*, direction, *f.*, conduite, *f.* — *way*, s. sillage, *m.*, chemin du vaisseau, *m.*

Steering, s. action *or* manière de gouverner, *f.*

Steersman, s. timonier, *m.*

Stem, s. tige, *f.*, tronc, *m.*, (*of a tree*) souche, *f.*, (*fruit*) queue, *f.*, (*fig.*) souche, *f.*, tige, *f.*, race, *f.*, (*of ships*) proue, *f.*, avant, *m.*, étrave, *f.*, (*of a glass*) patte, *f.* *From — to stern*, de l'avant à l'arrière

Stem, va. éviter . . . ., lutter contre, aller contre, résister à

Stench, s. mauvaise odeur, *f.*, puanteur, *f.*

Stenographic, Stenographical, adj. sténographique

Stentorian, adj. de stentor

Step, s. pas, *m.*, (*staircase*) marche, *f.*, degré, *m.*, gradin, *m.* —*s*, pl. (*carriage*) marchepied, *m.*, (*of a ladder*) échelon, *m.*, (*door*) seuil, *m.*, (*gait*) pas, *m.*, démarche, *f.*, allure, *f.* (*dancing*) pas, *m.*, (*progress*) acheminement, *m.*, progrès, *m.* — *by* —, pas à pas. *To take a* —, faire un pas. — *-ladder*, s. échelle d'appartement, *f.* *To take an important* —, faire une démarche importante

Step- . . . ., (*in compounds*). — *-brother*, s., — *-sister*, s. fils, fille du premier lit d'un beau-père ou d'une belle-mère. — *-child*, s. enfant d'un autre lit. — *-daughter*, s. belle-fille. — *-father*, s. beau-père. — *-mother*, s., — *-dame*, s. belle-mère. — *-son*, s. beau-fils

Step, vn. faire un pas, marcher, aller, suivre, venir. *To — upon*, mettre le pied sur. *To — after*, suivre, courir après. *To — aside*, se retirer à l'écart, s'écarter. *To — back*, reculer d'un pas, rebrousser chemin. *To — forward*, faire un pas en avant, (*fig.*) se mettre en avant. *To — in*, entrer, monter en voiture, intervenir. *To — out*, sortir, allonger le pas. *To — over*, franchir, enjamber. *To — up*, monter, s'avancer (vers), s'approcher (de)

Steppe, s. steppe, *m.*

Stepping, s. pas, *m.* — *-stone*, s. marchepied, *m.*

Stereoscope, s. stéréoscope, *m.*

Stereotype, s. stéréotypie, *f.*, cliché, *m.*, clichage, *m.*

Stereotype, va. stéréotyper

Stereotyping, s. stéréotypie, *f.*, clichage, *m.*

Sterile, adj. stérile

Sterility, s. stérilité, *f.*

Sterling, adj. sterling, (*fig.*) pur, de bon aloi, vrai, véritable

Stern, adj. sévère, austère, (*hard*) rigoureux, dur

Stern, s. (*nav.*) poupe, *f.*, arrière, *m.* — *-post*, s. étambot, *m.*

Sternal, adj. sternal

Sternly, adv. sévèrement, rudement, durement

Sternmost, adj. (le) plus en arrière, dernier

Sternness, s. sévérité, *f.*, austérité, *f.*, rudesse, *f.*, dureté, *f.*

Stethoscope, s. stéthoscope, *m.*

Stew, s. étuvée, *f.*, ragoût, *m.*, fricassée, *f.*, (*fruit*) compote, *f.*, (*fig.*) confusion, *f.*, embarras, *m.* — *-pan*, s. casserole, *f.* *Mutton* —, s. ragoût de mouton, *m.*

Stew, va. cuire à l'étuvée, arranger *or* mettre en ragoût, faire un ragoût, une compote de. —*ed eels*, matelote d'anguilles. —*ed fowl*, fricassée de poulet. —*ed fruit*, —*ed pigeons*, compote de fruits, de pigeons — vn. cuire à l'étuvée, (*fig.*) cuire dans sa peau

Steward, s. maître d'hôtel, *m.*, intendant, *m.*, régisseur, *m.*, (*college*) économe, *m.*, (*ball, &c.*) commissaire, *m.*, (*nav.*) commis aux vivres, *m.*

Stewardship, s. place de maître d'hôtel, *f.*, intendance, *f.*

Stewing, s. cuisson à l'étuvée, *f.*

Stick, s. bâton, *m.*, (*rod*) baguette, *f.*, (*tree*) branche, *f.*, (*walking*) canne, *f.*, (*wax, &c.*) bâton, *m.*, (*fiddle*) archet, *m.*

Stick, s. (*in compounds*) baguette de . . . ., manche de . . .

Stick, va. percer, frapper, piquer, (*drive in*) enfoncer, piquer, (*to fasten*) attacher, coller, fixer, mettre, appliquer, ajouter. *To — on*, attacher, coller. *To — out*, mettre en saillie, faire dépasser. *To — up*, coller, afficher. *Stuck all over with*, bien garni de, couvert de, armé de. — vn. se fixer, se coller, tenir, adhérer, (*in*, dans) rester, demeurer, s'arrêter, (*to be caught*) s'empêtrer, rester pris *or* engagé, (*to be puzzled*) s'arrêter, être embarrassé, hésiter. *To — at*, s'arrêter devant, hésiter, se faire scrupule de. *To — by*, s'attacher à, rester fidèle à, soutenir. *To — close*, s'attacher, adhérer, tenir bien, (*to*, à) s'attacher à, travailler d'arrache-pied à. *To — fast*, rester collé, tenir bien, s'embourber, se trouver pris. *To — on or upon*, adhérer (à), tenir (à). *To — out*, faire saillie, sortir, dépasser, (*fig.*) persister, soutenir (que). *To — to*, persévérer dans, s'attacher à, s'appliquer à, soutenir, s'obstiner dans, persister dans

Sticker, s. qui colle, qui affiche

Stickiness, s. viscosité, *f.*, ténacité, *f.*

Sticking, adj. qui fixe, qui colle. — *-place*, s. point d'arrêt, *m.* — *-plaster*, s. taffetas d'Angleterre, *m.*

Stickle, vn. hésiter, disputer

Stickleback, s. épinoche, *f.*

Stickler, s. partisan, *m.*, champion, *m.*

Sticky, adj. collant, gluant, visqueux

Stiff, adj. roide, dur, (*strong*) fort, (*obstinate*) roide, inflexible, obstiné, tout d'une pièce, (*formal*) gêné, froid, contraint. *He has got a — neck*, il a un torticolis. *To grow —, to get —*, se roidir. — *-necked*, adj. obstiné, endurci. — *-neckedness*, s. obstination, *f.*

Stiffen, va. roidir, durcir, rendre ferme, engourdir; — vn. se roidir, devenir roide, s'endurcir

Stiffly, adv. avec roideur

Stiffness, s. roideur *f.*, rigidité, *f.*, (*numbness*) torpeur, *f.*, engourdissement, *m.*

Stifle, va. étouffer, suffoquer, (*fig.*) réprimer, supprimer; — vn. étouffer

Stigma, s. stigmate, *m.*, flétrissure, *f.*, marque, *f.*, note d'infamie, *f.*

Stigmatize, va. stigmatiser, flétrir, noter d'infamie

Stile, s. barrière, *f.*, aiguille, *f.*, style, *m.*

Stiletto, s. stylet, *m.*, poinçon, *m.*

Still, va. tranquilliser, calmer, apaiser, distiller, amoupir

Still, adj. silencieux, sans bruit, doux, immobile, en repos, tranquille, paisible, calme. *Keep —, stand —, sit —*, restez tranquille, ne bougez pas. — *waters*, des eaux paisibles. — *life*, nature morte. — *-born*, mort-né

Still, adv. encore, toujours, (*nevertheless*) cependant, néanmoins, toutefois

Still, s. calme, *m.*, (*chemistry*) alambic, *m.*, distillerie, *f.*

Stillness, s. tranquillité, *f.*, calme, *m.*, repos, *m.*, paix, *f.*

Stilt, s. échasse, *f.*

Stilted, adj. guindé

Stimulant, adj. stimulant

Stimulate, va. stimuler, aiguillonner, exciter

Stimulation, s. excitation, *f.*, impulsion, *f.*, stimulation, *f.*

Stimulative, *see* STIMULANT

Stimulus, s. stimulant, *m.*

Sting, va. piquer, (*blow*) cingler, (*anger*) fâcher, irriter, (*grieve*) navrer, affliger

Sting, s. piqûre, *f.*, aiguillon, *m.*

Stingily, adv. sordidement, mesquinement, chichement

Stinginess, s. ladrerie, *f.*, avarice, *f.*, mesquinerie, *f.*

Stingy, adj. avare, ladre, sordide, mesquin, chiche

Stink, vn. puer, sentir mauvais

Stink, s. puanteur, *f.*, odeur fétide, *f.*, mauvaise odeur, *f.*

Stint, va. restreindre, borner, limiter, rogner, retrancher, réduire

Stint, s. restriction, *f.*, limite, *f.*, borne, *f.*

Stipend, s. salaire, *m.*

Stipendiary, adj. salarié, stipendié

Stipulate, va. stipuler

Stipulation, s. stipulation, *f.*

Stir, va. remuer, bouger, faire mouvoir, agiter, (*fig.*) exciter, soulever, irriter, réduire. — *the fire*, tisonnez le feu. — vn. bouger, remuer, se remuer, se mettre en mouvement, (*fig.*) s'agiter, se présenter. *To — about*, se donner du mouvement. *To — abroad*, sortir de chez soi

Stir, s. émoi, *m.*, mouvement, *m.*, remue-ménage, *m.*, agitation, *f.*, tumulte, *m.*, trouble, *m.*

Stirrer, s. moteur, *m.*, fauteur, *m.*

Stirring, s. excitation, *f.*, agitation, *f.*, impulsion, *f.*

Stirrup, s. étrier, *m.* — *-cup*, s. coup de l'étrier, *m.* — *-leather*, s., — *-strap*, s. étrivière, *f.* — *-oil*, s. huile de cotret, *f.*

Stitch, va.n. piquer, coudre, (*books*) brocher

Stitch, s. point, *m.*, (*knitting*) maille, *f.*, (*in the side*) point de côté, *m.*

Stitching, s. action de piquer, *f.*, couture, *f.*, (*of books*) brochage, *m.*

Stoat, s. hermine d'été, *f.*

Stock, s. (*tree*) tronc, *m.*, souche, *f.*, branche, *f.*, tige, *f.*, (*family*) tronc, *m.*, souche, *f.*, race, *f.*, famille, *f.*, (*wood*) bloc, *m.*, bûche, *f.*, (*fig.*) sot, *m.*, souche, *f.*, bûche, *f.*, (*handle*) manche, *m.*, (*of a gun*) monture, *f.*, (*in trade*) capital, *m.*, fonds, *m.pl.*, (*goods*) marchandises en magasin, *f.pl.*, assortiment, *m.*, (*punish.*) bloc, *m.*, (*cravat*) col, *m.*, (*funds*) fonds publics, *m.pl.*, fonds de l'État, *m.pl.*, rentes, *f.pl.*, effets, *m.pl.*, effets publics, *m.pl.*, (*shares*) actions, *f.pl.*, (*quantity*) provisions, *f.pl.*, quantité, *f.*, (*indust.*) matériel, *m.*, (*agric.*) mobilier, *m.*, (*bot.*) giroflée, *f.*, (*wheel*) moyeu, *m.* — *in trade*, marchandises en magasin, *f.pl.* (*fig.*) capital, *m.* *Rolling* —, s. matériel roulant, *m.* *Surplus* —, s. solde, *m.* *Working* —, s. matériel, *m.* *To take* —, inventorier. *To be sold the desirable business and — in trade of* . . ., à vendre le fonds de commerce et l'excellente clientèle de . . . *Miscellaneous* —, s. (*books*) livres d'assortiment, *m.pl.*, (*other goods*) marchandises d'assortiment, *f.pl.* *To sell* —, vendre des rentes réaliser. *Railroad* —, actions de chemin de fer. —*s are rising*, les fonds sont en hausse. —*s have fallen*, il y a eu baisse à la bourse. *To have — by* *oneself*, avoir des fonds *or* des provisions en réserve. *To lay in —, to take — of*, faire provision de, s'approvisionner de. *A — of wood*, une provision de bois. *His — of cash*, son argent (comptant). *A good — of impudence, of patience*, un bon fonds d'impudence, de patience. *Farming —*, matériel, mobilier d'exploitation

Stock . . ., (*in compounds*). *—-broker*, s. agent de change, *m.*, courtier de bourse, *m.* *—-exchange*, s. bourse, *f.* *—-fish*, s. morue salée, *f.* *—-holder*, s. actionnaire, *m.*, rentier, *m.*, rentière, *f.* *—-jobber*, s. courtier marron, *m.*, agioteur, *m.* *—-jobbing*, s. agiotage, *m.* *—-list*, s. cours de la bourse, *m.* *—-piece*, s. pièce du répertoire, *f.* *—-taking*, s. inventaire, *m.*

Stock, va. peupler, remplir, (*a pond*) empoissonner, (*with, de*) pourvoir, fournir, approvisionner, (*com.*) assortir, (*to put by*) amasser, mettre en réserve, (*punish*) mettre au pilori. *Well —ed*, bien pourvu, bien assorti

Stockade, s. palissade, *f.*

Stocking, s. bas, *m.* *—-frame*, s. métier à bas, *m.*

Stoic, s. stoïcien, *m.*, -ne, *f.*

Stoic, Stoical, adj. stoïcien, stoïque

Stoically, adv. stoïquement

Stoicalness, Stoicism, s. stoïcisme, *m.*

Stoker, s. chauffeur, *m.*

Stole, s. étole, *f.*

Stolid, adj. stupide, lourd, sot

Stolidity, s. stolidité, *f.*

Stomach, s. estomac, *m.*, (*fig.*) appétit, *m.*, inclination, *f.*, (*when sick*) cœur, *m.* *—-ache*, s. douleurs d'estomac

Stomach, va. s'irriter, se fâcher de, digérer

Stomacher, s. corsage, *m.*

Stomachic, adj. stomachique

Stone, s. pierre, *f.*, (*paving*) pavé, *m.*, (*hone, mill*) meule, *f.*, (*med.*) pierre, *f.*, calcul, *m.*, (*fruit*) noyau, *m.*, (*grape*) pepin, *m.*, (*weight*) six kilos. *To leave no — unturned*, mettre tout en œuvre, remuer ciel et terre. *Rolling — gathers no moss*, pierre qui roule n'amasse pas de mousse. *Atlantic —*, pierre atlantique, ivoire des îles. *Bristol —*, cristal de roche, *m.* *Pebble —*, caillou, *m.* *Rough —*, moellon, *m.*

Stone, adj. de pierre, en pierre, de grès. *— bottle*, s. bouteille de grès, *f.* *—-blind*, adj. complètement aveugle. *—-cutter*, s. tailleur de pierres, *m.*, marbrier, *m.* *—-cutting*, s. taille des pierres, *f.* *—-dead*, adj. roide mort. *—-fruit*, s. fruit à noyau, *m.* *—-pit*, s., *—-quarry*, s. carrière, *f.*

Stone, va. lapider, (*fruit*) ôter les noyaux de, (*road*) empierrer

Stoning, s. lapidation, *f.*, empierrement, *m.*, (*of fruit*) vidage, *m.*

Stony, adj. de pierre, en pierre, pierreux, (*fig.*) de rocher, inexorable, dur

Stool, s. tabouret, *m.*, escabeau, *m.*, sellette, *f.*, (*med.*) selle, *f.*

Stoop, vn. se baisser, se pencher, (*in walking*) se tenir courbé, (*to yield*) se soumettre, courber la tête, (*birds*) s'abattre, fondre. *To — down*, se baisser. *To — forward*, se pencher (en avant). *To — in walking, to have a —ing gait*, marcher courbé. *To — (with age)*, se tenir tout courbé. *He made the foe to —*, il fit courber la tête à *or* il fit plier l'ennemi. *The giant —s and totters*, le géant plie et chancelle. *She —s to conquer*, elle s'abaisse pour vaincre. *To — to folly*, s'oublier dans la folie

Stoop, s. inclination, *f.*, (*fig.*) abaissement, *m.*, action de fondre, de s'abattre, *f.* *To have a —*, avoir le dos légèrement voûté, marcher courbé. *To make a — at*, fondre sur. *To avoid the — of the kite*, pour éviter l'attaque rapide du milan. *Wooden —s*, perrons en bois, *m.pl.*

Stop, va. arrêter, (*hinder*) empêcher, (*breath*) couper, gêner, entraver, (*to close*) boucher, fermer, (*wages*) faire une retenue sur, (*game*) tenir en arrêt, (*tooth*) plomber. *To — up*, boucher, fermer, obstruer. — vn. s'arrêter, arrêter, cesser (de), (*wait*) attendre, (*dwell*) rester, demeurer, loger, (*payment*) suspendre ses payements, (*indust.*) chômer

Stop, s. halte, *f.*, pause, *f.*, repos, *m.*, point d'arrêt, *m.*, obstacle, *m.*, empêchement, *m.*, hésitation, *f.*, interruption, *f.*, (*punctuate*) point, *m.*, signe de ponctuation, *m.* *—s*, pl. points et virgules, *m.pl.* (*organ*) registre, *m.*, jeu d'orgue, *m.* *To bring to a —*, arrêter. *To come to a dead —*, s'arrêter court, faire une halte subite, (*hunt*) tomber en arrêt. *To put a — to*, arrêter, mettre fin à. *—-gap*, s. bouche-trou, *m.* *A full —*, un point

Stoppage, s. action d'arrêter, *f.*, cessation de mouvement, *f.*, (*obstruction*) action de boucher, *f.*, fermeture, *f.*, obstruction, *f.*, (*liquids*) engorgement, *m.*, (*vehicle*) encombrement, *m.*, temps d'arrêt, *m.*, repos, *m.*, interruption, *f.*, pause, *f.*, halte, *f.*, (*work*) chômage, *m.*, (*on a salary*) retenue sur les appointements, *f.*, (*law*) saisie-arrêt, *f.*

Stopper, s. qui arrête, qui bouche, etc., (*bottle*) bouchon, *m.*, (*of rage, &c.*) tampon, *m.*

Stopping, s. action d'arrêter, *f.*, de boucher, *f.*, etc., obstruction, *f.*, (*indust.*) chômage, *m.*

Stopple, s. bouchon, *m.*

Store, s. provision, *f.*, abondance, *f.*, (*fig.*) réserve, *f.*, fonds, *m.pl.*, (*milit.*) matériel, *m.*, munitions, *f.pl.*, (*food*) provisions, *f.pl.*, vivres, *m.pl.*, (*warehouse*) magasin, *m.*, entrepôt, *m.* *To hold, to keep in —*, tenir *or* garder en réserve, réserver. *To be in — for*, être réservé à, être en réserve pour. *A — of science*, un fonds de science. *—-house*, s., *—-room*, s. magasin, *m.*, entrepôt, *m.*, dépôt, *m.* *—-keeper*, s. garde-magasin, *m.* *—-ship*, s. transport de vivres, *m.*

Store, va. approvisionner, munir, pourvoir, (*fig.*) enrichir, orner, embellir. *To — up*, amasser, mettre en réserve

Storied, adj. historié, (*houses*) à . . . étages

Stork, s. cigogne, *f.*

Storm, s. orage, *m.*, tempête, *f.*, (*milit.*) assaut, *m.* *A — of rain*, une tempête de pluie. *To carry, to take by —*, emporter, prendre d'assaut

Storm, va. donner l'assaut à, prendre *or* emporter d'assaut; — vn. (*fig.*) tempêter

Storminess, s. état orageux, *m.*

Storming, s. assaut, *m.*, prise d'assaut, *f.*, (*fig.*) violence, *f.*, emportements, *m.pl.* *—-party*, s. colonne d'assaut, *f.*

Stormy, adj. orageux, tempêtueux

Story, s. récit, *m.*, conte, *m.*, histoire, *f.*, (*lie*) mensonge, *m.*, menterie, *f.*, (*of a house*) étage, *m.* *—-teller*, s. conteur, *m.*, (*liar*) menteur, *m.*, -euse, *f.* *Idle stories*, contes frivoles. *A — of one's own invention*, conte fait à plaisir. *Funny —*, plaisante histoire. *A true —*, histoire véritable. *Little —*, historiette. *The — of a pin*, l'histoire d'une épingle. *As my — goes*, à ce que dit mon histoire. *That is quite another —*, c'est une tout autre chose. *The best of the — is*, le plus beau de l'histoire c'est . . . *My travels' —*, l'histoire de mes voyages. *The — of my life*, l'histoire de ma vie. *To tell a —*, dire un mensonge, une menterie, mentir

Stot, s. bœuf, *m.*

Stout, s. bière brune, *f.*

Stout, adj. fort, vigoureux, ferme, solide, (*brave*) hardi, brave, vaillant, intrépide, (*obstinate*) opiniâtre, obstiné, acharné, (*fat*) gros, corpulent, puissant

Stoutly, adv. vigoureusement, fortement, solidement, hardiment, vaillamment, résolûment, obstinément, avec acharnement

Stoutness, s. vigueur, *f.*, force, *f.*, solidité, *f.*, bravoure, *f.*, intrépidité, *f.*, fermeté, *f.*, opiniâtreté, *f.*, acharnement, *m.*, corpulence, *f.*, embonpoint, *m.*, grosseur, *f.*

Stove, s. poêle, *m.*, cheminée à l'anglaise, *f.*, grille, *f.*, (*for cooking*) fourneau de cuisine, *m.*, (*hortic.*) serre chaude, *f.* *Hot air —*, s. calorifère, *m.* *—-builder*, s. poêlier, *m.*

Stow, va. mettre en place, serrer, arranger, (*nav.*) arrimer

Stowage, s. arrangement, *m.*, mise en place, *f.*, (*nav.*) arrimage, *m.*, cargaison, *f.*, chargement, *m.*

Strabism, s. strabisme, *m.*

Straddle, vn. écarter les jambes, marcher les jambes écartées. *To — over*, or *to —*, va. enjamber, enfourcher

Straggle, vn. s'écarter, se séparer, s'éloigner, être dispersé, errer, rôder

Straggler, s. personne qui s'écarte, rôdeur, *m.*, -euse, *f.*, (*mil.*) traînard, *m.*

Straggling, adj. écarté, séparé, éparpillé, isolé, épars. *A — house*, une maison isolée. *A — party*, une troupe isolée une bande de rôdeurs, de traînards

Straight, adj. droit, direct, équitable, juste, (*narrow*) étroit, serré. *— as an arrow*, droit comme un I. *In a — line*, en droite ligne, en ligne directe. *The — road*, le droit chemin. *To make —*, dresser, (*fig.*) arranger

Straight, adv. droit, directement, tout de suite, sur-le-champ

Straighten, va. rendre droit, redresser

Straightforward, adj. droit, direct, (*pers.*) juste, probe, franc

Straightforwardly, adv. avec droiture, sans détour, franchement

Straightforwardness, s. droiture, *f.*, franchise, *f.*

Straightway, adv. **Straightways,** adv. sur-le-champ, aussitôt

Strain, va n. tendre, (*sprain*) fouler, se fouler, (*endeavour*) faire faire un effort *or* des efforts à, (*compel*) contraindre, forcer, (*filter*) passer, filtrer, couler. *To — one's eyes*, se fatiguer la vue. *To — oneself*, s'efforcer, se fatiguer. *To — a point*, faire un effort. *To — the law, a text*, faire violence à la loi, forcer un texte

Strain, s. tension, *f.*, effort, *m.*, (*sprain*) entorse, *f.*, foulure, *f.*, (*song*) accords, *m.pl.*, accents, *m.pl.*, chant, *m.*, (*style*) style, *m.*, ton, *m.*, caractère, *m.*

Strainer, s. filtre, *m.*, passoire, *f.*

Straining, s. tension, *f.*, efforts, *m.pl.*, (*filtering*) filtrage, *m.*

Strait, adj. étroit, (*tight*) resserré. — *-jacket*, s., — *-waistcoat*, s. camisole de force, *f.* — *-laced*, adj. lacé serré, (*fig.*) collet monté, guindé, formel

Strait, s. (*geog.*) détroit, *m.*, pas, *m.*, chenal, *m.*, défilé, *m.*, (*difficulty*) gêne, *f.*, embarras, *m.*, difficulté, *f.*

Straiten, va. resserrer, rendre étroit, rétrécir, embarrasser, restreindre, (*tighten*) tendre, roidir, (*distress*) gêner, mettre dans la gêne, embarrasser

Straitened, past part. embarrassé, gêné. *In — circumstances*, dans la gêne

Straitly, adv. étroitement, intimement, strictement

Straitness, s. étroitesse, *f.*, rigueur, *f.*, sévérité, *f.*, gêne, *f.*, embarras, *m.*

Strand, s. rive, *f.*, plage, *f.*, grève, *f.*

Strand, va.n. échouer, briser

Strange, adj. étrange, (*foreign*) étranger, inconnu, timide

Strangely, adv. étrangement

Strangeness, s. étrangeté, *f.*, singularité, *f.*, nouveauté, *f.*

Stranger, s. étranger, *m.*, étrangère, *f.* *You are quite a —*, vous êtes rare comme les beaux jours. *You are making a — of me*, vous me traitez comme si j'étais compagnie. *I was no — to the original*, je connaissais bien l'original. *A room for —s*, une chambre d'amis. *—s' gallery*, (*polit.*) tribune publique, *f.*

Strangle, va. étrangler, étouffer

Strangles, s. pl. gourme, *f.*

Strangling, **Strangulation**, s. étranglement, *m.*

Strap, s. courroie, *f.*, lanière, *f.*, (*razor*) cuir, *m.*, (*techn.*) étrier, *m.*, bride, *f.*, (*trousers*) sous-pied, *m.*, (*milit.*) épaulette, *f.*, attache d'épaulette, *f.*

Strap, va. donner des coups d'étrivières à, attacher avec une courroie

Strappado, s. estrapade, *f.*

Strapping, adj. bien découplé, gros

Stratagem, s. stratagème, *m.*

Strategist, s. stratégiste, *m.*

Strategy, s. stratégie, *f.*

Stratum, s. stratum, *m.*, couche, *f.*

Straw, s. paille, *f.*, (*fig.*) fétu, *m.*, obole, *f.*, rien, *m.*, vétille, *f.* *To put — bottoms to*, empailler

Straw, adj. de paille, en paille. — *-bed*, s. paillasse, *f.* — *-bonnet*, s., — *-hat*, s. chapeau de paille, *m.* — *-bottomed*, adj. à fond de paille. — *-built*, adj. de paille. — *-cutter*, s. hache-paille, *m.*

Strawberry, s. fraise, *f.* — *-bush*, s., — *-plant*, s. fraisier, *m.* — *-tree*, s. arbousier, *m.*

Stray, vn. errer, vaguer, (*from the way*) s'égarer, dévier

Stray, s. bête épave, *f.*

Stray, adj. égaré, perdu, (*law*) épave

Streak, s. raie, *f.*, rayure, *f.*, bande, *f.*, bigarrure, *f.*, panachure, *f.*

Streak, va. rayer, strier, bigarrer

Streaked, **Streaky**, adj. rayé, (*meat*) entrelardé

Stream, s. cours d'eau, *m.*, courant, *m.*, fleuve, *m.*, rivière, *f.*, ruisseau, *m.*, fil de l'eau, *m.*, courant, *m.*, (*words*) flux, *m.*, torrent, *m.*, (*light*) jet, *m.*, (*people*) flots, *m.pl.* *Large —s*, de grands cours d'eau. *To go against the —*, remonter le courant, (*fig.*) résister au torrent. *To go with the —*, suivre le courant. — *-anchor*, s., — *-cable*, s. ancre, *f.*, câble de touée, *m.* *A — of ice*, un banc de glace flottante

Stream, vn. couler, ruisseler, (*light*) jaillir, (*wave*) flotter

Streamer, s. banderole, *f.*, banniere, *f.*

Streamy, adj. coupé par des ruisseaux, par des cours d'eau, qui ruisselle, qui jaillit

Street, s. rue, *f.* — *-door*, s. porte de la rue, *f.* — *-door-key*, s. passe-partout, *m.* — *-sweeper*, s. balayeur, *m.*, balayeuse de rues, *f.* — *-walker*, s. prostituée, *f.*

Strength, s. force, *f.*, (*of the frame*) forces, *f.pl.*, vigueur, *f.*, énergie, *f.*, influence, *f.*, (*mil.*) forces, *f.pl.*; troupes, *f.pl.*, (*mechan.*) effort, *m.*, résistance, *f.* *By — of*, à force de. *To gather — from*, se fortifier par, se renforcer par, prendre *or* trouver de nouvelles forces dans. *The — of the tea*, la force du thé. *— of arm*, la force du bras. *His — was fast failing him*, ses forces s'épuisaient rapidement. *The — of his blows*, la vigueur de ses coups. *I feel new —*, je sens une nouvelle vigueur. *Above my —*, au-dessus de mes forces. *Upon the — of their past successes*, se fiant à leurs succès passés. *On the — of this argument*, sous l'influence de, cédant à la force de cet argument. *On the — of having invited a guest*, sous prétexte qu'il avait invité quelqu'un

Strengthen, va. fortifier, renforcer, raffermir, affermir

Strengthener, s. qui fortifie, *m.*, fortifiant, *m.*

Strenuous, adj. vigoureux, énergique, courageux, vaillant, ardent, zélé

Strenuously, adv. vigoureusement, fortement

Strenuousness, s. vigueur, *f.*, énergie, *f.*, ardeur, *f.*, zèle, *m.*

Stress, s. force, *f.*, violence, *f.*, effort, *m.*, tension, *f.*, importance, *f.*, emphase, *f.*, (*gram.*) accent, *m.* *By — of weather*, par le mauvais temps, par la tempête. *To lay a great — upon*, attacher de l'importance à

Stretch, va. tendre, étendre, déployer, allonger, élargir, étirer, outrer, exagérer. *To — forth*, *to — out*, tendre, étendre, déployer. *To — oneself out at full length*, s'étendre tout de son long. *His arm is —ed out over us*, son bras est étendu sur nous. — vn. s'étendre, (*gloves*) prêter, s'élargir, (*pers.*) s'étirer

Stretch, s. tension, *f.*, effort, *m.*, étendue, *f.*, déploiement, *m.*, haleine, *f.*, coup, *m.* *At a —*, d'un trait, tout d'une haleine, sans s'arrêter

Stretcher, s. brancard, *m.*, civière, *f.* *Boot —*, s. forme brisée, *f.* *Glove —*, s. baguette à gants, *f.*

Strew, va. joncher, parsemer, éparpiller, couvrir

Striated, past. part. strié

Strict, adj. strict, exact, sévère, rigide

Strictly, adv. strictement, étroitement, sévèrement, rigoureusement. *What is — necessary*, le strict nécessaire de la vie

Strictness, s. exactitude, *f.*, précision, *f.*, sévérité, *f.*, rigueur, *f.*

Stricture, s. censure, *f.*, critique, *f.*, remarque critique, *f.*, (*med.*) resserrement, *m.*, étranglement, *m.*

Stride, s. grand pas, *m.*, enjambée, *f.*

Stride, va.n. marcher *or* avancer à grands pas, écarter les jambes, se mettre à califourchon, enjamber, (*a horse*) enfourcher, monter

Strife, s. lutte, *f.*, dispute, *f.*, contestation, *f.*, querelle, *f.*, opposition, *f.*, désaccord, *m.*

Strike, va. frapper, battre, heurter, cogner, (*blow*) frapper, asséner, porter, (*drum*) battre, (*hour*) sonner, (*dumb, &c.*) rendre, (*with fear*) saisir, frapper, (*idea*) venir à, frapper, venir à l'esprit de, paraître à, (*bargain*) conclure, (*balance*) établir, (*nav.*) abaisser, (*sails*) amener, (*tents*) plier, lever. *He struck me on the cheek*, il m'a frappé à la joue. *Without striking a blow*, sans coup férir. *You — deadly hard, man*, vous n'y allez pas de main morte, mon brave. *To — the ear*, frapper l'oreille. *The oak —s its roots deep into the ground*, le chêne enfonce profondément ses racines dans le sol. *To — one's head against*, se heurter la tête contre. *He struck him to the ground*, il le jeta à terre, il le renversa. *To — dead*, frapper à mort, tuer roide. *To — fire from*, faire jaillir des étincelles de. *To — terror through*, répandre la terreur de. *It struck me*, *the thought struck me that*, l'idée me vint que. *It —s me that you are not far wrong*, il me paraît que vous n'avez pas trop tort. *As it —s me*, comme il me paraît, selon moi. *To — hands with*, conclure un marché avec. *To — down*, abattre, renverser, jeter à terre. *To — off*, abattre enlever, couper, trancher, (*print.*) tirer. *To — out*, produire, faire jaillir, créer, imaginer, effacer, rayer, biffer. *To — through*, traverser. *To — up*, (*instrument*) commencer à jouer, (*song*) entonner. — vn. frapper, donner des coups, (*against*, contre) heurter, frapper, donner, (*hour*) sonner, (*into*, dans) entrer, pénétrer, s'enfoncer, (*through*) percer (à travers), pénétrer (dans), (*on*, de) toucher (de), jouer, (*drum*) battre, (*nav.*) toucher, échouer, amener son pavillon, se rendre, (*indust.*) faire grève, se mettre en grève. *To — in with*, s'accorder avec. *To — out*, s'écarter, nager vigoureusement, (*into*, dans) se jeter, s'élancer. *To — up*, jouer, commencer à jouer, se faire entendre

Strike, s. coup, *m.*, racloire, *f.*, (*workmen*) grève, *f.*

Striking, adj. frappant, saisissant, remarquable. *The most — part of beauty*, ce qui dans la beauté vous frappe le plus

Strikingly, adv. d'une manière frappante, remarquablement

String, s. corde, *f.*, ficelle, *f.*, filet, *m.*, cordon, *m.*, ruban, *m.*, (*bonnet*) bride, *f.*, (*mus.*) corde, *f.*, (*nerve*) nerf, *m.*, fibre, *f.*, (*of the tongue*) filet, *m.*, (*bot.*) fibre, *f.*, filament, *m.*, filandre, *f.*, (*pearls*) fil, *m.*, (*fig.*) enfilade, *f.*, kyrielle, *f.*, (*archit.*) cordon, *m.*

String, va. garnir de cordes, de nerfs, etc., (*mus.*) accorder, (*pearls*) enfiler, (*strengthen*) raffermir

Stringed, adj. à cordes

Stringent, adj. strict, sévère, dur. — *necessity*, la dure nécessité

Stringless, adj. sans cordes

Stringy, adj. fibreux, nerveux, filandreux

Strip, va. ôter, enlever, déshabiller, dépouiller, (*trees*) écorcer. *To — off*, dépouiller de, enlever, ôter. — vn. se déshabiller

Strip, s. lambeau, *m.*

Stripe, va. rayer
Stripe, s. raie, *f.*, barre, *f.*, (*lash*) marque, *f.*, coup, *m.*, (*milit.*) chevron, *m.*
Striped, adj. rayé, à raies
Stripling, s. jeune homme, *m.*, adolescent, *m.*
Strive, vn. s'efforcer de, chercher à, vouloir, essayer, (*with, against*) lutter (contre), combattre, le disputer (à), (*with*) rivaliser (avec). *In vain he strove to get away*, il se débattait en vain. *To —for*, essayer d'obtenir, chercher, se disputer. *To — hard*, faire tous ses efforts. *I strove hard not to kick him out of doors*, je fis un effort sur moi-même, je me tenais à quatre pour ne pas le jeter dehors
Striving, s. effort, *m.*, lutte, *f.*
Stroke, s. coup, *m.*, (*dash*) trait, *m.*, (*piston*) coup, *m.*, (*wit*) trait, *m.*, (*oar*) coup, *m.*, (*swimming*) brassée, *f.*, coup, *m.* *The finishing —*, le dernier coup. *A good, bold, lucky —*, un beau coup, un coup hardi, heureux. *With* or *at one — of his axe*, d'un coup de sa hache. *To do a good — of business*, faire de bonnes affaires. *Little —s fell great oaks*, petit à petit l'oiseau fait son nid, maille à maille se fait l'haubergeon. *With a — of his pen*, d'un trait de plume. *Thin —*, s., *— up —*, s. délié, *m.* *Thick —*, s., *down —*, s. plein, *m.* *With bold and rapid —s*, à grands trait. *Length of — of the piston*, course du piston, jeu du piston, *— -oar*, s. brigadier, *m.* *At one —, at a single —*, d'un seul coup, d'un seul trait, en une fois
Stroke, va. caresser
Stroll, vn. errer, flâner, rôder, courir le pays. *To — about*, errer çà et là, (*in the streets*) flâner dans. *To — out*, sortir pour se promener
Stroll, s. promenade, *f.*, flânerie, *f.* *To go out for a —*, sortir faire une promenade. *To take a —*, *to have a —*, faire une petite promenade. *To take a — down* or *through the vale*, aller doucement, se promener dans or par le vallon
Stroller, s. flâneur, *m.*, coureur, *m.*, -euse, *f.*, vagabond, *m.*, -e, *f.*, comédien ambulant, *m.*
Strolling, adj. ambulant, *— player*, s. comédien ambulant, *m.*, (*in company*) cabotin, *m.*
Strong, adj. vigoureux, robuste, fort, puissant, énergique, impétueux, (*wines*) capiteux, (*butter*) rance. *An army seven thousand —*, une armée forte de sept mille hommes. *— to labour*, fort pour le travail. *To be — of arm*, avoir le bras fort. *— in the back*, aux reins forts. *Not to be — enough*, n'avoir pas les reins assez forts. *To grow —*, de venir fort, prendre des forces, se fortifier, se raffermir. *To grow —er*, se renforcer, se raffermir
Strong, adv. fort, fortement
Strong- . . . . (*in compounds*) fort, solide, fortement. *— -box*, s. coffre-fort, *m.* *— -fisted*, adj. au poignet solide. *— -hand*, s. vive force, *f.* *— -handed*, adj. au poignet solide. *— -minded*, adj. décidé, résolu, de grand sens. *— -set*, adj. solide, fortement construit
Stronghold, s. forteresse, *f.*
Strongly, adv. fortement
Strop, s. cuir, *m.*
Strop, va. passer sur le cuir
Strophe, s. strophe, *f.*
Structure, s. structure, *f.*, construction, *f.*, édifice, *m.*
Struggle, vn. lutter, se débattre, s'agiter, se démener
Struggle, **Struggling**, s. lutte, *f.*, violent effort, *m.*, agitation, *f.*
Strum, vn. (*on*, sur) tapoter, taper
Strut, vn. se pavaner, se prélasser
Strut, **Strutting**, s. majesté affectée, *f.*, démarche fière, *f.*
Strychnia, s. strychnine, *f.*
Stub, s. souche, *f.*, bloc, *m.*
Stubble, s. chaume, *m.*
Stubborn, adj. entêté, obstiné, volontaire, têtu, rétractaire, (*fig.*) positif, irrécusable
Stubbornly, adv. obstinément, avec entêtement, opiniâtrement
Stubbornness, s. entêtement, *m.*, opiniâtreté, *f.*
Stubby, adj. encombré de souches
Stucco, s. stuc, *m.*
Stucco, adj. de stuc
Stud, s. (*constr.*) montant, *m.*, étai, *m.*, (*nail*) clou, *m.*, (*shirt —*) bouton double, *m.*, (*horses*) écurie, *f.*, haras, *m.*
Stud, va. (*nails*) garnir de clous, (*to strew*) parsemer, semer
Student, s. étudiant, *m.*, savant, *m.* *Law —*, s., *medical —*, s. étudiant en droit, en médecine, *m.*
Studied, adj. étudié, habile, expert, (*affected*) recherché
Studio, s. atelier, *m.*
Studious, adj. studieux, appliqué, empressé, diligent, attentif (à)
Studiously, adv. studieusement, soigneusement, avec empressement
Studiousness, s. empressement, *m.*, attention, *f.*
Study, s. étude, *f.*, méditation, *f.*, rêverie, *f.*, (*room*) cabinet, *m.*
Study, vn.a. étudier, travailler, piocher, réfléchir, méditer, s'appliquer à trouver, (*to*, à) s'étudier, s'appliquer, travailler
Studying, s. action d'étudier
Stuff, s. (*cloth*) étoffe, *f.*, matériaux *m.pl.*, matière, *f.*, effets, *m.pl.*, (*rubbish*) drogue, *f.*, (*nonsense*) fatras, *m.*, balivernes, *f.pl.*, chansons, *f.pl.*, sottises, *f.pl.*, niaiseries, *f.pl.* *Bread —*, s. provisions de bouche, *f.pl.* *— and nonsense*, balivernes que tout cela. *What wretched —!* quelle drogue! quel fatras!
Stuff, va. (*seats*) rembourrer, bourrer, (*fill*) garnir, remplir, (*meat*) farcir, (*birds*) empailler, (*to force in*) faire entrer, fourrer, serrer, tasser, (*obstruct*) boucher, obstruer. *To — out*, rembourrer, gonfler, enfler. *—* vn. se bourrer, goinfrer
Stuffing, s. action de remplir, *f.*, bourre, *f.*, (*cook*) farce, *f.*, (*of dead animals*) empaillage, *m.*, (*eating*) goinfrerie, *f.*
Stultify, va. hébéter, (*th.*) neutraliser, infirmer, annuler
Stumble, vn. broncher, trébucher, (*on*, à) se heurter (à), (*fig.*) rencontrer par hasard, trouver par hasard
Stumble, s. faux pas, *m.*
Stumbling, s. faux pas, *m.* *— -block*, s., *— -stone*, s. pierre d'achoppement, *f.*
Stumbling, adj. trébuchant, qui trébuche
Stump, s. souche, *f.*, tronçon, *m.*, (*limb*) moignon, *m.*, (*tooth*) chicot, *m.*, (*pen*) trognon, *m.*, (*leg*) quille, *f.*, (*drawing*) estompe, *f.* *— -orator*, s., *— -speaker*, s. orateur public, *m.* *Stir your —s*, remuez-vous
Stump, va. couper, estomper, (*puzzle*) mettre à quia. *To — it*, faire des discours publics
Stumpy, adj. plein de souches, (*short, stout*) trapu
Stun, va. étourdir, assourdir, abasourdir
Stunt, va. empêcher de croître
Stupefaction, s. stupéfaction, *f.*
Stupefy, va. stupéfier, engourdir
Stupendous, adj. prodigieux, étonnant, stupéfiant
Stupendously, adv. prodigieusement
Stupid, adj. stupide, sot, insensé
Stupidity, **Stupidness**, s. stupidité, *f.*
Stupidly, adv. stupidement
Stupor, s. stupeur, *f.*
Sturdily, adv. résolûment, fermement, hardiment
Sturdiness, s. résolution, *f.*, hardiesse, *f.*, fermeté, *f.*, opiniâtreté, *f.*, vigueur, *f.*
Sturdy, adj. résolu, hardi, ferme, opiniâtre, vigoureux
Sturgeon, s. esturgeon, *m.*
Stutter, va.n. bégayer, être bègue
Stutter, **Stuttering**, s. bégayement, *m.*, bégaiement, *m.*
Stutterer, s. bègue, *m.f.*
Sty, s. toit à porcs, *m.*, étable à cochons, *f.*, (*fig.*) taudis, *m.*
Sty, va. enfermer dans une étable
Stye, s. compère-loriot, *m.*, orgelet, *m.*
Style, s. style, *m.*, manière, *f.*, genre, *m.*, ton, *m.*, (*title*) titre, *m.*, stylet, *m.* *In —*, dans le grand style, comme il faut
Style, va. appeler, nommer, donner le titre de
Stylish, adj. élégant, distingué, dans le grand genre, brillant
Suavity, s. suavité, *f.*
Subaltern, adj. s. subalterne
Subcommittee, s. souscomité, *m.*
Subdivide, va. subdiviser; *—* vn. se subdiviser
Subdivision, s. subdivision, *f.*
Subdue, va. subjuguer, soumettre, dompter, (*disease*) maîtriser, vaincre, comprimer, réprimer
Subduer, s. vainqueur, *m.*
Sub-editor, s. gérant, *m.*
Sub-editorship, s. gérance, *f.*
Subject, va. soumettre, assujettir, vaincre, asservir, exposer
Subject, adj. inférieur, soumis, asservi, sujet, exposé
Subject, s. sujet, *m.*, -te, *f.* *— -matter*, s. sujet, *m.*
Subjection, s. soumission, *f.*, assujettissement, *m.*, sujétion, *f.*, asservissement, *m.*
Subjoin, va. ajouter, joindre
Subjugate, va. subjuguer, réduire, assujettir
Subjugation, s. assujettissement, *m.*
Subjunctive, s. subjonctif, *m.*
Sublieutenant, s. souslieutenant, *m.*
Sublimate, va. sublimer
Sublimate, s. sublimé, *m.*
Sublimation, s. sublimation, *f.*
Sublime, adj. élevé, (*fig.*) sublime
Sublime, s. sublime, *m.*
Sublimely, adv. d'une manière sublime, majestueusement
Sublimity, s. sublimité, *f.*
Sublunary, adj. sublunaire, terrestre
Submarine, adj. sousmarin
Submediant, s. sous médiante, *f.*
Submerge, **Submerse**,

va. submerger, plonger sous l'eau

Submersion, s. submersion, *f.*

Submission, s. soumission, *f.*, déférence, *f.*

Submissive, adj. soumis, docile

Submissively, adv. avec soumission, d'un air *or* d'un ton soumis

Submissiveness, s. soumission, *f.*

Submit, va. soumettre; — vn. se soumettre, se résigner, consentir

Subordinate, adj. s. subordonné, inférieur, subalterne

Subordinate, va. subordonner

Subordinately, adv. d'une manière subordonnée, en sous-ordre

Subordination, s. subordination, *f.*

Suborn, va. suborner

Subornation, s. subornation, *f.*

Suborner, s. suborneur, *m.*

Subpœna, s. citation, *f.*, assignation, *f.*

Subpœna, va. citer, assigner

Subscribe, va.n. souscrire, signer, consentir (à), admettre (. . .), (*to a journal*) abonner. *To cease to* —, se désabonner

Subscriber, s. souscripteur, *m.*, signataire, *m.f.*, abonné, *m.*

Subscription, s. souscription, *f.*, signature, *f.*, abonnement, *m.*

Subsequent, adj. subséquent, postérieur

Subsequently, adv. postérieurement, subséquemment

Subserve, va. servir à, avancer; — vn. obéir, servir en sous-ordre

Subserviency, s. dépendance, *f.*, subordination, *f.*

Subservient, adj. inférieur, de sous-ordre, secondaire

Subside, vn. tomber au fond, baisser, se calmer, s'abaisser

Subsidence, Subsidency, s. action de déposer, affaissement, *m.*, (*fig.*) apaisement, *m.*

Subsidiary, adj. subsidiaire

Subsidize, va. payer des subsides à, subventionner

Subsidy, s. subside, *m.*, subvention, *f.*

Subsist, vn. subsister, exister, demeurer, rester, vivre

Subsistence, s. existence, *f.*, (*means of support*) subsistance, *f.*, entretien, *m.*

Subsoil, s. sous-sol, *m.*

Substance, s. substance, *f.*, avoir, *m.*, bien, *m.*

Substantial, adj. substantiel, réel, solide, (*pers.*) aisé, ayant du bien, gros

Substantially, adv. en substance, substantiellement, réellement, solidement, (*comfortably*) dans l'aisance

Substantiate, va. établir, prouver

Substantive, s. substantif, *m.*

Substantif, adj. substantif, -ve

Substantively, adv. substantivement

Substitute, va. substituer, remplacer

Substitute, s. (*pers.*) remplaçant, *m.*, substitut, *m.*, (*things*) qui remplace, (*theat.*) doublure, *f.*

Substitution, s. substitution, *f.*, remplacement, *m.*

Substratum, s. couche inférieure, *m.*, sous-sol, *m.*

Substruction, s. substruction, *f.*

Subterfuge, s. subterfuge, *m.*

Subterranean, adj. souterrain

Subtile, adj. subtil, (*fine*) fin, délié, (*sly*) adroit, fin, rusé

Subtilely, adv. subtilement

Subtileness, Subtility, s. subtilité, *f.*, ruse, *f.*, finesse, *f.*

Subtilize, va.n. subtiliser

Subtle, adj. subtil, artificieux, (*sly*) fin, rusé

Subtleness, Subtlety, s. subtilité, *f.*, finesse, *f.*, ruse, *f.*

Subtly, adv. subtilement

Subtract, va.n. défalquer, soustraire

Subtraction, s. soustraction, *f.*, déduction, *f.*

Suburb, s. faubourg, *m.* —*s*, pl. alentours, *m.pl.*, environs, *m.pl.*, banlieue, *f.*

Suburban, adj. de faubourg, suburbain, de la banlieue

Subversion, s. subversion, *f.*

Subversive, adj. subversif

Subvert, va. subvertir, renverser

Subverter, s. destructeur, *m.*, -trice, *f.*

Succeed, vn. (*to follow*) succéder (à), suivre, (*to be successful*) réussir

Succeeding, adj. suivant, subséquent

Success, s. succès, *m.*, réussite, *f.* *I wish you all* —, bonne chance!

Successful, adj. heureux, qui réussit

Successfully, adv. heureusement, avec succès

Successfulness, s. succès, *m.*

Succession, s. succession, *f.*, suite, *f.*, (*to the throne*) avénement, *m.* *In* —, successivement

Successive, adj. successif

Successively, adv. successivement

Successor, s. successeur, *m.*

Succinct, adj. succinct

Succinctly, adv. succinctement

Succour, va. secourir, assister, aider

Succour, s. secours, *m.pl.*

Succulence, Succulency, s. goût succulent, *m.*, suc, *m.*

Succulent, adj. succulent

Succumb, vn. succomber, céder, se soumettre

Such, adj. pron. tel, pareil, semblable, (*these, those*) ceux, celles, ceux-là, celles-là, les . . .

Such, adv. si, tellement, aussi. — *a service*, un tel service, un pareil service. *Mr.* — *a one*, M. un tel. — *words*, de telles paroles. *For* — *and* — *a reason*, pour telle et telle raison. *And* — *like*, et d'autres gens pareils, et d'autres choses semblables. *No* — *thing*, rien de la sorte, rien de semblable. *In* — *a way*, d'une pareille façon. — *a long journey*, un aussi long voyage. — *as*, tel que, pareil à, semblable à, ceux qui, celles qui, les . . . qui, aussi . . . que. *I give it you* — *as it is*, je vous le donne tel quel. *Help* — *as need help*, aidez ceux qui ont besoin d'aide. — *an honest man as he is*, un aussi honnête homme que lui

Suck, va.n. sucer, (*the breast*) teter, (*absorb, &c.*) absorber, (*inhale*) aspirer, humer. *To* — *down*, entrainer, attirer au fond. *To* — *in*, sucer, aspirer, humer. *To* — *out, to* — *up*, sucer, pomper, aspirer

Suck, s. sucement, *m.*, succion, *f.*

Sucker, s. suceur, *m.*, (*pumps*) piston, *m.*, (*bot.*) branche gourmande, *f.*, (*insects*) suçoir, *m.*

Sucking, adj. qui suce, qui tette. — *-bottle*, s. biberon, *m.* — *-pig*, s. cochon de lait, *m.* — *-pump*, s. pompe aspirante, *f.*

Suckle, va. allaiter, donner le sein à, nourrir

Suckling, s. nourrisson, *m.*, enfant à la mamelle, *m.*, allaitement, *m.*

Suction, s. succion, *f.*, aspiration, *f.* — *-pipe*, s. tuyau d'aspiration, *m.* — *-pump*, s. pompe aspirante, *f.*

Sudden, adj. subit, soudain, inattendu, inopiné. *On a* —, *upon a* —, *all of a* — *see* SUDDENLY

Suddenly, adv. soudain, tout à coup, subitement, à l'improviste

Suddenness, s. soudaineté, *f.*, promptitude, *f.*

Sudorific, adj. sudorifique

Suds, s. pl. eau de savon, *f.* *To be in the* —*s*, être dans l'embarras. *Soap* —, s. eau de savon, *f.*

Sue, va.n. poursuivre, actionner, solliciter, implorer, poursuivre

Suet, s. graisse, *f.*, suif, *m.*

Suffer, va.n. (*to undergo*) subir, éprouver, souffrir, endurer, supporter, (*allow*) permettre, laisser, tolérer. *To* — *oneself to be deceived*, se laisser tromper. *To* — *pain, hunger, punishment*, souffrir de la douleur, la faim, subir un châtiment. *He will* — *for it*, il en portera la peine

Sufferable, adj. supportable

Sufferance, s. souffrance, *f.*, tolérance, *f.* *On* —, par tolérance

Sufferer, s. personne qui souffre, patient, *m.*, -e, *f.*, victime, *f.*

Suffering, s. souffrance, *f.*

Suffice, vn. suffire (à)

Sufficiency, s. suffisance, *f.*, quantité suffisante, *f.*, (*fortune*) aisance, *f.*, (*capacity*) aptitude, *f.*, talent, *m.*

Sufficient, adj. suffisant, qui suffit, assez. *To be* —, suffire à. *To be all*- —, suffire à tout

Sufficiently, adv. suffisamment

Suffocate, va. suffoquer, étouffer, asphyxier

Suffocating, adj. suffocant, étouffant

Suffocation, s. suffocation, *f.*, étouffement, *m.*, asphyxie, *f.*

Suffragan, s. adj. suffragant, *m.*

Suffrage, s. suffrage, *m.*

Suffuse, va. couvrir, répandre

Suffusion, s. suffusion, *f.*, épanchement, *m.*

Sugar, s. sucre, *m.* *Cane* —, s., *colonial* —, s. sucre de canne, *m.* *Brown* —, *moist* —, s. cassonade, *f.* *Raw* —, s. sucre brut, *m.*

Sugar, adj. de sucre, à sucre. — *-baker*, s. raffineur de sucre, *m.* — *-basin*, s. sucrier, *m.* — *-candy*, s. sucre candi, *m.* — *-cane*, s. canne à sucre, *f.* — *-house*, s. sucrerie, *f.* — *-mill*, s. moulin à cannes, *m.* — *-plum*, s. dragée, *f.* — *-refiner*, s. raffineur de sucre, *m.* — *-refinery*, s. raffinerie de sucre, *f.*, sucrerie, *f.* — *-tongs*, s. pinces à sucre, *f.pl.*

Sugar, va. sucrer

Sugary, adj. sucré

Suggest, va. suggérer, inspirer, insinuer, proposer, conseiller, prévenir

Suggestion, s. suggestion, *f.*, instigation, *f.*, avis, *m.*, conseil, *m.*

Suggestive, adj. qui inspire, qui suggère

Suicidal, adj. de suicide

Suicide, s. suicide, *m.* *To commit* —, se suicider

Suit, s. suite, *f.*, (*set*) assortiment, *m.*, collection complète, *f.*, (*clothes*) habit complet, *m.*, (*at cards*) couleur, *f.*, (*request*) prière, *f.*, sollicitation, *f.*, requête, *f.*, demande, *f.*, (*in marriage*) recherche, *f.*, (*law*) procès, *m.*, action, *f.*, poursuite, *f.*

Suit, va. adapter, accommoder, approprier, convenir à, aller à, satisfaire, plaire à, contenter; — vn. s'accorder (avec), seoir (à), aller (à)

Suitable, adj. approprié, adapté, qui convient, convenable, propre, sortable

Suitableness, s. convenance, *f.*, rapport, *m.*

Suitably, adv. convenablement

Suite, s. suite, *f.* '*A — of rooms*, un appartement. — *of furniture*, ameublement, *m.*

Suitor, s. (*petitioner*) solliciteur, *m.*, -euse, *f.*, (*lover*) prétendant, *m.*, (*law*) plaideur, *m.*, -euse, *f.*

Sulk, vn. bouder

Sulkily, adv. d'un ton boudeur

Sulkiness, **Sulking**, s. bouderie, *f.*, maussaderie, *f.*

Sulks, s.pl. bouderie, *f.* *To be in the* —, bouder

Sulky, adj. boudeur, maussade

Sullen, adj. morose, chagrin, maussade, sombre, boudeur, triste

Sullenly, adv. tristement, d'un ton maussade, de mauvaise humeur, maussadement

Sullenness, s. humeur morose, *f.*, maussaderie, *f.*, mauvaise humeur, *f.*, air sombre *or* lugubre, *m.*

Sully, va. souiller, ternir, salir

Sulphate, s. sulfate, *m.*

Sulphur, s. soufre, *m.*

Sulphurate, va. soufrer

Sulphuretted, adj. sulfuré

Sulphuric, adj. sulfurique

Sultan, s. sultan, *m.*

Sultana, s. sultane, *f.*

Sultriness, s. chaleur étouffante, *f.*

Sultry, adj. étouffant, accablant, lourd, brûlant

Sum, s. somme, *f.*, total, *m.*, masse, *f.*, (*abstract*) résumé, *m.*, substance, *f.*, sommaire, *m.*, (*arithm.*) règle, *f.*, problème, *m.*

Sum, va. calculer, compter, additionner, résumer. *To — up*, additionner, (*fig.*) résumer

Sumac, s. sumac, *m.*

Summarily, adv. sommairement

Summary, adj. sommaire

Summary, s. sommaire, *m.*, résumé, *m.*

Summer, s. été, *m.* *In the middle of* —, au fort de l'été. —*-house*, s. pavillon d'été, *m.*, kiosque, *m.*

Summer, adj. d'été

Summing, s. addition, *f.*, calcul, *m.* — *up*, s. addition, *f.*, résumé, *m.*

Summit, s. sommet, *m.*, cime, *f.*, faîte, *m.*

Summon, va. appeler, convoquer, mander, (*law*) citer, (*witnesses*) assigner, (*courage*) rappeler, (*mil.*) sommer, (*to bid*) sommer. *To — up*, rappeler, exciter, animer

Summoner, s. huissier, *m.*

Summons, s. appel, *m.*, convocation, *f.*, (*law*) citation, *f.*, assignation, *f.*, mandat de comparution, *m.*

Sumptuary, adj. somptuaire

Sumptuous, adj. somptueux

Sumptuously, adv. somptueusement

Sumptuousness, s. somptuosité, *f.*

Sun, s. soleil, *m.* —*-bright*, adj., —*-clad*, adj. brillant, resplendissant, radieux. —*-dial*, s. cadran solaire, *m.* —*-flower*, s. tournesol, *m.* —*-light*, s. clarté *or* lumière du soleil, *f.* —*-proof*, adj. impénétrable au soleil. —*-stroke*, s. coup de soleil, *m.*

Sunbeam, s. rayon de soleil, *m.*

Sunburnt, adj. brûlé par le soleil, hâlé

Sunday, s. dimanche, *m.* *On —, on —s*, le dimanche, les dimanches. *To put on one's — clothes*, mettre ses habits de dimanche, s'endimancher

Sunder, va. séparer, éloigner; — vn. se séparer

Sundries, s. pl. diverses choses, *f.pl.*, (*expenses*) faux frais, *m.pl.*

Sundry, adj. divers

Sunless, adj. sans soleil

Sunny, adj. exposé au soleil, riant, du soleil, brillant, radieux, (*fig.*) riant, heureux

Sunrise, **Sunrising**, s. le lever du soleil, le soleil levant

Sunset, **Sunsetting**, s. coucher du soleil, *m.*, soleil couchant, *m.*

Sunshine, s. soleil, *m.*, clarté du soleil, *f.*, (*fig.*) éclat, *m.*

Sunshiny, adj. de soleil, beau, brillant

Sup, va. (*to sip*) boire à petites gorgées, siroter, (*drink*) humer

Sup, s. gorgée, *f.*

Superabound, vn. surabonder

Superabounding,

Superabundant, adj. surabondant

Superabundance, s. surabondance, *f.*

Superabundantly, adv. surabondamment

Superadd, va. ajouter, surajouter

Superaddition, s. surcroît, *m.*

Superannuate, va. rendre suranné, (*to pension off*) mettre à la retraite

Superannuated, adj. suranné (*pensioned*) en retraite. *To be* —, être affaibli par l'âge, prendre sa retraite

Superannuation, s. retraite, *f.*

Superb, adj. superbe

Superbly, adv. superbement

Supercargo, s. subrécargue, *m.*

Supercilious, see Arrogant

Supereminence, s. prééminence, *f.*

Supereminent, adj. prééminent, suréminent

Supereminently, adv. très-éminemment

Supererogation, s. surérogation, *f.*

Supererogatory, adj. surérogatoire

Superficial, adj. superficiel

Superficially, adv. superficiellement

Superficies, s. superficie, *f.*

Superfine, adj. superfin

Superfluity, **Superfluousness**, s. superfluité, *f.*, superflu, *m.*

Superfluous, adj. superflu

Superfluously, adv. avec superfluité, surabondamment

Superhuman, adj. surhumain

Superintend, va. diriger, surveiller

Superintendence, s. surveillance, *f.*, direction, *f.*

Superintendent, s. surveillant, *m.*, -e, *f.*, inspecteur, *m.*, -trice, *f.*, directeur, *m.*, -trice, *f.*, surintendant, *m.*, -e, *f.*, (*railway*) chef de gare, *m.*, (*police*) commissaire de police, *m.*

Superior, adj.s. supérieur, -e

Superiority, s. supériorité, *f.*

Superlative, adj. suprême

Superlative, s. superlatif, *m.*

Superlatively, adv. superlativement, au suprême degré

Superlativeness, s. suprême degré, *m.*

Supernatural, adj. surnaturel

Supernaturally, adv. surnaturellement

Supernumerary, adj. surnuméraire, (*things*) supplémentaire

Supernumerary, s. surnuméraire, *m.f.*, (*theatre*) comparse, *m.*, figurant, *m.*, -e, *f.*

Superscribe, va. adresser, mettre une suscription

Superscription, s. suscription, *f.*, inscription, *f.*, adresse, *f.*

Supersede, va. annuler, supprimer, infirmer, écarter, (*law*) surseoir à

Supersedeas, s. sursis, *m.*

Superstition, s. superstition, *f.*

Superstitious, adj. superstitieux

Superstitiously, adv. superstitieusement

Superstructure, s. édifice, *m.*

Supervene, vn. s'ajouter, survenir

Supervise, va. surveiller, diriger

Supervision, s. surveillance, *f.*, inspection, *f.*

Supervisor, s. inspecteur, *m.*, surveillant, *m.*

Supine, adj. couché sur le dos, étendu, en pente, indolent, négligent, nonchalant

Supine, s. supin, *m.*

Supinely, adv. couché sur le dos, nonchalamment

Supineness, s. position d'être couché sur le dos, *f.*, négligence, *f.*, nonchalance, *f.*, indolence, *f.*

Supper, s. souper, *m.* *Last —, the Lord's* —, la (sainte) Cène

Supperless, adj. sans souper

Supplant, va. évincer, supplanter

Supple, adj. souple, flexible

Supple, va. assouplir

Supplement, s. supplément, *m.*

Supplemental, **Supplementary**, adj. supplémentaire

Suppleness, s. souplesse, *f.*

Suppliant, **Supplicant**, adj. s. suppliant, de supplication

Suppliantly, adv. en suppliant, -e

Supplicate, va n. supplier, implorer

Supplication, s. supplication, *f.*

Supplicatory, adj. suppliant

Supplier, s. pourvoyeur, *m.*, -euse, *f.*

Supply, va. pourvoir (de), fournir (de), approvisionner (de), alimenter, (*com.*) fournir, être le fournisseur de, (*wants*) fournir à, pourvoir à, subvenir à, (*to take the place of*) suppléer à, remplacer, suppléer, (*a vacancy*) remplir

Supply, s. approvisionnement, *m.*, provision, *f.*, (*fig.*) fonds, *m.pl.*, ressource, *f.* —*ies*, pl. fonds, *m.pl.*, subsides, *m. pl.* *Demand and* —, (*polit. econom.*) l'offre et la demande. *To lay in a — of*, s'approvisionner de

Support, va. soutenir, supporter, porter, appuyer, (*suffer*) supporter, endurer, soutenir, (*maintain*) fournir à, subvenir à, entretenir, faire subsister

Support, s. soutien, *m.*, support, *m.*, appui, *m.*, (*build.*) soutènement, *m.*, (*help*) soutien, *m.*, appui, *m.*, support, *m.*, entretien, *m.*, subsistance, *f.*

Supportable, adj. supportable

Supporter, s. support, *m.*, aide, *m.*, soutien, *m.*, appui, *m.*, partisan, *m.*, fauteur, *m.*

Supposable, adj. supposable

Suppose, va.n. supposer, s'imaginer

Supposed, adj. supposé

Supposition, s. supposition, *f.*

Supposititious, adj. supposé

Suppress, va. réprimer, détruire, (*complaints, &c.*) étouffer, (*voice*) baisser, (*sedition*) réprimer, contenir, (*book*) supprimer

Suppression, s. répression, *f.*, suppression, *f.*

Suppurate, vn. suppurer; — va. faire suppurer

Suppuration, s. suppuration, *f.*

Supremacy, s. suprématie, *f.*

Supreme, adj. suprême, souverain

Supremely, adv. suprêmement, souverainement

Sure, adj. sûr, assuré, infaillible, certain. *To be —*, assurément, certainement, à coup sûr, parbleu! *Be — and not fall*, prenez garde de tomber. *To make — of*, s'assurer de, se croire sûr de. *— of foot*, qui a le pied sûr. *—-footed*, adj. au pied sûr

Sure, Surely, adv. assurément, sûrement, à coup sûr

Sureness, s. sûreté, *f.*, certitude, *f.*

Surety, s. sûreté, *f.*, sécurité, *f.*, salut, *m.*, (*payment*) garantie, *f.*, (*law*) caution, *f.*, répondant, *m.*, garant, *m.* *To be a — for*, être caution de, répondre de

Suretyship, s. qualité de caution, *f.*

Surf, s. ressac, *m.*

Surface, s. surface, *f.*, superficie, *f.*

Surfeit, va. rassasier, satisfaire, gorger, (*fig.*) blaser (sur), dégoûter (de); — vn. être rassasié, se gorger, se repaître

Surfeit, s. rassasiement, *m.*, excès, *m.*, indigestion, *f.*, dégoût, *m.*, satiété, *f.*

Surge, s. houle, *f.*, vague, *f.*, flot, *m.*

Surge, vn. s'enfler, se grossir

Surgeon, s. chirurgien, *m.* *Army —*, s. chirurgien-major, *m.*

Surgery, s. chirurgie, *f.*, (*place*) pharmacie, *f.*

Surgical, adj. chirurgical, de chirurgie

Surgy, adj. houleux, agité

Surlily, adv. d'un ton bourru, de mauvaise humeur

Surliness, s. caractère bourru, *m.*, morosité, *f.*

Surly, adj. morose, bourru, hargneux, revêche

Surmise, va. soupçonner, supposer

Surmise, s. conjecture, *f.*, soupçon, *m.*

Surmount, va. surmonter, triompher de

Surmountable, adj. surmontable

Surname, s. surnom, *m.*

Surname, va. surnommer

Surpass, va. surpasser, l'emporter sur

Surpassing, adj. éminent, rare

Surpassingly, adv. incomparablement, éminemment

Surplice, s. surplis, *m.* *— fees*, s. casuel, *m.*

Surplus, s. surplus, *m.*, excédant, *m.*

Surplusage, s. surplus, *m.*, (*law*) superfluité, *f.*

Surprise, s. surprise, *f.*

Surprise, va. surprendre, étonner

Surprising, adj. surprenant, étonnant

Surprisingly, adv. étonnamment

Surrender, va. rendre, livrer, (*yield*) abandonner, renoncer à. *To — oneself*, se constituer prisonnier, se livrer

Surrender, s. reddition, *f.*, abandon, *m.*

Surreption, s. subreption, *f.*

Surreptitious, adj. subreptice

Surreptitiously, adv. subrepticement

Surrogate, s. délégué, *m.*

Surround, va. entourer, environner, (*milit.*) cerner

Survey, va. considérer, regarder, examiner, (*to measure land*) lever le plan de, arpenter, toiser, (*to value*) expertiser

Survey, s. vue, *f.*, examen, *m.*, inspection, *f.*, levée de plans, *f.*, (*of land*) arpentage, *m.*, études topographiques, *f.pl.*, cadastre, *m.* *To take a — of*, contempler, considérer, lever le plan de

Surveying, s. examen, *m.*, inspection, *f.*, surveillance, *f.*, arpentage, *m.*, lever des plans, *m.*

Surveyor, s. inspecteur, *m.*, surveillant, *m.*, (*of land*) arpenteur, *m.*, géomètre, *m.*, employé du cadastre, *m.*

Surveyorship, s. inspection, *f.*

Survival, s. survivance, *f.*

Survive, va.n. survivre

Survivor, s. survivant, *m.*, -e, *f.*

Survivorship, s. survivance, *f.*

Susceptible, adj. susceptible

Suspect, va.n. soupçonner, (*to apprehend*) se douter de, (*to doubt*) se méfier de, tenir pour suspect

Suspend, va. suspendre; — vn. cesser ses payements

Suspense, s. incertitude, *f.*, indécision, *f.*, répit, *m.* *In —*, en suspens

Suspension, s. suspension, *f.* *— -bridge*, s. pont suspendu, *m.*

Suspensor, Suspensory, s. suspensoir, *m.*

Suspicion, s. soupçon, *m.*, (*law*) suspicion, *f.*

Suspicious, adj. soupçonneux, méfiant, (*doubtful*) suspect

Suspiciously, adv. d'une manière suspecte, avec méfiance

Suspiciousness, s. nature suspecte, *f.*, nature soupçonneuse, *f.*

Sustain, va. soutenir, supporter, (*to feed*) entretenir, nourrir, (*endure*) endurer, souffrir, subir, éprouver

Sustainable, adj. soutenable

Sustainer, s. soutien, *m.*

Sustenance, s. soutien, *m.*, entretien, *m.*, subsistance, *m.*

Sutler, s. cantinier, *m.*, -ère, *f.*, vivandier, *m.*, -ère, *f.*

Sutling-booth, s. cantine, *f.*, buvette, *f.*

Suzerain, s. suzerain, *m.*, -e, *f.*

Suzerainty, s. suzeraineté, *f.*

Swab, s. faubert, *m.*

Swaddle, *see* Swathe

Swagger, vn. faire le bravache, le fanfaron

Swagger, Swaggering, s. fanfaronnade, *f.*, crânerie, *f.*

Swaggerer, s. bravache, *m.*, matamore, *m.*, tranche-montagne, *m.*

Swain, s. jeune homme, *m.*, jeune garçon, *m.*, berger, *m.*, paysan, *m.*

Swallow, s. hirondelle, *f.* *— -tail*, s. queue d'aronde, *f.* *— -tailed*, adj. à queue d'aronde, (*throat, &c.*) gosier, *m.*

Swallow, va. avaler, engloutir, (*to believe*) avaler, gober

Swamp, s. marais, *m.*, marécage, *m.*

Swamp, va. submerger, engloutir, faire chavirer, remplir d'eau, (*fig. and fam.*) détruire, enfoncer

Swampy, adj. marécageux

Swan, s. cygne, *m.* *—'s down*, s. duvet de cygne, *m.* *— skin*, s. molleton, *m.*

Swap, va. échanger

Sward, s. gazon, *m.*, pelouse, *f.*

Swarm, s. essaim, *m.*, (*fig.*) foule, *f.*

Swarm, vn. essaimer, (*fig.*) s'assembler, s'attrouper, se presser, (*with*, de) fourmiller, être rempli, abonder

Swarthiness, s. couleur basanée, *f.*

Swarthy, adj. basané, hâlé

Swash-buckler, s. ferrailleur, *m.*

Swath, s. fauchée, *f.*, coup de faux, *m.*

Swathe, s. lange, *f.*, maillot, *m.*

Swathe, va. emmailloter, envelopper

Sway, va.n. balancer, agiter, ballotter, manier, détourner, gouverner, régir, diriger, (*lean*) se pencher, incliner

Sway, s. (*of a weapon*) coup vigoureux, *m.*, balance, *f.*, poids, *m.pl.*, prépondérance, *f.*, empire, *m.*, puissance, *f.*, pouvoir, *m.*, autorité, *f.*, sceptre, *m.*

Swear, vn.a. jurer, faire serment, promettre, (*blaspheme*) jurer, blasphémer, (*law*) prêter serment, (*a person*) faire prêter serment à, (*declare*) déclarer sous la foi du serment, déposer. *To — in*, faire prêter serment à

Swearer, s. jureur, *m.*, blasphémateur, *m.*

Swearing, s. action de jurer, *f.*, serments, *m.pl.*, prestation de serment, *f.*, (*blasphemy*) jurons, *m.pl.*, jurements, *m.pl.*, blasphèmes *m.pl.*

Sweat, Sweating, s. sueur, *f.*, transpiration, *f.*, fatigue, *f.*

Sweat, vn. suer, transpirer, (*fig.*) se fatiguer, s'exténuer, travailler péniblement

Sweating, s. action de faire transpirer, *f.*, transpiration, *f.*, humidité, *f.*, sueur, *f.*

Sweaty, adj. couvert de sueur, en sueur, (*fig.*) pénible

Sweep, va. balayer, (*chimney*) ramoner, (*carry off*) entraîner, emporter, enlever, (*at a play*) rafler, (*glide*) effleurer, parcourir rapidement, (*look at*) parcourir, embrasser, (*a lyre, &c.*) toucher, frapper, (*nav.*) draguer. *To — away*, balayer, (*carry*) emporter, enlever, rafler. *To — up*, balayer en tas, ramasser. *To — round*, passer rapidement autour de, passer majestueusement

Sweep, s. (*pers.*) balayeur, *m.*, -euse, *f.*, (*chimney —*) ramoneur, *m.*, (*of a broom*) coup de balai, *m.*, (*motion*) mouvement, *m.*, passage, *m.*, (*at play*) coup, *m.*, (*extent*) étendue, *f.*, (*course*) parcours, *m.*, marche, *f.*, (*fig.*) essor, *m.*, (*of a vault*) ouverture, *f.*, (*avenue*) grande avenue, *f.*

Sweeper, s. balayeur, *m.*, -euse, *f.*, ramoneur, *m.*

Sweeping, s. balayage, *m.*, ramonage, *m.*, enlèvement, *m.* *—s*, pl. balayures, *f.pl.*

Sweeping, adj. entraînant, impétueux, irrésistible, sans exception, général

Sweepstakes, s. course par enjeux, *f.*

Sweepy, adj. rapide, ondulé, ondoyant

Sweet, adj. doux, sucré, (*to the taste*) suave, doux, (*pleasant*) doux, charmant, agréable, (*fresh*) frais. *My tea is too —*, mon thé est trop sucré. *To have a — tooth*, être friand, (*fam.*) aimer les chatteries. *— sounds*, doux accords. *To smell —*, sentir doux, exhaler un doux parfum. *To be — upon*, faire les yeux doux à. *A — place*, un endroit charmant. *— waters*, des eaux douces. *— -briar*, s. églantier odorant, *m.* *— -pea*, s. pois de senteur, *m.* *— -scented*, *— -smelling*, adj. odorant, au doux parfum, parfumé

Sweet, s. douceur, *f.*, (*pers.*) chéri, *m.*, -e, *f.* *—s*, pl. sucreries, *f.pl.*, friandises, *f.pl.*

Sweetbread, s. ris de veau, *m.*

Sweeten, va. adoucir, sucrer, (*pharmac.*) édulcorer, purifier

Sweetener, s. adoucissant, *m.*

Sweetening, s. adoucissement, *m.*

Sweetheart, s. amoureux, *m.*, -euse, *f.*

Sweetish, adj. douceâtre

Sweetishness, s. goût sucré, *f.*

Sweetly, adv. doucement, mélodieusement, agréablement

Sweetmeat, s. bonbon, *m.*, sucrerie, *f.*, plat sucré, *m.*

Sweetness, s. douceur, *f.*, goût sucré, *m.*, fraîcheur, *f.*, suavité, *f.*

Swell, vn. s'enfler, enfler, gonfler, (*flesh*) bouffir, boursoufler, (*increase*) grossir, (*dresses*) bouffer, (*to*) s'élever (à), devenir, s'agrandir, (*with*, de) s'enfler, gonfler, bouffir. *His arm was swollen*, il avait le bras enflé. *Swollen veins*, veines gonflées. *The river —s*, le fleuve grossit. *The sound —s*, le son grossit. *Eyes swollen with tears*, des yeux gros or gonflés de larmes. *To — to a large sum*, s'élever à une forte somme. — va. gonfler, enfler, faire bouffir, (*a river*) grossir. (*a fault*) augmenter, (*dress*) faire bouffer, (*into*) faire devenir, changer (en), gonfler. *To — out*, *to — up*, enfler, gonfler, augmenter, agrandir

Swell, s. gonflement, *m.*, enflure, *f.*, renflement, *m.*, (*sea*) houle, *f.*, lames, *f.pl.*, vagues grossissantes, *f.pl.*, (*land*) élévation, *f.*, ondulation, *f.*, (*mus.*) renflement, *m.*, (*organ*) son grave, *m.*, (*person*) élégant, *m.*, fashionable de mauvais goût. *To cut a —*, faire le fashionable, faire de l'étalage. *The — mob*, les filous de la haute

Swelling, s. enflure, *m.*, gonflement, *m.*, bouffissure, *f.*, renflement, *m.*, mouvement, *m.*, transport, *m.*

Swelter, vn. étouffer de chaleur, transpirer fortement; — va. accabler de chaleur

Swerve, vn. s'écarter, se détourner, (*horse*) faire un écart. *To — from one's duty*, s'écarter, dévier du devoir

Swerving, s. écart, *m.*, déviation, *f.*

Swift, adj. prompt, rapide

Swiftly, adv. rapidement

Swiftness, s. rapidité, *f.*, vitesse, *f.*, célérité, *f.*

Swill, va. boire avidement, (*intoxicate*) s'enivrer

Swill, s. grand trait, *m.*, coup, *m.*, (*wash*) eaux grasses, *f.pl.*

Swim, vn.a. nager, (*float*) surnager, flotter, (*be dizzy*) tourner. *To — across*, *to — over*, *to — through*, traverser or passer à la nage

Swim, s. vessie natatoire, *f.*

Swimmer, s. nageur, *m.*, -euse, *f.*

Swimming, s. natation, *f.*, (*dizziness*) vertiges, *m.pl.*, étourdissement, *m.* *— -girdle*, s. ceinture de natation, *f.* *— -school*, s. école de natation, *f.*

Swimmingly, adv. admirablement, à merveille, (*fam.*) comme sur des roulettes

Swindle, va. escroquer, voler

Swindle, s. escroquerie, *f.*, vol, *m.*

Swindler, s. escroc, *m.*

Swindling, s. escroquerie, *f.*

Swine, s. pourceau, *m.*, porc, *m.*, cochon, *m.* *— -herd*, s. porcher, *m.*

Swing, vn. se balancer, osciller, être pendu; — va. balancer, agiter, ballotter, remuer, brandir

Swing, s. balancement, *m.*, vibration, *f.*, oscillation, *f.*, (*of bells*) branle, *m.*, (*see-saw*) balançoire, *f.*, escarpolette, *f.*, (*scope*) cours, *m.*, carrière, *f.*, force d'impulsion, *f.*, essor, *m.*, portée, *f.*, (*tendency*) penchant, *m.*, tendance, *f.* *— -bridge*, s. pont tournant, *m.* *— -door*, s. porte battante, *f.* *To be in full —*, être en branle

Swinish, adj. de pourceau, grossier, sale

Swipes, s.pl. petite bière, *f.*

Switch, s. baguette, *f.*, badine, *f.*, houssine, *f.*, (*railway*) aiguille, *f.* *— -man*, s. aiguilleur, *m.*

Switch, va. houspiller, cingler

Swivel, s. tourniquet, *m.*, (*milit.*) canon à pivot, *m.* *— -gun*, s. canon à pivot, *m.*

Swoon, vn. s'évanouir, se trouver mal

Swoon, s. évanouissement, *m.*, syncope, *f.*

Swoop, va. s'abattre sur. *To — down*, s'abattre

Swoop, s. action de s'abattre, *f.*, attaque, *f.* *At one fell —*, d'un seul coup

Sword, s. épée, *f.*, sabre, *m.*, glaive, *m.*, (*poet.*) fer, *m.* *— in hand*, l'épée à la main. *At the —'s point*, à la pointe de l'épée. *To draw one's —*, tirer son épée, dégainer. *To put to the —*, passer au fil de l'épée. *— -bayonet*, s. sabre-poignard. *— -bearer*, s. porte-glaive, *m.* *— -belt*, s. ceinturon, *m.* *— -cane*, s., *— -stick*, s. canne à épée, *f.* *— -cutler*, s. armurier, *m.* *— -fish*, s. espadon, *m.* *— -knot*, s. dragonne, *f.*

Swordsman, s. tireur, *m.*, lame, *f.*, épée, *f.* *A clever —*, une fine lame

Sworn, adj. assermenté, intime

Sybarite, s. sybarite, *m.f.*

Sycamore, s. sycomore, *m.*

Sycophancy, s. flatterie *f.*, adulation, *f.*

Sycophant, s. sycophante, *m.*, adulateur, *m.*

Syllabic, **Syllabical**, adj. syllabique

Syllabication, s. division en syllabes

Syllable, s. syllabe, *f.*

Syllabus, s. sommaire, *m.*

Syllepsis, s. syllepse, *f.*

Syllogism, s. syllogisme, *m.*

Syllogistic, **Syllogistically**, adv. en forme de syllogisme

Syllogize, vn. syllogiser

Sylph, **Sylphid**, s. sylphe, *m.*, sylphide, *f.*

Sylvan, adj. des forêts, champêtre, agreste

Symbol, s. symbole, *m.*, emblème, *m.*, attribut, *m.*

Symbolic, **Symbolical**, adj. symbolique

Symbolically, adv. d'une manière symbolique

Symbolization, s. symbolisation, *f.*

Symbolize, va. représenter par un symbole, regarder comme un symbole; — vn. symboliser, avoir du rapport or de la conformité avec

Symmetrian, **Symmetrist**, s. observateur or amateur de la symétrie, *m.*

Symmetrical, adj. symétrique

Symmetrically, adv. symétriquement

Symmetrize, va. rendre symétrique

Symmetry, s. symétrie, *f.*

Sympathetic, **Sympathetical**, adj. sympathique

Sympathetically, adv. avec sympathie

Sympathize, vn. sympathiser (avec), (*pity*) compatir (à)

Sympathy, s. sympathie, *f.*

Symphonious, adj. harmonieux, mélodieux

Symphony, s. symphonie, *f.*

Symposiac, adj. de table

Symposium, s. symposie, *f.*, festin, *m.*, banquet, *m.*

Symptom, s. symptôme, *m.*

Symptomatic, adj. symptomatique

Synæresis, s. synérèse, *f.*

Synagogue, s. synagogue, *f.*

Synchronical, **Synchronal**, adj. synchronique

Synchronism, s. synchronisme, *m.*

Syncopate, va. faire une syncope, une élision, (*mus.*) syncoper

Syncopation, s. syncope, *f.*

Synchronism, s. synchronisme, *m.*

Syncope, s. syncope, *f.*

Syndic, s. syndic, *m.*

Syndicate, s. syndicat, *m.*

Synecdoche, s. synecdoche, *f.*

Syngenesia, s. syngénésie, *f.*

Synod, s. synode, *m.*

Synodal, **Synodic**, **Synodical**, adj. synodal, synodique

Synomos, s. confrérie, *f.*, confraternité, *f.*

Synonyme, s. synonyme, *m.*

Synonymist, s. synonymiste, *m.*

Synonymous, adj. synonyme

Synonymously, adv. synonymiquement

Synonymy, s. synonymie, *f.*

Synopsis, s. tableau synoptique, *m.*, sommaire, *m.*

Synoptic, **Synoptical**, adj. synoptique

Synoptically, adv. en abrégé

Syntactic, **Syntactical**, adj. syntaxique, rangé en ordre

Syntactically, adv. d'après les lois de la syntaxe

Syntax, s. syntaxe, *f.*

Synthesis, s. synthèse, *f.*

Synthetic, **Synthetical**, adj. synthétique

Synthetically, adv. synthétiquement

Syringa, s. seringat, *m.*

Syringe, s. seringue, *f.*, petite pompe, *f.* *Exhausting —*, s. pompe à faire le vide, *f.*

Syringe, va. seringuer, injecter, faire des injections avec une seringue

Syrinx, s. flûte de Pan, *m.*

Syrt, **Syrtis**, s. syrtes, *f.pl.*, fondrière, *f.*

Syrup, s. sirop, *m.*

System, s. système, *m.*, régime, *m.*, économie, *f.*, constitution, *f.* *To make a — of*, se faire, faire un système de

Systematic, **Systematical**, adj. systématique

Systematically, adv. systématiquement

Systematist, s. auteur d'un système, *m.*, partisan d'un système

Systematize, va. systématiser, réduire en système

Systematizer, s. auteur d'un système, qui réduit en système

T

T, s. T, t, *m.* *To a T*, parfaitement, trait pour trait

Tab, s. patte, *f.*

Tabaret, s. satin rayé, *m.*

Tabby, adj. tacheté, tavelé, rayé

Tabernacle, s. tabernacle, *m.*

Table, s. table, *f.*, (*board*) tableau, *m.*, (*prices*) tarif, *m.*, (*tablet*) tablette, *f.* *To lay out a* —, dresser une table. *To rise from the* —, quitter la table. *He keeps a good* —, sa table est excellente, on fait bonne chère chez lui. *To drink to the whole* —, boire à la santé de tous. *From the — of my memory*, des tablettes de ma mémoire. — *of prices*, tarif des prix. *To play at —s*, jouer au trictrac. *To turn the —s on*, battre un adversaire avec ses propres armes. — *-bed*, s. lit-table, *m.* — *-beer*, s. petite bière, *f.* — *-book*, s. tablettes, *f.pl.* — *-cloth*, s., — *-cover*, s. nappe, *f.* — *-flap*, s. feuille de table, *f.* — *-land*, s. plateau, *m.* — *-linen*, s. linge de table, *m.* — *-spoon*, s. cuiller à soupe, *f.* — *-talk*, s. propos de table, *m.*

Tablet, s. tablette, *f.*, (*plate*) plaque, *f.*

Taboo, s. indardiction, *f.*

Taboo, va. interdire, mettre en quarantaine

Tabour, s. tambourin, *m.*, tambour de basque, *m.*

Tabour, vn. jouer du tambourin. (*upon*, sur) tambouriner

Tabourer, s. joueur de tambourin, *m.*

Tabourine, s. tambourin, *m.*

Tabular, adj. en forme de table, synoptique

Tacit, adj. tacite, muet, implicite

Tacitly, adv. tacitement

Taciturn, adj. taciturne, silencieux

Taciturnity, s. taciturnité, *f.*

Tack, s. petit clou, *m.*, broquette, *f.*, (*of ships*) bordée, *f.*, point du vent, *m.*, (*of sails*) armure, *f.*

Tack, va. attacher, (*stitch*) bâtir, faufiler, (*to add*) ajouter, (*to nail*) clouer, (*nav.*) faire virer de bord, virer; — vn. (*nav.*) virer de bord, louvoyer. *To — about*, virer de bord, courir des bordées, louvoyer

Tackle, s. poulie, *f.*, appareil, *m.*, ustensiles, *m.pl.*, instruments, *m.pl.*, (*nav.*) cordages, *m.pl.*, palan, *m.*

Tackle, va. garnir, fournir, munir

Tact, s. toucher, *m.*, tact, *m.*

Tactic, adj. de tactique

Tactician, s. tacticien, *m.*

Tactics, s.pl. tactique, *f.*, évolutions, *f.pl.*

Tadpole, s. têtard, *m.*

Taffrail, s. couronnement, *m.*

Taffeta, s. taffetas, *m.*

Tag, s. ferret, *m.*, fer, *m.*, pointe, *f.* — *-rag and bobtail*, canaille, *f.*

Tag, va. ferrer, (*join*) ajouter à, coudre à. *To — on*, coudre

Tail, s. queue, *f.*, (*end*) fin, *f.*, bout, *m.*, (*coin*) revers, *m.*, (*fam.*) pile, *f.*, (*coat*) pan, *m.*, basque, *f.* *To turn* —, montrer les talons, s'enfuir. — *of a steelyard*, fléau d'une romaine. *Head or* —, pile ou face. *I can make neither head nor — of it*, je n'eu peux faire ni queue ni tête. — *-board*, s. derrière de charrette, *m.* — *-piece*, s. cul-de-lampe, *m.*

. . . -Tailed, adj. à . . . queue

Tailor, s. tailleur, *m.*

Tailoring, s. ouvrage de tailleur, *m.*

Taint, va. corrompre, gâter, infecter, empoisonner, souiller, ternir, entacher

Taint, s. infection, *f.*, corruption, *f.*, dépravation, *f.*, souillure, *f.*, flétrissure, *f.*, tache, *f.*, faute, *f.*

Take, va. prendre, accepter, (*to seize*) s'emparer de, enlever, (*to please*) attirer, captiver, plaire à, (*to understand*) entendre, comprendre, (*to follow*) adopter, suivre, (*to copy*) peindre, saisir, imiter, (*a joke*) entendre, (*refuge*) se réfugier, (*a house*) prendre, louer, (*to attest*) prendre, invoquer, attester, (*to lead*) mener, emmener, (*to carry*) porter. *When —n to be well shaken*, agitez avant de prendre. — *any shape but that*, prends toute autre forme que celle-là. *To — food and drink*, manger et boire. *He was —n with a fever*, la fièvre le prit. *He took it from me*, il me le prit. — *three from five*, ôtez trois de cinq. *To — a fox*, prendre un renard. *To — a disease*, gagner une maladie. *To — the public*, attirer le public. *You — me right*, vous me comprenez bien. *Charity —n in its largest extent*, la charité entendue dans son sens le plus large. *I took you for a clergyman*, je vous croyais ecclésiastique. *He was —n for another*, on le prit pour un autre. *What o'clock do you — it to be!* quelle heure croyez-vous qu'il soit? *As I — it*, selon moi. *It —s three feet to make a yard*, il faut trois pieds pour faire un yard. *Shall you — your son with you!* est-ce que vous emmenerez votre fils avec vous? *He took him into his house*, il le reçut dans sa maison. — *this book to him*, portez-lui ce livre. *To — again*, reprendre, reconduire. *To — along*, emmener, conduire, emporter. *To — away*, emmener, enlever, emporter, (*table*) desservir, (*steal*) soustraire. *What —s you away so soon!* qu'est ce qui vous fait partir de si bonne heure? *To — back*, reprendre, remporter, remmener, reconduire. *To — down*, descendre, (*fig.*) faire descendre, (*pride*) rabaisser, rabattre, (*swallow*) avaler, prendre, (*pull down*) abattre, démolir, (*write*) prendre par écrit. *To — in*, faire rentrer, rentrer, prendre, recevoir, admettre, (*load*) prendre un chargement de, charger, (*understand*) embrasser, comprendre, (*surround*) enclore, entourer, (*sails*) serrer, carguer, (*shorten*) raccourcir, (*provisions*) prendre, faire sa provision de, (*journal*) être abonné à, recevoir, (*cheat*) mettre dedans, attraper, duper. *To — off*, ôter, enlever, écarter, couper, retrancher, (*attention*) détourner, (*swallow*) avaler, boire, (*imitate*) imiter, copier, contrefaire. *To — oneself off*, partir, s'en aller, décamper. *To — off from*, amoindrir. *To — on oneself*, se charger de. *To — out*, retirer, tirer, (*tooth*) extraire, arracher, (*stain*) enlever, (*for a walk*) emmener, faire sortir, prendre, se faire délivrer, obtenir. *To — up*, prendre, lever, soulever, ramasser, (*buy*) acheter, (*borrow*) emprunter, se procurer, (*begin*) commencer, (*a song, &c.*) entonner, (*surgery*) rattacher, faire une ligature, (*seize*) absorber, prendre, accaparer, (*arrest*) arrêter, mettre en prison, (*adopt*) accepter, adopter, (*scold*) reprendre, relever, réprimander, (*continue*) reprendre, occuper, prendre, (*quarrel*) épouser, (*time*) comprendre, (*profession*) embrasser, (*taxes*) faire rentrer, percevoir, (*a note*) payer, recevoir. *To — a person up to*, conduire quelqu'un à. *To — upon oneself*, prendre sur soi, se charger. — vn. (*to go*) se diriger, aller (à), se réfugier (dans), (*to give oneself up*) s'adonner (à), s'attacher (à), se mettre (à), prendre de mauvaises habitudes, (*to, . . .*) prendre en affection, en amitié, avoir du goût (pour), mordre (à), (*succeed*) prendre, réussir, avoir du succès. *He took to his bed*, il se mit au lit. *To — to evil courses*, s'adonner, se livrer à une vie de désordre. *To — to writing verses*, se mettre à, se mêler de faire des vers. *To — to business*, se mettre dans les affaires. *The play will never* —, la pièce n'aura jamais de succès, ne prendra pas. *To — after*, copier, imiter, ressembler. *To — in with*, s'attacher à. *To — off*, s'enlever, s'ôter. *To — on*, gémir, s'affliger. *To — up*, s'arrêter, s'amender. *To — up with*, se contenter de, s'accommoder de, fréquenter, vivre avec. *To — with*, contenter, plaire à

Take, s. pêche, *f*

Take-in, s. duperie, *f.*, trompeur, *m.*

Take-off, s. imitation, *f.*, charge, *f.*

Taker, s. preneur, *m.*, -euse, *f.*

Taking, adj. séduisant, attrayant, contagieux

Taking, s. action de prendre, *f.*, prise, *f.*, capture, *f.*

Talc, s. talc, m.

Tale, s. conte, m., histoire, f., nouvelle, f., (*lie*) mensonge, m., fable, f., (*disclosure*) rapport, m., (*number*) compte, m., nombre, m. *The — of the castle*, les veillées du château. *Idle —s*, contes frivoles, contes en l'air, contes bleus, sornettes. *So ends my —*, ainsi finit mon histoire. *— of a tub*, conte d'un tonneau. *To tell a —*, conter une histoire. *To tell —s*, rapporter. *— -bearer*, s. rapporteur, m., -euse, f., mauvaise langue, f. *— -bearing*, s. rapports, m.pl. *— -bearers are as bad as — -makers*, ceux qui colportent des médisances ne valent pas mieux que ceux qui les inventent

Talent, s. talent, m.

Talented, adj. de talent

Talisman, s. talisman, m.

Talk, vn. parler, (*of, about*, de, *to*, à), causer, converser, (*private*) babiller, bavarder. *It was not much —ed of*, on n'en parla pas beaucoup. *To — away, to — on*, continuer de parler, parler toujours. *To — away the night, to — the night through*, passer la nuit à parler, à causer. *It's —ing for —ing sake*, c'est là parler pour parler. *To be —ing with*, être en conversation. *To — sensibly*, parler raison. *To — to oneself*, se parler à soi-même. *To — to each other*, se parler (l'un à l'autre), causer ensemble. *To — to the purpose*, parler juste. *To — about music*, causer musique. *To — about one thing and the other*, causer de choses et d'autres. — va. parler, dire. *To — down*, réduire au silence. *To — into*, persuader de faire quelque chose, produire un effet quelconque par la parole. *He will — himself into prison*, ses discours imprudents le feront mettre en prison. *My friend —ed me out of my resolution*, les arguments de mon ami me firent changer de résolution. *To — over*, causer de, discuter, parler de, raconter. *To — up*, monter la tête à, enjôler, entortiller. *To — oneself hoarse*, s'enrouer à force de parler

Talk, s. conversation, f., causerie, f., entretien, m., discours, m., propos, m.pl., bruit, m., rumeur, f. *To have a long — with*, causer, s'entretenir longuement avec. *Our pleasant —*, nos si douces causeries. *There is a — of*, on parle de. *It is the — of the whole town*, il n'est bruit que de cela dans la ville

Talkative, adj. bavard, causeur, babillard

Talkativeness, s. bavardage, m., loquacité, f.

Talker, s. causeur, m., bavard, m., parleur, m., discoureur, m., (*boaster*) hâbleur, m.

Talking, s. causerie, f., bavardage, m.

Tall, adj. de haute taille, élevé, haut

Tallness, s. taille, f., stature, f.

Tallow, s. suif, m. *— -candle*, s. chandelle, f. *— -chandler*, s. fabricant or marchand de chandelles, m. *— -face*, s. face blême, face de carême, f. *— -faced*, au visage blême. *— -trade*, s. commerce de suifs, m.

Tallow, va. graisser, suifer

Tallowy, adj. de suif, graisseux

Tally, s. (*baker's*) taille, f., pendant, m., pareil, m. *— -man*, s. marchand qui donne huit jours de crédit, m. *— -shop*, s. boutique où l'on achète avec un crédit de huit jours, f.

Tally, va.n. marquer, adapter, ajuster, cadrer, correspondre, s'accorder

Tally-ho! interj. taïaut!

Talmud, s. Talmud, m.

Talmudical, adj. du Talmud

Talon, s. serre, f.

Tamable, adj. domptable

Tamarind, s. tamarin, m. *— -tree*, s. tamarin, m.

Tamarisk, s. tamarisc, m.

Tambour, s. tambour de basque, m., (*arts*) tambour, m.

Tambourine, s. tambourin, m., tambour de basque, m.

Tame, adj. apprivoisé, doux, domestique, soumis, (*fig.*) faible, mou, terne, plat, pâle. *To grow —*, s'apprivoiser. *Made — to fortune's blows*, dompté par une fortune ennemie. *— -spirited*, adj. mou, sans énergie, faible

Tame, va. dompter, apprivoiser, humilier

Tamely, adv. doucement, avec soumission, (*fig.*) lâchement

Tameness, s. domesticité, f., douceur, f., soumission, f., mollesse, f., lâcheté, f.

Tamer, s. dompteur, m.

Tamper, vn. (*with*) se mêler (de), toucher (à), s'occuper (de), faire de petites expériences (avec), (*try to bribe*) pratiquer, suborner, chercher à corrompre. *To — with witnesses*, suborner des témoins

Tampering, s. expériences, f.pl., intrigues, f.pl., menées sourdes, f.pl.

Tamtam, s. tam-tam, m.

Tan, s. tan, m. *— -bed*, s. couche de tan, f. *— -house*, s., *— -yard*, s. tannerie, f.

Tan, va. tanner, (*complexion*) brûler, bronzer, hâler

Tandem, s. tandem, m.

Tangent, s. tangente, f. *To fly off, to go off, to run off at a —*, s'échapper par la tangente

Tangible, adj. tangible, perceptible, palpable

Tangle, s. nœud, m., pêle-mêle, m., enchevêtrement, m., confusion, f.

Tangle, va. emmêler, embrouiller, enchevêtrer

Tank, s. citerne, f., bassin, m., réservoir, m.

Tankard, s. pot, m.

Tanner, s. tanneur, m.

Tannery, s. tannerie, f.

Tannin, s. tannin, m.

Tanning, s. tannage, m.

Tansy, s. tanaisie, f.

Tantalize, va. tourmenter, exciter les désirs

Tantamount, adj. équivalent. *To be — to*, équivaloir à. *That is — to saying*, c'est comme si l'on disait

Tantivy, adv. à toute bride, f., à fond de train, f.

Tap, s. tape, f., petit coup, m., (*casks*) robinet, m., cannelle, f., (*room*) salle des buveurs, f., (*borer*) taraud, m. *To give a — at the door*, frapper doucement à la porte. *— -house*, s. cabaret, m. *— -room*, s. salle des buveurs, f. *— -root*, s. racine pivotante, f.

Tap, va.n. taper, frapper doucement, percer, mettre en perce, (*draw*) tirer, pivoter, (*a tree*) inciser, (*surgery*) faire la ponction

Tape, s. ruban de fil, m. *— -worm*, s. ver solitaire, m. *Red —*, s. bureaucratie, f.

Taper, s. bougie, f., flambeau, m., (*churches*) cierge, m., lumière, f.

Taper, Tapering, adj. élancé, pointé, conique, en pyramide, effilé, de fuseau

Taper, vn. s'effiler, se terminer en pointe, s'élancer. *The —ing spire*, l'aiguille du clocher. *Her —ing masts*, ses mâts élancés. *—ing top*, sommet en pointe. *—ing away*, s'élevant en pointe. — va. effiler, terminer en pointe

Tapestry, s. tapisserie, f. *— -carpet*, s. tapisserie, f. *— -worker*, s. ouvrier en tapisserie, m. *To make —*, faire de la tapisserie. *To hang with —*, tapisser

Tapioca, s. tapioca, m.

Tapir, s. tapir, m.

Tapping, s. (*surg.*) ponction, f., mise en perce, f.

Tapster, s. garçon, m., cabaretier, m.

Tar, s. goudron, m., (*sailor*) matelot, m., loup de mer, m. *Coal —*, s. goudron de houille, m. *Mineral —*, s. bitume, m. *— -water*, s. eau de goudron, f. *— -barrel*, s. baril de goudron, m.

Tar, va. goudronner

Tarantula, s. tarentule, f.

Tardily, adv. lentement, tardivement

Tardiness, s. lenteur, f., retard, m.

Tardy, adj. (*slow*) lent, (*late*) tardif, en retard

Tare, s. (*weed*) ivraie, f., (*bot.*) vesce, f., (*com.*) tare, f.

Target, s. cible, f. *— -practice*, s. tir à la cible, m.

Tariff, s. tarif, m.

Tarlatan, s. tarlatane, f.

Tarnish, va. ternir, flétrir. *To be —ed*, être terni, se ternir. — vn. se ternir, se flétrir

Tarpauling, s. toile goudronnée, f.

Tarragon, s. estragon, m.

Tarry, vn. s'arrêter, rester, demeurer, séjourner, (*delay*) tarder, se faire attendre, (*wait*) attendre

Tarry, adj. de goudron

Tart, adj. aigre, acide, âpre, (*keen*) mordant, piquant, (*temper*) acariâtre, revêche. *A — reply*, une réponse aigre, une réplique acerbe. *A — rebuke*, une verte réprimande

Tart, s. tarte, f., tourte, f. *— -dish*, s. tourtière, f.

Tartan, s. tartan, m., (*nav.*) tartane, f.

Tartar, s. (*salt*) tartre, m., (*pers.*) personne irritable, f., Turc, m. *To catch a —*, trouver à qui parler

Tartish, adj. aigrelet

Tartlet, adj. tartelette, f.

Tartly, adv. aigrement, vertement

Tartness, s. acidité, f., aigreur, f., acerbité, f., humeur revêche, f. *The — of his face*, son visage acerbe

Task, s. tâche, f., (*schools*) devoir, m., (*punishment*) pensum, m. *— -master*, s. maître, m. *To take to —*, quereller, réprimander. *I have set him his —*, je lui ai donné sa tâche. *Give the boy a — to do*, donnez aux élèves un devoir à faire

Task, va. donner *or* imposer *or* assigner une tâche à, (*require to do*) réclamer, exiger l'emploi de

Tassel, s. gland, m., (*books*) signet, m., (*archit.*) tasseau, m.

Tasseled, adj. orné de glands

Taste, va. goûter, déguster, (*experience*) éprouver, connaître, subir, (*enjoy*) jouir de. *I made him — it, I gave him to —*, je le lui fis goûter. *To — the sweets of sleep*, goûter les douceurs du sommeil. *To — death*, connaître la mort. — vn. avoir un goût, jouir, (*of, . . .*) avoir le goût de. *It makes things — bitter*, cela donne aux choses un goût amer. *To — delicious*, avoir un goût délicieux. *To — like honey*, avoir un goût de miel

Taste, s. goût, m., saveur, f., (*small quantity*) peu, m., goutte, f., gorgée, f., (*act of tasting*) gustation, f. *Bees have —*, les abeilles ont le sens du goût. *Of exquisite —*, d'un goût exquis. *He has no — for anything*, il ne prend goût à rien. — *is everything*, le goût est la loi suprême. *It is a matter of* —, c'est affaire de goût. *To dispute about* —, disputer des goûts. *Of great* —, plein de goût. *In point of* —, en matière de goût, pour ce qui est du goût. *In good* —, *in bad* —, de bon goût, de mauvais goût. *In the best* — du *or* dans le meilleur goût. *Quite out of* —, *of no* —, *without any* —, sans goût aucun, tout à fait de mauvais goût. *There is no accounting for* —*s*, il ne faut point disputer des goûts. *Is it to your* —? est-ce à votre goût? *To have a* — *for*, *a great* — *for*, avoir du goût pour, beaucoup de goût pour. *To have no* — *for*, n'avoir pas de goût pour, n'avoir pas le goût de

Tasteful, adj. agréable au goût, savoureux. *Highly* —, plein de goût, d'un goût rare

Tastefully, adv. avec goût

Tastefulness, s. goût, m.

Tasteless, adj. sans goût, insipide, fade. *To be* —, n'avoir aucun goût, être insipide

Tastelessly, adv. sans goût

Tastelessness, s. insipidité, f., fadeur, f., (*fig.*) manque de goût, m.

Taster, s. dégustateur, m., (*for cheese*) sonde, f.

Tastily, adv. avec goût

Tasting, s. action de goûter, f., dégustation, f.

Tasty, adj. de bon goût

Tatter, s. haillon, m., lambeau, m., guenille, f. *All in* —*s*, tout déguenillé. *To tear to* —*s*, mettre en lambeaux

Tatterdemalion, s. gueux, m.

Tattered, adj. déguenillé, en haillons

Tattle, s. babil, m., babillage, m., caquet, m., bavardage, m. *The* — *of the day*, les cancans du jour

Tattle, vn. babiller, caqueter, bavarder, jaser. *The French language is extremely proper to* — *in*, la langue française convient surtout aux causeries familières

Tattler, s. babillard, m., -e, f., (*tell-tale*) bavard, m., -e, f., rapporteur, m., -euse, f.

Tattoo, s. (*milit.*) retraite, f., (*paint.*) tatouage, m. *To beat a* —, battre le tambour, battre du tambour

Tattoo, va. tatouer

Tattooing, s. tatouage, m.

Taunt, s. reproche, m., sarcasme, m., raillerie, f., insulte, f.

Taunt, va. reprocher à, se moquer, railler, insulter

Taunter, s. railleur, m., -euse, f.

Tauntingly, adv. d'un ton insultant, injurieusement

Taurus, s. Taureau, m., (*geog.*) le mont Taurus, m.

Tautological, adj. tautologique

Tautology, s. tautologie, f.

Tavern, s. taverne, f., cabaret, m., auberge, f. —*-keeper*, s., —*-man*, s. cabaretier, m., tavernier, m. —*-haunter*, s. pilier de cabaret, m.

Taw, va. mégisser

Taw, s. bille, f.

Tawdrily, adv. avec prétention et sans goût

Tawdriness, s. clinquant, m., faux brillant, m.

Tawdry, adj. prétentieux, voyant, de mauvais goût. —*colours*, s. couleurs criardes, f.pl.

Tawny, adj. (*pers.*) basané, (*animals*) fauve. — *complexion*, teint basané

Tax, s. impôt, m., taxe, f., imposition, f., contribution, f., tribut, m., (*fig.*) exigence, f. *Additional* —, s. surtaxe, f. *To lay heavy* —*es upon*, frapper de lourds impôts. *To pay one's* —*es*, payer ses impositions. —*-gatherer*, s. percepteur de contributions, m. —*-free*, adj. exempté d'impôts. —*-cart*, s. voiture suspendue, f. —*-payer*, s. contribuable, m.f.

Tax, va. taxer, imposer, (*fig.*) exiger, demander à, mettre à l'épreuve, (*with*) accuser (de), reprocher (à)

Taxable, adj. imposable

Taxation, s. taxe, f., impôts, m.pl., taxation, f.

Taxer, s. taxateur, m.

Tea, s. thé, m., (*plant*) tisane, f. *To take* —, prendre le thé. *Black* —, s. thé noir, m. *Green* —, s. thé vert, m. *Cup of* —, s. tasse de thé, f. —*-cake*, s. gâteau à thé, m. —*-chest*, s. caisse à thé, f. —*-cup*, tasse à thé, f. —*-kettle*, s. bouilloire, f. —*-plant*, s. arbre à thé, m. —*-party*, s. thé, m. —*-board*, s. plateau, m. —*-caddy*, s., —*-canister*, s. boîte à thé, f. —*-garden*, s. guinguette, m. —*-service*, s., —*-set*, s., —*-things*, s. service à thé, m., cabaret, m. —*-pot*, s. théière, f. —*-spoon*, s. petite cuiller, f., cuiller à café. —*-trade*, s. commerce de thé, m. —*-urn*, s. fontaine à thé, f.

Teach, va. instruire, enseigner, apprendre, faire apprendre, accoutumer, inculquer à. *To* — *the nations*, instruire les nations. *I was taught French and German*, on m'apprit le français et l'allemand. *There I taught grammar*, j'y enseignai la grammaire. *She taught me my lessons*, elle me faisait apprendre mes leçons. *I have taught him his lesson*, (*fig.*) je lui ai fait sa leçon, je l'ai endoctriné. — vn. enseigner, être professeur

Teachable, adj. docile

Teachableness, s. docilité, f., aptitude, f.

Teacher, s. maître, m., instituteur, m., maîtresse, f., institutrice, f., précepteur, m. — *of English*, maître, maîtresse *or* professeur d'anglais. *The profession of a* —, la carrière de l'enseignement

Teaching, s. enseignement, m., instruction, f.

Teak, s. bois de teck, m.

Teal, s. sarcelle, f.

Team, s. attelage, m.

Tear, s. larme, f., pleurs, m.pl. *To drop a* —, laisser tomber une larme. *All in* —*s*, tout en larmes, tout en pleurs. *All drowned in* —*s*, les yeux noyés de larmes. *Even to* —*s*, jusqu'aux larmes. *With* —*s*, avec des larmes. *She came with* —*s in her eyes*, elle vint les larmes aux yeux *or* les yeux pleins de larmes. —*s gushed into his eyes*, les larmes lui vinrent aux yeux. —*s stood in his eyes*, les larmes brillèrent dans ses yeux, il avait des larmes aux yeux

Tear, s. déchirure, f.

Tear, va. déchirer, lacérer, (*pull*) arracher, enlever. *His clothes were all torn*, il était tout déchiré. *Torn from all I love*, arraché à tout ce que j'aime. *To* — *oneself from*, s'arracher à. *To* — *one's hair, each other's hair*, s'arracher les cheveux. *To* — *asunder*, déchirer en deux. *To* — *away, down, off, out, up*, arracher. — vn. déchirer, (*run*) courir, aller vite

Tearful, adj. plein de larmes, en pleurs

Tearing, s. déchirement, m.

Tearless, adj. sans larmes

Tease, va. (*wool, cloth*) peigner, carder, chardonner, (*to annoy*) taquiner, ennuyer, tourmenter, importuner. *To* — *a person into doing a thing*, faire faire quelque chose à quelqu'un à force d'importunités

Teasel, s. chardon, m.

Teaser, s. taquin, m., taquine, f.

Teasing, s. cardage, m., taquinerie, f., importunité, f.

Teat, s. mamelle, f., teton, m.

Technical, adj. technique

Technicality, s. détail technique, m., mot technique, m.

Technically, adv. d'une manière technique

Technological, adj. technologique

Technology, s. technologie, f.

Tedious, adj. ennuyeux, fatigant, pénible

Tediously, adv. ennuyeusement, d'une manière fatigante

Tediousness, s. **Tedium**, s. ennui, m., fatigue, f., prolixité, f., lenteur, f.

Teem, vn.a. être fécond (en), enfanter, être rempli *or* plein (de), être gros (de), abonder (en), produire

Teeming, adj. fécond, fertile, abondant

Teens, s.pl. âge de treize ans à dix-neuf. *A beauty in her* —*s*, une beauté dans son printemps. *In one's* —*s*, n'avoir pas son vingt

Teeth, vn. faire ses dents

Teething, s. dentition, f.

Teetotal, adj. de tempérance

Teetotaler, s. buveur d'eau, m.

Teetotalism, s. abstinence complète de spiritueux, f.

Teetotum, s. toton, m.

Telegram, s. télégramme, m., dépêche, f.

Telegraph, s. télégraph, m. *Electric, electro-magnetic* —, télégraphe électrique. *Submarine* —, télégraphe sous-marin

Telegraph, va. télégraphier

Telegraphic, adj. télégraphique

Telegraphy, s. télégraphie, f.

Telescope, s. télescope, m., lunette d'approche, f. —*-table*, s. table à rallonges, f.

Telescopic, adj. télescopique

Tell, va. dire, exprimer, (*relate*) raconter, conter, (*teach*) apprendre, montrer, (*converse*) entretenir, (*confess*) avouer, faire connaître, dévoiler, révéler, (*publish*) publier, proclamer, (*reckon*) compter, (*distinguish*) distinguer, discerner. *I am told, we are told that*, on me dit, on nous dit que. *Now I'll* — *you what*, maintenant écoutez-moi bien. *Tush! never* — *me*, bah! ne venez pas me dire cela. *To think one thing and* — *another*, penser d'une façon et parler d'une autre. *I have told you so over and over again*, je vous l'ai dit et redit. *How can I* —! comment dire, que sais-je! *He told me his misfortune*, il me raconta son malheur. *I was told it by my uncle*, je l'ai appris de mon oncle. *I will* — *you how to set the trap*, je vous montrerai à dresser le piége. *He told me of it*, il me l'a dit, il m'en a parlé. *To* — *the stars*, compter les étoiles. *To* — *down, to* — *off, to* — *out, to* — *over*, compter. — vn. dire, (*take effect*) porter, porter coup, produire, faire de l'effet, se dessiner, se voir. *Blush not to say I cannot* —, ne rougissez pas de dire, je ne puis le dire *or* je ne sais pas. *Every line* —*s*, chaque ligne porte coup. *Every shot told*, chaque coup porta. *The distance began to* — *upon the horse*, la distance produisait son effet sur le cheval. *That* —*s well in the world*, cela fait un bon effet dans le monde.

Teller, s. diseur, m., diseuse, f., narrateur, m., conteur, m., (*of votes*) scrutateur, m.

Telling, adj. qui porte coup, qui produit son effet, énergique, efficace. *A* —

blow, un coup qui porte. *A — speech*, un discours où chaque mot portait. *With — effect*, avec grand effet

Telltale, s.adj. rapporteur, *m.*, -euse, *f.*, bavard, *m.*, -e, *f.*, (*mach.*) compteur, *m.*

Temerity, s. témérité, *f.*

Temper, s. combinaison, *f.*, mélange, *m.*, tempérament, *m.*, constitution, *f.*, disposition, *f.*, caractère, *m.*, calme, *m.*, modération, *f.*, humeur, *f.*, irritation, *f.*, (*of metals*) trempe, *f.* *To lose one's —*, se fâcher, s'emporter, perdre patience. *To be, to put out of —*, être, mettre de mauvaise humeur. *To keep one's —*, ne pas se fâcher, garder son sang-froid

Temper, va. adoucir, tempérer, (*mix*) mélanger, combiner, mêler, (*steel*) tremper, (*colours*) délayer, détremper

Temperament, s. tempérament, *m.*

Temperance, s. tempérance, *f.*

Temperate, adj. tempéré, modéré, tempérant, sobre, patient

Temperature, s. température, *f.*

Tempered, adj. d'humeur . . ., de caractère . . ., (*steel*) trempé. *A good- — fellow*, un garçon d'un bon caractère

Tempest, s. tempête, *f.*, orage, *m.*

Tempestuous, adj. orageux

Templar, s. templier, *m.*, (*student*) étudiant en droit, *m.*

Temple, s. temple, *m.*, (*anat.*) tempe, *f.*

Temporal, adj. temporel

Temporalities, s.pl. temporel, *m.*, revenus temporels, *m.pl.*

Temporally, adv. temporellement

Temporarily, adv. temporairement, momentanément

Temporariness, s. état temporaire *or* provisoire, *m.*

Temporary, adj. temporaire

Temporization, s. temporisation, *f.*

Temporize, vn. temporiser, transiger (avec)

Temporizer, s. temporiseur, *m.*

Temporizing, s. temporisation, *f.*, versatilité, *f.*

Tempt, va. tenter, éprouver, (*incite*) exciter, pousser, porter

Temptation, s. tentation, *f.*

Tempter, Temptress, s. tentateur, *m.*, -trice, *f.*, séducteur, *m.*, -trice, *f.*

Tempting, adj. tentant, séduisant, attrayant

Temptingly, adv. d'une manière tentante

Ten, adj. dix

Ten, s. dix, *m.*, dizaine, *f.* *By —s*, par dizaines

Tenable, adj. (*milit.*) tenable, (*fig.*) soutenable

Tenacious, adj. tenace. *To be — of*, tenir à

Tenaciously, adv. d'une manière tenace, obstinément

Tenacity, s. ténacité, *f.*

Tenancy, s. tenure, *f.*, location, *f.*

Tenant, s. locataire, *m.*, tenancier, *m.*, fermier, *m.*

Tenant, va. louer, habiter, occuper

Tenantable, adj. logeable, habitable

Tenantless, adj. inhabité

Tenantry, s. tenanciers, *m.pl.*, fermiers, *m.pl.*

Tench, s. tanche, *f.*

Tend, va. garder, veiller sur, veiller, soigner; — vn. aller, venir, tendre (à), contribuer, aboutir

Tendency, s. tendance, *f.*

Tender, va. offrir, proposer, (*law*) déférer; — vn. soumissionner

Tender, s. (*locomotive*) tender, *m.*, (*nav.*) allége, *f.*, (*offer*) offre, *f.*, soumission, *f.*

Tender, adj. tendre, indulgent, compatissant, doux, sensible, faible, délicat, scrupuleux, (*of*, de) jaloux. — *-hearted*, adj. tendre, sensible, compatissant

Tenderly, adv. tendrement, mollement, délicatement

Tenderness, s. (*of meat*) tendreté, *f.*, (*pain*) sensibilité, *f.*, (*gentleness*) tendresse, *f.*, soin, *m.*, égard, *m.*, sollicitude, *f.*

Tendon, s. tendon, *m.*

Tendril, s. vrille, *f.*

Tenement, s. habitation, *f.*, maison, *f.*

Tenet, s. dogme, *m.*, principe, *m.*, doctrine, *f.*, opinion, *f.*

Tenfold, adj. décuple

Tennis, s. paume, *m.* *To play at —*, jouer à la paume. *— -ball*, s. balle du jeu de paume, *f.* *— -court*, s. jeu de paume, *f.*

Tenon, s. tenon, *m.*

Tenor, s. ténor, *m.*, (*instr.*) alto, *m.*

Tenour, s. teneur, *f.*, tendance, *f.*, sens, *m.*, portée, *f.*, esprit, *m.* *They kept the noiseless — of their way*, ils suivirent sans bruit le chemin qui leur était tracé

Tense, s. temps, *m.*

Tense, adj. tendu, roide

Tension, s. tension, *f.*

Tent, s. tente, (*wine*) vin de Malaga, *m.* *— bedstead*, s. lit de camp, *m.* *— -bed*, s. lit à colonnes, *m.* *— -cloth*, s. coutil, *m.* *— -maker*, s. fabricant de tentes, *m.*

Tent, vn. camper, vivre sous la tente

Tentative, adj. d'essai, expérimental

Tented, adj. couvert de tentes

Tenter, s. (*for drying*) séchoir, *m.*, crochet, *m.* *To be on —s or on — -hooks*, être dans des transes. *To keep on the — -hooks*, faire languir

Tenth, adj. s. dixième, dix. *One —*, un dixième. *Louis the —*, Louis dix. *On the — of June*, le dix juin

Tenthly, adv. dixièmement

Tenuity, s. ténuité, *f.*, simplicité, *f.*

Tenuous, adj. ténu, mince, rare, subtil

Tenure, s. tenure, *f.*, redevance, *f.*, possession, *f.*, durée, *f.*

Tepid, adj. tiède

Tepidity, s. tiédeur, *f.*

Teredo, s. taret, *m.*

Tergiversation, s. tergiversation, *f.*

Term, s. terme, *m.*, limite, *f.*, borne, *f.*, temps, *m.*, durée, *f.*, (*univ.*) semestre, *m.*, session, *f.*, mot, *m.*, (*charge*) conditions, *f.pl.*, prix, *m.* *To bring to —s*, amener à un arrangement, faire capituler. *To come to —s*, faire un arrangement, tomber d'accord. *I am on good —s with him*, je suis bien avec lui

Term, va. appeler, nommer, dire

Termagant, s. mégère, *f.*, femme acariâtre, *f.*

Terminate, va. terminer, déterminer, mettre un terme à; — vn. se terminer, finir

Termination, s. limite, *f.*, extrémité, *f.*, fin, *f.*, conclusion, *f.*, (*gram.*) terminaison, *f.*, désinence, *f.*

Terminus, s. embarcadère, *m.*, débarcadère, *m.*, gare, *f.*

Terrace, s. terrasse, *f.*

Terrace, va. bâtir en terrasse

Terraced, adj. à terrasse

Terra-cotta, s. terre cuite

Terrestrial, adj. terrestre

Terrible, adj. terrible, effrayant

Terribly, adv. terriblement

Terrier, s. terrier, *m.*

Terrific, adj. terrible, effrayant

Terrifically, adv. d'une manière effrayante, terriblement

Terrify, va. terrifier, épouvanter

Territorial, adj. territorial

Territory, s. territoire, *m.*

Terror, s. terreur, *f.*, frayeur, *f.*, épouvante, *f.*

Terse, adj. élégant, pur, bien

Tersely, adv. élégamment

Terseness, s. élégance, *f.*

Tertian, s. fièvre tierce, *f.*

Tertiary, adj. tertiaire

Tessellate, va. marqueter, faire en marqueterie

Tessellated, adj. marqueté, en mosaïque

Test, s. (*trial*) essai, *m.*, épreuve, *f.*, (*chem.*) réactif, *m.*, coupelle, *f.*

Test, va. essayer, éprouver, mettre à l'épreuve, (*chem.*) coupeller

Testacea, s. testacés, *m. plur.*

Testaceous, adj. testacé

Testament, s. testament, *m.*

Testamentary, adj. testamentaire

Testator, s. testateur, *m.*

Testatrix, s. testatrice, *f.*

Tester, s. baldaquin, *m.*, ciel de lit, *m.*

Testifier, s. témoin, *m.*

Testify, vn.a. témoigner, rendre *or* porter témoignage (de), (*law*) déposer

Testily, adv. avec humeur

Testimonial, s. témoignage, *m.*, attestation, *f.*, certificat, *m.*, souvenir, *m.*

Testimony, s. témoignage, *m.*, affirmation, *f.* *To bear — to*, rendre témoignage de, attester. *In — of which*, en foi de quoi

Testiness, s. humeur, *f.*, colère, *f.*, pétulance, *f.*

Testy, adj. irritable, emporté, bourru

Tetanus, s. tétanos, *m.*

Tether, s. attache, *f.*

Tether, va. mettre à l'attache

Tetter, s. dartre, *f.*

Teutonic, adj. teutonique

Text, s. texte, *m.* *— -book*, s. livre de classe, *m.*, manuel, *m.* *— -hand*, s., *large —*, s. écriture en gros

Textile, adj. textile

Textile, s. matière textile, *f.*

Textual, adj. textuel

Texture, s. tissage, *m.*, (*of cloth*) tissu, *m.*, toile, *f.*, (*fig.*) contexture, *f.*

Than, conj. que, (*before numerals*) de

Thank, va. remercier, rendre grâces. *— God!* Dieu merci! *— heaven!* grâces au ciel! *— you!* merci! *I will — you for*, voudriez vous bien me donner

Thankful, adj. reconnaissant

Thankfully, adv. avec reconnaissance

Thankfulness, s. reconnaissance, *f.*, gratitude, *f.* *Out of — to God*, par reconnaissance envers Dieu

Thankless, adj. ingrat, méconnu, oublié

Thanklessness, s. ingratitude, *f.*

Thanks, s. pl. grâces, *f.pl.*, actions de grâces, *f.pl.*, remercîments, *m.pl.* *Many —*, bien des remercîments. *To give, to return —*, remercier. *To give many — to*, faire bien des remercîments à. *— -offering*, s. sacrifice d'actions de grâces, *f.* *— -giving*, s. actions de grâces, *f.*

That, adj. dem. ce, cet, cette, ce . . . là. *— -way*, par là

That, pron. celui-là, celle-là, cela. *— is*, c'est-à-dire. *— is something new*, voilà du nouveau. *— one*, celui-là, celle-là. *For all —*, malgré tout, néanmoins

That, conj. que, pour que, afin que, parce que. *So* —, de sorte que. *I will know your business*, — *I will*, je saurai ce que vous faites, je vous le jure
That, pron. *see* Who, Whom, While.
Thatch, s. chaume, *m.*
Thatch, va. couvrir de chaume. —*ed cottage*, s. chaumière, *f.*
Thatcher, s. couvreur, *m.*
Thaw, va.n. dégeler, fondre
Thawing, s. dégel, *m.*
The, def. art. le, la, les, ce, cette, ces
Theatre, s. théâtre, *m.*, spectacle, *m.*
Theatrical, adj. de théâtre, théâtral, scénique
Theatricals, s. pl. spectacle, *m.* *Private* —, s. comédie de salon, *f.*
Thee, pers. pron. sing. te, toi. *To* —*thou*, tutoyer
Theft, s. vol, *m.*, larcin, *m.*, objet volé, *m.* *Guilty of* —, coupable de vol
Their, adj. leur, leurs
Theirs, pron. le leur, la leur, les leurs, à eux, à elles
Theism, s. théisme, *m.*
Theist, s. théiste, *m.*
Them, pers. pron. les, eux, elles, leur, à eux, à elles
Theme, s. thème, *m.*, sujet, *m.*, texte, *m.*
Themselves, pron. se, eux-mêmes, elles-mêmes, mêmes
Then, adv. alors, pour lors, dans ce temps-là, (*afterwards*) ensuite, puis, (*therefore*) donc, alors, par conséquent. — *and there*, sans désemparer, sur-le-champ. *Ever since* —, dès lors, dès ce temps-là. *Now* . . ., — . . ., tantôt . . ., tantôt . . . *What* — *!* et après? eh bien! après!
Then, adj. d'alors, du moment
Thence, adv. de là, en, dès lors, depuis lors, depuis ce temps
Thenceforth, **Thenceforward**, adv. dès lors, depuis lors, de là
Theocracy, s. théocratie, *f.*
Theocratic, adj. théocratique
Theodicy, s. théodicée, *f.*
Theologian, s. théologien, *m*
Theological, adj. théologique
Theologically, adv. théologiquement
Theorem, s. théorème, *m.*
Theoretical, adj. théorique, spéculatif
Theoretically, adv. théoriquement, en théorie
Theorist, s. théoricien, *m.*
Theory, s. théorie, *f.*
Therapeutics, s. pl. thérapeutique, *f.*
There, adv. là, y, voilà, (*before an impers. verb*) il, en cela, là. *He is* —, il y est. — *they are*, les voilà. — *is*, il y a, il est. — *are*, il y a
Thereabout, **Thereabouts**, adv. près de là, environ, à peu près, ensuite
Thereafter, adv. d'après cela, en conséquence, conformément
Thereat, adv. par là, à cet endroit
Thereby, adv. par là, par ce moyen
Therefore, conj. adv. donc, c'est pourquoi, aussi, par conséquent
Therefrom, adv. en, de là
Therein, adv. là-dedans, y, là, en cela
Thereof, adv. en, de cela, d'eux, d'entre eux
Thereto, **Thereunto**, adv. y, à cela
Thereupon, adv. là-dessus
Therewith, adv. en, avec cela
Thermal, adj. thermal
Thermometer, s. thermomètre, *m.*
Thermometric, adj. thermométrique
These, pl. *of* This, dem. adj. ces . . ., ci. —, dem. pron. ceux-ci, celles-ci
Thesis, s. thèse, *f.*
They, pers. pron. ils, eux, elles, ceux, celles, on
Thick, adj. épais, gros, fort, (*muddy, &c.*) trouble, (*close*) dru, nombreux, (*speech*) épais, embarrassé, indistinct, gras, (*hearing*) dur, (*stupid*) grossier, stupide, (*intimate*) intime, lié
Thick, s. partie épaisse, *f.*, (*middle*) épais, *m.*, fort, *m.* *The—of the leg*, le gras de la jambe. *To go through — and thin*, surmonter tous les obstacles, (*fam.*) employer le vert et le sec
Thick, adv. rapidement, à coups pressés, dru, en troupe, en foule. *To speak* —, grasseyer. —*-head*, s. —*-skulls*, s. sot, *m.*, lourdaud, *m.* —*-headed*, adj., —*-skulled*, adj. épais, stupide, à tête dure. —*-lipped*, adj. lippu, aux grosses lèvres. —*-necked*, adj. au gros cou. —*-set*, adj. touffu, (*pers.*) trapu. —*-sown*, adj. semé dru, serré
Thicken, va. épaissir, donner de la consistance à, (*make close*) serrer, renforcer; — vn. s'épaissir, s'obscurcir, prendre de la consistance, grossir, augmenter
Thickening, s. épaississement, *m.*, (*cook*) liaison, *f.*
Thicket, s. fourré, *m.*, hallier, *m.*, taillis, *m.*
Thickly, adv. épais, dru, nombreux, profondément
Thickness, s. épaisseur, *f.*, consistance, *f.*, (*of wine*) état trouble, *f.*, (*of hearing*) dureté, *f.*, parole épaisse, *f.*, difficulté *f.*, (*of speech*) grasseyement, *m.*
Thief, s. voleur, *m.*, -euse, *f.*, larron, *m.*, (*candl:*) champignon, *m.* *Stop thief!* au voleur! *Set a — to catch a* —, à corsaire corsaire et demi.
—*-catcher*, s. agent de police, *m.*
Thieve, vn. voler
Thievish, adj. de voleur, adonné au vol
Thievishness, s. penchant au vol, *m.*
Thigh, s. cuisse, *f.*
Thill, s. limon, *m.*, timon, *m.*, brancard, *m.* —*-horse*, *thiller*, s. limonier, *m.*
Thimble, s. dé, *m.*, gobelet, *m.* —*-rig*, s., —*-rigging*, s. le jeu des gobelets, *m.* —*-rigger*, s. joueur de gobelets, *m.*
Thimbleful, s. plein un dé, un doigt
Thin, adj. mince, (*liquid*) clair, léger, (*gas, air*) raréfié, subtil, (*grass*) maigre, rare, (*pers.*) maigre, (*voice*) grêle, léger, (*fig.*) maigre, pauvre, insuffisant
Thin, adv. en petit nombre. —*-bodied*, adj. au corsage fluet, (*wine*) léger
Thin, va. amincir, éclaircir, réduire, raréfier, faire maigrir
Thine, posses. pron. à toi, le tien, la tienne, les tiens, les tiennes
Thing, s. chose, *f.*, objet, *m.*, affaire, *f.*, (*pers., fam.*) être, *m.*, créature, *f.*, petit, *m.*, petite, *f.* *That's the very* —, c'est cela même. *Not to be quite the* —, n'être pas précisément ce qu'il faut
Think, vn. penser, croire, s'imaginer, (*judge*) juger, (*about, of, on*, à) penser, réfléchir, songer, (*imagine, &c.*) s'aviser (de), imaginer, (*esteem*) faire cas (de), avoir une idée de. *My way of* —*ing*, mon avis. *I — so*, je crois que oui. *I — not*, je pense que non. *I — I can*, je crois pouvoir le faire. *I — I hear*, il me semble entendre. *To — with oneself*, réfléchir à part soi. — va. penser, penser à, imaginer, concevoir, regarder comme, juger. *To — much*, faire difficulté, regarder comme grand'chose. *To — much of*, *nothing of*, faire grand cas de, ne faire aucun cas de
Thinker, s. penseur, *m.*
Thinking, adj. raisonnable, réfléchi, pensant
Thinking, s. pensée, *f.*, réflexion, *f.*, méditation, *f.*, avis, *m.*, jugement, *m.*
Thinly, adv. maigrement, peu nombreux, clair-semé
Thinness, s. manque d'épaisseur, *m.*, ténuité, *f.*, raréfaction, *f.*, fluidité, *f.*, rareté, *f.*, petit nombre, *m.*
Third, adj. s. troisième, trois, tierce. *A — person*, un tiers
Third, s. tiers, *m.*, (*mus.*) tierce, *f.*
Thirdly, adv. troisièmement
Thirst, s. soif, *f.*
Thirst, vn. avoir soif
Thirsty, adj. altéré, (*land*) aride, desséché
Thirteen, adj. treize
Thirteenth, adj. treizième, treize
Thirtieth, adj. trentième, trente
Thirty, adj. trente
This, adj. *and* pron. ce, cet, cette, voici, celui-ci, celle-ci, ceci. —*way*, par ici. —*way and that*, de côté et d'autre. *By — time*, à l'heure qu'il est. *I have taken no snuff for — month*, il y a un mois que je n'ai prisé
Thistle, s. chardon, *m.* —*-down*, le duvet du chardon
Thither, adv. là, y
Thong, s. courroie, *f.*, lanière, *f.*, sangle, *f.*
Thorn, s. épine, *f.*, (*prickle*) piquant, *m.* —*-back*, s. raie bouclée, *f.*
Thorny, adj. épineux, piquant
Thorough, adj. consommé, parfait, (*accomplished*) accompli, vrai, complet, (*in contempt*) fieffé, achevé
Thorough, adv. complètement, à fond, à outrance, de part en part. —*-bass*, s. (*mus.*) harmonie, *f.*, basse continue, *f.* —*-bred*, adj. (*pers.*) accompli, parfait, (*horse*) pur sang. —*-going*, déterminé, à outrance. —*-paced*, adj. consommé, parfait, accompli
Thoroughfare, s. rue, *f.*, voie de passage, *f.* *No* —, on ne passe pas, rue barrée
Thoroughly, adv. complètement, entièrement, tout à fait
Thoroughness, s. état parfait *or* complet
Those, *see* That
Thou, pers. pron. tu, toi
Though, conj. quoique, bien que, encore que, (*subj.*) quand même, si, (*adv.*) pourtant, tout de même, malgré cela. *Even* —, quand même, quand bien même, quand. *As* —, comme si. *Did he, — ?* vraiment, il a fait cela?
Thought, s. pensée, *f.*, idée, *f.*, rêverie, *f.*, réflexion, *f.*, méditation, *f.*, (*care*) souci, *m.*, inquiétude, *f.*, (*small quantity*) idée, *f.*, tantinet, *m.* *He always speaks his* —, il dit toujours ce qu'il pense. *Want of* —, irréflexion, *f.* *To take* —, s'inquiéter. *I am a — better*, je vais un tantinet mieux
Thoughtful, adj. méditatif, réfléchi, rêveur, pensif, attentif, soigneux, soucieux
Thoughtfully, adj. avec réflexion, tout pensif, tout rêveur, avec prévenance
Thoughtfulness, s. méditation, *f.*, rêverie, *f.*, recueillement, *m.*, humeur pensive, *f.*, soins, *m.pl.*, sollicitude, *f.*, prévenance, *f.*
Thoughtless, adj. irréfléchi, insouciant, négligent, léger, dissipé
Thoughtlessly, adv. avec insouciance, étourdiment, inconsidérément

Thoughtlessness, s. insouciance, *f.*, irréflexion, *f.*, attention, *f.*, étourderie, *f.*, négligence, *f.*
Thousand, s. millier, *m.*, mille, *m.*
Thousand, adj. (*num.*) mille, (*in dates*) mil
Thousandth, s. adj. (*num.*) millième
Thraldom, s. esclavage, *m.*, servitude, *f.*
Thrall, s. esclave, *m.*, serf, *m.*
Thrash, va. (*corn*) battre, (*person*) rosser, étriller
Thrashing, s. battage, *m.*, (*of persons*) volée, *f.*, raclée, *f.* — *-floor*, s. aire, *f.* — *-machine*, s. (*agr.*) batteuse, *f.*
Thread, s. fil, *m.*, (*in plants*) filament, *m.*, (*of a screw*) filet, *m.*, (*razor*) fil, *m.*, tranchant, *m.*
Thread, va. enfiler, traverser, passer
Threadbare, adj. usé jusqu'à la corde, râpé, (*argument, &c.*) rebattu
Thready, adj. fibreux, plein de fils
Threat, s. menace, *f.*
Threaten, va. menacer
Threatener, s. qui menace
Threatening, s. menaces, *f.pl.*
Threateningly, adv. avec menace, d'un air menaçant
Three, adj. (*num.*) trois, (*in compounds*) à trois . . . — *-cornered*, adj. à trois cornes. — *-decker*, vaisseau à trois ponts
Threefold, adj. triple
Threshold, s. seuil, *m.*, pas, *m.*
Thrice, adv. trois fois
Thrift, s. épargne, *f.*, économie, *f.*, frugalité, *f.*, prospérité, *f.*
Thriftily, adv. avec économie, avec épargne
Thriftiness, s. épargne, *f.*, économie, *f.*
Thriftless, adj. prodigue, extravagant
Thrifty, adj. frugal, économe, ménager
Thrill, s. (*fear*) frémissement, *m.*, (*joy*) tressaillement, *m.*
Thrill, va. percer, forer, pénétrer, faire tressaillir, faire frémir;—vn. frémir, tressaillir
Thrilling, adj. perçant, pénétrant, saisissant
Thrive, vn. s'enrichir, prospérer, réussir, (*grow*) venir bien, profiter, grossir
Thriving, adj. (*pers.*) qui prospère, qui s'enrichit, qui réussit, (*plants*) qui vient bien, qui profite, vigoureux, (*made in*) florissant, prospère
Thrivingly, adv. heureusement, d'une manière prospère
Throat, s. gorge, *f.*, gosier, *m.*, (*of bottles, &c.*) entrée, *f.* — *band*, s. sous gorge, *f.*, *Sore* —, s. mal de gorge, *m.*
Throb, s. battement, *m.*, palpitation, *f.*, pulsation, *f.*, (*pain*) élancement, *m.*
Throb, vn. battre, palpiter, élancer
Throbbing, adj. palpitant. *A — pain*, une douleur lancinante
Throbbing, s. battement *m.*, palpitation, *f.*, agitation, *f.*
Throe, s. douleur, *f.*, angoisse, *f.*, mal, *m.*
Throne, s. trône, *m.*
Throng, s. foule, *f.*, multitude, *f.*
Throng, vn. se presser, s'assembler, accourir en foule, s'attrouper; — va. presser, entourer en foule
Throttle, s. trachée-artère, *f.* — *valve*, s. soupape d'étranglement, *f.*
Throttle, va. étrangler, suffoquer
Through, prep. à travers, au travers de, par, (*in the middle*) dans, (*by means of*) au moyen de, par suite de, à cause de
Through, adv. de part en part, d'un bout à l'autre, complètement, entièrement
Through, adj. (*in compounds*). — *-passage*, s. tout le voyage. — *-ticket*, s. billet pour l'entier parcours. — *-train*, s. train direct
Throughout, prep. partout en, dans tout, pendant tout
Throughout, adv. d'un bout à l'autre, entièrement
Throw, va. jeter, rejeter, lancer, mettre, (*overturn*) renverser, terrasser, (*silk*) tordre, organsiner, (*from a horse*) désarçonner. *To — away*, jeter, (*spend*) perdre, gaspiller. *To — back*, rejeter en arrière, (*accusation, ball*) renvoyer. *To — down*, jeter en bas, jeter à terre, renverser, démolir. *To — off*, rejeter, (*habits, &c.*) renoncer à, perdre. *To — out*, jeter dehors, lancer, rejeter, expulser, chasser, exclure, (*force*) exercer, (*utter*) pousser, émettre (*see* HINT), (*bill*) rejeter. *To — up*, jeter en l'air, (*milit.*) élever, (*vomit*) rejeter, (*a window*) ouvrir, (*resign*) se démettre de
Throw, s. jet, *m.*, action de jeter, *m.*, (*dice*) coup de dés, *m.*, (*stroke*) coup, *m.*, (*effort*) élan, *m.*
Thrum, vn. jouer mal, (*on the fiddle*) râcler
Thrush, s. grive, *f.*, (*med.*) aphthes, *m.pl.*
Thrust, va. pousser, enfoncer, faire entrer, introduire, fourrer, (*fig.*) faire accepter, forcer de prendre, imposer. *To — away*, repousser, rejeter, écarter violemment. *To — down*, pousser en bas, précipiter, fourrer. *To — in*, faire entrer, introduire. *To — out*, expulser, chasser. *To — through*, transpercer. — vn. se jeter, fondre, attaquer, s'introduire, se mettre, se fourrer
Thrust, s. coup, *m.*, attaque, *f.*, (*fencing*) botte, *f.*, poussée, *f.* *Home* —, coup bien appliqué
Thumb, s. pouce, *m.* — *-screw*, s. vis de pression, *f.* — *-stall*, s. poucier, *m.*, doigtier, *m.*
Thumb, va. manier gauchement, salir, user. *To — over*, feuilleter
Thump, s. coup, *m.*, coup de poing, *m.*
Thump, va. battre, frapper, cogner, donner des coups de poing à
Thumping, adj. lourd, gros
Thunder, s. tonnerre, *m.*, foudre, *f.* — *-storm*, s. orage accompagné de tonnerre, *m.*
Thunder, vn.a. tonner, (*fig.*) tonner, retentir, (*to threat*) fulminer
Thundering, adj. de tonnerre, tonnant, retentissant
Thundering, s. tonnerre, *m.*, (*fig.*) grands coups, *m.pl.*
Thunderstrike, va. atterrer, confondre
Thursday, s. jeudi, *m.*
Thus, adv. ainsi, de cette manière. — *far*, jusqu'ici, jusque-là. — *much*, autant, autant que cela, c'est assez
Thwack, s. coup vigoureux, *m.*
Thwack, va. frapper, battre
Thwart, va. traverser, couper, (*fig.*) contrecarrer, contrarier
Thy, adj. pron. ton, ta, tes
Thyme, s. thym, *m.*
Thyrsus, s. thyrse, *m.*
Thyself, refl. pron. toi-même, te
Tiara, s. tiare, *f.*
Tick, s. crédit, *m.*, (*insect*) tique, *f.*, (*stuff*) coutil, *m.*, toile, *f.*, (*noise*) tic-tac, *m.* *To buy upon* —, *to go on* —, acheter à crédit
Tick, vn. prendre à crédit, faire crédit, se fier, (*to make a noise*) faire tic-tac
Ticket, s. billet, *m.*, (*order for goods*), bon, *m.*, (*pawning*) reconnaissance, *f.* (*label*) étiquette, *f.*, (*badge*) plaque, *f.*, numéro, *m.*, (*luggage*) bulletin, *m.* — *of leave*, s. permission, *f.* *Return* —, s. billet d'aller et de retour, billet de retour. *Season* —, s. billet de saison, *m.* *Free* —, s. billet de faveur, *m.* — *-porter*, s. commissionnaire, *m.* *That's the* —, à la bonne heure, voilà l'affaire
Ticket, va. étiqueter, numéroter
Ticking, s. (*noise*) tic-tac, *m.*, (*stuff*) coutil, *m.*, toile, *f.*
Tickle, va. chatouiller, (*fig.*) charmer, flatter
Tickling, s. chatouillement, *m.*
Ticklish, adj. chatouilleux, chancelant, mal assuré, difficile, scabreux, délicat, susceptible
Ticklishness, s. état critique, *f.*, difficulté, *f.*, nature scabreuse, *f.*
Tidal, adj. de marée, de la marée. — *harbour*, s. port où l'on n'entre qu'à la marée haute
Tide, s. marée, *f.*, (*time*) saison, *f.*, temps, *m.*, époque, *f.*, (*stream*) courant, cours d'eau, *m.*, flots, *m.pl.*, (*course*) *m.*, cours, *m.*, courant, *m.* — *-gate*, s. écluse, *f.* — *-waiter*, s. officier de douane, *m.*
Tide, va. entraîner ou pousser par la marée. *To — over*, passer par dessus, surmonter. — vn. aller avec la marée. *To — it up, down*, monter, descendre à la faveur de la marée
Tidily, adv. proprement
Tidiness, s. propreté, *f.*, bon ordre, *m.*
Tidings, s.pl. nouvelle, *f.*, nouvelles, *f.pl.*
Tidy, adj. propre, bien tenu, bien arrangé, soigné, soigneux
Tie, va. lier, attacher, nouer, (*oblige*) astreindre, assujettir. *To — down*, astreindre, assujettir. *To — up*, lier, attacher, nouer, (*dog*) mettre à l'attache. *Fig.* lier, obliger
Tie, s. attache, *f.*, lien, *m.*, nœud, *m.*, cravate, *f.*, (*shoes*) cordon, *m.*, tirant, *m.*, (*archit.*) crampon, tirant, *m.*, (*mus.*) liaison, *f.*
Tier, s. rangée, *f.*, rang, *m.*, (*nav.*) batterie, *f.* — *of boxes*, rang de loges, *m.*
Tiff, s. goutte, *f.*, coup, *m.*, (*quarrel*) querelle, *f.*, bouderie, *f.*, pique, *f.*
Tiffany, s. gaze de soie, *f.*
Tiger, s. tigre, *m.*, (*servant*) groom, *m.*
Tight, adj. (*shut*) bien clos, bien fermé, imperméable, (*clothes*) étroit, serré, collant, (*boots*) étroit, (*stretched*) tendu, roide, (*miserly*) dur à la détente, serré, avare, regardant
Tight, adv. fort, fortement, bien
Tighten, va. serrer, resserrer, tendre
Tightly, adv. ferme, fortement, étroitement, serré, proprement, lestement
Tightness, s. imperméabilité, *f.*, étroitesse, *f.*, roideur, *f.*, tension, *f.*, propreté, *f.*, activité, *f.*, prestesse, *f.*, (*of money*) parcimonie, *f.*, lésinerie, *f.*
Tights, s.pl. pantalon collant, *m.*
Tigress, s. tigresse, *f.*
Tilbury, s. tilbury, *m.*
Tile, s. tuile, *f.* carreau, *m.*, (*hat*) couvre-chef, *m.* — *-kilns*, s. tuilerie, *f.* *Drain-* — s. tuile à drainage, *f.* — *-maker*, s. tuilier, *m.*
Tile, va. couvrir de tuiles
Tiler, s. couvreur, *m.*
Tiling, s. recouvrement en tuiles, *m.*, toiture en tuiles, *f.*
Till, s. caisse, *f.*, tiroir, *m.*

Till, prep. jusqu'à
Till, conj. jusqu'à ce que, avant que, avant de
Till, va. labourer, cultiver
Tillable, adj. labourable
Tillage, s. labourage, m., culture, f.
Tiller, s. laboureur, m., cultivateur, m., (*nav.*) barre, f., (*shoot*) rejeton, m.
Tilt, s. (*carriage*) bâche, f., banne, f., (*nav.*) petite tente, f., (*of a lance*) coup, m., (*fight*) joute, f., tournoi, m., (*incline*) pente, f., inclinaison, f.
Tilt, va. couvrir d'une tente or d'une bâche, (*a lance*) diriger, frapper, (*incline*) faire pencher en avant
Tilt, vn. jouter, (*fight*) ferrailler (avec), (*float*) être ballotté, voguer, (*incline*) pencher, incliner, tomber
Tilter, s. jouteur, m., champion, m.
Tilth, s. culture, f.
Tilting, s. joute, f.
Timber, s. bois, m., bois de charpente, m. — *work*, s. charpente, f. — *yard*, s. chantier, m.
Timber, va. boiser, planter d'arbres
Time, s. temps, m., époque, f., saison, f., (*instant*) moment, m., (*opportunity*) occasion, f., (*by the clock*) heure, f., (*mus.*) temps, m., mesure, f., (*mil.*) pas, m. *Out of* —, prématurément, hors de saison. *In* —, à temps, avec le temps. *In no* —, en un clin d'œil. *In good* —, à propos, au bon moment. *From* — *to* —, de temps en temps. *To take one's* —, prendre son temps. *She was near her* —, elle était près d'accoucher. *For a* —, à terme. *For a short* —, à court terme. *Between* —*s*, de temps en temps. *Some* — *or other*, un jour ou l'autre. *As* —*s go*, par le temps qui court. *What* — *is it?* quelle heure est-il? *The* — *of day*, l'heure qu'il est. *Four at a* —, quatre à la fois. *At* —*s*, quelquefois, tantôt. *Every* —, chaque fois, chaque fois que. *To keep* —, aller en mesure. — *-bill*, s., — *-table*, s. indicateur, m. — *-book*, s. registre du travail des ouvriers. — *-keeper*, s. (*pers.*) qui marque le temps, régulateur des départs, m., (*thing*) chronomètre, m., montre, f. — *-piece*, s. pendule, f. — *-server*, — *-serving*, (adj.) servile, complaisant, s. lâche complaisance, f., servilité, f.
Time, va. faire à propos, choisir le bon moment pour faire, (*regulate*) régler, mesurer
Timed, adj. *Well* —, opportun, fait à propos, réglé
Timeliness, s. à-propos, m.
Timely, adj. opportun, fait à propos, de bonne heure
Timely, adv. de bonne heure, à propos
Timid, adj. timide, peureux, craintif
Timidity, s. timidité, f., crainte, f.
Timidly, adv. timidement
Timorous, adj. timoré, timide
Timorously, adv. timidement
Timorousness, s. nature timorée, f., timidité, f.
Tin, s. étain, m. (*latten*) fer-blanc, m., (*mould*) moule en fer-blanc, m., (*money*) argent, m.
Tin, adj. d'étain, en étain, de fer-blanc, en fer-blanc
Tin, va. étamer
Tincture, s. teinte, f. (*notion*) teinture, f., (*taste*) léger goût, m., (*pharm.*) teinture
Tincture, va. teindre, (*imbue*) imprégner
Tinder, s. amadou, m.
Tinge, s. *see* Tincture
Tingle, vn. tinter, vibrer, (*feeling*) brûler, picoter, démanger, cuire. *My ears* —*d* les oreilles me tintaient
Tingling, s. tintement, m., chaleur, f., picotement, m., tressaillement, m.
Tinker, s. chaudronnier ambulant, m., étameur, m.
Tinker, va. raccommoder, étamer
Tinkering, s. métier de chaudronnier, m., raccommodage, m., étamage, m.
Tinkle, vn. tinter ;— va. faire tinter
Tinkling, adj. retentissant, sonore
Tinkling, s. tintement, m.
Tinman, s. ferblantier, m.
Tinsel, s. clinquant, m., oripeau, m.
Tinsel, adj. de clinquant, faux
Tinsel, va. orner de clinquant or d'oripeaux, donner un faux éclat à
Tint, s. teinte, f., couleur, f., nuance, f. *Uniform* — teinte plate
Tint, va. teinter, nuancer
Tiny, adj. petit, chétif
Tip, s. (*ear, nose, fringe*) bout, m., extrémité, f., (*foot*) pointe, f., (*gift*) présent d'argent, m., cadeau, m.
Tip, va. mettre une pointe à, garnir le bout, couvrir la pointe, (*strike*) effleurer, toucher légèrement, (*gift*) donner, (*with iron*) ferrer
Tip, vn. tomber, se renverser. *To* — *off*, (*fam.*) mourir. *To* — *over*, se renverser, verser
Tipcat, s. bâtonnet, m.
Tippet, s. pèlerine, f., palatine, f.
Tipple, vn. boire, se griser
Tipple, s. boisson, f.
Tippler, s. ivrogne, m., buveur, m.
Tippling, s. ivrognerie, f.
Tipstaff, s. huissier, m., recors, m., (*staff*) verge, f.
Tipsy, adj. gris, ivre
Tiptoe, s. pointe du pied, f. *To be, to stand on* —, se tenir, s'élever, se dresser sur la pointe des pieds
Tiptop, s. sommet, m., faîte, m., comble, m.
Tiptop, adj. excellent, parfait, suprême, huppé
Tire, s. appareil, m., parure, f., atours, m., (*wheels*) bande, f.
Tire, va. fatiguer, lasser, épuiser, ennuyer, impatienter. *To* — *out*, fatiguer complètement, épuiser de fatigue, assommer. — vn. fatiguer, (*of*, de) se fatiguer, se lasser
Tired, adj. las, fatigué, ennuyé
Tiresome, adj. ennuyeux, fatigant, assommant
Tiresomeness, s. nature fatigante, f., fatigue, f., ennui, m.
Tiring-room, s. loge d'acteur, f.
Tissue, s. tissu, m., brocart, m. — *-paper*, s. papier de soie
Tissue, va. brocher, broder
Tit, s. (*pony*) bidet, m., haridelle, f., (*fig.*) femme, f., (*bird*) mésange, f. *To give* — *for tat*, rendre la pareille
Titbit, s. morceau friand, m.
Tithe, s. dîme, f.
Tithe, va. lever la dîme sur
Titlark, s. alouette des prés, f.
Title, s. titre, m., (*name*) nom, m. — *-deed*, s. titre, m.
Title, va. intituler, nommer, donner un titre à
Titled, adj. titré
Titmouse, s. mésange, f.
Titter, **Tittering**, s. rire, m., ricanement, m.
Titter, va. rire en cachette, ricaner
Tittle, s. point, m., iota, m., bagatelle, f.
Tittle-tattle, s. caquets, m pl., bavardage, m., babil, m., cancans, m.pl.
Titular, adj. titulaire
To, prep. à, vers, sur, jusqu'à, en, (*in order to*) afin de, pour, (*in comparison with*) auprès de, en comparaison de, à. *Even* —, jusqu'à. *From house* — *house*, de maison en maison
Toad, s. crapaud, m. — *-eater*, s. flagorneur, m., -euse, f., flatteur, m., -euse, f., parasite, m.
Toadstone, s. crapaudine, f.
Toadstool, s. champignon, m.
Toady, s. flagorneur, m., -euse, f.
Toady, va. flagorner
Toadyism, s. adulation, f., flagornerie, f., servilité, f.
Toast, va. faire griller, faire rôtir, (*drink the health*) porter un toast à
Toast, s. pain grillé, m., rôtie, f., (*health*) toast, m., santé, f. *Dipped* —, s. rôtie au beurre. *Dry* —, s. rôtie sans beurre. — *-rack*, s. porte-rôties, m. — *and water*, eau panée, f.
Toaster, s. gril, m. fourchette à rôties, f.
Tobacco, s. tabac, m. — *-box*, s. boîte à tabac, f. — *-pouch*, blague, f. — *-stopper*, s. fouloir, m.
Tobacconist, s. marchand de tabac, m.
To-day, s. adv. aujourd'hui
Toddle, va. chanceler, aller à petits pas
Toe, s. doigt de pied, m., orteil, m., (*horse*) pince, f. *Big* —, gros orteil
Toga, s. toge, f.
Together, adv. ensemble, (*in concert*) de concert, (*at the same time*) dans le même temps, (*consecutively*) de suite. — *with*, en même temps que, ainsi que
Toggery, s. attirail, m., accoutrement, m., habits, m.pl.
Toil, s. travail, m., labeur, m., peine, f., fatigue, f., (*net, snare*) rets, m., filet, m., toiles, f.pl.
Toil, vn. travailler, se fatiguer, se donner de la peine. *To* — *and moil*, s'exténuer de fatigue, suer sang et eau
Toiler, s. travailleur, m., -euse, f.
Toilet, s. toilette, f.
Toilsome, adj. pénible, fatigant, laborieux
Toilsomeness, s. peine, f., fatigue, f., labeur, m.
Token, s. gage, m., souvenir, m. signe, m., indice, m., marque, f., (*coin*) jeton, m., liard, m.
Tolerable, adj. supportable, tolérable, passable
Tolerably, adv. d'une manière supportable, passablement
Tolerant, adj. tolérant, indulgent
Tolerate, va. tolérer, souffrir
Toleration, s. tolérance, f.
Toll, s. (*roads*) péage, m., (*duty*) droit, m., impôt, m., (*of a bell*) son, m., tintement, m., — *-bar*, s. — *gate*, s. barrière de péage, f. — *-free*, adj. exempt de péage
Toll, va. sonner, tinter
Tolling, s. tintement, m.
Tom, s. (*in comp.*) — *-boy*, s. gamine, tapageuse, f., — *-cat*, s. matou, m., chat, m. — *-fool*, — *-noddy*, s. dadais, m., nigaud, m. — *-foolery*, s. niaiserie, f., — *-tit*, s. mésange, f.
Tomahawk, s. tomahawk, m., casse-tête, m.
Tomato, s. tomate, f., pomme d'amour, f.
Tomb, s. tombe, f., tombeau, m., sépulcre, m. — *-stone*, s. pierre tumulaire, f.
Ton, s. tonneau, m., tonne, f.
Tone, s. ton, m., son, m., (*of the voice*) timbre, m., ton, m., accent, m.
Tongs, s.pl. pincette, f., pinces, f.pl., (*of smiths*) tenailles, f.pl., pinces, f.pl.

Tongue, s. langue, *f.*, parole, *f.*, (*of scales*) languette, *f.*, (*of a buckle*) ardillon, *m.*, (*of a bell*) battant, *m.* *To hold one's* —, se taire. —*-tied*, adj. qui a le filet, interdit, muet

Tongued, adj. à la langue

Tongueless, adj. sans langue, muet

Tonic, adj. tonique

Tonic, s. tonique, *m.*, (*mus.*) tonique, *f.*

Tonnage, s. (*nav.*), tonnage, *m.*

Tonsils, s.pl. amygdales, *f.pl.*

Tonsure, s. tonsure, *f.*

Too, adv. trop, par trop, (*also*) aussi, en outre, de plus

Tool, s. outil, *m.*, instrument, *m.*, (*agent*) instrument, *m.*, agent, *m.*, âme damnée, *f.*

Tooth, s. dent, *f.*, goût, *m.*, palais, *m.* *First teeth*, dents de lait. *Wisdom teeth*, dents de sagesse. —*-ache*, s. mal de dents, *m.* —*-brush*, s. brosse à dents, *f.* —*-pick*, s. cure-dents, *m.* — *and nail*, à belles dents. *To be at* — *and nail*, être aux prises. *To his teeth*, face à face, en face. *To cast in one's teeth*, jeter à la face de

Toothed, adj. (*in compos.*) aux dents, denté

Toothless, adj. sans dents, édenté

Toothsome, adj. friand

Toothsomeness, s. goût agréable, *m.*

Top, s. haut, *m.*, sommet, *m.*, cime, *f.*, faîte, *m.*, (*buildings*) comble, *m.*, couronnement, *m.*, haut, *m.*, (*surface*) surface, *f.*, (*table*) haut bout, *m.*, (*height*) comble, *m.*, (*head*) tête, *f.*, (*chief*) chef, *m.*, (*boots*) revers, *m.*, bottes à revers, *f.pl.*, (*plant*) tête, *f.*, (*toy*) toupie, *f.*, sabot, *m.*, (*nav.*) hune, *f.* *From* — *to bottom*, du haut en bas. *The* — *of the morning to you*, bien le bonjour. *From* — *to toe*, de la tête aux pieds

Top, adj. supérieur, d'en haut, principal

Top, vn. s'élever, dominer, surpasser les autres. *To* — *over*, verser;—va. couvrir, s'élever sur, dominer, couronner, surpasser, être plus grand que, (*crop*) étêter, couper la tête à, (*climb*) gravir le sommet de

Topaz, s. topaze, *f.*

Tope, vn. boire sec

Toper, s. buveur, *m.*, ivrogne, *m.*

Topful, adj. plein jusqu'aux bords

Topic, s. sujet, *m.*, matière, *f.*, (*med.*,) topique, *m.*

Topmost, adj. le plus haut, le plus élevé

Topographer, s. topographe, *m.*

Topographic, Topographical, adj. topographique

Topography, s. topographie, *f.*

Topple, Topple down, vn. tomber, s'écrouler, dégringoler. *To* — *over*, pencher et tomber

Topsy-turvy, adv. sens dessus dessous

Torch, s. torche, *f.*, flambeau, *m.*

Torment, s. tourment, *m.*, supplice, *m.*, torture, *f.*, souffrance, *f.*

Torment, va. tourmenter, faire souffrir, vexer

Tormentor, s. bourreau, *m.*

Tornado, s. cyclone, *m.*, ouragan, *m.*, trombe, *f.*

Torpedo, s. torpille, *f.*

Torpid, adj. engourdi, inerte

Torpor, s. torpeur, *m.*, engourdissement, *m.*

Torrent, s. torrent, *m.*

Torrid, adj. brûlé, desséché, (*zone*) torride

Tortoise, s. tortue, *f.*

Tortuous, adj. tortueux

Torture, s. torture, *f.*, tourment, *m.*, supplice, *m.*

Torture, va. torturer, mettre à la torture

Tory, s. adj. tory

Toss, va. jeter, lancer, envoyer, secouer, brandir, ballotter, (*in a blanket*) berner. *To* — *up*, lancer en l'air, (*play*) jouer à pile *or* face;—vn. s'agiter, être ballotté. *Let us* — *up for it*, jouons-le à pile *or* face. *To* — *about*, s'agiter

Toss, s. jet, *m.*, secousse, *f.*, mouvement, *m.*, (*of head*) hochement, *m.*, (*at play*) coup, *m.* *All a* — *up*, pur hasard

Total, adj. total, entier, complet

Total, s. total, *m.*, somme, *f.*

Totality, s. totalité, *f.*, tout, *m.*

Totally, adv. totalement, entièrement, complètement

Totter, vn. chanceler, vaciller

Tottering, adj. chancelant, tremblant, vacillant

Touch, va. toucher, atteindre, (*nav.*) toucher à, aborder à, (*to corrode*) mordre sur, (*interest*) intéresser, concerner. *To* — *off*, esquisser rapidement, finir, retoucher. *To* — *up*, retoucher, corriger, rehausser, rafraîchir;—vn. se toucher, toucher. *To* — *upon*, (*nav.*) toucher à, (*a subject*) effleurer, (*fam.*) friser

Touch, s. (*feeling*) toucher, *m.*, tact, *m.*, (*touching*) *f.*, attouchement, *m.*, léger coup, *m.*, tape, *f.*, (*paint*) touche, *f.*, trait, *m.*, (*mus.*) toucher, *m.*, (*metals*) touche, *f.*, (*illness*) accès, *m.*, attaque, atteinte, *f.* —*-hole*, s. lumière, *f.* —*-stone*, pierre de touche, *f.*, épreuve, *f.* —*-wood*, s. amadou, *m.*

Touchiness, s. irritabilité, *f.*, susceptibilité, *f.*

Touchy, adj. susceptible, irritable, irascible

Tough, adj. dur, tenace, résistant, souple, (*strong*) solide, vigoureux, (*meat*) coriace, dur, (*difficult*) difficile, épineux

Toughen, va. durcir, roidir

Toughness, s. dureté, *f.*, ténacité, *f.*, nature coriace, *f.*, solidité, *f.*, force, *f.*, trempe, *f.*, roideur, *f.*, rudesse, inflexibilité, *f.*

Tour, s. tour, *m.*, voyage, *m.*

Tourist, s. touriste, *m.*

Tournament, s. tournoi, *m.*

Tout, vn. chercher des pratiques. *To* — *for*, solliciter

Touter, s. racoleur, *m.*, solliciteur

Tow, s. étoupe, *f.*, filasse, *f.*, (*boats*) remorque, *f.* *To take in* —, prendre à la remorque. — *-path*, s. chemin de halage *m.*

Tow, va. remorquer, haler, touer

Towage, s. remorque, *f.*, halage, *m.*, touage, *m.*

Toward, Towards, prep. vers, du côté de, (*behaviour*) envers, à l'égard de, pour, afin de, vers, environ

Towel, s. serviette, *f.*, essuiemains, *m.*

Towelling, s. toile pour serviettes, *f.*

Tower, s. tour, *f.*

Tower, vn. s'élever, monter, planer

Towering, adj. sublime, orgueilleux, superbe, violent, furieux

Town, s. ville, *m.*, bourg, *m.*, capitale, *f.* *A man of the* —, *on town, about* —, roué, viveur, *m.*, — *-clerk*, s. greffier municipal, *m.*, secrétaire du conseil municipal, *m.* — *-crier*, crieur public, *m.* — *-hall* — *house*, s. hôtel de ville, *m.* *Towns-people, towns-folk*, s.pl., habitants de la ville, *m.pl.*, bourgeois, *m.pl.* — *-talk*, s. sujet de toutes les conversations, *m.*

Township, s. territoire d'une ville, commune

Townsman, s. bourgeois, *m.*, habitant de la ville, *m.*

Toy, s. jouet, *m.*, joujou, *m.*, (*bauble*) hochet, *m.*, babiole, *f.*, colifichet, *m.*, (*trifle*) niaiserie, *f.*

Toy, vn. jouer, badiner, folâtrer

Toyman, s. marchand de jouets, *m.*, bimbelotier, *m.*

Toyshop, s. magasin de jouets, *m.*, boutique de bimbelotier, *f.*

Trace, s. trace, *f.*, trait, (*harness*) harnais, *m.*

Trace, va. tracer, (*follow*) suivre à la trace, suivre la trace de, suivre à la piste (*draw*) calquer, (*investigate*) trouver, découvrir, faire remonter

Trachea, s. trachée-artère, *f.*

Track, s. trace, *f.*, piste, *f.*, (*nav.*) sillage, *m.*, (*road*) route, *f.*, chemin, *m.*, sentier, *m.*, (*rails*) voie, *f.*, (*astr.*) orbite, *f.m.*, (*wheels*) ornière, *f.*, (*hunt*) piste, *f.*

Track, va. suivre à la trace, dépister, (*nav.*) haler

Trackless, adj. où il n'y a pas de traces, inexploré, impraticable

Tract, s. étendue, *f.*, espace, *m.*, terre, *f.*, région, *f.*, (*treatise*) traité, *m.*, brochure, *f.*

Tractableness, s. douceur, *f.* docilité, *f.*, humeur traitable, *f.*

Tractable, adj. traitable, docile, doux

Tractably, adj. docilement

Tractarian, s. Puseyite, *m.*

Traction, s. traction, *f.* —*-engine*, s. machine à vapeur locomobile, *f.*

Trade, s. commerce, *m.*, négoce, *m.*, trafic, *m.*, (*calling*) métier, *m.*, emploi, *m.*, occupation, *f.*, profession, *f.*, (*guild*) corps de métiers, *m.* — *-union*, compagnonnage, association ouvrière, *f.* — *-unionist*, compagnon, *m.* — *-winds*, s. vents alizés, *m.pl.* — *-mark*, s. marque, *f.* — *-price*, s. prix marchand, *m.*

Trade, vn. trafiquer, faire le commerce, commercer. — *on, upon*, spéculer

Trader, s. commerçant, *m.*, négociant, *m.*

Tradesman, s. marchand, *m.*, commerçant, *m.*, fournisseur, *m.*

Trading, adj. commercial, commerçant, marchand

Trading, s. commerce, *m.*, négoce, *m.*, trafic, *m.*

Tradition, s. tradition, *f.*

Traditional, adj. traditionnel

Traditionally, adv. traditionnellement

Traduce, *See* SLANDER

Traffic, s. trafic, *m.*, commerce, *m.*, marchandises, *f.pl.*, denrées, *f.pl.*, (*on roads*) transport, *m.*, roulage, *m.*, (*rails*) recettes, *f.pl.* — *-return*, compte des recettes, *m.* — *-manager*, chef du mouvement, *m.*

Traffic, vn. trafiquer, faire le commerce, *m.*

Trafficker, s. trafiquant, *m.*

Tragedian, s. tragédien, *m.*, -ne, *f.*

Tragedy, s. tragédie, *f.*

Tragic, Tragical, adj. tragique

Tragically, adv. tragiquement

Tragicalness, s. tragique, *m.*, nature tragique, *f.*

Tragi-comedy, s. tragicomédie, *f.*

Tragi-comic, Tragi-comical, adj. tragi-comique

Trail, s. (*train*) traînée, *f.*, trait, *m.*, (*of comet*) queue, *f.*, (*trace*) piste, *f.*, trace, *f.*

Trail, va. suivre à la piste, traîner

Train, va. trainer, (*teach*) élever, instruire, (*break in*) dresser, (*race horses*) entrainer, (*hortic.*) mettre en espalier, dresser, faire grimper

Train, s. (*powder*) trainée, *f.* (*retinue*) suite, *f.*, cortége, *m.* (*dress*) queue, *f.* (*series*) suite, *f.*, enchainement, *m.*, succession, *f.*, (*course*) train, cours, *m.*, (*rail*) train, *m.*, convoi, *m.*, (*artillery*) train, *m.*, équipage, *m.* — *-bearer*, page, *m.*, porte-queue, *m.* *Down* —, train descendant, *up* —, train montant. *Fast* —, *slow* —, train de grande vitesse, de petite vitesse. *Goods* —, *luggage* —, train de marchandises. *Parliamentary*.—, train à prix réduits. *Passenger* —, train de voyageurs. *Stopping* —, train s'arrêtant aux stations. — *-road*, voie de fer, *f.* *See*; Express, Excursion, Through, *etc.*

Trainband, s. milice bourgeoise, *f.*

Trainer, s. maître, *m.*, (*race horses*) entraineur, *m.*

Training, s. éducation, *f.*, instruction, *f.* (*horses*) entrainement, *m.*, (*mil.*) exercice, *m.*

Train-oil, s. huile de baleine, *f.*

Traitor, s. adj. traître, *m.*

Traitorous, adj. traître, perfide, déloyal, sans foi

Traitorously, adv. traîtreusement, déloyalement, en traître

Traitress, s. traîtresse, *f.*

Tram, s. chariot à houille, *m.* — *-way*, s. — *-road*, s. voie ferrée, *f.*, chemin de fer américain, *m.* — *-plate*, s. rail plat, *m.* — *-rail*, s. rail à ornières, *m.*

Trammel, s. (*net*) tramail, *m.*, (*shackle*) entrave, *f.*

Trammel, va. embarrasser, entraver

Tramp, s. marche pesante, *f.*, pas lourd, *m.*, piétinement, *m.*, (*pers.*) vagabond, *m.*, -e, *f.*, coureur, *m.*, -euse, *f.*

Trample, va. fouler aux pieds, marcher sur

Trampling, s. piétinement, *m.*, bruit de pas, *m.*

Trance, s. extase, *f.*, (*med.*) catalepsie, *f.*

Tranced, adj. ravi, en extase

Tranquil, adj. tranquille

Tranquillity, s. tranquillité, *f.*, calme, *m.*

Tranquilly, adv. tranquillement, paisiblement

Transact, va. faire, accomplir, négocier, traiter. *To — business*, être en affaires. (avec)

Transaction, s. négociation, *f.*, gestion, *f.*, conduite, *f.*, affaire, *f.*, (*event*) événement, *m.*, travaux, *m.pl.*, (*of societies*) procès-verbaux des séances, *m.pl.*

Transactor, s. administrateur, *m.* négociateur, *m.*

Transalpine, adj. transalpin

Transatlantic, adj. transatlantique

Transcend, va. surmonter, dépasser, outrepasser

Transcendency, s. supériorité marquée, *f.*, mérite transcendant, *m.*

Transcendent, adj. transcendant

Transcendently, adv. éminemment, d'une manière transcendante

Transcribe, va. transcrire, copier

Transcriber, s. copiste, *m.*, transcripteur, *m.*

Transcript, s. transcription, *f.*, copie, *f.*, double, *m.*

Transcription, s. transcription, *f.*

Transept, s. transept, *m.*

Transfer, va. transporter, transférer, céder

Transfer, s. transport, *m.*, (*law*) transfert, *m.*, cession, *f.*

Transferable, adj. transportable, transférable

Transferrer, s. cédant, *m.*, -e, *f.*

Transfiguration, s. transfiguration, *f.*

Transfigure, va. transfigurer, transformer

Transform, va. transformer; — vn. se transformer

Transformation, s. transformation, *f.*, métamorphose, *f.*

Transgress, va. outrepasser, dépasser, violer, enfreindre

Transgression, s. transgression, *f.*, violation, *f.*, (*pers.*) péché, *m.*

Transgressor, s. transgresseur, *m.*

Transient, adj. passager, fugitif, transitoire

Transiently, adv. en passant

Transientness, s. brièveté, *f.*, nature passagère *or* éphémère, *f.*

Transit, s. (*comm.*) transit, *m.*, (*astr.*) passage, *m.* — *-instrument*, s. lunette méridienne, *f.*

Transition, s. transition, *f.*

Transitive, adj. (*gramm.*) transitif, actif

Transitively, adv. transitivement

Transitoriness, s. brièveté, *f.*

Transitory, adj. *See* Transient

Translatable, adj. traduisible

Translate, va. (*bishop*) transférer, (*language*) traduire

Translation, s. (*of a bishop, etc.*) translation, *f.*, (*language*) traduction, version, *f.*

Translator, s. traducteur, *m.*, -trice, *f.*

Transmarine, adj. d'outre-mer

Transmigration, s. transmigration, *f.*, metempsycose, *f.*

Transmissible, adj. transmissible

Transmission, s. transmission, *f.*

Transmit, va. transmettre

Transmutability, s. transmutabilité, *f.*

Transmutable, adj. transmuable

Transmutation, s. transmutation, *f.*, conversion, *f.*

Transmute, va. (*metals*) transmuer, (*fig.*) convertir, transformer

Transom, s. traverse, *f.*

Transparency, s. transparence, *f.*, diaphanéité, *f.*, (*paint*) transparent, *m.*

Transparent, adj. transparent, diaphane

Transparently, adv. avec transparence, clairement

Transpire, vn. transpirer, se répandre

Transplant, va. transplanter

Transplantation, s. transplantation, *f.*

Transport, s. transport, *m.*, (*pers.*) déporté, *m.* — *-ship*, — *vessel*, bâtiment de transport, *m.*

Transport, va. transporter, (*criminals*) déporter

Transportable, adj. transportable, (*crim.*) sujet à la déportation

Transportation, s. transport, *m.*, transmission, *f.*, (*crim.*) déportation, *f.*

Transporting, adj. ravissant

Transpose, va. transposer

Transposition, s. transposition, *f.*

Transubstantiate, va. transsubstantier

Transubstantiation, s. transsubstantiation, *f.*

Transverse, adj. transversal

Transversely, adv. transversalement

Trap, s. piége, *m.*, trappe, *f.*, traquenard, *m.*, panneau, *m.*, ruse, *f.*, (*ball*) balle à la volée, *f.* —*s*, pl. effets, *m.pl.* (*carriage*) voiture, *f.* — *-door*, s. trappe, *f.*

Trap, va. attrapper, prendre dans un piége

Trappings, s. pl., harnachement, *m.*, harnais, *m.*, (*persons*) atours, *m.pl.*, ornements, *m.pl.*

Trappist, s. trappiste, *m.*

Trash, s. chose de rien, *f.*, bagatelle, *f.*, rebut, *m.*, cochonnerie, *f.*

Trashy, adj. vil, sans valeur, méchant

Travel, vn. a. voyager, aller, faire route, se diriger, cheminer. *To — about*, voyager de côté et d'autre. *To — over*, *to — through*, parcourir, voyager dans

Travel, s. voyage, *m.* —*s*, pl. voyages, *m.pl.*

Traveller, s. voyageur, *m.*, -euse, *f.*, (*com.*) commis-voyageur, *m.*

Travelling, s. voyages, *m.pl.*, voyager, *m.*

Travelling, adj. de voyage, voyageur. — *expenses*, s. pl. frais de voyage, *m. pl.*

Traverse, va. croiser, traverser, contrarier

Travesty, adj. travesti

Travesty, s. parodie, *f.*, traduction burlesque, *f.*

Travesty, va. parodier

Tray, s. plateau, *m.*, (*trough*) auge, *f.*

Treacherous, adj. perfide, traître, déloyal

Treacherously, adv. traîtreusement, en traître, déloyalement

Treacherousness, s. perfidie, *f.*

Treachery, s. trahison, *f.*, perfidie, *f.*, déloyauté, *f.*

Treacle, s. mélasse, *f.*

Tread, vn. marcher, aller, avancer; — va. fouler, marcher sur *or* dans, parcourir, (*fig.*) fouler aux pieds, (*birds*) féconder. *To — down*, *to — under*, fouler aux pieds

Tread, s. pas, *m.*, marche, *f.*, allure, *f.*, (*birds*) fécondation, *f.*

Treadle, s. marche, *f.*, (*of eggs*) cordon albumineux, *m.*,

Treadmill, s. moulin de discipline, *m.*

Treason, s. trahison, *f.* *High* —, haute trahison, lèse-majesté

Treasonable, adj. traître, de trahison, de lèse-majesté

Treasonably, adv. par trahison

Treasure, s. trésor, *m.*

Treasure, va. amasser, entasser, thésauriser, accumuler, (*fig.*) conserver précieusement

Treasurer, s. trésorier, *m.*

Treasurership, s. trésorerie, *f.*

Treasury, s. trésor, *m.*, trésorerie, *f.*

Treat, va. n. traiter, en user avec, agir envers, (*with*, *to*) régaler

Treat, s. festin, *m.*, régal, *m.*

Treater, s. négociateur, *m.*, amphitryon, *m.*

Treatise, s. traité, *m.*

Treatment, s. traitement, *m.*, manière d'agir, *f.*

Treaty, s. traité, *m.*, négociation, *f.*

Treble, adj. triple, (*voice*) aigu, (*mus.*) de dessus

Treble, s. triple, *m.*, (*mus.*) dessus, *m.*

Treble, va. n. tripler

Trebly, adv. triplement

Tree, s. arbre, *m.*, (*cross*) croix, *f.* *The — of a saddle*, s. pontet, *m.*

Tree, va. faire grimper sur un arbre, prendre dans l'arbre; — vn. se réfugier sur un arbre

Trefoil, s. trèfle, *m.* *Spanish* —, s. luzerne, *f.*

Trellis, s. treillis, *m.*, treillage, *m.*, jalousie, *f.*

Trellis, va. treillisser

Tremble, s. tremblement, *m.*, frisson, *m.*
Tremble, vn. trembler, frissonner, trembloter
Trembler, s. trembleur, *m.*, poltron, *m.*
Trembling, adj. tremblant
Trembling, s. tremblement, *m.*
Tremendous, adj. terrible, effroyable, épouvantable
Tremendously, adv. terriblement
Tremour, s. tremblement, *m.*, tremblotement, *m.*
Tremulous, adj. tremblant, frémissant, tremblotant
Tremulously, adv. en tremblant, timidement
Trench, s. tranchée, *f.*, fossé, *m.*
Trench, va. creuser une tranchée, faire un fossé, couper
Trench, vn. (*on*, sur) empiéter
Trenchant, adj. tranchant
Trencher, s. tranchoir, *m.*, tailloir, *m.*, assiette, *f.*, table, *f.*, mets, *m.*
Trepan, s. trépan, *m.*
Trepan, va. trépaner
Trepidation, s. tremblement, *m.*, vibration, *f.*, effroi, *m.*
Trespass, vn. (*encroach*) empiéter (sur), (*intrude*) abuser (de), (*of land*) s'introduire *or* entrer sans droit, se mettre en contravention, (*to sin*) transgresser, pécher. — *against*, offenser, enfreindre, violer
Trespass, s. offense, *f.*, transgression, *f.*, faute, *f.*, (*law*) contravention, *f.*, délit, *m.*, outrage, *m.*, violation d'une propriété, *f.*
Trespasser, s. pécheur, *m.*, délinquant, *m.*, intrus, *m.*, personne en contravention, *f.*
Tress, s. tresse, *f.*
Tressed, adj. tressé, en tresses
Trestle, s. tréteau, *m.*, support, *m.* — *-bed*, s. lit de sangle, *m.*
Trial, s. essai, *m.*, épreuve, *f.*, expérience, *f.*, (*suffering*) épreuve, *f.*, (*law*) jugement, *m.*, procès, *m.*, mise en jugement, *f.* *To take on* —, prendre à l'essai. *To put to a hard* —, mettre à de rudes épreuves. *To bring to* —, *to put upon* —, mettre *or* faire passer en jugement. *To take one's* —, passer en jugement
Triangle, s. triangle, *m.*
Triangular, adj. triangulaire
Triangulation, s. triangulation, *f.*
Tribe, s. tribu, *f.*, peuplade, *f.*, horde, *f.*
Tribulation, s. tribulation, *f.*
Tribunal, s. tribunal, *m.*
Tribune, s. (*pers.*) tribun, *m.*, (*th.*) tribune, *f.*
Tribunate, s. tribunat, *m.*
Tributary, s. adj. tributaire, *m.*, affluent, *m.*
Tribute, s. tribut, *m.*
Trice, s. clin d'œil, *m.*, instant, *m.*
Trick, s. tour, *m.*, artifice, *m.*, fraude, *f.*, supercherie, *f.*, ruse, *f.*, (*juggle*) tour, *m.*, (*child's*) malice, *f.*, (*habit*) habitude, *f.*, manière, *f.*, tic, *m.*, (*cards*) levée, *f.*
Trick, va. mettre dedans, (*adorn*) attifer, orner, parer, habiller, (*draw*) peindre. *To — one's self up* or *out in*, s'attifer dans, s'affubler de
Trickery, s. fourberie, *f.*
Trickish, adj. fin, finaud, trompeur, fourbe
Trickishness, s. fourberie, *f.*
Trickle, vn. dégoutter, couler, ruisseler
Trickster, s. trompeur, *m.*, fourbe, *m.*
Tricolour, s. drapeau tricolore, *m.*
Tricoloured, adj. tricolore
Trident, s. trident, *m.*
Tried, adj. éprouvé
Triennial, adj. triennal
Triennially, adv. tous les trois ans
Trier, s. examinateur, *m.*, expert, *m.*, essayeur, *m.*, expérimentateur, (*test*) épreuve, *f.*, pierre de touche, *f.*
Trifle, s. bagatelle, *f.*, babiole, *f.*, colifichet, *m.*, niaiserie, *f.*, sottise, *f.*, badinage, *m.*, chose aisée, *f.* *To stand upon* — *s*, s'arrêter à des vétilles
Trifle, vn. s'amuser, dire des riens, baguenauder, badiner. *To — away*, perdre à des riens, gaspiller, employer follement. *To — with*, se jouer de, badiner avec, amuser
Trifler, s. badin, *m.*, personne frivole, *f.*, lanternier, *m.*, baguenaudier, *m.*
Trifling, adj. léger, frivole, léger, peu important
Trifling, s. légèreté, *f.*, frivolité, *f.*, badinage, *m.*
Triflingly, adv. légèrement, en badinant
Trigger, s. détente, *f.*
Trigonometry, s. trigonométrie, *f.*
Trilateral, adj. trilatéral
Trill, s. trille, *m.*, cadence, *f.*
Trill, va.n. chanter en cadence, cadencer. *To — forth*, chanter, gazouiller
Trim, adj. bien fait, gentil, propret, coquet
Trim, s. arrangement, *m.*, parure, *f.*, ornement, *m.*, costume, *m.*, (*of a ship*) arrimage, *m.*
Trim, va. arranger, disposer, mettre en ordre, (*dress*) habiller, parer, orner, (*to line*) garnir, border, (*hair*) couper, (*trees*) tailler, émonder, élaguer, (*nav.*) arrimer, (*sails*) orienter, (*stow*) tancer, gronder, (*lamp*) arranger; — vn. hésiter, balancer, tergiverser
Trimestrial, adj. trimestriel
Trimly, adv. proprement, bien, gentiment
Trimmer, s. décorateur, *m.*, (*polit.*) girouette, *f.*
Trimming, s. garniture, *f.*, bordure, *f.*, (*scold*) réprimande, *f.*, (*trade*) passementerie, *f.*
Trimness, s. propreté, *f.*, bonne mine, *f.*, bon état, *m.*, coquetterie, *f.*
Trinity, s. Trinité, *f.*
Trinket, s. petit bijou, *m.*, colifichet, *m.*, breloque, *f.*, bagatelle, *f.*
Trio, s. trio, *m.*
Trip, s. croc-en-jambe, *m.*, (*false step*) faux pas, *m.*, (*mistake*) faute, *f.*, erreur, *f.*, (*excursion*) voyage, *m.*, tour, *m.*
Trip, vn. broncher, trébucher, (*fig.*) faire une faute, se tromper, se mettre en défaut, (*tongue*) fourcher à, (*to walk*) aller d'un pas léger *or* de son pied léger, courir légèrement; — va. (*pers.*) faire tomber, donner un croc-en-jambe à, (*th.*) faire trébucher, faire broncher, (*fig.*) supplanter. *To — up the heels of*, donner un croc-en-jambe à
Tripe, s. tripes, *f.pl.*, gras-double, *m.*, — *-man*, s., — *-seller*, s. tripier, *m.* — *-stall*, s. triperie, *f.*
Triple, va. tripler; vn. se tripler
Triple, adj. triple, troisième
Triplet, s. réunion de trois, *m.*, tercet, *m.*
Tripod, s. trépied, *m.*
Tripos, s. grand concours, *m.*
Tripping, s. croc-en-jambe, *m.*, faux pas, *m.*, pas léger, *m.*
Trippingly, adv. légèrement, agilement
Trireme, s. trirème, *f.*
Trite, adj. banal, usé, rebattu, trivial, vulgaire
Triteness, s. banalité, *f.*
Triton, s. triton, *m.*
Triturate, va. triturer
Trituration, s. trituration, *f.*
Triumph, s. triomphe, *m.*
Triumph, vn. triompher
Triumphal, adj. de triomphe, triomphal
Triumphant, adj. triomphant, triomphateur
Triumphantly, adv. en triomphe, avec triomphe, triomphalement
Triumvirate, s. triumvirat, *m.*
Triune, adj. un en trois personnes
Trivet, s. trépied, *m.*
Trivial, adj. trivial
Triviality, s. trivialité, *f.*
Trivially, adv. trivialement
Troat, vn. bramer
Trochee, s. trochée, *m.*
Troll, va. faire circuler, rouler, tourner
Trollop, s. négligente, *f.*, souillon, *f.*
Trombone, s. trombone, *m.*
Troop, s. troupe, *f.*, bande, *f.*, foule, *f.*, (*milit.*) compagnie de cavalerie, *f.*
Troop, vn. se rassembler, accourir en foule, marcher en troupe
Trooper, s. cavalier, *m.*
Trope, s. trope, *m.*
Trophied, adj. orné de trophées
Trophy, s. trophée, *m.*
Tropic, s. tropique, *m.* — *-bird*, s. paille-en-queue, *f.*
Tropic, Tropical, adj. tropical, des tropiques, (*lit.*) figuré
Tropically, adv. figurativement
Trot, vn. trotter, aller le trot
Trot, s. trot, *m.* *At full* —, *at a jog* —, au grand trot, au petit trot
Troth, s. foi, *f.*
Trotter, s. trotteur, *m.*, -euse, *f.*, (*meat*) pied de mouton, *m.*
Trouble, va. troubler, agiter, jeter dans le désordre, (*give trouble*) mettre en peine, tourmenter, importuner, déranger, embarrasser, charger. *I will — you for a cup more tea*, je vous demanderai encore une tasse de thé. *May I — you with this parcel?* oserai je vous charger de ce paquet?
Trouble, s. peine, *f.*, embarras, *m.*, (*mental*) trouble, *m.*, perplexité, *f.*, inquiétude, *f.*, tourment, *m.*, (*annoyance*) peine, *f.*, ennui, *m.*, (*pain*) chagrin, *m.*, mal, *m.*, tourment, *m.*, affliction, *f.* *To be at some* —, *to have some* — *to*, avoir peine à, avoir de la peine à. *All the — in the world*, toutes les peines du monde
Troubled, adj. agité, troublé, (*water*) trouble
Troublesome, adj. ennuyeux, importun, fatigant, tourmentant
Troublesomeness, s. ennui, *m.*, embarras, *m.*, importunité, *f.*
Troublous, adj. agité, orageux, de troubles
Trough, s. auge, *f.*, auget, *m.*, (*for kneading*) huche, *f.*, (*of the sea*) entredeux, *m.*
Trounce, va. fouetter, étriller
Trousers, s.pl. *See* Trowsers
Trout, s. truite, *f.*
Trowel, s. truelle, *f.*
Trowsers, s.pl. pantalon, *m.* *A pair of* —, un pantalon
Truant, s. adj. élève qui fait l'école buissonnière, paresseux, *m.*, -euse, *f.*, vagabond, *m.*
Truce, s. trêve, *f.*
Truck, va.n. faire le trafic troquer

Truck, s. (*cart*) voiture à bras, *f.*, camion, *m.*, (*rails*) truc, *m.*, (*artil.*) roue d'affût, *f.*, wagon, *m.*

Truckle, vn. ployer, s'abaisser, flatter bassement, ramper, s'humilier. *To — under*, se soumettre

Truckle, s. roulette, *f.* — *-bed*, s. grabat, *m.*

Truculent, adj. féroce, barbare, cruel, sanguinaire

Trudge, vn. aller à pied, marcher (péniblement)

True, adj. vrai, véritable, véridique, sincère, loyal, fidèle, honnête, intègre, conforme. — *-born*, adj. vrai, véritable. — *-bred*, adj. par sang, vrai, véritable. — *-hearted*, adj. sincère. — *-love*, s. bien-aimé, *m.* -ée, *f.* —! int. c'est vrai!

Truffle, s. truffe, *f.* — *-ground*, s. truffière, *f.* *To stuff with —s*, truffer

Truffled, adj. . . . . aux truffes

Truism, s. vérité banale, *f.*

Truly, adv. vraiment, véritablement, véridiquement, sincèrement, fidèlement, loyalement, honnêtement, exactement

Trump, s. trompe, trompette, *f.*, (*at cards*) atout, *m.*, (*fig.*) brave cœur. — *-card*, s. retourne, *f.*

Trump, va. (*at cards*) couper, (*to deceive*) tromper, se jouer de. *To — up*, inventer

Trumpery, s. choses de rebut, *f.pl.*, vieilleries, *f.pl.*, oripeaux, *m.pl.*, friperie, *f.*, (*nonsense*) fadaises, *f.pl.*, farce, *f.*

Trumpery, adj. sans valeur, mesquin, méchant

Trumpet, s. trompette, *f.*, trompe, *f.* *speaking —*, s. cornet acoustique, *m.*, (*pers.*) trompette, *m.*

Trumpet, va. publier à son de trompe, proclamer, publier

Trumpeter, s. trompette, *m.*

Truncate, va. tronquer

Truncheon, s. bâton, *m.*

Trundle, s. roulette, *f.*, camion, *m.*

Trundle, va. rouler, faire aller

Trunk, s. tronc, *m.*, corps, *m.*, (*arts*) torse, *m.*, (*of elephants, insects*) trompe, *f.* (*box*) malle, *f.*, coffre, *m.*, (*tube*) sarbacane, *f.* — *-line*, s. ligne principale, *f.* — *-maker*, s. layetier, *m.*

Trunnion, s. tourillon, *m.*

Truss, s. (*hay*) botte, *f.*, (*packet*) paquet, *m.*, trousse, *f.*, (*surg.*) bandage herniaire, *m.* — *-maker*, bandagiste, *m.*

Truss, va. (*fowls*) trousser, (*to pack*) empaqueter, lier, (*hay*) mettre en bottes

Trust, s. confiance, *f.*, (*hope*) espérance, *f.*, attente, *f.*, (*deposit*) dépôt, *m.*, (*care*) soin, *m.*, garde, *f.*, (*com.*) crédit, *m.*, (*law*) fidéicommis, *m.* *To buy or sell on, upon, —*, vendre, acheter de confiance, à crédit. *In —*, par fidéicommis, fiduciaire. — *-deed*, s. acte fiduciaire, *m.*

Trust, va.n. se fier à, se confier à, mettre sa confiance dans, (*believe*) croire à, ajouter foi à, (*intrust*) confier (*venture*) risquer, hasarder, (*com.*) faire crédit à, (*to hope*) espérer, compter

Trustee, s. gardien, dépositaire, *m.*, administrateur, *m.*, (*law*) commissaire, *m.*, (*of orphans*) fidéicommissaire, *m.* *Board of —s*, conseil d'administration, *m.*

Trusteeship, s. qualité de tuteur, *m.*, -rice, *f.*

Trustily, adv. fidèlement

Trustiness, s. fidélité, *f.*, loyauté, *f.*, honnêteté, *f.*

Trustworthy, Trusty, adj. fidèle, honnête, loyal, digne de confiance

Truth, s. vérité, *f.*, véracité, *f.*, fidélité, *f.*, vrai, *m.* *Of a —, in —*, en vérité, véritablement. *To speak or to tell the —, the whole —*, dire la vérité, toute la vérité

Truthful, adj. véridique, vrai

Truthfully, adv. véridiquement, sincèrement

Truthfulness, s. véracité, *f.*, sincérité, *f.*

Try, vn. essayer, tenter (de), (*endeavour*) chercher (à), s'efforcer (de). *To — after, for*, tâcher d'obtenir; — va. essayer, éprouver, faire l'expérience de, (*sight*) fatiguer, (*law*) juger, faire le procès à, (*metals*) raffiner. *To — on*, (*clothes*) essayer

Trying, adj. critique, pénible, difficile, fatigant, ennuyeux

Tub, baquet, *m.*, cuve, *f.*, tonneau, *m.*, (*plants*) caisse, *f.*

Tube, s. tube, *m.*, tuyau, *m.*, (*anat., bot.*) tube, *m.*, canal, *m.*, conduit, *m.*

Tubercle, Tubercule, s. tubercule, *m.*

Tuberose, s. tubéreuse, *f.*

Tuberous, adj. tubéreux

Tubular, Tubulated, adj. tubulaire. *Tubular bridge*, s. pont tube, *m.*

Tuck, s. (*sword*) rapière, *f.*, estoc, *m.*, (*in cloth, etc.*) pli, *m.*, faux pli, *m.* — *-out*, s. bombance, *f.*, festin, *m.*

Tuck, va. relever, retrousser, (*a bed*) border. *To — in*, rentrer, border (*to eat*) avaler, engloutir. *To — up*, relever, retrousser

Tucker, s. chemisette, *f.*, tour de gorge, *m.*

Tuesday, s. mardi, *m.*

Tuft, s. touffe, *f.*, (*of birds*) huppe, *f.*, aigrette, *f.*, (*trees*) bouquet, *m.*, touffe, *f.*, (*wool*) flocon, *m.*, (*milit.*) pompon, *m.* — *-hunter*, s. parasite, courtisan, *m.*

Tuft, va. former en touffes, orner or couvrir de touffes

Tufted, adj. touffu, en touffes, huppé, portant une aigrette, semé de bouquets d'arbres

Tug, va.n. tirer, tirailler, arracher, (*tow*) remorquer

Tug, s. action de tirer, *f.*, tiraillement, *m.*, secousse, *f.*, effort, *m.*, lutte, *f.*, (*boat*) bateau remorqueur, *m.*

Tuition, s. instruction, *f.*, éducation, *f.*, leçons, *f.pl.* enseignement, *m.*, (*fees*) prix de la pension, *m.*

Tulip, s. tulipe, *f.*

Tumble, vn. rouler, se rouler, être ballotté, se tourner, s'agiter, (*fall*) tomber, (*fam.*) dégringoler, (*things*) s'écrouler, (*fig.*) tomber comme grêle, pleuvoir. *To — down*, tomber, se laisser choir, dégringoler, faire la culbute, s'écrouler. *To — in*, entrer vivement. *To — out of bed*, sauter à bas du lit. *To — into bed*, se jeter dans son lit. *To — up*, monter lestement; — va. tourner, retourner, (*throw*) jeter, lancer, précipiter, (*put out of order*) déranger, bouleverser, bousculer, chiffonner

Tumble, s. chute, *f.*, dégringolade, *f.*, culbute, *f.* — *down*, *adj.* délabré, en ruines

Tumbler, s. bateleur, *m.*, saltimbanque, *m.*, sauteur, *m.*, (*glass*) verre à boire, *m.*, (*of fire arms*) noix, *f.*

Tumbrel, s. tombereau, *m.*, (*mil.*) fourgon, *m.*

Tumefy, va. tuméfier; — vn. se tuméfier

Tumour, s. tumeur, *f.*

Tumult, s. tumulte, *m.*

Tumultuous, adj. tumultueux

Tumultuously, adv. tumultueusement

Tun, s. tonne, *f.*, tonneau, *m.*, fût, *m.*, (*drunkard*) ivrogne, *m.*

Tunable, adj. qu'on peut accorder, harmonieux, musical

Tune, s. air, *m.*, ton, *m.*, accord, *m.*, (*fig.*) harmonie, *f.*, concorde, *f.*, train, *m.*, verve, *f.*

Tune, va. accorder, mettre d'accord

Tuneful, adj. harmonieux

Tuneless, adj. discordant

Tuner, s. accordeur, *m.*

Tuning, s. chant, *m.*, accord, *m.* — *-fork*, s. diapason, *m.* — *-hammer*, s. — *-key*, s. clé, *f.*

Tunnel, s. tunnel, *m.*, souterrain, *m.*

Tunnel, va. percer

Tunny, s. thon, *m.*

Turban, s. turban, *m.*

Turbid, adj. trouble, bourbeux

Turbine, s. turbine, *f.*

Turbot, s. turbot, *m.*

Turbulence, s. turbulence, *f.*, tumulte, *m.*, agitation, *f.*

Turbulent, adj. turbulent, remuant

Tureen, s. terrine, *f.*, soupière, *f.*

Turf, s. gazon, *m.*, herbe, *f.*, (*fuel*) tourbe, *f.*, (*race-ground*) turf, *m.*, terrain de course, *m.*, courses, *f.pl.*

Turf, va. gazonner

Turfing, s. gazonnement, *m.*

Turfy, adj. couvert de gazon, vert, (*of peat*) tourbeux

Turgid, adj. gonflé, (*fig.*) ampoulé, boursouflé

Turgidity, Turgidness, s. gonflement, *m.*, (*fig.*) boursouflure, *f.*

Turk, s. (*shrew*), mégère, *f.* —*'s head*, (*brush*) s. tête de loup, *f.*

Turkey, s. dindon, *m.*, coq d'Inde, *m.*, dinde, *f.* — *-cock*, dindon, *m.* — *-hen*, dinde, *f.* — *-poult*, dindonneau, *m.*

Turmeric, s. safran d'Inde, *m.*

Turmoil, s. tumulte, *m.*, agitation, *f.*, désordre, *m.*

Turn, va. tourner, faire tourner, (*nav.*) virer, diriger, (*change*) changer, (*at a lathe*) tourner, (*to make*) façonner au tour, (*translate*) traduire, tourner, (*the stomach*) faire soulever, (*the brain*) déranger, (*to apply*) tourner, diriger, appliquer, (*revolve*) retourner, repasser, rouler, agiter, (*a decree*) renverser, révoquer, (*milk, fruit*) tourner, aigrir. *To — about*, retourner. *To — aside*, écarter, détourner. *To — away*, détourner, renvoyer, remercier, congédier, chasser. *To — back*, faire retourner, renvoyer. *To — down*, retourner, (*a page*) faire un pli, marquer, (*collar*) rabattre, (*a bed*) faire, défaire. *To — in*, tourner en dedans, faire rentrer, rentrer. *To — off*, renvoyer, remercier, congédier, chasser, (*wife*) répudier, (*to give up*) renoncer à, détourner, divertir, distraire, (*a tap*) fermer, lâcher, laisser couler, (*question*) tourner. — *on a tap*, ouvrir, lâcher. — *out*, tourner en dehors, retourner, montrer, faire sortir, (*dismiss*) chasser, mettre à la porte, expulser, remercier, renvoyer, mettre dehors, (*hunting*) lancer. — *over*, retourner, (*think*) réfléchir à, (*convey*) transférer, (*attribute*) renvoyer, référer, (*a book*) examiner, feuilleter. *To — over and over*, tourner et retourner, retourner en tous sens. *To — up*, retourner, tourner, (*tuck up*) retrousser, trousser; — vn. tourner, se tourner, se retourner, (*from*, de) se détourner, recourir (à), s'adresser (à), (*upon*) rouler (sur), tourner (sur), (*nav.*) virer, (*into*, en) se changer, se tourner, devenir, se faire, se repentir, (*milk*) tourner, s'aigrir. — *to*, (*on, upon*, de), dépendre. *To — back*, se retourner, retourner sur ses pas. *To — in*, rentrer, se recourber, se ployer, (*to go to bed*) se mettre au lit. — *off*, se détourner, changer de route, (*things*) faire un détour, changer de direction. — *out*, tourner en dehors, se dévier, sortir, (*guard*) prendre les armes, (*to get up*) se lever, sortir du lit, (*happen*) arriver, se trouver, être, (*pers.*) devenir, finir par être, paraître. *The thing has —ed out well*, l'affaire s'est bien tournée, a bien tourné. *To — out right*, finir bien, réussir. *As it —ed out*, comme il arriva. *And so it —ed out*, et c'est ainsi que les choses se passèrent. *It —ed out that it was all untrue*, il se trouva que tout cela était faux. *It —s out now that he is the man*, il se trouve maintenant que c'est lui. *To — over*, se retourner, se renverser, culbuter, (*carriage*) verser, tourner la page. *To — up*, tourner, se retourner, se relever, se retrousser, (*cards*) retourner, (*happen*) arriver, se présenter

Turn, s. tour, *m.*, (*turning*) détour, *m.*, coude *m.*, révolution, *f.*, (*change*) changement, *m.*, vicissitude, *f.*, (*direction*) tournure, *f.*, (*service*) tour, service, *m.*, (*tendency*) tendance, *f.*, (*inclination*) goût, *m.* *Half a —*, un demi tour. *To take a — in the park*, faire un tour au parc. *By —s, in —*, tour à tour, à tour de rôle. *To take one's —, to take —s*, prendre son tour. *At every —*, à tout propos, à tout moment, à tout bout de champ. *To do an ill — to*, jouer un mauvais tour à. *To do a good —, a kind — to*, rendre service à. *The — of life*, le retour de l'âge.

Turncoat, s. déserteur, *m.*, renégat, *m.*, traître, *m.*

Turncock, s. fontainier, *m.*

Turner, s. tourneur, *m.*

Turning, s. mouvement, *m.*, détour, *m.*, changement, *m.*, déviation, *f.*, art du tourneur, *m.*, (*street*) rue, *f.*

Turning, adj. tournant. — *-point*, s. détour, *m.*, moment critique, *m.*

Turnip, s. navet, *m.*

Turnkey, s. porte-clefs, *m.*, geôlier, *m.*, guichetier, *m.*

Turnout, s. (*rails*) voie d'évitement *f.*, (*workmen*) grève *f.*, (*carriage*) équipage, *m.*, voiture, *f.*

Turnpike, s. barrière, *f.*, tourniquet, *m.*, — *-keeper*, s. garde-barrière, *m.*

Turnscrew, s. tournevis, *m.*

Turnspit, s. tournebroche, *m.*

Turnstile, s. tourniquet, *m.*

Turpentine, s. térébenthine, *f.*

Turpitude, s. turpitude, *f.*

Turquoise, s. turquoise, *f.*

Turret, s. tourelle, *f.*

Turreted, adj. garni de tourelles, à tourelles.

Turtle, s. (*bird*) tourtereau, *m.*, tourterelle, *f.* (*tortoise*) tortue, *f.*, tortue de mer, *f.*

Tush! interj. bah! fi donc!

Tusk, s. défense, *f.*, croc, *m.*

Tusked, adj. armé de défenses, armé de crocs.

Tussle, s. lutte, *f.*, bataille, *f.*

Tut! interj. bah! fi donc! assez!

Tutelage, s. tutelle *f.*, protection, *f.*

Tutelar, adj. tutélaire.

Tutor, s. précepteur, *m.*, instituteur, *m.*, maître, *m.*, répétiteur, *m.*

Tutoress, s. institutrice, *f.*

Tutorship, s. emploi de précepteur, *m.*

Twaddle, s bavardage, *m.*, caquetage, *m.*, niaiseries, *f. pl.*, fadaises, *f. pl.*, sottises, *f. pl.*

Twaddle, vn. caqueter, débiter des niaiseries, jacasser.

Twain, s. adj. deux, couple, *m.*

Twang, vn. retentir, rendre un son aigu; — va. faire retentir.

Twang, s. son, *m.*, bruit, *m.*, nasillement, *m.*, ton nasillard, *m.*

Tweezers, s. pl. petites pinces, *f.* *Tweezer-case*, s. étui, *m.*

Twelfth, adj. douzième, douze; — s. douzième, *m.*; — *-cake*, s. gâteau des Rois, *m.*

Twelve, adj. s. douze.

Twelvemonth, s. an, *m.*, année, *f.* *On this day —*, d'aujourd'hui en un an.

Twentieth, adj. vingtième, vingt.

Twenty, s. adj. vingt.

Twice, adj. deux fois.

Twig, s. petite branche, *f.*, baguette, *f.* brindille, *f.*

Twilight, s. crépuscule, *m.*, demi-jour, *m.*

Twilled, adj. croisé.

Twill, s. étoffe croisée, *f.*, croisé, *m.*

Twin, s. jumeau, *m.*, jumelle, *f.*; — s. *pl.* (*astron.*) (les) Gémeaux.

Twine, va. tordre, (*weave*) tisser, ouvrer, (*gird*) ceindre, entourer, — vn. s'entrelacer, s'enrouler, s'enlacer, tourner, serpenter, se plier.

Twine, s. ficelle, *f.*, (*fold, etc.*) repli, *m.*, embrassement, *m.*

Twinge, va. torturer, causer une douleur; — vn. élancer.

Twinge, s. douleur cuisante, *f.*, élancement, *m.*, tiraillement, *m.*

Twinkle, vn. scintiller, étinceler, (*eyes*) cligner de l'œil, clignoter

Twinkle, Twinkling, s. scintillement, *m.*, clignement de l'œil, *m.*, signe de l'œil, *m.*, (*fig.*) clin d'œil, *m.*, instant, *m.*

Twirl, va. tourner rapidement, faire tourner, (*with a stick*) pirouetter

Twirl, s. tour, *m.*, révolution, *f.*, pirouette, *f.*, enroulement, *m.* *Give a —*, faire tourner, faire le moulinet

Twist, va. tordre, tisser, courber, entourer, enlacer, enrouler, tourner autour de, fabriquer, tisser, ourdir, entortiller; — vn. s'entrelacer, s'enlacer, s'enrouler, s'entortiller, se tortiller, (*things*) se tordre, se contourner

Twist, s. enroulement, *m.*, contorsion, *f.*, tortillement, *m.*, repli, *m.*, tresse, *f.*, natte, *f.*, (*string*) cordon, *m.*, corde, *f.*, cordonnet, *m.*, (*indust.*) torsion, *f.*, tordage, *m.* détour, *m.*, (*of tobacco*) carotte, *f.*, (*prejudice*) préjugé, *m.*

Twisted, adj. tordu, (*thread*) tors, -e. — *fringe*, s. torsade, *f.*

Twit, va reprocher, accuser, (de)

Twitch, va. tirer brusquement, saisir, arracher; — *up*; — vn. se contracter

Twitch, Twitching, s. (*inst.*) action de tirer, *f.*, secousse, *f.*, mouvement de la main, *m.*, spasme, *m.*, contraction, *f.*, (*pain*) élancement, *m.*, vive douleur, *f.*

Twitter, vn. gazouiller

Twitter, s. gazouillement, *m.*

Two, adj. s. deux, (*in compounds*) à deux

Twofold, adj. double

Twofold, adv. doublement, deux fois

Tympan, s. tympan, *m.*

Type, s. type, *m.*, (*print.*) type, caractère, *m.*; — *-founder*, s. fondeur en caractères, *m.*; — *-metal*, s. fonte, *f.*; — *-foundry*, s. fonderie de caractères, *f.*

Typhoid, adj. typhoïde

Typhoon, s. typhon, *m.* trombe, *f.*

Typhus, s. typhus, *m.*

Typic, Typical, adj. typique, symbolique, allégorique

Typically, adj. d'une manière symbolique

Typify, va. représenter d'une manière symbolique, figurer

Typographer, s. typographe, *m.*

Typographic, Typographical, adj. typographique, symbolique

Typography, s. typographie, *f.*

Tyrannical, adj. tyrannique

Tyrannically, adv. tyranniquement, en tyran

Tyrannize, vn. tyranniser

Tyranny, s. tyrannie, *f.*

Tyrant, s. tyran, *m.*

Tyro, s. commençant *m.*, écolier, *m.*

U

U, s. U, u, *m.*

Udder, s. pis, *m.*

Ugliness, s. laideur, *f.*

Ugly, adj. laid, vilain

Ulcer, s. ulcère, *m.*; — *in the mouth*, aphte, *m.*

Ulcerate, vn. s'ulcérer; — va. ulcérer

Ulceration, s. ulcération, *f.*

Ulcerous, adj. ulcéré

Ulterior, adj. ultérieur

Ultimate, adj. dernier, extrême, définitif, final

Ultimately, adv. à la fin, finalement, définitivement

Ultimatum, s. ultimatum, *m.*

Ultra, s. ultra, *m.*, extrême, *m.*

Ultramontane, adj. ultramontain

Umber, s. ombre, *f.*, terre d'ombre, *f.*

Umbrage, s. ombre, *f.*, ombrage, *m.*

Umbrella, s. parapluie, *m.* — *-case*, s. fourreau de parapluie, *m.* — *-stand*, s. porte-parapluie, *m.*

Umpirage, s. arbitrage, *m.*

Umpire, s. arbitre, *m.*

Umpireship, s. arbitrage, *m.*

Umquhile, adj. d'autrefois

Un-, (*in comp.*) non...., in....., peu...., dés...., dé....

Unabated, adj. nullement diminué, toujours, égal

Unable, adj. incapable, ne pouvant pas, impuissant, impotent. *To be — to move*, ne pas pouvoir bouger

Unaccented, adj. non accentué, sans accent

Unacceptable, adj. inacceptable, désagréable

Unaccepted, adj. qu'on n'accepte pas

Unaccommodating, adj. peu accommodant

Unaccompanied, adj. seul, sans être accompagné

Unaccomplished, adj. inachevé, incomplet

Unaccountable, adj. inexplicable, inconcevable

Unaccountably, adv. inconcevablement, étrangement

Unaccredited, adj. non accrédité, sans pouvoir

Unaccustomed, adj. inaccoutumé, peu habitué

Unacknowledged, adj. non reconnu, non avoué, non confessé

Unacquainted, adj. qui ne connaît pas, qui ignore, peu habitué. *To be — with*, ignorer, ne pas connaître

Unadjusted, adj. non ajusté, (*law*) en litige

Unadorned, adj. sans ornement, sans parure

Unadulterated, adj. pur, non falsifié, non frelaté

Unadvisable, adj. peu sage, imprudent

Unadvised, adj. imprudent, peu sage, irréfléchi, inconsidéré

Unadvisedly, adv. imprudemment, sans réflexion, précipitamment

Unaffected, adj. sans affectation, sincère, vrai, simple, naturel

Unaffectedly, adv. sans affectation, réellement, simplement, naturellement

Unaffecting, adj. peu émouvant

Unaided, adj. sans aide, sans secours

Unalloyed, adj. sans alliage, sans mélange, pur

Unalterable, adj. inaltérable, invariable

Unaltered, adj. sans changement, pas changé

Unambitious, adj. sans ambition, pas ambitieux, sans prétention

Unanimity, s. unanimité, *f.*

Unanimous, adj. unanime

Unanimously, adv. à l'unanimité, unanimement

Unanswerable, adj. sans réplique, incontestable

Unanswerably, adv. irréfutablement

Unanswered, adj. sans réponse

Unappalled, adj. sans être effrayé, sans pâlir, sans effroi

Unappeasable, adj. implacable

Unappeased, adj. non apaisé

Unapprehensible, adj. *See* INAPPREHENSIBLE

Unapprised, adj. sans être informé

Unapproachable, adj. inabordable, inaccessible

Unappropriated, adj. sans application, sans emploi, non approprié

Unapproved, adj. non approuvé

Unarmed, adj. désarmé, sans armes

Unasked, adj. sans qu'on demande, sans être invité

Unaspiring, adj. peu ambitieux

Unassailable, adj. inattaquable

Unassisted, adj. sans aide, sans secours

Unassorted, adj. non assorti

Unassuming, adj. sans prétentions, modeste, simple

Unassured, adj. non assuré

Unatoned, adj. non expié, sans expiation

Unattached, adj. indépendant, en disponibilité

Unattainable, adj. impossible à atteindre, inaccessible

Unattained, adj. non atteint, manqué

Unattempted, adj. sans être essayé

Unattended, adj. sans suite, seul, sans être accompagné, non suivi, négligé

Unattested, adj. qui n'est pas attesté

Unauthenticated, adj. dont l'authenticité n'est pas prouvée, *or* reconnue, non légalisé

Unauthorized, adj. sans autorisation, sans autorité

Unavailable, **Unavailing**, adj. inutile, non valable, inefficace

Unavenged, adj. non vengé, sans vengeance

Unavoidable, adj. inévitable

Unavoidably, adv. inévitablement

Unaware, adj. qui ignore, inattentif

Unawares, adv. à l'improviste, au dépourvu, (*by mistake*) par mégarde, par inadvertance

Unawed, adj. sans crainte, sans se laisser intimider par, hardi

Unbacked, adj. sans être appuyé, sans appui

Unbaked, adj. non cuit

Unballasted, adj. sans lest, léger, frivole

Unbaptized, adj. sans être baptisé

Unbar, va. enlever la barre de, débarrer

Unbarricade, va. ôter les barricades, débarricader

Unbearable, adj. insupportable

Unbecoming, adj. inconvenant, malséant, déplacé, (*clothes*) qui ne va pas bien

Unbecomingly, adv. d'une manière inconvenante

Unbecomingness, s. inconvenance, *f.*

Unbefitting, adj. *See* **Unbecoming**

Unbefriended, adj. sans amis

Unbelief, s. incrédulité, *f.*, manque de foi, *m.*

Unbeliever, s. incrédule, *m.*, *f.*, infidèle, *m.*, *f.*

Unbelieving, adj. incrédule, infidèle, mécréant

Unbend, va. détendre, desserrer (*a bow*) débander, (*to rest*) délasser (*the brow*) dérider (*weaken*), relâcher, affaiblir. — vn. se détendre, se dérider

Unbending, adj. inflexible, roide

Unbenefited, adj. sans avantage, sans bénéfice

Unbiassed, adj. sans préventions, sans préjugés, impartial

Unbidden, adj. sans être invité, spontané

Unbigoted, adj. libéral, peu fanatique

Unbind, va. délier, détacher, desserrer, débander

Unbleached, adj. non blanchi, écru

Unblemished, adj. sans tache, pur

Unblessed, **Unblest**, adj. non béni, sans être béni, maudit, infortuné

Unblighted, adj. non flétri, frais, dans sa fraîcheur

Unblown, adj. non encore épanoui, en bouton

Unblushing, adj. qui ne rougit point, déhonté

Unbolt, va. tirer les verrous de, ouvrir

Unbolted, adj. pas verrouillé, ouvert, (*flour*) non bluté

Unboned, adj. désossé

Unborn, adj. encore à naître, futur

Unborrowed, adj. non emprunté, naturel

Unbosom, va. confier, découvrir, révéler ; — *oneself to*, s'ouvrir à

Unbought, adj. non acheté

Unbound, adj. délié, déchaîné, dénoué, libre, flottant, (*books*) non relié

Unbounded, adj. sans bornes, sans limites, illimité

Unboundedly, adv. sans bornes

Unbrace, va. délier, relâcher, détendre, ouvrir, défaire, énerver, affaiblir

Unbred, adj. mal élevé

Unbribed, adj. qui n'est pas acheté, libre

Unbridle, va. débrider

Unbridled, adj. débridé, effréné, sans frein

Unbroken, adj. non brisé, non interrompu, continu, incessant, (*animals*) indomptable, (*promise*) non violé, tenu, observé, non enfreint

Unbrotherly, adj. indigne d'un frère, peu fraternel

Unbuckle, va. déboucler

Unbuilt, adj. à bâtir

Unburden, va. décharger

Unburied, adj. sans sépulture

Unburnt, adj. sans être brûlé

Unbury, va. déterrer

Unbutton, va. déboutonner

Uncage, va. lâcher, délivrer

Uncalled, adj. sans être appelé ; — *for*, gratuit, inutile

Uncancelled, adj. sans être annulé

Uncandid, adj. non sincère, peu sincère

Uncap, va. découvrir, (*foils*) démoucheter

Uncared, adj. (*for*, ...) négligé, dans l'abandon, abandonné

Uncarpeted, adj. sans tapis

Unceasing, adj. incessant, sans relâche, continuel

Unceasingly, adv. sans cesse, sans relâche, incessamment

Unceremonious, adj. peu cérémonieux, brusque, sans façon, sans cérémonie

Unceremoniously, adv. sans façon

Uncertain, adj. incertain, peu sûr

Uncertainty, s. incertitude, *f.*

Uncertified, adj. non certifié

Unchain, va. déchaîner

Unchangeable, adj. immuable, invariable, inaltérable

Unchangeableness, s. immutabilité, *f.*

Unchanged, adj. sans être changé, le même

Unchanging, adj. qui ne change pas, invariable, constant

Unchangingly, adv. immuablement

Uncharitable, adj. peu charitable

Uncharitableness, s. manque de charité, *m.*

Uncharitably, adv. sans charité

Unchaste, adj. peu chaste, impudique

Unchastity, s. incontinence, *f.*

Unchecked, adj. sans frein, effréné

Unchewed, adj. sans être mâché

Unchristian, adj. peu chrétien, contraire aux doctrines chrétiennes

Uncircumspect, adj. peu circonspect

Uncivil, adj. malhonnête, impoli, incivil

Uncivilized, adj. non civilisé ; (*rude*) grossier

Uncivilly, adv. malhonnêtement, peu poliment

Unclad, adj. sans vêtement, nu

Unclaimed, adj. non réclamé

Unclasp, va. ouvrir, dégrafer, défaire

Uncle, s. oncle, *m.*, (*pawnbroker*) tante, *f.*

Unclean, adj. malpropre, sale, immonde, impur, libertin

Uncleanliness, s. malpropreté, *f.*, saleté, *f.*, impureté, *f.*

Uncleanly, adj. malpropre, impur

Unclench, va. desserrer, ouvrir

Unclipped, adj. (*coins*) non rogné, non coupé, (*fleeces*) non tondu

Unclog, va. dégager, débarrasser

Unclose, va. ouvrir

Unclouded, adj. sans nuages, serein, pur

Uncock, va. désarmer

Uncoil, va. dérouler

Uncoined, adj. non monnayé

Uncoloured, adj. incoloré, sans couleur

Uncombed, adj. non peigné, en désordre

Uncomeliness, s. manque de grâce, *m.*, mine disgracieuse, *f.*, laideur, *f.*, inconvenance, *f.*

Uncomely, adj. peu avenant, disgracieux, laid, malséant

Uncomfortable, adj. peu comfortable, peu commode, incommode, mal à son aise, gêné, (*sad*) malheureux

Uncomfortableness, s. incommodité, *f.*, peu d'agrément *or* de commodité, *m.*, gêne, *f.*, malaise, *m.*, ennui, *m.*, inquiétude, *f.*

Uncomfortably, adv. mal à l'aise, à la gêne, gêné, avec inquiétude, malheureux

Uncommon, adj. rare, extraordinaire, peu commun, singulier

Uncommonly, adv. extraordinairement, peu souvent, rarement

Uncommonness, s. rareté, *f.*

Uncommunicable, adj. incommunicable

Uncompleted, adj. incomplet, inachevé

Uncompounded, adj. simple, non composé

Uncompromising, adj. inflexible, ferme, opiniâtre, intraitable

Uncompromisingly, adv. fermement

Unconcern, s. indifférence, *f.*

Unconcerned, adj. indifférent

Unconcernedly, adv. avec indifférence

Unconditional, adj. sans condition, sans réserve

Unconditionally, adv. sans condition

Unconfined, adj. libre, non renfermé, illimité, sans bornes

Unconfirmed, adj. non confirmé

Unconformable, adj. non conforme, contraire

Unconnected, adj. sans rapport (avec), étranger (à), sans liaison, sans relation

Unconquerable, adj. indomptable, invincible

Unconquered, adj. invaincu, indompté, invincible

Unconscious, adj. sans conscience (de), sans le sentiment (de), ignorant, qui ne sait pas, sans connaissance, ayant perdu connaissance

Unconsciously, adv. sans le savoir, à son insu, par inadvertance

Unconsciousness, s. ignorance, *f.*, insensibilité, *f.*

Unconsecrated, adj. non consacré, non sacré, non béni

Unconstitutional, adj. inconstitutionnel

Unconstrained, adj. spontané, volontaire, libre

Unconstraint, s. liberté, *f.*

Uncontaminated, adj. sans souillure, pur

Uncontested, adj. sans contestation

Uncontradicted, adj. non contredit

Uncontrollable, adj. indomptable, effréné, irrésistible

Uncontrolled, adj. sans contrôle, sans frein, effréné

Uncontroverted, adj. incontesté, admis sans contestation

Unconversant, adj. peu versé (dans), peu familier (avec)

Unconverted, adj. non converti

Unconvinced, adj. non convaincu, pas persuadé

Unconvincing, adj. peu convaincant

Uncork, va. déboucher

Uncorrected, adj. pas corrigé

Uncorrupted, adj. non corrompu, intègre

Uncouple, va. découpler, détacher

Uncourteous, adj. peu courtois, peu affable

Uncourteously, adv. peu courtoisement, impoliment

Uncourtliness, s. rudesse, *f.*, gaucherie, *f.*

Uncourtly, adv. rude, rustique, gauche, commun

Uncouth, adj. étrange, bizarre, singulier, baroque, grossier

Uncouthly, adv. bizarrement

Uncouthness, s. étrangeté, *f.*, bizarrerie, *f.*

Uncover, va. découvrir, ôter le couvercle de; — vn. se découvrir

Uncritical, adj. sans discernement, peu judicieux

Uncropped, adj. non récolté

Unction, s. onction, *f.*

Unctuous, adj. onctueux

Unctuousness, s. on[ctuosité], tuosité, *f.*

Uncultivated, adj. i[n]culte

Uncurbed, adj. indompt[é], sans frein

Uncurl, va. déboucler, d[é]friser; — vn. se défaire, dérouler

Uncut, adj. non taillé, n[on] coupé

Undamaged, adj. n[on] endommagé, intact, en b[on] état, (*com.*) non avarié

Undaunted, adj. *See* I[N]TREPID

Undazzled, adj. n[on] ébloui

Undeceive, va. désabuse[r], détromper

Undecided, adj. indéc[is], irrésolu, incertain

Undecked, adj. sans orn[e]ments, dépouillé, (*nav.*) n[on] ponté

Undeclined, adj. inva[ri]able

Undefaced, adj. pas d[é]figuré, non effacé

Undefended, adj. sa[ns] défense, pas défendu

Undefiled, adj. sans sou[il]lure, pur

Undefinable, adj. ind[é]finissable, indéterminé

Undefined, adj. indéfin[i]

Undeluded, adj. désabu[sé]

Undeniable, adj. qu'[on] ne peut nier, incontestable

Undeniably, adv. inco[n]testablement

Under, prep. sous, au-d[essous] de, (*less*) moins de, sa[ns] (*with the help of*) à l'aide d[e], avec, à, (*in*) dans, en

Under, adv. dessous, a[u]-dessous, (*fig.*) soumis, da[ns] un état d'assujettissement d'infériorité, (*for less*) moins

Under, adj. de dessous, i[n]férieur, sous-. . . aide-, . . inférieur, subalterne. *T[he] — part, the — side*, le d[es]sous. *— -agent*, s. agent i[n]férieur, *m.* *— -secretary*, sous-secrétaire, *m.* *— -hou[se]maid*, s. deuxième bonne, *— -actor*, s. (*theat.*), doublu[re], *f.* *To — -bid*, offrir moi[ns] que. *— -cut*, s. (*of meat*) fil[et], *m.*

Under-foot, adv. sous [les] pieds; — adj. abject. *— -ga[r]dener*, s. aide-jardinier, *m*. *— -graduate*, s. étudiant, *— -ground*, s. souterrain, *m*. sous-sol, *m.*; — adj. sout[er]rain; — adv. sous terre. *-growth*, s. broussailles, *f.*; *To — let*, va. sous-louer, lou[er à] vil prix. *To — -line*, souligne[r]. *— -part* s. dessous, *m.*, acc[es]soire, *m.*, incident, *m.* *-plot*, s. complot secret, *To — praise*, louer trop p[eu]. *To — -prize*, déprécier. *— -prop*, soutenir, étay[er]. *To — sell*, vendre meille[ur] marché que

Underdone, adj. peu cu[it], pas assez cuit

Undergo, va. subir, so[uffrir]

Undescribed, adj. non décrit

Undescried, adj. inaperçu

Undeserved, adj. immérité, qu'on n'a point mérité

Undeservedly, adv. sans l'avoir mérité, injustement

Undeserving, adj. (*th.*) peu méritoire (*pers. and th.*) indigne de, qui mérite peu, sans mérite

Undesigned, adj. fait sans intention, involontaire

Undesigning, adj. sans intention, sincère, innocent, de bonne foi

Undesirable, adj. peu désirable, peu à désirer

Undetected, adj. sans être découvert

Undetermined, adj. (*pers.*) indécis, irrésolu (*th.*) indéterminé, indéfini

Undeviating, adj. qui ne dévie pas, direct, ferme, constant

Undigested, adj. sans être digéré, non digéré

Undignified, adj. sans dignité, bas, grossier

Undiminished, adj. nullement diminué, sans diminution

Undimmed, adj. non obscurci, pur, brillant

Undirected, adj. sans être dirigé, non guidé, (*letters*) sans adresse

Undiscerned, adj. inaperçu

Undiscernible, adj. imperceptible

Undiscerning, adj. sans discernement, peu judicieux

Undisciplined, adj. indiscipliné, sans discipline

Undiscoverable, adj. qu'on ne peut découvrir, introuvable

Undiscovered, adj. non découvert, caché, secret, inaperçu

Undisguised, adj. sans déguisement, franc, ouvert, sincère, sans fard

Undismayed, adj. sans terreur, ferme

Undisposed, adj. — *of*, dont on n'a pas disposé

Undisputed, adj. incontesté, sans conteste

Undissembled, adj. non simulé, sincère

Undistinguishable, adj. indistinct, méconnaissable, insaisissable, imperceptible

Undisturbed, adj. paisible, tranquille, calme

Undivided, adj. non divisé, entier, sans partage

Undivulged, adj. non divulgué, caché

Undo, va. défaire, ouvrir, effacer, annuler, détruire, perdre, ruiner. *To come undone*, se défaire. *To leave undone*, ne pas faire. *I am undone*, c'est fait de moi, je suis perdu *or* ruiné

Undoubted, adj. hors de doute, incontestable, certain, incontesté

Undoubtedly, adv. indubitablement, sans (aucun) doute, incontestablement

Undoubting, adj. certain, convaincu

Undress, va. déshabiller, dévêtir; — vn. se déshabiller

Undress, s. deshabillé, *m.*, négligé, *m.*, (*milit.*) petite tenue, *f.*, demi-tenue, *f.*

Undressed, adj. déshabillé, en négligé, (*food, comm.*) non apprêté

Undue, adj. non dû, qu'on ne doit pas, injuste, illégal, excessif

Undulate, vn. onduler, ondoyer, flotter

Undulating, adj. ondoyant, flottant, (*land*) accidenté

Undulation, s. ondulation, *f.*

Unduly, adv. irrégulièrement, mal à propos, à tort, à l'excès, trop

Undutiful, adj. désobéissant, peu soumis, peu respectueux

Undutifully, adv. irrespectueusement

Undutifulness, s. désobéissance, *f.*

Undying, adj. qui ne meurt pas, impérissable, immortel

Unearned, adj. qu'on n'a pas gagné, immérité

Unearth, va. déterrer

Unearthly, adj. qui n'est pas de ce monde, surhumain, surnaturel

Uneasily, adj. mal à son aise, avec inquiétude, malaisément, avec peine

Uneasiness, s. malaise, *m.*, gêne *f.*, inquiétude, *f.*, peine, *f.* chagrin, *m.*

Uneasy, adj. inquiet, sans repos; d'inquiétude, de tourment, (*pers.*) mal à son aise, gêné, incommodé; (*th.*) incommode, (*constrained*) gêné, guindé, contraint

Unedifying, adj. peu édifiant

Uneducated, adj. sans éducation, ignorant

Unembarrassed, adj. non embarrassé, (*fortune*) claire, nette, (*property*) libre, sans dettes

Unemployed, adj. sans occupation, sans travail, désœuvré, inactif

Unencumbered, adj. non embarrassé

Unendowed, adj. qui n'est pas doué, (*not portioned*) non doté

Un-English, adj. peu anglais, indigne d'un anglais

Unenjoyed, adj. dont on n'a pas joui

Unenlightened, adj. peu éclairé, ignorant, grossier

Unenslaved, adj. non asservi, libre

Unenterprising, adj. peu entreprenant

Unentertaining, adj. peu amusant, ennuyeux

Unenviable, adj. peu digne d'envie, peu désirable

Unenvied, adj. peu envié

Unequal, adj. inégal, inférieur, au-dessous

Unequalled, adj. sans égal, qui n'a pas de rival

Unequally, adv. inégalement

Unequivocal, adj. non équivoque

Unerring, adj. infaillible, sûr

Unerringly, adv. infailliblement

Uneven, adj. inégal, peu uni, raboteux, (*numbers*) impair

Unevenly, adv. inégalement

Unevenness, s. inégalité, *f.*

Unexaggerated, adj. nullement exagéré

Unexamined, adj. sans examen

Unexampled, adj. sans exemple

Unexceptionable, adj. irréprochable, irrécusable

Unexecuted, adj. non exécuté

Unexemplified, adj. sans exemple

Unexercised, adj. peu exercé, non exercé

Unexhausted, adj. non épuisé

Unexpected, adj. inattendu, imprévu

Unexpectedly, adv. d'une manière inattendue, à l'improviste, inopinément

Unexpectedness, s. nature inattendue *or* imprévue, *f.*, soudaineté, *f.*

Unexpired, adj. non fini

Unexplained, adj. non expliqué

Unexplored, adj. inexploré, inconnu

Unexposed, adj. caché, secret

Unfaded, adj. dans toute sa fraîcheur, non fané, non flétri

Unfading, adj. qui ne se fane pas, qui ne se flétrit pas

Unfailing, adj. inépuisable, intarissable, infaillible, immanquable

Unfair, adj. injuste, de mauvaise foi

Unfairly, adv. injustement, déloyalement, avec mauvaise foi

Unfairness, s. injustice, *f.*, partialité, *f.*, déloyauté, *f.*, mauvaise foi, *f.*

Unfaithful, adj. etc. *See* FAITHLESS, etc.

Unfaltering, adj. sans hésitation, assuré, ferme

Unfamiliar, adj. peu familier, peu connu

Unfashionable, adj. (*things*) qui n'est pas de mode, qui n'est pas à la mode

Unfashionableness, s. inélégance, *f.*

Unfashionably, adv. pas à la mode

Unfashioned, adj. non façonné, informe

Unfasten, va. défaire, détacher, desserrer, lâcher

Unfatherly, adj. peu paternel, indigne d'un père

Unfathomable, Unfathomed, adj. insondable, sans fond

Unfavourable, adj. défavorable, contraire

Unfavourably, adv. défavorablement

Unfeasible, adj. impraticable

Unfeathered, adj. sans plumes

Unfed, adj. non nourri, non entretenu

Unfeeling, adj. insensible, impitoyable, dur, cruel

Unfeelingly, adv. avec cruauté, sans pitié

Unfeelingness, s. insensibilité, *f.*, cruauté, *f.*

Unfeigned, adj. vrai, sincère

Unfeignedly, adv. sans feinte, sincèrement, réellement

Unfelt, adj. non senti, qu'on ne sent pas

Unfenced, adj. sans clôture

Unfermented, adj. non fermenté, (*bread*) sans levain

Unfetter, va. ôter les fers à, délivrer, dégager

Unfettered, adj. libre, sans entraves

Unfilial, adj. peu filial

Unfilled, adj. non rempli, inoccupé, vacant

Unfinished, adj. incomplet, inachevé, pas fini

Unfit, adj. impropre (à), peu propre (à), peu fait (pour), (*to*) peu fait (pour), incapable (de), (*to, de*) hors de propos, déplacé, peu favorable, qui ne convient guère. — *for service*, hors de service

Unfit, va. rendre incapable (de), mettre hors d'état (de)

Unfitly, adv. mal à propos, à tort

Unfitness, s. inaptitude, *f.*, inconvenance, *f.*

Unfitting, adj. inconvenant

Unfix, va. détacher, délier

Unflagging, adj. soutenu, infatigable

Unfledged, adj. sans plumes, frais, éclos, (*pers.*) jeune, novice, inexpérimenté

Unflinching, adj. qui ne recule pas, résolu, ferme, intrépide

Unfold, va. ouvrir, déplier, développer, révéler, dévoiler, découvrir, dénoncer, exposer, dire, déclarer, étaler, (*sheep*) déparquer

Unforbidden, adj. permis

Unforced, adj. libre, naturel, aisé, prompt, spontané

Unforeseen, adj. imprévu

Unforgiving, adj. qui ne pardonne pas, implacable

Unfortified, adj. non fortifié

Unfortunate, adj. malheureux, infortuné

Unfortunately, adv. malheureusement

Unfought, adj. non combattu, sans lutte

Unfounded, adj. sans fondements, controuvé, faux

Unframed, adj. non façonné, (*pictures*) sans cadre

Unfrequent, adj. rare

Unfrequented, adj. peu fréquenté, solitaire, retiré, écarté

Unfrequently, adv. peu souvent, rarement

Unfriended, adj. sans amis

Unfriendliness, s. froideur, *f.*, défaut de bienveillance, *m.*

Unfriendly, adj. peu amical, peu bienveillant, froid

Unfrock, va. défroquer

Unfrozen, adj. non gelé

Unfruitful, adj. stérile, infécond

Unfruitfulness, s. stérilité, *f.*

Unfulfilled, adj. non accompli

Unfunded, adj. non consolidé

Unfurl, va. déployer, (*nav.*) déferler

Unfurnish, va. dépouiller, priver, dégarnir, démeubler

Unfurnished, adj. non meublé, sans meubles, non garni, (*deprived of*) non pourvu

Ungainly, adj. gauche, maladroit, dégingandé, déhanché

Ungallant, adj. peu galant, peu courtois

Ungarnished, adj. dégarni, sans garniture

Ungarrisoned, adj. sans garnison

Ungathered, adj. non cueilli

Ungenerous, adj. peu généreux, sans générosité

Ungenerously, adv. d'une manière peu généreuse, sans générosité

Ungenial, adj. âpre, rude, rigoureux, peu naturel, triste, peu généreux

Ungenteel, adj. mal élevé, de mauvais ton, pas élégant, de mauvais goût

Ungentle, adj. dur, rude, sévère

Ungentlemanly, adj. vulgaire, commun, peu distingué, peu comme il faut, malhonnête, de mauvais ton, déshonorable

Ungentleness, s. dureté, *f.*, rudesse, *f.*, brusquerie, *f.*

Ungently, adv. durement

Ungifted, adj. peu doué

Ungilded, adj. non doré

Ungird, va. (*horses*) dessangler, ôter la ceinture de

Unglazed, adj. sans vitres, sans vitrage, (*unvarnished*) non verni, non vernissé, non glacé

Unglue, va. décoller

Ungodliness, s. impiété, *f.*

Ungodly, adj. impie

Ungovernable, adj. indisciplinable, indomptable, effréné, (*extravagant*) désordonné, déréglé

Ungoverned, adj. sans lois, (*fig.*) désordonné, déréglé

Ungraceful, adj. sans grâce, disgracieux

Ungracefully, adv. sans grâce

Ungracefulness, s. mauvaise grâce, *f.*

Ungracious, adj. peu gracieux, dur, déplaisant, fâcheux, odieux

Ungraciously, adv. d'une manière peu gracieuse

Ungrammatical, adj. peu grammatical, incorrect

Ungrammatically, adv. incorrectement

Ungrateful, adj. ingrat, déplaisant, désagréable

Ungratefully, adv. avec ingratitude, d'une manière désagréable

Ungratefulness, s. ingratitude, *f.*, nature déplaisante, *f.*

Ungrounded, adj. *see* **Groundless**

Ungrudgingly, adv. de bon cœur, volontiers

Unguarded, adj. mal gardé, sans garde, sans défense, qui n'est pas sur ses gardes, imprudent, indiscret

Unguided, adj. sans guide

Unhallowed, adj. profane, impie

Unhand, va. lâcher, laisser aller

Unhandsome, adj. petit, mesquin, peu généreux, déloyal

Unhandsomely, adv. mesquinement, petitement, sans générosité

Unhandy, adj. gauche, maladroit, difficile à manier, incommode, gênant

Unhang, va. dépendre, descendre, démonter, détendre

Unhappily, adv. malheureusement, par malheur

Unhappiness, s. malheur, *m.*

Unhappy, adj. malheureux, infortuné, funeste

Unharboured, adj. sans port, sans asile

Unharmed, adj. sans blessure, sain et sauf

Unharmonious, adj. discordant

Unharness, va. déharnacher, dételer, désarmer

Unhatched, adj. pas encore éclos

Unhealthy, adj. malsain, insalubre, (*pers.*) maladif

Unhealthiness, s. insalubrité, *f.*, état maladif, *m.*

Unheard, adj. sans être entendu, (*doings*) inouï, (*pers. and th.*) dont on n'a pas entendu parler, inconnu, ignoré

Unheeded, adj. inaperçu, négligé, méprisé

Unheedful, adj. **Unheeding**, adj. etc. *See* **Heedless**, etc.

Unhelped, adj. sans aide, sans être aidé

Unhesitating, adj. qui n'hésite pas, prompt, ferme, résolu

Unhesitatingly, adv. sans hésiter

Unhewn, adj. non taillé, brut

Unhindered, adj. sans empêchement

Unhinge, va. ôter de ses gonds, décrocher, (*fig.*) bouleverser, troubler, déranger

Unholy, adj. profane, impie

Unhonoured, adj. sans honneurs, dédaigné, méprisé

Unhook, va. décrocher, dégrafer

Unhoped (for), adj. inespéré, inattendu

Unhorse, va. désarçonner, démonter

Unhurt, adj. intact, sans blessure, sain et sauf

Unicorn, s. licorne, *f.*

Uniform, adj. uniforme

Uniform, s. uniforme, *m.* *In full* —, en grand uniforme, en grande tenue

Uniformity, s. uniformité, *f.*

Uniformly, adv. uniformément, d'une manière uniforme

Unimaginable, adj. inimaginable

Unimpaired, adj. entier, intact

Unimpeachable, adj. irréprochable, irrécusable

Unimpeached, adj. non accusé, incontesté, sans reproche

Unimportant, adj. sans importance, insignifiant, sans prétention

Unimproved, adj. non amélioré, qui n'est pas devenu meilleur, qui n'a rien appris, ignorant, dont on ne profite pas, dont on ne se sert pas, inculte

Uninformed, adj. qui ne sait pas, ignorant

Uninhabitable, adj. inhabitable

Uninhabited, adj. inhabité

Uninitiated, adj. non initié

Uninjured, adj. *See* **Unharmed**

Uninscribed, adj. non inscrit, sans inscription

Uninspired, adj. qui n'est pas inspiré

Uninstructed, adj. sans instruction, ignorant

Uninstructive, adj. peu instructif

Uninsured, adj. peu assuré

Unintelligible, adj. inintelligible

Unintelligibly, adv. inintelligiblement

Unintended, **Unintentional**, adj. fait sans dessein, involontaire

Unintentionally, adv. sans le vouloir

Uninteresting, adj. peu intéressant

Uninterrupted, adj. sans interruption, continuel

Uninterruptedly, adv. sans interruption

Uninvited, adj. sans être invité, sans invitation

Uninviting, adj. peu attrayant

Union, s. union, *f.*, (*nav.*) pavillon, *m.* — *-jack*, s. — *-flag*, s. pavillon anglais, *m.*

Unionist, s. unioniste, *m.*

Unique, adj. unique

Unison, s. unisson, *m.* *In* —, à l'unisson

Unit, s. unité, *f.*

Unitarian, adj. s. unitaire, *m., f.*

Unite, va. unir, réunir, joindre; — vn. s'unir, se réunir, se joindre

United, adj. uni, réuni, joint

Unitedly, adv. ensemble, d'accord

Unity, s. unité, *f.*, union, *f.*, harmonie, *f.*

Universal, adj. universel

Universality, s. universalité, *f.*

Universally, adv. universellement

Universe, s. univers, *m.*

University, s. université, *f.* — *-man*, s. universitaire, *m.*

Unjust, adj. injuste

Unjustifiable, adj. injustifiable, inexcusable

Unjustifiably, adv. d'une manière injustifiable *or* inexcusable

Unjustified, adj. non justifié, sans excuse

Unjustly, adv. injustement

Unkennel, va. lancer, (*stag*) débucher

Unkept, adj. non gardé, non retenu, (*festival, etc.*) non célébré

Unkind, adj. peu bienveillant, peu aimable, désobligeant, (*hard*) dur, cruel

Unkindly, adj. malveillant, contraire (à)

Unkindly, adv. désobligeamment, d'une manière peu aimable, durement, cruellement

Unkindness, s. peu de bienveillance, *m.*, désobligeance, *f.*, dureté, *f.*, cruauté, *f.*

Unknit, va. dénouer, défaire, délier, (*the brow*) dérider

Unknowable, adj. qu'on ne peut connaître, impénétrable

Unknowingly, adv. sans le savoir

Unknown, adj. inconnu, ignoré, inappréciable, (*without the knowledge of*) à l'insu (de), sans qu'on le sache. *He did it — to me*, il le fit à mon insu

Unlace, va. délacer

Unlade, va. décharger

Unladylike, adj. peu distingué, peu digne d'une dame, peu comme il faut

Unlamented, adj. sans être pleuré, sans laisser de regrets

Unlatch, va. ouvrir, lever le loquet

Unlawful, adj. illégal, illicite, illégitime

Unlawfully, adv. illégalement, illégitimement, illicitement

Unlawfulness, s. illégalité, *f.*, (*of birth*) illégitimité, *f.*

Unlearn, va. désapprendre

Unlearned, adj. ignorant, illettré

Unleavened, adj. sans levain

Unless, conj. à moins que . . . ne, (*with subj.*), à moins de, à moins de, (*with infin.*) sans que, (*subj.*), si . . . ne . . . pas, (*indic.*), à moins d'être

Unlettered, adj. illettré, ignorant

Unlevelled, adj. non nivelé

Unlicensed, adj. illicite, non autorisé, sans autorisation, (*hunt.*) sans permis, (*com.*) non patenté, (*brokers*) non breveté, marron

Unlicked, adj. mal léché

Unlighted, adj. non allumé, non éclairé

Unlike, adj. qui ne ressemble pas (à), différent (de). *It is not — him*, cela lui ressemble assez

Unlikelihood, Unlikeliness, s. invraisemblance, *f.*, improbabilité, *f.*

Unlikely, adj. invraisemblable, improbable, qui a peu de chances de succès, peu profitable

Unlikely, adv. invraisemblablement

Unlikeness, s. dissemblance, *f.*, différence, *f.*

Unlimited, adj. illimité, sans bornes

Unlimitedly, adv. sans bornes

Unlink, va. détacher, défaire, dénouer

Unlively, adj. pesant, sans vivacité

Unload, va. décharger, (*thoughts, cares*) épancher, confier

Unloading, s. déchargement, *m.*

Unlock, va. ouvrir

Unlooked-for, adj. inattendu, imprévu

Unloose, va. délier, détacher, desserrer

Unluckily, adv. malheureusement

Unluckiness, s. malheur, *m.*, mauvais présage, *m.*

Unlucky, adj. malheureux, malencontreux, (*ill-omened*) sinistre

Unmake, va. défaire

Unman, dégrader, amollir, abattre, décourager, (*ship*) désarmer, (*deprive of men*) dégarnir d'hommes

Unmanageable, adj. intraitable, indocile, indomptable, ingouvernable, indisciplinable, (*unwieldy*) peu maniable. *To become —*, (*horse*) s'emporter

Unmanly, adj. indigne d'un homme, lâche, pusillanime, efféminé, mou

Unmanfully, adv. d'une manière indigne d'un homme

Unmanliness, s. manque de fermeté, *m.*, lâcheté, *f.*, indignité, *f.*

Unmannerliness, s. grossièreté, *f.*

Unmannerly, adj. (*pers.*) grossier, mal appris, mal élevé ; (*th.*) grossier, de mauvais ton

Unmannerly, adv. grossièrement

Unmanufactured, adj. non fabriqué

Unmarked, adj. non marqué, (*unobserved*) inaperçu

Unmarried, adj. non marié, célibataire. *An — man*, un célibataire. *An — woman*, une demoiselle

Unmask, va. démasquer, dévoiler; — vn. se démasquer

Unmasked, adj. sans masque, à découvert

Unmastered, adj. indompté, non maîtrisé

Unmeaning, adj. insignifiant, qui n'a pas de sens

Unmeaningness, s. insignifiance, *f.*, manque de signification, *m.*

Unmeant, adj. involontaire

Unmeasured, adj. sans mesure, immense, sans bornes

Unmeditated, adj. non médité

Unmeet, adj. peu convenable, inconvenant

Unmelted, adj. non fondu, (*fig.*) inflexible

Unmentioned, adj. dont on ne parle pas

Unmerciful, adj. impitoyable, sans miséricorde, inhumain

Unmercifully, adj. sans miséricorde

Unmercifulness, s. barbarie, *f.*, cruauté, *f.*

Unmerited, adj. non mérité, immérité

Unmilitary, adj. non militaire

Unmindful, adj. inattentif (à), oublieux, insouciant

Unmindfully, adj. négligemment

Unmingled, adj. sans mélange, pur

Unmistakeable, adj. clair, évident

Unmistakeably, adv. clairement, évidemment

Unmolested, adj. sans être molesté *or* inquiété *or* tourmenté; en paix

Unmoor, va. démarrer, lever l'ancre

Unmotherly, adj. peu digne d'une mère

Unmounted, adj. sans être monté, démonté, à pied

Unmoved, adj. immobile, fixe, sans être déplacé, inébranlable, ferme, inexorable, impassible, insensible

Unmuffle, va. découvrir

Unmusical, adj. qui n'est pas musical, peu harmonieux, discordant

Unmuzzle, va. démuseler

Unnamed, adj. non nommé. *Who shall go —*, que je ne nommerai pas

Unnail, va. déclouer

Unnatural, adj. contre nature, (*pers.*) dénaturé, (*lit.*) forcé

Unnaturally, adv. contre nature

Unnecessarily, adv. sans nécessité

Unnecessary, adj. inutile

Unneighbourly, adj. qui n'est pas d'un bon voisin. — adv. en mauvais voisin

Unnerve, va. énerver, affaiblir, décourager, ôter le courage

Unnoticed, adj. inaperçu, passé sous silence, négligé, traité sans égards

Unnumbered, adj. sans nombre, innombrable

Unobjectionable, adj. irrécusable, irréprochable, excellent

Unobserved, adj. *see* UNNOTICED

Unobstructed, adj. non obstrué

Unobtainable, adj. qu'on ne peut obtenir

Unobtruding, Unobtrusive, adj. pas importun, modeste, discret

Unobtrusively, adv. modestement, discrètement

Unoccupied, adj. (*idle*) inoccupé, sans occupation, de loisir, (*place*) disponible, non occupé, vacant

Unoffending, adj. inoffensif

Unofficial, adj. pas officiel

Unopened, adj. non ouvert, fermé

Unopposed, adj. sans opposition

Unornamented, adj. sans ornement

Unostentatious, adj. sans faste, sans ostentation, simple, modeste

Unostentatiously, adv. sans ostentation, sans faste, simplement

Unostentatiousness, s. simplicité, *f.*

Unpack, va. déballer, défaire, décharger

Unpacking, s. déballage, *m.*

Unpaid, adj. non payé, (*soldiers*) sans solde, (*letters*) non affranchi

Unpalatable, adj. désagréable au goût, désagréable

Unparalleled, adj. sans pareil, sans égal, incomparable

Unpardonable, adj. impardonnable

Unpardonably, adv. d'une manière impardonnable

Unpardoned, adj. non pardonné, sans pardon

Unpatriotic, adj. peu patriotique

Unpaved, adj. non pavé

Unpensioned, adj. sans pension

Unpeople, va. dépeupler

Unperceived, adj. inaperçu

Unperformed, adj. inexécuté

Unphilosophical, adj. peu philosophique

Unpin, va. défaire, détacher

Unpitied, adj. qu'on ne plaint pas

Unpitying, adj. sans pitié

Unplaced, adj. non placé, sans place

Unplausible, adj. peu plausible

Unpleasant, adj. désagréable, déplaisant

Unpleasantly, adv. désagréablement

Unpleasantness, s. désagrément, *m.*

Unpledged, adj. pas engagé

Unpliant, adj. inflexible

Unploughed, adj. non labouré, inculte

Unpoetic, Unpoetical, adj. peu poétique

Unpoetically, adv. d'une manière peu poétique

Unpolished, adj. non poli, mat, dépoli, (*rude*) peu civilisé, brut, grossier, (*boots*) non ciré

Unpolluted, adj. non souillé, pur

Unpopular, adj. impopulaire

Unpopularity, s. impopularité, *f.*

Unportioned, adj. sans dot

Unpractised, adj. peu exercé, inexpérimenté, novice

Unprecedented, adj. sans exemple, sans précédent

Unprejudiced, Unprepossessed, adj. sans préjugés, non prévenu, exempt de préjugés, impartial

Unpremeditated, adj. non prémédité, fait sans préméditation, improvisé

Unprepared, adj. non préparé, sans être préparé, qui n'est pas préparé

Unprepossessing, adj. peu engageant, peu prévenant, disgracieux, désagréable

Unpresuming, Unpresumptuous, Unpretending, adj. modeste, sans présomption

Unprincely, adj. indigne d'un prince

Unprincipled, adj. sans principes

Unproductive, adj. improductif, stérile

Unprofitable, adj. sans profit aucun, qui ne rapporte rien, inutile, vain

Unprofitableness, s. inutilité, *f.*, vanité, *f.*

Unprofitably, adv. sans profit, inutilement

Unpromising, adj. qui

promet peu, qui ne promet guère, qui s'annonce mal

Unpropitious, adj. peu propice, contraire, ennemi

Unproportioned, adj. disproportionné

Unprosperous, adj. malheureux

Unprosperously, adv. sans succès

Unprotected, adj. sans défense, sans abri, sans protection

Unprovided, adj. dépourvu, pris au dépourvu, qui n'est pas préparé

Unprovoked, adj. injuste, immérité

Unpublished, adj. (*book*) non publié, inédit, (*unknown*) inconnu, secret, non divulgué

Unpunctual, adj. inexact

Unpunctuality, s. inexactitude, *f.*

Unpunished, adj. impuni

Unpurified, adj. non purifié

Unqualified, adj. peu propre (à), incapable (de), qui n'a pas les qualités requises (pour), qui n'a pas qualité (pour), formel, entier, complet, sans restriction aucune

Unqualify, va. *see* To DISQUALIFY

Unquenchable, adj. inextinguible

Unquenched, adj. non éteint

Unquestionable, adj. incontestable

Unquestionably, adv. sans contredit

Unquestioned, adj. qu'on ne met pas en question, incontesté, incontestable

Unquiet, adj. inquiet, turbulent, agité

Unransomed, adj. qui n'a pas été racheté, sans rançon

Unravel, va. débrouiller, démêler, dénouer, (*fig.*) éclaircir

Unreached, adj. non atteint

Unread, adj. sans être lu, (*pers.*) ignorant, illettré

Unreadable, adj. illisible

Unready, adj. (*not ready*) qui n'est pas prêt, mal préparé, (*slow*) lent, irrésolu, indolent, (*awkward*) gauche, maladroit

Unreal, adj. sans réalité, feint, idéal, chimérique, vain, immatériel

Unreasonable, adj. déraisonnable, extravagant, absurde, immodéré

Unreasonableness, s. nature déraisonnable *or* extravagante, *f.*, extravagance, *f.*, absurdité, *f.*, déraison, *f.*

Unreasonably, adv. déraisonnablement, sans raison, avec extravagance, à l'excès

Unreasoning, adj. qui ne raisonne pas

Unreclaimed, adj. non corrigé, non réformé

Unrecompensed, adj. *see* UNREWARDED

Unreconciled, adj. irréconcilié

Unrecorded, adj. non enregistré

Unrecovered, adj. non recouvré, qui n'est pas rétabli

Unredeemed, non racheté

Unredressed, adj. non redressé

Unrefined, adj. non raffiné, non épuré, brut, (*not polished*) grossier, rude

Unreflecting, adj. irréfléchi

Unreformed, adj. non réformé

Unregarded, adj. dédaigné, négligé

Unregistered, adj. non registré, oublié, (*of letters*) non chargé

Unrelenting, adj. implacable, inflexible, inexorable, impitoyable, acharné

Unrelieved, adj. sans secours

Unremarked, adj. non remarqué, inaperçu

Unremedied, adj. auquel on n'a pas remédié, non guéri, irrémédiable

Unremitting, adj. incessant, sans relâche, soutenu, constant

Unremittingly, adv. sans relâche

Unremoved, adj. qu'on n'a pas changé de place, non éloigné, non écarté

Unrepealed, adj. non rapporté

Unrepentant, **Unrepenting**, adj. impénitent, sans se repentir

Unrepining, adj. **Unrepiningly**, adv. sans se plaindre, sans murmurer

Unrepressed, adj. non réprimé

Unreproached, adj. sans être réprimandé, sans reproches

Unrequited, adj. sans récompense

Unresented, adj. sans ressentiment, enduré, pardonné

Unreserved, adj. sans restriction, franc, ouvert, sans réserve

Unreservedly, adv. sans réserve

Unreservedness, s. franchise, *f.*, abandon, *m.*

Unresisting, adj. qui ne résiste pas

Unresolved, adj. irrésolu, indécis

Unrestored, adj. non rendu, (*fig.*) non rétabli, non remis

Unrestrained, adj. (*licentious*) sans frein, désordonné, déréglé, (*free*) sans gêne, sans contrainte, sans limites

Unrestricted, adj. sans restriction

Unrevealed, adj. non révélé

Unrevenged, adj. sans être vengé

Unrevised, adj. non revu, non revisé

Unrevoked, adj. non révoqué

Unrewarded, adj. sans récompense, méconnu

Unriddle, va. expliquer, résoudre

Unrifled, adj. (*gun*) non rayé, lisse

Unrig, va. dégréer

Unrighteous, adj. injuste, inique, méchant, impie

Unrighteously, adv. injustement

Unrighteousness, s. iniquité, *f.*, injustice, *f.*

Unripe, adj. pas mûr, vert, précoce, prématuré

Unripened, adj. imparfait

Unripeness, s. défaut de maturité, *m.*, verdeur, *f.*

Unrivalled, adj. sans rival, sans égal, incomparable

Unroll, va. dérouler

Unroof, va. enlever la toiture de, découvrir

Unroot, va. déraciner

Unruffle, va. se calmer

Unruffled, adj. calme, tranquille

Unruliness, s. turbulence, *f.*

Unruly, adj. turbulent, ingouvernable, désordonné, (*horse*) fougueux

Unrumple, va. défroisser, défriper

Unsaddle, va. desseller, désarçonner

Unsafe, adj. peu sûr, dangereux

Unsafely, adj. peu sûrement

Unsaleable, adj. invendable

Unsalted, adj. non salé

Unsanctified, adj. impie, profane

Unsanctioned, adj. non sanctionné

Unsatisfactorily, adv. d'une manière peu satisfaisante

Unsatisfactory, adj. peu satisfaisant, insuffisant

Unsatisfied, adj. non satisfait, mécontent

Unsatisfying, adj. insuffisant

Unsavouriness, s. fadeur, *f.*, mauvaise odeur, *f.*

Unsavoury, adj. fade, insipide, désagréable

Unsay, va. rétracter, se dédire de

Unschooled, adj. illettré, ignorant

Unscientific, adj. peu scientifique

Unscrew, va. dévisser

Unscriptural, adj. antibiblique

Unscrupulous, adj. peu scrupuleux

Unscrupulously, adv. sans scrupule

Unscrupulousness, s. indélicatesse, *f.*, caractère peu scrupuleux, *m.*

Unseal, va. desceller, décacheter

Unsealed, adj. qui ne porte pas ouvert

Unsearchable scrutable, impéné

Unseasonable portun, peu conv mal à propos, déplacé, hors de sa avancé, indu, tar

Unseasonably à propos

Unseasoned, assaisonné

Unseat, va. ren arçonner, faire siége à, *or* annule d'un membre de p

Unseconded, condé

Unsecured, a suré, sans garanti

Unseemliness venance, *f.*

Unseemly, ad inconvenant

Unseen, adj. in n'est pas vu, sans visible

Unselfish, adj. désintéressé

Unsent, adj. sans être envoy qu'on n'a pas env

Unserviceabl USELESS

Unsettle, va. d traquer, agiter, bouleverser

Unsettled, ad peu ferme, mal assis, ébranlé, ag irrésolu, incerta irrégulier, varia geant, trouble

Unsettlednes bilité, *f.*, agitatio *m.*, hésitation, *f.*, *f.*, incertitude, ment, *m.*, irrégul constance, *f.*, ét *m.*

Unsew, va. déc

Unshackle, v affranchir

Unshaded, ad brage, sans ombr

Unshaken, ad pas ébranlé, inébr muable

Unshaven, ad rasé

Unsheath, v fourreau, dégaine

Unsheltered, abri

Unship, va. (*un* quer, (*oars*) déma

Unshod, adj. sure, nu, (*horses*) déferré

Unshrinking reculer, intrépide

Unsightlines *f.*

Unsightly, ad plaisant, vilain

Unsisterly, ad d'une sœur

Unsized, adj. n

Unskid, va. dé

Unskilful, U adj. inhabile (à), (à), inexpériment

Unskilfully, adv. maladroitement, sans adresse, sans art

Unskilfulness, s. inhabileté, *f.*, maladresse, *f.*

Unslaked, adj. non éteint, — *lime*, s. chaux vive, *f.*

Unsmoked, adj. pas fumé

Unsociable, Unsocial, adj. insociable, réservé, sauvage

Unsoiled, adj. sans souillure, sans tache

Unsold, adj. non vendu

Unsoldierlike, Unsoldierly, adj. indigne d'un soldat, peu martial

Unsolved, adj. non résolu, insoluble

Unsophisticated, adj. see UNADULTERATED

Unsought, adj. qu'on n'a pas cherché, inexploré

Unsound, adj. malsain, gâté, corrompu, pourri, peu solide, (*sickly*) infirme, maladif, mauvais, (*doctrines*) hétérodoxe, vicieux, faux, erroné, (*deceitful*) malhonnête, sans probité, (*sleep*) troublé, agité, (*mind*) dérangé, (*glass*) fêlé

Unsoundness, s. état malsain, *m.*, mauvais état, *m.*, peu de solidité, *m.*, faiblesse, *f.*, erreur, *f.*, fausseté, *f.*, hétérodoxie, *f.*, défaut, *m.*, vice, *m.*

Unsown, adj. non ensemencé

Unsparing, adj. libéral, prodigue, impitoyable, cruel

Unsparingly, adv. avec profusion, sans pitié

Unspeakable, adj. indicible, (*rapturous*) ineffable, inexprimable

Unspeakably, adv. d'une manière indicible

Unspecified, adj. non spécifié

Unspent, adj. non épuisé, non dépensé

Unspotted, adj. etc. see SPOTLESS etc.

Unstable, adj. peu stable, chancelant, inconstant, changeant

Unstained, adj. qui n'est pas taché, sans tache, blanc, (*not dyed*) non teint

Unstamped, adj. non marqué, (*letters*) non timbré, (*law*) non sujet au timbre

Unsteadfast, adj. see UNSTABLE

Unsteadily, adv. sans fixité, d'une manière mal assurée, inconsidérément, avec légèreté

Unsteadiness, s. manque de fixité, *m.*, instabilité, *f.*, mobilité, *f.*, inconstance, *f.*, irrégularité, *f.*

Unsteady, adj. peu stable, non fixe, mobile, vacillant, toujours en mouvement, mal assuré, tremblant, chancelant, inconstant, changeant, variable, irrégulier

Unstirred, adj. non remué, non agité

Unstitch, va. découdre

Unstop, va. déboucher, ouvrir

Unstrained, adj. aisé, naturel, non filtré

Unstrengthened, adj. non renforcé

Unstrewed, adj. non jonché

Unstring, va. détendre, relâcher, (*untie*) défaire, (*pearls*) désenfiler

Unstudied, adj. sans apprêt, naturel

Unstuffed, adj. non rembourré, vide

Unsubdued, adj. non subjugué, non soumis, indomptable

Unsubmissive, adj. insoumis, indocile

Unsubstantial, adj. immatériel, sans corps, imaginaire, chimérique, idéal, (*food*) peu substantiel

Unsuccessful, adj. malheureux, infructueux, sans succès

Unsuccessfully, adv. sans succès

Unsuccessfulness, s. insuccès, *m.*

Unsuccoured, adj. sans aide

Unsuitable, adj. peu convenable, qui ne convient pas, mal approprié, mal adapté, déplacé

Unsuitableness, s. peu de convenance, *m.*, inaptitude, *f.*, incapacité, *f.*

Unsuitably, adv. peu convenablement

Unsuited, adj. peu adapté, peu approprié, peu fait (pour)

Unsullied, adj. sans tache, pur

Unsupplied, adj. non pourvu, dépourvu, non approvisionné

Unsupported, adj. sans appui, sans soutien

Unsurpassed, adj. non surpassé

Unsuspected, adj. non soupçonné, non suspect

Unsuspecting, Unsuspicious, adj. confiant, franc, ouvert

Unsuspectingly, Unsuspiciously, adv. sans méfiance, sans soupçons

Unsustained, adj. etc. see UNSUPPORTED, etc.

Unswathe, va. démailloter

Unswept, adj. non balayé, (*chimney*) non ramonée

Unsymmetrical, adj. sans symétrie

Untack, va. détacher, défaire

Untainted, adj. frais, non corrompu, non vicié, non taché, non souillé

Untameable, adj indomptable, inapprivoisable

Untamed, adj. non apprivoisé, indompté

Untarnished, adj. non terni, sans tache

Untasted, adj. non goûté, à quoi on ne touche pas

Untaught, adj. ignorant, illettré, (*things*) naturel

Unteachable, adj. incapable, indocile, peu doué

Untenable, adj. qui n'est pas tenable, insoutenable

Untenantable, adj. pas habitable

Untenanted, adj. inhabité, sans habitants

Untested, adj. pas mis à l'épreuve, non éprouvé

Unthanked, adj. sans remerciments, méconnu

Unthankful, adj. ingrat

Unthankfully, adv. sans reconnaissance

Unthankfulness, s. ingratitude, *f.*

Unthawed, adj. non dégelé, encore gelé

Unthinking, adj. irréfléchi, inconsidéré

Unthought, adj. — *of*, à qui l'on ne pense pas, oublié, inattendu, imprévu

Unthread, va. désenfiler, détacher

Unthrifty, adj. prodigue, dépensier, qui ne réussit pas

Untidiness, s. manque d'ordre *or* de soin, *m.*, désordre, *m.*, malpropreté, *f.*

Untidy, adj. malpropre, mal tenu, en désordre, peu soigneux

Untie, va. détacher, délier, dénouer, défaire

Until, conj. jusqu'à ce que, que, avant que

Until, prep. jusqu'à, jusques à, avant

Untilled, adj. inculte, en friche

Untimely, adj. inopportun, prématuré, hâtif, précoce

Untimely, adv. prématurément, de bonne heure, mal à propos

Untiring, adj. infatigable

Untitled, adj. sans titre

Untold, adj. qu'on ne dit pas, tenu secret, non compté

Untouched, adj. non touché, intact, non atteint

Untoward, adj. difficile, mutin, indocile, pervers, revêche, (*inconvenient*) fâcheux, malencontreux, incommode, peu maniable

Untowardly, adv. avec indocilité, malencontreusement, disgracieusement

Untowardness, s. perversité, *f.*, maladresse, *f.*

Untraced, adj. non tracé, (*of roads*) non frayé

Untracked, adj. non suivi, non frayé

Untrained, adj. pas dressé, peu exercé, inhabile, indiscipliné

Untrammelled, adj. sans entraves, sans être entravé

Untransferable, adj. non transférable, (*law*) inaliénable

Untranslatable, adj. intraduisible

Untranslated, adj. non traduit

Untravelled, adj. inexploré, (*pers.*) qui n'a pas voyagé

Untried, adj. non essayé, non éprouvé, non mis à l'épreuve

Untrimmed, adj. sans garniture, non garni, sans parure, non ajusté, non arrangé, en désordre

Untrod, Untrodden, adj. non foulé aux pieds, non frayé

Untroubled, adj. calme, paisible, tranquille

Untrue, adj. pas vrai, faux, controuvé, inexact, infidèle

Untruly, adv. faussement, inexactement

Untrustiness, s. perfidie, *f.*

Untrustworthy, adj. indigne de confiance

Untrusty, adj. peu fidèle, déloyal

Untruth, s. fausseté, *f.*, mensonge, *m.*, contre-vérité, *f.*

Untruthful, adj. faux, mensonger, qui ne dit pas la vérité, peu loyal

Untune, va. mettre la discorde dans, désaccorder

Untuned, adj. discordant, peu harmonieux

Untutored, adj. ignorant, sans instruction

Untwine, Untwist, va. détordre

Unurged, adj. sans être excité, spontanément

Unused, adj. non employé, peu habitué, inaccoutumé, étranger

Unusual, adj. rare, extraordinaire, insolite

Unusually, adv. rarement, peu souvent, extraordinairement

Unutterable, adj. indicible, ineffable, inexprimable

Unvalued, adj. dédaigné, inestimable, sans prix

Unvaried, adj. invariable, uniforme

Unvarnished, adj. non verni, non vernissé, simple, sans ornement

Unvarying, invariable, constant

Unveil, va. ôter *or* lever le voile de, dévoiler

Unventilated, adj. non ventilé, mal aéré

Unversed, adj. peu versé

Unviolated, adj. non violé, non enfreint, intact, sans atteinte, pur

Unwaked, Unwakened, adj. non réveillé, endormi

Unwalled, adj. non clos de murs, ouvert

Unwarily, adv. étourdiment, imprudemment, sans précaution

Unwariness, s. imprudence, *f.*, étourderie, *f.*, imprévoyance, *f.*

Unwarlike, adj. peu belliqueux, efféminé

Unwarned, adj. non averti

Unwarrantable, adj. injustifiable, inexcusable

Unwarranted, adj. non garanti, incertain, non autorisé, sans motifs, injustifiable

Unwary, adj. imprévoyant, imprudent, étourdi, naïf, simple

Unwashed, adj. non lavé

Unwasting, adj. inépuisable

Unwatered, adj. non arrosé, (*stuffs*) non moiré

Unweaned, adj. qui n'est pas sevré

Unwearable, adj. qu'on ne peut plus porter

Unwearied, adj. non fatigué, non lassé, infatigable

Unweariedly, adv. sans se lasser

Unwearying, adj. qui jamais ne se lasse, infatigable

Unweave, va. défaire, détisser, (*linen*) effiler, érailler, (*tresses*) détresser

Unwedded, adj. non marié

Unweighed, adj. non pesé, (*fig.*) inconsidérée

Unwelcome, adj. mal venu, fâcheux, désagréable

Unwell, adj. indisposé, mal portant, souffrant

Unwholesome, adj. malsain, insalubre, nuisible

Unwholesomeness, s. insalubrité, *f.*

Unwieldily, adv. pesamment

Unwieldiness, s. lourdeur, *f.*, pesanteur, *f.*

Unwieldy, adj. difficile à manier, lourd, pesant, énorme, corpulent

Unwilling, adj. ne voulant pas, peu disposé, de mauvaise volonté

Unwillingly, adv. à contre-cœur, à regret, malgré soi, avec répugnance

Unwillingness, s. répugnance, *f.*, mauvaise volonté, *f.*, mauvais vouloir, *m.*

Unwind, va. dévider, dérouler, démêler, débrouiller; — vn. se dérouler

Unwise, adj. pas sage, peu sage, imprudent, insensé, mal avisé

Unwisely, adv. peu sagement

Unwished (for), adj. qu'on n'a pas désiré, peu désiré

Unwithered, adj. non flétri, non fané, encore dans sa fraîcheur

Unwitnessed, adj. sans témoin, qui n'a pas été vu

Unwittily, adv. sans esprit

Unwittingly, adj. à son insu

Unwonted, adj. inaccoutumé, rare, peu commun, peu habituel, insolite, étrange

Unworn, adj. non usé

Unworthily, adv. indignement

Unworthiness, s. indignité, *f.*, peu de mérite, *m.*

Unworthy, adj. indigne, peu digne, sans mérite

Unwrap, va. ôter l'enveloppe de, défaire, ôter, se débarrasser de

Unwrinkled, adj. sans rides

Unwritten, adj. non écrit, blanc, en blanc

Unwrought, adj. non travaillé

Unyielding, adj. qui ne cède pas, inflexible

Unyoke, va. ôter le joug à, dételer

Unyoked, adj. non mis sous le joug, non attelé, dételé

Up, adv. en haut, vers le haut, haut, qui monte, (*standing*) debout, levé, sur pied, (*excited*) excité, animé, emporté, (*ended*) fini, terminé, expiré, (*fig.*) coulé, fini, c'en est fait de, (*knowing*) au fait de, qui sait. — *there*, là haut. — *and down*, en haut et en bas, de haut en bas, de long en large, en tous sens, va-et-vient, en avant et en arrière; — prep. partout, çà et là; — *to*, prep. jusqu'à, qui remonte à, conformément à, selon. *To be — to*, être capable de, être de force à, être au courant *or* au fait de, voir où l'on veut en venir, deviner. — *with*, avec, sur un pied d'égalité avec, auprès de. *To be — with, to come — with*, atteindre. *Time is —*, c'est l'heure. *It is all — with him*, c'est un homme coulé, c'en est fait de lui; — interj. debout! — *with . . . !* debout! levez! haut! montez! (*nav.*) hisse! — *with the helm!* la barre au vent! — prep. vers le haut de, en montant, au haut de, sur. — *the river*, en remontant la rivière, en amont

Upas, s. (*bot.*) upas, *m.*

Upbear, va. soutenir, supporter, porter, élever

Upbraid, va. *see* Reproach

Upbraidingly, adv. avec reproche, d'un ton de reproche

Upheave, va. soulever

Uphill, adj. en montant, (*fig.*) ardu, difficile, pénible, rude, fatigant

Uphold, va. lever, élever, (en l'air) soutenir, maintenir, pourvoir à l'entretien de, entretenir

Upholder, s. soutien, *m.*, appui, *m.*

Upholsterer, s. tapissier, *m.*, marchand de meubles, *m.*

Upholstery, s. meubles, *m.pl.* articles d'ameublement, *m.pl.*

Upland, s. montagne, *f.*

Upland, adj. montagneux, élevé, escarpé

Uplift, va. élever, lever, soulever

Upon, prep. sur

Upper, adj. supérieur, de dessus, au-dessus, haut, (*géogr.*) haut. *The —-hand*, le dessus, la supériorité, l'avantage. *The — end*, le haut bout. — *-crust*, croûte de dessus, *f.*, (*pop.*) les richards, *m.pl.* *The — ten, the — ten-thousand*, l'aristocratie, *f.*, les riches, *m. pl.*

Uppermost, adj. (le), plus haut, le plus élevé, en dessus, au-dessus

Uppish, adj. fier

Upraise, va. *see* Uplift

Uprear, va. élever, soulever, dresser

Upright, adj. debout, droit, vertical, d'aplomb, (*fig.*) juste, droit. *To stand —*, se tenir droit *or* debout. *To sit —*, se mettre sur son séant

Upright, s. ligne perpendiculaire, *f.*, (*constr.*) montant, *m.*

Uprightly, adv. droit, debout, avec droiture, droitement, honnêtement

Uprightness, s. perpendicularité, *f.*, (*fig.*) droiture, *f.*, intégrité, *f.*, justice, *f.*

Uproar, s. tumulte, *m.*, vacarme, *m.*, brouhaha, *m.*, tapage, *m.*, désordre, *m.*

Uproarious, adj. bruyant

Uproariously, adv. bruyamment

Uproot, va. déraciner

Ups, s.pl. hauts, *m.pl.* *The — and downs of life*, les hauts et les bas de la vie, les vicissitudes de la vie

Upset, va. renverser, mettre sens dessus dessous, bouleverser, (*carriage*) verser, faire verser, (*boat*) faire chavirer; — vn. se renverser, (*carriage*) verser, (*boat*) chavirer

Upshot, s. conclusion, *f.*, fin, *f.*, résumé, *m.*, fin mot, *m.*

Upside, s. dessus, *m.* *To turn — down*, mettre sens dessus dessous

Upstart, s. parvenu, *m.*, -e, *f.*

Upward, adj. vers le haut, qui s'élève, (*eyes*) levé

Upward, Upwards, adv. vers le haut, en haut, vers le ciel, par le haut, dans la partie supérieure, (*time*) en remontant vers la source, (*more*) plus

Urbanity, s. urbanité, *f.*

Urchin, s. bambin, *m.*, marmot, *m.*, (*pop.*) gamin, *m.*, mômе, *m.*

Urethra, s. urètre, *m.*

Urge, va. porter, exciter, engager, pousser, hâter, presser, mettre en mouvement, (*follow close*) suivre de près, succéder rapidement à, (*solicit*) presser, solliciter, importuner, prier fortement, conseiller fortement (de), (*petition*) présenter, faire avec instance, (*argument*) insister sur, alléguer, avancer, mettre en avant

Urgency, s. nécessité urgente, *f.*, besoin pressant, *m.*, urgence, *f.*, instances, *f.pl.*, importunité, *f.*, sollicitations pressantes, *f.pl.*

Urgent, adj. urgent, pressant, qui insiste

Urgently, adv. d'une manière pressante, avec instance, instamment, avec urgence

Urinal, s. urinal, *m.*, vase de nuit, *m.*

Urinary, adj. urinaire

Urine, s. urine, *f.*

Urn, s. urne, *f.*

Ursine, adj. d'ours

Us, pron. plur. nous

Usage, s. traitement, *m.*, usage, *m.*, coutume, *f.*, habitude, *f.*

Usance, s. usance, *f.*

Use, s. emploi, *m.*, usage, *m.*, utilité, *f.*, profit, *m.*, avantage, *m.*, (*need*) besoin, *m.*, occasion, *f.*, habitude, *f.*, coutume, *f.* —*s*, pl. us, *m.pl.*, (*of money*) intérêt, *m.*, (*law*) jouissance, *f.*, usufruit, *m.* *To be in —, in —*, être en usage. *To bring again into —*, remettre en usage. *To be out of —*, ne plus servir, être hors d'usage, être vieilli. *To make — of*, se servir de, employer, user de. *For the — of*, à l'usage de. *To be of — to*, servir à, profiter à, être utile à. *Of what use is it?* à quoi sert-il? *To be of no — whatever*, ne servir à rien *or* de rien, n'être d'aucune utilité. *To turn to some — or other*, faire servir à quelque chose. *To turn to good —*, utiliser. *To make a good — of*, mettre à profit. *I have no further — for it*, je n'en ai plus besoin

Use, va. employer, se servir de, faire usage de, (*accustom*) habituer, accoutumer, (*to behave*) en user à l'égard de, traiter, en agir avec, exercer, se comporter. *To — up*, employer tout, consommer, épuiser, excéder, fatiguer; — vn. avoir l'habitude, avoir coutume, être dans l'usage, être d'usage

Useful, adj. utile, avantageux

Usefully, adv. utilement

Usefulness, s. utilité, *f.*

Useless, adj. inutile

Uselessly, adv. inutilement

Uselessness, s. inutilité, *f.*

Usher, s. huissier, *m.*, (*in school*) sous-maître, *m.*, maître répétiteur, *m.*

Usher, va. (— *in*) faire entrer, introduire, précéder, être l'avant-courrier de. *To — out*, faire sortir, reconduire

Usual, adj. ordinaire, usuel, habituel, d'usage, fréquent, usité. *As —*, à l'ordinaire, comme à l'ordinaire

Usually, adv. ordinairement, habituellement, d'ordinaire

Usurer, s. usurier, *m.*

Usurious, adj. qui fait l'usure, usuraire, d'usure

Usurp, va. usurper, s'emparer de, envahir

Usurpation, s. usurpation, *f.*

Usurper, s. usurpateur, *m.*, -trice, *f.*

Usurpingly, adv. par usurpation

Usury, s. usure, *f.*

Utensil, s. ustensile, *m.*, instrument, *m.*, vase, *m.*

Kitchen —s, s. batterie de cuisine, *f.*
Uterine, adj. utérin
Utility, s. utilité, *f.*
Utilize, va. utiliser
Utmost, adj. extrême, plus grand, dernier, plus éloigné
Utmost, s. ce qu'il y a de plus, tout ce qui est possible. *To do one's —*, faire de son mieux, faire tout son possible. *To the — of my power*, de tout mon pouvoir, autant qu'il m'est possible. *At the —*, au plus
Utopia, s. utopie, *f.*
Utopian, adj. chimérique
Utopist, s. utopiste, *m.*
Utter, adj. extrême, dernier, entier, complet, absolu, formel
Utter, va. prononcer, proférer, articuler, dire, débiter, (*cries*) pousser, faire entendre, (*divulge*) révéler, divulguer, débiter, (*coin*) émettre, mettre en circulation
Utterable, adj. qu'on peut prononcer or dire
Utterance, s. prononciation, *f.*, articulation, *f.*, émission, *f.*, parole, *f.*, débit, *m.*, expression, *f.*, élocution, *f.*, éloquence, *f.*
Utterer, s. celui, celle qui prononce, (*of bad money*) émissionnaire, *m.*
Utterly, adv. complètement, entièrement, tout à fait
Uttermost, adj. extrême, (le) plus grand, (le) plus éloigné, (le) plus reculé
Uvula, s. luette, *f.*

V

Vacancy, s. vide, *m.*, lacune, *f.*, (*of office*) vacance, *f.*, (*leisure*) loisir, *m.*, repos, *m.*, cessation, *f.*, interruption, *f.*, (*of thought*) vide de la pensée, *m.*
Vacant, adj. vide, vacant, (*office*) vacant, (*time*) libre, déchargé, (*pers.*) qui a du loisir, inoccupé, libre, (*look etc.*) indifférent, insouciant, inoccupé, (*thoughtless*) distrait
Vacate, va. vider, laisser vacant, annuler, invalider
Vacation, s. (*courts*) vacation, *f.*, (*schools*) vacances, *f. pl.*
Vaccinate, va. vacciner
Vaccination, s. vaccination, *f.*
Vaccinator, s. vaccinateur, *m.*
Vaccine, adj. de vache. *— matter*, s. vaccin, *m.*
Vacillation, s. vacillation, *f.*, chancellement, *m.*
Vacillate, vn. vaciller, chanceler, flotter
Vacillation, s. vacillation, *f.*
Vacuity, s. vide, *m.*, vacuité, *f.*, néant, *m.*
Vacuum, s. vide, *m.*
Vagabond, s. vagabond, *m.* *To be a —*, être vagabond, vagabonder
Vagary, s. fantaisie, *f.*, quinte, *f.*, bizarrerie, *f.*, caprice, *m.*
Vagrancy, s. vagabondage, *m.*
Vagrant, adj. see Vagabond
Vague, adj. vague
Vaguely, adv. vaguement
Vails, s. profits, *m. pl.*, gratification, *f.*, pourboire, *m.*
Vain, adj. vain, inutile, infructueux, vaniteux, orgueilleux. *In —*, vainement, en vain. *—-glory*, s. la vaine gloire, *f.*, gloriole, *f.*
Vainly, adv. vainement, en vain, avec vanité
Valance, s. draperie, *f.*
Vale, s. val, *m.*, vallon, *m.*, vallée, *f.*
Valerian, s. valériane, *f.*
Valet, valet, *m.*
Valetudinarian, adj. s. valétudinaire, *m.*, *f.*
Valiant, adj. vaillant, brave
Valiantly, adv. vaillamment
Valid, adj. valide, valable
Validity, s. validité, *f.*
Validly, adv. validement, valablement
Valley, s. vallée, *f.*, val, *m.*
Valorous, adj. valeureux, brave, vaillant, intrépide
Valorously, adv. vaillamment
Valour, s. valeur, *f.*, vaillance, *f.*, bravoure, *f.*, intrépidité, *f.*
Valuable, adj. de grande valeur, précieux, de prix. *—s*, s. pl. objets de prix, *m. pl.*
Valuation, s. évaluation, *f.*, estimation, *f.*
Valuator, s. estimateur, *m.*
Value, s. valeur, *f.*, prix, *m.*, cours, *m.* *To set great — on*, faire grand cas de, attacher de la valeur à
Value, va. estimer, apprécier, évaluer, fixer le prix, considérer, respecter
Valueless, adj. sans valeur
Valuer, s. estimateur, *m.*, appréciateur, *m.*, priseur, *m.*
Valve, s. soupape, *f.*
Valved, adj. à valves
Vamp, s. empeigne, *f.* *The outer —*, l'avant-pied, *m.*
Vamp, va. mettre une empeigne à, remonter, rapiécer, réparer
Vampire, s. vampire, *m.*
Van, s. (*mil. nav.*) front, *m.*, première ligne, *f.*, avant-garde, *f.*, (*mines*) nettoyage du minerai, *m.* (*for goods*) fourgon, *m.*, tapissière, *f.*, voiture de déménagements, *f.*, *—-guard*, s. avant-garde, *f.*
Vandal, s. vandale, *m.*
Vandalism, s. vandalisme, *m.*
Vane, s. girouette, *f.*, (*of quills*) barbes, *f. pl.*
Vanilla, s. vanille, *f.* *—-tree*, s. vanillier, *m.*
Vanish, vn. disparaître, s'évanouir, passer, se perdre
Vanity, s. vanité, *f.*, inutilité, *f.*, inanité, *f.*
Vanquish, va. vaincre, surmonter, dompter
Vanquisher, s. vainqueur, *m.*
Vantage, s. supériorité, *f.*, avantage, *m.* *—-ground*, s. haute position, *f.*, avantage, *m.*
Vapid, adj. insipide, fade, plat, (*vin*) éventé, plat
Vapidness, **Vapidity**, s. insipidité, *f.*, fadeur, *f.*, (*of wine*) évent, *m.*
Vaporous, adj. rempli de vapeurs, vain, chimérique, venteux, flatueux
Vapour, s. vapeur, *f.*, humidité, *f.*
Variable, adj. variable, changeant, inconstant
Variableness, **Variability**, s. variabilité, *f.*, inconstance, *f.*
Variably, adv. d'une manière changeante
Variance, s. différend, *m.*, désaccord, *m.*, désunion, *f.*, (*law*) brouillerie, *f.*, contestation, *f.*, variation, *f.* *To be at —*, être en désaccord, en contestation, avoir un différend. *To set at —*, mettre en désaccord, amener le désaccord entre
Variation, s. variation, *f.*, changement, *m.*, différence, *f.*, déviation, *f.*
Varicose Vein, s. varice, *f.*
Variegate, va. varier, diaprer, nuancer, émailler
Variegation, s. diversité, *f.*, bigarrure, *f.*
Variety, s. variété, *f.*
Various, adj. divers, différent, varié, changeant, inconstant, incertain
Variously, adv. diversement
Varnish, vernis, *m.*
Varnish, va. vernir, polir, vernisser
Varnisher, s. vernisseur, *m.*
Varnishing, s. vernissure, *f.*
Vary, va. varier, faire des changements à, changer, diversifier, bigarrer, nuancer; — vn. varier, changer, être inconstant, ne pas se ressembler, être changeant, se succéder, se suivre, être en dissentiment, n'être pas d'accord, dévier, s'écarter
Varying, adj. changeant, qui change, qui varie, divers
Vase, s. vase, *m.*, (*hort.*) calice, *m.*
Vassal, s. vassal, *m.*, vassale, *f.*
Vassalage, s. vasselage, *m.*, dépendance, *f.*, sujétion, *f.*
Vast, adj. vaste, immense, puissant
Vastly, adv. immensément, extrêmement, énormément, puissamment
Vastness, s. immensité, *f.*, étendue, *f.*, grandeur, *f.*, puissance, *f.*
Vat, s. cuve, *f.*, cuvier, *m.*
Vault, s. voûte, *f.*, cellier, *m.*, cave, *f.*, caveau, *m.*, (*leap*) voltige, *f.*
Vault, va. voûter; — vn. sauter, s'élancer, voltiger
Vaulter, s. voltigeur, *m.*, acrobate, *m.*
Vaunt, vn. see Boast
Veal, s. veau, *m.* *—-cutlet*, côtelette de veau, *f.*
Veer, vn. (*nav.*) virer, tourner, changer
Vegetable, s. végétal, *m.*, plante, *f.*, légume, *m.* *—-garden*, s. jardin potager, *m.*
Vegetable, adj. végétal, végétable. *—-marrow*, s. courge à la moelle, *f.* *To live on — diet*, vivre de légumes
Vegetarian, s. légumiste, *m.*
Vegetate, vn. végéter
Vegetation, s. végétation, *f.*
Vegetative, adj. végétatif, végétant
Vehemence, **Vehe-**

mency, s. véhémence, *f.*, impétuosité, *f.*
Vehement, adj. véhément, violent
Vehemently, adv. avec véhémence
Vehicle, s. voiture, *f.* (*fig.*) véhicule, *m.*
Vehicled, adj. voituré
Veil, s. voile, *m.*, rideau, *m.* (*fig.*) déguisement, *m.*, apparence, *f.* *Small* —, s. voilette, *f.*
Veil, va. voiler, couvrir d'un voile, (*fig.*) voiler, dissimuler, masquer
Vein, s. veine, *f.*
Veined, **Veiny**, adj. veiné, veineux, vasculeux
Vellum, vélin, *m.*
Velocipede, s. vélocipède, *m.*
Velocity, s. vélocité, *f.*, rapidité, *f.*, vitesse, *f.*
Velvet, s. velours, *m.*, *Terry* —, velours épinglé, — *down*, — *lace*, velouté, *m.*, — *-flower*, amarante, *f.*
Velvet, **Velvety**, adj. de velours, velouté, (*fig.*) doux uni, délicat
Velveteen, s. velours de coton, *m.*
Venal, adj. vénal, mercenaire
Venality, s. vénalité, *f.*
Vend, va. vendre
Vender, **Vendor**, s. vendeur, *m.*, marchand, *m.*, marchande, *f.*
Veneer, va. plaquer
Veneer, s. feuille pour placage, *f.*
Veneering, s. placage, *m.*
Venerable, adj. vénérable
Venerably, adv. vénérablement
Venerate, va. vénérer, révérer, avoir en vénération
Veneration, s. vénération, *f.*
Venereal, adj. vénérien, aphrodisiaque
Vengeance, s. vengeance, *f.*, vindicte, *f.*, emportement, *m.* *To do with a* —, s'emporter. *With a* —, (*pop.*) en diable, furieusement, à l'excès
Venial, adj. pardonnable, excusable, véniel
Venially, adv. véniellement
Venison, s. venaison, *f.*
Venom, s. venin, *m.*, poison, *m.*
Venomous, adj. venimeux, (*plants*) vénéneux
Venomousness, s. nature venimeuse, *f.*, venin, *m.*
Venous, adj. veineux
Vent, s. air, *m.*, vent, *m.*, (*issue*) ouverture, *f.*, (*casks*) trou, *m.*, fausset, *m.*, (*feelings*) cours, *m.*, carrière, *f.*, liberté, *f.* — *-hole*, s. ouverture, *f.* — *-peg*, s. fausset, *m.* *To give* — *to*, donner de l'air à, percer, laisser échapper, donner issue, *or* cours à
Vent, va. donner issue, laisser partir, laisser échapper, donner cours à, divulguer, rendre public
Ventilate, va. éventer, aérer, donner de l'air à, ventiler, (*winnow*) vanner, (*discuss*) élucider, discuter, examiner
Ventilation, s. ventilation, *f.*, aération, *f.* (*com.*) ventage, *m.*, (*winnowing*) vannage, *m.*, (*fig.*) examen, *m.*, élucidation, *f.*
Ventilator, s. ventilateur, *m.*
Ventricle, s. ventricule, *m.*
Ventriloquism, **Ventriloquy**, s. ventriloquie, *f.*
Ventriloquist, s. ventriloque, *m.*
Venture, s. aventure, *f.*, entreprise hasardeuse, *f.*, risque, *m.*, hasard, *m.*, chance, *f.*, (*com.*) pacotille, *f.*, cargaison, *f.* *At a* —, à l'aventure, au hasard, en péril
Venture, vn. s'aventurer, se hasarder, s'exposer, s'avancer, se risquer, oser, (*at*, *on*,...) entreprendre. — *upon*, essayer, prendre sur soi de, *To* — *out of*, oser sortir de, — va. aventurer, hasarder, risquer, oser, exposer, mettre en péril. *Nothing* — *nothing have*, qui ne risque rien n'a rien
Venturer, s. qui hasarde, qui risque
Venturesome, **Venturous**, adj. entreprenant, aventureux, osé
Venturesomely, adv. d'une manière hasardeuse, hardiment
Venturesomeness, s. caractère aventureux, *m.*, esprit aventureux, *m.*, hardiesse, *f.*
Veracious, adj. véridique, vrai
Veraciously, adv. avec véracité
Veracity, s. véracité, *f.*
Veranda, s. véranda, *f.*
Verb, s. verbe, *m.*
Verbal, adj. verbal, oral, littéral, mot à mot
Verbally, adv. verbalement, mot pour mot
Verbatim, adv. mot pour mot
Verbena, s. verveine, *f.*
Verbose, adj. verbeux, diffus, prolixe
Verbosity, s. verbosité, *f.*, prolixité, *f.*, rédondance, *f.*
Verdant, adj. verdoyant, vert, frais
Verdict, s. verdict, *m.*, jugement, *m.*, décision, *f.*, avis, *m.*, opinion, *f.*
Verdigris, s. vert-de-gris, *m.*
Verdure, s. verdure, *f.*, couleur verte, *f.*
Verge, s. verge, *f.*, (*edge*) extrémité, *f.*, limite, *f.*, lisière, *f.*, bordure, *f.* *On*, *upon*, *to the* — *of*, au bord de, sur le bord de, (*fig.*) à la veille de, sur le point de
Verge, vn. pencher, incliner, s'abaisser, approcher (de), être sur le bord (de), s'approcher
Verger, s. bedeau, *m.*, huissier à verge, *m.*, massier, *m.*
Verification, s. vérification, *f.*, preuve, *f.*
Verify, va. vérifier, confirmer, prouver
Verily, adv. en vérité, vraiment
Verjuice, s. verjus, *m.*
Vermicelli, s. vermicelle, *m.*
Vermicular, adj. vermiculaire, vermiculé
Vermifuge, s. vermifuge, *m.*
Vermilion, s. vermillon
Vermilion, va. vermillonner
Vermin, s. vermine, *f.*
Vernacular, adj. national, indigène. *Our* — *tongue*, notre langue maternelle
Vernal, adj. printanier, du printemps
Veronica, s. véronique, *f.*
Versatile, adj. versatile, changeant, inconstant
Versatility, **Versatileness**, s. versatilité, *f.*
Verse, s. vers, *m.*, poésie, *f.*, versification, *f.*, (*litur.*) verset, *m.*, (*stanza*) stance, *f.*
Versed, adj. versé, expérimenté, familier
Versification, s. versification, *f.*
Versifier, s. versificateur, *m.*
Versify, vn. faire des vers, mettre en vers
Version, s. traduction, *f.*, version, *f.*
Verst, s. verste, *f.*
Versus, prep. contre
Vertebra, s. vertèbre, *f.*
Vertebral, adj. vertébral
Vertebrate, **Vertebrated**, adj. vertébré
Vertex, s. haut, *m.*, sommet, *m.*
Vertical, adj. vertical
Vertically, adv. verticalement
Vertiginous, adj. à mouvement circulaire, vertigineux
Vertigo, s. vertiges, *m.pl.*
Vervain, s. verveine, *f.*
Very, adj. même, vrai, véritable, tout entier, en personne, tout. *In* — *deed*, en vérité. *The* — *thing!* la chose même! *interj.* c'est cela même
Very, adv. très, fort, bien, tout à fait, vraiment, extrêmement. *So bright*, *so* — *bright*, si brillant, d'un brillant si extraordinaire
Vesicle, s. vésicule, *f.*
Vesper, s. soir, *m.* —*s*, *pl.* vêpres, *m.pl.*
Vessel, s. vaisseau, *m.*, vase, *m.*
Vest, s. veste, *f.*, gilet, *m.*
Vest, va. vêtir, revêtir, mettre en possession
Vesta, s. allumette en cire, *f.*
Vestal, s. vestale, *f.*
Vestige, s. vestige, *m.*
Vestment, s. vêtement, *m.*, habit, *m.*
Vestry, s. sacristie, *f.*, vestiaire, *m.*, (*meeting*) assemblée paroissiale, *f.* — *-board*, s., conseil de fabrique, *m.* — *-clerk*, s., sacristain, *m.*, secrétaire de l'assemblée paroissiale, *m.* — *-man*, s., fabricien, *m.* — *-pew*, s., banc de l'œuvre, *m.* — *-meeting*, s., assemblée paroissiale, *f.*, réunion du conseil, *f.*
Vesture, s. vêtement, *m.*, habit, *m.*, manteau, *m.*
Vetch, s. vesce, *f.*
Veteran, adj. ancien, vieux, aguerri, expérimenté
Veteran, s. vétéran, *m.* — *troops*, de vieilles troupes
Veterinary, adj. vétérinaire
Veto, s. véto, *m.*
Veto, va. mettre son véto à
Vex, va. irriter, contrarier, fâcher, vexer, tourmenter troubler, agiter
Vexation, s. vexation, *f.*, peine, *f.*, contrariété, *f.*, ennui, *f.*, chagrin, *m.*, déplaisir, *m.*, tracasserie, *f.*, taquinerie, *f.*
Vexatious, adj. vexatoire, contrariant, fâcheux, ennuyeux, déplaisant, inquiétant, tourmentant
Vexatiously, adv. d'une manière fâcheuse, pour contrarier
Vexing, adj. contrariant, fâcheux, vexant
Vexingly, adv. de manière à contrarier, pour vexer
Via, adv. par la voie de, *f.* — *England*, par voie d'Angleterre
Viaduct, s. viaduc, *m.*
Vial, s. fiole, *f.*
Viand, s.pl. mets, *m.pl.*, viande, *f.*
Viaticum, s. viatique, *m.*
Vibrate, vn. osciller, vibrer
Vibration, s. vibration, *f.*
Viburnum, s. viorne, *f.*
Vicar, s. curé, *m.* vicaire, *m.*, ministre, *m.*
Vicarage, s. cure, *f.* presbytère, *m.*
Vicarship, s. vicariat, *m.*, cure, *f.*
Vice, s. vice, *m.*, défaut, *m.*, imperfection, *f.*, (*screw*) étau, *m.*, presse à vis, *f.*
Vice-... (*in compounds*) vice-... — *-admiral*, s., vice-amiral, *m.* — *-admiralty*, s. vice-amirauté, *f.*, — *consul*, s. vice-consul, *m.*
Viceroy, s. vice-roi, *m.*
Viceroyalty, s. vice-royauté, *f.*
Viciate, va. vicier, corrompre, gâter, altérer, rendre défectueux, débaucher
Vicinity, s. voisinage, *m.*, proximité, *f.*
Vicious, adj. vicieux
Viciously, adv. vicieusement
Viciousness, s. nature vicieuse, *f.*
Vicissitude, s. vicissitude, *f.*
Victim, s. victime, *f.*

Victimize, va. victimer
Victor, s. vainqueur, m.
Victorious, adj. victorieux, vainqueur
Victoriously, adv. victorieusement
Victory, s. victoire, f.
Victual, va. approvisionner, (milit.) avitailler, ravitailler
Victualler, s. munitionnaire, m., fournisseur, m., économe, m., pourvoyeur, m., (licensed) maître d'hôtel, m., aubergiste, m., cabaretier, m.
Victualling, s. avitaillement, m., approvisionnement, m.
Victuals, s. pl. aliments, m.pl., vivres, m.pl., (fam.) victuaille, f., provisions f.pl.
Videlicet, adv. c'est à savoir, savoir, c'est-à-dire
Vie, vn. rivaliser (avec), le disputer (à), faire à l'envi (de), (le) disputer (à), lutter (avec). *To — in beauty with*, le disputer en beauté avec. *To — with each other in splendour*, rivaliser de splendeur l'un avec l'autre
View, va. porter sa vue *or* ses regards sur, regarder, contempler, voir, apercevoir
View, s. vue, f., regard m., aspect, m., apparence, f., présence, f., coup d'œil, m., examen, m., perspective, f., étendue, f., intention, f., (*idea*) opinion, f., avis, m., point de vue, m., manière de voir f. *Dissolving —s*, fantasmagorie, f., *On —*, exposition publique, f.
Vigil, s. veille, f., insomnie, f., vigile, f.
Vigilance, s. vigilance, f.
Vigilant, adj. vigilant
Vigorous, adj. vigoureux
Vigorously, adv. vigoureusement, avec vigueur
Vigour, s. vigueur, f., force, f., énergie, f.
Vile, adj. bas, obscur, vil, abject, méprisable
Vilely, adv. vilement, bassement, ignoblement
Vileness, s. bassesse, f., obscurité, f., dégradation, f.
Vilification, s. avilissement, m., diffamation, f.
Vilifier, s. diffamateur, m.
Vilify, va. calomnier, vilipender, décrier
Villa, s. maison de campagne, f., villa, f.
Village, s. village, m.
Villager, s. villageois, m.
Villain, s. scélérat, m., misérable, m., gredin, m., malheureux, m.
Villanous, adj. scélérat, infâme, (*wicked*) méchant, mauvais, vilain
Villanously, adv. vilement, bassement
Villany, s. scélératesse, f., atrocité, f., infamie, f.
Villein, s. vilain, m., serf, m.
Villenage, s. servage, m.
Vindicate, va. défendre, justifier, maintenir
Vindication, s. défense, f., justification, f., apologie, f.
Vindicatory, adj. vengeur, justificatif
Vindictive, adj. vindicatif
Vindictively, adv. par (esprit de) vengeance, pour se venger
Vine, s. vigne, f. *—-branch*, s. pampre, m., sarment, m. *—-dresser*, s. vigneron, m. *—-estate*, s. vignoble, m., cru, m. *—-grower*, s. propriétaire de vignes, m. *—-growing*, adj. vinicole, vignoble. *—-leaf*, s. feuille de vigne, f. *—-stick*, s. échalas, m. *—-plant*, s., *—-stock*, s. cep de vigne, m. *Faggot of —-branches*, s. sarments, m.pl.
Vinegar, s. vinaigre, m.
Vinegar, adj. de vinaigre, aigre, sûr. *—-cruet*, s. vinaigrier, m., burette à vinaigre, f. *—-maker*, s. vinaigrier, m. *—-sauce*, s. vinaigrette, f.
Vinery, s. serre à vigne, f.
Vineyard, s. clos de vigne, m., vigne, f., vignes, f.pl., vignoble, m.
Vinosity, s. qualité vineuse, f., vinosité, f.
Vinous, adj. vineux
Vintage, s. vendange, f.
Vintager, s. vendangeur, m., vendangeuse, f.
Vintner, s. marchand de vin, m., cabaretier, m.
Violate, va. violer
Violation, s. violation, f.
Violator, s. violateur, m., -trice, f., perturbateur, m., -trice, f.
Violence, s. violence, f.
Violent, adj. violent (*pain*) violent, aigu
Violently, adv. violemment, avec violence
Violet, s. violette, f.
Violet, adj. violet
Violin, s. violon, m. *—-player*, *Violinist*, s. violoniste, m.
Violoncellist, s. violoncelliste, m.
Violoncello, s. violoncelle, m., basse, f.
Viper, s. vipère, f.
Viperine, **Viperous**, adj. vipérin, venimeux
Virago, s. virago, f., dragon, m.
Virgin, s. vierge, f.
Virgin, adj. vierge, virginal, modeste
Virginal, adj. virginal
Virginity, s. virginité, f.
Virile, adj. viril, mâle
Virility, s. virilité, f.
Virtu, s. goût artistique, m., sentiment de l'art, m. *Articles of —*, objets d'art, m.pl.
Virtual, adj. virtuel
Virtually, adv. virtuellement, de fait
Virtue, s. vertu, f., force, f., vigueur, f. *By* or *in —*, en vertu de
Virtuoso, s. virtuose, m., connaisseur, m., amateur, m., curieux, m.
Virtuous, adj. vertueux
Virtuously, adv. vertueusement
Virulence, s. virulence, f.
Virulent, adj. virulent
Virulently, adv. avec virulence
Virus, s. virus, m.
Visage, s. visage, m.
Visaged, adj. à visage, à face, à l'aspect
Viscera, s. viscères, m.pl.
Viscid, adj. visqueux, glutineux
Viscidity, **Viscosity**, s. viscosité, f.
Viscount, s. vicomte, m.
Viscountess, s. vicomtesse, f.
Viscounty, s. vicomté, f.
Viscous, adj. *see* Viscid
Visibility, s. visibilité, f.
Visible, adj. visible
Visibly, adv. visiblement
Vision, s. vision, f., vue, f.
Visionary, adj. s. visionnaire, m.f.
Visit, va. visiter, faire une visite à, (*vent upon*) châtier, se venger de (sur), attribuer, — vn. faire des visites, rendre des visites
Visit, s. visite, f., inspection, f., examen, m., perquisition, f.
Visitant, s. visiteur, m.
Visitation, s. visite, f., (*eccles.*) inspection, f., tournée, f., (*trial*) épreuve, f.
Visiting, s. visite, f., visites, f.pl. *—-cards*, s.pl. cartes de visite, f. pl.
Visitor, s. visiteur, m., -euse, f., inspecteur, m. *District —*, s. dame de charité, f., inspecteur, m., inspectrice, f., de canton
Visor, s. visière, f., masque, m.
Visored, adj. masqué, déguisé
Vista, s. vue, f., perspective, f., percée, f., éclaircie, f., avenue, f.
Visual, adj. visuel
Vital, adj. vital, important, essentiel. *Vitals*, s. pl. les organes essentiels à la vie, m. pl. les parties nobles, f.pl.
Vitality, s. vitalité, f.
Vitiate, *see* Viciate, etc.
Vitreous, adj. vitreux, vitré
Vitrifaction, s. vitrification, f.
Vitrifiable, adj. vitrifiable
Vitrify, va. vitrifier; — vn. se vitrifier
Vitriol, s. vitriol, m., couperose, f.
Vivacious, adj. vif, animé, enjoué
Vivaciousness, **Vivacity**, s. vivacité, f.
Vivaciously, adv. avec vivacité
Vivarium, s. vivier, m., (*for rabbits*) garenne, f., parc, m., réserve, f.
Vivid, adj. vif, frais, animé
Vividly, adv. vivement
Vividness, s. vivacité, f.
Vivification, s. vivification, f.
Vivify, va. n. vivifier, animer
Viviparous, adj. vivipare
Vivisection, s. vivisection, f.
Vixen, s. renarde, f., (*fig.*) femme acariâtre, f., mégère, f.
Viz, adv. *see* Videlicet
Vizier, s. vizir, m.
Vocabulary, s. vocabulaire, m.
Vocal, adj. vocal, de la voix
Vocalist, s. chanteur, m., cantatrice, f.
Vocalization, s. vocalisation, f.
Vocation, s. vocation, f.
Vocative, adj. s. vocatif, m.
Vociferate, vn. a. vociférer
Vociferation, s. vocifération, f.
Vociferous, adj. bruyant
Vociferously, adv. en vociférant
Vogue, s. vogue, f.
Voice, s. voix, f.
Voiced, adj. à la voix .... qui a une voix
Void, adj. vide, (*place*) désert, inhabité, (*null*) nul, sans force, annulé, (*free from*) libre, exempt, pur, *null and —*, nul et non avoué
Void, s. vide, m.
Void, va. vider, quitter, évacuer
Volatile, adj. qui vole, volatil, (*light*) vif, gai, folâtre, (*fickle*) léger, volage, inconstant
Volatility, s. volatilité, f., légèreté, f., inconstance, f.
Volatilization, s. volatilisation, f.
Volatilize, va. volatiliser
Volcanic, adj. volcanique
Volcano, s. volcan, m.
Vole, s. vole, f.
Volley, s. volée, f., décharge, f., (*firing of cannon*) salve, f., volée, f. *Fire a —*, faire une décharge générale, tirer une salve
Voltaic, adj. voltaïque
Volubility, s. volubilité, f.
Voluble, adj. (*tongue*) déliée, bien pendue, (*speech*) vif, facile, aisé, coulant, abondant
Volubly, adv. avec volubilité
Volume, s. volume, m., dimensions, f. pl., masse, f., (*books*) volume, m., tome, m., (*smoke*) tourbillon, m.
Voluminous, adj. gros, volumineux
Voluntarily, adv. volontairement, spontanément
Voluntary, adj. volontaire
Voluntary, s. prélude, m., improvisation, f.
Volunteer, s. adj. volontaire, m.
Volunteer, va. offrir *or* donner volontairement; — vn. s'engager, s'offrir, se présenter
Voluptuary, s. voluptueux, m.
Voluptuous, adj. voluptueux

Voluptuously, adv. voluptueusement

Voluptuousness, s. volupté, *f.*

Volute, s. volute, *f.*

Vomica, s. vomique, *f.*

Vomit, va.n. vomir

Vomit, s. matière vomie, *f.*, (*medicine*) vomitif, *m.*

Vomiting, s. vomissement, *m.*

Vomitive, adj. vomitif

Voracious, adj. vorace

Voraciously, adv. avec voracité

Voraciousness, Voracity, s. voracité, *f.*

Vortex, s. tourbillon, *m.*

Votary, s. adorateur, *m.*, sectateur, *m.*, partisan, *m.*, ami, *m.*

Votary, adj. votif

Vote, s. vote, *m.* *To come, to put to the* —, aller, mettre aux voix. *To pass a* — *of thanks*, voter des remerciments. *To have a* —, voter

Vote, vn.a. voter, donner sa voix, élire, nommer, déclarer, proclamer

Voter, s. votant, *m.*

Voting, s. action de voter, *f.*, vote, *m.* — *-paper*, s. bulletin, *m.*

Votive, adj. votif

Vouch, va. prendre à témoin, attester, affirmer, assurer, garantir; — vn. repondre (de), prouver

Voucher, s. (*pers.*) garant, *m.*, témoin, *m.*, (*things*) garantie, *f.*, gage, *m.*, pièce justificative, *f.*, titre, *m.*

Vouchsafe, va. accorder, donner, octroyer, envoyer; — vn. daigner, condescendre (à)

Vow, s. vœu, *m.*

Vow, va. vouer, consacrer, faire vœu de; — vn. faire un vœu *or* des vœux, promettre, jurer

Vowel, s. voyelle, *f.*

Voyage, s. voyage, *m.*, *sea* —, traversée, *f.*

Voyage, *see* Travel

Voyager, s. voyageur, *m.*

Vulcanize, va. vulcaniser

Vulgar, adj. vulgaire, commun, populaire, ordinaire, grossier, trivial, bas

Vulgarism, s. expression vulgaire, *f.*

Vulgarity, s. vulgarité, *f.*, air commun, *m.*

Vulgarize, va. vulgariser, rendre vulgaire

Vulgarly, adv. vulgairement, communément, grossièrement

Vulnerable, adj. vulnérable

Vulnerary, adj. vulnéraire

Vulpine, adj. de renard

Vulture, s. vautour, *m.*

Vulturine, adj. de vautour

W

W, s. W, w, *m.*

Wad, s. (*straw*) bouchon, *m.*, (*of a gun*) bourre, *f.* — *-hook*, s. tire-bourre, *m.*

Wad, va. bourrer, (*garments*) ouater

Wadded, adj. en bourre, ouaté

Wadding, s. bourre, *f.*, ouate, *f.*

Waddle, vn. se dandiner

Waddling, s. dandinement, *m.*

Wade, vn. (*ford*) passer à gué, guéer, (*walk with difficulty*) marcher (dans), s'avancer péniblement (dans, à travers). *To — through*, examiner, (*fig.*) venir à bout

Wafer, s. (*pastry*) gaufre, *f.*, (*host*) hostie, *f.*, pain à cacheter, *m.*

Waffle, s. gaufre, *f.* — *-iron*, s. gaufrier, *m.*

Waft, va. porter, transporter; — vn. flotter

Waft, s. corps flottant, *m.*

Wag, va.n. remuer, secouer, agiter

Wag, s. plaisant, *m.*, (*fam.*) farceur, *m.*

Wage, va. faire

Wager, s. pari, *m.*, gageure, *f.* *To lay, to take a* —, faire, tenir une gageure *or* un pari

Wager, va.n. parier, gager

Wagerer, s. parieur, *m.*

Wages, s. pl. gages, *m.pl.* (*of artisans*) salaire, *m.*, paye, *f.*

Waggery, s. plaisanterie, *f.*, (*trick*) espièglerie, *f.*

Waggish, adj. plaisant, comique, facétieux. — *trick*, espièglerie, *f.*, farce, *f.*

Waggishly, adv. plaisamment

Waggishness, s. plaisanterie, *f.*

Waggle, vn. *see* Waddle

Waggling, s. remuement, *m.*

Waggon, Wagon, s. voiture de roulage, *f.*, chariot, *m.*, (*milit.*) fourgon, *m.*, caisson, *m.*, (*rail*) voiture, *f.*, wagon, *m.* — *office*, s. bureau de roulage, *m.* *Ammunition* —, s. fourgon, *m.*, caisson, *m.* — *-master*, s. conducteur de train de marchandises, *m.*

Waggoner, s. roulier, *m.*, voiturier, *m.*

Wagtail, s. hochequeue, *m.*, bergeronnette, *f.*

Waif, s. épave, *f.*

Wail, va. gémir sur *or* de, pleurer, lamenter, déplorer; — vn. gémir

Wail, Wailing, s. gémissement, *m.*, plainte, *f.*, lamentation, *f.*

Wailing, adj. gémissant, plaintif, lamentable

Wain, s. *see* Waggon

Wainscot, s. boiserie, *f.*, lambris, *m.*

Wainscot, va. lambrisser, boiser

Wainscoting, s. lambrissage, *m.* boiserie, *f.*

Waist, s. taille, *f.*, ceinture, *f.*

Waistband, s. ceinture, *f.*

Waistcoat, s. gilet, *m.*

Wait, vn.a. attendre, rester, tarder, différer, (*at table*) servir. *To — for*, attendre. *To keep waiting*, faire attendre. *To — on or upon*, se présenter chez, (*to call*) passer chez, se rendre auprès de, présenter ses respects à, (*to serve*) servir, donner des soins à, soigner, (*accompany*) accompagner, suivre

Wait, s. embûches, *f.pl.* embuscade, *f.*, piége, *m.*, guet-apens, *m.*, (*at Christmas*) musiciens nocturnes, *m.pl.* *To lay — for*, dresser des embûches à. *In* —, aux aguets, en embuscade. *To lie in* —, se tenir en embuscade, être aux aguets

Waiter, s. garçon, *m.*, (*tray*) plateau, *m.*

Waiting, s. attente, *f.*, (*attendance*) service, *m.* *In* —, de service. *Lady in* —, s. dame d'honneur, *f.* — *-room*, s. salle d'attente, *f.* — *-maid*, s. — *-woman*, s. femme de chambre, *f.*, soubrette, *f.*

Waitress, s. fille de service, *f.*

Waive, va. abandonner, renoncer à, se désister de, mettre de côté, écarter, ne pas insister sur, ne pas parler de

Wake, vn. veiller, ne pas dormir, être éveillé, s'éveiller, se réveiller, passer la nuit. *To — up*, s'éveiller, se réveiller; — va. éveiller, réveiller, animer, rappeler à la vie, ranimer. *To — up*, réveiller

Wake, s. veille, *f.*, insomnie, *f.*, veillée, *f.*, (*nav.*) sillage, *m.*, eaux, *f.pl.* (*fair*) fête de village, *f.*

Wakeful, adj. éveillé, vigilant

Wakefully, adv. avec vigilance

Waken, v. *see* Wake

Waking, adj. éveillé, de veille

Waking, s. réveil, *m.*, veille, *f.*

Wale, s. (*weal*) marque, *f.*, trace, *f.*, (*of cloth*) côte, *f.*

Walk, vn. a. marcher, (*go on foot*) aller à pied, aller, (*take a walk*) se promener, (*in riding*) aller au pas *To — after*, suivre. *To — by*, passer, passer devant. *To — down*, descendre, *To — in*, entrer, *To — off*, partir, s'en aller, s'éloigner. *To — out*, sortir, se promener. *To — up*, monter, gravir. *To — up and down*, se promener de long en large; — va. parcourir en tous sens; — va. parcourir, marcher dans, se promener dans, fouler, arpenter, courir, aller à pied, (*a horse*) mettre au pas. *To — the rounds*, faire la ronde

Walk, s. marche, *f.*, (*for pleasure*) promenade, *f.*, (*gait*) marche, *f.*, allure, *f.*, (*place*) promenade, *f.*, allée, *f.*, avenue, *f.*, chemin, *m.*, (*space*) carrière, *f.*, sphère, *f.*, (*rounds*) tournée. *To take a* —, faire une promenade, se promener. *To go for a* —, aller se promener

Walker, s. marcheur, *m.* -euse, *f.*, piéton, *m.*, promeneur, *m.*, -euse, *f.*

Walking, s. marche, *f.*, promenade à pied, *f.*

Walking, adj. de marche, de promenade. — *-stick*, s. canne, *f.*

Wall, s. mur, *m.*, muraille, *f.*, paroi, *f.* *To give, to take the* —, donner, prendre le haut du pavé. *To go to the* —, être serré de près, être réduit à se défendre, être mis à l'écart

Wall, adj. de muraille, de mur. — *-creeper*, s. grimpereau, *m.* — *-eye*, s. œil vairon, *m.* — *-eyed*, adj. à l'œil vairon. — *-flower*, s. giroflée, *f.* — *-fruit*, s. fruit d'espalier, *m.* — *-tree*, arbre en espalier, *m.*

Wall, va. entourer *or* ceindre de murs. *To — up*, murer

Wallet, s. valise, *f.*, sac, *m.*, havre-sac, *m.*, besace, *f.*

Wallow, vn. se vautrer, se rouler, croupir

Walnut, s. noix, *f.*, bois de noyer, *m.* *Young —s*, des cerneaux, *m.pl.* — *-tree*, s. noyer, *m.* — *-wood*, s. noyer, *m.*, bois de noyer, *m.*

Walrus, s. morse, *m.*, cheval marin, *m.*

Waltz, s. valse, *f.*

Waltz, vn. valser

Waltzer, s. valseur, *m.* -euse, *f.*

Waltzing, s. valse, *f.*

Wan, adj. pâle, blême

Wand, s. baguette, *f*.
Wander, vn. errer, (*deviate*) s'égarer, errer à l'aventure, s'écarter (de), (*mind*) s'égarer, avoir le délire, battre la campagne
Wanderer, s. vagabond, *m*., vagabonde, *f*., voyageur, *m*., voyageuse, *f*., rôdeur, *m*., fugitif, *m*.
Wandering, s. action d'errer, *f*., voyage, *m*., course vagabonde, *f*., égarement, *m*., absence, *f*., inattention, *f*., distraction, *f*., délire, *m*.
Wane, vn. décroître, s'écouler, diminuer, baisser, décliner
Wane, s. déclin, *m*., décours, *m*., décroissement, *m*.
Wanness, s. pâleur, *f*., teint blême, *m*.
Want, s. manque, *m*., faute, *f*., défaut, *m*., (*need*) besoin, *m*., nécessité, *f*., indigence, *f*., misère, *f*., dénûment, *m*. *To stand in — of*, avoir besoin de. *For — of*, faute de. *To be in — of*, manquer de. *To be in —*, être dans le besoin
Want, va. manquer de, n'avoir pas, n'être pas pourvu de, faire défaut à, manquer à, avoir besoin de, vouloir, désirer, chercher. *To — mending*, avoir besoin de réparations. *You sadly — a new coat*, il vous faut un habit neuf, vous avez grand besoin d'un habit neuf; — vn. manquer (de), faire défaut à, être dénué (de), être absent, manquer. *To be —ing in*, manquer de. *To — for*, manquer de
Wanting, adj. manquant, absent, qui manque, qui est de trop peu
Wanton, adj. flottant, libre, léger, folâtre, enjoué, gai, joyeux, étourdi, (*licentious*) licencieux, dissolu, libertin, déréglé, (*mischievous*) fait de gaieté de cœur, libre, (*superabundant*) exubérant, luxuriant, surabondant
Wanton, s. libertin, *m*.
Wanton, vn. flotter, se jouer, folâtrer, s'ébattre
Wantonly, adv. en se jouant, en folâtrant, capricieusement, de gaieté de cœur, (*lasciviously*) lascivement, en libertin
Wantonness, s. folâtrerie, *f*., enjouement, *m*., caractère folâtre *or* enjoué, *m*., abandon, *m*., dérèglement, *m*., licence, *f*., caprice, *m*., gaieté de cœur, *f*., libertinage, *m*.
War, s. guerre, *f*. *To make — on* or *against*, faire la guerre à. *To be at — with*, être en guerre avec. *To carry on —*, faire la guerre, guerroyer. *— to the knife*, guerre à mort, *f*. *The — office* le ministère *or* le bureau de la guerre. *On the — establishment*, sur le pied de guerre, *— -cry*, s. cri de guerre, *m*. *— -dance*, s. danse guerrière, *f*. *— -department*, s. ministère de la guerre, *m*. *— -horse*, s. cheval de bataille, *m*. *— -insurance*, s. prime de guerre, *f*.
War, vn. faire la guerre (à), guerroyer (contre), combattre
Warble, va. n. chanter, moduler, gazouiller, faire résonner
Warbler, s. chanteur, *m*., (*bird*) fauvette, *f*.
Warbling, s. gazouillement, *m*., ramage, *m*., chant, *m*.
Ward, va. *To — off*, parer, détourner, repousser, écarter
Ward, s. garde, *f*., défense, *f*., (*orphans*) tutelle, *f*., (*an orphan*) pupille, *m*. *f*., (*towns*) quartier, *m*., district, *m*., arrondissement, *m*., (*hospitals*) salle, *f*.
Warden, s. garde, *m*., gardien, *m*., conservateur, *m*., gouverneur, *m*., (*university*) directeur, *m*., recteur, *m*.
Warder, s. garde, *m*., gardien, *m*.
Wardmote, s. conseil de quartier, *m*.
Wardrobe, s. garde-robe, *f*.
Wardroom, s. grande chambre, *f*., carré des officiers, *m*.
Wardship, s. tutelle, *f*.
Ware, s. denrée, *f*., marchandise, *f*.
Warehouse, s. magasin, *m*., entrepôt, *m*. *— -keeper*, s. entreposeur, *m*.
Warehouse, va. emmagasiner
Warehouseman, s. (*servant*) garde-magasin, *m*., garçon de magasin, (*merchant*) marchand en gros. *Italian —*, s. marchand de comestibles, *m*.
Warehousing, s. emmagasinage, *m*., magasinage, *m*., mise en entrepôt, *f*.
Warfare, s. guerre, *f*.
Warily, adv. avec prudence, avec circonspection
Wariness, s. circonspection, *f*., prudence, *f*.
Warlike, adj. guerrier, belliqueux, martial, aguerri, de guerre
Warm, adj. chaud, chaleureux, ardent, plein de feu, zélé, généreux, violent, emporté, (*rich*) riche, (*fam.*) cossu, qui a de quoi. *To be —*, avoir chaud, faire chaud. *To get —*, s'échauffer, (*weather, etc.*) commencer à faire chaud. *To grow —*, s'échauffer
Warm, va. chauffer, réchauffer, (*bed*) bassiner. *To — up*, réchauffer; — vn. chauffer, se chauffer, se réchauffer
Warmer, s. réchaud, *m*.
Warming, adj. qui chauffe. — s. chauffage, *m*. *— -apparatus*, s. calorifère, *m*. *— -pan*, s. bassinoire, *f*.
Warmly, adv. chaudement, avec chaleur, chaleureusement
Warmth, s. chaleur, *f*., ardeur, *f*., zèle, *m*.
Warn, va. prévenir, avertir, instruire, faire savoir à, (*against, of*, contre) prémunir, précautionner
Warning, s. avertissement, *m*., avis, *m*., leçon, *f*., (*notice to leave*) congé, *m*.
Warp, s. chaîne, *f*., (*nav.*) touée, *f*.
Warp, vn. se déjeter, travailler, se tourmenter, gauchir, se cambrer, (*fig.*) s'écarter, dévier, se détourner, (*nav.*) louvoyer, (*to weave*) touer, assembler, ourdir
Warrant, va. garantir, répondre de, être garant de, affirmer, certifier, attester, autoriser
Warrant, s. autorisation, *f*., justification, *f*., excuse, *f*., garantie, *f*., garant, *m*., ordre, *m*., (*law*) mandat, *m*., mandat d'arrêt, *m*., (*nav.*) brevet, *m*. *— of attorney*, s. procuration, *f*. *Out of —*, illégal. *— -officer*, sous-officier, *m*.
Warrantable, adj. autorisé, justifiable
Warrantor, s. garant, *m*.
Warranty, s. garantie, *f*., droit, *m*.
Warren, s. garenne, *f*.
Warrener, s. garde-chasse, *m*., garennier, *m*.
Warrior, s. guerrier, *m*., militaire, *m*., soldat, *m*.
Wart, s. verrue, *f*., poireau, *m*. *— -wort*, s. réveille-matin, *m*., euphorbe, *m*.
Warty, adj. couvert de verrues *or* de poireaux, verruqueux
Wary, adj. circonspect, prudent, avisé
Wash, va. laver, (*linen*) laver, blanchir, (*wet*) humecter, mouiller, baigner, (*overflow*) baigner, laver. *To — away or out*, laver, effacer, se laver de, emporter, nettoyer. *To — down*, faire descendre, emporter, entraîner. *To — over*, inonder, submerger, passer sur. *To — up*, rejeter, (*dishes*) laver, — vn. se laver, faire ses ablutions, (*clothes*) blanchir, faire la lessive
Wash, s. lavage, *m*., drainage, *m*., marais, *m*., marécage, *m*., étang, *m*., rivage, *m*., (*for the face*) cosmétique, *m*., lotion, *f*., (*of clothes*) lessive, *f*., (*kitchen*) lavure, *f*., (*drink*) lavasse, *f*., (*for houses, walls, etc.*) enduit, *m*., (*paint*) lavis, *m*. *— -house*, s. lavoir, *m*., blanchisserie, *f*. *— -leather*, s. peau de chamois, *f*. *— -pot*, s. cuvette, *f*. *— -hand-stand*, s. *— -stand*, s. lavabo, *m*. *— -hand-basin*, s. cuvette, *f*. *— -tub*, s. baquet, *m*.
Washer, s. laveur, *m*., -euse, *f*.
Washerman, s. blanchisseur, *m*.
Washerwoman, s. blanchisseuse, *f*.
Washing, s. lavage, *m*., (*linen*) blanchissage, *m*., lessive, *f*. *I pay my own —*, je me blanchis. *— -machine*, machine à laver, *f*.
Washy, adj. humide, (*fig.*) faible, fade, insipide
Wasp, s. guêpe, *f*. *—'s nest*, guêpier, *m*.
Waspish, adj. irascible, irritable
Waste, va. user, consumer, épuiser, faire dépérir, amaigrir, perdre, gaspiller, dissiper, prodiguer, (*time*) passer, consumer, (*a country*) ravager, dévaster, (*law*) dévaster, détériorer. *To — away*, user, consumer, épuiser, amaigrir
Waste, (AWAY) vn. s'user, s'épuiser, se consumer, dépérir, se dissiper, se perdre, se gaspiller
Waste, adj. dévasté, ravagé, désolé, désert, inculte, vague, superflu, perdu, inutile, (*worthless*) de rebut, sans valeur. *To lay —*, ravager, dévaster. *— lands*, terres vaines et vagues, *f.pl.* *— paper*, papier de rebut, *m*. *— -book*, brouillard, *m*., main courante, *f*. *— -pipe*, tuyau de dégagement, *m*.
Waste, s. perte, *f*., gaspillage, *m*., dépense inutile, *f*., consommation, *f*., dévastation, *f*., ravages, *m.pl.*, désolation, *f*., ruines, *f.pl.*, terre inculte, *f*., désert, *m*., espace, *m*., étendue, *f*., immensité, *f*., (*comm.*) déchet, *m*., rebut, *m*., (*law*) dégât, *m*., dégradation, *f*., (*mines*) remplissage, *m*., vieux travaux, *m.pl.*
Wasteful, adj. s. destructeur, *m*., qui ravage, prodigue, *m*., dissipateur, *m*.
Wastefully, adv. avec prodigalité, en dissipateur
Wastefulness, s. prodigalité, *f*., dissipation, *f*., gaspillage, *m*.
Waster, s. dissipateur, *m*.
Watch, s. vigilance, *f*., veille, *f*., état de veille, *m*., attention, *f*., observation, *f*., surveillance, *f*., guet, *m*., aguets, *m.pl.*, (*guard*) garde, *f*., poste, *m*., ronde, *f*., sentinelle, *f*., faction, *f*., (*nav.*) quart, *m*., vigie, *f*., (*time-piece*) montre, *f*. *Lever —*, s. montre à échappement, *f*. *To keep close — upon*, surveiller de près. *To keep —*, faire le guet. *To be on the —*, être au guet *or* aux aguets *or* à l'affût, avoir l'œil au guet. *To cry out, watch!* crier à la garde
Watch, (*in compounds*). *— -barrel*, s. cylindre de montre, *m*. *— -bell*, s. (*nav.*) cloche, *m*. *— -box*, s. guérite, *f*. *— -case*, s. boîte de montre, *f*., étui de montre, *m*. *— -coat*, s. capote, *f*. *— -dog*, s. chien de garde, *m*. *— -fire*, s. feu de bivouac, *m*. *— -guard*, s. cordon de montre, *m*., chaîne (de sûreté) de montre, *f*. *— -gun*, s. coup de canon de retraite, *m*., diane, *f*. *— -house*, s. corps de garde, *m*., violon, *m*. *— -key*, s. clef de montre, *f*. *— -light*, s. veilleuse, *f*.

— -*maker*, s. horloger, *m.* — -*tower*, s. tour du guetteur, *f.* — -*word*, s. mot d'ordre, mot de passe, *m.*, consigne, *f.*

Watch, vn. veiller, être de garde *or* de faction, faire sentinelle, (*fig.*) veiller sur, attendre, épier, guetter, se tenir aux aguets, observer, épier. *To — over*, veiller sur. *To — for*, guetter, attendre; — va. veiller, garder, surveiller, guetter, épier, attendre, examiner

Watchful, adj. vigilant, attentif, sur ses gardes, (*against*, contre) en garde, en éveil

Watchfully, adv. avec vigilance, attentivement, soigneusement

Watchfulness, s. vigilance, *f.*

Watching, s. guet, *m.*, garde, *f.*, observation, *f.*, surveillance, *f.*, insomnie, *f.*, veilles, *f.pl.*

Watchman, s. garde, *m.*, veilleur de nuit, *m.*

Water, s. eau, *f.*, (*tide*) marée, *f.*, eaux, *f.pl.*, (*merit*) (*fig.*) trempe, *f.*, force, *f.*, volée, *f.*, rang, *m.*, mérite, *m.* *Ditch —*, s. eau croupie. *To hold —*, être étanche, (*fig.*) être solide, endurer. *To come above — again*, revenir sur l'eau. *To go across the —*, traverser la mer, (*fig.*) être déporté. *By —*, par eau. *Under —*, sous l'eau, submergé. *To be in hot —*, être dans l'embarras. *To take in* (*fresh*) —, (*nav.*), faire de l'eau. *To drink the —s*, prendre les eaux. *Strong —s*, les spiritueux. *To make —*, lâcher de l'eau, uriner

Water, (*in compounds*) d'eau, à eau, à l'eau, dans l'eau, sur l'eau, aquatique, hydraulique. — -*bottle*, s. carafe, *f.* — -*carrier*, s. porteur, *m.*, *or* porteuse d'eau, *f.* — -*cart*, s. voiture pour l'arrosage, *f.* — -*closet*, s. cabinet (d'aisances), *m.*, lieux à l'anglaise, *m.pl.* — -*cock*, s. robinet à eau, *m.* — -*colour*, — -*colours*, s.pl. aquarelle, *f.*, gouache, *f.* — -*course*, s. cours d'eau, *m.*, chute d'eau, *f.* — -*cress*, s. cresson (de fontaine), *m.* — -*cure*, s. hydrothérapie, *f.* — *dog*, barbet, *m.* — -*gauge*, s. flotteur, *m.* — -*gruel*, s. gruau, *m.* — -*level*, s. niveau d'eau, *m.* — -*lily*, s. nénuphar, *m.* — -*line*, s. ligne de flottaison, *f.* — -*logged*, adj. engagé d'eau, rempli d'eau. — -*mark*, s. niveau des eaux, *m.*, étiage, *m.*, (*on paper*) filigrane, *m.* — -*melon*, melon d'eau, *m.* — -*mill*, s. moulin à eau, *m.* — -*nymph*, naïade, *f.* — -*proof*, adj. imperméable. — -*shed*, s. versant, *m.* — -*side*, s. bord de l'eau, *m.* — -*spout*, gargouille, *f.* tuyau, *m.*, trombe, *f.*, typhon, *m.* — -*wheel*, s. roue de moulin, *f.*, roue hydraulique, *f.* — -*works*, s.pl. eaux, *f.pl.*, machine hydraulique, *f.*, réservoir principal, *m.*, établissement pour la distribution des eaux, *m.*

Water, va. arroser, mouiller, baigner, (*wine*) mettre de l'eau dans, tremper, (*cattle*) abreuver, (*silk*) moirer; — vn. pleurer, répandre des larmes, s'humecter, se mouiller de larmes, (*nav.*) faire de l'eau, se remplir d'eau. *To make one's mouth —*, faire venir l'eau à la bouche de

Waterage, s. transport par eau, *m.*

Waterer, s. qui arrose

Waterfall, s. chute d'eau, *f.*, cascade, *f.*

Watering, s. action d'arroser, *f.*, arrosement, *m.*, arrosage, *m.*, irrigation, *f.*, (*supply*) distribution des eaux, *f.*, (*cattle*) abreuvage, *m.*, (*nav.*) action de faire de l'eau, *f.*, (*silks*) moirage, *m.*, moiré, *m.* — -*engine*, s. pompe d'arrosage *or* d'irrigation, *f.* — -*place*, eaux, *f.pl.*, bains de mer, *m. pl.*, (*trough*) abreuvoir, *m.*, (*nav.*) aiguade, *f.* — -*pot*, s. arrosoir, *m.*

Watery, adj. d'eau, liquide, aqueux, humide, mouillé

Wattle, s. (*hurdle*) claie, *f.*, (*twig*) petit rameau, *m.*, baguette, *f.*, (*of cocks*) barbe, *f.*, etc.

Wattle, va. (*bind*) lier, (*twist*) tresser, entrelacer

Wattling, s. natte, *f.*, tresse, *f.*

Wave, s. vague, *f.*, flot, *m.*, lame, *f.*, (*poet.*) onde, *f.*, (*of ground*) pli de terrain, *m.*, (*gesticulation*) geste, *m.*, mouvement, *m.*

Wave, vn. flotter, ondoyer, onduler, s'agiter, flotter, se jouer; — va. faire flotter, agiter, faire signe de

Waver, vn. s'agiter, flotter, hésiter, balancer, vaciller, être incertain, chanceler

Waverer, s. irrésolu, *m.*, indécis, *m.*, esprit vacillant, *m.*

Wavering, adj. vacillant, flottant, hésitant, indécis, irrésolu, incertain, chancelant

Wavering, s. hésitation, *f.*, indécision, *f.*, irrésolution, *f.*, incertitude, *f.*

Wavy, adj. houleux, s'élevant en vagues, onduleux, ondulé

Wax, s. cire, *f.*, (*shoemakers*) poix, *f.*, (*of the ears*) cérumen, *m.*

Wax, (*in compounds*) de cire, en cire. — -*flowers*, s.pl. fleurs en cire, *f.pl.* — -*candle*, bougie, *f.* — -*chandler*, s. fabricant de bougies, *m.* — -*cloth*, s. toile cirée, *f.* — *doll*, s. poupée en cire, *f.* — -*light*, s. bougie de cire, *f.* — -*painting*, s. encaustique, *m.* — -*taper*, s. bougie, *f.* (*eccles.*) cierge, *m.*, rat de cave, *m.* — -*work*, s. ouvrage fait en cire, *m.*, figure de cire, *f.*

Wax, va. cirer, enduire de cire; — vn. (*to grow*) grandir, croître, devenir, se faire

Waxen, adj. de cire

Waxy, adj. comme de la cire, mou, visqueux

Way, s. chemin, *m.*, passage, *m.*, route, *f.*, voie, *f.*, sentier, *m.*, distance, *f.*, course, *f.*, trajet, *m.*, (*direction*) côté, *m.*, direction, *f.*, progrès, *m.*, tendance, *f.*, cours, *m.*, sens, *m.*, (*own will*) volonté, *f.*, tête, *f.*, guise, *f.*, idée, *f.*, manière de voir, *f.*, (*means*) moyen, *m.*, méthode, *f.*, manière, *f.*, façon, *f.*, position, *f.*, embarras, *m.*, (*nav.*) marche, *f.*, progrès, *m.* *Right of —*, s. droit de passage, *m.* *To give —*, faire place, fléchir, céder. *To make —*, faire place (à), laisser passer, forcer *or* frayer un passage. *To make one's —* (*through*, à travers), se frayer un chemin, forcer un passage. *To make but little —*, ne faire que peu de progrès. *To be on one's — to*, être en route pour. *All the —*, tout le long de la route. *By the —*, chemin faisant, en route, (*fig.*) soit dit en passant, en passant. *In the —*, sur la route, en route. *To be in the —*, être sur la route, (*th.*) être sous la main, (*to annoy*) gêner, embarrasser. *To throw in the — of*, faire rencontrer, faire trouver, présenter. *On* or *upon the —*, en chemin, en route, chemin faisant. *To be out of the —*, être écarté, n'être pas là, n'être pas à la portée. *To go the right —*, *the wrong —*, *the longest —*, prendre le bon chemin, ne pas prendre le bon chemin. — *in*, entrée, *f.* — *out*, sortie, *f.* — *up*, chemin, *m.* — *down*, chemin. *To go a little —*, faire un peu de chemin, (*fig.*) avoir peu d'effet *or* d'influence, être peu utile. *To go a great —*, faire beaucoup de chemin, aller loin, (*fig.*) aller loin, avoir beaucoup d'influence, être fort utile. *Every —*, de tous les côtés. *I am going your —*, *another —*, *this —*, *that—*, je vais de votre côté, d'un autre côté, par ici *or* de ce côté-ci, par là *or* de ce côté-là. *Over the —*, de l'autre côté de la rue *or* de la route. *To make one's —*, faire son chemin, réussir. *To have one's own —*, faire à sa tête, à sa guise, à sa volonté. *To live one's own —*, vivre à sa guise. *—s and means*, voies et moyens. *Committee of —s and means*, commission du budget. *In some other —*, de qq. autre manière. *Some — or other*, de manière ou d'autre. *No —*, *no —s*, nullement, en aucune façon. *The — in which*, la manière dont. *To go or set about it the right —*, *the wrong —*, s'y prendre bien, s'y prendre mal. *By — of*, en guise de, par manière de, comme. *In the — of business*, comme affaire. *We are quite out of the —*, nous faisons fausse route. *He was in such a — about it*, il était si en colère. *To be under —*, commencer à marcher. *To get under —*, se mettre en route

Wayfarer, s. voyageur, *m.*

Wayfaring, s.adj. voyage, *m.*, qui voyage, voyageur, *m.*, en voyage

Waylay, va. tendre un guet-apens *or* une embûche à, guetter au passage

Wayward, adj. volontaire, obstiné, entêté, capricieux

We, pron. pl. nous

Weak, adj. faible, débile

Weaken, va. affaiblir

Weakening, adj. qui affaiblit, énervant; — s. affaiblissement, *m.*

Weakly, adv. faiblement, avec faiblesse

Weakly, adj. faible, débile

Weakness, s. faiblesse, *f.*, débilité, *f.*

Weal, s. bien, *m.*, bien-être, *m.*, bonheur, *m.*, prospérité, *f.*, marque, *f.*, trace, *f.*

Wealth, s. bonheur, *m.*, opulence, *f.*, richesse, *f.*, fortune, *f.*, biens, *m.pl.*

Wealthily, adv. richement

Wealthiness, s. opulence, *f.*

Wealthy, adj. opulent, riche

Wean, va. sevrer, détacher, (*fig.*) détourner, éloigner, priver

Weaning, s. sevrage, *m.*

Weanling, s. enfant en sevrage, *m.*, agneau en sevrage, *m.*

Weapon, s. arme, *f.*

Weaponless, adj. sans armes

Wear, va. (*have on*) porter, avoir sur soi, se mettre, (*to use*) user, consumer, ronger, effacer, faire disparaître, faire oublier, (*time*) passer. *To — away*, user, consumer, miner, effacer, détruire, faire oublier. *To — off*, effacer, faire disparaître. *To — out*, user, mettre hors de service, épuiser, (*time*) passer péniblement, (*patience*) excéder, mettre à bout; — vn. s'user, se porter, se consumer. *To — well*, être d'un bon user, être durable. *To — on*, s'écouler, se passer

Wear, s. user, *m.*, usage, *m.*, usure, *f.* *Much the worse for —*, fort détérioré par l'usage. — *and tear*, usure, *f.*

Wearable, adj. qu'on peut porter, mettable

Weariness, s. fatigue, *f.*, lassitude, *f.*, dégoût, *m.*

Weary, adj. fatigué, las, lassé, (*tedious*) fatigant, pénible, fastidieux, ennuyeux. — *bed*, s. lit de douleur, *m.*

Weary, va. fatiguer, lasser

Weasel, s. belette, *f.*

Weather, s. temps, *m.*, (*storm*) tempête, *f.*, orage, *m.*,

How is the —? quel temps fait-il? *It is bad —,* il fait mauvais temps. — *permitting,* si le temps le permet

Weather, adj. du côté du vent. — *-beaten,* adj. battu par la tempête, (*fig.*) fatigué, harassé, usé. — *-bound,* adj. retenu par le mauvais temps. — *-driven,* poussé par la tempête. — *-gage,* s. (*nav.*) avantage du vent, *m.* — *-glass,* s. baromètre, *m.* — *-proof,* adj. à l'épreuve du temps. — *-side,* s. côté du vent, *m.* — *-wise,* adj. qui sait prévoir le temps

Weather, va. doubler, résister à, supporter, lutter contre

Weathercock, s. girouette, *f.*

Weathermost, adj. plus au vent

Weave, va. tisser, tresser, entrelacer, enlacer, entremêler

Weaver, s. tisserand, *m.*, tisseur, *m.*

Weaving, s. tissage, *m.*

Web, s. tissu, *m.*, (*spider's*) toile, *f.*, (*on the eye*) taie, *f.*, (*of birds*) palmure, *f.*, membrane, *f.* — *-footed,* adj. palmipède

Webbed, adj. palmé

Wed, va. épouser, (*unite*) unir, marier, (*fig.*) lier, enchainer, attacher

Wedded, adj. conjugal, légitime, (*fig.*) uni, entiché (de) attaché (à)

Wedding, s. noce, *f.* noces, *f.pl.*, mariage, *m.*

Wedding, adj. de noces, nuptial. — *-cake,* s. gâteau de noces, *m.* — *-card,* s. carte des nouveaux mariés, *f.* — *-day,* jour des noces, *m.* — *-favour,* s. faveur, *f.* — *-feast,* s. repas de noces, *m.* — *-guest,* s. invité de la noce, *m.*, -e, *f.* *The — party,* s. les gens de la noce, *m.pl.*, la noce, *f.* — *-ring,* s. alliance, *f.*

Wedge, s. coin, *m.*, (*of gold*) lingot, *m.*

Wedge, va. enfoncer, pousser, serrer, presser, (*fix*) caler, assujettir, fixer, attacher

Wedlock, s. mariage, *m.*, hyménée, *f.*, hymen, *m.*

Wednesday, s. mercredi, *m.*

Weed, s. mauvaise herbe, *f.*, herbe, *f.*, (*pop.*) tabac, *m.*, cigare, *m.* — s.pl. (*dress*) habits *or* vêtements de deuil, *m.pl.*

Weed, va. arracher les mauvaises herbes de, sarcler, (*fig.*) extirper, débarrasser, purger, délivrer

Weeder, s. sarcleur, *m.*, -euse, *f.*, (*fig.*) extirpateur, *m.*

Weeding, s. sarclage, *m.*, épuration, *f.* — *-hook,* s. — *-tool,* s. — *-fork,* s. — *-iron,* s. sarcloir, *m.*

Weedy, adj. plein de mauvaises herbes

Week, s. semaine, *f.*, huit jours, *m.pl.*, huitaine, *f.* *By the —,* à la semaine. *A — ago,* il y a huit jours. — *in,* — *out,* *from —'s end to —'s end,* d'un bout de la semaine à l'autre. *In a —'s time,* dans une huitaine. — *-day,* jour de la semaine, *m.*, jour non férié, *m.*

Weekly, adj. de la semaine, hebdomadaire

Weep, vn.a. pleurer, répandre *or* verser des larmes, verser des pleurs

Weeper, s. pleureur, *m.*, -euse, *f.*

Weeping, adj. qui pleure. — *-willow,* s. saule pleureur, *m.*

Weevil, s. charançon, *m.*, calandre, *f.*

Weft, s. trame, *f.*

Weigh, va. peser, (*anchor*) lever, (*consider*) peser, considérer, examiner. *To — down,* l'emporter en poids sur, peser plus que, surcharger, (*fig.*) accabler, attrister, abattre; — vn. peser, avoir du poids, avoir de la valeur *or* de l'importance, (*upon*) peser (sur), être à charge (à), accabler (...) attrister. *To — down,* pencher, s'affaisser, s'enfoncer

Weigh, s. poids, *m.* — *-bridge,* s. pont à bascule, *m.*, bascule, *f.*

Weighing, s. pesage, *m.*, pesée, *f.* — *-house,* s. bureau de pesage, *m.* — *-machine,* s. bascule, *f.*

Weight, s. poids, *m.*, pesanteur, *f.*, pesant, *m.*

Weight, va. attacher un poids à, charger d'un poids, (*a stick*) plomber

Weightily, adv. pesamment

Weightiness, s. pesanteur, *f.*, poids, *m.*, importance, *f.*, gravité, *f.*

Weighty, adj. pesant, de poids, important, sévère

Weir, s. barrage, *m.*, nasse, *f.*

Welcome, s. bienvenue, *f.*, bon accueil, *m.*, gracieuse réception, *f.*

Welcome! interj. bienvenu! soyez le bienvenu!

Welcome, va. souhaiter *or* donner la bienvenue à, saluer, bien accueillir, recevoir gracieusement

Weld, va. souder

Welding, s. soudure, *f.*

Welfare, s. bien-être, *m.*, bien, *m.*, bonheur, *m.*

Well, s. puits, *m.*, source, *f.*, fontaine, *f.*, (*pump*) réservoir, *m.* — *-sinker,* s. puisatier, *m.*, fonceur de puits, *m.* —, s.pl. eaux minérales, *f.pl.*

Well, adv. bien, fort. — *enough,* assez bien. — *nigh,* presque, près de. *Well done,* bien fait. — *and good,* c'est bien. *As —,* aussi bien, autant. *As — as,* aussi bien que, ainsi que, de même que, tant ... que, ... *As — as may be,* tant bien que mal

Well! interj. eh bien! soit!

Well, adj. bien, bien portant, (*happy*) heureux, (*with,* avec) bien, en bons termes, en bons rapports, en faveur. *To be — off,* être dans l'aisance, être à son aise

Well, (*in compounds*) bien, — *-bred,* bien élevé. — *-mannered,* aux bonnes manières, poli. — *-meant,* fait à bonne intention. — *-met,* bien rencontré. — *-wisher of,* ami de, qui veut du bien à, qui porte intérêt à

Well, vn. jaillir, couler. *To — up from,* sourdre de, surgir de

Welsh, adj. gallois. — *flannel,* flanelle fine. — *-rabbit, see* Rabbit

Welt, s. bordure, *f.*, trépointe, *f.*

Welter, vn. rouler, (*in blood*) nager, être baigné, (*in mud*) se vautrer

Wen, s. loupe, *f.*, (*in the neck*) goitre, *m.*

Wench, s. jeune fille, *f.*, fillette, *f.*

Wend, vn.a. aller, poursuivre

West, s. ouest, *m.*, occident, *m.*, couchant, *m.*

West, adj. de l'ouest, de l'occident, occidental, du couchant

West, adv. vers l'ouest, à l'ouest

Westerly, adj. de l'ouest, occidental, vers l'ouest

Westerly, adv. vers l'ouest

Western, adj. de l'ouest, occidental, d'occident, ouest, à l'ouest, vers l'ouest, vers le couchant

Westward, Westwardly, adv. vers l'ouest

Wet, adj. mouillé, humide, (*weather*) pluvieux, de pluie, (*fig.*) mouillé, arrosé. *To be quite — through* or *— to the skin,* être mouillé jusqu'aux os. — *dock,* s. bassin de port, *m.* — *-nurse,* s. nourrice, *f.* — *weather,* s. temps de pluie, *m.*

Wet, s. humidité, *f.*, pluie, *f.*

Wet, va. mouiller, tremper, humecter, arroser, baigner. *To — one's whistle,* s'humecter le gosier

Wether, s. mouton, *m.*

Wetness, s. humidité, *f.*

Whack, va. battre, rosser

Whacking, s. roulée, *f.*

Whale, s. baleine, *f.*, cétacé, *m.* — *-boat,* s. bateau baleinier, *m.* — *-bone,* s. baleine, *f.*

Whaler, s. baleinier, *m.*

Wharf, s. quai, *m.*, (*for goods*) entrepôt, *m.*

Wharfage, s. quayage, *m.*

Wharfinger, s. maître du quai, *m.*, propriétaire d'entrepôt, *m.*

What, rel. pron. ce qui, ce que, le, la, les ... qui, celui qui, quoi, que; — adj. pron. quel; — interrog. que? quoi? qu'est-ce que? — adj. interrog. quel? lequel? qu'arriverait-il? — exclam. quel! quoi que (ce soit), — indef. une chose, quelque chose, ce, cette; — (repeated) partie ... partie ... tant ... tant; — interj. comment! quoi! *You don't know what it is!* vous ne savez pas ce que c'est! (*fam.*) vous en parlez bien à votre aise! *I'll teach you what's —,* je vous apprendrai ce que c'est. *To know —'s —,* être fin. *And — not,* et bien d'autres choses encore, et cætera. —? — *did you say?* plaît-il? comment? quoi? *Did you see —'s his name?* avez-vous vu chose? — *if,* si. — *though,* qu'importe que. — *else?* quelle autre chose? *Do, say — we will,* quoi que nous fassions, disions

Whatever, pron. tout ce qui, tout ce que, quoi que, quoi que ce soit qui, quoi que ce soit que, quelconque, quel que ... — *I do,* quoi que je fasse. *I had no share — in it,* je n'y pris aucune part. — *your opinion may be,* quelle que soit votre opinion

Whatnot, s. étagère, *f.*

Whatsoever, pron. *see* Whatever

Wheal, s. pustule, *f.*, bouton, *m.*

Wheat, s. froment, *m.*, blé, *m.* — *-sheaf,* s. gerbe de blé, *f.*

Wheedle, va.n. cajoler, enjôler, amadouer

Wheedler, s. cajoleur, *m.*, -euse, *f.*

Wheedling, s. cajolerie, *f.*, câlinerie, *f.*

Wheedling, adj. câlin, de cajoleur

Wheel, s. roue, *f.* *Catherine —,* soleil, *m.* — *-horse,* s. cheval de brancard, *m.* — *-house,* s. tambour de roue, *m.* — *-work,* s. rouages, *m.pl.*

Wheel, vn. rouler, tourner, se tourner, se retourner, avancer, (*milit.*) faire une conversion, pivoter. *To wheel about,* faire une pirouette, faire volte-face, (*horse*) caracoler, (*mil.*) faire volte-face. *To — round,* faire volte-face, se retourner. *Right —,* à droite, conversion. *Left — into line,* à gauche, en bataille; — va. faire tourner, rouler, approcher quelque chose en le roulant, brouetter, voiturer. *To — about one's horse,* faire caracoler son cheval

Wheelbarrow, s. brouette, *f.*

Wheeled, adj. à roues

Wheeler, s. cheval de brancard, *m.*

Wheeling, s. roulage, *m.*, (*mil.*) conversion, *f.*

Wheelwright, s. charron, *m.*

Wheeze, vn. souffler, être poussif

Wheezing, Wheezy, adj. poussif, asthmatique, court d'haleine

Wheezing, s. sifflement

asthmatique, *m.*, respiration bruyante, *f.*

Whelm, va. submerger, couvrir, ensevelir

Whelp, s. petit, *m.*, (*fig.*) fils, *m.*, drôle, *m.*

Whelp, vn. mettre bas

When, adv. quand, lorsque, où, que, et alors, alors, lors, ce temps là. *Till* —, jusques à quand? jusqu'à ce que. *On the eve of the day* — . . . , la veille du jour où . . . *Since* —, depuis lors

When! interj. allons!

Whence, adv. d'où. *From* —, d'où

Whencesoever, adv. de quelque endroit que, de quelque part que

Whenever, Whensoever, adv. toutes les fois que, quand, n'importe à quel moment que

Where, adv. où, là où, tandis que

Whereabout, Whereabouts, adv. où, au sujet de quoi *or* duquel. *Leaving no clue to his* —*s*, ne laissant aucun indice du lieu où il se trouvait

Whereas, conj. tandis que, au lieu que, (*law*) attendu que, vu que

Whereat, adv. à quoi, de quoi, sur quoi, ce dont, ce de quoi

Whereby, adv. par où, par lequel, par laquelle, par lesquels, *etc.*, au moyen de quoi

Wherefore, conj. adv. c'est pourquoi, donc, aussi, par conséquent, pourquoi

Wherein, adv. où, dans lequel, *etc.*, en quoi?

Whereof, adv. dont, de quoi, duquel, *etc.*, ce . . . de quoi

Whereon, adv. sur quoi, sur lequel, *etc.* là-dessus

Wheresoever, adv. *see* WHEREVER

Whereto, Whereunto, adv. à quoi, ce à quoi, où, auquel, *etc.*

Whereupon, adv. *see* WHEREON

Wherever, adv. partout où, n'importe où, en quelque lieu que ce soit que

Wherewith, Wherewithal, adv. avec lequel, avec laquelle, *etc.*, avec quoi, de quoi, dont

Wherry, s. canot, *m.*, bac, *m.*

Whet, va. aiguiser, donner le fil à, affiler, affûter, (*fig.*) stimuler, inciter, éveiller

Whet, s. action d'aiguiser, etc., *f.*, repassage, *m.*, (*fig.*) stimulant, *m.*

Whether, conj. si, soit que . . . , ou . . . , soit . . . , ou . . .

Whetstone, s. pierre à aiguiser, *f.*, (*fig.*) stimulant, *m.*, aiguillon, *m.*

Whey, s. petit lait, *m.*, sérum, *m.*

Which, rel. pron. qui, que, lequel, laquelle, *etc.*, ce qui, ce que; — interrog. qui? lequel? laquelle? *etc.*, ce, cette, etc. *Of* —, dont, de quoi, duquel, *etc.*, ce dont, ce de quoi. *For — reason*, et pour cette raison. *At — time*, et à ce moment

Whichever, Whichsoever, pron. quelque . . . que, l'un ou l'autre, celui

Whiff, s. bouffée, *f.*

Whiff, va. n. lancer des bouffées, lancer avec une bouffée

Whig, s. whig, *m.*, libéral, *m.*

While, s. instant, *m.*, moment, *m.*, espace de temps, *m.*, temps, *m.* *One* —, dans un moment. *The* —, pendant un instant. *It is not worth* —, *worth your — telling him*, cela ne vaut pas la peine de le lui dire. *What a — you have been!* quel temps vous y avez mis! *A long — ago*, il y a longtemps. *All the* —, pendant tout le temps, en même temps

While, adv. pendant que, tant que, en même temps que

While, vn. flâner. *To* — *away*, passer, faire passer, perdre

Whilst, adv. *see* WHILE

Whim, s. caprice, *m.*, fantaisie, *f.*, lubie, *f.*

Whimper, vn. pleurnicher; — va. dire en pleurnichant

Whimperer, s. pleurnicheur, *m.*, -euse, *f.*

Whimpering, s. adj. pleurnicheries, *f.pl.* pleurnichement, *m.*, (*pers.*) pleurnicheur, *m.*

Whimsical, adj. fantasque, capricieux, bizarre

Whin, s. ajonc, *m.*

Whine, vn. glapir, crier, gémir, geindre, pleurnicher

Whine, s. glapissement, *m.*, plainte, *f.*, cri dolent, *m.*, gémissement, *m.*

Whining, adj. glapissant, dolent

Whip, va. n. fouetter, donner des coups de fouet à, battre du fouet, (*grain*) battre, (*cream*) fouetter, battre, (*to sew*) faufiler, bâtir, (*take up*) enlever, prendre vivement, (*nav.*) hisser, raffermir. — *behind*, tapez derrière! *To — open*, ouvrir vivement. *To — from*, enlever vivement. *To — into*, passer *or* faire entrer vivement dans. *To — up*, enlever vivement. *To — back*, faire retourner à coup de fouet. *To — down*, descendre vivement. *To — on*, faire avancer à coups de fouet. *To* — *off*, chasser à coups de fouet, enlever vivement

Whip, s. fouet, *m.*, (*fam.*) cocher, *m.*, (*nav.*) palan, *m.* *A long* —, une chambrière, *f.*, — *and spur*, bride abattue, ventre à terre. — *-cord*, s. fouet, *m.* — *-handle*, s. manche de fouet, *m.* — *-lash*, s. mèche de fouet, *f.* — *-saw*, s. passant, *m.* — *-staff*, s. manivelle de la barre du gouvernail, *f.* — *stick*, — *stock*, s. manche de fouet, *m.* — *stitch*, s. tailleur, *m.*, ouvrage fait à la hâte, *m.*

Whipper, s. qui fouette, fouetteur, *m.* — *-in*, (*hunt.*) piqueur, *m.*, (*in Engl. Parl.*) celui qui rassemble les votants d'un parti. — *-snapper*, s. vaurien, *m.*, gamin, *m.*

Whipping, s. coups de fouet, *m.pl.*, action de fouetter, *f.*, le fouet, *m.*, flagellation, *f.* — *post*, s. poteau des condamnés au fouet. — *-top*, s. sabot, *m.*

Whipple-tree, s. palonnier, *m.*

Whirl, vn. tourner rapidement, tournoyer, passer rapidement; — va. faire tourner, faire tourbillonner, faire tournoyer, faire pirouetter

Whirl, s. tournoiement, *m.*, tourbillonnement, *m.*, tourbillon, *m.*, mouvement rapide, *m.*

Whirligig, s. pirouette, *f.*

Whirlpool, s. tourbillon, *m.*

Whirlwind, s. tourbillon, *m.*, trombe, *f.*

Whisk, s. petit balai, *m.*, vergette, *f.*

Whisk, va. épousseter, balayer, agiter vivement, mouvoir rapidement, (*eggs*) battre, (*cream*) fouetter

Whiskers, s.pl. favoris, *m.pl.*, (*cat's*) moustaches, *f.pl.*

Whisper, vn. dire tout bas (à), chuchoter (à), parler tout bas (à), parler à l'oreille (de), (*wind*) murmurer, soupirer. *To — against*, parler en secret contre; — va. dire tout bas, dire à l'oreille, chuchoter, murmurer, parler en secret à

Whisper, s. chuchotement, *m.*, murmure, *m.*, (*fig.*) doux murmure, *m.*, soupir, *m.*, bruit qui court, *m.*, rumeur, *f.* *In a* —, tout bas, à voix basse

Whisperer, s. chuchoteur, *m.*, -euse, *f.*

Whispering, s. chuchotement, *m.*, chuchoterie, *f.*, bruit, *m.*, rumeur, *f.*

Whist, s. whist, *m.*

Whistle, vn.a. siffler

Whistle, s. sifflet, *m.*, coup de sifflet, *m.*, (*wind*) sifflement, *m.*

Whistler, s. siffleur, *m.*

Whistling, s. sifflement, *m.*, coup de sifflet, *m.*

Whit, s. peu, *m.*, brin, *m.*, point, *m.*, iota, *m.*, rien, *m.* *Not a* —, pas le moins du monde, pas du tout

White, s. blanc, *m.*, couleur blanche, *f.*

White, adj. blanc, (*pale*) blême, pâle, (*old*) gris. *To grow* —, blanchir. — *man*, blanc, *m.* — *woman*, blanche, *f.* *To turn — with fear*, pâlir, devenir pâle de frayeur. *As* — *as a sheet*, blanc comme linge. — *-bait* s. blanquette, *f.* — *-lead*, s. plomb de céruse, *m.*, céruse, *f.* — *-lime*, s. blanc de chaux, *m.* — *-limed*, adj. blanchi à la chaux. — *-livered*, adj. envieux, lâche, poltron. — *-smith*, s. ferblantier, *m.*

Whiten, va. blanchir; — vn. blanchir, se blanchir

Whiteness, s. blancheur, *f.*, pâleur, *f.*

Whitening, s. blanc d'Espagne, *m.*, action de blanchir, *f.*

Whitewash, s. cosmétique, *m.*, eau de toilette, *f.*, (*for houses*) badigeon, *m.*, lait de chaux, *m.* *To give a coat of* —, badigeonner

Whitewash, va. badigeonner, blanchir

Whitewasher, s. badigeonneur, *m.*

Whitewashing, s. badigeonnage, *m.*

Whither, adv. où

Whiting, s. (*fish*) merlan, *m.*, (*polish*) blanc d'Espagne, *m.*

Whitish, adj. blanchâtre, tirant sur le blanc

Whitlow, s. panaris, *m.*, mal d'aventure, *m.*

Whitsunday, s. dimanche de la Pentecôte, *m.*

Whitsuntide, s. Pentecôte, *f.*, fêtes de la Pentecôte, *f.pl.*

Whittle, va. couper

Whiz, vn. siffler

Whiz, s. sifflement, *m.*

Who, rel. pron. qui, lequel, laquelle, lesquels, lesquelles

Whoever, pron. quiconque, qui que ce soit, quel que soit, quel que soit celui qui. — *he may be*, quel qu'il soit

Whole, adj. entier, tout, tout entier, complet, (*well*) sain, bien portant, guéri, rétabli, remis. *The — world*, le monde entier. *Our — hope*, tout notre espoir. *To be made* —, guérir

Whole, s. tout, *m.*, tout ensemble, *m.*, somme, *f.*, totalité, *f.* *On the* —, somme toute, en somme, à tout prendre, après tout

Wholesale, s. vente en gros, *f.*, gros, *m.*, masse, *f.* *By* —, en gros

Wholesale, adj. adv. en gros

Wholesome, adj. sain, salubre

Wholesomely, adv. sainement, salutairement

Wholesomeness, s. salubrité, *f.*, nature saine, *f.*

Wholly, adv. entièrement, complètement

Whom, rel. pron. que, lequel, laquelle, *etc.*, qui

Whomsoever, pron. *see* WHOEVER

Whoop, s. cri, *m.*, huée, *f.*, (*ornith.*) huppe, *f.*

Whoop, va. n. pousser un cri, crier, huer

Whooping, s. cri, *m.*, huée, *f.* — *cough*, s. coqueluche, *f.*

Whopper, s. qui bat,

(*wonder*) chose énorme, *f.*, (*a lie*) mensonge énorme, *m.*, bourde, *f.*

Whose, rel. pron. dont le, dont la, dont les, le, la, les... duquel, etc. (*followed by a possessive*) que, quel, à qui? *The mother to — heart you speak*, la mère au cœur de laquelle vous parlez. *Philosophy, — end is to instruct us*, la philosophie, dont le but est de nous instruire. *They — riches make them proud*, ceux que leurs richesses enorgueillissent. *Remember — hand it is inflicts the blow*, rappelez-vous quelle est la main qui frappe le coup. *— castle is this!* à qui est ce château?

Whosoever, pron. *see* WHOEVER

Why, adv. pourquoi? pour lequel, *etc.* *— not!* pourquoi pas? *— so!* pourquoi cela? *For —!* et pourquoi? *The reason —*, la raison pour laquelle

Why, interj. mais! eh bien!

Wick, s. mèche, *f.*

Wicked, adj. méchant, mauvais, malfaisant

Wickedly, adv. méchamment, mal, avec méchanceté

Wickedness, s. méchanceté, *f.*, perversité, *f.*

Wicker, s. osier, *m.*, *— basket*, panier d'osier, *m.*

Wickered, adj. d'osier, clissé

Wicket, s. guichet, *m.*, petite porte, *f.*

Wide, adj. vaste, immense, grand, large, (*far*) loin, éloigné. *To be three feet —*, avoir trois pieds de large, avoir une largeur de trois pieds, être large de trois pieds. *Rather — of the mark*, loin de la vérité

Wide, adv. loin, au loin, largement, bien écarté, tout à fait, complétement. *— open*, grand ouvert, (*eyes*) écarquillés, grand ouverts. *— -awake*, bien éveillé. *— -awake*, s. (chapeau de) feutre à larges bords, *m.* *— -spread*, adj. répandu, immense, qui s'étend au loin

Widely, adv. loin, au loin, à une grande distance, largement, bien, beaucoup

Widen, va. élargir, agrandir, étendre, dilater; — vn. s'élargir, s'agrandir, s'étendre, se dilater

Wideness, s. largeur, *f.*, ampleur, *f.*, étendue, *f.*

Widening, s. élargissement, *m.*, agrandissement, *m.*

Widgeon, s. sarcelle, *f.*

Widow, s. veuve, *f.* *— -hunter*, s. coureur de veuves, *m.*

Widow, va. rendre veuve *or* veuf

Widowed, adj. veuf, veuve, solitaire

Widower, s. veuf, *m.*

Widowhood, s. veuvage, *m.*

Width, s. largeur, *f.*

Wield, va. manier, se servir de, tenir

Wife, s. femme, *f.*, épouse, *f.*

Wig, s. perruque, *f.* *— -maker*, s. perruquier, *m.*, fabricant de perruques, *m.*

Wight, s. être, *m.*, individu, *m.*

Wild, adj. (*places*) sauvage, inculte, désert, (*persons*) sauvage, barbare, farouche, désordonné, furieux, dissipé, déréglé, (*weather*) déchaîné, orageux, (*look*) égaré, effaré, (*speech*) incohérent. *To run —*, (*pers.*) se déranger, se jeter dans la débauche, (*passions, mind*) se déchaîner. *He had been — in his youth*, il avait eu une jeunesse orageuse. *— child*, s. enfant turbulent, *m.*, démon, *m.*

Wild, **Wilderness**, s. désert, *m.*, lieu sauvage, *m.*, solitude, *f.*

Wildfire, s. feu grégeois, *m.* *To spread like —*, se répandre rapidement

Wilding, s. pomme sauvage, *f.*, sauvageon, *m.*

Wildly, adv. sans culture, dans l'état sauvage, d'un air farouche, avec égarement, d'un air égaré, furieusement, avec fureur, follement, capricieusement, d'une manière désordonnée, dans le déréglement, d'une manière incohérente

Wildness, s. état sauvage, *m.*, nature sauvage *or* inculte, *f.*, nature agreste, *f.*, férocité, *f.*, fureur, *f.*, violence, *f.*, impétuosité, *f.*, déchaînement, *m.*, turbulence, *f.*, tumulte, *m.*, emportement, *m.*, déréglement, *m.*, (*look*) égarement, *m.*, (*mind*) dérangement, *m.*, folie, *f.*

Wile, s. artifice, *m.*, ruse, *f.*

Wilful, adj. volontaire, obstiné, opiniâtre, (*horse*) rétif, (*premeditated*) prémédité, fait avec préméditation

Wilfully, adv. obstinément, avec entêtement, volontairement, à dessein, (*law*) avec préméditation

Wilfulness, s. obstination, *f.*, entêtement, *m.*, perversité, *f.*

Wiliness, s. astuce, *f.*, nature astucieuse, *f.*

Will, s. volonté, *f.*, gré, *m.*, bon plaisir, *m.*, vouloir, *m.*, intention, *f.*, désir, *m.*, souhait, *m.*, testament, *m.*, volonté dernière, *f.* *Where there's a — there's a way*, vouloir c'est pouvoir. *He has a — of his own*, ce qu'il veut, il le veut bien. *Good —*, bonne volonté, *f.*, bienveillance, *f.*, bon vouloir, *m.*, (*custom*) clientèle, *f.* *At one's —*, à son gré. *Against one's —*, contre son gré. *Take the — for the deed*, prendre l'intention pour le fait. *What's your —?* que désirez-vous? *To have one's —*, avoir ce qu'on désire, faire à sa tête. *To make one's —*, faire son testament

Will, va.n. vouloir, commander, ordonner, disposer de... par testament. *Go on and I — follow thee*, marchez et je vous suivrai. *I — tell you*, je vous dirai. *Do as you —*, fais comme tu voudras, faites comme vous voudrez. *— ye, will ye*, bon gré, mal gré. *Be that as it —*, que ce soit comme cela voudra

Willing, adj. bien disposé (à), prêt (à), empressé (de), désireux (de), complaisant, volontaire, spontanément, volontiers, de bon cœur. *To be — to do*, vouloir bien faire. *Who is both able and willing to relieve*, qui a à la fois le pouvoir et la volonté de secourir. *Ever — to oblige*, toujours prêt à obliger

Willingly, adv. volontiers, de son plein gré, de bon cœur, volontairement, avec empressement, sans répugnance

Willingness, s. bonne volonté, *f.*, bon vouloir, *m.*, disposition, *f.*, empressement, *m.*, consentement, *m.*

Willow, s. saule, *m.* *— -plot*, s. saussaie, *f.*

Willowed, **Willowy**, adj. planté de saules

Will-o'-the-wisp, s. feu follet, *m.*

Wily, adj. rusé, astucieux, fin

Wimble, s. vilebrequin, *m.*, tarière, *f.*

Win, vn. gagner, (*victory*) remporter, obtenir, (*to induce*) attirer, séduire, engager, persuader. *To — over to*, gagner à, attirer à; — va. gagner, remporter la victoire, (*on, upon, sur*) empiéter, gagner, faire du progrès

Wince, vn. tressaillir, frémir, faire un mouvement, faire une légère grimace, (*fig.*) hésiter, reculer, (*to kick*) ruer

Winch, s. manivelle, *f.*, vireveau, *m.*

Wind, s. vent, *m.*, souffle, *m.*, (*breath*) respiration, *f.*, haleine, *f.*, (*med.*) vent, *m.*, flatuosité, *f.* *Between — and water*, à fleur d'eau, à la flottaison. *To get —, to take —*, (*fig.*) s'ébruiter, s'éventer. *There's some mischief, something in the —*, il se machine *or* il se prépare quelque chose. *To snuff the —*, prendre vent. *To get the — of*, avoir vent de. *To have in the —, to have the — of*, avoir le vent sur, avoir le dessus de. *To raise the —*, être aux expédients, trouver de l'argent. *— -bound*, adj. retenu par les vents contraires. *— -broken*, adj. poussif. *— -mill*, s. moulin à vent, *m.*

Wind, va. faire tourner, tourner, monter, enrouler, rouler, (*silk, etc.*) dévider, (*wrap up*) entourer de, enlacer, diriger, manier, insinuer, glisser, (*road*) suivre, suivre les détours, (*a horn*) sonner de, donner de. *To — its way through*, serpenter dans. *— one's way*, poursuivre son chemin. *— off*, dévider, dérouler. *— out*, retirer. *— up*, mettre en pelote, enrouler, dévider, (*watch*) monter, (*fig.*) préparer, arranger, disposer, (*comm.*) terminer, liquider; — vn. s'enrouler, s'enlacer, s'entortiller, (*road etc.*) serpenter, tourner, faire des détours, (*pers.*) faire des détours, suivre les détours, monter, descendre (*en tournant*). *To — down*, descendre en serpentant, descendre. *To — out of*, sortir de, se retirer de. *To — up*, terminer, conclure

Windage, s. vent, *m.*

Winded, adj. à vent, à haleine. *see* LONG, SHORT, *etc.*

Winder, s. dévideur, *m.*, -euse, *f.*, (*instr.*) dévidoir, *m.*

Windfall, s. fruit tombé, *m.*, arbre abattu par le vent, *m.*, (*fig.*) bonne aubaine, *f.*, bonne fortune, *f.*

Windiness, s. temps venteux, *m.*, (*med.*) flatuosité, *f.*

Winding, s. détour, *m.*, sinuosité, *f.*, méandre, *m.*, (*road*) tour, *m.*, coude, *m.* *— off*, dévidage, *m.*, (*horn*) son, *m.*; — adj. tortueux, sinueux, plein de détours, qui serpente. *— -stairs*, s. escalier en spirale, *m.* *— -engine*, s. cylindre, *m.*, treuil, *m.* *— -machine*, s. dévidoir, *m.* *— -sheet*, s. linceul, *m.* *— -tackle*, s. gros palan tournant, *m.*

Windingly, adv. tortueusement, en serpentant

Windlass, s. cabestan, *m.*, treuil, *m.*

Window, s. fenêtre, *f.*, croisée, *f.*, vitres, *f.pl.* (*church*) vitraux, *m.pl.*, (*comm.*) montre, *f.*, étalage, *m.* *— -blind*, s. store, *m.*, jalousie, *f.* *— -curtain*, s. rideau de fenêtre, *m.* *— -fastening*, s. espagnolette, *f.* *— -frame*, s. châssis de fenêtre, *m.*, boiserie de fenêtre, *f.* *— -glass*, s. carreaux de vitre, *m.pl.* *— -pane*, s. carreau de fenêtre, *m.* *— -sash*, s. châssis de fenêtre, *m.* *— -seat*, s. banquette, *f.* *— -shade*, s. store extérieur, *m.* *— -shutter*, s. volet, *m.* *— -sill*, rebord de fenêtre, *m.* *— -tax*, s. impôt des fenêtres, *m.* *In the —*, à la montre, à l'étalage

Windpipe, s. trachée-artère, *f.*, (*fam.*) gosier, *m.*, sifflet, *m.*

Windward, adv. au vent, s. côté du vent, *m.*, endroit d'où vient le vent, *m.* *The — islands*, s.pl. les îles du Vent, *f.pl.* *To the — of*, au vent de

Windy, adj. de vent, orageux, tempétueux, (*empty*) vain, vide, creux, qui n'est que du vent, (*med.*) venteux, flatueux

Wine, s. vin, *m.*, ivresse, *f.* *Heavy —*, du gros vin. *— and water*, s. de l'eau rougie, *f.*, (*at school*) de l'abondance, *f.* —*-bag*, s. outre à vin, *f.* —*-bibber*, s. ivrogne, *m.*, buveur, *m.* —*-cask*, s. fût, *m.* —*-cellar*, s. cave (à vin), *f.* —*-cooler*, s. seau à frapper, *m.* —*-country*, s. pays vignoble, *m.* —*-coloured*, adj. —*-colour*, adj. vineux. —*-glass*, s. verre à vin, *m.* —*-grower*, s. propriétaire de vignobles, *m.*, vigneron, *m.* —*-measure*, s. mesure pour le vin, *f.*, mesures pour les liquides, *f.pl.* —*-merchant*, s. négociant en vins, *m.*, marchand de vin, *m.* —*-press*, s. pressoir, *m.* —*-pitcher*, s. pot à vin, *m.* —*-producing*, adj. vignoble, vinicole. —*-stone*, s. tartre (du vin), *m.* —*-shop*, s. boutique de marchand de vin, *f.* *At the —-shop*, chez le marchand de vin. —*-taster*, s. dégustateur de vins, *m.*, gourmet, *m.* —*-vaults*, s. caves, *f.pl.* cabaret, *m.*

Wing, s. aile *f.*, (*fig.*) vol, *m.*, essor, *m.*, (*theat.*) coulisse, *f.* *On the* —, au vol. *To take* —, prendre son vol. *From — to* —, d'une aile à l'autre. *To have a breadth* or *spread of* —, avoir une envergure de. —*-case*, s. —*-shell*, s. élytre, *m.* —*-footed*, adj. aux pieds ailés. —*-stroke*, s. coup d'aile, *m.* —*-swift*, adj. au vol rapide. —*-transom*, s. barre d'arcasse supérieure, *f.*

Wing, va. munir d'ailes, donner *or* prêter des ailes à, porter *or* transporter (en volant), ajouter une aile *or* des ailes à, (*mil.*) flanquer (de), protéger (par), (*hunting*) blesser à l'aile. *To — one's flight*, prendre son vol, prendre son essor

Winged, adj. ailé, muni d'ailes, rapide, ailé

Wink, va. cligner de l'œil, faire un signe de l'œil, clignoter, fermer les yeux, (*at*,...) regarder du coin de l'œil, regarder, (*fig.*) fermer les yeux sur

Wink, s. clignement d'œil, *m.*, clin d'œil, *m.*, regard, *m.*, œillade, *f.* *None of us slept a* —, pas un de nous ne ferma l'œil. *To give a — to, to tip the* —, faire signe de l'œil à

Winker, s. œillère, *f.*

Winking, s. clignement d'œil, *m.*, clignotement, *m.*; — adj. clignotant, (*light*) tremblant, vacillant

Winner, s. gagnant, *m.*, celui, celle qui gagne

Winning, adj. gagnant, qui gagne, sûr, sûr du succès, (*fig.*) attrayant, plein d'attraits, séduisant. —*-post*, s. poteau d'arrivée, *m.*, but, *m.*

Winning, s. action de gagner, *f.* — s.pl. gain, *m.*

Winnow, va. vanner, éventer, (*examine*) éplucher, examiner

Winnower, s. vanneur, *m.*

Winnowing, s. vannage, *m.*, (*fig.*) triage, *m.*, examen, *m.*, épuration, *f.*

Winsome, adj. gai, riant, joyeux, charmant, agréable

Winter, s. hiver, *m.*; — adj. d'hiver

Winter, vn. hiverner, passer l'hiver; — va. conserver dans l'hiver

Winterly, adj. d'hiver, brumeux

Wintry, adj. d'hiver, des frimas, froid, brumeux

Wipe, va. essuyer, nettoyer, effacer. *To — away, to — off*, — *out*, essuyer, enlever, ôter, effacer. *To — off old scores*, régler un vieux compte

Wipe, s. action d'essuyer, d'épousseter, de nettoyer, *etc.*, *f.*, coup de torchon *or* d'éponge, *etc.*, *m.*, (*pop.*) mouchoir, *m.*, (*fig.*) coup de langue, *m.*, lardon, *m.*

Wire, s. fil de fer, *m.*, fil, *m.*, (*fig.*) télégraphe électrique, *m.* —*-cloth*, s., —*-gauze*, s. toile métallique, *f.* —*-drawer*, s. tréfileur, *m.*, tireur d'or *or* d'argent, *m.* —*-drawing*, action de tréfiler *or* de tirer. —*-drawing machine*, s. tréfilerie, *f.*, filière, *f.* —*-iron*, s. fer à tréfiler, *m.* —*-mark*, s. filigrane, *f.* —*-mill*, s. tréfilerie, *f.* —*-rope*, s. corde en fil métallique, *f.* —*-sieve*, s. crible à fond de fil de fer, *m.* —*-worker*, s. ouvrier en fil métallique, *m.*, treillageur, *m.*

Wiredraw, va. tréfiler, tirer, filer

Wiry, adj. de fil de fer, (*pers.*) maigre, effilé, nerveux

Wisdom, s. sagesse, *f.* —*-tooth*, s. dent de sagesse, *f.*

Wise, adj. sage, habile, capable, prudent. *You'll be none* or *never the wiser for it*, vous n'en saurez pas davantage, vous n'en serez pas plus avancé

Wise, s. façon, *f.*, manière, *f.*, sorte, *f.*, guise, *f.*

Wiseacre, s. pédant, *m.*, sot, *m.*, benêt, *m.*

Wisely, adv. sagement, avec sagesse

Wish, va.n. souhaiter, désirer, vouloir, désirer que, vouloir que, demander, souhaiter pour. *To — away*, désirer le départ de, la disparition de, vouloir voir partir *or* disparaître. *To — time away*, vouloir hâter le cours du temps. *To — for*, souhaiter, désirer, vouloir. *The long-wished-for day*, le jour tant désiré. *I — to say a word*, je désire dire un mot. *To — well to*, vouloir du bien à, être bien disposé pour. *To — ill to*, en vouloir à, être mal disposé pour

Wish, s. souhait, *m.*, désir, *m.*, vœu, *m.*, demande, *f.* *To form a* —, faire un souhait

Wishful, adj. désireux, avide. *A — eye*, un regard avide

Wishfully, adv. avidement, ardemment, passionnément

Wisp, s. bouchon, *m.*, touffe, *f.*

Wistful, adj. pensif, attentif, sérieux, désireux, ardent, de regret

Wistfully, adv. attentivement, fixement, ardemment, avec désir, avec regret

Wit, vn. à savoir, savoir

Wit, s. esprit, *m.*, (*pers.*) bel esprit, *m.*, homme d'esprit, *m.*, femme d'esprit, *f.*, jugement, *m.*, bon sens, *m.* *To be at one's —'s* or *wits' end*, être au bout de son rouleau *or* de son latin, être à bout d'expédients. *To have lost one's —s*, avoir perdu l'esprit. *To be out of one's —s*, avoir perdu la tête, l'esprit, la raison. *To frighten one out of one's —s*, faire perdre la tête de frayeur

Witch, s. sorcière, *f.*

Witchcraft, s. sorcellerie, *f.*, magie, *f.*, charmes, *m. pl.*, sortilèges, *m.pl.*, maléfices, *m.pl.*

Witchery, s. sorcellerie, *f.*, magie, *f.*, charme, *m.*, sortilège, *m.*

With, prep. avec, de, avec, (*fig.*) par, à, entre les mains de, (*by striking*) à coups de, avec, contre, (*in*) chez, parmi, à la maison de, à la cour de, (*near*) auprès de. — *one another*, l'un avec l'autre. *One — the other*, l'un avec l'autre, l'un portant l'autre. *Filled* —, rempli de, plein de. *To fight — swords*, se battre à l'épée, — *a stick*, avec un bâton, à coups de bâton

Withal, adv. avec tout cela, en outre, aussi, d'ailleurs, de plus, en même temps

Withdraw, va. retirer, rappeler, ôter, éloigner, enlever. *To — one's self from*, se retirer de; — vn. se retirer, s'éloigner (de), s'en aller (de), quitter (...)

Withdrawal, s. retraite, *f.*, action de retirer, *f.*, (*law*) départ, *m.*, retrait, *m.*

Withe, s. osier, *m.*, hart, *f.*

Wither, vn. se dessécher, se flétrir, se faner, dépérir, languir; — va. dessécher, flétrir, faner

Withering, adj. qui se fane, qui se flétrit, qui flétrit, qui dessèche, mortel, foudroyant, (*look*) méprisant

Witheringly, adv. en se fanant, de manière à dessécher *or* à flétrir, (*fig.*) d'une manière foudroyante

Withers, s.pl. garrot, *m.*

Withhold, va. retenir, empêcher, arrêter, comprimer, refuser, écarter, retirer, (*information*) cacher

Withholder, s. celui, celle qui retient, *m.*, détenteur, *m.*

Within, prep. en dedans de, dans, dans les limites de, dans les bornes de, en deçà de, à la portée de, à moins de, à, avant, il y a, depuis, dans le cœur de. — *the frontier*, en deçà des frontières. — *a short distance*, à peu de distance. — *a few hours*, dans quelques heures. — *ten days' sail of*, à dix jours de navigation de

Within, adv. à l'intérieur, en dedans, dedans, à la maison, chez soi, (*fig.*) dans l'âme, dans le cœur. *From* —, de l'intérieur, du dedans. *Is he* —? est-il à la maison *or* chez lui?

Without, prep. en dehors de, hors de, au dehors de, à l'extérieur de, au delà de, en dehors de, sans, sans que, à moins de. — *doors*, au dehors, hors de la maison. — *my knowing it*, à mon insu. — *being mad*, à moins d'être fou

Without, adv. en dehors, au dehors, extérieurement, à l'extérieur. *From* —, du dehors

Without, conj. à moins que, sans que

Withstand, va. résister à, s'opposer à, combattre

Withstander, s. qui résiste, adversaire, *m.* antagoniste, *m.*

Withy, adj. d'osier, flexible, souple

Witless, adj. sot, imbécile

Witling, s. petit esprit, *m.*, (*ironic.*) bel esprit, *m.*

Witness, s. témoignage, *m.*, évidence, *f.*, (*pers.*) témoin, *m.*, déposant, *m.* *To bear — to*, porter *or* rendre témoignage de, témoigner de, attester, être témoin. *False* —, faux témoignage, *m.*, faux témoin, *m.* *In — whereof*, en témoignage de quoi. *To call* or *take to* —, prendre à témoin, attester, appeler en témoignage. *To take as a* —, prendre pour témoin. *God is my* —, Dieu m'est témoin. *In the —-box*, sur le banc des témoins. — *for the prosecution, crown* —, s. témoin à charge, *m.* — *for the prisoner*, s. témoin à décharge, *m.*

Witness, va. témoigner de, porter *or* rendre témoignage de, attester, signer, comme témoin, attester, être témoin *or* spectateur de, voir, assister à, contempler. — *my hand and seal*, donné sous mon seing et mon sceau; — vn. témoigner, porter témoignage, certifier véritable

Witted, adj. à l'esprit, à l'intelligence

Witticism, s. bon mot, *m.*, trait spirituel, *m.*, saillie, *f.*, pointe, *f.*

Wittily, adv. avec esprit, spirituellement, ingénieusement

Wittiness, s. esprit, *m.*, sel, *m.*

Wittingly, adv. sciemment, intentionnellement, à dessein

Witty, adj. spirituel, d'esprit, qui a de l'esprit, intelligent

Wizard, s. sorcier, *m.*, magicien, *m.*, (*juggler*) physicien, *m.*, prestidigitateur, *m.*

Woad, s. guède, *f.*, pastel, *m.*

Wo, Woe, s. malheur, *m.*, douleur, *f.*, chagrin, *m.*, peine, *f.* — *-begone*, adj. pitoyable, accablé de douleur, vaincu par le malheur. — *be to...!* malheur à...! — *is me!* malheureux que je suis!

Woful, Woeful, adj. malheureux, triste, pitoyable, piteux, douloureux

Woefully, adv. tristement, douloureusement, piteusement, pitoyablement

Woefulness, s. misère, *f.*, tristesse, *f.*, douleur, *f.*, infortune, *f.*, malheur, *m.*

Wold, s. bois, *m.*, forêt, *f.*, campagne, *f.*

Wolf, s. loup, m. *She* —, s. louve, *f.* —*'s cub*, louveteau. — *-hunting*, s. chasse au loup, *f.* — *-dog*, s. chien de berger, *m.*, chien loup, *m.* —*'s claw*, s. lycopode, *m.*

Wolfish, adj. de loup, (*fig.*) de loup, rapace, avide

Woman, s. femme, *f.* — *-cook*, s. cuisinière, *f.* — *-hater*, s. mysogyne, *m.*, ennemi des femmes, *m.*

Womanhood, s. âge de femme, *m.*, condition *or* qualité de femme, *f.*

Womanish, adj. de femme, féminin, efféminé, mou, faible, pusillanime

Womankind, s. femmes, *f.pl.* sexe, *m.*

Womanly, adv. *see* WOMANISH

Womb, s. matrice, *f.*, (*fig.*) sein, *m.*, flancs, *m.pl.*

Wonder, s. étonnement, *m.*, surprise, *f.*, ébahissement, *m.*, admiration, *f.*, chose étonnante, *f.*, merveille, *f.*, prodige, *m.*, miracle, *m.* — *-struck*, adj. frappé d'étonnement, émerveillé. *To do or work —s*, faire des merveilles *or* des prodiges, faire merveille. — *-worker*, s. faiseur de prodiges. — *-working*, qui fait des prodiges

Wonder, vn. s'étonner, s'émerveiller, être surpris, s'ébahir, vouloir savoir, être curieux de savoir, se demander. *I — whether he will come*, je voudrais savoir s'il viendra. *I — how he knew it*, je suis curieux de savoir comment il l'a appris

Wonderful, adj. étonnant, merveilleux, surprenant, prodigieux

Wonderfully, adv. étonnamment, merveilleusement, d'une manière surprenante, prodigieusement. — *well*, à merveille, merveilleusement bien

Wondering, adj. étonné

Wondrous, adj. *see* WONDERFUL

Wont, vn. *see* USE

Wont, s. habitude, *f.*, coutume, *f.*

Won't, *see* WILL NOT

Wonted, adj. accoutumé, habituel, ordinaire

Woo, va. faire la cour à, courtiser, rechercher en mariage, (*fig.*) inviter, solliciter, appeler, demander; — vn. faire la cour, se faire la cour

Wood, s. bois, *m.*, forêt, *f.*, (*cask*) fût, *m.*, pièce, *f.* — *-cut*, s. gravure sur bois, *f.*, vignette, *f.* — *-cutter*, s. bûcheron, *m.* — *-engraver*, s. graveur sur bois, *m.* — *-engraving*, s. gravure sur bois, *f.* — *-lark*, s. alouette des bois, *f.* — *-louse*, s. cloporte, *m.*, mille-pieds, *m.* — *-mouse*, s. mulot, *m.* — *-pigeon*, s. pigeon ramier, *m.* — *-seller*, s. marchand de bois, *m.* — *-sorrel*, s. oseille des bois, *f.* — *-spite*, s. pic vert, *m.* — *-work*, s. boiserie, *f.* — *-yard*, s. chantier, *m.*

Wood, adj. de bois

Woodbine, s. chèvrefeuille, *m.*

Woodcock, s. bécasse, *f.*

Wooded, adj. boisé

Wooden, adj. de bois, en bois

Woodiness, s. nature boisée, *f.*

Woodland, s. pays boisés, *m.pl.* bois, *m.pl.*, forêts, *f.pl.*, terre de bruyère, *f.*

Woodland, adj. de bois, boisé, (*fig.*) agreste, rustique

Woodman, s. garde forestier, *m.*, (*hunter*) chasseur des bois, *m.*, (*cutter*) bûcheron, *m.*

Woodpecker, Woodpeck, s. pic, *m.*, pic vert, *m.*, pivert, *m.*

Woodruff, s. petit muguet des bois, *m.*, aspérule, *f.*

Woody, adj. boisé, couvert de bois, de bois, ligneux, sylvain, agreste

Wooer, s. amant, *m.*, soupirant, *m.*, prétendant, *m.*

Woof, s. trame, *f.*, tissu, *m.*

Wooing, s. cour, *f.*

Wool, s. laine, *f.*, lainage, *m.*, duvet, *m.* — *-comber*, s. cardeur de laine, *m.* — *-combing*, s. cardage *or* peignage de laine, *m.* — *-combing machine*, s. peigneuse, *f.* — *-broker*, s. commissionnaire en laine, *m.* — *-driver*, s. marchand de laine, *m.* — *-dyed*, adj. teint en laine. — *-gathering*, s. rêvasserie, *f.*, sotte entreprise, *f.*, chimère, *f.* — *-grower*, s. éleveur de bêtes à laine, *m.* — *-hall*, s. marché aux laines, *m.* — *-pack*, s. ballot de laine, *m.* — *-packer*, — *-winder*, s. emballeur de laine, *m.* — — *-sack*, s. sac *or* ballot de laine, *m.* — *-staple*, s. marché aux laines, *m.* — *-stapler*, s. négociant en laines, *m.* — *-trade*, s. commerce des laines, *m.*

Woollen, adj. de laine, à laine. — *-cloth*, s. drap, *m.* — *-goods*, — *-stuffs*, s.pl. étoffes de laine, *f.pl.*, lainages, *m.pl.*, draperie, *f.* — *-draper*, s. marchand drapier, *m.*

Woolly, adj. laineux, de laine, couvert, (*hair*) crépu, laineux

Word, s. mot, *m.*, parole, *f.*, (*theol.*) Verbe, *m.*, —*s*, *in anger*, paroles irritées, *f.pl.*, discussion, *f.*, (*promise*) affirmation, *f.*, parole, *f.*, promesse, *f.*, (*watch*) mot d'ordre, *m.*, signal, *m.*, (*news*) nouvelle, *f.* *The next* —, le mot qui suit. *In a few —s*, en quelques mots. *A — with you, sir*, un mot, monsieur. *Not to say a* —, ne dire mot. — *for* —, mot pour mot, mot à mot. *A — to the wise*, à bon entendeur salut. *To take a person at one's* —, prendre qq.'un au mot. — *-book*, s. vocabulaire, *m.*, dictionnaire, *m.* — *-catcher*, s. chicaneur, *m.*, éplucheur de mots, *m.* *In — and deed*, en parole et en action. *Full of —s*, plein de discours, verbeux. *A man of few —s*, un homme sobre en paroles. *Don't drop a — of that*, ne soufflez pas un mot de cela. *By — of mouth*, de vive voix. *To have (high) —s*, se prendre de paroles. *High —s*, des paroles irritées, de gros mots. *You may take my — for it*, vous pouvez en croire ma parole. *Upon my* —, sur ma parole. *He is a man of his* —, il est homme de parole. *He is as good as his* —, il n'a qu'une parole. *To break, to keep one's* —, manquer à, tenir sa parole. *Give the — through*, faites passer le mot d'ordre. *To bring* — (*to*, à), faire savoir à, apporter la nouvelle *or* l'avis, donner avis, prévenir

Word, va. exprimer, énoncer, rendre, exposer, rédiger par écrit

Wordily, adv. avec verbosité

Wordiness, s. verbosité, *f.*, prolixité, *f.*

Wording, s. expression, *f.*, énonciation, *f.*, (*of a letter*) termes, *m.pl.*, (*of a problem*) énoncé, *m.*

Wordless, adj. sans paroles

Wordy, adj. prolixe, verbeux

Work, vn. travailler, (*mechan.*) fonctionner, jouer, aller, agir, s'agiter, (*on, upon*, sur) agir, opérer, avoir de l'effet, (*liquids*) travailler, fermenter, être en fermentation, (*the sea*) s'agiter, se soulever, (*wood*) travailler. *To — hard, well*, travailler ferme, bien travailler. *To — with a will*, avoir du cœur à l'ouvrage, travailler de tout cœur. *The lock works well*, la serrure joue bien. *The charm works*, le charme opère. *To — to windward*, louvoyer. *To — against*, travailler contre, s'opposer à, entraver. *To — about*, s'agiter, se démener. *To — at*, travailler à, s'occuper de. *To — down*, faire descendre. *To — into*, entrer dans, s'insinuer dans, (*mech.*) engrener. *To — into each other*, s'engrener. *To — out*, sortir peu à peu, se dégager peu à peu. *To — round*, tourner, virer lentement. *To — through*, traverser avec peine *or* à force de travail. *To — up*, s'élever avec peine *or* à force de travail. *To — upon*, travailler à, agir sur, exciter, travailler, agiter, émouvoir; — va. travailler, faire travailler, façonner, mettre en œuvre, (*indust.*) exploiter, (*result*) produire, faire naître, (*one's way*) se faire, se frayer, s'ouvrir, se créer, (*arithm.*) faire (à), faire fonctionner, faire jouer, faire aller, mettre en mouvement, (*machine*), agiter, remuer, faire aller, (*nav.*) manœuvrer, (*linen*) broder, ouvrager, (*stones*) tailler, (*print*) tirer. *To — one's passage* or *way home*, travailler pour payer son voyage de retour. *To — one's way*, (*up to*, jusqu'à) se frayer un chemin, s'ouvrir un passage, (*into*, dans) s'insinuer. *To — down*, réduire. *To — in or into*, faire entrer, tisser dans, entrelacer dans, broder, (*fig.*) insinuer, donner. *To — into a fever*, donner la fièvre. *To — off*, écarter, éloigner, se débarrasser de... par le travail, (*a debt*) s'acquitter en travaillant. *To — out*, travailler à, accomplir, effacer, payer par son travail, (*a problem*) résoudre. *To — up*, façonner, travailler, employer, user, consommer, épuiser, (*fig.*) exciter, soulever, porter, faire arriver, monter

Work, s. travail, *m.*, ouvrage, *m.*, tâche, *f.*, besogne, *f.*, œuvre, *f.*, production, *f.*, manière d'agir, *f.*, traitement, *m.*, — s.pl., (*mil.*) ouvrages, *m.pl.*, travaux, *m.pl.*, usine, *f.*, manufacture, *f.*, fabrique, *f.*, rouages, *m.pl.*, mécanisme, *m.*, (*nav.*) œuvres, *f.pl.* *Servant of all* —, s., domestique à tout faire, *f.* *A good day's* —, une bonne journée. *A piece of* —, un ouvrage, (*fam.*) un chef-d'œuvre, de la belle besogne, (*noise*) du tapage. *To be at* —, être au travail *or* à l'ouvrage, travailler. *To have hard — of it*, avoir du mal. *To leave off* —, cesser le travail. *To set to* —, mettre, se mettre à l'ouvrage, à l'œuvre. *To take in* —, prendre de l'ouvrage chez soi. *To throw out of* —, priver de travail, faire chômer. *He made sad — of it*, il fit de la triste besogne. *How did you go to* —? comment vous y êtes-vous pris?

Work-... adj. de travail, à ouvrage. — *-bag*, s. sac à ouvrage, *m.* — *-box*, s. boîte à ouvrage, *f.*, nécessaire, *m.* *The — -people*, — *-folk*, s. les ouvriers, *m.pl.* les travailleurs, *m.pl.* —-*table*, s. table à ouvrage, *f.* —-*woman*, s. couturière, *f.*, ouvrière, *f.*

Work-day, s. jour de travail, *m.*, jour ouvrable, *m.* *My* —-*day clothes*, mes habits de travail

Worker, s. travailleur, *m.*, -euse, *f.* ouvrier, *m.*, -ère, *f.*

Workhouse, s. atelier, *m.*, maison des pauvres, *f.*, asile, *m.*, pénitencier, *m.*

Working, s. travail, *m.*, (action de) travailler *f.*, exploitation, *f.*, œuvre, *f.*, (*of machines*) jeu, *m.*, fonction, *f.*, opération, *f.*, mouvement, *m.*, (*features*) contraction, *f.*, (*of the soul*) aspirations, *f.pl.*, (*liquids*) fermentation, *f.*, (*print.*) tirage, *m.*

Working, adj. laborieux, ouvrier qui travaille, de travail, d'exploitation, (*mach.*) en mouvement, qui fonctionne, (*fig.*) vivant, animé, en mouvement. *The — classes*, les classes ouvrières. —-*place*, s. —-*stock*, s. champ, *m.*, matériel d'exploitation, *m.* —-*gear*, s. pièce de manœuvre, *f.* —-*wheels*, s. roues motrices, *f.pl.*

Workman, s. ouvrier, *m.*, artisan, *m.*, travailleur, *m.*

Workmanship, s. ouvrage, *m.*, travail, *m.*, œuvre, *f.*, façon, *f.*

Workshop, s. atelier, *m.*

World, s. monde, *m.*, univers, *m.* *All the* —, le monde entier, tout le monde. *For all the* —, pour tout au monde, (*fam.*) absolument. *All over the* —, (dans) le monde entier. *To the —'s end*, au bout du monde. *The old* —, *the new* —, l'ancien monde, le nouveau monde. *For the* —, *for the whole* —, pour tout le monde. *In the* —, dans le monde, *All the precautions in the* —, toute la prudence du monde. *Nothing in the* —, rien au monde. *To know the* —, savoir le monde, avoir du monde. *It's the way of the* —, ainsi va le monde. *To begin the* —, débuter dans le monde, entrer dans la vie. — *of sighs*, tout un monde de soupirs. — *without end*, jusqu'à la fin des siècles. —-*wide*, adj. vaste comme le monde, vaste

Worldliness, s. nature mondaine, *f.*, caractère mondain, *m.*, mondanité, *f.*, frivolité, *f.*, prudence (mondaine), *f.*

Worldling, s. mondain, *m.*, -e, *f.*, âme mondaine, *f.*, homme mondain, *m.*, femme mondaine, *f.*

Worldly, adj. de ce monde, du monde, d'ici-bas, terrestre, humain, séculier, temporel, mondain, attaché au monde, égoïste, frivole

Worm, s. ver, *m.*, ver de terre, *m.*, vermisseau, *m.*, chenille, *f.*, larve, *f.*, (*remorse*) ver rongeur, *m.*, (*screws*) filet de vis, *m.*, filière, *f.*, tarand, *m.*, (*distill.*) serpentin, *m.*, (*artill.*) tire-bourre, *m.* —-*eaten*, adj. mangé, piqué, rongé par les vers, vermoulu. —-*fence*, s. clôture en zigzag, *f.* —-*like*, adj. comme un ver, vermiculaire, en spirale, (*anat.*) verniforme. —-*oil*, s. huile vermifuge, *f.*, —-*powder*, s. poudre vermifuge, *f.* —-*wheel*, s. roue à dents tarandées, *f.* —-*screw*, s. tire-bourre, *m.* —-*drawer*, s. tire-étoupes, *m.*

Worm, vn. ramper, (*fig.*) s'insinuer, travailler sourdement; — va. miner, pousser lentement, insinuer, (*a dog*) éverrer. *To — one's self into*, s'insinuer dans, se glisser dans. *I'll — it out of him*, je saurai lui tirer les vers du nez

Wormwood, s. absinthe, *f.*

Wormy, adj. plein de vers, (*fig.*) terrestre, vil, grossier

Worrier, s. personne tourmentante, *f.*, taquin, *m.*, -e, *f.*

Worry, va. harceler, (*fam.*) tarabuster, tourmenter, taquiner, tracasser, fatiguer, ennuyer, (*dogs*) déchirer, mordre; — vn. se tourmenter, se plaindre

Worry, s. tracasserie, *f.*, agitation, *f.*, fatigue, *f.*, ennui, *m.*, (*pers.*) ennuyeux, *m.*

Worse, adj. pire, plus mauvais, plus malade, plus mal, plus méchant. *To be — than useless*, être plus qu'inutile. *To be the — for, all the — for the rain*, valoir moins, avoir perdu de sa valeur par suite de la pluie. *He was (much) the — for liquor*, il avait bu, il était ivre. *You are none the — for that*, vous n'êtes pas plus malheureux pour cela, vous n'en êtes pas moins avancé. *Are you any the — for it?* vous en trouvez-vous plus mal? — *and* —, de plus en plus mauvais, de pis en pis, de plus en plus malade, de plus en plus mal, de plus en plus méchant. *To grow* —, *to get* —, *to become* —, devenir pire *or* plus mauvais, s'empirer, s'aggraver, (*pers.*) aller plus mal, aller de plus en plus mal, aller de mal en pis. *To think the — of*, avoir plus mauvaise opinion de. *For the* —, *to the* —, en mal. *To alter all things for the* —, changer tout en mal. *What is* —? qui est pis? *For better and* —, quoi qu'il advienne. *To take for better and* —, épouser. — *off*, plus malheureux, moins riche

Worse, adv. pis, plus mal. — *than ever*, pis que jamais. *So much the* —, tant pis. — *and* —, de pis en pis, de plus en plus mal

Worship, s. dignité, *f.*, éminence, *f.*, honneur, *m.*, considération, *f.* *His* —, son Honneur. *Please your* —, n'en déplaise à votre Honneur. *Divine* —, le culte divin

Worship, va.n. adorer, rendre un culte à, (*fig.*) respecter, honorer

Worshipful, adj. honorable. *The — mayor*, l'honorable maire, M. le maire

Worshipper, s. adorateur, *m.*, -trice, *f.*

Worst, adj. (le) plus mauvais, (le) pire, (le) plus malade, (le) plus méchant. *To have the — part* or *share*, être le plus mal partagé

Worst, s. pis, *m.*, plus mal, *m.*, pire, *m.*, pis aller, *m.*, dessous, *m.*, désavantage, *m.* *If the — come to the* —, *suppose the* —, si les choses en viennent au pis, pour prendre *or* mettre les choses au pis, au pis aller. *The — of it is that...*, le pis c'est que... *At the* —, *in the event of the* —, au pis aller. *He is at the* —, il est au plus mal. *Do your* —, faites ce que vous voudrez. *To have the — of it*, avoir le dessous

Worst, va. mettre en déroute, battre, défaire, vaincre. *To be worsted*, être mis en déroute, *etc.*, avoir le dessous

Worsted, s. laine, *f.* —-*stockings*, s. bas de laine, *m.* —-*yarn*, s. fil de laine peignée, *m.*

Worsted, adj. de laine

Wort, s. herbe, *f.*, herbe à..., chou, *m.*, (*malt*) moût, *m.*

Worth, s. valeur, *f.*, prix, *m.*, mérite, *m.*, vertu, *f.*

Worth, adj. qui vaut, qui a la valeur de, qui mérite, qui est digne. *To be* —, valoir. *To be — nothing*, ne rien valoir ne valoir rien. *Not to be — much*, valoir bien peu. *To be — money*, (*th.*) avoir de la valeur, (*pers.*) avoir de l'argent. *It is — any money*, cela n'a pas de prix, c'est impayable. *It is — a pound if it is — a penny*, cela vaut vingt francs comme un sou. *What is he* —, combien a-t-il de fortune? — *notice*, digne d'attention. *It is not — mentioning, seeing*, cela ne vaut pas la peine qu'on en parle, d'être vu. *Anything — knowing or having*, tout ce qui vaut la peine qu'on le sache ou qu'on le possède

Worthily, adv. dignement, à juste titre

Worthiness, s. mérite, *m.*

Worthless, adj. sans valeur, sans mérite, sans valeur, indigne, méprisable. *A — fellow*, un vaurien, *m.*

Worthlessness, s. manque de valeur, *m.*, (*fig.*) manque de mérite, *m.*, indignité, *f.*, nature méprisable, *f.*, bassesse, *f.*

Worthy, adj. digne (de), qui mérite, de mérite

Worthy, s. grand homme, *m.*, héros, *m.*, (*fam.*) sommités, *f.pl.*, élite, *f.*

Would, (*sign of the condit.*) ..., rais, etc., (*exclam.*) plût à ... *He — pay it now, if he could*, il le payerait maintenant, s'il le pouvait. *He — have paid it, if ...*, il l'aurait or il l'eût payé, si ..., *I don't think he — do it*, je ne pense pas qu'il le fasse. *The lock — go wrong, do all he could*, la serrure ne voulait pas aller *or* persistait à ne pas aller, quoi qu'il fît. — *to God*, — *to heaven that...!* plût à Dieu que...! plût au ciel que ...!

Would-be, adj. prétendu, soi-disant. *A — wit*, un prétendu bel esprit

Wound, s. blessure, *f.*, plaie, *f.* *To give a — to, to inflict a — upon*, faire une blessure à

Wound, va. blesser, faire une blessure or des blessures à, porter atteinte à, (*fig.*) blesser, offenser

Wrangle, vn. se disputer, se quereller, se chamailler. *To — on*, continuer à se quereller

Wrangle, Wrangling, s. querelle, *f.*, dispute, *f.*

Wrangler, s. querelleur, *m.*, -euse, *f.*, (*univ.*) élève de la première série. *Senior* —, premier sorti

Wrap, va. rouler, enrouler, entortiller, envelopper, (*fig.*) envelopper, entourer, comprendre, contenir, ravir, transporter

Wrapper, s. (*pers.*) qui enveloppe, (*things*) enveloppe, *f.*, toile, *f.*, papier, *m.*, (*pamphlet*) couverture, *f.*, (*papers*) chemise, *f.*, (*dressing-gown*) robe-de-chambre, *f.*, douillette, *f.*, peignoir, *m.*, (*for the face*) cache-nez, *m.*

Wrath, s. courroux, *m.*, fureur, *f.*, colère, *f.* *To rouse the — of*, exciter le courroux de, courroucer

Wrathful, adj. courroucé, en colère, irrité, furieux, emporté. *To grow* —, se courroucer

Wrathfully, adv. avec courroux

Wreak, va. accomplir, exécuter, assouvir, satisfaire, venger, châtier. *To — one's resentment on*, se venger de, tirer vengeance de

Wreath, s. guirlande, *f.*, couronne, *f.*, tresse, *f.*

Wreathe, va. tresser, entrelacer, entortiller, enrouler, arranger en guirlandes, enguirlander, entourer, couronner; — vn. s'entrelacer, s'enrouler

Wreathed, adj. entrelacé, festonné, (*archit.*) torse

Wreck, s. naufrage, *m.*, navire qui a fait naufrage, *m.*, navire perdu, *m.*, débris, *m.*, (*law*) épave *f.*, (*fig.*) ruine, *f.*, destruction, *f.*, perte, *f.* *To suffer* —, faire naufrage

A mere —, un vrai débris. *To go to* —, se perdre

Wreck, va. faire faire naufrage à, (*fig.*) ruiner, perdre

Wrecker, s. ravageur, *m.*, pilleur d'épaves, *m.*

Wren, s. roitelet, *m.*

Wrench, va. arracher, enlever, tordre, (*fig.*) forcer, fausser

Wrench, s. effort violent, *m.*, violente secousse, *f.*, arrachement, *m.*, (*key*) clef anglaise, *f.*, clef à dévisser, *f.*

Wrest, va. arracher, enlever, extorquer, (*sense*) forcer, fausser, tordre

Wrest, s. torsion, *f.*, effort violent, *m.*, violente secousse, *f.*, (*fig.*) action de forcer *or* de fausser, *f.*

Wrestle, vn. lutter, combattre, disputer (à)

Wrestler, s. lutteur, *m.*, athlète, *m.*

Wrestling, s. lutte, *f.* —*-match*, s. lutte, *f.*, assaut, *m.*

Wretch, s. malheureux, *m.*, -euse, *f.*, infortuné, *m.*, -e, *f.*, pauvre hère, *m.*, pauvre diable, *m.*, misérable, *m.*, scélérat, *m.*, -e, *f.*

Wretched, adj. misérable, malheureux, -se, infortuné, pauvre, souffrant, (*stupid*) ridicule, pitoyable. *He looked so* —, tant il faisait peine à voir

Wretchedly, adv. misérablement, malheureusement, pauvrement, mal, indignement

Wretchedness, s. misère, *f.*, malheur, *m.*, infortune, *f.*, maux, *m.pl.*, pauvreté, *f.*, caractère misérable *or* pitoyable, *m.*, nature mesquine, *f.*

Wriggle, vn. se tortiller, se démener, s'agiter, se remuer, frétiller, dérailler; — va. tortiller, remuer, (*into*, dans) faire entrer, insinuer. *To* — *one's self into*, s'insinuer dans, se faufiler dans. *To* — *one's self out of*, sortir de, se tirer de

Wriggler, s. qui se tortille, *etc.*

Wriggling, s. tortillement, *m.*, mouvement continuel, *m.*, frétillement, *m.*, oscillation, *f.*

Wright, s. ouvrier, *m.*

Wring, va. tordre, se tordre, (*out of*, de) exprimer, faire sortir, presser, (*hands*) serrer, presser, (*from*) arracher (à), extorquer (de), (*heart*) torturer, mettre à la torture, (*sense*) fausser, altérer. *To* — *off*, arracher. *To* — *one's hands in despair*, se tordre les mains de désespoir

Wringing, s. action de tordre, *f.*, torsion, *f.*, (*fig.*) remords, *m.*, tourment, *m.*

Wringing, adj. rapace

Wrinkle, s. ride, *f.*, faux pli, *m.*, pli, *m.*

Wrinkle, va. rider, plisser, (*eye-brows*) froncer, (*stuff*) plisser, chiffonner. *To* — *up*, rider, plisser; — vn. se rider

Wrist, s. poignet, *m.*

Wristband, s. poignet, *m.*

Writ, s. écriture, *f.*, écrit, *m.*, ouvrage, *m.*, (*law*) ordonnance, *f.*, mandat, *m.*, ordre, *m.*, assignation, *f.*, prise de corps, *f.*, (*parl.*) lettre de convocation, *f.* *Holy* —, les saintes Ecritures, la parole de Dieu. *To serve a* — *upon*, *to serve with a* —, signifier un mandat *or* une assignation à. — *of error*, recours pour cause d'erreur, *m.*

Write, va. écrire, mettre en écrit, graver, tracer. *To* — *a good hand*, avoir une belle main, une belle écriture. *To* — *one's self*, se signer. *To* — *back*, répondre. *To* — *down*, écrire, mettre par écrit, prendre note de, dire qu'on est, proclamer, faire taire, écraser par la plume. *To* — *one's self down*, se dire, se proclamer, s'avilir par ses écrits. *To* — *off*, écrire rapidement, écrire. *To* — *out*, écrire d'un bout à l'autre, retranscrire, copier; — vn. écrire, faire sa correspondance, faire son courrier. *To* — *small*, *large*, écrire fin, gros. *To* — *for*, mander par écrit, faire venir, écrire à la place de *or* en faveur de. *To* — *off to*, écrire tout de suite à. *To* — *on*, continuer d'écrire. *To* — *up to*, s'élever par ses écrits jusqu'à

Writer, s. personne qui écrit, *f.*, écrivain, *m.*, auteur, *m.*, commis aux écritures, *m.*

Writership, s. charge d'avoué, *f.*

Writhe, vn. se tordre, souffrir cruellement; — va. tordre, torturer, fausser

Writing, s. écriture, *f.*, écrit, *m.*, document, *m.*, ouvrage, *m.*, style, *m.*, (*law*) document, *m.*, acte, *m.*, inscription, *f.*

Writing, adj. d'écriture, à écrire. —*-book*, s. cahier d'écriture, *m.* —*-desk*, s. pupitre, *m.*, bureau, *m.* —*-master*, s. maître d'écriture, *m.* —*-paper*, s. papier à écrire, *m.* —*-school*, s. classe d'écriture, *f.* —*-table*, s. bureau, *m.*, table à écrire, *f.*

Wrong, adj. mal, injuste, mauvais, impropre, faux, incorrect, erroné, inexact, qui a tort. *That is* —, voilà qui est mal. —*-doing*, s. mal, *m.*, injustice, *f.* *The* — *door*, *volume*, la porte, le volume qu'il ne fallait pas, une autre porte, un autre volume. *The* — *side out*, à l'envers. *It went down the* — *way*, j'ai avalé de travers. *A* — *expression*, une expression impropre. — *ideas*, de fausses idées. *The* — *meaning*, un sens inexact. *To be* —, *very* —, avoir tort, avoir grand tort. *To set* —, égarer, tromper, mettre en désaccord

Wrong, s. mal, *m.*, injustice, *f.*, tort, *m.*, dommage, *m.*, préjudice, *m.*, injure, *f.*, atteinte, *f.*, erreur, *f.*, faute, *f.* *To do* — *to*, être injuste pour *or* envers, faire injure à, outrager, faire du tort à, faire *or* causer du dommage à, porter atteinte à, avoir tort de. *To be in the* —, avoir tort, être dans l'erreur, être dans son tort

Wrong, adv. mal, à tort, injustement

Wrong, va. faire du tort à, léser, nuire à, être injuste pour *or* envers, outrager, faire injure à

Wrongful, adj. injuste, inique, déloyal, nuisible

Wrongfully, Wrongly, adv. injustement, d'une manière inique, à tort, à faux

Wrongheaded, adj. entêté, obstiné, opiniâtre, têtu, qui a l'esprit de travers

Wrought, past part. adj. travaillé, façonné, ciselé, forgé

Wry, adj. tordu, de travers, oblique, tors, tortu, (*fig.*) détourné du vrai sens, faux, fausse, altéré. *To have a* — *neck*, *a* — *mouth*, avoir le cou tors, la bouche de travers. *To make a* — *face*, — *faces*, faire la grimace, des grimaces

Wryneck, s. torticoli, *m*

X

X, s. X, x, *m.*, dix

Xebeck, s. chébec, *m.*

Y

Y, s. Y, y, *m.*

Yacht, s. yacht, *m.* *The* — *club*, le club des yachts

Yachting, s. excursion à bord d'un yacht, *f.*, voyage en yacht, *m.*

Yam, s. igname, *f.*

Yard, s. mètre, *m.*, (*nav.*) vergue, *f.*, (*archit.*) poutre, *f.*, carré, *m.* *Man the* —*s!* sur les vergues! —*-arm*, s. bout de vergue, *m.*, (*court*) cour, *f.*, préau, *m.*, cour de prison, *f.*, (*work*) chantier, *m.*

Yarn, s. fil, *m.* *Rope* —, s. fil de caret, *m.* *Spun-* —, s. bitord, *m.* *To spin a long* —, *long* —*s*, débiter une longue histoire, de longues histoires, (*pop.*) en dégoiser

Yarrow, s. mille-feuille, *f.*

Yataghan, s. yatagan, *m.*

Yawl, s. yole, *f.*

Yawn, vn. bâiller, s'ouvrir béant, s'entr'ouvrir, (*after*, *at*, après) bayer

Yawn, Yawning, s. bâillement, *m.*, ouverture, *f.*, faire un bâillement

Yawning, adj. bâillant

Yea, adv. oui, en vérité, oui vraiment

Yean, vn. mettre bas, agneler

Year, s. année, *f.*, an, *m.* —*-book*, s. annuaire, *m.* *A* —, un an, par an. *At forty pounds a* —, à quarante livres sterling par an. *By the* —, à l'année. — *after* —, *for* —*s together*, une année après une autre, plusieurs années de suite. — *in*, — *out*, *from year's end to year's end*, d'un bout de l'année à l'autre. *One* — *with another*, bon an, mal an, année commune *or* moyenne, une année dans l'autre

To be in —*s*. être (fort) âgé, être chargé d'ans. *Of late* —*s*, dans ces dernières années, depuis quelques années

Yearling, s. adj. (agneau, veau, cheval, *etc.*) d'un an

Yearly, adj. annuel, de chaque année, de tous les ans

Yearly, adv. chaque année, annuellement

Yearn, vn. s'émouvoir, être ému de tendresse (pour), se sentir attiré (vers), soupirer (pour), souhaiter (. . .)

Yearning, s. élan, *m.*, émotion, *f.*, tendresse, *f.*, compassion, *f.*, (*fig.*) désir ardent (de), *m.*, élan de l'âme (vers), *m.*, aspiration (pour), *f.*

Yeast, s. levûre, *f.*, ferment, *m.*

Yell, vn. hurler, pousser des hurlements, crier

Yell, s. hurlement, *m.*, cri sauvage, *m.*, cri, *m.*, vocifération, *f.*

Yelling, s. hurlement, *m.*

Yellow, adj. s. jaune, *m.*

Yellowish, adj. jaunâtre

Yellowness, s. couleur jaune, *f.*

Yellows, s.pl. jaunisse, *f.*

Yelp, vn. glapir, japper, aboyer

Yelping, s. glapissement, *m.*, jappement, *m.*, aboiement, *m.*

Yeoman, s. fermier propriétaire, *m.*, garde national à cheval, *m.* (petit) officier de la maison du roi, *m.*, cent-garde, *m.*

Yeomanry, s. francs tenanciers, *m.pl.*, garde nationale à cheval, *f.*

Yes, adv. oui, si, si fait, oui vraiment

Yesterday, adv. hier, s. le jour d'hier, *m.* *The day before* —, avant-hier

Yet, conj. cependant, pourtant, néanmoins, encore

Yet, adv. encore, toutefois, réellement, même. *As* —, jusqu'ici, jusqu'à présent, jusqu'aujourd'hui. *Not as* —, pas encore

Yew, s. if, *m.*, bois d'if, *m.* — *-tree*, s. if, *m.*

Yield, va. produire, donner, rapporter, offrir, présenter, (*scent*) exhaler, émettre, (*give up*) céder, abandonner, livrer, renoncer à, (*to* à), rendre, remettre, livrer, (*passage*) laisser, livrer, (*grant*) reconnaître comme, admettre, accorder. *To* —, céder, abandonner, livrer, renoncer à, s'en rapporter à quelqu'un pour, céder à (quelqu'un), (*milit.*), rendre, remettre, livrer, (*ghost*) rendre; —vn. se rendre, (*th.*) céder, consentir, se laisser fléchir, (*to*, à) céder à, se laisser aller à, obéir

Yield, s. récolte, *f.*, rendement, *m.*

Yielding, s. soumission, *f.*

Yielding, adj. qui se rend, soumis, docile, facile

Yoke, s. joug, *m.*, (*of two*) paire, *f.*, attelage, *m.* — *-elm*, s. charme, *m.* — *-fellow*, s. — *-mate*, s. compagnon, *m.*, compagne, *f.*, époux, *m.*, épouse, *f.* *To pass under the* —, passer sous le joug

Yoke, va. atteler, (*fig.*) unir, asservir, assujettir

Yolk, s. jaune (d'œuf), *m.*

Yon, **Yonder**, adj. ce, cette, ces . . . là-bas

Yore, adv. jadis, autrefois. *Of* —, jadis, au temps jadis, autrefois, des anciens temps. *In times of* —, *in days of* —, au temps jadis, dans les anciens temps

You, pers. pron. vous, tu, toi, à vous, te, à toi, vous autres

Young, adj. jeune, petit, (*fig.*) jeune, neuf, novice, peu avancé

Young, s.pl. jeunes, jeunes gens, petits, *m.pl.*

Youngish, adj. assez jeune

Youngster, **Younker**, s. jeune homme, *m.*, (*contempt*) nigaud, *m.*, blanc-bec, *m.*

Your, poss. pron. votre, vos, ton, ta, tes

Yours, poss. pron. le vôtre, la vôtre, les vôtres, à vous. *Is this house* —*?* cette maison est-elle à vous? *You have my book, I have* —, vous avez mon livre, j'ai le vôtre. *Most truly* —, votre tout dévoué, tout à vous de cœur. — *very faithfully*, très-sincèrement à vous

Yourself, pron. vous-même, vous, toi-même, toi, vous-mêmes, vous

Youth, s. jeunesse, *f.*, adolescence, *f.*

Youthful, adj. jeune, de jeunesse, des jeunes gens, frais, vif, vigoureux

Youthfully, adv. en jeune homme, en jeune fille, comme un jeune homme, comme une jeune fille

Z

Z., s. Z, z, *m.*

Zany, s. bouffon, *m.*, nigaud, *m.*

Zeal, s. zèle, *m.*, enthousiasme, *m.*, ardeur, *f.*

Zealot, s. zélateur, *m.*, partisan, *m.*

Zealotry, s. fanatisme, *m.*

Zealous, adj. zélé, qui a du zèle

Zealously, adv. avec zèle

Zealousness, s. zèle, *m.*

Zebra, s. zèbre, *m.*

Zebu, s. zébu, *m.*

Zenith, s. zénith, *m.*

Zephyr, s. zéphyr, *m.*

Zero, s. zéro, *m.*

Zest, s. zeste, *m.*, (*fig.*) goût, *m.*, saveur, *f.*

Zigzag, s. zigzag, *m.*

Zigzag, adj. adv. en zigzag

Zigzag, va.t tracer, en zigzag; —vn. aller en zigzag, former des zigzags

Zinc, s. zinc, *m.* *Of* —, de zinc, en zinc. — *-worker*, s. zingueur, *m.*

Zodiac, s. zodiaque, *m.*

Zodiacal, adj. zodiacal

Zone, s. zone, *f.*, (*fig.*) ceinture, *f.*

Zoological, adj. zoologiqus. — *-gardens*, s.pl., jardins zoologiques, *m.pl.*

Zoologist, s. zoologiste, *m.*

Zoophyte, s. zoophyte, *m.*

Zymotic, adj. zymotique

DICTIONNAIRE GÉOGRAPHIQUE,

CONTÉNANT

LES NOMS DES NATIONS, VILLES, PROVINCES, FLEUVES, MONTAGNES,

LES PLUS USITÉS, QUI S'ÉCRIVENT DIFFÉREMMENT DANS LES DEUX LANGUES.

A

Abdera, s. Abdère
Abderite, s. Abdéritain
Abruzzo, s. Abruzze. *The Abruzzi*, les Abruzzes
Abyssinia, s. l'Abyssinie, *f.*
Abyssinian, adj. Abyssinien, -enne
Acadia, s. l'Acadie, *f.*
Acarnania, s. l'Acarnanie, *f.*
Achaia, s. l'Achaïe, *f.*
Achean, s. Achéen, -enne
Acre, s. St.-Jean d'Acre
Admiralty Islands, s. les îles de l'Amirauté
Adriatic, adj. Adriatique. *The* —, la mer Adriatique
Ægean, adj. Egée. *The — sea*, la mer Egée
Africa, s. l'Afrique, *f.*
African, s. adj. Africain
Agincourt, s. Azincourt, *m.*
Agrigentum, s. Agrigente, *f.*
Alba, s. Albe, *f.*
Alban, adj. s. Albain, *m.*, -e, *f.*
Albania, s. l'Albanie, *f.*
Albanese, adj. s. Albanais
Albigenses, s. pl. (les) Al-Albigeois
Alderney, s. Aurigny, *m.*
Aleutian, adj. Aléoutien
Aleppo, s. Alep, *m.*
Alexandria, s. Alexandrie, *f.*
Algarva, s. les Algarves, *f.pl.*
Algeria, s. l'Algérie, *f.*
Algerian, Algerine, s. adj. Algérien, *m.*, -enne, *f.*, d'Alger
Algiers, s. Algèr, *m.*
Alicant, s. Alicante
Alps, s. pl. (les) Alpes, *f.pl.*
Alsatia, s. l'Alsace, *f.*
Alsatian, s. adj. Alsacien, -ne
Amalekite, s. Amalécite
Amazon (The), s. (l')Amazone, *m.*
Amazonia, s. le pays des Amazones
Amazonian, adj. du pays des Amazones
Amboyna, s. Amboine, *f.*
America, s. l'Amérique. *British* —, l'Amérique anglaise
American, s. adj. Américain, -e
Anatolia, s. l'Anatolie, *f.*
Ancona, s. Ancône, *f.*
Andalusia, s. l'Andalousie, *f.*
Andalusian, adj. s. Andalous, -e
Andorra (The valley of), s. val d'Andorre
Angiers, s. Angers. *A native of* —, un Angevin
Antigua, s. Antigoa, Antigue, *f.*
Antioch, s. Antioche, *f.*
Antwerp, s. Anvers, *m.*
Aonian, adj. d'Aonie
Apennines (The), s.pl. (les) Apennins, *m.pl.*
Appalachian, adj. des Appalaches
Apulia, s. l'Apulie, *f.*, la Pouille, *f.*
Aquileia, s. Aquilée, *f.*
Aquitain, s. l'Aquitaine, *f.*
Arabia, Araby, s. l'Arabie, *f.* — *Deserta*, l'Arabie Déserte. — *Felix*, l'Arabie Heureuse. — *Petræa*, *Stony* —, l'Arabie Pétrée
Arabian, adj. Arabe. *The — gulf*, le golfe Arabique
Arbela, s. Arbèles, *f.*
Arcadia, s. l'Arcadie, *f.*
Arcadian, s. adj. Arcadien, *m.*, de l'Arcadie
Archipelago (The), s. (l') Archipel, *m.*
Argive, s. adj. Argien, d'Argos
Argolis, s. l'Argolide, *f.*
Armenia, s. l'Arménie, *f.*
Armenian, s. adj. Arménien, -ne
Armorica, s. l'Armorique, *f.*
Asia, s. l'Asie, *f.* — *minor*, *Lesser* —, l'Asie Mineure
Asiatic, adj. Asiatique
Asoph, s. Azof, Azow, *m.* *The sea of* —, la mer d'Azof
Asphaltites Lake, s. le lac Asphaltite, la mer Morte
Assyria, s. l'Assyrie, *f.*
Assyrian, adj. Assyrien, -ne
Asturias (The), s.pl. (les) Asturies, *f.pl.*
Athens, s. Athènes, *f.*
Athenian, s. adj. Athénien, -ne, d'Athènes
Atlantic, s.adj. Atlantique
Atlantis, s. l'Atlantide, *f.*
Attica, s. l'Attique, *f.*
Attic, adj. Attique
Augsburg, s. Augsbourg
Aulis, s. l'Aulide, *f.*
Australia, s. l'Australie, *f.*
Australian, s. adj. Australien, -ne, d'Australie, de l'Australie
Austrasia, s. l'Austrasie, *f.*
Austria, s. l'Autriche, *f.*
Austrian, s. adj. Autrichien, -ne, d'Autriche
Aventine, adj. Aventin. *The — hill*, le mont Aventin
Avernus (The),
Averno, s. (l') Averne, *m.*
Azores (The), s.pl. (les) Açores, *f.pl.*

B

Babylon, s. Babylone, *f.*
Babylonian, s. adj. Babylonien, -ne, de Babylone
Bactria, s. Bactre, *f.*
Bactriana, s. la Bactriane
Bactrian, s. adj. Bactrien, -ne
Baden, s. Bade, *m.*
Baffin's Bay, s. la baie *or* la mer de Baffin
Balearic, adj. *The — Islands*, les îles Baléares
Baltic (The), s. (la) Baltique
Barbadoes, s. la Barbade
Barbary, s. la Barbarie. *The states of* —, les États Barbaresques
Barbuda, s. la Barboude
Barcelona, s. Barcelone, *f.*
Bashan, s. Basan, *m.*
Batavia, s. la Batavie
Bavaria, s. la Bavière
Bavarian, s. adj. Bavarois, -e, de Bavière
Beer-sheba, s. Bersabée, *f.*
Belgian, s. adj. Belge, de la Belgique
Belgium, s. la Belgique
Benevento, s. Bénévent, *m.*
Bengal, s. Bengale, *m.*, le Bengale. *The Bay of* —, le golfe du Bengale
Bengalee, Bengalese, s. adj. Bengalais, -e
Beotia, s. la Béotie
Beotian, s. adj. Béotien, -ne
Bergamo, s. Bergame, *m.*
Bermuda, s. adj. *The — Islands, the —s*, les îles Bermudes
Bern, s. Berne, *f.*
Bessarabia, s. la Bessarabie
Bethany, s. Béthanie, *f.*
Bethlehem, s. Bethléem
Betica, s. la Bétique
Biscay, s. la Biscaye. *The Bay of* —, le golfe de Gascogne *or* de Biscaye
Biscayan, s. adj. Basque
Bithynia, s. la Bithynie
Bohemia, s. la Bohême

Bohemian, s. adj. Bohémien, -ne

Bologna, s. Bologne, *f.*

Bolognese, s. adj. Bolonnais, -e

Bordeaux, s. Bordeaux. *Native of —*, Bordelais, -e

Borysthenes (The), s. (le) Borysthène

Bosnia, s. Bosnie

Bosnian, s. adj. Bosniaque

Bosphorus (The), s. (le) Bosphore

Bothnia, s. la Bothnie

Braganza, s. Bragance, *f.*

Brahmapootra, s. Brahmapoutra, *m.*

Brandenburg, s. Brandebourg, *m.*

Brazil, s. Brésil, *m.*

Brazilian, s. adj. Brésilien, -ne, du Brésil

Bremen, s. Brême, *m.*

Brindisi, s. Brindes, *m.*

Britain, s. Brétagne

Britannia, s. Brétagne

Britannic, adj. Britannique

British, adj. s. Britannique, Bréton, Anglais. *The — Channel*, la Manche. *The — Isles*, les îles Britanniques

Briton, s. adj. Bréton, -ne

Brittany, s. Brétagne, *f.*

Brussels, s. Bruxelles, *f.*

Bucharia, s. Boukharie, *f.*

Buda, s. Bude, *f.*

Bugia, s. Bougie, *f.*

Bulgaria, s. Bulgarie, *f.*

Bulgarian, s. adj. Bulgare

Burgundian, s. adj. Bourguignon, -ne, de Bourgogne

Burgundy, s. Bourgogne, *f.*

Bursa, s. Brousse, *f.*

Byzantine, adj. Byzantin

Byzantium, s. Byzance, *f.*

C

Cadiz, s. Cadix, *m.*

Cæsarea, s. Césarée

Caffraria, s. Cafrérie, *f.*

Cairo, s. Caire

Calabria, s. Calabre, *f.*

Calabrian, adj. Calabrais

Caledonia, s. Calédonie, *f.*

Caledonian, adj. s. Calédonien

California, s. Californie. *Upper —, New —*, la Haute, la Nouvelle-Californie. *Old —, Lower —*, la Vieille, la Basse-Californie. *The Gulf of —*, le golfe de Californie, la mer Vermeille

Calmuck, s. adj. Calmouk

Cambodia, Camboge, s. Camboge

Campagna di Roma, Campagne de Rome, *f.*

Campania, s. Campanie, *f.*

Canadian, s. adj. Canadien, -ne

Canaan, s. Chanaan, *m.*

Canaanite, s. adj. Chananéen, -ne

Canary, s. Canarie, *f.* *The Canaries*, les Canaries. *The — Islands*, les îles Canaries

Candia, s. l'île de Candie, *f.*

Canea, s. Canée, *f.*

Cannæ, s. Cannes

Canterbury, s. Cantorbéry

Cape, s. Cap, *m.*

Capernaum, s. Capharnaum, *m.*

Cappadocia, s. Cappadoce, *f.*

Cappadocian, s. adj. Cappadocien, -ne

Capua, s. Capoue, *f.*

Caria, s. Carie, *f.*

Caribbean, Caribbee, adj. Caraïbe. *The — Islands*, les îles Caraïbes

Carinthia, s. Carinthie, *f.*

Carnatic (The), Carnatique

Carolina, s. Caroline, *f.*

Carpathian, adj. Carpathes. *The — Mountains*, les monts Carpathes *or* Crapacks

Carthagena, s. Carthagène

Carthaginian, adj. s. Carthaginois, -e

Cashmere, s. adj. Cachemire, de Cachemire

Caspian, adj. *The — sea*, la mer Caspienne

Castile, s. Castille, *f.*

Castilian, adj. s. Castillan, -e

Catalonia, s. Catalogne, *f.*

Catalonian, adj. s. Catalan, -e

Catania, s. Catane

Caucasus, s. Caucase, *m.*

Caucasian, adj. Caucasien, du Caucase. —, s. Caucasien, -ne

Celt, s. Celte

Celtiberia, s. Celtibérie, *f.*

Celtic, adj. Celtique

Ceylon, s. Ceylon

Chæronea, s. Chéronée

Chalcedonia, s. Chalcédoine

Chaldaic, s. adj. Chaldéen, chaldaïque

Chaldea, s. Chaldée, *f.*

Chaldean, adj. s. Chaldéen, -ne

Channel (The), s. (la) Manche. *The — Islands*, les îles de la Manche

Chersonesus, s. la Chersonèse. *— Cimbrica*, la Chersonèse Cimbrique. *— Taurica*, la Chersonèse Taurique. *Thracian —*, la Chersonèse de Thrace

China, s. Chine, *f.*

Chinese, s. adj. Chinois, -e. *The —*, les Chinois

Cilicia, s. Cilicie, *f.*

Cilician, adj. s. Cilicien, -e

Cimbri, s. pl. Cimbres

Cimbrian, adj. Cimbre

Circassia, s. Circassie, *f.*

Circassian, s. adj. Circassien, -ne

Cithæron, s. Cithéron

Cochin-China, s. Cochinchine, *f.*

Cochin-Chinese, s. adj. Cochin-chinois

Cocytus (The), s. (le) Cocyte

Coimbra, s. Coïmbre

Colchis, s. Colchide, *f.*

Columbia, s. Colombie

Compostella, s. Compostelle. *St.-Jago of —*, Saint-Jacques de Compostelle

Copenhagen, s. Copenhague

Cordilleras (The), s. pl. (les) Cordillères, *f.*

Cordova, s. Cordoue

Corea, s. Corée, *f.*

Corfu, s. Corfou

Corinth, s. Corinthe. *The Isthmus of —*, l'isthme de Corinthe

Cornwall, s. Cornouailles

Corsica, s. Corse, *f.*

Corsican, adj. s. Corse

Corunna, s. Corogne, *f.*

Cossak, s. adj. Cosaque

Courland, s. Courlande, *f.*

Cracow, s. Cracovie

Cremona, s. Crémone

Cretan, s. adj. Crétois

Crimea (The), s. (la) Crimée

Croatia, s. Croatie, *f.*

Croatian, s. adj. Croate

Cuma, s. Cume

Cumæ, s. Cumes

Cyprus, s. (l'île de) Chypre

Cyrenaica, s. Cyrénaïque

Cyrenean, adj. s. Cyrénéen, -ne

Cythera, s. Cythère

D

Dacia, s. Dacie, *f.*

Dacian, adj. s. Dace

Dalecarlia, s. Dalécarlie *f.*

Dalecarlian, adj. s. Dalécarlien, -ne

Dalmatia, s. Dalmatie, *f.*

Dalmatian, adj. s. Dalmate

Damascus, s. Damas

Damietta, s. Damiette

Dane, s. Danois, -e

Danish, adj. Danois

Dauphiny, s. Dauphiné, *m.*

Davis's Straits, s. pl. le détroit de Davis

Deccan, s. Dekhan, *m.*

Delphi, Delphos, s. Delphes

Denmark, s. Danemark, *m.*

Dominica, s. Dominique

Dominican, adj. s. Dominicain, -e

Doris, s. Doride

Dorian, adj. s. Dorien, -ne

Doric, adj. s. dorique

Dover, Dovor, s. Douvres. *The Straits of —*, le Pas de Calais

Dresden, s. Dresde

Dunkirk, s. Dunkerque

E

Ebro (The), s. (l') Èbre

Ecbatana, s. Ecbatane

Edinburg, s. Édimbourg

Egypt, s. Égypte. *Lower —*, la Basse-Égypte. *Middle —*, la Moyenne-Égypte. *Upper —*, la Haute-Égypte

Egyptian, adj. s. Égyptien, -ne

Elba, s. (l'île d') Elbe

Elis, s. l'Élide, *f.*

Elsinore, s. Elseneur

Emathia, s. Émathie, *f.*

England, s. Angleterre, *f.*

Ephesus, s. Éphèse

Ephesian, adj. s. Éphésien, -ne

Epirus, s. Épire, *f.*

Erebus, s. Érèbe

Erin, s. Irlande, *f.* *— go bragh!* vive l'Irlande, *f.*

Equator, s. Équateur. *The Republic of the —*, la république de l'Équateur

Estramadura, s. l'Estramadure

Ethiop, s. Éthiopien, -ne

Ethiopia, s. Éthiopie, *f.*

Ethiopian, adj. s. Éthiopien, -ne

Etruria, s. Étrurie, *f.*

Etrurian, adj. s. Étrusque

Eubœa, s. Eubée

Euphrates (The), s. (l') Euphrate

European, adj. s. Européen, -ne, d'Europe

Euxine (The), s. (le) Pont Euxin

F

Færoe, Faroe, Feroe, adj. *The — Islands*, les îles Féroé

Falkland, adj. s. *The — Islands, the —s*, les îles Malouines

Ferrara, s. Ferrare

Ferrarese, s. Ferrarais, *m.* duché de Ferrare

Ferro, s. Fer, l'île de Fer

Figueras, s. Figuières

Fez, Fezzan, s. Fez

Finisterra, s. *Cape —*, le cap Finisterre (*in Spain*)

Finisterre, s. *Cape —*, le cap Finistère (*in France*)

Finland, s. Finlande, *f.*

Finlander, s. Finlandais, -e

Flanders, s. Flandre, *f.*

Flemish, adj. Flamand, -e. *The —*, les Flamands

Florida, s. Floride, *f.*

Flushing, s. Flessingue

Fontarabia, s. Fontarabie

Formosa, s. (l'île) Formose

Forth, s. *The Frith of —*, le golfe du Forth

Frankfort, s. Francfort. *— on the Main, — on the Oder*, Francfort-sur-le Mein, Francfort-sur-l'Oder

Franconia, s. Franconie, *f.*

Freyburg, Friburg, s. Fribourg

Friuli, s. Frioul, *m.*

Friesland, s. Frise, *f.*

Frontignac, s. Frontignan

G

Gael, s. Celte, Gaël

Gaelic, adj. gaëlique. — s. le gaëlique, la langue gaëlique *or* celtique

G

Gaeta, s. Gaëte
Galatia, s. (la) Galatie
Galatian, adj. s. Galate
Galicia, s. (la) Galice (*in Spain*) (la) Galicie (*in Austria*)
Gambia (The), (la) Gambie
Ganges (The), s. (le) Gange
Gascony, s. (la) Gascogne
Gaul, s. (la) Gaule
Gaul, adj. s. Gaulois, -e
Gaunt, s. *John of —*, Jean de Gand
Genoa, s. Gênes
Genoese, adj. s. Génois, -e
Geneva, s. Genève
Genevese, adj. s. Génevois
Georgia, s. (la) Géorgie
Georgian, adj. s. Géorgien, -ne
Germany, s. l'Allemagne, (*anc. hist.*) la Germanie
German, adj. s. Allemand, -e, (*anc. hist.*) Germain, -e, l'Allemand, la langue Allemande
Ghauts (The), s. pl. (les) Ghattes
Ghent, s. Gand
Gibeon, s. Gabaon
Gilead, s. Galaad
Golconda, s. Golconde
Gold Coast, s. (la) Côte-d'Or
Goshen, s. Gessen. *The Land of —*, la Terre de Gessen
Gothia, Gothland, s. (la) Gothie
Gottingen, s. Gœttingue
Grain-Coast, s. la côte des Graines
Granicus (The), s. (le) Granique
Granada, s. Grenade. *New —*, la Nouvelle-Grenade
Greece, s. (la) Grèce
Greenland, s. (le) Groënland
Greenlander, s. Groënlandais, -e
Guadalupe, s. (la) Guadeloupe
Guelders, s. Gueldre
Guernsey, s. Guernsey
Guiana, s. Guyane. *British —*, la Guyane anglaise. *Dutch —*, la Guyane hollandaise. *French —*, la Guyane française
Guinea, s. Guinée. *New —*, la Nouvelle-Guinée
Guzerat, s. (le) Goudjérate

H

Hague (The), s. (la) Haye
Hainault, s. (le) Hainaut
Halicarnassus, s. Halicarnasse
Hamburgh, s. Hambourg
Hanover, s. (le) Hanovre
Hanoverian, adj. s. Hanovrien, -ne
Hanse, adj. Hanséatique, Anséatique. *The — towns*, les villes Hanséatiques
Hants, s. le Comté de Hampshire
Hapsburg, s. (le) Hapsbourg
Havannah, s. (la) Havane
Hayti, s. Haïti
Helvetia, s. Helvétie
Helvetian, adj. s. Helvétien, -ne
Heraclea, s. Héraclée
Herculaneum, s. Herculanum
Hercules' Pillars, s. pl. Colonnes d'Hercule
Hesperia, s. Hespérie
Hessian, adj. s. Hessois, -e. *— boots*, bottes à l'écuyère
Hibernia, s. Hibernie
Hindostan, s. Hindoustan, Hindostan, Indostan
Hindoo, adj. s. Hindou, -e
Holland, s. Hollande. *New —*, la Nouvelle-Hollande
Holy Land (The), s. (la) Terre Sainte, (la) Palestine
Homburg, s. Hombourg
Hudson's Bay, s. la baie d'Hudson, la mer d'Hudson
Hungary, s. (la) Hongrie
Hungarian, adj. s. Hongrois, -e
Hydaspes (The), s. (l') Hydaspe
Hyrcania, s. Hyrcanie
Hyrcanian, adj. Hyrcanie

I

Iberia, s. Ibérie
Icaria, s. Icarie
Icarian, adj. *The — sea*, la mer Icarienne, la mer d'Icare
Iceland, s. Islande
Icelander, s. Islandais, -e
Idalia, s. Idalie
Idumea, s. Idumée
Illyria, Illyricum, s. Illyrie
Illyrian, adj. s. Illyrien, -ne
India, s. l'Inde, les Indes. *British —*, l'Inde anglaise. *— beyond the Ganges, Farther —*, l'Inde au delà du Gange, l'Inde Transangétique. *— within* or *on this side the Ganges*, l'Inde en deçà du Gange, l'Inde Cisangétique. *The Indies*, les Indes. *The East Indies*, les Indes Orientales, les Grandes Indes. *The West Indies*, les Indes occidentales, les Antilles
Indian, adj. s. Indien, -ne. *The — Ocean*, la mer des Indes, l'océan Indien
Indo-China, s. Indo-Chine
Indus (The), s. (*anc. geog.*) l'Indus, (*mod. geog.*) (le) Sindh
Ionia, s. Ionie
Ionian, adj. s. Ionien, -ne, d'Ionie. *The — Islands*, les Îles Ioniennes
Ireland, s. Irlande
Irish, adj. s. Irlandais, -e. *The — sea*, la mer d'Irlande. *An — man*, un Irlandais. *An — woman*, une Irlandaise
Ishmaelite, adj. s. Ismaélite
Isle, s. île, *f.*
Istria, s. Istrie
Italian, adj. s. Italien, -ne
Italy, s. Italie
Ithaca, s. Ithaque
Ivory, adj. *The — coast*, la côte d'Ivoire

J

Jamaica, s. (la) Jamaïque
Japan, s. (le) Japon
Japanese, adj. s. Japonais, -e, du Japon
Javanese, adj. s. Javanais, -e
Jena, s. Iéna
Jordan (The), s. (le) Jourdain
Judea, s. (la) Judée

K

Kuriles (The), s. pl. (les) îles Kouriles, (les) Kouriles

L

Laccadives, s. pl. (les îles) Laquedives
Lacedæmon, s. Lacédémone
Lacedæmonian, adj. s. Lacédémonien, -ne
Laconia, s. (la) Laconie
Ladrones (The), s. (les îles des) Larrons
La Mancha, s. la Manche
Lampsacus, s. Lampsaque
Lancaster, s. (le) Lancastre
Laodicea, s. Laodicée
Lapitha (The), s. pl. (les) Lapithes
Lapland, s. (la) Laponie
Laplander, s. Lapon, -ne
Larissa, s. Larisse
Latakia, s. Latakieh
Latian, adj. du Latium, latin
Lebanon, s. (le) Liban
Leghorn, s. Livourne. *— bonnet*, chapeau de paille d'Italie
Lepanto, s. Lépante
Lerna, s. Lerne. *The Lernæan Hydra*, Hydre de Lerne
Lestrygones, s. pl. Lestrygons
Leuctra, s. Leuctres
Levantine, adj. s. Levantin, -e
Leyden, s. Leyde
Libya, s. (la) Libye
Liguria, s. (la) Ligurie
Ligurian, adj. s. Ligurien, -ne, de la Ligurie
Lisbon, s. Lisbonne
Lithuania, s. (la) Lithuanie
Lithuanian, adj. s. Lithuanien, -ne
Livonia, s. (la) Livonie
Locris, s. (la) Locride
Locust-eaters, s. pl. Lotophages
Lombard, adj. s. Lombard, -e. *Lombardo-Venitian*, Lombard Vénitien
Lombardy, s. (la) Lombardie
London, s. Londres. — adj. de Londres
Londoner, s. habitant, habitante de Londres
Loretto, s. Lorette
Louisiana, s. (la) Louisiane
Lucaya, s. *The — Islands*, les Lucayes
Lucca, s. Lucques
Lusatia, s. (la) Lusace
Lusitania, s. (la) Lusitanie
Lusitanian, adj. de la Lusitanie
Lycia, s. (la) Lycie
Lycian, adj. s. Lycien, -ne
Lydia, s. (la) Lydie
Lydian, adj. s. Lydien, -ne, de Lydie
Lyons, s. Lyon. — adj. de
Lyonese, s. Lyonnais, -e

M

Macedon, Macedonia, s. (la) Macédoine
Macedonian, adj. s. Macédonien, -ne
Madeira, s. Madère
Main (The), s. (le) Mein
Majorca, s. Majorque
Malay, s. Malais, -e
Malaya, Malaysia, s. (la) Malaisie
Malta, s. Malte
Maltese, adj. s. Maltaise, -e
Manilla, s. Manille
Mantinea, s. Mantinée
Mantua, s. Mantoue
Manx, adj. de l'Île de Man
Mariania, adj. *The — Islands*, les Îles des Larrons, les îles Mariannes
Marmora, s. Marmara
Marquesas, s. pl. *The — Islands*, les îles Marquises
Marseilles, s. Marseille. *Inhabitant of —*, Marseillais, -e
Martinico, s. (la) Martinique
Mauritania, s. (la) Mauritanie
Mauritius, s. l'Île Maurice
Mecca, s. (la) Mecque
Mechlin, s. Malines
Mede, s. Mède
Media, s. (la) Médie
Medina, s. Médine
Mediterranean (The), s. (la) mer Méditerranée
Megara, s. Mégare
Menai Straits, s. pl. détroit de Menai
Mesopotamia, s. (la) Mésopotamie
Messenia, s. (la) Messénie
Messenian, adj. s. Messénien, -ne
Messina, s. Messine. *The Straits of —*, le phare de Messine
Mexican, adj. s. Mexicain, -e, du Mexique
Mexico, s. Mexico, (*country*) le Mexique
Milanese, adj. s. Milanais, -e
Miletus, s. Milet
Mingrelia, s. (la) Mingrélie
Minorca, s. Minorque
Minturna, s. Minturnes. *The — Marches*, les marais de Minturnes

M

Modena, s. Modène
Modenese, s. Modénais, -e
Mogul, s. (le) Mogol
Moldavia, s. (la) Moldavie
Moor, s. Maure, Marocain, -e
Moorish, adj. Maure, Mauresque
Moravia, s. (la) Moravie
Morea (The), s. (la) Morée
Morocco, s. (le) Maroc
Moscow, s. Moscou
Mosul, s. Moussoul
Murcia, s. (la) Murcie
Mysia, s. (la) Mysie
Mysore, s. (le) Mysore

N

Natolia, s. Anatolie
Nauplia, s. Nauplie
Navarino, s. Navarin
Nemea, s. Némée
Negroland, s. (la) Nigritie
Netherlands (The), s. (les) Pays Bas
Neustria, s. (la) Neustrie
Neustrian, adj. s. Neustrien, -ne
Newfoundland, s. Terre Neuve
Nicomedia, s. Nicomédie
Nile (The), s. (le) Nil
Nimeguen, s. Nimègue
Nineveh, s. Ninive
Norman, adj. s. Normand, -e
Normandy, s. (la) Normandie
North, adj. du Nord, septentrional
Norway, s. (la) Norvége
Nova Zembla, s. Nouvelle Zemble
Nubia, s. (la) Nubie
Nubian, adj. s. Nubien, -ne
Numantia, s. Numance
Numidia, s. (la) Numidie

O

Oceania, s. Océanie
Olympus, s. Olympe. *Mount* —, le mont Olympe
Olynthus, s. Olynthe
Olynthian, s. Olynthien, -ne
Oporto, s. Porto
Orinoco (The), s. (l') Orénoque
Orkney, adj. s. *The — Islands, the —s*, les Orcades
Ostend, s. Ostende
Otaheite, s. Taïti, Otahiti
Otranto, s. Otrante
Owhyhee, s. Hawaii

P

Pacifique, adj. s. Pacifique *The —, the — Ocean*, l'Océan Pacifique, la mer Pacifique, la mer du Sud, le grand Océan

Palatinate (The), s. (le) Palatinat
Palermo, s. Palerme
Palmyra, s. Palmyre
Palus Meotis, s. Palus Méotides
Pampeluna, s. Pampelune
Papua, s. la Terre des Papous
Parnassus, s. Parnasse *Mount* —, le mont Parnasse
Parthia, s. (la) Parthie
Parthian, adj. s. Parthe, des Parthes
Patagonia, s. (la) Patagonie
Patagonian, s. Patagon
Pausilippo, s. Pausilippe
Pavia, s. Pavie
Pelasgi (The), **Pelasgians (The)**, s. (les) Pélasges
Pelew, s. *The — Islands*, les îles Pelew, les îles Palos
Peloponnesus, s. (le) Péloponnèse
Pensylvania, s. (la) Pensylvanie
Pergamus, s. Pergame
Permessus, s. Permesse
Persia, s. Perse
Persian, adj. persan. — s. Perse, Persan, -e. *The — gulf*, le golfe Persique
Peru, s. (le) Pérou
Peruvian, adj. s. Péruvien, -ne
Petersburg, s. St.-Petersbourg
Pharsalia, s. Pharsale
Phasis (The), s. (le) Phase
Philadelphia, s. Philadelphie
Philippi, s. Philippes
Philippine, adj. s. *The — Islands, the Philippines*, les îles Philippines
Philipsburg, s. Philipsbourg
Philistine, adj. s. Philistin, -e
Phocea, s. (la) Phocée
Phocean, s. Phocéen, -ne
Phocide, s. (la) Phocide
Phœnicia, s. (la) Phénicie
Phœnician, adj. s. Phénicien, -ne
Phrygia, s. (la) Phrygie
Phrygian, adj. s. Phrygien, -ne
Picardy, s. (la) Picardie. *A native of* —, un Picard
Piedmont, s. (le) Piémont
Piedmontese, adj. s. Piémontais, -e
Pindus, (le) s. Pinde
Piræus, s. (le) Pirée
Pisa, s. Pise
Piacenza, **Piacencia**, s. Plaisance
Platea, s. Platée
Poland, s. (la) Pologne
Pole, s. Polonais, -e
Polish, adj. Polonais, -e
Polynesia, s. (la) Polynésie
Pomerania, s. (la) Poméranie
Pompeii, s. Pompéies
Pontine, adj. *The — Marshes*, les marais Pontins
Port, adj. de Porto. — *wine*, vin de Porto
Portuguese, adj. s. Portugais, -e
Potidæa, s. Potidée
Poyas, adj. *The — Mountains*, les monts Poyas, les monts Ourals
Propontis, s. (la) Propontide
Prussia, s. (la) Prusse
Prussian, adj. s. Prussien, -ne
Pyrenean, adj. pyrénéen, -ne
Pyrenees (The), s. pl. (les) Pyrénées

R

Ragusa, s. Raguse
Ratisbon, s. Ratisbonne
Ravenna, s. Ravenne
Rhetia, s. (la) Rhétie
Rhine (The), s. (le) Rhin. *The Lower* — le Bas-Rhin. *The Upper Rhine*, le Haut-Rhin. *The Provinces of the* —, les provinces rhénanes
Riphean, adj. *The — Mountains*, les monts Riphées
Romagna, s. Romagne
Roman, adj. s. Romain, -e
Romelia, s. (la) Romélie
Rosetta, s. Rosette
Russia, s. (la) Russie. — *in Europe*, Russie d'Europe. — *in Asia, Asiatic* —, Russie d'Asie. *Great* —, Grande Russie. *Black* —, Russie Noire. *Little* —, petite Russie. *New* —, nouvelle Russie. *Red* —, Russie Rouge. *White* —, Russie Blanche
Russian, adj. s. Russe. — *America*, l'Amérique russe. *The — Empire*, l'Empire russe. *The — s*, les Russes

S

Sabina, s. (la) Sabine
Sabine, adj. s. Sabin, -e. *The Rape of the —s*, l'enlèvement des Sabines
Saguntum, s. Sagonte
Saigon, s. Saigon
St. Domingo, **San Domingo**, s. St.-Domingue
St. George's Channel, s. le canal St.-George
St. Helena, s. (l'île de) Ste.-Hélène
St. Kitts, s. St.-Christophe
St. Laurence (The), s. (le) St. Laurent
St. John of Acre, s. *see* ACRE
St. Lucia, s. Ste. Lucie
Salamanca, s. Salamanque
Salamis, s. Salamine
Sallee, s. Salé
Salentum, s. Salente
Salerno, s. Salerne
Salonica, s. Salonique
Salop, s. (le) Shropshire
Samaria, s. (la) Samarie
Samaritan, adj. s. Samaritain, -e
Samothracia, **Samothraki**, s. (la) Samothrace
Samoyedes (The), s. pl. (les) Samoyèdes
Saragossa, s. Saragosse
Sardinia, s. (la) Sardaigne
Sardinian, adj. s. Sarde
Sardis, s. Sardes
Sarmatia, s. (la) Sarmatie
Sarmatian, adj. s. Sarmate
Savoy, s. (la) Savoie. *A native of* —, Savoisien, -ne, Savoyard, -e
Saxon, adj. s. Saxon, -ne
Saxony, s. (la) Saxe
Scamander (The), s. (le) Scamandre
Scandinavia, s. (la) Scandinavie
Scania, s. (la) Scanie
Schaffhausen, s. Schaffhouse
Scilly, adj. *The — Islands*, les îles Sorlingues
Scythia, s. (la) Scythie
Scythian, adj. s. Scythe
Sea, s. mer, *f.* *The Dead* —, la mer Morte. *The North* —, la mer du Nord. *The Red* —, la mer Rouge. *The South* —, la mer du Sud. *The White* —, la mer Blanche. *The Yellow* —, la mer Jaune
Segovia, s. Ségovie
Seleucis, s. (la) Séleucide
Senegambia, s. (la) Sénégambie
Servia, s. (la) Servie
Servian, adj. s. Serbe
Severn (The), s. (la) Saverne
Sevilla, s. Séville
Sheba, s. Saba
Schechem, s. Sichem
Shiloh, s. Siloh
Siamese, adj. s. Siamois, du Siam. *The* —, les Siamois
Siberia, s. (la) Sibérie
Sicilian, adj. s. Sicilien, -ne
Sicily, s. (la) Sicile. *The Two Sicilies*, les Deux-Siciles
Sicyon, s. Sicyone
Sienna, s. Sienne
Silesia, s. (la) Silésie
Siloa, s. Siloé
Singhalese, s. natif de Ceylan. *The* —, les natifs de Ceylan
Smyrna, s. Smyrne
Society, adj. *The — Islands* or *Isles*, les îles de la Société
Sodom, s. Sodome
Sogdiana, s. (la) Sogdiane
Solyma, s. Solyme
Sorrento, s. Sorrente
Sound, s. (le) Sund
Spain, s. l'Espagne
Spaniard, s. Espagnol
Sparta, s. Sparte
Spartan, adj. s. Spartiate
Spitzbergen, s. (le) Spitzberg
Stagyra, s. Stagyre
Steenkirk, s. Steinkerque
Strasburg, s. Strasbourg
Stuttgard, s. Stuttgart
Styria, s. (la) Styrie
Suabia, s. (la) Souabe
Sunda, adj. *The — Isles*, les îles de la Sonde
Superior, s. *Lake* —, le lac Supérieur
Surat, s. Surate

S

Susa, s. Suse
Susiana, s. (la) Susiane
Swede, s. Suédois, -e
Sweden, s. (la) Suède
Swedish, adj. suédois, -e
Switzerland, s. (la) Suisse
Swiss, adj. s. Suisse. *The* —, les Suisses. *A — woman*, une Suissesse
Syria, s. (la) Syrie
Syrian, adj. s. Syrien, -ne

T

Tabriz, s. (la) Tauride
Tagus (The), s. (le) Tage
Tahiti, s. Taiti
Tangiers, s. Tanger
Tarentum, s. Tarente
Tarpeian, adj. Tarpéin, -ne
Tarsus, s. Tarse
Tartar, adj. s. Tartare
Tartary, (la) s. Tartarie
Tauris, s. (la) Tauride
Tasmania, s. (la) Tasmanie, la Terre de Van Diémen
Terceira, s. Tercère
Terracina, s. Terracine
Terra del Fuego, s. la Terre de Feu
Terra Firma, s. la Terre Ferme
Thames (The), s. (la) Tamise
Thebais, s. (la) Thébaïde
Theban, adj. s. Thébain, -e
Thessaly, s. (la) Thessalie
Thessalonian, adj. s. Thessalonien, -ne
Thessalonica, s. Thessalonique
Thurgovia, s. Thurgovie
Thuringia, s. (la) Thuringe
Tiber (The), s. (le) Tibre
Tigris (The), s. (le) Tigre
Timbuctoo, s. Tombouctou
Toledo, s. Tolède
Tortosa, s. Tortose
Transylvania, s. (la) Transylvanie
Trasimenus, s. (le) lac Trasimène
Trebia (The), s. (la) Trébie
Trebisond, s. Trébizonde
Trent, s. Trente
Trincomalee, s. Trincomale, Trinquemale
Trinidad, s. Trinité, l'île de la Trinité
Troas, s. (la) Troade
Troy, s. Troie
Turcomania, s. (la) Turcomanie
Turc, s. Turc
Turkey, s. Turquie. — *in Asia*, la Turquie d'Asie. — *in Europe*, la Turquie d'Europe
Turkish, adj. turc, turque
Tuscany, s. (la) Toscane
Tuscan, adj. s. Toscan, -e
Tyre, s. Tyr
Tyrian, adj. s. Tyrien, -e

U

Umbria, s. Ombrie
Ural, adj. Oural. *The — Mountains*, les monts Ourals
Ushant, s. Ouessant
Utica, s. Utique

V

Van Diemen's Land, s. (la) Terre de Van Diémen, (la) Tasmanie
Valetta, s. Valette
Valtellina, s. (la) Valteline
Venetia, s. (la) Vénétie
Venetian, adj. s. Vénitien, -ne
Venice, s. Venise
Verona, s. Vérone
Vesuvius, s. (le) Vésuve
Vicenza, s. Vicence
Vienna, s. Vienne
Virgin, s. *The — Islands*, les îles Vierges
Virginia, s. (la) Virginie
Vistula (The), s. (la) Vistule
Volsci, s. Volsques
Volscian, adj. s. Volsque
Vulturnus (The), s. (le) Vulturne

W

Wales, s. le pays de Galles. *North* —, la Galles du nord. *South* —, la Galles du sud. *New South* —, la Nouvelle Galles du sud
Wallachia, s. (la) Valachie
Wallachian, adj. s. Valaque
Warsaw, s. Varsovie
Warsovian, adj. s. Varsovien, -ne
Welsh, adj. s. Gallois, -e, du pays de Galles, habitant du pays de Galles
Western Islands (The), s. pl. (les) Hébrides
Westphalia, s. (la) Westphalie
White Sea (The), s. (la) mer Blanche
Wurtemburgher, s. Wurtembergeois, -e

X

Xanthus (The), s. (le) Xanthe
Xeres, s. Xérès

Z

Zealand, s. (la) Zélande. *New* —, Nouvelle-Zélande

DICTIONNAIRE

DES NOMS PROPRES MYTHOLOGIQUES ET HISTORIQUES.

DONT L'ORTHOGRAPHE VARIE DANS LES DEUX LANGUES.

A

Abdolonymus, s. Abdolonyme
Absalom, s. Absalon
Acestes, s. Aceste
Achates, s. Achate
Achilles, s. Achille
Actæon, s. Actéon
Admetus, s. Admète
Adrian, s. Adrien
Æacus, s. Éaque
Ægeus, s. Égée
Ægisthus, s. Égisthe
Æneas, s. Énée
Æolus, s. Éole
Æschines, s. Eschine
Æschylus, s. Eschyle
Æsculapius, s. Esculape
Æsop, s. Ésope
Agathocles, s. Agathocle
Agesilaus, s. Agésilas
Agrippina, s. Agrippine
Ahab, s. Achab
Ahasuerus, s. Assuérus
Albano, s. l'Albane
Alcæus, s. Alcée
Alcibiades, s. Alcibiade
Alcides, s. Alcide, Hercule
Alcmena, s. Alcmène
Alexander, s. Alexandre
Amalek, s. Amalec
Amalthæa, s. Amalthée
Americus Vespucius, s. Améric Vespuce
Ammianus, s. Ammien
Anaxagoras, s. Anaxagore
Anchises, s. Anchise
Andromache, s. Andromaque
Andromeda, s. Andromède
Antæus, s. Antée
Antigonus, s. Antigone
Antisthenes, s. Antisthène
Antoninus, s. Antonin. — *Pius*, Antonin le Pieux
Apelles, s. Apelle
Apollodorus, s. Apollodore
Apollo, s. Apollon. — *Belvidere*, l'Apollon du Belvédère
Apollyon, s. Lucifer, Satan
Appian, s. Appien. *The — way*, la voie Appienne
Apuleius, s. Apulée
Aquinas, s. d'Aquin
Archimedes, s. Archimède
Arethusa, s. Aréthuse
Argonauts (The), s. pl. (les) Argonautes
Ariadne, s. Ariane
Ariovistus, s. Arioviste
Ariosto, s. l'Arioste
Aristarchus, s. Aristarque
Aristæus, s. Aristée
Aristides, s. Aristide
Aristophanes, s. Aristophane

Aristotle, s. Aristote
Aroun, s. *see* HAROUN
Arsaces, s. Arsace
Artaxerxes, s. Artaxercès. — *Longimanus*, Artaxercès Longue-Main
Artemisia, s. Artémise
Ascanius, s. Ascagne
Asmodæus, s. Asmodée
Aspasia, s. Aspasie
Astræa, s. Astrée
Astyages, s. Astyage
Atalanta, s. Atalante
Athaliah, s. Athalie
Atreus, s. Atrée
Atrides, s. fils d'Atrée. *The* —, les Atrides, les fils d'Atrée
Augustus, s. Auguste
Augustulus, s. Augustule
Aulus Gellius, s. Aulu-Gelle
Aurelius, s. Aurèle
Aurelian, s. Aurélien

B

Bajazeth, s. Bajazet
Baldwin, s. Baudouin
Barbarossa, s. Barberousse
Bede, s. Bède
Belisarius, s. Bélisaire
Bellona, s. Bellone
Beelzebub, s. Belzébuth
Bethsheba, s. Bethsabé
Boadicea, s. Boadicée
Boccacio, s. Boccace
Boethius, s. Boèce
Boreas, s. Borée
Boas, Booz
Briareus, s. Briarée
Brunechild, s. Brunechild, Brunehaut
Bucephalus, s. Bucéphale

C

Cæsar, s. César. *Julius* —, Jules César. *Octavius* —, César Octave
Caiaphas, s. Caïphe
Callicrates, s. Callicrate
Candaules, s. Candaule
Canute, s. Canut
Capitolinus, s. Capitolin
Cassander, s. Cassandre
Cassandra, s. Cassandre
Cato, s. Caton. — *the Elder*, Caton l'Ancien. — *of Utica*, Caton l'Utique
Catullus, s. Catulle
Celsus, s. Celse
Cephalus, s. Céphale
Cerberus, s. Cerbère
Ceres, s. Cérès
Charles, s. Charles. — *the Bald*, Charles le Chauve. — *the Bold*, Charles le Téméraire. — *the Fair*, Charles le Bel. — *the Fat*—, Charles le Gros. — *the Fifth* (*of Germany*), Charles-Quint. — *the First*, Charles Premier. — *the Hammerer*, Charles Martel. — *the Second*, Charles Deux. — *the Simple*, Charles le Simple
Cicero, s. Cicéron
Claudius, s. Claude
Cleopatra, s. Cléopâtre
Clytemnestra, s. Clytemnestre
Collatinus, s. Collatin
Columbus, s. Colomb. *Christopher* —, Christophe Colombe
Commodus, s. Commode
Comnena, s. Comnène. *Anna* —, Anne Comnène
Constantius, s. Constance
Constantine, s. Constantin
Copernicus, s. Copernic
Corinna, s. Corinne
Coriolanus, s. Coriolan
Cornelia, s. Cornélie
Cosmus, s. Cosme (de Médicis)
Creusa, s. Créuse
Crœsus, s. Crésus
Cupid, s. Cupidon
Curiatius, s. Curiace
Cybela, **Cybele**, s. Cybèle
Cyclop, s. Cyclope

D

Danaids, **Danaides**, s. pl. Danaïdes
Dædalus, s. Dédale
Dejanira, s. Déjanire
Democrates, s. Démocrate
Demosthenes, s. Démosthène
Dionysius, s. Denis. — *the Elder*, Denis l'Ancien. — *the Younger*, Denis le Jeune
Diana, **Dian**, s. Diane
Dido, s. Didon
Diocletian, s. Dioclétien
Diodorus, s. Diodore
Diogenes, s. Diogène
Diomedes, **Diomed**, s. Diomède
Dives, s. le Riche, le mauvais Riche
Dominichino, s. le Dominiquin, Zampiéri
Draco, s. Dracon
Draconian, adj. de Dracon

E

Egeria, s. Égérie
Electra, s. Électre
Elijah, s. Élie
Elisha, s. Élisée
Enoch, Hénoch
Epictetus, s. Épictète
Epicurus, s. Épicure
Epigoni (The), s. (les) Épigones
Epimenides, s. Épiménide
Erasmus, s. Érasme
Erastus, s. Éraste
Eratosthenes, s. Ératosthène
Eratostratus, s. Ératostrate
Euclid, s. Euclide
Eumæus, s. Eumée
Eumenes, s. Eumène
Euripides, s. Euripide
Europa, s. Europe
Euryalus, s. Euryale
Eurystheus, s. Eurysthée
Eusebius, s. Eusèbe
Evander, s. Évandre
Ezekiel, s. Ézéchiel

F

Faustus, s. Faust
Faustina, s. Faustine
Flavian, s. Flavien
Flora, s. Flore
Fulvia, s. Fulvie

G

Galathea, s. Galatée
Galileo, s. Galilée
Gideon, Gédéon
Gordian, adj. *The — knot*, le nœud Gordien
Gracchi (The), s. pl. (les) Gracques

H

Habakkuk, s. Habacuc
Hagar, s. Agar
Haggai, s. Aggée
Hannibal, s. Annibal
Ham, s. Cham
Hamilcar, s. Hamilcar
Haroun-al-Raschid, s. Haroun-al-Raschid
Harpocrates, s. Harpocrate
Hebe, s. Hébé
Hecate, s. Hécate
Hecuba, **Hecube**, s. Hécube
Hegesippus, s. Hégésippe
Helen, s. Hélène
Heliodorus, Héliodore
Heliogabalus, s. Héliogabale
Hercules, s. Hercule
Herod, s. Hérode
Herodotus, s. Hérodote
Hesiod, s. Hésiode
Hesperus, s. Hespérus, Hesper, Vesper
Hezekiah, s. Ézéchias
Hiero, s. Hiéron
Hippocrates, s. Hippocrate
Hippolyta, s. Hippolyte
Hippolytus, s. Hippolyte
Hippomenes, s. Hippomène
Homer, s. Homère
Horace, s. Horace
Hosea, s. Osée
Hystaspes, s. Hystaspe

I

Icarus, s. Icare
Idomeneus, s. Idoménée
Iphigenia, s. Iphigénie
Isaiah, s. Isaïe
Ishmael, s. Ismaël
Isocrates, s. Isocrate

J

Jehoiada, s. Joïada
Jehoshaphat, s. Josaphat
Jephtha, s. Jephté
Jeremiah, s. Jérémie
Joan of Arc, Jeanne d'Arc
Jocasta, s. Jocaste
Josephus, s. Josèphe
Josiah, s. Josias
Joshua, s. Josué
Jove, s. Jupiter, *Olympian* —, Jupiter Olympien
Jovian, Jovien
Judah, s. Juda
Juno, s. Junon
Justinian, s. Justinien

L

Lactantius, s. Lactance
Laertes, s. Laërte
Laertius, s. Laerce
Laodomia, s. Laodomie
Lapithæ, s. pl. Lapithes
Latona, s. Latone
Lazarus, s. Lazare
Leander, s. Léandre
Lepidus, s. Lépide
Lewis, s. Louis
Linnæus, s. Linnée
Livia, s. Livie
Livy, s. Tite-Live
Longinus, s. Longin
Louis, s. Louis. — *the Ninth*, Louis neuf. — *the Fat*, Louis le Gros. — *the Great*, Louis le Grand. — *the Headstrong*, Louis le Hutin. — *the Stammerer*, Louis le Bègue
Lucan, s. Lucain
Lucian, s. Lucien
Lucretia, s. Lucrèce
Lucretius, s. Lucrèce
Lycurgus, s. Lycurgue
Lysander, s. Lysandre
Lysimachus, s. Lysimaque
Lysippus, s. Lysippe

M

Machabeus, s. Machabée
Machabees, s. pl. Machabées
Macrobius, s. Macrobe
Mahomet, **Mahomed**, s. Mahomet
Manasseh, s. Manassé
Mark-Antony, s. Marc-Antoine
Marcus-Aurelius, s. Marc-Aurèle
Methuselah, s. Mathusalem
Mausolus, s. Mausole
Maximian, s. Maximien
Maximilian, s. Maximilien
Mecænas, s. Mécène
Medea, s. Médée
Medusa, s. Méduse. *The —'s head*, la tête de Méduse
Melchizedech, s. Melchisédech
Menelaus, s. Ménélas
Mercury, s. Mercure
Messalina, s. Messaline

Metastasio, s. Métastase
Micah, s. Michée
Michael-Angelo, s. Michel-Ange
Milo, s. Milon
Miltiades, s. Miltiade
Minerva, s. Minerve
Mithridates, s. Mithridate
Mordecai, s. Mardochée
Moses, s. Moïse
Morpheus, s. Morphée
More (Sir Thomas), s. Thomas Morus
Musæus, s. Musée

N

Naomi, s. Noémie
Narcissus, s. Narcisse
Nazarite, Nazarene, s. Nazaréen
Nebuchadnezzar, s. Nabuchodonosor
Nehemiah, s. Néhémie
Neoptolemus, s. Néoptolème
Nereus, s. Nérée
Nero, s. Néron
Niobe, s. Niobé
Noah, s. Noé

O

Obadiah, s. Abdias
Oceanus, s. Océan
Octavius, s. Octave
Octavia, s. Octavie
Octavianus, s. Octavien
Odoacer, s. Odoacre
Œdipus, s. Œdipe
Orestes, s. Oreste
Origen, s. Origène
Orpheus, s. Orphée
Otho, s. Othon
Ovid, s. Ovide

P

Palæologus, s. Paléologue
Pandora, s. Pandore
Parmenio, s. Parménion
Patroclus, s. Patrocle
Paul, s. Paul. Paolo. — *of Venice*, Fra Paolo
Paulus Æmilius, s. Paul Emile
Pegasus, s. Pégase
Pelagius, s. Pélage
Peleus, s. Pélée
Penthesilea, s. Penthésilée
Perseus, s. Persée
Persius, s. Perse
Petrarch, s. Pétrarque
Petronius, s. Pétrone
Phædrus, s. Phèdre
Phædra, s. Phèdre
Pharaoh, s. Pharaon
Philip, s. Philippe
Philoctetes, s. Philoctète
Philomela, s. Philomèle
Phineas, s. Phinée
Phœbus, s. Phébus
Pindar, s. Pindare
Pisistratus, s. Pisistrate
Pius, s. Pie
Plato, s. Platon
Plautus, s. Plaute
Pliny, s. Pline. — *the Elder*, Pline l'Ancien. — *the Younger*, Pline le Jeune
Plutarch, s. Plutarque
Pluto, s. Pluton
Polybius, s. Polybe
Polycrates, s. Polycrate
Pontius Pilate, s. Ponce Pilate
Polymnia, s. Polymnie
Polyphemus, s. Polyphème
Pomona, s. Pomone
Pompey, s. Pompée
Potiphar, s. Putiphar
Praxiteles, s. Praxitèle
Priapus, s. Priape
Procopius, s. Procope
Prometheus, s. Prométhée
Propertius, s. Properce
Protesilaus, s. Protésilas
Proteus, s. Protée
Psyche, s. Psyché
Ptolemy, s. Ptolémée
Pylades, s. Pylade
Pyramus, s. Pyrame
Pythagoras, s. Pythagore

Q

Quintus Curtius, s. Quinte-Curce
Quintilian, s. Quintilien
Quixote (Don), s. Don Quichotte

R

Rhadamanthus, s. Rhadamanthe
Rhea, s. Rhéa

S

Sallust, s. Salluste
Sardanapalus, s. Sardanapale
Sappho, s. Sapho
Saturn, s. Saturne
Saturninus, s. Saturnin
Scipio, s. Scipion. — *Africanus*, Scipion l'Africain. — *Asiaticus*, Scipion l'Asiatique
Sejanus, s. Séjan
Seneca, s. Sénèque
Septimius, s. Septime. — *Severus*, Septime Sévère
Sextus, s. Sixte. *Pope — the Fifth*, le Pape Sixte-Quint
Sforza, s. Sforce
Shem, s. Sem
Sigismund, s. Sigismond
Silenus, s. Silène
Simonides, s. Simonide
Sisyphus, s. Sisyphe
Smintheus, s. Sminthée
Socrates, s. Socrate
Solomon, s. Solomon
Sophocles, s. Sophocle
Statius, s. Stace
Stilicho, s. Stilichon
Strabo, s. Strabon
Suetonius, s. Suétone
Symmachus, s. Symmaque

T

Tacitus, s. Tacite
Tamerlane, s. Tamerlan
Tantalus, s. Tantale
Tarquin, s. Tarquin. *The Elder —, Tarquinius Priscus*, Tarquin l'Ancien. — *the Proud*, Tarquin le Superbe
Tartarus, s. Tartare
Tasso, Tasse
Telemachus, s. Télémaque
Tereus, s. Térée
Tertullian, s. Tertullien
Thalia, s. Thalie
Themistocles, s. Thémistocle
Theocritus, s. Théocrite
Theodosius, s. Théodose
Theophrastus, s. Théophraste
Theseus, s. Thésée
Thersites, Thersite
Thucydides, s. Thucydide
Thyestes, s. Thyeste
Tiberius, s. Tibère
Titus, s. Titus
Tithonus, s. Tithon
Titian, s. Titien
Tobias, Toby, s. Tobie
Tribonian, s. Tribonien
Triptolemus, s. Triptolème
Tullia, s. Tullie
Tully, s. Cicéron
Tydeus, s. Tydée
Tydides, s. fils de Tydée
Tyndarus, s. Tyndare
Tyrtæus, s. Tyrtée

U

Ulysses, s. Ulysse
Urania, s. Uranie

V

Valentinian, s. Valentinien
Valerian, s. Valérien
Valerius, s. Valère. — *Maximus*, Valère-Maxime
Valkyriur, s. Valkyrie
Varro, s. Varron
Vertumnus, s. Vertumne
Vespasian, s. Vespasien
Virgil, s. Virgil
Vitruvius, s. Vitruve
Vulcan, s. Vulcain

X

Xantippus, s. Xantippe
Xenocrates, s. Xenocrate
Xenophon, s. Xenophon

Z

Zacharie, s. Zacharie
Zampieri, s. le Dominiquin, Zampiéri
Zedekiah, s. Sédécias
Zeno, s. Zénon
Zenobia, s. Zénobie
Zephyrus, s. Zéphire
Zoilus, s. Zoïle
Zoroaster, s. Zoroastre

DICTIONNAIRE

DES NOMS DE BAPTEME DE L'HOMME ET FEMME

DONT L'ORTHOGRAPHE VARIE DANS LES DEUX LANGUES

A

Adah, s. Ada
Adolphus, s. Adolphe
Agatha, s. Agathe
Allen, s. Alain
Alphonso, s. Alphonse
Annabel, s. Aimée
Ambrose, s. Ambroise
Amedeus, s. Amédée
Amelia, s. Amélie
Amy, s. Aimée
Anastasius, s. Anastase
Andrew, s. André
Angelo, s. Ange
Ann, Anna, Anne, s. Anne, Anna
Anselm, Anselmo, s. Anselme
Anthony, Antony, s. Antoine
Arabella, s. Arabelle
Athanasius, s. Athanase
Augustus, s. Auguste
Augustine, s. Augustin
Aurelia, s. Aurélie
Aurora, s. Aurore

B

Betsy, Bessy, Bess, s. Betsie, Babet, Élisabeth
Barbara, s. Barbara
Bartholomew, s. Barthélemy
Baldwin, s. Baudouin
Beatrice, s. Béatrix
Bella, s. Isabelle
Benedict, s. Benoît
Ben, s. Benjamin
Bertha, s. Berthe
Bertram, s. Bertrand
Blanch, s. Blanche
Bridget, s. Brigitte
Bill, Billa, s. William, Guillaume
Bob, s. Robert, Robin

C

Camilla, s. Camille
Cecilia, Cecily, s. Cécile
Celestine, s. Celestin
Celia, s. Célie
Charley, s. Charlot
Christian, s. Chrétien
Christina, s. Christine
Christopher, s. Christophe
Clara, s. Clara, Claire
Clarissa, s. Clarisse
Claud, s. Claude
Claudia, s. Claudie
Cleanthus, s. Cléanthe
Clelia, s. Clélie
Clementina, s. Clémentine
Clotilda, s. Clotilde
Cordelia, s. Cordélie
Crispin (Saint), s. Saint-Crépin

D

Dan, s. Daniel
Dick, s. Richard
Dominick, s. Dominique
Dorothea, s. Dorothée
Dorrit, s. Dorothée

E

Edmund, s. Edmond
Edward, s. Édouard
Eleanor, s. Éléonore
Elisa, s. Élise, Élisa
Elisabeth, s. Élisabeth
Emily, s. Émilie
Eugene, s. Eugène
Eugenia, s. Eugénie

F

Fabian, s. Fabien
Fanny, s. Fanny, Fanchon, Fanchette
Felicita, s. Félicité
Felicia, s. Félicie
Flora, s. Flore
Frances, s. Fanny, Françoise
Francis, s. Francis, François
Frederick, Fred, s. Frédéric

G

Geoffrey, s. Geoffroy
George, s. Georges
Giles, s. Gilles
Gregory, s. Grégoire
Gustavus, s. Gustave

H

Helen, Helena, s. Hélène, *f.*
Harry, s. Henri
Harrietta, s. Henriette
Henry, s. Henri
Hetty, s. Esther
Hortensia, s. Hortense

I

Ignatius, s. Ignace
Isabel, Isabella, s. Isabelle, Isabeau

J

Jack, s. Jean
James, s. Jacques
Jane, s. Jeanne
Janet, s. Jeanette
Jem, Jemmy, s. Jacques
Jenny, s. Jenny, Jeanne, Jeannette
Joan, s. Jeanne, Jacqueline
Joe, s. Joseph
John, s. Jean
Julia, s. Julie
Juliana, s. Julienne
Juliet, s. Juliette
Julius, s. Jules
Justina, s. Justine

K

Kate, Katie, Kitty, s. Catherine

L

Launcelot, s. Lancelot
Laura, s. Laure
Laurence, s. Laurent
Lewis, s. Louis
Lizzy, s. Lisette, Elise, Elisa, Elisabeth
Louisa, Loo, s. Louise, Louisette, Louison
Lucian, s. Lucien
Lucy, s. Lucie
Luke, s. Luc

M

Mabel, s. Mabel, Aimée
Madge, Meg, s. Margot, Marguerite

M

Magdalen, s. Madaleine
Margaret, s. Marguerite, Margot
Mark, s. Marc
Mary, s. Marie. *Mary Anne*, Marianne
Martha, s. Marthe
Matilda, s. Mathilde
Mathew, s. Mathieu
Maud, s Mathilde, Madeleine, Madelon
Michael, s. Michel
Montague, s. Montaigu

N

Nancy, s. Nancy, Nannette
Ned, Neddy, s. Edouard
Nell, Nelly, s. Eléonore
Nicodemus, s. Nicodème
Nicholas, s. Nick, Nicolas

O

Oliver, s. Olivier
Olivia, s. Olivie
Olympia, s. Olympe
Onesimus, s. Onésime
Ophelia, s. Ophélie

P

Patrick, s. Patrice
Peter, s. Pierre
Poll, Polly, s. Marie
Priscilla, s. Priscille

R

Randol, Randolph, s. Randolphe
Ralph, s. Ralph, Raoul
Richard, s. Richard. — *the Lion-Hearted*, Richard Cœur-de-Lion
Robert, s. Robert
Reuben, s. Ruben
Rodolph, s. Rodolphe
Rosamund, s. Rosamonde
Rowland, s. Roland. *To give a — for an Oliver*, à bon chat bon rat

S

Sabina, s. Sabine
Sally, s. Sara
Sam, s. Samuel
Silvester, s. Silvestre
Sophia, Sophy, s. Sophie
Susan, s. Susanne
Sylvia, s. Sylvie

T

Teophelus, s. Théophile
Theresa, s. Thérèse
Tom, Tommy, s. Thomas, Tom
Timothy, Tim, s. Thimothée
Tony, s. Antoine

U

Urban, s. Urbain
Ursula, s. Ursule

V

Valentine, s. Valentin, *m.*, Valentine, *f.*
Veronica, s. Véronique
Virginia, s. Virginie
Vivian, s. Vivien

W

Walter, Wat, s. Walter, Gauthier
William, Will, Willy, s. William, Guillaume
Wilhelmina, s. Wilhelmine

A LIST OF THE

PRINCIPAL DIVERGING DERIVATIONS (DOUBLETS)

IN THE FRENCH LANGUAGE.

Taken from M. A. Brachet's DICTIONNAIRE DES DOUBLETS.

Abrégeur—abréviateur: *abbreviatorem.*
Acre—aigre: *acris.*
Adjudant—aidant: (*Sp.*) *ayudante*; (*adjutantem*).
Advenir—avenir: *advenire.*
Adverse—averse: *adversus.*
Affaiter—affecter: *adfectare;* **affaiter** (*v.a.*), *term of falconry: to tame.*
Affaité—affecté—affété: *affectatum.*
Affermer—affirmer: *adfirmare.*
Agraire—agrier: *agrarium;* **agrier** (*s.m.*), *old law term: ground-rent.*
Agrégat—agrégé: *aggregatus.*
Aigage—aquatique: *aquaticum;* **aigage** (*s.m.*), *old law term: right of constructing an aqueduct upon another person's property.*
Aiglon—aquilon: *aquilonem.*
Aiguière—évier: *aquarium.*
Aimant—diamant: *adamantem.*
Aimé—amé: *amatus.*
Aire—are: *area.*
Aisselle—axille: *axilla;* **axille** (*s.f.*), *that which refers to the axis of a plant.*
Ajouter—ajuster: (*ad*) *juxtare* (*L.L. ajustare*).
Album—aube: *alba.*
Alguazil—argousin: (*Sp.*) *alguazil.*
Altesse—hautesse: (*It.*) *altezza* (*L.L. altitia*).
Amande—amydale: *amydala.*
Amant—aimant: *amantem.*
Anche—hanche: (*O.H.G.*) *ancha.*
Ange—angelus: *angelus.*
Anglé—angulé: *angulatus.*
Annate—année: *annata.*
Antienne—antiphone: *antiphona.*
Août—auguste: *augustus.*
Apothicaire—boutiquier: *apothecarium.*
Appas—appât: *adpastum.*
Appeau—appel: (*L.L.*) *appellum.*
Apprehender—apprendre: *apprehendere.*
Apreté—aspérité: *asperitatem.*
Aptitude—attitude: (*It.*) *attitudine* (*aptitudinem*).
Arc—arche: *arcus.*
Arcade—archée: *arcata;* **archée** (*s.f.*), *a bow-shot.*
Archer—arquer: *arcare.*
Armature—armure: *armatura.*
Article—orteil: *articulus.*
Asséner—assigner: *assignare.*
Assoupir—assouvir: *assopire.*
Astre—âtre: *astrum.*
Attacher—attaquer: (*Fr.*) *tacher.*
Augure—heur: *augurium.*
Auréole—loriot: *aureolum.*
Auriculaire—oreiller: *auricularius.*
Ausculter—écouter: *auscultare.*
Avocat—avoué: *advocatus.*
Bagne—bain: (*It.*) *bagno* (*balneum*).
Balance—bilan: (*It.*) *bilancio* (*bilancem*).
Banc—banque: (*It.*) *banca* (*bancus*).
Bandière—bannière: (*It.*) *bandiera* (*L.L. bandaria*).
Bandit—banni: (*It.*) *bandito* (*banditus*).
Barrette—béret: (*Prov.*) *barretta* (*birrettum*).
Basilique—basoche: *basilica;* *the basoche* (*s.f.*) *was an old court established in Paris for the purpose of settling the disputes which arose between lawyers' clerks.*
Bastille—bâtie: (*Prov.*) *bastida* (*L.L. bastita*); **bastide,** *a small country house in Provence.*
Bayant—béant: (*L.L.*) *badare.*
Beauvoir—belvédère: (*It.*) *bel vedere* (*bellum videre*).
Belladone—belle dame: (*It.*) *bella donna* (*bella domina*).
Benêt—béni—bénit—benoit: *benedictus.*
Bénir—bien dire: *bene dicere.*
Besogne—besoin: (*It.*) *bisogna.*
Béton—bitume: *bitumen;* **béton,** *a mixture of sand, lime, and gravel.*
Bill—bulle: (*Eng.*) *bill, bull* (*bulla*).
Blâmer—blasphémer: *blasphemare.*
Blanchette—blanquette: (*L.L.*) *blanchetum.*
Blockhaus—blocus: (*G.*) *block haus.*
Border—broder: (*O.H.G.*) *bordon.*
Bosquet—bouquet: (*L.L.*) *boscus.*
Bouffer—bouffir—pouffer (?): (*It.*) *buffare.*
Bouter—butor: (*O.H.G.*) *bozen.*
Bras—brasse: *brachium.*
Brigade—briguée: (*It.*) *brigata.*
Bruire—rugir (?): *rugire.*
Cabâne—cabine: (*Eng.*) *cabin* (*capanna*).
Cabale—gabelle: (*Heb.*) *alcabala.*
Cabriole—chevreuil: (*It.*) *capriola* (*capreolus*).
Cadenas—chaine: (*Sp.*) *cadena* (*catena*).
Cadence—chance: (*It.*) *cadenza* (*cadentia*).
Cadran—quarrant: *quadrantem;* **quarrant,** *O.F. for cadran.*
Cahier—casorne—quaterne: *quaternum.*

Cailler—coaguler: *coagulare.*
Caisse—châsse—casse: *capsa.*
Calandre—cylindre: *cylindrus.*
Caleçon—chausse—chausson: (*It.*) *calzone* (*calceus*).
Calleux—galeux: *callosus.*
Camarade—chambrée: (*It.*) *camerata;* (*Sp.*) *camarada* (*camerata*).
Cambrer—chambrer: *camerare.*
Camérier—chambrier: (*It.*) *cameriere* (*camerarius*).
Camp—champ: *campus.*
Campagne—champagne: *campania.*
Canaille—chiennaille: (*It.*) *canaglia* (*L.L. canacula*); chiennaille, *O.F. for canaille.*
Canal—chenal: *canalis.*
Cancre—chancre—cancer: *cancer.*
Canonique—chanoine: *canonicus.*
Cantate—chantée: (*It.*) *cantata* (*cantata*).
Cantine—quintaine: *quintana.*
Cap—chef: (*Prov.*) *cap* (*caput*).
Capitaine—capitan: (*Sp.*) *capitan* (*L.L. capitaneus*).
Capital—cheptel: *capitale.*
Capitoul—capitule—chapitre: *capitulum.*
Capituler—chapitrer: *capitulare.*
Capon—chapon: (*It.*) *capone* (*caponem*).
Cappe—chappe: *cappa.*
Captif—chétif: *captivus.*
Carbonade—charbonnée: (*Prov.*) *carbonada* (*carbonata*).
Carême—quadragésime: *quadragesima.*
Carguer—charger: (*Prov.*) *cargar* (*carricare*).
Carnier—charnier: *carnarium*
Carogne—charogne: (*L.L.*) *caronia.*
Carrer—cadrer: *quadrare.*
Carrure—quadrature: *quadratura.*
Carte—charta: *charta.*
Cartulaire—chartrier: *cartularium.*
Case—chez: (*Sp.*) *casa* (*casa*).
Castel—château: (*It.*) *castello* (*castellum*).
Castrat—châtré: (*It.*) *castrato* (*castratus*).
Catafalque—échafaud: (*It.*) *catafalco* (*L.L. catafalcus*).
Cause—chose: *causa.*
Cavalcade—chevauchée: (*It.*) *cavalcata* (*L.L. caballicata*).
Cavale—cheval: (*It.*) *cavallo* (*caballus*).
Cavalerie—chevalerie: (*It.*) *cavalleria.*
Cavalier—chevalier: (*It.*) *cavaliere* (*L.L. caballerius*).
Cément—ciment: *cœmentum.*
Cendrier—cinéraire: *cinerarius.*
Centenaire—centenier: *centenarium.*
Centième—centime: *centesimus.*
Cep—cippe: *cippus.*
Cérat—ciré: *ceratum.*
Cercelle—sarcelle: *querquedula,* cercelle=sarcelle.
Cercler—circuler: *circulare.*
Cercueil—sarcophage: *sarcophagus.*
Cerise—kirsch: *cerasus.*
Chainon—chignon: (*L.L.*) *catenionem.*
Chaire—chaise: *cathedra.*
Châlet—châtelet: (*L.L.*) *castelletum.*
Chanteur—chantre: *cantorem.*
Charbon—carbone: *carbonem.*
Charité—cherté: *caritatem.*
Charrier—charroyer: *carricare.*
Cheville—clavicule: *clavicula.*
Chiffre—zéro: (*Ar.*) *cifran.*
Chœur—chorus: *chorus.*
Cholera—colère—colle: *cholera.*
Chômer—calmer: (*It.*) *cauma* (*calmare*).
Chrétien—crétin: *christianus.*
Cingler—sangler: *cingulare.*
Cithare—guitare: (*Sp.*) *guitarra* (*cithara*).
Claire—glaire (?): *clara.*
Classique—glas: *classicum.*
Clause—close: *clausa.*
Coccinelle—cochenille: (*Sp.*) *cochinilla* (*coccinella*).
Coction—cuisson: *coctionem.*
Code—codex: *codex.*
Coffre—coffin: *cophinus.*
Cohorte—cour: *cohortem.*
Coi—quitte: *quietus.*
Col—cou: *collum.*
Collecte—cueillette: *collecta.*
Colliger—cueillir: *colligere.*
Colloquer—coucher: *collocare.*
Colorer—colorier: *colorare.*
Comble—combre (en-combre, dé-combre)—**cumul:** *cumulus.*
Combler—cumuler: *cumulare.*
Comité—comté—comtat: *comitatus.*
Communier—communiquer: *communicare.*
Compote—composite: *compositus.*
Composteur—compositeur: *compositorem.*
Confiance—confidence: *confidentia.*
Conque—coque: *concha.*
Constant—coûtant: *constantem.*
Contenance—continence: *continentia.*
Contracte—contrat: *contractum.*
Copule—couple: *copula.*
Copuler—coupler: *copulare.*
Coq—queux: (*Eng.*) **cook** (*coquus*).
Cor—corne: *cornu.*
Corsaire—coursier: *corsarius* (*It. corsare*).
Costume—coutume: (*It.*) *costume* (*L.L. costuma*).
Courir—courre: *currere.*
Crasse—gras: *crassus.*
Cravate—Croate: *Croate* (*proper name*).
Créance—crédence—croyance: *credentia.*
Créper—crisper—crépir: *crispare.*
Croisade—croisée: (*It.*) *crociata* (*L.L. cruciata*).
Croissant—crescendo: (*It.*) *crescendo* (*crescentem*).
Crypte—grotte: *crypta.*
Cucurbite—gourde: *cucurbita.*
Cuistre—custode: *custodem.*
Dactyle—datte: *dactylus.*
Dais—disque: *discus.*
Dame—dom: *dominus;* **dame!** (*exclam.*) *comp.* (*O.F.*) *Dame-Dieu!*
Dé—doigt: *digitus.*
Décadence—déchéance: *decadentia.*
Décanat—doyenné: *decanatus.*
Décime—dîme—dixième: *decima.*
Délayer—dilater: *dilatare.*
Délectant—dilettante: (*It.*) *dilettante* (*delectantem*).
Délié—délicat: *delicatus.*
Demoiselle—donzelle: (*L.L.*) *dominicella.*
Denaire—denier: *denarium;* **denaire,** *which has ten numbers.*
Dentier—dentaire: *dentarius.*
Dénudé—dénué: *denudatus.*
Dépenser—dispenser: *dispensare.*
Déprécier—dépriser: *depretiare.*

Désigner—dessiner: *designare.*
Dessein—dessin: *designum.*
Détroit—district: *districtus.*
Deux—duo: *duo.*
Dévier—dévoyer: *de, ex, viare.*
Dicton—dit: *dictum.*
Dé—digitale (?): *digitale.*
Direct—droit: *directus.*
Diurnal—journal: *diurnale;* **diurnal** (*s.m.*), *a kind of breviary.*
Diurne—jour: *diurnum.*
Divan—douane: (*It.*) *dogana, doana.*
Divin—devin: *divinus.*
Diviser—deviser: *divisare.*
Doge—duc: (*It.*) *doge* (*dux*).
Dorade—dorée: (*Prov.*) *dorada* (*L.L. de-aurata*).
Doter—douer: *dotare.*
Douille—ductile: *ductilis;* douille (*s.f.*), *a socket; also a cartridge for breech-loading rifles.*
Drac—dragon—estragon: *draconem;* drac, *O.F. nominat. of* dragon.
Drogman—truchement: (*Ar.*) *torgoman.*
Ducat—duché: (*It.*) *ducato* (*ducatus*).
Duègne—dame: (*Sp.*) *dueña* (*domina*).
Écaille—écale: (*O.H.G.*) *skalja.*
Echalier—escalier: *scalarium;* échalier (*s.m.*), *an enclosure for cattle.*
Échappée—escapade: (*It.*) *scappata* (*L.L. ex-cappata*).
Écharpe—escarpe: (*It.*) *scarpa.*
Échelle—escale: (*It.*) *scala* (*scala*).
Échine—esquine: (*O.H.G.*) *skina.*
Écolier—scholaire: *scholaris.*
Écorce noire—scorsonère: (*It.*) *scorza nera.*
Écorcer—écorcher: *corticare.*
Écrouelle—scrofule: *scrofula.*
Effeuiller—exfolier: *exfoliare.*
Embuscade—embusquée: (*L.L.and It.*) *imboscata.*
Émeute—émue: *ex, mota.*
Emplette—implicite: *implicita.*
Employer—impliquer: *implicare.*
Empreindre—imprimer: *imprimere.*
Enclaver—enclouer: *inclavare.*
Enclore—inclure: *includere.*
Encrasser—engraisser: *incrassare.*
Encroûter—incruster: *incrustare.*
Endroit—indirect: *indirectus.*
Enduire—induire: *inducere.*
Enduré—induré: *induratus;* induré, *medical expression: hardened.*
Enfant—infant: (*Sp.*) *infante* (*infantem*).
Enfermer—infirmer: *infirmare.*
Enjambe—ingambe: (*It.*) *ingamba.*
Enluminer—illuminer: *illuminare.*
Enquêteur—inquisiteur: *inquisitorem.*
Enrôler—enrouler: *inrotulare.*
Enseigne—insigne: *insignia* (?).
Entendant—intendant: *intendentem.*
Entier—intègre: *integer.*
Entreposer—interposer: *interpausare.*
Envers—inverse: *inversus.*
Épagneul—espagnol: (*Sp.*) *Español* (*Hispaniolus*).
Épaule—spatule: *spatula.*
Épée—spathe: *spatha;* spathe (*bot.*), *a foliaceous envelope.*
Épice—espèce: *species.*
Épingle—spinule: *spinula.*

Épiscopat—évêché: *episcopatus.*
Épistolaire—épistolier: *epistolarium:* Balzac grand *épistolier.*
Éployé—expliqué: *explicatus.*
Équerre—escadre—escouade: (*It.*) *squadra* (*exquadra*).
Esclandre—scandale: *scandalum.*
Esprit—spirite.
Essaim—examen: *examen.*
Étage—stage: (*It.*) *staggio* (*L.L. staticum*).
Étain—tain: *stannum.*
Étal—stalle: (*L.L.*) *stallum.*
Étinceler—scintiller: *scintillare.*
Étioler—stipuler: *stipulare.*
Étique—hectique: *hecticus.*
Étroit—strict: *strictus.*
Exaucer—exhausser: (*L.L.*) *exaltiare.*
Exhalaison—exhalation: *exhalationem.*
Explicite—exploit: *explicitus.*
Fabrique—forge: *fabrica.*
Façon—faction: *factionem.*
Factice—fétiche: *factitius.*
Factum—fait: *factum.*
Fade—fat: *fatuus.*
Faible—flébile: *flebilis.*
Faillir—falloir: *fallere.*
Faine—fouine: *fagina.*
Falquer—faucher: (*L.L.*) *falcare.*
Fantasque—fantastique: *phantasticus.*
Farouche—féroce: *ferocem.*
Faucheur—faucheux: (*L.L.*) *falcatorem.*
Féal—fidèle: *fidelis;* féal (*O.F.*) = fidèle.
Férie—foire: *feria;* férie (*s.f.*), *holiday.*
Feutre—filtre: (*L.L.*) *filtrum.*
Filateur—fileur—filou: *filatorem.*
Flairer—fleurer: *flagrare.*
Flamant—flambant: *flammantem.*
Fleurir—florir: *florere.*
Flottaison—fluctuation: *fluctuationem.*
Foison—fusion: *fusionem.*
For—fur: *forum:* au *fur* et à mesure.
Forçat—forcé: (*L.L.*) *fortiatus.*
Format—formé: *formatus.*
Fors—hors: *foris:* Tout est perdu, *fors* (excepté) l'honneur.
Fouace (*s.f. a kind of cake*)—fougasse (*s.f. a s*-*mine*, une *fougasse* de poudre): (*L.L.*) *focac*
Fragile—frêle: *fragilis.*
Frais—fresque: (*It.*) *fresco.*
Friction—frisson: *frictionem.*
Fugue—fuite: (*It.*) *fuga* (*fuga*).
Gai—geai: (*Sp.*) *gayo.*
Garenne—varenne: (*O.H.G.*) *waron.*
Gaudir—jouer: *gaudir* (*O.F.*) = *to rejoice.*
Gazon—vase: (*L.L.*) *waso.*
Geindre—gémir: *gemere.*
Gémeau—jumeau: *gemellus.*
Gêne—géhenne: γέεννα.
Golfe—gouffre: κόλφος.
Goule—gueule: *gula.*
Grammaire—grimoire: (*L.L.*) *grammaria.*
Grave—grief: *gravis.*
Grecque—grièche—grègue: *Græca:* "Pie-gri
Grenade—grenée: *granata.*
Grenouille—renoncule: *ranuncula.*
Grincer—grincher: grincher (*v.n.*) *is said of* *when the crust has risen too much:* (*O. grimmison.*

vre—vipère: *vipera.*
iter—hanter: *habitare.*
angue—rang: (*O.H.G.*) *hring.*
éditaire—héritier: *hereditarius.*
isson—oursin: (*L.L.*) *ericionem.*
mine—Arménie: *Armenia.*
nme—on: *hominem.*
chet—jonchet: *juncus.*
ital—hôtel: *hospitale.*
ppe—huppe: *upupa.*
cinthe—jacinthe: *hyacinthum.*
le: *ille.*
oste—impôt: (*It.*) *imposta* (*imposita*).
rnat—incarné: *incarnatus.*
inaison—inclination: *inclinationem.*
go—indique (*belonging to India*): *indicus.*
uet—jockey: (*Fr.*) *Jacques, of which* jacquet *the diminutive.*
e—joue: *gabata.*
ger—qualifier: *qualificare.*
te—junte: *juncta.*
e—jury—jurat: *juratus.*
esse—justice: *justitia.*
her—laisser: *laxare.*
ne—lagune: (*It.*) *laguna* (*lacuna*).
e—Lazare: *Lazarus.*
-laïque: *laicus.*
beau—lambel: (*L.L.*) *labellus;* lambel *erald.*) *label.*
e—largue: (*L.L.*) *larga.*
l—loyal: *legalis.*
lité—loyauté: *legalitatem.*
t—légué: *legatus.*
son—légation: *legationem.*
e—lien: *ligamen.*
ration—livraison: *liberationem.*
rer—livrer: *liberare.*
—liguer: *ligare.*
nge—louange: (*Pr.*) *lauzenga* (*L.L. laudemia*).
-loto: (*O.H.G.*) *hloz;* loto, *a kind of game.*
aron—macaroni: (*It.*) *macarone.*
hellier—maxillaire: *maxillaris.*
her—mastiquer: *masticare;* mastiquer, *to tty, to cement.*
ule—maille: *macula.*
ame—madone: (*It.*) *ma donna* (*mea domina*).
ister—maître: *magister.*
istral—mistral: *magistrale.*
e—major—majeur: *majorem.*
che—manique: *manica;* manique (*s.f.*), *hand ther.*
dat—mandé: *mandatus.*
her—marquer: (*Goth.*) *marka.*
guillier—matriculaire: *matricularius.*
teau—martel: (*L.L.*) *martellus.*
ian—moyen: *medianus.*
er—miner: *minare.*
estrel—ministériel: *ministerialis.*
ue—minute: *minuta.*
curiale—mercuriel: *mercurialis.*
er—ministère: *ministerium.*
ble—mobile: *mobilis.*
lière—molaire: *molaris.*
ésime—millième: *millesimus.*
eur—moindre: *minorem.*
—messe—mets: *missa.*
ule—moule: *modulus.*
Mol—mou: *mollis.*
Morceau—museau: (*L.L.*) *morcellus.*
Monastere—moutier: *monasterium.*
Muguet—muscat: *muscatus.*
Muscade—musquée: *muscata.*
Muscle—moule: *musculus.*
Nager—naviguer: *navigare.*
Naïf—natif: *nativus.*
Natal—noel: *natalis.*
Nausée—noise: *nausea.*
Nègre—noir: *niger.*
Niche—nique: (*O.H.G.*) *nyck.*
Nombre—numéro: *numero.*
Nombril—ombilic: *umbilicus.*
Nourrisson—nutrition: *nutritionem.*
Oblat—oublie: *oblata.*
Œuvre—opéra: *opera.*
Official—officiel: *officialis.*
Oignon—union: *unionem.*
Onglé—ongulé: *ungulatus.*
Opérer—ouvrer: *operare.*
Orbitaire—ornière: *orbitaria.*
Organe—orgue: *organum.*
Pagne—pan—panne: (*Sp.*) *paño* (*pannus*).
Pal—pieu: *palus.*
Paladin—palatin: *palatinus.*
Palme—paume: *palma.*
Panade—panée: (*Prov.*) *panada* (*L.L. panata*).
Panser—penser—peser: *pensare.*
Papier—papyrus: *papyrus.*
Papillon—pavillon: *papilionem.*
Par—part: *partem.*
Parabole—parole: *parabola.*
Parade—parée: (*It.*) *parata* (*parata*).
Paradis—parvis: *paradisus.*
Parafe—paragraphe: *παραγραφός.*
Partial—partiel: *partialis.*
Pasteur—pâtre: *pastorem.*
Pastille—pastel: (*It.*) *pastello.*
Pause—pose: *pausa.*
Pêche—presse: *persica.*
Pedicule—pou: *pediculum.*
Pensum—poids: *pensum.*
Pépie—pituite: *pituita.*
Perronnelle—Petronille: *Petronilla.*
Pétale—poêle: *petalum.*
Piano—plain—plane: (*It.*) *piano* (*L. planus*).
Piété—pitié: *pietatem.*
Plaid—plait: *placitum.*
Plaine—plane: *plana.*
Plaire—plaisir: *placere.*
Platane—plane: *platanus.*
Plate—plie: *plata.*
Plier—ployer: *plicare.*
Poinçon—ponction: *punctionem.*
Pointer—ponctuer: (*L.L.*) *punctuare.*
Poison—potion: *potionem.*
Poivrade—poivrée—purée: (*L.L.*) *piperata.*
Police—pouillé: *polypticum;* (police *in the sense of an insurance deed;*) pouille (*s.m.*), *a statement of the landed property belonging to an abbey, etc.*
Polype—poulpe: *polypus.*
Prebende—provende: *præbenda.*
Précaire—prière: *precaria.*
Prêcheur—prédicateur: *prædicatorem.*
Préhension—prison: *prehensionem.*
Premier—primaire: *primarius.*

Presbytère—prêtre: *presbyter.*
Préséance—présidence: *presidentia.*
Preste—prêt: (*It.*) *presto* (*præstus*).
Probable—prouvable: *probabilis.*
Provençal—provincial: *provincialis.*
Psaltérion—psautier: *psalterium.*
Quatre—quatuor: *quatuor.*
Questeur—quêteur: *quæstorem.*
Raboter—rebouter: (*O.H.G.*) *bozen;* rebouter (*v.a.*), *to set a bone.*
Radié—rayé: *radiatus.*
Rage—rêve: *rabies.*
Raison—ration: *rationem.*
Rançon—rédemption: *redemptionem.*
Rapprocher—reprocher: (*L.L.*) *repropiare.*
Ras—rez: *rasus.*
Rasade—rasée: (*Prov.*) *razada* (*rasata*).
Récollet—recueilli: *recollectus.*
Recouvrer—récupérer: *recuperare.*
Récuser—ruser: *recusare.*
Redoute—réduit: (*It.*) *ridotto* (*reductus*).
Régale—royale: *regalis.*
Régleur—régulateur: *regulatorem.*
Relâcher—relaxer: *relaxare.*
Renégat—renié: *renegatus.*
Répit—respect: *respectum.*
Replier—répliquer—reployer: *replicare.*
Réseau—résille: *retiolum.*
Rétracter—retraiter: *retractare.*
Revêche—revers: (*It.*) *revescio* (*reversus*).
Rhythme—rime: *rhythmus.*
Rigide—roide: *rigidus.*
Roder—rouer: (*Prov.*) *rodar* (*rotare*).
Rôle—rotule: *rotula.*
Ronde—rotonde: *rotonda.*
Rosaire—rosier: *rosarium.*
Rosat—rosé: *rosatus.*
Roture—rupture: *ruptura.*
Rustique—rustre: *rusticus.*
Sacrement—serment: *sacramentum.*
Salade—salée: (*Sp.*) *salada* (*salata*).
Salaire—salière: *salarium.*
Sanglier—singulier: *singularis.*
Sauterelle—saltarelle: (*It.*) *saltarella.*
Savonnerie—saponaire: (*L.L.*) *saponaria;* savonnerie (*s.f.*), *soap-house.*
Schiste—zeste: (*It.*) *zesto* (*schistus*).
Scieur—sécateur: *secatorem;* sécateur (*s.m.*), *pruning-shears.*
Sèche—seiche—sépia: *sepia.*
Seigneur—sieur—sire: *seniorem.*
Sein—sinus: *sinus.*
Seing—signe: *signum.*
Sembler—simuler: *simulare.*
Soc—socque: *soccus.*
Soda—soude: (*It.*) *soda* (*solida*).
Soldat—soldé—soudé: *solidatus.*
Solder—souder: *solidare.*
Solide—sou: *solidus.*
Solliciter—soucier: *sollicitare.*
Sommaire—sommier: *summarium.*
Sonate—sonnee: (*It.*) *sonata* (*sonata*).
Soubresaut—sursaut: (*It.*) *sobresalto*(*super,sal*
Soupçon—suspicion: *suspicionem.*
Sourdre—surgir: *surgere.*
Subrécargue—surcharge: (*It.*) *sobrecarga* (*su*
L.L. carrica).
Suçon—suction: (*L.L.*) *suctionem.*
Table—tôle: *tabula.*
Tâcher—tasser: *taxare.*
Taillade—taillée: (*It.*) *tagliata.*
Tempérer—tremper: *temperare.*
Teneur—ténor: (*It.*) *tenore* (*tenorem*).
Têt—tête: *testa.*
Tépide—tiède: *tepidus.*
Territoire—terroir: *territorium.*
Thyrse—torse—trou (de chou): *thyrsum.*
Tibia—tige: *tibia.*
Timbale—tympan—timbre: *tympanum.*
Toison—tonsion: *tonsionem;* tonsion (*s.f.*), *art of shearing.*
Toquer—toucher: (*L.L.*) *toccare.*
Tradition—trahison: *traditionem.*
Trognon—tronçon: *truncus.*
Vaillant—valant: *valentem.*
Variole—vérole: *variola.*
Veillant—vigilant: *vigilantem.*
Veille—vigile: *vigilia.*
Venteux—ventouse: *ventosus.*
Verge—vergue: *virga.*
Vermicelle—vermisseau: (*It.*) *vermicello* (*ve*
cellus).
Verre—vitre: *vitrum.*
Veuve—vide: *vidua.*
Viatique—voyage: *viaticum.*
Vicaire—viguier: *vicarius.*
Vocale—voyelle: *vocalis.*
Volte—voûte: (*It.*) *volta* (*voluta*).
Voter—vouer: *votare.*

www.ingramcontent.com/pod-product-compliance
Lightning Source LLC
Chambersburg PA
CBHW022136300426
44115CB00006B/205
9783337016364